Merriam-Webster's Intermediate Thesaurus

Merriam-Webster's Intermediate Thesaurus

Merriam-Webster, Incorporated
Springfield, Massachusetts

A GENUINE MERRIAM-WEBSTER

The name *Webster* alone is no guarantee of excellence. It is used by a number of publishers and may serve mainly to mislead an unwary buyer.

Merriam-Webster™ is the name you should look for when you consider the purchase of dictionaries or other fine reference books. It carries the reputation of a company that has been publishing since 1831 and is your assurance of quality and authority.

Library of Congress Cataloging-in-Publication Data

Merriam-Webster's intermediate thesaurus.
  p. cm.
 ISBN-13: 978-0-87779-076-1
 ISBN-10: 0-87779-076-0 (alk. paper)
 1. English language—Synonyms and antonyms—Juvenile literature. I. Title: Intermediate thesaurus. II. Merriam-Webster, Inc.
 PE1591.M4788 2004
 423′.12—dc22

                  2004017813

Made in the United States of America

07 NK:QWV 08

A powerful agent is the right word: it lights the reader's way and makes it plain; a close approximation to it will answer, and much traveling is done in a well-enough fashion by its help, but we do not welcome it and applaud it and rejoice in it as we do when the right one blazes out on us. Whenever we come upon one of those intensely right words in a book or a newspaper the resulting effect is physical as well as spiritual, and electrically prompt: it tingles exquisitely around through the walls of the mouth and tastes as tart and crisp and good as the autumn-butter that creams the sumac-berry.

—Mark Twain

Preface

Merriam-Webster's Intermediate Thesaurus is specially designed for students aged 11 to 14 who want to enlarge their vocabularies and learn more about the rich variety of the English language. The vocabulary of the thesaurus is based upon that of *Merriam-Webster's Intermediate Dictionary*, which is likewise intended for use primarily by middle-school students. We hope and expect that students will readily turn to the dictionary whenever they need a better understanding of the meaning of any word used in the thesaurus.

In creating this thesaurus, Merriam-Webster editors have drawn on years of experience with a thesaurus format that is at once easy to use, broad in its scope, and especially helpful to the user in the selection of the right word. We also believe that this thesaurus will prove to be highly useful as a vocabulary builder. We have parted ways with the more traditional approach of presenting long, undifferentiated lists of words that are tied to some topic or intellectual concept. Instead, we present a strictly alphabetical ordering of entries. These entries consist of lists of words that are centered on a specific—and specified—meaning. Main entries consist of lists of synonyms and related words, as well as antonyms and near antonyms whenever applicable. Phrases and idioms that function as synonyms are occasionally offered as well.

The purpose of the differentiated lists is to accommodate the various purposes for which a thesaurus is used. People use a thesaurus generally because they are dissatisfied with the word they already have in mind. They want a different word. The question is: how different?

If users of this thesaurus are trying to avoid a boring repetition of the same word, or are seeking to vary and enrich their vocabulary, then they will wish to select from the list of synonyms a word that shares the same basic meaning as the one they already have but differs from it in suggestion and tone. If they are seeking a word that is different from but still related to what they already have, then they will want to scan the lists of related words for a rewarding journey through the variety of possibilities that English offers.

If users are seeking a word that is to some degree opposite in meaning to what they have, then they will want to consult the lists of antonyms or near antonyms. By specifying the meaning under consideration, and by making distinctions between words that are truly synonymous and those that are only somewhat synonymous, we hope that we have given users the guidance they desire. We believe that our system minimizes the need to guess and to grope.

What makes *Merriam-Webster's Intermediate Thesaurus* unique, even among other thesauri published by Merriam-Webster, is the content of the separate entries for each and every word appearing in the lists of synonyms. Since a user's search for the right word may start anywhere, the thesaurus is arranged so that any member of a synonym group can serve as the starting point. An entry for a listed synonym consists of a restatement of the meaning common to all the members of the group and—most significantly—an illustration of how that particular synonym is used. A user who happens to start at a main entry should go to a synonym's own-place entry to see how it is distinctively used. A user who happens to use a particular synonym as a starting point should follow the cross-reference to the main entry for the complete listing of synonyms, related words, and any antonyms or near antonyms.

The thesaurus format is intended to encourage and facilitate students in finding the right word, which results in writing of greater precision and clarity. The word *thesaurus* literally means "treasury" in Latin, and we hope that the treasure trove of words contained in these pages will enhance the user's interest in and appreciation of the English language. We urge both students and teachers to read carefully the following sections entitled Introduction and Using Your Thesaurus in order to make the most of what the book has to offer. The Introduction contains an informative discussion of what distinguishes a synonym from a related word, an antonym from a near antonym. The Using Your Thesaurus section explains in detail the organization of the thesaurus and discusses the differences between the two basic types of entries. Study of this section is especially important.

The editor of *Merriam-Webster's Intermediate Thesaurus* has been ably assisted in its composition by the editors Rose Martino Bigelow, Daniel B. Brandon, Adam Groff, Kory L. Stamper, and Deanna Stathis. The entire project was supervised by Madeline L. Novak, and Robert D. Copeland served as editor in charge of production. Stephen J. Perrault devised ways to facilitate the creation of the manuscript electronically. The difficult task of cross-referencing the text was accomplished by Christopher Chapin Connor and Allison S. Crawford. Credit for proofreading the text goes to Ilya A. Davidovich, Donna L. Rickerby, Maria Sansalone, Adrienne M. Scholz, Peter A. Sokolowski, Emily A. Vezina, and Judy Yeh. Michael D. Roundy acted as a consultant on miscellaneous scientific questions. Finally, John M. Morse, Merriam-Webster's President and Publisher, must be acknowledged and thanked for his unfailing support for the Thesaurus.

Michael G. Belanger,
Editor

Introduction

Synonyms

The English language contains a wealth of words, and perhaps no other language has as many synonyms as English. Synonyms give color, precision, and variety to a person's writing, breaking up the dullness that can come from too many overused words.

So, just what are synonyms? Put simply, synonyms are words that mean the same thing. Words that are only somewhat similar in meaning—but do not mean the same thing—are not true synonyms. They are merely related words, and they belong in a different category. In this thesaurus a word is classified as a synonym if and only if it shares with another word at least one basic meaning.

Here's an example of how we arrived at a basic meaning shared by one group of words. The word *freight* is defined in *Merriam-Webster's Intermediate Dictionary* as "goods or cargo carried by ship, train, truck, or airplane." We can break up the definition like this:

$$\left.\begin{array}{c} goods \\ cargo \end{array}\right\} carried\ by \left\{\begin{array}{l} ship \\ train \\ truck \\ airplane \end{array}\right.$$

Since a person using *freight* as the starting point in his or her search for the right word is probably dissatisfied with that term, the word that he or she is seeking will most likely come under a broader or more basic meaning. We can phrase that more basic meaning as: "a mass or quantity of something taken up and carried, conveyed, or transported." The list of synonyms for *freight—burden, cargo, draft, haul, lading, load, loading, payload, weight*—can all be said to share this basic meaning.

If a word is more limited in scope than the basic meaning given at a main entry, then it cannot be regarded as a synonym. Hence, *truckload*, which refers specifically to the load carried by a truck, cannot be a synonym of *freight* and the other members of *freight's* synonym group. Likewise, the words *mass* and *quantity* cannot themselves be regarded as synonyms because the notion of being carried, conveyed, or transported is not an essential part of their meaning.

Related Words

Oftentimes thesaurus users are not looking for something that means exactly the same as the word they already have. To help in this situation, this thesaurus includes lists of related words, which are words whose meanings are close enough to the synonymy group to be of interest to the user. These related words do not qualify as synonyms because they have meanings that differ from the basic meaning shared by the synonymy group in some significant way.

For example, the word *funny* has the meaning of "causing or intended to cause laughter." A person who is making "funny faces" is causing, or at least trying to cause, others to laugh. *Witty*, which is certainly closely related to *funny*, has a slightly different meaning: "given to or marked by mature intelligent humor." A witty person is someone who has a habit of making clever remarks that display a grown-up sense of humor. Thus, *funny* and *witty* are related, but the words are not synonymous. Because of the close relationship between two words like *funny* and *witty*, all of the words listed as synonyms at *witty* are given as related words at *funny*.

The lists of related words at a main entry in the thesaurus may be likened to the hyperlinks that connect one Web site to another on the Internet. Following the links between Web sites often takes one to new and unexpected places. Thesaurus users are encouraged to go from one related entry to another in their search for just the right word.

Some words are not true synonyms of anything, but because they are so fundamentally useful, they have been included in this thesaurus among the lists of related words and in places where they are likely to be most helpful. For example, the word *ballast*, which refers to any type of "heavy material used to make a ship steady," is too narrow in meaning to have any synonyms of its own. It is related to the more general term *load*, however, and so, fittingly, it is included as a related word at the entry for *load*.

Antonyms

An antonym is a word whose meaning is directly opposite to another word's meaning. In this thesaurus, an antonym is a word that has a meaning that completely cancels out another word's meaning. *Short* and *tall* are complete opposites. Something cannot be both short and tall at the same time, and both words suggest about the same degree of difference from the norm or average in height. *Good* and *evil* are another pair of exact opposites. Logically, something cannot be both *good* and *evil* in the same way and at the same time.

Words that are only opposite in some aspect of their meaning cannot be said to be true antonyms. For example, *sad*, which means "causing unhappiness," is not a true antonym of *funny*, which means "causing or intended to cause laughter." The opposite of unhappiness is happiness, and so the opposite of sad is happy. There are things, like a frowning clown, that can be both funny and sad, so these words can't be antonyms. Pairs of words like *sad* and *funny* are better regarded as near antonyms.

Near Antonyms

Near antonyms are words that do not qualify as antonyms under the strict definition used for this thesaurus but that clearly have meanings in marked contrast with the members of a synonym group. For example, *afraid* is not so exactly opposite to *courageous* as *cowardly* is, but *afraid* and *courageous* certainly have markedly contrasting meanings and so are considered near antonyms. And just as a user may not be seeking a word that is exactly synonymous with another, he or she may likewise not be seeking a word that is exactly opposite. The user may simply want a word that lies somewhere on the opposite side of the range of meaning.

Phrases

This thesaurus also includes phrases that, taken as a whole, are synonymous with individual words. Within this category are some words that are commonly used in combination with one another but are not necessarily included as entry words in most dictionaries. Some of these fixed phrases represent virtually the only way in which the word is used in contemporary English. For example, *in jeopardy* appears as a synonymous phrase at *liable* because a person exposed to something dangerous or undesirable is a person in jeopardy. The word *jeopardy* is generally only used in the phrase *in jeopardy*.

Idioms constitute the other major class of word combinations that are entered under the heading of Phrases. Idioms are phrases that have a special meaning that is different from the literal meaning that a person would get if adding together the individual meanings of the components of the phrase. For example, the phrase *make good* is virtually meaningless if one attempts to piece together the literal meanings of *make* and *good*. As a fixed phrase, however, *make good* means "to reach a desired level of accomplishment" and is a synonym of *succeed*.

What this thesaurus does not enter are phrases that are simple restatements of the basic meaning shared by the members of the synonym group. The verb *remark*, for example, might be defined as "to express as an opinion." Such rewordings of a basic definition have no place in a thesaurus because they contribute nothing useful to the user's vocabulary.

Choosing the Right Word—Using Your Dictionary

Even after you have mastered all of these categories, deciding which word in a thesaurus entry is best for your purposes is not always easy. The basic meaning shared by the members of a synonym group cannot tell you everything you need to know in order to choose the word that best suits your needs.

Something that is "very pleasing to look at" can be described as *attractive, beauteous, beautiful, bonny, comely, cute, fair, gorgeous, handsome, knockout, lovely, pretty, ravishing, sightly, stunning,* or *taking*, but which word is best for describing a sunset? A city? Should you use *knockout* to describe a cathedral or *ravishing* for a sports car?

Sometimes, of course, your own experience can tell you when one word is better than another, but that's not always the case. That's when the verbal illustrations in this thesaurus can be of help. Verbal illustrations can help by showing how each synonym is typically used:

⟨sunsets in Hawaii are just *gorgeous*⟩

⟨the glass-topped table was a *handsome* addition to the room⟩

⟨a *knockout* sports car that's the talk of the neighborhood⟩

⟨with her red curls falling around her shoulders, she looked *ravishing* in her green dress⟩

If after reviewing the verbal illustrations for all of the synonyms, you decide that you still have not found the right word, then you have the list of related words to consider:

> **related words** alluring, appealing, charming, delightful, eye-catching, glamorous (*also* glamourous), prepossessing; elegant, exquisite, glorious, resplendent, splendid, statuesque, sublime, superb; flawless, perfect, radiant; dainty, delicate; personable, presentable

Now you have 38 words that mean the same thing or nearly the same thing as *beautiful*. Here's where you need a good dictionary. You can consult the dictionary to get a precise definition of any word in the lists, and perhaps an example of its use. The vocabulary in *Merriam-Webster's Intermediate Thesaurus* is based on *Merriam-Webster's Intermediate Dictionary*, which contains words within the range likely to be useful to you. Whether you use the Intermediate Dictionary or some other age-appropriate dictionary, *you should always use this thesaurus along with a reliable dictionary.*

Using Your Thesaurus

Every user of this thesaurus should read this section of the book carefully in order to use it effectively.

A thesaurus consists mostly of lists of words, and it is often difficult to know which word is best for a particular purpose. Because the English language has so many different ways of combining words with different shades of meaning, *you should always use this thesaurus along with a good age-appropriate dictionary*.

Entry Order

The first word of a thesaurus entry is called a **headword**. Headwords are printed in boldface type and are in alphabetical order. Alphabetization is by first letter, then second letter, and so on, regardless of any spaces or hyphens that may appear in them:

make *vb*

make–believe *adj*

make out *vb*

make over *vb*

Maker *n*

makeshift *adj*

When a headword contains a numeral, the numeral is alphabetized as though it were a spelled-out word:

anywise *adv*

A1 *adj*

apace *adv*

Homographs are words that are spelled the same, but each is a different part of speech or has a different etymology (word origin). Homographs that are different parts of speech are separate headwords:

hail *n* 1 a heavy fall of objects

hail *vb* 1 to declare enthusiastic approval of

Homographs that have a different etymology, even when they are the same part of speech, are entered as separate headwords. Those that are the same part of speech are grouped together and numbered in sequence:

¹**list** *n* a record of a series of items (as names or titles) usually arranged according to some system

²**list** *n* the act of positioning or an instance of being positioned at an angle

³**list** *n* a long narrow piece of material

¹**list** *vb* 1 to make a list of

²**list** *vb* to set or cause to be at an angle

Verbs that are used in combination with a preposition or an adverb are entered with the verb in boldface type followed by the preposition or adverb in parentheses in lightface type. Such combinations immediately follow the base verb in alphabetical order:

go *vb*

go (for) *vb*

go (on) *vb*

go (to) *vb*

When main entries are compound words, a closed form is entered before a hyphenated form and a hyphenated form is entered before a form that contains spaces:

nosedive *n*

nose–dive *vb*

open–air *adj*

open air *n*

Plural Nouns

Some nouns are always pluralized when they are used a certain way. When there are no thesaurus entries which include the singular form of a such a noun, the plural form is given as the headword:

leavings *n pl* a remaining group or portion ⟨the *leavings* of the banquet were packed up and delivered to a shelter for the homeless⟩ — see REMAINDER 1

When a noun is usually, but not always, used in plural form in a certain sense, the singular form is the headword, and the plural follows the label *usually*:

habiliment *n, usually* **habiliments** *pl* covering for the human body ⟨the lady's rich *habiliments* and haughty manner had the host's servants thinking she was someone important⟩ — see CLOTHING

Such nouns are followed by *s* in parentheses in the synonym list:

clothing *n* covering for the human body ⟨a store that sells both men's and women's *clothing*⟩
synonyms apparel, attire, clothes, dress, duds, habiliment(s), rags, raiment, togs, wear

When a noun is used in the singular form in one sense and in the plural form in another, the singular form is given as the headword. The plural form is indicated at the individual sense or senses:

provision *n* **1** something upon which the carrying out of an agreement or offer depends ⟨loaned them the car with the *provision* that they refill the gas tank before returning it⟩ — see CONDITION 2
2 provisions *pl* substances intended to be eaten ⟨gave them ample *provisions* so they would not get hungry on the trip⟩ — see FOOD

Variants

An alternate spelling or form of a headword is called a **variant**. Variants are shown in boldface after the headword and are preceded by *or* or *also*. The label *or* means that the variant is as common or nearly as common as the headword. The headword is usually the form that comes first alphabetically:

egotistic *or* **egotistical** *adj*

lighted *or* **lit** *adj*

OK *or* **okay** *vb*

However, if one of the spellings or forms is used slightly more frequently, the more common one is entered first even though it may not fall first alphabetically:

gizmo *or* **gismo** *n*

A variant that is preceded by the label *also* is not as common as the headword:

among *also* **amongst** *prep*

facade *also* **façade** *n*

naught *also* **nought** *n*

When two variants are separated from the headword by *also* but from each other by *or*, it means that they are both less common than the headword:

bogey *also* **bogy** *or* **bogie** *n*

Variants are also given in the word lists:

zero *n* the numerical symbol 0 or the absence of number or quantity represented by it ⟨anything multiplied by *zero* comes out to zero⟩
synonyms aught, cipher, goose egg, naught (*or* nought), nil, nothing, oh, zilch, zip

Parts of Speech

Every headword is followed by a part-of-speech label. The abbreviations for the parts of speech are *adj* (adjective), *adv* (adverb), *conj* (conjunction), *interj* (interjection), *n* (noun), *prep* (preposition), *pron* (pronoun), and *vb* (verb).

Kinds of Entries

There are two kinds of entries: main entries and secondary entries. Every headword with its part-of-speech label is followed by either one or more main entries, one or more secondary entries, or a combination of the two. If there is more than one entry, each one begins on a new line introduced by a boldface sense number. Main entries come first. A **main entry** consists of the meaning shared by the members of the synonym group, a verbal illustration, and lists of synonyms as well as any related words, phrases, near antonyms, and antonyms:

eagerness *n* urgent desire or interest ⟨students with an *eagerness* to learn⟩
synonyms appetite, ardor, avidity, desirousness, enthusiasm, excitement, hunger, impatience, keenness, thirst
related words alacrity, quickness; ambition, gusto, zest
near antonyms unconcern; aloofness, detachment; impassivity, languor
antonyms apathy, indifference

A **secondary entry** consists of the same shared meaning that is shown at the main entry along with a verbal illustration for that particular synonym. The secondary entry does not contain lists of synonyms, antonyms, related words, phrases, or near antonyms. Instead, at the end of the entry, there is a direction to "see" the appropriate main entry at another headword. Secondary entries follow any main entries at a headword:

gain *vb* **1** to increase in ⟨as the car coasted downhill, it gradually *gained* speed and momentum⟩

synonyms build (up), gather, grow (in), pick up . . .
2 to receive as return for effort ⟨*gained* her affections with his polite manner⟩ — see EARN 1
3 to become healthy and strong again after illness or weakness ⟨is *gaining* after his bout with the flu and will be back on his feet soon⟩ — see CONVALESCE

fade *vb* **1** to cease to be visible ⟨the departing ship gradually *faded* over the horizon⟩ — see DISAPPEAR
2 to make white or whiter by removing color ⟨years of harsh sunlight had *faded* the car, which was once fire-engine red⟩ — see WHITEN

Cross-References

The direction at the end of every secondary entry to see another entry is called a **cross-reference**. The cross-reference tells you where the main entry for a word's synonym group is located. No matter which member of a synonym group you used to begin your search, you can always find your way to the entry that has the lists of all the synonyms and any related words, phrases, near antonyms, or antonyms. If there is more than one sense at the headword referred to in the cross-reference, the cross-reference will also include a sense number. If the headword has more than one numbered homograph, the cross-reference will send you to the right homograph number as well:

pain *vb* to feel or cause physical pain ⟨my poor head was *paining* so from all that racket⟩ — see HURT 1

ranking *n* **1** a scheme of rank or order ⟨in one *ranking* of the best places to live, San Francisco surpassed all the other cities in the U.S.⟩ — see ³SCALE 1

If a headword appears as more than one part of speech, the cross-reference is sending you to the same part of speech as the word you looked up. The cross-reference in the **ranking** example above tells you that the main entry where you will find *ranking* as a member of the synonym group with the shared meaning "a scheme of rank or order" is at sense 1 of the noun entry ³**scale**:

³**scale** *n* **1** a scheme of rank or order ⟨a student who scored very highly on a standard intelligence *scale*⟩
synonyms graduation, ladder, ordering, ranking

Special Usage Labels

You will find special usage labels in italics after a headword whenever they apply. The labels are *chiefly British, British, chiefly Scottish, Scottish, Australian, chiefly dialect, chiefly Southern & Midland*, and *slang*. These labels are placed directly after the part-of-speech label when the word has only one sense or when the label applies to all the senses:

afore *prep, chiefly dialect* **1**

bairn *n, chiefly Scottish*

bobby *n, British*

dis *vb, slang* **1**

The label comes after the sense number when the word has more than one sense and the label applies only to that sense:

jack *n* **1** *slang* something (as pieces of stamped metal or printed paper) customarily and legally used as a medium of exchange, a measure of value, or a means of payment ⟨I'd buy that watch, but I don't have the *jack*⟩ — see MONEY

Special usage labels also appear in the word lists:

before *prep* **1** earlier than ⟨since I'm a faster runner, I got there *before* him⟩
synonyms afore [*chiefly dialect*], ahead of, ere, of, previous to, prior to, to

Shared Meanings

The shared meaning follows the sense number when there is more than one sense and the part-of-speech label when there is only one sense. It is a meaning shared equally by the headword and the other members of the synonym group. This shared meaning is the "thing" that is referred to when we say that two or more words "mean the same thing" and thus are synonyms.

Sometimes there are words in parentheses within a shared meaning:

district *n* an area (as of a city) set apart for some purpose or having some special feature ⟨Independence Hall in Philadelphia's historic *district*⟩
synonyms neighborhood, quarter, section
related words belt, zone; department, . . .

In the shared meaning at **district**, the words in parentheses indicate that *district, neighborhood, quarter*, and *section* are synonyms when they refer to an area of a city or something like that, and that the words in the related words list also refer specifically to this type of area.

For information regarding the use and purpose of parentheses around certain words in entries for verbs, read below.

Some Notes about Verbs

A boldface verb headword followed by a lightface word in parentheses tells you to use the parenthetical word with the verb:

comply (with) *vb* **1** to act according to the commands of ⟨the guards ran to *comply with* their ruler's orders⟩

hold off (on) *vb* to assign to a later time ⟨*held off on* accepting the invitation in the hopes that something better would come along⟩

knock (about) *vb* to move about from place to place aimlessly ⟨we *knocked about* from town to town⟩

If there are two words inside the parentheses and they are separated by *or*, then either word can be used with the verb:

fit (in *or* into) *vb* to put among or between others ⟨do you think you can *fit* this picture *into* the album?⟩ ⟨I can *fit* you *in* between my two o'clock and three o'clock appointments⟩

These verbs appear in the synonym lists followed by their customary adverb or preposition in parentheses. These entries are treated this way in the thesaurus because such verb combinations are not the usual form of dictionary entries, but it is only when the verb is used with the adverb or preposition that it matches the shared meaning of its synonym group.

When the meaning of a verb requires a direct object, all of the words in the synonym list take a direct object. If a verb does not take an object, none of the synonyms will take an object.

If you can't figure out from the shared meaning whether a word should have a direct object, or what kind of direct object it should have, you can look at how the verb is used in the verbal illustration.

Verbal Illustrations

Every synonym in this thesaurus is illustrated with an example of its typical use. The **verbal illustration**, as it is called, follows the shared meaning, is enclosed in angle brackets, and italicizes the synonym:

fight *vb* **1** to oppose (someone) in physical conflict ⟨a proud people who have fiercely *fought* all invaders of their homeland⟩

hold back *vb* to create difficulty for the work or activity of ⟨the only thing *holding* Joe *back* from joining the swim team is lack of transportation⟩

rich *adj* **1** having goods, property, or money in abundance ⟨Tanya's dad works as a chauffeur for the *richest* man in town, a big oil baron⟩

Words in parentheses after a boldface headword are italicized in the verbal illustration:

stick (to *or* with) *vb* to give steadfast support to ⟨thanks for *sticking with* me when all my other so-called friends have turned their backs⟩

Some verbal illustrations in the Thesaurus are complete sentences and others are only sentence fragments. Though it may look a little odd, for the sake of consistency, all verbal illustrations in this thesaurus begin with a lowercase letter unless the initial word is normally capitalized. Question marks and exclamation points are used when appropriate at the end of a verbal illustration, but otherwise no ending punctuation is used.

A Word about Synonyms

If a word is used as the defining term in a shared meaning, it will not be listed as one of the synonyms. Since words can only be defined in terms of other words, the result of this restriction is that some terms that might be rightly regarded as synonyms do not appear in the synonym lists. Here is an example:

go *vb* . . .
  2 to leave a place often for another ⟨will *go* on vacation at the end of the year⟩ ⟨decided it would be better to *go* before she got any angrier⟩
  synonyms begone, clear out, depart, exit, get, get off, move, pull (out), quit, sally (forth), shove (off), take off, walk out

Leave, used as the defining term, could be considered another synonym, but it is not entered as such in this thesaurus because it has been used as a defining term.

Related Words

You will see that in most cases there are more related words than synonyms. That is because there is much more flexibility in choosing words for these lists. They do not have to match the shared meaning: they only need to relate to some aspect of it. Related words are often divided into subgroups separated by a semicolon. Words within each subgroup are generally closer in meaning to each other than to the members of the following subgroups. The subgroups tend to be presented in order of most relevant to least relevant.

> **object** *n* **1** something material that can be perceived by the senses ⟨I kept tripping over countless little *objects* scattered about the darkened room⟩
> **synonyms** thing
> **related words** article, item, piece; being, entity, substance; commodity, good, ware; accessory, accompaniment; bauble, curio, knickknack, spangle, token, trinket

Phrases

Listed in alphabetical order after the heading **phrases** at some of the main entries are expressions that are synonymous with the headword and the other members of the synonym group. Although they have essentially the same meaning as the synonyms, these phrases tend to be used only in certain ways, and you should be careful about substituting one of them for a word in the synonym list. Since phrases are not entered as headwords in the thesaurus, they do not come with verbal illustrations. It's a good idea to look them up in a dictionary before considering them.

Near Antonyms

Just as related words are not exact synonyms, near antonyms are not exact antonyms. Not every synonym group has near antonyms. As is the case with related words, when there are near antonyms, they are often divided into subgroups separated by a semicolon, with the members of each subgroup listed alphabetically.

> **have** *vb* **1** to keep, control, or experience as one's own ⟨Aunt Chloe *has* 31 pairs of red shoes⟩
> **synonyms** command, enjoy, hold, occupy, own, possess, retain
> **related words** keep, reserve, withhold; bear, carry; boast, show off, sport
> **near antonyms** abandon, cede, disclaim, disown, hand over, relinquish, renounce, surrender, yield; discard, dump; decline, reject, repudiate, spurn; need, require
> **antonyms** lack, want

Antonyms

The words in the antonym lists are the exact opposites of the headword and the words in the

synonym lists. Not every synonym group has antonyms, and antonym lists tend to be shorter than near antonym lists. Antonyms are listed alphabetically, just as synonyms are. They appear as boldface headwords at their own alphabetical places in the thesaurus only if they are part of a synonym group elsewhere.

Ordinarily, all the words in an antonym list are synonyms of each other. Sometimes, however, a semicolon in an antonym list divides words which, while they are exact opposites of the words in the synonym group, are not synonyms of each other. Here is an example:

> **present** *adj* **1** existing or in progress right now ⟨I am very busy at the *present* moment⟩
> **synonyms** current, extant, ongoing, present-day
> **antonyms** ago, past; future

The opposite of "existing or in progress right now" is "*not* existing or in progress right now." All three of the words in the antonyms list fit that meaning. *Ago* and *past*, separated by a comma, are synonyms of each other; they both can mean "earlier than the present time." But *ago* and *past* are not synonyms of *future*, which means, of course, "occurring at a later time."

A Note about the Lists: Word Duplication

No word appears in more than one list at any single main entry. Some words have slight variations in meaning. If they are used one way, they are synonymous with a headword; if they are used another way, they are merely closely related. To avoid confusion, such words have been entered in a main entry's synonym list only. For example, *nice* is in the synonym list at *pleasant* where the shared meaning is "giving pleasure or contentment to the mind or senses." *Nice* is also in the synonym list at *amiable*, where the shared meaning is "having an easygoing and pleasing manner especially in social situations." If you go back to *pleasant*, you will find *amiable* among the related words. So it would stand to reason that *nice*, having the same meaning as *amiable*, would also be entered in the related word list at *pleasant*. Since it's already in the synonym list, however, it was left out of the related words.

Some words can have two meanings that are opposite of each other—or nearly so. *Nervy* can mean both "fearless" and "fearful, timid." Thus, at the thesaurus entry for *bold*, where the shared meaning is "inclined or willing to take risks," *nervy* might qualify as both a synonym and an antonym (or near antonym). And, indeed, *nervy* appears as a synonym, along with *adventuresome, adventurous, audacious, daring, dashing, emboldened, enterprising, gutsy, hardy, nerved, venturesome,* and *venturous.* Although the near antonym list contains *fearful* and *timid* as expected, *nervy* is left off the list. Again, this is to avoid confusion.

Guide Words

The two boldface words separated by a dot at the top of each page are **guide words**, and they show the alphabetical range of entries on the page. You can use them to find a word more quickly. The first guide word is the headword of the first entry beginning on that page, and the second guide is the headword of the last entry on the page.

Merriam-Webster's Intermediate Thesaurus

A

aback *adv* without warning ⟨completely taken *aback* by the neighbors' announcement that they were moving⟩ — see UNAWARES

abaft *adv* near, toward, or in the stern of a ship or the tail of an aircraft ⟨the lookout in the crow's nest warned that there was an enemy frigate *abaft* and bearing down hard on their ship⟩ — see AFT

abaft *prep* at, to, or toward the rear of ⟨a school of porpoises swam *abaft* the fishing boat⟩ — see BEHIND 1

abandon *n* carefree freedom from constraint ⟨added spices to the stew with complete *abandon*⟩
synonyms abandonment, ease, lightheartedness, naturalness, spontaneity, unrestraint
related words ardor, enthusiasm, exuberance, fervor, spirit, warmth, zeal; carelessness, heedlessness, impulsiveness, indiscretion, insouciance, recklessness, thoughtlessness; excess, excessiveness, immoderacy, incontinence, indulgence, intemperance, licentiousness, permissiveness, wantonness, wildness
near antonyms embarrassment, reserve, reticence, self-consciousness, uneasiness; inhibition, repression, self-restraint, suppression; carefulness, discreetness, discretion, heedfulness; discipline, self-control, self-discipline, willpower
antonyms constraint, restraint

abandon *vb* to cause to remain behind ⟨*abandoned* the group that he had been hiking with and struck out on his own⟩ — see LEAVE 1

abandoned *adj* left unoccupied or unused ⟨Marlene avoided walking past the *abandoned* house, with its broken windows and sagging porch⟩
synonyms derelict, deserted, disused, forgotten, forsaken, rejected, vacated
related words ignored, neglected, unattended, untended; castaway, cast-off, discarded, jettisoned, junked; desolate, godforsaken, miserable, shabby, wretched; empty, idle, vacant
near antonyms reclaimed, recovered, redeemed, rescued, retrieved, salvaged, saved; reconditioned, rehabilitated, restored; repeopled

abandonment *n* 1 carefree freedom from constraint ⟨sang at the top of her lungs with complete *abandonment* in the shower⟩ — see ABANDON
2 the act of abandoning ⟨the law says *abandonment* by the owner of any building for more than a year entitles the city to sell it⟩ — see DERELICTION 1

abase *vb* 1 to lower in character or dignity ⟨was unwilling to *abase* himself by pleading guilty to a crime that he did not commit⟩ — see DEBASE 1
2 to reduce to a lower standing in one's own eyes or in others' eyes ⟨I certainly don't *abase* myself when I do good, honest manual labor⟩ — see HUMBLE

abash *vb* to throw into a state of self-conscious distress ⟨felt terribly *abashed* when she walked into the wrong hotel room⟩ — see EMBARRASS 1

abashment *n* the emotional state of being made self-consciously uncomfortable ⟨his friends shared his *abashment* when his mom scolded him right in front of them⟩ — see EMBARRASSMENT 1

abate *vb* 1 to grow less in scope or intensity especially gradually ⟨interest in the author's home *abated* as her novels waned in popularity⟩ — see DECREASE 2
2 to make smaller in amount, volume, or extent ⟨a couple of aspirin should *abate* the pain⟩ — see DECREASE 1

abatement *n* 1 something that is or may be subtracted ⟨entitled to a tax *abatement* for child care expenses⟩ — see DEDUCTION 1
2 the amount by which something is lessened ⟨there's been a significant *abatement* in noise from the floor above since the upstairs neighbors installed carpets⟩ — see DECREASE

abbey *n* a residence for men under religious vows ⟨the monks in the *abbey* grow all their own vegetables⟩ — see MONASTERY

abbreviate *vb* to make less in extent or duration ⟨had to *abbreviate* his vacation in France in order to travel to Oslo to receive the Nobel Prize⟩ — see SHORTEN

abbreviation *n* a shortened version of a written work ⟨a recording of musical *abbreviations* that introduces the listener to the great composers⟩ — see ABRIDGMENT

abdicate *vb* to give up (as a position of authority) formally ⟨the revolutionary government forced Nicholas II to *abdicate* the Russian throne⟩
synonyms abnegate, cede, relinquish, renounce, resign, step down (from), surrender
related words abjure, deny, disavow, disclaim, disown, waive; forsake, give up, hand over, yield; abandon, desert, quit, vacate
near antonyms appropriate, arrogate, assume, claim, confiscate; seize, take over, usurp, wrest; defend, guard, protect, safeguard, secure

abdomen *n* the part of the body between the chest and the pelvis ⟨showed us a tiny tattoo on her *abdomen*, right next to her belly button⟩ — see STOMACH

abduct *vb* to carry a person away by unlawful force or against his or her will ⟨the gangsters planned to *abduct* a rich young woman and demand a huge ransom from her family⟩ — see KIDNAP

aberrant *adj* 1 being out of the ordinary ⟨a year of *aberrant* weather—record rainfall in the summer, record heat in the autumn⟩ — see EXCEPTIONAL
2 departing from some accepted standard of what is normal ⟨*aberrant* behavior can be a sign of rabies in a wild animal⟩ — see DEVIANT

aberration *n* a serious mental disorder that prevents one from living a safe and normal life ⟨Joan of Arc was certain the voices she heard were not a manifestation of some sort of *aberration*⟩ — see INSANITY 1

abet *vb* 1 to cause or encourage the development of ⟨the belief that violent entertainment *abets* violent behavior in the people who partake of it⟩ — see INCITE 1
2 to provide (someone) with what is useful or necessary to achieve an end ⟨car thieves are often unwittingly *abetted* by owners foolishly leaving the keys in the ignition⟩ — see HELP 1

abettor *also* **abetter** *n* 1 one associated with another in wrongdoing ⟨the man who drove the getaway car in the bank robbery was arrested as an aider and *abettor*⟩ — see ACCOMPLICE
2 someone associated with another to give assistance or moral support ⟨without all the neighborhood kids as *abettors*, I would never have gotten all my chickens back in their coop⟩ — see ALLY

abeyance *n* a state of temporary inactivity ⟨our weekend plans were held in *abeyance* until we could get a weather forecast⟩
synonyms doldrums, dormancy, latency, quiescence, suspense, suspension
related words inaction, inertia, inertness, motionlessness; impasse, standstill; coma, hibernation, hypnosis, repose, rest, sleep, slumber, torpor; recession, remission; idleness
near antonyms recommencement, renewal, resumption, resuscitation
antonyms continuance, continuation

abhor *vb* to dislike strongly ⟨*abhors* the way people leave their trash at the picnic sites in the park⟩ — see HATE

abhorrence *n* something or someone that is hated ⟨one of the changes in American society that remains a particular *abhorrence* of social conservatives⟩ — see HATE 2
2 a very strong dislike ⟨my firm *abhorrence* of all forms of hypocrisy⟩ — see HATE 1

abhorrent *adj* causing intense displeasure, disgust, or resentment ⟨he considers it *abhorrent* the way she keeps her dogs penned up all the time⟩ — see OFFENSIVE 1

abide *vb* **1** to continue to be in a place for a significant amount of time ⟨refused to *abide* where it was clear that he wasn't wanted⟩ — see STAY 1
2 to have a home ⟨believes that fairies *abide* in the cup-shaped flowers dotting the woodland floor⟩ — see LIVE 1
3 to put up with (something painful or difficult) ⟨cannot *abide* being in huge crowds⟩ — see BEAR 2
4 to remain indefinitely in existence or in the same state ⟨the once-honored ways no longer *abide* and now exist only in the memory of a few elders⟩ — see CONTINUE 1

ability *n* the physical or mental power to do something ⟨as a result of the accident he lost the *ability* to walk⟩
synonyms capability, capacity, competence, competency, faculty
related words aptitude, aptness, endowment, facility, gift, knack, talent; adroitness, deftness, dexterity, prowess, skill; gray matter, instinct, intelligence, reason, understanding; potency, staying power, stuff; adequacy, effectiveness, effectualness, fitness, form, influence, resourcefulness, usefulness; means, resources, wherewithal
near antonyms helplessness, impotence, paralysis, powerlessness, weakness; defectiveness, deficiency, inadequacy, ineffectiveness, ineffectualness, uselessness; debilitation, disablement, impairment, incapacitation
antonyms disability, inability, incapability, incapacity, incompetence, incompetency, ineptitude, ineptness

abjure *vb* to solemnly or formally reject or go back on (as something formerly adhered to) ⟨*abjured* some long-held beliefs when she converted to another religion⟩
synonyms recant, renounce, retract, take back, unsay, withdraw
related words contradict, deny, disavow, disclaim, disown, gainsay, negate, negative, repudiate; abandon, abnegate, forsake, give up, relinquish, spurn, surrender; controvert, disagree (with), disprove, dispute, rebut, refute; back down, back off, backtrack; disallow, recall, renege, revoke
near antonyms acknowledge, admit, affirm, assert, avow, claim, contend, declare, maintain, proclaim, profess, state; back, confirm, defend, endorse (*also* in-

dorse), espouse, maintain, support, uphold; accept, adopt, embrace
antonyms adhere (to)

ablaze *adj* **1** being on fire ⟨the entire block was *ablaze* by the time fire fighters arrived⟩
synonyms afire, aflame, blazing, burning, combusting, fiery, flaming, ignited, inflamed, kindled, lighted (*or* lit)
related words aglow, alight, flaring, flickering, glowing, live, smoldering; broiling, hot, piping hot, red-hot, roasting, scalding, scorching, searing, sizzling; burnt, charred, incinerated, scorched, seared, singed
near antonyms choked, damped, dead, doused, extinguished, quenched, smothered, snuffed (out), stamped (out), suffocated
2 filled with much light ⟨that night the ballroom, *ablaze* with light, looked very different from the curtained room it usually was by day⟩ — see BRIGHT 2

able *adj* having the required skills for an acceptable level of performance ⟨looking for an *able* and reliable assistant⟩ — see COMPETENT

able–bodied *adj* enjoying health and vigor ⟨every *able-bodied* young man in the village was sent off to fight in the war⟩ — see HEALTHY 1

ably *adv* in a skillful or expert manner ⟨*ably* maneuvered the boat up to the dock⟩ — see WELL 3

abnegate *vb* to give up (as a position of authority) formally ⟨*abnegated* all claims to the deceased lord's domain⟩ — see ABDICATE

abnegation *n* the act or practice of giving up or rejecting something once enjoyed or desired ⟨what the ailing executive found most difficult was the *abnegation* of all her corporate responsibilities⟩ — see RENUNCIATION

abnormal *adj* **1** being out of the ordinary ⟨a completely *abnormal* school day, because half of the kids were out sick⟩ — see EXCEPTIONAL
2 departing from some accepted standard of what is normal ⟨noticed his *abnormal* breathing and took him to the emergency room⟩ — see DEVIANT

abnormality *n* a person, thing, or event that is not normal ⟨the *abnormalities* in the tree's leaves are caused by disease⟩ — see FREAK 1

abode *n* the place where one lives ⟨welcome to my humble *abode*⟩ — see HOME 1

abolish *vb* to put an end to by formal action ⟨the U.S. *abolished* slavery by constitutional amendment on December 6, 1865⟩
synonyms abrogate, annul, cancel, dissolve, invalidate, negate, nullify, quash, repeal, rescind, void
related words countermand, override, overrule, overturn, veto; retract, reverse, revoke, suspend, withdraw; ban, enjoin, forbid, outlaw, prohibit; disallow, dismiss, reject; eliminate, eradicate, erase, liquidate, remove, throw out, write off
phrases do away with
near antonyms establish, found, institute; formalize, legalize, legitimate, legitimize, validate; pass, ratify; allow, approve, authorize, clear, endorse (*also* indorse), permit, sanction, warrant; command, decree, mandate, prescribe, order

abominable *adj* causing intense displeasure, disgust, or resentment ⟨your table manners are *abominable*!⟩ — see OFFENSIVE 1

abominate *vb* to dislike strongly ⟨we *abominate* jokes that make fun of people who have mental or physical disabilities⟩ — see HATE

abomination *n* something or someone that is hated ⟨although once common, torture is now an *abomination* to the civilized peoples of the earth⟩ — see HATE 2

2 a very strong dislike 〈the townspeople have such an *abomination* of taxes that they have even voted down increases that would have given their schools badly needed funds〉 — see HATE 1

aboriginal *adj* belonging to a particular place by birth or origin 〈the *aboriginal* peoples of northern Alaska are known as *Inupiats*, which in their language literally means "real people"〉 — see NATIVE 1

abort *vb* to put an end to (something planned or previously agreed to) 〈had to *abort* the mission to Mars when they lost contact with the satellite〉 — see CANCEL 1

abortion *n* the act of putting an end to something planned or previously agreed to 〈the *abortion* of the space mission caused the whole space program to be reexamined〉 — see CANCELLATION

abortive *adj* producing no results 〈an *abortive* attempt to recover the sunken pirate ship〉 — see FUTILE

abounding *adj* possessing or covered with great numbers or amounts of something specified 〈a city *abounding* with parks〉 — see RIFE

about *adv* **1** on all sides or in every direction 〈people standing *about* waiting for a sales clerk to assist them〉 — see AROUND 1

2 toward the opposite direction 〈turned *about* and saw the dog following him〉 — see AROUND 2

3 very close to but not completely 〈*about* as many boys as girls signed up for home economics〉 — see ALMOST

about *prep* **1** having to do with 〈a story *about* a young man who goes off to war〉

synonyms apropos of, concerning, of, on, regarding, respecting, toward (*or* towards)

related words as to, over

phrases as regards

2 close to 〈*about* the hedge there was a picket fence〉 — see AROUND 1

3 in random positions within the boundaries of 〈sparrows hopping *about* the playground〉 — see AROUND 2

above *prep* higher than 〈one minute our kite was *above* the telephone wires; the next minute it was tangled in them〉

synonyms over

related words atop

near antonyms underneath

antonyms below, beneath, under

above *adv* to or in a higher place 〈we eventually got used to the planes constantly flying *above*〉

synonyms aloft, over, overhead, skyward

near antonyms underneath

antonyms below, beneath, under

abrade *vb* **1** to damage or diminish by continued friction 〈ropes *abraded* by the rocks were a huge danger to the climbers〉

synonyms chafe, erode, fray, fret, gall, rub, wear

related words file, gnaw, grate, graze, grind, nibble, rasp, sandblast, sandpaper, scour, scrape, scuff, shave; erase, reduce, rub out, wear out, wipe (away); bite, break down, break up, chew, corrode, decompose, disintegrate, dissolve, eat; hone, sharpen, whet

2 to make sore by continued rubbing 〈the prisoner's manacles *abraded* his wrists and ankles until they bled〉 — see CHAFE 1

3 to damage by rubbing against a sharp or rough surface 〈the yacht's once-flawless wooden hull had been badly *abraded* by years of rough dockings〉 — see SCRAPE 2

abreast *adj* having information especially as a result of study or experience 〈keeping *abreast* of the latest fashion trends〉 — see FAMILIAR 2

abridge *vb* to make less in extent or duration 〈the library's hours have been drastically *abridged* to cut costs〉 — see SHORTEN

abridgment *or* **abridgement** *n* a shortened version of a written work 〈this Italian-English pocket dictionary is an *abridgment* of the hardback edition〉

synonyms abbreviation, condensation, digest

related words abstract, brief, outline, overview, précis, recap, recapitulation, résumé (*or* resume *also* resumé), review, sketch, sum, summarization, summary, summation, survey, syllabus, synopsis, wrap-up

near antonyms amplification, elaboration, enlargement, expansion

abrogate *vb* to put an end to by formal action 〈the U.S. Congress can *abrogate* old treaties that are unfair to Native Americans〉 — see ABOLISH

abrupt *adj* **1** being or characterized by direct, brief, and potentially rude speech or manner 〈the policeman's *abrupt* manner discouraged me from trying to claim that I hadn't seen the red light〉 — see BLUNT 1

2 having an incline approaching the perpendicular 〈the gentle, rolling hills gradually give way to high mountains with *abrupt* sides〉 — see STEEP 1

abruptly *adv* with great suddenness 〈the car in front stopped *abruptly*, and we almost hit it〉 — see SHORT

abscond *vb* to get free from a dangerous or confining situation 〈the burglar was trying to *abscond* with the jewels when he tumbled down the stairs〉 — see ESCAPE 1

absence *n* **1** a state of being without something necessary, desirable, or useful 〈the *absence* of volunteers to be troop leaders is putting the scouting program in real jeopardy〉 — see NEED 1

2 the fact or state of being absent 〈in the *absence* of ferry service to the island, they had to charter a plane〉 — see LACK 1

absent *adj* **1** not at a certain place 〈three students were *absent* because of the flu〉

synonyms away, missing, out

related words AWOL, truant; departed, gone, retired; abroad, vacationing

near antonyms accompanying, attending, participating

antonyms here, present

2 not present or in evidence 〈the usual stir of activity was *absent* in the city due to the report of an escaped lion from the zoo〉

synonyms lacking, missing, nonexistent, wanting

related words dead, departed, extinct, lost, perished, vanished; defunct, done, expired, finished, lapsed, obsolete, over, passé; inadequate, insufficient, rare, scarce, sparse, uncommon

near antonyms active, alive, animate, living, thriving; current, going, prevailing, uncanceled; common, prevalent; apparent, conspicuous, evident, obvious, plain

antonyms existent, present

3 lost in thought and unaware of one's surroundings or actions 〈seemed *absent* when I told him you were coming because he nodded but didn't say anything〉 — see ABSENTMINDED 1

absentminded *adj* **1** lost in thought and unaware of one's surroundings or actions 〈the grieving woman was so *absentminded* that she left her key in the lock after opening the door〉

synonyms absent, abstracted, preoccupied

related words absorbed, daydreaming, distracted, dreaming, dreamy, engrossed, faraway, intent, pensive, rapt; heedless, inattentive, insensible, oblivious, unaware, unconscious, unheeding, unknowing, unmindful, unobservant, unobserving, unperceiving, unperceptive, unseeing, unthinking, unwary, unwitting, vacant; befogged, befuddled, bemused, bewildered, confused, dazed, flighty, foggy, forgetful, forgetting, hazy, muddled, scatterbrained, unfocused

near antonyms alive, attentive, aware, conscious, heedful, mindful, observant, observing, open-eyed, sharp, vigilant, wary, watchful, wide-awake; clearheaded, unconfused

antonyms alert

2 inclined to forget what one has learned or to do what one should ⟨an *absentminded* aunt who some years sends me two birthday checks⟩ — see FORGETFUL

absolute *adj* **1** exercising power or authority without interference by others ⟨the *absolute* monarchy of Russia ended when Czar Nicholas II promised to share power with a legislative body⟩

synonyms autocratic, despotic, dictatorial, tyrannical (*also* tyrannic), tyrannous

related words authoritarian, totalitarian; arbitrary, high-handed, magisterial; domineering, imperious, masterful; all-powerful, almighty, omnipotent; autonomous, self-governing, sovereign; unconditional, unlimited

near antonyms circumscribed, restrained, restricted; constitutional, lawful

antonyms limited

2 having no exceptions or restrictions ⟨ironing is an *absolute* bore⟩ ⟨I want the *absolute* truth⟩

synonyms all-out, arrant, categorical (*also* categoric), complete, consummate, dead, downright, flat, out-and-out, outright, perfect, profound, pure, regular, sheer, simple, stark, thorough, thoroughgoing, total, unadulterated, unalloyed, unconditional, unequivocal, unmitigated, utter

related words authentic, classic, genuine, real, veritable; constant, endless, eternal, perpetual, undying, unremitting; extreme, rank, unrestricted; confirmed, habitual, hopeless, inveterate; deadly, extraordinary, frightful, horrible, huge, main, superlative, supreme, surpassing, terrible, terrific

near antonyms doubtful, dubious, equivocal, qualified, questionable, restricted, uncertain

3 being entirely without fault or flaw ⟨a room decorated with *absolute* taste⟩ — see PERFECT 1

4 free from added matter ⟨*absolute* alcohol⟩ — see PURE 1

5 serving to put an end to all debate or questioning ⟨*absolute* proof of her innocence⟩ — see CONCLUSIVE 1

absolution *n* release from the guilt or penalty of an offense ⟨the jury's verdict of "not guilty" was *absolution* in the eyes of the law, but the verdict would always be "guilty" in the court of public opinion⟩ — see PARDON

absolve *vb* to free from a charge of wrongdoing ⟨no amount of remorse will *absolve* shoplifters who are caught, and all cases will be prosecuted to the full extent of the law⟩ — see EXCULPATE

absorb *vb* **1** to take in (something liquid) through small openings ⟨most of the spilled water was *absorbed* by the tablecloth⟩

synonyms drink, imbibe, soak (up), sponge, suck (up)

related words gulp, guzzle, quaff, sip, slurp, swallow, swig, swill

2 to hold the attention of ⟨chatting on the phone doesn't *absorb* me so much that I can't do something else at the same time⟩ — see ENGAGE 1

absorbed *adj* having the mind fixed on something ⟨Lori was so *absorbed* in her book that she didn't hear the bell ring⟩ — see ATTENTIVE

absorbing *adj* holding the attention or provoking interest ⟨shell collecting can be so *absorbing* that you don't notice the tide coming in⟩ — see INTERESTING

absorption *n* a focusing of the mind on something ⟨forgot to return the phone call due to his *absorption* in setting up the new computer system⟩ — see ATTENTION 1

abstain (from) *vb* to resist the temptation of ⟨had to *abstain from* solid food before her surgery⟩ — see FORBEAR

abstract *adj* **1** dealing with or expressing a quality or idea ⟨the book deals with *abstract* matters such as honesty and integrity on the job as well as practical subjects such as asking for a raise⟩

synonyms conceptual, theoretical (*also* theoretic)

related words conjectural, hypothetical, speculative; intellectual, mental, spiritual; ethereal, immaterial, incorporeal, insubstantial, metaphysical, nonmaterial, nonphysical, unsubstantial; impalpable, imperceptible, insensible, intangible, invisible; impractical, romantic, transcendent, transcendental, unreal, utopian, visionary

near antonyms material, physical; appreciable, detectable, discernable, noticeable, observable, palpable, perceptible, sensible, substantial, tangible, visible; defined, definite, distinct; actual, factual, real

antonyms concrete

2 using elements of form (as color, line, or texture) with little or no attempt at creating a realistic picture ⟨Cubism is a style of *abstract* art in which natural forms are broken up into geometric shapes⟩

synonyms nonrealistic

related words impressionist, impressionistic; symbolist, symbolistic

near antonyms lifelike, natural

antonyms realistic, representational

abstract *n* a short statement of the main points ⟨the scientist wrote an *abstract* of his research and conclusions⟩ — see SUMMARY

abstract *vb* to make into a short statement of the main points (as of a report) ⟨took the 135-page report and *abstracted* it in three short paragraphs⟩ — see SUMMARIZE

abstracted *adj* lost in thought and unaware of one's surroundings or actions ⟨the man on the train seemed somewhat *abstracted*, and he did indeed forget to get off at his stop⟩ — see ABSENTMINDED 1

abstruse *adj* difficult for one of ordinary knowledge or intelligence to understand ⟨you're not the only one who finds Einstein's theory of relativity *abstruse*⟩ — see PROFOUND 1

absurd *adj* **1** conceived or made without regard for reason or reality ⟨*absurd* claims of having been abducted by UFO's⟩ — see FANTASTIC 1

2 showing or marked by a lack of good sense or judgment ⟨an *absurd* rule that bicycles are not allowed in the park⟩ — see FOOLISH 1

3 so foolish or pointless as to be worthy of scornful laughter ⟨it's *absurd* to expect an A if you haven't done any of the homework⟩ — see RIDICULOUS 1

absurdity *n* **1** a foolish act or idea ⟨to say men can't cook as well as women is of course an *absurdity*⟩ — see FOLLY 1

2 lack of good sense or judgment ⟨the *absurdity* of expecting a 98-year-old woman to babysit four six-year-olds⟩ — see FOOLISHNESS 1

abundance *n* **1** a considerable amount ⟨an *abundance* of flowers for the wedding⟩ ⟨grew up with an *abundance* of cousins⟩ — see LOT 2

2 an amount or supply more than sufficient to meet one's needs ⟨we have an *abundance* of food, so eat as much as you want⟩ — see PLENTY 1

abundant *adj* being more than enough without being excessive ⟨claimed that the needy were already receiving *abundant* help from both the government and charitable organizations⟩ — see PLENTIFUL

abuse *n* **1** harsh insulting language ⟨spectators hurled *abuse* at the visiting team⟩

synonyms fulmination, invective, vitriol, vituperation

related words blasphemy, curse, execration, imprecation, malediction, profanity; epithet, insult, put-down, slur; expletive, swearword; aspersion, bad-mouthing, belittlement, disparagement, revilement, vilification; castigation, chastisement, criticism, excoriation, opprobrium, rebuke, reprimand, reproof; broadside, diatribe, harangue, polemic, tirade

near antonyms acclaim, applause, commendation, praise; compliments, congratulations, endearments, felicitations; adulation, blarney, flattery, overpraise, soft soap

2 incorrect or improper use ⟨the furniture received a lot of *abuse* from the ten kids in the family⟩ — see MISUSE

abuse *vb* **1** to inflict physical or emotional harm upon ⟨if you *abuse* your pet, he will always have an ugly disposition⟩

synonyms ill-treat, ill-use, maltreat, manhandle, mishandle, mistreat, misuse

related words molest, outrage, violate; harass, harm, hurt, injure, oppress, persecute, torment, torture, victimize, wrong

near antonyms care (for), cherish, foster, nurture; baby, cater (to), coddle, favor, gratify, humor, indulge, mollycoddle, pamper, spoil

2 to criticize harshly and usually publicly ⟨a demanding, difficult patient who *abuses* the nurses and aides⟩ — see ATTACK 2

3 to put to a bad or improper use ⟨if you *abuse* your baseball bat by using it to hammer nails, don't expect it to last long⟩ — see MISAPPLY

4 to take unfair advantage of ⟨*abused* his parents' trust, pilfering small amounts from them that he hoped they wouldn't notice⟩ — see EXPLOIT 2

abut *vb* to be adjacent to ⟨our land *abuts* a nature preserve, so we see a lot of wildlife⟩ — see ADJOIN 1

abutting *adj* having a border in common ⟨erected fences between their property and the *abutting* properties⟩ — see ADJACENT

abysmal *adj* extending far downward or inward ⟨a cry echoing from the *abysmal* reaches of the cave⟩ — see DEEP 1

abyss *n* an immeasurable depth or space ⟨looking down at the dark ocean from the ship's rail, Malcolm felt as though he was staring into an *abyss*⟩

synonyms chasm, gulf

related words cleft, crevasse, crevice, fissure; cavern, hole, hollow, pit; breadth, expanse, extent, reach, spread, stretch; emptiness, nothingness, vacuity, vacuum, void

academic *adj* of or relating to schooling or learning especially at an advanced level ⟨"If you spent more time in *academic* pursuits and less time in social ones, you could easily make good grades," the dean told Valerie⟩

synonyms educational, scholarly, scholastic

related words bookish, pedantic, professorial; curricular; educative, instructive; collegiate, graduate, postgraduate

near antonyms extracurricular; noncollegiate

antonyms nonacademic, unacademic

academy *n* a place or establishment for teaching and learning ⟨a military *academy*⟩ ⟨an *academy* of the fine arts⟩ — see SCHOOL

accelerate *vb* to cause to move or proceed fast or faster ⟨we *accelerated* preparations for the hurricane when the weather reports said it had gained speed⟩ — see HURRY 1

accent *n* a special notice or importance given to something ⟨although we carried binoculars on our bird walk, the *accent* was on recognizing them by their song⟩ — see EMPHASIS 1

accent *vb* to indicate the importance of by giving prominent display ⟨the town's promotional literature *accents* its vital role in American history⟩ — see EMPHASIZE

accentuate *vb* to indicate the importance of by giving prominent display ⟨let's *accentuate* the saxophones during this piece by having the sax players stand up⟩ — see EMPHASIZE

accentuation *n* a special notice or importance given to something ⟨the school's *accentuation* on math skills has made our students among the highest math scorers in the state⟩ — see EMPHASIS 1

accept *vb* **1** to agree to receive whether willingly or reluctantly ⟨some merchants in town will *accept* Canadian coins⟩ — see TAKE 2

2 to have a favorable opinion of ⟨her husband feels that he has never been *accepted* by his wife's family⟩ — see APPROVE (OF)

3 to regard as right or true ⟨refused to *accept* that her friend had said those mean things⟩ — see BELIEVE 1

4 to take to or upon oneself ⟨*accepted* the responsibility of sending out the invitations⟩ — see ASSUME 1

acceptability *n* the quality or state of meeting one's needs adequately ⟨the *acceptability* of a broken key or two on the piano might depend on which keys are broken⟩ — see SUFFICIENCY

acceptable *adj* of a level of quality that meets one's needs or standards ⟨told the bike rental man that a bicycle with four broken gears was not *acceptable*⟩ — see ADEQUATE

acceptably *adv* in a satisfactory way ⟨the boys left the kitchen *acceptably* clean⟩ — see WELL 1

accepting *adj* showing or expressing acceptance or approval ⟨his parents are very *accepting* of his decision to join the military⟩ — see POSITIVE

access *n* the means or right of entering or participating in ⟨in the evening the only *access* to the building is through the side door⟩ — see ENTRANCE 1

access *vb* to go or come in or into ⟨could not *access* the bank vault because the lock was controlled by a timer⟩ — see ENTER 1

accessible *adj* **1** possible to get ⟨the phone line is not *accessible* without your personal identification number⟩ — see AVAILABLE 1

2 situated within easy reach ⟨with the elevator broken, the second floor is not *accessible* to people in wheelchairs⟩ — see CONVENIENT

accessory *adj* available to supply something extra when needed ⟨most phone services offer *accessory* features such as call-waiting⟩ — see AUXILIARY

accessory *n* **1** something that is not necessary in itself but adds to the convenience or performance of the main piece of equipment ⟨bought a new car with lots of high-tech *accessories*⟩
synonyms accoutrement (*or* accouterment), adjunct, appendage, attachment
related words accompaniment, additive, complement, supplement; auxiliary, subsidiary; amenity, extra, filler, frill, incidental, luxury, nonessential, nonnecessity; equipment, furnishings, paraphernalia, trappings; adornment, decoration, embellishment, enhancement, garnish, ornament, trim
near antonyms essential, necessity, requirement, requisite
2 one associated with another in wrongdoing ⟨two *accessories*, the driver of the getaway car and the dishonest bank teller, were charged in the robbery case⟩ — see ACCOMPLICE

accident *n* **1** a chance and usually sudden event bringing loss or injury ⟨was involved in an *accident* on her way home from work⟩
synonyms casualty, mischance, mishap
related words calamity, cataclysm, catastrophe, cropper, deathblow, disaster, tragedy; bummer, knock, misadventure, misfortune; collision, crack-up, crash, smashup, wreck
near antonyms boon, break, fluke, godsend, miracle, strike, windfall; fortune, luck, serendipity
2 the uncertain course of events ⟨you shouldn't leave it to *accident* to decide where you'll be lodging in the course of your trip across the country⟩ — see CHANCE 1

accidental *adj* happening by chance ⟨finding the gold was all the more remarkable because its discovery was entirely *accidental*⟩
synonyms casual, chance, fluky, fortuitous, inadvertent, incidental, unintended, unintentional, unplanned, unpremeditated, unwitting
related words coincidental; freak, odd; aimless, arbitrary, desultory, haphazard, random; uncertain, unexpected, unforeseeable, unforeseen; coerced, forced, involuntary; unconscious, unexpected, unprompted
near antonyms certain, destined, expected, fixed, foreordained, foreseeable, foreseen, inevitable, predestined, predetermined, predictable, preordained, prescribed, sure; conscious, freewill, knowing, unforced, voluntary, volunteer, willful (*or* wilful)
antonyms deliberate, intended, intentional, planned, premeditated

acclaim *n* public acknowledgment or admiration for an achievement ⟨many people were involved in the search, but the person who actually found the missing girl got all the *acclaim*⟩ — see GLORY 1

acclaim *vb* to declare enthusiastic approval of ⟨she was *acclaimed* by the critics for her realistic acting⟩
synonyms applaud, cheer, crack up, hail, laud, praise, salute, tout
related words ballyhoo; approve, commend, endorse (*also* indorse), favor, recommend, support; celebrate, emblazon, eulogize, extol (*also* extoll), glorify, sing; adulate, flatter, overpraise; deify, idolize
near antonyms belittle, disparage, put down; blame, censure, reprehend, reprobate; admonish, chide, criticize, rebuke, reprimand, reproach, reprove; castigate, excoriate, lambaste
antonyms knock, pan, slam

acclamation *n* enthusiastic and usually public expression of approval ⟨the young piano prodigy has received *ac-*

clamation from audiences worldwide⟩ — see APPLAUSE

acclimate *vb* to change (something) so as to make it suitable for a new use or situation ⟨never could *acclimate* himself to a nine-to-five office job⟩ — see ADAPT

acclimatize *vb* to change (something) so as to make it suitable for a new use or situation ⟨had lived several years in the north before she fully *acclimatized* her wardrobe⟩ — see ADAPT

accolade *n* **1** a formal expression of praise ⟨for their bravery the firefighters received *accolades* from both local and national officials⟩ — see ENCOMIUM
2 public acknowledgment or admiration for an achievement ⟨winning the Nobel Prize for Physics is generally regarded as the highest *accolade* for a physicist⟩ — see GLORY 1

accommodate *vb* **1** to make or have room for ⟨the back seat *accommodates* three people comfortably⟩
synonyms fit, hold, take
related words carry, contain, seat; enclose (*also* inclose), encompass; harbor, house
2 to bring to a state free of conflicts, inconsistencies, or differences ⟨*accommodate* the difference in their voices by moving the mike closer to Sarah, whose voice is softer⟩ — see HARMONIZE 2
3 to change (something) so as to make it suitable for a new use or situation ⟨*accommodated* the lectern to the height of the guest speaker, who turned out to be quite short⟩ — see ADAPT
4 to do a service or favor for ⟨couldn't *accommodate* everyone who wanted a free T-shirt⟩ — see OBLIGE 1
5 to provide with living quarters or shelter ⟨regards the tent as entirely inadequate for *accommodating* them through the winter⟩ — see HOUSE 1

accommodation *n* the act or practice of each side giving up something in order to reach an agreement ⟨the twins each made an *accommodation*: Jane agreed to Joan's pink curtains and Joan agreed to Jane's purple rug⟩ — see CONCESSION 1

accompaniment *n* something that is found along with something else ⟨the sound of crickets was the perfect *accompaniment* to our summer evenings on the porch⟩
synonyms companion, concomitant
related words accessory, adjunct, appendage; complement, supplement; counterpart, fellow, mate; consequence, corollary, follow-up; fixings, trimmings

accompany *vb* to go along with in order to provide assistance, protection, or companionship ⟨children must be *accompanied* by a parent at all times⟩
synonyms attend, chaperone (*or* chaperon), convoy, escort, squire
related words associate, consort, pal (around), team (up); defend, guard, protect; bring, conduct, guide, lead, pilot, see, steer, usher; follow, shadow, tag, tag along, tail; hang (around), hover (over)
near antonyms abandon, desert, ditch, dump, forsake

accompanying *adj* present at the same time and place ⟨doesn't mind if I play video games, but without the *accompanying* sound effects⟩ — see COINCIDENT

accomplice *n* one associated with another in wrongdoing ⟨the thief and his *accomplices* were eventually caught and brought to justice⟩
synonyms abettor (*also* abetter), accessory, cohort, confederate
related words collaborator, collaborationist, informant, informer; companion, comrade, crony, henchman, partner; conspirator, plotter, traitor; gangster, mobster, racketeer

accomplish *vb* to carry through (as a process) to completion ⟨you've *accomplished* your assigned task with your usual efficiency and good grace⟩ — see PERFORM 1

accomplished *adj* having or showing exceptional knowledge, experience, or skill in a field of endeavor ⟨an *accomplished* performance of a difficult violin concerto⟩ ⟨a delicate eye operation that only the most *accomplished* surgeon would attempt⟩ — see PROFICIENT

accomplishment *n* **1** a successful result brought about by hard work ⟨Jared's biggest *accomplishment* this week was finishing his art project⟩

synonyms achievement, attainment, coup, success, triumph

related words blockbuster, hit, jackpot, megahit, smash, winner; conquest, gain, victory, win; acquirement, skill; deed, feat, performance; completion, consummation, culmination, execution, fruition, fulfillment, implementation, realization

phrases a feather in one's cap

near antonyms botch, mess, muddle, shambles; bummer, bust, catastrophe, debacle (*also* débâcle), dud, failure, fiasco, fizzle, flop, washout; disappointment, letdown, loss, setback

2 the doing of an action ⟨your prompt *accomplishment* of this urgent project is much appreciated⟩ — see COMMISSION 2

3 the state of being actual or complete ⟨a long, difficult project whose *accomplishment* we wondered if we would ever see⟩ — see FRUITION

accord *n* **1** a formal agreement between two or more nations or peoples ⟨hoped to bring about a peace *accord* between the warring nations⟩ — see TREATY

2 a state of consistency ⟨the map doesn't seem to be in *accord* with the current layout of the streets⟩ — see CONFORMITY 1

3 an arrangement about action to be taken ⟨the judges have reached an *accord*: the match will have to be replayed⟩ — see AGREEMENT 2

4 the act or fact of being of one opinion about something ⟨is everyone in *accord* about where to go for lunch?⟩ — see AGREEMENT 1

5 the act or power of making one's own choices or decisions ⟨did not move to a different classroom of her own *accord*⟩ — see FREE WILL

accord *vb* **1** to be in agreement on every point ⟨claims that the newspaper's quote does not *accord* with what he actually said⟩ — see CHECK 1

2 to give the ownership or benefit of (something) formally or publicly ⟨women were finally *accorded* the right to vote in 1920⟩ — see CONFER 1

accordance *n* a state of consistency ⟨make sure the fundraiser is in *accordance* with the school rules⟩ — see CONFORMITY 1

accordingly *adv* for this or that reason ⟨the application deadline was yesterday; *accordingly*, only applications mailed before midnight can be considered⟩ — see THEREFORE

account *n* **1** a relating of events usually in the order in which they happened ⟨newspaper reporters must strive to provide an accurate *account* of what happened⟩

synonyms chronicle, history, narrative, record, report, story

related words version; deposition, documentation, testament, testimonial, testimony, witness; annals, diary, journal, log, logbook, memoir; anecdote, tale, yarn; epic, saga; recital, recitation

2 a record of goods sold or services performed together with the costs due ⟨please add this meal to my restaurant *account*⟩ — see ¹BILL 1

3 a sum of money set aside for a particular purpose ⟨after paying the tuition, there was still money left for books in her special *account* for college expenses⟩ — see FUND 1

4 the capacity for being useful for some purpose ⟨all the planning came to no *account* when the event was cancelled⟩ — see USE 2

5 the relative usefulness or importance of something as judged by specific qualities ⟨the position of publicity agent for a star is of considerable *account* in Hollywood⟩ — see WORTH 1

account *vb* to think of in a particular way ⟨*account* themselves lucky to be alive⟩ — see CONSIDER 1

account (for) *vb* to give the reason for or cause of ⟨could not *account for* the huge difference in price between the two practically identical handbags⟩ — see EXPLAIN 2

accountable *adj* being the one who must meet an obligation or suffer the consequences for failing to do so ⟨the owner was held *accountable* for his dog's biting of the child⟩ — see RESPONSIBLE 1

accoutre *or* **accouter** *vb* to provide (someone) with what is needed for a task or activity ⟨hikers *accoutred* with walking sticks, water bottles, trail maps, and compasses⟩ — see FURNISH 1

accoutrement *or* **accouterment** *n* **1** something that is not necessary in itself but adds to the convenience or performance of the main piece of equipment ⟨this vacuum cleaner has all of the *accoutrements* for cleaning furniture as well as floors⟩ — see ACCESSORY 1

2 accoutrements *or* **accouterments** *pl* items needed for the performance of a task or activity ⟨has all the *accoutrements* that the home pastry chef could ever want⟩ — see EQUIPMENT

accredit *vb* **1** to explain (something) as being the result of something else ⟨*accredits* his good choice of movies to reading a reviewer who seldom steers him wrong⟩ — see CREDIT 1

2 to give official or legal power to ⟨took a course that *accredited* her to teach first aid⟩ — see AUTHORIZE 1

accreditation *n* the granting of power to perform various acts or duties ⟨the only body empowered with the *accreditation* of medical schools in the state⟩ — see COMMISSION 1

accretion *n* something added (as by growth) ⟨*accretions* of lime have thickened the cave's stalactites and stalagmites over the centuries⟩ — see INCREASE 1

accrual *n* something added (as by growth) ⟨had an *accrual* of $100 through interest in my savings account last year⟩ — see INCREASE 1

accumulate *vb* **1** to become greater in extent, volume, amount, or number ⟨the number of complaints about that mail order firm is really *accumulating*⟩ — see INCREASE 2

2 to bring together in one body or place ⟨finally *accumulated* enough donated books to hold a book sale⟩ — see GATHER 1

3 to gradually form into a layer, pile, or mass ⟨clouds *accumulating* on the western horizon⟩ — see COLLECT 2

accumulating *n* the act or process of becoming greater in number ⟨the *accumulating* of newspapers in the basement over the years is really getting out of hand⟩ — see MULTIPLICATION

accumulation *n* **1** a mass or quantity that has piled up or that has been gathered ⟨a vast *accumulation* of evidence about the dangers of smoking⟩
  synonyms assemblage, collection, gathering
  related words agglomerate, assortment, conglomerate, conglomeration, hodgepodge, hotchpotch, jumble, medley, mélange, mishmash, mix, mixture, motley, potpourri; agglomeration, clutter, hash, heap, litter, mass, pile; aggregate, aggregation, sum, totality; cache, fund, hoard, inventory, nest egg, reserve, stock, stockpile, store, supply
  2 the act or process of becoming greater in number ⟨the *accumulation* of leaves on the ground is proceeding at a much faster rate than my raking⟩ — see MULTIPLICATION

accuracy *n* the quality or state of being very accurate ⟨obviously, with brain surgery the *accuracy* of the incision is incredibly important⟩ — see PRECISION

accurate *adj* **1** being in agreement with the truth or a fact or a standard ⟨an *accurate* count of the number of people coming to the wedding reception⟩ — see CORRECT 1
  2 following an original exactly ⟨an *accurate* translation of the original story⟩ — see FAITHFUL 2
  3 meeting the highest standard of accuracy ⟨an *accurate* thermometer⟩ ⟨*accurate* measurements⟩ — see PRECISE 1

accuse *vb* to make a claim of wrongdoing against ⟨she was *accused* of cheating on the test⟩
  synonyms charge, impeach, incriminate, indict
  related words blame, castigate, censure, condemn, criticize, damn, denounce, fault, impugn, reproach, reprobate; chide, rebuke, reprove, tax; arraign, book, cite, summon; prosecute, sue, try; frame, implicate, inform (against), report; recriminate, retaliate
  near antonyms advocate, champion, defend; excuse, forgive, justify, pardon, remit, shrive
  antonyms absolve, acquit, clear, exculpate, exonerate, vindicate

accustomed *adj* being in the habit or custom ⟨Josh felt uncomfortably full, as he was not *accustomed* to eating so much⟩
  synonyms given, habituated, used, wont
  related words apt, inclined, liable, prone; hardened, inured; experienced, practiced (*or* practised), seasoned, veteran; addicted, hooked
  near antonyms averse, disinclined, opposed; inexperienced, new, unseasoned
  antonyms unaccustomed, unused

ace *adj* having or showing exceptional knowledge, experience, or skill in a field of endeavor ⟨an *ace* computer programmer⟩ — see PROFICIENT 1

ace *n* **1** a person with a high level of knowledge or skill in a field ⟨took a few lessons with a tennis *ace* to improve his backhand⟩ — see EXPERT
  2 a very small amount ⟨not an *ace* of truth in what she said⟩ — see PARTICLE 1
  3 a very small distance or degree ⟨came within an *ace* of being chosen for the part⟩ — see HAIR 1

ache *n* a sharp unpleasant sensation usually felt in some specific part of the body ⟨a dull pounding *ache* in his head⟩ — see PAIN 1

ache *vb* to feel or cause physical pain ⟨my feet *ache* from all that walking⟩ — see HURT 1

ache (for) *vb* to have an earnest wish to own or enjoy ⟨*aching for* some quiet time to his own⟩ — see DESIRE

achievable *adj* capable of being done or carried out ⟨I think that a B in math is an *achievable* goal⟩ — see POSSIBLE 1

achieve *vb* **1** to obtain (as a goal) through effort ⟨finally *achieved* stardom⟩
  synonyms attain, hit, make, score, win
  related words acquire, capture, carry, draw, garner, get, land, make, obtain, procure, realize, secure; amount (to), approach, equal, match, measure up (to), meet, rival, tie, touch; beat, excel, outdo, surpass, top
  near antonyms fall short (of); fail (at); lose
  2 to carry through (as a process) to completion ⟨finally *achieved* his purpose, which was to form a first-class boys' choir made up of inner-city kids⟩ — see PERFORM 1

achievement *n* **1** a successful result brought about by hard work ⟨this improvement in your reading score is quite an *achievement!*⟩ — see ACCOMPLISHMENT 1
  2 the doing of an action ⟨what you're asking is the *achievement* of a miracle⟩ — see COMMISSION 2
  3 the state of being actual or complete ⟨you should be proud of the *achievement* of your goals⟩ — see FRUITION

aching *adj* causing or feeling bodily pain ⟨my poor, *aching* back⟩ — see PAINFUL 1

acid *adj* causing or characterized by the one of the four basic taste sensations that is produced chiefly by acids ⟨an *acid*-tasting medicine⟩ — see SOUR 1

acidic *adj* causing or characterized by the one of the four basic taste sensations that is produced chiefly by acids ⟨the *acidic* flavor of lemon goes nicely with broiled fish⟩ — see SOUR 1

acidity *n* **1** a harsh or sharp quality ⟨detected a certain *acidity* in the way he responded⟩ — see EDGE 1
  2 biting sharpness of feeling or expression ⟨the *acidity* of their relationship was well known to their mutual acquaintances⟩ — see ACRIMONY 1

acidness *n* biting sharpness of feeling or expression ⟨the *acidness* in his remarks hurt her to the core⟩ — see ACRIMONY 1

acknowledge *vb* to accept the truth or existence of (something) usually reluctantly ⟨finally had to *acknowledge* that she'd outgrown her favorite jacket⟩ — see ADMIT

acknowledgment *also* **acknowledgement** *n* **1** a formal recognition of an achievement or praiseworthy deed ⟨an *acknowledgment* to the food committee for the delicious refreshments⟩ — see COMMENDATION 1
  2 an open declaration of something (as a fault or the commission of an offense) about oneself ⟨a surprising *acknowledgment* that he had been faking sickness to stay home⟩ — see CONFESSION

acme *n* the highest part or point ⟨the *acme* of their basketball season was their hard-won victory over last year's state champs⟩ — see HEIGHT 1

acoustic *or* **acoustical** *adj* of, relating to, or experienced through the sense of hearing ⟨is a bird's *acoustic* organ similar to a human's?⟩ — see AUDITORY

acquaint *vb* **1** to impart knowledge of a new thing or situation to ⟨Mr. King spent the first week of class *acquainting* everyone with the new computers⟩
  synonyms familiarize, initiate, introduce, orient, orientate
  related words apprise, brief, clue (in), fill in, inform; educate, enlighten, ground, instruct, school, train; expose, present, subject; advise, tell, tip off, warn, wise up

2 to give information to ⟨his sailor friend *acquainted* him with the latest navigational aids for weekend yachtsmen⟩ — see ENLIGHTEN 1

3 to make (one person) known (to another) socially ⟨hoping that someone would *acquaint* them with the new neighbors⟩ — see INTRODUCE 1

acquaintance *n* knowledge gained by personal experience ⟨Tiffany's *acquaintance* with cows is limited to a visit to a petting zoo when she was three⟩
synonyms cognizance, familiarity
related words association, experience, exposure, intimacy, involvement; initiation, introduction; awareness, comprehension, conception, inkling, notion, understanding; education, enlightenment, grounding, information, instruction, learning, schooling, training
near antonyms callowness, greenness, ignorance, inexperience
antonyms unfamiliarity

acquainted *adj* having information especially as a result of study or experience ⟨would like to see students become *acquainted* with all the library services⟩ — see FAMILIAR 2

acquiescent *adj* receiving or enduring without offering resistance ⟨was not as *acquiescent* about sharing her room as her parents seemed to think she should be⟩ — see PASSIVE

acquirable *adj* possible to get ⟨is a decent bagel *acquirable* in this town?⟩ — see AVAILABLE 1

acquire *vb* **1** to come to have gradually ⟨from years of working two jobs, he has *acquired* the ability to get by on only a few hours of sleep a day⟩ — see DEVELOP 2

2 to receive as return for effort ⟨*acquired* a reputation for always arriving at his friends' house just as they were sitting down to dinner⟩ — see EARN 1

acquisitive *adj* having or marked by an eager and often selfish desire especially for material possessions ⟨*acquisitive* developers are trying to tear down the historic home and build a shopping mall⟩ — see GREEDY 1

acquisitiveness *n* an intense selfish desire for wealth or possessions ⟨the queen's *acquisitiveness* would not be satisfied until she owned the largest diamond in the world⟩ — see GREED

acquit *vb* **1** to free from a charge of wrongdoing ⟨*acquitted* of the robbery charge after proving he was nowhere near the scene of the crime⟩ — see EXCULPATE

2 to manage the actions of (oneself) in a particular way ⟨the king promised a handsome reward to those who *acquitted* themselves well in the battle⟩ — see BEHAVE

acrid *adj* **1** having or showing deep-seated resentment ⟨there have been *acrid* relations between the two families ever since they fought over that strip of land⟩ — see BITTER 1

2 marked by the use of wit that is intended to cause hurt feelings ⟨Phillipa's *acrid* comments about the new girl's clothes were met by laughter from everyone at the table⟩ — see SARCASTIC

acridness *n* **1** a harsh or sharp quality ⟨an *acridness* in her voice when she said she hoped that we would get what we deserve⟩ — see EDGE 1

2 biting sharpness of feeling or expression ⟨over the years the *acridness* he felt toward his stepfather softened somewhat⟩ — see ACRIMONY 1

acrimonious *adj* having or showing deep-seated resentment ⟨an *acrimonious* parting between the two former friends⟩ — see BITTER 1

acrimoniousness *n* a harsh or sharp quality ⟨*acrimoniousness* showed through his words, which on their face seemed harmless enough⟩ — see EDGE 1

acrimony *n* **1** biting sharpness of feeling or expression ⟨she responded with such *acrimony* that he never brought the subject up again⟩
synonyms acidity, acidness, acridness, asperity, bitterness, cattiness, tartness, virulence, vitriol
related words gruffness, harshness, hostility, relentlessness, severity, sternness, vehemence; coldness, crossness, discourteousness, iciness, impoliteness, incivility, nastiness, rudeness, sourness, surliness, ungraciousness; anger, animosity, bile, jaundice, malevolence, malice, rancor, scorn, spite, spleen, venom; jealousy, pique, resentment
near antonyms civility, cordiality, courtesy, diplomacy, geniality, graciousness, politeness, tactfulness; compassion, softness, sweetness, sympathy, tenderness, warmth; oiliness, smoothness, suaveness, unctuousness, urbanity

2 a harsh or sharp quality ⟨the *acrimony* of his parting words shocked everyone⟩ — see EDGE 1

across *adv* from one side to the other of an intervening space ⟨will you go *across* to the Bentleys and see if their phone is working?⟩ — see OVER 1

across *prep* to the opposite side of ⟨we swam *across* the lake and visited the other summer camp⟩
synonyms athwart, over, through
related words around, round; beyond, past

act *n* **1** a display of emotion or behavior that is insincere or intended to deceive ⟨was putting on an *act* when she said she didn't mind being left out of the outing⟩ — see MASQUERADE

2 a rule of conduct or action laid down by a governing authority and especially a legislator ⟨the Americans with Disabilities *Act* requires public buildings to have wheelchair access⟩ — see LAW 1

3 something done by someone ⟨it's *acts* such as this—locking your little brother outside—that make me feel I can't trust you⟩ — see ACTION 1

act *vb* **1** to present a portrayal or performance of ⟨a very talented student *acted* the part of Tiny Tim in our production of *A Christmas Carol*⟩
synonyms impersonate, perform, play, portray
related words depict, dramatize, enact, pantomime, render, represent, role-play, take on; overact, underplay; ape, clown, ham, imitate, masquerade, mime, mimic, pose (as); star (in)

2 to produce a desired effect ⟨the painkiller *acted* quickly⟩
synonyms operate, perform, take, work
related words behave, react, respond; affect, influence, sway; pan out, redound, result
phrases take effect
near antonyms backfire; fizzle

3 to give the impression of being ⟨always *acting* helpless, just to get attention⟩ — see SEEM

4 to have a certain purpose ⟨the tail feathers of woodpeckers *act* as props while the birds excavate tree trunks for insects⟩ — see FUNCTION

act (toward) *vb* to behave toward in a stated way ⟨I would never *act toward* my teacher that way⟩ — see TREAT 1

action *n* **1** something done by someone ⟨judge people by their *actions*, not by their words⟩
synonyms act, deed, doing, exploit, feat, thing
related words accomplishment, achievement, attainment; adventure, experience; enterprise, initiative, undertaking; handiwork, performance, work; stunt, trick; activity, dealing; maneuver, measure, move, operation, procedure, proceeding, step, tactic

2 a court case for enforcing a right or claim ⟨filed an *action* in county court to recover his lawnmower from his neighbor, who claims he "gave" it to her⟩ — see LAWSUIT

3 active fighting during the course of a war ⟨the battalion saw *action* soon after it arrived in France⟩ — see COMBAT 1

4 actions *pl* the way or manner in which one conducts oneself ⟨observing the *actions* of mice in various controlled settings helps scientists understand the effects of certain drugs⟩ — see BEHAVIOR

activate *vb* to cause to function ⟨the thermostat is set to *activate* the heating system only when the temperature drops below 65 degrees⟩

synonyms actuate, crank (up), drive, move, propel, run, set off, spark, start, touch off, trigger, turn on

related words charge, electrify, energize, fire, fuel, generate, power, push; discharge, launch, release, switch, trip; reactivate, recharge; arouse, excite, stimulate, vitalize; incite, instigate, provoke, quicken, stir up; accelerate, catalyze, speed up, step up

near antonyms arrest, brake, chock, cut off, draw up, halt, jam, stall, stick, stop; decelerate, repress, slow, stunt, suppress

antonyms cut, deactivate, kill, shut off, turn off

active *adj* **1** being in effective operation ⟨the abandoned factory had not been *active* for years⟩

synonyms alive, functional, functioning, going, living, on, operating, operational, operative, running, working

related words effective, effectual; employable, operable, usable, viable, workable; performing, producing, productive, serving, useful, yielding; astir, bustling, busy, dynamic, flourishing, humming, roaring, thriving

phrases in commission

near antonyms deactivated, decommissioned; ineffective, ineffectual, useless; inoperable, unusable, unworkable; arrested, asleep, dormant, fallow, idle, inert, latent, lifeless, nonproductive, quiescent, sleepy, stagnating, unproductive, vegetating

antonyms broken, dead, inactive, inoperative, nonfunctional, nonfunctioning, nonoperating

2 having much high-spirited energy and movement ⟨the fish are *active* today, but we still haven't caught anything⟩ — see LIVELY 1

3 involved in often constant activity ⟨all morning the crowd at the coffeehouse kept Marion and her helper pretty *active*⟩ — see BUSY 1

activity *n* energetic movement of the body for the sake of physical fitness ⟨had to restrict his *activity* after the surgery, which meant letting the weeds take over the garden⟩ — see EXERCISE 1

actor *n* one who acts professionally (as in a play, movie, or television show) ⟨my sister went to drama school to become an *actor*⟩

synonyms impersonator, mummer, player, trouper

related words barnstormer, entertainer, performer; actress, starlet; lead, leading lady, leading man, star; monologuist (*or* monologist); prima donna, scenestealer, understudy; comedian, tragedian; ape, aper, ham, imitator, impressionist, masquerader, mime, mimic, pantomime, pantomimist, poser; buffoon, clown, harlequin, stooge, zany

actual *adj* existing in fact and not merely as a possibility ⟨the *actual* outcome of the election was quite different from what everybody expected⟩

synonyms concrete, existent, factual, real, true, very

related words attested, authenticated, confirmed, demonstrated, established, proven, substantiated, vali-

dated, verified; incontestable, incontrovertible, indisputable, indubitable, inescapable, irrefutable, undeniable, unquestionable; believable, convincing, literal, realistic, unmistakable, verifiable; authentic, bona fide, genuine, real-life; absolute, certain, final, hard, palpable, positive, substantial, tangible; authoritative, certifiable, certified

near antonyms alleged, assumed, reputed, supposed; conceived, envisaged, imagined, pictured, visualized; chimerical, fabled, fanciful, fictional, fictitious, legendary, illusory; fabricated, fake, imaginary, invented, made-up, make-believe, pretend, romantic; abstract, unreal

antonyms conjectural, hypothetical, ideal, nonexistent, possible, potential, theoretical (*also* theoretic)

actuality *n* **1** the fact of being or of being real ⟨the *actuality* of the Abominable Snowman is not taken seriously by scientists⟩ — see EXISTENCE

2 the quality of being actual ⟨the *actuality* of equal opportunity depends on more than just having laws that supposedly ensure it⟩ — see FACT 1

3 the state of being actual or complete ⟨the *actuality* of a manned flight to the moon would never have been believed a hundred years ago⟩ — see FRUITION

actually *adv* **1** to tell the truth ⟨*actually*, I'd rather spend the evening at home⟩

synonyms forsooth, frankly, honestly, really, truly, truthfully, verily

related words absolutely, certainly, indisputably, indubitably, positively, realistically, undoubtedly, unquestionably, veritably

phrases in point of fact, in reality, in truth

2 in actual fact ⟨I call her Aunt Emily, but she is *actually* my cousin, not my aunt⟩ — see VERY 2

actuate *vb* **1** to cause to function ⟨a light *actuated* by a motion detector⟩ ⟨the alarm system *actuates* the door locks⟩ — see ACTIVATE

2 to set or keep in motion ⟨hearing depends on sound vibrations that *actuate* the complex mechanism of that sensory organ, the ear⟩ — see MOVE 2

act up *vb* **1** to behave badly ⟨two-year-old Jennifer was *acting up* in church, so her dad had to take her outside⟩ — see MISBEHAVE

2 to engage in attention-getting playful or boisterous behavior ⟨you should have seen the boys *acting up* when they put on their aprons⟩ — see CUT UP

acute *adj* **1** able to sense slight impressions or differences ⟨dogs, with their *acute* sense of smell, are used for finding toxic substances undetectable by humans⟩

synonyms delicate, keen, perceptive, sensitive, sharp

related words accurate, clear, discerning, fine, good, piercing, precise, quick, receptive, sensible, subtle; hypersensitive, oversensitive, supersensitive

near antonyms bad, deadened, dimmed, dull, dulled, fading; dead, imperceptive, insensible, insensitive, numb; imprecise, inaccurate

2 needing immediate attention ⟨famine caused by an *acute* shortage of grain⟩

synonyms critical, crying, dire, imperative, imperious, instant, pressing, urgent

related words compelling, demanding, extreme, immediate, insistent, intense, overriding; crucial, desperate, grave, life-and-death, serious, severe, vital; dangerous, explosive, hazardous, perilous, precarious, unstable

near antonyms incidental, low-pressure, minor, negligible, trivial, unimportant; nonthreatening, safe, stable

antonyms noncritical, nonurgent

3 causing intense mental or physical distress ⟨the *acute* pain in his side was quickly diagnosed as appendicitis⟩ — see SHARP 2

4 having a high musical pitch or range ⟨the *acute* sound of a siren⟩ — see SHRILL

acuteness *n* a harsh or sharp quality ⟨judging by the *acuteness* in his tone when he congratulated me, I think he was actually quite resentful that I won⟩ — see EDGE 1

ad *n* a published statement informing the public of a matter of general interest ⟨did you see the *ads* in the paper for cheap round-trip flights to Florida?⟩ — see ANNOUNCEMENT

adage *n* an often stated observation regarding something from common experience ⟨that old *adage*, "the early bird gets the worm"⟩ — see SAYING

adamant *adj* sticking to an opinion, purpose, or course of action in spite of reason, arguments, or persuasion ⟨remained *adamant* about getting the actor's autograph even after he had disappeared backstage⟩ — see OBSTINATE

adamantine *adj* sticking to an opinion, purpose, or course of action in spite of reason, arguments, or persuasion ⟨the *adamantine* opposition of his parents to his marriage to a girl from a poor family⟩ — see OBSTINATE

adapt *vb* to change (something) so as to make it suitable for a new use or situation ⟨it always takes freshmen a little while to *adapt* themselves to high school⟩

synonyms acclimate, acclimatize, accommodate, adjust, condition, conform, fit, shape

related words readapt, readjust; customize, tailor; attune, harmonize, reconcile, suit, tune; establish, root, settle; acquaint, familiarize, orient, orientate; equip, prepare, prime, rehearse; harden, inure, season, toughen; alter, convert, make over, modify, redo, refashion, refit, remake, remodel, revamp, revise, rework, transform

adaptable *adj* **1** able to do many different kinds of things ⟨an activities director who's *adaptable* to any kind of situation⟩ — see VERSATILE

2 capable of being readily changed ⟨the caterer's menu is *adaptable* to specific dietary needs, such as vegan, kosher, or low-fat⟩ — see FLEXIBLE 1

add *vb* **1** to join (something) to a mass, quantity, or number so as to bring about an overall increase ⟨the band recently *added* a saxophonist and a keyboard player to its ranks⟩ ⟨*add* another cup of flour to the mixture⟩

synonyms adjoin, annex, append, tack (on)

related words affix, attach, fasten, fix, graft, hitch, tie; infuse, inject, insert, introduce

near antonyms detach, disconnect, disjoin, separate, unfasten; amputate, cut, excise, lop off, sever

antonyms deduct, remove, subtract, take

2 to combine (numbers) into a single sum ⟨when she *added* all the phone charges she discovered an error in her bill⟩

synonyms foot (up), sum, total

related words calculate, cast, cipher, compute, figure, reckon, tally; count, enumerate, number

add (to) *vb* to make greater in size, amount, or number ⟨the need to be back home before 5:00 p.m. *adds to* the difficulty of arranging the trip⟩ — see INCREASE 1

added *adj* resulting in an increase in amount or number ⟨ever since his mother got sick, he's had the *added* responsibility of getting his little sister ready for school⟩ — see ADDITIONAL

addendum *n* something added (as by growth) ⟨an *addendum* at the end of the online news article that was essentially an update on the story⟩ — see INCREASE 1

addict *n* **1** a person who regularly uses drugs especially illegally ⟨an inspiring story about *addicts* who seek help and manage to kick their habit⟩ — see DOPER

2 a person with a strong and habitual liking for something ⟨all his friends are science-fiction *addicts*⟩ — see FAN

addition *n* **1** a smaller structure added to a main building ⟨a new *addition* to the library providing space for an expanded video collection⟩ — see ANNEX

2 something added (as by growth) ⟨the cache of old stamps I found in the discarded desk was a huge *addition* to my stamp collection⟩ — see INCREASE 1

3 the act or process of becoming greater in number ⟨how do you account for the *addition* of more paint stains on your shirt after you put on a smock?⟩ — see MULTIPLICATION

additional *adj* resulting in an increase in amount or number ⟨there turned out to be *additional* reasons for her absence besides those she had given⟩

synonyms added, another, else, farther, further, more, other

related words accessory, collateral, extraneous, side, supplemental, supplementary; fresh, new; extra, plus, spare, surplus

near antonyms fewer, less

additionally *adv* in addition to what has been said and ⟨the diet recommends fruit juice for breakfast and, *additionally*, fresh fruit once a day⟩ — see MORE 1

additive *adj* produced by a series of additions of identical or similar things ⟨certain drugs have *additive* effects when taken in conjunction with each other that one doesn't see when any one is used alone⟩ — see CUMULATIVE

addle *vb* to throw into a state of mental uncertainty ⟨after slipping on the ice, Bethany was so *addled* that she left her books where they'd fallen⟩ — see CONFUSE 1

addled *adj* having undergone organic breakdown ⟨*addled* eggs found on a long abandoned hen's nest⟩ — see ROTTEN 1

address *n* a usually formal discourse delivered to an audience ⟨George Washington's Farewell *Address*⟩ ⟨a papal *address*⟩ — see SPEECH 1

address *vb* to occupy (oneself) diligently or with close attention ⟨please *address* yourself to what I'm saying and not to what the boys are doing in the hall⟩ — see APPLY 2

adduce *vb* to give as an example ⟨in support of a 12-month school year, the committee *adduced* data from other school districts⟩ — see QUOTE 1

add up (to) *vb* **1** to be the same in meaning or effect ⟨whether we take the 4:00 train or the 4:15 bus, it *adds up to* the same thing: they both get us back too late⟩ — see AMOUNT (TO) 2

2 to have a total of ⟨even if we pool all our money, it won't *add up to* enough for a medium pizza⟩ — see AMOUNT (TO) 1

adept *adj* having or showing exceptional knowledge, experience, or skill in a field of endeavor ⟨he's an *adept* pitcher, and the team is lucky to have him⟩ — see PROFICIENT

adept *n* a person with a high level of knowledge or skill in a field ⟨if you want to know which works are the classics of science fiction, Jason and his friends are the *adepts*⟩ — see EXPERT

adeptly *adv* in a skillful or expert manner ⟨*adeptly* sank the ball in the basket with a hook shot⟩ — see WELL 3

adeptness *n* subtle or imaginative ability in inventing, devising, or executing something ⟨his *adeptness* at thinking on his feet makes him a fantastic debater⟩ — see SKILL 1

adequacy *n* the quality or state of meeting one's needs adequately ⟨the fire department sent someone to determine the *adequacy* of the school's evacuation plan⟩ — see SUFFICIENCY

adequate *adj* of a level of quality that meets one's needs or standards ⟨this old computer is probably *adequate* if you just want to type a book report⟩

synonyms acceptable, all right, decent, fine, OK (*or* okay), passable, respectable, satisfactory, tolerable

related words agreeable, bearable, endurable, sufferable; average, fair, mediocre, middling, minimal, unexceptional; appropriate, correct, due, fitting, good, meet, proper, right, seemly, suitable, useful, worthy; gratifying, satisfying

near antonyms disreputable, improper, indecent, objectionable, unfit, unsuitable, unworthy, useless; bad, defective, faulty, imperfect, incomplete, lamentable, pitiful; dissatisfying, unsatisfying; insufficient, meager, mean, miserly, niggardly, poor, scanty, shabby, short, skimpy, spare, stingy; insufferable, intolerable, unbearable, unendurable; exceptional, exquisite, extreme, first-class, matchless, maximized, maximum, optimal, optimum, peerless, preeminent, superior, supreme, unmatched, unparalleled, unsurpassed

antonyms deficient, inadequate, lacking, unacceptable, unsatisfactory, wanting

adequately *adv* **1** in a satisfactory way ⟨we weren't completely bowled over by the performance, but the band certainly played more than *adequately*⟩ — see WELL 1
2 in or to a degree or quantity that meets one's requirements or satisfaction ⟨*adequately* provided with candles and fresh water in case of a power outage⟩ — see ENOUGH 1

adhere *vb* to hold to something firmly as if by adhesion ⟨everyone started calling her "Cookie" when she was little and the name *adhered*⟩ — see STICK 1

adhere (to) *vb* to give steadfast support to ⟨our coach *adheres to* the belief that we can win this game if we just have a positive attitude⟩

synonyms cling (to), hew (to), keep (to), stick (to *or* with)

related words cleave (to), hang on (to); back, confirm, defend, endorse (*also* indorse), espouse, support, uphold; accept, adopt, cherish, cultivate, embrace, follow, foster, heed

phrases abide by, live up to, stand by

near antonyms abandon, desert, forsake, give up, relinquish, spurn, surrender; abjure, disavow, disclaim, disown, recall, recant, reconsider, renege, renounce, retract, revoke, take back, unsay, withdraw

antonyms defect (from)

adherence *n* a physical sticking to as if by glue ⟨you'd think these refrigerator magnets would have better *adherence*—they fall off every time I open the door⟩ — see ADHESION

adherent *n* one who follows the opinions or teachings of another ⟨the Flat Earth Society surely doesn't have many *adherents*⟩ — see FOLLOWER

adhesion *n* a physical sticking to as if by glue ⟨mom prefers photo albums that keep the pictures in place by *adhesion* to the pages⟩

synonyms adherence, bonding

related words agglutination, clumping, cohesion; adhesiveness, attachment, cohesiveness, tenacity; cementing, glueing

adhesive *adj* being of such a thick consistency as to readily cling to objects upon contact ⟨walked barefoot through *adhesive*, clayey mud⟩ — see STICKY 1

adhesive *n* a substance used to stick things together ⟨prefers postage stamps coated with *adhesive* so that she doesn't have to do any licking⟩ — see GLUE

adieu *n* an expression of good wishes at parting ⟨we bid our *adieus* and were off⟩ — see GOOD-BYE

adipose *adj* containing animal fat especially in unusual amounts ⟨seals have a thick layer of *adipose* tissue that acts as insulation against the cold and contributes to buoyancy⟩ — see FATTY

adiposity *n* the condition of having an excess of body fat ⟨a sedentary lifestyle contributes to *adiposity*⟩ — see CORPULENCE

adjacent *adj* having a border in common ⟨Crystal's house is *adjacent* to a wooded park⟩

synonyms abutting, adjoining, bordering, contiguous, flanking, fringing, joining, juxtaposed, skirting, touching, verging

related words close, closest, immediate, near, nearest, nearby, neighboring, next, next-door, nigh; attached, communicating, connecting, interconnecting, linked; bounding, embracing, encircling, enclosing, fencing, rimming, surrounding; marginal, peripheral, tangent, tangential

near antonyms apart, detached, free-standing, removed, separate, unattached, unconnected, unlinked; away, distant, far, far-off, farthest, remote; discontinuous, noncontinuous

antonyms nonadjacent

adjoin *vb* **1** to be adjacent to ⟨Colleen, whose bedroom *adjoins* her little brother's room, sometimes hears him talking in his sleep⟩

synonyms abut, border (on), flank, fringe, join, skirt, touch, verge (on)

related words attach (to), communicate (with), connect (with), link (with); bound, embrace, encircle, enclose (*also* inclose), fence, line, rim, surround; contact, converge, meet, neighbor

2 to join (something) to a mass, quantity, or number so as to bring about an overall increase ⟨after the dictionary writer's talk, the principal *adjoined* a few remarks about her own love of words⟩ — see ADD 1

adjoining *adj* having a border in common ⟨the cows had broken through the fence and were grazing in the *adjoining* field⟩ — see ADJACENT

adjourn *vb* to bring to a formal close for a period of time ⟨the meeting was *adjourned* by the chairperson until further notice⟩

synonyms recess, suspend

related words break off, discontinue, intermit, interrupt; defer, hold off, postpone, put off, reserve, shelve, table; abort, call off, cancel, dissolve, terminate; break up, close, conclude, wind up, wrap up

near antonyms inaugurate, launch, open; carry on, continue, draw out, extend, proceed, prolong; renew, reopen, resume; convene, convoke

adjudge *vb* to give an opinion about (something at issue or in dispute) ⟨his version of what had happened was generally *adjudged* to be completely fictitious⟩ — see JUDGE 1

adjudicate *vb* to give an opinion about (something at issue or in dispute) ⟨when we asked the sales clerk to *ad-*

judicate our disagreement, she agreed with me that the white shoes looked better⟩ — see JUDGE 1

adjunct *n* something that is not necessary in itself but adds to the convenience or performance of the main piece of equipment ⟨you can spend a lot on camera accessories, but this nifty little battery recharger is the one *adjunct* that will pay for itself⟩ — see ACCESSORY 1

adjure *vb* to issue orders to (someone) by right of authority ⟨in light of the seriousness of the gas explosion, the authorities have *adjured* all residents to evacuate the area⟩ — see COMMAND 1

adjust *vb* to change (something) so as to make it suitable for a new use or situation ⟨after going on the night shift, he found it difficult to *adjust* his sleep schedule⟩ ⟨*adjust* the amount of sugar in the recipe to your taste⟩ — see ADAPT

adjustable *adj* capable of being readily changed ⟨quantities that are easily *adjustable* to provide for a larger crowd⟩ — see FLEXIBLE 1

adjutant *n* a person who helps a more skilled person ⟨the senator's *adjutants* and aides always arrive ahead of him on the campaign trail⟩ — see HELPER

ad–lib *adj* made or done without previous thought or preparation ⟨not bad for an *ad-lib* comedy routine⟩ — see EXTEMPORANEOUS

ad–lib *vb* to perform, make, or do without preparation ⟨had to *ad-lib* constructing a piñata because she'd never actually seen it being done⟩ — see IMPROVISE

administer *vb* 1 to give out (something) in appropriate amounts or to appropriate individuals ⟨the principal *administers* discipline fairly when students break the rules⟩

synonyms allocate, apportion, deal (out), dispense, distribute, dole (out), mete (out), parcel (out), portion, prorate

related words allot, allow, appropriate, assign, dish (out), divide, measure (out), ration, redistribute, split; bestow, disburse, furnish, issue, provide, share, supply; circulate, disperse, disseminate, scatter, spread; chip in, contribute, donate, pledge

near antonyms begrudge, deny, deprive (of), pinch, refuse, skimp, stint, withhold

2 to carry out effectively ⟨local officials should see that the fair housing laws are rigorously *administered*⟩ — see ENFORCE

3 to look after and make decisions about ⟨the lieutenant governor *administers* the affairs of the state in the absence of the governor⟩ — see CONDUCT 1

administration *n* 1 lawful control over the affairs of a political unit (as a nation) ⟨the fair and just *administration* of the U.S. territories⟩ — see RULE 2

2 the act or activity of looking after and making decisions about something ⟨*administration* of the funds was left in the hands of a committee⟩ — see CONDUCT 1

administrative *adj* suited for or relating to the directing of things ⟨among his other *administrative* duties is the appointment of certain officials⟩ — see EXECUTIVE

administrator *n* a person who manages or directs ⟨school *administrators*⟩ ⟨a hospital *administrator*⟩ — see EXECUTIVE

admirable *adj* deserving of high regard or great approval ⟨it's *admirable* the way Kory helps her grandmother with chores and errands every Saturday⟩

synonyms commendable, creditable, laudable, meritorious, praiseworthy

related words awesome, distinctive, distinguished, excellent, honorable, noteworthy, noticeable, outstanding, reputable, worthy; invaluable, precious, priceless, valuable; delightful, enjoyable, pleasing, satisfying

near antonyms contemptible, deplorable, infamous, notorious, sorry, unlikable, unworthy, worthless; disgraceful, dishonorable, disreputable, low, mean, scandalous, seamy, shady, shameful, shocking, sordid, unsavory

antonyms censurable, discreditable, reprehensible

admiration *n* 1 a feeling of great approval and liking ⟨my *admiration* for Yoko increased when I discovered she had learned English only since coming to the U.S.⟩

synonyms appreciation, esteem, estimation, favor, regard, respect

related words acclamation, adoration, approbation, deference, homage, honor, praise, reverence, veneration, worship; delight, enjoyment, fancy; amazement, awe, wonder, wonderment

near antonyms condemnation, disapproval, disdain, opprobrium, scorn; disappointment, discontent, disenchantment, disgruntlement, disillusionment, displeasure, indignation, unhappiness; aversion, contempt, disgust, dislike, disregard, distaste

antonyms disfavor

2 the rapt attention and deep emotion caused by the sight of something extraordinary ⟨gaped in *admiration* as one flower-bedecked float after another paraded past them⟩ — see WONDER 2

admire *vb* to think very highly or favorably of ⟨I *admire* the way you handled such a touchy situation⟩

synonyms appreciate, esteem, regard, respect

related words acclaim, accredit, applaud, approve, commend, compliment, credit, praise; delight (in), drink (in), enjoy, relish, revel (in), savor; dig, fancy, favor, groove (on), like, love; adore, deify, idolize, revere, reverence, venerate, worship; cherish, prize, treasure, value

phrases set store by (*or* on)

near antonyms condemn, decry, deplore, disapprove, discount, discountenance, disdain, disfavor, dislike, dismiss, disregard, frown (on), scorn

admiring *adj* expressing approval ⟨the smartly dressed couple drew *admiring* glances⟩ — see FAVORABLE 1

admissible *adj* that may be permitted ⟨using direct quotations without naming your source is not *admissible*⟩ — see PERMISSIBLE

admission *n* 1 an open declaration of something (as a fault or the commission of an offense) about oneself ⟨by her own *admission*, her cooking is not the greatest⟩ — see CONFESSION

2 the means or right of entering or participating in ⟨no *admission* unless accompanied by an adult⟩ — see ENTRANCE 1

admit *vb* to accept the truth or existence of (something) usually reluctantly ⟨Eliza readily *admitted* she hadn't read the assignment⟩ ⟨you can't bring yourself to *admit* your mistakes⟩

synonyms acknowledge, agree, allow, concede, confess, grant, own (up)

related words disburden, unburden, unload; affirm, avow, confirm, profess; accept, recognize, yield; announce, break, broadcast, communicate, declare, disclose, divulge, impart, publish, reveal, spill, tell, unveil; betray, blab, expose, give away, inform, leak, rat, squeal, talk, tattle, tip off, warn, wise up; breathe, whisper

near antonyms disallow, disavow, disclaim, disown; contradict, dispute, gainsay, negate, negative; rebut, re-

fute, reject, repudiate; conceal, cover (up), hide, obscure, veil
antonyms deny

admittance *n* the means or right of entering or participating in ⟨*admittance* to the honor society requires a recommendation from one of your teachers⟩ — see ENTRANCE 1

admixture *n* a distinct entity formed by the combining of two or more different things ⟨an *admixture* of rose petals and lavender for a fragrant potpourri⟩ — see BLEND

admonish *vb* to criticize (someone) usually gently so as to correct a fault ⟨*admonished* her for tossing her candy wrapper on the sidewalk⟩ — see REBUKE 1

admonishing *adj* serving as or offering a warning ⟨shot an *admonishing* glance at me just as I was about to spill the beans⟩ — see CAUTIONARY

admonition *n* the act or an instance of telling beforehand of danger or risk ⟨ignored the ranger's *admonitions* and took the road over the mountain, only to be stranded by the blizzard⟩ — see WARNING 1

admonitory *adj* serving as or offering a warning ⟨*admonitory* articles abound around Halloween, warning parents of the hazards of trick-or-treating⟩ — see CAUTIONARY

adolescent *adj* **1** being in the early stage of life, growth, or development ⟨an *adolescent* sheepdog, who hasn't quite gotten the hang of keeping the sheep huddled together⟩ — see YOUNG
2 having or showing the annoying qualities (as silliness) associated with children ⟨would hope that college students had outgrown such *adolescent* behavior⟩ — see CHILDISH
3 lacking in adult experience or maturity ⟨took a group of *adolescent* recruits and turned them into professional warriors⟩ — see CALLOW

adopt *vb* to take for one's own use (something originated by another) ⟨the family *adopted* the American tradition of having turkey for Thanksgiving after they moved to the U.S.⟩
synonyms borrow, embrace, take up
related words domesticate, naturalize; appropriate, arrogate, take over, usurp; absorb, assimilate, incorporate; cherish, prize, treasure; cultivate, follow, heed, honor; use, utilize; bring up, foster, nurture, raise, rear; affect, assume, copy, imitate, pretend, put on, simulate
near antonyms abandon, forsake, give up, relinquish, surrender; abjure, abnegate, disown; reject, renounce, repudiate, spurn; discard, jettison, junk, throw away, throw out

adorable *adj* having qualities that tend to make one loved ⟨what an *adorable* old lady⟩ ⟨an *adorable* little cottage⟩ — see LOVABLE

adore *vb* **1** to feel passion, devotion, or tenderness for ⟨oh, Priscilla, my love, my all, how I *adore* you!⟩ — see LOVE 2
2 to love or admire too much ⟨*adores* her older sister so much that she cannot see her considerable faults⟩ — see IDOLIZE
3 to offer honor or respect to (someone) as a divine power ⟨the Roman soldier was beheaded for *adoring* the Christian god⟩ — see WORSHIP 1
4 to take pleasure in ⟨I *adore* those earrings—wherever did you get them?⟩ — see ENJOY 1

adoring *adj* **1** feeling or showing love ⟨*adoring* grandparents who love to spoil their grandchildren⟩ — see LOVING

2 reflecting great admiration or devotion ⟨the *adoring* attention of the girls' gymnastics team when our local Olympic hero spoke to them⟩ — see WORSHIPFUL

adorn *vb* to make more attractive by adding something that is beautiful or becoming ⟨the Sultan's tent was richly *adorned* with thick tapestries and gleaming gold candlesticks⟩ — see DECORATE

adorning *adj* serving to add beauty ⟨*adorning* garlands of greenery can be seen all over the mansion at Christmastime⟩ — see DECORATIVE

adornment *n* something that decorates or beautifies ⟨the only *adornment* in the sparely furnished bedroom was a small portrait of the poet Walt Whitman⟩ — see DECORATION 1

adroit *adj* accomplished with trained ability ⟨with an *adroit* flick of the wrist, flipped the omelet into the air and landed it squarely back in the pan⟩ — see SKILLFUL

adroitness *n* **1** mental skill or quickness ⟨shows a remarkable *adroitness* in identifying birds the moment they land at the feeder⟩ — see DEXTERITY 1
2 subtle or imaginative ability in inventing, devising, or executing something ⟨with the *adroitness* of a magician, she twisted the balloons to look like a monkey⟩ — see SKILL 1

adulate *vb* **1** to love or admire too much ⟨it's ridiculous how she *adulates* that good-for-nothing big sister of hers⟩ — see IDOLIZE
2 to praise too much ⟨a business executive who unwisely surrounds herself with incompetent assistants who spend all their time *adulating* her⟩ — see FLATTER 1

adulation *n* **1** excessive admiration of or devotion to a person ⟨the pathetic *adulation* of the leader of the cult by her misguided followers⟩ — see WORSHIP
2 excessive praise ⟨more objective critics have observed that the artist never deserved the *adulation* heaped upon her mediocre paintings⟩ — see FLATTERY

adulatory *adj* **1** overly or insincerely flattering ⟨an office flunky who can be counted on to make an *adulatory* response to the boss's every suggestion⟩ — see FULSOME
2 reflecting great admiration or devotion ⟨an *adulatory* eulogy delivered at a beloved teacher's retirement party⟩ — see WORSHIPFUL

adult *adj* fully grown or developed ⟨insects that are butterflies in their *adult* stage⟩ — see MATURE 1

adult *n* a fully grown person ⟨at the beach, the *adults* sat under broad umbrellas while the children splashed in the water⟩
synonyms grown-up
related words ancient, elder, graybeard, oldster, oldtimer, senior, senior citizen
near antonyms kid, moppet, tad, toddler, tot, tyke; baby, infant; adolescent, juvenile, minor, youngster, youth; preteen, teenager, teenybopper
antonyms child

adulterant *n* something that is or that makes impure ⟨*adulterants* in the town's water supply coming from the discharge from the factory⟩ — see IMPURITY

adulterate *vb* to alter (something) for the worse with the addition of foreign or lower-grade substances ⟨the company was fined for *adulterating* its "all beef" frankfurters with cereal⟩
synonyms dilute, thin, water (down), weaken
related words befoul, contaminate, corrupt, defile, dirty, foul, infect, poison, pollute, soil, spoil, sully, taint; cheapen, debase, degrade; manipulate, misrepre-

sent, tamper (with); counterfeit, fake, falsify, fudge; doctor, spike

near antonyms fertilize, lard; augment, supplement; clarify, clean, cleanse, distill, filter, flush, leach, pasteurize, purge, purify, refine; better, enhance, improve

antonyms enrich, fortify, richen, strengthen

adulterated *adj* containing foreign or lower-grade substances ⟨the food poisoning was traced to *adulterated* ground beef⟩ — see IMPURE

adulthood *n* the state of being fully grown or developed ⟨the period between childhood and *adulthood* is called adolescence⟩ — see MATURITY

advance *n* **1** forward movement in time or place ⟨during her long convalescence, Penny was barely aware of the *advance* of the seasons⟩

synonyms advancement, furtherance, going, headway, march, onrush, passage, process, procession, progress, progression

related words current, drift, flow, flux, stream, way; advent, approach, arrival, coming, nearing; bound, jump, leap, step, stride; impetus, momentum

near antonyms backwash, ebb, reflux; retraction, retreat, return, reversal, reverse; about-face, turnabout, turnaround

antonyms recession, regression, retrogression

2 an instance of notable progress in the development of knowledge, technology, or skill ⟨with her new violin teacher, Nadia has made noticeable *advances* in her technique in just a few weeks⟩

synonyms advancement, breakthrough, enhancement, improvement, refinement

related words amelioration, boost, heightening, increase, melioration, strengthening, upgrade, uplift, upswing, uptrend, upturn; betterment, evolution, maturation, perfection, ripening; civilization, edification, education, enlightenment; renaissance, renascence, revival; discovery, find, windfall; innovation, invention

near antonyms breakdown, collapse, crash; hindrance, impediment, stumbling block; decline, decrease, deterioration, diminishment, failing, flagging, languishment, lapse, lessening, reduction, sinking, slowing, weakening, worsening; detriment, disablement, drawback, glitch, impairment, shortcoming

antonyms setback

advance *vb* **1** to give to another for temporary use with the understanding that it or a like thing will be returned ⟨*advanced* her some cash with the understanding that the amount would be deducted from her first paycheck⟩ — see LEND

2 to help the growth or development of ⟨great thinkers who did much to *advance* modern science⟩ — see FOSTER 1

3 to move forward along a course ⟨as the technology *advances*, electronic devices keep getting smaller and doing more⟩ — see GO 1

4 to move higher in rank or position ⟨within six months was *advanced* to the position of head waiter, to the dismay of the waiters who had been there much longer⟩ — see PROMOTE 1

5 to set before the mind for consideration ⟨let me explain my reasons for *advancing* this proposal⟩ — see PROPOSE 1

6 to move closer to ⟨*advanced* cautiously toward the snarling dog⟩ — see COME 1

advanced *adj* **1** being far along in development ⟨an *advanced* civilization, among the first anywhere to use the

plow, developed on the banks of the Nile River thousands of years ago⟩

synonyms developed, evolved, high, higher, improved, progressive, refined

related words full-blown, full-fledged, full-grown, full-scale; aged, grown, mature, matured, perfected, ripe, ripened; civilized, educated, enhanced, enlightened; contemporary, latest, modern, newest, newfangled, new-fashioned, novel, recent, up-to-date; early, precocious

near antonyms green, immature, underdeveloped, undersized, underweight, unripe, unripened; uncivilized, uneducated; early, primeval, primordial; antediluvian, antiquated, Neanderthal, oldfangled, old-fashioned

antonyms backward, low, lower, nonprogressive, primitive, retarded, rudimentary, undeveloped

2 being at a higher level than average ⟨a two-year-old who is *advanced* for his age⟩ ⟨*advanced* mathematics⟩ — see HIGH 2

advancement *n* **1** a raising or a state of being raised to a higher rank or position ⟨Paul's rapid *advancement* in the company came as no surprise to those who knew he was the president's nephew⟩

synonyms ascent, elevation, preferment, promotion, rise, upgrade

related words aggrandizement, ennoblement, exaltation, glorification

near antonyms deposition, dethronement, dismissal, expulsion, impeachment, ouster, overthrow, removal, suspension, unmaking, unseating; downfall, fall

antonyms abasement, demotion, downgrade, reduction

2 an instance of notable progress in the development of knowledge, technology, or skill ⟨science has made huge *advancements* in the field of genetics in recent years⟩ — see ADVANCE 2

3 forward movement in time or place ⟨wondered why we hadn't made any *advancement* in the long checkout line for at least ten minutes⟩ — see ADVANCE 1

advantage *n* **1** the more favorable condition or position in a competition ⟨your experience volunteering at the hospital will put you at an *advantage* when you're applying for a job there⟩

synonyms better, drop, edge, jump, upper hand, vantage

related words allowance, head start, lead, margin, odds, start; ascendancy, command, dominance, mastery, predominance, superiority, supremacy, transcendence; favoritism, nepotism, precedence, preference, privilege, seniority; break, foothold, opportunity

near antonyms detriment, drawback, penalty, stranglehold; disparity, imbalance, inequality, unevenness; disability, impairment, shortcoming

antonyms disadvantage, handicap, liability

2 a thing that helps ⟨had all the *advantages* of being born into a wealthy and powerful family⟩ — see HELP 2

advantageous *adj* conferring benefits; promoting or contributing to personal or social well-being ⟨a trade agreement that is *advantageous* to both countries⟩ — see BENEFICIAL

advent *n* the act of coming upon a scene ⟨with the *advent* of the mass-produced automobile, the need for a better system of roads and highways soon became apparent⟩ — see ARRIVAL

adventitious *adj* not being a vital part of or belonging to something ⟨the point of view that art should be for art's sake and that moral considerations are *adventitious* to the study of art⟩ — see EXTRINSIC

adventure *n* an exciting or noteworthy event that one experiences firsthand ⟨our quiet hike turned into quite an *adventure* when we encountered a bear and her cub⟩

synonyms experience, happening, time

related words escapade, lark; act, action, deed, doing, exploit; episode, occasion; baptism, ordeal, test, trial, tribulation; enterprise, risk, venture; expedition, exploration, feat, mission, performance, quest, stunt

near antonyms bore, bummer, bust, drag

adventure *vb* to place in danger ⟨*adventured* all his savings in a very risky investment scheme⟩ — see ENDANGER

adventuresome *adj* inclined or willing to take risks ⟨not inclined to be *adventuresome* when it comes to foreign travel, preferring guided bus tours⟩ — see BOLD 1

adventurous *adj* inclined or willing to take risks ⟨let's be *adventurous* and take a bus into the city for New Year's Eve this year⟩ — see BOLD 1

adversary *n* **1** one that is hostile toward another ⟨our old cat seemed to consider the new kitten an *adversary*⟩ — see ENEMY

2 one that takes a position opposite another in a competition or conflict ⟨our *adversaries* in tomorrow's meet are from one of the top schools in the league⟩ — see OPPONENT 1

adverse *adj* **1** opposed to one's interests ⟨all the *adverse* publicity really caused the movie star's popularity to suffer⟩

synonyms counter, disadvantageous, hostile, inimical, negative, prejudicial, unfavorable, unfriendly, unsympathetic

related words bad, baleful, baneful, evil; damaging, deleterious, destructive, detrimental, fatal, harmful, hurtful, injurious, lethal, murderous, poisonous, ruinous, threatening, troublesome, unhealthy, wounding; dangerous, hazardous, imperiling, jeopardizing, parlous, perilous, risky, unsafe; defamatory, detractive, offensive, scathing, slanderous; antagonistic, antipathetic, inhospitable, intolerant, uncongenial, uncooperative; competing, conflicting, counteracting, countering, opposing, resistant, resisting

near antonyms beneficial, good, helpful, propitious, useful; harmless, innocent, innocuous, inoffensive, nondestructive, nonfatal, nonlethal, nonthreatening; unresisting, unresistant; tolerant, understanding; agreeable, affable, amiable, amicable, benign, benignant, congenial, cordial, complying, friendly, hospitable

antonyms advantageous, favorable, friendly, positive, supportive, sympathetic, well-disposed

2 causing or capable of causing harm ⟨the *adverse* effects of the drug are too severe to allow it to be marketed⟩ — see HARMFUL

adversity *n* **1** bad luck or an example of this ⟨many people came face-to-face with life-altering *adversity* when the stock market crashed⟩ — see MISFORTUNE

2 something that is a cause for suffering or special effort especially in the attainment of a goal ⟨some overcame all the *adversities* of the Great Depression and rebuilt their fortunes⟩ — see DIFFICULTY 1

advert (to) *vb* to make reference to or speak about briefly but specifically ⟨when our hosts *adverted to* the lateness of the hour we took the hint, and prepared to leave⟩ — see MENTION 1

advertise *vb* to make known openly or publicly ⟨I wouldn't *advertise* my F in art to the whole world if I were you⟩ — see ANNOUNCE

advertisement *n* a published statement informing the public of a matter of general interest ⟨an *advertisement* for special low fares to Florida and Cancun during spring break⟩ — see ANNOUNCEMENT

advice *n* an opinion suggesting a wise or proper course of action ⟨Stephanie got some good *advice* from the vet about dealing with her dog's habit of chasing cars⟩

synonyms counsel, guidance

related words recommendation, suggestion; hint, pointer, tip; data, feedback, information; answer, solution; advisement, consideration, thought; admonishment, admonition, caution, cautioning, expostulation, remonstration, urging, warning; judgment (*or* judgement), observation, verdict; assistance, briefing, coaching, direction, instruction, mentoring, priming, prompting, teaching, tutoring; interference, kibitzing, meddling; moralizing, pontificating, preaching; exhortation, lecture, lesson, sermon, speech

advisable *adj* suitable for bringing about a desired result under the circumstances ⟨it's never *advisable* to ride double on a bicycle⟩ — see EXPEDIENT

advise *vb* **1** to give advice to ⟨a popular guidance counselor who has been *advising* students about their college plans for two decades⟩

synonyms counsel

related words admonish, caution, warn; brief, clue (in), fill in, inform, wise (up); coach, direct, lead, guide, instruct, mentor, teach, tutor; acquaint, apprise, familiarize; convince, encourage, induce, persuade, talk (into); beg, exhort, implore, prevail (upon), urge; propose, recommend, suggest

2 to put forward as one's choice for a wise or proper course of action ⟨she *advised* calling ahead for a reservation at the new restaurant⟩

synonyms counsel, recommend, suggest

related words advocate, back, favor, support; exhort, urge; advance, propose, submit

3 to exchange viewpoints or seek advice for the purpose of finding a solution to a problem ⟨the doctor *advised* with his partner before recommending the patient's treatment⟩ — see CONFER 2

4 to give information to ⟨*advised* her as to the best way to get to the art museum by public transportation⟩ — see ENLIGHTEN 1

advised *adj* decided on as a result of careful thought ⟨wanting to make an *advised* decision, he consulted with his lawyer⟩ — see DELIBERATE 1

adviser *or* **advisor** *n* a person who gives advice especially professionally ⟨her English teacher, who is also her *adviser*, thinks she should enter the writing contest⟩ — see CONSULTANT

advocate *n* **1** a person who actively supports or favors a cause ⟨Mark Twain, Noah Webster, and President Theodore Roosevelt are among past *advocates* of a reformed spelling system⟩ — see EXPONENT

2 a person whose profession is to conduct lawsuits for clients or to advise about legal rights and obligations ⟨engage an *advocate* knowledgeable in property law if you want to dispute a land claim⟩ — see LAWYER

advocate *vb* to promote the interests or cause of ⟨environmentalists *advocating* agricultural methods designed to slow the destruction of rain forests⟩ — see SUPPORT 1

aegis *n* means or method of defending ⟨having no claim to the land under the *aegis* of the law, the cattle baron decided to claim it by force⟩ — see DEFENSE 1

aeon *or* **eon** *n* a long or seemingly long period of time ⟨it's been *aeons* since I saw a movie at the multiplex⟩ ⟨glaciers that formed *aeons* ago⟩ — see AGE 2

aerodrome *n, British* a place from which aircraft operate that usually has paved runways and a terminal ⟨landed at the *aerodrome* in Surrey, south of London⟩ — see AIRPORT

affability *n* the state or quality of having a pleasant or agreeable manner in socializing with others ⟨First Lady Dolley Madison was beloved by the nation for her *affability* toward people from all walks of life⟩ — see AMIABILITY 1

affable *adj* **1** having a relaxed, casual manner ⟨likes hanging around her grandfather's *affable* ranch hands, who are never too busy to pay attention to her⟩ — see EASYGOING 1
2 having an easygoing and pleasing manner especially in social situations ⟨everyone likes having *affable* Jeremy at dinner parties to keep the conversation flowing⟩ — see AMIABLE
3 showing a natural kindness and courtesy especially in social situations ⟨although First Lady Lucretia Hayes didn't particularly enjoy her role as White House hostess, she was always *affable*⟩ — see GRACIOUS 1

affair *n* **1** a brief romantic relationship ⟨an *affair* between two teenagers spending the summer at the same beach resort⟩
synonyms love affair, romance
related words amour, intrigue; attachment, infatuation; entanglement, fling, flirtation; liaison, passion
2 a social gathering ⟨the annual country club dance is a really fancy *affair*⟩ — see PARTY 1
3 something produced by physical or intellectual effort ⟨the lead float in the parade was a pretty impressive *affair*, a giant eagle's head with equally huge wings⟩ — see PRODUCT 1
4 something that happens ⟨the whole *affair* from start to finish took a total of 15 minutes⟩ — see EVENT 1
5 something to be dealt with ⟨it's none of your *affair* whom I'm going out with tonight⟩ — see MATTER 2

¹affect *vb* **1** to act upon (a person or a person's feelings) so as to cause a response ⟨Gary claims that scary movies don't *affect* him in the least⟩
synonyms impact, impress, influence, move, strike, sway, tell (on), touch
related words bias, color; inspire, stir; carry, engage, interest, involve, penetrate, pierce; afflict, agitate, bother, discomfort, discompose, disquiet, distress, disturb, fluster, harass, harry, perturb, pester, plague, smite, strain, stress, trouble, try, upset, worry, wring; allure, attract, bewitch, captivate, charm, dazzle, enchant
phrases get to
near antonyms bore, jade, pall, tire, weary
2 to be the business or affair of ⟨fortunately, hurricane season doesn't *affect* the West Coast⟩ — see CONCERN 2

²affect *vb* to present a false appearance of ⟨she *affected* complete unawareness that we were talking about her, though she must have overheard⟩ — see FEIGN

affectation *n* the quality or state of appearing or trying to appear more important or more valuable than is the case ⟨a woman of great *affectation* at social gatherings⟩ — see PRETENSE 1

affected *adj* **1** lacking in natural or spontaneous quality ⟨*affected* laughter at the principal's jokes⟩ ⟨an *affected* southern accent⟩ — see ARTIFICIAL 1
2 self-consciously trying to present an appearance of grandeur or importance ⟨with her pinkie extended, the four-year-old held her tiny teacup in that *affected* manner that some women have⟩ — see PRETENTIOUS 1

affectedness *n* the quality or state of appearing or trying to appear more important or more valuable than is the case ⟨bowed and sat down at the piano with much *affectedness* but didn't play very well⟩ — see PRETENSE 1

affecting *adj* having the power to affect the feelings or sympathies ⟨the *affecting* final scene in the play, when the children are reunited with their father⟩ — see MOVING

¹affection *n* a feeling of strong or constant regard for and dedication to someone ⟨show their *affection* for each other by little acts of kindness⟩ — see LOVE 1

²affection *n* an abnormal state that disrupts a plant's or animal's normal bodily functioning ⟨born with a heart *affection*⟩ — see DISEASE

affectionate *adj* feeling or showing love ⟨an *affectionate* child who gives hugs and kisses freely⟩ — see LOVING

affianced *adj* pledged in marriage ⟨the *affianced* couple are much-sought-after guests for this year's holiday parties⟩ — see ENGAGED

affiliate *n* a local unit of an organization ⟨our local Humane Society is an *affiliate* of a national organization⟩ — see CHAPTER

affiliated *adj* having a close connection like that between family members ⟨costuming and set design are *affiliated* arts, both requiring research into the period of the play or film⟩ — see RELATED

affiliation *n* the state of having shared interests or efforts (as in social or business matters) ⟨the Little League team, despite its name, the Northern Dynamites, has no *affiliation* with the Northern Dynamite Company⟩ — see ASSOCIATION 1

affirm *vb* **1** to state as a fact usually forcefully ⟨unwilling to *affirm* without further study that the painting is an original Rembrandt⟩ — see CLAIM 1
2 to state clearly and strongly ⟨he *affirmed* his trust in us, and we in turn promised not to let him down⟩ — see ASSERT 1

affirmation *n* a solemn and often public declaring of the truth or existence of something ⟨a sworn *affirmation* that he had never acted as a spy for the enemy⟩ — see PROTESTATION

affirmative *adj* showing or expressing acceptance or approval ⟨the proposal received an *affirmative* vote from all the members of the school committee⟩ — see POSITIVE

affix *vb* to cause (something) to hold to another ⟨*affix* a first-class stamp to the envelope⟩ — see FASTEN 1

afflict *vb* to cause persistent suffering to ⟨the South was *afflicted* by a severe drought⟩ ⟨he's been *afflicted* by nightmares ever since the accident⟩
synonyms agonize, bedevil, curse, harrow, martyr, persecute, plague, rack, torment, torture
related words assail, attack, beset, set upon; badger, dog, hound, ride; agitate, annoy, bother, distress, disturb, harass, harry, irk, molest, pester; discomfort, discompose, disquiet, fluster, perturb, strain, stress, trouble, try, upset, vex, worry; crush, oppress, overpower, overwhelm, smite, strike, tyrannize; pain, prick, stab, sting, wring

near antonyms abet, aid, assist, help; deliver, release, relieve, reprieve; comfort, console, solace, soothe, succor

afflicting *adj* hard to accept or bear especially emotionally ⟨the *afflicting* sight of so many earthquake victims was too much even for some hardened rescue workers⟩ — see BITTER 2

affliction *n* **1** a state of great suffering of body or mind ⟨she listened with deep *affliction* as her daughter told her about the latest trouble she was in⟩ — see DISTRESS 1

2 deep sadness especially for the loss of someone or something loved ⟨felt such great *affliction* over the destruction of the beautiful old home⟩ — see SORROW

affluent *adj* having goods, property, or money in abundance ⟨his parents are *affluent* and can afford to send him to the best schools⟩ — see RICH 1

affray *n* a rough and often noisy fight usually involving several people ⟨an *affray* broke out in the parking lot when someone shouted a racial slur⟩ — see BRAWL 1

affright *vb* to strike with fear ⟨a ghastly sight that would *affright* any person⟩ — see FRIGHTEN

affrighted *adj* filled with fear or dread ⟨the *affrighted* villagers ran in all directions at the first sight of the monster⟩ — see AFRAID 1

affront *n* an act or expression showing scorn and usually intended to hurt another's feelings ⟨took it as an *affront* that she wasn't asked to help cook Thanksgiving dinner⟩ — see INSULT

affront *vb* to cause hurt feelings or deep resentment in ⟨did not mean to *affront* you when I told you I didn't need your help⟩ — see INSULT

aficionado *n* a person with a strong and habitual liking for something ⟨a Harry Potter *aficionado*, who has seen all the movies several times⟩ — see FAN

afield *adv* off the desired or intended path or course ⟨how did we get so far *afield* from the subject we intended to discuss?⟩ — see WRONG 1

afire *adj* being on fire ⟨looked down upon the city, which was all *afire* from the bombing⟩ — see ABLAZE 1

aflame *adj* being on fire ⟨the kindling in the wood stove was *aflame* as soon as I held a match to it⟩ — see ABLAZE 1

aflutter *adj* feeling or showing uncomfortable feelings of uncertainty ⟨Jonathan was all *aflutter* about proposing to Shelley that evening⟩ — see NERVOUS 1

afoot *adj* being in progress or development ⟨plans are *afoot* for a new sports stadium⟩ — see ONGOING 1

afore *adv, chiefly dialect* so as to precede something in order of time ⟨some young boys raced *afore* to tell onlookers that there were elephants in the circus parade⟩ — see AHEAD 1

afore *prep, chiefly dialect* **1** earlier than ⟨my father, his father, and even his father *afore* him farmed this land⟩ — see BEFORE 1

2 preceding in space ⟨a majestic sailing ship going full speed *afore* the wind⟩ — see BEFORE 2

afraid *adj* **1** filled with fear or dread ⟨Melissa is *afraid* of flying, so she takes a train from Boston to visit her brother in Chicago⟩

synonyms affrighted, aghast, alarmed, fearful, frightened, horrified, scared, spooked, terrified, terrorized

related words fainthearted, fearsome, shrinking, shy, timid, timorous, tremulous; agitated, anxious, apprehensive, disconcerted, disquieted, disturbed, jittery, jumpy, nervous, panicky, perturbed, skittish, uneasy, upset, worried; appalled, dismayed, shocked, startled; cowed, daunted, intimidated, unnerved; coward, cow-

ardly, craven, gutless, lily-livered, pusillanimous; careful, cautious, heedful, prudent, unadventurous, wary

near antonyms adventuresome, adventurous, audacious, bold, daredevil, daring, dashing, gutsy, plucky, spirited, spunky, venturesome, venturous; brave, courageous, gallant, hardy, heroic, intrepid, lionhearted, manful, stalwart, stout, stouthearted, valiant, valorous; assured, collected, composed, confident, cool, sanguine, sure, unperturbed; dauntless, resolute, undaunted

antonyms fearless, unafraid

2 having doubts about the wisdom of doing something ⟨not *afraid* to show his feelings⟩ — see HESITANT

afresh *adv* yet another time ⟨the shooting broke out *afresh* when the bandits reappeared at the crest of the hill⟩ — see AGAIN 1

aft *adv* near, toward, or in the stern of a ship or the tail of an aircraft ⟨after transferring the controls to the copilot, the captain went *aft* to see what the disturbance was⟩

synonyms abaft, astern

related words after, back, backward, behind, posteriorly, rearward (*also* rearwards), rearwardly

near antonyms anteriorly; ahead, before

antonyms fore, forward

after *adj* being, occurring, or carried out at a time after something else ⟨in *after* years the government set up a special fund for disabled veterans of the war⟩ — see SUBSEQUENT

after *adv* following in time or place ⟨upon seeing *The Nutcracker* for the first time, and for a long time *after*, Irma wanted to play the part of the Mouse King⟩

synonyms afterward (*or* afterwards), later, subsequently, thereafter

related words next; by and by, hereafter, presently, since, soon, then, thereupon

near antonyms antecedently, formerly; heretofore, theretofore

antonyms afore [*chiefly dialect*], before, beforehand, earlier, previously

after *prep* subsequent to in time or order ⟨the high school band came right *after* the mayor in the parade⟩

synonyms behind, following

related words next; since

near antonyms of, to, toward (*or* towards)

antonyms afore [*chiefly dialect*], ahead of, before, ere, previous to, prior to

aftereffect *n* a condition or occurrence traceable to a cause ⟨in the U.S. slavery was abolished in 1865, but its *aftereffects* remained keenly felt long afterwards⟩ — see EFFECT 1

afterlife *n* unending existence after death ⟨hoping to join her deceased parents in the *afterlife*⟩ — see ETERNITY 2

aftermath *n* a condition or occurrence traceable to a cause ⟨the surgery was successful, but she now had to deal with its *aftermath*: a huge bill⟩ — see EFFECT 1

afterward *or* **afterwards** *adv* following in time or place ⟨we'll go to the play, then have supper *afterward*⟩ — see AFTER

again *adv* **1** yet another time ⟨now I have to mop the floor *again* because you didn't wipe your feet⟩

synonyms afresh, anew, over

related words always, constantly, continuously, endlessly, ever, evermore, perpetually; frequently, often; recurrently, repeatedly; freshly, newly

near antonyms ne'er, never

antonyms nevermore

2 in addition to what has been said ⟨a green pillow will go fine with my living room; *again*, the best colors are blues and greens⟩ — see MORE 1

3 just the opposite being true ⟨I might take swimming lessons this summer; then *again*, I might not⟩ — see CONTRARIWISE

against *prep* in or into contact with ⟨he leaned *against* the fence and it collapsed⟩ ⟨unwittingly rubbed his leg *against* some poison ivy⟩
synonyms on, upon
related words alongside, next, next to

agape *adj* having or showing signs of eagerly awaiting something ⟨at the sound of the sleigh bells the children were all *agape*, waiting for Santa to appear⟩ — see EXPECTANT 1

age *n* **1** an extent of time associated with a particular person or thing ⟨the Bronze *Age* marks the beginning of the use of metal by ancient peoples⟩
synonyms day, epoch, era, period, time
related words cycle, generation, year; span, spell, stretch, while
2 a long or seemingly long period of time ⟨it took *ages* for the clerk to ring up three items⟩
synonyms aeon (*or* eon), cycle, eternity
related words infinity; lifetime
near antonyms flash, instant, jiffy, minute, moment, second, trice, twinkle, twinkling, wink; microsecond, nanosecond

age *vb* to become mature ⟨as your cat *ages* and becomes less active, you should change her diet⟩ — see MATURE

aged *adj* **1** being of advanced years and especially past middle age ⟨all the young men went to fight in the war; and only the *aged* and infirm remained behind⟩ — see ELDERLY
2 dating or surviving from the distant past ⟨a forest of *aged* and gnarled oaks⟩ — see ANCIENT 1

agency *n* something used to achieve an end ⟨by what *agency* do you plan to acquire this fortune?⟩ — see AGENT 1

agenda *n* a listing of things to be presented or considered (as at a concert or play) ⟨unless your proposal is on the meeting's *agenda*, it won't be addressed⟩ — see PROGRAM 1

agent *n* **1** something used to achieve an end ⟨the whitening *agent* in the detergent is chlorine bleach⟩ ⟨the Church has been the traditional *agent* for social justice in impoverished countries⟩
synonyms agency, instrument, instrumentality, machinery, means, medium, organ, vehicle
related words determinant, expedient, factor, influence, ingredient, mechanism, tool; activator, catalyst, driver, energizer, executor, generator, instigator, launcher, mover, power, stimulus, trigger
2 a person who acts or does business for another ⟨the sports *agent* negotiated a record-breaking contract for the baseball player⟩
synonyms attorney, commissary, delegate, deputy, envoy, factor, procurator, proxy, representative
related words ambassador, emissary, foreign minister, legate, minister; alternate, backup, pinch hitter, relief, replacement, stand-in, sub, substitute, surrogate, understudy; informer, operative, spy; broker, distributor, manager; arbiter, arbitrator, go-between, intercessor, intermediary, interposer, liaison, mediator, middleman; mouthpiece, spokesperson

age–old *adj* dating or surviving from the distant past ⟨*age-old* customs and beliefs⟩ — see ANCIENT 1

agglomerate *vb* to form into a round compact mass ⟨breakfast cereal consisting of *agglomerated* clusters of wheat, rice, and nuts stays crunchy in milk⟩ — see WAD

aggrandize *vb* **1** to enhance the status of ⟨a movie that *aggrandizes* the bad guys and makes the cops look like dopes⟩ — see EXALT
2 to make greater in size, amount, or number ⟨a generous grant, enabling the library to significantly *aggrandize* its collection of books on tape⟩ — see INCREASE 1

aggravate *vb* to disturb the peace of mind of (someone) especially by repeated disagreeable acts ⟨it really *aggravates* me when I arrive ten minutes before the stated closing time, and they're closed already⟩ — see IRRITATE 1

aggravating *adj* **1** causing annoyance ⟨there's nothing so *aggravating* as a blaring car alarm that no one is paying any attention to⟩ — see ANNOYING

aggravation *n* **1** something that is a source of irritation ⟨the constant *aggravation* of having to get up and adjust the TV picture⟩ — see ANNOYANCE 3
2 the act of making unwelcome intrusions upon another ⟨the neighbors' constant *aggravations* prompted us to move out of town⟩ — see ANNOYANCE 1
3 the feeling of impatience or anger caused by another's repeated disagreeable acts ⟨mom informed us she didn't need the extra *aggravation* of hearing us fight in the back seat while we were stuck in traffic⟩ — see ANNOYANCE 2

aggregate *n* a complete amount of something ⟨Jon's absences, taken in the *aggregate*, amount to almost two months of school time⟩ — see WHOLE

aggression *n* **1** an inclination to fight or quarrel ⟨Japanese *aggression* in the years preceding the attack on Pearl Harbor had strained relations with the U.S.⟩ — see BELLIGERENCE
2 the act or action of setting upon with force or violence ⟨Japan's act of *aggression*—the attack on Pearl Harbor—brought the U.S. into World War II⟩ — see ATTACK 1

aggressive *adj* **1** having or showing a bold forcefulness in the pursuit of a goal ⟨if you don't take a more *aggressive* approach to this yard pretty soon, the weeds are going to take over completely⟩
synonyms ambitious, assertive, enterprising, fierce, go-getting, high-pressure, in-your-face, militant, self-assertive
related words dynamic, energetic, gung ho, hustling, scrappy, strenuous, vigorous; emphatic, obtrusive; adventuresome, adventurous, venturesome, venturous; audacious, bold, brash, brassy, cheeky, cocksure, cocky, confident, determined, forward, impudent, insolent, overconfident, presumptuous, unapologetic, unsubdued, unyielding; dominating, domineering, imperious, lordly, magisterial, overbearing
near antonyms easygoing, laid-back, relaxed; acquiescent, compliant, deferential, resigned, submissive, yielding; cowering, cringing, groveling (*or* grovelling), shrinking; bashful, diffident, meek, mousy (*or* mousey), overmodest, passive, quiet, reserved, retiring, shy, subdued, timid, unobtrusive
antonyms low-pressure, unaggressive, unambitious, unassertive, unenterprising
2 feeling or displaying eagerness to fight ⟨a kindergarten teacher who discourages *aggressive* behavior, like pushing, by rewarding those children who wait their turn⟩ — see BELLIGERENT

3 marked by or uttered with forcefulness ⟨an *aggressive* campaign to win the African-American vote⟩ — see EMPHATIC 1

aggressiveness *n* **1** readiness to engage in daring or difficult activity ⟨because of the mayor's *aggressiveness* in tackling problems, there have been a lot of changes for the better⟩ — see ENTERPRISE 2
2 the quality or state of being forceful (as in expression) ⟨Gregory has the *aggressiveness* one needs to run for class president⟩ — see VEHEMENCE 1
3 an inclination to fight or quarrel ⟨male bettas, known for their *aggressiveness*, are best raised alone⟩ — see BELLIGERENCE

aggressor *n* one that starts armed conflict against another especially without reasonable cause ⟨the countries formed an alliance to deter potential *aggressors*⟩
synonyms invader, raider
related words initiator, instigator; ambuscader, assailant, attacker, pillager, plunderer; hawk, militarist, warmonger; belligerent, combatant
near antonyms defender; dove, pacifist, peacemaker; nonbelligerent

aggrieved *adj* having a feeling that one has been wronged or thwarted in one's ambitions ⟨a line of *aggrieved* ticket-holders, demanding a refund for the cancelled concert⟩ — see DISCONTENTED

aghast *adj* filled with fear or dread ⟨I stood there, *aghast*, as the vile monster made its way toward me⟩ — see AFRAID 1

agile *adj* moving easily ⟨*agile* dancers⟩ ⟨*agile* herons wading in the marsh⟩ — see GRACEFUL 1

agility *n* ease and grace in physical activity ⟨a gymnast whose *agility* on the parallel bars has won him several medals⟩ — see DEXTERITY 2

aging *adj* being of advanced years and especially past middle age ⟨more and more middle-aged adults must care for *aging* parents⟩ — see ELDERLY

agitate *vb* **1** to cause (as a liquid) to move about in a circle especially repeatedly ⟨this room could use a ceiling fan to *agitate* the stuffy air a bit⟩ — see STIR 1
2 to trouble the mind of; to make uneasy ⟨there's no need to *agitate* Aunt Lydia about little things⟩ — see DISTURB 1
3 to make a series of small irregular or violent movements ⟨set the washing machine so it will *agitate* for four minutes before going into the rinse cycle⟩ — see SHAKE 1

agitated *adj* **1** being in a state of increased activity or agitation ⟨all ferry crossings were cancelled because of the *agitated* waters around the islands⟩ — see FEVERISH 1
2 feeling overwhelming fear or worry ⟨by the time they finally showed up, long after midnight, we'd become so *agitated* that we never did get to sleep that night⟩ — see FRANTIC 1

agitating *adj* marked by or causing agitation or uncomfortable feelings ⟨no more *agitating* waits to find out sports scores—get them instantly online!⟩ — see NERVOUS 2

agitation *n* **1** a state of wildly excited activity or emotion ⟨knew immediately, from the horses' *agitation*, that something terrible was happening⟩ — see FRENZY
2 an uneasy state of mind usually over the possibility of an anticipated misfortune or trouble ⟨experienced a great deal of *agitation* over whether she had an appropriate dress for her husband's inauguration⟩ — see ANXIETY 1

agitator *n* a person who stirs up public feelings especially of discontent ⟨a political *agitator* who led an unsuccessful revolt against the government⟩
synonyms demagogue (*also* demagog), exciter, firebrand, fomenter, incendiary, inciter, instigator, rabble-rouser
related words demonstrator, marcher, objector, picketer, protester (*or* protestor); advocate, champion, exponent, persuader, promoter, reformer, supporter; alarmist, extremist, insurgent, insurrectionist, radical, rebel, revolter, revolutionary, revolutionist, subversive, troublemaker

aglow *adj* having or being an outward sign of good feelings (as of love, confidence, or happiness) ⟨all *aglow* as she was awarded first place in the spelling bee⟩ — see RADIANT 1

agog *adj* **1** having or showing signs of eagerly awaiting something ⟨parents *agog* for the latest news from the children away at college⟩ — see EXPECTANT 1
2 showing urgent desire or interest ⟨all *agog* to get started on their journey⟩ — see EAGER

agonize *vb* **1** to cause persistent suffering to ⟨got into more trouble, further *agonizing* her poor mother⟩ — see AFFLICT
2 to feel deep sadness or mental pain ⟨*agonized* for days over whether she'd done the right thing⟩ — see GRIEVE

agonizing *adj* **1** hard to accept or bear especially emotionally ⟨*agonizing* cries rose up from the dungeon⟩ — see BITTER 2
2 intensely or unbearably painful ⟨died an *agonizing* death⟩ — see EXCRUCIATING 1
3 causing intense mental or physical distress ⟨*agonizing* back pain that bothered me for months⟩ — see SHARP 2

agonizingly *adv* with feelings of bitterness or grief ⟨*agonizingly* made the decision to have her beloved cat put to sleep⟩ — see HARD 2

agony *n* **1** a situation or state that causes great suffering and unhappiness ⟨waiting all those hours to hear if he'd survived the plane crash was pure *agony*⟩ — see HELL 2
2 a state of great suffering of body or mind ⟨the *agony* of never knowing what happened to her son⟩ — see DISTRESS 1
3 a sudden intense expression of strong feeling ⟨the announcement that the war was over unleashed a mass *agony* of joy⟩ — see OUTBURST 1

agrarian *adj* engaged in or concerned with agriculture ⟨an *agrarian* community⟩ ⟨the nation's *agrarian* history⟩ — see AGRICULTURAL

agree *vb* **1** to have or come to the same opinion or point of view ⟨since we couldn't *agree*, we tossed a coin to decide the matter⟩
synonyms coincide, concur
related words accede (to), accept, acquiesce, assent (to), comply (with), consent (to), go (by), subscribe; affiliate, ally, associate, unite; collaborate, cooperate, get along
phrases see eye to eye
near antonyms clash, collide, conflict; bicker, counter, dispute, dissent, diverge, fall out, object, oppose, protest, quarrel, resist, rival; dissociate, separate, split
antonyms differ, disagree
2 to accept the truth or existence of (something) usually reluctantly ⟨finally *agreed* that the paint job was sloppy and would have to be redone⟩ — see ADMIT

3 to be in agreement on every point ⟨the robber's story didn't *agree* with the cop's report on the incident⟩ — see CHECK 1

4 to form a pleasing relationship ⟨this warm climate seems to *agree* with you⟩ — see HARMONIZE 1

agreeable *adj* **1** being to one's liking ⟨is the zoo an *agreeable* alternative for everyone, since the aquarium is closed?⟩ — see SATISFACTORY 1

2 giving pleasure or contentment to the mind or senses ⟨put on some *agreeable* music for dinner⟩ — see PLEASANT

3 having an easygoing and pleasing manner especially in social situations ⟨an *agreeable* art teacher who lets me do pretty much whatever I want⟩ — see AMIABLE

4 having or marked by agreement in feeling or action ⟨the belief that these new security measures are not *agreeable* with our core concepts of personal freedom⟩ — see HARMONIOUS 3

agreeableness *n* the state or quality of having a pleasant or agreeable manner in socializing with others ⟨the impression that the couple give to first-time visitors is one of well-bred *agreeableness*⟩ — see AMIABILITY 1

agreeably *adv* in a pleasing way ⟨an *agreeably* warm day, just right for a picnic⟩ — see WELL 5

agreement *n* **1** the act or fact of being of one opinion about something ⟨I only had the energy to nod in *agreement* when Cheryl said we'd never worked so hard in all our lives⟩

synonyms accord, concurrence, consensus, unanimity, unison

related words accession, assent, consent; acceptance, acquiescence, compliance, concession, conformity; approbation, approval, favor; alliance, collaboration, collusion, complicity, conspiracy; concord, consonance, harmony, oneness, solidarity, understanding, union; empathy, rapport, sympathy

near antonyms conflict, discord, dissension; opposition, resistance; disapprobation, disapproval, disfavor

antonyms disagreement, dissent

2 an arrangement about action to be taken ⟨we finally reached an *agreement* regarding a fair division of the housework⟩

synonyms accord, bargain, compact, contract, convention, covenant, deal, pact, settlement, understanding

related words charter, treaty; pledge, promise; alliance, association, league, partnership; acceptance, approval, assent, concurrence, consent, OK (*or* okay)

3 a state of consistency ⟨the amount in column A needs to be in *agreement* with the total receipts minus expenses⟩ — see CONFORMITY 1

agricultural *adj* engaged in or concerned with agriculture ⟨he grew up in an *agricultural* community⟩

synonyms agrarian, farming

related words pastoral, rural

near antonyms metropolitan, urban; industrial, industrialized

antonyms nonagricultural

agriculture *n* the science or occupation of cultivating the soil, producing crops, and raising livestock ⟨the forest was cut down, and the land given over to *agriculture*⟩

synonyms farming, husbandry

related words agronomy; animal husbandry

agriculturist *or* **agriculturalist** *n* a person who cultivates the land and grows crops on it ⟨*agriculturists* who adhere to the organization's standards of organic farming⟩ — see FARMER

agronomist *n* a person who cultivates the land and grows crops on it ⟨went from being a simple soybean farmer to an *agronomist* specializing in soil management⟩ — see FARMER

aground *adj* resting on the shore or bottom of a body of water ⟨the villagers came to stare at the foreign ship that was *aground* on their beach and at the strangely dressed sailors on board⟩

synonyms beached, grounded, stranded

related words landed; alongshore

near antonyms offshore

antonyms afloat

ah *interj* how surprising, doubtful, or unbelievable ⟨*ah*—so that's the way it is!⟩ — see NO

aha *interj* how surprising, doubtful, or unbelievable ⟨*aha*! so the money was never missing in the first place!⟩ — see NO

ahead *adv* **1** so as to precede something in order of time ⟨we were cautioned not to fill out any of the test answers *ahead* of time⟩ ⟨call *ahead* for reservations⟩

synonyms afore [*chiefly dialect*], antecedently, anteriorly, before, beforehand, previously

related words formerly

phrases in advance

near antonyms behind, by and by, next, presently, subsequently

antonyms after, afterward (*or* afterwards), later

2 toward a point ahead in space or time ⟨sent me *ahead* to get a place in the check-out line while she went to get the eggs and milk⟩ — see ONWARD 1

3 toward or at a point lying in advance in space or time ⟨the line moved *ahead* at a snail's pace⟩ — see ALONG

ahead of *prep* **1** earlier than ⟨always arrives at school *ahead of* the bus⟩ — see BEFORE 1

2 preceding in space ⟨the three lost children emerged from the forest, with the family dog walking proudly *ahead of* them⟩ — see BEFORE 2

aid *n* **1** a person who helps a more skilled person ⟨Jack is his mother's preferred *aid* in the kitchen, as his sister Janice is clumsy when it comes to chopping and peeling⟩ — see HELPER

2 a thing that helps ⟨a dictionary is a handy *aid* for working crossword puzzles⟩ — see HELP 2

3 an act or instance of helping ⟨the clerk asked if she needed any *aid* carrying out her purchases⟩ — see HELP 1

aid *vb* to provide (someone) with what is useful or necessary to achieve an end ⟨sought to *aid* her in her search for a dachshund puppy by looking online⟩ — see HELP 1

aide *n* a person who helps a more skilled person ⟨the nurse's *aide* will bring you an extra pillow⟩ ⟨served as an *aide* in his father's senatorial campaign⟩ — see HELPER

ailing *adj* **1** chronically or repeatedly suffering from poor health ⟨when his *ailing* wife had to go to a nursing home, he visited her every day⟩ — see SICKLY 1

2 temporarily suffering from a disorder of the body ⟨he was *ailing* from some sort of infection in his eye that made it look all red and puffy⟩ — see SICK 1

ailment *n* an abnormal state that disrupts a plant's or animal's normal bodily functioning ⟨people who have AIDS are more susceptible to other *ailments* as well⟩ — see DISEASE

aim *n* something that one hopes or intends to accomplish ⟨the main *aim* of a trip to the city is to shop for school clothes, but we always go to the artisan's market, too⟩ — see GOAL

aim *vb* **1** to point or turn (something) toward a target or goal ⟨the anti-drug campaign was *aimed* primarily at preteens⟩
synonyms bend, cast, direct, head, level, set, train
related words bear, face; concentrate, focus; incline, orient, steer
near antonyms avert, curve, deflect, detour, divert, rechannel, shunt, sidetrack
2 to have in mind as a purpose or goal ⟨*aimed* to have his paper all done in time to go to the movies⟩ — see INTEND

aimless *adj* lacking a definite plan, purpose, or pattern ⟨this *aimless* walking through stores isn't going to get your Christmas shopping done⟩ — see RANDOM

aimlessly *adv* without definite aim, direction, rule, or method ⟨Snow White fled *aimlessly* through the forest until she was hopelessly lost⟩ — see HIT OR MISS

air *n* **1** a rhythmic series of musical tones arranged to give a pleasing effect ⟨played a lively *air* on his fiddle⟩ — see MELODY
2 a slight or gentle movement of air ⟨we sailed into the bay on a light *air* and just in time to enjoy a spectacular sunset⟩ — see BREEZE 1
3 a special quality or impression associated with something ⟨Naomi's the only person I know who can wear old jeans and a T-shirt with an *air* of elegance⟩ — see AURA
4 airs *pl* a display of emotion or behavior that is insincere or intended to deceive ⟨ever since she joined the country club she's been putting on *airs* of being too "high society" for us ordinary folks⟩ — see MASQUERADE

air *vb* to make known (as an idea, emotion, or opinion) ⟨suggested we *air* any complaints about the seating arrangements to the person who actually planned the event⟩ — see EXPRESS 1

airdrome *n* a place from which aircraft operate that usually has paved runways and a terminal ⟨helicopters taking off from a military *airdrome* near Moscow⟩ — see AIRPORT

airfield *n* a place from which aircraft operate that usually has paved runways and a terminal ⟨the passenger jet made an emergency landing at an abandoned *airfield*⟩ — see AIRPORT

airman *n* one who flies or is qualified to fly an aircraft or spacecraft ⟨her father was an *airman* who was shot down in Vietnam⟩ — see PILOT

airport *n* a place from which aircraft operate that usually has paved runways and a terminal ⟨the *airport* nearest us has plane service on only one major airline⟩
synonyms aerodrome [*British*], airdrome, airfield
related words air base, heliport; airstrip, landing field, landing strip, runway; launchpad, pad

airy *adj* **1** resembling air in lightness ⟨Aunt Helen's lemon pies are famous for their *airy* meringues⟩
synonyms ethereal, fluffy, gossamer, gossamery, light
related words dainty, delicate, downy, feathery, flimsy, insubstantial, tender, wispy; buoyant, lighter-than-air, lightweight, rarefied, unsubstantial, weightless
near antonyms firm, solid, substantial; bulky, burdensome, cumbersome, hefty, hulking, lumpish, ponderous, unwieldy, weighty
antonyms heavy, leaden
2 having little weight ⟨wondered what could be inside such an *airy* package⟩ — see ¹LIGHT 1
3 located at a greater height than average or usual ⟨*airy* mountain villages⟩ — see HIGH 3

akin *adj* **1** having a close connection like that between family members ⟨foxes are closely *akin* to dogs⟩ — see RELATED
2 having qualities in common ⟨mathematics and computer programming are *akin* in that they both require logical thinking⟩ — see ALIKE

alacritous *adj* having or showing the ability to respond without delay or hesitation ⟨his *alacritous* response to every request is "Right away, mate!"⟩ — see QUICK 1

alacrity *n* cheerful readiness to do something ⟨having just acquired his driver's license that morning, Sam agreed with *alacrity* to drive his cousin to the airport⟩
synonyms amenability, gameness, goodwill, willingness
related words celebrity, quickness, rapidity, speed, speediness, swiftness; dispatch, promptitude, promptness; ardor, avidity, eagerness, enthusiasm, exuberance, fervor, gusto, keenness, relish, zeal, zest; agreeableness, geniality, good-naturedness, heartiness, warmth; open-mindedness, receptivity, responsiveness
near antonyms leisureliness, pokiness, slowness, sluggishness; apathy, disinterestedness, halfheartedness, indifference, lukewarmness, perfunctoriness; delay, dilatoriness, doubt, equivocation, hesitance, hesitancy, hesitation, reluctance, reservation, uncertainty, vacillation; disinclination, indisposition, recalcitrance, resistance, unwillingness; antipathy, averseness, aversion

à la mode *also* **a la mode** *adj* being in the latest or current fashion ⟨Sylvia discovered that what is *à la mode* for teens to wear in the U.S. isn't all that different from what they wear in Europe⟩ — see STYLISH

alarm *n* **1** suspicion or fear of future harm or misfortune ⟨observed with *alarm* the man staggering toward the edge of the cliff⟩ — see APPREHENSION 1
2 the act or an instance of telling beforehand of danger or risk ⟨in a daring midnight ride Paul Revere gave the *alarm* that British troops were approaching⟩ — see WARNING 1
3 the emotion experienced in the presence or threat of danger ⟨filled with *alarm* when the flood waters reached their front steps⟩ — see FEAR

alarm *vb* to strike with fear ⟨I don't want to *alarm* you, but I think you should know there's a bear on your back porch⟩ — see FRIGHTEN

alarmed *adj* filled with fear or dread ⟨the Mohawks were his friends, so he was not the least bit *alarmed* at the sight of the band of Mohawk hunters⟩ — see AFRAID 1

alarming *adj* causing fear ⟨an *alarming* rise in her fever, causing the doctor to fear the worst⟩ — see FEARFUL 1

albeit *conj* in spite of the fact that ⟨she felt that her script was still too long, *albeit* it was much shorter than any of her previous scripts⟩ — see ALTHOUGH

album *n* a collection of writings ⟨a special anniversary *album* of his poetry published 100 years after his death⟩ — see ANTHOLOGY

alcohol *n* a fermented or distilled beverage that can make a person drunk ⟨once he joined the swim team, Sergei never again touched *alcohol*⟩
synonyms booze, drink, grog, intoxicant, liquor, moonshine, spirits
related words ale, beer, mead, sake (*or* saki), table wine, wine; brandy, gin, mescal, rum, tequila, vodka, whiskey (*or* whisky)

alcove *n* a hollowed-out space in a wall ⟨an ancient vase in an *alcove* and a sculpture of Achilles on a stand in the museum's Greek Hall⟩ — see NICHE 1

alert *adj* **1** paying close attention usually for the purpose of anticipating approaching danger or opportunity

⟨Susan needed to stay *alert* throughout the train ride so as not to miss her stop⟩
synonyms attentive, awake, open-eyed, vigilant, watchful, wide-awake
related words alive, aware, conscious, sensitive; heedful, mindful, observant, observing, sharp, sharp-eyed; sleepless, wakeful; careful, cautious, chary, wary; prepared, ready
phrases on guard, on the alert
near antonyms absent, absentminded, absorbed, abstracted, daydreaming, dazed, distracted, dreaming, dreamy, engrossed, faraway, insensible, oblivious, preoccupied; asleep, sleeping, unaware, unconscious, unknowing, unperceiving, unseeing, unwitting; careless, heedless, inattentive, unheeding, unmindful, unobservant, unobserving, unthinking, unwary; unprepared, unready
2 having or showing a close attentiveness to avoiding danger or trouble ⟨warned us to be *alert* to the presence of pickpockets on the crowded bus⟩ — see CAREFUL 1
3 having or showing quickness of mind ⟨an *alert* and well-trained sheep dog who can handle difficult situations⟩ — see INTELLIGENT 1
4 having or showing the ability to respond without delay or hesitation ⟨an *alert* force of commandos, ready to go on a mission at a moment's notice⟩ — see QUICK 1
alert *n* the act or an instance of telling beforehand of danger or risk ⟨the white flash of the doe's raised tail, giving the "danger" *alert* to her fawns⟩ — see WARNING 1
alert *vb* to give notice to beforehand especially of danger or risk ⟨*alerted* us to the possibility that the roads would be flooded and we might have to take a detour⟩ — see WARN
alertness *n* **1** a close attentiveness to avoiding danger ⟨drove through the fog with extra *alertness*, as the road signs repeatedly warned of deer and moose crossings⟩ — see CAUTION 1
2 the act or state of being constantly attentive and responsive to signs of opportunity, activity, or danger ⟨we observed the U.S. border patrol's intensified *alertness* for drug smugglers at the border stations⟩ — see VIGILANCE
alias *n* **1** a descriptive or familiar name given instead of or in addition to the one belonging to an individual ⟨a dressmaker whom everyone knows as "Bet," her adopted *alias* in the dressmaking business that she named after Betsy Ross⟩ — see NICKNAME
2 a fictitious or assumed name ⟨the English author Eric Blair, better known under the *alias* of George Orwell⟩ — see PSEUDONYM
alibi *n* an explanation that frees one from fault or blame ⟨a student who always has a very creative *alibi* for undone homework or late papers⟩ — see EXCUSE
alien *adj* **1** being, relating to, or characteristic of a country other than one's own ⟨new immigrants with customs *alien* to the community where they have settled⟩ — see FOREIGN 1
2 not being a vital part of or belonging to something ⟨it's completely *alien* to her nature to wish evil of anyone⟩ — see EXTRINSIC
alienate *vb* **1** to cause to change from friendly or loving to unfriendly or uncaring ⟨Jessica's constant badmouthing of Daniele completely *alienated* Daniele's other friends⟩ — see ESTRANGE

2 to give over the legal possession or ownership of ⟨a landowner has a right to *alienate* his right of ownership—in other words, he can sell the land if he wants to⟩ — see TRANSFER 1
alienation *n* the loss of friendship or affection ⟨after years of *alienation* from her family, she became reconciled with them when her father fell ill⟩ — see ESTRANGEMENT
alight *adj* filled with much light ⟨we approached the clearing, *alight* with torches, and observed a reenactment of ancient rites by Druids⟩ — see BRIGHT 2
alight *vb* to come to rest after descending from the air ⟨a flock of eight swans circled above, then *alighted* on the pond⟩
synonyms land, light, perch, roost, settle, touch down
related words belly-land, crash-land
near antonyms arise, ascend, climb, rise; float, fly, glide, plane, soar, wing; hang, hover
antonyms take off
alike *adj* having qualities in common ⟨all the houses in the neighborhood are *alike* in that they all have a one-car garage and a fenced-in backyard⟩
synonyms akin, analogous, comparable, correspondent, corresponding, like, matching, parallel, resembling, similar, such, suchlike
related words commensurate, proportionate; tantamount, virtual; allied, kindred, related; approaching, approximating, close, coextensive, coincident, conformable, conforming, consistent, consonant, equal, equivalent, identical, indistinguishable, interchangeable, same, selfsame, synonymous, twin; homogeneous, unchanging, uniform, unvaried, unvarying
phrases on the order of
near antonyms disparate, distinct, distinguishable; variable, varied, varying; imprecise, inaccurate, inexact; unallied, unconnected, unrelated
antonyms different, dissimilar, diverse, unlike
alike *adv* in like manner ⟨disapproved of by teachers and students *alike*⟩ — see ALSO 1
alikeness *n* the quality or state of having many qualities in common ⟨since they're identical twins, you shouldn't be so surprised at the *alikeness* of their personal tastes⟩ — see SIMILARITY 1
alive *adj* **1** having or showing life ⟨after crashing into the plate glass window the little bird was not only still *alive*, it seemed merely dazed⟩
synonyms animate, breathing, live, living
related words active, animated, dynamic, lively, thriving, vibrant, vital, vivacious; current, existent, existing, extant, going, prevailing, surviving
near antonyms dying, fading, moribund; stillborn; absent, extinct, fallen, finished, gone, lapsed, lost, nonexistent, perished, terminated, vanished, wiped out; barren, desert
antonyms breathless, dead, deceased, defunct, departed, expired, inanimate, lifeless, nonliving
2 marked by much life, movement, or activity ⟨the mall was *alive* with holiday shoppers⟩
synonyms animated, astir, bustling, busy, buzzing, flourishing, humming, lively, thriving, vibrant
related words abounding, crowded, overflowing, populous, swarming, teeming, thronging
antonyms asleep, dead, inactive, lifeless, sleepy
3 being in effective operation ⟨kept the cause of peace *alive* despite severe setbacks in relations between the two nations⟩ — see ACTIVE 1

4 having being at the present time ⟨insists that her new boyfriend is the handsomest guy *alive*⟩ — see EXTANT 1

5 having specified facts or feelings actively impressed on the mind ⟨*alive* to the need for major improvements in the school system⟩ — see CONSCIOUS

all *adj* not divided or scattered among several areas of interest or concern ⟨you need to focus *all* your attention on this matter⟩ — see WHOLE 1

all *adv* **1** to a full extent or degree ⟨we are *all* out of milk⟩ ⟨I was *all* ready to leave at least ten minutes ago⟩ — see FULLY 1

2 for each one ⟨the score is three *all*⟩ — see APIECE

all *pron* every person ⟨a joyous holiday to one and *all!*⟩ — see EVERYBODY

Allah *n* the being worshipped as the creator and ruler of the universe ⟨Muslims worship *Allah*⟩ — see DEITY 2

all–around *also* **all–round** *adj* **1** not limited or specialized in application or purpose ⟨an *all-around* garden rake that adjusts for any raking task, from raking lawns to delicate flower beds⟩ — see GENERAL 4

2 relating to the main elements and not to specific details ⟨this saw has the top rating for *all-around* performance, but for small detail work it might not be your best choice⟩ — see GENERAL 2

3 able to do many different kinds of things ⟨an *all-around* player, as skilled on the pitcher's mound as he is at the batting plate⟩ — see VERSATILE

allay *vb* **1** to free from distress or disturbance ⟨something that should *allay* your anxieties⟩ — see CALM 1

2 to make more bearable or less severe ⟨a gentle breeze would *allay* the heat⟩ — see HELP 2

allege *vb* to state as a fact usually forcefully ⟨*alleged* that the restaurant chain was engaging in discriminatory hiring practices⟩ — see CLAIM 1

allegiance *n* adherence to something to which one is bound by a pledge or duty ⟨torn between his *allegiance* to his native country and the opportunities a sports career in the U.S. could offer⟩ — see FIDELITY

allegory *n* a story intended to teach a basic truth or moral about life ⟨Dr. Seuss's story "The Sneetches" is an *allegory* about tolerance for people's differences⟩
   synonyms fable, parable
   related words morality play; legend, myth, narrative, tale

allergic *adj* having a natural dislike for something ⟨a lover of the outdoors who claims to be *allergic* to desk jobs⟩ — see ANTIPATHETIC

allergy *n* a strong feeling of not liking or approving ⟨independent-minded people who seem to have an *allergy* to any control from the government⟩ — see DISLIKE 1

alleviate *vb* to make more bearable or less severe ⟨a carpool *alleviates* some of the stress of driving the kids to and from school every day⟩ — see HELP 2

alleviation *n* reduction of or freedom from pain ⟨hoping a couple of aspirin would provide some *alleviation* of the pain in his shoulder⟩ — see EASE 1

alliance *n* **1** a formal agreement between two or more nations or peoples ⟨the smaller countries signed an *alliance* pledging to protect one another against the belligerent behemoth in their midst⟩ — see TREATY

2 an association of persons, parties, or states for mutual assistance and protection ⟨an *alliance* between the French and the Algonquians to check Iroquois advances into their territory⟩ — see CONFEDERACY

3 the state of having shared interests or efforts (as in social or business matters) ⟨in *alliance* with book-

sellers, the nation's schools are promoting National Reading Month⟩ — see ASSOCIATION 1

allied *adj* having a close connection like that between family members ⟨people with foreign language fluency and an *allied* skill such as the ability to relate to people from different cultures⟩ — see RELATED

all–important *adj* impossible to do without ⟨that *all-important* item for a successful birthday party: a fancily decorated cake with candles⟩ — see ESSENTIAL 1

allocate *vb* **1** to give as a share or portion ⟨not enough computers to *allocate* one to every student⟩ — see ALLOT

2 to give out (something) in appropriate amounts or to appropriate individuals ⟨*allocated* the housework in such a way that the older kids got more than the younger ones⟩ — see ADMINISTER 1

3 to keep or intend for a special purpose ⟨crushed the strawberries after first *allocating* all the nicest ones for the top of the cake⟩ — see DEVOTE 1

allocation *n* **1** a sum of money allotted for a specific use by official or formal action ⟨recognizing the importance of the arts in the health of a city, the council increased the *allocation* for the city's annual jazz festival⟩ — see APPROPRIATION

2 the act or process of giving out something to each member of a group ⟨the *allocation* of Halloween candy became my job when I was too old to go trick-or-treating⟩ — see DISTRIBUTION 1

allot *vb* to give as a share or portion ⟨each speaker was *allotted* five minutes to present his or her opinion in the debate⟩
   synonyms allocate, allow, apportion, assign, ration
   related words deal, dispense, distribute, divide, dole (out), measure, mete (out), parcel (out), portion, pro-rate, reserve; accord, award, grant; chip in, contribute, donate
   near antonyms begrudge, deny, deprive (of); keep, retain, stint, withhold; appropriate, arrogate, confiscate

allotment *n* **1** a sum of money allotted for a specific use by official or formal action ⟨the library budget was reduced, while *allotments* for city officials' travel expenses were increased⟩ — see APPROPRIATION

2 something belonging to, due to, or contributed by an individual member of a group ⟨every kindergartner received colored paper, scissors, and an *allotment* of paste to make paper chains⟩ — see SHARE 1

all–out *adj* **1** having no exceptions or restrictions ⟨Grandpa got the *all-out* support of the family when he decided to remarry at age 72⟩ — see ABSOLUTE 2

2 trying all possibilities ⟨an *all-out* effort to break open the door⟩ — see EXHAUSTIVE

all out *adv* with all power or resources being used ⟨went *all out* for her New Year's Eve party—she even had fireworks!⟩ — see FULL BLAST

all over *adv* in every place or in all places ⟨I've looked *all over*—even outside—and I can't find my other shoe⟩ — see EVERYWHERE

allow *vb* **1** to give permission for or to approve of ⟨flash photography is not *allowed* inside the church⟩
   synonyms have, permit, suffer
   related words authorize, commission, license (*also* licence); accede (to), acquiesce, agree (to), assent (to), consent (to), OK (*or* okay), warrant; accord, concede, grant, sanction, vouchsafe; admit, brook, condone, countenance, endure, support, tolerate
   near antonyms hinder, impede, obstruct; censure, disallow, disapprove, deny, interdict, refuse, reject, revoke, suppress, withhold; deplore, discountenance,

dislike, disfavor, frown (at *or* on); check, curb, repress, restrain

antonyms ban, enjoin, forbid, prohibit, proscribe, veto
2 to give permission to ⟨Cindy's parents sometimes *allow* her to take the bus by herself downtown⟩
synonyms let, permit, suffer
related words authorize, commission, empower, license (*also* licence); approve, endorse (*also* indorse), sanction; free, liberate, release; cater (to), give in (to), humor, indulge
near antonyms deter, discourage; bar, block, constrain, curb, frustrate, hold back, impede, inhibit, obstruct, prevent
antonyms enjoin, forbid, prohibit
3 to accept the truth or existence of (something) usually reluctantly ⟨I'll *allow* I probably said more than I should have⟩ — see ADMIT
4 to give as a share or portion ⟨*allowed* each camper one match to light his fire⟩ — see ALLOT
5 to make able or possible ⟨a patient's cancelled appointment *allowed* the doctor to squeeze in a few extra phone calls⟩ — see ENABLE 1

allowable *adj* that may be permitted ⟨homework that's not typed isn't *allowable*⟩ — see PERMISSIBLE

allowance *n* **1** something belonging to, due to, or contributed by an individual member of a group ⟨as the war progressed, each family's *allowance* of sugar and flour was reduced⟩ — see SHARE 1
2 the approval by someone in authority for the doing of something ⟨without the official *allowance* of the school board, no organization can hold its meetings on school property⟩ — see PERMISSION

alloyed *adj* containing foreign or lower-grade substances ⟨*alloyed* aluminum, containing either copper or silicon, is much stronger than pure aluminum for cookware⟩ — see IMPURE

all–powerful *adj* having unlimited power or authority ⟨that country's monarch was never an *all-powerful* ruler, but one who shared power with a parliament⟩ — see OMNIPOTENT

all–purpose *adj* not limited or specialized in application or purpose ⟨there's nothing wrong with *all-purpose* flour for baking bread, but flour with more gluten is better⟩ — see GENERAL 4

all right *adj* **1** being to one's liking ⟨it's *all right* with me if you wear jeans to the party⟩ — see SATISFACTORY 1
2 not exposed to the threat of loss or injury ⟨as soon as we heard the rescue helicopter, we knew we were *all right*⟩ — see SAFE 1
3 of a level of quality that meets one's needs or standards ⟨it wasn't a great meal, but it was *all right*⟩ — see ADEQUATE

all right *adv* **1** in a satisfactory way ⟨if everything goes *all right*, I should be back in a day or two⟩ — see WELL 1
2 used to express agreement ⟨*all right*, I'll try one tiny bite of octopus⟩ — see YES

allude *vb* to convey an idea indirectly ⟨Mrs. Simons *alluded* to some health problems, without being specific⟩ — see HINT

allure *n* the power of irresistible attraction ⟨the *allure* of America's Wild West attracts vacationers to ghost towns⟩ — see CHARM 2

allure *vb* **1** to attract or delight as if by magic ⟨was so *allured* by his daughter's fiancé that he offered him a partnership in his business even before the couple got married⟩ — see CHARM 1
2 to lead away from a usual or proper course by offering some pleasure or advantage ⟨*allured* by a cottage

made of gingerbread, Handsel and Gretel almost ended up as witch's stew⟩ — see LURE

allurement *n* **1** something that persuades one to perform an action for pleasure or gain ⟨for him the *allurement* of gambling is not the prospect of getting rich but rather the excitement of the game⟩ — see LURE 1
2 the act or pressure of giving in to a desire especially when ill-advised ⟨difficult to ignore the *allurements* of the sideshow posters at the carnival⟩ — see TEMPTATION 1

alluring *adj* having an often mysterious or magical power to attract ⟨the *alluring* beauty of the swans on the lake held us spellbound⟩ — see FASCINATING 1

ally *n* someone associated with another to give assistance or moral support ⟨in trying to convince his parents to send him to soccer camp, Toby had a real *ally* in his coach⟩
synonyms abettor (*also* abetter), backer, confederate, supporter, sympathizer
related words well-wisher; accessory, accomplice, collaborationist, collaborator; adjunct, assistant, coadjutor, helper; associate, cohort, colleague, fellow, partner; buddy, chum, companion, comrade, confidant, crony, familiar, friend, intimate, mate, pal
near antonyms belittler, detractor; adversary, enemy, foe, opponent

ally *vb* to form or enter into an association that furthers the interests of its members ⟨the area's small grape growers have *allied* and formed a cooperative that will help them get the best prices⟩
synonyms associate, band, club, confederate, conjoin, cooperate, federate, league, unite
related words collaborate, gang (up), team (up); incorporate, organize, unionize; affiliate; amalgamate, combine, conglomerate, consolidate, converge, group, join, merge; knot, link, tie, wed
near antonyms detach, disengage, dissolve, disunite; divorce, part, segregate, separate, sever, split, sunder; alienate, estrange, fall out
antonyms break up, disband

almighty *adj* having unlimited power or authority ⟨when we are young, we want our parents to be *almighty* and to be able to make everything right when something goes wrong⟩ — see OMNIPOTENT

Almighty *n* the being worshipped as the creator and ruler of the universe ⟨the missionaries gave thanks to the *Almighty* for their miraculous deliverance from death⟩ — see DEITY 2

almost *adv* very close to but not completely ⟨we were *almost* finished with dinner when Uncle Richard showed up⟩ ⟨there were *almost* enough seats for everybody on the bus⟩
synonyms about, more or less, most, much, near, nearly, next to, nigh, practically, some, virtually, wellnigh
related words appreciably, by and large, chiefly, largely, mainly, mostly; partially, partly, somewhat
phrases as good as
near antonyms absolutely, altogether, completely, entirely, fully, plumb [*chiefly dialect*], quite, thoroughly; totally, utterly, wholly; barely, hardly, scarcely

alms *n* a gift of money or its equivalent to a charity, humanitarian cause, or public institution ⟨believes that giving *alms* to the poor is a moral duty⟩ — see CONTRIBUTION

almsgiving *n* the giving of necessities and especially money to the needy ⟨good works such as *almsgiving*, tending the sick and visiting the imprisoned〉 — see CHARITY 1

aloft *adv* to or in a higher place 〈the ease with which he can hold a ballerina *aloft* with one hand is awesome〉 — see ABOVE

alone *adj* 1 not being in the company of others 〈no one realized Jeff was *alone* in his room so they all left for the movies without him〉
synonyms lone, lonely, lonesome, solitary, solo, unaccompanied
related words unattended, unchaperoned; forlorn, friendless; cloistered, insulated, isolated, remote, retired, secluded, withdrawn; quarantined, segregated, separated, sequestered; separate, unattached, unconnected, unlinked; detached, disconnected, disjointed, dissociated, disunited, divided, fractionated; abandoned, adrift, deserted, desolate, forgotten, forsaken, lorn, neglected
near antonyms attended, chaperoned, escorted; adjacent, adjoining, communicating, contiguous, neighboring, next-door; attached, connected, coupled, linked
antonyms accompanied
2 being the one or ones of a class with no other members 〈he is *alone* among the actors of his generation in his exceptional ability to play both comedic and serious parts〉 — see ONLY 2

alone *adv* 1 without aid or support 〈Rebecca managed to find her way home *alone*〉
synonyms independently, single-handedly, singly, solely, unaided, unassisted
related words individually, separately
phrases by oneself
near antonyms collectively, conjointly, cooperatively, jointly, mutually, together; en masse
2 for nothing other than 〈would willingly play professional baseball for the sheer enjoyment *alone*〉 — see SOLELY 1

along *adv* toward or at a point lying in advance in space or time 〈traffic was inching *along* at a snail's pace〉 〈work on the project is moving right *along*〉
synonyms ahead, forth, forward, on, onward (*also* onwards)
related words before
near antonyms back, backward (*or* backwards), behind, rearward (*or* rearwards)

aloof *adj* having or showing a lack of friendliness or interest in others 〈the new kid was really not so *aloof* as we thought him at first, just painfully shy〉 — see COOL 1

aloud *adv* with one's normal voice speaking the words 〈Mr. Gripp likes to call on the sleepiest-looking students to read *aloud* from the textbook〉
synonyms audibly, out, out loud
related words clearly, discernibly, distinctly, distinguishably, perceptibly, plainly; blatantly, boisterously, clamorously, loudly, lustily, mightily, noisily, resoundingly, stridently, thunderously, uproariously, vociferously
near antonyms faintly, feebly, low, noiselessly, quietly, softly
antonyms inaudibly, silently, soundlessly

alp *n* an elevation of land higher than a hill 〈an adventurer who has scaled *alps*, explored ocean depths, and flown into the stratosphere〉 — see MOUNTAIN 1

alpha *n* the point at which something begins 〈money is not the *alpha* and omega—the beginning and end—of life's purpose〉 — see BEGINNING

alright *adj* 1 being to one's liking 〈an *alright* movie, but I wouldn't pay to see it again〉 — see SATISFACTORY 1
2 not exposed to the threat of loss or injury 〈we got the plane's nose back up, and after that we were *alright*〉 — see SAFE 1

alright *adv* used to express agreement 〈*alright*, you can buy me lunch, but next time it's my treat〉 — see YES

also *adv* 1 in like manner 〈we stayed at an historic London hotel, the same establishment that had *also* welcomed our grandparents many years ago〉
synonyms alike, correspondingly, likewise, similarly, so
related words equally, equivalently, identically
near antonyms contrarily, conversely, inversely, oppositely, vice versa; diversely, unequally, variously
antonyms differently, dissimilarly, otherwise
2 in addition to what has been said 〈I'd like a bicycle for my birthday; *also*, I'd like a new CD player〉 — see MORE 1

alter *vb* 1 to make different in some way 〈can't you *alter* your plans just slightly so we can leave ten minutes earlier?〉 — see CHANGE 1
2 to remove the sex organs of 〈contends that cats and dogs that have been *altered* make better pets〉 — see NEUTER

alterable *adj* capable of being readily changed 〈if my vacation plans were *alterable*, I'd change them〉 — see FLEXIBLE 1

alteration *n* the act, process, or result of making different 〈there's been an *alteration* in the intended route of our bird walk〉 — see CHANGE

altercation *n* an often noisy or angry expression of differing opinions 〈judging from all the slamming and banging, I'd say there was some sort of *altercation* going on next door〉 — see ARGUMENT 1

alternative *n* the power, right, or opportunity to choose 〈there's no *alternative*: we must cross the stream to reach our destination〉 — see CHOICE 1

although *also* **altho** *conj* in spite of the fact that 〈*although* I've been to his house several times, I still can't remember how to get there〉
synonyms albeit, howbeit, though, when, while, whilst [*chiefly British*]
related words but, whereas

altitude *n* 1 the distance of something or someone from bottom to top 〈the *altitude* of the highest mountain in the U.S. is only about two thirds that of the highest mountain in the world〉 — see HEIGHT 3
2 the most extreme or advanced point 〈a man whose arrogance continues to reach new *altitudes*〉 — see HEIGHT 2
3 *usually* **altitudes** *pl* an area of high ground 〈the air is thinner at higher *altitudes*〉 — see HEIGHT 4

altogether *adv* 1 for the most part 〈*altogether*, I'd say we had a pretty good time〉 — see CHIEFLY
2 to a full extent or degree 〈I was not *altogether* prepared for such bad news〉 — see FULLY 1

altruistic *adj* having or showing a concern for the welfare of others 〈I'm not being *altruistic* in giving you these books, since I was going to have to lug them with me if you hadn't come along〉 — see CHARITABLE 1

always *adv* 1 on every relevant occasion 〈Aunt Trina *always* insists we stay for dinner〉
synonyms consistently, constantly, continually, ever, forever, incessantly, invariably, perpetually, unfailingly
related words commonly, frequently, oft, often, oftentimes (*or* ofttimes), recurrently, repeatedly; continuously, steadily, uninterruptedly; dependably, normally,

ordinarily, regularly, routinely, typically, usually; inevitably; eternally, everlastingly

near antonyms intermittently, occasionally, periodically, sometimes, sporadically; infrequently, rarely, seldom, unusually

antonyms ne'er, never

2 for all time ⟨I will love you *always*⟩ — see EVER 1

amalgam *n* a distinct entity formed by the combining of two or more different things ⟨a church that is an *amalgam* of traditional and modern architectural styles⟩ — see BLEND

amalgamate *vb* **1** to mix thoroughly so that the things mixed cannot be recognized ⟨four local school districts *amalgamated* into one regional district⟩ — see BLEND 1

2 to turn into a single mass that is more or less the same throughout ⟨silver *amalgamated* with mercury is used for tooth fillings⟩ — see BLEND 1

amalgamated *adj* made from the joining of two or more parts or elements ⟨the *Amalgamated* Clothing and Textile Workers Union was formed from the merger of the clothing workers' and textile workers' unions⟩ — see COMPOSITE

amalgamation *n* a distinct entity formed by the combining of two or more different things ⟨an *amalgamation* of peat moss and vermiculite is a good medium for starting vegetable seedlings⟩ — see BLEND

amass *vb* to bring together in one body or place ⟨*amassed* a truckload of donations in the course of their canned food drive⟩ — see GATHER 1

amateur *adj* lacking or showing a lack of expert skill ⟨in every room there were *amateur* watercolors, apparently the work of the innkeeper's wife⟩ — see AMATEURISH

amateur *n* a person who regularly or occasionally engages in an activity without being or becoming an expert at it ⟨a homemade doghouse that looked like it was built by an *amateur* who hadn't mastered basic carpentry⟩

synonyms dabbler, dilettante, potterer, putterer

related words apprentice, trainee; beginner, freshman, greenhorn, learner, neophyte, newcomer, novice, rookie, tenderfoot, tyro; hobbyist, tinkerer, trifler; layman, nonprofessional

near antonyms authority, pro, professional; maestro, virtuoso, whiz, wizard; artisan, artist, craftsman, workman; initiate, journeyman; specialist, technician; old hand, old-timer, vet, veteran

antonyms ace, adept, crackerjack, expert, master, past master

amateurish *adj* lacking or showing a lack of expert skill ⟨that's an *amateurish* wallpapering job—the pattern doesn't match at the seams⟩

synonyms amateur, dilettante, inexperienced, inexpert, nonprofessional, unprofessional, unskilled, unskillful

related words primitive, self-taught, uninitiated, unprepared, unqualified, unschooled, untaught, untrained, untutored; clumsy, crude, defective, faulty, flawed, unfinished, unpolished; beginning, green, new, raw, unpracticed, unseasoned, untested, untried; incapable, incompetent, unable, unfit, ungifted, untalented

near antonyms able, accomplished, capable, competent, dexterous (*also* dextrous), gifted, proficient, skilled, skillful, talented; experienced, practiced (*or* practised), seasoned, veteran; educated, fitted, initiated, knowledgeable, prepared, qualified, schooled,

taught, trained, tutored, versed; all-around (*also* all-round), versatile, well-rounded; finished, polished

antonyms ace, adept, consummate, crackerjack, expert, master, masterful, masterly, professional, virtuoso

amatory *adj* of, relating to, or expressing sexual attraction ⟨*amatory* letters that kept their love alive during the years they were separated by war⟩ — see EROTIC

amaze *vb* to make a strong impression on (someone) with something unexpected ⟨your ability to remember names and faces *amazes* me⟩ — see SURPRISE 1

amazed *adj* **1** affected with sudden and great wonder or surprise ⟨you'd be *amazed* at the destruction one small squirrel can cause inside a house⟩ — see THUNDERSTRUCK

2 filled with amazement or wonder ⟨a visitor cannot help but be *amazed* by the size of the Great Pyramid⟩ — see OPENMOUTHED

amazement *n* **1** the rapt attention and deep emotion caused by the sight of something extraordinary ⟨Israelites watched in *amazement* as the Red Sea parted so that they could cross on dry land⟩ — see WONDER 2

2 the state of being strongly impressed by something unexpected or unusual ⟨imagine Dorothy's *amazement* when she discovered that the Wizard of Oz was just an ordinary man⟩ — see SURPRISE 2

amazing *adj* **1** causing a strong emotional reaction because unexpected ⟨it was rather *amazing* that the store let me return the sweater after I'd worn and even washed it⟩ — see SURPRISING 1

2 causing wonder or astonishment ⟨the *amazing* feats of the circus acrobats simply enthralled the audience⟩ — see MARVELOUS 1

ambassador *n* a person sent on a mission to represent another ⟨a beloved entertainer who has often been sent abroad by the president as his country's goodwill *ambassador*⟩

synonyms delegate, emissary, envoy, minister, legate, representative

related words agent, attaché, consul, deputy, diplomat, foreign minister, nuncio, procurator, proxy; apostle, evangelist, missionary; deputation, detachment, legation; courier, messenger; mouthpiece, spokesperson

ambiguity *n* the quality or state of having a veiled or uncertain meaning ⟨the *ambiguity* of the clairvoyant's messages from the deceased allowed the grieving relatives to interpret them however they wished⟩ — see OBSCURITY 1

ambiguous *adj* having an often intentionally veiled or uncertain meaning ⟨the exact reason for the change in plans is *ambiguous*, but I suspect it has something to do with money⟩ — see OBSCURE 1

ambiguousness *n* the quality or state of having a veiled or uncertain meaning ⟨the *ambiguousness* of her "I'll come if I can" left us wondering if we should find someone to take her place⟩ — see OBSCURITY 1

ambition *n* **1** eager desire for personal advancement ⟨"Talent without *ambition* will not make you a star," McKenzie's dance instructor liked to remind her⟩

synonyms aspiration, go-getting

related words determination, diligence, drive, energy, enterprise, go, hustle, industry, initiative, motivation, push; opportunism; aggression, assertiveness, daring, spirit; ardor, avidity, eagerness, keenness, passion; avarice, greed

near antonyms apathy, indifference, unconcern; idleness, indolence, inertia, laziness, lethargy, shiftlessness, sloth

2 readiness to engage in daring or difficult activity ⟨the *ambition* shown by the undersea explorers of the Mariana Trench, the deepest in the world⟩ — see ENTERPRISE 2

3 something that one hopes or intends to accomplish ⟨his *ambition* is to study international business, then get a job overseas⟩ — see GOAL

ambitious *adj* **1** having a strong desire for personal advancement ⟨an *ambitious* child actor and his even more ambitious mother, who will do anything to get him in commercials⟩

synonyms aspiring, go-getting, self-seeking

related words determined, diligent, driving, dynamic, enterprising, gung ho, hustling, industrious, motivated, scrappy, venturesome, venturous; animated, lively, spirited; ardent, avid, eager, energetic, impassioned, keen, raring, vigorous; aggressive, assertive, opportunistic, pushy, self-assertive

near antonyms apathetic, disinterested, indifferent, uneager, unenthusiastic, unexcited, uninterested; casual, easygoing, lackadaisical; halfhearted, lukewarm, tepid; lazy, lethargic, listless, shiftless, sluggish, spiritless; unaggressive, unassertive

2 having or showing a bold forcefulness in the pursuit of a goal ⟨cleaning up the vacant lot in one weekend was an *ambitious* undertaking⟩ — see AGGRESSIVE 1

ambrosial *adj* **1** having a pleasant smell ⟨the *ambrosial* air of a greenhouse filled with orchids⟩ — see FRAGRANT

2 very pleasing to the sense of taste ⟨a platter heaped with exotic and *ambrosial* tropical fruits⟩ — see DELICIOUS 1

ambuscade *n* a scheme in which hidden persons wait to attack by surprise ⟨warned by one of their scouts of an Apache *ambuscade*, the Comanches took a different path through the mountains⟩ — see AMBUSH 1

ambush *n* **1** a scheme in which hidden persons wait to attack by surprise ⟨revolutionaries laid an *ambush* for the king along the route his carriage would travel⟩

synonyms ambuscade, surprise, trap

related words assault, attack, charge, sally; capture, entrapment, snare; hunting, stalking

2 a device or scheme for capturing another by surprise ⟨thinking that he was getting into his assigned limousine, the diplomat did not realize that he was the victim of an *ambush* as he was being lured into his captor's car⟩ — see TRAP 1

ambush *vb* to lie in wait for and attack by surprise ⟨the king's enemies planned to *ambush* the royal coach on the way to Paris and capture the king⟩

synonyms surprise, waylay

related words assail, assault, attack, storm, strike; jump, pounce (on), tackle; charge, sally; capture, ensnare, entrap, net, snare, trap; hunt, prey (on *or* upon), stalk

phrases lay for

ameliorate *vb* to make better ⟨social legislation that must be given credit for *ameliorating* the lot of millions of deprived people⟩ — see IMPROVE

amenability *n* **1** a desire or disposition to please ⟨our circle of friends tends to take advantage of Will's *amenability*, usually not even bothering to ask him what he wants to do⟩ — see COMPLAISANCE

2 cheerful readiness to do something ⟨our cat Figaro hasn't shown much *amenability* to going outside now that the weather's cold⟩ — see ALACRITY

amenable *adj* **1** having a desire or inclination (as for a specified course of action) ⟨whatever you decide to do, I'm *amenable*—just let me know⟩ — see WILLING 1

2 readily giving in to the command or authority of another ⟨Grandma doesn't think my little brother is difficult, as he's perfectly *amenable* whenever he's with her⟩ — see OBEDIENT

amend *vb* **1** to make better ⟨trying to *amend* the situation of the striking workers by supplying them with minimal food supplies⟩ — see IMPROVE

2 to remove errors, defects, deficiencies, or deviations from ⟨the Bill of Rights was adopted in an effort to *amend* a constitution that seemed to many to be deficient in guaranteeing individual rights⟩ — see CORRECT 1

amendment *n* a change designed to correct or improve a written work ⟨the article as written requires only one factual *amendment*⟩ — see CORRECTION 1

amenity *n* **1** an act or utterance that is a customary show of good manners ⟨an unhappy, bickering couple who, at least in public, observe all the *amenities* of polite behavior⟩ — see CIVILITY 1

2 something adding to pleasure or comfort but not absolutely necessary ⟨we don't need an expensive hotel with all the *amenities*—just a place to sleep⟩ — see LUXURY 1

3 something that adds to one's ease ⟨that campground has so many of the *amenities* of home that it is best left to those who only like to pretend they are camping⟩ — see COMFORT 2

4 the state or quality of having a pleasant or agreeable manner in socializing with others ⟨at the nursing home Mr. Crawford's natural *amenity* charms the ladies and puts the men at ease⟩ — see AMIABILITY 1

American Indian *n* a member of any of the native peoples of the western hemisphere usually not including the Eskimos ⟨Jeremy's great-grandfather was an *American Indian*, a member of the Shoshones⟩

synonyms Amerindian (*also* Amerind), Indian, Native American

related words mestizo

Amerindian *also* **Amerind** *n* a member of any of the native peoples of the western hemisphere usually not including the Eskimos ⟨a basketry design unique among *Amerindians* in the Southwest⟩ — see AMERICAN INDIAN

amiability *n* **1** the state or quality of having a pleasant or agreeable manner in socializing with others ⟨the waitress's *amiability* is what makes eating at the diner so much fun⟩

synonyms affability, agreeableness, amenity, amiableness, geniality, good-naturedness, good-temperedness, graciousness, niceness, pleasantness, sweetness

related words amenability, complaisance; amicability, amity, cordiality, friendliness; benignity, gentleness, kindness; cheerfulness, cheeriness, sunniness; civility, comity, considerateness, consideration, courteousness, courtesy, politeness, thoughtfulness; attractiveness, delightfulness, enjoyableness

near antonyms boorishness, discourtesy, impoliteness, incivility, rudeness, ungraciousness; biliousness, cantankerousness, churlishness, crankiness, fussiness, grouchiness, grumpiness, irascibility, irritability, peevishness, petulance, testiness; contentiousness, contrariness, orneriness, querulousness; hostility, unfriendliness

antonyms disagreeableness, unpleasantness

2 a desire or disposition to please ⟨we had expected our rich cousin to be pushy and snobby, so we were pleasantly surprised by her *amiability*⟩ — see COMPLAISANCE

amiable *adj* having an easygoing and pleasing manner especially in social situations ⟨the owner of the inn is an *amiable*, talkative widow who treats guests like family⟩
synonyms affable, agreeable, genial, good-natured, good-tempered, gracious, nice, sweet, well-disposed
related words amicable, cordial, friendly, neighborly; benign, gentle, kind; cheerful, cheery, sunny; companionable, sociable; civil, considerate, courteous, polite, thoughtful; accommodating, amenable, obliging; attractive, delightful, enjoyable
near antonyms boorish, discourteous, ill-mannered, impolite, inconsiderate, rude, surly, uncivil, unmannerly; bearish, bilious, cantankerous, choleric, churlish, crabby, cranky, dyspeptic, fussy, grouchy, grumpy, ill-humored, irascible, irritable, peevish, petulant, quick-tempered, snappish, testy, touchy; argumentative, contentious, contrary, ornery, querulous; unappealing, unattractive
antonyms disagreeable, ill-natured, ill-tempered, ungracious, unpleasant

amiableness *n* the state or quality of having a pleasant or agreeable manner in socializing with others ⟨the dance instructor's natural *amiableness* puts new students immediately at ease⟩ — see AMIABILITY 1

amicable *adj* **1** having or marked by agreement in feeling or action ⟨the contract negotiations between the hotel workers and management were reasonably *amicable*⟩ — see HARMONIOUS 3
2 having or showing kindly feeling and sincere interest ⟨Victoria finds the kids at her new school just as *amicable* as she ever could have hoped⟩ — see FRIENDLY 1

amid *or* **amidst** *prep* in or into the middle of ⟨having grown up *amid* farmers and ranchers, Keith still thinks of himself as a country boy at heart⟩ — see AMONG

amiss *adv* **1** in a mistaken or inappropriate way ⟨I hope that my suggestion that you might be more comfortable in a larger chair was not taken *amiss*⟩ — see WRONGLY
2 off the desired or intended path or course ⟨the reenactment of the Wright Brothers' first flight went *amiss* when the wind died on the makeshift runway and the plane stopped short in a mud puddle⟩ — see WRONG 1

amity *n* kindly concern, interest, or support ⟨a youth club fostering *amity* among the city's many and diverse ethnic groups⟩ — see GOODWILL 1

ammunition *n* means or method of defending ⟨be certain that all of your accusations are true, lest you just give them *ammunition* to claim that all of them are false⟩ — see DEFENSE 1

amnesty *n* release from the guilt or penalty of an offense ⟨the president of France traditionally grants *amnesty* to specially selected prisoners on Bastille Day⟩ — see PARDON

amok *or* **amuck** *adv* in a confused and reckless manner ⟨returned to the classroom to find an escaped snake and her students running *amok*⟩ — see HELTER-SKELTER 1

among *also* **amongst** *prep* in or into the middle of ⟨a gull landed *among* the burgers-and-fries eaters at the outdoor snack bar, clearly looking for handouts⟩
synonyms amid (*or* amidst), mid, midst, through
related words between, betwixt
phrases in the thick of

near antonyms from, out of

amorous *adj* of, relating to, or expressing sexual attraction ⟨male birds engage in *amorous* behavior—nest-building, singing, showing off their finery—in order to attract females⟩ — see EROTIC

amorphous *adj* having no definite or recognizable form ⟨*amorphous* lumps of clay magically transformed by a skilled potter's hands into works of art⟩ — see FORMLESS

amount *n* a given or particular mass or aggregate of matter ⟨is this small *amount* of food supposed to feed the whole hockey team?⟩
synonyms measure, quantity, volume
related words body, portion; many, number

amount (to) *vb* **1** to have a total of ⟨the expenses of the trip *amounted to* nearly double what we'd budgeted for⟩
synonyms add up (to), come (to), number, sum (to *or* into), total
related words average, equal, measure, reach; aggregate, comprise
2 to be the same in meaning or effect ⟨it makes no difference whether you're going to the game or to the movies, for it *amounts to* your unavailability for babysitting⟩
synonyms add up (to), come (to), correspond (to), equal
related words approach, match, measure (up), meet, rival, touch; connote, denote, express, import, mean, signify, smack (of), spell, suggest

ample *adj* **1** being more than enough without being excessive ⟨there's *ample* time to order a pizza before the show⟩ — see PLENTIFUL
2 more than adequate or average in capacity ⟨a husky fellow, he always heads for the most *ample* chair in the room⟩ — see SPACIOUS

amplify *vb* **1** to express more fully and in greater detail ⟨after filing a report of missing luggage, he was asked to *amplify* a bit as to the circumstances⟩ — see EXPAND 1
2 to make greater in size, amount, or number ⟨the number of blood volunteers was significantly *amplified* by the promise of thank-you gifts to donors⟩ — see INCREASE 1
3 to make markedly greater in measure or degree ⟨a fox's large ears serve to *amplify* such sounds as little critters skittering among stones⟩ — see INTENSIFY

amplitude *n* an area over which activity, capacity, or influence extends ⟨the *amplitude* of Thomas Jefferson's interests—government, architecture, agriculture, science, philosophy—is truly awesome⟩ — see RANGE 2

amulet *n* something worn or kept to bring good luck or keep away evil ⟨a small cross made of goat bone was worn in the Middle Ages as an *amulet* to ward off evil⟩ — see CHARM 1

amuse *vb* to cause (someone) to pass the time agreeably occupied ⟨Christie *amused* her four-year-old sister at the family reunion by showing her off to all the relatives⟩
synonyms disport, divert, entertain, regale
related words absorb, busy, distract, engage, engross, immerse, interest, involve, occupy; beguile, bewitch, captivate, charm, delight, enchant, enthrall (*or* enthral), fascinate; grip, hypnotize, intrigue, mesmerize; coddle, gratify, humor, indulge, mollycoddle, pamper, please, pleasure, spoil; appease, comfort, conciliate, console, content, mollify, oblige, pacify, placate, propitiate, soothe

near antonyms bore, jade; drain, enervate, exhaust, fatigue, tire, wear, wear out, weary; aggravate, annoy, bother, bug, chafe, disturb, exasperate, fret, gall, grate, harass, harry, irk, nettle, peeve, perturb, pester, pique, upset, vex

amusement *n* the act or activity of providing pleasure or amusement especially for the public ⟨with the opening of Disneyland in 1955, the film producer Walt Disney greatly expanded his *amusement* empire⟩ — see ENTERTAINMENT 1

amusing *adj* providing amusement or enjoyment ⟨Grandma told an *amusing* story about Dad when he was little⟩ — see FUN

analgesic *n* something (as a drug) that relieves pain ⟨the doctor prescribed an *analgesic* and rest for my injured knee⟩ — see PAINKILLER

analogous *adj* having qualities in common ⟨bad-mouthing her is *analogous* to slapping her in the face—it's just as bad⟩ — see ALIKE

analysis *n* **1** the separation and identification of the parts of a whole ⟨investigators took the mysterious powder to the lab for *analysis*⟩
synonyms anatomizing, assay, breakdown, dissection
related words assessment, evaluation, examination, inspection, investigation, scrutiny; arrangement, assortment, cataloging (*or* cataloguing), categorization, classification, codification, indexing; enumeration, inventory, itemization, tabulation; division, reduction, segmentation, separation, subdivision
near antonyms agglomeration, aggregation, amalgamation, assimilation, coalescence, conglomeration, consolidation, integration, synthesis, unification
2 a series of explanations or observations on something (as an event) ⟨gave a thorough *analysis* of the main character's motives⟩ — see COMMENTARY

analytic *or* **analytical** *adj* according to the rules of logic ⟨presented a very *analytical* argument for the defendant's guilt⟩ — see LOGICAL 1

analyze *vb* to identify and examine the basic elements or parts of (something) especially for discovering interrelationships ⟨*analyze* the park's ecosystem before deciding whether hunting should be allowed⟩
synonyms anatomize, assay, break down, dissect
related words assess, evaluate, examine, inspect, investigate, scrutinize; arrange, assort, catalog (*or* catalogue), categorize, classify, codify, diagram, index, order, schematize, sort, tabulate; divide, reduce, segment, separate, subdivide
near antonyms agglomerate, aggregate, amalgamate, assimilate, coalesce, conglomerate, consolidate, integrate, synthesize, unify

anarchic *adj* not restrained by or under the control of legal authority ⟨the city-wide blackouts caused *anarchic* looting and rioting⟩ — see LAWLESS

anarchy *n* a state in which there is widespread wrongdoing and disregard for rules and authority ⟨the *anarchy* that the country experienced after the dictator drained the treasury and fled the country⟩
synonyms lawlessness, misrule
related words commotion, tumult, uproar; chaos, confusion, disarray, disorder, disorderliness, disorganization; disruption, disturbance, havoc, riot, strife, turbulence, turmoil, unrest, upheaval; mutiny, rebellion, revolution, uprising; criminality, outlawry
near antonyms law, lawfulness, legality, legitimacy, rule; calmness, harmony, order, orderliness, peace, peacefulness, quiet, tranquillity (*or* tranquility)

anathema *n* **1** a prayer that harm will come to someone ⟨uttered an *anathema* before driving him from the room⟩ — see CURSE 1
2 something or someone that is hated ⟨the use of animals in the testing of cosmetics is *anathema* to animal-rights activists⟩ — see HATE 2

anatomize *vb* to identify and examine the basic elements or parts of (something) especially for discovering interrelationships ⟨if you *anatomize* the problem, you'll see it stems from a combination of her bad behavior and your unwillingness to speak to her about it⟩ — see ANALYZE

anatomizing *n* the separation and identification of the parts of a whole ⟨your *anatomizing* of the situation is quite insightful⟩ — see ANALYSIS 1

ancestor *n* **1** a person who is several generations earlier in an individual's line of descent ⟨Bridie's Irish *ancestors* immigrated to the United States in the 19th century during the Great Potato Famine⟩
synonyms father, forebear (*also* forebear), forefather, grandfather
related words grandmother, matriarch, patriarch; ancestry, antecedents
near antonyms children, issue, offspring, posterity, progeny, seed; heir, inheritor, son, successor
antonyms descendant (*or* descendent)
2 something belonging to an earlier time from which something else was later developed ⟨pinball machines—the *ancestors* of today's video games—go back to the 19th century⟩
synonyms antecedent, foregoer, forerunner, precursor, predecessor
related words archetype, model, original, prototype; father, mother
near antonyms by-product, derivative, offshoot, outgrowth, spin-off; daughter, son
antonyms descendant (*or* descendent)

ancestry *n* the line of ancestors from whom a person is descended ⟨a Cambodian immigrant who can trace her Khmer *ancestry* as far back as the 16th century⟩
synonyms birth, blood, bloodline, breeding, descent, extraction, family tree, genealogy, line, lineage, origin, parentage, pedigree, stock, strain
related words heredity, succession; family, house; kin, kindred, relations, relatives; race
near antonyms offspring; child, heir, inheritor, son, successor
antonyms issue, posterity, progeny, seed

anchor *n* one who reads and introduces news reports on a news program ⟨the news *anchor* coordinated the reports of the correspondents from around the state⟩ — see ANCHORPERSON

anchor *vb* **1** to put securely in place or in a desired position ⟨used ropes and sandbags to *anchor* the hot-air balloon to the ground⟩ — see FASTEN 2
2 to stop at or near a place along the shore ⟨we'll *anchor* at Praia, Cape Verde⟩ — see LAND 1

anchorage *n* a part of a body of water protected and deep enough to be a place of safety for ships ⟨sailed into a quiet *anchorage* to wait out the storm⟩ — see HARBOR 1

anchorite *n* a person who lives away from others ⟨many Christian saints were *anchorites* who removed themselves from the world to focus on their spirituality⟩ — see RECLUSE

anchorperson *n* one who reads and introduces news reports on a news program ⟨the new *anchorperson* did an

admirable job of dealing with the late-breaking news story⟩
synonyms anchor
related words anchorman, anchorwoman; broadcaster, newscaster, telecaster; correspondent, interviewer, reporter; journalist, newsman

ancient *adj* **1** dating or surviving from the distant past ⟨Rome's *ancient* ruins are carefully preserved in the midst of the bustle of the modern city⟩
synonyms aged, age-old, antediluvian, antique, dateless, hoar, hoary, old, venerable
related words aging, mature; antiquated, obsolete, outmoded, out-of-date, passé; old-fashioned, old-time, old-world; durable, enduring, lasting, long-lived, permanent; ageless, hallowed, time-honored, timeless, time-tested, traditional, tried, tried-and-true; classic, classical; prehistoric, primeval, primordial
near antonyms fresh, young, youthful; contemporary, current, latest, mod, novel, present-day, ultramodern; untested, untried; brand-new, unused, unworn
antonyms modern, new, recent
2 being of advanced years and especially past middle age ⟨used to think that age 40 was *ancient* until my mom turned 40⟩ — see ELDERLY
3 relating to or occurring near the beginning of a process, series, or time period ⟨the *ancient* Inca built a vast network of roads⟩ — see EARLY 1
ancient *n* a person of advanced years ⟨*ancients* in the tribe are accorded great respect and valued for their wisdom⟩ — see SENIOR CITIZEN
anecdote *n* a brief account of something interesting that happened especially to one personally ⟨told us once again that *anecdote* about the dog and the bike⟩ — see STORY 2
anesthetic *n* something (as a drug) that relieves pain ⟨the dentist waited until the *anesthetic* took effect⟩ — see PAINKILLER
anew *adv* yet another time ⟨junked what he had written and began the essay *anew*⟩ — see AGAIN 1
angel *n* **1** an innocent or gentle person ⟨her child is a perfect *angel*⟩ — see LAMB
2 one that announces or indicates the later arrival of another ⟨looking forward to seeing those red-breasted *angels* of the spring—robins⟩ — see FORERUNNER 1
anger *n* an intense emotional state of displeasure with someone or something ⟨Dave stifled his *anger* when the kids on the bus made fun of him⟩
synonyms angriness, furor, fury, indignation, irateness, ire, outrage, rage, spleen, wrath, wrathfulness
related words aggravation, annoyance, exasperation, irritation, vexation; animosity, antagonism, antipathy, bile, bitterness, contempt, enmity, grudge, hostility, rancor; envy, jaundice, jealousy, pique, resentment; malevolence, malice, spite, venom, virulence, vitriol; belligerence, contentiousness, contrariness, disputatiousness, orneriness, pugnacity, querulousness; blowup, flare-up, outburst; dander, dudgeon, huff, pet, rise, ruffle, temper; delirium, heat, passion, warmth
near antonyms calmness, forbearance, patience
antonyms delight, pleasure
anger *vb* to make angry ⟨it's virtually impossible to *anger* Mrs. Peterson—she's the most easygoing person I've ever known⟩
synonyms antagonize, enrage, incense, inflame, infuriate, madden, outrage, rankle, rile, roil
related words affront, aggravate, annoy, cross, exasperate, get, irritate, nettle, offend, peeve, pique, provoke, put out, ruffle, vex; embitter, envenom

phrases get one's goat, rub the wrong way
near antonyms allay, assuage, relieve; comfort, console, soothe; appease, conciliate, mollify, pacify, placate; calm, lull, quiet, settle; beguile, bewitch, captivate, charm, disarm, enchant
antonyms delight, gratify, please
angered *adj* feeling or showing anger ⟨*angered* residents demanded to know why their street hadn't been plowed⟩ — see ANGRY
angle *n* **1** a certain way in which something appears or may be regarded ⟨from this *angle*, that car looks gray, not brown⟩ — see ASPECT 1
2 a way of looking at or thinking about something ⟨what's your *angle* on the problem?⟩ — see POINT OF VIEW
3 something that curves or is curved ⟨the road around the peninsula is all *angles* and hairpin turns⟩ — see BEND 1
angle *vb* to set or cause to be at an angle ⟨*angle* the camera this way and the Leaning Tower of Pisa will look straight⟩ — see LEAN 1
angling *n* the act of positioning or an instance of being positioned at an angle ⟨his *angling* of the picture made everything else on the wall look crooked⟩ — see TILT
angriness *n* an intense emotional state of displeasure with someone or something ⟨his constant *angriness* makes him unpleasant to work with⟩ — see ANGER
angry *adj* feeling or showing anger ⟨my sister gets really *angry* and practically throws a tantrum if her soccer team loses⟩
synonyms angered, apoplectic, enraged, foaming, fuming, furious, incensed, indignant, inflamed, infuriated, irate, ireful, mad, outraged, rabid, riled, roiled, shirty [*chiefly British*], sore, steaming, wrathful, wroth
related words ranting, raving, stormy; bristling, burning, cross, huffy, livid, seething, smoldering, worked up, wrought (up); acrid, acrimonious, antagonistic, antipathetic, bitter, embittered, inimical, malevolent, piqued, rancorous, resentful, spiteful, vindictive, virulent; antisocial, cold, cool, disagreeable, disapproving, distant, frigid, icy, ill-tempered, sulky, unfriendly, unpleasant; aggravated, annoyed, bearish, bilious, cantankerous, choleric, churlish, crabby, cranky, dyspeptic, exasperated, fretful, fussy, grouchy, grumpy, ill-humored, irascible, irritable, peevish, perturbed, petulant, put out, quick-tempered, snappish, testy, touchy; argumentative, belligerent, contentious, contrary, disputatious, ornery, pugnacious, quarrelsome, querulous
near antonyms accepting, accommodating, obliging; agreeable, amenable, complaisant; amicable, cordial, friendly; content, happy, satisfied; empathetic, sympathetic, tolerant, understanding; calm, pacific, peaceable, placid, serene, tranquil; affable, amiable, easygoing, genial, good-natured, good-tempered, kind, pleasant, sweet
antonyms delighted, pleased
anguish *n* **1** a state of great suffering of body or mind ⟨was in *anguish* over the decision to report the cheating⟩ — see DISTRESS 1
2 deep sadness especially for the loss of someone or something loved ⟨words can't express my *anguish* at losing my cat⟩ — see SORROW
anguished *adj* expressing or suggesting mourning ⟨an *anguished* cry⟩ ⟨the military's explanation of the accident did nothing to console the *anguished* widow⟩ — see MOURNFUL 1
animal *adj* of or relating to the human body ⟨had intellectual as well as *animal* needs⟩ — see PHYSICAL 1

animal *n* one of the lower animals as distinguished from human beings ⟨we saw a lot of *animals* at the wildlife refuge—cranes, alligators, deer, a fox, even an armadillo⟩
synonyms beast, brute, creature, critter
related words varmint, vermin; biped, quadruped; carnivore, herbivore, insectivore; invertebrate, vertebrate

animate *adj* **1** having much high-spirited energy and movement ⟨an *animate* dance routine that will really get the blood pumping⟩ — see LIVELY 1
2 having or showing life ⟨had a dream about a sandwich that becomes *animate*⟩ — see ALIVE 1

animate *vb* to give life, vigor, or spirit to ⟨Mr. Clark *animates* history for his sixth graders by frequently showing up for class dressed like some famous historical figure⟩
synonyms brace, energize, enliven, fire, invigorate, jazz (up), liven (up), pep (up), quicken, stimulate, vitalize, vivify
related words arouse, awake, awaken, raise, rouse, stir, wake (up); activate, actuate, drive, impel, motivate, move, propel; charge, electrify, galvanize; excite, ferment, foment, incite, inflame, instigate, kindle, provoke, set off, spark, trigger, turn on, whip (up); abet, boost, buoy, cheer, embolden, fortify, hearten, inspire, lift, rally, steel, strengthen; reactivate, reanimate, reawake, reawaken, recharge, recreate, reenergize, refresh, regenerate, rejuvenate, rekindle, renew, resurrect, resuscitate, revitalize, revive
near antonyms burn out, debilitate, do in, drain, enervate, enfeeble, exhaust, fag, fatigue, sap, tucker (out), undermine, weaken, wear, wear out; check, curb, inhibit, jade, quell, quench, repress, restrain, slow, still, stunt, suppress; daunt, demoralize, discourage, dishearten, dispirit
antonyms damp, dampen, deaden, dull

animated *adj* **1** having much high-spirited energy and movement ⟨an *animated* group of girls loudly running down the hall⟩ — see LIVELY 1
2 marked by much life, movement, or activity ⟨an *animated* marketplace full of vendors and holiday shoppers⟩ — see ALIVE 2

animatedly *adv* in a quick and spirited manner ⟨*animatedly* raced into the living room to open Christmas presents⟩ — see GAILY 2

animately *adv* in a quick and spirited manner ⟨began talking *animately* about her favorite subject: horses⟩ — see GAILY 2

animation *n* the quality or state of having abundant or intense activity ⟨the *animation* of any city depends upon an abundance of street-level restaurants, shops, and places of entertainment⟩ — see VITALITY 1

animosity *n* a deep-seated ill will ⟨his open *animosity* towards us made our meeting very uncomfortable⟩ — see ENMITY

annalist *n* a student or writer of history ⟨new book by the country's best-known *annalist* of the Civil War⟩ — see HISTORIAN

annals *n pl* an account of important events in the order in which they happened ⟨his *annals* of the reigns of English kings was used as a source by Shakespeare⟩ — see HISTORY 1

annex *n* a smaller structure added to a main building ⟨a new *annex* that will serve as the permanent home for the school library⟩
synonyms addition, extension, penthouse
related words arm, ell, wing

annex *vb* to join (something) to a mass, quantity, or number so as to bring about an overall increase ⟨plans to *annex* the supply room so as to make our classroom bigger⟩ — see ADD 1

annihilate *vb* **1** to destroy all traces of ⟨the family's attempts to *annihilate* the roach population in their apartment had met with little success⟩
synonyms blot out, efface, eradicate, expunge, exterminate, extirpate, liquidate, obliterate, root (out), rub out, snuff (out), stamp (out), wipe out
related words decimate, demolish, destroy, devastate; dismantle, flatten, mow (down), raze, tear down; ruin, total, waste, wreck; blast, blow up, dash, dynamite, smash; atomize, consume, devour, dissolve, fragment, powder, pulverize, shatter, splinter; doom, finish, kill, terminate, zap; cancel, cut, discard, ditch, eject, excise, expel, jettison, oust, throw out
near antonyms conserve, preserve, protect, save; build, construct, create, fabricate, fashion, forge, form, frame, make, manufacture, shape; fix, mend, patch, rebuild, recondition, reconstruct, renew, renovate, repair, restore, revamp
2 to bring to a complete end the physical soundness, existence, or usefulness of ⟨the tornado simply *annihilated* the family's home⟩ — see DESTROY 1

annihilation *n* the state or fact of being rendered nonexistent, physically unsound, or useless ⟨idealists who seek the *annihilation* of all forms of prejudice⟩ — see DESTRUCTION

announce *vb* to make known openly or publicly ⟨Jeannie *announced* to everyone within hearing distance that she didn't care if she failed the test⟩
synonyms advertise, blaze, broadcast, declare, enunciate, placard, post, proclaim, promulgate, publicize, publish, sound
related words advise, apprise, inform, notify; communicate, impart, intimate; disclose, divulge, report, reveal; disseminate, spread
near antonyms conceal, hush (up), silence, suppress, withhold; recall, recant, retract, revoke

announcement *n* a published statement informing the public of a matter of general interest ⟨an *announcement* was in today's paper regarding the merger of the two banks⟩
synonyms ad, advertisement, bulletin, notice, notification, posting, release
related words broadside, circular, flier (*or* flyer), handbill, handout; bill, billboard, placard, poster, sign; broadcast, newscast, telecast; advertising, commercial, message, spot, word; communication, dispatch, report; ballyhoo, boost, buildup, campaign, plug, promotion, propaganda, publicity

annoy *vb* to disturb the peace of mind of (someone) especially by repeated disagreeable acts ⟨*annoyed* my older sister by shooting rubber bands at her⟩ — see IRRITATE 1

annoyance *n* **1** the act of making unwelcome intrusions upon another ⟨they have an unlisted number in the hopes that it will reduce the constant *annoyance* by telephone salespeople⟩
synonyms aggravation, bedevilment, bothering, bugging, disturbance, harassment, harrying, pestering, teasing, vexation
related words molestation, offense (*or* offence), persecution, provocation, torment, torture
2 the feeling of impatience or anger caused by another's repeated disagreeable acts ⟨Carlene made known

her *annoyance* at having to pick up her sister's dirty clothes⟩
synonyms aggravation, bother, exasperation, frustration, irritation, vexation
related words agitation, anger, angriness, discomfort, displeasure, distress, disturbance, indignation, irateness, ire, outrage, perturbation, resentment; dander, dudgeon, huff, peeve, pet, pique, umbrage, upset
near antonyms delight, pleasure
3 something that is a source of irritation ⟨flashing ads, visual clutter, and other *annoyances* that are the price for free information on the Internet⟩
synonyms aggravation, bother, exasperation, frustration, hassle, headache, inconvenience, irritant, nuisance, peeve, pest, problem, thorn
related words affront, insult, offense; upset, worry; affliction, cross, curse, menace, plague; plight, predicament, trial, tribulation; annoyer, disturber, offender
near antonyms delight, joy, pleasure
4 one who is obnoxiously annoying ⟨younger brothers can be an *annoyance* sometimes⟩ — see NUISANCE 1
annoyer *n* one who is obnoxiously annoying ⟨a bratty *annoyer* who wouldn't leave me alone⟩ — see NUISANCE 1
annoying *adj* causing annoyance ⟨Sheldon has the *annoying* habit of eating all the pickles and leaving a jar full of pickle juice in the refrigerator⟩
synonyms aggravating, bothersome, disturbing, exasperating, frustrating, galling, irksome, irritating, maddening, nettling, peeving, pesty, rankling, riling, vexatious, vexing
related words burdensome, discomforting, displeasing, disquieting, distressing, importunate, inconveniencing; angering, enraging, infuriating; mischievous, offensive, pesky, troublesome, upsetting; stressful, tiresome, troubling, trying, worrisome
near antonyms delightful, pleasing
annuity *n* a sum of money allotted for a specific use by official or formal action ⟨his grandfather's will provided him with an *annuity* of $5,000 a year to be used for school expenses⟩ — see APPROPRIATION
annul *vb* **1** to balance with an equal force so as to make ineffective ⟨unfortunately, his arrogant attitude *annuls* the many generous favors he does for people⟩ — see OFFSET
2 to put an end to by formal action ⟨plans to *annul* their short-lived, ill-advised marriage⟩ — see ABOLISH
anoint *vb* to rub an oily or sticky substance over ⟨*anoint* the wound with antiseptic to prevent infection⟩ — see SMEAR 1
anomalous *adj* departing from some accepted standard of what is normal ⟨an *anomalous* burst of anger from this usually easygoing person⟩ — see DEVIANT
anomaly *n* a person, thing, or event that is not normal ⟨snow in July is an *anomaly* in most of the northern hemisphere⟩ — see FREAK 1
anon *adv* at or within a short time ⟨be ready—we will begin our Yuletide Boar's Head Feast *anon*⟩ — see SHORTLY 2
anonymity *n* the quality or state of being mostly or completely unknown ⟨oddly enough we like the *anonymity* of being a part of an enormous crowd⟩ — see OBSCURITY 2
anonymous *adj* **1** known but not named ⟨I heard the news from a person who will remain *anonymous*⟩ — see CERTAIN 1

2 not named or identified by a name ⟨a beautiful manuscript illuminated by an *anonymous* medieval monk⟩ — see NAMELESS 1
3 not widely known ⟨loved the *anonymous* sculpture she came across in a back corner of the museum⟩ — see OBSCURE 2
another *adj* resulting in an increase in amount or number ⟨add *another* thing to the shopping list⟩ — see ADDITIONAL
answer *n* **1** something spoken or written in reaction especially to a question ⟨the standard *answer* of "Nothing" when asked, "What did you do in school today?"⟩
synonyms comeback, rejoinder, reply, response, retort, return
related words banter, persiflage, repartee; acknowledgment (*also* acknowledgement), comment, communication, correspondence, feedback, observation, reaction, remark; defense, explanation, justification, rebuttal, refutation
near antonyms challenge, cross-examination, grilling, interrogation, quiz; poll, questionnaire, survey
antonyms inquiry, query, question
2 something attained by mental effort and especially by computation ⟨the *answers* to the odd-numbered problems are at the back of the book⟩
synonyms result, solution
related words conclusion, determination, explanation, finding; clue, key
answer *vb* **1** to speak or write in reaction to a question or to another reaction ⟨Ryan didn't *answer* right away when Mrs. Jacobs asked him where he'd been for the last three hours⟩
synonyms rejoin, reply, respond, retort, return
related words acknowledge, comment, communicate, correspond, react, remark; explain, rebut, refute
near antonyms challenge, cross-examine, examine, grill, interrogate, pump, quiz; poll, query, survey
antonyms inquire, question
2 to be in agreement on every point ⟨sorry, I haven't seen anyone *answering* to that description⟩ — see CHECK 1
3 to do what is required by the terms of ⟨I don't have a box cutter as such, but will this knife *answer* the purpose?⟩ — see FULFILL 1
4 to find an answer for through reasoning ⟨try to *answer* this riddle⟩ — see SOLVE
answerable *adj* **1** being the one who must meet an obligation or suffer the consequences for failing to do so ⟨you are *answerable* for your own conduct at all times⟩ — see RESPONSIBLE 1
2 capable of having the reason for or cause of determined ⟨they say this equation is not *answerable*⟩ — see SOLVABLE
antagonism *n* a deep-seated ill will ⟨the *antagonism* between them was so bad they couldn't even sit near each other⟩ — see ENMITY
antagonist *n* **1** one that is hostile toward another ⟨please name the novel's hero and his *antagonist*⟩ — see ENEMY
2 one that takes a position opposite another in a competition or conflict ⟨his *antagonist* in the boxing match⟩ — see OPPONENT 1
antagonistic *adj* marked by opposition or ill will ⟨countries that have been *antagonistic* towards each other for centuries⟩ — see HOSTILE 1
antagonize *vb* **1** to implant bitter feelings in ⟨spread malicious gossip just to *antagonize* her classmates against the girl⟩ — see EMBITTER

2 to make angry ⟨your poking will only *antagonize* that dog⟩ — see ANGER

antecedent *adj* going before another in time or order ⟨I'd like to follow up on an *antecedent* question from another reporter⟩ — see PREVIOUS

antecedent *n* **1** someone or something responsible for a result ⟨what are the *antecedents* of the American Revolutionary War?⟩ — see CAUSE 1
2 something belonging to an earlier time from which something else was later developed ⟨the typewriter is the *antecedent* of the computer keyboard⟩ — see ANCESTOR 2

antecedently *adv* so as to precede something in order of time ⟨make credit card payments *antecedently* to their due date just in case there's a delay in mail delivery⟩ — see AHEAD 1

antedate *vb* to go or come before in time ⟨dinosaurs *antedate* cavemen by millions of years⟩ — see PRECEDE

antediluvian *adj* dating or surviving from the distant past ⟨found evidence in the Middle East of an *antediluvian* people previously unknown to history⟩ — see ANCIENT 1

antediluvian *n* a person with old-fashioned ideas ⟨an *antediluvian* who thought women shouldn't work outside the home⟩ — see FOGY

anterior *adj* going before another in time or order ⟨fossils from an *anterior* geologic age⟩ — see PREVIOUS

anteriorly *adv* so as to precede something in order of time ⟨archaeological artifacts are all that we have of those ancient people who flourished *anteriorly* of the invention of writing⟩ — see AHEAD 1

anthem *n* a religious song ⟨sang an *anthem* of praise to the Lord⟩ — see HYMN

anthology *n* a collection of writings ⟨an *anthology* of American short stories⟩
synonyms album, compilation, miscellany
related words archives; digest

antic *adj* **1** causing or intended to cause laughter ⟨*antic* shenanigans that made me nearly fall over with laughter⟩ — see FUNNY 1
2 given to good-natured joking or teasing ⟨an *antic* group of kids at summer camp⟩ — see PLAYFUL

antic *n* a playful or mischievous act intended as a joke ⟨we'll have no more of your *antics*, so just settle down⟩ — see PRANK

anticipate *vb* **1** to believe in the future occurrence of (something) ⟨I *anticipate* that we'll be seeing you for New Year's⟩ — see EXPECT
2 to realize or know about beforehand ⟨I *anticipated* this unhelpful response⟩ — see FORESEE

anticipated *adj* being in accordance with the prescribed, normal, or logical course of events ⟨the *anticipated* date of delivery is July 14th⟩ — see DUE 2

anticipatory *adj* having or showing signs of eagerly awaiting something ⟨couldn't control his *anticipatory* excitement on Christmas morning⟩ — see EXPECTANT 1

antipathetic *adj* having a natural dislike for something ⟨a series of adventure books that turned boys who had been *antipathetic* to reading into avid readers⟩
synonyms allergic, averse
related words disinclined, loath (*or* loth), reluctant, unwilling; adverse, antagonistic, hostile, intolerant, negative, opposed, opposing, resistant, resisting, uncongenial, unfriendly, unsympathetic; disgusted, nauseated, repelled, repulsed, revolted, shocked, squeamish, turned off

near antonyms friendly, sympathetic, tolerant, understanding; admiring, appreciative, charmed, delighted, fond, pleased, tickled

antipathy *n* **1** a deep-seated ill will ⟨I feel no *antipathy* towards any of my opponents in the tournament⟩ — see ENMITY
2 something or someone that is hated ⟨cruelty to animals is one of my most deeply felt *antipathies*⟩ — see HATE 2

antipodal *adj* being as different as possible ⟨love is *antipodal* to hate⟩ — see OPPOSITE

antipode *n* something that is as different as possible from something else ⟨my jock brother is an *antipode* to my bookworm sister⟩ — see OPPOSITE

antipodean *adj* being as different as possible ⟨since freedom and equality are often *antipodean* goals, a democratic society must find ways of striking a balance between the two⟩ — see OPPOSITE

antiquated *adj* having passed its time of use or usefulness ⟨saw an *antiquated* hand-cranked rope-making machine at the textiles museum⟩ — see OBSOLETE

antique *adj* **1** dating or surviving from the distant past ⟨studied shards from *antique* pots made by the Pueblos of the Southwest⟩ — see ANCIENT 1
2 pleasantly reminiscent of an earlier time ⟨loved to collect *antique* sugar tongs⟩ — see OLD-FASHIONED 1

antique *n* something belonging to or surviving from an earlier period ⟨Shamika's house is filled with *antiques*, including a collection of 19th-century African masks⟩
synonyms relic
related words artifact, fossil; antiquities, ruins; remains, remnant, trace, vestige

antisocial *adj* having or showing a lack of friendliness or interest in others ⟨she's not *antisocial*, just extremely shy⟩ — see COOL 1

antithesis *n* something that is as different as possible from something else ⟨true love for another is the *antithesis* of the desire to control that person's life⟩ — see OPPOSITE

antithetical *adj* being as different as possible ⟨spiritual concerns and ideals that are *antithetical* to the materialism embraced by modern society⟩ — see OPPOSITE

anxiety *n* **1** an uneasy state of mind usually over the possibility of an anticipated misfortune or trouble ⟨Dorothy's *anxiety* about her brother's operation kept her awake all night⟩
synonyms agitation, anxiousness, apprehension, apprehensiveness, care, concern, disquiet, nervousness, perturbation, solicitude, uneasiness, worry
related words strain, stress, tension; alarm, anguish, consternation, desperation, desperateness, discomfort, discomposure, dismay, distraction, distress, disturbance, edginess, jitters, jumpiness; fear, fearfulness, torment, upset, vexation; doubt, dread, foreboding, incertitude, misgiving, presentiment, suspense, uncertainty
near antonyms calm, calmness, content, contentment, ease, peace, placidity, quiet, quietude, serenity, tranquillity (*or* tranquility); comfort, consolation, relief, solace
2 the emotion experienced in the presence or threat of danger ⟨the newly discovered virus is creating considerable *anxiety* in the public at large⟩ — see FEAR

anxious *adj* **1** feeling or showing uncomfortable feelings of uncertainty ⟨was *anxious* about the play tryouts scheduled for the following day⟩ — see NERVOUS 1
2 marked by or causing agitation or uncomfortable feelings ⟨the whole crowd seemed to make an *anxious*

gasp as the home team almost fumbled the ball⟩ — see NERVOUS 2

3 showing urgent desire or interest ⟨I'm *anxious* for my birthday party⟩ — see EAGER

anxiousness *n* an uneasy state of mind usually over the possibility of an anticipated misfortune or trouble ⟨don't be overcome with *anxiousness* about things that may never happen⟩ — see ANXIETY 1

any *adj* being one of a group ⟨*any* person who comes in the store today is eligible for the discount⟩ — see EACH

anyhow *adv* **1** in spite of everything ⟨even though it's raining, I'm going to the amusement park *anyhow*⟩ — see REGARDLESS

2 without definite aim, direction, rule, or method ⟨clothes that were hurriedly stuffed *anyhow* into the suitcase⟩ — see HIT OR MISS

anymore *adv* at the present time ⟨they don't sell that kind of sandwich *anymore*⟩ — see NOW 1

anyway *adv* **1** in spite of everything ⟨I know I really can't afford it, but I'm buying the new CD *anyway*⟩ — see REGARDLESS

2 without definite aim, direction, rule, or method ⟨do it *anyway* you feel like⟩ — see HIT OR MISS

anywise *adv* **1** in any way or respect ⟨nor is it *anywise* important what you wear to the party⟩ — see AT ALL

2 without definite aim, direction, rule, or method ⟨just stuffed his cleaned clothes *anywise* back into the drawers⟩ — see HIT OR MISS

A1 *adj* of the very best kind ⟨an *A1* mom deserves only the very best Mother's Day card⟩ — see EXCELLENT

apace *adv* with great speed ⟨the end of the year is hastening *apace*⟩ — see FAST 1

apart *adv* into parts or to pieces ⟨the fancy new adjustable rake came *apart* the first time Chad tried to use it⟩

synonyms asunder, piecemeal

antonyms together

apartment *n* **1** a room or set of rooms in a private house or a block used as a separate dwelling place ⟨a spacious six-room *apartment* that occupies the entire upper floor of a two-family house⟩

synonyms flat, lodgings, suite, tenement

related words condominium, duplex, penthouse, salon, studio, triplex; apartment house, tenement house, walk-up

2 an area within a building that has been set apart from surrounding space by a wall ⟨the museum sets aside this large central *apartment* to display special exhibitions⟩ — see ROOM 2

apathetic *adj* **1** having or showing a lack of interest or concern ⟨people of conscience cannot be *apathetic* about suffering in the world⟩ — see INDIFFERENT 1

2 not feeling or showing emotion ⟨gave nothing more than an *apathetic* gaze to his interrogators⟩ — see IMPASSIVE 1

apathy *n* **1** a lack of emotion or emotional expressiveness ⟨the *apathy* of the people of that war-torn country comes from their having seen too many horrors⟩

synonyms impassivity, insensibility, numbness, phlegm

related words callousness, coldness, coolness, hardheartedness, hardness, heartlessness, insensitivity, obduracy; blankness, deadness, emptiness, vacancy; aloofness, detachment, indifference, unconcern; stiffness, woodenness

near antonyms compassion, empathy, pity, sympathy; responsiveness, sensitivity; solicitude, tenderness, un-

derstanding, warmth; histrionics, hysteria, hysterics, melodrama

antonyms emotion, feeling, sensibility

2 lack of interest or concern ⟨her poor grades are proof enough of her *apathy* concerning all matters academic⟩ — see INDIFFERENCE

ape *vb* to use (someone or something) as the model for one's speech, mannerisms, or behavior ⟨was caught *aping* the substitute teacher's thick accent⟩ — see IMITATE 1

aper *n* a person who adopts the appearance or behavior of another especially in an obvious way ⟨they're just no-talent *apers* of whatever rock band has the current number one record⟩ — see COPYCAT

aperture *n* a place in a surface allowing passage into or through a thing ⟨you can adjust the *aperture* on this camera's lens by pushing this button⟩ — see HOLE 1

apex *n* **1** the highest part or point ⟨she reached the *apex* of fame, only to find it wasn't what she expected⟩ — see HEIGHT 1

2 the last and usually sharp or tapering part of something long and narrow ⟨the *apex* of the spear⟩ — see POINT 2

aphorism *n* **1** an idea or statement about all of the members of a group or all the instances of a situation ⟨the *aphorism* that nerds can't play sports is wrong⟩ — see GENERALIZATION

2 an often stated observation regarding something from common experience ⟨what does the *aphorism* "Hindsight is 20/20" mean?⟩ — see SAYING

aphoristic *adj* marked by the use of few words to convey much information or meaning ⟨retorted with the *aphoristic* comment, "No one said life is fair"⟩ — see CONCISE

apiece *adv* for each one ⟨when you figure that it comes to six dollars *apiece*, it's too much to pay for used CDs⟩

synonyms all, each, per capita

related words apart, independently, individually, respectively, separately, singly

near antonyms altogether, collectively, together

apish *adj* using or marked by the use of something else as a basis or model ⟨whenever I smiled, the baby would respond with an *apish* grin⟩ — see IMITATIVE

aplomb *n* **1** evenness of emotions or temper ⟨you've handled a difficult situation with perfect *aplomb*⟩ — see EQUANIMITY

2 great faith in oneself or one's abilities ⟨carried herself with the dignity and *aplomb* of a born leader⟩ — see CONFIDENCE 1

apologetic *adj* feeling sorrow for a wrong that one has done ⟨was *apologetic* after accidentally breaking a treasured plate⟩ — see CONTRITE 1

apoplectic *adj* feeling or showing anger ⟨the coach was so *apoplectic* when the player missed the free throw that he threw his clipboard onto the court⟩ — see ANGRY

apostate *n* one who betrays a trust or an allegiance ⟨became an *apostate* to liberalism after he had gotten wealthy⟩ — see TRAITOR

apostle *n* a person who actively supports or favors a cause ⟨a fervent *apostle* of universal health care⟩ — see EXPONENT

apothecary *n* a person who prepares drugs according to a doctor's prescription ⟨in olden days the *apothecary* had few drugs that actually cured anything, most substances being little more than pain relievers⟩ — see DRUGGIST

appall *vb* to cause an often unpleasant surprise for ⟨the dead snake caught in the rake *appalled* my mom, who ran screaming into the house⟩ — see SHOCK 1

appalling *adj* **1** causing intense displeasure, disgust, or resentment ⟨opening your mouth to show me your half-chewed food is absolutely *appalling*⟩ — see OFFENSIVE 1
2 extremely disturbing or repellent ⟨*appalling* crimes against humanity⟩ — see HORRIBLE 1

appanage *n* **1** something granted as a special favor ⟨use of the grounds was just one *appanage* he gave the caretakers of his estate⟩ — see PRIVILEGE
2 something to which one has a just claim ⟨wealthy people who believe that political power is their natural *appanage*⟩ — see RIGHT 1

apparatus *n* items needed for the performance of a task or activity ⟨the hospital's operating rooms boast the very latest medical *apparatus*⟩ — see EQUIPMENT

apparel *n* covering for the human body ⟨a sale on summer *apparel* for women⟩ — see CLOTHING

apparel *vb* to outfit with clothes and especially fine or special clothes ⟨a designer who regularly *apparels* several of the presenters at the Oscar ceremonies⟩ — see CLOTHE 1

apparent *adj* **1** appearing to be true on the basis of evidence that may or may not be confirmed ⟨at the start of the investigation, the *apparent* cause of the plane crash was mechanical failure⟩
synonyms assumed, evident, ostensible, presumed, reputed, seeming, supposed
related words external, outward, visible; conceivable, plausible; likely, probable; clear, distinct, manifest, obvious, plain; deceptive, delusive, delusory, illusive, illusory, imaginary; misleading, specious; fake, faked, feigned, phony (*also* phoney), pretended, pseudo, put-on; alleged, professed, purported, so-called
near antonyms authenticated, confirmed, corroborated, established, real, substantiated, valid, validated, verified
2 capable of being seen ⟨as the fog lifts, the town in the valley below us will become more *apparent*⟩ — see VISIBLE
3 not subject to misinterpretation or more than one interpretation ⟨it's *apparent* from the smile on her face that she got a part in the play⟩ — see CLEAR 2

apparently *adv* to all outward appearances ⟨*apparently*, Phil didn't know the cake was for the raffle, since he helped himself to a piece⟩
synonyms evidently, ostensibly, presumably, seemingly, supposedly
related words externally, outwardly, visibly; believably, credibly; maybe, mayhap, perchance, perhaps, possibly, professedly; allegedly, reputedly; clearly, distinctly, obviously, plainly; assuredly, positively, surely
near antonyms implausibly, impossibly, improbably, incredibly

apparition *n* the soul of a dead person thought of especially as appearing to living people ⟨an eccentric who claimed to have photographed an *apparition* in her very own house⟩ — see GHOST

appeal *n* **1** an earnest request ⟨made an *appeal* to the public to donate desperately needed blood⟩ — see PLEA 1
2 the power of irresistible attraction ⟨that hot new actress has a lot of *appeal*⟩ — see CHARM 2

appeal (to) *vb* to make a request to (someone) in an earnest or urgent manner ⟨when Mom said no, we *appealed* to Dad⟩ — see BEG

appealing *adj* having an often mysterious or magical power to attract ⟨the idea of living on Mars is *appealing* to space enthusiasts⟩ — see FASCINATING 1

appear *vb* **1** to come into view ⟨a police car *appeared* just as Michael ran a red light⟩
synonyms come out, materialize, show up, turn up
related words reappear, resurface; bulk, loom; arrive, come; dawn, debut; arise, break, break out, emanate, erupt, issue, rise, spring (up), surface; happen, occur
near antonyms depart, leave, retire, withdraw
antonyms clear, disappear, dissolve, evanesce, evaporate, fade, go (away), melt (away), vanish
2 to give the impression of being ⟨it *appears* that he doesn't hear you⟩ — see SEEM

appearance *n* **1** the outward form of someone or something especially as indicative of a quality ⟨the dignified *appearance* of this church leader⟩ ⟨the country club's manicured lawns and well-groomed *appearance* in general⟩
synonyms aspect, look, mien, presence
related words air, attitude, bearing, behavior, comportment, demeanor, deportment, manner, poise, pose; carriage, posture, stance; color, complexion; countenance, face, features, physiognomy, visage
2 outward and often deceptive indication ⟨can't you at least give the *appearance* of listening to what I say?⟩
synonyms face, guise, name, semblance, show
related words affectation, display, fiction, imposture, make-believe, pose, pretense (*or* pretence), simulation; cloak, disguise, exterior, facade (*also* façade), front, mask, masquerade, shell, surface
3 the act of coming upon a scene ⟨his *appearance* at the party caused considerable speculation⟩ — see ARRIVAL

appease *vb* to lessen the anger or agitation of ⟨candy *appeases* an upset toddler⟩ — see PACIFY

appeasing *adj* tending to lessen or avoid conflict or hostility ⟨we had been feuding with the people next door, so inviting them to the party was intended as an *appeasing* gesture⟩ — see PACIFIC 1

appellation *n* a word or combination of words by which a person or thing is regularly known ⟨a twisting road that deserved the *appellation* "Sidewinder Lane"⟩ — see NAME 1

append *vb* to join (something) to a mass, quantity, or number so as to bring about an overall increase ⟨*append* the prefix "un-" to each of these words⟩ — see ADD 1

appendage *n* something that is not necessary in itself but adds to the convenience or performance of the main piece of equipment ⟨pasta makers became the must-have *appendage* for tabletop mixers⟩ — see ACCESSORY 1

appertain *vb* **1** to be the property of a person or group of persons ⟨the doctrine that the swath of land between the Atlantic and the Pacific naturally *appertained* to the United States⟩ — see BELONG 2
2 to have a relation or connection ⟨list some of the things *appertaining* to public health⟩ — see APPLY 1

appetite *n* **1** a need or desire for food ⟨don't eat before dinner, as it will spoil your *appetite*⟩ — see HUNGER 1
2 a strong wish for something ⟨an *appetite* for adventure⟩ — see DESIRE
3 positive regard for something ⟨his girlfriend has expensive *appetites*⟩ — see LIKING
4 urgent desire or interest ⟨an athlete with an *appetite* for in-your-face competition⟩ — see EAGERNESS

appetizing *adj* very pleasing to the sense of taste ⟨that dish looks very *appetizing*⟩ — see DELICIOUS 1

applaud *vb* to declare enthusiastic approval of ⟨I *applaud* your decision to take that advanced course⟩ — see ACCLAIM

applauding *adj* expressing approval ⟨a student encouraged by his teacher's *applauding* comments⟩ — see FAVORABLE 1

applause *n* enthusiastic and usually public expression of approval ⟨a design for a memorial for the victims of the attack that has received nothing but *applause* from officials, commentators, and the general public⟩
synonyms acclamation, cheering, cheers, ovation, plaudit(s), rave(s)
related words clapping; bravo, hallelujah, hosanna; acclaim, accolade, citation, commendation, compliment, encomium, eulogy, homage, paean, panegyric, salutation, tribute
near antonyms boo, hiss, hoot, jeer, raspberry, smirk, sneer, snicker, snigger, snort, whistle; gibe (*or* jibe), put-down, taunt
antonyms booing, hissing

appliance *n* an interesting and often novel device with a practical use ⟨since the invention of the cork, all manner of *appliances* have been invented for the extraction of these sometimes troublesome stoppers⟩ — see GADGET

applicability *n* the fact or state of being pertinent ⟨we have to question the *applicability* of much of the information he has included in his report⟩ — see PERTINENCE

applicable *adj* **1** capable of being put to use or account ⟨is that information *applicable* in this case?⟩ — see PRACTICAL 1
2 having to do with the matter at hand ⟨that comment isn't *applicable* to our discussion⟩ — see PERTINENT
3 meeting the requirements of a purpose or situation ⟨a knack for selecting the most *applicable* word⟩ — see FIT 1

applicant *n* one who seeks an office, honor, position, or award ⟨have numerous *applicants* for the job⟩ — see CANDIDATE

application *n* the act or practice of employing something for a particular purpose ⟨fixing a snag in pantyhose is not the intended *application* of nail polish, but it's a handy one⟩ — see USE 1

apply *vb* **1** to have a relation or connection ⟨does your rule about calling home *apply* to me as well?⟩
synonyms appertain, bear, pertain, refer, relate
related words affect, concern, interest, involve, touch; associate, connect, couple, interrelate, link, tie in; deal (with), treat
phrases have to do with
2 to occupy (oneself) diligently or with close attention ⟨Sam *applied* himself to writing thank-you letters to everyone who'd helped sponsor him for the jamboree⟩
synonyms address, bend, buckle, devote, give
related words readdress, reapply; knuckle down, set (to), settle (down); busy, commit, concern, engage, involve; exert, exhaust, put out, spend, strain, stress, tax, trouble, wear out; carry on, pitch in, plunge (in); grind, hump, hustle, peg (away), plod, plow, plug (away), work
near antonyms dally, dawdle, dillydally, fiddle, fool (around), idle, mess (around), monkey (around), play, potter, putter, trifle
3 to put a layer of on a surface ⟨*apply* the ointment liberally⟩ — see SPREAD 2
4 to put into action or service ⟨*apply* the laws of motion to this physics problem⟩ — see USE 1

5 to bring to bear especially forcefully or effectively ⟨*apply* pressure to the area to stop the bleeding⟩ — see EXERT
6 to carry out effectively ⟨a police officer *applying* the law⟩ — see ENFORCE

appoint *vb* **1** to decide upon (the time or date for an event) usually from a position of authority ⟨at the *appointed* hour we were in our places⟩
synonyms designate, fix, name, set
related words adopt, assign, choose, determine, establish, opt (for), pick, pin down, prefer, select, settle, single (out), specify; arrange, coordinate, orchestrate; advertise, announce, declare, publish
2 to pick (someone) by one's authority for a specific position or duty ⟨Igor was *appointed* hall monitor for May⟩
synonyms assign, attach, commission, constitute, designate, detail, name
related words authorize, delegate, depute, deputize; inaugurate, induct, install, instate, ordain, invest; crown, enthrone, throne; choose, elect, handpick, nominate, select, single (out), vote (in)
near antonyms depose, dethrone, displace, eject, oust, overthrow, remove, throw out, uncrown, unmake
antonyms discharge, dismiss, expel, fire

appointment *n* **1** the state or fact of being chosen for a position or duty ⟨the *appointment* of the mayor's husband to the Board of Health came as a surprise⟩
synonyms assignment, commission, designation
related words billet, job, office, place, position, situation, spot, station; authorization, delegation, deputation, placement, ranking; induction, installation, installment (*or* instalment), instating, investiture, investment, ordination; choosing, election, nomination, picking, selection, singling out
near antonyms deposition, dethronement, ejection, ouster, overthrow, rejection, removal
antonyms discharge, dismissal, expulsion, firing
2 an agreement to be present at a specified time and place ⟨I have a dental *appointment* for two o'clock tomorrow afternoon⟩ — see ENGAGEMENT 2
3 an assignment at which one regularly works for pay ⟨loved her latest *appointment* as an aide at the governor's office⟩ — see JOB 1
4 appointments *pl* the movable articles in a room ⟨the yacht's staterooms have the most luxurious *appointments* imaginable⟩ — see FURNITURE

apportion *vb* **1** to give as a share or portion ⟨*apportioned* the profits according to years of service with the company⟩ — see ALLOT
2 to give out (something) in appropriate amounts or to appropriate individuals ⟨*apportioned* the grant money to the winners of the competition⟩ — see ADMINISTER 1

apportionment *n* the act or process of giving out something to each member of a group ⟨the *apportionment* of the estate will happen this Friday⟩ — see DISTRIBUTION 1

apposite *adj* having to do with the matter at hand ⟨enriched his essays on patriotism with some very *apposite* quotations from famous people on the subject⟩ — see PERTINENT

appraisal *n* **1** an opinion on the nature, character, or quality of something ⟨gave us a positive *appraisal* of his artistic talents⟩ — see ESTIMATION 1
2 the act of placing a value on the nature, character, or quality of something ⟨the *appraisal* of the house's value took place yesterday⟩ — see ESTIMATE 1

appraise *vb* to make an approximate or tentative judgment regarding ⟨take a moment to *appraise* the current situation⟩ — see ESTIMATE 1

appraisement *n* **1** an opinion on the nature, character, or quality of something ⟨offered us her *appraisement* of the band's latest album⟩ — see ESTIMATION 1
2 the act of placing a value on the nature, character, or quality of something ⟨was too harsh in his *appraisement* of us⟩ — see ESTIMATE 1

appreciable *adj* able to be perceived by a sense or by the mind ⟨there doesn't seem to be any *appreciable* difference between this piece and that one⟩ — see PERCEPTIBLE

appreciate *vb* **1** to become greater in extent, volume, amount, or number ⟨the value of that antique should *appreciate* over time⟩ — see INCREASE 2
2 to hold dear ⟨I *appreciate* my parents more than I can express⟩ — see LOVE 1
3 to recognize the meaning of ⟨I hope you *appreciate* just how much that collector's CD costs⟩ — see COMPREHEND 1
4 to think very highly or favorably of ⟨many great artists and musicians have not been *appreciated* in their own lifetimes⟩ — see ADMIRE

appreciation *n* **1** a feeling of great approval and liking ⟨my *appreciation* of her great contributions to women's sports⟩ — see ADMIRATION 1
2 acknowledgment of having received something good from another ⟨if you can do that, you'll have our heartfelt *appreciation*⟩ — see THANKS
3 the knowledge gained from the process of coming to know or understand something ⟨a course intended to give students an *appreciation* of abstract art⟩ — see COMPREHENSION

appreciative *adj* **1** expressing approval ⟨his latest novel has received a number of *appreciative* reviews⟩ — see FAVORABLE 1
2 feeling or expressing gratitude ⟨very *appreciative* after we helped him change his flat tire⟩ — see GRATEFUL 1

appreciativeness *n* acknowledgment of having received something good from another ⟨a note expressing their *appreciativeness* of all that we had done for them⟩ — see THANKS

apprehend *vb* **1** to recognize the meaning of ⟨do you *apprehend* the importance of this discovery?⟩ — see COMPREHEND 1
2 to take or keep under one's control by authority of law ⟨the agency charged with *apprehending* criminals who have violated federal law⟩ — see ARREST 1

apprehended *adj* taken and held prisoner ⟨an *apprehended* crime lord who can easily post the million-dollar bail⟩ — see CAPTIVE

apprehension *n* **1** suspicion or fear of future harm or misfortune ⟨Erica entered the dark cave with a great deal of *apprehension*⟩
synonyms alarm, apprehensiveness, dread, foreboding, misgiving
related words agitation, anxiousness, concern, disquiet, distress, disturbance, fearfulness, perturbation, solicitude, uneasiness; scruple, worry; doubt, incertitude, suspense, uncertainty, wariness; defeatism, pessimism; foreknowledge, premonition, presage, presentiment
near antonyms anticipation, excitement, hope, hopefulness; confidence, optimism, sanguinity

2 the act of taking or holding under one's control by authority of law ⟨the robber's *apprehension* set us all at ease⟩ — see ARREST
3 the emotion experienced in the presence or threat of danger ⟨still had a lingering *apprehension* of snakes after being bitten by one⟩ — see FEAR
4 an uneasy state of mind usually over the possibility of an anticipated misfortune or trouble ⟨suddenly had the weirdest *apprehension* about the children's safety⟩ — see ANXIETY 1
5 the knowledge gained from the process of coming to know or understand something ⟨a good *apprehension* of how computer systems work⟩ — see COMPREHENSION

apprehensiveness *n* **1** an uneasy state of mind usually over the possibility of an anticipated misfortune or trouble ⟨her *apprehensiveness* about starting college is keeping her awake at night⟩ — see ANXIETY 1
2 suspicion or fear of future harm or misfortune ⟨my *apprehensiveness* of raw fish is keeping me from even trying sushi and having it disagree with me⟩ — see APPREHENSION 1

apprentice *n* a person who helps a more skilled person ⟨decided to be an *apprentice* to an electrician after he graduated⟩ — see HELPER

apprise *vb* to give information to ⟨let me *apprise* you of the current situation⟩ — see ENLIGHTEN 1

approach *n* **1** an established course for traveling from one place to another ⟨will take the standard landing *approach* from the south⟩ — see PASSAGE 1
2 the means or procedure for doing something ⟨that's a different *approach* to knitting, but it seems to work⟩ — see METHOD

approach *vb* **1** to come near or nearer ⟨The parade's *approaching*! I can hear the band playing!⟩
synonyms close, draw on, near
related words arrive, attain, come, gain, hit, land, make, reach, show up, turn up; adjoin, border, touch, verge
near antonyms clear out, depart, exit, go, leave, light out, pull (out), quit, remove, run away, shove (off), take off, walk out
antonyms back (up *or* away), recede, retire, retreat, withdraw

2 to move closer to ⟨*approach* the bull with caution⟩ — see COME 1
3 to come near or nearer to in character or quality ⟨his store-bought dessert doesn't even *approach* your homemade version of it⟩ — see APPROXIMATE

approaching *adj* being soon to appear or take place ⟨the *approaching* holiday has everyone in a state of excitement⟩ — see FORTHCOMING

approbation *n* an acceptance of something as satisfactory ⟨that plan has the *approbation* of the school board⟩ — see APPROVAL 1

appropriate *adj* meeting the requirements of a purpose or situation ⟨I don't think jeans and a T-shirt are *appropriate* attire for a wedding⟩ — see FIT 1

appropriate *vb* **1** to take or make use of without authority or right ⟨archaeologists once *appropriated* artifacts excavated at ancient African sites for their museums in Europe⟩
synonyms arrogate, commandeer, preempt, usurp
related words annex, claim, confiscate, expropriate, preoccupy, sequester; grab, grasp, seize, snatch, steal, take over, wrench, wrest; encroach, infringe, invade, trespass

2 to take (something) without right and with an intent to keep ⟨you can't just *appropriate* somebody's term paper and put your name on it!⟩ — see STEAL 1

appropriately *adv* in a manner suitable for the occasion or purpose ⟨make sure you greet your elders *appropriately*⟩ — see PROPERLY

appropriateness *n* the quality or state of being especially suitable or fitting ⟨Mrs. Bryce-Jones remarked on the *appropriateness* of window boxes on the cottage, noting they gave it a quaint, cheerful look⟩

synonyms aptness, felicitousness, fitness, fittingness, rightness, seemliness, suitability, suitableness

related words agreeableness, compatibility, congruity, harmoniousness; applicability, bearing, connection, materiality, pertinence, relevance; acceptability, adequacy, adequateness, satisfactoriness, serviceableness, usefulness

near antonyms inapplicability, irrelevance; meaninglessness, pointlessness; incompatibility, incongruity

antonyms inappropriateness, inaptness, infelicity, unfitness

appropriation *n* a sum of money allotted for a specific use by official or formal action ⟨the National Park Service received an increased *appropriation* for wildlife management⟩

synonyms allocation, allotment, annuity, grant, subsidy

related words advance, allowance, benefit, endowment, fund, stipend, trust

approval *n* an acceptance of something as satisfactory ⟨Does this dress I bought for the wedding meet with your *approval*?⟩

synonyms approbation, blessing, favor, imprimatur, OK (*or* okay)

related words backing, endorsement, sanction, support; benediction, goodwill; agreement, assent, concurrence, consent; countenance, liking, satisfaction

near antonyms refusal, rejection, repudiation; dislike, dissatisfaction; censure, condemnation, criticism, denunciation, deprecation, depreciation, disparagement, opprobrium, reprehension, reproach, reprobation

antonyms disapprobation, disapproval, disfavor

approve *vb* to give official acceptance of something as satisfactory ⟨as soon as the pond project was *approved*, the bulldozers were at the site⟩

synonyms authorize, clear, OK (*or* okay), ratify, sanction, warrant

related words accept, acknowledge, affirm, confirm; accredit, certify, endorse (*also* indorse), validate; initial, sign; allow, license (*or* licence), permit; reapprove

near antonyms ban, enjoin, forbid, interdict, prohibit; disregard, ignore, neglect, overlook; rebuff, rebut, refuse, spurn

antonyms decline, deny, disallow, disapprove, negative, reject, turn down

approve (of) *vb* to have a favorable opinion of ⟨Mrs. Pinkerton doesn't *approve of* people who stand in the "12 items or less" lane with 13 items⟩

synonyms accept, care (for), countenance, favor, OK (*or* okay), subscribe (to)

related words acclaim, applaud, laud, praise, salute; back (up), stand by, support, sustain, uphold; bear, endure, tolerate; assent (to), concur (with), consent (to); commend, recommend; enjoy, like

phrases go for, hold with

near antonyms censure, condemn, criticize, damn, denounce, deprecate, depreciate, disparage, reprehend,

reprobate; detest, dislike, hate, loathe; object (to), oppose

antonyms disapprove (of), discountenance, disfavor, frown (on *or* upon)

approving *adj* **1** expressing approval ⟨the play did not receive a single *approving* notice⟩ — see FAVORABLE 1

2 showing or expressing acceptance or approval ⟨gave me an *approving* smile⟩ — see POSITIVE

approximate *adj* being such only when compared to something else ⟨the movie's an *approximate* success, if you can overlook the overblown publicity that preceded it⟩ — see COMPARATIVE

approximate *vb* to come near or nearer to in character or quality ⟨Rob's violin performance last night didn't even *approximate* what he's really capable of when he's not feeling sick⟩

synonyms approach, compare (with), measure up (to), stack up (against *or* with)

related words add up (to), amount (to), come (to); duplicate, equal, match; mirror, parallel, reflect; border (on), touch (on), verge (on)

apropos *adj* having to do with the matter at hand ⟨the actor announced to reporters that he would regard as *apropos* only questions about the movie and would ignore inquiries about his love life⟩ — see PERTINENT

apropos of *prep* having to do with ⟨*apropos of* our earlier conversation, here's that file I mentioned⟩ — see ABOUT 1

apt *adj* **1** having a tendency to be or act in a certain way ⟨that dog is *apt* to run off if you don't put him on a leash⟩ — see PRONE 1

2 meeting the requirements of a purpose or situation ⟨"gingerbread" is certainly an *apt* description for that house with all the ornate trim⟩ — see FIT 1

aptitude *n* a special and usually inborn ability ⟨has an *aptitude* for math⟩ — see TALENT

aptness *n* **1** an established pattern of behavior ⟨an unfortunate *aptness* to interrupt people in mid sentence⟩ — see TENDENCY 1

2 the quality or state of being especially suitable or fitting ⟨I'd question the *aptness* of that goofy sympathy card⟩ — see APPROPRIATENESS

aquatic *adj* living, lying, or occurring below the surface of the water ⟨a lifelong fascination with sharks and other fearsome *aquatic* creatures⟩ — see UNDERWATER

aqueduct *n* an open man-made passageway for water ⟨marvelled at the ancient Roman *aqueducts* that still carry water to distant villages⟩ — see CHANNEL 1

arbiter *n* a person who impartially decides or resolves a dispute or controversy ⟨forced to take their contract dispute to an *arbiter*⟩ — see JUDGE 1

arbitrary *adj* **1** having or showing a tendency to force one's will on others without any regard to fairness or necessity ⟨an *arbitrary* piano teacher who makes all her students do the same exercises over and over again⟩

synonyms dictatorial, high-handed, imperious, peremptory, willful (*or* wilful)

related words arrogant, commanding, demanding, dominant, domineering, haughty, imperative, lordly, masterful, overbearing, presumptuous; authoritarian, autocratic, despotic, totalitarian, tyrannical (*also* tyrannic), tyrannous; capricious, changeable, erratic, mercurial, whimsical; biased, inequitable, partisan, prejudiced, unequal, unfair, unjust, unreasonable; unconscionable, unethical, unprincipled, unscrupulous

near antonyms balanced, disinterested, dispassionate, equal, equitable, evenhanded, fair, impartial, just, nonpartisan, objective; rational, reasonable, understanding; unbiased, unprejudiced; ethical, honorable, irreproachable, law-abiding, moral, principled, unimpeachable

2 lacking a definite plan, purpose, or pattern ⟨the order of the names of the ten semifinalists is entirely *arbitrary*⟩ — see RANDOM

arbitrate *vb* to give an opinion about (something at issue or in dispute) ⟨will *arbitrate* the dispute between the company and the labor union⟩ — see JUDGE 1

arbitrator *n* a person who impartially decides or resolves a dispute or controversy ⟨in order to avert a strike, the *arbitrator* forced each side to compromise on certain issues⟩ — see JUDGE 1

arc *n* something that curves or is curved ⟨the stars seemed to align themselves into one vast glittering *arc*⟩ — see BEND 1

arc *vb* to turn away from a straight line or course ⟨the ball *arced* toward the batter and nearly hit him⟩ — see CURVE 1

arch *adj* **1** coming before all others in importance ⟨Lex Luthor is Superman's *arch* enemy⟩ — see FOREMOST 1

2 displaying or marked by rude boldness ⟨was so *arch* as to ask him outright if he was wearing a toupee⟩ — see NERVY 1

arch *n* something that curves or is curved ⟨the limestone *arch* is a natural formation that is the product of many years of erosion⟩ — see BEND 1

arch *vb* **1** to cause to turn away from a straight line ⟨the cat *arched* her back⟩ — see BEND 1

2 to turn away from a straight line or course ⟨the path *arches* off into the woods⟩ — see CURVE 1

archaic *adj* having passed its time of use or usefulness ⟨"thou" and "thee" are usually considered *archaic* words⟩ — see OBSOLETE

archetypal *adj* **1** constituting, serving as, or worthy of being a pattern to be imitated ⟨St. Peter's basilica in Rome is considered by some art historians to be the *archetypal* structure in the baroque style⟩ — see MODEL

2 having or showing the qualities associated with the members of a particular group or kind ⟨the movie's hero is pretty *archetypal*, lacking in any distinctive qualities that would distinguish him from countless other masked avengers⟩ — see TYPICAL 1

archetype *n* something from which copies are made ⟨*Beowulf* is considered by some to be the *archetype* for medieval British heroic tales⟩ — see ORIGINAL

archive *n* a place where books, periodicals, and records are kept for use but not for sale ⟨asked that the book be brought from the *archive*⟩ ⟨sent the novelist's letters to the *archive* for preservation⟩ — see LIBRARY

arctic *adj* having a low or subnormal temperature ⟨the *arctic* air of deep winter⟩ — see COLD 1

ardent *adj* **1** having or expressing great depth of feeling ⟨made *ardent* declarations of love to the woman he hoped to marry⟩ — see FERVENT

2 showing urgent desire or interest ⟨an *ardent* science-fiction fan who has read virtually all of his favorite author's many works⟩ — see EAGER

ardor *n* **1** depth of feeling ⟨candidates for citizenship reciting the oath of allegiance to the United States with all the *ardor* that they could muster⟩

synonyms emotion, fervency, fervidness, fervor, heat, intensity, passion, vehemence, warmth

related words histrionics, mawkishness, melodrama, sappiness, sentimentality; eagerness, earnestness, enthusiasm, excitement, gusto, zest; fanaticism, fever, fire, hot-bloodedness, infatuation, mania, obsession, zeal; compassion, responsiveness, sympathy, tenderness

near antonyms aloofness, calmness, coldness, collectedness, composure, coolness, detachedness, dryness, phlegm, reserve, reservedness, reticence, taciturnity; apathy, indifference, unconcern; stiffness, woodenness

antonyms impassivity

2 urgent desire or interest ⟨in my *ardor* to get started on the hike, I forgot to pack a canteen⟩ — see EAGERNESS

arduous *adj* **1** requiring considerable physical or mental effort ⟨climbing Mt. Everest is an *arduous*, exhausting challenge⟩ — see HARD 2

2 requiring much time, effort, or careful attention ⟨the *arduous* task of doing the research for my term paper⟩ — see DEMANDING 1

arduously *adv* with great effort or determination ⟨*arduously* fought his way to the top of his profession⟩ — see HARD 1

area *n* **1** a part or portion having no fixed boundaries ⟨I last saw your dog over in that general *area*⟩ — see REGION 1

2 a region of activity, knowledge, or influence ⟨a top researcher in the *area* of human genetics⟩ — see FIELD 2

arena *n* **1** a large room or building for enclosed public gatherings ⟨watched the hockey game in the new sports *arena*⟩ — see HALL 3

2 a region of activity, knowledge, or influence ⟨has a lot of influence in the local business *arena*⟩ — see FIELD 2

argot *n* the special terms or expressions of a particular group or field ⟨used the *argot* of figure skaters⟩ — see TERMINOLOGY

argue *vb* **1** to state (something) as a reason in support of or against something under consideration ⟨Luis *argued* that a bake sale would make a lot less money than a car wash⟩

synonyms assert, contend, maintain, plead, reason

related words claim, insist; affirm, aver, avouch, avow; advance, offer, propose, submit; advise, counsel, recommend, suggest, urge; convince, persuade; advocate, champion, espouse, support; explain, justify, rationalize; consider, debate, discuss; counter, disprove, rebut, refute

2 to express different opinions about something often angrily ⟨Francesca didn't *argue* with her little brother the whole time they were at Walt Disney World⟩

synonyms bicker, brawl, dispute, fall out, fight, hassle, quarrel, row, scrap, spat, squabble, wrangle

related words challenge, dare, defy; clash, contend, contest; cavil, fuss, nitpick, quibble; consider, debate, discuss; kick, object, protest

phrases bandy words, fall foul

near antonyms coexist, get along; accept, agree, assent, concur, consent

3 to cause (someone) to agree with a belief or course of action by using arguments or earnest requests ⟨*argued* my parents into letting me go to the movie⟩ — see PERSUADE

4 to talk about (an issue) usually from various points of view and for the purpose of arriving at a decision or opinion ⟨candidates *arguing* gun control in the televised debate⟩ — see DISCUSS

arguer *n* a person who takes part in a dispute ⟨called each side's primary *arguer* up to the front to begin the debate⟩ — see DISPUTANT

argument *n* **1** an often noisy or angry expression of differing opinions ⟨the couple's *arguments* were often loud enough to be heard all over the neighborhood⟩
synonyms altercation, bicker, brawl, cross fire, disagreement, dispute, falling-out, fight, hassle, misunderstanding, quarrel, row, scrap, spat, squabble, tiff, wrangle
related words clash, run-in, skirmish, tussle; feud, vendetta; attack, contention, dissension; controversy, debate; fuss, objection, protest, protestation; affray, feud, fisticuffs, fracas, fray, free-for-all, melee
2 a statement given to explain a belief or act ⟨gave a solid *argument* for the redeeming value of the violent movie⟩ — see REASON 1
3 an exchange of views for the purpose of exploring a subject or deciding an issue ⟨the president of the Senate has allotted a week for the *argument* of the treaty⟩ — see DISCUSSION 1
4 an idea or opinion that is put forth in a discussion or debate ⟨it's my *argument* that we shouldn't be assigned homework on Friday⟩ — see CONTENTION
argumentative *adj* **1** given to arguing ⟨Ryan's *argumentative* nature is such that he's always insisting he didn't make the fouls that the referee calls⟩
synonyms contentious, disputatious, quarrelsome, scrappy
related words bellicose, belligerent, combative, pugnacious, truculent; balky, contrary, ornery, perverse, restive, wayward; disobedient, froward, insubordinate, intractable, recalcitrant, refractory; hardheaded, headstrong, mulish, obdurate, obstinate, pigheaded, resistant, self-willed, stubborn, unbending, uncompromising, uncooperative, unreasonable, unyielding, willful (*or* wilful)
near antonyms acquiescent, agreeable, amenable, complaisant, compliant, complying, conciliatory, cooperative, obliging; docile, obedient, submissive, tractable
2 feeling or displaying eagerness to fight ⟨an *argumentative* gang of bullies always looking for a fight⟩ — see BELLIGERENT
arid *adj* marked by little or no precipitation or humidity ⟨*arid* wastelands unfit for human habitation⟩ — see DRY 1
arise *vb* **1** to leave one's bed ⟨the travelers *arose* before dawn and were on their way as the sun came up⟩
synonyms get up, rise, uprise
related words arouse, awake, awaken, bestir, stir, wake
near antonyms doze, drop (off), nap, nod, sleep, slumber; bunk, perch, roost, settle; couch, lie (down), recline
antonyms bed (down), retire, turn in
2 to come to one's attention especially gradually or unexpectedly ⟨note in your report any problems that *arise* while you are conducting the experiment⟩
synonyms crop (up), emerge, materialize, spring (up), surface
related words appear, come out, show up, turn up; chance, come, come about, fall out, go (on), go off, hap, happen, occur, pass, transpire; interfere, interpose, intervene, intrude
3 to come into existence ⟨it is not known exactly how mammals *arose*, but scientists date the earliest mammals to the Triassic period⟩ — see BEGIN 2
4 to move or extend upward ⟨slowly the hot-air balloon *arose*, and the round-the-world flight was begun⟩ — see ASCEND
aristocracy *n* the highest class in a society ⟨at one time in China only the *aristocracy* could own land⟩

synonyms gentry, upper class, upper crust
related words elect, elite, establishment, gentlefolk, jet set, nobility, quality, royalty, society
near antonyms commoners, (the) crowd, (the) masses, peasantry, peonage, (the) people, plebeians, (the) populace, (the) public, rank and file; bourgeoisie, middle class, working class; dregs, (the) herd, (the) mob, rabble, riffraff, scum, trash
antonyms proletarians, proletariat
aristocrat *n* a man of high birth or social position ⟨could trace my lineage to an English *aristocrat* of the 17th century⟩ — see GENTLEMAN 1
aristocratic *adj* of high birth, rank, or station ⟨an impoverished dowager who never lets people forget about her *aristocratic* origins⟩ — see NOBLE 1
arithmetic *n* the act or process of performing mathematical operations to find a value ⟨she's terrible in writing but fantastic at *arithmetic*⟩ — see CALCULATION
¹arm *n* a portable weapon from which a shot is discharged by gunpowder ⟨soldiers grabbing their *arms* and helmets and heading into battle⟩ — see GUN 1
²arm *n* **1** an area of land that juts out into a body of water ⟨Maine has so many long, narrow *arms* that jut out into the ocean that early coastal settlers found it much easier to travel by sea⟩ — see ²CAPE
2 the right or means to command or control others ⟨few criminals manage to permanently escape the long *arm* of the law⟩ — see POWER 1
armada *n* a group of vehicles traveling together or under one management ⟨an *armada* of ships sailing up the coast⟩ — see FLEET
armed forces *n pl* the combined army, air force, and navy of a nation ⟨our nation's *armed forces* are stationed throughout the world⟩
synonyms military, service, troops
related words GI's (*or* GIs), men-at-arms, rank and file, servicemen, servicewomen, soldiers, soldiery; militia, reserves; armor, defense
near antonyms civilians, noncombatants
armistice *n* a temporary stopping of fighting ⟨each side in the conflict agreed to an *armistice* during the solemn holy days⟩ — see TRUCE
armor *n* **1** means or method of defending ⟨the skunk's primary *armor* is the foul-smelling fluid that it can eject⟩ — see DEFENSE 1
2 something that encloses another thing especially to protect it ⟨the crab's *armor* makes it difficult prey for some smaller predators⟩ — see ¹CASE
armory *n* a place where military arms are stored ⟨the soldier was sent to the *armory* to get a replacement weapon for the one that had been stolen⟩
synonyms arsenal, depot, dump, magazine
related words fort, fortress, stronghold; repository, storehouse, warehouse
army *n* **1** a large body of men and women organized for land warfare ⟨In 218 B.C., Hannibal marched into Italy with an *army* of 26,000, and even a few elephants, after crossing the Alps⟩
synonyms battalion, host, legion
related words infantry, ranks, regulars, soldiers, troops, troopers
2 a great number of persons or things gathered together ⟨a vast *army* of loyal fans in line for the band's farewell concert⟩ — see CROWD 1
aroma *n* a sweet or pleasant smell ⟨love the *aroma* of bread baking in the oven⟩ — see FRAGRANCE
aromatic *adj* having a pleasant smell ⟨beautiful and *aromatic* flowers⟩ — see FRAGRANT

around *adv* **1** on all sides or in every direction ⟨he looked *around*⟩ ⟨butterflies were flying all *around*⟩

synonyms about, round

related words all over, everyplace, everywhere; abroad, afloat, hereabouts (*or* hereabout)

2 toward the opposite direction ⟨she turned *around* and saw him⟩

synonyms about, back, round

related words backward (*or* backwards), behind, down, downward, rearward (*or* rearwards); across, athwart, counter, counterclockwise

3 at, within, or to a short distance or time ⟨stay *around* the yard while you're playing⟩ ⟨he'll be getting in *around* 6:00⟩ — see NEAR 1

4 from beginning to end ⟨a team that plays all year *around*⟩ — see THROUGH 1

around *prep* **1** close to ⟨I wouldn't stand *around* those rocks—there could be snakes under them⟩

synonyms about, by, near, next to

related words alongside, beside; across, along, at; circa

2 in random positions within the boundaries of ⟨huge, strangely shaped rocks were scattered *around* the canyon floor⟩

synonyms about, over, round, through, throughout

related words on

arouse *vb* **1** to cause to stop sleeping ⟨the rooster's crow *aroused* me from my deep sleep⟩ — see WAKE 1

2 to cease to be asleep ⟨set the alarm so we would *arouse* at 5:00 a.m.⟩ — see WAKE 2

3 to rouse to strong feeling or action ⟨the court's controversial decision *aroused* many to protest and to lobby the legislature for a constitutional amendment⟩ — see PROVOKE 1

arrange *vb* **1** to come to an agreement or decision concerning the details of ⟨*arrange* a time for the meeting⟩ ⟨*arrange* money matters for your trip⟩

synonyms decide, fix, set, settle

related words agree, contract, pledge, promise; draft, frame, hammer (out), intrigue, lay out, maneuver, map (out), plan, program, schematize, scheme, shape, square away, work out; affirm, approve, authorize, clear, confirm, OK (*or* okay), sanction, warrant; close, complete, conclude, end, finalize, finish, round (off *or* out), wind up, wrap up; bargain, chaffer, deal, dicker, haggle, horse-trade, negotiate

phrases dispose of

2 to put into a particular arrangement ⟨*arrange* the flowers so that the taller ones are at the center of the bouquet⟩ — see ORDER 1

3 to bring about through discussion and compromise ⟨I'll *arrange* your free movie pass with the cinema's manager⟩ — see NEGOTIATE 1

4 to work out the details of (something) in advance ⟨we need to *arrange* our European vacation so that we can get the best deals⟩ — see PLAN 1

arrangement *n* **1** a method worked out in advance for achieving some objective ⟨will work out a visitation *arrangement* in court⟩ — see PLAN 1

2 the way in which something is sized, arranged, or organized ⟨an artistic *arrangement* of the vases on the shelf⟩ — see FORMAT 1

3 the way in which the elements of something (as a work of art) are arranged ⟨the close *arrangement* of the figures in the family portrait is meant to be symbolic of their close emotional attachment⟩ — see COMPOSITION 3

4 the way objects in space or events in time are arranged or follow one another ⟨the *arrangement* of

works in the piano recital resulted in pieces of similar mood being played back-to-back⟩ — see ORDER 1

arrant *adj* having no exceptions or restrictions ⟨that statement is complete and *arrant* nonsense⟩ — see ABSOLUTE 2

array *n* **1** a number of things considered as a unit ⟨an *array* of baseball gloves in the corner of his room⟩ — see GROUP 1

2 a usually small number of persons considered as a unit ⟨a motley *array* of travelers waiting for the bus⟩ — see GROUP 2

3 dressy clothing ⟨dressed in festive *array* for the city's annual New Year's Eve celebration⟩ — see FINERY

4 the way objects in space or events in time are arranged or follow one another ⟨a marching band's carefully choreographed *array*⟩ — see ORDER 1

array *vb* **1** to make more attractive by adding something that is beautiful or becoming ⟨a door *arrayed* with a beautiful evergreen wreath⟩ — see DECORATE

2 to outfit with clothes and especially fine or special clothes ⟨*arrayed* in a wedding dress that has been handed down in the family for generations⟩ — see CLOTHE 1

3 to put into a particular arrangement ⟨*arrayed* his baseball cards in order of their rarity and consequent monetary value⟩ — see ORDER 1

arrest *n* the act of taking or holding under one's control by authority of law ⟨there have been only two *arrests* for driving while intoxicated in the county in the last six months⟩

synonyms apprehension, pinch

related words bust [*slang*], raid; capture, entrapment, seizure; captivity, confinement, detention, enchainment, immurement, imprisonment, incarceration, restraint

near antonyms emancipation, liberation, release

antonyms discharge

arrest *vb* **1** to take or keep under one's control by authority of law ⟨the inept robber was promptly *arrested* by the off-duty policeman he had tried to hold up⟩

synonyms apprehend, bust [*slang*], nab, pick up, pinch, restrain, seize

related words bag, capture, catch, collar, get, grab, grapple, hook, land, nail, snare, snatch, trap; confine, detain, hold, immure, imprison, incarcerate, intern, jail, lock (up); bind, enchain, fetter, handcuff, manacle, shackle, trammel

near antonyms emancipate, free, liberate, loose, loosen, release, spring; unbind, unchain

antonyms discharge

2 to bring (something) to a standstill ⟨cryogenics is based on the idea that extreme cold can almost *arrest* molecular motion⟩ — see ¹HALT 1

3 to hold the attention of as if by a spell ⟨the sight of the daredevil walking a tightrope between high-rises *arrested* area pedestrians and motorists alike⟩ — see ENTHRALL 1

arrested *adj* taken and held prisoner ⟨*arrested* suspects waiting to be booked on a variety of charges⟩ — see CAPTIVE

arresting *adj* **1** holding the attention or provoking interest ⟨an *arresting* film about tribal traditions in Africa⟩ — see INTERESTING

2 likely to attract attention ⟨at seven feet tall, he's an *arresting* figure⟩ — see NOTICEABLE

arrival *n* the act of coming upon a scene ⟨spring's late *arrival* meant we were still skiing in mid-April⟩ ⟨the

groom blamed his belated *arrival* for the wedding on a huge traffic snarl⟩
synonyms advent, appearance
related words approach, entrance, ingress; beginning, birth, commencement, dawn, dawning, debut, genesis, inception, morning, onset, start
near antonyms dissipation, dissolution, evaporation, fading, melting, passing, vanishing; clearing out, egress, exit, exiting, leaving, retirement, withdrawal
antonyms departing, departure, disappearance, going
arrive *vb* to get to a destination ⟨when will the guests *arrive*?⟩ — see COME 2
arrogance *n* an exaggerated sense of one's importance that shows itself in the making of excessive or unjustified claims ⟨in his *arrogance* the president of the club made all the arrangements for the annual banquet without consulting the members⟩
synonyms haughtiness, imperiousness, loftiness, lordliness, masterfulness, peremptoriness, pompousness, presumptuousness, pretense (*or* pretence), pretension, pretentiousness, self-importance, superciliousness, superiority
related words authoritativeness, bossiness, dominance, high-handedness; condescension, disdain, scorn; snobbery, snobbishness, snobbism, snootiness; cheek, cheekiness, impertinence, impudence, sauciness; boastfulness, bombast, braggadocio, swagger, vaingloriousness, vainglory; cockiness, complacence, conceit, egoism, egotism, pride, pridefulness, self-centeredness, self-conceit, self-satisfaction, smugness, vanity
near antonyms bashfulness, demureness, retiringness, shyness; diffidence, self-doubt, timidity; meekness, passiveness, passivity, submissiveness; quietness, reserve, reservedness
antonyms humility, modesty
arrogant *adj* having a feeling of superiority that shows itself in an overbearing attitude ⟨the *arrogant* young lawyer elbowed his way to the head of the line of customers, declaring that he was too busy to wait like everybody else⟩
synonyms cavalier, haughty, highfalutin, high-handed, high-hat, imperious, important, lofty, lordly, masterful, overweening, peremptory, pompous, presumptuous, pretentious, supercilious, superior, uppish, uppity
related words authoritarian, bossy, dominant, dominating, domineering, magisterial, pontificating; condescending, disdainful, patronizing; impertinent, impudent, saucy; snobbish, snobby, snooty; boastful, bombastic, braggart, bragging, cocky, swaggering, vain, vainglorious; complacent, conceited, egocentric, egoistic, egotistic (*or* egotistical), prideful, proud, self-centered, self-conceited, self-satisfied, smug, stuck-up
near antonyms bashful, cowering, cringing, demure, diffident, mousy (*or* mousey), overmodest, self-doubting, shrinking, shy, subdued, timid; acquiescent, compliant, deferential, meek, passive, submissive, unaggressive, unassertive, unassuming, unobtrusive, yielding; quiet, reserved, retiring
antonyms humble, modest
arrogate *vb* to take or make use of without authority or right ⟨*arrogated* the corner office without obtaining prior approval⟩ — see APPROPRIATE 1
arsenal *n* a place where military arms are stored ⟨sent the ordnance officer to the *arsenal* for weapons⟩ — see ARMORY
arsonist *n* a person who deliberately and unlawfully sets fire to a building or other property ⟨they finally caught the *arsonist*, but only after he'd set fire to four barns⟩

synonyms firebug, incendiary
related words igniter (*or* ignitor)
art *n* subtle or imaginative ability in inventing, devising, or executing something ⟨while some people see it simply as exercise, there is an *art* to skateboarding⟩ — see SKILL 1
artery *n* a passage cleared for public vehicular travel ⟨there's an accident on the main *artery* into town, so I'll be late⟩ — see WAY 1
artful *adj* **1** clever at attaining one's ends by indirect and often deceptive means ⟨the lawyer, by her *artful* questioning, got the witness to admit he had been lying⟩
synonyms beguiling, cagey (*also* cagy), crafty, cunning, devious, foxy, guileful, slick, sly, subtle, wily
related words astute, cute, facile, glib, sharp, shrewd; crooked, deceitful, deceptive, dishonest, insidious, insinuating, Machiavellian, shady, shifty, slippery, sneaky, treacherous, tricky, underhand, underhanded, unscrupulous; backhanded, double-dealing, hypocritical, insincere, mealymouthed, smooth-tongued, two-faced; circuitous, circular, roundabout; clandestine, concealed, covert, furtive, hugger-mugger, secret, stealthy, surreptitious, undercover; calculating, designing, scheming, plotting
near antonyms obvious, open, patent, plain, public, unconcealed; aboveboard, candid, direct, forthright, frank, honest, natural, outspoken, plainspoken, real, simple, sincere, straightforward, unaffected, unpretending
antonyms artless, guileless, ingenuous
2 showing a use of the imagination and creativity especially in inventing ⟨the *artful* inventor who came up with the vacuum bottle⟩ — see CLEVER 1
3 accomplished with trained ability ⟨that was an *artful* way to handle a very delicate situation⟩ — see SKILLFUL
artfulness *n* **1** skill in achieving one's ends through indirect, subtle, or underhanded means ⟨with well-practiced *artfulness*, he convinced his mother he was sick enough to stay home from school but not sick enough for a visit to the doctor's office⟩ — see CUNNING 1
2 subtle or imaginative ability in inventing, devising, or executing something ⟨building a ship model requires an *artfulness* I don't have⟩ — see SKILL 1
article *n* a short piece of writing typically expressing a point of view ⟨read an *article* extolling the benefits of vegetarianism⟩ — see ESSAY 1
articulate *adj* able to express oneself clearly and well ⟨the television crew covering the science fair were looking for photogenic and *articulate* students to explain their projects on the air⟩
synonyms eloquent, fluent, well-spoken
related words facile, glib, smooth-tongued, voluble; expressive, outspoken, verbal, vocal; blabby, chatty, garrulous, loquacious, talkative, verbose; unfaltering, unhesitating
near antonyms faltering, halting, hesitant, maundering, mumbling, muttering, sputtering, stammering, stumbling, stuttering; mute, speechless, tongue-tied, voiceless
antonyms inarticulate
articulate *vb* **1** to utter clearly and distinctly ⟨uses a very measured tone and *articulates* every syllable when issuing scoldings⟩
synonyms enunciate
related words express, pronounce, say, verbalize, vocalize, voice; speak out, speak up

near antonyms falter, grunt, halt, hesitate, maunder, sputter, stammer, stumble, stutter; mouth, mumble, murmur, mutter, whisper

2 to convey in appropriate or telling terms ⟨an essay that masterfully *articulates* the case for a greater commitment to space exploration⟩ — see PHRASE

3 to express (a thought or emotion) in words ⟨I'm not *articulating* my thoughts very well⟩ — see SAY 1

articulateness *n* the art or power of speaking or writing in a forceful and convincing way ⟨a public speaker should strive for *articulateness*⟩ — see ELOQUENCE

articulation *n* **1** an act, process, or means of putting something into words ⟨his *articulation* of his feelings for her was long overdue⟩ — see EXPRESSION 1

2 the clear and accurate pronunciation of words especially in public speaking ⟨you will have to work on your *articulation* if you want to be an announcer on TV⟩ — see DICTION 1

artifice *n* **1** a clever often underhanded means to achieve an end ⟨used the *artifice* of saying his grandmother had died so that he could get the last seat on the plane⟩ — see TRICK 1

2 skill in achieving one's ends through indirect, subtle, or underhanded means ⟨using their *artifice*, the Greeks crafted a hollow wooden horse to hide inside and thereby gained entry into the city of Troy⟩ — see CUNNING 1

3 subtle or imaginative ability in inventing, devising, or executing something ⟨a painting that could only have been created with the *artifice* of a master⟩ — see SKILL 1

4 the inclination or practice of misleading others through lies or trickery ⟨a crook who is a master of *artifice* and manipulation⟩ — see DECEIT

5 the use of clever underhanded actions to achieve an end ⟨a wise counselor who can see through any knave's *artifice*⟩ — see TRICKERY

artificer *n* a person whose occupation requires skill with the hands ⟨the oil tycoon insisted that the best stone masons, cabinetmakers, and *artificers* in every other craft be employed to create a mansion of unequalled splendor⟩ — see ARTISAN

artificial *adj* **1** lacking in natural or spontaneous quality ⟨the beauty-pageant contestants' *artificial* smiles looked like they were glued on their faces⟩

synonyms affected, assumed, bogus, contrived, factitious, fake, false, feigned, forced, mechanical, mock, phony (*also* phoney), pretended, pseudo, put-on, sham, simulated, spurious, strained, unnatural

related words automatic, canned, concocted, fabricated, labored, manufactured, unauthentic, unreal, unrealistic; empty, facile, hollow, hypocritical, insincere, left-handed; exaggerated, histrionic, melodramatic, overacted, overdone, theatrical; cute, cutesy, goody-goody, mincing, overrefined, simpering; conventional, formal, impersonal, inflexible, rigid, stiff, stylized, wooden; artful, calculated, conscious, cultivated, deliberate, premeditated, studied

near antonyms authentic, bona fide, real, realistic, true; honest, ingenuous, sincere, unpretending; easy, effortless, smooth; extemporaneous, impromptu, impulsive, instinctive, unconscious, unprompted, unrehearsed

antonyms artless, genuine, natural, spontaneous, unaffected, unfeigned, unforced

2 not being or expressing what one appears to be or express ⟨the familiar sight of the award winner accepting the *artificial* congratulations of the other nominees⟩ — see INSINCERE

3 being such in appearance only and made with or manufactured from usually cheaper materials ⟨*artificial* lemon flavor⟩ — see IMITATION

artillery *n* large firearms (as cannon or rockets) ⟨during the *artillery* attack families hid in their cellars⟩

synonyms guns, ordnance

related words ammunition, armament, arms, munitions, weaponry, weapons

artisan *n* a person whose occupation requires skill with the hands ⟨we visited a re-created 19-century New England village that features an array of *artisans*—a cooper, a carpenter, a blacksmith, a potter, a glass-blower⟩

synonyms artificer, craftsman, handicrafter, tradesman

related words artist, maker; journeyman, master; mechanic, smith, technician, wright; handyman

artist *n* a person with a high level of knowledge or skill in a field ⟨a pitcher who is a strikeout *artist*⟩ — see EXPERT

artistic *adj* of or relating to the fine arts ⟨funding for *artistic* endeavors is crucial if the city is to survive and prosper⟩ — see CULTURAL

artistry *n* subtle or imaginative ability in inventing, devising, or executing something ⟨the high level of *artistry* involved in painting miniatures⟩ — see SKILL 1

artless *adj* **1** free from any intent to deceive or impress others ⟨a genuine and *artless* girl⟩ — see GUILELESS

2 hastily or roughly constructed ⟨pulled together an *artless* lean-to and hoped it would stay up overnight⟩ — see RUDE 1

artlessly *adv* without any attempt to impress by deception or exaggeration ⟨*artlessly* commented that the dress looked good⟩ ⟨informed his host rather *artlessly* that the food was okay but not fantastic⟩ — see NATURALLY 3

artlessness *n* the quality or state of being simple and sincere ⟨the *artlessness* of children should be cherished while it lasts⟩ — see NAÏVETÉ 1

as *conj* for the reason that ⟨had his meals delivered to him *as* he couldn't navigate the icy sidewalk with his walker⟩ — see SINCE

ascend *vb* to move or extend upward ⟨the path *ascended* so steeply at one point that we had to scramble up on our hands and knees⟩

synonyms arise, climb, lift, mount, rise, soar, up, uprise, upsweep, upturn

related words boost, elevate, raise, uplift, upraise; take off, zoom; crest, scale, surmount, top

near antonyms dive, nose-dive, plummet, plunge, sink, slide

antonyms decline, descend, dip, drop, fall (off)

ascendancy *n* controlling power or influence over others ⟨a book chronicling the *ascendancy* of fascism⟩ — see SUPREMACY 1

ascension *n* the act or an instance of rising or climbing up ⟨her *ascension* from the freshman to the varsity team was evidence of how much she had improved in one season⟩ — see ASCENT 1

ascent *n* **1** the act or an instance of rising or climbing up ⟨our plane broke through some heavy low clouds during its *ascent* and leveled off once we were above them⟩

synonyms ascension, climb, rise, rising, soar

related words boost, hike, increase, raise; elevation, levitation, lift-off, raising, takeoff; heave, upheaval, up-

lifting, upraising, upsurge, upsweep, upswing, uptrend, upturn, upwelling
near antonyms dive, nosedive, plop, plummeting, plunge, sinking; decline, decrease
antonyms descent, dip, drop, fall
2 an upward slope ⟨we'd reached the final *ascent* of the trail to the summit⟩
synonyms rise, upgrade
related words grade, incline; climb, hump, mound, ridge, swell
near antonyms basin, depression, hollow
antonyms declension, decline, declivity, descent, downgrade
3 a raising or a state of being raised to a higher rank or position ⟨his long, gradual *ascent* into the ranks of management⟩ — see ADVANCEMENT 1

ascertain *vb* **1** to come to an awareness ⟨was immediately able to *ascertain* that the girl was uncomfortable talking about her life at home⟩ — see DISCOVER 1
2 to come upon after searching, study, or effort ⟨*ascertained* that their old colonial house had once functioned as a tavern⟩ — see FIND 1

ascribe *vb* to explain (something) as being the result of something else ⟨*ascribed* their stunning military victory to good intelligence beforehand⟩ — see CREDIT 1

aseptic *adj* free from filth, infection, or dangers to health ⟨patients with damaged immune systems must be treated in *aseptic* environments⟩ — see SANITARY

ashamed *adj* suffering from or expressive of a feeling of responsibility for wrongdoing ⟨was *ashamed* that she had lied to the interviewer⟩ ⟨wearing a very *ashamed* look⟩ — see GUILTY 2

ashen *adj* lacking a healthy skin color ⟨still looking *ashen* from his bout with the flu⟩ — see PALE 2

ashes *n pl* the portion or bits of something left over or behind after it has been destroyed ⟨sifted through the *ashes* of the campfire⟩ — see REMAINS 1

ashy *adj* lacking a healthy skin color ⟨paramedics knew she was in shock because she was *ashy* and shaking⟩ — see PALE 2

aside from *prep* not including ⟨*aside from* the C in geometry, he made all A's this term⟩ — see EXCEPT

as if *conj* the way it would be or one would do if ⟨she looked *as if* she wanted to ask one more question before we left⟩
synonyms as though, like

asinine *adj* showing or marked by a lack of good sense or judgment ⟨it was *asinine* to run into the street like that⟩ — see FOOLISH 1

asininity *n* **1** a foolish act or idea ⟨I will not take part in the *asininity* of throwing eggs at police cars⟩ — see FOLLY 1
2 lack of good sense or judgment ⟨the *asininity* of your sassing a teacher is beyond belief⟩ — see FOOLISHNESS 1

ask *vb* **1** to put a question or questions to ⟨my grandfather *asked* me all about my trip⟩
synonyms inquire (of), interrogate, query, question, quiz
related words cross-examine, examine, grill, pump; poll, survey
near antonyms rejoin, retort; comment, observe, remark
antonyms answer, reply, respond
2 to make a request of ⟨*ask* the sales clerk for assistance⟩
synonyms request, solicit

related words appeal (to), beg, beseech, entreat, implore, importune, invoke, petition, pray, supplicate; demand, enjoin, exact, press, require
phrases call on (*or* upon)
3 to set or receive as a price ⟨they are only *asking* $300 for that antique grandfather clock⟩ — see CHARGE 1

ask (for) *vb* **1** to make a request for ⟨don't be afraid to *ask for* help if you need it⟩
synonyms call (for), plead (for), quest, request, seek, solicit, sue (for)
related words apply (for), beg (for), clamor (for), urge; demand, enjoin, exact, insist (on), require, requisition
2 to act so as to make (something) more likely ⟨you are *asking for* trouble⟩ — see COURT 1
3 to give a request or demand for ⟨the surgeon *asked for* the scalpel⟩ — see ORDER 2

askance *adv* with distrust ⟨we looked *askance* at the dealer's assertion that the car had never been in an accident⟩
synonyms distrustfully, doubtfully, doubtingly, dubiously, mistrustfully, skeptically, suspiciously
related words hesitantly, hesitatingly, incredulously, questioningly, quizzically, unbelievingly; charily, guardedly, warily; captiously, critically, cynically, deprecatingly, disapprovingly, disparagingly, negatively, reproachfully, unfavorably; anxiously, apprehensively, uncomfortably, uneasily
phrases with a grain of salt
near antonyms approvingly, favorably, positively; confidently, sanguinely; credulously, uncritically
antonyms trustfully, trustingly

askew *adj* inclined or twisted to one side ⟨his hat was *askew* because of the wind⟩ — see AWRY

aslant *adj* inclined or twisted to one side ⟨that picture is *aslant*—would you mind straightening it?⟩ — see AWRY

asleep *adj* **1** being in a state of suspended consciousness ⟨Paul was *asleep* when the earthquake struck⟩
synonyms dormant, dozing, napping, resting, sleeping, slumbering
related words drowsy, nodding, sleepy, slumberous (*or* slumbrous), somnolent; dreaming, reposing; hypnotized, mesmerized, semiconscious
near antonyms aware, conscious; sleepless; aroused, astir, up
antonyms awake, wakeful, wide-awake
2 lacking in sensation or feeling ⟨after sitting cross-legged all afternoon, I arose only to discover that my right foot was *asleep*⟩ — see NUMB

aspect *n* **1** a certain way in which something appears or may be regarded ⟨depending on what *aspect* of college life you consider most important, there are several colleges which might be good for you⟩
synonyms angle, facet, hand, phase, side
related words air, appearance, character, color, complexion, condition, face, look, semblance, shape, state, visage; period, stage, step; point of view, position, posture, stance, standpoint, view, viewpoint; interpretation, reading, rendering, translation, version; article, case, component, count, detail, element, factor, instance, item, matter, part, particular, point, regard, respect
2 the outward form of someone or something especially as indicative of a quality ⟨he has the *aspect* of a man used to giving orders and seeing them obeyed⟩ — see APPEARANCE 1

asperity *n* **1** a harsh or sharp quality ⟨doesn't like the *asperity* of most experimental music⟩ — see EDGE 1

2 biting sharpness of feeling or expression ⟨she said no with such *asperity* that we knew she was deeply offended by the question⟩ — see ACRIMONY 1

3 something that is a cause for suffering or special effort especially in the attainment of a goal ⟨as a physically challenged person, he has encountered more than his share of *asperities* on the road to success⟩ — see DIFFICULTY 1

asperse *vb* to make untrue and harmful statements about ⟨how dare you *asperse* the character of our dedicated pastor!⟩ — see SLANDER

aspersing *n* the making of false statements that damage another's reputation ⟨she has refused to take part in the *aspersing* in which so many political candidates indulge⟩ — see SLANDER

aspirant *n* one who seeks an office, honor, position, or award ⟨a bevy of ever-smiling *aspirants* for the Miss America title⟩ — see CANDIDATE

aspiration *n* **1** eager desire for personal advancement ⟨a combination of *aspiration* and hard work made her the top female athlete in the state⟩ — see AMBITION 1

2 something that one hopes or intends to accomplish ⟨college is his immediate *aspiration* after he graduates from high school⟩ — see GOAL

aspire *vb* to have in mind as a purpose or goal ⟨*aspire* to great deeds, and you have a better chance of doing good deeds⟩ — see INTEND

aspiring *adj* having a strong desire for personal advancement ⟨an *aspiring* young pianist eager to win the prestigious competition⟩ — see AMBITIOUS 1

ass *n* a sturdy and patient domestic mammal that is used especially to carry things ⟨the farm kept a few *asses* for hauling hay in and out of the field⟩ — see DONKEY 1

assail *vb* **1** to criticize harshly and usually publicly ⟨the union organizers *assailed* the company for failing to provide a safe working environment⟩ — see ATTACK 2

2 to take sudden, violent action against ⟨a band of robbers *assailed* the lone traveler⟩ — see ATTACK 1

assassin *n* a person who kills another person ⟨shot down by an unknown *assassin*⟩

   synonyms killer, murderer

   related words butcher, executioner, slaughterer, slayer

assault *n* the act or action of setting upon with force or violence ⟨was arrested for his *assault* of the bystander⟩ — see ATTACK 1

assault *vb* to take sudden, violent action against ⟨*assaulted* his enemies with gusto⟩ — see ATTACK 1

assay *n* the separation and identification of the parts of a whole ⟨a metallurgist did an *assay* on the metal and determined it contained nickel⟩ — see ANALYSIS 1

assay *vb* **1** to identify and examine the basic elements or parts of (something) especially for discovering interrelationships ⟨the company *assayed* a sample of the rock to see if it contained gold in quantities worth mining⟩ — see ANALYZE

2 to make an effort to do ⟨*assaying* the task of writing his autobiography⟩ — see ATTEMPT

assemblage *n* **1** a body of people come together in one place ⟨an *assemblage* of onlookers at the construction site⟩ — see GATHERING 1

2 a mass or quantity that has piled up or that has been gathered ⟨tried to sort through the *assemblage* of ripped wrapping paper and boxes for the missing toy⟩ — see ACCUMULATION 1

3 a number of things considered as a unit ⟨an *assemblage* of brass candlesticks on the table⟩ — see GROUP 1

4 an organized group of objects acquired and maintained for study, exhibition, or personal pleasure ⟨donated his *assemblage* of 18th-century miniature paintings to the museum⟩ — see COLLECTION 1

assemble *vb* **1** to come together into one body or place ⟨the graduates were told to *assemble* in the cafeteria an hour before the ceremony⟩

   synonyms cluster, collect, concentrate, conglomerate, congregate, convene, converge, forgather (*or* foregather), gather, meet, rendezvous

   related words affiliate, ally, associate, band (together), club, collaborate, confederate, conjoin, consolidate, consort, cooperate, couple, federate, gang (up), join, merge, unite

   near antonyms depart, leave, take off; disjoin, dissociate, disunite

   antonyms break up, disband, disperse, split up

2 to form by putting together parts or materials ⟨it took a lot more time to *assemble* the model train set than the box said it would⟩ — see BUILD

3 to bring together in assembly by or as if by command ⟨we *assembled* the club members to decide who would be traveling with whom on the trip⟩ — see CONVOKE

4 to bring together in one body or place ⟨*assembled* an assortment of fancy desserts for the reception⟩ — see GATHER 1

assembly *n* **1** a body of people come together in one place ⟨an *assembly* of early morning commuters waiting at the train station⟩ — see GATHERING 1

2 a body of persons gathered for religious worship ⟨the preacher spoke to the *assembly* in somber tones⟩ — see CONGREGATION 1

3 a coming together of a number of persons for a specified purpose ⟨attendance at the awards *assembly* is mandatory⟩ — see MEETING 1

assert *vb* **1** to state clearly and strongly ⟨Mrs. Cartwright is never afraid to *assert* her allegiance to flag and country⟩

   synonyms affirm, aver, avouch, avow, declare, lay down, profess

   related words advance, advertise, boost, plug, promote, publicize; announce, blaze, call, proclaim, pronounce, say; accent, accentuate, emphasize, stress, underline, underscore; advocate, champion, defend, espouse, support, uphold; assure, convince, persuade; explain, justify, rationalize

   near antonyms minimize, understate; disregard, ignore, neglect, overlook

2 to state (something) as a reason in support of or against something under consideration ⟨*asserted* that a new roof would be necessary if the church was to remain open⟩ — see ARGUE 1

3 to state as a fact usually forcefully ⟨vigorously *asserted* that he was innocent of all the charges⟩ — see CLAIM 1

assertion *n* **1** a solemn and often public declaring of the truth or existence of something ⟨the *assertion* that all men have certain unalienable rights is set forth in the Declaration of Independence⟩ — see PROTESTATION

2 an idea or opinion that is put forth in a discussion or debate ⟨made the unlikely *assertion* that gravity affects light⟩ — see CONTENTION

assertive *adj* **1** having or showing a bold forcefulness in the pursuit of a goal ⟨some reef fish are *assertive* in defending their territory⟩ — see AGGRESSIVE 1

2 marked by or uttered with forcefulness ⟨after months of *assertive* declarations that he would not run for president, he announced he was running⟩ — see EMPHATIC 1

assertiveness *n* the quality or state of being forceful (as in expression) ⟨the *assertiveness* with which he voices his opinions intimidates some people⟩ — see VEHEMENCE 1

assess *vb* **1** to establish or apply as a charge or penalty ⟨the utility company will *assess* a fee if your payment is late⟩ — see IMPOSE

2 to make an approximate or tentative judgment regarding ⟨step back and *assess* the situation⟩ — see ESTIMATE 1

assessment *n* **1** a charge usually of money collected by the government from people or businesses for public use ⟨hated paying the annual *assessment* on his car⟩ — see TAX

2 an opinion on the nature, character, or quality of something ⟨I'm far too quiet, in the *assessment* of my new boss⟩ — see ESTIMATION 1

3 the act of placing a value on the nature, character, or quality of something ⟨we may have been too hasty in our *assessment* of the value of the property⟩ — see ESTIMATE 1

assets *n pl* the total of one's money and property ⟨the college's *assets* grew dramatically over the course of the decade⟩ — see WEALTH 1

assiduity *n* attentive and persistent effort ⟨this project was successful only through the *assiduity* of a lot of people⟩ — see DILIGENCE

assiduous *adj* involved in often constant activity ⟨*assiduous* ants carrying food into the anthill⟩ — see BUSY 1

assiduously *adv* with great effort or determination ⟨*assiduously* pursued a spot on the volleyball team⟩ — see HARD 1

assiduousness *n* attentive and persistent effort ⟨with painstaking *assiduousness* investigators finally cracked the case of the stolen works of art⟩ — see DILIGENCE

assign *vb* **1** to give a task, duty, or responsibility to ⟨*assigned* the class with the task of finding something in the state constitution they felt needed changing⟩ — see ENTRUST 1

2 to give as a share or portion ⟨each camper was *assigned* a bunk and a chest⟩ — see ALLOT

3 to give over the legal possession or ownership of ⟨*assigned* all rights to and royalties from the song to the Boy Scouts⟩ — see TRANSFER 1

4 to pick (someone) by one's authority for a specific position or duty ⟨the principal *assigned* me as hall monitor⟩ — see APPOINT 2

assignment *n* **1** a piece of work that needs to be done regularly ⟨his *assignment* was sweeping the shop every day⟩ — see CHORE 1

2 a specific task with which a person or group is charged ⟨the spy team's *assignment* was to steal the plans for the nuclear reactor⟩ — see MISSION

3 something assigned to be read or studied ⟨have you read the *assignment* for tomorrow?⟩ — see LESSON

4 the state or fact of being chosen for a position or duty ⟨her *assignment* to the board of directors was a point of pride for her⟩ — see APPOINTMENT 1

assimilate *vb* to make a part of a body or system ⟨social workers will need time to *assimilate* the new arrivals into the community⟩ — see EMBODY 1

assist *n* an act or instance of helping ⟨with an *assist* from my dad, I built a doghouse any canine would be proud to call home⟩ — see HELP 1

assist *vb* to provide (someone) with what is useful or necessary to achieve an end ⟨you can *assist* families in

need by donating old clothes in good condition⟩ — see HELP 1

assistance *n* an act or instance of helping ⟨thank you for your *assistance* in helping me change my flat tire⟩ — see HELP 1

assistant *n* a person who helps a more skilled person ⟨the *assistant* to the director⟩ — see HELPER

associate *n* **1** a person frequently seen in the company of another ⟨after he took up skateboarding, Michael gained a whole new set of *associates*⟩

synonyms cohort, companion, comrade, crony, fellow, hobnobber, mate

related words colleague, coworker, equal, peer, workmate; accomplice, affiliate, ally, collaborator, confederate, partner; buddy, chum, confidant, familiar, friend, hearty, intimate, pal; compatriot, countryman; classmate, housemate, messmate, playmate, roommate, schoolmate, shipmate, teammate; attendant, escort; hanger-on, leech, parasite

2 a fellow worker ⟨my *associates* at the office⟩ — see COLLEAGUE

associate *vb* **1** to come or be together as friends ⟨a boy who would *associate* only with other hard-core basketball fans⟩

synonyms chum, consort, fraternize, hang around, hobnob, pal (around)

related words affiliate, ally, attach, band, bond, club, collaborate, collude, confederate, conjoin, connect, cooperate, couple, gang, get along, group, hook, interrelate, join, knot, league, link, mingle, mix, rally, relate, side, socialize, team, tie, wed

phrases rub elbows (with), rub shoulders (with), take up with

near antonyms avoid, cold-shoulder, shun, snub; alienate, estrange; break up, disband, disperse, split up; disjoin, dissociate, disunite, divorce, sever, split, sunder

2 to think of (something) in combination ⟨Kelly *associates* getting shots with ice cream cones, her treat every time she goes to the doctor⟩

synonyms connect, correlate, identify, link, relate

related words compare, equate, liken; group, join, lump (together), tie (together)

near antonyms contrast, differentiate, discriminate, distinguish, separate, set off

3 to come together to form a single unit ⟨the elements hydrogen and oxygen *associate* to form molecules of water⟩ — see UNITE 1

4 to form or enter into an association that furthers the interests of its members ⟨nations deciding to *associate* in order to remove trade barriers⟩ — see ALLY

5 to take part in social activities ⟨you should try to *associate* with people your own age⟩ — see SOCIALIZE

association *n* **1** the state of having shared interests or efforts (as in social or business matters) ⟨Rita was honored for her long *association* with the Montgomery Benevolent Society⟩

synonyms affiliation, alliance, collaboration, confederation, connection, cooperation, hookup, liaison, linkup, partnership, relation, relationship, tie-up, union

related words business, dealings, interaction; exchange, interconnection, interrelation, mutualism, reciprocity, symbiosis; incorporation, integration, merger, unification; affinity, attachment, closeness, intimacy, rapport, sympathy; kinship, oneness, solidarity, togetherness, unity; companionship, company, fellowship

near antonyms breakup, dissolution, disunion; division, parting, separation, severance, split; alienation, divorce, estrangement
antonyms dissociation
2 a group of persons formally joined together for some common interest ⟨all *associations* meeting on school property must be registered with and approved by the principal's office⟩
synonyms brotherhood, club, college, congress, council, fellowship, fraternity, guild (*also* gild), institute, institution, junto, league, order, organization, society, sodality
related words collective, commune, community, cooperative; alliance, bloc, coalition, partnership; body, group; circle, clan, clique, coterie, lot, set; crew, outfit, party, squad, team; branch, chapter, local; faithful, fold, membership; sisterhood, sorority; cabal, confederacy, conspiracy; band, gang, ring; cartel, combine, syndicate
3 the fact or state of having something in common ⟨what's the *association* between cat hair and my allergic reaction to certain proteins?⟩ — see CONNECTION 1
assort *vb* to arrange or assign according to type ⟨*assort* these butterfly specimens according to geographic origin⟩ — see CLASSIFY 1
assorted *adj* consisting of many things of different sorts ⟨a box of *assorted* chocolates⟩ — see MISCELLANEOUS
assortment *n* **1** an unorganized collection or mixture of various things ⟨an *assortment* of nails in the bottom of my tool box⟩ — see MISCELLANY 1
2 the quality or state of being composed of many different elements or types ⟨we were disappointed in the small clothing store's lack of *assortment*⟩ — see VARIETY 1
assuage *vb* **1** to make more bearable or less severe ⟨a mother cooing to her toddler and *assuaging* his fear of the dark⟩ — see HELP 2
2 to put a complete end to (a physical need or desire) ⟨that huge meal certainly *assuaged* my hunger⟩ — see SATISFY 1
assume *vb* **1** to take to or upon oneself ⟨Josh promised to *assume* responsibility for any damage to the flower beds caused by the volleyball game in the backyard⟩
synonyms accept, bear, shoulder, take over, undertake
related words adopt, embrace; back, endorse (*also* indorse), espouse, stand by, support, uphold; accede, acquiesce, agree, assent, consent
near antonyms abjure, recant, renounce, retract, take back; decline, refuse, reject, spurn, turn down; abstain, forbear, refrain; avoid, bypass, detour
antonyms disavow, disclaim, disown, repudiate
2 to take as true or as a fact without actual proof ⟨everyone *assumed*, wrongly, that someone else was bringing dessert⟩
synonyms postulate, premise, presume, presuppose, suppose
related words accept, believe, credit, swallow; conclude, deduce, gather, judge, infer, take; conjecture, figure, guess, reckon [*chiefly dialect*], surmise, suspect, think; conceive, dream, fancy, imagine, perceive, preconceive; hypothesize, speculate, theorize; affirm, allege, assert, aver, avouch, avow, claim, contend, declare, insist, maintain, profess
phrases take for granted
near antonyms challenge, disbelieve, discount, discredit, dispute, distrust, doubt, mistrust, question, suspect, wonder (about); deny, disavow, disclaim, disown, reject, repudiate; confute, disprove, rebut, refute

3 to form an opinion from little or no evidence ⟨as I just *assumed* it was too late to go out, I didn't think to ask⟩ — see GUESS 1
4 to present a false appearance of ⟨she *assumed* an air of nonchalance even though she was wildly ecstatic she could go⟩ — see FEIGN
assumed *adj* **1** appearing to be true on the basis of evidence that may or may not be confirmed ⟨an *assumed* connection between the two species that has yet to be confirmed by fossil findings⟩ — see APPARENT 1
2 lacking in natural or spontaneous quality ⟨the salesclerk's *assumed* friendliness vanished as soon as I assured her I was just looking⟩ — see ARTIFICIAL 1
assumption *n* something taken as being true or factual and used as a starting point for a course of action or reasoning ⟨the widespread *assumption* that violent entertainment leads to violent behavior in children⟩ ⟨your argument is faulty because it's based on erroneous *assumptions*⟩
synonyms postulate, premise, presumption, presupposition, supposition
related words hypothesis, proposition, theory, thesis; axiom, truism, verity; belief, canon, doctrine, dogma, gospel, law; precept, principle, rule, standard, tenet; basis, foundation, ground; conclusion, deduction, inference; affirmation, assertion, avouchment, declaration
assurance *n* **1** a state of mind in which one is free from doubt ⟨I can state with complete *assurance* that no harm will ever come to you⟩ — see CONFIDENCE 2
2 great faith in oneself or one's abilities ⟨her *assurance* was evident in the way she carried herself onto the playing field⟩ — see CONFIDENCE 1
assure *vb* **1** to ease the grief or distress of ⟨a minister choosing just the right words to *assure* the grieving parents of the fallen soldier⟩ — see COMFORT 1
2 to make sure, certain, or safe ⟨security measures that *assured* our safety⟩ — see ENSURE
assured *adj* **1** having or showing a mind free from doubt ⟨a man who seemed very *assured* of the outcome⟩ — see CERTAIN 2
2 having or showing great faith in oneself or one's abilities ⟨an *assured* athlete on the field⟩ — see CONFIDENT 1
assuredly *adv* without any question ⟨I am most *assuredly* the person you are looking for⟩ — see INDEED 1
assuredness *n* a state of mind in which one is free from doubt ⟨the complete *assuredness* with which the cocky jock would ask for dates⟩ — see CONFIDENCE 2
astern *adv* near, toward, or in the stern of a ship or the tail of an aircraft ⟨if you turn around and look *astern*, you'll see dolphins following the boat⟩ — see AFT
as though *conj* the way it would be or one would do if ⟨the applause was so great it was *as though* the toddler's dance class had been the Bolshoi Ballet⟩ — see AS IF
astir *adj* marked by much life, movement, or activity ⟨the mall was *astir* with throngs of holiday shoppers⟩ — see ALIVE 2
astonish *vb* to make a strong impression on (someone) with something unexpected ⟨the news that you and she broke up absolutely *astonishes* me⟩ — see SURPRISE 1
astonished *adj* **1** affected with sudden and great wonder or surprise ⟨was *astonished* at seeing a cow wandering down Main Street⟩ — see THUNDERSTRUCK

2 filled with amazement or wonder ⟨grandparents *astonished* at how much their grandchildren had grown in the past year⟩ — see OPENMOUTHED

astonishing *adj* **1** causing a strong emotional reaction because unexpected ⟨gave us the *astonishing* news she was getting married⟩ — see SURPRISING 1

2 causing wonder or astonishment ⟨an *astonishing* view of the Grand Canyon that few tourists get to see⟩ — see MARVELOUS 1

astonishment *n* **1** the rapt attention and deep emotion caused by the sight of something extraordinary ⟨the Midwesterner's *astonishment* at seeing the ocean for the first time⟩ — see WONDER 2

2 the state of being strongly impressed by something unexpected or unusual ⟨the suddenness of the thunderstorm left the picnickers in a state of *astonishment*⟩ — see SURPRISE 2

astound *vb* to make a strong impression on (someone) with something unexpected ⟨it *astounds* me that you flew all the way out here just for my birthday⟩ — see SURPRISE 1

astounded *adj* **1** affected with sudden and great wonder or surprise ⟨was *astounded* to learn his grandmother was 99 years old⟩ — see THUNDERSTRUCK

2 filled with amazement or wonder ⟨the *astounded* look on their faces when the police ordered them to leave the country immediately⟩ — see OPENMOUTHED

astounding *adj* **1** causing a strong emotional reaction because unexpected ⟨the *astounding* sight of their cat returning home after being missing for two years⟩ — see SURPRISING 1

2 causing wonder or astonishment ⟨experiencing the *astounding* sight of the aurora borealis for the first time⟩ — see MARVELOUS 1

astral *adj* of or relating to the stars ⟨asked the astronomy students to chart *astral* movement for the next month⟩ — see STELLAR 1

astray *adv* off the desired or intended path or course ⟨the Big Bad Wolf tried to lead Little Red Riding Hood *astray*⟩ — see WRONG 1

astronomical *also* **astronomic** *adj* unusually large ⟨a googol is an *astronomical* number⟩ — see HUGE

astronomically *adv* to a large extent or degree ⟨their battalion was *astronomically* outnumbered by enemy forces⟩ — see GREATLY 2

astute *adj* having or showing a practical cleverness or judgment ⟨a guidance counselor known to be an *astute* judge of character⟩ — see SHREWD

asunder *adv* into parts or to pieces ⟨the youth organization was torn *asunder* by bitter rivalries⟩ — see APART

as well as *prep* in addition to ⟨we offer electronic toys *as well as* rent out video games⟩ — see BESIDES 1

asylum *n* **1** a place where insane people are cared for ⟨volunteered to play piano for the residents of the state *asylum* on weekends⟩ — see MADHOUSE 1

2 something (as a building) that offers cover from the weather or protection from danger ⟨the embassy serves as an *asylum* for that country's nationals in need of help⟩ — see SHELTER

at all *adv* in any way or respect ⟨Ted wasn't *at all* pleased with the way his mother's birthday cake came out⟩
synonyms anywise, ever, half
related words somehow, someway; remotely
phrases by any means

athirst *adj* showing urgent desire or interest ⟨was *athirst* for any news at all about family members serving in the war zone⟩ — see EAGER

athwart *adv* in a line or direction running from corner to corner ⟨we hung the twisted strips of crepe paper *athwart* to the floor and ceiling so that they formed giant crosses on all four walls⟩ — see CROSSWISE

athwart *prep* to the opposite side of ⟨*athwart* the road was farmland⟩ — see ACROSS

atmosphere *n* **1** a special quality or impression associated with something ⟨the fireplace and cozy armchairs give the bookstore the *atmosphere* of a comfortable home⟩ — see AURA

2 the circumstances, conditions, or objects by which one is surrounded ⟨liked the quiet and scholarly *atmosphere* of his prep school⟩ — see ENVIRONMENT

atom *n* a very small piece ⟨give me just one *atom* of information⟩ — see BIT 1

atomic *adj* very small in size ⟨made *atomic* adjustments to the clock's mechanism to keep it from whirring as it ran⟩ — see TINY

atomize *vb* to reduce to fine particles ⟨this medication for athlete's foot is *atomized* so that it can be sprayed on from an aerosol can⟩ — see POWDER

atone (for) *vb* to make up for (an offense) ⟨tried to *atone* for yelling at his sister by helping her with her homework and her household chores⟩ — see EXPIATE

atrocious *adj* **1** extremely disturbing or repellent ⟨showed the jury *atrocious* photos of the bludgeoned body⟩ — see HORRIBLE 1

2 extremely unsatisfactory ⟨the picture quality on the pirated videocassette was *atrocious*⟩ — see WRETCHED 1

atrociousness *n* **1** the quality of inspiring intense dread or dismay ⟨George Orwell's novel *1984* captures the *atrociousness* of tyranny⟩ — see HORROR 1

2 the state or quality of being utterly evil ⟨the *atrociousness* of the mass murderer's crimes shocked the courtroom⟩ — see ENORMITY 1

atrocity *n* **1** the quality of inspiring intense dread or dismay ⟨the *atrocity* of the forced march of Cherokees known as the Trail of Tears⟩ — see HORROR 1

2 the state or quality of being utterly evil ⟨was appalled by the *atrocity* of Stalin's mass executions⟩ — see ENORMITY 1

attach *vb* **1** to cause (something) to hold to another ⟨you can *attach* the buttons to the puppet with fabric glue⟩ — see FASTEN 1

2 to pick (someone) by one's authority for a specific position or duty ⟨*attached* the colonel to the new regiment⟩ — see APPOINT 2

attached *adj* having a liking or affection ⟨was rather *attached* to my old stuffed animals⟩ — see FOND 1

attachment *n* **1** a feeling of strong or constant regard for and dedication to someone ⟨I doubt that there's any permanent *attachment* between the two teenagers⟩ — see LOVE 1

2 something that is not necessary in itself but adds to the convenience or performance of the main piece of equipment ⟨bought a grinder *attachment* for the kitchen mixer⟩ — see ACCESSORY 1

attack *n* **1** the act or action of setting upon with force or violence ⟨The USS Constitution was nicknamed "Old Ironsides" after its oaken hull successfully withstood a British *attack*⟩
synonyms aggression, assault, blitzkrieg, charge, descent, offense (*or* offence), offensive, onset, onslaught, raid, rush, strike
related words ambuscade, ambush; counterattack, counteroffensive, sally, sortie; foray, incursion, invasion; pillage, ravage, sack; air raid, blitz, bombardment; siege, storm

near antonyms defense, defensive, guard, shield; opposition, resistance; protection, security, shelter
2 a sudden experiencing of a physical or mental disorder ⟨malaria is characterized by periodic *attacks* of chills and fever⟩
synonyms bout, case, fit, seizure, siege, spell
related words recurrence, relapse; brainstorm, convulsion, pang, paroxysm, spasm, throe; breakdown, collapse, prostration
near antonyms arrest, relief, remission
attack *vb* **1** to take sudden, violent action against ⟨my dog unexpectedly *attacked* the mailman, sinking his teeth into the startled man's leg⟩
synonyms assail, assault, beset, charge, descend (on *or* upon), jump (on), pounce (on *or* upon), raid, rush, storm, strike
related words gang (up on), mob, swarm; mug, rob; ambuscade, ambush, surprise, waylay; blitz, bomb, bombard; beleaguer, besiege; harry, loot, pillage, plunder, ravage, sack; foray, invade, overrun
phrases fly at, give it to, go at, set upon
near antonyms cover, defend, guard, protect, secure, shield
2 to criticize harshly and usually publicly ⟨the mayor and all his aides were *attacked* mercilessly in the press when the scandal erupted⟩
synonyms abuse, assail, belabor, blast, castigate, excoriate, jump (on), lambaste (*or* lambast), scathe, slam, vituperate
related words berate, harangue, harass, harry, revile, scold; blaspheme, curse, execrate, imprecate, profane; affront, insult, slur; asperse, bad-mouth, belittle, disparage, put down; libel, slander, traduce; chastise, chide, criticize, rebuke, reprimand, reproof; fulminate, lash (out)
near antonyms acclaim, commend, compliment, laud, praise
3 to start work on energetically ⟨Courtney *attacked* the huge mess in her room with determination and enthusiasm⟩
synonyms tackle, wade (into)
related words address, approach, face; buckle (down to), concentrate (on), focus (on), knuckle down (to), zero in (on); fall (to), pitch in, plunge (in), settle (down); pursue, take up, undertake
phrases go at, have at, sail into
near antonyms avoid, evade, shun; dally, dawdle, dillydally, fiddle, fool, idle, lag, mess, monkey, play, poke, potter, putter, trifle
attain *vb* **1** to obtain (as a goal) through effort ⟨Napoleon had *attained* mastery of much of Europe⟩ — see ACHIEVE 1
2 to receive as return for effort ⟨with hard work she will *attain* success in her chosen profession⟩ — see EARN 1
attainable *adj* **1** capable of being done or carried out ⟨set *attainable* goals, not impracticable ones⟩ — see POSSIBLE 1
2 possible to get ⟨I don't know if those blue jeans are *attainable* overseas⟩ — see AVAILABLE 1
attainment *n* **1** a successful result brought about by hard work ⟨first place in the state journalism competition is quite an *attainment*⟩ — see ACCOMPLISHMENT 1
2 the state of being actual or complete ⟨the *attainment* of man's dream of flying was realized in 1903 by Orville and Wilbur Wright⟩ — see FRUITION

attempt *n* an effort to do or accomplish something ⟨it took several *attempts* before we made good ice cream with an old-fashioned hand-cranked ice cream freezer⟩
synonyms crack, endeavor, essay, fling, go, pass, shot, stab, trial, try, whack
related words bid, striving, struggle, throes, undertaking; trial and error
attempt *vb* to make an effort to do ⟨after *attempting*—and failing—to start the lawn mower on my own, I finally succeeded with Dad's help⟩ ⟨don't even *attempt* walking on your broken foot⟩
synonyms assay, endeavor, essay, seek, strive, try
related words fight, strain, struggle, toil, trouble, work; aim, aspire, hope; assume, take up, undertake
phrases have a go at
near antonyms drop, give up, quit
attend *vb* **1** to go along with in order to provide assistance, protection, or companionship ⟨a passel of assistants *attend* the movie star wherever she goes⟩ — see ACCOMPANY
2 to pay attention especially through the act of hearing ⟨I'm sorry, but all the noise means I'm having a hard time *attending* to the conversation⟩ — see LISTEN
3 to take charge of especially on behalf of another ⟨tired of *attending* other people's children, the nanny was eager to have a child of her own⟩ — see ²TEND 1
attendant *adj* **1** coming as a result ⟨dreaded the coming flu season and the *attendant* flood of school absences⟩ — see RESULTANT
2 present at the same time and place ⟨the movie stars' divorce and the *attendant* press coverage about it⟩ — see COINCIDENT
attendant *n* one that accompanies another for protection, guidance, or as a courtesy ⟨let the hotel *attendant* help them with their bags⟩ — see ESCORT
attending *adj* **1** being within the confines of a specified place ⟨arrested the operator of the illegal gambling joint and all *attending* employees⟩ — see PRESENT 2
2 present at the same time and place ⟨dislikes flying and all of its *attending* inconveniences⟩ — see COINCIDENT
attention *n* **1** a focusing of the mind on something ⟨I need your full *attention* right now⟩
synonyms absorption, concentration, engrossment, enthrallment, immersion
related words fixation, obsession, preoccupation; alertness, application, awareness, consciousness, consideration, heedfulness, intentness, raptness
near antonyms absence, absentmindedness, abstractedness, abstraction, detachment, distraction, obliviousness, remoteness, unawareness, unconsciousness, withdrawal; disinterest, indifference, mindlessness, unconcern; befuddlement, bemusement, bewilderment, confusion
antonyms inattention
2 a state of being aware ⟨several mothers brought to the committee's *attention* the deplorable condition of the playground⟩
synonyms awareness, cognizance, ear, eye, heed, notice, observance, observation
related words advisement, care, concern, consideration, regard, watch; apprehension, discernment, grasp, mind, perception, recognition, thought, understanding
near antonyms disregard, neglect, obliviousness, unawareness
attentive *adj* **1** having the mind fixed on something ⟨Susan became particularly *attentive* when the sportscaster turned to field hockey, her favorite sport⟩

synonyms absorbed, engrossed, enthralled, focused (*also* focussed), immersed, intent, observant, rapt
related words interested, intrigued, involved; hypnotized, mesmerized; alert, alive, conscious, open-eyed, watchful, wide-awake
near antonyms daydreaming, dreamy, faraway, foggy, hazy, oblivious, preoccupied, remote; apathetic, disinterested, uninterested
antonyms absent, absentminded, abstracted, distracted, inattentive, unabsorbed, unfocused (*also* unfocussed), unobservant
2 given to or made with heedful anticipation of the needs and happiness of others ⟨an *attentive* neighbor who helps out whenever and wherever she spots a need⟩ — see THOUGHTFUL 1
3 paying close attention usually for the purpose of anticipating approaching danger or opportunity ⟨if only for your own safety, you need to stay *attentive* when you are hunting⟩ — see ALERT 1
attentiveness *n* the act or state of being constantly attentive and responsive to signs of opportunity, activity, or danger ⟨your *attentiveness* prevented a potentially bad accident⟩ — see VIGILANCE
attest *vb* **1** to declare (something) to be true or genuine ⟨the appraiser *attests* that the lamp is an original Tiffany⟩ — see CERTIFY 1
2 to make a solemn declaration under oath for the purpose of establishing a fact ⟨an eyewitness who will *attest* to my innocence⟩ — see TESTIFY
attestation *n* something presented in support of the truth or accuracy of a claim ⟨the fact that he spent hours standing in line for the sequel should be *attestation* enough that he's a true fan of the movie series⟩ — see PROOF
attire *n* covering for the human body ⟨needed some snazzy *attire* for the job interview⟩ — see CLOTHING
attire *vb* to outfit with clothes and especially fine or special clothes ⟨men *attired* in tuxedos for the awards banquet⟩ — see CLOTHE 1
attorney *n* **1** a person who acts or does business for another ⟨talked to the count's *attorney* about buying land from his estate⟩ — see AGENT 2
2 a person whose profession is to conduct lawsuits for clients or to advise about legal rights and obligations ⟨finished law school and became an *attorney*⟩ — see LAWYER
attraction *n* something that attracts interest ⟨a park with the world's fastest roller coaster and other *attractions*⟩ — see MAGNET
attractive *adj* **1** having an often mysterious or magical power to attract ⟨world travel has always been very *attractive* to me⟩ — see FASCINATING 1
2 very pleasing to look at ⟨generally the star of a TV commercial is an *attractive* person⟩ — see BEAUTIFUL
attractiveness *n* **1** the power of irresistible attraction ⟨she had a certain *attractiveness* that came from her witty conversation⟩ — see CHARM 1
2 the qualities in a person or thing that as a whole give pleasure to the senses ⟨the *attractiveness* of the Greek countryside has inspired poets since ancient times⟩ — see BEAUTY 1
attribute *n* something that sets apart an individual from others of the same kind ⟨list the *attributes* of a mammal⟩ — see CHARACTERISTIC
attribute *vb* to explain (something) as being the result of something else ⟨*attributed* the quick rescue to the well-trained police force⟩ — see CREDIT 1

attrition *n* a gradual weakening, loss, or destruction ⟨took the machinery out of operation since *attrition* had led to the main mechanism's breaking⟩ — see CORROSION
atypical *adj* **1** being out of the ordinary ⟨the postal service delivered the package with *atypical* speed⟩ — see EXCEPTIONAL
2 departing from some accepted standard of what is normal ⟨since that's an *atypical* response for an infant, you might want to have her hearing tested⟩ — see DEVIANT
audacious *adj* inclined or willing to take risks ⟨*audacious* adventurers risking all⟩ — see BOLD 1
audacity *n* shameless boldness ⟨I can't believe she had the *audacity* to tell me to shut up!⟩ — see EFFRONTERY
audibly *adv* with one's normal voice speaking the words ⟨don't whisper your lines—speak *audibly* so the audience can hear you⟩ — see ALOUD
audit *n* a close look at or over someone or something in order to judge condition ⟨an energy *audit* of our house showed that we were losing lots of heat and needed to upgrade the insulation⟩ — see INSPECTION
audit *vb* to look over closely (as for judging quality or condition) ⟨*audited* the equipment to make sure that everything was in working order⟩ — see INSPECT
auditorium *n* a large room or building for enclosed public gatherings ⟨will hold the pep rally in the *auditorium*⟩ — see HALL 3
auditory *adj* of, relating to, or experienced through the sense of hearing ⟨I have a bad *auditory* memory—unless I see a word in writing, and not just hear it, I forget it easily⟩
synonyms acoustic (*or* acoustical), aural, auricular
related words audible, clear, discernible, distinct, distinguishable, heard, perceptible
near antonyms faint, feeble, imperceptible, inaudible, indistinguishable, indistinct; low, noiseless, quiet, silent, soft, soundless
aught *n* the numerical symbol 0 or the absence of number or quantity represented by it ⟨for dates, the year is automatically listed as a pair of *aughts*, so the user has to scroll down to the correct figure⟩ — see ZERO 1
augment *vb* to make greater in size, amount, or number ⟨our volleyball team was *augmented* by some of the exchange team's players⟩ — see INCREASE 1
augmentation *n* something added (as by growth) ⟨the new course offerings were a valuable *augmentation* to the history department⟩ — see INCREASE 1
augur *n* one who predicts future events or developments ⟨ancient Roman *augurs* who predicted the future by reading the flight of birds⟩ — see PROPHET
augur *vb* **1** to show signs of a favorable or successful outcome ⟨the long interview *augurs* well for your acceptance into that school⟩ — see BODE
2 to tell of or describe beforehand ⟨the fortune-teller *augured* nothing but bad news for me⟩ — see FORETELL
auguring *n* a declaration that something will happen in the future ⟨it's a good thing that people don't remember the tabloid's *augurings* a year later, since very few come to pass⟩ — see PREDICTION
augury *n* something believed to be a sign or warning of a future event ⟨some people believe that a broken mirror is an *augury* of bad luck for seven years⟩ — see OMEN
august *adj* **1** having or showing a serious and reserved manner ⟨unsurprisingly, the head of the bank is an *august* old man⟩ — see DIGNIFIED

2 large and impressive in size, grandeur, extent, or conception ⟨an *august* golden anniversary celebration for the company⟩ — see GRAND 1

augustness *n* **1** a dignified bearing or appearance befitting royalty ⟨the opera star carries herself with the *augustness* of a queen⟩ — see MAJESTY 1

2 impressiveness of beauty on a large scale ⟨the *augustness* of the Lincoln Memorial in our nation's capital⟩ — see MAGNIFICENCE

auld lang syne *n* the events or experience of former times ⟨let us bid farewell to *auld lang syne* and welcome in the new year⟩ — see PAST

aura *n* a special quality or impression associated with something ⟨the monastery perched high on a mountaintop had an *aura* of unreality and mystery about it⟩
synonyms air, atmosphere, climate, flavor, mood, note, temper
related words feel, feeling, sensation, sense, spirit; attribute, character, characteristic, image, mark, notion, peculiarity, picture, property, trait; color, illusion, overtone, semblance, suggestion, tone

aural *adj* of, relating to, or experienced through the sense of hearing ⟨a quiet room for people seeking relief from *aural* stimulus⟩ — see AUDITORY

au revoir *n* an expression of good wishes at parting ⟨the noise of the street was so loud that the quieter *au revoirs* of her friends went unheard⟩ — see GOOD-BYE

auricular *adj* of, relating to, or experienced through the sense of hearing ⟨had *auricular* proof that the sun was up, as the birds began chirping⟩ — see AUDITORY

aurora *n* the first appearance of light in the morning or the time of its appearance ⟨a gorgeous pink *aurora* aroused us out of our slumber⟩ — see DAWN 1

auspice *n* something believed to be a sign or warning of a future event ⟨took the teacher's smile as an *auspice* that he would get an A on his presentation⟩ — see OMEN

auspicious *adj* **1** having qualities which inspire hope ⟨told him she couldn't dance with him just then, but her *auspicious* smile encouraged him to ask again later⟩ — see HOPEFUL 1

2 pointing toward a happy outcome ⟨began the season with an *auspicious* win against their strongest football rival⟩ — see FAVORABLE 2

austere *adj* **1** given to exacting standards of discipline and self-restraint ⟨an *austere* conductor who is as tough on himself as he is on the orchestra⟩ — see SEVERE 1

2 harsh and threatening in manner or appearance ⟨an *austere* fortress at the top of the cliffs⟩ — see GRIM 1

authentic *adj* **1** being exactly as appears or as claimed ⟨found an *authentic* Native American arrowhead⟩
synonyms bona fide, genuine, real, right, true
related words actual, historical, original; lawful, legal, legitimate; identifiable, recognizable, verifiable; proven, substantiated, validated, verified; incontestable, incontrovertible, indisputable, indubitable, irrefutable, undeniable, undoubted, unmistakable, unquestionable; veritable, very; accurate, correct, proper; pure, unadulterated, unalloyed
near antonyms artificial, factitious, imitation, manmade, simulated, synthetic, unnatural; concocted, fabricated, manufactured; deceptive, delusive, delusory, misleading; unauthenticated, unverified
antonyms bogus, counterfeit, fake, false, mock, phony (*also* phoney), pseudo, sham, spurious, unauthentic, unreal

2 following an original exactly ⟨an *authentic* reconstruction of the Parthenon as it is believed to have looked when first built⟩ — see FAITHFUL 2

authentically *adv* in actual fact ⟨people are surprised to learn that he is an *authentically* certified graduate of clown college⟩ — see VERY 2

authenticate *vb* to declare (something) to be true or genuine ⟨a jeweler *authenticated* the diamond as real⟩ — see CERTIFY 1

author *n* **1** a person who creates a written work ⟨a brilliant novel by a first-time *author*⟩
synonyms penman, writer
related words coauthor, ghostwriter, hack, scribbler; autobiographer, biographer; novelist; essayist, pamphleteer; dramatist, playwright, scenarist, screenwriter, scriptwriter; bard, poet, rhymer (*or* rimer); columnist, journalist, newspaperman, reporter, sportswriter

2 a person who establishes a whole new field of endeavor ⟨the *author* of modern genetics⟩ — see FATHER 2

author *vb* to compose and set down on paper the words of ⟨*authored* a new biography on Thomas Jefferson⟩ — see WRITE 1

authoritarian *adj* **1** fond of ordering people around ⟨an *authoritarian* older sister who thought she was queen of the world⟩ — see BOSSY

2 given to exacting standards of discipline and self-restraint ⟨an *authoritarian* coach who runs football practice like it's boot camp⟩ — see SEVERE 1

authoritative *adj* **1** being the most accurate and apparently thorough ⟨this book is considered the most *authoritative* source on that subject⟩ — see DEFINITIVE 1

2 having power over the minds or behavior of others ⟨after a couple of *authoritative* critics panned the movie, the other reviewers rushed to say how awful it was⟩ — see INFLUENTIAL 1

authority *n* **1** a person with a high level of knowledge or skill in a field ⟨the leading *authority* on neural anatomy⟩ — see EXPERT

2 lawful control over the affairs of a political unit (as a nation) ⟨the sheriff had *authority* over the whole county⟩ — see RULE 2

3 the power to direct the thinking or behavior of others usually indirectly ⟨speaks with a persuasive *authority* on matters of public health⟩ — see INFLUENCE 1

4 the right or means to command or control others ⟨by the *authority* vested in me, I now pronounce you married⟩ — see POWER 1

authorization *n* **1** the approval by someone in authority for the doing of something ⟨need the *authorization* of the council before you can act⟩ — see PERMISSION

2 the granting of power to perform various acts or duties ⟨his *authorization* to go ahead with the project was finally given⟩ — see COMMISSION 1

3 the right to act or move freely ⟨granted *authorization* to enter the facility⟩ — see FREEDOM 2

authorize *vb* **1** to give official or legal power to ⟨only the school nurse is *authorized* to give any necessary shots⟩
synonyms accredit, certify, commission, empower, enable, invest, license (*or* licence), qualify
related words approve, clear, endorse (*also* indorse), OK (*or* okay), sanction; affirm, confirm, validate; inaugurate, induct, initiate, install, instate, swear in; allow, let, permit; enfranchise, entitle, privilege
near antonyms ban, bar, block, constrain, deny, disallow, disbar, discourage, disenfranchise, disfranchise, disqualify, exclude, hinder, hold back, impede, inhibit,

obstruct, prevent, shut out, stop; enjoin, forbid, interdict, outlaw, prohibit, proscribe, veto

2 to give a right to ⟨this pass will *authorize* you to go backstage⟩ — see ENTITLE 1

3 to give official acceptance of something as satisfactory ⟨a system for sound reproduction that has been *authorized* as meeting the electronic industry's highest standards⟩ — see APPROVE

authorized *adj* ordered or allowed by those in authority ⟨an *authorized* biography of the former president⟩ — see OFFICIAL

auto *n* a self-propelled passenger vehicle on wheels ⟨the *auto* gave people a level of mobility that they had never known before⟩ — see CAR

autocracy *n* a system of government in which the ruler has unlimited power ⟨the Magna Carta is historically important because it signified the British rejection of *autocracy* and the first formal restraining of the power of the monarch⟩ — see DESPOTISM

autocrat *n* **1** a person who uses power or authority in a cruel, unjust, or harmful way ⟨a military tribunal to bring the former *autocrat* to justice⟩ — see DESPOT

2 one who rules over a people with a sole, supreme, and usually hereditary authority ⟨European *autocrats* once commonly believed that they had received the right to rule directly from God⟩ — see MONARCH

autocratic *adj* **1** exercising power or authority without interference by others ⟨democracy is supposed to protect the people against the rise of *autocratic* rulers⟩ — see ABSOLUTE 1

2 fond of ordering people around ⟨an *autocratic* Boy Scout leader who thought that he was still an army colonel⟩ — see BOSSY

autograph *vb* to write one's name on (as a document) ⟨asked the baseball player to *autograph* the bill of his cap⟩ — see SIGN

automated *adj* designed to replace or decrease human labor and especially physical labor ⟨an *automated* facility in which you can get your car washed without having encountered a single human being⟩ — see LABORSAVING

automatic *adj* **1** done instantly and without conscious thought or decision ⟨Carl's *automatic* use of the brakes prevented a serious accident⟩

synonyms instinctive, instinctual, involuntary, mechanical, spontaneous

related words conditioned, natural, reactive, reflex, simple, subliminal, unconscious, unforced; blind, inadvertent, unintended, unintentional, unwilling, unwitting; abrupt, quick, ready, sudden; ad-lib, extemporaneous, extempore, impromptu, improvised, offhand, offhanded, snap, spur-of-the-moment, unconsidered, unplanned, unpremeditated, unprepared, unprompted, unreasoned, unrehearsed, unstudied; casual, chance, chancy, haphazard, hasty, hit-or-miss, impetuous, impulsive, perfunctory, random, rash

near antonyms calculated, conscious, cultivated, deliberate, designed, intended, intentional, predetermined, prepared, projected, refined, rehearsed, volitional, voluntary, willed, willful (*or* wilful); advised, aforethought, careful, considered, foresighted, forethoughtful, measured, meticulous, reasoned, studied, thoughtful

2 designed to replace or decrease human labor and especially physical labor ⟨liked the ease of an *automatic* CD changer⟩ — see LABORSAVING

automobile *n* a self-propelled passenger vehicle on wheels ⟨browsed the classified ads for used *automobiles* for sale⟩ — see CAR

automobile *vb* to travel by a motorized vehicle ⟨would rather *automobile* across the country than fly over it at 35,000 feet⟩ — see DRIVE 2

automobilist *n* a person who travels by automobile ⟨with the introduction of affordable, mass-produced cars, more and more people left their horses at home and became *automobilists*⟩ — see MOTORIST

autonomous *adj* not being under the rule or control of another ⟨Native American nations are regarded as *autonomous* in many respects and thus not subject to a number of state and local laws⟩ — see FREE 1

autonomy *n* the state of being free from the control or power of another ⟨finding the mother country's treatment of them oppressive and intolerable, the thirteen British colonies made the momentous decision to seek *autonomy*⟩ — see FREEDOM 1

autopsy *n* examination of a dead body especially to find out the cause of death ⟨the *autopsy* revealed an advanced stage of cancer⟩

synonyms postmortem, postmortem examination

related words dissection

near antonyms biopsy, vivisection

auxiliary *adj* available to supply something extra when needed ⟨the auditorium has an *auxiliary* cooling system used only on particularly sweltering days⟩

synonyms accessory, peripheral, supplemental, supplementary

related words backup, makeshift, substitute; added, additional, another, further; complementary, contributory; assistant, assisting, helping, supportive, tributary; secondary, subordinate, subservient, subsidiary; dispensable, excess, nonessential, superfluous, surplus, unessential

near antonyms basic, fundamental, primary, prime; all-important, essential, imperative, indispensable, integral, necessary, needed, needful, required, requisite, vital

antonyms chief, main, principal

avail *n* the capacity for being useful for some purpose ⟨your help would be of little *avail* in this situation⟩ — see USE 2

avail *vb* to provide with something useful or desirable ⟨all your begging will not *avail* you in the least⟩ — see BENEFIT

available *adj* **1** possible to get ⟨the nursery's orchids are *available* by mail order only⟩ ⟨fare information is readily *available* by using the toll-free number⟩

synonyms accessible, acquirable, attainable, obtainable, procurable

related words purchasable, rentable; furnished, provided, supplied; common, omnipresent, prevalent, ubiquitous, universal, widespread; free, free-for-all, open, public, unrestricted

phrases on hand

near antonyms limited, off-limits, restricted; deficient, lacking, missing, rare, scarce, uncommon

antonyms inaccessible, unattainable, unavailable, unobtainable

2 capable of or suitable for being used for a particular purpose ⟨my car is *available* should you need a way to get to the mall⟩ — see USABLE 1

avarice *n* an intense selfish desire for wealth or possessions ⟨the bank official's embezzlement was motivated by pure *avarice*⟩ — see GREED

avaricious *adj* having or marked by an eager and often selfish desire especially for material possessions ⟨an *avaricious* scheme to con the elderly couple out of thousands of dollars⟩ — see GREEDY 1

avariciousness *n* an intense selfish desire for wealth or possessions ⟨their all-consuming *avariciousness* blinds them to the suffering of people just beyond their doorstep⟩ — see GREED

avenge *vb* to punish in kind the wrongdoer responsible for ⟨a play about a prince who struggles to *avenge* his father's death⟩

synonyms requite, retaliate, revenge

related words castigate, fix, get, penalize, punish, scourge; chasten, chastise, correct, discipline; redress, right; compensate, pay (back), recompense, repay

phrases get even (for)

near antonyms absolve, condone, excuse, forgive, pardon, remit

avenger *n* one who inflicts punishment in return for an injury or offense ⟨a novel about a man who becomes the obsessed *avenger* of his sister's death⟩ — see NEMESIS 1

avenue *n* 1 a passage cleared for public vehicular travel ⟨a city famous for its broad, tree-lined *avenues*⟩ — see WAY 1

2 an established course for traveling from one place to another ⟨the two main *avenues* available to those joining in the California gold rush were the trail across the Southwest desert or the hazard-filled loop around Central and South America⟩ — see PASSAGE 1

aver *vb* 1 to state as a fact usually forcefully ⟨was tearfully *averring* his innocence⟩ — see CLAIM 1

2 to state clearly and strongly ⟨*averred* that she didn't need any help choosing her own clothes⟩ — see ASSERT 1

average *adj* 1 being about midway between extremes of amount or size ⟨since a Chihuahua seems as impractical as a Saint Bernard, let's get a dog of more *average* dimensions⟩ — see MIDDLE 2

2 being of the type that is encountered in the normal course of events ⟨just an *average* day at school⟩ — see ORDINARY 1

3 having or showing the qualities associated with the members of a particular group or kind ⟨the company's marketing people want to interview *average* teenagers to see what kinds of clothes appeal to them⟩ — see TYPICAL 1

average *n* what is typical of a group, class, or series ⟨my cat's a cut above the *average* when it comes to being a finicky eater⟩

synonyms norm, normal, par, standard

related words golden mean, mean, median, middle; commonplace, ordinary, rule, run, status quo, usual; exemplar, representative

near antonyms abnormality, anomaly, deviation, exception, rarity

averse *adj* having a natural dislike for something ⟨I'm not *averse* to broccoli if it's cooked right⟩ — see ANTIPATHETIC

averseness *n* a strong feeling of not liking or approving ⟨our dog's strong *averseness* to getting a bath⟩ — see DISLIKE 1

aversion *n* 1 a dislike so strong as to cause stomach upset or queasiness ⟨I simply have this ingrained *aversion* to the sight of bloodshed⟩ — see DISGUST

2 a strong feeling of not liking or approving ⟨couldn't overcome her *aversion* to cucumbers and excused herself to the bathroom when they were served⟩ — see DISLIKE 1

3 something or someone that is hated ⟨clichés should be the pet *aversion* of every good writer⟩ — see HATE 2

avert *vb* to keep from happening by taking action in advance ⟨her careful planning *averted* disaster⟩ — see PREVENT

averting *n* the act or practice of keeping something from happening ⟨the *averting* of forest fires can be helped by the clearing of dry underbrush⟩ — see PREVENTION

aviator *n* one who flies or is qualified to fly an aircraft or spacecraft ⟨the solo flight from New York to Paris by the *aviator* Charles Lindbergh captured the imagination of people around the world⟩ — see PILOT

avid *adj* 1 having or marked by an eager and often selfish desire especially for material possessions ⟨stared at the array of jewels with an *avid* glint in his eye⟩ — see GREEDY 1

2 showing urgent desire or interest ⟨an *avid* baseball card collector⟩ — see EAGER

avidity *n* 1 an intense selfish desire for wealth or possessions ⟨an advanced case of *avidity* that led to shoplifting at the age of 13⟩ — see GREED

2 urgent desire or interest ⟨in her *avidity* to express her opinions, she frequently and unthinkingly interrupts people⟩ — see EAGERNESS

avoid *vb* to get or keep away from (as a responsibility) through cleverness or trickery ⟨trying to *avoid* writing thank-you notes for the gifts he didn't like⟩ — see ESCAPE 2

avoidance *n* the act or a means of getting or keeping away from something undesirable ⟨her habitual *avoidance* of conflict makes talking about problems with her difficult⟩ — see ESCAPE 2

avoirdupois *n* the state or quality of being heavy ⟨told his patient that he had to do something about his *avoirdupois* and that exercising would be a good start⟩ — see WEIGHTINESS 1

avouch *vb* 1 to declare (something) to be true or genuine ⟨a note from my doctor *avouching* that my medical condition did indeed disqualify me from gym class⟩ — see CERTIFY 1

2 to state as a fact usually forcefully ⟨*avouched* that he had never cheated on a test in his life⟩ — see CLAIM 1

3 to state clearly and strongly ⟨she tends to *avouch* her opinions in such a way as to imply that anyone who thinks otherwise is an idiot⟩ — see ASSERT 1

avouchment *n* a solemn and often public declaring of the truth or existence of something ⟨your *avouchment* of his good intentions means he won't be disciplined⟩ — see PROTESTATION

avow *vb* 1 to state as a fact usually forcefully ⟨*avowed* that the colonization of Mars is not only possible but probable⟩ — see CLAIM 1

2 to state clearly and strongly ⟨*avowed* their undying love for each other⟩ — see ASSERT 1

avowal *n* 1 a solemn and often public declaring of the truth or existence of something ⟨with jingoism rampant, the peace candidate felt compelled to make an *avowal* of his patriotism⟩ — see PROTESTATION

2 an open declaration of something (as a fault or the commission of an offense) about oneself ⟨her own *avowal* that she was to blame for the accident⟩ — see CONFESSION

await *vb* 1 to believe in the future occurrence of (something) ⟨members of the sect are confidently *awaiting* the imminent end of the world⟩ — see EXPECT

2 to remain in place in readiness or expectation of something 〈I *await* your reply〉 — see WAIT

awaited *adj* being in accordance with the prescribed, normal, or logical course of events 〈at the *awaited* moment the President walked up to the lectern and began his address to the nation〉 — see DUE 2

awake *adj* **1** not sleeping or able to sleep 〈was *awake* until 3:00 a.m.〉 — see WAKEFUL

2 paying close attention usually for the purpose of anticipating approaching danger or opportunity 〈*awake* to the possibility of trouble at the demonstration〉 — see ALERT 1

awake *vb* **1** to cause to stop sleeping 〈*awoke* the boys for breakfast〉 — see WAKE 1

2 to cease to be asleep 〈she *awoke* with a start〉 — see WAKE 2

awaken *vb* **1** to cause to stop sleeping 〈be quiet or you'll *awaken* the kids〉 — see WAKE 1

2 to cease to be asleep 〈*awaken* to the smell of fresh pancakes〉 — see WAKE 2

award *n* something given in recognition of achievement 〈Faye received the highest *award* in the 16 and under category for her poem〉

synonyms decoration, distinction, honor, plume, premium, prize

related words badge, crown, cup, laurel, medal, order, ribbon, trophy; accolade, applause, bravo, encomium, eulogy, hallelujah, homage, paean, panegyric, plaudit, tribute; citation, commendation, compliment

award *vb* **1** to give something as a token of gratitude or admiration for a service or achievement 〈we will *award* the top three contestants in the essay competition〉 — see REWARD

2 to give the ownership or benefit of (something) formally or publicly 〈custody was *awarded* to the grandparents〉 — see CONFER 1

aware *adj* having specified facts or feelings actively impressed on the mind 〈as she came out of surgery, she was *aware* that her parents were in the room〉 — see CONSCIOUS

awareness *n* a state of being aware 〈while in the big city maintain an *awareness* of what's going on around you〉 — see ATTENTION 2

awash *adj* containing, covered with, or thoroughly penetrated by water 〈the streets were *awash* from the heavy rains〉 — see WET

away *adj* **1** not close in time or space 〈the store is far *away* from here〉 〈Passover is still three months *away*〉 — see DISTANT 1

2 not at a certain place 〈he's *away* right now, but he should be back at the office next week〉 — see ABSENT 1

away *adv* from this or that place 〈don't walk *away* while I'm still talking to you〉

synonyms hence, off

related words apart, aside, elsewhere; abroad, afar, afield, astray

awe *n* the rapt attention and deep emotion caused by the sight of something extraordinary 〈was in *awe* of the sinewy Olympic runners〉 — see WONDER 2

awed *adj* filled with amazement or wonder 〈gave the nationally known skateboarder an *awed* look〉 — see OPENMOUTHED

awesome *adj* causing wonder or astonishment 〈the *awesome* power of the sun〉 — see MARVELOUS 1

awestruck *adj* **1** affected with sudden and great wonder or surprise 〈the crowds were *awestruck* by the rap group's stellar performance〉 — see THUNDERSTRUCK

2 filled with amazement or wonder 〈*awestruck* by the majesty of the Sierra Nevada Mountains〉 — see OPENMOUTHED

awful *adj* **1** causing intense displeasure, disgust, or resentment 〈that's an *awful* thing to say about someone〉 — see OFFENSIVE 1

2 causing wonder or astonishment 〈the *awful* power of Niagara Falls〉 — see MARVELOUS 1

3 extremely disturbing or repellent 〈spare me the *awful* details of the murder〉 — see HORRIBLE 1

4 extremely unsatisfactory 〈I can't believe I spent good money to see that movie—it was *awful*〉 — see WRETCHED 1

awful *adv* to a great degree 〈that's *awful* sweet of you〉 — see VERY 1

awfully *adv* to a great degree 〈I'm *awfully* sorry〉 — see VERY 1

awfulness *n* the quality of inspiring intense dread or dismay 〈the *awfulness* of the car accident can scarcely be described〉 — see HORROR 1

awkward *adj* **1** lacking social grace and assurance 〈preteens feeling *awkward* at their first formal dance〉

synonyms clumsy, gauche, graceless, inelegant, roughhewn, stiff, stilted, uncomfortable, uneasy, ungraceful, wooden

related words gawky, lubberly, ungainly; boorish, clownish, uncouth; abashed, discomfited, discomforted, discomposed, disconcerted, discountenanced, embarrassed; agitated, bothered, chagrined, dismayed, disquieted, distressed, disturbed, fazed, flustered, jittery, jumpy, mortified, nervous, nonplussed (*also* nonplused), perturbed, rattled, unhinged, unsettled, upset; diffident, insecure, meek, modest, self-doubting, timid, unassertive, unassuming, unpretentious

near antonyms assured, calm, collected, composed, confident, cool, placid, poised, serene, secure, self-assured, self-confident, self-possessed, tranquil, undisturbed, unperturbed

antonyms graceful, suave, urbane

2 showing or marked by a lack of skill and tact (as in dealing with a situation) 〈her *awkward* handling of the seating arrangements at the wedding reception resulted in many hurt feelings〉

synonyms botched, bungling, clumsy, fumbled, inept, inexpert, maladroit

related words amateur, amateurish, crude, green, incompetent, ineffectual, inefficient, inexperienced, unpolished, unprofessional, unskilled, unskillful; careless, sloppy, tacky, tactless, undiplomatic; ill-advised, ineffective, ineffectual, misdirected, misguided

near antonyms able, accomplished, adept, capable, clever, competent, consummate, crackerjack, expert, masterful, masterly, polished, professional, proficient, skilled, skillful, talented; diplomatic, easy, effortless, gracious, smooth, tactful

antonyms adroit, deft, dexterous (*also* dextrous), facile

3 causing embarrassment 〈the *awkward* situation of having to listen in as your teacher talks about you to your parents〉

synonyms discomfiting, disconcerting, disturbing, embarrassing, flustering, uncomfortable

related words confusing, difficult, disagreeable, impossible, inconvenient, intolerable, troublesome, unpleasant, unwieldy; debasing, degrading, demeaning, humbling, humiliating, mortifying

near antonyms agreeable, comfortable, convenient, pleasing

4 causing difficulty, discomfort, or annoyance ⟨our surprise guests came at a very *awkward* time⟩ — see INCONVENIENT 1

5 difficult to use or operate especially because of size, weight, or design ⟨that manual can opener is *awkward* to hold⟩ — see CUMBERSOME

6 lacking in physical ease and grace in movement or in the use of the hands ⟨an *awkward* person who is always tripping over herself⟩ — see CLUMSY 1

awning *n* a raised covering over something for decoration or protection ⟨stayed under the *awning* outside the shop during the rainstorm⟩ — see CANOPY

awry *adj* inclined or twisted to one side ⟨the shutters that still remained on the run-down old house were all *awry*⟩

    synonyms askew, aslant, cockeyed, crooked, listing, lopsided, oblique, skewed, slanted, slanting, slantwise, tilted, tipping, uneven

    related words asymmetrical (*or* asymmetric), unbalanced, unsymmetrical; contorted, disordered, distorted, irregular

    near antonyms ordered, orderly, regular, uniform; balanced, symmetrical (*or* symmetric)

    antonyms even, level, straight

awry *adv* off the desired or intended path or course ⟨their plans for an outdoor wedding went *awry* when they got a freak hailstorm the night before⟩ — see WRONG 1

¹aye *also* **ay** *adv* for all time ⟨a friendship that will *aye* endure⟩ — see EVER 1

²aye *also* **ay** *adv* used to express agreement ⟨*aye*, you're right about that⟩ — see YES

B

babble *n* unintelligible or meaningless talk ⟨the baby's good-natured *babble* and random gurglings were cute, but no one could tell what he wanted⟩ — see GIBBERISH

babble *vb* **1** to speak rapidly, inarticulately, and usually unintelligibly ⟨in such a rush to tell us the news that she just *babbled*⟩
   synonyms chatter, drivel, gabble, gibber, jabber, prattle, sputter
   related words gab, jaw, patter, prate, rattle, run on; maunder, mouth, mumble, murmur, mutter; stammer, stutter; chat, converse, palaver, rap, visit; discourse; screech, shout, shriek
   near antonyms articulate, enunciate, pronounce
   2 to engage in casual or rambling conversation ⟨the little girls *babbled* contentedly about school for the whole ride home⟩ — see CHAT

babbler *n* a person who talks constantly ⟨spending too much time with that *babbler* gives me a headache⟩ — see CHATTERBOX

babe *n* a recently born person ⟨a *babe* in arms, too young even to crawl⟩ — see BABY

babel *n* a place of uproar or confusion ⟨on opening day the school was an incredible *babel*⟩ — see MADHOUSE 2

babushka *n* a scarf worn on the head ⟨an elderly Russian woman with a *babushka*⟩ — see BANDANNA

baby *n* a recently born person ⟨the *baby* is just learning to sit up, so be careful⟩
   synonyms babe, child, infant, newborn
   related words cherub; foundling, nursling, suckling; papoose; kid, moppet, toddler, tot, tyke; boy, nipper, tad; juvenile, minor, youngster, youth; brat, imp, squirt, urchin, whippersnapper; girl, hoyden, tomboy
   phrases babe in arms
   near antonyms adult, grown-up; elder, graybeard, oldster, old-timer, senior citizen

baby *vb* to treat with great or excessive care ⟨he *babied* his car, faithfully washing it every week⟩
   synonyms coddle, dandle, mollycoddle, nurse, pamper, spoil
   related words cater (to), humor, indulge; gratify, mother, oblige, please, satisfy
   near antonyms control, discipline, restrain; oppress; neglect, overlook, slight
   antonyms abuse, ill-treat, ill-use, maltreat, mishandle, mistreat, misuse

babyish *adj* having or showing the annoying qualities (as silliness) associated with children ⟨the boy now thinks that playing with blocks is a rather *babyish* activity⟩ — see CHILDISH

babysitter *n* a girl or woman employed to care for a young child or children ⟨a *babysitter* who is a great favorite with the kids because she's always thinking of fun things to do⟩ — see NURSE

back *adj* being at or in the part of something opposite the front part ⟨she carried all the presents in the *back* door, as the children were playing in the front yard⟩
   synonyms hind, hindmost, posterior, rear, rearward
   antonyms anterior, fore, forward, front

back *adv* toward the opposite direction ⟨turned *back* for one last comment⟩ — see AROUND 2

back *vb* **1** to promote the interests or cause of ⟨she enthusiastically *backed* the plan to renovate the school⟩ — see SUPPORT 1
   2 to provide (someone) with what is useful or necessary to achieve an end ⟨a number of people have already agreed to *back* the candidate⟩ — see HELP 1

back away *vb* to move back or away (as from something difficult, dangerous, or disagreeable) ⟨*backed away* from the snake very slowly and carefully⟩ — see RETREAT 1

backbone *n* **1** a column of bones supporting the trunk of a vertebrate animal ⟨found the *backbone* of a fish lying on the beach⟩ — see SPINE
   2 the strength of mind that enables a person to endure pain or hardship ⟨it takes *backbone* to stand up to the kind of suffering that some cancer patients must endure⟩ — see FORTITUDE

back down *vb* to break a promise or agreement ⟨if you *back down* about dinner again, I'm not going to agree to another date⟩ — see RENEGE

backdrop *n* the physical conditions or features that form the setting against which something is viewed ⟨visitors dine at the restaurant with a dramatic stretch of the Pacific Ocean as a *backdrop*⟩ — see BACKGROUND 1

backer *n* **1** a person who actively supports or favors a cause ⟨*backers* of prison reform held a rally in front of the statehouse⟩ — see EXPONENT
   2 a person who takes the responsibility for some other person or thing ⟨all financial *backers* will be expected to offer some input into the company's decisions⟩ — see SPONSOR
   3 someone associated with another to give assistance or moral support ⟨the student's *backers* spoke at the school board meeting on her behalf⟩ — see ALLY

background *n* **1** the physical conditions or features that form the setting against which something is viewed ⟨they got married on a mountain top with the sunset as *background*⟩
   synonyms backdrop, ground
   related words scene, scenery, set, stage; environment, milieu, setting, surroundings
   near antonyms foreground; center, focal point, focus, heart
   2 the place and time in which the action for a portion of a dramatic work (as a movie) is set ⟨the *background* of that movie is the World War II era⟩ — see SCENE 1

backhanded *adj* not being or expressing what one appears to be or express ⟨"you throw okay, for a girl" is a bit of a *backhanded* compliment⟩ — see INSINCERE

backing *n* an act or instance of helping ⟨the teacher's *backing* on the project was invaluable⟩ — see HELP 1

back of *prep* at, to, or toward the rear of ⟨the equipment shed is a concrete structure *back of* the school⟩ — see BEHIND 1

back off *vb* to break a promise or agreement ⟨you'd better not *back off* on your promise to do all the planning for the big dance⟩ — see RENEGE

backpack *n* a soft-sided case designed for carrying belongings especially on the back ⟨stuffed her *backpack* so full of books that she could barely walk⟩ — see PACK 1

backside *n* the part of the body upon which someone sits ⟨the teacher ordered: "Put your *backsides* in those chairs now!"⟩ — see BUTTOCKS

backslider *n* a person who has sunk below the normal moral standard ⟨he was no *backslider*: he was always defending his faith and living up to it⟩ — see DEGENERATE

backstage *adj or adv* off or away from the part of the stage visible to the audience ⟨walked *backstage* to change costumes⟩ — see OFFSTAGE

back talk *n* disrespectful or argumentative talk given in response to a command or request ⟨his mother sent him to his room because of his constant *back talk*⟩
synonyms cheek, impertinence, impudence, insolence, sass, sauce
related words comeback, rejoinder, retort, riposte, wisecrack; discourtesy, disrespect, impoliteness, rudeness, tactlessness; audaciousness, audacity, boldness, brazenness; coarseness, crassness, crudity, vulgarity; abruptness, bluffness, bluntness, brusqueness, crossness, curtness, gruffness, surliness
near antonyms civility, cordiality, courtesy, diplomacy, politeness, tactfulness; consideration, gallantry, gentility, graciousness, smoothness, suaveness; deference, respect; affability

backup *adj* taking the place of one that came before ⟨a *backup* amplifier in case the first one breaks onstage⟩ — see NEW 1

backup *n* a person or thing that takes the place of another ⟨you didn't get the lead position, but you can be the *backup* to the chosen singer⟩ — see SUBSTITUTE

backward *adj* directed, turned, or done toward the back ⟨a *backward* turn on ice skates is hard to learn, because you can't see where you're going⟩
synonyms rearward, retrograde
related words reversed; hind, posterior, rear
near antonyms forward

backwater *n* a rural region that forms the edge of the settled or developed part of a country ⟨a distant *backwater* that didn't even have electricity⟩ — see FRONTIER 2

backwoods *n* a rural region that forms the edge of the settled or developed part of a country ⟨lived far out in the *backwoods* and raised hogs⟩ — see FRONTIER 2

bad *adj* **1** falling short of a standard ⟨a *bad* first attempt at making meat loaf resulted in a soggy inedible mess⟩
synonyms deficient, inferior, lousy, off, poor, punk, rotten, substandard, unacceptable, ungodly, unsatisfactory, wanting, wretched, wrong
related words defective, faulty, flawed; execrable, lesser, low-grade, mediocre, reprehensible, second-rate, unspeakable; bum, useless, valueless, worthless; inadequate, insufficient, lacking; astray; scurrilous, villainous
phrases below (*or* under) par
near antonyms choice, excellent, exceptional, first-class, first-rate, premium, prime, superior; adequate, sufficient
antonyms acceptable, satisfactory
2 not conforming to a high moral standard; morally unacceptable ⟨stealing is just plain *bad*⟩
synonyms black, evil, immoral, iniquitous, nefarious, rotten, sinful, unethical, unrighteous, unsavory, vicious, vile, villainous, wicked, wrong
related words base, contemptible, despicable, dirty, disreputable, evil-minded, ignoble, ill, infernal, low, mean; atrocious, cruel, nasty; blamable, blameworthy, censurable, reprehensible; corrupt, debased, debauched, degenerate, depraved, dissolute, libertine,

loose, perverted, reprobate; banned, barred, condemned, discouraged, forbidden, interdicted, outlawed, prohibited, proscribed, unauthorized, unclean; disallowed; execrable, lousy, miserable, wretched; erring, fallen, unprincipled, unscrupulous; improper, incorrect, indecent, indecorous, unbecoming
near antonyms high-minded, honest, honorable, law-abiding, legitimate, principled, reputable, right-minded, scrupulous, straight, upright; allowed, authorized, legal, licensed, permissible, permitted; approved, endorsed, sanctioned; abetted, encouraged, promoted, supported; clean, correct, decent, decorous, exemplary, proper, seemly; blameless, commendable, creditable, guiltless; chaste, immaculate, innocent, irreproachable, lily-white, perfect, pure, spotless
antonyms good, ethical, moral, right, righteous, virtuous
3 causing or capable of causing harm ⟨sitting too close to the television is said to be *bad* for the eyes⟩ — see HARMFUL
4 engaging in or marked by childish misbehavior ⟨the children were *bad*, so they didn't get dessert⟩ — see NAUGHTY
5 feeling unhappiness ⟨losing always makes him feel *bad*⟩ — see SAD 1
6 having a fault ⟨a *bad* video connection that is causing some picture loss⟩ — see FAULTY
7 having undergone organic breakdown ⟨I think the milk has turned *bad*⟩ — see ROTTEN 1
8 not giving pleasure to the mind or senses ⟨the air in the damp basement had a very *bad* smell⟩ — see UNPLEASANT
9 of low quality ⟨*bad* shoes that fell apart within a week⟩ — see CHEAP 2
10 temporarily suffering from a disorder of the body ⟨I've been feeling *bad* all week with this cold⟩ — see SICK 1

bad *n* that which is morally unacceptable ⟨there's *bad* and good in people of every race and nationality⟩ — see EVIL

badly *adv* in an unsatisfactory way ⟨I'm afraid you performed quite *badly* in our last rehearsal⟩
synonyms inadequately, poorly, unacceptably, unsatisfactorily
related words rottenly; intolerably, unbearably; inappropriately, incorrectly, indecently, rakishly, unsuitably; naughtily
near antonyms appropriately, congruously, correctly, decently, decorously, felicitously, fittingly, genteelly, rightly, seemly, suitably
antonyms acceptably, adequately, all right, fine, good, palatably, passably, so-so, tolerably

bad–mouth *vb* to express scornfully one's low opinion of ⟨*bad-mouthed* that awful movie to everyone she knew⟩ — see DECRY 1

badness *n* the state or quality of being utterly evil ⟨the villain's complete *badness* made him a good foil for the unfailingly virtuous hero⟩ — see ENORMITY 1

baffle *vb* **1** to prevent from achieving a goal ⟨the language barrier *baffled* everyone and kept us from doing our joint project efficiently⟩ — see FRUSTRATE
2 to throw into a state of mental uncertainty ⟨she was *baffled* by the wording of the problem⟩ — see CONFUSE 1

bafflement *n* a state of mental uncertainty ⟨his complete *bafflement* by the joke was itself funny⟩ — see CONFUSION 1

bag *n* **1** a container made of a flexible material (as paper or plastic) ⟨she carries her towel and other supplies to the beach in a bright, colorful *bag* slung over her arm⟩
synonyms poke [*chiefly Southern & Midland*], pouch, sack
related words carryall, portmanteau, traveling bag; bundle, pack, package, packet, parcel; backpack, duffel bag, haversack, knapsack, rucksack; handbag, pocketbook, purse, tote bag
2 a container for carrying money and small personal items ⟨a very carefully dressed woman who makes sure that her *bag* always matches the color of her shoes⟩ — see PURSE
bag *vb* **1** to extend outward beyond a usual point ⟨the shirt *bagged* at the waist⟩ — see BULGE
2 to take physical control or possession of (something) suddenly or forcibly ⟨*bagged* a deer while hunting last weekend⟩ — see CATCH 1
bail out *vb* to remove from danger or harm ⟨the government *bailed out* the savings and loan industry⟩ — see SAVE 2
bairn *n, chiefly Scottish* a young person who is between infancy and adulthood ⟨at the Scottish festival there were traditional contests of strength and endurance, Celtic fiddlers, and groups of *bairns* performing Highland flings⟩ — see CHILD 1
bait *n* **1** something used to attract animals to a hook or into a trap ⟨cheese is the traditional *bait* for trapping mice⟩
synonyms decoy, lure
related words ambush, trap; hook, snare, troll; appeal, attraction, call, draw, incentive, pull; enticement, seduction, temptation
near antonyms repellent
2 something that persuades one to perform an action for pleasure or gain ⟨the promise of free vacation is surefire *bait* to get people to agree to be chaperones for school trips⟩ — see LURE 1
bait *vb* to attack repeatedly with mean put-downs or insults ⟨the bullies regularly *baited* smaller children, calling them "stupid" and "weakling"⟩ — see TEASE 2
baiter *n* **1** a person who causes repeated emotional pain, distress, or annoyance to another ⟨vowed revenge someday on the *baiters* who were making his life miserable⟩ — see TORMENTOR
2 one that tries to get a person to give in to a desire ⟨my sister is quite the mischievous *baiter*, always offering candy even though she knows I'm on a diet⟩ — see TEMPTER
balance *n* **1** a condition in which opposing forces are equal to one another ⟨in order to determine the weight of that beaker, you need to get the two pans of the scale in perfect *balance*⟩
synonyms equilibrium, equipoise, poise
related words counterbalance, counterpoise; firmness, fixedness, security, stability, steadiness
near antonyms changeability, fluctuation, inconstancy, insecurity, instability, mutability, precariousness, shakiness, unsteadiness, volatility
antonyms imbalance
2 a balanced, pleasing, or suitable arrangement of parts ⟨the *balance* of the landscaping is in keeping with the symmetry of so many 18th-century mansions⟩ — see HARMONY 1
3 a device for measuring weight ⟨use a *balance* to make sure you get the amounts precisely correct⟩ — see ¹SCALE

4 a force or influence that makes an opposing force ineffective or less effective ⟨the *balance* to the mountain of complaints are the many letters of praise that we also receive⟩ — see COUNTERBALANCE
5 a remaining group or portion ⟨and the *balance* of the contestants should stand in that last corner⟩ — see REMAINDER 1
balance *vb* to make equal in amount, degree, or status ⟨tried to *balance* the amount of money everyone earned for the same work⟩ — see EQUALIZE
balanced *adj* **1** having full use of one's mind and control over one's actions ⟨no *balanced* person would believe that their dog's bark was actually the voice of God⟩ — see SANE
2 having the parts agreeably related ⟨a *balanced* arrangement of the furniture made the room look more spacious⟩ — see HARMONIOUS 2
bald *adj* **1** lacking a usual or natural covering ⟨trees that are *bald* in the winter aren't the best for giving a home year-round privacy⟩ — see NAKED 2
2 free from all additions or embellishment ⟨try to avoid the *bald* statement "you're wrong" when trying to reason with someone⟩ — see PLAIN 1
baleful *adj* **1** being or showing a sign of evil or calamity to come ⟨a dark, *baleful* sky portending a tornado⟩ — see OMINOUS
2 causing or capable of causing harm ⟨contends that the violent content of so much of popular entertainment is a *baleful* influence on our society⟩ — see HARMFUL
3 likely to cause or capable of causing death ⟨a medicine that is beneficial in small doses but *baleful* in large⟩ — see DEADLY
balk *vb* to prevent from achieving a goal ⟨a young man with big dreams who refused to be *balked* by the daily obstacles of his inner-city existence⟩ — see FRUSTRATE
balky *adj* given to resisting authority or another's control ⟨a *balky* toddler who only seemed to know the word "no" when told to do something⟩ — see DISOBEDIENT
¹ball *n* **1** a more or less round body or mass ⟨the little rubber *ball* used in racquetball⟩ ⟨a *ball* of string⟩
synonyms globe, orb, sphere
related words egg, oval; circle, ring, round; chunk, clump, gob, hunk, lump, nugget, wad
near antonyms block, cube, rectangle, square
2 a usually round or cone-shaped little piece of lead made to be fired from a firearm ⟨found a cache of musket *balls* while excavating the old fort⟩ — see BULLET
²ball *n* a social gathering for dancing ⟨a *ball* to celebrate the inauguration⟩ — see DANCE
ball *vb* to form into a round compact mass ⟨*balled* up the paper and threw it at the garbage can⟩ — see WAD
ballad *n* a short musical composition for the human voice often with instrumental accompaniment ⟨a haunting *ballad* about lost love and loneliness⟩ — see SONG 1
balloon *vb* **1** to become greater in extent, volume, amount, or number ⟨the number of students who stay home sick *balloons* every winter⟩ — see INCREASE 2
2 to extend outward beyond a usual point ⟨the paper bag *ballooned* and blew away as the wind lifted it skyward⟩ — see BULGE
ballot *n* a piece of paper indicating a person's preferences in an election ⟨we collected all of the *ballots* from the students voting for class president⟩
synonyms vote

related words aye (*also* ay), nay, no, yea; blackball; referendum; ticket

ballyhoo *n* newsworthy information released to the media that is designed to gain public attention or support for a person, business, or cause ⟨*ballyhoo* intended to lure people to the summer blockbuster⟩ — see PUBLICITY

ballyhoo *vb* **1** to praise or publicize lavishly and often excessively ⟨that reviewer always *ballyhoos* any book by one of his pet authors⟩ — see TOUT 1
2 to provide publicity for ⟨the TV networks usually spend the summer months *ballyhooing* their new fall shows⟩ — see PUBLICIZE 1

balminess *n* lack of good sense or judgment ⟨only sheer *balminess* would possess someone to jump off a bridge simply because their friends suggested it⟩ — see FOOLISHNESS 1

balmy *adj* **1** having or showing a very abnormal or sick state of mind ⟨a completely *balmy* but harmless old man who talked intently to plants and believed they answered back⟩ — see INSANE 1
2 marked by temperatures that are neither too high nor too low ⟨a *balmy* spring day⟩ — see CLEMENT
3 not harsh or stern especially in manner, nature, or effect ⟨a pleasant, *balmy* breeze was all that stirred the wildflowers growing near the shore⟩ — see GENTLE 1
4 showing or marked by a lack of good sense or judgment ⟨the *balmy* notion that such blatant cheating on the test would go unnoticed⟩ — see FOOLISH 1

balustrade *n* a protective barrier consisting of a horizontal bar and its supports ⟨an ornately carved *balustrade* for the staircase⟩ — see RAILING

ban *n* an order that something not be done or used ⟨a quiet seaside resort with a *ban* on the drinking of alcohol in public places⟩ — see PROHIBITION 2

ban *vb* **1** to order not to do or use or to be done or used ⟨the school absolutely *bans* smoking on school property⟩ — see FORBID
2 to prevent the participation or inclusion of ⟨the school *banned* those caught in the cheating scandal from graduation ceremonies⟩ — see EXCLUDE

banal *adj* **1** lacking in qualities that make for spirit and character ⟨the man was pleasant but *banal*, unlike his spirited sister⟩ — see WISHY-WASHY 1
2 used or heard so often as to be dull ⟨please find new ways of phrasing your thoughts instead of relying on *banal* expressions⟩ — see STALE

banality *n* an idea or expression that has been used by many people ⟨a *banality* that everyone seems to be saying lately⟩ — see COMMONPLACE

bananas *adj* having or showing a very abnormal or sick state of mind ⟨people say the woman just went *bananas* after the death of her beloved husband⟩ — see INSANE 1

¹band *n* **1** a circular strip ⟨a *band* of cloth tied around his wrist⟩ — see RING 2
2 something that physically prevents free movement ⟨the dog was forced to wear a *band* around its muzzle until it learned not to nip people⟩ — see BOND 1
3 a line or long narrow section differing in color from the background ⟨skunks have a *band* of white down their backs⟩ — see STRIPE

²band *n* **1** a usually large group of musicians playing together ⟨that traveling *band* needs to find a new singer⟩
synonyms orchestra, philharmonic, symphony, symphony orchestra
related words brass band; brasses, strings, woodwinds; combo, ensemble, group; company, troupe; duo, octet,

quartet (*also* quartette), quintet, septet (*also* septette), sextet, trio
2 a group of people working together on a task ⟨a *band* of volunteer searchers found the lost child⟩ — see GANG 1

band *vb* **1** to encircle or bind with or as if with a belt ⟨*banded* the waist of the dress with a speckled belt⟩ — see GIRD 1
2 to form or enter into an association that furthers the interests of its members ⟨small farmers *banded* together to oppose the interests of the agricultural giants⟩ — see ALLY
3 to gather into a tight mass by means of a line or cord ⟨*banded* the newspapers together for delivery⟩ — see TIE 1
4 to make stripes on ⟨*banded* the sleeves of the robe with strips of contrasting material⟩ — see STRIPE

bandage *vb* to cover with a bandage ⟨her mother always *bandages* her scraped knees very carefully⟩
synonyms bind, dress
related words care (for), doctor, medicate, minister (to), nurse, treat; mend, heal

bandanna *or* **bandana** *n* a scarf worn on the head ⟨she uses her colorful print *bandanna* to keep the hair out of her eyes⟩
synonyms babushka, handkerchief, kerchief, mantilla
related words shawl

bandwagon *n* a series of activities undertaken to achieve a goal ⟨tried to get everyone on the *bandwagon* about forming a language club⟩ — see CAMPAIGN

bandy *vb* to talk about (an issue) usually from various points of view and for the purpose of arriving at a decision or opinion ⟨*bandied* around the idea of going out to dinner for their anniversary⟩ — see DISCUSS

bane *n* a substance that by chemical action can kill or injure a living thing ⟨a plant that is believed to be the *bane* of the wolf⟩ — see POISON

baneful *adj* causing or capable of causing harm ⟨the incredibly *baneful* effect that drug dealing has on so many inner-city neighborhoods⟩ — see HARMFUL

bang *n* **1** a hard strike with a part of the body or an instrument ⟨delivered a sharp *bang* that rattled the door⟩ — see ¹BLOW
2 a loud explosive sound ⟨a sudden *bang* made the cat jump⟩ — see CLAP 1
3 a pleasurably intense stimulation of the feelings ⟨tried to get the most *bang* for her money at the fair⟩ — see THRILL

bang *vb* **1** to come into usually forceful contact with something ⟨the toy car *banged* into the wall and stopped⟩ — see HIT 2
2 to deliver a blow to (someone or something) usually in a strong vigorous manner ⟨idly *banged* trees with a stick⟩ — see HIT 1
3 to shove into a closed position with force and noise ⟨stomped off to his room and *banged* the door⟩ — see SLAM 1

bangle *n* an ornament worn on a chain around the neck or wrist ⟨wore a bracelet with small silver *bangles* on it⟩ — see PENDANT

bang–up *adj* of the very best kind ⟨you did a *bang-up* job on this report⟩ — see EXCELLENT

banish *vb* **1** to force to leave a country ⟨in the old days, criminals were sometimes *banished*⟩
synonyms deport, displace, exile, expatriate, transport
related words dismiss, eject, eliminate, evict, exclude, expel, oust, throw out; excommunicate, ostracize, reject, repudiate, spurn; dispossess

near antonyms naturalize, repatriate; accept, admit, receive, take in; entertain, harbor, house, shelter

2 to drive or force out ⟨permanently *banished* the troublemakers from the youth recreational center⟩ — see EJECT 1

banishment *n* the forced removal from a homeland ⟨some members of the tribe of Native Americans believe they are still owed payment for their *banishment* from their homeland⟩ — see EXILE 1

banister *n* a protective barrier consisting of a horizontal bar and its supports ⟨a much-needed new *banister* for the rickety staircase⟩ — see RAILING

¹**bank** *n* **1** a number of things considered as a unit ⟨a *bank* of telephones set up for the telethon⟩ — see GROUP 1

2 a series of people or things arranged side by side ⟨a *bank* of elevators⟩ — see ROW 1

²**bank** *n* a pile or ridge of granular matter (as sand or snow) ⟨he likes to play on the *bank* of dirt the construction workers left⟩

synonyms bar, drift, mound

related words snowbank, snowdrift; embankment, sandbar; heap, hill, mass, mountain, stack

bank *vb* **1** to form into a pile or ridge of earth ⟨*banked* sand into little mounds on the beach⟩ — see MOUND 1

2 to put in an account ⟨she always *banks* half of her paycheck⟩ — see DEPOSIT 1

bank note *n* a piece of printed paper used as money ⟨the new nation immediately printed up its own *bank notes*⟩ — see ¹BILL 2

bankroll *n* available money ⟨my total *bankroll* right now is $20⟩ — see FUND 2

bankrupt *vb* to cause to lose one's fortune and become unable to pay one's debts ⟨several bad investments *bankrupted* him⟩ — see RUIN 1

banned *adj* that may not be permitted ⟨you'll have to change out of that *banned* T-shirt⟩ — see IMPERMISSIBLE

banner *adj* of the very best kind ⟨it's been a *banner* year for business⟩ — see EXCELLENT

banner *n* a piece of cloth with a special design that is used as an emblem or for signaling ⟨the boat flew a bright red *banner* for the seaport's harbor festival⟩ — see FLAG 1

banning *n* the act of ordering that something not be done or used ⟨the *banning* of foul language on school property was long overdue⟩ — see PROHIBITION 1

banquet *n* a large fancy meal often accompanied by ceremony or entertainment ⟨prepared a celebratory *banquet* for the graduating class⟩ — see FEAST

banquet *vb* to entertain with a fancy meal ⟨*banqueted* the returning troops at the military base⟩ — see FEAST

bantam *adj* of a size that is less than average ⟨a *bantam* comedian who is known to fellow performers for his oversize ego⟩ — see SMALL 1

banter *n* good-natured teasing or exchanging of clever remarks ⟨those particular students are known for their brilliant and witty *banter* at lunchtime⟩

synonyms chaff, give-and-take, jesting, joshing, persiflage, raillery, repartee

related words barb, crack, dig, gag, jest, joke, quip, sally, wisecrack, witticism; facetiousness, humorousness; fooling, kidding, mocking, razzing, ribbing, ridiculing; humor, wit, wordplay; chatter, chitchat, gossip, small talk

banter *vb* to make jokes ⟨the teacher *bantered* pleasantly with the students at the school dance⟩ — see JOKE

bantering *adj* marked by or expressive of mild or good-natured teasing ⟨the gently *bantering* tone of the couple's conversation⟩ — see QUIZZICAL

baptism *n* the process or an instance of being formally placed in an office or organization ⟨the *baptism* of the new members of the college fraternity⟩ — see INSTALLATION 1

baptize *vb* **1** to give a name to ⟨*baptized* the child "Anne"⟩ — see NAME 1

2 to put into an office or welcome into an organization with special ceremonies ⟨the new sisters will be *baptized* with special initiation rites at the sorority house⟩ — see INSTALL 1

bar *n* **1** a straight piece (as of wood or metal) that is longer than it is wide ⟨all of the prison's windows are partially covered with steel *bars*⟩

synonyms billet, rod

related words beam, board; band, strip; ingot, slab, stick

2 a line or long narrow section differing in color from the background ⟨the cat had a *bar* of white down her throat⟩ — see STRIPE

3 a pile or ridge of granular matter (as sand or snow) ⟨a *bar* of snow along the edge of the parking lot⟩ — see ²BANK

4 a place of business where alcoholic beverages are sold to be consumed on the premises ⟨a *bar* that serves meals as well as drinks⟩ — see BARROOM

5 an assembly of persons for the administration of justice ⟨was admitted to the *bar* last year⟩ — see COURT 3

6 something that makes movement or progress more difficult ⟨the complication of the molecule is the biggest *bar* to reproducing it⟩ — see ENCUMBRANCE

bar *prep* not including ⟨everyone is invited, *bar* none⟩ — see EXCEPT

bar *vb* **1** to make stripes on ⟨*barred* the fence with white strips⟩ — see STRIPE

2 to order not to do or use or to be done or used ⟨hitting and shoving is *barred* in this school⟩ — see FORBID

3 to prevent the participation or inclusion of ⟨rowdy teenagers are *barred* from using the playground⟩ — see EXCLUDE

barb *n* an act or expression showing scorn and usually intended to hurt another's feelings ⟨delivered a last *barb* to his ex-girlfriend as he stalked away⟩ — see INSULT

barbarian *n* an uncivilized person ⟨in those times European explorers tended to regard any people having a different language, culture, or religion as a race of *barbarians*⟩ — see HEATHEN 2

barbaric *adj* having or showing the desire to inflict severe pain and suffering on others ⟨a *barbaric* dictator who tortured his own people with no qualms⟩ — see CRUEL 1

barbarity *n* the willful infliction of pain and suffering on others ⟨more than one reluctant dental patient has been tempted to level the charge of *barbarity* against their dentist⟩ — see CRUELTY

barbarous *adj* **1** having or showing the desire to inflict severe pain and suffering on others ⟨the *barbarous* treatment of the native peoples of the New World by those bent on conquest at any cost⟩ — see CRUEL 1

2 not civilized ⟨an aunt who abhors *barbarous* behavior such as eating with your fingers⟩ — see SAVAGE 1

bard *n* a person who writes poetry ⟨a *bard* best known for a series of love poems to his beloved⟩ — see POET

bare *adj* **1** being this and no more ⟨impoverished people who can no longer afford the *bare* necessities⟩ — see MERE

2 free from all additions or embellishment ⟨do you want to know the *bare* truth?⟩ — see PLAIN 1

3 lacking a usual or natural covering ⟨the ground was *bare*, without any grass at all⟩ — see NAKED 2

4 lacking or shed of clothing ⟨the toddler liked to run around *bare*⟩ — see NAKED 1

5 lacking contents that could or should be present ⟨the cupboard was *bare*—not a thing to eat⟩ — see EMPTY 1

bare *vb* to make known (as information previously kept secret) ⟨finally *bared* the secret that she had kept to herself for so long⟩ — see REVEAL 1

barely *adv* by a very small margin ⟨we *barely* made it on time⟩ — see JUST 2

bareness *n* the quality or state of being empty ⟨the *bareness* of the refrigerator suggested it was time to go shopping⟩ — see VACANCY 2

bargain *n* **1** something bought or offered for sale at a desirable price ⟨those shoes were a *bargain* because the store was going out of business⟩

synonyms buy, steal

related words markdown; bonus, freebie, gift, giveaway, premium, present; sale; boon, windfall

near antonyms overcharge, rip-off; markup; extravagance, luxury

2 an arrangement about action to be taken ⟨made a *bargain* that one would help the other next week⟩ — see AGREEMENT 2

bargain *vb* to talk over or dispute the terms of a purchase ⟨they *bargained* with the car salesman for half an hour before settling on a price⟩

synonyms chaffer, deal, dicker, haggle, horse-trade, negotiate, palter

related words argue, bicker, clash, quibble, squabble, wrangle; comparison shop, shop (around); barter, exchange, trade; hawk, peddle; buy, purchase

barge *vb* to move heavily or clumsily ⟨the big man *barged* into the room⟩ — see LUMBER 1

bark *n* a boat equipped with one or more sails ⟨took a small *bark* out on the lake⟩ — see SAILBOAT

¹bark *vb* to remove the natural covering of ⟨*barking* a tree will probably kill it⟩ — see PEEL

²bark *vb* to speak sharply or irritably ⟨please don't *bark* at your sister, as it's not her fault you can't find your shoes⟩ — see SNAP 1

baron *n* a person of rank, power, or influence in a particular field ⟨a railroad *baron*⟩ — see MAGNATE

baronial *adj* large and impressive in size, grandeur, extent, or conception ⟨a *baronial* mansion with dozens of spacious, luxurious rooms⟩ — see GRAND 1

barrage *n* a rapid or overwhelming outpouring of many things at once ⟨the teacher's rapid-fire *barrage* of homework assignments went by too fast for me to write them all down⟩

synonyms bombardment, cannonade, fusillade, hail, salvo, shower, storm, volley

related words broadside, burst, deluge, flood, flood tide, flush, gush, inundation, outburst, outflow, outpouring, overflow, spate, surge, torrent; current, river, stream, tide; excess, glut, overabundance, overage, overkill, overmuch, oversupply, superabundance, superfluity, surfeit, surplus

near antonyms dribble, drip, trickle

barred *adj* **1** having stripes ⟨a tabby is a *barred* cat, often with black stripes⟩ — see STRIPED

2 that may not be permitted ⟨smoking is *barred* inside the restaurant⟩ — see IMPERMISSIBLE

barrel *n* **1** a considerable amount ⟨a *barrel* of laughs⟩ — see LOT 2

2 a metal container in the shape of a cylinder ⟨a trash *barrel*⟩ — see CAN

3 an enclosed wooden vessel for holding beverages ⟨*barrels* of fine wine aging in the winery's cellar⟩ — see CASK

barrel *vb* to proceed or move quickly ⟨*barreled* through the project at a furious pace⟩ — see HURRY 2

barren *adj* **1** producing inferior or only a small amount of vegetation ⟨if tobacco fields aren't allowed to lie idle once every few years, they will become *barren*⟩

synonyms impoverished, infertile, poor, stark, unproductive, waste

related words bleak, dead, desolate, inhospitable, lifeless; bankrupted, consumed, debilitated, depleted, diminished, drained, dried up, enfeebled, exhausted, expended, lessened, reduced, spent, used up; arid, desert, dry

near antonyms arable, tillable; green, verdant

antonyms fertile, fruitful, lush, luxuriant, productive, rich

2 not able to produce fruit or offspring ⟨the pear tree appears to be *barren*⟩ — see STERILE 1

barren *n* land that is uninhabited or not fit for crops ⟨lived out in the *barrens* where it was impossible to grow anything⟩ — see WASTELAND

barricade *n* a physical object that blocks the way ⟨the police put up *barricades* to block off the parade route⟩ — see BARRIER

barrier *n* a physical object that blocks the way ⟨there was a big *barrier* plastered with signs saying "Keep Out" around the trash compactor⟩

synonyms barricade, fence, hedge, wall

related words bar, encumbrance, handicap, hindrance, hurdle, impediment, obstacle, obstruction, roadblock, stop; fetter, hobble, manacle, shackle; constraint, curb, restraint, snag

near antonyms door, doorway, entrance, entry, entryway, gate, portal

barring *n* the act of ordering that something not be done or used ⟨the *barring* of slogan-emblazoned clothing to reduce distractions and friction in the classroom⟩ — see PROHIBITION 1

barring *prep* not including ⟨we'll be there, *barring* rain or some other unexpected problem⟩ — see EXCEPT

barroom *n* a place of business where alcoholic beverages are sold to be consumed on the premises ⟨her mother didn't like her even to walk past the *barroom* because she was worried that there might be drunk people inside⟩

synonyms bar, café (*also* cafe), groggery, grogshop, pub, public house [*chiefly British*], saloon, tavern

related words cabaret, dive, joint, nightclub, roadhouse, speakeasy; package store

barter *n* a giving or taking of one thing of value in return for another ⟨I think the *barter* of your shoes for some candy was a bit foolish of you⟩ — see EXCHANGE 1

base *adj* not following or in accordance with standards of honor and decency ⟨a *base* and sneaky act that is a clear violation of international law⟩ — see IGNOBLE 2

base *n* **1** an immaterial thing upon which something else rests ⟨the firm belief that complete trust between husband and wife is the *base* of any successful marriage⟩

synonyms basis, bedrock, cornerstone, footing, foundation, ground, groundwork, keystone, underpinning

related words buttress, framework, prop, substructure, support; assumption, justification, premise, presumption, presupposition, theory, thesis, warrant; center, core, eye, focus, heart, hub, nucleus, seat; essence, quintessence, soul

2 a place from which an advance (as for military operations) is made ⟨the Army's *base* of attack was kept top secret until the battle began⟩
synonyms bridgehead, foothold
related words beachhead, center, front, headquarters; bastion, fastness, fortress, stronghold

3 a thing or place that is of greatest importance to an activity or interest ⟨the *base* of the industry is California's Silicon Valley⟩ — see CENTER 1

4 the lowest part, place, or point ⟨the *base* of the mountain extends over a huge area⟩ — see BOTTOM 3

5 the place from which a commander runs operations ⟨the army *base* is three miles down the road⟩ — see COMMAND 3

base *vb* to find a basis ⟨she *based* her argument against the death penalty on careful research⟩
synonyms ground, predicate, rest
related words establish, found; assume, postulate, premise, presume, presuppose, suppose

baseborn *adj* **1** belonging to the class of people of low social or economic rank ⟨in the Middle Ages, a *baseborn* person simply had to accept his or her station in life⟩ — see IGNOBLE 1

2 born to a father and mother who are not married ⟨a *baseborn* child who didn't even know his father's name⟩ — see ILLEGITIMATE 1

basement *n* a room or set of rooms below the surface of the ground ⟨we store our bicycles in the *basement* during the winter⟩ — see CELLAR

bash *vb* **1** to come into usually forceful contact with something ⟨the car *bashed* into the tree with glass-shattering force⟩ — see HIT 2

2 to deliver a blow to (someone or something) usually in a strong vigorous manner ⟨you have to *bash* that door hard in order to get it open⟩ — see HIT 1

3 to strike repeatedly ⟨the angry child kept *bashing* her toy with a hammer until it broke⟩ — see BEAT 1

bashful *adj* not comfortable around people ⟨a *bashful* child who hid in his room when visitors came over⟩ — see SHY 2

basic *adj* of or relating to the simplest facts or theories of a subject ⟨you'll work on learning *basic* math in first grade⟩ — see ELEMENTARY

basically *adv* for the most part ⟨your answer is *basically* correct⟩ — see CHIEFLY

basics *n pl* general or basic truths on which other truths or theories can be based ⟨if you don't learn the *basics* of algebra now, you'll never master calculus⟩ — see PRINCIPLES 1

basis *n* an immaterial thing upon which something else rests ⟨the sole *basis* for the rumor is someone's overactive imagination⟩ — see BASE 1

bask *vb* to refrain from labor or exertion ⟨*basked* at the seashore over the long holiday⟩ — see REST 1

bass *adj* having a low musical pitch or range ⟨a man with an impressive *bass* voice⟩ — see DEEP 2

bastard *adj* born to a father and mother who are not married ⟨Alexander Hamilton appears to have been bothered by the fact that he was a *bastard* child⟩ — see ILLEGITIMATE 1

bastion *n* a structure or place from which one can resist attack ⟨the army retreated to its *bastion* in the mountains to regroup⟩ — see FORT

bat *n* **1** a hard strike with a part of the body or an instrument ⟨a sharp *bat* with a rolled-up newspaper and that fly was a goner⟩ — see [1]BLOW

2 a heavy rigid stick used as a weapon or for punishment ⟨riot policemen armed with *bats* and tear gas⟩ — see CLUB 2

bat *vb* **1** to deliver a blow to (someone or something) usually in a strong vigorous manner ⟨*batted* the lamp off the table with one strike⟩ — see HIT 1

2 to strike repeatedly ⟨*batted* the piñata until it finally broke open⟩ — see BEAT 1

batch *n* **1** a number of things considered as a unit ⟨a *batch* of essays to correct⟩ — see GROUP 1

2 a usually small number of persons considered as a unit ⟨send in the next *batch* of applicants⟩ — see GROUP 2

bath *n* a room furnished with a fixture for flushing body waste ⟨retired to the *bath* to freshen up⟩ — see TOILET

bathe *vb* to make wet ⟨*bathe* your contact lens with the solution before inserting them⟩ — see WET

bathed *adj* containing, covered with, or thoroughly penetrated by water ⟨covered the victim's burns with *bathed* bandages⟩ — see WET

bathroom *n* a room furnished with a fixture for flushing body waste ⟨everyone should use the *bathroom* before we leave on the long trip⟩ — see TOILET

battalion *n* a large body of men and women organized for land warfare ⟨the nation's *battalions* were forced to fight on two fronts simultaneously⟩ — see ARMY 1

batter *vb* to strike repeatedly ⟨*battered* the door until it fell down⟩ — see BEAT 1

battery *n* **1** a number of things considered as a unit ⟨a *battery* of tests to determine the cause of the medical disorder⟩ — see GROUP 1

2 a usually small number of persons considered as a unit ⟨a *battery* of specialists worked on the problem until it was fixed⟩ — see GROUP 2

battle *n* **1** a forceful effort to reach a goal or objective ⟨passing the class was an uphill *battle*, but she succeeded⟩ — see STRUGGLE 1

2 a physical dispute between opposing individuals or groups ⟨a *battle* between rival gangs left two people injured⟩ — see FIGHT 1

3 active fighting during the course of a war ⟨the *battle* of Bunker Hill was actually fought on a nearby hill⟩ — see COMBAT 1

4 an earnest effort for superiority or victory over another ⟨the chess game was a real *battle* between two of the world's best players⟩ — see CONTEST 1

battle *vb* **1** to engage in a contest ⟨basketball players *battled* on the court for the state championship⟩ — see COMPETE

2 to enter into contest or conflict with ⟨the tennis players *battled* each other for almost three hours⟩ — see ENGAGE 2

3 to oppose (someone) in physical conflict ⟨she *battled* her sister over the toy until both of them ended up crying⟩ — see FIGHT 1

4 to strive to reduce or eliminate ⟨we must *battle* hunger and poverty wherever they exist⟩ — see FIGHT 2

batty *adj* having or showing a very abnormal or sick state of mind ⟨a *batty* old lady who lives with 100 cats⟩ — see INSANE 1

bauble *n* a small object displayed for its attractiveness or interest ⟨picked up some cheap *baubles* at the fair⟩ — see KNICKKNACK

bawdiness *n* the quality or state of being obscene ⟨the *bawdiness* of the song makes it inappropriate for children⟩ — see OBSCENITY 1

bawdy *adj* 1 depicting or referring to sexual matters in a way that is unacceptable in polite society ⟨a *bawdy* comment about someone you work with could get you fired⟩ — see OBSCENE 1

2 hinting at or intended to call to mind matters regarded as indecent ⟨a *bawdy* limerick that mischievous storytellers love to recite⟩ — see SUGGESTIVE 1

bawl *vb* 1 to shed tears often while making meaningless sounds as a sign of pain or distress ⟨he *bawled* for days after his dog died⟩ — see CRY 1

2 to speak so as to be heard at a distance ⟨Mom was always forced to *bawl* for us to come home for dinner whenever we played down the block⟩ — see CALL 1

bay *n* 1 a part of a body of water that extends beyond the general shoreline ⟨the boats drifted aimlessly in the *bay*⟩ — see GULF 1

2 one of the parts into which an enclosed space is divided ⟨the garage has three separate *bays* for cars⟩ — see COMPARTMENT

bay *vb* to make a long loud mournful sound ⟨the beagle *bayed* whenever someone walked by⟩ — see HOWL 1

bazaar *n* an establishment where goods are sold to consumers ⟨we wandered around the *bazaar* looking to buy gifts⟩ — see SHOP 1

be *vb* 1 to have life ⟨stories that begin with the familiar line "once upon a time there *was* a beautiful maiden"⟩
synonyms breathe, exist, live, subsist
related words abide, continue, endure, last, lead, persist, survive; move; flourish, prosper, thrive
near antonyms disappear, evaporate, vanish; cease, end, stop
antonyms depart, die, expire, pass away, perish, succumb

2 to occupy a place or location ⟨we'll *be* there waiting for you⟩ — see STAND 1

3 to take or have a certain position within a group arranged in vertical classes ⟨our school's football team *is* first in its division⟩ — see RANK 1

4 to take place ⟨the party *is* next Saturday⟩ — see HAPPEN

be (to) *vb* to behave toward in a stated way ⟨you need to *be* nice *to* your brother⟩ — see TREAT 1

beach *n* the usually sandy or gravelly land bordering a body of water ⟨she loves walking along the *beach*, looking for shells that the waves cast up⟩
synonyms shore, strand
related words seaboard, seacoast, seashore, seaside; coast, coastline, shoreline; waterfront; bank, riverbank, riverside; esplanade; littoral

beached *adj* resting on the shore or bottom of a body of water ⟨the *beached* whale had to be helped back out to sea⟩ — see AGROUND

beacon *n* something that provides illumination ⟨the floodlit skyscraper is one of the city's most beloved nighttime *beacons*⟩ — see LIGHT 2

beak *n* the jaws of a bird together with their hornlike covering ⟨the bird cracked the walnut shell with its *beak* and ate its nut⟩
synonyms bill, nib
related words mouth; muzzle; mandible, maw, maxilla

beam *n* a narrow sharply defined line of light radiating from an object ⟨we'll need a flashlight that casts a broader *beam* in order to really see anything⟩ — see SHAFT 1

beam *vb* 1 to emit rays of light ⟨a lighthouse has *beamed* from this site since the 1790s⟩ — see SHINE 1

2 to express an emotion (as amusement) by curving the lips upward ⟨my father *beamed* when I showed him my great report card⟩ — see SMILE 1

beaming *adj* 1 giving off or reflecting much light ⟨the orchestra began its season of outdoor concerts under a *beaming* moon⟩ — see BRIGHT 1

2 having or being an outward sign of good feelings (as of love, confidence, or happiness) ⟨Mom's *beaming* face shone with love as we all gathered for a family photo⟩ — see RADIANT 1

bear *n* an irritable and complaining person ⟨you've been a real *bear* lately—are you having a bad week?⟩ — see GROUCH

bear *vb* 1 to bring forth from the womb ⟨luckily, she turned out to be able to *bear* children after all⟩
synonyms drop, have, produce
related words deliver; create; breed, multiply, propagate, reproduce, spawn; beget, father, generate, get, mother, sire
phrases to give birth to
near antonyms abort, lose, miscarry

2 to put up with (something painful or difficult) ⟨I can't *bear* having to eat my vegetables in order to have ice cream⟩
synonyms abide, brook, countenance, endure, meet, stand, stick out, stomach, support, sustain, take, tolerate
related words accept, allow, permit, suffer, swallow; acquiesce, agree (with *or* to), assent (to), capitulate, consent (to), respect, submit (to), yield (to)
near antonyms decline, dismiss, refuse, reject, repudiate, spurn, turn down; combat, contest, fight, oppose, resist; avoid, bypass, circumvent, dodge, elude, escape, evade, miss; abstain, forbear, refrain

3 to have a relation or connection ⟨I just found another fact that *bears* on this issue⟩ — see APPLY 1

4 to go on a specified course or in a certain direction ⟨the road *bears* left after the second traffic light⟩ — see HEAD 1

5 to hold up or serve as a foundation for ⟨the wooden bridge will only *bear* one truck at a time⟩ — see SUPPORT 3

6 to keep in one's mind or heart ⟨I'm not one to *bear* grudges⟩ — see HARBOR 1

7 to manage the actions of (oneself) in a particular way ⟨she *bore* herself well in her first public speaking event⟩ — see BEHAVE

8 to support and take from one place to another ⟨the rescue team came *bearing* much-needed food and supplies⟩ — see CARRY 1

9 to take to or upon oneself ⟨I *bear* some responsibility for the mishap⟩ — see ASSUME 1

10 to wear or have on one's person ⟨the right to *bear* arms⟩ — see CARRY 2

bearable *adj* capable of being endured ⟨the pain from a sprained ankle is annoying but *bearable*⟩
synonyms endurable, sufferable, supportable, sustainable, tolerable
related words livable (*also* liveable); acceptable, allowable, reasonable
near antonyms agonizing, appalling, awful, bad, cruel, dire, dreadful, excruciating, ghastly, harrowing, harsh, horrible, nasty, painful, rotten, terrible, tormenting, torturous, unfortunate, vicious, vile, wretched; unacceptable; acute, extreme, intense, piercing

antonyms insufferable, insupportable, intolerable, unbearable, unendurable, unsupportable

beard *vb* to oppose (something hostile or dangerous) with firmness or courage ⟨a man of integrity who was never afraid to *beard* the lion in his den⟩ — see FACE 2

bear down on *vb* to push steadily against with some force ⟨you need to *bear down on* that cap a bit to get it to latch tightly⟩ — see PRESS 1

bearing *n* **1** the fact or state of being pertinent ⟨these new facts have some *bearing* on the case⟩ — see PERTINENCE

2 the fact or state of having something in common ⟨I don't see any *bearing* between your weekly allowance and your grades, even if they are good⟩ — see CONNECTION 1

3 the way or manner in which one conducts oneself ⟨always retained his military *bearing*, even after he entered politics⟩ — see BEHAVIOR

bearish *adj* having or showing a habitually bad temper ⟨a *bearish* recluse who yelled at everyone to stay off his lawn⟩ — see ILL-TEMPERED

bear out *vb* to give evidence or testimony to the truth or factualness of ⟨the newly discovered papers *bore out* the truth of the long-rumored story about the president⟩ — see CONFIRM

beast *n* **1** a mean, evil, or unprincipled person ⟨she's a real *beast* to anyone who makes the mistake of crossing her⟩ — see VILLAIN

2 a person whose behavior is offensive to others ⟨he always has to act like a *beast* whenever he loses a game⟩ — see JERK 1

3 one of the lower animals as distinguished from human beings ⟨the *beasts* are all kept in the barn during extremely frigid weather⟩ — see ANIMAL

beastly *adv* to a great degree ⟨it's *beastly* hot today⟩ — see VERY 1

beat *adj* depleted in strength, energy, or freshness ⟨can we pick this up tomorrow, because I'm *beat*?⟩ — see WEARY 1

beat *n* **1** a hard strike with a part of the body or an instrument ⟨delivered one hard *beat* on the drums⟩ — see ¹BLOW

2 a rhythmic expanding and contracting ⟨a single *beat* of the heart is said to be all that separates the vice president from the presidency⟩ — see PULSATION

3 the recurrent pattern formed by a series of sounds having a regular rise and fall in intensity ⟨moved to the *beat* of the music⟩ — see RHYTHM

beat *vb* to strike repeatedly ⟨they attacked and *beat* him, but fortunately he'll be fine⟩

synonyms bash, bat, batter, belt, bludgeon, buffet, bung (up), club, drub, flog, hammer, hide, lace, lambaste (*or* lambast), lick, maul, pelt, pommel, pound, pummel, thrash, thump, wallop, whale, whip

related words assail, attack, box, bust, cane, chop, clobber, clout, crack, cudgel, cuff, hit, horsewhip, knock, lam, lash, lay on, paste, punch, slap, smack, smash, sock, spank, swat, swipe, thwack, whack; gore, lacerate, wound; maim, mangle, mutilate

2 to achieve a victory over ⟨she always *beats* everyone at checkers, but she's not as good at chess⟩

synonyms best, clobber, conquer, crush, defeat, drub, lick, master, overbear, overcome, overmatch, prevail (over), rout, skunk, subdue, surmount, thrash, trim, triumph (over), trounce, wallop, whip, win (against), worst

related words nose out; excel, flourish, score, succeed; overpower, overthrow, subjugate, vanquish; exceed, outdo, surpass

phrases get around, get the better of

near antonyms fail

antonyms lose (to)

3 to be greater, better, or stronger than ⟨I *beat* her at tennis, but she always wins board games⟩ — see SURPASS 1

4 to expand and contract in a rhythmic manner ⟨the patient's heart *beats* roughly 60 times per minute⟩ — see PULSATE

5 to move or cause to move with a striking motion ⟨the bird's wings *beat* strongly as it soared in the air⟩ — see FLAP

6 to prevent from achieving a goal ⟨you *beat* me to it⟩ — see FRUSTRATE

7 to shape with a hammer ⟨the artisans who *beat* iron into exquisite swords⟩ — see HAMMER 1

8 to shine with a bright harsh light ⟨the tropical sun *beat* down on our heads without mercy⟩ — see GLARE 1

9 to strike or cause to strike lightly and usually rhythmically ⟨*beat* the drum in a marching rhythm⟩ — see ¹TAP

beater *n* one that defeats an enemy or opponent ⟨no one likes to see the *beater* of our team in the play-offs⟩ — see VICTOR 1

beating *n* failure to win a contest ⟨took a *beating* and ended up in second place⟩ — see DEFEAT 1

beau *n* a male romantic companion ⟨her *beau* brought flowers when he picked her up for their date⟩ — see BOYFRIEND

beau ideal *n* **1** someone of such unequaled perfection as to deserve imitation ⟨she is the *beau ideal* of the beautiful but unassuming film actress⟩ — see IDEAL 1

2 the most perfect type or example ⟨Frank Lloyd Wright's most famous architectural creation, Falling Water, is widely regarded as the *beau ideal* of a building in harmony with its setting⟩ — see QUINTESSENCE 1

beauteous *adj* very pleasing to look at ⟨a *beauteous* woman in a ball gown⟩ — see BEAUTIFUL

beauteousness *n* the qualities in a person or thing that as a whole give pleasure to the senses ⟨the *beauteousness* of the starlit evening put the couple in a very romantic mood⟩ — see BEAUTY 1

beautiful *adj* very pleasing to look at ⟨a strikingly *beautiful* child who is being eagerly pursued by all the modeling agencies⟩

synonyms attractive, beauteous, bonny [*chiefly British*], comely, cute, fair, gorgeous, handsome, knockout, lovely, pretty, ravishing, sightly, stunning, taking

related words alluring, appealing, charming, delightful, eye-catching, glamorous (*also* glamourous), prepossessing; elegant, exquisite, glorious, resplendent, splendid, statuesque, sublime, superb; flawless, perfect, radiant; dainty, delicate; personable, presentable

near antonyms abhorrent, abominable, bad, disagreeable, disgusting, dreadful, foul, frightful, ghastly, hideous, horrible, loathsome, nasty, nauseating, objectionable, offensive, repellent, repugnant, repulsive, revolting, shocking, sickening, terrible; unappealing, unappetizing, unpleasant, unpleasing, unprepossessing

antonyms homely, ill-favored, plain, ugly, unattractive, unbeautiful, unhandsome, unlovely, unpretty, unsightly

beautify *vb* to make more attractive by adding something that is beautiful or becoming ⟨*beautified* the roadside landscape by planting flowers⟩ — see DECORATE

beautifying *adj* serving to add beauty ⟨added one last *beautifying* ornament to the wreath and hung it on the door⟩ — see DECORATIVE

beauty *n* **1** the qualities in a person or thing that as a whole give pleasure to the senses ⟨her *beauty* was enough to take your breath away⟩

synonyms attractiveness, beauteousness, comeliness, cuteness, fairness, gorgeousness, handsomeness, looks, loveliness, prettiness

related words allure, appeal, attraction, glamour (*also* glamor); charm, elegance, exquisiteness, flawlessness, gloriousness, perfection, radiance, resplendence; desirability, desirableness

near antonyms dreadfulness, foulness, ghastliness, grotesqueness, hideousness, loathsomeness, nastiness, offensiveness, repellency, repulsiveness, unattractiveness; blemish, flaw, imperfection

antonyms homeliness, plainness, ugliness, unsightliness

2 a lovely woman ⟨she was quite a *beauty* in her younger days⟩

synonyms eyeful, goddess, knockout, stunner

related words belle, charmer, honey

near antonyms hag, horror, witch

3 something very good of its kind ⟨that fish is a *beauty*⟩ — see JIM-DANDY

because *conj* for the reason that ⟨I can't go to school *because* I don't feel well today⟩ — see SINCE

because of *prep* as the result of ⟨I was late for school *because of* the snowstorm, which made driving very hazardous⟩

synonyms due to, owing to, through, with

beckon *vb* to direct or notify by a movement or gesture ⟨*beckoned* the child to come closer⟩ — see MOTION

becloud *vb* **1** to make (something) unclear to the understanding ⟨don't *becloud* the discussion by raising unrelated issues⟩ — see CONFUSE 2

2 to make dark, dim, or indistinct ⟨the smog from the city's steel mills was once so great that it *beclouded* the local landscape even at noon⟩ — see CLOUD 1

beclouded *adj* **1** covered over by clouds ⟨a gloomy, *beclouded* sky that matched our mood⟩ — see OVERCAST

2 filled with or dimmed by fine particles (as of dust or water) in suspension ⟨the water was so *beclouded* by mud that I couldn't see the bottom⟩ — see HAZY 1

become *vb* to eventually have as a state or quality ⟨many people *became* sick with the flu⟩ ⟨with autumn the days *become* crisper and breezier⟩

synonyms come, get, go, grow, run, turn, wax

related words alter, change, metamorphose, modify, mutate, transfigure, transform, transmute

near antonyms abide, be, continue, linger, remain, stay

becoming *adj* meeting the requirements of a purpose or situation ⟨that's a particularly *becoming* dress for the dance⟩ — see FIT 1

bed *n* **1** a place set aside for sleeping ⟨the sofa in the living room will be your *bed* for the night⟩

synonyms bunk, pad, sack

related words bedstead, mattress, pallet; cot, couch, daybed, feather bed, four-poster, hammock, sofa, sofa bed, studio couch, trundle bed, water bed; bassinet, cradle, crib

2 the surface upon which a body of water lies ⟨some prospectors found gold in the *bed* of that mountain stream⟩ — see BOTTOM 2

bed *vb* to go to one's bed in order to sleep ⟨the campers all *bedded* down for the night around 9 pm⟩

synonyms retire, turn in

related words bunk, perch, roost, settle; doze, drop (off), nap, nod, sleep, slumber, snooze; couch, lie (down), recline

near antonyms arouse, awake, awaken, rouse, wake, waken; bestir, stir, wake; reawake, reawaken; shift, stir

antonyms arise, get up, rise, uprise

bedaub *vb* to rub an oily or sticky substance over ⟨the toddler delightedly *bedaubed* herself with her mother's makeup⟩ — see SMEAR 1

bedazzle *vb* to overpower with light ⟨the enormous chandelier *bedazzled* me⟩ — see DAZZLE

bedazzling *adj* giving off or reflecting much light ⟨*bedazzling* Christmas decorations⟩ — see BRIGHT 1

bedeck *vb* to make more attractive by adding something that is beautiful or becoming ⟨*bedecked* the house with hundreds of little lights for the party⟩ — see DECORATE

bedevil *vb* to cause persistent suffering to ⟨a lingering cold *bedeviled* me for over a month⟩ — see AFFLICT

bedevilment *n* the act of making unwelcome intrusions upon another ⟨constant *bedevilments* from my little brother kept me from finishing my work⟩ — see ANNOYANCE 1

bedim *vb* to make dark, dim, or indistinct ⟨the view from the mountain's summit is often *bedimmed* by haze⟩ — see CLOUD 1

bedizen *vb* to make more attractive by adding something that is beautiful or becoming ⟨an elderly actress *bedizening* herself with makeup and jewelry⟩ — see DECORATE

bedizened *adj* elaborately and often excessively decorated ⟨a *bedizened* dress that looked more like a Christmas tree than an article of clothing⟩ — see ORNATE

bedlam *n* a place of uproar or confusion ⟨there's no way I can get my homework done in this *bedlam*, so I'm going to the library⟩ — see MADHOUSE 2

bedrock *n* an immaterial thing upon which something else rests ⟨my religious faith is the *bedrock* of my life⟩ — see BASE 1

bedspread *n* a decorative cloth used as a top covering for a bed ⟨a beautiful *bedspread* that is a reproduction of an 18th-century design⟩ — see COUNTERPANE

beef *n* an expression of dissatisfaction, pain, or resentment ⟨an angry customer with a *beef* about our service⟩ — see COMPLAINT 1

beef *vb* to express dissatisfaction, pain, or resentment usually tiresomely ⟨he tends to stand around and *beef* for hours about any slight, real or imagined⟩ — see COMPLAIN

beef (up) *vb* **1** to increase the ability of (as a muscle) to exert physical force ⟨*beefed up* the walls with iron bars⟩ — see STRENGTHEN 1

2 to make markedly greater in measure or degree ⟨will *beef up* security for the next few days while the president is in town⟩ — see INTENSIFY

beefy *adj* strongly and heavily built ⟨a *beefy* man who worked in a warehouse all his life⟩ — see ¹HUSKY

beetle *vb* to extend outward beyond a usual point ⟨houses in the town commonly have second stories that *beetle* over the ground floors, and the overhang is known as a "bump"⟩ — see BULGE

befall *vb* to take place ⟨whatever *befalls*, we'll make the best of it⟩ — see HAPPEN

befit *vb* to be fitting or proper ⟨spoke politely of the deceased, as *befitted* the occasion⟩ — see DO 1

befitting *adj* meeting the requirements of a purpose or situation ⟨a *befitting* reply to a civil question⟩ — see FIT 1

befog *vb* 1 to make (something) unclear to the understanding ⟨the teacher's explanation only *befogged* the textbook's presentation of this scientific principle⟩ — see CONFUSE 2
2 to make dark, dim, or indistinct ⟨the morning murk *befogged* our view of the harbor⟩ — see CLOUD 1
3 to throw into a state of mental uncertainty ⟨completely *befogged* by the sudden change of subject⟩ — see CONFUSE 1

befogged *adj* filled with or dimmed by fine particles (as of dust or water) in suspension ⟨the *befogged* air of the construction site was so clogged with dust that I starting coughing⟩ — see HAZY 1

before *adv* so as to precede something in order of time ⟨their arrival was completely expected because a messenger had gone *before*⟩ — see AHEAD 1

before *prep* 1 earlier than ⟨since I'm a faster runner, I got there *before* him⟩
synonyms afore [*chiefly dialect*], ahead of, ere, of, previous to, prior to, to
related words till, until, up to
phrases in advance of
near antonyms next, next to, since
antonyms after, following
2 preceding in space ⟨the children always insisted on running *before* their parents⟩
synonyms afore [*chiefly dialect*], ahead of
related words against
phrases in advance of, in front of
antonyms after, following

beforehand *adv* 1 before the usual or expected time ⟨if you arrive *beforehand*, we won't be entirely prepared yet⟩ — see EARLY
2 so as to precede something in order of time ⟨if you get ready *beforehand*, you won't be late this time⟩ — see AHEAD 1

befoul *vb* 1 to make dirty ⟨mud and slush *befouls* the family car every winter⟩ — see DIRTY
2 to make unfit for use by the addition of something harmful or undesirable ⟨the enemy had *befouled* the water in all of the area's wells with animal carcasses⟩ — see CONTAMINATE

befuddle *vb* to throw into a state of mental uncertainty ⟨most of the class was *befuddled* by the wording of one of the questions on the test⟩ — see CONFUSE 1

befuddled *adj* suffering from mental confusion ⟨the *befuddled* professor was always forgetting where she'd left her glasses⟩ — see DIZZY 2

befuddlement *n* a state of mental uncertainty ⟨the library patron was in obvious *befuddlement* over where to find the appropriate references⟩ — see CONFUSION 1

beg *vb* to make a request to (someone) in an earnest or urgent manner ⟨she *begged* her mother to let her go on the Girl Scout camporee⟩
synonyms appeal (to), beseech, conjure, entreat, implore, importune, petition, plead (to), pray, solicit, supplicate
related words mooch, sponge; ask, desire, invoke, request, sue; claim, coerce, command, compel, demand, force, insist, require
phrases call on (*or* call upon)
near antonyms hint, imply, intimate, suggest; appease, conciliate, gratify, mollify, oblige, pacify, placate, please, satisfy; comfort, console, content, quiet

beget *vb* to become the father of ⟨the racehorse *begot* several Kentucky Derby winners⟩ — see FATHER

begetter *n* a person who establishes a whole new field of endeavor ⟨Michael Faraday is widely hailed as one of the *begetters* of electromagnetism, the field of study that sparked a technological revolution⟩ — see FATHER 2

beggar *n* a person who lives by public begging ⟨the poor *beggars* that are such a common sight in underdeveloped countries⟩
synonyms mendicant, panhandler
related words bum, drifter, hobo, tramp, vagabond, vagrant; pauper; hanger-on, leech, moocher, parasite, sponge, sponger; dependent; deadbeat, derelict, idler, ne'er-do-well

beggared *adj* lacking money or material possessions ⟨the family was completely *beggared* after the stock market crash⟩ — see POOR 1

beggary *n* the state of lacking sufficient money or material possessions ⟨too many people are homeless and living in *beggary* in this country⟩ — see POVERTY 1

begin *vb* 1 to take the first step in (a process or course of action) ⟨she *began* walking to school⟩
synonyms commence, embark (on *or* upon), enter (into *or* upon), get off, kick off, launch, open, start, strike (into)
related words create, generate, inaugurate, initiate, innovate, invent, originate; adopt, embrace, take on, take up; establish, father, found, institute, organize, pioneer, set up, spawn
phrases get to, set about
near antonyms cease, desist, discontinue, halt, lay off, quit, stop; close, complete; abandon, forsake, leave; abolish, demolish, destroy, exterminate, extinguish, phase out
antonyms conclude, end, finish, terminate
2 to come into existence ⟨the storm *began* late in the day and lasted all night⟩
synonyms arise, commence, dawn, form, materialize, originate, set in, spring, start
related words be, breathe, exist, live, subsist; appear, arrive, emerge; continue, endure, last, persist, survive
near antonyms conclude, desist, discontinue, finish, halt, quit, terminate; disappear, dissolve, evaporate, vanish; depart, die, expire, pass away, perish
antonyms cease, end, stop

beginner *n* a person who is just starting out in a field of activity ⟨although he is only a *beginner* at swimming, he is making excellent progress⟩
synonyms colt, fledgling, freshman, greenhorn, neophyte, newcomer, novice, recruit, rookie, tenderfoot, tyro
related words apprentice, cub; boot, novitiate; amateur, dilettante; learner, student, trainee; candidate, entrant, probationer
near antonyms expert, master, pro, professional
antonyms old hand, old-timer, vet, veteran

beginning *n* the point at which something begins ⟨the actual *beginning* of the universe is still under debate, with some scientists believing in the big bang theory⟩
synonyms alpha, birth, commencement, dawn, genesis, inception, incipiency, launch, morning, onset, outset, start, threshold
related words creation, inauguration, initiation, institution, origination; cradle, fountainhead, origin, root, source, spring, well, wellspring; dawning, opening; appearance, arrival, emergence; infancy

near antonyms cessation, closing, closure, completion, finale, finish, period, stop, termination, windup
antonyms close, conclusion, end, ending

begone *vb* to leave a place often for another ⟨in his frustration cried out, "*Begone* and let me finish my homework!"⟩ — see GO 2

begrime *vb* to make dirty ⟨years of spattered mud had *begrimed* the mailbox by the side of the road⟩ — see DIRTY

beguile *vb* **1** to attract or delight as if by magic ⟨the magician *beguiled* and amazed the children⟩ — see CHARM 1
2 to cause to believe what is untrue ⟨*beguiled* her into believing that yet another worthless item would enhance her life⟩ — see DECEIVE
3 to lead away from a usual or proper course by offering some pleasure or advantage ⟨was *beguiled* by the promise of easy money as a drug dealer⟩ — see LURE

beguiling *adj* **1** clever at attaining one's ends by indirect and often deceptive means ⟨a smart and *beguiling* child who can manipulate her parents with alarming ease⟩ — see ARTFUL 1
2 tending or having power to deceive ⟨the *beguiling* allure of a life of crime⟩ — see DECEPTIVE 1

behave *vb* to manage the actions of (oneself) in a particular way ⟨if she *behaves* herself properly and sits quietly during church, she will get ice cream afterward⟩
synonyms acquit, bear, comport, conduct, demean, deport, quit
related words check, collect, compose, constrain, contain, control, curb, handle, inhibit, quiet, repress, restrain; moderate, modulate, temper; act, impersonate, play
near antonyms act up, carry on, cut up, misbehave, misconduct

behavior *n* the way or manner in which one conducts oneself ⟨he promised to be on his best *behavior* for the party⟩
synonyms actions, bearing, comportment, conduct, demeanor, deportment
related words etiquette, form, manners, mores, proprieties; amenity, civility, courtesy, decorum, politeness; air, attitude, carriage, poise, pose, posture, presence; aspect, look, mien; formality, protocol, rules; custom, habit, pattern, practice (*also* practise), trick, wont; convention, fashion, form, mode, style; affectation, attribute, characteristic, mark, trait; distinctiveness, oddity, peculiarity, singularity, strangeness, uniqueness, weirdness

behead *vb* to cut off the head of ⟨Mary, Queen of Scots, was *beheaded* for plotting against Queen Elizabeth⟩ — see DECAPITATE

behemoth *n* something that is unusually large and powerful ⟨the newest car is a gas-guzzling *behemoth* that doesn't even fit in parking spaces⟩ — see GIANT

behest *n* a statement of what to do that must be obeyed by those concerned ⟨I only made the change at his *behest*⟩ — see COMMAND 1

behind *adj* not arriving, occurring, or settled at the due, usual, or proper time ⟨the required work was *behind*, so now we're running late⟩ — see LATE 1

behind *prep* **1** at, to, or toward the rear of ⟨she preferred to be *behind* the lead hikers, who were always too much in a rush to enjoy the scenery⟩
synonyms abaft, back of
near antonyms ahead of
antonyms before, in front of

2 subsequent to in time or order ⟨we arrived *behind* them⟩ — see AFTER

behindhand *adj* not arriving, occurring, or settled at the due, usual, or proper time ⟨the response was *behindhand*, just like everything else the company did⟩ — see LATE 1

behold *vb* to make note of (something) through the use of one's eyes ⟨I opened the window and *beheld* snow everywhere⟩ — see SEE 1

being *n* **1** a member of the human race ⟨no one has the right to enslave another *being*⟩ — see HUMAN
2 one that has a real and independent existence ⟨new parents are typically in awe at having created this separate *being*⟩ — see ENTITY

belabor *vb* to criticize harshly and usually publicly ⟨there's no need to *belabor* other people's flaws when you're hardly perfect yourself⟩ — see ATTACK 2

belated *adj* not arriving, occurring, or settled at the due, usual, or proper time ⟨a *belated* birthday card⟩ — see LATE 1

belatedness *n* the quality or state of being late ⟨the *belatedness* of the payment resulted in us being charged overdue fees⟩ — see LATENESS

belch *vb* to throw out or off (something from within) often violently ⟨the volcano *belched* lava and ash for days⟩ — see ERUPT 1

beldam *or* **beldame** *n* a mean or ugly old woman ⟨knocking on the *beldam's* door on Halloween was once an annual ritual for the kids in the neighborhood⟩ — see CRONE

beleaguer *vb* to surround (as a fortified place) with armed forces for the purpose of capturing or preventing commerce and communication ⟨*beleaguered* the castle for months⟩ — see BESIEGE

belie *vb* **1** to give a false idea of ⟨his bright smile *belied* his actual mood, which was really one of great sadness⟩
synonyms misrepresent
related words contradict; camouflage, cloak, conceal, counterfeit, disguise, hide, mask, obscure; color, deceive, distort, falsify, garble, mislead, twist; dissemble, feign, pretend
near antonyms bare, demonstrate, disclose, discover, exhibit, expose, evince, reveal; flaunt, parade, show off
antonyms betray, represent
2 to prove to be false ⟨the latest information *belies* the old theory⟩ — see DISPROVE

belief *n* **1** mental conviction of the truth of some statement or the reality of some being or phenomenon ⟨a *belief* in unicorns led him to look for them every time he walked through the woods⟩
synonyms credence, credit, faith
related words axiom, law, precept, principle, tenet; assurance, certainty, certitude, conviction, positiveness, sureness; confidence, dependance, reliance, trust; hope; doctrine, dogma, philosophy; dogmatism, fanaticism, insistence
near antonyms distrust, mistrust, skepticism, suspicion, uncertainty
antonyms disbelief, discredit, doubt, unbelief
2 an idea that is believed to be true or valid without positive knowledge ⟨it's my *belief* that the sky is blue because our eyes perceive the color blue easily⟩ — see OPINION 1

believable *adj* worthy of being accepted as true or reasonable ⟨she had a *believable* story for why her homework was late, so she didn't receive any punishment⟩
synonyms credible, likely, plausible, probable

related words acceptable, conceivable, imaginable, possible, practical, reasonable; dependable, reliable, trustworthy

near antonyms absurd, doubtful, dubious, fantastic, flimsy, outlandish, preposterous, questionable, ridiculous; impossible, inconceivable, unimaginable, unthinkable; skeptical, suspect, suspicious, uncertain, unsure; hopeless, unworkable, useless

antonyms far-fetched, implausible, improbable, incredible, unbelievable, unlikely

believe vb **1** to regard as right or true ⟨the teacher *believed* the student's explanation that the assignment was late because she was sick, even though she didn't bring in a note from the doctor⟩

synonyms accept, credit, swallow, trust

related words account, accredit, understand; assume, presume, suppose; conclude, deduce, infer

phrases set store by (*or* on)

near antonyms distrust, doubt, mistrust, question, suspect; challenge, dispute

antonyms disbelieve, discredit, reject

2 to have as an opinion ⟨he *believed* that his favorite tennis player was the best in the world⟩

synonyms consider, deem, feel, figure, guess, hold, imagine, reckon [*chiefly dialect*], suppose, think

related words esteem, regard, view; accept, conceive, perceive; depend, rely, trust; assume, presume, presuppose; conclude, deduce, infer

near antonyms distrust, doubt, mistrust, question, suspect; disbelieve, discredit, reject

belittle vb to speak scornfully one's low opinion of ⟨*belittled* the new kid's abilities as a basketball player⟩ — see DECRY 1

belittlement n the act of making a person or a thing seem little or unimportant ⟨the teacher's public *belittlement* of her artistic talents made her cry⟩ — see DEPRECIATION

belittling adj intended to make a person or thing seem of little importance or value ⟨there's no need for *belittling* comments about your brother's trumpet playing⟩ — see DEROGATORY

bellicose adj feeling or displaying eagerness to fight ⟨*bellicose* hockey players who always seemed to be in a fight⟩ — see BELLIGERENT

bellicosity n an inclination to fight or quarrel ⟨the *bellicosity* of the countries on the Balkan Peninsula over the centuries⟩ — see BELLIGERENCE

belligerence n an inclination to fight or quarrel ⟨among the Native American tribes of the Colonial period, the Iroquois were known for their *belligerence*⟩

synonyms aggression, aggressiveness, bellicosity, combativeness, contentiousness, disputatiousness, fight, militancy, pugnacity, scrappiness, truculence

related words antagonism, fierceness, hostility, unfriendliness; acidity, biliousness, crabbiness, crankiness, crossness, disagreeableness, fretfulness, grouchiness, grumpiness, huffiness, irascibility, irritability, irritableness, orneriness, peevishness, pettishness, petulance, querulousness, rudeness, surliness, testiness, waspishness

phrases chip on one's shoulder

near antonyms affability, amiability, amicability, benevolence, complaisance, cordiality, friendliness, geniality, graciousness, pleasantness, sociability; gentleness, kindliness, mildness

antonyms pacifism

belligerent adj feeling or displaying eagerness to fight ⟨the coach became quite *belligerent* and spit on an umpire after being thrown out of the game⟩

synonyms aggressive, argumentative, bellicose, combative, contentious, discordant, disputatious, gladiatorial, militant, pugnacious, quarrelsome, scrappy, truculent, warlike

related words antagonistic, fierce, hostile, hot-tempered; acidic, bearish, bilious, choleric, crabby, cranky, cross, disagreeable, dyspeptic, fretful, grouchy, grumpy, huffy, ill-humored, ill-natured, ill-tempered, irascible, irritable, ornery, peevish, pettish, petulant, querulous, rude, snappish, snappy, surly, testy, touchy, ugly, waspish; battling, fighting, warring

phrases on the warpath

near antonyms affable, amiable, amicable, benevolent, complaisant, conciliatory, cordial, easygoing, friendly, genial, good-natured, good-tempered, gracious, ingratiating, obliging, pleasant, sociable; calm, quiet, relaxed, serene, tranquil; benign, gentle, kindly, mild

antonyms nonbelligerent, pacific, peaceable, peaceful

bellow vb to make a long loud deep noise or cry ⟨the cow *bellowed* for her calf⟩ — see ROAR

belly n the part of the body between the chest and the pelvis ⟨a baby with a round little *belly*⟩ — see STOMACH

belly vb to extend outward beyond a usual point ⟨the sails slowly *bellied* as the wind picked up⟩ — see BULGE

bellyache n abdominal pain especially when focused in the digestive organs ⟨eating too many apples will give you a *bellyache*⟩ — see STOMACHACHE

bellyache vb to express dissatisfaction, pain, or resentment usually tiresomely ⟨I'm tired of the whole class *bellyaching* that I assign too much homework⟩ — see COMPLAIN

belong vb **1** to have or be in a usual or proper place ⟨your shoes *belong* in the closet, not out on the floor where people will trip on them⟩

synonyms go

related words place, stay; fit (in)

2 to be the property of a person or group of persons ⟨those textbooks *belong* to the school system, and you have to give them back at the end of the year⟩

synonyms appertain, pertain

related words have, hold, own, possess

belongings n pl transportable items that one owns ⟨packed up all his *belongings* and moved across the country⟩ — see POSSESSION 2

beloved adj granted special treatment or attention ⟨her *beloved* cat sleeps in its own little bed⟩ — see DARLING 1

beloved n a person with whom one is in love ⟨he is planning to ask his *beloved* to marry him⟩ — see SWEETHEART

below adv **1** in or to a lower place ⟨he climbed *below* to fix the engine⟩

synonyms beneath, under, underneath

related words beside, near, nearby

near antonyms aloft, overhead

antonyms up

2 toward or in a lower position ⟨when rock climbing I know that if I look *below*, I'll become paralyzed with fear⟩ — see DOWN

below prep in a lower position than ⟨she sat *below* everyone else, on the floor⟩

synonyms beneath, under

related words underneath
antonyms above, over

¹**belt** *n* a hard strike with a part of the body or an instrument ⟨delivered a shattering *belt* to the rock with a hammer⟩ — see ¹BLOW

²**belt** *n* a strip of flexible material (as leather) worn around the waist ⟨he loves his fancily decorated *belt*, but only gets to wear it on special occasions⟩
synonyms cincture, cummerbund, girdle, sash
related words band, waistband; circle, loop, ribbon, ring; baldric, bandolier (*or* bandoleer)
2 a broad geographical area ⟨that part of the country is sometimes called a "farm *belt*" because of the number of farms there⟩ — see REGION 2

belt *vb* **1** to deliver a blow to (someone or something) usually in a strong vigorous manner ⟨*belted* the baseball out of the park⟩ — see HIT 1
2 to encircle or bind with or as if with a belt ⟨*belted* the pants tightly so they would stay up⟩ — see GIRD 1
3 to strike repeatedly ⟨*belted* the punching bag over and over⟩ — see BEAT 1

bemoan *vb* **1** to feel or express sorrow for ⟨*bemoaned* the death of his pet goldfish⟩ — see LAMENT 1
2 to feel sorry or dissatisfied about ⟨there's no reason to *bemoan* your workload, since others have more⟩ — see REGRET

bemoaning *adj* expressing or suggesting mourning ⟨one parishioner who always seems to have a *bemoaning* expression on her face⟩ — see MOURNFUL 1

bemuse *vb* to throw into a state of mental uncertainty ⟨the stage mishap momentarily *bemused* the actress⟩ — see CONFUSE 1

bench *n* a public official having authority to decide questions of law ⟨appealed to the *bench* for leniency⟩ — see JUDGE 2

benchmark *n* something set up as an example against which others of the same type are compared ⟨this prize-winning essay will be the *benchmark* against which all others will be judged in future years⟩ — see STANDARD 1

bend *n* **1** something that curves or is curved ⟨it's hard to see around that *bend* in the road, so be careful⟩
synonyms angle, arc, arch, bow, crook, curvature, curve, turn, wind
related words kink, warp; circle, ring, ringlet, round; coil, curl, curlicue (*also* curlycue), flexure, fold, loop, spiral, swirl, twist; decline, inclination, incline, slope; corner, turnoff
antonyms straight line
2 the act of positioning or an instance of being positioned at an angle ⟨did knee *bends* for exercise⟩ — see TILT

bend *vb* **1** to cause to turn away from a straight line ⟨she *bent* the knife when she got it stuck in the drawer⟩
synonyms arch, crook, curve, hook, swerve
related words arc, bow, round; deflect, divert; entwine, kink, swirl, turn, twine, twist, veer, warp; coil, curl, loop, spiral; dent, dimple; meander, weave, wind; decline, incline, slope
antonyms straighten, unbend, uncurl
2 to occupy (oneself) diligently or with close attention ⟨*bent* herself to the task for the rest of the day⟩ — see APPLY 2
3 to point or turn (something) toward a target or goal ⟨*bent* all of his efforts toward winning the science award⟩ — see AIM 1
4 to turn away from a straight line or course ⟨the stream *bends* slightly to the east⟩ — see CURVE 1

bending *adj* marked by a long series of irregular curves ⟨the river takes a long *bending* path to the sea⟩ — see CROOKED 1

beneath *adv* in or to a lower place ⟨a ranch house with all of the rooms on one floor and a combined basement and garage *beneath*⟩ — see BELOW 1

beneath *prep* in a lower position than ⟨sat *beneath* him, on the floor⟩ — see BELOW

benediction *n* a prayer calling for divine care, protection, or favor ⟨the priest offered a *benediction* for the lost children⟩ — see BLESSING 1

benefaction *n* a gift of money or its equivalent to a charity, humanitarian cause, or public institution ⟨the generous *benefaction* from an anonymous donor meant the animal shelter could stay open⟩ — see CONTRIBUTION

benefactor *n* one that helps another with gifts or money ⟨an anonymous *benefactor* gave our school a dozen new computers⟩
synonyms donator, donor, patron
related words almsgiver, philanthropist; contributor, giver; subscriber, supporter, helper

beneficence *n* a gift of money or its equivalent to a charity, humanitarian cause, or public institution ⟨the library stays open primarily through *beneficences* from concerned residents⟩ — see CONTRIBUTION

beneficent *adj* **1** having or marked by sympathy and consideration for others ⟨a *beneficent* couple who are regular volunteers at a homeless shelter⟩ — see HUMANE 1
2 having or showing a concern for the welfare of others ⟨a *beneficent* effort to help out the needy during the holidays⟩ — see CHARITABLE 1

beneficial *adj* conferring benefits; promoting or contributing to personal or social well-being ⟨tutoring can often be as *beneficial* and rewarding for the tutor as for the student receiving the help⟩
synonyms advantageous, favorable, helpful, profitable, salutary
related words gratifying, rewarding, satisfying; promising, propitious; advisable, desirable, healthful, healthy, salubrious, wholesome
near antonyms bad, damaging, deleterious, harmful, injurious, unfavorable, unhelpful
antonyms disadvantageous, unfavorable, unhelpful

benefit *n* **1** a thing that helps ⟨it would be a real *benefit* if you could keep track of what you have already bought⟩ — see HELP 2
2 something that provides happiness or does good for a person or thing ⟨the meal service is a great *benefit* to invalids and the elderly⟩ — see BLESSING 2

benefit *vb* to provide with something useful or desirable ⟨his summer job *benefited* him in two ways: by giving him spending money and by offering some work experience⟩
synonyms avail, profit, serve
related words succeed, work (for); aid, assist, help, improve; content, delight, gladden, gratify, please, satisfy; bless
near antonyms hinder, impede; damage, harm, hurt, impair, injure; afflict, distress, upset

benevolence *n* kindly concern, interest, or support ⟨her *benevolence* towards her employees was such that she let one live in her home⟩ — see GOODWILL 1

benevolent *adj* **1** having or marked by sympathy and consideration for others ⟨a *benevolent* teacher would accept that a death in the family is grounds for an extension⟩ — see HUMANE 1

2 having or showing a concern for the welfare of others ⟨a *benevolent* businessman who has donated money and time to helping inner-city youths⟩ — see CHARITABLE 1

benighted *adj* lacking in education or the knowledge gained from books ⟨the poor *benighted* souls who do not know the joys of reading⟩ — see IGNORANT 1

benign *adj* not harsh or stern especially in manner, nature, or effect ⟨a *benign* sun on a day in early spring⟩ — see GENTLE 1

benignant *adj* having or marked by sympathy and consideration for others ⟨a *benignant* person would not be cold to strangers⟩ — see HUMANE 1

benison *n* a prayer calling for divine care, protection, or favor ⟨during the harbor festival the parish priest offered a *benison* for the local fishermen⟩ — see BLESSING 1

bent *n* a habitual attraction to some activity or thing ⟨a person of a literary *bent*⟩ — see INCLINATION 1

bent (*on or* upon) *adj* fully committed to achieving a goal ⟨she was so *bent on* completing her science project that she stayed up all night⟩ — see DETERMINED

benumb *vb* to reduce or weaken in strength or feeling ⟨a succession of personal tragedies *benumbed* him to all grief⟩ — see DULL 1

benumbed *adj* lacking in sensation or feeling ⟨my *benumbed* ears took a few minutes to warm up after the frigid air outside⟩ — see NUMB

bequeath *vb* to give by means of a will ⟨he *bequeathed* his house to his local church⟩ — see LEAVE 2

bequest *n* something that is or may be inherited ⟨left small *bequests* to all of her nieces and nephews⟩ — see INHERITANCE

berate *vb* to criticize (someone) severely or angrily especially for personal failings ⟨there's no need to *berate* someone for making a mistake during the first day on the job⟩ — see SCOLD

bereaved *adj* suffering the death of a loved one ⟨the *bereaved* parents cried often in the first year⟩
synonyms bereft
related words orphaned, widowed; distressed, grieving, melancholy, miserable, mournful, mourning, sad, sorrowing, suffering, unhappy, upset; bemoaning, crying, lamenting, wailing, weeping

bereft *adj* **1** suffering the death of a loved one ⟨she was *bereft* when her grandfather died⟩ — see BEREAVED
2 utterly lacking in something needed, wanted, or expected ⟨a cheap motel completely *bereft* of all amenities⟩ — see DEVOID 1

berserk *adv* in a confused and reckless manner ⟨the familiar scene in horror movies where everyone runs *berserk* as the monster destroys everything in sight⟩ — see HELTER-SKELTER 1

berth *n* an assignment at which one regularly works for pay ⟨found a *berth* at a travel agency⟩ — see JOB 1

beseech *vb* to make a request to (someone) in an earnest or urgent manner ⟨Sarah *beseeched* her boss to let her leave work early to attend to personal business⟩ — see BEG

beseeching *adj* asking humbly ⟨a *beseeching* letter from his parents asking him to pay them a visit⟩ — see SUPPLIANT

beset *vb* to take sudden, violent action against ⟨the tourists were suddenly *beset* by robbers⟩ — see ATTACK 1

beside *prep* **1** in addition to ⟨I'll need one more helper *beside* all of you⟩ — see BESIDES 1

2 not including ⟨I need four books *beside* this one⟩ — see EXCEPT

besides *adv* in addition to what has been said ⟨"*Besides*," Dan exclaimed, "I don't even play on the team!"⟩ — see MORE 1

besides *prep* **1** in addition to ⟨*besides* me, there are five people working on this project⟩
synonyms as well as, beside, over and above
related words plus; including
phrases along with, together with
near antonyms except (*also* excepting); less, minus
2 not including ⟨your essays should be three pages long *besides* the bibliography⟩ — see EXCEPT

besiege *vb* to surround (as a fortified place) with armed forces for the purpose of capturing or preventing commerce and communication ⟨the army *besieged* the fort for six months before it finally surrendered⟩
synonyms beleaguer, blockade, invest
related words barricade, block, cut off, dam, encircle; assail, assault, attack, beset; confine, insulate, isolate, quarantine
phrases lay siege to
near antonyms emancipate, free, liberate, release, rescue

besmear *vb* to rub an oily or sticky substance over ⟨*besmeared* the mirror with jelly⟩ — see SMEAR 1

besmirch *vb* to make dirty ⟨*besmirched* the white bedsheets with their dirty feet⟩ — see DIRTY

besmirched *adj* not clean ⟨wiped the toddler's *besmirched* face with a damp cloth⟩ — see DIRTY 1

bespatter *vb* to wet or soil by striking with something liquid or mushy ⟨vehicle after passing vehicle *bespattered* the sides of my once-clean car with that wintry slush⟩ — see SPLASH 2

bespeak *vb* **1** to arrange to have something (as a hotel room) held for one's future use ⟨*bespoke* the rental car weeks in advance of their trip⟩ — see RESERVE 1
2 to make known (something abstract) through outward signs ⟨her expression throughout the meeting *bespoke* great boredom⟩ — see SHOW 2

best *n* **1** dressy clothing ⟨a mother who still believes that you should wear your *best* to church⟩ — see FINERY
2 individuals carefully selected as being the best of a class ⟨only the *best* will go on to the finals⟩ — see ELITE

best *vb* to achieve a victory over ⟨at last she *bested* her card-playing mother at the game of hearts⟩ — see BEAT 2

bestow *vb* to make a present of ⟨*bestowed* a new car on their son for graduation⟩ — see GIVE 1

bestowal *n* something given to someone without expectation of a return ⟨the *bestowal* of holiday bonuses was a nice touch⟩ — see GIFT 1

bestrew *vb* to cover by or as if by scattering something over or on ⟨the flower girl *bestrewed* the aisle with rose petals⟩ — see SCATTER 2

bet *n* the money or thing risked on the outcome of an uncertain event ⟨she offered the *bet* of a free lunch if her team won the World Series⟩
synonyms stake, wager
related words collateral; jackpot, kitty, pot

bet *vb* to risk (something) on the outcome of an uncertain event ⟨he *bet* a month's allowance on the World Series⟩
synonyms gamble, go, lay, stake, wager
related words bid, offer; adventure, chance, hazard, speculate, venture; endanger, imperil, jeopardize

bête noire *n* **1** something or someone that causes fear or dread especially without reason ⟨as with so many students, her *bête noire* has always been the algebra test⟩ — see BOGEY 1

2 something or someone that is hated ⟨in the minds of that organization, society's biggest *bête noire* should be the drunk driver of a motor vehicle⟩ — see HATE 2

betide *vb* to take place ⟨we will be happy in our new home, whatever may *betide*⟩ — see HAPPEN

betray *vb* **1** to be unfaithful or disloyal to ⟨childhood friends of movie stars often *betray* them by telling their secrets to the supermarket tabloids⟩

synonyms cross, double-cross, sell (out)

related words give away; inform (on), rat (on), snitch (on), split (on) [*British*], tell (on)

phrases go back on

near antonyms defend, guard, protect, safeguard, save, shield

2 to make known (something abstract) through outward signs ⟨his face *betrayed* his exasperation with his nosy neighbor⟩ — see SHOW 2

betrayal *n* the act or fact of violating the trust or confidence of another ⟨the terrible *betrayal* of having her best friend reveal her confidences to others⟩

synonyms disloyalty, double cross, faithlessness, falseness, falsity, infidelity, perfidy, sellout, treachery, treason, unfaithfulness

related words abandonment, desertion; deceit, deception, double-dealing, duplicity, guile; fraud, informing, lying, snitching, talebearing, trickery

near antonyms dependability, reliability, trustworthiness; allegiance, devotion, faithfulness, fealty, fidelity, loyalty, staunchness, steadfastness; defense, protection, safeguard, shield

betrayer *n* **1** a person who provides secret information about another's wrongdoing ⟨the arrested drug dealer vowed that he would get his revenge on his *betrayer*⟩ — see INFORMER

2 one who betrays a trust or an allegiance ⟨the *betrayer* of Anne Frank's family in Amsterdam has never been identified for certain⟩ — see TRAITOR

betrothal *n* the act or state of being engaged to be married ⟨the couple's *betrothal* lasted four years⟩ — see ENGAGEMENT 1

betrothed *adj* pledged in marriage ⟨a splendid party in honor of the *betrothed* couple⟩ — see ENGAGED

betrothed *n* the person to whom one is engaged to be married ⟨he gazed lovingly at his *betrothed* throughout dinner⟩

synonyms fiancé, fiancée, intended

related words admirer, beau, beloved, boyfriend, darling, dear, favorite, fellow, flame, girlfriend, honey, love, lover, steady, swain, sweet, sweetheart, valentine; bride, groom

better *adv* to a greater or higher extent ⟨he knows this material *better* than anyone else⟩ — see MORE 2

better *n* **1** one who is above another in rank, station, or office ⟨be polite to your *betters* and to your inferiors in equal measure⟩ — see SUPERIOR

2 the more favorable condition or position in a competition ⟨she got the *better* of her opponents very early in the race⟩ — see ADVANTAGE 1

better *vb* **1** to be greater, better, or stronger than ⟨this year's profits should *better* last year's by a wide margin⟩ — see SURPASS 1

2 to make better ⟨social workers and reformers trying to *better* the lives of inner-city residents⟩ — see IMPROVE

bettor *or* **better** *n* one that bets (as on the outcome of a contest or sports event) ⟨*bettors* on the horse race have to place their bets at least 20 minutes before the start of the race⟩

synonyms gambler, wagerer

related words dicer; speculator

beverage *n* a liquid suitable for drinking ⟨would anyone like a *beverage* with their snack?⟩ — see DRINK 1

bewail *vb* to feel or express sorrow for ⟨he spent more time *bewailing* his predicament than trying to fix it⟩ — see LAMENT 1

bewailing *adj* expressing or suggesting mourning ⟨the doctor assured us that my father was not in any danger of dying, hence those *bewailing* looks on our faces were uncalled-for⟩ — see MOURNFUL 1

beware (of) *vb* to be cautious of or on guard against ⟨*beware of* that parrot because it bites⟩

synonyms guard (against), mind, watch out (for)

related words attend, heed, mark, note, notice; behold, discern, observe, perceive, see, watch

phrases be on the lookout for, look out for

near antonyms discount, disregard, ignore, miss, overlook

bewilder *vb* to throw into a state of mental uncertainty ⟨the change in policy seems to have *bewildered* many of our customers⟩ — see CONFUSE 1

bewildered *adj* suffering from mental confusion ⟨the *bewildered* child wandered aimlessly around the playground⟩ — see DIZZY 2

bewilderment *n* a state of mental uncertainty ⟨the slightest change in her daily routine leaves her in complete *bewilderment*⟩ — see CONFUSION 1

bewitch *vb* **1** to cast a spell on ⟨a wicked fairy *bewitched* Sleeping Beauty so that she would sleep for a hundred years⟩

synonyms charm, enchant, hex, spell

related words curse, jinx, possess; attract, beguile, captivate, fascinate, mesmerize, spellbind; entice, lure, seduce, tempt

near antonyms bless

2 to attract or delight as if by magic ⟨an animated film that *bewitches* children and adults alike⟩ — see CHARM 1

bewitched *adj* being or appearing to be under a magic spell ⟨the *bewitched* princess could not be awakened but by a kiss from the prince who will marry her⟩ — see ENCHANTED

bewitching *adj* having an often mysterious or magical power to attract ⟨a *bewitching* woman who never lacked for suitors⟩ — see FASCINATING 1

bewitchment *n* **1** a spoken word or set of words believed to have magic power ⟨the hope that there was some *bewitchment* that would turn their jerky son-in-law into a prince⟩ — see SPELL 1

2 the power to control natural forces through supernatural means ⟨while stuck in traffic, I could have used a bit of *bewitchment* to clear the road of other drivers⟩ — see MAGIC 1

beyond *adv* at or to a greater distance or more advanced point ⟨the dream that someday we will explore the outer reaches of our solar system and *beyond*⟩ — see FARTHER

beyond *prep* **1** on or to the farther side of ⟨the arrow flew *beyond* the fence and in the woods⟩

synonyms over, past

related words outside

near antonyms inside

2 out of the reach or sphere of ⟨although the school can keep you from screaming during school hours, making someone be quiet after school is *beyond* their authority⟩
synonyms outside, outside of, without
related words except (*also* excepting)
near antonyms inside
antonyms within

bias *n* an attitude that always favors one way of feeling or acting especially without considering any other possibilities ⟨he had a powerful *bias* towards doing all math problems by the same method, regardless of the problem⟩
synonyms favor, one-sidedness, partiality, partisanship, prejudice
related words favoritism, nepotism; bent, inclination, leaning, penchant, predilection, predisposition, proclivity, propensity, tendency; preconception, prejudgment
near antonyms calm, detachment, dispassion, indifference; aversion, dislike, distaste
antonyms impartiality, neutrality, objectivity, openmindedness

bias *vb* to cause to have often negative opinions formed without sufficient knowledge ⟨bad reviews *biased* her against the movie, even though it starred one of her favorite actors⟩ — see PREJUDICE

biased *adj* inclined to favor one side over another ⟨the *biased* judge always gave much harder sentences to minorities⟩ — see PARTIAL 1

Bible *n* a book made up of the writings accepted by Christians as coming from God ⟨she received a lovely *Bible* as a First Communion gift⟩
synonyms Book, Good Book, Holy Writ, Scripture

bicker *n* an often noisy or angry expression of differing opinions ⟨after a prolonged *bicker*, they finally chose a movie both of them were interested in seeing⟩ — see ARGUMENT 1

bicker *vb* to express different opinions about something often angrily ⟨if you two don't stop *bickering* about where to go to eat, we're not going out at all!⟩ — see ARGUE 2

bid *vb* to issue orders to (someone) by right of authority ⟨the servants were expected to do exactly as they were *bidden*⟩ — see COMMAND 1

bide *vb* to remain in place in readiness or expectation of something ⟨she *bided* for a while outside the store until it opened⟩ — see WAIT

big *adj* **1** having great meaning or lasting effect ⟨there will be a *big* meeting to resolve the issue⟩ — see IMPORTANT 1
2 of a size greater than average of its kind ⟨bought a *big* apple to quench his raging appetite⟩ — see LARGE

bight *n* a part of a body of water that extends beyond the general shoreline ⟨the *bight* known as the Bay of Fundy is known for its fast-running tides⟩ — see GULF 1

bigness *n* the quality or state of being large in size ⟨the sheer *bigness* of the fifty-pound pumpkin made us want to buy it⟩ — see LARGENESS

bigoted *adj* unwilling to grant other people social rights or to accept other viewpoints ⟨*bigoted* people once believed that black people were naturally inferior and unqualified to vote⟩ — see INTOLERANT 2

bilious *adj* having or showing a habitually bad temper ⟨a *bilious* old dog who snaps at everyone⟩ — see ILL-TEMPERED

biliousness *n* readiness to show annoyance or impatience ⟨her *biliousness* was such that most people simply avoided her⟩ — see PETULANCE

¹bill *n* **1** a record of goods sold or services performed together with the costs due ⟨luckily, the amount due on our electric *bill* wasn't too high this month, because we finally convinced everyone to stop wasting electricity⟩
synonyms account, check, invoice, statement, tab
related words receipt, reckoning; document, record; charge, cost, expense, fee, price, rate, toll; score, tally
2 a piece of printed paper used as money ⟨the United States twenty-dollar *bill* has a picture of Andrew Jackson on the front⟩
synonyms bank note, greenback, note
related words paper money, scrip; buck, dollar; cash, chips, currency, dough, legal tender, lucre, money, pelf; check, draft, money order
3 a sheet bearing an announcement for posting in a public place ⟨posted a *bill* advertising the new play⟩ — see POSTER
4 the amount owed at a bar or restaurant or the slip of paper stating the amount ⟨Dad always pays the *bill* when we go out to eat⟩ — see CHECK 1

²bill *n* **1** the jaws of a bird together with their hornlike covering ⟨parrots have very strong *bills* so they can break open nuts⟩ — see BEAK
2 the projecting front part of a hat or cap ⟨the hat was blue, but the *bill* was red⟩ — see VISOR

¹billet *n* a straight piece (as of wood or metal) that is longer than it is wide ⟨a stack of gold *billets* in the vault⟩ — see BAR 1

²billet *n* an assignment at which one regularly works for pay ⟨found a *billet* at one of the leading brokerage houses in New York⟩ — see JOB 1

billet *vb* to provide with living quarters or shelter ⟨every colonial household was expected to *billet* a British soldier⟩ — see HOUSE 1

bill of fare *n* a list of foods served at or available for a meal ⟨most restaurants in the resort town post their *bill of fare* outside the front door so tourists know what to expect⟩ — see MENU 1

billow *n* a moving ridge on the surface of water ⟨the great *billows* created by the ocean storm threatened to swamp the fishing boat⟩ — see WAVE

billow *vb* to extend outward beyond a usual point ⟨the curtains in the open windows *billowed* in the summer wind⟩ — see BULGE

billy *n* a heavy rigid stick used as a weapon or for punishment ⟨police officers carry a *billy* for protection⟩ — see CLUB 1

binary *adj* consisting of two members or parts that are usually joined ⟨a *binary* star is a system of two stars that revolve around each other under their mutual gravitation⟩ — see DOUBLE 1

bind *vb* **1** to confine or restrain with or as if with chains ⟨prisons tend to *bind* convicted criminals for transport⟩ ⟨Angie feels *bound* to her boyfriend by love and loyalty⟩
synonyms chain, enchain, fetter, handcuff, manacle, shackle, trammel
related words lash, pinion, secure, tie, truss; attach, fasten, join, link; confine, constrain, curb, hamper, hinder, limit, restrict; entangle, tangle
near antonyms emancipate, free, liberate, loose, release, rescue; undo, unfasten, untangle, untie; detach, disengage
antonyms unbind, unfetter

2 to cover with a bandage ⟨*bind* the wound to stop the bleeding⟩ — see BANDAGE

3 to gather into a tight mass by means of a line or cord ⟨*bind* the asparagus spears carefully before packing the bunches⟩ — see TIE 1

binge *n* a time or instance of carefree fun ⟨a shopping *binge* at the mall⟩ — see FLING 1

biography *n* a history of a person's life ⟨an unauthorized *biography* of the actor made him very unhappy⟩

synonyms life, memoir

related words autobiography; chronicle, history, past, story; obituary; character sketch

bipartite *adj* consisting of two members or parts that are usually joined ⟨separated the *bipartite* rock⟩ — see DOUBLE 1

birch *vb* to strike repeatedly with something long and thin or flexible ⟨students at the private school were once routinely *birched* for violating the rules⟩ — see WHIP 1

bird *n* a member of the human race ⟨they're a couple of tough old *birds* who can manage without any interference from their grandchildren⟩ — see HUMAN

birdman *n* one who flies or is qualified to fly an aircraft or spacecraft ⟨in the early days of aviation, *birdmen* would travel around the country in their biplanes, putting on flying shows⟩ — see PILOT

bird's–eye *adj* relating to the main elements and not to specific details ⟨a *bird's-eye* look at the current situation in that part of the world⟩ — see GENERAL 2

birth *n* **1** the act or instance of being born ⟨biology class will be showing a movie of the *birth* of kittens⟩

synonyms nativity

related words creation, genesis, origination, rise; bearing, childbearing, labor, parturition; begetting, breeding, fathering, generation, mothering, reproduction, siring, spawning; fatherhood, maternity, motherhood, parenthood, paternity

near antonyms abortion, miscarriage

2 the line of ancestors from whom a person is descended ⟨a man of noble *birth*⟩ — see ANCESTRY

3 the point at which something begins ⟨that 12-second flight by Orville Wright marked the *birth* of aviation⟩ — see BEGINNING

birthright *n* **1** something that is or may be inherited ⟨believed that the house was her *birthright*⟩ — see INHERITANCE

2 something to which one has a just claim ⟨the promotion is his *birthright*, after the work he put in⟩ — see RIGHT 1

bisect *vb* to divide by passing through or across ⟨the infamous concrete wall that once *bisected* the city of Berlin, Germany⟩ — see INTERSECT

bit *n* **1** a very small piece ⟨she left only a *bit* of the broccoli on her plate, so she was allowed to have dessert⟩

synonyms atom, crumb, fleck, flyspeck, grain, granule, molecule, morsel, mote, nubbin, particle, patch, scrap, scruple, snippet, speck, tittle

related words ace, dab, glimmer, hint, hoot, iota, jot, lick, little, mite, modicum, ounce, peanuts, pinch, ray, shade, shred, smidgen (*also* smidgeon *or* smidgin), spot, strain, streak, suspicion, taste, touch, trace, whisper, whit; dash, driblet, drop; fragment, part, portion, section; bite, mouthful, nibble; handful, scattering, smattering, sprinkling; dose, shot; damn, darn; chip, flake, shard, shiver, sliver, splinter; clipping, paring, shaving; smithereens

near antonyms chunk, gob, lump, hunk, slab; abundance, barrel, bucket, bushel, deal, heaps, loads, mass, mountain, much, peck, pile, plenty, pot, profusion, quantity, raft, scads, stack, volume, wad, wealth

2 a broken or irregular part of something that often remains incomplete ⟨*bits* of cookie scattered on the table⟩ — see FRAGMENT

3 a very small amount ⟨I'll have only a *bit* of food right now⟩ — see PARTICLE 1

4 an indefinite but usually short period of time ⟨this will only take a *bit*⟩ — see WHILE 1

bite *n* **1** a harsh or sharp quality ⟨the fall winds had a real *bite*⟩ — see EDGE 1

2 a small piece or quantity of food ⟨had only a *bite* to eat before rushing off⟩ — see MORSEL 1

3 an uncomfortable degree of coolness ⟨weather with a *bite* that suggested winter was right around the corner⟩ — see CHILL

bite (at) *vb* to consume or wear away gradually ⟨the waves were *biting at* the sand castle I had worked so hard on⟩ — see EAT 2

bite (on) *vb* to crush or grind with the teeth ⟨she likes to *bite on* her pencils when she thinks hard⟩

synonyms champ, chew, chomp (on), crunch (on), gnaw (on), masticate, nibble

related words lap, lick, munch; consume, eat, ingest, swallow; bolt, devour, gobble (up *or* down), gorge, gulp, scarf, scoff, snack, wolf; peck (at), pick (at)

biting *adj* **1** causing intense discomfort to one's skin ⟨a *biting* wind that only the toughest football fans were willing to endure⟩ — see CUTTING 1

2 causing intense mental or physical distress ⟨a *biting* criticism that left the student in tears⟩ — see SHARP 2

3 marked by the use of wit that is intended to cause hurt feelings ⟨the *biting* comments by the popular girls about the new kid in class⟩ — see SARCASTIC

bitter *adj* **1** having or showing deep-seated resentment ⟨a *bitter* attitude about always having to work on Saturday⟩ ⟨she's still *bitter* about the way her boyfriend broke up with her⟩

synonyms acrid, acrimonious, embittered, hard, rancorous, resentful, sore

related words disaffected, discontented, disgruntled, malcontent; contemptuous, cynical, disdainful, scornful; angry, cruel, harsh, irritated, mad, rough, savage, vicious; acid, caustic, cutting, mordant, sarcastic, trenchant

near antonyms caring, forgiving, gentle, kind, loving, sweet, sympathetic, tender, warm, warmhearted

2 hard to accept or bear especially emotionally ⟨discovering that he had been cut from the team was a *bitter* disappointment⟩

synonyms afflicting, agonizing, cruel, excruciating, galling, grievous, harrowing, harsh, heartrending, hurtful, painful, tormenting, torturous

related words insufferable, insupportable, intolerable, unacceptable, unbearable, unendurable, unsupportable; appalling, awful, bad, dire, dreadful, ghastly, horrible, miserable, nasty, rotten, terrible, vile, wretched; acute, extreme, intense, piercing

near antonyms bearable, endurable, supportable, sustainable, tolerable; livable (*also* liveable), sufferable, survivable; acceptable, allowable, reasonable

antonyms gratifying, pleasing, sweet

3 causing intense discomfort to one's skin ⟨a *bitter* wind was stinging the faces of the skiers⟩ — see CUTTING 1

4 difficult to endure ⟨a *bitter* lesson about money and friendship⟩ — see HARSH 1

5 having a low or subnormal temperature ⟨a *bitter* February day for this part of the country⟩ — see COLD 1
6 uncomfortably cool ⟨a *bitter*, rainy day⟩ — see CHILLY 1

bitterly *adv* with feelings of bitterness or grief ⟨cried *bitterly* after her grandmother died⟩ — see HARD 2

bitterness *n* **1** a deep-seated ill will ⟨he still harbored *bitterness* against the company that had fired him⟩ — see ENMITY
2 a harsh or sharp quality ⟨the *bitterness* of the coffee suggested that it had been reheated⟩ — see EDGE 1
3 an uncomfortable degree of coolness ⟨there's a *bitterness* in the air, so let's build a fire in the fireplace⟩ — see CHILL
4 biting sharpness of feeling or expression ⟨complained with great *bitterness* about the ill treatment he had always received from his in-laws⟩ — see ACRIMONY 1

bitty *adj* very small in size ⟨a little *bitty* kitten⟩ — see TINY

bivouac *n* a place where a group of people live for a short time in tents or cabins ⟨soldiers setting up a *bivouac* by the stream⟩ — see CAMP 1

bivouac *vb* to live in a camp or the outdoors ⟨the army *bivouacked* for the night by the lake⟩ — see CAMP

bizarre *adj* **1** conceived or made without regard for reason or reality ⟨a *bizarre* invention that no one could figure out how to use⟩ — see FANTASTIC 1
2 different from the ordinary in a way that causes curiosity or suspicion ⟨a *bizarre* tattoo that suggested he might be a member of a gang⟩ — see ODD 2

blab *vb* **1** to engage in casual or rambling conversation ⟨frequently calls her best friend and *blabs* for an hour⟩ — see CHAT
2 to relate sometimes questionable or secret information of a personal nature ⟨he *blabs* a lot, so never share a secret with him⟩ — see GOSSIP

blabber *n* **1** a person who talks constantly ⟨a *blabber* who always wastes my time with drivel⟩ — see CHATTERBOX
2 unintelligible or meaningless talk ⟨his boasting about having skied in the Alps was just a lot of *blabber*⟩ — see GIBBERISH

black *adj* **1** having the color of soot or coal ⟨a little *black* dress blends into the night very well⟩
synonyms ebony, pitch-black, pitch-dark, pitchy, raven, sable
related words dark, dusky, inky; blackish, brunet (*or* brunette)
near antonyms bright, brilliant, light, pale
antonyms white
2 causing or marked by an atmosphere lacking in cheer ⟨the Friday of the stock market crash was a *black* day for the country⟩ — see GLOOMY 1
3 not conforming to a high moral standard; morally unacceptable ⟨the *black* deeds of the brigands along the Scottish border⟩ — see BAD 2

black art *n* the power to control natural forces through supernatural means ⟨a secretive fellow who claims to have mastered the *black art*⟩ — see MAGIC 1

blackball *vb* to reject by or as if by a vote ⟨the club secretly *blackballs* applicants who belong to that religion⟩ — see NEGATIVE 1

blacken *vb* **1** to make dirty ⟨*blackened* the towels with their dirty hands⟩ — see DIRTY
2 to make untrue and harmful statements about ⟨the politician maliciously *blackened* his opponent's reputation⟩ — see SLANDER

3 to make dark, dim, or indistinct ⟨thick smoke from the forest fires *blackened* the sky for many miles⟩ — see CLOUD 1

blackened *adj* not clean ⟨the church's *blackened* ceiling is the result of centuries of candle smoke⟩ — see DIRTY 1

blackening *n* the making of false statements that damage another's reputation ⟨*blackening* of the senator's good name disgusted voters⟩ — see SLANDER

black magic *n* the power to control natural forces through supernatural means ⟨tried to use *black magic* to summon a storm⟩ — see MAGIC 1

blackmailer *n* a person who gets money from another by using force or threats ⟨the *blackmailer* threatened to tell the press about the mayor's arrest as a teenager⟩ — see RACKETEER

blackness *n* a time or place of little or no light ⟨strange nocturnal noises emanated from the *blackness* of the forest⟩ — see DARK 1

blackout *n* a temporary or permanent state of unconsciousness ⟨even though you experienced only a brief *blackout*, you still ought to be checked by a doctor⟩ — see FAINT

black out *vb* to lose consciousness ⟨*blacked out* after hitting her head on the beam⟩ — see FAINT

blade *n* **1** a hand weapon with a length of metal sharpened on one or both sides and usually tapered to a sharp point ⟨dueled with *blades* rather than guns⟩ — see SWORD
2 an instrument with a sharp edge for cutting ⟨used a small *blade* to cut the rope⟩ — see KNIFE

blamable *adj* **1** deserving reproach or blame ⟨an honest mistake is hardly a *blamable* offense⟩ — see BLAMEWORTHY
2 responsible for a wrong ⟨all costs for the accident will be paid by the insurance company of the *blamable* party⟩ — see GUILTY 1

blame *n* **1** responsibility for wrongdoing or failure ⟨willingly accepted the *blame* for not seeing that the kitchen was properly cleaned⟩
synonyms culpability, fault, guilt, rap
related words regret, remorse, self-reproach, shame; accountability, liability; complicity; blameworthiness, reprehensibleness, sinfulness; censure, condemnation, denunciation
near antonyms acclaim, plaudits, praise; achievement, success
antonyms blamelessness, faultlessness, guiltlessness, innocence
2 the state of being held as the cause of something that needs to be set right ⟨the *blame* is yours, so you have to fix this⟩ — see RESPONSIBILITY 1

blame *vb* to express one's unfavorable opinion of the worth or quality of ⟨*blamed* her for not being attentive enough to his needs⟩ — see CRITICIZE

blameless *adj* free from guilt or blame ⟨a *blameless* baby shouldn't have to suffer for his parents' mistakes⟩ — see INNOCENT 1

blamelessness *n* the quality or state of being free from guilt or blame ⟨your *blamelessness* in this incident is clear, so you won't be punished⟩ — see INNOCENCE 1

blameworthy *adj* deserving reproach or blame ⟨copying another student's work was certainly a *blameworthy* act⟩
synonyms blamable, censurable, culpable, reprehensible, reproachable
related words bad, guilty, sinful, wicked; foolish, irresponsible, reckless; chargeable, impeachable, in-

dictable, punishable; criminal, illegal, illicit, unlawful; illegitimate, improper, wrongful

phrases at fault

near antonyms flawless, perfect, pure; guiltless, innocent

antonyms blameless, faultless, impeccable, irreproachable

blanch *vb* to make white or whiter by removing color ⟨a good washing with bleach should *blanch* these yellowed sheets⟩ — see WHITEN

blanched *adj* lacking a healthy skin color ⟨looking *blanched* and feeble after a long illness⟩ — see PALE 2

bland *adj* not harsh or stern especially in manner, nature, or effect ⟨*bland* food that was good for babies and invalids⟩ — see GENTLE 1

blandish *vb* to get (someone) to do something by gentle urging, special attention, or flattery ⟨*blandished* her into doing their work for them by complimenting her shamelessly⟩ — see COAX

blank *adj* **1** not expressing any emotion ⟨the teacher knew no one was paying attention when she looked out and saw all those *blank* faces⟩

synonyms deadpan, expressionless, impassive, inexpressive, stolid, vacant

related words dull, empty, vacuous, vapid; enigmatic (*also* enigmatical), impenetrable, inscrutable, mysterious; dead, inactive, quiescent, sleepy, sluggish; indolent, languorous, lazy, lethargic, listless; motionless, static, still, wooden; reserved, restrained, reticent, taciturn; aloof, apathetic, detached, indifferent, phlegmatic; cold, cool

near antonyms active, alive, animated, bright, busy, dynamic, effervescent, energetic, expansive, exuberant, lively, vigorous, vital, vivacious; eloquent, revealing, revelatory, significant, vivid; emotional, melodramatic, theatrical, unreserved, unrestrained

antonyms demonstrative, expressive

2 lacking contents that could or should be present ⟨the page of instructions actually turned out to be *blank*⟩ — see EMPTY 1

blank *n* **1** a piece of paper with information written or to be written on it ⟨handed him an employment *blank* to fill out⟩ — see FORM 2

2 empty space ⟨a *blank* on the form for the patient's insurance policy number⟩ — see VACANCY 1

blanket *adj* belonging or relating to the whole ⟨a *blanket* promise of amnesty for everyone with overdue library books⟩ — see GENERAL 1

blanket *vb* **1** to form a layer over ⟨leaves *blanketed* the land around the house⟩ — see COVER 2

2 to keep secret or shut off from view ⟨*blanketed* the secret memo from the news media⟩ — see ¹HIDE 2

blankness *n* empty space ⟨*blankness* surrounded the figure of the woman, for the artist meant to suggest her isolation and loneliness⟩ — see VACANCY 1

blaring *adj* marked by a high volume of sound ⟨drove by and woke us up with *blaring* music⟩ — see LOUD 1

blarney *n* excessive praise ⟨laid the *blarney* on thick in order to get special treatment from the waitress⟩ — see FLATTERY

blarney *vb* **1** to get (someone) to do something by gentle urging, special attention, or flattery ⟨attendants at the nursing home sometimes have to *blarney* the patients to take their medicine⟩ — see COAX

2 to praise too much ⟨an eager, young assistant who *blarneys* the boss shamelessly⟩ — see FLATTER 1

blaspheme *vb* to use offensive or indecent language ⟨shocked that someone would *blaspheme* in church, of all places⟩ — see SWEAR 1

blasphemous *adj* not showing proper reverence for the holy or sacred ⟨Catholics used to believe that anyone but a priest touching the consecrated wafers was *blasphemous*⟩ — see IRREVERENT

blasphemy *n* an act of great disrespect shown to God or to sacred ideas, people, or things ⟨in the 17th century the Quakers were persecuted for beliefs and practices that older churches regarded as *blasphemies*⟩

synonyms defilement, desecration, impiety, irreverence, sacrilege

related words cursing, profanity, swearing; affront, insult; violation; contamination, corruption, debasement, pollution; sin, trespass

near antonyms consecration, purification, sanctification; reverence, veneration

antonyms adoration, glorification, worship

blast *n* **1** a loud explosive sound ⟨a sharp *blast* of the horn startled the other driver⟩ — see CLAP 1

2 a sudden brief rush of wind ⟨a surprise *blast* stole the umbrella right out of his hands⟩ — see GUST 1

3 the act or an instance of exploding ⟨the *blast* destroyed the building completely⟩ — see EXPLOSION 1

blast *vb* **1** to cause to break open or into pieces by or as if by an explosive ⟨the highway engineers will have to *blast* that hill in order to put a road through it⟩

synonyms blow up, burst, demolish, explode, pop, shatter, smash

related words dynamite; annihilate, decimate, destroy; ruin, wreck; detonate, discharge; fragment, splinter

near antonyms collapse, implode

2 to cause (a projectile) to be driven forward with force ⟨artillery that could *blast* cannonballs from hundreds of yards⟩ — see SHOOT 1

3 to cause a weapon to release a missile with great force ⟨they were all *blasting* away at the target range⟩ — see SHOOT 2

4 to criticize harshly and usually publicly ⟨*blasted* the new governor for every little misstep⟩ — see ATTACK 2

blasting *adj* marked by a high volume of sound ⟨carried a *blasting* radio wherever he went⟩ — see LOUD 1

blasting *n* a directed propelling of a missile by a firearm or artillery piece ⟨the next *blasting* by the artillery scored a direct hit⟩ — see SHOT

blatant *adj* **1** engaging in or marked by loud and insistent cries especially of protest ⟨a *blatant* clamor for the impeachment of the scandal-plagued governor⟩ — see VOCIFEROUS

2 very noticeable especially for being incorrect or bad ⟨I take off points for *blatant* spelling errors⟩ — see EGREGIOUS

blaze *n* the steady giving off of the form of radiation that makes vision possible ⟨temporarily blinded by the *blaze* of dozens of camera lights⟩ — see LIGHT 1

blaze *vb* **1** to be on fire especially brightly ⟨the house *blazed* for over three hours in the late-night fire⟩ — see BURN 1

2 to make known openly or publicly ⟨the White House didn't waste a minute in *blazing* the lower unemployment figures⟩ — see ANNOUNCE

3 to shine with a bright harsh light ⟨the spotlight *blazed* through my window⟩ — see GLARE 1

blazing *adj* **1** being on fire ⟨the *blazing* logs in the fireplace cast a warm glow on our holiday party⟩ — see ABLAZE 1

2 having or expressing great depth of feeling ⟨a *blazing* speech affirming the value of every individual⟩ — see FERVENT

bleach *vb* to make white or whiter by removing color ⟨*bleached* the stained shirt back to its original white⟩ — see WHITEN

bleak *adj* **1** causing or marked by an atmosphere lacking in cheer ⟨a *bleak* outlook for the team for the rest of the season⟩ — see GLOOMY 1
2 marked by wet and windy conditions ⟨it was a dark and *bleak* wintry day⟩ — see FOUL 1
3 uncomfortably cool ⟨a *bleak* December morning⟩ — see CHILLY 1

bleakness *n* an uncomfortable degree of coolness ⟨the morning *bleakness* prompted me to get a fire going⟩ — see CHILL

bleary *adj* not seen or understood clearly ⟨the *bleary* outline of a fishing boat could just be seen through the fog⟩ — see FAINT 1

bleed *vb* **1** to feel deep sadness or mental pain ⟨her heart *bleeds* for the homeless people she sees on her way to work⟩ — see GRIEVE
2 to flow forth slowly through small openings ⟨pitch was *bleeding* from cuts in the tree bark⟩ — see EXUDE
3 to remove (liquid) gradually or completely ⟨*bleed* water from the radiators⟩ — see DRAIN 1
4 to rob by the use of trickery or threats ⟨the confidence men *bled* the elderly couple of their life savings⟩ — see FLEECE

bleed (for) *vb* to have sympathy for ⟨he *bleeds for* his friend, who just lost his father⟩ — see PITY

blemish *n* something that spoils the appearance or completeness of a thing ⟨a slight *blemish* on the mirror was the only break in the gleaming surface⟩
synonyms defect, deformity, disfigurement, fault, flaw, imperfection, mark, pockmark, scar
related words abnormality, distortion, irregularity, malformation; bug, glitch, kink; blot, blotch, spot, stain; failing, vice, weakness
near antonyms adornment, decoration, embellishment, enhancement, ornament

blemish *vb* **1** to affect slightly with something morally bad or undesirable ⟨a single indiscretion *blemished* his reputation for years⟩ — see TAINT 1
2 to reduce the soundness, effectiveness, or perfection of ⟨a scratch *blemished* the finish on the car⟩ — see DAMAGE 1

¹blench *vb* to draw back in fear, pain, or disgust ⟨she *blenched* from the horrible sight⟩ — see FLINCH

²blench *vb* to make white or whiter by removing color ⟨*blench* the sheets with bleach to restore that snow-white look⟩ — see WHITEN

blend *n* a distinct entity formed by the combining of two or more different things ⟨that fabric is a cotton and polyester *blend*, so it shouldn't shrink as much as pure cotton⟩
synonyms admixture, amalgam, amalgamation, combination, composite, compound, fusion, intermixture, mix, mixture
related words coalescence, concoction, incorporation, intermingling, mingling; assortment, hash, hodgepodge, hotchpotch, jumble, medley, mélange, mishmash, motley, patchwork, potpourri, variety; accumulation, aggregation, conglomeration
near antonyms component, constituent, element, ingredient

blend *vb* **1** to turn into a single mass that is more or less the same throughout ⟨she *blended* the ingredients for the brownies very thoroughly to eliminate lumps in the batter⟩
synonyms amalgamate, combine, commingle, fuse, incorporate, integrate, intermingle, intermix, merge, mingle, mix
related words fold, stir, toss; coalesce, compound, conjoin, join, link, unite
near antonyms cleave, disjoin, disunite, divide, divorce, part, rupture, sever, sunder; disperse, dissolve, scatter; detach, disengage, split
antonyms break down, break up, separate
2 to form a pleasing relationship ⟨the colors *blend* nicely in that rug⟩ — see HARMONIZE 1

bless *vb* **1** to make holy through prayers or ritual ⟨the priest *blessed* the water, thus allowing it to be used as holy water for various rites⟩
synonyms consecrate, hallow, sanctify
related words cleanse, purify; commit, dedicate, devote; reconsecrate
near antonyms defile, desecrate, profane; dirty, foul, pollute, soil, taint; curse, damn, execrate; cast out, condemn, damn, punish
2 to proclaim the glory of ⟨*bless* the name of God⟩ — see PRAISE 1

blessed *adj* **1** of, relating to, or being God ⟨a prayer to the *blessed* Savior⟩ — see HOLY 3
2 set apart or worthy of veneration by association with God ⟨statues honoring an array of *blessed* saints are scattered throughout the cathedral⟩ — see HOLY 2

blessedness *n* **1** a feeling or state of well-being and contentment ⟨they can scarcely describe the *blessedness* of having four healthy children⟩ — see HAPPINESS 1
2 the quality or state of being spiritually pure or virtuous ⟨Mother Teresa's renowned *blessedness* made her an obvious candidate for sainthood⟩ — see HOLINESS

blessing *n* **1** a prayer calling for divine care, protection, or favor ⟨that rabbi also always ends the service with a short *blessing*⟩
synonyms benediction, benison
related words Godspeed; appeal, entreaty, grace, invocation, orison, petition, plea, prayer, supplication; sanctification
antonyms anathema, curse, execration, imprecation, malediction
2 something that provides happiness or does good for a person or thing ⟨finding money on the sidewalk just when he needed to buy new sneakers was an unexpected *blessing*⟩
synonyms benefit, boon, felicity, godsend, good, manna, windfall
related words bonus, extra, lagniappe; advantage, aid, assistance, gift, help, relief, support; comfort, consolation, solace; delight, joy, pleasure
near antonyms hex, hoodoo, jinx; bother, irritant, nuisance, pest
antonyms affliction, bane, curse, evil, plague, scourge
3 an acceptance of something as satisfactory ⟨Mr. Roberts promptly gave his *blessing* to his daughter's choice of husband⟩ — see APPROVAL 1
4 the act of making something holy through religious ritual ⟨traditionally, worshippers kneel during the *blessing* of the communion wafers⟩ — see CONSECRATION

blind *adj* lacking the power of sight ⟨our old *blind* cat kept walking into walls and furniture⟩
synonyms eyeless, sightless, stone blind
related words unobservant, unobserving; blinded, purblind

near antonyms observant, observing
antonyms sighted

blind *vb* to overpower with light ⟨the bright lights in the TV studio momentarily *blinded* the quiz show contestants⟩ — see DAZZLE

blink *vb* **1** to shine with light at regular intervals ⟨she loves to sit in the dark and watch the lights on the Christmas tree *blink* in ever-changing patterns⟩
synonyms flash, twinkle, wink
related words flicker, glance, glimmer, glint, glisten, glister, glitter, scintillate, shimmer, sparkle; beam, gleam, irradiate, radiate
2 to rapidly open and close one's eyes ⟨I *blinked* for a few seconds after the camera flashed⟩ — see WINK 1

bliss *n* a feeling or state of well-being and contentment ⟨the wedded *bliss* of a happily married couple⟩ — see HAPPINESS 1

blissful *adj* experiencing pleasure, satisfaction, or delight ⟨a *blissful* cat being stroked⟩ — see GLAD 1

blissfulness *n* a feeling or state of well-being and contentment ⟨the *blissfulness* that only a full stomach and a warm bed can bring⟩ — see HAPPINESS 1

blithe *adj* **1** having or showing a good mood or disposition ⟨a *blithe*, obedient child⟩ — see CHEERFUL 1
2 indicative of or marked by high spirits or good humor ⟨a *blithe* remark that good food enjoyed with good company make good wine seem even better⟩ — see MERRY

blithesome *adj* **1** having or showing a good mood or disposition ⟨a *blithesome* girl who never seems to be sad or angry⟩ — see CHEERFUL 1
2 indicative of or marked by high spirits or good humor ⟨a *blithesome* and silly joke⟩ — see MERRY

blitz *vb* to use bombs or artillery against ⟨in 1940 and 1941 the German air force *blitzed* London night after horrible night⟩ — see BOMBARD

blitzkrieg *n* the act or action of setting upon with force or violence ⟨the war began with a *blitzkrieg* that was designed to shock the enemy into submission⟩ — see ATTACK 1

blob *n* **1** a small uneven mass ⟨flicked a *blob* of jelly on the toast and began to spread it around⟩ — see LUMP 1
2 the quantity of fluid that falls naturally in one rounded mass ⟨got a *blob* of honey on his sweater⟩ — see DROP 1

bloc *n* **1** a group of people acting together within a larger group ⟨a whole *bloc* of students got together to complain⟩ — see FACTION
2 an association of persons, parties, or states for mutual assistance and protection ⟨the *bloc* that the United States and most of western Europe formed during the Cold War⟩ — see CONFEDERACY

block *n* **1** a number of things considered as a unit ⟨bought a *block* of stocks⟩ — see GROUP 1
2 something that makes movement or progress more difficult ⟨constant bickering that is only a *block* to the completion of the project⟩ — see ENCUMBRANCE

block *vb* **1** to close up so that no empty spaces remain ⟨*block* up the opening in the wall where the old window was⟩ — see FILL 2
2 to prevent passage through ⟨a fallen tree is *blocking* the road⟩ — see CLOG 1

blockade *n* the cutting off of an area by military means to stop the flow of people or supplies ⟨it was the *blockade* of all the enemy's major ports that finally won the war⟩
synonyms investment, siege

related words encompassment, encirclement; confinement, insulation, isolation, quarantine, seclusion, segregation, sequestration; incarceration, internment
near antonyms emancipation, freedom, liberation, release, rescue

blockade *vb* to surround (as a fortified place) with armed forces for the purpose of capturing or preventing commerce and communication ⟨*blockaded* the city until it surrendered⟩ — see BESIEGE

blockbuster *n* **1** a person or thing that is successful ⟨the movie is expected to be the biggest *blockbuster* of the summer⟩ — see HIT 1
2 something that is unusually large and powerful ⟨a *blockbuster* of a fighter plane⟩ — see GIANT

blockhead *n* a stupid person ⟨only a real *blockhead* would not be able to tie a shoe⟩ — see IDIOT

bloke *n, chiefly British* an adult male human being ⟨a couple of friendly *blokes* offered to show us the sights of London⟩ — see MAN 1

blond *or* **blonde** *adj* of a pale yellow or yellowish brown color ⟨the little boy's *blond* hair darkened to brown as he grew older⟩
synonyms fair, flaxen, golden, sandy, straw, tawny
related words gold, light, white
near antonyms brunet (*or* brunette), dark, swarthy; black, ebony, raven
antonyms dark

blood *n* **1** a group of persons who come from the same ancestor ⟨in his mind, *blood* came before anything else, and he would not betray his criminal brother to the police⟩ — see FAMILY 1
2 the line of ancestors from whom a person is descended ⟨the language expert was certain that a young woman with such an upper-class accent had to be of royal *blood*⟩ — see ANCESTRY

bloodline *n* the line of ancestors from whom a person is descended ⟨came from a famous *bloodline*⟩ — see ANCESTRY

bloodstained *adj* containing, smeared, or stained with blood ⟨had to throw away the *bloodstained* washcloth after having a nosebleed⟩ — see BLOODY 1

bloodthirsty *adj* eager for or marked by the shedding of blood, extreme violence, or killing ⟨the Goths were a wild and *bloodthirsty* people⟩
synonyms bloody, homicidal, murdering, murderous, sanguinary, sanguine
related words barbaric, barbarous, cruel, heartless, inhumane, sadistic, savage, vicious, wanton; antagonistic, fierce, gladiatorial, hostile; aggressive, assertive, bellicose, belligerent, combative, contentious, discordant, pugnacious, quarrelsome, scrappy, truculent, violent; merciless, pitiless, ruthless; fell, ferocious, grim; despiteful, hateful, malevolent, malicious, malign, malignant, mean, nasty, spiteful; destructive, devastating, ruinous
near antonyms appeasing, conciliatory, disarming, dovish, mollifying, pacific, pacifying, peaceable, peaceful, peacemaking, placating, propitiatory; unaggressive, unassertive; benign, benignant, compassionate, good-hearted, humane, kind, kindhearted, sympathetic, tenderhearted; tender, warm, warmhearted; clement, lenient, merciful; affable, amiable, amicable, benevolent, gentle, kindly; submissive, surrendering, yielding

bloody *adj* **1** containing, smeared, or stained with blood ⟨after the fight, her shirt was all *bloody*⟩
synonyms bloodstained, gory

related words carmine, crimson, red, ruby, sanguine; bloodthirsty, sanguinary

2 eager for or marked by the shedding of blood, extreme violence, or killing ⟨a *bloody* battle⟩ ⟨a *bloody* movie that is unsuitable for children⟩ — see BLOODTHIRSTY

bloom *n* **1** a state or time of great activity, thriving, or achievement ⟨a handsome young man in the full *bloom* of youth⟩
synonyms blossom, flower, flush, heyday, prime
related words acme, apex, climax, meridian, peak, pinnacle, summit, zenith; glory, grandeur, splendor; haleness, heartiness; energy, force, potency, power, vigor
near antonyms decline; bottom, nadir; feebleness, fragility, frailty, weakness; illness, infirmity, sickness; shriveling, wilting, withering

2 a rosy appearance of the cheeks ⟨after a snowball fight, she came inside with a *bloom*⟩
synonyms blush, flush
related words brightness, brilliance, glow; pinkness, rosiness

3 the usually showy plant part that produces seeds ⟨the rosebush produces *blooms* only in midsummer⟩ — see FLOWER 1

bloom *vb* **1** to produce flowers ⟨forsythias only *bloom* at the beginning of spring⟩
synonyms blossom, blow, burgeon, flower, unfold
related words leaf, leave; bud; open
near antonyms dry (up), fade, shrivel, wilt, wither; die, drop, expire, perish

2 to develop a rosy facial color (as from excitement or embarrassment) ⟨*bloomed* when she realized she'd said something so silly⟩ — see BLUSH

blooming *adj* having a healthy reddish skin tone ⟨the *blooming* faces of children at play in the great outdoors⟩ — see RUDDY

blossom *n* **1** a state or time of great activity, thriving, or achievement ⟨in the full *blossom* of her career as a writer⟩ — see BLOOM 1

2 the usually showy plant part that produces seeds ⟨the marigolds are finally showing *blossoms*⟩ — see FLOWER 1

blossom *vb* to produce flowers ⟨the fruit tree seemed to *blossom* overnight once the warm spring weather arrived⟩ — see BLOOM

blot *n* a mark of guilt or disgrace ⟨the bribery scandal was a *blot* on his reputation⟩ — see STAIN 1

blotch *n* a small area that is different (as in color) from the main part ⟨a dog with a single small *blotch* of black⟩ — see SPOT 1

blotch *vb* **1** to mark with blotches especially of different colors or shades ⟨*blotched* the bedroom walls with various shades of blue to give them a textured effect⟩ — see MOTTLE 1

2 to mark with small spots especially unevenly ⟨my pen leaked and *blotched* my shirt pocket⟩ — see SPOT 1

blotched *adj* having blotches of two or more colors ⟨a *blotched* black-and-white rabbit⟩ — see PIED

blot out *vb* **1** to destroy all traces of ⟨*blotted out* all evidence of tampering with the explosive device⟩ — see ANNIHILATE 1

2 to keep secret or shut off from view ⟨bushes *blotted out* the shed from our view⟩ — see ¹HIDE 2

¹blow *n* a hard strike with a part of the body or an instrument ⟨he was dizzy for the rest of the day after the *blow* to his head⟩
synonyms bang, bat, beat, belt, bop, box, buffet, bust, chop, clap, clip, clout, crack, cuff, hit, hook, knock,

lick, pound, punch, rap, slam, slap, slug, smack, smash, sock, spank, stroke, swat, swipe, thud, thump, thwack, wallop, whack
related words flick, jab, poke, roundhouse, stab; beating, battering, bludgeoning, clobbering, drubbing, hammering, lambasting, licking, pasting, pounding, pummeling, thrashing; flogging, walloping, whipping

²blow *n* a sudden brief rush of wind ⟨the ocean *blows* that sweep over the islands are so strong that only the hardiest shrubs can grow there⟩ — see GUST 1

¹blow *vb* **1** to breathe hard, quickly, or with difficulty ⟨that horse was really *blowing* after the race⟩ — see GASP

2 to use up carelessly ⟨often *blows* his entire allowance on toys⟩ — see WASTE 1

²blow *vb* to produce flowers ⟨longing for a grassy field where the wildflowers *blow*⟩ — see BLOOM

blow (out) *vb* to let or force out of the lungs ⟨*blew out* a smoke ring and began to tell us a good yarn⟩ — see EXHALE 1

blowout *n* a social gathering ⟨staged a huge *blowout* for Halloween⟩ — see PARTY 1

blowup *n* an outburst or display of excited anger ⟨the boss had a *blowup* when someone fouled up the copy machine⟩ — see TANTRUM

blow up *vb* **1** to become very angry ⟨she *blew up* at everybody after a very long and very bad day⟩
synonyms flare (up), flip
related words fulminate, rant, vituperate; bristle, burn, foam, fume, rage, seethe; burst, explode; enrage, incense, inflame, infuriate, madden; aggravate, anger, annoy, bother, bug, displease, distress, exasperate, gall, get, irk, irritate, nettle, peeve, pique, provoke, put out, rile, vex; agitate, disturb, perturb, upset
phrases fly into a rage, fly off the handle, forget oneself, lose one's temper
near antonyms appease, conciliate, mollify, pacify, placate; comfort, console, quiet, soothe
antonyms calm (down)

2 to break open or into pieces usually because of internal pressure ⟨the building *blew up* because of a gas leak⟩ — see EXPLODE 1

3 to cause to break open or into pieces by or as if by an explosive ⟨*blew up* the biggest rocks and then cleared them away⟩ — see BLAST 1

blowy *adj* marked by strong wind or more wind than usual ⟨a *blowy* day that knocked most of the fall foliage off the trees⟩ — see WINDY 1

blubber *vb* to shed tears often while making meaningless sounds as a sign of pain or distress ⟨the child was *blubbering* because she had fallen and skinned her knee⟩ — see CRY 1

bludgeon *n* a heavy rigid stick used as a weapon or for punishment ⟨guards armed with *bludgeons*⟩ — see CLUB 1

bludgeon *vb* **1** to deliver a blow to (someone or something) usually in a strong vigorous manner ⟨*bludgeoned* the door with an iron bar in a senseless act of vandalism⟩ — see HIT 1

2 to strike repeatedly ⟨*bludgeoned* the victim to death⟩ — see BEAT 1

blue *adj* feeling unhappiness ⟨cold, dreary winter always leaves me *blue*⟩ — see SAD 1

blue *n* **1** the expanse of air surrounding the earth ⟨the plane flew off into the *blue* and was never seen again⟩ — see SKY

2 the whole body of salt water that covers nearly three-fourths of the earth ⟨pirate ships that sailed the *blue* in search of treasure⟩ — see OCEAN

blueprint *n* a method worked out in advance for achieving some objective ⟨an ambitious young man with a remarkably detailed *blueprint* for becoming a millionaire by the age of 25⟩ — see PLAN 1

blueprint *vb* to work out the details of (something) in advance ⟨*blueprinted* the schedule of events for the festival right down to the last detail⟩ — see PLAN 1

blues *n pl* a state or spell of low spirits ⟨failing the test gave me the *blues* for the rest of the day⟩ — see SADNESS

bluff *adj* being or characterized by direct, brief, and potentially rude speech or manner ⟨he's a *bluff* but good-hearted teacher⟩ — see BLUNT 1

bluff *n* a steep wall of rock, earth, or ice ⟨fossils embedded in a stone *bluff* that date from the Jurassic period⟩ — see CLIFF

bluff *vb* to cause to believe what is untrue ⟨I *bluffed* my teacher into believing that I could really speak French and thus would be the perfect exchange student⟩ — see DECEIVE

blunder *n* an unintentional departure from truth or accuracy ⟨fixed a minor *blunder* in the advertising flier⟩ — see ERROR 1

blunt *adj* **1** being or characterized by direct, brief, and potentially rude speech or manner ⟨he values honesty and is quite *blunt* about telling people their flaws⟩
synonyms abrupt, bluff, brusque, crusty, curt, downright, snippy
related words gruff, rough, short; hearty, honest, sincere; candid, direct, forthright, foursquare, frank, free-spoken, open, outspoken, plain, plainspoken, straightforward; discourteous, disrespectful, impertinent, impolite, inconsiderate, rude, tactless, undiplomatic; closemouthed, laconic, reserved, reticent, terse, tight-lipped; artless, earnest, sincere; coarse, crass, crude, low, uncouth, vulgar
near antonyms civil, considerate, courteous, diplomatic, gracious, polite, politic, smooth, suave, tactful; loquacious, talkative, voluble; long-winded, prolix, verbose; courtly, cultivated, gallant, genteel, polished, refined
antonyms circuitous, mealymouthed
2 lacking sharpness of edge or point ⟨a *blunt* knife won't open that package⟩ — see DULL 1

blunt *vb* to reduce or weaken in strength or feeling ⟨the mushy music *blunted* the effect of the movie's final tragic scene⟩ — see DULL 1

blunted *adj* lacking sharpness of edge or point ⟨the *blunted* saw was worthless for fine woodworking⟩ — see DULL 1

blur *vb* **1** to make (something) unclear to the understanding ⟨an article for the layman that *blurs* the distinction between the two kinds of cholesterol⟩ — see CONFUSE 2
2 to make dark, dim, or indistinct ⟨evening shadows *blurred* the view of the valley⟩ — see CLOUD 1

blurt (out) *vb* to utter with a sudden burst of strong feeling ⟨"I'm very sad!" the toddler *blurted out*⟩ — see EXCLAIM

blush *n* a rosy appearance of the cheeks ⟨a baby with a healthy *blush*⟩ — see BLOOM 2

blush *vb* to develop a rosy facial color (as from excitement or embarrassment) ⟨she *blushed* when she realized she had walked into the boys' bathroom by mistake⟩

synonyms bloom, color, crimson, flush, glow, redden
related words rouge; abash, chagrin, discomfit, disconcert, embarrass, faze, humiliate, mortify

bluster *n* **1** boastful speech or writing ⟨all the *bluster* in the campaign speech was intended to hide a lack of specifics⟩ — see BOMBAST 1
2 loud, confused, and usually unharmonious sound ⟨I can't work with all the *bluster* in here⟩ — see NOISE 1

bluster *vb* to talk loudly and wildly ⟨the rude customer *blustered* and yelled about lawsuits, but eventually left⟩ — see RANT

blustery *adj* marked by strong wind or more wind than usual ⟨it can be a bit risky to drive across the bridge on a *blustery* day⟩ — see WINDY 1

board *n* a leg-mounted piece of furniture with a broad flat top designed for the serving of food ⟨arranged the fancy dishes and silverware on the inn's finest *board*⟩ — see TABLE 1

board *vb* **1** to provide food or meals for ⟨housed and *boarded* many foster children over the years⟩ — see FEED 1
2 to provide with living quarters or shelter ⟨*boarded* the stray cat until a permanent home was found⟩ — see HOUSE 1

boarder *n* one who rents a room or apartment in another's house ⟨a *boarder* who paid $100 per week for a room and meals⟩ — see TENANT

boast *n* an asset that brings praise or renown ⟨the school's *boast* was a winning football team⟩ — see GLORY 2

boast *vb* to praise or express pride in one's own possessions, qualities, or accomplishments often to excess ⟨he *boasted* that he was the best hockey goalie in the whole school⟩
synonyms brag, crow, swagger
related words puff (up); pride; gush; exult, glory, rejoice; brandish, display, exhibit, expose, flaunt, parade, show off; magnify, maximize
near antonyms bad-mouth, belittle, decry, deprecate, depreciate, diminish, discount, disparage, minimize; bemoan, lament, mourn, regret

boat *n* **1** a small buoyant structure for travel on water ⟨paddling the little *boat* across the lake is great exercise, but tiring⟩
synonyms bottom, craft, vessel, watercraft
related words canoe, catamaran, catboat, cockleshell, coracle, dinghy, dory, dugout, flatboat, float, gig, gondola, houseboat, ironclad, kayak, launch, life boat, longboat, motorboat, outrigger, pirogue, pontoon, punt, raft, rowboat, sail, sampan, scow, scull, shallop, shell, sloop, tender, umiak; bark, brig, brigantine, caravel, clipper, galleon, galley, junk, ketch, pinnace, sailboat, schooner, ship, square-rigger, windjammer, xebec, yacht; corvette, cutter, destroyer, fireship, flagship, gunboat, landing craft, privateer, torpedo boat, warship; argosy, barge, coaster, collier, containership, ferryboat, icebreaker, lighter, lightship, liner, merchantman, merchant ship, packet, revenuer, riverboat, showboat, steamboat, steamer, supertanker, taxi, towboat, trader, tugboat; sealer, shrimper, trawler, whaler; derelict, hulk, tub; air-cushion vehicle, hovercraft; hydrofoil, hydroplane
2 a large craft for travel by water ⟨you'll have to take a passenger *boat* to get to the island⟩ — see SHIP

boat *vb* to travel on water in a vessel ⟨*boated* to the picnic site on an island in the bay⟩ — see SAIL 1

¹**bob** *vb* to make (as hair) shorter with or as if with the use of shears ⟨*bobbed* her waist-length hair herself on her 18th birthday⟩ — see CLIP

²**bob** *vb* to make short up-and-down movements ⟨a family of ducks *bobbing* on the water⟩ — see NOD

bobble *vb* **1** to make or do (something) in a clumsy or unskillful way ⟨the first baseman *bobbled* the catch, so the runner was safe⟩ — see BOTCH

2 to make short up-and-down movements ⟨the little doll's head *bobbled* when you poked it⟩ — see NOD

bobby *n, British* a member of a force charged with law enforcement at the local level ⟨asked a passing London *bobby* for directions⟩ — see OFFICER 1

bobby–soxer *n* a young usually unmarried woman ⟨Granny showed us how young people danced when she was a *bobby-soxer*⟩ — see GIRL 1

bode *vb* to show signs of a favorable or successful outcome ⟨her natural gift for reading *boded* well for her future in school⟩
synonyms augur, forebode (*also* forbode), promise
related words forecast, foretell, predict, presage, prognosticate, prophesy; forewarn, warn; anticipate, divine, foreknow, foresee; foreshadow, portend, prefigure; allude, connote, hint, imply, insinuate, intimate, suggest
phrases bid fair, give promise of

bodiless *adj* not composed of matter ⟨ghosts are supposed to be *bodiless*⟩ — see IMMATERIAL 1

bodily *adj* of or relating to the human body ⟨the old man suffered from a number of *bodily* ailments⟩ — see PHYSICAL 1

boding *n* something believed to be a sign or warning of a future event ⟨among some ancient peoples, solar eclipses were often seen as celestial *bodings* of earthly calamities⟩ — see OMEN

body *n* **1** the main or greater part of something as distinguished from its appendages ⟨the *body* of the novel was quite good, even if the beginning was a bit slow⟩
synonyms bulk, core, generality, main, mass, staple, weight
related words majority; aggregate, amount, entirety, sum, sum total, total, totality, whole; bottom, essence, essentiality, marrow, nature, quintessence, soul, stuff, substance; center, heart, hub, middle, nucleus, seat; affair, argument, burden, crux, focus, gist, kernel, nub, pitch, point, purport; matter, motif, subject, text, theme, topic
near antonyms accessory, adjunct, appendage, extension, offshoot; component, constituent, element, ingredient; division, part, piece, section, segment; angle, aspect, facet, feature, quality, side

2 a distinct and separate portion of matter ⟨the Atlantic is a gigantic *body* of water⟩
synonyms mass
related words aggregate, amount, bulk, quantity, volume; item, object, thing; material, stuff, substance; entirety, totality, whole

3 a group of people acting together within a larger group ⟨the class walked out as a *body* in protest⟩ — see FACTION

4 a group of people sharing a common interest and relating together socially ⟨running for president of the student *body*⟩ — see GANG 2

5 a member of the human race ⟨the most intelligent *body* in this entire place⟩ — see HUMAN

6 a usually small number of persons considered as a unit ⟨a *body* of security men accompany the president at all times⟩ — see GROUP 2

bog *n* spongy land saturated or partially covered with water ⟨got a shoe stuck in the *bog*⟩ — see SWAMP

bog (down) *vb* to place in conflict or difficulties ⟨we were *bogged down* by the endless changes, and of course finished late⟩ — see EMBROIL

bogey *also* **bogy** *or* **bogie** *n* **1** something or someone that causes fear or dread especially without reason ⟨math and math tests have long been *bogeys* for many students⟩
synonyms bête noire, bugaboo, bugbear, hobgoblin, ogre
related words apparition, ghost, phantasm, phantom, poltergeist, shade, specter (*or* spectre), spirit, spook, wraith; banshee, bogeyman, demon, devil, fiend, imp, incubus; fright, horror, monster, monstrosity, terror; bane, curse, plague, scourge, torment; abomination, anathema

2 the soul of a dead person thought of especially as appearing to living people ⟨the child believed *bogeys* lived in the closet⟩ — see GHOST

bogus *adj* **1** being such in appearance only and made with or manufactured from usually cheaper materials ⟨for that price, you're only going to get furniture covered in *bogus* leather and not the real stuff⟩ — see IMITATION

2 being such in appearance only and made or manufactured with the intention of committing fraud ⟨the "designer" watches sold on the street are usually *bogus*⟩ — see COUNTERFEIT

3 lacking in natural or spontaneous quality ⟨there was often a lot of *bogus* conviviality at the company's parties⟩ — see ARTIFICIAL 1

bohemian *n* a person who does not conform to generally accepted standards or customs ⟨he spent a few years living as a *bohemian* in the artists' quarter of the city⟩ — see NONCONFORMIST 1

boil *vb* **1** to be excited or emotionally stirred up with anger ⟨she was *boiling* at the thought of her so-called best friend trying to steal her boyfriend⟩
synonyms burn, fume, rage, seethe, steam
related words fulminate, rant, rave; smolder; bristle, flare (up); chafe, fret, stew; agitate, convulse, shake; disturb, perturb, upset

2 to cook in a liquid heated to the point that it gives off steam ⟨*boil* the potatoes very well before you try to mash them⟩
synonyms coddle, parboil, poach, simmer, stew
related words scald; braise, fricassee, pressure-cook, steam; reboil

3 to be in a state of violent rolling motion ⟨the sea *boiled* and frothed during the storm⟩ — see SEETHE 1

boisterous *adj* being rough or noisy in a high-spirited way ⟨the fans at the baseball game became particularly *boisterous* after the home run⟩
synonyms knockabout, rambunctious, raucous, rowdy
related words rampageous, riotous, stormy, tempestuous, turbulent, violent; disorderly, raffish, ruffianly; headstrong, intractable, obstreperous, recalcitrant, uncontrollable, uncontrolled, undisciplined, ungovernable, uninhibited, unmanageable, unruly, wild, willful (*or* wilful); bubbly, buoyant, effervescent, exuberant, high-spirited, impassioned, lively, passionate, sprightly, vivacious; clamorous, loudmouthed, noisy, strident, vociferous; howling, screaming, yelling
near antonyms sedate, sober, solemn, somber (*or* sombre), staid; decorous, dignified, proper, seemly; calm, hushed, noiseless, peaceful, placid, quiet, restrained, serene, silent, soundless, tranquil; collected, composed,

constrained, controlled, imperturbable, inhibited, repressed, self-controlled, unflappable, unruffled; moderate, reasonable, subdued, temperate; impassive, phlegmatic, stoic (*or* stoical), stolid; depressed; aloof, detached, indifferent
antonyms orderly

bold *adj* **1** inclined or willing to take risks 〈our youngest brother was the *boldest* one in the family, instantly taking to everything from skiing to skateboarding〉
synonyms adventuresome, adventurous, audacious, daring, dashing, emboldened, enterprising, gutsy, hardy, nerved, nervy, venturesome, venturous
related words brash, daredevil, foolhardy, heedless, hotheaded, impetuous, imprudent, impulsive, incautious, madcap, overbold, overconfident, rash, reckless, spirited, thoughtless, wild; brave, courageous, dauntless, fearless, gallant, greathearted, heroic, intrepid, lionhearted, stalwart, stout, stouthearted, unafraid, undaunted, valiant, valorous; gritty, plucky, spirited, spunky; hasty, headlong, precipitate; absurd, asinine, balmy, brainless, crazy, foolish, half-witted, harebrained, insane, lunatic, mad, nutty, scatterbrained, silly, wacky, witless; unnecessary; dumb, idiotic, moronic, stupid; irrational, unreasonable
near antonyms chickenhearted, coward, cowardly, craven, lily-livered, pusillanimous, shy, timid, timorous; careful, cautious, heedful, prudent, wary; overcareful, overcautious; affrighted, afraid, alarmed, fainthearted, fearful, frightened, horrified, scared, shocked, spooked, startled, terrified, terrorized; unnerved; calm, cool, levelheaded, rational, reasonable, sage, sane, sensible, sound, wise; appalled, concerned, dismayed, upset, worried
antonyms unadventurous, unenterprising
2 displaying or marked by rude boldness 〈you're a *bold* little brat for trying to steal my stuff while I'm right here〉 — see NERVY 1
3 likely to attract attention 〈an interior decorator who likes to use *bold* colors〉 — see NOTICEABLE
4 showing a lack of proper social reserve or modesty 〈a *bold* child who interrupts the adults at his parents' parties〉 — see PRESUMPTUOUS 1
5 having an incline approaching the perpendicular 〈the advanced climbers chose a *bold* cliff to test themselves〉 — see STEEP 1

bold–faced *adj* displaying or marked by rude boldness 〈the child proceeded to tell a *bold-faced* lie despite the evidence right in front of us〉 — see NERVY 1

bolster *vb* to hold up or serve as a foundation for 〈used additional facts to *bolster* the claim〉 — see SUPPORT 3

bolt *n* something that makes a strong impression because it is so unexpected 〈the news was a *bolt* from the blue〉 — see SURPRISE 1

bolt *vb* **1** to move suddenly and sharply (as in surprise) 〈I *bolted* as I read the winning lottery numbers〉 — see START 1
2 to proceed or move quickly 〈the cat *bolted* for the food dish the minute he spied it〉 — see HURRY 2
3 to hasten away from something dangerous or frightening 〈the rabbit *bolted* when it saw the fox〉 — see RUN 2
4 to utter with a sudden burst of strong feeling 〈*bolted* out the bad word without thinking〉 — see EXCLAIM

bomb *vb* to use bombs or artillery against 〈the enemy has *bombed* the city again〉 — see BOMBARD

bombard *vb* to use bombs or artillery against 〈the Allies *bombarded* Germany for a great many months during World War II〉

synonyms blitz, bomb, shell
related words rake, strafe; assail, assault, attack, devastate, hit, pound, ravage, strike

bombardment *n* a rapid or overwhelming outpouring of many things at once 〈the *bombardment* of so many instructions meant that I missed some of the information〉 — see BARRAGE

bombast *n* **1** boastful speech or writing 〈filling a speech with *bombast* about one's unique qualifications for student council is usually a bad idea〉
synonyms bluster, brag, braggadocio, gas, grandiloquence, hot air, rant
related words rhapsody, rhetoric; babble, blab, chatter, drivel, gabble, gibber, jabber, prattle; jawing, patter, prating, yammering; egotism, self-conceit, self-importance
2 language that is impressive-sounding but not meaningful or sincere 〈you need less *bombast* and more evidence in this paper〉 — see RHETORIC 1

bombastic *adj* marked by the use of impressive-sounding but mostly meaningless words and phrases 〈a *bombastic* speech intended to impress voters〉 — see RHETORICAL

bombshell *n* something that makes a strong impression because it is so unexpected 〈discovering that I had a sister I never knew was an absolute *bombshell*〉 — see SURPRISE 1

bona fide *adj* being exactly as appears or as claimed 〈a *bona fide* war hero〉 — see AUTHENTIC 1

bond *n* **1** something that physically prevents free movement 〈before they could release the captive, they had to undo a number of *bonds*〉
synonyms band, bracelet, chain, fetter, handcuff(s), irons, ligature, manacle, shackle
related words confinement, constraint, curb, hamper, hindrance, restraint, restriction; entanglement, net, trammel, trap; collar, straitjacket (*also* straightjacket); hobble, tie
2 a uniting or binding force or influence 〈the *bond* of love between them was so strong that even death could not break it〉
synonyms cement, knot, ligature, link, tie
related words attachment, connection, entanglement, fastening, joint, linkage; affection, fondness, sympathy; fetter, handcuff, manacle, shackle, trammel; constraint, curb, hampering, limit, limitation, restraint, restriction
near antonyms detaching, disengaging, parting, separation; unbinding, unfastening, unfettering, untying; emancipation, freedom, liberation, release
3 a formal agreement to fulfill an obligation 〈signed a *bond* to repay the money〉 — see GUARANTEE 1

bondage *n* the state of being a slave 〈the Civil War ended over 200 years of *bondage* for black Africans in America〉 — see SLAVERY 1

bonding *n* a physical sticking to as if by glue 〈this epoxy has good *bonding* for glass and ceramics〉 — see ADHESION

bondman *n* a person who is considered the property of another person 〈would rather die as an insurgent than live as a *bondman*〉 — see SLAVE 1

bondsman *n* a person who is considered the property of another person 〈*bondsmen* were once not allowed to vote〉 — see SLAVE 1

bone *n, usually* **bones** *pl* a small cube marked on each side with one to six spots and usually played in pairs in various games 〈threw the *bones* to see how to move〉 — see DIE

bone (up) *vb* to use the mind to acquire knowledge ⟨I suggest you *bone up* a bit before the next vocabulary quiz⟩ — see STUDY 1

bonny *adj, chiefly British* very pleasing to look at ⟨a *bonny* child dressed in traditional Scottish clothing⟩ — see BEAUTIFUL

bonus *n* something given in addition to what is ordinarily expected or owed ⟨this job offers a nice Christmas *bonus* in addition to the salary⟩
   synonyms dividend, extra, gratuity, gravy, lagniappe, perquisite, tip
   related words fillip; bestowal, presentation; benefaction, benevolence, bounty, charity, generosity, largess (*or* largesse), philanthropy; contribution, donation, gift, offering, present; grant, subsidy; boon, manna, windfall; favor, freebie (*or* freebee), giveaway, premium; award, prize, reward; fringe benefit

bon voyage *n* an expression of good wishes at parting ⟨everyone said their *bon voyages* as the happy couple left on a cruise for their honeymoon⟩ — see GOOD-BYE

boo *n* a vocal sound made to express scorn or disapproval ⟨the referee's call was greeted with a chorus of *boos*⟩ — see CATCALL

booby *n* a person who lacks good sense or judgment ⟨what kind of *booby* goes out into the snow barefoot?⟩ — see FOOL 1

boobytrap *vb* to place hidden explosive devices in or under ⟨*boobytrapped* the field bordering the army's camp⟩ — see MINE

booby trap *n* **1** a usually concealed explosive device designed to go off when disturbed ⟨luckily, the bomb squad didn't find any *booby traps*⟩
   synonyms mine
   related words bomb, explosive; pitfall, snare, trap; ambush
   2 a danger or difficulty that is hidden or not easily recognized ⟨he noticed the *booby trap* in the last question on the test just a little too late⟩ — see PITFALL 1

book *n* **1** a set of printed sheets of paper bound together between covers and forming a work of fiction or nonfiction ⟨I bought another new *book* yesterday, and I can't wait to read it⟩
   synonyms tome, volume
   related words hardback, paperback, pocket book; folio, quarto; guidebook, handbook, manual; catalog (*or* catalogue), dictionary, encyclopedia; booklet, brochure, circular, flier (*or* flyer), folder, leaflet, magazine, pamphlet, program; textbook, tract, treatise; novel, novelette, pulp
   2 *cap* a book made up of the writings accepted by Christians as coming from God ⟨offered to swear on the *Book* that everything had happened just as he said⟩ — see BIBLE

book *vb* to arrange to have something (as a hotel room) held for one's future use ⟨we *booked* a conference room for the meeting next week⟩ — see RESERVE 1

bookish *adj* suggestive of the vocabulary used in books ⟨*fealty* is a *bookish* synonym for *loyalty*⟩
   synonyms erudite, learned, literary
   related words academic, pedantic, scholastic; highbrow, intellectual; educated, schooled; formal
   near antonyms chatty, conversational; familiar, informal; slangy
   antonyms colloquial, nonliterary

booklet *n* a short printed publication with no cover or with a paper cover ⟨there's an instruction *booklet* next to the computer⟩ — see PAMPHLET

bookworm *n* a person slavishly devoted to intellectual or academic pursuits ⟨a *bookworm* who prefers to read rather than to go outside⟩ — see NERD

boom *n* a loud explosive sound ⟨the *boom* of a car backfiring⟩ — see CLAP 1

boom *vb* to make a long loud deep noise or cry ⟨the cannons *boomed* throughout the night⟩ — see ROAR

booming *adj* **1** marked by a high volume of sound ⟨a *booming* bass drum⟩ — see LOUD 1
   2 marked by vigorous growth and well-being especially economically ⟨a *booming* business that has grown every year since it was founded⟩ — see PROSPEROUS 1

boon *adj* likely to seek or enjoy the company of others ⟨I and my *boon* companions celebrated that afternoon's victory on the gridiron with a night at a local dance club⟩ — see CONVIVIAL

boon *n* **1** a thing that helps ⟨the couple's generous donation was a great *boon* to the school band's fund-raising campaign⟩ — see HELP 2
   2 an act of kind assistance ⟨a softhearted man who finds it hard to deny any *boon*, whether it be for friend or stranger⟩ — see FAVOR 1
   3 something granted as a special favor ⟨at the prep school, seniors are given certain *boons* that make them the envy of underclassmen⟩ — see PRIVILEGE
   4 something that provides happiness or does good for a person or thing ⟨the rain was a *boon* for the farmers who had been struggling with drought⟩ — see BLESSING 2

boor *n* a person whose behavior is offensive to others ⟨a *boor* who embarrassed his family at every social event they attended⟩ — see JERK 1

boorish *adj* having or showing crudely insensitive or impolite manners ⟨*boorish* behavior, such as yelling for service in restaurants⟩ — see CLOWNISH

boost *n* **1** an act or instance of helping ⟨she always liked to give struggling families in the neighborhood a *boost*⟩ — see HELP 1
   2 something added (as by growth) ⟨a sudden *boost* in sales⟩ — see INCREASE 1
   3 something that arouses action or activity ⟨according to the president, a tax cut is just the *boost* that the economy needs⟩ — see IMPULSE

boost *vb* **1** to lift with effort ⟨*boosted* the child into her car seat⟩ — see HEAVE 1
   2 to make greater in size, amount, or number ⟨a promotion that *boosted* the number of interested customers in the showroom⟩ — see INCREASE 1
   3 to make markedly greater in measure or degree ⟨*boost* the volume on the radio so everyone can hear⟩ — see INTENSIFY
   4 to move from a lower to a higher place or position ⟨*boosted* the box onto the top shelf⟩ — see RAISE 1
   5 to provide publicity for ⟨*boosted* the singer's latest release with a round of appearances on all the talk and entertainment shows⟩ — see PUBLICIZE 1

booster *n* a person who actively supports or favors a cause ⟨*boosters* for the school's sports program will be having a bake sale so the teams can get some sorely needed equipment⟩ — see EXPONENT

boot (out) *vb* to drive or force out ⟨the theater manager *booted out* the kids who were making a disturbance⟩ — see EJECT 1

bootleg *n* illegally produced liquor ⟨getting caught with *bootleg* during Prohibition could lead to a jail sentence⟩ — see MOONSHINE 1

bootless *adj* producing no results ⟨a *bootless* effort to get tickets to the sold-out game⟩ — see FUTILE

booty *n* valuables stolen or taken by force ⟨no one knows where Captain Kidd hid his *booty*, but that hasn't deterred hopeful adventurers from looking for it for the last 300 years⟩ — see LOOT

booze *n* a fermented or distilled beverage that can make a person drunk ⟨this will be a party without *booze*⟩ — see ALCOHOL

bop *n* a hard strike with a part of the body or an instrument ⟨a *bop* to the television set sometimes fixes it⟩ — see ¹BLOW

bop *vb* to deliver a blow to (someone or something) usually in a strong vigorous manner ⟨*bopped* the dog on the nose to discourage bad behavior⟩ — see HIT 1

border *n* 1 the line or relatively narrow space that marks the outer limit of something ⟨a rug with a fancily embroidered *border*⟩
synonyms bound, boundary, brim, circumference, compass, confines, edge, end, fringe, margin, perimeter, periphery, rim, skirt, verge
related words crest, hem, lip; ceiling, maximum; demarcation, extent, limitation, measure, restriction, termination; borderland, frontier, march, pale
near antonyms center; inner, inside, interior
2 a region along the dividing line between two countries ⟨people who live on an international *border* get used to carrying a passport⟩ — see FRONTIER 1

border *vb* to serve as a border for ⟨that velvet *bordered* the sleeves on this shirt, until it fell off⟩
synonyms bound, fringe, margin, rim, skirt
related words edge, hem, trim; circumscribe, define, delineate, demarcate, frame, outline; circle, compass, encircle, girdle, girth, loop, ring, round, surround; check, confine, control, curb, limit, restrain, restrict

border (on) *vb* 1 to come very close to being ⟨that comment *borders on* insubordination, and you should be more careful in the future⟩
synonyms verge (on)
related words approach, near; appear, look, resemble, seem, suggest
2 to be adjacent to ⟨the state *borders* two others⟩ — see ADJOIN 1

bordering *adj* having a border in common ⟨a country given to constant disagreements with *bordering* nations⟩ — see ADJACENT

borderland *n* a region along the dividing line between two countries ⟨I grew up on the *borderland*, so I speak both languages⟩ — see FRONTIER 1

bore *n* someone or something boring ⟨the graduation speaker was a real *bore*⟩ — see DRAG 1

¹bore *vb* to make a hole or series of holes in ⟨some woodpecker *bored* holes in our tree in the backyard⟩ — see PERFORATE

²bore *vb* to make weary and restless by being dull or monotonous ⟨the teacher's lifeless and unimaginative teaching style *bored* the students to death⟩
synonyms jade, tire, weary
related words pall; drain, enervate, exhaust, fatigue, wear, wear out; debilitate, disable, enfeeble; deject, demoralize, discourage, dishearten, dispirit
phrases put to sleep
near antonyms animate, energize, enliven, excite, galvanize, invigorate, stimulate, vitalize; amuse, entertain; allure, attract, beguile, bewitch, captivate, charm, enchant, enthrall (*or* enthral), fascinate, hypnotize, mesmerize; monopolize, preoccupy; busy, immerse, involve, occupy; rally, rouse, stir
antonyms absorb, engage, engross, grip, interest, intrigue

bored *adj* having one's patience, interest, or pleasure exhausted ⟨I was completely *bored* during that class⟩ — see WEARY 2

boredom *n* the state of being bored ⟨she spends that whole class in a state of complete *boredom*, waiting for lunch⟩
synonyms doldrums, ennui, listlessness, restlessness, tedium, tiredness, weariness
related words cheerlessness, dispiritedness, joylessness, melancholy; languor, lassitude, lethargy, lifelessness, torpor; dullness (*also* dulness), monotonousness, monotony, sameness; apathy, indifference, unconcern
near antonyms beguilement, bewitchment, captivation, enchantment, fascination; absorption, engagement, engrossment, immersion, involvement; animation, enlivenment, excitement, invigoration, stimulation; amusement, entertainment

boring *adj* causing weariness, restlessness, or lack of interest ⟨I wish this book weren't so *boring*; I keep falling asleep whenever I try to read it⟩
synonyms drab, dreary, dry, dull, flat, heavy, humdrum, jading, leaden, monotonous, pedestrian, ponderous, stodgy, stuffy, stupid, tame, tedious, tiresome, tiring, unanimated, uninteresting, wearisome, weary, wearying
related words undramatic, unentertaining, uneventful, unexciting, uninspiring, unnewsworthy, unrewarding, unsatisfying, unsensational, unspectacular; annoying, bothersome, irksome, irritating; drudging, palling, draining, enervating, exhausting, fatiguing, wearing; debilitating, enfeebling; demoralizing, discouraging, disheartening, dispiriting; common, commonplace, ordinary, stale, unexceptional; lumbering, plodding, slow
near antonyms amazing, astonishing, astounding, awesome, eye-opening, fabulous, marvelous (*or* marvellous), sensational, spectacular, surprising, wonderful, wondrous; animating, energizing, enlivening, exciting, galvanizing, invigorating, stimulating; amusing, diverting, entertaining; alluring, attracting, attractive, beguiling, bewitching, captivating, charming, enchanting, enthralling, entrancing, fascinating; mesmerizing
antonyms absorbing, engaging, engrossing, gripping, interesting, intriguing, involving

born *adj* 1 being such from birth or by nature ⟨a *born* artist and largely self-taught, John Singleton Copley was producing accomplished portraits by the time he was in his late teens⟩ — see NATURAL 1
2 belonging to a particular place by birth or origin ⟨a *born* Texan and very proud of it⟩ — see NATIVE 1

borrow *vb* to take for one's own use (something originated by another) ⟨*borrowed* the basic plot from a book of tales, but put her personal stamp on the story⟩ — see ADOPT

bosom *adj* closely acquainted ⟨promised to remain *bosom* friends for the rest of their lives⟩ — see FAMILIAR 1

boss *adj, slang* of the very best kind ⟨that's a really *boss* stereo you've got⟩ — see EXCELLENT

boss *n* the person (as an employer or supervisor) who tells people and especially workers what to do ⟨every morning the *boss* hands out a list of top-priority tasks⟩
synonyms captain, chief, foreman, head, headman, helmsman, kingpin, leader, master, taskmaster
related words administrator, commander, director, executive, general, manager, overseer, principal, standard-bearer, straw boss, superintendent, superior, supervisor; dominator, lord, overlord, potentate, ruler;

figurehead; slave driver; baron, czar (*also* tsar *or* tzar), king, magnate, mogul, president, prince
near antonyms dependent, inferior, secondary, subject, subordinate, underling
boss *vb* **1** to be in charge of ⟨she *bossed* that project for years, until she was promoted again⟩
synonyms captain, head, oversee, superintend, supervise
related words command, control, direct, guide, manage, order, run, shepherd, show, steer; quarterback; administer; monitor; govern, reign, rule
2 to exercise authority or power over ⟨*bossed* the entire job site for a year⟩ — see GOVERN 1
3 to serve as leader of ⟨*bossed* the entire gang of electricians on the construction project⟩ — see LEAD 2
boss (around) *vb* to issue orders to (someone) by right of authority ⟨that teacher likes to *boss* people *around*—even other teachers⟩ — see COMMAND 1
bossy *adj* fond of ordering people around ⟨I don't want to work with him because he's so *bossy* and always runs roughshod over me⟩
synonyms authoritarian, autocratic, despotic, dictatorial, domineering, imperious, masterful, overbearing, peremptory, tyrannical (*also* tyrannic), tyrannous
related words arrogant, disdainful, haughty, lofty, lordly, proud, supercilious, superior; commanding, dictating; arbitrary, high-handed, imperial; authoritative, directorial, magisterial; aggressive, assertive, self-assertive; conceited, narcissistic, pompous, vain; all-powerful, almighty, omnipotent; firm, stern
near antonyms humble, meek, modest, unassuming; amenable, docile, obedient, tractable; indecisive, irresolute; acquiescent, compliant, passive, resigned, submissive, yielding
botch *vb* to make or do (something) in a clumsy or unskillful way ⟨the first time we tried to make a cake, we *botched* the job completely⟩
synonyms bobble, bungle, butcher, flub, foozle, foul up, fumble, louse up, mangle, mess (up), muff, murder
related words blunder, goof (up), gum (up); blemish, blight, damage, flaw, harm, hurt, impair, injure, mar, mutilate, ruin, spoil, vitiate; destroy, wreck; mishandle, mismanage
near antonyms ameliorate, better, enhance, help, improve, meliorate, rectify, refine, reform, remedy
botched *adj* showing or marked by a lack of skill and tact (as in dealing with a situation) ⟨a *botched* attempt to mend relations with our disaffected European allies⟩ — see AWKWARD 2
bother *n* **1** a state of noisy, confused activity ⟨the whole household was in a *bother*, as our overnight guests were expected to arrive any minute⟩ — see COMMOTION
2 one who is obnoxiously annoying ⟨my little sister is such a *bother*—always following me around!⟩ — see NUISANCE 1
3 something that is a source of irritation ⟨that task is a real *bother*⟩ — see ANNOYANCE 3
4 the feeling of impatience or anger caused by another's repeated disagreeable acts ⟨never let his personal *bothers* interfere with his responsibilities at work⟩ — see ANNOYANCE 2
bother *vb* **1** to thrust oneself upon (another) without invitation ⟨I am never going to get this work done if people don't stop wandering into the room and *bothering* me⟩
synonyms bug, chivy, disturb, intrude (upon), pester
related words inconvenience, trouble; aggravate, anger, annoy, bedevil, devil, exasperate, fret, gall, get,

gnaw, hassle, irritate, nettle, peeve, pique, put out, rile, torment, vex, worry; beleaguer, beset, besiege; distress, plague; afflict, harass, torment; grate, inflame, provoke; enrage, incense, inflame, infuriate, madden; agitate, perturb
near antonyms ignore, leave; appease, conciliate, mollify, oblige, placate; delight, gladden, gratify, please, satisfy; comfort, console, content
2 to disturb the peace of mind of (someone) especially by repeated disagreeable acts ⟨it *bothers* me when obviously sick people go to concerts and spend the whole time coughing and sneezing⟩ — see IRRITATE 1
3 to experience concern or anxiety ⟨just get the basic concept right and don't *bother* about the details⟩ — see WORRY 1
4 to trouble the mind of; to make uneasy ⟨the stranger lurking outside the school building *bothered* her⟩ — see DISTURB 1
bothering *n* the act of making unwelcome intrusions upon another ⟨one more *bothering*, and I'm going to kick you out of here⟩ — see ANNOYANCE 1
bothersome *adj* causing annoyance ⟨a *bothersome* habit of dropping trash on the floor right next to the garbage can⟩ — see ANNOYING
bottom *n* **1** the side or part facing downward from something ⟨that side of the shelf is supposed to be the *bottom*, so turn it over before you assemble the bookcase⟩
synonyms underbelly, underbody, underside, undersurface
related words belly, sole; base, floor, foot, ground, seat, underpinning
near antonyms acme, apex, crest, crown, height, peak, pinnacle, roof, summit; cusp, head, point, tip
antonyms face, top
2 the surface upon which a body of water lies ⟨my missing fishing pole is probably lying on the *bottom* of the lake⟩
synonyms bed, floor
related words riverbed; base, basement, foundation, ground
near antonyms surface
3 the lowest part, place, or point ⟨sliding all the way to the *bottom* of the snow-covered slope⟩
synonyms base, foot, rock bottom
related words basis, bed, bedrock, foundation, ground, groundwork, keystone, seat, underpinning
near antonyms acme, apex, climax, crest, face, height, peak, pinnacle, summit, tip-top, zenith
antonyms head, top
4 the part of the body upon which someone sits ⟨the baby fell backwards onto her *bottom*⟩ — see BUTTOCKS
5 a small buoyant structure for travel on water ⟨the cargo will be carried by a local *bottom*⟩ — see BOAT 1
bottomless *adj* extending far downward or inward ⟨the killer threw the gun into what he thought was a *bottomless* pit⟩ — see DEEP 1
bough *n* a major outgrowth from the main stem of a woody plant ⟨a tree *bough* fell on my car during the windstorm⟩ — see BRANCH 1
boulevard *n* a passage cleared for public vehicular travel ⟨the city is celebrated for its broad, tree-lined *boulevards*⟩ — see WAY 1
bounce *n* active strength of body or mind ⟨the new pop singer has real *bounce* that serves her well in her videos⟩ — see VIGOR 1
bounce *vb* **1** to drive or force out ⟨the bar doesn't hesitate to *bounce* customers for getting rowdy⟩ — see EJECT 1

2 to strike and fly off at an angle ⟨most of my shots *bounce* off the rim of the basket⟩ — see GLANCE 1

bouncing *adj* **1** enjoying health and vigor ⟨a *bouncing* new baby in the family⟩ — see HEALTHY 1
2 having much high-spirited energy and movement ⟨a *bouncing* dance routine that should be good for an aerobics class⟩ — see LIVELY 1

bound *adj* fully committed to achieving a goal ⟨I am *bound* and determined to write a novel before I'm out of my teens⟩ — see DETERMINED 1

¹bound *n* **1** a real or imaginary point beyond which a person or thing cannot go ⟨the player ran out of *bounds*⟩ — see LIMIT
2 the line or relatively narrow space that marks the outer limit of something ⟨colored outside the *bounds* of the drawing⟩ — see BORDER 1

²bound *n* an act of leaping into the air ⟨the kangaroo took one giant *bound* and was gone⟩ — see JUMP 1

¹bound *vb* **1** to mark the limits of ⟨the country is *bounded* by water on two sides⟩ — see LIMIT 2
2 to serve as a border for ⟨being *bounded* on all sides by the Alps has helped Switzerland maintain its neutrality⟩ — see BORDER

²bound *vb* **1** to move with a light bouncing step ⟨the child giggled and *bounded* off to play with her friends⟩ — see SKIP 1
2 to propel oneself upward or forward into the air ⟨a rabbit *bounded* away⟩ — see JUMP 1

boundary *n* **1** a real or imaginary point beyond which a person or thing cannot go ⟨parents have to set *boundaries* for their children, and the children want them to⟩ — see LIMIT
2 the line or relatively narrow space that marks the outer limit of something ⟨that chalk line marks the *boundary* of our playing field⟩ — see BORDER 1

bounded *adj* having distinct or certain limits ⟨in their paintings the Impressionists played down *bounded* figures and concentrated on the subtle, fleeting effects of light⟩ — see LIMITED 1

boundless *adj* being or seeming to be without limits ⟨her *boundless* energy and enthusiasm make her a natural for the cheerleading squad⟩ — see INFINITE

bounteous *adj* giving or sharing in abundance and without hesitation ⟨a *bounteous* king who made sure all his subjects were well-fed⟩ — see GENEROUS 1

bountiful *adj* **1** being more than enough without being excessive ⟨a *bountiful* supply of apples for the harvest festival⟩ — see PLENTIFUL
2 giving or sharing in abundance and without hesitation ⟨a *bountiful* host who makes sure that everyone has plenty to eat at his dinners⟩ — see GENEROUS 1

bountifully *adv* in a generous manner ⟨Grandma makes sure that everyone in the family is *bountifully* supplied with her hand-knit sweaters and scarves⟩ — see WELL 2

bountifulness *n* the quality or state of being generous ⟨because of the restaurant owner's *bountifulness*, a number of homeless people were fed that day⟩ — see LIBERALITY

bounty *n* **1** something offered or given in return for a service performed ⟨a *bounty* was offered for information leading to the capture of the criminal⟩ — see REWARD
2 the quality or state of being generous ⟨her *bounty* at Halloween was known throughout the neighborhood⟩ — see LIBERALITY

bouquet *n* **1** a bunch of flowers ⟨I bought my mother a nice *bouquet* for her birthday⟩

synonyms nosegay, posy
related words boutonniere, corsage; arrangement; garland, lei
2 a sweet or pleasant smell ⟨this wine has a good *bouquet*⟩ — see FRAGRANCE

bout *n* **1** a competitive encounter between individuals or groups carried on for amusement, exercise, or in pursuit of a prize ⟨undoubtedly the school's best wrestler, he hasn't lost a *bout* yet⟩ — see GAME 1
2 a sudden experiencing of a physical or mental disorder ⟨currently suffering from a *bout* of the flu⟩ — see ATTACK 2

bow *n* something that curves or is curved ⟨her full lips form a perfect *bow*⟩ — see BEND 1

¹bow *vb* **1** to cease resistance (as to another's arguments, demands, or control) ⟨finally *bowed* to the principal's insistence that she change her outfit⟩ — see YIELD 3
2 to give up and cease resistance (as to a liking, temptation, or habit) ⟨*bowed* to the craving for fresh coffee⟩ — see YIELD 1

²bow *vb* to turn away from a straight line or course ⟨the river *bows* gently to the north before it reaches the sea⟩ — see CURVE 1

bowed *adj* bending downward or forward ⟨the *bowed* branches of the weeping willow offered some protection from the rain⟩ — see NODDING

bowing *adj* bending downward or forward ⟨the *bowing* blossoms indicated that the petunia plant desperately needed water⟩ — see NODDING

bowl *n* a large usually roofless building for sporting events with tiers of seats for spectators ⟨a new *bowl* for the college football team⟩ — see STADIUM

bowl *vb* **1** to move or proceed smoothly and readily ⟨*bowling* along in my spiffy new car⟩ — see FLOW 2
2 to proceed or move quickly ⟨*bowled* through the test and was the first one to hand in the booklet⟩ — see HURRY 2

bowl (down *or* over) *vb* to strike (someone) so forcefully as to cause a fall ⟨the exuberant dog *bowled over* several children⟩ — see FELL 1

bowl (over) *vb* **1** to cause an often unpleasant surprise for ⟨he was *bowled over* by the discovery that he had flunked the test⟩ — see SHOCK 1
2 to make a strong impression on (someone) with something unexpected ⟨she was *bowled over* to learn that she had a long-lost sister⟩ — see SURPRISE 1

bowled over *adj* affected with sudden and great wonder or surprise ⟨I was *bowled over* when the appraiser told me what the painting was worth⟩ — see THUNDERSTRUCK

¹box *n* a covered rectangular container for storing or transporting things ⟨filled a whole *box* with books⟩ — see CHEST

²box *n* a hard strike with a part of the body or an instrument ⟨the vicious bully delivered a *box* to the child's ear⟩ — see ¹BLOW

boxer *n* one that engages in the sport of fighting with the fists ⟨that *boxer* is quite famous for being the youngest heavyweight champion ever⟩
synonyms fighter, prizefighter, pugilist
related words bantamweight, featherweight, flyweight, heavyweight, light heavyweight, lightweight, middleweight, welterweight

boy *n* a male person who has not yet reached adulthood ⟨a giggling little *boy* ran by⟩
synonyms lad, laddie, nipper, shaver, sonny, stripling, tad, youth

related words adolescent, juvenile, kid, minor, moppet, teenager, youngster; brat, gamin, hobbledehoy, imp, squirt, urchin, whippersnapper; schoolboy

boyfriend *n* a male romantic companion ⟨her *boyfriend* always brings her flowers for Valentine's Day⟩
synonyms beau, fellow, man, swain
related words admirer, crush, steady; gallant, suitor, wooer; beloved, darling, dear, favorite, flame, honey, love, lover, sweet, sweetheart, valentine; date, escort; groom, husband; fiancé, intended

brace *n* **1** something that holds up or serves as a foundation for something else ⟨wore a *brace* for the injured knee⟩ — see SUPPORT 1
2 two things of the same or similar kind that match or are considered together ⟨caught a *brace* of pheasants⟩ — see PAIR

brace *vb* **1** to give life, vigor, or spirit to ⟨the pep talk *braced* the team up for the second half⟩ — see ANIMATE
2 to hold up or serve as a foundation for ⟨several boards *braced* the wall⟩ — see SUPPORT 3
3 to prepare (oneself) mentally or emotionally ⟨she *braced* herself for the college interview⟩ — see FORTIFY 1

bracelet *n* something that physically prevents free movement ⟨putting the handcuffs on the jewel thief, the detective asked him how he liked those *bracelets*⟩ — see BOND 1

bracing *adj* having a renewing effect on the state of the body or mind ⟨a chilly but *bracing* day⟩ — see TONIC

bracket *n* one of the units into which a whole is divided on the basis of a common characteristic ⟨they're in the same income *bracket*⟩ — see CLASS 2

bracket *vb* to describe as similar ⟨I wouldn't exactly *bracket* your paintings with those of Michelangelo and Leonardo da Vinci⟩ — see COMPARE 1

brag *n* boastful speech or writing ⟨for all his *brag* about diving, he actually does very little⟩ — see BOMBAST 1

brag *vb* to praise or express pride in one's own possessions, qualities, or accomplishments often to excess ⟨she *bragged* that she was richer than anyone else in the class⟩ — see BOAST

braggadocio *n* boastful speech or writing ⟨his *braggadocio* hid the fact that he felt really inadequate⟩ — see BOMBAST 1

braid *n* a length of something formed of three or more strands woven together ⟨until she was fifteen, she had a *braid* that reached to her knees⟩
synonyms lace, lacing, plait
related words rickrack (*or* ricrac), stripe; pigtail

braid *vb* to form into a braid ⟨they taught each other how to *braid* yarn into bracelets⟩
synonyms plait, pleat
related words interlace, interweave, weave

brain *n* **1** a very smart person ⟨the *brains* all sit together at lunch⟩ — see GENIUS 1
2 *often* **brains** *pl* the ability to learn and understand or to deal with problems ⟨you have the *brains* to figure out that problem⟩ — see INTELLIGENCE 1

brainless *adj* **1** not having or showing an ability to absorb ideas readily ⟨there are no *brainless* students in this class⟩ — see STUPID 1
2 showing or marked by a lack of good sense or judgment ⟨a *brainless* decision to cheat on a test right in front of the teacher⟩ — see FOOLISH 1

brainlessness *n* **1** lack of good sense or judgment ⟨had the *brainlessness* to sell his car for half of what it was worth⟩ — see FOOLISHNESS 1

2 the quality or state of lacking intelligence or quickness of mind ⟨the turkey is one bird that has often been cited for its *brainlessness*⟩ — see STUPIDITY 1

brainstorm *vb* to engage in an exchange of information or ideas ⟨they *brainstormed* about ways to raise money for their club⟩ — see COMMUNICATE 2

brainy *adj* having or showing quickness of mind ⟨a *brainy* child who was always first with the correct answer⟩ — see INTELLIGENT 1

brake *n* a thick patch of shrubbery, small trees, or underbrush ⟨built a small shelter in the *brake* to watch for deer⟩ — see THICKET

brake *vb* to cause to move or proceed at a less rapid pace ⟨*braked* the car sharply when someone pulled out in front of us⟩ — see SLOW 1

braking *n* a usually gradual decrease in the pace or level of activity of something ⟨there's always a *braking* in sales after lunch⟩ — see SLOWDOWN

brambly *adj* likely to cause a scratch ⟨be careful of the *brambly* blackberry bushes⟩ — see SCRATCHY 1

branch *n* **1** a major outgrowth from the main stem of a woody plant ⟨I loved climbing among the *branches* of that old tree⟩
synonyms bough, limb
related words offshoot, outgrowth, shoot; spray, sprig, twig
2 a local unit of an organization ⟨a bank with many neighborhood *branches*⟩ — see CHAPTER

branch *vb* to extend outwards from or as if from a central point ⟨threads *branched* from the center of the spider web⟩ — see RADIATE 1

branch (out) *vb* to go or move in different directions from a central point ⟨the vine *branched out* across the wall⟩ — see SEPARATE 2

brand *n* **1** a device (as a word) identifying the maker of a piece of merchandise and legally reserved for the exclusive use of that person or company ⟨a company sued for using a name that was very similar to a rival's *brand*⟩ — see TRADEMARK 1
2 a mark of guilt or disgrace ⟨believed that shabby clothes showed the *brand* of poverty⟩ — see STAIN 1

brand–new *adj* **1** being in an original and unused or unspoiled state ⟨his car is so well cared for that three years later it still looks *brand-new*⟩ — see FRESH 1
2 recently made and never used before ⟨a *brand-new* disk still in its original packaging⟩ — see NEW 3

brash *adj* **1** displaying or marked by rude boldness ⟨a *brash* request to get something for free⟩ — see NERVY 1
2 foolishly adventurous or bold ⟨that *brash* motorcyclist likes to show off by riding on only one wheel⟩ — see FOOLHARDY 1

brashness *n* shameless boldness ⟨the *brashness* of the student's excuse was amazing⟩ — see EFFRONTERY

brass *n* shameless boldness ⟨had the *brass* to demand a refund for something they had broken themselves!⟩ — see EFFRONTERY

brassiness *n* shameless boldness ⟨the *brassiness* with which he would blame his mistakes on others left me speechless⟩ — see EFFRONTERY

brassy *adj* displaying or marked by rude boldness ⟨a *brassy* customer insisted on arriving late and still being taken first⟩ — see NERVY 1

brave *adj* feeling or displaying no fear by temperament ⟨the *brave* little boy sat still for the flu shot⟩
synonyms courageous, dauntless, doughty, fearless, gallant, greathearted, heroic, intrepid, lionhearted,

manful, stalwart, stout, stouthearted, undaunted, valiant, valorous

related words determined, firm, game, plucky, resolute, undeterred, undismayed, unflinching, unswerving; mettlesome, spirited, spunky; adventuresome, adventurous, audacious, bold, daring, dashing, gutsy, hardy, venturesome, venturous; crazy, foolish, half-witted, insane, lunatic, mad, nutty; brash, brazen, daredevil, foolhardy, heedless, hotheaded, impetuous, imprudent, impulsive, incautious, madcap, overbold, overconfident, rash, reckless, thoughtless, wild; hasty, headlong, precipitate; comforted, emboldened, encouraged, heartened, reassured, unafraid

near antonyms mousy (*or* mousey), scary, shy, skittish, timid, timorous; anxious, apprehensive, nervous; careful, cautious, heedful, prudent, unadventurous; afraid, agitated, disconcerted, disquieted, disturbed, frightened, horrified, panicked, perturbed, scared, shocked, spooked, startled, terrified, terrorized, unnerved, upset; appalled, concerned, dismayed, worried

antonyms chicken, chickenhearted, coward, cowardly, craven, fainthearted, fearful, lily-livered, pusillanimous

brave *vb* to oppose (something hostile or dangerous) with firmness or courage ⟨a soldier who *braved* enemy fire to rescue her wounded comrade⟩ — see FACE 2

bravery *n* **1** dressy clothing ⟨children in their Sunday *bravery*⟩ — see FINERY

2 strength of mind to carry on in spite of danger ⟨it took great *bravery* to rescue the baby trapped in the burning building⟩ — see COURAGE

brawl *n* **1** a rough and often noisy fight usually involving several people ⟨they were thrown out of the party after starting a *brawl*⟩

synonyms affray, fracas, fray, free-for-all, melee, row, ruckus, ruction

related words battle, clash, combat, conflict, contest, fight, fisticuffs, scrap, scrimmage, scuffle, struggle, tussle; horseplay, roughhousing; altercation, argument, dispute, quarrel, spat, squabble, tiff, wrangle

2 an often noisy or angry expression of differing opinions ⟨the student drama society's decision to put on the controversial play prompted a *brawl* at the school board meeting⟩ — see ARGUMENT 1

brawl *vb* to express different opinions about something often angrily ⟨the Wilsons were always loudly *brawling*, and the neighbors were always shutting their windows⟩ — see ARGUE 2

brawn *n* muscular strength ⟨an actor who is more famous for his *brawn* than for his talent⟩ — see MUSCLE 1

brawny *adj* **1** having muscles capable of exerting great physical force ⟨they always asked the *brawniest* person there to do the heavy lifting⟩ — see STRONG 1

2 marked by a well-developed musculature ⟨*brawny* arms that weren't developed in the gym but by years of work in the construction business⟩ — see MUSCULAR 1

3 strongly and heavily built ⟨a tough little boy who's going to be a *brawny* man⟩ — see ¹HUSKY

brazen *adj* displaying or marked by rude boldness ⟨a *brazen* demand for special treatment just because she's rich⟩ — see NERVY 1

brazen *vb* to oppose (something hostile or dangerous) with firmness or courage ⟨a principal willing to *brazen* the opposition from parents that such a decision was sure to bring⟩ — see FACE 2

brazenness *n* shameless boldness ⟨she had the *brazenness* to expect me to let her cheat⟩ — see EFFRONTERY

breach *n* **1** a failure to uphold the requirements of law, duty, or obligation ⟨the president's deliberate misstatements were widely seen as a *breach* of the public trust⟩

synonyms infraction, infringement, transgression, trespass, violation

related words offense, sin, wrong; disregard, forgetting, ignoring, nonobservance, overlooking; delinquency, dereliction, neglect; intrusion, invasion

near antonyms respecting, upholding

antonyms nonviolation, observance

2 a breaking of a moral or legal code ⟨cheating on the exam was a serious *breach* of the school's honor code⟩ — see OFFENSE 1

3 an open space in a barrier (as a wall or hedge) ⟨the cat got out of the yard through a *breach* in the hedge⟩ — see GAP 1

breach *vb* to fail to keep ⟨a builder being sued by a homeowner for *breaching* a contract⟩ — see VIOLATE 1

bread *n* **1** *slang* something (as pieces of stamped metal or printed paper) customarily and legally used as a medium of exchange, a measure of value, or a means of payment ⟨I'll buy that tomorrow, when I get some *bread*⟩ — see MONEY

2 substances intended to be eaten ⟨supplied his charges with *bread* and a place to stay⟩ — see FOOD

breadbasket *n, slang* the part of the body between the chest and the pelvis ⟨got hit right in the *breadbasket*⟩ — see STOMACH

breadth *n* **1** a wide space or area ⟨a great *breadth* of land awaited those who were brave enough to settle it⟩ — see EXPANSE

2 an area over which activity, capacity, or influence extends ⟨the *breadth* of his knowledge on the subject is awesome⟩ — see RANGE 2

break *n* **1** a momentary halt in an activity ⟨the gym teacher called a *break* when he noticed Timmy was being pelted with basketballs⟩ — see PAUSE

2 a period during which the usual routine of school or work is suspended ⟨most of the students at the boarding school are going home for Christmas *break*⟩ — see VACATION

3 an open space in a barrier (as a wall or hedge) ⟨the rancher repaired the *break* in the fence where the horse had gotten through⟩ — see GAP 1

break *vb* **1** to cause to separate into pieces usually suddenly or forcibly ⟨I hated admitting to Mom that I had *broken* her favorite glass vase⟩

synonyms bust, fracture, fragment

related words blast, blow up, burst, detonate, explode; pop, shatter, shiver, smash; sliver, splinter, split; collapse, implode; demolish, destroy, ruin, wreck

near antonyms fix, heal, mend, patch, rebuild, reconstruct, repair

2 to bring (as an action or operation) to an immediate end ⟨the final vote *broke* the deadlock⟩ — see STOP 1

3 to bring to a lower grade or rank ⟨the captain was *broken* to lieutenant commander for disobeying a direct order of his group commander⟩ — see DEMOTE

4 to change (as a secret message) from code into ordinary language ⟨Alan Turing and the Bletchley Park mathematicians *broke* the Enigma code being used by the Nazis⟩ — see DECODE

5 to come to a temporary halt in one's activity ⟨she *broke* from her ruminations to find that it was already six o'clock⟩ — see PAUSE

6 to cut into and turn over the sod of (a piece of land) using a bladed implement ⟨farmers once *broke* fields with horse-drawn plows⟩ — see PLOW 1

7 to fail to keep ⟨John was furious when he found that Louis had *broken* his promise not to blab about his crush on Sarah⟩ — see VIOLATE 1

8 to find an answer for through reasoning ⟨Professor Bates *broke* the problem when she realized that it was possible to synthesize the necessary compounds⟩ — see SOLVE

9 to reduce the soundness, effectiveness, or perfection of ⟨Jason *broke* a tooth on the hard candy⟩ — see DAMAGE 1

10 to stop functioning ⟨after working for 30 years, the pump simply *broke* one day⟩ — see FAIL 1

11 to hasten away from something dangerous or frightening ⟨the herd of gazelles *broke* when they saw the lions racing toward them from the ridge above⟩ — see RUN 2

breakable *adj* easily broken ⟨elderly people's bones can be highly *breakable* if they haven't gotten enough calcium during their lifetimes⟩ — see FRAGILE 1

breakdown *n* **1** the process by which dead organic matter separates into simpler substances ⟨the *breakdown* of the body was arrested by the embalming process⟩ — see CORRUPTION 1

2 the separation and identification of the parts of a whole ⟨a demographic *breakdown* revealed that the ethnic composition of the area had changed significantly since the last census⟩ — see ANALYSIS 1

break down *vb* **1** to arrange or assign according to type ⟨when presented with the pile of files, the first thing he did was to *break* them *down* by month, order within the month, and region⟩ — see CLASSIFY 1

2 to go through decomposition ⟨the enamel of a human tooth will begin to *break down* when exposed to sugar for too long⟩ — see DECAY 1

3 to identify and examine the basic elements or parts of (something) especially for discovering interrelationships ⟨if we *break* the problem *down* into what appear to be three aspects of it, we'll have a better chance of solving it⟩ — see ANALYZE

4 to stop functioning ⟨the computer finally *broke down* and had to be replaced⟩ — see FAIL 1

5 to yield to mental or emotional stress ⟨Martin began to *break down* when he realized that he had no more money left in his bank account⟩ — see CRACK 2

break in *vb* **1** to enter a house or building by force usually with illegal intent ⟨the burglars *broke in* by smashing a window⟩
synonyms burglarize
related words invade, trespass; hold up, loot, plunder, rip off, rob, stick up; ransack, rifle; despoil, devastate, maraud, pillage, ravage, sack

2 to cause a disruption in a conversation or discussion ⟨he rudely *broke in* to mention that he had indeed saved several hundred dollars by shopping carefully⟩ — see INTERRUPT

breakneck *adj* moving, proceeding, or acting with great speed ⟨the *breakneck* production of naval vessels during World War II⟩ — see FAST 1

break off *vb* **1** to bring (as an action or operation) to an immediate end ⟨the judge *broke off* court proceedings until after lunch⟩ — see STOP 1

2 to come to an end ⟨talks between the two sides *broke off* when one began making unreasonable demands⟩ — see CEASE 1

break out *vb* to develop suddenly and violently ⟨in the wake of news reports of deaths from the flu, panic *broke out*, and there was a mad rush for flu shots⟩ — see ERUPT 2

breakthrough *n* an instance of notable progress in the development of knowledge, technology, or skill ⟨Alexander Fleming's discovery of penicillin was one of medicine's great *breakthroughs*, for penicillin became the first antibiotic to successfully combat bacterial infections in humans⟩ — see ADVANCE 2

breakup *n* the act or process of a whole separating into two or more parts or pieces ⟨the *breakup* of the Soviet Union and the collapse of communism pretty much signaled the end of the Cold War⟩ — see SEPARATION 1

break up *vb* **1** to cease to exist or cause to cease to exist as a group or organization ⟨the band *broke up* when their arguments over money grew too stressful⟩ — see DISBAND 1

2 to come to an end ⟨the meeting *broke up* when all the business for the day had been completed⟩ — see CEASE 1

3 to set or force apart ⟨he *broke up* the rocks in the old stone wall with a crowbar, sending them tumbling to the ground⟩ — see SEPARATE 1

breast *n* the seat of one's deepest thoughts and emotions ⟨deep in his *breast*, he knew that his father had a great love for him that did not need to be expressed in words⟩ — see CORE 1

breast *vb* to oppose (something hostile or dangerous) with firmness or courage ⟨*breasted* the medical crisis calmly and without hesitation⟩ — see FACE 2

breath *n* **1** a momentary halt in an activity ⟨let's all take a *breath* before continuing⟩ — see PAUSE

2 a slight or gentle movement of air ⟨a sweet *breath* caressed her cheek as she sat in the garden⟩ — see BREEZE 1

breathe *vb* **1** to inhale and exhale air ⟨sometimes it gets so hot in here that it's hard to even *breathe*⟩
synonyms respire
related words expire, inspire; gasp, huff, pant, puff, wheeze; sniff, snore, snort, snuffle; yawn
near antonyms asphyxiate, choke, gag, smother, suffocate; garrotte (*or* garotte), stifle, strangle, throttle

2 to have life ⟨as long as I *breathe*, you will have a place to stay⟩ — see BE 1

breathe (out) *vb* to let or force out of the lungs ⟨*breathed out* the smoke⟩ — see EXHALE 1

breather *n* a momentary halt in an activity ⟨took a *breather* from the seemingly endless task of sorting through years of stuff stored in the attic⟩ — see PAUSE

breathing *adj* having or showing life ⟨realized that he didn't need a comic-book superhero, since he had a real, *breathing* hero in his father⟩ — see ALIVE 1

breathless *adj* **1** lacking fresh air ⟨the room was hot and *breathless*⟩ — see STUFFY 1

2 moving, proceeding, or acting with great speed ⟨ran at a *breathless* pace to get help⟩ — see FAST 1

3 no longer living ⟨carried the *breathless* body of his beloved dog back home⟩ — see DEAD 1

breathtaking *adj* causing great emotional or mental stimulation ⟨a truly *breathtaking* view of the majestic waterfall⟩ — see EXCITING 1

breech *n* **1** the part of the body upon which someone sits ⟨plant yourselves on your *breeches* on that bench and listen to what I have to say⟩ — see BUTTOCKS

2 breeches *pl* an outer garment covering each leg separately from waist to ankle ⟨the mounted riders look striking in their red coats and white *breeches*⟩ — see PANTS

breed *n* a number of persons or things that are grouped together because they have something in common

⟨some people say that honest politicians are a rare *breed*⟩ — see SORT 1

breed *vb* **1** to bring forth offspring ⟨rabbits will *breed* very frequently unless they're kept separated⟩ — see PROCREATE

2 to bring to maturity through care and education ⟨he was *bred* to a life in the military by his father, himself an army captain⟩ — see BRING UP 1

breeding *n* the line of ancestors from whom a person is descended ⟨a family of good *breeding* that is well respected in the community⟩ — see ANCESTRY

breeze *n* **1** a slight or gentle movement of air ⟨a warm spring *breeze* ruffled our hair⟩

synonyms air, breath, puff, waft, zephyr

related words draft, whiff; land breeze, sea breeze; blast, blow, flurry, gale, northeaster, norther, northwester, southeaster, southwester, westerly, wind; squall, tempest, tornado, windstorm; airflow

near antonyms calm

2 something that is easy to do ⟨that assignment will be a *breeze*⟩ — see CINCH

breeze *vb* **1** to move or proceed smoothly and readily ⟨she *breezed* through the spelling test⟩ — see FLOW 2

2 to proceed or move quickly ⟨the doctor *breezed* past the people in the waiting room, apparently on his way to an emergency⟩ — see HURRY 2

breezy *adj* **1** having a relaxed, casual manner ⟨a *breezy*, fun teacher⟩ — see EASYGOING 1

2 marked by strong wind or more wind than usual ⟨a *breezy* day is best for flying a kite⟩ — see WINDY 1

brevity *n* **1** the condition of being short ⟨the best quality a graduation speech can have is *brevity*⟩

synonyms briefness, conciseness, shortness

related words abbreviation, abridgment (*or* abridgement), compression, condensation, contraction, curtailment; decreasing, diminishing, lessening, reducing, shortening, shrinking; abruptness, brusqueness, curtness; pithiness, succinctness, terseness; littleness, minuteness, smallness, tininess

near antonyms extensiveness; elongating, elongation, extending, extension, prolongation, prolonging, protraction, stretching; expansion, growth, spread; diffuseness, prolixity, talkativeness, verboseness, volubility, wordiness; bigness, bulkiness, greatness, heftiness, largeness

antonyms lengthiness

2 the quality or state of being marked by or using only few words to convey much meaning ⟨the importance of the lecture was matched only by its *brevity*⟩ — see SUCCINCTNESS

brew *vb* to be about to happen ⟨there's trouble *brewing* in the school⟩ — see LOOM

bribable *adj* open to improper influence and especially bribery ⟨corruption in that country is so widespread that there are few public officials who are not *bribable*⟩ — see VENAL

bribe *n* something given or promised in order to improperly influence a person's conduct or decision ⟨that judge refused a huge *bribe* to dismiss the charges against the wealthy defendant⟩

synonyms fix, sop

related words incentive, incitement, motivation, spur, stimulation, stimulus; boost, goad, inducement; allurement, bait, enticement, lure, temptation; flattery, persuasion; decoy, snare, trap

bribe *vb* to influence someone with a bribe ⟨meat inspectors were *bribed*, and the contaminated beef was sold to the public⟩

synonyms have, square

related words fix, tamper (with); corrupt, debase, defile, dishonor, taint; allure, bait, entice, lure, tempt; motivate, provoke, spur, stimulate; goad, induce; flatter, persuade; snare, trap

bridal *n* a ceremony in which two people are united in matrimony ⟨an old-fashioned country *bridal*⟩ — see WEDDING

bridgehead *n* a place from which an advance (as for military operations) is made ⟨established a *bridgehead* on the beach before beginning the land invasion⟩ — see BASE 2

bridle *vb* to keep from exceeding a desirable degree or level (as of expression) ⟨try to *bridle* your criticism next time so that it is helpful and not hurtful⟩ — see CONTROL 1

brief *adj* **1** marked by the use of few words to convey much information or meaning ⟨a *brief* but crucial admonition to keep quiet⟩ — see CONCISE

2 not lasting for a considerable time ⟨fortunately, the meeting was *brief*⟩ — see SHORT 2

brief *vb* to give information to ⟨the lieutenant *briefed* his superior officers on the state of the enemy's fortifications⟩ — see ENLIGHTEN 1

briefly *adv* in a few words ⟨tell us *briefly* why you chose this class⟩ — see SHORTLY 1

briefness *n* **1** the condition of being short ⟨the *briefness* of the instructions rendered them less than helpful⟩ — see BREVITY 1

2 the quality or state of being marked by or using only few words to convey much meaning ⟨in this case the *briefness* of the essay is not a drawback because it says all that needs to be said and does so with eloquence⟩ — see SUCCINCTNESS

brig *n* a place of confinement for persons held in lawful custody ⟨the captain ordered that the prisoner be thrown into the *brig* immediately⟩ — see JAIL

bright *adj* **1** giving off or reflecting much light ⟨in the desert the sun was so *bright* that it hurt my eyes⟩ ⟨the moon is *bright* tonight⟩

synonyms beaming, bedazzling, brilliant, dazzling, effulgent, glowing, incandescent, lambent, lucent, lucid, luminous, lustrous, radiant, refulgent, shining, shiny

related words blazing, burning, combusting, fiery, flaming; agleam, aglitter, blinding, flaring, flashing, flickering, glaring, gleaming, glimmering, glinting, glistening, glittering, scintillating, shimmering, sparkling, twinkling; burnished, polished; sunny

near antonyms blackened, dark, darkened, darkish, darkling, darksome, dimmed, dusky, gloomy, murky, obscure, obscured, pitch-black, pitch-dark, somber, sunless; cloudy, shadowy, shady; gray (*also* grey), leaden, pale

antonyms dim, dull, lackluster

2 filled with much light ⟨the display windows of department stores are especially *bright* at Christmastime⟩

synonyms ablaze, alight, brightened, illuminated, illumined, light, lighted (*or* lit)

related words floodlit (*or* floodlighted), highlighted, spotlighted (*or* spotlit); kindled, ignited

near antonyms gloomy, somber (*or* sombre), sunless; cloudy, murky, obscured, shadowy; gray (*also* grey), leaden, pale

antonyms blackened, dark, darkened, darkish, darkling, dimmed, dusky, pitch-black, pitch-dark

3 having or showing a good mood or disposition ⟨always walks into work with a *bright* smile on his face⟩ — see CHEERFUL 1

4 having or showing quickness of mind ⟨a *bright* student who always has her hand up first⟩ — see INTELLIGENT 1

5 having qualities which inspire hope ⟨predicted a *bright* future for the young math whiz⟩ — see HOPEFUL 1

6 pointing toward a happy outcome ⟨all the signs are *bright* right now for an economic boom⟩ — see FAVORABLE 2

7 serving to lift one's spirits ⟨a *bright* and beautiful morning to begin planting our garden⟩ — see CHEERFUL 2

brighten *vb* to become glad or hopeful ⟨the glum soccer player started to *brighten* the minute we told him we were taking him out for ice cream⟩ — see CHEER (UP) 1

brightened *adj* filled with much light ⟨the *brightened* room is now a much more cheerful place for the recuperating patients⟩ — see BRIGHT 2

brightness *n* the quality or state of having or giving off light ⟨the *brightness* of the sunshine made me squint after an afternoon spent in a darkened movie theater⟩ — see BRILLIANCE 1

brilliance *n* **1** the quality or state of having or giving off light ⟨the *brilliance* of the flash from the camera was so intense that I was blinded for a moment afterwards⟩
synonyms brightness, brilliancy, dazzle, effulgence, illumination, lightness, lucidity, luminosity, radiance, refulgence, splendor
related words blaze, flare, flicker, light; fluorescence, incandescence, luminescence; burnish, gloss, luster, polish, sheen, shine; fire, flame, glare, glow; flash, gleam, glimmer, glint, glisten, glitter, scintillation, shimmer, sparkle, twinkle
near antonyms dimness, dullness (*also* dulness), gloominess, somberness; cloudiness, haziness, murkiness, obscurity; colorlessness, grayness, paleness
antonyms blackness, dark, darkness, duskiness
2 impressiveness of beauty on a large scale ⟨the *brilliance* of the palace is really quite staggering⟩ — see MAGNIFICENCE

brilliancy *n* the quality or state of having or giving off light ⟨the *brilliancy* of the diamond is shown to good effect by the museum's lighting⟩ — see BRILLIANCE 1

brilliant *adj* **1** giving off or reflecting much light ⟨a *brilliant* chandelier graces the hotel lobby⟩ — see BRIGHT 1
2 having or showing quickness of mind ⟨a *brilliant* boy who left for college at the age of 16⟩ — see INTELLIGENT 1

brilliant *n* a usually valuable stone cut and polished for ornament ⟨the diamond cutter set out an array of *brilliants* to show the various ways the diamond could be cut⟩ — see GEM 1

brim *n* **1** the line or relatively narrow space that marks the outer limit of something ⟨the *brim* of the cup was banded with gold⟩ — see BORDER 1
2 the projecting front part of a hat or cap ⟨touched the *brim* of his cap by way of salute⟩ — see VISOR

brimful *adj* containing or seeming to contain the greatest quantity or number possible ⟨a book *brimful* of stories about people who overcome childhood adversities to achieve great things⟩ — see FULL 1

brimming *adj* containing or seeming to contain the greatest quantity or number possible ⟨bins *brimming*

with coffee beans from a wide array of tropical localities⟩ — see FULL 1

brine *n* the whole body of salt water that covers nearly three-fourths of the earth ⟨for hundreds of years people from Atlantic Canada have made their living from the *brine*⟩ — see OCEAN

bring *vb* to have a price of ⟨the antique will probably *bring* at least $1000 at auction⟩ — see COST

bring about *vb* to be the cause of (a situation, action, or state of mind) ⟨I promise: making one mistake will not *bring about* the Apocalypse⟩ — see EFFECT

bring up *vb* **1** to bring to maturity through care and education ⟨it takes an immense commitment and a lot of love to *bring up* a child properly⟩
synonyms breed, foster, raise, rear
related words father, mother; attend, care (for), cultivate, mind, minister (to), nurse, nurture, watch; discipline, educate, instruct, mentor, school, teach, train, tutor; edify, enlighten, indoctrinate; feed, nourish, provide (for), supply; advance, forward, further, promote; prepare; direct, guide, lead, shepherd, show
near antonyms abuse, ill-treat, ill-use, maltreat, mishandle, mistreat; ignore, neglect; harm, hurt, injure
2 to present or bring forward for discussion ⟨I hate to *bring* this *up*, but we're running short of money⟩ — see INTRODUCE 2

brininess *n* the quality or state of being salty ⟨the *brininess* of the soup rendered it inedible⟩ — see SALTINESS

briny *adj* of, relating to, or containing salt ⟨a *briny* liquid that is often used to make pickles⟩ — see SALTY 1

brisk *adj* **1** having much high-spirited energy and movement ⟨a *brisk* exercise that many athletes use to warm up⟩ — see LIVELY 1
2 moving, proceeding, or acting with great speed ⟨moved at a *brisk* walk through the exhibit⟩ — see FAST 1

briskly *adv* with great speed ⟨strode off *briskly* to deal with the problem⟩ — see FAST 1

briskness *n* the quality or state of having abundant or intense activity ⟨the *briskness* of the shopping scene at the mall makes it a good candidate for our next store⟩ — see VITALITY 1

bristle *vb* to express one's anger usually violently ⟨the man *bristled* at the accusation, and threatened to file a lawsuit⟩ — see RAGE 1

bristly *adj* covered with or as if with hair ⟨although pigs look hairless, they're actually *bristly*⟩ — see HAIRY 1

brittle *adj* having a texture that readily breaks into little pieces under pressure ⟨a *brittle* cracker that turned into crumbs in my pocket⟩ — see CRISP 1

broach *vb* **1** to penetrate the surface (as of water) from below ⟨the immense whales *broaching* was a magnificent sight⟩
synonyms surface
related words break, emerge, rise
near antonyms dive, drop, founder, plunge, sink, submerge, submerse
2 to present or bring forward for discussion ⟨*broached* the topic of plans for next year's parade⟩ — see INTRODUCE 2

broad *adj* **1** having a greater than usual measure across ⟨a *broad* expanse of water in the island-dotted lake⟩ — see WIDE 1
2 having considerable extent ⟨her *broad* knowledge of American politics makes her a much-sought-after guest on talk shows⟩ — see EXTENSIVE

3 not subject to misinterpretation or more than one interpretation ⟨gave them a *broad* hint that it was time to leave⟩ — see CLEAR 2

4 relating to the main elements and not to specific details ⟨a *broad* overview of the topic⟩ — see GENERAL 2

broadcast *vb* **1** to cause to be known over a considerable area or by many people ⟨*broadcast* the information only to people who needed to know⟩ — see SPREAD 1

2 to make known openly or publicly ⟨please don't *broadcast* this news, as it's not being publicly announced yet⟩ — see ANNOUNCE

broadly *adv* to a large extent or degree ⟨the new policy is *broadly* applicable⟩ — see GREATLY 2

broad–minded *adj* **1** not bound by traditional ways or beliefs ⟨a *broad-minded* social policy⟩ — see LIBERAL 1

2 willing to consider new or different ideas ⟨my mother always votes for the most *broad-minded* candidate in the race⟩ — see OPEN-MINDED 1

broadside *adv* with one side faced forward ⟨one car hit the other *broadside* and crushed the passenger door⟩ — see SIDEWAYS

brochure *n* a short printed publication with no cover or with a paper cover ⟨handed out *brochures* giving practical hints about environment-friendly practices that every family can adopt⟩ — see PAMPHLET

broiling *adj* having a notably high temperature ⟨the classroom was *broiling* because the air conditioning was on the blink⟩ — see HOT 1

broke *adj* lacking money or material possessions ⟨too *broke* to afford even a used car⟩ — see POOR 1

broken *adj* **1** having an uneven edge or outline ⟨the *broken* rim of the antique vase greatly reduces its value⟩ — see RAGGED 1

2 not having a level or smooth surface ⟨that portion of the hiking trail consists of a long, *broken* mountain ridge⟩ — see UNEVEN 1

brokenhearted *adj* feeling unhappiness ⟨she was *brokenhearted* at losing the contest⟩ — see SAD 1

brood *vb* to cover and warm eggs to hatch them ⟨don't disturb the hen while she's *brooding*⟩ — see SET 1

brook *n* a natural body of running water smaller than a river ⟨there are tiny fish and frogs in that *brook*⟩ — see CREEK 1

brook *vb* to put up with (something painful or difficult) ⟨I will not *brook* insults from my students⟩ — see BEAR 2

brooklet *n* a natural body of running water smaller than a river ⟨a little *brooklet* trickled past the house⟩ — see CREEK 1

brotherhood *n* **1** a group of persons formally joined together for some common interest ⟨they're a *brotherhood* of retired war veterans⟩ — see ASSOCIATION 2

2 the body of people in a profession or field of activity ⟨a family that has been part of the *brotherhood* of police officers for four generations⟩ — see CORPS

brotherly *adj* of, relating to, or befitting brothers ⟨the *brotherly* love that exists between the members of the scout troop⟩ — see FRATERNAL

browbeat *vb* to make timid or fearful by or as if by threats ⟨*browbeat* the younger child until he cried⟩ — see INTIMIDATE

brownie *n* an imaginary being usually having a small human form and magical powers ⟨some people believe that *brownies* will clean your house if you leave them milk⟩ — see FAIRY

browse *vb* **1** to feed on grass or herbs ⟨cows *browsing* in fields are a common sight along that stretch of the road⟩ — see GRAZE

2 to take a quick or hasty look ⟨*browsed* through the stacks looking for interesting books⟩ — see ¹GLANCE 2

bruise *n* a bodily injury in which small blood vessels are broken but the overlying skin is not ⟨she got quite a big *bruise* from walking into the corner of the table⟩ — see CONTUSION

bruit (about) *vb* to make (as a piece of information) the subject of common talk without any authority or confirmation of accuracy ⟨please don't *bruit* accusations *about* without confirming them first⟩ — see RUMOR

brush *n* a brief clash between enemies or rivals ⟨the two advance parties had a *brush*, but no one was wounded⟩ — see ENCOUNTER

brush *vb* to pass lightly across or touch gently especially in passing ⟨spiderwebs *brushed* her cheek as she walked through the basement⟩

synonyms graze, kiss, nudge, shave, skim

related words bump, contact, scrape, strike, sweep, swipe, touch; bounce, carom, glance, rebound, ricochet, sideswipe, skip; caress, cuddle, fondle, pet, stroke

near antonyms clash, collide, hit, knock, punch, slap, smack, smash, thwack, whack

brush (aside *or* off) *vb* to overlook or dismiss as of little importance ⟨*brushed off* their complaints as the whining of people who were never satisfied⟩ — see EXCUSE 1

brush–off *n* treatment that is deliberately unfriendly ⟨the politician tends to give anyone under voting age the *brush-off*⟩ — see COLD SHOULDER

brushwood *n* a thick patch of shrubbery, small trees, or underbrush ⟨cleared away the *brushwood* in order to build a shed⟩ — see THICKET

brusque *adj* being or characterized by direct, brief, and potentially rude speech or manner ⟨a *brusque* and unhelpful reply from the clerk in the hardware store⟩ — see BLUNT 1

brutal *adj* **1** difficult to endure ⟨*brutal* hard labor in the hot sun⟩ — see HARSH 1

2 having or showing the desire to inflict severe pain and suffering on others ⟨a *brutal* child who liked to torture animals⟩ — see CRUEL 1

brutality *n* the willful infliction of pain and suffering on others ⟨the police were accused of *brutality* for using excessive force in making arrests⟩ — see CRUELTY

brute *n* **1** one of the lower animals as distinguished from human beings ⟨it is a fundamental sense of right and wrong that separates us from the *brutes*⟩ — see ANIMAL

2 a mean, evil, or unprincipled person ⟨only a *brute* would deliberately break someone's arm⟩ — see VILLAIN

bubble *vb* to flow in a broken irregular stream ⟨soapy water *bubbled* down the drain⟩ — see GURGLE

bubbly *adj* joyously unrestrained ⟨offered a *bubbly* congratulations to the expectant parents⟩ — see EXUBERANT

buccaneer *n* someone who engages in robbery of ships at sea ⟨*buccaneers* who preyed upon the treasure-laden ships in the Caribbean⟩ — see PIRATE

buck *n* **1** a man extremely interested in his clothing and personal appearance ⟨a vain *buck* who spends an hour before the bathroom mirror every morning⟩ — see DANDY 1

2 an adult male human being ⟨found some strong, young *bucks* to help out⟩ — see MAN 1

buck *vb* **1** to move or cause to move with a sharp quick motion ⟨the car *bucked* and stalled⟩ — see JERK 1

2 to refuse to give in to ⟨*bucked* the trend and wore the same clothes they always had⟩ — see RESIST

buckaroo *n* a hired hand who tends cattle or horses at a ranch or on the range ⟨a *buckaroo* teaches riding lessons at that dude ranch⟩ — see COWBOY

bucket *n* **1** a considerable amount ⟨made *buckets* of money in the stock market⟩ — see LOT 2

2 a round container that is open at the top and outfitted with a handle ⟨carried water from the well in a *bucket*⟩ — see PAIL

buckle *vb* to occupy (oneself) diligently or with close attention ⟨*buckled* himself down and finished the assignment in record time⟩ — see APPLY 2

bucolic *adj* of, relating to, associated with, or typical of open areas with few buildings or people ⟨a *bucolic* region where farms were still common⟩ — see RURAL

buddy *n* a person who has a strong liking for and trust in another ⟨my *buddy* is the one person I can always turn to⟩ — see FRIEND 1

budge *vb* **1** to cease resistance (as to another's arguments, demands, or control) ⟨despite hours of intense pressure, she refused to *budge* from her position⟩ — see YIELD 3

2 to change one's position ⟨he finally *budged* from his beach blanket when the tide started swirling up around him⟩ — see MOVE 3

3 to change the place or position of ⟨the bureau was so heavy that two people couldn't *budge* it⟩ — see MOVE 1

budget *n* **1** a sum of money set aside for a particular purpose ⟨we've spent a little more than our *budget* this year⟩ — see FUND 1

2 the number of individuals or amount of something available at any given time ⟨they had a whole *budget* of complaints⟩ — see SUPPLY

buff *n* a person with a strong and habitual liking for something ⟨he's such a film *buff* that he owns over 3,000 movies⟩ — see FAN

buff *vb* **1** to make smooth by friction ⟨she learned to *buff* semiprecious stones to make her own jewelry⟩ — see GRIND 1

2 to make smooth or glossy usually by repeatedly applying surface pressure ⟨the janitor *buffed* the gym floor until it shone⟩ — see POLISH

buffed *adj* having a shiny surface or finish ⟨a beautiful, *buffed* antique table⟩ — see GLOSSY

buffer *n* something that serves as a protective barrier ⟨the excelsior acts as an additional *buffer* for the marble bust during shipping⟩ — see CUSHION

buffer *vb* to lessen the shock of ⟨an umbrella and thick coat *buffered* the freezing rain⟩ — see CUSHION

¹buffet *n* a hard strike with a part of the body or an instrument ⟨delivered a powerful *buffet* to the side of the prisoner's head⟩ — see ¹BLOW

²buffet *n* a storage case typically having doors and shelves ⟨a *buffet* completed the kitchen set⟩ — see CABINET

buffet *vb* to strike repeatedly ⟨fierce winds *buffeted* the small sailboat⟩ — see BEAT 1

buffoon *n* a comically dressed performer (as at a circus) who entertains with playful tricks and ridiculous behavior ⟨children giggled at the *buffoon's* silly tricks⟩ — see CLOWN 1

bug *n* **1** a person with a strong and habitual liking for something ⟨a camera *bug* who loves taking pictures⟩ — see FAN

2 an abnormal state that disrupts a plant's or animal's normal bodily functioning ⟨I can't go to school today because I've caught some *bug* that's going around⟩ — see DISEASE

bug *vb* **1** to attack repeatedly with mean put-downs or insults ⟨my big sister *bugs* me constantly⟩ — see TEASE 2

2 to disturb the peace of mind of (someone) especially by repeated disagreeable acts ⟨these incessant phone calls are really starting to *bug* me⟩ — see IRRITATE 1

3 to thrust oneself upon (another) without invitation ⟨I hate to *bug* you, but could you help me move this table?⟩ — see BOTHER 1

bugaboo *n* something or someone that causes fear or dread especially without reason ⟨final exams are some students' *bugaboo*⟩ — see BOGEY 1

bugbear *n* something or someone that causes fear or dread especially without reason ⟨communism was once the nation's biggest *bugbear*⟩ — see BOGEY 1

bugging *n* the act of making unwelcome intrusions upon another ⟨this perpetual *bugging* while I'm trying to concentrate is driving me nuts!⟩ — see ANNOYANCE

build *n* the type of body that a person has ⟨she has a slender *build*⟩ — see PHYSIQUE

build *vb* to form by putting together parts or materials ⟨he spent hours *building* a model airplane from a kit⟩

synonyms assemble, construct, erect, fabricate, make, make up, piece, put up, raise, rear, set up

related words fashion, forge, frame, manufacture, mold, produce, shape; prefabricate; begin, coin, create, generate, inaugurate, initiate, innovate, invent, originate; constitute, establish, father, found, institute, organize; conceive, concoct, contrive, cook up, design, devise, imagine, think (up); rebuild; rig up

phrases put together

near antonyms dismember; demolish, destroy, devastate, flatten, pulverize, raze, ruin, shatter, smash, wreck; blow up, explode

antonyms disassemble, dismantle, take down

build (up) *vb* **1** to become greater in extent, volume, amount, or number ⟨static electricity *built up* on the cat's fur⟩ — see INCREASE 2

2 to increase in ⟨the roller coaster *built up* momentum⟩ — see GAIN 1

3 to produce or bring about especially by long or repeated effort ⟨the stock broker worked hard to *build up* a clientele⟩ — see HAMMER (OUT)

building *n* something built as a dwelling, shelter, or place for human activity ⟨English class will be in that big stone *building* over there⟩

synonyms edifice, structure

related words construction, erection; bungalow, cabin, chalet, cottage, house, lodge, summerhouse; hovel, hut, shack, shanty, shed; castle, château, estate, hall, manor, mansion, palace, villa; skyscraper, tower

bulge *n* a part that sticks out from the general mass of something ⟨several *bulges* in the old vinyl flooring in the dingy bathroom⟩

synonyms jut, overhang, projection, protrusion, protuberance

related words dome; blob, bump, knob, lump, nub, swelling; block, piece, portion, section; enlargement, escalation, expansion, increase

near antonyms cavity, crater, hole; basin, dip, valley

antonyms concavity, dent, depression, hollow, indentation, pit

bulge *vb* to extend outward beyond a usual point ⟨the sides of the returning camper's suitcase *bulged* with a month's worth of dirty laundry⟩

synonyms bag, balloon, beetle, belly, billow, jut, overhang, poke, project, protrude, stand out, start, stick out

related words dome; blow up, inflate; distend, expand, swell; mushroom, snowball; elongate, extend, lengthen, stretch

near antonyms compress, condense, constrict, contract, shrink

bulk *n* the main or greater part of something as distinguished from its appendages ⟨the cookie lost a few crumbs, but the *bulk* of it remained⟩ — see BODY 1

bulkiness *n* the quality or state of being large in size ⟨the box wasn't heavy, but its *bulkiness* made it awkward to carry⟩ — see LARGENESS

bulky *adj* of a size greater than average of its kind ⟨*bulky* packages might cost more to mail⟩ — see LARGE

bull *n, slang* a member of a force charged with law enforcement at the local level ⟨put one of his best *bulls* on the missing person case⟩ — see OFFICER 1

bulldoze *vb* to force one's way ⟨*bulldozed* through the crowd at the arena to find the bathroom⟩ — see PRESS 4

bullet *n* a usually round or cone-shaped little piece of lead made to be fired from a firearm ⟨it is possible to make your own *bullets*, but it takes a lot of patience and some extra money⟩

synonyms ball, pellet

related words ammunition, cannonball, cap, cartridge, charge, gunshot, lead, load, missile, pop, projectile, round, shell, shot, slug; twenty-two

near antonyms blank

bulletin *n* a published statement informing the public of a matter of general interest ⟨a Web site that allows visitors to read the latest news *bulletins* free of charge⟩ — see ANNOUNCEMENT

bully *n* 1 a person who teases, threatens, or hurts smaller or weaker persons ⟨the *bully* spent most of the afternoon in detention for pushing people down on the playground⟩

synonyms intimidator

related words antagonist, enemy; harrier, nuisance, persecutor, pest, tease, teaser; heckler; goon, hood, hoodlum, punk, rough, roughneck, rowdy, ruffian, thug, tough; cutthroat, felon, gangster, gunman, mobster, racketeer

2 a violent, brutal person who is often a member of an organized gang ⟨the local loan shark and his *bullies* have ways of making people pay up⟩ — see HOODLUM

bully *vb* to make timid or fearful by or as if by threats ⟨the older boys *bullied* him until he was afraid to walk home alone⟩ — see INTIMIDATE

bulwark *n* something that holds up or serves as a foundation for something else ⟨a strong democratic government is the *bulwark* of freedom⟩ — see SUPPORT 1

bum *adj* of low quality ⟨that was *bum* advice that you got from that chat room⟩ — see CHEAP 2

bum *n* a homeless wanderer who may beg or steal for a living ⟨I feel sorry for *bums* and occasionally give them money⟩ — see TRAMP

bummer *n* 1 something (as a situation or event) that is depressing ⟨boy, breaking your leg right before summer vacation is a *bummer*⟩ — see DOWNER

2 something that disappoints ⟨the cancellation of the party was a total *bummer*⟩ — see DISAPPOINTMENT 2

3 something that has failed ⟨that Internet business proved to be a real *bummer*⟩ — see FAILURE 3

bump *n* 1 a small rounded mass of swollen tissue ⟨that's a nasty *bump* on your arm where you hit the table⟩

synonyms knot, lump, node, nodule, swelling

related words growth, tumor, wart; hump, hunch; bruise, contusion; blob, chunk, clod, clump, gob, gobbet, hunk, knob, nub, nubble, nugget, wad

2 a forceful coming together of two things ⟨I felt the *bump* of the other car, but there was no damage to either vehicle⟩ — see IMPACT 1

bump *vb* to come into usually forceful contact with something ⟨he *bumped* into me and should have apologized⟩ — see HIT 2

bumper *adj* unusually large ⟨a *bumper* crop of pumpkins that year⟩ — see HUGE

bumper *n* something that serves as a protective barrier ⟨cars have *bumpers* to protect them from damage in minor collisions⟩ — see CUSHION

bumpkin *n* an awkward or simple person especially from a small town or the country ⟨the *bumpkin* was overwhelmed by the city's confusing subway system⟩ — see HICK

bumpy *adj* 1 marked by a series of sharp quick motions ⟨a *bumpy* ride over a rutted road⟩ — see JERKY 1

2 not having a level or smooth surface ⟨the *bumpy* road made the jeep bounce all over⟩ — see UNEVEN 1

bunch *n* 1 a group of people sharing a common interest and relating together socially ⟨that *bunch* goes out to lunch together every Friday⟩ — see GANG 2

2 a number of things considered as a unit ⟨bought a *bunch* of grapes⟩ — see GROUP 1

3 a usually small number of persons considered as a unit ⟨a small *bunch* of people were sent to clean up the place⟩ — see GROUP 2

bunch *vb* to gather into a closely packed group ⟨the slow service caused the customers at the pick-up counter to *bunch* up⟩ — see PRESS 3

bundle *n* a wrapped or sealed case containing an item or set of items ⟨a *bundle* of newspapers⟩ — see PACKAGE 1

bung *vb* to close up so that no empty spaces remain ⟨we had *bunged* up the moving van so much that we couldn't have possibly squeezed in one more thing⟩ — see FILL 2

bungle *vb* to make or do (something) in a clumsy or unskillful way ⟨*bungled* the job the first time she tried to do it⟩ — see BOTCH

bungling *adj* showing or marked by a lack of skill and tact (as in dealing with a situation) ⟨I refuse to let that *bungling* incompetent insult me again⟩ — see AWKWARD 2

¹**bunk** *n* a place set aside for sleeping ⟨crawled into their *bunks* and went to sleep immediately⟩ — see BED 1

²**bunk** *n* 1 language, behavior, or ideas that are absurd and contrary to good sense ⟨the idea that the moon is made of green cheese is pure *bunk*⟩ — see NONSENSE 1

2 unintelligible or meaningless talk ⟨mumbled some *bunk* about having to be elsewhere⟩ — see GIBBERISH

bunk *vb* to provide with living quarters or shelter ⟨*bunked* the guest in the spare room⟩ — see HOUSE 1

buoy (up) *vb* to fill with courage or strength of purpose ⟨the sudden improvement in his health *buoyed* him *up*⟩ — see ENCOURAGE 1

buoyant *adj* 1 having or showing a good mood or disposition ⟨all the fans were *buoyant* the day after the big win⟩ — see CHEERFUL 1

2 joyously unrestrained ⟨gave him a *buoyant* hug and kiss upon meeting him at the airport⟩ — see EXUBERANT

burden *n* **1** a mass or quantity of something taken up and carried, conveyed, or transported ⟨the early settlers often used horses to carry their *burdens*⟩ — see LOAD 1

2 a part of a song or hymn that is repeated every so often ⟨had some trouble coming up with a *burden* for the song⟩ — see CHORUS 2

3 something one must do because of prior agreement ⟨the *burden* of homework prevented me from joining my friends at the game⟩ — see OBLIGATION

burden *vb* **1** to place a weight or burden on ⟨*burdened* the dog with a little backpack⟩ — see LOAD 1

2 to make sad ⟨refuses to let everyday problems *burden* her⟩ — see DEPRESS 1

burdensome *adj* **1** difficult to endure ⟨the *burdensome* living conditions that the early settlers had to endure⟩ — see HARSH 1

2 requiring much time, effort, or careful attention ⟨the *burdensome* task of finishing the tax return⟩ — see DEMANDING 1

bureau *n* a large unit of a governmental, business, or educational organization ⟨the federal revenue *bureau*⟩ — see DIVISION 2

bureaucrat *n* a worker in a government agency ⟨the *bureaucrats* at the town hall seem to think that we need a building permit to build a tree house⟩

synonyms functionary, public servant

related words clerk, officeholder, official; employee, underling, worker

burg *n* a thickly settled, highly populated area ⟨moved from a small town into a much bigger *burg*⟩ — see CITY

burgeon *vb* **1** to become greater in extent, volume, amount, or number ⟨the trout population in the stream is *burgeoning* now that the water is clean⟩ — see INCREASE 2

2 to grow vigorously ⟨the spring flowers *burgeoned* once the warm weather set in for good⟩ — see THRIVE 1

3 to produce flowers ⟨chrysanthemums usually *burgeon* in early fall⟩ — see BLOOM

burgher *n* a person who lives in a town on a permanent basis ⟨many of the college students are regarded by the local *burghers* as obnoxious louts⟩

synonyms citizen, townie, villager

related words denizen, dweller, habitant, homeowner, inhabitant, national, native, occupant, resident, resider; town, townsfolk, townspeople; suburbanite, urbanite

near antonyms foreigner, guest, tourist, transient, visitor

burglarize *vb* **1** to enter a house or building by force usually with illegal intent ⟨the Watergate scandal began when Republican operatives *burglarized* the Democratic Party's headquarters in Washington, D.C.⟩ — see BREAK IN 1

2 to remove valuables from (a place) unlawfully ⟨before they were caught, the thieves had *burglarized* dozens of houses around the city⟩ — see ROB

burial *n* the act or ceremony of putting a dead body in its final resting place ⟨the children wanted to give the dead bird a proper *burial* in the backyard⟩

synonyms burying, entombing, entombment, interment, interring, sepulture

related words embalmment, funeral

near antonyms cremation

antonyms disinterment, exhumation, unearthing

burlesque *n* a work that imitates and exaggerates another work for comic effect ⟨it is interesting to note

that the first novel ever written in English was followed by a *burlesque* of it⟩ — see PARODY 1

burlesque *vb* to copy or exaggerate (someone or something) in order to make fun of ⟨*burlesquing* the teacher's nervous tic isn't very nice⟩ — see MIMIC 1

burly *adj* strongly and heavily built ⟨a *burly* delivery man brought the furniture⟩ — see ¹HUSKY

burn *vb* **1** to be on fire especially brightly ⟨all evening long we just sat there, contentedly watching the Yule log *burn*⟩

synonyms blaze, combust, flame, glow

related words fire, ignite, kindle; flare (up), light (up); flicker, gutter, waver; bake, broil, char, cook, melt, roast, scorch, swelter; smolder, spark, sputter; beam, brighten, radiate; beat (down), flash, glare, gleam, glimmer, glint, glisten, glitter, scintillate, shimmer, shine, sparkle, twinkle

2 to set (something) on fire ⟨it is not a good idea to try to *burn* old papers in the sink⟩

synonyms fire, ignite, inflame, kindle, light

related words char, scorch; bake, cremate, incinerate, kiln; brighten, illumine, illuminate, irradiate, lighten, radiate; scald, scathe, sear; rekindle, relight

near antonyms choke, smother, suffocate; stamp (out); blacken, darken, dim, dull, obscure

antonyms douse, extinguish, put out, quench, snuff (out)

3 to be excited or emotionally stirred up with anger ⟨the child came home *burning* with anger because of a reprimand in class⟩ — see BOIL 1

4 to shine with a bright harsh light ⟨the streetlight outside our motel *burned* all night long⟩ — see GLARE 1

burnable *adj* capable of catching or being set on fire ⟨don't put something so *burnable* as a towel next to the stove⟩ — see COMBUSTIBLE

burned–out *or* **burnt–out** *adj* depleted in strength, energy, or freshness ⟨I'm feeling so *burned-out* that I can't wait for vacation⟩ — see WEARY 1

burning *adj* **1** being on fire ⟨a fire fighter must be that rare soul who rushes into a *burning* house, not away from it⟩ — see ABLAZE 1

2 having a notably high temperature ⟨a *burning* sauna seems like a welcome retreat after a day of shoveling snow⟩ — see HOT 1

3 having or expressing great depth of feeling ⟨the *burning* enthusiasm of that candidate's campaign workers⟩ — see FERVENT

burnish *vb* to make smooth or glossy usually by repeatedly applying surface pressure ⟨*burnished* the floor of the ballroom⟩ — see POLISH

burnished *adj* having a shiny surface or finish ⟨bright *burnished* metal is used extensively in that boutique's decor⟩ — see GLOSSY

burnout *n* a complete depletion of energy or strength ⟨people in that job often suffer *burnout* and have to retire at a relatively early age⟩ — see FATIGUE

burn out *vb* to use up all the physical energy of ⟨working 12-hour days at that job just *burned* me *out*⟩ — see EXHAUST 1

burro *n* a sturdy and patient domestic mammal that is used especially to carry things ⟨used a *burro* to carry the supplies⟩ — see DONKEY 1

burrow *n* the shelter or resting place of a wild animal ⟨the chipmunk retreated to its *burrow* to have its babies⟩ — see DEN 1

burst *n* **1** a sudden and usually temporary growth of activity ⟨a sudden *burst* of industriousness whenever the teacher appeared⟩ — see OUTBREAK

2 a sudden intense expression of strong feeling ⟨a *burst* of anger that startled the other members on the panel⟩ — see OUTBURST 1

burst *vb* **1** to break open or into pieces usually because of internal pressure ⟨the turnover's crust *burst* when the filling expanded⟩ — see EXPLODE 1

2 to cause to break open or into pieces by or as if by an explosive ⟨finally *burst* the piñata open with one mighty swing of the bat⟩ — see BLAST 1

burst (forth) *vb* to develop suddenly and violently ⟨hives *burst forth* on the child's arms and face whenever she goes near that plant⟩ — see ERUPT 2

bursting *adj* containing or seeming to contain the greatest quantity or number possible ⟨the store was *bursting* with bargain hunters on the day of the big sale⟩ — see FULL 1

bursting *n* the act or an instance of exploding ⟨narrowly escaped the *bursting* of the car's gas tank⟩ — see EXPLOSION 1

bury *vb* **1** to place (a dead body) in the earth, a tomb, or the sea ⟨he died on Tuesday and was *buried* on Friday⟩
synonyms entomb, inter
related words enshrine; conceal, cover, ensconce, hide; obscure, shade, shield; cloak, curtain, enshroud, shroud
near antonyms burn, cremate; bare, disclose, discover, display, exhibit, expose, reveal, show
antonyms disinter, exhume, unearth

2 to put into a hiding place ⟨*buried* his face in his hands as his wife recounted the embarrassing incident⟩ — see ¹HIDE 1

burying *n* the act or ceremony of putting a dead body in its final resting place ⟨all the grandchildren attended the *burying* of their grandfather in his homeland⟩ — see BURIAL

bush *n* a rural region that forms the edge of the settled or developed part of a country ⟨a guide who specializes in taking adventurous tourists through the *bush*⟩ — see FRONTIER 2

bushed *adj* depleted in strength, energy, or freshness ⟨I'm *bushed* after a day of moving boxes from the cellar to the attic⟩ — see WEARY 1

bushel *n* a considerable amount ⟨picked up a *bushel* of decorations at the after-Christmas sale⟩ — see LOT 2

business *n* **1** a commercial or industrial activity or organization ⟨most of the local *businesses* belong to the association⟩ — see ENTERPRISE 1

2 something to be dealt with ⟨we have one piece of *business* remaining for today's meeting⟩ — see MATTER 2

3 the buying and selling of goods especially on a large scale and between different places ⟨this bookstore is a place of *business*, not a free library, so please do your reading elsewhere⟩ — see COMMERCE

bust *n* **1** a hard strike with a part of the body or an instrument ⟨delivered a *bust* to the boxer's chops⟩ — see ¹BLOW

2 something that has failed ⟨the first movie was a hit, but the sequel was a *bust*⟩ — see FAILURE 3

bust *vb* **1** to bring to a lower grade or rank ⟨the commander threatened to *bust* her for failing to salute⟩ — see DEMOTE

2 to cause to lose one's fortune and become unable to pay one's debts ⟨gambling is a dangerous habit that has *busted* many unfortunate souls⟩ — see RUIN 1

3 to cause to separate into pieces usually suddenly or forcibly ⟨the butterfingered husband had *busted* more plates than he cared to remember⟩ — see BREAK 1

4 to deliver a blow to (someone or something) usually in a strong vigorous manner ⟨*busted* the storekeeper on the nose and was promptly arrested for it⟩ — see HIT 1

5 *slang* to take or keep under one's control by authority of law ⟨the police *busted* the revelers for drinking in public⟩ — see ARREST 1

bustle *n* a state of noisy, confused activity ⟨I couldn't concentrate in all the *bustle*⟩ — see COMMOTION

bustling *adj* marked by much life, movement, or activity ⟨a *bustling* shopping center during the Christmas season⟩ — see ALIVE 2

busy *adj* **1** involved in often constant activity ⟨the deadline is in two days, so everyone at work has been extremely *busy*⟩
synonyms active, assiduous, diligent, employed, engaged, industrious, laborious, occupied, sedulous, working
related words absorbed, concentrating, engrossed, focused (*also* focussed), immersed, intent, preoccupied; alive, functional, functioning, going, living, operating, operational, operative, running; energetic, vigorous; indefatigable, tireless, untiring
near antonyms asleep, dormant, latent, quiescent, sleepy; inert, passive; dead, dull, slow; inoperative, nonoperating
antonyms idle, inactive, unemployed, unengaged, unoccupied

2 marked by much life, movement, or activity ⟨the *busy*, often hectic floor of the New York Stock Exchange⟩ — see ALIVE 2

busy *vb* to hold the attention of ⟨the puzzle *busied* the child for hours⟩ — see ENGAGE 1

busybody *n* a person who meddles in the affairs of others ⟨that *busybody* across the street is always telling me how to tend to my own garden⟩
synonyms interferer, interloper, intruder, kibitzer, meddler
related words peeper, peeping Tom, snoop, snooper, spy; blabber, discloser, gossip, gossiper, prattler, revealer, teller; betrayer, talebearer, tattletale; snake, sneak; informer, snitcher, squealer, stool pigeon

but *adv* nothing more than ⟨the accused is *but* a child and should be tried as a child⟩ — see JUST 3

but *conj* **1** if it were not for the fact that ⟨I would have said something *but* I was too chicken⟩ — see EXCEPT

2 in spite of that ⟨we're running late, *but* we're still coming to the party⟩ — see HOWEVER

but *prep* not including ⟨brought everything *but* the kitchen table⟩ — see EXCEPT

butcher *vb* **1** to kill on a large scale ⟨the barbarians *butchered* the monks in the monasteries without mercy⟩ — see MASSACRE

2 to make or do (something) in a clumsy or unskillful way ⟨the new piano student *butchered* the song⟩ — see BOTCH

butchery *n* the killing of a large number of people ⟨*butchery* on a scale that horrified the civilized world⟩ — see MASSACRE

¹butt *n* the part of the body upon which someone sits ⟨park your *butts* in the seats and keep quiet, or I'm turning this car around⟩ — see BUTTOCKS

²butt *n* **1** a person or thing that is made fun of ⟨the social outcast got tired of being the *butt* of everyone's jokes⟩ — see LAUGHINGSTOCK

2 a person or thing that is the object of abuse, criticism, or ridicule ⟨usually the president is the *butt* of the radio commentator's scathing wit⟩ — see TARGET 1

butt in *vb* to interest oneself in what is not one's concern 〈stop *butting in* on my personal life〉 — see INTERFERE

buttocks *n pl* the part of the body upon which someone sits 〈she slipped in the mud puddle and hit the ground square on her *buttocks*〉
synonyms backside, bottom, breech, butt, fanny, hams, haunches, posterior, rear, rump, seat

buttress *n* **1** something or someone to which one looks for support 〈my mother has always been the *buttress* of our family in trying times〉 — see DEPENDENCE 2
2 something that holds up or serves as a foundation for something else 〈the state's unspoiled natural beauty is the very *buttress* of its vital tourist industry〉 — see SUPPORT 1

buttress *vb* to hold up or serve as a foundation for 〈all the facts *buttress* the case for adopting the measure〉 〈a brace *buttressed* the wall〉 — see SUPPORT 3

buy *n* something bought or offered for sale at a desirable price 〈four half gallons of ice cream for four dollars is a real *buy*〉 — see BARGAIN 1

buy *vb* to get possession of (something) by giving money in exchange for 〈I really want to *buy* that new book, but I don't have enough money right now〉
synonyms pick up, purchase, take
related words acquire, get, obtain, procure, secure; finance, pay (for), spring (for); barter (for), deal (for), exchange (for), trade (for); bargain (with), chaffer (with), dicker (over), horse-trade (with), negotiate (about), palter (with); bid, offer; rebuy, repurchase

buzz *n* **1** a communication by telephone 〈give me a *buzz* when you decide〉 — see CALL 3
2 a monotonous sound like that of an insect in motion 〈the motor made a soft *buzz*〉 — see HUM

buzz *vb* to fly, turn, or move rapidly with a fluttering or vibratory sound 〈the little plane *buzzed* past the crowd〉 — see WHIRR

buzzing *adj* marked by much life, movement, or activity 〈the arena is really *buzzing* tonight〉 — see ALIVE 2

by *adv* at, within, or to a short distance or time 〈the library is close *by*〉 — see NEAR 1

by *prep* **1** along the way of 〈went *by* the woods to get to the summer cottage〉
synonyms through, via
related words across, along, alongside, beyond, near, nearby, over; below, beneath, under, underneath; outside, past
phrases by way of
2 using the means or agency of 〈try to convince them *by* reason alone, if possible〉
synonyms per, through, with
phrases by means of, by (*or* in) virtue of, through the medium of
3 close to 〈that house is right *by* the ocean〉 — see AROUND 1

by–and–by *n* time that is to come 〈we shall meet again in the *by-and-by*〉 — see FUTURE 1

by and large *adv* for the most part 〈*by and large*, that information is accurate〉 — see CHIEFLY

bygone *adj* no longer existing 〈elderly people reminiscing about *bygone* fashions〉 — see EXTINCT

bylaw *n* a statement spelling out the proper procedure or conduct for an activity 〈the club's *bylaws* bar any member whose annual dues remain unpaid from voting in the election〉 — see RULE 1

bypass *vb* to avoid by going around 〈we can *bypass* the traffic jam if we take this other road〉 — see DETOUR 1

by–product *n* something that naturally develops or is developed from something else 〈hydrogen is one *by-product* of that chemical reaction〉 — see DERIVATIVE

byword *n* an often stated observation regarding something from common experience 〈Mom's favorite *byword* is "you can get more flies with honey than with vinegar"〉 — see SAYING

C

cab *n* an automobile that carries passengers for a fare usually determined by the distance traveled ⟨called a *cab* to get back to the hotel⟩ — see TAXICAB

cabal *n* a group involved in secret or criminal activities ⟨rumors about the existence of a *cabal* devoted to world domination⟩ — see RING 1

cabaret *n* a bar or restaurant offering special nighttime entertainment (as music, dancing, or comedy acts) ⟨a singing superstar who got her start singing in the *cabarets* of New York City⟩ — see NIGHTCLUB

cabin *n* 1 a small, simply constructed, and often temporary dwelling ⟨a small *cabin* that hikers along the Appalachian Trail use for overnight stays⟩ — see SHACK
2 an often small house for recreational or seasonal use ⟨kept a *cabin* in the mountains for vacations during skiing season⟩ — see COTTAGE
3 one of the parts into which an enclosed space is divided ⟨an airplane *cabin*⟩ — see COMPARTMENT

cabinet *n* a storage case typically having doors and shelves ⟨the most precious knickknacks were kept in a *cabinet* with glass doors⟩
synonyms buffet, closet, cupboard, hutch, locker, sideboard
related words bookcase, secretary; shelving; console

cabinetwork *n* the movable articles in a room ⟨18th-century *cabinetwork* from Newport, Rhode Island, is among the most prized of all American furniture⟩ — see FURNITURE

cable *n* a length of braided, flexible material that is used for tying or connecting things ⟨a mass of *cables* connecting the audio and video components⟩ — see CORD

cache *n* 1 a collection of things kept available for future use or need ⟨a *cache* of medical supplies in case of emergency⟩ — see STORE 1
2 a supply stored up and often hidden away ⟨the squirrel kept a *cache* of nuts in the hollow of the tree⟩ — see HOARD 1

cache *vb* 1 to put (something of future use or value) in a safe or secret place ⟨*cached* money in odd places, such as under the boards of the floor⟩ — see HOARD
2 to put into a hiding place ⟨*cached* the fugitive slaves in their cellar until they could make their way to Canada⟩ — see ¹HIDE 1

caching *n* the placing of something out of sight ⟨the *caching* of holiday gifts in the weeks before Christmas⟩ — see CONCEALMENT 1

cackle *n* an explosive sound that is a sign of amusement ⟨let out a belly-shaking *cackle* at the joke⟩ — see LAUGH 1

cackle *vb* to engage in casual or rambling conversation ⟨*cackled* on the phone with her friends about the latest soap opera plots⟩ — see CHAT

cackler *n* a person who talks constantly ⟨avoids the *cackler* in the lunchroom who doesn't mind wasting other people's time⟩ — see CHATTERBOX

cacophony *n* loud, confused, and usually unharmonious sound ⟨the *cacophony* of a pet store full of animals⟩ — see NOISE 1

cad *n* a person whose behavior is offensive to others ⟨he's a *cad* who bad-mouths every girl who's ever dumped him⟩ — see JERK 1

cadaver *n* a dead body ⟨medical students who train by using *cadavers*⟩ — see CORPSE

cadaverous *adj* 1 lacking a healthy skin color ⟨everyone always looks *cadaverous* in the winter⟩ — see PALE 2
2 suffering extreme weight loss as a result of hunger or disease ⟨a *cadaverous* cancer patient living out his final days with dignity and courage⟩ — see EMACIATED

caddy *n* a covered rectangular container for storing or transporting things ⟨an antique tea *caddy* from the colonial period⟩ — see CHEST

cadence *n* the recurrent pattern formed by a series of sounds having a regular rise and fall in intensity ⟨the soothing *cadence* of the lecturer's voice nearly put me to sleep⟩ — see RHYTHM

cadenced *adj* marked by or occurring with a noticeable regularity in the rise and fall of sound ⟨a very *cadenced* voice of the instructor in the meditation class⟩ — see RHYTHMIC

café *also* **cafe** *n* 1 a bar or restaurant offering special nighttime entertainment (as music, dancing, or comedy acts) ⟨the *café* presents nationally known jazz performers in an intimate setting⟩ — see NIGHTCLUB
2 a place of business where alcoholic beverages are sold to be consumed on the premises ⟨a speakeasy that became a fashionable *café* with the repeal of prohibition⟩ — see BARROOM
3 a public establishment where meals are served to paying customers for consumption on the premises ⟨they met at a little *café* in Paris⟩ — see RESTAURANT

cage *n* an enclosure with an open framework for keeping animals ⟨the dogs and cats at the animal shelter looked so sad in their *cages*⟩
synonyms coop, corral, pen, pound
related words fence; cote, dovecote, fold; aquarium, terrarium

cage *vb* to close or shut in by or as if by barriers ⟨*caged* the rabbit at night so she wouldn't wake everyone up⟩ — see ENCLOSE 1

cagey *also* **cagy** *adj* clever at attaining one's ends by indirect and often deceptive means ⟨a *cagey* old politician who is skilled at getting federal money for his district⟩ — see ARTFUL 1

caginess *n* skill in achieving one's ends through indirect, subtle, or underhanded means ⟨the lawyer's celebrated *caginess* makes her the first choice of the hopelessly guilty⟩ — see CUNNING 1

cajole *vb* to get (someone) to do something by gentle urging, special attention, or flattery ⟨*cajoled* her into doing his homework for him⟩ — see COAX

cake *n* a small usually rounded mass of minced food that has been fried ⟨the rich, tender *cakes* of crabmeat had been lightly fried⟩
synonyms croquette, cutlet, fritter, patty (*also* pattie)
related words finger, stick

cake *vb* to cover with a hardened layer ⟨shoes *caked* with dried mud⟩ — see ENCRUST

calamitous *adj* 1 bringing about ruin or misfortune ⟨a *calamitous* decision to sell only online ruined the business⟩ — see FATAL 1
2 causing or tending to cause destruction ⟨a *calamitous* flood that destroyed the town's central business district⟩ — see DESTRUCTIVE 1

calamity *n* a sudden violent event that brings about great loss or destruction ⟨this breakdown of the car is inconvenient, but not a *calamity*⟩ — see DISASTER

calculate *vb* **1** to determine (a value) by doing the necessary mathematical operations ⟨the family has been *calculating* what a week at the beach resort would end up costing⟩
synonyms compute, figure, reckon, work out
related words conjecture, estimate, guess, judge, suppose; add up, sum, tally, total; add, cipher, divide, multiply, subtract; calibrate, gauge (*also* gage), measure, scale; ascertain, discover, dope (out), figure out, find out; recompute, refigure
2 to decide the size, amount, number, or distance of (something) without actual measurement ⟨I *calculate* that this job will take another two days to finish⟩ — see ESTIMATE 2
3 to work out the details of (something) in advance ⟨*calculated* the best route to take to the coast⟩ — see PLAN 1
calculated *adj* decided on as a result of careful thought ⟨took a *calculated* risk⟩ — see DELIBERATE 1
calculation *n* the act or process of performing mathematical operations to find a value ⟨by my *calculation*, it should take me a month to save up for the sneakers⟩
synonyms arithmetic, ciphering, computation, figures, figuring, reckoning
related words mathematics; addition, division, multiplication, subtraction; appraisal, assessment, estimation, evaluation, judgment (*or* judgement)
calendar *n* a listing of things to be presented or considered (as at a concert or play) ⟨the *calendar* of upcoming events at the state fair will be available tomorrow⟩ — see PROGRAM 1
caliber *or* **calibre** *n* degree of excellence ⟨musicians of the highest *caliber* perform at that concert hall⟩ — see QUALITY 1
call *n* **1** a natural vocal sound made by an animal ⟨a ranger who could immediately identify the *call* of every creature in the forest⟩
synonyms cry, note
related words bark, bay, bellow, bleat, bray, caterwaul, caw, cheep, chirp, grunt, hoot, howl, low, meow, moo, neigh, peep, roar, screech, squawk, squeak, squeal, twitter, whinny, yap, yelp, yip, yowl
2 a coming to see another briefly for social or business reasons ⟨we paid a *call* on the new neighbors the day after they moved in⟩
synonyms visit, visitation
related words meeting, rendezvous, tryst; stopover
3 a communication by telephone ⟨give me a *call* as soon as you arrive, so I'll know you got there safely⟩
synonyms buzz, ring
related words callback; toll call; message
4 an act or instance of asking for information ⟨put out a *call* for the answer to the question⟩ — see QUESTION 2
5 an entitlement to something ⟨you have no *call* to insult people⟩ — see CLAIM 1
call *vb* **1** to speak so as to be heard at a distance ⟨we could hear someone *calling* for help from the other side of the wall⟩
synonyms bawl, cry, holler, shout, vociferate, yell
related words bellow, roar; whoop; scream, screech, shriek, shrill, squeak, squeal; caterwaul, howl, wail, yawp (*or* yaup), yowl
near antonyms breathe, mumble, murmur, mutter, whisper
2 to make a telephone call to ⟨use this cell phone to *call* me if there's an emergency⟩

synonyms dial, phone, ring (up) [*chiefly British*], telephone
related words beep, buzz
3 to make a brief visit ⟨the hospital posts the hours during which friends and relatives may *call*⟩
synonyms drop (by *or* in), pop (in), stop (by *or* in), visit
related words barge (in); look up, see; frequent, hang around (in), hang out (at), haunt, resort (to)
4 to put an end to (something planned or previously agreed to) ⟨the game was *called* on account of rain⟩ — see CANCEL 1
5 to think of in a particular way ⟨I wouldn't quite *call* that cheating, but it's not entirely ethical either⟩ — see CONSIDER 1
6 to utter one's distinctive animal sound ⟨the dog *called* whenever it flushed a quail⟩ — see CRY 2
7 to bring together in assembly by or as if by command ⟨*called* all the night workers in for a meeting⟩ — see CONVOKE
8 to decide the size, amount, number, or distance of (something) without actual measurement ⟨let's *call* that five feet for now, and we'll measure it out later⟩ — see ESTIMATE 2
9 to demand or request the presence or service of ⟨rushed to *call* a repairman when the furnace broke⟩ — see SUMMON 1
10 to give a name to ⟨we've decided to *call* the kitten "Molly"⟩ — see NAME 1
call (for) *vb* **1** to ask for (something) earnestly or with authority ⟨the manager *called for* additional waiters⟩ — see DEMAND 1
2 to make a request for ⟨*called for* someone to help with planning the club's party⟩ — see ASK (FOR) 1
call (on *or* upon) *vb* to make a social call upon ⟨lots of people *called on* the new mother in the weeks following the birth of her first child⟩ — see VISIT 1
caller *n* a person who visits another ⟨a number of *callers* have been by since they heard you weren't feeling well⟩ — see GUEST 1
calligraphy *n* writing done by hand ⟨she has beautiful *calligraphy*⟩ — see HANDWRITING 2
calling *n* **1** the act of putting an end to something planned or previously agreed to ⟨the *calling* of the match was a disappointment to both players⟩ — see CANCELLATION
2 the activity by which one regularly makes a living ⟨I think my true *calling* will be as a commercial artist⟩ — see OCCUPATION
calling off *n* the act of putting an end to something planned or previously agreed to ⟨the *calling off* of the dance is not going to go over well⟩ — see CANCELLATION
call off *vb* to put an end to (something planned or previously agreed to) ⟨*called off* the party after half of those invited couldn't make it⟩ — see CANCEL 1
callous *adj* having or showing a lack of sympathy or tender feelings ⟨the *callous* comment "it's just a fish," when his pet died, made him cry⟩ — see HARD 1
callow *adj* lacking in adult experience or maturity ⟨a story about a *callow* youth who learns the value of hard work and self-reliance⟩
synonyms adolescent, green, immature, inexperienced, juvenile, puerile, raw, unfledged, unripe, unripened
related words babyish, childish, infantile; boyish, girlish, maidenly, virginal, youthful; ingenuous, innocent, naive (*or* naïve); unpracticed, unseasoned, untrained, untried

near antonyms advanced, precocious; knowing, sophisticated, worldly-wise

antonyms adult, experienced, grown-up, mature, ripe

calm *adj* **1** free from storms or physical disturbance ⟨after a stormy night of high winds and driving rains, the day dawned on a *calm* sea⟩

synonyms halcyon, hushed, peaceful, placid, quiet, serene, still, stilly, tranquil, untroubled

related words calming, pacific, restful, soothing; inactive, inert, quiescent, reposing, resting; smooth, unruffled; clear, cloudless, fair, rainless, sunny, sunshiny

near antonyms bleak, cloudy, dirty, foul, nasty, overcast, rainy, raw, rough, squally

antonyms agitated, angry, stormy, turbulent

2 free from emotional or mental agitation ⟨bystanders tried to help the injured person remain *calm* while they waited for the ambulance to arrive⟩

synonyms collected, composed, cool, coolheaded, placid, self-possessed, serene, tranquil, undisturbed, unperturbed, unshaken, untroubled, unworried

related words imperturbable, nerveless, unflappable, unshakable; disciplined, self-contained, self-controlled; affable, breezy, devil-may-care, easygoing, happy-go-lucky, laid-back, low-pressure; carefree, nonchalant, unconcerned; assured, confident, self-assured; aloof, detached, dispassionate, indifferent; impassive, phlegmatic, stolid

near antonyms anxious, bothered, distressed, worried; jittery, jumpy, nervous, skittish, tense; high-strung, uptight

antonyms agitated, discomposed, disturbed, flustered, perturbed, upset

3 free from disturbing noise or uproar ⟨the room became much *calmer* once the rowdy tour group had left⟩ — see QUIET 1

calm *n* a state of freedom from storm or disturbance ⟨vacationing city dwellers who are tired of the hustle and bustle enjoy the *calm* of the secluded mountain village⟩

synonyms calmness, hush, peace, peacefulness, placidity, quiet, quietness, quietude, repose, restfulness, sereneness, serenity, still, stillness, tranquillity (*or* tranquility)

related words lull, pause, respite; silence; comity, concord, harmony

near antonyms clamor, din, noise, racket

antonyms bustle, commotion, hubbub, hurly-burly, pandemonium, tumult, turmoil, uproar

calm *vb* **1** to free from distress or disturbance ⟨the president's reassuring words did much to *calm* the public during the national emergency⟩

synonyms allay, compose, quiet, settle, soothe, still, tranquilize (*also* tranquillize)

related words alleviate, assuage, ease, mitigate, relieve; appease, conciliate, mollify, pacify, placate; lull, relax, stupefy

near antonyms aggravate, heighten, intensify; arouse, excite, foment, incite, rouse, stir (up)

antonyms agitate, discompose, disquiet, disturb, perturb, upset

2 to gain emotional or mental control of ⟨he *calmed* himself before continuing the eulogy⟩ — see COLLECT 1

calm (down) *vb* to become still and orderly ⟨the sea finally *calmed down* once the storm had passed⟩ — see QUIET 1

calming *adj* tending to calm the emotions and relieve stress ⟨a *calming* glass of warm milk⟩ — see SOOTHING 1

calmness *n* **1** a state of freedom from storm or disturbance ⟨the *calmness* of the lake made it possible to see the bottom clearly⟩ — see CALM

2 evenness of emotions or temper ⟨her *calmness* in a crisis serves her well as a nurse in the emergency room⟩ — see EQUANIMITY

camaraderie *n* the feeling of closeness and friendship that exists between companions ⟨the students have developed a real *camaraderie* after spending three years in the same classes⟩ — see COMPANIONSHIP

camouflage *n* clothing put on to hide one's true identity or imitate someone or something else ⟨the soldiers must wear protective jungle *camouflage* while on patrol⟩ — see DISGUISE

camouflage *vb* to change the dress or looks of so as to conceal true identity ⟨*camouflaged* the military camp as a native village⟩ — see DISGUISE

camp *n* **1** a place where a group of people live for a short time in tents or cabins ⟨the war forced people to flee their homes and to live in crowded *camps* along the border⟩

synonyms bivouac, campground, campsite, encampment

related words barracks; colony, plantation, settlement; shantytown; concentration camp, prison camp

2 a small, simply constructed, and often temporary dwelling ⟨a hunter's *camp* deep in the woods⟩ — see SHACK

3 an often small house for recreational or seasonal use ⟨years ago the wealthy industrialists built some rather grand *camps* along the lake⟩ — see COTTAGE

camp *vb* to live in a camp or the outdoors ⟨rather than stay in motels, my family usually *camps* when we're on vacation⟩

synonyms bivouac, encamp

related words tent; backpack

phrases rough it

campaign *n* a series of activities undertaken to achieve a goal ⟨an all-out *campaign* to bring a minor league baseball team to the city⟩

synonyms bandwagon, cause, crusade, drive, movement

related words attack, march, offensive

campaigner *n* one who seeks an office, honor, position, or award ⟨an experienced *campaigner* who knows that one televised mistake can put an end to one's candidacy⟩ — see CANDIDATE

camper *n* a motor vehicle that is specially equipped for living while traveling ⟨the family loaded up the *camper* and headed off for the tour of several national parks⟩

synonyms caravan, mobile home, motor home, trailer

related words van

campground *n* a place where a group of people live for a short time in tents or cabins ⟨the weary vacationers pulled into a *campground* for the night⟩ — see CAMP 1

campsite *n* a place where a group of people live for a short time in tents or cabins ⟨the *campsite* at least offers shower and bathroom facilities⟩ — see CAMP 1

can *vb* **1** *slang* to bring (as an action or operation) to an immediate end ⟨*can* the chatter, or I'm kicking you out of this library⟩ — see STOP 1

2 to let go from office, service, or employment ⟨the cashier was *canned* for stealing from the registers⟩ — see DISMISS 1

can *n* a metal container in the shape of a cylinder ⟨the shelter stores huge *cans* of water for an emergency⟩
synonyms barrel, drum
related words tube; tin

canal *n* an open man-made passageway for water ⟨the Panama *Canal* opened a much easier and shorter passageway from the Atlantic to the Pacific⟩ — see CHANNEL 1

cancel *vb* **1** to put an end to (something planned or previously agreed to) ⟨please call to *cancel* your appointment with the dentist if you can't make it⟩
synonyms abort, call, call off, drop, recall, repeal, rescind, revoke
related words abrogate, annul, invalidate, nullify, void, write off; recant, retract, take back, withdraw; countermand, reverse; end, halt, stop, terminate; give up, relinquish, surrender
near antonyms engage, pledge, promise; begin, commence, initiate, start; take on, take up, undertake
antonyms continue, keep
2 to put an end to by formal action ⟨the agreement can be *canceled* by either side with a formal written notice⟩ — see ABOLISH
3 to show (something written) to be no longer valid by drawing a cross over or a line through it ⟨*canceled* the check and wrote a new one⟩ — see X (OUT)

cancel (out) *vb* to balance with an equal force so as to make ineffective ⟨at least your recent efforts will *cancel out* the past failing grades⟩ — see OFFSET

canceler *or* **canceller** *n* a force or influence that makes an opposing force ineffective or less effective ⟨his dispassionate manner can be a welcome *canceler* of his wife's emotional response to every little thing⟩ — see COUNTERBALANCE

cancellation *n* the act of putting an end to something planned or previously agreed to ⟨the misbehavior of a few bad apples at the end of the football game resulted in the *cancellation* of the victory party⟩
synonyms abortion, calling, calling off, dropping, recall, repeal, rescission, revocation
related words annulment, invalidation, neutralization, nullification; abolishment, abolition, ending, halting, stopping, termination; giving up, relinquishment, surrender
near antonyms beginning, commencement, initiation; engagement, undertaking
antonyms continuation

candid *adj* free in expressing one's true feelings and opinions ⟨a *candid* woman who never hesitates to say what's on her mind⟩ — see FRANK

candidate *n* one who seeks an office, honor, position, or award ⟨each *candidate* for student council was allowed to speak at the school assembly⟩
synonyms applicant, aspirant, campaigner, contender, hopeful, prospect, seeker
related words competitor, contestant, entrant; also-ran, dark horse, favorite, finisher, has-been, runner-up; nominee; claimant, pretender
near antonyms incumbent, officeholder; dropout

candor *n* the free expression of one's true feelings and opinions ⟨an interview in which the members of the rock band speak with *candor* about their recent squabbling⟩
synonyms directness, forthrightness, frankness, openheartedness, openness, plainness, straightforwardness
related words earnestness, sincerity, sobriety; artlessness, genuineness, naïveté (*also* naivete), simplicity, un-sophistication; bluffness, bluntness, brusqueness; freedom, license (*or* licence), unrestraint
near antonyms inhibition, reserve, restraint; diplomacy, tact
antonyms dissembling, pretense (*or* pretence)

cane *n* a heavy rigid stick used as a weapon or for punishment ⟨in those days corporal punishment was common, and the *cane* was regarded as another one of the schoolmaster's educational tools⟩ — see CLUB 1

canine *n* a domestic mammal that is related to the wolves and foxes ⟨in the minds of some, the winner of this prestigious dog show has a fair claim to the title of King of the *Canines*⟩ — see DOG

canniness *n* skill in achieving one's ends through indirect, subtle, or underhanded means ⟨the *canniness* with which she negotiated her contract as spokesperson for the shoe manufacturer⟩ — see CUNNING 1

cannonade *n* a rapid or overwhelming outpouring of many things at once ⟨the director of the sporting event was greeted at the scene with a *cannonade* of complaints⟩ — see BARRAGE

canny *adj* having or showing a practical cleverness or judgment ⟨a *canny* card player, good at psyching out his opponents⟩ — see SHREWD

canon *n* **1** a statement or body of statements concerning faith or morals proclaimed by a church ⟨Christian *canon* states that Jesus rose from the dead⟩ — see DOCTRINE 1
2 a record of a series of items (as names or titles) usually arranged according to some system ⟨the *canon* of plays that are attributed to William Shakespeare⟩ — see ¹LIST

canonize *vb* **1** to declare to be a saint and worthy of public respect ⟨a martyr who was *canonized* a hundred years after his death⟩ — see SAINT
2 to love or admire too much ⟨a singing star so *canonized* by his fans that they refuse to believe anything bad about him⟩ — see IDOLIZE

canopy *n* a raised covering over something for decoration or protection ⟨trees line both sides of the garden path, with their foliage forming a leafy *canopy* for walkers⟩
synonyms awning, ceiling, roof, tent
related words screen, shade, shelter, shield, sunshade; canvas, fly

¹cant *n* the degree to which something rises up from a position level with the horizon ⟨a steep *cant* of the riverbank at that turn in the river⟩ — see SLANT

²cant *n* **1** the pretending of having virtues, principles, or beliefs that one does not have ⟨many accused the evangelist of *cant*, since his lifestyle seemed to bear little resemblance to what he was preaching⟩ — see HYPOCRISY
2 the special terms or expressions of a particular group or field ⟨the *cant* used by movie producers and publicity agents in Hollywood⟩ — see TERMINOLOGY

cant *vb* to set or cause to be at an angle ⟨carefully *canted* the ladder against the wall⟩ — see LEAN 1

cantankerous *adj* having or showing a habitually bad temper ⟨a *cantankerous* old woman who insisted that nothing should ever be allowed to change⟩ — see ILL-TEMPERED

canted *adj* running in a slanting direction ⟨an odd little house, built with deliberately *canted* windows and not one right angle⟩ — see DIAGONAL

canticle *n* a religious song ⟨the monks offered up a *canticle* at dawn on Easter morning⟩ — see HYMN

canvas *n* a picture created with usually oil paint ⟨one *canvas* by Picasso is worth more money than most of us can imagine⟩ — see PAINTING

canvass *vb* to go around and approach (people) with a request for opinions or information ⟨we *canvassed* people all over town, asking if they would be interested in participating in a recycling program⟩
synonyms poll, solicit, survey
related words interrogate, interview, question; feel (out), sound (out)
near antonyms report

canyon *also* **cañon** *n* a narrow opening between hillsides or mountains that can be used for passage ⟨as the scouts made their way through the *canyon*, they marveled at the sheer walls of rock on both sides⟩
synonyms defile, flume, gap, gorge, gulch, gulf, notch, pass, ravine
related words abyss, chasm, cirque, cleft, crevasse, crevice, fissure; dale, glen, hollow, vale, valley; basin, floodplain, plain; arroyo, coulee, gully, gutter, wash [*Western*]

cap *n* **1** a covering for the head usually having a shaped crown ⟨grabbed a *cap* and plopped it on his head⟩ — see HAT
2 a piece placed over an open container to hold in, protect, or conceal its contents ⟨I can't find the *cap* to the milk bottle⟩ — see COVER 1

capability *n* **1** a skill, an ability, or knowledge that makes a person able to do a particular job ⟨a pilot lacking the *capability* to fly jet fighters⟩ — see QUALIFICATION 1
2 the physical or mental power to do something ⟨the natural *capability* some people seem to have for teaching⟩ — see ABILITY

capable *adj* having the required skills for an acceptable level of performance ⟨a *capable* and efficient editor⟩ — see COMPETENT

capably *adv* in a skillful or expert manner ⟨performed almost any task at the television station *capably* and quickly⟩ — see WELL 3

capacious *adj* more than adequate or average in capacity ⟨that car has a *capacious* trunk that makes it a good choice for families⟩ — see SPACIOUS

capacity *n* **1** the largest number or amount that something can hold ⟨the seating *capacity* of the school auditorium is 800 people⟩
synonyms complement, content
related words area, room, space, volume; fill, load, measure
2 an assignment at which one regularly works for pay ⟨served in the *capacity* of the network's White House reporter for a year⟩ — see JOB 1
3 the action for which a person or thing is specially fitted or used or for which a thing exists ⟨offered advice in his *capacity* as a lawyer⟩ — see ROLE
4 the physical or mental power to do something ⟨not everyone has the *capacity* for learning higher math⟩ — see ABILITY

caparison *n* **1** dressy clothing ⟨wore their costliest *caparison* to the party⟩ — see FINERY
2 something that decorates or beautifies ⟨horses dressed in fancy *caparison* for the parade⟩ — see DECORATION 1

caparison *vb* to outfit with clothes and especially fine or special clothes ⟨used to seeing him in a T-shirt and jeans, we were startled by the sight of Brad *caparisoned* for the prom in a tuxedo⟩ — see CLOTHE 1

¹cape *n* a sleeveless garment worn so as to hang over the shoulders, arms, and back ⟨the mysterious figure wrapped his *cape* tightly around his shoulders⟩
synonyms cloak, mantle, roquelaure
related words frock, gown, robe; shawl, stole, wrap; poncho, serape (*or* sarape)

²cape *n* an area of land that juts out into a body of water ⟨residents fled the *cape* as the hurricane roared up the coast⟩
synonyms arm, headland, peninsula, point, promontory, spit
related words breakwater, jetty

caper *n* a playful or mischievous act intended as a joke ⟨the students got in trouble for their midnight *caper*, but it was undeniably funny⟩ — see PRANK

caper *vb* to play and run about happily ⟨children *capered* and laughed on the beach as the summer drew to a close⟩ — see FROLIC 1

capital *adj* of the very best kind ⟨a truly *capital* book that I highly recommend⟩ — see EXCELLENT

capital *n* **1** a thing or place that is of greatest importance to an activity or interest ⟨during the 1980s Silicon Valley became the *capital* of the computer industry⟩ — see CENTER 1
2 the total of one's money and property ⟨invested nearly all of their *capital* in the new business⟩ — see WEALTH

capitalize *vb* to provide money for ⟨several investors agreed to *capitalize* the new venture⟩ — see FINANCE 1

capitalize (on) *vb* to take unfair advantage of ⟨*capitalized on* a coworker's absence to take full credit for the joint project⟩ — see EXPLOIT 1

capitol *n* the building in which a state legislature meets ⟨the legislators were called to the *capitol* for an emergency session⟩
synonyms state house
related words meetinghouse; chamber, hall

capitulate *vb* **1** to cease resistance (as to another's arguments, demands, or control) ⟨one side finally *capitulated* when it became clear that they couldn't win the argument⟩ — see YIELD 3
2 to yield to the control or power of enemy forces ⟨the city *capitulated* to the invaders after a three-day siege⟩ — see FALL 2

capitulating *n* the usually forced yielding of one's person or possessions to the control of another ⟨the tug-of-war will continue until the *capitulating* of one side or the other⟩ — see SURRENDER

capitulation *n* the usually forced yielding of one's person or possessions to the control of another ⟨her sudden *capitulation* surprised everyone; she usually debated for hours⟩ — see SURRENDER

caprice *n* a sudden impulsive and apparently unmotivated idea or action ⟨an out-of-character *caprice* led him to take the day off from work and go to the beach⟩ — see WHIM

capricious *adj* **1** likely to change frequently, suddenly, or unexpectedly ⟨*capricious* weather that was balmy one day and freezing cold the next⟩ — see FICKLE 1
2 prone to sudden illogical changes of mind, ideas, or actions ⟨a *capricious* woman who changed her mind dozens of times about what color to paint the bathroom⟩ — see WHIMSICAL

capriciousness *n* an inclination to sudden illogical changes of mind, ideas, or actions ⟨the client's *capriciousness* frustrated the building contractor to no end⟩ — see WHIMSICALITY

capsize *vb* to turn on one's side or upside down ⟨a huge wave out of nowhere caused our little sailboat to *capsize*⟩
synonyms overturn, upset
related words invert, topple; keel over; heel, list, tilt; founder, sink, swamp
phrases turn turtle
antonyms right

capsule *n* 1 a small mass containing medicine to be taken orally ⟨took an antibiotic *capsule* three times a day for a week⟩ — see PILL
2 something that encloses another thing especially to protect it ⟨a *capsule* containing all sorts of items from our day that is to be opened 100 years from now⟩ — see ¹CASE 1

captain *n* 1 a person in overall command of a ship ⟨the *captain* is responsible for everything that happens to his ship in the course of a voyage⟩
synonyms commander, skipper
related words master; commanding officer; admiral, commodore, vice admiral
2 one in official command especially of a military force or base ⟨the *captain* of the largest army ever marshaled for battle in this country⟩ — see COMMANDER 1
3 the person (as an employer or supervisor) who tells people and especially workers what to do ⟨we only do what the *captain* tells us to, so it's not our fault when things don't work out⟩ — see BOSS

captain *vb* 1 to be in charge of ⟨if you do well on this, you'll be asked to *captain* the next mission⟩ — see BOSS 1
2 to exercise authority or power over ⟨*captained* the project for a few days while the boss was out of town⟩ — see GOVERN 1
3 to serve as leader of ⟨you did a good job of *captaining* the team⟩ — see LEAD 2

caption *n* 1 an explanation or description accompanying a pictorial illustration ⟨for the school yearbook, funny *captions* were written for snapshots showing a typical day at school⟩
synonyms legend
related words key; subtitle, translation; motto, tag line
2 a word or series of words often in larger letters placed at the beginning of a passage or at the top of a page in order to introduce or categorize ⟨the textbook features cleverly worded *captions* to capture the reader's attention⟩ — see HEADING

captious *adj* given to making or expressing unfavorable judgments about things ⟨a *captious* and cranky eater who's never met a vegetable he didn't hate⟩ — see CRITICAL 1

captivate *vb* to attract or delight as if by magic ⟨the clown *captivated* the toddlers with his balloon tricks⟩ — see CHARM 1

captivating *adj* having an often mysterious or magical power to attract ⟨a *captivating* performance by the young singing sensation⟩ — see FASCINATING 1

captivation *n* the power of irresistible attraction ⟨by some mysterious method of *captivation*, the therapist is able to evoke a response from even the shiest of children⟩ — see CHARM 2

captive *adj* taken and held prisoner ⟨the *captive* soldiers were treated humanely by the guards⟩
synonyms apprehended, arrested, captured, caught, imprisoned, incarcerated, interned, jailed
related words bound, enslaved, indentured; subdued, subjugated

near antonyms emancipated, enfranchised, freed, liberated, released
antonyms free

captive *n* one that has been taken and held in confinement ⟨the *captives* in the concentration camp had devised a daring plan of escape⟩
synonyms capture, internee, prisoner
related words convict, jailbird; parolee
near antonyms custodian, guard, guardian, jailer (*or* jailor), keeper, warden
antonyms captor

captivity *n* the act of confining or the state of being confined ⟨the wildlife refuge raises endangered species in *captivity* and then releases them into the wild⟩ — see INTERNMENT

capture *n* one that has been taken and held in confinement ⟨the Spanish treasure ship was the most valuable *capture* taken by that privateer⟩ — see CAPTIVE

capture *vb* 1 to receive as return for effort ⟨the movie's producers *captured* several awards for their work⟩ — see EARN 1
2 to take physical control or possession of (something) suddenly or forcibly ⟨*captured* the cat just as it was about to escape out the front door⟩ — see CATCH 1

captured *adj* taken and held prisoner ⟨a *captured* princess held for ransom⟩ — see CAPTIVE

car *n* a self-propelled passenger vehicle on wheels ⟨every teenager's dream of getting a driver's license and a first *car*⟩
synonyms auto, automobile, machine, motor, motorcar, motor vehicle
related words bus, coach, minibus; beach buggy, brougham, compact, convertible, coupe, dune buggy, fastback, gas-guzzler, hardtop, hatchback, hot rod, jeep, limousine, roadster, sedan, sports car, station wagon, stock car, subcompact, van; flivver, jalopy

caravan *n* 1 a group of vehicles traveling together or under one management ⟨a funeral *caravan* slowly making its way down the street⟩ — see FLEET
2 a motor vehicle that is specially equipped for living while traveling ⟨bought a *caravan* and drove cross-country to California⟩ — see CAMPER

caravansary *or* **caravanserai** *n* a place that provides rooms and usually a public dining room for overnight guests ⟨a *caravansary* designed specifically for self-styled cheapskates⟩ — see HOTEL

carbon copy *n* 1 something or someone that strongly resembles another ⟨the child is a *carbon copy* of his father⟩ — see IMAGE 1
2 something that is made to look exactly like something else ⟨a clothing company that makes *carbon copies* of designer duds⟩ — see COPY

carcass *n* a dead body ⟨the *carcass* of a squirrel that had been run over⟩ — see CORPSE

card *n* a person (as a writer) noted for or specializing in humor ⟨you're really a *card*, but save the jokes for after class⟩ — see HUMORIST

cardinal *adj* coming before all others in importance ⟨the *cardinal* rule of medicine: do no harm⟩ — see FOREMOST 1

care *n* 1 strict attentiveness to what one is doing ⟨that's an extremely valuable violin, so handle it with *care*⟩
synonyms carefulness, conscientiousness, heed, heedfulness, pains, scrupulousness
related words exactness, meticulousness, particularity, punctiliousness; dutifulness, responsibility; bother, effort, trouble; alertness, vigilance, watchfulness

antonyms carelessness, heedlessness

2 a close attentiveness to avoiding danger ⟨take *care* while crossing the street⟩ — see CAUTION 1

3 an uneasy state of mind usually over the possibility of an anticipated misfortune or trouble ⟨on vacation, without a *care* in the world⟩ — see ANXIETY 1

4 responsibility for the safety and well-being of someone or something ⟨while you're under my *care*, you'll do as you're told⟩ — see CUSTODY

5 the duty or function of watching or guarding for the sake of proper direction or control ⟨you'll have *care* of the project from its beginning to its completion⟩ — see SUPERVISION 1

care *vb* to have an interest or concern for ⟨a teacher who *cares* what happens to her students long after they leave her classroom⟩

synonyms mind, watch

related words attend, heed, regard; note, notice, observe; empathize (with), feel (for), sympathize (with)

phrases look out for

near antonyms disregard, ignore, overlook

care (for) *vb* **1** to take charge of especially on behalf of another ⟨will you *care for* the lawn while we're gone?⟩ — see ²TEND 1

2 to attend to the needs and comforts of ⟨he is *caring for* his mother while she's sick⟩ — see NURSE 1

3 to have a favorable opinion of ⟨I don't really *care for* what you're doing with that dog⟩ — see APPROVE (OF)

4 to wish to have ⟨I don't particularly *care for* rice cereal, but I'll eat it⟩ — see LIKE 1

careen *vb* **1** to make a series of unsteady side-to-side motions ⟨the sled *careened* as it barreled down the hill⟩ — see ROCK 1

2 to move forward while swaying from side to side ⟨he *careened* unsteadily to the couch after hitting his head⟩ — see STAGGER 1

career *vb* to proceed or move quickly ⟨she *careered* off to the class she'd almost forgotten⟩ — see HURRY 2

carefree *adj* having or showing a lack of concern or seriousness ⟨passengers on a luxury cruise ship enjoying a *carefree* vacation⟩ ⟨*carefree* college students on spring break⟩

synonyms careless, cavalier, devil-may-care, easygoing, gay, happy-go-lucky, insouciant, lighthearted, unconcerned

related words breezy, nonchalant; casual, informal, laid-back, low-pressure, relaxed; heedless, irresponsible, lackadaisical, negligent, reckless

near antonyms earnest, grave, serious, somber (*or* sombre); careful, cautious, heedful, wary; concerned, upset, worried; long-suffering, overburdened, sorrowful

antonyms careworn

careful *adj* **1** having or showing a close attentiveness to avoiding danger or trouble ⟨*careful* drivers slow down on slick or icy roadways⟩

synonyms alert, cautious, circumspect, considerate, gingerly, guarded, heedful, safe, wary

related words attentive, chary, observant, vigilant, watchful; foresighted, forethoughtful, provident; cagey (*also* cagy), noncommittal; calculating, scheming, shrewd; considerate, thoughtful; deliberate, slow

near antonyms bold, impetuous, rash, reckless; inattentive, unobservant; inconsiderate, thoughtless; lax, neglectful, negligent; imprudent, indiscreet, injudicious

antonyms careless, heedless, incautious, unguarded, unsafe, unwary

2 taking great care and effort ⟨that furniture maker was known to be a most *careful* worker, so his output was small⟩ — see PAINSTAKING

carefulness *n* **1** a close attentiveness to avoiding danger ⟨her natural *carefulness* keeps her from having accidents⟩ — see CAUTION 1

2 strict attentiveness to what one is doing ⟨a degree of *carefulness* is required to get the details just right⟩ — see CARE 1

careless *adj* **1** not paying or showing close attention especially for the purpose of avoiding trouble ⟨a *careless* reporter who often doesn't get his facts straight⟩ ⟨a *careless* mistake that caused the plane to crash⟩

synonyms heedless, incautious, mindless, unguarded, unsafe, unwary

related words bold, impetuous, rash, reckless; inattentive, unobservant; blithe, inconsiderate, thoughtless; absentminded, forgetful, unmindful; lax, neglectful, negligent, remiss; imprudent, indiscreet, injudicious; inadvertent, unintentional, unplanned

near antonyms attentive, chary, observant, vigilant, watchful; foresighted, forethoughtful, provident; calculating, scheming, shrewd; considerate, thoughtful

antonyms alert, cautious, circumspect, gingerly, guarded, heedful, safe, wary

2 failing to give proper care and attention ⟨a *careless* effort that made an unnecessary mess⟩ — see NEGLIGENT

3 having or showing a lack of concern or seriousness ⟨a *careless* attitude toward schoolwork⟩ — see CAREFREE

carelessness *n* failure to take the care that a cautious person usually takes ⟨the only errors you made were from *carelessness*, not lack of knowledge⟩ — see NEGLIGENCE 1

caress *vb* to touch or handle in a tender or loving manner ⟨gently *caressed* her hair⟩ — see FONDLE

caretaker *n* a person who takes care of a property sometimes for an absent owner ⟨hired a *caretaker* for the mansion during the winter months⟩ — see CUSTODIAN 1

cargo *n* a mass or quantity of something taken up and carried, conveyed, or transported ⟨we put all of our *cargo* on the pack animals and began our journey through the canyon⟩ — see LOAD 1

caricature *n* **1** a poor, insincere, or insulting imitation of something ⟨the TV network's reporting is a mere *caricature* of real journalism⟩ — see MOCKERY 1

2 a work that imitates and exaggerates another work for comic effect ⟨the artist creates *caricatures* of famous paintings by replacing humans with cats⟩ — see PARODY 1

3 the representation of something in terms that go beyond the facts ⟨the politician presented only a *caricature* of his opponent's views⟩ — see EXAGGERATION

caricature *vb* to copy or exaggerate (someone or something) in order to make fun of ⟨*caricatured* the principal's distinctive walk⟩ — see MIMIC 1

carnage *n* the killing of a large number of people ⟨the appalling *carnage* in that country requires that the outside world intervene⟩ — see MASSACRE

carnal *adj* **1** having to do with life on earth especially as opposed to that in heaven ⟨the preacher warned that those who were interested only in *carnal* pursuits would not see the kingdom of heaven⟩ — see EARTHLY

2 of or relating to the human body ⟨a missionary who tends to the *carnal* needs of the people as well as their spiritual concerns⟩ — see PHYSICAL 1

3 pleasing to the physical senses ⟨*carnal* attractions of that gambling mecca in the desert⟩ — see SENSUAL

carnival *n* a time or program of special events and entertainment in honor of something ⟨a Fourth of July *carnival*⟩ — see FESTIVAL

carol *n* a religious song ⟨sang *carols* at the Christmas service⟩ — see HYMN

carol *vb* to produce musical sounds with the voice ⟨she *caroled* with glee when she heard the good news⟩ — see SING 1

caroler *or* **caroller** *n* one who sings ⟨those feathered *carolers* outside my window every morning⟩ — see SINGER

carom *vb* to strike and fly off at an angle ⟨a ball *caromed* off the wall⟩ — see GLANCE 1

carousal *n* a bout of drinking ⟨came home tired and sick after a *carousal* with his friends⟩ — see CAROUSE

carouse *n* a bout of drinking ⟨the Old West custom of heading to the saloon at night for a *carouse* and some poker playing⟩

synonyms carousal, drunk, wassail

related words binge, jag, spree; blowout, orgy

carp *vb* **1** to express dissatisfaction, pain, or resentment usually tiresomely ⟨someone who *carps* and whines about everything is not very much fun to be around⟩ — see COMPLAIN

2 to make often peevish criticisms or objections about matters that are minor, unimportant, or irrelevant ⟨*carped* about the order of names on the wedding invitations⟩ — see QUIBBLE

carper *n* a person given to harsh judgments and to finding faults ⟨eventually, almost everyone learned to avoid the ski school's resident *carper*⟩ — see CRITIC 1

carpet *vb* to form a layer over ⟨leaves *carpeted* the lawn⟩ — see COVER 2

carping *adj* given to making or expressing unfavorable judgments about things ⟨a peevish and *carping* old woman who is not a favorite at the nursing home⟩ — see CRITICAL 1

carriage *n* **1** a horse-drawn wheeled vehicle for carrying passengers ⟨a museum with a large collection of beautiful, old *carriages*⟩

synonyms equipage, rig

related words brougham, buckboard, cab, chaise, coach, hackney, hansom, surrey

2 a general way of holding the body ⟨her *carriage* was upright and regal⟩ — see POSTURE 1

carry *vb* **1** to support and take from one place to another ⟨each camper must be able to *carry* his or her own backpack⟩

synonyms bear, cart, convey, ferry, haul, lug, pack, tote, transport

related words deliver, hand over, transfer; forward, send, ship, transmit; bring, fetch, take; move, remove, shift

2 to wear or have on one's person ⟨I always *carry* a camera with me so as to never miss a great shot⟩

synonyms bear, pack

related words flaunt, show off, sport; display, exhibit, parade, show

3 to bring before the public in performance or exhibition ⟨all of the television networks will *carry* the president's speech⟩ — see PRESENT 1

4 to have as part of a whole ⟨the idea *carries* with it a number of other concepts⟩ — see INCLUDE

5 to hold up or serve as a foundation for ⟨massive pillars *carry* the arch⟩ — see SUPPORT 3

6 to receive as return for effort ⟨*carried* off the award for best picture of the year⟩ — see EARN 1

carryall *n* a bag carried by hand and designed to hold a traveler's clothing and personal articles ⟨took only a small *carryall* on the plane⟩ — see TRAVELING BAG

carry away *vb* **1** to fill with overwhelming emotion (as wonder or delight) ⟨the beauty of the music *carried* him *away*⟩ — see ENTRANCE

2 to subject to incapacitating emotional or mental stress ⟨the family was completely *carried away* by the shocking news of the death of their eldest son⟩ — see OVERWHELM 1

carry on *vb* **1** to behave badly ⟨a toddler crying and *carrying on* in the store⟩ — see MISBEHAVE

2 to continue despite difficulties, opposition, or discouragement ⟨she bravely *carried on* despite the loss of her husband⟩ — see PERSEVERE

3 to look after and make decisions about ⟨*carries on* a business and still manages to run the household⟩ — see CONDUCT 1

carry out *vb* to carry through (as a process) to completion ⟨*carried out* the task efficiently and well⟩ — see PERFORM 1

cart *n* a wheeled usually horse-drawn vehicle used for hauling ⟨an old *cart* piled up with hay⟩

synonyms wagon, wain

related words barrow, pushcart, wheelbarrow; oxcart

cart *vb* to support and take from one place to another ⟨*carted* a knapsack filled with books from class to class⟩ — see CARRY 1

cartel *n* a number of businesses or enterprises united for commercial advantage ⟨a *cartel* of oil-producing nations that controls production and influences prices⟩

synonyms combination, combine, syndicate, trust

related words chain, conglomerate, multinational; association, organization, pool

cartoon *n* **1** a picture using lines to represent the chief features of an object or scene ⟨a political *cartoon* mocking the state legislature⟩ — see DRAWING

2 a series of drawings that tell a story or part of a story ⟨reading the *cartoons* in the Sunday newspaper⟩ — see COMIC STRIP

carve *vb* to create a three-dimensional representation of (something) using solid material ⟨*carved* a statue out of rare marble⟩ — see SCULPT

carve (out) *vb* to produce or bring about especially by long or repeated effort ⟨finally *carved out* a niche for the sport in the school's athletic program⟩ — see HAMMER (OUT)

cascade *n* a fall of water usually from a great height ⟨it would be foolhardy to try to go over the *cascade* in a barrel⟩ — see WATERFALL

¹case *n* **1** something that encloses another thing especially to protect it ⟨those binoculars come with their own *case*⟩

synonyms armor, capsule, casing, cocoon, cover, covering, housing, husk, jacket, pod, sheath, shell

related words bark, crust; mail, plate, plating, shield; hide, skin; envelope, wrapper; backing, coating, facing

2 a covered rectangular container for storing or transporting things ⟨a handy little cosmetics *case* that matches the rest of her luggage⟩ — see CHEST

²case *n* **1** an individual awaiting or under medical care and treatment ⟨her doctor wishes that all of his *cases* were as cooperative as she is⟩ — see PATIENT

2 one of a group or collection that shows what the whole is like ⟨this is a perfect *case* of people jumping to the wrong conclusion before all the facts are known⟩ — see EXAMPLE

3 something that actually exists ⟨this has never been the *case* before⟩ — see FACT 2

4 a statement given to explain a belief or act ⟨you'll get a chance to make your *case*, but unless you're very convincing, you'll probably be punished⟩ — see REASON 1

5 a sudden experiencing of a physical or mental disorder ⟨a young boy suffering from a *case* of chicken pox⟩ — see ATTACK 2

6 something that might happen ⟨that may be the *case* that the cause of the fire will forever remain a mystery⟩ — see EVENT 2

7 something that requires thought and skill for resolution ⟨that's a tough *case* to solve⟩ — see PROBLEM 1

cash *n* something (as pieces of stamped metal or printed paper) customarily and legally used as a medium of exchange, a measure of value, or a means of payment ⟨went to the bank to get more *cash*⟩ — see MONEY

cashier *vb* to let go from office, service, or employment ⟨was abruptly *cashiered* after money was found missing⟩ — see DISMISS 1

cash in (on) *vb* to take unfair advantage of ⟨some people thought the lawyers were *cashing in on* the tragedy⟩ — see EXPLOIT 1

casing *n* something that encloses another thing especially to protect it ⟨the egg of this bird has an unusually hard *casing*⟩ — see ¹CASE 1

cask *n* an enclosed wooden vessel for holding beverages ⟨*casks* of wine that had been in the castle for many years⟩
synonyms barrel, firkin, hogshead, keg, pipe, puncheon
related words tub, vat; can, drum

casket *n* **1** a box for holding a dead body ⟨bought a beautiful *casket* when her grandmother died⟩ — see COFFIN

2 a covered rectangular container for storing or transporting things ⟨a small *casket* of jewels⟩ — see CHEST

cast *n* **1** a declaration that something will happen in the future ⟨offered an optimistic *cast* for the coming year⟩ — see PREDICTION

2 a property that becomes apparent when light falls on an object and by which things that are identical in form can be distinguished ⟨the walls had a slight yellowish *cast*⟩ — see COLOR 1

3 an instance of looking especially briefly ⟨a mischievous *cast* in his eye when we asked what our destination would be⟩ — see LOOK 2

4 facial appearance regarded as an indication of mood or feeling ⟨his face took on a somewhat sad *cast*⟩ — see LOOK 1

5 the outward appearance of something as distinguished from its substance ⟨the lovely *cast* of the baby's features⟩ — see FORM 1

cast *vb* **1** to get rid of as useless or unwanted ⟨*cast* off all the old junk in the attic⟩ — see DISCARD

2 to point or turn (something) toward a target or goal ⟨*cast* her eyes skyward for any sign of the rescue plane⟩ — see AIM 1

3 to put (something) into proper and usually carefully worked out written form ⟨carefully *cast* the letter of complaint as politely as possible⟩ — see COMPOSE 1

4 to send through the air especially with a quick forward motion of the arm ⟨*cast* a rock into the stream⟩ — see THROW

cast (off) *vb* to throw or give off ⟨a small lamp *casting off* some dim light⟩ — see EMIT 1

cast (out) *vb* to drive or force out ⟨*cast* them *out* of the tribe for violating sacred traditions⟩ — see EJECT 1

cast about (for) *vb* to go in search of ⟨*cast about for* an answer to the question why so many people had ignored the victim's cries for help⟩ — see SEEK 1

cast around (for) *vb* to go in search of ⟨*cast around for* a last minute replacement for the lead actor in the movie⟩ — see SEEK 1

castaway *n* one who is cast out or rejected by society ⟨one theory is that Easter Island was first settled by *castaways* from Polynesia⟩ — see OUTCAST

caste *n* one of the segments of society into which people are grouped ⟨a member of the upper *caste*⟩ — see CLASS 1

castigate *vb* **1** to criticize (someone) severely or angrily especially for personal failings ⟨*castigated* him for his constant tardiness⟩ — see SCOLD

2 to criticize harshly and usually publicly ⟨a newspaper editorial *castigating* the city council for approving the project in the first place⟩ — see ATTACK 2

3 to inflict a penalty on for a fault or crime ⟨a judge who believes in *castigating* criminals to the full extent of the law⟩ — see PUNISH

castigating *adj* inflicting, involving, or serving as punishment ⟨a *castigating* task that succeeds in doing nothing more than making the lives of the inmates miserable⟩ — see PUNITIVE

castigation *n* suffering, loss, or hardship imposed in response to a crime or offense ⟨the loss of his father's trust was the harshest *castigation* that the boy could have possibly received for having told the lie⟩ — see PUNISHMENT

castigator *n* **1** a person given to harsh judgments and to finding faults ⟨even Broadway's most famously caustic *castigator* liked the play⟩ — see CRITIC 1

2 one who inflicts punishment in return for an injury or offense ⟨the principal seems to enjoy his role as the tireless *castigator* of classroom pranksters⟩ — see NEMESIS 1

castle *n* a large impressive residence ⟨the tycoon built a magnificent *castle* on the hill overlooking the town⟩ — see MANSION

castoff *n* one who is cast out or rejected by society ⟨a *castoff* who later became a famous poet⟩ — see OUTCAST

casual *adj* **1** not designed for special occasions ⟨a restaurant where people in *casual* clothes are always welcome⟩
synonyms everyday, informal, workaday
related words sporty; shabby, sloppy, slovenly, unkempt
near antonyms best, Sunday; chic, elegant, fashionable, smart, stylish; neat, tidy, trim; semiformal
antonyms dressy, formal

2 happening by chance ⟨a *casual* meeting with the next-door neighbors on a beach in Hawaii⟩ — see ACCIDENTAL

3 having or showing a lack of interest or concern ⟨only a *casual* examination of the bicycle before buying it⟩ — see INDIFFERENT 1

4 lacking in steadiness or regularity of occurrence ⟨a *casual* attendance at their son's hockey games⟩ — see FITFUL

casualness *n* lack of interest or concern ⟨her *casualness* distressed everyone who took the issue seriously⟩ — see INDIFFERENCE

casualty *n* **1** a person or thing harmed, lost, or destroyed ⟨the real *casualties* in the war against drugs are millions of innocent children⟩
synonyms fatality, loss, victim
related words failure, loser
near antonyms gainer, victor, winner
2 a chance and usually sudden event bringing loss or injury ⟨*casualties* at sea that sometimes resulted in great losses of men or even of entire ships⟩ — see ACCIDENT 1

cat *n* **1** a small domestic animal known for catching mice ⟨the family's *cat* did a good job of keeping the house and yard free of all rodents⟩
synonyms feline, house cat, kitty, puss, pussy
related words mouser; kit, kitten; tabby, tomcat
2 *slang* an adult male human being ⟨a cool *cat* driving around in his new sports car⟩ — see MAN 1

cataclysm *n* **1** a great flow of water or of something that overwhelms ⟨an ancient *cataclysm* that may have been the basis for the Flood described in the Bible⟩ — see FLOOD
2 a sudden violent event that brings about great loss or destruction ⟨the earthquake that struck Lisbon in 1755, killing 30,000 people, was one of the greatest *cataclysms* ever recorded⟩ — see DISASTER
3 a violent disturbance (as of the political or social order) ⟨a social *cataclysm* that gave rise to a new world order⟩ — see CONVULSION

cataclysmal *or* **cataclysmic** *adj* **1** bringing about ruin or misfortune ⟨a *cataclysmal* decision to plunge the nation into war⟩ — see FATAL 1
2 causing or tending to cause destruction ⟨a *cataclysmal* landslide that virtually wiped out the village⟩ — see DESTRUCTIVE 1
3 marked by sudden or violent disturbance ⟨the French Revolution was one of the great *cataclysmal* events in modern history⟩ — see CONVULSIVE

catacomb *n*, *usually* **catacombs** *pl* an underground burial chamber ⟨explored the *catacombs* looking for evidence about burial customs of that ancient society⟩ — see CRYPT

catalog *or* **catalogue** *n* a record of a series of items (as names or titles) usually arranged according to some system ⟨a *catalog* of music album titles⟩ — see ¹LIST

catalog *or* **catalogue** *vb* to put (someone or something) on a list ⟨*cataloged* the latest additions to the collection⟩ — see ¹LIST 2

catamount *n* a large tawny cat of the wild ⟨found the footprints of a *catamount* on the mountain trail⟩ — see COUGAR

catapult *vb* to send through the air especially with a quick forward motion of the arm ⟨*catapulted* a pumpkin into the next yard⟩ — see THROW

cataract *n* **1** a fall of water usually from a great height ⟨the roaring *cataract* is one of the park's most majestic sights⟩ — see WATERFALL
2 a great flow of water or of something that overwhelms ⟨in spring the melting snows usually produce a *cataract* that inundates the valley⟩ — see FLOOD

catastrophe *n* **1** a sudden violent event that brings about great loss or destruction ⟨more than one natural *catastrophe* has threatened to destroy their farm over the years⟩ — see DISASTER
2 something that has failed ⟨the movie was a *catastrophe*, nearly bankrupting the studio that produced it⟩ — see FAILURE 3

catastrophic *adj* bringing about ruin or misfortune ⟨a *catastrophic* tornado destroyed the hamlet's only house of worship⟩ — see FATAL 1

catcall *n* a vocal sound made to express scorn or disapproval ⟨the band's sloppy playing produced only *catcalls* from the crowd⟩
synonyms boo, hiss, hoot, jeer, raspberry, snort
related words smirk, sneer, snicker, snigger; gibe (*or* jibe), put-down, taunt; whistle
near antonyms applause, clapping
antonyms cheer

catch *n* **1** a danger or difficulty that is hidden or not easily recognized ⟨the *catch* is that you have to come up with the money by tomorrow⟩ — see PITFALL 1
2 someone or something unusually desirable ⟨everyone thought the captain of the football team was a real *catch*⟩ — see PRIZE 1
3 the total amount collected or obtained especially at one time ⟨the total *catch* for our day at the creek was six fish and a crab⟩ — see HAUL 1

catch *vb* **1** to take physical control or possession of (something) suddenly or forcibly ⟨we tried to *catch* the kitten before she could sneak out the door⟩
synonyms bag, capture, collar, corral, get, grab, grapple, hook, land, nab, nail, seize, snap (up), snare, snatch, trap
related words lasso, rope; apprehend, arrest, detain; clasp, clutch, grasp, grip, hold, secure; rend, wrest; ensnare, entangle, entrap; abduct, kidnap, spirit (away *or* off)
phrases lay hold of
near antonyms discharge, free, liberate, release; drop, loosen
antonyms miss
2 to become affected with (a disease or disorder) ⟨you'll *catch* the flu for sure if you don't get a shot⟩ — see CONTRACT 1
3 to bring (something) to a standstill ⟨I *caught* myself just as I was about to step into the freshly poured concrete⟩ — see ¹HALT 1
4 to put securely in place or in a desired position ⟨*caught* back her hair with a barrette⟩ — see FASTEN 2
5 to recognize the meaning of ⟨I didn't *catch* the point you were making about our nation's foreign policy⟩ — see COMPREHEND 1

catching *adj* **1** capable of being passed by physical contact from one person to another ⟨a cold is often *catching* before the symptoms even begin⟩ — see CONTAGIOUS 1
2 exciting a similar feeling or reaction in others ⟨a *catching* smile that instantly puts patients at ease⟩ — see CONTAGIOUS 2

catch on *vb* to come to an awareness ⟨she *caught on* to the fact that they were planning a surprise party⟩ — see DISCOVER 1

catch on (to) *vb* to recognize the meaning of ⟨he finally *caught on to* the concept of phototaxis⟩ — see COMPREHEND 1

catch up (with) *vb* to move fast enough to get even with ⟨I walked faster to *catch up with* my friends⟩ — see OVERTAKE

catchy *adj* **1** likely to attract attention ⟨will need a *catchy* slogan to sell the new product, which is actually pretty boring⟩ — see NOTICEABLE
2 requiring exceptional skill or caution in performance or handling ⟨Mr. Hartman's tests always include at least one *catchy* question⟩ — see TRICKY

categorical *also* **categoric** *adj* having no exceptions or restrictions ⟨a *categorical* denial of the rumors that the celebrities were planning to get married⟩ — see ABSOLUTE 2

categorize *vb* to arrange or assign according to type ⟨*categorized* the questions by topic⟩ — see CLASSIFY 1

category *n* one of the units into which a whole is divided on the basis of a common characteristic ⟨divide the essays into *categories* based on difficulty of comprehension⟩ — see CLASS 2

cater *vb* to provide food or meals for ⟨a local firm will *cater* the awards banquet for high school athlete of the year⟩ — see FEED 1

cater (to) *vb* to give in to (a desire) ⟨the gooey dessert *catered to* the children's sweet tooth⟩ — see INDULGE

catnap *n* a short sleep ⟨a *catnap* left me refreshed enough to face the rest of the day⟩ — see ¹NAP

catnap *vb* **1** be in a state of sleep ⟨Dad's *catnapping*, so please call back later⟩ — see SLEEP 1
2 to sleep lightly or briefly ⟨*catnapped* for ten minutes and then went back to work⟩ — see NAP 1

catnapping *n* a natural periodic loss of consciousness during which the body restores itself ⟨indulged in some quick *catnapping* between appointments with patients⟩ — see SLEEP 1

cattily *adv* in a mean or spiteful manner ⟨commented *cattily* that the woman onstage was wearing an ugly dress⟩ — see NASTILY

cattiness *n* **1** biting sharpness of feeling or expression ⟨the *cattiness* of the commentary for the televised awards was neither nice nor necessary⟩ — see ACRIMONY 1
2 the desire to cause pain for the satisfaction of doing harm ⟨there's no reason for saying such hurtful things except sheer *cattiness*⟩ — see MALICE

catty *adj* having or showing a desire to cause someone pain or suffering for the sheer enjoyment of it ⟨a *catty* remark that served its only purpose: to make someone cry⟩ — see HATEFUL

caught *adj* taken and held prisoner ⟨after seeing how the *caught* soldiers were treated, we resolved never to be taken alive⟩ — see CAPTIVE

cause *n* **1** someone or something responsible for a result ⟨the much-debated *causes* of the American Civil War⟩
synonyms antecedent, occasion, reason
related words consideration, determinant, factor; impetus, incentive, inspiration, instigation, stimulus; mother, origin, root, source, spring
near antonyms ramification; denouement, repercussion; conclusion, end; by-product, side effect
antonyms aftereffect, aftermath, consequence, corollary, development, effect, fate, fruit, issue, outcome, outgrowth, product, result, resultant, sequel, sequence, upshot
2 a series of activities undertaken to achieve a goal ⟨joined the freedom fighters' *cause* as a young man⟩ — see CAMPAIGN

cause *vb* to be the cause of (a situation, action, or state of mind) ⟨the ice storm *caused* a massive power outage⟩ — see EFFECT

caustic *adj* marked by the use of wit that is intended to cause hurt feelings ⟨*caustic* movie reviews that serve mainly to show how clever the reviewer is⟩ — see SARCASTIC

caution *n* **1** a close attentiveness to avoiding danger ⟨the extreme *caution* with which the zookeeper handled the snake⟩

synonyms alertness, care, carefulness, cautiousness, circumspection, heedfulness, wariness
related words attentiveness, chariness, vigilance, watchfulness; foresight, foresightedness, providence; calculation, canniness, deliberateness, deliberation, shrewdness
near antonyms abruptness, hastiness, impetuousness, precipitousness, rashness, suddenness; inconsideration, thoughtlessness
antonyms brashness, carelessness, heedlessness, incautiousness, recklessness, unwariness
2 something extraordinary or surprising ⟨how she manages to drive her car without destroying the neighborhood is a *caution*⟩ — see WONDER 1
3 something that tells of approaching danger or risk ⟨this is just a *caution* that the following paragraph practically gives away the plot of the entire movie⟩ — see WARNING 2
4 the act or an instance of telling beforehand of danger or risk ⟨we heeded the police officer's *caution* about the road ahead⟩ — see WARNING 1

caution *vb* to give notice to beforehand especially of danger or risk ⟨the doctor *cautioned* that I should still be careful using my sprained wrist for the next several days⟩ — see WARN

cautionary *adj* serving as or offering a warning ⟨the story of King Midas is a *cautionary* tale about the perils of wishing for something—you just might get it⟩
synonyms admonishing, admonitory, cautioning, warning
related words didactic, moralistic, moralizing; advisory, counseling (*or* counselling); punishing, punitive

cautioning *adj* serving as or offering a warning ⟨a *cautioning* story about how envy can destroy a friendship⟩ — see CAUTIONARY

cautious *adj* having or showing a close attentiveness to avoiding danger or trouble ⟨a *cautious* approach to everyday living⟩ — see CAREFUL 1

cautiousness *n* a close attentiveness to avoiding danger ⟨the *cautiousness* of drivers on the icy roadways was largely responsible for the accident-free day⟩ — see CAUTION 1

cavalcade *n* **1** a group of vehicles traveling together or under one management ⟨the longest *cavalcade* of floats in the history of the parade⟩ — see FLEET
2 a staged presentation often with music that consists of a procession of narrated or enacted scenes ⟨a *cavalcade* presenting major events in the town's history⟩ — see PAGEANT

cavalier *adj* **1** having a feeling of superiority that shows itself in an overbearing attitude ⟨a *cavalier* and pompous boss, indifferent to the feelings of her subordinate⟩ — see ARROGANT
2 having or showing a lack of concern or seriousness ⟨a *cavalier* approach to work got her fired from her first summer job⟩ — see CAREFREE

cavalier *n* an honorable and courteous man ⟨a novel about the dashing *cavaliers* and gracious ladies of the South before the Civil War⟩
synonyms gentleman
related words knight, prince; blade, buck, dandy, fop, gallant; charmer, smoothy (*or* smoothie); aristocrat, patrician

cave *n* a naturally formed underground chamber with an opening to the surface ⟨Kentucky's Mammoth *Cave* is actually a series of large chambers on five levels⟩
synonyms cavern, grot, grotto

related words abyss, chasm, gulf, hollow; subway, tunnel; excavation, mine, pit, shaft, well; bunker, dugout, foxhole; burrow, covert, den, hole, lair, lodge, shelter

cave (in) *vb* to fall down or in as a result of physical pressure ⟨the wall *caved in* when a tree fell on it⟩ — see COLLAPSE 1

cavern *n* a naturally formed underground chamber with an opening to the surface ⟨a *cavern* with beautiful stalactites⟩ — see CAVE

cavil *vb* to make often peevish criticisms or objections about matters that are minor, unimportant, or irrelevant ⟨*caviled* for hours about a single sentence⟩ — see QUIBBLE

caviler *or* **caviller** *n* a person given to harsh judgments and to finding faults ⟨the chronic *cavilers* who are going to complain no matter what the principal does⟩ — see CRITIC 1

caviling *or* **cavilling** *adj* given to making or expressing unfavorable judgments about things ⟨a *caviling* teacher who has yet to read a theme she likes⟩ — see CRITICAL 1

cavity *n* a sunken area forming a separate space ⟨a *cavity* in the lawn where a tree stump had been removed⟩ — see HOLE 2

cavort *vb* to play and run about happily ⟨children *cavorting* on the first sunny day of spring⟩ — see FROLIC 1

cease *vb* **1** to come to an end ⟨the rain finally *ceased*, and we were able to continue the baseball game⟩
synonyms break off, break up, close, conclude, die, discontinue, elapse, end, expire, finish, halt, lapse, leave off, let up, pass, quit, stop, terminate, wind up
related words desist (from), lay off (of), refrain (from); knock off; break down, conk (out), cut out, stall; pause, stay, suspend
near antonyms draw out, extend, prolong, protract
antonyms continue, hang on, persist
2 to bring (as an action or operation) to an immediate end ⟨*cease* chattering and get down to work, please⟩ — see STOP 1

cease–fire *n* a temporary stopping of fighting ⟨the two armies declared a *cease-fire* for the holiday⟩ — see TRUCE

ceaseless *adj* **1** going on and on without any interruptions ⟨there has been *ceaseless* rain for three days⟩ — see CONTINUOUS
2 lasting forever ⟨promised her *ceaseless* happiness if she would only marry him⟩ — see EVERLASTING

cede *vb* **1** to give (something) over to the control or possession of another usually under duress ⟨she reluctantly *ceded* her position as leader⟩ — see SURRENDER 1
2 to give over the legal possession or ownership of ⟨Spain *ceded* Puerto Rico to the United States as part of the settlement of the Spanish-American War⟩ — see TRANSFER 1
3 to give up (as a position of authority) formally ⟨the President officially *cedes* his position on the January 20th immediately following the presidential election⟩ — see ABDICATE

ceiling *n* **1** a real or imaginary point beyond which a person or thing cannot go ⟨there's a *ceiling* on prices⟩ — see LIMIT
2 a raised covering over something for decoration or protection ⟨we sat around the campfire under a *ceiling* of stars⟩ — see CANOPY

celebrant *n* one who engages in merrymaking especially in honor of a special occasion ⟨all of the *celebrants* at the birthday party received a favor to take home⟩
synonyms celebrator, merrymaker, reveler (*or* reveller), roisterer
related words carouser, wassailer; cutup, skylarker
antonyms killjoy, party pooper

celebrate *vb* to act properly in relation to ⟨a mixed family that *celebrates* both the Christian and Jewish religious holidays⟩ — see KEEP 1

celebrated *adj* widely known ⟨a *celebrated* author making an appearance on a talk show⟩ — see FAMOUS

celebration *n* a time or program of special events and entertainment in honor of something ⟨a *celebration* of the school's 100th anniversary⟩ — see FESTIVAL

celebrator *n* one who engages in merrymaking especially in honor of a special occasion ⟨some rowdy Super Bowl *celebrators* had to be given friendly warnings by the police⟩ — see CELEBRANT

celebrity *n* **1** a person who is widely known and usually much talked about ⟨*celebrities* from sports and entertainment attended the opening ceremonies of the Olympic Games⟩
synonyms figure, light, luminary, notable, personage, personality, somebody, standout, star, superstar, VIP
related words favorite, hero, idol; demigod, dignitary, eminence, immortal, pillar, worthy; baron, big shot, bigwig, magnate, mogul, nabob
near antonyms lightweight, mediocrity; has-been
antonyms nobody
2 the fact or state of being known to the public ⟨an actor who feels very uncomfortable with his *celebrity*⟩ — see FAME

celerity *n* a high rate of movement or performance ⟨a journalist who writes his well-crafted stories with remarkable *celerity*⟩ — see SPEED

celestial *adj* of, relating to, or suggesting heaven ⟨movie scenes depicting life after death are usually accompanied by *celestial* music⟩
synonyms Elysian, empyreal, empyrean, heavenly, supernal
related words ethereal, supernatural, transcendent, transcendental, unearthly, unworldly; angelic, beatific, blissful; Olympian, utopian; cosmic, stellar
near antonyms earthly, mundane, terrestrial, worldly
antonyms hellish, infernal

cell *n* **1** an area within a building that has been set apart from surrounding space by a wall ⟨a jail *cell*⟩ — see ROOM 2
2 one of the parts into which an enclosed space is divided ⟨*cells* in a honeycomb⟩ — see COMPARTMENT

cellar *n* a room or set of rooms below the surface of the ground ⟨an amazing variety of interesting things were found in the *cellar* of the old house⟩
synonyms basement
related words bunker, crawlway, foundation, hold

cement *n* **1** a substance used to stick things together ⟨what kind of *cement* works best on glass and pottery?⟩ — see GLUE
2 a uniting or binding force or influence ⟨she is the *cement* that holds that often quarrelsome group together⟩ — see BOND 2

cemetery *n* a piece of land used for burying the dead ⟨many of the soldiers who died in the battle are buried in a *cemetery* nearby⟩
synonyms graveyard, potter's field

related words catacombs, churchyard; crypt, grave, mausoleum, sepulcher (*or* sepulchre), sepulture, tomb, vault

censor *vb* to remove objectionable parts from ⟨the producers were told that they would have to *censor* their movie if they wanted a PG rating⟩
synonyms clean (up), expurgate
related words cleanse, purge, purify; abbreviate, edit, shorten; cut (out), delete, excise, expunge; repress, silence, suppress; censure, condemn, denounce; examine, review, screen, scrutinize
near antonyms approve, authorize, sanction

censurable *adj* **1** deserving reproach or blame ⟨*censurable* conduct that should get that student expelled⟩ — see BLAMEWORTHY
2 provoking or likely to provoke protest ⟨the *censurable* language on the poster resulted in it being taken down⟩ — see OBJECTIONABLE

censure *n* an often public or formal expression of disapproval ⟨a rare *censure* of a senator by the full United States Senate for misconduct⟩
synonyms condemnation, denunciation, rebuke, reprimand, reproach, reproof, stricture
related words admonishment, admonition, castigation, chastisement, punishment; belittlement, criticism, deprecation, depreciation, disparagement
near antonyms acclamation, honor, tribute; encomium, eulogy, panegyric, plaudit(s), praise; approval, blessing, sanction
antonyms citation, commendation, endorsement

censure *vb* **1** to express public or formal disapproval of ⟨a vote to *censure* the President for conduct that was unbecoming to his office⟩
synonyms condemn, denounce, rebuke, reprimand, reproach, reprove
related words admonish, castigate, chastise, punish; belittle, criticize, deprecate, depreciate, disparage
near antonyms acclaim, applause, honor; eulogize, laud, praise; approve, bless, sanction
antonyms cite, commend, endorse (*also* indorse)
2 to declare to be morally wrong or evil ⟨our society generally *censures* the taking of another person's life⟩ — see CONDEMN 1
3 to express one's unfavorable opinion of the worth or quality of ⟨critics have striven to outdo each other in *censuring* the author's latest work⟩ — see CRITICIZE

censurer *n* a person given to harsh judgments and to finding faults ⟨there's more malicious fun in being a *censurer* than in being a celebrator, so many theater critics are the latter⟩ — see CRITIC 1

center *n* **1** a thing or place that is of greatest importance to an activity or interest ⟨a stretch of coastline that has long been the area's *center* of tourism⟩
synonyms base, capital, core, cynosure, eye, focus, heart, hub, mecca, nucleus, seat
related words focus, headquarters; kernel, nub, pith; deep, thick; essence, quintessence, soul; attraction, lodestone, magnet
2 an area or point that is an equal distance from all points along an edge or outer surface ⟨the *center* of the earth⟩
synonyms core, middle, midpoint, midst
related words inside, interior
antonyms perimeter, periphery

center *vb* to bring (something) to a central point or under a single control ⟨*centered* administrative duties under the command of a single person⟩ — see CENTRALIZE

central *adj* coming before all others in importance ⟨the *central* theme of the book⟩ — see FOREMOST 1

centralize *vb* to bring (something) to a central point or under a single control ⟨the company decided to *centralize* all of its operations at its Ohio plant⟩
synonyms center, compact, concentrate, consolidate, unify, unite
related words coordinate, harmonize, integrate, orchestrate; blend, coalesce, combine, fuse, incorporate, merge; conjoin, join, link; assemble, collect, gather; reunify, reunite
near antonyms segregate, separate
antonyms decentralize, spread (out)

cerebral *adj* **1** much given to learning and thinking ⟨a *cerebral* lawyer who has given much thought to what makes our nation's constitution work⟩ — see INTELLECTUAL 1
2 of or relating to the mind ⟨a young man given more to *cerebral* pursuits than to sporting activities⟩ — see MENTAL 1

cerebrum *n* the part of a person that feels, thinks, perceives, wills, and especially reasons ⟨you'll need the patience of a saint and the *cerebrum* of a rocket scientist to figure out the solution to this brainteaser⟩ — see MIND 1

ceremonial *adj* following or agreeing with established form, custom, or rules ⟨a *ceremonial* presentation of the ambassador's credentials⟩ — see FORMAL 1

ceremonial *n* an oft-repeated action or series of actions performed in accordance with tradition or a set of rules ⟨a baptism *ceremonial*⟩ — see RITE

ceremonious *adj* **1** marked by or showing careful attention to set forms and details ⟨a century ago everyday life was much more *ceremonious* than in our anything-goes era⟩
synonyms correct, decorous, formal, proper, starchy
related words sober, solemn, stately; chivalrous, courtly, gallant; genteel, polished, refined; civil, courteous, polite, red-carpet
near antonyms improper, indecorous, unmannerly; discourteous, impolite, rude
antonyms casual, easygoing, informal, laid-back
2 following or agreeing with established form, custom, or rules ⟨the *ceremonious* regalia of the Swiss Guards, the pope's traditional body guards⟩ — see FORMAL 1

ceremony *n* an oft-repeated action or series of actions performed in accordance with tradition or a set of rules ⟨a beautiful, old-fashioned wedding *ceremony*⟩ — see RITE

certain *adj* **1** known but not named ⟨a *certain* person told me that today is your birthday⟩
synonyms anonymous, one, some, unidentified, unnamed, unspecified
related words particular, specific
near antonyms known, named, specified
2 having or showing a mind free from doubt ⟨I'm *certain* that they'll arrive on time⟩
synonyms assured, clear, cocksure, confident, doubtless, positive, sanguine, sure
related words self-assured, self-conceited, self-confident; decisive, resolute, unfaltering, unhesitating, unwavering
near antonyms hesitant, indecisive, wavering; diffident, unassuming
antonyms doubtful, dubious, uncertain, unsure
3 having been established and usually not subject to change ⟨a *certain* percentage of the profits will go to charity⟩ — see FIXED 1

4 impossible to avoid or evade ⟨as he got older, the athlete began to feel the *certain* effects of the aging process on his body⟩ — see INEVITABLE

5 not likely to fail ⟨chicken soup is grandma's *certain* cure for pretty much whatever ails you⟩ — see INFALLIBLE 2

certainly *adv* without any question ⟨*certainly*, you can come to the party⟩ — see INDEED 1

certainty *n* a state of mind in which one is free from doubt ⟨I have full *certainty* that I'll pass the test⟩ — see CONFIDENCE 2

certificate *n* a written or printed paper giving information about or proof of something ⟨a *certificate* will be awarded to each person who completes the course in lifesaving⟩

synonyms document, instrument

related words credentials; diploma, parchment; warrant, writ; warranty; coupon, voucher

certify *vb* **1** to declare (something) to be true or genuine ⟨experts *certified* the letter as indeed having been written by Abraham Lincoln⟩

synonyms attest, authenticate, avouch, testify (to), vouch (for), witness

related words guarantee, warrant; affirm, assert, aver, avow, profess

2 to give official or legal power to ⟨*certified* her as a teacher⟩ — see AUTHORIZE 1

certitude *n* a state of mind in which one is free from doubt ⟨believes with *certitude* that he is the best candidate for the job⟩ — see CONFIDENCE 2

cessation *n* the stopping of a process or activity ⟨the *cessation* of the snowstorm was a relief⟩ — see END 1

chafe *vb* **1** to make sore by continued rubbing ⟨ill-fitting boots that had badly *chafed* my heels⟩

synonyms abrade, gall, irritate

related words graze, scrape, scratch; burn, inflame; flay, peel, skin

2 to damage or diminish by continued friction ⟨constant stepping on a rope will gradually *chafe* it, rendering it unsafe for rock climbing⟩ — see ABRADE 1

3 to disturb the peace of mind of (someone) especially by repeated disagreeable acts ⟨the constantly ringing phone *chafed* him while he was trying to study⟩ — see IRRITATE 1

chaff *n* **1** discarded or useless material ⟨there's a lot of *chaff* in this book, and the reader should be on the alert for it⟩ — see GARBAGE

2 good-natured teasing or exchanging of clever remarks ⟨I got no end of *chaff* about my accent at the new school⟩ — see BANTER

chaff *vb* to make fun of in a good-natured way ⟨*chaffed* her about the brightly colored shirt she had received as a gift⟩ — see TEASE 1

chaffer *vb* to talk over or dispute the terms of a purchase ⟨in that country you're expected to *chaffer* with the vendors at the bazaar⟩ — see BARGAIN

chaffing *adj* marked by or expressive of mild or good-natured teasing ⟨a *chaffing* tone to Dad's discussion of my sister's new boyfriend⟩ — see QUIZZICAL

chaffy *adj* having no usefulness ⟨a *chaffy* book that is basically a collection of old interviews with celebrities⟩ — see WORTHLESS

chain *n* **1** a series of things linked together ⟨the *chain* of events that led the American colonies to seek independence from Great Britain⟩

synonyms concatenation, progression, sequence, string, train

related words chain reaction; belt, circle, cycle; continuum, gamut, scale, spectrum; flow, river, stream; file, line, queue, row, succession

2 something that makes movement or progress more difficult ⟨this community will grow and prosper only after it has thrown off the *chains* of ignorance and prejudice⟩ — see ENCUMBRANCE

3 something that physically prevents free movement ⟨*chains* on the prisoner's ankles⟩ — see BOND 1

chain *vb* **1** to confine or restrain with or as if with chains ⟨*chaining* up the dog in the backyard⟩ — see BIND 1

2 to put or bring together so as to form a new and longer whole ⟨the prosecutor *chained* all the evidence together in his closing argument⟩ — see CONNECT 1

chair *n* **1** a person in charge of a meeting ⟨all questions and comments should be directed to the *chair*⟩

synonyms chairman, chairperson, moderator, president, speaker

related words chairwoman

2 the place of leadership or command ⟨the *chair* of the English department at the university⟩ — see HEAD 2

chairman *n* a person in charge of a meeting ⟨the *chairman* called the meeting to order⟩ — see CHAIR 1

chairperson *n* a person in charge of a meeting ⟨the *chairperson* will determine the order in which people will speak⟩ — see CHAIR 1

chalet *n* an often small house for recreational or seasonal use ⟨a mountain *chalet* for weekend getaways⟩ — see COTTAGE

challenge *n* a feeling or declaration of disapproval or dissent ⟨there were no *challenges* to the legislative bill, so it passed easily⟩ — see OBJECTION

challenge *vb* **1** to demand proof of the truth or rightness of ⟨don't hesitate to *challenge* any statement that generalizes about people⟩

synonyms contest, dispute, query, question

related words doubt, mistrust; kick (about), object (to), protest; combat, fight, oppose, resist

near antonyms back, defend, support; advocate, champion, promote; abide, endure, stomach, tolerate

antonyms accept, believe, embrace, swallow

2 to invite (someone) to take part in a contest or to perform a feat ⟨I *challenge* you to swim to the other side of the pond⟩

synonyms dare, defy, stump

related words beard, brave, brazen, breast, confront, face, outbrave

challenged *adj* deprived of the power to perform one or more natural bodily activities ⟨all parts of the sports complex are fully accessible to the physically *challenged*⟩ — see DISABLED

challenger *n* one who strives for the same thing as another ⟨the third-party *challenger* in the presidential election⟩ — see COMPETITOR

challenging *adj* requiring much time, effort, or careful attention ⟨a *challenging* test designed to whittle down the number of contestants⟩ — see DEMANDING 1

chamber *n* **1** an area within a building that has been set apart from surrounding space by a wall ⟨the inner *chamber* is the president's private office⟩ — see ROOM 2

2 one of the parts into which an enclosed space is divided ⟨if the camera doesn't work, check to see that the battery has been properly installed in its *chamber*⟩ — see COMPARTMENT

chamber *vb* to provide with living quarters or shelter ⟨*chambered* the lost hikers in the barn until the next morning⟩ — see HOUSE 1

champ *n* the person who comes in first in a competition ⟨the wrestling *champ*⟩ — see CHAMPION 1

champ *vb* to crush or grind with the teeth ⟨kept *champing* a cigar as he barked out orders⟩ — see BITE (ON)

champion *n* **1** the person who comes in first in a competition ⟨the *champion* of the national spelling bee⟩
synonyms champ, victor, winner
related words finalist, semifinalist; medalist, prizewinner; star, superstar
near antonyms loser
2 a person who actively supports or favors a cause ⟨she's the biggest *champion* of budget reform in the congress⟩ — see EXPONENT

champion *vb* to promote the interests or cause of ⟨he has always *championed* the protection of abused animals⟩ — see SUPPORT 1

championship *n* the position occupied by the one who comes in first in a competition ⟨the Yankees have won the *championship* many times⟩ — see CROWN 2

chance *adj* happening by chance ⟨a *chance* advantage that I immediately recognized and made full use of⟩ — see ACCIDENTAL

chance *n* **1** the uncertain course of events ⟨rather than leave everything to *chance*, let's plan how we're going to spend our time in New York City⟩
synonyms accident, circumstance, hap, hazard, luck
related words fortuitousness, randomness, uncertainty; fluke; destiny, doom, fate, fortune, lot; danger, peril, risk
near antonyms intent, intention, purpose; design, outline, plan, scheme
2 a favorable combination of circumstances, time, and place ⟨this is my one *chance* to succeed⟩ — see OPPORTUNITY
3 a measure of how often an event will occur instead of another ⟨the *chance* of being struck by lightning is very low⟩ — see PROBABILITY 2
4 a risky undertaking ⟨it's a *chance*, but I think the business will be profitable⟩ — see GAMBLE

chance *vb* **1** to take a chance on ⟨I don't think we should *chance* driving in this snowstorm⟩ — see RISK 1
2 to take place ⟨there *chanced* to be a beautiful day when we were touring that part of Scotland⟩ — see HAPPEN

chance (upon) *vb* **1** to come upon face-to-face or as if face-to-face ⟨*chanced upon* my archenemy as I rounded a corner⟩ — see MEET
2 to come upon unexpectedly or by chance ⟨I *chanced upon* your mother in the grocery store yesterday⟩ — see HAPPEN (ON OR UPON)

change *n* the act, process, or result of making different ⟨the positive *change* in our students' attitude toward people who are somehow different was a long and gradual process⟩
synonyms alteration, difference, modification, redoing, refashioning, remaking, remodeling, revamping, revise, revision, reworking, variation
related words amendment, correction, rectification; conversion, deformation, distortion, metamorphosis, mutation, transfiguration, transformation; fluctuation, oscillation, shift; displacement, replacement, substitution; adjustment, modulation, regulation
antonyms fixation, stabilization

change *vb* **1** to make different in some way ⟨Mother has *changed* the look of our living room more times than we care to remember⟩
synonyms alter, make over, modify, recast, redo, refashion, remake, remodel, revamp, revise, rework, vary

related words deform, metamorphose, mutate; revolutionize, transfigure, transform, transmute; commute, convert, exchange
antonyms fix, freeze, set, stabilize
2 to pass from one form, state, or level to another ⟨the weather in New England is constantly *changing*⟩
synonyms fluctuate, mutate, shift, vary
related words metamorphose, transmute; better, improve; deteriorate, worsen; seesaw, teeter, vacillate, waver
antonyms stabilize
3 to give up (something) and take something else in return ⟨would you mind *changing* your seat so my friends can sit together?⟩
synonyms commute, exchange, shift, substitute, swap, switch, trade
related words interchange; displace, replace, supersede; cede, surrender, yield

changeable *adj* **1** capable of being readily changed ⟨an easily *changeable* color scheme for the nursery⟩ — see FLEXIBLE 1
2 likely to change frequently, suddenly, or unexpectedly ⟨the *changeable* nature of the business is such that you either have too much or too little to do⟩ — see FICKLE 1

changeful *adj* likely to change frequently, suddenly, or unexpectedly ⟨a *changeful* attitude toward his so-called best friend⟩ — see FICKLE 1

changeless *adj* not undergoing a change in condition ⟨apparently *changeless* mountains⟩ — see CONSTANT 1

changelessness *n* the state of continuing without change ⟨the *changelessness* of the scenery is actually an illusion⟩ — see CONSTANCY 1

changeover *n* a change in form, appearance, or use ⟨the region's *changeover* from an agricultural economy to one based on manufacturing⟩ — see CONVERSION

changing *adj* not staying constant ⟨a *changing* wind made sailing a challenge⟩ — see UNEVEN 2

channel *n* **1** an open man-made passageway for water ⟨water was drained from the swamp through a specially constructed *channel*⟩
synonyms aqueduct, canal, conduit, flume, raceway, watercourse, waterway
related words millrace, millstream; river, rivulet, stream
2 a narrow body of water between two land masses ⟨the world record for swimming the *channel* between France and Great Britain⟩
synonyms narrows, sound, strait
related words arm, bay, gulf, inlet; roads, roadstead; reach, stretch
3 a direct way of passing along information or supplies ⟨you need to make arrangements through the proper *channels*⟩ — see PIPELINE
4 a long hollow cylinder for carrying a substance (as a liquid or gas) ⟨had to replace the main water *channel*⟩ — see PIPE 1

channel *vb* to cause to move to a central point or along a restricted pathway ⟨an athletic youth who *channeled* all of his energy into sports⟩
synonyms channelize, conduct, direct, funnel, pipe, siphon
related words carry, convey, transmit; concentrate, consolidate, focus

channelize *vb* to cause to move to a central point or along a restricted pathway ⟨*channelized* all of his resources into winning that state's crucial primary⟩ — see CHANNEL

chant *vb* **1** to utter in musical or drawn out tones ⟨the frustrated crowd at the rock concert started to *chant*, "We want the show to start!"⟩
synonyms intone, sing
related words bellow, belt, roar; chime, chorus
2 to produce musical sounds with the voice ⟨monks *chanting* fervently at matins⟩ — see SING 1

chaos *n* a state in which everything is out of order ⟨your room is in such *chaos* that it looks as though a tornado had struck⟩
synonyms confusion, disarrangement, disarray, disorder, disorganization, havoc, hell, jumble, mess, muddle, shambles
related words anarchy, lawlessness, misrule; knot, snarl, tangle; labyrinth, maze, web; maelstrom, storm; clutter, litter, mishmash, shuffle; hodgepodge, medley, miscellany, motley
near antonyms method, pattern, plan, system
antonyms order, orderliness

chaotic *adj* lacking in order, neatness, and often cleanliness ⟨a *chaotic* cellar sorely in need of some straightening up⟩ — see MESSY

chap *n, chiefly British* an adult male human being ⟨a couple of *chaps* gave us directions to Buckingham Palace⟩ — see MAN 1

chaparral *n* a thick patch of shrubbery, small trees, or underbrush ⟨the rabbit darted into the *chaparral*⟩ — see THICKET

chaperone *or* **chaperon** *vb* to go along with in order to provide assistance, protection, or companionship ⟨three parents will *chaperone* the students on the school trip⟩ — see ACCOMPANY

chapter *n* a local unit of an organization ⟨our *chapter* of the 4-H Club came in first in the competition⟩
synonyms affiliate, branch, local
related words arm, division, wing; offshoot; lodge, post

char *vb* to burn on the surface ⟨I'd like my hamburger *charred*, but not cooked through⟩ — see SCORCH

character *n* **1** a written or printed mark that is meant to convey information to the reader ⟨the pictorial *characters* of the ancient Egyptians were long a mystery⟩
synonyms sign, symbol
related words cipher, letter, numeral; hieroglyph, pictogram, pictograph; rune
2 a person of odd or whimsical habits ⟨the junk dealer is certainly a *character*, but he's a really nice man⟩ — see ECCENTRIC
3 conduct that conforms to an accepted standard of right and wrong ⟨we need more people of sound *character* in public office⟩ — see MORALITY 1
4 overall quality as seen or judged by people in general ⟨the general *character* of the business appears to be good⟩ — see REPUTATION
5 something that sets apart an individual from others of the same kind ⟨one of the distinguishing *characters* of mammals⟩ — see CHARACTERISTIC
6 the set of qualities that make a person different from other people ⟨she regards each of her children as having a distinctive *character* that should be valued for what it is⟩ — see INDIVIDUALITY
7 the set of qualities that makes a person, a group of people, or a thing different from others ⟨the basic *character* of the work requires that an employee be able to work quietly and independently⟩ — see NATURE 1

characteristic *adj* **1** serving to identify as belonging to an individual or group ⟨the *characteristic* taste of licorice⟩
synonyms classic, distinct, distinctive, distinguishing, identifying, individual, peculiar, proper, symptomatic, typical
related words idiosyncratic; identifiable, pronounced, unmistakable; general, generic; common, normal, regular, usual; particular, special, specific; archetypal, model, paradigmatic
antonyms atypical, nontypical
2 having or showing the qualities associated with the members of a particular group or kind ⟨the *characteristic* wit and good-naturedness of the Irish⟩ — see TYPICAL 1

characteristic *n* something that sets apart an individual from others of the same kind ⟨the ability to fashion tools and other *characteristics* that distinguish human beings from other animals⟩
synonyms attribute, character, feature, mark, peculiarity, point, property, quality, trait
related words badge, indication, sign; emblem, symbol, token; excellence, merit, virtue; individuality, singularity, uniqueness

characterize *vb* **1** to point out the chief quality or qualities of an individual or group ⟨how would you *characterize* the mission of this environmental organization?⟩
synonyms define, depict, describe, portray, represent
related words categorize, classify, pigeonhole, type; identify, indicate, name, specify; distinguish, individualize, mark, particularize, stamp
2 to be an important feature of ⟨an unsightly rash *characterizes* chicken pox⟩
synonyms distinguish, mark
related words differentiate; customize, individualize, particularize

characterless *adj* lacking strength of will or character ⟨a *characterless* person who never has an opinion of his own⟩ — see WEAK 2

charade *n* a display of emotion or behavior that is insincere or intended to deceive ⟨put on a *charade* to keep her from knowing about the surprise party⟩ — see MASQUERADE

charge *n* **1** a formal claim of criminal wrongdoing against a person ⟨*charges* of burglary and armed robbery that have yet to be proved⟩
synonyms complaint, count, indictment, rap
related words accusation, allegation; arraignment, impeachment; implication, innuendo, insinuation; censure, condemnation, denunciation; incrimination
2 a specific task with which a person or group is charged ⟨your *charge* is to keep everyone else organized and busy⟩ — see MISSION
3 a statement of what to do that must be obeyed by those concerned ⟨we've received an official *charge* about how to handle the situation⟩ — see COMMAND 1
4 something one must do because of prior agreement ⟨the first *charge* of our armed forces is to defend this country against enemy attack⟩ — see OBLIGATION
5 the act or action of setting upon with force or violence ⟨the famously disastrous *charge* led by General George Pickett at Gettysburg⟩ — see ATTACK 1
6 the amount of money that is demanded as payment for something ⟨the *charge* for the book will be five dollars⟩ — see PRICE 1
7 the duty or function of watching or guarding for the sake of proper direction or control ⟨was given *charge* of the business during the owner's absence⟩ — see SUPERVISION 1

charge *vb* **1** to set or receive as a price ⟨any shop would *charge* $100 to repair that thing⟩

synonyms ask, command, demand
related words overcharge, undercharge; bring, fetch, sell (for); discount, mark down, mark up; assess, price, value
2 to establish or apply as a charge or penalty ⟨*charges* a fee of $200 for a standard office visit⟩ — see IMPOSE
3 to give a task, duty, or responsibility to ⟨we're *charging* you with the care of your little sister while we're gone for the evening⟩ — see ENTRUST 1
4 to issue orders to (someone) by right of authority ⟨*charged* the soldier to keep watch over the prisoner⟩ — see COMMAND 1
5 to make a claim of wrongdoing against ⟨he has not yet been *charged* with any crime⟩ — see ACCUSE
6 to put into (something) as much as can be held or contained ⟨*charge* a blast furnace with iron ore⟩ — see FILL 1
7 to take sudden, violent action against ⟨plans to *charge* the enemy's fortification at daybreak⟩ — see ATTACK 1
charged *adj* having or expressing great depth of feeling ⟨a very *charged* speech that got everyone worked up⟩ — see FERVENT
charisma *n* the power of irresistible attraction ⟨a movie star with great *charisma*⟩ — see CHARM 2
charitable *adj* **1** having or showing a concern for the welfare of others ⟨a *charitable* couple who have donated a sizable chunk of their fortune to the local university⟩
synonyms altruistic, beneficent, benevolent, humanitarian, philanthropic
related words selfless, self-sacrificing; bounteous, bountiful, free, freehanded, generous, greathearted, handsome, liberal, magnanimous, munificent, openhanded, openhearted, unselfish, unsparing; compassionate, humane, kind
near antonyms self-indulgent, self-seeking; cheap, closefisted, miserly, niggardly, parsimonious, stingy, tight, tightfisted; hardhearted, pitiless, unfeeling
antonyms self-centered, selfish
2 giving or sharing in abundance and without hesitation ⟨a *charitable* woman who helped everyone who needed it⟩ — see GENEROUS 1
charity *n* **1** the giving of necessities and especially money to the needy ⟨after amassing a fortune in the computer industry, they devoted themselves to *charity*⟩
synonyms almsgiving, philanthropy
related words altruism, humanitarianism; beneficence, benevolence, goodwill; alms, benefaction, contribution, donation; dole, relief, welfare; endowment, fund, grant, subsidy
2 a gift of money or its equivalent to a charity, humanitarian cause, or public institution ⟨gave his mansion and all of its land as a *charity* to the people of his beloved home state⟩ — see CONTRIBUTION
3 kind, gentle, or compassionate treatment especially towards someone who is undeserving of it ⟨can't you show a little *charity* to a guy who's the first to admit he's not perfect?⟩ — see MERCY 1
4 the capacity for feeling for another's unhappiness or misfortune ⟨his *charity* is such that he's a sucker for every panhandler's tale of woe⟩ — see HEART 1
charlatan *n* one who makes false claims of identity or expertise ⟨the famous doctor turned out to be a *charlatan*⟩ — see IMPOSTOR
charley horse *n* a painful sudden tightening of a muscle ⟨had to stop and rest because of a *charley horse* in his leg⟩ — see CRAMP

charm *n* **1** something worn or kept to bring good luck or keep away evil ⟨an old cap that I use as a *charm* for whenever I play softball⟩
synonyms amulet, fetish (*also* fetich), mascot, mojo, phylactery, talisman
related words emblem, symbol, token, totem
near antonyms curse, hex, spell
antonyms hoodoo, jinx
2 the power of irresistible attraction ⟨a young singer with the kind of *charm* that turns a performer into a star⟩
synonyms allure, appeal, attractiveness, captivation, charisma, enchantment, fascination, glamour (*also* glamor), magic, magnetism, seductiveness, witchery
related words allurement, attraction, call, lure, seduction; agreeableness, delightfulness, desirableness, niceness, pleasantness, sweetness
near antonyms disagreeableness, distastefulness, obnoxiousness, offensiveness, unpleasantness
antonyms repulsion, repulsiveness
3 a spoken word or set of words believed to have magic power ⟨recited a *charm* to make the prince fall in love with her⟩ — see SPELL 1
4 an ornament worn on a chain around the neck or wrist ⟨a dangling *charm* in the figure of a horse on her bracelet⟩ — see PENDANT
charm *vb* **1** to attract or delight as if by magic ⟨a quaint seaside village that *charms* all who visit it⟩
synonyms allure, beguile, bewitch, captivate, enchant, fascinate, magnetize, wile
related words disarm, draw, entice, lure, pull, seduce, tempt; delight, gratify, please; arrest, enrapture, enthrall (*or* enthral), entrance; appeal (to), interest, intrigue; beckon, court, invite, solicit, woo
near antonyms disgust, offend, repel, revolt; annoy, displease, irk; bore, tire, weary
2 to cast a spell on ⟨a vengeful fairy *charmed* Sleeping Beauty so that she would sleep for a hundred years⟩ — see BEWITCH 1
charmed *adj* being or appearing to be under a magic spell ⟨you must be living a *charmed* life if you haven't caught the flu that's going around⟩ — see ENCHANTED
charmer *n* a person skilled in using supernatural forces ⟨the legendary *charmer* known as the Pied Piper of Hamelin⟩ — see MAGICIAN 1
charming *adj* having an often mysterious or magical power to attract ⟨a *charming* man who had no problem winning women's hearts⟩ — see FASCINATING 1
chart *n* an illustration of certain features of a geographical area ⟨a *chart* of that section of the coastline will show any possible hazards⟩ — see MAP
chart *vb* to work out the details of (something) in advance ⟨*charted* the entire campaign for class president before she even agreed to run⟩ — see PLAN 1
charter *vb* to take or get the temporary use of (something) for a set sum ⟨*charter* a boat⟩ — see HIRE 1
charwoman *n* a female domestic servant ⟨the couple finally hired a *charwoman* because they were just too busy to clean⟩ — see MAID 1
chase *n* **1** an animal that is hunted or killed ⟨the gazelle is a favorite *chase* of lions⟩ — see PREY
2 the act of going after or in the tracks of another ⟨a high-speed car *chase*⟩ — see PURSUIT
chase *vb* **1** to drive or force out ⟨*chased* the cat out of the garden⟩ — see EJECT 1
2 to go after or on the track of ⟨a dog that likes to *chase* cars⟩ — see FOLLOW 2

3 to seek out (game) for food or sport ⟨owls often *chase* mice in the dark⟩ — see HUNT 1

chasing *n* the act of going after or in the tracks of another ⟨after a prolonged *chasing*, the rabbit got away⟩ — see PURSUIT

chasm *n* an immeasurable depth or space ⟨a *chasm* in the ocean floor⟩ — see ABYSS

chaste *adj* free from any trace of the coarse or indecent ⟨as one would expect, the minister's small talk is always *chaste*, even though he likes a joke as much as the next person⟩

synonyms clean, decent, immaculate, modest, pure

related words spotless, stainless, unblemished, undefiled, unsoiled, unspotted, unstained, unsullied, untainted, untarnished; decorous, proper, seemly; cultivated, refined, tasteful; harmless, innocent, innocuous, inoffensive

near antonyms blemished, defiled, soiled, spotted, stained, sullied, tainted, tarnished; improper, indecorous, ribald, unseemly; crude, tacky, tasteless, unrefined

antonyms coarse, dirty, filthy, immodest, impure, indecent, obscene, smutty, unchaste, unclean, vulgar

chastely *adv* with purity of thought and deed ⟨for living so *chastely* Kateri Tekakwitha became known as the "Lily of the Mohawks"⟩ — see PURELY

chasten *vb* to inflict a penalty on for a fault or crime ⟨*chastened* the child with five minutes of sitting in the corner⟩ — see PUNISH

chasteness *n* the quality or state of being morally pure ⟨her *chasteness* is one reason she was made a saint⟩ — see CHASTITY

chastening *adj* inflicting, involving, or serving as punishment ⟨a *chastening* hour spent cleaning floors should discourage them from further pranks⟩ — see PUNITIVE

chastise *vb* to inflict a penalty on for a fault or crime ⟨the teacher *chastised* two students for failing to hand in their work⟩ — see PUNISH

chastisement *n* suffering, loss, or hardship imposed in response to a crime or offense ⟨missing the field trip should be sufficient *chastisement* for the schoolyard fight⟩ — see PUNISHMENT

chastiser *n* one who inflicts punishment in return for an injury or offense ⟨the highway patrolman who is the committed *chastiser* of those motorists who regard speed limits as no more than suggestions⟩ — see NEMESIS 1

chastising *adj* inflicting, involving, or serving as punishment ⟨a *chastising* lecture on the proper care and feeding of the dog⟩ — see PUNITIVE

chastity *n* the quality or state of being morally pure ⟨a saint who is often held up as a model of *chastity*⟩

synonyms chasteness, modesty, purity

related words goodness, righteousness, virtuousness; morality, probity, rectitude; decency, decorum, propriety, seemliness

near antonyms badness, evil, sinfulness, unrighteousness, wickedness; impropriety, indecency

antonyms immodesty, impurity, unchastity

chat *n* friendly, informal conversation or an instance of this ⟨short *chats* between parents and teachers during the school's open house⟩

synonyms chatter, chitchat, gabfest, gossip, palaver, rap, small talk, table talk, talk, tête-à-tête

related words colloquy, conference, discourse, parley, powwow, symposium; debate, dialogue (*or* dialog), exchange, give-and-take

chat *vb* to engage in casual or rambling conversation ⟨the coffeehouse is a great place to meet friends and *chat* for hours⟩

synonyms babble, blab, cackle, chatter, converse, gab, gabble, gas, jabber, jaw, palaver, patter, prate, prattle, rap, rattle, run on, talk, twitter, visit

related words gossip, tattle; descant, discuss, expatiate

phrases shoot the breeze

chat (with) *vb* to communicate with by means of spoken words ⟨*chatting with* a classmate before the start of class⟩ — see TALK 1

château *n* a large impressive residence ⟨a gorgeous *château* on a hill⟩ — see MANSION

chattel *n* **1** a person who is considered the property of another person ⟨at one time, the children of black slaves were also considered *chattel*⟩ — see SLAVE 1

2 chattels *pl* transportable items that one owns ⟨packed up all her *chattels* and moved to a new state⟩ — see POSSESSION 2

chatter *n* friendly, informal conversation or an instance of this ⟨pleasant *chatter* over coffee⟩ — see CHAT

chatter *vb* **1** to engage in casual or rambling conversation ⟨*chattered* idly while waiting in line⟩ — see CHAT

2 to speak rapidly, inarticulately, and usually unintelligibly ⟨the parrot *chatters* all day⟩ — see BABBLE 1

chatterbox *n* a person who talks constantly ⟨my seat companion was a *chatterbox* who never once shut up during the whole trip⟩

synonyms babbler, blabber, cackler, chatterer, conversationalist, gabbler, jabberer, magpie, prattler, talker

related words blabbermouth, gossip, gossiper, talebearer, tattler, tattletale; converser

chatterer *n* a person who talks constantly ⟨the little boy is a real *chatterer*⟩ — see CHATTERBOX

chatty *adj* **1** having the style and content of everyday conversation ⟨a time when campers were expected to write a *chatty* letter to their folks every week⟩

synonyms colloquial, conversational, gossipy, newsy

related words casual, familiar, informal, intimate; digressive, discursive, rambling; communicative, expansive, garrulous, talkative

near antonyms ceremonious, dignified, elevated, formal, solemn, stately

antonyms bookish, literary

2 fond of talking or conversation ⟨a *chatty* older woman who talked to everyone that walked by⟩ — see TALKATIVE

chauvinism *n* excessive favoritism towards one's own country ⟨their *chauvinism* blinded them to their country's faults⟩

synonyms jingoism, nationalism

related words loyalty, patriotism; xenophobia

near antonyms internationalism

chauvinist *n* one who shows excessive favoritism towards his or her own country ⟨*chauvinists* who express their patriotism by plastering flag decals all over their cars⟩ — see NATIONALIST

cheap *adj* **1** costing little ⟨e-mail is so popular because it's a *cheap* way to send messages⟩

synonyms cut-rate, inexpensive, low, reasonable

related words moderate, popular; discounted, lowered, reduced; wholesale

near antonyms precious, priceless, valuable; increased, inflated

antonyms costly, dear, expensive, high, premium

2 of low quality ⟨a *cheap* sweater that started to unravel almost as soon as I bought it⟩

synonyms bad, bum, cheesy, coarse, common, cut-rate, execrable, inferior, junky, lousy, low-grade, mediocre, miserable, poor, rotten, rubbishy, second-rate, shoddy, sleazy, terrible, trashy, trumpery, wretched
related words useless, valueless, worthless; flashy, garish, gaudy, meretricious, showy, tawdry; seedy, shabby, tacky; counterfeit, fake, phony (*also* phoney), sham
near antonyms elegant, handsome, tasteful; hand-crafted, polished, refined
antonyms excellent, fine, first-class, first-rate, good, high-grade, superior, top-notch
3 giving or sharing as little as possible ⟨a *cheap* coworker who never contributes to the collections taken up in the office⟩ — see STINGY 1

cheapen *vb* to lower the price or value of ⟨a glutted market *cheapened* cranberries to the point where they were selling for less than what it cost to grow them⟩ — see DEPRECIATE 1

cheapness *n* the quality of being overly sparing with money ⟨his chronic *cheapness* is such that he never takes vacations or replaces old, worn-out household goods⟩ — see PARSIMONY

cheapskate *n* a mean grasping person who is usually stingy with money ⟨a *cheapskate* who lived like a pauper, she was reputedly the wealthiest woman in the U.S. at the time of her death⟩ — see MISER

cheat *n* a dishonest person who uses clever means to cheat others out of something of value ⟨a *cheat* at cards⟩ — see TRICKSTER 1

cheat *vb* **1** to use dishonest methods to achieve a goal ⟨students who *cheat* on tests end up never knowing anything⟩
synonyms fudge
related words distort, falsify, misrepresent, twist; doctor, fake, tamper (with); color, elaborate, embellish, embroider, exaggerate, magnify, pad, stretch; dodge, evade, hedge
2 to fall short in satisfying the expectation or hope of ⟨the daredevil survived his plunge over the falls with barely a scratch, having *cheated* death once again⟩ — see DISAPPOINT
3 to rob by the use of trickery or threats ⟨a despicable confidence man who *cheated* elderly people out of their savings⟩ — see FLEECE

cheater *n* a dishonest person who uses clever means to cheat others out of something of value ⟨gambling casinos have very elaborate means of detecting *cheaters*⟩ — see TRICKSTER 1

check *n* **1** the amount owed at a bar or restaurant or the slip of paper stating the amount ⟨diners at the fancy restaurant often look shocked when they receive the *check*⟩
synonyms bill, tab
related words invoice, receipt; account, record, statement; charge, fee; score, tally
2 a close look at or over someone or something in order to judge condition ⟨made a careful *check* of the antique table before buying it⟩ — see INSPECTION
3 a record of goods sold or services performed together with the costs due ⟨request a detailed *check* from the company before sending any money⟩ — see ¹BILL 1
4 a small sheet of plastic, paper, or paperboard showing that the bearer has a claim to something (as admittance) ⟨handed over a *check* for his coat⟩ — see TICKET 1
5 something that limits one's freedom of action or choice ⟨the Supreme Court is intended to be a *check* on

the executive and legislative branches of government⟩ — see RESTRICTION 1

check *vb* **1** to be in agreement on every point ⟨their story of what happened *checks* with the report of the eyewitness⟩
synonyms accord, agree, answer, cohere, coincide, comport, conform, correspond, dovetail, fit, go, harmonize, jibe, square, tally
related words equal, match, parallel
near antonyms contradict, dispute, gainsay; negate, nullify; clash, conflict, jar
antonyms differ (from), disagree (with)
2 to bring (something) to a standstill ⟨a tree finally *checked* the skidding car⟩ — see ¹HALT 1
3 to keep from exceeding a desirable degree or level (as of expression) ⟨*check* your enthusiasm a bit, and think before you marry someone you just met⟩ — see CONTROL 1

check (out) *vb* to look over closely (as for judging quality or condition) ⟨*check out* the house and let me know if you think it's worth buying⟩ — see INSPECT

checklist *n* a record of a series of items (as names or titles) usually arranged according to some system ⟨a *checklist* of things to do before the flight⟩ — see ¹LIST 1

checkmate *vb* to prevent from achieving a goal ⟨finally *checkmated* the billionaire in his attempt to take over the company⟩ — see FRUSTRATE

checkup *n* a close look at or over someone or something in order to judge condition ⟨the vet gave the kitten a *checkup*, then declared her in fine health⟩ — see INSPECTION

cheek *n* **1** disrespectful or argumentative talk given in response to a command or request ⟨any more *cheek* in this classroom and you'll get a detention⟩ — see BACK TALK
2 shameless boldness ⟨she had the *cheek* to blame me for the fact that she had forgotten her homework⟩ — see EFFRONTERY

cheekiness *n* shameless boldness ⟨the *cheekiness* of the restaurant's demand that we pay for unordered food was breathtaking⟩ — see EFFRONTERY

cheeky *adj* displaying or marked by rude boldness ⟨a *cheeky* comment about something that was none of her business⟩ — see NERVY 1

cheep *vb* to make a short sharp sound like a small bird ⟨the toaster *cheeps* to indicate that the toast is done⟩ — see CHIRP

cheer *n* **1** a mood characterized by high spirits and amusement and often accompanied by laughter ⟨a birthday celebration filled with amusement and *cheer*⟩ — see MIRTH
2 a feeling of ease from grief or trouble ⟨the visiting general had some words of *cheer* for each of the recuperating soldiers⟩ — see COMFORT 1
3 a state of mind dominated by a particular emotion ⟨be of good *cheer* in this Christmas season⟩ — see MOOD 1
4 **cheers** *pl* enthusiastic and usually public expression of approval ⟨all three movies in the series received *cheers* from fans of the novels⟩ — see APPLAUSE

cheer *vb* **1** to declare enthusiastic approval of ⟨critics and fans alike have *cheered* the latest addition to the author's series of fantasy novels⟩ — see ACCLAIM
2 to ease the grief or distress of ⟨let's hope that these flowers will *cheer* my ailing aunt at least a little⟩ — see COMFORT 1

cheer (up) *vb* **1** to become glad or hopeful ⟨*cheer up* —things are bound to get better⟩

synonyms brighten, perk (up)
related words rejoice; liven (up), revive; beam, glow, radiate, sparkle; encourage, gladden, hearten
near antonyms despair, despond; brood, fret, mope
antonyms darken, sadden
2 to fill with courage or strength of purpose ⟨the general's speech *cheered up* the troops tremendously⟩ — see ENCOURAGE 1
cheerful *adj* **1** having or showing a good mood or disposition ⟨a *cheerful* person who is always fun to work with and a pleasure to be around⟩
synonyms blithe, blithesome, bright, buoyant, cheery, chipper, gay, gladsome, lightsome, sunny, upbeat
related words hopeful, optimistic, sanguine; jaunty, lively, perky, sprightly, vivacious; carefree, careless, cavalier, devil-may-care, easygoing, happy-go-lucky, insouciant, lighthearted, unconcerned; boon, jolly, jovial, merry, mirthful; glad, happy, pleased
near antonyms dull, lethargic, listless, sluggish, torpid; blue, dejected, depressed, heavyhearted, melancholy, sorrowful; discontented, disgruntled, unhappy
antonyms dour, gloomy, glum, morose, saturnine, sulky, sullen
2 serving to lift one's spirits ⟨a hospital with sunny, *cheerful* rooms that are designed to make a patient's stay as pleasant as possible⟩
synonyms bright, cheering, cheery, gay, glad
related words gladdening, heartening, heartwarming; gleaming, radiant, sparkling
near antonyms discouraging, disheartening; colorless, drab, dull, lackluster, lusterless
antonyms bleak, cheerless, dark, depressing, dismal, dreary, gloomy, gray (*also* grey)
cheerfully *adv* in a cheerful or happy manner ⟨*cheerfully* announced, "It's a beautiful morning!"⟩ — see GAILY 1
cheerfulness *n* a mood characterized by high spirits and amusement and often accompanied by laughter ⟨his constant *cheerfulness* makes him a pleasure to be around⟩ — see MIRTH
cheeriness *n* a mood characterized by high spirits and amusement and often accompanied by laughter ⟨a moment of *cheeriness* interrupted the solemn discussion⟩ — see MIRTH
cheering *adj* **1** making one feel good inside ⟨a *cheering* sight of a child being reunited with a pet that had been lost⟩ — see HEARTWARMING
2 serving to lift one's spirits ⟨*cheering* words from the doctor that the worst was over⟩ — see CHEERFUL 2
cheering *n* enthusiastic and usually public expression of approval ⟨a raucous *cheering* welcomed the newlyweds⟩ — see APPLAUSE
cheerless *adj* causing or marked by an atmosphere lacking in cheer ⟨a dank and *cheerless* castle⟩ — see GLOOMY 1
cheery *adj* **1** having or showing a good mood or disposition ⟨a *cheery* grin on the host of the holiday party⟩ — see CHEERFUL 1
2 serving to lift one's spirits ⟨a *cheery*, unexpected compliment can really make another person's day⟩ — see CHEERFUL 2
cheesy *adj* **1** marked by an obvious lack of style or good taste ⟨*cheesy* plastic knickknacks lined the fireplace mantel⟩ — see TACKY 1
2 of low quality ⟨a *cheesy* toy that broke the first day I played with it⟩ — see CHEAP 2
chef *n* a person who prepares food by some manner of heating ⟨the restaurant hired a famous *chef* to raise the quality of its cuisine⟩ — see COOK

cherish *vb* **1** to feel passion, devotion, or tenderness for ⟨promised to love and *cherish* her husband forever⟩ — see LOVE 2
2 to hold dear ⟨we shall always *cherish* the keepsakes that our grandmother left us⟩ — see LOVE 1
3 to keep in one's mind or heart ⟨still *cherishes* the memory of her first summer romance⟩ — see HARBOR 1
cherished *adj* granted special treatment or attention ⟨a *cherished* heirloom that has been in the family for generations⟩ — see DARLING 1
chest *n* a covered rectangular container for storing or transporting things ⟨a *chest* containing almost every tool that the home do-it-yourselfer is likely to need⟩
synonyms box, caddy, case, casket, locker, trunk
related words crate; footlocker; coffer, safe, safe-deposit box, strongbox; coffin; compartment, vault
chesterfield *n* a long upholstered piece of furniture designed for several sitters ⟨bought a huge new *chesterfield* for the living room⟩ — see COUCH
chew *vb* to crush or grind with the teeth ⟨please *chew* your food thoroughly so you don't choke⟩ — see BITE (ON)
chew out *vb* to criticize (someone) severely or angrily especially for personal failings ⟨the coach *chews out* anyone who doesn't show up for practice⟩ — see SCOLD
chew over *vb* **1** to give serious and careful thought to ⟨*chewing over* the idea of running for president⟩ — see PONDER
2 to talk about (an issue) usually from various points of view and for the purpose of arriving at a decision or opinion ⟨the panelists *chewed over* the latest political scandal for a while⟩ — see DISCUSS
chewy *adj* not easily chewed ⟨a *chewy* piece of meat⟩ — see TOUGH 1
chic *adj* being in the latest or current fashion ⟨a *chic* new hairstyle that makes her look very sophisticated⟩ — see STYLISH
chicanery *n* the use of clever underhanded actions to achieve an end ⟨that candidate only won the election through *chicanery*⟩ — see TRICKERY
chick *n, slang* a young usually unmarried woman ⟨a place where *chicks* often congregate⟩ — see GIRL 1
chicken *adj* having or showing a shameful lack of courage ⟨too *chicken* to go through with the stunt⟩ — see COWARDLY
chicken *n* a person who shows a shameful lack of courage in the face of danger ⟨it's not true that only a *chicken* would refuse to play in traffic⟩ — see COWARD
chickenhearted *adj* having or showing a shameful lack of courage ⟨that *chickenhearted* soldier deserted under fire⟩ — see COWARDLY
chide *vb* to criticize (someone) usually gently so as to correct a fault ⟨Mom *chided* me for forgetting to offer our guests some refreshments⟩ — see REBUKE 1
chief *adj* **1** coming before all others in importance ⟨our *chief* priority this year will be the budget⟩ — see FOREMOST 1
2 highest in rank or authority ⟨the *chief* administrator will be retiring soon⟩ — see HEAD
chief *n* the person (as an employer or supervisor) who tells people and especially workers what to do ⟨our *chief* is out on a business trip right now⟩ — see BOSS
chiefly *adv* for the most part ⟨our video collection consists *chiefly* of comedies, but we have a few horror movies⟩

synonyms altogether, basically, by and large, generally, largely, mainly, mostly, overall, predominantly, primarily, principally, substantially

related words nearly, practically, virtually; approximately, broadly, roughly; commonly, frequently, normally, ordinarily, usually; incompletely, partially, partly

phrases in general, on the whole

near antonyms completely, entirely, fully, totally, wholly; barely, hardly, marginally, minimally, scarcely

child *n* **1** a young person who is between infancy and adulthood ⟨an imaginative animated film that appeals to adults as well as to *children*⟩

synonyms bairn [*chiefly Scottish*], cub, juvenile, kid, youngster, youth

related words adolescent, minor; schoolboy, schoolchild, schoolgirl; moppet, nestling, toddler, tot, tyke; brat, imp, squirt, urchin, whippersnapper; cherub; preteen, subteen, teenager, teenybopper; lad, nipper, shaver, stripling, tad; bobby-soxer, hoyden, tomboy

near antonyms golden-ager, oldster, senior citizen

antonyms adult, grown-up

2 a recently born person ⟨wrapped the *child* in a blanket before taking him outside in the cold⟩ — see BABY

childbearing *n* the act or process of giving birth to children ⟨many women died in *childbearing* in the old days⟩ — see CHILDBIRTH

childbirth *n* the act or process of giving birth to children ⟨women who choose to undergo *childbirth* without the use of anesthetics and other drugs⟩

synonyms childbearing, delivery, labor, parturition

related words pains; pregnancy; abortion, miscarriage; cesarean section (*also* cesarian section)

childhood *n* the state or time of being a child ⟨enjoy your *childhood*—it won't last forever⟩

synonyms youth

related words boyhood, girlhood; adolescence, minority; immaturity, juvenility; babyhood, infancy

near antonyms majority

antonyms adulthood

childish *adj* having or showing the annoying qualities (as silliness) associated with children ⟨you almost spoiled the ceremony for everyone with your *childish* giggling⟩

synonyms adolescent, babyish, immature, infantile, juvenile, kiddish, puerile

related words boyish, girlish; childlike, innocent, naive (*or* naïve), simple, unsophisticated

near antonyms experienced, sophisticated, worldly-wise

antonyms adult, grown-up, mature

child's play *n* **1** something of little importance ⟨the injury is *child's play*, just a scratch⟩ — see TRIFLE

2 something that is easy to do ⟨winning the game against those guys will be *child's play*⟩ — see CINCH

chill *adj* **1** lacking in friendliness or warmth of feeling ⟨were met with a *chill* gaze when they arrived home late from the party⟩ — see COLD 2

2 uncomfortably cool ⟨this *chill* weather is making my teeth chatter⟩ — see CHILLY 1

chill *n* an uncomfortable degree of coolness ⟨there's a *chill* in the air, so you'd better wear a sweater⟩

synonyms bite, bitterness, bleakness, chilliness, nip, rawness, sharpness

related words briskness, crispness; coldness, frigidity, frigidness, frostiness, iciness; cold, freeze, snap

near antonyms balminess, warmth

chill *vb* to cause to lose heat ⟨*chill* the gelatin for two hours, until it sets⟩ — see COOL 1

chilliness *n* an uncomfortable degree of coolness ⟨the *chilliness* in the church prompted everyone to put on jackets⟩ — see CHILL

chilling *adj* uncomfortably cool ⟨a Southern visitor who was unused to the *chilling* air of a Northeast winter⟩ — see CHILLY 1

chilly *adj* **1** uncomfortably cool ⟨those *chilly* nights when a warm fire can be especially comforting⟩

synonyms bitter, bleak, chill, chilling, nippy, raw, sharp

related words brisk, crisp; arctic, cold, freezing, frigid, frosty, icy

near antonyms balmy, warm

2 lacking in friendliness or warmth of feeling ⟨a *chilly* glare directed at the person who tried to go to the head of the line⟩ — see COLD 2

chime *vb* to make the clear sound heard when metal vibrates ⟨the doorbell *chimed* as we were sitting down to eat⟩ — see RING 1

chime *n, usually* **chimes** *pl* a series of short high ringing sounds ⟨the *chimes* on our doorbell⟩ — see TINKLE

chime in *vb* to cause a disruption in a conversation or discussion ⟨"I don't like that show at all," my friend *chimed in*⟩ — see INTERRUPT

chimera *n* a conception or image created by the imagination and having no objective reality ⟨a monster in the closet would not have been the first *chimera* that the boy had seen⟩ — see FANTASY 1

chimerical *adj* not real and existing only in the imagination ⟨for the time being, interplanetary travel remains a *chimerical* feature of life in the 21st century⟩ — see IMAGINARY

chine *n* a column of bones supporting the trunk of a vertebrate animal ⟨uncovered the *chine* of some animal while digging in the backyard⟩ — see SPINE

chink *n* an irregular usually narrow break in a surface created by pressure ⟨plugged the *chinks* in the walls with mortar⟩ — see CRACK 1

chink *vb* to make a repeated sharp light ringing sound ⟨the flag's chain *chinked* against the flagpole⟩ — see JINGLE

chip *n* **1** a small flat piece separated from a whole ⟨wood *chips* were spread over the ground between the plants⟩

synonyms flake, sliver, splint, splinter

related words bit, disk (*or* disc), fragment, particle, scrap, shard; shiver, smithereens; shred, tatter; clipping, paring, shaving, snippet; leaf, sheet, slice; chunk, hunk, lump, slab

2 a V-shaped cut usually on an edge or a surface ⟨watch out for the *chip* on the rim of that drinking glass⟩ — see NOTCH 1

3 **chips** *pl* something (as pieces of stamped metal or printed paper) customarily and legally used as a medium of exchange, a measure of value, or a means of payment ⟨was in the *chips* after buying a winning lottery ticket⟩ — see MONEY

chip in *vb* to make a donation as part of a group effort ⟨we all *chipped in* and bought flowers for the teacher⟩ — see CONTRIBUTE 1

chipper *adj* **1** enjoying health and vigor ⟨a sturdy, *chipper* older man⟩ — see HEALTHY 1

2 having or showing a good mood or disposition ⟨you're awfully *chipper* this morning⟩ — see CHEERFUL 1

chirp *vb* to make a short sharp sound like a small bird ⟨the sparrows were *chirping* up a storm in the backyard⟩

synonyms cheep, chirrup, peep, pipe, tweet, twitter

related words cackle, chatter, jabber; sing, trill, warble

chirr *n* a monotonous sound like that of an insect in motion ⟨the *chirr* of dragonflies⟩ — see HUM

chirrup *vb* to make a short sharp sound like a small bird ⟨the kitten *chirruped* insistently for her dinner⟩ — see CHIRP

chisel *vb* to rob by the use of trickery or threats ⟨deftly *chiseled* other students out of their lunch money⟩ — see FLEECE

chitchat *n* friendly, informal conversation or an instance of this ⟨a bit of *chitchat* over lunch with people we hadn't seen in a while⟩ — see CHAT

chivalrous *adj* having, characterized by, or arising from a dignified and generous nature ⟨still engages in *chivalrous* behavior, such as holding doors for people⟩ — see NOBLE 2

chivy *vb* to thrust oneself upon (another) without invitation ⟨a boss with a reputation for *chivying* the workers about every little thing⟩ — see BOTHER 1

chock–full *or* **chockful** *adj* containing or seeming to contain the greatest quantity or number possible ⟨a plate *chock-full* of food⟩ — see FULL 1

choice *adj* having qualities that appeal to a refined taste ⟨*choice* chocolates for which chocolate lovers are willing to pay extra⟩

synonyms dainty, delicate, elegant, exquisite, rare, select

related words elite, exclusive; excellent, outstanding, premium, prime, superior

near antonyms coarse, gross, vulgar; commercial, mass-produced, popular; common, ordinary; average, mediocre, run-of-the-mill, second-rate

choice *n* **1** the power, right, or opportunity to choose ⟨you have no *choice*: you have to go to school⟩

synonyms alternative, discretion, option, pick, preference, way

related words say, voice, vote; inclination, liking, partiality, penchant, predilection, proclivity, propensity, tendency; discernment, judgment (*or* judgement), perspicacity

near antonyms coercion, duress, force; duty, obligation

2 a person or thing that is chosen ⟨my *choice* for best song of all time⟩

synonyms pick, selection

related words favorite, like, liking, preference; elective, option; appointment, designation, nomination; appointee, candidate, nominee

3 individuals carefully selected as being the best of a class ⟨that school accepts only the *choice* of the city's crop of high school students⟩ — see ELITE

4 the act or power of making one's own choices or decisions ⟨the prisoner had no *choice* but to do what he was told⟩ — see FREE WILL

5 the act or process of selecting ⟨you'll have to make a *choice* eventually⟩ — see SELECTION 1

choir *n* an organized group of singers ⟨joined the *choir* for next year⟩ — see CHORUS 1

choke *vb* **1** to keep (someone) from breathing by exerting pressure on the windpipe ⟨let go of my throat—you're *choking* me!⟩

synonyms garrote (*or* garotte), strangle, throttle

related words asphyxiate, smother, suffocate

near antonyms restore, resuscitate, revive

2 to experience complete or partial blockage of the windpipe ⟨the recommended procedure for helping someone who is *choking*⟩

synonyms gag

related words heave, retch, throw up, vomit; asphyxiate, smother, suffocate

near antonyms breathe, respire

3 to be or cause to be killed by lack of breathable air ⟨thick, black smoke *choked* the trapped fire fighters⟩ — see SMOTHER 1

4 to prevent passage through ⟨overgrown bushes *choked* the narrow alleyway between the buildings⟩ — see CLOG 1

choke (back) *vb* to refrain from openly showing or uttering ⟨*choked back* a sarcastic reply⟩ — see SUPPRESS 2

choker *n* an ornamental chain or string (as of beads) worn around the neck ⟨a pearl *choker* closely wrapped around her throat⟩ — see NECKLACE

choleric *adj* easily irritated or annoyed ⟨watch out for the *choleric* librarian at the reference desk⟩ — see IRRITABLE

chomp (on) *vb* to crush or grind with the teeth ⟨loudly *chomped on* popcorn during the movie⟩ — see BITE (ON)

choose *vb* **1** to decide to accept (someone or something) from a group of possibilities ⟨*choose* a computer that best suits your needs⟩

synonyms cull, elect, handpick, name, opt (for), pick, prefer, select, single (out), take

related words appoint, designate, nominate, tab; accept, adopt, embrace, espouse

near antonyms discard, jettison, throw away, throw out

antonyms decline, refuse, reject, turn down

2 to see fit ⟨you can wear whatever you *choose* to the party⟩

synonyms like, want, will, wish

related words crave, desire, fancy, hanker (for), hunger (for), long (for), yearn (for); decide, determine, resolve

3 to come to a judgment after discussion or consideration ⟨*chose* to write on a controversial topic for the school newspaper⟩ — see DECIDE 1

chooser *n* someone with the right or responsibility for making a selection ⟨the *chooser* for today will be your sister; you'll get your turn tomorrow⟩ — see SELECTOR

choosing *n* the act or process of selecting ⟨the *choosing* of a new mayor is often left to a few voters, unfortunately⟩ — see SELECTION 1

choosy *or* **choosey** *adj* **1** hard to please ⟨a *choosy* dog who refuses all but the fanciest food⟩ — see FINICKY

2 tending to select carefully ⟨a *choosy* man when it came to clothes⟩ — see SELECTIVE

chop *n* a hard strike with a part of the body or an instrument ⟨delivered a sharp *chop* to his opponent's neck⟩ — see ¹BLOW

chop *vb* to cut into small pieces ⟨*chop* the onions before adding them to the pot⟩

synonyms dice, hash, mince

related words chip, grind, mash, puree, slice

chop (down) *vb* to bring down by cutting ⟨we have to *chop down* that tree out front before it falls on the house⟩ — see FELL 2

choppy *adj* lacking in steadiness or regularity of occurrence ⟨a sharp, *choppy* wind⟩ — see FITFUL

chorale *n* **1** a religious song ⟨practiced a *chorale* to perform in church⟩ — see HYMN

2 an organized group of singers ⟨a *chorale* that is regarded as being among the best in the state⟩ — see CHORUS 1

chore *n* **1** a piece of work that needs to be done regularly ⟨everyone in this household is expected to do weekly *chores*⟩
synonyms assignment, duty, job, stint, task
related words endeavor, enterprise, project, undertaking; care, charge, commission, responsibility; function, mission, office; errand; circuit, round, route
2 a dull, unpleasant, or difficult piece of work ⟨cleaning everything out of the attic was a real *chore*⟩
synonyms headache, labor
related words drudgery, grind; effort, strain, sweat; burden, load, weight; bother, nuisance, trouble
near antonyms breeze, child's play, cinch, duck soup, snap

chortle *n* an explosive sound that is a sign of amusement ⟨the joke provoked a sudden *chortle* from a bystander⟩ — see LAUGH 1

chorus *n* **1** an organized group of singers ⟨the annual Christmas program presented by the school's *chorus*⟩
synonyms choir, chorale, glee club
related words ensemble; minstrelsy
2 a part of a song or hymn that is repeated every so often ⟨the whole congregation will join in for the *chorus*⟩
synonyms burden, refrain
related words repeat

chosen *adj* singled out from a number or group as more to one's liking ⟨the *chosen* few who are invited to a gathering at the headmaster's house at the end of the year⟩ — see SELECT 1

chow *n* **1** food eaten or prepared for eating at one time ⟨that evening's *chow* was pretty basic because we were in a hurry⟩ — see MEAL
2 substances intended to be eaten ⟨there's always at least some *chow* in the house⟩ — see FOOD

christen *vb* to give a name to ⟨*christened* the new baby "Ophelia"⟩ — see NAME 1

Christian name *n* a name that is placed before one's family name ⟨although his *Christian name* is ordinary, his last name is quite distinctive⟩ — see FORENAME

Christmastime *n* the season celebrating Christmas ⟨there are always lots of lights on the neighborhood's houses around *Christmastime*⟩ — see YULETIDE

chronic *adj* being such by habit and not likely to change ⟨a *chronic* smoker who has quit—many, many times⟩ — see HABITUAL 1

chronicle *n* **1** a relating of events usually in the order in which they happened ⟨a *chronicle* of their adventure on the river⟩ — see ACCOUNT 1
2 an account of important events in the order in which they happened ⟨only sketchy information about King Arthur can be found in the *chronicles* of ancient England⟩ — see HISTORY 1

chronicler *n* a student or writer of history ⟨*chroniclers* who gave often conflicting accounts of what the king did or commanded⟩ — see HISTORIAN

chronometer *n* a device to measure time ⟨a fancy new *chronometer* that is light-years more advanced than your average wristwatch⟩ — see TIMEPIECE

chubbiness *n* the condition of having an excess of body fat ⟨a bit of *chubbiness* is normal in very small children⟩ — see CORPULENCE

chubby *adj* having an excess of body fat ⟨the *chubby* baby slimmed down by the time she was a toddler⟩ — see FAT 1

chuck *vb* to send through the air especially with a quick forward motion of the arm ⟨*chucked* a wad of paper at his friend's back⟩ — see THROW

chuckle *n* an explosive sound that is a sign of amusement ⟨a quick *chuckle* at the funny comment⟩ — see LAUGH 1

chum *n* a person who has a strong liking for and trust in another ⟨school *chums*⟩ — see FRIEND 1

chum *vb* to come or be together as friends ⟨they always *chum* around together⟩ — see ASSOCIATE 1

chumminess *n* the state of being in a very personal or private relationship ⟨my *chumminess* with Susan made it easy to work on group projects with her⟩ — see FAMILIARITY 1

chummy *adj* closely acquainted ⟨they know each other but are hardly *chummy*⟩ — see FAMILIAR 1

chump *n* one who is easily deceived or cheated ⟨it's not polite to say that someone who disagrees with you is a *chump*⟩ — see DUPE

chunk *n* a small uneven mass ⟨a little *chunk* of dirt⟩ — see LUMP 1

chunky *adj* **1** having small pieces or lumps spread throughout ⟨*chunky* peanut butter adds an interesting layer of texture when paired with jelly⟩
synonyms clumpy, curdy, lumpy, nubbly, nubby
related words ropy, thick, viscous; clabbered [*dialect*], clotted, coagulated, congealed, curdled, gelled, thickened
antonyms smooth
2 being compact and broad in build and often short in stature ⟨a *chunky* little toddler⟩ — see STOCKY
3 having or being of relatively great depth or extent from one surface to its opposite ⟨a *chunky* piece of bread⟩ — see THICK 1

church *n* **1** a building for public worship and especially Christian worship ⟨a city that is noted for its many historic *churches*⟩
synonyms kirk [*chiefly Scottish*], tabernacle, temple
related words abbey, bethel, cathedral, chapel, oratory, sanctuary, shrine; meetinghouse; mosque, pagoda, synagogue (*or* synagog)
2 a body of persons gathered for religious worship ⟨spoke to the whole *church* at once⟩ — see CONGREGATION 1

churchly *adj* of or relating to a church ⟨refused to discuss *churchly* matters except on Sundays⟩ — see ECCLESIASTICAL

churl *n* a person whose behavior is offensive to others ⟨a *churl* who gets thrown out of parties with remarkable regularity⟩ — see JERK 1

churlish *adj* having or showing crudely insensitive or impolite manners ⟨any *churlish* behavior will result in going to bed without dinner⟩ — see CLOWNISH

churn *vb* **1** to be in a state of violent rolling motion ⟨a *churning* sea made getting to the island a risky undertaking⟩ — see SEETHE 1
2 to cause (as a liquid) to move about in a circle especially repeatedly ⟨*churn* the cream until it turns into butter⟩ — see STIR 1

chutzpah *also* **chutzpa** *or* **hutzpah** *or* **hutzpa** *n* shameless boldness ⟨had the *chutzpah* to demand that he be treated as a special case and be given more time to finish his science project⟩ — see EFFRONTERY

cinch *n* something that is easy to do ⟨the clear instructions made setting up the audiovisual system a *cinch*⟩
synonyms breeze, child's play, duck soup, picnic, pushover, snap
related words nothing; sitting duck
phrases piece of cake
near antonyms bother, nuisance, trouble

antonyms chore, headache, labor

cinch *vb* to make sure, certain, or safe ⟨the team's latest victory *cinches* a trip to the play-offs⟩ — see ENSURE

cincture *n* a strip of flexible material (as leather) worn around the waist ⟨wrapped a *cincture* around the dress as a stylish accessory⟩ — see ²BELT

cinema *n* 1 the art or business of making a movie ⟨felt that the *cinema* was one of the most challenging and fulfilling forms of artistic expression⟩ — see MOVIE 2
2 a building or part of a building where movies are shown ⟨got a job cleaning the *cinemas* at the multiplex⟩ — see THEATER 1

cipher *n* the numerical symbol 0 or the absence of number or quantity represented by it ⟨remember to put the *cipher* after the decimal point⟩ — see ZERO 1

ciphering *n* the act or process of performing mathematical operations to find a value ⟨he wasn't very good at *ciphering*, but he had excellent language skills⟩ — see CALCULATION

circle *n* 1 something with a perfectly round circumference ⟨a *circle* of columns surrounds the memorial to the fallen heroes⟩
synonyms ring, round
related words circlet; ellipse, loop, oval; ball, globe, orb, sphere
2 a circular strip ⟨a little *circle* of silver on the rim of the commemorative plate for their 25th wedding anniversary⟩ — see RING 2
3 a group of people sharing a common interest and relating together socially ⟨got together with her social *circle* once a week⟩ — see GANG 2
4 a series of events or actions that repeat themselves regularly and in the same order ⟨with the birth of a child coming so soon after the death of a grandparent, we were once again reminded of the *circle* of life⟩ — see CYCLE 1

circle *vb* 1 to form a circle around ⟨everyone *circled* the lectern and waited their turn to read from the Bible⟩ — see SURROUND
2 to pass completely around ⟨the equator is an imaginary line that *circles* the globe⟩ — see ENCIRCLE 1

circuitous *adj* 1 not straightforward or direct ⟨we took a *circuitous* route to the airport so as to avoid the massive traffic jam on the highway⟩ — see INDIRECT
2 using or containing more words than necessary to express an idea ⟨a *circuitous* explanation for what seems like a fairly basic concept⟩ — see WORDY

circular *adj* not straightforward or direct ⟨a rather *circular* discussion of the problem that never addresses it directly⟩ — see INDIRECT

circular *n* a short printed publication with no cover or with a paper cover ⟨promptly tosses out those advertising *circulars* that come in the newspaper⟩ — see PAMPHLET

circulate *vb* 1 to cause to be known over a considerable area or by many people ⟨*circulate* the plans for the new stadium around town to get people's reaction⟩ — see SPREAD 1
2 to make (as a piece of information) the subject of common talk without any authority or confirmation of accuracy ⟨*circulated* a rumor that someone was about to be fired⟩ — see RUMOR

circumference *n* 1 the distance around a round body ⟨the *circumference* of the earth at the equator⟩
synonyms girth
related words waistline; equator; diameter, perimeter
2 the line or relatively narrow space that marks the outer limit of something ⟨a silly little affair that's of interest to no one beyond the *circumference* of this campus⟩ — see BORDER 1

circumlocution *n* the use of too many words to express an idea ⟨your papers have to be five pages long, but that's five pages of substance, not *circumlocution*⟩ — see VERBIAGE

circumlocutory *adj* using or containing more words than necessary to express an idea ⟨the studio's statement that "the film's earnings did not live up to expectations" was a *circumlocutory* admission that the movie was a flop⟩ — see WORDY

circumnavigate *vb* to pass completely around ⟨the first ship to *circumnavigate* the globe⟩ — see ENCIRCLE 1

circumscribe *vb* 1 to set bounds or an upper limit for ⟨*circumscribed* his enthusiasm so as not to make the losing side feel worse⟩ — see LIMIT 1
2 to mark the limits of ⟨Lake Michigan *circumscribes* the city of Chicago on the east⟩ — see LIMIT 2

circumscribed *adj* having distinct or certain limits ⟨the powers of that state's governor are so sharply *circumscribed* that often his hands are tied by the state legislature⟩ — see LIMITED 1

circumspect *adj* having or showing a close attentiveness to avoiding danger or trouble ⟨she has a reputation for being quiet and *circumspect* in investigating charges of child abuse⟩ — see CAREFUL 1

circumspection *n* a close attentiveness to avoiding danger ⟨*circumspection* is always good when considering charging someone with cheating⟩ — see CAUTION 1

circumstance *n* 1 a state or end that seemingly has been decided beforehand ⟨the condemned murderer seemed indifferent to his *circumstance*⟩ — see FATE 1
2 something that happens ⟨due to unexpected *circumstances*, the test will be postponed⟩ — see EVENT 1
3 the uncertain course of events ⟨I was a victim of *circumstance*, for nothing that I could have done would have made a difference⟩ — see CHANCE 1

circumstantial *adj* including many small descriptive features ⟨the *circumstantial* account of his surgery told us more than we really wanted to know about the stomach⟩ — see DETAILED 1

circumvent *vb* 1 to avoid having to comply with (something) especially through cleverness ⟨students who try to *circumvent* the school's dress code⟩
synonyms dodge, sidestep, skirt
related words avoid, duck, elude, escape, eschew, evade, shake, shun; disobey, disregard, flout, ignore
phrases get around
near antonyms accede (to), acquiesce (to), assent (to)
antonyms comply (with), follow, keep, obey, observe
2 to avoid by going around ⟨*circumvented* the traffic jam by taking an alternate route⟩ — see DETOUR 1

circus *n* 1 a large usually roofless building for sporting events with tiers of seats for spectators ⟨the Roman *circus* is believed to have held 50,000 spectators in ancient times⟩ — see STADIUM
2 a place of uproar or confusion ⟨with seven kids in the house, it's a *circus* most of the time⟩ — see MADHOUSE 2

citadel *n* a structure or place from which one can resist attack ⟨a massive stone *citadel* continues to command the city of Halifax, Nova Scotia⟩ — see FORT

citation *n* 1 a formal expression of praise ⟨the *citation* for the Nobel Prize winner noted his major contributions to quantum theory⟩ — see ENCOMIUM
2 a formal recognition of an achievement or praiseworthy deed ⟨a police officer who has received several

citations for his work with troubled youths in the city⟩ — see COMMENDATION 1

3 a passage referred to, repeated, or offered as an example ⟨in your paper be sure to include *citations* to back up any points you make about the play⟩ — see QUOTATION

cite *vb* **1** to give as an example ⟨*cited* several experts' opinions to back up her argument⟩ — see QUOTE 1

2 to make reference to or speak about briefly but specifically ⟨*cited* a number of similar instances⟩ — see MENTION 1

citify *vb* to accustom to the ways of the city ⟨we've become so *citified* that many people have no idea where their food comes from⟩

synonyms urbanize

related words civilize, cultivate

citizen *n* **1** a person who owes allegiance to a government and is protected by it ⟨conscientious *citizens* who regard voting as a duty as well as a right⟩

synonyms national, subject

related words compatriot, countryman; inhabitant, native, nonimmigrant, resident

near antonyms foreigner, stranger; immigrant, nonnative

antonyms alien, noncitizen

2 a person who lives in a town on a permanent basis ⟨claimed that the good *citizens* of the town were sick of high property taxes⟩ — see BURGHER

city *n* a thickly settled, highly populated area ⟨commuters who drive every day between their homes in the suburbs and their jobs in the *city*⟩

synonyms burg, megalopolis, metropolis, municipality, town

related words borough; conurbation; urban sprawl; suburbia

civil *adj* **1** of or relating to a nation ⟨the country was not destroyed by outside enemies but by a series of *civil* wars⟩ — see NATIONAL

2 showing consideration, courtesy, and good manners ⟨please try to be *civil* to Aunt Mabel, even though you don't like her⟩ — see POLITE 1

civility *n* **1** an act or utterance that is a customary show of good manners ⟨after the usual *civilities*, the parents and the principal had a serious talk about the boy⟩

synonyms amenity, courtesy, formality, gesture

related words ceremony, observance, rite, ritual; etiquette, manners, proprieties; greetings, regards, respects; favor, grace, kindness

2 speech or behavior that is a sign of good breeding ⟨treated people from all walks of life with the same unfailing *civility*⟩ — see POLITENESS

civilization *n* **1** the way people live at a particular time and place ⟨a study unit on the advanced *civilization* created by the Mayas over a thousand years ago⟩

synonyms culture, life, lifestyle, society

related words customs, manners, mores, values; folklore, heritage, tradition

2 a high level of taste and enlightenment as a result of extensive intellectual training and exposure to the arts ⟨by the 18th century Boston had reached a level of *civilization* sufficiently advanced to support a circle of portrait painters⟩ — see CULTURE 1

civilized *adj* having or showing a taste for the fine arts and gracious living ⟨a *civilized* older couple who are celebrated for holding dinner parties that are attended by the city's best and brightest⟩ — see CULTIVATED

clack *vb* to make a series of short sharp noises ⟨her teeth *clacked* because she was freezing while waiting for the bus⟩ — see RATTLE 1

claim *n* **1** an entitlement to something ⟨I'm announcing my *claim* to that last slice of pizza⟩

synonyms call, pretense (*or* pretence), pretension, right

related words birthright, prerogative; favor, privilege; refusal

2 a legal right to participation in the advantages, profits, and responsibility of something ⟨a shareholder has a *claim* in the business⟩ — see INTEREST 1

3 a solemn and often public declaring of the truth or existence of something ⟨Galileo's *claim* that the moon has a very irregular surface and thus is not the perfect sphere that the ancients had imagined⟩ — see PROTESTATION

4 something that someone insists upon having ⟨young children make great *claims* on their parents' time⟩ — see DEMAND 1

claim *vb* **1** to state as a fact usually forcefully ⟨people who *claim* that they have been kidnapped by aliens from other worlds⟩

synonyms affirm, allege, assert, aver, avouch, avow, contend, declare, insist, maintain, profess, protest, warrant

related words announce, broadcast, proclaim; argue, rationalize, reason; confirm, justify, vindicate; defend, support, uphold

near antonyms disavow, disclaim, disown; challenge, dispute, question; confute, disprove, rebut, refute; contradict

antonyms deny, gainsay

2 to ask for (something) earnestly or with authority ⟨after many years had passed, he suddenly appeared to *claim* his inheritance⟩ — see DEMAND 1

clairvoyance *n* the power of seeing or knowing about things that are not present to the senses ⟨people who claim to have *clairvoyance* are sometimes asked to help locate missing persons⟩

synonyms extrasensory perception, sixth sense

related words foreknowledge, foresight, prescience; telepathy

clamber *vb* to move (as up or over something) often with the help of the hands in holding or pulling ⟨*clambered* over a wall and was never seen again⟩ — see CLIMB 1

clamor *n* **1** a violent shouting ⟨a *clamor* arose from the crowd as the prisoner was brought forward⟩

synonyms howl, hubbub, hue and cry, hullabaloo, noise, outcry, roar, tumult, uproar

related words clangor, din, jangle, racket

near antonyms mumble, mumbling, murmur, murmuring, rumble, rumbling

2 loud, confused, and usually unharmonious sound ⟨the *clamor* of a dozen kids practicing the trumpet at once⟩ — see NOISE 1

clamor (for) *vb* to ask for (something) earnestly or with authority ⟨*clamored for* ice cream for dessert⟩ — see DEMAND 1

clamorous *adj* **1** engaging in or marked by loud and insistent cries especially of protest ⟨a *clamorous* objection to the play that the students have chosen to put on this year⟩ — see VOCIFEROUS

2 full of or characterized by the presence of noise ⟨a *clamorous* kindergarten classroom that would try the patience of any sane adult⟩ — see NOISY 2

3 marked by a high volume of sound ⟨a rock band whose *clamorous* concerts will rattle your bones⟩ — see LOUD 1

clamp *vb* to put securely in place or in a desired position ⟨*clamped* the headphones to her ears⟩ — see FASTEN 2

clamp down (on) *vb* to put a stop to (something) by the use of force ⟨*clamp down on* petty crime⟩ — see QUELL 1

clam up *vb* to stop talking ⟨the little girl *clammed up* when her big brother came into the room⟩ — see SHUT UP

clan *n* **1** a group of people sharing a common interest and relating together socially ⟨that *clan* of football fans has parties every weekend on which the New England Patriots play⟩ — see GANG 2
2 a group of persons who come from the same ancestor ⟨the whole *clan* gets together only for holidays⟩ — see FAMILY 1

clandestine *adj* undertaken or done so as to escape being observed or known by others ⟨I took a *clandestine* peek at my neighbor's test paper⟩ — see SECRET 1

clang *n* the loud sound made when metal strikes metal ⟨the horseshoe hit the stake with a satisfying *clang*⟩
synonyms clangor, clank, clash
related words chime, dingdong, peal, ring; clink, jangle, jingle, tinkle; clap, clop, crack, crash

clangor *n* **1** loud, confused, and usually unharmonious sound ⟨the *clangor* of a battle in the Middle Ages, as steel hit against steel a thousand times⟩ — see NOISE 1
2 the loud sound made when metal strikes metal ⟨the child created a terrible *clangor* when she banged the two pots together⟩ — see CLANG

clangorous *adj* **1** full of or characterized by the presence of noise ⟨a *clangorous* but warmhearted household⟩ — see NOISY 2
2 making loud, confused, and usually unharmonious sounds ⟨the teen's *clangorous* efforts to learn to play the drums⟩ — see NOISY 1
3 marked by a high volume of sound ⟨a *clangorous* train factory⟩ — see LOUD 1

clank *n* the loud sound made when metal strikes metal ⟨the car is making a funny *clank*, and this can't be good⟩ — see CLANG

clannish *adj* bound together by feelings of very close association ⟨a *clannish* family that can be rather cool to outsiders⟩ — see CLOSE-KNIT

clap *n* **1** a loud explosive sound ⟨a *clap* of thunder that woke the whole house up⟩
synonyms bang, blast, boom, crack, crash, pop, report, slam, smash, snap, thwack, whack
related words clang, clangor, clank, clash; knock, rap, tap; clamor, howl, hubbub, hue and cry, hullabaloo, outcry, roar, tumult, uproar
2 a hard strike with a part of the body or an instrument ⟨a sharp *clap* to the head of the disrespectful youth⟩ — see ¹BLOW

clap *vb* to deliver a blow to (someone or something) usually in a strong vigorous manner ⟨*clapped* him on the back as a friendly gesture⟩ — see HIT 1

claptrap *n* **1** language, behavior, or ideas that are absurd and contrary to good sense ⟨the idea that you can get a cold from not dressing warmly is *claptrap*⟩ — see NONSENSE 1
2 unintelligible or meaningless talk ⟨picked up the phone and heard only *claptrap*⟩ — see GIBBERISH

clarification *n* a statement that makes something clear ⟨after that *clarification*, I find I actually agree with you⟩ — see EXPLANATION 1

clarify *vb* **1** to remove usually visible impurities from ⟨*clarify* the melted butter by skimming off the milky bits⟩
synonyms clear, distill, filter, purify
related words process, refine; clean, cleanse, purge; extract, leach; screen, sieve, sift
near antonyms cloud, dull, muddy; contaminate, dirty, soil
2 to make plain or understandable ⟨it would help if you could *clarify* your position for us⟩ — see EXPLAIN 1

clarity *n* **1** the state or quality of being easily seen through ⟨mountain streams with water of incredible *clarity*⟩
synonyms clearness, limpidity, limpidness, transparency
related words lucidity, lucidness, translucency; brightness, brilliance, effulgence, luminosity, luminousness; definition, resolution, sharpness
near antonyms fogginess, haziness, murkiness
antonyms cloudiness, opacity, opaqueness
2 clearness of expression ⟨this essay on civic responsibility is a marvel of *clarity*⟩ — see SIMPLICITY 2

clash *n* **1** a physical dispute between opposing individuals or groups ⟨a *clash* between rival gangs that resulted in some serious injuries⟩ — see FIGHT 1
2 the loud sound made when metal strikes metal ⟨the *clash* of cymbals⟩ — see CLANG

clash *vb* to be out of harmony or agreement usually noticeably ⟨the colors of your shirt and pants *clash*⟩ ⟨Mom's idea of proper dress often *clashes* with mine⟩
synonyms collide, conflict, jar
related words mismatch; battle, combat, fight, war (against); chafe, gall, grate, jangle; differ, disagree
near antonyms agree, coincide, correspond
antonyms blend, harmonize, match

clash (with) *vb* to oppose (someone) in physical conflict ⟨he often *clashed with* the other children when he was young⟩ — see FIGHT 1

clashing *adj* not being in agreement or harmony ⟨freedom and equality are often a *clashing* set of ideals⟩ — see INCONSISTENT

clasp *n* the act or manner of holding ⟨be careful that your *clasp* on the cat isn't too tight, or she could get hurt⟩ — see HOLD 1

clasp *vb* **1** to put one's arms around and press tightly ⟨*clasped* his long-lost sister and cried without restraint⟩ — see EMBRACE 1
2 to reach for and take hold of by embracing with the fingers or arms ⟨*clasped* a crayon and began drawing⟩ — see TAKE 1

class *n* **1** one of the segments of society into which people are grouped ⟨a politician who appeals to people of every *class*⟩
synonyms caste, estate, folk, order, stratum
related words bracket, echelon, grade, layer, level, tier; place, position, rank, standing, status; grouping, hierarchy, stratification; clan, family, people, race, tribe
2 one of the units into which a whole is divided on the basis of a common characteristic ⟨a new *class* of wireless devices that could be used for Internet access as well as personal communication⟩
synonyms bracket, category, division, family, grade, group, kind, order, rank(s), set, species, type
related words description, feather, ilk, nature, sort; branch, section, subdivision, subgroup, variety; breed, race; classification, heading, label, rubric, title

3 a number of persons or things that are grouped together because they have something in common ⟨only a particular *class* of burglar would do that⟩ — see SORT 1

4 a series of lectures on a subject ⟨took a *class* on modern art⟩ — see COURSE 2

5 degree of excellence ⟨only horses of great *class* are allowed to enter the Kentucky Derby⟩ — see QUALITY 1

6 dignified or restrained beauty of form, appearance, or style ⟨an old mansion with tremendous *class* that puts today's gaudy behemoths to shame⟩ — see ELEGANCE

7 high position within society ⟨the woman exudes an aura of *class* and breeding⟩ — see RANK 2

class *vb* to arrange or assign according to type ⟨I would *class* that suggestion as helpful, so let's make a note of it⟩ — see CLASSIFY 1

classic *adj* **1** constituting, serving as, or worthy of being a pattern to be imitated ⟨*classic* designs in furniture that never go out of style⟩ — see MODEL

2 of the very best kind ⟨one of the really *classic* comedies in the history of movies⟩ — see EXCELLENT

3 serving to identify as belonging to an individual or group ⟨the anthropologist noted the *classic* facial features of the inhabitants of those islands⟩ — see CHARACTERISTIC 1

classic *n* **1** someone of such unequaled perfection as to deserve imitation ⟨among women who have devoted themselves to a life of scientific inquiry, Marie Curie is one of the acknowledged *classics*⟩ — see IDEAL 1

2 something (as a work of art) that is a great achievement and often its creator's greatest achievement ⟨the works of Michelangelo are regarded as *classics* of the sculptor's art⟩ — see MASTERPIECE

3 the most perfect type or example ⟨his journey of discovery was a *classic* of arduous effort and fierce determination⟩ — see QUINTESSENCE 1

classical *adj* based on customs usually handed down from a previous generation ⟨the *classical* preparation of a ham for Easter⟩ — see TRADITIONAL 1

classify *vb* **1** to arrange or assign according to type ⟨*classify* the baseball cards in your collection on the basis of rarity⟩

synonyms assort, break down, categorize, class, grade, group, peg, place, range, rank, separate, sort

related words arrange, order, organize, systematize; alphabetize, catalog (*or* catalogue), codify, file, index, list; pigeonhole, shelve; distinguish, identify, recognize; cull, screen, sift, winnow

near antonyms confuse, disarrange, jumble, lump, mix (up), scramble

2 to put into a particular arrangement ⟨*classify* the information you got from the Internet by source⟩ — see ORDER 1

clatter *n* a state of noisy, confused activity ⟨the *clatter* of a crowded cafeteria⟩ — see COMMOTION

clatter *vb* to make a series of short sharp noises ⟨horses' hooves *clattering* on the pavement⟩ — see RATTLE 1

clattering *adj* full of or characterized by the presence of noise ⟨a huge, *clattering* warehouse⟩ — see NOISY 2

clattery *adj* full of or characterized by the presence of noise ⟨a *clattery* cafeteria serving hordes of hungry students⟩ — see NOISY 2

clean *adj* **1** free from dirt or stain ⟨although the soccer team always starts out with *clean* uniforms, they don't stay that way for long⟩

synonyms immaculate, spick-and-span (*or* spic-and-span), spotless, stainless, unsoiled, unsullied

related words pure, taintless, undefiled, unpolluted, untainted, wholesome; cleanly, hygienic, sanitary; bleached, cleansed, purified, whitened; milky, snowy, white; flawless, unblemished; bright, shiny, sparkling

near antonyms dingy, greasy, grimy, mucky, muddy; defiled, polluted, tainted; blackened, discolored

antonyms besmirched, dirty, filthy, foul, grubby, soiled, spotted, stained, sullied, unclean

2 following or according to the rules ⟨a *clean* check from the other hockey player⟩ — see FAIR 3

3 free from any trace of the coarse or indecent ⟨only *clean* songs will be permitted for the performances on the last night of summer camp⟩ — see CHASTE

4 trying all possibilities ⟨police made a *clean* sweep of the area before the governor's arrival⟩ — see EXHAUSTIVE

clean *adv* to a full extent or degree ⟨the thief got *clean* away⟩ — see FULLY 1

clean *vb* **1** to make clean ⟨we *cleaned* the clothes before donating them to charity⟩

synonyms cleanse

related words decontaminate, purge, purify; disinfect, sanitize; brush, dry-clean, dust, launder, mop, rinse, scour, scrub, sweep, wash, wipe; brighten, deodorize, freshen, spruce (up), sweeten; pick up, straighten (up), tidy

near antonyms begrime, muddy; defile, pollute, taint; blacken, discolor

antonyms besmirch, dirty, foul, soil, spot, stain, sully

2 to take the internal organs out of ⟨*cleaned* the rabbit before cooking it⟩ — see GUT

clean (out) *vb* to make complete use of ⟨in anticipation of the snowstorm, shoppers *cleaned out* the store's supplies of milk and bread⟩ — see DEPLETE

clean (up) *vb* to remove objectionable parts from ⟨*cleaned up* the book before publishing it for school use⟩ — see CENSOR

cleaner *n* a substance used for cleaning ⟨a kitchen shelf loaded with household *cleaners*⟩

synonyms cleanser, detergent, soap

related words disinfectant, purifier, solvent

cleanse *vb* **1** to free from moral guilt or blemish especially ceremonially ⟨the priestess *cleansed* all supplicants in one ceremony⟩ — see PURIFY 1

2 to make clean ⟨*cleanse* the wound with soap and water before applying the bandage⟩ — see CLEAN 1

cleanser *n* a substance used for cleaning ⟨a bathroom *cleanser*⟩ — see CLEANER

cleansing *n* the act or fact of freeing from sin or moral guilt ⟨underwent a *cleansing* before he could enter the temple's most sacred chamber⟩ — see PURIFICATION

clear *adj* **1** easily seen through ⟨the *clear* glass walls of the aquarium's giant ocean tank⟩

synonyms limpid, liquid, lucent, pellucid, transparent

related words colorless, uncolored; lucid, translucent; crystal, crystalline, glassy, sparkling; bright, brilliant, effulgent, luminous

near antonyms foggy, hazy, misty, murky, smoky (*also* smokey)

antonyms cloudy, nontransparent, opaque

2 not subject to misinterpretation or more than one interpretation ⟨the meaning of her broad smile was *clear* to the whole class⟩

synonyms apparent, broad, clear-cut, decided, distinct, evident, lucid, manifest, obvious, open-and-shut, palpable, patent, perspicuous, plain, transparent, unambiguous, unequivocal, unmistakable *related words* comprehendible, comprehensible, decipherable, fathomable, graspable, intelligible, knowable, understandable; self-evident, self-explanatory; simple, uncomplicated; overt, undisguised; appreciable, perceptible, recognizable, sensible, tangible; discernible, noticeable, observable, visible

near antonyms incomprehensible, unfathomable, unintelligible, unknowable; imperceptible, inappreciable, insensible; delicate, subtle

antonyms dark, enigmatic, indistinct, mysterious, obscure, unclear; ambiguous, equivocal

3 having or showing a mind free from doubt ⟨I need to be absolutely *clear* about what you're saying⟩ — see CERTAIN 2

4 not stormy or cloudy ⟨novice pilots can only fly on *clear* days⟩ — see FAIR 1

5 serving to put an end to all debate or questioning ⟨the evidence is *clear*: he's innocent⟩ — see CONCLUSIVE 1

6 allowing passage without obstruction ⟨flooding was widespread, and only some roads are *clear* so far⟩ — see OPEN 1

7 free from guilt or blame ⟨slept with a *clear* conscience⟩ — see INNOCENT 2

clear *vb* **1** to rid the surface of (as an area) from things in the way ⟨the early settlers worked hard to *clear* the land for crops⟩

synonyms free, open, unblock

related words ease, facilitate, loosen (up), smooth, unclog, unstop

near antonyms clog, dam, obstruct, plug, stop

antonyms block

2 to set (a person or thing) free of something that encumbers ⟨*cleared* the woods of brush⟩ — see RID

3 to give what is owed for ⟨finally *cleared* the last debt⟩ — see PAY 2

4 to remove the contents of ⟨*cleared* a drawer so there would be a place to store his clothes⟩ — see EMPTY

5 to remove usually visible impurities from ⟨*cleared* the car windows⟩ — see CLARIFY 1

6 to set free from entanglement or difficulty ⟨*cleared* himself of any involvement in the matter⟩ — see EXTRICATE

7 to arrange clear passage of (something) by removing obstructions ⟨plows promptly *cleared* the roads of snow⟩ — see OPEN 2

8 to free from a charge of wrongdoing ⟨she was accused of embezzlement, but an investigation by the bank *cleared* her⟩ — see EXCULPATE

9 to give official acceptance of something as satisfactory ⟨the administration *cleared* the plan, and building should begin shortly⟩ — see APPROVE

10 to take away from a place or position ⟨*cleared* the dishes from the table⟩ — see REMOVE 2

clear (up) *vb* to make plain or understandable ⟨a simple explanation *cleared* the matter *up*⟩ — see EXPLAIN 1

clearance *n* the approval by someone in authority for the doing of something ⟨we'll need official *clearance* before publishing this⟩ — see PERMISSION

clear-cut *adj* **1** not subject to misinterpretation or more than one interpretation ⟨a *clear-cut* case of plagiarism⟩ — see CLEAR 2

2 so clearly expressed as to leave no doubt about the meaning ⟨*clear-cut* instructions that even an idiot should be able to follow⟩ — see EXPLICIT

cleared *adj* allowing passage without obstruction ⟨for safety reasons, there must be a *cleared* staircase at all times⟩ — see OPEN 1

clearheaded *adj* **1** having full use of one's mind and control over one's actions ⟨waited until she was *clearheaded* to make the decision⟩ — see SANE

2 not having one's mind affected by alcohol ⟨woke up *clearheaded* and alert the next morning⟩ — see SOBER 1

clearing *n* a small area of usually open land ⟨deer browsing in a *clearing* in the woods⟩ — see FIELD 1

clearness *n* the state or quality of being easily seen through ⟨the *clearness* of a diamond is one of the factors used to judge its quality⟩ — see CLARITY 1

clear out *vb* **1** to cause (members of a group) to move widely apart ⟨police used tear gas to *clear out* the demonstrators⟩ — see SCATTER 1

2 to get free from a dangerous or confining situation ⟨everyone *cleared out* quickly when the fire alarm went off⟩ — see ESCAPE 1

3 to leave a place often for another ⟨the lunch crowd *cleared out* to get back to class⟩ — see GO 2

clear-sighted *adj* **1** having or showing a practical cleverness or judgment ⟨a *clear-sighted* businessman who doesn't let sentimentality or compassion affect his decisions⟩ — see SHREWD

2 having unusually keen vision ⟨a *clear-sighted* person could see for almost 20 miles from the observatory⟩ — see SHARP-EYED

cleave *vb* to hold to something firmly as if by adhesion ⟨you should resolutely *cleave* to the facts in your report⟩ — see STICK 1

cleft *n* an irregular usually narrow break in a surface created by pressure ⟨my fishing line managed to get wedged in a *cleft* in the rocks⟩ — see CRACK 1

clemency *n* kind, gentle, or compassionate treatment especially towards someone who is undeserving of it ⟨the judge chose to show *clemency* to the truly repentant prisoner⟩ — see MERCY 1

clement *adj* marked by temperatures that are neither too high nor too low ⟨Hawaii is known for its delightfully *clement* climate⟩

synonyms balmy, equable, gentle, mild, moderate, temperate

related words clear, cloudless, fair, rainless, sunny, sunshiny; calm, halcyon, peaceful, placid, tranquil; delightful, fine, pleasant

near antonyms blustering, blustery, breezy, gusty; foggy, hazy, misty; bleak, cloudy, dirty, foul, nasty, overcast, rainy, raw, rough, squally, stormy, sunless

antonyms harsh, inclement, intemperate, severe

clench *vb* to have or keep in one's hands ⟨*clenched* a tissue in his hands as he told his story of misfortune⟩ — see HOLD 1

clergyman *n* a person specially trained and authorized to conduct religious services in a Christian church ⟨a special memorial service that attracted *clergymen* from all over the city⟩

synonyms cleric, deacon, divine, dominie, ecclesiastic, father, minister, padre, parson, preacher, priest, reverend

related words evangelist, missionary; deaconess, priestess; dean, pastor, rector, vicar; chaplain, confessor; canon, curate; friar, mendicant, monastic, monk, religious

antonyms layman

cleric *n* a person specially trained and authorized to conduct religious services in a Christian church ⟨*clerics* were sharply divided on the issue of whether the war was morally justified⟩ — see CLERGYMAN

clerical *adj* of, relating to, or characteristic of the clergy ⟨*clerical* duties such as providing spiritual counseling and leading classes in Bible study⟩
synonyms ministerial, pastoral, priestly, sacerdotal
related words evangelical, missionary; apostolic, canonical, episcopal, papal, patriarchal, pontifical; churchly, ecclesiastical (*or* ecclesiastic); divine, holy, religious, sacramental; rabbinic (*or* rabbinical)
antonyms lay, nonclerical

clerk *n* **1** a person whose job is to keep records ⟨you'll need to get a copy of your birth certificate from the office of the town *clerk*⟩
synonyms register, registrar, scribe
related words archivist, bookkeeper, recorder; annalist, chronicler
2 a person employed to sell goods or services especially in a store ⟨the *clerk* suggested a different brand⟩ — see SALESPERSON

clever *adj* **1** showing a use of the imagination and creativity especially in inventing ⟨an inventor who was constantly coming up with *clever* devices for doing everyday chores⟩
synonyms artful, creative, imaginative, ingenious
related words innovative, novel, original; convenient, handy, practical, useful; complex, sophisticated; adroit, deft, dexterous (*also* dextrous); brainy, intelligent, sharp, smart
near antonyms dull, pedestrian, stodgy
antonyms uncreative, unimaginative
2 having or showing quickness of mind ⟨a *clever* student figured out a trick to do the assignment faster⟩ — see INTELLIGENT 1
3 skillful with the hands ⟨the Shakers were *clever* artisans who created many ingenious and highly useful devices⟩ — see DEXTEROUS 1
4 given to or marked by mature intelligent humor ⟨a *clever* joke that requires a little bit of thought on the part of the listener⟩ — see WITTY

cleverness *n* **1** mental skill or quickness ⟨it takes real *cleverness* to find a way around the rules⟩ — see DEXTERITY 1
2 subtle or imaginative ability in inventing, devising, or executing something ⟨the *cleverness* of the negotiator getting each side to believe that they had won⟩ — see SKILL 1

cliché *n* an idea or expression that has been used by many people ⟨try to write the story without resorting to *clichés*⟩ — see COMMONPLACE

click *vb* **1** to form a close personal relationship ⟨we just *clicked* from the moment we met⟩ — see COMMUNE
2 to turn out as planned or desired ⟨sometimes an idea simply *clicks*⟩ — see SUCCEED 1

client *n* a person who buys a product or uses a service from a business ⟨a law firm soliciting new *clients* through television advertising⟩ — see CUSTOMER 1

cliff *n* a steep wall of rock, earth, or ice ⟨the *cliff* rises 200 feet from the island's south shore⟩
synonyms bluff, crag, escarpment, palisade, precipice, scarp
related words tor; bulwark, embankment

climate *n* **1** a special quality or impression associated with something ⟨a new school designed to encourage a *climate* of learning⟩ — see AURA
2 the circumstances, conditions, or objects by which one is surrounded ⟨it's hard to concentrate in this hectic *climate*⟩ — see ENVIRONMENT

climax *n* **1** a point in a chain of events at which an important change (as in one's fortunes) occurs ⟨the cli-max of the story occurs when the hero discovers the identity of his father⟩ — see TURNING POINT
2 the highest part or point ⟨the *climax* of her career as a performer⟩ — see HEIGHT 1

climax *vb* to bring to a triumphant conclusion ⟨*climaxed* the county fair with a pie-eating contest⟩ — see CROWN

climb *n* the act or an instance of rising or climbing up ⟨a long hard *climb* up the mountain⟩ — see ASCENT 1

climb *vb* **1** to move (as up or over something) often with the help of the hands in holding or pulling ⟨visitors should use caution when *climbing* over the wet rocks along the shore⟩
synonyms clamber, scramble
related words shin, shinny; inch; mount, scale, surmount; claw, struggle
2 to move or extend upward ⟨smoke from the cabin *climbing* in the still mountain air⟩ — see ASCEND

clinch *vb* to make final, definite, or beyond dispute ⟨the rain *clinched* the matter: we would have the party indoors⟩
synonyms decide, settle
related words demonstrate, determine, establish, prove, show; clarify, clear (up), illuminate; conclude, end, finish
near antonyms confuse, muddle, muddy

clincher *n* something (as a fact or argument) that is decisive or overwhelming ⟨the fact that the resort had tennis courts was the *clincher* in our deciding to stay there⟩
synonyms crusher, topper
related words deathblow, knockout; coup

cling *vb* to hold to something firmly as if by adhesion ⟨a dozen magnets *clinging* to the refrigerator⟩ — see STICK 1

cling (to) *vb* **1** to give steadfast support to ⟨continued to *cling to* the old ideas long after they had gone out of fashion⟩ — see ADHERE
2 to have or keep in one's hands ⟨*clung to* a pole in the subway car to keep from falling as it lurched along⟩ — see HOLD 1

clink *vb* to make a repeated sharp light ringing sound ⟨coins *clinking* in his pocket as he traipsed down the street⟩ — see JINGLE

clip *n* a hard strike with a part of the body or an instrument ⟨an unexpectedly low branch dealt him a *clip* to the head⟩ — see ¹BLOW

clip *vb* to make (as hair) shorter with or as if with the use of shears ⟨toddlers are often fearful the first time they get their hair *clipped*⟩
synonyms bob, crop, curtail, cut, cut back, dock, lop (off), nip, pare, prune, shave, shear, snip, trim
related words manicure, mow; abbreviate, abridge, shorten
near antonyms elongate, extend, lengthen

clique *n* a group of people sharing a common interest and relating together socially ⟨that *clique* refuses to even talk to outsiders at their lunch table⟩ — see GANG 2

cloak *n* **1** something that covers or conceals like a piece of cloth ⟨the *cloak* of mystery that surrounds the royal family⟩
synonyms curtain, hood, mantle, mask, shroud, veil
related words cover, screen, shield; facade (*also* façade), face, veneer
2 a sleeveless garment worn so as to hang over the shoulders, arms, and back ⟨threw a *cloak* around his shoulders⟩ — see ¹CAPE

cloak *vb* **1** to change the dress or looks of so as to conceal true identity ⟨a celebrity *cloaked* in anonymity⟩ — see DISGUISE

2 to keep secret or shut off from view ⟨*cloaked* their maneuvers in secrecy⟩ — see ¹HIDE 2

clobber *vb* **1** to deliver a blow to (someone or something) usually in a strong vigorous manner ⟨he *clobbered* the ball, sending it in a high arc toward the back wall⟩ — see HIT 1

2 to defeat by a large margin ⟨they *clobbered* the opposing team⟩ — see WHIP 2

3 to achieve a victory over ⟨I *clobbered* that test⟩ — see BEAT 2

clock *n* a device to measure time ⟨the *clock* reads 5:00 p.m.⟩ — see TIMEPIECE

clod *n* **1** a big clumsy often slow-witted person ⟨he's no simple *clod*⟩ — see OAF

2 a small uneven mass ⟨a *clod* of dirt stuck to the bottom⟩ — see LUMP 1

cloddish *adj* having or showing crudely insensitive or impolite manners ⟨the *cloddish* behavior of an unfeeling brute⟩ — see CLOWNISH

clodhopper *n* an awkward or simple person especially from a small town or the country ⟨*clodhoppers* visiting the city for the first time⟩ — see HICK

clog *n* something that makes movement or progress more difficult ⟨a *clog* in the arteries⟩ — see ENCUMBRANCE

clog *vb* **1** to prevent passage through ⟨the discovery that a ton of hair was *clogging* the drain in the tub⟩

synonyms block, choke, close (off), congest, dam, jam, obstruct, plug (up), stop (up), stuff

related words bung, fill, pack; flood, glut, inundate, overwhelm, swamp

near antonyms excavate, hollow (out), scoop (out); empty, lighten

antonyms clear, free, open (up), unclog

2 to create difficulty for the work or activity of ⟨a court system *clogged* by frivolous suits⟩ — see HAMPER

cloister *n* a residence for men under religious vows ⟨monks living in a *cloister* in the country⟩ — see MONASTERY

cloistered *adj* hidden from view ⟨a *cloistered* cottage deep in the woods⟩ — see SECLUDED

close *adj* **1** having little space between items or parts ⟨the soldiers marched in *close* formation against the enemy⟩

synonyms compact, crowded, dense, jam-packed, packed, serried, thick, tight

related words airtight, snug; compacted, compressed, condensed; firm, hard, solid; impenetrable, impermeable, impervious

near antonyms commodious, roomy, spacious

antonyms loose, uncrowded

2 not being distant in time, space, or significance ⟨my birthday is *close* to Christmas⟩ ⟨a shopping mall that is very *close* to the highway⟩ ⟨these words are *close* synonyms⟩

synonyms immediate, near, nearby, neighboring, next-door, nigh

related words abutting, adjacent, adjoining, bordering, contiguous; approaching, coming, forthcoming, oncoming, upcoming; accessible, convenient, handy

phrases at hand

near antonyms divorced, removed, separated

antonyms away, distant, far, faraway, far-off, remote

3 showing little difference in the standing of the competitors ⟨the election results were so *close* that the votes had to be recounted⟩

synonyms narrow, nip and tuck, tight

related words crowded

4 closely acquainted ⟨*close* friends⟩ — see FAMILIAR 1

5 given to keeping one's activities hidden from public observation or knowledge ⟨she was as *close* as a stone⟩ — see SECRETIVE

6 giving or sharing as little as possible ⟨folks who are very *close* when charity calls⟩ — see STINGY 1

7 lacking fresh air ⟨a room with an uncomfortably *close* atmosphere⟩ — see STUFFY 1

8 meeting the highest standard of accuracy ⟨a *close* study of the item⟩ — see PRECISE 1

close *adv* at, within, or to a short distance or time ⟨they drew *close* for reassurance⟩ — see NEAR 1

¹close *n* an open space wholly or partly enclosed (as by buildings or walls) ⟨a garden in a *close* at the center of the complex⟩ — see COURT 2

²close *n* **1** the stopping of a process or activity ⟨at the *close* of the evening⟩ — see END 1

2 the last part of a process or action ⟨conduct the negotiations to a satisfactory *close*⟩ — see FINALE

close *vb* **1** to position (something) so as to prevent passage through an opening ⟨be sure to *close* the gate when you leave⟩

synonyms shut

related words bar, batten (down), bolt, chain, fasten, latch, lock; plug, seal, stopper; secure; bang, clap, slam

near antonyms unbar, unbolt, unchain, unfasten, unlatch, unlock, unseal

antonyms open

2 to stop the operations of ⟨the merchant will *close* the store if business doesn't improve⟩

synonyms shut

related words phase out, turn off; extinguish, quell, suppress; gag, muzzle, silence; fail, fold

near antonyms build, expand

antonyms open, start

3 to bring (an event) to a natural or appropriate stopping point ⟨we'll *close* the assembly with the singing of our national anthem⟩

synonyms conclude, end, finish, round (off *or* out), terminate, wind up, wrap up

related words climax, crown; complete, consummate, perfect; halt, stop, suspend

antonyms begin, commence, inaugurate, open, start

4 to come to an end ⟨the services *closed* with a short prayer⟩ — see CEASE 1

5 to come near or nearer ⟨the two groups *closed* with each other from opposite sides of the field⟩ — see APPROACH 1

close (off) *vb* to prevent passage through ⟨*close off* the street⟩ — see CLOG 1

closefisted *adj* giving or sharing as little as possible ⟨*closefisted* administrators objecting to expenses⟩ — see STINGY 1

close–knit *adj* bound together by feelings of very close association ⟨a *close-knit* family that constantly keeps in touch⟩

synonyms clannish

related words bosom, chummy, close, familiar, friendly, intimate, thick; exclusive, snobbish, snobby; forbidding, inhospitable, unfriendly

closely *adv* to a close degree ⟨*closely* resembling a normal outfit⟩ — see NEAR 2

closemouthed *adj* **1** given to keeping one's activities hidden from public observation or knowledge ⟨he remained *closemouthed* about their activities⟩ — see SECRETIVE

2 tending not to speak frequently (as by habit or inclination) ⟨encourage the *closemouthed* children to speak up and not be shy⟩ — see SILENT 2

closeness *n* **1** the practice or habit of keeping secrets or keeping one's affairs secret ⟨we tried to penetrate her *closeness* and discover her secret⟩ — see SECRECY

2 the quality of being overly sparing with money ⟨rebelled against his parents' *closeness* with his allowance⟩ — see PARSIMONY

3 the quality or state of being very accurate ⟨examined it with *closeness* and exactness⟩ — see PRECISION

4 the state of being in a very personal or private relationship ⟨the *closeness* of the best of friends⟩ — see FAMILIARITY 1

5 the state or condition of being near ⟨we were surprised by the *closeness* of the local grocery store⟩ — see PROXIMITY

closer *adj* being the less far of two ⟨the *closer* gas station was also more expensive⟩ — see NEAR 1

closet *n* **1** a storage case typically having doors and shelves ⟨a linen *closet*⟩ — see CABINET

2 an area within a building that has been set apart from surrounding space by a wall ⟨kept old clothes in the back of the *closet*⟩ — see ROOM 2

closet *vb* to close or shut in by or as if by barriers ⟨he *closeted* himself in a phone booth⟩ — see ENCLOSE 1

closing *adj* following all others of the same kind in order or time ⟨his *closing* arguments⟩ — see LAST

closing *n* the last part of a process or action ⟨in *closing*, I'd just like to say thanks once again⟩ — see FINALE

closure *n* the stopping of a process or activity ⟨business *closures*⟩ — see END 1

clot *vb* to turn from a liquid into a substance resembling jelly ⟨scabs form over cuts when your blood starts to *clot*⟩ — see COAGULATE

cloth *n* a woven or knitted material (as of cotton or nylon) ⟨cotton canvas was the *cloth* traditionally used for a ship's sails⟩

synonyms fabric, textile

related words fiber, thread, yarn

clothe *vb* **1** to outfit with clothes and especially fine or special clothes ⟨they liked to *clothe* the twins in identical outfits just to confuse people⟩

synonyms apparel, array, attire, caparison, costume, deck, dress, garb, garment, gown, invest, rig (out), robe, suit

related words cloak, mantle; drape, swaddle, swathe; accoutre (*or* accouter), equip, furnish, outfit

near antonyms divest, uncover, undrape, unveil

antonyms disrobe, strip, unclothe, undress

2 to convey in appropriate or telling terms ⟨regulations *clothed* in obscure terminology⟩ — see PHRASE

clothes *n pl* covering for the human body ⟨put on your warmest *clothes* to go out into the blizzard⟩ — see CLOTHING

clothing *n* covering for the human body ⟨a store that sells both men's and women's *clothing*⟩

synonyms apparel, attire, clothes, dress, duds, habiliment(s), raiment, togs, wear

related words garment, vestment; array, bravery, finery; tatters; costume, garb, getup, guise, outfit, rig, wardrobe; haberdashery

cloud *vb* **1** to make dark, dim, or indistinct ⟨unfortunately, smog *clouds* the view of the city from the hilltop⟩

synonyms becloud, bedim, befog, blacken, blur, darken, dim, fog, haze, mist, obscure, overcast, overcloud, overshadow, shadow, shroud

related words blot out, conceal, hide, screen, shade; camouflage, cloak, cover, curtain, disguise, mask, veil; distort, falsify, garble, misrepresent

near antonyms expose, reveal, uncover, unveil; clarify, clear, purify; highlight, spotlight

antonyms brighten, illuminate, illumine, light (up), lighten

2 to make (something) unclear to the understanding ⟨*cloud* the issue with obscure statistics⟩ — see CONFUSE 2

cloudburst *n* a steady falling of water from the sky in significant quantity ⟨the weatherman warned of possible *cloudbursts* in the afternoon⟩ — see RAIN 1

clouded *adj* **1** covered over by clouds ⟨*clouded* skies⟩ — see OVERCAST

2 filled with or dimmed by fine particles (as of dust or water) in suspension ⟨*clouded* water⟩ — see HAZY 1

cloudless *adj* not stormy or cloudy ⟨playing in the park on a *cloudless* summer day⟩ — see FAIR 1

cloudy *adj* **1** having visible particles in liquid suspension ⟨the water coming out of the faucet was unusually *cloudy*⟩

synonyms muddy, roiled, turbid

related words dingy, filmy, hazy, unfiltered; inky, murky; nontransparent, opaque

near antonyms clarified, filtered, purified

antonyms clear

2 covered over by clouds ⟨the skies grew *cloudy* and we headed home⟩ — see OVERCAST

3 filled with or dimmed by fine particles (as of dust or water) in suspension ⟨the room grew *cloudy* with smoke from the fire⟩ — see HAZY 1

clout *n* **1** a hard strike with a part of the body or an instrument ⟨gave the stubborn handle a solid *clout* to make it turn⟩ — see ¹BLOW

2 the power to direct the thinking or behavior of others usually indirectly ⟨has a great deal of *clout* in the industry⟩ — see INFLUENCE 1

clout *vb* to deliver a blow to (someone or something) usually in a strong vigorous manner ⟨*clouted* the nail with the hammer and drove it all the way into the wood⟩ — see HIT 1

clown *n* **1** a comically dressed performer (as at a circus) who entertains with playful tricks and ridiculous behavior ⟨a *clown* wearing big floppy shoes and a red wig⟩

synonyms buffoon, harlequin, zany

related words cutup, madcap; fool, jester, motley; mime, mummer; comedian, comedienne, comic, joker, jokester, wag

2 a person whose behavior is offensive to others ⟨you should stay away from that *clown*⟩ — see JERK 1

clown (around) *vb* to engage in attention-getting playful or boisterous behavior ⟨he was always *clowning around* in the classroom⟩ — see CUT UP

clowning *n* wildly playful or mischievous behavior ⟨her *clowning* was distracting, but fun to watch⟩ — see HORSEPLAY

clownish *adj* having or showing crudely insensitive or impolite manners ⟨the *clownish* antics of some of the teenagers at the wedding reception⟩

synonyms boorish, churlish, cloddish, loutish, uncouth

related words coarse, ill-bred, uncultivated, unpolished, unrefined; tasteless, vulgar; beastly, bestial; doltish, oafish, stupid; discourteous, impolite, rude, uncivil

near antonyms cultivated, polished, refined, well-bred; courtly, genteel, gentlemanly, ladylike; civil, courteous, polite

club *n* **1** a heavy rigid stick used as a weapon or for punishment ⟨hit the prisoner with a *club* if he tries anything funny⟩

synonyms bat, billy, bludgeon, cane, cudgel, nightstick, rod, shillelagh, staff, truncheon

related words blackjack, mace; birch, switch; hammer, mallet, maul; walking stick

2 the meeting place of an organization ⟨the Scouts gather at their *club* every Monday evening⟩

synonyms clubhouse, lodge

related words den, hangout, haunt, hideaway, hideout, lair; camp, headquarters; meetinghouse

3 a group of persons formally joined together for some common interest ⟨an alumni *club*⟩ — see ASSOCIATION 2

club *vb* **1** to form or enter into an association that furthers the interests of its members ⟨*clubbed* together to share their love of model rockets⟩ — see ALLY

2 to strike repeatedly ⟨he *clubbed* an inoffensive weed into submission in his frustration⟩ — see BEAT 1

clubhouse *n* the meeting place of an organization ⟨meet at the *clubhouse* each week⟩ — see CLUB 2

clue *n* a slight or indirect pointing to something (as a solution or explanation) ⟨searched for a *clue* to the answer⟩ — see HINT 1

clue *vb* to give information to ⟨*clue* him in on the plan⟩ — see ENLIGHTEN 1

clump *n* **1** a number of things considered as a unit ⟨a *clump* of cheerleaders in front of the gym⟩ — see GROUP 1

2 a small uneven mass ⟨a *clump* of dirt⟩ — see LUMP 1

clump *vb* to move heavily or clumsily ⟨*clumping* along the side of the road⟩ — see LUMBER 1

clumpy *adj* having small pieces or lumps spread throughout ⟨the soil was a little too *clumpy* to make a good garden⟩ — see CHUNKY 1

clumsy *adj* **1** lacking in physical ease and grace in movement or in the use of the hands ⟨diamond cutting is no job for a *clumsy* person⟩

synonyms awkward, gawky, graceless, heavy-handed, lubberly, lumbering, lumpish, ungainly, unhandy

related words butterfingered, uncoordinated; oafish; bungling, gauche, inept, inexpert, maladroit, unskilled, unskillful; cumbersome, unwieldy

near antonyms expert, masterly, skilled, skillful; lissome (*also* lissom), lithe, nimble; light, light-footed, surefooted

antonyms deft, dexterous (*also* dextrous), graceful, handy

2 lacking social grace and assurance ⟨felt *clumsy* in the unfamiliar uniform⟩ — see AWKWARD 1

3 showing or marked by a lack of skill and tact (as in dealing with a situation) ⟨a *clumsy* joke⟩ — see AWKWARD 2

4 difficult to use or operate especially because of size, weight, or design ⟨a *clumsy* contraption, but it got the job done⟩ — see CUMBERSOME

5 hastily or roughly constructed ⟨a *clumsy* mock-up of the real thing⟩ — see RUDE 1

cluster *n* **1** a number of things considered as a unit ⟨a *cluster* of stars in the southern sky⟩ — see GROUP 1

2 a usually small number of persons considered as a unit ⟨a small *cluster* of reporters waited by the courthouse door⟩ — see GROUP 2

cluster *vb* **1** to come together into one body or place ⟨the mice *clustered* together into a small burrow⟩ — see ASSEMBLE 1

2 to gather into a closely packed group ⟨*cluster* the tents together⟩ — see PRESS 3

clutch *n* **1** a time or state of affairs requiring prompt or decisive action ⟨come through in the *clutch*⟩ — see EMERGENCY

2 the right or means to command or control others ⟨living in the *clutch* of a cruel tyrant⟩ — see POWER 1

clutch *vb* to have or keep in one's hands ⟨he *clutched* the eggs carefully so he wouldn't drop them⟩ — see HOLD 1

clutter *n* an unorganized collection or mixture of various things ⟨the floor was covered in random *clutter*⟩ — see MISCELLANY 1

cluttered *adj* lacking in order, neatness, and often cleanliness ⟨keeping a *cluttered* workshop makes it hard to find the right tool⟩ — see MESSY

coach *n* a person who trains performers or athletes ⟨a *coach* who is highly respected by all of the baseball players⟩

synonyms trainer

related words instructor, teacher; driller, drillmaster; adviser (*or* advisor), counselor (*or* counsellor), mentor

coach *vb* to give advice and instruction to (someone) regarding the course or process to be followed ⟨carefully *coached* her through the process⟩ — see GUIDE 1

coadjutor *n* a person who helps a more skilled person ⟨he was appointed *coadjutor* to the president⟩ — see HELPER

coagulate *vb* to turn from a liquid into a substance resembling jelly ⟨the blood *coagulated*, and a scab formed on the wound⟩

synonyms clot, congeal, gel, jell, jelly, set

related words concrete, firm (up), freeze, harden, solidify, stiffen; condense, thicken; curdle, lump (up)

near antonyms deliquesce, flux, fuse, liquefy, melt, thaw

coalesce *vb* to come together to form a single unit ⟨several small townships have *coalesced* into a single metropolis⟩ — see UNITE 1

coalition *n* **1** a group of people acting together within a larger group ⟨rival *coalitions* struggling for control⟩ — see FACTION

2 an association of persons, parties, or states for mutual assistance and protection ⟨they formed a *coalition* with the theater owners⟩ — see CONFEDERACY

coarse *adj* **1** made up of large particles ⟨*coarse* rock salt was sprinkled on the icy walkway⟩

synonyms grainy, granular, granulated

related words rough; unfiltered, unrefined; gravelly, gritty, sandy; pebbly, rocky, stony (*also* stoney); lumpy, mealy

near antonyms smooth; filtered, pulverized, refined

antonyms dusty, fine, floury, powdery

2 lacking in refinement or good taste ⟨the hockey player's *coarse* manners turned his date off completely⟩

synonyms common, crass, crude, gross, ill-bred, low, lowbred, lowbrow, raffish, rough, roughhewn, rude, tasteless, uncouth, uncultivated, uncultured, unpolished, unrefined, vulgar *related words* boorish, churlish, cloddish, clownish, loutish, ungentlemanly; clumsy, lubberly, lumpish, oafish; inconsiderate, insensitive, thoughtless; countrified (*also* countryfied), provincial, rustic; graceless, inelegant, tacky

near antonyms aristocratic, courtly, patrician; elegant, graceful, gracious; considerate, sensitive, thoughtful; citified, sophisticated, urbane

antonyms cultivated, cultured, genteel, polished, refined, smooth, tasteful, well-bred

3 depicting or referring to sexual matters in a way that is unacceptable in polite society ⟨offended by its *coarse* humor⟩ — see OBSCENE 1

4 harsh and dry in sound ⟨a *coarse* laugh⟩ — see HOARSE

5 not having a level or smooth surface ⟨the *coarse* surface of the sandpaper⟩ — see UNEVEN 1

6 of low quality ⟨*coarse* imitations of quality merchandise⟩ — see CHEAP 2

coarseness *n* **1** the quality or state of being obscene ⟨she took offense at his *coarseness*⟩ — see OBSCENITY 1

2 the quality or state of lacking refinement or good taste ⟨learned to overcome her *coarseness* and fit into high society⟩ — see VULGARITY 1

coast *vb* to move or proceed smoothly and readily ⟨*coasting* along easily⟩ — see FLOW 2

coat *n* the hairy covering of a mammal especially when fine, soft, and thick ⟨a poodle's *coat* is often extremely curly⟩ — see FUR 1

coat *vb* to form a layer over ⟨thicken the sauce until it will *coat* the back of a spoon⟩ — see COVER 2

coax *vb* to get (someone) to do something by gentle urging, special attention, or flattery ⟨trying to *coax* Dad into taking us on a ski trip, we mentioned what a great skier he is⟩

synonyms blandish, blarney, cajole, soft-soap, wheedle

related words adulate, flatter, overpraise; compliment, praise; beguile, charm, woo; beg, importune, urge; bug, nag, pester

near antonyms browbeat, bulldoze, bully, cow, intimidate; coerce, compel, constrain, force, oblige

cobble (together) *vb* to make or assemble roughly or hastily ⟨the stranded hikers *cobbled together* a rickety shelter for the night⟩

synonyms patch (together), throw up

related words dash (off)

phrases knock together

near antonyms craft, handcraft; fashion, forge, hammer (out), pound (out)

¹cock *n* a fixture for controlling the flow of a liquid ⟨an automobile radiator *cock*⟩ — see FAUCET

²cock *n* a quantity of things thrown or stacked on one another ⟨a *cock* of hay⟩ — see ¹PILE 1

³cock *n* the act of positioning or an instance of being positioned at an angle ⟨a *cock* of the head⟩ — see TILT

cock *vb* to set or cause to be at an angle ⟨*cocked* his head to the side as he listened to her quizzically⟩ — see LEAN 1

cockcrow *n* the first appearance of light in the morning or the time of its appearance ⟨have to wake up every morning at *cockcrow*⟩ — see DAWN 1

cockeyed *adj* **1** inclined or twisted to one side ⟨wears his hat a little *cockeyed*⟩ — see AWRY

2 showing or marked by a lack of good sense or judgment ⟨a *cockeyed* scheme⟩ — see FOOLISH 1

cocksure *adj* having or showing a mind free from doubt ⟨you're always so *cocksure* about everything⟩ — see CERTAIN 2

cocky *adj* displaying or marked by rude boldness ⟨a *cocky* young actor⟩ — see NERVY 1

cocoon *n* something that encloses another thing especially to protect it ⟨wrapped in a *cocoon* of blankets⟩ — see ¹CASE 1

coddle *vb* **1** to cook in a liquid heated to the point that it gives off steam ⟨*coddled* eggs⟩ — see BOIL 2

2 to treat with great or excessive care ⟨accused the court of *coddling* criminals⟩ — see BABY

code *n* a collection or system of rules of conduct ⟨Hammurabi was an ancient king of Babylon with a famous *code* of laws⟩

synonyms decalogue, law

related words constitution

codger *n* a person of odd or whimsical habits ⟨just an old *codger*⟩ — see ECCENTRIC

codify *vb* to put into a particular arrangement ⟨the rules for the game were *codified* over a hundred years ago⟩ — see ORDER 1

coequal *adj* resembling another in every respect ⟨*coequal* branches of government⟩ — see SAME 1

coerce *vb* to cause (a person) to give in to pressure ⟨was *coerced* into agreeing⟩ — see FORCE

coerced *adj* not made or done willingly or by choice ⟨*coerced* cooperation that couldn't last⟩ — see INVOLUNTARY 1

coercion *n* the use of power to impose one's will on another ⟨a promise obtained by *coercion* is never binding⟩ — see FORCE 2

coeval *adj* existing or occurring at the same period of time ⟨two stars thought to be *coeval*⟩ — see CONTEMPORARY 1

coeval *n* a person who lives at the same time or is about the same age as another ⟨an actor more popular than his *coevals*⟩ — see CONTEMPORARY

coexist *vb* to occur or exist at the same time ⟨able to *coexist* without conflict⟩ — see COINCIDE 1

coexistence *n* the occurrence or existence of several things at once ⟨everyone together in peaceful *coexistence*⟩ — see CONCURRENCE 1

coexistent *adj* **1** existing or occurring at the same period of time ⟨two *coexistent* varieties⟩ — see CONTEMPORARY 1

2 present at the same time and place ⟨*coexistent* dialects spoken in the same town⟩ — see COINCIDENT

coexisting *adj* **1** existing or occurring at the same period of time ⟨*coexisting* populations⟩ — see CONTEMPORARY 1

2 present at the same time and place ⟨*coexisting* beliefs⟩ — see COINCIDENT

coextensive *adj* existing or occurring at the same period of time ⟨a performance fortunately *coextensive* with the time available⟩ — see CONTEMPORARY 1

coffer *n* a specially reinforced container to keep valuables safe ⟨kept the jewels in a locked *coffer*⟩ — see SAFE

coffin *n* a box for holding a dead body ⟨*coffins* are said to be the preferred sleeping places of vampires⟩

synonyms casket

related words sarcophagus, vault; urn; sepulcher (*or* sepulchre), sepulture

cogency *n* **1** the capacity to persuade ⟨the *cogency* of Thomas Paine's case for American independence⟩

synonyms effectiveness, force, forcefulness, persuasiveness

related words impact, punch, strength; soundness, validity; pertinence, relevance

near antonyms invalidity, unsoundness; weakness
antonyms ineffectiveness
2 the quality of an utterance that provokes interest and produces an effect ⟨satirical comments of great *cogency*⟩ — see ¹PUNCH 1

cogent *adj* having the power to persuade ⟨the results of the DNA fingerprinting were the most *cogent* evidence for acquittal⟩
synonyms compelling, conclusive, convincing, decisive, effective, forceful, persuasive, satisfying, strong, telling
related words sound, valid, well-founded; important, significant, weighty; material, pertinent, relevant
near antonyms groundless, invalid, unfounded, unsound; inconsequential, insignificant, unimportant; immaterial, irrelevant
antonyms inconclusive, indecisive, ineffective, unconvincing

cogitate *vb* to give serious and careful thought to ⟨*cogitate* carefully about her choices⟩ — see PONDER

cognizance *n* **1** a state of being aware ⟨take *cognizance* of what is happening⟩ — see ATTENTION 2
2 knowledge gained by personal experience ⟨seemed to have no *cognizance* of last night's events⟩ — see ACQUAINTANCE

cognizant *adj* having specified facts or feelings actively impressed on the mind ⟨not fully *cognizant* of the details⟩ — see CONSCIOUS

cognomen *n* **1** a descriptive or familiar name given instead of or in addition to the one belonging to an individual ⟨earned the *cognomen* of "Butterfingers"⟩ — see NICKNAME
2 a word or combination of words by which a person or thing is regularly known ⟨known by their full *cognomen* rather than a nickname⟩ — see NAME 1

cohere *vb* to be in agreement on every point ⟨the account *coheres*⟩ — see CHECK 1

coherence *n* a balanced, pleasing, or suitable arrangement of parts ⟨a jumbled mess that lacks *coherence*⟩ — see HARMONY 1

coherent *adj* according to the rules of logic ⟨a *coherent* argument⟩ — see LOGICAL 1

cohort *n* **1** a person frequently seen in the company of another ⟨went with a few *cohorts* to the party⟩ — see ASSOCIATE 1
2 one associated with another in wrongdoing ⟨her *cohorts* in crime⟩ — see ACCOMPLICE

coil *vb* to follow a circular or spiral course ⟨a vine *coiling* around a pillar⟩ — see WIND

coiling *adj* turning around an axis like the thread of a screw ⟨the *coiling* strands of rope⟩ — see SPIRAL

coinage *n* something (as a device) created for the first time through the use of the imagination ⟨his *coinage* of the word over a hundred years ago⟩ — see INVENTION 1

coincide *vb* **1** to occur or exist at the same time ⟨the heaviest snowfall of the season *coincided* with the start of our week-long ski vacation⟩
synonyms coexist, concur
related words chance, happen, transpire
near antonyms antedate, precede, predate; follow, succeed
2 to be in agreement on every point ⟨the two lists *coincide*⟩ — see CHECK 1
3 to have or come to the same opinion or point of view ⟨their wishes *coincide* exactly with my desire⟩ — see AGREE 1

coincidence *n* the occurrence or existence of several things at once ⟨the *coincidence* of the last note of the violin with the sound of the bell⟩ — see CONCURRENCE 1

coincident *adj* present at the same time and place ⟨the hard economic times and the *coincident* increase in crime were a double strain on the city's social services⟩
synonyms accompanying, attendant, attending, coexistent, coexisting, coincidental, concomitant, concurrent
related words contemporaneous, contemporary, simultaneous, synchronous; associated, collateral, connected, linked, related; consequent, resultant, resulting; ensuing, following, subsequent; accidental, casual, chance, fluky, fortuitous, freak, incident, incidental
near antonyms unassociated, unconnected, unrelated

coincidental *adj* present at the same time and place ⟨two *coincidental* events happening simultaneously⟩ — see COINCIDENT

coincidentally *adv* at one and the same time ⟨the final stages of the Napoleonic Wars were fought *coincidentally* with the U.S.-British conflict known as the War of 1812⟩ — see TOGETHER 1

coincidently *adv* at one and the same time ⟨the outdoor concert is timed so that its rousing finale occurs *coincidently* with the setting of the summer sun⟩ — see TOGETHER 1

coitus *n* sexual union involving penetration of the vagina by the penis ⟨the act of *coitus* is the natural method by which conception occurs⟩ — see SEXUAL INTERCOURSE

cold *adj* **1** having a low or subnormal temperature ⟨the *cold* climate of the Yukon⟩ ⟨an unusually *cold* spring that was followed by a sweltering summer⟩
synonyms arctic, bitter, cool, coolish, freezing, frigid, frosty, glacial, ice-cold, icy, nipping, nippy, numbing, polar, shivery, snappy, wintry
related words subfreezing, subzero; cutting, keen, penetrating, piercing, sharp; bracing, brisk, crisp, invigorating, rigorous; chilled, cooled, frosted, frozen, iced, refrigerated, unheated
near antonyms lukewarm, tepid; heated, warmed
antonyms broiling, burning, fiery, hot, piping hot, red-hot, roasting, scalding, scorching, searing, sultry, summery, sweltering, torrid, tropical, warm, warming
2 lacking in friendliness or warmth of feeling ⟨the prisoners got only a *cold* stare when they tried to befriend the guard⟩
synonyms chill, chilly, cold-blooded, cool, frigid, frosty, glacial, icy, unfriendly, unsympathetic, wintry
related words hardhearted, heartless, pitiless, uncaring, unfeeling; reserved, soulless, undemonstrative, unemotional, unresponsive; apathetic, indifferent, unenthusiastic, uninterested; aloof, detached, impersonal
near antonyms compassionate, kind, kindhearted; demonstrative, emotional, expressive; eager, enthusiastic, passionate
antonyms cordial, friendly, genial, hearty, sympathetic, warm, warm-blooded, warmhearted
3 having or showing a lack of friendliness or interest in others ⟨received a *cold* reception from the hostess⟩ — see COOL 1
4 having lost consciousness ⟨the boxer was out *cold* for a few minutes⟩ — see UNCONSCIOUS 1

cold *n* a weather condition marked by low temperatures ⟨the *cold* will stay with us for another day, then temperatures should rise⟩
synonyms freeze, snap
related words frost; glaciation, ice age; bite, chill, nip, wintriness
near antonyms heat wave; dog days

cold–blooded *adj* **1** having or showing a lack of sympathy or tender feelings ⟨a *cold-blooded* criminal who never once showed an ounce of mercy to his victims⟩ — see HARD 1
2 lacking in friendliness or warmth of feeling ⟨the *cold-blooded* selfishness shown by the miser when confronted by people in need⟩ — see COLD 2
3 not feeling or showing emotion ⟨a *cold-blooded* assessment of the situation showed that the company needed either to lay off workers or go bankrupt⟩ — see IMPASSIVE 1

cold–shoulder *vb* to deliberately ignore or treat rudely ⟨*cold-shouldered* by his old friends after his family had lost all of its money⟩ — see SNUB 1

cold shoulder *n* treatment that is deliberately unfriendly ⟨at the party the two former friends gave each other the *cold shoulder*⟩
synonyms brush-off, rebuff, repulse, snub
related words dismissal, rejection; banishment, ostracism
near antonyms welcome

coliseum *n* a large usually roofless building for sporting events with tiers of seats for spectators ⟨the local *coliseum* is a standard stop for rock bands on tour⟩ — see STADIUM

collaborate *vb* to participate or assist in a joint effort to accomplish an end ⟨they *collaborated* to finish the job more quickly⟩ — see COOPERATE 1

collaboration *n* **1** the state of having shared interests or efforts (as in social or business matters) ⟨our *collaboration* with the other departments⟩ — see ASSOCIATION 1
2 the work and activity of a number of persons who individually contribute toward the efficiency of the whole ⟨our *collaboration* produced a better result than any of us could have achieved alone⟩ — see TEAMWORK

collapse *n* **1** a complete depletion of energy or strength ⟨suffered a mental *collapse* under the strain⟩ — see FATIGUE
2 a falling short of one's goals ⟨the plan suffered a *collapse* with the first obstacle⟩ — see FAILURE 2

collapse *vb* **1** to fall down or in as a result of physical pressure ⟨the motel balcony *collapsed* under the weight of so many people⟩
synonyms cave (in), crumple, give, go, yield
related words deflate, flatten, melt; break, break down, conk (out), crash, die, fail, give out, stall; burst, shatter, smash; crack, pop, snap
phrases give way
near antonyms inflate, rise, swell
2 to be unsuccessful ⟨the legal case *collapsed* in the face of the opposition's evidence⟩ — see FAIL 2

collar *vb* to take physical control or possession of (something) suddenly or forcibly ⟨she *collared* the boy before he could get into the cookies⟩ — see CATCH 1

colleague *n* a fellow worker ⟨on her first day at work her *colleagues* went out of their way to make her feel welcome⟩
synonyms associate, coworker

related words equal, fellow, peer; accomplice, ally, cohort, collaborator, confederate, partner; buddy, chum, companion, comrade, crony, pal; compatriot, countryman

collect *vb* **1** to gain emotional or mental control of ⟨applicants should *collect* their thoughts while waiting to be interviewed⟩
synonyms calm, compose, contain, control, re-collect, settle
related words allay, lull, quiet, soothe, still, tranquilize (*also* tranquillize)
phrases pull oneself together
2 to gradually form into a layer, pile, or mass ⟨dust has been *collecting* under my bed for years⟩
synonyms accumulate, conglomerate, gather, heap, pile (up)
related words bank, drift, ridge
near antonyms disperse, dissipate, scatter
3 to bring together from several sources into a single volume or list ⟨*collected* information together to make a report⟩ — see COMPILE
4 to bring together in one body or place ⟨she *collects* antique silverware⟩ — see GATHER 1
5 to come together into one body or place ⟨a crowd *collected* at the beach as the sun came out⟩ — see ASSEMBLE 1

collected *adj* free from emotional or mental agitation ⟨stayed calm and *collected*⟩ — see CALM 2

collection *n* **1** an organized group of objects acquired and maintained for study, exhibition, or personal pleasure ⟨his stamp *collection* has become quite valuable⟩
synonyms assemblage, library
related words cache, hoard, repertory, reserve, stock, stockpile, store, supply; accumulation, gathering, heap, pile; clutter, jumble, litter
2 a mass or quantity that has piled up or that has been gathered ⟨a *collection* of lint underneath the dryer⟩ — see ACCUMULATION 1
3 a number of things considered as a unit ⟨a *collection* of similar houses in each neighborhood⟩ — see GROUP 1

collective *adj* used or done by a number of people as a group ⟨the cleanup of the neighborhood park was a *collective* effort for which many people should be thanked⟩
synonyms combined, common, communal, concerted, conjoint, joint, mutual, public, shared, united
related words cooperative, reciprocal, symbiotic; mass, popular; general, generic, universal
near antonyms personal, private; independent, separate; particular, special, specialized
antonyms individual, single, sole

college *n* a group of persons formally joined together for some common interest ⟨a *college* of craftsmen⟩ — see ASSOCIATION 2

collide *vb* **1** to be out of harmony or agreement usually noticeably ⟨*colliding* cultures⟩ — see CLASH
2 to come into usually forceful contact with something ⟨fortunately, I wasn't hurt when my bike *collided* with that fence⟩ — see HIT 2

collision *n* **1** a forceful coming together of two things ⟨the *collision* of two opposing philosophies⟩ — see IMPACT 1
2 the violent coming together of two bodies into destructive contact ⟨a car *collision* on the highway⟩ — see CRASH 1

colloquial *adj* **1** used in or suitable for speech and not formal writing ⟨the new kid's rudeness soon began—to use a *colloquial* expression—to rub me the wrong way⟩
synonyms conversational, informal, nonliterary, unliterary, vernacular, vulgar
related words dialectal, dialectical, nonstandard, substandard, uneducated; slang, slangy
near antonyms educated, standard; correct, genteel, grammatical, proper
antonyms bookish, formal, learned, literary
2 having the style and content of everyday conversation ⟨*colloquial* English⟩ — see CHATTY 1

colloquy *n* **1** a meeting featuring a group discussion ⟨attended a *colloquy* on international politics⟩ — see FORUM
2 an exchange of views for the purpose of exploring a subject or deciding an issue ⟨the two old friends engaged in a spirited *colloquy* on the nature of the universe⟩ — see DISCUSSION 1
3 talking or a talk between two or more people ⟨a casual *colloquy* between two colleagues⟩ — see CONVERSATION

collusion *n* a secret agreement or cooperation between two parties for an illegal or dishonest purpose ⟨there was *collusion* between the two companies to fix prices⟩
synonyms complicity, connivance, conspiracy
related words chicanery, foul play, skulduggery (or skullduggery); double-dealing, duplicity; cover-up, frame-up; intrigue, plot, scheme

colonist *n* a person who settles in a new region ⟨the *colonists* began to desire separation from the old country⟩ — see FRONTIERSMAN

colonizer *n* a person who settles in a new region ⟨the first *colonizers* of the uncharted isle faced many challenges⟩ — see FRONTIERSMAN

colony *n* **1** a settlement in a new country or region ⟨the early history of New York City when it was a Dutch *colony*⟩
synonyms plantation
related words outpost; dependency, mandate, possession, protectorate, territory
2 a group of people with a common interest living in one place ⟨a *colony* of artists⟩ — see COMMUNITY 2

color *n* **1** a property that becomes apparent when light falls on an object and by which things that are identical in form can be distinguished ⟨a shirt that is available in every *color* of the rainbow⟩
synonyms cast, hue, shade, tinge, tint, tone
related words complementary color, primary color, secondary color; brightness, saturation, value; coloration, coloring
2 a substance used to color other materials ⟨added some red *color* to the base paint⟩ — see PIGMENT
3 the hue or appearance of the skin and especially of the face ⟨good *color* in her cheeks⟩ — see COMPLEXION 1
4 colors *pl* a piece of cloth with a special design that is used as an emblem or for signaling ⟨flew their country's *colors* atop the highest mast on the ship⟩ — see FLAG 1

color *vb* **1** to give color or a different color to ⟨she's *colored* her hair for so long and so often that no one knows what her natural color is⟩
synonyms dye, paint, stain, tinge, tint
related words brighten, lighten; darken, tone (down); daub
near antonyms blanch, bleach, whiten

antonyms decolorize
2 to add to the interest of by including made-up details ⟨he gave a highly *colored* version of what really happened⟩ — see EMBROIDER
3 to change so much as to create a wrong impression or alter the meaning of ⟨his story is *colored* by his prejudices⟩ — see GARBLE
4 to develop a rosy facial color (as from excitement or embarrassment) ⟨she *colored* after hearing the nasty remarks⟩ — see BLUSH

colorful *adj* marked by a variety of usually vivid colors ⟨the *colorful* robes and blankets of the Native Americans of the Southwest⟩
synonyms motley, multicolored, polychromatic, polychrome, varicolored, variegated
related words brave, bright, brilliant, gay; flashy, garish, gaudy, loud, showy, splashy; deep, rich, unbleached; checkered, dotted, plaid, striped; colored, pigmented; dappled, shaded; marbled, mottled, piebald, pied, pinto; flecked, spotted, streaked; specked, speckled; banded, barred, brindled (or brindle)
near antonyms achromatic; bleached, decolorized, faded, washed out; dull, faint, gray (*also* grey), neutral, pale, pallid
antonyms colorless; monochromatic, solid

coloring *n* **1** a substance used to color other materials ⟨added more *coloring* to get the perfect shade of blue⟩ — see PIGMENT
2 the hue or appearance of the skin and especially of the face ⟨the pale *coloring* of people of Irish descent⟩ — see COMPLEXION 1
3 the representation of something in terms that go beyond the facts ⟨the bare facts were given a sensational *coloring* in the local news⟩ — see EXAGGERATION

colorless *adj* lacking an addition of color ⟨since we can't decide what color to paint the doghouse, our latest home project remains *colorless* for the time being⟩
synonyms uncolored, undyed, unpainted, unstained, white
related words clear, limpid, liquid, lucent, pellucid, transparent; bleached, faded, washed; dull, faint, gray (*also* grey), neutral, pale, pallid
near antonyms colorful, multicolored, polychromatic, polychrome, varicolored, variegated
antonyms colored, dyed, painted, stained, tinged, tinted

colossal *adj* unusually large ⟨a *colossal* statue of the town's founder⟩ — see HUGE

colossally *adv* to a large extent or degree ⟨the most *colossally* rude person she had ever met⟩ — see GREATLY 2

colosseum *n* a large usually roofless building for sporting events with tiers of seats for spectators ⟨run ten laps around the *colosseum*⟩ — see STADIUM

colossus *n* something that is unusually large and powerful ⟨he was a *colossus* in the art world⟩ — see GIANT

colt *n* a person who is just starting out in a field of activity ⟨a *colt* who looked to the more experienced players for advice⟩ — see BEGINNER

coltish *adj* given to good-natured joking or teasing ⟨*coltish* antics⟩ — see PLAYFUL

column *n* **1** a series of persons or things arranged one behind another ⟨a *column* of ants stretched between the fallen hot dog and the ant hill⟩ — see LINE 1
2 an upright shaft that supports an overhead structure ⟨engraved *columns* supported the arch on either side⟩ — see PILLAR 1

coma *n* a temporary or permanent state of unconsciousness ⟨she was in a *coma* for three days after the accident⟩ — see FAINT

comb *vb* to look through (as a place) carefully or thoroughly in an effort to find or discover something ⟨*combed* the library for the missing book⟩ — see SEARCH 1

combat *n* **1** active fighting during the course of a war ⟨a soldier who served through the war without actually seeing *combat*⟩

  synonyms action, battle

  related words attack, fire; hostilities, operations, warfare; duty, service

  2 a physical dispute between opposing individuals or groups ⟨the two stags entered a furious *combat* for dominance of the herd⟩ — see FIGHT 1

  3 an earnest effort for superiority or victory over another ⟨fierce ideological *combat*⟩ — see CONTEST 1

combat *vb* **1** to oppose (someone) in physical conflict ⟨*combat* fiercely with an enemy⟩ — see FIGHT 1

  2 to strive to reduce or eliminate ⟨*combat* disease⟩ — see FIGHT 2

combative *adj* feeling or displaying eagerness to fight ⟨channeling the natural *combative* impulses into sports⟩ — see BELLIGERENT

combativeness *n* an inclination to fight or quarrel ⟨the boxer was known more for his *combativeness* than his skill⟩ — see BELLIGERENCE

combination *n* **1** a distinct entity formed by the combining of two or more different things ⟨his chief advantage was a *combination* of luck and planning⟩ — see BLEND

  2 the act or an instance of joining two or more things into one ⟨the *combination* of mint and chocolate in a delicious dessert⟩ — see UNION 1

  3 a number of businesses or enterprises united for commercial advantage ⟨the businesses formed a *combination* in an attempt to establish a monopoly⟩ — see CARTEL

  4 an association of persons, parties, or states for mutual assistance and protection ⟨a *combination* of citizens dedicated to fighting higher property taxes⟩ — see CONFEDERACY

combine *n* **1** a number of businesses or enterprises united for commercial advantage ⟨a football *combine*⟩ — see CARTEL

  2 an association of persons, parties, or states for mutual assistance and protection ⟨one of the most notorious *combines* in the history of criminal gangs⟩ — see CONFEDERACY

combine *vb* **1** to come together to form a single unit ⟨distinct pieces *combine* to form a harmonious whole⟩ — see UNITE 1

  2 to turn into a single mass that is more or less the same throughout ⟨*combine* the sugar and flour in a bowl⟩ — see BLEND 1

combined *adj* used or done by a number of people as a group ⟨a *combined* effort on the part of all of the members⟩ — see COLLECTIVE

combining *n* the act or an instance of joining two or more things into one ⟨abhors the *combining* of business and pleasure⟩ — see UNION 1

combust *vb* to be on fire especially brightly ⟨the gasoline *combusted* quickly when a spark was applied⟩ — see BURN 1

combustible *adj* capable of catching or being set on fire ⟨don't store oily rags and other *combustible* materials in a hot attic⟩

  synonyms burnable, flammable, ignitable, inflammable

  related words explosive, incendiary

  near antonyms nonexplosive

  antonyms fireproof, incombustible, noncombustible, nonflammable, noninflammable

combusting *adj* being on fire ⟨*combusting* logs in the fireplace⟩ — see ABLAZE 1

come *vb* **1** to move closer to ⟨*come* here and sit by the fire⟩

  synonyms advance, approach, near

  related words drop (in), enter, pop (in)

  near antonyms depart, exit, leave

  antonyms go, retreat, withdraw

  2 to get to a destination ⟨when do you think they'll *come*?⟩

  synonyms arrive, land, show up, turn up

  related words hit, make, reach; pull (in), touch down; debark, disembark; barge (in), breeze (in), burst (in *or* into), waltz (in)

  antonyms go

  3 to eventually have as a state or quality ⟨your dreams can *come* true⟩ — see BECOME

  4 to take place ⟨no harm will *come* to you⟩ — see HAPPEN

come (to) *vb* **1** to have a total of ⟨your bill *comes to* $53.74⟩ — see AMOUNT (TO) 1

  2 to be the same in meaning or effect ⟨it all *comes to* nothing in the end⟩ — see AMOUNT (TO) 2

come about *vb* to take place ⟨how did all this *come about*?⟩ — see HAPPEN

come around *vb* to gain consciousness again ⟨she *came around* rapidly after falling off the horse⟩ — see COME TO

comeback *n* **1** a quick witty response ⟨always ready with a *comeback* for every insult⟩ — see RETORT 1

  2 something spoken or written in reaction especially to a question ⟨his *comebacks* to the press were always well thought out⟩ — see ANSWER 1

  3 the process or period of gradually regaining one's health and strength ⟨trying to make a *comeback* after a career-threatening injury⟩ — see CONVALESCENCE

comedian *n* a person (as a writer) noted for or specializing in humor ⟨made his living as a *comedian* in night clubs, trying to make people laugh⟩ — see HUMORIST

comedown *n* a loss of status ⟨after a rapid rise to stardom, the rock band's *comedown* was just as quick⟩

  synonyms decline, descent, down, downfall, fall

  related words breakdown, collapse, crash, meltdown, ruin, undoing; defeat, disappointment, reversal, setback; bottom, nadir

  near antonyms advance, headway, progress; flower, heyday, prime

  antonyms aggrandizement, ascent, exaltation, rise, up

come down (with) *vb* to become affected with (a disease or disorder) ⟨*come down with* a cold⟩ — see CONTRACT 1

comedy *n* humorous entertainment ⟨presented a night of *comedy* as part of the week-long celebrations⟩

  synonyms farce, humor, slapstick

  related words burlesque, parody, satire; banter, persiflage, wit; foolery, fun, horseplay, monkeyshines, shenanigans

comeliness *n* the qualities in a person or thing that as a whole give pleasure to the senses ⟨the *comeliness* of the idyllic country town⟩ — see BEAUTY 1

comely *adj* very pleasing to look at ⟨the *comely* grace of a dancer⟩ — see BEAUTIFUL

come out *vb* **1** to come to be ⟨in the end everything *came out* OK⟩
synonyms pan out, prove, turn out
related words develop, emerge, evolve, play out, unfold, work out
2 to come into view ⟨*come out, come out* wherever you are!⟩ — see APPEAR 1
3 to become known ⟨his pride *came out* in his refusal to accept help⟩ — see GET OUT 1
come round *vb* to gain consciousness again ⟨she waved smelling salts under his nose until he *came round*⟩ — see COME TO
come to *vb* to gain consciousness again ⟨after being in a coma for months, the patient suddenly *came to*⟩
synonyms come around, come round, revive
related words pull through, rally, recover; awake, awaken, wake up
near antonyms black out, faint, pass out
comfort *n* **1** a feeling of ease from grief or trouble ⟨the mourners found *comfort* in their pastor's words⟩
synonyms cheer, consolation, relief, solace
related words encouragement, inspiration, uplift; assurance, reassurance; alleviation, assuagement, mitigation; contentment, gladness, happiness; commiseration, empathy, sympathy
near antonyms anguish, distress, heartache, heartbreak, torment, torture
2 something that adds to one's ease ⟨a family campground with all the *comforts* of home⟩
synonyms amenity, convenience, luxury
related words extra; benefit, help, service; delight, indulgence, joy, pleasure
antonyms burden, millstone, weight
3 reduction of or freedom from pain ⟨a life of *comfort*⟩ — see EASE 1
4 something adding to pleasure or comfort but not absolutely necessary ⟨an array of domestic *comforts*⟩ — see LUXURY 1
comfort *vb* **1** to ease the grief or distress of ⟨the minister did his best to *comfort* the victims of the terrible tornado⟩
synonyms assure, cheer, console, reassure, solace, soothe
related words commiserate, condole, empathize, sympathize; boost, buoy (up), elevate, lift, uplift; allay, alleviate, assuage, relieve; calm, quiet, relax, tranquilize (*also* tranquillize)
near antonyms demoralize, discourage, dishearten; fret, upset, worry; aggravate, intensify, worsen; annoy, irk, irritate; harass, pester
antonyms distress, torment, torture, trouble
2 to fill with courage or strength of purpose ⟨*comforted* by the cheerful melody⟩ — see ENCOURAGE 1
comfortable *adj* **1** providing physical comfort ⟨a large, overstuffed chair that is very *comfortable*⟩
synonyms cozy, cushy, easy, snug, soft
related words relaxing, reposeful, restful; genial, hospitable, inviting, pleasant; commodious, roomy, spacious; homelike, homely, homey
near antonyms hard, harsh, severe; inhospitable, uninviting, unpleasant
antonyms uncomfortable
2 enjoying physical comfort ⟨make yourself *comfortable* in the living room while I fix us some snacks⟩
synonyms cozy, relaxed, snug
related words content, contented, pleased, satisfied; peaceful, resting; easygoing, laid-back; undisturbed, unperturbed, untroubled

phrases at ease, at home
near antonyms discontented, displeased, dissatisfied; agitated, disturbed, perturbed, troubled
antonyms uncomfortable
3 being more than enough without being excessive ⟨a *comfortable* income⟩ — see PLENTIFUL
comforting *adj* **1** making one feel good inside ⟨the *comforting* smell of fresh bread⟩ — see HEARTWARMING
2 tending to calm the emotions and relieve stress ⟨a long *comforting* soak in a hot bath⟩ — see SOOTHING 1
comforting *n* the giving of hope and strength in times of grief, distress, or suffering ⟨the *comforting* of the sick has always been regarded as one of the major acts of charity⟩ — see CONSOLATION 1
comfortless *adj* **1** causing discomfort ⟨a *comfortless* sofa⟩ — see UNCOMFORTABLE 1
2 causing or marked by an atmosphere lacking in cheer ⟨spent a night in a sleazy *comfortless* hotel⟩ — see GLOOMY 1
comic *adj* causing or intended to cause laughter ⟨a *comic* monologue⟩ — see FUNNY 1
comic *n* **1** a person (as a writer) noted for or specializing in humor ⟨a well-known TV *comic*⟩ — see HUMORIST
2 a series of drawings that tell a story or part of a story ⟨posted a *comic* by the water cooler⟩ — see COMIC STRIP
comical *adj* **1** causing or intended to cause laughter ⟨the *comical* antics of the clown⟩ — see FUNNY 1
2 so foolish or pointless as to be worthy of scornful laughter ⟨the *comical* expression on his face⟩ — see RIDICULOUS 1
comic strip *n* a series of drawings that tell a story or part of a story ⟨a *comic strip* that is beloved by both children and adults⟩
synonyms cartoon, comic, funny
related words comic book, funny paper(s); animated cartoon, animation; caricature
coming *adj* **1** being soon to appear or take place ⟨*coming* attractions⟩ — see FORTHCOMING
2 being the one that comes immediately after another ⟨in the *coming* year⟩ — see NEXT
3 of a time after the present ⟨over the *coming* weeks⟩ — see FUTURE
comity *n* peaceful coexistence ⟨group activities promoting *comity*⟩ — see HARMONY 2
command *n* **1** a statement of what to do that must be obeyed by those concerned ⟨the captain's *commands* were followed without question⟩
synonyms behest, charge, commandment, decree, dictate, direction, directive, edict, instruction, order, word
related words demand, requirement; injunction, mandate; law, precept, rule; ordinance, regulation, statute
near antonyms appeal, entreaty, petition, plea, urging; proposal, recommendation, suggestion
2 a highly developed skill in or knowledge of something ⟨a *command* of French that is the result of a year spent in France as an exchange student⟩
synonyms mastership, mastery, proficiency
related words virtuosity; fluency, literacy; experience, expertise, know-how, practice (*also* practise), skill(s); acquaintance, familiarity, intimacy
near antonyms incompetence, incompetency; ignorance, illiteracy, unfamiliarity
3 the place from which a commander runs operations ⟨the general set up his *command* in the old port city⟩
synonyms base, headquarters
related words home, seat

4 a place from which authority is exercised ⟨central *command*⟩ — see SEAT 1

5 the right or means to command or control others ⟨the army officer in *command*⟩ — see POWER 1

command *vb* **1** to issue orders to (someone) by right of authority ⟨the general *commanded* the troops to advance⟩

synonyms adjure, bid, boss (around), charge, direct, enjoin, instruct, order, tell

related words ask, petition, request; beg, beseech, entreat; advise, counsel, warn; appoint, assign, authorize, commission; oversee, superintend, supervise; conduct, control, lead, manage; coerce, compel, constrain, force, oblige, require

near antonyms comply (with), follow, keep, observe

antonyms mind, obey

2 to give an order ⟨the governor has *commanded* that all state flags be flown at half-mast⟩

synonyms decree, dictate, direct, ordain, order

related words ask, petition, request; demand, require

phrases call for

3 to ask for (something) earnestly or with authority ⟨*command* loyalty from her subordinates⟩ — see DEMAND 1

4 to exercise authority or power over ⟨the general ultimately *commands* all the troops in the nation⟩ — see GOVERN 1

5 to keep, control, or experience as one's own ⟨*commands* many resources⟩ — see HAVE 1

6 to look down on ⟨a hill that *commands* the city⟩ — see OVERLOOK 1

7 to serve as leader of ⟨*command* the entire department⟩ — see LEAD 2

8 to set or receive as a price ⟨*commands* a high fee⟩ — see CHARGE 1

commandant *n* one in official command especially of a military force or base ⟨the *commandant* of a naval district⟩ — see COMMANDER 1

commandeer *vb* **1** to take control of (a vehicle) by force ⟨an airliner *commandeered* by terrorists⟩

synonyms hijack (*also* highjack)

related words appropriate, confiscate, expropriate, seize

2 to take or make use of without authority or right ⟨*commandeer* his entire family to help clean the garage⟩ — see APPROPRIATE 1

commander *n* **1** one in official command especially of a military force or base ⟨a surrender of the fort by the *commander* without a single shot having been fired⟩

synonyms captain, commandant, commanding officer

related words commissioned officer

phrases commander in chief

2 a person in overall command of a ship ⟨*commander* of the USS Enterprise⟩ — see CAPTAIN 1

commanding *adj* highest in rank or authority ⟨he sought a *commanding* position in all he did⟩ — see HEAD

commanding officer *n* one in official command especially of a military force or base ⟨reported directly to the *commanding officer*⟩ — see COMMANDER 1

commandment *n* a statement of what to do that must be obeyed by those concerned ⟨according to tradition, Moses brought ten *commandments* from God down from the mountain⟩ — see COMMAND 1

commemorate *vb* **1** to be a memorial of ⟨a stone obelisk *commemorates* the Battle of Bunker Hill⟩

synonyms memorialize

related words celebrate, keep, observe, remember; enshrine, exalt, glorify, honor; bless, consecrate, sanctify, solemnize

near antonyms disgrace, dishonor

2 to act properly in relation to ⟨*commemorate* Memorial Day with the laying of wreaths⟩ — see KEEP 1

commemorating *adj* serving to preserve the memory of a person, thing, or an event ⟨a *commemorating* festival in honor of the victory⟩ — see COMMEMORATIVE

commemorative *adj* serving to preserve the memory of a person, thing, or an event ⟨*commemorative* stamps for the stars of American popular music⟩

synonyms commemorating, memorial, memorializing

related words dedicatory, testimonial; enshrining, glorifying, honorary

commemorative *n* something that serves to keep alive the memory of a person or event ⟨a coin was issued as a *commemorative* of the event⟩ — see MEMORIAL

commence *vb* **1** to take the first step in (a process or course of action) ⟨*commence* the festivities⟩ — see BEGIN 1

2 to come into existence ⟨the games *commenced* early in the morning⟩ — see BEGIN 2

commencement *n* the point at which something begins ⟨there was a large turnout at the *commencement* of the conference, but the numbers dwindled as it progressed⟩ — see BEGINNING

commend *vb* to put (something) into the possession or safekeeping of another ⟨I *commend* my fate into your hands⟩ — see GIVE 2

commendable *adj* deserving of high regard or great approval ⟨a *commendable* attitude toward studying⟩ — see ADMIRABLE

commendation *n* **1** a formal recognition of an achievement or praiseworthy deed ⟨a firefighter who has been awarded several *commendations* for bravery⟩

synonyms acknowledgment (*also* acknowledgement), citation

related words decoration, medal, ribbon; accolade, award, prize, tribute; dedication

2 a formal expression of praise ⟨a new novel that has received *commendations* from most of the critics⟩ — see ENCOMIUM

commendatory *adj* expressing approval ⟨on the basis of several *commendatory* letters from his teachers, the student was admitted to the advanced studies program⟩ — see FAVORABLE 1

commensurate *adj* corresponding in size, amount, extent, or degree ⟨was given a job *commensurate* with her abilities and experience⟩ — see PROPORTIONAL

comment *n* **1** a briefly expressed opinion ⟨just ate the food without offering even a single *comment*⟩ — see REMARK

2 **comments** *pl* a series of explanations or observations on something (as an event) ⟨gave his *comments* on the political events of the previous week⟩ — see COMMENTARY

comment *vb* to make a statement of one's opinion ⟨*commenting* on recent developments⟩ — see REMARK 1

commentary *n* a series of explanations or observations on something (as an event) ⟨the TV anchors provided a running *commentary* on the parade⟩

synonyms analysis, comment, exposition

related words annotation, explication; note, observation, remark; report, review, write-up

commerce *n* the buying and selling of goods especially on a large scale and between different places ⟨a gov-

ernment agency in charge of regulating interstate *commerce*⟩
synonyms business, marketplace, trade, traffic
related words free trade; dealings, horse-trading; merchandising, retailing, wholesaling; bartering
commercial *adj* fit or likely to be sold especially on a large scale ⟨the *commercial* fare produced by the Hollywood movie studios⟩
synonyms marketable, salable (*or* saleable)
related words mass-produced, wholesale
antonyms noncommercial, nonsalable, uncommercial, unmarketable, unsalable
commingle *vb* to turn into a single mass that is more or less the same throughout ⟨*commingled* the remaining dry ingredients before adding them to the batter⟩ — see BLEND 1
commiserate (with) *vb* to have sympathy for ⟨we *commiserated with* him but there was little we could do to make him feel better⟩ — see PITY
commiseration *n* 1 sorrow or the capacity to feel sorrow for another's suffering or misfortune ⟨letters of *commiseration* sent to the hospitalized student⟩ — see SYMPATHY 1
2 the capacity for feeling for another's unhappiness or misfortune ⟨a heartless businessman with no *commiseration* for the less fortunate⟩ — see HEART 1
commissary *n* a person who acts or does business for another ⟨serve as *commissary* of the whole diocese⟩ ⟨a *commissary* judge⟩ — see AGENT 2
commission *n* 1 the granting of power to perform various acts or duties ⟨President Jefferson's *commission* to Lewis and Clark to explore the Louisiana Territory⟩
synonyms accreditation, authorization, delegation, license (*or* licence), mandate
related words commendation, consignment, entrustment; facilitation, fostering, promotion; commanding, directing, ordering
2 the doing of an action ⟨a single burglar was responsible for the *commission* of all the break-ins⟩
synonyms accomplishment, achievement, discharge, enactment, execution, fulfillment, implementation, performance, perpetration
related words dispatch, expedition; administration, direction, handling, management; application, operation, practice (*also* practise)
antonyms nonfulfillment, nonperformance
3 a select group of persons assigned to consider or take action on some matter ⟨reported to a UN *commission*⟩ — see COMMITTEE
4 the state or fact of being chosen for a position or duty ⟨her *commission* as head of the investigation⟩ — see APPOINTMENT 1
commission *vb* 1 to appoint as one's representative ⟨*commission* a deputy⟩ — see DELEGATE 1
2 to give official or legal power to ⟨was *commissioned* lieutenant⟩ — see AUTHORIZE 1
3 to give a task, duty, or responsibility to ⟨was *commissioned* to do the biography⟩ — see ENTRUST 1
4 to pick (someone) by one's authority for a specific position or duty ⟨*commissioned* him to paint a mural⟩ — see APPOINT 2
commit *vb* 1 to carry through (as a process) to completion ⟨accused of *committing* a felony⟩ — see PERFORM 1
2 to obligate by prior agreement ⟨we were *committed* to finishing the project⟩ — see PLEDGE 1

3 to put (something) into the possession or safekeeping of another ⟨*commit* only some power to each official⟩ — see GIVE 2
4 to put in or as if in prison ⟨*committed* the criminal to prison⟩ — see IMPRISON
commitment *n* something one must do because of prior agreement ⟨they made a *commitment* to pay their bill when they received their order⟩ — see OBLIGATION
committee *n* a select group of persons assigned to consider or take action on some matter ⟨a *committee* in charge of planning the organization's annual Christmas party⟩
synonyms commission, panel
related words subcommittee; delegation, mission; assembly, body, congress, convocation, council, synod
commodious *adj* more than adequate or average in capacity ⟨a *commodious* closet⟩ — see SPACIOUS
commodities *n pl* products that are bought and sold in business ⟨*commodities* such as sugar or oil⟩ — see MERCHANDISE
common *adj* 1 often observed or encountered ⟨horse ranches are a *common* sight in that part of the state⟩
synonyms commonplace, everyday, familiar, frequent, garden, household, ordinary, routine, ubiquitous, usual
related words normal, regular, standard; general, universal; ceaseless, constant, continual, continuous, incessant, unceasing; popular, prevailing, prevalent, rampant; perennial, recurrent, repeated
near antonyms aberrant, abnormal, irregular, unnatural; intermittent, occasional, sporadic
antonyms extraordinary, infrequent, rare, uncommon, unfamiliar, unusual
2 being of the type that is encountered in the normal course of events ⟨a common *sparrow*⟩ — see ORDINARY 1
3 belonging or relating to the whole ⟨facts of *common* knowledge⟩ — see GENERAL 1
4 belonging to the class of people of low social or economic rank ⟨the *common* folk⟩ — see IGNOBLE 1
5 held by or applicable to a majority of the people ⟨the *common* good⟩ — see GENERAL 3
6 used or done by a number of people as a group ⟨had several features in *common*⟩ — see COLLECTIVE
7 of average to below average quality ⟨a *common* ordinary blanket⟩ — see MEDIOCRE 1
8 of low quality ⟨*common* unskilled labor⟩ — see CHEAP 2
9 lacking in refinement or good taste ⟨*common* manners⟩ — see COARSE 2
commoners *n pl* the body of the community as contrasted with the elite ⟨the British nobles used to believe that they were fundamentally better than the *commoners*⟩ — see MASS 1
commonly *adv* according to the usual course of things ⟨they can *commonly* be found hanging around the mall⟩ — see NATURALLY 2
commonness *n* 1 the fact or state of happening often ⟨as much *commonness* as the rising of the sun⟩ — see FREQUENCY
2 the quality or state of lacking refinement or good taste ⟨the socialites were appalled by the newcomer's *commonness*⟩ — see VULGARITY 1
commonplace *adj* 1 being of the type that is encountered in the normal course of events ⟨a *commonplace* occurrence⟩ — see ORDINARY 1
2 often observed or encountered ⟨the large mergers that had become *commonplace*⟩ — see COMMON 1

3 used or heard so often as to be dull ⟨the *commonplace* plot twist of the evil twin⟩ — see STALE

commonplace *n* an idea or expression that has been used by many people ⟨the familiar summertime *commonplace* that "it's not the heat, it's the humidity"⟩
synonyms banality, cliché, platitude, shibboleth, truism
related words inanity; generality, generalization, simplification; adage, proverb, saw, saying; old wives' tale, stereotype
near antonyms profundity

commonsense *adj* based on sound reasoning or information ⟨the *commonsense* interpretation⟩ — see GOOD 1

common sense *n* the ability to make intelligent decisions especially in everyday matters ⟨*common sense* should tell you not to meet face-to-face with someone who is just an online acquaintance⟩
synonyms discreetness, discretion, horse sense, levelheadedness, prudence, sense, sensibleness, wisdom, wit
related words street smarts; farsightedness, foresight, foresightedness, judgment (*or* judgement); brains, gray matter, intelligence; logicalness, practicality, rationality; discernment, discrimination, insight, sagacity, sapience; acumen, astuteness, keenness, penetration, perspicacity, shrewdness; care, caution, circumspection, precaution, premeditation
near antonyms shortsightedness; brainlessness, foolishness, idiocy, senselessness, stupidity; carelessness, heedlessness
antonyms imprudence, indiscretion

commonwealth *n* a body of people composed of one or more nationalities usually with its own territory and government ⟨the *Commonwealth* of Massachusetts⟩ — see NATION

commotion *n* a state of noisy, confused activity ⟨the *commotion* created when the nation's top rock band arrived in town⟩
synonyms bother, bustle, clatter, disturbance, furor, furore, fuss, hubbub, hullabaloo, hurly-burly, pandemonium, pother, row, ruckus, ruction, rumpus, shindy, squall, stew, stir, storm, to-do, tumult, turmoil, uproar, welter, whirl
related words cacophony, clamor, din, howl, hue and cry, outcry, noise, racket, roar; disorder, unrest, upheaval; eruption, flare-up, flurry, outbreak, outburst; brawl, fracas, fray, hassle, melee, scuffle; dither, fever, fret, lather, tizzy
near antonyms calm, hush, peace, quiet, quietude, rest, stillness, tranquillity (*or* tranquility); order, orderliness

communal *adj* used or done by a number of people as a group ⟨*communal* property⟩ — see COLLECTIVE

commune *vb* to form a close personal relationship ⟨after a week in the wilderness, the scouts were really starting to *commune* with nature⟩
synonyms click, relate
related words bond; befriend

communicable *adj* capable of being passed by physical contact from one person to another ⟨*communicable* diseases⟩ — see CONTAGIOUS 1

communicate *vb* **1** to cause (something) to pass from one to another ⟨the infected cook unknowingly *communicated* the disease to hundreds of people⟩
synonyms convey, impart, spread, transfer, transfuse, transmit
related words deliver, hand over, surrender, turn over; broadcast, diffuse, disseminate, propagate; contaminate, infect, poison

near antonyms catch, come down (with), contract
2 to engage in an exchange of information or ideas ⟨for decades the two medical centers have been *communicating* about cancer research⟩
synonyms brainstorm, intercommunicate
related words correspond; converse, talk; bond, commune, relate; accost, approach, contact

communicate (with) *vb* to transmit information or requests to ⟨*communicating with* other ham radio enthusiasts⟩ — see CONTACT

communication *n* a piece of conveyed information ⟨the latest *communication* from the crew of the space station⟩
synonyms dispatch, message
related words bulletin, communiqué, report; memo, memorandum, notice; epistle, letter, missive, note; electronic mail, e-mail; intelligence, news, tidings, word; command, directive, instruction, order

communion *n* a friendly relationship marked by ready communication and mutual understanding ⟨a feeling of *communion* with her peer group⟩ — see RAPPORT

community *n* **1** the people living in a particular area ⟨the whole *community* rallied to the aid of the family who had lost its home⟩
synonyms neighborhood
related words city, commune, town, village; denizens, dwellers, inhabitants, residents; citizenry, culture, people, populace, public, society
2 a group of people with a common interest living in one place ⟨a picturesque seacoast village that is known for its sizable *community* of artists⟩
synonyms colony
related words circle, clique, coterie, set, society; band, company, troop; clan, family
3 a group of people sharing a common interest and relating together socially ⟨a *community* of retired people⟩ — see GANG 2
4 the body of people in a profession or field of activity ⟨members of the professional *community*⟩ — see CORPS
5 the quality or state of having many qualities in common ⟨*community* of interests⟩ — see SIMILARITY 1

commutation *n* a giving or taking of one thing of value in return for another ⟨the international *commutation* of experts⟩ — see EXCHANGE 1

commute *vb* to give up (something) and take something else in return ⟨*commuting* foreign money to domestic⟩ — see CHANGE 3

compact *adj* **1** having a consistency that does not easily yield to pressure ⟨a *compact* foam core⟩ — see FIRM 2
2 having little space between items or parts ⟨*compact* soil⟩ — see CLOSE 1
3 marked by the use of few words to convey much information or meaning ⟨*compact* prose⟩ — see CONCISE

compact *n* **1** a formal agreement between two or more nations or peoples ⟨a five-nation *compact* to control drug traffic⟩ — see TREATY
2 an arrangement about action to be taken ⟨a *compact* with the devil⟩ — see AGREEMENT 2

compact *vb* **1** to bring (something) to a central point or under a single control ⟨racial and religious similarities helped *compact* the tribes into a great nation⟩ — see CENTRALIZE
2 to reduce in size or volume by or as if by pressing parts or members together ⟨*compact* the snow into a tight ball for throwing⟩ — see COMPRESS 1

compacting *n* the act or process of reducing the size or volume of something by or as if by pressing ⟨the *compacting* of wool fibers into felt⟩ — see COMPRESSION

compactly *adv* in a few words ⟨write the instructions as *compactly* as possible⟩ — see SHORTLY 1

compactness *n* the quality or state of being marked by or using only few words to convey much meaning ⟨the *compactness* of his prose made it easy to read quickly, but harder to understand fully⟩ — see SUCCINCTNESS

companion *n* 1 a person frequently seen in the company of another ⟨the *companions* of one's youth⟩ — see ASSOCIATE 1

2 one that accompanies another for protection, guidance, or as a courtesy ⟨took a *companion* to the ball⟩ — see ESCORT

3 either of a pair matched in one or more qualities ⟨a sketch that is a *companion* to the original drawing⟩ — see MATE 1

4 something that is found along with something else ⟨the report and its *companion* recommendations⟩ — see ACCOMPANIMENT

companionable *adj* 1 having or showing kindly feeling and sincere interest ⟨*companionable* laughter⟩ — see FRIENDLY 1

2 likely to seek or enjoy the company of others ⟨*companionable* friends⟩ — see CONVIVIAL

companionship *n* the feeling of closeness and friendship that exists between companions ⟨the widow's pet cats provided her with her only *companionship*⟩

synonyms camaraderie, company, comradeship, fellowship, society

related words amity, benevolence, cordiality, friendliness, friendship, goodwill, kindliness; civility, comity, concord, harmony, rapport; charity, generosity; affinity, compassion, empathy, sympathy; chumminess, familiarity, inseparability, intimacy, nearness; affection, devotion, fondness, love

near antonyms forlornness, loneliness, lonesomeness

company *n* 1 an organized group of stage performers ⟨a city that is fortunate enough to have two thriving opera *companies*⟩

synonyms troop, troupe

related words stock company; cast, dramatis personae, ensemble

2 a group of people working together on a task ⟨a *company* of horsemen⟩ — see GANG 1

3 a commercial or industrial activity or organization ⟨she works for a construction *company*⟩ — see ENTERPRISE 1

4 the feeling of closeness and friendship that exists between companions ⟨enjoying each other's *company*⟩ — see COMPANIONSHIP

comparable *adj* having qualities in common ⟨two *comparable* selections that are hard to choose between⟩ — see ALIKE

comparative *adj* being such only when compared to something else ⟨if you consider the multimillionaire's yearly income, we're living in *comparative* poverty⟩

synonyms approximate, near, relative

related words alike, comparable, similar; equal, equivalent

near antonyms genuine, real, true

antonyms absolute, complete, downright, out-and-out, outright, perfect, pure, unqualified

compare *vb* 1 to describe as similar ⟨reviews that *compared* the adventure movie to a thrilling ride on a roller coaster⟩

synonyms bracket, equate, liken

related words associate, connect, couple, link; allude, refer, relate; equal, match, parallel

antonyms contrast

2 to regard or represent as equal or comparable ⟨*compared* the restaurant's food to the nectar of the gods⟩ — see EQUATE 1

compare (with) *vb* to come near or nearer to in character or quality ⟨nothing *compares with* you⟩ — see APPROXIMATE

compartment *n* one of the parts into which an enclosed space is divided ⟨a backpack with many handy *compartments* for storing your camping gear⟩

synonyms bay, cabin, cell, chamber, cubicle

related words cubbyhole, pigeonhole, snuggery [*chiefly British*]; alcove, niche, nook, recess; cabinet, drawer; cavity, hole, hollow; booth, crib, stall; crypt, vault

compass *n* 1 an area over which activity, capacity, or influence extends ⟨within the *compass* of my voice⟩ — see RANGE 2

2 the line or relatively narrow space that marks the outer limit of something ⟨within the *compass* of the city walls⟩ — see BORDER 1

compass *vb* 1 to carry through (as a process) to completion ⟨attempting more than his abilities could *compass*⟩ — see PERFORM 1

2 to pass completely around ⟨*compass* the earth⟩ — see ENCIRCLE 1

compassion *n* 1 sorrow or the capacity to feel sorrow for another's suffering or misfortune ⟨treats the homeless with great *compassion*⟩ — see SYMPATHY 1

2 the capacity for feeling for another's unhappiness or misfortune ⟨had a great deal of *compassion* for his situation⟩ — see HEART 1

compassionate *adj* 1 having or marked by sympathy and consideration for others ⟨a *compassionate* friend⟩ — see HUMANE 1

2 having or showing the capacity for sharing the feelings of another ⟨a *compassionate* smile⟩ — see SYMPATHETIC 1

compatibility *n* peaceful coexistence ⟨*compatibility* between church and state⟩ — see HARMONY 2

compatible *adj* 1 having or marked by agreement in feeling or action ⟨*compatible* as friends⟩ — see HARMONIOUS 3

2 not having or showing any apparent conflict ⟨*compatible* theories⟩ — see CONSISTENT

compatriot *n* a person living in or originally from the same country as another ⟨an appeal to all of his *compatriots* to come to their country's aid in its hour of need⟩

synonyms countryman

related words nationalist, patriot; citizen, national, subject; aborigine, native; homeboy, resident

near antonyms alien, foreigner, immigrant, outsider

compel *vb* to cause (a person) to give in to pressure ⟨public opinion *compelled* her to make the decision⟩ — see FORCE

compelling *adj* having the power to persuade ⟨made a *compelling* argument⟩ — see COGENT

compendious *adj* 1 covering everything or all important points ⟨her *compendious* knowledge of the subject⟩ — see ENCYCLOPEDIC

2 marked by the use of few words to convey much information or meaning ⟨a *compendious* summary⟩ — see CONCISE

compensate *vb* **1** to provide (someone) with a just payment for loss or injury ⟨you'll have to *compensate* the neighbors for cutting down their tree⟩
synonyms indemnify, recompense, recoup, remunerate, requite
related words refund, reimburse, repay; redress, remedy, repair; discharge, pay, quit
2 to give (someone) the sum of money owed for goods or services received ⟨*compensate* them for their efforts⟩ — see PAY 1

compensate (for) *vb* to balance with an equal force so as to make ineffective ⟨*compensating for* the evil done with comparable good⟩ — see OFFSET

compensation *n* **1** payment to another for a loss or injury ⟨a warehouse worker who received a large *compensation* for his crippling injury while on the job⟩
synonyms damages, indemnification, indemnity, quittance, recompense, recoupment, redress, remuneration, reparation, requital, restitution, satisfaction
related words amends, atonement, expiation; refund, reimbursement, repayment; adjustment, settlement; punishment, reprisal, retaliation
2 something (as money) that is given or received in return for goods or services ⟨fair *compensation* for his work on the project⟩ — see PAYMENT 2
3 the act of offering money in exchange for goods or services ⟨his *compensation* was greatly appreciated⟩ — see PAYMENT 1

compete *vb* to engage in a contest ⟨prizefighters *competing* for the world heavyweight championship⟩
synonyms battle, contend, fight, race, vie
related words challenge, engage, play; jockey, maneuver; go out, try out; train, work

competence *n* the physical or mental power to do something ⟨tried to determine his *competence* to finish the task without help⟩ — see ABILITY

competency *n* the physical or mental power to do something ⟨she handled all of her assignments with a great deal of *competency*⟩ — see ABILITY

competent *adj* having the required skills for an acceptable level of performance ⟨any *competent* mechanic should be able to fix that⟩
synonyms able, capable, fit, good, qualified, suitable
related words accomplished, ace, adept, experienced, expert, master, masterful, masterly, practiced (*or* practised), proficient, seasoned, skilled, skillful, veteran; prepared, schooled, trained
near antonyms inexperienced, inexpert, unseasoned, unskilled, unskillful; unprepared, unschooled, untrained; beginning, green, new, raw, untested, untried
antonyms incompetent, inept, poor, unfit, unqualified

competently *adv* in a skillful or expert manner ⟨performed at least *competently* if not superbly⟩ — see WELL 3

competition *n* **1** a competitive encounter between individuals or groups carried on for amusement, exercise, or in pursuit of a prize ⟨a *competition* between two fierce rivals⟩ — see GAME 1
2 one who strives for the same thing as another ⟨tried to analyze his *competition*⟩ — see COMPETITOR

competitor *n* one who strives for the same thing as another ⟨the *competitors* for the science award come from the best high schools in the country⟩
synonyms challenger, competition, contender, contestant, rival
related words finalist, semifinalist; entrant, player; adversary, antagonist, opponent

compilation *n* a collection of writings ⟨she bound a *compilation* of her best work into a single volume⟩ — see ANTHOLOGY

compile *vb* to bring together from several sources into a single volume or list ⟨*compiled* the best short stories ever written into one fat book⟩
synonyms collect
related words edit, redraft, revamp, revise, rework; accumulate, amass, assemble, gather, group

complacence *n* an often unjustified feeling of being pleased with oneself or with one's situation or achievements ⟨the *complacence* of some of the rich kids at the exclusive private school⟩
synonyms complacency, conceit, conceitedness, ego, egotism, pompousness, pride, pridefulness, self-admiration, self-conceit, self-esteem, self-importance, self-satisfaction, smugness, vaingloriousness, vainglory, vainness, vanity
related words assurance, confidence, self-assurance, self-confidence; self-righteousness; arrogance, disdainfulness, haughtiness, imperiousness, lordliness, self-assertion, snobbishness, superciliousness, superiority; overconfidence, presumption; pretense (*or* pretence), pretension, pretentiousness; egoism, self-centeredness, selfishness; self-respect
near antonyms diffidence, self-doubt; altruism, unselfishness; bashfulness, demureness, shyness, timidity, timidness; passiveness, passivity
antonyms humbleness, humility, modesty

complacency *n* an often unjustified feeling of being pleased with oneself or with one's situation or achievements ⟨a momentary *complacency* that was quickly dispelled by reality⟩ — see COMPLACENCE

complacent *adj* having too high an opinion of oneself ⟨they grew *complacent* and reacted badly to unexpected events⟩ — see CONCEITED

complain *vb* to express dissatisfaction, pain, or resentment usually tiresomely ⟨the time-honored tradition of students *complaining* about the food in the cafeteria⟩
synonyms beef, bellyache, carp, crab, croak, fuss, gripe, grouse, growl, grumble, kick, moan, murmur, mutter, repine, squawk, wail, whine, yammer
related words object (to), protest, quarrel (with); cavil, quibble; fret, stew, worry; blubber, cry, sob; bemoan, bewail, deplore, lament
near antonyms accept, bear, countenance, endure, tolerate; applaud, cheer, commend
antonyms rejoice

complainant *n* the person in a legal proceeding who makes a charge of wrongdoing against another ⟨the *complainant* charged that the defendant had broken the ironclad contract that both had signed⟩
synonyms plaintiff, suer
related words accuser; litigant, party, suitor; appellant, petitioner, pleader
near antonyms accused
antonyms defendant

complainer *n* **1** a person who makes frequent complaints usually about little things ⟨she unfortunately got a reputation as a *complainer* after finding fault with the food⟩ — see CRYBABY
2 an irritable and complaining person ⟨a chronic *complainer*⟩ — see GROUCH

complaint *n* **1** an expression of dissatisfaction, pain, or resentment ⟨a warning that if there were any more *complaints*, we were turning around and not going to the beach after all⟩

synonyms beef, fuss, grievance, gripe, grumble, murmur, plaint, squawk

related words challenge, demur, expostulation, kick, objection, protest, quibble, remonstrance

near antonyms commendation, compliment, plaudit; acclaim, applause, praise; approval, endorsement, sanction

2 a feeling or declaration of disapproval or dissent ⟨we proceeded despite the *complaints* of the authorities⟩ — see OBJECTION

3 a formal claim of criminal wrongdoing against a person ⟨filed a *complaint* in court⟩ — see CHARGE 1

4 an abnormal state that disrupts a plant's or animal's normal bodily functioning ⟨various medicines for his many *complaints*⟩ — see DISEASE

complaisance *n* a desire or disposition to please ⟨the *complaisance* of his girlfriend is such that she goes along with everything he says⟩

synonyms amenability, amiability, good-naturedness

related words affability, amicability, congeniality, cordiality, friendliness, geniality, sociability; agreeableness, graciousness, pleasantness; kindheartedness, kindliness, warmheartedness; compliance, docility, passivity, submissiveness

near antonyms disagreeableness, sullenness, surliness, ungraciousness; disobedience, intractability, recalcitrance

complement *n* **1** something that serves to complete or make up for a deficiency in something else ⟨with his practicality and her refreshing enthusiasm, they are perfect *complements* to each other⟩

synonyms supplement

related words addendum, addition, appendix; adjunct, annex, appendage, extension; accessory, appliance, attachment; additive, filler

2 the largest number or amount that something can hold ⟨a full *complement* of sailors on the ship⟩ — see CAPACITY 1

complement *vb* to serve as a completing element to ⟨this cap *complements* your Boy Scout uniform⟩

synonyms complete, round (off *or* out)

related words finish (off), flesh (out); adorn, beautify, decorate, embellish; better, enhance, improve; constitute, form, make up

complementary *adj* related to each other in such a way that one completes the other ⟨the *complementary* contributions of the cooking and cleanup committees were essential to the success of the church barbecue⟩

synonyms reciprocal, supplementary

related words cooperative, mutual, symbiotic; collective, combined, common, communal, conjoint, joint, shared, united

antonyms noncomplementary, nonreciprocal

complete *adj* **1** not lacking any part or member that properly belongs to it ⟨a *complete* deck of cards⟩

synonyms comprehensive, entire, full, grand, intact, integral, perfect, plenary, total, whole

related words unabridged, uncut, undiminished; all-out, exhaustive, extensive; full-blown, full-fledged, full-scale

near antonyms abbreviated, abridged, cut, diminished, reduced

antonyms imperfect, incomplete, partial

2 brought or having come to an end ⟨your education is never *complete*—there's always something more to learn⟩

synonyms completed, concluded, done, down, ended, finished, over, terminated, through, up

related words accomplished, achieved, attained, compassed, realized; dead, defunct, extinct, obsolete; expired

antonyms continuing, incomplete, ongoing, uncompleted, unfinished

3 covering everything or all important points ⟨*complete* coverage of the sporting events⟩ — see ENCYCLOPEDIC

4 having no exceptions or restrictions ⟨he's a *complete* lunatic⟩ — see ABSOLUTE 2

5 trying all possibilities ⟨a *complete* search of the computer file⟩ — see EXHAUSTIVE

complete *vb* **1** to bring (something) to a state where nothing remains to be done ⟨*complete* the assignment with time to spare⟩ — see FINISH 1

2 to serve as a completing element to ⟨the bird's beautiful song *completes* its charm⟩ — see COMPLEMENT

completed *adj* brought or having come to an end ⟨hand in your *completed* assignments⟩ — see COMPLETE 2

completely *adv* **1** to a full extent or degree ⟨she waited until we were *completely* finished before starting the next part⟩ — see FULLY 1

2 with attention to all aspects or details ⟨an allegation that was *completely* investigated and found to be groundless⟩ — see THOROUGHLY 1

complex *adj* **1** having many parts or aspects that are usually interrelated ⟨this camera is a *complex* instrument that requires careful handling⟩ ⟨*complex* issues regarding free speech and school discipline⟩

synonyms complicated, convoluted, elaborate, intricate, involved, knotty, labyrinthine, sophisticated

related words composite, compound, heterogeneous, mixed, multifarious, varied; challenging, difficult, tough; impenetrable, incomprehensible, inexplicable, unfathomable, unintelligible

near antonyms oversimplified, simplified; homogeneous, uniform, univaried

antonyms plain, simple, uncomplicated

2 made or done with great care or with much detail ⟨a *complex* recipe⟩ — see ELABORATE 1

complex *n* **1** a structure that is designed and built for a particular purpose ⟨an apartment *complex*⟩ — see FACILITY

2 something made up of many interdependent or related parts ⟨a *complex* of government programs⟩ — see SYSTEM 1

complexion *n* **1** the hue or appearance of the skin and especially of the face ⟨a sunscreen for people with very light *complexions*⟩

synonyms color, coloring

related words shade, tint, tone; features, lineaments, looks; countenance, face, visage

2 the set of qualities that makes a person, a group of people, or a thing different from others ⟨changing the *complexion* of the department to reflect the new trends⟩ — see NATURE 1

complexity *n* **1** the state or quality of having many interrelated parts or aspects ⟨the *complexity* of the company's computer system is such that a full-time repairman is needed⟩

synonyms complicatedness, elaborateness, intricacy, involution, sophistication

related words diversity, heterogeneousness; impenetrability, incomprehensibility, inexplicability

near antonyms simplification; homogeneity, uniformity

antonyms plainness, simpleness, simplicity

2 something that makes a situation more complicated or difficult ⟨the political *complexities* of his office⟩ — see COMPLICATION 1

compliance *n* **1** a readiness or willingness to yield to the wishes of others ⟨a strong-willed pop star who is not known for her *compliance*⟩
synonyms compliancy, deference, docility, obedience, submissiveness
related words amenability, amiability, complaisance, good-naturedness; servility, slavishness, subservience, subserviency; conformity; cooperativeness, receptiveness, receptivity; humoring, indulgence; acceptance, acquiescence, assent, consent; capitulation, submission, surrender; affability, amicability, congeniality, cordiality, friendliness, geniality, sociability
near antonyms animosity, antipathy, enmity, hostility, ill will
antonyms defiance, disobedience, intractability, recalcitrance
2 a bending to the authority or control of another ⟨we appreciate your *compliance* with our wishes in this matter⟩ — see OBEDIENCE 1

compliancy *n* a readiness or willingness to yield to the wishes of others ⟨*compliancy* with local regulations⟩ — see COMPLIANCE 1

compliant *adj* readily giving in to the command or authority of another ⟨a corrupt regime aided by a *compliant* press⟩ — see OBEDIENT

complicate *vb* to make complex or difficult ⟨the need to go to both a soccer game and band practice really *complicates* tonight's schedule⟩
synonyms perplex, sophisticate
related words develop, elaborate, expand; intensify, magnify; confound, confuse, mess (up), mix (up), muddle; entangle, snarl, tangle
near antonyms abbreviate, cut, shorten; ease, facilitate; disentangle, straighten (out), untangle; oversimplify
antonyms simplify, streamline

complicated *adj* **1** having many parts or aspects that are usually interrelated ⟨a *complicated* apparatus⟩ — see COMPLEX 1
2 made or done with great care or with much detail ⟨*complicated* plans for world domination⟩ — see ELABORATE 1

complicatedness *n* the state or quality of having many interrelated parts or aspects ⟨the *complicatedness* of the instructions made them very hard to understand⟩ — see COMPLEXITY 1

complication *n* **1** something that makes a situation more complicated or difficult ⟨the food allergies of the guests were just another *complication* for the couple trying to plan their wedding reception⟩
synonyms complexity, difficulty, intricacy
related words aftereffect, ramification, side effect; subtlety, technicality; annoyance, bother, headache, inconvenience, matter, trouble
phrases fly in the ointment
2 an abnormal state that disrupts a plant's or animal's normal bodily functioning ⟨*complications* set in after the surgery⟩ — see DISEASE

complicity *n* a secret agreement or cooperation between two parties for an illegal or dishonest purpose ⟨salesmen acting in *complicity* to drive up the prices⟩ — see COLLUSION

compliment *vb* to express to (someone) admiration for his or her success or good fortune ⟨*complimented* her on her victory⟩ — see CONGRATULATE

complimentary *adj* **1** expressing approval ⟨the novel received *complimentary* reviews⟩ — see FAVORABLE 1
2 not costing or charging anything ⟨the airline gave out *complimentary* soft drinks on the flight⟩ — see FREE 4

compliments *n pl* best wishes ⟨please extend our *compliments* to the chef for a great meal⟩
synonyms congratulations, felicitations, greetings, regards, respects
related words approval, blessing, endorsement; acknowledgment (*also* acknowledgement), citation, commendation; adulation, flattery, praise
near antonyms dig, gibe (*or* jibe), insult, put-down, taunt

comply (with) *vb* **1** to act according to the commands of ⟨the guards ran to *comply with* their ruler's orders⟩ — see OBEY
2 to do what is required by the terms of ⟨the businessmen agreed to *comply with* the contract⟩ — see FULFILL 1

component *n* one of the parts that make up a whole ⟨each set is composed of several distinct *components*⟩ — see ELEMENT 1

comport *vb* **1** to be in agreement on every point ⟨actions that *comport* with policy⟩ — see CHECK 1
2 to manage the actions of (oneself) in a particular way ⟨*comport* ourselves with dignity and style⟩ — see BEHAVE

comportment *n* the way or manner in which one conducts oneself ⟨the *comportment* of a gentleman⟩ — see BEHAVIOR

compose *vb* **1** to put (something) into proper and usually carefully worked out written form ⟨the whole class *composed* a request to the governor asking that the endangered species be adopted as the official state animal⟩
synonyms cast, craft, draft, draw (up), formulate, frame, prepare
related words fabricate, fashion, form, mold, sculpture, shape; couch, express, phrase, state, verbalize, word; author, pen, write; conceive, concoct, devise; build, construct, make; assemble, compound, piece (together)
phrases put together
2 to be all the substance of ⟨the earth's crust is *composed* of mostly silicon with several other elements in smaller amounts⟩ — see CONSTITUTE 1
3 to free from distress or disturbance ⟨*composed* himself after hearing the terrible news⟩ — see CALM 1
4 to gain emotional or mental control of ⟨she took a deep breath and *composed* herself⟩ — see COLLECT 1

composed *adj* free from emotional or mental agitation ⟨stayed *composed* and focused despite all of the distractions⟩ — see CALM 2

composer *n* a person who writes musical compositions ⟨a versatile *composer* whose works include operas, symphonies, concertos, and sonatas⟩
synonyms musician, songwriter
related words arranger, scorer; librettist

composite *adj* made from the joining of two or more parts or elements ⟨the movie's special effects included the use of many *composite* photographs⟩
synonyms amalgamated, compound
related words blended, combined, commingled, mingled, mixed; fused, integrated; interlaced, intermixed, intertwined, interwoven
near antonyms uncombined, unmixed
antonyms simple

composite *n* a distinct entity formed by the combining of two or more different things ⟨a *composite* of two separate images⟩ — see BLEND

composition *n* **1** a literary, musical, or artistic production ⟨the *compositions* of Michelangelo include the dome of St. Peter's, the ceiling of the Sistine Chapel, and his monumental statue of David⟩

synonyms opus, piece, work

related words classic, magnum opus, masterpiece, pièce de résistance, showpiece; model, outline, sketch; étude

2 a short piece of writing done as a school exercise ⟨a teacher who is fond of having her class write *compositions*⟩

synonyms paper, theme

related words article, essay, story

3 the way in which the elements of something (as a work of art) are arranged ⟨student photographers learn the importance of *composition* in creating striking images⟩

synonyms arrangement, configuration, design, form, format, layout, makeup, pattern

related words motif, theme

4 a short piece of writing typically expressing a point of view ⟨submitted a *composition* to the local newspaper⟩ — see ESSAY 1

composure *n* evenness of emotions or temper ⟨kept his *composure* no matter what happened⟩ — see EQUANIMITY

compound *adj* made from the joining of two or more parts or elements ⟨a *compound* substance⟩ — see COMPOSITE

compound *n* a distinct entity formed by the combining of two or more different things ⟨mixed the chemicals together to form a new *compound*⟩ — see BLEND

compound *vb* **1** to make greater in size, amount, or number ⟨we *compounded* our error with further mistakes⟩ — see INCREASE 1

2 to put or bring together so as to form a new and longer whole ⟨*compound* ingredients for a medicine⟩ — see CONNECT 1

comprehend *vb* **1** to recognize the meaning of ⟨the age at which children can *comprehend* the difference between right and wrong⟩

synonyms appreciate, apprehend, catch, catch on (to), dig [*slang*], get, grasp, make, make out, perceive, see, seize, tumble (to), understand

related words absorb, assimilate, digest, take in; know, realize, sense; fathom, penetrate

near antonyms misapprehend, misconstrue, misinterpret, misunderstand

antonyms miss

2 to have a practical understanding of ⟨it took me a while to *comprehend* algebra⟩ — see KNOW 1

3 to have as part of a whole ⟨his system *comprehends* all of history⟩ — see INCLUDE

comprehension *n* the knowledge gained from the process of coming to know or understand something ⟨the president's *comprehension* of the current situation in the Middle East⟩

synonyms appreciation, apprehension, grasp, grip, perception, understanding

related words absorption, assimilation, uptake; conception, visualization; awareness, consciousness, realization

near antonyms misapprehension, misinterpretation, misunderstanding

comprehensive *adj* **1** covering everything or all important points ⟨a *comprehensive* overview of the subject⟩ — see ENCYCLOPEDIC

2 not lacking any part or member that properly belongs to it ⟨a *comprehensive* listing of all the paintings generally attributed to the Dutch artist Rembrandt⟩ — see COMPLETE 1

3 trying all possibilities ⟨*comprehensive* plans for covering just about any conceivable terrorist attack⟩ — see EXHAUSTIVE

comprehensively *adv* with attention to all aspects or details ⟨no period in American history has been as *comprehensively* studied as the Civil War⟩ — see THOROUGHLY 1

compress *vb* **1** to reduce in size or volume by or as if by pressing parts or members together ⟨a science textbook that *compresses* a lot of information about human reproduction into a few short chapters⟩

synonyms compact, condense, constrict, contract, squeeze

related words cram, crowd, jam, jam-pack, pack; abbreviate, abridge, curtail, shorten; downsize, shrink; concentrate, consolidate; simplify, streamline; decrease, diminish, lessen

near antonyms disperse, dissipate, scatter; distend, inflate, swell

antonyms expand, open, outspread, outstretch

2 to become smaller in size or volume through the drawing together of particles of matter ⟨the material can *compress* under pressure⟩ — see CONTRACT 2

compression *n* the act or process of reducing the size or volume of something by or as if by pressing ⟨the *compression* of a long, complicated story into a two-hour movie is never easy⟩

synonyms compacting, condensation, constriction, contraction, squeezing

related words abbreviation, abridgment (*or* abridgement), curtailment, shortening; concentration, consolidation; simplification, streamlining; decreasing, diminishment, lessening

near antonyms dispersion, dissipation, scattering; distension (*or* distention), inflation, swelling

antonyms expansion

comprise *vb* **1** to be made up of ⟨the mall *comprises* three department stores and eighty smaller shops selling specialized goods⟩

synonyms consist (of), contain

related words embrace, encompass, entail, include, involve, take in; assimilate, embody, incorporate

2 to be all the substance of ⟨at the time, about 100,000 fighting men and women *comprised* our military force in that country⟩ — see CONSTITUTE 1

compromise *n* the act or practice of each side giving up something in order to reach an agreement ⟨eventually we reached a *compromise* on the number of hours per week that would be devoted to piano practice⟩ — see CONCESSION 1

compromise *vb* to place in danger ⟨officials at the state department were concerned that his statements would *compromise* national security⟩ — see ENDANGER

compulsion *n* the use of power to impose one's will on another ⟨in that class I read books under *compulsion* that I ordinarily wouldn't have considered⟩ — see FORCE 2

compulsive *adj* caused by or suggestive of an irresistible urge ⟨his *compulsive* clowning around can sometimes be annoying⟩

synonyms impulsive, obsessive

related words uncontrollable, irrepressible; automatic, instinctive, involuntary, reflex, spontaneous; conditioned, mechanical; unconscious, unthinking, unwitting

near antonyms unforced, voluntary, willful (*or* wilful); controllable, manageable, resistible

compulsory *adj* forcing one's compliance or participation by or as if by law 〈*compulsory* retirement at age 70〉 — see MANDATORY

compunction *n* an uneasy feeling about the rightness of what one is doing or going to do 〈throughout her school years she cheated without *compunction*〉 — see QUALM

computation *n* the act or process of performing mathematical operations to find a value 〈we were able to divide the dinner bill fairly with a little *computation*〉 — see CALCULATION

compute *vb* to determine (a value) by doing the necessary mathematical operations 〈for the test we were required to *compute* the answers without using a calculator〉 — see CALCULATE 1

comrade *n* 1 a person frequently seen in the company of another 〈the boy, and two others who are known to be his *comrades*, are wanted for questioning by the police〉 — see ASSOCIATE 1

2 a person who has a strong liking for and trust in another 〈we expect to be *comrades* for the rest of our lives〉 — see FRIEND 1

comradely *adj* having or showing kindly feeling and sincere interest 〈a *comradely* handshake from an old friend whom he hadn't seen in years〉 — see FRIENDLY 1

comradeship *n* the feeling of closeness and friendship that exists between companions 〈nursing home residents are able to offer each other support and *comradeship*〉 — see COMPANIONSHIP

con *vb* to commit to memory 〈usually candidates *con* their entire campaign speech, right down to the jokes they supposedly ad-lib〉 — see MEMORIZE

concatenate *vb* to put together into a series by means of or as if by means of a thread 〈the movie actually *concatenates* into one extended narrative several episodes from various books in the series〉 — see THREAD 2

concatenation *n* a series of things linked together 〈a complicated *concatenation* of events leading to the freak accident〉 — see CHAIN 1

concave *adj* curved inward 〈a *concave* lens〉 — see HOLLOW

concavity *n* a sunken area forming a separate space 〈water collected in a shallow *concavity*〉 — see HOLE 2

conceal *vb* 1 to put into a hiding place 〈*conceal* the documents in a drawer beneath a false bottom〉 — see ¹HIDE 1

2 to keep secret or shut off from view 〈tried to *conceal* her true intentions〉 — see ¹HIDE 2

concealment *n* 1 the placing of something out of sight 〈your choice of the oven for the *concealment* of the money was unwise〉

synonyms caching, hiding, secretion, stashing

related words burial, burying, entombment, interment, interring

near antonyms disinterment, unearthing

antonyms display, exhibition, exposure, parading, showing

2 a place where a person goes to hide 〈cave-riddled mountains that offer a multitude of *concealments*

where a fugitive could hide indefinitely〉 — see HIDE-OUT

concede *vb* 1 to accept the truth or existence of (something) usually reluctantly 〈she grudgingly *conceded* his point〉 — see ADMIT

2 to cease resistance (as to another's arguments, demands, or control) 〈he *conceded* as soon as it became clear that he could not win〉 — see YIELD 3

conceit *n* 1 an elaborate or fanciful way of expressing something 〈the *conceit* that the crowd at the outdoor rock concert was a vast sea of people waving to the beat of the music〉

synonyms metaphor

related words analogy, circumlocution, euphemism, simile

phrases figure of speech

2 a conception or image created by the imagination and having no objective reality 〈his dream of swimming in the Olympics is nothing more than a *conceit*〉 — see FANTASY 1

3 an often unjustified feeling of being pleased with oneself or with one's situation or achievements 〈even though her novels are enormously popular, the writer is more prone to insecurity than to *conceit*〉 — see COMPLACENCE

conceited *adj* having too high an opinion of oneself 〈a *conceited* basketball player who was always too busy even to sign autographs〉

synonyms complacent, egoistic, egotistic (*or* egotistical), important, overweening, pompous, prideful, proud, self-conceited, self-important, self-satisfied, smug, stuck-up, vain, vainglorious

related words boastful, braggart, bragging; arrogant, cavalier, disdainful, haughty, lordly, self-assertive, snobbish, supercilious, superior, uppity; domineering, high-handed, imperious; highfalutin, pretentious; overconfident, presumptuous; confident, self-assured, self-confident; self-centered, selfish

near antonyms diffident, self-doubting; meek, unassertive; down-to-earth, unassuming, unpretentious; bashful, retiring, shy

antonyms humble, modest

conceitedness *n* an often unjustified feeling of being pleased with oneself or with one's situation or achievements 〈she was annoyed by his persistent air of *conceitedness*〉 — see COMPLACENCE

conceivably *adv* it is possible 〈we could *conceivably* finish next week〉 — see PERHAPS

conceive *vb* to form a mental picture of 〈it takes an idealist to *conceive* a world without war, and an activist to make it happen〉 — see IMAGINE 1

concentrate *vb* 1 to increase the amount of (a substance in a mixture) by removing other substances 〈prolonged boiling is required to *concentrate* the sap when making maple syrup〉

synonyms condense

related words distill (*or* distil), purify, refine; compact, harden, solidify; deepen, enhance, heighten, intensify; evaporate, extract, remove

near antonyms weaken

antonyms dilute, water (down)

2 to fix (as one's attention) steadily toward a central objective 〈a president who will try to *concentrate* public attention on the problems of inner cities〉

synonyms fasten, focus, rivet, train

related words aim, direct, level, point, zero (in on); attend, heed, mind

3 to bring (something) to a central point or under a single control ⟨*concentrate* our efforts on the most important issues⟩ — see CENTRALIZE

4 to bring together in one body or place ⟨*concentrate* your forces on the right side of the battlefield⟩ — see GATHER 1

5 to come together into one body or place ⟨recent immigrants tend to *concentrate* in port cities⟩ — see ASSEMBLE 1

concentrated *adj* **1** having an abundance of some characteristic quality (as flavor) ⟨a *concentrated* mixture of lemonade and iced tea⟩ — see FULL-BODIED

2 not divided or scattered among several areas of interest or concern ⟨when you get a private conference with that teacher, you get nothing but his *concentrated* attention⟩ — see WHOLE 1

concentration *n* a focusing of the mind on something ⟨the noise from the party next door threatened to disturb her *concentration*⟩ — see ATTENTION 1

concept *n* something imagined or pictured in the mind ⟨a *concept* for a new kind of automobile that could revolutionize the industry⟩ — see IDEA

conception *n* something imagined or pictured in the mind ⟨our changing *conceptions* of what constitutes art⟩ — see IDEA

conceptual *adj* dealing with or expressing a quality or idea ⟨*conceptual* thinking is often the most demanding kind of mental activity⟩ — see ABSTRACT 1

concern *n* **1** a commercial or industrial activity or organization ⟨several banking *concerns* in the area⟩ — see ENTERPRISE 1

2 an uneasy state of mind usually over the possibility of an anticipated misfortune or trouble ⟨the recent crime wave has caused a great deal of *concern* in the neighborhood⟩ — see ANXIETY 1

concern *vb* **1** to have (something) as a subject matter ⟨the book *concerns* the challenges faced by children growing up in single-parent households⟩

synonyms cover, deal (with), pertain (to), treat (of)

related words appertain (to), bear (on *or* upon), refer (to), relate (to); allude (to), glance (upon), mention, touch (upon); offer, present; contain, embrace, encompass, entail, include, incorporate

phrases have to do with

near antonyms exclude, omit; disregard, ignore, neglect, overlook, pass over, slight

2 to be the business or affair of ⟨the problems of air and water pollution that *concern* all of us⟩

synonyms affect, involve, touch

related words apply (to), relate (to); embroil, ensnare, entangle, implicate

3 to trouble the mind of; to make uneasy ⟨we were greatly *concerned* by reports that yet another previously unknown virus is now posing a threat⟩ — see DISTURB 1

concerning *prep* having to do with ⟨we had a meeting with the principal today *concerning* the new policy on student-run organizations⟩ — see ABOUT 1

concert *n* an entertainment featuring singing or the playing of musical instruments ⟨during the summer various groups give *concerts* on the town green⟩

synonyms musicale

related words performance, presentation; recital; hootenanny, jam session, sing, songfest; festival

concert *vb* **1** to bring about through discussion and compromise ⟨warned that the rain forests are in danger of extinction unless the world's industrial powers *concert*

a plan to prevent such an occurrence⟩ — see NEGOTIATE 1

2 to participate or assist in a joint effort to accomplish an end ⟨he refuses to consult his business partners or to *concert* with them⟩ — see COOPERATE 1

concerted *adj* used or done by a number of people as a group ⟨a victory like that results only from the *concerted* effort of the entire team⟩ — see COLLECTIVE

concession *n* **1** the act or practice of each side giving up something in order to reach an agreement ⟨when trying to get a raise in your allowance, it's good to know the art of *concession*⟩

synonyms accommodation, compromise, give-and-take, negotiation

related words arrangement, bargain, deal, understanding; agreement, settlement

2 an open declaration of something (as a fault or the commission of an offense) about oneself ⟨a *concession* of guilt from the governor is the only thing that will save her political career⟩ — see CONFESSION

3 something granted as a special favor ⟨a *concession* to sell their T-shirts at the village fair⟩ — see PRIVILEGE

conciliate *vb* **1** to bring to a state free of conflicts, inconsistencies, or differences ⟨it is hard to *conciliate* the views of labor and management regarding health benefits⟩ — see HARMONIZE 2

2 to lessen the anger or agitation of ⟨a principal trying to *conciliate* the parents who did not receive their tickets to graduation ceremonies⟩ — see PACIFY

conciliating *adj* tending to lessen or avoid conflict or hostility ⟨small *conciliating* acts designed to win the trust of the new neighbors⟩ — see PACIFIC 1

conciliator *n* one who works with opposing sides in order to bring about an agreement ⟨his genius as a *conciliator* is that he is able to convince both sides that they got everything they wanted⟩ — see MEDIATOR

conciliatory *adj* tending to lessen or avoid conflict or hostility ⟨eased the tension with *conciliatory* remarks⟩ — see PACIFIC 1

concise *adj* marked by the use of few words to convey much information or meaning ⟨a *concise* article on violence in the media that manages to say more than most books on the subject⟩

synonyms aphoristic, brief, compact, compendious, crisp, epigrammatic, laconic, pithy, succinct, summary, terse

related words abrupt, blunt, brusque, curt, short, snippy; abbreviated, abridged, condensed, shortened; meaty, substantial; meaningful, significant

near antonyms redundant, repetitious, tautological; enlarged, expanded, supplemented; embellished, embroidered, exaggerated

antonyms diffuse, long-winded, prolix, rambling, verbose, wordy

concisely *adv* in a few words ⟨since there's little room on the form, you'll have to state *concisely* the reason why you're returning the merchandise⟩ — see SHORTLY 1

conciseness *n* **1** the condition of being short ⟨we were disappointed by the *conciseness* of the presentation, since we wanted more details⟩ — see BREVITY 1

2 the quality or state of being marked by or using only few words to convey much meaning ⟨many have admired the *conciseness* of Emily Dickinson's poetry⟩ — see SUCCINCTNESS

conclude *vb* **1** to bring (an event) to a natural or appropriate stopping point ⟨a brief reminder of tonight's game *concluded* the announcements⟩ — see CLOSE 3

2 to come to an end ⟨the concert *concluded* late in the evening⟩ — see CEASE 1

3 to bring about through discussion and compromise ⟨*concluded* an economic agreement among the world's leading industrial nations⟩ — see NEGOTIATE 1

4 to come to a judgment after discussion or consideration ⟨he *concluded* that it could wait until later⟩ — see DECIDE 1

5 to form an opinion through reasoning and information ⟨*concluded* that only the murderer could possibly have known that information⟩ — see INFER 1

concluded *adj* brought or having come to an end ⟨with another recently *concluded* summer at camp behind us, we are now ready to start school⟩ — see COMPLETE 2

concluding *adj* following all others of the same kind in order or time ⟨the *concluding* statement will be read by the secretary⟩ — see LAST

conclusion *n* **1** an opinion arrived at through a process of reasoning ⟨the detective's *conclusion* that the murderer had to be left-handed⟩
synonyms deduction, determination, inference
related words decision, judgment (*or* judgement), ruling, verdict; conjecture, guess, surmise; assumption, presumption, supposition

2 a position arrived at after consideration ⟨came to the *conclusion* that we couldn't go on vacation while the dog was sick⟩ — see DECISION 1

3 a condition or occurrence traceable to a cause ⟨all their efforts came to no practical *conclusion*⟩ — see EFFECT 1

4 the last part of a process or action ⟨the *conclusion* of the speech was a brief summary⟩ — see FINALE

5 the stopping of a process or activity ⟨a bell signaled the *conclusion* of the event⟩ — see END 1

conclusive *adj* **1** serving to put an end to all debate or questioning ⟨the archeological discovery was *conclusive* proof that the Vikings had indeed settled in North America around 1000 A.D.⟩
synonyms absolute, clear, decisive, definitive
related words incontestable, incontrovertible, indisputable, indubitable, irrefutable, undeniable, unquestionable; unchallenged, uncontested, undisputed; unambiguous, unequivocal; certain, definite, positive, sure
near antonyms debatable, disputable, questionable, refutable; ambiguous, equivocal
antonyms inconclusive, indecisive, unclear

2 having the power to persuade ⟨a *conclusive* argument for allowing the students to put on a play of their own choosing⟩ — see COGENT

concoct *vb* to create or think of by clever use of the imagination ⟨trying to *concoct* an explanation for how the lamp got broken by itself⟩ — see INVENT

concoction *n* something (as a device) created for the first time through the use of the imagination ⟨the first submarine must have seemed like the looniest *concoction* ever to spring from the human mind⟩ — see INVENTION 1

concomitant *n* something that is found along with something else ⟨disease is all too often one of the *concomitants* of poverty⟩ — see ACCOMPANIMENT

concomitant *adj* present at the same time and place ⟨an improvement in the facilities led to a *concomitant* improvement in morale⟩ — see COINCIDENT

concord *n* peaceful coexistence ⟨living in *concord* with people of different races and religions⟩ — see HARMONY 2

concourse *n* a typically long narrow way connecting parts of a building ⟨airline passengers had to pass through the security checkpoints before being allowed in the *concourse*⟩ — see HALL 2

concrete *adj* **1** existing in fact and not merely as a possibility ⟨*concrete* evidence, and not just a theory, must be presented at a trial⟩ — see ACTUAL

2 relating to or composed of matter ⟨*concrete* objects like rocks and trees⟩ — see MATERIAL 1

concrete *vb* to become physically firm or solid ⟨the mortar slowly *concreted* in the mold⟩ — see HARDEN 1

concur *vb* **1** to have or come to the same opinion or point of view ⟨I *concur* with your assessment of the situation⟩ — see AGREE 1

2 to occur or exist at the same time ⟨the lively 1960s, a decade in which the Cold War, the race to the moon, the Vietnam War, and the civil rights movement all *concurred*⟩ — see COINCIDE 1

concurrence *n* **1** the occurrence or existence of several things at once ⟨the *concurrence* of my birthday and the concert by my favorite rock band made my preference for a birthday present pretty obvious⟩
synonyms coexistence, coincidence
related words development, happening, occurrence

2 the act or fact of being of one opinion about something ⟨looked for *concurrence* among the delegates to the conference⟩ — see AGREEMENT 1

3 the approval by someone in authority for the doing of something ⟨we needed the *concurrence* of the boss before proceeding with the project⟩ — see PERMISSION

concurrent *adj* **1** existing or occurring at the same period of time ⟨*concurrent* expeditions to the Antarctic that were in a race to reach the South Pole⟩ — see CONTEMPORARY 1

2 present at the same time and place ⟨the postwar period of prosperity and the *concurrent* baby boom are the major topics in this history of the 1950s⟩ — see COINCIDENT

concurrently *adv* at one and the same time ⟨two major trade shows running *concurrently* at the convention center⟩ — see TOGETHER 1

concussion *n* a forceful coming together of two things ⟨the *concussion* of the airliner slamming into the skyscraper was felt for several blocks in all directions⟩ — see IMPACT 1

condemn *vb* **1** to declare to be morally wrong or evil ⟨it is a sign of human progress that slavery, which was once common, is now universally *condemned*⟩
synonyms censure, damn, decry, denounce, execrate, reprehend, reprobate
related words attack, blast, criticize, knock, pan, slam; belittle, deprecate, disparage; doom, sentence; convict; blacklist, excommunicate, ostracize; rebuke, reprimand, reproach; admonish, chide, reprove; berate, lambaste (*or* lambast), scold, upbraid; curse, imprecate; abhor, abominate, detest, hate, loathe, revile
near antonyms approve, endorse (*also* indorse), sanction; eulogize, exalt, extol (*also* extoll), glorify, laud, praise; acclaim, applaud, commend, hail; consecrate, hallow, sanctify; honor, revere, venerate
antonyms bless

2 to express one's unfavorable opinion of the worth or quality of ⟨a report that *condemns* the working conditions in the factories of many developing countries⟩ — see CRITICIZE

3 to express public or formal disapproval of ⟨the philosopher's works were once *condemned* by the church and placed on its list of forbidden books⟩ — see CENSURE 1

4 to find or pronounce guilty ⟨he was *condemned* by the news media even before the trial began⟩ — see CONVICT

5 to impose a judicial punishment on ⟨a stern judge who does not hesitate to *condemn* a prisoner to life behind bars⟩ — see SENTENCE

condemnation *n* an often public or formal expression of disapproval ⟨a *condemnation* of the war by the conference of bishops⟩ — see CENSURE

condensation *n* **1** a shortened version of a written work ⟨a *condensation* of the opinion issued by the state's supreme court⟩ — see ABRIDGMENT

2 the act or process of reducing the size or volume of something by or as if by pressing ⟨a staff employed in the *condensation* of magazine articles⟩ — see COMPRESSION

condense *vb* **1** to become smaller in size or volume through the drawing together of particles of matter ⟨over time the once-fluffy material in the pillow had *condensed* into a lumpy wad⟩ — see CONTRACT 2

2 to reduce in size or volume by or as if by pressing parts or members together ⟨*condense* the information into as brief a report as possible⟩ — see COMPRESS 1

3 to increase the amount of (a substance in a mixture) by removing other substances ⟨added *condensed* milk to the mix⟩ — see CONCENTRATE 1

condensed *adj* not lasting for a considerable time ⟨a *condensed* lecture⟩ — see SHORT 2

condescend *vb* **1** to descend to a level that is beneath one's dignity ⟨I will not *condescend* to answer the sore loser's charge that I cheated in order to win the race⟩
   synonyms deign, stoop
   related words debase, degrade, demean, humble, humiliate, lower
   near antonyms rise

2 to assume or treat with an air of superiority ⟨wealthy people who tend to be *condescending* toward their poor relations⟩
   synonyms lord (it over), patronize
   related words cold-shoulder, cut, high-hat, snub

condiment *n* something used to enhance the flavor of cooked or prepared food ⟨the cafeteria's self-serve table has a full array of *condiments*⟩
   synonyms seasoning
   related words herb, savory, spice; relish, sauce; flavoring

condition *n* **1** a state of being or fitness ⟨a car that was ten years old but in still good *condition*⟩
   synonyms estate, fettle, form, kilter, order, repair, shape, trim
   related words practice (*also* practise); pass, phase, stage
   near antonyms disorder, disrepair

2 something upon which the carrying out of an agreement or offer depends ⟨you'll get a raise in your allowance with the *condition* that you'll do a better job of keeping your room clean⟩
   synonyms provision, proviso, qualification, reservation, stipulation
   related words strings, terms; prerequisite, requirement, requisite; limitation, modification, restriction; exception, exemption; essential, must, necessity

3 an abnormal state that disrupts a plant's or animal's normal bodily functioning ⟨a skin *condition* that prevents me from staying out in the sun for very long⟩ — see DISEASE

4 something necessary, indispensable, or unavoidable ⟨water is a *condition* for life on Earth⟩ — see ESSENTIAL 1

5 something that limits one's freedom of action or choice ⟨my parents placed several *conditions* on our weekend plans⟩ — see RESTRICTION 1

condition *vb* **1** to bring to a proper or desired state of fitness ⟨the length of time that it takes for runners to *condition* their bodies for a marathon⟩
   synonyms season, train
   related words fit, prepare, ready; acclimate, acclimatize, break in, orient, orientate; accustom, familiarize, habituate; harden, inure

2 to change (something) so as to make it suitable for a new use or situation ⟨an immigrant family that must *condition* its traditional attitudes regarding child rearing to the realities of modern American life⟩ — see ADAPT

conditional *adj* determined by something else ⟨the sale of the house is *conditional* upon the approval of a mortgage for the prospective buyer⟩ — see DEPENDENT 2

conditioning *n* energetic movement of the body for the sake of physical fitness ⟨the actor went through months of *conditioning* in order to play the role in the action film⟩ — see EXERCISE 1

condole (with) *vb* to have sympathy for ⟨*condole with* them in their hour of grief⟩ — see PITY

condone *vb* to overlook or dismiss as of little importance ⟨Roger is too quick to *condone* his friend's faults⟩ — see EXCUSE 1

conduct *n* **1** the act or activity of looking after and making decisions about something ⟨the president was happy to leave the *conduct* of foreign affairs to his secretary of state⟩
   synonyms administration, control, direction, governance, government, guidance, handling, management, operation, oversight, regulation, running, superintendence, supervision
   related words care, custody, guardianship, protection, tutelage; engineering, machination, manipulation

2 the way or manner in which one conducts oneself ⟨a child who has often been scolded for poor *conduct* in public⟩ — see BEHAVIOR

conduct *vb* **1** to look after and make decisions about ⟨the company's president continues to *conduct* the everyday affairs of the software firm he founded many years ago⟩
   synonyms administer, carry on, control, direct, govern, guide, handle, manage, operate, oversee, regulate, run, superintend, supervise
   related words care (for), keep, mind, tend, watch; lead, pilot, steer; guard, protect, safeguard

2 to cause to move to a central point or along a restricted pathway ⟨the gutter *conducts* water to the curb, thus protecting the house's basement⟩ — see CHANNEL

3 to manage the actions of (oneself) in a particular way ⟨*conducted* themselves at the party like perfect ladies and gentlemen⟩ — see BEHAVE

4 to point out the way for (someone) especially from a position in front ⟨a job *conducting* tourists through the historical museum⟩ — see LEAD 1

conduit *n* **1** a long hollow cylinder for carrying a substance (as a liquid or gas) ⟨the major *conduit* for carrying water to the military base⟩ — see PIPE 1

2 an open man-made passageway for water ⟨water flowed along the *conduit* to the fountain⟩ — see CHANNEL 1

confection *n* a food having a high sugar content ⟨following the main course there were assorted *confections* so delicious-looking as to tempt even determined dieters⟩ — see SWEET 1

confederacy *n* an association of persons, parties, or states for mutual assistance and protection ⟨a *confederacy* of several small nations who had promised to come to one another's aid if any were attacked⟩
synonyms alliance, bloc, coalition, combination, combine, confederation, federation, league, union
related words cabal, conspiracy, junto; cartel, syndicate, trust; faction, side, wing; association, group, organization; affiliation, cooperative, partnership

confederate *n* **1** one associated with another in wrongdoing ⟨the police were able to track down his *confederates* once the thief started talking⟩ — see ACCOMPLICE
2 someone associated with another to give assistance or moral support ⟨relied on her *confederates* in the medical community for support⟩ — see ALLY

confederate *vb* to form or enter into an association that furthers the interests of its members ⟨the nations *confederated* in order to lower international trade barriers⟩ — see ALLY

confederation *n* **1** an association of persons, parties, or states for mutual assistance and protection ⟨the small nations formed a *confederation* out of self-defense⟩ — see CONFEDERACY
2 the state of having shared interests or efforts (as in social or business matters) ⟨the big-budget movie was produced by the studio in *confederation* with another in order to lower the risk⟩ — see ASSOCIATION 1

confer *vb* **1** to give the ownership or benefit of (something) formally or publicly ⟨the British monarch continues to *confer* knighthood on those who are outstanding in their fields⟩
synonyms accord, award, grant
related words bestow, contribute, donate, give, present; furnish, provide, supply; extend, offer, proffer; allocate, appropriate, assign
near antonyms rescind, revoke
2 to exchange viewpoints or seek advice for the purpose of finding a solution to a problem ⟨my parents are going to *confer* with a financial advisor about saving for my college education⟩
synonyms advise, consult, counsel, parley, powwow, treat
related words debate, deliberate, discuss, hash (over); coach, guide, tutor; recommend, suggest; direct, refer (to)

conference *n* **1** a body of people come together in one place ⟨the *conference* voted to conclude that day's meeting and to resume discussions the next morning⟩ — see GATHERING 1
2 a coming together of a number of persons for a specified purpose ⟨a *conference* of teachers for the discussion of the state's new policy of mandatory testing⟩ — see MEETING 1
3 a meeting featuring a group discussion ⟨a *conference* on the need for international cooperation in combating emerging viruses⟩ — see FORUM
4 an exchange of views for the purpose of exploring a subject or deciding an issue ⟨a parent-teacher *conference* to discuss a student having trouble in school⟩ — see DISCUSSION 1

confess *vb* to accept the truth or existence of (something) usually reluctantly ⟨political prisoners, under threat of torture, forced to *confess* their guilt⟩ — see ADMIT

confession *n* an open declaration of something (as a fault or the commission of an offense) about oneself ⟨a *confession* that he had been lying all along⟩
synonyms acknowledgment (*also* acknowledgement), admission, avowal, concession
related words allowance; betrayal, disclosure, divulgence, revelation; announcement, declaration, proclamation; contrition, regret, remorse, repentance

confidant *n* a person who has a strong liking for and trust in another ⟨she's my *confidant*; I tell her everything without reservation⟩ — see FRIEND 1

confidence *n* **1** great faith in oneself or one's abilities ⟨a lifelong *confidence* that enabled her to achieve great things despite powerful obstacles⟩
synonyms aplomb, assurance, self-assurance, self-confidence, self-esteem
related words cockiness, complacence, complacency, conceit, conceitedness, ego, egotism, overconfidence, pompousness, pride, self-admiration, self-conceit, self-importance, self-satisfaction, smugness, vainglory, vanity; calmness, composure, coolness, equanimity; self-possession
near antonyms apprehension, doubt, misgiving
antonyms diffidence, self-doubt
2 a state of mind in which one is free from doubt ⟨the *confidence* with which the game show contestant answered every question⟩
synonyms assurance, assuredness, certainty, certitude, conviction, positiveness, sureness
related words authoritarianism, dogmatism; decisiveness, firmness, resolution
near antonyms hesitancy, hesitation, indecisiveness, irresolution
antonyms doubt, incertitude, nonconfidence, uncertainty
3 firm belief in the integrity, ability, effectiveness, or genuineness of someone or something ⟨as players, we have complete *confidence* in our coach⟩ — see TRUST 1
4 information shared only with another or with a select few ⟨accused him of betraying a *confidence*⟩ — see SECRET 1

confidence game *n* a scheme in which the victim is cheated out of his money after first gaining his trust ⟨the old *confidence game* in which the victims are told that they must pay a fee in order to collect their prize money⟩
synonyms hustle, racket, swindle
related words double cross, fix; gyp, rip-off; squeeze; ruse, subterfuge, trick

confidence man *n* a dishonest person who uses clever means to cheat others out of something of value ⟨taken in by a persuasive *confidence man* using the Internet⟩ — see TRICKSTER 1

confident *adj* **1** having or showing great faith in oneself or one's abilities ⟨you'll need to be *confident*—even in the face of rejection—if you want to pursue a career in show business⟩
synonyms assured, secure, self-assured, self-confident
related words hopeful, optimistic, rosy, sanguine, upbeat; complacent, conceited, egoistic, egotistic (*or* egotistical), important, overweening, pompous, prideful, proud, self-conceited, self-important, self-satisfied, smug, stuck-up, vain, vainglorious; calm, collected,

composed, cool, placid, self-possessed, serene, tranquil, undisturbed, unperturbed
near antonyms meek, timid, unassertive; modest, unassuming, unpretentious; jittery, jumpy, nervous
antonyms diffident, insecure, self-doubting
2 having or showing a mind free from doubt ⟨we were *confident* that the directions we had been given were accurate⟩ — see CERTAIN 2

confidential *adj* not known or meant to be known by the general populace ⟨someone leaked *confidential* government information to the press⟩ — see PRIVATE 1

confiding *adj* having or showing trust in another ⟨a very *confiding* child who is a little too eager to trust total strangers⟩ — see TRUSTING 1

configuration *n* **1** the arrangement of parts that gives something its basic form ⟨the basic *configuration* of the building is that of a geodesic dome⟩ — see FRAME 1
2 the way in which something is sized, arranged, or organized ⟨a small business computer system in its simplest *configuration*⟩ — see FORMAT 1
3 the way in which the elements of something (as a work of art) are arranged ⟨his photographs have an intentionally loose *configuration*, with no single object intended as the primary center of interest⟩ — see COMPOSITION 3
4 the outward appearance of something as distinguished from its substance ⟨a cake in the *configuration* of a top hat⟩ — see FORM 1

confine *vb* **1** to set bounds or an upper limit for ⟨will *confine* my remarks to the subject we came here to discuss⟩ — see LIMIT 1
2 to put in or as if in prison ⟨the accused was *confined* until the trial could take place⟩ — see IMPRISON

confinement *n* **1** the act of confining or the state of being confined ⟨some wild animals take to *confinement* very poorly⟩ — see INTERNMENT
2 the act or practice of keeping something (as an activity) within certain boundaries ⟨the *confinement* of commercial development to one stretch of roadway is intended to help preserve the town's rural character⟩ — see RESTRICTION 2

confines *n pl* **1** a real or imaginary point beyond which a person or thing cannot go ⟨within the *confines* of the city⟩ — see LIMIT
2 the line or relatively narrow space that marks the outer limit of something ⟨outside the *confines* of the school walls⟩ — see BORDER 1

confirm *vb* to give evidence or testimony to the truth or factualness of ⟨several eyewitnesses who can *confirm* the youngster's account of what happened⟩
synonyms bear out, corroborate, substantiate, support, validate, verify, vindicate
related words attest, authenticate, avouch, certify, testify (to), vouch (for), witness; guarantee, warrant; affirm, assert, aver, avow, profess
near antonyms contradict, gainsay; deny, disavow, disclaim
antonyms disprove, rebut, refute

confirmable *adj* capable of being proven as true or real ⟨the theory was not *confirmable*, and eventually it had to be discarded in favor of one that was⟩ — see VERIFIABLE

confirmation *n* something presented in support of the truth or accuracy of a claim ⟨regards the finding as a *confirmation* of the theory that extraterrestrial impacts were responsible for the demise of the dinosaurs⟩ — see PROOF

confirmatory *adj* serving to give support to the truth or factualness of something ⟨a *confirmatory* test for pregnancy⟩ — see CORROBORATIVE

confirmed *adj* **1** being such by habit and not likely to change ⟨a *confirmed* grouch who never seems to smile⟩ — see HABITUAL 1
2 firmly established over time ⟨a *confirmed* tendency to exaggerate⟩ — see INVETERATE 1

confirming *adj* serving to give support to the truth or factualness of something ⟨a *confirming* glance at the readout⟩ — see CORROBORATIVE

confiscate *vb* to take ownership or control of (something) by right of one's authority ⟨anything that might be used as a weapon will be *confiscated* by the security guards⟩
synonyms expropriate, sequester
related words appropriate, arrogate, preempt, usurp; commandeer, seize, take over
near antonyms release, relinquish, surrender, yield

conflagration *n* a destructive burning ⟨the school burned to the ground in a horrible *conflagration*⟩ — see FIRE

conflict *n* **1** a lack of agreement or harmony ⟨the *conflict* between absolute freedom and personal responsibility⟩ — see DISCORD
2 a physical dispute between opposing individuals or groups ⟨an armed *conflict* between strikers and strikebreakers⟩ — see FIGHT 1
3 a state of armed violent struggle between states, nations, or groups ⟨the United Nations strives to prevent international *conflicts*⟩ — see WAR 1
4 an earnest effort for superiority or victory over another ⟨the eternal *conflict* between the forces of good and evil⟩ — see CONTEST 1

conflict *vb* to be out of harmony or agreement usually noticeably ⟨his statement *conflicts* with the facts⟩ — see CLASH

conflicting *adj* not being in agreement or harmony ⟨*conflicting* reports from the witnesses at the scene⟩ — see INCONSISTENT

confluence *n* the coming together of two or more things to the same point ⟨a happy *confluence* of beautiful weather and spectacular scenery during our vacation⟩ — see CONVERGENCE

conform *vb* **1** to be in agreement on every point ⟨the list *conforms* with the contents of the trunk⟩ — see CHECK 1
2 to form a pleasing relationship ⟨last-minute changes in the schedule that *conform* with our plans nicely⟩ — see HARMONIZE 1
3 to bring to a state free of conflicts, inconsistencies, or differences ⟨we'll have to *conform* this new rule with existing policy regarding after-school activities⟩ — see HARMONIZE 2
4 to change (something) so as to make it suitable for a new use or situation ⟨I can be funny or serious, for I always *conform* my behavior to the situation⟩ — see ADAPT

conform (to) *vb* to act according to the commands of ⟨an independent-minded person who refuses to *conform to* the dictates of society⟩ — see OBEY

conformable *adj* readily giving in to the command or authority of another ⟨one of the more *conformable* inmates in a prison that's filled with unruly ones⟩ — see OBEDIENT

conformable (to) *adj* not having or showing any apparent conflict ⟨student conduct must be at all times *con-*

formable to the principles and values of the school⟩ — see CONSISTENT

conformation *n* **1** the outward appearance of something as distinguished from its substance ⟨an ice sculpture in the *conformation* of a swan⟩ — see FORM 1

2 the way in which something is sized, arranged, or organized ⟨the regular *conformation* of particles in a crystal⟩ — see FORMAT 1

conformity *n* **1** a state of consistency ⟨the simple lifestyle of the Amish is in *conformity* with their ascetic religious beliefs⟩

synonyms accord, accordance, agreement, congruity, consonance, harmony, tune

related words assimilation, integration; oneness, solidarity, togetherness; affinity, empathy, sympathy

near antonyms discrepancy, disparity, dissimilarity

antonyms conflict, disagreement

2 a bending to the authority or control of another ⟨a rebellious artist who has never shown any interest in *conformity* to social custom⟩ — see OBEDIENCE 1

confound *vb* **1** to throw into a state of mental uncertainty ⟨we were *confounded* by the unexpectedly difficult questions on the quiz⟩ — see CONFUSE 1

2 to throw into a state of self-conscious distress ⟨his renewed popularity has *confounded* the critics who said his singing career was dead⟩ — see EMBARRASS 1

confront *vb* to oppose (something hostile or dangerous) with firmness or courage ⟨you must *confront* your fear in order to conquer it⟩ — see FACE 2

confrontation *n* an earnest effort for superiority or victory over another ⟨the softball rivals met in an epic *confrontation* on the last weekend of the summer⟩ — see CONTEST 1

confuse *vb* **1** to throw into a state of mental uncertainty ⟨the similar-sounding words "censure" and "censor" often *confuse* people⟩

synonyms addle, baffle, befog, befuddle, bemuse, bewilder, confound, disorient, muddle, muddy, mystify, perplex, puzzle

related words stick, stump; abash, discomfit, disconcert, discountenance, embarrass, faze, fluster, mortify, nonplus, rattle; agitate, bother, chagrin, discomfort, discompose, dismay, disquiet, distress, disturb, perturb, stun, unhinge, unsettle, upset; deceive, misguide, mislead

near antonyms assure, reassure, satisfy; enlighten, inform

2 to make (something) unclear to the understanding ⟨stop *confusing* the issue with irrelevant facts⟩

synonyms becloud, befog, blur, cloud, fog, muddy

related words complicate, perplex, sophisticate; entangle, snarl, tangle; disorder, jumble, mess (up), mix (up)

near antonyms simplify, streamline; disentangle, straighten (out), untangle

antonyms clarify

3 to throw into a state of self-conscious distress ⟨she was *confused* by the shocking bluntness of his marriage proposal⟩ — see EMBARRASS 1

4 to undo the proper order or arrangement of ⟨vandals had hopelessly *confused* the papers in the office files⟩ — see DISORDER

confused *adj* **1** lacking in order, neatness, and often cleanliness ⟨the cans were lying in a *confused* jumble in the basement⟩ — see MESSY

2 suffering from mental confusion ⟨she was briefly *confused* after her fall from the horse⟩ — see DIZZY 2

confusion *n* **1** a state of mental uncertainty ⟨the farmer's driving directions to the fairground just left us in total *confusion*⟩

synonyms bafflement, befuddlement, bewilderment, distraction, muddle, mystification, perplexity, puzzlement, whirl

related words abashment, discomfiture, embarrassment, fluster, mortification; agitation, chagrin, discomfort, dismay, disquiet, distress, disturbance, perturbation, upset

near antonyms assurance, certainty, certitude, confidence, conviction, positiveness, sureness

2 a state in which everything is out of order ⟨it was hard to find anything in that *confusion* in the attic⟩ — see CHAOS

3 the emotional state of being made self-consciously uncomfortable ⟨thrown into speechless *confusion* by the wild accusations⟩ — see EMBARRASSMENT 1

confute *vb* to prove to be false ⟨theories which will eventually be confirmed or *confuted* by experience⟩ — see DISPROVE

congeal *vb* **1** to become physically firm or solid ⟨the surface of the pond *congealed* after several days of frigid temperatures⟩ — see HARDEN 1

2 to turn from a liquid into a substance resembling jelly ⟨the gravy had already started to *congeal* by the time the waiter served our dinners⟩ — see COAGULATE

congenial *adj* **1** giving pleasure or contentment to the mind or senses ⟨a *congenial* atmosphere of the luxury health spa⟩ — see PLEASANT

2 having or marked by agreement in feeling or action ⟨*congenial* traveling companions who made our tour of Italy even more enjoyable⟩ — see HARMONIOUS 3

congenital *adj* being such from birth or by nature ⟨a *congenital* liar⟩ — see NATURAL 1

congest *vb* to prevent passage through ⟨the usual weekend traffic *congested* the highways⟩ — see CLOG 1

conglomerate *n* a group of businesses or enterprises under one control ⟨the huge media *conglomerate* owns TV and radio stations, a cable company, and a movie studio⟩

synonyms empire

related words multinational; cartel, combination, syndicate, trust; chain; association, corporation, organization, pool

conglomerate *vb* **1** to come together into one body or place ⟨people *conglomerated* in the hallway in an impromptu victory celebration⟩ — see ASSEMBLE 1

2 to gradually form into a layer, pile, or mass ⟨over the years the town's discarded junk *conglomerated* at the bottom of the river⟩ — see COLLECT 2

congratulate *vb* to express to (someone) admiration for his or her success or good fortune ⟨let me be the first to *congratulate* you on winning the award⟩

synonyms compliment, felicitate

related words applaud, cheer, commend, hail; extol (*also* extoll), glorify, laud, praise

near antonyms bad-mouth, belittle, decry, disparage, put down; jeer, mock, ridicule, taunt, tease

congratulations *n pl* best wishes ⟨a gift for you with our *congratulations*⟩ — see COMPLIMENTS

congregate *vb* to come together into one body or place ⟨travelers have *congregated* in the town's historic square for centuries⟩ — see ASSEMBLE 1

congregation *n* **1** a body of persons gathered for religious worship ⟨the whole *congregation* began to sing with great fervor⟩

synonyms assembly, church
related words laity, parish; communion, denomination, fold, sect
2 a body of people come together in one place ⟨a *congregation* of journalists were at the hotel bar, discussing the latest developments⟩ — see GATHERING 1
congress *n* **1** the highest lawmaking body of a political unit ⟨the national emergency required a special session of *congress*⟩
synonyms parliament
related words assembly, chamber, council, diet, house, legislature
2 a coming together of a number of persons for a specified purpose ⟨following World War I a great *congress* of world leaders took place in Paris to plan the postwar world⟩ — see MEETING 1
3 a group of persons formally joined together for some common interest ⟨the Canada Trades and Labor *Congress*⟩ — see ASSOCIATION 2
congruity *n* a state of consistency ⟨there's little *congruity* between your thought, which is ambitious, and your action, which is nonexistent⟩ — see CONFORMITY 1
congruous *adj* **1** having the parts agreeably related ⟨the *congruous* layout of the mansion's formal gardens conveys a sense of both grandeur and intimacy⟩ — see HARMONIOUS 2
2 not having or showing any apparent conflict ⟨when performing his official duties, the president must be dressed in clothes that are *congruous* with his high position⟩ — see CONSISTENT
congruously *adv* in a manner suitable for the occasion or purpose ⟨in a *congruously* solemn voice, he recited the oath of office⟩ — see PROPERLY
conjectural *adj* existing only as an assumption or speculation ⟨a necessarily *conjectural* account of Shakespeare's life, since there is so little hard information⟩ — see THEORETICAL 1
conjecture *n* an opinion or judgment based on little or no evidence ⟨the many *conjectures* about the true identity of Jack the Ripper⟩
synonyms guess, supposition, surmise
related words hypothesis, theory, thesis; guesswork, speculation; hunch, intuition; belief, faith
conjecture *vb* **1** to decide the size, amount, number, or distance of (something) without actual measurement ⟨he *conjectured* that the theater could seat 1000 people⟩ — see ESTIMATE 2
2 to form an opinion from little or no evidence ⟨she only *conjectures* that he was the culprit⟩ — see GUESS 1
conjoin *vb* **1** to come together to form a single unit ⟨several streets *conjoin* to form the crossroads known as New York's Times Square⟩ — see UNITE 1
2 to form or enter into an association that furthers the interests of its members ⟨small farmers had to *conjoin* in order to compete with the agricultural conglomerates⟩ — see ALLY
conjoint *adj* used or done by a number of people as a group ⟨only through the *conjoint* effort of the troop could we have accomplished this⟩ — see COLLECTIVE
conjointly *adv* in or by combined action or effort ⟨the two departments worked *conjointly* to finish the project in half the time⟩ — see TOGETHER 2
conjugal *adj* of or relating to marriage ⟨newlyweds still in a rapturous state of *conjugal* happiness⟩ — see MARITAL
conjugate *vb* **1** to come together to form a single unit ⟨biological cells *conjugating* under a microscope⟩ — see UNITE 1

2 to put or bring together so as to form a new and longer whole ⟨*conjugate* polymers in a chemistry lab⟩ — see CONNECT 1
conjunction *n* the coming together of two or more things to the same point ⟨the *conjunction* of the two major highways creates a massive influx of cars into the city⟩ — see CONVERGENCE
conjuration *n* a spoken word or set of words believed to have magic power ⟨he claimed he could raise the spirits of the dead with a mystical *conjuration*⟩ — see SPELL 1
conjure *vb* to make a request to (someone) in an earnest or urgent manner ⟨I *conjure* you to hear my plea⟩ — see BEG
conjure (up) *vb* to call into being through the use of one's inner resources or powers ⟨managed to *conjure up* the courage to tell the bully to back off⟩ — see SUMMON 2
conjurer *or* **conjuror** *n* **1** a person skilled in using supernatural forces ⟨in the book the *conjurer* battles a barbarian swordsman⟩ — see MAGICIAN 1
2 one who practices tricks and illusions for entertainment ⟨a *conjurer* in Las Vegas who must make audiences believe in the impossible eight shows a week⟩ — see MAGICIAN 2
conjuring *n* **1** the power to control natural forces through supernatural means ⟨his attempts at *conjuring* demonstrated the vanity of human wishes⟩ — see MAGIC 1
2 the art or skill of performing tricks or illusions for entertainment ⟨she's so good at *conjuring* that she's a much-sought-after entertainer at children's parties⟩ — see MAGIC 2
conk (out) *vb* to stop functioning ⟨the engine *conked out* just as we were approaching the exact middle of nowhere⟩ — see FAIL 1
connect *vb* **1** to put or bring together so as to form a new and longer whole ⟨*connect* all the sets of lights and attach them to the branches of the Christmas tree⟩
synonyms chain, compound, conjugate, couple, hitch, hook, join, link, yoke
related words dovetail; concatenate, string; cement, coalesce, combine, fuse, unite
near antonyms divide, part, split
antonyms disconnect, disjoin, separate, unchain, uncouple, unhitch, unlink, unyoke
2 to come together to form a single unit ⟨the two interstate highways *connect*, so a driver can go from one corner of the state to the other without much trouble⟩ — see UNITE 1
3 to think of (something) in combination ⟨opera is popularly *connected* with high society⟩ — see ASSOCIATE 2
connecting *n* the act or an instance of joining two or more things into one ⟨the *connecting* of the truck to the trailer was easily accomplished⟩ — see UNION 1
connection *n* **1** the fact or state of having something in common ⟨the endless debate about the *connection* between crime and poverty⟩
synonyms association, bearing, kinship, liaison, linkage, relation, relationship
related words correlation, interrelation; materiality, pertinence, relevance; bond, link, tie; affiliation, alliance, union; likeness, resemblance, similarity
2 a place where two or more things are united ⟨there's a problem at the *connection* where the outside wire is hooked up to the inside wiring⟩ — see JOINT 1

3 an acquaintance who has influence especially in the business or political world ⟨I have a *connection* in Hollywood who might be able to get you a part in a movie⟩ — see CONTACT

4 the act or an instance of joining two or more things into one ⟨that bridge is the only *connection* between the island and the mainland⟩ — see UNION 1

5 the fact or state of being pertinent ⟨that last comment of yours has no *connection* with what we've been talking about for the last hour⟩ — see PERTINENCE

6 the state of having shared interests or efforts (as in social or business matters) ⟨in a truly secular society there is no *connection* between church and state⟩ — see ASSOCIATION 1

connivance *n* a secret agreement or cooperation between two parties for an illegal or dishonest purpose ⟨was able to sneak out at night with the *connivance* of a camp counselor⟩ — see COLLUSION

connive *vb* to secretly sympathize with or pretend ignorance of something improper or unlawful ⟨the principal *connived* at all the school absences that were recorded on the day of the city's celebration of its Super Bowl victory⟩
synonyms wink
related words condone, disregard, excuse, ignore, overlook, tolerate
near antonyms disapprove (of), frown (on *or* upon); deny, disallow, refuse

connoisseur *n* a person having a knowledgeable and fine appreciation of the arts ⟨a forthcoming exhibit at the art museum that is eagerly awaited by *connoisseurs* of ancient Greek pottery⟩
synonyms dilettante
related words adept, authority, expert, master; critic, reviewer; amateur, dabbler; collector
near antonyms materialist, philistine

connubial *adj* of or relating to marriage ⟨a happy couple celebrating half a century of *connubial* bliss⟩ — see MARITAL

conquer *vb* **1** to bring under one's control by force of arms ⟨before his final defeat, Napoleon had managed to *conquer* much of Europe⟩
synonyms dominate, overpower, subdue, subject, subjugate, vanquish
related words beat, crush, defeat, drub, lick, mow (down), rout, smash, thrash, trounce; enslave; break, put down, quell, suppress
near antonyms emancipate, free, liberate, manumit, release

2 to achieve a victory over ⟨love *conquers* all, or so romance novels would have us believe⟩ — see BEAT 2

3 to achieve victory (as in a contest) ⟨a coach who demands that his team *conquer*, whatever the cost⟩ — see WIN 1

conqueror *n* one that defeats an enemy or opponent ⟨hailed as *conqueror* of the barbarian forces⟩ — see VICTOR 1

conquest *n* the act or process of bringing someone or something under one's control ⟨the *conquest* of much of North and South America by the Spanish during the 16th century⟩
synonyms dominating, domination, overpowering, subduing, subjecting, subjection, subjugating, subjugation, vanquishing
related words triumph, victory, winning; beating, defeat, drubbing, licking, trouncing; enslavement
near antonyms emancipation, freeing, liberation, manumission, release

conscientious *adj* **1** guided by or in accordance with one's sense of right and wrong ⟨operated on the belief that most people are *conscientious*, the unattended farm stand has a price list and a money drawer for customers to leave payment for their purchases⟩
synonyms ethical, honest, honorable, just, moral, principled, scrupulous
related words good, righteous, upright, virtuous; dutiful, observant, respectful; overconscientious; reliable, trustworthy, trusty
near antonyms unreliable, untrustworthy
antonyms cutthroat, dishonest, dishonorable, immoral, unethical, unjust, unprincipled, unscrupulous

2 taking great care and effort ⟨a guidance counselor who serves students by first being a *conscientious* listener⟩ — see PAINSTAKING

conscientiousness *n* strict attentiveness to what one is doing ⟨finished the last details with as much *conscientiousness* as the first⟩ — see CARE 1

conscious *adj* having specified facts or feelings actively impressed on the mind ⟨*conscious* of the fact that my hands were sweating the whole time that I was making my presentation⟩
synonyms alive, aware, cognizant, mindful, sensible, sentient
related words attentive, heedful, observant, regardful, vigilant, watchful
near antonyms inattentive, unheeding, unobservant, unobserving
antonyms insensible, unaware, unconscious, unmindful

consciously *adv* with full awareness of what one is doing ⟨she *consciously* chose to take the more dangerous route down the mountain⟩ — see INTENTIONALLY

conscript *n* a person forced or required to enroll in military service ⟨as the war continued, the body of enlisted soldiers was supplemented by an increasing number of *conscripts*⟩
synonyms draftee, inductee
related words recruit, rookie

conscript *vb* to pick especially for required military service ⟨was *conscripted* into the army shortly after turning 18⟩ — see DRAFT 1

consecrate *vb* **1** to keep or intend for a special purpose ⟨a philanthropist who *consecrated* his fortune to charitable causes⟩ — see DEVOTE 1

2 to make holy through prayers or ritual ⟨plans to *consecrate* the altar in the new church with great ceremony⟩ — see BLESS 1

consecrated *adj* set apart or worthy of veneration by association with God ⟨built the cemetery on *consecrated* ground⟩ — see HOLY 2

consecration *n* the act of making something holy through religious ritual ⟨the *consecration* of the Host during Communion⟩
synonyms blessing, hallowing, sanctification
related words dedication
near antonyms defilement, desecration, profanation

consecutive *adj* following one after another without others coming in between ⟨the team's winning streak has lasted for seven *consecutive* games⟩
synonyms sequential, succeeding, successional, successive
related words serial; constant, continuous, uninterrupted; ensuing, following, later, next, subsequent

consensus *n* the act or fact of being of one opinion about something ⟨reached a *consensus* on how to spend the money that the club had raised⟩ — see AGREE-MENT 1

consent *n* the approval by someone in authority for the doing of something ⟨we had to get our parents' *consent* in order to go on the field trip⟩ — see PERMISSION

consequence *n* **1** a condition or occurrence traceable to a cause ⟨the flood was an inevitable *consequence* of the prolonged, heavy rains⟩ — see EFFECT 1
2 the quality or state of being important ⟨a mistake that was of no great *consequence*⟩ — see IMPORTANCE

consequent *adj* coming as a result ⟨her new job and *con-sequent* relocation⟩ — see RESULTANT

consequential *adj* **1** coming as a result ⟨his high-fat diet and the *consequential* weight gain⟩ — see RESULTANT
2 having great meaning or lasting effect ⟨the American Civil War is often regarded as the nation's most *conse-quential* event since its founding⟩ — see IMPORTANT 1

consequently *adv* for this or that reason ⟨taxes were lowered, and *consequently* complaints were fewer⟩ — see THEREFORE

conservation *n* **1** the careful maintaining and protection of something valuable especially in its natural or origi-nal state ⟨everyone has a duty to aid in the *conservation* of our nation's wilderness areas⟩
synonyms preservation
related words care, maintenance, upkeep; salvation, saving; guardianship, protection, safeguarding, safe-keeping; economy, husbandry, management
near antonyms neglect, squandering, waste; destruc-tion, ruin; damage, injury
2 the act or activity of keeping something in an existing and usually satisfactory condition ⟨the *conservation* of the nation's monuments and memorials⟩ — see MAIN-TENANCE

conservative *adj* **1** tending to favor established ideas, conditions, or institutions ⟨*conservative* baseball fans consider the new ballpark too modern-looking and plain ugly⟩
synonyms old-fashioned, orthodox, reactionary, tradi-tional, unprogressive
related words conventional; faithful, loyal, steadfast, true-blue
near antonyms extremist, radical, revolutionary; non-conformist
antonyms liberal, nonorthodox, nontraditional, pro-gressive, unorthodox
2 not excessively showy ⟨dressing in *conservative* out-fits so as to make a good impression at job interviews⟩ — see QUIET 2

conservative *n* a person whose political beliefs are cen-tered on tradition and keeping things the way they are ⟨proposed legislation that was opposed by *conservatives* throughout the state⟩
synonyms reactionary, rightist
related words conformist
near antonyms extremist, radical, revolutionary, revo-lutionist
antonyms leftist, liberal, progressive

conservatory *n* a glass-enclosed building for growing plants ⟨the college's *conservatory* is entirely devoted to cultivating and displaying orchids⟩
synonyms greenhouse, hothouse
related words cold frame; nursery

conserve *vb* to keep in good condition ⟨*conserve* our na-tional parks so that they may be enjoyed by future gen-erations⟩ — see MAINTAIN 1

conserving *n* the act or activity of keeping something in an existing and usually satisfactory condition ⟨the con-

serving of such national treasures as the flag that flew over Fort McHenry during its famous bombardment⟩ — see MAINTENANCE

consider *vb* **1** to think of in a particular way ⟨I *consider* him a very good friend⟩
synonyms account, call, count, esteem, hold, rate, reckon, regard, take (for)
related words believe, feel, sense, think; conceive, fancy, imagine
phrases look on (*or* upon)
2 to give serious and careful thought to ⟨carefully *con-sidering* our options⟩ — see PONDER
3 to have as an opinion ⟨*consider* the price too high⟩ — see BELIEVE 2

considerable *adj* **1** sufficiently large in size, amount, or number to merit attention ⟨the *considerable* number of auto accidents that resulted from the surprise snow-storm⟩
synonyms good, goodly, good-sized, healthy, largish, respectable, significant, sizable (*or* sizeable), substan-tial, tidy
related words big, colossal, enormous, gigantic, great, huge, immense, mammoth
near antonyms piddling, puny, trivial, unimportant; marginal, meager, slight; little, small, tiny
antonyms inconsiderable, insignificant, insubstantial
2 of a size greater than average of its kind ⟨a house with a *considerable* barn in back⟩ — see LARGE

considerably *adv* to a large extent or degree ⟨home elec-tronic devices that have fallen *considerably* in price⟩ — see GREATLY 2

considerate *adj* **1** given to or made with heedful antici-pation of the needs and happiness of others ⟨a kindly woman who is very *considerate* of other people's feel-ings⟩ — see THOUGHTFUL 1
2 having or showing a close attentiveness to avoiding danger or trouble ⟨you need to develop a more *consid-erate* temperament and learn to think before you speak⟩ — see CAREFUL 1

considerately *adv* with good reason or courtesy ⟨he *con-siderately* made breakfast for all of the exhausted res-cue workers⟩ — see WELL 4

consideration *n* **1** a careful weighing of the reasons for or against something ⟨after much *consideration* we de-cided to make an offer on the house⟩
synonyms debate, deliberation, thought
related words cogitation, contemplation, meditation, pondering, rumination; introspection, reflection; ago-nizing, hesitation, indecision
2 something (as money) that is given or received in re-turn for goods or services ⟨a *consideration* paid for le-gal services⟩ — see PAYMENT 2

considered *adj* decided on as a result of careful thought ⟨my *considered* opinion is that this is the best movie I've ever seen⟩ — see DELIBERATE 1

consign *vb* **1** to cause to go or be taken from one place to another ⟨*consigned* the prisoner to the dungeon⟩ — see SEND
2 to put (something) into the possession or safekeeping of another ⟨the deliveryman had *consigned* our pack-age to a next-door neighbor⟩ — see GIVE 2

consist (of) *vb* to be made up of ⟨those cookies *consist of* flour, butter, sugar, chocolate, and vanilla⟩ — see COMPRISE 1

consistency *n* the degree to which a fluid can resist flow-ing ⟨beat the egg whites until they take on the *consis-tency* of whipped cream⟩

synonyms density, thickness, viscosity
related words compactness, firmness, solidity; ropiness, stickiness

consistent *adj* not having or showing any apparent conflict ⟨the clothes you wear to class must be *consistent* with the school's dress code⟩
synonyms compatible, conformable (to), congruous, consonant, correspondent (with *or* to), harmonious, nonconflicting
related words appropriate, fitting, meet, suitable
phrases of a piece
antonyms conflicting, incompatible, incongruous, inconsistent, inharmonious, unharmonious

consistently *adv* on every relevant occasion ⟨he *consistently* brings a sandwich for lunch⟩ — see ALWAYS 1

consolation *n* **1** the giving of hope and strength in times of grief, distress, or suffering ⟨the *consolation* of the grieving family by their pastor⟩
synonyms comforting, consoling, solace, solacing
related words commiseration, condolence, sympathy; counseling (*or* counselling)
2 a feeling of ease from grief or trouble ⟨the *consolation* that our favorite foods give us when we're having a bad day⟩ — see COMFORT 1

console *vb* to ease the grief or distress of ⟨the military officer who must *console* the bereaved at a soldier's funeral⟩ — see COMFORT 1

consolidate *vb* **1** to bring (something) to a central point or under a single control ⟨plans to *consolidate* several schools into one regional high school⟩ — see CENTRALIZE
2 to make markedly greater in measure or degree ⟨another win would *consolidate* their hold on first place in their division⟩ — see INTENSIFY

consolidation *n* the act or an instance of joining two or more things into one ⟨the *consolidation* of several intelligence agencies into one super agency⟩ — see UNION 1

consoling *n* the giving of hope and strength in times of grief, distress, or suffering ⟨the responsibility for the *consoling* of the families of the firefighters fell to the mayor⟩ — see CONSOLATION 1

consonance *n* **1** a balanced, pleasing, or suitable arrangement of parts ⟨at present, the living room lacks *consonance* because all of the furniture is on one side⟩ — see HARMONY 1
2 a state of consistency ⟨in good writing there is always *consonance* of thought and expression, as the use of simple words for simple thoughts⟩ — see CONFORMITY 1

consonant *adj* **1** having the parts agreeably related ⟨the temples and palaces of ancient Greece are among the most *consonant* buildings in architectural history⟩ — see HARMONIOUS 2
2 not having or showing any apparent conflict ⟨his gentle behavior is *consonant* with his expressed belief in pacifism⟩ — see CONSISTENT

consort *n* the person to whom another is married ⟨it is the queen's eldest son and not her *consort* who is next in line for the throne⟩ — see SPOUSE

consort *vb* to come or be together as friends ⟨*consorting* with other boys having similar interests⟩ — see ASSOCIATE

conspicuous *adj* **1** likely to attract attention ⟨the seven-foot-tall basketball player is *conspicuous* in any crowd⟩ — see NOTICEABLE

2 very noticeable especially for being incorrect or bad ⟨*conspicuous* bureaucratic waste that drives taxpayers crazy⟩ — see EGREGIOUS

conspiracy *n* **1** a group involved in secret or criminal activities ⟨members of the *conspiracy* recognized each other by a secret handshake⟩ — see RING 1
2 a secret agreement or cooperation between two parties for an illegal or dishonest purpose ⟨a *conspiracy* among the leading manufacturers to fix prices⟩ — see COLLUSION
3 a secret plan for accomplishing evil or unlawful ends ⟨several generals were engaged in a *conspiracy* to overthrow the government⟩ — see PLOT 1

conspire *vb* to engage in a secret plan to accomplish evil or unlawful ends ⟨*conspired* to replace the leader with someone more easily influenced⟩ — see PLOT

constable *n* a member of a force charged with law enforcement at the local level ⟨reported the crime to the local *constable*⟩ — see OFFICER 1

constabulary *n* a body of officers of the law ⟨all members of the local *constabulary* were on the alert for the escaped convict⟩ — see POLICE 2

constancy *n* **1** the state of continuing without change ⟨the mistaken notion that there is *constancy* in language—words do indeed change their meanings over time⟩
synonyms changelessness, fixedness, immutability, invariability, stability, steadiness, unchangeableness
related words consistency, regularity, sameness, uniformity; durability, lastingness, permanence
near antonyms inconsistency, irregularity, unevenness; evanescence, impermanence
antonyms changeability, changeableness, instability, mutability, unsteadiness, variability
2 adherence to something to which one is bound by a pledge or duty ⟨soldiers serving with *constancy* and devotion⟩ — see FIDELITY

constant *adj* **1** not undergoing a change in condition ⟨change is the only *constant* thing in the world of fashion⟩
synonyms changeless, stable, stationary, steady, unchanging, unvarying
related words fast, fixed, hard-and-fast, immutable, inflexible, invariable, unalterable, unchangeable; established, set, settled; durable, enduring, lasting, permanent
near antonyms alterable, changeable, flexible, mutable, variable; ephemeral, evanescent, fleeting, momentary, transient, transitory
antonyms changeful, changing, fluctuating, inconstant, unstable, unsteady, varying
2 appearing or occurring repeatedly from time to time ⟨I get *constant* headaches during humid weather⟩ — see REGULAR 1
3 firm in one's allegiance to someone or something ⟨*constant* friends during times both good and bad⟩ — see FAITHFUL 1

constantly *adv* **1** many times ⟨a crackpot who *constantly* wrote angry letters to the local newspaper⟩ — see OFTEN
2 on every relevant occasion ⟨stay *constantly* on guard until the danger is past⟩ — see ALWAYS 1

consternation *n* the emotion experienced in the presence or threat of danger ⟨stared at the unexpected obstacle in utter *consternation*⟩ — see FEAR

constituent *n* one of the parts that make up a whole ⟨the soil contained all of the necessary *constituents* for growing crops⟩ — see ELEMENT 1

constitute *vb* **1** to be all the substance of ⟨nine players *constitute* a baseball team⟩
synonyms compose, comprise, form, make up
related words embody, incorporate, integrate; complement, complete, supplement; fill out, flesh (out)
2 to be responsible for the creation and early operation or use of ⟨a fund was *constituted* to help needy students attend the prep school⟩ — see FOUND
3 to pick (someone) by one's authority for a specific position or duty ⟨the legally *constituted* authorities with jurisdiction in this matter⟩ — see APPOINT 2

constitution *n* **1** the set of qualities that makes a person, a group of people, or a thing different from others ⟨the question of whether violent conflict is part of the *constitution* of human society⟩ — see NATURE 1
2 the type of body that a person has ⟨that marathon runner is known more for her strong *constitution* than for her speed⟩ — see PHYSIQUE

constitutional *n* a relaxed journey on foot for exercise or pleasure ⟨went for my evening *constitutional* in the park⟩ — see WALK

constitutionally *adv* by natural character or ability ⟨I'm afraid that I'm *constitutionally* incapable of carrying a tune⟩ — see NATURALLY 1

constrain *vb* **1** to cause (a person) to give in to pressure ⟨*constrained* by conscience to tell only the truth⟩ — see FORCE
2 to keep from exceeding a desirable degree or level (as of expression) ⟨*constrained* his anger at the needless interruption⟩ — see CONTROL 1

constraint *n* **1** the checking of one's true feelings and impulses when dealing with others ⟨in civilized society people do not just say or do whatever they feel like—they exercise some *constraint*⟩
synonyms inhibition, repression, reserve, restraint, self-control, self-restraint, suppression
related words control, discipline, self-denial, self-discipline; composure, self-possession; aloofness, detachedness, distance; bashfulness, modesty, shyness; reticence, silence, taciturnity
near antonyms self-indulgence; bluntness, candor, frankness
2 something that limits one's freedom of action or choice ⟨put legal *constraints* on the board's activities⟩ — see RESTRICTION 1
3 the use of power to impose one's will on another ⟨parental *constraint* can take several different forms, including a denial of the approval that children usually seek from their parents⟩ — see FORCE 2

constrict *vb* **1** to become smaller in size or volume through the drawing together of particles of matter ⟨the vessel *constricted*, thereby reducing the flow of blood⟩ — see CONTRACT 2
2 to reduce in size or volume by or as if by pressing parts or members together ⟨*constricted* the opening with a clamp⟩ — see COMPRESS 1

constriction *n* the act or process of reducing the size or volume of something by or as if by pressing ⟨tried to ease the tie's *constriction* of his neck⟩ — see COMPRESSION

construct *vb* to form by putting together parts or materials ⟨*constructed* a dam across the river⟩ — see BUILD

construction *n* **1** something put together by arranging or connecting an array of parts ⟨the swing set turned out to be a more complicated *construction* than the "some assembly required" warning suggested⟩
synonyms erection, structure

related words arrangement, assembly; frame, framework, skeleton
2 a statement that makes something clear ⟨could you give us your *construction* of this passage in the Bible?⟩ — see EXPLANATION 1

constructive *adj* having a role in deciding something's final form ⟨his experiences as an exchange student played a *constructive* part in the course that his life would take⟩ — see FORMATIVE

construe *vb* to make plain or understandable ⟨the role of the justices of the supreme court in *construing* the constitution⟩ — see EXPLAIN 1

consult *vb* to exchange viewpoints or seek advice for the purpose of finding a solution to a problem ⟨will *consult* with several experts before deciding which course of treatment to pursue⟩ — see CONFER 2

consultant *n* a person who gives advice especially professionally ⟨a *consultant* in public relations to a number of large corporations⟩
synonyms adviser (*or* advisor), counselor (*or* counsellor)
related words authority, expert, professional; confidant

consume *vb* **1** to destroy all trace of ⟨massive fires had *consumed* hundreds of square miles of forest⟩
synonyms devour, eat (up)
related words gut; deplete, exhaust, use up; raze, ruin, waste; annihilate, extinguish
2 to make complete use of ⟨*consumed* all of the local mineral resources⟩ — see DEPLETE
3 to take in as food ⟨hungry enough to *consume* a large portion of pie⟩ — see EAT 1

consummate *adj* **1** having or showing exceptional knowledge, experience, or skill in a field of endeavor ⟨*consummate* cabinetmakers, they produced desks and chests of drawers that are now regarded as masterpieces of American furniture⟩ — see PROFICIENT
2 having no exceptions or restrictions ⟨a *consummate* liar who has practically made mendacity an art⟩ — see ABSOLUTE 2
3 of the greatest or highest degree or quantity ⟨a ballerina renowned for her *consummate* grace⟩ — see ULTIMATE 1

consummate *vb* to bring (something) to a state where nothing remains to be done ⟨willing to do whatever it takes to *consummate* a business deal⟩ — see FINISH 1

consummation *n* **1** the last part of a process or action ⟨the signing of the contract marked the *consummation* of the negotiations⟩ — see FINALE
2 the state of being actual or complete ⟨the opening of the performing arts center brought to *consummation* years of planning⟩ — see FRUITION

contact *n* an acquaintance who has influence especially in the business or political world ⟨an intern who got her summer job in the governor's office through *contacts*⟩
synonyms connection
related words big shot, bigwig, somebody, VIP; go-between, intermediary, mediator

contact *vb* to transmit information or requests to ⟨you can *contact* me at this number⟩
synonyms communicate (with), reach
related words apprise, fill in, inform, notify; buzz, call, phone, ring [*chiefly British*], telephone
phrases get (*or* keep) in touch with

contagious *adj* **1** capable of being passed by physical contact from one person to another ⟨chicken pox,

measles, German measles, and other *contagious* diseases⟩
synonyms catching, communicable, transmittable
related words infectious, infective
near antonyms noninfectious
antonyms noncommunicable
2 exciting a similar feeling or reaction in others ⟨the enthusiasm of the new club members was *contagious*⟩
synonyms catching, infectious, spreading
related words palpable, perceptible, tangible; irresistible, overpowering, overwhelming; fetching, inviting, winning
contain *vb* **1** to have within ⟨the top drawer of the cabinet *contains* my stamp collection⟩
synonyms hold
related words accommodate, fit; encase, enclose (*also* inclose), encompass; harbor, house, lodge, shelter
2 to have as part of a whole ⟨the contract *contains* several new clauses⟩ — see INCLUDE
3 to be made up of ⟨the recipe *contains* several parts⟩ — see COMPRISE 1
4 to gain emotional or mental control of ⟨could hardly *contain* herself when she heard that she had won the scholarship⟩ — see COLLECT 1
5 to keep from exceeding a desirable degree or level (as of expression) ⟨*contain* the spread of the disease⟩ — see CONTROL 1
container *n* something into which a liquid or smaller objects can be put for storage or transportation ⟨save the plastic *containers* from the deli for other uses⟩
synonyms holder, receptacle, vessel
related words cartridge; bin, box, carton, case, crate; bag, pocket, sack; cooler, warmer
contaminant *n* something that is or that makes impure ⟨a filter to remove *contaminants* from the drinking water⟩ — see IMPURITY
contaminate *vb* to make unfit for use by the addition of something harmful or undesirable ⟨a supply of drinking water that was *contaminated* by a toxic waste dump⟩
synonyms befoul, defile, foul, poison, pollute, taint
related words infect; besmirch, dirty, soil, sully; corrupt, rot, spoil; adulterate, doctor; dilute, water (down)
near antonyms clean, cleanse, purge; filter; disinfect, sanitize
antonyms decontaminate, purify
contaminated *adj* containing foreign or lower-grade substances ⟨the hospitals had to throw out the *contaminated* blood supply⟩ — see IMPURE
contemplate *vb* **1** to give serious and careful thought to ⟨she *contemplated* the problem for several hours before reaching a decision⟩ — see PONDER
2 to have in mind as a purpose or goal ⟨he waited patiently, *contemplating* revenge all the while⟩ — see INTEND
contemplation *n* long or deep thinking about spiritual matters ⟨the decision to enter a monastery and to spend one's life in prayer and *contemplation*⟩
synonyms meditation
related words introspection, reflection, retrospection; cogitation, deliberation, musing, pondering, rumination
contemplative *adj* given to or marked by long, quiet thinking ⟨a *contemplative* person who likes to go on solitary walks⟩ ⟨the *contemplative* life of the monks at the abbey⟩
synonyms meditative, melancholy, pensive, reflective, ruminant, thoughtful

related words introspective, retrospective; earnest, serious, sober, somber (*or* sombre); analytic (*or* analytical), logical, rational; deliberate, purposeful
near antonyms flighty, flippant, frivolous; brainless, mindless, silly, thoughtless, unthinking
antonyms unreflective
contemporaneous *adj* existing or occurring at the same period of time ⟨*contemporaneous* accounts of the battle from officers on both sides⟩ — see CONTEMPORARY 1
contemporaneously *adv* at one and the same time ⟨Mozart was writing music *contemporaneously* with Haydn⟩ — see TOGETHER 1
contemporary *adj* **1** existing or occurring at the same period of time ⟨the absurd notion that early cave dwellers were *contemporary* with the dinosaurs⟩
synonyms coeval, coexistent, coexisting, coextensive, concurrent, contemporaneous, simultaneous, synchronous
related words accompanying, attendant, attending, coincident, concomitant
antonyms noncontemporary
2 being or involving the latest methods, concepts, information, or styles ⟨a magazine devoted to *contemporary* fashions⟩ — see MODERN
contemporary *n* a person who lives at the same time or is about the same age as another ⟨Abraham Lincoln and Charles Darwin were exact *contemporaries*, actually being born on the same day in 1809⟩
synonyms coeval
related words accompaniment, companion, concomitant; equal, peer
contempt *n* open dislike for someone or something considered unworthy of one's concern or respect ⟨my undying *contempt* for people who abuse animals⟩
synonyms despite, despitefulness, disdain, scorn
related words abhorrence, abomination, execration, hate, hatred, loathing; cattiness, hatefulness, invidiousness, malevolence, malice, maliciousness, malignancy, malignity, meanness, spite, spitefulness; aversion, disgust, distaste, horror, odium, repugnance, repulsion, revulsion; animosity, antagonism, antipathy, bitterness, enmity, grudge, hostility, jealousy, pique, resentment; bile, jaundice, rancor, spleen, venom, virulence, vitriol
near antonyms acceptance, tolerance; adoration, veneration, worship; affection, fondness, liking
antonyms admiration, esteem, regard, respect
contemptible *adj* **1** arousing or deserving of one's loathing and disgust ⟨the *contemptible* thieves who stole the Christmas gifts intended for needy children⟩
synonyms despicable, lousy, nasty, pitiable, pitiful, scabby, scummy, scurvy, sorry, wretched
related words abhorrent, abominable, detestable, execrable, hateful, loathsome, odious; disgusting, repugnant, repulsive; disgraceful, dishonorable, shameful; base, ignoble, low, mean; shabby, sordid, squalid, vile; cowardly, craven, dastardly
near antonyms high-minded, honorable, noble, principled; commendable, creditable, laudable, praiseworthy
antonyms admirable
2 deserving pitying scorn (as for inadequacy) ⟨a *contemptible* attempt at science fiction⟩ — see PITIFUL 1
3 not following or in accordance with standards of honor and decency ⟨the *contemptible* behavior of the students who took part in the hazing⟩ — see IGNOBLE 2
contemptuous *adj* **1** feeling or showing open dislike for someone or something regarded as undeserving of re-

spect or concern ⟨loutish tourists who are *contemptuous* of the ways and traditions of their host countries⟩
synonyms disdainful, scornful
related words discourteous, disrespectful, impudent, insolent; arrogant, cavalier, high-handed; haughty, lofty, lordly, prideful, sniffish, snobbish, supercilious; pompous, self-important, superior
near antonyms deferential, respectful; accepting, tolerant; courteous, polite
antonyms admiring, appreciative
2 intended to make a person or thing seem of little importance or value ⟨*contemptuous* comments about the baseball team's poor efforts of late⟩ — see DEROGATORY

contend *vb* **1** to engage in a contest ⟨two traditional rivals *contending* for the championship⟩ — see COMPETE
2 to state (something) as a reason in support of or against something under consideration ⟨*contended* that the senator's considerable experience made him the best candidate⟩ — see ARGUE 1
3 to state as a fact usually forcefully ⟨*contended* that he was wrong about practically everything⟩ — see CLAIM 1

contend (with) *vb* **1** to deal with (something) usually skillfully or efficiently ⟨many problems to *contend with*⟩ — see HANDLE 1
2 to strive to reduce or eliminate ⟨medical missionaries who daily *contend with* disease and poverty⟩ — see FIGHT 2

contender *n* **1** one who seeks an office, honor, position, or award ⟨a *contender* for the mayoral position⟩ — see CANDIDATE
2 one who strives for the same thing as another ⟨several *contenders* competing for the title of the city's best Italian restaurant⟩ — see COMPETITOR

content *adj* feeling that one's needs or desires have been met ⟨are you *content* with your present allowance?⟩
synonyms contented, gratified, happy, pleased, satisfied
related words delighted, glad, joyful, joyous, jubilant; ecstatic, elated, enraptured, euphoric, overjoyed, rapturous, thrilled; appeased, mollified, pacified, placated
near antonyms disaffected, disgruntled; discouraged, disheartened, dispirited
antonyms discontent, discontented, displeased, dissatisfied, malcontent, unhappy

¹**content** *n* **1** a major object of interest or concern (as in a discussion or artistic composition) ⟨although I appreciate the poem's lyrical qualities, I don't understand its *content*⟩ — see MATTER 1
2 the amount of something (as subject matter) included ⟨judging from the table of *contents*, I'd have to say that this book covers most of the major topics in American history⟩ — see COVERAGE
3 the largest number or amount that something can hold ⟨the oil can has a *content* of four liters⟩ — see CAPACITY 1

²**content** *n* the feeling experienced when one's wishes are met ⟨slept to her heart's *content* on weekends⟩ — see PLEASURE 1

content *vb* to give satisfaction to ⟨a person easily *contented* by life's simple pleasures⟩ — see PLEASE

contented *adj* feeling that one's needs or desires have been met ⟨having had her fill of candy, the *contented* girl sank back into the easy chair and dozed off⟩ — see CONTENT

contentedness *n* the feeling experienced when one's wishes are met ⟨went to bed that night with a feeling of *contentedness*⟩ — see PLEASURE 1

contention *n* an idea or opinion that is put forth in a discussion or debate ⟨my *contention* is that today's lower batting averages are the result of better pitching⟩
synonyms argument, assertion, thesis
related words hypothesis, theory; proposal, proposition; assumption, presupposition, supposition; position, stand

contentious *adj* **1** feeling or displaying eagerness to fight ⟨the Tartars were a *contentious* people who terrorized much of Asia and eastern Europe during the Middle Ages⟩ — see BELLIGERENT
2 given to arguing ⟨a tiresomely *contentious* person who likes to argue for the sake of arguing⟩ — see ARGUMENTATIVE 1

contentiousness *n* an inclination to fight or quarrel ⟨his natural tendency towards *contentiousness* made him a poor choice for a diplomat⟩ — see BELLIGERENCE

contentment *n* the feeling experienced when one's wishes are met ⟨a couple of golden-agers looking over their life together with a feeling of *contentment* and accomplishment⟩ — see PLEASURE 1

contest *n* **1** an earnest effort for superiority or victory over another ⟨the eternal *contest* between the forces of good and the forces of evil⟩
synonyms battle, combat, conflict, confrontation, duel, face-off, rivalry, struggle, tug-of-war, warfare
related words showdown; contention, discord, friction, strife; controversy, debate, disagreement
near antonyms concord, harmony, peace
2 a competitive encounter between individuals or groups carried on for amusement, exercise, or in pursuit of a prize ⟨a *contest* for the gold medal in diving⟩ — see GAME 1
3 a physical dispute between opposing individuals or groups ⟨what mighty *contests* have been waged on trivial matters⟩ — see FIGHT 1

contest *vb* to demand proof of the truth or rightness of ⟨vowed to *contest* the claim in court⟩ — see CHALLENGE 1

contestant *n* one who strives for the same thing as another ⟨three *contestants* will compete on live TV for the cash prize⟩ — see COMPETITOR

contiguity *n* the state or condition of being near ⟨because of the *contiguity* of the mall to the border, it attracts many shoppers from out of state⟩ — see PROXIMITY

contiguous *adj* having a border in common ⟨Connecticut and Massachusetts are *contiguous* states⟩ — see ADJACENT

continent *n* one of the great divisions of land on the globe or the main part of such a division ⟨Europe and Asia are sometimes considered together to be one *continent*⟩ — see MAINLAND

contingency *n* something that might happen ⟨agencies trying to provide for every *contingency* in a national emergency⟩ — see EVENT 2

contingent *n* a body of persons chosen as representatives of a larger group ⟨our Scout troop sent a large *contingent* to the jamboree⟩
synonyms delegation
related words embassy, legation, mission; crew, detachment, gang, outfit, squad

contingent (on *or* upon) *adj* determined by something else ⟨the train's scheduled departure is *contingent on* the prompt fixing of the mechanical fault⟩ — see DE-PENDENT 2

continual *adj* **1** going on and on without any interrup-tions ⟨the castaways hoped that the *continual* broad-cast of the distress signal would eventually attract attention⟩ — see CONTINUOUS

2 occurring or appearing at intervals ⟨a history of *con-tinual* invasions from countries to the west⟩ — see IN-TERMITTENT 1

continually *adv* **1** many times ⟨we were *continually* being told to mind our manners⟩ — see OFTEN

2 on every relevant occasion ⟨the computer program *continually* updated the file with new information⟩ — see ALWAYS 1

continuance *n* **1** continuing existence ⟨annoyed by the *continuance* of the cold weather⟩ — see PERSISTENCE 1

2 uninterrupted or lasting existence ⟨the *continuance* of hunger in the world despite some valiant efforts to solve the problem⟩ — see CONTINUATION

continuation *n* uninterrupted or lasting existence ⟨the *continuation* of high unemployment has cost the gov-ernment much support⟩

synonyms continuance, duration, endurance, persis-tence, subsistence

related words elongation, extension, lengthening, pro-longation

near antonyms abridgment (*or* abridgement), curtail-ment, shortening

antonyms ending, termination

continue *vb* **1** to remain indefinitely in existence or in the same state ⟨the heavy snow *continued* throughout the night⟩

synonyms abide, endure, hold (up), hold on, keep up, last, persist, run on

related words linger, remain, stay, stick around, tarry

near antonyms abate, die (down), ebb, let up, moder-ate, subside, wane

antonyms cease, desist, discontinue, quit, stop

2 to begin again or return to after an interruption ⟨we'll *continue* this discussion after we've eaten⟩ — see RESUME

continuous *adj* going on and on without any interrup-tions ⟨a city that has been under *continuous* bombard-ment for three days⟩

synonyms ceaseless, continual, incessant, unbroken, unceasing, uninterrupted, unremitting

related words endless, eternal, everlasting, inter-minable, perpetual, unending; changeless, constant, stable, steady, unchanging, unvarying

near antonyms intermittent, periodic, recurrent, re-curring

antonyms noncontinuous

contort *vb* to twist (something) out of a natural or nor-mal shape or condition ⟨the acrobat is able to *contort* his body so that it almost looks like a pretzel⟩

synonyms deform, distort, screw, squinch, warp

related words deface, disfigure; wrench, wrest, wring; coil, curl, twine, wind, wreathe

contortion *n* the twisting of something out of its natural or normal shape or condition ⟨the comedian is renowned for his seemingly endless variety of facial *contortions*⟩

synonyms deformation, distortion, screwing, squinch-ing, warping

related words defacement, disfigurement

contour *n* a line that traces the outer limits of an object or surface ⟨a car with flowing *contours*⟩ — see OUT-LINE 1

contract *n* **1** a formal agreement to fulfill an obligation ⟨accused her of breaking their *contract* by not com-pleting the decorating job on budget⟩ — see GUARAN-TEE 1

2 an arrangement about action to be taken ⟨a *contract* outlining what needed to be done by each person⟩ — see AGREEMENT 2

contract *vb* **1** to become affected with (a disease or dis-order) ⟨before vaccines were invented, people lived in fear of *contracting* polio⟩

synonyms catch, come down (with), get, sicken (with), take

related words break out (with); die (from), succumb (to); fail, sink, weaken

near antonyms recover (from), shake (off)

2 to become smaller in size or volume through the drawing together of particles of matter ⟨metal *con-tracts* at low temperatures⟩

synonyms compress, condense, constrict, shrink

related words collapse, deflate; dry (up), shrivel, wither; decrease, diminish, dwindle, lessen; recede, re-treat, withdraw

near antonyms accumulate, grow, increase; balloon, inflate, puff (up)

antonyms expand, swell

3 to reduce in size or volume by or as if by pressing parts or members together ⟨*contract* the calf muscles in your legs⟩ — see COMPRESS 1

contraction *n* the act or process of reducing the size or volume of something by or as if by pressing ⟨most sub-stances undergo *contraction* when cooled⟩ — see COM-PRESSION

contradict *vb* **1** to make an assertion that is contrary to one made by (another) ⟨no matter what I say, you al-ways have to *contradict* me⟩

synonyms disagree (with), gainsay

related words challenge, contest, dispute, question; confute, rebut, refute; cross, fight, oppose, resist

near antonyms concur (with); confirm, corroborate, substantiate, verify

antonyms agree (with)

2 to declare not to be true ⟨his account *contradicted* the story that they had gotten earlier⟩ — see DENY 1

contradiction *n* **1** someone or something with qualities or features that seem to conflict with one another ⟨a loving father as well as a ruthless killer, the gangster is a living *contradiction*⟩

synonyms incongruity, paradox

related words conundrum, enigma, mystery, puzzle, riddle

2 a refusal to confirm the truth of a statement ⟨the ac-tress's *contradiction* of the marriage rumor caused quite a stir⟩ — see DENIAL 2

contradictory *adj* being as different as possible ⟨*contra-dictory* predictions regarding stock prices that were of no help to investors at all⟩ — see OPPOSITE

contraption *n* an interesting and often novel device with a practical use ⟨built a *contraption* for automatically buttering toast⟩ — see GADGET

contrariness *n* refusal to obey ⟨cursed the *contrariness* of the mutt when it refused to come back inside the house⟩ — see DISOBEDIENCE

contrariwise *adv* just the opposite being true ⟨the rock singer is hardly a carouser; *contrariwise*, he totally ab-stains from alcohol⟩

synonyms again, conversely

phrases on the contrary

near antonyms even, indeed, nay, truly, verily, yea

contrary *adj* **1** being as different as possible ⟨the other jurors seemed sure the defendant was guilty, but I came to the *contrary* conclusion⟩ — see OPPOSITE
2 engaging in or marked by childish misbehavior ⟨a *contrary* child who wouldn't behave⟩ — see NAUGHTY
3 given to resisting authority or another's control ⟨the *contrary* soldier is facing a court-martial for insubordination⟩ — see DISOBEDIENT

contrary *n* something that is as different as possible from something else ⟨the admonition that we should not return hate with hate, but rather with its *contrary*—love⟩ — see OPPOSITE

contrast *n* the quality or state of being different ⟨the *contrast* between the two approaches to the problem of overeating could not be greater⟩ — see DIFFERENCE 1

contribute *vb* **1** to make a donation as part of a group effort ⟨would you like to *contribute* to the Thanksgiving fund for needy families?⟩
synonyms chip in, kick in, pitch in
related words bestow, donate, give, present
2 to make a present of ⟨*contributes* money to a variety of worthy causes⟩ — see GIVE 1

contribution *n* a gift of money or its equivalent to a charity, humanitarian cause, or public institution ⟨*contributions* for the victims of the earthquake began pouring in⟩
synonyms alms, benefaction, beneficence, charity, donation, philanthropy
related words offering, tithe; bequest, endowment, legacy; aid, assistance, relief, welfare; grant, subsidy

contrite *adj* **1** feeling sorrow for a wrong that one has done ⟨being *contrite* is not enough to spare you an arrest if you're caught shoplifting⟩
synonyms apologetic, penitent, regretful, remorseful, repentant, rueful, sorry
related words sad, grieving, mournful, sorrowful, woeful
near antonyms merciless, pitiless, ruthless
antonyms impenitent, remorseless, unapologetic, unrepentant
2 suffering from or expressive of a feeling of responsibility for wrongdoing ⟨her *contrite* expression made them take her apology more seriously⟩ — see GUILTY 2

contriteness *n* a feeling of responsibility for wrongdoing ⟨his determination to make things right again were seen as a sign of his *contriteness*⟩ — see GUILT 1

contrition *n* a feeling of responsibility for wrongdoing ⟨tearful expressions of *contrition*⟩ — see GUILT 1

contrivance *n* **1** an interesting and often novel device with a practical use ⟨a new *contrivance* for cleaning computer keyboards⟩ — see GADGET
2 something (as a device) created for the first time through the use of the imagination ⟨despite the many modern *contrivances* for saving time and labor, we seem to have less leisure and energy than ever before⟩ — see INVENTION 1

contrive *vb* **1** to create or think of by clever use of the imagination ⟨*contrived* abstract metal sculptures using old household utensils⟩ — see INVENT
2 to engage in a secret plan to accomplish evil or unlawful ends ⟨the mischievous boys were always *contriving* and trying to pull the prank that would be the talk of the school⟩ — see PLOT
3 to plan out usually with subtle skill or care ⟨*contrived* a way of helping the needy family without their knowing it⟩ — see ENGINEER

contrived *adj* lacking in natural or spontaneous quality ⟨the *contrived* applause of a TV studio audience that has been told when to clap⟩ — see ARTIFICIAL 1

contriver *n* one who creates or introduces something new ⟨a *contriver* of yet another piece of exercise equipment guaranteed to take off the pounds⟩ — see INVENTOR

control *n* **1** a mechanism for adjusting the operation of a device, machine, or system ⟨the *controls* for the player are well marked⟩
synonyms regulator
related words button, dial, key, knob, lever, push button, switch
2 the ability to direct the course of something ⟨after the tail fell off, the plane went out of the pilot's *control*⟩ ⟨firefighters keeping *control* of the blaze⟩
synonyms grasp, hand(s)
related words clutch, grip, hold, mastery; command, dominion, helm; authority, jurisdiction, might, power
3 the act or activity of looking after and making decisions about something ⟨*control* of operations was given to a new manager with new ideas⟩ — see CONDUCT 1
4 the fact or state of having (something) at one's disposal ⟨took *control* of the process of selecting candidates for the scholarship⟩ — see POSSESSION 1
5 the right or means to command or control others ⟨teachers are responsible for the students under their *control*⟩ — see POWER 1

control *vb* **1** to keep from exceeding a desirable degree or level (as of expression) ⟨you must learn to *control* your temper⟩
synonyms bridle, check, constrain, contain, curb, govern, hold in, inhibit, regulate, rein (in), restrain, tame
related words bottle (up), repress, suppress; arrest, interrupt, stop; block, hinder, impede, obstruct; gag, muzzle, silence
near antonyms liberate, loose, loosen, unleash; air, express, take out, vent
2 to gain emotional or mental control of ⟨he *controlled* himself only with the greatest difficulty in the face of his opponent's insulting remarks⟩ — see COLLECT 1
3 to exercise authority or power over ⟨circumstances often *control* the choices we can make⟩ — see GOVERN 1
4 to look after and make decisions about ⟨during the period that she *controlled* the company it was highly profitable⟩ — see CONDUCT 1

controversy *n* variance of opinion on a matter ⟨there is considerable *controversy* regarding the assassination of President Kennedy⟩ — see DISAGREEMENT 1

contusion *n* a bodily injury in which small blood vessels are broken but the overlying skin is not ⟨*contusions* occurred as a result of a car accident⟩
synonyms bruise
related words black eye; discoloration

conundrum *n* something hard to understand or explain ⟨the *conundrum* of how an ancient people were able to build such massive structures without the benefit of today's knowledge and technology⟩ — see MYSTERY

convalesce *vb* to become healthy and strong again after illness or weakness ⟨the long months that the soldier spent in the hospital slowly *convalescing*⟩
synonyms gain, heal, mend, rally, recover, recuperate, snap back
related words come around, come round, come to, improve, pick up, revive; cheer (up), perk (up); pull through, survive; recruit

near antonyms ail, collapse, come down, sicken; decline, degenerate, deteriorate, fade, fail, languish, sink, waste (away), weaken, wilt, wither, worsen; relapse

convalescence *n* the process or period of gradually regaining one's health and strength ⟨her release from the hospital was followed by a long *convalescence* at home⟩
synonyms comeback, healing, mending, rally, recovery, recuperation, rehabilitation, snapback
related words resuscitation, revival; survival
near antonyms decline, deterioration, failing, languishing, sinking, wasting (away), weakening

convene *vb* **1** to bring together in assembly by or as if by command ⟨*convened* the members of the council for an emergency session⟩ — see CONVOKE
2 to come together into one body or place ⟨the students *convened* in the auditorium to hear the guest speaker⟩ — see ASSEMBLE 1

convenience *n* something that adds to one's ease ⟨a house with all the modern *conveniences* that buyers have come to expect⟩ — see COMFORT 2

convenient *adj* situated within easy reach ⟨the shopping mall is *convenient* to all of the area's major highways⟩
synonyms accessible, handy, reachable
related words close, near, nigh; abutting, adjacent, adjoining
near antonyms distant, far, remote
antonyms inaccessible, inconvenient, unhandy, unreachable

convention *n* **1** a coming together of a number of persons for a specified purpose ⟨attended a *convention* of mathematicians in California⟩ — see MEETING 1
2 a formal agreement between two or more nations or peoples ⟨an international *convention* banning the spread of nuclear weapons⟩ — see TREATY
3 an arrangement about action to be taken ⟨the Geneva *Convention* details treatment of prisoners of war⟩ — see AGREEMENT 2
4 an inherited or established way of thinking, feeling, or doing ⟨the bride decided to follow *convention* and to have her father give her away⟩ — see TRADITION 1

conventional *adj* **1** accepted, used, or practiced by most people ⟨*conventional* wisdom holds that an incumbent president has an overwhelming advantage over his opponent⟩ — see CURRENT 1
2 based on customs usually handed down from a previous generation ⟨tried to break from the *conventional* attitudes regarding the proper roles for men and women⟩ — see TRADITIONAL 1
3 following or agreeing with established form, custom, or rules ⟨*conventional* courtesy demands that the bridal couple send written thank-you notes for their gifts⟩ — see FORMAL 1

converge *vb* to come together into one body or place ⟨hungry students *converged* on the cafeteria almost as soon as the class bell rang⟩ — see ASSEMBLE 1

convergence *n* the coming together of two or more things to the same point ⟨the *convergence* of the city's major arteries on a single rotary⟩
synonyms confluence, conjunction, meeting
related words joining, juncture, merging, union
antonyms divergence

conversant *adj* having information especially as a result of study or experience ⟨a world traveler who is highly *conversant* with the customs of foreign cultures⟩ — see FAMILIAR 2

conversation *n* talking or a talk between two or more people ⟨Thomas Jefferson was celebrated for his bril-

liant, wide-ranging *conversations* with a host of friends and acquaintances⟩
synonyms colloquy, dialogue (*also* dialog), discourse, discussion, exchange
related words banter, cross fire, give-and-take, repartee; conference, parley, powwow; babble, chat, chatter, chitchat, gabfest, gossip, palaver, prate, prattle, rap, small talk, table talk; roundtable, symposium; debate, deliberation

conversational *adj* **1** fond of talking or conversation ⟨feeling *conversational* after a good meal with good friends⟩ — see TALKATIVE
2 having the style and content of everyday conversation ⟨struck a very *conversational* tone in his reports of his travels in foreign countries⟩ — see CHATTY 1
3 used in or suitable for speech and not formal writing ⟨uses *conversational* language instead of more stilted expressions in her speeches⟩ — see COLLOQUIAL 1

conversationalist *n* a person who talks constantly ⟨she was known as a compulsive *conversationalist*, so much so that it was often impossible to stop her once she got going⟩ — see CHATTERBOX

converse *vb* to engage in casual or rambling conversation ⟨jurors are not allowed to *converse* while the attorneys go off to one side to confer with the judge⟩ — see CHAT

converse (with) *vb* to communicate with by means of spoken words ⟨in a press conference, the president is not just addressing reporters—he's *conversing with* the public⟩ — see TALK (TO)

conversely *adv* just the opposite being true ⟨she cannot stand sugary food; *conversely*, he is fond of sweets⟩ — see CONTRARIWISE

conversion *n* a change in form, appearance, or use ⟨the *conversion* of the spare bedroom into a home office was easily accomplished⟩
synonyms changeover, metamorphosis, transfiguration, transformation
related words shift, transition; adjustment, alteration, modification; redoing, refashioning, remaking, remodeling, revamping, revision, reworking, variation; deformation, disfigurement, distortion, mutation, transmutation; displacement, replacement, substitution, supplantation

convert *n* **1** a person who has recently been persuaded to join a religious sect ⟨the *converts* were the most vocal and fervent worshippers in the church⟩
synonyms proselyte
related words newcomer, novice, recruit
2 one who follows the opinions or teachings of another ⟨the British biologist T. H. Huxley was one of the earliest *converts* to Darwin's theory of evolution⟩ — see FOLLOWER

convert *vb* **1** to persuade to change to one's religious faith ⟨young missionaries who go door-to-door trying to *convert* people⟩
synonyms proselytize
related words brainwash, influence, sway; propagate
near antonyms dissuade
2 to change in form, appearance, or use ⟨the old factory was *converted* into an apartment building⟩
synonyms make over, metamorphose, transfigure, transform
related words adjust, alter, modify; redo, refashion, remake, remodel, revamp, revise, rework, vary; deform, disfigure, distort, mutate, transmute; displace, replace, substitute, supplant

convey *vb* **1** to cause (something) to pass from one to another ⟨intends to *convey* a message to the governor⟩ — see COMMUNICATE 1

2 to support and take from one place to another ⟨*conveying* a package to his relatives⟩ — see CARRY 1

conveyance *n* something used to carry goods or passengers ⟨the covered wagon was the major *conveyance* that transported settlers and their belongings across the frontier⟩

synonyms transport, transportation, vehicle

related words carrier, hauler, mover; transit

convict *n* a person convicted as a criminal and serving a prison sentence ⟨a warning that the three escaped *convicts* were armed and dangerous⟩

synonyms jailbird

related words captive, capture, inmate, internee, prisoner

convict *vb* to find or pronounce guilty ⟨an accused person is presumed innocent until *convicted* in a court of law⟩

synonyms condemn

related words censure, denounce, rebuke, reprimand, reproach, reprove; admonish, castigate, chastise; penalize, punish, sentence

near antonyms cite, commend, endorse (*also* indorse); approve, bless, sanction

antonyms absolve, acquit, clear, exonerate, vindicate

conviction *n* **1** a state of mind in which one is free from doubt ⟨spoke with *conviction* about her political beliefs⟩ — see CONFIDENCE 2

2 an idea that is believed to be true or valid without positive knowledge ⟨held deep *convictions* about religion⟩ — see OPINION 1

convince *vb* to cause (someone) to agree with a belief or course of action by using arguments or earnest requests ⟨we *convinced* him to keep silent about our activities until we could spring the surprise⟩ — see PERSUADE

convincing *adj* having the power to persuade ⟨*convincing* evidence for the guilt of the accused⟩ — see COGENT

convincing *n* the act of reasoning or pleading with someone to accept a belief or course of action ⟨it will take a great deal of *convincing* to make them see our point of view⟩ — see PERSUASION 1

convivial *adj* likely to seek or enjoy the company of others ⟨the hiking club attracts a wide range of *convivial* people who share a love of the outdoors⟩

synonyms boon, companionable, extroverted (*also* extraverted), gregarious, outgoing, sociable, social

related words cordial, friendly, hospitable; affable, genial, gracious; animated, lively, sprightly, vivacious; communicative, expansive, garrulous, talkative

near antonyms misanthropic; aloof, reserved, standoffish; reticent, silent, taciturn

antonyms antisocial, introverted, reclusive, unsociable

conviviality *n* **1** joyful or festive activity ⟨fondly remembers the many evenings spent in *conviviality* with her teammates⟩ — see MERRYMAKING

2 the quality or state of being social ⟨his *conviviality*, warmth, and good nature are irresistible⟩ — see SOCIABILITY

convocation *n* **1** a body of people come together in one place ⟨the first speaker to address the *convocation*⟩ — see GATHERING 1

2 a coming together of a number of persons for a specified purpose ⟨called for a *convocation* of all the people affected by the decision⟩ — see MEETING 1

convoke *vb* to bring together in assembly by or as if by command ⟨*convoked* the leading experts on juvenile delinquency to study the situation⟩

synonyms assemble, call, convene, muster, summon

related words amass, collect, gather, group, round up

near antonyms break up, dissolve

convoluted *adj* having many parts or aspects that are usually interrelated ⟨a *convoluted* explanation that left the listeners even more confused than they were before⟩ — see COMPLEX 1

convoy *vb* to go along with in order to provide assistance, protection, or companionship ⟨will *convoy* the shipment to its destination in the war zone⟩ — see ACCOMPANY

convulse *vb* to make a series of small irregular or violent movements ⟨*convulsing* with silent laughter as the inept pianist blithely played on⟩ — see SHAKE 1

convulsion *n* a violent disturbance (as of the political or social order) ⟨the Russian Revolution was one of the major *convulsions* of the 20th century⟩

synonyms cataclysm, paroxysm, storm, tempest, tumult, upheaval, uproar

related words overthrow, overturn, revolution, subversion, upset; fit, seizure, spasm; eruption, flare-up, outbreak, outburst; commotion, furor, fuss, hubbub, hullabaloo, row, ruckus, stew, turmoil; quaking, rocking, shaking, trembling

convulsive *adj* marked by sudden or violent disturbance ⟨the assassination of Martin Luther King was one of the most *convulsive* events of the 1960s⟩

synonyms cataclysmal (*or* cataclysmic), stormy, tempestuous, tumultuous

related words fitful, spasmodic, sporadic

near antonyms calm, peaceful, serene, tranquil

cook *n* a person who prepares food by some manner of heating ⟨the hearty meals prepared by the *cook* at summer camp⟩

synonyms chef, cooker

related words baker

cook (up) *vb* to create or think of by clever use of the imagination ⟨*cooked up* a scheme to get out of doing the dishes⟩ — see INVENT

cooker *n* **1** an appliance that prepares food for consumption by heating it ⟨a portable gas-fired *cooker* that's perfect for camping trips⟩

synonyms cookstove, range

related words broiler, fryer (*also* frier), microwave oven, oven, roaster, rotisserie, stove, toaster, toaster oven

2 a person who prepares food by some manner of heating ⟨Dad was the traditional *cooker* for breakfast⟩ — see COOK

cookery *n* the art or style of preparing food (as in a specified region) ⟨tacos represented my introduction to Mexican *cookery*⟩

synonyms cooking, cuisine

cooking *n* the art or style of preparing food (as in a specified region) ⟨a TV show that teaches viewers the basics of French *cooking*⟩ — see COOKERY

cookstove *n* an appliance that prepares food for consumption by heating it ⟨a small *cookstove* that would be appropriate for an apartment⟩ — see COOKER 1

cool *adj* **1** having or showing a lack of friendliness or interest in others ⟨the locals were *cool* towards outsiders⟩ ⟨the schoolmaster's *cool* manner did not encourage chitchat⟩

synonyms aloof, antisocial, cold, detached, distant, frosty, remote, standoffish, unsociable *related words* introverted, reclusive, reserved, withdrawn; misanthropic; apathetic, indifferent, unconcerned; disinterested, incurious, uninterested; reticent, silent, taciturn; diffident, shy, timid

near antonyms companionable, convivial, extroverted (*also* extraverted), gregarious, outgoing; communicative, expansive, garrulous, talkative

antonyms cordial, friendly, sociable, warm

2 free from emotional or mental agitation ⟨in a crisis keep a *cool* head, even if no one else is⟩ — see CALM 2

3 having a low or subnormal temperature ⟨a *cool* basement that would be perfect for storing wine⟩ — see COLD 1

4 lacking in friendliness or warmth of feeling ⟨directed a *cool* glance at the student who was sneaking into class late⟩ — see COLD 2

cool *vb* **1** to cause to lose heat ⟨*cool* your drinks in the icy mountain stream⟩

synonyms chill, refrigerate

related words air-condition; freeze, ice, quick-freeze, supercool; air-cool, ventilate

near antonyms bake, boil, broil, steam

antonyms heat, warm

2 to become still and orderly ⟨after the recess, tempers had *cooled*, and we could have a civil, rational discussion⟩ — see QUIET 1

coolheaded *adj* free from emotional or mental agitation ⟨a *coolheaded* response to the crisis⟩ — see CALM 2

coolheadedness *n* evenness of emotions or temper ⟨*coolheadedness* in the classroom is a necessary quality in a teacher⟩ — see EQUANIMITY

coolish *adj* having a low or subnormal temperature ⟨made the mistake of wearing shorts on a *coolish* day⟩ — see COLD 1

coolness *n* evenness of emotions or temper ⟨his *coolness* under pressure makes him everyone's first choice to handle sudden problems⟩ — see EQUANIMITY

coop *n* an enclosure with an open framework for keeping animals ⟨a chicken *coop*⟩ — see CAGE

coop (up) *vb* to close or shut in by or as if by barriers ⟨restless kids *cooped up* in the house on a rainy day⟩ — see ENCLOSE 1

cooperate *vb* **1** to participate or assist in a joint effort to accomplish an end ⟨conservation groups *cooperated* with state authorities to find a humane way to manage the area's overpopulation of deer⟩

synonyms collaborate, concert, join, team (up)

related words connive, conspire; affiliate, ally, associate, band, combine, confederate, league, unite

phrases play ball

2 to form or enter into an association that furthers the interests of its members ⟨several industrialized nations *cooperated* in a trade agreement to reduce or eliminate tariffs⟩ — see ALLY

cooperation *n* **1** the state of having shared interests or efforts (as in social or business matters) ⟨a series of televised announcements made in *cooperation* with the tobacco companies warning teenagers about the hazards of smoking⟩ — see ASSOCIATION 1

2 the work and activity of a number of persons who individually contribute toward the efficiency of the whole ⟨everyone's *cooperation* will make the project go much faster⟩ — see TEAMWORK

coordinate *n* one that is equal to another in status, achievement, or value ⟨the Nobel Memorial Award for Economic Science is universally regarded as the *coordinate* of the original Nobel Prizes for peace, literature, medicine, physics, and chemistry⟩ — see EQUAL

coordinate *vb* **1** to bring to a state free of conflicts, inconsistencies, or differences ⟨*coordinating* the plans for the surprise party⟩ — see HARMONIZE 2

2 to form a pleasing relationship ⟨a very meticulous hostess, who makes sure that every aspect of her dinner parties—table settings, food, flowers—*coordinate* right down to the last detail⟩ — see HARMONIZE 1

coordination *n* the work and activity of a number of persons who individually contribute toward the efficiency of the whole ⟨an operation requiring precise *coordination* among all branches of the armed forces⟩ — see TEAMWORK

cop *n* a member of a force charged with law enforcement at the local level ⟨a *cop* stopped her for speeding⟩ — see OFFICER 1

copacetic *also* **copasetic** *or* **copesetic** *adj* being to one's liking ⟨don't worry, because I assure you that everything's *copacetic*⟩ — see SATISFACTORY 1

cope *vb* to meet one's day-to-day needs ⟨a young man learning to *cope* on his own at college⟩ — see GET ALONG 1

cope (with) *vb* to deal with (something) usually skillfully or efficiently ⟨*coped with* the latest foul-up gracefully⟩ — see HANDLE 1

copious *adj* pouring forth in great amounts ⟨a *copious* rush of words just poured out of the two friends who hadn't seen each other in years⟩ — see PROFUSE

cop–out *n* the act or a means of getting or keeping away from something undesirable ⟨I think that saying you're sick is just a *cop-out* to get out of going to school⟩ — see ESCAPE 2

cop out *vb* to break a promise or agreement ⟨don't *cop out* on your promise to watch your little brother⟩ — see RENEGE

coppice *n* a thick patch of shrubbery, small trees, or underbrush ⟨the deer bounded off into the *coppice*⟩ — see THICKET

copse *n* a thick patch of shrubbery, small trees, or underbrush ⟨a small *copse* of trees shaded the back of the house⟩ — see THICKET

copulate *vb* to engage in sexual intercourse ⟨the time of year when deer in the wild are likely to *copulate*⟩

synonyms mate, sleep

related words fornicate

copulating *n* sexual union involving penetration of the vagina by the penis ⟨our Puritan forebears imposed severe penalties for *copulating* outside of marriage⟩ — see SEXUAL INTERCOURSE

copulation *n* sexual union involving penetration of the vagina by the penis ⟨laws against *copulation* between an adult and one who has not reached the legal age of consent⟩ — see SEXUAL INTERCOURSE

copy *n* something that is made to look exactly like something else ⟨a *copy* of the famous painting "Washington Crossing the Delaware"⟩

synonyms carbon copy, duplicate, duplication, facsimile, imitation, reduplication, replica, replication, reproduction

related words counterfeit, fake, forgery, phony (*also* phoney), sham; dummy, mock-up, simulation; reconstruction, re-creation; image, likeness, semblance, shadow; impression, imprint, print

antonyms original

copy *vb* **1** to make an exact likeness of ⟨for the movie, set designers *copied* the Oval Office in the White House down to the smallest detail⟩

synonyms duplicate, imitate, reduplicate, replicate, reproduce

related words counterfeit, fake, forge; simulate; reconstruct, re-create

near antonyms create, imagine, initiate, invent

antonyms originate

2 to use (someone or something) as the model for one's speech, mannerisms, or behavior ⟨she shamelessly *copies* her idol's hairstyle and fashion choices⟩ — see IMITATE 1

copycat *n* a person who adopts the appearance or behavior of another especially in an obvious way ⟨every rock singer who makes it big soon has a whole cluster of *copycats*⟩

synonyms aper, copyist, imitator

related words parrot

copyist *n* a person who adopts the appearance or behavior of another especially in an obvious way ⟨she prides herself on being an innovator in fashion, and not a mere *copyist*⟩ — see COPYCAT

coquettish *adj* affecting shyness or modesty in order to attract masculine interest ⟨an 18th-century painting of a *coquettish* maiden dallying with a young moonstruck gallant⟩ — see COY 1

cord *n* a length of braided, flexible material that is used for tying or connecting things ⟨a vacuum cleaner with an extra long *cord*⟩

synonyms cable, lace, lacing, line, rope, string, wire

related words guy, lanyard, stay

cordial *adj* **1** having or showing kindly feeling and sincere interest ⟨a *cordial* inquiry about her mother's health⟩ — see FRIENDLY 1

2 showing a natural kindness and courtesy especially in social situations ⟨a *cordial* hostess who makes sure everyone is comfortable⟩ — see GRACIOUS 1

cordiality *n* kindly concern, interest, or support ⟨everyone appreciated the *cordiality* and thoughtfulness of the welcoming committee⟩ — see GOODWILL 1

core *n* **1** the seat of one's deepest thoughts and emotions ⟨in my very *core* I knew that an injustice was being committed⟩

synonyms breast, heart, quick, soul

related words conscience, mind

phrases bottom of one's heart

2 a thing or place that is of greatest importance to an activity or interest ⟨the capitol building is the *core* of the political life of the state⟩ — see CENTER 1

3 the central part or aspect of something under consideration ⟨at last, we come to the *core* of the issue that has been dividing us⟩ — see CRUX

4 the main or greater part of something as distinguished from its appendages ⟨a starfish can even survive the division of its *core* into two parts; both halves then regenerate⟩ — see BODY 1

5 an area or point that is an equal distance from all points along an edge or outer surface ⟨the mountain rises from ground that is almost precisely at the island's *core*⟩ — see CENTER 2

corker *n* something very good of its kind ⟨that last race was a real *corker!*⟩ — see JIM-DANDY

corkscrew *adj* turning around an axis like the thread of a screw ⟨a child with beautiful *corkscrew* curls⟩ — see SPIRAL

corn *n* something (as a work of literature or music) that is too sentimental ⟨a story about a lost puppy that was pure *corn*⟩

synonyms mush, schmaltz (*also* schmalz)

related words claptrap, drivel, rubbish, slush

corner *n* **1** a difficult, puzzling, or embarrassing situation from which there is no easy escape ⟨the writers have

gotten themselves into a *corner* on that TV show⟩ — see PREDICAMENT

2 a place where roads meet ⟨we'll meet at the *corner* tomorrow⟩ — see CROSSROAD 1

cornerstone *n* an immaterial thing upon which something else rests ⟨a concern for basic human rights was the *cornerstone* of the president's foreign policy⟩ — see BASE 1

cornet *n* something shaped like a hollow cone and used as a container ⟨*cornets* of pastry dough that were baked and later filled with cream⟩

synonyms cornucopia, horn

related words funnel, tube

cornucopia *n* something shaped like a hollow cone and used as a container ⟨a *cornucopia* filled with fruits and vegetables in celebration of the harvest⟩ — see CORNET

corny *adj* appealing to the emotions in an obvious and tiresome way ⟨*corny* violin music during the movie's love scenes⟩

synonyms maudlin, mawkish, mushy, saccharine, sappy, schmaltzy, sentimental, sloppy, sugarcoated, sugary

related words dreamy, moonstruck, nostalgic; flat, insipid, tasteless, vapid, watery

near antonyms unadulterated, unvarnished; cynical, hard-boiled, hardheaded

antonyms unsentimental

corollary *n* a condition or occurrence traceable to a cause ⟨one *corollary* of the attack was that no one trusted them thereafter⟩ — see EFFECT 1

coronet *n* a decorative band or wreath worn about the head as a symbol of victory or honor ⟨the prince wore a small gold *coronet* to denote his rank⟩ — see CROWN 1

corporal *adj* of or relating to the human body ⟨started to suffer the *corporal* ailments that come with advancing age⟩ — see PHYSICAL 1

corporeal *adj* of or relating to the human body ⟨*corporeal* cravings such as hunger and thirst⟩ — see PHYSICAL 1

corps *n* the body of people in a profession or field of activity ⟨a reporter who is widely respected throughout the press *corps*⟩

synonyms brotherhood, community, fellowship, fraternity

related words calling, profession; association, club, federation, guild (*also* gild), organization, society, sodality

corpse *n* a dead body ⟨the discovery of a *corpse* required a call to the police⟩

synonyms cadaver, carcass, remains

related words deceased, decedent

corpulence *n* the condition of having an excess of body fat ⟨the doctor warned that *corpulence* is unhealthy and not just unattractive⟩

synonyms adiposity, chubbiness, fatness, fleshiness, grossness, obesity, plumpness, portliness, pudginess, rotundity

related words bulkiness, heaviness; huskiness, stoutness; brawniness, burliness

near antonyms fitness, trimness; scrawniness, skinniness

antonyms leanness, slenderness, slimness, thinness

corpulent *adj* having an excess of body fat ⟨a *corpulent*, elegantly dressed opera singer came out and sang, and we knew it was over⟩ — see FAT 1

corral *n* an enclosure with an open framework for keeping animals 〈the horses live in our *corral*, along with a cow〉 — see CAGE

corral *vb* **1** to close or shut in by or as if by barriers 〈*corralled* everyone in the gym for a speech by the principal〉 — see ENCLOSE 1

2 to take physical control or possession of (something) suddenly or forcibly 〈*corralled* a scattering of stray pens and quickly stuffed them in the drawer to tidy the desk〉 — see CATCH

correct *adj* **1** being in agreement with the truth or a fact or a standard 〈a real brainteaser with only one *correct* solution to it〉

synonyms accurate, exact, precise, proper, right, so, true

related words legitimate, logical, valid; errorless, faultless, flawless, impeccable, letter-perfect, perfect; rigorous, strict, stringent

near antonyms defective, faulty, flawed, imperfect

antonyms false, improper, inaccurate, incorrect, inexact, untrue, wrong

2 following the established traditions of refined society and good taste 〈painfully *correct* dress for the White House dinner〉 — see PROPER 1

3 marked by or showing careful attention to set forms and details 〈the *correct* method for folding the American flag〉 — see CEREMONIOUS 1

correct *vb* **1** to remove errors, defects, deficiencies, or deviations from 〈students who never take the time to *correct* their own compositions before handing them in〉

synonyms amend, debug, emend, rectify, reform, remedy

related words redraft, redraw, restyle, revise, rework, rewrite; redress, right; ameliorate, better, improve; perfect, polish, touch up; fix, mend, repair; adjust, modulate, regulate; alter, change, modify

near antonyms damage, harm, hurt, impair, injure, mar, spoil; aggravate, worsen

2 to balance with an equal force so as to make ineffective 〈the young inventor tried to be even more serious to *correct* his partner's extreme enthusiasm〉 — see OFFSET

3 to inflict a penalty on for a fault or crime 〈a teacher who liked to *correct* students by forcing them to write "I will not..." 100 times〉 — see PUNISH

correctable *adj* capable of being corrected 〈a horse with some minor, *correctable* faults〉 — see REMEDIABLE

correcting *adj* inflicting, involving, or serving as punishment 〈a *correcting* assignment to write an essay stating why the use of racial and ethnic insults is wrong〉 — see PUNITIVE

correction *n* **1** a change designed to correct or improve a written work 〈here's your theme back with the *corrections* marked in blue〉

synonyms amendment, emendation

related words cut, deletion; addition, amplification, supplement; alteration, modification, revision; improvement, renovation; clarification, explanation, explication

2 suffering, loss, or hardship imposed in response to a crime or offense 〈received a severe *correction* after the third offense〉 — see PUNISHMENT

correctional *adj* inflicting, involving, or serving as punishment 〈threatened to take *correctional* measures if the household chores were not done〉 〈the state's largest *correctional* institution〉 — see PUNITIVE

corrective *adj* **1** serving to raise or adjust something to some standard or proper condition 〈eyeglasses are called *corrective* lenses by the department of motor vehicles〉

synonyms rectifying, remedial, remedying, reformative, reformatory

related words curative, medicinal, therapeutic; reparative, restorative; beneficial, helpful, salutary, wholesome

2 inflicting, involving, or serving as punishment 〈a *corrective* sentence of five years' hard labor〉 — see PUNITIVE

corrective *n* something that corrects or counteracts something undesirable 〈the only *corrective* to bad behavior is good discipline〉 — see CURE 1

correctly *adv* in a manner suitable for the occasion or purpose 〈dressed *correctly* for an appearance in court〉 — see PROPERLY

correlate *vb* to think of (something) in combination 〈I always *correlate* the color blue with my mother, for some reason〉 — see ASSOCIATE 2

correspond *vb* **1** to engage in an exchange of written messages 〈old friends who have been *corresponding* for years〉

synonyms write

related words communicate, intercommunicate; airmail, e-mail, telegraph; mail, post; answer, reply

2 to be in agreement on every point 〈the menu for the wedding banquet *corresponds* exactly with everyone's requests〉 — see CHECK 1

correspond (to) *vb* **1** to be the exact counterpart of 〈the British chancellor of the exchequer *corresponds* to the U.S. secretary of the treasury〉 — see MATCH 1

2 to be the same in meaning or effect 〈"shut up" and "please be quiet" may *correspond to* each other in meaning, but please use the more polite phrase〉 — see AMOUNT (TO) 2

correspondence *n* **1** a point which two or more things share in common 〈the *correspondence* in hair color is about all that the siblings have in common〉 — see SIMILARITY 2

2 the quality or state of having many qualities in common 〈the best friends' *correspondence* in looks is so striking that they could pass for twins〉 — see SIMILARITY 1

correspondent *n* a person employed by a newspaper, magazine, or radio or television station to gather, write, or report news 〈a foreign *correspondent* just filed a new report〉 — see REPORTER

correspondent *adj* having qualities in common 〈reading and writing are actually *correspondent* activities〉 — see ALIKE

correspondent (with *or* **to)** *adj* not having or showing any apparent conflict 〈the new regulation regarding cell phones is *correspondent with* existing policy on the use of electronic devices〉 — see CONSISTENT

corresponding *adj* having qualities in common 〈solving a crime and diagnosing a disease are *corresponding* tasks: they both require a careful looking for clues〉 — see ALIKE

correspondingly *adv* in like manner 〈if you're nice to someone, they'll probably be *correspondingly* polite〉 — see ALSO 1

corridor *n* a typically long narrow way connecting parts of a building 〈kids scurrying down the *corridors* to class〉 — see HALL 2

corroborate *vb* to give evidence or testimony to the truth or factualness of ⟨the witnesses *corroborated* the policeman's testimony⟩ — see CONFIRM

corroborating *adj* serving to give support to the truth or factualness of something ⟨*corroborating* information on the activities of the terrorists⟩ — see CORROBORATIVE

corroboration *n* something presented in support of the truth or accuracy of a claim ⟨that's a serious charge, so you certainly should have *corroboration* for it⟩ — see PROOF

corroborative *adj* serving to give support to the truth or factualness of something ⟨the results of the DNA fingerprinting was all the *corroborative* evidence the jury needed to convict⟩

synonyms confirmatory, confirming, corroborating, corroboratory, substantiating, supporting, supportive, verifying, vindicating

related words auxiliary, supplementary; beneficial, helpful

near antonyms contradictory, contrary, counter, opposing

antonyms confuting, disproving, refuting

corroboratory *adj* serving to give support to the truth or factualness of something ⟨offered *corroboratory* testimony for the defendant's alibi⟩ — see CORROBORATIVE

corrode *vb* to consume or wear away gradually ⟨water slowly *corrodes* iron⟩ — see EAT 2

corrosion *n* a gradual weakening, loss, or destruction ⟨the *corrosion* of family values that is often brought on by great wealth⟩

synonyms attrition, erosion

related words breakdown, decay, decomposition, disintegration, dissolution

near antonyms gain, increase

antonyms buildup

corrupt *adj* having or showing lowered moral character or standards ⟨*corrupt* businessmen who are out to fleece the public⟩ ⟨*corrupt* business practices that should be investigated⟩

synonyms debased, debauched, decadent, degenerate, degraded, demoralized, depraved, dissipated, dissolute, perverse, perverted, reprobate, warped

related words crooked, cutthroat, dishonest, unethical, unprincipled, unscrupulous; contaminated, spoiled, tainted; bad, evil, immoral, iniquitous, nefarious, sinful, vicious, wicked

near antonyms incorruptible, uncorruptible; ethical, honest, principled; good, moral, righteous, virtuous

antonyms uncorrupted

corrupt *vb* **1** to go through decomposition ⟨a dead mouse *corrupting* in the walls produced a terrible smell⟩ — see DECAY 1

2 to lower in character or dignity ⟨some observers believe that grossly violent movies *corrupt* the people who watch them as well as the people who make them⟩ — see DEBASE 1

corrupted *adj* having undergone organic breakdown ⟨*corrupted* corpses that sickened the animal control officers sent to investigate⟩ — see ROTTEN 1

corruptible *adj* open to improper influence and especially bribery ⟨there's a rumor that that judge is *corruptible*⟩ — see VENAL

corruption *n* **1** the process by which dead organic matter separates into simpler substances ⟨the ancient Egyptians used special preservatives to spare their dead from complete *corruption*⟩

synonyms breakdown, decay, decomposition, putrefaction, rot, spoilage

related words crumbling, disintegration, dissolution; curdling, fermentation, moldering, souring

near antonyms growth, maturation, ripening

2 a sinking to a state of low moral standards and behavior ⟨the *corruption* of the upper classes eventually led to the fall of the Roman empire⟩

synonyms corruptness, debasement, debauchery, decadence, degeneracy, degeneration, degradation, demoralization, depravity, dissipatedness, dissipation, dissoluteness, perversion

related words evil, immorality, nefariousness, sinfulness, wickedness

near antonyms goodness, morality, righteousness, virtue

3 immoral conduct or practices harmful or offensive to society ⟨Socrates was put to death because the ancient Athenians believed he was spreading *corruption* to their youth⟩ — see VICE 1

corruptness *n* a sinking to a state of low moral standards and behavior ⟨such *corruptness* in government would horrify George Washington⟩ — see CORRUPTION 2

corsair *n* someone who engages in robbery of ships at sea ⟨no one knows where the *corsair's* treasure-filled ship finally sank⟩ — see PIRATE

cortege *also* **cortège** *n* **1** a body of employees or servants who accompany and wait on a person ⟨the movie star's *cortege* included her hair stylist, makeup artist, personal assistant, and press agent⟩

synonyms following, retinue, suite, train

related words crew, personnel, staff; assistant, attendant, helper, retainer

2 a body of individuals moving along in an orderly and often ceremonial way ⟨the funeral *cortege* of mourners stretched for three city blocks⟩

synonyms parade, procession

related words column, line, string, train

cosmetics *n pl* preparations intended to beautify the face or hair ⟨I need to buy some fresh *cosmetics* to use for the wedding⟩ — see MAKEUP 1

cosmic *adj* unusually large ⟨predicted that the war would forever be regarded as a *cosmic* error⟩ — see HUGE

cosmopolitan *adj* having a wide and refined knowledge of the world especially from personal experience ⟨her younger brother thought she was terribly mature and *cosmopolitan* after the trip to Europe⟩ — see WORLDLY-WISE

cosmopolitan *n* a person with the outlook, experience, and manners thought to be typical of big city dwellers ⟨as someone who had lived in Paris for a year as an exchange student, she seemed very much the *cosmopolitan* to her old classmates⟩

synonyms metropolitan, sophisticate

related words urbanite; worldling

antonyms bumpkin, hick, provincial, rustic, yokel

cosmos *n* the whole body of things observed or assumed ⟨an essay that ponders the place of humankind in the vast *cosmos*⟩ — see UNIVERSE

cost *n* **1** a payment made in the course of achieving a result ⟨they spared no *cost* in building the kitchen of their dreams⟩ — see EXPENSE

2 the amount of money that is demanded as payment for something ⟨we can't afford the *cost* of a house just yet, so we're renting an apartment⟩ — see PRICE 1

3 the loss or penalty involved in achieving a goal ⟨they won the war, but at a terrible *cost* in lives⟩ — see PRICE 2

cost *vb* to have a price of ⟨the raffle tickets *cost* a dollar each⟩
synonyms bring, fetch, go (for), sell (for)
related words amount (to), come (to), total; command, exact; ask, demand

costly *adj* commanding a large price ⟨running is one sport that does not require a lot of *costly* equipment⟩
synonyms dear, expensive, high, precious, premium, valuable
related words exorbitant, extravagant, overpriced, prohibitive, steep, stiff, unreasonable; invaluable, priceless
near antonyms moderate, reasonable; valueless, worthless; discounted
antonyms cheap, inexpensive

costume *n* **1** clothing chosen as appropriate for a specific situation ⟨a tuxedo is the only acceptable *costume* for men attending a formal event⟩ — see OUTFIT 1
2 clothing put on to hide one's true identity or imitate someone or something else ⟨her Halloween *costume* will give her—she hopes—the appearance of a terrifying spider⟩ — see DISGUISE

costume *vb* to outfit with clothes and especially fine or special clothes ⟨I'm going to *costume* the girls in full dresses for Easter Sunday⟩ — see CLOTHE 1

coterie *n* a group of people sharing a common interest and relating together socially ⟨a *coterie* of old friends who attend all of the home games of the high school basketball team⟩ — see GANG 2

cotillion *n* a social gathering for dancing ⟨young men hoping to meet the women of their dreams at the *cotillion*⟩ — see DANCE

cottage *n* an often small house for recreational or seasonal use ⟨for a month every summer we rent a *cottage* on the ocean⟩
synonyms cabin, camp, chalet, lodge
related words bungalow, cot; hut, shack, shanty

cottony *adj* smooth or delicate in appearance or feel ⟨fluffy, *cottony* hair⟩ — see SOFT 2

couch *n* a long upholstered piece of furniture designed for several sitters ⟨find yourself a place on the *couch* and make yourself at home⟩
synonyms chesterfield, davenport, divan, lounge, settee, sofa
related words love seat; day bed, sofa bed; bench

couch *vb* to convey in appropriate or telling terms ⟨I'm trying to *couch* this delicately: I don't think we should date anymore⟩ — see PHRASE

cougar *n* a large tawny cat of the wild ⟨in many areas suburban developments have encroached upon the habitat of the *cougar*⟩
synonyms catamount, mountain lion, panther, puma

council *n* **1** a coming together of a number of persons for a specified purpose ⟨a war *council* attended by the top commanders of each of the armed services⟩ — see MEETING 1
2 a group of persons formally joined together for some common interest ⟨the neighborhood *council* decided to campaign for a new park⟩ — see ASSOCIATION 2
3 a meeting featuring a group discussion ⟨summoned to a *council* to discuss ways that the state could improve medical care for the elderly⟩ — see FORUM

counsel *n* **1** a person whose profession is to conduct lawsuits for clients or to advise about legal rights and obligations ⟨if you cannot afford *counsel*, one will be provided for you⟩ — see LAWYER

2 an opinion suggesting a wise or proper course of action ⟨I suggest you take the teacher's *counsel*⟩ — see ADVICE

counsel *vb* **1** to exchange viewpoints or seek advice for the purpose of finding a solution to a problem ⟨parents *counseling* about the problem of substance abuse⟩ — see CONFER 2
2 to give advice and instruction to (someone) regarding the course or process to be followed ⟨the admissions officer *counsels* thousands of students a year about the process of applying to college⟩ — see GUIDE 1
3 to give advice to ⟨perhaps a psychologist would be better qualified to *counsel* you⟩ — see ADVISE 1
4 to put forward as one's choice for a wise or proper course of action ⟨I would *counsel* caution and deliberation⟩ — see ADVISE 2

counselor *or* **counsellor** *n* **1** a person who gives advice especially professionally ⟨a young couple going to a marriage *counselor*⟩ — see CONSULTANT
2 a person whose profession is to conduct lawsuits for clients or to advise about legal rights and obligations ⟨get the best *counselor* that money can buy, especially if you're guilty⟩ — see LAWYER

count *n* **1** a total number obtained or recorded by noting each thing as it was being added ⟨my *count* for the number of bird species and subspecies that visited the sanctuary that weekend was 43⟩
synonyms tally
related words score; amount, gross, sum, total, whole
2 a formal claim of criminal wrongdoing against a person ⟨she's been charged with two *counts* of larceny⟩ — see CHARGE 1

count *vb* **1** to find the sum of (a collection of things) by noting each one as it is being added ⟨*count* the baseball gloves in the storage locker to see if there are enough to go around⟩
synonyms enumerate, number, tell
related words add (up), tally, total; calculate, compute, reckon, table, tabulate; check, mark, tick (off)
2 to be of importance ⟨spelling and grammar *count* in the grading of these essays⟩ — see MATTER
3 to place reliance or trust ⟨I'm *counting* on you to show up tomorrow to help me move⟩ — see DEPEND 2
4 to think of in a particular way ⟨I'm not sure I'd *count* that as a real effort⟩ — see CONSIDER 1

countenance *n* **1** facial appearance regarded as an indication of mood or feeling ⟨a pleasant *countenance* that puts visitors at ease⟩ — see LOOK 1
2 the front part of the head ⟨a fairly pretty *countenance*⟩ — see FACE 1

countenance *vb* **1** to have a favorable opinion of ⟨I don't *countenance* such behavior in children of any age⟩ — see APPROVE (OF)
2 to put up with (something painful or difficult) ⟨*countenanced* the delays and inconveniences of traveling by air with good grace⟩ — see BEAR 2

counter *adj* opposed to one's interests ⟨was unprepared for such a strong *counter* campaign by opponents of the legislative bill⟩ — see ADVERSE 1

counter *vb* to strive to reduce or eliminate ⟨efforts to *counter* poverty in every sector of our country⟩ — see FIGHT 2

counteract *vb* to balance with an equal force so as to make ineffective ⟨this medication will *counteract* the symptoms⟩ — see OFFSET

counteraction *n* a force or influence that makes an opposing force ineffective or less effective ⟨the wind serves as a *counteraction* to gravity, making it possible for a kite to remain airborne⟩ — see COUNTERBAL-ANCE

counterattack *n* an attack made to counter an enemy's attack ⟨suddenly the tide of battle turned, and the rebels, who had been falling back, made a furious *counterattack*⟩
synonyms counteroffensive
related words sally, sortie; blitzkrieg, charge; assault, attack, offensive, onslaught

counterbalance *n* a force or influence that makes an opposing force ineffective or less effective ⟨charitable giving is usually a good *counterbalance* to the self-indulgent commercialism of the Christmas season⟩
synonyms balance, canceler (*or* canceller), counteraction, counterpoise, counterweight, equipoise, neutralizer, offset
related words trade-off

counterbalance *vb* to balance with an equal force so as to make ineffective ⟨a hearty dinner might *counterbalance* missing lunch⟩ — see OFFSET

counterfeit *adj* being such in appearance only and made or manufactured with the intention of committing fraud ⟨*counterfeit* money that had been passed all over town⟩
synonyms bogus, fake, false, forged, inauthentic, phony (*also* phoney), sham, spurious, unauthentic
related words artificial, factitious, imitation, manmade, mimic, mock, simulated, substitute, synthetic; dummy, nonfunctioning, ornamental; cultured, fabricated, manufactured; deceptive, delusive, misleading
near antonyms natural; actual, true, valid
antonyms authentic, bona fide, genuine, real

counterfeit *n* an imitation that is passed off as genuine ⟨the will as well as the other documents turned out to be *counterfeits*⟩ — see FAKE 1

counterfeit *vb* 1 to imitate or copy especially in order to deceive ⟨an expert at *counterfeiting* money⟩ — see FAKE 1
2 to present a false appearance of ⟨managing to *counterfeit* a happy expression while visiting a sick friend⟩ — see FEIGN

counteroffensive *n* an attack made to counter an enemy's attack ⟨the army launched a *counteroffensive* at dawn⟩ — see COUNTERATTACK

counterpane *n* a decorative cloth used as a top covering for a bed ⟨a beautiful *counterpane* that was a family heirloom⟩
synonyms bedspread, coverlet, spread
related words comforter, puff, quilt; bedclothes, bedding

counterpart *n* 1 one that is equal to another in status, achievement, or value ⟨she worked with her *counterpart* in the other office to get the job done⟩ — see EQUAL
2 something or someone that strongly resembles another ⟨the daughter is her mother's *counterpart* in somewhat reduced form⟩ — see IMAGE 1

counterpoise *n* a force or influence that makes an opposing force ineffective or less effective ⟨the happiness of a new baby was a timely *counterpoise* to the grief occasioned by a death in the family⟩ — see COUNTERBALANCE

counterpoise *vb* to balance with an equal force so as to make ineffective ⟨her overall health largely *counterpoised* her bout of the flu⟩ — see OFFSET

countersign *n* a word or phrase that must be spoken by a person in order to pass a guard ⟨the guard demanded the *countersign*⟩ — see PASSWORD

counterweight *n* a force or influence that makes an opposing force ineffective or less effective ⟨hard work can often be a *counterweight* to modest intelligence⟩ — see COUNTERBALANCE

countless *adj* too many to be counted ⟨I've told you *countless* times not to do that⟩
synonyms innumerable, numberless, uncountable, uncounted, unnumbered, untold
related words endless, infinite, unlimited, vast; many, multitudinous, numerous
near antonyms finite, limited
antonyms countable

count out *vb* to prevent the participation or inclusion or ⟨I don't feel well, so *count* me *out* for the party tonight⟩ — see EXCLUDE

country *adj* of, relating to, associated with, or typical of open areas with few buildings or people ⟨stories that are about the joys of plain *country* living among unpretentious people⟩ — see RURAL

country *n* 1 the land of one's birth, residence, or citizenship ⟨a great love for my *country*⟩
synonyms fatherland, home, homeland, motherland, sod
related words old country; community, neighborhood
2 the open rural area outside of big towns and cities ⟨out in the *country*, where the air is fresh and the rivers are clean⟩
synonyms countryside, sticks
related words exurbia, backwater, backwoods, bush, frontier, hinterland, up-country; wild, wilderness
near antonyms conurbation, megalopolis, urban sprawl
3 a body of people composed of one or more nationalities usually with its own territory and government ⟨usually in time of war, the whole *country* unites behind the president⟩ — see NATION

countryman *n* 1 a person living in or originally from the same country as another ⟨met a fellow Canadian *countryman* while traveling in France⟩ — see COMPATRIOT
2 an awkward or simple person especially from a small town or the country ⟨though neither well-educated nor well-dressed, the *countryman* presented the farmers' case before the state legislature⟩ — see HICK

countryseat *n* a large impressive residence ⟨for four generations the family of media moguls has maintained a *countryseat* overlooking a wide swath of the ocean⟩ — see MANSION

countryside *n* the open rural area outside of big towns and cities ⟨everyone hates to see the *countryside* ruined by new developments⟩ — see COUNTRY 2

coup *n* a successful result brought about by hard work ⟨winning that big contract was a real *coup*⟩ — see ACCOMPLISHMENT 1

couple *n* two things of the same or similar kind that match or are considered together ⟨a *couple* of socks⟩ — see PAIR

couple *vb* 1 to come together to form a single unit ⟨at Pittsburgh, the Allegheny and Monongahela Rivers *couple* to form the Ohio⟩ — see UNITE 1
2 to put or bring together so as to form a new and longer whole ⟨if you *couple* the two extension cords, the connection should be long enough to reach the next room⟩ — see CONNECT 1

coupling *n* 1 a place where two or more things are united ⟨the *coupling* between two train cars⟩ — see JOINT 1
2 the act or an instance of joining two or more things into one ⟨credited with the *coupling* of several existing ideas into a single thesis⟩ — see UNION 1

coupon *n* a small sheet of plastic, paper, or paperboard showing that the bearer has a claim to something (as admittance) ⟨a book of discount *coupons*⟩ — see TICKET 1

courage *n* strength of mind to carry on in spite of danger ⟨the moral *courage* to speak out against injustice when no one else will⟩

  synonyms bravery, courageousness, daring, dauntlessness, doughtiness, fearlessness, gallantry, greateartedness, guts, hardihood, heart, heroism, intrepidity, intrepidness, nerve, stoutness, valor

  related words backbone, fiber, fortitude, grit, gumption, mettle, pluck, spunk; determination, perseverance, resolution; endurance, stamina, tenacity; audacity, boldness, brazenness, cheek, effrontery, gall, temerity

  near antonyms faintheartedness, fearfulness, timidity, timorousness; feebleness, softness, weakness; impotence, ineffectualness; hesitation, indecision, indecisiveness, irresolution

  antonyms cowardice, cowardliness, cravenness, dastardliness, spinelessness, yellowness

courageous *adj* feeling or displaying no fear by temperament ⟨the *courageous* decision to quit rather than obey an illegal order⟩ — see BRAVE

courageousness *n* strength of mind to carry on in spite of danger ⟨the soldiers' *courageousness* saved the mission from near disaster⟩ — see COURAGE

courier *n* one that carries a message or does an errand ⟨a *courier* just delivered a package for you⟩ — see MESSENGER

course *n* 1 a way of acting or proceeding ⟨the president's usual *course* has been to obtain advice from several people and then make up his own mind⟩

  synonyms line, policy, procedure, program

  related words blueprint, design, plan, scheme, strategy; intent, intention, purpose; approach, direction, path, pathway, tack

  2 a series of lectures on a subject ⟨a *course* on American history from the colonial period to the present⟩

  synonyms class

  related words elective, refresher, seminar; core, curriculum

  3 a usually fixed or ordered series of actions or events leading to a result ⟨set out on the *course* that would lead to a college degree⟩ — see PROCESS 1

  4 the direction along which something or someone moves ⟨the river follows a southeasterly *course* to the ocean⟩ — see PATH 1

course *vb* to proceed or move quickly ⟨horses *coursing* along the track⟩ — see HURRY 2

court *n* 1 the residence of a ruler ⟨Hampton *Court* was the residence of King Henry VIII⟩

  synonyms palace

  related words castle, château, estate, mansion, villa

  2 an open space wholly or partly enclosed (as by buildings or walls) ⟨the art museum boasts a glass-sided *court* that is filled with an array of greenery and sculpture⟩

  synonyms close, courtyard, enclosure (*also* inclosure), patio, quadrangle, yard

  related words place, plaza, square; deck, terrace

  3 an assembly of persons for the administration of justice ⟨this *court* is now called to order⟩

  synonyms bar, tribunal

  related words judiciary; court-martial; inquisition, kangaroo court

4 a public official having authority to decide questions of law ⟨if it please the *court*, I'd like to approach the bench⟩ — see JUDGE 1

court *vb* 1 to act so as to make (something) more likely ⟨you're *courting* disaster if you keep playing with matches⟩

  synonyms ask (for), invite, woo

  related words angle (for), fish (for); hunt, search, seek

  phrases look for

  2 to go on dates that may eventually lead to marriage ⟨they *courted* for a year before getting married⟩

  synonyms date

  related words romance, spark, woo; escort, see, take out

  phrases go steady, make love

courteous *adj* showing consideration, courtesy, and good manners ⟨always offers a *courteous* reply, even to rude people⟩ — see POLITE 1

courteously *adv* with good reason or courtesy ⟨*courteously* suggested that we try a different bookstore⟩ — see WELL 4

courteousness *n* speech or behavior that is a sign of good breeding ⟨a gentleman of unfailing *courteousness*⟩ — see POLITENESS

courtesy *n* 1 an act of kind assistance ⟨did me the *courtesy* of loaning me yesterday's notes⟩ — see FAVOR 1

  2 an act or utterance that is a customary show of good manners ⟨the greeting "How are you?" is often intended as no more than a *courtesy*⟩ — see CIVILITY 1

  3 speech or behavior that is a sign of good breeding ⟨a woman who responded to every situation with *courtesy* and kindness⟩ — see POLITENESS

courting *n* the series of social engagements shared by a couple looking to get married ⟨after two years of *courting*, they finally married⟩ — see COURTSHIP

courtship *n* the series of social engagements shared by a couple looking to get married ⟨a long-married couple who look back on their whirlwind *courtship* with fondness and laughter⟩

  synonyms courting, dating

  related words affair, love affair, romance; betrothal, engagement

courtyard *n* an open space wholly or partly enclosed (as by buildings or walls) ⟨it's such a nice day that we'll be having class in the *courtyard* today⟩ — see COURT 2

cove *n* a part of a body of water that extends beyond the general shoreline ⟨a secluded *cove* that smugglers once used⟩ — see GULF 1

covenant *n* 1 a formal agreement between two or more nations or peoples ⟨the two countries signed a peace *covenant* that, it was hoped, would put an end to decades of bitter conflict⟩ — see TREATY

  2 a formal agreement to fulfill an obligation ⟨I had to sign a *covenant* that I would return the rental car on time⟩ — see GUARANTEE 1

  3 an arrangement about action to be taken ⟨the *covenant* that existed among neighbors in olden times whereby they would quickly respond to the call to help put out one another's house fires⟩ — see AGREEMENT 2

covenant *vb* to make a solemn declaration of intent ⟨the home buyers had to *covenant* that they would restore and keep the house for at least ten years in order to receive a low mortgage rate⟩ — see PROMISE 1

cover *n* 1 a piece placed over an open container to hold in, protect, or conceal its contents ⟨where's the *cover* for the cookie jar?⟩

synonyms cap, lid, top

related words dome, hood, roof; capsule, case, casing, covering, housing, jacket, sheath, shell

2 means or method of defending ⟨provided *cover* while their comrades ran for safety⟩ — see DEFENSE 1

3 something that encloses another thing especially to protect it ⟨put the restaurant menus in clear plastic *covers* so that they would last longer⟩ — see ¹CASE 1

cover *vb* **1** to serve as a replacement usually for a time only ⟨a friend *covered* for me as a hospital volunteer while my family went on vacation⟩

synonyms fill in, pinch-hit, stand in, sub, substitute, take over

related words understudy; relieve, spell; double (as)

2 to form a layer over ⟨by morning a foot of snow *covered* the ground⟩

synonyms blanket, carpet, coat, overlay, overlie, overspread, sheet

related words enclose (*also* inclose), enshroud, envelop, enwrap, mantle, shawl, shroud, swathe, wrap; cloak, clothe, curtain, veil; circle, encircle, encompass

3 to place a protective layer over ⟨*cover* your skin with sunblock so you won't get sunburned⟩

synonyms screen, shield

related words cloak, clothe, veil; disguise, mask, obscure

near antonyms bare, expose, uncover

4 to have (something) as a subject matter ⟨this section of the book *covers* both multiplication and fractions⟩ — see CONCERN 1

5 to keep secret or shut off from view ⟨*covered* the hole with grass and leaves⟩ — see ¹HIDE 2

6 to make one's way through, across, or over ⟨we usually manage to *cover* a lot of ground in a single day⟩ — see TRAVERSE

7 to pay continued close attention to (something) for a particular purpose ⟨I'll *cover* this section while you take a break⟩ — see MONITOR

8 to drive danger or attack away from ⟨*covered* the wounded soldier until he could be rescued⟩ — see DEFEND 1

cover (up) *vb* to keep from being publicly known ⟨the governor vainly tried to *cover up* the scandal⟩ — see SUPPRESS 1

coverage *n* the amount of something (as subject matter) included ⟨the biographical dictionary's *coverage* is limited to people no longer living⟩

synonyms content

related words compass, gamut, range, scope, sweep; membership, participation

covering *n* something that encloses another thing especially to protect it ⟨the plastic *coverings* on lamp shades should be removed⟩ — see ¹CASE 1

coverlet *n* a decorative cloth used as a top covering for a bed ⟨bought a beautiful new *coverlet* to match the sheets⟩ — see COUNTERPANE

covert *adj* **1** hidden from view ⟨a *covert* little hideaway that provides a lot of privacy⟩ — see SECLUDED

2 undertaken or done so as to escape being observed or known by others ⟨a *covert* operation to provide aid to the rebels⟩ — see SECRET 1

covert *n* **1** a place where a person goes to hide ⟨set up a *covert* from which to watch wildlife without being detected⟩ — see HIDEOUT

2 a thick patch of shrubbery, small trees, or underbrush ⟨the rabbit rushed to the safety of the nearest *covert*⟩ — see THICKET

covet *vb* to have an earnest wish to own or enjoy ⟨all the other kids could not hide the fact that they *coveted* her new toy⟩ — see DESIRE

coveting *adj* having or marked by an eager and often selfish desire especially for material possessions ⟨cast a *coveting* glance at her friend's diamond necklace⟩ — see GREEDY 1

covetous *adj* **1** having or marked by an eager and often selfish desire especially for material possessions ⟨one aggressive bargain hunter rushed to make a *covetous* grab for the last marked-down TV⟩ — see GREEDY 1

2 having or showing mean resentment of another's possessions or advantages ⟨a *covetous* child who must destroy what he cannot have⟩ — see ENVIOUS

covetousness *n* **1** a painful awareness of another's possessions or advantages and a desire to have them too ⟨his *covetousness* for his neighbors' things spoils any enjoyment he might have of his own possessions⟩ — see ENVY

2 an intense selfish desire for wealth or possessions ⟨*covetousness* made her work long hours so that she could afford expensive things⟩ — see GREED

cow *vb* to make timid or fearful by or as if by threats ⟨a sharp glare *cowed* the child into being quiet⟩ — see INTIMIDATE

coward *n* a person who shows a shameful lack of courage in the face of danger ⟨the soldiers who ran as soon as the first shots were fired were branded as *cowards*⟩

synonyms chicken, craven, dastard, poltroon, recreant, sissy

related words defeatist, quitter; pushover, weakling, wimp; snake, sneak

near antonyms daredevil

antonyms hero, stalwart, valiant

cowardice *n* a shameful lack of courage in the face of danger ⟨the *cowardice* shown by political leaders who were willing to give the Nazis whatever they wanted⟩

synonyms cowardliness, cravenness, dastardliness, spinelessness, yellowness

related words diffidence, faintheartedness, fearfulness, timidity, timorousness; carefulness, cautiousness, wariness; bashfulness, shyness; feebleness, softness, weakness

near antonyms audacity, boldness, brazenness; backbone, fiber, fortitude, grit, gumption, mettle, pluck, spunk; determination, perseverance, resolution; endurance, stamina, tenacity

antonyms bravery, courage, courageousness, daring, dauntlessness, doughtiness, fearlessness, gallantry, greatheartedness, guts, hardihood, heart, heroism, intrepidity, intrepidness, nerve, stoutness, valor

cowardliness *n* a shameful lack of courage in the face of danger ⟨the soldier was court-marshaled for *cowardliness* under fire⟩ — see COWARDICE

cowardly *adj* having or showing a shameful lack of courage ⟨a *cowardly* bully who picks on much smaller kids⟩ ⟨vile charges that were made in a *cowardly*, unsigned letter⟩

synonyms chicken, chickenhearted, craven, dastardly, lily-livered, pusillanimous, recreant, spineless, unheroic, yellow

related words diffident, fainthearted, fearful, timid, timorous; afraid, frightened, scared; careful, cautious, wary; bashful, coy, shy; feeble, soft, weak

near antonyms audacious, bold, brazen, cheeky, nervy; plucky, spirited, spunky; determined, resolute

antonyms brave, courageous, daring, dauntless, doughty, fearless, gallant, greathearted, gutsy, hardy, heroic, intrepid, lionhearted, stalwart, stout, stout-hearted, valiant, valorous

cowboy *n* a hired hand who tends cattle or horses at a ranch or on the range ⟨*cowboys* were rounding up the cattle for branding⟩
synonyms buckaroo, cowhand, cowman, cowpoke, cowpuncher
related words cowgirl; gaucho, vaquero; horseman, horsewoman, wrangler; cattleman, rancher; herdsman

cower *vb* to draw back or crouch down in fearful submission ⟨the abused dog always *cowered* in the presence of its master⟩
synonyms cringe, grovel, quail
related words flinch, recoil, shrink, squinch; blanch, blench, whiten; fawn, kowtow, toady

cowhand *n* a hired hand who tends cattle or horses at a ranch or on the range ⟨we need to hire a new *cowhand* to help out⟩ — see COWBOY

cowhide *vb* to strike repeatedly with something long and thin or flexible ⟨was *cowhiding* the horse until a police officer intervened⟩ — see WHIP 1

cowman *n* a hired hand who tends cattle or horses at a ranch or on the range ⟨an expert *cowman* who can round up the livestock in no time⟩ — see COWBOY

coworker *n* a fellow worker ⟨my *coworkers* and I often play jokes on each other⟩ — see COLLEAGUE

cowpoke *n* a hired hand who tends cattle or horses at a ranch or on the range ⟨it takes a long time to train a good *cowpoke*⟩ — see COWBOY

cowpuncher *n* a hired hand who tends cattle or horses at a ranch or on the range ⟨*cowpunchers* hanging out and telling stories during branding time⟩ — see COWBOY

coy *adj* 1 affecting shyness or modesty in order to attract masculine interest ⟨not wanting him to know that she was interested in him, she acted very *coy* at the dance⟩
synonyms coquettish, demure, kittenish
related words flirtatious; goody-goody, overmodest, priggish, prim, prudish
2 not comfortable around people ⟨a *coy* toddler who hid whenever anyone tried to say hi⟩ — see SHY 2

cozen *vb* 1 to cause to believe what is untrue ⟨*cozened* several elderly ladies into believing that he was intending marriage⟩ — see DECEIVE
2 to rob by the use of trickery or threats ⟨*cozened* scores of people by persuading them to hand over funds that he would "invest"⟩ — see FLEECE

cozener *n* a dishonest person who uses clever means to cheat others out of something of value ⟨he was a "career" *cozener* who had worked one racket or another his whole life⟩ — see TRICKSTER 1

cozy *adj* 1 enjoying physical comfort ⟨the cat looked very *cozy*, all cuddled up into the blankets⟩ — see COMFORTABLE 2
2 providing physical comfort ⟨a coffeehouse with soft, *cozy* chairs⟩ — see COMFORTABLE 1

crab *n* an irritable and complaining person ⟨you're always such a *crab* in the mornings!⟩ — see GROUCH

crab *vb* to express dissatisfaction, pain, or resentment usually tiresomely ⟨the two-year-old whined and *crabbed* for the whole car trip⟩ — see COMPLAIN

crabby *adj* 1 easily irritated or annoyed ⟨a *crabby* old dog who snapped at passersby⟩ — see IRRITABLE
2 given to complaining a lot ⟨a bunch of *crabby* kids who don't want to do any work⟩ — see FUSSY 1

crack *adj* having or showing exceptional knowledge, experience, or skill in a field of endeavor ⟨known as one

of the college's *crack* tennis players⟩ — see PROFICIENT

crack *n* 1 an irregular usually narrow break in a surface created by pressure ⟨a pebble struck the car's windshield and left a *crack* in it⟩
synonyms chink, cleft, cranny, crevice, fissure, rift, split
related words craze, hairline; fracture, rupture; breach, gap, opening; cut, gash, incision, slit
2 a hard strike with a part of the body or an instrument ⟨a disciplinary *crack* on the hand with a ruler⟩ — see ¹BLOW
3 a loud explosive sound ⟨the tree fell with a sharp *crack*⟩ — see CLAP 1
4 an effort to do or accomplish something ⟨this is my first *crack* at painting⟩ — see ATTEMPT
5 something said or done to cause laughter ⟨a whispered *crack* made the whole back row start laughing⟩ — see JOKE 1

crack *vb* 1 to break suddenly with an explosive sound ⟨the tree branch unexpectedly *cracked* under our weight⟩
synonyms pop, snap
related words crackle, hiss, sizzle, sputter; burst, explode, shatter; clack, click, clatter
2 to yield to mental or emotional stress ⟨after hours of tough questioning the suspect finally *cracked* and blurted out a confession⟩
synonyms break (down), flip, freak (out)
phrases go to pieces
3 to change (as a secret message) from code into ordinary language ⟨the United States used the Navajo language as a code during the war, and no one ever *cracked* it⟩ — see DECODE
4 to deliver a blow to (someone or something) usually in a strong vigorous manner ⟨*cracked* him on the bottom with a paddle⟩ — see HIT 1
5 to find an answer for through reasoning ⟨I've been studying this riddle, but I can't *crack* it⟩ — see SOLVE

crackbrain *n* 1 a person judged to be legally or medically insane ⟨once a brilliant dancer, he died a *crackbrain* in a mental institution⟩ — see LUNATIC 1
2 a person of odd or whimsical habits ⟨a *crackbrain* who wore bedroom slippers to the grocery shop⟩ — see ECCENTRIC

crackbrained *adj* having or showing a very abnormal or sick state of mind ⟨had the *crackbrained* idea that he was receiving radio signals from outer space⟩ — see INSANE 1

crack down (on) *vb* to put a stop to (something) by the use of force ⟨the government *cracked down on* political demonstrations⟩ — see QUELL 1

cracked *adj* having or showing a very abnormal or sick state of mind ⟨are you completely *cracked*?⟩ — see INSANE 1

crackerjack *adj* 1 having or showing exceptional knowledge, experience, or skill in a field of endeavor ⟨a *crackerjack* photographer who gets the news photo that is reprinted around the world⟩ — see PROFICIENT
2 of the very best kind ⟨a *crackerjack* book on the history of rock music⟩ — see EXCELLENT

crackerjack *n* 1 a person with a high level of knowledge or skill in a field ⟨a *crackerjack* on the baseball diamond⟩ — see EXPERT
2 something very good of its kind ⟨the band's new song is a real *crackerjack*⟩ — see JIM-DANDY

crackpot *n* a person of odd or whimsical habits ⟨everyone is tolerant of the town *crackpot*, a man who never hurt anyone⟩ — see ECCENTRIC

crack–up *n* the violent coming together of two bodies into destructive contact ⟨two people were injured in a serious *crack-up* on the interstate⟩ — see CRASH 1

crack up *vb* **1** to declare enthusiastic approval of ⟨that sports car isn't all it's *cracked up* to be⟩ — see ACCLAIM
2 to praise or publicize lavishly and often excessively ⟨the movie is being *cracked up* as the blockbuster of the summer⟩ — see TOUT 1

craft *n* **1** an occupation requiring skillful use of the hands ⟨the *craft* of cabinetmaking was much admired in colonial times⟩
synonyms handcraft, handicraft, trade
related words art, skill; calling, occupation, profession, vocation
2 a small buoyant structure for travel on water ⟨borrowed a *craft* to get across the river⟩ — see BOAT 1
3 the inclination or practice of misleading others through lies or trickery ⟨never hesitated to resort to *craft* to get what she wanted in life⟩ — see DECEIT
4 skill in achieving one's ends through indirect, subtle, or underhanded means ⟨celebrated in political circles for his *craft*, he's the legislator who knows how to get bills passed⟩ — see CUNNING 1
5 subtle or imaginative ability in inventing, devising, or executing something ⟨a really ingenious household appliance that shows a lot of *craft* on the part of its inventors⟩ — see SKILL 1

craft *vb* to put (something) into proper and usually carefully worked out written form ⟨spent hours *crafting* the perfect letter of recommendation for her prize student⟩ — see COMPOSE 1

craftiness *n* **1** skill in achieving one's ends through indirect, subtle, or underhanded means ⟨other antique dealers envied her for her *craftiness* in getting people to sell their treasures for a song⟩ — see CUNNING 1
2 the inclination or practice of misleading others through lies or trickery ⟨according to the confidence man's credo of *craftiness*, "there's a sucker born every minute"⟩ — see DECEIT

craftsman *n* a person whose occupation requires skill with the hands ⟨if you want good work, hire a *craftsman*⟩ — see ARTISAN

crafty *adj* clever at attaining one's ends by indirect and often deceptive means ⟨a *crafty* real estate broker who got people to sell their property at bargain prices⟩ — see ARTFUL 1

crag *n* a steep wall of rock, earth, or ice ⟨a menacing *crag* overhangs the trail⟩ — see CLIFF

craggy *adj* having an uneven edge or outline ⟨goats scrambled nimbly up the *craggy* side of the mountain⟩ — see RAGGED 1

cram *vb* **1** to fit (something) into a tight space ⟨tried to *cram* one more book into the backpack⟩ — see CROWD 1
2 to put into (something) as much as can be held or contained ⟨*crammed* his mouth with candy⟩ — see FILL 1

crammed *adj* containing or seeming to contain the greatest quantity or number possible ⟨the auditorium is usually *crammed* when that candidate makes an appearance⟩ — see FULL 1

cramp *n* a painful sudden tightening of a muscle ⟨I was suddenly awakened by a *cramp* in my leg⟩
synonyms charley horse, crick, spasm
related words contraction, jerk, stitch, twinge, twitch

cramp *vb* to create difficulty for the work or activity of ⟨having to constantly entertain guests at the summer cottage really *cramped* my writing efforts⟩ — see HAMPER

crane *vb* to move from a lower to a higher place or position ⟨*craned* her head to see the roof⟩ — see RAISE 1

cranium *n* the case of bone that encloses the brain and supports the jaws of vertebrates ⟨the *cranium* of a Neanderthal is striking for its brow ridges⟩ — see SKULL

crank *n* **1** a person of odd or whimsical habits ⟨she's a bit of a *crank*, but still a nice woman⟩ — see ECCENTRIC
2 an irritable and complaining person ⟨he's always a *crank* until he has his coffee⟩ — see GROUCH

crank (up) *vb* to cause to function ⟨*crank up* the CD player so we can dance⟩ — see ACTIVATE

crankiness *n* readiness to show annoyance or impatience ⟨overtired children are often prone to *crankiness*⟩ — see PETULANCE

cranky *adj* **1** difficult to use or operate especially because of size, weight, or design ⟨that old typewriter is handy sometimes, but rather *cranky* these days⟩ — see CUMBERSOME
2 easily irritated or annoyed ⟨the baby was *cranky* after not being fed for hours⟩ — see IRRITABLE
3 given to complaining a lot ⟨if *cranky* children don't appreciate what they have, then they won't get anything at all!⟩ — see FUSSY 1

cranny *n* an irregular usually narrow break in a surface created by pressure ⟨one shoe got wedged into a *cranny* in the face of the cliff⟩ — see CRACK 1

crash *n* **1** the violent coming together of two bodies into destructive contact ⟨the fiery *crash* of two jumbo jet airplanes in midair⟩
synonyms collision, crack-up, smash, smashup, wreck
related words accident; demolishment, destruction, ruin
2 a falling short of one's goals ⟨refused to be discouraged by the *crash* of hairdressing business⟩ — see FAILURE 2
3 a loud explosive sound ⟨the *crash* of cymbals⟩ — see CLAP 1
4 a forceful coming together of two things ⟨the *crash* of a baseball through the window⟩ — see IMPACT 1

crash *vb* **1** to cause to break with violence and much noise ⟨*crashed* the vase against the wall⟩ — see SMASH 1
2 to come into usually forceful contact with something ⟨the speeding car *crashed* into the tree with horrifying results⟩ — see HIT 2
3 to stop functioning ⟨the computer *crashed* again⟩ — see FAIL 1

crass *adj* lacking in refinement or good taste ⟨a loudmouthed jerk given to rude jokes and *crass* comments⟩ — see COARSE 2

crassness *n* the quality or state of lacking refinement or good taste ⟨the *crassness* of the observation shocked everyone into silence⟩ — see VULGARITY 1

crave *vb* to have an earnest wish to own or enjoy ⟨*craves* ice cream at all hours of the day⟩ — see DESIRE

craven *adj* having or showing a shameful lack of courage ⟨a *craven* refusal to deliver the unwelcome news personally⟩ — see COWARDLY

craven *n* a person who shows a shameful lack of courage in the face of danger ⟨a *craven* who ran away and left everyone else behind to deal with the crisis⟩ — see COWARD

cravenness *n* a shameful lack of courage in the face of danger ⟨it was sheer *cravenness* to avoid the consequences of your actions⟩ — see COWARDICE

craving *n* a strong wish for something ⟨a pregnant woman with a *craving* for pickles⟩ — see DESIRE

crawl *vb* **1** to move slowly with the body close to the ground ⟨the time we had to *crawl* through a narrow passageway from one cave to another⟩
synonyms creep, grovel, slither, snake, worm, wriggle
related words crouch, squat; slide; edge, inch, nose; skulk, sneak, steal, tiptoe
2 to move slowly ⟨the weekend traffic on the road to the beach just *crawled*⟩
synonyms creep, drag, inch, plod, poke
related words lumber, shamble, shuffle, tramp, trudge
near antonyms float, glide, sail; hurry, tear
antonyms fly, race, speed, whiz (*or* whizz), zip
3 to move or act slowly ⟨the deadline is fast approaching, so this is no time to *crawl*⟩ — see DELAY 1

crawler *n* someone who moves slowly or more slowly than others ⟨he's always the *crawler* who makes everyone else late⟩ — see SLOWPOKE

crawling *adj* moving or proceeding at less than the normal, desirable, or required speed ⟨traffic is really *crawling* today⟩ — see SLOW 1

craze *n* a practice or interest that is very popular for a short time ⟨if history is any guide, this latest diet for losing weight is just another *craze*⟩ — see FAD

craze *vb* to cause to go insane or as if insane ⟨soldiers who had been *crazed* by months of combat and chaos in the countryside⟩
synonyms derange, madden, unbalance, unhinge, unstring
related words agitate, bother, confuse, discompose, disquiet, distract, disturb, perturb, unsettle, upset; annoy, irritate, vex
near antonyms calm, quiet, relax, settle, soothe, tranquilize (*or* tranquillize)

crazed *adj* having or showing a very abnormal or sick state of mind ⟨the inmate's *crazed* and disturbing stare⟩ — see INSANE 1

craziness *n* lack of good sense or judgment ⟨this latest example of *craziness* does not incline us to trust you⟩ — see FOOLISHNESS 1

crazy *adj* **1** conceived or made without regard for reason or reality ⟨the mansion is a *crazy* construction of several different styles⟩ — see FANTASTIC 1
2 having or showing a very abnormal or sick state of mind ⟨a *crazy* woman who tried to throw her baby out of a window⟩ — see INSANE 1
3 showing or marked by a lack of good sense or judgment ⟨a *crazy* plan to climb Mount Everest without proper equipment⟩ — see FOOLISH 1
4 showing urgent desire or interest ⟨*crazy* for the latest entertainment news⟩ — see EAGER

crazy (*about or* over) *adj* filled with an intense or excessive love for ⟨he's just *crazy about* that new drummer⟩ — see ENAMORED (OF)

creak *n* a harsh grating sound ⟨the *creak* of a floorboard⟩ — see RASP

creak *vb* to make a short shrill noise ⟨the old house always *creaks* and groans at night⟩ — see SQUEAK

cream *n* individuals carefully selected as being the best of a class ⟨this advanced studies program only accepts the *cream* of the applicants⟩ — see ELITE

crease *n* a small fold in a soft and otherwise smooth surface ⟨carefully ironed a *crease* into the pants⟩ — see WRINKLE 1

crease *vb* to develop creases or folds ⟨her face *creased* with worry⟩ — see WRINKLE 1

create *vb* to be the cause of (a situation, action, or state of mind) ⟨it was your negligence that *created* this mess⟩ — see EFFECT

creation *n* **1** something (as a device) created for the first time through the use of the imagination ⟨Dr. Frankenstein was very proud of his *creation*, at least at first⟩ — see INVENTION 1
2 the whole body of things observed or assumed ⟨there are still many things in *creation* that are unknown⟩ — see UNIVERSE

creative *adj* **1** having the skill and imagination to create new things ⟨Thomas Edison's status as perhaps America's greatest *creative* genius⟩
synonyms imaginative, ingenious, innovative, inventive, original
related words gifted, inspired, talented; resourceful; fecund, fertile, fruitful, productive, prolific
near antonyms imitative, uninspired; infertile, unproductive
antonyms uncreative, unimaginative, unoriginal
2 showing a use of the imagination and creativity especially in inventing ⟨looking for *creative* and skillful writing in students' themes⟩ — see CLEVER 1

creativeness *n* the skill and imagination to create new things ⟨a child with the *creativeness* to build his own figure of a superhero out of the parts of several toys⟩ — see CREATIVITY 1

creativity *n* **1** the skill and imagination to create new things ⟨the arts and crafts fair showed the remarkable *creativity* of local artists and artisans⟩
synonyms creativeness, imaginativeness, ingeniousness, ingenuity, invention, inventiveness, originality
related words resourcefulness; fecundity, fertility, fruitfulness, productiveness, productivity; freshness, newness, novelty; genius, inspiration, talent
near antonyms dryness, dullness (*also* dulness)
2 the ability to form mental images of things that either are not physically present or have never been conceived or created by others ⟨while his imaginary friend is a little annoying, you have to admire his *creativity* in thinking her up⟩ — see IMAGINATION

creator *n* **1** a person who establishes a whole new field of endeavor ⟨although some people see Freud as the *creator* of psychology, that isn't really true⟩ — see FATHER 2
2 *cap* the being worshipped as the creator and ruler of the universe ⟨we must all give thanks to the *Creator* for our very existence⟩ — see DEITY 2

creature *n* **1** a member of the human race ⟨we must try to be kind to our fellow *creatures*⟩ — see HUMAN
2 one of the lower animals as distinguished from human beings ⟨he loved birds and other small *creatures*⟩ — see ANIMAL

credence *n* **1** firm belief in the integrity, ability, effectiveness, or genuineness of someone or something ⟨I'm afraid I don't put much *credence* in common gossip⟩ — see TRUST 1
2 mental conviction of the truth of some statement or the reality of some being or phenomenon ⟨a foolish theory that once had wide *credence* among educated people⟩ — see BELIEF 1

credentials *n pl* a skill, an ability, or knowledge that makes a person able to do a particular job ⟨she certainly has the *credentials* for the position⟩ — see QUALIFICATION 1

credible *adj* worthy of being accepted as true or reasonable ⟨it's at least a *credible* explanation⟩ — see BELIEVABLE

credit *n* **1** the right to take possession of goods before paying for them ⟨because of their reputation for not paying their bills, no store will extend the family *credit*⟩
synonyms trust
related words installment plan, layaway
2 an asset that brings praise or renown ⟨your intelligence and dedication are a *credit* to you, our choice for teacher of the year⟩ — see GLORY 2
3 mental conviction of the truth of some statement or the reality of some being or phenomenon ⟨I give full *credit* to his report on the prevalence of cheating among students today⟩ — see BELIEF 1
4 public acknowledgment or admiration for an achievement ⟨she deserves all the *credit*, since she did all the work⟩ — see GLORY 1

credit *vb* **1** to explain (something) as being the result of something else ⟨has to *credit* his success in picking winning lottery numbers to pure luck⟩
synonyms accredit, ascribe, attribute, impute
related words blame, pin (on); associate, connect, link
2 to regard as right or true ⟨I simply cannot *credit* that story about the boy who was supposedly raised by wolves⟩ — see BELIEVE 1

creditable *adj* deserving of high regard or great approval ⟨a *creditable* effort, even if it didn't succeed completely⟩ — see ADMIRABLE

credo *n* **1** a body of beliefs and practices regarding the supernatural and the worship of one or more deities ⟨the *credo* of the ancient Egyptians was a variety of polytheism⟩ — see RELIGION 1
2 the basic beliefs or guiding principles of a person or group ⟨we must work by the simple *credo* that "the customer is always right"⟩ — see CREED 1

credulity *n* readiness to believe the claims of others without sufficient evidence ⟨the quack pushing the phony medicine was taking advantage of the *credulity* of people hoping for miracle cures⟩
synonyms credulousness, gullibility, naïveté (*also* naivete)
related words artlessness, simplicity, unsophistication; trust, unwariness
near antonyms sophistication, worldliness; distrust, mistrust, suspicion, wariness; doubt, uncertainty
antonyms incredulity, skepticism

credulousness *n* readiness to believe the claims of others without sufficient evidence ⟨her inveterate *credulousness* makes her an easy target for practical jokes⟩ — see CREDULITY

creed *n* **1** the basic beliefs or guiding principles of a person or group ⟨central to the *creed* of this organization of medical volunteers is the belief that health care is a basic human right⟩
synonyms credo, doctrine, gospel, ideology, philosophy
related words manifesto
2 a body of beliefs and practices regarding the supernatural and the worship of one or more deities ⟨the Amish live by a strict *creed* that rejects many of the values and practices of modern society⟩ — see RELIGION 1

creek *n* **1** a natural body of running water smaller than a river ⟨the shallow *creek* that runs in back of our house⟩
synonyms brook, brooklet, rill, rivulet, run [*chiefly Midland*], streamlet
related words freshet, runoff; river, stream, watercourse, waterway; canal, millrace, millstream, race
2 *chiefly British* a part of a body of water that extends beyond the general shoreline ⟨explored many of the *creeks* along the Cornwall coast of England⟩ — see GULF 1

creep *n* a person whose behavior is offensive to others ⟨he's a *creep*, so don't listen to him⟩ — see JERK 1

creep *vb* **1** to advance gradually beyond the usual or desirable limits ⟨water *crept* slowly over the top of the tub and onto the floor⟩ — see ENCROACH
2 to move or act slowly ⟨*creeping* like a snail because she dreaded going to school that day⟩ — see DELAY 1
3 to move slowly with the body close to the ground ⟨the kitten *crept* silently across the floor before suddenly pouncing on the mouse⟩ — see CRAWL 1
4 to move slowly ⟨the class hour seems to *creep* by⟩ — see CRAWL 2

creeper *n* someone who moves slowly or more slowly than others ⟨the youngest child is still the *creeper* in the family⟩ — see SLOWPOKE

creeping *adj* moving or proceeding at less than the normal, desirable, or required speed ⟨at this *creeping* pace of progress we'll never have the float ready for the parade⟩ — see SLOW 1

creepy *adj* fearfully and mysteriously strange or fantastic ⟨a fascinating but *creepy* stage show by an offbeat magician⟩ — see EERIE

crest *n* the line formed when two sloping surfaces come together along their topmost edge ⟨the hiking party finally reached the *crest* of the mountain⟩ — see RIDGE

crestfallen *adj* feeling unhappiness ⟨they were *crestfallen* to learn that the highest grade on the quiz was a 68%⟩ — see SAD 1

cretin *n* **1** a person whose behavior is offensive to others ⟨a *cretin* who was constantly blurting out unkind remarks about the students performing on stage⟩ — see JERK 1
2 a stupid person ⟨it's ridiculous to call your sister a *cretin* just because she's too young to read⟩ — see IDIOT

crevice *n* an irregular usually narrow break in a surface created by pressure ⟨steam escaped from a long *crevice* in the volcano⟩ — see CRACK 1

crew *n* a group of people working together on a task ⟨we'll need the whole *crew* to stay late tomorrow⟩ — see GANG 1

crick *n* a painful sudden tightening of a muscle ⟨got a *crick* in my neck from sleeping while sitting up⟩ — see CRAMP

crime *n* **1** activities that are in violation of the laws of the state ⟨a promise by the president to step up the war against *crime*⟩
synonyms criminality, lawbreaking, lawlessness
related words malfeasance, misconduct; wrongdoing; evil, immorality, sin, wickedness; corruption, depravity; malefaction, misdeed, misdoing, offense (*or* offence), transgression, trespass
2 a regrettable or blameworthy act ⟨it's a *crime* to waste food, so give the rest of the pizza to me⟩
synonyms disgrace, pity, shame, sin
related words outrage, scandal
3 a breaking of a moral or legal code ⟨anyone who commits a *crime* can expect to go to jail⟩ — see OFFENSE 1

4 a cause of shame ⟨her only *crime* was saying the wrong thing at the wrong time⟩ — see DISGRACE 2

criminal *adj* contrary to or forbidden by law ⟨people should know with certainty that *criminal* behavior will be punished⟩ — see ILLEGAL 1

criminal *n* a person who has committed a crime ⟨car thieves, pickpockets, burglars, and other *criminals*⟩
synonyms crook, culprit; felon, lawbreaker, malefactor, offender
related words desperado, outlaw; convict, jailbird; perpetrator; evildoer, sinner, transgressor, trespasser, wrongdoer; gangster, gunman, hoodlum, mobster, racketeer, thug; backslider, relapser, repeater

criminality *n* activities that are in violation of the laws of the state ⟨*criminality* and physical violence often go hand in hand⟩ — see CRIME 1

crimp *n* **1** a small fold in a soft and otherwise smooth surface ⟨put *crimps* in her hair for the party⟩ — see WRINKLE 1
2 something that makes movement or progress more difficult ⟨the strike could put a real *crimp* in production⟩ — see ENCUMBRANCE

crimson *vb* to develop a rosy facial color (as from excitement or embarrassment) ⟨he *crimsoned* when he realized the foolishness of what he'd said⟩ — see BLUSH

cringe *vb* to draw back or crouch down in fearful submission ⟨the puppy *cringed*, knowing he shouldn't have gnawed on the shoe⟩ — see COWER

crinkle *n* a small fold in a soft and otherwise smooth surface ⟨little *crinkles* at the corners of his mouth showed when he smiled⟩ — see WRINKLE 1

crinkle *vb* **1** to create (as by crushing) an irregular mass of creases in ⟨*crinkled* the candy wrapper up and threw it away⟩ — see CRUMPLE 1
2 to develop creases or folds ⟨her forehead *crinkled* with confusion⟩ — see WRINKLE 1

cripple *vb* **1** to cause severe or permanent injury to ⟨the car crash may have *crippled* two people for life⟩ — see MAIM
2 to reduce the soundness, effectiveness, or perfection of ⟨the collision so severely *crippled* the ship that it had to be towed into port⟩ — see DAMAGE 1
3 to render powerless, ineffective, or unable to move ⟨a wave of strikes *crippled* that nation's steel industry⟩ — see PARALYZE

crisis *n* a time or state of affairs requiring prompt or decisive action ⟨the governor responded swiftly and surely to the *crisis*⟩ — see EMERGENCY

crisp *adj* **1** having a texture that readily breaks into little pieces under pressure ⟨the bag of *crisp* cookies had a lot of crumbs on the bottom⟩
synonyms brittle, crispy, crumbly, flaky, friable, short
related words crunchy; breakable, delicate, fragile
near antonyms elastic, flexible, pliable, pliant, resilient; strong, sturdy, tough
2 being clean and in good order ⟨a pretty, *crisp* bedspread⟩ — see NEAT 1
3 marked by the use of few words to convey much information or meaning ⟨a *crisp* suggestion about what they could do with their boom box⟩ — see CONCISE

crisply *adv* in a few words ⟨the principal *crisply* commanded rubbernecking students back to classes⟩ — see SHORTLY 1

crispness *n* the quality or state of being marked by or using only few words to convey much meaning ⟨the *crispness* of the writing is such that this writer says more in nine paragraphs than some others say in nine pages⟩ — see SUCCINCTNESS

crispy *adj* having a texture that readily breaks into little pieces under pressure ⟨the *crispy* potato chips snapped satisfyingly in my mouth⟩ — see CRISP 1

crisscross *vb* to make one's way through, across, or over ⟨the children had to *crisscross* the park in order to play with the swings⟩ — see TRAVERSE

criterion *n* something set up as an example against which others of the same type are compared ⟨one important *criterion* for grading these essays will be their conformity to proper grammar⟩ — see STANDARD 1

critic *n* **1** a person given to harsh judgments and to finding faults ⟨the president's hard-core *critics* are going to criticize him no matter what he does⟩
synonyms carper, castigator, caviler (*or* caviller), censurer, faultfinder, nitpicker, railer, scold
related words belittler, derider, detractor; pettifogger, quibbler; complainer, crybaby, fusser, whiner
2 a person who makes or expresses a judgment on the quality of offerings in some field of endeavor ⟨the restaurant *critic* said that the fries at that fast-food outlet were the worst that she had ever eaten⟩
synonyms reviewer
related words analyst, columnist, commentator; appraiser, evaluator, judge

critical *adj* **1** given to making or expressing unfavorable judgments about things ⟨adults tend to be *critical* of teenagers' taste in music and movies⟩
synonyms captious, carping, caviling (*or* cavilling), faultfinding, hypercritical, overcritical
related words discerning, discriminating, judicious; demanding, exacting, fastidious, finicky, fussy, particular
near antonyms undiscerning
antonyms uncritical
2 needing immediate attention ⟨this problem isn't *critical*, so we can go home now and tend to it in the morning⟩ — see ACUTE 2
3 of the greatest possible importance ⟨this is the *critical* exam that will largely determine your college career⟩ — see CRUCIAL

criticism *n* an essay evaluating or analyzing something ⟨every *criticism* of the movie has noted that there are major holes in its plot⟩
synonyms notice, review
related words rave; appraisal, assessment, evaluation; analysis, examination, study

criticize *vb* to express one's unfavorable opinion of the worth or quality of ⟨the students who feel the need to *criticize* every single idea by the principal for improving the school⟩
synonyms blame, censure, condemn, denounce, dis [*slang*], fault, knock, pan, reprehend
related words assail, attack, blast, slam, slash; beef, bellyache, carp, complain, crab, croak, fuss, gripe, grouse, growl, grumble, kick, moan, murmur, mutter, repine, squawk, wail, whine, yammer; admonish, chide, rebuke, reprimand, reproach, reprove; berate, castigate, crucify, excoriate, flay, lambaste (*or* lambast), lash, pillory, scold, upbraid; bad-mouth, belittle, disparage, put down
phrases find fault (with), take to task
near antonyms approve, endorse (*also* indorse), recommend, sanction
antonyms extol (*also* extoll), laud, praise

critter *n* one of the lower animals as distinguished from human beings ⟨she's so fond of little *critters* that she wants to be a veterinarian⟩ — see ANIMAL

croak *vb* **1** to express dissatisfaction, pain, or resentment usually tiresomely ⟨the cranky patient was always *croaking* to the nurses about something〉 — see COM-PLAIN

2 *slang* to stop living 〈it's not polite to say that your great-grandmother "*croaked*" the other day!〉 — see DIE 1

3 *slang* to deprive of life 〈the boy bragged that he'd *croaked* several frogs〉 — see KILL 1

croaker *n* an irritable and complaining person 〈she becomes a real *croaker* when she's overtired〉 — see GROUCH

croaking *adj* harsh and dry in sound 〈a *croaking* voice from smoking too many cigarettes〉 — see HOARSE

crockery *n* articles made of baked clay 〈a display of beautifully hand-painted *crockery* on the kitchen countertop〉
  synonyms earthenware, pottery, stoneware
  related words ceramics; china, porcelain

crone *n* a mean or ugly old woman 〈a run-down house that was inhabited by a cantankerous *crone* who kept to herself〉
  synonyms beldam (*or* beldame), hag, witch
  related words grandam (*or* grandame); harpy, shrew, virago

crony *n* **1** a person frequently seen in the company of another 〈the criminal's *cronies* were also closely questioned about the illegal gambling operation〉 — see ASSOCIATE 1

2 a person who has a strong liking for and trust in another 〈only my *cronies* can call me by my nickname〉 — see FRIEND 1

crook *n* **1** a person who has committed a crime 〈they nabbed the *crook* who robbed the bank〉 — see CRIMINAL

2 something that curves or is curved 〈carried the baby in the *crook* of her arm〉 — see BEND 1

crook *vb* **1** to cause to turn away from a straight line 〈*crooked* a finger〉 — see BEND 1

2 to turn away from a straight line or course 〈the road suddenly *crooked* to the left〉 — see CURVE 1

crooked *adj* **1** marked by a long series of irregular curves 〈a long, *crooked* line of people had formed in front of the ticket booth〉
  synonyms bending, curled, curling, curved, curving, devious, serpentine, sinuous, tortuous, twisted, twisting, winding
  related words zigzag, zigzagging; circling, coiled, coiling, corkscrew, looping, spiral, spiraling (*or* spiralling), swirling; circuitous, indirect, roundabout; meandering, rambling, wandering
  near antonyms direct, linear
  antonyms straight, straightaway

2 given to or marked by cheating and deception 〈the common belief that gambling casinos are often *crooked* businesses〉 — see DISHONEST 2

3 inclined or twisted to one side 〈the photo on that wall is *crooked*〉 — see AWRY

4 marked by, based on, or done by the use of dishonest methods to acquire something of value 〈a *crooked* scheme to bill the government for medical services never performed〉 — see FRAUDULENT 1

crookedness *n* the inclination or practice of misleading others through lies or trickery 〈someone finally caught on to the car dealer's *crookedness* and turned him in〉 — see DECEIT

crop *n* **1** the quantity of an animal or vegetable product gathered at the end of a season 〈the wheat *crop* is going to be exceptionally large this year〉

  synonyms harvest
  related words return, yield

2 a usually small number of persons considered as a unit 〈the school's latest *crop* of graduates is its most academically gifted〉 — see GROUP 2

crop *vb* **1** to look after or assist the growth of by labor and care 〈a family that's been *cropping* potatoes on that piece of land for generations〉 — see GROW 1

2 to make (as hair) shorter with or as if with the use of shears 〈the toddler *cropped* her own hair with scissors when no one was looking〉 — see CLIP

crop (up) *vb* to come to one's attention especially gradually or unexpectedly 〈a new issue has just *cropped up* in the campaign〉 — see ARISE 2

cropper *n* a falling short of one's goals 〈several people were glad to see the smug skater come a *cropper* at the national championships〉 — see FAILURE 2

croquette *n* a small usually rounded mass of minced food that has been fried 〈a fish *croquette*〉 — see CAKE

cross *adj* easily irritated or annoyed 〈she was *cross* all day because of a nagging headache〉 — see IRRITABLE

cross *n* **1** a test of faith, patience, or strength 〈this learning disability is just my *cross* to bear〉 — see TRIAL 1

2 an offspring of parents with different genes especially when of different races, breeds, species, or genera 〈the mare is an Arabian-Thoroughbred *cross*〉 — see HYBRID

cross *vb* **1** to be unfaithful or disloyal to 〈people who *cross* the local mob boss usually are found floating in the river〉 — see BETRAY 1

2 to divide by passing through or across 〈that street *crosses* Main Street after about a mile from its beginning〉 — see INTERSECT

3 to make one's way through, across, or over 〈you may have to *cross* some woods on the way〉 — see TRAVERSE

cross (out) *vb* to show (something written) to be no longer valid by drawing a cross over or a line through it 〈*cross out* the old phone number and write in the new one〉 — see X (OUT)

crossbred *adj* being offspring produced by parents of different races, breeds, species, or genera 〈a beautiful *crossbred* dog who had the pleading eyes of a beagle and the body of a greyhound〉 — see MIXED 1

crossbreed *n* an offspring of parents with different genes especially when of different races, breeds, species, or genera 〈a Siamese *crossbreed* who was atypically black, but had the body type and the voice of a Siamese〉 — see HYBRID

cross fire *n* an often noisy or angry expression of differing opinions 〈viewers tune in to witness the weekly *cross fire* between the liberal and conservative commentators〉 — see ARGUMENT 1

crossing *n* **1** a journey over water in a vessel 〈an uneventful *crossing* from the United States to Britain〉 — see SAIL

2 a place where roads meet 〈turn left at the next *crossing*〉 — see CROSSROAD 1

crossness *n* readiness to show annoyance or impatience 〈a librarian who had a reputation for chronic *crossness*〉 — see PETULANCE

crossroad *n* **1** *usually* **crossroads** *pl* a place where roads meet 〈the fast-food chain has a restaurant at practically every *crossroads*〉
  synonyms corner, crossing, intersection
  related words overpass, underpass

2 *usually* **crossroads** *pl* a time or state of affairs requiring prompt or decisive action 〈we've come to a *crossroads*, and we have to make a decision⟩ — see EMERGENCY

cross section *n* a number of things selected from a group to stand for the whole ⟨a television ratings service that monitors the viewing of a representative *cross section* of the general population⟩ — see SAMPLE 1

crossways *adv* in a line or direction running from corner to corner ⟨lines running horizontally and not *crossways*⟩ — see CROSSWISE

crosswise *adv* in a line or direction running from corner to corner ⟨first cut the sandwiches *crosswise* and then trim the crusts⟩
synonyms athwart, crossways, obliquely, transversely

crotchet *n* an odd or peculiar habit ⟨her one *crotchet* is a fondness for eating cookies while soaking in the tub⟩ — see IDIOSYNCRASY

crotchetiness *n* readiness to show annoyance or impatience ⟨the understandable *crotchetiness* of an overworked teacher⟩ — see PETULANCE

crotchety *adj* easily irritated or annoyed ⟨I get *crotchety* after a long day at work⟩ — see IRRITABLE

crouch *vb* to lie low with the limbs close to the body ⟨the cat *crouched* in the bushes, waiting for the right moment to pounce on the chipmunk⟩
synonyms huddle, hunch, scrunch, squat, squinch
related words curl up

crow *vb* **1** to feel or express joy or triumph ⟨people clapped and *crowed* at the announcement that our school had placed first in the math competition⟩ — see EXULT
2 to praise or express pride in one's own possessions, qualities, or accomplishments often to excess ⟨please don't *crow* about your "A" in science to your sister⟩ — see BOAST

crowd *n* **1** a great number of persons or things gathered together ⟨a huge *crowd* of fans was on hand to greet the returning Super Bowl champions⟩
synonyms army, crush, drove, flock, horde, host, legion, mob, multitude, press, swarm, throng
related words masses, rabble, riffraff; gaggle, herd; heap, mountain, pile
2 a group of people sharing a common interest and relating together socially ⟨the fashionable *crowd* at the polo tournament⟩ — see GANG 2

crowd *vb* **1** to fit (something) into a tight space ⟨*crowded* all the boats into the harbor before the storm struck⟩
synonyms cram, jam, ram, sandwich, squeeze, stuff, wedge
related words fill, heap, jam-pack, load, pack
2 to move upon or fill (something) in great numbers ⟨cars *crowded* the roads over the long holiday weekend⟩
synonyms flock, mob, swarm, throng
related words beset, infest, invade, overrun; clog, dam, obstruct, plug (up)
3 to gather into a closely packed group ⟨everyone *crowded* around to see the baby being shown off by his proud parents⟩ — see PRESS 3

crowded *adj* **1** containing or seeming to contain the greatest quantity or number possible ⟨a *crowded* parking lot at a mall⟩ — see FULL 1
2 having little space between items or parts ⟨a *crowded* design that made the bedroom wallpaper a little overwhelming⟩ — see CLOSE 1

crown *n* **1** a decorative band or wreath worn about the head as a symbol of victory or honor ⟨the *crown* of laurel leaves that is traditionally placed on the winner of the marathon⟩

synonyms coronet, diadem
related words tiara; garland, laurel
2 the position occupied by the one who comes in first in a competition ⟨his lifelong dream of someday winning the heavyweight boxing *crown*⟩
synonyms championship, title
3 the highest part or point ⟨covered in mud from the soles of his feet to the *crown* of his head⟩ — see HEIGHT 1

crown *vb* to bring to a triumphant conclusion ⟨the Olympic Games were *crowned* by spectacular closing ceremonies⟩
synonyms climax, culminate
related words complete, conclude, finish, round (off *or* out), terminate, wrap up

crucial *adj* of the greatest possible importance ⟨water is *crucial* to our survival⟩
synonyms critical, key, pivotal, vital
related words decisive, life-and-death; basic, elementary, fundamental; essential, indispensable, necessary, requisite; pressing, urgent
near antonyms inconsequential, insignificant, trivial, unimportant

crucible *n* a test of faith, patience, or strength ⟨soldiers who had withstood the *crucible* of war⟩ — see TRIAL 1

crude *adj* **1** being such as found in nature and not altered by processing or refining ⟨a spill of *crude* oil along a coastline is the worst kind of environmental disaster⟩
synonyms native, natural, raw, undressed, unprocessed, unrefined, untreated
related words undeveloped; roughhewn, unfinished, unpolished; unbaked, uncooked; impure, unfiltered, unpurified
phrases in the rough
near antonyms filtered, pure, purified
antonyms dressed, processed, refined, treated
2 belonging to or characteristic of an early level of skill or development ⟨the *crude* stone tools that those prehistoric peoples used⟩ — see PRIMITIVE 1
3 depicting or referring to sexual matters in a way that is unacceptable in polite society ⟨*crude* jokes can be considered sexual harassment⟩ — see OBSCENE 1
4 lacking in refinement or good taste ⟨any discussion of one's money is considered *crude* by the club's members⟩ — see COARSE 2
5 hastily or roughly constructed ⟨a *crude* hut that was constructed by some shipwrecked sailors⟩ — see RUDE 1

crudeness *n* **1** the quality or state of being obscene ⟨the *crudeness* of the remark first made him blush and then made him angry⟩ — see OBSCENITY 1
2 the quality or state of lacking refinement or good taste ⟨the *crudeness* of the commentary at the fashion show horrified her⟩ — see VULGARITY 1

cruel *adj* **1** having or showing the desire to inflict severe pain and suffering on others ⟨a *cruel* dictator who tortured anyone who dared to speak out against him⟩ ⟨*cruel* and unusual punishments are forbidden by the U.S. Constitution⟩
synonyms barbaric, barbarous, brutal, heartless, inhumane, sadistic, savage, vicious, wanton
related words cutthroat, merciless, pitiless, ruthless; fell, ferocious, grim; bloodthirsty, murderous, sanguinary, sanguine; catty, despiteful, hateful, malevolent, malicious, malign, malignant, mean, nasty, spiteful

near antonyms tender, warm, warmhearted; charitable, clement, lenient, merciful, pitying; pacific, peaceable, peaceful

antonyms benign, benignant, compassionate, goodhearted, humane, kind, kindhearted, sympathetic, tenderhearted

2 difficult to endure ⟨the *cruel* climate of the Arctic⟩ — see HARSH 1

3 hard to accept or bear especially emotionally ⟨the *cruel* situation of being orphaned at an early age⟩ — see BITTER 2

4 having or showing a desire to cause someone pain or suffering for the sheer enjoyment of it ⟨the bully was fond of making *cruel* little jabs at his victim's sore points⟩ — see HATEFUL

cruelness *n* the willful infliction of pain and suffering on others ⟨far from being healers, the doctors in the Nazi death camps were notable for their senseless *cruelness*⟩ — see CRUELTY

cruelty *n* the willful infliction of pain and suffering on others ⟨centuries after he ravaged Europe, Attila the Hun remains notorious for his *cruelty*⟩

synonyms barbarity, brutality, cruelness, heartlessness, inhumanity, sadism, savageness, savagery, viciousness, wantonness

related words mercilessness, ruthlessness; ferocity, fierceness; bloodthirstiness, sanguinity; cattiness, despitefulness, hatefulness, malevolence, maliciousness, malignity, meanness, nastiness, spitefulness

near antonyms tenderness, warmheartedness, warmth; clemency, leniency, mercifulness, mercy, pity

antonyms benignity, compassion, good-heartedness, humanity, kindheartedness, kindness, sympathy

cruise *n* a journey over water in a vessel ⟨took a *cruise* for their first wedding anniversary⟩ — see SAIL

cruise *vb* to travel on water in a vessel ⟨*cruised* to the Bahamas in their yacht⟩ — see SAIL 1

crumb *n* **1** a very small amount ⟨a neglected dog who is desperate for *crumbs* of affection⟩ — see PARTICLE 1

2 a very small piece ⟨eating pretzels in bed got *crumbs* between the sheets⟩ — see BIT 1

crumble *vb* to become worse or of less value ⟨the stock *crumbled* after the revelations of fraud and mismanagement⟩ — see DETERIORATE

crumbly *adj* having a texture that readily breaks into little pieces under pressure ⟨a *crumbly* shortbread cookie⟩ — see CRISP 1

crumple *vb* **1** to create (as by crushing) an irregular mass of creases in ⟨*crumpled* the piece of paper and angrily threw it in the wastebasket⟩

synonyms crinkle, rumple, scrunch, wrinkle

related words corrugate, crease, crimp, fold, furrow, pleat; ripple, ruffle; disarrange, jumble, mess (up), muss (up)

antonyms iron out, smooth

2 to fall down or in as a result of physical pressure ⟨the box *crumpled* when I accidentally dropped a brick on it⟩ — see COLLAPSE 1

crunch *n* a time or state of affairs requiring prompt or decisive action ⟨she's always good in a *crunch*, like when we need a goal to win the soccer match⟩ — see EMERGENCY

crunch *vb* to press or strike against or together so as to make a scraping sound ⟨I could hear the bicycle gears *crunch* as I shifted the derailleur⟩ — see GRIND 2

crunch (on) *vb* to crush or grind with the teeth ⟨people who *crunch on* hard candies during movies really annoy me⟩ — see BITE (ON)

crusade *n* a series of activities undertaken to achieve a goal ⟨a *crusade* for spending more money on our public schools⟩ — see CAMPAIGN

crusader *n* one who is intensely or excessively devoted to a cause ⟨a *crusader* for improved safety in the workplace⟩ — see ZEALOT

crush *n* **1** a strong but often short-lived liking for another person ⟨the *crush* that she had on a boy whom she had met over the summer⟩

synonyms infatuation, passion

related words fixation, obsession; affection, devotion, fondness, love; craze, fad, rage, vogue

2 a great number of persons or things gathered together ⟨the huge *crush* in the store must have far exceeded safety limits⟩ — see CROWD 1

crush *vb* **1** to cause to become a pulpy mass ⟨dark-colored grapes that will be *crushed* to make red wine⟩

synonyms mash, pulp, squash

related words press, squeeze; beat, pound, powder, pulverize

2 to achieve a victory over ⟨our team *crushed* their traditional rivals in last night's game⟩ — see BEAT 2

3 to put a stop to (something) by the use of force ⟨the government is attempting to *crush* the latest guerrilla uprising⟩ — see QUELL 1

4 to reduce to fine particles ⟨*crushed* the baby's medicine tablet and mixed it with applesauce⟩ — see POWDER

5 to subject to incapacitating emotional or mental stress ⟨the terrible news simply *crushed* the entire family⟩ — see OVERWHELM 1

6 to apply external pressure on so as to force out the juice or contents of ⟨after *crushing* the grapes, let the skins soak in the juice in order to extract some color⟩ — see PRESS 2

crusher *n* something (as a fact or argument) that is decisive or overwhelming ⟨the *crusher* was that we would be out of town that weekend in any event⟩ — see CLINCHER

crusty *adj* being or characterized by direct, brief, and potentially rude speech or manner ⟨a *crusty* old fisherman who doesn't care to have his picture taken with silly tourists⟩ — see BLUNT 1

crux *n* the central part or aspect of something under consideration ⟨the *crux* of the problem is that the school's current budget is totally inadequate⟩

synonyms core, gist, heart, nub, pith, pivot

related words course, direction, drift, tenor; body, essence, substance

cry *n* **1** a loud vocal expression of strong emotion ⟨a *cry* of despair⟩ — see SHOUT

2 a natural vocal sound made by an animal ⟨the *cry* of a coyote⟩ — see CALL 1

3 an attention-getting word or phrase used to publicize something (as a campaign or product) ⟨"a chance to change America" was the *cry* on which the candidate was hoping to win the White House⟩ — see SLOGAN

4 an earnest request ⟨the king was deaf to their *cries*⟩ — see PLEA 1

cry *vb* **1** to shed tears often while making meaningless sounds as a sign of pain or distress ⟨some kids started to *cry* even before the doctor had given them their shot⟩

synonyms bawl, blubber, sob, weep

related words grieve, keen, lament, mourn; howl, scream, squall, wail, yowl; pule, whimper, whine; sniffle, snivel; groan, moan, sigh

2 to utter one's distinctive animal sound ⟨we knew that we were getting very close to the ocean when we could hear sea gulls *crying*⟩
synonyms call, sing

3 to speak so as to be heard at a distance ⟨Mom *cried* that it was time for dinner⟩ — see CALL 1

cry (out) *vb* to utter with a sudden burst of strong feeling ⟨"I can't stand it!" he *cried out*⟩ — see EXCLAIM

crybaby *n* a person who makes frequent complaints usually about little things ⟨car trips that were often spoiled by a couple of *crybabies* in the back seat⟩
synonyms complainer, fusser, griper, growler, grumbler, whiner
related words malcontent; carper, critic, faultfinder, nitpicker, squawker; bawler, wailer, weeper

cry down *vb* to express scornfully one's low opinion of ⟨she *cried down* any party to which she wasn't invited⟩ — see DECRY 1

crying *adj* needing immediate attention ⟨a *crying* need for more activities for young people in this town⟩ — see ACUTE 2

crypt *n* an underground burial chamber ⟨the old church's *crypt* is the final resting place for the president and his beloved wife⟩
synonyms catacomb(s), vault
related words mausoleum, sepulcher (*or* sepulchre), tomb

cryptic *adj* **1** being beyond one's powers to know, understand, or explain ⟨puzzled by the *cryptic* e-mail message left on his computer⟩ — see MYSTERIOUS 1

2 having an often intentionally veiled or uncertain meaning ⟨the oracle offered only *cryptic* predictions that could be interpreted any number of different ways⟩ — see OBSCURE 1

crystallize *vb* to take on a definite form ⟨after months of planning, the project is finally starting to *crystallize*⟩ — see FORM 1

cub *n* a young person who is between infancy and adulthood ⟨assigned to teach a bunch of young *cubs* how to play baseball⟩ — see CHILD 1

cubicle *n* one of the parts into which an enclosed space is divided ⟨workers busily typing in *cubicles*⟩ — see COMPARTMENT

cuckoo *adj* **1** having or showing a very abnormal or sick state of mind ⟨a *cuckoo* woman who wandered around town carefully gathering up useless trash⟩ — see INSANE 1

2 showing or marked by a lack of good sense or judgment ⟨offered a completely *cuckoo* suggestion for raising money for the school band⟩ — see FOOLISH 1

cuddle *vb* **1** to lie close ⟨kittens *cuddling* in a basket⟩ — see NUZZLE

2 to sit or recline comfortably or cozily ⟨they like to *cuddle* on the couch while watching TV⟩ — see SNUGGLE 1

cudgel *n* a heavy rigid stick used as a weapon or for punishment ⟨a farmer armed with a *cudgel* drove us off his land⟩ — see CLUB 1

cue *n* **1** a series of persons or things arranged one behind another ⟨the *cue* to get tickets to the concert moved with agonizing slowness⟩ — see LINE 1

2 a slight or indirect pointing to something (as a solution or explanation) ⟨a teacher should avoid offering *cues* to the answers⟩ — see HINT 1

cuff *n* a hard strike with a part of the body or an instrument ⟨the mama cat would give her kittens a *cuff* with a paw whenever they played too rough⟩ — see ¹BLOW

cuisine *n* the art or style of preparing food (as in a specified region) ⟨Italian *cuisine*⟩ — see COOKERY

cull *n* something separated from a group or lot for not being as good as the others ⟨the unbruised apples will be packed in bags, and the *culls* will be used for cider⟩
synonyms discard, reject, rejection
related words second, throwaway

cull *vb* to decide to accept (someone or something) from a group of possibilities ⟨*cull* the best short stories from the author's body of writings⟩ — see CHOOSE 1

culminate *vb* to bring to a triumphant conclusion ⟨*culminated* the school year with a joyous celebration⟩ — see CROWN

culmination *n* the highest part or point ⟨this is the *culmination* of all my hard work⟩ — see HEIGHT 1

culpability *n* responsibility for wrongdoing or failure ⟨she refused to accept *culpability* for someone else's mistake⟩ — see BLAME 1

culpable *adj* **1** deserving reproach or blame ⟨you're *culpable* for risking other people's lives needlessly, even though no one got hurt⟩ — see BLAMEWORTHY

2 responsible for a wrong ⟨find the *culpable* person for this prank!⟩ — see GUILTY 1

culprit *n* a person who has committed a crime ⟨the police caught the *culprit* two blocks away from the scene of the crime⟩ — see CRIMINAL

cult *n* **1** a group of people showing intense devotion to a cause, person, or work (as a film) ⟨long after it had gone off the air, the TV series continued to have a huge *cult*⟩
synonyms following
related words discipleship

2 a body of beliefs and practices regarding the supernatural and the worship of one or more deities ⟨an ancient *cult* that centered on the worship of the earth as the source of all life⟩ — see RELIGION 1

cultivate *vb* **1** to come to have gradually ⟨*cultivated* a taste for opera⟩ — see DEVELOP 2

2 to help the growth or development of ⟨*cultivated* an enduring interest in learning among his students over the years⟩ — see FOSTER 1

3 to look after or assist the growth of by labor and care ⟨I plan to *cultivate* beans and peas this year⟩ — see GROW 1

4 to work by plowing, sowing, and raising crops on ⟨we ought to *cultivate* the field out back⟩ — see FARM

cultivated *adj* having or showing a taste for the fine arts and gracious living ⟨the museum's annual gala for charity usually attracts a *cultivated* crowd⟩
synonyms civilized, cultured, genteel, polished, refined
related words cerebral, highbrow, intellectual; educated, erudite, knowledgeable, learned, literate, scholarly, well-read; civil, courteous, mannerly, polite, well-bred; cosmopolitan, sophisticated, urbane
near antonyms ignorant, illiterate, uneducated, unlettered; lowbrow, unintelligent; coarse, ill-bred, ill-mannered; provincial, rustic, unsophisticated; boorish, churlish, cloddish, clownish, crude, uncouth, vulgar
antonyms philistine, uncivilized, uncultured, unpolished, unrefined

cultivation *n* a high level of taste and enlightenment as a result of extensive intellectual training and exposure to the arts ⟨the *cultivation* of a graduate from a top university should be quite impressive⟩ — see CULTURE 1

cultivator *n* a person who cultivates the land and grows crops on it ⟨the *cultivator* of that field intends to harvest next week⟩ — see FARMER

cultural *adj* of or relating to the fine arts ⟨with its many museums, theaters, and opera and ballet companies, the city is a *cultural* paradise⟩
　synonyms artistic
　related words aesthetic, tasteful
culture *n* **1** a high level of taste and enlightenment as a result of extensive intellectual training and exposure to the arts ⟨because of its wide reputation as a place of *culture*, Boston became known as "the Athens of America"⟩
　synonyms civilization, cultivation, polish, refinement
　related words education, erudition, learning, literacy, scholarship; sophistication, urbanity; breeding, gentility, manners; class, elegance, grace, taste; civility, courtesy, politeness
　near antonyms ignorance, illiteracy; parochialism, provincialism, unsophistication; boorishness, churlishness, clownishness, coarseness, crudeness, vulgarity
　antonyms philistinism
　2 the way people live at a particular time and place ⟨a study of ancient Anasazi *culture* as it existed in the canyons of the American Southwest⟩ — see CIVILIZATION 1
culture *vb* to look after or assist the growth of by labor and care ⟨*culture* bacteria in laboratory dishes⟩ — see GROW 1
cultured *adj* having or showing a taste for the fine arts and gracious living ⟨an interior decorator who takes into account the *cultured* preferences of her wealthy clients⟩ — see CULTIVATED
cumbersome *adj* difficult to use or operate especially because of size, weight, or design ⟨a long-handled wrench that is too *cumbersome* for tight spots, like under the sink⟩
　synonyms awkward, clumsy, cranky, cumbrous, ungainly, unhandy, unwieldy
　related words uncontrollable, unmanageable; bulky, heavy, massive; impracticable, impractical
　near antonyms functional, practicable, practical, serviceable, useful
　antonyms handy
cumbrous *adj* difficult to use or operate especially because of size, weight, or design ⟨it took two people to haul the *cumbrous* machine into the garage⟩ — see CUMBERSOME
cummerbund *n* a strip of flexible material (as leather) worn around the waist ⟨a *cummerbund* is the perfect accessory for a man's tuxedo⟩ — see ²BELT
cumulative *adj* produced by a series of additions of identical or similar things ⟨a *cumulative* weight gain of 20 pounds over the course of a year⟩
　synonyms additive, incremental
　related words gradual, step-by-step
cunning *adj* **1** clever at attaining one's ends by indirect and often deceptive means ⟨a *cunning*, underhanded plan to win the election by preying on people's fears and prejudices⟩ — see ARTFUL 1
　2 skillful with the hands ⟨only the most *cunning* cabinetmaker could have crafted such a beautifully proportioned chest of drawers⟩ — see DEXTEROUS 1
cunning *n* **1** skill in achieving one's ends through indirect, subtle, or underhanded means ⟨the *cunning* with which Tom Sawyer was able to get others to whitewash the fence for him⟩
　synonyms artfulness, artifice, caginess, canniness, craft, craftiness, deviousness, foxiness, guile, slickness, slyness, sneakiness, subtleness, subtlety, wiliness

related words calculation, care, design; savvy, sharpness, shrewdness; cleverness, ingeniousness, ingenuity, inventiveness; ease, facility, finesse; deceitfulness, duplicity, shiftiness
　2 subtle or imaginative ability in inventing, devising, or executing something ⟨the *cunning* required to create an airworthy airplane without even so much as a kit⟩ — see SKILL 1
　3 the inclination or practice of misleading others through lies or trickery ⟨used *cunning* and subterfuge to work her way up the corporate ladder⟩ — see DECEIT
cup *n* a round vessel equipped with a handle and designed for drinking ⟨a large *cup* that can hold almost a pint of hot chocolate⟩
　synonyms mug
　related words stein, tankard; demitasse, noggin; teacup
cupboard *n* a storage case typically having doors and shelves ⟨dishes go in the *cupboard* next to the sink⟩ — see CABINET
cupidity *n* an intense selfish desire for wealth or possessions ⟨reports of great treasure in the Indies inflamed the *cupidity* of Columbus's crew⟩ — see GREED
cur *n* a person whose behavior is offensive to others ⟨only a *cur* would tell his girlfriend that, yes, a certain outfit did make her look fat⟩ — see JERK 1
curb *n* something that limits one's freedom of action or choice ⟨these international regulations act as a *curb* on the plundering of a nation's archaeological treasures⟩ — see RESTRICTION 1
curb *vb* to keep from exceeding a desirable degree or level (as of expression) ⟨try to *curb* your curiosity when it comes to your neighbors' business⟩ — see CONTROL 1
curdy *adj* having small pieces or lumps spread throughout ⟨*curdy* cottage cheese⟩ — see CHUNKY 1
cure *n* **1** something that corrects or counteracts something undesirable ⟨a fun hobby is always a good *cure* for boredom⟩
　synonyms corrective, remedy
　related words cure-all, elixir, panacea; answer, solution; aid, help, relief, succor; balm, palliative
　2 a substance or preparation used to treat disease ⟨researchers tirelessly working to find a *cure* for cancer⟩ — see MEDICINE
cure *vb* **1** to bring about recovery from ⟨do you have anything that will *cure* my headache?⟩
　synonyms heal, remedy
　related words allay, alleviate, assuage, relieve; palliate, salve, soothe; ease, lighten, moderate, temper; doctor, treat
　near antonyms aggravate, worsen
　2 to restore to a healthy condition ⟨the antibiotic *cured* the sick boy of the bacterial infection⟩ — see HEAL 1
cure–all *n* something that cures all ills or problems ⟨raising a young person's self-esteem is not the *cure-all* that some people think⟩
　synonyms elixir, panacea
　related words corrective, cure, remedy
curio *n* **1** a small object displayed for its attractiveness or interest ⟨be careful of the fragile *curios* on the end tables⟩ — see KNICKKNACK
　2 something strange or unusual that is an object of interest ⟨a museum's collection of *curios* brought back from the Far East by 19th-century traders⟩ — see CURIOSITY 2
curiosity *n* **1** an eager desire to find out about things that are often none of one's business ⟨the neighbors' *curios-*

ity about what we paid for our new car was really offensive⟩
synonyms curiousness, inquisitiveness, nosiness
related words attentiveness, concern, interest, regard; inquiry, interrogation, questioning; intrusiveness, obtrusiveness, officiousness; eavesdropping, rubbernecking
near antonyms apathy, disinterestedness, disregard, indifference, unconcern
2 something strange or unusual that is an object of interest ⟨the museum's *curiosities* include items constructed entirely out of toothpicks⟩
synonyms curio, exotic, oddity, rarity
related words marvel, prodigy, wonder; abnormality, anomaly, freak, monster, monstrosity; malformation, mutant, mutation
3 a small object displayed for its attractiveness or interest ⟨an assortment of *curiosities* from around the world that the family picked up during various vacations⟩ — see KNICKKNACK
curious *adj* **1** interested in what is not one's own business ⟨*curious* neighbors peered out of their windows as the new people moved in⟩
synonyms inquisitive, nosy (*or* nosey), prying, snoopy
related words interfering, intrusive, meddlesome, meddling, obtrusive, officious; inquisitional, inquisitorial; concerned, interested
near antonyms apathetic, disinterested, indifferent, unconcerned, uninterested
antonyms incurious, uncurious
2 different from the ordinary in a way that causes curiosity or suspicion ⟨that's a *curious* argument to make in favor of legalizing certain drugs⟩ — see ODD 2
3 noticeably different from what is generally found or experienced ⟨a *curious* hairstyle for a young girl⟩ — see UNUSUAL 1
curiousness *n* an eager desire to find out about things that are often none of one's business ⟨the *curiousness* of their new neighbors was a little annoying to the young couple⟩ — see CURIOSITY 1
curl *n* a length of hair that forms a loop or series of loops ⟨a young girl with beautiful golden *curls*⟩
synonyms ringlet
related words kink, wave; lock, tress
curl *vb* to follow a circular or spiral course ⟨an inviting path for joggers *curls* around the reservoir⟩ — see WIND
curled *adj* **1** forming or styled into loops ⟨a *curled* vine can add interest to a garden wall⟩ — see CURLY
2 marked by a long series of irregular curves ⟨a *curled* and complicated route through a series of caves⟩ — see CROOKED 1
curling *adj* marked by a long series of irregular curves ⟨a *curling* labyrinth designed to discourage grave robbers from ever finding the inner burial chamber⟩ — see CROOKED 1
curl up *vb* to sit or recline comfortably or cozily ⟨I love to *curl up* in a big chair with a book⟩ — see SNUGGLE 1
curly *adj* forming or styled into loops ⟨the boy's naturally *curly* hair⟩
synonyms curled
related words frizzy, kinky, waved, wavy
near antonyms lank, limp
antonyms straight
curmudgeon *n* an irritable and complaining person ⟨only a *curmudgeon* would object to the nursing home's holiday decorations⟩ — see GROUCH

currency *n* something (as pieces of stamped metal or printed paper) customarily and legally used as a medium of exchange, a measure of value, or a means of payment ⟨I prefer to carry only paper *currency*, as coins are too heavy⟩ — see MONEY
current *adj* **1** accepted, used, or practiced by most people ⟨the *current* theories on parenting favor allowing children lots of self-expression⟩
synonyms conventional, customary, going, popular, prevailing, prevalent, standard, stock, usual
related words average, common, everyday, normal, ordinary; regular, routine; ubiquitous, universal, widespread; accustomed, wonted; fashionable, in, modish, stylish
near antonyms abnormal, exceptional, extraordinary, uncommon
antonyms nonstandard, unconventional, unpopular, unusual
2 being or involving the latest methods, concepts, information, or styles ⟨*current* therapies for treating cancer have success rates that were undreamed of only a few decades ago⟩ — see MODERN
3 existing or in progress right now ⟨the *current* fundraising effort⟩ — see PRESENT 1
current *n* **1** a prevailing or general movement or inclination ⟨the *currents* of fashion are always changing⟩ — see TREND 1
2 noticeable movement of air in a particular direction ⟨curtains that were being lightly lifted by a fresh *current* from the open window⟩ — see ¹WIND 1
currently *adv* at the present time ⟨we're *currently* working on three separate projects⟩ — see NOW 1
curse *n* **1** a prayer that harm will come to someone ⟨the victim's *curse* that the man who robbed her never receive any pleasure from her money⟩
synonyms anathema, execration, imprecation, malediction
related words censure, condemnation, damnation, denunciation; hex, spell
near antonyms citation, commendation, endorsement
antonyms benediction, benison, blessing
2 a disrespectful or indecent word or expression ⟨started muttering *curses* after hitting his thumb with the hammer⟩ — see SWEARWORD
curse *vb* **1** to ask a divine power to send harm or evil upon ⟨I *curse* the guy who had the idea of having annoying salespeople call up innocent people to sell them things they don't want⟩
synonyms imprecate
related words condemn, damn, denounce, execrate, reprobate; hex, jinx; fulminate (against), rail (against), revile
near antonyms applaud, commend, congratulate
antonyms bless
2 to cause persistent suffering to ⟨misfortunes and problems seem to have *cursed* everyone ever associated with that house⟩ — see AFFLICT
3 to use offensive or indecent language ⟨you'll have to put a quarter in the jar every time you *curse*⟩ — see SWEAR 1
cursorily *adv* with excessive or careless speed ⟨*cursorily* glanced over the report before tossing it to one side⟩ — see HASTILY 1
cursory *adj* acting or done with excessive or careless speed ⟨your essays require more than a *cursory* effort at proofreading⟩ — see HASTY 1
curt *adj* being or characterized by direct, brief, and potentially rude speech or manner ⟨she was offended by

the *curt* reply to her well-meaning question⟩ — see BLUNT 1

curtail *vb* **1** to make (as hair) shorter with or as if with the use of shears ⟨this season designers have once again *curtailed* skirts so that they fall above the knees⟩ — see CLIP

2 to make less in extent or duration ⟨*curtailed* the school day because of the stormy weather⟩ — see SHORTEN

curtain *n* **1** something that covers or conceals like a piece of cloth ⟨there has long been a *curtain* of secrecy surrounding that religious sect⟩ — see CLOAK 1

2 curtains *pl* pieces of cloth hung to darken, decorate, or divide a room ⟨the kittens keep climbing the *curtains*⟩ — see DRAPERY

curtain *vb* to keep secret or shut off from view ⟨she dropped her head and in shame *curtained* her face with her hair⟩ — see ¹HIDE 2

curvature *n* something that curves or is curved ⟨*curvature* of the spine is called scoliosis⟩ — see BEND 1

curve *n* something that curves or is curved ⟨the bold *curve* of the racing yacht's hull⟩ — see BEND 1

curve *vb* **1** to turn away from a straight line or course ⟨after following a straight path most of the way down the mountain, the ski trail abruptly *curves* to the right⟩
synonyms arc, arch, bend, bow, crook, hook, round, sweep, swerve, wheel
related words circle, coil, curl, loop, spiral; turn, twist, wind; deviate, veer
antonyms straighten

2 to cause to turn away from a straight line ⟨*curved* the wood to make a bow⟩ — see BEND 1

curved *adj* marked by a long series of irregular curves ⟨a *curved* strip of metal that had sheared off during the collision⟩ — see CROOKED 1

curving *adj* marked by a long series of irregular curves ⟨the *curving* shoreline on the island's south side is a beachcomber's paradise⟩ — see CROOKED 1

cushion *n* something that serves as a protective barrier ⟨used a blanket as a *cushion* between the two tables in the moving van⟩
synonyms buffer, bumper, fender, pad
related words baffle, muffler; padding; safeguard, shield; barricade, cordon

cushion *vb* to lessen the shock of ⟨a substantial nest egg helped to *cushion* the sudden loss of her job⟩
synonyms buffer, gentle, soften
related words baffle, dampen, deaden, dull; moderate, modulate, temper; allay, alleviate, assuage, ease; lighten, mitigate, relieve
near antonyms heighten, intensify, sharpen

cushy *adj* providing physical comfort ⟨a big *cushy* chair that's perfect for watching television⟩ — see COMFORTABLE 1

cusp *n* the last and usually sharp or tapering part of something long and narrow ⟨the *cusp* of a fang⟩ — see POINT 2

cuss *n* a disrespectful or indecent word or expression ⟨a man who has never uttered a single *cuss*⟩ — see SWEARWORD

cuss *vb* to use indecent or indecent language ⟨the little girl clapped her hands over her ears when her brother started *cussing*⟩ — see SWEAR 1

custodian *n* **1** a person who takes care of a property sometimes for an absent owner ⟨the *custodian* made his usual rounds of the building to make sure that everything was OK⟩

synonyms caretaker, guardian, janitor, keeper, warden, watchman
related words curator; sexton; steward

2 a person or group that watches over someone or something ⟨the proud *custodian* of the clan's Celtic traditions⟩ — see GUARD 1

3 someone that protects ⟨he will be his niece's *custodian* until she reaches legal age⟩ — see PROTECTOR

custody *n* responsibility for the safety and well-being of someone or something ⟨the divorcing parents will share *custody* of the children⟩
synonyms care, guardianship, keeping, safekeeping, trust, ward
related words control, governorship, management, superintendence, supervision

custom *adj* made or fitted to the needs or preferences of a specific customer ⟨the business tycoon wears only *custom* suits⟩ — see CUSTOM-MADE

custom *n* **1** a usual manner of behaving or doing ⟨it is my *custom* to have half a bagel and coffee for breakfast⟩ — see HABIT

2 an inherited or established way of thinking, feeling, or doing ⟨the *custom* around here is that the bride's family pays for the wedding⟩ — see TRADITION 1

customary *adj* **1** accepted, used, or practiced by most people ⟨the *customary* response to the greeting "How are you?" is "Fine, thanks"⟩ — see CURRENT 1

2 based on customs usually handed down from a previous generation ⟨the *customary* toasting of the bride and groom at their wedding reception⟩ — see TRADITIONAL 1

customer *n* **1** a person who buys a product or uses a service from a business ⟨the store greatly values its regular *customers*⟩
synonyms client, guest, patron
related words consumer, end user, user; buyer, purchaser; browser, prospect, shopper, window-shopper
near antonyms merchant, seller, vendor (*also* vender)

2 a member of the human race ⟨he's one tough *customer*, so you'd better not cross him⟩ — see HUMAN

customized *adj* made or fitted to the needs or preferences of a specific customer ⟨a *customized* car for a physically challenged person⟩ — see CUSTOM-MADE

custom–made *adj* made or fitted to the needs or preferences of a specific customer ⟨an odd-sized window that will require the purchase of *custom-made* curtains⟩
synonyms custom, customized, tailored, tailor-made
related words particular, special, specialized; handcrafted, handmade
antonyms mass-produced, ready-made

cut *n* **1** a piece that has been separated from the whole by cutting ⟨choose *cuts* of meat that have very little visible fat⟩
synonyms cutting, slice
related words chop, cutlet; chunk, hunk, lump; clipping, paring, shaving, snippet; sliver, splinter

2 an individual part of a process, series, or ranking ⟨a *cut* above the rest in intelligence⟩ — see DEGREE 1

3 something belonging to, due to, or contributed by an individual member of a group ⟨received my *cut* of the profits from the garage sale⟩ — see SHARE 1

cut *vb* **1** to penetrate with a sharp edge (as a knife) ⟨I *cut* my hand on a piece of broken glass⟩
synonyms gash, incise, rip, slash, slice, slit
related words saw, scissor; cleave, rive, split; pierce, stab; bruise, hack, lacerate, mangle; rend, tear; butcher, carve, dissect; chop, dice, mince; amputate, cut off, sever

2 to fail to attend ⟨a warning that she had been *cutting* too many classes without valid excuses⟩
synonyms miss, skip
related words ignore, neglect, pass over
phrases absent oneself, play hooky
antonyms attend, show up (for)
3 to deliberately ignore or treat rudely ⟨the snobbish lady *cut* anyone who didn't meet her standards of wealth and social standing⟩ — see SNUB 1
4 to make (as hair) shorter with or as if with the use of shears ⟨*cut* her hair back to shoulder length⟩ — see CLIP
5 to shorten the standing leafy plant cover of ⟨you need to *cut* the lawn very soon—before it becomes a jungle⟩ — see MOW 1
cut (across) *vb* to make one's way through, across, or over ⟨*cut across* the field on the way to school⟩ — see TRAVERSE
cut (down) *vb* to bring down by cutting ⟨we need to *cut down* that dying tree⟩ — see FELL 2
cut (out) *vb* to bring (as an action or operation) to an immediate end ⟨now *cut* that *out*, or I'm turning this car around!⟩ — see STOP 1
cut back *vb* **1** to make (as hair) shorter with or as if with the use of shears ⟨Dad *cut back* the bushes a bit yesterday⟩ — see CLIP
2 to make less in extent or duration ⟨*cut back* the assembly so everyone could leave early⟩ — see SHORTEN
cute *adj* very pleasing to look at ⟨a *cute* baby that no one could resist cooing over⟩ — see BEAUTIFUL
cuteness *n* the qualities in a person or thing that as a whole give pleasure to the senses ⟨that kitten's *cuteness* is simply overwhelming!⟩ — see BEAUTY 1
cut in *vb* to cause a disruption in a conversation or discussion ⟨a stranger *cut in* with unsolicited advice on how we could fix our relationship⟩ — see INTERRUPT
cutlet *n* a small usually rounded mass of minced food that has been fried ⟨a breaded veal *cutlet*⟩ — see CAKE
cut off *vb* to set or keep apart from others ⟨the dog *cut off* the one sheep that had to be sheared⟩ — see ISOLATE
cut out *vb* to stop functioning ⟨the engine abruptly *cut out*⟩ — see FAIL 1
cut–rate *adj* **1** costing little ⟨opted for a *cut-rate* insurance policy because we didn't need anything more⟩ — see CHEAP 1
2 of low quality ⟨a *cut-rate* motel that looked like the kind at which people in horror movies always end up⟩ — see CHEAP 2
cutter *n* an instrument with a sharp edge for cutting ⟨a fabric *cutter*⟩ — see KNIFE
cutthroat *adj* not guided by or showing a concern for what is right ⟨*cutthroat* business practices intended to drive competitors out of business⟩ — see UNPRINCIPLED
cutting *adj* **1** causing intense discomfort to one's skin ⟨a frigid day with a *cutting* wind that made it seem even colder⟩
synonyms biting, bitter, keen, penetrating, piercing, raw, sharp, smarting, stinging

related words brisk, invigorating, nippy, snappy; needlelike, prickly, tingling; caustic, corrosive
near antonyms balmy, gentle, mild, soothing
2 having an edge thin enough to cut or pierce something ⟨the *cutting* side of the sword blade⟩ — see SHARP 1
3 marked by the use of wit that is intended to cause hurt feelings ⟨her *cutting* comments serve only one purpose: to make someone cry⟩ — see SARCASTIC
cutting *n* a piece that has been separated from the whole by cutting ⟨a bag full of grass *cuttings*⟩ — see CUT 1
cut up *vb* to engage in attention-getting playful or boisterous behavior ⟨high-spirited cousins who *cut up* at every family gathering⟩
synonyms act up, clown (around), fool (around), horse (around), monkey (around), show off, skylark
related words carry on, misbehave; roughhouse; caper, cavort, disport, frisk, frolic, gambol, lark, rollick, romp; carouse, revel, wassail
cycle *n* **1** a series of events or actions that repeat themselves regularly and in the same order ⟨the *cycle* of birth, growth, decline, and death that is experienced by all life forms⟩
synonyms circle, round
related words pattern, syndrome; course, development, progression, run; circuit, loop, ring; rotation, revolution, turn; chain, sequence, series, string, succession, train
2 a long or seemingly long period of time ⟨it's been *cycles* since I last saw you⟩ — see AGE 2
cynic *n* a person who distrusts other people and believes that everything is done for selfish reasons ⟨a *cynic* who believes that nobody does a good deed without expecting something in return⟩
synonyms misanthrope, pessimist
related words misogynist; doubter, skeptic; belittler, derider, detractor, scoffer; malcontent; defeatist, quitter
near antonyms optimist; idealist; sentimentalist
cynical *adj* having or showing a deep distrust of human beings and their motives ⟨so *cynical* that he can't understand why anyone would volunteer to help out at a homeless shelter⟩
synonyms misanthropic, pessimistic
related words distrustful, mistrustful, skeptical, suspicious; derisive, mocking, sardonic, scornful; defeatist, fatalistic, negative; ironic (*or* ironical), sarcastic; jaded, sophisticated, worldly-wise; hard-bitten, hard-boiled, unsentimental
near antonyms trustful, trusting, unsuspicious; cheerful, optimistic, rose-colored; ingenuous, innocent, naive (*or* naïve), unsophisticated; idealistic, impractical, romantic; maudlin, mushy, saccharine, sappy, sentimental
cynosure *n* a thing or place that is of greatest importance to an activity or interest ⟨that company is the *cynosure* for anyone wishing to make it in the music business⟩ — see CENTER 1
czar *also* **tsar** *or* **tzar** *n* a person of rank, power, or influence in a particular field ⟨a show biz *czar* who is said to be able to make or break a career⟩ — see MAGNATE

D

¹dab *n* a quick thrust ⟨one more quick *dab* of the brush and he would be finished with his painting⟩ — see ¹POKE

²dab *n* a very small amount ⟨she added a *dab* of sesame oil to the dressing before pouring it on the salad⟩ — see PARTICLE 1

dabbler *n* a person who regularly or occasionally engages in an activity without being or becoming an expert at it ⟨he was a *dabbler*, learning the basics of many arts but mastering none⟩ — see AMATEUR

dad *n* a male human parent ⟨my *dad* does most of the cooking for us because he gets home earlier than my mom⟩ — see FATHER 1

daddy *n* a male human parent ⟨I stopped calling my father "*Daddy*" because I thought it sounded childish⟩ — see FATHER 1

daffy *adj* **1** having or showing a very abnormal or sick state of mind ⟨court-appointed psychiatrists agreed that the criminal was clearly *daffy*⟩ — see INSANE 1
2 showing or marked by a lack of good sense or judgment ⟨their *daffy* antics made generations of movie audiences laugh⟩ — see FOOLISH 1

daft *adj* **1** having or showing a very abnormal or sick state of mind ⟨the king was clearly *daft*, talking to trees and rocks as if they were people⟩ — see INSANE 1
2 showing or marked by a lack of good sense or judgment ⟨a *daft* plan doomed to wretched failure and merciless ridicule⟩ — see FOOLISH 1

daftness *n* lack of good sense or judgment ⟨his dithery *daftness* makes him unfit for any position but that of class clown⟩ — see FOOLISHNESS 1

daily *adj* occurring, done, produced, or appearing every day ⟨they made their *daily* stop at the coffee shop after work to relax before dinner⟩
synonyms day-to-day, diurnal
related words alternate, cyclical, intermittent, periodic, recurrent, recurring, regular; continuous, frequent, incessant
near antonyms nightly, nocturnal; monthly, weekly, yearly; erratic, infrequent, irregular; occasional, spasmodic, sporadic; interrupted

daintiness *n* the state or quality of having a delicate structure ⟨we were less impressed by the *daintiness* of the etching on the crystal vase than by the heftiness of its price⟩ — see DELICACY 2

dainty *adj* **1** hard to please ⟨you can't afford to be *dainty* about food when you're starving⟩ — see FINICKY
2 having qualities that appeal to a refined taste ⟨the *dainty* hors d'oeuvres were delicious, but not terribly filling⟩ — see CHOICE
3 satisfying or pleasing because of fineness or mildness ⟨a set of *dainty* teacups that would be perfect for an elderly lady⟩ — see DELICATE 1

dainty *n* something that is pleasing to eat because it is rare or a luxury ⟨she plied her suitor with *dainties* and endless glasses of sherry⟩ — see DELICACY 1

dais *n* a level usually raised surface ⟨the speaker took his place at the front of the *dais*⟩ — see PLATFORM

dale *n* an area of lowland between hills or mountains ⟨a hunting lodge in a secluded *dale* in the country⟩ — see VALLEY

dalliance *n* activity engaged in to amuse oneself ⟨an extremely serious scientist who is not much given to *dalliance* or idle chitchat⟩ — see PLAY 1

dallier *n* someone who moves slowly or more slowly than others ⟨the *dalliers* began to hurry when they realized a violent storm was brewing⟩ — see SLOWPOKE

dally *vb* **1** to engage in activity for amusement ⟨he spent his college years *dallying*, seemingly determined to acquire as little knowledge as possible⟩ — see PLAY 1
2 to move or act slowly ⟨don't *dally* on the way to school⟩ — see DELAY 1
3 to show a liking for someone of the opposite sex just for fun ⟨she spent the summer *dallying* with a boy from out of town⟩ — see FLIRT
4 to spend time doing nothing ⟨I kept *dallying* at my desk until I couldn't put off doing my homework any longer⟩ — see IDLE

dallying *adj* moving or proceeding at less than the normal, desirable, or required speed ⟨the *dallying* diners seemed oblivious to the fact that other customers were impatiently waiting for tables⟩ — see SLOW 1

dam *n* a bank of earth constructed to control water ⟨the river backed up behind the *dam* until it formed a new lake⟩
synonyms dike, embankment, levee
related words breakwater, jetty, seawall; breastwork, bulwark, earthwork, rampart; canal, channel, ditch, gutter, trough; lock; barricade, barrier, block; floodgate, sluice

dam *vb* **1** to prevent passage through ⟨ice floes were *damming* the river⟩ — see CLOG 1
2 to close up so that no empty spaces remain ⟨*dam* up the pipes⟩ — see FILL 2

damage *n* **1** something that causes loss or pain ⟨the collision did a great deal of *damage* to her car⟩ — see INJURY 1
2 damages *pl* a sum of money to be paid as a punishment ⟨ordered by the court to pay $1000 in *damages*⟩ — see FINE
3 damages *pl* payment to another for a loss or injury ⟨the company was forced to pay millions in *damages* to the permanently injured worker⟩ — see COMPENSATION 1

damage *vb* **1** to reduce the soundness, effectiveness, or perfection of ⟨the explosion in the sewers *damaged* the entire city's water supply⟩
synonyms blemish, break, cripple, deface, disfigure, flaw, harm, hurt, impair, injure, mar, spoil, vitiate
related words enfeeble, undermine, weaken; erode, scour, wash out, wear (away); blight, tarnish; dent, dint; botch, gum (up); lacerate, wound; maim, mangle, mutilate, torment, torture; annihilate, crush, dash, decimate, demolish, destroy, devastate, pulverize, raze, ruin, scourge, shatter, smash, tear down, waste, wipe out, wreck
near antonyms cure, heal, help, rectify, remedy; edit, remodel, revise; ameliorate, better, enhance, improve, meliorate
antonyms fix, mend, patch, rebuild, recondition, reconstruct, renovate, repair, revamp
2 to cause bodily damage to ⟨his knee was badly *damaged* in the accident, and he walked with a limp for months⟩ — see INJURE 1

damaging *adj* causing or capable of causing harm ⟨the *damaging* effects of the sun on unprotected skin⟩ — see HARMFUL

dame *n* **1** a dignified usually elderly woman of some rank or authority ⟨as the grand *dames* of local society, they determined which charities received support⟩ — see MATRIARCH

2 a woman of high birth or social position ⟨the lords and *dames* of the shire eagerly awaited the royal visit⟩ — see GENTLEWOMAN

damn *vb* **1** to declare to be morally wrong or evil ⟨a heresy that was quickly *damned* by a hastily called church council⟩ — see CONDEMN 1

2 to impose a judicial punishment on ⟨*damned* him to life in prison without the possibility of parole⟩ — see SENTENCE

damp *adj* slightly or moderately wet ⟨marks can usually be removed with a *damp* cloth⟩ — see MOIST

damp *vb* to reduce or weaken in strength or feeling ⟨nothing seemed to *damp* the unwelcome attentions of her suitor⟩ — see DULL 1

dampen *vb* **1** to make or become slightly or moderately wet ⟨*dampen* a paper towel with water and use it to clean up the mess⟩ — see MOISTEN

2 to reduce or weaken in strength or feeling ⟨the oppressive heat *dampened* our spirits⟩ — see DULL 1

damper *n* a device on a musical instrument that deadens or softens its tone ⟨the pianist used the *damper* pedal on the piano for the quiet passages⟩ — see MUTE

dampness *n* the amount of water suspended in the air in tiny droplets ⟨the *dampness* in the air made a mess of my new hairstyle⟩ — see MOISTURE

damsel *n* a young usually unmarried woman ⟨knights are celebrated in fairy tales for rescuing *damsels* in distress⟩ — see GIRL 1

dance *n* a social gathering for dancing ⟨who are you taking to the *dance* Saturday night?⟩
    synonyms ball, cotillion, formal, hop, prom
    related words blowout, celebration, event, festival, festivity, fete (*or* fête), gala, masquerade, mixer, party, reception, shindig, soiree (*or* soirée)

dance *vb* **1** to perform a series of usually rhythmic bodily movements to music ⟨she liked to *dance* to her favorite rock bands⟩
    synonyms foot (it), hoof (it), step
    related words prance, strut, trip; gavotte, jig, jitterbug, jive, mambo, polka, tango, tap-dance, waltz; tread
    2 to make an irregular series of quick, sudden movements ⟨the lithe boxer *danced* around the ring, staying just out of the reach of his opponent⟩ — see FLIT

dandle *vb* to treat with great or excessive care ⟨the college president is used to *dandling* wealthy alumni⟩ — see BABY

dandy *adj* of the very best kind ⟨that's a *dandy* new racing bike⟩ — see EXCELLENT

dandy *n* **1** a man extremely interested in his clothing and personal appearance ⟨that *dandy* was willing to spend all day and hundreds of dollars just to get the perfect pair of shoes⟩
    synonyms buck, dude, fop, gallant
    related words coxcomb, popinjay; blade, cavalier; swell; clotheshorse
    near antonyms slattern, slob, sloven, slut
    2 something very good of its kind ⟨that new computer system is a *dandy*⟩ — see JIM-DANDY

danger *n* **1** the state of not being protected from injury, harm, or evil ⟨he knew he was in *danger* when he received the threatening phone calls at home⟩
    synonyms distress, endangerment, imperilment, jeopardy, peril, risk, trouble
    related words exposure, liability, vulnerability; precariousness, threat
    near antonyms preservation, salvation; defense, protection; exemption, immunity, impunity
    antonyms safeness, safety, security
    2 something that may cause injury or harm ⟨she was willing to face the *dangers* of the construction site in order to get her Frisbee back⟩
    synonyms hazard, menace, peril, pitfall, risk, threat, trouble
    related words snare, trap
    near antonyms guard, protection, safeguard, shield, ward

dangerous *adj* involving potential loss or injury ⟨the soldiers were commanded to go on a *dangerous* mission behind enemy lines⟩
    synonyms grave, grievous, hazardous, jeopardizing, menacing, parlous, perilous, risky, serious, threatening, unhealthy, unsafe, venturesome
    related words insecure, precarious, treacherous, uncertain; chance, haphazard, random; distressing, sickening, unpleasant; ugly, wicked; adverse, bad, baleful, baneful, deleterious, detrimental, evil, harmful, hurtful, ill, inimical, injurious, malignant, nasty, noxious, pernicious, pestilent; deadly, deathly, destructive, dire, fatal, fateful, fell, killer, lethal, mortal, murderous
    near antonyms advantageous, beneficial, good
    antonyms harmless, innocent, innocuous, safe

dangle *vb* to place on an elevated point without support from below ⟨he *dangled* the string in front of the cat, hoping that it was in the mood for play⟩ — see HANG 1

dangling *adj* extending freely from a support from above ⟨there was a *dangling* banner in one corner of the room⟩ — see DEPENDENT 1

dank *adj* slightly or moderately wet ⟨vegetables tended to go bad quickly in the *dank* cellar⟩ — see MOIST

dapper *adj* being strikingly neat and trim in style or appearance ⟨the *dapper* gentleman drew admiring glances from all over the ballroom⟩ — see SMART 1

dapple *n* a small area that is different (as in color) from the main part ⟨the clouds threw *dapples* of shadow over the eerily quiet street⟩ — see SPOT 1

dapple *vb* to mark with small spots especially unevenly ⟨a roan horse is a dark-colored horse *dappled* with small pale spots⟩ — see SPOT

dappled *also* **dapple** *adj* **1** marked with spots ⟨a *dappled* fawn⟩ — see SPOTTED 1

2 having blotches of two or more colors ⟨the *dappled* foliage of autumn⟩ — see PIED

dare *vb* **1** to invite (someone) to take part in a contest or to perform a feat ⟨I *dare* you to repeat that to my face!⟩ ⟨he *dared* his friend to race to the end of the block⟩ — see CHALLENGE 2

2 to oppose (something hostile or dangerous) with firmness or courage ⟨every day the old fisherman *dared* the elements to make his meager living⟩ — see FACE 2

daredevil *adj* **1** foolishly adventurous or bold ⟨his *daredevil* stunts are sure to end in disaster someday⟩ — see FOOLHARDY 1

2 having or showing a lack of concern for the consequences of one's actions ⟨a *daredevil* driver who thinks that drag racing on city streets is a harmless game⟩ — see RECKLESS 1

daring *adj* inclined or willing to take risks ⟨*daring* acrobats who risk life and limb every day for the entertainment of the crowds at the circus⟩ — see BOLD 1

daring *n* strength of mind to carry on in spite of danger ⟨the *daring* that the early explorers of Oceania must have had⟩ — see COURAGE

dark *adj* **1** being without light or without much light ⟨a *dark* alley that most people wisely avoided⟩
synonyms darkened, darkish, darkling, darksome, dim, dimmed, dusky, gloomy, murky, obscure, obscured, pitch-black, pitch-dark, somber (*or* sombre)
related words moonless, sunless; cloudy, dull, dulled, lackluster; shadowy, shady; gray (*also* grey), leaden, pale
near antonyms beaming, effulgent, glowing, lambent, radiant, shining; glossy, lustrous, shiny
antonyms bright, brightened, brilliant, illuminated, illumined, light, lighted (*or* lit), lucent, lucid, luminous
2 causing or marked by an atmosphere lacking in cheer ⟨her mind was filled with *dark* thoughts as she waited for the results of the medical test⟩ — see GLOOMY 1
3 given to keeping one's activities hidden from public observation or knowledge ⟨the actor was always quite *dark* about his life before his arrival in Hollywood⟩ — see SECRETIVE
4 having an often intentionally veiled or uncertain meaning ⟨a troubled kid who was always muttering *dark* threats that someday they'd all be sorry⟩ — see OBSCURE 1
5 lacking in education or the knowledge gained from books ⟨a *dark* period in European history when people lived in ignorance, fear, and want⟩ — see IGNORANT 1

dark *n* **1** a time or place of little or no light ⟨I have a bad habit of running into tables in the *dark*⟩
synonyms blackness, darkness, dusk, gloaming, gloom, murk, night, semidarkness, shade, shadows, twilight, umbra
related words blackout, brownout; shadiness; dullness (*also* dulness), somberness; cloudiness, fogginess, haziness, mistiness, murkiness; dimness, faintness, gloominess, grayness, paleness
near antonyms moonlight, starlight, sunlight; effulgence, radiance, shine, sunshine; incandescence, luminescence, luminosity
antonyms blaze, brightness, brilliance, day, daylight, glare, glow, light, lightness
2 the time from sunset to sunrise when there is no visible sunlight ⟨we were going to wait until *dark* to go trick-or-treating⟩ — see NIGHT 1

darken *vb* **1** to take on a gloomy or forbidding look ⟨his face slowly *darkened* as we told him the sad news⟩
synonyms gloom, glower, lower (*also* lour)
related words frown, scowl; glare, stare; brood, mope, pout, sulk; anger, fume, rage, steam; intimidate, menace, threaten
antonyms brighten, cheer (up), lighten, perk (up)
2 to make dark, dim, or indistinct ⟨years of accumulated grime have *darkened* the painting until it can barely be seen⟩ — see CLOUD 1

darkened *adj* being without light or without much light ⟨wanting to surprise her, we waited in the *darkened* room for her to get home⟩ — see DARK 1

darkening *adj* causing or marked by an atmosphere lacking in cheer ⟨a *darkening* sky that seemed to match our downcast spirits⟩ — see GLOOMY 1

darkish *adj* being without light or without much light ⟨the *darkish* galleries do not show off the museum's paintings to their best advantage⟩ — see DARK 1

darkling *adj* **1** being beyond one's powers to know, understand, or explain ⟨an intelligence agency feared for its secret files and *darkling* plots⟩ — see MYSTERIOUS 1
2 being without light or without much light ⟨the *darkling* valleys of Transylvania, where tales of vampires have long existed⟩ — see DARK 1
3 having an often intentionally veiled or uncertain meaning ⟨*darkling* glances cast across a dimly lit room⟩ — see OBSCURE 1

darkness *n* **1** a time or place of little or no light ⟨the raiding party snuck up under cover of *darkness*⟩ — see DARK 1
2 the quality or state of having a veiled or uncertain meaning ⟨the *darkness* of certain passages in the book of Revelation⟩ — see OBSCURITY 1
3 the time from sunset to sunrise when there is no visible sunlight ⟨let's wait for *darkness* before telling ghost stories⟩ — see NIGHT 1

darksome *adj* being without light or without much light ⟨a pile of *darksome* ruins in the heart of the forest⟩ — see DARK 1

darling *adj* **1** granted special treatment or attention ⟨they poured gifts and affection on their *darling* child⟩
synonyms beloved, cherished, dear, favored, favorite, loved, pet, precious, special, sweet
related words admired, adored, appreciated, esteemed, relished, revered; prized, treasured; preferred
near antonyms despised, detested, disdained, disfavored, disliked, execrated, hated, loathed; abandoned, forgotten, ignored
2 having qualities that tend to make one loved ⟨a *darling* child that any couple would want to adopt⟩ — see LOVABLE
3 giving pleasure or contentment to the mind or senses ⟨what a *darling* set of dishes!⟩ — see PLEASANT

darling *n* **1** a person or thing that is preferred over others ⟨for a while that candidate was the *darling* of the news media and could do no wrong⟩ — see FAVORITE
2 a person with whom one is in love ⟨anything you say, *darling*⟩ — see SWEETHEART

darn *vb* to close up with a series of interlacing stitches ⟨in the old days, holes in socks had to be *darned* by hand⟩ — see SEW

dart *n* an act or expression showing scorn and usually intended to hurt another's feelings ⟨the *darts* flew fast and furiously when the two former friends bumped into each other at the party⟩ — see INSULT

dart *vb* to make an irregular series of quick, sudden movements ⟨the housefly *darted* about the room until it found an open window and flew out⟩ — see FLIT

dash *n* active strength of body or mind ⟨the cavalry officer's *dash* and enthusiasm inspired his men to follow him into battle⟩ — see VIGOR 1

dash *vb* **1** to go at a pace faster than a walk ⟨one sprinter *dashed* to the finish line in record-breaking time⟩ — see RUN 1
2 to proceed or move quickly ⟨we *dashed* about in a panic, trying to get everything organized before the guests were scheduled to arrive⟩ — see HURRY 2
3 to send through the air especially with a quick forward motion of the arm ⟨she *dashed* water in his face in an attempt to wake him up⟩ — see THROW
4 to wet or soil by striking with something liquid or mushy ⟨our clothes were *dashed* with the mud of passing cars⟩ — see SPLASH 2

dashing *adj* inclined or willing to take risks ⟨the *dashing* heroes in stories about the American West⟩ — see BOLD 1

dashingly *adv* **1** in a bright and showy way ⟨the Christmas tree was decorated *dashingly* with lots of lights and colorful ornaments⟩ — see GAILY 3

2 in a strikingly neat and trim manner ⟨a young man *dashingly* dressed in a tuxedo for the prom⟩ — see SMARTLY

dastard *n* a person who shows a shameful lack of courage in the face of danger ⟨the villain of the story is a *dastard* indeed⟩ — see COWARD

dastardliness *n* a shameful lack of courage in the face of danger ⟨the *dastardliness* of the enemy's surprise attack⟩ — see COWARDICE

dastardly *adj* having or showing a shameful lack of courage ⟨his *dastardly* conduct haunted him for the rest of his life⟩ — see COWARDLY

date *n* **1** an agreement to be present at a specified time and place ⟨I have a *date* to meet my math tutor at the library at seven o'clock⟩ — see ENGAGEMENT 2

2 the period during which something exists, lasts, or is in progress ⟨the embarrassingly short *date* of most of his romances⟩ — see DURATION 1

date *vb* **1** to go on a social engagement with ⟨I don't want to *date* him—I'd rather just be friends⟩

synonyms take out

related words accompany, escort, see; court, woo

2 to go on dates that may eventually lead to marriage ⟨we *dated* for two years before we got engaged⟩ — see COURT 2

dated *adj* having passed its time of use or usefulness ⟨his jokes are awfully *dated*, referring to things that happened years ago⟩ — see OBSOLETE

dateless *adj* **1** dating or surviving from the distant past ⟨*dateless* artifacts left by an obscure people of the distant past⟩ — see ANCIENT 1

2 lasting forever ⟨the *dateless* cycle of the seasons⟩ — see EVERLASTING

dating *n* the series of social engagements shared by a couple looking to get married ⟨their *dating* had been going on for so long that she was starting to wonder if she'd ever take that trip down the aisle⟩ — see COURTSHIP

datum *n* a single piece of information ⟨let's begin our discussion of this matter with a *datum* from actual experience⟩ — see FACT 3

daub *vb* to rub an oily or sticky substance over ⟨he begins his nightly transformation into a circus clown by *daubing* greasepaint on his face⟩ — see SMEAR 1

daunt *vb* to lessen the courage or confidence of ⟨the raging inferno didn't *daunt* the firefighters for a moment⟩ — see DISCOURAGE 1

dauntless *adj* feeling or displaying no fear by temperament ⟨*dauntless* heroes who are inclined to rush to danger, not away from it⟩ — see BRAVE

dauntlessness *n* strength of mind to carry on in spite of danger ⟨the *dauntlessness* of the soldiers who led the charge up the hill⟩ — see COURAGE

davenport *n* a long upholstered piece of furniture designed for several sitters ⟨we seated ourselves on the *davenport* while we waited for him to get ready⟩ — see COUCH

dawdle *vb* **1** to move or act slowly ⟨if you continue to *dawdle*, we'll be late for sure⟩ — see DELAY 1

2 to spend time doing nothing ⟨accused the city council of *dawdling* even as the crime rate was going out of control⟩ — see IDLE

dawdler *n* someone who moves slowly or more slowly than others ⟨we encouraged the *dawdlers* to pick up the pace⟩ — see SLOWPOKE

dawdling *adj* moving or proceeding at less than the normal, desirable, or required speed ⟨the *dawdling* pace of the movie was really making us restless⟩ — see SLOW 1

dawn *n* **1** the first appearance of light in the morning or the time of its appearance ⟨we stayed up talking until *dawn*⟩

synonyms aurora, cockcrow, dawning, daybreak, daylight, morn, morning, sunrise, sunup

related words day, daytime, light; twilight; forenoon

near antonyms dark, darkness, night, nighttime; afternoon, dusk, evening, gloaming

antonyms nightfall, sundown, sunset

2 the point at which something begins ⟨the *dawn* of civilization⟩ — see BEGINNING

dawn *vb* to come into existence ⟨a smile *dawned* on his face as he got the joke⟩ — see BEGIN 2

dawn (on) *vb* to come into the mind of ⟨it finally *dawned on* me that I had been going the wrong way⟩ — see OCCUR (TO)

dawning *n* the first appearance of light in the morning or the time of its appearance ⟨the cold, gray *dawning* of a wintry day⟩ — see DAWN 1

day *n* **1** the hours of light between one night and the next ⟨during the *day*, we like to go play ball in the park⟩

synonyms daylight, daytime

related words light, sunlight, sunshine; dawn, dawning, daybreak, morn, morning, sunrise, sunset; dusk, evening, gloaming, nightfall, sundown, twilight

near antonyms dark, darkness

antonyms night, nighttime

2 an extent of time associated with a particular person or thing ⟨the brief but glorious *day* of the clipper ship⟩ — see AGE 1

daybreak *n* the first appearance of light in the morning or the time of its appearance ⟨I seem to wake up at *daybreak* regardless of what the clock says⟩ — see DAWN 1

daydream *n* a conception or image created by the imagination and having no objective reality ⟨hoped that one day world peace would be a reality and not just a *daydream*⟩ — see FANTASY 1

daydreaming *n* the state of being lost in thought ⟨if you're bored while traveling, *daydreaming* is a perfectly normal state to be in, regardless of what the road signs say⟩ — see REVERIE

daylight *n* **1** the first appearance of light in the morning or the time of its appearance ⟨*daylight* was just breaking when we stumbled out of bed⟩ — see DAWN 1

2 the hours of light between one night and the next ⟨there isn't a lot of *daylight* left, so we'd better get home soon⟩ — see DAY 1

daytime *n* the hours of light between one night and the next ⟨it's a lot easier to find your way through a strange neighborhood in the *daytime*⟩ — see DAY 1

day–to–day *adj* occurring, done, produced, or appearing every day ⟨the *day-to-day* routine of going to school⟩ — see DAILY

daze *n* a state of mental confusion ⟨she was in a *daze* for a minute after being hit on the head by a volleyball⟩ — see HAZE 2

daze *vb* **1** to make senseless or dizzy by a blow ⟨the fall *dazed* him for a moment, causing him to become disoriented⟩ — see STUN 1

2 to overpower with light ⟨a skier *dazed* by the glare from the snow⟩ — see DAZZLE

dazed *adj* suffering from mental confusion ⟨the *dazed* goalie could only watch as the winning point went flying past him⟩ — see DIZZY 2

dazzle *n* the quality or state of having or giving off light ⟨the *dazzle* of the stars on a cold but clear winter's night⟩ — see BRILLIANCE 1

dazzle *vb* to overpower with light ⟨skiers were *dazzled* by the glare off of the slopes of freshly packed snow⟩
synonyms bedazzle, blind, daze
related words confuse, overpower, overwhelm, stun

dazzling *adj* giving off or reflecting much light ⟨the attraction that the *dazzling* lights of Broadway have for many young performers⟩ — see BRIGHT 1

deacon *n* a person specially trained and authorized to conduct religious services in a Christian church ⟨my cousin was married by his uncle, who is also a *deacon* in his church⟩ — see CLERGYMAN

dead *adj* **1** no longer living ⟨I inherited this heirloom from my *dead* great-grandfather⟩
synonyms breathless, deceased, defunct, departed, fallen, gone, late, lifeless
related words extinct; dying, fading, moribund; stillborn; finished, lapsed, terminated; barren, desert; inanimate, insensate, nonliving, unanimated
phrases bitten the dust, passed away, passed on
near antonyms animate, animated; dynamic, lively, thriving, vibrant, vital, vivacious; active, functioning, operative, running
antonyms alive, breathing, going, living
2 depleted in strength, energy, or freshness ⟨a long day of traveling left them just *dead*⟩ — see WEARY 1
3 having no exceptions or restrictions ⟨there was a *dead* silence following that incredibly moving performance⟩ — see ABSOLUTE 2
4 lacking in sensation or feeling ⟨my foot was *dead* after I absentmindedly sat on it for an hour⟩ — see NUMB
5 no longer existing ⟨the *dead* Babylonian culture⟩ — see EXTINCT
6 not being in a state of use, activity, or employment ⟨local coal mines that have been *dead* for years⟩ — see INACTIVE 2
7 of, relating to, or suggestive of death ⟨fell into a *dead* faint upon hearing the news⟩ — see DEATHLY 1

dead *adv* **1** in a direct line or course ⟨the finish line is *dead* ahead⟩ — see DIRECTLY 1
2 to a full extent or degree ⟨I'm *dead* certain that's the one I want⟩ — see FULLY 1

deaden *vb* to reduce or weaken in strength or feeling ⟨a couple of aspirins *deadened* the headache⟩ — see DULL 1

dead heat *n* a situation in which neither participant in a contest, competition, or struggle comes out ahead of the other ⟨the horses crossed the finish line in a *dead heat*⟩ — see TIE 1

deadlock *n* a point in a struggle where neither side is capable of winning or willing to give in ⟨the jury sent a note to the judge that it was hopelessly stuck in a *deadlock*⟩ — see IMPASSE

deadly *adj* likely to cause or capable of causing death ⟨the doctors were alarmed about the outbreak of the *deadly* new virus⟩
synonyms baleful, deathly, fatal, fell, killer, lethal, mortal, murderous, pestilent, vital
related words baneful, destructive, harmful, noxious, pernicious; poisonous, toxic, virulent; dangerous, grave, grievous, hazardous, jeopardizing, menacing, parlous, perilous, risky, serious, threatening, ugly, un-

healthy, unsound; capital; bloody, internecine, sanguinary, sanguine
near antonyms beneficial, restorative; nonpoisonous, nontoxic, safe
antonyms healthful, healthy, nonfatal, nonlethal, wholesome

deadly *adv* to a great degree ⟨I'm *deadly* serious about passing this test⟩ — see VERY 1

deadness *n* the state of being dead ⟨the sheer *deadness* of the corpse was the creepiest thing about it⟩ — see DEATH 2

deadpan *adj* not expressing any emotion ⟨he delivered the joke in such a *deadpan* voice that we thought at first that he was serious⟩ — see BLANK 1

deadwood *n* discarded or useless material ⟨much of the material in the file cabinets is just *deadwood*⟩ — see GARBAGE

deafening *adj* marked by a high volume of sound ⟨a boom box blasting *deafening* music⟩ — see LOUD 1

¹deal *n* a considerable amount ⟨there is a great *deal* of waste in government⟩ — see LOT 2

²deal *n* **1** an arrangement about action to be taken ⟨we made a *deal* to cooperate on the next assignment⟩ — see AGREEMENT 2
2 the transfer of ownership of something from one person to another for a price ⟨we closed the *deal* for the house last week⟩ — see SALE

deal *vb* **1** to carry on the business of buying and selling goods or other property ⟨that store *deals* in used furniture⟩ — see TRADE 1
2 to talk over or dispute the terms of a purchase ⟨you're going to have to learn how to *deal* if you want to buy a car at a fair price⟩ — see BARGAIN

deal (in) *vb* to offer for sale to the public ⟨the company *deals in* virtually all types of insurance⟩ — see MARKET

deal (out) *vb* to give out (something) in appropriate amounts or to appropriate individuals ⟨he *dealt out* a packet of emergency supplies to each earthquake victim⟩ — see ADMINISTER 1

deal (with) *vb* **1** to behave toward in a stated way ⟨it's important to *deal with* others fairly⟩ — see TREAT 1
2 to have (something) as a subject matter ⟨this textbook *deals with* the history of France⟩ — see CONCERN 1

dealer *n* **1** a buyer and seller of goods for profit ⟨a *dealer* in fine fabrics⟩ — see MERCHANT
2 the person in a business deal who hands over an item in exchange for money ⟨if both the *dealer* and the buyer are happy, then the item sold at a fair price⟩ — see VENDOR

dealings *n pl* doings between individuals or groups ⟨I've had *dealings* with those guys before⟩ — see RELATION 1

dean *n* the senior member of a group ⟨the *dean* of the Aspen ski instructors oversaw the training of the rescue team⟩
synonyms elder, elder statesman, senior
related words better, superior
near antonyms inferior, subordinate, underling; beginner, freshman, newcomer, rookie
antonyms baby

dear *adj* **1** commanding a large price ⟨caviar has always been among the *dearest* of foods⟩ — see COSTLY
2 granted special treatment or attention ⟨spared no expense when caring for and feeding her *dear* little dog⟩ — see DARLING 1
3 having qualities that tend to make one loved ⟨a *dear* friend that I would do anything for⟩ — see LOVABLE

dear *n* a person with whom one is in love ⟨I love you, *dear*⟩ — see SWEETHEART

dearth *n* **1** a falling short of an essential or desirable amount or number ⟨there was a *dearth* of usable firewood at the campsite⟩ — see DEFICIENCY

2 the fact or state of being absent ⟨the *dearth* of salesclerks at the store annoyed us⟩ — see LACK 1

death *n* **1** the permanent stopping of all the vital bodily activities ⟨we were all saddened by the *death* of our teacher⟩

synonyms decease, demise, doom, end, passing, quietus

related words casualty, fatality; martyrdom, self-destruction, suicide; annihilation, destruction, ending, expiration, extermination, ruin

near antonyms existence, life; creation

antonyms birth

2 the state of being dead ⟨*death* is one of the few constants in the universe⟩

synonyms deadness, lifelessness, sleep

antonyms existence, life

3 the act of ceasing to exist ⟨the *death* of the Soviet economic system in the wake of the breakup of the USSR⟩

synonyms demise, expiration, termination

related words dispersion, dissolution; shutdown; decease, doom, end, ending, passing, quietus; suicide; annihilation, destruction, ruin

near antonyms existence

antonyms beginning, creation, start

deathless *adj* lasting forever ⟨an author who craved *deathless* fame⟩ — see EVERLASTING

deathlike *adj* of, relating to, or suggestive of death ⟨special makeup that gave his face a *deathlike* appearance on Halloween⟩ — see DEATHLY 1

deathly *adj* **1** of, relating to, or suggestive of death ⟨his *deathly* pallor suggested that any attempt to find a pulse would be futile⟩

synonyms dead, deathlike, mortal

related words ghostly, phantom, spectral; inactive, inert, inoperative, lifeless, quiescent, still; macabre; baleful, fatal, fateful, fell, killer, lethal, murderous, pestilent

near antonyms active, alive, living; animated, energetic, lively, vigorous, vivacious; hale, healthy, hearty, robust, sound

2 likely to cause or capable of causing death ⟨smallpox is one *deathly* disease that medical science has been able to conquer⟩ — see DEADLY

debacle *also* **débâcle** *n* **1** a sudden violent event that brings about great loss or destruction ⟨the financial *debacle* that was the stock market crash of 1929⟩ — see DISASTER

2 something that has failed ⟨the movie, which some had predicted would be a blockbuster, turned out to be the summer's biggest *debacle* at the multiplexes⟩ — see FAILURE 3

debar *vb* to prevent the participation or inclusion of ⟨the judge *debarred* all of the reporters from the courtroom⟩ — see EXCLUDE

debark *vb* to go ashore from a ship ⟨the passengers *debarked* as soon as the ship dropped anchor⟩ — see DISEMBARK

debase *vb* **1** to lower in character or dignity ⟨we *debased* ourselves when we cheated on the test⟩

synonyms abase, corrupt, debauch, degrade, demean, deprave, pervert, poison, profane, prostitute, subvert, warp

related words contaminate, pollute, taint; descend; disgrace, humble, humiliate; blemish, damage, deface, destroy, flaw, harm, hurt, impair, mar, ruin, spoil, stain, tarnish, vitiate, wreck; depreciate, downgrade

near antonyms dignify, exalt, honor; amend, improve; cleanse, purify, restore; respect

antonyms elevate, ennoble, uplift

2 to reduce to a lower standing in one's own eyes or in others' eyes ⟨our failure to win a single game completely *debased* us⟩ — see HUMBLE

debased *adj* having or showing lowered moral character or standards ⟨a book that examines the *debased* character of the criminal mind⟩ — see CORRUPT

debasement *n* a sinking to a state of low moral standards and behavior ⟨the *debasement* of professional sports to a shamelessly commercial enterprise⟩ — see CORRUPTION 2

debatable *adj* **1** open to question or dispute ⟨it's always *debatable* which college football team is really number one, since there's more than one ranking system⟩

synonyms disputable, doubtable, doubtful, moot, questionable

related words refutable; controversial, debated, disputed; dubious, inconclusive, indecisive, problematic (*also* problematical), uncertain; academic, hypothetical, speculative, theoretical (*also* theoretic); ambiguous, equivocal

near antonyms irrefutable; certain, definite, positive, sure; unambiguous, unequivocal; absolute, clear, conclusive, decisive; uncontested, undisputed

antonyms incontestable, incontrovertible, indisputable, indubitable, undeniable, unquestionable

2 giving good reason for being doubted, questioned, or challenged ⟨the *debatable* wisdom of going back for another helping from the buffet⟩ — see DOUBTFUL 2

debate *n* **1** a careful weighing of the reasons for or against something ⟨after much *debate*, I decided to get the chocolate ice cream⟩ — see CONSIDERATION 1

2 variance of opinion on a matter ⟨there was a great deal of *debate* over the need for cutting the school's music program⟩ — see DISAGREEMENT 1

debate *vb* **1** to give serious and careful thought to ⟨still *debating* what to do⟩ — see PONDER

2 to talk about (an issue) usually from various points of view and for the purpose of arriving at a decision or opinion ⟨we *debated* the advantages versus the disadvantages of the new school policy⟩ — see DISCUSS

debater *n* a person who takes part in a dispute ⟨the *debater* was unable to come up with a convincing rebuttal for his opponent's argument⟩ — see DISPUTANT

debauch *vb* to lower in character or dignity ⟨the long stay on a tropical isle had *debauched* the ship's crew to the point where they no longer acted liked naval professionals⟩ — see DEBASE 1

debauched *adj* having or showing lowered moral character or standards ⟨the *debauched* philanderer was the talk of the town⟩ — see CORRUPT

debaucher *n* a person who has sunk below the normal moral standard ⟨in his youth the man had been a *debaucher* of the worst sort⟩ — see DEGENERATE

debauchery *n* **1** immoral conduct or practices harmful or offensive to society ⟨the fraternity brothers indulged in shameless *debauchery* all weekend⟩ — see VICE 1

2 a sinking to a state of low moral standards and behavior ⟨the minister decried what he called the *debauchery* of today's society⟩ — see CORRUPTION 2

debilitate *vb* to diminish the physical strength of ⟨the heart surgery *debilitated* the athlete beyond his worst fears⟩ — see WEAKEN 1

debilitated *adj* lacking bodily strength ⟨the *debilitated* prisoners could barely stand⟩ — see WEAK 1

debilitation *n* **1** a gradual sinking and wasting away of mind or body ⟨the *debilitation* that all the prisoners of war had experienced⟩ — see DECLINE 1
2 the quality or state of lacking physical strength or vigor ⟨attributed the patient's general *debilitation* to an iron deficiency⟩ — see WEAKNESS 1

debility *n* the quality or state of lacking physical strength or vigor ⟨our grandmother's *debility* is due in large part to her advanced age⟩ — see WEAKNESS 1

debonair *adj* having or showing very polished and worldly manners ⟨the *debonair* gentleman charmed all of the ladies in the room⟩ — see SUAVE

debris *n* the portion or bits of something left over or behind after it has been destroyed ⟨the demolition workers cleared away all of the *debris* from the demolished building⟩ — see REMAINS 1

debt *n* a breaking of a moral or legal code ⟨forgive us our *debts*⟩ — see OFFENSE 1

debug *vb* to remove errors, defects, deficiencies, or deviations from ⟨the computer program ran much faster after it was *debugged*⟩ — see CORRECT 1

debunk *vb* to reveal the true nature of ⟨the investigative reporter easily *debunked* the charlatan's claims of clairvoyance⟩ — see EXPOSE 1

decadence *n* **1** a change to a lower state or level ⟨a symbol of the *decadence* of their once-mighty civilization⟩ — see DECLINE 2
2 a sinking to a state of low moral standards and behavior ⟨clergymen striving to combat *decadence* and sin in their communities⟩ — see CORRUPTION 2

decadent *adj* **1** having lost forcefulness, courage, or spirit ⟨he claimed that their culture had become *decadent* and weak⟩ — see EFFETE 1
2 having or showing lowered moral character or standards ⟨opponents of gambling casinos claim that gambling is a *decadent* form of entertainment⟩ — see CORRUPT

decadent *n* a person who has sunk below the normal moral standard ⟨a *decadent* who was trying to reform himself⟩ — see DEGENERATE

decalogue *n* a collection or system of rules of conduct ⟨the *decalogue* for scouting known as the Scout Oath⟩ — see CODE

decamping *n* the act of leaving a place ⟨the mass *decamping* for the mountains or the shore by city dwellers that occurs every summer weekend⟩ — see DEPARTURE

decampment *n* the act of leaving a place ⟨the simultaneous *decampment* of tens of thousands of sports fans from the stadium created the inevitable traffic jam⟩ — see DEPARTURE

decapitate *vb* to cut off the head of ⟨he started *decapitating* wildflowers with his walking stick as they strolled through the park⟩
synonyms behead, guillotine
related words prune, shorten, trim; scalp

decay *n* **1** a gradual sinking and wasting away of mind or body ⟨middle-aged people who fervently hope that daily exercise will arrest the physical *decay* that usually accompanies advancing age⟩ — see DECLINE 1
2 the process by which dead organic matter separates into simpler substances ⟨the cycle by which the *decay* of dead plants on the forest floor provides soil and nu-

trients for the next generation of plants⟩ — see CORRUPTION 1

decay *vb* **1** to go through decomposition ⟨the logs *decayed* on the rain forest floor⟩ ⟨the atom of plutonium *decayed* in the test chamber⟩
synonyms break down, corrupt, decompose, disintegrate, molder, putrefy, rot, spoil
related words sour, turn; contaminate, defile, pollute, taint; curdle, ferment; crumble, degenerate, deteriorate
phrases go to seed, run to seed
near antonyms develop, grow, mature, ripen; refresh, renew, restore; cleanse, purify; assemble, compose, integrate
2 to become worse or of less value ⟨the restaurant's standards for food and service had *decayed* over the years⟩ — see DETERIORATE
3 to lose bodily strength or vigor ⟨since reaching her 80s, the woman could sense that her body was *decaying*⟩ — see WEAKEN 2

decayed *adj* **1** having lost forcefulness, courage, or spirit ⟨a candidate who vehemently rejects the idea that liberalism is a *decayed* political philosophy⟩ — see EFFETE 1
2 having undergone organic breakdown ⟨we routinely throw all *decayed* or unwanted organic matter into our compost heap⟩ — see ROTTEN 1

decaying *n* a gradual sinking and wasting away of mind or body ⟨the *decaying* of the bone mass that is so regrettably common in elderly women⟩ — see DECLINE 1

decease *n* the permanent stopping of all the vital bodily activities ⟨in the event of the *decease* of the president, the vice president will immediately assume his duties⟩ — see DEATH 1

decease *vb* to stop living ⟨no one knows what happened to the family fortune after the spinster *deceased*⟩ — see DIE 1

deceased *adj* no longer living ⟨the recently *deceased* tenant was found by a neighbor⟩ — see DEAD 1

deceit *n* the inclination or practice of misleading others through lies or trickery ⟨the evil queen in the story was full of *deceit*⟩
synonyms artifice, craft, craftiness, crookedness, cunning, deceitfulness, dishonesty, dissembling, dissimulation, double-dealing, duplicity, fakery, foxiness, guile, wiliness
related words equivocation, prevarication; chicanery, skulduggery (*or* skullduggery), subterfuge, trickery; hypocrisy, insincerity; deviousness, shrewdness; treacherousness, underhandedness, unscrupulousness; covertness, furtiveness, secrecy, shadiness, sneakiness, stealthiness; oiliness, shiftiness, slickness, slipperiness, slyness, smoothness
near antonyms candidness, candor, directness, frankness, ingenuousness, openness, plainness; honesty, probity; reliability, trustworthiness
antonyms artlessness, forthrightness, good faith, guilelessness, sincerity

deceitful *adj* **1** marked by, based on, or done by the use of dishonest methods to acquire something of value ⟨charged the store owner with such *deceitful* practices as inflating the list prices for items only so he could put them on sale at drastically reduced prices⟩ — see FRAUDULENT 1
2 tending or having power to deceive ⟨the *deceitful* salesman neglected to mention some important information about the used car⟩ — see DECEPTIVE 1

deceitfulness *n* **1** the inclination or practice of misleading others through lies or trickery ⟨her *deceitfulness* about the long-term effects of her weight-loss program was finally exposed⟩ — see DECEIT

2 the tendency to tell lies ⟨his lifelong *deceitfulness* began when he was just a toddler⟩ — see DISHONESTY 1

deceive *vb* to cause to believe what is untrue ⟨he went to great lengths to *deceive* his younger brother about the nature of his new job at the mall⟩

synonyms beguile, bluff, cozen, delude, dupe, fool, gull, have, hoax, hoodwink, humbug, misguide, misinform, mislead, snow, string along, take in, trick

related words cheat, chisel, defraud, fleece, gyp, hustle, rook, swindle

near antonyms debunk, expose, reveal, show up, uncloak, uncover, unmask; disclose, divulge, tell, unveil; disabuse, disenchant, disillusion; edify, enlighten

antonyms undeceive

deceiving *adj* tending or having power to deceive ⟨the *deceiving* nature of most flat maps of the globe causes some people to believe erroneously that Greenland is actually bigger than South America⟩ — see DECEPTIVE 1

decelerate *vb* to cause to move or proceed at a less rapid pace ⟨Mom *decelerated* the car as we entered the school zone⟩ — see SLOW 1

deceleration *n* a usually gradual decrease in the pace or level of activity of something ⟨demand for our product is dropping, so I have ordered a *deceleration* of production⟩ — see SLOWDOWN

decency *n* **1** socially acceptable behavior ⟨the standards of basic *decency* demanded that they help the old lady with her groceries⟩

synonyms decorum, form, propriety

related words civility, courtesy, politeness; dignity, grace, refinement; discretion, prudence; correctness, decorousness, fitness, rightness, seemliness; attention, attentiveness, care, carefulness; goodness, high-mindedness, honesty, morality, probity, rectitude, righteousness, straightness, uprightness, virtue, virtuousness

near antonyms coarseness, crudeness, gracelessness; discourtesy, impoliteness, incivility; imprudence, indiscretion; badness, evil, immorality, wickedness

antonyms impropriety, indecency, indecorum

2 conduct that conforms to an accepted standard of right and wrong ⟨expected all of the scouts in his troop to be models of *decency*⟩ — see MORALITY 1

decent *adj* **1** conforming to a high standard of morality or virtue ⟨as *decent* and kind a couple as you could ever hope to meet⟩ — see GOOD 2

2 following the accepted rules of moral conduct ⟨demanded nothing less than *decent* behavior by the troops serving overseas⟩ — see HONORABLE 1

3 following the established traditions of refined society and good taste ⟨*decent* clothing for someone attending a funeral, if only as a friend of a friend⟩ — see PROPER 1

4 free from any trace of the coarse or indecent ⟨students were warned that their skits could be funny but still had to remain *decent*⟩ — see CHASTE

5 of a level of quality that meets one's needs or standards ⟨he did a *decent* job on his homework, but there's still room for improvement⟩ — see ADEQUATE

deceptive *adj* **1** tending or having power to deceive ⟨in his *deceptive* answer about the vehicle's history, the salesman said that the used car had never been hit by another car⟩

synonyms beguiling, deceitful, deceiving, deluding, delusive, delusory, fallacious, false, misleading, specious

related words devious, guileful, shady, shifty, sly, sneaking, sneaky, trick, tricky, underhand, underhanded; inaccurate, incorrect, wrong; bewildering, confounding, distracting, perplexing, puzzling; crooked, dishonest, double-dealing, faithless, fast, fraudulent, knavish, lying, mendacious, untrustworthy, untruthful; insidious, perfidious, treacherous; artificial, backhanded, feigned, hypocritical, insincere, left-handed, two-faced

near antonyms candid, frank, open, plain; clarifying, elucidative, explanatory, illuminating; revealing, revelatory; honest, trustworthy, truthful

antonyms aboveboard, forthright, straightforward

2 given to or marked by cheating and deception ⟨a mail-order firm indicted for *deceptive* business practices⟩ — see DISHONEST 2

decide *vb* **1** to come to a judgment after discussion or consideration ⟨they *decided* to go out for pizza after the movie was over⟩

synonyms choose, conclude, determine, figure, opt, resolve

related words decree, rule; cull, elect, handpick, pick, prefer, select, single (out), take

phrases make up one's mind

near antonyms abstain, decline, refuse, reject, turn down; delay, hesitate, stall, temporize; shilly-shally, vacillate, waver

2 to give an opinion about (something at issue or in dispute) ⟨the judge *decided* that the defendant was not liable for damages⟩ — see JUDGE 1

3 to come to an agreement or decision concerning the details of ⟨we waited for our parents to *decide* our fate⟩ — see ARRANGE 1

4 to make final, definite, or beyond dispute ⟨the huge sum that they were offering *decided* the matter: we would sell the house⟩ — see CLINCH

decided *adj* not subject to misinterpretation or more than one interpretation ⟨a *decided* hint of perfume on her skin⟩ — see CLEAR 2

decidedness *n* firm or unwavering adherence to one's purpose ⟨for two years he pursued the presidential nomination with an undeviating *decidedness*⟩ — see DETERMINATION 1

decimate *vb* to bring to a complete end the physical soundness, existence, or usefulness of ⟨the army's attack *decimated* the enemy's defenses beyond repair⟩ — see DESTROY 1

decimation *n* the state or fact of being rendered nonexistent, physically unsound, or useless ⟨the virtual *decimation* of the coastal town by the hurricane⟩ — see DESTRUCTION

decipher *vb* to change (as a secret message) from code into ordinary language ⟨we *deciphered* the hidden message to find out when we were supposed to meet⟩ — see DECODE

decision *n* **1** a position arrived at after consideration ⟨after much deliberation, we made a *decision* about what to have on our pizza⟩

synonyms conclusion, deliverance, determination, diagnosis, judgment (*or* judgement), opinion, resolution, verdict

related words decree, mandate, order; say-so; doom, finding, ruling, sentence; choice, option, selection

near antonyms deadlock, draw, stalemate, standoff, tie

2 firm or unwavering adherence to one's purpose ⟨acted with swift *decision*⟩ — see DETERMINATION 1

decisive *adj* **1** fully committed to achieving a goal ⟨only a team with a *decisive* attitude is going to win a state championship⟩ — see DETERMINED 1

2 having the power to persuade ⟨a lawyer who knows how to construct the kind of *decisive* argument that sways a jury⟩ — see COGENT

3 serving to put an end to all debate or questioning ⟨the *decisive* finding of the coroner regarding the cause of death⟩ — see CONCLUSIVE 1

decisiveness *n* firm or unwavering adherence to one's purpose ⟨moved with speed and *decisiveness* in investigating the charges of the use of excessive force by the police⟩ — see DETERMINATION 1

deck *vb* **1** to make more attractive by adding something that is beautiful or becoming ⟨*deck* the halls with boughs of holly⟩ — see DECORATE

2 to outfit with clothes and especially fine or special clothes ⟨all *decked* out in our finest outfits for the wedding⟩ — see CLOTHE 1

declaim *vb* **1** to give a formal often extended talk on a subject ⟨over the last two centuries some of the most illustrious personages of their times have *declaimed* in the town's historic lyceum⟩ — see TALK 1

2 to talk as if giving an important and formal speech ⟨he *declaimed* at some length about the nation's obligation to spread democratic values around the world⟩ — see ORATE 1

declamation *n* a usually formal discourse delivered to an audience ⟨inspired *declamations* about the global triumph of democracy within our lifetimes⟩ — see SPEECH 1

declaration *n* a solemn and often public declaring of the truth or existence of something ⟨once the delegates had made the *declaration* that the colonies were henceforth independent of Great Britain, their fate was sealed⟩ — see PROTESTATION

declare *vb* **1** to make known openly or publicly ⟨they chose to *declare* war⟩ — see ANNOUNCE

2 to state as a fact usually forcefully ⟨she *declared* her innocence to the whole world⟩ — see CLAIM 1

3 to state clearly and strongly ⟨our guest *declared* that the pie was the best he had ever eaten⟩ — see ASSERT 1

declension *n* **1** a gradual sinking and wasting away of mind or body ⟨a noticeable *declension* of the fitness of the baseball players over the winter⟩ — see DECLINE 1

2 a change to a lower state or level ⟨a *declension* in her acting career from leading roles to cameos eventually⟩ — see DECLINE 2

decline *n* **1** a gradual sinking and wasting away of mind or body ⟨her sad *decline* from a robust athlete to an old woman with arthritis⟩

synonyms debilitation, decay, decaying, declension, degeneration, descent, deterioration, ebbing, enfeeblement, weakening

related words atrophy; exhaustion; drooping, flagging; limping; relapse, setback

near antonyms invigoration, strengthening; progress

antonyms improvement, recovery, revitalization

2 a change to a lower state or level ⟨the *decline* of the Roman Empire⟩

synonyms decadence, declension, degeneracy, degeneration, degradation, descent, deterioration, downfall, downgrade, fall

related words decay, rotting, spoiling; breakup, crumbling, decomposition, disintegration, dissolution; abasement, debasement; depreciation, lessening; decimation, demolishment, demolition, desolation, destruction, havoc, ruin, ruination; abatement, decrease, decrement, de-escalation, deflation, diminishment, diminution, dip, drop, fall, loss, lowering, reduction, sag, shrinkage

near antonyms advancement, development, evolution, growth; blossoming, flourishing, flowering; renewal, restoration, revitalization; heightening; accretion, accrual, addendum, addition, augmentation, boost, enhancement, gain, increase, increment, raise, supplement

antonyms ascent, rise, upswing

3 a loss of status ⟨the engagement at the small club was an unmistakable sign of the rock band's *decline*⟩ — see COMEDOWN

4 the amount by which something is lessened ⟨a huge *decline* in the value of the artwork after its authenticity was questioned⟩ — see DECREASE

decline *vb* **1** to show unwillingness to accept, do, engage in, or agree to ⟨he *declined* the invitation to the party⟩ ⟨she *declined* to participate in the soccer game⟩

synonyms disapprove, negative, refuse, reject, repudiate, spurn, turn down

related words overrule, veto; forbid, prohibit, proscribe; dismiss; abstain, forbear, refrain; deny, dispute, gainsay; balk, stick; abjure, renounce; avoid, bypass, detour

near antonyms condone, countenance, swallow, tolerate; adopt, embrace, receive, take; accede, acquiesce, agree, assent, consent; choose, select; espouse, support

antonyms accept, agree (to), approve

2 to be unwilling to grant ⟨*declined* our request to hold a party in the school gym⟩ — see DENY 2

3 to go to a lower level ⟨new-car sales *declined* to their lowest level in years⟩ — see DROP 2

4 to become worse or of less value ⟨his reputation as a writer began to *decline* not long after his death⟩ — see DETERIORATE

5 to grow less in scope or intensity especially gradually ⟨the winds should *decline* as soon as the cold front passes⟩ — see DECREASE 2

6 to lead or extend downward ⟨the bike path *declines* toward the riverbank and then follows the river for several miles⟩ — see DESCEND 1

declined *adj* bending downward or forward ⟨we awaited our punishment with *declined* heads⟩ — see NODDING

declining *adj* bending downward or forward ⟨the *declining* flowers perked up with the gentle rainfall⟩ — see NODDING

decode *vb* to change (as a secret message) from code into ordinary language ⟨the agents worked into the night to *decode* the transmission from the enemy spy⟩

synonyms break, crack, decipher

related words render, translate; dope (out), figure out, puzzle (out), solve, unravel, work, work out

antonyms cipher, code, encode

decolorize *vb* to make white or whiter by removing color ⟨the sample was *decolorized* before being examined under a microscope⟩ — see WHITEN

decompose *vb* to go through decomposition ⟨detectives needed to know how long it would take a corpse to *decompose* to that condition⟩ — see DECAY 1

decomposed *adj* having undergone organic breakdown ⟨the *decomposed* remains of an old tree trunk⟩ — see ROTTEN 1

decomposition *n* the process by which dead organic matter separates into simpler substances ⟨the unmistakable smell of *decomposition* led us to some fruit that

had fallen behind the refrigerator⟩ — see CORRUP-
TION 1

decorate *vb* to make more attractive by adding something that is beautiful or becoming ⟨they *decorated* the
hallway with paintings and tapestries⟩
synonyms adorn, array, beautify, bedeck, bedizen,
deck, do, dress, embellish, enrich, garnish, grace, ornament, trim
related words doll up, dress up, trick (out); brighten,
freshen, smarten, spruce (up); boss, chase, emboss; embroider, figure, flounce, fringe, garland, hang, lace,
wreathe; gild, paint; redecorate, redo
near antonyms simplify, streamline; bare, denude, dismantle, display, divest, expose, reveal, strip, uncover
antonyms blemish, deface, disfigure, mar, scar, spoil

decoration *n* **1** something that decorates or beautifies
⟨they put lots of *decorations* on and around the Christmas tree⟩
synonyms adornment, caparison, embellishment, frill,
garnish, ornament, trim
related words finery, frippery; flounce, flourish, furbelow, ruffle; enhancement, enrichment, improvement;
embossment, embroidery, fancywork; gilt, glitter; design, figure, pattern; furnishings, regalia, trappings
near antonyms blemish, defacement, disfigurement,
scar; blot, spot, stain
2 something given in recognition of achievement ⟨an
army veteran proudly wearing his old military *decorations*⟩ — see AWARD

decorative *adj* serving to add beauty ⟨they planted *decorative* flowers all along the path to the cottage⟩
synonyms adorning, beautifying, embellishing, ornamental
related words alluring, appealing, attractive, charming,
delightful, glamorous (*also* glamourous), pleasing, prepossessing; beauteous, beautiful, bonny, comely, fair,
gorgeous, handsome, lovely, pretty, stunning; detailed,
elaborate, fancy, ornate
antonyms functional, utilitarian

decorous *adj* **1** following the established traditions of refined society and good taste ⟨we were asked to be on
our most *decorous* behavior at the formal event⟩ — see
PROPER 1
2 marked by or showing careful attention to set forms
and details ⟨the *decorous* standards of a royal court⟩ —
see CEREMONIOUS 1

decorum *n* socially acceptable behavior ⟨high standards
of *decorum* are usually required when attending the
opera⟩ — see DECENCY 1

decoy *n* something used to attract animals to a hook or
into a trap ⟨we floated the *decoy* in the water and from
the blind waited for the ducks to arrive⟩ — see BAIT 1

decoy *vb* to lead away from a usual or proper course by
offering some pleasure or advantage ⟨tacky souvenir
shops to which first-time tourists had been *decoyed*
into spending their hard-earned money⟩ — see LURE

decrease *n* the amount by which something is lessened
⟨the average *decrease* in the price of milk was five
cents per gallon⟩
synonyms abatement, decline, decrement, diminishment, diminution, drop, fall, loss, reduction, shrinkage
related words deduction, dent, depression; slip, slump;
curtailment, cut, cutback
near antonyms accretion, accrual, accumulation, addition, supplement; continuation, extension; upswing,
uptrend, upturn
antonyms boost, enlargement, gain, increase, increment, raise, rise

decrease *vb* **1** to make smaller in amount, volume, or extent ⟨they *decreased* the amount of water flowing
through the pipes in order to prevent an overflow⟩
synonyms abate, de-escalate, diminish, downsize,
dwindle, lessen, lower, reduce
related words compress, condense, constrict, contract;
abbreviate, abridge, clip, crop, curtail, cut, cut back,
cut down, dock, pare, prune, retrench, shorten, slash,
trim, truncate, whittle; deflate, shrink; moderate, modify, modulate, qualify
near antonyms blow up, dilate, distend, inflate, swell;
elongate, extend, lengthen, prolong, protract; add (to),
complement, supplement; enhance, heighten, intensify
antonyms aggrandize, amplify, augment, boost, enlarge, escalate, expand, increase, raise
2 to grow less in scope or intensity especially gradually
⟨the force of the wind slowly *decreased* until the flowers were standing upright again⟩
synonyms abate, decline, de-escalate, die (down), diminish, dwindle, ebb, fall, lessen, let up, lower, moderate, recede, relent, remit, shrink, subside, taper, taper
off, wane
related words compress, condense, constrict, contract;
evaporate, fade (away), give out, melt (away), peter
(out), vanish; slacken, slow (down); alleviate, ease, relax; flag, sink, weaken; cave (in), collapse, deflate, give
out
near antonyms appear, emerge, show up; blow up, distend, elongate, lengthen
antonyms accumulate, balloon, build, burgeon, enlarge, escalate, expand, grow, increase, intensify,
mount, mushroom, pick up, rise, snowball, soar, swell,
wax

decree *n* **1** a statement of what to do that must be
obeyed by those concerned ⟨the boss doesn't give out
many *decrees*, but he does expect those that are issued
to be fully obeyed⟩ — see COMMAND 1
2 an order publicly issued by an authority ⟨a *decree* issued by the court to the state legislature⟩ — see
EDICT 1

decree *vb* to give an order ⟨he *decreed* that thenceforth
coffee breaks would have a 15-minute limit⟩ — see
COMMAND 2

decrement *n* the amount by which something is lessened
⟨each *decrement* in amount is limited to one third of
the previous total⟩ — see DECREASE

decry *vb* **1** to express scornfully one's low opinion of
⟨scientists were quick to *decry* the claims of the psy-
chic⟩
synonyms bad-mouth, belittle, cry down, deprecate,
depreciate, diminish, discount, disparage, minimize,
put down, write off
related words abuse, scold; disapprove (of), dislike;
censure, condemn, criticize, denounce, reprehend,
reprobate; asperse, defame, malign, slander, traduce,
vilify; discredit, disgrace
near antonyms approve, countenance, endorse (*also*
indorse), favor, recommend, sanction; commend, compliment, eulogize
antonyms acclaim, applaud, exalt, extol (*also* extoll),
glorify, laud, magnify, praise
2 to declare to be morally wrong or evil ⟨a statement
by the church *decrying* modern society's liberal attitude regarding marriage and divorce⟩ — see CON-
DEMN 1

decrying *adj* intended to make a person or thing seem of
little importance or value ⟨*decrying* remarks about the
farm boy's personal appearance⟩ — see DEROGATORY

dedicate *vb* to keep or intend for a special purpose ⟨a young attorney who has decided to *dedicate* her career to helping the poor receive justice⟩ — see DEVOTE 1

dedication *n* adherence to something to which one is bound by a pledge or duty ⟨her *dedication* to the ideals of the organization is admirable⟩ — see FIDELITY

deduce *vb* to form an opinion through reasoning and information ⟨I can *deduce* through an analysis of your behavior that you're trying to hide something from me⟩ — see INFER 1

deducible *adj* being or provable by reasoning in which the conclusion follows necessarily from given information ⟨the killer's identity is clearly *deducible* from the clues scattered throughout the novel⟩ — see DEDUCTIVE

deduct *vb* to take away (an amount or number) from a total ⟨after *deducting* taxes, what's left is your net pay for the week⟩ — see SUBTRACT

deduction *n* **1** something that is or may be subtracted ⟨contestants get a *deduction* from their scores for every incorrect guess⟩
synonyms abatement, discount, reduction
related words kickback, rebate; dent, depreciation; decline, decrement, diminishment, diminution, drop, fall, loss; forfeit, forfeiture, penalty
near antonyms accretion, accrual, augmentation, boost, gain, increase, increment, raise, rise; appreciation
antonyms accession, addition
2 the act or an instance of taking away from a total ⟨the *deduction* of the amount awarded to the plaintiff in order to pay the legal fees⟩ — see SUBTRACTION
3 an opinion arrived at through a process of reasoning ⟨his impressive *deduction* of the correct answer from only a few hints⟩ — see CONCLUSION 1

deductive *adj* being or provable by reasoning in which the conclusion follows necessarily from given information ⟨using *deductive* reasoning we must conclude that since everyone eventually dies, sooner or later it's going to be our turn⟩
synonyms deducible, derivable, inferable, reasoned
related words conjectural, hypothetical, purported, supposed, suppositional; academic, speculative, theoretical (*also* theoretic); logical, rational
near antonyms inducible, inductive; absolute, categorical (*also* categoric), definite, explicit, express; instinctive, intuitive; illogical, irrational

deed *n* **1** an act of notable skill, strength, or cleverness ⟨heroes are celebrated for their great *deeds*⟩ — see FEAT 1
2 something done by someone ⟨be virtuous not only in word but also in *deed*⟩ — see ACTION 1

deed *vb* to give over the legal possession or ownership of ⟨the philanthropist *deeded* his entire fortune to the animal shelter⟩ — see TRANSFER 1

deem *vb* to have as an opinion ⟨I *deem* it fitting that she be placed in charge of this project⟩ — see BELIEVE 2

deep *adj* **1** extending far downward or inward ⟨they dropped their bucket down a *deep* well⟩ ⟨the knife made a *deep* cut into the wood⟩
synonyms abysmal, bottomless
related words abyssal, unfathomable; boundless, endless, immeasurable, inestimable, infinite, limitless, measureless, unlimited, vast
near antonyms depthless, two-dimensional; even, flat, flush, horizontal, level, plane, smooth; confined, finite, limited, measured, restricted

antonyms shallow, shoal, skin-deep, superficial, surface
2 having a low musical pitch or range ⟨the tour guide had a very *deep* voice⟩
synonyms bass, low, throaty
related words gruff, hoarse, husky, rough
near antonyms squeaking, squeaky, squealing, thin; earsplitting, penetrating, piercing, strident; peeping, tinny
antonyms acute, high, high-pitched, piping, sharp, shrill, treble
3 being beyond one's powers to know, understand, or explain ⟨a *deep*, dark secret that he took to his grave⟩ — see MYSTERIOUS 1
4 difficult for one of ordinary knowledge or intelligence to understand ⟨her poetry is now regarded as sentimental and not very *deep*⟩ — see PROFOUND 1
5 having an often intentionally veiled or uncertain meaning ⟨one of those *deep* passages in the Bible that can be interpreted in any number of different ways⟩ — see OBSCURE 1
6 extreme in degree, power, or effect ⟨fell into a *deep* sleep after taking the potion⟩ — see INTENSE

deep *n* **1** the most intense or characteristic phase of something ⟨the kind of cold weather that we usually have only in the *deep* of winter⟩ — see THICK
2 the whole body of salt water that covers nearly three-fourths of the earth ⟨sailors exploring the farther reaches of the briny *deep*⟩ — see OCEAN

deepen *vb* to make markedly greater in measure or degree ⟨this book really *deepens* our knowledge of how the brain works⟩ — see INTENSIFY

deep–rooted *adj* firmly established over time ⟨he had a *deep-rooted* fear of the dark ever since he was a small child⟩ — see INVETERATE 1

deep–seated *adj* firmly established over time ⟨*deep-seated* convictions about religion that no one is ever going to change⟩ — see INVETERATE 1

de–escalate *vb* **1** to make smaller in amount, volume, or extent ⟨the mediator tried to *de-escalate* the tension in the room⟩ — see DECREASE 1
2 to grow less in scope or intensity especially gradually ⟨the fighting *de-escalated* as the peace talks progressed⟩ — see DECREASE 2

deface *vb* **1** to deliberately cause the damage or destruction of another's property ⟨the principal was eager for any information about the person who *defaced* the statue in front of the school⟩ — see VANDALIZE 1
2 to reduce the soundness, effectiveness, or perfection of ⟨years of wear had *defaced* the fine engraving on the coins⟩ — see DAMAGE 1

defacement *n* deliberate damaging or destroying of another's property ⟨the *defacement* of the school's property ended up costing hundreds of dollars⟩ — see VANDALISM

defacer *n* a person who damages or destroys property on purpose ⟨the police are eager to learn the identity of the *defacer* of the street signs⟩ — see VANDAL

defamation *n* the making of false statements that damage another's reputation ⟨accused him of *defamation* of character⟩ — see SLANDER

defamatory *adj* causing or intended to cause unjust injury to a person's good name ⟨*defamatory* remarks that were published in the newspaper⟩ — see LIBELOUS

defame *vb* to make untrue and harmful statements about ⟨of course I want to win the election, but I refuse to *defame* my opponent in order to do so⟩ — see SLANDER

defaming *n* the making of false statements that damage another's reputation ⟨the *defaming* of the popular actress by the unscrupulous tabloid reporter⟩ — see SLANDER

default *n* the nonperformance of an assigned or expected action ⟨a *default* on a bank loan⟩ — see FAILURE 1

defeat *n* **1** failure to win a contest ⟨sore losers griping about their *defeat* in the basketball game earlier that week⟩
synonyms beating, drubbing, licking, loss, overthrow, rout, shellacking, trimming, trouncing, whipping
related words collapse, debacle (*also* débâcle), failure, fizzle, flop, nonsuccess, setback, upset, washout; lurch, shutout
near antonyms accomplishment, achievement; landslide, sweep
antonyms success, triumph, victory, win
2 a falling short of one's goals ⟨truly disheartened by the *defeat* of his plans⟩ — see FAILURE 2

defeat *vb* to achieve a victory over ⟨they *defeated* their arch rivals easily and moved into the next round of the play-offs⟩ — see BEAT 2

defeatist *adj* emphasizing or expecting the worst ⟨your *defeatist* attitude is depressing everyone else on the team!⟩ — see PESSIMISTIC 1

defeatist *n* one who emphasizes bad aspects or conditions and expects the worst ⟨we told her that if she was going to be such a *defeatist*, she should keep her thoughts to herself⟩ — see PESSIMIST 1

defect *n* something that spoils the appearance or completeness of a thing ⟨the statue has a slight *defect* on the base, so it's being sold at a discount⟩ — see BLEMISH

defect (from) *vb* to leave (a cause or party) often in order to take up another ⟨many soldiers *defected from* the rebel army as soon as they realized the uprising was hopeless⟩
synonyms desert, rat (on)
related words abandon, abdicate, abjure, cut off, disown, forsake, quit, reject, renounce, repudiate, spurn; renege; depart, go, leave, withdraw
phrases go back on, walk out on
near antonyms adhere (to), cling (to), stick (to *or* with); cherish, cultivate, foster

defective *adj* having a fault ⟨we took the *defective* microwave oven back to the store for a replacement⟩ — see FAULTY

defector *n* a person who abandons a cause or organization usually without right ⟨the *defector* demanded political asylum in exchange for information about his former associates⟩ — see RENEGADE

defend *vb* **1** to drive danger or attack away from ⟨a solemn oath to *defend* the country at any cost⟩
synonyms cover, guard, protect, safeguard, screen, secure, shield, ward
related words avert, prevent; fend (off), oppose, resist, withstand; battle, contend, fight, war; conserve, keep, preserve, save; buffer, palisade, picket, wall
phrases look out for, stand up for
near antonyms bombard, storm; beset, besiege, overrun; capitulate, cave, submit, yield
antonyms assail, assault, attack
2 to continue to declare to be true or proper despite opposition or objections ⟨she will *defend* any claim regardless of all evidence to the contrary⟩ — see MAINTAIN 2

defendable *adj* capable of being defended with good reasoning against verbal attack ⟨that excuse is hardly *defendable* given your past record⟩ — see TENABLE 2

defender *n* someone that protects ⟨one of the traditional roles of an older brother is that of *defender*⟩ — see PROTECTOR

defense *n* **1** means or method of defending ⟨thorns are a rose's *defense* against grazing animals⟩
synonyms aegis, ammunition, armor, cover, guard, protection, safeguard, screen, security, shield, wall, ward
related words arm, armament, munitions, weapon, weaponry; fastness, fort, fortress, palisade, stronghold
near antonyms aggression, assault, attack, offense (*or* offence), offensive
2 an explanation that frees one from fault or blame ⟨there's absolutely no *defense* for your actions⟩ — see EXCUSE

defenseless *adj* lacking protection from danger or resistance against attack ⟨the lack of heat left them *defenseless* against the cold⟩ — see HELPLESS 1

defenselessness *n* the quality or state of having little resistance to some outside agent ⟨we worked to overcome our *defenselessness* against the rising floodwaters⟩ — see SUSCEPTIBILITY

defensible *adj* capable of being defended with good reasoning against verbal attack ⟨there's simply no *defensible* reason for dropping out of school⟩ — see TENABLE 1

defensive *adj* intended to resist or prevent attack or aggression ⟨a *defensive* alliance against the aggressors⟩
synonyms protective, self-protective
related words deterrent, preventive; safe, secure
near antonyms aggressive, bellicose, belligerent, combative, contentious, militant, pugnacious, quarrelsome, scrappy, truculent, warlike
antonyms offensive

defensive *n* a position or readiness to oppose actual or expected attack ⟨their harsh words put him on the *defensive*⟩
synonyms guard
related words alert, watch
antonyms offensive

defer *vb* to assign to a later time ⟨we agreed to *defer* the discussion of the issue until we had more information⟩ — see POSTPONE

deference *n* a readiness or willingness to yield to the wishes of others ⟨we always treat our grandparents with *deference* and courtesy⟩ — see COMPLIANCE 1

deferential *adj* marked by or showing proper regard for another's higher status ⟨the man had the *deferential* attitude of someone who had been a servant his entire life⟩ — see RESPECTFUL

deferentially *adv* in a manner showing no signs of pride or self-assertion ⟨behaved *deferentially* when approaching someone in authority⟩ — see LOWLY

defiance *n* **1** refusal to obey ⟨any *defiance* of our parents would have dire consequences⟩ — see DISOBEDIENCE
2 the inclination to resist ⟨the troubled youth seems to have had an ingrained *defiance* to authority of any sort⟩ — see RESISTANCE 1

defiant *adj* given to resisting authority or another's control ⟨the *defiant* puppy refused to let go of the football⟩ — see DISOBEDIENT

deficiency *n* a falling short of an essential or desirable amount or number ⟨there was a *deficiency* of fresh food in the house⟩
synonyms dearth, deficit, failure, famine, inadequacy, insufficiency, lack, paucity, poverty, scantiness, scarceness, scarcity, shortage, want

related words absence, omission; meagerness, poorness, skimpiness; necessity, need, privation
near antonyms bountifulness, copiousness; excess, overabundance, oversupply, surfeit, surplus
antonyms abundance, adequacy, amplitude, plenitude, plenty, sufficiency

deficient *adj* **1** lacking some necessary part ⟨a diet *deficient* in calcium can lead to weak bones⟩ — see INCOMPLETE
2 falling short of a standard ⟨*deficient* eyesight kept him out of military service⟩ — see BAD 1
3 not coming up to a usual standard or meeting a particular need ⟨*deficient* in morality⟩ — see SHORT 3

deficit *n* a falling short of an essential or desirable amount or number ⟨a budget *deficit* that will require either the cutting of programs or the raising of taxes⟩ — see DEFICIENCY

defile *n* a narrow opening between hillsides or mountains that can be used for passage ⟨the cattle, trapped in the *defile*, were quickly rounded up⟩ — see CANYON

defile *vb* **1** to make unfit for use by the addition of something harmful or undesirable ⟨the bucolic landscape was being *defiled* by ugly factories⟩ — see CONTAMINATE
2 to treat (a sacred place or object) shamefully or with great disrespect ⟨art experts were careful not to do anything that might *defile* the holy relic⟩ — see DESECRATE

defilement *n* **1** an act of great disrespect shown to God or to sacred ideas, people, or things ⟨for two centuries the Christian monasteries in England suffered *defilements* at the hands of Viking invaders⟩ — see BLASPHEMY
2 something that is or that makes impure ⟨souvenir shops, observation towers, and other tacky *defilements* on Civil War battlefields that should be considered hallowed ground⟩ — see IMPURITY

define *vb* **1** to draw or make apparent the outline of ⟨the glass skyscraper's sleek silhouette was strikingly *defined* by the setting sun to its west⟩ — see OUTLINE 1
2 to mark the limits of ⟨the river *defines* the town on the south⟩ — see LIMIT 2
3 to point out the chief quality or qualities of an individual or group ⟨a student who is *defined* by her unswerving loyalty to her friends⟩ — see CHARACTERIZE 1
4 to give the rules about (something) clearly and exactly ⟨let me *define* the task so that there is no doubt in your minds about what needs to be done⟩ — see PRESCRIBE

defined *adj* having distinct or certain limits ⟨well *defined* guidelines on the range of activities in which student organizations can engage⟩ — see LIMITED 1

definite *adj* **1** having distinct or certain limits ⟨there should be a *definite* scope to your paper on the campaign for women's rights because you obviously cannot cover the whole history in five pages⟩ — see LIMITED 1
2 so clearly expressed as to leave no doubt about the meaning ⟨a *definite* instruction not to let anyone in the house while our parents were out for the evening⟩ — see EXPLICIT

definitely *adv* without any question ⟨that is *definitely* the kind of dog we're looking to adopt⟩ — see INDEED 1

definitive *adj* **1** being the most accurate and apparently thorough ⟨the *definitive* work on the attack on Pearl Harbor⟩
synonyms authoritative
related words conclusive, decisive; official; accurate, correct; complete, thorough

2 serving to put an end to all debate or questioning ⟨a *definitive* answer that put an immediate end to the discussion⟩ — see CONCLUSIVE 1
3 so clearly expressed as to leave no doubt about the meaning ⟨the insurance company's *definitive* statement on the types of surgical operations that are covered⟩ — see EXPLICIT

deflect *vb* to change the course or direction of (something) ⟨the wind *deflected* the Frisbee just as I was about to lunge for it⟩ — see TURN 2

deform *vb* to twist (something) out of a natural or normal shape or condition ⟨a cynic whose face seems to be permanently *deformed* by a sneer⟩ — see CONTORT

deformation *n* the twisting of something out of its natural or normal shape or condition ⟨the *deformation* of the steel girders under the enormous weight of the bridge⟩ — see CONTORTION

deformed *adj* badly or imperfectly formed ⟨his first sculpture looked more like a *deformed* rabbit than a galloping horse⟩ — see MALFORMED

deformity *n* something that spoils the appearance or completeness of a thing ⟨a primitive culture that cast aside infants born with *deformities* and allowed them to die of exposure to the elements⟩ — see BLEMISH

defraud *vb* to rob by the use of trickery or threats ⟨we were too smart to fall for the fast-talking salesman's attempts to *defraud* us⟩ — see FLEECE

defrauder *n* a dishonest person who uses clever means to cheat others out of something of value ⟨the state's department of consumer protection has to contend with *defrauders* of every ilk⟩ — see TRICKSTER 1

defrauding *adj* marked by, based on, or done by the use of dishonest methods to acquire something of value ⟨every new technology has brought with it a raft of *defrauding* schemes that make full use of it⟩ — see FRAUDULENT 1

defrosted *adj* freed from a frozen state by exposure to warmth ⟨I tossed a *defrosted* steak under the broiler for dinner⟩ — see THAWED

deft *adj* skillful with the hands ⟨the *deft* jeweler quickly attached the diamond to its mount on the gold band⟩ — see DEXTEROUS 1

deftness *n* **1** ease and grace in physical activity ⟨the effortless *deftness* with which he plays the piano⟩ — see DEXTERITY 2
2 subtle or imaginative ability in inventing, devising, or executing something ⟨with *deftness* and aplomb she managed to keep the bickering relatives apart for the duration of the reception⟩ — see SKILL 1

defunct *adj* **1** no longer existing ⟨a stack of brochures and a few faded placards are all that remain of the *defunct* organization⟩ — see EXTINCT
2 no longer living ⟨a *defunct* species that we know only through fossil remains⟩ — see DEAD 1

defy *vb* **1** to go against the commands, prohibitions, or rules of ⟨we knew we'd get in trouble if we *defied* our parents' curfew⟩ — see DISOBEY
2 to invite (someone) to take part in a contest or to perform a feat ⟨after missing the target, she *defied* him to do better⟩ — see CHALLENGE 1
3 to oppose (something hostile or dangerous) with firmness or courage ⟨a rescue team willing to *defy* the oncoming storm⟩ — see FACE 2
4 to refuse to give in to ⟨a bicyclist who regularly *defies* illness and infirmity in order to compete in races⟩ — see RESIST

degeneracy *n* **1** a change to a lower state or level ⟨the *degeneracy* of the old neighborhood into a slum⟩ — see DECLINE 2

2 a sinking to a state of low moral standards and behavior ⟨the *degeneracy* of the family into a gang of petty thieves⟩ — see CORRUPTION 2

degenerate *adj* **1** having lost forcefulness, courage, or spirit ⟨a *degenerate* society in which people had no sense of being citizens, only consumers⟩ — see EFFETE 1

2 having or showing lowered moral character or standards ⟨a movie about a gang of *degenerate* drug dealers⟩ — see CORRUPT

degenerate *n* a person who has sunk below the normal moral standard ⟨the *degenerate* would stop at nothing to get satisfaction⟩

synonyms backslider, debaucher, decadent, libertine, pervert, profligate

related words delinquent, derelict, incorrigible; blackguard, cad, heel, knave, rascal, miscreant, reprobate, rogue, scoundrel, villain; playboy, satyr

near antonyms saint

degenerate *vb* to become worse or of less value ⟨over the years the community-minded organization *degenerated* into a club for loafers⟩ — see DETERIORATE

degeneration *n* **1** a change to a lower state or level ⟨the organization's *degeneration* from a movement for political reform to just another political party⟩ — see DECLINE 2

2 a gradual sinking and wasting away of mind or body ⟨the troubling *degeneration* of his memory since he reached middle age⟩ — see DECLINE 1

3 a sinking to a state of low moral standards and behavior ⟨the general *degeneration* that characterized so many old mining towns, which had only drinking and gambling for entertainment⟩ — see CORRUPTION 2

degradation *n* **1** a change to a lower state or level ⟨their English teacher bemoaned the *degradation* of the language that e-mail and instant messaging have allegedly brought about⟩ — see DECLINE 2

2 a sinking to a state of low moral standards and behavior ⟨the belief that moral *degradation* is an unmistakable sign of a nation in decline⟩ — see CORRUPTION 2

degrade *vb* **1** to bring to a lower grade or rank ⟨the view that such a system *degrades* doctors to the status of medical employees who ultimately are not in charge of their patients' health care⟩ — see DEMOTE

2 to lower in character or dignity ⟨*degrading* the school's animal mascot with a silly costume⟩ — see DEBASE 1

3 to reduce to a lower standing in one's own eyes or in others' eyes ⟨the players *degraded* themselves with their crude antics off the field⟩ — see HUMBLE

degraded *adj* having or showing lowered moral character or standards ⟨many observers deplored the fact that the city's festivities for Mardi Gras had become a *degraded*, drunken celebration⟩ — see CORRUPT

degrading *adj* intended to make a person or thing seem of little importance or value ⟨made *degrading* comments about his so-called friend behind his back⟩ — see DEROGATORY

degree *n* **1** an individual part of a process, series, or ranking ⟨they completed the project by *degrees*⟩

synonyms cut, grade, inch, notch, peg, phase, point, stage, step

related words amount, measure, plane; decrement, increment

2 the placement of someone or something in relation to others in a vertical arrangement ⟨a Freemason of the 32nd *degree*⟩ — see RANK 1

dehydrate *vb* to make dry ⟨bought a dehumidifier in order to *dehydrate* the damp basement⟩ — see DRY 1

deification *n* excessive admiration of or devotion to a person ⟨the instant *deification* by the press of the country's newest war hero⟩ — see WORSHIP

deify *vb* **1** to love or admire too much ⟨materialistic people who *deify* money⟩ — see IDOLIZE

2 to offer honor or respect to (someone) as a divine power ⟨some ancient pagans *deified* such objects of nature as trees and rivers⟩ — see WORSHIP 1

deifying *adj* reflecting great admiration or devotion ⟨the *deifying* descriptions of military heroes that are often published in wartime⟩ — see WORSHIPFUL

deign *vb* to descend to a level that is beneath one's dignity ⟨I wouldn't *deign* to answer that absurd accusation⟩ — see CONDESCEND 1

deity *n* **1** a being having superhuman powers and control over a particular part of life or the world ⟨to the ancient Greeks, Zeus was the *deity* who ruled over the sky and weather, and Poseidon was god of the sea⟩

synonyms divinity, god

related words angel, demigod, demon (*or* daemon), devil, spirit, supernatural

2 *cap* the being worshipped as the creator and ruler of the universe ⟨we prayed to the *Deity* for salvation⟩

synonyms Allah, Almighty, Creator, Divinity, Father, God, Godhead, Jehovah, Lord, Maker, Providence, Supreme Being

3 the quality or state of being divine ⟨the repudiation of the claim of *deity* by the Japanese emperor after the end of World War II⟩ — see DIVINITY

dejected *adj* feeling unhappiness ⟨the *dejected* players slowly made their way back to the locker room, where they could mourn their defeat in private⟩ — see SAD 1

dejection *n* a state or spell of low spirits ⟨ice cream often works when trying to cure someone of *dejection*⟩ — see SADNESS

delay *n* an instance or period of being prevented from going about one's business ⟨there was a *delay* for our boarding while the airplane unloaded incoming passengers⟩

synonyms detainment, holdup, wait

related words deferment, postponement; reprieve, respite; hesitation, lag, pause, setback, slowdown

near antonyms haste, rush; dispatch, promptness

delay *vb* **1** to move or act slowly ⟨she told them to stop *delaying* and get to bed⟩

synonyms crawl, creep, dally, dawdle, dillydally, drag, lag, linger, loiter, poke, tarry

related words hang around, hang out, idle, loaf, loll, lounge; amble, ease, inch, lumber, plod, saunter, shuffle, stagger, stroll; decelerate, slow (down *or* up); filibuster, procrastinate, stall, temporize

phrases mark time

near antonyms bowl, breeze, dart, hump, hurtle, hustle, scramble, stampede; gallop, jog, run, sprint, trot; accelerate, quicken, speed up; catch up, fast-forward, outpace, outrun, outstrip, overtake

antonyms barrel, bolt, career, course, dash, fly, hasten, hotfoot (it), hurry, race, rip, rocket, run, rush, scoot, scud, scurry, speed, tear, whirl, whisk, whiz (*or* whizz), zip

2 to assign to a later time ⟨our guests *delayed* their departure until after dinner⟩ — see POSTPONE

3 to create difficulty for the work or activity of ⟨bad weather has repeatedly *delayed* the construction project⟩ — see HAMPER

delectable *adj* **1** giving pleasure or contentment to the mind or senses ⟨a *delectable* melody to listen to after a hard day⟩ — see PLEASANT

2 very pleasing to the sense of taste ⟨a *delectable* roast turkey lay on the table⟩ — see DELICIOUS 1

delectably *adv* in a pleasing way ⟨a *delectably* witty comedy⟩ — see WELL 5

delectation *n* **1** a source of great satisfaction ⟨tourists enjoying the *delectations* of this tropical paradise for the first time⟩ — see DELIGHT 1

2 the feeling experienced when one's wishes are met ⟨a musical concert was presented for the *delectation* of the guests⟩ — see PLEASURE 1

delegate *n* **1** a person sent on a mission to represent another ⟨the *delegate* had a list of concerns to discuss with the country's new ruler⟩ — see AMBASSADOR

2 a person who acts or does business for another ⟨the real estate developer sent a *delegate* to the meeting to represent his interests⟩ — see AGENT 2

delegate *vb* **1** to appoint as one's representative ⟨he *delegated* his son to go pick up the tickets for him⟩
synonyms commission, depute, deputize
related words assign, charge; appoint, designate, name, nominate
near antonyms abrogate; abdicate

2 to put (something) into the possession or safekeeping of another ⟨a manager who is reluctant to *delegate* authority to subordinates⟩ — see GIVE 2

delegation *n* **1** a body of persons chosen as representatives of a larger group ⟨a *delegation* from the local scout troop is being sent to the national jamboree⟩ — see CONTINGENT

2 the granting of power to perform various acts or duties ⟨the *delegation* by the president to the secretary of state of complete control of the nation's foreign policy⟩ — see COMMISSION 1

delete *vb* to show (something written) to be no longer valid by drawing a cross over or a line through it ⟨the teacher *deleted* the last line of the student's essay, feeling that it lessened the impact⟩ — see X (OUT)

deleterious *adj* causing or capable of causing harm ⟨nicotine has long been recognized as a *deleterious* substance⟩ — see HARMFUL

deletion *n* something left out ⟨one of the *deletions* in the final version of the movie turned out to be my one line of dialogue⟩ — see OMISSION

deliberate *adj* **1** decided on as a result of careful thought ⟨the judge made a *deliberate* decision to impose the maximum sentence⟩
synonyms advised, calculated, considered, measured, reasoned, studied, thoughtful, weighed
related words aforethought, premeditated; educated, informed; intentional, purposeful; designed, intended, planned, projected; careful, meticulous; foresighted, forethoughtful, provident, prudent
near antonyms ill-advised; chance, haphazard, hit-or-miss, random; aimless, desultory, purposeless; hasty, hurried, rushed; abrupt, impetuous, sudden; automatic, extemporaneous, impromptu, instinctive, spontaneous
antonyms casual

2 made, given, or done with full awareness of what one is doing ⟨a *deliberate* act of vandalism⟩ — see INTENTIONAL

deliberate *vb* to give serious and careful thought to ⟨the jury *deliberated* the case for three days before returning a verdict⟩ — see PONDER

deliberately *adv* with full awareness of what one is doing ⟨*deliberately* chose to break the rules⟩ — see INTENTIONALLY

deliberation *n* **1** a careful weighing of the reasons for or against something ⟨gave the matter full *deliberation* before reaching a decision⟩ — see CONSIDERATION 1

2 an exchange of views for the purpose of exploring a subject or deciding an issue ⟨there was a great deal of *deliberation* among the representatives about the wording of the public statement⟩ — see DISCUSSION 1

delicacy *n* **1** something that is pleasing to eat because it is rare or a luxury ⟨they were given a plate of *delicacies* while they waited for the queen⟩
synonyms dainty, goody, tidbit (*also* titbit), treat
related words morsel; candy, dessert, junket, sweet, sweetmeat

2 the state or quality of having a delicate structure ⟨they marvelled at the *delicacy* of a snowflake⟩
synonyms daintiness, delicateness, exquisiteness, fineness, fragility
related words flimsiness, insubstantiality, wispiness
near antonyms firmness, solidity; strength
antonyms coarseness, crudeness, crudity, roughness, rudeness

3 the tendency to be or state of being squeamish ⟨the urgent need for blood prompted many people to overcome their habitual *delicacy* and become first-time donors⟩
synonyms qualmishness, queasiness, squeamishness
related words daintiness, fastidiousness, finickiness, fussiness
near antonyms boldness
antonyms indelicacy

4 the quality or state of being very accurate ⟨the *delicacy* of the watch movement is incredible⟩ — see PRECISION

5 the quality or state of lacking physical strength or vigor ⟨all of her life the shy poet gave the appearance of extreme *delicacy*⟩ — see WEAKNESS 1

delicate *adj* **1** satisfying or pleasing because of fineness or mildness ⟨a heavy sauce would spoil the *delicate* flavor of this fish⟩
synonyms dainty, exquisite, refined, subtle
related words choice, elegant, extraordinary, incomparable, peerless, preeminent, prime, rare, select, superior, superlative, supreme, transcendent, unsurpassed; picked, selected; fine, fragile, frail
near antonyms coarse, crude, rough; common, ordinary; average, fair, indifferent, mediocre, medium, middling, run-of-the-mill, second-rate
antonyms robust, strong, sturdy

2 able to sense slight impressions or differences ⟨only a person with *delicate* taste buds could tell the difference between these two wines⟩ — see ACUTE 1

3 accomplished with trained ability ⟨the *delicate* handling of a difficult diplomatic situation⟩ — see SKILLFUL

4 easily broken ⟨*delicate* glassware that must be carefully wrapped for shipping⟩ — see FRAGILE 1

5 easily injured without careful handling ⟨the *delicate* ecosystem of the wetlands⟩ — see TENDER 1

6 hard to please ⟨a person of *delicate* tastes⟩ — see FINICKY

7 having qualities that appeal to a refined taste ⟨*delicate* perfumes that only a connoisseur of scents would appreciate⟩ — see CHOICE

8 lacking bodily strength ⟨a *delicate* child who was never allowed to play sports⟩ — see WEAK 1

9 made or done with extreme care and accuracy ⟨*delicate* measurements that are only possible with the latest medical technology⟩ — see FINE 2

10 meeting the highest standard of accuracy ⟨*delicate* instruments such as an atomic clock⟩ — see PRECISE 1

11 not harsh or stern especially in manner, nature, or effect ⟨a *delicate* breeze was floating in from the open window⟩ — see GENTLE 1

12 requiring exceptional skill or caution in performance or handling ⟨the *delicate* situation of inviting two people who don't like each other to the same party⟩ — see TRICKY

delicateness *n* **1** the quality or state of lacking physical strength or vigor ⟨the *delicateness* of his condition worried the doctors⟩ — see WEAKNESS 1

2 the state or quality of having a delicate structure ⟨he was amazed by the *delicateness* of the elaborate crystal sculpture⟩ — see DELICACY 2

delicious *adj* **1** very pleasing to the sense of taste ⟨the family sat down to a *delicious* Thanksgiving dinner⟩

synonyms ambrosial, appetizing, delectable, flavorful, luscious, palatable, savory, scrumptious, tasty, toothsome, yummy

related words digestible, eatable, edible; delightful, heavenly, pleasing; agreeable, gratifying, pleasant; satisfying; choice, dainty, delicate, exquisite, rare

near antonyms banal, boring, commonplace, tedious; noisome, smelly, stinky; noxious, unwholesome; miserable, wretched; abhorrent, abominable, awful, detestable, disagreeable, disgusting, distasteful, foul, horrid, nauseating, offensive, repellent, repugnant, repulsive, sickening, unpleasant

antonyms flat, flavorless, insipid, stale, tasteless, unappetizing, unpalatable

2 giving pleasure or contentment to the mind or senses ⟨a *delicious* breeze gave us some relief from the tropical heat⟩ — see PLEASANT

deliciously *adv* in a pleasing way ⟨a *deliciously* prepared meal⟩ — see WELL 5

deliciousness *n* the quality of being delicious ⟨the fancy feast was *deliciousness* itself⟩

synonyms lusciousness, savor, savoriness, tastiness

delight *n* **1** a source of great satisfaction ⟨the school play was a *delight* for the parents⟩

synonyms delectation, gas [*slang*], joy, kick, manna, pleasure, treat

related words amusement, diversion, entertainment, fun, recreation; comfort, relief, solace; gratification, indulgence; ambrosia

2 someone or something that provides amusement or enjoyment ⟨with his great sense of humor and bubbly personality, he is a *delight* to be around⟩ — see FUN 1

3 the feeling experienced when one's wishes are met ⟨we were filled with *delight* at the sight of everyone in the family gathered together for the holidays⟩ — see PLEASURE 1

delight *vb* **1** to feel or express joy or triumph ⟨I *delighted* in seeing my schoolyard tormentor get his just deserts⟩ — see EXULT

2 to give satisfaction to ⟨the news *delighted* us⟩ — see PLEASE

delight (in) *vb* to take pleasure in ⟨I've been *delighting in* your company, so I was wondering if we might have another date⟩ — see ENJOY 1

delighted *adj* experiencing pleasure, satisfaction, or delight ⟨we're *delighted* to meet you finally!⟩ — see GLAD 1

delightful *adj* **1** giving pleasure or contentment to the mind or senses ⟨a *delightful* rendition of our favorite song⟩ — see PLEASANT

2 providing amusement or enjoyment ⟨we had a *delightful* time at the party⟩ — see FUN

delightfully *adv* in a pleasing way ⟨a *delightfully* silly song about dancing bears⟩ — see WELL 5

delimit *vb* to mark the limits of ⟨the highway *delimits* the eastern edge of the downtown area⟩ — see LIMIT 2

delineate *vb* **1** to draw or make apparent the outline of ⟨the man's roly-poly shape was softly *delineated* by the glow of the fire⟩ — see OUTLINE 1

2 to give a representation or account of in words ⟨the story does a remarkable job of *delineating* the emotions that immigrants feel upon their arrival in a strange country⟩ — see DESCRIBE 1

delineated *adj* producing a mental picture through clear and impressive description ⟨the finely *delineated* characters of the novel will seem real to the reader⟩ — see GRAPHIC 1

delineation *n* **1** a picture using lines to represent the chief features of an object or scene ⟨his simple but striking *delineations* of Dutch landscapes⟩ — see DRAWING

2 a vivid representation in words of someone or something ⟨a finely wrought *delineation* of a young woman's first experience with romantic love⟩ — see DESCRIPTION 1

delinquency *n* **1** the nonperformance of an assigned or expected action ⟨we received a notice in the mail informing us of our *delinquency* in paying our utility bill⟩ — see FAILURE 1

2 the quality or state of being late ⟨*delinquency* of our mortgage payment meant that we would have to pay a surcharge⟩ — see LATENESS

delinquent *adj* not arriving, occurring, or settled at the due, usual, or proper time ⟨the bank was annoyed because our check was *delinquent*⟩ — see LATE 1

deliquesce *vb* to go from a solid to a liquid state ⟨a rotting tomato slowly *deliquescing* in the hot summer sun⟩ — see LIQUEFY

delirious *adj* **1** feeling overwhelming fear or worry ⟨we were *delirious* with anxiety when the boy failed to return home⟩ — see FRANTIC 1

2 marked by great and often stressful excitement or activity ⟨rushing about in a *delirious* state⟩ — see FURIOUS 1

delirium *n* a state of wildly excited activity or emotion ⟨shoppers running around in a *delirium* the day before Christmas⟩ — see FRENZY

deliver *vb* **1** to free from the penalties or consequences of sin ⟨*deliver* us from evil⟩ — see SAVE 1

2 to remove from danger or harm ⟨the doomed passengers kept hoping that a ship would miraculously appear and *deliver* them⟩ — see SAVE 2

3 to give (something) over to the control or possession of another usually under duress ⟨*delivered* up the ransom money⟩ — see SURRENDER 1

4 to put (something) into the possession of someone for use or consumption ⟨the company promises to *deliver* all orders in time for Christmas⟩ — see FURNISH 2

5 to put (something) into the possession or safekeeping of another 〈*delivered* the prisoners to the sheriff〉 — see GIVE 2

6 to turn out as planned or desired 〈finally, a summer blockbuster that *delivers*〉 — see SUCCEED 1

deliverance *n* **1** the saving from danger or evil 〈looked to the European powers for *deliverance* from their country's cruel tyrant〉 — see SALVATION

2 a position arrived at after consideration 〈the jury's *deliverance* shocked the courtroom〉 — see DECISION 1

deliverer *n* **1** a person who delivers goods to customers usually over a regular local route 〈we took the food and tipped the *deliverer*〉 — see DELIVERYMAN

2 one that saves from danger or destruction 〈the surviving passengers thanked their *deliverers* profusely〉 — see SAVIOR

delivery *n* **1** a freeing from an obligation or responsibility 〈the school bell signaled their *delivery* from the tortures of math class〉 — see RELEASE 1

2 the act or process of giving birth to children 〈her second *delivery* took only three hours〉 — see CHILDBIRTH

deliveryman *n* a person who delivers goods to customers usually over a regular local route 〈the *deliveryman* dropped off a package for us while we were at the store〉

synonyms deliverer

related words bearer, carrier, courier, go-between, liaison, messenger

delude *vb* to cause to believe what is untrue 〈we *deluded* ourselves into thinking that the ice cream wouldn't affect our diet〉 — see DECEIVE

deluding *adj* tending or having power to deceive 〈the *deluding* appearance of the surface of the river, which is actually quite polluted〉 — see DECEPTIVE 1

deluge *n* **1** a great flow of water or of something that overwhelms 〈a *deluge* of thanks and appreciation for the returning troops〉 — see FLOOD

2 a steady falling of water from the sky in significant quantity 〈the exiting moviegoers were caught in the *deluge* without umbrellas〉 — see RAIN 1

deluge *vb* to cover or become filled with a flood 〈*deluged* with requests for help〉 — see FLOOD

delusion *n* a conception or image created by the imagination and having no objective reality 〈her idea that he is a long lost prince is surely just a *delusion*〉 — see FANTASY 1

delusive *adj* tending or having power to deceive 〈*delusive* promises of reward〉 — see DECEPTIVE 1

delusory *adj* tending or having power to deceive 〈the *delusory* importance of money〉 — see DECEPTIVE 1

deluxe *adj* showing obvious signs of wealth and comfort 〈the classy hotel gave us *deluxe* accommodations〉 — see LUXURIOUS

delve (into) *vb* to search through or into 〈we uncovered many interesting stories as we *delved into* the history of the building〉 — see EXPLORE 1

delving *n* a systematic search for the truth or facts about something 〈we didn't want to pry and did as little personal *delving* as possible〉 — see INQUIRY 1

demagogue *also* **demagog** *n* a person who stirs up public feelings especially of discontent 〈that politician is just a *demagogue* who preys upon people's fears and prejudices〉 — see AGITATOR

demand *n* **1** something that someone insists upon having 〈the terrorists presented their list of *demands*〉

synonyms claim, dun, requisition, ultimatum

related words desire, request, want, wish; drive, need, requirement, stipulation; basic, essential, must; imposition; condition, provision

2 something necessary, indispensable, or unavoidable 〈we are very confident that our new employee is fully equal to the *demands* of the job〉 — see ESSENTIAL 1

demand *vb* **1** to ask for (something) earnestly or with authority 〈the losing party *demanded* a recount of the votes cast in the election〉

synonyms call (for), claim, clamor (for), command, enjoin, exact, insist (on), press (for), quest, stipulate (for)

related words ask, plead (for), request, want; cry (for), necessitate, need, require, take, warrant; requisition; impose; badger, dun, hound

near antonyms give up, relinquish, surrender, yield

2 to have as a requirement 〈a task that *demands* one's unremitting attention〉 — see NEED 1

3 to set or receive as a price 〈superstars who *demand* millions for appearing in a movie〉 — see CHARGE 1

demanding *adj* **1** requiring much time, effort, or careful attention 〈the *demanding* assignment kept them working all night〉

synonyms arduous, burdensome, challenging, exacting, grueling (*or* gruelling), laborious, onerous, taxing, toilsome

related words difficult, formidable, hard, herculean, rough, rugged, stiff, strenuous, tough; oppressive, trying; rigid, rigorous, severe, stern, strict, stringent

near antonyms easy, effortless, facile, simple, smooth
antonyms light, undemanding

2 hard to please 〈will play before a *demanding* audience of music critics, who are not easily impressed〉 — see FINICKY

3 requiring considerable physical or mental effort 〈the *demanding* task of reading and grading student compositions〉 — see HARD 2

demarcate *vb* to mark the limits of 〈a yellow line *demarcated* the county on the road map〉 — see LIMIT 2

demarcation *n* the state of being kept distinct 〈the lines of *demarcation* between art and entertainment are often blurry〉 — see SEPARATION 2

¹demean *vb* **1** to lower in character or dignity 〈it *demeans* the political process to demand that candidates make promises that everyone knows are unrealistic〉 — see DEBASE 1

2 to reduce to a lower standing in one's own eyes or in others' eyes 〈we were *demeaned* by our shabby appearance at the funeral〉 — see HUMBLE

²demean *vb* to manage the actions of (oneself) in a particular way 〈I shall endeavor to *demean* myself with utmost respect when our pastor comes to visit〉 — see BEHAVE

demeaning *adj* intended to make a person or thing seem of little importance or value 〈demanded an apology from the men's football coach for his *demeaning* comments on women athletes〉 — see DEROGATORY

demeanor *n* the way or manner in which one conducts oneself 〈the director of the opera company has a haughty *demeanor* that can be irritating〉 — see BEHAVIOR

demented *adj* having or showing a very abnormal or sick state of mind 〈a poor, *demented* animal that had obviously suffered years of abuse〉 — see INSANE 1

dementia *n* a serious mental disorder that prevents one from living a safe and normal life 〈doctors were able to treat the patient's *dementia* with drugs and thus allow him to function on his own〉 — see INSANITY 1

demerit *n* a defect in character ⟨as a typist she has the advantage of speed but the *demerit* of inaccuracy⟩ — see FAULT 1

demesne *n* **1** a part or portion having no fixed boundaries ⟨the vast and frozen *demesne* of the northern tundra⟩ — see REGION 1
2 a region of activity, knowledge, or influence ⟨the view that the issue is not in the *demesne* of the courts and is something that should be decided by the state legislature⟩ — see FIELD 2
3 the area around and belonging to a building ⟨the mansion's huge *demesne* covers more than 100 acres⟩ — see GROUND 1

demilitarization *n* the reduction or elimination of a country's armed forces or weapons ⟨the *demilitarization* of some formerly warlike nations that occurred in the aftermath of World War II⟩ — see DISARMAMENT

demilitarize *vb* to reduce the size and strength of the armed forces of ⟨the two nations agreed to *demilitarize* themselves reciprocally⟩ — see DISARM 1

demise *n* **1** the permanent stopping of all the vital bodily activities ⟨inherited all of the estate upon the *demise* of his grandfather⟩ — see DEATH 1
2 the act of ceasing to exist ⟨the gradual *demise* of the Roman Empire over the course of several centuries⟩ — see DEATH 3

democracy *n* government in which the supreme power is held by the people and used by them directly or indirectly through representation ⟨under our *democracy* the people have some control over their lives by being able to decide who their political leaders will be⟩
synonyms republic, self-government, self-rule
related words home rule, self-determination; autonomy, sovereignty
near antonyms despotism, dictatorship, monarchy, totalitarianism, tyranny

democratic *adj* of, relating to, or favoring political democracy ⟨the *democratic* system ensured that every citizen's voice was heard⟩
synonyms popular, republican, self-governing, self-ruling
related words representative; libertarian
near antonyms autocratic, despotic, dictatorial, monarchal (*or* monarchial), monarchical (*also* monarchic), tyrannical (*also* tyrannic)
antonyms undemocratic

demolish *vb* **1** to destroy (as a building) completely by knocking down or breaking to pieces ⟨they *demolished* the old warehouse to make room for the new shopping mall⟩
synonyms raze, tear down
related words blow up, dynamite; abolish, annihilate, crack up, crush, dash, decimate, destroy, devastate, devour, dissolve, do in, eradicate, extirpate, finish, flatten, obliterate, overturn, pulverize, ravage, ruin, scourge, smash, total, unmake, waste, wipe out, wreck
near antonyms build, construct, erect, put up, raise; rebuild, renew, renovate, restore; create, fabricate, fashion, forge, form, make, manufacture, shape
2 to bring to a complete end the physical soundness, existence, or usefulness of ⟨most of the buildings in the town had been *demolished* in the bombing raid⟩ — see DESTROY 1
3 to cause to break open or into pieces by or as if by an explosive ⟨the concrete wall was *demolished* by the powerful bomb⟩ — see BLAST 1

demolishment *n* the state or fact of being rendered nonexistent, physically unsound, or useless ⟨in the aftermath of its *demolishment* by the tornado, the house looked like a discarded plaything⟩ — see DESTRUCTION

demolition *n* the state or fact of being rendered nonexistent, physically unsound, or useless ⟨several condemned buildings around the city are undergoing *demolition* right at this very moment⟩ — see DESTRUCTION

demon *or* **daemon** *n* an evil spirit ⟨only in rare cases is the ancient rite of exorcism performed to cast out a troublesome *demon*⟩
synonyms devil, fiend, ghoul, imp, incubus
related words apparition, bogey (*also* bogy *or* bogie), familiar, ghost, phantasm, phantom, poltergeist, shade, shadow, specter (*or* spectre), spirit, spook, vision, wraith; brownie, dwarf, elf, faerie (*also* faery), fairy, fay, gnome, goblin, gremlin, hobgoblin, leprechaun, pixie (*also* pixy), puck, sprite, troll; monster, ogre
near antonyms angel

demoniac *also* **demoniacal** *adj* of, relating to, or worthy of an evil spirit ⟨the murderer seemed possessed by a *demoniac* wish to destroy life⟩ — see FIENDISH

demonic *adj* of, relating to, or worthy of an evil spirit ⟨the villain in the movie cackled with *demonic* laughter⟩ — see FIENDISH

demonstrable *adj* capable of being proven as true or real ⟨as a serious scientist, she is only interested in *demonstrable* phenomena⟩ — see VERIFIABLE

demonstrate *vb* **1** to gain full recognition or acceptance of ⟨you must *demonstrate* your scientific thesis before a jury of your professional peers⟩ — see ESTABLISH 1
2 to show the existence or truth of by evidence ⟨the paleontologist hopes to *demonstrate* that dinosaurs once existed in central Peru by unearthing fossil remains⟩ — see PROVE 1
3 to make known (something abstract) through outward signs ⟨the babysitter's actions during the emergency *demonstrate* her underlying dependability⟩ — see SHOW 2
4 to make plain or understandable ⟨a few facts should *demonstrate* the complex nature of our topic⟩ — see EXPLAIN 1
5 to show or make clear by using examples ⟨the visiting physicist *demonstrated* very graphically several basic scientific principles⟩ — see ILLUSTRATE 1

demonstration *n* **1** a mass meeting for the purpose of displaying or arousing support for a cause or person ⟨disgruntled students organized a *demonstration* to protest the new policies⟩ — see RALLY 2
2 an outward and often exaggerated indication of something abstract (as a feeling) for effect ⟨a grand *demonstration* of her love for her husband on Valentine's Day⟩ — see SHOW 1

demonstrative *adj* showing feeling freely ⟨my grandmother was always very *demonstrative* when we visited, showering us with hugs and kisses⟩
synonyms effusive, emotional, uninhibited, unreserved, unrestrained
related words dramatic, histrionic, melodramatic, theatrical; gushing, maudlin, mawkish, mushy, schmaltzy, sentimental; communicative, expansive; extroverted (*also* extraverted), outgoing; affectionate, feeling, intense, loving, passionate, sensitive, soulful, warm; blunt, candid, frank, outspoken, plain
near antonyms constrained; quiet, reticent, silent, taciturn; bashful, modest, retiring, shy; introverted, self-directed; aloof, detached, dispassionate, impassive, indifferent, phlegmatic, stolid, unconcerned, unfeeling;

chilly, cold, frigid, glacial, hard-boiled, hardhearted, icy, unfriendly
antonyms inhibited, reserved, restrained, undemonstrative, unemotional

demoralization *n* **1** a sinking to a state of low moral standards and behavior ⟨a general state of *demoralization* prevailed at every level of the government⟩ — see CORRUPTION 2
2 the state of being discouraged ⟨the officers struggled to combat the *demoralization* of the troops as their tour of duty grew longer⟩ — see DISCOURAGEMENT

demoralize *vb* **1** to deprive of courage or confidence ⟨the forbidding cliffs *demoralized* the climbers⟩ — see UNNERVE 1
2 to lessen the courage or confidence of ⟨we refused to be *demoralized* by our humiliating defeat and vowed to come roaring back the following week⟩ — see DISCOURAGE 1

demoralized *adj* having or showing lowered moral character or standards ⟨a *demoralized* nation that had forgotten the values that once made it great⟩ — see CORRUPT

demote *vb* to bring to a lower grade or rank ⟨the courtmartial's decision was to *demote* the officer responsible for the failed mission⟩
synonyms break, bust, degrade, downgrade, reduce
related words can, dismiss, fire, lay off, sack; abase, debase, demean, humble, humiliate, lower
near antonyms hire
antonyms advance, elevate, promote, raise

demount *vb* to take apart ⟨soldiers were expected to be able to *demount* and reassemble their weapons⟩ — see DISASSEMBLE

demur *n* a feeling or declaration of disapproval or dissent ⟨we accepted his offer to pay for our dinners without *demur*⟩ — see OBJECTION

demur *vb* to present an opposing opinion or argument ⟨don't hesitate to *demur* to the idea if you have any qualms⟩ — see OBJECT

demure *adj* **1** affecting shyness or modesty in order to attract masculine interest ⟨the previously *demure* maiden began making some surprisingly shocking remarks⟩ — see COY 1
2 not comfortable around people ⟨hesitant and *demure*, she hardly spoke a word at the banquet table⟩ — see SHY 2
3 not having or showing any feelings of superiority, self-assertiveness, or showiness ⟨wore a very *demure* outfit to the interview for the job at the church's headquarters⟩ — see HUMBLE 1

demureness *n* the absence of any feelings of being better than others ⟨her excessive *demureness* will be to her disadvantage if she wants a career in show business⟩ — see HUMILITY

den *n* **1** the shelter or resting place of a wild animal ⟨the foxes hid in their *den* until the bear left the area⟩
synonyms burrow, hole, lair, lodge
related words nest
2 a place where a person goes to hide ⟨an abandoned building that is often used as a *den* by the city's petty criminals⟩ — see HIDEOUT

denial *n* **1** an unwillingness to grant something asked for ⟨our principal's *denial* of our request to come to school on Halloween dressed in costumes⟩
synonyms disallowance, nay, no, refusal, rejection
related words decline, rebuff, repudiation; negative
near antonyms acceptance, accession, consent, leave, permission, sufferance

antonyms allowance, grant
2 a refusal to confirm the truth of a statement ⟨the senator issued a flat *denial* of the accusation against her⟩
synonyms contradiction, disallowance, disavowal, disclaimer, negation, rejection, repudiation
related words disproof, rebuttal, refutation; negative
near antonyms confession; affirmation, assertion, declaration
antonyms acknowledgment (*also* acknowledgement), admission, avowal, confirmation

denizen *n* one who lives permanently in a place ⟨the polar bear is a *denizen* of the snowy arctic⟩ — see INHABITANT

denominate *vb* to give a name to ⟨stargazing is nothing more than that, and *denominating* it as astrology does not make it a science⟩ — see NAME 1

denomination *n* a word or combination of words by which a person or thing is regularly known ⟨a variety of creative works that today come under the *denomination* of "art"⟩ — see NAME 1

denotation *n* **1** a word or combination of words by which a person or thing is regularly known ⟨"soul" is the common *denotation* for that mysterious force within the human body that gives it life and yet is separate from it⟩ — see NAME 1
2 the idea that is conveyed or intended to be conveyed to the mind by language, symbol, or action ⟨although most people exercise for fitness, the *denotation* of the term "fitness" varies from exerciser to exerciser⟩ — see MEANING 1

denotative *adj* indicating something ⟨a string of absences from this course will be seen as *denotative* of the student's lack of interest in it⟩ — see INDICATIVE

denote *vb* to communicate or convey (as an idea) to the mind ⟨a flashing red light that *denotes* danger⟩ — see MEAN 1

denoting *adj* indicating something ⟨an arrow is a common *denoting* symbol for direction⟩ — see INDICATIVE

denounce *vb* **1** to declare to be morally wrong or evil ⟨the church council *denounced* the bishop's teachings, officially declaring them to be heresy⟩ — see CONDEMN 1
2 to express one's unfavorable opinion of the worth or quality of ⟨*denounced* the shoddy merchandise that the local shops were foisting on tourists⟩ — see CRITICIZE
3 to express public or formal disapproval of ⟨the governor has *denounced* the court's decision and vows to press for a constitutional amendment⟩ — see CENSURE 1

dense *adj* **1** having little space between items or parts ⟨the *dense* soil in the garden⟩ — see CLOSE 1
2 not having or showing an ability to absorb ideas readily ⟨she accused him of being *dense* when he didn't seem to understand her at first⟩ — see STUPID 1

denseness *n* the quality or state of lacking intelligence or quickness of mind ⟨we were appalled by the *denseness* of the other students⟩ — see STUPIDITY 1

density *n* **1** the degree to which a fluid can resist flowing ⟨in our science experiment we learned that molasses has greater *density* than room-temperature water⟩ — see CONSISTENCY
2 the quality or state of lacking intelligence or quickness of mind ⟨the new teacher was concerned by the *density* shown by some of her students⟩ — see STUPIDITY 1

dent *n* a sunken area forming a separate space ⟨there was a big *dent* in the car's hood where something had hit it⟩ — see HOLE 2

dented *adj* curved inward ⟨the *dented* car fender bore silent testament to an accident that no one in the family was owning up to⟩ — see HOLLOW

denuded *adj* lacking a usual or natural covering ⟨the *denuded* trees left behind after the forest fire had passed⟩ — see NAKED 2

denunciation *n* an often public or formal expression of disapproval ⟨the official *denunciation* of the congresswoman's actions before the full house⟩ — see CENSURE

deny *vb* 1 to declare not to be true ⟨the congressman *denied* all charges of wrongdoing⟩
synonyms contradict, disallow, disavow, disclaim, gainsay, negate, negative, reject, repudiate
related words disown, renounce; challenge, confute, disprove, rebut, refute; disagree (with), dispute
near antonyms accept, adopt, embrace, espouse; affirm, announce, assert, aver, claim, declare, maintain, profess, submit; authenticate, corroborate, substantiate, validate, verify
antonyms acknowledge, admit, allow, avow, concede, confirm, own
2 to be unwilling to grant ⟨he *denied* access to the top secret files to the nosy reporters⟩
synonyms decline, disallow, refuse, reject, withhold
related words rebuff, repel, spurn; check, constrain, hold, keep, restrain, restrict
near antonyms afford, furnish, give, provide, supply
antonyms allow, concede, grant, let, permit

depart *vb* 1 to leave a place often for another ⟨I'll sing one more song before I *depart*⟩ — see GO 2
2 to stop living ⟨we held a little service for our hamster, who recently *departed*⟩ — see DIE 1

departed *adj* 1 no longer existing ⟨a few crumbling ruins are all that remain of that *departed* civilization⟩ — see EXTINCT
2 no longer living ⟨our dear *departed* friend⟩ — see DEAD 1

departing *n* the act of leaving a place ⟨his *departing* was filled with tears and farewells⟩ — see DEPARTURE

department *n* 1 a large unit of a governmental, business, or educational organization ⟨the *Department* of the Interior⟩ — see DIVISION 2
2 a region of activity, knowledge, or influence ⟨that's not my *department*, but maybe I can help you anyway⟩ — see FIELD 2

departure *n* the act of leaving a place ⟨his sudden *departure* left them wondering if they'd upset him⟩
synonyms decamping, decampment, departing, exit, exiting, farewell, going, leave-taking, lighting out, parting, quitting, walking out
related words flight, retirement, retreat, running away, withdrawal; emigration, evacuation, exodus; egress; abandonment, forsaking, relinquishment
near antonyms advent, coming; entrance, ingress
antonyms arrival

depend *vb* 1 to be determined by, based on, or subject (to) ⟨whether or not we play baseball will *depend* on how much rain we get⟩
synonyms hang, hinge
related words base, establish, found, rest, stay; ground
2 to place reliance or trust ⟨I know I can always *depend* on you for help when I really need it⟩
synonyms count, lean, reckon, rely
related words commit, confide, entrust, trust
phrases bank on, figure on
near antonyms distrust, mistrust

dependability *n* worthiness as the recipient of another's trust or confidence ⟨her *dependability* as a friend, in good times and bad, is legendary⟩ — see RELIABILITY

dependable *adj* worthy of one's trust ⟨Boy Scouts are supposed to be always *dependable*⟩
synonyms good, reliable, responsible, safe, solid, steady, sure, tried, tried-and-true, true, trustworthy, trusty
related words constant, devoted, faithful, fast, loyal, staunch (*or* stanch), steadfast; honest, sincere, single-minded; infallible, unerring; firm, sound, strong; effective, telling; attested, authenticated, confirmed, proven, valid, validated, verified; blameless, irreproachable, unimpeachable, unquestionable
near antonyms disloyal, faithless, false, unfaithful; deceitful, dishonest; doubtful, dubious, questionable, suspect, uncertain, unsound; hazardous, risky; unauthenticated, unconfirmed, untried, unverified
antonyms irresponsible, undependable, unreliable, untrustworthy

dependence *n* 1 the quality or state of needing something or someone ⟨a baby's total *dependence* upon his or her parents for every one of life's needs⟩
synonyms dependency, reliance
related words reciprocity, relativity; confidence, faith, stock, trust
near antonyms autonomy, sovereignty
antonyms independence, self-reliance
2 something or someone to which one looks for support ⟨ultimately rice became the chief *dependence* in that state⟩
synonyms buttress, mainstay, pillar, reliance, standby, support
related words backbone, spine; crutch, prop, stay

dependency *n* the quality or state of needing something or someone ⟨she was concerned with his *dependency* on coffee to get him moving in the morning⟩ — see DEPENDENCE 1

dependent *adj* 1 extending freely from a support from above ⟨the *dependent* willow branches swayed in the gentle breeze⟩
synonyms dangling, hanging, pendent (*or* pendant), pendulous
2 determined by something else ⟨our going to the movies tonight is *dependent* on whether or not we have any money left after we eat out⟩
synonyms conditional, contingent (on *or* upon), subject (to), tentative
related words liable, open, susceptible; limited, modified, qualified, restricted; doubtful, iffy, problematic (*also* problematical), questionable, uncertain
near antonyms absolute, categorical (*also* categoric), ultimate; basal, basic, fundamental, primary
antonyms independent, unconditional

depict *vb* 1 to give a representation or account of in words ⟨this letter from an eyewitness *depicts* the battle in greater detail than any other account⟩ — see DESCRIBE 1
2 to point out the chief quality or qualities of an individual or group ⟨the report *depicted* him as a reliable assistant and an employee who could be entrusted with any task⟩ — see CHARACTERIZE 1
3 to present a picture of ⟨the painting *depicts* a pastoral landscape on a summer day⟩ — see PICTURE 1

depiction *n* a vivid representation in words of someone or something ⟨his story presented a *depiction* of the battle that made us feel like we were there⟩ — see DESCRIPTION 1

deplete *vb* to make complete use of ⟨miners *depleted* the vein of copper ore after months of working⟩
synonyms clean (out), consume, drain, exhaust, expend, spend, use up
related words decrease, diminish, lessen, reduce; eat, use; bankrupt, impoverish; cripple, debilitate, disable, enfeeble, sap, undermine, weaken; dry up, empty; dissipate, squander, waste
near antonyms augment, enlarge, increase; bolster, fortify, reinforce, strengthen; rebuild, repair, restore, revive
antonyms renew, replace

deplorable *adj* of a kind to cause great distress ⟨condemned the *deplorable* conditions in which the family was living⟩ — see REGRETTABLE

deplore *vb* **1** to feel or express sorrow for ⟨a statement from the bishops *deploring* the loss of life in the war overseas⟩ — see LAMENT 1
2 to feel sorry or dissatisfied about ⟨*deplored* the fact that his guests were seeing his apartment at its messiest⟩ — see REGRET

deploring *adj* expressing or suggesting mourning ⟨a *deploring* look on his face long after the funeral had ended⟩ — see MOURNFUL 1

deport *vb* **1** to force to leave a country ⟨*deported* them back to their country of birth⟩ — see BANISH 1
2 to manage the actions of (oneself) in a particular way ⟨*deported* herself with grace and propriety at the country club cotillion⟩ — see BEHAVE

deportation *n* the forced removal from a homeland ⟨the *deportation* of the Jews from Spain in 1492⟩ — see EXILE 1

deportee *n* a person forced to emigrate for political reasons ⟨the *deportee* vowed that he would someday return to a liberated nation⟩ — see ÉMIGRÉ 1

deportment *n* the way or manner in which one conducts oneself ⟨her *deportment* during the bitter divorce was a model of self-restraint and class⟩ — see BEHAVIOR

depose *vb* **1** to remove from a position of prominence or power (as a throne) ⟨they *deposed* the dictator after he had bankrupted the country⟩
synonyms dethrone, oust, uncrown, unmake, unseat, unthrone
related words discharge, dismiss; overthrow, usurp, subvert, topple; eject, throw out
near antonyms inaugurate, induct, install, instate, invest; appoint, designate, elect
antonyms crown, enthrone, throne
2 to make a solemn declaration under oath for the purpose of establishing a fact ⟨she was nervous when the time to *depose* before the jury finally arrived⟩ — see TESTIFY

deposit *n* **1** matter that settles to the bottom of a body of liquid ⟨a *deposit* of silt on the river bed⟩
synonyms deposition, dregs, grounds, precipitate, sediment
related words lees; ooze, sludge; dross, slag, waste
2 a collection of things kept available for future use or need ⟨a *deposit* of ammunition under lock and key⟩ — see STORE 1
3 a sum of money set aside for a particular purpose ⟨made a *deposit* at the bank every week⟩ — see FUND 1

deposit *vb* **1** to put in an account ⟨we *deposited* the check in a bank account⟩
synonyms bank
related words cache, hoard, lay away, reserve, salt away, save, squirrel (away), stash, store, stow; invest

near antonyms remove, take out; disburse, expend, lay out, spend
antonyms withdraw
2 to arrange something in a certain spot or position ⟨*deposited* their luggage at the foot of the hotel bed⟩ — see PLACE 1

deposition *n* matter that settles to the bottom of a body of liquid ⟨several types of *deposition* on the bottom of the lake⟩ — see DEPOSIT 1

depository *n* a building for storing goods ⟨a book *depository*⟩ — see STOREHOUSE

depot *n* **1** a building for storing goods ⟨a distribution *depot* for auto parts⟩ — see STOREHOUSE
2 a place where military arms are stored ⟨the guns and ammunition were stored in a *depot* in Concord⟩ — see ARMORY

deprave *vb* to lower in character or dignity ⟨the belief that pornography *depraves* society as a whole⟩ — see DEBASE 1

depraved *adj* having or showing lowered moral character or standards ⟨the *depraved* actions of madmen who had gained control of an entire nation⟩ — see CORRUPT

depravedness *n* the state or quality of being utterly evil ⟨the prosecutor argued that the murders in their utter *depravedness* called for nothing less the death penalty⟩ — see ENORMITY 1

depravity *n* **1** a sinking to a state of low moral standards and behavior ⟨regards the widespread acceptance of gambling as another sign of the *depravity* of today's society⟩ — see CORRUPTION 2
2 immoral conduct or practices harmful or offensive to society ⟨a section of the city long known as den of *depravity*⟩ — see VICE 1
3 the state or quality of being utterly evil ⟨the *depravity* of the demons and devils in many tales of horror⟩ — see ENORMITY 1

deprecate *vb* **1** to express scornfully one's low opinion of ⟨movie critics tried to outdo one another in *deprecating* the comedy as the stupidest movie of the year⟩ — see DECRY 1
2 to hold an unfavorable opinion of ⟨*deprecates* TV sitcoms as childish and simpleminded⟩ — see DISAPPROVE (OF)

deprecation *n* **1** refusal to accept as right or desirable ⟨a teacher's *deprecation* of his students' casual attitude toward their schoolwork⟩ — see DISAPPROVAL
2 the act of making a person or a thing seem little or unimportant ⟨she had low self-esteem, so she made up for it with a near-constant *deprecation* of other people⟩ — see DEPRECIATION

depreciate *vb* **1** to lower the price or value of ⟨a faded finish will really *depreciate* your car when you decide to trade it in⟩
synonyms cheapen, depress, mark down, write off
related words underrate, undervalue; abate, abridge, compress, contract, de-escalate, deflate, diminish, dwindle, lessen, lower, moderate, reduce, shrink
near antonyms bloat, blow up, inflate; add, aggrandize, amplify, augment, balloon, boost, dilate, enlarge, escalate, expand, extend, heighten, increase, maximize, raise, swell
antonyms appreciate, mark up
2 to express scornfully one's low opinion of ⟨dared to *depreciate* Shakespeare, saying his works have no relevance for modern audiences⟩ — see DECRY 1

depreciation *n* the act of making a person or a thing seem little or unimportant ⟨the boys' *depreciation* of the girls' basketball victories only showed how jealous they were⟩

synonyms belittlement, deprecation, detraction, diminishment, disparagement, put-down

related words aspersion, backbiting, defamation, libel, slander, vilification; derision, mockery, ridicule; abuse, invective, vituperation; censure, condemnation, denunciation

near antonyms acclaim, praise; approbation, approval, commendation

antonyms aggrandizement, ennoblement, exaltation, glorification, magnification

depreciative *adj* intended to make a person or thing seem of little importance or value ⟨the usual *depreciative* comments about the food in the cafeteria⟩ — see DEROGATORY

depreciatory *adj* intended to make a person or thing seem of little importance or value ⟨a customer making *depreciatory* remarks about the quality of the service at the restaurant⟩ — see DEROGATORY

depress *vb* 1 to make sad ⟨the thought of failing the test *depressed* me⟩

synonyms burden, oppress, sadden

related words ail, distress, trouble; afflict, torment, torture; discourage, dishearten, dispirit; bother, disquiet, disturb, perturb, upset

near antonyms animate, enliven, invigorate; comfort, console, solace; excite, inspire, stimulate; elate, exhilarate; encourage, hearten; delight, gratify, please

antonyms brighten, buoy, cheer, gladden

2 to cause to fall intentionally or unintentionally ⟨construction workers *depressed* the roadbed in order to make way for an overpass⟩ — see DROP 1

3 to lower the price or value of ⟨the glut of wheat on the market has *depressed* that commodity for most of the past year⟩ — see DEPRECIATE 1

4 to push steadily against with some force ⟨*depressed* the lever to start the machine⟩ — see PRESS 1

depressed *adj* 1 curved inward ⟨the *depressed* sections of the highway under the overpasses constantly get flooded during heavy rainstorms⟩ — see HOLLOW

2 feeling unhappiness ⟨I was *depressed* and didn't feel much like going to the party⟩ — see SAD 1

depressing *adj* 1 causing or marked by an atmosphere lacking in cheer ⟨the *depressing* atmosphere of the funeral⟩ — see GLOOMY 1

2 causing unhappiness ⟨more *depressing* news about the famine overseas⟩ — see SAD 2

depression *n* 1 a period of decreased economic activity ⟨during the 1930s the U.S. suffered a great *depression*⟩

synonyms recession, slump

related words crash, panic; stagnation

near antonyms development, growth; advancement, progress

antonyms boom

2 a state or spell of low spirits ⟨we threw our friend a party just to jar him out of his *depression*⟩ — see SADNESS

3 a sunken area forming a separate space ⟨the water generally collects in the patchwork of *depressions* in the city plaza⟩ — see HOLE 2

deprivation *n* the state of being robbed of something normally enjoyed ⟨the concern of some that there has been a *deprivation* of rights since the passing of laws to combat the threat of terrorism⟩ — see PRIVATION

deprived *adj* kept from having the necessities of life or a healthful environment ⟨*deprived* children growing up in the slums⟩

synonyms disadvantaged, underprivileged

related words impoverished, needy, poor

near antonyms fortunate, lucky; affluent, rich, wealthy; coddled, indulged, pampered, spoiled

antonyms privileged

depth *n* 1 distance measured from the top to the bottom of something ⟨be sure to check the *depth* of the water before diving off the dock⟩

synonyms drop

related words lowness; draft, sounding

near antonyms shallowness; altitude, elevation, height

2 the quality of being great in extent (as of insight) ⟨the *depth* of the poet's understanding of human nature has given his works a timeless appeal⟩

synonyms profoundness, profundity

related words discernment, sense, wisdom; brain, intellect, intelligence; acuteness, keenness, sharpness

near antonyms shallowness, superficiality; smattering

3 the most intense or characteristic phase of something ⟨I was in the *depths* of profound thought when I was rudely interrupted⟩ — see THICK

4 the most extreme or advanced point ⟨in the *depth* of her despondency she even contemplated suicide⟩ — see HEIGHT 2

depthless *adj* lacking significant physical depth ⟨three inches of water may seem rather *depthless*, but unattended babies have drowned in bathtubs with that amount⟩ — see SHALLOW 1

depute *vb* to appoint as one's representative ⟨the governor has the authority to *depute* anyone he wants⟩ — see DELEGATE 1

deputize *vb* to appoint as one's representative ⟨he *deputized* a local citizen to take charge of the situation while he went for reinforcements⟩ — see DELEGATE 1

deputy *n* 1 a person who acts or does business for another ⟨the club president sent a *deputy* to the conference to vote on our behalf⟩ — see AGENT 2

2 a person who helps a more skilled person ⟨a *deputy* to help out with simpler tasks⟩ — see HELPER

derange *vb* 1 to cause to go insane or as if insane ⟨the stranded motorist was half *deranged* from fright⟩ — see CRAZE

2 to undo the proper order or arrangement of ⟨the house was all *deranged* by the earthquake, and it took hours to sort out things⟩ — see DISORDER

deranged *adj* having or showing a very abnormal or sick state of mind ⟨a *deranged* prisoner who had been in that rat-infested hole for 20 years⟩ — see INSANE 1

derangement *n* 1 a serious mental disorder that prevents one from living a safe and normal life ⟨given drugs to treat his *derangement*⟩ — see INSANITY 1

2 an act or instance of the order of things being disturbed ⟨the *derangement* of the carefully organized event by a freak accident⟩ — see UPSET

derelict *adj* 1 failing to give proper care and attention ⟨the guards were judged *derelict* in their duty⟩ — see NEGLIGENT

2 left unoccupied or unused ⟨an old *derelict* mansion that was rumored to be haunted⟩ — see ABANDONED

dereliction *n* 1 the act of abandoning ⟨the family's shameful *dereliction* of their pets at the end of the summer season⟩

synonyms abandonment, desertion, forsaking

related words defection; discard, dumping, jettison

near antonyms retention

antonyms reclamation

2 failure to take the care that a cautious person usually takes ⟨the ski area was not held responsible for the in-

jury on account of the skier's own manifest *dereliction*⟩ — see NEGLIGENCE 1

3 the nonperformance of an assigned or expected action ⟨both sentries were to be court-marshaled for *dereliction* of duty⟩ — see FAILURE 1

deride *vb* to make (someone or something) the object of unkind laughter ⟨my brothers *derided* our efforts, but were forced to eat their words when we won first place⟩ — see RIDICULE

derision *n* the making of unkind jokes as a way of showing one's scorn for someone or something ⟨her absurd behavior on the awards show became a source of *derision* for comedians⟩ — see RIDICULE

derisive *adj* so foolish or pointless as to be worthy of scornful laughter ⟨the *derisive* performances of some of the singers on the talent show⟩ — see RIDICULOUS 1

derisory *adj* so foolish or pointless as to be worthy of scornful laughter ⟨the pawnbroker offered only a *derisory* amount for the diamond ring⟩ — see RIDICULOUS 1

derivable *adj* being or provable by reasoning in which the conclusion follows necessarily from given information ⟨the solution was easily *derivable* from the clues we were given⟩ — see DEDUCTIVE

derivative *adj* taken or created from something original or basic ⟨a *derivative* style that she took from earlier and better painters⟩ — see SECONDARY 1

derivative *n* something that naturally develops or is developed from something else ⟨the whole field of industrial robots is a *derivative* of technology developed for the space program⟩
synonyms by-product, offshoot, outgrowth, spin-off
related words descendant (*or* descendent); aftermath, consequence, result; aftereffect, side effect; copy, duplicate, facsimile, replica, reproduction
near antonyms archetype, original, prototype; antecedent, cause, determinant
antonyms origin, root, source

derogatory *adj* intended to make a person or thing seem of little importance or value ⟨fans made a steady stream of *derogatory* remarks about the players on the visiting team⟩
synonyms belittling, contemptuous, decrying, degrading, demeaning, depreciative, depreciatory, disdainful, disparaging, scornful, slighting, uncomplimentary
related words aspersing, defamatory, detractive, insulting, libelous, maligning, slandering, slanderous, vilifying; abusive, opprobrious, scurrilous; despiteful, malevolent, malicious, spiteful
near antonyms admiring, adulatory, laudatory; appreciative, respectful
antonyms commendatory, complimentary

descant *vb* **1** to give a formal often extended talk on a subject ⟨the professor loves to *descant* on his beloved Shakespeare⟩ — see TALK 1

2 to produce musical sounds with the voice ⟨the soprano *descanted* above the melody line⟩ — see SING 1

descend *vb* **1** to lead or extend downward ⟨the pathway *descends* to the river bank⟩
synonyms decline, dip, drop, fall, plunge
related words cant, incline, lean, list, recline, slant, slope, tilt, tip
near antonyms even, flatten, level, straighten
antonyms ascend, climb, rise

2 to become worse or of less value ⟨the family's economic fortunes *descended* to the point where they were finally homeless⟩ — see DETERIORATE

3 to go to a lower level ⟨leaves slowly *descended* from the branches in the gentle autumn wind⟩ — see DROP 2

descend (on *or* upon) *vb* to take sudden, violent action against ⟨the troops *descended on* the village without warning⟩ — see ATTACK 1

descendant *or* **descendent** *adj* bending downward or forward ⟨the *descendant* branches of a weeping willow⟩ — see NODDING

descending *adj* bending downward or forward ⟨with *descending* heads the mourners made their way to the burial site⟩ — see NODDING

descent *n* **1** the act or process of going to a lower level or altitude ⟨the airplane began its gradual *descent* to the landing field⟩
synonyms dip, dive, down, drop, fall, nosedive, plunge
related words comedown, downfall, downgrade; sinking
near antonyms advance, headway, progress, progression; betterment, improvement
antonyms ascent, climb, rise, upswing, upturn

2 a gradual sinking and wasting away of mind or body ⟨the family patriarch's heartbreaking *descent* into infirmity and senility⟩ — see DECLINE 1

3 a change to a lower state or level ⟨the nation's rapid *descent* into anarchy after the revolution⟩ — see DECLINE 2

4 a loss of status ⟨for throwing the game, the ball player underwent a huge *descent* in the eyes of the fans⟩ — see COMEDOWN

5 a sudden attack on and entrance into hostile territory ⟨the lightning *descent* of the invading army on that unsuspecting border town⟩ — see RAID 1

6 the act or action of setting upon with force or violence ⟨the *descent* of the locusts on the wheat fields⟩ — see ATTACK 1

7 the line of ancestors from whom a person is descended ⟨a person of Finnish *descent*⟩ — see ANCESTRY

describe *vb* **1** to give a representation or account of in words ⟨he tried to *describe* the dream he had last night as accurately as he could⟩
synonyms delineate, depict, draw, image, paint, picture, portray, sketch
related words characterize, qualify, represent; demonstrate, illustrate; narrate, recite, recount, relate; display, exhibit, show; hint, suggest; draft, outline
near antonyms color, distort, falsify, garble, misrepresent, pervert, twist, warp

2 to give an oral or written account of in some detail ⟨a biography of Washington that *describes* the Battle of Yorktown at great length⟩ — see TELL 1

3 to point out the chief quality or qualities of an individual or group ⟨how would you *describe* the Inupiat people you encountered in Alaska?⟩ — see CHARACTERIZE 1

description *n* **1** a vivid representation in words of someone or something ⟨we recognized his cousin from his *description*⟩
synonyms delineation, depiction, picture, portrait, portrayal, sketch
related words account, chronicle, narrative, report, story, tale; demonstration, exemplification, illustration

2 a number of persons or things that are grouped together because they have something in common ⟨fixes small appliances and other things of that *description*⟩ — see SORT 1

descry *vb* **1** to come upon after searching, study, or effort ⟨we couldn't *descry* the reasons for his sudden departure⟩ — see FIND 1
2 to make note of (something) through the use of one's eyes ⟨could just *descry* the ship coming over the horizon⟩ — see SEE 1
desecrate *vb* to treat (a sacred place or object) shamefully or with great disrespect ⟨vandals *desecrated* the cemetery last night with graffiti⟩
synonyms defile, profane, violate
related words blaspheme, curse, swear; befoul, contaminate, foul, pollute; affront, insult, offend; crush, decimate, demolish, destroy, devastate, ravage, raze, ruin, waste, wreck; despoil, loot, pillage, plunder, raid, ransack, rob, sack, spoil, strip
near antonyms bless, consecrate, dedicate, hallow, sanctify; honor, respect; cleanse, purify
desecration *n* an act of great disrespect shown to God or to sacred ideas, people, or things ⟨they were aghast at the *desecration* of the altar⟩ — see BLASPHEMY
¹desert *n* land that is uninhabited or not fit for crops ⟨we were lost in the *desert* for days without food⟩ — see WASTELAND
²desert *n* suffering, loss, or hardship imposed in response to a crime or offense ⟨the robbers got their just *deserts*⟩ — see PUNISHMENT
desert *vb* **1** to leave (a cause or party) often in order to take up another ⟨the volunteer became disillusioned with his candidate and *deserted* to a political rival⟩ — see DEFECT
2 to cause to remain behind ⟨*deserted* the kids at the food court⟩ — see LEAVE 1
deserted *adj* left unoccupied or unused ⟨we had the *deserted* beach all to ourselves⟩ — see ABANDONED
deserter *n* a person who abandons a cause or organization usually without right ⟨we had orders to find and capture the *deserters* before they could reveal our secrets⟩ — see RENEGADE
desertion *n* the act of abandoning ⟨the soldiers were imprisoned for *desertion* of their posts⟩ — see DERELICTION 1
deserve *vb* to be or make worthy of (as a reward or punishment) ⟨the team really *deserved* that victory after the way they played⟩ — see EARN 2
deserved *adj* being what is called for by accepted standards of right and wrong ⟨a well *deserved* promotion for a hard worker⟩ — see JUST 1
deserving *adj* having sufficient worth or merit to receive one's honor, esteem, or reward ⟨gifts donated to *deserving* children every Christmas⟩ — see WORTHY
desex *vb* to remove the sex organs of ⟨*desex* the baby chickens destined for market⟩ — see NEUTER
design *n* **1** a method worked out in advance for achieving some objective ⟨she always achieves her objective by *design* rather than by luck⟩ — see PLAN 1
2 a secret plan for accomplishing evil or unlawful ends ⟨the adventurer had *designs* on her fortune⟩ — see PLOT 1
3 something that one hopes or intends to accomplish ⟨the immigrant laborer had ambitious *designs* in mind for his daughter⟩ — see GOAL
4 a unit of decoration that is repeated all over something (as a fabric) ⟨the curtains have a lovely floral *design*⟩ — see PATTERN 1
5 the way in which the elements of something (as a work of art) are arranged ⟨the *design* of the building's lobby encourages the free flow of traffic⟩ — see COMPOSITION 3

design *vb* **1** to have in mind as a purpose or goal ⟨she *designed* to a top executive in a major insurance company⟩ — see INTEND
2 to work out the details of (something) in advance ⟨he *designed* a better layout for the factory floor to improve efficiency⟩ — see PLAN 1
designate *vb* **1** to decide upon (the time or date for an event) usually from a position of authority ⟨the *designated* time for the meeting⟩ — see APPOINT 1
2 to pick (someone) by one's authority for a specific position or duty ⟨he has yet to *designate* his successor as head of the firm⟩ — see APPOINT 2
3 to give a name to ⟨he was *designated* "Air Jordan" by his fans⟩ — see NAME 1
designation *n* **1** a word or combination of words by which a person or thing is regularly known ⟨we've never given the homemade gadget a proper *designation*⟩ — see NAME 1
2 the state or fact of being chosen for a position or duty ⟨his surprising *designation* as the running mate raised a few eyebrows⟩ — see APPOINTMENT 1
designedly *adv* with full awareness of what one is doing ⟨the puzzle was *designedly* difficult to decipher⟩ — see INTENTIONALLY
designer *n* one who creates or introduces something new ⟨the *designer* of the first sneaker specifically intended for distance running⟩ — see INVENTOR
desirable *adj* suitable for bringing about a desired result under the circumstances ⟨a *desirable* location for the new house⟩ — see EXPEDIENT
desire *n* a strong wish for something ⟨a *desire* for adventure and excitement prompted him to travel to Africa⟩
synonyms appetite, craving, drive, hankering, hunger, itch, longing, lust, passion, pining, thirst, urge, yearning, yen
related words compulsion, impulse, urge, will, zeal; liking, love, taste; eagerness, impatience; wish, want; necessity, need, requirement; avarice, cupidity, greed, rapacity
near antonyms abhorrence, aversion, disfavor, disgust, dislike, distaste, hatred, repugnance, repulsion; apathy, indifference, unconcern
desire *vb* to have an earnest wish to own or enjoy ⟨he greatly *desired* a new mountain bike for his next birthday⟩
synonyms ache (for), covet, crave, die (for), hanker (for *or* after), hunger (for), itch (for), long (for), lust (for *or* after), pant (after), pine (for), repine (for), sigh (for), thirst (for), want, wish (for), yearn (for)
related words delight (in), enjoy, fancy, like, relish
near antonyms abhor, abominate, detest, hate, loathe; decline, refuse, reject, spurn
desirous *adj* showing urgent desire or interest ⟨*desirous* of finishing the project and going to bed⟩ — see EAGER
desirousness *n* urgent desire or interest ⟨her *desirousness* for advancement in the corporation is such that she'll stamp on anyone in her way⟩ — see EAGERNESS
desist (from) *vb* to bring (as an action or operation) to an immediate end ⟨ordered to *desist from* all attempts to contact her⟩ — see STOP 1
desk *n* a large unit of a governmental, business, or educational organization ⟨the city *desk* of a prominent newspaper⟩ — see DIVISION 2
desolate *adj* **1** causing or marked by an atmosphere lacking in cheer ⟨a *desolate* house abandoned many years ago⟩ — see GLOOMY 1

2 sad from lack of companionship or separation from others ⟨her boyfriend has been *desolate* since she left for the summer⟩ — see LONESOME 1

desolate *vb* to bring to a complete end the physical soundness, existence, or usefulness of ⟨*desolated* the city with aerial bombs⟩ — see DESTROY 1

desolation *n* **1** a state or spell of low spirits ⟨his *desolation* after his brother left for college was incurable⟩ — see SADNESS

2 land that is uninhabited or not fit for crops ⟨looked out over the vast untamed *desolation* to the north⟩ — see WASTELAND

3 the state of being unattended to or not cared for ⟨the *desolation* of the abandoned garden⟩ — see NEGLECT 1

4 the state or fact of being rendered nonexistent, physically unsound, or useless ⟨the attack resulted in a scene of utter *desolation*⟩ — see DESTRUCTION

despair *n* **1** utter loss of hope ⟨the endless drought drove the farmers to *despair*⟩

synonyms desperation, despondency, forlornness, hopelessness

related words blues, depression, dejection, desolation, doldrums, dolor, downheartedness, dumps, gloom, melancholy, mopes, oppression, sadness, sorrow, unhappiness; cynicism, pessimism; acceptance, resignation

near antonyms cheer, cheerfulness, sunniness; optimism

antonyms hope, hopefulness

2 the state of being discouraged ⟨the other team's temporary lead caused some momentary *despair*⟩ — see DISCOURAGEMENT

despair *vb* to lose all hope or confidence ⟨we *despaired* when we saw how little time we had left to complete our project⟩

synonyms despond

related words give up, surrender, yield; darken, sadden; grieve, mourn, sorrow; discourage, dishearten, dispirit

near antonyms assure, encourage, hearten, reassure; hope

antonyms brighten, cheer (up), perk (up)

despairing *adj* emphasizing or expecting the worst ⟨*despairing* predictions that we would not finish before time ran out⟩ — see PESSIMISTIC 1

desperation *n* utter loss of hope ⟨her *desperation* drove her to do things she wouldn't have normally considered⟩ — see DESPAIR 1

despicable *adj* **1** arousing or deserving of one's loathing and disgust ⟨condemned for his *despicable* actions during the crisis⟩ — see CONTEMPTIBLE 1

2 not following or in accordance with standards of honor and decency ⟨the cad's *despicable* behavior toward women⟩ — see IGNOBLE 2

3 deserving pitying scorn (as for inadequacy) ⟨a *despicable* attempt at making a movie comedy⟩ — see PITIFUL 1

despise *vb* **1** to dislike strongly ⟨I *despise* anchovies on pizza, and I refuse to eat them!⟩ — see HATE

2 to ignore in a disrespectful manner ⟨a traitor hated and *despised* by the whole community⟩ — see SCORN 2

despite *n* **1** open dislike for someone or something considered unworthy of one's concern or respect ⟨pointedly ignored his false friend out of *despite*⟩ — see CONTEMPT

2 the desire to cause pain for the satisfaction of doing harm ⟨sheer *despite* was the sole reason for her hurtful comments⟩ — see MALICE

despite *prep* without being prevented by ⟨we went to the party *despite* the bad weather outside⟩

synonyms notwithstanding, with

phrases in despite of, in spite of

despiteful *adj* having or showing a desire to cause someone pain or suffering for the sheer enjoyment of it ⟨*despiteful* treatment of his poor relations during their visit⟩ — see HATEFUL

despitefully *adv* in a mean or spiteful manner ⟨behaved *despitefully* toward the school nerds⟩ — see NASTILY

despitefulness *n* open dislike for someone or something considered unworthy of one's concern or respect ⟨the *despitefulness* with which she treated girls with no fashion sense⟩ — see CONTEMPT

despoil *vb* to search through with the intent of committing robbery ⟨the burglars *despoiled* the art museum in search of treasures they could sell to a fence⟩ — see RANSACK 1

despond *vb* to lose all hope or confidence ⟨we should not *despond* even though we lost⟩ — see DESPAIR

despondency *n* **1** a state or spell of low spirits ⟨in *despondency* because he couldn't get a date to the dance⟩ — see SADNESS

2 the state of being discouraged ⟨in their *despondency* they forgot that losing teams can become winning teams in a single season⟩ — see DISCOURAGEMENT

3 utter loss of hope ⟨never once gave into *despondency* during her long recovery from her injuries in the car crash⟩ — see DESPAIR 1

despondent *adj* feeling unhappiness ⟨feeling *despondent* over being fired from his job⟩ — see SAD 1

despot *n* a person who uses power or authority in a cruel, unjust, or harmful way ⟨the *despot* threw anyone who dared to criticize his rule into jail⟩

synonyms autocrat, dictator, oppressor, potentate, tyrant

related words dominator, master, overlord, ruler; king, lord, monarch, prince, queen, sovereign; baron, czar (*also* tsar *or* tzar), magnate, mogul, tycoon; authoritarian, disciplinarian, discipliner, martinet

despotic *adj* **1** exercising power or authority without interference by others ⟨the *despotic* monarch quickly became the target of assassination plots⟩ — see ABSOLUTE 1

2 fond of ordering people around ⟨the *despotic* coach demands that his players obey him without question⟩ — see BOSSY

despotism *n* a system of government in which the ruler has unlimited power ⟨by the end of the 20th century many countries around the world had rejected *despotism* in favor of democracy⟩

synonyms autocracy, dictatorship, totalitarianism, tyranny

related words monarchy; authoritarianism, fascism; domination, oppression

near antonyms democracy; freedom; anarchy

destine *vb* to determine the fate of in advance ⟨his extreme height seemed to *destine* him for a career in basketball⟩

synonyms doom, fate, foredoom, foreordain, ordain, predestine, predetermine

related words forecast, foretell, predict, prognosticate, prophesy; preconceive, prejudge; condemn, sentence

destiny *n* a state or end that seemingly has been decided beforehand ⟨we knew that it wasn't our *destiny* to end up in a dead-end job⟩ — see FATE 1

destitute *adj* **1** lacking money or material possessions ⟨many families were left *destitute* by the horrible fire⟩ — see POOR 1

2 utterly lacking in something needed, wanted, or expected ⟨a lingering drought and a sky *destitute* of rain clouds⟩ — see DEVOID 1

destitution *n* the state of lacking sufficient money or material possessions ⟨widespread *destitution* in Third World countries⟩ — see POVERTY 1

destroy *vb* **1** to bring to a complete end the physical soundness, existence, or usefulness of ⟨they practically *destroyed* the safe in order to get at the money inside⟩ ⟨their poor scores on the final exam *destroyed* any chance they might have had to pass the course⟩

synonyms annihilate, decimate, demolish, desolate, devastate, do in, extinguish, pulverize, raze, ruin, shatter, smash, tear down, waste, wreck

related words gut; beat, best, clobber, conquer, crush, defeat, lick, master, overbear, overcome, prevail (over), scotch, subdue, surmount, thrash, triumph (over), win (against); blow up, break, damage, deface, disintegrate, dynamite, mangle, mar, mutilate, spoil, vitiate; erode, scour, wash out, wear (away); dismantle, undo, unmake; blot out, eradicate, exterminate, extirpate, obliterate, remove, rub out, stamp (out), wipe out; despoil, loot, pillage, plunder, ravage, sack, vandalize; assassinate, butcher, cut down, dispatch, execute, kill, massacre, murder, slaughter, slay, zap

near antonyms create, invent; fabricate, fashion, forge, form, make, manufacture, shape; bring about, establish, found, institute, organize; conserve, preserve, protect, save; rebuild, reconstruct, remodel, renovate, restore

antonyms build, construct, erect, put up, raise

2 to bring destruction to (something) through violent action ⟨wildfires *destroyed* thousands of acres in forests across the state⟩ — see RAVAGE

3 to deprive of life ⟨the veterinarian was forced to *destroy* the injured horse⟩ — see KILL 1

destruction *n* the state or fact of being rendered nonexistent, physically unsound, or useless ⟨the violent storm resulted in the *destruction* of their tree house⟩

synonyms annihilation, decimation, demolishment, demolition, desolation, devastation, extermination, extinction, havoc, loss, obliteration, ruin, ruination, wastage, wreckage

related words depredation, despoilment, despoliation; breakup, disintegration, dissolution; assassination, execution, killing, massacre, slaughter

near antonyms conservation, preservation, protection; reconstruction, re-creation, remodeling, renovation, restoration

antonyms building, construction, erection, raising

destructive *adj* **1** causing or tending to cause destruction ⟨the *destructive* storm blew down trees all over town, and blew the roof off our neighbor's house⟩

synonyms calamitous, cataclysmal (*or* cataclysmic), devastating, disastrous, ruinous

related words deadly, fatal, lethal, mortal, vital; deleterious, detrimental, harmful, pernicious

near antonyms preservative, protective; creative, formative; harmless, innocuous, inoffensive, nondestructive; ameliorative, helpful, useful

antonyms constructive

2 bringing about ruin or misfortune ⟨technology used for *destructive* ends⟩ — see FATAL 1

desultorily *adv* without definite aim, direction, rule, or method ⟨sat watching the movie, *desultorily* eating popcorn⟩ — see HIT OR MISS

desultory *adj* **1** lacking a definite plan, purpose, or pattern ⟨a *desultory* search for something of interest on TV⟩ — see RANDOM

2 passing from one topic to another ⟨a *desultory* discussion about the news of the day⟩ — see DISCURSIVE

detached *adj* **1** having or showing a lack of friendliness or interest in others ⟨a *detached* observer at company parties⟩ — see COOL 1

2 not physically attached to another unit ⟨a *detached* garage on the side of the house⟩ — see SEPARATE 2

detachment *n* **1** lack of favoritism toward one side or another ⟨the judge showed great *detachment* when deciding the controversial case⟩

synonyms disinterestedness, impartiality, neutrality, objectivity

related words equitableness, fairness; apathy, indifference, unconcern; broad-mindedness, open-mindedness, tolerance

near antonyms chauvinism, nepotism; subjectivity; bent, inclination, leaning, penchant, predilection, predisposition, proclivity, propensity, tendency; preconception, prejudgment

antonyms bias, favor, favoritism, one-sidedness, partiality, partisanship, prejudice

2 a small military unit with a special task or function ⟨the general sent a *detachment* ahead to scout the enemy's position⟩

synonyms detail

related words commando, firing squad, paratroops, patrol, picket; battalion, command, company, corps, division, platoon, regiment, squad, troop, wing

detail *n* **1** a separate part in a list, account, or series ⟨every *detail* was accounted for⟩ — see ITEM 1

2 a single piece of information ⟨didn't leave out a single *detail* in his story⟩ — see FACT 3

3 a small military unit with a special task or function ⟨the officer sent out a *detail* to patrol the perimeter⟩ — see DETACHMENT 2

detail *vb* **1** to assign to a place or position ⟨once again he was *detailed* to guard duty⟩ — see ²POST

2 to pick (someone) by one's authority for a specific position or duty ⟨Anne was *detailed* to accompany the boss on the business trip⟩ — see APPOINT 2

3 to specify one after another ⟨*detailed* all of the reasons that the plan was a bad idea⟩ — see ENUMERATE 1

detailed *adj* **1** including many small descriptive features ⟨a *detailed* report on all the activities that their Scout troop had been involved in over the past year⟩

synonyms circumstantial, elaborate, full, minute, particularized, thorough

related words enumerated, inventoried, itemized, listed; delineated, specific, specified; abundant, copious; comprehensive, exhausting, exhaustive, thoroughgoing; accurate, exact, precise; complete, entire, replete; distinct, explicit, precise, sharp; inclusive, mapped (out); descriptive, graphic (*also* graphical), picturesque, vivid

near antonyms concise, pithy, short, succinct; abbreviated, abridged, curtailed, cut, pruned, shortened, trimmed; indeterminate, nebulous, nondescript, sketchy, vague; bird's-eye, broad, general, nonspecific, overall, unspecified

antonyms compendious, summary

2 made or done with great care or with much detail ⟨a *detailed* miniature of the royal palace⟩ — see ELABORATE 1

detailedly *adv* with attention to all aspects or details ⟨went over the proposal more *detailedly* than he had the first time⟩ — see THOROUGHLY 1

detainment *n* an instance or period of being prevented from going about one's business ⟨their *detainment* at the border only lasted a few minutes⟩ — see DELAY

detect *vb* to come upon after searching, study, or effort ⟨I can *detect* just a hint of lemon in the soup⟩ — see FIND 1

detectable *adj* able to be perceived by a sense or by the mind ⟨there was a barely *detectable* hum coming from the refrigerator⟩ — see PERCEPTIBLE

detection *n* the act or process of sighting or learning the existence of something for the first time ⟨my *detection* of the scent of baked apple pie led me to the kitchen⟩ — see DISCOVERY 1

detective *n* a person whose business is solving crimes and catching criminals or gathering information that is not easy to get ⟨the *detective* tracked the criminals to an abandoned warehouse on the south side of town⟩
synonyms investigator, operative, plainclothesman, shadow, sleuth, tail
related words Federal, G-man, narc (*or* nark) [*slang*]

detector *n* a device that detects some physical quantity and responds usually with a transmitted signal ⟨a motion *detector* to thwart burglaries⟩ — see SENSOR

deter *vb* to steer (a person) from an activity or course of action ⟨we tried to *deter* him from his crazy plan⟩ — see DISCOURAGE 2

detergent *n* a substance used for cleaning ⟨add the *detergent* to the washing machine before putting in the clothes⟩ — see CLEANER

deteriorate *vb* to become worse or of less value ⟨the garden slowly *deteriorated* after months of neglect⟩
synonyms crumble, decay, decline, degenerate, descend, ebb, rot, sink, worsen
related words recede, wane; decompose, degrade, disintegrate; sour, spoil; lessen, lower, reduce; debilitate, undermine, weaken
phrases go to pot
near antonyms better, upgrade; enhance, enrich, fortify, heighten, intensify, strengthen; advance, develop, progress
antonyms ameliorate, improve, meliorate

deterioration *n* **1** a gradual sinking and wasting away of mind or body ⟨muscle *deterioration* resulting from prolonged disuse⟩ — see DECLINE 1
2 a change to a lower state or level ⟨a *deterioration* in the quality of food in the cafeteria⟩ — see DECLINE 2

determinate *adj* **1** having been established and usually not subject to change ⟨a *determinate* order of succession to the throne⟩ — see FIXED 1
2 having distinct or certain limits ⟨contestants have a *determinate* length of time to answer the questions⟩ — see LIMITED 1

determination *n* **1** firm or unwavering adherence to one's purpose ⟨the *determination* with which the pioneers settled the land despite many hardships and setbacks⟩
synonyms decidedness, decision, decisiveness, firmness, granite, purposefulness, resoluteness, resolution, resolve
related words doggedness, obstinacy, perseverance, persistence, stubbornness, tenaciousness, tenacity; backbone, fortitude, grit, pluck

near antonyms uncertainty
antonyms hesitation, indecision, irresolution, vacillation
2 a position arrived at after consideration ⟨a *determination* by the judge regarding an appropriate sentence⟩ — see DECISION 1
3 an opinion arrived at through a process of reasoning ⟨his *determination* of the truth⟩ — see CONCLUSION 1

determine *vb* **1** to give an opinion about (something at issue or in dispute) ⟨a three-member panel will *determine* the case⟩ — see JUDGE 1
2 to come to a judgment after discussion or consideration ⟨trying to *determine* which direction we were facing⟩ — see DECIDE 1
3 to come upon after searching, study, or effort ⟨we failed to *determine* the answer to the riddle⟩ — see FIND 1

determined *adj* **1** fully committed to achieving a goal ⟨his *determined* opponent would not be bluffed or shaken⟩
synonyms bent (on *or* upon), bound, decisive, firm, intent, purposeful, resolute, resolved, set
related words certain, cocksure, positive, sure; earnest, serious; steady, unfaltering, unhesitating, unswerving, unwavering
near antonyms doubtful, dubious, uncertain, unsure
antonyms faltering, hesitant, indecisive, irresolute, undetermined, unresolved, vacillating, wavering
2 showing no signs of slackening or yielding in one's purpose ⟨a runner who was *determined* to finish first in the race⟩ — see UNYIELDING 1

determinedly *adv* with great effort or determination ⟨running *determinedly* for the goal line⟩ — see HARD 1

deterrent *n* something that makes movement or progress more difficult ⟨the homeowner put up a fence around his garden as a *deterrent* for animals⟩ — see ENCUMBRANCE

detest *vb* to dislike strongly ⟨I *detest* pepperoni, and wouldn't eat it if you paid me!⟩ — see HATE

detestable *adj* not following or in accordance with standards of honor and decency ⟨the *detestable* actions of a nasty little man⟩ — see IGNOBLE 2

dethrone *vb* to remove from a position of prominence or power (as a throne) ⟨the last monarch was *dethroned* in a popular uprising many years ago⟩ — see DEPOSE 1

detonate *vb* to break open or into pieces usually because of internal pressure ⟨the bomb *detonated* with a noise that could be heard for blocks in all directions⟩ — see EXPLODE 1

detonation *n* the act or an instance of exploding ⟨there was a series of *detonations* around the base of the condemned building, causing it to come crashing down in a matter of minutes⟩ — see EXPLOSION 1

detour *vb* **1** to avoid by going around ⟨we had to *detour* the construction zone in order to get to the stadium⟩
synonyms bypass, circumvent, skirt
related words circumnavigate; avoid, dodge, duck, elude, escape, eschew, evade, shake, shun
near antonyms confront, face, meet; accept, court, embrace, pursue, seek, welcome
2 to change one's course or direction ⟨we had to *detour* for a few miles around the section of highway under construction⟩ — see TURN 3

detraction *n* the act of making a person or a thing seem little or unimportant ⟨her constant *detraction* of every new idea is annoying to the other club members⟩ — see DEPRECIATION

detriment *n* something that causes loss or pain ⟨opponents of casino gambling claim that it is a *detriment* to society at large⟩ — see INJURY 1

detrimental *adj* causing or capable of causing harm ⟨there were concerns that the factory's waste was *detrimental* to the local environment⟩ — see HARMFUL

devastate *vb* **1** to bring destruction to (something) through violent action ⟨the city was *devastated*, first by the earthquake and then by fires⟩ — see RAVAGE
2 to bring to a complete end the physical soundness, existence, or usefulness of ⟨the explosion *devastated* an entire city block⟩ — see DESTROY 1
3 to subject to incapacitating emotional or mental stress ⟨we were *devastated* by the awful news⟩ — see OVERWHELM 1

devastating *adj* causing or tending to cause destruction ⟨a *devastating* blow to our morale⟩ — see DESTRUCTIVE 1

devastation *n* the state or fact of being rendered nonexistent, physically unsound, or useless ⟨the sheer *devastation* of the housing development after the forest fire had passed⟩ — see DESTRUCTION

develop *vb* **1** to gradually become clearer or more detailed ⟨as the story of the bombing *developed*, the scope of the tragedy became more apparent⟩
synonyms evolve, unfold
related words advance, proceed, progress; mature, ripen; materialize
2 to come to have gradually ⟨they *developed* a taste for green olives⟩
synonyms acquire, cultivate, form
related words gain, get, obtain; achieve, attain, reach; foster, nourish, nurture, promote
antonyms lose
3 to become mature ⟨the roses are *developing* nicely in the garden⟩ — see MATURE
4 to express more fully and in greater detail ⟨they *developed* the initial idea into a complete plan⟩ — see EXPAND 1

developed *adj* being far along in development ⟨a highly *developed* society with a rigid class system⟩ — see ADVANCED 1

developer *n* one who creates or introduces something new ⟨the *developer* of software that is used the world over⟩ — see INVENTOR

development *n* **1** the act or process of going from the simple or basic to the complex or advanced ⟨the *development* of an idea into a marketable product⟩
synonyms elaboration, evolution, expansion, growth, progress, progression
related words advancement, betterment, improvement, perfection, refinement; maturation
near antonyms decadence, decay, decaying, declension, decline, degeneration, descent, deterioration, downgrade, ebbing, weakening
antonyms regression, retrogression
2 a condition or occurrence traceable to a cause ⟨a *development* that the writers of the law never anticipated or intended⟩ — see EFFECT 1
3 the process of becoming mature ⟨a tulip's *development* from a bulb into a flower⟩ — see MATURATION

deviant *adj* departing from some accepted standard of what is normal ⟨some studies show that many violent criminals begin exhibiting *deviant* behavior in early childhood⟩
synonyms aberrant, abnormal, anomalous, atypical, irregular, unnatural

related words extraordinary, preternatural; rare, uncommon, uncustomary, unusual, unwonted; odd, peculiar, strange, weird
near antonyms common, familiar, ordinary; customary, usual, wonted
antonyms natural, normal, regular, standard, typical

deviant *n* a person who does not conform to generally accepted standards or customs ⟨branded as social *deviants* by a society that did not value self-expression⟩ — see NONCONFORMIST 1

deviate *vb* to change one's course or direction ⟨sailors forced to *deviate* from their course in order to avoid the storm⟩ — see TURN 3

device *n* **1** a clever often underhanded means to achieve an end ⟨used every *device* and stratagem he knew to prevent their marriage⟩ — see TRICK 1
2 an article intended for use in work ⟨the salesclerk tried to sell me a new *device* for grooming cats⟩ — see IMPLEMENT
3 devices *pl* a habitual attraction to some activity or thing ⟨left to her own *devices* she'd eat at a fast-food restaurant every night of the week⟩ — see INCLINATION 1

devil *n* **1** *cap* the supreme personification of evil often represented as the ruler of Hell ⟨the *Devil* is traditionally seen as a being who relentlessly tempts people to commit evil⟩
synonyms Lucifer, Satan
related words deuce, dickens
phrases Prince of Darkness
2 an evil spirit ⟨acted as if possessed by some *devil*⟩ — see DEMON
3 a member of the human race ⟨that poor *devil* never did achieve his dream⟩ — see HUMAN
4 an appealingly mischievous person ⟨why, you little *devil*!⟩ — see SCAMP 1
5 a mean, evil, or unprincipled person ⟨he's a *devil* to everyone he does business with⟩ — see VILLAIN

devilfish *n* any of several extremely large rays ⟨they saw a *devilfish* when they went scuba diving in the Caribbean, but it swam away quickly⟩
synonyms devil ray, manta, manta ray, sea devil
related words ray, skate

devilish *adj* **1** going beyond a normal or acceptable limit in degree or amount ⟨that's a *devilish* amount of bad luck for any person to have to endure⟩ — see EXCESSIVE
2 of, relating to, or worthy of an evil spirit ⟨a *devilish* plan to sabotage the other party's political convention⟩ — see FIENDISH
3 tending to or exhibiting reckless playfulness ⟨a *devilish* grin that told us he was up to something⟩ — see MISCHIEVOUS 1

devilishly *adv* beyond a normal or acceptable limit ⟨a *devilishly* clever scheme to make money⟩ — see TOO 1

devilishness *n* playful, reckless behavior that is not intended to cause serious harm ⟨the children always concoct some sort of *devilishness* on Halloween⟩ — see MISCHIEF 1

devil–may–care *adj* **1** having a relaxed, casual manner ⟨a *devil-may-care* golfer who knows that it's only a game⟩ — see EASYGOING 1
2 having or showing a lack of concern or seriousness ⟨a *devil-may-care* outlook on life⟩ — see CAREFREE
3 having or showing a lack of concern for the consequences of one's actions ⟨the *devil-may-care* speed with which he drives his sports car is going to cause a lot of grief someday⟩ — see RECKLESS 1

devilment *n* playful, reckless behavior that is not intended to cause serious harm ⟨his *devilment* at school remains the stuff of local legend⟩ — see MISCHIEF 1

devil ray *n* any of several extremely large rays ⟨you can recognize a *devil ray* by its flat body and long thin tail⟩ — see DEVILFISH

devilry *or* **deviltry** *n* playful, reckless behavior that is not intended to cause serious harm ⟨children always getting into some *devilry*⟩ — see MISCHIEF 1

devious *adj* 1 clever at attaining one's ends by indirect and often deceptive means ⟨we always left it to our most *devious* friends to find out the latest information⟩ — see ARTFUL 1
2 marked by a long series of irregular curves ⟨a *devious* trail through the swampland⟩ — see CROOKED 1

deviousness *n* skill in achieving one's ends through indirect, subtle, or underhanded means ⟨his *deviousness* was almost as awesome as his lack of scruples⟩ — see CUNNING 1

devise *vb* to create or think of by clever use of the imagination ⟨she quickly *devised* a new scheme when the first one failed⟩ — see INVENT

deviser *n* one who creates or introduces something new ⟨Melvil Dewey was the *deviser* of a new system for organizing books⟩ — see INVENTOR

devoid *adj* 1 utterly lacking in something needed, wanted, or expected ⟨the so-called comedy is totally *devoid* of intelligence, originality, and even laughs⟩
synonyms bereft, destitute, void
related words bare, barren, blank, empty, lacking, stark, vacant, wanting; deficient, fragmental, fragmentary, incomplete, partial; absent, missing
near antonyms filled, full; furnished, provided, supplied
antonyms replete
2 lacking contents that could or should be present ⟨the picnic jug was completely *devoid* of juice after only a few minutes⟩ — see EMPTY 1

devote *vb* 1 to keep or intend for a special purpose ⟨he *devoted* several hours every weekend to playing with his dog⟩
synonyms allocate, consecrate, dedicate, earmark, reserve, save
related words hallow, sanctify; commit, confide, consign, entrust
phrases set apart, set aside
2 to occupy (oneself) diligently or with close attention ⟨she plans to *devote* herself to the study of foreign languages in college⟩ — see APPLY

devoted *adj* 1 feeling or showing love ⟨a *devoted* couple who enjoy sharing their lives with one another⟩ — see LOVING
2 firm in one's allegiance to someone or something ⟨remembered her most *devoted* servants in her will⟩ — see FAITHFUL 1

devotedness *n* 1 a feeling of strong or constant regard for and dedication to someone ⟨the heartwarming *devotedness* that the newlywed couple felt for each other⟩ — see LOVE 1
2 adherence to something to which one is bound by a pledge or duty ⟨the *devotedness* that only a dog can show for its master⟩ — see FIDELITY

devotee *n* a person with a strong and habitual liking for something ⟨a *devotee* of stamp collecting⟩ — see FAN

devotion *n* 1 a feeling of strong or constant regard for and dedication to someone ⟨Albert Schweitzer was world-renowned for his *devotion* to his fellow man⟩ — see LOVE 1

2 adherence to something to which one is bound by a pledge or duty ⟨the knight's fierce *devotion* to his lord⟩ — see FIDELITY
3 belief and trust in and loyalty to God ⟨a people of deep spirituality and indomitable *devotion*⟩ — see FAITH 1

devotional *adj* of, relating to, or used in the practice or worship services of a religion ⟨a religious bookstore with an extensive stock of *devotional* literature⟩ — see RELIGIOUS 1

devour *vb* to destroy all trace of ⟨a series of devastating storms *devoured* the beach on the south side of the island⟩ — see CONSUME 1

devout *adj* showing a devotion to God and to a life of virtue ⟨*devout* monks living a life of prayer and solitude⟩ — see HOLY 1

devoutness *n* the quality or state of being spiritually pure or virtuous ⟨a figure of such *devoutness* that a campaign for her canonization was begun shortly after her death⟩ — see HOLINESS

dexterity *n* 1 mental skill or quickness ⟨the ambassador showed great *dexterity* in his handling of the touchy situation⟩
synonyms adroitness, cleverness, finesse, sleight
related words ability, prowess, talent; competence, efficiency, expertise, know-how, proficiency; ingeniousness, ingenuity, resourcefulness
near antonyms inadequacy, ineptitude, ineptness; slowness, stupidity
2 ease and grace in physical activity ⟨the juggler needed lots of *dexterity* in order to keep all five balls in the air at the same time⟩
synonyms agility, deftness, nimbleness, sleight, spryness
related words coordination
antonyms awkwardness, clumsiness, gawkiness

dexterous *also* **dextrous** *adj* 1 skillful with the hands ⟨the *dexterous* watchmaker was able to repair the tiny gears and parts in the antique watch⟩
synonyms clever, cunning, deft, handy
related words agile, flexible, graceful, limber, lissome (*also* lissom), lithe, nimble, spry; coordinated; adept, competent, expert, masterful, masterly, proficient, skilled, skillful; double-jointed, loose-jointed
near antonyms awkward, bungling, clumsy, fumbling, gawky; uncoordinated; incompetent, inept, maladroit
antonyms butterfingered, heavy-handed, unhandy
2 accomplished with trained ability ⟨*dexterous* handling of a potentially embarrassing situation⟩ — see SKILLFUL

diabolical *or* **diabolic** *adj* of, relating to, or worthy of an evil spirit ⟨the police quickly mobilized to track down the *diabolical* killer⟩ — see FIENDISH

diadem *n* a decorative band or wreath worn about the head as a symbol of victory or honor ⟨a fairy princess with a crystal *diadem* on her brow⟩ — see CROWN 1

diagnosis *n* a position arrived at after consideration ⟨my *diagnosis* of the situation is that immediate action needs to be taken⟩ — see DECISION 1

diagonal *adj* running in a slanting direction ⟨the *diagonal* design ran up the wall all the way from the lower left to the upper right-hand corner⟩
synonyms canted, inclined, leaning, listing, oblique, pitched, slanted, slantwise, sloped, sloping, tilted, tilting
near antonyms horizontal, vertical; parallel, perpendicular

diagonal *n* the degree to which something rises up from a position level with the horizon ⟨the ramp was set at a low *diagonal* to make it easier for physically challenged patrons⟩ — see SLANT

diagram *n* something that visually explains or decorates a text ⟨the explanation of the process is accompanied by a very useful *diagram*⟩ — see ILLUSTRATION 1

dial *vb* to make a telephone call to ⟨*dialed* the operator and asked for the police⟩ — see CALL 2

dialect *n* the special terms or expressions of a particular group or field ⟨the promotional team for the new computer used a *dialect* full of acronyms that the press found difficult to follow⟩ — see TERMINOLOGY

dialogue *also* **dialog** *n* talking or a talk between two or more people ⟨coworkers having a short *dialogue* about politics before heading back to work⟩ — see CONVERSATION

diametric *or* **diametrical** *adj* being as different as possible ⟨war and peace are *diametric* states⟩ — see OPPOSITE

diatribe *n* a long angry speech or scolding ⟨he was forced to sit through a long *diatribe* after he came home late once too often⟩ — see TIRADE

dice *n* a small cube marked on each side with one to six spots and usually played in pairs in various games ⟨she anxiously rolled the *dice*, hoping to win the jackpot⟩ — see DIE

dice *vb* to cut into small pieces ⟨quickly *diced* some peppers and onions and threw them into the stew⟩ — see CHOP

dicker *vb* to talk over or dispute the terms of a purchase ⟨they *dickered* over the price of the car for a few minutes⟩ — see BARGAIN

dictate *n* a statement of what to do that must be obeyed by those concerned ⟨a *dictate* from on high concerning the company's dress code⟩ — see COMMAND 1

dictate *vb* to give an order ⟨*dictated* that the terms of surrender be negotiated by his senior staff⟩ — see COMMAND 2

dictator *n* a person who uses power or authority in a cruel, unjust, or harmful way ⟨the *dictator* had a stranglehold on the country, keeping its people in poverty and ignorance⟩ — see DESPOT

dictatorial *adj* 1 exercising power or authority without interference by others ⟨a *dictatorial* leader with total control over people's lives⟩ — see ABSOLUTE 1

2 fond of ordering people around ⟨the *dictatorial* manager is highly unpopular among employees⟩ — see BOSSY

3 having or showing a tendency to force one's will on others without any regard to fairness or necessity ⟨even the teachers hated the *dictatorial* attitude of the principal⟩ — see ARBITRARY 1

dictatorship *n* a system of government in which the ruler has unlimited power ⟨a revolution that only ended up replacing one *dictatorship* with another⟩ — see DESPOTISM

diction *n* 1 the clear and accurate pronunciation of words especially in public speaking ⟨the actors had very good *diction*, clearly speaking every single word of the Shakespearean play that they were performing⟩
synonyms articulation, enunciation
related words elocution; speech, wording

2 the way in which something is put into words ⟨our teacher promises to take off points for careless *diction* in the essays⟩ — see WORDING

dictionary *n* a reference book giving information about the meanings, pronunciations, uses, and origins of words listed in alphabetical order ⟨try to develop the habit of going to the *dictionary* whenever you encounter an unfamiliar word⟩
synonyms lexicon, wordbook
related words glossary, thesaurus, vocabulary

die *n* a small cube marked on each side with one to six spots and usually played in pairs in various games ⟨he rolled the *die*, hoping for a six⟩
synonyms bone(s), dice

die *vb* 1 to stop living ⟨the king *died* of old age after ruling for many years⟩
synonyms croak [*slang*], decease, depart, expire, pass (on), pass away, perish, succumb
related words disappear, fade
phrases bite the dust
near antonyms be, exist, subsist; flourish, prosper, thrive
antonyms breathe, live

2 to come to an end ⟨the storm *died* just as the dawn was breaking over the horizon⟩ — see CEASE 1

3 to stop functioning ⟨fortunately, the engine *died* when we were only two blocks away from home⟩ — see FAIL 1

die (down) *vb* to grow less in scope or intensity especially gradually ⟨the fuss gradually *died down* as people found other things with which to concern themselves⟩ — see DECREASE 2

die (for) *vb* to have an earnest wish to own or enjoy ⟨I'd *die for* some ice cream right now⟩ — see DESIRE

differ *vb* 1 to be unlike; to not be the same ⟨my brother and I *differ* in looks⟩
synonyms disagree, vary
related words clash, conflict, jar; distinguish, divide, separate
near antonyms blend, harmonize
antonyms accord, agree, conform, correspond

2 to have a different opinion ⟨after much arguing, we simply have agreed to *differ* about the issue⟩ — see DISAGREE 1

difference *n* 1 the quality or state of being different ⟨there's a great *difference* between claiming to care about the environment and living like you really do⟩
synonyms contrast, disagreement, discrepancy, disparateness, disparity, dissimilarity, distinction, distinctiveness, distinctness, diverseness, diversity, unlikeness
related words deviance, divergence; change, modification, variation; conflict, discord, discordance, dissension, dissent, dissidence, disunity, friction, strife; variability, variance; incompatibility, incongruity, incongruousness; disproportion
near antonyms identicalness, identity; analogy, similitude; accordance, agreement, conformity, congruity, correspondence; equality, equivalence, equivalency; parallelism
antonyms alikeness, community, likeness, resemblance, sameness, similarity

2 variance of opinion on a matter ⟨we must try to settle our *differences* without fighting⟩ — see DISAGREEMENT 1

3 the act, process, or result of making different ⟨it won't make any *difference* which one you choose⟩ — see CHANGE

different *adj* 1 being not of the same kind ⟨apples are *different* from oranges⟩
synonyms disparate, dissimilar, distinct, distinctive, distinguishable, diverse, other, unalike, unlike
related words divers, miscellaneous, several, sundry, variant, varied, various; individual, particular, peculiar, single; unequal; disproportionate

near antonyms identical, selfsame; equal, equivalent, tantamount; akin, analogous, comparable, related; homogeneous, uniform
antonyms alike, indistinguishable, like, parallel, same, similar
2 not the same or shared ⟨my brother and I sleep in *different* rooms when we travel⟩ — see SEPARATE 1
differential *adj* favoring, applying, or being unequal treatment of different classes of people ⟨did away with *differential* pay scales for men and women doing the same work⟩ — see DISCRIMINATORY
differentiate *vb* to understand or point out the difference ⟨it was hard at first to *differentiate* between the two styles of music⟩ — see DISTINGUISH 1
differently *adv* in a different way ⟨we do things *differently* around here⟩ — see OTHERWISE
difficult *adj* **1** requiring considerable physical or mental effort ⟨*difficult* questions on the exam that required analytical thinking⟩ — see HARD 2
2 requiring exceptional skill or caution in performance or handling ⟨it's a *difficult* situation when two of your friends are fighting and you're trying to stay out of it⟩ — see TRICKY
difficulty *n* **1** something that is a cause for suffering or special effort especially in the attainment of a goal ⟨the many *difficulties* that he encountered on the road from poor orphan to head of a major corporation⟩
synonyms adversity, asperity, hardness, hardship, rigor
related words discomfort, inconvenience, nuisance; affliction, trial, tribulation; knock, misfortune, mishap, tragedy; bar, catch, check, clog, crimp, embarrassment, handicap, hindrance, hitch, hurdle, impediment, interference, let, manacle, obstacle, obstruction, rub, shackle, snag, stop, trammel; block, chain, deterrent, encumbrance, fetter, inhibition; hump
near antonyms advantage, break, opportunity
2 something that makes a situation more complicated or difficult ⟨there was a minor *difficulty* when we realized that the store had already closed⟩ — see COMPLICATION 1
diffident *adj* not comfortable around people ⟨for someone who makes a living performing for other people, the actress is remarkably *diffident* in real life⟩ — see SHY 2
diffuse *adj* using or containing more words than necessary to express an idea ⟨a *diffuse* speech that took a great deal of time to make a very small point⟩ — see WORDY
diffuseness *n* the use of too many words to express an idea ⟨I was bored by the *diffuseness* of the Victorian novel I was trying to read⟩ — see VERBIAGE
dig *n* **1** a quick thrust ⟨gave him a *dig* in the ribs with my elbow⟩ — see ¹POKE
2 an act or expression showing scorn and usually intended to hurt another's feelings ⟨got in a couple of *digs* about lawyers at my friend's expense⟩ — see INSULT
dig *vb* **1** to hollow out or form (something) by removing earth ⟨a backhoe *dug* a hole in the backyard to make a swimming pool⟩
synonyms excavate, shovel
related words dredge; burrow, claw, grub; dig in; scoop, spade; delve; mine, quarry
near antonyms fill (in); smooth (out *or* over)
2 to take pleasure in ⟨I really *dig* the CD I just bought⟩ — see ENJOY 1

3 *slang* to recognize the meaning of ⟨can you *dig* what I'm saying?⟩ — see COMPREHEND 1
dig (into) *vb* to search through or into ⟨we *dug into* the old records in search of information about the abandoned house⟩ — see EXPLORE 1
dig (through) *vb* to look through (as a place) carefully or thoroughly in an effort to find or discover something ⟨I roughly *dug through* the closet looking for my shoes⟩ — see SEARCH 1
dig (up) *vb* to come upon after searching, study, or effort ⟨she tried to *dig up* any information she could for the report on sharks⟩ — see FIND 1
digest *n* **1** a short statement of the main points ⟨a *digest* of yesterday's meeting⟩ — see SUMMARY
2 a shortened version of a written work ⟨on the ballot there will be a *digest* of the proposed law that is be submitted for voter approval⟩ — see ABRIDGMENT
digest *vb* to make into a short statement of the main points (as of a report) ⟨I *digested* the results of my experiments into a few pages⟩ — see SUMMARIZE
diggings *n pl* the place where one lives ⟨he hasn't been seen around these *diggings* lately⟩ — see HOME 1
digit *n* a character used to represent a mathematical value ⟨you only need to fill in the last two *digits* of the year in which you were born⟩ — see NUMBER
dignified *adj* having or showing a serious and reserved manner ⟨the chief justice of the U.S. Supreme Court is always very *dignified* when swearing in the new president⟩ ⟨*dignified* funeral services for the fallen firemen⟩
synonyms august, imposing, solemn, staid, stately
related words decorous, formal, proper, seemly; grim, sober, somber (*or* sombre); aristocratic, lordly, majestic, noble
near antonyms coarse, crass, crude, improper, indecent, uncouth, unseemly, vulgar
antonyms flighty, frivolous, giddy, goofy, silly, undignified
dignify *vb* to enhance the status of ⟨our graduation ceremony was *dignified* by a visit from the mayor⟩ — see EXALT
dignity *n* high position within society ⟨the archbishop is very conscious of his *dignity*⟩ — see RANK 2
digression *n* a departure from the subject under consideration ⟨the teacher's *digression* took up half of the allotted class time⟩ — see TANGENT
digressive *adj* passing from one topic to another ⟨a *digressive* lecture on current events around the world⟩ — see DISCURSIVE
dike *n* **1** a bank of earth constructed to control water ⟨the story about the little boy who plugged a hole in the *dike* with his finger⟩ — see DAM
2 a long narrow channel dug in the earth ⟨water flowed along the *dike* to the small pond⟩ — see DITCH
dilapidated *adj* showing signs of advanced wear and tear and neglect ⟨a *dilapidated* car that had seen better days⟩ — see SHABBY 1
dilapidation *n* the state of being unattended to or not cared for ⟨the *dilapidation* of the abandoned movie theater was almost beyond repair⟩ — see NEGLECT 1
dilatory *adj* moving or proceeding at less than the normal, desirable, or required speed ⟨he was *dilatory* in delivering the message⟩ — see SLOW 1
dilemma *n* a situation in which one has to choose between two or more equally unsatisfactory choices ⟨they were faced with a *dilemma*: either they could spend the night out in the cold or they could walk back into their house and face their father⟩

synonyms quandary
related words deadlock, halt, impasse, quagmire, stalemate, standoff; knot, problem; difficulty, fix, hole, jam, pickle, pinch, plight, predicament, spot
near antonyms breeze, cinch, duck soup, snap

dilettante *adj* lacking or showing a lack of expert skill ⟨many *dilettante* efforts to be seen at the sidewalk art show⟩ — see AMATEURISH

dilettante *n* **1** a person having a knowledgeable and fine appreciation of the arts ⟨she writes about art not from the point of view of an artist but from that of a committed *dilettante*⟩ — see CONNOISSEUR
2 a person who regularly or occasionally engages in an activity without being or becoming an expert at it ⟨a *dilettante* at heart, she was never willing to commit the time and effort that ballet demands⟩ — see AMATEUR

diligence *n* attentive and persistent effort ⟨through the *diligence* and ingenuity of a single detective, the gang's ringleader was finally caught⟩
synonyms assiduity, assiduousness, industriousness, industry
related words application, concentration; doggedness, perseverance, persistence, tenacity, tirelessness
near antonyms carelessness; idleness, indolence, laziness

diligent *adj* involved in often constant activity ⟨a student who has been unceasingly *diligent* in pursuit of a degree in mathematics⟩ — see BUSY 1

diligently *adv* with great effort or determination ⟨working *diligently* to finish his science project on time⟩ — see HARD 1

dillydally *vb* **1** to move or act slowly ⟨don't *dillydally* on the way to the store⟩ — see DELAY 1
2 to spend time doing nothing ⟨restaurant employees who, during the slow periods, would rather be doing something instead of just *dillydallying*⟩ — see IDLE

dillydallying *adj* moving or proceeding at less than the normal, desirable, or required speed ⟨the *dillydallying* congress hadn't passed any legislation, and the term was almost over⟩ — see SLOW 1

dilute *adj* **1** not containing very much of some important element ⟨a *dilute* acid that was safe to handle in the classroom⟩ — see WEAK 3
2 containing foreign or lower-grade substances ⟨a *dilute* solution of ammonia⟩ — see IMPURE

dilute *vb* to alter (something) for the worse with the addition of foreign or lower-grade substances ⟨the pharmacist was convicted of *diluting* prescription drugs in order to increase profits⟩ — see ADULTERATE

diluted *adj* **1** not containing very much of some important element ⟨a glass of *diluted* wine for the children on special occasions only⟩ — see WEAK 3
2 containing foreign or lower-grade substances ⟨a *diluted* solution of sulfuric acid⟩ — see IMPURE

dim *adj* **1** being without light or without much light ⟨a *dim* room in the basement that is very depressing⟩ — see DARK 1
2 lacking a surface luster or gloss ⟨*dim* colors that were all wrong for a room that will be a nursery⟩ — see MATTE
3 not seen or understood clearly ⟨have only a *dim* knowledge of the subject⟩ — see FAINT 1

dim *vb* to make dark, dim, or indistinct ⟨the storm clouds *dimmed* our view of the city from the airplane⟩ — see CLOUD 1

dimension *n* **1** the total amount of measurable space or surface occupied by something ⟨the mansion is great in *dimension* but not in splendor⟩ — see ¹SIZE

2 dimensions *pl* an area over which activity, capacity, or influence extends ⟨the vast *dimensions* of the subject will require years of study⟩ — see RANGE 2

diminish *vb* **1** to express scornfully one's low opinion of ⟨tends to *diminish* any rival's accomplishments with snide remarks⟩ — see DECRY 1
2 to make smaller in amount, volume, or extent ⟨they vowed that their friendship would never be *diminished* by time⟩ — see DECREASE 1
3 to grow less in scope or intensity especially gradually ⟨the sound of the train *diminished* as our distance from it increased⟩ — see DECREASE 2

diminishment *n* **1** the act of making a person or a thing seem little or unimportant ⟨she resented the *diminishment* of her achievements by the theater critics⟩ — see DEPRECIATION
2 the amount by which something is lessened ⟨there was a sharp *diminishment* in our checking account after Christmas shopping season⟩ — see DECREASE

diminution *n* the amount by which something is lessened ⟨a *diminution* of 60 percent over the course of the month⟩ — see DECREASE

diminutive *adj* of a size that is less than average ⟨a single *diminutive* shrub on the edge of the lawn⟩ — see SMALL 1

diminutive *n* a living thing much smaller than others of its kind ⟨if we get a horse, it's going to have to be a *diminutive*, such as a Shetland pony⟩ — see DWARF 1

diminutiveness *n* the quality or state of being little in size ⟨the *diminutiveness* of jockeys prompts some people to make them the butt of jokes⟩ — see SMALLNESS

dimmed *adj* being without light or without much light ⟨a *dimmed* lounge where students like to rest and sleep⟩ — see DARK 1

din *n* loud, confused, and usually unharmonious sound ⟨there's always a great *din* from the cafeteria during lunch⟩ — see NOISE 1

din *vb* to say or state again ⟨lessons *dinned* into us over and over⟩ — see REPEAT 1

dine *vb* **1** to take a meal ⟨they *dined* elegantly at the city's finest restaurant before taking in an opera downtown⟩
synonyms eat, fare, feed
related words banquet, feast, fete (*or* fête); board, mess; breakfast, lunch, sup; picnic
2 to entertain with a fancy meal ⟨the advertising agency lavishly wines and *dines* prospective clients⟩ — see FEAST

diner *n* a public establishment where meals are served to paying customers for consumption on the premises ⟨we'll just grab a quick hamburger at the local *diner*⟩ — see RESTAURANT

dinghy *n* a boat equipped with one or more sails ⟨we went sailing on the calm lake in a little two-person *dinghy*⟩ — see SAILBOAT

dinginess *n* the state or quality of being dirty ⟨she was appalled by the *dinginess* of the old curtains and took them all down to be cleaned⟩ — see DIRTINESS 1

dingy *adj* not clean ⟨the bed sheets were pretty *dingy* so we threw them in the laundry pile⟩ — see DIRTY 1

dinky *adj* of a size that is less than average ⟨a *dinky* computer that's not good for very much⟩ — see SMALL 1

dinner *n* a large fancy meal often accompanied by ceremony or entertainment ⟨there will be a celebratory *dinner* at a local restaurant for the entire team⟩ — see FEAST

dinnerware *n* dishes used for eating or serving food or drink ⟨he told his kids to help set the *dinnerware* out on the table while he made the food⟩ — see TABLE-WARE 2

dinning *adj* making loud, confused, and usually unharmonious sounds ⟨*dinning* honks and beeps arose from cars stuck in the massive traffic jam⟩ — see NOISY 1

dint *n* a sunken area forming a separate space ⟨left a small *dint* in the car's fender⟩ — see HOLE 2

dip *n* the act or process of going to a lower level or altitude ⟨the city's population has take a slight *dip* since the last census⟩ — see DESCENT 1

dip *vb* 1 to sink or push (something) briefly into or as if into a liquid ⟨he went to *dip* a paper towel in water and clean off the window⟩ ⟨she *dipped* a hand into her pocket and pulled out a piece of candy⟩
synonyms douse, duck, dunk, immerse, souse, submerge, submerse
related words drench, flood, soak, wet; plunge, thrust
2 to lift out with something that holds liquid ⟨they *dipped* water from the bucket to pour into the kettle⟩
synonyms lade, ladle, scoop, spoon
related words bail; deplete, drain, eliminate, exhaust; bleed, draw (off); dish; draw, siphon
near antonyms pour; fill
3 to go to a lower level ⟨the temperature *dipped* a bit in the evening⟩ — see DROP 2
4 to lead or extend downward ⟨slow down, the road *dips* here⟩ — see DESCEND 1
5 to take a quick or hasty look ⟨I *dipped* into the book, but I didn't have a chance to study it thoroughly⟩ — see GLANCE 2

diplomacy *n* the ability to deal with others in touchy situations without offending them ⟨that candidate is thought to lack the *diplomacy* necessary in dealing with people of power and influence⟩ — see TACT

diplomatic *adj* having or showing tact ⟨a *diplomatic* attempt at preventing any hurt feelings⟩ — see TACTFUL

dipper *n* a utensil with a bowl and a handle that is used especially in cooking and serving food ⟨she accidentally left the metal *dipper* in the stew pot, and it quickly grew too hot to touch⟩ — see SPOON

dire *adj* 1 being or showing a sign of evil or calamity to come ⟨a *dire* forecast of a plunge in stock prices⟩ — see OMINOUS
2 causing fear ⟨a series of *dire* tremors that hinted at a huge volcanic eruption⟩ — see FEARFUL
3 needing immediate attention ⟨a *dire* need for food and medicine in the famine-stricken country⟩ — see ACUTE 2

direct *adj* 1 done or working without something else coming in between ⟨a zoologist whose works are based entirely on her *direct* observation of animals in the wild⟩ ⟨the virus was the *direct* cause of the disease⟩
synonyms firsthand, immediate, primary
related words clinical
antonyms indirect, secondhand
2 free in expressing one's true feelings and opinions ⟨our coach is very *direct*, never hesitating for a moment to tell a player he isn't performing well⟩ — see FRANK
3 going straight to the point clearly and firmly ⟨clear and *direct* instructions that left no room for misinterpretation⟩ — see STRAIGHTFORWARD 1

direct *adv* in a direct line or course ⟨flew *direct* to the coast⟩ — see DIRECTLY 1

direct *vb* 1 to cause to move to a central point or along a restricted pathway ⟨the aqueduct *directed* the water into an artificial lake⟩ — see CHANNEL

2 to issue orders to (someone) by right of authority ⟨our teacher *directed* us to wait in front of the building until she got there⟩ — see COMMAND 1
3 to give an order ⟨she *directed* that all of the windows had to be closed before we left⟩ — see COMMAND 2
4 to look after and make decisions about ⟨the music teacher *directs* both the student orchestra and the marching band⟩ — see CONDUCT 1
5 to point or turn (something) toward a target or goal ⟨we *directed* our attention toward the noise coming from the rear⟩ — see AIM 1
6 to point out the way for (someone) especially from a position in front ⟨the guide *directed* the tour through the museum with commendable efficiency and expertise⟩ — see LEAD 1

direction *n* 1 a statement of what to do that must be obeyed by those concerned ⟨we were given very specific *directions* for the first part of the exam⟩ — see COMMAND 1
2 the act or activity of looking after and making decisions about something ⟨working under the close *direction* of the engineering supervisor⟩ — see CONDUCT 1

directive *n* 1 a statement of what to do that must be obeyed by those concerned ⟨the company president regularly issues *directives* intended for all staff members⟩ — see COMMAND 1
2 an order publicly issued by an authority ⟨a *directive* issued by the archbishop that is to be read during Sunday services at every parish⟩ — see EDICT 1
3 a written communication giving information or directions ⟨a growing stack of unread *directives* from the company vice president⟩ — see MEMORANDUM 1

directly *adv* 1 in a direct line or course ⟨we went *directly* to the school without stopping⟩
synonyms dead, direct, due, plumb, plump, right, straight
phrases as the crow flies
near antonyms circuitously, deviously
antonyms indirectly
2 in an honest and direct manner ⟨she deals with her art students *directly*, always telling them the plain truth⟩ — see STRAIGHTFORWARD
3 in the same words ⟨quoted *directly* from the encyclopedia⟩ — see VERBATIM
4 without delay ⟨in case of a medical emergency, do not try to contact your doctor but instead go *directly* to the hospital⟩ — see IMMEDIATELY

directness *n* the free expression of one's true feelings and opinions ⟨his *directness* is much appreciated by his patients⟩ — see CANDOR

director *n* a person who manages or directs ⟨the new *director* of the company plans to make a number of changes in daily operations⟩ — see EXECUTIVE

directorial *adj* suited for or relating to the directing of things ⟨an applicant with a number of *directorial* positions on his résumé⟩ — see EXECUTIVE

direful *adj* causing fear ⟨the *direful* howling of the wolves during the night⟩ — see FEARFUL 1

dirge *n* a composition expressing one's grief over a loss ⟨sang a heartrending *dirge* at the funeral⟩ — see LAMENT 2

dirt *n* 1 the loose surface material in which plants naturally grow ⟨dig into the *dirt* to a depth of about three inches⟩
synonyms earth, ground, soil
related words clay, duff, dust, gravel, humus, loam, loess, marl, mud, sand, silt, subsoil, topsoil

2 the solid part of our planet's surface as distinguished from the sea and air ⟨at the first sound of gunfire we hit the *dirt*⟩ — see EARTH 2

3 foul matter that mars the purity or cleanliness of something ⟨there's some *dirt* on your shoes⟩ — see FILTH 1

4 the quality or state of being obscene ⟨appalled by the *dirt* in the author's novels⟩ — see OBSCENITY 1

dirtiness *n* **1** the state or quality of being dirty ⟨when the maid arrived, she exclaimed over the *dirtiness* of the china⟩
synonyms dinginess, dustiness, filthiness, foulness, griminess, grubbiness, nastiness, squalidness, uncleanliness, uncleanness
related words impurity; messiness, sloppiness, untidiness; shabbiness; squalor; smuttiness, sootiness
near antonyms purity
antonyms cleanliness, immaculateness, spotlessness

2 the quality or state of being obscene ⟨the *dirtiness* of the film demanded an adult rating⟩ — see OBSCENITY 1

dirty *adj* **1** not clean ⟨after playing in the mud all day, his clothes were very *dirty*⟩
synonyms besmirched, blackened, dingy, dusty, filthy, foul, grimy, grubby, grungy, mucky, muddy, nasty, smutty, soiled, sordid, stained, sullied, unclean, uncleanly
related words contaminated, defiled, impure, polluted, tainted; uncleaned, unsanitary, unsterile, unsterilized, unwashed; discolored; bedraggled, draggled; chaotic, cluttered, confused, disarranged, disarrayed, disheveled (*or* dishevelled), disordered, jumbled, littered, messed, messy, muddled, mussed, mussy, rumpled, scruffy, sloppy, slovenly, unkempt, untidy; shabby, sleazy, squalid, smoky (*also* smokey), sooty
near antonyms clear, limpid, pure; cleaned, cleansed, combed, groomed, neat, ordered, orderly, tidy; bleached, purified, whitened; bright, flawless, perfect, shiny, sparkling, unspotted, untouched; taintless, unblemished, undefiled, unpolluted, untainted, wholesome
antonyms clean, cleanly, immaculate, spick-and-span (*or* spic-and-span), spotless, stainless, unsoiled, unstained, unsullied

2 depicting or referring to sexual matters in a way that is unacceptable in polite society ⟨some radio stations refused to play the song because of the *dirty* lyrics⟩ — see OBSCENE 1

3 marked by wet and windy conditions ⟨a forecast of *dirty* weather along the coast⟩ — see FOUL 1

4 not being in accordance with the rules or standards of what is fair in sport ⟨the school is known for the *dirty* football it plays⟩ — see FOUL 2

5 not following or in accordance with standards of honor and decency ⟨accused the other campaign of playing *dirty* tricks⟩ — see IGNOBLE 2

dirty *vb* to make dirty ⟨she *dirtied* her new shoes when she splashed in the puddle⟩
synonyms befoul, begrime, besmirch, blacken, foul, grime, mire, muddy, smirch, smudge, soil, stain, sully
related words contaminate, defile, pollute, taint; discolor; confuse, disarrange, disarray, dishevel, disorder, jumble, mess, muddle
near antonyms decontaminate, purge, purify; disinfect, sanitize; brush, dry-clean, dust, launder, mop, rinse, scour, scrub, sweep, wash, wipe; brighten, deodorize, freshen, renew, spruce (up); straighten (up), tidy (up)

antonyms clean, cleanse

dis *vb, slang* **1** to cause hurt feelings or deep resentment in ⟨are you *dissing* me?⟩ — see INSULT

2 to express one's unfavorable opinion of the worth or quality of ⟨never *dis* a person's style of clothing in front of her friends⟩ — see CRITICIZE

disable *vb* **1** to cause severe or permanent injury to ⟨a promising athlete who was *disabled* in a plane crash⟩ — see MAIM

2 to render powerless, ineffective, or unable to move ⟨*disabled* the controls for unauthorized users⟩ — see PARALYZE

disabled *adj* deprived of the power to perform one or more natural bodily activities ⟨the *disabled* man was unable to climb the stairs without help⟩
synonyms challenged, incapacitated
related words blind, deaf, mute; halt, lame, paralyzed, quadriplegic; immobile, immobilized; ailing, diseased, ill, sick, unfit, unhealthy, unsound, unwell
near antonyms bouncing, chipper, fit, hale, healthy, hearty, robust, sound, well, whole, wholesome
antonyms able-bodied, nondisabled

disabuse *vb* to free from mistaken beliefs or foolish hopes ⟨let me *disabuse* you of your foolish notions about married life⟩ — see DISILLUSION

disadvantage *n* a feature of someone or something that creates difficulty for achieving success ⟨their lack of height was a *disadvantage* on the basketball court⟩
synonyms drawback, handicap, liability, minus, penalty, strike
related words stranglehold; detriment, disability, impairment; failing, shortcoming; bar, catch, check, clog, crimp, embarrassment, hindrance, hitch, hurdle, impediment, interference, let, manacle, obstacle, obstruction, rub, shackle, stop, trammel
near antonyms vantage; head start, jump, lead, margin, start; ascendancy, better, command, control, drop, mastery, predominance, superiority, supremacy, transcendence, upper hand; prerogative, privilege; break, opportunity; aid, assistance, help
antonyms advantage, asset, edge, plus

disadvantaged *adj* kept from having the necessities of life or a healthful environment ⟨*disadvantaged* families struggling to get by in the inner city⟩ — see DEPRIVED

disadvantageous *adj* opposed to one's interests ⟨such an arrangement with the wholesalers would be *disadvantageous* for small farmers⟩ — see ADVERSE 1

disaffect *vb* **1** to cause to change from friendly or loving to unfriendly or uncaring ⟨a *disaffected* boyfriend was responsible for the vandalism to her home⟩ — see ESTRANGE

2 to make discontented ⟨the troops were *disaffected* by the extension of their tours of duty⟩ — see DISCONTENT

disaffection *n* the loss of friendship or affection ⟨widespread *disaffection* with the governor's administration⟩ — see ESTRANGEMENT

disagree *vb* **1** to have a different opinion ⟨she thought we were still headed north on the trail, but I *disagreed*⟩
synonyms differ, dissent
related words clash, collide, conflict, contrast; counter, debate, object, oppose, protest, resist; contest, dispute; argue, bicker, fall out, quarrel
near antonyms accede, accept, acquiesce, comply, consent, subscribe; affiliate, ally, associate, collaborate, collude, compromise, cooperate, get along, side
antonyms agree, assent, concur

2 to be unlike; to not be the same ⟨the two versions of the legend *disagree* in several ways⟩ — see DIFFER 1

disagree (with) *vb* to make an assertion that is contrary to one made by (another) ⟨she *disagreed with* me when I said that the jacket was dark blue⟩ — see CONTRADICT 1

disagreeable *adj* **1** having or showing a habitually bad temper ⟨a *disagreeable* old grouch with no friends⟩ — see ILL-TEMPERED

2 not giving pleasure to the mind or senses ⟨a *disagreeable* smell coming from the closet⟩ — see UNPLEASANT

disagreeing *adj* not being in agreement or harmony ⟨the teenagers' *disagreeing* accounts of what happened that night make me wonder if either is telling the truth⟩ — see INCONSISTENT

disagreement *n* **1** variance of opinion on a matter ⟨there was some *disagreement* about what the color of the missing sweater actually was⟩
synonyms controversy, debate, difference, disputation, dispute, dissension
related words clash, collision, conflict, contention, discord, strife; discussion; altercation, argument, bicker, falling-out, fight, quarrel
near antonyms acceptance, compliance; concord, peace
antonyms accord, agreement, consensus, harmony, unanimity

2 an often noisy or angry expression of differing opinions ⟨a loud *disagreement* started as soon as we tried to order pizza for everyone⟩ — see ARGUMENT 1

3 the quality or state of being different ⟨there is some *disagreement* between the Gospels on the sequence of events⟩ — see DIFFERENCE 1

disallow *vb* **1** to declare not to be true ⟨*disallowing* the philosophical concept of free will⟩ — see DENY 1

2 to be unwilling to grant ⟨*disallowed* the defendant's request for a new trial⟩ — see DENY 2

disallowance *n* **1** an unwillingness to grant something asked for ⟨the taxpayer was notified of the *disallowance* of his claim for medical expenses⟩ — see DENIAL 1

2 a refusal to confirm the truth of a statement ⟨a categorical *disallowance* of all charges⟩ — see DENIAL 2

disappear *vb* to cease to be visible ⟨the stranger *disappeared* into the mists, never to be seen again⟩
synonyms dissolve, evanesce, evaporate, fade, flee, go (away), melt, vanish
related words clear, dissipate
near antonyms arrive, break out, come out, emerge, issue, loom, show up
antonyms appear, materialize

disappoint *vb* to fall short in satisfying the expectation or hope of ⟨they were *disappointed* by the outcome of the big game⟩
synonyms cheat, dissatisfy, fail, let down
related words discontent, disgruntle, displease; disenchant, disillusion
near antonyms gladden
antonyms satisfy

disappointment *n* **1** the emotion felt when one's expectations are not met ⟨we felt *disappointment* after failing a test that we thought would be easy⟩
synonyms dismay, dissatisfaction, frustration, letdown
related words disenchantment, disillusionment; blues, dejection, depression, desolateness, desolation, despondency, disconsolateness, distress, doldrums, dolefulness, dolor, downheartedness, dreariness, dumps, gloom, gloominess, joylessness, melancholy, mopes,

oppression, sadness, sorrow, unhappiness; alarm, concern, consternation; chagrin, discomfiture
near antonyms bliss, felicity, gladness, happiness, joy
antonyms contentment, gratification, satisfaction

2 something that disappoints ⟨after all the publicity and high expectations, the sequel to the movie blockbuster was a *disappointment*⟩
synonyms bummer, letdown
related words anticlimax, failure, fiasco, fizzle; lemon, loser
near antonyms success, winner; relief

disapprobation *n* refusal to accept as right or desirable ⟨there was widespread *disapprobation* of their marriage in that narrow-minded community⟩ — see DISAPPROVAL

disapproval *n* refusal to accept as right or desirable ⟨thus far, every one of her boyfriends has met with her parents' *disapproval*⟩
synonyms deprecation, disapprobation, disfavor, dislike, displeasure
related words blame, censure, criticism, condemnation, denunciation, dressing down, opprobrium, reproach, reprobation; antagonism, antipathy, hostility; belittlement, disparagement, opposition
near antonyms acclaim, commendation, praise; endorsement, sanction; empathy, sympathy
antonyms approbation, approval, favor

disapprove *vb* to show unwillingness to accept, do, engage in, or agree to ⟨*disapproved* the first set of blueprints submitted by the firm⟩ — see DECLINE 1

disapprove (of) *vb* to hold an unfavorable opinion of ⟨my sister *disapproves of* smoking and refuses to date anyone who thinks it's cool⟩
synonyms deprecate, discountenance, disfavor, dislike, frown (on), reprove
related words blame, censure, condemn, criticize, denounce, reprehend, reprobate; chide, rebuke, reproach, scold
near antonyms endorse (*also* indorse), sanction, support; adore, delight (in), dig, enjoy, fancy, groove (on), love, relish, revel (in)
antonyms approve, favor, like

disarm *vb* **1** to reduce the size and strength of the armed forces of ⟨the defeated nation was *disarmed* so that it would never again be a threat to international order⟩
synonyms demilitarize
related words demobilize
near antonyms equip, mobilize
antonyms arm, militarize

2 to lessen the anger or agitation of ⟨her future father-in-law was *disarmed* by her easy charm⟩ — see PACIFY

disarmament *n* the reduction or elimination of a country's armed forces or weapons ⟨the ambassador spoke at length about the possible unilateral *disarmament* of his country⟩
synonyms demilitarization
related words demobilization
near antonyms mobilization
antonyms militarization

disarming *adj* **1** having qualities that tend to make one loved ⟨a thoroughly *disarming* little rascal who can talk his way out of any trouble⟩ — see LOVABLE

2 likely to win one's affection ⟨there's a *disarming* lack of pretension about the girl⟩ — see INGRATIATING

3 tending to lessen or avoid conflict or hostility ⟨the secretary's *disarming* smile made me forget why I was angry⟩ — see PACIFIC 1

disarrange *vb* to undo the proper order or arrangement of 〈the wind had hopelessly *disarranged* my hair〉 — see DISORDER

disarranged *adj* lacking in order, neatness, and often cleanliness 〈a *disarranged* collection of sports memorabilia scattered about the room〉 — see MESSY

disarrangement *n* a state in which everything is out of order 〈the *disarrangement* of the files makes it almost impossible to find anything〉 — see CHAOS

disarray *n* a state in which everything is out of order 〈the boys' bedroom was in its usual *disarray*〉 — see CHAOS

disarray *vb* to undo the proper order or arrangement of 〈he had accidentally *disarrayed* his brother's CDs, leaving a telltale sign of borrowing without permission〉 — see DISORDER

disarrayed *adj* lacking in order, neatness, and often cleanliness 〈a *disarrayed* pile of rugs in the attic〉 — see MESSY

disassemble *vb* to take apart 〈they had to *disassemble* the television set in order to replace the wiring〉
synonyms demount, dismantle, dismember, knock down, strike, take down
related words detach, disengage; disconnect, disjoin, disunite, divide, separate
near antonyms build, erect; combine, unite
antonyms assemble, construct, put together

disaster *n* a sudden violent event that brings about great loss or destruction 〈hurricanes are natural *disasters*〉
synonyms calamity, cataclysm, catastrophe, debacle (*also* débâcle), tragedy
related words collapse, crash, meltdown; convulsion, paroxysm, upheaval; accident, casualty, fatality; misadventure, mischance, misfortune, mishap, woe; bummer, downer
near antonyms godsend, manna, windfall

disastrous *adj* **1** bringing about ruin or misfortune 〈a split-second, *disastrous* decision that I would forever regret〉 — see FATAL 1
2 causing or tending to cause destruction 〈a *disastrous* fire from which the town never fully recovered〉 — see DESTRUCTIVE 1

disavow *vb* **1** to declare not to be true 〈*disavowed* her testimony earlier in the trial〉 — see DENY 1
2 to refuse to acknowledge as one's own or as one's responsibility 〈the government will *disavow* any knowledge of your mission〉 — see DISCLAIM 1

disavowal *n* a refusal to confirm the truth of a statement 〈the official's *disavowal* of the rumor put our minds at rest〉 — see DENIAL 2

disband *vb* **1** to cease to exist or cause to cease to exist as a group or organization 〈they *disbanded* the committee after the report had been submitted〉 〈the rock group *disbanded* upon finishing the tour〉
synonyms break up, disperse, dissolve
near antonyms incorporate; consolidate
antonyms band, join, unite
2 to cause (members of a group) to move widely apart 〈police *disbanded* the rioters with tear gas〉 — see SCATTER 1

disbandment *n* an act or process in which something scatters or is scattered 〈the *disbandment* of the crowd at the end of the outdoor rock concert〉 — see SCATTERING 1

disbelief *n* refusal to accept as true 〈their story explaining their absence was met with frank *disbelief*〉
synonyms incredulity, unbelief
related words distrust, doubt, mistrust, skepticism, suspicion, uncertainty; denial, rejection, repudiation
near antonyms acceptance, faith; trust
antonyms belief, credence, credit

disbelieve *vb* to think not to be true or real 〈many *disbelieved* the medium's claims that she could communicate with the spirits of the dead〉
synonyms discredit, negate
related words deny, reject, repudiate; distrust, doubt, mistrust, suspect; debunk, disprove; deride, pooh-pooh, scoff (at)
near antonyms trust
antonyms accept, believe, credit, swallow

disbeliever *n* a person who is always ready to doubt or question the truth or existence of something 〈the usual *disbelievers* refused to accept the president's claim that he was acting only in the public interest〉 — see SKEPTIC

disbelieving *adj* inclined to doubt or question claims 〈the senator stated her case before a *disbelieving* press corps〉 — see SKEPTICAL 1

disburden *vb* **1** to empty or rid of cargo 〈*disburdened* the oil tanker before it could leak any more oil〉 — see UNLOAD 1
2 to set (a person or thing) free of something that encumbers 〈a place where we could *disburden* ourselves of our cares〉 — see RID

disburse *vb* to hand over or use up in payment 〈the foundation *disburses* money to many worthy causes〉 — see SPEND 1

disbursement *n* **1** a payment made in the course of achieving a result 〈*disbursements* for research and development〉 — see EXPENSE
2 the act of offering money in exchange for goods or services 〈the *disbursement* of the foundation's funds to several cancer research centers〉 — see PAYMENT 1

discard *n* something separated from a group or lot for not being as good as the others 〈toss all of your *discards* in the garbage〉 — see CULL

discard *vb* to get rid of as useless or unwanted 〈*discard* an old, torn sweater〉
synonyms cast, ditch, dump, fling (off *or* away), jettison, junk, lose, reject, scrap, shed, shuck (off), slough (*also* sluff), throw away, throw out, unload
related words abandon, desert, forsake; dismiss; abolish, annihilate, eliminate, eradicate, expunge, exterminate, extinguish, extirpate, liquidate, remove, root (out), stamp (out), wipe out
phrases dispose of, set aside
near antonyms adopt, embrace, take on; employ, use, utilize; hold, hold back, keep, retain

discarding *n* the getting rid of whatever is unwanted or useless 〈the *discarding* of all unwanted material〉 — see DISPOSAL 1

discern *vb* **1** to make note of (something) through the use of one's eyes 〈barely able to *discern* the gate through the mist〉 — see SEE 1
2 to understand or point out the difference 〈*discern* between right and wrong〉 — see DISTINGUISH 1

discernible *adj* able to be perceived by a sense or by the mind 〈*discernible* differences in the two authors' writing styles〉 — see PERCEPTIBLE

discerning *adj* having or showing deep understanding and intelligent application of knowledge 〈a *discerning* critic of modern art〉 — see WISE 1

discernment *n* the ability to understand inner qualities or relationships 〈the *discernment* to know when someone is a true friend〉 — see WISDOM 1

discharge *n* **1** a directed propelling of a missile by a firearm or artillery piece ⟨the thunderous *discharge* of the cannons⟩ — see SHOT
2 a freeing from an obligation or responsibility ⟨a full *discharge* from responsibility for the accident⟩ — see RELEASE 1
3 the termination of the employment of an employee or a work force often temporarily ⟨she was resentful over what she felt was a wrongful *discharge*⟩ — see LAYOFF
4 the doing of an action ⟨aided in the *discharge* of his duties by a capable assistant⟩ — see COMMISSION 2
discharge *vb* **1** to cause (a projectile) to be driven forward with force ⟨*discharge* a rocket⟩ — see SHOOT 1
2 to empty or rid of cargo ⟨docks for *discharging* cargo ships⟩ — see UNLOAD 1
3 to give what is owed for ⟨*discharge* a debt in full⟩ — see PAY 2
4 to set free (as from slavery or confinement) ⟨*discharged* the prisoners upon the signing of the peace treaty⟩ — see FREE 1
5 to throw or give off ⟨the mighty river *discharges* its waters into the ocean⟩ — see EMIT 1
6 to cause a weapon to release a missile with great force ⟨felt a strong recoil as the rifle *discharged*⟩ — see SHOOT 2
disciple *n* one who follows the opinions or teachings of another ⟨a circle of *disciples* who wrote down everything the prophet said⟩ — see FOLLOWER
disciplinary *adj* inflicting, involving, or serving as punishment ⟨*disciplinary* actions in response to the outrageous behavior⟩ — see PUNITIVE
discipline *n* **1** a region of activity, knowledge, or influence ⟨you must choose a *discipline* to focus on in college⟩ — see FIELD 2
2 suffering, loss, or hardship imposed in response to a crime or offense ⟨harsh *discipline* imposed to keep order within the ranks⟩ — see PUNISHMENT
discipline *vb* to inflict a penalty on for a fault or crime ⟨the pranksters were severely *disciplined* for their actions⟩ — see PUNISH
disciplining *adj* inflicting, involving, or serving as punishment ⟨*disciplining* actions taken in response to the rowdiness⟩ — see PUNITIVE
disclaim *vb* **1** to refuse to acknowledge as one's own or as one's responsibility ⟨the prisoner *disclaimed* any part in the prank⟩
synonyms disavow, disown, repudiate
related words contradict, deny, disallow, gainsay, negate, negative, refuse, reject; challenge, confute, criticize, disprove, rebut, refute; dispute, question
near antonyms accept, adopt, embrace, espouse; admit, concede, confess, grant; affirm, announce, assert, aver, declare, maintain, profess, submit; authenticate, confirm, corroborate, substantiate, validate, verify
antonyms acknowledge, avow, claim, own, recognize
2 to declare not to be true ⟨*disclaimed* the marriage rumor in the press⟩ — see DENY 1
disclaimer *n* a refusal to confirm the truth of a statement ⟨the intelligence agency's *disclaimer* of any involvement in the assassination plot⟩ — see DENIAL 2
disclose *vb* to make known (as information previously kept secret) ⟨the informer *disclosed* all sorts of details about the secret organization⟩ — see REVEAL 1
disclosure *n* the act or an instance of making known something previously unknown or concealed ⟨he offered full *disclosure* of the government files⟩ — see REVELATION

disco *n* a bar or restaurant offering special nighttime entertainment (as music, dancing, or comedy acts) ⟨that night we went to a downtown *disco* to dance⟩ — see NIGHTCLUB
discomfit *vb* to throw into a state of self-conscious distress ⟨he was *discomfited* by the awkward situation of having his ex-girlfriend meet his current one⟩ — see EMBARRASS 1
discomfiting *adj* causing embarrassment ⟨the *discomfiting* scrutiny of an audience of music critics⟩ — see AWKWARD 3
discomfiture *n* the emotional state of being made self-consciously uncomfortable ⟨blushed and lowered her eyes in evident *discomfiture*⟩ — see EMBARRASSMENT 1
discomfort *vb* to trouble the mind of; to make uneasy ⟨the harsh criticism of his talent did not *discomfort* him in the least⟩ — see DISTURB 1
discomforting *adj* **1** causing discomfort ⟨a *discomforting* perch on the thin balcony rail⟩ — see UNCOMFORTABLE 1
2 causing worry or anxiety ⟨a *discomforting* situation for the workers who depend on the factory for a living⟩ — see TROUBLESOME
discommode *vb* to cause discomfort to or trouble for ⟨the breakdown of her car didn't *discommode* her seriously⟩ — see INCONVENIENCE
discommoding *adj* causing difficulty, discomfort, or annoyance ⟨the thoroughly unpleasant and *discommoding* experience of changing a flat tire in the rain⟩ — see INCONVENIENT 1
discompose *vb* **1** to trouble the mind of; to make uneasy ⟨*discomposed* by the loss of his beloved wife⟩ — see DISTURB 1
2 to undo the proper order or arrangement of ⟨the wind ruffled her hair and *discomposed* her carefully arranged papers⟩ — see DISORDER
discomposing *adj* causing worry or anxiety ⟨a *discomposing* response to our query about her health⟩ — see TROUBLESOME
disconcert *vb* to throw into a state of self-conscious distress ⟨we were *disconcerted* by the unexpected changes to the program⟩ — see EMBARRASS 1
disconcerting *adj* causing embarrassment ⟨a *disconcerting* habit of chewing with his mouth open⟩ — see AWKWARD 3
disconnect *vb* to set or force apart ⟨*disconnected* the two parts of the light fixture⟩ — see SEPARATE 1
disconnected *adj* **1** not clearly or logically connected ⟨a *disconnected* narrative of her time in a mental hospital⟩ — see INCOHERENT 1
2 not physically attached to another unit ⟨a *disconnected* computer terminal⟩ — see SEPARATE 2
disconsolate *adj* feeling unhappiness ⟨she was utterly *disconsolate* when her best friend moved away⟩ — see SAD 1
disconsolateness *n* a state or spell of low spirits ⟨his *disconsolateness* threatened to last forever⟩ — see SADNESS
discontent *adj* having a feeling that one has been wronged or thwarted in one's ambitions ⟨she was *discontent* with her grades and vowed to work harder⟩ — see DISCONTENTED
discontent *n* the condition of being dissatisfied with one's life or situation ⟨the rebels tried to stir up *discontent* among the citizens⟩
synonyms discontentedness, discontentment, disgruntlement, displeasure, dissatisfaction

related words bitterness, resentment; disquiet, perturbation, uneasiness; blues, dejection, depression, desolateness, desolation, despondency, disconsolateness, doldrums, dolefulness, dolor, downheartedness, dreariness, dumps; misery, sadness, sorrow, unhappiness, wretchedness

near antonyms bliss, felicity, gladness, happiness, joy, lightheartedness; elatedness, exultation, jubilation, triumph

antonyms contentedness, contentment, pleasure, satisfaction

discontent *vb* to make discontented ⟨the ongoing lack of decent food *discontented* and demoralized the soldiers in the rebel army⟩

synonyms disaffect, disgruntle, displease, dissatisfy

related words alienate, estrange; agitate, discompose, disquiet, disturb, perturb, upset; annoy, irk, irritate, nettle, peeve; depress, sadden

near antonyms delight, gladden, tickle; calm, soothe, tranquilize (*also* tranquillize)

antonyms content, gratify, please, satisfy

discontented *adj* having a feeling that one has been wronged or thwarted in one's ambitions ⟨he was *discontented* with his small role in the school play⟩

synonyms aggrieved, discontent, disgruntled, displeased, dissatisfied, malcontent

related words disappointed, frustrated, unfulfilled; disquieted, disturbed, perturbed, upset; dejected, depressed, despairing, despondent, disconsolate, doleful, down, downcast, downhearted, forlorn, hangdog, inconsolable, joyless, low-spirited, miserable, mournful, sad, sorrowful, unhappy

near antonyms blissful, delighted, glad, happy, joyful, joyous; elated, exultant, jubilant, triumphant

antonyms content, contented, gratified, pleased, satisfied

discontentedness *n* the condition of being dissatisfied with one's life or situation ⟨he was left with a vague feeling of *discontentedness* after he got the car he had always wanted⟩ — see DISCONTENT

discontentment *n* the condition of being dissatisfied with one's life or situation ⟨*discontentment* with the way the club was being run⟩ — see DISCONTENT

discontinuance *n* the stopping of a process or activity ⟨the possible *discontinuance* of one of the town's big holiday traditions⟩ — see END 1

discontinue *vb* **1** to bring (as an action or operation) to an immediate end ⟨the editors were told to *discontinue* the printing of rumors in the student paper immediately⟩ — see STOP 1

2 to stop doing (something) permanently ⟨we have *discontinued* the manufacture of that item⟩ — see QUIT 2

3 to come to an end ⟨publication of the magazine will *discontinue* at the end of the year⟩ — see CEASE 1

discontinuity *n* **1** an open space in a barrier (as a wall or hedge) ⟨microscopic *discontinuities* in the connecting wires⟩ — see GAP 1

2 a break in continuity ⟨a *discontinuity* in the flow of the story⟩ — see GAP 2

discontinuous *adj* lacking in steadiness or regularity of occurrence ⟨*discontinuous* showers throughout the day⟩ — see FITFUL

discord *n* a lack of agreement or harmony ⟨the *discord* between the two scout leaders threatened to tear our troop apart⟩

synonyms conflict, discordance, dissension, dissent, dissidence, disunity, friction, schism, strife, variance, war, warfare

related words clash, collision, competition, contention; altercation, argument, bicker, brawl, debate, disagreement, dispute, falling-out, fight, hassle, jar, quarrel, row, run-in, scrap, spat, squabble, tiff, wrangle; incompatibility, incongruity, inconsistency, inconsonance; animosity, antagonism, antipathy, enmity, hostility, ill will, rancor

near antonyms concurrence, cooperation

antonyms accord, agreement, concord, concordance, harmony, peace

discordance *n* **1** a lack of agreement or harmony ⟨there was a real *discordance* between the tough guys that the actor played in the movies and the wimp that he was in real life⟩ — see DISCORD

2 loud, confused, and usually unharmonious sound ⟨the jarring *discordance* coming from the garage where the band was rehearsing⟩ — see NOISE 1

discordant *adj* **1** marked by or producing a harsh combination of sounds ⟨the *discordant* tones coming from the poorly tuned instrument⟩ — see DISSONANT

2 making loud, confused, and usually unharmonious sounds ⟨the *discordant* cries of sea gulls fighting over the fishing boat's castoffs⟩ — see NOISY 1

3 feeling or displaying eagerness to fight ⟨a troubled, *discordant* family that would benefit from professional counseling⟩ — see BELLIGERENT

4 not being in agreement or harmony ⟨his views on the proper role of women are certainly *discordant* with most contemporary opinions on the subject⟩ — see INCONSISTENT

discotheque *n* a bar or restaurant offering special nighttime entertainment (as music, dancing, or comedy acts) ⟨a popular *discotheque* that features nightly dancing to recorded music⟩ — see NIGHTCLUB

discount *n* something that is or may be subtracted ⟨a *discount* of 20% from the original price⟩ — see DEDUCTION 1

discount *vb* to express scornfully one's low opinion of ⟨shouldn't *discount* their contributions to our fund-raising efforts⟩ — see DECRY 1

discountenance *vb* **1** to hold an unfavorable opinion of ⟨a social philosopher who *discountenanced* all programs for helping the needy, claiming that society should encourage survival of the fittest⟩ — see DISAPPROVE (OF)

2 to throw into a state of self-conscious distress ⟨the political party was *discountenanced* by the actions of a few of its overly zealous members⟩ — see EMBARRASS 1

discourage *vb* **1** to lessen the courage or confidence of ⟨I didn't let losing *discourage* me from trying again⟩

synonyms daunt, demoralize, dishearten, dismay, dispirit, unman, unnerve

related words browbeat, bully, cow, intimidate; depress, sadden, weigh; afflict, try; damp, dampen, deaden; distress, trouble; bother, irk, vex, worry; debilitate, enfeeble, undermine, weaken; frighten, horrify, scare

near antonyms buoy (up), cheer, gladden; animate, enliven, invigorate; fortify, reinforce, strengthen; assure, reassure; boost, energize, excite, galvanize, inspire, lift, provoke, quicken, rally, stimulate, stir

antonyms embolden, encourage, hearten, nerve, steel

2 to steer (a person) from an activity or course of action ⟨the higher fines may help *discourage* drivers from speeding on the highway⟩

synonyms deter, dissuade, inhibit

related words divert

near antonyms egg (on), exhort, goad, prod, urge; impel, induce, prompt

antonyms encourage, persuade

discouragement *n* the state of being discouraged ⟨we tried to avoid *discouragement* after failing the test twice⟩

synonyms demoralization, despair, despondency, disheartenment, dismay, dispiritedness

related words blues, dejection, depression, dumps, gloom, melancholy, mopes; defeatism, pessimism, resignation

near antonyms optimism, sanguinity

antonyms encouragement

discourse *n* **1** an exchange of views for the purpose of exploring a subject or deciding an issue ⟨a *discourse* on the lingering effects of imperialism⟩ — see DISCUSSION 1

2 talking or a talk between two or more people ⟨Thomas Jefferson is said to have been able to participate in knowledgeable *discourse* on a breathtaking array of subjects⟩ — see CONVERSATION

discourse *vb* **1** to give a formal often extended talk on a subject ⟨*discoursed* at some length on the long-term results of the war⟩ — see TALK 1

2 to talk as if giving an important and formal speech ⟨*discoursed* as though he was an expert on every subject⟩ — see ORATE 1

discourteous *adj* showing a lack of manners or consideration for others ⟨wouldn't tolerate any *discourteous* behavior in classroom discussions⟩ — see IMPOLITE

discourteousness *n* rude behavior ⟨a campaign to try to remedy the increasing *discourteousness* of the state's drivers⟩ — see DISCOURTESY

discourtesy *n* rude behavior ⟨the courtiers shuddered at the *discourtesy* shown to the king⟩

synonyms discourteousness, disrespect, impertinence, impoliteness, impudence, incivility, inconsideration, insolence, rudeness, ungraciousness

related words audacity, boldness, brashness, brassiness, sauciness, shamelessness; boorishness, churlishness, clownishness, crudeness, loutishness, vulgarity; abruptness, bluntness, brusqueness, crustiness, curtness, gruffness, sharpness; crabbedness, crossness, disagreeableness, grumpiness, sullenness, surliness; impropriety, inappropriateness, incorrectness, indecency, unfitness, unsuitability; arrogance, conceit, conceitedness, presumption, pretense (*or* pretence), pretension, pretentiousness

near antonyms humility, meekness, modesty; deference, dutifulness, respectfulness, submissiveness; acceptability, appropriateness, correctness, decency, decorousness, fitness, goodness, propriety, respectability, respectableness, rightness, seemlineness, suitability; affability, cordiality, friendliness, geniality, hospitality; felicitousness, grace, gracefulness

antonyms civility, considerateness, consideration, courtesy, genteelness, gentility, graciousness, politeness, thoughtfulness

discover *vb* **1** to come to an awareness ⟨I was startled to *discover* that my keys were missing⟩

synonyms ascertain, catch on, find out, hear, learn, realize, see

related words hit (on *or* upon), tumble (to); descry, detect, encounter, espy, spot; dope (out), figure out, puzzle (out); discern, note, observe, perceive; divine

near antonyms miss, overlook; disregard, ignore; forget, unlearn; blanket, blot out, cloak, conceal, cover,

curtain, enshroud, hide, mask, occult, screen, shroud, veil

2 to come upon after searching, study, or effort ⟨we hope to *discover* the real reason for his odd behavior⟩ — see FIND 1

3 to make known (as information previously kept secret) ⟨*discovered* to his friend how people whom he had trusted had betrayed him⟩ — see REVEAL 1

discovery *n* **1** the act or process of sighting or learning the existence of something for the first time ⟨the *discovery* of a new species of starfish⟩

synonyms detection, finding, spotting, unearthing

related words disclosure, exposure, revelation, uncovering, unveiling; creation, invention; exploration; rediscovery

near antonyms concealment, hiding

2 something discovered ⟨his many zoological *discoveries* included several species of birds⟩

synonyms find

related words pay dirt, strike, treasure trove; breakthrough

discredit *n* the state of having lost the esteem of others ⟨to his everlasting *discredit*, the coach was found to have placed bets against his own team⟩ — see DISGRACE 1

discredit *vb* **1** to reduce to a lower standing in one's own eyes or in others' eyes ⟨attempted to *discredit* her political opponents by deliberately spreading false rumors⟩ — see HUMBLE

2 to think not to be true or real ⟨I *discredit* the story that the old inn is haunted⟩ — see DISBELIEVE

discreditable *adj* not respectable ⟨the *discreditable* conduct of drunken college students celebrating a win by their team⟩ — see DISREPUTABLE

discreet *adj* having or showing good judgment and restraint especially in conduct or speech ⟨he was very *discreet*, only saying what was necessary⟩

synonyms judicious, prudent

related words cautious, chary, circumspect; foresighted, forethoughtful; discerning, discriminating, sage, sane, sapient, sensible, wise; canny, provident; astute, perspicacious, sagacious, shrewd

near antonyms careless, heedless; improvident, shortsighted; foolish, unwise

antonyms imprudent, indiscreet, injudicious

discreetness *n* the ability to make intelligent decisions especially in everyday matters ⟨I appreciated her *discreetness* in keeping quiet about my inability to pay for our date⟩ — see COMMON SENSE

discrepancy *n* the quality or state of being different ⟨the *discrepancy* of the calculations of my bill by the hotel and myself was a matter of concern⟩ — see DIFFERENCE 1

discrepant *adj* not being in agreement or harmony ⟨widely *discrepant* conclusions on the impact the real estate development would have on the local environment⟩ — see INCONSISTENT

discrete *adj* not physically attached to another unit ⟨several *discrete* sections to this vast medical complex, including a college of pharmacology and a research center⟩ — see SEPARATE 2

discreteness *n* the state of being kept distinct ⟨the original *discreteness* of the various modules for the International Space Station⟩ — see SEPARATION 2

discretion *n* **1** the ability to make intelligent decisions especially in everyday matters ⟨we'll rely on your *discretion* in handling this accusation of cheating⟩ — see COMMON SENSE

2 the power, right, or opportunity to choose ⟨ambassadorships are generally regarded as subject to the president's *discretion*⟩ — see CHOICE 1

discretionary *adj* subject to one's freedom of choice ⟨*discretionary* spending on luxuries dropped dramatically last year⟩ — see OPTIONAL

discriminate *vb* to understand or point out the difference ⟨the human eye can *discriminate* a vast number of different colors⟩ — see DISTINGUISH 1

discriminating *adj* favoring, applying, or being unequal treatment of different classes of people ⟨accused of *discriminating* practices in the hiring of employees⟩ — see DISCRIMINATORY

discrimination *n* the state of being kept distinct ⟨in her mind there did not exist a *discrimination* between the imaginary and the real⟩ — see SEPARATION 2

discriminational *adj* favoring, applying, or being unequal treatment of different classes of people ⟨are you guilty of *discriminational* behavior toward people unlike yourself?⟩ — see DISCRIMINATORY

discriminative *adj* favoring, applying, or being unequal treatment of different classes of people ⟨fighting laws which were grossly *discriminative*⟩ — see DISCRIMINATORY

discriminatory *adj* favoring, applying, or being unequal treatment of different classes of people ⟨a company that was fined for its *discriminatory* practices in the hiring of women⟩
  synonyms differential, discriminating, discriminational, discriminative
  related words biased, inequitable, partial, partisan, prejudiced, prejudicial, unequal, unfair, unjust
  near antonyms equal, equitable, fair, just; impartial, neutral, objective, unbiased, uncolored, unprejudiced
  antonyms nondiscriminatory

discursive *adj* passing from one topic to another ⟨the speaker's *discursive* style made it difficult to understand his point⟩
  synonyms desultory, digressive, leaping, maundering, rambling
  related words circuitous, deviating, devious, roundabout
  near antonyms focused (*also* focussed)

discuss *vb* to talk about (an issue) usually from various points of view and for the purpose of arriving at a decision or opinion ⟨we *discussed* the new proposal for the school stadium⟩
  synonyms argue, bandy, chew over, debate, dispute, hash (over), moot, talk over
  related words descant (on), lecture (on *or* about), speak (about), talk (about); broach, introduce; forge, hammer (out), thrash (out); consider, deliberate, weigh; reason (with)

discussion *n* **1** an exchange of views for the purpose of exploring a subject or deciding an issue ⟨the *discussion* about the club budget went on for hours⟩
  synonyms argument, colloquy, conference, deliberation, discourse, give-and-take, parley, talk
  related words debate, dialogue (*also* dialog); forum, meeting, powwow, roundtable, seminar, symposium; chat, conversation, rap
  2 talking or a talk between two or more people ⟨*discussions* around the water cooler at work⟩ — see CONVERSATION

disdain *n* open dislike for someone or something considered unworthy of one's concern or respect ⟨showing undisguised *disdain* for the other students⟩ — see CONTEMPT

disdain *vb* to show contempt for ⟨*disdained* him as a coward⟩ — see SCORN 1

disdainful *adj* **1** feeling or showing open dislike for someone or something regarded as undeserving of respect or concern ⟨a *disdainful* attitude toward people who work as waiters and waitresses⟩ — see CONTEMPTUOUS 1
  2 having or displaying feelings of scorn for what is regarded as beneath oneself ⟨*disdainful* of manual labor of any kind⟩ — see PROUD 1
  3 intended to make a person or thing seem of little importance or value ⟨*disdainful* remarks regarding the cheap clothes that the local people were wearing⟩ — see DEROGATORY

disease *n* an abnormal state that disrupts a plant's or animal's normal bodily functioning ⟨they caught a rare *disease* while they were traveling in Africa and were sick for weeks⟩
  synonyms affection, ailment, bug, complaint, complication, condition, disorder, fever, ill, illness, infirmity, malady, sickness, trouble
  related words contagion, contagious disease; infection, infectious disease; deficiency disease; attack, bout, fit, spell; debility, decrepitude, feebleness, frailness, lameness, weakness; malaise, matter; pest, pestilence, plague
  near antonyms fitness, healthiness, heartiness, robustness, soundness, wholeness, wholesomeness
  antonyms health, wellness

disembark *vb* to go ashore from a ship ⟨the cruise passengers *disembarked* as soon as they got to the terminal in Miami⟩
  synonyms debark, land
  related words beach; anchor, dock, put in
  near antonyms board, get (on); weigh (anchor)
  antonyms embark

disembowel *vb* to take the internal organs out of ⟨ancient Roman prophets would *disembowel* animals in order to read the future from their entrails⟩ — see GUT

disenchant *vb* to free from mistaken beliefs or foolish hopes ⟨if you thought that you could pass this course without doing any work, let me be the first to *disenchant* you⟩ — see DISILLUSION

disencumber *vb* **1** to empty or rid of cargo ⟨we *disencumbered* our pack animals as soon as we made camp that night⟩ — see UNLOAD 1
  2 to set (a person or thing) free of something that encumbers ⟨a simple statement of the terms of the contract *disencumbered* of legal jargon⟩ — see RID

disencumbered *adj* no longer burdened with something unpleasant or painful ⟨the paying off of my loan left me feeling delightfully *disencumbered*⟩ — see FREE 2

disengage *vb* to set free from entanglement or difficulty ⟨sought to *disengage* myself from the embarrassing situation⟩ — see EXTRICATE

disentangle *vb* **1** to separate the various strands of ⟨it took forever to *disentangle* the knot⟩ — see UNRAVEL 1
  2 to set free from entanglement or difficulty ⟨the years that it took to *disentangle* ourselves from our troubles after someone starting using our social security number⟩ — see EXTRICATE

disfavor *n* **1** a strong feeling of not liking or approving ⟨made no attempt to hide his *disfavor* of his wife's relatives⟩ — see DISLIKE 1
  2 refusal to accept as right or desirable ⟨their suggestion was met with *disfavor* by virtually all of the other club members⟩ — see DISAPPROVAL

disfavor *vb* **1** to feel dislike for ⟨a style of stage acting that is *disfavored* by most theatergoers today⟩ — see DISLIKE 1

2 to hold an unfavorable opinion of ⟨polls showing that this political candidate is highly *disfavored* by most voters⟩ — see DISAPPROVE (OF)

disfigure *vb* to reduce the soundness, effectiveness, or perfection of ⟨the statue was seriously *disfigured* by falling rubble during the earthquake⟩ — see DAMAGE 1

disfigurement *n* something that spoils the appearance or completeness of a thing ⟨a plastic surgeon who occasionally donates his services to treat the *disfigurements* of needy children⟩ — see BLEMISH

disgorge *vb* to throw out or off (something from within) often violently ⟨the volcano *disgorged* lava in a spectacular nighttime show⟩ — see ERUPT 1

disgrace *n* **1** the state of having lost the esteem of others ⟨the players who threw the game were in *disgrace* with their schoolmates⟩

synonyms discredit, dishonor, disrepute, ignominy, infamy, odium, opprobrium, reproach, shame

related words contempt, disdain, scorn; deprecation, disapprobation, disapproval, disfavor; abasement, debasement, debasing, degradation, humbling, humiliation; blot, brand, slur, smirch, spot, stain, stigma

near antonyms admiration, regard; awe, fear, reverence; fame, glory, renown, repute

antonyms esteem, honor, respect

2 a cause of shame ⟨the exposure of his criminal activities was a huge *disgrace* for the councilman⟩

synonyms crime, dishonor, reflection, reproach, scandal

related words brand, smirch, spot, stain, stigma

antonyms credit, honor

3 a regrettable or blameworthy act ⟨it's a *disgrace* to let all the leftover food from the banquet go to waste, so let's deliver it to the homeless shelter⟩ — see CRIME 2

disgrace *vb* to reduce to a lower standing in one's own eyes or in others' eyes ⟨*disgraced* by the shameful actions of their leader⟩ — see HUMBLE

disgraceful *adj* not respectable ⟨*disgraceful* disruptions at the graduation ceremonies⟩ — see DISREPUTABLE

disgruntle *vb* **1** to cause to change from friendly or loving to unfriendly or uncaring ⟨an employee, *disgruntled* by the restaurant owner's unfair treatment, turned him in to the IRS⟩ — see ESTRANGE

2 to make discontented ⟨a crew *disgruntled* by a long voyage that provided no opportunity for recreation onshore⟩ — see DISCONTENT

disgruntled *adj* having a feeling that one has been wronged or thwarted in one's ambitions ⟨a *disgruntled* postal worker was responsible for the vandalism⟩ — see DISCONTENTED

disgruntlement *n* **1** the condition of being dissatisfied with one's life or situation ⟨a survey showing the extent of people's satisfaction—or *disgruntlement*— with their marriages⟩ — see DISCONTENT

2 the loss of friendship or affection ⟨feelings of neglect that inevitably lead to *disgruntlement* among employees⟩ — see ESTRANGEMENT

disguise *n* clothing put on to hide one's true identity or imitate someone or something else ⟨Mardi Gras revelers dressed in a colorful array of outlandish *disguises*⟩

synonyms camouflage, costume, guise

related words domino, mask, veil, vizard; dress, getup, outfit, rig; coloring, cosmetic, makeup, paint

disguise *vb* to change the dress or looks of so as to conceal true identity ⟨the spies *disguised* themselves as harmless tourists⟩

synonyms camouflage, cloak, dress up, mask

related words blanket, blot out, conceal, cover, curtain, enshroud, hide, obscure, occult, screen, shroud, veil; affect, assume, counterfeit, dissemble, dissimulate, feign, pose, pretend, sham, simulate

near antonyms display, exhibit, expose, flaunt, parade, show, uncover, unmask; betray, disclose, discover, reveal

disgust *n* a dislike so strong as to cause stomach upset or queasiness ⟨we turned from the grisly scene with *disgust*⟩

synonyms aversion, distaste, loathing, nausea, repugnance, repulsion, revulsion

related words abhorrence, abomination, execration, hate, hatred; disapproval, disfavor, disinclination, dislike, disliking, displeasure

near antonyms appetite, bent, fondness, like, liking, partiality, penchant, predilection, preference, propensity, taste

disgust *vb* to cause to feel disgust ⟨the usual school lunch *disgusted* us, so we started bringing our lunches from home⟩

synonyms nauseate, repel, repulse, revolt, sicken, turn off

related words displease, distress; appall, horrify; affront, insult, offend, outrage, shock

near antonyms attract, charm, entice, tempt; delight, gratify, please, rejoice, tickle

disgusted *adj* filled with disgust ⟨the *disgusted* diners refused to patronize the restaurant ever again⟩ — see SICK 2

dish *n* a usually circular utensil for holding something (as food) ⟨we threw all of the ingredients for the salsa into a *dish* and mixed them together⟩

synonyms vessel

related words bowl, casserole, charger, cup, plate, platter, salver, saucer, tray

dishearten *vb* to lessen the courage or confidence of ⟨we were *disheartened* by the news that our grandmother was seriously ill⟩ — see DISCOURAGE 1

disheartenment *n* the state of being discouraged ⟨our excusable *disheartenment* in the face of overwhelming odds against winning the game⟩ — see DISCOURAGEMENT

dishevel *vb* to undo the proper order or arrangement of ⟨decorations for the garden wedding that had been *disheveled* by the wind⟩ — see DISORDER

disheveled *or* **dishevelled** *adj* lacking in order, neatness, and often cleanliness ⟨a slovenly woman with *disheveled* hair and a cigarette hanging out of her mouth⟩ — see MESSY

dishonest *adj* **1** telling or containing lies ⟨*dishonest* kids who lie about their ages in order to get into R-rated movies⟩ ⟨*dishonest* statements about the fight in the locker room⟩

synonyms lying, mendacious, untruthful

related words erroneous, fallacious, false, misleading; double-dealing, hypocritical, two-faced

near antonyms candid, open, straightforward; earnest, sincere, true

antonyms honest, truthful, veracious

2 given to or marked by cheating and deception ⟨*dishonest* car dealers who roll back mileage gauges⟩ ⟨*dishonest* business deals that landed him in jail⟩

synonyms crooked, deceptive, fast, fraudulent, shady, sharp, shifty, underhand, underhanded

related words unconscionable, unethical, unprincipled, unscrupulous; deceitful, deceiving, deluding, delusive, delusory; artful, cunning; devious, furtive, sneaking, sneaky, tricky; insidious, perfidious, treacherous

near antonyms conscientious, honorable, just, scrupulous, upright; forthright, straightforward

antonyms aboveboard, honest, straight

3 marked by, based on, or done by the use of dishonest methods to acquire something of value ⟨*dishonest* appraisals of art works that were part of an elaborate scheme to defraud insurance companies⟩ — see FRAUDULENT 1

dishonesty *n* **1** the tendency to tell lies ⟨if you gain a reputation for *dishonesty*, no one will believe you even when you're telling the truth⟩

synonyms deceitfulness, mendacity, untruthfulness

related words artifice, craft, craftiness, crookedness, cunning, deceit, dissembling, dissimulation, double-dealing, duplicity, fakery, foxiness, guile, wiliness; falseness; hypocrisy

near antonyms honor, incorruptibility; candidness, candor, frankness, good faith, sincerity, straightforwardness; dependability, reliability, reliableness, trustworthiness; accuracy, objectivity; authenticity, correctness, genuineness; credibility

antonyms honesty, integrity, probity, truthfulness, veracity, verity

2 the inclination or practice of misleading others through lies or trickery ⟨a religious cult that recruits members through *dishonesty* and subterfuge⟩ — see DECEIT

dishonor *n* **1** the state of having lost the esteem of others ⟨a person of integrity who would prefer death to *dishonor*⟩ — see DISGRACE 1

2 a cause of shame ⟨your expulsion from the academy for cheating is a *dishonor* to this family⟩ — see DISGRACE 2

dishonor *vb* to reduce to a lower standing in one's own eyes or in others' eyes ⟨*dishonored* herself and the school by fixing the results of the class election⟩ — see HUMBLE

dishonorable *adj* **1** not following or in accordance with standards of honor and decency ⟨resorted to *dishonorable* tactics in order to win first place in the science fair⟩ — see IGNOBLE 2

2 not respectable ⟨*dishonorable* conduct shown by some students on the class trip⟩ — see DISREPUTABLE

disillusion *vb* to free from mistaken beliefs or foolish hopes ⟨we were *disillusioned* when we saw how the movie star acted in real life⟩

synonyms disabuse, disenchant, undeceive

related words debunk, expose, show up, uncloak, uncover, unmask; disclose, divulge, tell, unveil

near antonyms beguile, bluff, cozen, delude, dupe, fool, gull, hoax, hoodwink, kid, misguide, misinform, mislead, misrepresent, snow, take in, trick

disinclination *n* **1** a lack of willingness or desire to do or accept something ⟨it's an understatement to say that our dog shows a *disinclination* to get into the car to go to the vet⟩ — see RELUCTANCE

2 a strong feeling of not liking or approving ⟨a *disinclination* for Brussels sprouts since birth⟩ — see DISLIKE 1

disinclined *adj* having doubts about the wisdom of doing something ⟨*disinclined* to go skateboarding in the middle of the night⟩ — see HESITANT

disintegrate *vb* to go through decomposition ⟨fallen leaves slowly *disintegrate* over the course of the winter⟩ — see DECAY 1

disinter *vb* to remove from place of burial ⟨the Egyptian mummy was carefully *disinterred* for further study⟩ — see EXHUME

disinterested *adj* **1** having or showing a lack of interest or concern ⟨the city's philistines, naturally *disinterested* in art, voted to cut the museum's budget⟩ — see INDIFFERENT 1

2 marked by justice, honesty, and freedom from bias ⟨a judge who is widely respected for his *disinterested* decisions⟩ — see FAIR 2

disinterestedness *n* **1** lack of favoritism toward one side or another ⟨the *disinterestedness* with which the newspaper reports stories earns it the respect and trust of the community⟩ — see DETACHMENT 1

2 lack of interest or concern ⟨the chorus of yawns was a fair indication of the students' *disinterestedness* in the proceedings⟩ — see INDIFFERENCE

disjoin *vb* to set or force apart ⟨*disjoined* the two glasses, which were stuck together, only with the greatest difficulty⟩ — see SEPARATE 1

disjoint *vb* to set or force apart ⟨*disjoint* the parts of a chicken for frying⟩ — see SEPARATE 1

disjointed *adj* not clearly or logically connected ⟨a *disjointed* harangue about an odd hodgepodge of things that are supposedly wrong with our society⟩ — see INCOHERENT 1

dislike *n* **1** a strong feeling of not liking or approving ⟨we have a strong *dislike* for olives and wouldn't eat them even if we were paid⟩

synonyms allergy, averseness, aversion, disfavor, disinclination, disliking

related words disgust, distaste, loathing, nausea, repugnance, repulsion, revulsion; abomination, antipathy, detestation, hate, hatred; deprecation, disapproval, displeasure, dissatisfaction; jaundice

near antonyms affection, attachment, love; bent, leaning, penchant, predilection, propensity, tendency

antonyms appetite, fondness, like, liking, partiality, preference, taste

2 refusal to accept as right or desirable ⟨the public's general *dislike* of negative campaign ads⟩ — see DISAPPROVAL

dislike *vb* **1** to feel dislike for ⟨the two dogs *disliked* each other the first time they met, and never did become friends⟩

synonyms disfavor

related words abhor, abominate, detest, hate, loathe; condemn, despise, scorn; disapprove (of), frown (on *or* upon), object (to)

near antonyms admire, appreciate, cherish, revere, venerate, worship; prize, treasure, value; drink (in), savor; dote (on), idolize; favor, prefer

antonyms adore, cotton (to), delight (in), dig, enjoy, fancy, groove (on), like, love, relish, revel (in)

2 to hold an unfavorable opinion of ⟨*dislike* the governor's heavy-handed way of doing things⟩ — see DISAPPROVE (OF)

disliking *n* a strong feeling of not liking or approving ⟨I had taken an instant *disliking* to them⟩ — see DISLIKE 1

dislocate *vb* **1** to change the place or position of ⟨*dislocated* his shoulder in the accident⟩ — see MOVE 1

2 to undo the proper order or arrangement of ⟨the country's entire social structure was *dislocated* by the war⟩ — see DISORDER

dislocation *n* an act or instance of the order of things being disturbed ⟨the slightest *dislocation* in her daily routine bothered the elderly woman⟩ — see UPSET

disloyal *adj* not true in one's allegiance to someone or something ⟨we knew that he was *disloyal* and would eventually turn on us⟩ — see FAITHLESS

disloyalty *n* **1** lack of faithfulness especially to one's husband or wife ⟨she was greatly pained by her husband's *disloyalty*⟩ — see INFIDELITY 1
2 the act or fact of violating the trust or confidence of another ⟨abuse of a young person by a clergyman is usually regarded as the ultimate *disloyalty*⟩ — see BETRAYAL

dismal *adj* **1** causing or marked by an atmosphere lacking in cheer ⟨a suitably *dismal* setting for a haunted house⟩ — see GLOOMY 1
2 causing unhappiness ⟨the *dismal* failure of our hopes for the championship⟩ — see SAD 2

dismantle *vb* to take apart ⟨*dismantle* the table for easier transport⟩ — see DISASSEMBLE

dismay *n* **1** the emotion felt when one's expectations are not met ⟨filled with *dismay* at not making the finals⟩ — see DISAPPOINTMENT 1
2 the state of being discouraged ⟨in my *dismay* I failed to realize that there would be other chances⟩ — see DISCOURAGEMENT

dismay *vb* to lessen the courage or confidence of ⟨the imposing climb *dismayed* us even before we got started⟩ — see DISCOURAGE 1

dismember *vb* to take apart ⟨*dismembered* the stage settings after the last performance⟩ — see DISASSEMBLE

dismiss *vb* **1** to let go from office, service, or employment ⟨the secretary was *dismissed* after it was discovered that she was stealing office supplies⟩
synonyms can, cashier, fire, muster out, remove, retire, sack
related words downsize, furlough, lay off; boot (out), bounce
near antonyms contract, subcontract
antonyms employ, hire
2 to drive or force out ⟨the sick boy's mother *dismissed* the visitors so he could get some rest⟩ — see EJECT 1

dismissal *n* the termination of the employment of an employee or a work force often temporarily ⟨numerous *dismissals* from the company during the economic slump⟩ — see LAYOFF

disobedience *n* refusal to obey ⟨they gave up on training the dog to fetch because of his constant *disobedience*⟩
synonyms contrariness, defiance, frowardness, insubordination, intractability, rebelliousness, recalcitrance, refractoriness, unruliness, willfulness
related words disrespect, impudence, insolence, rudeness; doggedness, hardheadedness, mulishness, obstinacy, pertinaciousness, pertinacity, perversity, stubbornness; mischievousness, naughtiness
near antonyms agreeability, amiability; slavishness, submissiveness, subservience
antonyms amenability, compliance, docility, obedience

disobedient *adj* given to resisting authority or another's control ⟨the *disobedient* child refused to eat his vegetables⟩
synonyms balky, contrary, defiant, froward, insubordinate, intractable, rebellious, recalcitrant, refractory,

restive, ungovernable, unruly, untoward, wayward, willful (or wilful)
related words insurgent, mutinous; dogged, hardheaded, headstrong, mulish, obdurate, obstinate, peevish, pertinacious, pigheaded, self-willed, stubborn, unyielding; obstreperous, uncontrollable, unmanageable, wild; perverse, resistant, wrongheaded; bad, disorderly, errant, misbehaving, mischievous, monkeying, monkeyish, naughty; undisciplined; dissident, nonconformist; disrespectful, ill-mannered, ill-natured, impolite, impudent, insolent, ornery, rude, uncouth
near antonyms acquiescent, agreeable, amiable, deferential, obliging; submissive, yielding; behaved, disciplined, well-bred; courteous, polite, respectful; servile, slavish, subservient; decorous, orderly, proper; controllable, governable, manageable
antonyms amenable, compliant, docile, obedient, tractable

disobey *vb* to go against the commands, prohibitions, or rules of ⟨students who *disobey* their teachers and use cell phones in class⟩ ⟨drivers who consistently *disobey* traffic laws⟩
synonyms defy, rebel (against)
related words mutiny (against), revolt (against); disregard, ignore, tune out; dismiss, flout, pooh-pooh, reject, scoff (at), scorn, shrug off; break, transgress, violate; combat, contest, dispute, fight, oppose, resist, withstand
near antonyms defer (to), serve, submit (to), surrender (to), yield (to); keep, observe; accede (to), acquiesce (to), agree (to), assent (to), comply (with), conform (to), oblige; attend, hear, heed, listen (to), mark, note, notice, regard, watch
antonyms follow, mind, obey

disoblige *vb* to cause discomfort to or trouble for ⟨didn't want to *disoblige* her relatives by spending the night⟩ — see INCONVENIENCE

disobliging *adj* causing difficulty, discomfort, or annoyance ⟨a friend with the *disobliging* habit of never having the cash to pay his fair share of the check⟩ — see INCONVENIENT 1

disorder *n* **1** a state in which everything is out of order ⟨the general *disorder* of the room after the guests finally left the party⟩ — see CHAOS
2 an abnormal state that disrupts a plant's or animal's normal bodily functioning ⟨afflicted all her life with a nervous *disorder*⟩ — see DISEASE

disorder *vb* to undo the proper order or arrangement of ⟨be careful not to *disorder* the carefully arranged contents of the dresser⟩
synonyms confuse, derange, disarrange, disarray, discompose, dishevel, dislocate, disorganize, disrupt, disturb, hash, jumble, mess (up), mix (up), muddle, muss, rumple, scramble, shuffle, tousle, tumble, upset
related words embroil, entangle, snarl, tangle; agitate, stir (up), unsettle
near antonyms align, line, line up; systematize; adjust, fix
antonyms arrange, array, draw up, marshal, order, organize, range, regulate, straighten (up), tidy

disordered *adj* lacking in order, neatness, and often cleanliness ⟨his *disordered* clothing was obviously thrown on in a hurry⟩ — see MESSY

disorderly *adj* **1** not restrained by or under the control of legal authority ⟨*disorderly* mobs roamed the streets after the fall of the city⟩ — see LAWLESS

2 lacking in order, neatness, and often cleanliness ⟨*disorderly* piles of clothes on various tables about the room⟩ — see MESSY

disorganization *n* a state in which everything is out of order ⟨all of her notes were in a state of *disorganization*⟩ — see CHAOS

disorganize *vb* to undo the proper order or arrangement of ⟨those unexpected problems that can *disorganize* an entire plan⟩ — see DISORDER

disorient *vb* to throw into a state of mental uncertainty ⟨troops *disoriented* by the sudden change in strategy⟩ — see CONFUSE 1

disown *vb* to refuse to acknowledge as one's own or as one's responsibility ⟨the angry father *disowned* his rebellious son⟩ — see DISCLAIM 1

disparage *vb* to express scornfully one's low opinion of ⟨*disparaged* polo as a game for the idle rich⟩ — see DECRY 1

disparagement *n* the act of making a person or a thing seem little or unimportant ⟨his predictable *disparagement* of the latest fashions among young people⟩ — see DEPRECIATION

disparaging *adj* intended to make a person or thing seem of little importance or value ⟨*disparaging* comments about the lack of talent among the musical performers⟩ — see DEROGATORY

disparate *adj* being not of the same kind ⟨*disparate* notions among adults and adolescents about when middle age begins⟩ — see DIFFERENT 1

disparateness *n* the quality or state of being different ⟨the *disparateness* of their notions of an ideal weekend may indicate that they would not make a compatible couple⟩ — see DIFFERENCE 1

disparity *n* the quality or state of being different ⟨an enormous *disparity* in the lives of the rich and the poor in that country⟩ — see DIFFERENCE 1

dispassionate *adj* marked by justice, honesty, and freedom from bias ⟨*dispassionate* refereeing is all that we ask⟩ — see FAIR 2

dispatch *n* **1** a message on paper from one person or group to another ⟨a soldier sending daily *dispatches* to friends and family back home⟩ — see LETTER

2 a piece of conveyed information ⟨a *dispatch* from headquarters regarding a change in battle plans⟩ — see COMMUNICATION

dispatch *vb* **1** to cause to go or be taken from one place to another ⟨*dispatched* a messenger with urgent news⟩ — see SEND

2 to deprive of life ⟨the exterminator *dispatched* the termites with professional efficiency⟩ — see KILL 1

3 to put to death deliberately ⟨during his reign of terror the dictator *dispatched* thousands without the slightest qualm⟩ — see MURDER 1

dispel *vb* to cause (members of a group) to move widely apart ⟨the morning sun *dispelled* the fog⟩ — see SCATTER 1

dispensable *adj* not needed by the circumstances or to accomplish an end ⟨a new invention that renders the old methods eminently *dispensable*⟩ — see UNNECESSARY

dispensation *n* the act or process of giving out something to each member of a group ⟨the emergency *dispensation* of medicine to the sick⟩ — see DISTRIBUTION 1

dispense *vb* to give out (something) in appropriate amounts or to appropriate individuals ⟨a pharmacist *dispenses* pills to people with prescriptions⟩ — see ADMINISTER 1

dispersal *n* an act or process in which something scatters or is scattered ⟨the *dispersal* of plant seeds in the forests through natural means⟩ — see SCATTERING 1

disperse *vb* **1** to cause (members of a group) to move widely apart ⟨the family of the missing woman *dispersed* searchers to all corners of the globe⟩ — see SCATTER 1

2 to cease to exist or cause to cease to exist as a group or organization ⟨the campaign staff *dispersed* almost immediately after the election⟩ — see DISBAND 1

dispersion *n* an act or process in which something scatters or is scattered ⟨the *dispersion* of energy from a source⟩ — see SCATTERING 1

dispirit *vb* to lessen the courage or confidence of ⟨*dispirited* by the overwhelming amount of information needed to write the report⟩ — see DISCOURAGE 1

dispiritedness *n* **1** a state or spell of low spirits ⟨experienced a period of general *dispiritedness* following the birth of her first child⟩ — see SADNESS

2 the state of being discouraged ⟨the *dispiritedness* of the losing team in the Super Bowl must be staggering⟩ — see DISCOURAGEMENT

displace *vb* **1** to change the place or position of ⟨the slight tremor *displaced* the dishes on the shelves, but didn't do any real damage⟩ — see MOVE 1

2 to force to leave a country ⟨World War II *displaced* people all over Europe⟩ — see BANISH 1

3 to take the place of ⟨inefficient methods *displaced* by newer ones⟩ — see REPLACE 1

displacement *n* the forced removal from a homeland ⟨the *displacement* of Jews from their homes⟩ — see EXILE 1

display *n* **1** a public showing of objects of interest ⟨a *display* of paintings by masters of French Impressionism⟩ — see EXHIBITION 1

2 an outward and often exaggerated indication of something abstract (as a feeling) for effect ⟨a *display* of sympathy that was totally phony⟩ — see SHOW 1

display *vb* **1** to present so as to invite notice or attention ⟨*display* the best items at the front of the showcase⟩ — see SHOW 1

2 to make known (something abstract) through outward signs ⟨an actress who can *display* a great range of emotion⟩ — see SHOW 2

displease *vb* to make discontented ⟨her coworkers malicious gossip *displeased* her⟩ — see DISCONTENT

displeased *adj* having a feeling that one has been wronged or thwarted in one's ambitions ⟨feeling *displeased* by the way his relationship with his girlfriend was going⟩ — see DISCONTENTED

displeasing *adj* not giving pleasure to the mind or senses ⟨*displeasing* behavior by their grandchildren⟩ — see UNPLEASANT

displeasure *n* **1** refusal to accept as right or desirable ⟨fans showed their *displeasure* by loudly booing the umpire⟩ — see DISAPPROVAL

2 the condition of being dissatisfied with one's life or situation ⟨his *displeasure* with his job intensified as the years wore on⟩ — see DISCONTENT

disport *vb* **1** to cause (someone) to pass the time agreeably occupied ⟨*disported* themselves with silly games while they waited in the airport⟩ — see AMUSE

2 to engage in activity for amusement ⟨children *disporting* in the playground at a variety of games⟩ — see PLAY 1

3 to play and run about happily ⟨the puppies *disported* in the backyard while we ate⟩ — see FROLIC 1

4 to present so as to invite notice or attention ⟨football fans *disported* the sports memorabilia they had just bought⟩ — see SHOW 1

disposal *n* **1** the getting rid of whatever is unwanted or useless ⟨trash *disposal* is on Wednesday in our neighborhood⟩

synonyms discarding, disposition, dumping, jettison, junking, removal, riddance, scrapping, throwing away

related words clearance, clearing; decimation, demolishment, demolition, destruction

near antonyms accumulation, acquirement, acquisition, collection, deposit

2 the way objects in space or events in time are arranged or follow one another ⟨the *disposal* of troops along the ridge⟩ — see ORDER 1

dispose *vb* **1** to arrange something in a certain spot or position ⟨looking for the perfect spot to *dispose* the new knickknack⟩ — see PLACE 1

2 to put into a particular arrangement ⟨*disposed* her tools within easy reach⟩ — see ORDER 1

disposed *adj* having a desire or inclination (as for a specified course of action) ⟨a dog that is *disposed* to bite⟩ — see WILLING 1

disposition *n* **1** one's characteristic attitude or mood ⟨he had a cheerful *disposition* and was very rarely depressed⟩

synonyms grain, nature, temper, temperament

related words cheer, frame, humor, mode, mood; attitude, outlook, perspective, point of view, standpoint, viewpoint; emotion, feeling, heart, passion, sentiment; strain; belief, conviction, mind, opinion, persuasion; expression, tone, vein; character, individuality, personality; responsiveness, sensibility, sensitiveness, sensitivity

2 a habitual attraction to some activity or thing ⟨a woman with a *disposition* to fuss about trivial matters⟩ — see INCLINATION 1

3 the getting rid of whatever is unwanted or useless ⟨found some means for the *disposition* of all of this junk⟩ — see DISPOSAL 1

4 the way objects in space or events in time are arranged or follow one another ⟨planned the *disposition* of events at her wedding with a precision that military commanders would envy⟩ — see ORDER 1

disprove *vb* to prove to be false ⟨Magellan's circumnavigation of the globe *disproved* any lingering notions that the earth is flat⟩

synonyms belie, confute, rebut, refute

related words overthrow, overturn

phrases give the lie to

near antonyms evidence, show; demonstrate, display, illustrate, manifest; argue, reason

antonyms confirm, prove, verify

disputable *adj* **1** giving good reason for being doubted, questioned, or challenged ⟨a speech full of *disputable* generalizations about people⟩ — see DOUBTFUL

2 open to question or dispute ⟨all *disputable* claims must be referred to the committee⟩ — see DEBATABLE 2

disputant *n* a person who takes part in a dispute ⟨there were only three *disputants* in the argument, but they made enough noise for a dozen⟩

synonyms arguer, debater, disputer, quarreler (*or* quarreller), squabbler, wrangler

related words advocate, defendant, plaintiff, pleader; nitpicker, pettifogger, quibbler

disputation *n* variance of opinion on a matter ⟨a heated *disputation* over the true authorship of the poem "The Night Before Christmas"⟩ — see DISAGREEMENT 1

disputatious *adj* **1** feeling or displaying eagerness to fight ⟨a long history of little wars waged by the *disputatious* countries occupying that European peninsula⟩ — see BELLIGERENT

2 given to arguing ⟨a *disputatious* professor who could give you an argument on just about anything⟩ — see ARGUMENTATIVE 1

disputatiousness *n* an inclination to fight or quarrel ⟨the stubborn *disputatiousness* of the committee members kept them from getting much accomplished⟩ — see BELLIGERENCE

dispute *n* **1** variance of opinion on a matter ⟨a *dispute* over the proper pronunciation of "nuclear"⟩ — see DISAGREEMENT 1

2 an often noisy or angry expression of differing opinions ⟨after much *dispute*, the school committee decided that all backpacks would have to be stored in lockers during class hours⟩ — see ARGUMENT 1

dispute *vb* **1** to demand proof of the truth or rightness of ⟨a whole slew of relatives eager to *dispute* his claim to being the sole heir⟩ — see CHALLENGE 1

2 to express different opinions about something often angrily ⟨hometown fans *disputing* with visiting fans over which had the better team⟩ — see ARGUE 2

3 to talk about (an issue) usually from various points of view and for the purpose of arriving at a decision or opinion ⟨in an extended session the city council *disputed* the need for a new high school⟩ — see DISCUSS

disputer *n* a person who takes part in a dispute ⟨in debate she's a dogged *disputer* who never gives an inch⟩ — see DISPUTANT

disquiet *n* **1** a disturbed or uneasy state ⟨a period of *disquiet* before the results of the close election were confirmed⟩ — see UNREST

2 an uneasy state of mind usually over the possibility of an anticipated misfortune or trouble ⟨was filled with *disquiet* as the hours passed without any sign of the missing children⟩ — see ANXIETY 1

disquiet *vb* to trouble the mind of; to make uneasy ⟨we were *disquieted* by the strange noises we heard outside our tent⟩ — see DISTURB 1

disquieting *adj* **1** causing worry or anxiety ⟨*disquieting* news of troubles downtown⟩ — see TROUBLESOME

2 marked by or causing agitation or uncomfortable feelings ⟨with a *disquieting* voice she asked me to investigate the strange noise coming from the basement⟩ — see NERVOUS 2

disregard *n* lack of interest or concern ⟨revelers firing guns in the air with complete *disregard* for the possible consequences⟩ — see INDIFFERENCE

disregard *vb* **1** to ignore in a disrespectful manner ⟨*disregarded* the wishes of his family in his choice of a bride⟩ — see SCORN 2

2 to fail to give proper attention to ⟨*disregarded* the posted warnings of avalanche danger and went skiing anyway⟩ — see NEGLECT 1

3 to overlook or dismiss as of little importance ⟨this essay is so good that I can safely *disregard* a couple of spelling errors⟩ — see EXCUSE 1

disrepair *n* the state of being unattended to or not cared for ⟨the old house was in such *disrepair* that the roof had caved in⟩ — see NEGLECT 1

disreputable *adj* not respectable ⟨a *disreputable* Internet retailer that had a record of hundreds of complaints for shoddy merchandise and slow refunds⟩

synonyms discreditable, disgraceful, dishonorable, ignominious, infamous, notorious, shameful

related words bad, immoral, seamy, shady, sordid, unethical, unsavory, wicked; base, contemptible, despicable, detestable, dirty, low, mean, vile, wretched

near antonyms ethical, good, moral

antonyms honorable, reputable, respectable

disrepute *n* the state of having lost the esteem of others ⟨a once proud name fallen into *disrepute*⟩ — see DISGRACE 1

disrespect *n* rude behavior ⟨treated the substitute teacher with awful *disrespect*⟩ — see DISCOURTESY

disrobe *vb* to remove clothing from ⟨the doctor instructed the patient to *disrobe* himself before the examination⟩ — see UNDRESS

disrobed *adj* lacking or shed of clothing ⟨a statue of a partially *disrobed* woman⟩ — see NAKED 1

disrupt *vb* to undo the proper order or arrangement of ⟨the arrival of a baby in the household would totally *disrupt* their established routine⟩ — see DISORDER

disruption *n* an act or instance of the order of things being disturbed ⟨the flat tire resulted in an unfortunate *disruption* of the schedule for our road trip⟩ — see UPSET

dissatisfaction *n* **1** the condition of being dissatisfied with one's life or situation ⟨our *dissatisfaction* with the poorly prepared meal⟩ — see DISCONTENT

2 the emotion felt when one's expectations are not met ⟨she felt keen *dissatisfaction* at the hurried job the house painters had done⟩ — see DISAPPOINTMENT 1

dissatisfied *adj* having a feeling that one has been wronged or thwarted in one's ambitions ⟨the store prides itself on never allowing a customer to walk away *dissatisfied*⟩ — see DISCONTENTED

dissatisfy *vb* **1** to fall short in satisfying the expectation or hope of ⟨a restaurant serving portions that will not *dissatisfy* even the heartiest eater⟩ — see DISAPPOINT

2 to make discontented ⟨an administrative assistant *dissatisfied* by her meager paycheck⟩ — see DISCONTENT

dissect *vb* to identify and examine the basic elements or parts of (something) especially for discovering interrelationships ⟨let's *dissect* the plot of this thriller to see what makes it thrilling⟩ — see ANALYZE

dissection *n* the separation and identification of the parts of a whole ⟨the book's *dissection* of the problem of obesity in this country⟩ — see ANALYSIS 1

dissemble *vb* to take on a false or deceptive appearance ⟨children learn to *dissemble* at a surprisingly early age⟩ — see PRETEND 1

dissembling *n* **1** the inclination or practice of misleading others through lies or trickery ⟨a crafty child given to frequent *dissembling* to get what she wants⟩ — see DECEIT

2 the pretending of having virtues, principles, or beliefs that one in fact does not have ⟨in the end the preacher's *dissembling* is discovered, and he is exposed as a fraud⟩ — see HYPOCRISY

disseminate *vb* to cause to be known over a considerable area or by many people ⟨missionaries sent by their church to *disseminate* their faith⟩ — see SPREAD 1

dissension *n* **1** a lack of agreement or harmony ⟨religious *dissension* threatened to split the colony⟩ — see DISCORD

2 variance of opinion on a matter ⟨continued *dissension* among historians on the exact spot of Columbus's first landing⟩ — see DISAGREEMENT 1

dissent *n* **1** a lack of agreement or harmony ⟨considerable *dissent* within the party's rank and file⟩ — see DISCORD

2 departure from a generally accepted theory, opinion, or practice ⟨the church reacted to any form of *dissent* by promptly excommunicating its proponents⟩ — see HERESY

dissent *vb* to have a different opinion ⟨anyone who *dissented* was encouraged to speak out while they had the chance⟩ — see DISAGREE 1

dissenter *n* a person who believes or teaches something opposed to accepted beliefs ⟨a society that prized conformity very highly and treated *dissenters* of any kind very harshly⟩ — see HERETIC

dissentient *adj* deviating from commonly accepted beliefs or practices ⟨the communist party did not look favorably on *dissentient* opinions⟩ — see HERETICAL

dissenting *adj* deviating from commonly accepted beliefs or practices ⟨*dissenting* views were ruthlessly suppressed under the dictatorship⟩ — see HERETICAL

disservice *n* unfair or inadequate treatment of someone or something or an instance of this ⟨you do a great *disservice* to the professionals at the day-care center when you refer to them as "babysitters"⟩

synonyms injury, injustice, raw deal, wrong

related words insult, offense, outrage; complaint, grievance

near antonyms cricket

antonyms justice

dissever *vb* to set or force apart ⟨placed the *dissevered* pieces of chicken in the roasting pan⟩ — see SEPARATE 1

dissidence *n* **1** a lack of agreement or harmony ⟨political *dissidence* had plagued the country for years⟩ — see DISCORD

2 departure from a generally accepted theory, opinion, or practice ⟨after abstract art became established, its proponents became just as intolerant of *dissidence* as earlier schools of art had been⟩ — see HERESY

dissident *adj* deviating from commonly accepted beliefs or practices ⟨*dissident* elements within the Catholic Church⟩ — see HERETICAL

dissident *n* a person who believes or teaches something opposed to accepted beliefs ⟨the conference drew political *dissidents* of every ilk⟩ — see HERETIC

dissimilar *adj* being not of the same kind ⟨a place where people with *dissimilar* backgrounds can interact⟩ — see DIFFERENT 1

dissimilarity *n* the quality or state of being different ⟨the effectiveness of a metaphor largely depends upon the superficial *dissimilarity* of the two things being compared⟩ — see DIFFERENCE 1

dissimulation *n* **1** the inclination or practice of misleading others through lies or trickery ⟨got whatever she wanted through shameless *dissimulation*⟩ — see DECEIT

2 the pretending of having virtues, principles, or beliefs that one in fact does not have ⟨teenagers indulging in *dissimulation* simply in order to be one of the in crowd⟩ — see HYPOCRISY

dissipate *vb* **1** to cause (members of a group) to move widely apart ⟨*dissipated* the enemy forces by unremitting artillery fire⟩ — see SCATTER 1

2 to use up carelessly ⟨*dissipated* the family fortune in reckless business ventures⟩ — see WASTE 1

dissipated *adj* having or showing lowered moral character or standards ⟨the *dissipated* and drunken son of the wealthiest man in the county⟩ — see CORRUPT

dissipatedness *n* a sinking to a state of low moral standards and behavior ⟨a novel chronicling the *dissipatedness* of a generation born to great wealth⟩ — see CORRUPTION 2

dissipation *n* **1** a sinking to a state of low moral standards and behavior ⟨wasting of a once promising life in *dissipation* and drunkenness⟩ — see CORRUPTION 2
2 an act or process in which something scatters or is scattered ⟨the *dissipation* of the clouds by the early morning winds⟩ — see SCATTERING 1

dissociate *vb* to set or force apart ⟨attempts to *dissociate* herself from her past⟩ — see SEPARATE 1

dissolute *adj* having or showing lowered moral character or standards ⟨literature dealing with the *dissolute* and degrading aspects of human experience⟩ — see CORRUPT

dissoluteness *n* a sinking to a state of low moral standards and behavior ⟨the *dissoluteness* of the Roman nobles as the empire declined⟩ — see CORRUPTION 2

dissolution *n* the act or process of a whole separating into two or more parts or pieces ⟨the *dissolution* of the empire into a patchwork of kingdoms⟩ — see SEPARATION 1

dissolve *vb* **1** to cease to be visible ⟨as the mist *dissolved* in the morning sun⟩ — see DISAPPEAR
2 to cease to exist or cause to cease to exist as a group or organization ⟨the company formally *dissolved* three months after declaring bankruptcy⟩ — see DISBAND 1
3 to put an end to by formal action ⟨the king simply *dissolved* parliament⟩ — see ABOLISH

dissonant *adj* marked by or producing a harsh combination of sounds ⟨a *dissonant* chorus of noises arose from the busy construction site⟩
synonyms discordant, inharmonious, unmelodious, unmusical
related words blaring, clanging, clashing, clattering, grating, harsh, jangling, jarring, metallic, raspy, raucous, scratching, screeching, shrill, squeaky, strident; disagreeable, unpleasant, unpleasing; atonal, off-key
near antonyms dulcet, euphonious, mellifluous, mellow, melodic, sweet, tuneful; resonant, sonorous; quavering, trilling, warbling; agreeable, appealing, pleasant; cadenced, lilting, lyric, lyrical, rhythmic (*or* rhythmical); chordal, harmonic, homophonic, orchestral, polyphonic, symphonic, tonal
antonyms harmonious, harmonizing, melodious, musical

dissuade *vb* to steer (a person) from an activity or course of action ⟨tried to *dissuade* her from her intention to drop out of college⟩ — see DISCOURAGE 2

distance *n* the space or amount of space between two points, lines, surfaces, or objects ⟨the *distance* between the earth and the sun is about 93 million miles⟩
synonyms lead, length, remove, spacing, spread, stretch, way
related words altitude, area, breadth, depth, height, rise, space, volume, width; extension, extent; cast, range, reach, scope, shot, sweep, throw; drop, fall, flight, haul; berth, clearance
phrases a far cry

distant *adj* **1** not close in time or space ⟨the *distant* towers were barely visible in the fog⟩
synonyms away, far, faraway, far-off, remote, removed
related words apart, isolated, obscure, outlying, out-of-the-way, retired, secluded, secret, sequestered
near antonyms adjacent, adjoining, contiguous

antonyms close, near, nearby, nigh
2 having or showing a lack of friendliness or interest in others ⟨was *distant* and distracted all throughout the interview⟩ — see COOL 1

distaste *n* a dislike so strong as to cause stomach upset or queasiness ⟨usually views the abstract paintings with *distaste*⟩ — see DISGUST

distasteful *adj* **1** disagreeable or disgusting to the sense of taste ⟨cod-liver oil is so *distasteful* that it's worse than anything it cures⟩
synonyms unappetizing, unpalatable, unsavory
related words abominable, awful, bad, filthy, foul, horrible, loathsome, nasty, nauseating, noisome, obnoxious, offensive, repellent, repugnant, repulsive, revolting, shocking, sickening; bland, flat, flavorless, insipid, savorless, tasteless
near antonyms appealing, attractive, flavorful, piquant, rich
antonyms appetizing, delectable, delicious, palatable, savory, tasty
2 not giving pleasure to the mind or senses ⟨she finds some recent musical trends *distasteful*⟩ — see UNPLEASANT
3 causing intense displeasure, disgust, or resentment ⟨the *distasteful* nature of his job as a bill collector⟩ — see OFFENSIVE 1

distill *vb* to remove usually visible impurities from ⟨*distill* the water before pouring it in the steam iron⟩ — see CLARIFY 1

distinct *adj* **1** being not of the same kind ⟨two *distinct* approaches to the same problem⟩ — see DIFFERENT 1
2 not subject to misinterpretation or more than one interpretation ⟨a person with a *distinct* Scottish accent⟩ — see CLEAR 2
3 of a particular or exact sort ⟨I left *distinct* instructions that my books were not to be touched⟩ — see EXPRESS 1
4 serving to identify as belonging to an individual or group ⟨one of the *distinct* traits of a preliterate society⟩ — see CHARACTERISTIC 1

distinction *n* **1** exceptionally high quality ⟨a shop selling native handicrafts of *distinction*⟩ — see EXCELLENCE 1
2 a quality that gives something special worth ⟨has the *distinction* of being the oldest house in the city⟩ — see EXCELLENCE 2
3 public acknowledgment or admiration for an achievement ⟨I did all of the work, and the other guy got all the *distinction*⟩ — see GLORY 1
4 the fact or state of being above others in rank or importance ⟨a number of physicians of *distinction* serve on the staff of the teaching hospital⟩ — see EMINENCE 1
5 something given in recognition of achievement ⟨won a number of *distinctions* in her long career as an actress⟩ — see AWARD
6 the quality or state of being different ⟨the *distinction* between the two photographic prints escapes me⟩ — see DIFFERENCE 1
7 the state of being kept distinct ⟨the *distinction* between liberty and license is often violated in today's society⟩ — see SEPARATION 2

distinctive *adj* **1** being not of the same kind ⟨she seems to alternate between two *distinctive* hairstyles⟩ — see DIFFERENT 1
2 serving to identify as belonging to an individual or group ⟨the *distinctive* odor of a barnyard⟩ — see CHARACTERISTIC 1

distinctiveness *n* the quality or state of being different ⟨the *distinctiveness* of his style of playing the violin⟩ — see DIFFERENCE 1

distinctness *n* the quality or state of being different ⟨the *distinctness* of Jane Austen's writing makes it easy to recognize on a test⟩ — see DIFFERENCE 1

distinguish *vb* 1 to understand or point out the difference ⟨even at such a young age, he could *distinguish* between right and wrong⟩
   synonyms differentiate, discern, discriminate, separate
   related words comprehend, grasp, know, understand; divide, part, sever; demarcate, mark (off), set off
   near antonyms confound, lump (together), mingle
   antonyms confuse, mistake, mix (up)
   2 to be an important feature of ⟨recipes *distinguished* by their ease and simplicity⟩ — see CHARACTERIZE 2
   3 to find out or establish the identity of ⟨learned at an early age to *distinguish* the sound of a piano in an orchestra⟩ — see IDENTIFY 1
   4 to make note of (something) through the use of one's eyes ⟨could barely *distinguish* the garden gate through the mist⟩ — see SEE 1

distinguishable *adj* 1 able to be perceived by a sense or by the mind ⟨a star easily *distinguishable* by the naked eye⟩ — see PERCEPTIBLE
   2 being not of the same kind ⟨snowflakes are *distinguishable* from each other under a microscope⟩ — see DIFFERENT 1

distinguished *adj* standing above others in rank, importance, or achievement ⟨a *distinguished* astronomer who is widely respected in the field⟩ — see EMINENT

distinguishing *adj* serving to identify as belonging to an individual or group ⟨a novice birder still learning the *distinguishing* features of various finches⟩ — see CHARACTERISTIC 1

distort *vb* 1 to change so much as to create a wrong impression or alter the meaning of ⟨the coach's message was so *distorted* after passing through so many people it was unintelligible⟩ — see GARBLE
   2 to twist (something) out of a natural or normal shape or condition ⟨if you keep *distorting* your face like that, someday it's going to freeze in that position⟩ — see CONTORT

distorted *adj* badly or imperfectly formed ⟨surgery to correct a *distorted* foot⟩ — see MALFORMED

distortion *n* the twisting of something out of its natural or normal shape or condition ⟨a *distortion* of the car chassis resulting from collision⟩ — see CONTORTION

distract *vb* 1 to draw the attention or mind to something else ⟨we were *distracted* from our homework by the noise outside⟩
   synonyms divert
   related words amuse, entertain; stray, wander
   near antonyms focus
   2 to trouble the mind of; to make uneasy ⟨*distracted* by the upcoming exam⟩ — see DISTURB 1

distraction *n* 1 a state of mental uncertainty ⟨in my *distraction* I forgot where I was⟩ — see CONFUSION 1
   2 a state of wildly excited activity or emotion ⟨driven to *distraction* by the constant screaming and bickering in the house⟩ — see FRENZY
   3 the act or activity of providing pleasure or amusement especially for the public ⟨a harmless *distraction* for children at the playground⟩ — see ENTERTAINMENT 1

distraught *adj* feeling overwhelming fear or worry ⟨*distraught* relatives waiting to learn whether there were any survivors of the crash⟩ — see FRANTIC 1

distress *n* 1 a state of great suffering of body or mind ⟨the upcoming final exam is causing us considerable *distress*⟩ ⟨the survivors were in extreme *distress* after having been stranded on the island for a week with no food⟩
   synonyms affliction, agony, anguish, misery, pain, strait(s), torment, torture, tribulation, woe
   related words discomfort; cross, crucible, trial; heartbreak, joylessness, sadness, sorrow, unhappiness; emergency, pinch; asperity, difficulty, hardship, rigor; ache, hurt, pang, smarting, soreness, stitch, throe, twinge; danger, jeopardy, trouble
   near antonyms comfort, consolation, solace; alleviation, assuagement, ease, relief; peace, security
   2 the state of not being protected from injury, harm, or evil ⟨a ship in *distress*⟩ — see DANGER 1

distress *vb* to trouble the mind of; to make uneasy ⟨don't let all the bad news *distress* you⟩ — see DISTURB 1

distressful *adj* 1 marked by or causing agitation or uncomfortable feelings ⟨the *distressful* period during which we waited to learn who had passed and who had failed⟩ — see NERVOUS 2
   2 of a kind to cause great distress ⟨a *distressful* situation⟩ — see REGRETTABLE

distressing *adj* 1 causing worry or anxiety ⟨*distressing* signs that another war might be imminent⟩ — see TROUBLESOME
   2 of a kind to cause great distress ⟨the *distressing* death of our favorite actor⟩ — see REGRETTABLE
   3 marked by or causing agitation or uncomfortable feelings ⟨the *distressing* habit of constantly fiddling with her hair⟩ — see NERVOUS 2

distribute *vb* to give out (something) in appropriate amounts or to appropriate individuals ⟨*distributed* pamphlets on recycling to everyone in the neighborhood⟩ — see ADMINISTER 1

distribution *n* 1 the act or process of giving out something to each member of a group ⟨we oversaw the *distribution* of medicine to the natives⟩
   synonyms allocation, apportionment, dispensation, division, issuance
   related words disbursement; reapportionment, redistribution
   2 the way objects in space or events in time are arranged or follow one another ⟨the *distribution* of those stars has long suggested the form of a dipper⟩ — see ORDER 1

district *n* an area (as of a city) set apart for some purpose or having some special feature ⟨Independence Hall in Philadelphia's historic *district*⟩
   synonyms neighborhood, quarter, section
   related words belt, zone; department, division, part; precinct, ward; area, locality, place, region; barrio, enclave, ghetto

distrust *n* a feeling or attitude that one does not know the truth, truthfulness, or trustworthiness of someone or something ⟨the psychic's bold claims were greeted with *distrust* and suspicion⟩ — see DOUBT

distrust *vb* to have no trust or confidence in ⟨we *distrusted* the stranger when he offered us free candy⟩
   synonyms doubt, mistrust, question, suspect
   related words disbelieve, discount, discredit, negate
   phrases look askance at
   near antonyms bank (on *or* upon), count (on *or* upon), depend (on *or* upon), rely (on *or* upon)
   antonyms trust

distrustful *adj* **1** inclined to doubt or question claims ⟨she was *distrustful* of his claim of having saved the kitten from a raging fire⟩ — see SKEPTICAL 1
2 not feeling sure about the truth, wisdom, or trustworthiness of someone or something ⟨naturally *distrustful* of politicians who claim to have all the answers⟩ — see DOUBTFUL 1

distrustfully *adv* with distrust ⟨to say that I read the stories in the tabloids *distrustfully* is putting it mildly⟩ — see ASKANCE

distrustfulness *n* a feeling or attitude that one does not know the truth, truthfulness, or trustworthiness of someone or something ⟨she usually listens to campaign promises with an air of *distrustfulness*⟩ — see DOUBT

disturb *vb* **1** to trouble the mind of; to make uneasy ⟨all that talk of war *disturbed* us⟩
   synonyms agitate, bother, concern, discomfort, discompose, disquiet, distract, distress, exercise, freak (out), perturb, undo, unhinge, unsettle, upset, worry
   related words aggravate, anger, annoy, bug, chafe, chivy, exasperate, fret, gall, get, grate, harass, harry, irk, irritate, nettle, peeve, pester, pique, put out, rile, vex; bedevil, haunt, plague; abash, confound, confuse, discomfit, disconcert, discountenance, embarrass, faze, fluster, mortify, nonplus, rattle; daunt, demoralize, discourage, dishearten, dismay, dispirit
   near antonyms allay, alleviate, assuage; appease, conciliate, mollify, pacify, placate, propitiate
   antonyms calm, compose, quiet, settle, soothe, tranquilize (*also* tranquillize)
2 to change the place or position of ⟨the items on her desk had been *disturbed*⟩ — see MOVE 1
3 to undo the proper order or arrangement of ⟨her careful filing system is sure to be *disturbed* during the move⟩ — see DISORDER
4 to thrust oneself upon (another) without invitation ⟨sorry to *disturb* you while you're working⟩ — see BOTHER 1
5 to cause discomfort to or trouble for ⟨the noisy lawnmower *disturbed* their sleep⟩ — see INCONVENIENCE

disturbance *n* **1** a state of noisy, confused activity ⟨went to investigate the *disturbance* outside⟩ — see COMMOTION
2 an act or instance of the order of things being disturbed ⟨caused a *disturbance* in the carefully ordered proceedings⟩ — see UPSET
3 the act of making unwelcome intrusions upon another ⟨she apologized for the *disturbance* and got straight to the point⟩ — see ANNOYANCE 1

disturbing *adj* **1** causing annoyance ⟨a *disturbing* visit by his little cousin while he was trying to study⟩ — see ANNOYING
2 causing embarrassment ⟨there was a *disturbing* silence as I struggled to remember her name⟩ — see AWKWARD 3
3 causing worry or anxiety ⟨a *disturbing* trend in the nation's energy consumption⟩ — see TROUBLESOME
4 marked by or causing agitation or uncomfortable feelings ⟨a *disturbing* pause in the normally smooth operation of the machinery⟩ — see NERVOUS 2

disunion *n* the act or process of a whole separating into two or more parts or pieces ⟨the *disunion* of Czechoslovakia into Slovakia and the Czech Republic⟩ — see SEPARATION 1

disunite *vb* to set or force apart ⟨attempted to *disunite* the members of the club by vicious gossip⟩ — see SEPARATE 1

disunited *adj* disagreeing with each other ⟨the *disunited* members of the committee⟩ — see DIVIDED

disunity *n* a lack of agreement or harmony ⟨troubling signs of *disunity* within the normally peaceful organization⟩ — see DISCORD

disuse *n* lack of use ⟨the old farmhouse showed signs of *disuse*⟩
   synonyms idleness, inactivity
   related words abandonment, desertion, neglect; dormancy, latency, quiescence
   antonyms use

disused *adj* left unoccupied or unused ⟨a *disused* warehouse that had become a den for drug dealers⟩ — see ABANDONED

ditch *n* a long narrow channel dug in the earth ⟨after skidding on the ice, our car went right into the *ditch*⟩
   synonyms dike, gutter, trench, trough
   related words culvert, drain, draw, gully, ravine; drill, furrow

ditch *vb* to get rid of as useless or unwanted ⟨we *ditched* the old table at the dump⟩ — see DISCARD

dither *n* **1** a state of nervous or irritated concern ⟨Grandma usually gets in a *dither* if I don't make my weekly call⟩ — see FRET
2 a sense of panic or extreme nervousness ⟨we were all in a *dither* while we waited for the test results⟩ — see JITTERS

dithery *adj* feeling or showing uncomfortable feelings of uncertainty ⟨an expectant father in a high state of *dithery* alarm⟩ — see NERVOUS 1

ditty *n* a short musical composition for the human voice often with instrumental accompaniment ⟨sung a little *ditty* in a minor key⟩ — see SONG 1

diurnal *adj* occurring, done, produced, or appearing every day ⟨a love as constant and certain as the *diurnal* tides⟩ — see DAILY

divan *n* a long upholstered piece of furniture designed for several sitters ⟨when I stayed over at their house I usually slept on the *divan* in the living room⟩ — see COUCH

dive *n* **1** an act or instance of diving ⟨the penguin took a *dive* off of the ice sheet⟩
   synonyms pitch, plunge
   related words dip, immersion, submersion; fall, slip, spill, stumble, tumble; descent, drop; belly flop, header, jackknife
   near antonyms jump, leap
2 the act or process of going to a lower level or altitude ⟨stock prices took a long, steady *dive*⟩ — see DESCENT 1

dive *vb* to cast oneself head first into deep water ⟨we watched her *dive* in after the drowning man⟩
   synonyms pitch, plunge, sound
   related words dip, immerse, submerge; belly flop
   near antonyms surface

diverge *vb* **1** to extend outwards from or as if from a central point ⟨light rays *diverge* after passing through a concave lens⟩ — see RADIATE 1
2 to go or move in different directions from a central point ⟨at that point the road and the railroad tracks *diverge*⟩ — see SEPARATE 2

divergence *n* a movement in different directions away from a common point ⟨a growing *divergence* of opinion about that U.S. president's place in history⟩
   synonyms separation
   related words difference, disagreement, discrepancy, disparateness, disparity, dissidence, dissimilarity, dis-

tinction, distinctiveness, distinctness, diversity, unlikeness

near antonyms accord, agreement; likeness, similarity

antonyms convergence

divers *adj* being of many and various kinds ⟨the state fair offers *divers* amusements for the whole family⟩ — see MANIFOLD

diverse *adj* being not of the same kind ⟨a movement supported by people with *diverse* interests but one common goal⟩ — see DIFFERENT 1

diverseness *n* **1** the quality or state of being composed of many different elements or types ⟨the *diverseness* of the science projects at the fair made judging a challenge⟩ — see VARIETY 1

2 the quality or state of being different ⟨the *diverseness* of the two top movies in the running for Best Picture could not be more striking⟩ — see DIFFERENCE 1

diversion *n* **1** someone or something that provides amusement or enjoyment ⟨a scavenger hunt was organized as a *diversion* for the guests at the party⟩ — see FUN 1

2 the act or activity of providing pleasure or amusement especially for the public ⟨movies and television became two of the most popular and influential *diversions* of the 20th century⟩ — see ENTERTAINMENT 1

diversity *n* **1** the quality or state of being composed of many different elements or types ⟨a *diversity* of opinions on where the senior class should go for its end-of-the-year trip⟩ — see VARIETY 1

2 the quality or state of being different ⟨there's considerable *diversity* in Jake's two choices for what he'd like to be someday: a clergyman or an acrobat⟩ — see DIFFERENCE 1

divert *vb* **1** to cause (someone) to pass the time agreeably occupied ⟨a light comedy to *divert* the tired business executive⟩ — see AMUSE

2 to change the course or direction of (something) ⟨the bike race was *diverted* around the construction zone⟩ — see TURN 2

3 to draw the attention or mind to something else ⟨trying to *divert* the child with a toy while the doctor was giving her a shot⟩ — see DISTRACT 1

diverting *adj* providing amusement or enjoyment ⟨some tall and *diverting* tales were told by the storyteller at the party⟩ — see FUN

divide *vb* **1** to set or force apart ⟨we *divided* the donated groceries into several dozen piles⟩ — see SEPARATE 1

2 to go or move in different directions from a central point ⟨the group *divided* based on those who wanted to go swimming and those who didn't⟩ — see SEPARATE 2

divided *adj* disagreeing with each other ⟨the club members were *divided* on the need for more fundraising⟩

synonyms disunited, split

phrases at loggerheads, at odds

antonyms undivided, united

dividend *n* something given in addition to what is ordinarily expected or owed ⟨the reward money was an unexpected *dividend* for our good deed⟩ — see BONUS

divider *n* something that divides, separates, or marks off ⟨placed a *divider* across the gym so we could have two activities going on at once⟩ — see DIVISION 1

divine *adj* **1** of the very best kind ⟨how about a piece of the most *divine* apple pie I've ever tasted!⟩ — see EXCELLENT

2 of, relating to, or being God ⟨for these *divine* gifts let us be truly thankful⟩ — see HOLY 3

divine *n* a person specially trained and authorized to conduct religious services in a Christian church ⟨the great influence exerted by the Puritan *divines* in the Massachusetts Bay Colony⟩ — see CLERGYMAN

divine *vb* to realize or know about beforehand ⟨it was easy to *divine* his intention of asking his girlfriend to marry him⟩ — see FORESEE

diviner *n* one who predicts future events or developments ⟨somehow the *diviner* failed to foresee her own misfortunes with the law⟩ — see PROPHET

divinity *n* **1** the quality or state of being divine ⟨Henry David Thoreau felt the presence of *divinity* in every part of nature⟩

synonyms deity, godhead, godhood

2 a being having superhuman powers and control over a particular part of life or the world ⟨a modest temple built for one of the minor *divinities* in ancient Greek mythology⟩ — see DEITY 1

3 *cap* the being worshipped as the creator and ruler of the universe ⟨worship of the *Divinity*⟩ — see DEITY 2

divisible *adj* capable of being split into two or more parts or pieces ⟨easily *divisible* into enough pieces for everyone⟩ — see SEPARABLE

division *n* **1** something that divides, separates, or marks off ⟨we poked our heads over the *division* between the yards to see what the fuss was about⟩

synonyms divider, partition

related words barrier, fence, wall; border, boundary, limit

2 a large unit of a governmental, business, or educational organization ⟨the complaints *division* handled all of the calls from the angry townsfolk⟩

synonyms bureau, department, desk, office

3 one of the units into which a whole is divided on the basis of a common characteristic ⟨one of the major *divisions* of birds⟩ — see CLASS 2

4 the act or process of a whole separating into two or more parts or pieces ⟨the assembly line was a major development in the *division* of labor among workers⟩ — see SEPARATION 1

5 the act or process of giving out something to each member of a group ⟨the person in charge of the *division* of the profits among the business partners⟩ — see DISTRIBUTION 1

divorce *vb* to set or force apart ⟨in your head you need to *divorce* your wishes and fantasies from realities of the world as it is⟩ — see SEPARATE 1

divulge *vb* to make known (as information previously kept secret) ⟨we tried to make him *divulge* the answers, but he wouldn't budge⟩ — see REVEAL 1

divulgence *n* the act or an instance of making known something previously unknown or concealed ⟨the government strictly prohibits the *divulgence* of classified information⟩ — see REVELATION

dizzy *adj* **1** having a feeling of being whirled about and in danger of falling down ⟨I felt very *dizzy* after I got off of the roller coaster⟩

synonyms giddy, light-headed, reeling, whirling

related words faint, weak; addled, befuddled, confused, dazed

near antonyms clearheaded; stable, steady

2 suffering from mental confusion ⟨he felt *dizzy* from trying to remember all of the dates and names that were sure to be asked on the test⟩

synonyms befuddled, bewildered, confused, dazed, stunned, stupefied

related words senseless, unconscious

phrases at sea

near antonyms alert, conscious

antonyms clearheaded, unconfused

3 moving, proceeding, or acting with great speed ⟨prices climbing at a *dizzy* rate⟩ — see FAST 1

do *vb* **1** to be fitting or proper ⟨Oh, that outfit just won't *do* for the opera⟩

synonyms befit, fit, go, serve, suit

related words satisfy, suffice; function, work

2 to be enough ⟨even half of that amount will *do*⟩ — see SERVE 2

3 to carry through (as a process) to completion ⟨*do* as much as you can⟩ — see PERFORM 1

4 to make more attractive by adding something that is beautiful or becoming ⟨*did* the living room in French provincial style⟩ — see DECORATE

5 to meet one's day-to-day needs ⟨I'm *doing* just fine⟩ — see GET ALONG 1

doable *adj* capable of being done or carried out ⟨the assigned paper was just barely *doable* in the time allowed⟩ — see POSSIBLE 1

docile *adj* readily giving in to the command or authority of another ⟨a *docile* young pony that went wherever it was led⟩ — see OBEDIENT

docility *n* a readiness or willingness to yield to the wishes of others ⟨dogs bred for *docility* instead of aggressiveness⟩ — see COMPLIANCE 1

dock *n* a structure used by boats and ships for taking on or landing cargo and passengers ⟨the boat remained tied up at the *dock* for a week, waiting for the weather to clear⟩

synonyms float, jetty, landing, levee, pier, quay, wharf

related words berth, mooring, slip; dockyard, marina, shipyard

¹**dock** *vb* to make (as hair) shorter with or as if with the use of shears ⟨the boxer's tail was *docked* soon after birth⟩ — see CLIP

²**dock** *vb* to stop at or near a place along the shore ⟨the cruise ship *docked* at the first port of call early the next morning⟩ — see LAND 1

docket *n* a listing of things to be presented or considered (as at a concert or play) ⟨on the Broadway *docket* for the early part of this season⟩ — see PROGRAM 1

dockworker *n* one who loads and unloads ships at a port ⟨the *dockworkers* spent all afternoon taking crates off of the ship⟩

synonyms longshoreman, stevedore

doctor *n* a person specially trained in healing human medical disorders ⟨we called a *doctor* as soon as we realized the baby was sick⟩

synonyms medic, physician

related words dermatologist, general practitioner, gynecologist, internist, neurologist, obstetrician, ophthalmologist, orthopedist, pediatrician, specialist, surgeon; intern, resident; nurse, paramedic

doctor *vb* **1** to give medical treatment to ⟨a pledge to *doctor* the burn victims until they were whole again⟩

synonyms treat

related words cure, heal, mend, rehabilitate, remedy; attend, care (for), dose, drug, minister (to), nurse

2 to put into good shape or working order again ⟨spends his spare time *doctoring* old clocks⟩ — see MEND 1

doctrine *n* **1** a statement or body of statements concerning faith or morals proclaimed by a church ⟨the Catholic Church's *doctrine* on the Eucharist⟩

synonyms canon, dogma

related words belief, conviction, tenet; credo, creed, ideology, philosophy, theology; axiom, precept, principle

2 the basic beliefs or guiding principles of a person or group ⟨the *doctrine* of quantum physicists⟩ — see CREED 1

document *n* **1** a piece of paper with information written or to be written on it ⟨filled out the *documents* for a bank loan⟩ — see FORM 2

2 a written or printed paper giving information about or proof of something ⟨have your *documents* ready as you approach the border⟩ — see CERTIFICATE

document *vb* to show the existence or truth of by evidence ⟨he tried in vain to *document* a link between ancient civilizations and extraterrestrials⟩ — see PROVE 1

documentary *adj* restricted to or based on fact ⟨a *documentary* film about the surprise attack on Pearl Harbor⟩ — see FACTUAL 1

documentation *n* something presented in support of the truth or accuracy of a claim ⟨the archaeologist presented *documentation* of her theory at the conference⟩ — see PROOF

dodder *vb* to move forward while swaying from side to side ⟨was *doddering* down the walk outside the nursing home⟩ — see STAGGER 1

dodge *n* a clever often underhanded means to achieve an end ⟨just another *dodge* to get out of working in the yard⟩ — see TRICK 1

dodge *vb* **1** to move suddenly aside or to and fro ⟨*dodging* through the crowd on his way to the exit⟩

synonyms duck, sidestep, zigzag

related words avoid, elude, escape, evade, parry, shirk, skirt; deflect, turn; slide, slip

2 to avoid having to comply with (something) especially through cleverness ⟨always trying to *dodge* the school's mandatory dress code⟩ — see CIRCUMVENT 1

3 to get or keep away from (as a responsibility) through cleverness or trickery ⟨*dodged* the draft by falsely claiming to be a conscientious objector⟩ — see ESCAPE 2

dodger *n* a dishonest person who uses clever means to cheat others out of something of value ⟨one of the most artful *dodgers* in the annals of American crime⟩ — see TRICKSTER 1

dodging *n* the act or a means of getting or keeping away from something undesirable ⟨Tom Sawyer's clever *dodging* of the onerous task of whitewashing the fence⟩ — see ESCAPE 2

dodo *n* **1** a person with old-fashioned ideas ⟨youngsters helping old *dodos* learn to use computers⟩ — see FOGY

2 a stupid person ⟨she called him a *dodo* after he lost the concert tickets⟩ — see IDIOT

doff *vb* to rid oneself of (a garment) ⟨the elderly gentleman *doffed* his hat as the lady passed by⟩ — see REMOVE 1

dog *n* a domestic mammal that is related to the wolves and foxes ⟨we got a *dog* from the pound to keep as a pet⟩

synonyms canine, doggy (*or* doggie), hound, pooch

related words cur, mongrel, mutt; bitch; lapdog, pup, puppy, whelp; bird dog, hunter, police dog, sheepdog, sled dog, watchdog, wolf dog, wolfhound

dog *vb* to go after or on the track of ⟨trouble seems to *dog* him wherever he goes⟩ — see FOLLOW 2

dog–eared *adj* showing signs of advanced wear and tear and neglect ⟨an old *dog-eared* copy of a beloved book⟩ — see SHABBY 1

dogged *adj* **1** continuing despite difficulties, opposition, or discouragement ⟨a madman who spent his life in *dogged* pursuit of power⟩ — see PERSISTENT

2 sticking to an opinion, purpose, or course of action in spite of reason, arguments, or persuasion ⟨a *dogged* reporter determined to get the real story⟩ — see OBSTINATE

3 showing no signs of slackening or yielding in one's purpose ⟨a *dogged* search for the missing piece of the puzzle⟩ — see UNYIELDING 1

doggedness *n* a steadfast adherence to an opinion, purpose, or course of action ⟨being a detective requires *doggedness* as well as cleverness⟩ — see OBSTINACY

dogging *n* the act of going after or in the tracks of another ⟨the merciless *dogging* of the Hollywood couple by the press⟩ — see PURSUIT

doggy *or* **doggie** *n* a domestic mammal that is related to the wolves and foxes ⟨what a good little *doggy!*⟩ — see DOG

dogma *n* a statement or body of statements concerning faith or morals proclaimed by a church ⟨the Catholic *dogma* of the bodily assumption of the Virgin Mary⟩ — see DOCTRINE 1

do in *vb* **1** to bring to a complete end the physical soundness, existence, or usefulness of ⟨a businessman *done in* by uncontrollable greed⟩ — see DESTROY 1

2 to deprive of life ⟨the early frost *did in* all of our tender plants⟩ — see KILL 1

3 to put to death deliberately ⟨somebody *did* the old man *in* late last night⟩ — see MURDER 1

4 to use up all the physical energy of ⟨the long day of hard work really *did* me *in*⟩ — see EXHAUST 1

doing *n* something done by someone ⟨is that mess in the kitchen your *doing?*⟩ — see ACTION 1

doldrums *n pl* **1** a state of temporary inactivity ⟨the theater scene is usually in the *doldrums* during the summer⟩ — see ABEYANCE

2 a state or spell of low spirits ⟨fighting the winter *doldrums* by taking up skiing⟩ — see SADNESS

3 the state of being bored ⟨in the *doldrums* while we waited for something to happen⟩ — see BOREDOM

dole (out) *vb* to give out (something) in appropriate amounts or to appropriate individuals ⟨my folks *dole out* my allowance only at the end of the week and not before⟩ — see ADMINISTER 1

doleful *adj* **1** expressing or suggesting mourning ⟨a *doleful* expression on their faces as they said good-bye to the friends they had made over the summer⟩ — see MOURNFUL 1

2 feeling unhappiness ⟨the visibly *doleful* players, heartbroken about their loss⟩ — see SAD 1

dolefulness *n* deep sadness especially for the loss of someone or something loved ⟨a period of *dolefulness* that seemed to last forever for the widower⟩ — see SORROW

doll *n* **1** a small figure often of a human being used especially as a child's plaything ⟨there was a row of *dolls* along the shelf in the bedroom⟩
synonyms dolly, puppet
related words rag doll; figure, figurine; plaything, toy
2 a young usually unmarried woman ⟨a beach resort famous for attracting cute guys and *dolls*⟩ — see GIRL 1

doll up *vb* to put on one's best or formal clothes ⟨got all *dolled up* for the party⟩ — see DRESS UP

dolly *n* a small figure often of a human being used especially as a child's plaything ⟨my kid sister's always playing with her *dollies*⟩ — see DOLL 1

dolor *n* deep sadness especially for the loss of someone or something loved ⟨her sad poems grew out of a deep *dolor* that lasted for weeks⟩ — see SORROW

dolorous *adj* expressing or suggesting mourning ⟨*dolorous* ballads of death and regret⟩ — see MOURNFUL 1

dolt *n* a stupid person ⟨he's always jokingly calling his best friend a *dolt*⟩ — see IDIOT

doltish *adj* not having or showing an ability to absorb ideas readily ⟨foolish and *doltish* behavior that was really beneath you⟩ — see STUPID 1

doltishness *n* the quality or state of lacking intelligence or quickness of mind ⟨she's usually quite bright, with only occasional moments of *doltishness*⟩ — see STUPIDITY 1

domain *n* a region of activity, knowledge, or influence ⟨a museum director who is one of the most powerful figures in the art *domain*⟩ — see FIELD 2

domestic *adj* **1** of or relating to a household or family ⟨the surest way to maintain *domestic* peace and harmony is to have everyone pitch in on chores⟩
synonyms familial, household
related words homelike, homely, homey; residential
2 changed from the wild state so as to become useful and obedient to humans ⟨*domestic* animals in a barnyard⟩ — see TAME 1

domestic *n* **1** a female domestic servant ⟨the couple paid the *domestic* a supplement for watching the children⟩ — see MAID 1

2 a person hired to perform household or personal services ⟨working as a team, the man and his wife hired themselves out as *domestics* for wealthy homeowners⟩ — see SERVANT

domesticated *adj* changed from the wild state so as to become useful and obedient to humans ⟨the *domesticated* horses are kept in a corral⟩ — see TAME 1

domicile *n* the place where one lives ⟨welcome to my *domicile*, humble though it may be⟩ — see HOME 1

domicile *vb* to provide with living quarters or shelter ⟨the university *domiciles* students in a variety of buildings in and around its urban campus⟩ — see HOUSE 1

dominance *n* **1** controlling power or influence over others ⟨although Napoleon had achieved *dominance* over the European continent, Great Britain still ruled the waves⟩ — see SUPREMACY 1

2 the fact or state of being above others in rank or importance ⟨the professor's *dominance* in the field of ancient Greek history⟩ — see EMINENCE 1

dominant *adj* coming before all others in importance ⟨the *dominant* authority on the English language⟩ — see FOREMOST 1

dominate *vb* **1** to bring under one's control by force of arms ⟨by 1941 Hitler had *dominated* much of Europe⟩ — see CONQUER 1

2 to look down on ⟨the ruined fortress *dominates* the town⟩ — see OVERLOOK 1

3 to serve as leader of ⟨it has been said that whoever *dominates* Germany controls Europe⟩ — see LEAD 2

dominating *n* the act or process of bringing someone or something under one's control ⟨the gradual *dominating* of Europe by a few ruling families⟩ — see CONQUEST

domination *n* the act or process of bringing someone or something under one's control ⟨the Spanish *domination* of the Americas in the 16th century⟩ — see CONQUEST

domineering *adj* fond of ordering people around ⟨the younger children in the family were controlled by a *domineering* older sister⟩ — see BOSSY

dominie *n* a person specially trained and authorized to conduct religious services in a Christian church ⟨a small village where the doctor and the *dominie* were the two pillars of society⟩ — see CLERGYMAN

dominion *n* **1** controlling power or influence over others ⟨in the Bible, man is given *dominion* over all the animals⟩ — see SUPREMACY 1
2 the right or means to command or control others ⟨was granted *dominion* over the household servants⟩ — see POWER 1

don *vb* to place on one's person ⟨she *donned* her best gown for the ball⟩ — see PUT ON 1

donate *vb* to make a present of ⟨we plan to *donate* all the profits from the rummage sale to charity⟩ — see GIVE 1

donation *n* **1** a gift of money or its equivalent to a charity, humanitarian cause, or public institution ⟨a generous *donation* to the orphanage⟩ — see CONTRIBUTION
2 something given to someone without expectation of a return ⟨gave the piano as a *donation* to the school's music program⟩ — see GIFT 1

donator *n* one that helps another with gifts or money ⟨a frequent *donator* of funds to research foundations⟩ — see BENEFACTOR

done *adj* brought or having come to an end ⟨the demanding job was finally *done*⟩ — see COMPLETE 2

done in *adj* depleted in strength, energy, or freshness ⟨I was *done in* after that exhausting hike⟩ — see WEARY 1

donkey *n* **1** a sturdy and patient domestic mammal that is used especially to carry things ⟨we put our bags on the *donkey* and headed down the canyon⟩
synonyms ass, burro, jackass
related words jack, jenny; hinny, mule; pack animal
2 a stupid person ⟨called him a *donkey* when he refused to go along with their plans⟩ — see IDIOT

donor *n* one that helps another with gifts or money ⟨a list of *donors* in the charitable foundation's annual report⟩ — see BENEFACTOR

doom *n* **1** a decision made by a court or tribunal regarding a case it has heard ⟨the judge solemnly pronounced his *doom* before a hushed courtroom⟩ — see SENTENCE
2 a state or end that seemingly has been decided beforehand ⟨it was her *doom* to be haunted by the memory of that terrible day⟩ — see FATE 1
3 the permanent stopping of all the vital bodily activities ⟨met his *doom* at the hands of a rampaging rhinoceros⟩ — see DEATH 1

doom *vb* **1** to determine the fate of in advance ⟨had always felt that he was *doomed* to remain single forever⟩ — see DESTINE
2 to impose a judicial punishment on ⟨*doomed* the murderer to life in prison without the possibility of parole⟩ — see SENTENCE

door *n* **1** a barrier by which an entry is closed and opened ⟨we locked the *door* to the room so that no one could get in⟩
synonyms gate, hatch, portal
related words Dutch door, French door, lattice, portcullis, postern, trapdoor, wicket
2 the opening through which one can enter or leave a structure ⟨a steady stream of visitors through the front *door*⟩
synonyms doorway, entrance, gate, gateway, way
related words hatch, hatchway

doorkeeper *n* a person who tends a door ⟨the *doorkeeper* held the door open for us so we didn't have to put down our packages⟩
synonyms doorman, gatekeeper, janitor, porter [*chiefly British*]

doorman *n* a person who tends a door ⟨we tipped the *doorman* on our way out of the hotel⟩ — see DOORKEEPER

doorway *n* **1** the means or right of entering or participating in ⟨the *doorway* to a life of luxury and leisure⟩ — see ENTRANCE 1
2 the opening through which one can enter or leave a structure ⟨he stood in the *doorway* until we finally invited him in⟩ — see DOOR 2

dope *n* **1** information not generally available to the public ⟨he gave us the *dope* on the deal taking place that night at the warehouse⟩
synonyms lowdown, scoop, tip
related words dirt, gossip, rumor, story; hint, pointer; information, intelligence, news, tidings, word
2 a stupid person ⟨that *dope* thought he could swim across the Colorado River at night⟩ — see IDIOT

dope (**out**) *vb* to find an answer for through reasoning ⟨tried to *dope out* the answer from the little information we had been given⟩ — see SOLVE

doper *n* a person who regularly uses drugs especially illegally ⟨the *doper* had to go straight, since he couldn't keep a steady job while using drugs⟩
synonyms addict, fiend, junkie (*also* junky), substance abuser, user
related words pothead

dopey *adj* not having or showing an ability to absorb ideas readily ⟨a *dopey* little dog who never learned any tricks⟩ — see STUPID 1

dopiness *n* the quality or state of lacking intelligence or quickness of mind ⟨amused by the sheer *dopiness* of the movie's plot⟩ — see STUPIDITY 1

dork *n, slang* a stupid person ⟨he tried to be suave, but she still thought he was a *dork*⟩ — see IDIOT

dorky *adj, slang* not having or showing an ability to absorb ideas readily ⟨she's always being embarrassed by her *dorky* little cousin⟩ — see STUPID 1

dormancy *n* **1** a state of temporary inactivity ⟨some volcanoes have eruptive cycles marked by long stretches of *dormancy*⟩ — see ABEYANCE
2 lack of action or activity ⟨a fighting force that could be roused instantly from *dormancy* to action⟩ — see INACTION

dormant *adj* **1** being in a state of suspended consciousness ⟨the bears lay *dormant* in their den during the winter⟩ — see ASLEEP 1
2 not being in a state of use, activity, or employment ⟨the engine lay *dormant* in the garage until we could find a use for it⟩ — see INACTIVE 2

dot *n* a small area that is different (as in color) from the main part ⟨there was just a *dot* on the tablecloth where the food had spattered⟩ — see SPOT 1

dot *vb* **1** to cover by or as if by scattering something over or on ⟨a hillside *dotted* with wildflowers⟩ — see SCATTER 2
2 to mark with small spots especially unevenly ⟨the practice of some chefs of positioning a small portion of food in the center and *dotting* the rest of the plate with sauce⟩ — see SPOT

dote (**on**) *vb* to love or admire too much ⟨*doted on* her only grandchild⟩ — see IDOLIZE

dotted *adj* marked with spots ⟨a *dotted* tie that didn't go with his striped shirt at all⟩ — see SPOTTED 1

dotty *adj* showing or marked by a lack of good sense or judgment ⟨*dotty* relatives that we have to endure only on Thanksgiving⟩ — see FOOLISH 1

double *adj* **1** consisting of two members or parts that are usually joined ⟨an egg with a *double* yolk⟩

synonyms binary, bipartite, dual, duplex, twin
related words mated, paired
antonyms single
2 being twice as great or as many ⟨after it was ranked the best in the country, the college had *double* the usual number of applicants⟩
synonyms twofold

double *adv* to two times the amount or degree ⟨raced to his side *double* quick⟩ — see DOUBLY

double *n* something or someone that strongly resembles another ⟨he looks so much like you that he could be your *double*⟩ — see IMAGE 1

double *vb* **1** to make twice as great or as many ⟨we *doubled* our efforts to find a solution to the problem⟩
synonyms duplicate, redouble
related words compound, multiply; accumulate, balloon, build (up), burgeon, enlarge, escalate, expand, increase, mount, mushroom, proliferate, rise, snowball, swell, wax
2 to lay one part over or against another part of ⟨*double* the wet cloth and place it on the victim's forehead⟩ — see FOLD 1

double–cross *vb* to be unfaithful or disloyal to ⟨she promised to help but then *double-crossed* us⟩ — see BETRAY 1

double cross *n* the act or fact of violating the trust or confidence of another ⟨politics is full of *double crosses* and backbiting⟩ — see BETRAYAL

double–crosser *n* one who betrays a trust or an allegiance ⟨we knew he was a *double-crosser* so we didn't tell him our real plans⟩ — see TRAITOR

double–dealing *adj* **1** marked by, based on, or done by the use of dishonest methods to acquire something of value ⟨*double-dealing* business practices that are being investigated by the state's attorney general⟩ — see FRAUDULENT 1
2 not being or expressing what one appears to be or express ⟨*double-dealing* statements of reassurance⟩ — see INSINCERE

double–dealing *n* the inclination or practice of misleading others through lies or trickery ⟨a go-between suspected of *double-dealing*⟩ — see DECEIT

doubly *adv* to two times the amount or degree ⟨we were *doubly* certain of her guilt after we read the article in the newspaper⟩
synonyms double, twice, twofold

doubt *n* a feeling or attitude that one does not know the truth, truthfulness, or trustworthiness of someone or something ⟨from the beginning I had my *doubts* about the new kid in school⟩
synonyms distrust, distrustfulness, incertitude, misgiving, mistrust, mistrustfulness, skepticism, suspicion, uncertainty
related words disbelief, incredulity, unbelief; anxiety, concern; compunction, qualm, scruple
near antonyms credence, faith
antonyms assurance, belief, certainty, certitude, confidence, conviction, sureness, surety, trust

doubt *vb* to have no trust or confidence in ⟨I *doubt* that you can do all you say⟩ — see DISTRUST

doubtable *adj* **1** giving good reason for being doubted, questioned, or challenged ⟨there was only some highly *doubtable* logic supporting her position⟩ — see DOUBTFUL 1
2 open to question or dispute ⟨that it happened at all is *doubtable*⟩ — see DEBATABLE 1

doubter *n* a person who is always ready to doubt or question the truth or existence of something ⟨there will al-

ways be some hard-core *doubters* of the government's denial of the UFO incident⟩ — see SKEPTIC

doubtful *adj* **1** not feeling sure about the truth, wisdom, or trustworthiness of someone or something ⟨he was *doubtful* about the decision to complete the project despite its mounting problems⟩
synonyms distrustful, dubious, mistrustful, skeptical, suspicious, uncertain, unconvinced, undecided, unsettled, unsure
related words diffident, insecure; hesitant, indecisive, irresolute, vacillating, wavering
phrases on the fence
near antonyms assured, confident, sanguine, self-assured; decisive, determined, resolute
antonyms certain, convinced, positive, sure
2 giving good reason for being doubted, questioned, or challenged ⟨the election results were highly *doubtful*, so an investigation was begun⟩
synonyms debatable, disputable, doubtable, dubious, equivocal, fishy, problematic (*also* problematical), questionable, shady, shaky, suspect, suspicious
related words moot; ambiguous, open, unclear; uncertain, undecided, undetermined; far-fetched, flimsy, improbable, unlikely
near antonyms decisive, definitive; clear, obvious, open-and-shut, positive
antonyms certain, incontestable, indisputable, indubitable, sure, undeniable, undoubted, unquestionable
3 not likely to be true or to occur ⟨our winning the championship increasingly looks like a *doubtful* outcome⟩ — see IMPROBABLE
4 open to question or dispute ⟨a *doubtful* claim to the property⟩ — see DEBATABLE 1

doubtfully *adv* with distrust ⟨we followed her *doubtfully*, keeping our eyes open at all times⟩ — see ASKANCE

doubting *adj* inclined to doubt or question claims ⟨a *doubting* Thomas who demands to see everything with his own eyes⟩ — see SKEPTICAL 1

doubtingly *adv* with distrust ⟨we looked at her *doubtingly* as she told the story of her life⟩ — see ASKANCE

doubtless *adj* having or showing a mind free from doubt ⟨another one of his *doubtless* predictions that will never come true⟩ — see CERTAIN 2

doubtless *adv* **1** without any question ⟨she is *doubtless* the one and only girl for me⟩ — see INDEED 1
2 without much doubt ⟨*doubtless* you have heard this story before, but I'll tell it anyway⟩ — see PROBABLY

dough *n* something (as pieces of stamped metal or printed paper) customarily and legally used as a medium of exchange, a measure of value, or a means of payment ⟨didn't have to spend a lot of *dough* for a new stereo⟩ — see MONEY

doughtiness *n* strength of mind to carry on in spite of danger ⟨a new recruit with all of the *doughtiness* of the finest soldiers who ever saw battle⟩ — see COURAGE

doughty *adj* feeling or displaying no fear by temperament ⟨the *doughty* heroes of old⟩ — see BRAVE

dour *adj* harsh and threatening in manner or appearance ⟨a *dour* prison guard who didn't look like he'd be very understanding⟩ — see GRIM 1

douse *vb* **1** to cause to cease burning ⟨*douse* the campfire before leaving in the morning⟩ — see EXTINGUISH 1
2 to make wet ⟨the rains *doused* the tourists strolling the town streets⟩ — see WET
3 to sink or push (something) briefly into or as if into a liquid ⟨*douse* the drapes in water to remove dust⟩ — see DIP 1

doused *adj* containing, covered with, or thoroughly penetrated by water ⟨shook the water out of her thoroughly *doused* hair⟩ — see WET

dove *n* 1 a person who opposes war or warlike policies ⟨the *doves* were in favor of using the money to improve the school system instead of the army⟩
synonyms pacifist
related words peacemaker
near antonyms militarist; chauvinist, nationalist
antonyms hawk, jingo, warmonger
2 an innocent or gentle person ⟨he's a *dove* who wouldn't hurt a fly⟩ — see LAMB

dovetail *vb* to be in agreement on every point ⟨the Union and the Confederate accounts of the battle don't *dovetail* at all⟩ — see CHECK 1

dowager *n* a dignified usually elderly woman of some rank or authority ⟨the *dowagers* frequently shake their heads over the younger generation⟩ — see MATRIARCH

dowdily *adv* in a careless or unfashionable manner ⟨dressed hurriedly and *dowdily* to go do her workout⟩ — see SLOPPILY

dowdy *adj* 1 lacking neatness in dress or person ⟨a *dowdy* old matron⟩ — see SLOPPY 1
2 marked by an obvious lack of style or good taste ⟨the *dowdy*, beat-up furniture at the cheap motel⟩ — see TACKY 1

down *adj* 1 brought or having come to an end ⟨eight *down* and two to go⟩ — see COMPLETE 2
2 directed down ⟨a *down* escalator⟩ — see DOWNCAST 1
3 feeling unhappiness ⟨feeling a bit *down*⟩ — see SAD 1
4 temporarily suffering from a disorder of the body ⟨*down* with the flu⟩ — see SICK 1

down *adv* toward or in a lower position ⟨the stairs went *down* to the basement⟩
synonyms below, downward, over
related words facedown; low; downgrade, downhill, downstairs
near antonyms aloft
antonyms up, upward (*or* upwards), upwardly

¹**down** *n* a soft airy substance or covering ⟨a comforter filled with goose *down*⟩ — see FUZZ

²**down** *n* 1 the act or process of going to a lower level or altitude ⟨suffered with a psychological disorder in which she alternated between emotional ups and *downs*⟩ — see DESCENT 1
2 a loss of status ⟨experienced the ups and *downs* of a career in show biz⟩ — see COMEDOWN

down *vb* 1 to strike (someone) so forcefully as to cause a fall ⟨*downed* his opponent with one stunning blow⟩ — see FELL 1
2 to take into the stomach through the mouth and throat ⟨*downing* slices of pizza and guzzling bottles of soda⟩ — see SWALLOW 1

downcast *adj* 1 directed down ⟨her *downcast* gaze made us realize that she was shy⟩
synonyms down, downward, lowered
near antonyms elevated, lifted, raised, uplifted, upward
2 feeling unhappiness ⟨I'm always a little *downcast* on rainy days⟩ — see SAD 1

downer *n* something (as a situation or event) that is depressing ⟨that math exam was a real *downer*⟩
synonyms bummer
related words bore, drag; accident, fatality, mishap, woe; calamity, catastrophe, debacle (*also* débâcle), misfortune, tragedy

near antonyms pick-me-up

downfall *n* 1 a change to a lower state or level ⟨the gradual *downfall* of the Roman Empire⟩ — see DECLINE 2
2 a loss of status ⟨an ill-advised speech that proved to be the cause of the candidate's *downfall*⟩ — see COMEDOWN

downgrade *n* a change to a lower state or level ⟨a singing career on the *downgrade*⟩ — see DECLINE 2

downgrade *vb* to bring to a lower grade or rank ⟨increased automation resulted in many jobs in the factory being *downgraded*⟩ — see DEMOTE

downhearted *adj* feeling unhappiness ⟨*downhearted* because the family of his best friend was moving out of state⟩ — see SAD 1

downheartedness *n* a state or spell of low spirits ⟨his *downheartedness* lasted until another girl came along and won his heart⟩ — see SADNESS

downpour *n* a steady falling of water from the sky in significant quantity ⟨the *downpour* was so heavy that we were soaked by the time we got to the car⟩ — see RAIN 1

downright *adj* 1 being or characterized by direct, brief, and potentially rude speech or manner ⟨rural folks are often known for their *downright* speech, as they are generally not ones to beat around the bush⟩ — see BLUNT 1
2 having no exceptions or restrictions ⟨that's a *downright* lie, and you know it⟩ — see ABSOLUTE 2

downs *n pl* a broad area of level or rolling treeless country ⟨hold a festival on the *downs*⟩ — see PLAIN

downsize *vb* to make smaller in amount, volume, or extent ⟨the company *downsized* its staff in an attempt to cut costs⟩ — see DECREASE 1

down–to–earth *adj* willing to see things as they really are and deal with them sensibly ⟨a *down-to-earth* guidance counselor who is frank in telling students which colleges they're likely to get into⟩ — see REALISTIC 1

downward *adv* toward or in a lower position ⟨at this point the river flows gently *downward* to the sea⟩ — see DOWN

downward *adj* directed down ⟨at that age where the *downward* pull of gravity on the body is obvious⟩ — see DOWNCAST 1

downwind *adj* being in the direction that the wind is blowing ⟨we were *downwind* of the deer, so it couldn't smell us⟩
synonyms leeward
antonyms upwind, windward

downy *adj* smooth or delicate in appearance or feel ⟨the *downy* surface of a ripe peach⟩ — see SOFT 2

doze *n* a short sleep ⟨a brief *doze* in the sun⟩ — see ¹NAP

doze *vb* 1 to be in a state of sleep ⟨likes to *doze* through those lazy summer afternoons⟩ — see SLEEP 1
2 to sleep lightly or briefly ⟨she *dozed* fitfully in the car but never fell completely asleep⟩ — see NAP 1

dozer *n* one who sleeps ⟨the crash abruptly wakened the *dozers* on the bus⟩ — see SLEEPER

dozing *adj* being in a state of suspended consciousness ⟨the *dozing* dog was running in his dream⟩ — see ASLEEP 1

dozing *n* a natural periodic loss of consciousness during which the body restores itself ⟨*dozing* is a natural response to the stifling heat of summer⟩ — see SLEEP 1

drab *adj* causing weariness, restlessness, or lack of interest ⟨the new city hall promises to be another *drab* pile of masonry for the town⟩ — see BORING

draft *n* **1** a mass or quantity of something taken up and carried, conveyed, or transported ⟨the *draft* of an average-sized oil tanker⟩ — see LOAD 1

2 the portion of a serving of a beverage that is swallowed at one time ⟨took a long *draft* of the beer before putting his mug down⟩ — see DRINK 2

3 noticeable movement of air in a particular direction ⟨do you feel a *draft* from beneath the door?⟩ — see ¹WIND 1

draft *vb* **1** to pick especially for required military service ⟨my grandfather was *drafted* to fight in the war, even though he didn't want to go⟩

synonyms conscript

related words impress, press; enlist, enroll (*also* enrol); sign up, volunteer

near antonyms discharge

2 to put (something) into proper and usually carefully worked out written form ⟨*draft* a letter to the local newspaper giving your views on the problem⟩ — see COMPOSE 1

draftee *n* a person forced or required to enroll in military service ⟨the massive mobilization required *draftees* to be rushed through training⟩ — see CONSCRIPT

drag *n* **1** someone or something boring ⟨that lecture was such a *drag* that half of the audience fell asleep⟩

synonyms bore

related words bummer, downer; pill

near antonyms gas [*slang*]

2 a passage cleared for public vehicular travel ⟨the main *drag* in town⟩ — see WAY 1

3 something that makes movement or progress more difficult ⟨the *drag* of overpopulation on raising the living standards of that developing country⟩ — see ENCUMBRANCE

4 the portion of a serving of a beverage that is swallowed at one time ⟨took a deep *drag* of the party punch⟩ — see DRINK 2

drag *vb* **1** to cause to follow by applying steady force on ⟨the deliveryman *dragged* the barrels over against the wall⟩ — see PULL 1

2 to move or act slowly ⟨one of the climbers was beginning to *drag*⟩ — see DELAY 1

3 to move slowly ⟨the play *dragged* and seemed to take forever to get to its predictable conclusion⟩ — see CRAWL 2

dragger *n* someone who moves slowly or more slowly than others ⟨we quickly left the *draggers* behind⟩ — see SLOWPOKE

dragging *adj* moving or proceeding at less than the normal, desirable, or required speed ⟨a mysterious, cloaked figure with a strange, *dragging* walk⟩ — see SLOW 1

drain *vb* **1** to remove (liquid) gradually or completely ⟨we *drained* the water from the tank before cleaning it⟩

synonyms bleed, draw (off), pump, siphon, tap

related words milk; suck; clear, empty, evacuate, exhaust, vacate, void

antonyms fill

2 to make complete use of ⟨virtually *drained* the country's natural resources⟩ — see DEPLETE

3 to use up all the physical energy of ⟨the long hike *drained* us⟩ — see EXHAUST 1

drained *adj* depleted in strength, energy, or freshness ⟨we were completely *drained* after shoveling snow all afternoon⟩ — see WEARY 1

drainpipe *n* a pipe or channel for carrying off water from a roof ⟨our *drainpipe* is always getting clogged with leaves⟩ — see GUTTER 1

drama *n* **1** the public performance of plays ⟨he has been interested in *drama* from the first time he ever saw a play⟩

synonyms dramatics, stage, theater (*or* theatre), theatricals

related words boards; acting, footlights; entertainment, show business

2 a written work in which the story is told through speech and action that is intended to be acted out on stage ⟨wrote a police *drama* that really captured the speech of cops and criminals⟩ — see PLAY 2

dramatic *adj* **1** having the general quality or effect of a stage performance ⟨the basketball player's *dramatic* announcement of his sudden retirement held everybody spellbound⟩

synonyms histrionic, melodramatic, theatrical

related words affected, emotional, sensational

near antonyms matter-of-fact, monotonous

antonyms undramatic, untheatrical

2 given to or marked by attention-getting behavior suggestive of stage acting ⟨oh, don't be so *dramatic*, and just tell us, without the pregnant pauses, what happened⟩ — see THEATRICAL 1

3 likely to attract attention ⟨a *dramatic* drop in the temperature overnight⟩ — see NOTICEABLE

dramatics *n pl* the public performance of plays ⟨took part in *dramatics* while a student at the local university⟩ — see DRAMA 1

dramatization *n* a written work in which the story is told through speech and action that is intended to be acted out on stage ⟨a *dramatization* of a true story⟩ — see PLAY 2

drapery *n* pieces of cloth hung to darken, decorate, or divide a room ⟨the *drapery* for the picture window matched the color of the furniture in the center of the room⟩

synonyms curtains, drapes

related words hanging(s), tapestry, window shade

drapes *n pl* pieces of cloth hung to darken, decorate, or divide a room ⟨we hung new *drapes* in the living room to match the new color scheme⟩ — see DRAPERY

draw *n* **1** a situation in which neither participant in a contest, competition, or struggle comes out ahead of the other ⟨the game ended in a *draw*⟩ — see TIE 1

2 something that attracts interest ⟨they hoped that the new waterfront development would be a big *draw* for tourists⟩ — see MAGNET

3 the act or an instance of applying force on something so that it moves in the direction of the force ⟨took a *draw* on his cigarette and immediately started coughing⟩ — see PULL 1

draw *vb* **1** to cause to follow by applying steady force on ⟨*draw* a chair up to the fire and sit with us⟩ — see PULL 1

2 to give a representation or account of in words ⟨a writer who *draws* characters well⟩ — see DESCRIBE 1

3 to receive as return for effort ⟨*draw* a weekly salary⟩ — see EARN 1

4 to take away from a place or position ⟨*draw* her aside so we can ask a quick question⟩ — see REMOVE 2

5 to take the internal organs out of ⟨hated the thought of having to pluck and *draw* a goose before cooking it⟩ — see GUT

draw (off) *vb* to remove (liquid) gradually or completely ⟨*drew off* the fat from the top of the drippings⟩ — see DRAIN 1

draw (up) *vb* to put (something) into proper and usually carefully worked out written form ⟨*draw up* a proposal and submit it to the committee for approval⟩ — see COMPOSE 1

drawback *n* a feature of someone or something that creates difficulty for achieving success ⟨this plan has only one *drawback*: it's unworkable⟩ — see DISADVANTAGE

drawing *n* a picture using lines to represent the chief features of an object or scene ⟨he made a *drawing* of the tree in his sketchpad while he was waiting for the bus⟩
synonyms cartoon, delineation, sketch
related words outline, silhouette; caricature, doodle, illustration; depiction, image, likeness, portrait, representation; engraving, etching; blueprint

drawing out *n* the act of making longer ⟨the tedious *drawing out* of wool into thread that was required before weaving⟩ — see EXTENSION 1

drawn *adj* stretched with little or no give ⟨properly *drawn* skins covered both ends of the drum⟩ — see TAUT

draw on *vb* to come near or nearer ⟨night *draws on*, so we should hurry home⟩ — see APPROACH 1

draw out *vb* to make longer ⟨the actor refused to *draw out* the interview any further⟩ — see EXTEND 1

draw up *vb* **1** to bring (something) to a standstill ⟨he *drew up* his horse outside the tavern⟩ — see ¹HALT 1
2 to put into a particular arrangement ⟨*drew up* the troops into a line along the ridge⟩ — see ORDER 1

dread *n* **1** suspicion or fear of future harm or misfortune ⟨the *dread* felt by people awaiting bad news⟩ — see APPREHENSION 1
2 the emotion experienced in the presence or threat of danger ⟨we were filled with *dread* when we saw the rapids we would be rafting down⟩ — see FEAR

dreadful *adj* **1** causing fear ⟨a *dreadful* storm⟩ — see FEARFUL 1
2 causing intense displeasure, disgust, or resentment ⟨a *dreadful* performance of a beautiful piece of music⟩ — see OFFENSIVE 1
3 extremely disturbing or repellent ⟨*dreadful* news of a crime wave in the neighborhood⟩ — see HORRIBLE 1

dreadfulness *n* the quality of inspiring intense dread or dismay ⟨the *dreadfulness* of an oncoming avalanche can scarcely be described⟩ — see HORROR 1

dream *n* **1** a series of often striking pictures created by the imagination during sleep ⟨I had a *dream* last night about flying without any support⟩
synonyms nightmare, vision
related words daydream, pipe dream, reverie (*also* revery); chimera, delusion, fancy, fantasy (*also* phantasy), figment, hallucination, illusion, mirage, phantasm
2 a conception or image created by the imagination and having no objective reality ⟨his invention is only a *dream* right now, but someday it might be a reality⟩ — see FANTASY 1
3 something that one hopes or intends to accomplish ⟨my *dream* is to open my own restaurant⟩ — see GOAL

dream *vb* to form a mental picture of ⟨I *dreamed* that I was living on an island in the South Pacific⟩ — see IMAGINE 1

dreamer *n* one whose conduct is guided more by the image of perfection than by the real world ⟨a *dreamer* who believes that war doesn't have to be part of the human condition⟩ — see IDEALIST

dreamily *adv* in a pleasing way ⟨our date at the restaurant went *dreamily*⟩ — see WELL 5

dreamy *adj* **1** giving pleasure or contentment to the mind or senses ⟨a beach resort that is a perfectly *dreamy* place to relax⟩ — see PLEASANT
2 tending to calm the emotions and relieve stress ⟨the kind of *dreamy* music I want after a hard day at work⟩ — see SOOTHING 1

drear *adj* **1** causing or marked by an atmosphere lacking in cheer ⟨it was a *drear* morning in January when I went to take my driving test⟩ — see GLOOMY 1
2 causing unhappiness ⟨a barren and *drear* existence in a remote village⟩ — see SAD 2

dreariness *n* a state or spell of low spirits ⟨my own *dreariness* seemed to match the dismal weather we were having⟩ — see SADNESS

dreary *adj* **1** causing or marked by an atmosphere lacking in cheer ⟨vowed that he would never take a desk job working in a *dreary* office⟩ — see GLOOMY 1
2 causing unhappiness ⟨decided to see a professional counselor in order to save their *dreary* marriage⟩ — see SAD 2
3 causing weariness, restlessness, or lack of interest ⟨another *dreary* social event to suffer through⟩ — see BORING

dredge *vb* to look through (as a place) carefully or thoroughly in an effort to find or discover something ⟨I've been *dredging* my memory bank, and I simply can't remember her name⟩ — see SEARCH 1

dregs *n pl* matter that settles to the bottom of a body of liquid ⟨poured the *dregs* into the trash⟩ — see DEPOSIT 1

drench *vb* **1** to make wet ⟨we were *drenched* by the sudden rainstorm⟩ — see WET
2 to wet thoroughly with liquid ⟨when using the carpet shampooer, wet but do not *drench* the carpet⟩ — see SOAK 1

drenched *adj* containing, covered with, or thoroughly penetrated by water ⟨the *drenched* tourists straggled into the visitors' center⟩ — see WET

dress *adj* relating to or suitable for wearing to an event requiring elegant dress and manners ⟨the naval commander wore his *dress* uniform to the ball⟩
synonyms dressy, formal
related words costume; chic, dapper, fashionable, modish, natty, sharp, smart, stylish; custom-made, fitted, tailored; state
near antonyms street; dowdy, unfashionable, unstylish
antonyms casual, informal, sporty

dress *n* **1** a garment with a joined blouse and skirt for a woman or girl ⟨what a lovely *dress* you're wearing today!⟩
synonyms frock, gown
related words chemise, granny, housedress, jumper, Mother Hubbard, muumuu (*or* mumu), overdress
2 clothing chosen as appropriate for a specific situation ⟨a bagpiper in full Scottish Highlander *dress*⟩ — see OUTFIT 1
3 covering for the human body ⟨a businessman who is very conservative in his *dress*⟩ — see CLOTHING

dress *vb* **1** to cover with a bandage ⟨first wash and then *dress* the wound⟩ — see BANDAGE
2 to make more attractive by adding something that is beautiful or becoming ⟨let's *dress* up the room with some greenery for the holiday party⟩ — see DECORATE
3 to make smooth or glossy usually by repeatedly applying surface pressure ⟨*dress* the granite block to be used as the headstone on all four sides⟩ — see POLISH

4 to outfit with clothes and especially fine or special clothes ⟨*dressed* the young girl in satin and lace⟩ — see CLOTHE 1

5 to put on one's best or formal clothes ⟨we don't usually *dress* for dinner⟩ — see DRESS UP

dress down *vb* to criticize (someone) severely or angrily especially for personal failings ⟨*dressed down* for boorish behavior at the dance⟩ — see SCOLD

dressing *n* **1** a medicated covering used to heal an injury ⟨nurses put a *dressing* over his cuts so they wouldn't get infected⟩
synonyms plaster, poultice
related words balm, cream, liniment, lotion, ointment, salve, unguent
2 a savory fluid food used as a topping or accompaniment to a main dish ⟨salad *dressing*⟩ — see SAUCE 1

dress up *vb* **1** to put on one's best or formal clothes ⟨we always like to *dress up* when going to parties⟩
synonyms doll up, dress
related words apparel, array, attire, bedeck, bedizen, caparison, clothe, costume, deck, garb, garment, invest, rig (out), robe
2 to change the dress or looks of so as to conceal true identity ⟨the war was a fiasco that the administration tried to *dress up* as a triumph⟩ — see DISGUISE

dressy *adj* relating to or suitable for wearing to an event requiring elegant dress and manners ⟨shopping for a *dressy* handbag for a New Year's Eve party⟩ — see DRESS

dribble *vb* **1** to fall or let fall in or as if in drops ⟨water *dribbling* over the lip of the fountain⟩ — see DRIP
2 to flow in a broken irregular stream ⟨water *dribbling* along the partially clogged gutter⟩ — see GURGLE
3 to let saliva or some other substance flow from the mouth ⟨picnickers *dribbling* in eager anticipation of the hamburgers on the grill⟩ — see DROOL

driblet *n* **1** a very small amount ⟨money doled out in *driblets* to the workers⟩ — see PARTICLE 1
2 the quantity of fluid that falls naturally in one rounded mass ⟨rain leaked through the roof in solitary *driblets* here and there⟩ — see DROP 1

drift *n* **1** a pile or ridge of granular matter (as sand or snow) ⟨deep *drifts* of snow blocked our driveway⟩ — see ²BANK
2 a prevailing or general movement or inclination ⟨the *drift* of the population away from large cities⟩ — see TREND 1
3 the idea that is conveyed or intended to be conveyed to the mind by language, symbol, or action ⟨you should expect a visit from the stork, if you get my *drift*⟩ — see MEANING 1

drift *vb* **1** to move or proceed smoothly and readily ⟨casual conversation *drifting* from one topic to another⟩ — see FLOW 2
2 to rest or move along the surface of a liquid or in the air ⟨the boat *drifted* along on the current⟩ — see FLOAT

drifter *n* a person who roams about without a fixed route or destination ⟨the *drifter* just packed up and moved on whenever he felt like it⟩ — see NOMAD

drill *n* something done over and over in order to develop skill ⟨doing vocabulary *drills* all afternoon in preparation for the test⟩ — see EXERCISE 2

¹drill *vb* **1** to make a hole or series of holes in ⟨*drill* a tooth⟩ — see PERFORATE
2 to strike with a missile from a gun ⟨*drilled* the target from 100 yards away⟩ — see SHOOT 3

²drill *vb* to put or set into the ground to grow ⟨he *drills* soybeans in the same rows with corn⟩ — see PLANT

drink *n* **1** a liquid suitable for drinking ⟨we went inside to have a *drink* after mowing the lawn⟩
synonyms beverage, libation, quencher
related words potion; pop, soda, soda pop, soft drink; alcohol, brew, intoxicant, liquor, spirits
2 the portion of a serving of a beverage that is swallowed at one time ⟨the thirsty scout took a long *drink* from his canteen⟩
synonyms draft, drag, gulp, nip, quaff, shot, sip, slug, snort, sup, swallow, swig, swill
3 a fermented or distilled beverage that can make a person drunk ⟨you can get *drinks* at the bar only if you show them a valid ID⟩ — see ALCOHOL

drink *vb* **1** to swallow in liquid form ⟨the doctor wants her to *drink* lots of water before the examination⟩
synonyms gulp, guzzle, imbibe, quaff, sip, slurp, sup, swig, swill, toss (down *or* off)
related words lap, lick; consume, down, mouth (down); tipple; toast, wine
2 to take in (something liquid) through small openings ⟨the hot surface of the porous rock *drank* water like a sponge⟩ — see ABSORB 1

drinkable *adj* suitable for drinking ⟨technically, that cheap stuff may be wine, but it's hardly *drinkable*⟩ — see POTABLE

drip *n* the quantity of fluid that falls naturally in one rounded mass ⟨the faucet leaked one *drip* after another no matter what I did to try to fix it⟩ — see DROP 1

drip *vb* to fall or let fall in or as if in drops ⟨water from the leaky roof was *dripping* all over the floor⟩ ⟨the cracked bottle *dripped* wine⟩
synonyms dribble, trickle
related words bleed, exude, ooze, seep, weep; discharge

dripping *adj* containing, covered with, or thoroughly penetrated by water ⟨*dripping* shoes left on the porch to dry⟩ — see WET

drive *n* **1** a passage cleared for public vehicular travel ⟨raced our motorcycles along the *drive*⟩ — see WAY 1
2 a series of activities undertaken to achieve a goal ⟨a fund-raising *drive* for the school's marching band⟩ — see CAMPAIGN
3 a strong wish for something ⟨a *drive* to succeed in the television news business⟩ — see DESIRE
4 active strength of body or mind ⟨senior citizens who exercise regularly are more likely to have the *drive* to keep up with their grandchildren⟩ — see VIGOR 1
5 readiness to engage in daring or difficult activity ⟨a great opportunity for a sales representative who is full of *drive*⟩ — see ENTERPRISE 2

drive *vb* **1** to urge, push, or force onward ⟨cowboys *drove* the herd of cattle from San Antonio to San Francisco⟩
synonyms herd, punch, run
related words shepherd; wrangle; egg, exhort, goad, prick, prod, spur, urge
2 to travel by a motorized vehicle ⟨I'm going to *drive* across the country—want to come?⟩
synonyms automobile, motor
related words roll, wheel; chauffeur, taxi; ride; drag, race
3 to apply force to (someone or something) so that it moves in front of one ⟨*drove* the plunger into the opening⟩ — see PUSH 1
4 to cause (a person) to give in to pressure ⟨the corrupt governor was *driven* out of office⟩ — see FORCE

5 to cause to function ⟨machinery *driven* by water-power⟩ — see ACTIVATE

6 to set or keep in motion ⟨this motor *drives* the gears, which then turn the shaft⟩ — see MOVE 2

drivel *n* **1** language, behavior, or ideas that are absurd and contrary to good sense ⟨that critic's reviews are nothing but *drivel*⟩ — see NONSENSE 1

2 unintelligible or meaningless talk ⟨she talks in her sleep, but it's just *drivel*⟩ — see GIBBERISH

drivel *vb* **1** to let saliva or some other substance flow from the mouth ⟨the panting dog *driveled* on my hand⟩ — see DROOL

2 to speak rapidly, inarticulately, and usually unintelligibly ⟨he *driveled* on about his family for what seemed like hours⟩ — see BABBLE 1

driver *n* a person who travels by automobile ⟨fans arriving by public transportation will find the south entrance most convenient, but *drivers* will have a choice of entrances⟩ — see MOTORIST

drizzle *n* a light or fine rain ⟨the intermittent *drizzle* was just heavy enough to spoil all of our outdoor activities⟩
synonyms mist, sprinkle
related words precipitation, rainfall, shower
near antonyms cloudburst, deluge, downpour, storm; rainstorm, thunderstorm; monsoon

droll *adj* causing or intended to cause laughter ⟨made a *droll* comment about the commencement speaker⟩ — see FUNNY 1

drollness *n* the amusing quality or element in something ⟨the radio host's dependable *drollness* ensures that listeners keep tuning in⟩ — see HUMOR 1

¹drone *n* a lazy person ⟨those *drones* just lie around while we do all the work⟩ — see LAZYBONES

²drone *n* a monotonous sound like that of an insect in motion ⟨heard the *drone* of an airplane overhead⟩ — see HUM

drone *vb* to fly, turn, or move rapidly with a fluttering or vibratory sound ⟨the sound of *droning* bees all around us⟩ — see WHIRR

drool *vb* to let saliva or some other substance flow from the mouth ⟨the dog *drooled* when we put the steak down on the floor⟩
synonyms dribble, drivel, salivate, slaver, slobber
related words water; expectorate, spit; foam, froth; sputter

droop *n* the extent to which something hangs or dips below a straight line ⟨tighten the line at the top of the banner so there won't be so much *droop*⟩ — see SAG

droop *vb* **1** to be limp from lack of water or vigor ⟨the flowers *drooped* on their stalks in the blazing sun⟩
synonyms flag, hang, loll, sag, wilt
related words slouch, slump; collapse, drop, fall, sink, subside
near antonyms distend, stiffen; rise, straighten

2 to lose bodily strength or vigor ⟨as the afternoon wore on, we started to *droop*⟩ — see WEAKEN 2

drooping *adj* bending downward or forward ⟨faded, *drooping* banners lining the walls of the hall⟩ — see NODDING

droopy *adj* **1** bending downward or forward ⟨the *droopy* heads of tired fans riding home on the bus⟩ — see NODDING

2 not stiff in structure ⟨a *droopy* stalk of celery⟩ — see LIMP 1

3 feeling unhappiness ⟨looking *droopy* and miserable while standing in the pouring rain⟩ — see SAD 1

drop *n* **1** the quantity of fluid that falls naturally in one rounded mass ⟨a *drop* of water fell from the leaky faucet every few seconds⟩
synonyms blob, driblet, drip, droplet, glob, globule
related words dewdrop, raindrop, tear; spatter; dribble, trickle

2 distance measured from the top to the bottom of something ⟨a *drop* of ten feet from the roof to the ground⟩ — see DEPTH 1

3 the act or process of going to a lower level or altitude ⟨the sudden *drop* of the plane really shook up the passengers⟩ — see DESCENT 1

4 the amount by which something is lessened ⟨a huge *drop* in pressure⟩ — see DECREASE

5 the more favorable condition or position in a competition ⟨got the *drop* on his opponent very early in the wrestling match⟩ — see ADVANTAGE 1

drop *vb* **1** to cause to fall intentionally or unintentionally ⟨I *dropped* the fly ball⟩ ⟨*drop* the anchor⟩
synonyms depress, lower
related words flatten, floor, level; bobble, bungle, foozle, fumble; immerse, sink, submerge
antonyms lift, pick up, raise

2 to go to a lower level ⟨although they start out high, prices for home electronics eventually *drop*⟩
synonyms decline, descend, dip, fall, lower, nose-dive, plummet, plunge, sink, tumble
related words decrease, diminish, lessen; recede, retreat
antonyms arise, lift, rise, soar

3 to bring (as an action or operation) to an immediate end ⟨*drop* what you're doing and come here⟩ — see STOP 1

4 to stop doing (something) permanently ⟨isn't it time you *dropped* that smoking habit and spent your money on better things?⟩ — see QUIT 2

5 to lead or extend downward ⟨the cable car tracks can *drop* suddenly, so be sure to hang onto something⟩ — see DESCEND 1

6 to put an end to (something planned or previously agreed to) ⟨*drop* that plan in favor of another⟩ — see CANCEL 1

7 to bring forth from the womb ⟨the cow *dropped* her calf⟩ — see BEAR 1

8 to strike (someone) so forcefully as to cause a fall ⟨*dropped* him in his tracks with a single well-aimed blow⟩ — see FELL 1

drop (by *or* in) *vb* to make a brief visit ⟨I just *dropped by* to say hello⟩ — see CALL 3

droplet *n* the quantity of fluid that falls naturally in one rounded mass ⟨there were only a few *droplets* left in the canteen⟩ — see DROP 1

dropping *n* **1** **droppings** *pl* solid matter discharged from an animal's alimentary canal ⟨the only bad part about owning a rabbit was cleaning the *droppings* out of the cage every night⟩
synonyms dung, excrement, excreta, feces, slops, waste
related words stool; dunghill, guano, manure, muck; spoor; sewage

2 the act of putting an end to something planned or previously agreed to ⟨the *dropping* of an act from the talent show should bring it in on time⟩ — see CANCELLATION

dross *n* discarded or useless material ⟨get rid of the *dross* before closing up the shop⟩ — see GARBAGE

droughty *adj* marked by little or no precipitation or humidity ⟨a *droughty* region that could never support settlements⟩ — see DRY 1

drove *n* **1** a great number of persons or things gathered together ⟨people flocked to the event in *droves*⟩ — see CROWD 1

2 a group of domestic animals assembled or herded together ⟨a *drove* of cattle⟩ — see HERD

drown *vb* **1** to cover or become filled with a flood ⟨villages *drowned* by the overflowing river⟩ — see FLOOD

2 to wet thoroughly with liquid ⟨*drowned* the fish in a rich sauce⟩ — see SOAK 1

drowse *n* a short sleep ⟨was just falling into a *drowse* when you called⟩ — see ¹NAP

drowse *vb* to sleep lightly or briefly ⟨picnickers *drowsing* in the shade of an oak tree⟩ — see NAP 1

drowsiness *n* the quality or state of desiring or needing sleep ⟨we tried to fight our *drowsiness* but fell asleep anyway⟩ — see SLEEPINESS

drowsy *adj* **1** desiring or needing sleep ⟨the *drowsy* students shuffled into class⟩ — see SLEEPY 1

2 tending to cause sleep ⟨listened to *drowsy* music while waiting in the dentist's office⟩ — see HYPNOTIC

drub *vb* **1** to strike repeatedly ⟨a crowd was *drubbing* the purse snatcher when the police arrived on the scene⟩ — see BEAT 1

2 to achieve a victory over ⟨determined to *drub* the enemy at any cost⟩ — see BEAT 2

3 to defeat by a large margin ⟨we *drubbed* our traditional football rivals so badly that it was basically no contest⟩ — see WHIP 2

drubbing *n* failure to win a contest ⟨took a terrible *drubbing* in last night's basketball game⟩ — see DEFEAT 1

drudge *n* a person who does very hard or dull work ⟨worked like a *drudge* at the low-paying job that had few benefits⟩ — see SLAVE 2

drudge *vb* to devote serious and sustained effort ⟨factory workers who must *drudge* all day at repetitive tasks⟩ — see LABOR

drudger *n* a person who does very hard or dull work ⟨a youth striving to become something more than just a *drudger* working at some dead-end job⟩ — see SLAVE 2

drudgery *n* very hard or unpleasant work ⟨in the "good old days" household servants led lives filled with much *drudgery* and little pleasure⟩ — see TOIL

drug *n* a substance or preparation used to treat disease ⟨prescribed a *drug* to treat the bacterial infection⟩ — see MEDICINE

druggist *n* a person who prepares drugs according to a doctor's prescription ⟨she got her prescription for antibiotics filled by the *druggist*⟩
synonyms apothecary, pharmacist
related words pharmacologist

drugstore *n* a retail store where medicines and miscellaneous articles are sold ⟨we picked up her medicine and some toothpaste at the *drugstore*⟩
synonyms pharmacy
related words dispensary

drum *n* a metal container in the shape of a cylinder ⟨an oil *drum*⟩ — see CAN

drum *vb* to strike or cause to strike lightly and usually rhythmically ⟨absentmindedly *drumming* his fingers on the table⟩ — see ¹TAP

drum (out) *vb* to drive or force out ⟨*drummed out* of the service for conduct unbecoming an officer⟩ — see EJECT 1

drunk *adj* being under the influence of alcohol ⟨several wedding guests who got a little *drunk*⟩

synonyms drunken, high, inebriate, inebriated, intoxicated, loaded [*slang*], soused, tipsy
related words maudlin; befuddled, stupefied; debauched, dissipated, dissolute
near antonyms abstemious, abstinent, temperate; clearheaded, cool, level, steady
antonyms sober

drunk *n* **1** a person who makes a habit of getting drunk ⟨you can't trust anything that old *drunk* says⟩
synonyms drunkard, inebriate, soak, sot, souse, tippler
related words alcoholic, substance abuser; drinker
near antonyms abstainer

2 a bout of drinking ⟨after a week-long *drunk* he was unable to remember anything⟩ — see CAROUSE

drunkard *n* a person who makes a habit of getting drunk ⟨accused him of being a no-good *drunkard* who needed professional help for his problem⟩ — see DRUNK 1

drunken *adj* being under the influence of alcohol ⟨the *drunken* revelers made sure to take taxis home instead of trying to drive⟩ — see DRUNK

dry *adj* **1** marked by little or no precipitation or humidity ⟨the *dry* climate of the American Southwest⟩
synonyms arid, droughty, sere, thirsty, waterless
related words baked, dehydrated, parched, sunbaked; rainless
near antonyms drenched, dripping, saturated, soaked, soaking, sodden, sopping, soppy, soused
antonyms damp, dank, humid, moist, wet

2 causing weariness, restlessness, or lack of interest ⟨a very *dry* topic for a lecture before a body of students⟩ — see BORING

dry *vb* **1** to make dry ⟨they *dried* the grapes to make raisins⟩
synonyms dehydrate, parch, sear
related words dehumidify; evaporate; shrivel, wither
near antonyms deluge, douse, drench, saturate, soak, sop, souse; damp, dampen, moisten; rehydrate
antonyms hydrate, wet

2 to lose liveliness, force, or freshness ⟨grapes *drying* on the vine in the scorching heat⟩ — see WITHER

dryad *n* a mythical goddess represented as a young girl and said to live outdoors ⟨*dryads* were said to live within trees, their lives ending when the life of the tree ended⟩ — see NYMPH 1

dry run *n* a private performance or session in preparation for a public appearance ⟨we had time for just one *dry run* of the play before opening night⟩ — see REHEARSAL

dual *adj* consisting of two members or parts that are usually joined ⟨*dual* axles⟩ — see DOUBLE 1

dub *vb* to give a name to ⟨I've *dubbed* my car the "Lone Ranger," although "Loan Raider" probably would have been more apt⟩ — see NAME 1

dubious *adj* **1** giving good reason for being doubted, questioned, or challenged ⟨any letter bearing the signature of Samoset would be of *dubious* authenticity, to say the least⟩ — see DOUBTFUL 2

2 having doubts about the wisdom of doing something ⟨I'm *dubious* about our plan to go hang gliding without having had any training⟩ — see HESITANT

3 not likely to be true or to occur ⟨made the *dubious* claim of being of royal blood⟩ — see IMPROBABLE

4 not feeling sure about the truth, wisdom, or trustworthiness of someone or something ⟨*dubious* about a diet that claims I can eat all I want and still lose weight⟩ — see DOUBTFUL 1

dubiously *adv* with distrust ⟨the young girl approached the camel *dubiously*⟩ — see ASKANCE

duck *vb* **1** to get or keep away from (as a responsibility) through cleverness or trickery ⟨don't try to *duck* your commitment to babysit by pretending you have to be someplace else⟩ — see ESCAPE 2

2 to move suddenly aside or to and fro ⟨*duck* behind a pillar before they see us⟩ — see DODGE 1

3 to sink or push (something) briefly into or as if into a liquid ⟨*ducked* the new camper in the lake as a joke⟩ — see DIP 1

ducking *n* the act or a means of getting or keeping away from something undesirable ⟨the disgraceful *ducking* of your duties to your family⟩ — see ESCAPE 2

duck soup *n* something that is easy to do ⟨with proper preparation, this test should be *duck soup*⟩ — see CINCH

duct *n* a long hollow cylinder for carrying a substance (as a liquid or gas) ⟨air *ducts* to provide ventilation⟩ — see PIPE 1

dud *n* **1** something that has failed ⟨our first attempt was a *dud* and we had to start over⟩ — see FAILURE 3

2 duds *pl* covering for the human body ⟨those are some pretty fancy *duds* you're wearing⟩ — see CLOTHING

dude *n* **1** a man extremely interested in his clothing and personal appearance ⟨a *dude* given to sporting expensive suits and flashy jewelry⟩ — see DANDY 1

2 an adult male human being ⟨OK, *dude*, whatever you say⟩ — see MAN 1

dudgeon *n* the feeling of being offended or resentful after a slight or indignity ⟨stomped off in high *dudgeon* after having his honor questioned⟩ — see PIQUE

due *adj* **1** having reached the date at which payment is required ⟨the loan is *due* next April⟩

synonyms mature

related words delinquent, outstanding, overdue, owed, owing, receivable, unpaid, unsettled; payable

2 being in accordance with the prescribed, normal, or logical course of events ⟨their train is *due* to arrive in half an hour⟩

synonyms anticipated, awaited, expected, scheduled, slated

near antonyms belated, delinquent, dilatory, latish, overdue, tardy

3 being what is called for by accepted standards of right and wrong ⟨all the participants in the trial are required to treat the judge with *due* respect⟩ — see JUST 1

due *adv* in a direct line or course ⟨a plane flying *due* east⟩ — see DIRECTLY 1

due (to) *adj* coming as a result ⟨success that is *due to* hard work⟩ — see RESULTANT

duel *n* an earnest effort for superiority or victory over another ⟨a *duel* for the title of captain of the team⟩ — see CONTEST 1

due to *prep* as the result of ⟨classes were cancelled *due to* heavy snow⟩ — see BECAUSE OF

dull *adj* **1** lacking sharpness of edge or point ⟨the *dull* knife just bounced off the skin of the tomato without cutting it⟩

synonyms blunt, blunted, dulled, obtuse

related words rounded

near antonyms cutting, edged, edgy, ground, honed, stropped; jagged, needlelike, prickly, spiked, spiky, spiny

antonyms keen, pointed, sharp, sharpened, whetted

2 causing weariness, restlessness, or lack of interest ⟨a *dull* dance recital that made us wish that we were someplace else⟩ — see BORING

3 covered over by clouds ⟨*dull* skies plagued most of our vacation at the beach⟩ — see OVERCAST

4 lacking a surface luster or gloss ⟨a good polish should restore that car's *dull* finish⟩ — see MATTE

5 lacking intensity of color ⟨that canvas shirt should fade to an attractive, *dull* red over time⟩ — see PALE 1

6 not having or showing an ability to absorb ideas readily ⟨the importance of the discovery was lost on the *dull* minds of his colleagues⟩ — see STUPID 1

7 not loud in pitch or volume ⟨a *dull* roar from the distance⟩ — see SOFT 1

8 slow to move or act ⟨a *dull* market for luxury goods⟩ — see INACTIVE 1

dull *vb* **1** to reduce or weaken in strength or feeling ⟨the aspirin *dulled* his headache and he was soon feeling better⟩

synonyms benumb, blunt, damp, dampen, deaden, numb

related words muffle, mute, tone (down); decrease, diminish, lessen, let up (on), reduce, subdue; debilitate, enfeeble, weaken; dwindle, recede, subside, taper (off), wane; alleviate, ease, lighten; abate, moderate

near antonyms amplify, beef (up), boost, consolidate, deepen, enhance, heighten, intensify, magnify, redouble, step up, strengthen; animate, arouse, stimulate

antonyms sharpen, whet

2 to make white or lighter by removing color ⟨the painting's once-vivid colors have been *dulled* by time⟩ — see WHITEN

dulled *adj* **1** lacking a surface luster or gloss ⟨it might be best to paint the exposed pipes with a *dulled* enamel⟩ — see MATTE

2 lacking intensity of color ⟨the *dulled* colors and brownish tones are characteristic of this painter's works⟩ — see PALE 1

3 lacking sharpness of edge or point ⟨the *dulled* blade of a knife that had been stored in a drawer of utensils⟩ — see DULL 1

dullness *also* **dulness** *n* the quality or state of lacking intelligence or quickness of mind ⟨the *dullness* of the characters in horror movies cannot be overstated⟩ — see STUPIDITY 1

dumb *adj* **1** deliberately refraining from speech ⟨the mayor has chosen to remain *dumb* about her activities that night⟩ — see SILENT 1

2 not having or showing an ability to absorb ideas readily ⟨don't call him *dumb* just because he makes the occasional mistake like the rest of us⟩ — see STUPID 1

dumbbell *n* a stupid person ⟨if we don't give him a shove, the poor *dumbbell* never will propose to her⟩ — see IDIOT

dumbfound *also* **dumfound** *vb* to make a strong impression on (someone) with something unexpected ⟨the surprise ending will *dumbfound* even the most seasoned mystery reader⟩ — see SURPRISE 1

dumbfounded *or* **dumfounded** *adj* **1** affected with sudden and great wonder or surprise ⟨the *dumbfounded* tourists gazed in awe at the spectacle⟩ — see THUNDERSTRUCK

2 filled with amazement or wonder ⟨*dumbfounded* visitors to the Grand Canyon⟩ — see OPENMOUTHED

dumbfounding *or* **dumfounding** *adj* causing a strong emotional reaction because unexpected ⟨the *dumbfounding* sight of the race car driver walking away from that horrific crash⟩ — see SURPRISING 1

dumbness *n* **1** incapacity for or restraint from speaking ⟨the determined *dumbness* of the accountants who tally the votes for the Academy Awards⟩ — see SI-LENCE 1

2 the quality or state of lacking intelligence or quickness of mind ⟨couldn't believe the *dumbness* of the people who fell for that scam⟩ — see STUPIDITY 1

dummy *n* **1** a stupid person ⟨only a *dummy* would think that the mechanical monster was real⟩ — see IDIOT

2 a three-dimensional representation of the human body used especially for displaying clothes ⟨the *dummies* were arranged in the store window as if they were acting out scenes⟩ — see MANNEQUIN 1

dump *n* **1** a place where discarded materials (as trash) are dumped ⟨all of the used packaging eventually ends up in the *dump*⟩

synonyms landfill, sanitary landfill

related words pigpen, pigsty

2 a place where military arms are stored ⟨a daring raid on the ammunition *dump*⟩ — see ARMORY

dump *vb* to get rid of as useless or unwanted ⟨*dump* the trash on the curb and go back inside⟩ — see DISCARD

dumping *n* the getting rid of whatever is unwanted or useless ⟨the *dumping* of last year's fashions by the garment manufacturers⟩ — see DISPOSAL 1

dumps *n pl* a state or spell of low spirits ⟨I've been down in the *dumps* all week⟩ — see SADNESS

dumpy *adj* being compact and broad in build and often short in stature ⟨*dumpy* little men trying to look like tough guys⟩ — see STOCKY

dun *n* something that someone insists upon having ⟨it's probably not a good idea to ignore a loan shark's *dun* for repayment⟩ — see DEMAND 1

dunce *n* a stupid person ⟨there are no *dunces* among my friends⟩ — see IDIOT

dung *n* solid matter discharged from an animal's alimentary canal ⟨researchers tracked the wild gorillas by following the piles of *dung*⟩ — see DROPPING 1

dunk *vb* to sink or push (something) briefly into or as if into a liquid ⟨*dunking* a doughnut in one's morning coffee⟩ — see DIP 1

duo *n* two things of the same or similar kind that match or are considered together ⟨the shy boy and his outgoing friend make an unlikely *duo*⟩ — see PAIR

dupe *n* one who is easily deceived or cheated ⟨the swindler was able to escape with all of the *dupe's* money⟩

synonyms chump, gull, pigeon, sap, sucker, tool

related words victim; schlemiel; butt, derision, laughingstock, mark, mock, mockery; booby, dodo, fool, goose, half-wit, jackass, lunatic, monkey, nincompoop, ninny, nitwit, simpleton, turkey; pushover; loser

near antonyms confidence man, shark, sharper, swindler, trickster

dupe *vb* to cause to believe what is untrue ⟨we were *duped* into thinking the dummy was a real alien⟩ — see DECEIVE

duplex *adj* consisting of two members or parts that are usually joined ⟨a *duplex* house with all of the bedrooms on the second floor⟩ — see DOUBLE 1

duplicate *adj* resembling another in every respect ⟨*duplicate* copies of the school lunch menu⟩ — see SAME 1

duplicate *n* **1** something or someone that strongly resembles another ⟨doll carriages that are *duplicates* of baby carriages⟩ — see IMAGE 1

2 something that is made to look exactly like something else ⟨a *duplicate* of a house key⟩ — see COPY 1

duplicate *vb* **1** to make an exact likeness of ⟨art students trying to *duplicate* paintings in the museum's collection as part of their training⟩ — see COPY 1

2 to make or do again ⟨we were unable to *duplicate* the experiment in our own lab⟩ — see REPEAT 4

3 to make twice as great or as many ⟨the recipe can be easily *duplicated* in order to feed a large family⟩ — see DOUBLE 1

duplication *n* **1** something or someone that strongly resembles another ⟨in adulthood he became sort of a living *duplication* of his late father⟩ — see IMAGE 1

2 something that is made to look exactly like something else ⟨a *duplication* of an ancient Chinese vase for the mass market⟩ — see COPY

3 the act of saying or doing over again ⟨let's avoid *duplication* of effort if we can⟩ — see REPEAT

duplicity *n* the inclination or practice of misleading others through lies or trickery ⟨we were lucky not to be taken in by his *duplicity*⟩ — see DECEIT

durability *n* continuing existence ⟨the *durability* of Shakespeare's reputation could scarcely have been imagined in Elizabethan England⟩ — see PERSISTENCE 1

duration *n* **1** the period during which something exists, lasts, or is in progress ⟨for the whole *duration* of the speech the bored audience fidgeted⟩

synonyms date, life, life span, lifetime, run, standing, time

related words spell, stretch; span, tenure, term; hitch, tour, turn

2 uninterrupted or lasting existence ⟨scientists warning that the very *duration* of our civilization depends upon finding a solution to this major environmental problem⟩ — see CONTINUATION

duress *n* the use of power to impose one's will on another ⟨complied with the order only under *duress*⟩ — see FORCE 2

during *prep* in the course of ⟨we wrote notes *during* the boring lecture⟩

synonyms over, through, throughout

dusk *n* **1** the time from when the sun begins to set to the onset of total darkness ⟨we stopped playing at *dusk*, since it was getting too dark to see the ball⟩

synonyms evening, eventide, gloaming, nightfall, sundown, sunset, twilight

related words dark, darkness, night, nighttime

near antonyms day, daytime, light

antonyms aurora, cockcrow, dawn, dawning, daybreak, daylight, morn, morning, sunrise, sunup

2 a time or place of little or no light ⟨legends of fearsome beasts living in the *dusk* of the great forest⟩ — see DARK 1

dusky *adj* being without light or without much light ⟨in the *dusky* depths of the dungeon⟩ — see DARK 1

dust *n* **1** discarded or useless material ⟨the piles of *dust* that future archaeologists will sift through for insights into our civilization⟩ — see GARBAGE

2 the solid part of our planet's surface as distinguished from the sea and air ⟨laid him out in the *dust* with one blow to the head⟩ — see EARTH 2

dustiness *n* the state or quality of being dirty ⟨we were glad for a shower after the *dustiness* of the hike⟩ — see DIRTINESS 1

dusty *adj* **1** consisting of very small particles ⟨*dusty* soil⟩ — see FINE 1

2 not clean ⟨old *dusty* clothes⟩ — see DIRTY 1

dutiful *adj* marked by or showing proper regard for another's higher status ⟨the family showed a *dutiful* deference to their minister when he came to dinner⟩ — see RESPECTFUL

duty *n* **1** a charge usually of money collected by the government from people or businesses for public use ⟨the *duty*-free shop at the airport⟩ — see TAX

2 a piece of work that needs to be done regularly ⟨the regular *duties* of a lifeguard⟩ — see CHORE 1

3 something one must do because of prior agreement ⟨I must obey the call of *duty* and serve my country⟩ — see OBLIGATION

dwarf *adj* of a size that is less than average ⟨a *dwarf* elephant⟩ — see SMALL 1

dwarf *n* **1** a living thing much smaller than others of its kind ⟨Shetland ponies are the *dwarfs* of the horse world⟩

   synonyms diminutive, midget, mite, peewee, pygmy, runt, scrub, shrimp

   related words mini, miniature

   near antonyms whale

   antonyms behemoth, colossus, giant, jumbo, leviathan, mammoth, monster, titan

2 an imaginary being usually having a small human form and magical powers ⟨Snow White and the seven *dwarfs*⟩ — see FAIRY

dwarf *vb* to hold back the normal growth of ⟨shrubs *dwarfed* by the lack of water⟩ — see STUNT

dwarfish *adj* of a size that is less than average ⟨a *dwarfish* people living deep in the rain forest⟩ — see SMALL 1

dwell *vb* **1** to continue to be in a place for a significant amount of time ⟨*dwelling* with a farm family as an exchange student in France⟩ — see STAY 1

2 to have a home ⟨the widow *dwells* in the valley by herself⟩ — see LIVE 1

dweller *n* one who lives permanently in a place ⟨the kinds of nuisances that city *dwellers* are all too familiar with⟩ — see INHABITANT

dwelling *n* the place where one lives ⟨the simple *dwellings* in which the Pilgrims spent the first winter at Plymouth⟩ — see HOME 1

dwindle *vb* **1** to make smaller in amount, volume, or extent ⟨the long winter *dwindled* our supply of firewood to practically nothing⟩ — see DECREASE 1

2 to grow less in scope or intensity especially gradually ⟨our hopes *dwindled* as the reports of more casualties came in⟩ — see DECREASE 2

dye *n* a substance used to color other materials ⟨soaked the fabric in blue *dye*⟩ — see PIGMENT

dye *vb* to give color or a different color to ⟨*dyed* her hair a startling red⟩ — see COLOR 1

dyestuff *n* a substance used to color other materials ⟨indigo is a *dyestuff* originally from India⟩ — see PIGMENT

dying *adj* nearly dead ⟨we watered the *dying* plants just in time⟩ — see MORIBUND

dynamic *adj* **1** having active strength of body or mind ⟨a *dynamic* new challenger for the title of heavyweight champion⟩ — see VIGOROUS 1

2 marked by or uttered with forcefulness ⟨a *dynamic* speech expressing her party's goals and values⟩ — see EMPHATIC 1

dyspeptic *adj* having or showing a habitually bad temper ⟨as might be expected, the newspaper's resident curmudgeon took a *dyspeptic* view of the whole affair⟩ — see ILL-TEMPERED

E

each *adj* being one of a group ⟨*each* park visitor receives a free souvenir⟩
synonyms any, every
related words all; several, various; particular; respective, specific
phrases each and every

each *adv* for each one ⟨raffle tickets selling for a dollar *each*⟩ — see APIECE

eager *adj* showing urgent desire or interest ⟨Tom was *eager* to try out his new pair of skis⟩
synonyms agog, anxious, ardent, athirst, avid, crazy, desirous, enthusiastic, excited, gung ho, hot, hungry, impatient, keen, nuts, raring, solicitous, thirsty, voracious
related words engaged, interested; hung up, obsessed; ambitious, covetous, craving, hankering, longing, pining; restive, restless; disposed, inclined, ready, unreluctant, willing
phrases champing at the bit
near antonyms incurious, unconcerned, uninterested; aloof, detached, disinterested; impassive, stolid; half-hearted, lackadaisical, languid, languorous, spiritless; averse, disinclined, hesitant, loath (*or* loth), reluctant, unwilling
antonyms apathetic, indifferent, uneager

eagerness *n* urgent desire or interest ⟨students with an *eagerness* to learn⟩
synonyms appetite, ardor, avidity, desirousness, enthusiasm, excitement, hunger, impatience, keenness, thirst
related words alacrity, quickness; ambition, gusto, zest
near antonyms unconcern; aloofness, detachment; impassivity, languor
antonyms apathy, indifference

ear *n* a state of being aware ⟨I'm trying to get Dad's *ear* in order to ask for a raise in my allowance⟩ — see ATTENTION 2

earliest *adj* coming before all others in time or order ⟨the *earliest* computers were massive machines that practically filled up a room⟩ — see FIRST 1

early *adj* **1** relating to or occurring near the beginning of a process, series, or time period ⟨*early* birds of the Jurassic period⟩
synonyms ancient, primal, primeval, primitive, primordial
related words aged, antediluvian, antiquated, antique, hoary
near antonyms advanced, complex
antonyms late
2 occurring before the usual or expected time ⟨we had an *early* dinner so as not to miss the concert⟩
synonyms inopportune, precocious, premature, unseasonable, untimely
related words unanticipated, unexpected; abrupt, sudden
near antonyms slow, tardy; anticipated, expected
antonyms late

early *adv* before the usual or expected time ⟨that year spring arrived *early*⟩
synonyms beforehand, inopportunely, precociously, prematurely, unseasonably
related words immediately, promptly, punctually; betimes, seasonably

near antonyms belatedly, tardily
antonyms late

earmark *vb* to keep or intend for a special purpose ⟨the earnings from my paper route have been *earmarked* for a digital camera⟩ — see DEVOTE 1

earn *vb* **1** to receive as return for effort ⟨for years I've *earned* pocket money by mowing lawns⟩
synonyms acquire, attain, capture, carry, draw, gain, garner, get, land, make, obtain, procure, realize, secure, win
related words clear, net; accomplish, achieve, notch (up), score; accumulate, draw, rack up; catch, pick up; occupy, take over; reacquire, recapture, regain, remake
phrases come by
near antonyms give up, hand over, part (with), relinquish, surrender, yield
antonyms forfeit, lose
2 to be or make worthy of (as a reward or punishment) ⟨you've *earned* the afternoon off after all that hard work⟩
synonyms deserve, merit, rate
related words entitle, qualify

earnest *adj* not joking or playful in mood or manner ⟨I'll accept only an *earnest* apology from you⟩ — see SERIOUS 1

earnestness *n* a mental state free of jesting or trifling ⟨practiced the art of acting with great *earnestness*⟩
synonyms gravity, intentness, seriousness, soberness, sobriety, solemnity
related words deliberation, determination, firmness, purposefulness, resolve; absorption, attentiveness, concentration, engrossment
near antonyms lightness, shallowness, superficiality; dalliance, dilettantism
antonyms frivolity, levity, lightheartedness

earnings *n pl* **1** an increase usually measured in money that comes from labor, business, or property ⟨*earnings* from her babysitting jobs that are being put away for college⟩ — see INCOME
2 the amount of money left when expenses are subtracted from the total amount received ⟨after subtracting what we spent on lemons, sugar, and paper cups, the *earnings* from our lemonade stand were still impressive⟩ — see PROFIT 1

earshot *n* range of hearing ⟨babysitters should remain within *earshot* of young children⟩
synonyms hearing, sound
related words volume; distance, sight

earsplitting *adj* marked by a high volume of sound ⟨the *earsplitting* noise coming from the jackhammers at the construction site⟩ — see LOUD 1

earth *n* **1** the celestial body on which we live ⟨environmentalists who are committed to preserving the *earth*⟩
synonyms globe, planet, world
related words cosmos, creation, universe; orb, sphere; macrocosm, microcosm
2 the solid part of our planet's surface as distinguished from the sea and air ⟨after nearly drowning, I was glad to feel the *earth* under my feet⟩
synonyms dirt, dust, ground, land, soil
related words continent, landmass; island, isthmus, mainland, peninsula

3 the loose surface material in which plants naturally grow ⟨set the plants deep enough into the *earth* so that they'll be sure to take root⟩ — see DIRT 1

earthenware *n* articles made of baked clay ⟨a wide array of hand-painted *earthenware* available at the craft fair⟩ — see CROCKERY

earthlike *adj* consisting or suggestive of earth ⟨the basket of garden-fresh mushrooms had that typically *earthlike* smell⟩ — see EARTHY 1

earthly *adj* having to do with life on earth especially as opposed to that in heaven ⟨a sermon against our obsession with *earthly* pursuits⟩
    synonyms carnal, fleshly, material, mundane, temporal, terrestrial, worldly
    related words bodily, corporal, corporeal, physical; daily, diurnal; unspiritual
    near antonyms celestial, empyreal, empyrean; divine, spiritual, utopian; extraterrestrial
    antonyms heavenly, nontemporal

earthquake *n* a shaking of the earth ⟨the San Andreas Fault is notorious for its *earthquakes*⟩
    synonyms quake, tremor
    related words shock; cataclysm, convulsion, upheaval

earthy *adj* **1** consisting or suggestive of earth ⟨the unmistakably *earthy* aroma of a greenhouse⟩
    synonyms earthlike, loamy
    related words clayey, dusty, muddy, sandy
    2 willing to see things as they really are and deal with them sensibly ⟨the dog trainer was *earthy*, nononsense, and blunt—with us, as well as our dog⟩ — see REALISTIC 1

ease *n* **1** reduction of or freedom from pain ⟨the sunburn medication brought me instant *ease*⟩
    synonyms alleviation, comfort, relief
    related words appeasement, assuagement, decrease, diminishment, moderation, mollification; calming, salving, soothing
    near antonyms discomfort, unrest; agony, anguish, pain
    2 carefree freedom from constraint ⟨a gymnast who can handle even the most demanding moves on the parallel bars with total *ease*⟩ — see ABANDON
    3 freedom from activity or labor ⟨the dream of every lottery player is a life of fabulous luxury and everlasting *ease*⟩ — see ¹REST 1

ease *vb* **1** to free from obstruction or difficulty ⟨measures intended to *ease* the flow of traffic during rush hour⟩
    synonyms facilitate, loosen (up), smooth, unclog
    related words accelerate, expedite, hasten, speed; advance, further, promote; aid, assist, help, improve
    phrases pave the way (for)
    near antonyms hinder, impede; retard
    antonyms complicate
    2 to make less taut ⟨the rock climber *eased* the rope a little so that his fellow climber had room to maneuver⟩ — see SLACKEN
    3 to make more bearable or less severe ⟨grandmother's belief that there are few ailments that chicken soup won't *ease*⟩ — see HELP 2

easily *adv* without difficulty ⟨a skater who *easily* executes even the most difficult jumps⟩
    synonyms effortlessly, facilely, fluently, freely, handily, lightly, painlessly, readily, smoothly
    related words ably, adeptly, adroitly, competently, dexterously, efficiently, expertly, proficiently, skillfully; instinctively, intuitively, naturally, spontaneously

    near antonyms awkwardly, clumsily, gracelessly, ineptly, maladroitly; painfully, painstakingly
    antonyms arduously, laboriously

easy *adj* **1** involving minimal difficulty or effort ⟨a minor problem with an *easy* solution⟩
    synonyms effortless, facile, fluent, fluid, light, painless, ready, simple, smooth, snap, soft
    related words apparent, clear, distinct, evident, manifest, obvious, plain; clear-cut, straightforward, uncomplicated
    near antonyms painful, troublesome; abstruse, complex, complicated, intricate, knotty
    antonyms arduous, difficult, hard, labored
    2 readily taken advantage of ⟨senior citizens who are *easy* prey for scam artists⟩
    synonyms exploitable, gullible, naive (*or* naïve), susceptible, trusting
    related words credulous, trustful, uncritical, unsuspecting, unsuspicious; artless, simple, unsophisticated
    near antonyms critical, cynical, mistrustful, skeptical, suspicious; sophisticated
    3 providing physical comfort ⟨my favorite *easy* chair for watching TV⟩ — see COMFORTABLE 1

easygoing *adj* **1** having a relaxed, casual manner ⟨counselors at the summer camp are pretty *easygoing*⟩
    synonyms affable, breezy, devil-may-care, happy-go-lucky, laid-back, low-pressure
    related words carefree, lackadaisical, nonchalant, unaffected, unconcerned; familiar, homey, informal; lax, lenient, permissive, soft
    near antonyms ceremonious, decorous, formal, rigid, strict
    antonyms uptight
    2 not bound by rigid standards ⟨boys are pretty *easygoing* about housekeeping⟩
    synonyms flexible, lax, loose, relaxed, slack, unrestrained, unrestricted
    related words careless, heedless, negligent, slipshod, sloppy, slovenly, unfussy
    near antonyms constrained, restrained, restricted, rigid, strict, tight; exact, fussy, meticulous, scrupulous
    antonyms rigorous
    3 having or showing a lack of concern or seriousness ⟨your *easygoing* attitude toward your schoolwork promises a bright future behind the counter at a fast-food restaurant⟩ — see CAREFREE

eat *vb* **1** to take in as food ⟨having gone all day without food, we greedily *ate* the hamburgers⟩
    synonyms consume, ingest
    related words digest, down, mouth (down), swallow; bolt, devour, gobble (up *or* down), gorge, gulp, wolf; chew, gnaw (at *or* on), lap, lick, nibble (on); relish, savor, taste; banquet, dine, feast, gormandize, pig out; dispatch, polish off; breakfast, lunch, sup; munch, snack
    2 to consume or wear away gradually ⟨the pot's protective coating was *eaten* away by the acid⟩
    synonyms bite (at), corrode, erode, fret
    related words break down, break up, decompose, disintegrate, dissolve; destroy, ruin, wreck
    3 to take a meal ⟨where's the best place to *eat* in this town?⟩ — see DINE 1

eat (up) *vb* to destroy all trace of ⟨the surf created by a powerful hurricane could really *eat up* what's left of the island's eastern beach⟩ — see CONSUME 1

eatable *adj* suitable for use as food ⟨a survival course in which you learn which wild plants are *eatable*⟩ — see EDIBLE

eatables *n pl* substances intended to be eaten ⟨the buffet table aboard the cruise ship always had a tempting array of *eatables*⟩ — see FOOD

eavesdrop (on) *vb* to listen to (another in private conversation) ⟨a nosy traveler who likes to *eavesdrop on* his fellow airline passengers⟩
synonyms listen in (on), overhear
related words bug, tap, wiretap; monitor, snoop, spy; hear, hearken

eaves trough *n* a pipe or channel for carrying off water from a roof ⟨rain so heavy that the *eaves trough* couldn't handle it⟩ — see GUTTER 1

ebb *vb* **1** to become worse or of less value ⟨the fortunes of the town slowly *ebbed* as factory after textile factory closed⟩ — see DETERIORATE
2 to grow less in scope or intensity especially gradually ⟨the howling winds *ebbed* as the hurricane moved into the interior⟩ — see DECREASE 2

ebbing *n* a gradual sinking and wasting away of mind or body ⟨seniors who stay active can keep at bay some of the inevitable *ebbing* of the memory that comes with advanced years⟩ — see DECLINE 1

ebony *adj* having the color of soot or coal ⟨the *ebony* loudspeakers on their chrome stands look very sleek and modern⟩ — see BLACK 1

eccentric *n* a person of odd or whimsical habits ⟨an *eccentric* who designed his house to look like a Scottish castle⟩
synonyms character, codger, crackbrain, crackpot, crank, kook, nut, oddball, screwball, weirdo
related words bohemian, maverick, nonconformist; coot, rarity; freak
near antonyms conformer, conformist, follower, sheep

eccentricity *n* an odd or peculiar habit ⟨one of the woman's *eccentricities* was her lifelong habit of reading while soaking in the bathtub for hours⟩ — see IDIOSYNCRASY

ecclesiastic *n* a person specially trained and authorized to conduct religious services in a Christian church ⟨as the leading *ecclesiastic* for his church in the state, the bishop must be beyond reproach in everything he does⟩ — see CLERGYMAN

ecclesiastical *or* **ecclesiastic** *adj* of or relating to a church ⟨*ecclesiastical* laws that have been in existence for centuries⟩
synonyms churchly
related words divine, holy, religious, sacramental; apostolic, canonical, clerical, episcopal, evangelical, ministerial, papal, pastoral, patriarchal, pontifical, priestly, rabbinical, sacerdotal
near antonyms lay, profane, secular, temporal

echo *vb* **1** to continue or be repeated in a series of reflected sound waves ⟨my calls for help *echoed* off the walls of the abandoned mine shaft⟩ — see REVERBERATE
2 to say after another ⟨the little brats sassed the babysitter by *echoing* in a singsong voice everything she said⟩ — see REPEAT 3

eclipse *vb* to be greater, better, or stronger than ⟨the brilliant young pianist now *eclipsed* even his own mentor in musical artistry⟩ — see SURPASS 1

economical *adj* careful in the management of money or resources ⟨we have to be *economical* in our use of the camp's limited supply of electricity⟩ — see FRUGAL

economize *vb* to avoid unnecessary waste or expense ⟨in tough times people learn how to *economize*⟩

synonyms save, scrimp, skimp
related words conserve, husband, manage; scrape; cut back, cut down, retrench
near antonyms dissipate, fritter (away), squander, throw away
antonyms waste

economizing *adj* careful in the management of money or resources ⟨*economizing* drivers aren't so affected by every hike in the price of gasoline⟩ — see FRUGAL

economy *n* careful management of material resources ⟨people on fixed incomes are used to practicing *economy*⟩
synonyms frugality, husbandry, providence, scrimping, skimping, thrift
related words conservation, saving; miserliness, stinginess; discretion, prudence
near antonyms extravagance, improvidence, lavishness, prodigality, squandering
antonyms wastefulness

ecstasy *n* a state of overwhelming usually pleasurable emotion ⟨actors are typically in *ecstasy* upon winning an Oscar⟩
synonyms elation, euphoria, exhilaration, heaven, intoxication, paradise, rapture, rhapsody, transport
related words exaltation; bliss, blissfulness, delight, enchantment, gladness, happiness, joy, joyfulness, pleasure; reverie, trance; inspiration; fervor, frenzy, madness, passion
near antonyms blues, dejection, despondency, doldrums, downheartedness, dumps, melancholy, mopes
antonyms depression

ecstatic *adj* experiencing or marked by overwhelming usually pleasurable emotion ⟨a football player who was *ecstatic* upon receiving a full athletic scholarship to the college of his choice⟩
synonyms elated, enraptured, entranced, euphoric, exhilarated, intoxicated, rapturous, rhapsodic (*also* rhapsodical)
related words exultant, jubilant, triumphant; enthusiastic, excited, gung ho, thrilled; blissful, delighted, glad, gratified, happy, joyful, joyous, pleased, satisfied, tickled
near antonyms blue, dejected, despondent, disconsolate, disheartened, downhearted, melancholy
antonyms depressed

Eden *n* a place or state of great happiness ⟨some of the first Europeans to explore Polynesia thought that they had discovered a tropical *Eden*⟩ — see PARADISE 1

edge *n* **1** a harsh or sharp quality ⟨the teacher's voice had a sarcastic *edge* as she welcomed the tardy student to class⟩
synonyms acidity, acridness, acrimoniousness, acrimony, acuteness, asperity, bite, bitterness, harshness, keenness, poignancy, pungency, roughness, sharpness, tartness
related words ginger, punch, spice, tang; severity, shrillness, virulence; pointedness, thorniness
2 the line or relatively narrow space that marks the outer limit of something ⟨the design along the *edge* of the plate is badly worn⟩ — see BORDER 1
3 the more favorable condition or position in a competition ⟨my big feet give me something of an *edge* in swimming⟩ — see ADVANTAGE 1

edge *vb* to make sharp or sharper ⟨if you *edge* the tip of that stick, it should be a fine skewer for roasting marshmallows⟩ — see SHARPEN

edged *adj* having an edge thin enough to cut or pierce something ⟨always store your finely *edged* knives in a knife block⟩ — see SHARP 1

edgewise *adv* with one side faced forward ⟨you can squeeze through the narrow passage between the two caves if you go *edgewise*⟩ — see SIDEWAYS

edginess *n* a state of nervousness marked by sudden jerky movements ⟨the *edginess* of the basketball players in the moments before the start of the tournament was apparent⟩ — see JUMPINESS

edgy *adj* **1** feeling or showing uncomfortable feelings of uncertainty ⟨with an *edgy* voice the spelling-bee contestant started to spell the tongue twister⟩ — see NERVOUS 1

2 having an edge thin enough to cut or pierce something ⟨be careful as you walk along the beach—those broken clam shells are *edgy* enough to cut your feet⟩ — see SHARP 1

edible *adj* suitable for use as food ⟨*edible* plant products⟩

synonyms eatable, esculent

related words absorbable, chewable, digestible; nourishing, nutritious, nutritive; appetizing, delicious, flavorful, palatable, savory, succulent, tasty, toothsome

near antonyms indigestible, nondigestible

antonyms inedible

edibles *n pl* substances intended to be eaten ⟨even if the storm turns out to be a blizzard, there are enough *edibles* in the refrigerator to last us a week⟩ — see FOOD

edict *n* **1** an order publicly issued by an authority ⟨the school board's *edict* put a new student dress code into effect⟩

synonyms decree, directive, fiat, ruling

related words call, decision, judgment (*or* judgement); announcement, declaration, dictum, manifesto, proclamation, pronouncement; canon, encyclical

2 a statement of what to do that must be obeyed by those concerned ⟨this household's *edict* of long standing: no television until all homework has been completed⟩ — see COMMAND 1

edifice *n* **1** a large, magnificent, or massive building ⟨the U.S. Capitol is one of our nation's most impressive *edifices*⟩

synonyms hall, palace, tower

related words construction, erection, structure; castle, château, estate, manor, mansion, villa; mausoleum, memorial, monument

2 something built as a dwelling, shelter, or place for human activity ⟨the first *edifices* built by the colonists were primitive huts with walls of dried mud and roofs covered with thatch⟩ — see BUILDING

edify *vb* to provide (someone) with moral or spiritual understanding ⟨a family-oriented show that tried to *edify* the television audience as well as entertain it⟩ — see ENLIGHTEN 2

edit *vb* to prepare for publication by correcting, rewriting, or updating ⟨the publisher *edited* a new version of its best-selling school dictionary⟩

synonyms redraft, revamp, revise, rework

related words amend, correct, emend, rectify; collect, compile; issue, print, publish

educate *vb* **1** to cause to acquire knowledge or skill in some field ⟨park rangers have tried to *educate* visitors about the dangers of feeding the bears⟩ — see TEACH

2 to provide (someone) with moral or spiritual understanding ⟨the belief that parents better *educate* their children by example than by sending them to Sunday school⟩ — see ENLIGHTEN 2

educated *adj* having or displaying advanced knowledge or education ⟨*educated* people are often more aware and tolerant of cultural and ethnic diversity⟩

synonyms erudite, knowledgeable, learned, literate, scholarly, well-read

related words civilized, cultivated, cultured; cerebral, highbrow, intellectual; polished, refined, well-bred; academic, bookish, didactic, pedantic, professorial; instructed, schooled, skilled, trained; homeschooled, self-educated, self-taught; briefed, enlightened, informed, versed

near antonyms uncivilized, uncultivated, uncultured; lowbrow, unintelligent; ill-bred, unpolished, unrefined; uninformed

antonyms ignorant, illiterate, uneducated

education *n* **1** the act or process of imparting knowledge or skills to another ⟨a teacher who devoted herself to the *education* of children with special needs⟩

synonyms instruction, schooling, teaching, training, tutelage, tutoring

related words coaching, conditioning, cultivation, preparation, readying; development, direction, guidance, nurturance, nurturing; edification, enlightenment, improvement

2 the understanding and information gained from being educated ⟨a person whose extensive *education* was obvious to all who met him⟩

synonyms erudition, knowledge, learnedness, learning, scholarship, science

related words culture, edification, enlightenment; literacy, reading; bookishness, pedantry

near antonyms ignorance, illiteracy

educational *adj* **1** providing useful information or knowledge ⟨we found the talk on easy ways for families to recycle household products very *educational*⟩ — see INFORMATIVE

2 of or relating to schooling or learning especially at an advanced level ⟨the community college strives to meet the *educational* needs of the residents of its urban location⟩ — see ACADEMIC

educative *adj* providing useful information or knowledge ⟨college students discover that what they experience outside the classroom can be just as *educative* as anything that happens within⟩ — see INFORMATIVE

educator *n* a person whose occupation is to give formal instruction in a school ⟨decided at a fairly young age that there is no more rewarding career than that of an *educator*⟩ — see TEACHER

educe *vb* to draw out (something hidden, latent, or reserved) ⟨the gift of a puppy finally *educed* a response from the shy boy⟩

synonyms elicit, evoke, raise

related words drag, dredge (up), extort, pull, wangle, wrest, wring; gain, get, obtain, procure, secure; expose, reveal, uncover

near antonyms miss, overlook, pass over

eerie *adj* fearfully and mysteriously strange or fantastic ⟨*eerie* noises would occasionally come from locked rooms in the castle⟩

synonyms creepy, haunting, spooky, uncanny, unearthly, weird

related words ghostly, spectral; odd, strange, uncommon, unusual; preternatural, supernatural; enigmatic (*also* enigmatical), inscrutable, mysterious, puzzling; dreadful, fearsome, horrible, horrifying, terrible, terrifying

near antonyms common, commonplace, everyday, normal, ordinary, usual

efface *vb* to destroy all traces of ⟨when the supply ship finally arrived, it discovered that virtually all evidence of the colony at Roanoke had been *effaced*⟩ — see ANNIHILATE 1

effect *n* **1** a condition or occurrence traceable to a cause ⟨better health is always one of the *effects* of improved hygiene⟩
synonyms aftereffect, aftermath, conclusion, consequence, corollary, development, fate, fruit, issue, outcome, outgrowth, product, result, resultant, sequel, sequence, upshot
related words ramification; denouement, repercussion; conclusion, end; by-product, side effect
phrases matter of course
near antonyms consideration, determinant, factor; base, basis, foundation, ground, groundwork
antonyms antecedent, cause, occasion, reason
2 the power to bring about a result on another ⟨religion has a profound *effect* on our lives⟩
synonyms impact, influence, mark, repercussion, sway
related words authority, clout, prestige, weight; command, domination, dominion; consequence, importance, significance
3 effects *pl* transportable items that one owns ⟨the family packed up its household *effects* and moved to Florida⟩ — see POSSESSION 2

effect *vb* to be the cause of (a situation, action, or state of mind) ⟨classroom discussions designed to *effect* a change in racial attitudes⟩
synonyms bring about, cause, create, effectuate, engender, generate, induce, make, produce, prompt, result (in), spawn, work, yield
related words decide, determine; begin, establish, father, found, inaugurate, initiate, institute, introduce, set, set up; advance, encourage, forward, foster, promote; enact, render, turn out
phrases bring forth, give rise to
near antonyms impede, limit, restrict; dampen, repress, smother, stifle, suppress; arrest, check, curb, restrain, retard; can, kill, snuff (out), still; abolish, demolish, destroy, extinguish, liquidate, quash, quell, quench

effective *adj* **1** producing or capable of producing a desired result ⟨an *effective* treatment of the once-dreaded disease⟩
synonyms effectual, efficacious, efficient, fruitful, potent, productive
related words adequate, capable, competent; adept, expert, masterly, proficient, skilled, skillful; cogent, convincing, killer, sound, striking, telling, valid; active, dynamic; operative, useful, working; feasible, practical, realizable, workable
near antonyms incapable, incompetent, inexpert, unqualified; abortive, bootless, futile, vain; empty, hollow, idle, pointless; inoperative, useless, worthless
antonyms fruitless, ineffective, ineffectual, inefficient, unproductive
2 having the power to persuade ⟨made an *effective* argument in favor of the proposal⟩ — see COGENT

effectiveness *n* **1** the capacity to persuade ⟨the "guilty" verdict was all the proof needed of the *effectiveness* of the prosecutor's closing argument⟩ — see COGENCY 1
2 the power to produce a desired result ⟨the huge upsurge in sales pretty much demonstrated the *effectiveness* of the new ad campaign⟩ — see EFFICACY
3 the quality of an utterance that provokes interest and produces an effect ⟨your writing lacks *effectiveness* be-

cause practically every sentence is in the passive voice⟩ — see ¹PUNCH 1

effectual *adj* producing or capable of producing a desired result ⟨acting like a jerk has generally not been a terribly *effectual* dating strategy⟩ — see EFFECTIVE 1

effectualness *n* the power to produce a desired result ⟨the *effectualness* of that new cancer treatment has yet to be proven⟩ — see EFFICACY

effectuate *vb* to be the cause of (a situation, action, or state of mind) ⟨the hope that the greater social interaction between native residents and the immigrants will *effectuate* greater understanding and harmony⟩ — see EFFECT

effeminate *adj* having or displaying qualities more suitable for women than for men ⟨a comedian deliberately affecting *effeminate* mannerisms⟩
synonyms feminine, girlish, sissy, unmanly, womanish, womanlike, womanly
related words old-maidish, overnice, spinsterish; dandyish, foppish, sappy
antonyms manlike, manly, mannish, masculine

effervescent *adj* joyously unrestrained ⟨candidates for positions on the cheerleading squad should have naturally *effervescent* personalities⟩ — see EXUBERANT

effete *adj* **1** having lost forcefulness, courage, or spirit ⟨the soft, *effete* society that marked the final years of the Roman empire⟩
synonyms decadent, decayed, degenerate, overripe, washed-up
related words decaying, declining, dying, failing, waning; soft, weak; dissolute, immoral
2 depleted in strength, energy, or freshness ⟨an *effete* rock band that had done too many concert tours and sung their old hits too many times⟩ — see WEARY 1
3 lacking bodily strength ⟨the Western ranch takes *effete* youths from comfortable suburbs and turns them into rugged wranglers⟩ — see WEAK 1
4 lacking strength of will or character ⟨the governor is too *effete* to take on the powerful special interests that really run this state⟩ — see WEAK 2

efficacious *adj* producing or capable of producing a desired result ⟨taking a cookie break while studying is one of the most *efficacious* ways of rejuvenating the mind that I have ever discovered⟩ — see EFFECTIVE 1

efficaciousness *n* the power to produce a desired result ⟨the debatable *efficaciousness* of many of the campaigns aimed at reducing smoking among teenagers⟩ — see EFFICACY

efficacy *n* the power to produce a desired result ⟨questioned the *efficacy* of the alarms in actually preventing auto theft⟩
synonyms effectiveness, effectualness, efficaciousness, efficiency, productiveness
related words ability, capability, capacity; potency, strength
near antonyms inability, inadequacy, incompetence
antonyms ineffectiveness, ineffectualness, inefficiency

efficiency *n* the power to produce a desired result ⟨the proven *efficiency* of citizen patrols in reducing crime in urban neighborhoods⟩ — see EFFICACY

efficient *adj* producing or capable of producing a desired result ⟨that manual lawn mower is not a very *efficient* tool for doing a huge yard⟩ — see EFFECTIVE 1

effort *n* the active use of energy in producing a result ⟨the finished parade float was well worth the *effort*⟩
synonyms elbow grease, exertion, expenditure, labor, pains, sweat, trouble, while, work

related words drudgery, grind, toil, travail; dint, energy; force, might, muscle, power, puissance; attempt, endeavor, essay
near antonyms adroitness, ease, facility, fluency, smoothness; idleness, inaction, inactivity, indolence, inertia, languor, laziness
effortless *adj* involving minimal difficulty or effort ⟨using an automatic dishwasher is not quite as *effortless* as I would like—you still have to put the dishes away⟩ — see EASY 1
effortlessly *adv* without difficulty ⟨the pizza worker flung the round of dough into the air and *effortlessly* caught it⟩ — see EASILY
effrontery *n* shameless boldness ⟨the little squirt had the *effrontery* to deny eating any cookies, even with the crumbs still on his lips⟩
synonyms audacity, brashness, brass, brassiness, brazenness, cheek, cheekiness, chutzpah (*also* chutzpa *or* hutzpah *or* hutzpa), gall, nerve, nerviness, pertness, presumption, presumptuousness, sauce, sauciness, temerity
related words arrogance, assurance, cockiness, confidence, overconfidence, sanguinity, self-assurance, self-confidence; impertinence, impudence, insolence, rudeness
near antonyms bashfulness, diffidence, hesitancy, modesty, shyness, timidity
effulgence *n* the quality or state of having or giving off light ⟨the exceptional *effulgence* of the harvest moon is always a striking sight⟩ — see BRILLIANCE 1
effulgent *adj* giving off or reflecting much light ⟨the stars always seem more *effulgent* when viewed in the country, far away from the distracting lights of the city⟩ — see BRIGHT 1
effusive *adj* showing feeling freely ⟨often *effusive* no matter what the occasion, my aunt is even more so at weddings and funerals⟩ — see DEMONSTRATIVE
egg (on) *vb* to try to persuade (someone) through earnest appeals to follow a course of action ⟨though exhausted, I was *egged on* by spectators to finish the marathon⟩ — see URGE
ego *n* **1** a reasonable or justifiable sense of one's worth or importance ⟨I have enough *ego* not to want to give up easily in any contest or competition⟩ — see PRIDE 1
2 an often unjustified feeling of being pleased with oneself or with one's situation or achievements ⟨the football team's *ego* after winning the state championship was unbearable⟩ — see COMPLACENCE
egocentric *adj* overly concerned with one's own desires, needs, or interests ⟨the cult attracts *egocentric* people who are preoccupied with reaching their potential as individuals⟩
synonyms egoistic, egotistic (*or* egotistical), self-centered, selfish, self-seeking
related words complacent, conceited, self-conceited, self-directed, self-important, self-indulgent, self-satisfied, smug, vain
near antonyms altruistic, generous, greathearted, magnanimous, self-sacrificing
antonyms selfless
egoism *n* excessive interest in oneself ⟨because of her *egoism*, she never gave a thought to asking how the others felt⟩
synonyms egotism, self-centeredness, self-interest, selfishness, self-regard
related words conceit, self-admiration, self-conceit, self-esteem, self-importance, self-indulgence, self-respect, self-satisfaction, self-sufficiency

near antonyms altruism, generosity, magnanimity, self-sacrifice
antonyms selflessness
egoistic *adj* **1** having too high an opinion of oneself ⟨unfortunately, the race car driver is so *egoistic* that he pats himself on the back before anyone else has a chance⟩ — see CONCEITED
2 overly concerned with one's own desires, needs, or interests ⟨they're too *egoistic* to even give a thought to becoming involved in something that benefits the whole community⟩ — see EGOCENTRIC
egotism *n* **1** an often unjustified feeling of being pleased with oneself or with one's situation or achievements ⟨for someone who has won a Nobel Prize in physics, he is remarkably without *egotism*⟩ — see COMPLACENCE
2 excessive interest in oneself ⟨*egotism* is not something that winners of the Nobel Prize for peace usually have time for⟩ — see EGOISM
egotistic *or* **egotistical** *adj* **1** having too high an opinion of oneself ⟨the *egotistic* pro quarterback was always too busy to sign autographs, forgetting that the fans had paid good money to see him play⟩ — see CONCEITED
2 overly concerned with one's own desires, needs, or interests ⟨the true spirit of the Christmas season is the resolve to be less *egotistic* and more altruistic⟩ — see EGOCENTRIC
egregious *adj* very noticeable especially for being incorrect or bad ⟨the student's theme was marred by a number of *egregious* errors in spelling⟩
synonyms blatant, conspicuous, flagrant, glaring, gross, obvious, patent, pronounced, rank, striking
related words clear, distinct, evident, notable, outstanding, plain, salient; absolute, arrant, downright, out-and-out, outright, sheer, stark, utter; abominable, atrocious, awful, deplorable, execrable, heinous, monstrous, outrageous, preposterous, shameful, shocking
near antonyms imperceptible, inconspicuous; insignificant, slight, trifling, trivial; concealed, hidden, invisible
egress *n* a place or means of going out ⟨the only *egress* from the nightclub was a dark, narrow stairway to the street below⟩ — see EXIT 1
ejaculate *vb* to utter with a sudden burst of strong feeling ⟨"Eureka!" the Greek mathematician Archimedes is said to have *ejaculated* upon discovering a method for determining the purity of gold⟩ — see EXCLAIM
eject *vb* **1** to drive or force out ⟨we quickly *ejected* the unwanted guest from our party⟩
synonyms banish, boot (out), bounce, cast (out), chase, dismiss, drum (out), expel, extrude, oust, rout, run off, throw out
related words deport, displace, dispossess, evict, exile, expatriate, ostracize, shut out; discharge, fire, sack
phrases send packing
near antonyms accept, admit, receive, take in; welcome; entertain, harbor, house, lodge, shelter
2 to throw out or off (something from within) often violently ⟨the malfunctioning VCR abruptly stopped rewinding and *ejected* the tape⟩ — see ERUPT 1
eke out *vb* to get with great difficulty ⟨*eked out* a living from the family's small farm⟩
synonyms scrape, scrounge, squeeze, wrest, wring
related words acquire, earn, gain, obtain, procure, secure
elaborate *adj* **1** made or done with great care or with much detail ⟨*elaborate* festivities for the 200th anniversary of the town's founding⟩

synonyms complex, complicated, detailed, fancy, intricate, involved, sophisticated

related words elegant, grand, ornate, magnificent, splendid; extravagant, flamboyant, frilly, grandiose, ostentatious, overwrought; labyrinthine

near antonyms modest, plain, uncomplicated, unsophisticated

antonyms simple

2 including many small descriptive features ⟨the *elaborate* world known as Middle Earth that J.R.R. Tolkien created in his novels⟩ — see DETAILED 1

3 having many parts or aspects that are usually interrelated ⟨plans for a huge mall that will actually be an *elaborate* center for sports, entertainment, and shopping⟩ — see COMPLEX 1

elaborate (on) *vb* **1** to add to the interest of by including made-up details ⟨my friend tends to *elaborate on* his hiking experiences, turning an ordinary walk in the woods into a hair-raising adventure⟩ — see EMBROIDER

2 to express more fully and in greater detail ⟨the candidate for governor refused to *elaborate on* how she would balance the state's budget⟩ — see EXPAND 1

elaborateness *n* the state or quality of having many interrelated parts or aspects ⟨the *elaborateness* of the parade is such that a virtual army of people spend the whole year working on it⟩ — see COMPLEXITY 1

elaboration *n* **1** the act or process of going from the simple or basic to the complex or advanced ⟨the *elaboration* of the Internet from an exclusive computer network into a worldwide communications network of colossal proportions⟩ — see DEVELOPMENT 1

2 the representation of something in terms that go beyond the facts ⟨the eyewitness was deemed unreliable because of his obvious *elaboration* of what he had actually seen⟩ — see EXAGGERATION

elapse *vb* to come to an end ⟨in those pay viewers at scenic areas your viewing time seems to *elapse* almost before it has begun⟩ — see CEASE 1

elastic *adj* **1** able to revert to original size and shape after being stretched, squeezed, or twisted ⟨*elastic* rubber bands⟩

synonyms flexible, resilient, rubberlike, rubbery, springy, stretch, stretchable, supple

related words adaptable, ductile, malleable, moldable, plastic, pliable, pliant; limber, lissome (*also* lissom), lithe

near antonyms firm, hard, solid; brittle, crisp, friable

antonyms inelastic, inflexible, nonelastic, rigid, stiff

2 capable of being readily changed ⟨when vacationing, we generally have very *elastic* daily sightseeing plans⟩ — see FLEXIBLE 1

elate *vb* to fill with great joy ⟨the winning of the state basketball championship *elated* the whole student body⟩

synonyms elevate, enrapture, exhilarate, overjoy, transport

related words excite, inspire, stimulate, uplift; delight, gladden, gratify, please

near antonyms demoralize, discourage, dishearten, dispirit; distress, oppress, sadden

antonyms depress

elated *adj* experiencing or marked by overwhelming usually pleasurable emotion ⟨she was *elated* upon learning that she had been accepted by her first-choice college⟩ — see ECSTATIC

elation *n* a state of overwhelming usually pleasurable emotion ⟨most people can't imagine the kind of *elation* that comes with winning a super lottery's grand prize, but they're dying to find out⟩ — see ECSTASY

elbow *vb* to force one's way ⟨the sort of greedy person who is always the first to *elbow* to the front of the buffet table at every party⟩ — see PRESS 4

elbow grease *n* the active use of energy in producing a result ⟨with a little polish and a lot of *elbow grease*, I was able to make the old silver teapot shine again⟩ — see EFFORT

elbowroom *n* an extent or area available for or used up by some activity or thing ⟨help me move the furniture so that we'll have enough *elbowroom* to do some aerobics⟩ — see ROOM 1

elder *n* **1** a person of advanced years ⟨in that Asian society *elders* are accorded great respect⟩ — see SENIOR CITIZEN

2 one who is above another in rank, station, or office ⟨as your *elder* in the company, he is within his rights to tell you what to do⟩ — see SUPERIOR

3 one who is older than another ⟨it wouldn't hurt to show a little more respect for your *elders*⟩ — see SENIOR 1

4 the senior member of a group ⟨as the *elder* of the contingent of living former presidents, he was accorded a place of honor at the ceremonies⟩ — see DEAN

elderly *adj* being of advanced years and especially past middle age ⟨*elderly* people who stay active are usually the healthiest and the happiest⟩

synonyms aged, aging, ancient, geriatric, long-lived, old, older, senior

related words adult, grown-up, mature, middle-aged; pensioned, retired, superannuated; matriarchal, patriarchal, venerable; doddering, senile, tottery

near antonyms youngish; adolescent, immature, juvenile, puerile

antonyms young, youthful

elder statesman *n* the senior member of a group ⟨the *elder statesman* of the White House correspondents is finally retiring after nearly a half century of service⟩ — see DEAN

elect *adj* singled out from a number or group as more to one's liking ⟨this *elect* body of students represents the best that the nation's high schools have to offer⟩ — see SELECT 1

elect *n* individuals carefully selected as being the best of a class ⟨the members of this all-American team are the *elect* of collegiate football⟩ — see ELITE

elect *vb* to decide to accept (someone or something) from a group of possibilities ⟨I've *elected* to study French as my foreign language⟩ — see CHOOSE 1

election *n* the act or process of selecting ⟨the *election* of a major is something that every college student has to do at some point⟩ — see SELECTION 1

elective *adj* subject to one's freedom of choice ⟨a plastic surgeon who mainly does face-lifting and other kinds of *elective* surgery⟩ — see OPTIONAL

electric *adj* causing great emotional or mental stimulation ⟨Dr. King's "I Have a Dream" speech was one of the truly *electric* moments in American oratory⟩ — see EXCITING 1

electrify *vb* to cause a pleasurable stimulation of the feelings ⟨Marian Anderson *electrified* audiences with her soaring operatic voice⟩ — see THRILL

electrifying *adj* causing great emotional or mental stimulation ⟨ranked the U.S. hockey team's victory in 1980 as one of the most *electrifying* moments in Olympic history⟩ — see EXCITING 1

elegance *n* dignified or restrained beauty of form, appearance, or style ⟨the *elegance* of the hotel's French furnishings⟩
  synonyms class, elegancy, grace, gracefulness, handsomeness, majesty, refinement, stateliness
  related words grandeur, lavishness, luxuriousness, magnificence, ornateness, richness, splendor; artfulness, chic, polish, sophistication, taste, tastefulness; choiceness, classicism, dignity, exquisiteness, restraint, simplicity; affectedness, grandiosity, pretentiousness
  near antonyms coarseness, crudeness, flashiness, garishness, gaudiness, gracelessness, grotesqueness, tastelessness, tawdriness

elegancy *n* dignified or restrained beauty of form, appearance, or style ⟨there's a certain *elegancy* about this hotel that other places in Las Vegas don't have⟩ — see ELEGANCE

elegant *adj* **1** having or showing elegance ⟨the most *elegant* First Lady in the nation's history⟩ ⟨the bride's *elegant* gown received nothing but praise⟩
  synonyms graceful, handsome, majestic, refined, stately, tasteful
  related words grand, lavish, luxurious, magnificent, ornate, rich, splendid; artful, genteel, polished, sophisticated; classic, exquisite, restrained, simple; chic, fashionable, posh, smart, stylish; affected, grandiose, pretentious
  near antonyms coarse, crude, flashy, garish, gaudy, grotesque, tacky, tawdry
  antonyms graceless, inelegant, tasteless, unhandsome
  2 having qualities that appeal to a refined taste ⟨prepared an *elegant* dinner for the honored guests⟩ — see CHOICE

elegiac *adj* causing or marked by an atmosphere lacking in cheer ⟨the sight of an old ruined church or castle can be a pleasantly *elegiac* experience⟩ — see GLOOMY 1

elegy *n* a composition expressing one's grief over a loss ⟨"O Captain! My Captain!" is Walt Whitman's *elegy* on the death of President Lincoln⟩ — see LAMENT 2

element *n* **1** one of the parts that make up a whole ⟨a free press is an essential *element* of a democracy⟩
  synonyms component, constituent, factor, ingredient, member
  related words detail, item, particular, point; aspect, characteristic, facet, feature, trait; division, fragment, particle, piece, portion, section, sector, segment
  near antonyms aggregate, composite, compound, sum, total, totality
  antonyms whole
  2 elements *pl* general or basic truths on which other truths or theories can be based ⟨the *elements* of mathematics can be traced back to Euclid⟩ — see PRINCIPLES 1

elemental *adj* of or relating to the simplest facts or theories of a subject ⟨even if you're not planning on becoming a scientist, you should have an *elemental* knowledge of chemistry⟩ — see ELEMENTARY

elementary *adj* of or relating to the simplest facts or theories of a subject ⟨students who do not have even an *elementary* knowledge of geography⟩
  synonyms basic, elemental, essential, fundamental, rudimentary, underlying
  related words primal, primary, prime; primitive; beginning, introductory, preliminary
  near antonyms complex, sophisticated; detailed, extensive, intricate

antonyms advanced

elephantine *adj* unusually large ⟨the wedding reception was held under an *elephantine* tent on the great lawn⟩ — see HUGE

elevate *vb* **1** to fill with great joy ⟨seeing their son ordained as a priest was one of the most *elevating* moments in their lives⟩ — see ELATE
  2 to move from a lower to a higher place or position ⟨the old trick of using a fat phone book to *elevate* a child to a more comfortable position at the table⟩ — see RAISE 1
  3 to move higher in rank or position ⟨the announcement that the pope will *elevate* several prelates to the rank of cardinal⟩ — see PROMOTE 1

elevated *adj* **1** being positioned above a surface ⟨an *elevated* monorail that transports visitors all over the theme park⟩
  synonyms lifted, raised, uplifted, upraised
  related words aerial, suspended; erect, upright
  near antonyms low-lying
  antonyms sunken
  2 very dignified in form, tone, or style ⟨the *elevated* language of Lincoln's Gettysburg Address⟩
  synonyms eloquent, formal, high-flown, lofty, majestic, stately, towering
  related words bombastic, declamatory, florid, flowery, grandiloquent, highfalutin, pompous, stilted
  near antonyms casual, colloquial, conversational, informal, slangy; coarse, crude, indecent, vulgar
  antonyms low, undignified
  3 being at a higher level than average ⟨for the next several days temperatures will be a little *elevated* for this time of year⟩ — see HIGH 2
  4 having, characterized by, or arising from a dignified and generous nature ⟨the offspring of this very wealthy family have been instilled with the *elevated* notion that they should devote their lives to public service⟩ — see NOBLE 2
  5 located at a greater height than average or usual ⟨from their *elevated* position the machine gunners had a commanding view of the whole battlefield⟩ — see HIGH 3

elevation *n* **1** a raising or a state of being raised to a higher rank or position ⟨the appointment of Sandra Day O'Connor marked the first *elevation* of a woman to the U.S. Supreme Court⟩ — see ADVANCEMENT 1
  2 an area of high ground ⟨Little Round Top is one of the most visited *elevations* in the entire Gettysburg National Military Park⟩ — see HEIGHT 4
  3 the distance of something or someone from bottom to top ⟨the *elevation* of Angel Falls is 979 meters, making it the world's highest waterfall⟩ — see HEIGHT 3
  4 the most extreme or advanced point ⟨some people contend that Western civilization reached its *elevation* in Greece five centuries before Christ⟩ — see HEIGHT 2

elf *n* an imaginary being usually having a small human form and magical powers ⟨*elves* are often portrayed as rather mischievous⟩ — see FAIRY

elfin *adj* having an often mysterious or magical power to attract ⟨the heroine in the story has an *elfin* beauty that men find irresistible⟩ — see FASCINATING 1

elfish *adj* given to good-natured joking or teasing ⟨an *elfish* comedian who often played lovable drunks and wisecracking sidekicks⟩ — see PLAYFUL

elicit *vb* to draw out (something hidden, latent, or reserved) ⟨the role *elicited* the actress's flair for comedy that previous directors had overlooked⟩ — see EDUCE

eliminate *vb* to prevent the participation or inclusion of ⟨the stiff entry fee is intended to *eliminate* less-than-serious competitors⟩ — see EXCLUDE

elite *n* individuals carefully selected as being the best of a class ⟨the winners of this science award represent the *elite* of our high schools⟩
synonyms best, choice, cream, elect, fat, flower, pick, prime, upper crust
related words aristocracy, (the) establishment, gentry, nobility, society, (the) top, upper class
phrases cream of the crop
near antonyms commoners, masses, rank and file

elixir *n* something that cures all ills or problems ⟨warned that casino gambling would not be an *elixir* for all of the region's economic woes⟩ — see CURE-ALL

elliptic *or* **elliptical** *adj* having the shape of an egg ⟨the villa's marble pool is surrounded by an *elliptic* arrangement of ancient Greek statuary⟩ — see OVAL

elocution *n* the art of speaking in public eloquently and effectively ⟨the oft-told story that he practiced *elocution* by learning to speak with a mouth full of pebbles⟩ — see ORATORY 1

elongate *vb* to make longer ⟨in his paintings the artist *elongated* the bodies of angels to give them a spiritual quality⟩ — see EXTEND 1

elongated *adj* of great extent from end to end ⟨the giraffe's *elongated* neck is thought to be the result of natural selection⟩ — see LONG 1

elongation *n* the act of making longer ⟨the *elongation* of artificial fibers in the manufacturing process⟩ — see EXTENSION 1

eloquence *n* the art or power of speaking or writing in a forceful and convincing way ⟨the *eloquence* of Martin Luther King's "I Have a Dream" speech⟩
synonyms articulateness, poetry, rhetoric
related words expression, expressiveness; declamation, elocution, oratory; forcefulness, meaningfulness, persuasiveness; ardor, fervor, passion, power

eloquent *adj* **1** able to express oneself clearly and well ⟨an *eloquent* writer and speaker, Elizabeth Cady Stanton was one of the founders of the women's rights movement⟩ — see ARTICULATE
2 clearly conveying a special meaning (as one's mood) ⟨in an *eloquent* gesture, the defeated general was graciously given back his sword at the surrender ceremonies⟩ — see EXPRESSIVE
3 very dignified in form, tone, or style ⟨President Kennedy's *eloquent* inaugural address is often credited with inspiring a whole generation⟩ — see ELEVATED 2

else *adj* resulting in an increase in amount or number ⟨is there anything *else* you would like to add to your list?⟩ — see ADDITIONAL

else *adv* in a different way ⟨if you could do it over again, how *else* would you have done it?⟩ — see OTHERWISE

elucidate *vb* to make plain or understandable ⟨colored charts that really help to *elucidate* the points made in the text⟩ — see EXPLAIN 1

elucidation *n* a statement that makes something clear ⟨the candidate issued what were supposed to be *elucidations* of his earlier statements, but they did little to quell the controversy⟩ — see EXPLANATION 1

elucidative *adj* serving to explain ⟨most editions of Shakespeare's plays now have *elucidative* footnotes to help the modern reader⟩ — see EXPLANATORY

elude *vb* to get or keep away from (as a responsibility) through cleverness or trickery ⟨the millionaire had been *eluding* his fair share of taxes for years before getting caught⟩ — see ESCAPE 2

eluding *n* the act or a means of getting or keeping away from something undesirable ⟨the bachelor's *eluding* of that dreaded trip to the altar came to an end when his girlfriend issued an ultimatum⟩ — see ESCAPE 2

elusive *adj* hard to find, capture, or isolate ⟨the giant squid is one of the ocean's most *elusive* inhabitants⟩
synonyms evasive, fugitive, slippery
related words cagey (*also* cagy), shifty; ephemeral, evanescent, fleeting, momentary, passing, short-lived, transitory; unavailable, unobtainable
near antonyms accessible, approachable, attainable, available, obtainable

elvish *adj* tending to or exhibiting reckless playfulness ⟨with *elvish* glee the fraternity brothers hazed the new members to the point of utter humiliation⟩ — see MISCHIEVOUS 1

Elysian *adj* of, relating to, or suggesting heaven ⟨the dream of retiring to a tropical isle and enjoying a life of *Elysian* ease⟩ — see CELESTIAL

Elysium *n* **1** a dwelling place of perfect bliss for the soul after death ⟨the mourners were comforted by their belief that the saintly woman was now experiencing the joys of *Elysium*⟩ — see HEAVEN 1
2 a place or state of great happiness ⟨the universal pipe dream that there exists somewhere an earthly *Elysium* where people live trouble-free lives⟩ — see PARADISE 1

emaciated *adj* suffering extreme weight loss as a result of hunger or disease ⟨the *emaciated* bodies of the survivors of the concentration camps⟩
synonyms cadaverous, gaunt, haggard, skeletal, wasted
related words bony, rawboned, scrawny, skinny, thin; starved, underfed, undernourished; shriveled, withered, wizened
near antonyms beefy, brawny, burly, fit, hale, healthy, hearty, husky; chubby, corpulent, fat, fleshy, heavyset, plump, portly, stocky, thickset

emancipate *vb* to set free (as from slavery or confinement) ⟨under the cover of darkness animal rights activists *emancipated* the inhabitants of the mink ranch⟩ — see FREE 1

emancipation *n* the act of setting free from slavery ⟨a book discussing the role that the *emancipation* of slaves played in the nation's history⟩ — see LIBERATION

emasculate *vb* to deprive of courage or confidence ⟨being eliminated early in one's very first tennis tournament can be an *emasculating* experience⟩ — see UNNERVE 1

embankment *n* a bank of earth constructed to control water ⟨the *embankment* is steep, so be careful walking along the ridge⟩ — see DAM

embargo *n* an order that something not be done or used ⟨there's a standing *embargo* against the use of foul language in this house⟩ — see PROHIBITION 2

embark (on *or* upon) *vb* to take the first step in (a process or course of action) ⟨she's eager to finish college and to *embark* upon a career⟩ — see BEGIN 1

embarrass *vb* **1** to throw into a state of self-conscious distress ⟨the young soldier was *embarrassed* by the public praise for his heroism⟩
synonyms abash, confound, confuse, discomfit, disconcert, discountenance, faze, fluster, mortify, nonplus, rattle
related words agitate, bother, chagrin, discomfort, discompose, dismay, disquiet, distress, disturb, perturb, unhinge, unsettle, upset; debase, degrade, demean, humble, humiliate

near antonyms calm, comfort, console, relieve, soothe; buoy, cheer, embolden, encourage, hearten; assure, reassure

2 to create difficulty for the work or activity of ⟨a lot of this paperwork is unnecessary and just *embarrasses* the organization⟩ — see HAMPER

embarrassing *adj* causing embarrassment ⟨an *embarrassing* fall marked my first appearance on stage⟩ — see AWKWARD 3

embarrassment *n* **1** the emotional state of being made self-consciously uncomfortable ⟨experienced the great *embarrassment* of tripping while on stage⟩

synonyms abashment, confusion, discomfiture, fluster, mortification

related words agitation, bother, chagrin, discomfort, discomposure, dismay, disquiet, distress, disturbance, perturbation, uneasiness, upset; debasement, degradation, humiliation

near antonyms aplomb, assurance, composure, confidence, coolness, equanimity, poise, self-assurance, self-confidence, self-possession

2 something that makes movement or progress more difficult ⟨a big suitcase filled with clothes proved to be more an *embarrassment* than a convenience on my trip⟩ — see ENCUMBRANCE

embed *also* **imbed** *vb* to set solidly in or as if in surrounding matter ⟨the nails were solidly *embedded* in those old plaster walls⟩ — see ENTRENCH

embellish *vb* **1** to add to the interest of by including made-up details ⟨the story of the comic marriage proposal was *embellished* as it passed from one generation to the next in the family⟩ — see EMBROIDER

2 to make more attractive by adding something that is beautiful or becoming ⟨the walls of the French restaurant are *embellished* with scenes of Parisian life⟩ — see DECORATE

embellishing *adj* serving to add beauty ⟨the chef tends to overuse sprigs of parsley and other *embellishing* garnishes on dishes that don't need them⟩ — see DECORATIVE

embellishment *n* **1** something that decorates or beautifies ⟨a colorful mobile is just the *embellishment* that the soon-to-be nursery needs⟩ — see DECORATION 1

2 the representation of something in terms that go beyond the facts ⟨the actor's penchant for *embellishment* suggests that his memoirs would be more appropriately shelved in the fiction section⟩ — see EXAGGERATION

embitter *vb* to implant bitter feelings in ⟨the family refused to allow their devastating collision with a drunk driver to permanently *embitter* them⟩

synonyms antagonize, envenom

related words aggravate, anger, enrage, incense, infuriate, madden; alienate, disaffect, disgruntle, estrange; sour

near antonyms endear, ingratiate; appease, assuage, mollify, pacify, placate, propitiate; sweeten

embittered *adj* having or showing deep-seated resentment ⟨gradually the *embittered* woman realized that her lingering feelings of hate were slowly destroying her⟩ — see BITTER 1

emblem *n* a device, design, or figure used as an identifying mark ⟨the oil company uses a scallop shell as its *emblem*⟩

synonyms hallmark, logo, symbol, trademark

related words icon, pictograph; badge, coat of arms, crest, insignia; monogram, stamp, token

emblematic *also* **emblematical** *adj* having the function or meaning of a symbol ⟨the dove is *emblematic* of the

organization's mission to bring some peace to a troubled world⟩ — see SYMBOLIC

embodiment *n* a visible representation of something abstract (as a quality) ⟨Mother Theresa was often regarded as the *embodiment* of selfless devotion to others⟩

synonyms epitome, incarnation, manifestation, personification

related words exemplification, incorporation, substantiation; essence, quintessence; archetype, exemplar, model, paradigm, pattern; acme, apex, culmination, peak, pinnacle, summit, zenith

embody *vb* **1** to make a part of a body or system ⟨concepts of moral behavior that we should *embody* into our daily life⟩

synonyms assimilate, incorporate, integrate

related words amalgamate, blend, combine, commingle, fuse, intermingle, merge, mingle

2 to represent in visible form ⟨George Washington *embodied* so many of the virtues that Americans hold dear⟩

synonyms epitomize, incarnate, manifest, materialize, personalize, personify, substantiate

related words actualize, realize; symbolize; exemplify, illustrate

embolden *vb* to fill with courage or strength of purpose ⟨his poor showing in his first swim meet just *emboldened* him to train even harder⟩ — see ENCOURAGE 1

emboldened *adj* inclined or willing to take risks ⟨not too surprisingly, rock climbing tends to attract the more *emboldened* seekers of outdoor adventure⟩ — see BOLD 1

embosom *vb* to surround or cover closely ⟨an old villa that has been *embosomed* by the verdant hills of northern Italy for three centuries⟩ — see ENFOLD 1

embower *vb* to surround or cover closely ⟨over the years grape vines have completely *embowered* the summerhouse in the garden⟩ — see ENFOLD 1

embrace *vb* **1** to put one's arms around and press tightly ⟨upon being finally reunited, the overjoyed father *embraced* his son⟩

synonyms clasp, enfold, grasp, hug

related words cling, cradle, grab, grip, hold; embosom, encircle, entwine, envelop; fold, lock, twine, wrap; cuddle, fondle, nestle, nuzzle, pat, pet, snuggle, stroke

2 to surround or cover closely ⟨the stone walls that *embrace* the monastery serve to symbolize its function as a retreat from an unquiet world⟩ — see ENFOLD 1

3 to take for one's own use (something originated by another) ⟨rap music came to be *embraced* by people who were far removed from the inner cities where it originated⟩ — see ADOPT

4 receive or accept gladly or readily ⟨the exchange student was gratified to be so quickly *embraced* by people of the small rural community⟩ — see WELCOME

5 to have as part of a whole ⟨a course in social studies can *embrace* everything from sociology to civics and economics⟩ — see INCLUDE

embroider *vb* to add to the interest of by including made-up details ⟨Dad likes to *embroider* his fishing stories⟩

synonyms color, elaborate (on), embellish, exaggerate, magnify, pad, stretch

related words amplify, enhance, enlarge (upon), expand, flesh (out); fudge, hedge; overdo, overdraw, overemphasize, overplay, overstate; caricature; satirize

near antonyms belittle, minimize, play (down), understate

embroidering *n* the representation of something in terms that go beyond the facts ⟨with considerable *embroidering* the owners of the bed-and-breakfast have turned a few odd incidents into a full-blown legend of ghostly apparitions⟩ — see EXAGGERATION

embroidery *n* decorative stitching done on cloth with the use of a needle ⟨she's been able to turn her skill at *embroidery* into a second business selling decorative cushions at craft fairs⟩ — see NEEDLEWORK

embroil *vb* to place in conflict or difficulties ⟨the town has been *embroiled* in controversy over the building of the huge shopping mall⟩
   synonyms bog (down), mire
   related words enmesh, ensnare, entangle, entrap, snare, tangle, trap
   near antonyms emancipate, free, liberate, release

emend *vb* to remove errors, defects, deficiencies, or deviations from ⟨the first printout quickly revealed that our computer program needed to be *emended*⟩ — see CORRECT 1

emendation *n* a change designed to correct or improve a written work ⟨my teacher's *emendations* made my returned theme look like a sea of blue ink⟩ — see CORRECTION 1

emerge *vb* to come to one's attention especially gradually or unexpectedly ⟨problems *emerged* almost as soon as the contractor began the excavation for the swimming pool⟩ — see ARISE 2

emergency *n* a time or state of affairs requiring prompt or decisive action ⟨an alert, quick-thinking girl who is good to have around in an *emergency*⟩
   synonyms clutch, crisis, crossroad(s), crunch, exigency, head, juncture, zero hour
   related words contingency, possibility; climax, landmark, milestone, turning point; condition, pass, situation, strait; deadlock, impasse, stalemate; corner, fix, hole, hot water, jam, pinch, predicament, scrape, spot

emigrant *n* one that leaves one place to settle in another ⟨a city teeming with *emigrants* from many lands⟩
   synonyms émigré (*also* emigré), immigrant, migrant, settler
   related words defector, deportee, evacuee, exile, expatriate, refugee; alien, foreigner, noncitizen, nonnative; colonist, newcomer, squatter
   near antonyms aborigine, native; citizen, inhabitant, national, resident
   antonyms nonimmigrant

émigré *also* **emigré** *n* **1** a person forced to emigrate for political reasons ⟨the revolution resulted in a flood of *émigrés* into neighboring countries⟩
   synonyms deportee, evacuee, exile, expatriate, refugee
   related words alien, fugitive; castoff, outcast, pariah; loyalist, patriot
   2 one that leaves one place to settle in another ⟨the *émigrés* had little understanding of what awaited them in America⟩ — see EMIGRANT

eminence *n* **1** the fact or state of being above others in rank or importance ⟨the *eminence* of the Nobel Prize in the field of awards and prizes⟩
   synonyms distinction, dominance, noteworthiness, preeminence, superiority
   related words celebrity, fame, famousness, glory, honor, renown, reputation, repute; authority, greatness, influence, power, weight
   near antonyms insignificance, unimportance; inferiority, mediocrity; obscurity

2 an area of high ground ⟨the old citadel sits on an *eminence* with a commanding view of the city⟩ — see HEIGHT 4

eminent *adj* standing above others in rank, importance, or achievement ⟨many *eminent* surgeons are on the hospital's staff⟩
   synonyms distinguished, illustrious, noble, notable, noteworthy, outstanding, preeminent, prestigious, signal, star, superior
   related words celebrated, famed, famous, glorious, honored, renowned, reputable; infamous, notorious; dominant, paramount, predominant
   near antonyms insignificant, minor, unimportant; average, inferior, mediocre; obscure, uncelebrated, unsung

emissary *n* a person sent on a mission to represent another ⟨most of the industrialized nations of the world sent *emissaries* to the conference on global warming⟩ — see AMBASSADOR

emit *vb* **1** to throw or give off ⟨the cabin's chimney *emitted* smoke⟩
   synonyms cast (off), discharge, exhale, expel, issue, release, shoot, vent
   related words eliminate, evacuate, excrete, exude, ooze, secrete; gush, pour, spew
   near antonyms absorb, inhale
   2 to send forth using the vocal chords ⟨I was so scared that I couldn't *emit* a sound⟩ — see UTTER 1

emolument *n* the money paid regularly to a person for labor or services ⟨the annual *emolument* for the director of the charity is officially only one dollar⟩ — see WAGE

emotion *n* **1** a subjective response to a person, thing, or situation ⟨my *emotions* after hearing the shocking news went from utter disbelief to overwhelming sorrow⟩ — see FEELING 1
   2 depth of feeling ⟨the *emotion* that the singer is able to instill in "Amazing Grace" is truly stirring⟩ — see ARDOR 1

emotional *adj* **1** having or expressing great depth of feeling ⟨worship at revival meetings often takes a markedly *emotional* form⟩ — see FERVENT
   2 having the power to affect the feelings or sympathies ⟨in one *emotional* scene in the movie the boy must say goodbye to his extraterrestrial friend⟩ — see MOVING
   3 showing feeling freely ⟨the fact that he is not a very *emotional* person does not mean that he is not a loving, caring father⟩ — see DEMONSTRATIVE

emphasis *n* **1** a special notice or importance given to something ⟨a prep school with a long-established *emphasis* on sports⟩
   synonyms accent, accentuation, stress, weight
   related words attention, concentration, consideration, heed, note, regard; value, worth; consequence, import, moment, significance; precedence, primacy, priority
   near antonyms apathy, disregard, indifference
   2 the quality or state of being forceful (as in expression) ⟨the *emphasis* with which my parents issued the warning about smoking left no doubt that they were serious⟩ — see VEHEMENCE 1

emphasize *vb* to indicate the importance of by giving prominent display ⟨supermarket tabloids that *emphasize* sensational news stories⟩
   synonyms accent, accentuate, feature, highlight, play (up), point (up), stress, underline, underscore
   related words focus, identify, pinpoint, spotlight; advertise, boost, plug, promote, publicize

near antonyms tone (down), understate; belittle, discount, disparage, minimize
antonyms play (down)

emphatic *adj* **1** marked by or uttered with forcefulness ⟨the governor issued an *emphatic* denial of all charges⟩
synonyms aggressive, assertive, dynamic, energetic, forceful, resounding, strenuous, vehement, vigorous
related words decided, insistent, marked, pointed; arresting, compelling, conspicuous, noticeable, striking; absolute, categorical (*also* categoric), clear, plain, unambiguous, unequivocal
near antonyms guarded, mild, weak, wishy-washy; ambiguous, equivocal; understated
antonyms unemphatic
2 likely to attract attention ⟨with all of the decorative fishing nets, lobster pots, and oars, the seafood restaurant's nautical theme was a little too *emphatic* for my taste⟩ — see NOTICEABLE

empire *n* a group of businesses or enterprises under one control ⟨the media mogul's *empire* consists of newspapers, TV stations, and cable companies⟩ — see CONGLOMERATE

empirical *adj* based on observation or experience ⟨guidelines for raising children that are based on *empirical* evidence⟩
synonyms experimental, objective, observational
related words actual, factual, genuine, hard, real; accepted, established, tried, tried-and-true; indisputable, undeniable; demonstrable, provable, verifiable
near antonyms conjectural, hypothetical, speculative; unproven, unsubstantiated, unverified
antonyms nonempirical, theoretical (*also* theoretic)

employ *n* the state of being provided with a paying job ⟨while you're under our *employ*, you can't do outside work for our competitors⟩ — see HIRE 1

employ *vb* **1** to provide with a paying job ⟨a new factory that will *employ* 500 people⟩
synonyms engage, hire, retain, take on
related words recruit, sign on; keep
near antonyms furlough, lay off
antonyms can, discharge, dismiss, fire, sack
2 to put into action or service ⟨Martha is looking for a job in which she can *employ* her writing skills⟩ — see USE 1

employable *adj* capable of or suitable for being used for a particular purpose ⟨this wall map of the bay is for decoration only—it's not *employable* for actual navigation⟩ — see USABLE 1

employed *adj* involved in often constant activity ⟨insisted that the children be *employed* in some useful activity, even during school vacations⟩ — see BUSY 1

employee *n* one who works for another for wages or a salary ⟨an employer who was loved and admired by generations of *employees*⟩
synonyms hand, hireling, jobholder, worker
related words assistant, cog, flunky (*also* flunkey), subordinate, underling, yes-man; drudge, grub, laborer, navvy [*chiefly British*], toiler, workingman, workman; associate, colleague, coworker
near antonyms boss, superior, supervisor
antonyms employer

employment *n* **1** the act or practice of employing something for a particular purpose ⟨the *employment* of the kitchen oven as a storage cupboard had predictably disastrous results⟩ — see USE 1
2 the activity by which one regularly makes a living ⟨his regular *employment* is that of a restaurant waiter,

but he always identifies himself as an actor⟩ — see OCCUPATION
3 the state of being provided with a paying job ⟨the parents tried to convey to their adult son the joys of steady *employment*⟩ — see HIRE 1

emporium *n* an establishment where goods are sold to consumers ⟨an *emporium* for home electronic equipment filled with stuff I didn't know I needed but now desperately want⟩ — see SHOP 1

empower *vb* to give official or legal power to ⟨the agency *empowered* to collect taxes⟩ — see AUTHORIZE 1

emptiness *n* **1** a need or desire for food ⟨the *emptiness* that usually sets in about three o'clock in the afternoon⟩ — see HUNGER 1
2 empty space ⟨there in the vast *emptiness* of the desert was a long-abandoned jeep⟩ — see VACANCY 1
3 the quality or state of being empty ⟨the *emptiness* of the interior of the isolated house just made it seem all the more eerie⟩ — see VACANCY 2

empty *adj* **1** lacking contents that could or should be present ⟨the refrigerator is *empty*, so we'll have to eat out⟩
synonyms bare, blank, devoid, stark, vacant, void
related words barren, hollow; available, clear, free, open; unfilled, unfurnished; unattended, uninhabited, unoccupied; abandoned, deserted, emptied, forsaken, vacated; depleted, drained, dry, exhausted
near antonyms complete; replete; furnished, provided, supplied; filled, occupied; flush, overflowing, packed, teeming
antonyms full
2 feeling a desire or need for food ⟨as the long car trip wore on, we all started to feel a little *empty*⟩ — see HUNGRY 1
3 having no meaning ⟨spare me your *empty* apologies because if you were truly sorry, you'd change⟩ — see MEANINGLESS
4 having no usefulness ⟨an *empty* task that was assigned just to keep us busy⟩ — see WORTHLESS
5 producing no results ⟨all of the leads in the missing-person case were turning up *empty*⟩ — see FUTILE

empty *vb* to remove the contents of ⟨*empty* the room before starting to paint the ceiling⟩
synonyms clear, evacuate, vacate, void
related words deplete, drain, eliminate, exhaust; bleed, draw (off); clean, flush, purge, scour, sweep
antonyms fill, load

empyreal *adj* of, relating to, or suggesting heaven ⟨a painting depicting the Deity as seated on an *empyreal* throne surrounded by saints and angels⟩ — see CELESTIAL

empyrean *adj* of, relating to, or suggesting heaven ⟨movie scenes set in heaven often suggest that harps are the favored instruments for *empyrean* music⟩ — see CELESTIAL

emulate *vb* to use (someone or something) as the model for one's speech, mannerisms, or behavior ⟨a pro athlete who has often said that children should *emulate* their parents—not him⟩ — see IMITATE 1

emulative *adj* using or marked by the use of something else as a basis or model ⟨right now she's an *emulative* singer, not having yet created a style of her own⟩ — see IMITATIVE

enable *vb* **1** to make able or possible ⟨my new glasses *enable* me to read⟩
synonyms allow, let, permit
related words fit, prepare, qualify, ready; approve, endorse (*also* indorse), sanction; condition, equip

near antonyms inhibit, preclude; disallow, enjoin, forbid, prohibit
antonyms prevent
2 to give official or legal power to 〈a law that would *enable* the authorities to use wiretaps without obtaining court orders〉 — see AUTHORIZE 1

enact *vb* to put into effect through legislative or authoritative action 〈Congress *enacts* all laws relating to foreign trade and immigration〉
synonyms lay down, legislate, make, pass
related words bring about, effect; allow, authorize, permit, sanction; decree, dictate, proclaim; administer, execute; approve, confirm, ratify
near antonyms abolish, abrogate, annul, cancel, invalidate, nullify; overturn, reverse
antonyms repeal, rescind, revoke

enactment *n* **1** a rule of conduct or action laid down by a governing authority and especially a legislator 〈as a result of an *enactment* by Congress, this breathtaking canyon will be permanently protected from development〉 — see LAW 1
2 the doing of an action 〈the *enactment* of the murder is never actually shown on screen〉 — see COMMISSION 2

enamored (of) *adj* filled with an intense or excessive love for 〈many teenage girls became *enamored of* the movie idol for his boyish good looks〉
synonyms crazy (about *or* over), enraptured (by), infatuated (with), mad (about), nuts (about)
related words hung up, obsessed; foolish, silly, wild; bewitched, captivated, charmed, enchanted, entranced, fascinated
phrases sweet on
near antonyms cool, detached, unimpressed; disenchanted, disillusioned

encamp *vb* **1** to live in a camp or the outdoors 〈the hike will take several days, and we plan to *encamp* along the trail〉 — see CAMP
2 to provide with living quarters or shelter 〈the stranded tourists were *encamped* overnight in the high school gym during the hurricane〉 — see HOUSE 1

encampment *n* a place where a group of people live for a short time in tents or cabins 〈a recreational area that will serve as this year's *encampment* for the Scouts' jamboree〉 — see CAMP 1

encapsulate *vb* to make into a short statement of the main points (as of a report) 〈can you *encapsulate* the president's speech in about a paragraph?〉 — see SUMMARIZE

encapsulation *n* a short statement of the main points 〈didn't have time to read the full news article, just the *encapsulation* on the second page〉 — see SUMMARY

encase *vb* to close or shut in by or as if by barriers 〈fear of the outside world can *encase* a person just as surely as stone walls〉 — see ENCLOSE 1

enchain *vb* to confine or restrain with or as if with chains 〈children who were *enchained* by an overprotective mother〉 — see BIND 1

enchant *vb* **1** to attract or delight as if by magic 〈the child actress *enchanted* audiences with her bubbly personality〉 — see CHARM 1
2 to cast a spell on 〈out of spite, the jealous queen *enchanted* her chief rival for the title of the fairest one of all〉 — see BEWITCH 1
3 to hold the attention of as if by a spell 〈the tales about the young wizard have *enchanted* children around the globe〉 — see ENTHRALL 1

enchanted *adj* being or appearing to be under a magic spell 〈an *enchanted* isle of the South Pacific〉
synonyms bewitched, charmed, entranced, magic, magical, spellbound
related words dreamy, fairy, fairylike; fantastic, miraculous, utopian, wondrous; hypnotized, mesmerized; captivated, fascinated

enchanter *n* a person skilled in using supernatural forces 〈in Shakespeare's play an *enchanter* creates a storm at sea that causes his rivals to be cast upon the shores of his magical isle〉 — see MAGICIAN 1

enchanting *adj* having an often mysterious or magical power to attract 〈visitors have long found the highlands of Scotland to be an *enchanting* place〉 — see FASCINATING 1

enchantment *n* **1** a spoken word or set of words believed to have magic power 〈eventually she realized that there wasn't an *enchantment* in the world that was going to turn her boyfriend into a prince〉 — see SPELL 1
2 the power of irresistible attraction 〈there's an *enchantment* about that handsome, young actor that women just adore〉 — see CHARM 2
3 the power to control natural forces through supernatural means 〈there are people even today who claim to be skilled in *enchantment*〉 — see MAGIC 1

enchantress *n* **1** a woman believed to have often harmful supernatural powers 〈when misfortune occurred, it was not uncommon for some unpopular woman of the village to be branded an *enchantress*〉 — see WITCH 1
2 a woman whom men find irresistibly attractive 〈Scarlett O'Hara is one of literature's most celebrated *enchantresses*〉 — see SIREN

encircle *vb* **1** to pass completely around 〈communication satellites *encircling* the earth〉
synonyms circle, circumnavigate, compass, girdle, girth, loop, orbit, ring, round
related words cross, perambulate, traverse
2 to form a circle around 〈immediately after announcing their engagement, the couple was *encircled* by their applauding friends〉 — see SURROUND

enclose *also* **inclose** *vb* **1** to close or shut in by or as if by barriers 〈dogs who spend the day *enclosed* in small cages〉
synonyms cage, closet, coop (up), corral, encase, envelop, fence (in), hedge, hem, house, immure, pen, wall (in)
related words bound, circumscribe, confine, contain, limit, restrict; encircle, encompass, ring, surround
2 to form a circle around 〈in a show of support, the women rushed to *enclose* their distraught friend〉 — see SURROUND
3 to surround or cover closely 〈the house was *enclosed* by a high hedge that shielded it from public view〉 — see ENFOLD 1

enclosure *also* **inclosure** *n* an open space wholly or partly enclosed (as by buildings or walls) 〈a fenced-in *enclosure* where the sheep are allowed to graze unattended〉 — see COURT 2

encomium *n* a formal expression of praise 〈the *encomiums* bestowed on a teacher at her retirement ceremonies〉
synonyms accolade, citation, commendation, eulogy, homage, paean, panegyric, salutation, tribute
related words award, decoration, honor, prize; acclaim, acclamation, approval, compliment, recommendation; applause, plaudits; bravo, hallelujah

near antonyms censure, condemnation, denunciation, indictment, rebuke, reprimand, reproof; admonition, correction, lecture, sermon

encompass *vb* **1** to form a circle around ⟨a necklace of sapphire-blue lakes *encompasses* the town⟩ — see SURROUND

2 to have as part of a whole ⟨textbooks on American history are now likely to *encompass* its social history as well as its political and military history⟩ — see INCLUDE

3 to surround or cover closely ⟨a fog of mystery has long *encompassed* this fraternal organization, which is known for its secret rituals⟩ — see ENFOLD 1

encounter *n* a brief clash between enemies or rivals ⟨survived an *encounter* with the school bully at the local park⟩

synonyms brush, hassle, run-in, scrape, skirmish

related words argument, fight, quarrel, row, spat, squabble, tiff; battle, brawl, fray, wrangle

encounter *vb* **1** to come upon face-to-face or as if face-to-face ⟨quite unexpectedly *encountered* our next-door neighbor while vacationing in Europe⟩ — see MEET 1

2 to come upon unexpectedly or by chance ⟨we *encountered* a host of unforeseen problems during the restoration of our 200-year-old house⟩ — see HAPPEN (ON *or* UPON)

3 to enter into contest or conflict with ⟨the troops *encountered* bands of guerrilla fighters as they made their way across the desert⟩ — see ENGAGE 2

encourage *vb* **1** to fill with courage or strength of purpose ⟨a pep talk that *encouraged* the team to get out there and win⟩

synonyms buoy (up), cheer (up), comfort, embolden, hearten, inspire, steel

related words animate, enliven, invigorate; fortify, reinforce, strengthen; assure, reassure; boost, energize, excite, galvanize, provoke, quicken, rally, stimulate, stir

near antonyms demoralize, depress, sadden; debilitate, enfeeble, undermine, weaken

antonyms daunt, discourage, dishearten, dispirit

2 to help the growth or development of ⟨asserted that the government should be *encouraging* small businesses, not smothering them with regulations⟩ — see FOSTER 1

3 to rouse to strong feeling or action ⟨the movie's cheap special effects will not *encourage* audiences to sit on the edge of their seats but to roll in the aisles with laughter⟩ — see PROVOKE 1

4 to try to persuade (someone) through earnest appeals to follow a course of action ⟨the pastor continues to *encourage* the couple to work out their problems and to save their marriage⟩ — see URGE

encouragement *n* something that arouses action or activity ⟨the huge rebates that the auto companies were offering was all the *encouragement* I needed to buy a new car⟩ — see IMPULSE

encouraging *adj* **1** having qualities which inspire hope ⟨*encouraging* signs that the economy is improving⟩ — see HOPEFUL 1

2 making one feel good inside ⟨the *encouraging* story of a young girl who overcame great social and physical obstacles to become an outstanding athlete⟩ — see HEARTWARMING

3 pointing toward a happy outcome ⟨we're off to an *encouraging* start on this project⟩ — see FAVORABLE 2

encroach *vb* to advance gradually beyond the usual or desirable limits ⟨each year the sea continues to *encroach* upon the island's beaches⟩

synonyms creep, inch, worm

related words snake, sneak; entrench (*also* intrench), impinge, infringe, intrude, invade; overpass, overreach, overrun, overshoot, overstep

encrust *also* **incrust** *vb* to cover with a hardened layer ⟨refrigerator shelves that were *encrusted* with the residue of many spills⟩

synonyms cake, rime

related words besmear, coat, smear, spread; cover, daub; coagulate, congeal, harden

encumber *vb* **1** to create difficulty for the work or activity of ⟨the claim that all of these regulations *encumber* doctors, taking time away from the actual practice of medicine⟩ — see HAMPER

2 to place a weight or burden on ⟨don't *encumber* your pack animal so much that it can hardly move⟩ — see LOAD 1

encumbrance *n* something that makes movement or progress more difficult ⟨without the *encumbrance* of a heavy backpack, I could sprint along the trail⟩

synonyms bar, block, chain, clog, crimp, deterrent, drag, embarrassment, fetter, handicap, hindrance, hurdle, impediment, inhibition, interference, let, manacle, obstacle, obstruction, shackles, stop, stumbling block, trammel

related words catch, hitch, rub, snag; hobble; arrest, check, constraint, curb, rein, restraint, stop; delay, holdup; burden, load; danger, hazard, peril; adversity, difficulty, disadvantage, hardship

near antonyms catalyst, goad, impetus, incentive, spur, stimulant, stimulus; advantage, edge; break

antonyms aid, assistance, benefit, help

encyclopedic *also* **encyclopaedic** *adj* covering everything or all important points ⟨a tour guide with an *encyclopedic* knowledge of New York City and its people⟩

synonyms compendious, complete, comprehensive, full, global, inclusive, in-depth, omnibus, panoramic, universal

related words broad, catholic, extensive, far-reaching, general, overall, sweeping, vast, wide; blanket, indiscriminate, unrestricted

near antonyms circumscribed, limited, narrow, restricted, specialized; exact, precise; individual, singular, specific

end *n* **1** the stopping of a process or activity ⟨the *end* of hostilities brought general rejoicing⟩

synonyms cessation, close, closure, conclusion, discontinuance, ending, expiration, finish, halt, lapse, shutdown, shutoff, stop, stoppage, surcease, termination

related words abeyance, interruption, moratorium, suspension

near antonyms extension, persistence, prolongation

antonyms continuation

2 a real or imaginary point beyond which a person or thing cannot go ⟨I'm at the *end* of my patience with these little brats⟩ — see LIMIT

3 an unused or unwanted piece or item typically of small size or value ⟨a couple of *ends* of wallpaper were all that was left after we finished papering the room⟩ — see ¹SCRAP 1

4 something that one hopes or intends to accomplish ⟨in this case the *ends* definitely do not justify the means⟩ — see GOAL

5 the last and usually sharp or tapering part of something long and narrow ⟨a child's pair of scissors with blunt *ends*⟩ — see POINT 2

6 the last part of a process or action ⟨the war wasn't yet over, but we were definitely at the beginning of the *end*⟩ — see FINALE

7 the line or relatively narrow space that marks the outer limit of something ⟨the *ends* of his shirt cuffs were badly frayed⟩ — see BORDER 1

8 the permanent stopping of all the vital bodily activities ⟨Henry Hudson and eight others were set adrift in the bay in a small boat, and how they met their *end* is unknown⟩ — see DEATH 1

end *vb* **1** to bring (an event) to a natural or appropriate stopping point ⟨let's *end* the meeting with a short prayer⟩ — see CLOSE 3

2 to bring (as an action or operation) to an immediate end ⟨unfortunately, an argument *ended* their date, and they're still not speaking to each other⟩ — see STOP 1

3 to come to an end ⟨a book so good that you hate to see it *end*⟩ — see CEASE 1

endanger *vb* to place in danger ⟨a reckless use of fireworks that *endangered* the lives of many people⟩

synonyms adventure, compromise, gamble (with), hazard, imperil, jeopardize, menace, risk, venture

related words intimidate, threaten; expose; subject; chance, wager

near antonyms guard, protect, shelter, shield; preserve, resume, save

endangered *adj* being in a situation where one is likely to meet with harm ⟨a daring attempt to rescue the *endangered* passengers from the burning boat⟩ — see LIABLE 1

endangerment *n* the state of not being protected from injury, harm, or evil ⟨I didn't think that I was in any *endangerment* while dangling my legs over the rock ledge⟩ — see DANGER 1

endearing *adj* **1** having qualities that tend to make one loved ⟨you have to wonder about people who don't find kittens and puppies *endearing*⟩ — see LOVABLE

2 likely to win one's affection ⟨his impish sense of humor is one of his more *endearing* traits⟩ — see INGRATIATING

endeavor *n* an effort to do or accomplish something ⟨the hope that this latest *endeavor* will yield much information about the atmosphere of the planet⟩ — see ATTEMPT

endeavor *vb* **1** to devote serious and sustained effort ⟨the trapped climber *endeavored* mightily to get the boulder to budge⟩ — see LABOR

2 to make an effort to do ⟨our club is forever *endeavoring* to find ways to raise more money for activities⟩ — see ATTEMPT

ended *adj* brought or having come to an end ⟨the recently *ended* season was one of the best that the baseball team ever had⟩ — see COMPLETE 2

endemic *adj* belonging to a particular place by birth or origin ⟨the fish is not an *endemic* species of the lake, and it is devouring the native trout population⟩ — see NATIVE 1

ending *n* **1** the last part of a process or action ⟨audiences generally prefer movies with happy *endings*⟩ — see FINALE

2 the stopping of a process or activity ⟨the best part about any dental procedure is its *ending*⟩ — see END 1

endless *adj* **1** being or seeming to be without limits ⟨from the promontory visitors can look out over an *endless* sea⟩ — see INFINITE

2 lasting forever ⟨the *endless* roar is what I remember most about Niagara Falls⟩ — see EVERLASTING

endorse *also* **indorse** *vb* to promote the interests or cause of ⟨an increase in the number of parents who *endorse* the idea of school uniforms⟩ — see SUPPORT 1

endow *vb* **1** to furnish with something freely or naturally ⟨a young performer *endowed* with a great singing voice⟩

synonyms endue, invest

related words equip, provide, supply; bestow, confer; accord, award, grant; empower, enable, enhance, enrich, heighten; bless, favor, grace; bequeath, will

near antonyms dispossess, divest, strip; deplete, drain, exhaust; skimp, stint

2 to furnish (as an institution) with a regular source of income ⟨a wealthy businessman who *endowed* several museums⟩

synonyms finance, fund, subsidize

related words establish, found, organize; bequeath, contribute, donate, subscribe, support; award, grant; back, promote, sponsor

near antonyms draw, receive; subsist

3 to provide money for ⟨the program to bring the arts to inner-city youths is *endowed* by a grant from the federal government⟩ — see FINANCE 1

endowment *n* a special and usually inborn ability ⟨it's a sin to waste one's God-given *endowments*⟩ — see TALENT

endue *vb* to furnish with something freely or naturally ⟨she's always been *endued* with an unquenchable optimism⟩ — see ENDOW 1

endurable *adj* capable of being endured ⟨a flu shot is never pleasant, but I find the momentary pain entirely *endurable*⟩ — see BEARABLE

endurance *n* **1** continuing existence ⟨the amazing *endurance* of the rumor that an alien spaceship crashed in that area⟩ — see PERSISTENCE 1

2 uninterrupted or lasting existence ⟨the *endurance* of his love for his wife was not arrested even by her death⟩ — see CONTINUATION

endure *vb* **1** to come to a knowledge of (something) by living through it ⟨an elderly couple who have *endured* the ups and downs of a half century of married life⟩ — see EXPERIENCE

2 to put up with (something painful or difficult) ⟨at some point we all have to *endure* the loss of a beloved pet⟩ — see BEAR 2

3 to remain indefinitely in existence or in the same state ⟨the fashion business is built on change, since nobody expects a particular clothing style to *endure*⟩ — see CONTINUE 1

enemy *n* one that is hostile toward another ⟨a beloved minister with no known *enemies*⟩

synonyms adversary, antagonist, foe, opponent

related words archenemy; (the) opposition; nemesis; bane, bête noire; assailant, attacker, combatant, invader; competitor, emulator, rival

near antonyms ally, collaborator, colleague, confederate, friendly, partner; adherent, disciple, follower; backer, benefactor, supporter

antonyms friend

energetic *adj* **1** having active strength of body or mind ⟨a lifelong fitness fanatic, he remained *energetic* well into his 80s⟩ — see VIGOROUS 1

2 having much high-spirited energy and movement ⟨trying to find the right music for an *energetic* aerobics routine⟩ — see LIVELY 1

3 marked by or uttered with forcefulness ⟨the salesperson gave us an *energetic* sales pitch, talking excitedly about the amazing features of this year's cars⟩ — see EMPHATIC 1

energetically *adv* in a vigorous and forceful manner ⟨the crew worked *energetically* to get the parade float done on time⟩ — see HARD 3

energize *vb* to give life, vigor, or spirit to ⟨our teacher knows how to *energize* history lessons, telling us little-known but interesting facts about long-ago people⟩ — see ANIMATE

energized *adj* made or become fresh in spirits or vigor ⟨after a refreshing lunch, we felt *energized* and ready to hit the bike trail once again⟩ — see NEW 4

energy *n* **1** active strength of body or mind ⟨for a woman of advanced years, she has remarkable *energy*⟩ — see VIGOR 1

2 something with a usable capacity for doing work ⟨some of the power needs of the house are provided by solar *energy*⟩ — see FUEL

3 the ability to exert effort for the accomplishment of a task ⟨I'm so tired that I don't think I have the *energy* to take another step⟩ — see POWER 2

enervate *vb* to diminish the physical strength of ⟨the surgery really *enervated* me for weeks afterwards⟩ — see WEAKEN 1

enervated *adj* **1** lacking bodily energy or motivation ⟨as the heat wave wore on, everyone really started to feel *enervated*⟩ — see LISTLESS

2 lacking bodily strength ⟨months of recovery in the hospital had rendered the soldiers *enervated* and unfit⟩ — see WEAK 1

enfeeble *vb* to diminish the physical strength of ⟨long periods of being confined to a hospital bed will *enfeeble* anyone⟩ — see WEAKEN 1

enfeebled *adj* lacking bodily strength ⟨the *enfeebled* old woman now needs a companion to help her with everyday tasks⟩ — see WEAK 1

enfeeblement *n* **1** a gradual sinking and wasting away of mind or body ⟨daily exercise can help to halt some of the *enfeeblement* that comes with advanced years⟩ — see DECLINE 1

2 the quality or state of lacking physical strength or vigor ⟨a lot of the *enfeeblement* I've experienced since the accident is being reduced by daily physical therapy⟩ — see WEAKNESS 1

enfold *vb* **1** to surround or cover closely ⟨darkness began to *enfold* the lonely house on the hill⟩
synonyms embosom, embower, embrace, enclose (*also* inclose), encompass, enshroud, envelop, enwrap, invest, lap, mantle, shroud, swathe, veil, wrap
related words curtain, drape; encase; swaddle; blanket, overlay, overspread; camouflage, cloak, disguise, mask; circle, encircle, encompass
near antonyms bare, denude, expose, strip
2 to put one's arms around and press tightly ⟨the winner *enfolded* the huge bouquet of roses in her arms and thanked the judges⟩ — see EMBRACE 1

enforce *vb* to carry out effectively ⟨the duty of the police is to *enforce* the law⟩
synonyms administer, apply, execute, implement
related words effect, effectuate; discharge, fulfil (*or* fulfill), render; cite, invoke; enact, legislate; honor, observe; prosecute; promulgate
near antonyms disregard, ignore, neglect

enfranchise *vb* to set free (as from slavery or confinement) ⟨in a way, modern labor-saving appliances en-

franchised people, giving them much more leisure time⟩ — see FREE 1

enfranchisement *n* **1** the act of setting free from slavery ⟨the Emancipation Proclamation was merely the first step in the full *enfranchisement* of African-Americans⟩ — see LIBERATION

2 the right to formally express one's position or will in an election ⟨a time when *enfranchisement* was limited to white males who owned property⟩ — see VOTE 1

engage *vb* **1** to hold the attention of ⟨the challenging jigsaw puzzle *engaged* us all evening⟩
synonyms absorb, busy, engross, enthrall (*or* enthral), fascinate, grip, immerse, interest, intrigue, involve, occupy
related words allure, attract, bewitch, captivate, charm, enchant; hypnotize, mesmerize; monopolize, preoccupy
near antonyms bore, jade, pall, tire, weary
2 to enter into contest or conflict with ⟨the daring young captain was eager to *engage* the enemy⟩
synonyms battle, encounter, face, meet, take on
related words emulate, rival; contend, fight, oppose
near antonyms elude, escape, evade; retreat
3 to obligate by prior agreement ⟨we can't go to the dance because we're already *engaged* to attend a piano recital⟩ — see PLEDGE 1
4 to provide with a paying job ⟨the wealthy couple are looking to *engage* a handyman to take care of the estate⟩ — see EMPLOY 1
5 to take or get the temporary use of (something) for a set sum ⟨my sister and her boyfriend have *engaged* a chauffeured limousine for the prom⟩ — see HIRE 1

engaged *adj* **1** involved in often constant activity ⟨I'm *engaged* right now, so call back some other time⟩ — see BUSY 1
2 pledged in marriage ⟨the *engaged* couple make a charming pair⟩
synonyms affianced, betrothed
related words committed
antonyms unengaged

engagement *n* **1** the act or state of being engaged to be married ⟨the fun couple recently announced their *engagement*⟩
synonyms betrothal, espousal, troth
antonyms disengagement
2 an agreement to be present at a specified time and place ⟨a lifelong practice of marking all of my *engagements* on a weekly calendar⟩
synonyms appointment, date, rendezvous, tryst
related words arrangement; invitation; interview; get-together, meeting; call, visit; schedule
3 the state of being provided with a paying job ⟨his *engagement* as a caddie at the golf club was his first work experience⟩ — see HIRE 1

engaging *adj* **1** having an often mysterious or magical power to attract ⟨movie stars often have an *engaging* aura that is hard to describe⟩ — see FASCINATING 1
2 holding the attention or provoking interest ⟨a movie with an *engaging* story that will hold your interest for a couple of hours⟩ — see INTERESTING

engender *vb* to be the cause of (a situation, action, or state of mind) ⟨a suggestion to go out for pizza that didn't seem to *engender* any interest⟩ — see EFFECT

engine *n* a device that changes energy into mechanical motion ⟨a car with a 200-horsepower *engine*⟩
synonyms machine, motor
related words converter, transformer; appliance, mechanism; equipment; mill

engineer *vb* to plan out usually with subtle skill or care ⟨the mayor *engineered* an agreement to have a major league team play in our city⟩

synonyms contrive, finagle, finesse, frame, machinate, maneuver, manipulate, mastermind, negotiate, wangle

related words intrigue, plot, scheme; connive; concoct, cook (up), hatch; captain, command, conduct, direct, handle, manage, quarterback, run; gerrymander

near antonyms blow, bobble, botch, bungle, butcher, flub, fumble, gum (up), louse up, mangle, mess (up), mishandle, muff

engrave *vb* **1** to cut (as letters or designs) on a hard surface ⟨*engraved* the birth and death dates on the tombstone⟩

synonyms etch, grave, incise, inscribe

related words carve, chisel, sculpt, sculpture; chase; score

2 to produce a vivid impression of ⟨a scar that forever *engraved* the killer's face in the witness's mind⟩

synonyms etch, impress, imprint, ingrain

related words imbue, implant, inculcate, infuse, instill

engross *vb* to hold the attention of ⟨a mystery story that will *engross* readers all the way to the surprise ending⟩ — see ENGAGE 1

engrossed *adj* having the mind fixed on something ⟨I was too *engrossed* in the book to notice the time⟩ — see ATTENTIVE

engrossing *adj* holding the attention or provoking interest ⟨an *engrossing* lecture on Native-American culture before the arrival of Europeans⟩ — see INTERESTING

engrossment *n* a focusing of the mind on something ⟨my *engrossment* in the video game made me lose track of time⟩ — see ATTENTION 1

engulf *vb* to cover or become filled with a flood ⟨high waves from the hurricane just *engulfed* the coastal community⟩ — see FLOOD

enhance *vb* **1** to make better ⟨some shrubbery would really *enhance* the looks of that house⟩ — see IMPROVE

2 to make markedly greater in measure or degree ⟨the right makeup would *enhance* the beauty of her eyes⟩ — see INTENSIFY

enhancement *n* an instance of notable progress in the development of knowledge, technology, or skill ⟨the phenomenal *enhancements* that have been made in home electronic equipment⟩ — see ADVANCE 2

enigma *n* something hard to understand or explain ⟨how Thomas Jefferson could be both a slaveholder and a champion of liberty remains an *enigma*⟩ — see MYSTERY

enigmatic *also* **enigmatical** *adj* **1** being beyond one's powers to know, understand, or explain ⟨the discovery of the abandoned ship in mid ocean remains one of the most *enigmatic* episodes in seafaring history⟩ — see MYSTERIOUS 1

2 having an often intentionally veiled or uncertain meaning ⟨the Mona Lisa's *enigmatic* smile⟩ — see OBSCURE 1

enjoin *vb* **1** to ask for (something) earnestly or with authority ⟨police *enjoined* the community's full cooperation in getting rid of the drug dealers⟩ — see DEMAND 1

2 to issue orders to (someone) by right of authority ⟨the captain *enjoined* his crew to sail at full speed into the mine-filled harbor⟩ — see COMMAND 1

3 to order not to do or use or to be done or used ⟨Quakerism *enjoins* the taking of human life⟩ — see FORBID

enjoining *n* the act of ordering that something not be done or used ⟨the *enjoining* of the use of all tobacco products by the director of the baseball camp⟩ — see PROHIBITION 1

enjoy *vb* **1** to take pleasure in ⟨TV and videos are OK, but we still *enjoy* seeing movies on the big screen⟩

synonyms adore, delight (in), dig, fancy, groove (on), like, love, relish, revel (in)

related words admire, appreciate, cherish, revere, venerate, worship; prize, treasure, value; devour, drink (in), savor; dote (on), idolize; cotton (to), favor, prefer

phrases be partial to, get a kick (*or* charge) out of, go for, have a soft spot for, take to

near antonyms abhor, abominate, detest, dislike, hate, loathe; condemn, despise, scorn

2 to keep, control, or experience as one's own ⟨a country where the people *enjoy* the highest living standards in the world⟩ — see HAVE 1

enjoyable *adj* **1** giving pleasure or contentment to the mind or senses ⟨the great food, service, and atmosphere made for a most *enjoyable* dinner⟩ — see PLEASANT

2 providing amusement or enjoyment ⟨the theme park's great variety of attractions mean that every member of the family will have an *enjoyable* time⟩ — see FUN

enjoyment *n* the feeling experienced when one's wishes are met ⟨this new video game should provide countless hours of *enjoyment*⟩ — see PLEASURE 1

enlarge *vb* **1** to become greater in extent, volume, amount, or number ⟨as the number of people with cell phones *enlarges*, more transmission towers will have to be built⟩ — see INCREASE 2

2 to make greater in size, amount, or number ⟨with a new member of the family on the way, Dad thinks maybe we should consider *enlarging* the house⟩ — see INCREASE 1

enlarge (on) *vb* to express more fully and in greater detail ⟨in your book report, don't just say that the story was interesting; *enlarge on* what you mean by that⟩ — see EXPAND 1

enlighten *vb* **1** to give information to ⟨the lecturer at the planetarium *enlightened* us about the latest astronomical discoveries⟩

synonyms acquaint, advise, apprise, brief, clue, familiarize, fill in, inform, instruct, tell, wise (up)

related words clarify, clear (up), construe, elucidate, explain, explicate, expound, illuminate, illustrate, interpret, spell out; announce, disclose, report; disabuse, disenchant, disillusion

near antonyms misinform, mislead

2 to provide (someone) with moral or spiritual understanding ⟨many people around the world have been *enlightened* by the teachings of Gautama Buddha⟩

synonyms edify, educate, nurture

related words elevate, ennoble, lift, uplift; better, improve, transform; exalt, glorify, transfigure

near antonyms confuse, perplex, puzzle; becloud, cloud, darken, obscure

enlist (in) *vb* to become a member of ⟨young men and women were *enlisting in* the navy in greater numbers⟩ — see ENTER 2

enliven *vb* to give life, vigor, or spirit to ⟨in most instances it's a good idea to *enliven* a speech with a joke or two⟩ — see ANIMATE

enmesh *vb* to catch or hold as if in a net ⟨soon after Eli Whitney had invented it, others copied his cotton gin, and he spent the rest of his life *enmeshed* in lawsuits trying to protect his invention⟩ — see ENTANGLE 2

enmity *n* a deep-seated ill will ⟨*enmity* had existed between the two families for generations⟩

synonyms animosity, antagonism, antipathy, bitterness, gall, grudge, hostility, jaundice, rancor

related words hate, hatred, loathing; vindictiveness, virulence, vitriol; alienation, disaffection, estrangement; abhorrence, aversion, repugnance, repulsion; disgust, horror; conflict, coolness, friction, strain, tension; discord, unfriendliness; malice, malignancy, malignity, spite, spitefulness, venom

near antonyms amiability, amicability, civility, cordiality, friendliness, hospitality, neighborliness; comity, empathy, friendship, goodwill, sympathy, understanding

antonyms amity

ennoble *vb* to enhance the status of ⟨the heroic actions of fire fighters during the terrorist attack did much to *ennoble* the profession of fire fighting in the public mind⟩ — see EXALT

ennui *n* the state of being bored ⟨the kind of *ennui* that comes from having too much time on one's hands and too little will to find something productive to do⟩ — see BOREDOM

enormity *n* **1** the state or quality of being utterly evil ⟨the *enormity* of the crimes committed by the Nazis⟩

synonyms atrociousness, atrocity, badness, depravedness, depravity, evilness, heinousness, monstrosity, nefariousness, sinfulness, vileness, wickedness

related words accursedness, baseness, devilishness, execrableness, fiendishness, hellishness; corruption, decadence, degeneracy; immorality; infamy, notoriety

near antonyms morality; chasteness, innocence, purity

antonyms goodness, righteousness, virtuousness

2 the quality or state of being very large ⟨the *enormity* of the canyon can only be grasped by taking a trip through its entire length⟩ — see IMMENSITY

enormous *adj* unusually large ⟨that pumpkin is so *enormous* that it has to be a record holder⟩ — see HUGE

enormously *adv* to a large extent or degree ⟨the neighbors have been *enormously* helpful in helping us to settle in⟩ — see GREATLY 2

enormousness *n* the quality or state of being very large ⟨the *enormousness* of the mall is such that one could shop at a different store for every day of the year⟩ — see IMMENSITY

enough *adv* **1** in or to a degree or quantity that meets one's requirements or satisfaction ⟨the elevator is big *enough* to hold everyone⟩

synonyms adequately, satisfactorily, sufficiently

related words acceptably, decently, fairly, moderately, passably, tolerably; abundantly, amply; commensurately, proportionately

antonyms inadequately, insufficiently, unsatisfactorily

2 to some degree or extent ⟨I can play the piano well *enough*, but I have no hope for a musical career⟩ — see FAIRLY

enrage *vb* to make angry ⟨the fact that the auto garage bungled the repair and then overcharged him simply *enraged* the customer⟩ — see ANGER

enraged *adj* feeling or showing anger ⟨the repair shop owner tore up the bill when saw the *enraged* look on the customer's face⟩ — see ANGRY

enrapture *vb* **1** to fill with great joy ⟨*enraptured* upon learning that he would be attending college on a full sports scholarship⟩ — see ELATE

2 to fill with overwhelming emotion (as wonder or delight) ⟨this classic ballet of the Christmas season never fails to *enrapture* audiences young and old⟩ — see ENTRANCE

enraptured *adj* experiencing or marked by overwhelming usually pleasurable emotion ⟨the *enraptured* look on the fans' faces during the band's concerts⟩ — see ECSTATIC

enraptured (by) *adj* filled with an intense or excessive love for ⟨her friends have noticed that she usually becomes totally *enraptured by* her latest boyfriend—for about a month⟩ — see ENAMORED (OF)

enrich *vb* **1** to make better ⟨a truly great book can *enrich* your life⟩ — see IMPROVE

2 to make more attractive by adding something that is beautiful or becoming ⟨the church's magnificent interior is *enriched* with stunningly beautiful murals⟩ — see DECORATE

enroll *also* **enrol** *vb* **1** to enter in a list or roll ⟨the school *enrolls* about 800 students⟩

synonyms inscribe, list, matriculate, register

related words catalog (*or* catalogue), itemize, tabulate, tally; file, index; book, log, post; program, schedule; check in

near antonyms cancel, delete, exclude, expel, expunge, reject; omit, overlook

2 to put (someone or something) on a list ⟨can I *enroll* you on the list of volunteers for the church supper?⟩ — see ¹LIST 2

enroll (in) *vb* to become a member of ⟨plans to *enroll in* the local chapter of the Girl Scouts⟩ — see ENTER 2

enrollment *n* the number of individuals registered ⟨the school's *enrollment* currently stands at 500⟩ — see REGISTRATION

ensconce *vb* **1** to establish or place comfortably or snugly ⟨the kids had contentedly *ensconced* themselves on the couch before the TV⟩

synonyms install, lodge, perch, roost, settle

related words curl up; park, plant; anchor, bivouac, camp; burrow; locate, situate

2 to put into a hiding place ⟨*ensconced* the spare house key in a place where no intruder would think to look⟩ — see ¹HIDE 1

enshrine *vb* to enhance the status of ⟨some teachers tend to *enshrine* their personal preferences as sacred rules of English grammar⟩ — see EXALT

enshroud *vb* **1** to keep secret or shut off from view ⟨the criminal organization uses a strictly enforced vow of silence to *enshroud* its villainous doings⟩ — see ¹HIDE 2

2 to surround or cover closely ⟨a dense fog *enshrouded* the bridge spanning the harbor⟩ — see ENFOLD 1

ensign *n* a piece of cloth with a special design that is used as an emblem or for signaling ⟨fittingly, the organization promoting the welfare of marine life features a dolphin on its *ensign*⟩ — see FLAG 1

enslavement *n* the state of being a slave ⟨having known the misery of *enslavement* first hand, Frederick Douglass went on devote his life to the cause of making others free⟩ — see SLAVERY 1

ensnare *vb* to catch or hold as if in a net ⟨parked just out of view, the state trooper was lying in wait to *ensnare* unwary speeders⟩ — see ENTANGLE 2

ensuing *adj* **1** being the one that comes immediately after another ⟨business was slow in the restaurant's first year, but the *ensuing* year saw a much-needed increase⟩ — see NEXT

2 being, occurring, or carried out at a time after something else ⟨the war and the *ensuing* famine caused unimaginable suffering⟩ — see SUBSEQUENT

ensure *vb* to make sure, certain, or safe ⟨regulations that *ensure* the wholesomeness of our food⟩

   synonyms assure, cinch, guarantee, guaranty, insure, secure

   related words attest, certify, vouch, warrant, witness; pledge, promise, swear

   near antonyms enfeeble, undermine, weaken

entail *vb* to have as part of a whole ⟨a lavish wedding *entails* extensive planning and often staggering expense⟩ — see INCLUDE

entangle *vb* **1** to twist together into a usually confused mass ⟨in the process of taking down the Christmas tree, we managed to *entangle* the string of lights into a hopeless mess of wires⟩

   synonyms interlace, intertwine, interweave, knot, snarl, tangle

   related words weave, wind, wreathe; braid, plait

   antonyms disentangle

2 to catch or hold as if in a net ⟨the young runaway gradually became *entangled* in a web of lies⟩

   synonyms enmesh, ensnare, entrap, mesh, snare, tangle, trap

   related words bag, capture, collar; embroil, implicate, involve, mire

   near antonyms extricate, untangle; detach, disengage; clear, free, liberate

   antonyms disentangle

entanglement *n* something that catches and holds ⟨this newest government regulation was only the latest *entanglement* for the fledgling business owner⟩ — see WEB 1

enter *vb* **1** to go or come in or into ⟨the hikers *entered* the cave with considerable caution⟩

   synonyms access, penetrate, pierce

   related words barge (in), breeze (in), burst (in *or* into), waltz (in); drop (in), pop (in)

   phrases set foot in, step in

   antonyms depart, exit, leave

2 to become a member of ⟨patriotic young men and women *entering* the armed services⟩

   synonyms enlist (in), enroll (in), join, sign on (for), sign up (for)

   related words reenlist, reenroll, reenter

3 to put (someone or something) on a list ⟨can I *enter* you among those pledging to contribute to the church building fund?⟩ — see ¹LIST 2

enter (into *or* upon) *vb* to take the first step in (a process or course of action) ⟨a series of counseling sessions intended to help young couples about to *enter into* the trials and tribulations of marriage⟩ — see BEGIN 1

enterprise *n* **1** a commercial or industrial activity or organization ⟨the booming economy witnessed the launch of many small *enterprises*⟩

   synonyms business, company, concern, establishment, firm, house, outfit

   related words conglomerate, corporation, multinational; association, cartel, chain, combine, syndicate, trust; agency, dealer, outlet

2 readiness to engage in daring or difficult activity ⟨the *enterprise* shown by the early developers and promoters of personal computers⟩

   synonyms aggressiveness, ambition, drive, go, hustle, initiative

   related words gumption, pluck, snap, spirit, spunk, starch; assertiveness, self-reliance; energy, hardihood, pep, vigor, vitality

   near antonyms inactivity, inertia, passivity; diffidence, faintheartedness, timidity; hesitation, reluctance; indolence, laziness, lethargy

3 a risky undertaking ⟨the general viewed the proposed invasion as a military *enterprise* that offered no easy way out⟩ — see GAMBLE

enterprising *adj* **1** having or showing a bold forcefulness in the pursuit of a goal ⟨the company is claiming that there will be huge financial rewards for *enterprising* sales representatives⟩ — see AGGRESSIVE 1

2 inclined or willing to take risks ⟨*enterprising* people of vision were responsible for the boom in technological industries⟩ — see BOLD 1

entertain *vb* **1** to cause (someone) to pass the time agreeably occupied ⟨*entertain* the kids while I go and prepare dinner⟩ — see AMUSE

2 to give serious and careful thought to ⟨have you ever *entertained* the thought that you could be wrong?⟩ — see PONDER

3 to keep in one's mind or heart ⟨I don't *entertain* the hope of ever getting a girl like that to go out with me⟩ — see HARBOR 1

entertaining *adj* providing amusement or enjoyment ⟨a list of *entertaining* things to do on a snow day⟩ — see FUN

entertainment *n* **1** the act or activity of providing pleasure or amusement especially for the public ⟨a variety show was staged as *entertainment* for the scouts at the jamboree⟩

   synonyms amusement, distraction, diversion, recreation

   related words show business; delectation, delight, enjoyment, joy, mirth; gratification, relaxation, relief, satisfaction; exhibition, performance, presentation, production, show, spectacle; escapism

2 someone or something that provides amusement or enjoyment ⟨what do you do for *entertainment* in this town?⟩ — see FUN 1

enthrall *or* **enthral** *vb* **1** to hold the attention of as if by a spell ⟨*enthralled* by the flickering fire in the hearth, we lost all track of time⟩

   synonyms arrest, enchant, fascinate, grip, hypnotize, mesmerize, spellbind

   related words enrapture, entrance, thrill; beguile, bewitch, charm; absorb, engage, engross, involve

   phrases cast a spell on

2 to fill with overwhelming emotion (as wonder or delight) ⟨for years these master magicians have been *enthralling* audiences with their astounding illusions⟩ — see ENTRANCE

3 to hold the attention of ⟨a play that will *enthrall* you for two hours⟩ — see ENGAGE 1

enthralled *adj* having the mind fixed on something ⟨gave her speech to several hundred *enthralled* listeners⟩ — see ATTENTIVE

enthralling *adj* holding the attention or provoking interest ⟨an *enthralling* account of life in the scientific community in Antarctica⟩ — see INTERESTING

enthrallment *n* a focusing of the mind on something ⟨the child's *enthrallment* with the new toy was short-lived indeed⟩ — see ATTENTION 1

enthuse *vb* to make an exaggerated display of affection or enthusiasm ⟨the neighbors invited us over just so we could *enthuse* over their new car⟩ — see GUSH 2

enthusiasm *n* **1** a practice or interest that is very popular for a short time ⟨this year's *enthusiasm* is often next year's laughingstock⟩ — see FAD

2 urgent desire or interest ⟨in my *enthusiasm* to get going, I forgot to pack any foul-weather clothing⟩ — see EAGERNESS

enthusiast *n* a person with a strong and habitual liking for something ⟨skiing *enthusiasts* can't wait for the first snowfall of the season⟩ — see FAN

enthusiastic *adj* showing urgent desire or interest ⟨as soon as the gates to the concert area opened, *enthusiastic* fans rushed to get the best seats⟩ — see EAGER

enthusiastically *adv* in an enthusiastic manner ⟨sports writers have praised this new pitching find so *enthusiastically* you'd think he's going to pitch nothing but no-hitters⟩ — see SKY-HIGH

entice *vb* to lead away from a usual or proper course by offering some pleasure or advantage ⟨every commercial seemed to be for some tempting snack specifically designed to *entice* me from my diet⟩ — see LURE

enticement *n* **1** something that persuades one to perform an action for pleasure or gain ⟨the hospital often offers T-shirts or caps as *enticements* for people to donate blood⟩ — see LURE 1

2 the act or pressure of giving in to a desire especially when ill-advised ⟨the *enticement* of the party buffet was just too great to ignore for very long⟩ — see TEMPTATION 1

entire *adj* **1** not divided or scattered among several areas of interest or concern ⟨this matter is important, so please give me your *entire* attention⟩ — see WHOLE 1

2 not lacking any part or member that properly belongs to it ⟨the *entire* team needs to be present for the photograph⟩ — see COMPLETE 1

entirely *adv* to a full extent or degree ⟨are you *entirely* aware of what you're doing with that thing?⟩ — see FULLY 1

entitle *vb* **1** to give a right to ⟨the card *entitles* my grandmother to the discount for senior citizens⟩

synonyms authorize, qualify

related words empower, enable, license (*also* licence); approve, endorse (*also* indorse); allow, let, permit; certify, ratify, sanction, validate

antonyms disqualify

2 to give a name to ⟨apart from the obvious, she couldn't decide what to *entitle* her painting of a vase with flowers⟩ — see NAME 1

entity *n* one that has a real and independent existence ⟨the question of whether extrasensory perception will ever be a scientifically recognized *entity*⟩

synonyms being, individual, object, something, substance, thing

related words body; material, matter, stuff

entomb *vb* to place (a dead body) in the earth, a tomb, or the sea ⟨a number of Boston's historic notables are *entombed* in the Old Granary Burying Ground⟩ — see BURY 1

entombing *n* the act or ceremony of putting a dead body in its final resting place ⟨the *entombing* of the pharaohs in the pyramids must have been a magnificent sight⟩ — see BURIAL

entombment *n* the act or ceremony of putting a dead body in its final resting place ⟨the *entombment* of President Kennedy in Arlington National Cemetery⟩ — see BURIAL

entrails *n pl* the internal organs of the body ⟨in ancient Rome predictions of future events would sometimes be based on an examination of the *entrails* of a sacrificial animal⟩ — see GUT 1

entrance *n* **1** the means or right of entering or participating in ⟨*entrance* to the club is by invitation only⟩

synonyms access, admission, admittance, doorway, entrée (*or* entree), entry, gateway

related words approval, certification, qualification

2 the opening through which one can enter or leave a structure ⟨when you come, use the *entrance* on the right side of the building⟩ — see DOOR 2

entrance *vb* to fill with overwhelming emotion (as wonder or delight) ⟨a production of *The Nutcracker* ballet that will *entrance* audiences⟩

synonyms carry away, enrapture, enthrall (*or* enthral), overjoy, ravish, transport

related words delight, gladden, gratify, please, satisfy; bewitch, captivate, charm, enchant, fascinate; elate, excite, exhilarate, stir

entranced *adj* **1** being or appearing to be under a magic spell ⟨the princess seems to attract a throng of *entranced* admirers wherever she goes⟩ — see ENCHANTED

2 experiencing or marked by overwhelming usually pleasurable emotion ⟨the *entranced* look on her face as she danced at the ball⟩ — see ECSTATIC

entrancing *adj* having an often mysterious or magical power to attract ⟨travelers to India say that it has an *entrancing* beauty that is hard to describe⟩ — see FASCINATING 1

entrap *vb* to catch or hold as if in a net ⟨a string of inconsistent statements and outright lies that finally *entrapped* the witness⟩ — see ENTANGLE 2

entreat *vb* to make a request to (someone) in an earnest or urgent manner ⟨the children *entreated* their parents to let them stay up past their bedtime just this once⟩ — see BEG

entreating *adj* asking humbly ⟨it was hard to refuse the *entreating* panhandler⟩ — see SUPPLIANT

entreaty *n* an earnest request ⟨our *entreaties* to give us another few minutes to answer the test questions fell on deaf ears⟩ — see PLEA 1

entrée *or* **entree** *n* the means or right of entering or participating in ⟨*entrée* to the country club is through sponsorship by someone who is already a member⟩ — see ENTRANCE 1

entrench *also* **intrench** *vb* to set solidly in or as if in surrounding matter ⟨a father who *entrenched* in our minds the belief that hard work pays off⟩

synonyms embed (*also* imbed), fix, implant, ingrain, lodge, root

related words imbue, infuse, instill; establish, place, put, settle, stick

near antonyms eliminate, eradicate; eject, expel; detach, disconnect, disengage, remove

antonyms dislodge, root (out), uproot

entrenched *also* **intrenched** *adj* firmly established over time ⟨I have an *entrenched* dislike of mimes⟩ — see INVETERATE 1

entrust *vb* **1** to give a task, duty, or responsibility to ⟨we *entrusted* our financial adviser with the investment of all of our savings⟩

synonyms assign, charge, commission, trust

related words confer, impose; commit, consign, delegate, relegate; allocate, allot; authorize, empower, invest

2 to put (something) into the possession or safekeeping of another ⟨we *entrusted* our pets to the care of our neighbor while we went on vacation⟩ — see GIVE 2

entry *n* **1** the entrance room of a building ⟨please wait in the *entry* while I get the person you want⟩ — see HALL 1

2 the means or right of entering or participating in ⟨believed that a college education was one's *entry* to a life of luxury⟩ — see ENTRANCE 1

entryway *n* the entrance room of a building ⟨a small *entryway* to receive visitors⟩ — see HALL 1

entwine *vb* to follow a circular or spiral course ⟨the quick-growing vine was soon *entwining* around the fence post⟩ — see WIND

enumerate *vb* **1** to specify one after another ⟨I proceeded to *enumerate* the reasons why my allowance needed raising⟩

synonyms detail, itemize, list, numerate, rehearse, tick (off)

related words outline; tabulate, tally; catalog (*or* catalogue), inventory; chart, diagram, graph; calculate, compute, estimate, figure, reckon; cite, mention, name

2 to find the sum of (a collection of things) by noting each one as it is being added ⟨there were more birds hovering about the bird feeder than I could possibly *enumerate*⟩ — see COUNT 1

3 to make a list of ⟨let's *enumerate* the top ten reasons why Top Ten lists have gotten out of hand⟩ — see ¹LIST 1

enunciate *vb* **1** to utter clearly and distinctly ⟨*enunciate* your words, and then you won't have to repeat them so often⟩ — see ARTICULATE 1

2 to make known openly or publicly ⟨today the president *enunciated* a new foreign policy⟩ — see ANNOUNCE

enunciation *n* the clear and accurate pronunciation of words especially in public speaking ⟨a radio announcer who is known for his very careful *enunciation*⟩ — see DICTION 1

envelop *vb* **1** to close or shut in by or as if by barriers ⟨a chronic mistrust of outsiders *envelops* that neighborhood, cutting it off from the rest of the city⟩ — see ENCLOSE 1

2 to surround or cover closely ⟨the truth of the presidential assassination is *enveloped* in a dense fog of myths and conspiracy theories⟩ — see ENFOLD 1

envenom *vb* to implant bitter feelings in ⟨thoughtless, self-indulgent antics that only managed to *envenom* his teammates⟩ — see EMBITTER

envenomed *adj* containing or contaminated with a substance capable of injuring or killing a living thing ⟨the *envenomed* spines of these tropical fishes make them a particular hazard of coral reefs⟩ — see POISONOUS

envious *adj* having or showing mean resentment of another's possessions or advantages ⟨a family that is *envious* of their neighbors' big house⟩

synonyms covetous, invidious, jaundiced, jealous, resentful

related words begrudging, grudging; avaricious, grasping, greedy; distrustful, suspicious; malicious, petty, spiteful

phrases green with envy

near antonyms generous, kind, kindhearted; altruistic, benevolent, charitable; well-meaning

enviousness *n* a painful awareness of another's possessions or advantages and a desire to have them too ⟨Lisa's *enviousness* of Debra's athletic achievements was obvious to all of their friends⟩ — see ENVY

environment *n* the circumstances, conditions, or objects by which one is surrounded ⟨the joys of growing up in the *environment* that a small town offers⟩

synonyms atmosphere, climate, environs, medium, milieu, setting, surroundings

related words backdrop, background, context; element; situation, status; habitat

environs *n pl* **1** the area around a city ⟨the city and its *environs* total about a million in population⟩

synonyms exurbia, outskirts, purlieu, suburbia

related words backwater, backwoods, hinterland

2 the circumstances, conditions, or objects by which one is surrounded ⟨growing up in the *environs* of the inner city wasn't easy, but he was determined to make something of himself⟩ — see ENVIRONMENT

envisage *vb* to form a mental picture of ⟨I'm trying to *envisage* you on a surfboard⟩ — see IMAGINE 1

envoy *n* **1** a person sent on a mission to represent another ⟨the president sent the secretary of state as his personal *envoy* to gain the support of the country's allies⟩ — see AMBASSADOR

2 a person who acts or does business for another ⟨one of the hostage takers was chosen as the group's *envoy* for all dealings with the authorities⟩ — see AGENT 2

envy *n* a painful awareness of another's possessions or advantages and a desire to have them too ⟨her *envy* of her neighbor's fancy clothes wrecked their friendship⟩

synonyms covetousness, enviousness, invidiousness, jealousy, resentment

related words animosity, enmity, hatred, ill will; malice, maliciousness, spitefulness

near antonyms benevolence, goodwill, kindness, sympathy

enwrap *vb* to surround or cover closely ⟨an air of serene self-satisfaction *enwraps* the leafy, well-to-do suburb⟩ — see ENFOLD 1

ephemeral *adj* lasting only for a short time ⟨the autumnal blaze of colors is always to be appreciated, if only because it is so *ephemeral*⟩ — see MOMENTARY

epicure *n* a person with refined tastes in food and wine ⟨Thomas Jefferson was one of America's first great *epicures*⟩

synonyms gourmand, gourmet

related words connoisseur, dilettante; savorer

near antonyms glutton, gorger, hog, trencherman

epigram *n* an often stated observation regarding something from common experience ⟨Benjamin Franklin's famous *epigram*, "Remember that time is money"⟩ — see SAYING

epigrammatic *adj* marked by the use of few words to convey much information or meaning ⟨Oscar Wilde's *epigrammatic* observation, "In America the young are always ready to give to those who are older than themselves the full benefits of their inexperience"⟩ — see CONCISE

episode *n* something that happens ⟨the *episode* in which the Native American Samoset walked into Plymouth Plantation and surprised the Pilgrims with the greeting, "Welcome, Englishman"⟩ — see EVENT 1

episodic *adj* appearing in parts or numbers that follow regularly ⟨the long novel was filmed for television as an *episodic* movie that was shown over the course of five evenings⟩ — see SERIAL

epistle *n* a message on paper from one person or group to another ⟨the *epistles* of Saint Paul to various communities of early Christians⟩ — see LETTER

epithet *n* **1** a descriptive or familiar name given instead of or in addition to the one belonging to an individual ⟨King Richard I of England was given the very laudatory *epithet* "the Lion-Hearted"⟩ — see NICKNAME

2 an act or expression showing scorn and usually intended to hurt another's feelings ⟨the school has a strict ban against the use of racial, ethnic, religious, and sexual *epithets*⟩ — see INSULT

epitome *n* **1** a short statement of the main points ⟨the golden rule is often cited as the *epitome* of moral conduct: "Do unto others as you would have them do unto you"⟩ — see SUMMARY

2 a visible representation of something abstract (as a quality) ⟨the prestigious prep school prides itself on being widely regarded as the *epitome* of tradition and old-fashioned values⟩ — see EMBODIMENT

3 the most perfect type or example ⟨Mahatma Gandhi is often cited as the *epitome* of resolute reformer who uses nonviolence to bring about social and political change⟩ — see QUINTESSENCE 1

epitomize *vb* **1** to make into a short statement of the main points (as of a report) ⟨his personal code of behavior on the playing field is *epitomized* by his favorite saying, "Nice guys finish last"⟩ — see SUMMARIZE

2 to represent in visible form ⟨the Parthenon in Athens *epitomizes* the ancient Greek ideal of architectural beauty⟩ — see EMBODY 2

epoch *n* an extent of time associated with a particular person or thing ⟨Sir Isaac Newton is usually credited with establishing the *epoch* of modern science⟩ — see AGE 1

equable *adj* marked by temperatures that are neither too high nor too low ⟨an area with an *equable* climate would be our first choice for a place in which to settle⟩ — see CLEMENT

equal *vb* **1** to produce something equal to (as in quality or value) ⟨no one has *equaled* Shakespeare's plays⟩

synonyms match, meet, tie

related words beat, excel, outdo, surpass, top; amount (to), approach, touch; measure (up), rival

2 to be the same in meaning or effect ⟨being confined to home for a whole weekend would *equal* a death sentence in the minds of a lot of teens⟩ — see AMOUNT (TO) 2

3 to be the exact counterpart of ⟨in the British system a public school *equals* an American prep school⟩ — see MATCH 1

equal *adj* **1** marked by justice, honesty, and freedom from bias ⟨the basic belief that everyone is entitled to *equal* opportunity in employment⟩ — see FAIR 2

2 resembling another in every respect ⟨as far as I can see, except for the high price, the store-brand jacket is *equal* to the jacket with the designer label⟩ — see SAME 1

equal *n* one that is equal to another in status, achievement, or value ⟨a basketball player who truly has no *equal* in his sport⟩

synonyms coordinate, counterpart, equivalent, fellow, like, match, parallel, peer, rival

related words analogue (*or* analog); double, mate, twin; associate, colleague, companion, partner; competitor

equality *n* the state or fact of being exactly the same in number, amount, status, or quality ⟨it's absurd to suggest that there's an *equality* in the evil committed by the Nazis and the crimes of the government of that Asian country⟩ — see EQUIVALENCE

equalize *vb* to make equal in amount, degree, or status ⟨a plan to *equalize* educational opportunities for all the state's children, rich and poor alike⟩

synonyms balance, equate, even, level

related words accommodate, adjust, compensate, fit; homogenize, normalize, regularize, standardize; democratize

equanimity *n* evenness of emotions or temper ⟨an Olympic diver who always displays remarkable *equanimity* on the platform⟩

synonyms aplomb, calmness, composure, coolheadedness, coolness, imperturbability, placidity, self-possession, serenity, tranquillity (*or* tranquility)

related words assurance, confidence, poise, self-assurance, self-confidence; apathy, detachment, indifference, phlegm

near antonyms alarm, anxiety, apprehension, disquiet; excitability, nervousness; disturbance

antonyms agitation, discomposure, perturbation

equate *vb* **1** to regard or represent as equal or comparable ⟨a value system that *equates* money with success⟩

synonyms compare, liken

related words associate, connect, join, link, match; group, lump (together)

near antonyms differentiate, discriminate, distinguish

2 to describe as similar ⟨you're being silly when you *equate* the talent of that pop star with the musical genius of Mozart⟩ — see COMPARE 1

3 to make equal in amount, degree, or status ⟨you'll stop running up debts when you start *equating* what you spend with what you earn⟩ — see EQUALIZE

equatorial *adj* being near the equator ⟨the lush *equatorial* rain forest that is threatened by development⟩ — see LOW 1

equilibrium *n* a condition in which opposing forces are equal to one another ⟨we must find an *equilibrium* between development and conservation of our natural treasures⟩ — see BALANCE 1

equine *n* a large hoofed domestic animal that is used for carrying or drawing loads and for riding ⟨one of the more esteemed *equines* of modern times was the racehorse Seabiscuit⟩ — see HORSE

equip *vb* **1** to make competent (as by training, skill, or ability) for a particular office or function ⟨years of service in the congress and in the cabinet *equipped* him better than most people for the office of the presidency⟩ — see QUALIFY 2

2 to provide (someone) with what is needed for a task or activity ⟨a visit to a ski shop to *equip* ourselves for a week of skiing in the Rockies⟩ — see FURNISH 1

equipage *n* a horse-drawn wheeled vehicle for carrying passengers ⟨for their old-fashioned wedding, the couple arrived at the church in a Victorian-era *equipage*, complete with costumed driver⟩ — see CARRIAGE 1

equipment *n* items needed for the performance of a task or activity ⟨the *equipment* for the polar expedition included ships, instruments, sleds, dogs, and provisions⟩

synonyms accoutrements (*or* accouterments), apparatus, gear, material(s), matériel (*or* materiel), outfit, paraphernalia, tackle

related words accessories, attachments, fittings; baggage, belongings, impedimenta; appliances, facilities, instruments, machinery, tools; apparel, attire, habiliments, raiment, trappings; battery

equipoise *n* **1** a condition in which opposing forces are equal to one another ⟨when participating in any dangerous sport, one should maintain an *equipoise* between fearless boldness and commonsense caution⟩ — see BALANCE 1

2 a force or influence that makes an opposing force ineffective or less effective ⟨her frugality is a much-needed *equipoise* to her husband's spendthrift ways⟩ — see COUNTERBALANCE

equitable *adj* marked by justice, honesty, and freedom from bias ⟨the will calls for an *equitable* distribution of the father's assets among his four children⟩ — see FAIR 2

equity *n* the act or practice of giving to others what is their due ⟨basic to the notion of *equity* is the principle that all people are of equal standing in the eyes of the law⟩ — see JUSTICE 1

equivalence *n* the state or fact of being exactly the same in number, amount, status, or quality ⟨moviegoers who mistakenly believe that there is an *equivalence* between the personality of an actor and that of his character⟩
synonyms equality, equivalency, par, parity, sameness
related words compatibility, correlation, correspondence; likeness, similarity; exchangeability, interchangeability
near antonyms difference, discrepancy, disparity, divergence; incompatibility; dissimilarity, unlikeness
antonyms inequality

equivalency *n* the state or fact of being exactly the same in number, amount, status, or quality ⟨as long as there's a rough *equivalency* in the armaments of the two countries, neither is likely to attack the other⟩ — see EQUIVALENCE

equivalent *n* one that is equal to another in status, achievement, or value ⟨that huge mansion is the *equivalent* of five ordinary houses⟩ — see EQUAL

equivocal *adj* **1** giving good reason for being doubted, questioned, or challenged ⟨the evidence that this latest diet really results in lasting weight loss is certainly *equivocal*⟩ — see DOUBTFUL 2
2 having an often intentionally veiled or uncertain meaning ⟨his demand that I promptly pay what I owe him ended with the *equivocal* threat "or else"⟩ — see OBSCURE 1

equivocalness *n* the quality or state of having a veiled or uncertain meaning ⟨the *equivocalness* of her warning that I would get what I had coming to me⟩ — see OBSCURITY 1

equivocate *vb* to avoid giving a definite answer or position ⟨the candidate *equivocated* as long as he could on controversial issues⟩
synonyms fudge, hedge, pussyfoot
related words dodge, duck, evade, sidestep, skirt; bypass, circumvent; cavil, quibble
phrases beat around (*or* about) the bush, dance around, hem and haw

equivocation *n* the quality or state of having a veiled or uncertain meaning ⟨the *equivocation* of the last line of the poem, "That is all ye know on earth, and all ye need to know"⟩ — see OBSCURITY 1

era *n* an extent of time associated with a particular person or thing ⟨the introduction of the mass production of cars on an assembly line ushered in the *era* of the automobile⟩ — see AGE 1

eradicate *vb* to destroy all traces of ⟨the successful effort to *eradicate* smallpox around the globe⟩ — see ANNIHILATE 1

ere *prep* earlier than ⟨an old typewriter that was a relic of the time *ere* the invention of word processors⟩ — see BEFORE 1

erect *adj* rising straight up ⟨a lone tree remained *erect* after the terrible tornado had passed⟩
synonyms perpendicular, plumb, raised, standing, upright, upstanding, vertical

related words elevated, lifted, upended, upraised; freestanding
near antonyms prostrate, supine; hanging, sagging, slanted, slanting
antonyms flat, recumbent

erect *vb* **1** to fix in an upright position ⟨the tribes of the Pacific Northwest *erected* totem poles in front of their dwellings⟩
synonyms pitch, put up, raise, rear, set up, upend, upraise
related words brace, buttress, prop (up), shore (up), support; elevate, hoist, lift
near antonyms demolish, flatten, knock down, level, raze, tear down
2 to form by putting together parts or materials ⟨we'd better *erect* some sort of shelter before these woods are in total darkness⟩ — see BUILD

erection *n* something put together by arranging or connecting an array of parts ⟨when it was brand-new, the Eiffel Tower was considered as ugly an *erection* as Europe had ever seen⟩ — see CONSTRUCTION 1

ergo *adv* for this or that reason ⟨according to that line of reasoning, the eyewitness couldn't identify the aircraft, *ergo* it must have been from another planet⟩ — see THEREFORE

erode *vb* **1** to consume or wear away gradually ⟨the fear that inflation will continue to *erode* people's savings⟩ — see EAT 2
2 to damage or diminish by continued friction ⟨the winds and desert sands have *eroded* much of the original surface of these ancient monuments⟩ — see ABRADE 1

erosion *n* a gradual weakening, loss, or destruction ⟨the *erosion* of the banks along the river worries flood experts⟩ — see CORROSION

erotic *adj* of, relating to, or expressing sexual attraction ⟨the *erotic* aspects of the story of Beauty and the Beast⟩
synonyms amatory, amorous, sexy
related words carnal, sensual, sensuous; bawdy, lascivious, lewd, lustful, obscene, prurient, spicy

err *vb* to commit an offense ⟨when we *err*, we must be willing to accept the consequences⟩ — see OFFEND 1

errant *adj* **1** engaging in or marked by childish misbehavior ⟨what he considers to be no more than *errant* conduct toward women would be regarded as sexual harassment by most people⟩ — see NAUGHTY
2 traveling from place to place ⟨the *errant* gunslinger as a standard character in western novels⟩ — see ITINERANT

erratic *adj* **1** lacking a definite plan, purpose, or pattern ⟨so far your effort to land a summer job has been very *erratic*⟩ — see RANDOM
2 lacking in steadiness or regularity of occurrence ⟨because of your *erratic* attendance at practice, you're in danger of being cut from the team⟩ — see FITFUL
3 not staying constant ⟨business at the fast-food restaurant has been so *erratic* lately that the manager never knows how much staff to have on hand⟩ — see UNEVEN 2

erratically *adv* without definite aim, direction, rule, or method ⟨the police officer pulled over the driver, who had been driving very *erratically*⟩ — see HIT OR MISS

erroneous *adj* not being in agreement with what is true ⟨a news article about the new virus that was filled with much *erroneous* information⟩ — see FALSE 1

erroneously *adv* in a mistaken or inappropriate way ⟨people *erroneously* believed that the disease was contagious⟩ — see WRONGLY

erroneousness *n* the quality or state of being false ⟨the *erroneousness* of so much that is printed in the tabloids is amazing⟩ — see FALLACY 2

error *n* **1** an unintentional departure from truth or accuracy ⟨a report on the earthquake contained several unfortunate *errors*⟩
synonyms blunder, fault, flub, fumble, goof, inaccuracy, lapse, miscue, misstep, mistake, oversight, slip, slipup, stumble
related words boner, howler; foul-up, muff; misapprehension, miscalculation, misconception, misjudgment, misstatement, misunderstanding
near antonyms accuracy, correctness, precision
2 a breaking of a moral or legal code ⟨we have all committed *errors* in our lives and strayed from the path of righteousness⟩ — see OFFENSE 1
3 a false idea or belief ⟨the church published a list of moral *errors* that it considers to be at odds with its teachings⟩ — see FALLACY 1

erstwhile *adj* having been such at some previous time ⟨my *erstwhile* friend ignored me when I ran into her at the mall⟩ — see FORMER

erudite *adj* **1** having or displaying advanced knowledge or education ⟨the most *erudite* people in medical research attended the conference⟩ ⟨an *erudite* lecture on the latest discoveries in astronomy⟩ — see EDUCATED
2 suggestive of the vocabulary used in books ⟨the *erudite* language of a textbook on philosophy⟩ — see BOOKISH

erudition *n* the understanding and information gained from being educated ⟨a theologian of impressive *erudition* but with a down-to-earth manner⟩ — see EDUCATION 2

erupt *vb* **1** to throw out or off (something from within) often violently ⟨the volcano *erupted* clouds of poisonous gas and tons of hot ash⟩
synonyms belch, disgorge, eject, expel, jet, spew, spout, spurt
related words gush, pour, stream, surge; emanate, issue, spring; discharge, emit, fire; cast, fling, heave, hurl, launch, pitch, toss
near antonyms bottle (up), contain, restrain, shut (in *or* up)
2 to develop suddenly and violently ⟨a fire *erupted*, and flames soon engulfed the room⟩
synonyms break out, burst (forth), explode, flame, flare (up)
related words burgeon, mushroom, snowball; blow up, detonate, touch off

eruption *n* **1** a sudden intense expression of strong feeling ⟨a great *eruption* of glee as it suddenly dawned on her that she had won⟩ — see OUTBURST 1
2 the act or an instance of exploding ⟨the *eruption* of the volcano Krakatoa was one of the most violent in global history⟩ — see EXPLOSION 1

escalate *vb* **1** to become greater in extent, volume, amount, or number ⟨as the war between the two countries *escalated*, it threatened to become a global conflict⟩ — see INCREASE 2
2 to make greater in size, amount, or number ⟨the president promised to *escalate* the government's program to combat the dreaded disease⟩ — see INCREASE 1

escalated *adj* being at a higher level than average ⟨for a time there was an *escalated* interest in the Titanic following the release of the blockbuster movie⟩ — see HIGH 2

escapade *n* a playful or mischievous act intended as a joke ⟨their *escapades* at the prep school became the stuff of boarding-school legend⟩ — see PRANK

escape *n* **1** the act or an instance of getting free from danger or confinement ⟨a daring prison *escape*⟩
synonyms flight, getaway, lam, slip
related words deliverance, liberation, redemption, release, rescue, salvation
near antonyms imprisonment, incarceration; custody, detention, hold, holding, retention; danger, hazard, jeopardy, peril, risk
2 the act or a means of getting or keeping away from something undesirable ⟨the reading of science fiction novels as an *escape* from boring reality⟩
synonyms avoidance, cop-out, dodging, ducking, eluding, eschewing, evasion, out, shaking, shunning
related words bypassing, circumvention; averting, deflection, prevention
near antonyms abidance, endurance, submission, toleration

escape *vb* **1** to get free from a dangerous or confining situation ⟨everyone managed to *escape* from the burning building in time⟩
synonyms abscond, clear out, flee, fly, get away, get out, lam, run away, run off
related words avoid, elude, evade, lose, shun; decamp, depart, exit, leave; disentangle, extricate; emancipate, free, liberate, redeem, release
phrases fly the coop, free oneself
near antonyms abide, linger, remain, stay, tarry; come back, return
2 to get or keep away from (as a responsibility) through cleverness or trickery ⟨a judge who is very determined not to let criminals *escape* punishment⟩
synonyms avoid, dodge, duck, elude, eschew, evade, shake, shirk, shun
related words miss; avert, deflect, divert, obviate, parry, prevent, ward (off); debar, exclude, preclude; bypass, circumvent, skirt; foil, frustrate, outwit, thwart
phrases get around, have nothing to do with, shy away from, steer clear of
near antonyms accept, court, embrace, pursue, seek, welcome; catch, contract, incur

escarpment *n* a steep wall of rock, earth, or ice ⟨the castle sits atop an *escarpment* that for hundreds of years made it virtually invulnerable to attack⟩ — see CLIFF

eschew *vb* to get or keep away from (as a responsibility) through cleverness or trickery ⟨the minister *eschews* involvement in local politics, since he doesn't want to diminish his moral authority in the community⟩ — see ESCAPE 2

eschewing *n* the act or a means of getting or keeping away from something undesirable ⟨the basketball coach's *eschewing* of favoritism has won her the team's wholehearted respect⟩ — see ESCAPE 2

escort *n* one that accompanies another for protection, guidance, or as a courtesy ⟨the mayor served as the First Lady's *escort* for her tour of the city⟩
synonyms attendant, companion, guard, guide
related words chaperone (*or* chaperon), squire; shadow, sidekick; conductor, leader, pilot

escort *vb* to go along with in order to provide assistance, protection, or companionship ⟨a student from the college *escorted* my parents and me on our tour of the campus⟩ — see ACCOMPANY

esculent *adj* suitable for use as food ⟨harvesting wild mushrooms is no business for amateurs, since some of the *esculent* ones closely resemble poisonous varieties⟩ — see EDIBLE

esoteric *adj* difficult for one of ordinary knowledge or intelligence to understand ⟨metaphysics is such an *esoteric* subject that most people are content to leave it to the philosophers⟩ — see PROFOUND 1

especial *adj* of a particular or exact sort ⟨with a very ordinary lawn, we don't have any *especial* need for a gardener⟩ — see EXPRESS 1

especially *adv* to a great degree ⟨that prep school is *especially* strong in the sciences⟩ — see VERY 1

espionage *n* the secret gathering of information on others ⟨the acts of *espionage* on behalf of the Confederacy carried on by Belle Boyd and Rose Greenhow⟩
synonyms spying
related words dope, goods, lowdown; counterintelligence, intelligence; observation, reconnaissance, surveillance; bugging, eavesdropping, wiretapping

espousal *n* **1** a ceremony in which two people are united in matrimony ⟨the expected *espousal* of the Hollywood actor and the singing superstar should attract the elite of show business⟩ — see WEDDING
2 the act or state of being engaged to be married ⟨considering how long her previous marriage lasted, she'd be wise to have an extended *espousal*⟩ — see ENGAGEMENT 1

espouse *vb* **1** to give in marriage ⟨a couple eager to *espouse* their eldest daughter⟩ — see MARRY 2
2 to take as a spouse ⟨heeded his father's advice to *espouse* someone with whom he had common interests⟩ — see MARRY 3

esprit *n* active strength of body or mind ⟨the dance company has an *esprit* that captivates audiences⟩ — see VIGOR 1

espy *vb* to make note of (something) through the use of one's eyes ⟨out of the corner of my eye I *espied* the squirrel making another raid on the bird feeder⟩ — see SEE 1

essay *n* **1** a short piece of writing typically expressing a point of view ⟨school *essays* on what it means to be a patriot⟩
synonyms article, composition, paper, theme
related words column, commentary, editorial, feature, report, review, write-up; dissertation, thesis; tract, treatise; discourse, discussion, exposition, study
2 an effort to do or accomplish something ⟨my first *essay* at baking a cake did not go well⟩ — see ATTEMPT

essay *vb* to make an effort to do ⟨he had been in gymnastics for some time before he even considered *essaying* that move⟩ — see ATTEMPT

essence *n* the quality or qualities that make a thing what it is ⟨the belief that power ultimately rests with the people is the very *essence* of democracy⟩
synonyms essentiality, nature, quintessence, soul, stuff, substance
related words heart, spirit; center, core, keynote, marrow, pith, seat; embodiment, epitome, incarnation, manifestation, personification; aspect, attribute, feature, property; gist, kernel, nub

essential *adj* **1** impossible to do without ⟨a well-stocked public library is *essential* for the well-being of a community⟩
synonyms all-important, imperative, indispensable, integral, necessary, needed, needful, required, requisite, vital

related words prerequisite; compulsory, mandatory, obligatory; important, momentous, significant; basic, central, fundamental, key, organic; insistent, persistent, pressing, urgent
near antonyms undesired, unwanted; inconsequential, insignificant, unimportant; excess, extra, superfluous, surplus
antonyms dispensable, needless, nonessential, unnecessary, unneeded
2 of or relating to the simplest facts or theories of a subject ⟨anyone with an *essential* knowledge of human biology can follow the documentary⟩ — see ELEMENTARY
3 being a part of the innermost nature of a person or thing ⟨an unquenchable belief in the *essential* goodness of most people⟩ — see INHERENT

essential *n* **1** something necessary, indispensable, or unavoidable ⟨the *essentials* for success include a willingness to work and the right attitude⟩
synonyms condition, demand, must, necessity, need, requirement, requisite
related words precondition, prerequisite; advantage, edge, plus
near antonyms extra, extravagance, frill, luxury, superfluity
antonyms nonessential, nonnecessity
2 *essentials pl* general or basic truths on which other truths or theories can be based ⟨this will be just an introduction to the *essentials* of computer programming⟩ — see PRINCIPLES 1

essentiality *n* the quality or qualities that make a thing what it is ⟨physical strength or endurance is the *essentiality* that makes activity a sport and not just a game⟩ — see ESSENCE

establish *vb* **1** to gain full recognition or acceptance of ⟨the teenagers accused of shoplifting were able to *establish* their innocence⟩
synonyms demonstrate, prove, show, substantiate
related words attest, authenticate, bear out, document, evidence, support, sustain, uphold; confirm, corroborate, justify, validate, verify
phrases prove beyond a reasonable doubt
near antonyms confute, discredit, invalidate, rebut, refute
antonyms disprove
2 to show the existence or truth of by evidence ⟨the developers haven't *established* that there's a need for another shopping center in town⟩ — see PROVE 1
3 to be responsible for the creation and early operation or use of ⟨*established* the first school for the education of Native Americans⟩ — see FOUND

establisher *n* a person who establishes a whole new field of endeavor ⟨Alfred Stieglitz is often credited as the *establisher* of photography as an art form⟩ — see FATHER 2

establishment *n* **1** a building, room, or suite of rooms occupied by a service business ⟨one of the best dining *establishments* in the city⟩ — see PLACE 2
2 a commercial or industrial activity or organization ⟨new business *establishments* sprang up all over in the postwar boom⟩ — see ENTERPRISE 1
3 a public organization with a particular purpose or function ⟨the proposed change in pollution standards was opposed by environmental *establishments* across the board⟩ — see INSTITUTION 1
4 a structure that is designed and built for a particular purpose ⟨the city boasts a host of outstanding medical *establishments*⟩ — see FACILITY

estate *n* **1** a large impressive residence ⟨the *estates* of multimillionaires line the shores of this ocean resort⟩ — see MANSION

2 a state of being or fitness ⟨the mayor pronounced the city's schools to be in their best *estate* ever⟩ — see CONDITION 1

3 one of the segments of society into which people are grouped ⟨the passionate belief that a society is judged by how well it treats and cares for those in the lowest *estate*⟩ — see CLASS 1

esteem *n* a feeling of great approval and liking ⟨an athlete who is held in great *esteem* by her peers⟩ — see ADMIRATION 1

esteem *vb* **1** to think of in a particular way ⟨I had *esteemed* the whole affair to be a colossal waste of time⟩ — see CONSIDER 1

2 to think very highly or favorably of ⟨although the works of the Impressionist painters are *esteemed* today, they met with scorn when they were introduced⟩ — see ADMIRE

esteemed *adj* having a good reputation especially in a field of knowledge ⟨concerned about his heart, my grandfather went to see an *esteemed* cardiac specialist⟩ — see RESPECTABLE 1

estimate *n* **1** the act of placing a value on the nature, character, or quality of something ⟨what we owe our war veterans is beyond *estimate*⟩

synonyms appraisal, appraisement, assessment, estimation, evaluation, reckoning, valuation

related words calculation, computation, measurement

2 an opinion on the nature, character, or quality of something ⟨the *estimate* of many art specialists that the painting is a fake⟩ — see ESTIMATION 1

estimate *vb* **1** to make an approximate or tentative judgment regarding ⟨experts *estimated* the value of the painting at a million dollars⟩

synonyms appraise, assess, evaluate, rate, set, value

related words adjudge, deem, judge; ascertain, determine, discover, learn; price, prize; decide, settle; analyze, assay, survey, test; reappraise, reassess, reevaluate, revalue

2 to decide the size, amount, number, or distance of (something) without actual measurement ⟨we *estimated* the snowfall to be about a foot⟩

synonyms calculate, call, conjecture, figure, gauge (*also* gage), guess, judge, make, place, put, reckon, suppose

near antonyms calibrate, measure, scale; compute

estimation *n* **1** an opinion on the nature, character, or quality of something ⟨the teacher's *estimation* of her student's scientific aptitude proved to be well-founded when he won a national science award⟩

synonyms appraisal, appraisement, assessment, estimate, evaluation, judgment (*or* judgement)

related words impression, notion, perception; confidence, faith, stock, trust

2 the act of placing a value on the nature, character, or quality of something ⟨I may have been a little too hasty in my *estimation* of his musical abilities⟩ — see ESTIMATE 1

3 a feeling of great approval and liking ⟨a show business superstar who enjoys the *estimation* of fans and fellow performers alike⟩ — see ADMIRATION 1

estrange *vb* to cause to change from friendly or loving to unfriendly or uncaring ⟨Carrie's tendency to tattle *estranged* her classmates⟩

synonyms alienate, disaffect, disgruntle, sour

related words antagonize, embitter, envenom; aggravate, anger, enrage, incense, infuriate, madden; disunite, divide, separate, sever, sunder; disappoint, disenchant, disillusion

near antonyms endear, ingratiate; appease, conciliate, mollify, pacify, propitiate

antonyms reconcile

estrangement *n* the loss of friendship or affection ⟨a silly quarrel that eventually resulted in a complete and lasting *estrangement* between the onetime friends⟩

synonyms alienation, disaffection, disgruntlement, souring

related words antagonism, embitterment, envenoming; aggravation, incensing, infuriation; disunion, division, divorce, schism, separation; disenchantment, disillusionment

near antonyms endearment, ingratiation; appeasement, conciliation, mollification, pacification, propitiation

antonyms reconciliation

estuary *n* a part of a body of water that extends beyond the general shoreline ⟨the city sits on the shores of a deep *estuary* where the Hudson River meets the Atlantic Ocean⟩ — see GULF 1

etch *vb* **1** to cut (as letters or designs) on a hard surface ⟨the artist *etched* his landscape on a copper plate⟩ — see ENGRAVE 1

2 to produce a vivid impression of ⟨in just a few pages the writer *etched* an unforgettable portrait of one of the more remarkable First Ladies⟩ — see ENGRAVE 2

eternal *adj* lasting forever ⟨the quest for some magic potion that promises *eternal* youth⟩ — see EVERLASTING

eternally *adv* for all time ⟨we will be *eternally* grateful for your kind generosity⟩ — see EVER 1

eternity *n* **1** endless time ⟨the question whether the universe will end someday or continue to exist in *eternity*⟩

synonyms infinity, perpetuity

related words boundlessness, endlessness, interminableness, permanence, timelessness

2 unending existence after death ⟨a firm belief in the *eternity* of the soul⟩

synonyms afterlife, hereafter, immortality

related words otherworld

phrases life after death

3 a long or seemingly long period of time ⟨we waited in line for tickets for an *eternity*⟩ — see AGE 2

ethereal *adj* resembling air in lightness ⟨the bakery's scrumptious pastries have a wonderfully *ethereal* consistency⟩ — see AIRY 1

ethical *adj* **1** conforming to a high standard of morality or virtue ⟨the *ethical* behavior expected of every member of the police force⟩ — see GOOD 2

2 following the accepted rules of moral conduct ⟨the *ethical* course of action for the senator who lied to congress would be to resign⟩ — see HONORABLE 1

3 guided by or in accordance with one's sense of right and wrong ⟨*ethical* writers do not use the words of other writers without giving them proper credit⟩ — see CONSCIENTIOUS 1

ethics *n pl* the code of good conduct for an individual or group ⟨the *ethics* of scouting require scouts to be loyal, clean, and reverent⟩

synonyms morality, morals, principles, standards

related words customs, etiquette, manners, mores; beliefs, dogma, faith, tenets

ethnic *adj* of, relating to, or reflecting the traits exhibited by a group of people with a common ancestry and culture ⟨children who were raised in a home where there was a strong *ethnic* consciousness⟩ — see RACIAL

etiquette *n* personal conduct or behavior as evaluated by an accepted standard of appropriateness for a social or professional setting ⟨the couple showed poor *etiquette* when they left the party without saying good-bye to the host and hostess⟩ — see MANNER 1

eulogy *n* a formal expression of praise ⟨several *eulogies* were given at the special assembly marking the retirement of the school's principal⟩ — see ENCOMIUM

euphonious *adj* **1** having a pleasantly flowing quality suggestive of music ⟨an opera singer with an appropriately *euphonious* name⟩ — see LYRIC 1
2 having a pleasing mixture of notes ⟨the doorbell had a noticeably *euphonious* chime⟩ — see HARMONIOUS 1

euphoria *n* a state of overwhelming usually pleasurable emotion ⟨a general *euphoria* seemed to engulf the city following the World Series win⟩ — see ECSTASY

euphoric *adj* experiencing or marked by overwhelming usually pleasurable emotion ⟨the *euphoric* winner was momentarily speechless⟩ — see ECSTATIC

evacuate *vb* to remove the contents of ⟨*evacuate* the cupboards completely before spraying the insecticide⟩ — see EMPTY

evacuee *n* a person forced to emigrate for political reasons ⟨*evacuees* by the thousands poured into the camps for displaced persons⟩ — see ÉMIGRÉ 1

evade *vb* to get or keep away from (as a responsibility) through cleverness or trickery ⟨people who use every loophole in the law to *evade* paying taxes⟩ — see ESCAPE 2

evaluate *vb* to make an approximate or tentative judgment regarding ⟨a trained assistant to *evaluate* the needs of the patients waiting to see the doctor⟩ — see ESTIMATE 1

evaluation *n* **1** an opinion on the nature, character, or quality of something ⟨what's your *evaluation* of her writing ability?⟩ — see ESTIMATION 1
2 the act of placing a value on the nature, character, or quality of something ⟨the *evaluation* of the defendant's mental condition was conducted by a team of psychiatrists⟩ — see ESTIMATE 1

evanesce *vb* to cease to be visible ⟨our rainy-day gloom *evanesced* the minute we heard that we were going out for ice cream⟩ — see DISAPPEAR

evanescent *adj* lasting only for a short time ⟨beauty that is as *evanescent* as a rainbow⟩ — see MOMENTARY

evaporate *vb* to cease to be visible ⟨by mid-morning the fog that had enshrouded the island had just *evaporated*⟩ — see DISAPPEAR

evasion *n* the act or a means of getting or keeping away from something undesirable ⟨pleading chronic back pain is my standard *evasion* for doing any heavy lifting⟩ — see ESCAPE 2

evasive *adj* hard to find, capture, or isolate ⟨believers in Bigfoot have never quite explained how such a large creature can be so *evasive*⟩ — see ELUSIVE

even *adj* **1** being neither more nor less than a certain amount, number, or extent ⟨the distance to town is an *even* mile⟩
synonyms exact, flat, precise, round
near antonyms approximate, comparative, relative
2 having a surface without bends, breaks, or irregularities ⟨let's find an *even* stretch of ground to pitch our tent⟩ — see LEVEL
3 resembling another in every respect ⟨the armies of the two countries are fairly *even*⟩ — see SAME 1

even *adv* not merely this but also ⟨the blue whale is a huge, *even* awesome animal by any measure⟩
synonyms indeed, nay, truly, verily, yea
related words assuredly, certainly, decidedly, definitely, positively, really, surely, undeniably, unquestionably
phrases in fact, in reality, in truth

even *vb* **1** to make free from breaks, curves, or bumps ⟨*even* the filling before adding the top layer of the cake⟩
synonyms flatten, level, plane, smooth
related words clip, crop, pare, prune, shave, trim; lay, spread; card, comb, rake
near antonyms coarsen, rumple, wrinkle
antonyms rough, roughen
2 to make equal in amount, degree, or status ⟨the contention that producing more arms will *even* us with the enemy and therefore more secure⟩ — see EQUALIZE

evening *n* the time from when the sun begins to set to the onset of total darkness ⟨in the *evening* a reddish glow often appears on the mountaintops⟩ — see DUSK 1

event *n* **1** something that happens ⟨dinnertime was devoted to talking over the day's *events*, not to watching television⟩
synonyms affair, circumstance, episode, hap, happening, incident, occasion, occurrence, thing
related words coincidence, fluke, freak; landmark, milestone, page, phenomenon, turning point; adventure, experience; accident, crisis, emergency, juncture; achievement, deed, exploit, feat; news, tidings
2 something that might happen ⟨in the *event* of rain, graduation ceremonies will be held indoors⟩
synonyms case, contingency, eventuality, possibility
related words probability; chance, risk
3 a competitive encounter between individuals or groups carried on for amusement, exercise, or in pursuit of a prize ⟨figure skating is usually one of the most popular *events* in the winter Olympics⟩ — see GAME 1
4 a social gathering ⟨the mayor's evenings are often tied up with one *event* after another⟩ — see PARTY 1

eventful *adj* having great meaning or lasting effect ⟨the first moon landing was universally regarded as an *eventful* moment in human history⟩ — see IMPORTANT 1

eventide *n* the time from when the sun begins to set to the onset of total darkness ⟨*eventide* was their favorite time for enjoying a quiet respite in the backyard⟩ — see DUSK 1

eventuality *n* **1** something that can develop or become actual ⟨we're preparing for every *eventuality* during a national emergency⟩ — see POTENTIAL
2 something that might happen ⟨a full-force hurricane on the day of the picnic was one *eventuality* that we hadn't planned on⟩ — see EVENT 2

eventually *adv* at a later time ⟨stop whining about how long it's taking us—we'll get there *eventually*⟩ — see YET 1

ever *adv* **1** for all time ⟨the name of Benedict Arnold will *ever* be linked with treason⟩
synonyms always, aye (*also* ay), eternally, everlastingly, evermore, forever, forevermore, permanently, perpetually
related words enduringly, long, perennially
phrases forever and a day, forever and ever, for good, to (*or* until) the end of time
antonyms never, nevermore

2 in any way or respect ⟨how can we *ever* repay what you've done for us?⟩ — see AT ALL

3 on every relevant occasion ⟨the boy and his *ever* present dog were a common sight around the village⟩ — see ALWAYS 1

everlasting *adj* lasting forever ⟨valentines typically express the giver's *everlasting* love and devotion⟩
synonyms ceaseless, dateless, deathless, endless, eternal, immortal, permanent, perpetual, undying, unending
related words durable, enduring, lasting, persistent; imperishable, indestructible; timeless; abiding, steadfast, steady, unfailing, unfaltering
near antonyms ephemeral, evanescent, fleeting, momentary, passing, short-lived, transitory
antonyms impermanent, mortal, temporary

everlastingly *adv* for all time ⟨the sacrifices made by our brave soldiers on this battlefield will be *everlastingly* remembered⟩ — see EVER 1

evermore *adv* for all time ⟨he promised to love her *evermore*, if only she would consent to be his wife⟩ — see EVER 1

every *adj* being one of a group ⟨*every* man here must decide for himself whether to go or to stay and fight⟩ — see EACH

everybody *pron* every person ⟨*everybody* must do what his or her conscience dictates⟩
synonyms all, everyone
phrases each and everyone, one and all
antonyms nobody

everyday *adj* **1** being of the type that is encountered in the normal course of events ⟨we're just an *everyday* family, with a dog and a cat and bills to pay⟩ — see ORDINARY 1

2 having to do with the practical details of regular life ⟨even the richest man in town has to do such *everyday* tasks as shaving his face and brushing his teeth⟩ — see MUNDANE 1

3 not designed for special occasions ⟨*everyday* clothes will be fine for this party⟩ — see CASUAL 1

4 often observed or encountered ⟨fortunately, murder is not an *everyday* event around here⟩ — see COMMON 1

everyone *pron* every person ⟨there's plenty of food for *everyone*⟩ — see EVERYBODY

everyplace *adv* in every place or in all places ⟨I can't be *everyplace* at once, so somebody has to help me⟩ — see EVERYWHERE

everywhere *adv* in every place or in all places ⟨freedom and happiness are the goals of people *everywhere*⟩
synonyms all over, everyplace, throughout
phrases all over the place (*or* map), far and near, far and wide, high and low, in every corner (*or* quarter)
antonyms nowhere

evidence *n* something presented in support of the truth or accuracy of a claim ⟨do you have any *evidence* that this bike is yours?⟩ — see PROOF

evident *adj* **1** appearing to be true on the basis of evidence that may or may not be confirmed ⟨the *evident* motive for the assault was robbery⟩ — see APPARENT 1

2 not subject to misinterpretation or more than one interpretation ⟨the man was discovered dead in his apartment, but there were no *evident* signs of foul play⟩ — see CLEAR 2

evidently *adv* to all outward appearances ⟨she was *evidently* dissatisfied with her job and abruptly quit⟩ — see APPARENTLY

evil *adj* **1** causing or capable of causing harm ⟨the contention that pornography is an *evil* influence on society⟩ — see HARMFUL

2 not conforming to a high moral standard; morally unacceptable ⟨their *evil* deeds rank among the worst in history⟩ — see BAD 2

evil *n* that which is morally unacceptable ⟨our free will allows us to choose between good and *evil*⟩
synonyms bad, evildoing, ill, immorality, iniquity, sin, villainy, wrong
related words atrociousness, badness, evilness, heinousness, nefariousness, sinfulness, vileness, wickedness; devilry (*or* deviltry), fiendishness; cancer, decay, rot, squalor; corruption, debauchery, degeneracy, depravity, indecency, perversion; abomination, anathema, taboo (*also* tabu)
near antonyms integrity, probity, rectitude, uprightness; goodness, righteousness, virtuousness
antonyms good, morality, right, virtue

evildoer *n* **1** a person who commits moral wrongs ⟨if good people stand by and do nothing, *evildoers* will triumph⟩
synonyms malefactor, sinner, wrongdoer
related words criminal, crook, felon, lawbreaker, miscreant, reprobate, transgressor, villain
near antonyms angel, saint

2 a mean, evil, or unprincipled person ⟨the novel's slave owner, Simon Legree, became one of the most notorious *evildoers* in all of literature⟩ — see VILLAIN

evildoing *n* that which is morally unacceptable ⟨a book that ponders the question of the presence of *evildoing* in a universe controlled by a benevolent Supreme Being⟩ — see EVIL

evilness *n* the state or quality of being utterly evil ⟨the *evilness* of the crimes committed by the mass murderer are beyond comprehension⟩ — see ENORMITY 1

evince *vb* to make known (something abstract) through outward signs ⟨the teenager caught shoplifting seemed to *evince* no remorse⟩ — see SHOW 2

eviscerate *vb* to take the internal organs out of ⟨the ancient Egyptians would *eviscerate* the bodies of the dead as part of the process of mummifying them⟩ — see GUT

evocative *adj* provoking a memory or mental association ⟨the Italian-American restaurant is decorated in a manner *evocative* of the charming outdoor cafés in Italy⟩ — see SUGGESTIVE 2

evoke *vb* to draw out (something hidden, latent, or reserved) ⟨the old family photographs we found in the attic *evoked* a lot of warm memories⟩ — see EDUCE

evolution *n* the act or process of going from the simple or basic to the complex or advanced ⟨the *evolution* of motion pictures from a peep-show novelty into an medium of mass entertainment and an art form⟩ — see DEVELOPMENT 1

evolve *vb* to gradually become clearer or more detailed ⟨as the governor's plans for the reform of state government *evolved*, objections from various groups inevitably arose⟩ — see DEVELOP 1

evolved *adj* being far along in development ⟨whether this is an *evolved* technology or one still in its infancy is a matter of debate⟩ — see ADVANCED 1

exact *adj* **1** being in agreement with the truth or a fact or a standard ⟨maybe I wasn't being very *exact* when I said I had done it a million times⟩ — see CORRECT 1

2 being neither more nor less than a certain amount, number, or extent ⟨the *exact* number of passengers on that airplane was 147⟩ — see EVEN 1

3 following an original exactly ⟨an *exact* replica of the notorious slave ship *Amistad*⟩ — see FAITHFUL 2

4 made or done with extreme care and accuracy ⟨the company stresses that its optical telescopes are *exact* instruments and should not be handled as toys⟩ — see FINE 2

5 meeting the highest standard of accuracy ⟨in order for the blind to fit properly, we must have the *exact* measurements of the window⟩ — see PRECISE 1

exact *vb* **1** to ask for (something) earnestly or with authority ⟨every war inevitably *exacts* the greatest sacrifice possible from some of the nation's best and brightest⟩ — see DEMAND 1

2 to establish or apply as a charge or penalty ⟨vowed to *exact* a heavy fine from any hockey player engaging in such outrageous behavior on the ice⟩ — see IMPOSE

3 to get (as money) by the use of force or threats ⟨the loan shark is sure to *exact* repayment of his loan by whatever means necessary⟩ — see EXTORT

exacting *adj* **1** hard to please ⟨Kyle was shocked when his normally *exacting* teacher complimented him on a well-written theme⟩ — see FINICKY

2 not allowing for any exceptions or loosening of standards ⟨the prep school's *exacting* standards for admission⟩ — see RIGID 1

3 requiring considerable physical or mental effort ⟨the new recruits had to adjust themselves to the *exacting* discipline of military life⟩ — see HARD 2

4 requiring much time, effort, or careful attention ⟨the task of writing is always an *exacting* one⟩ — see DEMANDING 1

exactitude *n* the quality or state of being very accurate ⟨our chemistry teacher demanded that we carry out our lab experiments with considerable *exactitude*⟩ — see PRECISION

exactly *adv* **1** as stated or indicated without the slightest difference ⟨we will meet at *exactly* six o'clock⟩
synonyms just, precisely, right, sharp, smack-dab, squarely
2 in a like manner ⟨he wants to be *exactly* like his father⟩ — see JUST 1
3 in the same words ⟨you copied the encyclopedia article *exactly*⟩ — see VERBATIM
4 without any relaxation of standards or precision ⟨follow the rules *exactly* and you won't get into trouble⟩ — see STRICTLY

exactness *n* the quality or state of being very accurate ⟨the *exactness* of the bathroom scale isn't such that you could use it in business⟩ — see PRECISION

exaggerate *vb* **1** to add to the interest of by including made-up details ⟨the American colonist John Smith is believed by historians to have *exaggerated* his adventures⟩ — see EMBROIDER

2 to describe or express in too strong terms ⟨it would be impossible to *exaggerate* the importance of this entrance exam⟩ — see OVERSTATE

exaggeration *n* the representation of something in terms that go beyond the facts ⟨their *exaggeration* was such that a rainstorm became a hurricane⟩
synonyms caricature, coloring, elaboration, embellishment, embroidering, hyperbole, magnification, overstatement, padding, stretching
related words amplification, enhancement; fabrication, misrepresentation; fudging, hedging
near antonyms belittlement, disparagement, minimizing
antonyms understatement

exalt *vb* to enhance the status of ⟨popular support and media hype have *exalted* Super Bowl Sunday to the level of a national holiday⟩
synonyms aggrandize, dignify, ennoble, enshrine, glorify, magnify
related words boost, elevate, lift, promote, raise, upgrade, uplift; heighten, intensify; idealize, romanticize, sanitize, sugarcoat; canonize, deify; acclaim, extol (*also* extoll), honor, laud, praise
near antonyms belittle, decry, depreciate, detract, disparage, minimize
antonyms abase, degrade, demean, humble, humiliate

exam *n* a set of questions or problems designed to assess knowledge, skills, or intelligence ⟨the *exam* will cover everything we have studied this term⟩ — see EXAMINATION 1

examination *n* **1** a set of questions or problems designed to assess knowledge, skills, or intelligence ⟨applicants to the prep school are required to take an *examination*⟩
synonyms exam, quiz, test
related words catechism; audition; final; checkup, inspection, review; inquiry, interrogation, investigation, probe, research
2 a systematic search for the truth or facts about something ⟨an *examination* into the extent and causes of juvenile delinquency in the community⟩ — see INQUIRY 1
3 a close look at or over someone or something in order to judge condition ⟨even a hasty *examination* will tell any jeweler that that is not a real diamond⟩ — see INSPECTION

examine *vb* **1** to put a series of questions to ⟨the defense attorney was eager to *examine* her star witness⟩
synonyms grill, interrogate, pump, query, question, quiz
related words debrief; cross-examine; catechize; annoy, harass, hound, pester
phrases give the third degree to
2 to look over closely (as for judging quality or condition) ⟨the customer *examined* the antique piece of furniture from top to bottom before purchasing it⟩ — see INSPECT

example *n* one of a group or collection that shows what the whole is like ⟨a war bonnet that is a fine *example* of Native American handicraft⟩
synonyms case, exemplar, illustration, instance, representative, sample, specimen
related words cross section; evidence, indication, manifestation, sign
phrases case in point

exasperate *vb* to disturb the peace of mind of (someone) especially by repeated disagreeable acts ⟨small children can *exasperate* their parents with endless questions about why this or that is so⟩ — see IRRITATE 1

exasperating *adj* causing annoyance ⟨those *exasperating* details that come with almost any job⟩ — see ANNOYING

exasperation *n* **1** something that is a source of irritation ⟨add people who use cell phones inconsiderately to the list of daily *exasperations*⟩ — see ANNOYANCE 3
2 the feeling of impatience or anger caused by another's repeated disagreeable acts ⟨my rising *exasperation* with these constant interruptions⟩ — see ANNOYANCE 2

excavate *vb* to hollow out or form (something) by removing earth ⟨workmen are *excavating* a long tunnel that will eventually replace the aboveground expressway⟩ — see DIG 1

exceed *vb* to go beyond the limit of ⟨by resorting to corporal punishment, the teacher had *exceeded* his authority⟩

synonyms overreach, overrun, overshoot, overstep, surpass

related words encroach, entrench (*also* intrench), infringe, invade, trespass; overdo, overuse, overwork

exceedingly *also* **exceeding** *adv* to a great degree ⟨the salesclerk was *exceedingly* patient with one customer who couldn't make up his mind⟩ — see VERY 1

excel *vb* to be greater, better, or stronger than ⟨the special effects in this new sci-fi adventure *excel* any that we've seen previously⟩ — see SURPASS 1

excellence *n* **1** exceptionally high quality ⟨the annual awards honor *excellence* in children's literature⟩

synonyms distinction, excellency, greatness, preeminence, superbness, superiority, supremacy

related words faultlessness, flawlessness, impeccability, perfection; goodness, value, worth; consequence, importance, notability

near antonyms averageness, badness, inferiority, mediocrity, ordinariness, worthlessness

2 a quality that gives something special worth ⟨the particular *excellence* of down in clothing and sleeping bags is its lightness⟩

synonyms distinction, excellency, merit, value, virtue

related words advantage, edge, superiority

near antonyms blemish, defect, failing, fault, flaw

antonyms deficiency

excellency *n* **1** a quality that gives something special worth ⟨claimed that granite has so many *excellencies* as material for countertops that it is worth the high price⟩ — see EXCELLENCE 2

2 exceptionally high quality ⟨the *excellency* of the violins made by Stradivarius is beyond dispute⟩ — see EXCELLENCE 1

excellent *adj* of the very best kind ⟨fast-food fans rate this chain's fries as *excellent*⟩

synonyms A1, bang-up, banner, boss [*slang*], capital, classic, crackerjack, dandy, divine, fabulous, fine, first-class, first-rate, grand, great, groovy, heavenly, jim-dandy, keen, marvelous (*or* marvellous), mean, neat, nifty, noble, par excellence, prime, sensational, splendid, stellar, sterling, superb, superior, superlative, supernal, swell, terrific, tip-top, top, top-notch, unsurpassed, wonderful

related words acceptable, adequate, all right, decent, good, OK, passable, satisfactory, tolerable; better, exceptional, fancy, high-grade, premium, special

phrases out of sight

near antonyms bad, inferior, low-grade, substandard, unsatisfactory; mediocre, second-class, second-rate; atrocious, execrable, vile, wretched

antonyms poor

except *also* **excepting** *conj* if it were not for the fact that ⟨I'd go, *except* it's too far⟩

synonyms but, only, saving, yet

except *also* **excepting** *prep* not including ⟨the store is open daily *except* Sundays⟩

synonyms aside from, bar, barring, beside, besides, but, except for, excluding, outside, outside of, save, saving

except *vb* to prevent the participation or inclusion of ⟨we'll have to *except* members who haven't paid their club dues from voting in the election⟩ — see EXCLUDE

except for *prep* not including ⟨*except for* newscasts, I hardly watch any television at all⟩ — see EXCEPT

exceptionable *adj* provoking or likely to provoke protest ⟨as long as the language is not *exceptionable*, people can discuss any topic they want in the chat room⟩ — see OBJECTIONABLE

exceptional *adj* being out of the ordinary ⟨an *exceptional* amount of snow fell in March⟩

synonyms aberrant, abnormal, atypical, extraordinary, freak, odd, peculiar, phenomenal, rare, singular, uncommon, uncustomary, unique, unusual, unwonted

related words conspicuous, notable, noticeable, outstanding, prominent, remarkable, salient, striking; bizarre, deviant, eccentric, outlandish, quaint, strange, weird; incomprehensible, inconceivable, incredible, unimaginable, unthinkable

near antonyms everyday, familiar, frequent

antonyms common, customary, normal, ordinary, typical, unexceptional, usual

excerpt *n* a part taken from a longer work ⟨we'll read an *excerpt* from the novel⟩

synonyms extract, passage

related words snippet; citation, quotation; context; selection

excess *adj* being over what is needed ⟨any *excess* food from the party will be donated to a shelter for the homeless⟩ — see SPARE 1

excess *n* the state or an instance of going beyond what is usual, proper, or needed ⟨a new television season with an *excess* of wisecracking teenagers⟩

synonyms fat, overabundance, overage, overflow, overkill, overmuch, oversupply, superabundance, superfluity, surfeit, surplus

related words abundance, bounty, plentitude, plenty, profusion, sufficiency; overproduction, overstock

near antonyms dearth, lack, scarcity

antonyms deficiency, deficit, insufficiency

excessive *adj* going beyond a normal or acceptable limit in degree or amount ⟨nerdy hackers who spend an *excessive* amount of time sitting in front of their computers⟩

synonyms devilish, exorbitant, extravagant, extreme, immoderate, inordinate, lavish, overmuch, overweening, steep, stiff, towering, unconscionable, undue

related words boundless, endless, immeasurable, infinite, limitless; intolerable, unbearable, unjustifiable, unwarranted; improper, inappropriate, thick, unseemly

near antonyms deficient, inadequate, insufficient; minimal, minimum

antonyms moderate, modest, reasonable, temperate

excessively *adv* beyond a normal or acceptable limit ⟨noise from the party was *excessively* loud⟩ — see TOO 1

exchange *n* **1** a giving or taking of one thing of value in return for another ⟨*exchanges* of commemorative pins are common among Olympic athletes⟩

synonyms barter, commutation, swap, trade, truck

related words replacement, substitution; reciprocation, recompense, requital; bargain, deal, horse trade, negotiation, transaction; bargaining, dealing, dickering, haggling, horse trading; logrolling

2 talking or a talk between two or more people ⟨we had a brief *exchange* with the pastor as we passed him on the way out of church⟩ — see CONVERSATION

exchange *vb* to give up (something) and take something else in return ⟨I'd like to *exchange* this sweater for one in a larger size⟩ — see CHANGE 3

excitable *adj* easily excited by nature ⟨an *excitable* child who needed a stable home life⟩

synonyms flighty, fluttery, high-strung, jittery, jumpy, nervous, skittish, spooky

related words hot-blooded, mercurial, temperamental, unstable, volatile, volcanic; anxious, edgy, jumpy, nervy, tense, uptight; emotional, hypersensitive, intense, sensitive, soulful; dramatic, histrionic, melodramatic; irascible, irritable, prickly, testy, touchy

near antonyms calm, collected, cool, serene, tranquil; easy, easygoing, laid-back, relaxed

antonyms unflappable

excite *vb* 1 to cause a pleasurable stimulation of the feelings ⟨for some reason the first snowfall of the season never fails to *excite* us⟩ — see THRILL

2 to rouse to strong feeling or action ⟨televised pictures of the victims of the famine that would *excite* any viewer to pity⟩ — see PROVOKE 1

excited *adj* 1 being in a state of increased activity or agitation ⟨*excited* trading on the stock exchange followed in the wake of the favorable economic report⟩ — see FEVERISH 1

2 showing urgent desire or interest ⟨everyone was *excited* about the upcoming family vacation at the ski resort⟩ — see EAGER

excitement *n* 1 something that arouses a strong response from another ⟨there were few *excitements* of any kind on our very uneventful trip back home⟩ — see PROVOCATION 1

2 urgent desire or interest ⟨in our *excitement* to get going, we forgot to make sure that all of the lights in the house had been turned off⟩ — see EAGERNESS

exciter *n* a person who stirs up public feelings especially of discontent ⟨many of the *exciters* of the so-called "tax revolt" were actually campaign workers for one of the gubernatorial candidates⟩ — see AGITATOR

exciting *adj* 1 causing great emotional or mental stimulation ⟨an *exciting*, come-from-behind victory for the underdogs in the last game of the World Series⟩

synonyms breathtaking, electric, electrifying, exhilarating, galvanizing, inspiring, rip-roaring, rousing, stimulating, stirring, thrilling

related words arresting, interesting, intriguing, provocative, tantalizing; absorbing, engrossing, gripping, riveting; moving, poignant, touching; enchanting, enthralling, fascinating, spellbinding

near antonyms boring, tedious, tiresome; dreary, dull, humdrum, monotonous, uninteresting

antonyms unexciting

2 serving or likely to arouse a strong reaction ⟨and what *exciting* news have you for us today?⟩ — see PROVOCATIVE

exclaim *vb* to utter with a sudden burst of strong feeling ⟨the whole team *exclaimed* with one voice, "We won!"⟩

synonyms blurt (out), bolt, cry (out), ejaculate

related words blunder, leak; bellow, bleat, crow, holler, hoot, howl, roar, shout, whoop, yowl; interject

exclude *vb* to prevent the participation or inclusion of ⟨troublemakers were *excluded* from the club⟩

synonyms ban, bar, count out, debar, eliminate, except, rule out

related words blackball, blacklist, ostracize; banish, deport, exile, expel, oust, throw out; block, hinder, impede, obstruct; cease, discontinue, halt, suspend; deter, stave off, ward (off)

near antonyms accept, entertain, receive, welcome

antonyms admit, include

excluding *prep* not including ⟨*excluding* me, plan on five guests for dinner tonight⟩ — see EXCEPT

exclusive *adj* 1 belonging only to the one person, unit, or group named ⟨residents of the apartment complex have *exclusive* use of the pool⟩ — see SOLE 1

2 not divided or scattered among several areas of interest or concern ⟨during interviews she gives the job applicant her *exclusive* attention⟩ — see WHOLE 1

exclusively *adv* for nothing other than ⟨his best paintings are the ones that he did *exclusively* for the sheer pleasure they gave him⟩ — see SOLELY 1

excoriate *vb* to criticize harshly and usually publicly ⟨the mayor had hardly been in office for a month before she was *excoriated* for problems of very long standing⟩ — see ATTACK 2

excrement *n* solid matter discharged from an animal's alimentary canal ⟨an ordinance that requires dog walkers to remove their animal's *excrement* from city streets⟩ — see DROPPING 1

excrescence *n* an abnormal mass of tissue ⟨concerned about the *excrescence* that seemed to be developing on his hand⟩ — see GROWTH 1

excreta *n pl* solid matter discharged from an animal's alimentary canal ⟨the cage badly needed to be cleaned of the rabbit's *excreta*⟩ — see DROPPING 1

excruciating *adj* 1 intensely or unbearably painful ⟨those who publicly disagreed with the government were subjected to *excruciating* torture⟩

synonyms agonizing, harrowing, racking, tormenting, torturing, torturous

related words acute, exquisite, extreme, fierce, intense, vehement, violent; piercing, sharp, shooting, stabbing, stinging, tearing, tingling

2 causing intense mental or physical distress ⟨the patient asked for something to relieve her *excruciating* pain⟩ — see SHARP 2

3 difficult to endure ⟨the *excruciating* heat that the settlers faced as they crossed the deserts of the Southwest⟩ — see HARSH 1

4 hard to accept or bear especially emotionally ⟨most *excruciating* of all was the endless wait for news of any survivors of the plane crash⟩ — see BITTER 2

exculpate *vb* to free from a charge of wrongdoing ⟨I will present evidence that will *exculpate* my client⟩

synonyms absolve, acquit, clear, exonerate, vindicate

related words atone (for), expiate; discharge, liberate, redeem, release, unburden; condone, excuse, forgive, pardon, remit; avenge, redress, revenge

near antonyms accuse, arraign, charge, impeach, indict; convict

antonyms incriminate

excursion *n* 1 a short trip for pleasure ⟨our weekend *excursions* have been to all parts of our home state⟩

synonyms jaunt, junket, outing, sally

related words journey, travel(s); circuit, tour; expedition, odyssey, safari; detour; hike, peregrination, trek, walk; pilgrimage

2 a departure from the subject under consideration ⟨the professor's frequent *excursions* in his lectures are the stuff of campus legend⟩ — see TANGENT

excursionist *n* a person who travels for pleasure ⟨a list of things to do for weekend *excursionists* in the city⟩ — see TOURIST

excusable *adj* worthy of forgiveness ⟨an *excusable* lapse of memory in a senior citizen⟩ — see VENIAL

excuse *n* an explanation that frees one from fault or blame ⟨a whole evening of must-see TV is no *excuse* for not having your homework done⟩

synonyms alibi, defense, justification, plea, reason
related words guise, pretense (*or* pretence), pretext, rationale, rationalization; cop-out, out; acknowledgment (*also* acknowledgement), apology, atonement, confession

excuse *vb* **1** to overlook or dismiss as of little importance ⟨the student's theme is so good that I'm willing to *excuse* the spelling errors⟩
synonyms brush (aside *or* off), condone, disregard, forgive, gloss (over), gloze (over), ignore, pardon, pass over, remit, shrug off, wink (at)
related words explain, justify, rationalize, whitewash; absolve, acquit, clear, exculpate, exonerate, vindicate
phrases forgive and forget
near antonyms heed, mark, mind, note, object (to)
2 to be an acceptable reason for ⟨having a female passenger in labor will generally *excuse* a little disregard for the speed limit⟩ — see JUSTIFY 1
3 to make (something) seem less bad by offering excuses ⟨he's always *excusing* his chronic lying by claiming everybody lies⟩ — see PALLIATE 1

execrable *adj* **1** extremely unsatisfactory ⟨her *execrable* singing finally brought a complaint from the neighbors⟩ — see WRETCHED 1
2 of low quality ⟨another souvenir shop selling *execrable* knickknacks⟩ — see CHEAP 2

execrate *vb* **1** to declare to be morally wrong or evil ⟨the President *execrated* the terrorists responsible for the bomb blast⟩ — see CONDEMN 1
2 to dislike strongly ⟨*execrated* anyone who would physically abuse children or animals⟩ — see HATE

execration *n* **1** a prayer that harm will come to someone ⟨upon discovering that someone had stolen his skateboard, he let loose a volley of *execrations*⟩ — see CURSE 1
2 a very strong dislike ⟨a betrayal that earned him the *execration* of all who had remained loyal to the cause⟩ — see HATE 1

execute *vb* **1** to carry out effectively ⟨the agency charged with *executing* the nation's drug laws⟩ — see ENFORCE
2 to carry through (as a process) to completion ⟨when you *execute* this dance step, try to keep your arms a little higher⟩ — see PERFORM 1
3 to put to death deliberately ⟨during the war those convicted of desertion were promptly *executed*⟩ — see MURDER 1

execution *n* the doing of an action ⟨the *execution* of this magic trick must be accomplished in one fluid motion⟩ — see COMMISSION 2

executive *adj* suited for or relating to the directing of things ⟨the *executive* skills needed to manage a large business office⟩
synonyms administrative, directorial, managerial, supervisory
related words bureaucratic, governmental, ministerial, official, parliamentary; regulatory; authoritarian, despotic, dictatorial

executive *n* a person who manages or directs ⟨a program that teaches company *executives* how to better manage their staffs⟩
synonyms administrator, director, manager, superintendent, supervisor
related words officer, official; commissioner, minister; boss, chief, head, leader, president

exemplar *n* **1** one of a group or collection that shows what the whole is like ⟨the village's Congregational church could serve as an *exemplar* of the white clapboard church with a steeple that is a fixture in old New England towns⟩ — see EXAMPLE
2 someone of such unequaled perfection as to deserve imitation ⟨few of history's heroes were quite the *exemplars* that generations of schoolteachers made them out to be⟩ — see IDEAL 1
3 the most perfect type or example ⟨the paintings of the French painter Claude Monet are often regarded as *exemplars* of Impressionism⟩ — see QUINTESSENCE 1

exemplary *adj* constituting, serving as, or worthy of being a pattern to be imitated ⟨as a hospital volunteer you have given *exemplary* service to your community⟩ — see MODEL

exemplify *vb* to show or make clear by using examples ⟨in your essay you need to *exemplify* your points with specific examples from the novel⟩ — see ILLUSTRATE 1

exemption *n* freedom from punishment, harm, or loss ⟨don't think that you can continue to flout the school's rules with *exemption*⟩ — see IMPUNITY

exercise *n* **1** energetic movement of the body for the sake of physical fitness ⟨the doctor ordered plenty of fresh air and *exercise*⟩
synonyms activity, conditioning, exertion
related words training, warm-up, workout; toning, trimming; aerobics, bodybuilding, calisthenics, isometrics, weight lifting; physical therapy
2 something done over and over in order to develop skill ⟨a young piano student dutifully going through the standard finger *exercises*⟩
synonyms drill, practice (*also* practise), routine, training, workout
related words assignment, homework, lesson
3 the act or practice of employing something for a particular purpose ⟨the observation that the best exercise for losing weight is the *exercise* of one's ability to say no to food⟩ — see USE 1

exercise *vb* **1** to bring to bear especially forcefully or effectively ⟨we asked Mom to *exercise* her influence to get Dad to change his mind about a dog⟩ — see EXERT
2 to do over and over so as to become skilled ⟨her regimen of physical therapy calls for her to *exercise* her leg muscles daily⟩ — see PRACTICE
3 to put into action or service ⟨the students *exercised* really good judgment in that emergency⟩ — see USE 1
4 to trouble the mind of; to make uneasy ⟨the slightest change in travel plans is enough to get him all *exercised*⟩ — see DISTURB 1

exert *vb* to bring to bear especially forcefully or effectively ⟨parental involvement has been shown to *exert* the most influence over a child's success in school⟩
synonyms apply, exercise, ply, put out, wield
related words employ, use, utilize

exertion *n* **1** energetic movement of the body for the sake of physical fitness ⟨often the television addict's greatest attempt at *exertion* was switching channels on the remote control⟩ — see EXERCISE 1
2 the active use of energy in producing a result ⟨the number of blueberries that we were finding was hardly worth the *exertion*⟩ — see EFFORT

exfoliate *vb* to cast (a natural bodily covering or appendage) aside ⟨a soap that promises to help me *exfoliate* all that dry, flaky skin I've been carrying around⟩ — see SHED 1

exhale *vb* **1** to let or force out of the lungs ⟨before answering, the suspect *exhaled* a cloud of cigarette smoke⟩
synonyms blow (out), breathe (out), expire

related words expectorate
antonyms inhale, inspire
2 to throw or give off ⟨the lilacs were *exhaling* a sweet fragrance that virtually filled the room⟩ — see EMIT 1

exhaust *vb* **1** to use up all the physical energy of ⟨the long day at the county fair had *exhausted* everyone⟩
synonyms burn out, do in, drain, fag, fatigue, tire, tucker (out), wash out, wear, wear out, weary
related words debilitate, enervate, enfeeble, sap, waste, weaken
phrases wear to a frazzle
near antonyms activate, energize, invigorate, strengthen, vitalize; relax, rest, unwind
2 to make complete use of ⟨we had been at the theme park barely for two hours, and we were on the verge of *exhausting* our spending money⟩ — see DEPLETE

exhausted *adj* depleted in strength, energy, or freshness ⟨the *exhausted* runner crossed the finish line and just collapsed⟩ — see WEARY 1

exhaustion *n* a complete depletion of energy or strength ⟨with all of the work and activity that the holiday season brings, Mom was on the point of *exhaustion*⟩ — see FATIGUE

exhaustive *adj* trying all possibilities ⟨after an *exhaustive* search of our house, we still hadn't found the cat⟩
synonyms all-out, clean, complete, comprehensive, full-scale, out-and-out, thorough, thoroughgoing, total
related words broad, extensive, far-reaching, in-depth, wide; general, global, inclusive
near antonyms aimless, desultory, haphazard, hit-or-miss, random; cursory, shallow, slipshod, superficial; limited, narrow, restricted

exhaustively *adv* with attention to all aspects or details ⟨the psychic's claims were *exhaustively* examined by scientific experts and found to be without merit⟩ — see THOROUGHLY 1

exhibit *n* a public showing of objects of interest ⟨a touring *exhibit* of national treasures from the Smithsonian Institution⟩ — see EXHIBITION 1

exhibit *vb* to present so as to invite notice or attention ⟨these naturalists take their birds of prey on tour and *exhibit* them before groups of schoolchildren⟩ — see SHOW 1

exhibition *n* **1** a public showing of objects of interest ⟨an *exhibition* of valuable and fascinating artifacts from a recovered pirate ship⟩
synonyms display, exhibit, exposition, fair, show
related words demonstration, performance, presentation, production; extravaganza, pageant, spectacle; auction, offering, sale
2 an outward and often exaggerated indication of something abstract (as a feeling) for effect ⟨for the benefit of the crowd, the professional wrestler made a great *exhibition* of ferocity⟩ — see SHOW 1

exhilarate *vb* **1** to cause a pleasurable stimulation of the feelings ⟨the *exhilarating* feeling of flying that hang gliding offers⟩ — see THRILL
2 to fill with great joy ⟨the climax of the graduation ceremonies usually *exhilarates* graduates and proud parents alike⟩ — see ELATE

exhilarated *adj* experiencing or marked by overwhelming usually pleasurable emotion ⟨the winner's *exhilarated* glow was seen in newspaper photographs around the globe⟩ — see ECSTATIC

exhilarating *adj* causing great emotional or mental stimulation ⟨no recording can capture the *exhilarating* feeling of being at a live rock concert⟩ — see EXCITING 1

exhilaration *n* **1** a pleasurably intense stimulation of the feelings ⟨the lavish spectacle results in one *exhilaration* after another⟩ — see THRILL
2 a state of overwhelming usually pleasurable emotion ⟨the *exhilaration* of victory that spectators get to witness at the Olympic Games⟩ — see ECSTASY

exhort *vb* to try to persuade (someone) through earnest appeals to follow a course of action ⟨the speaker *exhorted* the graduating students to go forth and try to make a difference in the world⟩ — see URGE

exhume *vb* to remove from place of burial ⟨the remains of John Paul Jones were *exhumed* in Paris and transported with great ceremony to the U.S. Naval Academy⟩
synonyms disinter, unearth
antonyms bury, entomb, inter

exigency *n* a time or state of affairs requiring prompt or decisive action ⟨the *exigencies* requiring snap decisions that traders on the stock exchange face every day⟩ — see EMERGENCY

exile *n* **1** the forced removal from a homeland ⟨the *exile* of French settlers from Nova Scotia resulted in the birth of the Cajun community in the U.S.⟩
synonyms banishment, deportation, displacement, expatriation, expulsion
related words ostracism; extradition; dispersion, scattering; emigration, migration; evacuation
near antonyms repatriation, return; immigration
2 a person forced to emigrate for political reasons ⟨after being overthrown in a coup, the dictator spent the remainder of his life as an *exile* in a string of countries⟩ — see ÉMIGRÉ 1

exile *vb* to force to leave a country ⟨with their conquest of the Moors complete, Ferdinand and Isabella next *exiled* the Jews from Spain⟩ — see BANISH 1

exist *vb* to have life ⟨strive to have a full, rich life rather than merely *exist*⟩ — see BE 1

existence *n* the fact of being or of being real ⟨the *existence* of UFOs is something that people continue to argue about⟩
synonyms actuality, reality, subsistence
related words genuineness, realness; activity, animation, life; currency, presence, prevalence
near antonyms absence, dearth, lack, want
antonyms nonexistence

existent *adj* **1** existing in fact and not merely as a possibility ⟨to some people, angels are as *existent* as aardvarks or astronomers⟩ — see ACTUAL
2 having being at the present time ⟨the coelacanth is one *existent* fish that was once thought to be entirely extinct⟩ — see EXTANT 1

existing *adj* having being at the present time ⟨*existing* breeds of the turkey that graces our Thanksgiving table are said to bear little resemblance to the gamy birds that the Pilgrims enjoyed⟩ — see EXTANT 1

exit *n* **1** a place or means of going out ⟨all of the building's *exits* were being watched by security guards⟩
synonyms egress, issue, outlet
related words escape, release; opening, passage, vent
near antonyms access, entrée (*or* entree)
antonyms entrance, entry, entryway, ingress
2 the act of leaving a place ⟨the movie star's quick *exit* through the back of the hotel went unnoticed by the horde of photographers waiting out front⟩ — see DEPARTURE

exit *vb* to leave a place often for another ⟨in case of fire, *exit* from the building in a calm and orderly fashion⟩ — see GO 2

exiting *n* the act of leaving a place 〈their *exiting* of the boring party was swiftly and quietly accomplished〉 — see DEPARTURE

exodus *n* a flowing or going out 〈the mass *exodus* from the cities for the beaches and the mountains on most summer weekends〉 — see OUTFLOW

exonerate *vb* to free from a charge of wrongdoing 〈the results of the DNA fingerprinting finally *exonerated* the man, but only after he had wasted ten years of his life in prison〉 — see EXCULPATE

exorbitant *adj* going beyond a normal or acceptable limit in degree or amount 〈the cost of our stay was so *exorbitant* you would have thought that we had bought the hotel and not just spent a few nights there〉 — see EXCESSIVE

exorbitantly *adv* beyond a normal or acceptable limit 〈the *exorbitantly* priced concert tickets had us wondering if we were personally footing the bill for the band's private jet〉 — see TOO 1

exotic *adj* excitingly or mysteriously unusual 〈the dream of someday traveling to *exotic* lands〉
synonyms fantastic, glamorous (*also* glamourous), marvelous (*or* marvellous), outlandish, romantic, strange
related words colorful, picturesque, quaint; alien, foreign; distant, faraway, remote; alluring, captivating, enchanting, fascinating

exotic *n* something strange or unusual that is an object of interest 〈the botanical garden boasts an array of horticultural *exotics* from around the world〉 — see CURIOSITY 2

expand *vb* 1 to express more fully and in greater detail 〈an article on the First Ladies that the author later *expanded* into a book〉
synonyms amplify, develop, elaborate (on), enlarge (on)
related words add (to), complement, supplement; discourse, expatiate, ramble, run on
near antonyms compress, contract; outline, summarize, sum up
antonyms abbreviate, abridge, condense, shorten
2 to make greater in size, amount, or number 〈we had to *expand* the list of wedding guests several times in order to accommodate all the relatives Mother wouldn't dream of excluding〉 — see INCREASE 1
3 to arrange the parts of (something) over a wider area 〈a spare leaf for those times when we have to *expand* the dining table to accommodate extra guests〉 — see OPEN 3
4 to become greater in extent, volume, amount, or number 〈water *expands* when it becomes frozen〉 — see INCREASE 2

expanse *n* a wide space or area 〈the great explorers who crossed the vast *expanse* of the ocean in small ships〉
synonyms breadth, extent, reach, spread, stretch
related words domain, field, sphere, territory; compass, range, scope, sweep; gamut, scale, spectrum; depth, emptiness, void; distance, extension, latitude, length, span; amplitude, immensity, magnitude

expansion *n* 1 something added (as by growth) 〈the museum's new wing is only the first in a series of *expansions* planned for the next decade〉 — see INCREASE 1
2 the act or process of going from the simple or basic to the complex or advanced 〈the *expansion* of remedial reading classes into a district-wide program using school volunteers for a variety of needs〉 — see DEVELOPMENT 1

expansive *adj* having considerable extent 〈as the river nears the end of its long journey to the sea it becomes quite *expansive*〉 — see EXTENSIVE

expatiate *vb* to give a formal often extended talk on a subject 〈the naturalist is known for her willingness to *expatiate* on any number of issues relating to wildlife and the environment〉 — see TALK 1

expatriate *n* a person forced to emigrate for political reasons 〈while in exile, the deposed king was accompanied by a small band of loyal *expatriates*〉 — see ÉMIGRÉ 1

expatriate *vb* to force to leave a country 〈members of the deposed dictator's once-feared political party were *expatriated* as well〉 — see BANISH 1

expatriation *n* the forced removal from a homeland 〈the brutal *expatriation* of thousands of Cherokees to Indian Territory is now commonly referred to as the Trail of Tears〉 — see EXILE 1

expect *vb* to believe in the future occurrence of (something) 〈we *expect* their arrival late this afternoon〉
synonyms anticipate, await, hope (for), watch (for)
related words bank on, count (on *or* upon), depend (on *or* upon), rely (on *or* upon); envisage, foresee; foretell, predict, prophesy; assume, presume, presuppose; contemplate, eye, view
phrases look for, look forward to
near antonyms doubt, question

expectant *adj* 1 having or showing signs of eagerly awaiting something 〈*expectant* crowds gathered at the spot where the President was scheduled to make an appearance〉
synonyms agape, agog, anticipatory
related words open-eyed, openmouthed; alert, vigilant, watchful; anxious, breathless, eager, enthusiastic, raring; impatient, restive, restless
near antonyms apathetic, indifferent, unconcerned, unimpressed, uninterested, unmoved
2 containing unborn young within the body 〈a medication that should not be taken by *expectant* women without permission from a doctor〉 — see PREGNANT 1

expected *adj* being in accordance with the prescribed, normal, or logical course of events 〈the children did their chores, but not without the *expected* whining〉 — see DUE 2

expedient *adj* suitable for bringing about a desired result under the circumstances 〈made the *expedient* decision to sell the land to whomever offered the most money〉
synonyms advisable, desirable, judicious, politic, prudent, tactical, wise
related words advantageous, beneficial, profitable; useful, utilitarian; feasible, possible, practicable, practical; opportune, seasonable, timely; opportunistic, self-seeking
near antonyms impractical, unfeasible, unprofitable; inopportune, unseasonable, untimely
antonyms imprudent, inadvisable, inexpedient, injudicious, unwise

expedient *n* 1 a temporary replacement 〈if you're a spectator caught without rainwear at a sporting event, then a plastic garbage bag makes an acceptable, if unfashionable, *expedient*〉 — see MAKESHIFT
2 an action planned or taken to achieve a desired result 〈he vowed to use any *expedient* available to get the project done on time〉 — see MEASURE 1
3 something that one uses to accomplish an end especially when the usual means is not available 〈since there wasn't a single bandage left in our backpacks, we

had to use a bandanna, our only *expedient*⟩ — see RE-SOURCE 1

expedition *n* a going from one place to another usually of some distance ⟨an avid mountain climber, always on an *expedition* to some far-off corner of the world⟩ — see JOURNEY

expeditious *adj* having or showing the ability to respond without delay or hesitation ⟨a company that is well-regarded for its *expeditious* handling of any request or complaint⟩ — see QUICK 1

expel *vb* **1** to drive or force out ⟨animal lover though I am, I was determined to *expel* the uninvited mouse from my room⟩ — see EJECT 1

2 to throw or give off ⟨something in a wastebasket was *expelling* a foul odor⟩ — see EMIT 1

3 to throw out or off (something from within) often violently ⟨ringing and flashing madly, the slot machine *expelled* a bucketful of quarters⟩ — see ERUPT 1

expend *vb* **1** to hand over or use up in payment ⟨redecoration will have to wait, since we've just *expended* our last dollar in buying the house⟩ — see SPEND 1

2 to make complete use of ⟨settlers had to be sure not to *expend* their supply of firewood before the end of the long winter⟩ — see DEPLETE

expenditure *n* **1** a payment made in the course of achieving a result ⟨you'll have to drastically cut back on your clothing *expenditures* if you hope to save anything⟩ — see EXPENSE

2 the active use of energy in producing a result ⟨the *expenditure* of the nation's military might on wars that may or may not involve the national interest⟩ — see EFFORT

expense *n* a payment made in the course of achieving a result ⟨they spared no *expense* in building the house of their dreams⟩

synonyms cost, disbursement, expenditure, outgo, outlay

related words overhead; outflow; spending money; charge, price, rate, tab, tariff, toll

expensive *adj* commanding a large price ⟨*expensive* clothing that only the truly wealthy can afford⟩ — see COSTLY

expensively *adv* in a luxurious manner ⟨the pop singer's *expensively* decorated mansion was a testament to her commercial success⟩ — see HIGH

experience *n* **1** knowledge gained by actually doing or living through something ⟨the hospital is looking for nurses with operating-room *experience*⟩

synonyms expertise, know-how, proficiency, savvy, skills

related words background; command, mastery; acquaintance, familiarity, intimacy

near antonyms ignorance, unawareness, unfamiliarity

antonyms inexperience

2 an exciting or noteworthy event that one experiences firsthand ⟨related in a book his *experiences* as a roving correspondent for network TV news⟩ — see ADVENTURE

experience *vb* to come to a knowledge of (something) by living through it ⟨eventually we all have to *experience* the loss of a loved one⟩

synonyms endure, feel, have, know, see, suffer, sustain, taste, undergo

related words encounter, meet; accept, receive

phrases go through

experienced *adj* having or showing exceptional knowledge, experience, or skill in a field of endeavor ⟨for this

delicate eye operation, seek out an *experienced* eye surgeon⟩ — see PROFICIENT

experiment *n* a procedure or operation carried out to resolve an uncertainty ⟨Benjamin Franklin's famous *experiment* in which he flew a kite in a thunderstorm to see if lightning and electricity were identical⟩

synonyms experimentation, test, trial

related words trial and error; dry run, shakedown; exercise, practice (*also* practise), rehearsal, tryout, workout; crucible, ordeal; attempt, effort, try

experimental *adj* **1** made or done as an experiment ⟨an *experimental* procedure for patients suffering from leukemia⟩

synonyms pilot, trial

related words developmental, investigative, preparatory; preliminary, provisional, temporary, tentative; conjectural, hypothetical, speculative, theoretical (*also* theoretic); untested, untried; unproved, unproven

near antonyms accepted, established, standard; tested, tried; advanced, developed; proved, proven; conclusive, decisive, definitive, final, permanent

2 based on observation or experience ⟨asserted that *experimental* knowledge is vastly superior to idle speculation and theorizing⟩ — see EMPIRICAL

experimentation *n* a procedure or operation carried out to resolve an uncertainty ⟨people who oppose *experimentations* involving animals for the testing of cosmetics intended for humans⟩ — see EXPERIMENT

expert *adj* **1** accomplished with trained ability ⟨to a collector the *expert* carving on the duck decoy justifies its high price⟩ — see SKILLFUL

2 having or showing exceptional knowledge, experience, or skill in a field of endeavor ⟨people interested in laser eye surgery are advised to seek out an *expert* practitioner⟩ — see PROFICIENT

expert *n* a person with a high level of knowledge or skill in a field ⟨*experts* at the crime lab were able to tell the sex, race, and approximate age of the murderer⟩

synonyms ace, adept, artist, authority, crackerjack, maestro, master, past master, scholar, shark, virtuoso, whiz, wizard

related words pro, professional; specialist; addict, aficionado, buff, devotee, enthusiast, fan; craftsman, journeyman; jack-of-all-trades

near antonyms apprentice, beginner, neophyte, novice; dabbler, dilettante; layman, nonprofessional

antonyms amateur

expertise *n* knowledge gained by actually doing or living through something ⟨new dog owners seeking someone with *expertise* in animal obedience⟩ — see EXPERIENCE 1

expertly *adv* in a skillful or expert manner ⟨the apple pie was a traditional but *expertly* made version of an old favorite⟩ — see WELL 3

expiate *vb* to make up for (an offense) ⟨Yom Kippur is the holy day on which Jews are expected to *expiate* sins committed during the past year⟩

synonyms atone (for)

related words compensate, recompense, reimburse, remunerate, repay; amend, correct, rectify, redress; propitiate

phrases make amends for, make good for

expiration *n* **1** the act of ceasing to exist ⟨directed that upon her *expiration* her splendid Italian-style villa be given to the public as a museum⟩ — see DEATH 3

2 the stopping of a process or activity ⟨with the *expiration* of all brain activity there was no point in keeping the patient alive⟩ — see END 1

expire *vb* **1** to come to an end ⟨speakers will not be allowed to continue after their allotted time has *expired*⟩ — see CEASE 1

2 to let or force out of the lungs ⟨he vows to hold on to that belief until he *expires* his last breath⟩ — see EXHALE 1

3 to stop living ⟨made one last visit to his homeland and *expired* not long afterwards⟩ — see DIE 1

expired *adj* no longer existing ⟨a wildlife organization dedicated to ensuring that the giant panda not be added to the list of *expired* species⟩ — see EXTINCT

explain *vb* **1** to make plain or understandable ⟨write an essay that *explains* the meaning of the poem⟩

synonyms clarify, clear (up), construe, demonstrate, elucidate, explicate, expound, illuminate, illustrate, interpret, spell out

related words decipher, decode; analyze, break down; disentangle, undo, unravel, unscramble, untangle; resolve, solve; define, specify

phrases get across

near antonyms befog, cloud; confound, confuse

antonyms obscure

2 to give the reason for or cause of ⟨can you *explain* your very odd behavior at the wedding reception?⟩

synonyms account (for), explain away, rationalize

related words condone, excuse, forgive, justify; absolve, acquit, exculpate, exonerate, vindicate

explainable *adj* capable of having the reason for or cause of determined ⟨investigators found that the so-called mysterious happenings at the house were entirely *explainable*⟩ — see SOLVABLE

explain away *vb* to give the reason for or cause of ⟨after the surprise attack military leaders struggled to *explain away* the nation's unpreparedness⟩ — see EXPLAIN 2

explanation *n* **1** a statement that makes something clear ⟨an *explanation* of photosynthesis that the whole class was able to understand⟩

synonyms clarification, construction, elucidation, explication, exposition, illumination, illustration, interpretation

related words paraphrase, restatement, translation; deciphering, decoding; disentanglement, unscrambling; analysis; definition, meaning; demonstration, enactment; justification, rationale, rationalization, reasoning

2 a statement given to explain a belief or act ⟨when questioned by authorities, the students were unable to give an *explanation* for their senseless vandalism⟩ — see REASON 1

explanatory *adj* serving to explain ⟨the *explanatory* section has as its heading "Using Your Dictionary"⟩

synonyms elucidative, expository, illuminative, illustrative, interpretive

related words analytic (*also* analytical), demonstrative, discursive; exculpatory

expletive *n* a disrespectful or indecent word or expression ⟨losing a game isn't adequate reason for spewing a slew of *expletives*⟩ — see SWEARWORD

explicable *adj* capable of having the reason for or cause of determined ⟨those strange noises were quite *explicable* once we realized that a colony of bats had taken up residence⟩ — see SOLVABLE

explicate *vb* to make plain or understandable ⟨the physicist did his best to *explicate* the wave theory of light for the audience of laymen⟩ — see EXPLAIN 1

explication *n* a statement that makes something clear ⟨any *explication* of Einstein's theory of relativity probably wouldn't help me much⟩ — see EXPLANATION 1

explicit *adj* so clearly expressed as to leave no doubt about the meaning ⟨*explicit* instructions about what to do in an emergency⟩

synonyms clear-cut, definite, definitive, express, specific, unambiguous, unequivocal

related words avowed, declared, stated; categorical (*also* categoric), complete, comprehensive, exhaustive, full; certain, sure, unmistakable; clear, distinct, lucid; exact, precise; direct, literal, plain, simple, straightforward; comprehensible, intelligible, understandable

near antonyms cryptic, dark, enigmatic (*also* enigmatical), obscure, unclear; imprecise, inaccurate, incorrect, inexact; incomprehensible, unintelligible

antonyms implicit, implied, inferred; ambiguous, circuitous; equivocal, indefinite

explicitness *n* **1** careful thoroughness of detail ⟨the *explicitness* of the instruction about human reproduction should be appropriate for the age of the students⟩ — see PARTICULARITY 1

2 clearness of expression ⟨the user's manual is written with such rare *explicitness* that the average consumer actually has a chance of understanding it⟩ — see SIMPLICITY 2

explode *vb* **1** to break open or into pieces usually because of internal pressure ⟨the building was wrecked when a powerful bomb *exploded*⟩

synonyms blow up, burst, detonate, go off, pop

related words fragment, shatter, smash, splinter; discharge, fire, shoot; balloon, burgeon, mushroom

near antonyms collapse, fizzle

antonyms implode

2 to cause to break open or into pieces by or as if by an explosive ⟨the bomb was so powerful that it *exploded* windows in neighboring buildings⟩ — see BLAST 1

3 to develop suddenly and violently ⟨the mayor's latest unpopular decision caused long-suppressed resentment to *explode* into open anger⟩ — see ERUPT 2

exploit *n* **1** an act of notable skill, strength, or cleverness ⟨the fanciful *exploits* of the giant lumberjack Paul Bunyan⟩ — see FEAT 1

2 something done by someone ⟨once famed as an actor, John Wilkes Booth is now remembered for a single *exploit*, his assassination of Lincoln⟩ — see ACTION 1

exploit *vb* **1** to take unfair advantage of ⟨a student who *exploits* his friend's good nature by always sponging off him⟩

synonyms abuse, capitalize (on), cash in (on), impose (on *or* upon), play (on *or* upon), use

related words manipulate, mistreat; bleed, cheat, fleece, overcharge, skin, soak, stick; commercialize

2 to control or take advantage of by artful, unfair, or insidious means ⟨she would *exploit* kids who weren't popular, pretending to be their friend just so they'd vote for her for student council⟩ — see MANIPULATE 1

3 to put into action or service ⟨it will be a shame if you don't *exploit* your artistic talent to the fullest⟩ — see USE 1

exploitable *adj* **1** capable of or suitable for being used for a particular purpose ⟨claimed that solar power is an *exploitable* form of energy that is being unfairly neglected⟩ — see USABLE 1

2 readily taken advantage of ⟨the group opposes commercials on TV shows for kids, believing that young viewers are too *exploitable* by advertisers⟩ — see EASY 2

exploration *n* a systematic search for the truth or facts about something ⟨an *exploration* into the disappearance of famed aviator Amelia Earhart⟩ — see IN-QUIRY 1

explore *vb* 1 to search through or into ⟨let's *explore* new ways of raising money for the school band⟩
synonyms delve (into), dig (into), inquire (into), investigate, look (into), probe, research
related words examine, inspect, sift, study, view; browse, peruse, scan, skim (through), thumb (through)
2 to go into or range over for purposes of discovery ⟨we must continue to *explore* the depths of the ocean⟩
synonyms hunt, probe, prospect, search
related words reconnoiter (*or* reconnoitre), scout; disclose, discover, reveal, unearth; fathom, plumb, sound

explosion *n* 1 the act or an instance of exploding ⟨the *explosion* of the first atomic bomb at Hiroshima⟩
synonyms blast, bursting, detonation, eruption
related words discharge, firing, shooting; blowout, flare-up; bang, boom, pop
antonyms implosion
2 a sudden intense expression of strong feeling ⟨the *explosion* of patriotic feeling that the country experienced after that event⟩ — see OUTBURST 1
3 an outburst or display of excited anger ⟨the tennis player's expletive-enriched *explosions* on the court tested the patience of officials⟩ — see TANTRUM

explosive *adj* 1 extreme in degree, power, or effect ⟨there's been an *explosive* interest in the sport since the Olympics⟩ — see INTENSE
2 marked by bursts of destructive force or intense activity ⟨one of the most *explosive* storms to hit that area of the coast in some time⟩ — see VIOLENT 1

exponent *n* a person who actively supports or favors a cause ⟨*exponents* of space exploration called for more missions to the outer reaches of the solar system⟩
synonyms advocate, apostle, backer, booster, champion, friend, promoter, proponent, supporter
related words loyalist, partisan, stalwart; adherent, cohort, disciple, follower; expounder, interpreter; cheerleader
near antonyms enemy, foe, rival; belittler, critic, faultfinder
antonyms adversary, antagonist, opponent

expose *vb* 1 to reveal the true nature of ⟨a well-researched article that *exposes* the UFO story as a hoax⟩
synonyms debunk, show up, uncloak, uncover, unmask
related words discredit, disprove; disclose, divulge, tell, unveil
near antonyms conceal, hide, secrete
antonyms camouflage, cloak, disguise, mask
2 to make known (as information previously kept secret) ⟨the documentary claims to *expose* how winners of beauty pageants are really picked⟩ — see REVEAL 1
3 to make known (something abstract) through outward signs ⟨the tight race for the championship *exposed* one team's mean streak⟩ — see SHOW 2
4 to present so as to invite notice or attention ⟨I didn't want to *expose* my ignorance in front of the others, so I kept silent⟩ — see SHOW 1

exposed *adj* 1 being in a situation where one is likely to meet with harm ⟨without our immune systems we'd be *exposed* to all sorts of deadly infections⟩ — see LIABLE 1
2 lacking a usual or natural covering ⟨the *exposed* electrical wires were a safety hazard⟩ — see NAKED 2
3 lacking protection from danger or resistance against attack ⟨the soldiers were so *exposed* in the open field that they were the proverbial sitting ducks⟩ — see HELPLESS 1

exposition *n* 1 a public showing of objects of interest ⟨an *exposition* of flying machines from the early days of aviation⟩ — see EXHIBITION 1
2 a series of explanations or observations on something (as an event) ⟨the nonstop *exposition* of the ceremonies by the TV newscasters was both unnecessary and irritating⟩ — see COMMENTARY
3 a statement that makes something clear ⟨the astronomer's *exposition* of white dwarfs was a little helpful⟩ — see EXPLANATION 1

expository *adj* serving to explain ⟨an *expository* piece on the workings of the internal-combustion engine⟩ — see EXPLANATORY

expostulate (with) *vb* to present an opposing opinion or argument ⟨the concerned parents tried to *expostulate with* their daughter whenever she pressed them about permission to start dating⟩ — see OBJECT

expostulation *n* a feeling or declaration of disapproval or dissent ⟨despite the earnest *expostulations* of her friends, Jessica continued to date the boy⟩ — see OBJECTION

exposure *n* 1 the state of being left without shelter or protection against something harmful ⟨some people avoid situations in which there is a high level of *exposure* to germs⟩
synonyms liability, openness, vulnerability
related words susceptibility; defenselessness, helplessness, weakness; danger, jeopardy, peril, risk
near antonyms protection, safeguarding, sheltering, shielding
2 the act or an instance of making known something previously unknown or concealed ⟨the *exposure* by the local newspaper of the kickback scheme in the public works department⟩ — see REVELATION

expound *vb* to make plain or understandable ⟨at the start of the trial the judge *expounded* the legal difference between libel and slander to the jury⟩ — see EXPLAIN 1

express *adj* 1 of a particular or exact sort ⟨a trip to the supermarket with the *express* purpose of buying milk⟩
synonyms distinct, especial, precise, set, special, specific
related words lone, only, separate, single, sole, solitary; distinctive, exclusive, individual, peculiar, unique; limited, restricted; specified
near antonyms general, generic, nonexclusive, universal
antonyms nonspecific
2 so clearly expressed as to leave no doubt about the meaning ⟨no one is allowed to leave the grounds during school hours unless they have *express* permission from the principal's office⟩ — see EXPLICIT

express *vb* 1 to make known (as an idea, emotion, or opinion) ⟨in a true democracy, a person can freely *express* his or her views⟩
synonyms air, give, look, sound, state, vent, ventilate, voice
related words advertise, announce, declare, enunciate, proclaim; broadcast, circulate, disseminate, publish; describe, write, write up; sound off, speak out, speak up; chime in; communicate, convey, put across, put over; offer, submit
phrases put forth
near antonyms censor, restrain, restrict
antonyms stifle, suppress

2 to apply external pressure on so as to force out the juice or contents of ⟨except as a fun event at festivals, people do not make wine by *expressing* grapes with their feet⟩ — see PRESS 2

3 to communicate or convey (as an idea) to the mind ⟨an upraised thumb is now universally recognized as a gesture *expressing* approval or encouragement⟩ — see MEAN 1

4 to convey in appropriate or telling terms ⟨could you *express* your opinion of the book in words a little more precise than "lousy"?⟩ — see PHRASE

expression *n* **1** an act, process, or means of putting something into words ⟨the poem is his *expression* of his grief upon the loss of his beloved dog⟩

synonyms articulation, formulation, statement, utterance, voice

related words outlet, vent; observation, reflection, remark, thought; speech, tongue

2 facial appearance regarded as an indication of mood or feeling ⟨we could tell by the fans' *expressions* that the Chicago Cubs had lost again⟩ — see LOOK 1

3 a pronounceable series of letters having a distinct meaning especially in a particular field ⟨the *expression* "John Doe" is used in legal proceedings to refer to a person whose actual name is either unknown or being withheld from the public⟩ — see WORD 1

4 a sequence of words having a specific meaning ⟨we had fun illustrating the popular *expression* "raining cats and dogs"⟩ — see PHRASE

expressionless *adj* not expressing any emotion ⟨veteran poker players invariably have *expressionless* faces, regardless of the hand they're holding⟩ — see BLANK 1

expressive *adj* clearly conveying a special meaning (as one's mood) ⟨the teacher's *expressive* sigh showed that she had heard that excuse many times before⟩

synonyms eloquent, meaning, meaningful, pregnant, revealing, significant, suggestive

related words graphic (*also* graphical), pictorial, vivid; evocative, redolent, reminiscent; sententious, weighty; flavorful, rich

expressway *n* a passage cleared for public vehicular travel ⟨a baffling maze of high-speed *expressways* encircles the city⟩ — see WAY 1

expropriate *vb* to take ownership or control of (something) by right of one's authority ⟨plans by the city to *expropriate* entire blocks of houses in order to bulldoze them for expansion of the airport⟩ — see CONFISCATE

expulsion *n* the forced removal from a homeland ⟨the ruthless *expulsion* of the French-speaking Acadians from Nova Scotia by the British⟩ — see EXILE 1

expunge *vb* to destroy all traces of ⟨time and the weather have *expunged* any evidence that a thriving community once existed here⟩ — see ANNIHILATE 1

expurgate *vb* to remove objectionable parts from ⟨the newspaper had to *expurgate* the angry speech that the criminal made upon being sentenced to life imprisonment⟩ — see CENSOR

exquisite *adj* **1** extreme in degree, power, or effect ⟨felt such *exquisite* anger at being betrayed by a so-called friend that she could hardly think straight⟩ — see INTENSE

2 having qualities that appeal to a refined taste ⟨*exquisite* pen-and-ink drawings of city scenes grace the walls of the formal restaurant⟩ — see CHOICE

3 satisfying or pleasing because of fineness or mildness ⟨waiters at the wedding reception served *exquisite* hors d'oeuvres from silver trays⟩ — see DELICATE 1

exquisiteness *n* the state or quality of having a delicate structure ⟨the *exquisiteness* of the lace on the bride's gown⟩ — see DELICACY 2

extant *adj* **1** having being at the present time ⟨a celebrated author who is generally regarded as America's greatest novelist *extant*⟩

synonyms alive, existent, existing, living

related words active, busy, flourishing, functioning, operating, working

near antonyms defunct, destroyed, exterminated; departed, gone, lost; nonexistent; idle, inactive, inert

antonyms dead, extinct

2 existing or in progress right now ⟨when people envisage the future, they often base their predictions on the assumption that *extant* trends will continue indefinitely⟩ — see PRESENT 1

extemporaneous *adj* made or done without previous thought or preparation ⟨caught by surprise, I had to make an *extemporaneous* speech at the awards banquet⟩

synonyms ad-lib, extempore, impromptu, improvised, offhand, offhanded, snap, spur-of-the-moment, unconsidered, unplanned, unpremeditated, unprepared, unrehearsed

related words automatic, impulsive, instinctive, involuntary, spontaneous; casual, informal, unauthorized

near antonyms deliberate, intended, intentional

antonyms considered, planned, premeditated, prepared, rehearsed

extempore *adj* made or done without previous thought or preparation ⟨after the election both candidates admitted that they had made a number of *extempore* remarks that they later regretted⟩ — see EXTEMPORANEOUS

extemporize *vb* to perform, make, or do without preparation ⟨a good talk show host has to be able to *extemporize* the interviews when things don't go as planned⟩ — see IMPROVISE

extend *vb* **1** to make longer ⟨our guests from out of town *extended* their visit by a week⟩

synonyms draw out, elongate, lengthen, prolong, protract, stretch

related words amplify, enlarge, expand, increase; attenuate, thin

near antonyms decrease, diminish, lessen, reduce; thicken

antonyms abbreviate, abridge, curtail, cut, cut back, shorten

2 to put before another for acceptance or consideration ⟨the couple *extended* an invitation to join them for a get-together at their house after the concert⟩ — see OFFER 1

3 to arrange the parts of (something) over a wider area ⟨you can *extend* that chaise lounge so that it lies completely flat⟩ — see OPEN 3

4 to be positioned along a certain course or in a certain direction ⟨our backyard *extends* all the way to that brook⟩ — see RUN 3

5 to make greater in size, amount, or number ⟨embarked on a series of wars intended to *extend* his empire⟩ — see INCREASE 1

extended *adj* **1** expressing one thing in terms normally used for another ⟨the word "snake" in its *extended* sense refers to a contemptible or treacherous person⟩ — see FIGURATIVE

2 having considerable extent ⟨an *extended* portion of the valley is now devoted to the growing of grapes for wine⟩ — see EXTENSIVE

3 lasting for a considerable time ⟨I've met her, but I have never had an *extended* conversation with her⟩ — see LONG 2

4 of great extent from end to end ⟨the two armies clashed along an *extended* line of battle that stretched for miles⟩ — see LONG 1

extended family *n* those who live as a family in one house ⟨their *extended family* includes a grandmother and widowed aunt⟩ — see HOUSEHOLD

extension *n* **1** the act of making longer ⟨the board's *extension* of the school year drew howls of protest⟩
synonyms drawing out, elongation, lengthening, prolongation, prolonging, stretching
antonyms abbreviation, abridgment (*or* abridgement), curtailment, cutback, shortening
2 a smaller structure added to a main building ⟨the new *extension* will connect the house with what is now a freestanding garage⟩ — see ANNEX

extensive *adj* having considerable extent ⟨a rock hound whose *extensive* reading enables him to identify just about any rock or mineral⟩
synonyms broad, expansive, extended, far-flung, far-reaching, wide, widespread
related words comprehensive, general, global, inclusive; boundless, endless, limitless, unlimited; capacious, commodious, roomy, spacious
near antonyms circumscribed, limited, restricted
antonyms narrow

extensively *adv* to a large extent or degree ⟨several beaches were *extensively* damaged by the hurricane⟩ — see GREATLY 2

extent *n* **1** a real or imaginary point beyond which a person or thing cannot go ⟨the coach exceeded the *extent* of his authority by exempting some of the players from the requirement⟩ — see LIMIT
2 a wide space or area ⟨the seemingly endless *extent* of the windswept prairies⟩ — see EXPANSE
3 an area over which activity, capacity, or influence extends ⟨the *extent* of this criminal investigation has widened considerably since it began⟩ — see RANGE 2
4 the total amount of measurable space or surface occupied by something ⟨looking at the *extent* of the stain on my shirt, you might think that I had spilled a gallon of coffee⟩ — see ¹SIZE

extenuate *vb* to make (something) seem less bad by offering excuses ⟨don't even try to *extenuate* their vandalism of the cemetery with the old refrain of "boys will be boys"⟩ — see PALLIATE 1

exterior *adj* situated on the outside or farther out ⟨the house's *exterior* walls badly need to be painted⟩ — see OUTER

exterior *n* an outer part or layer ⟨the *exterior* of the tooth consists of very hard enamel⟩
synonyms face, outside, skin, surface, veneer
related words facade (*also* façade), front, top; cover, covering, facing; appearance, disguise, guise, mask, semblance, show
antonyms inside, interior

exterminate *vb* to destroy all traces of ⟨hope that the fumigant *exterminates* the whole colony of cockroaches, for any survivors may be resistant to any poison⟩ — see ANNIHILATE 1

extermination *n* the state or fact of being rendered nonexistent, physically unsound, or useless ⟨the virtual *extermination* of the native tribes by the colonizers⟩ — see DESTRUCTION

external *adj* situated on the outside or farther out ⟨the *external* chambers of the ancient tomb gave little indication of the magnificence of the innermost chamber⟩ — see OUTER

extinct *adj* no longer existing ⟨a few overgrown ruins are all that remain of that once mighty but now *extinct* civilization⟩
synonyms bygone, dead, defunct, departed, expired, gone, vanished
related words nonexistent; dying, faded, moribund; collapsed, fallen, overthrown; antiquated, dated, obsolete, passé; finished, lapsed, terminated; lost, missing
near antonyms active, dynamic, thriving, vibrant
antonyms alive, existent, existing, extant, living

extinction *n* the state or fact of being rendered nonexistent, physically unsound, or useless ⟨the state's population of moose has been replenished, having once been hunted almost to *extinction*⟩ — see DESTRUCTION

extinguish *vb* **1** to cause to cease burning ⟨the fire in the skillet was quickly *extinguished* by slamming the lid on⟩
synonyms douse, put out, quench, snuff (out)
related words choke, smother, suffocate; stamp (out)
antonyms fire, ignite, inflame, kindle
2 to bring to a complete end the physical soundness, existence, or usefulness of ⟨a fatal blunder that *extinguished* all hope that the team would actually win the play-offs⟩ — see DESTROY 1

extirpate *vb* to destroy all traces of ⟨the triumph of modern medicine in *extirpating* certain diseases⟩ — see ANNIHILATE 1

extol *also* **extoll** *vb* to proclaim the glory of ⟨campaign literature *extolling* the candidate's military record⟩ — see PRAISE 1

extort *vb* to get (as money) by the use of force or threats ⟨a school bully who was used to *extorting* lunch money from weaker kids⟩
synonyms exact, wrest, wring
related words bleed, fleece, gouge, milk, skin, squeeze; cheat, gyp, racketeer, swindle; coerce, compel, force

extortioner *n* a person who gets money from another by using force or threats ⟨*extortioners* threatened to beat up the shop owner if he didn't pay the bribe⟩ — see RACKETEER

extortionist *n* a person who gets money from another by using force or threats ⟨tortured by a gang of *extortionists* into revealing the combination for the money vault⟩ — see RACKETEER

extra *adj* being over what is needed ⟨always has *extra* food on hand in the event that unexpected company drops by⟩ — see SPARE 1

extra *adv* to a great degree ⟨the children tried to be *extra* quiet while their mother was recovering⟩ — see VERY 1

extra *n* **1** an interchangeable part or piece of equipment that is kept on hand for replacement of an original ⟨that portable player runs through batteries incredibly fast, so I always keep plenty of *extras* on hand⟩ — see SPARE
2 something adding to pleasure or comfort but not absolutely necessary ⟨the motel is clean and comfortable, but there are no *extras*⟩ — see LUXURY 1
3 something given in addition to what is ordinarily expected or owed ⟨as an *extra*, the dealer filled the tank of my new car⟩ — see BONUS

extract *n* a part taken from a longer work ⟨the anthology includes a long *extract* from the epic poem⟩ — see EXCERPT

extract *vb* to draw out by force or with effort ⟨*extracted* a splinter from my hand⟩

synonyms prize, pry, pull, root (out), tear (out), uproot, wrest, yank

related words remove, take (out), withdraw

near antonyms implant, insert, install, instill; cram, jam, ram, stuff, wedge

extraction *n* the line of ancestors from whom a person is descended ⟨a family of Italian *extraction*⟩ — see ANCESTRY

extraneous *adj* **1** not being a vital part of or belonging to something ⟨the architect's streamlined modern style shuns any sort of *extraneous* ornamentation⟩ — see EXTRINSIC

2 not having anything to do with the matter at hand ⟨the professor would have covered all of the course material if she had refrained from her *extraneous* remarks on just about everything⟩ — see IRRELEVANT

extraneousness *n* the quality or state of not having anything to do with the matter at hand ⟨the *extraneousness* of the commentators' remarks became more pronounced as the broadcast dragged on⟩ — see IRRELEVANCE

extraordinary *adj* **1** being out of the ordinary ⟨the marine is being cited for *extraordinary* courage⟩ — see EXCEPTIONAL

2 noticeably different from what is generally found or experienced ⟨no one noticed anything *extraordinary* about the airline passenger⟩ — see UNUSUAL 1

extrapolate *vb* to form an opinion through reasoning and information ⟨we can *extrapolate* from past economic recessions the probable course of the current one⟩ — see INFER 1

extrasensory perception *n* the power of seeing or knowing about things that are not present to the senses ⟨discouraged by the lack of progress in the case, the police were willing to listen to a woman claiming *extrasensory perception*⟩ — see CLAIRVOYANCE

extravagance *n* **1** the quality or fact of being free or wasteful in the expenditure of money ⟨Hollywood stars are famous for the *extravagance* of their parties⟩

synonyms lavishness, prodigality, wastefulness

related words bountifulness, generosity, liberality; improvidence, squandering; indulgence, overindulgence, self-indulgence; excess, immoderacy, overkill

near antonyms austerity, moderation, restraint, temperance

antonyms economy, frugality

2 an instance of spending money or resources without care or restraint ⟨the purchase of a fur coat was simply the latest of his wife's *extravagances*⟩ — see WASTE 1

extravagant *adj* **1** given to spending money freely or foolishly ⟨the billionaire's son is the typically *extravagant* playboy who hasn't earned any of what he spends⟩ — see PRODIGAL

2 going beyond a normal or acceptable limit in degree or amount ⟨the book doesn't quite merit the *extravagant* praise that it has received⟩ — see EXCESSIVE

extravagantly *adv* in a luxurious manner ⟨the ancient Roman emperors lived as *extravagantly* as any rulers in history⟩ — see HIGH

extreme *adj* **1** most distant from a center ⟨spacecraft that is specially designed to explore the *extreme* edge of our solar system⟩

synonyms farthermost, farthest, furthermost, furthest, outermost, outmost, remotest, ultimate, utmost

near antonyms intermediate, medial, median, mid, middle, middlemost, midmost

antonyms inmost, innermost, nearest

2 being very far from the center of public opinion ⟨their *extreme* political views attracted only a small band of followers⟩

synonyms extremist, fanatic (*or* fanatical), rabid, radical, revolutionary, revolutionist, ultra

related words subversive, violent, wild; reactionary

near antonyms conservative, moderate, temperate; conventional, orthodox, traditional

antonyms middle-of-the-road

3 going beyond a normal or acceptable limit in degree or amount ⟨in their *extreme* zeal the members of the cult are willing to do whatever their leader dictates⟩ — see EXCESSIVE

extremely *adv* to a great degree ⟨an *extremely* hot day⟩ — see VERY 1

extremist *adj* being very far from the center of public opinion ⟨their *extremist* views on religious issues set them apart from the rest of the community⟩ — see EXTREME 2

extremist *n* a person who favors rapid and sweeping changes especially in laws and methods of government ⟨*extremists* wanted to do away with everything, even though they had no thought-out plan for what to do afterwards⟩ — see RADICAL

extremity *n* the most extreme or advanced point ⟨at its *extremity* the fever was actually life-threatening⟩ — see HEIGHT 2

extricate *vb* to set free from entanglement or difficulty ⟨you've woven such a web of lies that it's hard to see how you can *extricate* yourself now⟩

synonyms clear, disengage, disentangle, free, liberate, release, untangle

related words deliver, redeem, rescue, save; disburden, disencumber, unburden; unravel, unsnarl, untie

near antonyms block, hamper, hinder, impede, obstruct; burden, encumber, load, weigh

antonyms embroil, entangle

extrinsic *adj* not being a vital part of or belonging to something ⟨the fact that the ring belonged to your grandmother is *extrinsic* to its value to a jeweler⟩

synonyms adventitious, alien, extraneous, foreign

related words exterior, external, outside; immaterial, inapplicable, insignificant, irrelevant; nonessential, unessential, unnecessary

near antonyms congenital, deep-seated, inborn, inbred; inside, interior, internal; basic, essential

antonyms inherent, innate, intrinsic

extroverted *also* **extraverted** *adj* likely to seek or enjoy the company of others ⟨a job in a research lab that is probably not well suited to an *extroverted* person⟩ — see CONVIVIAL

extrude *vb* to drive or force out ⟨the sort of person who is determined to *extrude* every last gob of toothpaste from the tube⟩ — see EJECT 1

exuberance *n* the quality or state of having abundant or intense activity ⟨the *exuberance* of the housing market was an encouraging economic indicator⟩ — see VITALITY 1

exuberant *adj* joyously unrestrained ⟨*exuberant* crowds rushed to greet the returning national champions in collegiate basketball⟩

synonyms bubbly, buoyant, effervescent, frolicsome, high-spirited, vivacious

related words extroverted (*also* extraverted), outgoing, uninhibited; carefree, insouciant, joyful, lighthearted, lively, sprightly; boisterous, raucous, rollicking, rowdy; giddy, light-headed, silly; ecstatic, euphoric, rapturous;

audacious, bold, brash, brazen, impertinent, impudent, insolent, saucy

near antonyms constrained, inhibited, repressed, restrained, subdued; impassive, phlegmatic, stoic (*or* stoical), stolid; depressed, dour, glum, morose, surly

antonyms low-spirited, noneffervescent, sullen

exuberantly *adv* **1** in a quick and spirited manner ⟨*exuberantly* raced up to the stage to collect his prize⟩ — see GAILY 2

2 in an enthusiastic manner ⟨her last employer sang her praises so *exuberantly* that we just had to hire her⟩ — see SKY-HIGH

exude *vb* to flow forth slowly through small openings ⟨a sticky resin *exudes* from the bark of the tree⟩

synonyms bleed, ooze, percolate, seep, strain, sweat, weep

related words dribble, drip, trickle; discharge, emit, give off, vent; emanate, flow, spring

near antonyms flood, gush, pour, stream, surge

exult *vb* to feel or express joy or triumph ⟨the winners of the Super Bowl spent the next week *exulting* in their victory⟩

synonyms crow, delight, glory, joy, rejoice, triumph

related words gloat; boast, brag; flaunt, parade, show off, strut, swagger

near antonyms bemoan, bewail, grieve, lament, weep

exultant *adj* having or expressing feelings of joy or triumph ⟨the *exultant* winner of the award for best country artist of the year⟩

synonyms exulting, glorying, jubilant, rejoicing, triumphant

related words ecstatic, elated, euphoric; arrogant, boastful, cocky; conquering, victorious, winning

near antonyms crestfallen, defeated, dejected, depressed, disconsolate, dispirited, downcast

exulting *adj* having or expressing feelings of joy or triumph ⟨with an *exulting* smile the winner of the beauty pageant waved to the cheering crowd⟩ — see EXULTANT

exurbia *n* the area around a city ⟨over the years the upper crust have abandoned the city for its *exurbia*⟩ — see ENVIRONS 1

eye *n* **1** a circular strip ⟨push the drawstring through the metal *eye* and knot it on one end⟩ — see RING 2

2 a state of being aware ⟨this young actor has the *eye* of every director in Hollywood⟩ — see ATTENTION 2

3 a thing or place that is of greatest importance to an activity or interest ⟨this wilderness area is at the *eye* of the controversy between conservation and development⟩ — see CENTER 1

4 an idea that is believed to be true or valid without positive knowledge ⟨in my *eye*, cats make better pets than dogs⟩ — see OPINION 1

5 an instance of looking especially briefly ⟨all of the guys cast an appreciative *eye* on the new girl as they passed her in the hall⟩ — see LOOK 2

6 the ability to see ⟨her *eyes* are diminishing with age⟩ — see EYESIGHT

eye *vb* **1** to keep one's eyes on ⟨a lot of his backyard bird watching was spent *eyeing* the squirrels as they depleted the bird feeder of seeds⟩ — see WATCH 1

2 to make note of (something) through the use of one's eyes ⟨I was starting to believe her tale of woe, until I *eyed* the diamond ring on her finger⟩ — see SEE 1

eye–catching *adj* likely to attract attention ⟨Brad needs an *eye-catching* slogan for his campaign for president of the student body⟩ — see NOTICEABLE

eyeful *n* a lovely woman ⟨they watched their teenage daughter, once something of an ugly duckling, blossom into quite an *eyeful*⟩ — see BEAUTY 2

eyeglasses *n pl* a pair of lenses set in a frame that is held in place with ear supports and which are usually worn to correct vision ⟨uses her *eyeglasses* only for reading⟩ — see GLASSES 1

eyeless *adj* lacking the power of sight ⟨his failing eyesight makes him fear that he may be *eyeless* in old age⟩ — see BLIND

eye–opening *adj* **1** causing a strong emotional reaction because unexpected ⟨hunting for a first apartment in a big city is an *eye-opening* experience for young people⟩ — see SURPRISING 1

2 causing wonder or astonishment ⟨that acclaimed animal-cum-magic act had a number of *eye-opening* moments⟩ — see MARVELOUS 1

eyesight *n* the ability to see ⟨the keen *eyesight* of a bird of prey⟩

synonyms eye, sight, vision

related words myopia, nearsightedness; farsightedness; astigmatism

eyesore *n* something unpleasant to look at ⟨the old abandoned house was a neighborhood *eyesore*⟩

synonyms fright, horror, mess, monstrosity, sight

related words blot, smear, smudge, spot, stain

eyespot *n* a small area that is different (as in color) from the main part ⟨a tie having *eyespots* of blue on a light gray background⟩ — see SPOT 1

F

fable *n* **1** a story intended to teach a basic truth or moral about life ⟨this classic Christmas film is essentially a *fable* showing how every person's life has meaning and touches the lives of others⟩ — see ALLEGORY

2 a traditional but unfounded story that gives the reason for a current custom, belief, or fact of nature ⟨according to an ancient *fable* the waters of the mountain spring are the tears of a woman weeping for her lost children⟩ — see MYTH 1

3 something that is the product of the imagination ⟨the stories of lost cities of gold may have been *fables* deliberately concocted by Native Americans to dupe the Spanish⟩ — see FICTION

fabled *adj* based on, described in, or being a myth ⟨the *fabled* unicorn continues to be a symbol of elusive and magical beauty⟩ — see MYTHICAL 1

fabric *n* a woven or knitted material (as of cotton or nylon) ⟨a *fabric* that is supposed to repel rain while at the same time allowing the wearer's perspiration to escape⟩ — see CLOTH

fabricate *vb* **1** to bring into being by combining, shaping, or transforming materials ⟨with a few inexpensive materials from a craft shop, we were able to *fabricate* our own holiday wreath⟩ — see MAKE 1

2 to create or think of by clever use of the imagination ⟨*fabricated* a daring plan to create an underground explosion that would take the enemy totally by surprise⟩ — see INVENT

3 to form by putting together parts or materials ⟨the house was essentially *fabricated* at the factory and then shipped to the site for assembly⟩ — see BUILD

4 to make a statement one knows to be untrue ⟨since he didn't have a good excuse for not having done his homework, he would have to *fabricate* one⟩ — see LIE 1

fabrication *n* **1** a statement known by its maker to be untrue and made in order to deceive ⟨her claim that she had been a nurse during the war proved to be a total *fabrication*⟩ — see LIE

2 something that is the product of the imagination ⟨the notion that the Colossus of Rhodes could straddle the harbor was a *fabrication* of medieval writers⟩ — see FICTION

fabricator *n* a person who tells lies ⟨he's been a *fabricator* for so long that it no longer occurs to him to tell the truth⟩ — see LIAR

fabulous *adj* **1** based on, described in, or being a myth ⟨the city of Phoenix is named after a *fabulous* bird that every 500 years destroys itself with fire, only to rise again from its own ashes⟩ — see MYTHICAL 1

2 causing wonder or astonishment ⟨the *fabulous* sites of dazzlingly lit Las Vegas⟩ — see MARVELOUS 1

3 not real and existing only in the imagination ⟨a story of a *fabulous* land where the people know nothing of war and live together in perfect harmony⟩ — see IMAGINARY

4 of the very best kind ⟨we had a *fabulous* time on our vacation⟩ — see EXCELLENT

facade *also* **façade** *n* **1** a forward part or surface ⟨all of the stores in the mall have *facades* that are in keeping with the style of an 19th-century American village⟩ — see FRONT 1

2 a display of emotion or behavior that is insincere or intended to deceive ⟨his interest in acting is just a *facade*—he joined the drama club to meet girls⟩ — see MASQUERADE

face *n* **1** the front part of the head ⟨the criminal hid his *face* from the news cameras as he slumped into the patrol car⟩

synonyms countenance, kisser [*slang*], mug, puss [*slang*], visage

related words appearance, features, lineaments, looks; expression, physiognomy

2 a forward part or surface ⟨the *face* of the store building has been altered many times over the years to meet changing tastes and needs⟩ — see FRONT 1

3 a twisting of the facial features in disgust or disapproval ⟨it's rude to make a *face* when your dinner hostess offers you broccoli⟩ — see GRIMACE

4 an outer part or layer ⟨a much-needed sandblasting revealed that the *face* of the old stone church is actually a pinkish granite⟩ — see EXTERIOR

5 facial appearance regarded as an indication of mood or feeling ⟨a rainy day is no excuse for just moping around with a long *face*, so let's do something⟩ — see LOOK 1

6 outward and often deceptive indication ⟨on the *face* of it, the country went to war for noble reasons⟩ — see APPEARANCE 2

face *vb* **1** to stand or sit with the face or front toward ⟨the house *faces* the sparkling blue waters of the Pacific Ocean⟩

synonyms front, look (toward), point (toward)

related words abut, adjoin, border, meet, neighbor, touch; command, dominate, overlook

2 to oppose (something hostile or dangerous) with firmness or courage ⟨movie superheroes who are ever ready to *face* danger without blinking an eye⟩

synonyms beard, brave, brazen, breast, confront, dare, defy, outbrave

related words encounter, meet; accost, approach; repel, resist, withstand; battle, combat, contend (with), fight, oppose, square (off)

phrases stand up to

near antonyms avoid, eschew, shun; elude, escape, evade

antonyms dodge, duck, shirk, sidestep

3 to cover with something that protects ⟨we decided to *face* our old frame house with aluminum siding⟩ — see SHEATHE

4 to enter into contest or conflict with ⟨the Boston Red Sox were eager to *face* their traditional rivals, the Yankees, in the play-offs⟩ — see ENGAGE 2

face–off *n* an earnest effort for superiority or victory over another ⟨the annual fall *face-off* between these traditional rivals is a big event for both football-mad colleges⟩ — see CONTEST 1

facet *n* a certain way in which something appears or may be regarded ⟨there are so many *facets* to Benjamin Franklin: statesman, scientist, inventor, American original⟩ — see ASPECT 1

facetious *adj* **1** given to or marked by mature intelligent humor ⟨the essay is a *facetious* commentary on the absurdity of war as a solution for international disputes⟩ — see WITTY

2 making light of something usually regarded as serious or sacred ⟨a *facetious* and tasteless remark about people in famine-stricken countries being spared the problem of overeating⟩ — see FLIPPANT

facetiousness *n* a lack of seriousness often at an improper time ⟨underage drinking is a serious problem and not a matter for *facetiousness* and lame jokes⟩ — see FRIVOLITY 1

face-to-face *adv* in person and usually privately ⟨I won't believe that accusation until I meet with him *face-to-face* and ask him myself⟩ — see TÊTE-À-TÊTE

facile *adj* **1** having or showing a lack of depth of understanding or character ⟨the movie takes a *facile* look at what happens when teens enter into serious romantic relationships⟩ — see SUPERFICIAL 2

2 involving minimal difficulty or effort ⟨a few early *facile* victories misled the country into thinking that the war would be short and relatively painless⟩ — see EASY 1

facilely *adv* without difficulty ⟨most TV sitcoms give the impression that family problems can be solved *facilely* and in less than 30 minutes⟩ — see EASILY

facilitate *vb* to free from obstruction or difficulty ⟨several religious organizations are involved in the effort to *facilitate* the settlement of the immigrants arriving in the area⟩ — see EASE 1

facility *n* a structure that is designed and built for a particular purpose ⟨the city is known for its outstanding medical *facilities*⟩
synonyms complex, establishment, installation
related words building, edifice; institute, institution; business, company, concern, outfit

facsimile *n* **1** something or someone that strongly resembles another ⟨the family resemblance is so strong that the boy is virtually a pint-size *facsimile* of his father⟩ — see IMAGE 1

2 something that is made to look exactly like something else ⟨this is not an antique copy of the Declaration of Independence but a modern *facsimile*⟩ — see COPY

fact *n* **1** the quality of being actual ⟨like other scientists, astronomers deal in the realm of *fact*, not speculation⟩
synonyms actuality, factuality, materiality, reality
related words authenticity, genuineness, truth
near antonyms fancy, fantasy (*also* phantasy), fiction; fictitiousness
antonyms unreality

2 something that actually exists ⟨once considered a wild fantasy, the Internet is now a *fact* of everyday life⟩
synonyms case, materiality, reality
related words certainty, inevitability; circumstance, event, occurrence, phenomenon; element, item, particular, thing
near antonyms eventuality, possibility, potentiality, probability
antonyms fantasy (*also* phantasy), fiction, illusion

3 a single piece of information ⟨a book of little-known *facts* about famous people⟩
synonyms datum, detail, nicety, particular, particularity, point
related words article, item; element, ingredient, part; aspect, facet, factor; evidence, exhibit; database, information, knowledge
near antonyms error, fallacy, falsehood, misconception, myth

faction *n* a group of people acting together within a larger group ⟨several *factions* within the environmental

movement have joined forces to save this wilderness area⟩
synonyms bloc, body, coalition, party, sect, set, side, wing
related words crew, gang, pack, team; denomination, persuasion, schism

factitious *adj* **1** being such in appearance only and made with or manufactured from usually cheaper materials ⟨presumably the statue is of *factitious* marble, because for that price you're not going to get the real stuff⟩ — see IMITATION

2 lacking in natural or spontaneous quality ⟨the *factitious* friendliness shown by the beauty-pageant contestants to one another⟩ — see ARTIFICIAL 1

factor *n* **1** a person who acts or does business for another ⟨the high bidder at the auction for the painting was actually a *factor* for a wealthy art collector⟩ — see AGENT 2

2 one of the parts that make up a whole ⟨price was only one *factor* in my decision to buy the car⟩ — see ELEMENT 1

factory *n* a building or set of buildings for the manufacturing of goods ⟨the new *factory* will create hundreds of much-needed jobs⟩
synonyms manufactory, mill, plant, shop, works, workshop
related words sweatshop; workroom; yard

factual *adj* **1** restricted to or based on fact ⟨a *factual* biography of George Washington that scoffs at the story about the cherry tree⟩
synonyms documentary, hard, historical, literal, matter-of-fact, nonfictional, objective, true
related words actual, authentic, genuine, real; documented, established; reliable, verifiable; demonstrable, provable; incontestable, incontrovertible, indisputable, irrefutable, undeniable, unquestionable; plain, simple, unexaggerated; certain, undoubted
near antonyms hypothetical, speculative, theoretical (*also* theoretic); fabulous, fanciful, imaginary, legendary, mythical (*or* mythic); embroidered, exaggerated
antonyms fictional, fictionalized, fictitious, nondocumentary, nonhistorical

2 existing in fact and not merely as a possibility ⟨a serious scientist, she is only interested in *factual* phenomena and lets others speculate about the hypothetical⟩ — see ACTUAL

factuality *n* **1** agreement with fact or reality ⟨some viewers complained that the TV docudrama was short on *factuality* and long on speculation⟩ — see TRUTH

2 the quality of being actual ⟨although this account of the murders seems like it must be fiction, its very *factuality* makes it all the more fascinating⟩ — see FACT 1

faculty *n* **1** a natural ability of the mind or body ⟨although they are well into their 80s, the mental *faculties* of this couple are as sharp as ever⟩ — see POWER 3

2 a special and usually inborn ability ⟨even when he was still at a young age, John Singleton Copley's artistic *faculties* were readily recognizable⟩ — see TALENT

3 the physical or mental power to do something ⟨the belief that if someone loses their sight, all of their other physical *faculties* are heightened⟩ — see ABILITY

fad *n* a practice or interest that is very popular for a short time ⟨once the *fad* for that kind of music had passed, nobody would have been caught dead listening to it⟩
synonyms craze, enthusiasm, fashion, go, last word, mode, rage, sensation, style, trend, vogue

related words crush, infatuation; fervor, passion; furor, fuss, hullabaloo, to-do, uproar; bandwagon, crusade, cult, movement; novelty, wrinkle; caprice, fancy, whim
near antonyms classic, standard

fade *vb* **1** to cease to be visible ⟨the departing ship gradually *faded* over the horizon⟩ — see DISAPPEAR
2 to make white or whiter by removing color ⟨years of harsh sunlight had *faded* the car, which was once fire-engine red⟩ — see WHITEN

faded *adj* lacking intensity of color ⟨rather than buy *faded* jeans, I get the dark blues and let time and the washing machine do their thing⟩ — see PALE 1

faerie *also* **faery** *n* an imaginary being usually having a small human form and magical powers ⟨in ancient folklore *faeries* were often portrayed as powerful beings who could wreak havoc on the lives of humans⟩ — see FAIRY

fag *n* a person who does very hard or dull work ⟨a rigid class system, with *fags* at the very bottom of it⟩ — see SLAVE 2

fag *vb* **1** to devote serious and sustained effort ⟨the road crew *fagged* mightily to move the boulder out of the way⟩ — see LABOR
2 to use up all the physical energy of ⟨the long hike up the mountain had *fagged* us out⟩ — see EXHAUST 1

fag end *n* an unused or unwanted piece or item typically of small size or value ⟨a patchwork quilt sown together from the *fag ends* of many bolts of cloth⟩ — see ¹SCRAP 1

fail *vb* **1** to stop functioning ⟨my video camera *failed* just as I was about to shoot the big moment⟩
synonyms break, break down, conk (out), crash, cut out, die, give out, stall
related words fizzle, sputter, wheeze; malfunction
antonyms start (up)
2 to be unsuccessful ⟨despite all the publicity, the movie *failed* miserably at the box office⟩
synonyms collapse, flop, flunk, fold, wash out
related words flounder, struggle; decline, slip, slump, wane
phrases fall flat
near antonyms flourish, prosper, thrive
antonyms succeed
3 to fall short in satisfying the expectation or hope of ⟨Boston Red Sox fans are pretty much used to having the team *fail* them⟩ — see DISAPPOINT
4 to lose bodily strength or vigor ⟨ever since she reached the age of 90, Grandma has been noticeably *failing*⟩ — see WEAKEN 2
5 to miss the opportunity or obligation ⟨*failed* to mention that he had already been paid for the job by the homeowner's wife⟩ — see NEGLECT 3

failing *n* a defect in character ⟨we could talk about your *failings*, but it would take all night⟩ — see FAULT 1

failure *n* **1** the nonperformance of an assigned or expected action ⟨your *failure* to check the batteries in the smoke detector could have tragic results⟩
synonyms default, delinquency, dereliction, neglect, negligence, oversight
related words carelessness, heedlessness, laxity
near antonyms compliance, discharge, fulfillment
2 a falling short of one's goals ⟨the *failure* of the school's fund-raising drive was a big disappointment to all⟩
synonyms collapse, crash, cropper, defeat, fizzle, nonsuccess

related words futility, uselessness; ineffectiveness, ineffectualness; deficiency, inadequacy, insufficiency; disappointment, letdown, setback
antonyms accomplishment, achievement, success
3 something that has failed ⟨the students' first attempt to build a homemade rocket was a disappointing *failure*⟩
synonyms bummer, bust, catastrophe, debacle (*also* débâcle), dud, fiasco, fizzle, flop, lemon, loser, turkey, washout
related words also-ran, disappointment, has-been; botch, hash, mess, muddle, shambles
near antonyms corker, crackerjack, dandy, jim-dandy, phenomenon
antonyms blockbuster, hit, smash, success, winner
4 a falling short of an essential or desirable amount or number ⟨the *failure* of the potato crop had a devastating effect on the population of Ireland⟩ — see DEFICIENCY

faint *adj* **1** not seen or understood clearly ⟨after wandering in the woods for hours, we had only a *faint* idea of where we were⟩
synonyms bleary, dim, foggy, fuzzy, hazy, indefinite, indistinct, indistinguishable, murky, nebulous, obscure, opaque, shadowy, unclear, undefined, undetermined, vague
related words dark, dusky, gloomy; impalpable, inappreciable, intangible, invisible; incomprehensible, inexplicable, mysterious, puzzling
near antonyms bright, distinct, evident, obvious; certain, firm, strong, sure
antonyms clear, definite
2 lacking bodily strength ⟨I was starting to feel a little *faint* after going so long without food⟩ — see WEAK 1

faint *n* a temporary or permanent state of unconsciousness ⟨shocking news can cause a person to fall into a *faint*⟩
synonyms blackout, coma, insensibility, knockout, swoon
related words daze, stupor, trance; drowsiness, narcosis, sleep, somnolence

faint *vb* to lose consciousness ⟨the kind of person who *faints* at the sight of blood⟩
synonyms black out, pass out, swoon
related words break down, collapse
antonyms come around, come round, come to, revive

fainthearted *adj* easily frightened ⟨the sport of river rafting is not for those who are *fainthearted*⟩ — see SHY 1

faintheartedness *n* lack of willingness to assert oneself and take risks ⟨his *faintheartedness* got the better of him, and he backed off from the ski trail for experts⟩ — see TIMIDITY

faintness *n* the quality or state of lacking physical strength or vigor ⟨after a year of increasing *faintness*, the old man quietly died in his sleep⟩ — see WEAKNESS 1

fair *adj* **1** not stormy or cloudy ⟨we prayed for *fair* weather during our vacation at the beach⟩
synonyms clear, cloudless, sunny, sunshiny, unclouded
related words balmy, clement, gentle, mild, temperate; calm, halcyon, peaceful, placid, tranquil; fine, pleasant
near antonyms harsh, inclement, severe; blustering, blustery, breezy, gusty; foggy, hazy, misty
antonyms bleak, cloudy, dirty, foul, nasty, overcast, rainy, raw, rough, squally, stormy, sunless

2 marked by justice, honesty, and freedom from bias ⟨a commanding officer who enjoyed the respect of his soldiers because his decisions were always *fair*⟩
synonyms disinterested, dispassionate, equal, equitable, impartial, just, nonpartisan, objective, square, unbiased, unprejudiced
related words candid, frank, forthright, open, straightforward; balanced, rational, reasonable
near antonyms deceitful, deceptive, dishonest; arbitrary, unconscionable, unreasonable
antonyms biased, inequitable, partisan, prejudiced, unequal, unjust
3 following or according to the rules ⟨a hockey player who is respected for his *fair* play⟩
synonyms clean, legal, sportsmanlike, sportsmanly
related words just, law-abiding; ethical, moral, principled; honorable, irreproachable, unimpeachable
near antonyms immoral, unethical, unprincipled, unscrupulous
antonyms dirty, foul, nasty, unfair, unsportsmanlike
4 of light complexion ⟨*fair* people tend to sunburn easily⟩
synonyms light
related words ashen, pale, pallid, pasty, peaked, sallow, wan, white
antonyms black, brunet (*or* brunette), dark, swarthy
5 having qualities which inspire hope ⟨as long as the team keeps playing as hard as they can, they have a *fair* chance of winning—no matter what the scoreboard says⟩ — see HOPEFUL 1
6 of a pale yellow or yellowish brown color ⟨the abundance of people with *fair* hair in Scandinavia⟩ — see BLOND
7 of average to below average quality ⟨for what they charged us, the painters should have done better than a *fair* job of painting the house⟩ — see MEDIOCRE 1
8 very pleasing to look at ⟨generally considered the *fairest* girl in town, she had no lack of boyfriends⟩ — see BEAUTIFUL
fair *n* a public showing of objects of interest ⟨a dazzling array of sleek cabin cruisers at the annual boat *fair*⟩ — see EXHIBITION 1
fairly *adv* to some degree or extent ⟨for someone without professional training, she sings *fairly* well⟩
synonyms enough, kind of, like, moderately, more or less, pretty, quite, rather, relatively, something, somewhat, sort of
related words acceptably, decently, passably, tolerably
near antonyms awfully, exceedingly (*also* exceeding), exceptionally, extremely, greatly, surpassingly, very
fairness *n* the qualities in a person or thing that as a whole give pleasure to the senses ⟨a city of incomparable *fairness*, Venice has enchanted travelers for centuries⟩ — see BEAUTY 1
fairy *n* an imaginary being usually having a small human form and magical powers ⟨*fairies* are part of the folklore of many countries and cultures⟩
synonyms brownie, dwarf, elf, faerie (*also* faery), fay, gnome, goblin, gremlin, hobgoblin, leprechaun, pixie (*also* pixy), puck, sprite, troll
related words changeling; imp; banshee, ghoul, ogre
fairy tale *n* a statement known by its maker to be untrue and made in order to deceive ⟨did you really see a bear, or are you telling us another one of your *fairy tales*?⟩ — see LIE
faith *n* **1** belief and trust in and loyalty to God ⟨a people who are known for their strong and steadfast *faith*⟩

synonyms devotion, piety, religion
related words devoutness, piousness, religiousness; adoration, reverence, veneration, worship
near antonyms disbelief, doubt, unbelief
antonyms atheism, godlessness
2 a body of beliefs and practices regarding the supernatural and the worship of one or more deities ⟨the city of Jerusalem is sacred to three *faiths*: Christianity, Islam, and Judaism⟩ — see RELIGION 1
3 adherence to something to which one is bound by a pledge or duty ⟨after they had to declare bankruptcy, the family found out how much *faith* their friends had⟩ — see FIDELITY
4 firm belief in the integrity, ability, effectiveness, or genuineness of someone or something ⟨never having had much *faith* in banks, the old miser kept his money under the mattress⟩ — see TRUST 1
5 mental conviction of the truth of some statement or the reality of some being or phenomenon ⟨she has complete *faith* that the universe is controlled by a benevolent Supreme Being with a master plan⟩ — see BELIEF 1
faithful *adj* **1** firm in one's allegiance to someone or something ⟨fans of the Chicago Cubs are famously *faithful*⟩
synonyms constant, devoted, fast, good, loyal, pious, staunch (*or* stanch), steadfast, steady, true, true-blue
related words dependable, dutiful, reliable, tried, trustworthy; unfaltering, unhesitating, unwavering; determined, intent, resolute; confirmed, dyed-in-the-wool, inveterate, sworn; ardent, fervent, fervid, impassioned, passionate
near antonyms undependable, unreliable, untrustworthy; faltering, hesitant, vacillating, wavering; dubious, irresolute, uncertain; apathetic, dispassionate, uninterested
antonyms disloyal, faithless, false, fickle, inconstant, perfidious, recreant, traitorous, treacherous, unfaithful, untrue
2 following an original exactly ⟨a *faithful* filming of Robert Louis Stevenson's novel *Treasure Island*⟩
synonyms accurate, authentic, exact, precise, right, strict, true, veracious
related words lifelike, realistic; careful, conscientious, meticulous, punctilious, scrupulous; authoritative; bona fide, genuine, real
near antonyms careless, slack, slipshod, slovenly
antonyms false, imprecise, inaccurate, inauthentic, inexact, loose, unfaithful
faithfulness *n* adherence to something to which one is bound by a pledge or duty ⟨put the *faithfulness* of his disciples to the test⟩ — see FIDELITY
faithless *adj* not true in one's allegiance to someone or something ⟨*faithless* friends who deserted him in his time of need⟩
synonyms disloyal, false, fickle, inconstant, perfidious, recreant, traitorous, treacherous, unfaithful, untrue
related words undependable, unreliable, untrustworthy; faltering, hesitant, vacillating, wavering; dubious, irresolute, uncertain; apathetic, dispassionate, uninterested
near antonyms dependable, reliable, tried, trustworthy; unfaltering, unhesitating, unwavering; determined, intent, resolute; confirmed, dyed-in-the-wool, inveterate, sworn; ardent, fervent, fervid, impassioned, passionate
antonyms constant, devoted, faithful, fast, loyal, staunch (*or* stanch), steadfast, steady, true

faithlessness *n* **1** lack of faithfulness especially to one's husband or wife ⟨a wife who long ago became resigned to the *faithlessness* of her husband⟩ — see INFIDELITY 1

2 the act or fact of violating the trust or confidence of another ⟨the former butler's *faithlessness* shocked and offended the royal family⟩ — see BETRAYAL

fake *adj* **1** being such in appearance only and made with or manufactured from usually cheaper materials ⟨opposed to the unnecessary killing of animals, she'll consider wearing only *fake* furs⟩ — see IMITATION

2 being such in appearance only and made or manufactured with the intention of committing fraud ⟨arrested for peddling designer watches that were *fake*⟩ — see COUNTERFEIT

3 lacking in natural or spontaneous quality ⟨the boss's pitiful attempts at humor were met with *fake* laughter⟩ — see ARTIFICIAL 1

fake *n* **1** an imitation that is passed off as genuine ⟨experts declared that one of the museum's prized paintings was actually a *fake*⟩

synonyms counterfeit, forgery, hoax, humbug, phony (*also* phoney), sham

related words copy, reproduction; dummy; fraud, imposture, swindle; simulation, synthetic

near antonyms original

2 one who makes false claims of identity or expertise ⟨a hidden-camera investigation revealed that the so-called psychic was a *fake*⟩ — see IMPOSTOR

fake *vb* **1** to imitate or copy especially in order to deceive ⟨pranksters *faked* giant footprints and then claimed that they had seen Bigfoot⟩

synonyms counterfeit, forge

related words simulate; crib, plagiarize; adulterate, doctor, fudge, juggle, manipulate, tamper (with); concoct, cook (up), fabricate, invent

2 to present a false appearance of ⟨while running for class president, Dan was not above *faking* friendship with people just to get their votes⟩ — see FEIGN

faker *n* one who makes false claims of identity or expertise ⟨the medium was exposed as a *faker* who was herself making the strange noises that she claimed were from the dead⟩ — see IMPOSTOR

fakery *n* the inclination or practice of misleading others through lies or trickery ⟨if the product were any good, the company wouldn't have to resort to *fakery* to get people to buy it⟩ — see DECEIT

fall *n* **1** the act of going down from an upright position suddenly and involuntarily ⟨a bad *fall* that resulted in several broken bones⟩

synonyms slip, spill, stumble, tumble

related words header, pratfall; trip; descent, dive, plunge, slide; free-fall

2 a change to a lower state or level ⟨last night's record *fall* in temperature was a sure sign that winter's coming, like it or not⟩ — see DECLINE 2

3 a loss of status ⟨being sent back to the minor leagues was quite a *fall* for the once-promising pitcher⟩ — see COMEDOWN

4 the act or process of going to a lower level or altitude ⟨there's usually a *fall* in gas prices after the end of the summer driving season⟩ — see DESCENT 1

5 the amount by which something is lessened ⟨that year the *fall* in prices was ten cents for a gallon of regular gas⟩ — see DECREASE

6 *usually* **falls** *pl* a fall of water usually from a great height ⟨tourists were shocked to see a man jump into the water and go over the *falls*⟩ — see WATERFALL

fall *vb* **1** to go down from an upright position suddenly and involuntarily ⟨better sand that walkway before somebody *falls* on the ice⟩

synonyms slip, stumble, topple, trip, tumble

related words collapse, crumple, drop, keel over, slump (over); nose-dive, plunge, precipitate

antonyms get up, rise, stand (up); uprise

2 to yield to the control or power of enemy forces ⟨the city *fell* after weeks of merciless bombardment⟩

synonyms capitulate, give up, knuckle under, submit, succumb, surrender

related words bow, buckle, cave (in), collapse; hand over, relinquish, yield; lose; fail, fold

near antonyms fight, oppose, resist, withstand; beat, overcome, win; prevail, triumph

antonyms stand

3 to go to a lower level ⟨word got out that the movie was no good, and box-office receipts *fell* like a rock⟩ — see DROP 2

4 to grow less in scope or intensity especially gradually ⟨manufacturing in the area is *falling*, and closing signs are going up all over⟩ — see DECREASE 2

5 to lead or extend downward ⟨the lake bottom *falls* sharply just a few feet from the shoreline, so be careful⟩ — see DESCEND 1

fallacious *adj* **1** not using or following good reasoning ⟨it's *fallacious* to say that something must exist because science hasn't proven its nonexistence⟩ — see ILLOGICAL

2 tending or having power to deceive ⟨consumers who harbor the *fallacious* belief that credit-card spending will never catch up with them⟩ — see DECEPTIVE 1

fallaciousness *n* the quality or state of being false ⟨the *fallaciousness* of that argument will be apparent as soon as we examine it⟩ — see FALLACY 2

fallacy *n* **1** a false idea or belief ⟨the once-common *fallacy* that girls just weren't any good at math⟩

synonyms error, falsehood, falsity, illusion, misconception, myth, old wives' tale, untruth

related words superstition; distortion, inaccuracy, misinterpretation, misrepresentation, misstatement, misunderstanding; sophism, sophistry; fib, lie, story, tale

antonyms truth, verity

2 the quality or state of being false ⟨the *fallacy* of the notion of spontaneous generation was demonstrated by the Dutch naturalist Leeuwenhoek⟩

synonyms erroneousness, fallaciousness, falseness, falsity, untruth

related words speciousness, spuriousness; deception, deceptiveness, delusion

near antonyms accuracy, correctness, factualness, genuineness

antonyms truth

fall back *vb* to move back or away (as from something difficult, dangerous, or disagreeable) ⟨resistance from native forces was greater than expected, and the invading army was forced to *fall back*⟩ — see RETREAT 1

fallen *adj* no longer living ⟨let's take a moment to remember our *fallen* comrades⟩ — see DEAD 1

fall guy *n* a person or thing taking the blame for others ⟨the sandlot ball players wanted the littlest kid to be the *fall guy* for the broken window, figuring that he'd have the best chance of escaping punishment⟩ — see SCAPEGOAT

falling-out *n* an often noisy or angry expression of differing opinions ⟨the two friends have been lonely and miserable since they had a *falling-out*⟩ — see ARGUMENT 1

fall out *vb* to express different opinions about something often angrily ⟨club members were soon *falling out* about how to spend the money they'd made washing cars⟩ — see ARGUE 2

fallow *adj* not being in a state of use, activity, or employment ⟨the coal mine has been lying *fallow* since the drop in prices made it unprofitable⟩ — see INACTIVE 2

false *adj* **1** not being in agreement with what is true ⟨early reports about the explosion contained much *false* information⟩
synonyms erroneous, inaccurate, incorrect, inexact, invalid, off, unsound, untrue, untruthful, wrong
related words specious, spurious; deceptive, delusive, delusory, distorted, fallacious, misleading; amiss, askew, awry; deceitful, dishonest, fraudulent, lying, mendacious, untruthful; unconfirmed, unproven, untested; fabricated, invented, made-up, trumped-up
near antonyms confirmed, demonstrated, established, proven, tested
antonyms accurate, correct, errorless, factual, right, sound, true, valid
2 being such in appearance only and made with or manufactured from usually cheaper materials ⟨George Washington's *false* teeth were not made of wood but of elephant ivory and cow's teeth⟩ — see IMITATION
3 being such in appearance only and made or manufactured with the intention of committing fraud ⟨arrested for selling *false* ID cards to teenagers⟩ — see COUNTERFEIT
4 lacking in natural or spontaneous quality ⟨so much of the sympathy that the widow received was *false* and hypocritical, since it came from people who never liked her husband in the first place⟩ — see ARTIFICIAL 1
5 marked by, based on, or done by the use of dishonest methods to acquire something of value ⟨*false* advertising that claimed that the vegetables were organically grown when they weren't⟩ — see FRAUDULENT 1
6 not true in one's allegiance to someone or something ⟨*false* friends who deserted the prizefighter when all his money was gone⟩ — see FAITHLESS
7 tending or having power to deceive ⟨it turned out that the con man had made *false* promises of marriage to a dozen women⟩ — see DECEPTIVE 1

falsehood *n* **1** a false idea or belief ⟨the possibility of a perpetual motion machine is one *falsehood* that has been disproved by modern physics⟩ — see FALLACY 1
2 a statement known by its maker to be untrue and made in order to deceive ⟨several *falsehoods* in the witness's testimony that may be grounds for perjury⟩ — see LIE

falseness *n* **1** lack of faithfulness especially to one's husband or wife ⟨so that their love would never know a moment of *falseness*, Thomas Jefferson promised his dying wife that he would never remarry⟩ — see INFIDELITY 1
2 the act or fact of violating the trust or confidence of another ⟨she could not believe that her best friend could ever be guilty of such *falseness*⟩ — see BETRAYAL
3 the quality or state of being false ⟨the *falseness* of your reasoning is so blatant that it's no wonder you reached that absurd conclusion⟩ — see FALLACY 2

falsify *vb* to change so much as to create a wrong impression or alter the meaning of ⟨taking that statement completely out of context essentially *falsifies* it, whether that's your intention or not⟩ — see GARBLE

falsity *n* **1** a false idea or belief ⟨a letter condemning secularism and other movements that the church considered to be *falsities* of the modern age⟩ — see FALLACY 1
2 a statement known by its maker to be untrue and made in order to deceive ⟨when questioned by his parents about his drug use, the teenager told one blatant *falsity* after another⟩ — see LIE
3 lack of faithfulness especially to one's husband or wife ⟨the *falsity* of Guinevere usually figures prominently in medieval and modern tellings of the legend of King Arthur⟩ — see INFIDELITY 1
4 the act or fact of violating the trust or confidence of another ⟨despite being offered a fortune to spill the president's secrets, the trusted aide declared that he'd sooner die than be guilty of such *falsity*⟩ — see BETRAYAL
5 the quality or state of being false ⟨the *falsity* of Columbus's estimate of the earth's circumference was pretty much demonstrated when he made a head-on collision with the western hemisphere⟩ — see FALLACY 2

falter *vb* **1** to show uncertainty about the right course of action ⟨William Lloyd Garrison never once *faltered* in his demand that slavery be unconditionally abolished⟩ — see HESITATE
2 to swing unsteadily back and forth or from side to side ⟨the cut tree seemed to *falter* for a moment before crashing to the ground⟩ — see TEETER 1

faltering *n* the act or an instance of pausing because of uncertainty about the right course of action ⟨when it's so clear that this is the right thing to do, there's no excuse for *faltering*⟩ — see HESITATION

fame *n* the fact or state of being known to the public ⟨many go to Hollywood in search of *fame* and fortune⟩
synonyms celebrity, notoriety, renown
related words infamy; name, report, reputation, repute; cachet, position, prestige, rank, standing, stature; distinction, eminence, glory, greatness, honor, illustriousness, note, preeminence, prominence; acclaim, acknowledgment (*also* acknowledgement), praise, recognition; adoration, idolization
near antonyms disgrace, dishonor, disrepute, ignominy, odium, opprobrium, shame; unimportance
antonyms anonymity, obscurity

famed *adj* widely known ⟨San Francisco's *famed* Golden Gate Bridge⟩ — see FAMOUS

familial *adj* of or relating to a household or family ⟨it's a *familial* duty as well as a tradition for everyone in my family to eat dinner together⟩ — see DOMESTIC 1

familiar *adj* **1** closely acquainted ⟨the little inside jokes that people who have long been *familiar* like to share⟩
synonyms bosom, chummy, close, friendly, intimate, thick
related words affable, boon, companionable, convivial, cordial, genial, gracious, hearty; gregarious, sociable, social; comfortable, cozy, easy, snug; amicable, neighborly; confidential, secretive; affectionate, dear, devoted, fond, loving, warm
near antonyms aloof, cold, cool, reserved, standoffish, unfriendly, unsociable, withdrawn
antonyms distant
2 having information especially as a result of study or experience ⟨book editors who are *familiar* with what is being taught in the schools⟩
synonyms abreast, acquainted, conversant, informed, knowledgeable, up, up-to-date, versed

related words aware, cognizant, conscious, heedful, mindful

phrases in the know

near antonyms unaware, unconscious, unmindful; blind, oblivious, unknowing, unwitting

antonyms ignorant, unacquainted, unfamiliar, uninformed

3 often observed or encountered ⟨the woman and her pair of Welsh corgis were a *familiar* sight in the quiet neighborhood⟩ — see COMMON 1

4 showing a lack of proper social reserve or modesty ⟨rather too *familiar* for a first-time guest in our home, the woman kept asking how much we paid for this or for that⟩ — see PRESUMPTUOUS 1

familiar *n* a person who has a strong liking for and trust in another ⟨with old *familiars* the normally reserved writer can be quite warm and funny⟩ — see FRIEND 1

familiarity *n* **1** the state of being in a very personal or private relationship ⟨the elderly couple enjoys a *familiarity* that is the result of many years of happy marriage⟩

synonyms chumminess, closeness, inseparability, intimacy, nearness

related words immediacy; affinity, kinship; commitment, devotion; affection, fondness, love; constancy, faithfulness, fidelity; amity, fellowship, friendship, goodwill; affability, conviviality, cordiality, geniality

near antonyms aloofness, coldness, coolness, reserve

antonyms distance

2 a socially improper or unsuitable act or remark ⟨placing his hand on my shoulder was just one *familiarity* by the car salesman that I did not appreciate⟩ — see IMPROPRIETY 2

3 knowledge gained by personal experience ⟨the restaurant critic's considerable *familiarity* with restaurant kitchens should stand her in good stead⟩ — see ACQUAINTANCE

familiarize *vb* **1** to give information to ⟨the general's day-to-day duties included *familiarizing* the president on international developments⟩ — see ENLIGHTEN 1

2 to impart knowledge of a new thing or situation to ⟨one office worker is assigned with the task of *familiarizing* new staffers with the use of electronic equipment around the office⟩ — see ACQUAINT 1

family *n* **1** a group of persons who come from the same ancestor ⟨the Adams *family* made remarkable contributions to American life for more than two centuries⟩

synonyms blood, clan, folks, house, kin, kindred, kinfolk, kinsfolk, line, lineage, people, race, stock, tribe

related words nuclear family; extended family, kith; brood; descendant (*or* descendent), issue, offspring, progeny, scion, seed; clansman, kinsman, kinswoman, relative; dynasty

near antonyms ancestry, birth, descent, extraction, origin, pedigree

2 one of the units into which a whole is divided on the basis of a common characteristic ⟨the flute, the clarinet, the oboe, and other members of the woodwind *family*⟩ — see CLASS 2

family tree *n* the line of ancestors from whom a person is descended ⟨his *family tree* includes writers, musical composers, and other notables in the arts⟩ — see ANCESTRY

famine *n* a falling short of an essential or desirable amount or number ⟨there's a *famine* of good general practitioners in many rural areas⟩ — see DEFICIENCY

famished *adj* feeling a desire or need for food ⟨after a full day of skiing, I was feeling absolutely *famished*⟩ — see HUNGRY 1

famishment *n* a need or desire for food ⟨there's something about outdoor activity that invariably increases one's *famishment*⟩ — see HUNGER 1

famous *adj* widely known ⟨a book about some of the most *famous* people of the last century⟩

synonyms celebrated, famed, noted, notorious, prominent, renowned, star, well-known

related words fabled, fabulous, legendary; infamous; distinguished, eminent, exceptional, great, illustrious, leading, notable, outstanding, prestigious, remarkable; important, significant; favorite, popular, preferred; estimable, honorable, reputable, respectable; formidable, redoubtable

near antonyms insignificant, unimportant; inconspicuous; undistinguished, unexceptional; unpopular

antonyms anonymous, obscure, unknown

fan *n* a person with a strong and habitual liking for something ⟨life-long *fans* of country and western music⟩

synonyms addict, aficionado, buff, bug, devotee, enthusiast, fanatic, fancier, fiend, freak, lover, maniac, nut

related words groupie; admirer, collector, connoisseur, dilettante; authority, expert; cultist, disciple, follower, votary; backer, patron, promoter, supporter; partisan, zealot; booster, rooter, well-wisher; faddist

near antonyms belittler, carper, critic, detractor

fan (out) *vb* **1** to arrange the parts of (something) over a wider area ⟨the accordionist smoothly *fanned out* the bellows of his instrument as he played⟩ — see OPEN 3

2 to extend outwards from or as if from a central point ⟨most of the city's subway lines *fan out* from this central station⟩ — see RADIATE 1

fanatic *n* **1** a person with a strong and habitual liking for something ⟨football *fanatics* are pretty much booked up for weekends from Labor Day to Super Bowl Sunday⟩ — see FAN

2 one who is intensely or excessively devoted to a cause ⟨the vandalism was blamed on *fanatics* within the environmental movement⟩ — see ZEALOT

fanatic *or* **fanatical** *adj* being very far from the center of public opinion ⟨because of her *fanatical* views, her friends know better than to discuss religion with her⟩ — see EXTREME 2

fancier *n* a person with a strong and habitual liking for something ⟨chocolate *fanciers* generally like their favorite confection without the addition of milk or a lot of sugar⟩ — see FAN

fanciful *adj* **1** conceived or made without regard for reason or reality ⟨she harbors the *fanciful* notion that she has a talent for singing⟩ — see FANTASTIC 1

2 not real and existing only in the imagination ⟨the *fanciful* creatures that J.R.R. Tolkien created for his Middle Earth novels⟩ — see IMAGINARY

fancy *adj* made or done with great care or with much detail ⟨we're having a little get-together after the concert—nothing *fancy*⟩ — see ELABORATE 1

fancy *n* **1** a conception or image created by the imagination and having no objective reality ⟨a writer with a prodigious talent for creating *fancies* that captivate readers young and old⟩ — see FANTASY 1

2 a sudden impulsive and apparently unmotivated idea or action ⟨is this a serious interest in music, or just your latest *fancy* that will be forgotten after a week?⟩ — see WHIM

3 positive regard for something ⟨now that he's rich he's taken a *fancy* to expensive sports cars⟩ — see LIKING

4 the ability to form mental images of things that either are not physically present or have never been conceived or created by others ⟨to fans of Lewis Carroll, the animal creations of his fertile *fancy* are as real as any creature to be found at the zoo⟩ — see IMAGINATION

fancy *vb* **1** to form a mental picture of ⟨try to *fancy*, if you can, our mother on an elephant⟩ — see IMAGINE 1
2 to take pleasure in ⟨the teacher didn't *fancy* the idea of failing a student, even if he was the class clown⟩ — see ENJOY 1

fanny *n* the part of the body upon which someone sits ⟨be careful on that icy walk, unless you want to fall on your *fanny*⟩ — see BUTTOCKS

fantastic *adj* **1** conceived or made without regard for reason or reality ⟨a *fantastic* scheme for getting rich quick⟩
synonyms absurd, bizarre, crazy, fanciful, foolish, insane, nonsensical, preposterous, unreal, wild
related words inconceivable, incredible, unbelievable; extravagant, grotesque; eccentric, odd, peculiar, strange, weird; farcical, laughable, ludicrous, ridiculous
antonyms realistic, reasonable
2 excitingly or mysteriously unusual ⟨to European explorers, the Far East was a *fantastic* land filled with unimaginable riches⟩ — see EXOTIC
3 not real and existing only in the imagination ⟨a science fiction writer who can conjure up *fantastic* worlds as make them seem as real as our own⟩ — see IMAGINARY
4 too extraordinary or improbable to believe ⟨concocted some *fantastic* story to try to explain why they had returned home so late⟩ — see INCREDIBLE

fantasy *also* **phantasy** *n* **1** a conception or image created by the imagination and having no objective reality ⟨a constant daydreamer who started to believe his own *fantasies*⟩
synonyms chimera, conceit, daydream, delusion, dream, fancy, figment, hallucination, illusion, phantasm, pipe dream, unreality, vision
related words mirage; brainchild, idea; concoction, fabrication, fiction, invention; envisaging, imaging, visualization
near antonyms actuality, fact, reality
2 the ability to form mental images of things that either are not physically present or have never been conceived or created by others ⟨the painter gave free rein to his *fantasy* to create pictures that capture the kind of reality we experience only in our dreams⟩ — see IMAGINATION
3 something that is the product of the imagination ⟨we were coming to the conclusion that the person Karen "saw" in the woods was another one of her *fantasies*⟩ — see FICTION

far *adj* **1** lasting for a considerable time ⟨the primitive rafts that ancient peoples built for their *far* journeys across the wide expanses of Oceania⟩ — see LONG 2
2 not close in time or space ⟨the dream of someday sending manned spacecraft to explore the *far* reaches of our solar system⟩ — see DISTANT 1

far *adv* to a great degree ⟨the solid advice that if you can't say something good about a person, it is *far* better to say nothing at all⟩ — see VERY 1

faraway *adj* not close in time or space ⟨growing up in a seaport instilled in the youth a restless desire to travel to *faraway* places⟩ — see DISTANT 1

farce *n* **1** a poor, insincere, or insulting imitation of something ⟨the recall of a duly elected official for a frivolous reason is not democracy in action but a *farce*⟩ — see MOCKERY 1
2 humorous entertainment ⟨the rubber-faced, loose-jointed comedian is a master of knockabout *farce*⟩ — see COMEDY

farcical *adj* **1** causing or intended to cause laughter ⟨the *farcical* behavior of the troupe of circus clowns⟩ — see FUNNY 1
2 so foolish or pointless as to be worthy of scornful laughter ⟨the *farcical* routine that a person has to go through to get a refund from that company⟩ — see RIDICULOUS 1

fare *n* substances intended to be eaten ⟨that restaurant is well-known for serving only fresh, seasonal *fare* from local suppliers⟩ — see FOOD

fare *vb* **1** to meet one's day-to-day needs ⟨residents of the flood-ravaged town are *faring* much better than one might have expected⟩ — see GET ALONG 1
2 to move forward along a course ⟨families can be seen *faring* along the road to the campground driving or towing all manner of conveyance⟩ — see GO 1
3 to take a meal ⟨diners at this charming country inn will *fare* sumptuously in an authentic colonial atmosphere⟩ — see DINE 1

farewell *adj* given, taken, or performed at parting ⟨the singer's *farewell* tour seemed to last almost as long as her entire career⟩ — see PARTING 1

farewell *n* **1** an expression of good wishes at parting ⟨the exchange student and her host family said their tearful *farewells*, promising to keep in touch⟩ — see GOODBYE
2 the act of leaving a place ⟨before making his final *farewell*, the company president personally spoke to as many employees as he could⟩ — see DEPARTURE
3 the act or process of two or more persons going off in different directions ⟨our *farewell* was rushed, and we didn't say all that we wanted to before heading off to colleges at opposite ends of the country⟩ — see PARTING

far–fetched *adj* not likely to be true or to occur ⟨an exciting thriller, but one with a *far-fetched* plot that no sensible person could believe⟩ — see IMPROBABLE

far–flung *adj* having considerable extent ⟨it could once be said that the sun never set on the *far-flung* British Empire⟩ — see EXTENSIVE

farm *n* a piece of land and its buildings used to grow crops or raise livestock ⟨a *farm* that has been in the same family for five generations⟩
synonyms farmstead, grange, ranch
related words cropland, farmland, farmyard; farmhouse, homestead, manor, plantation; croft [*chiefly British*], station; garden, orchard

farm *vb* to work by plowing, sowing, and raising crops on ⟨we're planning on *farming* 50 acres the first year⟩
synonyms cultivate, tend, till
related words crop, plant; harvest, reap; harrow, hoe

farmer *n* a person who cultivates the land and grows crops on it ⟨a young *farmer* whose family has been growing wheat for many generations⟩
synonyms agriculturist (*or* agriculturalist), agronomist, cultivator, grower, planter, tiller
related words farmhand, gleaner, harvester, reaper; crofter [*chiefly British*], cropper, sharecropper; homesteader, nester [*West*]; granger; rancher, ranchero, ranchman

farming *adj* engaged in or concerned with agriculture ⟨years of drought had a devastating impact on the region's *farming* communities⟩ — see AGRICULTURAL

farming *n* the science or occupation of cultivating the soil, producing crops, and raising livestock ⟨since an ancestor settled there in the 19th century, *farming* has been the only occupation for six generations of the family⟩ — see AGRICULTURE

farmstead *n* a piece of land and its buildings used to grow crops or raise livestock ⟨many of the area's proud, old *farmsteads* have been bulldozed by developers to make way for condominiums⟩ — see FARM

far–off *adj* not close in time or space ⟨many a young person has joined the military with the hope of traveling to *far-off* places⟩ ⟨the impossibility of predicting what life will be like in the *far-off* future⟩ — see DISTANT 1

far–out *adj* different from the ordinary in a way that causes curiosity or suspicion ⟨the religious sect's *far-out* clothes and practices made them the talk of the small town⟩ — see ODD 2

far–reaching *adj* having considerable extent ⟨to the pioneers the *far-reaching* prairies seemed like an endless sea of grass⟩ — see EXTENSIVE

farsighted *adj* having or showing awareness of and preparation for the future ⟨*farsighted* conservationists long ago realized that wilderness areas of breathtaking beauty needed to be protected from future development⟩ — see FORESIGHTED

farsightedness *n* concern or preparation for the future ⟨thanks to our parents' *farsightedness*, we had sufficient emergency supplies when the storm knocked out our power⟩ — see FORESIGHT 2

farther *adj* resulting in an increase in amount or number ⟨for *farther* information on this condition, you should consult your family physician⟩ — see ADDITIONAL

farther *adv* at or to a greater distance or more advanced point ⟨they had traveled *farther* down the Colorado River than any previous explorers⟩
synonyms beyond, further, yon, yonder

farthermost *adj* most distant from a center ⟨it's a long trip to a major hospital for residents of the *farthermost* corners of the state⟩ — see EXTREME 1

farthest *adj* most distant from a center ⟨for privacy and quiet, we requested a hotel room that was *farthest* from the elevator⟩ — see EXTREME 1

fascinate *vb* 1 to attract or delight as if by magic ⟨for years the zoo's family of giant pandas have *fascinated* visitors⟩ — see CHARM 1
2 to hold the attention of as if by a spell ⟨I can gaze at the sea for hours, *fascinated* by the never-ending waves crashing upon the shore⟩ — see ENTHRALL 1
3 to hold the attention of ⟨the subject of artificial intelligence *fascinates* me⟩ — see ENGAGE 1

fascinating *adj* 1 having an often mysterious or magical power to attract ⟨the *fascinating* cities and peoples of central Asia have been intriguing travelers at least since the time of Marco Polo⟩
synonyms alluring, appealing, attractive, bewitching, captivating, charming, elfin, enchanting, engaging, entrancing, fetching, glamorous (*also* glamourous), luring, magnetic, seductive
related words enthralling, gripping, hypnotizing, mesmerizing, riveting, spellbinding; enticing, tantalizing, tempting; exciting, haunting, interesting, intriguing, titillating; beckoning, inviting, winning; darling, delightful, pleasing

near antonyms boring, irksome, tedious, tiresome; abhorrent, distasteful, invidious, loathsome, obnoxious, offensive
antonyms repellant, repelling, repugnant, repulsive, revolting
2 holding the attention or provoking interest ⟨the *fascinating*—but dubious—legend that Pocahontas rescued John Smith from certain death⟩ — see INTERESTING

fascination *n* the power of irresistible attraction ⟨the *fascination* that the subject of dinosaurs has for most children⟩ — see CHARM 2

fashion *n* 1 a practice or interest that is very popular for a short time ⟨during the 1990s tattoos once again became a hot *fashion* especially for young men⟩ — see FAD
2 a distinctive way of putting ideas into words ⟨when angry, he tends to express himself in a *fashion* that shows that he has a mastery of all of the expletives in which the English language abounds⟩ — see STYLE 1
3 a usual manner of behaving or doing ⟨it has long been my *fashion* to rise early⟩ — see HABIT
4 the means or procedure for doing something ⟨you can mix the ingredients in any *fashion* you choose—by hand or by machine⟩ — see METHOD

fashion *vb* to bring into being by combining, shaping, or transforming materials ⟨for the Christmas pageant my mother was able to *fashion* the length of fabric into something that could pass as a shepherd's outfit⟩ — see MAKE 1

fashionable *adj* 1 being in the latest or current fashion ⟨a shopping district filled with expensive boutiques selling *fashionable* clothing from the top designers⟩ — see STYLISH
2 enjoying widespread favor or approval ⟨that breed of dog became *fashionable* after it became the preferred dog among Hollywood celebrities⟩ — see POPULAR 1

fashionableness *n* the state of enjoying widespread approval ⟨the *fashionableness* of that look took a nosedive after it began to show up on some very unfashionable people⟩ — see POPULARITY

fast *adj* 1 moving, proceeding, or acting with great speed ⟨the *fast* pace of construction resulted in our new house being done ahead of schedule⟩
synonyms breakneck, breathless, brisk, dizzy, fleet, fleet-footed, flying, hasty, lightning, nippy, quick, rapid, rapid-fire, rattling, snappy, speedy, swift, whirlwind
related words expeditious, prompt, ready; hurried, quickened; breathtaking; energetic, strenuous, strong, vigorous
near antonyms crawling, dawdling, laggard, lingering, plodding, poky (*or* pokey), slowish, sluggish, unhurried; deliberate, leisurely, measured; dilatory, late
antonyms slow
2 firm in one's allegiance to someone or something ⟨the two girls soon became *fast* and inseparable friends⟩ — see FAITHFUL 1
3 firmly positioned in place and difficult to dislodge ⟨the rusty, old screws are so *fast* in the fitting that there's no hope of getting them out⟩ — see TIGHT 2
4 given to or marked by cheating and deception ⟨rolling back odometers was just one of the *fast* practices that the used-car dealer was guilty of⟩ — see DISHONEST 2
5 marked by the ability to withstand stress without structural damage or distortion ⟨as the storm approached, we checked to see that every thing on the

outside of the house was *fast* and locked in position⟩ — see STABLE 1

fast *adv* **1** with great speed ⟨run as *fast* as you can to get help⟩

synonyms apace, briskly, fleetly, full tilt, hastily, posthaste, presto, pronto, quick, quickly, rapidly, snappily, soon, speedily, swift, swiftly

related words immediately, promptly, readily; impetuously, impulsively, rashly, recklessly; abruptly, suddenly; energetically, vigorously

phrases at full tilt, by leaps and bounds, in short order

near antonyms laggardly, lingeringly, ploddingly, sluggishly; deliberately, leisurely

antonyms slow, slowly

2 to a full extent or degree ⟨the camp was *fast* asleep within minutes of hitting the sack⟩ — see FULLY 1

fasten *vb* **1** to cause (something) to hold to another ⟨use this paperclip to *fasten* your picture to the application form⟩

synonyms affix, attach, fix

related words adhere, bolt, clamp, clasp, clinch, clip, glue, hang, harness, lace, lash, latch, nail, paste, pin, rivet, screw, staple, stick, strap, tack, tie, yoke; connect, join, link, unite; reattach, refasten, refix

near antonyms part, separate, sever; loose, loosen

antonyms detach, undo, unfasten

2 to put securely in place or in a desired position ⟨don't forget to *fasten* all the lines on your tent⟩

synonyms anchor, catch, clamp, fix, hitch, moor, secure, set

related words embed (*also* imbed), entrench (*also* intrench), implant, ingrain, lodge, wedge

near antonyms extract, pry, yank

antonyms loose, loosen, unfasten, unloose, unloosen

3 to fix (as one's attention) steadily toward a central objective ⟨if you could *fasten* your attention on one task for more than a minute, you just might get something done⟩ — see CONCENTRATE 2

fastidious *adj* hard to please ⟨Jared is very *fastidious* about how he arranges his music collection, and woe to anyone who dares to mess around with it⟩ — see FINICKY

fastness *n* **1** a high rate of movement or performance ⟨the *fastness* with which the boy took his shower had us wondering if he'd used any water⟩ — see SPEED

2 a structure or place from which one can resist attack ⟨the guerillas retreated to their network of hidden *fastnesses* deep within the mountains⟩ — see FORT

3 adherence to something to which one is bound by a pledge or duty ⟨his *fastness* to the cause of freedom was beyond question⟩ — see FIDELITY

fat *adj* **1** having an excess of body fat ⟨the popular image of Santa Claus as a *fat* man in a red suit⟩

synonyms chubby, corpulent, fleshy, full, gross, obese, overweight, plump, portly, pudgy, roly-poly, rotund, round, tubby

related words beefy, bulky, chunky, heavy, heavyset, stocky, stout, thick, thickset, weighty; brawny, burly, husky; dumpy, squat, stubby; paunchy, potbellied; flabby, soft; buxom

near antonyms angular, bony, gaunt, lank, lanky, rawboned, sinewy, skinny; cadaverous, haggard, skeletal, wasted; puny, scraggy, scrawny, slight; reedy, twiggy, willowy

antonyms lean, slender, slim, spare, thin

2 containing or seeming to contain the greatest quantity or number possible ⟨the lake is so *fat* with trout

that you probably could catch fish with a bare hook⟩ — see FULL 1

3 having a greater than usual measure across ⟨a set of *fat* encyclopedia volumes took up the whole shelf⟩ — see WIDE 1

4 having or being of relatively great depth or extent from one surface to its opposite ⟨the splendid sight of a *fat*, juicy steak cooked to perfection⟩ — see THICK 1

5 producing abundantly ⟨the *fat* soil in the river's delta⟩ — see FERTILE

6 yielding a profit ⟨the highly sought-after baseball player signed a *fat* contract that set a record for the major leagues⟩ — see PROFITABLE 1

fat *n* **1** individuals carefully selected as being the best of a class ⟨makers of fine wine will pay very high prices for grapes that are the *fat* of the harvest⟩ — see ELITE

2 the state or an instance of going beyond what is usual, proper, or needed ⟨claimed that there was absolutely no *fat* in the military's budget⟩ — see EXCESS

fatal *adj* **1** bringing about ruin or misfortune ⟨I made the *fatal* mistake of sharing my secret with the school's biggest blabbermouth⟩

synonyms calamitous, cataclysmal (*or* cataclysmic), catastrophic, destructive, disastrous, fateful, ruinous, unfortunate

related words hapless, ill-fated, ill-starred, luckless

near antonyms fluky, fortuitous, fortunate, happy, lucky, providential; auspicious, bright, encouraging, golden, heartening, hopeful, promising, propitious

2 likely to cause or capable of causing death ⟨that snake's venom is *fatal* unless the victim is given the antidote almost immediately⟩ — see DEADLY

fatality *n* a person or thing harmed, lost, or destroyed ⟨the grim reminder that every holiday weekend inevitably results in a slew of highway *fatalities*⟩ — see CASUALTY 1

fate *n* **1** a state or end that seemingly has been decided beforehand ⟨the belief that it was this country's *fate* to extend from sea to sea⟩

synonyms circumstance, destiny, doom, fortune, lot, portion

related words accident, chance, hazard, luck; predestination; consequence, effect, issue, outcome, result, upshot

2 a condition or occurrence traceable to a cause ⟨the *fate* of the presidential election hinged on a few thousand votes in a single state⟩ — see EFFECT 1

fate *vb* to determine the fate of in advance ⟨the warning that the lack of an advanced education will *fate* a person to a lifetime of below-average earnings⟩ — see DESTINE

fateful *adj* bringing about ruin or misfortune ⟨a *fateful* encounter with a confidence man that they would long regret⟩ — see FATAL 1

fathead *n* a stupid person ⟨so who's the *fathead* who messed around with my movie collection?⟩ — see IDIOT

father *n* **1** a male human parent ⟨the special relationship that exists between *fathers* and sons⟩

synonyms dad, daddy, old man, pa, papa, pop

related words patriarch

2 a person who establishes a whole new field of endeavor ⟨Sir Isaac Newton is regarded by many as the *father* of modern science⟩

synonyms author, begetter, creator, establisher, founder, generator, inaugurator, initiator, instituter (*or* institutor), originator

related words conceiver, contriver, designer, formulator, innovator, inventor, spawner; builder, maker, producer; developer, pioneer, researcher; organizer, promoter; encourager, inspiration, inspirer
near antonyms disciple, follower, supporter
3 a person specially trained and authorized to conduct religious services in a Christian church ⟨a request that the *fathers* at the oratory remember the soul of a deceased relative in their prayers⟩ — see CLERGYMAN
4 a person who is several generations earlier in an individual's line of descent ⟨our *fathers* founded this nation on the fundamental belief that no person is entitled to rule by divine right⟩ — see ANCESTOR 1
5 *cap* the being worshipped as the creator and ruler of the universe ⟨let us ask humbly for the blessings of our *Father* in heaven⟩ — see DEITY 2
father *vb* to become the father of ⟨Paul Revere somehow found room in his small house for the large family he had *fathered*⟩
synonyms beget, get, sire
related words breed, multiply, procreate, propagate, reproduce, spawn; bear, engender, generate, produce
fatherland *n* the land of one's birth, residence, or citizenship ⟨though they had lived in their adopted country for many years, the immigrant families never broke their ties with the *fatherland* entirely⟩ — see COUNTRY 1
fathom *vb* to measure the depth of (as a body of water) typically with a weighted line ⟨the pilot had to continually *fathom* the river, which drought conditions had lowered to unprecedented levels⟩ — see ²SOUND 1
fatigue *n* a complete depletion of energy or strength ⟨the day-long battle against the blaze left firefighters in a state of utter *fatigue*⟩
synonyms burnout, collapse, exhaustion, lassitude, prostration, tiredness, weariness
related words debilitation, enervation, faintness, feebleness, weakness; languor, lethargy, listlessness; sluggishness, slumber, stupor, torpor; apathy, inertia, passivity
near antonyms energy, go, liveliness, pep, vigor, vitality; might, potency, strength
antonyms refreshment, rejuvenation, revitalization
fatigue *vb* to use up all the physical energy of ⟨the rescue workers pressed on, though their efforts to reach the miners had almost completely *fatigued* them⟩ — see EXHAUST 1
fatigued *adj* depleted in strength, energy, or freshness ⟨the *fatigued* hikers paused for some much-needed fun and frolic in the woodland stream⟩ — see WEARY 1
fatness *n* the condition of having an excess of body fat ⟨advised his patient that her *fatness* wasn't just unsightly—it was unhealthy⟩ — see CORPULENCE
fatty *adj* containing animal fat especially in unusual amounts ⟨*fatty* ground beef that was the cheapest available⟩
synonyms adipose
related words greasy, oily
near antonyms fibrous, gristly, stringy, tough; nonfat
antonyms lean
fatuity *n* **1** a foolish act or idea ⟨building another mall in an area that seems to already have a surplus of them seems like a gross *fatuity*⟩ — see FOLLY 1
2 lack of good sense or judgment ⟨the *fatuity* of the homeowner who used gasoline to burn a pile of brushwood⟩ — see FOOLISHNESS 1
3 the quality or state of lacking intelligence or quickness of mind ⟨the stupidity of the characters on that

TV sitcom is probably nothing in comparison to the *fatuity* of its creators⟩ — see STUPIDITY 1
fatuous *adj* **1** not having or showing an ability to absorb ideas readily ⟨the *fatuous* questions that the audience members asked after the lecture suggested to the oceanographer that they had understood little⟩ — see STUPID 1
2 showing or marked by a lack of good sense or judgment ⟨ignoring the avalanche warnings, the *fatuous* skiers continued on their course⟩ — see FOOLISH 1
faucet *n* a fixture for controlling the flow of a liquid ⟨don't forget to turn off the *faucet*⟩
synonyms cock, gate, spigot, stopcock, tap, valve
related words hydrant, spout
fault *n* **1** a defect in character ⟨the common *fault* of being quick to judge others⟩
synonyms demerit, failing, foible, frailty, shortcoming, vice, weakness
related words blot, spot, stain; blemish, deficiency, flaw; Achilles' heel; corruption, depravity, evil, immorality, sinfulness, wickedness
near antonyms excellence, perfection; goodness, integrity, morality, probity, rectitude, righteousness
antonyms merit, virtue
2 an unintentional departure from truth or accuracy ⟨there's a *fault* somewhere in the program⟩ — see ERROR 1
3 responsibility for wrongdoing or failure ⟨getting the time of the performance wrong was entirely my *fault*⟩ — see BLAME 1
4 something that spoils the appearance or completeness of a thing ⟨the minor *faults* in the leather are entirely natural and are what gives it a look different from vinyl⟩ — see BLEMISH
5 the state of being held as the cause of something that needs to be set right ⟨the auto accident was entirely the other driver's *fault*⟩ — see RESPONSIBILITY 1
fault *vb* to express one's unfavorable opinion of the worth or quality of ⟨you should look at your own work before *faulting* what others have done⟩ — see CRITICIZE
faultfinder *n* a person given to harsh judgments and to finding faults ⟨no sooner had we finished decorating the church than the parish *faultfinder* decided that she didn't like it⟩ — see CRITIC 1
faultfinding *adj* given to making or expressing unfavorable judgments about things ⟨publishers now have to produce textbooks that pass muster with a slew of *faultfinding* committees⟩ — see CRITICAL 1
faultily *adv* in a mistaken or inappropriate way ⟨discovered that the foreign ambassador's statement had been *faultily* translated⟩ — see WRONGLY
faultless *adj* **1** being entirely without fault or flaw ⟨this 18th-century chest of drawers is considered a *faultless* example of early American craftsmanship⟩ — see PERFECT 1
2 free from guilt or blame ⟨I may have broken my share of things in the past, but in this instance I am entirely *faultless*⟩ — see INNOCENT 2
faultlessly *adv* without any flaws or errors ⟨at the recital the young piano student performed the sonata *faultlessly*⟩ — see PERFECTLY 1
faultlessness *n* the quality or state of being free from guilt or blame ⟨the parents sought to assure the children of their complete *faultlessness* in the breakup of the marriage⟩ — see INNOCENCE 1
faulty *adj* having a fault ⟨the cause of the plane crash was traced to *faulty* wiring⟩

synonyms bad, defective, flawed, imperfect
related words fallible; blemished, broken, damaged, defaced, disfigured, impaired, injured, marred, spoiled; deficient, inadequate, incomplete, insufficient, wanting
near antonyms complete, entire, intact, whole; undamaged, unimpaired, unspoiled
antonyms faultless, flawless, impeccable, perfect

favor *n* **1** an act of kind assistance ⟨a good and generous friend who is always doing *favors* for others⟩
synonyms boon, courtesy, grace, indulgence, kindness, mercy, service, turn
related words dispensation, waiver; advantage, benefit, blessing, godsend, manna; liberty, license (*or* licence), privilege
near antonyms hindrance, impediment, obstacle
2 a feeling of great approval and liking ⟨entertainers often learn that the *favor* of the public can be fickle indeed⟩ — see ADMIRATION 1
3 an acceptance of something as satisfactory ⟨over the years that kind of movie fell out of *favor* with the mass audience⟩ — see APPROVAL 1
4 an attitude that always favors one way of feeling or acting especially without considering any other possibilities ⟨although his own son is on the hockey team that he coaches, Mr. Watkins conscientiously avoids any show of *favor*⟩ — see BIAS
5 positive regard for something ⟨was willing to do just about anything to keep the boss's *favor*⟩ — see LIKING
6 the state of enjoying widespread approval ⟨after that rock band fell out of *favor*—almost overnight—the stores couldn't give their CDs away⟩ — see POPULARITY

favor *vb* **1** to do a service or favor for ⟨although she was at the party as a guest, the singer *favored* us with a song⟩ — see OBLIGE 1
2 to have a favorable opinion of ⟨if this measure will reduce our property taxes, then I *favor* it⟩ — see APPROVE (OF)
3 to show partiality toward ⟨older moviegoers tend to *favor* films that have certain extras—like a plot and developed characters⟩ — see PREFER 1

favorable *adj* **1** expressing approval ⟨*favorable* reviews for the movie were few⟩
synonyms admiring, applauding, appreciative, approving, commendatory, complimentary, friendly, good, positive
related words eulogistic, laudatory, praiseful; respectful, supportive; adulatory, worshipful
near antonyms captious, carping, caviling (*or* cavilling), censuring, hypercritical, overcritical
antonyms adverse, disapproving, negative, unappreciative, uncomplimentary, unfavorable, unfriendly
2 pointing toward a happy outcome ⟨*favorable* conditions for opening a new business⟩
synonyms auspicious, bright, encouraging, golden, heartening, hopeful, promising, propitious
related words fortunate, happy, lucky, providential; advantageous, beneficial, profitable
near antonyms unfortunate, unhappy, unlucky; calamitous, catastrophic, disastrous, fatal, ruinous
antonyms discouraging, disheartening, futureless, hopeless, inauspicious, unfavorable, unpromising
3 conferring benefits; promoting or contributing to personal or social well-being ⟨moved to a region with a milder climate with the hope that it would be more *favorable* to his health⟩ — see BENEFICIAL
4 showing or expressing acceptance or approval ⟨a *favorable* reply to our request⟩ — see POSITIVE

favorably *adv* in a pleasing way ⟨Carla's violin teacher has been *favorably* impressed with her progress⟩ — see WELL 5
favored *adj* **1** granted special treatment or attention ⟨the youngest child, he was also the most *favored*—much to the envy of his siblings⟩ — see DARLING 1
2 singled out from a number or group as more to one's liking ⟨for a *favored* few, the restaurant always has a table available, no matter how busy it is⟩ — see SELECT 1
favorite *adj* granted special treatment or attention ⟨that teacher claims not to have any *favorite* students, although many in the class would disagree⟩ — see DARLING 1
favorite *n* a person or thing that is preferred over others ⟨the youngest child was always Mother's *favorite*⟩
synonyms darling, minion, pet, preference
related words beloved, dear; jewel, prize, treasure
near antonyms abomination, anathema, bête noire, bugbear
fawn *vb* to use flattery or the doing of favors in order to win approval especially from a superior ⟨a student who could not wait to *fawn* over the new teacher⟩
synonyms fuss, kowtow, toady
related words drool, gush, slaver, slobber; endear, ingratiate; court, woo; adulate, idolize, worship; blandish, cajole, coax, flatter, soft-soap; cower, cringe, grovel; abase, debase, demean; defer, submit, yield
phrases curry favor
near antonyms despise, disdain, scorn; gibe (*or* jibe), jeer, scoff; brave, challenge, defy
fawner *n* a person who flatters another in order to get ahead ⟨having surrounded himself with *fawners* who gave him only good news, the governor had no idea of the true state of affairs⟩ — see SYCOPHANT
fay *adj* given to good-natured joking or teasing ⟨with her slight build and perky manner, the actress was usually cast as the *fay* young woman who charms all the men in town⟩ — see PLAYFUL
fay *n* an imaginary being usually having a small human form and magical powers ⟨in the tale a *fay* appears in the form of a beautiful and serene woman with an angelic air and a billowy gown⟩ — see FAIRY
faze *vb* to throw into a state of self-conscious distress ⟨the collapse of part of the scenery didn't *faze* the actors one bit, and they just carried on⟩ — see EMBARRASS 1
fealty *n* adherence to something to which one is bound by a pledge or duty ⟨as much as I wanted to back my friend up, my *fealty* to the truth was greater, and I could not lie for him⟩ — see FIDELITY
fear *n* the emotion experienced in the presence or threat of danger ⟨the sight of the headless horseman filled the schoolmaster with *fear*⟩
synonyms alarm, anxiety, apprehension, consternation, dread, fearfulness, fright, horror, panic, terror, trepidation
related words phobia; creeps, jitters, nervousness, willies; pang, qualm, twinge; agitation, discomposure, disquiet, perturbation; concern, dismay, worry; cowardice, faintheartedness, timidity, timorousness
near antonyms aplomb, assurance, boldness, confidence, self-assurance, self-confidence; courage, dauntlessness, fearlessness, fortitude
fear *vb* to experience concern or anxiety ⟨Morgan's friends *feared* that she was dating a guy who was all wrong for her⟩ — see WORRY 1

fearful *adj* 1 causing fear ⟨the *fearful* roar of a lion⟩
  synonyms alarming, dire, direful, dreadful, fearsome, forbidding, formidable, frightening, frightful, hair-raising, horrendous, horrible, horrifying, intimidating, redoubtable, scary, shocking, terrible, terrifying
  related words daunting, disconcerting, discouraging, dismaying, disquieting, distressing, disturbing, perturbing, startling, threatening, troubling, trying; creepy, eerie (*also* eery), weird; ghastly, gruesome, nightmarish
  near antonyms comforting, consoling, inviting, reassuring, soothing; nonthreatening
  2 easily frightened ⟨the stray cat that we took in is still *fearful*, even around us⟩ — see SHY 1
  3 extreme in degree, power, or effect ⟨the *fearful* wind and cold simply made being outside a miserable experience⟩ — see INTENSE
  4 filled with fear or dread ⟨*fearful* of venturing out onto the dark highway, the stranded motorist decided to wait in the car for help⟩ — see AFRAID 1

fearfulness *n* the emotion experienced in the presence or threat of danger ⟨the *fearfulness* felt by hostages can scarcely be imagined⟩ — see FEAR

fearless *adj* feeling or displaying no fear by temperament ⟨skydiving is one sport that tends to attract *fearless* types⟩ — see BRAVE

fearlessness *n* strength of mind to carry on in spite of danger ⟨the *fearlessness* shown by the pioneers of the civil rights movement⟩ — see COURAGE

fearsome *adj* causing fear ⟨at night the child would always imagine that there were *fearsome* monsters lurking under his bed⟩ — see FEARFUL 1

feasible *adj* capable of being done or carried out ⟨would it be *feasible* to build a cabin in so short a time?⟩ — see POSSIBLE 1

feast *n* a large fancy meal often accompanied by ceremony or entertainment ⟨some 90 Native Americans showed up for the *feast* put on by the Pilgrims at Plymouth⟩
  synonyms banquet, dinner, feed, spread
  related words chow, repast; blowout, festival, fete (*or* fête), gala, party, shindig; festivity; barbecue, clambake, cookout, fry, luau, roast

feast *vb* to entertain with a fancy meal ⟨the returning war heroes were *feasted* all over the country⟩
  synonyms banquet, dine, junket, regale
  related words cater, feed; fete (*or* fête), honor

feat *n* 1 an act of notable skill, strength, or cleverness ⟨Washington's legendary *feat* of tossing a silver dollar across the Rappahannock River⟩
  synonyms deed, exploit, stunt, trick
  related words accomplishment, achievement, coup; adventure; performance
  2 something done by someone ⟨famously rich, the oil magnate is today remembered less for his *feats* than for his finances⟩ — see ACTION 1

feather *n* 1 a number of persons or things that are grouped together because they have something in common ⟨the two brothers are sports-obsessed jocks, and most of their friends are of the same *feather*⟩ — see SORT 1
  2 dressy clothing ⟨prom couples strutted into the ballroom in full *feather*⟩ — see FINERY

featherbrained *adj* lacking in seriousness or maturity ⟨some *featherbrained* youngsters giggled through the graduation ceremonies⟩ — see GIDDY 1

feathery *adj* having little weight ⟨the apple pie had a wonderfully *feathery* crust⟩ — see ¹LIGHT 1

feature *n* something that sets apart an individual from others of the same kind ⟨perhaps the most striking *feature* of that house is the way it was constructed to fit into its hillside site⟩ — see CHARACTERISTIC

feature *vb* to indicate the importance of by giving prominent display ⟨a restaurant *featuring* an extensive list of American wines to complement its creative American cuisine⟩ — see EMPHASIZE

feces *n pl* solid matter discharged from an animal's alimentary canal ⟨examined the animal's *feces* for signs of intestinal parasites⟩ — see DROPPING 1

fecund *adj* producing abundantly ⟨the Franklin stove, bifocals, and the lightning rod are just a few of the inventions that we owe to the *fecund* creativity of Benjamin Franklin⟩ — see FERTILE

fed up *adj* having one's patience, interest, or pleasure exhausted ⟨*fed up* with the noise and bustle of the big city, the family decided to try country life⟩ — see WEARY 2

federate *vb* to form or enter into an association that furthers the interests of its members ⟨in the years following World War II, the U.S. and the nations of western Europe made the decision to *federate* as the North Atlantic Treaty Organization⟩ — see ALLY

federation *n* an association of persons, parties, or states for mutual assistance and protection ⟨the new organization is a *federation* of existing organizations that were all dedicated to preserving Civil War battlefields⟩ — see CONFEDERACY

fee *n* the amount of money that is demanded as payment for something ⟨my dentist's *fees* seem to increase with every visit⟩ — see PRICE 1

feeble *adj* lacking bodily strength ⟨*feeble* members of the congregation are not expected to stand or kneel during services⟩ — see WEAK 1

feebleness *n* the quality or state of lacking physical strength or vigor ⟨the patient felt a lingering *feebleness* in the weeks following her heart surgery⟩ — see WEAKNESS 1

feed *n* 1 a large fancy meal often accompanied by ceremony or entertainment ⟨the company barbecue was an elaborate *feed* that was enlivened by country music and dancing⟩ — see FEAST
  2 food eaten or prepared for eating at one time ⟨after soccer practice we were all ready for a hot shower and a satisfying *feed*⟩ — see MEAL

feed *vb* 1 to provide food or meals for ⟨a charity dedicated to *feeding* the hungry⟩
  synonyms board, cater, provision
  related words serve, wait; nourish, nurture; banquet, dine, feast, regale; mess
  2 to put (something) into the possession of someone for use or consumption ⟨all week long Dad's been *feeding* me ideas for a science project⟩ — see FURNISH 2
  3 to take a meal ⟨an all-you-can-eat buffet where families can *feed* heartily and fairly inexpensively⟩ — see DINE 1

feed (on) *vb* to seize and eat (something) as prey ⟨the flycatcher is a bird that—as its name suggests—*feeds on* winged insects in midair⟩ — see PREY

feel *n* an indefinite physical response to a stimulus ⟨the warm *feel* that fine cashmere gives⟩ — see SENSATION 1

feel *vb* 1 to have a vague awareness of ⟨I *feel* trouble brewing in the town⟩
  synonyms perceive, scent, see, sense, smell, taste
  related words behold, discern, observe, view; ascertain, discover, learn; anticipate, expect, foresee

2 to come into bodily contact with (something) so as to perceive a slight pressure on the skin ⟨*feel* this blanket and perceive how soft it is⟩ — see TOUCH 1

3 to come to a knowledge of (something) by living through it ⟨with the birth of their first child the couple came to *feel* true happiness for the first time⟩ — see EXPERIENCE

4 to have as an opinion ⟨I just *feel* that we haven't explored all of our options for raising funds⟩ — see BELIEVE 2

5 to search for something blindly or uncertainly ⟨the sudden blackout had us *feeling* around in the dark for a flashlight⟩ — see GROPE

feel (for) *vb* to have sympathy for ⟨a reminder that during the holidays we should all *feel for* those families who have members serving in the military abroad⟩ — see PITY

feeling *n* **1** a subjective response to a person, thing, or situation ⟨an overall *feeling* of happiness about their new home⟩
synonyms emotion, passion, sentiment
related words impression, perception, sense; attitude, outlook, perspective, viewpoint; belief, opinion, view; responsiveness, sensibility, sensitiveness, sensitivity
2 feelings *pl* general emotional condition ⟨a remark that thoughtlessly hurt her *feelings*⟩
synonyms heartstrings, passions, sensibilities
related words cheer, frame, humor, mode, mood, temper
3 an idea that is believed to be true or valid without positive knowledge ⟨an interesting essay in which the student expressed her *feelings* about our nation's most pressing problems⟩ — see OPINION 1
4 an indefinite physical response to a stimulus ⟨that odd *feeling* of forward movement you get when the parked car next to you backs out⟩ — see SENSATION 1
5 sorrow or the capacity to feel sorrow for another's suffering or misfortune ⟨a rich person without much *feeling* for those who are less fortunate⟩ — see SYMPATHY 1
6 the capacity for feeling for another's unhappiness or misfortune ⟨a woman of great *feeling*, the princess wanted to use her status and influence to help the needy⟩ — see HEART 1

feign *vb* to present a false appearance of ⟨I would never *feign* illness just to get out of a test⟩
synonyms affect, assume, counterfeit, fake, pretend, profess, put on, sham, simulate
related words act, dissemble, impersonate, masquerade; forge, imitate; camouflage, conceal, disguise, mask; bluff, feint; malinger

feigned *adj* **1** lacking in natural or spontaneous quality ⟨the *feigned* applause that polite people give after a bad concert⟩ — see ARTIFICIAL 1
2 not being or expressing what one appears to be or express ⟨the *feigned* looks of innocence I got when I asked who had broken the lamp⟩ — see INSINCERE

felicitate *vb* to express to (someone) admiration for his or her success or good fortune ⟨the other contestants rushed to *felicitate* the winner of the spelling bee⟩ — see CONGRATULATE

felicitations *n pl* best wishes ⟨our heartfelt *felicitations* on the start of your new business⟩ — see COMPLIMENTS

felicitous *adj* **1** giving pleasure or contentment to the mind or senses ⟨a *felicitous* accompaniment to dinner is provided by a harpist on weekends at the restaurant⟩ — see PLEASANT

2 meeting the requirements of a purpose or situation ⟨the museum's restaurant is featuring a French menu as a *felicitous* complement to the current show on French Impressionism⟩ — see FIT 1

felicitously *adv* in a pleasing way ⟨the evening passed quietly but *felicitously* as we chatted with the other guests at the inn⟩ — see WELL 5

felicitousness *n* the quality or state of being especially suitable or fitting ⟨guests remarked on the *felicitousness* of the rose garden as a site for a June wedding⟩ — see APPROPRIATENESS

felicity *n* **1** a feeling or state of well-being and contentment ⟨told his friends that marriage had brought him a *felicity* that he had never known before⟩ — see HAPPINESS 1
2 something that provides happiness or does good for a person or thing ⟨in their old age their grandchildren were their most cherished *felicities*⟩ — see BLESSING 2

feline *n* a small domestic animal known for catching mice ⟨the commercial claims that the product will please the palate of even the most finicky *feline*⟩ — see CAT 1

fell *adj* **1** likely to cause or capable of causing death ⟨planning in the event that the enemy resorted to biological warfare and released some *fell* virus on the civilian population⟩ — see DEADLY
2 violently unfriendly or aggressive in disposition ⟨Captain Cook died in a scuffle with some *fell* natives of the Hawaiian Islands⟩ — see FIERCE 1

fell *vb* **1** to strike (someone) so forcefully as to cause a fall ⟨a boxer who was often *felled* in the first round⟩
synonyms bowl (down *or* over), down, drop, floor, knock (down *or* over), level
related words hit, jab, poke, punch, smite, sock, strike, whack
2 to bring down by cutting ⟨the settlers began the daunting task of *felling* the mighty trees that blanketed the island⟩
synonyms chop (down), cut (down), hew, mow
related words bulldoze, flatten, level, raze, tear down
3 to deprive of life ⟨the quest for a cure for malaria, the disease that *felled* so many during the digging of the Panama Canal⟩ — see KILL 1

fellow *n* **1** a male romantic companion ⟨most of the women were bringing their *fellows* to the banquet after the tournament⟩ — see BOYFRIEND
2 a person frequently seen in the company of another ⟨the singer's *fellows* were rumored to have ties to organized crime⟩ — see ASSOCIATE 1
3 an adult male human being ⟨what does a *fellow* have to do to get waited on around here?⟩ — see MAN 1
4 either of a pair matched in one or more qualities ⟨one ice skate isn't much good without its *fellow*⟩ — see MATE 1
5 one that is equal to another in status, achievement, or value ⟨he is well regarded as a chemist by his *fellows* in the field⟩ — see EQUAL

fellowship *n* **1** a friendly relationship marked by ready communication and mutual understanding ⟨the new counselor is eager to develop a trustful *fellowship* with the troubled teens at the center⟩ — see RAPPORT
2 a group of persons formally joined together for some common interest ⟨a *fellowship* of physicians dedicated to administering medical aid without regard to politics⟩ — see ASSOCIATION 2
3 kindly concern, interest, or support ⟨this music festival would not have been a success without the *fellow-*

ship of many people in the community⟩ — see GOOD-
WILL 1

4 the body of people in a profession or field of activity
⟨violated just about every ethical principle that the legal *fellowship* holds dear⟩ — see CORPS

5 the feeling of closeness and friendship that exists between companions ⟨the *fellowship* that exists among
members of a college fraternity⟩ — see COMPANION-
SHIP

female *adj* of, relating to, or marked by qualities traditionally associated with women ⟨*female* standards of
housekeeping imposed by the women at the vacation
cottage weren't especially popular with the men⟩ —
see FEMININE 1

female *n* an adult female human being ⟨the prospect of
being in close company with *females* was the main reason why some males joined the amateur theater
troupe⟩ — see WOMAN

feminine *adj* **1** of, relating to, or marked by qualities traditionally associated with women ⟨the *feminine* furnishings suggested that the bedroom was intended for a
girl⟩
  synonyms female, womanish, womanlike, womanly
  related words effeminate, girlish, sissy, unmanly; ladylike; distaff, petticoat
  near antonyms boyish, hoydenish, tomboyish; gentlemanly
  antonyms male, manlike, manly, mannish, masculine

2 having or displaying qualities more suitable for
women than for men ⟨Roger had a *feminine* giggle that
was an endless source of teasing from his buddies⟩ —
see EFFEMINATE

fen *n* spongy land saturated or partially covered with water ⟨a day spent trudging through the *fens* in quest of
game birds⟩ — see SWAMP

fence *n* a physical object that blocks the way ⟨the only
way to prevent motorists from trying to use that unsafe
bridge is to put a *fence* across the road leading to it⟩ —
see BARRIER

fence (in) *vb* to close or shut in by or as if by barriers
⟨*fencing in* the yard would keep our dog in as well as
keep unwanted stray dogs out⟩ — see ENCLOSE 1

fend (off) *vb* to drive back ⟨several bystanders rushed to
help the woman *fend off* the mugger⟩ — see REPEL 1

fender *n* something that serves as a protective barrier
⟨not wanting our brand-new cabin cruiser to get
scratched, we put thick rubber *fenders* between it and
the dock⟩ — see CUSHION

feral *adj* living outdoors without taming or domestication by humans ⟨animal experts discourage homeowners from trying to adopt *feral* animals as pets⟩ — see
WILD 1

ferment *n* a disturbed or uneasy state ⟨the city was in
ferment as its residents nervously awaited the airborne
invasion that was sure to come⟩ — see UNREST

ferment *vb* to cause or encourage the development of
⟨the various social and economic factors that *fermented* the major cultural change in the U.S. in the
1960s⟩ — see INCITE 1

ferocious *adj* **1** extreme in degree, power, or effect ⟨the
ferocious appetite that athletic teenagers have been
known to display⟩ — see INTENSE

2 marked by bursts of destructive force or intense activity ⟨*ferocious* forest fires threatened to destroy hundreds of homes in the scrubland⟩ — see VIOLENT 1

3 violently unfriendly or aggressive in disposition
⟨Captain Bligh and his castaways bypassed numerous

Pacific islands, so afraid were they of the *ferocious*
tribesmen⟩ — see FIERCE 1

ferry *vb* to support and take from one place to another
⟨there are shuttle buses to *ferry* visitors from the parking lots to the fairground⟩ — see CARRY 1

fertile *adj* producing abundantly ⟨the *fertile* mind of
Leonardo da Vinci explored art, architecture, engineering, mathematics, and many other fields⟩
  synonyms fat, fecund, fruitful, luxuriant, productive,
prolific, rich
  related words bearing, producing, yielding; abounding,
abundant, bountiful; copious, plenteous, plentiful;
blooming, bursting, flourishing, swarming, teeming,
thriving; creative, inventive, original
  near antonyms meager (*or* meagre), scant, scanty,
skimpy, spare, sparse
  antonyms barren, infertile, sterile, unfruitful, unproductive

fervency *n* depth of feeling ⟨the guest soloist was able to
infuse the familiar hymn with a moving *fervency*⟩ —
see ARDOR 1

fervent *adj* having or expressing great depth of feeling ⟨a
fervent speech that called for tolerance and compassion
for those who are different⟩
  synonyms ardent, blazing, burning, charged, emotional, fervid, feverish, fiery, flaming, glowing, hot-
blooded, impassioned, passionate, red-hot, vehement,
warm, warm-blooded
  related words gushing, maudlin, mawkish, mushy, sentimental; histrionic, melodramatic; enthusiastic, gung
ho, zealous; enamored, infatuated, obsessed
  phrases on fire
  near antonyms detached, dry, impersonal, objective;
reserved, undemonstrative
  antonyms cold, cool, dispassionate, impassive, unemotional

fervid *adj* having or expressing great depth of feeling ⟨at
the school board meeting the librarian delivered a *fervid* speech defending the classic novel against would-be
censors⟩ — see FERVENT

fervidness *n* depth of feeling ⟨the *fervidness* that the actor brought to the part of Romeo made the play fresh
all over again⟩ — see ARDOR 1

fervor *n* depth of feeling ⟨surprised by the *fervor* that her
parents' old love letters contained when she discovered
them in the attic⟩ — see ARDOR 1

festival *n* a time or program of special events and entertainment in honor of something ⟨tourists flock to the
town for its annual strawberry *festival*⟩
  synonyms carnival, celebration, festivity, fete (*or* fête),
fiesta, gala, jubilee
  related words jamboree, jollification, merrymaking,
revel, revelry; exhibit, exhibition, exposition, fair,
show; exercises, honors

festive *adj* indicative of or marked by high spirits or
good humor ⟨we arrived at the Christmas party to find
everyone already in a *festive* mood, perhaps owing in
part to the punch⟩ — see MERRY

festivity *n* **1** a mood characterized by high spirits and
amusement and often accompanied by laughter
⟨rather than mourn our friend's death we celebrated
his life, and his memorial service was more notable for
its *festivity* than its funereal gloom⟩ — see MIRTH

2 a time or program of special events and entertainment in honor of something ⟨year-long *festivities* will
mark the 300th anniversary of the city's founding⟩ —
see FESTIVAL

3 joyful or festive activity ⟨in keeping with their habit of doing everything in a big way, the couple's wedding will entail a whole weekend of *festivity*⟩ — see MERRY-MAKING

fetch *vb* to have a price of ⟨those old toys that we tossed away are now *fetching* big bucks as antiques⟩ — see COST

fetching *adj* having an often mysterious or magical power to attract ⟨the woman's *fetching* smile has long made the painting a favorite with visitors to the museum⟩ — see FASCINATING 1

fetch up *vb* to bring (something) to a standstill ⟨the driver *fetched up* the horse-drawn carriage in front of the church⟩ — see ¹HALT 1

fete *or* **fête** *vb* to show appreciation, respect, or affection for (someone) with a public celebration ⟨the returning servicemen and servicewomen were *feted* with a week's worth of celebrations⟩ — see HONOR

fete *or* **fête** *n* **1** a social gathering ⟨the heiress wanted to do something with her life other than shuttle from *fete* to *fete*⟩ — see PARTY 1
2 a time or program of special events and entertainment in honor of something ⟨the island's annual *fete* is a celebration of the daffodil in all of its springtime beauty⟩ — see FESTIVAL

fetid *adj* having an unpleasant smell ⟨that *fetid* cheese from Belgium is definitely an acquired taste⟩ — see MALODOROUS

fetish *also* **fetich** *n* **1** something about which one is constantly thinking or concerned ⟨dieting seems to be a *fetish* with some people⟩ — see FIXATION
2 something worn or kept to bring good luck or keep away evil ⟨an archaeologist discovering an old animal tooth that may have been worn as a *fetish*⟩ — see CHARM 1

fetter *n* **1** something that limits one's freedom of action or choice ⟨a time-honored tradition is fine as long as it doesn't become a *fetter* that prevents us from trying something new⟩ — see RESTRICTION 1
2 something that makes movement or progress more difficult ⟨claims that government regulations are unnecessary *fetters* that keep him from achieving his business goals⟩ — see ENCUMBRANCE
3 something that physically prevents free movement ⟨considered a seat belt a pointless *fetter*—until one saved his life in an auto accident⟩ — see BOND 1

fetter *vb* **1** to confine or restrain with or as if with chains ⟨museum artifacts that serve as somber reminders of the days when slaves were *fettered* with irons⟩ — see BIND 1
2 to create difficulty for the work or activity of ⟨the belief that too many rules and restrictions *fetter* children's creativity⟩ — see HAMPER

fettle *n* a state of being or fitness ⟨a visit to the relatives on the other side of the state revealed them all to be in fine *fettle*⟩ — see CONDITION 1

fever *n* an abnormal state that disrupts a plant's or animal's normal bodily functioning ⟨before the days of modern medicine, when death remained a mystery, people said that someone died of a *fever* and left it at that⟩ — see DISEASE

feverish *adj* **1** being in a state of increased activity or agitation ⟨scary stories that were the product of a *feverish* imagination⟩
synonyms agitated, excited, frenzied, heated, hectic, overactive, overwrought
related words ardent, burning, fervent, fiery, impassioned; high-strung, jittery, jumpy, nervous

phrases keyed up
near antonyms calm, composed, cool, serene, tranquil
2 having or expressing great depth of feeling ⟨the desperate prisoner made a *feverish* appeal for mercy⟩ — see FERVENT
3 marked by great and often stressful excitement or activity ⟨working at a *feverish* pace to get the project done on time⟩ — see FURIOUS 1

few *n* a small number ⟨a *few* of the songs on the album are good, but most are forgettable⟩
synonyms handful, scattering, smattering, sprinkle, sprinkling
related words minority
near antonyms majority, most; abundance, excess, plenty, surplus
antonyms army, crowd, flock, horde, host, legion, many, mountain, multitude

fiancé *n* the person to whom one is engaged to be married ⟨couldn't wait to show off her *fiancé* to all of her relatives⟩ — see BETROTHED

fiancée *n* the person to whom one is engaged to be married ⟨his *fiancée* is insisting on an elaborate wedding⟩ — see BETROTHED

fiasco *n* something that has failed ⟨undaunted by his early *fiascoes*, he continued to experiment⟩ — see FAILURE 3

fiat *n* an order publicly issued by an authority ⟨the school principal issued a *fiat* that caps were not to be worn inside the school, and that was that⟩ — see EDICT 1

fib *n* a statement known by its maker to be untrue and made in order to deceive ⟨the claim that everyday living would be impossible without at least a few innocent *fibs*⟩ — see LIE

fib *vb* to make a statement one knows to be untrue ⟨*fibbed* and said that he had remembered to water her plants while she was away⟩ — see LIE 1

fibber *n* a person who tells lies ⟨research that shows that children learn to become *fibbers* at a remarkably early age⟩ — see LIAR

fiber *n* the strength of mind that enables a person to endure pain or hardship ⟨a person of lesser *fiber* would not have spoken out against such an injustice⟩ — see FORTITUDE

fibrous *adj* resembling or having the texture of a mass of strings ⟨thick, *fibrous* hair that was not easy to comb⟩ — see STRINGY

fickle *adj* **1** likely to change frequently, suddenly, or unexpectedly ⟨a *fickle* friendship that was on and off over the years⟩
synonyms capricious, changeable, changeful, flickery, fluctuating, fluid, inconstant, mercurial, mutable, temperamental, uncertain, unpredictable, unsettled, unstable, unsteady, variable, volatile
related words aimless, erratic, haphazard, irregular, random; hesitating, shilly-shallying, vacillating, wavering; undependable, unreliable, untrustworthy; adaptable, mobile, protean, versatile
near antonyms equable, even, uniform; abiding, durable, lasting, permanent, persistent; dependable, reliable, trustworthy
antonyms certain, changeless, constant, immutable, invariable, settled, stable, steady, unchangeable
2 not true in one's allegiance to someone or something ⟨when the family's fortune disappeared, so did their *fickle* friends⟩ — see FAITHLESS

fiction *n* something that is the product of the imagination ⟨most stories about famous outlaws of the Old

West are *fictions* that have little or nothing to do with fact〉
synonyms fable, fabrication, fantasy (*also* phantasy), figment, invention
related words anecdote, narrative, novel, story, tale, yarn; falsehood, fib, lie, misrepresentation, untruth
near antonyms actuality, reality
antonyms fact

fictional *adj* not real and existing only in the imagination 〈the events in the horror movie seemed so real to some fans that they could not believe that the whole thing was *fictional*〉 — see IMAGINARY

fictitious *adj* not real and existing only in the imagination 〈his wartime exploits turned out to be entirely *fictitious*, as he had never even been in the military〉 — see IMAGINARY

fiddle *vb* to make jerky or restless movements 〈the executive *fiddled* with a pen as she impatiently waited for the meeting to begin〉 — see FIDGET

fiddle (around) *vb* to spend time in aimless activity 〈we spent the snow day just *fiddling around*〉
synonyms fool (around), mess (around), monkey (around), play, potter (around), putter (around), trifle
related words dally, dawdle, dillydally, hang around, hang out, idle, loaf, loll, lounge; clown (around), horse (around); tinker
near antonyms buckle (down)

fiddle (with) *vb* to handle thoughtlessly, ignorantly, or mischievously 〈I could tell that someone had been *fiddling with* the carefully set controls on my entertainment system〉 — see TAMPER

fiddlesticks *n pl* language, behavior, or ideas that are absurd and contrary to good sense 〈some people have one word for the game of golf: *fiddlesticks!*〉 — see NONSENSE 1

fidelity *n* adherence to something to which one is bound by a pledge or duty 〈they have never wavered in their *fidelity* to the cause of freedom〉
synonyms allegiance, constancy, dedication, devotedness, devotion, faith, faithfulness, fastness, fealty, loyalty, steadfastness
related words affection, attachment, fondness; determination, firmness, resolution; dependability, reliability, trustworthiness
near antonyms alienation, disaffection, estrangement, separation
antonyms disloyalty, faithlessness, falseness, inconstancy, infidelity, perfidiousness, perfidy, treachery

fidget *vb* to make jerky or restless movements 〈small children are likely to *fidget* in church〉
synonyms fiddle, jerk, squirm, toss, twitch, wiggle, wriggle, writhe
related words flit, flutter, twitter; quake, quiver, shake, shiver, tremble; pace
near antonyms relax, rest, unwind

fidgets *n pl* a state of nervousness marked by sudden jerky movements 〈one dental patient in the waiting room had a bad case of the *fidgets*〉 — see JUMPINESS

fie *interj* how surprising, doubtful, or unbelievable 〈*fie!* you expect me to believe that sorry excuse?〉 — see NO

field *n* 1 a small area of usually open land 〈a *field* that is the frequent site of neighborhood softball games〉
synonyms clearing, ground, lot, parcel, plat, plot, tract
related words common(s); grass, green, greensward, lawn; glade, grassland, heath, lea, meadow, moor, pasture
2 a region of activity, knowledge, or influence 〈the first woman to enter the *field* of medicine〉

synonyms area, arena, demesne, department, discipline, domain, line, province, realm, specialty, sphere
related words study, subject; territory, turf; business, occupation, profession, pursuit, racket, vocation
3 a part or portion having no fixed boundaries 〈if you set your camera lens to small aperture, the *field* of sharp focus will be quite large〉 — see REGION 1

fiend *n* 1 a mean, evil, or unprincipled person 〈even the utter horror of the terrorist attack did not deter some *fiends* from going on a looting spree〉 — see VILLAIN
2 a person who regularly uses drugs especially illegally 〈the miserable, wasted lives of narcotic *fiends*〉 — see DOPER
3 a person with a strong and habitual liking for something 〈comic-book *fiends* seem to have their own little world〉 — see FAN
4 an evil spirit 〈the legend that a *fiend* continues to haunt what was once the castle's torture chamber〉 — see DEMON

fiendish *adj* of, relating to, or worthy of an evil spirit 〈a *fiendish* delight in playing cruel tricks〉
synonyms demoniac (*also* demoniacal), demonic, devilish, diabolical (*or* diabolic), satanic
related words hellish, infernal; baleful, evil, sinister; malevolent, malicious, malignant; heinous, monstrous; barbarous, cruel, ferocious, inhuman, savage, vicious
near antonyms celestial, heavenly; beneficent, benevolent, benign, benignant; godly, holy, saintly
antonyms angelic

fierce *adj* 1 violently unfriendly or aggressive in disposition 〈the Vikings had a well-earned reputation for being *fierce* warriors〉
synonyms fell, ferocious, grim, savage, vicious
related words bellicose, belligerent, pugnacious, warlike; contentious, quarrelsome, truculent; menacing, threatening; bestial, brute, inhuman, inhumane; barbaric, uncivilized, wild; heartless, implacable, merciless, pitiless, relentless, ruthless, unrelenting, wanton; bloodthirsty, bloody, murderous; rapacious, ravenous, voracious
near antonyms amicable, congenial, friendly; compliant, submissive, tame, unaggressive; compassionate, kind, merciful; pacific, peaceable, peaceful; amiable, complaisant, obliging; human, humane; civilized, cultured
antonyms gentle, mild
2 extreme in degree, power, or effect 〈a *fierce* wind made the frigid temperatures seem even worse〉 — see INTENSE
3 harsh and threatening in manner or appearance 〈the *fierce* faces of the players on the opposing hockey team〉 — see GRIM 1
4 having or showing a bold forcefulness in the pursuit of a goal 〈a social reformer of *fierce* and fearless determination〉 — see AGGRESSIVE 1
5 marked by bursts of destructive force or intense activity 〈*fierce* fighting raged in the streets of the war-torn city〉 — see VIOLENT 1
6 marked by great and often stressful excitement or activity 〈*fierce* early-morning trading sent stocks soaring〉 — see FURIOUS 1

fierceness *n* the quality or state of being forceful (as in expression) 〈the *fierceness* of her denial prompted many people to wonder if maybe she was innocent after all〉 — see VEHEMENCE 1

fiery *adj* 1 being on fire 〈the *fiery* Yule log made a splendid backdrop for our holiday party〉 — see ABLAZE 1

2 having a notably high temperature ⟨the long, dangerous trek across the *fiery* desert⟩ — see HOT 1

3 having or expressing great depth of feeling ⟨the *fiery* preacher held the members of the revival meeting spellbound⟩ — see FERVENT

4 marked by a lively display of strong feeling ⟨the controversial editorial sparked a page's worth of *fiery* letters to the editor⟩ — see SPIRITED 1

fiesta *n* a time or program of special events and entertainment in honor of something ⟨the city's Latinos have a series of *fiestas* throughout the summer⟩ — see FESTIVAL

fight *n* **1** a physical dispute between opposing individuals or groups ⟨a troubled youth who got into one *fight* after another⟩

synonyms battle, clash, combat, conflict, contest, fracas, fray, hassle, scrap, scrimmage, scuffle, skirmish, struggle, tussle

related words pitched battle; brawl, free-for-all, melee; fisticuffs; confrontation, duel, face-off; altercation, argument, disagreement, quarrel, row, wrangle

2 a forceful effort to reach a goal or objective ⟨the mayoral candidate pledged to lead a successful *fight* to improve the city's schools⟩ — see STRUGGLE 1

3 an inclination to fight or quarrel ⟨a tough, streetwise kid with a lot of *fight* in him⟩ — see BELLIGERENCE

4 an often noisy or angry expression of differing opinions ⟨the couple have their share of *fights*, but they quickly get over them⟩ — see ARGUMENT 1

fight *vb* **1** to oppose (someone) in physical conflict ⟨a proud people who have fiercely *fought* all invaders of their homeland⟩

synonyms battle, clash (with), combat, scrimmage (with), skirmish (with), war (against)

related words duel; bash, batter, beat, buffet, hit, punch, slug, strike; box, spar; brawl; grapple, scuffle, tussle, wrestle; bump, collide

phrases fall foul (of)

near antonyms give up, submit, surrender

2 to strive to reduce or eliminate ⟨a civil rights leader who dedicated his life to *fighting* prejudice⟩

synonyms battle, combat, contend (with), counter, oppose

related words baffle, foil, frustrate, resist, thwart, withstand; confront, defy, face, meet

near antonyms abide, bear, endure, suffer; advocate, back, support, uphold

antonyms advance, encourage, foster, further, promote

3 to engage in a contest ⟨we're all *fighting* to see who can sell the most boxes of candy for the school band⟩ — see COMPETE

4 to express different opinions about something often angrily ⟨if you continue to *fight*, I'm turning this car around and we're heading back home⟩ — see ARGUE 2

5 to refuse to give in to ⟨I tried to *fight* the temptation to eat another cookie—and lost⟩ — see RESIST

fighter *n* **1** a person engaged in military service ⟨the debate whether more *fighters* are needed to bring order to that war-torn country⟩ — see SOLDIER

2 one that engages in the sport of fighting with the fists ⟨a program at the community center for training local youths as *fighters*⟩ — see BOXER

figment *n* **1** a conception or image created by the imagination and having no objective reality ⟨unable to find any tracks in the snow the next morning, I was forced to conclude that the man had been a *figment* of my imagination⟩ — see FANTASY 1

2 something that is the product of the imagination ⟨thus far, the invisible human being has been nothing more than a *figment* of fantasy writers⟩ — see FICTION

figurative *adj* expressing one thing in terms normally used for another ⟨the *figurative* meaning of "allergy" is "a feeling of dislike"⟩

synonyms extended, metaphorical

related words allegorical, emblematic (*also* emblematical), symbolic (*also* symbolical); euphemistic

near antonyms nonsymbolic

antonyms literal, nonfigurative

figure *n* **1** a character used to represent a mathematical value ⟨no doubt the *figures* on the price tags at the jewelry store are so small because the zeroes are so many⟩ — see NUMBER

2 a line that traces the outer limits of an object or surface ⟨we could gradually see the *figure* of a ship coming our way through the fog⟩ — see OUTLINE 1

3 a person who is widely known and usually much talked about ⟨*figures* from the worlds of sport and entertainment will be guests at the White House dinner⟩ — see CELEBRITY 1

4 a small statue ⟨painted wooden *figures* by untrained artists can be quite valuable on today's antique market⟩ — see FIGURINE

5 a three-dimensional representation of the human body used especially for displaying clothes ⟨the museum features a collection of *figures* strikingly attired in suits of medieval armor⟩ — see MANNEQUIN 1

6 a unit of decoration that is repeated all over something (as a fabric) ⟨upholstered the chair with a fabric embossed with *figures* of fleur-de-lis⟩ — see PATTERN 1

7 something that visually explains or decorates a text ⟨the layout editor could have done a better job of getting the *figures* on the same page as the portion of text they illustrate⟩ — see ILLUSTRATION 1

8 the amount of money that is demanded as payment for something ⟨a number of the paintings at the auction sold at *figures* far higher than had been estimated⟩ — see PRICE 1

9 the outward appearance of something as distinguished from its substance ⟨the ice sculpture at the banquet was in the *figure* of an eagle spreading its wings⟩ — see FORM 1

10 the type of body that a person has ⟨Martha has such a slender *figure* that just about anything looks good on her⟩ — see PHYSIQUE

11 figures *pl* the act or process of performing mathematical operations to find a value ⟨a person with a good head for *figures*⟩ — see CALCULATION

figure *vb* **1** to come to a judgment after discussion or consideration ⟨we *figured* that we had better arrive early at the concert in order to get good seats⟩ — see DECIDE 1

2 to decide the size, amount, number, or distance of (something) without actual measurement ⟨let's *figure* the juice in the pan to be about a cup and just add it to the mix⟩ — see ESTIMATE 2

3 to determine (a value) by doing the necessary mathematical operations ⟨the car dealer *figured* that our monthly car payment would be $357⟩ — see CALCULATE 1

4 to have as an opinion ⟨the father *figures* that girls should have the same athletic opportunities as boys and supports his daughter's interest in soccer⟩ — see BELIEVE 2

figure out *vb* to find an answer for through reasoning ⟨a book of brainteasers that even a really clever person won't have an easy time *figuring out*⟩ — see SOLVE

figurine *n* a small statue ⟨his collection of *figurines* includes toy soldiers from every war that America has fought⟩
synonyms figure, statuette
related words doll, marionette, puppet; bust, figurehead; carving, model, sculpture; dummy, form, mannequin
antonyms colossus

figuring *n* the act or process of performing mathematical operations to find a value ⟨the *figuring* of the cost of the car repair was rushed, and so it bears little resemblance to the actual result⟩ — see CALCULATION

filch *vb* to take (something) without right and with an intent to keep ⟨too hungry to wait until the party had started, he *filched* a cookie from the buffet table when no one was looking⟩ — see STEAL 1

file *n* a series of persons or things arranged one behind another ⟨a long *file* of people waiting to get tickets to the game⟩ — see LINE 1

¹**file** *vb* to make smooth by friction ⟨beautifully *filed* nails that obviously had been done by a manicurist⟩ — see GRIND 1

²**file** *vb* to move along with a steady regular step especially in a group ⟨to the strains of that familiar music, this year's graduating class *filed* into the auditorium⟩ — see MARCH 1

fill *n* soft material that is used to fill the hollow parts of something ⟨we ripped the tag off years ago, so we have no idea what the *fill* in that pillow is⟩ — see FILLING

fill *vb* **1** to put into (something) as much as can be held or contained ⟨*fill* the basket with apples⟩
synonyms charge, cram, heap, jam, jam-pack, load, pack, stuff
related words flood, glut, swamp; crowd, crush, press, ram, shove, squash, squeeze; refill, reload, repack
near antonyms lighten
antonyms empty
2 to close up so that no empty spaces remain ⟨before starting to paint, *fill* all the cracks with putty⟩
synonyms block, bung, dam, pack, plug, stop, stuff
related words choke, clog, obstruct; caulk, chink
near antonyms excavate, hollow (out), scoop (out)
3 to do what is required by the terms of ⟨orders received by this date will be *filled* in time for Christmas delivery of the merchandise⟩ — see FULFILL 1

filled *adj* containing or seeming to contain the greatest quantity or number possible ⟨*filled* baskets of every variety of apple were available at the farmers' market⟩ — see FULL 1

filler *n* soft material that is used to fill the hollow parts of something ⟨the vase was packed in Styrofoam *filler* to protect it during shipping⟩ — see FILLING

fill in *vb* **1** to give information to ⟨the friend quickly *filled* me *in* on the portion of the movie that I had missed⟩ — see ENLIGHTEN 1
2 to serve as a replacement usually for a time only ⟨she's only *filling in* while the regular secretary is on vacation⟩ — see COVER 1

filling *n* soft material that is used to fill the hollow parts of something ⟨the *filling* for the parka is goose down⟩
synonyms fill, filler, padding, stuffing
related words interlining, lining, wadding; cushion

film *n* **1** a story told by means of a series of continuously projected pictures and a sound track ⟨watched a *film* on the Hopi Indians during our social studies class⟩ — see MOVIE 1
2 the art or business of making a movie ⟨learned about some of the special-effects techniques used in *film*⟩ — see MOVIE 2

filmy *adj* **1** being of a material lacking in sturdiness or substance ⟨*filmy* cobwebs covering the entry⟩ — see FLIMSY 1
2 very thin and easy to see through ⟨those *filmy* curtains don't block out enough light⟩ — see SHEER 1

filter *vb* **1** to pass through a filter ⟨steep the tea and then *filter* it to get rid of the leaves⟩ — see STRAIN 2
2 to remove usually visible impurities from ⟨after frying the chicken, Mother *filtered* the oil and kept it in the refrigerator to use again⟩ — see CLARIFY 1

filth *n* **1** foul matter that mars the purity or cleanliness of something ⟨the *filth* in the restaurant's kitchen was unbelievable⟩
synonyms dirt, grime, muck, smut, soil
related words scum, sewage, slime, sludge, swill; garbage, refuse, trash; soot; dirtiness, filthiness, foulness, griminess, grubbiness, nastiness, squalidness, uncleanliness, uncleanness
near antonyms cleanliness, cleanness
2 the quality or state of being obscene ⟨films full of *filth* and violence⟩ — see OBSCENITY 1

filthiness *n* **1** the quality or state of being obscene ⟨the book was banned primarily because of the *filthiness* of the language⟩ — see OBSCENITY 1
2 the state or quality of being dirty ⟨the *filthiness* of the oven in the vacated apartment⟩ — see DIRTINESS 1

filthy *adj* **1** depicting or referring to sexual matters in a way that is unacceptable in polite society ⟨you simply cannot use *filthy* language in this school⟩ — see OBSCENE 1
2 not clean ⟨you can't go to the concert unless you clean this *filthy* room first⟩ — see DIRTY 1

finagle *vb* to plan out usually with subtle skill or care ⟨let me look at my schedule and see if I can't *finagle* a visit to the museum⟩ — see ENGINEER

final *adj* **1** following all others of the same kind in order or time ⟨this will be my *final* order⟩ — see LAST
2 having been established and usually not subject to change ⟨the wedding date is *final*⟩ — see FIXED 1

finale *n* the last part of a process or action ⟨the *finale* to the festivities was a grand display of fireworks⟩
synonyms close, closing, conclusion, consummation, end, ending, finis, finish, windup
related words apex, climax, crescendo, culmination, peak, summit, zenith; aftermath, anticlimax, coda, epilogue, postscript; tag end, tail end
near antonyms introduction, overture, prelude, prologue
antonyms beginning, dawn, opening, start

finalize *vb* to bring (something) to a state where nothing remains to be done ⟨we're still *finalizing* our travel plans but hope to have finished making them by the end of the week⟩ — see FINISH 1

finally *adv* at a later time ⟨we're making steady progress and may *finally* finish this project⟩ — see YET 1

finance *vb* **1** to provide money for ⟨a local business kindly *financed* the high school band's trip to New York City⟩
synonyms capitalize, endow, fund, stake, subsidize, underwrite
related words grubstake; aid, back, patronize, sponsor, support

2 to furnish (as an institution) with a regular source of income ⟨established a fund to *finance* a visiting lecturer position at the local college⟩ — see ENDOW 2

finances *n pl* available money ⟨will have to take a look at our *finances* to see if we can afford it⟩ — see FUND 2

financial *adj* of or relating to money, banking, or investments ⟨the *financial* world was watching the stock market closely⟩

synonyms fiscal, monetary, pecuniary

related words capitalist (*or* capitalistic), commercial, economic

find *n* something discovered ⟨that antique plate was a great garage sale *find*⟩ — see DISCOVERY 2

find *vb* **1** to come upon after searching, study, or effort ⟨we finally *found* the information after searching dozens of Internet sites⟩

synonyms ascertain, descry, detect, determine, dig (up), discover, find out, get, hit (on *or* upon), hunt (down *or* up), learn, locate, run down, scare up, scout (up), track (down)

related words espy, sight, spot; look for, search (for *or* out), seek

near antonyms lose, mislay, misplace

antonyms miss, overlook, pass over

2 to come upon unexpectedly or by chance ⟨hey, I *found* my notebook!⟩ — see HAPPEN (ON *or* UPON)

finding *n* **1** a decision made by a court or tribunal regarding a case it has heard ⟨the Supreme Court's *finding* was that the state law was unconstitutional⟩ — see SENTENCE

2 the act or process of sighting or learning the existence of something for the first time ⟨the scientists were thrilled with the *finding* of the new fossil⟩ — see DISCOVERY 1

find out *vb* **1** to come to an awareness ⟨that was around the time that I *found out* I was adopted⟩ — see DISCOVER 1

2 to come upon after searching, study, or effort ⟨*found out* where she lived by checking the phone book⟩ — see FIND 1

fine *adj* **1** consisting of very small particles ⟨the *fine* sand found on the island's beaches⟩

synonyms dusty, floury, powdery

related words smooth; filtered, pulverized, refined

near antonyms rough; unfiltered, unrefined; gravelly, gritty, sandy; pebbly, rocky, stony (*also* stoney); lumpy, mealy

antonyms coarse, grainy, granular, granulated

2 made or done with extreme care and accuracy ⟨the *fine* distinction between bravery and recklessness⟩

synonyms delicate, exact, hairline, hairsplitting, minute, nice, refined, subtle

related words nitpicking, quibbling; petty, piddling, trifling, trivial; fastidious, finicky, fussy, particular

near antonyms apparent, clear, obvious; broad, indefinite; careless, slapdash, slipshod, sloppy

antonyms coarse, inexact, rough

3 being of less than usual width ⟨use a *fine* line for the outline of the facial features you intend to carve into the pumpkin⟩ — see NARROW 1

4 being to one's liking ⟨that is *fine* with me⟩ — see SATISFACTORY 1

5 free from added matter ⟨that silver is .9600 *fine*⟩ — see PURE 1

6 meeting the highest standard of accuracy ⟨making the final *fine* adjustments on the car⟩ — see PRECISE 1

7 of a level of quality that meets one's needs or standards ⟨the wine steward declared that the complaint

was unjustified and that the wine was *fine*⟩ — see ADEQUATE

8 of a size that is less than average ⟨read the *fine* print⟩ — see SMALL 1

9 of the very best kind ⟨a *fine* performance of a classic ballet⟩ — see EXCELLENT

fine *adv* in a satisfactory way ⟨you did just *fine*⟩ — see WELL 1

fine *n* a sum of money to be paid as a punishment ⟨a $50 *fine* for speeding⟩

synonyms damages, forfeit, forfeiture, mulct, penalty

related words reparations; award, compensation; indemnity

fine *vb* to establish or apply as a charge or penalty ⟨I'll have to *fine* you for driving with one headlight out⟩ — see IMPOSE

fineness *n* **1** the quality or state of being little in size ⟨the *fineness* of the grains of sand enhances the appeal of the beach⟩ — see SMALLNESS

2 the quality or state of being very accurate ⟨the *fineness* of the telescope's lens and mirror⟩ — see PRECISION

3 the state or quality of having a delicate structure ⟨the *fineness* of the cat's bones⟩ — see DELICACY 2

finery *n* dressy clothing ⟨the guests arrived at the wedding in all their *finery*⟩

synonyms array, best, bravery, caparison, feather, frippery, full dress, gaiety (*also* gayety), regalia

related words apparel, attire, costume, duds, raiment

near antonyms rags, tatters

finesse *n* mental skill or quickness ⟨maneuvered his opponent into checkmate with his customary *finesse*⟩ — see DEXTERITY 1

finesse *vb* to plan out usually with subtle skill or care ⟨had to *finesse* the schedule a bit to fit in another patient that afternoon⟩ — see ENGINEER

finicky *adj* hard to please ⟨cats have a reputation for being *finicky* eaters⟩

synonyms choosy (*or* choosey), dainty, delicate, demanding, exacting, fastidious, fussy, nice, old-maidish, particular, picky

related words discerning, discriminating, insightful, knowledgeable; carping, critical; careful, meticulous, punctilious, scrupulous; queasy (*also* queazy), squeamish; peevish, petulant, prickly, touchy

near antonyms affable, breezy, devil-may-care, happy-go-lucky, laid-back; flexible, lax, loose; lenient, permissive; uncritical

antonyms undemanding, unfussy

finis *n* the last part of a process or action ⟨if the two countries keep up their arms race, the inevitable *finis* to their rivalry will be their mutual destruction⟩ — see FINALE

finish *n* **1** the last part of a process or action ⟨a pie-eating contest is the fair's traditional *finish*⟩ — see FINALE

2 the stopping of a process or activity ⟨an all-out fight right to the *finish*⟩ — see END 1

finish *vb* **1** to bring (something) to a state where nothing remains to be done ⟨we should *finish* the painting of the house by tomorrow⟩

synonyms complete, consummate, finalize, perfect

related words follow through, see out, stick out; accomplish, achieve, effect; discharge, execute, fulfill (*or* fulfil), perform; machine, polish, refine, round (off *or* out), shine, touch up

near antonyms abandon, desert, drop, forsake, quit

2 to bring (an event) to a natural or appropriate stopping point ⟨we'll *finish* the concert before dark⟩ — see CLOSE 3

3 to come to an end ⟨the three-day race *finished* yesterday⟩ — see CEASE 1

finished *adj* brought or having come to an end ⟨the frosting isn't *finished* until you've added all of the decorative roses⟩ — see COMPLETE 2

finite *adj* **1** having a limit ⟨our nation's natural resources are abundant, but they are also *finite*⟩
synonyms limited
related words confined, restricted; definable, defined, definite, determinate; decided, established, fixed, set; exact, precise, specific
near antonyms unconfined, unrestricted; indefinite, indeterminate, undefinable, undefined
antonyms boundless, infinite, unbounded, unlimited
2 having distinct or certain limits ⟨we have a *finite* number of options to consider⟩ — see LIMITED 1

fire *n* a destructive burning ⟨a number of suspicious *fires* in the neighborhood recently⟩
synonyms conflagration, holocaust, inferno
related words blaze, flare-up; backfire, bonfire, forest fire, wildfire; arson

fire *vb* **1** to cause (a projectile) to be driven forward with force ⟨police officers *firing* rubber bullets⟩ — see SHOOT 1
2 to cause a weapon to release a missile with great force ⟨soldiers *fired* at the enemy in panic-stricken disorder⟩ — see SHOOT 2
3 to give life, vigor, or spirit to ⟨the trip to the zoo managed to *fire* up the bored schoolchildren⟩ — see ANIMATE
4 to let go from office, service, or employment ⟨*fired* the secretary for incompetence⟩ — see DISMISS 1
5 to send through the air especially with a quick forward motion of the arm ⟨*fired* a pass to the running back⟩ — see THROW
6 to set (something) on fire ⟨lit some kindling before attempting to *fire* the logs⟩ — see BURN 2

fire (up) *vb* to rouse to strong feeling or action ⟨the dynamic speaker *fired* the audience *up*⟩ — see PROVOKE 1

firearm *n* a portable weapon from which a shot is discharged by gunpowder ⟨need a permit to carry a *firearm*⟩ — see GUN 1

firebrand *n* a person who stirs up public feelings especially of discontent ⟨a *firebrand* who urged crowds to riot during the blackouts⟩ — see AGITATOR

firebug *n* a person who deliberately and unlawfully sets fire to a building or other property ⟨after the second suspicious fire, police set a trap for the *firebug*⟩ — see ARSONIST

fireproof *adj* incapable of being burned ⟨remember to store valuable papers in a *fireproof* box⟩ — see INCOMBUSTIBLE

fireside *n* the place where one lives ⟨couldn't wait to get off the plane and back to his comfortable *fireside*⟩ — see HOME 1

fireworks *n pl* an outburst or display of excited anger ⟨can we have a calm, rational discussion without the usual *fireworks*?⟩ — see TANTRUM

firing *n* a directed propelling of a missile by a firearm or artillery piece ⟨found a flaw in the gun's *firing*⟩ — see SHOT

firkin *n* an enclosed wooden vessel for holding beverages ⟨the innkeeper opened up a *firkin* of his special ale for the weary travelers⟩ — see CASK

firm *adj* **1** not showing weakness or uncertainty ⟨a friendly fellow with a ready smile and a *firm* handshake⟩
synonyms forceful, hearty, iron, lusty, robust, solid, stout, strong, sturdy, vigorous
related words mighty, powerful, tough, unyielding; animated, energetic, lively, spirited; certain, confident, sanguine, sure
near antonyms feeble, fragile, frail; limp, listless, spiritless
antonyms uncertain, weak
2 having a consistency that does not easily yield to pressure ⟨cold butter that was too *firm* to spread⟩
synonyms compact, hard, rigid, solid, stiff, unyielding
related words case-hardened, compacted, compressed, hardened, indurated, stiffened, tempered; close, dense, heavy, thick, thickset; inelastic, inflexible, ramrod, unbending; compressed, condensed; sturdy, substantial; impenetrable, impermeable, nonporous
near antonyms loose, scattered, thin; bendable, elastic, flexible, malleable, pliable; flaccid, floppy, limp, slack; airy, light; permeable, porous
antonyms flabby, soft, spongy, squashy, squishy
3 firmly positioned in place and difficult to dislodge ⟨was *firm* in the saddle during the canter⟩ — see TIGHT 2
4 fully committed to achieving a goal ⟨asked him to reconsider, but he was *firm* in his commitment to the project⟩ — see DETERMINED 1
5 having been established and usually not subject to change ⟨the selling price of the house is *firm*, so there'll be no dickering⟩ — see FIXED 1
6 marked by the ability to withstand stress without structural damage or distortion ⟨built on a *firm* foundation, so the house hasn't settled⟩ — see STABLE 1

firm *n* a commercial or industrial activity or organization ⟨merged with another *firm* to form a larger business⟩ — see ENTERPRISE 1

firm (up) *vb* to become physically firm or solid ⟨wait for the modeling clay to *firm up* before handling the finished pot⟩ — see HARDEN 1

firmament *n* the expanse of air surrounding the earth ⟨the stars in the *firmament* twinkled ever so brightly⟩ — see SKY

firmly *adv* in a vigorous and forceful manner ⟨stomped his feet *firmly* to get the snow off his boots⟩ — see HARD 3

firmness *n* **1** firm or unwavering adherence to one's purpose ⟨a woman of remarkable *firmness* in the achievement of the goals she has set for herself⟩ — see DETERMINATION 1
2 the ability to withstand force or stress without being distorted, dislodged, or damaged ⟨test the *firmness* of the concrete before parking the car on it⟩ — see STABILITY 1

first *adj* **1** coming before all others in time or order ⟨the much-studied *first*—and last—voyage of the *Titanic*⟩
synonyms earliest, inaugural, initial, maiden, original, pioneer, premier
related words ancient, early, primal, primary, primeval, primitive, primordial; antecedent, preceding, previous
near antonyms advanced, late; ensuing, following, subsequent, succeeding
antonyms final, last, terminal, ultimate
2 coming before all others in importance ⟨there are a number of reasons you can't go, but the *first* is that we don't have the money⟩ — see FOREMOST 1

3 highest in rank or authority ⟨auditioned and got *first* clarinet in the band⟩ — see HEAD

first *adv* **1** as a substitute ⟨eat peas? I'd eat cockroaches *first*⟩ — see INSTEAD

2 by choice or preference ⟨we will not give in, but will fight for our freedom *first*⟩ — see RATHER 1

first–class *adj* of the very best kind ⟨a *first-class* production of a classic American musical⟩ — see EXCELLENT

firsthand *adj* done or working without something else coming in between ⟨had *firsthand* knowledge of the events of that evening⟩ — see DIRECT 1

firstly *adv* in the beginning ⟨*firstly*, gather all the ingredients together⟩ — see ORIGINALLY

first–rate *adj* of the very best kind ⟨wanted a *first-rate* bike and not the cheap model she had been using⟩ — see EXCELLENT

firth *n* a part of a body of water that extends beyond the general shoreline ⟨the *Firth* of Forth in Scotland⟩ — see GULF 1

fiscal *adj* of or relating to money, banking, or investments ⟨gained some *fiscal* knowledge by taking an economics course⟩ — see FINANCIAL

fish *vb* to search for something blindly or uncertainly ⟨*fish* for some change to drop in the donation box⟩ — see GROPE

fishy *adj* giving good reason for being doubted, questioned, or challenged ⟨something's *fishy* about the way he's acting⟩ — see DOUBTFUL 2

fissure *n* an irregular usually narrow break in a surface created by pressure ⟨lava flows up through a *fissure* in the earth's crust⟩ — see CRACK 1

fit *adj* **1** meeting the requirements of a purpose or situation ⟨clothing that is *fit* for horseback riding⟩

synonyms applicable, appropriate, apt, becoming, befitting, felicitous, fitting, good, happy, meet, proper, right, suitable

related words just, justified; needed, required, requisite; able, capable, competent, qualified, trained; acceptable, adequate, decent, satisfactory, tolerable; correct, decorous, respectable, seemly

near antonyms incompetent, unqualified, untrained; inadequate, intolerable, unacceptable, unsatisfactory; incorrect, indecorous, unseemly

antonyms improper, inapplicable, inappropriate, inapt, infelicitous, unhappy, unsuitable, wrong

2 being in a state of fitness for some experience or action ⟨*fit* for military service⟩ — see READY 1

3 capable of or suitable for being used for a particular purpose ⟨I don't think those bald tires are *fit* for winter driving⟩ — see USABLE 1

4 enjoying health and vigor ⟨eat well and stay *fit*⟩ — see HEALTHY 1

5 having the required skills for an acceptable level of performance ⟨need to hire someone whose language skills make them *fit* for the job⟩ — see COMPETENT

fit *n* **1** a sudden experiencing of a physical or mental disorder ⟨without her medication, she'd have an epileptic *fit*⟩ — see ATTACK 2

2 a sudden intense expression of strong feeling ⟨helpless *fits* of laughter from the audience⟩ — see OUTBURST 1

3 an outburst or display of excited anger ⟨found out he couldn't go to the amusement park and threw a *fit*⟩ — see TANTRUM

fit *vb* **1** to be fitting or proper ⟨we hardly know them, so for Christmas a simple card will *fit*⟩ — see DO 1

2 to be in agreement on every point ⟨now that you've explained your absence to me, my records and the office's *fit*⟩ — see CHECK 1

3 to change (something) so as to make it suitable for a new use or situation ⟨I can undo the hem on these old culottes and *fit* them into a skirt⟩ — see ADAPT

4 to make competent (as by training, skill, or ability) for a particular office or function ⟨that final computer course should *fit* him for a career in programming⟩ — see QUALIFY 2

5 to make or have room for ⟨we can *fit* you in the booth if the rest of us squeeze closer together⟩ — see ACCOMMODATE 1

6 to make ready in advance ⟨I won't have time to *fit* the spare room for the guests⟩ — see PREPARE 1

fit (in *or* into) *vb* to put among or between others ⟨do you think you can *fit* this picture *into* the album?⟩ ⟨I can *fit* you *in* between my two o'clock and three o'clock appointments⟩ — see INSERT

fit (out) *vb* to provide (someone) with what is needed for a task or activity ⟨*fitted* the hikers *out* with good boots and heavy socks⟩ — see FURNISH 1

fitful *adj* lacking in steadiness or regularity of occurrence ⟨a night of *fitful* sleep did not leave me feeling well rested the next morning⟩

synonyms casual, choppy, discontinuous, erratic, intermittent, irregular, occasional, spasmodic, sporadic, spotty, unsteady

related words convulsive, sudden, violent; broken, disconnected, fragmentary, interrupted; desultory, haphazard, hit-or-miss, random; changing, fluctuating, unstable, varying, wavering; changeable, fickle, variable

near antonyms equable, even, stable, uniform; unchanging, unvarying, unwavering; methodical, orderly, systematic

antonyms constant, continuous, regular, steady

fitness *n* **1** the condition of being sound in body ⟨a gymnastics program promoting *fitness* and agility in school-aged children⟩ — see HEALTH

2 the quality or state of being especially suitable or fitting ⟨I have to question the *fitness* of wearing a bright red dress to a funeral⟩ — see APPROPRIATENESS

fitting *adj* meeting the requirements of a purpose or situation ⟨it is only *fitting* that you should be the one to take her back to the airport since she flew out to see you⟩ — see FIT 1

fittingly *adv* in a manner suitable for the occasion or purpose ⟨he was dressed *fittingly* for the prom—all decked out in a spiffy tux⟩ — see PROPERLY

fittingness *n* the quality or state of being especially suitable or fitting ⟨trusted their judgment and didn't have to worry about the *fittingness* of their choice for a school play⟩ — see APPROPRIATENESS

fix *n* **1** a difficult, puzzling, or embarrassing situation from which there is no easy escape ⟨what a *fix* we're in!⟩ — see PREDICAMENT

2 something given or promised in order to improperly influence a person's conduct or decision ⟨caught the judge on video accepting the *fix* from the mob boss⟩ — see BRIBE

fix *vb* **1** to arrange something in a certain spot or position ⟨*fixed* my hair so that it would stop falling in my eyes⟩ — see PLACE 1

2 to cause (something) to hold to another ⟨first, you need to *fix* those pieces of wood together⟩ — see FASTEN 1

3 to come to an agreement or decision concerning the details of ⟨make sure to *fix* the number of guests with the bride's family before drawing up a list of people from the groom's side⟩ — see ARRANGE 1

4 to decide upon (the time or date for an event) usually from a position of authority ⟨have we *fixed* a day for the party yet?⟩ — see APPOINT 1

5 to make ready in advance ⟨would you mind *fixing* dinner tonight?⟩ — see PREPARE 1

6 to put into good shape or working order again ⟨have to *fix* the car before we can go⟩ — see MEND 1

7 to put securely in place or in a desired position ⟨*fixed* the mittens to the child's snowsuit⟩ — see FASTEN 2

8 to set solidly in or as if in surrounding matter ⟨the image of what Santa Claus looks like is solidly *fixed* in our minds⟩ — see ENTRENCH

fixable *adj* capable of being corrected ⟨don't worry, that mistake is *fixable*⟩ — see REMEDIABLE

fixation *n* something about which one is constantly thinking or concerned ⟨their weight is an unfortunate *fixation* for many teenagers⟩
   synonyms fetish (*also* fetich), idée fixe, mania, obsession, preoccupation, prepossession
   related words complex, hang-up, problem; compulsion, craving, enthusiasm, fascination, infatuation, passion; idiosyncrasy, quirk; penchant, predilection, proclivity
   near antonyms apathy, indifference, unconcern

fixed *adj* **1** having been established and usually not subject to change ⟨the baseball card dealer's prices were *fixed*, so bargaining was not an option⟩
   synonyms certain, determinate, final, firm, flat, frozen, hard, hard-and-fast, set, settled, stable
   related words nonadjustable, nonnegotiable, unchangeable; constant, steady, unchanging, uniform, unwavering; definite, exact, explicit, specific; stated, stipulated
   near antonyms adjustable, changeable, negotiable; indefinite, unspecified

2 not capable of changing or being changed ⟨interest accrues at a *fixed* rate⟩ — see INFLEXIBLE 1

fixedness *n* the state of continuing without change ⟨wasn't comfortable with the *fixedness* of her stare⟩ — see CONSTANCY 1

fizz *n* a sound similar to the speech sound \s\ stretched out ⟨the light bulb burned out with a quick *fizz*⟩ — see HISS 1

fizz *vb* to make a sound like that of stretching out the speech sound \s\ ⟨soda pop *fizzing* in the glass⟩ — see HISS

fizzle *n* **1** a falling short of one's goals ⟨the home team's unexpected *fizzle* in that last game cost them the championship⟩ — see FAILURE 2

2 something that has failed ⟨the play was a *fizzle*, opening and closing the same night⟩ — see FAILURE 3

fjord *or* **fiord** *n* a part of a body of water that extends beyond the general shoreline ⟨took a cruise through some of the larger *fjords* along the coast of Norway⟩ — see GULF 1

flabbergast *vb* to make a strong impression on (someone) with something unexpected ⟨your decision to drop out of school *flabbergasts* me⟩ — see SURPRISE 1

flabbergasted *adj* **1** affected with sudden and great wonder or surprise ⟨was *flabbergasted* when we heard she was moving out of the state⟩ — see THUNDERSTRUCK

2 filled with amazement or wonder ⟨met the news of his arrival with a *flabbergasted* gasp⟩ — see OPEN-MOUTHED

flabbergasting *adj* causing a strong emotional reaction because unexpected ⟨the *flabbergasting* sight of the mess caused by the children⟩ — see SURPRISING 1

flabby *adj* giving easily to the touch ⟨his daughter playfully poked at his *flabby* belly⟩ — see SOFT 3

flaccid *adj* not stiff in structure ⟨the *flaccid* stems of flowers wilting in the heat⟩ — see LIMP 1

flag *n* **1** a piece of cloth with a special design that is used as an emblem or for signaling ⟨the *flags* of both countries were prominently displayed at the treaty signing⟩
   synonyms banner, colors, ensign, guidon, jack, pennant, pennon, standard, streamer
   related words bunting; black flag, Jolly Roger, union jack, white flag; semaphore, signaler; badge, coat of arms, crest, insignia

2 an object intended to give public notice or warning ⟨road crews using hand-held stop signs as *flags* at both ends of the highway construction zone⟩ — see SIGNAL 1

¹flag *vb* **1** to be limp from lack of water or vigor ⟨flowers *flagging* in the heat⟩ — see DROOP

2 to lose bodily strength or vigor ⟨we *flagged* as we neared the end of the long mountain trail⟩ — see WEAKEN 2

²flag *vb* to direct or notify by a movement or gesture ⟨*flagged* the cars into the other parking lot⟩ — see MOTION

flagellate *vb* to strike repeatedly with something long and thin or flexible ⟨some medieval monks believed it was important to *flagellate* themselves to keep their desires in check⟩ — see WHIP 1

flagon *n* a handled container for holding and pouring liquids that usually has a lip or a spout ⟨brought a *flagon* of wine to the table⟩ — see PITCHER

flagrant *adj* very noticeable especially for being incorrect or bad ⟨that was a *flagrant* violation of the rules⟩ — see EGREGIOUS

flail *vb* **1** to move or cause to move with a striking motion ⟨started to *flail* his arms when he saw the bat in the house⟩ — see FLAP

2 to strike repeatedly with something long and thin or flexible ⟨gruesome evidence that the prisoner had been *flailed*⟩ — see WHIP 1

flair *n* a special and usually inborn ability ⟨he has a *flair* for the dramatic⟩ — see TALENT

flake *n* a small flat piece separated from a whole ⟨sprinkle the cake with coconut *flakes*⟩ — see CHIP 1

flaky *adj* having a texture that readily breaks into little pieces under pressure ⟨a tender but *flaky* crust on the pastry⟩ — see CRISP 1

flamboyance *n* excessive or unnecessary display ⟨the *flamboyance* of her costume almost guaranteed she'd win the masquerade pageant⟩ — see OSTENTATION

flamboyant *adj* **1** likely to attract attention ⟨has a *flamboyant* gesture that he uses whenever he's upset⟩ — see NOTICEABLE

2 excessively showy ⟨Las Vegas dancers wearing *flamboyant* headdresses⟩ — see GAUDY

flamboyantly *adv* in a bright and showy way ⟨mummers dressed *flamboyantly* for the holiday parade⟩ — see GAILY 3

flame *n* a person with whom one is in love ⟨decided to look up an old *flame* when she was in town⟩ — see SWEETHEART

flame *vb* **1** to be on fire especially brightly ⟨guests gathered around as the Yule log *flamed* brightly in the inn's great stone fireplace⟩ — see BURN 1

2 to develop suddenly and violently ⟨my anger *flamed* when the usher told my friend to shut up⟩ — see ERUPT 2

3 to shine with a bright harsh light ⟨the noonday sun *flamed* down on the desert travelers⟩ — see GLARE 1

4 to shoot forth bursts of light ⟨the actress's ruby necklace *flamed* dazzlingly under the bright lights⟩ — see FLASH 1

flaming *adj* **1** being on fire ⟨a fancy restaurant serving eye-catching *flaming* desserts⟩ — see ABLAZE 1

2 having or expressing great depth of feeling ⟨a *flaming* champion of soccer as the world's greatest sport⟩ — see FERVENT

flammable *adj* capable of catching or being set on fire ⟨avoid wearing loose *flammable* clothing when using the blowtorch⟩ — see COMBUSTIBLE

flank *n* a place, space, or direction away from or beyond a central point or line ⟨painted the name of the ship along its *flank*⟩ — see SIDE 1

flank *vb* to be adjacent to ⟨the tackles *flank* the center on a football team's offensive line⟩ — see ADJOIN 1

flanking *adj* having a border in common ⟨*flanking* farms that share the same water source⟩ — see ADJACENT

flap *vb* to move or cause to move with a striking motion ⟨the stirring sight of a huge flock of geese *flapping* their wings⟩

  synonyms beat, flail, flop, flutter, whip

  related words bang, batter, buffet, knock, pound, smack, spank, thump; flick, flicker, flit; oscillate, sway, swing; undulate, wave; palpitate, pulse, throb

flapjack *n* a flat cake made from thin batter and cooked on both sides (as on a griddle) ⟨for breakfast, there's bacon and *flapjacks* with syrup⟩ — see PANCAKE

flare *n* **1** a sudden and usually temporary growth of activity ⟨a *flare* in antacid sales around the holidays⟩ — see OUTBREAK

2 a sudden intense expression of strong feeling ⟨ended the quarrel with a *flare* of swearwords⟩ — see OUTBURST 1

3 the steady giving off of the form of radiation that makes vision possible ⟨solar *flares*⟩ — see LIGHT 1

flare *vb* to shine with a bright harsh light ⟨floodlights *flaring* into the forbidding empty spaces surrounding the prison⟩ — see GLARE 1

flare (out) *vb* to arrange the parts of (something) over a wider area ⟨can we *flare out* the umbrella a little more so that more of the picnic table is sheltered⟩ — see OPEN 3

flare (up) *vb* **1** to become very angry ⟨naturally I *flared up* when he insulted my girlfriend⟩ — see BLOW UP

2 to develop suddenly and violently ⟨her cold sores *flared up* again when she got the flu⟩ — see ERUPT 2

flare–up *n* **1** a sudden and usually temporary growth of activity ⟨took medication to prevent a *flare-up* of her disease⟩ — see OUTBREAK

2 a sudden intense expression of strong feeling ⟨there's no need for a *flare-up*, as we'll take care of the problem immediately⟩ — see OUTBURST 1

flash *adj* lasting only for a short time ⟨*flash* floods in the local area⟩ — see MOMENTARY

flash *n* **1** a sudden and usually temporary growth of activity ⟨a *flash* of last-minute trips to the video store before the big snowstorm⟩ — see OUTBREAK

2 a sudden intense expression of strong feeling ⟨a much-needed *flash* of humor during the otherwise boring lecture⟩ — see OUTBURST 1

3 a very small space of time ⟨it will be over in a *flash*⟩ — see INSTANT

4 something extraordinary or surprising ⟨the new goalie for our hockey team was apparently quite a *flash* in his hometown⟩ — see WONDER 1

flash *vb* **1** to shoot forth bursts of light ⟨the actress's diamond necklace *flashed* as she hurried on stage to accept the award⟩

  synonyms flame, glance, gleam, glimmer, glint, glisten, glister, glitter, scintillate, shimmer, sparkle, twinkle, wink

  related words beam, radiate, shine; bedazzle, blind, daze, dazzle; blaze, burn, flare, glare, glow

2 to present so as to invite notice or attention ⟨*flashed* a wad of cash as he paid for his coffee⟩ — see SHOW 1

3 to shine with light at regular intervals ⟨the disco lights *flashed,* and the revelers danced⟩ — see BLINK 1

flashily *adv* in a bright and showy way ⟨*flashily* decorated houses during the holiday season⟩ — see GAILY 3

flashiness *n* excessive or unnecessary display ⟨his *flashiness* in wearing expensive, specially tailored suits⟩ — see OSTENTATION

flashy *adj* **1** attractively eye-catching in style ⟨I bought the CD for its *flashy* cover design⟩ — see JAZZY 1

2 excessively showy ⟨wore *flashy* rings on almost all the fingers of his left hand⟩ — see GAUDY

flat *adj* **1** being neither more nor less than a certain amount, number, or extent ⟨industrial growth has been a *flat* two percent for each of the last four quarters⟩ — see EVEN 1

2 causing weariness, restlessness, or lack of interest ⟨a *flat* portrayal of Benjamin Franklin in the new TV series⟩ — see BORING

3 having a surface without bends, breaks, or irregularities ⟨preferred riding her bike on a *flat* road⟩ — see LEVEL

4 having been established and usually not subject to change ⟨charged a *flat* rate for overseas calls⟩ — see FIXED 1

5 having no exceptions or restrictions ⟨a *flat* denial of the charges⟩ — see ABSOLUTE 2

6 lacking a surface luster or gloss ⟨*flat* paint for the interior walls⟩ — see MATTE

7 lacking in qualities that make for spirit and character ⟨a *flat* and dull person⟩ — see WISHY-WASHY 1

8 lacking in taste or flavor ⟨this dish tastes a little *flat*⟩ — see INSIPID 1

flat *adv* to a full extent or degree ⟨I am *flat* broke⟩ — see FULLY 1

flat *n*, *chiefly British* a room or set of rooms in a private house or a block used as a separate dwelling place ⟨had to take a third roommate on in order to afford the bigger *flat*⟩ — see APARTMENT 1

flatten *vb* to make free from breaks, curves, or bumps ⟨*flattened* out the wrinkled paper⟩ — see EVEN 1

flatter *vb* **1** to praise too much ⟨the billionaire had an army of assistants who *flattered* him at every opportunity⟩

  synonyms adulate, blarney, overpraise, soft-soap

  related words blandish, cajole, coax, wheedle; fawn, kowtow, toady; idolize, worship; eulogize, extol (*also* extoll), laud, praise; applaud, commend, compliment; congratulate, felicitate; drool, gush, slaver, slobber; endear, ingratiate; court, woo

  near antonyms bad-mouth, belittle, decry, depreciate, disparage, put down

2 to think highly of (oneself) ⟨I *flatter* myself that no one had thought of that idea before⟩ — see PRIDE

flattery *n* excessive praise ⟨a talk show host who is known for charming her guests with *flattery*⟩

synonyms adulation, blarney, overpraise, soft soap
related words allurements, blandishments, endearments; compliments, congratulations, felicitations, greetings, regards, respects; adoration, idolatry, worship; cajolery, endearment, ingratiation; acclaim, applause, commendation, praise
near antonyms bad-mouthing, belittlement, depreciation, detraction, disparagement, put-down

flatware *n* eating and serving utensils ⟨asked for glasses and *flatware* for their wedding⟩ — see TABLEWARE 1

flaunt *vb* to present so as to invite notice or attention ⟨she *flaunted* her engagement ring in all of her coworkers' faces⟩ — see SHOW 1

flaunting *n* an outward and often exaggerated indication of something abstract (as a feeling) for effect ⟨at first, her *flaunting* of her affection for her boyfriend was funny, but after a while it became tiresome⟩ — see SHOW 1

flavor *n* **1** a special quality or impression associated with something ⟨a birthday party whose Caribbean decorations gave it a tropical *flavor*⟩ — see AURA
2 something (as a spice or herb) that adds an agreeable or interesting taste to food ⟨with natural and artificial *flavors*⟩ — see SEASONING 1
3 the property of a substance that can be identified by the sense of taste ⟨loved the *flavor* of strawberries⟩ — see TASTE 1

flavor *vb* to make more pleasant to the taste by adding something intensely flavored ⟨try *flavoring* the beans with salt and oregano⟩ — see SEASON 1

flavorful *adj* very pleasing to the sense of taste ⟨makes a *flavorful* broth⟩ — see DELICIOUS 1

flavoring *n* something (as a spice or herb) that adds an agreeable or interesting taste to food ⟨soup made with beef *flavoring*⟩ — see SEASONING 1

flavorless *adj* lacking in taste or flavor ⟨a *flavorless* fruitcake that must have been given as a gift many times over⟩ — see INSIPID 1

flaw *n* something that spoils the appearance or completeness of a thing ⟨noted the *flaw* in the diamond before I bought it⟩ — see BLEMISH

flaw *vb* to reduce the soundness, effectiveness, or perfection of ⟨that crack has *flawed* the vase to the extent its value is greatly reduced⟩ — see DAMAGE 1

flawed *adj* having a fault ⟨a *flawed* paint job that resulted in some peeling almost as soon as the paint had dried⟩ — see FAULTY

flawless *adj* being entirely without fault or flaw ⟨a *flawless* performance of the piano concerto⟩ — see PERFECT 1

flawlessly *adv* without any flaws or errors ⟨*flawlessly* recited the first 100 digits of pi⟩ — see PERFECTLY 1

flaxen *adj* of a pale yellow or yellowish brown color ⟨fields of *flaxen* wheat waving in the wind⟩ — see BLOND

flay *vb* **1** to criticize (someone) severely or angrily especially for personal failings ⟨her father *flayed* her constantly for her incessant shopping⟩ — see SCOLD
2 to remove the natural covering of ⟨*flayed* their kill right in the forest and took the meat and skin home⟩ — see PEEL

fleck *n* **1** a small area that is different (as in color) from the main part ⟨tile that is brown with *flecks* of white⟩ — see SPOT 1
2 a very small piece ⟨wiped a *fleck* of cookie off his jacket⟩ — see BIT 1

fleck *vb* to mark with small spots especially unevenly ⟨*fleck* the canvas with the paint simply by flicking the brush close to the surface to achieve the right effect⟩ — see SPOT

flecked *adj* marked with spots ⟨liked that beautiful *flecked* blue writing paper⟩ — see SPOTTED 1

fledgling *n* a person who is just starting out in a field of activity ⟨at hockey he's still a *fledgling* and needs to work on his ice skating⟩ — see BEGINNER

flee *vb* **1** to cease to be visible ⟨the fog *fled* with the arrival of the dawn⟩ — see DISAPPEAR
2 to get free from a dangerous or confining situation ⟨a murderer who *fled* on foot⟩ — see ESCAPE 1
3 to hasten away from something dangerous or frightening ⟨a toddler who *fled* when the ladybug he had been quietly watching suddenly began flying around the room⟩ — see RUN 2

fleece *n* the hairy covering of a mammal especially when fine, soft, and thick ⟨learning how to shear the *fleece* off a sheep⟩ — see FUR 1

fleece *vb* to rob by the use of trickery or threats ⟨swindlers who use the telephone to *fleece* senior citizens out of their savings⟩
synonyms bleed, cheat, chisel, cozen, defraud, gyp, hustle, mulct, rook, shortchange, skin, squeeze, stick, sting, swindle, victimize
related words extort, wrench, wrest, wring; gouge, overcharge, soak; exploit, milk; deceive, dupe, fool, gull, trick; rope (in); betray, double-cross

fleecy *adj* covered with or as if with hair ⟨there were signs of the family's *fleecy* poodle all over the upholstery⟩ — see HAIRY 1

fleet *adj* moving, proceeding, or acting with great speed ⟨a jewel thief said to be light of heart and *fleet* of foot⟩ — see FAST 1

fleet *n* a group of vehicles traveling together or under one management ⟨a *fleet* of buses rolling down the highway⟩
synonyms armada, caravan, cavalcade, line, motorcade, train
related words convoy, flotilla, navy; column, cortege (*also* cortège), parade, procession

fleet–footed *adj* moving, proceeding, or acting with great speed ⟨the Roman god Mercury was the *fleet-footed* messenger of the gods⟩ — see FAST 1

fleeting *adj* lasting only for a short time ⟨had a *fleeting* desire to jump into the cool lake but kept on hiking⟩ — see MOMENTARY

fleetly *adv* with great speed ⟨horses galloping *fleetly* across the plain⟩ — see FAST 1

fleetness *n* a high rate of movement or performance ⟨clipper ships were renowned for their *fleetness*⟩ — see SPEED

flesh *n* animal and especially mammal tissue used as food ⟨eats no *flesh* of any kind, only vegetables⟩ — see MEAT 1

fleshiness *n* **1** the condition of having an excess of body fat ⟨the *fleshiness* of the foreign tourists was in sharp contrast to the gauntness of the native Africans⟩ — see CORPULENCE
2 the quality or state of being full of juice ⟨loves the *fleshiness* of ripe watermelon⟩ — see SUCCULENCE

fleshly *adj* **1** having to do with life on earth especially as opposed to that in heaven ⟨don't focus on *fleshly* concerns, but instead on spiritual matters⟩ — see EARTHLY
2 of or relating to the human body ⟨the *fleshly* eye sees the only finished painting, but the mind's eye sees the genius behind its creation⟩ — see PHYSICAL 1

3 pleasing to the physical senses ⟨returning campers looking forward to all *fleshly* pleasures, including warm baths⟩ — see SENSUAL

fleshy *adj* **1** full of juice ⟨*fleshy* apples⟩ — see JUICY

2 having an excess of body fat ⟨the *fleshy* man slowly heaved himself out of his chair⟩ — see FAT 1

flexible *adj* **1** capable of being readily changed ⟨fortunately, Mom has a very *flexible* schedule for her office job⟩

synonyms adaptable, adjustable, alterable, changeable, elastic, fluid, malleable, modifiable, variable

related words changing, fluctuating, inconstant, unstable, unsteady, varying

near antonyms constant, stable, steady, unchanging, uniform, unvarying

antonyms established, fixed, immutable, inelastic, inflexible, invariable, nonmalleable, ramrod, set, unalterable, unchangeable

2 not bound by rigid standards ⟨has a *flexible* attitude when it comes to bedtime⟩ — see EASYGOING 2

3 able to bend easily without breaking ⟨the tent was held up by two *flexible* rods threaded through the top⟩ — see WILLOWY

4 able to revert to original size and shape after being stretched, squeezed, or twisted ⟨used a *flexible* plastic for the toy⟩ — see ELASTIC 1

flick *vb* to make an irregular series of quick, sudden movements ⟨the horse's tail *flicked* in restless irritation⟩ — see FLIT

flicker *n* a sudden and usually temporary growth of activity ⟨usually there's a *flicker* in car sales when the new models come out⟩ — see OUTBREAK

flicker *vb* to make an irregular series of quick, sudden movements ⟨a dragonfly *flickering* above the salt marsh⟩ — see FLIT

flickery *adj* likely to change frequently, suddenly, or unexpectedly ⟨wise political leaders don't try to govern according to *flickery* public opinion⟩ — see FICKLE 1

flier *or* **flyer** *n* **1** a risky undertaking ⟨willing to take a *flier* on the bold, new venture⟩ — see GAMBLE

2 one who flies or is qualified to fly an aircraft or spacecraft ⟨a hot-air balloon *flier*⟩ — see PILOT

3 a short printed publication with no cover or with a paper cover ⟨came out of the store and saw a *flier* for a restaurant on my windshield⟩ — see PAMPHLET

¹flight *n* the act or an instance of getting free from danger or confinement ⟨was struck by the illustration depicting the ancient Israelites' *flight* from Egypt⟩ — see ESCAPE 1

²flight *n* travel through the air by the use of wings ⟨for centuries people had been fascinated by the *flight* of birds⟩

synonyms flying

related words aviation; aeronautics; ballooning, gliding, skydiving, soaring

flightiness *n* **1** a lack of seriousness often at an improper time ⟨wouldn't tolerate her *flightiness* at the honor society ceremony⟩ — see FRIVOLITY 1

2 a state of nervousness marked by sudden jerky movements ⟨his *flightiness* before exams was so bad that he nearly made himself sick⟩ — see JUMPINESS

flighty *adj* **1** easily excited by nature ⟨you have to be quiet while the deer are grazing, as they are *flighty* animals and will run if they hear you⟩ — see EXCITABLE

2 lacking in seriousness or maturity ⟨*flighty* and giggly preteens at their first dance⟩ — see GIDDY 1

flimsy *adj* **1** being of a material lacking in sturdiness or substance ⟨a *flimsy* scarf that was more for decoration than for warmth⟩

synonyms filmy, gauzy, gossamer, gossamery, insubstantial, unsubstantial

related words dainty, delicate, fine; feeble, fragile, frail; sheer, transparent

near antonyms durable, lasting, tough; coarse, heavy, rough, rude

antonyms sturdy, substantial

2 not likely to be true or to occur ⟨"the dog ate my homework" is a pretty *flimsy* and tired excuse⟩ — see IMPROBABLE

flinch *vb* to draw back in fear, pain, or disgust ⟨there are some patients who *flinch* at the mere sight of a needle⟩

synonyms blench, quail, recoil, shrink, wince

related words blanch, pale, whiten; quake, quiver, shake, shudder, tremble; crouch, squinch; jerk, start, twitch; recede, retire, retreat, withdraw; falter, hesitate, reel, waver

near antonyms advance, approach, near; confront, challenge, defy, face

fling *n* **1** a time or instance of carefree fun ⟨most families spend Labor Day weekend having one last summer *fling*⟩

synonyms binge, frolic, gambol, lark, revel, rollick, romp, spree

related words caper, escapade, prank; antic, monkeyshine(s), shenanigans; field day; festivity, merriment, merrymaking; enjoyment, indulgence, pleasure, self-indulgence; amusement, diversion, entertainment, recreation

2 an effort to do or accomplish something ⟨take a *fling* at water-skiing⟩ — see ATTEMPT

fling *vb* to send through the air especially with a quick forward motion of the arm ⟨*flinging* rocks into the pond just for the fun of it⟩ — see THROW

fling (off *or* away) *vb* to get rid of as useless or unwanted ⟨he *flung away* the broken toy⟩ ⟨*flinging off* dirty clothes⟩ — see DISCARD

flinty *adj* **1** given to exacting standards of discipline and self-restraint ⟨a *flinty* warrior hardened by years of battle⟩ — see SEVERE 1

2 harsh and threatening in manner or appearance ⟨wrestling opponents intimidating each other with *flinty* stares⟩ — see GRIM 1

flip *adj* making light of something usually regarded as serious or sacred ⟨made some *flip* comment about the marriage of the old man and young woman⟩ — see FLIPPANT

flip *vb* **1** to become very angry ⟨when Mom saw that I had broken her great-grandmother's vase, she *flipped*⟩ — see BLOW UP

2 to change the position of (an object) so that the opposite side or end is showing ⟨*flip* the coin over⟩ — see REVERSE 2

3 to yield to mental or emotional stress ⟨a movie about a submarine captain who *flips* when there's an emergency, leaving the crew to deal with it themselves⟩ — see CRACK 2

flippancy *n* a lack of seriousness often at an improper time ⟨no one appreciates your *flippancy* during our religious services⟩ — see FRIVOLITY 1

flippant *adj* making light of something usually regarded as serious or sacred ⟨his *flippant* comment that the poor save on taxes offended many people⟩

synonyms facetious, flip, pert, smart, smart-alecky (*or* smart-aleck)

related words flighty, frivolous; cheeky, cocky, cute, fresh, impertinent, impish, impudent, mischievous, playful, roguish, sassy, saucy, waggish; disrespectful, rude; breezy, casual, glib, inappropriate, thoughtless

near antonyms grave, serious, sober, solemn, somber (*or* sombre)

antonyms earnest, sincere

flirt *vb* to show a liking for someone of the opposite sex just for fun ⟨the servers at that restaurant *flirt* with all the customers⟩

synonyms dally, frivol, trifle

related words josh, kid, put on, razz, rib, tease; fool, lead on, string along; play (with), toy (with)

flit *vb* to make an irregular series of quick, sudden movements ⟨bargain hunters at the flea market *flitted* from table to table like hummingbirds in a garden⟩

synonyms dance, dart, flick, flicker, flutter, zip

related words dash, fly, sail, shoot, speed, sprint, zoom; scamper, scud, scurry, scuttle, skip, skitter; meander, ramble, roam, wander

near antonyms float, hang, hover

float *n* a structure used by boats and ships for taking on or landing cargo and passengers ⟨the crew put the cargo on the *float* before heading back down the river⟩ — see DOCK

float *vb* to rest or move along the surface of a liquid or in the air ⟨a canoe *floating* down the river⟩ ⟨particles of dust *floating* in the air⟩

synonyms drift, glide, hang, hover, poise, ride, sail, waft

related words bob, dangle, suspend; buoy; balloon, raft

near antonyms dive, lunge, plunge; dip, immerse, submerge, submerse

antonyms settle, sink

flock *n* **1** a great number of persons or things gathered together ⟨a *flock* of reporters at the press conference⟩ — see CROWD 1

2 a group of domestic animals assembled or herded together ⟨a *flock* of sheep lazily crossing the road⟩ — see HERD

flock *vb* to move upon or fill (something) in great numbers ⟨vacationers *flocked* to the towns along the shore⟩ — see CROWD 2

flog *vb* **1** to strike repeatedly with something long and thin or flexible ⟨a movie scene showing a sailor being *flogged* by the captain for disobeying orders⟩ — see WHIP 1

2 to strike repeatedly ⟨was fined heavily for *flogging* a horse⟩ — see BEAT 1

flogger *n* a long thin or flexible tool for striking ⟨a horseman who believes that *floggers* should be used sparingly⟩ — see WHIP

flood *n* a great flow of water or of something that overwhelms ⟨a *flood* nearly wiped out the town⟩ ⟨a *flood* of messages on my computer⟩

synonyms cataclysm, cataract, deluge, flood tide, inundation, overflow, spate, torrent

related words current, river, stream, tide; discharge, flush, gush, outflow, outpouring; flux, inflow, influx; engulfment, washout; avalanche; cascade, waterfall; excess, glut, overabundance, overage, overkill, overmuch, oversupply, superabundance, superfluity, surfeit, surplus

near antonyms dribble, drip, trickle

antonyms drought

flood *vb* to cover or become filled with a flood ⟨the lowlands were completely *flooded*⟩ ⟨angry calls *flooded* the radio station⟩

synonyms deluge, drown, engulf, inundate, overflow, overwhelm, submerge, submerse, swamp

related words overcome, overrun; flow, flush, gush, pour, sluice, spout, spurt, stream; douse, drench, soak, wet

near antonyms dehydrate, dry, parch

antonyms drain

flood tide *n* a great flow of water or of something that overwhelms ⟨let's collect shells before the *flood tide* comes in and covers the beach⟩ — see FLOOD

floor *n* the surface upon which a body of water lies ⟨discovered a new species of crab living on the ocean *floor*⟩ — see BOTTOM 2

floor *vb* **1** to cause an often unpleasant surprise for ⟨that you would say such a rude thing to my mother *floors* me⟩ — see SHOCK 1

2 to make a strong impression on (someone) with something unexpected ⟨winning the lottery simply *floored* us⟩ — see SURPRISE 1

3 to strike (someone) so forcefully as to cause a fall ⟨the boxer *floored* his opponent in the second round and won the fight by a knockout⟩ — see FELL 1

4 to subject to incapacitating emotional or mental stress ⟨the pushing and shoving at the clearance sale absolutely *floored* me, and I had to leave⟩ — see OVERWHELM 1

flop *n* something that has failed ⟨the movie is such a *flop* that theaters showing it are the loneliest places in town⟩ — see FAILURE 3

flop *vb* **1** to throw or set down clumsily or casually ⟨they *flopped* themselves onto the couch to watch the game⟩ ⟨*flopped* the bag of groceries onto the counter⟩

synonyms plop, plump, plunk

related words fling, heave, sling, toss; ensconce, install, plant, settle

2 to be unsuccessful ⟨the attempt to run the ball into the end zone *flopped*, and our team lost by five points⟩ — see FAIL 2

3 to move or cause to move with a striking motion ⟨a fish *flopping* around on the dock⟩ — see FLAP

floppy *adj* not stiff in structure ⟨my bassett hound is always tripping over her long, *floppy* ears⟩ — see LIMP 1

flora *n* green leaves or plants ⟨loved the *flora* of the South⟩ — see GREENERY 1

floral *adj* of or relating to flowers ⟨wallpaper with a *floral* pattern for the bedroom⟩

synonyms flowered, flowery

related words florid; abloom

florid *adj* **1** elaborately and often excessively decorated ⟨a *florid*, gilded mirror that took up most of the wall⟩ — see ORNATE

2 full of fine words and fancy expressions ⟨gave a *florid* welcome speech to the visiting queen⟩ — see FLOWERY 1

3 having a healthy reddish skin tone ⟨a jolly fat man with a *florid* complexion⟩ — see RUDDY

floss *n* a soft airy substance or covering ⟨made an angel ornament with gold paper wings and clouds of cotton *floss*⟩ — see FUZZ

flounce *n* a strip of fabric gathered or pleated on one edge and used as trimming ⟨a prom dress with a small *flounce* at the hem⟩ — see RUFFLE

flounder *vb* **1** to make progress in a clumsy, struggling manner ⟨unprepared choristers who *floundered* helplessly through the musical number⟩

synonyms limp, lumber, plod, stumble, trudge

related words shamble, shuffle; wallow, welter; falter, lurch, reel, stagger, sway, teeter, totter; blunder, fumble, muddle

near antonyms coast, fly, glide, sail, zip, zoom

2 to move heavily or clumsily ⟨the car *floundered* through the heavy wet snow, constantly getting stuck⟩ — see LUMBER 1

flourish *vb* **1** to grow vigorously ⟨that plant *flourishes* in cool, wet weather⟩ — see THRIVE 1

2 to reach a desired level of accomplishment ⟨the arts program *flourished* once it received adequate funding⟩ — see SUCCEED 2

flourishing *adj* **1** having attained a desired end or state of good fortune ⟨a *flourishing* actor⟩ — see SUCCESSFUL 1

2 marked by much life, movement, or activity ⟨a *flourishing* market in sports memorabilia⟩ — see ALIVE 2

3 marked by vigorous growth and well-being especially economically ⟨the job market is *flourishing*⟩ — see PROSPEROUS 1

floury *adj* consisting of very small particles ⟨old books covered with *floury* dust⟩ — see FINE 1

flout *vb* to ignore in a disrespectful manner ⟨disciplined a student who was *flouting* the regulation against offensive language in the halls⟩ — see SCORN 2

flow *vb* **1** to move in a stream ⟨water was *flowing* over the dam at a tremendous rate⟩

synonyms pour, roll, run, stream

related words arise, emanate, issue, spring; course, race, rush; gush, spout, spurt; deluge, engulf, flood, inundate, overflow, swamp; cascade, dribble, drip, gutter, riffle, ripple, trickle; flush, wash out

near antonyms clot, coagulate, congeal, gel, harden, set

antonyms back up

2 to move or proceed smoothly and readily ⟨as everyone relaxed, the conversation really started to *flow*⟩

synonyms bowl, breeze, coast, drift, glide, roll, sail, skim, slide, slip, stream, sweep, whisk

related words fly, race, rush, speed

near antonyms limp, lumber, plod, stumble, trudge; shamble, shuffle; stamp, stomp, stump, tramp; labor, toil

antonyms flounder, struggle

flower *n* **1** the usually showy plant part that produces seeds ⟨*flowers* are always a thoughtful gift⟩

synonyms bloom, blossom

related words bud, floret; bouquet, nosegay, posy; arrangement, boutonniere, corsage, garland, lei, spray, wreath

2 a state or time of great activity, thriving, or achievement ⟨skiing season is in full *flower* by Christmas⟩ — see BLOOM 1

3 individuals carefully selected as being the best of a class ⟨the *flower* of this year's graduating class will be going to top colleges⟩ — see ELITE

flower *vb* to produce flowers ⟨the plant will keep *flowering* if you water it and cut off the dead flower heads⟩ — see BLOOM

flowered *adj* of or relating to flowers ⟨a pretty tablecloth with a *flowered* border⟩ — see FLORAL

flowery *adj* **1** full of fine words and fancy expressions ⟨the *flowery* verses that always appear on valentines⟩

synonyms florid, grandiloquent, highfalutin, highflown, high-sounding

related words affected, grandiose, inflated, pompous, pretentious, stilted; excessive, flattering, fulsome; boastful, bombastic; elevated, eloquent, lofty

near antonyms prosaic, unpoetic; bald, direct, matter-of-fact, plain, plainspoken, simple, stark, straightforward, unadorned; natural, unaffected, unpretentious

2 of or relating to flowers ⟨Mother's Day cards typically have a *flowery* design on the cover⟩ — see FLORAL

flowing *adj* capable of moving like a liquid ⟨a *flowing* silk scarf⟩ — see FLUID 1

flub *n* an unintentional departure from truth or accuracy ⟨when she was told her information was wrong, she apologized for the *flub* and immediately corrected it⟩ — see ERROR 1

flub *vb* to make or do (something) in a clumsy or unskillful way ⟨added too much flour and *flubbed* the gravy⟩ — see BOTCH

fluctuate *vb* to pass from one form, state, or level to another ⟨temperatures will *fluctuate* between the low and high 50s today⟩ — see CHANGE 2

fluctuating *adj* **1** likely to change frequently, suddenly, or unexpectedly ⟨a *fluctuating* stock market makes it hard for investors to know what to do⟩ — see FICKLE 1

2 not staying constant ⟨our speed was constantly *fluctuating*, so the figure of 50 miles per hour is just an average⟩ — see UNEVEN 2

fluent *adj* **1** able to express oneself clearly and well ⟨a very *fluent* speaker who always communicates his points well⟩ — see ARTICULATE

2 capable of moving like a liquid ⟨heated the wax until it was *fluent*, then poured it into the mold⟩ — see FLUID 1

3 involving minimal difficulty or effort ⟨a *fluent* performance of the magic trick⟩ — see EASY 1

fluently *adv* without difficulty ⟨skied *fluently* down the hill⟩ — see EASILY

fluff *n* a soft airy substance or covering ⟨picked the *fluff* off his sweater⟩ — see FUZZ

fluffy *adj* resembling air in lightness ⟨big *fluffy* pillows⟩ — see AIRY 1

fluid *adj* **1** capable of moving like a liquid ⟨warm the jam until it is *fluid*, then spread it over the cake⟩

synonyms flowing, fluent, liquid

related words diluted, thin, watery, weak

near antonyms clotted, coagulated, gelatinous, gelled, jelled, jellied, thick; gluey, glutinous, gooey, gummy, viscous

antonyms hard, solid

2 capable of being readily changed ⟨the script is *fluid*, so be prepared for last-minute rewrites⟩ — see FLEXIBLE 1

3 involving minimal difficulty or effort ⟨the dance looked smooth and *fluid*, though backstage we could see the dancer gasping for breath and sweating from the effort⟩ — see EASY 1

4 likely to change frequently, suddenly, or unexpectedly ⟨his arrival plans are *fluid*, so expect him anytime⟩ — see FICKLE 1

fluky *adj* **1** coming or happening by good luck especially unexpectedly ⟨a *fluky* coincidence that kept me home when the blizzard hit⟩ — see FORTUNATE 1

2 happening by chance ⟨the *fluky* selection of consecutive numbers on consecutive days of the lottery⟩ — see ACCIDENTAL

flume *n* **1** a narrow opening between hillsides or mountains that can be used for passage ⟨hiked through the *flume* and into the meadow beyond it⟩ — see CANYON

2 an open man-made passageway for water ⟨built a *flume* next to the road for runoff⟩ — see CHANNEL 1

flunk *vb* to be unsuccessful ⟨you're going to *flunk* if you don't shape up⟩ — see FAIL 2

flunky *also* **flunkey** *n* **1** a person hired to perform household or personal services ⟨since I'm just the *flunky* who files his papers, I've no idea where he is⟩ — see SERVANT

2 a person who flatters another in order to get ahead ⟨a rock star who saw through the phonies and the *flunkies*⟩ — see SYCOPHANT

fluorescence *n* the steady giving off of the form of radiation that makes vision possible ⟨studied the *fluorescence* of certain elements⟩ — see LIGHT 1

flurry *n* **1** a sudden and usually temporary growth of activity ⟨a *flurry* of activity on the stock market as soon as the news spread⟩ — see OUTBREAK

2 a sudden brief rush of wind ⟨garbage cans blown over by the *flurry*⟩ — see GUST 1

flush *adj* **1** having a healthy reddish skin tone ⟨was *flushed* after getting out of the hot bath⟩ — see RUDDY

2 having a surface without bends, breaks, or irregularities ⟨the *flush* paneling on the door makes it very plain and dull⟩ — see LEVEL

3 having active strength of body or mind ⟨a *flush*, healthy man of 65⟩ — see VIGOROUS 1

4 having goods, property, or money in abundance ⟨she's very *flush* now that she has her inheritance⟩ — see RICH 1

5 possessing or covered with great numbers or amounts of something specified ⟨a field *flush* with flowers⟩ — see RIFE

flush *n* **1** a rosy appearance of the cheeks ⟨looked for a *flush* on her cheeks as evidence of a fever⟩ — see BLOOM 2

2 a state or time of great activity, thriving, or achievement ⟨was in the *flush* of his youth⟩ — see BLOOM 1

3 a sudden intense expression of strong feeling ⟨a *flush* of patriotic pride⟩ — see OUTBURST 1

flush *vb* **1** to pour liquid over or through in order to cleanse ⟨use this cleaner to *flush* the drain in the sink⟩

synonyms irrigate, rinse, sluice, wash

related words deluge, engulf, flood, inundate, swamp; flow, gush, rush, stream; douche, hose; drench, saturate, soak; douse, slosh, splash

2 to develop a rosy facial color (as from excitement or embarrassment) ⟨he *flushed* deeply when she complimented him⟩ — see BLUSH

fluster *n* **1** a state of nervous or irritated concern ⟨all the yelling on the bus put the driver in a *fluster*⟩ — see FRET

2 the emotional state of being made self-consciously uncomfortable ⟨there was a general *fluster* in the group when I asked my awkward question⟩ — see EMBARRASSMENT 1

fluster *vb* to throw into a state of self-conscious distress ⟨was *flustered* when her parents dragged out her baby pictures for her new boyfriend⟩ — see EMBARRASS 1

flustering *adj* causing embarrassment ⟨a *flustering* situation that left us all silent⟩ — see AWKWARD 3

flutter *n* a sudden and usually temporary growth of activity ⟨saw a *flutter* of construction last month, but nothing's happening now⟩ — see OUTBREAK

flutter *vb* **1** to make an irregular series of quick, sudden movements ⟨a butterfly *fluttering* across the lawn⟩ — see FLIT

2 to move or cause to move with a striking motion ⟨*fluttered* my eyelashes as I struck up a conversation with the new guy at school⟩ — see FLAP

fluttery *adj* easily excited by nature ⟨a *fluttery* bus driver who made us all nervous⟩ — see EXCITABLE

flux *n* a flowing or coming in ⟨January brings a great *flux* of returns to department stores⟩ — see INFLUX

flux *vb* to go from a solid to a liquid state ⟨the solid will *flux* sooner under pressure⟩ — see LIQUEFY

fly *vb* **1** to move through the air with or as if with outstretched wings ⟨the Wright brothers realized mankind's age-old wish to *fly*⟩

synonyms glide, plane, soar, wing

related words drift, float, hang, hover, waft; coast, cruise, sail, sweep; dart, flit, flutter; catapult, jet, orbit, rocket

2 to get free from a dangerous or confining situation ⟨you must *fly* to safety immediately⟩ — see ESCAPE 1

3 to proceed or move quickly ⟨*flew* down the hall to class⟩ — see HURRY 2

4 to hasten away from something dangerous or frightening ⟨no one in the movies ever thinks to *fly* from the ax murderer and call the police⟩ — see RUN 2

flying *adj* **1** acting or done with excessive or careless speed ⟨a *flying* attempt at finishing the work⟩ — see HASTY 1

2 moving, proceeding, or acting with great speed ⟨that car was *flying*⟩ — see FAST 1

flying *n* travel through the air by the use of wings ⟨most birds travel by *flying*, but some flightless species have to walk⟩ — see ¹FLIGHT

flyspeck *n* a very small piece ⟨removed a *flyspeck* of dirt from the china⟩ — see BIT 1

foam *n* a light mass of fine bubbles formed in or on a liquid ⟨a steaming cup of hot cocoa with a sprinkling of marshmallows drifting through the *foam*⟩

synonyms froth, head, lather, spume, suds, surf

related words mousse; mist, spindrift, spray; scum

foaming *adj* feeling or showing anger ⟨was so upset he was *foaming*⟩ — see ANGRY

foamy *adj* covered with, consisting of, or resembling foam ⟨*foamy* milk shakes⟩

synonyms frothy, lathery, sudsy

related words bubbly, effervescent, fizzy, sparkling; soapy

focus *n* a thing or place that is of greatest importance to an activity or interest ⟨the *focus* of the conference is on genetics⟩ — see CENTER 1

focus *vb* to fix (as one's attention) steadily toward a central objective ⟨try to *focus* on the task at hand⟩ — see CONCENTRATE 2

focused *also* **focussed** *adj* **1** having the mind fixed on something ⟨was *focused* on the football game and didn't hear me knock⟩ — see ATTENTIVE

2 not divided or scattered among several areas of interest or concern ⟨a *focused* effort to provide shelter for the homeless during the winter⟩ — see WHOLE 1

foe *n* one that is hostile toward another ⟨are you friend or *foe*?⟩ — see ENEMY

fog *n* **1** a state of mental confusion ⟨didn't get enough sleep and now I'm in a *fog*⟩ — see HAZE 2

2 an atmospheric condition in which suspended particles in the air rob it of its transparency ⟨the *fog* lifted once the sun was out⟩ — see HAZE 1

fog *vb* **1** to make (something) unclear to the understanding ⟨time will *fog* memories⟩ — see CONFUSE 2

2 to make dark, dim, or indistinct ⟨the steam from the water *fogged* my glasses⟩ — see CLOUD 1

foggy *adj* **1** filled with or dimmed by fine particles (as of dust or water) in suspension ⟨it's pretty *foggy* outside, so be careful driving home⟩ — see HAZY 1

2 not seen or understood clearly ⟨could only see a *foggy* outline in the dark⟩ — see FAINT 1

fogy *also* **fogey** *n* a person with old-fashioned ideas ⟨old *fogies* who said that rap music would never last⟩
  synonyms antediluvian, dodo, fossil, fuddy-duddy, reactionary, stick-in-the-mud
  related words conservative, rightist, tory; old hand, old-timer, veteran; old maid
  near antonyms liberal, progressive, radical
  antonyms modern

foible *n* a defect in character ⟨could tolerate his *foibles* because we loved him⟩ — see FAULT 1

foil *vb* to prevent from achieving a goal ⟨the hero will always *foil* the villain's plans⟩ — see FRUSTRATE

foist *vb* to offer (something fake, useless, or inferior) as genuine, useful, or valuable ⟨shopkeepers who *foist* shoddy souvenirs on unsuspecting tourists⟩
  synonyms palm off, pass off
  related words force, impose, inflict; counterfeit, fake, forge; distort, falsify, misrepresent

fold *n* a group of people sharing a common interest and relating together socially ⟨ready to welcome their old Liberal friend back into the *fold*⟩ — see GANG 2

fold *vb* **1** to lay one part over or against another part of ⟨*fold* the blanket so that it will fit inside the trunk⟩
  synonyms double
  related words overlap, overlay, overlie; collapse, telescope; close, shut
  antonyms extend, open, spread, unfold
  2 to be unsuccessful ⟨the business *folded* after just two months⟩ — see FAIL 2

folder *n* a short printed publication with no cover or with a paper cover ⟨I promised Mom I'd read the *folder* on safe driving⟩ — see PAMPHLET

foliage *n* green leaves or plants ⟨decided the office needed more *foliage* and bought a few plants⟩ — see GREENERY 1

folk *n* **1 folks** *pl* a group of persons who come from the same ancestor ⟨she's gone back home to live with her *folks*⟩ — see FAMILY 1
  2 one of the segments of society into which people are grouped ⟨the working-class *folk*⟩ — see CLASS 1
  3 folks *pl* human beings in general ⟨c'mon, *folks*, let's get to work⟩ — see PEOPLE 1

folklore *n* the body of customs, beliefs, stories, and sayings associated with a people, thing, or place ⟨the Scottish Highlands are rich in *folklore*⟩
  synonyms legend, lore, myth, mythology, tradition
  related words information, knowledge, wisdom; anecdote, fable, folktale, old wives' tale, yarn

follow *vb* **1** to come after in time ⟨a wrap-up always *follows* the Super Bowl broadcast⟩
  synonyms postdate, succeed, supervene
  related words displace, replace, supersede, supplant; ensue
  antonyms antedate, precede, predate
  2 to go after or on the track of ⟨let's *follow* the boys to their hiding place⟩
  synonyms chase, dog, hound, pursue, shadow, tag, tail, trace, track, trail
  related words accompany, chaperone (*or* chaperon), escort; hunt, search (for), seek; eye, observe, watch
  near antonyms head
  antonyms guide, lead, pilot
  3 to act according to the commands of ⟨*follow* me, and you'll do OK⟩ — see OBEY
  4 to make one's way through, across, or over ⟨*followed* the path into the garden⟩ — see TRAVERSE

5 to take notice of and be guided by ⟨don't *follow* his advice⟩ — see HEED 1

follower *n* one who follows the opinions or teachings of another ⟨the *followers* of Gandhi have spread his philosophy of nonviolence all over the world⟩
  synonyms adherent, convert, disciple, partisan, pupil, votary
  related words apostle; faithful, loyalist; advocate, backer, champion, supporter; scholar, student; ideologist, sectarian; admirer, cultist, devotee, enthusiast, fan, idolater (*or* idolator), worshipper (*or* worshiper), zealot; flunky (*also* flunkey), hanger-on, henchman, lackey, satellite, stooge, sycophant, toady, yes-man
  near antonyms apostate, defector, renegade, traitor, turncoat
  antonyms leader

following *prep* subsequent to in time or order ⟨*following* the concert, there will be refreshments in the lobby⟩ — see AFTER

following *adj* being the one that comes immediately after another ⟨the *following* morning, I found the cat was gone⟩ — see NEXT

following *n* **1** a body of employees or servants who accompany and wait on a person ⟨a prince with a large *following* to do practically everything for him⟩ — see CORTEGE 1
  2 a group of people showing intense devotion to a cause, person, or work (as a film) ⟨that rock star attracts quite a *following*⟩ — see CULT 1
  3 the act of going after or in the tracks of another ⟨took part in the *following* of the coyote⟩ — see PURSUIT

follow through *vb* to carry through (as a process) to completion ⟨make sure you *follow through* with your promise to take her out for ice cream⟩ — see PERFORM 1

folly *n* **1** a foolish act or idea ⟨the American purchase of Alaska was originally considered a grand *folly*⟩
  synonyms absurdity, asininity, fatuity, foolery, idiocy, imbecility, inanity, insanity, lunacy, stupidity
  related words absurdness, craziness, foolishness, madness, senselessness, witlessness; monkeyshine(s), shenanigans, tomfoolery; drivel, humbug, nonsense, twaddle; blunder, bungle, flub, goof, howler
  near antonyms discretion, forethought, prudence, sagacity, wisdom; brainstorm, inspiration
  2 lack of good sense or judgment ⟨in all my *folly*, I didn't think about how my actions would hurt my father⟩ — see FOOLISHNESS 1
  3 language, behavior, or ideas that are absurd and contrary to good sense ⟨enough of this *folly* about moving to the North Pole⟩ — see NONSENSE 1

foment *vb* to cause or encourage the development of ⟨John Adams's wife, Abigail, told him that if women were not remembered by the new American government, they would "*foment* a Rebellion and will not hold ourselves bound by any Laws in which we have no voice or Representation"⟩ — see INCITE 1

fomenter *n* a person who stirs up public feelings especially of discontent ⟨sent the *fomenter* of the riot to prison⟩ — see AGITATOR

fond *adj* **1** having a liking or affection ⟨even lots of city people are *fond* of country music⟩
  synonyms attached, inclined, partial
  related words crazy (about *or* over), enamored, enraptured, gone (on), infatuated, mad (about), nuts (about); desirous, eager, enthusiastic, excited, gung ho, keen

near antonyms apathetic, cool, indifferent, uninterested; contemptuous, disdainful, scornful; antagonistic, antipathetic, hostile; alienated, disaffected, disenchanted, estranged

antonyms allergic, averse, disinclined

2 feeling or showing love ⟨gave me a *fond* embrace upon parting⟩ — see LOVING

fondle *vb* to touch or handle in a tender or loving manner ⟨a cat who enjoys being *fondled* by his loving owners⟩

synonyms caress, love, pat, pet, stroke

related words cuddle, nestle, nose, nuzzle, snuggle; cradle, embrace, enfold, hug; bounce, dandle; knead, massage; baby, coddle, indulge, mollycoddle, pamper, spoil

fondness *n* **1** a feeling of strong or constant regard for and dedication to someone ⟨my *fondness* for you will never fail⟩ — see LOVE 1

2 positive regard for something ⟨I have a *fondness* for expensive chocolate⟩ — see LIKING

food *n* substances intended to be eaten ⟨a simple, little restaurant with excellent *food*⟩

synonyms bread, chow, eatables, edibles, fare, foodstuffs, grub, meat, provender, provisions, table, viands, victuals, vittles

related words rations; aliment, nutriment; diet, nurture, sustenance; mess, pap; feed, fodder, forage, slop, swill; feast, meal, refreshments, repast, spread; board; dish, plate, serving

near antonyms poison

foodstuffs *n pl* substances intended to be eaten ⟨stocked up on candles and *foodstuffs* before the hurricane⟩ — see FOOD

fool *n* **1** a person who lacks good sense or judgment ⟨only a *fool* would attempt to climb that mountain unprepared⟩

synonyms booby, goose, half-wit, jackass, lunatic, nincompoop, ninny, nitwit, nut, simpleton, turkey, yo-yo

related words daredevil; madman, madwoman; blockhead, cretin, dodo, dolt, dope, dumbbell, dummy, dunce, idiot, imbecile, moron; featherbrain, scatterbrain; butt, dupe, laughingstock, mockery, monkey; chump, loser, schlemiel

near antonyms sage, thinker; brain, genius

2 a person formerly kept in a royal or noble household to amuse with jests and pranks ⟨a king's *fool* could get away with saying things that others in the palace couldn't⟩

synonyms jester, motley

related words buffoon, clown, comedian, comedienne, comic, cutup, harlequin, zany

fool *vb* **1** to cause to believe what is untrue ⟨I *fooled* him into thinking that we were driving to the store, not to his surprise birthday party⟩ — see DECEIVE

2 to make jokes ⟨a comedian *fooling* with the audience⟩ — see JOKE

fool (around) *vb* **1** to engage in attention-getting playful or boisterous behavior ⟨quit *fooling around* on the jungle gym, or you'll get hurt⟩ — see CUT UP

2 to spend time in aimless activity ⟨spent the afternoon listening to music and *fooling around*⟩ — see FIDDLE (AROUND)

fool (with) *vb* to handle thoughtlessly, ignorantly, or mischievously ⟨not a good idea to *fool with* the power tools in the garage without supervision⟩ — see TAMPER

foolery *n* **1** a foolish act or idea ⟨it's *foolery* to expect me to let you shoplift that DVD⟩ — see FOLLY 1

2 wildly playful or mischievous behavior ⟨let the kids have a little *foolery* once in a while⟩ — see HORSEPLAY

foolhardy *adj* **1** foolishly adventurous or bold ⟨hikers who were *foolhardy* enough to remain on the summit during a thunderstorm⟩

synonyms brash, daredevil, madcap, overbold, overconfident, reckless

related words adventuresome, adventurous, audacious, bold, daring, venturesome, venturous; brave, courageous, dauntless, fearless, intrepid, lionhearted, stouthearted, undaunted, valiant; hotheaded; impetuous, impulsive, rash; brainless, foolish, harebrained, scatterbrained; careless, heedless, thoughtless; hasty, headlong, precipitate

near antonyms unadventurous, unambitious; fainthearted, timid, timorous; calm, cool, levelheaded, sensible; alert, intelligent, quick-witted, sharp

antonyms careful, cautious, heedful, prudent

2 having or showing a lack of concern for the consequences of one's actions ⟨it's *foolhardy* to go hiking during late fall without warm clothes⟩ — see RECKLESS 1

fooling *adj* marked by or expressive of mild or good-natured teasing ⟨bothered him with *fooling* comments about the girl he had a crush on⟩ — see QUIZZICAL

foolish *adj* **1** showing or marked by a lack of good sense or judgment ⟨*foolish* people who thought that the world would end in the year 2000⟩ ⟨a *foolish* scheme that was supposed to make us all rich⟩

synonyms absurd, asinine, balmy, brainless, cockeyed, crazy, cuckoo, daffy, daft, dotty, fatuous, harebrained, half-witted, insane, jerky, kooky, loony (*also* looney), lunatic, mad, nonsensical, nutty, preposterous, sappy, screwball, senseless, silly, simpleminded, stupid, unwise, wacky, weak-minded, witless, zany

related words dumb, idiotic, imbecilic, moronic; fallacious, illogical, invalid, irrational, unreasonable; farcical, laughable, ludicrous, ridiculous

near antonyms brainy, bright, clever, intelligent, smart; logical, rational, reasonable, valid

antonyms judicious, prudent, sage, sane, sapient, sensible, sound, wise

2 conceived or made without regard for reason or reality ⟨it's *foolish* to make plans for the year 2500, since you won't even be around⟩ — see FANTASTIC 1

foolishness *n* **1** lack of good sense or judgment ⟨the *foolishness* of going off to search for the fountain of youth⟩

synonyms absurdity, asininity, balminess, brainlessness, craziness, daftness, fatuity, folly, inanity, insanity, lunacy, madness, nonsensicalness, nuttiness, preposterousness, senselessness, silliness, simplicity, wackiness, witlessness, zaniness

related words idiocy, imbecility, stupidity; fallacy, irrationality, unreasonableness; laughableness, ludicrousness, ridiculousness

near antonyms logicalness, rationality, reasonableness, validity

antonyms prudence, sageness, sanity, sapience, sensibleness, soundness, wisdom

2 language, behavior, or ideas that are absurd and contrary to good sense ⟨couldn't listen to another second of their *foolishness*, so I told them to be quiet⟩ — see NONSENSE 1

3 the quality or state of lacking intelligence or quickness of mind ⟨you didn't fail the test because of any innate *foolishness* but because of a lack of preparation⟩ — see STUPIDITY 1

foot *n* the lowest part, place, or point ⟨the *foot* of the pedestal⟩ — see BOTTOM 3

foot *vb* to give what is owed for ⟨I'll *foot* the bill for dinner⟩ — see PAY 2

foot (it) *vb* **1** to go on foot ⟨after the car broke down, we had to *foot it* to the movie⟩ — see WALK

2 to perform a series of usually rhythmic bodily movements to music ⟨got out onto the dance floor and *footed it* like crazy⟩ — see DANCE 1

foot (up) *vb* to combine (numbers) into a single sum ⟨please *foot up* the expenses from this month⟩ — see ADD 2

foothold *n* a place from which an advance (as for military operations) is made ⟨don't let the opposing team push us back down the field and gain a *foothold*⟩ — see BASE 2

footing *n* **1** an immaterial thing upon which something else rests ⟨your donations help provide the charity with a firm financial *footing* for its work⟩ — see BASE 1

2 position with regard to conditions and circumstances ⟨our two high schools are on a friendly *footing*⟩ — see SITUATION 1

3 the placement of someone or something in relation to others in a vertical arrangement ⟨work hard to get a better *footing* in the company⟩ — see RANK 1

footloose *adj* **1** not bound, confined, or detained by force ⟨after serving a detention, the students were *footloose* and free to go home⟩ — see FREE 3

2 not held back by rules, duties, or worries ⟨wished I could be as carefree as that *footloose* toddler⟩ — see FREEWHEELING

footpath *n* a rough course or way formed by or as if by repeated footsteps ⟨found the *footpath* leading down into the valley⟩ — see TRAIL 1

footprint *n* the mark or impression made by a foot ⟨mysterious *footprints* along the beach⟩

synonyms footstep, step

related words hoofprint; spoor, track; sign, trace, vestige

footstep *n* the mark or impression made by a foot ⟨saw *muddy* footsteps on the cleaned stairs⟩ — see FOOTPRINT

foozle *vb* to make or do (something) in a clumsy or unskillful way ⟨*foozled* the attempt to move the couch into the apartment and tore the fabric on the arms⟩ — see BOTCH

fop *n* a man extremely interested in his clothing and personal appearance ⟨such a *fop* that he drives nearly 50 miles just to get his hair cut by Monsieur Louis⟩ — see DANDY 1

for *conj* for the reason that ⟨it should have been graded, *for* I turned it in on time⟩ — see SINCE

forage *vb* to feed on grass or herbs ⟨cows *foraging* in the pasture⟩ — see ¹GRAZE

forage (for) *vb* to go in search of ⟨went *foraging for* change for the parking meter⟩ — see SEEK 1

foray *n* a sudden attack on and entrance into hostile territory ⟨made a nighttime *foray* into the enemy camp and took their command post⟩ — see RAID 1

foray (into) *vb* to enter for conquest or plunder ⟨Vikings *foraying into* the village⟩ — see INVADE

forbear *vb* to resist the temptation of ⟨she's old enough to make her own decisions, so we must *forbear* criticizing her taste in clothes⟩

synonyms abstain (from), forgo (*also* forego), keep (from), refrain (from)

related words avoid, eschew, shun; check, constrain, curb, inhibit; deny, refuse, withhold; buck, combat, fight

near antonyms capitulate, knuckle under, submit, surrender

antonyms give in (to), succumb (to), yield (to)

forbearance *n* the capacity to endure what is difficult or disagreeable without complaining ⟨we thank you for your *forbearance* while we attend to the technical difficulties interrupting the TV program⟩ — see PATIENCE

forbearing *adj* accepting pains or hardships calmly or without complaint ⟨was inspired by the *forbearing* patients of the intensive care unit⟩ — see PATIENT 1

forbid *vb* to order not to do or use or to be done or used ⟨smoking is *forbidden* throughout the building⟩ ⟨we *forbid* you to see him⟩

synonyms ban, bar, enjoin, interdict, outlaw, prohibit, proscribe

related words deter, discourage, dissuade; repress, suppress; halt, preclude, prevent, stop; embargo, exclude, rule out, shut out; debar, deprive, disallow, reject, veto; check, curb, inhibit, restrain; block, hinder, impede, obstruct

near antonyms approve, endorse (*also* indorse), sanction; authorize, license (*also* licence); abet, encourage, promote, support; bid, command, order; abide, bear, endure, tolerate

antonyms allow, let, permit, suffer

forbidden *adj* that may not be permitted ⟨trespassing is *forbidden*⟩ — see IMPERMISSIBLE

forbidding *adj* **1** causing fear ⟨a dark, *forbidding* house reputed to be haunted⟩ — see FEARFUL 1

2 harsh and threatening in manner or appearance ⟨told us in a *forbidding* voice to stop⟩ — see GRIM 1

forbidding *n* the act of ordering that something not be done or used ⟨the landlord's *forbidding* of loud music after 10:00 p.m.⟩ — see PROHIBITION 1

force *n* **1** a body of persons at work or available for work ⟨the nation's labor *force*⟩

synonyms help, manpower, personnel, pool, staff

related words labor, proletariat, rank and file; band, company, crew, gang, outfit, party, team; employee, helper, hireling, worker

2 the use of power to impose one's will on another ⟨a cruel tyrant who disbanded the parliament and ruled by *force*⟩

synonyms coercion, compulsion, constraint, duress, pressure

related words browbeating, bulldozing, bullying; fear, intimidation, menace, sword, terror, terrorism, threat, violence; might, muscle, strength; hardheadedness, self-will, willfulness; strain, stress

near antonyms agreement, approval, consent, permission; persuasion, reason

3 the ability to exert effort for the accomplishment of a task ⟨got through the college board exams by sheer *force* of will⟩ — see POWER 2

4 the capacity to persuade ⟨surely you were influenced by the *force* of his arguments?⟩ — see COGENCY 1

5 the quality of an utterance that provokes interest and produces an effect ⟨felt the full *force* of her denunciation of war as a moral option⟩ — see ¹PUNCH 1

6 the use of brute strength to cause harm to a person or property ⟨threatened to resort to *force* if he wouldn't listen to reason⟩ — see VIOLENCE

force *vb* to cause (a person) to give in to pressure ⟨*forced* the natives to sell their land⟩ ⟨hunger *forced* the refugees to steal⟩

synonyms coerce, compel, constrain, drive, make, muscle, obligate, oblige, press, pressure

related words browbeat, bulldoze, bully; high-pressure, intimidate, menace, terrorize, threaten

near antonyms allow, let, permit; convince, induce, persuade

forced *adj* **1** forcing one's compliance or participation by or as if by law ⟨*forced* attendance at school assemblies⟩ — see MANDATORY

2 lacking in natural or spontaneous quality ⟨wasn't too excited about the plans and so gave them a *forced* smile⟩ — see ARTIFICIAL 1

3 not made or done willingly or by choice ⟨participation in the program was *forced*⟩ — see INVOLUNTARY 1

forceful *adj* **1** having the power to persuade ⟨made a very *forceful* argument against going to war⟩ — see COGENT

2 marked by or uttered with forcefulness ⟨he kept asking me out until I gave him a very *forceful* and blunt "no"⟩ — see EMPHATIC 1

3 not showing weakness or uncertainty ⟨took a *forceful* stand on the issue⟩ — see FIRM 1

4 having power over the minds or behavior of others ⟨a *forceful* speaker whose words moved the audience to tears⟩ — see INFLUENTIAL 1

forcefully *adv* in a vigorous and forceful manner ⟨shut the door *forcefully*⟩ — see HARD 3

forcefulness *n* **1** the capacity to persuade ⟨the *forcefulness* of his argument is indisputable⟩ — see COGENCY 1

2 the quality of an utterance that provokes interest and produces an effect ⟨delivered the punch line with *forcefulness*⟩ — see ¹PUNCH 1

3 the quality or state of being forceful (as in expression) ⟨her clenched teeth only added to the *forcefulness* of her words⟩ — see VEHEMENCE 1

forcibly *adv* in a vigorous and forceful manner ⟨after getting in the ref's face once too often, he was *forcibly* ejected from the game⟩ — see HARD 3

ford *n* a place where a body of water (as a sea or river) is shallow ⟨didn't attempt getting the horses across the stream until we had reached the *ford*⟩ — see SHOAL

forearm *vb* to prepare (oneself) mentally or emotionally ⟨*forearmed* themselves for the championship game with the help of a sports psychologist⟩ — see FORTIFY 1

forebear *also* **forbear** *n* a person who is several generations earlier in an individual's line of descent ⟨his *forebears* came to America on the *Mayflower*⟩ — see ANCESTOR 1

forebode *also* **forbode** *vb* to show signs of a favorable or successful outcome ⟨that police car parked outside the house doesn't *forebode* well⟩ — see BODE

foreboding *adj* being or showing a sign of evil or calamity to come ⟨*foreboding* thunderclouds began to gather⟩ — see OMINOUS

foreboding *n* **1** a feeling that something bad will happen ⟨I have this strange *foreboding* that your ski vacation will not turn out well, so be extra careful⟩ — see PREMONITION

2 something believed to be a sign or warning of a future event ⟨used to think that if he saw a blackbird fly over his left shoulder it was a *foreboding* of harm⟩ — see OMEN

3 suspicion or fear of future harm or misfortune ⟨a pessimist who is always overcome by a sense of *foreboding* before flying on an airplane⟩ — see APPREHENSION 1

forecast *n* a declaration that something will happen in the future ⟨want to catch the weather *forecast* so I'll know kind of clothes to pack for the trip tomorrow⟩ — see PREDICTION

forecast *vb* to tell of or describe beforehand ⟨the station's meteorologist *forecasts* sun for the next five days⟩ — see FORETELL

forecaster *n* one who predicts future events or developments ⟨a financial *forecaster* who is widely followed by small investors⟩ — see PROPHET

forecasting *n* a declaration that something will happen in the future ⟨the construction company's *forecasting* of a September 1 completion date for the new school was wildly optimistic⟩ — see PREDICTION

foredoom *vb* to determine the fate of in advance ⟨since the dawn of the ages he was *foredoomed* to be king⟩ — see DESTINE

forefather *n* a person who is several generations earlier in an individual's line of descent ⟨our *forefathers* bought this farm, and our family has worked it for three generations⟩ — see ANCESTOR 1

forefront *n* the leading or most important part of a movement ⟨a politician who was in the *forefront* of women's rights⟩

synonyms vanguard

related words spearhead

near antonyms rank and file

forego *vb* to go or come before in time ⟨if the sparse crowds are any indication of the public's interest in the presidential candidate, then his reputation obviously *foregoes* him⟩ — see PRECEDE

foregoer *n* **1** one that announces or indicates the later arrival of another ⟨a nearly November snowfall that appears to be a disconcerting *foregoer* of the harsh winter facing us⟩ — see FORERUNNER 1

2 something belonging to an earlier time from which something else was later developed ⟨not many people still have manual typewriters, the *foregoers* to word processors⟩ — see ANCESTOR 2

foregoing *adj* going before another in time or order ⟨your *foregoing* statement contradicts your latest one⟩ — see PREVIOUS

forehanded *adj* having or showing awareness of and preparation for the future ⟨was *forehanded* enough to stock up on batteries for winter storms⟩ — see FORESIGHTED

foreign *adj* **1** being, relating to, or characteristic of a country other than one's own ⟨more Americans should take an interest in *foreign* languages⟩

synonyms alien, nonnative

related words imported, introduced, naturalized, transplanted; international, multicultural, multinational; distant, far-off, overseas, remote; bizarre, exotic, outlandish, strange

near antonyms endemic, local; aboriginal, indigenous

antonyms domestic, native

2 not being a vital part of or belonging to something ⟨pediatricians often have to remove peas or other *foreign* bodies from inside the ears of curious toddlers⟩ — see EXTRINSIC

foreigner *n* a person who is not native to or known to a community ⟨can tell by your accent you're a *foreigner* in these parts⟩ — see STRANGER

foreknow *vb* to realize or know about beforehand ⟨what couple can possibly *foreknow* the trials and tribulations that marriage will bring?⟩ — see FORESEE

foreknowledge *n* the special ability to see or know about events before they actually occur ⟨a suspenseful story about a man who has a frightening *foreknowledge* of disasters⟩ — see FORESIGHT 1

foreman *n* the person (as an employer or supervisor) who tells people and especially workers what to do ⟨asked the shift *foreman* if he could take a break⟩ — see BOSS

foremost *adj* **1** coming before all others in importance ⟨Albert Einstein is regarded by many as the *foremost* figure of the 20th century⟩
synonyms arch, cardinal, central, chief, dominant, first, grand, greatest, highest, key, leading, main, paramount, predominant, preeminent, premier, primary, principal, sovereign, supreme
related words distinguished, eminent, notable, noteworthy, illustrious, outstanding, prestigious, stellar, superior; important, major, momentous, significant; incomparable, matchless, unequaled (*or* unequalled), unparalleled, unsurpassed
near antonyms inconsequential, insignificant, minor, trivial, unimportant; collateral, inferior, secondary, subordinate, subsidiary
antonyms last, least
2 highest in rank or authority ⟨wanted to speak to the *foremost* supervisor in our department⟩ — see HEAD

forename *n* a name that is placed before one's family name ⟨a long string of *forenames* was given to the latest addition to the royal family⟩
synonyms Christian name, given name
related words appellation, denomination, designation; epithet, handle, nickname, sobriquet (*also* soubriquet); alias, nom de plume, pen name, pseudonym

forenoon *n* the time from sunrise until noon ⟨enjoy the relatively cool *forenoon*, for the afternoon promises to be a scorcher⟩ — see MORNING 1

foreordain *vb* to determine the fate of in advance ⟨we are such good friends, it's almost like we were *foreordained* to meet⟩ — see DESTINE

forepart *n* a forward part or surface ⟨moved to the *forepart* of the machine to check the mechanism⟩ — see FRONT 1

forerunner *n* **1** one that announces or indicates the later arrival of another ⟨the return of the swallows is traditionally regarded as a *forerunner* of spring⟩
synonyms angel, foregoer, harbinger, herald, precursor
related words foreboder, foreshadower, foretaste, forewarning; advertiser, announcer, crier, proclaimer; courier, messenger, runner; augury, omen, portent, presage; mark, sign, symptom; bellwether
2 something belonging to an earlier time from which something else was later developed ⟨enjoyed the demonstration of the simple hand loom that was the *forerunner* of today's computer-controlled looms⟩ — see ANCESTOR 2

foresee *vb* to realize or know about beforehand ⟨a freak accident that no one could possibly have *foreseen*⟩
synonyms anticipate, divine, foreknow
related words augur, forecast, foretell, presage, prognosticate, prophesy; envisage, foreshadow, prefigure, visualize; forewarn; preview; descry, discern, perceive; apprehend, dread, fear

foreseeing *adj* having or showing awareness of and preparation for the future ⟨some years ago the senator wrote a *foreseeing* essay on the threat of global terrorism⟩ — see FORESIGHTED

foreseer *n* one who predicts future events or developments ⟨in Greek mythology Cassandra was a *foreseer* who always accurately predicted misfortune but was never believed⟩ — see PROPHET

foreshadow *vb* to give a slight indication of beforehand ⟨a series of small tremors that *foreshadowed* the massive earthquake the next day⟩
synonyms prefigure
related words anticipate, foreknow, foresee; forecast, foretell, predict, prognosticate, prophesy; forewarn; augur, bode, forebode (*also* forbode), portend, presage, promise; connote, hint, imply, insinuate, intimate, suggest

foreshadowing *n* something believed to be a sign or warning of a future event ⟨the hero's strange encounter with a grave digger is often seen as a *foreshadowing* of his own death⟩ — see OMEN

foresight *n* **1** the special ability to see or know about events before they actually occur ⟨a mysterious woman who claims to have the gift of *foresight*⟩
synonyms foreknowledge, prescience
related words premonition, presentiment; clairvoyance, extrasensory perception, sixth sense; omniscience; divination
2 concern or preparation for the future ⟨had the *foresight* to realize the global importance of the Internet⟩
synonyms farsightedness, foresightedness, forethought, prescience, providence
related words precaution, premeditation; discretion, insight, prudence, sagacity, wisdom
near antonyms hindsight
antonyms improvidence, shortsightedness

foresighted *adj* having or showing awareness of and preparation for the future ⟨the *foresighted* conservationists who worked to create the national park system⟩
synonyms farsighted, forehanded, foreseeing, forethoughtful, prescient, provident
related words careful, cautious; insightful, perceptive, prudent, sage, wise
near antonyms careless, heedless, incautious
antonyms improvident, shortsighted

foresightedness *n* concern or preparation for the future ⟨thanks to your *foresightedness*, we have enough ice and food to last through the blackout⟩ — see FORESIGHT 2

forest *n* a dense growth of trees and shrubs covering a large area ⟨the endless *forest* that the first European settlers encountered⟩
synonyms timber, timberland, wood(s), woodland
related words coppice, copse, grove, scrubland, stand, thicket; greenwood, wildwood; woodlot

forestall *vb* to keep from happening by taking action in advance ⟨you can often *forestall* skidding on the ice simply by driving more slowly⟩ — see PREVENT

forestallment *n* the act or practice of keeping something from happening ⟨by raising the necessary funds, the historical society was able to effect a last-minute *forestallment* of the demolition of the town's oldest house⟩ — see PREVENTION

foretell *vb* to tell of or describe beforehand ⟨a 16th century astrologer who, some claim, accurately *foretold* 20th century events⟩
synonyms augur, forecast, predict, presage, prognosticate, prophesy
related words forewarn; bode, forebode (*also* forbode), portend; anticipate, divine, foreknow, foresee; announce, declare, proclaim
near antonyms recount, relate, report

foreteller *n* one who predicts future events or developments ⟨some regard that 16th-century astrologer as an uncanny *foreteller* of some of the most disastrous events of the 20th century⟩ — see PROPHET

foretelling *n* a declaration that something will happen in the future ⟨the ludicrous *foretellings* of self-styled psychics at the end of each year⟩ — see PREDICTION

forethought *n* concern or preparation for the future ⟨in an unusual show of *forethought*, he did his homework promptly on Friday night so he could have the weekend free⟩ — see FORESIGHT 2

forethoughtful *adj* having or showing awareness of and preparation for the future ⟨doctors encouraging people to be *forethoughtful* and get their flu shots in advance of the flu season⟩ — see FORESIGHTED

forever *adv* **1** for all time ⟨we'll be best friends *forever*⟩ — see EVER 1

2 on every relevant occasion ⟨he is *forever* reminding me to wear my hat and gloves in cold weather⟩ — see ALWAYS 1

forevermore *adv* for all time ⟨a hero that will be praised *forevermore* for his great deeds⟩ — see EVER 1

forewarn *vb* to give notice to beforehand especially of danger or risk ⟨I should *forewarn* you before you come to visit that we have a dog⟩ — see WARN

forewarning *n* the act or an instance of telling beforehand of danger or risk ⟨heeded the *forewarning* to stay off the ice until the town had checked to see if it was thick enough⟩ — see WARNING 1

foreword *n* a short section (as of a book) that leads to or explains the main part ⟨the editor makes some good points in the *foreword* about the author's life, so be sure to read it⟩ — see INTRODUCTION

forfeit *n* a sum of money to be paid as a punishment ⟨the *forfeit* for each baseball player involved in the brawl was $5,000⟩ — see FINE

forfeiture *n* a sum of money to be paid as a punishment ⟨the *forfeiture* for early withdrawal of the investment savings will be an amount equal to ten percent of the investment⟩ — see FINE

forgather *or* **foregather** *vb* to come together into one body or place ⟨asked the townsfolk to *forgather* at the flagpole for the Memorial Day ceremony⟩ — see ASSEMBLE 1

¹**forge** *vb* **1** to imitate or copy especially in order to deceive ⟨got in trouble for *forging* my dad's signature on the permission slip⟩ — see FAKE 1

2 to produce or bring about especially by long or repeated effort ⟨both sides labored mightily to *forge* a peace treaty⟩ — see HAMMER (OUT)

3 to shape with a hammer ⟨loved the dented look of that hand-*forged* copper pot⟩ — see HAMMER 1

²**forge** *vb* to move forward along a course ⟨*forged* ahead despite the bad weather⟩ — see GO 1

forged *adj* being such in appearance only and made or manufactured with the intention of committing fraud ⟨a *forged* ancient document that didn't fool experts in cartography⟩ — see COUNTERFEIT

forgery *n* an imitation that is passed off as genuine ⟨that is a cheap *forgery*, not an authentic Ming Dynasty vase⟩ — see FAKE 1

forget *vb* **1** to be unable to recall or think of ⟨I *forget* exactly on which street that the house is⟩

    synonyms unlearn

    related words lose, miss; blank; disregard, ignore, neglect, overlook

    near antonyms reminisce; remind

    antonyms mind [*chiefly dialect*], recall, recollect, remember

2 to fail to give proper attention to ⟨promised not to *forget* her high school friends after she went off to college⟩ — see NEGLECT 1

3 to leave undone or unattended to especially through carelessness ⟨*forgot* the pot boiling on the stove⟩ — see NEGLECT 2

4 to miss the opportunity or obligation ⟨I *forgot* to call on his birthday⟩ — see NEGLECT 3

forgetful *adj* inclined to forget what one has learned or to do what one should ⟨we become more *forgetful* as we get older⟩

    synonyms absentminded

    related words absent, abstracted, lost, oblivious, preoccupied, unmindful; amnesiac, senile; lax, neglectful, negligent, remiss, slack; careless, heedless, inconsiderate, thoughtless

    near antonyms alert, keen, sharp; careful, conscientious, heedful, thoughtful

    antonyms retentive

forgetfulness *n* a state of being disregardful or unconscious of one's surroundings, concerns, or obligations ⟨welcomed the *forgetfulness* of one's worries that only sleep can bring⟩ — see OBLIVION

forgivable *adj* worthy of forgiveness ⟨accidentally spilling your milk on my paper is certainly a *forgivable* mishap⟩ — see VENIAL

forgive *vb* **1** to cease to have feelings of anger or bitterness toward ⟨it is not easy to *forgive* those who have hurt us⟩

    synonyms pardon

    related words absolve, acquit, clear, exculpate, exonerate, vindicate; remit, shrive; condone, disregard, excuse, ignore, pass over, shrug off

    near antonyms smart; despise, detest, dislike, hate, loathe; avenge, redress, revenge

    antonyms resent

2 to overlook or dismiss as of little importance ⟨he has so many good qualities that I guess we can *forgive* a slight penchant for exaggeration⟩ — see EXCUSE 1

forgiveness *n* release from the guilt or penalty of an offense ⟨asked her *forgiveness* for failing to invite her to the party⟩ — see PARDON

forgo *also* **forego** *vb* to resist the temptation of ⟨I'll *forgo* dessert tonight—I'm trying to lose weight⟩ — see FORBEAR

forgotten *adj* left unoccupied or unused ⟨a *forgotten* doll under the bed⟩ ⟨a long-*forgotten* house down a winding dirt road⟩ — see ABANDONED

fork *vb* to go or move in different directions from a central point ⟨the road *forks* up ahead and you'll want to take the right fork⟩ — see SEPARATE 2

forlorn *adj* **1** feeling unhappiness ⟨was *forlorn* when she found out the trip had been cancelled⟩ — see SAD 1

2 sad from lack of companionship or separation from others ⟨a *forlorn* wanderer far from home⟩ — see LONESOME 1

forlornness *n* **1** a state or spell of low spirits ⟨seemingly nothing could relieve the losing team's *forlornness*⟩ — see SADNESS

2 utter loss of hope ⟨gave into *forlornness* and abandoned his quest⟩ — see DESPAIR 1

form *n* **1** the outward appearance of something as distinguished from its substance ⟨carved the block of wood into the *form* of a duck⟩

    synonyms cast, configuration, conformation, figure, geometry, shape *related words* contour, outline, profile, silhouette; framework, skeleton, situation; arrangement, layout, organization, pattern, plan, setup

near antonyms composition, material, matter, stuff, substance

2 a piece of paper with information written or to be written on it ⟨I filled out all the *forms* for applying to the school⟩

synonyms blank, document, paper

related words instrument, writ

3 personal conduct or behavior as evaluated by an accepted standard of appropriateness for a social or professional setting ⟨it's bad *form* to throw a tantrum on the court when you lose a tennis match⟩ — see MANNER 1

4 a state of being or fitness ⟨after a long season off, the football team is back in good *form*⟩ — see CONDITION 1

5 a three-dimensional representation of the human body used especially for displaying clothes ⟨put the dress on the *form* to finish pinning it together⟩ — see MANNEQUIN 1

6 an oft-repeated action or series of actions performed in accordance with tradition or a set of rules ⟨we'll use the second *form* in our church missals for today's Lenten service⟩ — see RITE

7 socially acceptable behavior ⟨displayed good *form* throughout the formal dinner⟩ — see DECENCY 1

8 the means or procedure for doing something ⟨there are established *forms* for voting on motions and amendments at meetings⟩ — see METHOD

9 the type of body that a person has ⟨has the big-boned *form* of a linebacker⟩ — see PHYSIQUE

10 the way in which the elements of something (as a work of art) are arranged ⟨liked the asymmetrical *form* of the mobile⟩ — see COMPOSITION 3

form *vb* **1** to take on a definite form ⟨my ideas on the subject are just starting to *form*⟩

synonyms crystallize, jell, shape (up), solidify

related words coalesce, cohere, fuse; combine, connect, join, unite

near antonyms break down, decompose, disintegrate

2 to be all the substance of ⟨this one sentence really *forms* the basis of your argument⟩ — see CONSTITUTE 1

3 to bring into being by combining, shaping, or transforming materials ⟨*formed* the pot out of the clay⟩ — see MAKE 1

4 to come into existence ⟨the new company *formed* from two smaller ones⟩ — see BEGIN 2

5 to come to have gradually ⟨I don't want you beginning skiers to *form* any bad habits⟩ — see DEVELOP 2

formal *adj* **1** following or agreeing with established form, custom, or rules ⟨a *formal* meeting of the school board⟩ ⟨a *formal* contract that was legally binding⟩

synonyms ceremonial, ceremonious, conventional, orthodox, regular, routine

related words authorized, certified, official; accepted, correct, decorous, proper; formalistic, ritual, ritualistic; methodical, orderly, systematic

near antonyms unauthorized, unofficial; improper, incorrect, indecorous

antonyms informal, irregular, unceremonious, unconventional, unorthodox

2 being something in name or form only ⟨was the *formal* head of the charitable organization though he never attended a single meeting⟩ — see NOMINAL 1

3 marked by or showing careful attention to set forms and details ⟨gave her a *formal* invitation to dinner⟩ — see CEREMONIOUS 1

4 relating to or suitable for wearing to an event requiring elegant dress and manners ⟨dress code is *formal* tonight⟩ ⟨a shop that rents out *formal* wear⟩ — see DRESS

5 very dignified in form, tone, or style ⟨the *formal* language of the coronation ceremony⟩ — see ELEVATED 2

formal *n* a social gathering for dancing ⟨asked her to the *formal* at the end of the year⟩ — see DANCE

formality *n* **1** an act or utterance that is a customary show of good manners ⟨bowing to your guest is a *formality* you don't need to perform for me⟩ — see CIVILITY 1

2 an oft-repeated action or series of actions performed in accordance with tradition or a set of rules ⟨loved the *formalities* of a traditional Christmas Eve candlelight service⟩ — see RITE

formalize *vb* to make agree with a single established standard or model ⟨we'll need to *formalize* our research results before we submit our study for review⟩ — see STANDARDIZE

format *n* **1** the way in which something is sized, arranged, or organized ⟨the book's *format* is very user-friendly⟩

synonyms arrangement, configuration, conformation, formation, layout, setup

related words design, plan, scheme; composition, constitution, makeup; build, construction, structure

2 the way in which the elements of something (as a work of art) are arranged ⟨this abstract painter bases the *format* of his works on color and its subtle gradations and not line or form⟩ — see COMPOSITION 3

formation *n* the way in which something is sized, arranged, or organized ⟨geese flying south in a V-*formation*⟩ — see FORMAT 1

formative *adj* having a role in deciding something's final form ⟨a teacher who was a *formative* influence on generations of students⟩

synonyms constructive, productive

related words causal, creative; consequential, influential

antonyms nonconstructive, nonproductive, unproductive

former *adj* having been such at some previous time ⟨the coach is a *former* professional baseball player⟩

synonyms erstwhile, late, old, onetime, past, sometime, whilom

related words bygone, dead, extinct

near antonyms contemporary, current, present; future, prospective

formidable *adj* **1** causing fear ⟨a *formidable*, irascible old man who frightened the neighborhood children⟩ — see FEARFUL 1

2 requiring considerable physical or mental effort ⟨running a marathon is a *formidable* undertaking⟩ — see HARD 2

formless *adj* having no definite or recognizable form ⟨a *formless* mass of clay that the potter transformed into an attractive bowl⟩

synonyms amorphous, shapeless, unformed, unshaped, unstructured

related words characterless, featureless, nondescript; chaotic, disorganized, incoherent, unordered, unorganized; fuzzy, hazy, indeterminate, indistinct, obscure, unclear, vague

near antonyms coherent, ordered, organized; clear, definite, distinct

antonyms formed, shaped, structured

formulaic *adj* using or marked by the use of something else as a basis or model ⟨she thought the plots of most action movies were pretty *formulaic*⟩ — see IMITATIVE

formulate *vb* **1** to convey in appropriate or telling terms ⟨trying to *formulate* a good way to tell her that she would need surgery⟩ — see PHRASE
2 to put (something) into proper and usually carefully worked out written form ⟨a writer planning to *formulate* a response to what he considered a very unfair review of his work⟩ — see COMPOSE 1

formulation *n* an act, process, or means of putting something into words ⟨his letter was a very accurate *formulation* of his thoughts on the matter⟩ — see EXPRESSION 1

formulator *n* one who creates or introduces something new ⟨the *formulator* of the microcomputer⟩ — see INVENTOR

forsake *vb* to cause to remain behind ⟨we evacuated for the hurricane and *forsook* most of our possessions⟩ — see LEAVE 1

forsaken *adj* left unoccupied or unused ⟨the *forsaken* paper mill was a rusting wreck⟩ — see ABANDONED

forsaking *n* the act of abandoning ⟨his hardhearted *forsaking* of his wife and children was truly unforgivable⟩ — see DERELICTION 1

forsooth *adv* **1** to tell the truth ⟨*forsooth*, the rumor is true: this lovely lass and I are getting married!⟩ — see ACTUALLY 1
2 without any question ⟨you're getting married without a penny to your name? a pretty story *forsooth*!⟩ — see INDEED 1

fort *n* a structure or place from which one can resist attack ⟨a series of *forts* along the frontier⟩
synonyms bastion, citadel, fastness, fortification, fortress, hold, stronghold
related words breastwork, bulwark, parapet, rampart; bunker, dugout

forte *n* something for which a person shows a special talent ⟨doing funny impressions of people has always been my *forte*⟩
synonyms speciality, specialty
related words area, demesne, department, discipline, domain, field, line, province, realm, sphere; element; aptness, bent, faculty, flair, genius, gift, knack, talent

forth *adv* **1** toward a point ahead in space or time ⟨from that day *forth* we were fast friends⟩ — see ONWARD 1
2 toward or at a point lying in advance in space or time ⟨go *forth* into the world with love and hope⟩ — see ALONG

forthcoming *adj* being soon to appear or take place ⟨everyone's excited about the *forthcoming* school vacation⟩
synonyms approaching, coming, imminent, impending, nearing, oncoming, pending, upcoming
related words future; anticipated, awaited, expected, foreseen, predicted
near antonyms bygone, former, past
antonyms late, recent

forthright *adj* **1** free in expressing one's true feelings and opinions ⟨sometimes was a little too *forthright* for her own good and ended up saying things that inadvertently offended people⟩ — see FRANK
2 going straight to the point clearly and firmly ⟨I appreciate your *forthright* explanation of the situation⟩ — see STRAIGHTFORWARD 1

forthrightly *adv* in an honest and direct manner ⟨*forthrightly* and unhesitatingly admitted his mistake⟩ — see STRAIGHTFORWARD

forthrightness *n* the free expression of one's true feelings and opinions ⟨valued her *forthrightness* in telling me she didn't like being called "Susie"⟩ — see CANDOR

forthwith *adv* without delay ⟨if the fire alarm rings, leave the building *forthwith*⟩ — see IMMEDIATELY

fortification *n* a structure or place from which one can resist attack ⟨defenders at the *fortifications* preparing for attack⟩ — see FORT

fortify *vb* **1** to prepare (oneself) mentally or emotionally ⟨Kelly *fortified* herself for the basketball tournament with a series of confidence-boosting exercises⟩
synonyms brace, forearm, nerve, ready, steel, strengthen
related words harden, inure, season, toughen; bolster, boost, buoy (up), buttress, prop (up), reinforce, support, sustain; embolden, encourage, hearten; rally, rouse, stir
near antonyms demoralize, discourage, dishearten, unnerve; debilitate, enfeeble, undermine, weaken
2 to increase the ability of (as a muscle) to exert physical force ⟨ate another granola bar to *fortify* himself for the rest of the bike ride⟩ — see STRENGTHEN 1
3 to make able to withstand physical hardship, strain, or exposure ⟨bought lots of warm clothing to *fortify* ourselves against the cold⟩ — see HARDEN 2

fortitude *n* the strength of mind that enables a person to endure pain or hardship ⟨it was only with the greatest *fortitude* that the Pilgrims were able to survive their first winter in Plymouth⟩
synonyms backbone, fiber, grit, guts, pluck, spunk
related words determination, purposefulness, resoluteness, resolution; bravery, courage, fearlessness, intrepidity; endurance, stamina, tolerance; heart, mettle, spirit; audacity, boldness, brass, cheek, chutzpah (*also* chutzpa *or* hutzpah *or* hutzpa), effrontery, hardihood, nerve, temerity
near antonyms indecisiveness, irresoluteness, irresolution, vacillation; cowardliness, cravenness, faintheartedness, timidity, timorousness
antonyms spinelessness

fortress *n* a structure or place from which one can resist attack ⟨built a snow *fortress* and then challenged the neighborhood kids to an in-your-face snowball fight⟩ — see FORT

fortuitous *adj* **1** coming or happening by good luck especially unexpectedly ⟨your arrival just before the thunderstorm was *fortuitous*⟩ — see FORTUNATE 1
2 happening by chance ⟨firmly believes that the creation of the universe was something other than just the *fortuitous* coming together of particles of matter⟩ — see ACCIDENTAL

fortunate *adj* **1** coming or happening by good luck especially unexpectedly ⟨in a *fortunate* turn of events, the motel had one last vacancy⟩
synonyms fluky, fortuitous, happy, lucky, providential
related words convenient, opportune, seasonable, timely; unexpected, unforeseen, unlooked-for; accidental, chance, coincidental; auspicious, bright, fair, promising, propitious; benign, favorable, golden, good; advantageous, beneficial, profitable
near antonyms inconvenient, inopportune, unseasonable, untimely; anticipated, expected, foreseen; deliberate, intentional, planned; inauspicious, unpromising
antonyms luckless, unfortunate, unhappy, unlucky

2 having good luck ⟨rabbits' feet are seen as making the carrier of them *fortunate*⟩ — see LUCKY 1

fortunateness *n* success that is partly the result of chance ⟨attributed his habitual *fortunateness* to the lucky penny he stuck in his shoe⟩ — see LUCK 1

fortune *n* **1** what is going to happen to someone in the time ahead ⟨the telephone psychic proceeded to tell me my *fortune*—at great length⟩

synonyms future

related words circumstance, destiny, doom, lot, portion; futurities, outlook, prospect

near antonyms present

antonyms past

2 a very large amount of money ⟨the billionaire's huge mansion must have cost a *fortune*⟩

synonyms king's ransom, mint, wad

related words heap, pile, pot; bonanza, mine, treasure trove; assets, property, riches, wealth

antonyms mite, pittance

3 a state or end that seemingly has been decided beforehand ⟨it was his *fortune* that he should wander in the wilderness before becoming king⟩ — see FATE 1

4 success that is partly the result of chance ⟨in a streak of good *fortune* won the lottery twice that year⟩ — see LUCK 1

5 the total of one's money and property ⟨the family *fortune* is mostly in rare paintings and real estate⟩ — see WEALTH 1

fortune–teller *n* one who predicts future events or developments ⟨if the carnival's *fortune-teller* had been on the level, she could have predicted that I'd pass right by⟩ — see PROPHET

forty winks *n pl* a short sleep ⟨after turning the boat over to the first mate, the captain went below decks for *forty winks*⟩ — see ¹NAP

forum *n* a meeting featuring a group discussion ⟨a public *forum* called to find out how residents felt about a large high school being built in their neighborhood⟩

synonyms colloquy, conference, council, panel, parley, powwow, roundtable, seminar, symposium

related words caucus, town meeting; assembly, conclave, congregation, congress, convention, convocation, synod; debate, deliberation; brainstorming

forward *adv* **1** toward or at a point lying in advance in space or time ⟨if you keep walking *forward*, you'll hit that wall⟩ — see ALONG

2 toward a point ahead in space or time ⟨from this day *forward*, our two nations will live in peace and harmony⟩ — see ONWARD 1

forward *adj* showing a lack of proper social reserve or modesty ⟨a stranger so *forward* as to ask what medication he was taking and what it was for⟩ — see PRESUMPTUOUS 1

forward *vb* to help the growth or development of ⟨their funds will help *forward* better relations between young people from those warring nations⟩ — see FOSTER 1

fossil *n* a person with old-fashioned ideas ⟨Dad is an old *fossil* who thinks that a boy and a girl shouldn't be together unsupervised until they are engaged⟩ — see FOGY

foster *vb* **1** to help the growth or development of ⟨the head librarian firmly declared that it is indeed the duty of local government to *foster* learning and a love of reading⟩

synonyms advance, cultivate, encourage, forward, further, nourish, nurture, promote

related words back, champion, support, uphold; endow, finance, fund, patronize, subsidize; abet, aid, as-

sist; advertise, boost, plug, publicize, tout; agitate (for), campaign (for), work (for)

near antonyms forbid, prevent, prohibit; battle, combat, counter, fight, oppose; repress, stifle, suppress; arrest, check, halt, retard

antonyms discourage, frustrate, hinder, inhibit

2 to bring to maturity through care and education ⟨a greathearted couple *fostering* two adopted children as well as three more of their own⟩ — see BRING UP 1

foul *adj* **1** marked by wet and windy conditions ⟨the *foul* weather brought out the windbreakers and rain slickers as everyone braced for a day of rough sailing⟩

synonyms bleak, dirty, inclement, nasty, raw, rough, squally, stormy, tempestuous, turbulent

related words blustering, blustery, breezy, gusty, windblown, windswept; cloudy, overcast, sunless; rainy, snowy; foggy, hazy, misty

near antonyms clear, cloudless, rainless, sunny; balmy, calm, halcyon, peaceful, placid

antonyms clement, fair

2 not being in accordance with the rules or standards of what is fair in sport ⟨an aggressive hockey player who is known for his *foul* play and readiness for a fight⟩

synonyms dirty, illegal, unfair, unsportsmanlike

related words dishonorable, shabby, shameful; ignoble, low, mean, ungentlemanly; immoral, unethical, unjust, unprincipled, unrighteous, unscrupulous

near antonyms just, law-abiding; ethical, moral, principled, righteous; honorable, irreproachable, unimpeachable

antonyms clean, fair, legal, sportsmanlike, sportsmanly

3 causing intense displeasure, disgust, or resentment ⟨a *foul* taste that made us gag⟩ — see OFFENSIVE 1

4 depicting or referring to sexual matters in a way that is unacceptable in polite society ⟨was sent to the principal's office for using *foul* language in class⟩ — see OBSCENE 1

5 having an unpleasant smell ⟨the *foul* fumes from the paper mill⟩ — see MALODOROUS

6 not clean ⟨I wouldn't play in the *foul* rainwater that's collected in the feeding trough⟩ — see DIRTY 1

foul *vb* **1** to make dirty ⟨*fouled* the bath towels with axle grease⟩ — see DIRTY

2 to make unfit for use by the addition of something harmful or undesirable ⟨industrial pollution *fouling* the water supply⟩ — see CONTAMINATE

foulness *n* **1** the quality or state of being obscene ⟨the *foulness* of your language means that it won't get on the Web site's bulletin board⟩ — see OBSCENITY 1

2 the state or quality of being dirty ⟨couldn't believe the *foulness* of her daughter's room and ordered her to clean it⟩ — see DIRTINESS 1

foul play *n* **1** the intentional and unlawful taking of another person's life ⟨the coroner ruled that there was no evidence of *foul play*⟩ — see HOMICIDE

2 the use of brute strength to cause harm to a person or property ⟨a long history of *foul play* and was once convicted on assault and battery charges⟩ — see VIOLENCE

foul–up *n* an instance of confusion ⟨there was a *foul-up* with our mail order, and not one item arrived as ordered⟩

synonyms mix-up

related words bobble, botch, bungle, fumble; blunder, error, flub, goof, mistake, slipup; chaos, confusion, disarrangement, disarray, disorder, hash, jumble, mess, muddle, shambles

foul up *vb* to make or do (something) in a clumsy or unskillful way ⟨tried not to *foul up* the football play⟩ — see BOTCH

found *vb* to be responsible for the creation and early operation or use of ⟨John Harvard did not actually *found* the university that now bears his name⟩
synonyms constitute, establish, inaugurate, initiate, innovate, institute, introduce, launch, pioneer, set up, start
related words author, father, originate; create, invent, produce; construct, erect, put up; develop, enlarge, expand; endow, finance, fund, subsidize; arrange, organize, systematize
near antonyms abolish, annihilate, annul, nullify; end, finish, stop, terminate
antonyms close (down), phase out, shut (up)

foundation *n* **1** a public organization with a particular purpose or function ⟨donated to a *foundation* that supported cancer research⟩ — see INSTITUTION 1
2 an immaterial thing upon which something else rests ⟨had a good enough *foundation* in math to pursue an economics degree⟩ — see BASE 1

founder *n* a person who establishes a whole new field of endeavor ⟨Maria Montessori was the *founder* of an educational system dedicated to maximizing a child's creative potential⟩ — see FATHER 2

foursquare *adj* **1** free in expressing one's true feelings and opinions ⟨when a woman wants to know if she looks fat in a certain outfit is not the time to be *foursquare*⟩ — see FRANK
2 going straight to the point clearly and firmly ⟨a *foursquare* evaluation of her performance that didn't mince words⟩ — see STRAIGHTFORWARD 1

foursquare *adv* in an honest and direct manner ⟨asked him *foursquare* if he was ever going to ask her to marry him⟩ — see STRAIGHTFORWARD

fox *vb* to get the better of through cleverness ⟨no confidence man will ever *fox* me and get my money⟩ — see OUTWIT

foxiness *n* **1** skill in achieving one's ends through indirect, subtle, or underhanded means ⟨his clever *foxiness* in getting you to reveal what he's getting for his birthday⟩ — see CUNNING 1
2 the inclination or practice of misleading others through lies or trickery ⟨an imposter of such formidable *foxiness* that a movie was made of his entertaining escapades⟩ — see DECEIT

foxy *adj* clever at attaining one's ends by indirect and often deceptive means ⟨the oft-told story of the *foxy* flatterer who works her way up the ladder of success by stepping on people as she goes⟩ — see ARTFUL 1

foyer *n* **1** a centrally located room in a building that serves as a gathering or waiting area or as a passageway into the interior ⟨theatergoers crowded the *foyer* during the play's intermission⟩
synonyms hall, lobby
related words entry, entryway, hallway, vestibule; concourse, corridor, gallery, passageway; antechamber, anteroom, waiting room
2 the entrance room of a building ⟨leave your muddy boots in the *foyer* and come into the house⟩ — see HALL 1

fracas *n* **1** a physical dispute between opposing individuals or groups ⟨broke up the *fracas* in the hall and sent both combatants to the office⟩ — see FIGHT 1

2 a rough and often noisy fight usually involving several people ⟨police preparing for any *fracas* that might follow the soccer game⟩ — see BRAWL 1

fractionation *n* the act or process of a whole separating into two or more parts or pieces ⟨originally conceived as one novel, *The Lord of the Rings* underwent a *fractionation* into a trilogy when its publisher feared it was too massive to sell as a single volume⟩ — see SEPARATION 1

fracture *vb* to cause to separate into pieces usually suddenly or forcibly ⟨*fractured* his arm in the fall⟩ — see BREAK 1

fragile *adj* **1** easily broken ⟨attaching the beautiful but *fragile* ornaments to the Christmas tree is always a touchy operation⟩
synonyms breakable, delicate, frail
related words dainty, fine, gossamer; flimsy, slight, tenuous; brittle, crisp, crumbly, flaky, friable, short; feeble, infirm, weak; inelastic, inflexible, stiff
near antonyms firm, solid, substantial; elastic, flexible, resilient
antonyms nonbreakable, strong, sturdy, tough, unbreakable
2 easily injured without careful handling ⟨babies are *fragile*, so remember to care for them gently⟩ — see TENDER 1

fragility *n* the state or quality of having a delicate structure ⟨marvelled at the *fragility* and the surprising strength of the bird's wing bones⟩ — see DELICACY 2

fragment *n* a broken or irregular part of something that often remains incomplete ⟨charred *fragments* of the exploded rocket were scattered over a huge area of ground⟩
synonyms bit, piece, scrap
related words shred, tatter; end, leftover, remainder, remnant; part, portion, section, segment

fragment *vb* to cause to separate into pieces usually suddenly or forcibly ⟨rough handling will *fragment* these delicate cookies, so take care or you'll have crumbs⟩ — see BREAK 1

fragmental *adj* lacking some necessary part ⟨will have to settle for a quick, *fragmental* explanation of what happened⟩ — see INCOMPLETE

fragmentary *adj* lacking some necessary part ⟨the historical record of this pharaoh's life and reign is *fragmentary* at best⟩ — see INCOMPLETE

fragrance *n* a sweet or pleasant smell ⟨the *fragrance* of lilac trees in full bloom⟩
synonyms aroma, bouquet, incense, perfume, redolence, scent, spice
related words odor
antonyms reek, stench, stink

fragrant *adj* having a pleasant smell ⟨the balsam fir is a favorite as a Christmas tree because it is so *fragrant*⟩
synonyms ambrosial, aromatic, perfumed, redolent, savory, scented, sweet
related words flowery, fruity, pungent, spicy; odoriferous, odorous; clean, fresh, pure
near antonyms odorless, unscented; fusty, musty, stale; gamy (*or* gamey)
antonyms fetid, foul, malodorous, noisome, putrid, rancid, rank, reeking, reeky, smelly, stinking, stinky, strong

frail *adj* **1** easily broken ⟨a *frail* eggshell⟩ — see FRAGILE 1
2 easily injured without careful handling ⟨be careful with your grandmother, as she's very *frail* and a fall would be disastrous⟩ — see TENDER 1

3 lacking bodily strength ⟨*frail* after a long battle with his bronchitis⟩ — see WEAK 1

4 lacking strength of will or character ⟨a *frail* person easily swayed by other's opinions⟩ — see WEAK 2

frailness *n* **1** the quality or state of lacking physical strength or vigor ⟨his *frailness* prevented him from playing football⟩ — see WEAKNESS 1

2 the quality or state of lacking strength of will or character ⟨don't take advantage of your younger sister's *frailness* of character and get her to lie for you⟩ — see WEAKNESS 2

frailty *n* **1** a defect in character ⟨selfishness is a common human *frailty*⟩ — see FAULT 1

2 the quality or state of lacking physical strength or vigor ⟨*frailty* doesn't affect all elderly people, for many are indeed healthy and strong⟩ — see WEAKNESS 1

3 the quality or state of lacking strength of will or character ⟨the *frailty* shown by the apostle Peter when he denied Jesus three times⟩ — see WEAKNESS 2

frame *n* **1** the arrangement of parts that gives something its basic form ⟨now that the *frame* has been built, we have a better idea of the size of our new house⟩

synonyms configuration, framework, shell, skeleton, structure

related words lattice, network; contour, figure, outline, profile, shape, silhouette; chassis

2 a state of mind dominated by a particular emotion ⟨was in a strange *frame* of mind after winning the lottery⟩ — see MOOD 1

3 the type of body that a person has ⟨a tall man with a big *frame*⟩ — see PHYSIQUE

frame *vb* **1** to bring into being by combining, shaping, or transforming materials ⟨*framed* a unique coffee table from an old, discarded chest of drawers⟩ — see MAKE 1

2 to plan out usually with subtle skill or care ⟨a composer *framing* the structure of a song⟩ — see ENGINEER

3 to put (something) into proper and usually carefully worked out written form ⟨you'll need to *frame* your argument well if you're going to win the debate⟩ — see COMPOSE 1

4 to work out the details of (something) in advance ⟨*framed* a schedule for the project⟩ — see PLAN 1

framework *n* the arrangement of parts that gives something its basic form ⟨you've got the *framework* of the story and just need to fill in the details⟩ — see FRAME 1

franchise *n* the right to formally express one's position or will in an election ⟨the Territory of Wyoming granted women the *franchise* in 1869, a full 51 years before the Nineteenth Amendment granted women the right to vote in all elections⟩ — see VOTE 1

frank *adj* free in expressing one's true feelings and opinions ⟨our ballet teacher is very *frank* about telling her students whether she thinks they have the talent for a career in dance⟩

synonyms candid, direct, forthright, foursquare, freespoken, honest, open, openhearted, outspoken, plain, plainspoken, straight, straightforward, unguarded, unreserved

related words artless, earnest, sincere; outgoing, uninhibited, unrestrained; vocal, vociferous; abrupt, bluff, blunt, brusque, curt, gruff, sharp; impolite, inconsiderate, rude, tactless, undiplomatic, unsubtle

near antonyms inhibited, reserved, restrained; closemouthed, reticent, tight-lipped; ambiguous, circuitous, equivocal, evasive; diplomatic, politic, tactful; civil, considerate, courteous, polite

antonyms dissembling

frankly *adv* to tell the truth ⟨*frankly*, I'd rather stay at home than go to the movies⟩ — see ACTUALLY 1

frankness *n* the free expression of one's true feelings and opinions ⟨considering her *frankness*, I knew she would tell me what she really thought of my dress⟩ — see CANDOR

frantic *adj* **1** feeling overwhelming fear or worry ⟨the *frantic* parents were searching all over the fairgrounds for their lost child⟩

synonyms agitated, delirious, distraught, frenzied, hysterical

related words alarmed, anxious, disquieted, disturbed, troubled, upset, worried, wrought (up); berserk, crazed, demented, deranged, mad, maniacal (*also* maniac); raging, ranting, raving

near antonyms calm, peaceful, serene, tranquil; cool, coolheaded, undisturbed, unperturbed, untroubled

antonyms collected, composed, self-possessed

2 marked by great and often stressful excitement or activity ⟨the holiday season seems to be moving along at a *frantic* pace⟩ — see FURIOUS 1

frantically *adv* in a confused and reckless manner ⟨ran *frantically* from room to room looking for the escaped hamster⟩ — see HELTER-SKELTER 1

fraternal *adj* of, relating to, or befitting brothers ⟨there was a *fraternal* bond between the two boys all throughout their school years⟩

synonyms brotherly

related words familial, sisterly; chummy, friendly, neighborly

fraternity *n* **1** a group of persons formally joined together for some common interest ⟨a firm believer in community service and a dedicated member of the local *fraternity* of Good Samaritans⟩ — see ASSOCIATION 2

2 the body of people in a profession or field of activity ⟨the *fraternity* of civil engineers⟩ — see CORPS

fraternize *vb* **1** to come or be together as friends ⟨don't *fraternize* just with people of the same race, religion, or social background⟩ — see ASSOCIATE 1

2 to take part in social activities ⟨a group of kids *fraternizing* together after school every day⟩ — see SOCIALIZE

fraud *n* one who makes false claims of identity or expertise ⟨the "blind" panhandler was just a *fraud* trying to con people out of their money⟩ — see IMPOSTOR

fraudulent *adj* **1** marked by, based on, or done by the use of dishonest methods to acquire something of value ⟨hoping to get millions from the insurance company, the man made the *fraudulent* claim that he had been seriously injured in the accident⟩

synonyms crooked, deceitful, defrauding, dishonest, double-dealing, false

related words deceptive, misleading, specious

near antonyms legitimate, true, valid

antonyms aboveboard, honest, truthful

2 given to or marked by cheating and deception ⟨*fraudulent* citizens who cheat on their taxes⟩ — see DISHONEST 2

fraught *adj* possessing or covered with great numbers or amounts of something specified ⟨every room in my childhood home is *fraught* with memories⟩ — see RIFE

fray *n* **1** a forceful effort to reach a goal or objective ⟨another generation of scientists entered the *fray* to find a cure for AIDS⟩ — see STRUGGLE 1

2 a physical dispute between opposing individuals or groups ⟨a troubled youth always getting into *frays* at school⟩ — see FIGHT 1

3 a rough and often noisy fight usually involving several people ⟨school officials broke up the *fray* and gave all guilty parties detention⟩ — see BRAWL 1

fray *vb* to damage or diminish by continued friction ⟨constant rubbing against the rock face has badly *frayed* our climbing rope⟩ — see ABRADE 1

frayed *adj* worn or torn into or as if into rags ⟨wore a beloved but badly *frayed* flannel shirt⟩ — see RAGGED 2

freak *adj* being out of the ordinary ⟨was surprised by a *freak* hailstorm⟩ — see EXCEPTIONAL

freak *n* **1** a person, thing, or event that is not normal ⟨that snowstorm in April was a *freak*, since our weather is usually much balmier by then⟩
synonyms abnormality, anomaly, monster, monstrosity
related words malformation, mutant, mutation; character, crackbrain, crackpot, eccentric, kook, oddball, screwball, weirdo; deviant; maverick, nonconformist
near antonyms sample, specimen; standard
antonyms average, norm
2 a person with a strong and habitual liking for something ⟨I'm a hockey *freak*⟩ — see FAN
3 a sudden impulsive and apparently unmotivated idea or action ⟨suddenly had the bizarre *freak* to take a road trip across the country⟩ — see WHIM

freak (out) *vb* **1** to trouble the mind of; to make uneasy ⟨don't say that, as it totally *freaks* me *out*⟩ — see DISTURB 1
2 to yield to mental or emotional stress ⟨the substitute teacher *freaked out* when she saw the frog we had slipped into her desk⟩ — see CRACK 2

freakish *adj* prone to sudden illogical changes of mind, ideas, or actions ⟨had a *freakish* roommate in college who once decided to drive all the way to Canada on the spur of the moment⟩ — see WHIMSICAL

freakishness *n* an inclination to sudden illogical changes of mind, ideas, or actions ⟨though some mistook his *freakishness* for mental illness, it was just a quirk of his personality and nothing more⟩ — see WHIMSICALITY

freckle *vb* to mark with small spots especially unevenly ⟨*freckled* the frosting with flakes of coconut⟩ — see SPOT

freckled *adj* marked with spots ⟨a tanned girl with a *freckled* face⟩ — see SPOTTED 1

free *adj* **1** not being under the rule or control of another ⟨the 20th century saw many African countries become *free* after many years of European rule⟩
synonyms autonomous, independent, self-governing, separate, sovereign
related words freeborn; delivered, emancipated, freed, liberated, manumitted, redeemed, released; unconquered, ungoverned, unruled, unsupervised; empowered, enfranchised; democratic, republican
near antonyms captive, conquered, enslaved, subdued, subjugated; inferior, subordinate, subservient
antonyms dependent, subject, unfree
2 no longer burdened with something unpleasant or painful ⟨after our son arrived home safely, we were grateful to be *free* from worry⟩
synonyms disencumbered, quit, unburdened
related words delivered, freed, liberated, released; unhampered, unimpeded
3 not bound, confined, or detained by force ⟨all of the animals in the game preserve are *free* to roam all over its vast area⟩
synonyms footloose, loose, unbound, unconfined, unrestrained

related words escaped; uncaged, unchained, unfettered, unleashed; uncaught; unanchored, unbolted, undone, unfastened, untied; clear, disengaged, unengaged
phrases at large, at liberty
near antonyms caught; caged, chained, leashed; anchored, bolted, fastened, shackled, tied
antonyms bound, confined, restrained, unfree
4 not costing or charging anything ⟨although the museum normally charges admission, on Wednesdays it is *free* to all⟩
synonyms complimentary, gratis, gratuitous
related words nominal; discretionary, freewill, optional, voluntary; honorary, uncompensated, unpaid
near antonyms paid
5 allowing passage without obstruction ⟨make sure the pass is *free* before you attempt the trip through the mountains this winter⟩ — see OPEN 1
6 giving or sharing in abundance and without hesitation ⟨was very *free* with his money⟩ — see GENEROUS 1
7 not being in a state of use, activity, or employment ⟨this computer terminal is *free* if you need to use it⟩ — see INACTIVE 2
8 showing a lack of proper social reserve or modesty ⟨she's a little too *free* with information about her social life⟩ — see PRESUMPTUOUS 1

free *vb* **1** to set free (as from slavery or confinement) ⟨a global crusade to *free* Nelson Mandela from a South African prison had emerged⟩
synonyms discharge, emancipate, enfranchise, liberate, loose, loosen, manumit, release, spring, unbind, uncage, unchain, unfetter
related words bail (out), deliver, parole, ransom, redeem, rescue; disengage, disentangle, extricate
near antonyms manacle, shackle, trammel; immure, imprison, incarcerate, intern, jail; conquer, enslave, subdue, subjugate
antonyms bind, confine, enchain, fetter, restrain
2 to arrange clear passage of (something) by removing obstructions ⟨we'll *free* the river by breaking up the ice jam⟩ — see OPEN 2
3 to rid the surface of (as an area) from things in the way ⟨would you mind *freeing* up the work area so I can work?⟩ — see CLEAR 1
4 to set (a person or thing) free of something that encumbers ⟨a phone call would *free* your parents from worry⟩ — see RID
5 to set free from entanglement or difficulty ⟨quickly *free* the animal from the trap⟩ — see EXTRICATE

freebie *or* **freebee** *n* something given to someone without expectation of a return ⟨got this CD as a *freebie* for buying a receiver⟩ — see GIFT 1

freebooter *n* someone who engages in robbery of ships at sea ⟨the ship was captured by *freebooters* who were looking for gold⟩ — see PIRATE

freedom *n* **1** the state of being free from the control or power of another ⟨we owe our *freedom* to the untold numbers of soldiers who have fought in our nation's wars since its founding⟩
synonyms autonomy, independence, liberty, self-government, sovereignty
related words emancipation, enfranchisement, liberation, manumission, release
near antonyms captivity, enchainment, enslavement, imprisonment, incarceration, subjugation
antonyms dependence, subjection

2 the right to act or move freely ⟨as special guests of the owners, the youngsters had full *freedom* of the resort and its private beach⟩
synonyms authorization, free hand, latitude, license (*or* licence), run
related words authority, mandate, power; range, room, space

free-for-all *adj* freely available for use or participation by all ⟨the public library has a *free-for-all* lending policy⟩ — see OPEN 2

free-for-all *n* a rough and often noisy fight usually involving several people ⟨during the play-offs, fans of the opposing teams clashed in the streets in several *free-for-alls*⟩ — see BRAWL 1

free hand *n* the right to act or move freely ⟨gave him *free hand* in managing the club⟩ — see FREEDOM 2

freehanded *adj* giving or sharing in abundance and without hesitation ⟨is very *freehanded* with her friends whenever she gets some extra money⟩ — see GENEROUS 1

freeing *n* the act of setting free from slavery ⟨the human rights group works for the *freeing* of political prisoners all over the world⟩ — see LIBERATION

freely *adv* **1** of one's own free will ⟨I will *freely* give my life for my country⟩ — see VOLUNTARILY
2 without difficulty ⟨the horse broke the halter rope quite *freely*⟩ — see EASILY

free-spoken *adj* free in expressing one's true feelings and opinions ⟨I pride myself on being *free-spoken* and feel no shame in telling you my honest opinion on just about anything⟩ — see FRANK

freestanding *adj* not physically attached to another unit ⟨a *freestanding* CD player that can easily be hooked up to your existing components⟩ — see SEPARATE 2

freeway *n* a passage cleared for public vehicular travel ⟨a new driver who's nervous about driving on the *freeway* for the first time⟩ — see WAY 1

freewheeling *adj* not held back by rules, duties, or worries ⟨James Bond has long been the model of the *freewheeling* hero who encounters danger and excitement in every corner of the globe⟩
synonyms footloose
related words easygoing, nonchalant, relaxed; unattached, uncommitted; unbridled, ungoverned, unrestrained; uninhibited, unsuppressed; self-assured, self-confident, self-reliant
near antonyms attached, committed
antonyms tied

freewill *adj* **1** made, given, or done with one's own free will ⟨a *freewill* confession of guilt made by the defendant during police interrogation⟩ — see INTENTIONAL 1
2 done, made, or given with one's own free will ⟨made a *freewill* offering for UNESCO⟩ — see VOLUNTARY 1

free will *n* the act or power of making one's own choices or decisions ⟨all of the workers at the homeless shelter are unpaid and are there of their own *free will*⟩
synonyms accord, choice, option, self-determination, volition, will
related words election, preference; inclination, penchant, predilection, predisposition
near antonyms coercion, compulsion, constraint, duress, force

freeze *n* a weather condition marked by low temperatures ⟨the Midwest will experience an intense *freeze* later in the week⟩ — see COLD

freeze *vb* to become physically firm or solid ⟨add antifreeze to the water in the radiator so it won't *freeze* and damage the engine⟩ — see HARDEN 1

freezing *adj* having a low or subnormal temperature ⟨why aren't you wearing a coat, as it's *freezing* outside?⟩ — see COLD 1

freight *n* a mass or quantity of something taken up and carried, conveyed, or transported ⟨shipped a large *freight* of steel to the manufacturer⟩ — see LOAD 1

frenetic *adj* marked by great and often stressful excitement or activity ⟨the *frenetic* rush to get every member of the cast in place before the curtain went up⟩ — see FURIOUS 1

frenzied *adj* **1** being in a state of increased activity or agitation ⟨the *frenzied* scene at the mall in the final week before Christmas⟩ — see FEVERISH 1
2 feeling overwhelming fear or worry ⟨*frenzied* rescue workers searched through the snow, looking for more victims of the avalanche⟩ — see FRANTIC 1
3 marked by great and often stressful excitement or activity ⟨the *frenzied* pace of the first week of the new school year⟩ — see FURIOUS 1

frenziedly *adv* in a confused and reckless manner ⟨the *frenziedly* scattering protestors were fleeing the tear gas⟩ — see HELTER-SKELTER 1

frenzy *n* a state of wildly excited activity or emotion ⟨in its *frenzy* to flee the danger the crowd became uncontrollable, and a number of people were trampled to death⟩
synonyms agitation, delirium, distraction, furor, furore, fury, hysteria, rage, rampage, uproar
related words chaos, confusion, disorder, turmoil; clamor, commotion, hubbub, hurly-burly, tumult
near antonyms calm, peacefulness, serenity, tranquillity (*or* tranquility)

frequency *n* the fact or state of happening often ⟨the *frequency* of twins in that family is remarkable⟩
synonyms commonness, prevalence
related words constancy, continualness, regularity; appearance, incidence, occurrence
antonyms infrequency, uncommonness, unusualness

frequent *adj* **1** appearing or occurring repeatedly from time to time ⟨our local multiplex usually has *frequent* showings of blockbusters, with starting times about every half hour⟩ — see REGULAR 1
2 often observed or encountered ⟨finches are *frequent* sights in this part of the country⟩ — see COMMON 1

frequent *vb* to go to or spend time in often ⟨like their counterparts elsewhere, the town's teenagers like to *frequent* the local malls⟩
synonyms hang around (in), hang out (at), haunt, resort (to), visit
related words attend, take in; infest, invade, swarm, overrun; drop (in *or* by), pop (in), run (in), stop (in *or* by); sojourn (at), stay (at), stop (over), tarry (in)
near antonyms elude, escape, evade
antonyms avoid, shun

frequenter *n* a person who visits another ⟨he's a regular *frequenter* of the corner restaurant⟩ — see GUEST 1

frequently *adv* many times ⟨our oddball uncle *frequently* lets himself into our house without knocking⟩ — see OFTEN

fresh *adj* **1** being in an original and unused or unspoiled state ⟨the restaurant uses only really *fresh* ingredients in all of its dishes⟩
synonyms brand-new, pristine, virgin
related words unaltered, unblemished, unbruised, uncontaminated, undamaged, undefiled, unharmed, un-

hurt, unimpaired, uninjured, unpolluted, unsoiled, unspoiled, unsullied, untainted, untouched, unused, unworn
near antonyms blemished, bruised, damaged, defiled, harmed, hurt, impaired, injured, soiled, sullied, tainted; faded, shopworn, used, worn; contaminated, polluted, spoiled
antonyms stale
2 displaying or marked by rude boldness ⟨if you are *fresh* with the art teacher, she'll give you a detention immediately⟩ — see NERVY 1
3 not known or experienced before ⟨a *fresh* look at the situation⟩ — see NEW 2
freshen *vb* to bring back to a former condition or vigor ⟨cool glasses of lemonade *freshened* us after a day of hard work outside⟩ — see RENEW 1
freshened *adj* made or become fresh in spirits or vigor ⟨the team came back from the locker room *freshened* and ready for the rest of the game⟩ — see NEW 4
freshly *adv* not long ago ⟨a *freshly*-paved road⟩ — see NEWLY
freshman *n* a person who is just starting out in a field of activity ⟨our senator is just a *freshman* in Congress⟩ — see BEGINNER
freshness *n* the quality or appeal of being new ⟨the *freshness* of that teacher's approach makes his classes fun and interesting⟩ — see NOVELTY 1
fret *n* a state of nervous or irritated concern ⟨one of my customers always gets into a *fret* if I'm so much as 15 minutes late delivering his newspaper⟩
synonyms dither, fluster, fuss, huff, lather, pother, stew, tizzy, twitter
related words dudgeon, pique; alarm, panic; ado, agitation, delirium, distraction, furor, hysteria, uproar; nervous breakdown
fret *vb* **1** to consume or wear away gradually ⟨over the span of thousands of years, the annual spring runoff *fretted* the rock, forming a deep channel⟩ — see EAT 2
2 to damage or diminish by continued friction ⟨don't let the girth *fret* the horse's belly or you won't be able to ride him⟩ — see ABRADE 1
3 to experience concern or anxiety ⟨don't *fret* over whether it will be sunny tomorrow, as there's nothing we can do about it⟩ — see WORRY 1
friable *adj* having a texture that readily breaks into little pieces under pressure ⟨sand dollars are *friable*, so handle them carefully⟩ — see CRISP 1
friary *n* a residence for men under religious vows ⟨the Franciscans left the chapel and went to the *friary* for rest⟩ — see MONASTERY
friction *n* a lack of agreement or harmony ⟨there was *friction* between the two sides of the family⟩ — see DISCORD
frictionless *adj* having or marked by agreement in feeling or action ⟨enjoys an easygoing and *frictionless* relationship with her mother-in-law⟩ — see HARMONIOUS 3
friend *n* **1** a person who has a strong liking for and trust in another ⟨really close *friends* who like to do everything together and are always sharing secrets⟩
synonyms buddy, chum, comrade, confidant, crony, familiar, intimate, pal
related words acquaintance; associate, cohort, colleague, companion, fellow, hearty, hobnobber, mate, partner, peer; brother, sister; accomplice, ally, collaborator, confederate; benefactor, supporter, sympathizer, well-wisher; friendly

near antonyms adversary, antagonist, opponent, rival; archenemy, nemesis
antonyms enemy, foe
2 a person who actively supports or favors a cause ⟨hopes that the new governor will be a *friend* to environmental causes⟩ — see EXPONENT
friendliness *n* kindly concern, interest, or support ⟨was overwhelmed with the *friendliness* of the welcoming committee⟩ — see GOODWILL 1
friendly *adj* **1** having or showing kindly feeling and sincere interest ⟨all of the kids at Stacy's new school seemed *friendly*⟩ ⟨as a *friendly* gesture, we presented our new neighbors with a plate of homemade cookies⟩
synonyms amicable, companionable, comradely, cordial, genial, hearty, neighborly, warm, warmhearted
related words affable, approachable, gracious; convivial, gregarious, hospitable, sociable, social; jolly, jovial, merry; extroverted (*also* extraverted), outgoing; brotherly, fraternal, sisterly; close, familiar, intimate; affectionate, devoted, loving
near antonyms cold, cool, frigid; bellicose, belligerent, contentious, quarrelsome
antonyms antagonistic, hostile, unfriendly
2 closely acquainted ⟨we're *friendly* with our neighbors⟩ — see FAMILIAR 1
3 expressing approval ⟨a *friendly* sign that our plan would be approved⟩ — see FAVORABLE 1
friendship *n* kindly concern, interest, or support ⟨I appreciate your *friendship* during this difficult time for my family⟩ — see GOODWILL 1
fright *n* **1** something unpleasant to look at ⟨people in our neighborhood think that that orange and green office building is a hideous *fright*⟩ — see EYESORE
2 the emotion experienced in the presence or threat of danger ⟨the earthquake so filled me with *fright* that I still have trouble sleeping⟩ — see FEAR
frighten *vb* to strike with fear ⟨around the campfire the campers tried to *frighten* one another with ghostly legends and grisly tales⟩
synonyms affright, alarm, horrify, panic, scare, shock, spook, startle, terrify, terrorize
related words appall, dismay; amaze, astound, awe; chill, daunt, demoralize, dispirit, unman, unnerve; discompose, disconcert, disquiet, disturb, perturb, upset
near antonyms cheer, comfort, console, solace, soothe; embolden, encourage, hearten
antonyms reassure
frightened *adj* filled with fear or dread ⟨I am *frightened* of the dark⟩ — see AFRAID 1
frightening *adj* causing fear ⟨a truly *frightening* movie⟩ — see FEARFUL 1
frightful *adj* **1** causing fear ⟨that *frightful* costume could actually scare your younger sister, so don't let her see you wearing it⟩ — see FEARFUL 1
2 extremely disturbing or repellent ⟨couldn't listen to the *frightful* details of the murder trial⟩ — see HORRIBLE 1
frightfully *adv* to a great degree ⟨that coat is *frightfully* expensive, so don't spill anything on it⟩ — see VERY 1
frightfulness *n* the quality of inspiring intense dread or dismay ⟨had heard stories about the *frightfulness* of the entrance exams⟩ — see HORROR 1
frigid *adj* **1** having a low or subnormal temperature ⟨the poor old woman was discovered shivering in a *frigid* apartment⟩ — see COLD 1
2 lacking in friendliness or warmth of feeling ⟨the innkeeper gave us a *frigid* and unnecessarily formal welcome⟩ — see COLD 2

frill *n* **1** a strip of fabric gathered or pleated on one edge and used as trimming ⟨just had to sew the *frill* onto the bottom of the skirt and the dress was finished⟩ — see RUFFLE

2 something adding to pleasure or comfort but not absolutely necessary ⟨didn't get any food or drinks on the no-*frills* flight⟩ — see LUXURY 1

3 something that decorates or beautifies ⟨a birthday cake decorated with *frills* like edible glitter⟩ — see DECORATION 1

fringe *n* the line or relatively narrow space that marks the outer limit of something ⟨was on the *fringes* of the crowd and couldn't see the speaker⟩ — see BORDER 1

fringe *vb* **1** to be adjacent to ⟨the orchestral pit *fringed* the edge of the stage⟩ — see ADJOIN 1

2 to serve as a border for ⟨neat rows of red brick *fringe* the estate's flower beds⟩ — see BORDER

fringing *adj* having a border in common ⟨*fringing* nations fighting over territory on their shared border⟩ — see ADJACENT

frippery *n* **1** dressy clothing ⟨dressed in *frippery* for the big gala at the symphony⟩ — see FINERY

2 something of little importance ⟨socialites whose lives were consumed by *fripperies*⟩ — see TRIFLE

frisk *vb* to play and run about happily ⟨carefree kids laughing and *frisking* about in their backyard⟩ — see FROLIC 1

friskiness *n* a natural disposition for playful behavior ⟨as your puppy grows older, her *friskiness* will diminish a bit, but this breed is generally very energetic and playful⟩ — see PLAYFULNESS

frisky *adj* **1** given to good-natured joking or teasing ⟨a *frisky* kid who keeps the class in stitches with his jokes⟩ — see PLAYFUL

2 having much high-spirited energy and movement ⟨the *frisky* colt didn't like to be kept in his stall⟩ — see LIVELY 1

fritter *n* a small usually rounded mass of minced food that has been fried ⟨loves eating corn *fritters* with maple syrup⟩ — see CAKE

fritter (away) *vb* to use up carelessly ⟨quit *frittering away* the afternoon playing video games and get some housework done!⟩ — see WASTE 1

frivol *vb* to show a liking for someone of the opposite sex just for fun ⟨my friends warned me not to *frivol* with that guy, as he was likely to take me seriously⟩ — see FLIRT

frivolity *n* a lack of seriousness often at an improper time ⟨the boys were scolded for joking during the funeral service, which was hardly the time for *frivolity*⟩

synonyms facetiousness, flightiness, flippancy, frivolousness, levity, light-headedness, lightness

related words cheerfulness, gaiety (*also* gayety), glee, high-spiritedness, lightheartedness, merriment, mirth

near antonyms gloom, melancholy, moroseness, sadness, sullenness

antonyms gravity, intentness, seriousness, soberness, sobriety

frivolous *adj* **1** lacking importance ⟨judges are getting sick of people bringing *frivolous* lawsuits⟩ — see UNIMPORTANT

2 lacking in seriousness or maturity ⟨when asked by the waiter if we wanted anything else that evening, we made a *frivolous* request for free drinks⟩ — see GIDDY 1

frivolousness *n* a lack of seriousness often at an improper time ⟨his childish *frivolousness* at the awards ceremony wasn't appreciated by anyone⟩ — see FRIVOLITY 1

frock *n* a garment with a joined blouse and skirt for a woman or girl ⟨please get into your nicest *frock* and come down for tea⟩ — see DRESS 1

frolic *n* **1** a playful or mischievous act intended as a joke ⟨listened to Grandpa share memories of *frolics* like tipping the outhouse over while people were inside⟩ — see PRANK

2 a time or instance of carefree fun ⟨took the long weekend as a three-day *frolic* and spent it at the beach⟩ — see FLING 1

3 activity engaged in to amuse oneself ⟨firmly believes that childhood should be a time of carefree *frolic*⟩ — see PLAY 1

frolic *vb* **1** to play and run about happily ⟨scores of swimmers were *frolicking* in the ocean surf along the beach⟩

synonyms caper, cavort, disport, frisk, gambol, lark, rollick, romp, sport

related words bound, leap, skip, spring, tumble; curvet, dance, prance; carouse, revel, roister; carry on, fool (around), horse (around); clown, cut up; joyride, roughhouse, skylark

phrases kick up one's heels

near antonyms mope, stew, sulk

2 to engage in activity for amusement ⟨would rather *frolic* than do chores or homework any day of the week⟩ — see PLAY 1

frolicking *n* activity engaged in to amuse oneself ⟨after he finished his homework, he joined the *frolicking* on the street outside⟩ — see PLAY 1

frolicsome *adj* **1** given to good-natured joking or teasing ⟨a *frolicsome* uncle who was a favorite among his relatives⟩ — see PLAYFUL

2 joyously unrestrained ⟨teachers smiling at the *frolicsome* students leaving school for summer vacation⟩ — see EXUBERANT

front *n* **1** a forward part or surface ⟨the *front* of the church features a magnificent stained-glass window⟩

synonyms facade (*also* façade), face, forepart

related words exterior, outside, skin, surface, veneer

near antonyms innards, inside, interior

antonyms back, rear, reverse

2 a display of emotion or behavior that is insincere or intended to deceive ⟨that smile is just a *front*—I don't think she actually likes me at all⟩ — see MASQUERADE

front *vb* to stand or sit with the face or front toward ⟨the apartment complex *fronts* the ocean⟩ — see FACE 1

frontier *n* **1** a region along the dividing line between two countries ⟨the Apaches were once feared on both sides of the U.S.-Mexico *frontier*⟩

synonyms border, borderland, march

related words no-man's-land

2 a rural region that forms the edge of the settled or developed part of a country ⟨Alaska has been called America's last *frontier*⟩

synonyms backwater, backwoods, bush, hinterland, up-country

related words country, countryside, sticks

frontiersman *n* a person who settles in a new region ⟨the *frontiersmen* were willing to brave harsh living conditions in order to achieve a better life⟩

synonyms colonist, colonizer, homesteader, pioneer, settler

related words explorer, pathfinder, trailblazer

frost *n* a covering of tiny ice crystals on a cold surface ⟨the wintertime routine of scraping the *frost* off the car's windshield every morning⟩

synonyms hoar, hoarfrost, rime
related words frostwork

frosty *adj* **1** having a low or subnormal temperature ⟨a *frosty* autumn that was a sign of the brutal winter that followed⟩ — see COLD 1

2 having or showing a lack of friendliness or interest in others ⟨her response was *frosty* enough to tell me she didn't appreciate the question⟩ — see COOL 1

3 lacking in friendliness or warmth of feeling ⟨gave the salesperson on the phone a *frosty* "No, thank you" and hung up⟩ — see COLD 2

froth *n* a light mass of fine bubbles formed in or on a liquid ⟨*froth* on the ocean waves⟩ — see FOAM

frothy *adj* covered with, consisting of, or resembling foam ⟨a *frothy* dessert made of whipped egg whites and fruit puree⟩ — see FOAMY

froward *adj* **1** engaging in or marked by childish misbehavior ⟨a *froward* prank not appropriate in the work place⟩ — see NAUGHTY

2 given to resisting authority or another's control ⟨*froward* students sent to the office for chronic disciplinary problems⟩ — see DISOBEDIENT

3 given to resisting control or discipline by others ⟨acting like a *froward* preschooler is not going to get you what you want⟩ — see UNCONTROLLABLE

frowardness *n* refusal to obey ⟨was disciplined for her *frowardness*⟩ — see DISOBEDIENCE

frown *n* a twisting of the facial features in disgust or disapproval ⟨it was clear from the *frown* on Mom's face that we were later than we had promised⟩ — see GRIMACE

frown *vb* to look with anger or disapproval ⟨the principal just stood there and *frowned* at the student who, once again, was in trouble⟩
synonyms glare, gloom, glower, lower (*also* lour), scowl
related words gape, gaze, ogle, stare; grimace, pout; growl, snarl, sneer
phrases look daggers
antonyms beam, smile

frown (on) *vb* to hold an unfavorable opinion of ⟨school officials *frown on* skipping class without a valid excuse⟩ — see DISAPPROVE (OF)

frowsy *or* **frowzy** *adj* lacking neatness in dress or person ⟨a *frowsy* family living in wretched poverty⟩ — see SLOPPY 1

frozen *adj* **1** firmly positioned in place and difficult to dislodge ⟨the car door was *frozen* ever since an accident had damaged the hinge⟩ — see TIGHT 2

2 having been established and usually not subject to change ⟨pay rates will remain *frozen* until the company does better financially⟩ — see FIXED 1

frugal *adj* careful in the management of money or resources ⟨by being *frugal*, the family is able to stretch its monthly budget⟩
synonyms economical, economizing, provident, scrimping, sparing, thrifty
related words conserving, preserving, saving; forehanded, foresighted, prudent; penny-wise; cheap, close, closefisted, miserly, niggardly, parsimonious, stingy, stinting, tight, tightfisted
near antonyms improvident, shortsighted; freehanded, generous, liberal, openhanded, unsparing; extravagant, indulgent, lavish
antonyms prodigal, wasteful

frugality *n* careful management of material resources ⟨her life-long *frugality* has enabled her to save enough money to go to college next year⟩ — see ECONOMY

fruit *n* **1** a condition or occurrence traceable to a cause ⟨one *fruit* of your faithfulness in carrying out your duties will be more rewarding responsibilities⟩ — see EFFECT 1

2 something produced by physical or intellectual effort ⟨medical apparatus that was the *fruit* of years of research and development⟩ — see PRODUCT 1

fruitful *adj* **1** producing abundantly ⟨a very *fruitful* tree that gives us plenty of apples every year⟩ — see FERTILE

2 producing or capable of producing a desired result ⟨I hope your efforts to find that missing package are *fruitful*⟩ — see EFFECTIVE 1

fruition *n* the state of being actual or complete ⟨when she landed the lead in a Broadway play, a lifelong dream was brought to *fruition*⟩
synonyms accomplishment, achievement, actuality, attainment, consummation, fulfillment, realization
antonyms naught (*also* nought), nonfulfillment

fruitless *adj* producing no results ⟨this argument is totally *fruitless*, as neither of us will change our position⟩ — see FUTILE

frustrate *vb* to prevent from achieving a goal ⟨a multitude of conflicting opinions *frustrated* me in my attempt to find a computer that best suits my needs⟩
synonyms baffle, balk, beat, checkmate, foil, thwart
related words bar, block, hinder, impede, obstruct; arrest, check, halt, stop; forestall, obviate, preclude; negate, neutralize, nullify; counteract, offset; conquer, defeat, overcome
near antonyms abet, aid, assist; ease, facilitate, smooth
antonyms advance, cultivate, encourage, forward, foster, further, nurture, promote

frustrating *adj* causing annoyance ⟨these daily traffic jams are *frustrating*⟩ — see ANNOYING

frustration *n* **1** something that is a source of irritation ⟨bad spelling is a constant *frustration* to language-arts teachers⟩ — see ANNOYANCE 3

2 the emotion felt when one's expectations are not met ⟨the kids couldn't hide their *frustration* when they couldn't get the electronic toy to work⟩ — see DISAPPOINTMENT 1

3 the feeling of impatience or anger caused by another's repeated disagreeable acts ⟨Mom's *frustration* over our constant whining became too much to bear, and she lashed out⟩ — see ANNOYANCE 2

fuddy–duddy *n* a person with old-fashioned ideas ⟨a *fuddy-duddy* who thought that anyone too young to vote shouldn't be out past 8:00 p.m.⟩ — see FOGY

fudge *n* **1** language, behavior, or ideas that are absurd and contrary to good sense ⟨I was starting to realize that Grandpa's tales about when he was a boy were a lot of *fudge*⟩ — see NONSENSE 1

2 unintelligible or meaningless talk ⟨baby talk is pure *fudge* to everyone but the mother of the child who is doing the talking⟩ — see GIBBERISH

fudge *vb* **1** to avoid giving a definite answer or position ⟨wouldn't say whether he was for or against gun control but just *fudged* on the issue⟩ — see EQUIVOCATE

2 to use dishonest methods to achieve a goal ⟨she *fudged* on the exam and was expelled when she was caught⟩ — see CHEAT 1

fuel *n* something with a usable capacity for doing work ⟨such fossil *fuels* as coal, petroleum, and natural gas⟩
synonyms energy, power
related words kindling, propellant

fugitive *adj* **1** hard to find, capture, or isolate ⟨that *fugitive* trait called creativity⟩ — see ELUSIVE

2 lasting only for a short time ⟨had *fugitive* thoughts of leaving town after finishing high school but never acted on them⟩ — see MOMENTARY

fulfill *or* **fulfil** *vb* **1** to do what is required by the terms of ⟨the football player must remain with the team one more year to *fulfill* his contract⟩

synonyms answer, comply (with), fill, keep, meet, redeem, satisfy

related words complete, conclude, finalize, finish; accomplish, achieve, bring about, bring off, effect; discharge, execute, perform

phrases abide by, make good

near antonyms disregard, ignore, neglect, overlook, slight

antonyms breach, break, violate

2 to carry through (as a process) to completion ⟨you have *fulfilled* your duties most admirably⟩ — see PERFORM 1

fulfilling *adj* making one feel good inside ⟨had a *fulfilling* job tutoring inner-city youths⟩ — see HEARTWARMING

fulfillment *n* **1** the doing of an action ⟨her prompt *fulfillment* of any assignment given her⟩ — see COMMISSION 2

2 the state of being actual or complete ⟨saw the entire project through, from initial idea to final *fulfillment*⟩ — see FRUITION

full *adj* **1** containing or seeming to contain the greatest quantity or number possible ⟨at the start of the game everyone was *full* of energy and hope⟩ ⟨the boy's bedroom is *full* of sports trophies and medals⟩

synonyms brimful, brimming, bursting, chock-full (*or* chockful), crammed, crowded, fat, filled, jammed, jampacked, loaded, packed, stuffed

related words overcrowded, overfilled, overflowing, overfull, overloaded, overstuffed; abounding, fraught, replete, rife, swarming, teeming

near antonyms deficient, incomplete, insufficient, short; depleted, drained, exhausted

antonyms bare, blank, devoid, empty, stark, vacant, void

2 of the highest degree ⟨even at the age of eighteen he hadn't reached his *full* height⟩ ⟨a boat going at *full* speed⟩

synonyms greatest, maximum, top, topmost, utmost

related words high

near antonyms low

antonyms least, lowest, minimal, minimum

3 having one's appetite completely satisfied ⟨even the heartiest eaters are sure to be *full* when they leave that restaurant⟩

synonyms sated, satiate, satiated, stuffed, surfeited

related words glutted, gorged, overfed, overfull, overstuffed

near antonyms underfed, undernourished

antonyms empty, hungry, starving

4 covering everything or all important points ⟨a *full* analysis of the problems facing our cities today⟩ — see ENCYCLOPEDIC

5 having an abundance of some characteristic quality (as flavor) ⟨the dessert had a rich, *full* chocolate flavor⟩ — see FULL-BODIED

6 having an excess of body fat ⟨she should have a hairdo that compliments her *full* face⟩ — see FAT 1

7 including many small descriptive features ⟨a very *full* description of the city's cultural offerings⟩ — see DETAILED 1

8 not lacking any part or member that properly belongs to it ⟨a *full* deck of cards⟩ — see COMPLETE 1

full *adv* **1** to a full extent or degree ⟨waited until it was *full* dark to launch the attack⟩ — see FULLY 1

2 to a great degree ⟨he knew *full* well that what he was doing was wrong⟩ — see VERY 1

full *n* a complete amount of something ⟨the account is now paid in *full*⟩ — see WHOLE

full blast *adv* with all power or resources being used ⟨Mom and Dad arrived home to find the stereo going *full blast* and the kitchen a mess⟩

synonyms all out, full steam ahead, full tilt, tooth and nail

related words completely, fully, totally; extremely, utterly

phrases in full career, to the hilt

full–blooded *adj* of unmixed ancestry ⟨a *full-blooded* American Indian⟩ — see PUREBRED

full–blown *adj* fully grown or developed ⟨before he became a *full-blown* literary sensation, he wrote articles for little journals that paid even littler money⟩ — see MATURE 1

full–bodied *adj* having an abundance of some characteristic quality (as flavor) ⟨after that huge Sunday brunch, Mom and Dad needed a *full-bodied* coffee⟩

synonyms concentrated, full, potent, rich, robust, strong

related words heavy; straight, undiluted, unmixed

near antonyms diluted, watered (down), watery

antonyms light, mild, thin, weak

full dress *n* dressy clothing ⟨suburban teens in *full dress* for the prom at the country club⟩ — see FINERY

full–fledged *adj* fully grown or developed ⟨it was years before he became a *full-fledged* star⟩ — see MATURE 1

full–grown *adj* fully grown or developed ⟨when you are *full-grown*, then you can set your own curfew⟩ — see MATURE 1

full–scale *adj* trying all possibilities ⟨a *full-scale* search and rescue for the victims of the rock slide⟩ — see EXHAUSTIVE

full steam ahead *adv* with all power or resources being used ⟨construction on the house is going *full steam ahead* and will probably be done ahead of schedule⟩ — see FULL BLAST

full tilt *adv* **1** with all power or resources being used ⟨during the war the nation's factories were going *full tilt*⟩ — see FULL BLAST

2 with great speed ⟨the fleeing robber ran *full tilt* down the hill⟩ — see FAST 1

fully *adv* **1** to a full extent or degree ⟨only with daybreak did we *fully* realize the extent of the damage from the storm⟩

synonyms all, altogether, clean, completely, dead, entirely, fast, flat, full, perfectly, plumb [*chiefly dialect*], quite, thoroughly, totally, utterly, well, wholly

related words absolutely, categorically, unqualifiedly; by and large, chiefly, generally, largely, mainly, more or less, mostly, predominately, primarily, principally

phrases at length, to pieces, to the hilt

near antonyms barely, hardly, just, scarcely

antonyms partially, partly

2 with attention to all aspects or details ⟨wanted to be *fully* involved in the project⟩ — see THOROUGHLY 1

fulminate *vb* to talk loudly and wildly ⟨was embarrassed when her dad began *fulminating* at the restaurant about what's wrong with today's kids⟩ — see RANT

fulmination *n* harsh insulting language ⟨players were told they had a right to be spared the *fulmination* of the hockey coach⟩ — see ABUSE 1

fulsome *adj* overly or insincerely flattering ⟨the player's *fulsome* praise for the coach showed just how hard he was trying to be named captain of the team⟩
synonyms adulatory, gushing, unctuous
related words drooling, slavering, slobbering; cloying, sickening; demonstrative, effusive, mushy; hypocritical, insincere, sanctimonious; endearing, ingratiating; extravagant, lavish, unrestrained; abundant, copious, profuse
near antonyms earnest, genuine, heartfelt, sincere, unfeigned

fumble *n* an unintentional departure from truth or accuracy ⟨played the entire piano piece without a single *fumble*⟩ — see ERROR 1

fumble *vb* **1** to make or do (something) in a clumsy or unskillful way ⟨*fumbled* the party plans by getting the time wrong on the invitations⟩ — see BOTCH
2 to search for something blindly or uncertainly ⟨*fumbled* for the light switch as she entered the dark room⟩ — see GROPE

fumbled *adj* showing or marked by a lack of skill and tact (as in dealing with a situation) ⟨shook his head over my *fumbled* attempt to compliment his daughter⟩ — see AWKWARD 2

fume *vb* **1** to be excited or emotionally stirred up with anger ⟨he silently *fumed* as his ex-girlfriend danced with her new beau⟩ — see BOIL 1
2 to express one's anger usually violently ⟨when she found out her driver's license was being suspended, she *fumed*, throwing papers across the room and shouting at the top of her lungs⟩ — see RAGE 1

fuming *adj* feeling or showing anger ⟨I was *fuming* after losing the game by a single point⟩ — see ANGRY

fun *adj* providing amusement or enjoyment ⟨there were so many *fun* things to do at summer camp that I really hated to leave⟩
synonyms amusing, delightful, diverting, enjoyable, entertaining, pleasurable
related words agreeable, beguiling, pleasant; funny, hilarious, humorous; gay, happy, jolly, merry; exciting, stimulating, thrilling
near antonyms disagreeable, unpleasant
antonyms boring, dull

fun *n* **1** someone or something that provides amusement or enjoyment ⟨theme parks with their rides, shows, and games are great *fun* for the whole family⟩
synonyms delight, diversion, entertainment, pleasure, recreation
related words binge, fling, frolic, gambol, lark, revel, rollick, romp, spree; carousing, festivity, gaiety (*also* gayety), hilarity, merrymaking, revelry; picnic; laugh, riot, scream
antonyms bore, bummer, downer, drag
2 an attitude or manner not to be taken seriously ⟨when I said that playing the piano like that could get you arrested, I only said it in *fun*⟩
synonyms game, jest, play, sport
related words facetiousness, flippancy, levity
near antonyms earnestness, gravity, seriousness
antonyms earnest
3 activity engaged in to amuse oneself ⟨came outside to where we were playing touch football and joined the *fun*⟩ — see PLAY 1

fun *vb* to make jokes ⟨old friends *funning* with each other⟩ — see JOKE

function *n* **1** a social gathering ⟨made a brief appearance at the annual holiday *function*⟩ — see PARTY 1

2 an assignment at which one regularly works for pay ⟨what's your *function* in this company?⟩ — see JOB 1
3 the action for which a person or thing is specially fitted or used or for which a thing exists ⟨that machine's *function* is to sort bolts by size⟩ — see ROLE

function *vb* to have a certain purpose ⟨the heart *functions* as a pump for the blood⟩
synonyms act, perform, serve, work
related words operate, run; control, direct, manage

functional *adj* **1** being in effective operation ⟨I don't think that pop machine is *functional*, so don't put money into it⟩ — see ACTIVE 1
2 capable of being put to use or account ⟨a *functional* knowledge of auto mechanics⟩ — see PRACTICAL 1
3 capable of or suitable for being used for a particular purpose ⟨a very *functional* kitchen utensil for peeling potatoes⟩ — see USABLE 1

functionary *n* **1** a person who holds a public office ⟨spoke to high-ranking *functionaries* at the embassy in the hopes that they could help⟩ — see OFFICIAL
2 a worker in a government agency ⟨the faceless *functionaries* at the Internal Revenue Service⟩ — see BUREAUCRAT

functioning *adj* being in effective operation ⟨looked for a *functioning* washing machine, but the few that weren't broken were in use⟩ — see ACTIVE 1

fund *n* **1** a sum of money set aside for a particular purpose ⟨our club has a *fund* for parties—which we like to have as often as possible⟩
synonyms account, budget, deposit, kitty, nest egg, pool
related words chest, coffer(s); assets, savings, savings account; bankroll, cache, collection, hoard, reserve, treasure; petty cash, pin money, pocket money, spending money
2 **funds** *pl* available money ⟨my *funds* were a little low, so I asked my favorite lending institution—Dad—for a small advance on my allowance⟩
synonyms bankroll, finances, pocket, resources, wherewithal
related words cash, money; assets, capital, means, wealth; purse, treasury
3 the number of individuals or amount of something available at any given time ⟨we have a deep *fund* of volunteers to call on when there is an unexpected need for help⟩ — see SUPPLY

fund *vb* **1** to furnish (as an institution) with a regular source of income ⟨her will *funded* a new science center at the college she attended⟩ — see ENDOW 2
2 to provide money for ⟨Dad advised me to get a job because he wasn't going to *fund* my social life forever⟩ — see FINANCE 1

fundamental *adj* of or relating to the simplest facts or theories of a subject ⟨the purpose of the course is to furnish students with *fundamental* knowledge of human reproduction⟩ — see ELEMENTARY

fundamentals *n pl* general or basic truths on which other truths or theories can be based ⟨all students at the school of music must take a course in the *fundamentals* of their chosen art⟩ — see PRINCIPLES 1

funeral *adj* expressing or suggesting mourning ⟨a slow and heavy *funeral* song⟩ — see MOURNFUL 1

funeral director *n* a person who manages funerals and prepares the dead for burial or cremation ⟨the *funeral director* instructed the pallbearers on how to proceed⟩
synonyms mortician, undertaker
related words embalmer

funereal *adj* causing or marked by an atmosphere lacking in cheer ⟨shivered with cold in the dark and *funereal* Victorian mansion⟩ — see GLOOMY 1

funnel *vb* to cause to move to a central point or along a restricted pathway ⟨*funneled* time and money into his misguided pet project⟩ — see CHANNEL

funniness *n* the amusing quality or element in something ⟨the *funniness* of the situation is often lost on the victim of the prank⟩ — see HUMOR 1

funning *adj* marked by or expressive of mild or good-natured teasing ⟨after he confided to his friends that he had a crush on his science lab partner, they made *funning* comments about the "chemistry" between the two sweethearts⟩ — see QUIZZICAL

funny *adj* 1 causing or intended to cause laughter ⟨a very *funny* movie that had audiences rolling in the aisles⟩
synonyms antic, comic, comical, droll, farcical, hilarious, humorous, hysterical, laughable, ludicrous, ridiculous, riotous, risible, screaming, side-splitting, uproarious
related words amusing, diverting, entertaining; clownish, slapstick, zany; facetious, flip, flippant, pert, smart, smart-alecky (*or* smart-aleck); jocular, playful, waggish; priceless, rich, whimsical, witty; gleeful, merry, mirthful
near antonyms grave, serious, sober, solemn, somber (*or* sombre); affecting, moving, poignant, touching, tragic; lachrymose, mournful, sad, tearful
antonyms humorless, lame, uncomic, unfunny
2 different from the ordinary in a way that causes curiosity or suspicion ⟨that's *funny*, for I could have sworn I put my keys right here yesterday⟩ — see ODD 2
3 noticeably different from what is generally found or experienced ⟨that's a *funny*-looking dog—what kind is it?⟩ — see UNUSUAL 1

funny *n* a series of drawings that tell a story or part of a story ⟨asked Dad if I could read the Sunday *funnies* when he was done⟩ — see COMIC STRIP

fur *n* 1 the hairy covering of a mammal especially when fine, soft, and thick ⟨the chinchilla is known for its exceptionally soft *fur*⟩
synonyms coat, fleece, hair, pelage, pile, wool
related words hide, pelt, skin
2 a soft airy substance or covering ⟨picked at the *fur* on the chenille pillows⟩ — see FUZZ
3 the outer covering of an animal removed for its commercial value ⟨furriers willing to pay good money for a lynx *fur*⟩ — see HIDE 1

furbelow *n* a strip of fabric gathered or pleated on one edge and used as trimming ⟨opted for a simple prom dress that did without all the frills and *furbelows*⟩ — see RUFFLE

furious *adj* 1 marked by great and often stressful excitement or activity ⟨everyone worked at a *furious* pace in order to get the float ready for the parade⟩
synonyms delirious, feverish, fierce, frantic, frenetic, frenzied, mad, rabid, violent, wild
related words concentrated, high-pressured, intense, vehement; excessive, extreme, inordinate; crazy, demented, insane, irrational
near antonyms calm, peaceful, quiet, subdued, tranquil; moderate, reasonable, temperate; casual, easygoing, low-pressure
antonyms relaxed
2 extreme in degree, power, or effect ⟨a *furious* hurricane virtually destroyed the seaside town⟩ — see INTENSE

3 feeling or showing anger ⟨a *furious* customer demanding to see the manager⟩ — see ANGRY
4 marked by bursts of destructive force or intense activity ⟨rioters went on a *furious* rampage, doing over two million dollars in damage⟩ — see VIOLENT 1

furlough *n* the termination of the employment of an employee or a work force often temporarily ⟨the landscaping company usually has to put most of its personnel on *furlough* during the extremely slow winter months⟩ — see LAYOFF

furnish *vb* 1 to provide (someone) with what is needed for a task or activity ⟨the students were *furnished* with brushes, crayons, pencils, and various other art supplies⟩
synonyms accoutre (*or* accouter), equip, fit (out), outfit, rig, supply
related words stock, store; bestow, donate, give, present; deal, dispense, distribute, dole (out); allocate, allot, assign
near antonyms deprive, dispossess, divest, strip
2 to put (something) into the possession of someone for use or consumption ⟨we'll gladly *furnish* the food for any out-of-town guests⟩
synonyms deliver, feed, give, hand, hand over, provide, supply
related words administer, dispense, distribute, dole (out), mete (out), parcel (out); cede, deed, transfer
near antonyms conserve, preserve, save
antonyms hold (back), keep (back), reserve, retain, withhold

furnishings *n pl* the movable articles in a room ⟨moved the *furnishings* out of the room so we could sand down and refinish the wood floors⟩ — see FURNITURE

furniture *n* the movable articles in a room ⟨we bought all new *furniture* for our new house⟩
synonyms appointments, cabinetwork, furnishings, movables (*or* moveables)
related words effects, goods, possessions
near antonyms fixtures

furor *n* 1 a state of noisy, confused activity ⟨the classroom was in a *furor* when the mice escaped from their cage⟩ — see COMMOTION
2 a state of wildly excited activity or emotion ⟨children in a gift-opening *furor* on Christmas morning⟩ — see FRENZY
3 an intense emotional state of displeasure with someone or something ⟨residents were in a *furor* about the new paper mill being constructed within city limits⟩ — see ANGER

furore *n* 1 a state of noisy, confused activity ⟨the store's going-out-of-business sale caused such a *furore* that security guards had to be called in to restore order⟩ — see COMMOTION
2 a state of wildly excited activity or emotion ⟨baseball fans in a *furore* as the game stretched to 11 innings⟩ — see FRENZY

furrow *n* a small fold in a soft and otherwise smooth surface ⟨the *furrows* in his usually unwrinkled brow suggested that he was very worried⟩ — see WRINKLE 1

furrow *vb* 1 to cut into and turn over the sod of (a piece of land) using a bladed implement ⟨had to *furrow* the field before we could plant the wheat⟩ — see PLOW 1
2 to develop creases or folds ⟨his brow *furrowed* in concentration as he tried to figure out the math problem⟩ — see WRINKLE 1

furry *adj* 1 covered with or as if with hair ⟨a *furry* teddy bear that would be so nice to cuddle up with⟩ — see HAIRY 1

2 made of or resembling hair ⟨green *furry* mold on old bread⟩ — see HAIRY 2

further *adj* resulting in an increase in amount or number ⟨I think *further* research is needed before we can say whether that treatment is safe or not⟩ — see ADDITIONAL

further *adv* **1** at or to a greater distance or more advanced point ⟨go *further* along this road and you'll see the sign for the highway⟩ — see FARTHER
2 in addition to what has been said ⟨I'll say nothing *further* at this time⟩ — see MORE 1

further *vb* to help the growth or development of ⟨worked hard to *further* her career⟩ — see FOSTER 1

furtherance *n* forward movement in time or place ⟨assigned her to oversee the *furtherance* of the construction on the new hospital wing⟩ — see ADVANCE 1

furthermore *adv* in addition to what has been said ⟨I'm not interested in what you are selling, and *furthermore*, I asked your company not to contact me again⟩ — see MORE 1

furthermost *adj* most distant from a center ⟨a satellite that will travel into the *furthermost* reaches of deep space⟩ — see EXTREME 1

furthest *adj* most distant from a center ⟨this belongs in the aisle *furthest* from the cash registers⟩ — see EXTREME 1

furtive *adj* **1** given to acting in secret and to concealing one's intentions ⟨a *furtive* guy who always seems to be up to something, and usually that something is no-good⟩ — see SNEAKY 1
2 undertaken or done so as to escape being observed or known by others ⟨gave each other *furtive* glances as we watched our friend open the booby-trapped soda⟩ — see SECRET 1

fury *n* **1** a bad-tempered scolding woman ⟨tradition has it that Socrates' wife was such a *fury* that the philosopher's death sentence by the authorities was not an entirely unwelcome fate⟩ — see SHREW
2 a state of wildly excited activity or emotion ⟨the sudden appearance of the celebrity whipped the crowd of onlookers into a *fury* of excitement⟩ — see FRENZY
3 an intense emotional state of displeasure with someone or something ⟨in his *fury* overturned the card table and claimed that the game was fixed⟩ — see ANGER

fuse *vb* **1** to come together to form a single unit ⟨our two local teams *fused* into a larger regional team⟩ — see UNITE 1
2 to go from a solid to a liquid state ⟨the lightning strike was so hot it caused the electrical wires to *fuse* and then drip onto the road⟩ — see LIQUEFY
3 to turn into a single mass that is more or less the same throughout ⟨the many foundries would daily *fuse* copper and zinc to create the brass that made the city famous⟩ — see BLEND 1

fusillade *n* a rapid or overwhelming outpouring of many things at once ⟨responded calmly to the *fusillade* of criticism leveled at his design for the memorial⟩ — see BARRAGE

fusion *n* a distinct entity formed by the combining of two or more different things ⟨a *fusion* of jazz and classical music⟩ — see BLEND

fuss *n* **1** a feeling or declaration of disapproval or dissent ⟨made a *fuss* over not being picked for the lead role in the play⟩ — see OBJECTION
2 a state of nervous or irritated concern ⟨the new parents are always in a *fuss* over whether the baby is dressed warmly enough⟩ — see FRET

3 a state of noisy, confused activity ⟨Mom heard us yelling and came racing into the room, asking what all the *fuss* was about⟩ — see COMMOTION
4 an expression of dissatisfaction, pain, or resentment ⟨none of the employees dared to make a *fuss* over having to come to work in the huge snowstorm⟩ — see COMPLAINT 1

fuss *vb* **1** to express dissatisfaction, pain, or resentment usually tiresomely ⟨the eldest daughter is always *fussing* that she gets stuck with all the chores around the house⟩ — see COMPLAIN
2 to make an exaggerated display of affection or enthusiasm ⟨fans *fussing* over their favorite rock guitarist⟩ — see GUSH 2
3 to make often peevish criticisms or objections about matters that are minor, unimportant, or irrelevant ⟨the picky eater who *fusses* over the arrangement of food on his plate or who won't eat the rice if it touches the salad⟩ — see QUIBBLE
4 to use flattery or the doing of favors in order to win approval especially from a superior ⟨given to *fussing* over her father whenever she wants a favor or some ready cash⟩ — see FAWN

fusser *n* **1** a person who makes frequent complaints usually about little things ⟨sat next to a *fusser* who whined during the entire bus trip⟩ — see CRYBABY
2 an irritable and complaining person ⟨a natural *fusser* who has never had a glimmer of gratitude for anything done for him⟩ — see GROUCH

fussy *adj* **1** given to complaining a lot ⟨the kids riding in the back were *fussy* passengers, always asking "Are we there yet?"⟩
synonyms crabby, cranky, grouchy, grumpy, querulous
related words fidgety, restive, restless, squirmy, uneasy; discontented, disgruntled, displeased, dissatisfied; fretful, nervous, worrisome; cantankerous, crotchety, irascible, irritable, ornery
near antonyms amiable, genial, good-humored, good-natured, good-tempered; accommodating, complaisant, obliging; easygoing, laid-back, relaxed
antonyms uncomplaining
2 hard to please ⟨cats have a well-deserved reputation for being *fussy* eaters⟩ — see FINICKY
3 taking great care and effort ⟨a *fussy* teacher who reads through papers two and even three times before issuing a grade⟩ — see PAINSTAKING

fusty *adj* having an unpleasant smell ⟨couldn't stay too long in the *fusty* attic without sneezing⟩ — see MALODOROUS

futile *adj* producing no results ⟨the prison is so well guarded that all attempts to escape have been *futile*⟩
synonyms abortive, bootless, empty, fruitless, ineffective, ineffectual, unavailing, unproductive, unprofitable, unsuccessful, useless, vain
related words hollow, idle, meaningless, pointless, worthless; hopeless, impossible; inadequate, insufficient
phrases in vain, of no avail
near antonyms meaningful, worthwhile; adequate, sufficient
antonyms effective, effectual, efficacious, efficient, fruitful, productive, profitable, successful

future *adj* of a time after the present ⟨we must preserve our national parks in all their glory so that *future* generations can experience the majesty of nature⟩
synonyms coming, unborn

related words approaching, forthcoming, imminent, impending, nearing, oncoming, pending, upcoming; later, posterior, subsequent; anticipated, awaited, expected, planned, predicted, projected; eventual, final, last, ultimate

near antonyms ancient, olden

antonyms bygone, past

future *n* **1** time that is to come ⟨in the *future*, there may be medical discoveries beyond our fondest dreams⟩

synonyms by-and-by, futurity, hereafter, offing

related words eventuality, finality; posterity

near antonyms yesterday, yesteryear; antiquity, old, yore

antonyms past

2 what is going to happen to someone in the time ahead ⟨with such a strong academic record, his *future* looks bright⟩ — see FORTUNE 1

futurist *n* one who predicts future events or develop-ments ⟨economic *futurists* predict a new world order in which information is the resource that drives a nation's economy⟩ — see PROPHET

futurity *n* time that is to come ⟨we can scarcely imagine what observers in some remote *futurity* will think of civilization as it existed at the dawn of the 21st century⟩ — see FUTURE 1

fuzz *n* a soft airy substance or covering ⟨a comfortable old sweater with clumps of *fuzz* all over it⟩

synonyms down, floss, fluff, fur, lint, nap, pile

related words batting

fuzzy *adj* **1** made of or resembling hair ⟨wore a *fuzzy* red wig at the Halloween party⟩ — see HAIRY 2

2 not clearly expressed ⟨the specifics of the program proposed by the candidate are rather *fuzzy*, perhaps intentionally so⟩ — see VAGUE 1

3 not seen or understood clearly ⟨saw a *fuzzy* outline through the fog⟩ — see FAINT 1

G

gab *vb* to engage in casual or rambling conversation ⟨spent the time that she should have been working *gabbing* with friends instead⟩ — see CHAT

gabble *n* unintelligible or meaningless talk ⟨he claimed he was speaking Arabic, but an Egyptian friend confided that all his murmurings were just *gabble*⟩ — see GIBBERISH

gabble *vb* **1** to engage in casual or rambling conversation ⟨the crowd of tourists met in the hotel lobby, *gabbling* politely before the bus arrived to take them to their next destination⟩ — see CHAT

2 to speak rapidly, inarticulately, and usually unintelligibly ⟨trying to cover up the fact that she hadn't learned the poem, she *gabbled* out a few half-remembered phrases and quickly sat down⟩ — see BABBLE 1

gabbler *n* a person who talks constantly ⟨was a real *gabbler* who never let you get a word in edgewise⟩ — see CHATTERBOX

gabby *adj* fond of talking or conversation ⟨a *gabby* talk-show host whose interviews were almost as much about herself as about her guests⟩ — see TALKATIVE

gabfest *n* friendly, informal conversation or an instance of this ⟨invited the neighbor over for coffee and a quick *gabfest*⟩ ⟨the slumber party was an all-night *gabfest* filled with gossip, giggling, and whispered secrets⟩ — see CHAT

gad (about) *vb* to move about from place to place aimlessly ⟨he *gads about* town every Saturday, flirting and gossiping with various shopkeepers and locals⟩ — see WANDER

gadabout *n* a person who roams about without a fixed route or destination ⟨she was a thoughtful *gadabout*, always remembering to pick up for a friend some unique souvenir from whichever European capital she happened to be in at the time⟩ — see NOMAD

gadfly *n* one who is obnoxiously annoying ⟨a loud sports commentator who was a tactless *gadfly* during post-game interviews with the losing team⟩ — see NUISANCE 1

gadget *n* an interesting and often novel device with a practical use ⟨she tried out a new *gadget* for weeding the garden⟩
synonyms appliance, contraption, contrivance, gimmick, gizmo (*or* gismo), jigger
related words implement, instrument, tool, utensil; ingenuity, innovation, invention; accessory, adjunct; mechanism, trick

gaffe *n* a socially improper or unsuitable act or remark ⟨committed a huge *gaffe* when she started drinking from the finger bowl⟩ — see IMPROPRIETY 2

gag *n* something said or done to cause laughter ⟨the movie featured a *gag* involving a chicken driving a car that audiences thought was hysterically funny⟩ — see JOKE 1

gag *vb* **1** to discharge the contents of the stomach through the mouth ⟨the terrible smell of rotting fish made me *gag*⟩ — see VOMIT

2 to experience complete or partial blockage of the windpipe ⟨took a bite that was too large and began to *gag*⟩ — see CHOKE 2

gage *n* something given or held to assure that the giver will keep a promise ⟨Dad had to give his credit card number as a *gage* for the boat rental⟩ — see PLEDGE 1

gaiety *also* **gayety** *n* **1** dressy clothing ⟨attendees of the masquerade ball arrived dressed in all their *gaiety*⟩ — see FINERY

2 joyful or festive activity ⟨loved the *gaiety* of the annual harvest festival⟩ ⟨the *gaiety* of the wedding reception⟩ — see MERRYMAKING

gaily *also* **gayly** *adv* **1** in a cheerful or happy manner ⟨we sat around the table, *gaily* teasing each other and laughing about the good old days⟩
synonyms cheerfully, happily, heartily, jocosely, jovially, merrily, mirthfully
related words blithely, blithesomely, breezily, brightly, buoyantly; cheerily, gladly, gladsomely, sanguinely, sunnily; good-humoredly, good-naturedly
near antonyms abjectly, dejectedly, despondently, disconsolately, dispiritedly, wretchedly; dolefully, dolorously, forlornly, mournfully, plaintively, sorrowfully; dourly, glumly, sternly, sulkily, sullenly; dismally, drearily, gloomily
antonyms bleakly, cheerlessly, darkly, heavily, miserably, morosely, unhappily

2 in a quick and spirited manner ⟨children *gaily* running to the buses on the last day of school⟩
synonyms animatedly, animately, exuberantly, high-spiritedly, jauntily, pertly, sprightly, trippingly
related words friskily, playfully, skittishly, sportively; briskly, crisply, snappily, springily; breezily, cockishly; allegro
near antonyms idly, indolently, lazily, slothfully; heavily, inactively, listlessly
antonyms dully, inanimately, sluggishly, tardily

3 in a bright and showy way ⟨the Mexican dancers were *gaily* dressed in lavish, bright costumes⟩
synonyms dashingly, flamboyantly, flashily, jauntily, rakishly, swankily
related words garishly, gaudily, loud, loudly, ostentatiously; fancily, gallantly, ornately; nattily, neatly, smartly; conspicuously, luridly, spectacularly, strikingly; gorgeously, splendidly
near antonyms inconspicuously, unobtrusively, unpretentiously; chastely, demurely, homely, modestly; plainly, simply; colorlessly, dirtily, drably, dully; bleakly, severely, somberly
antonyms conservatively, plain, quietly

gain *n* **1** something added (as by growth) ⟨saw a 15 percent *gain* in the number of students applying to our school⟩ — see INCREASE 1

2 the amount of money left when expenses are subtracted from the total amount received ⟨the company posted a substantial 4th-quarter *gain*, signaling an end to their money-losing ventures⟩ — see PROFIT 1

3 gains *pl* an increase usually measured in money that comes from labor, business, or property ⟨after a year of hard work, we finally saw some *gains* in the family business and can now afford to expand⟩ — see INCOME

gain *vb* **1** to increase in ⟨as the car coasted downhill, it gradually *gained* speed and momentum⟩
synonyms build (up), gather, grow (in), pick up

related words accrue, accumulate, amass; excite, stimulate; enhance, enrich, maximize; boost, jack (up), mount, step up

near antonyms abate, diminish (in), dip, dwindle, fall (in), lessen, taper, taper off

antonyms decrease (in), lose

2 to receive as return for effort ⟨*gained* her affections with his polite manner⟩ — see EARN 1

3 to become healthy and strong again after illness or weakness ⟨is *gaining* after his bout with the flu and will be back on his feet soon⟩ — see CONVALESCE

gainful *adj* yielding a profit ⟨graduated from school and went looking for *gainful* employment⟩ — see PROFITABLE 1

gainsay *vb* **1** to declare not to be true ⟨it can't be *gainsaid* that most people wish they had more time and money⟩ — see DENY 1

2 to make an assertion that is contrary to one made by (another) ⟨repeatedly tried to *gainsay* me, though every point I made was backed up by facts⟩ — see CONTRADICT 1

gal *n* **1** a woman with whom one is in love ⟨after years of dating, Fred finally asked his *gal* to marry him⟩ — see GIRLFRIEND

2 a young usually unmarried woman ⟨a club for single guys and *gals*⟩ — see GIRL 1

gala *n* a time or program of special events and entertainment in honor of something ⟨attended the *gala* celebrating the reopening of the museum⟩ — see FESTIVAL

gale *n* a sudden intense expression of strong feeling ⟨the audience responded to the comedian's joke with *gales* of laughter⟩ — see OUTBURST 1

gall *n* **1** a deep-seated ill will ⟨mortal enemies filled with *gall* for each other⟩ — see ENMITY

2 shameless boldness ⟨I can't believe he had the *gall* to ask me how much I weighed⟩ — see EFFRONTERY

gall *vb* **1** to damage or diminish by continued friction ⟨move that rope so the sharp edge of the hull doesn't *gall* it⟩ — see ABRADE 1

2 to disturb the peace of mind of (someone) especially by repeated disagreeable acts ⟨humming through your nose like that absolutely *galls* me⟩ — see IRRITATE 1

3 to make sore by continued rubbing ⟨tie your shoes so they don't *gall* your heels sliding on and off like that⟩ — see CHAFE 1

gallant *adj* **1** feeling or displaying no fear by temperament ⟨a *gallant* firefighter, rushing into the burning house to save the children⟩ ⟨a *gallant* rescue⟩ — see BRAVE

2 having, characterized by, or arising from a dignified and generous nature ⟨a *gallant* knight⟩ ⟨the members of that service club are known for their *gallant* service to the community⟩ ⟨the *gallant* courtesies of the king⟩ — see NOBLE 2

3 large and impressive in size, grandeur, extent, or conception ⟨a great and *gallant* sailing ship⟩ — see GRAND 1

gallant *n* **1** a man extremely interested in his clothing and personal appearance ⟨he was quite a *gallant*, primping more than either of his sisters⟩ — see DANDY 1

2 a man who courts a woman usually with the goal of marrying her ⟨she had a whole host of *gallants* vying for her hand in marriage⟩ — see SUITOR 1

gallantly *adv* in a manner befitting a person of the highest character and ideals ⟨a man who *gallantly* offers everything he has to the poor⟩ — see GREATLY 1

gallantry *n* strength of mind to carry on in spite of danger ⟨commended the rescuers for their *gallantry* in bringing the lost and injured hiker back to camp in spite of the life-threatening weather conditions⟩ — see COURAGE

gallery *n* **1** a building or part of a building in which objects of interest are displayed ⟨visited an array of small art and photography *galleries* while on vacation⟩ — see MUSEUM

2 a typically long narrow way connecting parts of a building ⟨asked us to take our shoes off in the *gallery* before stepping onto the white carpet of the living room⟩ — see HALL 2

galling *adj* **1** causing annoyance ⟨these stupid unsolicited e-mails are *galling*⟩ — see ANNOYING

2 hard to accept or bear especially emotionally ⟨losing in the last round of play-offs was *galling* to our home team⟩ — see BITTER 2

gallivant *also* **galavant** *vb* to move about from place to place aimlessly ⟨*gallivanted* about the country before returning to school in the fall⟩ — see WANDER

gallivanting *also* **galavanting** *adj* traveling from place to place ⟨the *gallivanting* entertainers stayed in town for a few days, then moved on⟩ — see ITINERANT

gallop *vb* to go at a pace faster than a walk ⟨wasn't watching where she was going and *galloped* straight into the principal⟩ — see RUN 1

galore *adj* pouring forth in great amounts ⟨there was food *galore* at our Thanksgiving meal⟩ — see PROFUSE

galvanize *vb* to cause a pleasurable stimulation of the feelings ⟨the thought that he might be the first in his family to go to college *galvanized* him⟩ — see THRILL

galvanizing *adj* causing great emotional or mental stimulation ⟨the presentation on the international aid organization was *galvanizing* and thought-provoking⟩ — see EXCITING 1

gamble *n* a risky undertaking ⟨would never take a *gamble* on such a poorly researched business deal⟩

synonyms chance, enterprise, flier (*or* flyer), speculation, venture

related words bet, hazard, stake, wager; liberty; dark horse, long shot, play

gamble *vb* to risk (something) on the outcome of an uncertain event ⟨a foolish man who *gambled* away his life savings on the lottery⟩ — see BET

gamble (on) *vb* to take a chance on ⟨a movie studio willing to *gamble on* a new actress for its summer blockbuster⟩ — see RISK 1

gamble (with) *vb* to place in danger ⟨you don't want to *gamble with* your life⟩ — see ENDANGER

gambler *n* one that bets (as on the outcome of a contest or sports event) ⟨marveled at the number of *gamblers* in the casino⟩ — see BETTOR

gambol *n* a time or instance of carefree fun ⟨the students headed off for one final *gambol* before the summer recess ended⟩ — see FLING 1

gambol *vb* to play and run about happily ⟨youngsters *gamboling* in the sunlit meadow⟩ — see FROLIC 1

game *adj* having a desire or inclination (as for a specified course of action) ⟨are you *game* for going out tonight?⟩ — see WILLING 1

game *n* **1** a competitive encounter between individuals or groups carried on for amusement, exercise, or in pursuit of a prize ⟨decided he would indulge in a friendly basketball *game* with his friends before dinner⟩

synonyms bout, competition, contest, event, match, meet, sweepstakes, tournament, tourney

related words athletics, sport; battle, conflict, scrimmage, skirmish, struggle, tug-of-war, tussle; championship, final, nightcap, play-off, semifinal; derby, field day, open; marathon, race; heat, round, run, set; rally, volley; rubber, runoff, sudden death; dead heat, photo finish, seesaw; classic

2 a method worked out in advance for achieving some objective ⟨the crook told his accomplice, "Here's the *game*: look surprised when the police ask about the money"⟩ — see PLAN 1

3 an attitude or manner not to be taken seriously ⟨there's no need to get upset, all our teasing is only a *game*⟩ — see FUN 2

gameness *n* cheerful readiness to do something ⟨his *gameness* to try new types of food has been fairly well demonstrated by his consumption of rattlesnake and squirrel⟩ — see ALACRITY

gamut *n* the distance or extent between possible extremes ⟨the actress's work ran the *gamut* from goofy comedies to serious historical dramas⟩ — see RANGE 3

gander *n* an instance of looking especially briefly ⟨took a *gander* at the classic car as we drove by⟩ — see LOOK 2

gang *n* **1** a group of people working together on a task ⟨a *gang* of neighborhood residents spent the weekend cleaning up the park⟩
synonyms band, company, crew, outfit, party, squad, team
related words army, battalion, brigade, corps, troop; force, host, posse, stable, troupe; administration, department, help, personnel, staff

2 a group of people sharing a common interest and relating together socially ⟨the whole *gang* went out for pizza⟩ ⟨the school's computer hackers had their own little *gang*⟩
synonyms body, bunch, circle, clan, clique, community, coterie, crowd, fold, lot, ring, set
related words bevy, covey, flock, herd, horde, mob, swarm, throng; club, college, fellowship, guild (*also* gild), league, organization, society; cohort, pack; camp, faction, sect, side, tribe; mess, squad; brotherhood, fraternity, order, sisterhood, sodality, sorority; commune; alliance, bloc, coalition, confederation, congress, council, federation, union
near antonyms loner; individualist

3 a group involved in secret or criminal activities ⟨politicians promising to stop the growth of inner-city *gangs*⟩ — see RING 1

gangling *adj* being tall, thin and usually loose-jointed ⟨the riders at the barn loved the *gangling* newborn colt⟩ — see LANKY

gangly *adj* being tall, thin and usually loose-jointed ⟨a *gangly* teenager who was born to play varsity basketball⟩ — see LANKY

gangster *n* a violent, brutal person who is often a member of an organized gang ⟨Al Capone is one of the most notorious *gangsters* in American history⟩ — see HOODLUM

gaol *n*, *chiefly British* a place of confinement for persons held in lawful custody ⟨inspectors from Scotland Yard visited the suspect being held in the county *gaol*⟩ — see JAIL

gap *n* **1** an open space in a barrier (as a wall or hedge) ⟨there were several visible *gaps* in the wall where the drywall had pulled away from the wall framing⟩
synonyms breach, break, discontinuity, gulf, hole, interval, opening, rent, rift, separation

related words chink, cleft, crack, cranny, crevice, fissure; notch, slit, slot, split; interspace, pore, space; abyss, aperture, cavity, chasm, gape, orifice; fracture, rupture, severance, sundering

2 a break in continuity ⟨there was a 15-minute *gap* between the two televised sporting events⟩
synonyms discontinuity, hiatus, interim, interlude, intermission, interruption, interval
related words caesura, pause, space; lapse, suspension; lull, recess, respite, rest
near antonyms continuum, run, stretch; procession, progression
antonyms continuation, continuity

3 a narrow opening between hillsides or mountains that can be used for passage ⟨thought they were stuck until they found a *gap* in the mountain range that they could hike through⟩ — see CANYON

gape *vb* to look long and hard in wonder or surprise ⟨she *gaped* openmouthed at the young man in the mall with purple and green hair⟩
synonyms gawk, gaze, goggle, peer, rubberneck, stare
related words glare, gloat, glower; eye, observe, watch; leer, ogle
near antonyms glance, glimpse, peek, peep; browse, dip (into), scan; blink, wink

garb *n* clothing chosen as appropriate for a specific situation ⟨decided to clothe himself in traditional Scottish *garb* for the celebration⟩ — see OUTFIT 1

garb *vb* to outfit with clothes and especially fine or special clothes ⟨firefighters *garbed* in protective gear⟩ — see CLOTHE 1

garbage *n* discarded or useless material ⟨the stray dogs were looking for leftover food in the family's *garbage*⟩
synonyms chaff, deadwood, dross, dust, junk, litter, refuse, riffraff, rubbish, scrap, trash, waste
related words offal, sewage, slop, swill, wash; debris, detritus, rubble, ruins; lumber, odds and ends; flotsam, jetsam; castoff, cull, discard, reject, throwaway; nothing, straw, two bits
near antonyms catch, treasure, treasure trove
antonyms find, prize

garble *vb* to change so much as to create a wrong impression or alter the meaning of ⟨the candidate complained that his views had been deliberately *garbled* by his opponent⟩
synonyms color, distort, falsify, misinterpret, misrepresent, misstate, pervert, twist, warp
related words belie, camouflage, disguise, mask, veil; complicate, confound, confuse, mix up; mystify, obscure, puzzle; equivocate, fib, lie, palter, prevaricate
near antonyms clarify, clear (up), explain, illuminate, illustrate, interpret, spell out; decipher

garden *adj* **1** being of the type that is encountered in the normal course of events ⟨just a *garden* variety earthworm⟩ — see ORDINARY 1

2 often observed or encountered ⟨we drove a *garden* variety four-door car⟩ — see COMMON 1

garish *adj* excessively showy ⟨the wedding guest's thick makeup was *garish* and unnecessary⟩ — see GAUDY

garishness *n* excessive or unnecessary display ⟨the *garishness* of the enormous statues in the small yard was almost funny⟩ — see OSTENTATION

garment *vb* to outfit with clothes and especially fine or special clothes ⟨a princess *garmented* in fine satins and silks⟩ — see CLOTHE 1

garner *vb* **1** to bring together in one body or place ⟨a prisoner *garnering* food bit by bit and hiding it in his pillow⟩ ⟨a group of music fans *garnered* from all over

the country by the promoters of the festival⟩ — see
GATHER 1

2 to receive as return for effort ⟨a novelist that *garnered* praise for consistently good work⟩ — see EARN 1

garnish *n* something that decorates or beautifies ⟨added a *garnish* of parsley to the plate before serving it⟩ — see DECORATION 1

garnish *vb* to make more attractive by adding something that is beautiful or becoming ⟨a chef who never served any dish without first *garnishing* it⟩ — see DECORATE

garrote *or* **garotte** *vb* to keep (someone) from breathing by exerting pressure on the windpipe ⟨the sinister villain threatened to *garrote* the hero with his own necktie⟩ — see CHOKE 1

garrulous *adj* fond of talking or conversation ⟨a *garrulous* boy who was in constant trouble for talking out of turn⟩ — see TALKATIVE

gas *n* **1** boastful speech or writing ⟨all that *gas* about being the best fisherman in the world is another exaggeration⟩ — see BOMBAST 1

2 language that is impressive-sounding but not meaningful or sincere ⟨the candidate's pledge that he'll fight for the common people is just a lot of *gas*⟩ — see RHETORIC 1

3 *slang* a source of great satisfaction ⟨that movie with the new special effects was a *gas*⟩ — see DELIGHT 1

gas *vb* to engage in casual or rambling conversation ⟨a group of kids in the mall, *gassing* about their favorite rockers⟩ — see CHAT

gaseous *adj* marked by the use of impressive-sounding but mostly meaningless words and phrases ⟨a pompous professor known for his *gaseous* lectures that often put students to sleep⟩ — see RHETORICAL

gash *n* a long deep cut ⟨got a *gash* in his knee that required four stitches⟩
synonyms incision, laceration, rent, rip, slash, slit, tear
related words abrasion, score, scrape, scratch; injury, wound

gash *vb* to penetrate with a sharp edge (as a knife) ⟨her face had been *gashed* by the rocks as she tumbled down the embankment⟩ — see CUT 1

gasp *vb* to breathe hard, quickly, or with difficulty ⟨the runner was *gasping* by the end of the marathon⟩
synonyms blow, hyperventilate, pant, puff, wheeze
related words choke, gulp, huff; exhale, expire
phrases to be out of breath

gassy *adj* marked by the use of impressive-sounding but mostly meaningless words and phrases ⟨a *gassy* politician whose jargon-filled speeches didn't fool the voters at all⟩ — see RHETORICAL

gate *n* **1** a barrier by which an entry is closed and opened ⟨be sure to latch the *gate* in the fence so that the dog can't sneak out of the yard⟩ — see DOOR 1

2 the opening through which one can enter or leave a structure ⟨passed through the *gates* of the walled city⟩ — see DOOR 2

3 a fixture for controlling the flow of a liquid ⟨open the *gate* in the lock so the ships can get through the canal⟩ — see FAUCET

gatekeeper *n* a person who tends a door ⟨the nightclub has a *gatekeeper* and a velvet rope to keep out people who aren't considered hip enough⟩ — see DOORKEEPER

gateway *n* **1** something that allows someone to achieve a desired goal ⟨my college degree is a *gateway* to a high-paying job⟩ — see PASSPORT

2 the means or right of entering or participating in ⟨Denver is the *gateway* to the West⟩ — see ENTRANCE 1

3 the opening through which one can enter or leave a structure ⟨the *gateway* of the museum was too small for our whole group to go through at once⟩ — see DOOR 2

gather *vb* **1** to bring together in one body or place ⟨he *gathered* the leftovers from the table and gave them to the dog⟩ ⟨let's *gather* the students and have them line up on the playground before going in from recess⟩
synonyms accumulate, amass, assemble, collect, concentrate, garner, group, lump, pick up, round up, scrape (together)
related words agglomerate, aggregate, ball, bunch, cluster, huddle; heap, pile, stack; muster, raise, rally; flock, herd, hive, pack, press, swarm, throng, troop; congregate, forgather (*or* foregather), meet, rendezvous; affiliate, ally, combine, connect, join, link, merge, unite; arrange, organize, systematize; regather, regroup
phrases get together
near antonyms break up, disband, disintegrate, dissolve, separate, sever, split (up); dismiss, send
antonyms dispel, disperse, dissipate, scatter

2 to catch or collect (a crop or natural resource) for human use ⟨July and August is when we *gather* the tomatoes and begin canning them for the winter⟩ — see HARVEST

3 to come together into one body or place ⟨a crowd *gathered* around the street musician⟩ ⟨ask the faculty to *gather* in the lounge for the meeting⟩ — see ASSEMBLE 1

4 to form an opinion through reasoning and information ⟨I *gather* that, since you are back so early, she didn't want to see you?⟩ — see INFER 1

5 to gradually form into a layer, pile, or mass ⟨the newspapers that had been allowed to *gather* on the front doorstep told thieves that the family was away on vacation⟩ — see COLLECT 2

6 to increase in ⟨the car *gathered* speed as it rolled down the hill⟩ — see GAIN 1

gather (up) *vb* to call into being through the use of one's inner resources or powers ⟨the runner came to a point where she had to *gather up* the strength to keep running the marathon⟩ — see SUMMON 2

gathering *n* **1** a body of people come together in one place ⟨the President spoke before the *gathering* of student leaders⟩
synonyms assemblage, assembly, conference, congregation, convocation, meeting, muster
related words aggregation, collection, conglomeration; company, coterie, gang, pack; caucus, forum, market, panel, rally, symposium, synod; crowd, flock, horde, legion, multitude, press, swarm, throng; crush, mob, rabble

2 a coming together of a number of persons for a specified purpose ⟨attended a *gathering* for descendants of people who came to America on the Mayflower⟩ — see MEETING 1

3 a mass or quantity that has piled up or that has been gathered ⟨a great *gathering* of dust under the bed⟩ — see ACCUMULATION 1

gauche *adj* lacking social grace and assurance ⟨his loud talking at the opera marked him as *gauche* and uncultured⟩ — see AWKWARD 1

gaud *n* a small object displayed for its attractiveness or interest ⟨some tacky little *gaud* that they had picked up at a souvenir stand at an amusement park⟩ — see KNICKKNACK

gaudiness *n* excessive or unnecessary display ⟨the *gaudiness* of the velvety wallpaper and cut-glass lamps made the guests giggle in amusement⟩ — see OSTENTATION

gaudy *adj* excessively showy ⟨the bright purple sequined miniskirt she wore to the wedding was *gaudy*⟩
synonyms flamboyant, flashy, garish, glitzy, loud, ostentatious, splashy, swank (*or* swanky), tawdry
related words meretricious, pretentious; graceless, inelegant, tacky, tasteless, vulgar; bedizened, extravagant, fancy, florid, glittery, spectacular; lurid, ornate, overdone, overwrought
near antonyms appropriate, fitting, proper; inconspicuous, muted, restrained, subdued, toned (down), unobtrusive; elegant, graceful, tasteful; modest, plain, simple, unpretentious
antonyms conservative, quiet, understated

gauge *also* **gage** *vb* **1** to decide the size, amount, number, or distance of (something) without actual measurement ⟨glance over the pattern and try to *gauge* how much fabric you'll need⟩ — see ESTIMATE 2
2 to find out the size, extent, or amount of ⟨very difficult to *gauge* how upset he is by his controlled reaction⟩ — see MEASURE

gaunt *adj* suffering extreme weight loss as a result of hunger or disease ⟨a *gaunt* patient suffering from the side effects of treatment⟩ — see EMACIATED

gauntlet *also* **gantlet** *n* a test of faith, patience, or strength ⟨before being adopted, school textbooks must often run the *gauntlet* of several local and state committees⟩ — see TRIAL

gauzy *adj* **1** being of a material lacking in sturdiness or substance ⟨the old and *gauzy* dress tore very easily⟩ — see FLIMSY 1
2 very thin and easy to see through ⟨*gauzy* curtains that let plenty of light through⟩ — see SHEER 1

gawk *n* a big clumsy often slow-witted person ⟨thought that the linebackers were dumb *gawks* until he got to know them better⟩ — see OAF

gawk *vb* to look long and hard in wonder or surprise ⟨don't *gawk* at that woman in the wheelchair⟩ — see GAPE

gawky *adj* lacking in physical ease and grace in movement or in the use of the hands ⟨some teenagers go through a stage where they are *gawky* and uncoordinated⟩ — see CLUMSY 1

gay *adj* **1** having much high-spirited energy and movement ⟨couples dancing a *gay*, fast-paced jig⟩ — see LIVELY 1
2 having or showing a lack of concern or seriousness ⟨a *gay*, thoughtless girl who didn't care whether her work was done or not⟩ — see CAREFREE
3 indicative of or marked by high spirits or good humor ⟨had a *gay* old time at the party⟩ — see MERRY
4 having or showing a good mood or disposition ⟨with a *gay* toss of his coat over his shoulder, the dapper old gentleman set off for the party⟩ — see CHEERFUL 1
5 serving to lift one's spirits ⟨the skylark's *gay* song lifted me out of my gloom⟩ — see CHEERFUL 2

gaze *vb* to look long and hard in wonder or surprise ⟨her teachers *gazed* at her in admiration as she read her valedictorian speech at graduation⟩ — see GAPE

gazette *n* a publication that appears at regular intervals ⟨picked up the monthly car-buyer's *gazette* when he was in town⟩ — see JOURNAL

gear *n* items needed for the performance of a task or activity ⟨grabbed his *gear*, threw on his pads, and headed out to the football field for practice⟩ — see EQUIPMENT

gel *vb* to turn from a liquid into a substance resembling jelly ⟨the jam should *gel* after you add the pectin⟩ — see COAGULATE

gelatinous *adj* being of such a thick consistency as to readily cling to objects upon contact ⟨brought a glob of *gelatinous* frog's eggs home from the pond⟩ — see STICKY 1

gem *n* **1** a usually valuable stone cut and polished for ornament ⟨a ring set with diamonds and other precious *gems*⟩
synonyms brilliant, gemstone, jewel
related words birthstone; baguette, cameo, scarab, solitaire, teardrop; paste, rhinestone, zircon
near antonyms rough
2 someone or something unusually desirable ⟨that new car is a real *gem*⟩ ⟨she's dating a real *gem* these days⟩ — see PRIZE 1

gemstone *n* a usually valuable stone cut and polished for ornament ⟨a shop that offered polished nuggets of various *gemstones* for collecting⟩ — see GEM 1

genealogy *n* the line of ancestors from whom a person is descended ⟨has a distinguished *genealogy* that traces back to William the Conqueror⟩ — see ANCESTRY

general *adj* **1** belonging or relating to the whole ⟨a *general* increase in postage rates⟩ ⟨there's been a *general* improvement in the economy⟩
synonyms blanket, common, generic, global, overall, universal
related words broad, collective, comprehensive, extensive, pervasive, sweeping, ubiquitous, wholesale, wide, widespread; complete, full, plenary; planetary, worldwide
near antonyms component, constituent; cross-sectional, divisional, fragmentary, partial; local, localized, regional, sectional
antonyms individual, particular
2 relating to the main elements and not to specific details ⟨gave the *general* impression of being kindhearted⟩ ⟨a *general* course of study in American history⟩
synonyms all-around (*also* all-round), bird's-eye, broad, nonspecific, overall
related words comprehensive, inclusive; absolute, boundless, expansive, extensive, infinite, panoramic, sweeping, vast, wide; indeterminate, nebulous, nondescript, vague; nonspecific, unlimited, unrestricted, unspecified
near antonyms limited, restricted, specified; distinct, explicit, precise, sharp; comprehensive, elaborate, full, mapped (out), thorough; enumerated, inventoried, itemized, listed; individual, singular; particular, peculiar
antonyms delineated, detailed, particularized, specific
3 held by or applicable to a majority of the people ⟨it was the *general* opinion that the politician was a liar⟩ ⟨the *general* mood of the nation was one of hope and optimism⟩
synonyms common, public, popular, prevailing, vulgar
related words unanimous, universal; pop; everyday, familiar, household, usual, well-known; contemporary, current, present; dominant, predominant, preponderant; characteristic, typical; pandemic, pervasive, prevalent, rife, widespread; communal, shared

near antonyms rare, strange, unknown, unusual; distinctive, especial, idiosyncratic, peculiar, special, unique; individual, separate, singular; nonpublic, personal, private
antonyms uncommon, unpopular
4 not limited or specialized in application or purpose ⟨a new kitchen tool of *general* usefulness⟩
synonyms all-around (*also* all-round), all-purpose, unlimited, unqualified, unrestricted, unspecialized
related words broad, wide; nonspecific, unspecified, vague
near antonyms bounded, circumscribed, confined, definite, demarcated, determinate, finite, qualified
antonyms limited, restricted, specialized, technical
generality *n* **1** an idea or statement about all of the members of a group or all the instances of a situation ⟨the idea that all boys are naturally messy is a gross *generality*⟩ — see GENERALIZATION
2 the main or greater part of something as distinguished from its appendages ⟨a great but little-known inventor whose work was never appreciated by the *generality* of the public⟩ — see BODY 1
generalization *n* an idea or statement about all of the members of a group or all the instances of a situation ⟨the *generalization* that children who like violent entertainment grow up to be violent criminals⟩
synonyms aphorism, generality, maxim, stereotype
related words concept, conception, notion; precept, rule, rule of thumb; adage, proverb, saw, saying; cliché, commonplace, platitude, truism; hypothesis, proposition, theory
generally *adv* **1** according to the usual course of things ⟨after lunch we *generally* have a history lesson⟩ — see NATURALLY 2
2 for the most part ⟨*generally* speaking, I don't like vegetables⟩ — see CHIEFLY
generate *vb* to be the cause of (a situation, action, or state of mind) ⟨his rabble-rousing speech *generated* a lot of controversy among local taxpayers⟩ — see EFFECT
generator *n* a person who establishes a whole new field of endeavor ⟨the French painter Paul Cézanne is considered to be one of the principal *generators* of modern art⟩ — see FATHER 2
generic *adj* belonging or relating to the whole ⟨a love of big things—big cars, big meals—seems to be a *generic* trait of the American people⟩ — see GENERAL 1
generosity *n* the quality or state of being generous ⟨a sidewalk beggar who benefited from the *generosity* of kindhearted passersby⟩ — see LIBERALITY
generous *adj* **1** giving or sharing in abundance and without hesitation ⟨a civic leader who is very *generous* with his money and time⟩
synonyms bounteous, bountiful, charitable, free, freehanded, liberal, munificent, openhanded, unselfish, unsparing
related words extravagant, handsome, lavish, profuse, unstinting; altruistic, beneficent, benevolent, hospitable, humanitarian, philanthropic; compassionate, good-hearted, greathearted, kindly, magnanimous, openhearted
near antonyms mean, petty, small; frugal, spare, sparing, thrifty; chary, stinting; acquisitive, avaricious, avid, coveting, covetous, desirous, grasping, hoggish, itchy, mercenary, rapacious; begrudging, envious, grudging, resentful

antonyms cheap, close, closefisted, miserly, niggardly, parsimonious, penurious, selfish, stingy, tight, tightfisted, uncharitable
2 being more than enough without being excessive ⟨mashed potatoes with a *generous* serving of butter⟩ — see PLENTIFUL
generously *adv* in a generous manner ⟨gave *generously* to several charities⟩ — see WELL 2
genesis *n* the point at which something begins ⟨was present at the meeting which was later considered the *genesis* of the new political movement⟩ — see BEGINNING
genetic *also* **genetical** *adj* genetically passed or capable of being passed from parent to offspring ⟨hemophilia and other *genetic* medical disorders⟩ — see HEREDITARY
genial *adj* **1** having an easygoing and pleasing manner especially in social situations ⟨was a *genial* host that spoke personally to every guest and set everyone at ease⟩ — see AMIABLE
2 having or showing kindly feeling and sincere interest ⟨*genial* new neighbors who helped us unpack boxes and brought us dinner our first night in the new place⟩ — see FRIENDLY 1
3 showing a natural kindness and courtesy especially in social situations ⟨his *genial* offer to give up his seat on the bus for the pregnant woman was noticed and approved by everyone⟩ — see GRACIOUS 1
geniality *n* the state or quality of having a pleasant or agreeable manner in socializing with others ⟨an outgoing person whose *geniality* never fails to draw fellow passengers into a conversation with her⟩ — see AMIABILITY 1
genius *n* **1** a very smart person ⟨the 16-year-old college graduate was considered to be a *genius*⟩
synonyms brain, intellect, thinker, whiz, wizard
related words egghead, highbrow, intellectual; master, virtuoso; ace, crackerjack, natural; sage, savant
near antonyms ignoramus, illiterate, know-nothing; ass, donkey, fool, jackass; beast, boor, cad, churl, clown, creep, cretin, cur, heel, jerk, louse, lout, skunk, snake, stinker
antonyms blockhead, dodo, dolt, dope, dumbbell, dummy, dunce, fathead, goon, half-wit, idiot, imbecile, knothead, moron, nitwit, numskull (*or* numbskull), pinhead
2 a special and usually inborn ability ⟨had a *genius* for remembering long strings of numbers⟩ — see TALENT
3 a habitual attraction to some activity or thing ⟨had a *genius* for saying the wrong thing no matter what the social situation⟩ — see INCLINATION 1
4 the set of qualities that makes a person, a group of people, or a thing different from others ⟨putting the needs of the individual before those of society is alien to the *genius* of the Japanese people⟩ — see NATURE 1
gent *n* an adult male human being ⟨ladies and *gents*⟩ — see MAN 1
genteel *adj* **1** following the established traditions of refined society and good taste ⟨those bygone days when young women were taught how to drink tea while wearing long gloves and other *genteel* ways of behaving⟩ — see PROPER 1
2 having or showing a taste for the fine arts and gracious living ⟨a *genteel* opera lover who relished the opportunity to play hostess to her favorite tenor⟩ — see CULTIVATED

3 of high birth, rank, or station ⟨the *genteel* ladies never mixed with the servants⟩ ⟨a princess of *genteel* birth⟩ — see NOBLE 1

4 showing consideration, courtesy, and good manners ⟨was impressed with his *genteel* gesture of holding the door for the group of ladies leaving the restaurant⟩ — see POLITE 1

gentile *n* a person who does not worship the God of the Bible ⟨a strict sect that believes that fellowship with *gentiles* should exist only for the purposes of conversion⟩ — see HEATHEN 1

gentility *n* speech or behavior that is a sign of good breeding ⟨was full of the same *gentility* and grace that marked the rest of the family⟩ — see POLITENESS

gentle *adj* **1** not harsh or stern especially in manner, nature, or effect ⟨use a *gentle* detergent on that delicate silk blouse⟩ ⟨the pastor had a *gentle* disposition that calmed everyone he met⟩
synonyms balmy, benign, bland, delicate, light, mellow, mild, soft, soothing, tender
related words sleek, slick, smooth; calm, pacific, peaceful, placid, quiet, serene, tranquil; clement, compassionate, easy, lenient, merciful; buffering, cushioning, softening
near antonyms exquisite, fierce, intense, powerful, severe; forceful, forcible, savage, violent; roughened, rugged, strong; abrading, irritating, roughening; grim, gruff, rude, stiff; heavy-handed, oppressive, tyrannical (*also* tyrannic)
antonyms abrasive, caustic, coarse, hard, harsh, rough, scathing, stern, ungentle
2 marked by temperatures that are neither too high nor too low ⟨whisk the egg yolks in a double boiler set over a *gentle* heat⟩ — see CLEMENT
3 of high birth, rank, or station ⟨loved reading about the days when *gentle* lords and ladies danced at fancy balls⟩ — see NOBLE 1

gentle *vb* to lessen the shock of ⟨adding a bit of sugar to the salsa will *gentle* the hot spiciness of the chili peppers⟩ — see CUSHION

gentleman *n* **1** a man of high birth or social position ⟨many of the signers of the Declaration of Independence were *gentlemen* who were risking everything⟩
synonyms aristocrat, grandee, noble, nobleman, patrician
related words squire; cavalier, knight; don, nawab, seigneur, seignior, sheikh (*or* sheik); baron, baronet, count, duke, earl, esquire, lord, marquess, marquis, prince, thane, viscount; czar (*also* tsar *or* tzar), magnate, mogul, nabob; socialite, swell
near antonyms boor, churl, cotter (*or* cottar), fellah, peasant, peon; commoner, plebeian; proletarian; toiler
2 an adult male human being ⟨ladies and *gentlemen* attending the ball⟩ — see MAN 1
3 an honorable and courteous man ⟨was such a *gentleman* that he offered to call a cab for me⟩ — see CAVALIER

gentlewoman *n* a woman of high birth or social position ⟨in the 19th century a number of American *gentlewomen* used their wealth and influence to further abolitionism, women's rights, and other worthy causes⟩
synonyms dame, lady, noblewoman
related words ladyship, madam; baroness, countess, duchess, marchioness; czarina (*also* tsarina *or* tzarina), empress, queen; dowager, matriarch, matron, mistress

gentry *n* the highest class in a society ⟨poor tenant farmers working for landed *gentry*⟩ — see ARISTOCRACY

genuine *adj* **1** being exactly as appears or as claimed ⟨had a *genuine* van Gogh painting hanging in their living room⟩ — see AUTHENTIC 1
2 free from any intent to deceive or impress others ⟨a woman so *genuine* she freely spoke her mind without fear of what others would think⟩ — see GUILELESS

genuinely *adv* in actual fact ⟨is *genuinely* fond of her older brother⟩ — see VERY 2

geometry *n* the outward appearance of something as distinguished from its substance ⟨the *geometry* of Sydney's famed opera house is that of some modernistic sailing ship⟩ — see FORM 1

geriatric *adj* being of advanced years and especially past middle age ⟨went into nursing to work with *geriatric* patients⟩ — see ELDERLY

germane *adj* having to do with the matter at hand ⟨my personal opinion isn't *germane* to our discussion of the facts of the case⟩ — see PERTINENT

germfree *adj* free from filth, infection, or dangers to health ⟨had to prepare the microscope slides in an isolated and *germfree* environment⟩ — see SANITARY

gestation *n* the state of containing unborn young within the body ⟨the length of *gestation* for the gray wolf is about 63 days⟩ — see PREGNANCY

gesticulation *n* a movement of the body or limbs that expresses or emphasizes an idea or feeling ⟨as the argument grew more heated, his *gesticulations* got bigger and wilder⟩ — see GESTURE 1

gesture *n* **1** a movement of the body or limbs that expresses or emphasizes an idea or feeling ⟨a teenager who often shrugs her shoulders in a *gesture* of indifference⟩
synonyms gesticulation, pantomime, sign, signal
related words beck, flourish, shrug, wave; body language, posture; indication, motion
2 an act or utterance that is a customary show of good manners ⟨sent a handwritten thank-you note as a *gesture* of his gratitude⟩ — see CIVILITY 1

gesture *vb* to direct or notify by a movement or gesture ⟨the police officer *gestured* me to the side of the road to tell me my headlight was out⟩ — see MOTION

get *vb* **1** to acquire complete knowledge, understanding, or skill in ⟨I'm not sure I *got* the math in our homework assignment⟩ — see LEARN 1
2 to become affected with (a disease or disorder) ⟨don't cough on me—I don't want to *get* your cold⟩ — see CONTRACT 1
3 to become the father of ⟨Abraham was quite old when he *got* Isaac, his only son⟩ — see FATHER
4 to cause (someone) to agree with a belief or course of action by using arguments or earnest requests ⟨tried to *get* our mother to let us go to the concert, but she refused⟩ — see PERSUADE
5 to come upon after searching, study, or effort ⟨redid the math problem until I *got* the right answer⟩ — see FIND 1
6 to disturb the peace of mind of (someone) especially by repeated disagreeable acts ⟨continuously clearing your throat like that is starting to *get* to me⟩ — see IRRITATE 1
7 to eventually have as a state or quality ⟨it's going to *get* colder as winter approaches⟩ — see BECOME
8 to receive as return for effort ⟨*got* an A on his final paper⟩ — see EARN 1
9 to recognize the meaning of ⟨even though I've studied this chapter all week, I still don't *get* it⟩ — see COMPREHEND 1

10 to take physical control or possession of (something) suddenly or forcibly ⟨the defense tackled the running back and *got* the ball⟩ — see CATCH 1

11 to leave a place often for another ⟨will *get* away to the Bahamas for a vacation⟩ — see GO 2

get along *vb* **1** to meet one's day-to-day needs ⟨most college students can *get along* with just a few hours of sleep at night⟩

synonyms cope, do, fare, get by, get on, make out, manage, shift

related words carry on, contrive, fend, handle, scrape (by *or* through), survive; eke out, scrape (out), scrounge, squeeze, wrest, wring; afford, swing

phrases make shift

near antonyms collapse, fail, fall short, fizzle, flounder; decline, peter (out), slump, wane; give up

2 to move forward along a course ⟨the preparations for the party are *getting along* just fine⟩ — see GO 1

getaway *n* the act or an instance of getting free from danger or confinement ⟨the bank robbers jumped into the car and made their *getaway*⟩ — see ESCAPE 1

get by *vb* to meet one's day-to-day needs ⟨working at night to pay for school allowed me to just *get by*⟩ — see GET ALONG 1

get off *vb* **1** to leave a place often for another ⟨told him to *get off* for home before it got dark⟩ — see GO 2

2 to take the first step in (a process or course of action) ⟨breakfast helps you *get off* to a good start in the morning⟩ — see BEGIN 1

get on *vb* to meet one's day-to-day needs ⟨despite his new job's low pay, he was still *getting on*⟩ — see GET ALONG 1

get out *vb* **1** to become known ⟨news of the rock star's secret wedding *got out* to the news media⟩

synonyms come out, leak (out), spread

related words break, develop, transpire, unfold; circulate, disclose, reveal, spill, tell

near antonyms hush (up), suppress; conceal, disguise, hide, mask; secrete

2 to get free from a dangerous or confining situation ⟨tried but couldn't *get out* of the old well without assistance⟩ — see ESCAPE 1

3 to produce and release for distribution in printed form ⟨an author who *got* a new book *out* every year⟩ — see PUBLISH 1

get-together *n* **1** a coming together of a number of persons for a specified purpose ⟨promised to meet friends for lunch after that morning's sales *get-together*⟩ — see MEETING 1

2 a social gathering ⟨was invited to a neighborhood *get-together*⟩ — see PARTY 1

getup *n* clothing chosen as appropriate for a specific situation ⟨went to the prom in some elaborately beaded *getup*⟩ — see OUTFIT 1

get up *vb* to leave one's bed ⟨you need to *get* right *up* when the alarm goes off in the morning⟩ — see ARISE 1

gewgaw *n* a small object displayed for its attractiveness or interest ⟨had a shelf devoted just to *gewgaws* featuring his favorite team's logo⟩ — see KNICKKNACK

ghastliness *n* the quality of inspiring intense dread or dismay ⟨the *ghastliness* of the Holocaust can scarcely be described⟩ — see HORROR 1

ghastly *adj* extremely disturbing or repellent ⟨a *ghastly* murder⟩ — see HORRIBLE 1

ghost *n* the soul of a dead person thought of especially as appearing to living people ⟨looked for *ghosts* in the graveyard on Halloween⟩

synonyms apparition, bogey (*also* bogy *or* bogie), phantasm, phantom, poltergeist, shade, shadow, specter (*or* spectre), spirit, spook, vision, wraith

related words banshee, demon (*or* daemon), familiar (*or* familiar spirit), genie, imp, incubus, puck; vampire, zombie

ghoul *n* an evil spirit ⟨in Arabic folklore, *ghouls* could change their shapes but had one unchanging feature: donkey's hooves for feet⟩ — see DEMON

giant *adj* unusually large ⟨the *giant* sycamore tree that dwarfs our house is almost 250 years old⟩ — see HUGE

giant *n* something that is unusually large and powerful ⟨the Great Pyramids of Egypt are *giants*⟩

synonyms behemoth, blockbuster, colossus, jumbo, leviathan, mammoth, monster, titan, whale, whopper

related words amazon; bulk, hulk; heavyweight

near antonyms lightweight, weakling, wimp, wisp; nonentity, twerp, whippersnapper

antonyms dwarf, midget, mini, miniature, peewee, pygmy, runt, shrimp

gibber *vb* to speak rapidly, inarticulately, and usually unintelligibly ⟨when we told the kindergarteners they had earned an extra recess, they began to laugh and *gibber* like monkeys⟩ — see BABBLE 1

gibberish *n* unintelligible or meaningless talk ⟨was so excited he could only talk *gibberish*⟩

synonyms babble, blabber, bunk, claptrap, drivel, fudge, gabble, gobbledygook (*also* gobbledegook), hogwash, jabber, jabberwocky, jazz, moonshine, mumbo jumbo, nonsense, piffle, prattle, rigmarole, rot

related words abracadabra; chatter, clatter, gab, gibber, prate, tattle, twaddle; double-talk, hocus-pocus, jive; gas, hot air, wind

gibe *or* **jibe** *vb* to make (someone or something) the object of unkind laughter ⟨teammates *gibing* each other when they foul up an important play⟩ — see RIDICULE

giddy *adj* **1** lacking in seriousness or maturity ⟨the *giddy* youngsters continued to laugh, joke, and make faces during the ceremonies⟩

synonyms featherbrained, flighty, frivolous, goofy, harebrained, light-headed, puerile, scatterbrained, silly

related words fatuous, foolish, inane, nonsensical, thoughtless, witless; crazy, daffy, daft, exuberant, flippant, fluttery, light, lighthearted, playful; sappy, shallow, superficial

near antonyms grave, melancholy, somber (*or* sombre), thoughtful; dignified, heavy, no-nonsense, sedate, severe, solemn, staid

antonyms earnest, serious, serious-minded, sober

2 having a feeling of being whirled about and in danger of falling down ⟨I love the *giddy* feeling you get riding roller coasters⟩ — see DIZZY 1

gift *n* **1** something given to someone without expectation of a return ⟨gave him a *gift* for his birthday⟩

synonyms bestowal, donation, freebie (*or* freebee), giveaway, lagniappe, largess (*or* largesse), present, presentation

related words alms, benefaction, beneficence, benevolence, charity, contribution, dole, generosity, offering, philanthropy; grant, subsidy; remembrance, tribute; bonus, boon, windfall; favor, valentine; gratuity, tip; award, prize, reward; bequest, legacy; sacrifice

near antonyms advance, loan; bribe, sop

2 a special and usually inborn ability ⟨has a *gift* for making guests feel right at home⟩ — see TALENT

gigantic *adj* unusually large ⟨a raccoon got into the trash and now there's a *gigantic* mess on our front lawn, the sidewalk, and half the street⟩ — see HUGE

giggle *n* an explosive sound that is a sign of amusement ⟨couldn't help but *giggle* at his joke⟩ — see LAUGH 1

gimmick *n* **1** a clever often underhanded means to achieve an end ⟨that free magazine subscription they offer is just a sales *gimmick* to get you to buy their product⟩ — see TRICK 1

2 an interesting and often novel device with a practical use ⟨a laptop equipped with a carrying handle and other neat *gimmicks*⟩ — see GADGET

ginger *n* active strength of body or mind ⟨a 60-year-old with the *ginger* to consider skydiving lessons⟩ — see VIGOR 1

gingerbread *adj* elaborately and often excessively decorated ⟨marvelled at all the woodwork on the historic *gingerbread* cottages that lined the coast⟩ — see ORNATE

gingerly *adj* having or showing a close attentiveness to avoiding danger or trouble ⟨his quiet compliments show a *gingerly* attempt at keeping her from whining that she feels fat⟩ — see CAREFUL 1

gingery *adj* **1** having active strength of body or mind ⟨a *gingery* old lobsterman who went out regardless of the weather⟩ — see VIGOROUS 1

2 marked by a lively display of strong feeling ⟨I got a *gingery* rebuke when I asked the spry old woman if she needed any help crossing the street⟩ — see SPIRITED 1

gird *vb* **1** to encircle or bind with or as if with a belt ⟨for the celebration of the heroes' return, well-wishers *girded* hundreds of trees with yellow ribbons⟩ ⟨she *girded* her waist with a delicate sash⟩
synonyms band, belt, girdle, girt, girth, wrap
related words tie up, truss; circle, loop, wind, wreathe; bandage, swathe; chain, cord, enchain, lash, rope, shackle, tape, wire
near antonyms loose, loosen, unbind, unchain, undo, unfasten, unlash, untie, unwind
antonyms unwrap

2 to gather into a tight mass by means of a line or cord ⟨*girded* the stack of papers with twine⟩ — see TIE 1

girdle *n* a strip of flexible material (as leather) worn around the waist ⟨drew a handkerchief from the *girdle* around her waist and offered it to the knight as a token of affection⟩ — see ²BELT

girdle *vb* **1** to encircle or bind with or as if with a belt ⟨trees *girdled* the campus, essentially hiding it from view⟩ ⟨wire *girdling* the bundle of firewood⟩ — see GIRD 1

2 to pass completely around ⟨an asteroid belt that *girdles* the inner planets of the solar system⟩ — see ENCIRCLE 1

girl *n* **1** a young usually unmarried woman ⟨a book that discusses the special challenges that *girls* face as they enter their teenage years⟩
synonyms bobby-soxer, chick [*slang*], damsel, doll, gal, lass, lassie, mademoiselle, maid, maiden, miss
related words gamine; hoyden, tomboy; hussy; ingenue; belle, deb, debutante, sylph; schoolgirl; teenybopper; senorita (*or* señorita)

2 a woman with whom one is in love ⟨sent her a note asking her to be his *girl*⟩ — see GIRLFRIEND

girlfriend *n* a woman with whom one is in love ⟨he proposed to his *girlfriend* of seven years⟩
synonyms gal, girl, ladylove
related words mistress; beloved, darling, dear, favorite, flame, honey, love, lover, sweet, sweetheart, valentine

girlish *adj* having or displaying qualities more suitable for women than for men ⟨told him not to walk on his toes because it made him look *girlish*⟩ — see EFFEMINATE

girt *vb* to encircle or bind with or as if with a belt ⟨a model of a Roman soldier with a sword *girted* to his leg⟩ — see GIRD 1

girth *n* the distance around a round body ⟨a fallen tree with a *girth* of some 26 feet making it wide enough for a full-grown man to walk through⟩ — see CIRCUMFERENCE 1

girth *vb* **1** to encircle or bind with or as if with a belt ⟨you'll need to make sure you *girth* the saddle tightly or you'll fall off the horse⟩ — see GIRD 1

2 to pass completely around ⟨his arms couldn't quite *girth* the stone column⟩ — see ENCIRCLE 1

gist *n* the central part or aspect of something under consideration ⟨didn't catch every word between them, but heard enough to get the *gist* of the conversation⟩ — see CRUX

give *vb* **1** to make a present of ⟨tutors *gave* their time to help students after school⟩
synonyms bestow, contribute, donate, present
related words chip in, kick in, pitch in; award, confer, dole (out); afford, furnish, provide; lavish, regale; aid, assist, benefit, help; administer, dispense, impart, issue, render; extend, offer, pay, proffer, tender; sacrifice
near antonyms hold, keep, pocket, retain, withhold; preserve, save; advance, lend, loan; sell

2 to put (something) into the possession or safekeeping of another ⟨*gave* my camera to my father to hold while I went swimming⟩
synonyms commend, commit, consign, delegate, deliver, entrust, hand over, leave, pass, transfer, transmit, trust, turn over, vest
related words confer, grant; assign, deal (out), dispense, disperse, distribute, divide; release, relinquish, submit, surrender, turn in, yield; bequeath, hand down, will; advance, lend, loan; furnish, supply
near antonyms detain, hold back, reserve, withhold; own, possess; accept, receive, take in; occupy, take, take over
antonyms hold, keep, retain

3 to bring before the public in performance or exhibition ⟨the author will *give* a reading from her latest work at 7:00 p.m.⟩ — see PRESENT 1

4 to fall down or in as a result of physical pressure ⟨they loaded the shopping cart with so much food it *gave* under all the weight⟩ — see COLLAPSE 1

5 to hand over or use up in payment ⟨I wouldn't *give* a nickel for such a run-down car⟩ — see SPEND 1

6 to make known (as an idea, emotion, or opinion) ⟨she *gave* her opinion on the matter very firmly and unmistakably⟩ — see EXPRESS 1

7 to occupy (oneself) diligently or with close attention ⟨totally *gave* himself to his studies in the hopes of winning a scholarship for next year⟩ — see APPLY 2

8 to produce as revenue ⟨a company that consistently *gives* $30 million in profits to the owner⟩ — see YIELD 2

9 to put (something) into the possession of someone for use or consumption ⟨*gave* him my e-mail address⟩ — see FURNISH 2

10 to put before another for acceptance or consideration ⟨she *gave* the committee her grant proposal⟩ — see OFFER 1

give–and–take *n* **1** an exchange of views for the purpose of exploring a subject or deciding an issue ⟨a *give-and-*

take about what we should do Saturday night⟩ — see DISCUSSION 1

2 the act or practice of each side giving up something in order to reach an agreement ⟨negotiating the terms of the deal will require some *give-and-take* on both sides⟩ — see CONCESSION 1

3 good-natured teasing or exchanging of clever remarks ⟨enjoyed the flirty *give-and-take* between the two romantic lead characters⟩ — see BANTER

giveaway *n* something given to someone without expectation of a return ⟨offering a Caribbean vacation *giveaway* to the millionth customer⟩ — see GIFT 1

give away *vb* to make known (something abstract) through outward signs ⟨the insincerity of his apology was *given away* by that slight smirk on his face⟩ — see SHOW 2

give in *vb* **1** to give up and cease resistance (as to a liking, temptation, or habit) ⟨*give in* and have some chocolate⟩ — see YIELD 1

2 to cease resistance (as to another's arguments, demands, or control) ⟨after withstanding hours of begging, Mom finally *gave in* and let us go to the amusement park⟩ — see YIELD 3

given *adj* **1** being in the habit or custom ⟨a quiet man not *given* to loud expressions of emotion⟩ — see ACCUSTOMED

2 having a tendency to be or act in a certain way ⟨she's *given* to exaggeration⟩ — see PRONE 1

given name *n* a name that is placed before one's family name ⟨everyone calls me Jack, but my *given name* is John⟩ — see FORENAME

give out *vb* to stop functioning ⟨waiting for the fuel pump in my old car to *give out*⟩ — see FAIL 1

give up *vb* **1** to give (something) over to the control or possession of another usually under duress ⟨was in so much debt he had to *give up* his house and move into a cheaper apartment⟩ — see SURRENDER 1

2 to stop doing (something) permanently ⟨I hope you won't *give up* playing the piano⟩ — see QUIT 2

3 to yield to the control or power of enemy forces ⟨with the prospect of a renewed enemy attack, the regiment decided to simply *give up*⟩ — see FALL 2

giving *n* the act of offering money in exchange for goods or services ⟨a diorama about pioneer life at the museum that depicts the *giving* of beads for clothes⟩ — see PAYMENT 1

gizmo *or* **gismo** *n* an interesting and often novel device with a practical use ⟨found all sorts of interesting woodworking *gizmos* in the garage⟩ — see GADGET

glacial *adj* **1** having a low or subnormal temperature ⟨a *glacial* weather front coming down from Canada will bring freezing temperatures this weekend⟩ — see COLD 1

2 lacking in friendliness or warmth of feeling ⟨her *glacial* manner stopped him from attempting further conversation⟩ — see COLD 2

glad *adj* **1** experiencing pleasure, satisfaction, or delight ⟨the husband was *glad* to see his wife again, after so long an absence⟩

synonyms blissful, delighted, gratified, happy, joyful, joyous, pleased, satisfied, tickled

related words beaming, blithe, blithesome, buoyant, cheerful, cheery, gay, gladsome, lighthearted, sunny, upbeat; gleeful, jocund, jolly, jovial, laughing, merry, mirthful, smiling; carried away, ecstatic, elated, enraptured, entranced, euphoric, exhilarated, intoxicated, rapturous, rhapsodic; exuberant, exultant, jubilant,

rapt, rejoicing, thrilled; hopeful, optimistic, rosy, sanguine

near antonyms abject, aggrieved, anguished, blue, brokenhearted, dejected, depressed, despondent, disconsolate, disheartened, downcast, downhearted, forlorn, melancholy; doleful, dolorous, lachrymose, mournful, plaintive, sorrowful, sorry, woeful; black, dark, desolate, dispirited, gloomy, glum, gray (*also* grey), grieved, heartbroken, heartsick, miserable, woebegone, wretched

antonyms displeased, joyless, sad, unhappy, unsatisfied

2 having a desire or inclination (as for a specified course of action) ⟨I am *glad* to do it⟩ — see WILLING 1

3 serving to lift one's spirits ⟨the doctor brought *glad* tidings to those awaiting news of her condition⟩ — see CHEERFUL 2

gladden *vb* to give satisfaction to ⟨it would *gladden* me to hear you sing again⟩ — see PLEASE

gladdening *adj* making one feel good inside ⟨the sudden change to warm, sunny weather is *gladdening*⟩ — see HEARTWARMING

gladiatorial *adj* feeling or displaying eagerness to fight ⟨*gladiatorial* boxers held apart by the referee until the bell rang⟩ — see BELLIGERENT

gladness *n* **1** a feeling or state of well-being and contentment ⟨felt nothing but *gladness* at seeing her friends after arriving back in the country⟩ — see HAPPINESS 1

2 the feeling experienced when one's wishes are met ⟨the children's *gladness* was evident as they opened their Christmas presents⟩ — see PLEASURE 1

gladsome *adj* having or showing a good mood or disposition ⟨a *gladsome* group of carolers⟩ ⟨a *gladsome* smile⟩ — see CHEERFUL 1

glamorize *also* **glamourize** *vb* to represent or think of as better than reality ⟨most people *glamorize* fame, not thinking of the lack of privacy that accompanies it⟩ — see IDEALIZE

glamorous *also* **glamourous** *adj* **1** excitingly or mysteriously unusual ⟨the *glamorous* sights and smells of a Turkish market⟩ — see EXOTIC

2 having an often mysterious or magical power to attract ⟨*glamorous* Hollywood celebrities whose every move is breathlessly recorded by the media⟩ — see FASCINATING 1

glamour *also* **glamor** *n* the power of irresistible attraction ⟨the *glamour* of the motion picture industry⟩ — see CHARM 2

glance *n* an instance of looking especially briefly ⟨she was about to say something rude, but her mother silenced her with a *glance*⟩ — see LOOK 2

glance *vb* **1** to strike and fly off at an angle ⟨the basketball *glanced* off the rim⟩ ⟨her wild pitch *glanced* off my shoulder and landed in the dugout⟩

synonyms bounce, carom, rebound, ricochet, skim, skip

related words brush, graze, nudge, shave, sweep; bump, contact, hit, kiss, touch; sideswipe; reflect

2 to take a quick or hasty look ⟨just *glanced* at the instructions before assembling the bike⟩ ⟨*glanced* over his shoulder to see if she was still there⟩

synonyms browse, dip, glimpse, peek, skim

related words peep; blink, squint; look over, scan

near antonyms examine, overlook, oversee, question, survey; study, view; peer, pry; gawk, goggle, rubberneck; leer, ogle

antonyms gaze, stare

3 to shoot forth bursts of light ⟨diamonds *glancing* in the display case⟩ — see FLASH 1

glare *n* the steady giving off of the form of radiation that makes vision possible ⟨the *glare* of headlights⟩ — see LIGHT 1

glare *vb* **1** to shine with a bright harsh light ⟨the spotlight *glared* down on the suspect as the police questioned him relentlessly⟩

synonyms beat, blaze, burn, flame, flare

related words beam, glow, radiate; flash, glance, gleam, glimmer, glint, glisten, glister, glitter, scintillate, shimmer, sparkle, twinkle; bedazzle, blind, daze, dazzle

2 to look with anger or disapproval ⟨don't *glare* at me like that when I tell you "no"⟩ — see FROWN

glaring *adj* very noticeable especially for being incorrect or bad ⟨no one missed the *glaring* spelling error in the title⟩ — see EGREGIOUS

glasses *n pl* a pair of lenses set in a frame that is held in place with ear supports and which are usually worn to correct vision ⟨I'm a little nearsighted, so I'm going to need *glasses*⟩

synonyms eyeglasses, specs, spectacles

related words bifocals; monocle, pince-nez; sunglasses; goggles; contact lens

gleam *n* the steady giving off of the form of radiation that makes vision possible ⟨the door opened a crack and let in a *gleam* of light from the hallway⟩ — see LIGHT 1

gleam *vb* to shoot forth bursts of light ⟨plates and glasses *gleaming* in the candlelight⟩ — see FLASH 1

glee *n* a mood characterized by high spirits and amusement and often accompanied by laughter ⟨students running down the halls in *glee* on the last day of school⟩ — see MIRTH

glee club *n* an organized group of singers ⟨sang with the *glee club* in college⟩ — see CHORUS 1

gleeful *adj* indicative of or marked by high spirits or good humor ⟨*gleeful* shouting when they found out they were getting a puppy⟩ — see MERRY

gleefulness *n* a mood characterized by high spirits and amusement and often accompanied by laughter ⟨the general *gleefulness* of the townsfolk during the holidays⟩ — see MIRTH

glide *vb* **1** to move or proceed smoothly and readily ⟨looking for a course that he could just *glide* through⟩ — see FLOW 2

2 to move through the air with or as if with outstretched wings ⟨a kite *gliding* on the breeze⟩ — see FLY 1

3 to rest or move along the surface of a liquid or in the air ⟨water striders *gliding* along the surface of the brook⟩ — see FLOAT

glimmer *n* a very small amount ⟨a *glimmer* of hope that there will be snow on Christmas⟩ — see PARTICLE 1

glimmer *vb* to shoot forth bursts of light ⟨the waters of the rippling brook *glimmered* in the sun⟩ — see FLASH 1

glimpse *n* an instance of looking especially briefly ⟨I only got a *glimpse* of him as we drove by⟩ — see LOOK 2

glimpse *vb* to take a quick or hasty look ⟨just *glimpsed* at the photo then turned his attention elsewhere⟩ — see GLANCE 2

glint *vb* to shoot forth bursts of light ⟨the cat's eyes *glinted* in the moonlight⟩ — see FLASH 1

glisten *vb* to shoot forth bursts of light ⟨this dull opal really *glistens* in full light⟩ — see FLASH 1

glistening *adj* having a shiny surface or finish ⟨a *glistening* marble table top⟩ — see GLOSSY

glister *vb* to shoot forth bursts of light ⟨the knight's armor *glistered* in the light of day⟩ — see FLASH 1

glitter *vb* to shoot forth bursts of light ⟨the queen's crown *glittered* under the glare of the TV lights⟩ — see FLASH 1

glitz *n* excessive or unnecessary display ⟨a nice dinner without all the *glitz* of fancy folded napkins and finger bowls⟩ — see OSTENTATION

glitzy *adj* excessively showy ⟨I think that rhinestone-studded outfit is a little too *glitzy* for church⟩ — see GAUDY

gloaming *n* **1** a time or place of little or no light ⟨couldn't see if her dog was hiding in the *gloaming* of the backyard woods⟩ — see DARK 1

2 the time from when the sun begins to set to the onset of total darkness ⟨watched the stars begin to come out during the *gloaming*⟩ — see DUSK 1

glob *n* **1** a small uneven mass ⟨found a *glob* of chewing gum under my seat⟩ — see LUMP 1

2 the quantity of fluid that falls naturally in one rounded mass ⟨add a *glob* or two of molasses to the batter⟩ — see DROP 1

global *adj* **1** belonging or relating to the whole ⟨do a *global* search and replace the misspelling throughout the whole document⟩ — see GENERAL 1

2 covering everything or all important points ⟨published a *global* report on the plight of Third World economies⟩ — see ENCYCLOPEDIC

3 having every part of the surface the same distance from the center ⟨thought of the space station as a *global* structure, more like a planet than a spaceship⟩ — see ROUND 1

globe *n* **1** a more or less round body or mass ⟨the glassblower shaped the molten mass into a *globe* of remarkable thinness and clarity⟩ — see ¹BALL 1

2 the celestial body on which we live ⟨New Year's celebrations around the *globe*⟩ — see EARTH 1

globule *n* the quantity of fluid that falls naturally in one rounded mass ⟨fat *globules* of hot wax dripping onto the table⟩ — see DROP 1

gloom *n* **1** a state or spell of low spirits ⟨has been in a perpetual *gloom* since his dog died⟩ — see SADNESS

2 a time or place of little or no light ⟨the *gloom* of a rainy night is the perfect setting for a mystery story⟩ — see DARK 1

gloom *vb* **1** to look with anger or disapproval ⟨his teacher *gloomed* at him as he passed notes across the room⟩ — see FROWN

2 to take on a gloomy or forbidding look ⟨he continued to *gloom* over the fact that he had been passed over for the captaincy of the football team⟩ — see DARKEN 1

gloominess *n* a state or spell of low spirits ⟨his *gloominess* seemed to spread to the other campers until everyone was sulking in their tents⟩ — see SADNESS

gloomy *adj* causing or marked by an atmosphere lacking in cheer ⟨the cold rain made for a *gloomy* day⟩

synonyms black, bleak, cheerless, comfortless, dark, darkening, depressing, desolate, dismal, drear, dreary, elegaic, funereal, glum, gray (*also* grey), miserable, morbid, morose, murky, saturnine, sepulchral, somber (*or* sombre), sullen, wretched

related words dejected, depressed, despondent, disconsolate, droopy, inconsolable, low, melancholy, sad, unhappy, woebegone, woeful; discomfiting, discouraging, disheartening, dismaying, dispiriting, distressful, distressing, upsetting; desperate, hopeless, pessimistic;

lamentable, lugubrious, mournful, sorrowful; cloudy, colorless, drab, dull; dour, grim, lowering (*also* louring), menacing, negative, oppressive, threatening
near antonyms blithe, blithesome, buoyant, gay, jocund, jolly, joyful, joyous, merry, mirthful; encouraging, hopeful, optimistic; lighthearted, lightsome
antonyms bright, cheerful, cheering, cheery, comforting, cordial, gay, festive, friendly, heartwarming, sunshiny
2 feeling unhappiness 〈has been *gloomy* ever since his girlfriend and her family moved away〉 — see SAD 1
3 being without light or without much light 〈that house would be less *gloomy* if some of the overgrown trees and shrubs were cleared away〉 — see DARK 1
glorify *vb* **1** to enhance the status of 〈that newly acquired Picasso painting will certainly *glorify* the college art museum〉 — see EXALT
2 to offer honor or respect to (someone) as a divine power 〈let us now *glorify* the Lord〉 — see WORSHIP 1
3 to praise or publicize lavishly and often excessively 〈fond parents who *glorify* everything that their precious offspring do〉 — see TOUT 1
4 to proclaim the glory of 〈the hillsides ablaze in red and gold silently *glorify* New England in the fall〉 — see PRAISE 1
5 to represent or think of as better than reality 〈don't let the job title "team spirit coordinator" fool you—he is nothing more than a *glorified* cheerleader〉 — see IDEALIZE
glorious *adj* large and impressive in size, grandeur, extent, or conception 〈the advent of the printing press in the West ushered in a *glorious* new era of learning〉 — see GRAND 1
gloriously *adv* in a pleasing way 〈for Easter services the full choir sang *gloriously*〉 — see WELL 5
gloriousness *n* impressiveness of beauty on a large scale 〈the *gloriousness* of the Taj Mahal〉 — see MAGNIFICENCE
glory *n* **1** public acknowledgment or admiration for an achievement 〈the drama teacher gave the stage crew all the *glory* for the successful production〉
synonyms acclaim, accolade, credit, distinction, homage, honor, laurels
related words celebrity, fame, renown, repute; compliment, encomium, eulogy, panegyric, toast, tribute; acclamation, ovation, plaudit, praise, rave, rhapsody; citation, commendation, note, recommendation; elevation, exaltation, glorification
2 an asset that brings praise or renown 〈the new computer lab was the *glory* of the middle school〉
synonyms boast, credit, honor, jewel, pride, treasure
related words pièce de résistance, showpiece; attraction, feature, highlight; distinction, excellence, merit, value, virtue
phrases a feather in one's cap
near antonyms disgrace, dishonor; blemish, blot, defect, shame, slur, smirch, smudge, stain, stigma; eyesore, fright, horror, mess
3 impressiveness of beauty on a large scale 〈was overwhelmed by the imperial *glory* of Rome〉 — see MAGNIFICENCE
glory *vb* to feel or express joy or triumph 〈the home team *gloried* in their come-from-behind victory〉 — see EXULT
glorying *adj* having or expressing feelings of joy or triumph 〈the *glorying* winners who brought home their trophies〉 — see EXULTANT

gloss *n* brightness created by light reflected from a surface 〈the surface had such a high *gloss*, you could see your face reflected in it〉 — see SHINE 1
gloss *vb* to make smooth or glossy usually by repeatedly applying surface pressure 〈the seal's fur was *glossed* by the water〉 — see POLISH
gloss (over) *vb* **1** to make (something) seem less bad by offering excuses 〈I don't want to *gloss over* her misbehavior, but keep in mind that she is under a lot of stress lately〉 — see PALLIATE 1
2 to overlook or dismiss as of little importance 〈this biographer tends to *gloss over* his subject's many character flaws〉 — see EXCUSE 1
glossy *adj* having a shiny surface or finish 〈the *glossy* finish on the gym floor〉 〈a sports car with an interior upholstered with *glossy* leather〉
synonyms buffed, burnished, glistening, lustrous, polished, rubbed, satin, satiny, sleek
related words silken, silky, slick, slippery; glassy, glazed, lacquered, shellacked, varnished; gleaming, glittering, reflective, shining
near antonyms lackluster
antonyms dim, dull, flat, lusterless, matte (*also* mat *or* matt)
glow *n* the steady giving off of the form of radiation that makes vision possible 〈was reading by the *glow* of the lamp〉 — see LIGHT 1
glow *vb* **1** to be on fire especially brightly 〈the coals *glowed* red-hot〉 — see BURN 1
2 to develop a rosy facial color (as from excitement or embarrassment) 〈when they found out he had won the tournament, his parents *glowed* with pride〉 — see BLUSH
glower *vb* **1** to look with anger or disapproval 〈baseball fans *glowering* at the TV as they watched their favorite team lose〉 — see FROWN
2 to take on a gloomy or forbidding look 〈the old man just sat in his rocking chair and silently *glowered* at the uninvited guests〉 — see DARKEN 1
glowing *adj* **1** giving off or reflecting much light 〈enjoyed the warmth of the *glowing* fire〉 — see BRIGHT 1
2 having a healthy reddish skin tone 〈was *glowing* after spending an afternoon outside splitting firewood〉 — see RUDDY
3 being or being an outward sign of good feelings (as of love, confidence, or happiness) 〈her *glowing* face made it evident she'd been offered the job〉 — see RADIANT 1
4 having or expressing great depth of feeling 〈*glowing* confessions of love〉 — see FERVENT
gloze (over) *vb* **1** to make (something) seem less bad by offering excuses 〈he tried to *gloze over* his own failing grade by pointing out that none of the others had received anything higher than a C〉 — see PALLIATE 1
2 to overlook or dismiss as of little importance 〈we're certainly willing to *gloze over* a couple of minor historical inaccuracies in an otherwise splendid movie〉 — see EXCUSE 1
glue *n* a substance used to stick things together 〈used *glue* to stick the photo in the album〉
synonyms adhesive, cement, size
related words epoxy, epoxy resin, library paste, mucilage, superglue; dope, goo, gum
gluey *adj* being of such a thick consistency as to readily cling to objects upon contact 〈don't over-beat the mashed potatoes or they will be thick and *gluey* instead of light and fluffy〉 — see STICKY 1

glum *adj* **1** causing or marked by an atmosphere lacking in cheer ⟨the usual *glum* waiting room at the tax collector's office⟩ ⟨a cold, *glum* day⟩ — see GLOOMY 1
2 feeling unhappiness ⟨how can you be *glum* after such a great day?⟩ — see SAD 1
3 given to or displaying a resentful silence and often irritability ⟨a *glum* and pouting child⟩ — see SULKY

glut *vb* to fill with food to capacity ⟨didn't like to watch those nature programs where all they show are predators *glutting* themselves on the kill⟩ — see GORGE 1

glutinous *adj* being of such a thick consistency as to readily cling to objects upon contact ⟨a bad horror movie from the 1950s about a *glutinous* blob that devoured Manhattan⟩ — see STICKY 1

glutton *n* one who eats greedily or too much ⟨he's such a *glutton* that he ate the whole cake⟩
synonyms gorger, gormandizer, gourmand, hog, overeater, stuffer, swiller
related words feaster, trencherman; muncher; guzzler
near antonyms dieter, nibbler, picker

gluttonous *adj* having a huge appetite ⟨*gluttonous* customers had practically emptied the all-you-can-eat buffet⟩ — see VORACIOUS 1

gnash *vb* to press or strike against or together so as to make a scraping sound ⟨dogs *gnashing* their teeth⟩ — see GRIND 2

gnaw (on) *vb* to crush or grind with the teeth ⟨please don't *gnaw on* that steak bone, it's very rude⟩ — see BITE (ON)

gnawer *n* one who is obnoxiously annoying ⟨a whiny *gnawer* who wouldn't quit mentioning that I had made a wrong turn and got us lost⟩ — see NUISANCE 1

gnome *n* an imaginary being usually having a small human form and magical powers ⟨in Europe, *gnomes* are thought to guard underground treasure, so perhaps that is why people have taken to putting statues of them in their gardens⟩ — see FAIRY

go *adj* being in a state of fitness for some experience or action ⟨all systems are *go*⟩ — see READY 1

go *n* **1** a practice or interest that is very popular for a short time ⟨snowboarding is all the *go*⟩ — see FAD
2 active strength of body or mind ⟨a healthy six-year-old full of *go*⟩ — see VIGOR 1
3 an effort to do or accomplish something ⟨it took several *goes* to get the car started⟩ — see ATTEMPT
4 readiness to engage in daring or difficult activity ⟨a young executive with the *go* to make this company grow⟩ — see ENTERPRISE 2

go *vb* **1** to move forward along a course ⟨everything is *going* according to our plans⟩
synonyms advance, fare, forge, get along, march, proceed, progress
related words accelerate, fast-forward, speed; approach, near; journey, pass, repair, run, travel, wend; actuate, drive, impel, propel, push; do, go off, take out
phrases gain ground
near antonyms arrest, balk, block, check, detain, halt, hinder, hold back, impede, nip, obstruct, slow (down *or* up), stem; repress, retard, stunt, suppress; delay, interrupt, stall; cramp, hamper, inhibit; cease, let up, pause; regress
antonyms remain, stand, stay, stop
2 to leave a place often for another ⟨will *go* on vacation at the end of the year⟩ ⟨decided it would be better to *go* before she got any angrier⟩
synonyms begone, clear out, depart, exit, get, get off, move, pull (out), quit, sally (forth), shove (off), take off, walk out

related words set out, start, strike out; abscond, decamp, escape, evacuate, flee, fly, get out, run away, scat, scram, skip; go out, light out, step out; abandon, desert, forsake, vacate; emigrate; remove, retire, retreat, withdraw
phrases beat it
near antonyms abide, dwell, lodge, remain, settle, stay, tarry; approach, close, near; hit, land, reach
antonyms arrive, come, show up, turn up
3 to be fitting or proper ⟨at Mardi Gras, just about anything *goes*⟩ — see DO 1
4 to be in agreement on every point ⟨your account of how the fire started doesn't *go* with what she said⟩ — see CHECK 1
5 to be positioned along a certain course or in a certain direction ⟨the highway *goes* right along the river⟩ — see RUN 3
6 to eventually have as a state or quality ⟨she *goes* crazy on the dance floor when they start playing her favorite music⟩ ⟨the room *went* dark⟩ — see BECOME 1
7 to fall down or in as a result of physical pressure ⟨watched the building *go* after the demolition crew detonated the charges⟩ — see COLLAPSE 1
8 to have or be in a usual or proper place ⟨these plates *go* in this cabinet⟩ — see BELONG 1
9 to lose bodily strength or vigor ⟨when you get old, your eyesight starts to *go*⟩ — see WEAKEN 2
10 to make one's way through, across, or over ⟨if you *go* down the river, you'll see the landing⟩ ⟨*go* along Main Street for another two miles, then turn left⟩ — see TRAVERSE
11 to occur within a continuous range of variation ⟨selling prices for houses in that neighborhood generally *go* between one and two million⟩ — see RUN 4
12 to risk (something) on the outcome of an uncertain event ⟨to play in this game of poker, you have to be willing to *go* at least five dollars per round⟩ — see BET

go (for) *vb* to have a price of ⟨those cars *go for* $25,000⟩ — see COST

go (on) *vb* to take place ⟨what in the world is *going on* in there?⟩ — see HAPPEN

go (to) *vb* to use or seek out as a source of aid, relief, or advantage ⟨when the sales representative refused to help us, we *went to* the store manager⟩ — see RESORT (TO) 1

goad *n* something that arouses action or activity ⟨bad grades are quite a *goad* for studying harder⟩ — see IMPULSE

goad *vb* **1** to try to persuade (someone) through earnest appeals to follow a course of action ⟨tried to *goad* me into auditioning for the play⟩ — see URGE
2 to urge or push forward with or as if with a pointed object ⟨*goading* the horse forward into the stall⟩ — see PROD 1

goal *n* something that one hopes or intends to accomplish ⟨graduating from high school with honors is one of my main *goals*⟩
synonyms aim, ambition, aspiration, design, dream, end, intent, intention, mark, meaning, object, objective, plan, pretension, purpose, target, thing
related words plot, project, scheme; desire, hope, wish; destination, terminus
near antonyms means, method, way

goat *n* a person or thing taking the blame for others ⟨you have to quit making your soccer practice the *goat* and take responsibility for not finishing your homework⟩ — see SCAPEGOAT

¹**gob** *n* **1** a small uneven mass ⟨grabbed a *gob* of clay from the block and threw it on the pottery wheel⟩ — see LUMP 1

2 gobs *pl* a considerable amount ⟨has *gobs* of money⟩ — see LOT 2

²**gob** *n* one who operates or navigates a seagoing vessel ⟨avast, ye *gobs*, and haul anchor!⟩ — see SAILOR

gobbet *n* a small uneven mass ⟨avoided stepping in a *gobbet* of spit on the sidewalk⟩ — see LUMP 1

gobbledygook *also* **gobbledegook** *n* unintelligible or meaningless talk ⟨that early in the morning, anything you try to say is just *gobbledygook*⟩ — see GIBBERISH

go–between *n* **1** one that carries a message or does an errand ⟨I won't act as *go-between* between you and the girl you want to ask out⟩ — see MESSENGER

2 one who works with opposing sides in order to bring about an agreement ⟨acted as *go-between* for the two warring nations during the peace process⟩ — see MEDIATOR

goblin *n* an imaginary being usually having a small human form and magical powers ⟨my shorter friend dressed up like a *goblin* for Halloween⟩ — see FAIRY

god *n* **1** a being having superhuman powers and control over a particular part of life or the world ⟨in some parts of the world, people believed that the wind and the sea were *gods* that controlled people's fortune⟩ — see DEITY 1

2 *cap* the being worshipped as the creator and ruler of the universe ⟨give thanks to *God*⟩ — see DEITY 2

goddess *n* a lovely woman ⟨like any guy in love, he thought his new girlfriend was a *goddess*⟩ — see BEAUTY 2

godhead *n* **1** the quality or state of being divine ⟨in some cultures, the ruler of the people has *godhead* and is worshipped accordingly⟩ — see DIVINITY

2 *cap* the being worshipped as the creator and ruler of the universe ⟨most Christians believe that there are three separate persons—Father, Son, and Holy Spirit—that make up the *Godhead*⟩ — see DEITY 2

godhood *n* the quality or state of being divine ⟨in Greek myth, Hercules was granted *godhood* after his death⟩ — see DIVINITY

godless *adj* lacking religious emotions, principles, or practices ⟨a *godless* atheist⟩ — see IRRELIGIOUS

godlike *adj* of, relating to, or being God ⟨the *godlike* splendor of creation⟩ — see HOLY 3

godliness *n* the quality or state of being spiritually pure or virtuous ⟨they say that cleanliness is next to *godliness*⟩ — see HOLINESS

godly *adj* showing a devotion to God and to a life of virtue ⟨a *godly* and humble man who will be richly rewarded in the next world⟩ — see HOLY 1

godsend *n* something that provides happiness or does good for a person or thing ⟨that extra job has proved to be a *godsend* for my bills⟩ — see BLESSING 2

Godspeed *n* an expression of good wishes at parting ⟨a hearty *Godspeed* was extended to all the departing troops⟩ — see GOOD-BYE

go–getter *n* an ambitious person who eagerly goes after what is desired ⟨a *go-getter* with his sights set on the presidency⟩

synonyms hummer, hustler, live wire, powerhouse, rustler, self-starter

related words dasher; doer, enterpriser; he-man

near antonyms dawdler, idler, loafer, lounger, putterer, trifler; goldbrick, malingerer, procrastinator, shirker, slacker; drone, lazybones, sluggard; dallier, laggard, lingerer, loiterer, slowpoke, stick-in-the-mud;

ignorer, ne'er-do-well, neglecter; daydreamer, dreamer; dropout, quitter

go–getting *adj* **1** having a strong desire for personal advancement ⟨this job is a great opportunity for some *go-getting* young person⟩ — see AMBITIOUS 1

2 having or showing a bold forcefulness in the pursuit of a goal ⟨a determined newcomer who made a *go-getting* bid for the governorship⟩ — see AGGRESSIVE 1

go–getting *n* eager desire for personal advancement ⟨with all his *go-getting*, he should move quickly up the corporate ladder⟩ — see AMBITION 1

goggle *vb* to look long and hard in wonder or surprise ⟨*goggled* at the elaborate costumes and floats in the parade⟩ — see GAPE

going *adj* **1** accepted, used, or practiced by most people ⟨what's the *going* price for a good used skateboard?⟩ — see CURRENT 1

2 being in effective operation ⟨he just can't keep the business *going*⟩ — see ACTIVE 1

3 having attained a desired end or state of good fortune ⟨our continued partnership with them is a *going* concern⟩ — see SUCCESSFUL 1

going *n* **1** forward movement in time or place ⟨tried to get up the hill, but it was slow *going*⟩ — see ADVANCE 1

2 the act of leaving a place ⟨was so absorbed in her TV show she didn't notice his comings or *goings*⟩ — see DEPARTURE

gold *n* something (as pieces of stamped metal or printed paper) customarily and legally used as a medium of exchange, a measure of value, or a means of payment ⟨pirates burying a chest full of Spanish *gold*⟩ — see MONEY

goldbrick *n* one who deliberately avoids work or duty ⟨the *goldbricks* among the colonists were warned: no work, no food⟩ — see SLACKER

golden *adj* **1** having qualities which inspire hope ⟨this may be your *golden* moment to impress a baseball scout, so don't blow it⟩ — see HOPEFUL 1

2 marked by conspicuously full and rich sounds or tones ⟨sang in a *golden* alto that filled the concert hall⟩ — see RESONANT

3 marked by vigorous growth and well-being especially economically ⟨the *golden* age of industrialization⟩ — see PROSPEROUS 1

4 of a pale yellow or yellowish brown color ⟨a *golden* retriever⟩ — see BLOND

5 pointing toward a happy outcome ⟨that new job is a *golden* opportunity⟩ — see FAVORABLE 2

golden–ager *n* a person of advanced years ⟨offered discounts and special tours for *golden-agers*⟩ — see SENIOR CITIZEN

golden mean *n* a middle point between extremes ⟨when it comes to money, the *golden mean* of saving but allowing yourself a modest spending allowance is the best⟩ — see MEAN 1

gone *adj* **1** no longer existing ⟨woolly mammoths have been long *gone*⟩ — see EXTINCT

2 no longer living ⟨doctors came to the waiting room to give the sad news that the operation wasn't successful and the heart patient was *gone*⟩ — see DEAD 1

3 no longer possessed ⟨I put my watch right here on the table, but now it's *gone*⟩ — see LOST

good *adj* **1** based on sound reasoning or information ⟨had enough information to make a *good* assessment of the situation⟩

synonyms commonsense, hard, informed, just, justified, levelheaded, logical, rational, reasonable, reasoned, sensible, sober, solid, valid, well-founded *related words* actual, real, true; certain, sure; certified, validated, verified; confirmed, corroborated, substantiated; cogent, convincing, credible

near antonyms unsubstantiated, unsupported, unwarranted; flimsy, implausible, unconvincing, weak; fallacious, false, misled

antonyms groundless, illogical, invalid, irrational, nonrational, nonsensical, nonvalid, unfounded, ungrounded, uninformed, unjustified, unreasonable, unsound

2 conforming to a high standard of morality or virtue ⟨a *good* person who seldom did wrong⟩ ⟨*good* behavior will earn you the respect of others⟩

synonyms decent, ethical, honest, honorable, just, moral, right, righteous, right-minded, straight, upright, virtuous

related words correct, decorous, proper, seemly; high-minded, noble, principled; commendable, creditable, exemplary, legitimate; esteemed, law-abiding, reputable, respected, upstanding, worthy; blameless, clean, guiltless, immaculate, incorruptible, innocent, inoffensive, irreproachable, unobjectionable; lily-white, pure, scrupulous, spotless, uncorrupted, unerring; goody-goody, moralistic, sanctimonious, self-righteous

near antonyms improper, incorrect, indecorous, naughty, unbecoming, unseemly; corrupt, debased, debauched, degenerate, depraved, dissolute, perverted, reprobate; unprincipled, unscrupulous; atrocious, infamous, villainous; base, low, mean, vicious, vile; blameworthy, objectionable, offensive; iniquitous, nefarious; errant, erring, fallen

antonyms bad, black, dishonest, dishonorable, evil, evil-minded, immoral, indecent, sinful, unethical, unrighteous, wicked, wrong

3 according to the rules of logic ⟨you don't need a *good* reason to stop doing that—it's because I said so⟩ — see LOGICAL 1

4 being to one's liking ⟨that band's music is *good*⟩ — see SATISFACTORY 1

5 expressing approval ⟨gave the restaurant a *good* review⟩ — see FAVORABLE 1

6 firm in one's allegiance to someone or something ⟨has a few *good* friends who stick by her when things get difficult⟩ — see FAITHFUL 1

7 giving pleasure or contentment to the mind or senses ⟨we had a *good* time at the movies⟩ — see PLEASANT

8 having or showing exceptional knowledge, experience, or skill in a field of endeavor ⟨he's *good* at math⟩ — see PROFICIENT

9 having sufficient worth or merit to receive one's honor, esteem, or reward ⟨she is *good* enough to win the scholarship⟩ — see WORTHY

10 having the required skills for an acceptable level of performance ⟨that electrician is *good* at what he does⟩ — see COMPETENT

11 meeting the requirements of a purpose or situation ⟨those rotten apples aren't *good* to eat⟩ — see FIT 1

12 showing or expressing acceptance or approval ⟨got *good* marks at the dog show⟩ — see POSITIVE

13 sufficiently large in size, amount, or number to merit attention ⟨had a *good* number of valuable baseball cards in his collection⟩ — see CONSIDERABLE 1

14 worthy of one's trust ⟨a car that should be *good* for another few years⟩ — see DEPENDABLE

good *adv* in a satisfactory way ⟨things are going *good* for us⟩ — see WELL 1

good *n* **1** something that provides happiness or does good for a person or thing ⟨let us praise God, from Whom all *goods* flow⟩ — see BLESSING 2

2 the state of doing well especially in relation to one's happiness or success ⟨I am doing this for your own *good*⟩ — see WELFARE

3 goods *pl* products that are bought and sold in business ⟨had a hard time selling leftover Easter *goods* that were still on the shelves by Mother's Day⟩ — see MERCHANDISE

Good Book *n* a book made up of the writings accepted by Christians as coming from God ⟨what does the *Good Book* say about temptation?⟩ — see BIBLE

good–bye *or* **good-by** *n* an expression of good wishes at parting ⟨said our *good-byes* and headed for home⟩

synonyms adieu, au revoir, bon voyage, farewell, Godspeed

related words leave-taking, send-off

near antonyms greeting(s), salutation, salute; welcome

antonyms hello

good–hearted *adj* having or marked by sympathy and consideration for others ⟨a *good-hearted* doctor who saw poor patients for free⟩ — see HUMANE 1

goodly *adj* **1** of a size greater than average of its kind ⟨$10,000 is a *goodly* reward to offer for a missing ring⟩ — see LARGE

2 sufficiently large in size, amount, or number to merit attention ⟨a *goodly* number of people gathered to watch the spectacle⟩ — see CONSIDERABLE 1

good–natured *adj* having an easygoing and pleasing manner especially in social situations ⟨the guests at the party were a *good-natured* bunch⟩ — see AMIABLE

good–naturedness *n* **1** a desire or disposition to please ⟨his *good-naturedness* made him an easy person to work with⟩ — see COMPLAISANCE

2 the state or quality of having a pleasant or agreeable manner in socializing with others ⟨the *good-naturedness* of her response to the teasing made her a hit with the guys⟩ — see AMIABILITY 1

goodness *n* conduct that conforms to an accepted standard of right and wrong ⟨a person displaying such *goodness* that others were inspired to lead better lives⟩ — see MORALITY 1

good–sized *adj* **1** of a size greater than average of its kind ⟨wanted a *good-sized* portion of green beans⟩ — see LARGE

2 sufficiently large in size, amount, or number to merit attention ⟨a *good-sized* crowd of volunteers turned out for the cleanup of the city's riverside park⟩ — see CONSIDERABLE 1

good–tempered *adj* having an easygoing and pleasing manner especially in social situations ⟨her children were *good-tempered* and well-behaved in public⟩ — see AMIABLE

good–temperedness *n* the state or quality of having a pleasant or agreeable manner in socializing with others ⟨the volunteer's general *good-temperedness* was infectious and lifted the spirits of those waiting to give blood⟩ — see AMIABILITY 1

goodwill *n* **1** kindly concern, interest, or support ⟨the long tradition of *goodwill* that exists between the United States and Canada⟩

synonyms amity, benevolence, cordiality, fellowship, friendliness, friendship, kindliness

related words camaraderie, community, companionship, comradeship; civility, comity, concord, harmony, rapport; charity, generosity, neighborliness; affinity, communion, empathy, sympathy, tolerance; altruism, philanthropy, selflessness

near antonyms disfavor, intolerance; animosity, antagonism, antipathy, enmity, hate, hatred, hostility, incivility, malice, rancor

antonyms ill will, malevolence

2 cheerful readiness to do something 〈took on the task of coaching the soccer team with lots of zeal and *goodwill*〉 — see ALACRITY 1

goody *n* something that is pleasing to eat because it is rare or a luxury 〈couldn't wait to sample the bonbons, tortes, and other *goodies*〉 — see DELICACY 1

gooey *adj* being of such a thick consistency as to readily cling to objects upon contact 〈that new hair gel is really *gooey*〉 — see STICKY 1

goof *n* an unintentional departure from truth or accuracy 〈that typo is just a *goof*〉 — see ERROR 1

go off *vb* to break open or into pieces usually because of internal pressure 〈specialists were able to deactivate the bomb before it *went off*〉 — see EXPLODE 1

goofy *adj* lacking in seriousness or maturity 〈it's not appropriate to be *goofy* at a funeral〉 — see GIDDY 1

goon *n* **1** a stupid person 〈called his opponents brainless *goons*〉 — see IDIOT

2 a violent, brutal person who is often a member of an organized gang 〈the crime boss threatened to send the *goons* after him if he talked〉 — see HOODLUM

goose *n* a person who lacks good sense or judgment 〈don't be such a silly *goose*; you know they received your application because they cashed the check for your application fee〉 — see FOOL 1

goose egg *n* the numerical symbol 0 or the absence of number or quantity represented by it 〈was such a bad bowler his final score was a big, fat *goose egg*〉 — see ZERO 1

go over *vb* to turn out as planned or desired 〈his sales pitch *went over* as expected and he saw a 200% increase in his commissions〉 — see SUCCEED 1

gore *vb* to penetrate or hold (something) with a pointed object 〈running with the bulls in Pamplona, Spain, may sound like fun, but the bulls have been known to *gore* runners who get too close〉 — see IMPALE

gorge *n* a narrow opening between hillsides or mountains that can be used for passage 〈walked the bridge over the *gorge*, marveling at the spectacular drop〉 — see CANYON

gorge *vb* **1** to fill with food to capacity 〈they *gorged* themselves on the four pies Aunt Martha brought for Thanksgiving〉

synonyms glut, sate, stuff, surfeit

related words gobble, gormandize, pig out; gulp, guzzle; cloy, fill; banquet, feast, regale

near antonyms diet, fast

2 to eat greedily or to excess 〈the kids *gorged* on Halloween candy when they got home from trick-or-treating〉

synonyms gormandize, overeat, pig out, swill

related words devour, glut, sate, stuff, surfeit, wolf; banquet, feast, regale; bolt, cram, gulp, guzzle

near antonyms nibble, peck, pick, taste

gorgeous *adj* very pleasing to look at 〈sunsets in Hawaii are just *gorgeous*〉 — see BEAUTIFUL

gorgeousness *n* the qualities in a person or thing that as a whole give pleasure to the senses 〈nothing compares to the *gorgeousness* of the first snow of the winter〉 — see BEAUTY 1

gorger *n* one who eats greedily or too much 〈a shark that is such a *gorger* it can't move after devouring a meal〉 — see GLUTTON

gormandize *vb* to eat greedily or to excess 〈everybody tends to *gormandize* on Thanksgiving—it's traditional!〉 — see GORGE 2

gormandizer *n* one who eats greedily or too much 〈a habitual *gormandizer* who eats his hosts out of house and home〉 — see GLUTTON

gory *adj* containing, smeared, or stained with blood 〈doesn't watch too many movies that feature *gory* violence〉 — see BLOODY 1

gospel *n* the basic beliefs or guiding principles of a person or group 〈her private *gospel* is to do good cheerfully and expect no reward〉 — see CREED 1

gossamer *adj* **1** being of a material lacking in sturdiness or substance 〈fairies are usually depicted as wearing *gossamer* or tattered clothing〉 — see FLIMSY 1

2 resembling air in lightness 〈the *gossamer* veil seemed to float about the bride as she walked down the aisle〉 — see AIRY 1

3 very thin and easy to see through 〈didn't see the *gossamer* spider webs until the sun hit them just right〉 — see SHEER 1

gossamery *adj* **1** being of a material lacking in sturdiness or substance 〈that *gossamery* dress should be washed gently by hand so it doesn't disintegrate〉 — see FLIMSY 1

2 resembling air in lightness 〈a *gossamery* feather floating on the breeze〉 — see AIRY 1

3 very thin and easy to see through 〈use this *gossamery* cheesecloth to strain the liquid out of the cottage cheese〉 — see SHEER 1

gossip *n* friendly, informal conversation or an instance of this 〈stayed at the water fountain for a little *gossip*〉 — see CHAT

gossip *vb* to relate sometimes questionable or secret information of a personal nature 〈likes to *gossip* with others about our neighbors' arguments〉

synonyms blab, talk, tattle

related words bandy (about), circulate, noise (about), rumor; disclose, divulge, reveal, tell; hint, imply, insinuate, intimate, let on, suggest; inform, report, snitch, squeal, tip (off); babble, spill; confide

phrases spill the beans

near antonyms clam up, shut up

gossipy *adj* having the style and content of everyday conversation 〈your research paper's tone is a little too *gossipy* for formal writing〉 — see CHATTY 1

gouge *vb* to charge (someone) too much for goods or services 〈because I forgot the sunscreen, I had to buy it from the concession stand at the beach, where they *gouged* me for it〉 — see OVERCHARGE 1

gourmand *n* **1** a person with refined tastes in food and wine 〈a finicky *gourmand* who vacationed in Europe every year simply for the wine〉 — see EPICURE

2 one who eats greedily or too much 〈a *gourmand* who swallows food without even tasting it〉 — see GLUTTON

gourmet *n* a person with refined tastes in food and wine 〈food critics have to be *gourmets* in order to write about food in an informed way〉 — see EPICURE

govern *vb* **1** to exercise authority or power over 〈the president is elected in order to *govern* the country〉

synonyms boss, captain, command, control, preside (over), rule

related words conduct, direct, head, lead; administer, manage, oversee, regulate, superintend, supervise; dictate, dominate, domineer, lord (it over), master, oppress, reign (over), tyrannize; conquer, subdue, subjugate

2 to keep from exceeding a desirable degree or level (as of expression) ⟨you need to *govern* your speech and be able to communicate your frustration without resorting to profanity⟩ — see CONTROL 1

3 to look after and make decisions about ⟨the student council's finances are *governed* by the treasurer⟩ — see CONDUCT 1

governance *n* **1** lawful control over the affairs of a political unit (as a nation) ⟨after World War II, the four Allied nations shared the *governance* of the territory of postwar Germany under the Allied Control Council⟩ — see RULE 2

2 the act or activity of looking after and making decisions about something ⟨while a counselor can be helpful, the *governance* of your academic career rests solely with you⟩ — see CONDUCT 1

government *n* **1** lawful control over the affairs of a political unit (as a nation) ⟨*government* by the people, for the people⟩ — see RULE 2

2 the act or activity of looking after and making decisions about something ⟨a board involved in the *government* of the distribution of benefits to veterans⟩ — see CONDUCT 1

gown *n* a garment with a joined blouse and skirt for a woman or girl ⟨a shopping trip to find the perfect *gown* for the prom⟩ — see DRESS 1

gown *vb* to outfit with clothes and especially fine or special clothes ⟨a queen *gowned* in exotic silks and satins⟩ — see CLOTHE 1

grab *n* an instance of theft ⟨a political activist who thinks the government's lease of public lands to logging companies amounts to an illegal land *grab*⟩ — see THEFT 2

grab *vb* to take physical control or possession of (something) suddenly or forcibly ⟨don't *grab* your brother like that⟩ — see CATCH 1

grace *n* **1** an act of kind assistance ⟨in Victor Hugo's novel, *Les Misérables*, Jean Valjean's decision to go to jail for the man mistaken for him is a *grace* that goes beyond thanks⟩ — see FAVOR 1

2 dignified or restrained beauty of form, appearance, or style ⟨a beautiful actress who was the epitome of *grace* during her too-brief career⟩ — see ELEGANCE

grace *vb* to make more attractive by adding something that is beautiful or becoming ⟨I hope that you will *grace* our gathering with your presence⟩ — see DECORATE

graceful *adj* **1** moving easily ⟨the *graceful* ballerina effortlessly leapt across the dance floor⟩
synonyms agile, light, light-footed, lissome (*also* lissom), lithe, lithesome, nimble, spry
related words flexible, limber, loose-jointed, pliable, pliant, supple; adroit, deft, dexterous (*also* dextrous); fleet-footed, surefooted
near antonyms inflexible, rigid, stiff; bungling, inept, maladroit
antonyms awkward, clumsy, gawky, graceless, lumbering, ungainly, ungraceful

2 having or showing elegance ⟨sat down in the old plantation home's very *graceful* parlor⟩ — see ELEGANT 1

gracefulness *n* dignified or restrained beauty of form, appearance, or style ⟨a home decorated with all of the *gracefulness* you'd expect of a fashion designer⟩ ⟨impressed by the *gracefulness* of the antebellum mansion⟩ — see ELEGANCE

graceless *adj* **1** lacking in physical ease and grace in movement or in the use of the hands ⟨a *graceless* person who was a butterfingered lout when it came to playing basketball⟩ — see CLUMSY 1

2 lacking social grace and assurance ⟨was a *graceless* preteen but grew up to be a confident teenager⟩ — see AWKWARD 1

3 not appropriate for a particular occasion or situation ⟨one guest made a *graceless* comment about the bride's hair⟩ — see INAPPROPRIATE

gracious *adj* **1** showing a natural kindness and courtesy especially in social situations ⟨a *gracious* teacher who made the new student feel welcome⟩
synonyms affable, cordial, genial, hospitable, sociable
related words agreeable, amiable, benignant, congenial, convivial, friendly, kind, kindly, neighborly; accommodating, obliging; considerate, courteous, polite, thoughtful; sophisticated, urbane; approachable, attentive, outgoing
near antonyms boorish, churlish; abrupt, blunt, brusque, curt, gruff, sharp, snippy; antisocial, disagreeable, discourteous, ill-mannered, impolite, rude, sullen, surly, uncivil, unfriendly, unkind, unmannerly; crabbed, crabby, cross, crusty, grumpy
antonyms inhospitable, ungracious, unsociable

2 having an easygoing and pleasing manner especially in social situations ⟨a *gracious* innkeeper whose jokes and laughter made weary travelers feel right at home⟩ — see AMIABLE

3 showing consideration, courtesy, and good manners ⟨he was a *gracious* man, habitually offering his seat on the bus to elderly women⟩ — see POLITE 1

graciousness *n* **1** speech or behavior that is a sign of good breeding ⟨at these private schools, young women would be taught upper-class *graciousness*⟩ — see POLITENESS

2 the state or quality of having a pleasant or agreeable manner in socializing with others ⟨his *graciousness* and wit kept the entire table entertained through the whole meal⟩ — see AMIABILITY 1

gradational *adj* proceeding or changing by steps or degrees ⟨*gradational* increases in altitude⟩ — see GRADUAL

gradationally *adv* by small steps or amounts ⟨by adding the white tint drop by drop, she *gradationally* changed the color from dark red to pink⟩ — see GRADUALLY

grade *n* **1** an individual part of a process, series, or ranking ⟨just one *grade* removed from completion⟩ — see DEGREE 1

2 degree of excellence ⟨only motor oil of the highest *grade* for his fancy sports car⟩ — see QUALITY 1

3 one of the units into which a whole is divided on the basis of a common characteristic ⟨there are various *grades* of wool to consider when selecting a fabric⟩ — see CLASS 2

4 something set up as an example against which others of the same type are compared ⟨that painting just doesn't make the *grade*⟩ — see STANDARD 1

5 the degree to which something rises up from a position level with the horizon ⟨the hill rises at a seven percent *grade*⟩ — see SLANT

grade *vb* **1** to arrange or assign according to type ⟨*grade* these apples "extra fancy" and those "fancy"⟩ — see CLASSIFY 1

2 to take or have a certain position within a group arranged in vertical classes ⟨that music *grades* pretty high with young teens⟩ — see RANK 1

gradient *n* the degree to which something rises up from a position level with the horizon ⟨the path goes up at a pretty steep *gradient* before leveling off⟩ — see SLANT

gradual *adj* proceeding or changing by steps or degrees ⟨a *gradual* drop in gas prices will take place over the next several months⟩

synonyms gradational, incremental, phased, piecemeal, step-by-step

related words progressive, stepped, tapered; imperceptible, inching

near antonyms abrupt, acute, sharp; changeable, dynamic, volatile

antonyms sudden

gradually *adv* by small steps or amounts ⟨*gradually* worked his way down the class roster⟩ ⟨add the sugar to the beaten egg whites *gradually* to make the meringue⟩

synonyms gradationally, little by little, piece by piece, piecemeal

related words hierarchically, increasingly, progressively; fractionally, imperceptibly; slowly

near antonyms acutely, sharply, steeply, unprogressively; hastily, precipitously

antonyms abruptly, suddenly

graduation *n* a scheme of rank or order ⟨had a *graduation* of testing levels we had to divide the students into⟩ — see ³SCALE 1

grain *n* 1 a very small piece ⟨just give me a *grain* of information about what to expect on the exam⟩ — see BIT 1

2 one's characteristic attitude or mood ⟨lying about that goes against my *grain*⟩ — see DISPOSITION 1

grainy *adj* made up of large particles ⟨*grainy* sand⟩ — see COARSE 1

grand *adj* 1 large and impressive in size, grandeur, extent, or conception ⟨the *grand* ceremonies that typically mark the opening of the Olympic Games⟩

synonyms august, baronial, gallant, glorious, grandiose, heroic, imposing, magnificent, majestic, monumental, noble, proud, regal, royal, splendid, stately

related words colossal, monstrous, prodigious, stupendous, tremendous; kingly, lordly, princely, queenly; awesome, awful, cosmic, sublime, wondrous; formidable, impressive, prepossessing, redoubtable; marvelous (*or* marvellous), superb, terrific, wonderful; extravagant, lavish, luxurious, opulent, sumptuous; gorgeous, resplendent, splendiferous; extraordinary, killer, remarkable, sensational, striking; celestial, divine, heavenly

near antonyms lowly, modest, unprepossessing; average, common, mediocre, ordinary, run-of-the-mill, second-rate; abject, mean, meretricious, shabby, sordid; insignificant, measly, paltry, petty, puny, trifling, trivial

antonyms humble, unheroic, unimposing, unimpressive

2 coming before all others in importance ⟨won the *grand* prize⟩ — see FOREMOST 1

3 not lacking any part or member that properly belongs to it ⟨the *grand* total comes to $350⟩ — see COMPLETE 1

4 of a size greater than average of its kind ⟨in the *grand* ring of the three-ring circus was the lion tamer⟩ — see LARGE

5 of high birth, rank, or station ⟨everyone wanted to be seen with society's *grand* dame⟩ — see NOBLE 1

6 of the very best kind ⟨that picnic in the mountains was simply *grand*⟩ — see EXCELLENT

7 unusually large ⟨when the cast came out to make their bows, the stage was completely filled with the members of the *grand* company⟩ — see HUGE

grandee *n* a man of high birth or social position ⟨only a Spanish *grandee*—and no one of lesser rank—can address comments to the king and queen of Spain⟩ — see GENTLEMAN 1

grandeur *n* impressiveness of beauty on a large scale ⟨struck by the *grandeur* of the setting sun on the Golden Gate Bridge⟩ — see MAGNIFICENCE

grandfather *n* a person who is several generations earlier in an individual's line of descent ⟨this tradition has been passed down from our pioneer *grandfathers*⟩ — see ANCESTOR 1

grandiloquence *n* 1 boastful speech or writing ⟨a heavyweight champion who was famous for his entertaining *grandiloquence* prior to every match⟩ — see BOMBAST 1

2 language that is impressive-sounding but not meaningful or sincere ⟨the *grandiloquence* of the speeches at a political convention⟩ — see RHETORIC 1

grandiloquent *adj* 1 full of fine words and fancy expressions ⟨poets in the 19th century tended to write poetry filled with *grandiloquent* phrases⟩ — see FLOWERY 1

2 marked by the use of impressive-sounding but mostly meaningless words and phrases ⟨at Independence Day celebrations *grandiloquent* speeches by local politicians are as traditional as fireworks⟩ — see RHETORICAL

grandiose *adj* 1 large and impressive in size, grandeur, extent, or conception ⟨a *grandiose* plan to upgrade the entire interstate highway system in ten years⟩ — see GRAND 1

2 self-consciously trying to present an appearance of grandeur or importance ⟨made some *grandiose* claim she was the descendant of a French princess⟩ — see PRETENTIOUS 1

grandiosity *n* the quality or state of appearing or trying to appear more important or more valuable than is the case ⟨I'd rather be thought of as a person with simple integrity, not a person given to *grandiosity* and exaggeration⟩ — see PRETENSE 1

grandly *adv* 1 in a luxurious manner ⟨we were staying at the Plaza Hotel in New York and living *grandly*⟩ — see HIGH

2 in a manner befitting a person of the highest character and ideals ⟨had *grandly* offered to pay the entire cost of the Christmas party at the children's hospital⟩ — see GREATLY 1

grandness *n* 1 impressiveness of beauty on a large scale ⟨wanted to see the Alps in all of their wintertime *grandness*⟩ — see MAGNIFICENCE

2 the quality or state of being large in size ⟨were impressed with the *grandness* of the movie set⟩ — see LARGENESS

grange *n* a piece of land and its buildings used to grow crops or raise livestock ⟨asked the community's farmers to meet at the Howard family *grange* to help raise a new barn⟩ — see FARM

granite *n* firm or unwavering adherence to one's purpose ⟨had the *granite* to see the project out to the end⟩ — see DETERMINATION 1

grant *n* a sum of money allotted for a specific use by official or formal action ⟨applied for a federal *grant* to restore the church, one of the oldest and architecturally significant in the state⟩ — see APPROPRIATION

grant *vb* 1 to accept the truth or existence of (something) usually reluctantly ⟨you will *grant* that she is difficult to work with⟩ — see ADMIT

2 to give the ownership or benefit of (something) formally or publicly ⟨by the power vested in me, I *grant* you the keys to the city⟩ — see CONFER 1

granting *n* the approval by someone in authority for the doing of something ⟨your *granting* of an interview for this job opening will be much appreciated⟩ — see PERMISSION

granular *adj* made up of large particles ⟨icy, *granular* snow makes for terrible skiing—if you can, ski on light, powdery snow⟩ — see COARSE 1

granulated *adj* made up of large particles ⟨don't use powdered sugar in that recipe, use *granulated* sugar⟩ — see COARSE 1

granule *n* a very small piece ⟨is there one *granule* of truth in that statement?⟩ — see BIT 1

graphic *also* **graphical** *adj* **1** producing a mental picture through clear and impressive description ⟨the report offered many *graphic* details about the huge earthquake that rocked the area⟩
   synonyms delineated, pictorial, picturesque, vivid
   related words depicted, descriptive, expressive; concrete, explicit, specific; faithful, lifelike, natural, realistic; fresh, incisive, sharp
   near antonyms indeterminate, nebulous, obscure, sketchy, unclear, vague; blurry, dark, dim, muddy, murky, shadowy
2 consisting of or relating to pictures ⟨got a degree in *graphic* design⟩ — see PICTORIAL 1

graphic *n* something that visually explains or decorates a text ⟨the use of *graphics* in the text of the dictionary helps to break up the visual monotony of the page⟩ — see ILLUSTRATION 1

grapple *n* the act or manner of holding ⟨was simply unable to break my opponent's viselike *grapple* and lost the wrestling match⟩ — see HOLD 1

grapple *vb* **1** to seize and attempt to unbalance one another for the purpose of achieving physical mastery ⟨two sumo wrestlers *grappling* like a pair of mammoth bears⟩ — see WRESTLE
2 to take physical control or possession of (something) suddenly or forcibly ⟨a crane *grappled* the sunken boat and hoisted it above water⟩ — see CATCH 1

grapple (with) *vb* to deal with (something) usually skillfully or efficiently ⟨the new teacher *grapples with* classroom discipline problems quite well⟩ — see HANDLE 1

grasp *n* **1** the ability to direct the course of something ⟨for a time it looked like most of Europe would be within Hitler's *grasp*⟩ — see CONTROL 2
2 the act or manner of holding ⟨during the roller coaster ride, she clutched my arm with a deathlike *grasp*⟩ — see HOLD 1
3 the knowledge gained from the process of coming to know or understand something ⟨I think I finally have a *grasp* on Spanish grammar⟩ — see COMPREHENSION 1

grasp *vb* **1** to have a practical understanding of ⟨he just doesn't *grasp* how important it is that he call when he'll be late⟩ — see KNOW 1
2 to put one's arms around and press tightly ⟨the departing soldier *grasped* his children a little closer than usual⟩ — see EMBRACE 1
3 to reach for and take hold of by embracing with the fingers or arms ⟨*grasped* my arm and steered me towards the door⟩ — see TAKE 1
4 to recognize the meaning of ⟨finally *grasped* what he was trying to tell her⟩ — see COMPREHEND 1

grasping *adj* having or marked by an eager and often selfish desire especially for material possessions ⟨a

grasping person who would rather buy another car than give money to the poor⟩ — see GREEDY 1

grassland *n* a broad area of level or rolling treeless country ⟨took pictures of the giraffes and zebras roaming the *grasslands* of Africa⟩ — see PLAIN

grate *vb* **1** to disturb the peace of mind of (someone) especially by repeated disagreeable acts ⟨you unintentionally say rude things that *grate* people⟩ — see IRRITATE 1
2 to pass roughly and noisily over or against a surface ⟨the sled *grated* along the bare ground⟩ — see SCRAPE 1
3 to press or strike against or together so as to make a scraping sound ⟨he *grated* the pieces of metal together⟩ — see GRIND 2

grateful *adj* **1** feeling or expressing gratitude ⟨was *grateful* for her neighbor's help after she broke her foot⟩
   synonyms appreciative, obliged, thankful
   related words beholden, indebted; gratified, pleased; thanking
   antonyms thankless, unappreciative, ungrateful, unthankful
2 giving pleasure or contentment to the mind or senses ⟨glad for the *grateful* warmth of the fire on such a cold day⟩ — see PLEASANT

gratefulness *n* acknowledgment of having received something good from another ⟨a note expressing her *gratefulness* for our help⟩ — see THANKS

gratification *n* the feeling experienced when one's wishes are met ⟨eating good chocolate gives me a sense of intense *gratification*⟩ — see PLEASURE 1

gratified *adj* **1** experiencing pleasure, satisfaction, or delight ⟨I am deeply *gratified* that you'll be able to come to the wedding⟩ — see GLAD 1
2 feeling that one's needs or desires have been met ⟨a good meal eaten in excellent company are enough to keep me *gratified*⟩ — see CONTENT

gratify *vb* **1** to give in to (a desire) ⟨just *gratify* this one whim⟩ — see INDULGE
2 to give satisfaction to ⟨your improved test scores will *gratify* your teachers⟩ — see PLEASE

gratifying *adj* **1** giving pleasure or contentment to the mind or senses ⟨a spectacular film that is *gratifying* to both the mind and the eyes⟩ — see PLEASANT
2 making one feel good inside ⟨your warm welcome sure is *gratifying*⟩ — see HEARTWARMING

grating *adj* **1** disagreeable to one's aesthetic or artistic sense ⟨the mix of colors in that painting is *grating*⟩ — see HARSH 2
2 harsh and dry in sound ⟨with a *grating* voice, she croaked a feeble "hello"⟩ — see HOARSE

gratis *adj* not costing or charging anything ⟨if you sign up today, you get a 13-inch TV *gratis*⟩ — see FREE 4

gratitude *n* acknowledgment of having received something good from another ⟨accept these flowers as a token of my *gratitude*⟩ — see THANKS

gratuitous *adj* **1** not costing or charging anything ⟨will throw in a *gratuitous* box of chocolates when you spend $30 in their shop⟩ — see FREE 4
2 not needed by the circumstances or to accomplish an end ⟨that violent scene was completely *gratuitous* and didn't need to be in the movie at all⟩ — see UNNECESSARY

gratuity *n* **1** a small sum of money given for a service over and above what is due ⟨for parties of eight or more, we automatically add a 15% *gratuity* onto the bill⟩ — see ²TIP 1

2 something given in addition to what is ordinarily expected or owed ⟨got a $100 *gratuity* in addition to regular pay⟩ — see BONUS

grave *adj* **1** having a matter of importance as its topic ⟨leaving gossip and celebrities to other magazines, this journal focuses on the *grave* issues of the day⟩ — see SERIOUS 2

2 involving potential loss or injury ⟨going over Niagara Falls poses a *grave* danger⟩ — see DANGEROUS

3 not joking or playful in mood or manner ⟨when I asked him how his dog was doing, he looked *grave* and said, "Not good"⟩ — see SERIOUS 1

grave *n* a final resting place for a dead person ⟨put flowers on his mother's *grave*⟩

synonyms sepulcher (*or* sepulchre), sepulture, tomb
related words catacomb, charnel, crypt, mausoleum, vault; cemetery, churchyard, graveyard, potter's field; barrow, mound, tumulus

grave *vb* to cut (as letters or designs) on a hard surface ⟨*graved* his initials into the rock face⟩ — see ENGRAVE 1

gravel *adj* harsh and dry in sound ⟨after his bout with laryngitis, he had a terribly *gravel* voice⟩ — see HOARSE

gravelly *adj* harsh and dry in sound ⟨his singing voice is a little *gravelly*, but otherwise he's a fine musician⟩ — see HOARSE

gravestone *n* a shaped stone laid over or erected near a grave and usually bearing an inscription to identify and preserve the memory of the deceased ⟨loved to tour old cemeteries to read the poetic inscriptions on the *gravestones*⟩ — see TOMBSTONE

graveyard *n* a piece of land used for burying the dead ⟨the neighborhood kids all think the *graveyard* up the street is haunted⟩ — see CEMETERY

gravid *adj* containing unborn young within the body ⟨the patient is a *gravid* woman in her seventh month⟩ — see PREGNANT 1

gravity *n* a mental state free of jesting or trifling ⟨the hospital waiting room was filled with the *gravity* that results from worry⟩ — see EARNESTNESS

gravy *n* **1** a savory fluid food used as a topping or accompaniment to a main dish ⟨order a large serving of fries with extra *gravy*⟩ — see SAUCE 1

2 something given in addition to what is ordinarily expected or owed ⟨you only pay for three CDs; the fourth one they give you is just *gravy*⟩ — see BONUS

gray *also* **grey** *adj* **1** of the color gray ⟨the *gray* elephant and the gaudily dressed circus performer created a striking contrast⟩

synonyms grayish, leaden, pewter, silver, silvery, slate, slaty, steely
related words achromatic, neutral; dirty, dull, faded, washed-out; ashen, ashy, chalky, livid, mousy (*or* mousey), pale, white, whitish; chocolate, dun, sandy, sepia; brindled, grizzled, hoar, hoary
near antonyms ablaze, bright, deep, gay, rich; chromatic, colored

2 causing or marked by an atmosphere lacking in cheer ⟨a *gray* rainy day⟩ — see GLOOMY 1

grayish *adj* of the color gray ⟨the black stallion and white mare produced a *grayish* filly⟩ — see GRAY 1

gray matter *n* the ability to learn and understand or to deal with problems ⟨she's got the *gray matter* to figure that equation out⟩ — see INTELLIGENCE 1

¹graze *vb* to feed on grass or herbs ⟨cows *grazing* in the meadow⟩

synonyms browse, forage, pasture
related words eat, feed, nibble

²graze *vb* **1** to damage by rubbing against a sharp or rough surface ⟨I *grazed* my elbow diving for the ball⟩ — see SCRAPE 2

2 to pass lightly across or touch gently especially in passing ⟨the volleyball just *grazed* my face, so I'm okay⟩ — see BRUSH

grease *vb* to coat (something) with a slippery substance in order to reduce friction ⟨make sure you *grease* the pan before you put the batter in⟩ — see LUBRICATE

greased *adj* having or being a surface so smooth as to make sliding or falling likely ⟨the floor was *greased* with condensation and we slid everywhere we went⟩ — see SLICK 1

greasy *adj* having or being a surface so smooth as to make sliding or falling likely ⟨that wet tarmac road is *greasy* enough to send the car into a skid⟩ — see SLICK 1

great *adj* **1** having or showing exceptional knowledge, experience, or skill in a field of endeavor ⟨one of the *great* anthropologists⟩ — see PROFICIENT

2 having, characterized by, or arising from a dignified and generous nature ⟨a *great* humanitarian⟩ ⟨*great* acts of charity⟩ — see NOBLE 2

3 lasting for a considerable time ⟨haven't seen them in a *great* while⟩ — see LONG 2

4 of a size greater than average of its kind ⟨saw a *great* moose calmly walking through our backyard⟩ — see LARGE

5 of the very best kind ⟨that cake is *great*⟩ — see EXCELLENT

greatcoat *n* a warm outdoor coat ⟨the men donned their *greatcoats* and got into the carriage⟩ — see OVERCOAT

greatest *adj* **1** coming before all others in importance ⟨the *greatest* achievement in the school's history⟩ — see FOREMOST 1

2 of the highest degree ⟨I have the *greatest* respect for the selfless medical missionaries working around the world⟩ — see FULL 2

greathearted *adj* **1** feeling or displaying no fear by temperament ⟨awarded the *greathearted* soldier a Congressional Medal for his bravery in battle⟩ — see BRAVE

2 having, characterized by, or arising from a dignified and generous nature ⟨a *greathearted* program to provide basic necessities to one million children in war-torn countries⟩ — see NOBLE 2

greateartedness *n* strength of mind to carry on in spite of danger ⟨the *greatheartedness* of firefighters rushing into the burning building⟩ — see COURAGE

greatly *adv* **1** in a manner befitting a person of the highest character and ideals ⟨as commander of the Union army's first black regiment, Robert Gould Shaw died as *greatly* as he had lived⟩

synonyms gallantly, grandly, heroically, high-mindedly, honorably, magnanimously, nobly
related words loftily, venerably; magnificently, majestically
near antonyms abominably, contemptibly, despicably, detestably, hatefully; degenerately
antonyms basely, dishonorably, ignobly

2 to a large extent or degree ⟨Todd has *greatly* increased the scope of his theme on civic responsibility⟩

synonyms astronomically, broadly, colossally, considerably, enormously, extensively, hugely, largely, massively, monstrously, much, sizably, stupendously, tremendously, utterly, vastly

related words appreciably, noticeably, significantly; abundantly, amply, copiously, healthily, plentifully
near antonyms modestly; fractionally; imperceptibly, infinitesimally, insignificantly, invisibly, microscopically, minutely, negligibly; barely, hardly, just, scarcely
antonyms little, slightly
3 to a great degree ⟨I'm not *greatly* bothered by this setback⟩ — see VERY 1

greatness *n* **1** exceptionally high quality ⟨a poet whose work is of enduring *greatness*⟩ — see EXCELLENCE 1
2 the quality or state of being large in size ⟨the overwhelming *greatness* of the canyon is what visitors first notice⟩ — see LARGENESS

greed *n* an intense selfish desire for wealth or possessions ⟨don't let *greed* for riches control you⟩
synonyms acquisitiveness, avarice, avariciousness, avidity, covetousness, cupidity, greediness, rapaciousness, rapacity
related words materialism, possessiveness; appetite, craving, hankering, hunger, itch, longing, lust, passion, ravenousness, thirst, voracity, yearning, yen
near antonyms contentment, fulfillment, satisfaction; bounteousness, bounty, charity, generosity, generousness, liberality, openhandedness, openheartedness, unselfishness

greediness *n* an intense selfish desire for wealth or possessions ⟨her *greediness* blinded her to how she hurt others in her attempts to get rich⟩ — see GREED

greedy *adj* **1** having or marked by an eager and often selfish desire especially for material possessions ⟨a young rocker who was *greedy* for fame and riches⟩ ⟨the *greedy* exploitation of the land by developers⟩
synonyms acquisitive, avaricious, avid, coveting, covetous, grasping, mercenary, rapacious
related words materialistic, philistine; desirous, eager, itchy, miserly; hoggish, piggish, swinish; devouring, gluttonous, gobbling, insatiable, ravenous, unquenchable, voracious; discontent, discontented, malcontent, unquenched, unsatisfied; begrudging, grudging, resentful
near antonyms bounteous, bountiful, charitable, freehanded, generous, greathearted, handsome, liberal, munificent, openhanded, openhearted, unselfish, unsparing; controlled, moderate, restrained, temperate; content, sated, satisfied
2 having a huge appetite ⟨he's so *greedy* you have to carefully watch your plate during dinner, lest he snatch food off it⟩ — see VORACIOUS 1

green *adj* **1** covered with a thick, healthy natural growth ⟨fields *green* with meadow grass⟩ — see LUSH 1
2 lacking in adult experience or maturity ⟨a new pitcher who's pretty *green*, even by rookie standards⟩ — see CALLOW
3 lacking in worldly wisdom or informed judgment ⟨in spite of her age, she's still *green* enough to be hoodwinked⟩ — see NAIVE 1
4 lacking the warm skin color indicative of or associated with good health ⟨after going on the fastest roller coaster in the world, we were all looking a little *green*⟩ — see SICKLY 2

green *n* green leaves or plants ⟨the lonely soldier dreamt of the fields of *green* that he had wandered in as a youth⟩ — see GREENERY 1

greenback *n* a piece of printed paper used as money ⟨threw a few *greenbacks* on the counter to pay for the pop⟩ — see ¹BILL 2

greenery *n* green leaves or plants ⟨Scottish highlands covered with lush *greenery*⟩

synonyms flora, foliage, green, herbage, leafage, vegetation, verdure
related words grassland, prairie; underbrush, undergrowth

greenhorn *n* a person who is just starting out in a field of activity ⟨go easy on him—he's just a *greenhorn* and doesn't have all the experience you do⟩ — see BEGINNER

greenhouse *n* a glass-enclosed building for growing plants ⟨needed to move the plants into the *greenhouse* before the first frost killed them⟩ — see CONSERVATORY

greenness *n* the quality or state of being simple and sincere ⟨was charmed by her *greenness* and child-like innocence⟩ — see NAÏVETÉ 1

greeting *n* **1** an expression of goodwill upon meeting ⟨the volunteer directed the conference participants towards the coffee after offering them a cheerful *greeting*⟩ — see HELLO
2 **greetings** *pl* best wishes ⟨when you see him, give him my *greetings*⟩ — see COMPLIMENT

gregarious *adj* likely to seek or enjoy the company of others ⟨a *gregarious* child who ran up to every person on the playground and wanted to be their friend⟩ — see CONVIVIAL

gregariousness *n* the quality or state of being social ⟨his *gregariousness* is a necessity: he works as a salesman⟩ — see SOCIABILITY

gremlin *n* an imaginary being usually having a small human form and magical powers ⟨during the World Wars, fighter pilots adopted the fanciful notion that *gremlins* were responsible for mechanical failures on their planes⟩ — see FAIRY

griddle cake *n* a flat cake made from thin batter and cooked on both sides (as on a griddle) ⟨my French grandmother used to serve buckwheat *griddle cakes* with strawberry butter⟩ — see PANCAKE

grief *n* deep sadness especially for the loss of someone or something loved ⟨felt a heartbreaking *grief* when the family dog died⟩ — see SORROW

grievance *n* **1** a lingering ill will towards a person for a real or imagined wrong ⟨this is no place to air your *grievances* against him⟩ — see GRUDGE 1
2 an expression of dissatisfaction, pain, or resentment ⟨decided to file a formal *grievance* against the company⟩ — see COMPLAINT 1

grieve *vb* to feel deep sadness or mental pain ⟨*grieved* over the lost cat⟩
synonyms agonize, bleed, hurt, mourn, sorrow, suffer
related words ache, long (for), pine (away); rack, torment, torture; bemoan, bewail, deplore, lament, rue; bawl, cry, groan, howl, keen, moan, take on, wail, weep, yammer
near antonyms beam, cheer, exult, joy, laugh, overjoy, ravish, rejoice; comfort, console

grieve (for) *vb* to feel or express sorrow for ⟨I *grieve for* our loss⟩ — see LAMENT 1

grieving *adj* expressing or suggesting mourning ⟨the *grieving* sobs of the widow could be heard throughout the funeral service⟩ — see MOURNFUL 1

grievous *adj* **1** difficult to endure ⟨the months of chemotherapy seemed almost as *grievous* an affliction as the cancer itself⟩ — see HARSH 1
2 hard to accept or bear especially emotionally ⟨the death of a spouse can be a *grievous* loss from which one never recovers⟩ — see BITTER 2

3 involving potential loss or injury ⟨a *grievous* wound that requires a doctor's immediate attention⟩ — see DANGEROUS

4 of a kind to cause great distress ⟨the *grievous* cost of the war in human lives weighed heavily on the president's mind⟩ — see REGRETTABLE

grievously *adv* with feelings of bitterness or grief ⟨I was *grievously* disappointed not to be invited⟩ — see HARD 2

grill *n* a public establishment where meals are served to paying customers for consumption on the premises ⟨headed down to the local bar and *grill* for a beer and a burger⟩ — see RESTAURANT

grill *vb* to put a series of questions to ⟨police *grilled* the suspect, but had to release him when it became clear he didn't have the information they were looking for⟩ — see EXAMINE 1

grim *adj* **1** harsh and threatening in manner or appearance ⟨a *grim* and desolate landscape⟩ ⟨a *grim* and short-tempered shopkeeper who didn't exactly invite friendly conversation⟩

synonyms austere, dour, fierce, flinty, forbidding, gruff, intimidating, lowering (*also* louring), rough, rugged, severe, stark, steely, stern, ungentle

related words bleak, cold, hostile, unfriendly; adamant, determined, firm, resolute, steadfast, unflinching; fixed, hard, immovable, implacable, inflexible, obdurate, rigid, set, stiff, unbending, uncompromising, unyielding; immutable, unchangeable; black, cheerless, dark, gloomy, glum, joyless, moody, morose, sulky, sullen, surly; brooding, grave, melancholy, serious, sober, solemn, somber (*or* sombre), unsmiling, weighty

near antonyms bland, meek, mellow, soft; easy, quiet, tranquil; agreeable, bright, cheerful, inviting, pleasant, pleasing, sweet; glad, happy, lighthearted, merry, mirthful, sunny; featherbrained, flighty, frivolous, giddy, goofy, light-headed, playful

antonyms benign, benignant, gentle, mild, tender

2 difficult to endure ⟨this winter is supposed to be particularly *grim*, so stock up on firewood⟩ — see HARSH 1

3 showing no signs of slackening or yielding in one's purpose ⟨with *grim* determination, the woman worked three jobs to put her fatherless children through college⟩ — see UNYIELDING 1

4 violently unfriendly or aggressive in disposition ⟨*grim* warriors heading into battle⟩ — see FIERCE 1

grimace *n* a twisting of the facial features in disgust or disapproval ⟨made a *grimace* when he tasted the medicine⟩

synonyms face, frown, lower (*also* lour), mouth, pout, scowl

related words flinch, squinch, wince; growl, snarl; simper, smirk; scoff, sneer; glare, glower, look, stare

near antonyms grin, smile

grimace *vb* to distort one's face ⟨*grimaced* at the actor's terrible attempt at a French accent⟩ — see MUG 1

grime *n* foul matter that mars the purity or cleanliness of something ⟨this new product really cuts through *grime*⟩ — see FILTH 1

grime *vb* to make dirty ⟨countless hours of work were needed to clean the floors of the old warehouse that had been *grimed* from a century of use⟩ — see DIRTY

griminess *n* the state or quality of being dirty ⟨disgusted by the *griminess* in which the previous tenant had left the appliances⟩ — see DIRTINESS 1

grimy *adj* not clean ⟨this mirror is so *grimy* you can barely see your reflection in it⟩ — see DIRTY 1

grin *vb* to express an emotion (as amusement) by curving the lips upward ⟨*grinned* at the kids' fooling around in the pool⟩ — see SMILE 1

grind *n* **1** a harsh grating sound ⟨the *grind* of ice in the blender sent the cat running from the room⟩ — see RASP

2 a person slavishly devoted to intellectual or academic pursuits ⟨don't be such a *grind*—go out with your friends and enjoy yourself⟩ — see NERD

3 very hard or unpleasant work ⟨yard work is a real *grind*⟩ — see TOIL

grind *vb* **1** to make smooth by friction ⟨after they are *ground* and polished, these stones can be used for jewelry⟩

synonyms buff, file, hone, rasp, rub, sand

related words plane, scrape; sandblast, scour; burnish, polish; sharpen, whet; regrind

near antonyms coarsen, roughen

2 to press or strike against or together so as to make a scraping sound ⟨everyone in the car winced when the driver *ground* the gears trying to shift into second⟩

synonyms crunch, gnash, grate, grit, scrape, scrunch

related words creak, groan, rasp, scratch; clash, jangle, jar

3 to make sharp or sharper ⟨better *grind* down that ax before you even think about trying to cut down that tree⟩ — see SHARPEN

4 to make smooth or glossy usually by repeatedly applying surface pressure ⟨used the finest polishing paper he could to *grind* down the facets of the diamond before dusting it with a soft cloth⟩ — see POLISH

5 to pass roughly and noisily over or against a surface ⟨*ground* the rock against the stone wall⟩ — see SCRAPE 1

6 to reduce to fine particles ⟨*grind* whole coffee beans if you want the freshest coffee⟩ — see POWDER

grind (out) *vb* to produce or bring about especially by long or repeated effort ⟨after several years of aborted attempts, the band finally *ground out* a new album⟩ — see HAMMER (OUT)

grinder *n* a large sandwich on a long split roll ⟨ordered a meatball *grinder* from the beach's concession stand⟩ — see SUBMARINE

grip *n* **1** a bag carried by hand and designed to hold a traveler's clothing and personal articles ⟨placed her *grip* in the train's overhead rack and seated herself comfortably⟩ — see TRAVELING BAG

2 the act or manner of holding ⟨get a better *grip* on the lid and try to open the jar again⟩ — see HOLD 1

3 the knowledge gained from the process of coming to know or understand something ⟨has a good *grip* on basic Spanish grammar and spelling⟩ — see COMPREHENSION

4 the right or means to command or control others ⟨a tyrant that keeps the masses tightly in his *grip*⟩ — see POWER 1

grip *vb* **1** to have or keep in one's hands ⟨*gripped* the handlebars tightly and raced down the hill⟩ — see HOLD 1

2 to hold the attention of as if by a spell ⟨that true crime story *gripped* me as much as any whodunit⟩ — see ENTHRALL 1

3 to hold the attention of ⟨that movie will *grip* any true sports car fan⟩ — see ENGAGE 1

4 to reach for and take hold of by embracing with the fingers or arms ⟨*gripped* my fingers and wouldn't let go⟩ — see TAKE 1

gripe *n* an expression of dissatisfaction, pain, or resentment ⟨would rather not listen to *gripes* about your younger brother⟩ — see COMPLAINT 1

gripe *vb* to express dissatisfaction, pain, or resentment usually tiresomely ⟨her tendency to *gripe* constantly drove everyone away⟩ — see COMPLAIN

griper *n* 1 a person who makes frequent complaints usually about little things ⟨a petty *griper* who drove us nuts with his merciless nitpicking⟩ — see CRYBABY
2 an irritable and complaining person ⟨driving across the country in four days would make anyone a confirmed *griper*⟩ — see GROUCH

gripping *adj* holding the attention or provoking interest ⟨I found the exhibit on the Holocaust intensely *gripping* and quite moving⟩ — see INTERESTING

grisliness *n* the quality of inspiring intense dread or dismay ⟨the *grisliness* of the crime scene was too much for the jury⟩ — see HORROR 1

grisly *adj* extremely disturbing or repellent ⟨recounted the visit to the murder scene in *grisly* detail⟩ — see HORRIBLE 1

grit *n* the strength of mind that enables a person to endure pain or hardship ⟨an athlete with true *grit*, continuing her training despite bad weather and an injury⟩ — see FORTITUDE

grit *vb* to press or strike against or together so as to make a scraping sound ⟨*gritted* his teeth as a way of coping with the pain⟩ — see GRIND 2

groan *n* 1 a crying out in grief ⟨when the underdog lost the playoffs, the *groans* of millions of disappointed fans were heard throughout the land⟩ — see LAMENT 1
2 a long low sound indicating pain or grief ⟨let out a *groan* when he tried to stand on the sprained ankle⟩ — see MOAN 1

groan *vb* to utter a moan ⟨*groaning* in pain⟩ — see MOAN 1

grog *n* a fermented or distilled beverage that can make a person drunk ⟨sailors clamoring for more *grog*⟩ — see ALCOHOL

groggery *n* a place of business where alcoholic beverages are sold to be consumed on the premises ⟨an area of the old seaport that was once filled with *groggeries* and other establishments catering to sailors⟩ — see BARROOM

grogshop *n* a place of business where alcoholic beverages are sold to be consumed on the premises ⟨last saw them heading down to the local *grogshop* for a pint of beer⟩ — see BARROOM

groomed *adj* being clean and in good order ⟨the front office is always carefully *groomed* in order to give customers a good first impression⟩ — see NEAT 1

groove *n* an established and often automatic or monotonous series of actions followed when engaging in some activity ⟨I can't get into the *groove* on Monday morning without a cup of coffee⟩ — see ROUTINE 1

groove *vb* to mark with or as if with a line or groove ⟨if you *groove* that piece of wood, we should be able to fit this smaller board into it⟩ — see SCORE 1

groove (on) *vb* to take pleasure in ⟨thrill-seekers who *groove on* skiing will love snowboarding⟩ — see ENJOY 1

groovy *adj* of the very best kind ⟨a great movie with *groovy* special effects⟩ — see EXCELLENT

grope *vb* to search for something blindly or uncertainly ⟨*groped* for her car keys⟩ ⟨*groping* for the right answer⟩
synonyms feel, fish, fumble

related words cast about, hunt, look, reach, seek (out); clutch, grab, scrabble, snatch

gross *adj* 1 depicting or referring to sexual matters in a way that is unacceptable in polite society ⟨was thrown out of class for making a *gross* gesture⟩ — see OBSCENE 1
2 having an excess of body fat ⟨a very *gross* man trying to squeeze into an airplane seat⟩ — see FAT 1
3 lacking in refinement or good taste ⟨refused to mix with what she called "the *gross* masses who are unappreciative of fine art"⟩ — see COARSE 2
4 very noticeable especially for being incorrect or bad ⟨a *gross* mistake that somebody should have caught⟩ — see EGREGIOUS

grossness *n* 1 the condition of having an excess of body fat ⟨had difficulty navigating the stairs because of his *grossness*⟩ — see CORPULENCE
2 the quality or state of being obscene ⟨a movie of such indisputable *grossness* that people who thought that they had seen everything were proven wrong⟩ — see OBSCENITY 1
3 the quality or state of lacking refinement or good taste ⟨the *grossness* of his table manners disgusted the other wedding guests⟩ — see VULGARITY 1

grot *n* a naturally formed underground chamber with an opening to the surface ⟨the famous Dead Sea Scrolls were discovered in a long-forgotten *grot* by a shepherd boy⟩ — see CAVE

grotesque *adj* 1 disagreeable to one's aesthetic or artistic sense ⟨the gaudy, overdecorated interior of the gambling casino was just too *grotesque* for my taste⟩ — see HARSH 2
2 unpleasant to look at ⟨that bloody Halloween mask is *grotesque*⟩ — see UGLY 1

grotto *n* a naturally formed underground chamber with an opening to the surface ⟨at the heart of the shrine is a small rocky *grotto* into which pilgrims can descend⟩ — see CAVE

grouch *n* an irritable and complaining person ⟨an uncle who is a real *grouch* when he's sick⟩
synonyms bear, complainer, crab, crank, croaker, curmudgeon, fusser, griper, grouser, growler, grumbler, grump, murmurer, mutterer, whiner
related words fulminator, malcontent, sorehead; killjoy, party pooper, spoilsport; defeatist, pessimist; faultfinder, kicker, nagger, nitpicker, quibbler
near antonyms optimist; rejoicer

grouchiness *n* readiness to show annoyance or impatience ⟨while some people thought that toddler's *grouchiness* was cute, it drove me nuts⟩ — see PETULANCE

grouchy *adj* 1 easily irritated or annoyed ⟨a lack of sleep would make anyone *grouchy*⟩ — see IRRITABLE
2 given to complaining a lot ⟨a *grouchy* kid who refuses to eat his vegetables⟩ — see FUSSY 1

ground *adj* having an edge thin enough to cut or pierce something ⟨a finely *ground* axe⟩ — see SHARP 1

ground *n* 1 **grounds** *pl* the area around and belonging to a building ⟨an escorted tour of the White House and its surrounding *grounds*⟩
synonyms demesne, park, premises, yard
related words acres, estate, land, lot, parcel, plot, property, real estate, realty; campus; backyard, churchyard, dooryard, schoolyard
2 **grounds** *pl* matter that settles to the bottom of a body of liquid ⟨strain the coffee to remove the *grounds*⟩ — see DEPOSIT 1

3 grounds *pl* something (as a belief) that serves as the basis for another thing ⟨your dislike of her haircut would be insufficient *grounds* for firing her⟩ — see REASON 2

4 a small area of usually open land ⟨I'll meet you at the parade *ground* in two hours⟩ — see FIELD 1

5 an immaterial thing upon which something else rests ⟨opposed to the notion that religious law should be used as a *ground* for civil law⟩ — see BASE 1

6 the loose surface material in which plants naturally grow ⟨stuck the shovel in the *ground* and went inside for a glass of water⟩ — see DIRT 1

7 the physical conditions or features that form the setting against which something is viewed ⟨take her picture against a blue *ground* in order to bring out her blue eyes⟩ — see BACKGROUND 1

8 the solid part of our planet's surface as distinguished from the sea and air ⟨one of the Nordic creation myths states that the *ground* was formed by the body of the giant Ymir when he was killed by Odin and his brothers⟩ — see EARTH 2

ground *vb* to find a basis ⟨you're *grounding* your entire case on circumstantial evidence⟩ — see BASE

grounded *adj* resting on the shore or bottom of a body of water ⟨once his boat was *grounded*, all he could do was wait for the tide to come back in and raise it off the sand bar⟩ — see AGROUND

groundless *adj* having no basis in reason or fact ⟨please stop making *groundless* accusations against the teachers you dislike⟩ ⟨fears of a strike proved *groundless*⟩

synonyms invalid, nonvalid, unfounded, ungrounded, unreasonable, unsubstantiated, unsupported, unwarranted

related words illogical, irrational, nonlogical, unconscionable, unsound; fallacious, false, misled, wrong; gratuitous, uncalled-for, unnecessary; flimsy, implausible, misleading, specious, unconvincing, unsatisfying, untenable, weak; ill-advised, unreasoned; inconsistent; absurd, asinine, foolish, meaningless, nonsensical, preposterous, senseless, silly; insane, nutty, mad, wacky

near antonyms certified, validated, verified; confirmed, corroborated; informed, logical, rational; commonsense, sane, sensible, sober, wise; actual, genuine, real, true; certain, sure; clear, cogent, compelling, convincing, credible, persuasive, plausible, satisfying, solid

antonyms good, hard, just, justified, reasonable, reasoned, substantiated, valid, well-founded

ground plan *n* a method worked out in advance for achieving some objective ⟨their *ground plan* is first to finish college and then get married⟩ — see PLAN 1

ground rule *n* a statement spelling out the proper procedure or conduct for an activity ⟨before the debate begins, let's lay out some *ground rules*⟩ — see RULE 1

groundwork *n* an immaterial thing upon which something else rests ⟨we've laid the *groundwork* for a new kind of art⟩ — see BASE 1

group *n* **1** a number of things considered as a unit ⟨car buffs stood around admiring a *group* of classic cars in the parking lot⟩

synonyms array, assemblage, bank, batch, battery, block, bunch, clump, cluster, collection, grouping, huddle, knot, lot, package, parcel, passel, set, suite

related words accumulation, aggregate, aggregation, conglomeration; agglomeration, assortment, hodgepodge, jumble, miscellany, mixture, odds and ends, sundries, variety; series, suit

phrases the whole kit and caboodle

near antonyms entity, item, single, unit

2 a usually small number of persons considered as a unit ⟨the next *group* of guests were being seated for dinner⟩

synonyms array, batch, battery, body, bunch, cluster, crop, grouping, huddle, knot, lot, parcel, party, passel

related words assembly, congregation, gathering, organization; circle, clan, clique, coterie, fellowship, gang, ring, set; faction, guild (*also* gild), order, school, sect; brigade, crew, outfit, platoon, posse; alliance, bloc, coalition, confederacy, confederation, federation, league, union; bevy, covey

phrases the whole kit and caboodle

near antonyms individual, single

3 one of the units into which a whole is divided on the basis of a common characteristic ⟨you'll find both good and bad in every ethnic *group*⟩ — see CLASS 2

group *vb* **1** to arrange or assign according to type ⟨first *group* the invertebrates by genus⟩ — see CLASSIFY 1

2 to bring together in one body or place ⟨*group* the kids together and we'll see who's missing⟩ — see GATHER 1

grouping *n* **1** a number of things considered as a unit ⟨the standard *grouping* for an average living room: sofa, matching wing chairs, and the inevitable coffee table⟩ — see GROUP 1

2 a usually small number of persons considered as a unit ⟨the next *grouping* of tourists can start the house tour as soon as the last bunch leaves⟩ — see GROUP 2

grouse *vb* to express dissatisfaction, pain, or resentment usually tiresomely ⟨hasn't stopped *grousing* since we started this vacation⟩ — see COMPLAIN

grouser *n* an irritable and complaining person ⟨had the misfortune of waiting on the table full of *grousers* who sent her back to the kitchen constantly and then refused to tip her⟩ — see GROUCH

grovel *vb* **1** to draw back or crouch down in fearful submission ⟨the way in which the abused dog would *grovel* whenever its owner came near⟩ — see COWER

2 to move slowly with the body close to the ground ⟨because of their anatomy, bats can only *grovel* while moving along the ground⟩ — see CRAWL 1

grow *vb* **1** to look after or assist the growth of by labor and care ⟨a dedicated home gardener who *grows* tomatoes in her small garden every summer⟩

synonyms crop, cultivate, culture, promote, raise, rear, tend

related words breed, produce, propagate; plant, sow; gather, glean, harvest, reap; germinate, quicken, root, sprout

near antonyms kill; dig, extirpate, pick, pluck, pull (up), uproot; cut, hay, mow

2 to become mature ⟨you've *grown* so much since we last saw each other⟩ — see MATURE

3 to eventually have as a state or quality ⟨he will *grow* angry if we don't answer his question⟩ — see BECOME

grow (in) *vb* to increase in ⟨you've *grown in* wisdom over the years⟩ — see GAIN 1

grower *n* a person who cultivates the land and grows crops on it ⟨orange *growers* in Florida were hard hit by the hurricane⟩ — see FARMER

growl *vb* **1** to express dissatisfaction, pain, or resentment usually tiresomely ⟨*growling* about how much work he had to do⟩ — see COMPLAIN

2 to make a long loud deep noise or cry ⟨the neighbor's dog *growls* every time we pass the house⟩ — see ROAR

3 to make a low heavy rolling sound ⟨sorry my stomach is *growling*, but I'm just really hungry⟩ — see RUMBLE

growler *n* **1** a person who makes frequent complaints usually about little things ⟨was such a *growler* that when we took her for ice cream, she complained they didn't have the flavor she wanted⟩ — see CRYBABY

2 an irritable and complaining person ⟨we can't figure out why our very happy and optimistic friend is dating that chronic *growler*⟩ — see GROUCH

grown–up *n* a fully grown person ⟨once you turn 12, you get to eat with the *grown-ups* at Thanksgiving⟩ — see ADULT

growth *n* **1** an abnormal mass of tissue ⟨found a *growth* on the dog's neck under her collar⟩

synonyms excrescence, lump, neoplasm, tumor

related words outgrowth; cancer, carcinoma, lymphoma, malignancy, melanoma; cyst, tubercle, wart

2 the act or process of going from the simple or basic to the complex or advanced ⟨the *growth* of the gambling industry into an economic mainstay in some locations⟩ — see DEVELOPMENT 1

3 the process of becoming mature ⟨her thoughts and behavior certainly demonstrate just how much emotional *growth* took place last summer⟩ — see MATURATION

grow up *vb* to become mature ⟨everyone has to *grow up* at some point in their lives⟩ — see MATURE

grub *n* substances intended to be eaten ⟨after the game, we headed to the diner for some hearty *grub*⟩ — see FOOD

grub *vb* to devote serious and sustained effort ⟨*grubbing* away at the yard work before the first snow of the season⟩ — see LABOR

grubber *n* a person who does very hard or dull work ⟨most of the inhabitants of the seedy town are just downtrodden *grubbers* living from paycheck to paycheck⟩ — see SLAVE 2

grubbiness *n* the state or quality of being dirty ⟨the *grubbiness* and general dilapidation of the old house discouraged potential buyers⟩ — see DIRTINESS 1

grubby *adj* not clean ⟨clean off those *grubby* hands before you touch anything⟩ — see DIRTY 1

grudge *n* **1** a lingering ill will towards a person for a real or imagined wrong ⟨he's had a *grudge* against her ever since she snubbed him at the dance⟩

synonyms grievance, resentment, score

related words condemnation; offense (*or* offence), umbrage; complaint; peeve, pique

2 a deep-seated ill will ⟨there's been a *grudge* between the two families for years⟩ — see ENMITY

grueling *or* **gruelling** *adj* **1** requiring considerable physical or mental effort ⟨running a marathon is *grueling*⟩ — see HARD 2

2 requiring much time, effort, or careful attention ⟨cutting diamonds can be *grueling* work⟩ — see DEMANDING 1

gruesome *adj* extremely disturbing or repellent ⟨didn't stick around to hear the *gruesome* details of the car accident⟩ — see HORRIBLE 1

gruesomeness *n* the quality of inspiring intense dread or dismay ⟨permanently scarred by the sheer *gruesomeness* of what she had witnessed during the war⟩ — see HORROR 1

gruff *adj* **1** harsh and dry in sound ⟨had a *gruff* speaking voice, but a surprisingly sweet singing voice⟩ — see HOARSE

2 harsh and threatening in manner or appearance ⟨didn't exchange one word with the *gruff* mountain man who sat next to me in the diner⟩ — see GRIM 1

grumble *n* an expression of dissatisfaction, pain, or resentment ⟨a Boy Scout troop full of moans and *grumbles* when they found out that the overnight camping trip had been cancelled⟩ — see COMPLAINT 1

grumble *vb* **1** to express dissatisfaction, pain, or resentment usually tiresomely ⟨*grumbled* about how sore his feet were after standing all day⟩ — see COMPLAIN

2 to make a low heavy rolling sound ⟨heavily loaded trucks *grumbling* as they passed over the steel bridge⟩ — see RUMBLE

grumbler *n* **1** a person who makes frequent complaints usually about little things ⟨how can you be such a *grumbler* when so much in your life is going well?⟩ — see CRYBABY

2 an irritable and complaining person ⟨the field trip would have been okay if I hadn't been paired up with a *grumbler* who whined through the whole thing⟩ — see GROUCH

grump *n* an irritable and complaining person ⟨a real *grump* in the morning⟩ — see GROUCH

grumpiness *n* readiness to show annoyance or impatience ⟨I don't want your *grumpiness* to spoil the evening⟩ — see PETULANCE

grumpy *adj* **1** easily irritated or annoyed ⟨a *grumpy* neighbor whose yard we had long ago learned not to trespass⟩ — see IRRITABLE

2 given to complaining a lot ⟨the baby's sure to be *grumpy* if she doesn't get her afternoon nap⟩ — see FUSSY 1

grungy *adj* **1** not clean ⟨after playing outside, the kids came in *grungy* and in need of a good washing⟩ — see DIRTY 1

2 showing signs of advanced wear and tear and neglect ⟨even though this *grungy* sweatshirt is falling apart, it's still my favorite⟩ — see SHABBY 1

grunt *n* speech that is not clear enough to be understood ⟨preoccupied with what he was doing, the mechanic gave only a *grunt* when I asked when the car would be ready⟩ — see MUMBLE

grunt *vb* to speak softly and unclearly ⟨was so absorbed with the video game that when asked what he wanted for dinner, he just *grunted*⟩ — see MUMBLE

grunting *n* speech that is not clear enough to be understood ⟨says he talks in his sleep, but really it's just snorts and *grunting*⟩ — see MUMBLE

guarantee *n* **1** a formal agreement to fulfill an obligation ⟨the contractors gave us a written *guarantee* that the work on the house would be done by Christmas⟩

synonyms bond, contract, covenant, guaranty, surety, warranty

related words oath, pledge, vow, word; bargain, compact, pact, treaty; assurance, insurance; bail, deposit, pawn, security

2 something given or held to assure that the giver will keep a promise ⟨you can keep my CDs as a *guarantee* that I'll bring your bike right back when I'm done⟩ — see PLEDGE 1

guarantee *vb* **1** to assume responsibility for the satisfactory quality or performance of ⟨the shop will *guarantee* all work done on the car for 30 days⟩ — see WARRANT 1

2 to make sure, certain, or safe ⟨I can *guarantee* that you'll feel better after using my product for 30 days⟩ — see ENSURE

guarantor *n* a person who takes the responsibility for some other person or thing ⟨the town police force is the *guarantor* of our safety⟩ — see SPONSOR

guaranty *n* **1** a formal agreement to fulfill an obligation ⟨this fridge comes with a money-back *guaranty* of complete customer satisfaction⟩ — see GUARANTEE 1
2 something given or held to assure that the giver will keep a promise ⟨couples exchange engagement rings as a symbolic *guaranty* that they will marry⟩ — see PLEDGE 1

guaranty *vb* to make sure, certain, or safe ⟨a house *guarantied* against termite damage⟩ — see ENSURE

guard *n* **1** a person or group that watches over someone or something ⟨checked in with the security *guard* at the gate⟩
synonyms custodian, guardian, keeper, lookout, picket, sentinel, sentry, warden, warder, watch, watchman
related words observer, patrol, spotter, watchdog; bodyguard, convoy, defender, escort, honor guard
2 a position or readiness to oppose actual or expected attack ⟨be on your *guard* against snakes in the swamp⟩ — see DEFENSIVE
3 a protective device (as on a weapon) to prevent accidental operation ⟨slid the *guard* into place over the chainsaw chain⟩ — see SAFETY 2
4 means or method of defending ⟨the boxer's sparring partner managed to get a blow in under his left *guard*⟩ — see DEFENSE 1
5 one that accompanies another for protection, guidance, or as a courtesy ⟨the honor *guards* raised their sabers as the happy couple descended the church steps⟩ — see ESCORT
6 someone that protects ⟨a battalion of burly *guards* surrounding the celebrity⟩ — see PROTECTOR

guard *vb* to drive danger or attack away from ⟨*guard* the quarterback so he doesn't get sacked⟩ — see DEFEND 1

guard (against) *vb* to be cautious of or on guard against ⟨unfortunately, you have to *guard against* theft while you're traveling⟩ — see BEWARE (OF)

guarded *adj* having or showing a close attentiveness to avoiding danger or trouble ⟨a *guarded* man who knew better than to reveal such delicate information⟩ ⟨*guarded* actions⟩ — see CAREFUL 1

guardian *n* **1** a person or group that watches over someone or something ⟨the state became his *guardian* when he was put into protective custody⟩ — see GUARD 1
2 a person who takes care of a property sometimes for an absent owner ⟨the *guardians* of the summer estate awaited the return of the tycoon⟩ — see CUSTODIAN 1

guardianship *n* responsibility for the safety and wellbeing of someone or something ⟨gave the *guardianship* of his estate to his children⟩ ⟨has *guardianship* of the dogs while I'm in the hospital⟩ — see CUSTODY

guardrail *n* a protective barrier consisting of a horizontal bar and its supports ⟨the car ran off the road, but fortunately only hit the *guardrail*⟩ — see RAILING

guardroom *n* a place of confinement for persons held in lawful custody ⟨hauled the prisoners of war into the *guardroom* and sent for the doctor on duty⟩ — see JAIL

guess *n* an opinion or judgment based on little or no evidence ⟨if you don't know the answer for sure, just make a *guess*⟩ — see CONJECTURE

guess *vb* **1** to form an opinion from little or no evidence ⟨though she does not speak with an accent, I would still *guess* that she is a foreigner⟩
synonyms assume, conjecture, presume, speculate, suppose, surmise, suspect, suspicion [*chiefly dialect*]
related words conclude, deduce, gather, infer; hypothesize, theorize; believe, conceive, expect, imagine, reckon [*chiefly dialect*], take, think

near antonyms demonstrate, establish, prove; ascertain, determine, find out
2 to decide the size, amount, number, or distance of (something) without actual measurement ⟨I would *guess* the road goes for about two miles before you have to take a left⟩ — see ESTIMATE 2
3 to have as an opinion ⟨I *guess* it will snow this afternoon⟩ — see BELIEVE 2

guest *n* **1** a person who visits another ⟨invited the afternoon *guests* to stay for dinner⟩
synonyms caller, frequenter, visitant, visitor
related words company; crasher, hanger-on
near antonyms denizen, dweller, habitant, inhabitant, occupant, resident, resider
2 a person who buys a product or uses a service from a business ⟨the headwaiter will seat the *guests* as soon as the waitress clears and sets a table for them⟩ — see CUSTOMER 1

guffaw *n* an explosive sound that is a sign of amusement ⟨managed to keep a straight face for a minute before he let loose with a loud *guffaw*⟩ — see LAUGH 1

guidance *n* **1** an opinion suggesting a wise or proper course of action ⟨sought career *guidance* from the college counselor⟩ — see ADVICE
2 the act or activity of looking after and making decisions about something ⟨felt secure under the president's cautious *guidance* of foreign affairs⟩ — see CONDUCT 1
3 the duty or function of watching or guarding for the sake of proper direction or control ⟨an adviser who undertakes the *guidance* of his students' academic careers⟩ — see SUPERVISION 1

guide *n* one that accompanies another for protection, guidance, or as a courtesy ⟨followed our *guide* through the dangerous mountain trails⟩ — see ESCORT

guide *vb* **1** to give advice and instruction to (someone) regarding the course or process to be followed ⟨the famous chef *guided* her through the creation of the wedding cake, showing her how to ice the layers, fashion the elaborate decorations, and assemble the whole shebang⟩
synonyms coach, counsel, lead, mentor, pilot, shepherd, show, tutor
related words direct, steer; accompany, escort, see; oversee, superintend, supervise; drill, train; brief, enlighten, inform; instruct, school, teach; inculcate, indoctrinate; cultivate, foster, nurture
2 to look after and make decisions about ⟨thought the new superintendent would *guide* the school system well⟩ — see CONDUCT 1
3 to point out the way for (someone) especially from a position in front ⟨would be happy to *guide* you folks to the historic part of town⟩ — see LEAD 1

guidon *n* a piece of cloth with a special design that is used as an emblem or for signaling ⟨each army command unit flew a different color *guidon*, though they were all the same shape⟩ — see FLAG 1

guild *also* **gild** *n* a group of persons formally joined together for some common interest ⟨after his apprenticeship, he was able to join the stonemasons' *guild*⟩ — see ASSOCIATION 2

guile *n* **1** skill in achieving one's ends through indirect, subtle, or underhanded means ⟨a shady salesman who usually relies on a combination of quick thinking and *guile*⟩ — see CUNNING 1
2 the inclination or practice of misleading others through lies or trickery ⟨a person so full of *guile* he

can't even be trusted to give you the correct time of day〉 — see DECEIT

guileful *adj* clever at attaining one's ends by indirect and often deceptive means 〈tried to fix the game with a *guileful* plot to sabotage the other team's bats, but the umpire caught them〉 — see ARTFUL 1

guileless *adj* free from any intent to deceive or impress others 〈she was an easy-going, *guileless* young woman who was comfortable just being herself〉
synonyms artless, genuine, honest, ingenuous, innocent, naive (*or* naïve), natural, real, simple, sincere, true, unaffected, unpretending, unpretentious
related words childlike, impressionable, inexperienced, malleable, persuadable, simpleminded, unsophisticated, unworldly; unforced, unstudied; candid, frank, free, openhearted, plain, plainspoken, single-minded; trustful, trusting
phrases on the level
near antonyms sophisticated, worldly, worldly-wise; crooked, deceitful, deceptive, devious, double-dealing, hypocritical, two-faced; arch, calculating, canny, crafty, cunning, designing, scheming, sharp, shifty, shrewd, slick, slippery, sly, tricky, underhanded, wily; flattering, mealymouthed, smooth, sycophantic, unctuous; feigned, forced, strained
antonyms affected, artful, artificial, assuming, dishonest, dissembling, dissimulating, fake, false, guileful, insincere, phony (*also* phoney), pretentious

guilelessly *adv* without any attempt to impress by deception or exaggeration 〈she's a naturally beautiful young woman, *guilelessly* unaware of the effect she has on men〉 — see NATURALLY 3

guilelessness *n* the quality or state of being simple and sincere 〈the small-town boy's *guilelessness* is endearing, but it may not serve him well in the ruthless big city〉 — see NAÏVETÉ 1

guillotine *vb* to cut off the head of 〈French Revolutionary forces captured and *guillotined* countless aristocrats in the chaotic period following the downfall of the monarchy〉 — see DECAPITATE

guilt *n* **1** a feeling of responsibility for wrongdoing 〈he was wracked with *guilt* after he accidentally broke his sister's antique grandfather clock〉
synonyms contriteness, contrition, penitence, regret, remorse, remorsefulness, repentance, rue, self-reproach, shame
related words compunction, misgiving, qualm, scruple; blame, fault, responsibility; chagrin, embarrassment; anguish, distress, grief, sadness, sorrow
antonyms impenitence, remorselessness
2 responsibility for wrongdoing or failure 〈he was saddled with the *guilt* for the company's failure〉 — see BLAME 1

guiltless *adj* free from guilt or blame 〈if the jury acquits him, he is *guiltless* in the eyes of the law〉 — see INNOCENT 2

guiltlessness *n* the quality or state of being free from guilt or blame 〈her *guiltlessness* is obvious, since she couldn't possibly have done it〉 — see INNOCENCE 1

guilty *adj* **1** responsible for a wrong 〈he was found *guilty* on all charges brought against him〉
synonyms blamable, culpable
related words blameworthy, censurable, impeachable, indictable, punishable, reprehensible, reproachable; accused, arraigned, impeached, implicated, indicted; accountable, answerable; condemned, convicted
phrases at fault

near antonyms absolved, acquitted, exonerated, vindicated; faultless, impeccable, irreproachable, unimpeachable
antonyms blameless, guiltless, innocent
2 suffering from or expressive of a feeling of responsibility for wrongdoing 〈she was burdened with a *guilty* conscience after stealing the newspaper from the newsstand〉
synonyms ashamed, contrite, hangdog, penitent, remorseful, repentant, shamed, shamefaced
related words apologetic, sorry; regretful, rueful; penitential; blushing, chagrined, embarrassed, sheepish
near antonyms unapologetic; brazen, cheeky, impudent
antonyms impenitent, remorseless, shameless, unashamed, unrepentant

guise *n* **1** a display of emotion or behavior that is insincere or intended to deceive 〈my new neighbor began seeking my company under the *guise* of friendship, but he turned out to be a member of a religious cult bent on conversion〉 — see MASQUERADE
2 clothing chosen as appropriate for a specific situation 〈felt as though she should be wearing some sort of Germanic *guise*, complete with dirndl, for the fall festival featuring traditional German food and drink〉 — see OUTFIT 1
3 clothing put on to hide one's true identity or imitate someone or something else 〈snuck into the castle to rescue Ivanhoe in the *guise* of a priest coming to give Ivanhoe his last rites〉 — see DISGUISE
4 outward and often deceptive indication 〈hazing rituals may have the *guise* of harmless fun, but often the reality is serious physical abuse〉 — see APPEARANCE 2

gulch *n* a narrow opening between hillsides or mountains that can be used for passage 〈the *gulch* floods in the spring with the runoff from the mountains, so wait until later in the summer to hike it〉 — see CANYON

gulf *n* **1** a part of a body of water that extends beyond the general shoreline 〈dipped our feet in the warm waters of the *gulf*〉
synonyms bay, bight, cove, creek [*chiefly British*], estuary, firth, fjord (*or* fiord), inlet, loch [*Scottish*]
related words harbor, port, road(s), roadstead; narrow, sound, strait; bayou
2 an immeasurable depth or space 〈the great *gulf* of time and space that separates us from the first inhabitants of North America〉 — see ABYSS
3 a narrow opening between hillsides or mountains that can be used for passage 〈the *gulf* was too wide to cross, so we had to hike down into it and go through it〉 — see CANYON
4 an open space in a barrier (as a wall or hedge) 〈a wide *gulf* in the defensive wall meant the city was in grave danger〉 — see GAP 1

gull *n* one who is easily deceived or cheated 〈that multimillionaire is enough of a *gull* to believe that it's his personality that attracts women〉 — see DUPE

gull *vb* to cause to believe what is untrue 〈we were *gulled* into believing that if we answered the e-mail, we'd somehow become millionaires, but instead we just got put on a list for junk mail〉 — see DECEIVE

gullibility *n* readiness to believe the claims of others without sufficient evidence 〈teased her about her well-known *gullibility* by repeatedly offering to sell her the Continental Divide〉 — see CREDULITY

gullible *adj* readily taken advantage of 〈he thought his grandmother was *gullible* simply because she was elderly, but she was sharper than he was in many ways⟩ — see EASY 2

gulp *n* the portion of a serving of a beverage that is swallowed at one time ⟨took a big *gulp* of water⟩ — see DRINK 2

gulp *vb* to swallow in liquid form ⟨*gulping* down the last of her tea before rushing out the door⟩ — see DRINK 1

gummy *adj* being of such a thick consistency as to readily cling to objects upon contact ⟨the outside of the salad oil bottle was *gummy* with old dribbles of oil⟩ — see STICKY 1

gun *n* **1** a portable weapon from which a shot is discharged by gunpowder ⟨while her father preferred hunting with a crossbow, she preferred a *gun*⟩
synonyms arm, firearm, piece, small arm
related words forty-five (*or* .45), gat [*slang*], handgun, pistol, revolver, rod [*slang*], six-gun, six-shooter, zip gun; blunderbuss, flintlock, harquebus (*or* arquebus), matchlock, musket, muzzle-loader, rifle, shotgun; automatic, machine gun, repeater, submachine gun, tommy gun; speargun
2 guns *pl* large firearms (as cannon or rockets) ⟨the field commander called for the big *guns* to be deployed for battle⟩ — see ARTILLERY

gun *vb* to strike with a missile from a gun ⟨traded stories of the Wild West, when outlaws *gunned* men down in broad daylight and in cold blood⟩ — see SHOOT 3

gung ho *adj* showing urgent desire or interest ⟨was *gung ho* about his accounting class⟩ — see EAGER

gurgle *vb* to flow in a broken irregular stream ⟨the tiny stream gently *gurgled* down the rocky slope⟩
synonyms bubble, dribble, lap, plash, ripple, splash, trickle, wash
related words eddy, purl, swirl; swash, swish, whish; drip, drop; gush, jet, rush, spout, spurt, squirt
near antonyms run
antonyms pour, roll, stream

gush *n* **1** a flowing or going out ⟨the dam burst with a stupendous *gush* of water⟩ — see OUTFLOW
2 a sudden intense expression of strong feeling ⟨with his customary *gush* of tears, he once again begged her to stay⟩ — see OUTBURST 1

gush *vb* **1** to flow out in great quantities or with force ⟨the dam cracked and water *gushed* from the break⟩
synonyms jet, pour, rush, spew, spout, spurt, squirt
related words cascade, issue, roll, run, stream; plash, slosh, splash; surge, swell; flush, sluice; deluge, engulf, flood, inundate, overflow, overwhelm, submerge, swamp
near antonyms spatter, sprinkle; exude, leak, ooze, seep, weep
antonyms dribble, drip, drop, trickle
2 to make an exaggerated display of affection or enthusiasm ⟨he *gushed* about his favorite basketball player, calling him "the best there ever was"⟩
synonyms enthuse, fuss, rave, rhapsodize, slobber
related words dote (on), fawn; emote

gushing *adj* **1** overly or insincerely flattering ⟨heaped disgustingly *gushing* praise on her cheerleading skills in the hopes it would induce her to go out with him⟩ — see FULSOME
2 pouring forth in great amounts ⟨the *gushing* water from the opened fire hydrant reduced water pressure to a dangerous level⟩ — see PROFUSE

gust *n* **1** a sudden brief rush of wind ⟨a *gust* tore her umbrella from her grip and blew it down the street⟩
synonyms blast, blow, flurry, williwaw
related words breeze, zephyr; air, breath, waft; puff, whiff; gale, hurricane, squall, tempest, tornado, windstorm; northeaster, norther, northerly, northwester, southeaster, southwester, westerly
2 a sudden intense expression of strong feeling ⟨cried out with a *gust* of emotion that we had never witnessed before⟩ — see OUTBURST 1

gusty *adj* marked by strong wind or more wind than usual ⟨watch out for *gusty* conditions as the storm blows in⟩ — see WINDY 1

gut *n* **1 guts** *pl* the internal organs of the body ⟨dissected the frog and looked at its *guts*⟩
synonyms entrails, innards, inside(s), viscera, vitals
related words bowel(s), intestine(s); giblet(s), variety meat
2 guts *pl* strength of mind to carry on in spite of danger ⟨it took a lot of *guts* to rush into that building and save her cat⟩ — see COURAGE
3 guts *pl* the strength of mind that enables a person to endure pain or hardship ⟨had the *guts* to keep running the race even though she felt like quitting⟩ — see FORTITUDE
4 the part of the body between the chest and the pelvis ⟨eating too many French fries will result in a substantial *gut*⟩ — see STOMACH

gut *vb* to take the internal organs out of ⟨you'll need to *gut* the fish and wash it out before you can cook it⟩
synonyms clean, disembowel, draw, eviscerate
related words bone, dress; cut, excise, extract, remove, withdraw; transplant

gutsy *adj* inclined or willing to take risks ⟨a *gutsy* coach willing to let her team improvise on the court⟩ — see BOLD 1

gutter *n* **1** a pipe or channel for carrying off water from a roof ⟨one of his chores is to clean leaves and sticks out of the *gutters* before winter sets in⟩
synonyms drainpipe, eaves trough, spout, trough, waterspout
related words drain, flume, sluice; conduit, duct
2 a long narrow channel dug in the earth ⟨rainwater running off the road into the *gutters*⟩ — see DITCH

guy *n* **1** a member of the human race ⟨hey *guys*! Let's get to class!⟩ — see HUMAN
2 an adult male human being ⟨was not the kind of *guy* she ever thought she'd date⟩ — see MAN 1

guzzle *vb* to swallow in liquid form ⟨*guzzled* my milk before I could stop him⟩ — see DRINK 1

gym *n* a building or room used for sports activities and exercising ⟨decided to get up early and go to the *gym* to lift weights⟩
synonyms gymnasium, spa
related words arena, bowl, coliseum, colosseum, stadium

gymnasium *n* a building or room used for sports activities and exercising ⟨since it was raining, the kids had recess in the *gymnasium*⟩ — see GYM

gyp *vb* to rob by the use of trickery or threats ⟨*gypped* them into spending a fortune on counterfeit jewels, not real diamonds⟩ — see FLEECE

gyrate *vb* to move in circles around an axis or center ⟨the gyroscope got its name for the way the disk inside the instrument *gyrates* around an axis⟩ — see SPIN 1

gyration *n* a rapid turning about on an axis or central point ⟨dizzy from the spirally *gyrations* of the roller coaster⟩ — see SPIN 1

H

habiliment *n, usually* **habiliments** *pl* covering for the human body 〈the lady's rich *habiliments* and haughty manner had the host's servants thinking she was someone important〉 — see CLOTHING

habit *n* a usual manner of behaving or doing 〈it was his *habit* to rise early〉
synonyms custom, fashion, pattern, practice (*also* practise), trick, way, wont
related words addiction; disposition; bent, inclination, proclivity, tendency, turn; convention, form, mode, style; usage; manners, mores; groove, rote, routine, rut; affectation, airs, pose; attribute, characteristic, mark, trait; oddity, peculiarity, quirk, singularity, tic; strangeness, weirdness

habitable *adj* suitable for living in 〈the frigid Arctic is not *habitable* for amphibians and reptiles—or for humans, either, for that matter〉 — see LIVABLE

habitant *n* one who lives permanently in a place 〈the *habitants* of Connecticut are nicknamed *Nutmeggers*〉 — see INHABITANT

habitat *n* the place where a plant or animal is usually or naturally found 〈a forest in California is set aside to preserve the unique brushy, rugged *habitat* required by nesting California condors〉 — see HOME 2

habitation *n* the place where one lives 〈even though he spends most of the year at boarding school in New York, Jake considers his parents' home in Vermont his permanent *habitation*〉 — see HOME 1

habitual *adj* **1** being such by habit and not likely to change 〈Sarah admits she's an *habitual* procrastinator, but she still manages to complete her assignments on time〉
synonyms chronic, confirmed, inveterate
related words incorrigible, unregenerate; born, natural; persistent, regular, steady, unfailing; addicted; accustomed, habituated, used; deep-rooted, entrenched (*also* intrenched), inbred, inherent, innate
near antonyms unaccustomed, unused; occasional
2 appearing or occurring repeatedly from time to time 〈if your tardiness becomes *habitual,* I will have to call your parents〉 — see REGULAR 1

habituated *adj* being in the habit or custom 〈not only did James become *habituated* to getting up early, he found he liked it〉 — see ACCUSTOMED

hacienda *n* a large impressive residence 〈from the wide porch of Maria's *hacienda,* the ranch stretches as far as the eye can see〉 — see MANSION

¹hack *n* a V-shaped cut usually on an edge or a surface 〈smallish *hacks* made in the bark of the trees blazed the trail through the forest〉 — see NOTCH 1

²hack *n* an automobile that carries passengers for a fare usually determined by the distance traveled 〈after a week of hailing *hacks* and inhabiting hotels, Harry was happy to be home〉 — see TAXICAB

hackney *adj* used or heard so often as to be dull 〈Mom just ignores *hackney* complaints like "It isn't fair" and "Why me?"〉 — see STALE

hackneyed *adj* used or heard so often as to be dull 〈it's *hackneyed*, but true—the more you save the more you earn〉 — see STALE

hag *n* **1** a mean or ugly old woman 〈how was poor Snow White to know that the *hag* with the apple was actually the jealous queen in disguise?〉 — see CRONE

2 a woman believed to have often harmful supernatural powers 〈in the dark forest the mossy trees looked to poor frightened Gretel like *hags,* who were sure to turn her into a stump〉 — see WITCH 1

haggard *adj* suffering extreme weight loss as a result of hunger or disease 〈*haggard* and worn after a week lost in the woods〉 — see EMACIATED

haggle *vb* to talk over or dispute the terms of a purchase 〈had to *haggle* to get his friend to sell his guitar for twenty bucks〉 — see BARGAIN

hail *n* **1** a heavy fall of objects 〈a *hail* of small stones warned them of the oncoming avalanche〉 — see RAIN 2
2 a rapid or overwhelming outpouring of many things at once 〈under the *hail* of angry questions, Jennifer stayed cool〉 — see BARRAGE

hail *vb* **1** to declare enthusiastic approval of 〈yesterday's lunch at school—so *hailed* by the school board members—wasn't exactly a typical school lunch〉 — see ACCLAIM
2 to demand or request the presence or service of 〈*hail* a taxi〉 〈*hail* the waiter for the check〉 — see SUMMON 1

hair *n* **1** a very small distance or degree 〈a race that was won by a *hair*〉
synonyms ace, hairbreadth (*or* hairsbreadth), inch
related words bit, crumb, jot, mite, particle, smidgen, trace, trifle
2 the hairy covering of a mammal especially when fine, soft, and thick 〈has no *hair*, but wears a wig〉 〈a coat made of camel's *hair*〉 — see FUR 1

hairbreadth *or* **hairsbreadth** *n* a very small distance or degree 〈just missed the bull's-eye by a *hairbreadth*〉 — see HAIR 1

hairline *adj* **1** being of less than usual width 〈a *hairline* crack in the mug, almost too small to notice, was enough to make the mug break when filled with hot tea〉 — see NARROW 1
2 made or done with extreme care and accuracy 〈a *hairline* distinction between her rating of certain things as "necessary" and others as "absolutely necessary"〉 — see FINE 2
3 meeting the highest standard of accuracy 〈an ultrasensitive telescope that requires *hairline* placement of the lenses〉 — see PRECISE 1

hair–raising *adj* causing fear 〈*hair-raising* stories of headless corpses and disembodied screams〉 — see FEARFUL 1

hairsplitting *adj* made or done with extreme care and accuracy 〈Mom ignored my *hairsplitting* complaint about Brian's piece of cake being bigger by two bites〉 — see FINE 2

hairy *adj* **1** covered with or as if with hair 〈a *hairy* spider〉
synonyms bristly, fleecy, furry, hirsute, rough, shaggy, unshorn, woolly (*also* wooly)
related words bearded, mustachioed, whiskered; downy, fluffy, fuzzy, nappy
near antonyms beardless, shaved, shaven
antonyms bald, furless, hairless, shorn, smooth
2 made of or resembling hair 〈enough *hairy* clumps around the house to make another cat〉 〈a *hairy* mass of fiberglass insulation〉

synonyms furry, fuzzy, rough, shaggy, woolly (*also* wooly)

related words downy, fluffy, nappy

halcyon *adj* free from storms or physical disturbance ⟨a *halcyon* sea⟩ ⟨a *halcyon* era of postwar peace⟩ — see CALM 1

hale *adj* enjoying health and vigor ⟨still *hale* and strong at 80, outdoing his younger acquaintances⟩ — see HEALTHY 1

hale *vb* to cause to follow by applying steady force on ⟨the sailors *haled* the huge net onto the deck of the ship⟩ — see PULL 1

half *adv* in any way or respect ⟨this cut on your arm isn't *half* as bad as it looks⟩ — see AT ALL

half *n* 1 one of two equal or nearly equal parts ⟨to be fair, we each get *half* the pie⟩

synonyms moiety

related words hemisphere, meridian, semicircle; component, division, fraction, part, piece, portion, section, segment

near antonyms aggregate, whole

2 either of a pair matched in one or more qualities ⟨it's the bottom *half* of the ninth inning, and the Yankees are up at bat⟩ — see MATE 1

halfhearted *adj* showing little or no interest or enthusiasm ⟨a *halfhearted* attempt to clean her room⟩ — see TEPID 1

halfway *adj* 1 lacking some necessary part ⟨when *halfway* measures, such as posting signs, failed to keep people off the property, a fence was erected⟩ — see INCOMPLETE

2 occupying a position equally distant from the ends or extremes ⟨by the time Leslie had reached the *halfway* point, she was ready to quit the marathon⟩ — see MIDDLE 1

half-wit *n* 1 a person who lacks good sense or judgment ⟨some *half-wit* had left the gate open, and all the sheep had gotten loose⟩ — see FOOL 1

2 a stupid person ⟨even a *half-wit* knows that ice cream melts if it's not in the freezer⟩ — see IDIOT

half-witted *adj* 1 not having or showing an ability to absorb ideas readily ⟨after the fall on his head, Paul could only give a *half-witted* stare when asked if he was okay⟩ — see STUPID 1

2 showing or marked by a lack of good sense or judgment ⟨had the *half-witted* idea to try to swim across the raging river, and would have drowned if someone hadn't rescued him⟩ — see FOOLISH 1

hall *n* 1 the entrance room of a building ⟨the guests hung their coats in the *hall*⟩

synonyms entry, entryway, foyer, lobby, vestibule

related words antechamber, anteroom, waiting room; doorway, entrance, threshold

2 a typically long narrow way connecting parts of a building ⟨the bedroom is at the end of the *hall*⟩

synonyms concourse, corridor, gallery, hallway, passage, passageway

related words arcade, breezeway, cloister

3 a large room or building for enclosed public gatherings ⟨the concert *hall* was full⟩

synonyms arena, auditorium, theater (*or* theatre)

related words amphitheater, hippodrome, house, playhouse; ballroom; lyceum; chamber, senate

4 a centrally located room in a building that serves as a gathering or waiting area or as a passageway into the interior ⟨from the main *hall* of the museum, turn left to see the pottery and turn right to see the mummies⟩ — see FOYER 1

5 a large impressive residence ⟨Lord Plentiworth has opened his family's hereditary home, Richley *Hall,* to visitors on Tuesdays⟩ — see MANSION

6 a large, magnificent, or massive building ⟨on your right, you will see Parliament *Hall,* a splendid example of Georgian architecture⟩ — see EDIFICE 1

hallmark *n* a device, design, or figure used as an identifying mark ⟨the *hallmark* of the Primrose Pottery Works is the small rose emblem etched on each piece⟩ — see EMBLEM

hallow *vb* to make holy through prayers or ritual ⟨Lincoln's memorable words at the Gettysburg battlefield, "we cannot dedicate—we cannot consecrate—we cannot *hallow*—this ground" ⟩ — see BLESS 1

hallowed *adj* 1 deserving honor and respect especially by reason of age ⟨the club's *hallowed* tradition of distributing Thanksgiving baskets to the needy⟩ — see VENERABLE 1

2 set apart or worthy of veneration by association with God ⟨a church erected on one of Christianity's most *hallowed* sites⟩ — see HOLY 2

hallowing *n* the act of making something holy through religious ritual ⟨the church's belief that the marriage ceremony is a *hallowing* of the union between a man and a woman⟩ — see CONSECRATION

hallucination *n* a conception or image created by the imagination and having no objective reality ⟨were the voices real, or merely a *hallucination,* caused by the wind?⟩ — see FANTASY 1

hallway *n* a typically long narrow way connecting parts of a building ⟨the *hallway* between the bedroom and bathroom was strewn with toys⟩ — see HALL 2

halt *n* 1 a point in a struggle where neither side is capable of winning or willing to give in ⟨negotiations are at a *halt,* with neither management nor the union budging on the issue of salary limits⟩ — see IMPASSE

2 the stopping of a process or activity ⟨our parents called a *halt* to our plans⟩ ⟨gardening came to a *halt* during the week of solid rain⟩ — see END 1

¹**halt** *vb* 1 to bring (something) to a standstill ⟨traffic was *halted* by the parade⟩

synonyms arrest, catch, check, draw up, fetch up, hold up, stall, stay, still, stop

related words balk, block, blockade, dam, detain, hinder, hold, hold back, impede, obstruct, stem; conclude, end, terminate; call, discontinue, suspend; clamp down, rein (in), squash, squelch, stamp, stanch (*also* staunch), stunt, suppress, turn back

near antonyms carry on, continue, follow through, keep on, keep up, run on; advance, fare, move, proceed, progress, wend; actuate, budge, drive, impel, propel, push, stir

2 to bring (as an action or operation) to an immediate end ⟨the private eye decided to *halt* his surveillance of the building after he was spotted by his subject⟩ — see STOP 1

3 to come to an end ⟨the filming *halted* when the star of the movie quit in a huff⟩ — see CEASE 1

²**halt** *vb* to walk while favoring one leg ⟨even with her twisted ankle, Carmen *halted* along to complete her Walk for Peace⟩ — see LIMP 1

hammer *vb* 1 to shape with a hammer ⟨medieval artisans *hammered* brass into bowls and trays which they embossed with elaborate designs⟩

synonyms beat, forge, pound

related words chase, fashion, form, knead, model, mold, work; coin, mint, stamp; carve, chisel, hew, sculpt, sculpture

2 to deliver a blow to (someone or something) usually in a strong vigorous manner ⟨*hammer* a nail⟩ ⟨*hammered* the ball for a home run⟩ — see HIT 1

3 to strike repeatedly ⟨tried *hammering* the door to wake them up⟩ ⟨the crops were *hammered* with hail⟩ — see BEAT 1

hammer (out) *vb* to produce or bring about especially by long or repeated effort ⟨the school committee *hammered out* a new sports-participation policy with input from students, parents, and administrators⟩

synonyms build (up), carve (out), forge, grind (out), work out

related words cobble (together *or* up), create, construct, fabricate, fashion, form, frame, manufacture, model, shape, tailor; conceive, concoct, contrive, cook (up), devise, hatch, invent, originate; bring forth, effect; accomplish, achieve, bring off

near antonyms demolish, destroy, dismantle, raze, tear down; ruin, undo, unmake, wreck

hamper *vb* to create difficulty for the work or activity of ⟨fallen branches *hampered* the hikers as they made their way along the narrow path⟩

synonyms clog, cramp, delay, embarrass, encumber, fetter, handicap, hinder, hobble, hold back, hold up, impede, inhibit, interfere (with), manacle, obstruct, shackle, tie up, trammel

related words arrest, brake, check, constrain, curb, rein, restrain, snag; bind, chain, handcuff, leash, muzzle, strap, tether, tie; barricade, block, blockade, dam, head (off), plug; balk, choke, hurt, repress, retard, stifle, straiten, strangle, stunt; baffle, foil, frustrate, interrupt, sabotage, thwart; bog (down), confine, hedge (in), hem (in), limit, tie (down)

phrases cramp one's style, give a hard time

near antonyms clear, make way, open, unclog, unplug, unstop; free, liberate, release, untie; loosen, smooth; further, promote

antonyms aid, assist, facilitate, help

hams *n pl* the part of the body upon which someone sits ⟨after sitting on my *hams* all day, I could use a good workout⟩ — see BUTTOCKS

hamstring *vb* to render powerless, ineffective, or unable to move ⟨the decorations committee was *hamstrung* by the new rule against hanging anything in the gym⟩ — see PARALYZE

hand *n* **1** a certain way in which something appears or may be regarded ⟨on the one *hand,* it's nice to rest your brain all summer, but on the other, you would forget less with a shorter break⟩ — see ASPECT 1

2 a place, space, or direction away from or beyond a central point or line ⟨tall buildings rose on either *hand*⟩ ⟨nothing but wide open space on either *hand*⟩ — see SIDE 1

3 an arrow-shaped piece on a dial or scale for registering information ⟨both *hands* of the clock pointed to 12⟩ — see POINTER 1

4 one who works for another for wages or a salary ⟨the first mate shouted, "All *hands* on deck!"⟩ — see EMPLOYEE

5 the form or style of a particular person's writing ⟨writes with a flowing, old-fashioned *hand*⟩ — see HANDWRITING 1

6 *usually* **hands** *pl* the ability to direct the course of something ⟨the final decision is in your *hands*⟩ — see CONTROL 2

7 hands *pl* the fact or state of having (something) at one's disposal ⟨I'd like to get my *hands* on some really cool posters⟩ — see POSSESSION 1

hand *vb* **1** to put (something) into the possession of someone for use or consumption ⟨was happy to *hand* her grandmother's cookie recipes to the parish ladies to put in their cookbook⟩ — see FURNISH 2

2 to shift possession of (something) from one person to another ⟨the clerk *handed* her change⟩ — see PASS 1

handbag *n* **1** a bag carried by hand and designed to hold a traveler's clothing and personal articles ⟨flies only with a *handbag* so he doesn't have to check his luggage⟩ — see TRAVELING BAG

2 a container for carrying money and small personal items ⟨Karen's *handbag* is just big enough to hold her favorite photos and wallet⟩ — see PURSE

handbook *n* a book used for instruction in a subject ⟨a *handbook* of grammar⟩ ⟨a tongue-in-cheek *handbook* on "how to live with siblings"⟩ — see TEXTBOOK

handcraft *n* an occupation requiring skillful use of the hands ⟨watched Native Americans engaged in traditional *handcrafts,* such as basketry and pottery-making⟩ — see CRAFT 1

handcuff *vb* to confine or restrain with or as if with chains ⟨wanted to take the trip, but was *handcuffed* by her responsibility to watch her little sisters⟩ — see BIND 1

handcuff *n, usually* **handcuffs** *pl* something that physically prevents free movement ⟨the man placidly held out his wrists so the policeman could snap on *handcuffs*⟩ — see BOND 1

handful *n* a small number ⟨only a *handful* of people signed up for the wintertime hike⟩ — see FEW

handicap *n* **1** a feature of someone or something that creates difficulty for achieving success ⟨her shyness was not a *handicap* when she played chess, and she went on to become the school chess champion⟩ — see DISADVANTAGE

2 something that makes movement or progress more difficult ⟨having to walk in high heels for the first time was a bit of a *handicap,* and Ariel preceded the bride very carefully⟩ — see ENCUMBRANCE

handicap *vb* to create difficulty for the work or activity of ⟨was not *handicapped* by his small size from becoming one of the best players on the team⟩ — see HAMPER

handicraft *n* an occupation requiring skillful use of the hands ⟨volunteers demonstrating early American *handicrafts,* such as blacksmithing, glassblowing, and weaving⟩ — see CRAFT 1

handicrafter *n* a person whose occupation requires skill with the hands ⟨a *handicrafter* who cards, spins, and weaves wool from the sheep she raises⟩ — see ARTISAN

handily *adv* without difficulty ⟨*handily* whipped up a fluffy meringue and spread it on the pie⟩ — see EASILY

handiwork *n* something produced by physical or intellectual effort ⟨Michael was proud of his *handiwork* and certain that the birdhouse would win first place in the "original" category⟩ — see PRODUCT 1

handkerchief *n* a scarf worn on the head ⟨tied a *handkerchief* around her head and set about cleaning out the dust-covered attic⟩ — see BANDANNA

handle *n* a word or combination of words by which a person or thing is regularly known ⟨likes to go by the *handle* "Champ"⟩ — see NAME 1

handle *vb* **1** to deal with (something) usually skillfully or efficiently ⟨as host of a live TV talk show, she must *handle* any situation that comes up⟩

synonyms contend (with), cope (with), grapple (with), manage, maneuver, manipulate, negotiate, swing, treat

related words bring off, carry out, pull, swing; command, direct, guide, steer; control, regulate, run

phrases have a grip on

near antonyms botch, bungle, goof (up), louse up, mess (up)

antonyms fumble, muddle (through)

2 to behave toward in a stated way ⟨*handles* all requests the same, whether they come from long-time customers or new ones⟩ — see TREAT 1

3 to control the mechanical operation of ⟨in shop we learned how to *handle* basic woodworking power tools⟩ — see OPERATE 1

4 to look after and make decisions about ⟨Mom takes care of the flower beds, and Dad *handles* all the lawn care⟩ — see CONDUCT 1

handling *n* the act or activity of looking after and making decisions about something ⟨the *handling* of proper order in the courtroom is the job of the sergeant at arms⟩ — see CONDUCT 1

hand over *vb* **1** to give (something) over to the control or possession of another usually under duress ⟨told him to *hand over* the donut that he'd snuck from the box⟩ — see SURRENDER 1

2 to put (something) into the possession of someone for use or consumption ⟨in response to a desperate plea, we *handed over* all our extra blankets and pillows to the shelter⟩ — see FURNISH 2

3 to put (something) into the possession or safekeeping of another ⟨*handed over* their valuables to the desk clerk who put them in the hotel safe⟩ — see GIVE 2

4 to shift possession of (something) from one person to another ⟨*hand over* that screwdriver, will you please?⟩ — see PASS 1

handpick *vb* to decide to accept (someone or something) from a group of possibilities ⟨*handpicked* what she considered to be the cutest kitten from the litter⟩ — see CHOOSE 1

handsome *adj* **1** having or showing elegance ⟨the glass-topped table was a *handsome* addition to the room⟩ — see ELEGANT 1

2 of a size greater than average of its kind ⟨receives a *handsome* allowance every week⟩ — see LARGE

3 very pleasing to look at ⟨a *handsome* and well-dressed man⟩ — see BEAUTIFUL

handsomely *adv* in a generous manner ⟨rewarded *handsomely* the kids who had found his lost dog⟩ — see WELL 2

handsomeness *n* **1** dignified or restrained beauty of form, appearance, or style ⟨a modern-style addition that detracts from the *handsomeness* of that neoclassic building⟩ — see ELEGANCE

2 the qualities in a person or thing that as a whole give pleasure to the senses ⟨she never had noticed his *handsomeness* until he got a more becoming haircut⟩ — see BEAUTY 1

hand–to–mouth *adj* less plentiful than what is normal, necessary, or desirable ⟨a *hand-to-mouth* income that came from any odd job that he could find⟩ — see MEAGER

handwriting *n* **1** the form or style of a particular person's writing ⟨she immediately recognized the *handwriting* on the envelope as that of her old college roommate⟩

synonyms hand, penmanship, script

related words scratch, scrawl, scribble; backhand, print; autograph, signature

2 writing done by hand ⟨most students are taught the value of good *handwriting*⟩

synonyms calligraphy, longhand, manuscript, penmanship, script

related words lettering; shorthand

antonyms print, type

handy *adj* **1** situated within easy reach ⟨keeps a box of tissue *handy* whenever she watches *Romeo and Juliet* on the VCR⟩ — see CONVENIENT

2 skillful with the hands ⟨*handy* with a needle and thread⟩ — see DEXTEROUS 1

hang *vb* **1** to place on an elevated point without support from below ⟨*hang* your coats on the coat rack in the hall⟩

synonyms dangle, sling, suspend, swing

related words hook, pin, tack; drape, festoon, garland, string; extend (out), jut, project, stick out; overhang, protrude; cascade, depend, fall

2 to be determined by, based on, or subject (to) ⟨our plan to go to the amusement park had all been worked out; now it just *hung* on the weather⟩ — see DEPEND 1

3 to be limp from lack of water or vigor ⟨as they neared the end of the long, hard march all but the most hardy were *hanging*, and some could barely put one foot in front of the other⟩ — see DROOP 1

4 to rest or move along the surface of a liquid or in the air ⟨*hanging* just above the horizon was a little pink cloud⟩ — see FLOAT

hang (over) *vb* to remain poised to inflict harm, danger, or distress on ⟨as long as the possibility of having to move again was *hanging over* them, the family couldn't really settle in⟩ — see THREATEN

hang around *vb* **1** to come or be together as friends ⟨she *hangs around* with her cousin⟩ — see ASSOCIATE 1

2 to continue to be in a place for a significant amount of time ⟨if you *hang around* until my dad gets home, you can meet him⟩ — see STAY 1

3 to spend time doing nothing ⟨*hung around* the house all day⟩ — see IDLE

hang around (in) *vb* to go to or spend time in often ⟨after school Thalia and her friends *hang around in* her mother's hair salon⟩ — see FREQUENT

hang back *vb* to show uncertainty about the right course of action ⟨even though Teresa wanted the job, she still *hung back* because she wasn't sure if she should take time from her studies⟩ — see HESITATE

hangdog *adj* suffering from or expressive of a feeling of responsibility for wrongdoing ⟨figured he'd be forgiven for breaking the window if he adopted a *hangdog* expression⟩ — see GUILTY 2

hanger–on *n* a person who is supported or seeks support from another without making an adequate return ⟨almost overnight, Bruce was star, and almost overnight, he was surrounded by *hangers-on* who wanted something⟩ — see LEECH

hanging *adj* **1** bending downward or forward ⟨*hanging* branches blocked our way for a good part of the trail⟩ — see NODDING

2 extending freely from a support from above ⟨a *hanging* plant⟩ ⟨*hanging* clusters of fruit⟩ ⟨*hanging* lanterns⟩ — see DEPENDENT 1

hang on (to) *vb* **1** to continue to have in one's possession or power ⟨likes to *hang on to* old T-shirts and sneakers because they come in handy when he's doing yard work or painting⟩ — see KEEP 2

2 to have or keep in one's hands ⟨*hang on to* my watch for me while I swim⟩ — see HOLD 1

hangout *n* a place for spending time or for socializing ⟨Jake's favorite *hangout* is the local community center⟩

synonyms haunt, rendezvous, resort

related words camp, canteen, club, clubhouse, den, harbor, haven, nest, refuge, retreat

hang out *vb* to spend time doing nothing ⟨spent the afternoon *hanging out* at his friend's house⟩ — see IDLE

hang out (at) *vb* to go to or spend time in often ⟨most summer afternoons, we'd *hang out* at the Yogurt Hut⟩ — see FREQUENT

hanker (for *or* after) *vb* to have an earnest wish to own or enjoy ⟨*hankering for* some company in his lonely mountain cabin⟩ ⟨*hanker after* a life of leisure⟩ — see DESIRE

hankering *n* a strong wish for something ⟨I've had a *hankering* for pizza with anchovies all afternoon⟩ — see DESIRE

hanky–panky *n* the use of clever underhanded actions to achieve an end ⟨had to resort to a certain amount of *hanky-panky* to sneak away from the house without his dog seeing him⟩ — see TRICKERY

hap *n* **1** something that happens ⟨we must make the best of both the good and the bad *haps* of life⟩ — see EVENT 1

2 the uncertain course of events ⟨by *hap* and circumstance, he ended up as a cartoonist in New York⟩ — see CHANCE 1

hap *vb* to take place ⟨what wondrous events hath *happed* this Christmas Day?⟩ — see HAPPEN

haphazard *adj* lacking a definite plan, purpose, or pattern ⟨considering the *haphazard* way you measured the ingredients, it's a wonder the cookies came out this good⟩ — see RANDOM

haphazard *adv* without definite aim, direction, rule, or method ⟨shoes were tossed *haphazard* into the closet⟩ — see HIT OR MISS

haphazardly *adv* without definite aim, direction, rule, or method ⟨you should not begin writing *haphazardly*; first make an outline⟩ — see HIT OR MISS

hapless *adj* having, prone to, or marked by bad luck ⟨the *hapless* prince was turned into a frog⟩ — see UNLUCKY

happen *vb* to take place ⟨did anything exciting *happen* over the summer?⟩

synonyms be, befall, betide, chance, come, come about, go (on), hap, occur, pass, transpire

related words arise, crop (up), develop, materialize, spring (up); intervene; fall out, go off, proceed, turn out

phrases come to pass

happen (on *or* upon) *vb* to come upon unexpectedly or by chance ⟨*happened on* the filming of a movie⟩

synonyms chance (upon), encounter, find, hit (upon), meet, stumble (on *or* onto)

related words confront, face; discover, turn up

phrases bump into, come across, run across, run into

happen (upon) *vb* to come upon face-to-face or as if face-to-face ⟨*happened upon* the hotel manager in the lobby and promptly complained about the room⟩ — see MEET 1

happening *n* **1** an exciting or noteworthy event that one experiences firsthand ⟨the President's visit to the school was a real *happening* for teachers and students alike⟩ — see ADVENTURE

2 something that happens ⟨gave a detailed account of all the *happenings* of the weekend⟩ — see EVENT 1

happily *adv* **1** in a cheerful or happy manner ⟨*happily* accepted the invitation to dinner⟩ — see GAILY 1

2 in a manner suitable for the occasion or purpose ⟨a desire to try rappelling does not *happily* combine with a natural fear of heights⟩ — see PROPERLY

happiness *n* **1** a feeling or state of well-being and contentment ⟨Marta's *happiness* was complete when she got her very own horse⟩

synonyms blessedness, bliss, blissfulness, felicity, gladness, joy

related words elatedness, elation, exhilaration, exultation, intoxication; ecstasy, euphoria, heaven, rapture, rapturousness; delectation, delight, enjoyment, pleasure; cheer, cheerfulness, exuberance, gaiety (*also* gayety), gladsomeness, glee, gleefulness, jollity, joyfulness, joyousness, jubilation, lightheartedness; content, contentedness, gratification, satisfaction

near antonyms anguish, desolation, joylessness, sorrow, woe, woefulness; blues, dejection, depression, despondency, disheartenment, dispiritedness, doldrums, downheartedness, gloom, gloominess, melancholy, mournfulness

antonyms misery, sadness, unhappiness, wretchedness

2 the feeling experienced when one's wishes are met ⟨finally found true *happiness* as a doctor in a poor rural area⟩ — see PLEASURE 1

happy *adj* **1** coming or happening by good luck especially unexpectedly ⟨a *happy* discovery, finding the letter that would prove her innocence⟩ — see FORTUNATE 1

2 experiencing pleasure, satisfaction, or delight ⟨made bread for the first time and was *happy* with the tasty result⟩ — see GLAD 1

3 feeling that one's needs or desires have been met ⟨has been much *happier* ever since she moved⟩ — see CONTENT

4 having good luck ⟨the *happy* person who is both appreciated and rewarded for all his hard work⟩ — see LUCKY 1

5 meeting the requirements of a purpose or situation ⟨gave us the *happy* advice to limit our luggage to what we could carry on board⟩ — see FIT 1

happy–go–lucky *adj* **1** having a relaxed, casual manner ⟨Martin is completely *happy-go-lucky* on fishing trips—if he catches something, fine; if he doesn't, that's fine, too⟩ — see EASYGOING 1

2 having or showing a lack of concern or seriousness ⟨went on her *happy-go-lucky* way, totally unaware that she was strewing litter behind her⟩ — see CAREFREE

harangue *n* **1** a long angry speech or scolding ⟨launched into a long *harangue* about tossing his newspaper in the bushes without realizing that I'm not even his paper girl!⟩ — see TIRADE

2 a usually formal discourse delivered to an audience ⟨the speaker who was to give an informative *harangue* on life in a Muslim country⟩ — see SPEECH 1

harangue *vb* **1** to give a formal often extended talk on a subject ⟨the eminent professor *harangued* for three hours on his favorite subject, the clash of East and West⟩ — see TALK 1

2 to talk as if giving an important and formal speech ⟨a talk-show guest using the interviewer's questions as an opportunity to *harangue* on a variety of pet peeves⟩ — see ORATE 1

harassment *n* the act of making unwelcome intrusions upon another ⟨Jack owes Joe a lot of money, so he shouldn't be surprised at Joe's constant *harassment* for a repayment⟩ — see ANNOYANCE 1

harbinger *n* one that announces or indicates the later arrival of another ⟨her father's successful job interview was seen as a *harbinger* of better times to come⟩ — see FORERUNNER 1

harbor *n* **1** a part of a body of water protected and deep enough to be a place of safety for ships ⟨the tanker stayed in Boston *harbor* three days to undergo repairs⟩
synonyms anchorage, harborage, haven, port
related words seaport; arm, bay, bight, cove, creek [*chiefly British*], estuary, firth, fjord (*or* fiord), gulf, inlet, loch [*Scottish*], narrow, roads, roadstead; canal, channel, sound, strait
2 something (as a building) that offers cover from the weather or protection from danger ⟨seeking a *harbor* from the drenching rain, we unfortunately chose a bank where a robbery was taking place⟩ — see SHELTER

harbor *vb* **1** to keep in one's mind or heart ⟨Grandpa *harbored* a grudge against his first boss for nearly 50 years⟩
synonyms bear, cherish, entertain, have, hold, nurse
related words cultivate, foster, nurture, sustain, support; carry, keep, maintain, preserve, remember, retain, treasure; cleave (to), cling (to), hang on (to), stick (to)
near antonyms disregard, drop, forget, ignore, neglect, overlook; abjure, decline, deny, disdain, refuse, reject, repudiate, scorn; abandon, desert, discard, forsake, give up, quit, renounce, throw out
2 to provide with living quarters or shelter ⟨the woods in our suburb *harbor* deer, foxes, raccoons, and skunks⟩ — see HOUSE 1
3 to be or provide a shelter for ⟨the little cabin is *harbored* from the wind by a thick growth of pines⟩ — see SHELTER 1

harborage *n* **1** a part of a body of water protected and deep enough to be a place of safety for ships ⟨the city boasts one of the best deepwater *harborages* on the Atlantic coast⟩ — see HARBOR 1
2 something (as a building) that offers cover from the weather or protection from danger ⟨the only *harborage* from the storm was a lone pine tree, which looked like it could get hit by lightning any minute⟩ — see SHELTER

hard *adj* **1** having or showing a lack of sympathy or tender feelings ⟨a *hard* man, who never had a kind word for anyone⟩
synonyms callous, cold-blooded, hard-boiled, hard-hearted, heartless, inhuman, inhumane, insensate, insensitive, merciless, obdurate, pitiless, ruthless, soulless, stony (*also* stoney), uncharitable, unfeeling, unmerciful, unsparing, unsympathetic
related words inconsiderate, thoughtless, uncaring, unfriendly, unloving, unthinking; grim, hard-bitten, harsh, heavy-handed, oppressive, rough, severe, stern, tough, ungentle; abusive, acrimonious, disagreeable, hateful, ill-natured, ill-tempered, malevolent, malicious, mean, rancorous, spiteful, surly, virulent; barbarous, bestial, brutal, brutish, cruel, evil-minded, savage, vicious
near antonyms benevolent, benignant, gentle, kind; clement, lenient, mild; cordial, friendly, good-natured, good-tempered, gracious; tolerant, understanding; affectionate, loving
antonyms charitable, compassionate, humane, merciful, sensitive, softhearted, sympathetic, tender, tenderhearted, warm, warmhearted
2 requiring considerable physical or mental effort ⟨clearing land is *hard* work⟩ ⟨a *hard* Spanish test⟩
synonyms arduous, demanding, difficult, exacting, formidable, grueling (*or* gruelling), herculean, killer,

laborious, murderous, rough, severe, stiff, strenuous, tall, toilsome, tough
related words abstract, abstruse, complex, complicated, insoluble, intricate, involved, knotty, problematic (*also* problematical), recondite, serious, spiny, thorny, ticklish, tricky, stubborn; burdensome, exhausting, labored, onerous, oppressive, problem, sore, stressful, taxing, tight, trying, uphill; annoying, bothersome, distressing, irksome, troublesome, vexatious; grievous, grim, heavy, strict, stringent; brutal, cruel, inhuman, painful
near antonyms achievable, clear, doable, elementary, manageable, uncomplicated; comforting, gentle, painless, relaxed, smooth, soothing
antonyms easy, effortless, facile, simple, soft, undemanding
3 able to withstand hardship, strain, or exposure ⟨they were forced to import sheep of a *harder* stock, one that could thrive in the harsh climate⟩ — see HARDY 1
4 based on sound reasoning or information ⟨do you have any *hard* evidence that this was once the site of a Native American village?⟩ — see GOOD 1
5 difficult to endure ⟨the *hard* life of a migrant farm worker⟩ — see HARSH 1
6 extreme in degree, power, or effect ⟨a carpet that withstood years of *hard* wear⟩ — see INTENSE
7 given to exacting standards of discipline and self-restraint ⟨a *hard* disciplinarian who is quick to punish the tiniest violation of the rules⟩ — see SEVERE 1
8 having a consistency that does not easily yield to pressure ⟨*hard* candies⟩ ⟨fell on the *hard* floor and bruised her arm⟩ — see FIRM 2
9 having been established and usually not subject to change ⟨there isn't always a *hard* line between right and wrong⟩ — see FIXED 1
10 having or showing deep-seated resentment ⟨maintained *hard* feelings toward those who had cheated him⟩ — see BITTER 1
11 sticking to an opinion, purpose, or course of action in spite of reason, arguments, or persuasion ⟨a woman with a *hard* will who won't budge from her chosen path⟩ — see OBSTINATE
12 restricted to or based on fact ⟨that newscast is strictly devoted to *hard* news, as the producers prefer to leave the gossip to others⟩ — see FACTUAL 1

hard *adv* **1** with great effort or determination ⟨we took a much-needed break after working *hard* all week⟩ ⟨a *hard*-won victory⟩
synonyms arduously, assiduously, determinedly, diligently, hardly, indefatigably, industriously, intensely, intensively, intently, laboriously, mightily, sedulously, slavishly, strenuously, tirelessly
related words actively, animatedly, briskly, busily, dynamically, energetically, feverishly, spiritedly, vehemently, vigorously, zealously; continuously, ploddingly, steadily, unabatedly, unrelentingly, unremittingly; ardently, attentively, conscientiously, earnestly, exhaustively, meticulously, painstakingly, seriously, thoroughly
near antonyms casually, desultorily, indolently, lackadaisically, languidly, lazily, listlessly, shiftlessly, sluggishly, spiritlessly, tiredly, wearily
2 with feelings of bitterness or grief ⟨took the news of their grandfather's death *hard*⟩
synonyms agonizingly, bitterly, grievously, hardly, mournfully, painfully, regretfully, resentfully, ruefully, sadly, sorely, sorrowfully, unhappily, woefully, wretchedly

related words abjectly, dejectedly, despondently, dispiritedly; blackly, darkly, distressfully, distressingly, forlornly, gloomily, miserably; acutely, harshly, keenly, poignantly, severely, sharply; cruelly, hurtfully, ill, rancorously

near antonyms cheerfully, cheerily, delightedly, gaily (*also* gayly), gleefully, good-naturedly, lightheartedly, merrily; blithely, calmly, casually, dispassionately, easily, indifferently, lightly, nonchalantly, unconcernedly; favorably, well

antonyms gladly, happily, joyfully, joyously

3 in a vigorous and forceful manner ⟨Terry hit the ball *hard* and it soared out of bounds⟩ ⟨the wind blew *hard* all day⟩

synonyms energetically, firmly, forcefully, forcibly, mightily, powerfully, stiffly, stoutly, strenuously, strongly, sturdily, vigorously

related words robustly, sharply, vehemently, violently; animatedly, briskly, crisply, dynamically, heartily, lustily, snappily, spiritedly, vivaciously; decidedly, determinedly, directly, emphatically, fast, fixedly, intensively, intently, resolutely, rigidly, smartly, solidly, soundly, squarely, steadfastly, steadily, surely; aggressively, assertively, manfully, potently

phrases with might and main

near antonyms delicately, faintly, frailly, shakily; indirectly, languidly, listlessly, spiritlessly; impotently, ineffectively, ineffectually, nervelessly, spinelessly, uncertainly

antonyms feebly, gently, softly, weakly

4 at, within, or to a short distance or time ⟨the groom stood *hard* by, ready to help, as the lady mounted the skittish horse⟩ — see NEAR 1

5 in a manner so as to cause loss or suffering ⟨the horse had been treated *hard* by his previous owner⟩ — see HARDLY 1

hard–and–fast *adj* **1** having been established and usually not subject to change ⟨*hard-and-fast* traditions that my mother insists on following every Thanksgiving⟩ — see FIXED 1

2 not capable of changing or being changed ⟨*hard-and-fast* beliefs that are the rock-solid foundation of their religion⟩ — see INFLEXIBLE 1

hard–bitten *adj* able to withstand hardship, strain, or exposure ⟨a *hard-bitten* Apache chief who could endure scorching heat of the Arizona desert⟩ — see HARDY 1

hard–boiled *adj* having or showing a lack of sympathy or tender feelings ⟨a *hard-boiled* Puritan schoolmaster who was as unyielding as New England granite⟩ — see HARD 1

hard–core *adj* firmly established over time ⟨the *hard-core* habits that generate our mountains of trash everyday will be extremely difficult to change⟩ — see INVETERATE 1

harden *vb* **1** to become physically firm or solid ⟨waited for the bubbly caramel-and-nut sauce to cool and *harden* into peanut brittle⟩

synonyms concrete, congeal, firm (up), freeze, set, solidify

related words cake, callus, encrust (*also* incrust); coagulate, clot, gel, jell, jelly, stiffen, thicken; calcify, crystallize, ossify, petrify; anneal, case harden, temper

near antonyms deliquesce, dissolve, flux, fuse, liquefy, melt, smelt, thaw

antonyms soften

2 to make able to withstand physical hardship, strain, or exposure ⟨pioneer women who had been *hardened* by years of living on the plains⟩

synonyms fortify, inure, season, steel, strengthen, toughen

related words acclimate, acclimatize, adapt, adjust; anneal, temper; invigorate, vitalize; immunize; bolster, boost, brace, buttress, forearm, prop (up), reinforce, support; break in, limber (up), train; accustom, condition, habituate, naturalize

near antonyms emasculate, enervate, enfeeble, exhaust, sap, weaken; cripple, debilitate, incapacitate; sensitize

antonyms soften

3 to increase the ability of (as a muscle) to exert physical force ⟨arm muscles that were *hardened* by all the years of casting and hauling his fishing nets⟩ — see STRENGTHEN 1

hardened *adj* **1** able to withstand hardship, strain, or exposure ⟨*hardened* from years of deprivation and grief, the man regarded the house fire as just another misfortune in a life filled with them⟩ — see HARDY 1

2 sticking to an opinion, purpose, or course of action in spite of reason, arguments, or persuasion ⟨*hardened* cynics regarded those TV shows as being anything but reality-based⟩ — see OBSTINATE

hardheaded *adj* **1** having or showing a practical cleverness or judgment ⟨even as a preteen, Tony showed the traits of a *hardheaded* businessman, refusing to extend credit to the customers on his paper route⟩ — see SHREWD

2 sticking to an opinion, purpose, or course of action in spite of reason, arguments, or persuasion ⟨Granny remained *hardheaded* about keeping her house and not moving into a nursing home⟩ — see OBSTINATE

3 willing to see things as they really are and deal with them sensibly ⟨a *hardheaded* minister who understands the difficulties teenagers face today⟩ — see REALISTIC 1

hardheadedness *n* a steadfast adherence to an opinion, purpose, or course of action ⟨the zoo had never used teen volunteers before, and if it weren't for Sylvia's *hardheadedness*, they probably still wouldn't⟩ — see OBSTINACY

hardhearted *adj* **1** having or showing a lack of sympathy or tender feelings ⟨a *hardhearted* brush-off to the homeless man asking for money⟩ — see HARD 1

2 sticking to an opinion, purpose, or course of action in spite of reason, arguments, or persuasion ⟨my *hardhearted* teacher won't listen to any excuses for late homework⟩ — see OBSTINATE

hardihood *n* **1** active strength of body or mind ⟨80-year-old Helen attributes her *hardihood* to having eaten a cup of yogurt every day for the past 50 years⟩ — see VIGOR 1

2 strength of mind to carry on in spite of danger ⟨what *hardihood* those musicians showed, continuing to perform even as the Titanic slipped into the sea⟩ — see COURAGE

hardly *adv* **1** in a manner so as to cause loss or suffering ⟨the new judge vowed to deal *hardly* with repeat offenders⟩

synonyms hard, harshly, ill, oppressively, roughly, severely, sternly, stiffly

related words callously, cold-bloodedly, hardheartedly, heartlessly, inhumanely, inhumanly, insensately, insensitively, mercilessly, obdurately, pitilessly, ruthlessly, tyrannically, uncharitably, unfeelingly, unmercifully, unsparingly; abusively, brutally, brutishly, savagely, viciously; aggressively, assertively, decidedly, determinedly, firmly, grimly, gruffly, resolutely, strongly, toughly

near antonyms benevolently, benignantly, considerately, cordially, graciously, kindly, lovingly, tenderly; charitably, compassionately, humanely, mercifully, softheartedly, sympathetically, tolerantly, understandingly

antonyms clemently, gently, leniently, lightly, mildly, softly

2 certainly not ⟨it's *hardly* surprising that our team won, considering how weak the opponents were⟩

synonyms no, none, no way, scarcely

related words near, never, nothing, nowhere, nowise

phrases by no means, nothing doing, on no account

near antonyms awful, awfully, enormously, exceedingly (*also* exceeding), extremely, greatly, highly, hugely, immensely, mighty, most, quite, terribly, very; assuredly, clearly, perfectly, plainly, positively, really, truly, unequivocally, unquestionably, utterly; doubtless, more or less, mostly, rather, slightly, somewhat

antonyms absolutely, certainly, completely, definitely, positively, surely

3 by a very small margin ⟨don't worry about shaving just yet—your beard is *hardly* there!⟩ — see JUST 2

4 with feelings of bitterness or grief ⟨his broker did not think that he would take his financial losses so *hardly*⟩ — see HARD 2

5 with great effort or determination ⟨their state championship was *hardly* won, and the basketball players were going to enjoy their victory to the fullest⟩ — see HARD 1

hardness *n* **1** something that is a cause for suffering or special effort especially in the attainment of a goal ⟨the test questions were rated for *hardness,* a rating of five indicating the most difficult⟩ — see DIFFICULTY 1

2 the quality or state of being demanding or unyielding (as in discipline or criticism) ⟨the aunt's *hardness* gave way under the influence of the little goat girl's endearing ways⟩ — see SEVERITY

hardship *n* something that is a cause for suffering or special effort especially in the attainment of a goal ⟨despite the new *hardship* of having to get up at five o'clock, Aaron still went to his old school after moving some distance away⟩ — see DIFFICULTY 1

hardy *adj* **1** able to withstand hardship, strain, or exposure ⟨chrysanthemums are *hardy* enough to survive a light frost⟩ ⟨the men and women who settled the West were a *hardy* lot⟩

synonyms hard, hard-bitten, hardened, inured, rugged, stout, strong, sturdy, tough, toughened, vigorous

related words flinty, leathery, resilient, stalwart; durable, enduring, everlasting, immortal, imperishable, lasting, permanent, stable, staunch (*or* stanch), staying, tenacious, unyielding; flourishing, prospering, thriving; able-bodied, brawny, muscular; fit, fortified, hale, healthy, husky, lusty, red-blooded, robust, sound, strapping, virile; annealed, seasoned, tempered

near antonyms emasculated, enervated, enfeebled, exhausted, run-down, sapped, wasted, weakened, worn, worn out; crippled, debilitated, diseased, incapacitated, infirm, unsound; fragile, frail, puny; resistless, sensitive, susceptible, unresistant, vulnerable, yielding; mortal, perishable, temporary, transient

antonyms delicate, nonhardy, soft, tender, weak

2 inclined or willing to take risks ⟨*hardy* souls, who pioneered new paths into outer space⟩ — see BOLD 1

harebrained *adj* **1** lacking in seriousness or maturity ⟨my *harebrained* sister decides at the last minute to go to a concert and then wonders why it's impossible to get tickets⟩ — see GIDDY 1

2 showing or marked by a lack of good sense or judgment ⟨a *harebrained* idea to go for a hike in an area where attacks by grizzly bears had recently been reported⟩ — see FOOLISH 1

hark *vb* to pay attention especially through the act of hearing ⟨upon hearing the offending ringing, the teacher sarcastically cried, "*Hark!* Could that possibly be a cell phone?"⟩ — see LISTEN

hark back (to) *vb* to bring back to mind ⟨while making the plans for her daughter's wedding, Marla kept *harking back to* her own wedding, over three decades ago⟩ — see REMEMBER

harlequin *n* a comically dressed performer (as at a circus) who entertains with playful tricks and ridiculous behavior ⟨among the court entertainers waiting to enter the grand hall were masked *harlequins* in brightly colored pantaloons⟩ — see CLOWN 1

harlot *n* a woman who engages in sexual activities for money ⟨the *harlot* promised the street evangelist that she would mend her ways⟩ — see PROSTITUTE

harlotry *n* the practice of engaging in sexual activities for money ⟨the preacher assured her that the Lord would forgive a life of *harlotry* if she repented⟩ — see PROSTITUTION

harm *n* something that causes loss or pain ⟨you were lucky to survive the fire without *harm*⟩ ⟨no *harm* in trying⟩ — see INJURY 1

harm *vb* **1** to cause bodily damage to ⟨though she wasn't *harmed* by the flying glass, she slipped and fell on a piece and cut her hand⟩ — see INJURE 1

2 to reduce the soundness, effectiveness, or perfection of ⟨Chris's chances of getting the part weren't *harmed* by the fact that he was a good friend of the person casting the play⟩ — see DAMAGE 1

harmful *adj* causing or capable of causing harm ⟨DDT has been proven extremely *harmful* to the environment⟩

synonyms adverse, bad, baleful, baneful, damaging, deleterious, detrimental, evil, hurtful, ill, injurious, mischievous, noxious, pernicious, prejudicial

related words hostile, inimical, unfriendly; contagious, deadly, infectious, pestilent, pestilential, poisonous, venomous; insidious, menacing, ominous, sinister, threatening; dangerous, hazardous, imperiling, jeopardizing, parlous, perilous, risky, unsafe, unsound; nasty, noisome, unhealthful, unhealthy, unwholesome; destructive, fatal, lethal, malignant, ruinous

near antonyms advantageous, beneficial, useful; favorable, good, propitious; curative, healthful, healthy, helpful, palliative, remedial, salubrious, salutary, wholesome; secure, sound; benign, benignant; noncorrosive, nondestructive, nonfatal, noninfectious, nonlethal, nonpoisonous, nonpolluting, nontoxic, nonvenomous

antonyms harmless, innocent, innocuous, inoffensive, safe

harmless *adj* not causing injury or hurt ⟨a perfectly *harmless* little spider⟩

synonyms innocent, innocuous, inoffensive, safe, white

related words healthful, healthy, salubrious, wholesome; benign, benignant; sound, trustworthy; gentle, gracious, mild; nonthreatening, painless, unobjectionable; noncorrosive, nondestructive, nonfatal, noninfectious, nonlethal, nonpoisonous, nonpolluting, nontoxic, nonvenomous

near antonyms poisonous, venomous; menacing, ominous, sinister, threatening; dangerous, hazardous, imperiling, jeopardizing, parlous, perilous, risky, unsafe, unsound; nasty, noisome, unhealthful, unhealthy, unwholesome; offensive, painful, scathing, wounding; deadly, fatal, lethal, ruinous; contaminated, corrosive, malignant, noxious, pestilent, polluted, tainted

antonyms adverse, bad, baleful, baneful, damaging, deleterious, detrimental, evil, harmful, hurtful, ill, injurious, mischievous, noxious, pernicious, prejudicial

harmonious *adj* **1** having a pleasing mixture of notes ⟨the naturally *harmonious* sounds of a forest glen in springtime⟩

synonyms euphonious, harmonizing, melodious, musical, symphonic, tuneful

related words blending, chiming, flowing, mellifluous; dulcet, mellow, melodic, sweet; echoing, resonant, sonorous; quavering, trilling, warbling; agreeable, appealing, pleasant; cadenced, lilting, lyric, lyrical, rhythmic (*or* rhythmical); chordal, harmonic, homophonic, orchestral, polyphonic, tonal

near antonyms blaring, clanging, clashing, clattering, grating, harsh, jangling, jarring, metallic, raspy, raucous, scratching, screeching, shrill, squeaky, strident; disagreeable, unpleasant, unpleasing; atonal, off-key

antonyms discordant, dissonant, inharmonious, unharmonious, unmelodious, unmusical

2 having the parts agreeably related ⟨a *harmonious* arrangement of archways and doorways in the palace courtyard⟩

synonyms balanced, congruous, consonant

related words even, proportioned, regular, symmetrical (*or* symmetric); aesthetic (*or* esthetic), artistic, becoming, elegant, graceful, tasteful; agreeable, felicitous, pleasant, pleasing, satisfying; compatible, coordinated, correspondent, matched, matching

near antonyms asymmetrical, disordered, irregular, skewed, unequal, uneven, unsymmetrical; distasteful, graceless, inartistic, inelegant, tasteless, unaesthetic, unbecoming, ungraceful, unlovely; disagreeable, displeasing, dissatisfying, infelicitous, unfortunate, unpleasant, unsightly; clashing, conflicting, disunited, incompatible, uncoordinated

antonyms incongruous, inharmonious, unbalanced

3 having or marked by agreement in feeling or action ⟨an unusually *harmonious* meeting among the leaders resulted in a quick peace agreement⟩

synonyms agreeable, amicable, compatible, congenial, frictionless, kindred, unanimous, united

related words pacific, peaceable, peaceful; collaborating, cooperative, symbiotic; noncompetitive, nonconflicting, uncompetitive; sympathetic, tolerant, understanding; affable, amiable, cordial, friendly, genial, neighborly; collaborating

near antonyms antagonistic, antipathetic, clashing, conflicting, hostile, inimical, unfriendly; belligerent, contentious, quarrelsome; contradicting, contradictory, contrary, opposing, opposite; competing, competitive, rivaling (*or* rivalling)

antonyms disagreeable, disunited, incompatible, inharmonious, uncongenial

4 not having or showing any apparent conflict ⟨no form of social discrimination can ever be *harmonious* with the basic principles and ideals of our nation⟩ — see CONSISTENT

harmonize *vb* **1** to form a pleasing relationship ⟨the color of the walls *harmonized* nicely with the blue tones in the carpet⟩

synonyms agree, blend, conform, coordinate

related words balance, correlate, correspond, dovetail, match; meet, parallel; bond, coalesce, cohere, conjoin, fuse, merge, square, tally

near antonyms contradict, contrast, counter, differ, diverge, jar; cancel (out), counteract, negate, offset

antonyms clash, collide, conflict

2 to bring to a state free of conflicts, inconsistencies, or differences ⟨an attempt to *harmonize* the New Testament version of events with the accounts of the ancient Romans⟩

synonyms accommodate, conciliate, conform, coordinate, key, reconcile

related words adapt, attune, tune; blend, combine, connect, correlate, dovetail, fit, fuse, integrate, join, match, merge, orchestrate, pair, square, suit, synchronize, synthesize, unify, unite; align, arrange, array, balance, equalize, even, order, proportion, regularize, standardize

near antonyms confuse, disarray, disorder, disorganize, disrupt, disturb, skew, upset

antonyms alienate, disjoin

3 to be in agreement on every point ⟨interrogated in separate rooms, the two burglary suspects gave stories that didn't *harmonize* at all⟩ — see CHECK 1

harmonizing *adj* having a pleasing mixture of notes ⟨a *harmonizing* chorus of chirps arose from the bird-laden trees⟩ — see HARMONIOUS 1

harmony *n* **1** a balanced, pleasing, or suitable arrangement of parts ⟨her face had an angelic *harmony* that fascinated the leading painters of her day⟩

synonyms balance, coherence, consonance, proportion, symmetry, symphony, unity

related words coordination, correlation, correspondence, equalization, equilibrium, evenness, order, orderliness, regularity, uniformity

near antonyms confusion, disorganization, dissonance, disturbance, tension; disconnectedness, disjointedness, incompatibility; irregularity, unevenness

antonyms asymmetry, discordance, disproportion, disunity, imbalance, incoherence

2 peaceful coexistence ⟨Mary Beth was determined to live in *harmony* with her new stepsister⟩

synonyms comity, compatibility, concord, peace

related words amity, congeniality, fellowship, fraternization, friendship; collaboration, reciprocity, symbiosis; consensus, unanimity, unity; affinity, connection, empathy, kinship, oneness, rapport, solidarity, sympathy, understanding; peacefulness, serenity, tranquillity (*or* tranquility)

near antonyms antagonism, antipathy, enmity, hatred, hostility, unfriendliness; alienation, breach, divorce, estrangement, rupture, schism, severance; dissent, dissidence; disturbance, strife, turmoil

antonyms conflict, discord, dissension

3 a state of consistency ⟨for once, the kids' idea of a vacation was in perfect *harmony* with their parents' notion of relaxation⟩ — see CONFORMITY 1

harness *vb* to put into action or service ⟨huge dams *harness* the power of water to produce electricity⟩ — see USE 1

harpoon *vb* to penetrate or hold (something) with a pointed object ⟨the Eskimo men *harpooned* seals, using kayaks to get up close to their prey⟩ — see IMPALE

harpy *n* a bad-tempered scolding woman ⟨in fairy tales stepmothers are often portrayed as *harpies* who make the lives of their stepchildren miserable⟩ — see SHREW

harrow *vb* to cause persistent suffering to ⟨a doctor *harrowed* by a hail of regulations and restrictions that kept him from his sole purpose—curing the sick⟩ — see AFFLICT

harrowing *adj* **1** hard to accept or bear especially emotionally ⟨a *harrowing* portrayal of the ravages of war⟩ — see BITTER 2

2 intensely or unbearably painful ⟨the *harrowing* amputations without any anesthetic that soldiers and sailors once were forced to endure⟩ see EXCRUCIATING 1

harrying *n* the act of making unwelcome intrusions upon another ⟨he'd had enough of the street gang's constant *harrying* as he made his way home from school⟩ — see ANNOYANCE 1

harsh *adj* **1** difficult to endure ⟨*harsh* conditions in the refugee camp⟩

synonyms bitter, brutal, burdensome, cruel, excruciating, grievous, grim, hard, heavy, inhuman, murderous, onerous, oppressive, rough, rugged, severe, stiff, tough, trying

related words austere, bleak, comfortless, discomforting, forbidding, hostile, inhospitable, Spartan, uncomfortable; biting, inclement, intemperate; rigorous, strict, stringent; agonizing, heartbreaking, heartrending, painful, wretched; crushing, grinding, overwhelming, wearing; insufferable, insupportable, intolerable, unbearable, unendurable; harrowing, torturous; bad, disagreeable, hostile, unfriendly, unpleasant

near antonyms comfortable, cozy, luxurious, snug; agreeable, friendly, genial, hospitable, pleasant; peaceful, relaxing, reposeful, restful; bearable, endurable, painless, tolerable; balmy, calm, clement, gentle, mild, moderate, temperate

antonyms easy, light, soft

2 disagreeable to one's aesthetic or artistic sense ⟨the *harsh* lighting in the cafeteria makes the food look slightly off-color⟩

synonyms grating, grotesque, jarring, unaesthetic

related words flashy, garish, gaudy, loud, tawdry; tacky, tasteless, vulgar; inartistic, unartistic; artless, clumsy, crude, graceless, inelegant, rude; uncouth, uncultured, unrefined; disgusting, gross, obscene, repugnant, repulsive, ugly; disagreeable, jolting, unpleasant, unpleasing; blaring, clashing, discordant, dissonant, inharmonious, off-key, jangling, raspy, raucous, unharmonious, unmelodious, unmusical; bizarre, kinky, odd, outlandish, shocking

near antonyms artful, artistic; attractive, beautiful, becoming, comely; agreeable, appealing, felicitous, good, harmonious, harmonizing, pleasing, seemly; calming, comforting, soothing; softened, subdued; cultured, elegant, graceful, gracious, polished, refined, tasteful

antonyms aesthetic (*or* esthetic)

3 causing discomfort ⟨the *harsh* northern climate⟩ — see UNCOMFORTABLE 1

4 given to exacting standards of discipline and self-restraint ⟨a *harsh* judge when it comes to drug users and especially drug pushers⟩ — see SEVERE 1

5 hard to accept or bear especially emotionally ⟨the *harsh* reality of failure⟩ ⟨*harsh* words of criticism from her favorite teacher⟩ — see BITTER 2

harshly *adv* in a manner so as to cause loss or suffering ⟨treated the prisoners *harshly,* and many died⟩ — see HARDLY 1

harshness *n* **1** a harsh or sharp quality ⟨the *harshness* in the vampire's laughter was enough to send shivers up your spine⟩ — see EDGE 1

2 the quality or state of being demanding or unyielding (as in discipline or criticism) ⟨was surprised at the *harshness* of the choirmaster's criticism, since he was usually pretty easygoing⟩ — see SEVERITY

harum–scarum *adv* in a confused and reckless manner ⟨tossed everything *harum-scarum* from the closet in a desperate attempt to find her shoes⟩ — see HELTERSKELTER 1

harvest *n* the quantity of an animal or vegetable product gathered at the end of a season ⟨we can thank the bountiful *harvest* of 1621 for our traditional turkey and cranberry sauce every November⟩ — see CROP 1

harvest *vb* to catch or collect (a crop or natural resource) for human use ⟨*harvest* salmon from nearby rivers⟩ ⟨every year we *harvest* corn from our own garden⟩

synonyms gather, pick, reap

related words clam, fish, seal, shrimp, whale; accumulate, garner; glean; cut, hay, mow; bag, capture, hunt, net, snare, trap; crop, grow, raise

near antonyms plant, seed, sow

hash *n* an unorganized collection or mixture of various things ⟨the docudrama was a *hash* of facts, half-truths, speculation, and pure fiction⟩ — see MISCELLANY 1

hash *vb* **1** to cut into small pieces ⟨he *hashed* some roast beef, put it in a pie shell, and overspread a layer of mashed potatoes⟩ — see CHOP 1

2 to undo the proper order or arrangement of ⟨the bookkeeper had so *hashed* the figures it took weeks to straighten out the accounts⟩ — see DISORDER

hash (over) *vb* to talk about (an issue) usually from various points of view and for the purpose of arriving at a decision or opinion ⟨after *hashing over* various options, the Ridleys decided to stay home for Christmas⟩ — see DISCUSS

hassle *n* **1** a brief clash between enemies or rivals ⟨the best way to avoid *hassles* with that bully is to ignore him⟩ — see ENCOUNTER

2 a physical dispute between opposing individuals or groups ⟨the moment the police arrived, the *hassle* broke up, and no one was hurt⟩ — see FIGHT 1

3 an often noisy or angry expression of differing opinions ⟨had a huge *hassle* with an airline representative before she got her ticket refunded⟩ — see ARGUMENT 1

4 something that is a source of irritation ⟨it's a *hassle* to find a parking space downtown⟩ — see ANNOYANCE 3

hassle *vb* **1** to attack repeatedly with mean put-downs or insults ⟨the other kids *hassled* him for smelling like fish because he often helped out on his father's shrimp boat⟩ — see TEASE 2

2 to express different opinions about something often angrily ⟨constantly *hassled* with the cook over the need to cook pork thoroughly⟩ — see ARGUE 2

haste *n* **1** a high rate of movement or performance ⟨made *haste* to get there on time⟩ — see SPEED

2 excited and often showy or disorderly speed ⟨*haste* makes waste⟩ ⟨in her *haste,* she forgot her keys⟩ — see HURRY 1

hasten *vb* **1** to cause to move or proceed fast or faster ⟨*hasten* the activation of yeast with heat⟩ — see HURRY 1

2 to proceed or move quickly ⟨*hastened* to get to church before the rain started⟩ — see HURRY 2

hastily *adv* **1** with excessive or careless speed ⟨the *hastily* put together report contained a lot of errors⟩
  synonyms cursorily, headlong, hotfoot, hurriedly, pell-mell, precipitately, precipitously, rashly
  related words headily, hotheadedly, impatiently, impetuously, impulsively, recklessly, thoughtlessly; automatically, glancingly, haphazardly; impromptu, spontaneously; abruptly, suddenly; offhand, offhandedly
  phrases on the spur of the moment
  near antonyms calculatingly, circumspectly, designedly; falteringly, hesitantly, hesitatingly, tentatively; leisurely, slowly
  antonyms deliberately, studiedly
  2 with great speed ⟨*hastily* cleaned up the mess before her parents walked in⟩ — see FAST 1
hastiness *n* excited and often showy or disorderly speed ⟨the *hastiness* with which she threw together the dress probably had something to do with why it fit funny⟩ — see HURRY 1
hasty *adj* **1** acting or done with excessive or careless speed ⟨Anna later regretted her *hasty* decision to sell her car⟩
  synonyms cursory, flying, headlong, hurried, pell-mell, precipitate, precipitous, rash, rushed
  related words breakneck, breathtaking; headstrong, heady, hotheaded, impatient, impetuous, impulsive, madcap, reckless, unadvised; quick, rapid, speedy, swift; impromptu, makeshift, offhand, offhanded, slapdash, snap, spontaneous, spur-of-the-moment; abrupt, sudden
  near antonyms calculated, calculating, measured; circumspect, foresighted, forethoughtful; drawn-out, extended, long-term, prolonged; faltering, hesitant, hesitating, tentative; dallying, dawdling, laggard, leisurely, poky (*or* pokey), shilly-shallying, slow
  antonyms deliberate, unhurried
  2 moving, proceeding, or acting with great speed ⟨we all wish our sick friend a *hasty* recovery⟩ — see FAST 1
hat *n* a covering for the head usually having a shaped crown ⟨Paul brought back warm fur *hats* for everyone from Russia⟩
  synonyms cap, headdress, headgear, headpiece, lid [*slang*]
  related words beret, biretta, boater, bonnet, bowler, derby, fedora, fez, hard hat, helm, helmet, homburg, hood, leghorn, miter, nightcap, panama, pillbox, poke bonnet, shako, skullcap, sombrero, sou'wester, Stetson, stocking cap, stovepipe, sunbonnet, tam-o'-shanter, top hat, topper, toque, turban; war bonnet; coronet, crown, diadem, headband, tiara; babushka, coif, kerchief, mantilla, scarf, shawl, tallith, veil, wimple
hatch *n* a barrier by which an entry is closed and opened ⟨holding onto the plane's open *hatch*, the parachutist turned a little green with anxiety⟩ — see DOOR 1
hatch *vb* to cover and warm eggs to hatch them ⟨Mother Hen regally *hatching* on her nest like the henhouse queen⟩ — see SET 1
hate *n* **1** a very strong dislike ⟨*hate* can sometimes be replaced with tolerance when people meet face to face⟩
  synonyms abhorrence, abomination, execration, hatred, loathing
  related words cattiness, despite, despitefulness, hatefulness, invidiousness, malevolence, malice, maliciousness, malignancy, malignity, meanness, spite, spitefulness; aversion, disgust, distaste, horror, odium, repugnance, repulsion, revulsion; animosity, antago-

nism, antipathy, bitterness, contempt, disdain, enmity, grudge, hostility, jealousy, pique, resentment, scorn; bile, jaundice, rancor, spleen, venom, virulence, vitriol
  near antonyms appetite, inclination, liking; adoration, veneration, worship; acceptance, tolerance; passion, relish, taste
  antonyms affection, devotion, fondness, love
  2 something or someone that is hated ⟨the Alaska pipeline is a pet *hate* of environmentalists⟩
  synonyms abhorrence, abomination, anathema, antipathy, aversion, bête noire
  related words dread, hang-up, horror, phobia; bogey (*also* bogy *or* bogie), bugaboo, bugbear; adversary, enemy; annoyance, grievance, hassle, nuisance, peeve
  near antonyms beloved, darling, dear, honey; delight, enjoyment, felicity, joy, pleasure; favorite, like, preference; treasure
  antonyms love
hate *vb* to dislike strongly ⟨Pete *hated* the farm and dreamed of working in the city⟩
  synonyms abhor, abominate, despise, detest, execrate, loathe
  related words deplore, deprecate, disapprove (of), discountenance, disdain, disfavor, scorn
  phrases have it in for
  near antonyms fancy, favor, like, prefer; enjoy, relish; adore, esteem, idolize, revere, venerate, worship; cherish, prize, treasure
  antonyms love
hateful *adj* having or showing a desire to cause someone pain or suffering for the sheer enjoyment of it ⟨a *hateful* bully who loved to pick on little kids⟩ ⟨Janet's *hateful* remarks drove Penny to tears⟩
  synonyms catty, cruel, despiteful, malevolent, malicious, malign, malignant, mean, nasty, spiteful, virulent
  related words devious, scoundrelly, scurvy, snakelike; acrimonious, bitter, envious, jaundiced, jealous, rancorous, resentful; contemptuous, deprecating, disdainful, obnoxious, opprobrious, scornful, snide, unkind, unkindly, unloving; baleful, baneful, evil; harsh, hostile, inimical; acrid, caustic, scathing, venomous
  near antonyms compassionate, good, good-hearted, kind, kindhearted, kindly, sympathetic, warm, warmhearted; affable, agreeable, amiable, cordial, friendly, genial, gracious, nice, pleasant; affectionate, amorous, sweet, tender, tenderhearted; altruistic, high-minded, humanitarian, magnanimous, noble, philanthropic
  antonyms benevolent, benign, benignant, loving, unmalicious
hatefully *adv* in a mean or spiteful manner ⟨glared *hatefully* at the person who cut in front of him, but didn't say anything⟩ — see NASTILY
hatefulness *n* the desire to cause pain for the satisfaction of doing harm ⟨it was just *hatefulness* that made her tell those lies about Ian, because it's not as if she gained anything by them⟩ — see MALICE
hatred *n* a very strong dislike ⟨a lifelong *hatred* of war that inspired him to join a peace movement⟩ — see HATE 1
haughtiness *n* an exaggerated sense of one's importance that shows itself in the making of excessive or unjustified claims ⟨her *haughtiness* after she made the team and I didn't was more than I could bear⟩ — see ARROGANCE
haughty *adj* **1** having a feeling of superiority that shows itself in an overbearing attitude ⟨the *haughty* waiter

smirked when I remarked that it was odd that a French restaurant didn't even have French fries on the menu⟩ — see ARROGANT

2 having or displaying feelings of scorn for what is regarded as beneath oneself ⟨the student reporter received a *haughty* letter in reply to his request for an interview with the governor⟩ — see PROUD 1

haul *n* **1** the total amount collected or obtained especially at one time ⟨the trick-or-treaters showed off their *haul*⟩

synonyms catch, take, yield

related words bag; earnings, gain, gross, income, net, payoff, proceeds, profit, receipts, return, revenue, winnings; booty, loot, plunder, spoils, swag; appropriation, collection

near antonyms deduction, loss, subtraction

2 a mass or quantity of something taken up and carried, conveyed, or transported ⟨several huge *hauls* of dirt were required to level the soccer field⟩ — see LOAD 1

3 the act or an instance of applying force on something so that it moves in the direction of the force ⟨the sharp *haul* strained the rope but didn't break it⟩ — see PULL 1

haul *vb* **1** to cause to follow by applying steady force on ⟨a pair of strong oxen *hauled* the plow⟩ — see PULL 1

2 to support and take from one place to another ⟨a vast army of trucks *haul* produce across America every day⟩ — see CARRY 1

haunches *n pl* the part of the body upon which someone sits ⟨squatted down on her *haunches* to get a better shot of the ducks with her camera⟩ — see BUTTOCKS

haunt *n* a place for spending time or for socializing ⟨one of their favorite after-school *haunts* is Joe's Pizza⟩ — see HANGOUT

haunt *vb* to go to or spend time in often ⟨much of her time is spent *haunting* antique shops in search of unique knobs for the curio cabinets she builds⟩ — see FREQUENT

haunting *adj* fearfully and mysteriously strange or fantastic ⟨the *haunting* tones of the Highland bagpipes⟩ — see EERIE

have *vb* **1** to keep, control, or experience as one's own ⟨Aunt Chloe *has* 31 pairs of red shoes⟩

synonyms command, enjoy, hold, occupy, own, possess, retain

related words keep, reserve, withhold; bear, carry; boast, show off, sport

near antonyms abandon, cede, disclaim, disown, hand over, relinquish, renounce, surrender, yield; discard, dump; decline, reject, repudiate, spurn; need, require

antonyms lack, want

2 to agree to receive whether willingly or reluctantly ⟨I agreed to *have* the job of calling everybody on the phone⟩ ⟨asked her to marry him, but she would not *have* him⟩ — see TAKE 2

3 to bring forth from the womb ⟨her grandmother *had* 11 children⟩ — see BEAR 1

4 to cause to believe what is untrue ⟨he'd been *had* —the painting was a fake, and he never saw the "art dealer" or his money again⟩ — see DECEIVE

5 to come to a knowledge of (something) by living through it ⟨*had* a great time at the party⟩ ⟨*had* three operations on her leg⟩ — see EXPERIENCE

6 to give permission for or to approve of ⟨I will not *have* any more nonsense⟩ — see ALLOW 1

7 to influence someone with a bribe ⟨the guard at the gate would not be *had*, no matter what anyone offered to pay him to let them join the celebrity gala⟩ — see BRIBE

8 to keep in one's mind or heart ⟨I have never *had* an unkind thought for him⟩ ⟨do you *have* an opinion?⟩ — see HARBOR 1

have (to) *vb* to be under necessity or obligation to ⟨I *have to* take out the trash before we can leave⟩ ⟨*has to* take medicine for her heart⟩ — see NEED 2

haven *n* **1** a part of a body of water protected and deep enough to be a place of safety for ships ⟨this picturesque cove is one of the most popular *havens* on all of the cape for weekend yachtsmen⟩ — see HARBOR 1

2 something (as a building) that offers cover from the weather or protection from danger ⟨the cross-country skiers hoped desperately to find a cave, as a *haven* from the blizzard⟩ — see SHELTER

havoc *n* **1** a state in which everything is out of order ⟨utter *havoc* as everyone tried to get out of the burning building⟩ — see CHAOS

2 the state or fact of being rendered nonexistent, physically unsound, or useless ⟨the powerful hurricane wreaked *havoc* all along the coast⟩ — see DESTRUCTION

hawk *n* one who urges or attempts to cause a war ⟨the *hawks* were claiming that without war there could be no peace⟩ — see WARMONGER

hawk *vb* to sell from place to place usually in small quantities ⟨*hawking* newspapers on the street corner⟩ — see PEDDLE

hawker *n* one who sells things outdoors ⟨at the sidewalk fair there were *hawkers* of everything from fake designer purses to original works of art⟩ — see PEDDLER

hazard *n* **1** something that may cause injury or harm ⟨the tumbledown old barn was considered a fire *hazard*⟩ — see DANGER 2

2 the uncertain course of events ⟨our nightly accommodations for each leg of the journey were entirely the result of *hazard* and not of any prearrangement⟩ — see CHANCE 1

hazard *vb* **1** to place in danger ⟨an emergency landing in the pasture would *hazard* only a few sheep⟩ — see ENDANGER

2 to take a chance on ⟨was unwilling to *hazard* landing the plane on the small island⟩ — see RISK 1

hazardous *adj* involving potential loss or injury ⟨a *hazardous* journey across the Arctic ice⟩ — see DANGEROUS

haze *n* **1** an atmospheric condition in which suspended particles in the air rob it of its transparency ⟨Jim could barely make out the tall buildings through the *haze*⟩

synonyms fog, mist, murk, reek, smog, soup

related words cloud, fume, miasma, smoke, steam

2 a state of mental confusion ⟨people wandered around in a *haze* in the days following the earthquake⟩

synonyms daze, fog, muddle, spin

related words reverie, stupor, trance; befuddlement, bewilderment, perplexity, puzzlement; delirium, malaise, paralysis; cloudiness, fogginess

near antonyms alertness, levelheadedness

haze *vb* to make dark, dim, or indistinct ⟨smog was *hazing* the view of the distant city skyline⟩ — see CLOUD 1

hazed *adj* covered over by clouds ⟨*hazed* skies made the flat landscape look even duller⟩ — see OVERCAST

hazy *adj* **1** filled with or dimmed by fine particles (as of dust or water) in suspension ⟨*hazy* skies made it dangerous to fly⟩ ⟨the *hazy* sunshine so common in August⟩

synonyms beclouded, befogged, clouded, cloudy, foggy, misty, murky, smoggy, soupy

related words overcast, rainy, stormy, thick; dirty, miry, mucky, muddy, slimy, slushy, turbid; smoky (*also* smokey), sooty; filmy, milky, opaque

near antonyms bright, clean; fair, rainless, sunny, sunshiny; translucent, transparent

antonyms clear, cloudless, limpid, pellucid, unclouded

2 covered over by clouds ⟨when taking landscape photographs, compensate for dull, *hazy* skies by emphasizing colorful features on the ground⟩ — see OVERCAST

3 not seen or understood clearly ⟨the meaning of "you should" here is *hazy* —does it mean "you are strongly urged" or "you are commanded"?⟩ — see FAINT 1

head *adj* highest in rank or authority ⟨Mr. Pendergast, *head* editor at the TV station for 17 years, has hired and fired innumerable staff members⟩

synonyms chief, commanding, first, foremost, high, lead, leading, managing, preeminent, premier, presiding, primary, prime, principal, supreme

related words high-level, senior; controlling, directing, officiating, overseeing, reigning, ruling, supervisory; main, major, paramount, predominant; dominant, grand, superior, topmost, upmost, upper, uppermost

phrases in charge

near antonyms inferior, last, lesser, lower, lowly, second, secondary, subordinate; assistant, assisting, coadjutor, deputy, junior, under

head *n* **1** the upper or front part of the body that contains the brain, the major sense organs, and the mouth ⟨I hit my *head* as I went through the low doorway⟩

synonyms noddle, noggin, pate, poll

related words cranium, crown, scalp, skull

2 the place of leadership or command ⟨every year a different parent is placed at the *head* of the troop's cookie drive⟩

synonyms chair, headship, helm, rein

related words chieftainship, commandership, directorship; forefront, lead, preferment; chairmanship, deanship, dictatorship, governorship, kingship, mastership, mastery, presidency, superintendency; dominance, dominion, jurisdiction, sovereignty, sway, upper hand; eminence, height, pedestal, pinnacle, seat, throne, top

near antonyms ranks

3 a light mass of fine bubbles formed in or on a liquid ⟨the *head* on the ice cream soda rose a good two inches above the rim of the glass⟩ — see FOAM

4 a member of the human race ⟨the tour guide counted *heads*, and everyone was present⟩ — see HUMAN

5 a time or state of affairs requiring prompt or decisive action ⟨the problems of building security came to a *head* when someone was robbed in broad daylight⟩ — see EMERGENCY

6 the beginning part of a stream ⟨Lake Itasca in Minnesota is the *head* of the Mississippi River⟩ — see HEADWATER

7 the highest part or point ⟨stood at the *head* of the stairs and looked down⟩ — see HEIGHT 1

8 the normal or healthy condition of the mental abilities ⟨you're out of your *head* if you think you can swim across that river⟩ — see MIND 2

9 the part of a person that feels, thinks, perceives, wills, and especially reasons ⟨a history teacher who asks us a lot of hard questions and really makes us use our *heads*⟩ — see MIND 1

10 the person (as an employer or supervisor) who tells people and especially workers what to do ⟨as *head* of the planning committee, he had the responsibility of appointing someone to look into the parking situation⟩ — see BOSS

head *vb* **1** to go on a specified course or in a certain direction ⟨the migrant workers were *heading* for California for the grape harvest⟩

synonyms bear, make

related words aim, bend, direct, point, turn; put, put out, set forth, set off, set out, strike, take off; face, orient, steer; about-face, back, come about, come round, cut, incline, put about, reverse, swerve, tack, veer, yaw, wheel

2 to be at the front of ⟨*heading* the procession at the dog show was a miniature poodle, followed by dogs seemingly of every breed⟩ — see LEAD 3

3 to be in charge of ⟨who *headed* the CIA when Ronald Reagan was president?⟩ — see BOSS 1

4 to be positioned along a certain course or in a certain direction ⟨the road to riches *heads* north, thought many, as off they went to Alaska to try their luck at panning gold⟩ — see RUN 3

5 to point or turn (something) toward a target or goal ⟨*headed* the car toward home⟩ — see AIM

6 to serve as leader of ⟨Robert LaSalle *headed* the expedition that claimed Louisiana for the French king⟩ — see LEAD 2

headache *n* **1** a dull, unpleasant, or difficult piece of work ⟨filling out all the required forms was a real *headache*⟩ — see CHORE 2

2 something that is a source of irritation ⟨one of the *headaches* of being a band teacher is never knowing if the school's music program will be cut⟩ — see ANNOYANCE 3

headdress *n* a covering for the head usually having a shaped crown ⟨most of the acrobats riding the horses and elephants wore some sort of fancy *headdress*⟩ — see HAT

headgear *n* a covering for the head usually having a shaped crown ⟨in some states a helmet is required *headgear* for motorcycle riders⟩ — see HAT

heading *n* a word or series of words often in larger letters placed at the beginning of a passage or at the top of a page in order to introduce or categorize ⟨Fran found the recipe for turkey gumbo under the *heading* "stews" rather than under "soups"⟩

synonyms caption, headline, rubric, title

related words guide word, legend; greeting, salutation; superscript, superscription; subhead, subheading, subtitle

headland *n* **1** an area of high ground jutting out into a body of water beyond the line of the coast ⟨the lighthouse, situated on a narrow, rocky *headland*, commands an expansive view of the coast⟩

synonyms point, promontory

related words cape, peninsula; breakwater, jetty, levee; spit

2 an area of land that juts out into a body of water ⟨navigation is notoriously difficult at the southernmost tip of South America, where ships must round the *headland* of Cape Horn⟩ — see ²CAPE

headline *n* a word or series of words often in larger letters placed at the beginning of a passage or at the top of a page in order to introduce or categorize ⟨Sherri usually just reads the *headlines* in the morning paper⟩ — see HEADING

headlong *adj* acting or done with excessive or careless speed ⟨terrified forest creatures in a *headlong* retreat from the rapidly spreading fire⟩ — see HASTY 1

headlong *adv* with excessive or careless speed ⟨plunged *headlong* into the crowd in pursuit of the purse snatcher⟩ — see HASTILY 1

headman *n* the person (as an employer or supervisor) who tells people and especially workers what to do ⟨as *headman* at the newspaper 20 years ago, he hired the then-promising young reporter who won this year's Pulitzer Prize for investigative reporting⟩ — see BOSS

headpiece *n* a covering for the head usually having a shaped crown ⟨the bride will be wearing a flowing veil fastened to a pearl-covered *headpiece*⟩ — see HAT

headquarters *n pl* **1** a place from which authority is exercised ⟨the *headquarters* of the newly established United States government was in New York City, the nation's first capital⟩ — see SEAT 1
2 the place from which a commander runs operations ⟨the scout went straight to the large tent in the center of the camp, correctly assuming that it served as the division's *headquarters*⟩ — see COMMAND 3

headship *n* **1** the duty or function of watching or guarding for the sake of proper direction or control ⟨while he was in the hospital, the CEO had his wife assume the temporary *headship* of the firm⟩ — see SUPERVISION 1
2 the place of leadership or command ⟨after the CEO died, the shareholders voted to put his wife at the *headship* of the firm⟩ — see HEAD 2

headstone *n* a shaped stone laid over or erected near a grave and usually bearing an inscription to identify and preserve the memory of the deceased ⟨many of the *headstones* were for children who had died during the influenza epidemic⟩ — see TOMBSTONE

headstrong *adj* **1** given to resisting control or discipline by others ⟨a *headstrong* child who likes to test the limits of his parents' patience⟩ — see UNCONTROLLABLE
2 sticking to an opinion, purpose, or course of action in spite of reason, arguments, or persuasion ⟨the tenants of the building remain *headstrong* in their determination not to be evicted by the developer⟩ — see OBSTINATE

headwater *n, usually* **headwaters** *pl* the beginning part of a stream ⟨the first exploration of the Missouri River from its mouth to its *headwaters* was made by Meriwether Lewis and William Clark in the early 1800s⟩
synonyms head, source
related words fountain, fountainhead, geyser, hot spring, spring, thermal spring, wellspring

headway *n* forward movement in time or place ⟨the ant was making little *headway* carrying a crumb that was about five times his size⟩ — see ADVANCE 1

heal *vb* **1** to restore to a healthy condition ⟨a low-fat vegetarian diet, moderate exercise, and stress management help *heal* a diseased heart⟩ ⟨*heal* the sick⟩
synonyms cure, mend, rehabilitate
related words attend (to), care (for), doctor, minister (to), nurse, treat; fortify, rejuvenate, renew, resuscitate, revive; alleviate, fix, relieve, remedy, repair
phrases take care of
near antonyms damage, disable, harm, hurt, impair, injure, lacerate, lame, maim, mangle, mutilate, wound; afflict, ail, debilitate, enervate, enfeeble, lay up, sap, sicken, waste, weaken
2 to become healthy and strong again after illness or weakness ⟨most of the soldiers could go home while they were still *healing* from their wounds⟩ — see CONVALESCE
3 to bring about recovery from ⟨time *heals* all wounds, even those of the heart⟩ — see CURE 1

healing *n* the process or period of gradually regaining one's health and strength ⟨the long period of *healing* following the operation⟩ — see CONVALESCENCE

health *n* the condition of being sound in body ⟨Sam gradually regained his *health* after a long bout with cholera⟩
synonyms fitness, healthiness, heartiness, robustness, soundness, wellness, wholeness, wholesomeness
related words fettle, shape; cleanliness, hygiene; hardiness, lustiness, ruggedness, stamina, strength, toughness, vigor, vigorousness, vitality; bloom, flush, flushness; activeness, agility, liveliness, spryness; weal, welfare, well-being
near antonyms debility, decrepitude, feebleness, frailness, infirmity, lameness, weakness; ailment, condition, disease, disorder, malady, trouble
antonyms illness, sickness, unhealthiness, unsoundness

healthful *adj* good for the health ⟨one of the most *healthful* forms of exercise is a brisk walk⟩
synonyms healthy, restorative, salubrious, salutary, wholesome
related words alleviative, corrective, curative, remedial, tonic; advantageous, beneficial, useful; antiseptic, clean, hygienic, sanitary; nonfattening, nonpoisonous, nontoxic
near antonyms deleterious, injurious, pernicious; infectious, poisonous, toxic; insanitary, unhygienic, unsanitary
antonyms insalubrious, noxious, unhealthful, unhealthy, unwholesome

healthiness *n* the condition of being sound in body ⟨healthy teeth are an indication of a horse's overall *healthiness*⟩ — see HEALTH

healthy *adj* **1** enjoying health and vigor ⟨always a hard worker, Grandma has remained *healthy* into her eighties⟩
synonyms able-bodied, bouncing, chipper, fit, hale, hearty, robust, sound, well, whole, wholesome
related words hardy, lusty, rugged, stalwart, strong, sturdy, tough; nondisabled, uncrippled; active, agile, lively, sprightly, spry, vigorous, vital; blooming, clean-cut, flourishing, flush, prospering, thriving; all right, good, right
phrases in fine fettle
near antonyms decrepit, enfeebled, feeble, infirm, rundown, sickened, sickly, weak, weakened, weakly, worn-out; challenged, crippled, debilitated, disabled, incapacitated, lame; delicate, fragile, frail; undernourished; afflicted, troubled; bad, poorly
antonyms ailing, diseased, ill, sick, unfit, unhealthy, unsound, unwell
2 good for the health ⟨the air in here isn't *healthy*⟩ ⟨ads that promote *healthy* eating habits⟩ — see HEALTHFUL
3 sufficiently large in size, amount, or number to merit attention ⟨a *healthy* turnout of volunteers to plant trees on Arbor Day⟩ — see CONSIDERABLE 1

heap *n* **1** a considerable amount ⟨she always has a *heap* of good ideas⟩ — see LOT 2
2 a quantity of things thrown or stacked on one another ⟨found her shoe under a *heap* of clothes on the floor⟩ — see ¹PILE 1

heap *vb* **1** to give readily and in large quantities ⟨all the teachers *heaped* homework on us this week⟩ — see RAIN 2
2 to gradually form into a layer, pile, or mass ⟨snow *heaping* against the side of the house as the blizzard raged on⟩ — see COLLECT 2

3 to lay or throw on top of one another ⟨*heaped* the stones in a corner of the yard⟩ — see PILE

4 to put into (something) as much as can be held or contained ⟨*heaped* her plate with spaghetti⟩ — see FILL 1

hear *vb* **1** to come to an awareness ⟨I *heard* your little sister is home from the hospital⟩ — see DISCOVER 1

2 to pay attention especially through the act of hearing ⟨at least *hear* what I have to say before you start disagreeing⟩ — see LISTEN

hearing *n* range of hearing ⟨let's make sure she's out of *hearing* before I tell you what I got her for her birthday⟩ — see EARSHOT

hearken *vb* to pay attention especially through the act of hearing ⟨*hearken!* I hear the distant beat of the hooves of many horses⟩ — see LISTEN

heart *n* **1** the capacity for feeling for another's unhappiness or misfortune ⟨when her parents refused her request for a puppy, Jessica asked, "Have you no *heart*?"⟩

synonyms charity, commiseration, compassion, feeling, humanity, kindheartedness, kindliness, kindness, mercy, pity, softheartedness, sympathy

related words responsiveness, sensitivity; affection, love, regard; affinity, empathy, rapport; altruism, benevolence, benignity, generosity, goodwill, humanitarianism, philanthropy

near antonyms callousness, coldness, indifference, unconcern; cruelty, harshness; animosity, antipathy, dislike, hatred, hostility

antonyms hardheartedness, inhumanity, mercilessness

2 the body of knowledge that has been retained in one's mind or the use of it ⟨Dan can recite the entire Declaration of Independence by *heart*⟩

synonyms memory, rote

related words association, conning, memorization

3 a thing or place that is of greatest importance to an activity or interest ⟨the *heart* of the village economy was the outdoor market⟩ — see CENTER 1

4 strength of mind to carry on in spite of danger ⟨never lost *heart* while she was lost in the woods⟩ — see COURAGE

5 the central part or aspect of something under consideration ⟨the *heart* of the problem is the school's outmoded computer system⟩ — see CRUX

6 the seat of one's deepest thoughts and emotions ⟨deep down in her *heart*, she knew he was telling the truth⟩ — see CORE 1

heartache *n* deep sadness especially for the loss of someone or something loved ⟨the *heartache* she felt when she saw the effects of the war⟩ — see SORROW

heartbreak *n* deep sadness especially for the loss of someone or something loved ⟨I understand the *heartbreak* you must feel over your grandmother's death⟩ — see SORROW

heartbreaking *adj* **1** causing unhappiness ⟨a *heartbreaking* story of a family split up by war⟩ — see SAD 2

2 of a kind to cause great distress ⟨the *heartbreaking* state of Main Street now that most of the businesses have closed⟩ — see REGRETTABLE

3 deserving of one's pity ⟨a *heartbreaking* attempt to escape that ends in disaster⟩ — see PATHETIC 1

heartbroken *adj* **1** feeling unhappiness ⟨not as *heartbroken* over missing out on the trip to New York as I thought she would be⟩ — see SAD 1

2 expressing or suggesting mourning ⟨was utterly *heartbroken* when his pet frog died⟩ — see MOURNFUL 1

hearten *vb* to fill with courage or strength of purpose ⟨thinking we were hopelessly lost, we were *heartened* by the sight of a familiar farmhouse⟩ — see ENCOURAGE 1

heartening *adj* **1** having qualities which inspire hope ⟨a *heartening* visit to the hospital, where the patient was alert and sitting up⟩ — see HOPEFUL 1

2 making one feel good inside ⟨hearing how his students still appreciated him after all those years was *heartening* to the music teacher⟩ — see HEARTWARMING

3 pointing toward a happy outcome ⟨the accomplishments of the first day were a *heartening* start to our renovation of the house⟩ — see FAVORABLE 2

hearth *n* the place where one lives ⟨all were welcome, friends and strangers alike, to their *hearth*⟩ — see HOME 1

hearthstone *n* the place where one lives ⟨after years abroad, the eldest son returned to the family *hearthstone*, the old house in Philadelphia⟩ — see HOME 1

heartily *adv* in a cheerful or happy manner ⟨greets the class *heartily* every morning⟩ — see GAILY 1

heartiness *n* the condition of being sound in body ⟨Granddad's *heartiness* put everyone else to shame—he wouldn't even hear of stopping to rest⟩ — see HEALTH

heartless *adj* **1** having or showing a lack of sympathy or tender feelings ⟨a *heartless* boss who would fire people who missed work, even if they were sick as a dog⟩ — see HARD 1

2 having or showing the desire to inflict severe pain and suffering on others ⟨his *heartless* whipping of runaway slaves virtually to the point of death shocked even other slave owners⟩ — see CRUEL 1

heartlessness *n* the willful infliction of pain and suffering on others ⟨the *heartlessness* with which the secret police tortured prisoners was beyond belief⟩ — see CRUELTY

heartrending *adj* **1** causing unhappiness ⟨*heartrending* photos of victims of the famine⟩ — see SAD 2

2 hard to accept or bear especially emotionally ⟨a *heartrending* choice between saving his daughter or his son⟩ — see BITTER 2

3 of a kind to cause great distress ⟨*heartrending* memories of all the terrible crimes he'd committed and was sorry for now⟩ — see REGRETTABLE

4 deserving of one's pity ⟨the *heartrending* way the starving child held out his hands for food⟩ — see PATHETIC 1

heartsick *adj* feeling unhappiness ⟨felt *heartsick* over having to give up the family farm⟩ — see SAD 1

heartsickness *n* a state or spell of low spirits ⟨could not begin to describe the *heartsickness* he felt when he sold the family farm⟩ — see SADNESS

heartsore *adj* feeling unhappiness ⟨a grandmother feeling *heartsore* and despondent when all her family left after the holidays⟩ — see SAD 1

heartstrings *n pl* general emotional condition ⟨always said she didn't care much for cats, but now the little kitten was tugging at her *heartstrings*⟩ — see FEELING 2

heartwarming *adj* making one feel good inside ⟨Sarah appreciated the *heartwarming* welcome she received from her relatives in Israel⟩

synonyms cheering, comforting, encouraging, fulfilling, gladdening, gratifying, heartening, rewarding, satisfying *related words* affecting, inspiring, moving, poignant, stirring, touching; edifying, elevating, uplifting; sympathetic, tender; kind, kindly, loving, warm; exciting, exhilarating, rousing, stimulating, thrilling; pleasing, welcoming

near antonyms cheerless, depressing, disappointing, discouraging, disgruntling, disheartening, displeasing, dissatisfying, saddening; cold, unfeeling, unfriendly, unkind, unloving, unpleasant

antonyms depressing, discouraging, disheartening, dispiriting

hearty *adj* **1** characterized by unqualified enthusiasm ⟨Frank expressed *hearty* approval of his aunt's suggestion to rendezvous in Tokyo⟩

synonyms wholehearted

related words single-minded; ardent, avid, eager, enthusiastic, excited, exuberant, gung ho, impassioned, keen, raring, vehement, warm, zealous; alacritous, immediate, prompt, ready, willing, unhesitating; animated, energetic, lively, spirited, vigorous; absolute, bona fide, genuine, unaffected, undisguised, unequivocal, unrestrained

near antonyms apathetic, disinterested, indifferent, uninterested; lackadaisical, listless, perfunctory, spiritless, uneager, unenthusiastic, unexcited; equivocal, hesitant, qualified, tentative, uncertain; delayed, dilatory, doubtful, hedging, hesitating; forced, reluctant, resistant, unwilling

antonyms grudging, halfhearted, lukewarm, tepid

2 enjoying health and vigor ⟨you're looking really *hearty* after that month in the clear mountain air!⟩ — see HEALTHY 1

3 having or showing kindly feeling and sincere interest ⟨the mayor gave our club his *hearty* permission to repair the bandstand on the town square⟩ — see FRIENDLY 1

4 not showing weakness or uncertainty ⟨gave the reins a *hearty* tug but the horse wouldn't budge⟩ — see FIRM 1

heat *n* depth of feeling ⟨informed the doctor, with considerable *heat,* that she had been kept waiting for three hours⟩ — see ARDOR 1

heat *vb* to cause to have or give off heat to a moderate degree ⟨*heat* water for tea⟩ ⟨*heat* the oven to 350 degrees before you put the cake in⟩ — see WARM 1

heated *adj* **1** being in a state of increased activity or agitation ⟨a *heated* discussion about who should pay for the pizza⟩ — see FEVERISH 1

2 having or giving off heat to a moderate degree ⟨early settlers put *heated* bricks under the blankets to keep warm⟩ — see WARM 1

heathen *adj* not civilized ⟨old missionaries who mistakenly thought that they were going off to China to tame the *heathen* hordes⟩ — see SAVAGE 1

heathen *n* **1** a person who does not worship the God of the Bible ⟨a missionary sent to distant lands to convert the *heathens*⟩

synonyms gentile, idolater (*or* idolator), pagan

related words atheist, infidel, nonbeliever, non-Christian, unbeliever; polytheist, theist

near antonyms Christian, Jew, Muslim

2 an uncivilized person ⟨European colonizers, who considered the New World peoples to be *heathens,* forced them to conform to European ways⟩

synonyms barbarian, savage

related words Neanderthal, primitive

heathenish *adj* not civilized ⟨believing that going to church in bare feet was *heathenish,* the missionaries made the natives wear shoes⟩ — see SAVAGE 1

heave *vb* **1** to lift with effort ⟨I *heaved* my duffel bag into the bus's overhead compartment⟩

synonyms boost, heft, hoist, jack (up)

related words elevate, hike, raise, rear, up, uplift, upraise

near antonyms drop, lower; sink, submerge, submerse

2 to discharge the contents of the stomach through the mouth ⟨*heaved* as soon as he stepped off the roller coaster⟩ — see VOMIT

3 to move from a lower to a higher place or position ⟨*heaved* the bucket from the bottom of the well⟩ — see RAISE 1

4 to send through the air especially with a quick forward motion of the arm ⟨*heaved* the brick over the fence⟩ — see THROW

heaven *n* **1** a dwelling place of perfect bliss for the soul after death ⟨prayed that the souls of the deceased would go to *heaven*⟩

synonyms Elysium, kingdom come, paradise

related words empyrean; glory; otherworld

phrases on high

near antonyms inferno; limbo, purgatory; hades, netherworld, underworld

antonyms hell, perdition

2 a place or state of great happiness ⟨compared to the old school, this new one is *heaven*⟩ — see PARADISE 1

3 a state of overwhelming usually pleasurable emotion ⟨she was in *heaven* the day she learned she was one of the finalists for the science scholarship⟩ — see ECSTASY

4 *usually* **heavens** *pl* the expanse of air surrounding the earth ⟨the starry *heavens*⟩ ⟨the space shuttle gradually disappeared into the *heavens*⟩ — see SKY

heavenly *adj* **1** of the very best kind ⟨had a *heavenly* time at the dance⟩ — see EXCELLENT

2 of, relating to, or being God ⟨do not concern yourself with material things, but with things *heavenly,* the prophet admonished⟩ — see HOLY 3

3 of, relating to, or suggesting heaven ⟨*heavenly* hosts singing "Alleluia!"⟩ — see CELESTIAL

4 giving pleasure or contentment to the mind or senses ⟨the *heavenly* aroma of chocolate fills the shop⟩ — see PLEASANT

heavily *adv* to a great degree ⟨*heavily* spiced sausage⟩ — see VERY 1

heaviness *n* **1** the amount that something weighs ⟨the numbers on the back of each sample indicate the *heaviness* of the carpeting material⟩ — see WEIGHT 1

2 the state or quality of being heavy ⟨the *heaviness* of this backpack is due to the four bottles of water⟩ — see WEIGHTINESS 1

heavy *adj* **1** having great weight ⟨this trunk full of books is much too *heavy* for one person to lift⟩

synonyms hefty, massive, ponderous, weighty

related words burdensome, leaden, lumpish; bulky, elephantine, outsize; overweight, top-heavy; solid, substantial

near antonyms airy, ethereal, feathery, gossamer, gossamery; flimsy, fluffy, insubstantial

antonyms light, lightweight, weightless

2 causing weariness, restlessness, or lack of interest ⟨history doesn't have to be all dull *heavy* reading and memorizing dates⟩ — see BORING

3 containing much seasoning, fat, or sugar ⟨avoid *heavy* desserts like cheesecake and pecan pie⟩ — see RICH 2

4 covered over by clouds ⟨*heavy* skies threatening rain⟩ — see OVERCAST

5 difficult to endure ⟨ignoring common sense, she drank the parasite-infested pond water and paid a *heavy* penalty for it⟩ — see HARSH 1

6 extreme in degree, power, or effect ⟨*heavy* rains⟩ ⟨*heavy* debt⟩ — see INTENSE

7 having a matter of importance as its topic ⟨got into a *heavy* discussion about death and the afterlife⟩ — see SERIOUS 2

heavy *n* a mean, evil, or unprincipled person ⟨Mom had to play the *heavy* and threaten all kinds of dire punishments if I didn't shape up⟩ — see VILLAIN

heavy–handed *adj* **1** given to exacting standards of discipline and self-restraint ⟨the gym teacher is *heavy-handed* with the boys and much more lenient with the girls⟩ — see SEVERE 1

2 lacking in physical ease and grace in movement or in the use of the hands ⟨felt *heavy-handed* and awkward when she held the newborn infant⟩ — see CLUMSY 1

heavyset *adj* being compact and broad in build and often short in stature ⟨has the *heavyset* build of a weight lifter⟩ — see STOCKY

heckle *vb* to attack repeatedly with mean put-downs or insults ⟨Cinderella was constantly *heckled* by her stepsisters⟩ — see TEASE 2

heckler *n* a person who causes repeated emotional pain, distress, or annoyance to another ⟨avoided the *hecklers* who hung out on the street corner making threatening remarks to passersby⟩ — see TORMENTOR

hectic *adj* being in a state of increased activity or agitation ⟨exhausted from a *hectic* day at the office⟩ — see FEVERISH 1

hectically *adv* in a confused and reckless manner ⟨a moth kept banging *hectically* against the screen, seeking the light on the other side⟩ — see HELTER-SKELTER 1

hector *vb* to make timid or fearful by or as if by threats ⟨the children used to constantly *hector* the poor dog, and now he growls at everybody⟩ — see INTIMIDATE

hedge *n* a physical object that blocks the way ⟨the messenger was confronted with a *hedge* of spears held aloft by the castle guards⟩ — see BARRIER

hedge *vb* **1** to avoid giving a definite answer or position ⟨she kept *hedging* whenever he asked her to go to the dance with him⟩ — see EQUIVOCATE

2 to close or shut in by or as if by barriers ⟨the prison was *hedged* by a high stone wall⟩ — see ENCLOSE 1

heed *n* **1** a state of being aware ⟨took *heed* of the student's learning disability to arrive at reasonable expectations for him⟩ — see ATTENTION 2

2 strict attentiveness to what one is doing ⟨pay *heed* to what you're doing with that knife while you're talking⟩ — see CARE 1

heed *vb* **1** to take notice of and be guided by ⟨if Paul had *heeded* his brother's advice, he might not have gotten lost⟩

synonyms follow, listen (to), mind, note, observe, regard, watch

related words consider, contemplate, mull, ponder, weigh; comply (with), keep, obey, respect; hark (to), hear, hearken (to); mark, notice, see

near antonyms brush (off), dismiss, pooh-pooh, scorn, shrug off; defy, flout; slight, snub

antonyms disregard, ignore, tune out

2 to pay attention especially through the act of hearing ⟨that boy never *heeds* when I caution him about running with his shoelaces untied⟩ — see LISTEN

heedful *adj* having or showing a close attentiveness to avoiding danger or trouble ⟨*heedful* of snakes, we watched our footing while walking through the tall grass to the lake's edge⟩ — see CAREFUL 1

heedfulness *n* **1** a close attentiveness to avoiding danger ⟨despite their *heedfulness,* even good drivers can get into accidents⟩ — see CAUTION 1

2 strict attentiveness to what one is doing ⟨always exercises extreme *heedfulness* when she handles her grandmother's china⟩ — see CARE 1

heedless *adj* not paying or showing close attention especially for the purpose of avoiding trouble ⟨*heedless* drivers who back out of parking spaces without looking⟩ — see CARELESS 1

heedlessness *n* failure to take the care that a cautious person usually takes ⟨the dog's lack of protection against rabies was purely due to his owner's *heedlessness*⟩ — see NEGLIGENCE 1

heel *n* a person whose behavior is offensive to others ⟨felt like a *heel* when she found out that she'd blamed the wrong person⟩ — see JERK 1

heel *vb* to set or cause to be at an angle ⟨the strong gust *heeled* the sailboat almost to the point of capsizing, but we managed to right it⟩ — see LEAN 1

heft *n* the amount that something weighs ⟨some modern fabrics are nice and warm, but I prefer wool because it has more *heft*⟩ — see WEIGHT 1

heft *vb* **1** to lift with effort ⟨*hefted* his growing son onto his shoulders⟩ — see HEAVE 1

2 to move from a lower to a higher place or position ⟨*heft* your baggy gym shorts a little higher—you're showing us more than we care to see⟩ — see RAISE 1

heftiness *n* **1** the quality or state of being large in size ⟨a restaurant known for the *heftiness* of its portions⟩ — see LARGENESS

2 the state or quality of being heavy ⟨clerks no longer have to deal with the *heftiness* of paper files now that everything is filed on computers⟩ — see WEIGHTINESS 1

hefty *adj* **1** having great weight ⟨that's a pretty *hefty* book bag for a tiny person like you⟩ — see HEAVY 1

2 of a size greater than average of its kind ⟨received a *hefty* donation from the Business Association for holiday lights along Main Street⟩ — see LARGE

height *n* **1** the highest part or point ⟨many regard the painting of the Sistine Chapel as the *height* of Michelangelo's career⟩

synonyms acme, apex, climax, crown, culmination, head, high-water mark, meridian, peak, pinnacle, summit, tip-top, top, zenith

related words bloom, flood tide, flower, glory, heyday; high; cap, ceiling, crest, roof; crescendo, extremity, maximum, tip, vertex

near antonyms abyss, base, foot; minimum

antonyms bottom, nadir

2 the most extreme or advanced point ⟨the student's defiant use of a cell phone during class was regarded by the teacher as the *height* of insolence⟩

synonyms depth, extremity, limit

related words consummation, epitome, quintessence, ultimate

3 the distance of something or someone from bottom to top ⟨the average *height* of the players on the volleyball team is well over six feet⟩

synonyms altitude, elevation, stature
related words rise; highness, loftiness, tallness
4 an area of high ground ⟨Gulliver, standing on a *height* near the shore, saw an island suspended above the sea⟩
synonyms altitude(s), elevation, eminence, highland, hill, mound, prominence, rise, upland
related words alp, mount, mountain, peak; butte, mesa, plateau, table, tableland; cliff, crag, precipice, tor; ridge, sierra; dome, sugarloaf; foothill, hillock, knob, knoll; down
near antonyms dale, dell, dingle, glen, hollow, vale, valley; basin, bottom, bottomland, fen, flat, floodplain, plain, tidewater
antonyms lowland
5 the most intense or characteristic phase of something ⟨at the very *height* of the storm, someone knocked on the door⟩ — see THICK

heighten *vb* **1** to make markedly greater in measure or degree ⟨several controversial measures have *heightened* parental awareness of the impact of school policy decisions⟩ — see INTENSIFY
2 to move from a lower to a higher place or position ⟨*heightened* the hem on her skirt just a couple of inches⟩ — see RAISE 1

heightened *adj* being at a higher level than average ⟨there were *heightened* levels of lead in the drinking water⟩ — see HIGH 2

heinousness *n* the state or quality of being utterly evil ⟨the *heinousness* of the Holocaust was only fully realized after the war⟩ — see ENORMITY 1

heir *n* a person who has the right to inherit property ⟨upon his death, Mr. Parkworth's property was divided evenly among his *heirs*, four sons and three daughters⟩
synonyms inheritor, legatee
related words claimant; heir apparent, successor; heiress; assignee, beneficiary, grantee; descendant (*or* descendent), scion (*also* cion)

helical *adj* turning around an axis like the thread of a screw ⟨Sirius, the brightest star in the heavens, travels a *helical* path through space⟩ — see SPIRAL

hell *n* **1** the place of punishment for the wicked after death ⟨condemned to *hell* for their sins⟩
synonyms perdition
related words inferno; purgatory; hades, netherworld, underworld
near antonyms empyrean; glory
antonyms Elysium, heaven, kingdom come, paradise
2 a situation or state that causes great suffering and unhappiness ⟨picking cotton under the hot summer sun was *hell*⟩
synonyms agony, horror, misery, murder, nightmare, torment, torture
related words cross, ordeal, trial, tribulation; gall, thorn; bummer, downer, drag
near antonyms delight, diversion, entertainment, fun, pleasure, recreation; lark, picnic, riot
antonyms heaven, paradise
3 a place of uproar or confusion ⟨the burning city was a fiery *hell*⟩ — see MADHOUSE 2
4 a state in which everything is out of order ⟨all *hell* broke loose when the jury's verdict was announced⟩ — see CHAOS

hellion *n* an appealingly mischievous person ⟨the little *hellions*—my brother and his friends—were tearing through the house squirting their water pistols⟩ — see SCAMP 1

hello *n* an expression of goodwill upon meeting ⟨we said our *hellos* and got right down to business⟩
synonyms greeting, salutation, salute, welcome
related words amenities, civilities, pleasantries; regards, respects, wishes
antonyms adieu, bon voyage, farewell, Godspeed, good-bye (*or* good-by)

helm *n* the place of leadership or command ⟨with a blind person at the *helm*, the city has made a lot of improvements for the physically challenged⟩ — see HEAD 2

helmsman *n* the person (as an employer or supervisor) who tells people and especially workers what to do ⟨had a complaint and demanded to talk to the *helmsman*, not some underling⟩ — see BOSS

help *n* **1** an act or instance of helping ⟨Andrew didn't get any *help* with his homework⟩
synonyms aid, assist, assistance, backing, boost, lift, support
related words advancement, encouragement, facilitation, forwarding, furtherance, furthering, nurturance; benefaction, patronage, promotion, sponsorship; advice, care, counsel, guidance, mentoring; attendance, attention, service; beneficence, charity, favor, kindness, philanthropy; relief, succor
near antonyms constraint, frustration, inhibition, interference, obstruction, repression, restraint; deterrence, discouragement
antonyms hindrance
2 a thing that helps ⟨the computer is a great *help* for writing reports⟩
synonyms advantage, aid, benefit, boon
related words lift, pick-me-up; support, sustenance; blessing, godsend, windfall; recourse, resort, resource; asset
near antonyms constraint, inhibitor, liability, obstacle, obstruction, restraint, stranglehold
antonyms disadvantage, drawback, hindrance, impediment
3 a body of persons at work or available for work ⟨it's so hard to get good *help* these days⟩ — see FORCE 1

help *vb* **1** to provide (someone) with what is useful or necessary to achieve an end ⟨Mary Beth flew to Chicago to *help* her dad when he moved into an apartment⟩
synonyms abet, aid, assist, back, prop (up), support
related words advance, facilitate, forward, foster, further; champion, endorse (*also* indorse), patronize, promote, sponsor; attend, care (for), comfort, minister (to), succor; bolster, boost, buttress, reinforce; advise, counsel, guide, mentor, nurture; bail out, deliver, rescue, save; embolden, encourage, hearten; benefit, favor, profit, serve
phrases to stand one in good stead
near antonyms balk, bar, block, constrain, hamper, hold back, impede, inhibit, obstruct, restrain, strangle; baffle, foil, frustrate, interfere, oppose, sabotage, thwart; desert, disappoint, fail, let down; discourage, dishearten; repress, retard, stifle, straiten, stunt; damage, harm, hurt, injure
antonyms hinder
2 to make more bearable or less severe ⟨the new ointment didn't *help* Josh's sunburn one bit⟩
synonyms allay, alleviate, assuage, ease, mitigate, mollify, palliate, relieve, soothe
related words abate, lighten, moderate, soften, temper; cure, heal, remedy; amend, correct, emend, fix, mend, rectify, reform, repair; ameliorate, better, enhance, enrich, improve, meliorate, perfect, refine

near antonyms harm, hurt, impair, injure; heighten, intensify, sharpen
antonyms aggravate
3 to keep from happening by taking action in advance ⟨they couldn't *help* the way things turned out⟩ — see PREVENT

helper *n* a person who helps a more skilled person ⟨over the summer Chris worked as a carpenter's *helper*⟩
synonyms adjutant, aid, aide, apprentice, assistant, coadjutor, deputy, helpmate, helpmeet, mate, sidekick
related words attendant, handmaiden (*also* handmaid), maid, maidservant, scullion, servant; auxiliary, subordinate, underling; employee, hand, help, hireling, laborer, worker

helpful *adj* conferring benefits; promoting or contributing to personal or social well-being ⟨it would be *helpful* to have more than one thesaurus in the classroom⟩ — see BENEFICIAL

helpless *adj* **1** lacking protection from danger or resistance against attack ⟨after the storm we found a *helpless* baby bird that had fallen out of its nest⟩
synonyms defenseless, exposed, susceptible, undefended, unguarded, unprotected, unresistant, unshielded, vulnerable
related words indefensible, untenable; uncovered, unsafe, unsheltered; overcome, preyed (on *or* upon); disarmed, passive, resistless, unarmed; feeble, frail, weak; abandoned, marooned
phrases in the lurch
near antonyms defensible; covered, fortified, safe, secure, screened, sheltered; armed, armored; immune, impenetrable, impregnable, invincible, strong, unassailable, unbeatable, unconquerable
antonyms guarded, invulnerable, protected, resistant, shielded
2 unable to act or achieve one's purpose ⟨the baby birds had fallen out of their nest, and their parents were *helpless*⟩ — see POWERLESS

helpmate *n* **1** a person who helps a more skilled person ⟨after many years as the sculptor's *helpmate* in his studio, she took the step of becoming a sculptress in her own right⟩ — see HELPER
2 the female partner in a marriage ⟨the man and his *helpmate* of 50 years decided that it was high time they took a trip around the world together⟩ — see WIFE

helpmeet *n* **1** a person who helps a more skilled person ⟨the army surgeon requested a *helpmeet* who wouldn't faint at the sight of blood⟩ — see HELPER
2 the female partner in a marriage ⟨chose for his *helpmeet* a woman who could share his passion for rock hunting⟩ — see WIFE

helter–skelter *adv* **1** in a confused and reckless manner ⟨the sheep ran *helter-skelter* inside their pen when the coyote appeared in their midst⟩
synonyms amok (*or* amuck), berserk, frantically, frenziedly, harum-scarum, hectically, madly, pell-mell, wild, wildly
related words agitatedly, confusedly, crazily, desperately, feverishly, skittishly, uncontrollably; heedlessly, hotheadedly, recklessly, wantonly; chaotically, riotously, tumultuously, turbulently; aimlessly, haphazardly, hit-or-miss
near antonyms calmly, collectedly, composedly, coolly, imperturbably, peacefully, placidly, serenely, unconcernedly; meekly, mildly, passively, tamely; methodically, orderly, systematically

2 without definite aim, direction, rule, or method ⟨goods arranged *helter-skelter* on the shelves of the variety store⟩ — see HIT OR MISS

hem *vb* to close or shut in by or as if by barriers ⟨a village *hemmed* in on all sides by mountains⟩ — see ENCLOSE 1

hence *adv* **1** for this or that reason ⟨an endangered orchid species, *hence* illegal to pick⟩ — see THEREFORE
2 from this or that place ⟨urged the princess to flee *hence,* if she wished to escape the wicked queen's spell⟩ — see AWAY

henceforth *adv* from this point on ⟨*henceforth,* there will be no more prolonged coffee breaks⟩
synonyms henceforward, hereafter

henceforward *adv* from this point on ⟨we swore to tell the truth in court, and *henceforward* we are bound by our oath⟩ — see HENCEFORTH

henpeck *vb* to subject (someone) to constant scoldings and sharp reminders ⟨neighbors say she *henpecked* him into selling his golf clubs⟩ — see NAG

herald *n* one that announces or indicates the later arrival of another ⟨the American robin—the *herald* of spring in the North⟩ — see FORERUNNER 1

herbage *n* green leaves or plants ⟨added some ferns and other *herbage* to the flower arrangement⟩ — see GREENERY 1

herculean *adj* **1** requiring considerable physical or mental effort ⟨the *herculean* task of grading 60 student essays over one weekend⟩ — see HARD 2
2 unusually large ⟨a *herculean* banquet table that took eight men to lift it⟩ — see HUGE

herd *n* **1** a group of domestic animals assembled or herded together ⟨the great *herds* of cattle that cowboys once drove across the plains⟩
synonyms drove, flock
related words colony, covey, gaggle, pack, school, swarm
2 the body of the community as contrasted with the elite ⟨aspire to achieve something, to distinguish yourself from the *herd*⟩ — see MASS 1

herd *vb* to urge, push, or force onward ⟨the guards briskly *herded* us through the museum to keep the crowd moving⟩ — see DRIVE 1

herder *n* a tender of livestock ⟨the nomadic reindeer *herders* of Siberia live in reindeer-skin tents⟩
synonyms herdsman
related words buckaroo, cowboy, cowgirl, cowhand, cowherd, cowman, cowpoke, cowpuncher, gaucho, ranchero, vaquero; shepherd, sheepherder, shepherdess; goatherd; wrangler; drover

herdsman *n* a tender of livestock ⟨a lone *herdsman* stood with his sheep and his dog on the hillside⟩ — see HERDER

hereafter *adv* from this point on ⟨he is giving up all his worldly goods and *hereafter* will devote his life to the poor⟩ — see HENCEFORTH

hereafter *n* **1** time that is to come ⟨Gordon apologized, promising there would be no recurrences of his behavior in the *hereafter*⟩ — see FUTURE 1
2 unending existence after death ⟨hoped to be reunited with his dead wife in the *hereafter*⟩ — see ETERNITY 2

hereditary *adj* genetically passed or capable of being passed from parent to offspring ⟨eye and hair color are *hereditary*⟩
synonyms genetic (*also* genetical), heritable, inborn, inheritable, inherited
related words congenital, inbred, inherent, innate, native, natural

near antonyms acquired

heresy *n* departure from a generally accepted theory, opinion, or practice ⟨the *heresy* of asserting that Shakespeare was not a great writer⟩

synonyms dissent, dissidence, heterodoxy, nonconformity

related words error, fallacy, falsehood, misbelief, misconception, myth; apostasy, defection, schism, sectarianism, separatism; deviance, deviation, unconventionality; disagreement, discord, dissension

near antonyms agreement, conformation, conventionality

antonyms conformity, orthodoxy

heretic *n* a person who believes or teaches something opposed to accepted beliefs ⟨Galileo was condemned as a *heretic* for supporting Copernicus's thesis that the earth revolves around the sun and not vice versa⟩

synonyms dissenter, dissident, nonconformist

related words apostate, defector, renegade; schismatic, sectarian, separatist; disbeliever, infidel, unbeliever; bohemian, individualist

near antonyms believer

antonyms conformer, conformist

heretical *adj* deviating from commonly accepted beliefs or practices ⟨the belief that women should be allowed to have careers outside the home was once considered *heretical*⟩

synonyms dissentient, dissenting, dissident, heterodox, nonconformist, nonorthodox, unconventional, unorthodox

related words nontraditional; apostate, defecting, renegade; schismatic, sectarian, separatist

antonyms conforming, conformist, conventional, orthodox

heretofore *adv* up to this or that time ⟨having been *heretofore* unwilling to fly, he made an exception for the wedding⟩ — see HITHERTO

heritable *adj* genetically passed or capable of being passed from parent to offspring ⟨*heritable* characteristics like skin and eye and hair color⟩ — see HEREDITARY

heritage *n* something that is or may be inherited ⟨this farm is my *heritage* from my father, as it was for him from my grandfather⟩ — see INHERITANCE

hermit *n* a person who lives away from others ⟨St. Jerome spent two years searching for inner peace as a *hermit* in the desert⟩ — see RECLUSE

hero *n* a large sandwich on a long split roll ⟨shared a foot-long meatball *hero* with his friend⟩ — see SUBMARINE

heroic *adj* **1** feeling or displaying no fear by temperament ⟨honored the *heroic* nurses who served in the war⟩ — see BRAVE

2 large and impressive in size, grandeur, extent, or conception ⟨an opera production of *heroic* proportions⟩ — see GRAND 1

3 unusually large ⟨a *heroic* statue of Alexander the Great astride his horse⟩ — see HUGE

heroically *adv* in a manner befitting a person of the highest character and ideals ⟨he *heroically* offered to give his concert tickets to his sister because she had lost hers⟩ — see GREATLY 1

heroism *n* strength of mind to carry on in spite of danger ⟨the *heroism* of the firefighters who risked their lives to save the people in the burning building⟩ — see COURAGE

hesitance *n* **1** a lack of willingness or desire to do or accept something ⟨it's with a certain amount of *hesitance*

that I'm letting you go to the movies, since you have a lot of homework⟩ — see RELUCTANCE

2 the act or an instance of pausing because of uncertainty about the right course of action ⟨she mistook my *hesitance* to mean I didn't like her poem, but I was trying to come up with appropriate words of praise⟩ — see HESITATION

hesitancy *n* **1** a lack of willingness or desire to do or accept something ⟨without any *hesitancy*, I recommend Sara as someone you can depend on⟩ — see RELUCTANCE

2 the act or an instance of pausing because of uncertainty about the right course of action ⟨his *hesitancy* in pulling over into the next lane while he had a chance resulted in him missing his turn⟩ — see HESITATION

hesitant *adj* having doubts about the wisdom of doing something ⟨Ivan was *hesitant* about lending CDs to his friends after he'd lost several of them that way⟩

synonyms afraid, disinclined, dubious, indisposed, loath (*or* loth), reluctant

related words uneager, unenthusiastic; averse, unwilling; doubtful, faltering, irresolute, questioning, uncertain, undecided, unsure, vacillating, wobbly; fainthearted, shy, timid

near antonyms eager, enthusiastic, glad, happy, keen; ready, willing; certain, decided, resolute, sure, unquestioning

antonyms disposed, inclined

hesitate *vb* to show uncertainty about the right course of action ⟨Keri didn't *hesitate* before answering the question⟩

synonyms falter, hang back, shilly-shally, stagger, teeter, vacillate, waver, wobble

related words haw, hem; dally, dawdle, delay, linger, procrastinate, pause, wait; back down, chicken (out); consider, debate, deliberate, ponder, weigh; oscillate; equivocate, hedge, pussyfoot

near antonyms budge, stir; advance, continue

antonyms dive (in), plunge (in)

hesitation *n* the act or an instance of pausing because of uncertainty about the right course of action ⟨one moment's *hesitation* on my part, and the elusive butterfly was lost to me forever⟩

synonyms faltering, hesitance, hesitancy, indecision, irresolution, shilly-shallying, vacillation, wavering, wobbling

related words delay, hawing, procrastination, waiting; consideration, debate, deliberation, doubt, incertitude, indetermination, uncertainty; avoidance, equivocation; aversion, disinclination, indisposition, reluctance, unwillingness; faintheartedness, shyness, timidness

near antonyms certainty, certitude, confidence, decisiveness, determination, firmness, resoluteness, resolution, sureness; alacrity, eagerness, readiness

heterodox *adj* deviating from commonly accepted beliefs or practices ⟨a Christian clergyman with a very *heterodox* opinion on the divinity of Jesus⟩ — see HERETICAL

heterodoxy *n* departure from a generally accepted theory, opinion, or practice ⟨Copernicus's theory that the earth revolved the sun was *heterodoxy* at a time when the earth was thought to be the center of the universe⟩ — see HERESY

heterogeneous *adj* consisting of many things of different sorts ⟨the seating in the hall was a *heterogeneous* collection of old school desk chairs, wood or metal folding chairs, and even a few plush theater seats⟩ — see MISCELLANEOUS

het up *adj* feeling or showing uncomfortable feelings of uncertainty ⟨it won't do you any good to get all *het up* before the tryouts and lose sleep⟩ — see NERVOUS 1

hew *vb* **1** to bring down by cutting ⟨*hewed* trees on their land to build their log cabin⟩ — see FELL 2

2 to hold to something firmly as if by adhesion ⟨*hewed* to the original plan rather than changing everything⟩ — see STICK 1

hew (to) *vb* to give steadfast support to ⟨no longer was able to *hew to* the beliefs of his political party and so he switched parties⟩ — see ADHERE

hex *n* **1** a woman believed to have often harmful supernatural powers ⟨people who used to believe that misfortune was caused by evil *hexes* and mischievous sprites⟩ — see WITCH 1

2 something that brings bad luck ⟨the wizard put a *hex* on the evil gnome that turned him to stone⟩ — see JINX

hex *vb* to cast a spell on ⟨I think our plans have been *hexed* from the start—everything is going wrong⟩ — see BEWITCH 1

heyday *n* a state or time of great activity, thriving, or achievement ⟨in its *heyday,* the circus was anticipated for weeks in advance of its arrival in town⟩ — see BLOOM 1

hiatus *n* a break in continuity ⟨a three-year *hiatus* before the fifth book in the series appeared⟩ — see GAP 2

hick *n* an awkward or simple person especially from a small town or the country ⟨city dwellers who looked down on their cousins from northern Maine as *hicks*⟩

synonyms bumpkin, clodhopper, countryman, hillbilly, provincial, rustic, yokel

related words boor, clod, gawk, lout, oaf; greenhorn, tenderfoot; peasant, peon; mountaineer

near antonyms slicker, smoothy (*or* smoothie); suburbanite, urbanite

antonyms cosmopolitan, sophisticate

hide *n* **1** the outer covering of an animal removed for its commercial value ⟨seal *hides* are used by Eskimos to make footwear, boats, shelters, bags, and clothing⟩

synonyms fur, leather, pelt, skin

related words badger, beaver, chamois, chinchilla, ermine, fisher, fox, mink, muskrat, otter, Persian lamb, rabbit, raccoon (*also* racoon), sable, seal, silver fox; bearskin, buckskin, calfskin, coonskin, cowhide, deerskin, doeskin, goatskin, horsehide, kidskin, lambskin, pigskin, rawhide, sealskin, sharkskin, sheepskin, snakeskin; fleece, mouton; alligator; cordovan, morocco, patent leather, suede

2 the hairless natural covering of an animal prepared for use ⟨boots made of shiny alligator *hide*⟩ — see LEATHER 1

¹**hide** *vb* **1** to put into a hiding place ⟨the thief *hid* the stolen jewelry under the floorboards⟩

synonyms bury, cache, conceal, ensconce, secrete

related words hoard, squirrel (away), stash; entomb, inter

near antonyms bare, expose, reveal, show, uncover, unmask, unveil, unwrap; flaunt, parade, show off; disinter, unearth

antonyms display, exhibit

2 to keep secret or shut off from view ⟨he tried to *hide* his criminal past⟩ ⟨she *hid* the cat's litter box behind a screen⟩

synonyms blanket, blot out, cloak, conceal, cover, curtain, enshroud, mask, obscure, occult, screen, shroud, veil

related words camouflage, cover (up), disguise, smother; gild, gloss (over), varnish, whitewash; be-

cloud, bedim, befog, cloud, darken, eclipse, overcast, overshadow, shade

near antonyms bring out, present; clarify, illuminate; advertise, air, broadcast, proclaim, publicize

antonyms bare, disclose, display, divulge, expose, reveal, show, uncloak, uncover, unmask, unveil

3 to strike repeatedly with something long and thin or flexible ⟨threatened to *hide* the boys with his cane if he ever found them on his property again⟩ — see WHIP 1

²**hide** *vb* to strike repeatedly ⟨the big boys that said they would beat him up were too chicken to *hide* anyone their own size⟩ — see BEAT 1

hideaway *n* a place where a person goes to hide ⟨he has a little *hideaway* in the country where he goes when he wants to write⟩ — see HIDEOUT

hideous *adj* **1** causing intense displeasure, disgust, or resentment ⟨the *hideous* way in which she treated her maid after she discovered her ring was missing⟩ — see OFFENSIVE 1

2 extremely disturbing or repellent ⟨a *hideous* crime that could not be fully described in the newspapers⟩ — see HORRIBLE 1

3 unpleasant to look at ⟨wearing a *hideous* Halloween mask that made us all jump with fright⟩ — see UGLY 1

hideousness *n* the quality of inspiring intense dread or dismay ⟨the *hideousness* of the two-headed giant made all who saw him faint from fear⟩ — see HORROR 1

hideout *n* a place where a person goes to hide ⟨they found the stolen jewels under the floorboards in the thief's *hideout,* a cabin deep in the woods⟩

synonyms concealment, covert, den, hideaway, lair, nest

related words blind, cover, nook, recess; hangout, harbor, haunt, haven, refuge, retreat, shelter

hiding *n* the placing of something out of sight ⟨fearing that soon the enemy would be upon them, the museum director oversaw the *hiding* of the most valuable works of art⟩ — see CONCEALMENT 1

higgledy-piggledy *adj* lacking in order, neatness, and often cleanliness ⟨the quilt was a *higgledy-piggledy* patchwork of odd-shaped fabric scraps, each of which held a fond memory⟩ — see MESSY

high *adj* **1** extending to a great distance upward ⟨Mt. Everest is the *highest* mountain in the world⟩

synonyms lofty, tall, towering

related words dominant, dominating, eminent, prominent; elevated, lifted, raised, uplifted, upswept; highrise, statuesque

near antonyms flat, stubby, stumpy

antonyms low, low-lying, short, squat

2 being at a higher level than average ⟨gasoline prices are *high* right now⟩ ⟨a *high* fever⟩ ⟨people with *high* incomes⟩

synonyms advanced, elevated, escalated, heightened, increased, jacked (up), raised, up

related words extreme, full, maximized, maximum, peaked, sky-high, utmost; inflated, over, overfilled, overflowing, overfull, overlarge, overloaded, oversize (*or* oversized)

near antonyms decreased, depressed, dropped, receded, under

antonyms down, low

3 located at a greater height than average or usual ⟨an eagle's nest *high* on the cliff⟩ ⟨an old house with *high* ceilings⟩

synonyms airy, elevated

related words aerial, ascendant, ascending, soaring; overhead, overlooking, raised, upheld, uplifted, upraised; topmost, upmost, upper, uppermost, upward
near antonyms depressed, descendant (*or* descendent), descending, down, dropped, fallen, grounded, lowered, sunken; lowermost, nethermost, undermost; abreast, even, level
antonyms low, low-lying
4 being far along in development ⟨diagnosing illness using *high* technology⟩ — see ADVANCED 1
5 being under the influence of alcohol ⟨not only has he never been *high,* he has never even tasted alcohol⟩ — see DRUNK
6 commanding a large price ⟨the tickets weren't cheap—you don't even want to know how *high* they were⟩ — see COSTLY
7 having, characterized by, or arising from a dignified and generous nature ⟨she had the *highest* intentions, but her "help" turned out to be a disaster⟩ — see NOBLE 2
8 highest in rank or authority ⟨*high* government officials⟩ ⟨lord *high* executioner⟩ — see HEAD
high *n* the expanse of air surrounding the earth ⟨V formations of honking geese on *high* mean winter will soon be here⟩ — see SKY
high *adv* in a luxurious manner ⟨after he won the lottery Philip lived *high* until all the money was gone⟩
synonyms expensively, extravagantly, grandly, lavishly, luxuriously, opulently, richly, sumptuously
related words imposingly, impressively, magnificently, splendidly; grandiosely, ostentatiously, pretentiously; affluently, comfortably, fine; immoderately, indulgently, intemperately, prodigally, wantonly, wastefully
near antonyms unassumingly, unpretentiously; cheaply, economically, frugally, inexpensively, meagerly, poorly, skimpily, sparely, sparingly, thriftily; conservatively, moderately, prudently, reasonably, restrainedly, sensibly, temperately
antonyms austerely, humbly, modestly, plainly, simply
highborn *adj* of high birth, rank, or station ⟨because his mother was not *highborn,* the prince could never inherit the throne⟩ — see NOBLE 1
highbrow *adj* much given to learning and thinking ⟨finally, a TV series that appeals to a *highbrow* audience⟩ — see INTELLECTUAL 1
higher *adj* being far along in development ⟨an institute of *higher* learning⟩ ⟨*higher* primates, such as the apes⟩ — see ADVANCED 1
highest *adj* **1** being at a point or level higher than all others ⟨the *highest* grade⟩ ⟨the *highest* flag on the pole⟩ — see TOP 1
2 coming before all others in importance ⟨turned to the *highest* authority for answers⟩ ⟨the *highest* official in the land⟩ — see FOREMOST 1
highfalutin *adj* **1** full of fine words and fancy expressions ⟨*highfalutin* speeches about the noble king and his glorious realm on the tenth anniversary of his reign⟩ — see FLOWERY 1
2 having a feeling of superiority that shows itself in an overbearing attitude ⟨her *highfalutin* relatives from New York made the snide remark that her little house "has that lived-in look"⟩ — see ARROGANT
3 having or displaying feelings of scorn for what is regarded as beneath oneself ⟨refused to be intimidated by the *highfalutin* manner of the sales staff in the fashionable boutique⟩ — see PROUD 1
4 self-consciously trying to present an appearance of grandeur or importance ⟨"fine Southern cuisine"

sounds a bit *highfalutin* for a barbecue shack⟩ — see PRETENTIOUS 1
high–flown *adj* **1** full of fine words and fancy expressions ⟨gave a *high-flown* reply instead of a simple "yes" or "no" answer⟩ — see FLOWERY 1
2 very dignified in form, tone, or style ⟨*high-flown* speeches about the nobleness of their cause⟩ — see ELEVATED 2
high–handed *adj* **1** having a feeling of superiority that shows itself in an overbearing attitude ⟨the *high-handed* members of the visiting team made it clear they thought our hockey players didn't have a chance⟩ — see ARROGANT
2 having or showing a tendency to force one's will on others without any regard to fairness or necessity ⟨the country club tends to be rather *high-handed* about who they let in and who they don't let in⟩ — see ARBITRARY 1
high–hat *adj* having a feeling of superiority that shows itself in an overbearing attitude ⟨several *high-hat* society types arrived after we did, but they got seated first⟩ — see ARROGANT
high–hat *vb* to show contempt for ⟨*high-hatted* by his former friends when the family lost all of its money⟩ — see SCORN 1
high jinks *n pl* wildly playful or mischievous behavior ⟨was finally suspended for his *high jinks* with the drinking fountain after it squirted the principal in the chest⟩ — see HORSEPLAY
highland *n* an area of high ground ⟨there are permanent glaciers in the cool, humid *highlands* of the Pacific Northwest⟩ — see HEIGHT 4
highlight *vb* to indicate the importance of by giving prominent display ⟨according to the TV schedule, this week's "Astronomy Today" *highlights* the accomplishments of Maria Mitchell⟩ — see EMPHASIZE
highly *adv* to a great degree ⟨though she didn't win, she was *highly* pleased to be selected as first runner-up⟩ — see VERY 1
high–minded *adj* having, characterized by, or arising from a dignified and generous nature ⟨*high-minded* efforts to change the lives of people who are less fortunate⟩ — see NOBLE 2
high–mindedly *adv* in a manner befitting a person of the highest character and ideals ⟨*high-mindedly* gave his colleagues all the credit for the successful completion of the project⟩ — see GREATLY 1
high noon *n* the middle of the day ⟨the ceremony began at *high noon* with a 21-gun salute⟩ — see NOON
high–pitched *adj* having a high musical pitch or range ⟨the *high-pitched* sound of a siren⟩ — see SHRILL
high–pressure *adj* having or showing a bold forcefulness in the pursuit of a goal ⟨a *high-pressure* salesman who wouldn't take "no" for an answer⟩ ⟨*high-pressure* advertising⟩ — see AGGRESSIVE 1
highroad *n* a passage cleared for public vehicular travel ⟨heard tales of outlaws who ambushed coaches traveling the *highroads*⟩ — see WAY 1
high–sounding *adj* full of fine words and fancy expressions ⟨*high-sounding* speeches full of promises that the candidates would never keep⟩ — see FLOWERY 1
high–spirited *adj* **1** joyously unrestrained ⟨a *high-spirited* crowd loudly cheering the team on⟩ — see EXUBERANT
2 marked by a lively display of strong feeling ⟨the band struck up a *high-spirited* march as the President's cavalcade approached⟩ — see SPIRITED 1

high–spiritedly *adv* in a quick and spirited manner ⟨the girls *high-spiritedly* donned clown costumes in preparation for the party they were giving at the Children's Hospital⟩ — see GAILY 2

high–strung *adj* easily excited by nature ⟨a dog that tends to be *high-strung* is not the best pet for young children⟩ — see EXCITABLE

high–water mark *n* the highest part or point ⟨the *high-water mark* of his acting career seems to have been when he played Tiny Tim⟩ — see HEIGHT 1

highway *n* a passage cleared for public vehicular travel ⟨the four-lane *highway* narrows to two lanes once you leave the city⟩ — see WAY 1

hijack *also* **highjack** *vb* to take control of (a vehicle) by force ⟨tried to *hijack* the plane with a toy gun⟩ — see COMMANDEER 1

hike *vb* to move from a lower to a higher place or position ⟨*hiked* his dad's trousers up above his waist⟩ — see RAISE 1

hilarious *adj* causing or intended to cause laughter ⟨*hilarious* cartoons that the whole family can enjoy⟩ ⟨the clown's *hilarious* antics⟩ — see FUNNY 1

hilariousness *n* the amusing quality or element in something ⟨the *hilariousness* of the situation only struck us later, and we had a good laugh⟩ — see HUMOR 1

hilarity *n* a mood characterized by high spirits and amusement and often accompanied by laughter ⟨*hilarity* is the last thing you expect to find at a funeral⟩ — see MIRTH

hill *n* **1** a quantity of things thrown or stacked on one another ⟨the ants made little *hills* of dirt⟩ — see ¹PILE 1
2 an area of high ground ⟨a town nestled in a valley surrounded by green *hills*⟩ — see HEIGHT 4

hill *vb* to form into a pile or ridge of earth ⟨*hilled* peat moss around the rosebushes to protect them from the freeze⟩ — see MOUND 1

hillbilly *n* an awkward or simple person especially from a small town or the country ⟨in the skit, he was a shy *hillbilly* in overalls in love with a city girl⟩ — see HICK

hind *adj* being at or in the part of something opposite the front part ⟨the frog's long *hind* legs⟩ ⟨the hawk's reddish *hind* feathers⟩ — see BACK

hinder *vb* to create difficulty for the work or activity of ⟨was not *hindered* by a lack of money because she could use what she had on hand⟩ — see HAMPER

hindmost *adj* **1** being at or in the part of something opposite the front part ⟨the dance teacher had to keep reminding us to kick our *hindmost* foot when we reversed direction⟩ — see BACK
2 following all others of the same kind in order or time ⟨the *hindmost* wagon in the caravan had the roughest ride because of the deep ruts and heavy dust created by the others⟩ — see LAST

hindrance *n* **1** something that makes movement or progress more difficult ⟨made a survey of all the *hindrances* to wheelchair access, such as curbs and stairs⟩ — see ENCUMBRANCE
2 something that stands in the way of one's progress or achievement ⟨would like to grow veggies, but lack of sunny yard space has been a *hindrance*⟩ — see OBSTACLE 1

hinge *vb* to be determined by, based on, or subject (to) ⟨my going *hinges* on whether or not I have a lot of homework⟩ — see DEPEND 1

hint *n* **1** a slight or indirect pointing to something (as a solution or explanation) ⟨can't you give me some *hint* as to where you're taking me?⟩
synonyms clue, cue, indication, inkling, intimation, lead, suggestion
related words breath, flicker, glimmer, glimpse, mention, scent, whiff, wind; hunch, idea, inspiration, notion; allusion, implication, inference, innuendo, insinuation; evidence, mark, overtone, pointer, sign, signal, telltale, token; assistance, nod, prompt, tip, tip-off, wink; feeling, foreboding, intuition, premonition, presentiment, suspicion; augury, foreshadower, foretaste, omen, portent, prefigurement, symptom
near antonyms answer, solution
2 a piece of advice or useful information especially from an expert ⟨some helpful *hints* for surviving middle school⟩ — see ¹TIP 1
3 a very small amount ⟨I detect just a *hint* of mint in the sauce⟩ — see PARTICLE 1

hint *vb* to convey an idea indirectly ⟨Cecilia kept *hinting* that she wanted an invitation to Patty's party⟩
synonyms allude, imply, indicate, infer, insinuate, intimate, suggest
related words advert, mention, point, refer, signal, signify; smack (of), smell (of)
near antonyms announce, declare, proclaim; elucidate, explain, spell out

hinterland *n* a rural region that forms the edge of the settled or developed part of a country ⟨the colonies hugged the coastline, while the *hinterland* remained largely unexplored⟩ — see FRONTIER 2

hip *adj* having inside information ⟨he wasn't *hip* to what the other boys were planning⟩ — see WISE 2

hire *n* **1** the state of being provided with a paying job ⟨college graduates seeking *hire* by big corporations⟩
synonyms employ, employment, engagement
related words appointment, assignment, conscription, enlistment, recruitment; incumbency, tenure; occupation, place, position, post, situation, work
near antonyms boot, discharge, dismissal, firing, removal, sack; demotion, suspension; furlough, layoff, leave, liberty, retirement
antonyms joblessness, unemployment
2 the money paid regularly to a person for labor or services ⟨used to mow lawns for *hire*⟩ — see WAGE

hire *vb* **1** to take or get the temporary use of (something) for a set sum ⟨the Young's *hired* a limousine for their daughter's wedding⟩
synonyms charter, engage, lease, rent
related words sublease, sublet; check out; arrange (for), bespeak, book, contract (for), order, reserve, sign up (for)
2 to provide with a paying job ⟨the farm *hires* teenagers to pick blueberries in the summer⟩ — see EMPLOY 1

hireling *n* one who works for another for wages or a salary ⟨demanded to speak to the store's owner and not one of his *hirelings*⟩ — see EMPLOYEE

hirsute *adj* covered with or as if with hair ⟨wore a *hirsute* mask and said he was a werewolf⟩ — see HAIRY 1

hiss *n* **1** a sound similar to the speech sound \s\ stretched out ⟨the *hiss* of air escaping from a balloon⟩
synonyms fizz, sizzle, swish, whish, whiz (*or* whizz)
related words wheeze, whistle, whoosh, zip; sibilant
2 a vocal sound made to express scorn or disapproval ⟨there were *hisses* and boos from the fans whenever the umpire called a foul⟩ — see CATCALL

hiss *vb* to make a sound like that of stretching out the speech sound \s\ ⟨the frightened kitten *hissed* at us when we tried to pick it up⟩
synonyms fizz, sizzle, swish, whish, whiz (*or* whizz)

related words wheeze, whistle, whoosh, zip; bubble, effervesce; buzz, drone, hum

historian *n* a student or writer of history ⟨*historians* are still trying to sort out fact from fiction in the story of Kateri Tekakwitha, the Lily of the Mohawks⟩
synonyms annalist, chronicler
related words autobiographer, biographer; archivist, chronologist, genealogist

historical *adj* restricted to or based on fact ⟨a *historical* novel that tells the story of Hannibal's crossing of the Alps through the eyes of a young boy⟩ — see FACTUAL 1

history *n* **1** an account of important events in the order in which they happened ⟨a *history* of the American civil rights movement during the 1960s⟩
synonyms annals, chronicle, record
related words autobiography, diary, journal, memoir, reminiscence(s); biography, life; epic, legend, narrative, saga, story, tale; archives, documentation, log, register, report; chronology, genealogy
2 a relating of events usually in the order in which they happened ⟨we heard the whole *history* of her illness and every last detail⟩ — see ACCOUNT 1
3 the events or experience of former times ⟨*history* has many lessons to teach us, if only we would listen⟩ — see PAST

histrionic *adj* **1** given to or marked by attention-getting behavior suggestive of stage acting ⟨a penchant for *histrionic* temper fits with lots of throwing of dishes and door slamming⟩ — see THEATRICAL 1
2 having the general quality or effect of a stage performance ⟨we never tired of his *histrionic* reenactment of how he found a chest of jewels⟩ — see DRAMATIC 1

hit *n* **1** a person or thing that is successful ⟨the new babysitter turned out to be a great *hit* with the kids⟩
synonyms blockbuster, megahit, smash, success, winner
related words corker, crackerjack, dandy, jim-dandy, pip, prizewinner; gem, jewel, treasure; marvel, phenomenon, sensation, wonder; coup, triumph, victory
near antonyms disappointment, fizzle, lemon, loser
antonyms bummer, bust, catastrophe, debacle (*also* débâcle), dud, failure, fiasco, flop, turkey, washout
2 a hard strike with a part of the body or an instrument ⟨the quarterback can't take too many more *hits* like that and escape permanent injury⟩ — see ¹BLOW

hit *vb* **1** to deliver a blow to (someone or something) usually in a strong vigorous manner ⟨a good carpenter *hits* a nail just two or three times to drive it in⟩
synonyms bang, bash, bat, belt, bludgeon, bop, bust, clap, clobber, clout, crack, hammer, knock, paste, pound, punch, rap, slam, slap, slog, slug, smack, smite, sock, strike, swat, swipe, thump, thwack, wallop, whack, whale, zap
related words batter, beat, buffet, bung, chop, drub, lace, lambaste (*or* lambast), lick, mangle, maul, pelt, pepper, pummel, rough; bunt, flick, stroke, tap; bump, butt, jab, jostle, kick, knee, poke, prod, push, shove, stamp; bowl (over), knock (down); cane, club, cudgel, flail, flog, lash, slash, spear, stab, switch, thrash, whip; brain
2 to come into usually forceful contact with something ⟨when she fell on the ice, she *hit* hard and badly bruised her elbow⟩
synonyms bang, bash, bump, collide, crash, impact, impinge, knock, ram, slam, smash, strike, swipe, thud
related words bounce, carom, glance, rebound, ricochet, skim, skip; contact, land, touch; brush, graze,

kiss, nudge, scrape, shave, sweep; bulldoze, jostle, muscle, press, push
near antonyms miss, skirt
3 to obtain (as a goal) through effort ⟨if a musical group or artist sells a million CDs, we say they *hit* "the big time"⟩ — see ACHIEVE 1

hit (on *or* upon) *vb* to come upon after searching, study, or effort ⟨the doctor finally *hit on* what was wrong with Aunt Phoebe⟩ — see FIND 1

hit (upon) *vb* to come upon unexpectedly or by chance ⟨Sir Isaac Newton is sometimes said to have *hit upon* his understanding of gravity when he saw an apple fall out of a tree⟩ — see HAPPEN (ON *or* UPON)

hitch *n* a fixed period of time during which a person holds a job or position ⟨signed on for a three-year *hitch* in the army⟩ — see TERM 1

hitch *vb* **1** to move or cause to move with a sharp quick motion ⟨kept *hitching* up his pants because they were too big in the waist⟩ — see JERK 1
2 to put or bring together so as to form a new and longer whole ⟨simply *hitching* rhyming lines together doesn't necessarily make a poem⟩ — see CONNECT 1
3 to put securely in place or in a desired position ⟨*hitched* the trailer to the back of the car⟩ — see FASTEN 2
4 to travel by securing free rides ⟨her brother *hitched* across the country after he graduated⟩ — see HITCHHIKE

hitcher *n* one who hitchhikes ⟨never stops for *hitchers* on interstates, where hitchhiking is illegal⟩ — see HITCHHIKER

hitchhike *vb* to travel by securing free rides ⟨Andrew *hitchhiked* from Baltimore to attend his sister's wedding in New Jersey⟩
synonyms hitch, thumb
related words bum; stow away; hijack (*also* highjack)

hitchhiker *n* one who hitchhikes ⟨on the highway out of town we picked up a *hitchhiker* who was trying to get to his sister's wedding⟩
synonyms hitcher
related words stowaway; hijacker

hither *adj* being the less far of two ⟨a boat was tied up on the *hither* bank⟩ — see NEAR 1

hitherto *adv* up to this or that time ⟨at the talent show Kyle revealed his *hitherto* unknown gift for doing impressions⟩
synonyms heretofore, theretofore, thus far, yet
related words before, formerly, previously
near antonyms afterward (*or* afterwards), later, subsequently; hereupon, thereupon
antonyms henceforth, henceforward, hereafter, thenceforth, thenceforward (*also* thenceforwards), thereafter

hit–or–miss *adj* lacking a definite plan, purpose, or pattern ⟨your *hit-or-miss* schedule for taking your medication is going to land you in the hospital again⟩ — see RANDOM

hit or miss *adv* without definite aim, direction, rule, or method ⟨Angelo was learning Spanish *hit or miss,* mostly just by hearing his friends speak it⟩
synonyms aimlessly, anyhow, anyway, anywise, desultorily, erratically, haphazard, haphazardly, helter-skelter, irregularly, randomly
related words capriciously, carelessly, casually, indiscriminately, informally, offhand, offhandedly, promiscuously, whimsically; accidentally, fortuitously, inadvertently, unconsciously, unintentionally, unwittingly; disconnectedly, disjointedly, fitfully, intermit-

tently, spottily, unpredictably; higgledy-piggledy, topsy-turvy

phrases at random

near antonyms carefully, formally, meticulously, orderly, punctiliously; deliberately, intentionally, purposefully, purposely

antonyms methodically, systematically

hoagie *n* a large sandwich on a long split roll ⟨had a steak-and-cheese *hoagie* for the first time in Philadelphia⟩ — see SUBMARINE

hoar *adj* dating or surviving from the distant past ⟨the *hoar* and crumbling stones of ruined temples⟩ — see ANCIENT 1

hoar *n* a covering of tiny ice crystals on a cold surface ⟨the *hoar*-covered meadow gleamed in the early-morning sun⟩ — see FROST

hoard *n* 1 a supply stored up and often hidden away ⟨Dad was upset when Mom put his entire *hoard* of empty yogurt containers in the recycling bin⟩

synonyms cache, stash, stockpile, store

related words coffers, deposit, funds, nest egg, savings, sinking fund, treasure; inventory, reserve, reservoir, stock; provisions, resources; accumulation, collection; repertory

2 a collection of things kept available for future use or need ⟨couldn't find one pencil with an eraser in her entire *hoard* of pencil stubs⟩ — see STORE 1

hoard *vb* to put (something of future use or value) in a safe or secret place ⟨Dad's been *hoarding* empty yogurt containers all winter, with the intention of using them to start seedlings in the spring⟩

synonyms cache, lay away, lay up, put by, salt away, squirrel (away), stash, stockpile, store, stow

related words accumulate, acquire, amass, assemble, collect, concentrate, garner, gather, round up, scrape (together); heap, pile, stack; conserve, husband, preserve; bank, deposit, hold, keep, reserve, retain, save, stock, withhold; conceal, ensconce, secrete

phrases set aside

near antonyms discard, dump, throw away, throw out; consume, squander, use up, waste; hand over, relinquish, surrender; blow, dissipate, fritter (away), lavish, misspend, run through, spend; deplete, exhaust, expend; dispel, disperse, dissipate, scatter

hoarfrost *n* a covering of tiny ice crystals on a cold surface ⟨the *hoarfrost* formed a delicate swirly pattern on the window⟩ — see FROST

hoarse *adj* harsh and dry in sound ⟨the dying man spoke in a *hoarse* whisper⟩

synonyms coarse, croaking, grating, gravel, gravelly, gruff, husky, rasping, raspy, scratchy, throaty

related words guttural; abrasive, cacophonous, discordant, grinding, jarring, rough, scraping, scratching; cawing, raucous, squawking, strident; choked, cracked, strained, strangled

near antonyms gentle, gliding, golden, liquid, mellifluous, mellow, sweet, tender; satiny, silken, smooth, soft, velvety

hoary *adj* dating or surviving from the distant past ⟨*hoary* oak trees with dripping moss and gnarled limbs, blocking out the sun⟩ — see ANCIENT 1

hoax *n* an imitation that is passed off as genuine ⟨the skeleton of the purported ancient hominid turned out to be a *hoax*⟩ — see FAKE 1

hoax *vb* to cause to believe what is untrue ⟨a smooth-talking confidence man who *hoaxes* elderly people and convinces them to trust him with their money⟩ — see DECEIVE

hoaxer *n* 1 a dishonest person who uses clever means to cheat others out of something of value ⟨if it sounds too good to be true, you're probably dealing with a *hoaxer*⟩ — see TRICKSTER 1

2 one who makes false claims of identity or expertise ⟨the new kid turned out be a complete *hoaxer* and not the son of a wealthy shipping tycoon he said he was⟩ — see IMPOSTOR

hob *n* playful, reckless behavior that is not intended to cause serious harm ⟨our indoor Frisbee game—my dog's and mine—played *hob* with a couple of lamps and a vase⟩ — see MISCHIEF 1

hobble *vb* 1 to create difficulty for the work or activity of ⟨*hobbled* by the snowstorm from getting out to do some Christmas shopping⟩ — see HAMPER

2 to walk while favoring one leg ⟨*hobbled* home with a twisted ankle⟩ — see LIMP 1

hobgoblin *n* 1 an imaginary being usually having a small human form and magical powers ⟨in Shakespeare's *Midsummer Night's Dream,* Puck is a *hobgoblin* who plays pranks such as spoiling milk and tripping old ladies⟩ — see FAIRY

2 something or someone that causes fear or dread especially without reason ⟨the fear of success and the pressures that come with it can be more of a *hobgoblin* than the possibility of failure⟩ — see BOGEY 1

hobnob *vb* 1 to come or be together as friends ⟨those two have been *hobnobbing* together since the first grade⟩ — see ASSOCIATE 1

2 to take part in social activities ⟨*hobnobbing* with the rich and famous⟩ — see SOCIALIZE

hobnobber *n* a person frequently seen in the company of another ⟨the actor's agent is a *hobnobber* with a lot of big movie producers⟩ — see ASSOCIATE 1

hobo *n* a homeless wanderer who may beg or steal for a living ⟨kind folks who always gave *hobos* who came to the farm a meal and then sent them on their way⟩ — see TRAMP

hock *vb* to leave as a guarantee of repayment of a loan ⟨the prince had to *hock* the family jewels to pay his debts⟩ — see PAWN

hodgepodge *n* an unorganized collection or mixture of various things ⟨the exhibit was a *hodgepodge* of mediocre art, bad art, and really bad art⟩ — see MISCELLANY 1

hog *n* one who eats greedily or too much ⟨Rob and his friends were *hogs* and didn't leave any cake and ice cream for the rest of us⟩ — see GLUTTON

hoggish *adj* having a huge appetite ⟨was feeling *hoggish* after the hike and ate the whole bag of cookies⟩ — see VORACIOUS 1

hogshead *n* an enclosed wooden vessel for holding beverages ⟨the ship's hold carried 164 *hogsheads* of molasses⟩ — see CASK

hogwash *n* 1 language, behavior, or ideas that are absurd and contrary to good sense ⟨told us a lot of *hogwash* about how you can go to jail for having overdue books⟩ — see NONSENSE 1

2 unintelligible or meaningless talk ⟨promises that are pure *hogwash,* because they know nothing's going to change⟩ — see GIBBERISH

hoist *vb* 1 to lift with effort ⟨*hoisted* all 164 barrels of molasses out of the ship's hold when it arrived in port⟩ — see HEAVE 1

2 to move from a lower to a higher place or position ⟨*hoisted* the flag on the flagpole⟩ — see RAISE 1

hold *n* **1** the act or manner of holding ⟨make sure you have a firm *hold* on the chain saw before you turn it on⟩

synonyms clasp, grapple, grasp, grip

related words anchorage, leverage, purchase; grab, seizure; foothold, footing, toehold; embrace, hug

near antonyms release, relinquishment

2 a structure or place from which one can resist attack ⟨the ruins of an ancient Roman *hold*⟩ — see FORT

3 the right or means to command or control others ⟨the government has no *hold* over where we live and work⟩ — see POWER 1

hold *vb* **1** to have or keep in one's hands ⟨this casserole dish is too hot to *hold,* so grab a potholder⟩

synonyms clench, cling (to), clutch, grip, hang on (to), hold on (to)

related words bear, carry; catch, grapple, nab, seize, snatch, take; feel, finger, handle, paw; clasp, embrace, grasp, hug

near antonyms drop, give, hand, unclasp, unhand; release, relinquish

2 to continue to have in one's possession or power ⟨she *held* the keys to the mysterious chest, and no one else knew what was inside⟩ — see KEEP 2

3 to have as an opinion ⟨"We *hold* these truths to be self-evident, that all men are created equal"⟩ — see BELIEVE 2

4 to have within ⟨the mysterious chest *held* an ancient book on magic spells and potions⟩ — see CONTAIN 1

5 to keep in one's mind or heart ⟨still *held* her close to his heart, though they had long parted⟩ — see HARBOR 1

6 to keep, control, or experience as one's own ⟨the same family has *held* this piece of land for over 300 years⟩ — see HAVE 1

7 to make or have room for ⟨needed to rent a hall that would *hold* 300 people⟩ — see ACCOMMODATE 1

8 to reach for and take hold of by embracing with the fingers or arms ⟨*hold* my arm on these slippery stairs⟩ — see TAKE 1

9 to think of in a particular way ⟨*held* to be the best blueberry pies in the state⟩ — see CONSIDER 1

hold (up) *vb* **1** to continue to operate or to meet one's needs ⟨the air conditioner *held up* this year, but it's not going to make it through another summer⟩ — see HOLD OUT

2 to remain indefinitely in existence or in the same state ⟨the storm's hurricane-force winds did not *hold up* once it hit the coast⟩ — see CONTINUE 1

hold back *vb* to create difficulty for the work or activity of ⟨the only thing *holding* Joe *back* from joining the swim team is lack of transportation⟩ — see HAMPER

holder *n* **1** one who has a legal or rightful claim to ownership ⟨the *holders* of the land gave us permission to camp on it⟩ — see PROPRIETOR

2 something into which a liquid or smaller objects can be put for storage or transportation ⟨her hat made a good *holder* for the shells she collected on the beach⟩ — see CONTAINER

hold in *vb* to keep from exceeding a desirable degree or level (as of expression) ⟨managed to *hold in* our laughter until we got outside⟩ — see CONTROL 1

holding *n* **1** a decision made by a court or tribunal regarding a case it has heard ⟨the *holding* of "not guilty" took everyone by surprise⟩ — see SENTENCE

2 *usually* **holdings** *pl* transportable items that one owns ⟨the museum's *holdings* of ancient manuscripts are among the rarest in the world⟩ — see POSSESSION 2

hold off (on) *vb* to assign to a later time ⟨*held off on* accepting the invitation in the hopes that something better would come along⟩ — see POSTPONE

hold on *vb* **1** to remain indefinitely in existence or in the same state ⟨the ancient beliefs still *held on* in remote mountain villages⟩ — see CONTINUE 1

2 to remain in place in readiness or expectation of something ⟨*hold on* a minute—it's not your turn⟩ — see WAIT

hold on (to) *vb* to have or keep in one's hands ⟨*hold on to* my fishing pole while I cut some more bait⟩ — see HOLD 1

hold out *vb* to continue to operate or to meet one's needs ⟨we hoped our supply of firewood would *hold out* until power was restored⟩ ⟨luckily, the old outboard motor *held out* till we made it to shore⟩

synonyms hold (up), last, keep up, prevail, survive

related words bear up, carry on, cope, endure, go, hang in, persevere; continue, draw out, hang on, linger, persist, remain, stretch

near antonyms break down, collapse, conk (out), crash, die, expire, stall, stop; run down, wane

antonyms fail, fizzle, give out, go out, peter (out), run out

holdup *n* an instance or period of being prevented from going about one's business ⟨a *holdup* in construction due to the weather⟩ — see DELAY

hold up *vb* **1** to assign to a later time ⟨*held up* mail delivery until we had a permanent address⟩ — see POSTPONE

2 to bring (something) to a standstill ⟨traffic was *held up* for miles by the accident⟩ — see ¹HALT 1

3 to create difficulty for the work or activity of ⟨if lack of transportation is the only thing *holding* you *up*, I can give you a ride⟩ — see HAMPER

hole *n* **1** a place in a surface allowing passage into or through a thing ⟨Mark was beside himself after seeing that his little sister had punched *holes* in his homework⟩

synonyms aperture, opening, orifice, perforation

related words chink, cleft, crack, cranny, crevice, cut, breach, break, fissure, gash, notch, rent, rift, rupture, slash, slit, split; gap, slot, space; exit, mouth, outlet, pore, vent; entrance, inlet, intake; pinprick, punch, puncture; armhole, buttonhole, knothole, peephole, pinhole, wormhole

near antonyms fill, filler, filling, patch, plug, seal, stopper; barrier, blockage, obstacle, obstruction

2 a sunken area forming a separate space ⟨Ann dug a *hole* big enough to plant the tree⟩

synonyms cavity, concavity, dent, depression, dint, hollow, indentation, pit, recess

related words burrow, cave, cavern, ditch, excavation, furrow, groove, trench, trough; basin, bowl, valley; alcove, cleft, niche, nook, opening, recess, socket; alveolus, dimple, gouge, notch, impression, pocket; chuckhole, crater, posthole, pothole, sinkhole, wallow, waterhole, well; abyss, chasm, gulf, vacuity, vacuum, void

near antonyms hill, mound, projection, rise; bump, lump, pimple, swell, swelling, tumor

antonyms bulge, convexity, protrusion, protuberance

3 a difficult, puzzling, or embarrassing situation from which there is no easy escape ⟨Bill dug himself into a *hole* by promising to be in two places at the same time⟩ — see PREDICAMENT

4 a dirty or messy place ⟨when people see my room, they often ask, "How can you live in this *hole*?"⟩ — see PIGPEN

5 an open space in a barrier (as a wall or hedge) ⟨found a *hole* in the chain-link fence big enough to squeeze through⟩ — see GAP 1

6 the shelter or resting place of a wild animal ⟨watched the snake slither into its *hole*⟩ — see DEN 1

hole *vb* to make a hole or series of holes in ⟨*holed* the target with a round of shots⟩ — see PERFORATE

holiday *n, chiefly British* a period during which the usual routine of school or work is suspended ⟨the member of parliament met his wife while on *holiday* in the south of France⟩ — see VACATION

holiday *vb* to take or spend a vacation ⟨saw a kangaroo while *holidaying* in Australia⟩ — see VACATION

holiness *n* the quality or state of being spiritually pure or virtuous ⟨known throughout the world for his *holiness*, the prophet was visited daily by hundreds of pilgrims⟩

synonyms blessedness, devoutness, godliness, piety, piousness, sainthood, saintliness, saintship, sanctity

related words asceticism, devotion, morality, prayerfulness, religiousness, spirituality; righteousness, virtuousness

near antonyms blasphemousness, irreverence, sacrilegiousness; depravity, sinfulness, wickedness

antonyms godlessness, impiety, ungodliness, unholiness

holler *n* a loud vocal expression of strong emotion ⟨heard a *holler* from somewhere in the woods and ran toward it⟩ — see SHOUT

holler *vb* to speak so as to be heard at a distance ⟨there's no need to *holler*; I'm in the next room⟩ — see CALL 1

hollow *adj* curved inward ⟨there's a *hollow* spot in the mattress where Jim sleeps⟩

synonyms concave, dented, depressed, indented, recessed, sunken

related words alveolar, cavernous, cuplike, cupped; dimpled, pockmarked; compressed, condensed, contracted, diminished, reduced

near antonyms ballooning, bloated, blown up, bulbous, distended, enlarged, expanded, extended, inflated, jutting, projecting, puffed (up), puffy, risen, swollen; domed, globular, rounded, spherical

antonyms bulging, convex, protruding, protuberant

hollow *n* **1** a sunken area forming a separate space ⟨made a little *hollow* in her mashed potatoes and filled it with gravy⟩ — see HOLE 2

2 an area of lowland between hills or mountains ⟨a quaint village nestled in a *hollow* among green hills⟩ — see VALLEY

holocaust *n* a destructive burning ⟨the *holocaust* caused by the ignited chemicals completely destroyed the factory and several surrounding homes⟩ — see FIRE

holy *adj* **1** showing a devotion to God and to a life of virtue ⟨the *holy* monk spent many hours on his knees in prayer⟩

synonyms devout, godly, pious, religious, sainted, saintly

related words ascetic, prayerful, reverent, reverential, spiritual, worshipful; beatified, blessed, canonized, venerable; angelic (*or* angelical), cherubic; chaste, pure, righteous, virtuous

near antonyms blasphemous, desecrating, irreverent, profane, sacrilegious, unspiritual; backsliding, unfaithful; sinful, sinning, wicked

antonyms faithless, godless, impious, irreligious, ungodly, unholy

2 set apart or worthy of veneration by association with God ⟨the Torah contains the *holy* writings of Judaism⟩

synonyms blessed, consecrated, hallowed, sacred, sacrosanct, sanctified

related words adored, enshrined, glorified, revered, venerated, worshipped (*also* worshiped); ceremonial, liturgical, priestly, religious, ritual, spiritual; biblical, scriptural

near antonyms nonreligious, unspiritual; earthly, mundane, secular, temporal, worldly

antonyms unconsecrated, unhallowed, unsanctified

3 of, relating to, or being God ⟨the *Holy* Trinity⟩

synonyms blessed, divine, godlike, heavenly, sacred, supernatural

related words eternal, everlasting, immortal; almighty, omnipotent, omniscient, supreme

near antonyms human, mortal

4 not to be violated, criticized, or tampered with ⟨the hour every Saturday she listens to her radio program is *holy* and you'd better not make her miss it⟩ — see SACRED 1

Holy Writ *n* a book made up of the writings accepted by Christians as coming from God ⟨quotes extensively from *Holy Writ* in his sermons⟩ — see BIBLE

homage *n* **1** a formal expression of praise ⟨the students paid *homage* to the retiring Mr. Byrnes with a poem of their own composition⟩ — see ENCOMIUM

2 public acknowledgment or admiration for an achievement ⟨the unique *homage* that we grant to Olympic athletes⟩ — see GLORY 1

hombre *n* an adult male human being ⟨two *hombres* sauntered into the bar and ordered . . . lemonade⟩ — see MAN 1

home *n* **1** the place where one lives ⟨as we entered his 34-room mansion, Ernest said, "Welcome to my humble *home*!"⟩

synonyms abode, diggings, domicile, dwelling, fireside, habitation, hearth, hearthstone, house, lodging, pad, place, quarters, residence, roof

related words accommodations, housing, nest, residency, shelter; bungalow, cabin, chalet, cottage; duplex, ranch, split level, town house, tract house, triplex; apartment, apartment house, condominium, flat, tenement, tenement house, walk-up; penthouse, salon, suite; barracks, boardinghouse, dorm, dormitory, lodgment (*or* lodgement), lodging house, room(s), rooming house; castle, château, country seat, estate, manor, manor house, mansion, palace, villa; farmhouse, grange, hacienda, homestead, ranch house; houseboat, mobile home, motor home, trailer; hermitage, manse, parsonage, vicarage; hovel, hut, shack

2 the place where a plant or animal is usually or naturally found ⟨the American south, the *home* of the armadillo⟩

synonyms habitat, niche, range, territory

related words element, environment, environs, haunt, locality, milieu, neighborhood, setting, surroundings

3 the land of one's birth, residence, or citizenship ⟨people who have a common *home*, traditions, language, and food tend to form their own communities in their adopted countries⟩ — see COUNTRY 1

homeboy *n* a violent, brutal person who is often a member of an organized gang ⟨the papers described the two accused of the robbery as *homeboys* whose street activities had been known to the police for some time⟩ — see HOODLUM

homeland *n* the land of one's birth, residence, or citizenship ⟨travels every year to Italy, her *homeland* for the first two decades of her life⟩ — see COUNTRY 1

homely *adj* unpleasant to look at ⟨Cinderella's stepsisters were about as *homely* as they come⟩ — see UGLY 1

homesteader *n* a person who settles in a new region ⟨in the 1800s *homesteaders* in search of cheap land and a new life headed to the West in droves⟩ — see FRONTIERSMAN

homicidal *adj* eager for or marked by the shedding of blood, extreme violence, or killing ⟨court-appointed psychiatrists described the accused as a *homicidal* maniac who should be put away for life⟩ — see BLOODTHIRSTY

homicide *n* the intentional and unlawful taking of another person's life ⟨the missing man was thought to be the victim of a *homicide*, but his body was never found⟩
synonyms foul play, murder, slaying
related words killing, manslaughter; bloodshed, butchery, carnage, decimation, destruction, massacre, slaughter; assassination, execution; euthanasia, mercy killing

homily *n* a public speech usually by a member of the clergy for the purpose of giving moral guidance or uplift ⟨last Sunday's *homily* was about being kind to your neighbors⟩ — see SERMON

homogenize *vb* to make agree with a single established standard or model ⟨plans to *homogenize* the science curriculum in public high schools throughout the state⟩ — see STANDARDIZE

Homo sapiens *n* the human race ⟨how far into outer reaches of the universe will *Homo sapiens* someday be able to go?⟩ — see MANKIND

hone *vb* 1 to make sharp or sharper ⟨*honed* the knife's blade to razor-like sharpness⟩ ⟨*honed* his crossword-puzzle skills by reading the dictionary as though it were a thrilling novel⟩ — see SHARPEN
2 to make smooth by friction ⟨*honed* the edge of the axe until it was amazingly sharp⟩ — see GRIND 1

honed *adj* having an edge thin enough to cut or pierce something ⟨using a finely *honed* butcher knife will make cutting meat easier⟩ — see SHARP 1

honest *adj* 1 being in the habit of telling the truth ⟨at least the weatherman is *honest* and doesn't pretend to be able to predict the unpredictable⟩ — see TRUTHFUL
2 conforming to a high standard of morality or virtue ⟨*honest* and industrious farm folk⟩ — see GOOD 2
3 following the accepted rules of moral conduct ⟨that rare, *honest* customer who doesn't hesitate to tell the cashier she's given him too much change⟩ — see HONORABLE 1
4 free from any intent to deceive or impress others ⟨the sort of person who helps others from an *honest* desire to do good, and not because she might need a favor from them someday⟩ — see GUILELESS
5 free in expressing one's true feelings and opinions ⟨appreciate your *honest* friends who tell you what you need to hear and not what you want to hear⟩ — see FRANK
6 guided by or in accordance with one's sense of right and wrong ⟨made an *honest* attempt to return the money she had found in the cafeteria⟩ — see CONSCIENTIOUS 1

honestly *adv* to tell the truth ⟨*honestly*, I haven't the slightest idea what you're talking about⟩ — see ACTUALLY 1

honesty *n* 1 devotion to telling the truth ⟨George Washington has gone down in history for his *honesty*⟩
synonyms integrity, probity, truthfulness, veracity, verity
related words honor, incorruptibility; candidness, candor, frankness, good faith, sincerity, straightforwardness; dependability, reliability, reliableness, trustworthiness; accuracy, objectivity; authenticity, correctness, genuineness; credibility
near antonyms deception, dissembling, dissimulation, duplicity, fakery, falseness, falsity, fraudulentness, hypocrisy, insincerity; beguilement, craftiness, cunning, furtiveness, guile, insidiousness, oiliness, slickness, slipperiness, slyness, smoothness, trickery, underhandedness, wiliness; equivocation, prevarication; exaggeration, inaccuracy
antonyms deceit, deceitfulness, dishonesty, lying, mendacity, untruthfulness
2 conduct that conforms to an accepted standard of right and wrong ⟨known for his *honesty* in business dealings⟩ — see MORALITY 1
3 faithfulness to high moral standards ⟨could count on her students' *honesty*, even if she left the classroom for a few moments during the test⟩ — see HONOR 1

honey *n* a person with whom one is in love ⟨gave his *honey* a dozen red roses on Valentine's Day⟩ — see SWEETHEART

honor *n* 1 faithfulness to high moral standards ⟨the mayor, a man of *honor*, never broke a promise to the voters⟩
synonyms honesty, integrity, probity, rectitude, righteousness, uprightness
related words blamelessness, character, conscientiousness, decency, fairness, high-mindedness, incorruptibility, justice, morality, nobility, reputability, respectability, scrupulousness, virtue, virtuousness
near antonyms corruptibility, corruption, corruptness, debasement, decadence, degeneracy, depravity, disgracefulness, disreputableness, dissipation, dissoluteness, looseness, perversion, profligacy, shamelessness, venality; blameworthiness, criminality, crookedness, dishonesty, immorality, unrighteousness, unscrupulousness; knavery, rascality, roguishness; meanness, reprehensibleness, rottenness, sinfulness, vileness, villainy, wretchedness
antonyms baseness, lowness
2 an asset that brings praise or renown ⟨a dedicated, caring teacher who is an *honor* to the teaching profession⟩ — see GLORY 2
3 public acknowledgment or admiration for an achievement ⟨the *honor* we give to our soldiers on Veterans Day⟩ — see GLORY 1
4 something given in recognition of achievement ⟨has received several *honors* from the Boy Scouts for his many years of service⟩ — see AWARD
5 something granted as a special favor ⟨it will be an *honor* for me to show your aunt around the city⟩ — see PRIVILEGE

honor *vb* to show appreciation, respect, or affection for (someone) with a public celebration ⟨the newlyweds were *honored* with a dinner given by the bride's grandmother⟩
synonyms fete (*or* fête), recognize
related words acknowledge, cite, commend, compliment, credit, thank; extol (*also* extoll), glorify, laud, praise; acclaim, applaud, cheer, hail, salute; celebrate, commemorate, memorialize, observe; congratulate, felicitate

near antonyms bad-mouth, defame, libel, malign, slander; boo, hiss, hoot, jeer; censure, condemn, damn, denounce, reprobate; mock, put down, ridicule, slight

honorable *adj* **1** following the accepted rules of moral conduct ⟨the only *honorable* thing to do is to admit that you were wrong and apologize⟩
synonyms decent, ethical, honest, just, noble, principled, respectable, righteous, upright, upstanding
related words decorous, proper, seemly; blameless, guiltless, irreproachable, unassailable, unimpeachable; chivalrous, high-minded, right-minded; conscientious, fair, good, incorruptible, moral, reputable, respected, scrupulous, uncorrupted, virtuous
near antonyms bad, blackguardly, corrupt, criminal, crooked, immoral, iniquitous, knavish, mean, rascally, reprehensible, roguish, rotten, scoundrelly, sinful; unfair, unscrupulous, vile, villainous, wicked, wretched; blamable, blameworthy, censurable; debased, debauched, decadent, degenerate, depraved, disgraceful, disreputable, dissipated, dissolute, libertine, loose, perverted, profligate, reprobate, shameful, unscrupulous, venal
antonyms base, dishonest, ignoble, low, unethical, unjust, unprincipled, unrighteous
2 conforming to a high standard of morality or virtue ⟨it was *honorable* of you to give all the credit to your friend⟩ — see GOOD 2
3 guided by or in accordance with one's sense of right and wrong ⟨the only *honorable* thing to do is to return the extra toaster the company sent to you by mistake⟩ — see CONSCIENTIOUS 1

honorably *adv* in a manner befitting a person of the highest character and ideals ⟨their sons died *honorably*, fighting a war to preserve freedom for future generations⟩ — see GREATLY 1

¹**hood** *n* a violent, brutal person who is often a member of an organized gang ⟨when a gang of *hoods* started hanging out in front of the store, customers went elsewhere⟩ — see HOODLUM

²**hood** *n* something that covers or conceals like a piece of cloth ⟨counterfeiters conducting their affairs under a *hood* of secrecy⟩ — see CLOAK 1

hoodlum *n* a violent, brutal person who is often a member of an organized gang ⟨a couple of *hoodlums* held up the convenience store⟩
synonyms bully, gangster, goon, homeboy, hood, mobster, mug, punk, roughneck, rowdy, ruffian, thug, tough, toughie
related words cutthroat, scoundrel, villain; assassin, bandit, bravo, brigand, criminal, crook, desperado, felon, gunman, highwayman, lawbreaker, mafioso, outlaw, perpetrator, pickpocket, racketeer, robber, swindler, thief

hoodoo *n* something that brings bad luck ⟨some *hoodoo* must be at work—I lost both sets of house keys⟩ — see JINX

hoodwink *vb* to cause to believe what is untrue ⟨Tom *hoodwinked* the other boys into thinking there was nothing more enjoyable than whitewashing a fence⟩ — see DECEIVE

hoof (it) *vb* **1** to go on foot ⟨*hoofed* it to the library to save bus fare⟩ — see WALK
2 to perform a series of usually rhythmic bodily movements to music ⟨*hoofs* it from seven to eight every Thursday night with other avid square dancers⟩ — see DANCE 1

hook *n* a hard strike with a part of the body or an instrument ⟨delivered a hard right *hook* that struck his opponent in the eye⟩ — see ¹BLOW

hook *vb* **1** to cause to turn away from a straight line ⟨the pitcher *hooked* the ball, and the batter missed⟩ — see BEND 1
2 to put or bring together so as to form a new and longer whole ⟨*hooked* up three short chains together to make a longer necklace⟩ — see CONNECT 1
3 to take (something) without right and with an intent to keep ⟨the monkey *hooked* four bananas from the basket and climbed out of reach with them⟩ — see STEAL 1
4 to take physical control or possession of (something) suddenly or forcibly ⟨*hooked* the shoplifter just as she was about to run out of the store⟩ — see CATCH 1
5 to turn away from a straight line or course ⟨hang the bird feeder on a branch that *hooks* upward⟩ — see CURVE 1

hookup *n* the state of having shared interests or efforts (as in social or business matters) ⟨the drama club's *hookup* with a local acting company provided several aspiring young actors with experience doing summer theater⟩ — see ASSOCIATION 1

hoop *n* a circular strip ⟨made Christmas garlands from *hoops* of red and green construction paper⟩ — see RING 2

hoosegow *n* a place of confinement for persons held in lawful custody ⟨ended up in the *hoosegow* for stealing a diamond necklace⟩ — see JAIL

hoot *n* **1** a loud vocal expression of strong emotion ⟨the class erupted in *hoots* of laughter⟩ — see SHOUT
2 a vocal sound made to express scorn or disapproval ⟨ignored the *hoots* and jeers coming from the back of the crowd and kept on speaking⟩ — see CATCALL
3 the smallest amount or part imaginable ⟨I don't give a *hoot* whether you want to go or not—you're going⟩ — see JOT

hop *n* **1** a social gathering for dancing ⟨saw Lindsay at the *hop* dancing with John⟩ — see DANCE
2 an act of leaping into the air ⟨made it across the rocky creek in two *hops*⟩ — see JUMP 1

hop *vb* **1** to move with a light bouncing step ⟨a rabbit *hopped* across the yard⟩ — see SKIP 1
2 to propel oneself upward or forward into the air ⟨the wagon stopped, Annie *hopped* on, and the driver continued on his way⟩ — see JUMP 1

hope (for) *vb* to believe in the future occurrence of (something) ⟨*hoping for* an A in English⟩ — see EXPECT

hopeful *adj* **1** having qualities which inspire hope ⟨economists are offering a *hopeful* forecast for a healthy economy in the coming year⟩
synonyms auspicious, bright, encouraging, fair, golden, heartening, likely, optimistic, promising, propitious, rose-colored, rosy, upbeat
related words cheering, comforting, reassuring; assured, confident, decisive, doubtless, positive, sure, unhesitating; bullish, favorable, good
near antonyms cheerless, comfortless; doubtful, dubious, uncertain; bearish, grim, negative, unfavorable
antonyms bleak, dark, desperate, discouraging, disheartening, dismal, dreary, gloomy, hopeless, inauspicious, pessimistic, unlikely, unpromising
2 pointing toward a happy outcome ⟨a *hopeful* response to the ad, several people calling to say they'd seen our lost cat⟩ — see FAVORABLE 2

hopeful *n* one who seeks an office, honor, position, or award ⟨the three mayoral *hopefuls* are going to debate on local TV⟩ — see CANDIDATE

hopeless *adj* **1** not capable of being cured or reformed ⟨a *hopeless* optimist who looked for the good in everyone and everything⟩ ⟨a *hopeless* criminal who spent most of his life in jail⟩
synonyms incorrigible, incurable, irrecoverable, irredeemable, irremediable, irretrievable, unrecoverable, unredeemable
related words irreparable, irreversible; unpromising; impenitent, unreformed, unregenerate, unrepentant
near antonyms reversible; promising; penitent, repentant; repairable, reparable, salvageable
antonyms correctable, curable, reclaimable, recoverable, redeemable, reformable, remediable, retrievable
2 emphasizing or expecting the worst ⟨feeling *hopeless* about ever finding her lost cat⟩ — see PESSIMISTIC 1
3 incapable of being solved or accomplished ⟨keeping this desk organized is *hopeless*⟩ — see IMPOSSIBLE

hopelessness *n* utter loss of hope ⟨felt utter *hopelessness* about ever returning to her native country⟩ — see DESPAIR 1

horde *n* a great number of persons or things gathered together ⟨a *horde* of mosquitoes⟩ ⟨*hordes* of shoppers crowding the stores the week before Christmas⟩ — see CROWD 1

horn *n* something shaped like a hollow cone and used as a container ⟨musketeers carrying their gunpowder in a powder *horn*⟩ — see CORNET

horrendous *adj* **1** causing fear ⟨a *horrendous* explosion shook the building⟩ — see FEARFUL 1
2 causing intense displeasure, disgust, or resentment ⟨a *horrendous* breach of good manners⟩ — see OFFENSIVE 1
3 extremely disturbing or repellent ⟨emergency room personnel must not flinch even from the most *horrendous* injuries⟩ — see HORRIBLE 1

horrible *adj* **1** extremely disturbing or repellent ⟨a *horrible* car accident that left eyewitnesses in a state of shock⟩
synonyms appalling, atrocious, awful, dreadful, frightful, ghastly, grisly, gruesome, hideous, horrendous, horrid, horrifying, lurid, macabre, monstrous, nightmarish, shocking, terrible
related words bloodcurdling, dire, direful, fearful, fearsome, forbidding, formidable, frightening, hair-raising, terrifying; abhorrent, deplorable, disagreeable, disgusting, distasteful, loathsome, nauseating, obnoxious, offensive, repugnant, repulsive, revolting, sickening; abominable, evil, foul, heinous, noxious, odious, unspeakable, vile
near antonyms agreeable, appealing, attractive, enticing, inviting; cheering, comforting, soothing
2 causing fear ⟨a *horrible* scream that made shivers go up and down our spines⟩ — see FEARFUL 1
3 causing intense displeasure, disgust, or resentment ⟨the *horrible* way she treated her stepdaughter⟩ — see OFFENSIVE 1

horrid *adj* **1** causing intense displeasure, disgust, or resentment ⟨accused him of stealing and said mean and *horrid* things about him⟩ — see OFFENSIVE 1
2 extremely disturbing or repellent ⟨died a *horrid* death in the fire⟩ — see HORRIBLE 1

horridness *n* the quality of inspiring intense dread or dismay ⟨imagine the *horridness* of not being able to escape from the path of lava spewing from a volcano⟩ — see HORROR 1

horrified *adj* filled with fear or dread ⟨sat rigid in his seat, *horrified* that the plane would crash⟩ — see AFRAID 1

horrify *vb* to strike with fear ⟨the news that the escaped convict was in her neighborhood *horrified* her⟩ — see FRIGHTEN

horrifying *adj* **1** causing fear ⟨received *horrifying* threats from the townspeople for his accusations of wrongdoing against the popular football coach⟩ — see FEARFUL 1
2 extremely disturbing or repellent ⟨the *horrifying* sight of children suffering from malnutrition⟩ — see HORRIBLE 1

horror *n* **1** the quality of inspiring intense dread or dismay ⟨it's difficult to even begin to comprehend the *horror* of the Holocaust⟩
synonyms atrociousness, atrocity, awfulness, dreadfulness, frightfulness, ghastliness, grisliness, gruesomeness, hideousness, horridness, monstrosity, repulsiveness
related words badness, baseness, diabolicalness, evil, foulness, heinousness, immorality, iniquity, invidiousness, nefariousness, ungodliness, viciousness, vileness, wickedness; accursedness, cursedness, deplorableness, despicableness, detestableness, execrableness, hatefulness, loathsomeness, reprehensibleness; creepiness, eeriness, fearfulness, fearsomeness, ghostliness, scariness; agony, hellishness, misery, torment, torture
near antonyms agreeableness, delightfulness, pleasantness; allurement, appeal, attraction, attractiveness, desirability, desirableness
2 a situation or state that causes great suffering and unhappiness ⟨had never experienced the *horrors* of war⟩ — see HELL 2
3 something unpleasant to look at ⟨are you really going to hang that *horror* on the wall?⟩ — see EYESORE
4 the emotion experienced in the presence or threat of danger ⟨imagine my *horror* at finding myself face to face with a lion on the loose⟩ — see FEAR

horse *n* a large hoofed domestic animal that is used for carrying or drawing loads and for riding ⟨the mounted police stable their *horses* in the city park⟩
synonyms equine, nag, steed
related words colt, filly, foal, gelding, mare, stallion; bronco, mustang, pony; charger, courser, cow pony, mount, palfrey, prancer, quarter horse, racehorse, saddle horse, trotter, war-horse, workhorse; bay, black, buckskin, chestnut, dun, palomino, pinto, roan, sorrel; cob, jade, plug

horse (around) *vb* to engage in attention-getting playful or boisterous behavior ⟨the boys were *horsing around* in the boat when one of them fell overboard⟩ — see CUT UP

horseplay *n* wildly playful or mischievous behavior ⟨when he saw us spraying each other with the hose instead of washing the car, Dad yelled, "Cut out the *horseplay!*"⟩
synonyms clowning, foolery, high jinks, horsing (around), monkeying, monkeyshines, roughhouse, roughhousing, shenanigans, skylarking, tomfoolery
related words buffoonery, clownishness, foolishness, funning, jesting, joking, nonsense, waggery; boisterousness, rowdiness; devilry (*or* deviltry), impishness, mischief, mischievousness, prankishness, roguishness, trickery; cavorting, frivolity, frolicking, gamboling (*or* gambolling), merrymaking, playfulness, revelry, roistering, romping, sporting, sportiveness

horse sense *n* the ability to make intelligent decisions especially in everyday matters ⟨pure *horse sense* should tell you not to stand so close to the space heater⟩ — see COMMON SENSE

horse–trade *vb* to talk over or dispute the terms of a purchase ⟨we *horse-traded*: I would give Jeff my guitar and guitar lessons, and he would give me 100 bucks and piano lessons⟩ — see BARGAIN

horsewhip *vb* to strike repeatedly with something long and thin or flexible ⟨the cruel guards *horsewhipped* the prisoners if they collapsed under the heavy loads they were forced to carry⟩ — see WHIP 1

horsing (around) *n* wildly playful or mischievous behavior ⟨the monitor made Phillip and his friends sit apart in the cafeteria for *horsing around*⟩ — see HORSEPLAY

hose *n* a close-fitting covering for the foot and leg ⟨dressed like Benjamin Franklin in waistcoat, breeches, and *hose*⟩ — see STOCKING

hospice *n* a place that provides rooms and usually a public dining room for overnight guests ⟨the monks run a *hospice* for travelers in their mountain retreat⟩ — see HOTEL

hospitable *adj* showing a natural kindness and courtesy especially in social situations ⟨Andy's aunt was extremely *hospitable* when he showed up at her door with his friends, inviting them to stay for dinner⟩ — see GRACIOUS 1

host *n* **1** a great number of persons or things gathered together ⟨a *host* of people of all faiths gathered in St. Peter's Square to see the Pope⟩ — see CROWD 1
2 a large body of men and women organized for land warfare ⟨the small band of defenders was no match for the enemy's *host* that bore down on them⟩ — see ARMY 1

hostel *n* a place that provides rooms and usually a public dining room for overnight guests ⟨in the old days, a traveler could spend the night at one of the *hostels* placed along the coach route⟩ — see HOTEL

hostelry *n* a place that provides rooms and usually a public dining room for overnight guests ⟨the knight spent the night at a small *hostelry* and then continued on his quest⟩ — see HOTEL

hostile *adj* **1** marked by opposition or ill will ⟨our landlord has a *hostile* attitude toward foreigners and refuses to rent to them⟩
synonyms antagonistic, inhospitable, inimical, jaundiced, negative, unfriendly, unsympathetic
related words adverse, bellicose, belligerent, clashing, conflicting, contentious, contrary, opposed, pugnacious, quarrelsome, resisting; antisocial, cold, cool, disagreeable, disapproving, distant, frigid, icy, biased, prejudiced; discourteous, impolite, rude, surly, uncivil, unfavorable, unkind, unpleasant, unsociable; acrimonious, antipathetic, bitter, hateful, malevolent, opprobrious, rancorous, spiteful, unloving, vindictive, virulent
near antonyms affable, amiable, amicable, companionable, convivial, cordial, civil, genial, gracious, gregarious, neighborly, pleasant, sociable, social, warm; affectionate, devoted, kind, loving, nice, sweet; accepting, agreeable, approving, benign, empathetic, favorable, understanding, warmhearted, welcoming
antonyms friendly, hospitable, sympathetic
2 opposed to one's interests ⟨the company's president vows to fight the *hostile* takeover by the giant corporation⟩ — see ADVERSE 1

hostility *n* **1** a deep-seated ill will ⟨felt no *hostility* toward the girl who had knocked her off the diving board because she was sure it had been an accident⟩ — see ENMITY
2 hostilities *pl* a state of armed violent struggle between states, nations, or groups ⟨both sides agreed to cease all *hostilities* for Hanukkah and Christmas⟩ — see WAR 1

hot *adj* **1** having a notably high temperature ⟨the casserole, just out of the oven, was too *hot* to eat⟩
synonyms broiling, burning, fiery, piping hot, red-hot, roasting, scalding, scorching, searing, sultry, superheated, sweltering, torrid
related words blazing, glowing, molten, sizzling; heated, overheated, reheated, warmed; snug, toasty, warm; feverish, flushed, inflamed; muggy, steamy, summery, tropical
near antonyms chilly, cool, frosty, nippy, snowy, subzero, wintry; cooled, refrigerated, unheated, unthawed; benumbed, numb, shivering; lukewarm, temperate, tepid
antonyms arctic, chill, chilled, cold, freezing, frigid, frozen, glacial, ice-cold, iced, icy
2 being or involving the latest methods, concepts, information, or styles ⟨this spring it's the cool shades of lipstick that are *hot*⟩ — see MODERN
3 enjoying widespread favor or approval ⟨was surprised to learn that American jazz has long been *hot* in Russia⟩ — see POPULAR 1
4 marked by bursts of destructive force or intense activity ⟨your *hot* temper is going to get you in trouble⟩ ⟨a *hot* battle for first place in the American League⟩ — see VIOLENT 1
5 showing urgent desire or interest ⟨*hot* to get the baseball game started and wished it would stop raining⟩ — see EAGER

hot air *n* **1** boastful speech or writing ⟨his taking credit for the rescue was mostly *hot air,* since the boat was actually saved by the Coast Guard⟩ — see BOMBAST 1
2 language that is impressive-sounding but not meaningful or sincere ⟨her campaign promise to "fight for the people" showed a taste for stale *hot air*⟩ — see RHETORIC 1

hot–blooded *adj* having or expressing great depth of feeling ⟨after watching the successful defense of Fort McHenry, Francis Scott Key quickly wrote the *hot-blooded* poem that later became known as "The Star-Spangled Banner"⟩ — see FERVENT

hotcake *n* a flat cake made from thin batter and cooked on both sides (as on a griddle) ⟨*hotcakes* and maple syrup will be served at the church breakfast⟩ — see PANCAKE

hotchpotch *n* an unorganized collection or mixture of various things ⟨the meal was a *hotchpotch* of leftovers⟩ — see MISCELLANY 1

hotel *n* a place that provides rooms and usually a public dining room for overnight guests ⟨for their 50th anniversary they stayed at one of the finest *hotels* in San Francisco⟩
synonyms caravansary (*or* caravanserai), hospice, hostel, hostelry, inn, lodge, public house, tavern
related words bed-and-breakfast; accommodations, lodgings, rest; motel, motor court, resort, spa, youth hostel; camp, campground; bunkhouse, dorm, dormitory; boardinghouse, lodging house, rooming house

hotfoot *adv* with excessive or careless speed ⟨lowered his plane *hotfoot* onto a pasture when the engine started to sputter⟩ — see HASTILY 1

hotfoot (it) *vb* to proceed or move quickly ⟨you'd better *hotfoot it* to the bus stop if you're going to catch the bus⟩ — see HURRY 2

hothouse *n* a glass-enclosed building for growing plants ⟨grows tomatoes in his *hothouse* all winter⟩ — see CONSERVATORY

hotness *n* the state of enjoying widespread approval ⟨the *hotness* of the movie's stars is the driving force behind all of the advance publicity⟩ — see POPULARITY

hot war *n* a state of armed violent struggle between states, nations, or groups ⟨fortunately, the cool relationship between the two nations never escalated into a *hot war*⟩ — see WAR 1

hound *n* a domestic mammal that is related to the wolves and foxes ⟨in the yard an old *hound* greeted us with a single bark⟩ — see DOG

hound *vb* **1** to go after or on the track of ⟨after she was publicly dumped by her boyfriend, the actress was *hounded* by reporters night and day⟩ — see FOLLOW 2
2 to subject (someone) to constant scoldings and sharp reminders ⟨kept *hounding* his mother to let him drive her car until she gave in⟩ — see NAG

hounding *n* the act of going after or in the tracks of another ⟨eventually couldn't take the constant *hounding* by reporters and fans⟩ — see PURSUIT

house *n* **1** a commercial or industrial activity or organization ⟨a publishing *house* that specializes in school textbooks⟩ — see ENTERPRISE 1
2 a group of persons who come from the same ancestor ⟨the present British royal family belongs to the *House* of Windsor⟩ — see FAMILY 1
3 the place where one lives ⟨come over to my *house* for supper so I can show you my new stove⟩ — see HOME 1
4 those who live as a family in one house ⟨the whole *house* is in a state of excited anticipation for the holidays⟩ — see HOUSEHOLD

house *vb* **1** to provide with living quarters or shelter ⟨some of the freshmen were temporarily *housed* in the gym while the new dorm was being finished⟩
synonyms accommodate, billet, board, bunk, chamber, domicile, encamp, harbor, lodge, put up, quarter, roof, shelter, take in
related words ensconce, home, roost, secure, stable, tent
near antonyms eject, evict
2 to close or shut in by or as if by barriers ⟨*housed* the stereo speakers in attractive walnut cabinets that match the furniture⟩ — see ENCLOSE 1

house cat *n* a small domestic animal known for catching mice ⟨the *house cat* at the Cheshire Cat Bookstore has the dual responsibility of being mascot and mouser⟩ — see CAT 1

household *adj* **1** of or relating to a household or family ⟨spent the weekend at home, helping with *household* chores⟩ — see DOMESTIC 1
2 often observed or encountered ⟨ozone is now a *household* word, thanks to global warming⟩ — see COMMON 1

household *n* those who live as a family in one house ⟨a *household* that consists of a single mom, her two kids, and her widowed mother⟩
synonyms extended family, house, ménage
related words folks, kin, kindred, kinfolk, kinsfolk, kith; brood; nuclear family; clan, community

housekeeper *n* a female domestic servant ⟨could afford to hire a *housekeeper* to cook and clean once he was established in his profession⟩ — see MAID 1

housemaid *n* a female domestic servant ⟨scrubbing floors fell to Lily, the lowliest *housemaid*⟩ — see MAID 1

housing *n* something that encloses another thing especially to protect it ⟨a camera with a waterproof *housing* for taking pictures of coral reefs and other underwater features⟩ — see ¹CASE 1

hovel *n* a small, simply constructed, and often temporary dwelling ⟨refugees living in crowded *hovels*⟩ — see SHACK

hover *vb* to rest or move along the surface of a liquid or in the air ⟨claimed that the UFO *hovered* a moment, then spun off into space at incredible speed⟩ — see FLOAT

hover (over) *vb* to remain poised to inflict harm, danger, or distress on ⟨after the first big layoff, the possibility of losing their jobs *hovered over* all the factory workers⟩ — see THREATEN

howbeit *adv* in spite of that ⟨I've never written a poem before; *howbeit*, I feel my first attempt is quite good⟩ — see HOWEVER

howbeit *conj* in spite of the fact that ⟨our visit to Niagara Falls was very pleasant, *howbeit* slightly shorter than we had planned⟩ — see ALTHOUGH

however *adv* in spite of that ⟨I'm all out of eggs; *however*, I can still make us a nice breakfast⟩
synonyms howbeit, nevertheless, nonetheless, notwithstanding, still, though, withal, yet
related words after all, anyhow, regardless

howl *n* **1** a crying out in grief ⟨the agonized *howl* of the grief-stricken parents rose toward heaven⟩ — see LAMENT 1
2 a loud vocal expression of strong emotion ⟨heard *howls* of laughter from the children watching the clown's silly antics⟩ — see SHOUT
3 a violent shouting ⟨the crowd raised a *howl* when the notorious criminal appeared at the door⟩ — see CLAMOR 1

howl *vb* **1** to make a long loud mournful sound ⟨several coyotes began *howling* close by as the sun went down⟩ ⟨the wind *howled* on the open plain⟩
synonyms bay, keen, wail, yowl
related words bawl, caterwaul, squall, yawp (*or* yaup), yell, yelp
2 to cry out loudly and emotionally ⟨*howled* in pain when his baby sister bit him⟩ — see SCREAM

hoydenish *adj* having qualities or traits that are traditionally considered inappropriate for a girl or woman ⟨a *hoydenish* woman, who smoked cigars and wore heavy work boots to town⟩ — see UNFEMININE

hub *n* a thing or place that is of greatest importance to an activity or interest ⟨Broadway is the *hub* of theater life in New York⟩ — see CENTER 1

hubbub *n* **1** a state of noisy, confused activity ⟨imagine all the *hubbub* at the zoo when the lion escaped⟩ — see COMMOTION
2 a violent shouting ⟨the people without tickets made a huge *hubbub* when they were told that the concert was all sold out⟩ — see CLAMOR 1

huckster *n* one who sells things outdoors ⟨*hucksters* outside the auditorium selling everything from key chains to life-size cutouts of the rock star⟩ — see PEDDLER

huddle *n* **1** a coming together of a number of persons for a specified purpose ⟨after an all-night *huddle*, the state legislature finally approved a budget for the coming year⟩ — see MEETING 1

2 a number of things considered as a unit ⟨saw a *huddle* of tents that turned out to be a Boy Scout encampment⟩ — see GROUP 1

3 a usually small number of persons considered as a unit ⟨in the lobby during intermission *huddles* of theatergoers were excitedly discussing the play⟩ — see GROUP 2

huddle *vb* **1** to gather into a closely packed group ⟨the puppies *huddled* together to keep warm⟩ — see PRESS 3

2 to lie low with the limbs close to the body ⟨*huddled* under her bed when she heard the thunder⟩ — see CROUCH

hue *n* a property that becomes apparent when light falls on an object and by which things that are identical in form can be distinguished ⟨suggested she wear brighter *hues* to complement her skin tone⟩ — see COLOR 1

hue and cry *n* a violent shouting ⟨the *hue and cry* in the classroom when someone let loose a snake⟩ — see CLAMOR 1

huff *n* **1** a state of nervous or irritated concern ⟨was in a *huff* because everyone was running late and the hot breakfast she had prepared was getting cold⟩ — see FRET

2 an outburst or display of excited anger ⟨gets all in a *huff* every time anyone makes the slightest criticism⟩ — see TANTRUM

3 the feeling of being offended or resentful after a slight or indignity ⟨left the restaurant in a *huff* after waiting 15 minutes to be seated⟩ — see PIQUE

huffiness *n* readiness to show annoyance or impatience ⟨there's no point in telling her what you think unless you want to put up with her *huffiness*⟩ — see PETULANCE

hug *vb* to put one's arms around and press tightly ⟨*hugged* the grandchildren good-bye⟩ — see EMBRACE 1

huge *adj* unusually large ⟨the old stadium was replaced by a *huge* new one that seats 100,000 spectators⟩

synonyms astronomical (*also* astronomic), bumper, colossal, cosmic, elephantine, enormous, giant, gigantic, grand, herculean, heroic, immense, jumbo, king-size (*or* king-sized), mammoth, massive, monster, monstrous, monumental, mountainous, prodigious, super, titanic, tremendous, vast, vasty, whacking, whopping

related words big, bulky, considerable, extensive, good, goodly, good-sized, great, gross, handsome, hefty, hulking, largish, major, sizable (*or* sizeable), substantial, voluminous; august, formidable, grandiose, imposing, lofty, majestic; cavernous, monolithic, overwhelming, staggering, stupendous, towering; boundless, cosmic, immeasurable, infinite

near antonyms little, petite, pint-size (*or* pint-sized), puny, small, smallish, undersized

antonyms bitty, diminutive, microscopic (*or* microscopical), midget, miniature, minute, pocket, pygmy, teeny, teeny-weeny, tiny, wee

hugely *adv* **1** to a great degree ⟨*hugely* mistaken about the people he had rented the house to⟩ — see VERY 1

2 to a large extent or degree ⟨the donation has added *hugely* to the library's collection of music⟩ — see GREATLY 1

hugeness *n* the quality or state of being very large ⟨can only appreciate the *hugeness* of the dome when you see how tiny the people standing under it look⟩ — see IMMENSITY

hugger–mugger *adj* **1** lacking in order, neatness, and often cleanliness ⟨a *hugger-mugger* presentation of the facts of the case that left everyone confused⟩ — see MESSY

2 undertaken or done so as to escape being observed or known by others ⟨a tale of *hugger-mugger* doings and international espionage⟩ — see SECRET 1

hulk *n* a big clumsy often slow-witted person ⟨big-boned Brianna felt like a *hulk* standing in line next to the slender, delicate girl⟩ — see OAF

hulking *adj* **1** of a size greater than average of its kind ⟨a heavy, *hulking* stone blocked the way⟩ — see LARGE

2 strongly and heavily built ⟨I need a strong *hulking* young man to carry out the television set⟩ — see ¹HUSKY

hull *vb* to remove the natural covering of ⟨*hull* pinto beans⟩ — see PEEL

hullabaloo *n* **1** a state of noisy, confused activity ⟨there was a lot of needless *hullabaloo* as the new millennium approached⟩ — see COMMOTION

2 a violent shouting ⟨there was such a *hullabaloo* in the room that he couldn't hear himself think⟩ — see CLAMOR 1

hum *n* a monotonous sound like that of an insect in motion ⟨we heard the *hum* of an outboard motor and a few minutes later the small craft came into sight⟩

synonyms buzz, chirr, drone, purr, thrum, whir (*also* whirr), whiz (*or* whizz), zoom

related words babble, coo, gurgle, hiss, moan, murmur, rustle, sigh, whisper; whish, zing, zip

near antonyms bawl, howl, roar, scream, screech, shriek

hum *vb* to fly, turn, or move rapidly with a fluttering or vibratory sound ⟨a helicopter *hummed* overhead⟩ — see WHIRR

human *adj* relating to or characteristic of human beings ⟨it's *human* nature to care about what people think of us⟩

synonyms mortal, natural

related words anthropoid, hominid, humanlike, humanoid

near antonyms angelic (*or* angelical), divine, godlike, superhuman, supernatural; immortal, omnipotent, omniscient; animal, beastly, bestial, brute; inhuman, robotic

antonyms nonhuman

human *n* a member of the human race ⟨*humans* are the only mammals not endowed with a natural defense against the elements, such as fur or a thick hide⟩

synonyms being, bird, body, creature, customer, devil, guy, head, individual, life, man, mortal, party, person, scout, sort, soul, specimen, thing, wight

related words hominid, homo, humanoid; brother, fellow, fellowman, neighbor; celebrity, personage, personality, self, somebody

near antonyms animal, beast, brute

humane *adj* **1** having or marked by sympathy and consideration for others ⟨*humane* guards who treated the prisoners decently⟩ ⟨the Geneva conventions spelled out standards for *humane* treatment of prisoners of war⟩

synonyms beneficent, benevolent, benignant, compassionate, good-hearted, kind, kindhearted, kindly, softhearted, sympathetic, tender, tenderhearted, warm-hearted

related words attentive, considerate, thoughtful; affable, benign, cordial, friendly, gentle, good, good-natured, good-tempered, gracious, mild, nice, pleasant;

clement, forbearing, forgiving, lenient, merciful, soft; patient, pitying, tolerant, understanding; altruistic, brotherly, charitable, generous, greathearted, humanitarian, magnanimous, noble, openhearted, philanthropic, unselfish, unsparing

near antonyms merciless, pitiless, ruthless; inconsiderate, insensitive, thoughtless, uncaring, unthinking; grim, hard-boiled, harsh, heavy-handed, severe, stern, tough, unsentimental; hateful, malevolent, malicious, mean, spiteful, virulent

antonyms barbarous, bestial, brutal, brutish, callous, cold-blooded, cruel, hardhearted, heartless, inhuman, inhumane, insensate, savage, unfeeling, unkind, unkindly, unsympathetic

2 having or showing the capacity for sharing the feelings of another ⟨the movie's *humane* depiction of people who are physically and mentally challenged⟩ — see SYMPATHETIC 1

humanitarian *adj* having or showing a concern for the welfare of others ⟨*humanitarian* efforts to aid the earthquake victims⟩ — see CHARITABLE 1

humanity *n* **1** human beings in general ⟨all *humanity* can learn from this tragedy⟩ — see PEOPLE 1
2 the capacity for feeling for another's unhappiness or misfortune ⟨a country known for the *humanity* of its liberal immigration policy⟩ — see HEART 1
3 the human race ⟨in Greek mythology, the gods display many of the weaknesses of *humanity,* such as jealousy, foolishness, and greed⟩ — see MANKIND

humankind *n* **1** human beings in general ⟨all *humankind* shares the desire for peace⟩ — see PEOPLE 1
2 the human race ⟨perhaps someday *humankind* will find the key that unlocks the mystery of the universe⟩ — see MANKIND

humble *adj* **1** not having or showing any feelings of superiority, self-assertiveness, or showiness ⟨a medical scientist who remained remarkably *humble* even after winning the Nobel Prize⟩ ⟨even though she'd been twice proven wrong, Janet's attitude was still far from *humble*⟩

synonyms demure, lowly, meek, modest, retiring, unassuming, unpretentious

related words acquiescent, compliant, deferential, resigned, submissive, unaggressive, unassertive, yielding; cowering, cringing, shrinking; ingenuous, naive (*or* naïve), plain, simple, unaffected; bashful, diffident, mousy (*or* mousey), overmodest, passive, quiet, reserved, shy, subdued, timid, unobtrusive

near antonyms aggressive, assertive, audacious, bold, brash, brassy, cheeky, forward; cocksure, cocky, confident, overconfident, self-confident; egocentric, egoistic, self-centered, self-satisfied; boastful, bombastic, vain, vainglorious; condescending, disdainful, dominant, dominating, domineering, imperious, lofty, lordly, magisterial, masterful, overbearing, patronizing, pontificating; flamboyant, flaunting, highfalutin, parading, ostentatious, showy

antonyms arrogant, conceited, egotistic (*or* egotistical), haughty, high-hat, pompous, presumptuous, pretentious, prideful, proud, self-assertive, self-conceited, self-important, stuck-up, supercilious, superior

2 belonging to the class of people of low social or economic rank ⟨a *humble* peasant girl who claimed she was chosen by God to restore the French king to his throne⟩ — see IGNOBLE 1

humble *vb* to reduce to a lower standing in one's own eyes or in others' eyes ⟨Philip was utterly *humbled* by a

crushing defeat in the first round of the state chess tournament⟩

synonyms abase, debase, degrade, demean, discredit, disgrace, dishonor, humiliate, lower, shame, smirch, take down

related words abash, discomfit, discountenance, embarrass, fluster, mortify; belittle, castigate, criticize, decry, depreciate, detract, disparage, minimize, put down, ridicule; bad-mouth, defame, defile, libel, malign, slander; affront, insult; censure, condemn, damn, denounce, reprobate

near antonyms acclaim, applaud, boast, celebrate, cite, commend, compliment, congratulate, decorate, eulogize, extol (*also* extoll), fete (*or* fête), hail, honor, laud, praise, salute, tout; acknowledge, recognize; highlight, play up, spotlight; dignify, ennoble, enshrine, glorify, magnify; lift, promote, raise, upgrade, uplift

antonyms aggrandize, elevate, exalt

humbleness *n* the absence of any feelings of being better than others ⟨in a display of true *humbleness* he gave much of the credit for his discovery to others⟩ — see HUMILITY

humbly *adv* in a manner showing no signs of pride or self-assertion ⟨*humbly* accepted the criticism⟩ — see LOWLY

humbug *n* **1** an imitation that is passed off as genuine ⟨tests showed that the "old" map of America was a cleverly made *humbug*⟩ — see FAKE 1
2 language, behavior, or ideas that are absurd and contrary to good sense ⟨those UFO stories are a lot of *humbug*⟩ — see NONSENSE 1
3 one who makes false claims of identity or expertise ⟨one *humbug* after another claimed to be the miraculously surviving daughter of the Russian czar⟩ — see IMPOSTOR

humbug *vb* to cause to believe what is untrue ⟨*humbugged* into believing that the bones were the skeleton of a prehistoric human being⟩ — see DECEIVE

humbuggery *n* language, behavior, or ideas that are absurd and contrary to good sense ⟨a lot of *humbuggery* about a mean old witch that lives in the woods⟩ — see NONSENSE 1

humdrum *adj* causing weariness, restlessness, or lack of interest ⟨leads a *humdrum* life that will never be made into a major motion picture⟩ ⟨a *humdrum* meal⟩ — see BORING

humid *adj* containing or characterized by an uncomfortable amount of moisture ⟨the air was so *humid* that our beach towels hanging on the line never really got dry⟩

synonyms muggy, sticky, sultry

related words summery, sweltering, torrid; semitropical (*also* semitropic), subtropical (*also* subtropic), tropic, tropical; close, heavy, oppressive, smothering, stifling, stuffy, suffocating; clammy, damp, dank, moist; drenched, dripping, soaked, sodden, soggy, sopping, soppy, waterlogged, wet

near antonyms bracing, cool, crisp, fresh, invigorating, refreshing; arid, baked, burned, burnt, dehydrated, desert, droughty, dusty, parched, scorched, seared, semiarid, sere, thirsty

antonyms dry

humidity *n* the amount of water suspended in the air in tiny droplets ⟨the *humidity* made the hot day seem even hotter⟩ — see MOISTURE

humiliate *vb* to reduce to a lower standing in one's own eyes or in others' eyes ⟨no student feels *humiliated* for not having the "right" clothes because everyone is wearing a school uniform⟩ — see HUMBLE

humility *n* the absence of any feelings of being better than others ⟨displaying genuine *humility*, the peace activist accepted the Nobel Prize on behalf of all who have worked to end the violence⟩
synonyms demureness, humbleness, lowliness, meekness, modesty, retiringness
related words acquiescence, compliance, deference, resignedness, submission, submissiveness; ingenuousness, naïveté (*also* naivete); directness, plainness, simpleness; bashfulness, diffidence, passiveness, passivity, quietness, reserve, reservedness, shyness, timidity, timidness
near antonyms aggressiveness, assertiveness; audaciousness, boldness, brashness, brassiness, cheek, cheekiness, cockiness, forwardness, overconfidence, presumptuousness, temerity; impudence, insolence, nerve; boastfulness, self-centeredness, self-satisfaction; vanity, vaingloriousness; condescension, disdain, imperiousness, lordliness, masterfulness; flamboyance, ostentation, ostentatiousness, showiness
antonyms arrogance, conceit, egoism, egotism, haughtiness, pompousness, pretense (*or* pretence), pretension, pretentiousness, pride, pridefulness, superciliousness, superiority

hummer *n* an ambitious person who eagerly goes after what is desired ⟨she's a real *hummer* when it comes to being the top seller in the annual cookie drive⟩ — see GO-GETTER

humming *adj* marked by much life, movement, or activity ⟨the new science center is usually *humming* with school groups on Thursdays⟩ — see ALIVE 2

humor *n* **1** the amusing quality or element in something ⟨Sarah failed to see any *humor* in being chased by the dog, but Tom thought it was quite funny⟩
synonyms drollness, funniness, hilariousness, humorousness, richness
related words amusement, enjoyment, fun, pleasure; absurdity, irony, laughableness, ludicrousness, ridiculousness; burlesque, caricature, comedy, farce, jest, lampoon, parody, satire, slapstick
near antonyms agony, anguish, heartache, misery, sorrow, woe
antonyms pathos
2 humorous entertainment ⟨a screenwriter best known for lowbrow *humor*⟩ — see COMEDY
3 a state of mind dominated by a particular emotion ⟨the prospect of going shopping after school put her in a good *humor* all day⟩ — see MOOD 1

humor *vb* to give in to (a desire) ⟨*humored* her grandfather by listening to his war stories for the hundredth time⟩ — see INDULGE

humorist *n* a person (as a writer) noted for or specializing in humor ⟨Mark Twain is perhaps America's most beloved *humorist*⟩
synonyms card, comedian, comic, jester, joker, jokester, wag, wit
related words comedienne, entertainer; banterer, cut up, kidder, practical joker, prankster, teaser, wisecracker; buffoon, clown, fool, harlequin, zany; caricaturist, lampooner, parodist, satirist

humorless *adj* not joking or playful in mood or manner ⟨*humorless* people who can't see the lighter side of life⟩ — see SERIOUS 1

humorous *adj* **1** causing or intended to cause laughter ⟨the *humorous* antics of the Three Stooges⟩ ⟨"most hu-

morous costume" went to the girl dressed as Little Bo Peep⟩ — see FUNNY 1
2 given to or marked by mature intelligent humor ⟨the movie's a *humorous* look at love and marriage⟩ — see WITTY

humorousness *n* the amusing quality or element in something ⟨the *humorousness* of falling on a banana peel is usually lost on the person who falls⟩ — see HUMOR 1

hump *vb* **1** to devote serious and sustained effort ⟨the farmers had to really *hump* to get the harvest in before the rains⟩ — see LABOR
2 to proceed or move quickly ⟨the boat was really *humping* before the motor started to sputter all of a sudden⟩ — see HURRY 2

hunch *vb* to lie low with the limbs close to the body ⟨he *hunched* next to a bush to avoid being seen⟩ — see CROUCH

hung *also* **hanged** *adj* bending downward or forward ⟨stood penitently before the principal with *hung* head while he scolded her⟩ — see NODDING

hunger *n* **1** a need or desire for food ⟨no amount of *hunger* would induce me to eat octopus⟩
synonyms appetite, emptiness, famishment
related words rapaciousness, ravenousness, voracity; malnutrition, starvation, undernourishment; craving, sweet tooth; stomach; famine, fast, hunger strike; gluttony, gourmandism, greed, hoggishness
near antonyms fill, fullness, glut, repletion, satiation, satiety, satisfaction
2 a strong wish for something ⟨a lonely girl with a *hunger* for love⟩ — see DESIRE
3 urgent desire or interest ⟨reads everything he can find on airplanes with a seemingly insatiable *hunger*⟩ — see EAGERNESS

hunger (**for**) *vb* to have an earnest wish to own or enjoy ⟨voters *hungering for* honest and upright leadership⟩ — see DESIRE

hungry *adj* **1** feeling a desire or need for food ⟨John was still *hungry* after eating only a muffin for breakfast⟩
synonyms empty, famished, starved, starving
related words rapacious, ravenous, voracious, wolfish; malnourished, underfed, undernourished; gluttonous, gormandizing, greedy, hoggish, insatiable, piggish
near antonyms engorged, glutted, gorged, overfed, overfull, replete, sated, satiated, stuffed, surfeited
antonyms full, satisfied
2 showing urgent desire or interest ⟨*hungry* for the latest news⟩ — see EAGER

hung up *adj* **1** having extreme or relentless concern ⟨Stephanie's parents are already *hung up* about her getting into a good college, and she's only six years old⟩
synonyms obsessed
related words absorbed, anxious, concerned, distracted, engaged, engrossed, full, involved, occupied, prepossessed, preoccupied, worried; ardent, crazy, fervent, fervid, foolish, impassioned, nuts, passionate, silly
near antonyms apathetic, cool, detached, dispassionate, unconcerned, unenthusiastic, uninterested, uninvolved
2 feeling or showing uncomfortable feelings of uncertainty ⟨so *hung up* about getting another C in math that she spends hours doing her homework⟩ — see NERVOUS 1

hunk *n* a small uneven mass ⟨what looked like a *hunk* of potato in her stew turned out to be a pebble⟩ — see LUMP 1

hunt *n* an act or process of looking carefully or thoroughly for someone or something ⟨soon the whole family was involved in the *hunt* for Mom's car keys⟩ — see SEARCH

hunt *vb* **1** to seek out (game) for food or sport ⟨Indians of the plains *hunted* buffalo for food, clothing, and shelter⟩

   synonyms chase, stalk

   related words capture, drag, net, snare, trap; ferret, dog, hawk, hound; pursue, run down, track, trail; gun (for), harpoon, kill, shoot; poach

   2 to go in search of ⟨I spent all afternoon *hunting* a job for the summer⟩ — see SEEK 1

   3 to go into or range over for purposes of discovery ⟨*hunts* the neighborhood for returnable bottles⟩ — see EXPLORE 2

hunt (down *or* up) *vb* to come upon after searching, study, or effort ⟨managed to *hunt down* his ancestors back to the 16th century⟩ — see FIND 1

hunt (through) *vb* to look through (as a place) carefully or thoroughly in an effort to find or discover something ⟨*hunted through* old birth and marriage records to trace the family tree⟩ — see SEARCH 1

hunter *n* a person who hunts game ⟨*hunters* must have a license to shoot deer⟩

   synonyms huntsman

   related words huntress, sportsman, sportswoman; archer, gunner; falconer, hawker; hunter-gatherer, trapper; poacher

huntsman *n* a person who hunts game ⟨the *huntsman* offered the king two pheasants for the royal table⟩ — see HUNTER

hurdle *n* something that makes movement or progress more difficult ⟨the many *hurdles* he had to overcome on the road to success⟩ — see ENCUMBRANCE

hurl *vb* to send through the air especially with a quick forward motion of the arm ⟨*hurled* snowballs at each other⟩ — see THROW

hurly-burly *n* a state of noisy, confused activity ⟨lost sight of his parents in all the *hurly-burly* of the fair⟩ — see COMMOTION

hurried *adj* acting or done with excessive or careless speed ⟨*hurried* shoppers who grab the wrong items⟩ ⟨ate a *hurried* meal⟩ — see HASTY 1

hurriedly *adv* with excessive or careless speed ⟨*hurriedly* dashed off a note to let them know she'd been called away for an emergency⟩ — see HASTILY 1

hurry *n* **1** excited and often showy or disorderly speed ⟨after all her *hurry* to get her history report done on time, Elizabeth learned that it wasn't due till the following week⟩

   synonyms haste, hastiness, hustle, precipitation, precipitousness, rush

   related words bustle, flurry, flutter, scurry, scuttle, stir, whirl; beeline, dash, scramble, stampede; hotheadedness, impetuosity, impetuousness, impulsiveness, rashness; fleetness, quickness, rapidity, rapidness, speed, speediness, swiftness; celerity, dispatch, expeditiousness, promptness

   near antonyms dilatoriness, lateness, pokiness, procrastination, slowness; languor, leisureliness, lethargy, sluggishness, torpor; inaction, inactivity, inertia, inertness, quiescence

   antonyms deliberateness, deliberation

   2 a high rate of movement or performance ⟨a person who does everything in a *hurry*⟩ — see SPEED

hurry *vb* **1** to cause to move or proceed fast or faster ⟨the new nursing staff was *hurried* through the orientation because they were so desperately needed on the ward⟩

   synonyms accelerate, hasten, quicken, rush, speed (up), whisk

   related words drive, goad, prod, propel, push, race, spur, stir, urge; advance, aid, dispatch, ease, encourage, expedite, facilitate, forward, further

   near antonyms delay, hamper, hinder, restrain; brake, check, stay

   antonyms decelerate, retard, slow (down)

   2 to proceed or move quickly ⟨if we *hurry,* we'll make the four o'clock train⟩

   synonyms barrel, bolt, bowl, breeze, career, course, dash, fly, hasten, hotfoot (it), hump, hurtle, hustle, pelt, race, rip, rocket, run, rush, rustle, scoot, scurry, scuttle, shoot, speed, step (along), tear, trot, whirl, whisk, zip, zoom

   related words dart, flit, scamper, scud, scuffle; stampede, streak, whiz (*or* whizz); gallop, jog, sprint; accelerate, quicken; catch up, fast-forward, outpace, outrun, outstrip, overtake

   phrases shake a leg

   near antonyms dally, dawdle, drag, lag, linger, loiter, tarry; amble, lumber, plod, saunter, shuffle, stroll; decelerate, slow (down *or* up)

   antonyms crawl, creep, poke

hurt *n* something that causes loss or pain ⟨the town suffered no significant *hurt* from the hurricane⟩ — see INJURY 1

hurt *vb* **1** to feel or cause physical pain ⟨a bad sprain that really *hurts*⟩ ⟨I *hurt* all over⟩

   synonyms ache, pain, smart

   related words bleed, bite, burn, chafe, cramp, fester, itch, nag, pinch, pound, rack, sting, swell, throb, tingle, twinge; agonize, suffer

   2 to reduce the soundness, effectiveness, or perfection of ⟨don't worry that you'll *hurt* the new lawn by walking across it⟩ — see DAMAGE 1

   3 to cause bodily damage to ⟨reading in poor light *hurts* your eyes⟩ — see INJURE 1

   4 to feel deep sadness or mental pain ⟨I know you must be *hurting* from the cruel words they said⟩ — see GRIEVE

hurtful *adj* **1** causing or capable of causing harm ⟨the most *hurtful* thing you can do to this silk dress is put it in the dryer⟩ — see HARMFUL

   2 hard to accept or bear especially emotionally ⟨he said *hurtful* things that she could never forgive⟩ — see BITTER 2

hurting *adj* causing or feeling bodily pain ⟨a *hurting* finger kept her from writing neatly⟩ — see PAINFUL 1

hurtle *vb* **1** to proceed or move quickly ⟨the satellite *hurtled* through space⟩ — see HURRY 2

   2 to send through the air especially with a quick forward motion of the arm ⟨*hurtled* his spear at the tiger as it leaped toward him⟩ — see THROW

husband *n* the male partner in a marriage ⟨she and her *husband* just celebrated their 50th wedding anniversary⟩

   synonyms man, old man

   related words consort, mate, partner, spouse; bridegroom, groom; widower

husbandry *n* **1** careful management of material resources ⟨in accordance with his practice of good *husbandry,* he never bought anything on credit⟩ — see ECONOMY

2 the science or occupation of cultivating the soil, producing crops, and raising livestock ⟨a family of winemakers whose tradition of vineyard *husbandry* went back several generations⟩ — see AGRICULTURE

hush *n* **1** a state of freedom from storm or disturbance ⟨the storm passed, and a *hush* fell over the sea⟩ — see CALM

2 the near or complete absence of sound ⟨a *hush* fell over the auditorium as the lights went down⟩ — see SILENCE 2

hush *vb* **1** to become still and orderly ⟨the whole class *hushed* when the teacher walked in⟩ — see QUIET 1

2 to stop talking ⟨the talkative lady next to me on the train never *hushed* once during the whole four-hour trip⟩ — see SHUT UP

3 to stop the noise or speech of ⟨tried to *hush* the baby by making a lot of silly faces⟩ — see SILENCE 1

hush (up) *vb* to keep from being publicly known ⟨the family was able to *hush up* the scandal so it never reached the papers⟩ — see SUPPRESS 1

hushed *adj* **1** free from disturbing noise or uproar ⟨entered the *hushed* interior of the church⟩ — see QUIET 1

2 free from storms or physical disturbance ⟨the *hushed* lake was smooth as glass the morning after the storm⟩ — see CALM 1

3 mostly or entirely without sound ⟨a *hushed* sickroom⟩ — see SILENT 3

4 not known or meant to be known by the general populace ⟨*hushed* negotiations between the two countries⟩ — see PRIVATE 1

husk *n* something that encloses another thing especially to protect it ⟨corn *husks*⟩ ⟨a high stone wall is the *husk* that protects her from prying curiosity seekers⟩ — see ¹CASE 1

husk *vb* to remove the natural covering of ⟨*husking* coconuts⟩ — see PEEL

¹husky *adj* strongly and heavily built ⟨a *husky* weight lifter⟩

synonyms beefy, brawny, burly, hulking

related words able-bodied, athletic, heavy, hefty, herculean, mighty, muscle-bound, muscular, powerful, robust, rugged, stalwart, strapping, strong, sturdy; chunky, compact, heavyset, solid, squat, squatty, stocky, thickset; dumpy, lumpish, portly, pudgy, stout

near antonyms lean, light, lightweight, slender, slight, slim, svelte, sylphlike, thin, willowy; bony, gangling, gangly, gaunt, gawky, lanky, scrawny, skinny, spare, twiggy; sinewy, spidery, wiry; delicate, emaciated, fragile, frail, puny, weakly

²husky *adj* harsh and dry in sound ⟨a voice *husky* from years of smoking⟩ — see HOARSE

hustle *n* **1** a scheme in which the victim is cheated out of his money after first gaining his trust ⟨finally got wise to his *hustle* and threatened to call the police⟩ — see CONFIDENCE GAME

2 excited and often showy or disorderly speed ⟨the *hustle* and bustle of the holiday season⟩ — see HURRY 1

3 readiness to engage in daring or difficult activity ⟨with his characteristic *hustle*, he had everything lined up in two days⟩ — see ENTERPRISE 2

hustle *vb* **1** to devote serious and sustained effort ⟨everyone really *hustled* to get the magazine out on schedule⟩ — see LABOR

2 to proceed or move quickly ⟨we'd better *hustle*, or we'll miss the train⟩ — see HURRY 2

3 to rob by the use of trickery or threats ⟨a customer *hustled* the cashier by getting her all confused while she was making change⟩ — see FLEECE

hustler *n* an ambitious person who eagerly goes after what is desired ⟨the ad for the sales job claims that for someone who's a real *hustler*, the sky's the limit⟩ — see GO-GETTER

hut *n* a small, simply constructed, and often temporary dwelling ⟨smoke rose from a fisherman's *hut* on the shore of the lake⟩ — see SHACK

hutch *n* **1** a small, simply constructed, and often temporary dwelling ⟨the whole family lives in a tiny *hutch* made of tin and cardboard⟩ — see SHACK

2 a storage case typically having doors and shelves ⟨keeps her best china in a *hutch* in the dining room⟩ — see CABINET

hybrid *adj* being offspring produced by parents of different races, breeds, species, or genera ⟨a *hybrid* rose called "American Beauty" was actually first developed in France⟩ — see MIXED 1

hybrid *n* an offspring of parents with different genes especially when of different races, breeds, species, or genera ⟨a tangelo is a *hybrid* of the tangerine and the grapefruit⟩

synonyms cross, crossbreed, mongrel

related words mulatto

near antonyms purebred, thoroughbred

hygienic *adj* free from filth, infection, or dangers to health ⟨food packaging done under *hygienic* conditions⟩ — see SANITARY

hymn *n* a religious song ⟨our Sunday church services always open with a *hymn*⟩

synonyms anthem, canticle, carol, chorale, psalm, spiritual

related words dirge, lament, requiem, threnody; Gloria Patri, hallelujah, paean; mass, oratorio; processional, recessional

hymnal *n* a book of hymns ⟨*hymnals* are distributed among the congregation before the church service so everyone can join in the singing⟩

synonyms hymnbook, psalmody

related words breviary, missal, Psalter, songster

hymnbook *n* a book of hymns ⟨knew the words of all the church songs and didn't need a *hymnbook*⟩ — see HYMNAL

hyperbole *n* the representation of something in terms that go beyond the facts ⟨"enough food to feed a whole army" is a common example of *hyperbole*⟩ — see EXAGGERATION

hypercritical *adj* given to making or expressing unfavorable judgments about things ⟨don't be so *hypercritical* of your sister's essay—you can't expect a third-grader to write as well as you do⟩ — see CRITICAL 1

hyperventilate *vb* to breathe hard, quickly, or with difficulty ⟨he was so nervous he began *hyperventilating*, and the extra oxygen made him dizzy⟩ — see GASP

hypnosis *n* the art or act of inducing in a person a sleeplike state during which he or she readily follows suggestions ⟨with *hypnosis* there's some question as to just how involuntary the actions of the hypnotized person really are⟩

synonyms hypnotism, mesmerism

related words bewitchment, enchantment, spellbinding

hypnotic *adj* tending to cause sleep ⟨her eyes soon grew heavy from the *hypnotic* rhythm of the train's wheels⟩

synonyms drowsy, narcotic, opiate, slumberous (*or* slumbrous)

related words depressant, relaxant, sedative, tranquilizing (*also* tranquillizing); calming, lulling, quieting, relaxing, restful, settling, soothing; analgesic, anesthetic, anesthetizing, benumbing, deadening, dulling, numbing; hypnotizing, mesmerizing, stupefying

near antonyms arousing, awakening, energizing, invigorating, rousing, stimulating, wakening, waking

antonyms stimulant

hypnotism *n* the art or act of inducing in a person a sleep-like state during which he or she readily follows suggestions ⟨some people have undergone *hypnotism* in order to induce them to give up their smoking habit⟩ — see HYPNOSIS

hypnotize *vb* to hold the attention of as if by a spell ⟨the crowd was *hypnotized* by the powerful, eloquent speaker⟩ — see ENTHRALL 1

hypocrisy *n* the pretending of having virtues, principles, or beliefs that one in fact does not have ⟨the *hypocrisy* of people who claim to care about the environment but ride around in gas-guzzlers⟩

synonyms cant, dissembling, dissimulation, insincerity, piousness, sanctimoniousness

related words deception, deceptiveness, dishonesty, falsity, pretense, pretension, pretentiousness, self-righteousness, self-satisfaction; duplicity, fakery, falseness, fraudulentness, shamming; artificiality, glibness, oiliness, smoothness, unctuousness

near antonyms candor, honesty, openness, probity, straightforwardness, truthfulness; artlessness, guilelessness, naturalness, unaffectedness

antonyms genuineness, sincerity

hypocritical *adj* not being or expressing what one appears to be or express ⟨it's *hypocritical* to says mean things behind Jill's back, and then to act nice when you want something from her⟩ — see INSINCERE

hypodermic *n* a slender hollow instrument by which material is put into or taken from the body through the skin ⟨he hardly felt it when the nurse stuck the *hypodermic* in his arm⟩ — see NEEDLE 1

hypodermic needle *n* a slender hollow instrument by which material is put into or taken from the body through the skin ⟨doesn't mind getting shots as long as he doesn't catch sight of the *hypodermic needle*⟩ — see NEEDLE 1

hypodermic syringe *n* a slender hollow instrument by which material is put into or taken from the body through the skin ⟨the nurse filled a different *hypodermic syringe* for each injection⟩ — see NEEDLE 1

hypothesis *n* an idea that is the starting point for making a case or conducting an investigation ⟨working on the *hypothesis* that teenagers function better in the late morning, some high schools are starting classes later⟩ — see THEORY

hypothetical *adj* existing only as an assumption or speculation ⟨we talked about what we would do in various *hypothetical* emergencies⟩ — see THEORETICAL 1

hysteria *n* a state of wildly excited activity or emotion ⟨the *hysteria* of the mother when she realized that she had lost her four-year-old son in the crowd⟩ — see FRENZY

hysterical *adj* 1 causing or intended to cause laughter ⟨some of the things my little sister says are *hysterical*⟩ — see FUNNY 1

2 feeling overwhelming fear or worry ⟨the police officer assured the mother that there was no need to get *hysterical,* for most children are found safe and sound⟩ — see FRANTIC 1

I

ice–cold *adj* having a low or subnormal temperature ⟨*ice-cold* hands from hours spent shoveling snow⟩ — see COLD 1

icy *adj* **1** having a low or subnormal temperature ⟨an *icy* drink that was especially refreshing on that hot afternoon⟩ — see COLD 1
2 lacking in friendliness or warmth of feeling ⟨she wondered why the salesclerk at the boutique gave her an *icy* glare⟩ — see COLD 2

idea *n* something imagined or pictured in the mind ⟨my *idea* of the perfect vacation spot is an unspoiled beach⟩
synonyms concept, conception, image, impression, notion, picture, thought
related words apprehension, premonition, presentiment; chimera, illusion, phantasm; caprice, conceit, fancy, freak, notion, vagary, whim; observation, perception, reflection; assumption, belief, conclusion, conviction; conjecture, guess, hunch, hypothesis, speculation, supposition, surmise, theory; brainstorm, inspiration
near antonyms actuality, fact, reality

ideal *adj* being entirely without fault or flaw ⟨for years she's been searching for a man who would make an *ideal* husband, and she's still looking⟩ — see PERFECT 1

ideal *n* **1** someone of such unequaled perfection as to deserve imitation ⟨she's our *ideal* of the concerned, caring physician⟩
synonyms beau ideal, classic, exemplar, model, nonpareil, paragon
related words role model; embodiment, epitome, incarnation, manifestation, personification; archetype, example, paradigm, pattern; guideline, principle, rule; gauge (*also* gage), standard, touchstone; essence, quintessence; acme, apex, culmination, peak, pinnacle, summit, zenith
2 the most perfect type or example ⟨the Taj Mahal in India is generally regarded as the *ideal* of Mogul architectural beauty⟩ — see QUINTESSENCE 1

idealist *n* one whose conduct is guided more by the image of perfection than by the real world ⟨an *idealist* sees the best in everyone, regardless of how they behave⟩
synonyms dreamer, romantic, romanticist, utopian, visionary
related words sentimentalist; daydreamer, optimist, theorist; perfectionist; thinker
near antonyms cynic, defeatist, pessimist
antonyms pragmatist, realist

idealize *vb* to represent or think of as better than reality ⟨he had a tendency to *idealize* his heroes and believe they could do no wrong⟩
synonyms glamorize (*also* glamourize), glorify, romanticize
related words daydream, imagine, romance, theorize, vision; better, perfect
near antonyms blame, condemn, criticize, denounce; worsen

ideally *adv* without any flaws or errors ⟨an *ideally* executed routine on the parallel bars that earned him perfect scores from the judges⟩ — see PERFECTLY 1

idée fixe *n* something about which one is constantly thinking or concerned ⟨had this *idée fixe* that people

were spying on her with electromagnetic waves⟩ — see FIXATION

identical *adj* **1** being one and not another ⟨both families wanted the *identical* puppy and weren't accepting the argument that its littermates were just as good⟩ — see SAME 2
2 resembling another in every respect ⟨*identical* dresses whose only difference is a designer label that fetches a high price⟩ — see SAME 1

identicalness *n* the state of being exactly alike ⟨the *identicalness* of your answers to your friend's suggests that someone copied⟩ — see IDENTITY 1

identify *vb* **1** to find out or establish the identity of ⟨with a quick look at everyone's tongue, Mom was able to *identify* the person who had sneaked a piece of blueberry pie⟩
synonyms distinguish, pinpoint, single (out)
related words diagnose; determine, find; locate, pick out, place, recognize, spot; check, examine, inspect, investigate, notice, observe, scrutinize; betray, disclose, discover, reveal
near antonyms camouflage, conceal, disguise, hide; counterfeit, feign, sham, simulate
2 to think of (something) in combination ⟨for some reason, he always *identified* the color red with flowers⟩ — see ASSOCIATE 2

identifying *adj* serving to identify as belonging to an individual or group ⟨the marching band's striking black-and-silver uniforms serve as its *identifying* mark for thousands of parade spectators⟩ — see CHARACTERISTIC 1

identity *n* **1** the state of being exactly alike ⟨although the covers of the two paperback editions of the novel are different, there's a complete *identity* in the texts⟩
synonyms identicalness, sameness
related words oneness; homogeneity, homology; equality, equivalence; accordance, agreement, conformity, congruity, correspondence, likeness, resemblance, similarity
near antonyms alteration, change, modification, variation; distinction, distinctiveness, distinctness, exoticness, individuality, separateness, separation, uniqueness, unusualness; deviance, divergence; variance; incompatibility, incongruity, incongruousness; contrast
antonyms difference, disagreement, discrepancy, disparateness, disparity, dissimilarity, unlikeness
2 the set of qualities that make a person different from other people ⟨children begin to form their own *identity* by the age of two⟩ — see INDIVIDUALITY

ideology *n* the basic beliefs or guiding principles of a person or group ⟨members of that sect follow an *ideology* of nonviolence and freely given cooperation⟩ — see CREED 1

idiocy *n* a foolish act or idea ⟨planning to throw a party while your parents were gone was pure *idiocy*⟩ — see FOLLY 1

idiom *n* a sequence of words having a specific meaning ⟨the English *idiom* "how are you doing?" is our version of a greeting that in some other languages can be translated as "how are you going?"⟩ — see PHRASE

idiosyncrasy *n* an odd or peculiar habit ⟨his only *idiosyncrasy* was collecting pencil erasers and making little dolls out of them⟩
synonyms crotchet, eccentricity, mannerism, oddity, peculiarity, quirk, singularity, trick
related words affectation, airs; attribute, characteristic, mark, property, trait; custom, habit, pattern, practice (*also* practise), way, wont; addiction; abnormality, perversion; disposition, genius, leaning, partiality; bent, inclination, penchant, predilection, predisposition, proclivity, propensity, tendency, turn; attitude, character, humor, identity, individuality, nature, personality, temperament
near antonyms conformity, sameness

idiot *n* a stupid person ⟨only an *idiot* would jump off a bridge just because their friends told them to⟩
synonyms blockhead, cretin, dodo, dolt, donkey, dope, dork [*slang*], dumbbell, dummy, dunce, fathead, goon, half-wit, ignoramus, imbecile, jackass, knothead, moron, nincompoop, ninny, nitwit, numskull (*or* numbskull), pinhead, simpleton, stock, turkey
related words booby, fool, goose, loony (*also* looney), lunatic, madman, nut, zany; loser; gawk; featherbrain, scatterbrain; beast, boor, cad, churl, clown, creep, cur, heel, jerk, skunk, snake, stinker, villain
near antonyms egghead, intellectual, sage, thinker
antonyms brain, genius

idle *vb* to spend time doing nothing ⟨she likes to *idle* during the summer even though her parents always tell her to get out and do something⟩
synonyms dally, dawdle, dillydally, hang around, hang out, loaf, loll, lounge
related words fiddle, fool, mess, monkey, play, potter, putter, trifle; estivate, hibernate; lag, linger, loiter, poke, relax, rest, tarry; amble, mosey, saunter, stroll; bum, furlough, goldbrick, malinger
phrases kill time, lie around, mark time, waste time
near antonyms drudge, grind, grub, hump, hustle, labor, moil, peg, plod, plow, plug, slave, sweat, toil, travail, work; apply, buckle (down); exert, put out

idle *adj* **1** not being in a state of use, activity, or employment ⟨the car was *idle* for two weeks while they went on vacation⟩ — see INACTIVE 2
2 not easily aroused to action or work ⟨an *idle* employee who always seems to be either on break or at lunch⟩ — see LAZY

idleness *n* **1** an inclination not to do work or engage in activities ⟨the brothers' innate *idleness* meant that neither did much, either inside or outside the house⟩ — see LAZINESS
2 lack of action or activity ⟨a day spent in *idleness* is nice, but a month of doing nothing is boring!⟩ — see INACTION
3 lack of use ⟨the *idleness* of the sewing machine was apparent by its thick layer of dust⟩ — see DISUSE

idler *n* a lazy person ⟨an *idler* will not do well in this class, which requires a lot of work⟩ — see LAZYBONES

idolater *or* **idolator** *n* a person who does not worship the God of the Bible ⟨some societies are more tolerant of *idolaters* than others⟩ — see HEATHEN 1

idolatry *n* excessive admiration of or devotion to a person ⟨my sister's *idolatry* of her favorite rock star is a bit disturbing⟩ — see WORSHIP

idolization *n* excessive admiration of or devotion to a person ⟨the mass *idolization* of the sports figure resulted in the public's refusal to believe that he could ever do wrong⟩ — see WORSHIP

idolize *vb* to love or admire too much ⟨she *idolized* her big sister⟩
synonyms adore, adulate, canonize, deify, dote (on), worship
related words appreciate, cherish, esteem, prize, treasure, value; fancy, favor, like, prefer; regard; respect, revere, venerate; approve, endorse (*also* indorse), support
near antonyms abhor, abominate, despise, detest, disdain, dislike, hate, loathe; belittle, deprecate, disparage, put down

idolizing *adj* reflecting great admiration or devotion ⟨gave his fiancée an *idolizing* glance⟩ — see WORSHIPFUL

ignitable *adj* capable of catching or being set on fire ⟨gasoline fumes are quite *ignitable*⟩ — see COMBUSTIBLE

ignite *vb* to set (something) on fire ⟨used kindling to *ignite* the logs in the fireplace⟩ — see BURN 2

ignited *adj* being on fire ⟨the *ignited* fireworks caused explosions that leveled the building⟩ — see ABLAZE 1

ignoble *adj* **1** belonging to the class of people of low social or economic rank ⟨an *ignoble* child cannot grow up to be king⟩
synonyms baseborn, common, humble, inferior, low, lower-class, lowly, mean, plebeian, proletarian, vulgar
related words bourgeois, middle-class; peasant, plain, poor, simple, working-class
near antonyms eminent, illustrious, notable, prominent
antonyms aristocratic, high, highborn, lofty, noble, wellborn
2 not following or in accordance with standards of honor and decency ⟨cheating on a test is an *ignoble* act and can get you expelled⟩
synonyms base, contemptible, despicable, detestable, dirty, dishonorable, low, mean, snide, sordid, vile, wretched
related words bad, black, evil, foul, immoral, iniquitous, wicked, wrong; cruel, nasty, vicious; blamable, blameworthy, censurable, reprehensible; corrupt, debased, debauched, degenerate, depraved, dissolute, perverted; atrocious, villainous; unethical, unprincipled, unscrupulous; discreditable, disgraceful, disreputable, ignominious, shameful
near antonyms ethical, honest, just, principled, righteous, right-minded, scrupulous; commendable, excellent, exemplary, good, moral, right; decent, proper, reputable, respectable, seemly; blameless, guiltless; incorruptible, irreproachable; uncorrupted, unerring
antonyms high, high-minded, honorable, lofty, noble, straight, upright, venerable, virtuous

ignominious *adj* not respectable ⟨some of his friends considered the job of janitor to be an *ignominious* fate for the laid-off executive⟩ — see DISREPUTABLE

ignominy *n* the state of having lost the esteem of others ⟨he spent the week in *ignominy* after being exposed as a cheat during the spelling bee⟩ — see DISGRACE 1

ignoramus *n* a stupid person ⟨only an *ignoramus* would be incapable of learning to tie their own shoes⟩ — see IDIOT

ignorance *n* **1** the state of being unaware or uninformed ⟨*ignorance* of the law is no excuse⟩
synonyms obliviousness, unawareness, unfamiliarity
related words callowness, greenness, inexperience, innocence, naïveté (*also* naivete), rawness, simpleness, unsophistication

near antonyms experience, know-how; sophistication

antonyms acquaintance, awareness, familiarity

2 the state of being unlearned ⟨with such vast sums spent on education, the level of *ignorance* among graduating seniors is a national disgrace⟩

synonyms illiteracy

related words brainlessness, dumbness, idiocy, imbecility, stupidity; philistinism; foolishness, mindlessness, senselessness, witlessness

near antonyms education, instruction, training; enlightenment, knowledge; erudition, scholarship

antonyms learning, literacy

ignorant *adj* **1** lacking in education or the knowledge gained from books ⟨the teacher was committed to educating the children of those poor, *ignorant* farmers⟩

synonyms benighted, dark, illiterate, nonliterate, simple, uneducated, uninstructed, unlearned, unlettered, unread, unschooled, untaught, untutored

related words lowbrow, uncultivated, uncultured; callow, green, inexperienced, innocent, naive (*or* naïve); unsophisticated; raw, untrained; brainless, dumb, idiotic, imbecilic, moronic, stupid, witless; foolish, senseless, silly

near antonyms brilliant, intelligent, smart; experienced, expert, trained; erudite, learned, scholarly; cultivated, cultured, highbrow, intellectual; sophisticated; acquainted, aware, familiar

antonyms educated, knowledgeable, literate, schooled

2 not informed about or aware of something ⟨he was *ignorant* of their plans⟩

synonyms oblivious, unacquainted, unaware, unconscious, ungrounded, uninformed, unknowing, unmindful, unwitting

related words uneducated, unschooled, untaught; absent, absentminded, abstracted, heedless, inattentive

near antonyms conversant, educated, knowledgeable, schooled, taught; heedful, observant; sensitive, sentient

antonyms acquainted, aware, cognizant, conscious, conversant, grounded, informed, knowing, mindful, witting

ignore *vb* **1** to fail to give proper attention to ⟨*ignoring* your homework is sure to lead to a failing grade⟩ — see NEGLECT 1

2 to overlook or dismiss as of little importance ⟨although your science project is worthy of a prize, we can't *ignore* the fact that you broke a couple of the entry rules⟩ — see EXCUSE 1

ilk *n* a number of persons or things that are grouped together because they have something in common ⟨we're looking for chestnuts and other items of that *ilk* for our autumn decorations⟩ — see SORT 1

ill *adj* **1** affected with nausea ⟨she grew *ill* from the constant rocking motion of the boat⟩ — see NAUSEOUS

2 causing or capable of causing harm ⟨one of the *ill* effects of winter weather is the rapid spread of germs as people spend more time together indoors⟩ — see HARMFUL

3 temporarily suffering from a disorder of the body ⟨since I'm *ill*, I guess that I'll just have to miss that math test⟩ — see SICK 1

ill *adv* in a manner so as to cause loss or suffering ⟨in those days society treated debtors very *ill*, even putting them in prison⟩ — see HARDLY 1

ill *n* **1** an abnormal state that disrupts a plant's or animal's normal bodily functioning ⟨chicken pox and the other common *ills* of childhood⟩ — see DISEASE

2 that which is morally unacceptable ⟨idealistic people who try to cure all of our society's *ills*⟩ — see EVIL

ill–advised *adj* showing poor judgment especially in personal relationships or social situations ⟨an *ill-advised* criticism of the principal before the entire student body⟩ — see INDISCREET

ill–bred *adj* **1** lacking in refinement or good taste ⟨the *ill-bred* habit of chewing with the mouth open⟩ — see COARSE 2

2 showing a lack of manners or consideration for others ⟨only an *ill-bred,* conceited person would demand that everyone cater to their whims⟩ — see IMPOLITE

illegal *adj* **1** contrary to or forbidden by law ⟨it is *illegal* to steal⟩

synonyms criminal, illegitimate, illicit, unlawful, wrongful

related words bad, evil, immoral, shameful, sinful, unethical, wicked, wrong; blamable, blameworthy, censurable, reprehensible; banned, barred, disallowed, discouraged, forbidden, interdicted, outlawed, prohibited, proscribed; unauthorized, unlicensed, unsanctioned; corrupt, unprincipled, unscrupulous, villainous

near antonyms ethical, good, just, principled, right, righteous, virtuous; allowed, permitted; authorized, licensed (*also* licenced); approved, endorsed, sanctioned; abetted, encouraged, promoted, suggested, supported; correct, decent, decorous, proper, seemly

antonyms lawful, legal, legitimate

2 not being in accordance with the rules or standards of what is fair in sport ⟨an *illegal* pass⟩ — see FOUL 2

illegitimate *adj* **1** born to a father and mother who are not married ⟨despite being *illegitimate,* Alexander Hamilton rose to greatness⟩

synonyms baseborn, bastard, misbegotten

related words fatherless, motherless; adopted, orphaned

antonyms legitimate

2 contrary to or forbidden by law ⟨an *illegitimate* ploy to get people to invest in their fledgling company⟩ — see ILLEGAL 1

ill–fated *adj* having, prone to, or marked by bad luck ⟨the *ill-fated* trip ended in disaster for all⟩ — see UNLUCKY

ill–favored *adj* unpleasant to look at ⟨an *ill-favored* and yapping little dog that reminded people a lot of its owner⟩ — see UGLY 1

ill–humored *adj* having or showing a habitually bad temper ⟨an *ill-humored* person should probably not take a job that requires dealing with the public⟩ — see ILL-TEMPERED

illicit *adj* contrary to or forbidden by law ⟨users of *illicit* drugs can go to jail⟩ — see ILLEGAL 1

illimitable *adj* being or seeming to be without limits ⟨the *illimitable* expanse of the universe⟩ — see INFINITE

illiteracy *n* the state of being unlearned ⟨far too many children are doomed to a lifetime of *illiteracy* in that country⟩ — see IGNORANCE 2

illiterate *adj* lacking in education or the knowledge gained from books ⟨offered menus with pictures, presumably for the many *illiterate* people who must eat there⟩ — see IGNORANT 1

ill–mannered *adj* showing a lack of manners or consideration for others ⟨an *ill-mannered* child who refuses to say "please" or "thank you"⟩ — see IMPOLITE

ill–natured *adj* having or showing a habitually bad temper ⟨an *ill-natured* and unpleasant old horse that sometimes bites⟩ — see ILL-TEMPERED

illness *n* **1** an abnormal state that disrupts a plant's or animal's normal bodily functioning ⟨suffered a prolonged *illness* that left her weak and tired all the time⟩ — see DISEASE

2 the condition of not being in good health ⟨his chronic *illness* rendered him unfit for military service⟩ — see SICKNESS 1

illogical *adj* not using or following good reasoning ⟨the *illogical* claim that playing basketball makes people taller because one sees so many tall players⟩ ⟨*illogical* people are likely to believe every sensational claim on TV⟩

synonyms fallacious, invalid, irrational, nonrational, unreasonable, unreasoning, unsound, weak

related words misleading, specious; ill-advised, unconsidered, unreasoned; inconsistent; absurd, asinine, foolish, meaningless, nonsensical, preposterous, senseless, silly; odd, peculiar, strange, unusual, weird; insane, mad, nutty, wacky; disordered, disorganized, rambling, random; unconvincing, unsatisfying; inexplicable, unaccountable, unexplainable

near antonyms commonsense, sane, sensible, sober, wise; enlightened, informed, just, justified, reasoned; ordered, organized; clear, cogent, compelling, convincing, credible, persuasive, plausible, satisfying, solid; certain, sure, true; confirmed, corroborated, demonstrated, established, substantiated, validated, well-founded

antonyms logical, rational, reasonable, sound, valid

ill–starred *adj* having, prone to, or marked by bad luck ⟨an *ill-starred* attempt to circumnavigate the earth in a balloon⟩ — see UNLUCKY

ill–tempered *adj* having or showing a habitually bad temper ⟨an *ill-tempered* cat will scratch⟩

synonyms bearish, bilious, cantankerous, disagreeable, dyspeptic, ill-humored, ill-natured, ornery, splenetic, surly

related words choleric, crabby, cranky, crotchety, fussy, grouchy, grumpy, querulous; irascible, irritable, peevish, petulant, quick-tempered, snappish, testy, touchy; argumentative, contentious, contrary; angry, exasperated, indignant, irate, mad, upset, uptight; depressed, dour, glum, morose, sullen

near antonyms agreeable, amicable, congenial, friendly, pleasant; benign, gentle, kind, nice, sweet; bubbly, cheerful, cheery, effervescent, exuberant, high-spirited, lighthearted, lively, joyful, vivacious; content, glad, happy; calm, placid, serene; long-suffering, patient, tolerant

antonyms amiable, good-natured, good-tempered

ill–treat *vb* to inflict physical or emotional harm upon ⟨anyone who *ill-treats* their pets should not be allowed to have any⟩ — see ABUSE 1

illuminate *vb* **1** to supply with light ⟨a floor lamp *illuminates* a living room rather nicely⟩

synonyms illumine, irradiate, light, lighten

related words brighten; beam, beat (down), radiate, shine; floodlight; highlight, spotlight; blaze, burn, fire, flame, glare, glow, ignite, incinerate, kindle; bedazzle, blind, daze, dazzle; gleam, glisten, glitter

near antonyms dim, dull, obscure; cover, shroud, veil; douse, extinguish, put out, quench, snuff (out)

antonyms blacken, darken

2 to make plain or understandable ⟨the teacher's demonstration of the refraction of light really *illuminated* the subject for us⟩ — see EXPLAIN 1

illuminated *adj* filled with much light ⟨an intensely *illuminated* room is usually needed for producing live television shows⟩ — see BRIGHT 2

illumination *n* **1** a statement that makes something clear ⟨the candidate's so-called *illuminations* of his views on a number of controversial issues left many voters in the dark⟩ — see EXPLANATION 1

2 the quality or state of having or giving off light ⟨in that clime the *illumination* of the full moon is such as you can practically read by it⟩ — see BRILLIANCE 1

3 the steady giving off of the form of radiation that makes vision possible ⟨a steady *illumination* from the flashlight was all I had while changing the tire⟩ — see LIGHT 1

illuminative *adj* serving to explain ⟨*illuminative* descriptions of the sights to be seen from the observatory gave us a much better idea of what we were looking at⟩ — see EXPLANATORY

illumine *vb* to supply with light ⟨small table lamps *illumine* the inn's dining room in a most romantic way⟩ — see ILLUMINATE 1

illumined *adj* filled with much light ⟨*illumined* display windows in the street's many shops add much to the holiday glow⟩ — see BRIGHT 2

ill–use *vb* to inflict physical or emotional harm upon ⟨the alcoholic *ill-used* his long-suffering wife for all of their married life⟩ — see ABUSE 1

illusion *n* **1** a conception or image created by the imagination and having no objective reality ⟨the magician specializes in creating *illusions,* so that people believe they have seen something when they really haven't⟩ — see FANTASY 1

2 a false idea or belief ⟨the idea that we can ever have perfect safety is an *illusion*⟩ — see FALLACY 1

illustrate *vb* **1** to show or make clear by using examples ⟨she *illustrated* her point with a story about her last experiment and the results it provided⟩

synonyms demonstrate, exemplify, instance

related words cite, mention, quote; name, specify; analyze, break down; clarify, clear (up), explain, explicate, expound; edify, elucidate, enlighten; illuminate; construe, interpret; simplify, spell out; detail, enumerate, list

near antonyms becloud, blur, cloud, darken, fog, muddy, obscure; confuse, perplex, puzzle

2 to make plain or understandable ⟨the devastating fire *illustrates* the need for improved safety codes⟩ — see EXPLAIN 1

illustration *n* **1** something that visually explains or decorates a text ⟨the book on birds had gorgeous *illustrations*⟩

synonyms diagram, figure, graphic, plate

related words drawing, illumination, image, pictogram, pictograph, picture; caption, key, legend; depiction, portrait, portrayal, representation; clarification, elucidation, explanation, explication, exposition

2 a statement that makes something clear ⟨forced to give several *illustrations* until she was understood⟩ — see EXPLANATION 1

3 a two-dimensional design intended to look like a person or thing ⟨the doctor sketched an *illustration* to explain the procedure to the patient⟩ — see PICTURE 1

4 one of a group or collection that shows what the whole is like ⟨chose one essay as an *illustration* of the high quality of the collection⟩ — see EXAMPLE

illustrative *adj* serving to explain ⟨an *illustrative* analogy in which the relationship between God and humanity is likened to that between a shepherd and his flock⟩ — see EXPLANATORY

illustrious *adj* standing above others in rank, importance, or achievement ⟨an *illustrious* scientist who is a sure bet for a Nobel Prize⟩ — see EMINENT

image *n* **1** something or someone that strongly resembles another ⟨the girl is growing up to be the perfect *image* of her mother⟩
synonyms carbon copy, counterpart, double, duplicate, duplication, facsimile, likeness, match, picture, replica, ringer, spit
related words effigy, portrait, portrayal; companion, counterpart, fellow, mate; equal, equivalent, identical twin; analogue (*or* analog), parallel
near antonyms antithesis, converse, opposite, reverse
2 a two-dimensional design intended to look like a person or thing ⟨drew an *image* of a bird⟩ — see PICTURE 1
3 something imagined or pictured in the mind ⟨a sentimental visit to her childhood home to see if it matched her mental *image* of the place⟩ — see IDEA

image *vb* **1** to present a picture of ⟨in the painting Sacagawea is *imaged* as an intrepid woman pointing the way for Lewis and Clark⟩ — see PICTURE 1
2 to give a representation or account of in words ⟨the brochure *images* a vacation at the resort in language that makes you want to make a reservation this instant⟩ — see DESCRIBE 1
3 to reproduce or show (an exact likeness) as a mirror would ⟨the burnished chrome fixtures *imaged* the jewelry store's glittery merchandise⟩ — see REFLECT

imaginary *adj* not real and existing only in the imagination ⟨his *imaginary* friend had purple hair⟩
synonyms chimerical, fabulous, fanciful, fantastic, fictional, fictitious, imagined, invented, made-up, make-believe, mythical (*or* mythic), phantasmal, phantom, pretend, unreal
related words fabled, legendary, romantic; abstract, hypothetical, theoretical (*also* theoretic); unbelievable, unconvincing, unlikely; conceived, envisaged, pictured, visualized; deceptive, delusional, delusive, hallucinatory, illusory; concocted, fabricated
near antonyms authentic, genuine, true; factual, verifiable, verified; believable, convincing, realistic; corporeal, material, physical, solid, substantial; palpable, tangible
antonyms actual, existent, existing, real

imagination *n* the ability to form mental images of things that either are not physically present or have never been conceived or created by others ⟨a cartoonist needs a good *imagination* in order to think up and draw interesting cartoons⟩
synonyms creativity, fancy, fantasy (*also* phantasy), imaginativeness, invention, inventiveness
related words brainstorm, brainstorming, inspiration; fecundity, fertility; ingenuity, originality; versatility; chimera, daydream, delusion, dream, figment, hallucination, illusion, mirage, phantasm, pipe dream; envisaging, visualization
near antonyms literalness

imaginative *adj* **1** having the skill and imagination to create new things ⟨an *imaginative* child who is always writing short stories about her pet cat⟩ — see CREATIVE 1
2 showing a use of the imagination and creativity especially in inventing ⟨an *imaginative* gadget that can grind the beans and heat the water to brew coffee⟩ — see CLEVER 1

imaginativeness *n* **1** the ability to form mental images of things that either are not physically present or have never been conceived or created by others ⟨what sets apart geniuses like Thomas Edison and Ben Franklin from the average person is their intelligence and restless *imaginativeness*⟩ — see IMAGINATION
2 the skill and imagination to create new things ⟨it took both *imaginativeness* and tireless dedication to invent the airplane⟩ — see CREATIVITY 1

imagine *vb* **1** to form a mental picture of ⟨she *imagined* meeting the members of her favorite rock band face-to-face⟩
synonyms conceive, dream, envisage, fancy, picture, vision, visualize
related words daydream, stargaze; hallucinate; reflect, relive, reminisce; contemplate, meditate, muse, ponder, ruminate; concoct, fabricate, invent, make up, manufacture, plan, project
2 to have as an opinion ⟨I *imagine* that's true, but you still have to prove it⟩ — see BELIEVE 2

imagined *adj* not real and existing only in the imagination ⟨got needlessly upset about *imagined* dangers⟩ — see IMAGINARY

imbecile *n* a stupid person ⟨only an *imbecile* would let the door slam on their own nose⟩ — see IDIOT

imbecility *n* a foolish act or idea ⟨was arrested for the *imbecility* of speeding down a dark road with no headlights on⟩ — see FOLLY 1

imbibe *vb* **1** to swallow in liquid form ⟨an array of colorful and tasty drinks for party guests to *imbibe*⟩ — see DRINK 1
2 to take in (something liquid) through small openings ⟨plants can *imbibe* water through their roots⟩ — see ABSORB 1

imbue *vb* to cause (as a person) to become filled or saturated with a certain quality or principle ⟨her training at the school for the deaf *imbued* her with a sense of purpose that she had never known before⟩ — see INFUSE

imitate *vb* **1** to use (someone or something) as the model for one's speech, mannerisms, or behavior ⟨teenage boys who *imitate* whichever rock stars are hot⟩
synonyms ape, copy, emulate, mime, mimic
related words burlesque, caricature, lampoon, mock, parody, travesty; impersonate, perform, play; pantomime
2 to copy or exaggerate (someone or something) in order to make fun of ⟨*imitating* someone's stutter and laughing at them is not a nice thing to do⟩ — see MIMIC 1
3 to make an exact likeness of ⟨a second-rate artist who was notorious for *imitating* the works of other painters⟩ — see COPY 1

imitation *adj* being such in appearance only and made with or manufactured from usually cheaper materials ⟨you have to be careful not to buy an *imitation* diamond passed off as the real thing⟩
synonyms artificial, factitious, bogus, fake, false, man-made, mimic, mock, sham, simulated, substitute, synthetic
related words dummy, phony (*also* phoney); cultured, manufactured; unauthentic; adulterated, doctored, fudged, juggled, manipulated, tampered (with); concocted, fabricated; counterfeit, deceptive, forged, fraudulent, misleading; affected, feigned, pseudo, spurious
near antonyms authentic, bona fide, legitimate, true; premium, quality, valuable; pure, unadulterated
antonyms genuine, natural, real

imitation *n* something that is made to look exactly like something else ⟨challenged me to tell the real roses from the silk *imitations*⟩ — see COPY

imitative *adj* using or marked by the use of something else as a basis or model ⟨your writing style tends to be *imitative* of whichever author you've recently read⟩
synonyms apish, emulative, formulaic, mimetic, mimic, slavish, unoriginal
related words copied, cribbed, plagiarized; artificial, bogus, factitious, fake, false, imitation, man-made, mock, sham, simulated, substitute, synthetic; duplicated, photocopied, reduplicated, reproduced, transcribed; backup; counterfeit, deceptive, forged, fraudulent, misleading; uninspired
near antonyms authentic, bona fide, legitimate, true; genuine, natural, real; classic, ideal, model
antonyms archetypal, original

imitator *n* **1** a person who adopts the appearance or behavior of another especially in an obvious way ⟨an Elvis *imitator* in a sequinned jumpsuit⟩ — see COPYCAT
2 a person who imitates another's voice and mannerisms for comic effect ⟨the comedian is a hilarious *imitator* of a surprising array of current celebrities⟩ — see MIMIC

immaculate *adj* **1** free from any trace of the coarse or indecent ⟨an *immaculate* soul⟩ — see CHASTE
2 free from dirt or stain ⟨somehow managed to keep the white carpet *immaculate*⟩ — see CLEAN 1

immaterial *adj* **1** not composed of matter ⟨it is only possible to study *immaterial* forces like gravity by observing their effects on the physical world⟩
synonyms bodiless, incorporeal, insubstantial, nonmaterial, nonphysical, spiritual, unsubstantial
related words metaphysical, supernatural; impalpable, insensible, intangible, invisible; airy, diaphanous, ethereal, tenuous, thin, vaporous
near antonyms animal, carnal, fleshly; detectable, discernable, noticeable, observable, palpable, sensible, tangible, visible; bulky, heavy, massive, solid
antonyms bodily, corporeal, material, physical, substantial
2 not having anything to do with the matter at hand ⟨while upsetting, that story is *immaterial* to the question of why you are late⟩ — see IRRELEVANT

immature *adj* **1** being in the early stage of life, growth, or development ⟨*immature* frogs are called "tadpoles"⟩ — see YOUNG
2 having or showing the annoying qualities (as silliness) associated with children ⟨an *immature* teenager who still threw tantrums⟩ — see CHILDISH
3 lacking in adult experience or maturity ⟨many high school students are still too *immature* to foresee the consequences of their actions⟩ — see CALLOW

immeasurable *adj* being or seeming to be without limits ⟨the *immeasurable* expanse of the ocean⟩ — see INFINITE

immediacy *n* the state or condition of being near ⟨the *immediacy* of Christmas is just beginning to dawn on many last-minute shoppers⟩ — see PROXIMITY

immediate *adj* **1** done or occurring without any noticeable lapse in time ⟨received an *immediate* response to the question⟩ — see INSTANTANEOUS
2 done or working without something else coming in between ⟨she is my *immediate* superior, so I report to her⟩ — see DIRECT 1
3 done, carried out, or given without delay ⟨*immediate* treatment saved the victim of the massive heart attack⟩ — see PROMPT 1

4 not being distant in time, space, or significance ⟨for the victims of the terrorist attack, the incident is as *immediate* as yesterday's news⟩ — see CLOSE 2

immediately *adv* without delay ⟨if you don't leave *immediately*, you'll be late for school and probably get in trouble⟩
synonyms directly, forthwith, instantly, now, promptly, pronto, right away, right now, straightaway, straightway
related words away, freely; anon, momentarily, shortly, soon; apace, briskly, fast, fleetly, full-tilt, posthaste, quick, quickly, rapidly, readily, snappily, speedily, swift, swiftly; abruptly, presto, suddenly, unexpectedly; hastily, impetuously, impulsively, rashly, recklessly; exactly, opportunely, punctually, seasonably
phrases at once, on the line, on the spot
near antonyms slowly; late, tardily

immense *adj* unusually large ⟨the elephant was simply *immense*, even as elephants go⟩ — see HUGE

immenseness *n* the quality or state of being very large ⟨the overwhelming *immenseness* of the building made me feel like an ant⟩ — see IMMENSITY

immensity *n* the quality or state of being very large ⟨the *immensity* of the mountain was awe-inspiring, especially up close⟩
synonyms enormity, enormousness, hugeness, immenseness, magnitude, massiveness, vastness
related words bigness, extensiveness, greatness, largeness, voluminousness, weightiness; awesomeness, grandness, stupendousness; excessiveness, extravagance, extremeness, immoderacy
near antonyms littleness, puniness, smallness; triviality, unimportance
antonyms diminutiveness, minuteness, tininess

immerse *vb* **1** to hold the attention of ⟨the documentary on human reproduction *immersed* the whole class for an hour⟩ — see ENGAGE 1
2 to sink or push (something) briefly into or as if into a liquid ⟨tried to *immerse* the balloon in the water⟩ — see DIP 1

immersed *adj* having the mind fixed on something ⟨the child was so *immersed* in a book that she didn't hear her mother calling⟩ — see ATTENTIVE

immersing *adj* holding the attention or provoking interest ⟨an *immersing* television program⟩ — see INTERESTING

immersion *n* a focusing of the mind on something ⟨a complete *immersion* in the lesson is the only way you're going to learn a foreign language⟩ — see ATTENTION 1

immigrant *n* one that leaves one place to settle in another ⟨America was founded by *immigrants*⟩ — see EMIGRANT

imminent *adj* **1** giving signs of immediate occurrence ⟨a storm is *imminent*, so you should seek shelter now⟩
synonyms impending, pending, threatening
related words approaching, coming, forthcoming, future, near, nearing, oncoming, upcoming; brewing, gathering; likely, possible, probable; inevitable, unavoidable; menacing, ominous, portentous; anticipated, awaited, expected, foreseen, predicted
near antonyms distant, far-off, remote; eventual, ultimate; bygone, former, past; late, recent
2 being soon to appear or take place ⟨an *imminent* development that should radically change how we treat the disease⟩ — see FORTHCOMING

immobile *adj* **1** fixed in a place or position ⟨the table saw is *immobile*, so we'll have to arrange the rest of the workshop around it⟩ — see STATIONARY 1
2 incapable of moving or being moved ⟨a huge, *immobile* tree of an endangered species that the creators of the theme park decided to make part of the design⟩ — see IMMOVABLE 1

immobilize *vb* to render powerless, ineffective, or unable to move ⟨town councils felt *immobilized* by the new state legislation⟩ — see PARALYZE

immoderate *adj* going beyond a normal or acceptable limit in degree or amount ⟨*immoderate* laughter that seemed to last for all fifteen minutes of the speech⟩ — see EXCESSIVE

immodest *adj* showing a lack of proper social reserve or modesty ⟨an *immodest* proposal for altering the town's character by an uppity newcomer⟩ — see PRESUMPTUOUS 1

immolate *vb* to give up as an offering to a god ⟨a ceremony in which they *immolated* their cherished possessions so that the gods would send rain⟩ — see SACRIFICE

immolation *n* something offered to a god ⟨offered an *immolation* of her hair to placate the god⟩ — see SACRIFICE

immoral *adj* **1** not conforming to a high moral standard; morally unacceptable ⟨blatantly *immoral* behavior by members of the clergy should not be tolerated⟩ — see BAD 2
2 not guided by or showing a concern for what is right ⟨stealing another's words, even over the Internet, is an *immoral* act⟩ — see UNPRINCIPLED

immorality *n* **1** immoral conduct or practices harmful or offensive to society ⟨religious denominations that regard drinking, smoking, and even dancing as examples of *immorality*⟩ — see VICE 1
2 that which is morally unacceptable ⟨a sermon about modern society's casual acceptance of or indifference to *immorality*⟩ — see EVIL

immortal *adj* lasting forever ⟨the universe is not *immortal*, although it will probably last for billions of years⟩ — see EVERLASTING

immortality *n* unending existence after death ⟨central to most religions is a belief in the *immortality* of the soul⟩ — see ETERNITY 2

immortalize *vb* to give eternal or lasting existence to ⟨*immortalized* the words "Call me Ishmael" in a famous novel⟩ — see PERPETUATE

immovable *adj* **1** incapable of moving or being moved ⟨that boulder is *immovable*, even with a bulldozer⟩
synonyms immobile, irremovable, nonmotile, nonmoving, unbudging, unmovable
related words motionless, moveless, static, stationary, still, unmoving; fast, fixed, rooted, steadfast, stuck, wedged
near antonyms portable, removable, transferable, transportable
antonyms mobile, motile, movable (*or* moveable), moving
2 sticking to an opinion, purpose, or course of action in spite of reason, arguments, or persuasion ⟨despite tears and pleading, the principal was *immovable* on the matter of automatic suspension for obscene language⟩ — see OBSTINATE

immunity *n* freedom from punishment, harm, or loss ⟨the suspect refused to name his partners unless he was granted *immunity*⟩ — see IMPUNITY

immure *vb* **1** to close or shut in by or as if by barriers ⟨scientists at the research station in Alaska are *immured* by the frozen wastelands that surround them⟩ — see ENCLOSE 1
2 to put in or as if in prison ⟨Rapunzel was *immured* in her tower by her evil stepmother⟩ — see IMPRISON

immurement *n* the act of confining or the state of being confined ⟨the *immurement* of the Japanese-Americans didn't end until after the war⟩ — see INTERNMENT

immutability *n* the state of continuing without change ⟨the *immutability* of the laws of physics is a myth, since refinements of those laws continue to be made⟩ — see CONSTANCY 1

immutable *adj* not capable of changing or being changed ⟨an *immutable* attitude of superiority toward others⟩ — see INFLEXIBLE 1

imp *n* **1** an appealingly mischievous person ⟨scooped up the little *imp* and took him to bed⟩ — see SCAMP 1
2 an evil spirit ⟨a story about a crumbling mansion infested with *imps*⟩ — see DEMON

impact *n* **1** a forceful coming together of two things ⟨the glass shattered on *impact* with the floor⟩
synonyms bump, collision, concussion, crash, jar, jolt, shock, smash, strike, wallop
related words blow, buffet, hit, knock, punch, rap, slap, thump; bashing, battering, bludgeoning, clobbering, hammering, lambasting, licking, pounding, pummelling, thrashing; contact, encounter, meeting, touch
2 the power to bring about a result on another ⟨the *impact* of the event was such that she became a crusader for prison reform⟩ — see EFFECT 2
3 the quality of an utterance that provokes interest and produces an effect ⟨the story has real dramatic *impact*⟩ — see ¹PUNCH 1

impact *vb* **1** to act upon (a person or a person's feelings) so as to cause a response ⟨the tragic loss of his father *impacted* him for the rest of his life⟩ — see ¹AFFECT 1
2 to come into usually forceful contact with something ⟨the damage sustained when a car going 40 miles an hour *impacts* with a brick wall⟩ — see HIT 2

impair *vb* to reduce the soundness, effectiveness, or perfection of ⟨*impaired* by a crack, the windshield shattered on impact⟩ — see DAMAGE 1

impale *vb* to penetrate or hold (something) with a pointed object ⟨*impale* a marshmallow or two on that stick and let's start toasting⟩
synonyms gore, harpoon, lance, pierce, puncture, skewer, spear, spike, stab, stick, transfix
related words spindle; perforate; jab, poke, prick, punch, thrust; cut, knife, slice

impalpable *adj* **1** not capable of being perceived by the sense of touch ⟨the rich colors used in the wall coverings and furniture give the room an *impalpable* warmth⟩ — see INTANGIBLE
2 not perceptible by a sense or by the mind ⟨any difference between the two sound systems is *impalpable* to all but the most discerning audiophiles⟩ — see IMPERCEPTIBLE

impart *vb* to cause (something) to pass from one to another ⟨*imparted* the latest information on the approaching snowstorm⟩ — see COMMUNICATE 1

impartial *adj* marked by justice, honesty, and freedom from bias ⟨an *impartial* teacher who doesn't assign grades on the basis of her fondness for a student⟩ — see FAIR 2

impartiality *n* lack of favoritism toward one side or another ⟨the lawyer questioned the *impartiality* of the judge⟩ — see DETACHMENT 1

impassable *adj* impossible to get through or into ⟨the road was *impassable* until snowplows cleared it⟩ — see IMPENETRABLE 1

impasse *n* a point in a struggle where neither side is capable of winning or willing to give in ⟨if we cannot ever agree on which movie to see tonight, we are at an *impasse*⟩
synonyms deadlock, halt, stalemate, standstill
related words dead end; bottleneck, corner, dilemma, fix, hole, jam, pickle, pinch, plight, predicament, quagmire, quandary, spot; difficulty; problem

impassioned *adj* having or expressing great depth of feeling ⟨an *impassioned* plea for justice⟩ — see FERVENT

impassive *adj* **1** not feeling or showing emotion ⟨she remained *impassive* as they told her the bad news⟩
synonyms apathetic, cold-blooded, phlegmatic, stoic (*or* stoical), stolid, undemonstrative, unemotional
related words cold, cool, dispassionate, unmoved; calm, collected, composed; imperturbable, unflappable; reserved, reticent, taciturn; blank, deadpan, dry, empty, expressionless, inexpressive, vacant, wooden; enigmatic (*also* enigmatical), impenetrable, inscrutable; aloof, detached, unconcerned, unsentimental; impersonal, objective, unresponsive; hardhearted, pitiless, unfeeling; inconsiderate, thoughtless
near antonyms blazing, burning, fiery, flaming, glowing, red-hot; ardent, enthusiastic, gung ho, zealous; gushing, maudlin, mawkish, mushy, sentimental; dramatic, histrionic, melodramatic; compassionate, responsive, sympathetic; reactive, sensitive
antonyms demonstrative, emotional, fervent, fervid, hot-blooded, impassioned, passionate
2 not expressing any emotion ⟨an *impassive* expression on the prisoner's face as his sentence was read⟩ — see BLANK 1

impassivity *n* a lack of emotion or emotional expressiveness ⟨the child's apparent *impassivity* after the trauma worried people⟩ — see APATHY 1

impatience *n* urgent desire or interest ⟨the child's *impatience* for Christmas morning is engaging⟩ — see EAGERNESS

impatient *adj* **1** showing urgent desire or interest ⟨she was *impatient* to give her presentation before the class⟩ — see EAGER
2 unable or unwilling to endure ⟨airline passengers who are so *impatient* of delays, even for the most obvious of reasons⟩ — see INTOLERANT 1

impeach *vb* to make a claim of wrongdoing against ⟨the company's president has been *impeached* by the Securities and Exchange Commission⟩ — see ACCUSE

impeccability *n* the quality or state of being free from guilt or blame ⟨the *impeccability* of the nun's moral character and untiring selflessness qualified her for sainthood⟩ — see INNOCENCE 1

impeccable *adj* **1** being entirely without fault or flaw ⟨the etiquette expert was famous for her absolutely *impeccable* manners⟩ — see PERFECT 1
2 free from guilt or blame ⟨a man of *impeccable* probity and honesty⟩ — see INNOCENT 2

impeccably *adv* without any flaws or errors ⟨she speaks French *impeccably*⟩ — see PERFECTLY 1

impecunious *adj* lacking money or material possessions ⟨they were so *impecunious* that they couldn't afford Christmas gifts⟩ — see POOR 1

impecuniousness *n* the state of lacking sufficient money or material possessions ⟨her claims of *impecuniousness*

rang false when we noticed the luxuries she had bought⟩ — see POVERTY 1

impede *vb* to create difficulty for the work or activity of ⟨the construction work *impeded* the teachers' efforts at maintaining classroom quiet⟩ — see HAMPER

impediment *n* something that makes movement or progress more difficult ⟨tough going for the mules, even without the added *impediment* of heavy loads⟩ — see ENCUMBRANCE

impel *vb* to set or keep in motion ⟨gasoline *impels* a car's engine⟩ — see MOVE 2

impend *vb* to be about to happen ⟨for pessimists some disaster always seems to be *impending*⟩ — see LOOM

impend (over) *vb* to remain poised to inflict harm, danger, or distress on ⟨a hurricane *impended over* the whole southeastern coast⟩ — see THREATEN

impending *adj* **1** being soon to appear or take place ⟨an *impending* celebration of the 100th anniversary of the school's founding⟩ — see FORTHCOMING
2 giving signs of immediate occurrence ⟨an aura of *impending* doom hung over the city⟩ — see IMMINENT 1

impenetrable *adj* **1** impossible to get through or into ⟨the ancient temple was surrounded by vast stretches of *impenetrable* jungle⟩
synonyms impassable, impermeable, impervious
related words close, compact, dense, thick; compressed, condensed; sturdy, substantial, tough; firm, frozen, hard, solid, stiff; inflexible, rigid, unbending, unyielding
near antonyms soft, squishy; bendable, elastic, flexible, giving, malleable, pliable, yielding; absorbent, porous
antonyms negotiable, passable, penetrable, permeable
2 being beyond one's powers to know, understand, or explain ⟨the mysteries of that religion are completely *impenetrable* to outsiders⟩ — see MYSTERIOUS 1
3 impossible to understand ⟨the textbook's language is completely *impenetrable*, at least to me⟩ — see INCOMPREHENSIBLE
4 not allowing penetration (as by gas, liquid, or light) ⟨the container of toxic waste has an *impenetrable* seal to prevent leaks⟩ — see TIGHT 1

impenitent *adj* not sorry for having done wrong ⟨an *impenitent* criminal who said he'd do it all over again, given the chance⟩ — see REMORSELESS

imperative *adj* **1** forcing one's compliance or participation by or as if by law ⟨reporting signs of physical abuse is now an *imperative* duty for hospital and school personnel⟩ — see MANDATORY
2 impossible to do without ⟨proper equipment is *imperative* for the success of this chemical experiment⟩ — see ESSENTIAL 1
3 needing immediate attention ⟨an *imperative* need for medical supplies in the earthquake-ravaged country⟩ — see ACUTE 2

imperceptible *adj* not perceptible by a sense or by the mind ⟨a slight difference in hue between the two glasses that's *imperceptible* unless they're placed side by side⟩
synonyms impalpable, inappreciable, indistinguishable, insensible
related words inaudible, intangible, invisible; inconspicuous, indistinct, unnoticeable, unseeable, unseen; faint, insignificant, slight, trivial; buried, concealed, covert, disguised, hidden, obscure, shrouded, unapparent, vague
near antonyms audible, observable, tangible, visible; clear, conspicuous, evident, eye-catching, manifest, no-

ticeable, obvious, plain, prominent, striking; apparent, distinct, significant, straightforward

antonyms appreciable, discernible, palpable, perceptible, sensible

imperfect *adj* having a fault ⟨an *imperfect* representation of the circumstances surrounding Paul Revere's famous ride⟩ — see FAULTY

imperfection *n* something that spoils the appearance or completeness of a thing ⟨the shirt was marked down because of a minor *imperfection*⟩ — see BLEMISH

imperil *vb* to place in danger ⟨a single mistake could *imperil* the lives of everyone⟩ — see ENDANGER

imperilment *n* the state of not being protected from injury, harm, or evil ⟨the city has reduced the number of its firefighters, to the *imperilment* of every homeowner⟩ — see DANGER 1

imperious *adj* 1 fond of ordering people around ⟨an *imperious* little boy who liked to tell his parents what to do⟩ — see BOSSY

2 having a feeling of superiority that shows itself in an overbearing attitude ⟨an *imperious* movie star who thinks she's some sort of goddess⟩ — see ARROGANT

3 having or showing a tendency to force one's will on others without any regard to fairness or necessity ⟨an office administrator with an *imperious* manner⟩ — see ARBITRARY 1

4 needing immediate attention ⟨as war casualties mounted, the need for trained nurses became *imperious*⟩ — see ACUTE 2

imperiousness *n* an exaggerated sense of one's importance that shows itself in the making of excessive or unjustified claims ⟨the *imperiousness* of the fashion designer irritates everyone around her⟩ — see ARROGANCE

imperishable *adj* impossible to destroy ⟨energy is *imperishable*⟩ — see INDESTRUCTIBLE

impermanent *adj* 1 intended to last, continue, or serve for a limited time ⟨built an *impermanent* structure to serve for the archaeologists' living quarters⟩ — see TEMPORARY 1

2 lasting only for a short time ⟨a summer romance that was an *impermanent* fancy, quickly forgotten⟩ — see MOMENTARY

impermeable *adj* 1 impossible to get through or into ⟨the wall of security people surrounding the rock band was *impermeable*⟩ — see IMPENETRABLE 1

2 not allowing penetration (as by gas, liquid, or light) ⟨an *impermeable* seal on the ancient tomb had preserved the artifacts exceptionally well⟩ — see TIGHT 1

impermissible *adj* that may not be permitted ⟨chewing gum is an *impermissible* activity in school⟩

synonyms banned, barred, forbidden, interdicted, outlawed, prohibited, proscribed, taboo (*also* tabu)

related words intolerable, unacceptable, unbearable, unendurable; illegal, illegitimate, illicit, improper, inappropriate, unadvisable, unauthorized, unlawful, unlicensed, unmentionable; unseemly, unsuitable; objectionable; disallowed, disapproved, discouraged; refused, rejected, revoked, unsanctioned, vetoed; repressed, suppressed; precluded, prevented, stopped; excluded, ruled out, shut out; blocked, hindered, impeded, obstructed

near antonyms acceptable, bearable, endurable, tolerable; accepted, accredited, allowed, appropriate, approved, authorized, certified, endorsed, lawful, legal, legitimate, licensed (*also* licenced), OK (*or* okay), permitted, warranted; accorded, granted, sanctioned, vouchsafed; brooked, condoned, countenanced; en-

couraged, promoted, supported; commanded, mandatory, ordered, required; proper, seemly, suitable, tolerated, unobjectionable

antonyms allowable, licensable, permissible, permissive, sufferable

impersonate *vb* 1 to pretend to be (what one is not) in appearance or behavior ⟨a school intruder was caught trying to *impersonate* a teacher⟩

synonyms masquerade (as), play, pose (as)

related words ape, copy, imitate, mime, mimic, mock, parody, travesty; act, perform, portray

2 to present a portrayal or performance of ⟨*impersonated* the character for the school play⟩ — see ACT 1

impersonator *n* 1 a person who imitates another's voice and mannerisms for comic effect ⟨a male *impersonator* who pretends to be a small galaxy of famous female stars⟩ — see MIMIC

2 one who acts professionally (as in a play, movie, or television show) ⟨a gifted *impersonator* who can convincingly portray both heroes and heels⟩ — see ACTOR

impertinence *n* 1 disrespectful or argumentative talk given in response to a command or request ⟨I won't tolerate such *impertinence* when I tell you to do something⟩ — see BACK TALK

2 rude behavior ⟨the *impertinence* of deliberately ignoring waiting customers⟩ — see DISCOURTESY

impertinent *adj* 1 displaying or marked by rude boldness ⟨the *impertinent* child talked back every time the babysitter made a request⟩ — see NERVY 1

2 showing a lack of manners or consideration for others ⟨*impertinent* salesmen who telephone people during the dinner hour⟩ — see IMPOLITE

imperturbability *n* evenness of emotions or temper ⟨her *imperturbability* in a crisis is legendary⟩ — see EQUANIMITY

imperturbable *adj* not easily panicked or upset ⟨he was *imperturbable* even when the kitchen caught on fire⟩ — see UNFLAPPABLE

impervious *adj* 1 not allowing penetration (as by gas, liquid, or light) ⟨the material for this coat is supposed to be *impervious* to rain⟩ — see TIGHT 1

2 impossible to get through or into ⟨the rain forest is *impervious* to all but the most dedicated explorers⟩ — see IMPENETRABLE 1

impetus *n* something that arouses action or activity ⟨the reward was an *impetus* to get good grades⟩ — see IMPULSE

impiety *n* an act of great disrespect shown to God or to sacred ideas, people, or things ⟨the unspeakable *impiety* of spitting at a church⟩ — see BLASPHEMY

impinge *vb* to come into usually forceful contact with something ⟨hail *impinging* upon the car hood and making quite a racket⟩ — see HIT 2

impious *adj* not showing proper reverence for the holy or sacred ⟨an *impious* act that horrified their pious mother⟩ — see IRREVERENT

impish *adj* tending to or exhibiting reckless playfulness ⟨*impish* children ran into the street, oblivious to the traffic⟩ — see MISCHIEVOUS 1

impishness *n* 1 a natural disposition for playful behavior ⟨her *impishness* means that no one is ever safe from her practical jokes⟩ — see PLAYFULNESS

2 playful, reckless behavior that is not intended to cause serious harm ⟨the *impishness* was easy to forgive, since it caused no real harm⟩ — see MISCHIEF 1

implacable *adj* 1 sticking to an opinion, purpose, or course of action in spite of reason, arguments, or persuasion ⟨an *implacable* judge who always hands down

the maximum sentence allowed by law⟩ — see OBSTI-
NATE

2 showing no signs of slackening or yielding in one's
purpose ⟨an *implacable* man who was determined to
avenge the murder of his brother⟩ — see UNYIELD-
ING 1

implant *vb* to set solidly in or as if in surrounding matter
⟨the gemstone was poorly *implanted* in the ring, so it
was constantly popping out⟩ — see ENTRENCH

implausible *adj* too extraordinary or improbable to believe ⟨I don't want to hear any more *implausible* stories
about why you didn't do the homework⟩ — see IN-
CREDIBLE

implement *n* an article intended for use in work ⟨gar-
dening *implements* such as hoes, spades, and pruners⟩
  synonyms device, instrument, tool, utensil
  related words apparatus, appliance, mechanism; contraption, contrivance, gadget, gizmo (*or* gismo), jigger

implement *vb* to carry out effectively ⟨*implemented* the
evacuation plan without a hitch⟩ — see ENFORCE

implementation *n* the doing of an action ⟨the *implementation* of the idea turned out to be harder than it
sounded⟩ — see COMMISSION 2

implicit *adj* understood although not put into words ⟨the
implicit agreement in the outing club is that every
member pays his or her own way on all trips⟩
  synonyms implied, tacit, unexpressed, unspoken, unvoiced, wordless
  related words inferred; unannounced, undeclared, un-
said, untold; hinted, intimated, suggested
  near antonyms apparent, blatant, evident, obvious,
plain, straightforward; unambiguous, unequivocal, unmistakable
  antonyms explicit, express, expressed, spoken, stated

implied *adj* understood although not put into words ⟨an
implied agreement is not legally enforceable⟩ — see
IMPLICIT

implore *vb* to make a request to (someone) in an earnest
or urgent manner ⟨the students *implored* the teacher
for more time to finish the test⟩ — see BEG

imploring *adj* asking humbly ⟨the *imploring* boy tearfully asked the veterinarian to do what he could to save
the life of his dog⟩ — see SUPPLIANT

imply *vb* to convey an idea indirectly ⟨you may have *implied* that you'd help, but you didn't actually say so⟩ —
see HINT

impolite *adj* showing a lack of manners or consideration
for others ⟨the librarian was shocked that anyone
could be so *impolite* as to continue talking despite repeated warnings to be quiet⟩
  synonyms discourteous, ill-bred, ill-mannered, impertinent, inconsiderate, rude, thoughtless, uncalled-for,
uncivil, ungracious, unmannerly
  related words audacious, bold, bold-faced, brash,
brassy, disrespectful, impudent, insolent, saucy,
shameless; boorish, churlish, clownish, loutish, uncouth, vulgar; undiplomatic, unsportsmanlike; abrupt,
blunt, brusque, crusty, curt, gruff, sharp, snippy; antisocial, crabbed, cross, disagreeable, grumpy, sullen,
surly; improper, inappropriate, incorrect, indecent, indecorous, unseemly; arrogant, conceited, presumptuous, pretentious
  near antonyms humble, meek, modest, unassertive;
deferential, dutiful, respectful, submissive, yielding; acceptable, appropriate, becoming, befitting, correct, decent, decorous, fit, fitting, good, meet, proper, respectable, right, seemly, suitable; affable, cordial,

friendly, genial, hospitable, sociable; felicitous, graceful
  antonyms civil, considerate, courteous, genteel, gracious, mannerly, polite, thoughtful, well-bred

impoliteness *n* rude behavior ⟨the hecklers were escorted out of the auditorium because of their flagrant
impoliteness⟩ — see DISCOURTESY

import *n* **1** the quality or state of being important ⟨I can't
overemphasize the *import* of this examination on your
future academic career⟩ — see IMPORTANCE

2 the idea that is conveyed or intended to be conveyed
to the mind by language, symbol, or action ⟨didn't understand all the words, but got the general *import* of
the speech⟩ — see MEANING 1

import *vb* **1** to be of importance ⟨it *imports* little whether
you like Grandma's gift; you should have graciously
thanked her⟩ — see MATTER

2 to communicate or convey (as an idea) to the mind
⟨the word "freedom" can *import* different things to different people⟩ — see MEAN 1

importance *n* the quality or state of being important ⟨a
final exam has great *importance*⟩
  synonyms consequence, import, magnitude, moment,
significance, weight, weightiness
  related words celebrity, distinction, eminence, fame,
note, noteworthiness, notoriety, preeminence, prominence, renown; store, substance, value, worth, worthiness; gravity, seriousness; authority, potency, power;
mark, name, report, reputation, repute; cachet, position, prestige, rank, standing, stature; glory, greatness,
honor, illustriousness
  near antonyms paltriness, pettiness, worthlessness; disgrace, dishonor, disrepute, ignominy, odium, opprobrium, shame; anonymity; obscurity
  antonyms insignificance, littleness, slightness, smallness, triviality, unimportance

important *adj* **1** having great meaning or lasting effect
⟨the discovery of penicillin was a very *important* event
in the history of medicine⟩
  synonyms big, consequential, eventful, major, material, meaningful, momentous, significant, substantial,
weighty
  related words decisive, fatal, fateful, strategic; earnest,
grave, serious, sincere; distinctive, exceptional, impressive, outstanding, prominent, remarkable; valuable,
worthwhile, worthy; distinguished, eminent, great, illustrious, preeminent, prestigious; famous, notorious,
renowned; all-important, critical, crucial
  near antonyms inconsiderable, minor, paltry, petty,
worthless; anonymous, nameless, obscure, uncelebrated, unknown
  antonyms insignificant, little, minor, slight, small, trivial, unimportant

2 having great power or influence ⟨Rachel Carson was
an *important* figure in the environmental movement⟩
  synonyms influential, mighty, potent, powerful, puissant, significant, strong
  related words high-level, senior, top; able, capable,
competent, effective, efficient; authoritarian, autocratic, despotic, dictatorial, magisterial, tyrannical
(*also* tyrannic); distinguished, dominant, eminent, famous, great, illustrious, notorious, preeminent, prestigious, renowned; dynamic, energetic, forceful, robust,
sturdy, tough, vigorous
  near antonyms feeble, flimsy, frail, infirm; anonymous, obscure; incapable, incompetent, ineffective, inept, unfit, useless

antonyms impotent, insignificant, little, powerless, unimportant, weak

3 having a feeling of superiority that shows itself in an overbearing attitude ⟨an *important* businessman who always expects special treatment wherever he goes⟩ — see ARROGANT

4 having too high an opinion of oneself ⟨oh, you're so *important*—you think the world revolves around you⟩ — see CONCEITED

importune *vb* to make a request to (someone) in an earnest or urgent manner ⟨she was always *importuning* people for favors, even when she had no right to ask⟩ — see BEG

impose *vb* to establish or apply as a charge or penalty ⟨every town *imposes* a fine for speeding⟩

   synonyms assess, charge, exact, fine, lay, levy, put

   related words dock, mulct, penalize, tax; extort, shake down, wrest, wring; bleed, fleece, gouge, milk, skin, squeeze; coerce, compel, force; inflict, wreak; set; reapply, reimpose, relay

   near antonyms abate, diminish, lessen; forgive, release

   antonyms remit

impose (on *or* upon) *vb* to take unfair advantage of ⟨thanks for offering your own bed, but I wouldn't dream of *imposing on* you and will be perfectly happy on the couch⟩ — see EXPLOIT 1

imposing *adj* **1** having or showing a serious and reserved manner ⟨the *imposing* principal soon made it clear that he hadn't called me to his office just to chat⟩ — see DIGNIFIED

2 large and impressive in size, grandeur, extent, or conception ⟨an *imposing* castle that suggested that the king was wealthy and powerful⟩ — see GRAND 1

imposition *n* a charge usually of money collected by the government from people or businesses for public use ⟨an *imposition* of 10% on imported goods⟩ — see TAX

impossible *adj* incapable of being solved or accomplished ⟨the seemingly *impossible* problem of world hunger⟩ ⟨fitting everything in my backpack seemed an *impossible* task⟩

   synonyms hopeless, unachievable, unattainable, unsolvable

   related words impracticable, impractical; doubtful, dubious, far-fetched, improbable, unlikely; implausible, inconceivable, incredible, unbelievable, unthinkable; futile, useless; absurd, fantastic, outlandish, preposterous, ridiculous

   near antonyms practicable, practical, reasonable; likely, probable; acceptable, believable, conceivable, credible, plausible

   antonyms achievable, attainable, doable, feasible, possible, realizable, workable

impost *n* a charge usually of money collected by the government from people or businesses for public use ⟨consumers steadfastly resisted any *impost* on merchandise purchased over the Internet⟩ — see TAX

impostor *or* **imposter** *n* one who makes false claims of identity or expertise ⟨the man who claimed to be a prince turned out to be an *impostor*⟩

   synonyms charlatan, fake, faker, fraud, hoaxer, humbug, mountebank, phony (*also* phoney), pretender, quack

   related words imitator, impersonator, mimic; actor, bluffer, counterfeiter, deceiver, dissembler, duper, feigner, misleader, trickster; poseur

   near antonyms adept, expert, master, professional, virtuoso, whiz, wizard

impotence *n* the lack of sufficient ability, power, or means ⟨the committee's *impotence* in military affairs frustrated the members⟩ — see INABILITY

impotent *adj* **1** not able to produce fruit or offspring ⟨most mules are *impotent*⟩ — see STERILE 1

2 unable to act or achieve one's purpose ⟨an *impotent* ruler who was just a figurehead⟩ — see POWERLESS

impoverished *adj* **1** lacking money or material possessions ⟨the hope that an *impoverished* family wins the lottery's big jackpot⟩ — see POOR 1

2 producing inferior or only a small amount of vegetation ⟨an *impoverished* field that had been overgrazed⟩ — see BARREN 1

impoverishment *n* the state of lacking sufficient money or material possessions ⟨they were left in *impoverishment* after some bad investments⟩ — see POVERTY 1

impracticable *adj* not capable of being put to use or account ⟨an *impracticable* plan for dealing with the recent intrusion of bears in the suburban neighborhood⟩ — see IMPRACTICAL

impractical *adj* not capable of being put to use or account ⟨the flimsy little toy shovel was cute, but completely *impractical* for digging up tree stumps⟩

   synonyms impracticable, inoperable, nonpractical, unusable, unworkable, useless

   related words unsuitable; inaccessible, unattainable, unavailable, unobtainable, unreachable; dead, dormant, fallow, free, idle, inactive, inert, inoperative, latent; arrested, interrupted, suspended; unrealistic

   near antonyms accessible, available, obtainable, reachable; all-around (*also* all-round), handy; active, alive, busy, employed, functioning, operating, operative, running, working

   antonyms applicable, feasible, functional, operable, operational, practicable, practical, usable, useful, workable

imprecate *vb* to ask a divine power to send harm or evil upon ⟨the witch *imprecated* the villagers for their relentless, superstitious persecution of her⟩ — see CURSE 1

imprecation *n* a prayer that harm will come to someone ⟨the prisoner hurled *imprecations* and insults at the guards⟩ — see CURSE 1

imprecise *adj* not precisely correct ⟨3.14 is an *imprecise* approximation of the value of pi⟩ — see INEXACT 1

impregnable *adj* incapable of being defeated, overcome, or subdued ⟨an *impregnable* fortress that had foiled one invader after another over the centuries⟩ — see INVINCIBLE

impregnate *vb* to wet thoroughly with liquid ⟨*impregnated* the cloth with bleach⟩ — see SOAK 1

impress *n* a perceptible trace left by pressure ⟨the stamp left a smudgy *impress* on the paper⟩ — see PRINT 1

impress *vb* **1** to act upon (a person or a person's feelings) so as to cause a response ⟨*impressed* him with the intensity of their musical performance⟩ — see ¹AFFECT 1

2 to produce a vivid impression of ⟨*impressed* the importance of the lesson on the students⟩ — see ENGRAVE 2

impression *n* **1** a perceptible trace left by pressure ⟨a shoe *impression* in the dirt that could lead police to the culprit⟩ — see PRINT 1

2 something imagined or pictured in the mind ⟨had a vague *impression* that the guide would be female⟩ — see IDEA

impressionist *n* a person who imitates another's voice and mannerisms for comic effect ⟨a celebrated *impres-*

sionist who can do enough rapid-fire imitations to populate an entire stage with characters⟩ — see MIMIC

impressive *adj* having the power to affect the feelings or sympathies ⟨an *impressive* play about a loving family attempting to lift themselves out of poverty⟩ — see MOVING

imprimatur *n* an acceptance of something as satisfactory ⟨could not begin the project without the teacher's *imprimatur*⟩ — see APPROVAL 1

imprint *n* **1** a mark or series of marks left on a surface by something that has passed along it ⟨found an *imprint* on the road where something apparently had been dragged⟩ — see TRACK 1

2 a perceptible trace left by pressure ⟨an *imprint* of a dinosaur's foot embedded in the limestone⟩ — see PRINT 1

imprint *vb* to produce a vivid impression of ⟨the lesson on the value of honesty permanently *imprinted* itself on my mind⟩ — see ENGRAVE 2

imprison *vb* to put in or as if in prison ⟨in this society, we try to *imprison* criminals so that they can't do any more harm⟩
synonyms commit, confine, immure, incarcerate, intern, jail, jug, lock (up)
related words constrain, limit, restrain, restrict, shut; apprehend, arrest, capture, catch, detain; impress, shanghai; hold, keep; enslave, subjugate
near antonyms emancipate, manumit
antonyms discharge, free, liberate, release

imprisoned *adj* taken and held prisoner ⟨the *imprisoned* hostages were eventually released without harm⟩ — see CAPTIVE

imprisonment *n* the act of confining or the state of being confined ⟨the offense is punishable by a fine or *imprisonment*⟩ — see INTERNMENT

improbable *adj* not likely to be true or to occur ⟨it is *improbable* that we will be allowed to stay out all night⟩
synonyms doubtful, dubious, far-fetched, flimsy, questionable, unapt, unlikely
related words implausible, impossible, inconceivable, incredible, last, unbelievable, unthinkable; absurd, outlandish, preposterous, ridiculous; outside, remote, slight
near antonyms believable, conceivable, credible, plausible; possible; liable
antonyms likely, probable

impromptu *adj* made or done without previous thought or preparation ⟨our guest thanked us with an *impromptu* song⟩ — see EXTEMPORANEOUS

improper *adj* not appropriate for a particular occasion or situation ⟨an *improper* comment for a serious moment⟩ — see INAPPROPRIATE

improperly *adv* in a mistaken or inappropriate way ⟨the manufacturer's warranty is no longer valid if the appliance is used *improperly*⟩ — see WRONGLY

impropriety *n* **1** the quality or state of not being socially proper ⟨the *impropriety* of the song that the campers sang for the visitors was embarrassing⟩
synonyms inappropriateness, incorrectness, indecency, unfitness
related words coarseness, crudeness; imprudence, indiscretion
near antonyms discretion, prudence; etiquette
antonyms appropriateness, correctness, decency, decorousness, fitness, propriety, rightness, seemliness, suitability

2 a socially improper or unsuitable act or remark ⟨such *improprieties* as asking people how much money they make⟩
synonyms familiarity, gaffe, indiscretion, solecism
related words blunder, error, flub, fumble, goof, lapse, miscue, misstep, mistake, slip, slipup, stumble; discourtesy, incivility, offense (*or* offence); boner, howler, screamer; foul-up, muff; misapprehension, miscalculation, misconception, misjudgment, misstatement, misunderstanding
near antonyms manners, proprieties
antonyms amenity, civility, courtesy, formality, gesture

improve *vb* to make better ⟨a little salt would *improve* this bland food⟩
synonyms ameliorate, amend, better, enhance, enrich, meliorate, perfect, refine
related words correct, emend, rectify, reform, remedy; help; edit, revise; upgrade; fortify, intensify, strengthen; retouch, touch up
near antonyms damage, harm, hurt, impair, injure, spoil, tarnish; blemish, blight, deface, disfigure, flaw, mar; diminish, lessen, lower, reduce
antonyms worsen

improved *adj* being far along in development ⟨an *improved* version of the software is now available⟩ — see ADVANCED 1

improvement *n* an instance of notable progress in the development of knowledge, technology, or skill ⟨there's been a great *improvement* in your handwriting—I can actually read it!⟩ — see ADVANCE 2

improvident *adj* not thinking about and providing for the future ⟨the *improvident* view that the wearing away of the ozone layer need not concern us⟩
synonyms myopic, shortsighted
related words careless, heedless, imprudent, incautious, injudicious, unwise; extravagant, prodigal, profligate, spendthrift, thriftless, unthrifty; indulgent, lavish, reckless, wasteful
near antonyms careful, judicious, prudent, sensible, wise; economical, economizing, frugal, scrimping, sparing, thrifty; conserving, preserving, saving
antonyms farsighted, forehanded, foreseeing, foresighted, forethoughtful, provident

improvise *vb* to perform, make, or do without preparation ⟨since the award was a complete surprise, I *improvised* an acceptance speech⟩
synonyms ad-lib, extemporize
related words concoct, contrive, cook (up), devise, hatch, invent, make up, think up; cobble (together *or* up), dash (off)
near antonyms arrange, prepare, ready; consider, contemplate, ponder, study, think; practice (*or* practise), rehearse

improvised *adj* made or done without previous thought or preparation ⟨an *improvised* reply to an unexpected question at the press conference⟩ — see EXTEMPORANEOUS

imprudent *adj* showing poor judgment especially in personal relationships or social situations ⟨a very sweet girl, but so *imprudent* that no one trusts her with a secret⟩ — see INDISCREET

impudence *n* **1** disrespectful or argumentative talk given in response to a command or request ⟨my mother will not tolerate *impudence* from any of us⟩ — see BACK TALK

2 rude behavior ⟨their *impudence* irritated everyone at the wedding reception⟩ — see DISCOURTESY

impudent *adj* displaying or marked by rude boldness ⟨the guest's *impudent* inquiries about the cost of just about everything we had in the house⟩ — see NERVY 1

impulse *n* something that arouses action or activity ⟨the new auto factory was just the *impulse* that the local economy needed⟩

synonyms boost, encouragement, goad, impetus, incentive, incitement, instigation, momentum, motivation, provocation, spur, stimulant, stimulus, yeast

related words inducement, invitation; cause, consideration, motive, reason

impulsive *adj* **1** caused by or suggestive of an irresistible urge ⟨an *impulsive* purchase of a very expensive jacket⟩ — see COMPULSIVE

2 prone to sudden illogical changes of mind, ideas, or actions ⟨an *impulsive* woman who never seems to have the same opinion about anything for longer than ten minutes⟩ — see WHIMSICAL

impulsiveness *n* an inclination to sudden illogical changes of mind, ideas, or actions ⟨his *impulsiveness* sometimes got him into trouble⟩ — see WHIMSICALITY

impunity *n* freedom from punishment, harm, or loss ⟨she mistakenly believed that she could insult people with *impunity*⟩

synonyms exemption, immunity

related words armor, defense, guard, protection, safeguard, safety, security, shield; buffer, bumper, screen; absolution, absolving, dispensation, forgiveness

near antonyms exposure, liability, susceptibility, vulnerability

impure *adj* containing foreign or lower-grade substances ⟨be careful, because *impure* motor oil can damage your car's engine⟩

synonyms adulterated, alloyed, contaminated, dilute, diluted, polluted, tainted, thinned, weakened

related words befouled, besmirched, corrupted, debased, defiled, dirtied, fouled, soiled, spoiled, sullied; blended, commingled, incorporated, intermingled, intermixed, merged, mingled, mixed; coalesced, combined, compounded; cheapened, doctored

near antonyms clarified, filtered, purified, refined; neat, plain, straight; concentrated, strong; uncombined; pasteurized

antonyms pure, unadulterated, unalloyed, uncontaminated, undiluted, unpolluted, untainted

impurity *n* something that is or that makes impure ⟨*impurities* in the water made it cloudy⟩

synonyms adulterant, contaminant, defilement, pollutant

related words blot, blotch, spot, stain, taint; dirt, filth, grime; blemish, defect, disfigurement, fault, flaw; abnormality, imperfection, irregularity

near antonyms clarifier, filter, purifier, refiner; cleanliness, immaculateness, purity

impute *vb* to explain (something) as being the result of something else ⟨people often *impute* his silence to unfriendliness and not to the shyness it really represents⟩ — see CREDIT 1

in *adj* **1** being in the latest or current fashion ⟨the *in* hairstyle this spring⟩ — see STYLISH

2 enjoying widespread favor or approval ⟨the *in* thing to do is not always the right thing to do⟩ — see POPULAR 1

in *adv* at, within, or to a short distance or time ⟨the fielders closed *in*⟩ — see NEAR 1

inability *n* the lack of sufficient ability, power, or means ⟨the apparent *inability* of young children to sit still⟩

synonyms impotence, inadequacy, incapability, incapacity, incompetence, ineptitude, powerlessness

related words inaptitude; ineffectiveness, ineffectualness, inefficiency

near antonyms aptitude, bent, flair, talent; effectiveness, effectualness, efficaciousness, efficiency; fitness, suitability; power, strength

antonyms ability, adequacy, capability, capacity, competence, potency

inaccessible *adj* hard or impossible to get to or get at ⟨my pen is *inaccessible* now that it's fallen down the crack behind my desk⟩

synonyms inconvenient, unapproachable, unattainable, unavailable, unobtainable, unreachable, untouchable

related words distant, far, faraway, far-off, remote, removed; apart, hidden, isolated, out-of-the-way, secluded

near antonyms close, near, nearby

antonyms accessible, approachable, attainable, convenient, obtainable, reachable

inaccuracy *n* an unintentional departure from truth or accuracy ⟨included an unfortunate *inaccuracy* in the report⟩ — see ERROR 1

inaccurate *adj* **1** not being in agreement with what is true ⟨claimed that the TV ratings were *inaccurate* because they didn't take into account all those viewers in health clubs⟩ — see FALSE 1

2 not precisely correct ⟨the estimate is *inaccurate*, but will do for our purposes⟩ — see INEXACT 1

inaccurately *adv* in a mistaken or inappropriate way ⟨*inaccurately* reported that she was absent that day⟩ — see WRONGLY

inaction *n* lack of action or activity ⟨as a result of the park department's *inaction*, the city's pools are not ready to open for the summer⟩

synonyms dormancy, idleness, inactivity, inertness, nonaction, quiescence

related words indolence, languor, lassitude, laziness, lethargy, listlessness, sleepiness, sloth, sluggishness

near antonyms animateness, briskness, liveliness, sprightliness; business, diligence, employment, industriousness, occupation

antonyms action, activeness, activity

inactive *adj* **1** slow to move or act ⟨it's easiest to catch snakes early in the morning, while they're still cold and *inactive*⟩

synonyms dull, inert, lethargic, quiescent, sleepy, sluggish, torpid

related words apathetic, indolent, languorous, lazy, lazyish, listless, slothful; dormant, inanimate, motionless, sedentary, static, still; dead; dopey, drugged

near antonyms busy, engaged, occupied, working; animated, dynamic, energetic, lively, sprightly, vigorous; assiduous, diligent, hardworking, industrious

antonyms active

2 not being in a state of use, activity, or employment ⟨an *inactive* oil well⟩

synonyms dead, dormant, fallow, free, idle, inert, inoperative, latent, off, vacant

related words arrested, interrupted, suspended; asleep, lifeless, quiescent, sleepy; inoperable, unusable, unworkable, useless; dead, dull, slow

phrases out of commission

near antonyms functional, operable, operational, workable; assiduous, industrious; energetic, vigorous; feasible, practical, usable, useful, viable

antonyms active, alive, busy, employed, functioning, on, operating, operative, running, working

inactivity *n* **1** lack of action or activity ⟨the *inactivity* outside the school led me to think that it must have been vacation week⟩ — see INACTION

2 lack of use ⟨after weeks of *inactivity*, the car wouldn't start⟩ — see DISUSE

inadequacy *n* **1** a falling short of an essential or desirable amount or number ⟨the *inadequacy* of our servings was soon apparent, as hungry guests started clamoring for seconds⟩ — see DEFICIENCY

2 the lack of sufficient ability, power, or means ⟨tried to lie to hide the obvious *inadequacy* of his leadership⟩ — see INABILITY

inadequate *adj* not coming up to a usual standard or meeting a particular need ⟨an *inadequate* amount of food on hand for so many unexpected guests⟩ — see SHORT 3

inadequately *adv* in an unsatisfactory way ⟨did the job quickly, but *inadequately*⟩ — see BADLY

inadvertent *adj* happening by chance ⟨an *inadvertent* encounter with a rattlesnake in the brush⟩ — see ACCIDENTAL

inadvisable *adj* showing poor judgment especially in personal relationships or social situations ⟨it's *inadvisable* to have public arguments in the hallways⟩ — see INDISCREET

inane *adj* having no meaning ⟨*inane* and useless phrases, such as "have a nice day"⟩ — see MEANINGLESS

inanity *n* **1** a foolish act or idea ⟨quickly realized that her suggestion was an *inanity* and withdrew it⟩ — see FOLLY 1

2 lack of good sense or judgment ⟨the *inanity* of the singer's comments on the award show⟩ — see FOOLISHNESS 1

inapplicability *n* the quality or state of not having anything to do with the matter at hand ⟨the sheer *inapplicability* of the comment made everyone else at the meeting stare⟩ — see IRRELEVANCE

inapplicable *adj* not having anything to do with the matter at hand ⟨the judge refused to allow mention of the defendant's conviction for shoplifting, ruling that it was *inapplicable* to the case at hand⟩ — see IRRELEVANT

inappreciable *adj* not perceptible by a sense or by the mind ⟨an *inappreciable* change in the temperature⟩ — see IMPERCEPTIBLE

inappropriate *adj* not appropriate for a particular occasion or situation ⟨a bathing suit is *inappropriate* dress for strolling the streets of this seaside village⟩

synonyms graceless, improper, inapt, incongruous, incorrect, indecorous, inept, infelicitous, unapt, unbecoming, unfit, unhappy, unseemly, unsuitable, wrong

related words inopportune, unfortunate, unseasonable, untimely; immaterial, irrelevant; incompatible, uncongenial, unharmonious; bad, naughty, sinful; blamable, blameworthy, censurable; banned, barred, disallowed; forbidden, interdicted, outlawed, prohibited, proscribed; awkward, gauche, ungraceful, unacceptable, unsatisfactory

near antonyms fortunate, opportune, seasonable, timely; apt, material, relevant; compatible, congenial, harmonious; allowed, authorized, permitted; approved, endorsed, licensed (*also* licenced), sanctioned; abetted, encouraged, promoted, supported; acceptable, adequate, satisfactory; commendable, creditable, exemplary; blameless, irreproachable

antonyms appropriate, becoming, befitting, correct, decorous, felicitous, fit, fitting, genteel, happy, meet, proper, right, seemly, suitable

inappropriately *adv* in a mistaken or inappropriate way ⟨*inappropriately* referred to my chaperone as my father, and not as my stepfather⟩ — see WRONGLY

inappropriateness *n* **1** the quality or state of being unsuitable or unfitting ⟨I cannot even begin to describe the *inappropriateness* of such language for the dinner table⟩

synonyms inaptness, incorrectness, infelicity, unfitness, wrongness

related words inadmissibility, inapplicability, extraneousness, inadequacy, irrelevance, meaninglessness, pointlessness, senselessness; inauspiciousness, intolerability, undesirability, undesirableness, unsatisfactorability, uselessness

near antonyms admissibility, applicability, bearing, connection, materiality, pertinence, pointedness, relevance

antonyms appropriateness, aptness, correctness, felicitousness, felicity, fitness, fittingness, rightness, seemliness, suitability, suitableness

2 the quality or state of not being socially proper ⟨the *inappropriateness* of belching in a restaurant should have been apparent even to you⟩ — see IMPROPRIETY 1

inapt *adj* not appropriate for a particular occasion or situation ⟨an *inapt* but well-meaning attempt to inject some humor into the proceedings⟩ — see INAPPROPRIATE

inaptly *adv* in a mistaken or inappropriate way ⟨the development was *inaptly* named Apple Orchard Condominiums, presumably in honor of what was destroyed in order to build them⟩ — see WRONGLY

inaptness *n* the quality or state of being unsuitable or unfitting ⟨the *inaptness* of the ski outfit made her stand out among the somberly dressed mourners⟩ — see INAPPROPRIATENESS 1

inarticulate *adj* unable to speak ⟨the sudden rumblings of the earthquake rendered people *inarticulate* with fear⟩ — see MUTE 1

inasmuch as *conj* for the reason that ⟨you should not use that source, *inasmuch as* it is out of date⟩ — see SINCE

inaugural *adj* coming before all others in time or order ⟨the *inaugural* event in the city's week-long festival honoring the sailing ships⟩ — see FIRST 1

inaugural *n* the process or an instance of being formally placed in an office or organization ⟨attended the *inaugural* of three mayors⟩ — see INSTALLATION 1

inaugurate *vb* **1** to be responsible for the creation and early operation or use of ⟨*inaugurated* the college's athletic program for women⟩ — see FOUND

2 to put into an office or welcome into an organization with special ceremonies ⟨*inaugurated* the newest member of the club with a welcoming speech⟩ — see INSTALL 1

inauguration *n* the process or an instance of being formally placed in an office or organization ⟨a presidential *inauguration*⟩ — see INSTALLATION 1

inaugurator *n* a person who establishes a whole new field of endeavor ⟨the *inaugurator* of the assembly line in the production of automobiles⟩ — see FATHER 2

inauspicious *adj* being or showing a sign of evil or calamity to come ⟨this many problems so early in the project is an *inauspicious* sign⟩ — see OMINOUS

inauthentic *adj* being such in appearance only and made or manufactured with the intention of committing fraud ⟨an *inauthentic* warbonnet that was probably made in a factory a few months ago⟩ — see COUNTERFEIT

inborn *adj* **1** being a part of the innermost nature of a person or thing ⟨an *inborn* talent for dancing⟩ — see INHERENT

2 genetically passed or capable of being passed from parent to offspring ⟨certain instincts are *inborn* in mice⟩ — see HEREDITARY

inbred *adj* being a part of the innermost nature of a person or thing ⟨an *inbred* desire to do good in the world⟩ — see INHERENT

incandescence *n* the steady giving off of the form of radiation that makes vision possible ⟨candles made from whale oil were once highly prized because they burned with an *incandescence* superior to that of other candles⟩ — see LIGHT 1

incandescent *adj* giving off or reflecting much light ⟨sitting in darkness, except for the *incandescent* coals of our campfire⟩ — see BRIGHT 1

incantation *n* a spoken word or set of words believed to have magic power ⟨hovering over the sick child, the witch doctor muttered mysterious *incantations*⟩ — see SPELL 1

incapability *n* the lack of sufficient ability, power, or means ⟨the *incapability* of the staff to deal with the crisis⟩ — see INABILITY

incapable *adj* lacking qualities (as knowledge, skill, or ability) required to do a job ⟨hired an *incapable* assistant who only made a mess of things⟩ — see INCOMPETENT

incapacitate *vb* to render powerless, ineffective, or unable to move ⟨the malfunctioning of a single component can *incapacitate* the engine⟩ — see PARALYZE

incapacitated *adj* deprived of the power to perform one or more natural bodily activities ⟨was temporarily *incapacitated* by the car accident⟩ — see DISABLED

incapacity *n* the lack of sufficient ability, power, or means ⟨her *incapacity* for decision-making doesn't make her a very good boss⟩ — see INABILITY

incarcerate *vb* to put in or as if in prison ⟨the state *incarcerated* 1900 people last year⟩ — see IMPRISON

incarcerated *adj* taken and held prisoner ⟨*incarcerated* residents of that state are still allowed to vote in elections⟩ — see CAPTIVE

incarceration *n* the act of confining or the state of being confined ⟨he was bored and frustrated by his *incarceration*⟩ — see INTERNMENT

incarnate *vb* to represent in visible form ⟨the general view that Hitler *incarnated* extreme egotism and indeed evil itself⟩ — see EMBODY 2

incarnation *n* a visible representation of something abstract (as a quality) ⟨she is the very *incarnation* of grace and tactfulness⟩ — see EMBODIMENT

incautious *adj* not paying or showing close attention especially for the purpose of avoiding trouble ⟨an *incautious* comment got her in trouble⟩ — see CARELESS 1

incautiousness *n* failure to take the care that a cautious person usually takes ⟨a moment of *incautiousness* can cause an accident⟩ — see NEGLIGENCE 1

incendiary *n* **1** a person who deliberately and unlawfully sets fire to a building or other property ⟨firefighters caught the *incendiary*, who was watching the effects of his handiwork⟩ — see ARSONIST

2 a person who stirs up public feelings especially of discontent ⟨blamed the protests on outside *incendiaries*

who were intent on overthrowing the government⟩ — see AGITATOR

incense *n* a sweet or pleasant smell ⟨the heavenly *incense* of spring flowers⟩ — see FRAGRANCE

incense *vb* to make angry ⟨the insult so *incensed* him that he had to be restrained from hitting the guy⟩ — see ANGER

incensed *adj* feeling or showing anger ⟨*incensed* residents demanded that the police apprehend the punks who vandalized the cemetery⟩ — see ANGRY

incentive *n* something that arouses action or activity ⟨the reward for the missing dog was an *incentive* for me to start looking⟩ — see IMPULSE

inception *n* the point at which something begins ⟨this seemed like a good program at its *inception*, but it isn't working out as planned⟩ — see BEGINNING

incertitude *n* a feeling or attitude that one does not know the truth, truthfulness, or trustworthiness of someone or something ⟨a growing *incertitude* about the honesty of the housekeeper they had just hired⟩ — see DOUBT

incessant *adj* going on and on without any interruptions ⟨the *incessant* noise from a repair crew was a real distraction during the test⟩ — see CONTINUOUS

incessantly *adv* on every relevant occasion ⟨she *incessantly* made the same suggestion for a Roman theme whenever anyone mentioned holding a party⟩ — see ALWAYS 1

inch *n* **1** a very small distance or degree ⟨give them an *inch,* and they'll take a mile⟩ — see HAIR 1

2 an individual part of a process, series, or ranking ⟨*inch* by *inch*, we're making progress toward our goal⟩ — see DEGREE 1

inch *vb* **1** to advance gradually beyond the usual or desirable limits ⟨every year the water *inches* further up the embankments, threatening to permanently engulf the island city⟩ — see ENCROACH

2 to move slowly ⟨the car *inched* carefully across the snow-covered causeway⟩ — see CRAWL 2

incident *n* something that happens ⟨the odd little *incident* was reported in the local paper⟩ — see EVENT 1

incidental *adj* happening by chance ⟨an *incidental* meeting of two ships in the middle of the Atlantic⟩ — see ACCIDENTAL

incipiency *n* the point at which something begins ⟨from its *incipiency* the city's month-long festival of the performing arts has been a great success⟩ — see BEGINNING

incise *vb* **1** to cut (as letters or designs) on a hard surface ⟨*incised* a pattern into the copper plate⟩ — see ENGRAVE 1

2 to penetrate with a sharp edge (as a knife) ⟨*incised* the tree with a sharp ax to get the sap flowing⟩ — see CUT 1

incision *n* a long deep cut ⟨the surgeon made a thin *incision* with the scalpel⟩ — see GASH

incite *vb* **1** to cause or encourage the development of ⟨the rock band's failure to show up *incited* a riot, as the crowd had waited for hours⟩

synonyms abet, ferment, foment, instigate, provoke, raise, stir (up), whip (up)

related words forward, foster, further, promote, sow, stimulate; set off, trigger; excite, galvanize, inflame, inspire, motivate, rouse; activate, energize, quicken, vitalize

near antonyms check, curb, discourage, inhibit, restrain; calm, soothe, subdue, tranquilize (*also* tranquilize)

2 to rouse to strong feeling or action ⟨the demagogue's speech *incited* the crowd to riot⟩ — see PROVOKE 1

incitement *n* **1** something that arouses a strong response from another ⟨the insulting remark was all the *incitement* that was needed for a fight to break out⟩ — see PROVOCATION 1

2 something that arouses action or activity ⟨the approaching deadline was certainly an *incitement* to get going on the assignment⟩ — see IMPULSE

inciter *n* a person who stirs up public feelings especially of discontent ⟨wild-eyed *inciters* had been whipping up mobs in the streets⟩ — see AGITATOR

inciting *adj* serving or likely to arouse a strong reaction ⟨a deliberately *inciting* comment started the brawl⟩ — see PROVOCATIVE

incivility *n* rude behavior ⟨I won't tolerate *incivility,* such as spitting at people in the schoolyard⟩ — see DISCOURTESY

inclement *adj* marked by wet and windy conditions ⟨the weather report warned that the holiday weekend would be spoiled by *inclement* weather⟩ — see FOUL 1

inclination *n* **1** a habitual attraction to some activity or thing ⟨her natural *inclination* to help people in need⟩
synonyms bent, devices, disposition, genius, leaning, partiality, penchant, predilection, predisposition, proclivity, propensity, tendency, turn
related words bias, prejudice; aptitude, faculty, flair, gift, knack, talent; addiction, fondness, liking; forte, speciality, specialty; convention, custom, habit, pattern, practice (*also* practise), routine, trick, way, wont; oddity, peculiarity, quirk, singularity
near antonyms aversion, dislike, distaste; impartiality, neutrality, objectivity; apathy, disinterestedness, indifference

2 the act of positioning or an instance of being positioned at an angle ⟨the photographer adjusted the *inclination* of her head⟩ — see TILT

3 the degree to which something rises up from a position level with the horizon ⟨the *inclination* of the hill is gentle, so walking up it isn't too bad⟩ — see SLANT

incline *n* the degree to which something rises up from a position level with the horizon ⟨the steep *incline* of the hill meant that it was impossible to ride a bicycle up it⟩ — see SLANT

incline *vb* **1** to set or cause to be at an angle ⟨carefully *inclined* the ladder against the house⟩ — see LEAN 1

2 to show a liking or proneness (for something) ⟨a good restaurant for diners who *incline* to spicy food⟩ — see LEAN 2

inclined *adj* **1** having a desire or inclination (as for a specified course of action) ⟨we couldn't have convinced her if she weren't already so *inclined*⟩ — see WILLING 1

2 having a liking or affection ⟨*inclined* towards loud music⟩ — see FOND 1

3 having a tendency to be or act in a certain way ⟨a kindly couple who are *inclined* to be helpful to strangers⟩ — see PRONE 1

4 running in a slanting direction ⟨the highway ramps and other *inclined* roadways were treacherous during the ice storm⟩ — see DIAGONAL

inclining *adj* bending downward or forward ⟨the *inclining* branches of the evergreens seemed almost ready to break under the weight of the heavy snow⟩ — see NODDING

include *vb* to have as part of a whole ⟨the test *included* some hard essay questions⟩

synonyms carry, comprehend, contain, embrace, encompass, entail, involve, number, take in
related words comprise, consist (of); have, hold, own, possess; admit, receive; compose, constitute, form, make; assimilate, embody, incorporate, integrate
near antonyms bar, debar, preclude, prevent, prohibit; deny, refuse, reject; eliminate, except, rule out; lose, mislay, misplace
antonyms exclude, omit

inclusive *adj* covering everything or all important points ⟨a butterfly expert with an *inclusive* knowledge of his subject⟩ — see ENCYCLOPEDIC

incognito *adj* not named or identified by a name ⟨an *incognito* source in the CIA was the source of the information⟩ — see NAMELESS 1

incoherent *adj* **1** not clearly or logically connected ⟨the thriller's *incoherent* plot left movie audiences wondering who did what⟩
synonyms disconnected, disjointed, unconnected
related words baffling, bewildering, confounding, confused, confusing, disordered, disorderly, disorganized, muddled, perplexing, puzzling; disconcerting, frustrating; fallacious, illogical, inconsistent, invalid, irrational, unsound; absurd, asinine, eccentric, foolish, odd, peculiar, strange, unreasonable, unusual, weird; meaningless, nonsensical, nutty, preposterous, ridiculous, senseless, silly; unconvincing, unsatisfying; inexplicable, unaccountable, unexplainable
near antonyms ordered, orderly, organized; logical, rational, reasonable, sensible, solid, sound, valid; cogent, compelling, convincing, persuasive, plausible, satisfying; clear, lucid, perspicuous
antonyms coherent, connected

2 consisting of particles that do not stick together ⟨a driveway covered with *incoherent* gravel⟩ — see LOOSE 2

incombustible *adj* incapable of being burned ⟨we keep our important papers in an *incombustible* safe in the basement⟩
synonyms fireproof, noncombustible, nonflammable, noninflammable, uninflammable
related words nonexplosive
near antonyms ablaze, afire, blazing, burning, fiery; consumable; explosive, incendiary, volcanic
antonyms burnable, combustible, flammable, ignitable, inflammable

income *n* an increase usually measured in money that comes from labor, business, or property ⟨her summer job gave her some extra *income*⟩
synonyms earnings, gain(s), proceeds, profit, return, revenue, yield
related words killing, windfall; salary, tips, wages; capital, finances, funds, money
near antonyms cost, expenditures, expenses, outgo, outlay

incommode *vb* to cause discomfort to or trouble for ⟨tried to hide how much the request *incommoded* them⟩ — see INCONVENIENCE

incommoding *adj* causing difficulty, discomfort, or annoyance ⟨such *incommoding* features of air travel as flight delays and time-consuming security screenings⟩ — see INCONVENIENT 1

incommunicable *adj* beyond the power to describe ⟨the vastness of the universe is *incommunicable*⟩ — see INDESCRIBABLE

incomparable *adj* having no equal or rival for excellence or desirability ⟨the *incomparable* jewel known as the Hope Diamond⟩ — see ONLY 1

incompatible *adj* not being in agreement or harmony ⟨the committee's *incompatible* goals—develop new projects and cut costs—meant that they got very little accomplished⟩ — see INCONSISTENT

incompetence *n* the lack of sufficient ability, power, or means ⟨the astounding *incompetence* of the new assistant⟩ — see INABILITY

incompetent *adj* lacking qualities (as knowledge, skill, or ability) required to do a job ⟨an *incompetent* carpenter had built the deck, and the railings were loose already⟩
synonyms incapable, inept, inexpert, unfit, unqualified, unskilled, unskillful
related words ineffective, ineffectual, inefficient; callow, green, inexperienced, raw; unequipped, unprepared, untrained; useless, worthless; ineligible; wanting
near antonyms prepared, ready, trained; experienced, practiced (*or* practised), seasoned, veteran
antonyms able, capable, competent, expert, fit, qualified, skilled, skillful

incomplete *adj* lacking some necessary part ⟨an *incomplete* puzzle that has several pieces missing⟩
synonyms deficient, fragmental, fragmentary, halfway, partial
related words broken, damaged, flawed, impaired, imperfect, injured, marred, spoiled; sketchy, uncompleted, unfinished
near antonyms flawless, perfect, unbroken, undamaged, unimpaired, uninjured, unmarred; completed, finished
antonyms complete, entire, full, intact, whole

incompletely *adv* in some measure or degree ⟨*incompletely* explained the concept⟩ — see PARTLY

incomprehensible *adj* impossible to understand ⟨rocket science is *incomprehensible* to most people⟩
synonyms impenetrable, unfathomable, unintelligible
related words abstruse, enigmatic (*also* enigmatical), esoteric, inscrutable, recondite; cryptic, mysterious, obscure; unanswerable, unknowable; baffling, bewildering, confounding, confusing, mystifying, perplexing, puzzling
near antonyms basic, elementary, rudimentary; easy, simple; coherent, connected, ordered, orderly, organized; clear, cogent, compelling, convincing, lucid, perspicuous, plain, straightforward
antonyms fathomable, intelligible, understandable

inconceivable *adj* too extraordinary or improbable to believe ⟨the *inconceivable* idea that aliens snatched your homework⟩ — see INCREDIBLE

incongruity *n* someone or something with qualities or features that seem to conflict with one another ⟨she's an *incongruity*: an impeccably groomed woman who keeps a messy house⟩ — see CONTRADICTION 1

incongruous *adj* **1** not appropriate for a particular occasion or situation ⟨wore an *incongruous* Halloween costume to the fancy party⟩ — see INAPPROPRIATE
2 not being in agreement or harmony ⟨*incongruous* theories about the origins of matter⟩ — see INCONSISTENT

inconsequential *adj* **1** lacking importance ⟨that's an *inconsequential* problem compared to the other issues⟩ — see UNIMPORTANT
2 so small or unimportant as to warrant little or no attention ⟨an *inconsequential* error that does nothing to lessen the value of the report⟩ — see NEGLIGIBLE

inconsiderable *adj* **1** lacking importance ⟨the duties of the club's vice president are *inconsiderable* by any standard⟩ — see UNIMPORTANT
2 so small or unimportant as to warrant little or no attention ⟨an *inconsiderable* number of complaints about the car seat⟩ — see NEGLIGIBLE 1

inconsiderate *adj* showing a lack of manners or consideration for others ⟨she was *inconsiderate* by nature, never bothering to hold the door for anyone⟩ — see IMPOLITE

inconsideration *n* rude behavior ⟨the *inconsideration* and self-centeredness of toddlers is fortunately temporary⟩ — see DISCOURTESY

inconsistent *adj* not being in agreement or harmony ⟨*inconsistent* theories make it difficult to settle on one explanation⟩
synonyms clashing, conflicting, disagreeing, discordant, discrepant, incompatible, incongruous, inharmonious
related words irreconcilable; antagonistic, antithetical, contradictory, contrary, opposing, opposite
near antonyms akin, like, similar
antonyms agreeing, compatible, congruous, consistent, consonant, harmonious, nonconflicting

inconsolable *adj* feeling unhappiness ⟨he was *inconsolable* after he failed to make the hockey team⟩ — see SAD 1

inconspicuous *adj* not readily seen or noticed ⟨left an *inconspicuous* scratch on the wall⟩ — see UNOBTRUSIVE

inconstancy *n* lack of faithfulness especially to one's husband or wife ⟨*inconstancy* is grounds for divorce in some states⟩ — see INFIDELITY 1

inconstant *adj* **1** likely to change frequently, suddenly, or unexpectedly ⟨an *inconstant* but always entertaining friend⟩ — see FICKLE 1
2 not true in one's allegiance to someone or something ⟨the *inconstant* soldier deserted as soon as the first shot was fired⟩ — see FAITHLESS

incontestable *adj* not capable of being challenged or proved wrong ⟨the *incontestable* statement that every contest has a winner and a loser⟩ — see IRREFUTABLE

incontestably *adv* without any question ⟨you are *incontestably* correct that tomorrow is another day⟩ — see INDEED 1

incontrovertible *adj* not capable of being challenged or proved wrong ⟨*incontrovertible* facts left the jury with no choice but to convict⟩ — see IRREFUTABLE

incontrovertibly *adv* without any question ⟨an *incontrovertibly* accurate measurement of the height of the mountain⟩ — see INDEED 1

inconvenience *n* something that is a source of irritation ⟨the *inconvenience* of having to walk everywhere until the car is fixed⟩ — see ANNOYANCE 3

inconvenience *vb* to cause discomfort to or trouble for ⟨he *inconvenienced* his sister by moving into her tiny apartment⟩
synonyms discommode, disoblige, disturb, incommode, trouble
related words burden, encumber, saddle, weigh; hamper, hamstring, hinder, hobble, impede; aggravate, anger, annoy, bother, bug, exasperate, gall, get, nettle, peeve, pique, put out, rile, vex; grate, inflame, provoke; agitate, perturb, upset
near antonyms aid, assist, help; ease, facilitate; appease, conciliate, mollify, pacify, placate; delight, gladden, gratify, please; comfort, console, content
antonyms accommodate, oblige

inconvenient *adj* **1** causing difficulty, discomfort, or annoyance ⟨the unexpected visitors showed up at an *inconvenient* time⟩
synonyms awkward, discommoding, disobliging, incommoding

related words bothersome, burdensome, onerous, troublesome; annoying, exasperating, irritating
near antonyms acceptable, bearable, tolerable; advantageous, desirable, good, helpful
antonyms convenient
2 hard or impossible to get to or get at ⟨for some reason, they placed the dishes in an *inconvenient* cabinet⟩ — see INACCESSIBLE

incorporate *vb* **1** to make a part of a body or system ⟨scientists had to *incorporate* the existence of Pluto into their scheme of the solar system after the tiny planet was discovered⟩ — see EMBODY 1
2 to turn into a single mass that is more or less the same throughout ⟨*incorporated* all the ingredients for the cheesecake mixture⟩ — see BLEND 1

incorporeal *adj* not composed of matter ⟨ghosts are supposed to be *incorporeal*⟩ — see IMMATERIAL 1

incorrect *adj* **1** having an opinion that does not agree with truth or the facts ⟨you're *incorrect* about the date of the final exam—it's next Tuesday, not Wednesday⟩
synonyms mistaken, wrong
related words confused, misguided, misled; erroneous, false; deceived, deluded, tricked
phrases all wet, full of it
near antonyms informed; accurate, exact, precise
antonyms correct, right
2 not appropriate for a particular occasion or situation ⟨chose the *incorrect* military uniform for the treaty ceremony⟩ — see INAPPROPRIATE
3 not being in agreement with what is true ⟨an *incorrect* but not intentionally deceitful statement⟩ — see FALSE 1

incorrectly *adv* in a mistaken or inappropriate way ⟨you *incorrectly* identified the part of speech of one of the words in the sentence⟩ — see WRONGLY

incorrectness *n* **1** the quality or state of being unsuitable or unfitting ⟨the issue of the *incorrectness* of the hat she wore to her daughter's wedding mattered only to gossips⟩ — see INAPPROPRIATENESS 1
2 the quality or state of not being socially proper ⟨the *incorrectness* of the use of such language in a church can scarcely be expressed⟩ — see IMPROPRIETY 1

incorrigible *adj* not capable of being cured or reformed ⟨an *incorrigible* criminal who should spend the rest of his life behind bars⟩ — see HOPELESS 1

increase *n* **1** something added (as by growth) ⟨shortly after he turned 12, he had a sudden height *increase*⟩
synonyms accretion, accrual, addendum, addition, augmentation, boost, expansion, gain, increment, plus, proliferation, raise, rise, supplement
related words accumulation; complement; appendix, continuation, extension, uptrend, upturn; jump
near antonyms deduction
antonyms abatement, decrease, diminishment, lessening, lowering, reduction
2 the act or process of becoming greater in number ⟨the *increase* in the number of students enrolled at the school was very gradual⟩ — see MULTIPLICATION

increase *vb* **1** to make greater in size, amount, or number ⟨if you *increase* the number by two, how much do you have now?⟩
synonyms add (to), aggrandize, amplify, augment, boost, compound, enlarge, escalate, expand, extend, multiply, raise, swell, up
related words skyrocket; blow up, dilate, distend, inflate; elongate, lengthen, prolong, protract; enhance, heighten, intensify, magnify; complement, supplement;

beef (up), reinforce, strengthen; maximize; accumulate, amass, collect; follow up, parlay
near antonyms abbreviate, abridge, curtail, shorten; compress, condense, constrict, cut back, retrench
antonyms abate, contract, decrease, diminish, lessen, lower, reduce, subtract (from)
2 to become greater in extent, volume, amount, or number ⟨the number of Internet users *increased* rapidly during the 1990s⟩
synonyms accumulate, appreciate, balloon, build (up), burgeon, enlarge, escalate, expand, mount, multiply, mushroom, proliferate, rise, snowball, swell, wax
related words rocket, skyrocket; heighten, intensify; blow up, distend, inflate; crest, peak, surge
antonyms contract, decrease, diminish, lessen, wane

increased *adj* being at a higher level than average ⟨an *increased* amount of sugar in the bloodstream⟩ — see HIGH 2

incredible *adj* too extraordinary or improbable to believe ⟨she came in on Monday with an *incredible* story about monsters eating her homework⟩
synonyms fantastic, implausible, inconceivable, unbelievable, unconvincing, unimaginable, unthinkable
related words doubtful, dubious, far-fetched, fishy, flimsy, questionable, suspect, unlikely, unreasonable; hopeless, impossible; absurd, outlandish, preposterous, ridiculous; indefensible, insupportable, untenable
near antonyms likely, possible, probable; reasonable
antonyms believable, conceivable, convincing, credible, imaginable, plausible

incredulity *n* refusal to accept as true ⟨the teacher's *incredulity* about the claims in the essay proved wellfounded⟩ — see DISBELIEF

incredulous *adj* inclined to doubt or question claims ⟨*incredulous* by nature, I'm of course very suspicious of anyone who claims to be able to communicate with the dead⟩ — see SKEPTICAL 1

increment *n* something added (as by growth) ⟨added another big *increment* to the sales total this quarter⟩ — see INCREASE 1

incremental *adj* **1** proceeding or changing by steps or degrees ⟨the *incremental* evolution of the collection from a specialized gallery into a comprehensive art museum⟩ — see GRADUAL
2 produced by a series of additions of identical or similar things ⟨the *incremental* total for my collection of baseball cards⟩ — see CUMULATIVE

incriminate *vb* to make a claim of wrongdoing against ⟨in exchange for a reduced sentence, the thief agreed to *incriminate* his accomplice⟩ — see ACCUSE

incubate *vb* to cover and warm eggs to hatch them ⟨the hen *incubated* her eggs for two weeks⟩ — see SET 1

incubus *n* an evil spirit ⟨according to medieval legend, the magician Merlin was fathered by an *incubus*⟩ — see DEMON

inculcate *vb* to cause (as a person) to become filled or saturated with a certain quality or principle ⟨dedicated teachers *inculcating* young minds with a love of learning⟩ — see INFUSE

incumbent *adj* forcing one's compliance or participation by or as if by law ⟨it is *incumbent* upon you to attend every meeting⟩ — see MANDATORY

incurable *adj* not capable of being cured or reformed ⟨an *incurable* flirt at school dances⟩ — see HOPELESS 1

incurious *adj* having or showing a lack of interest or concern ⟨a quick *incurious* glance at the pile of junk mail⟩ — see INDIFFERENT 1

incursion *n* a sudden attack on and entrance into hostile territory ⟨there were *incursions* from the border every summer⟩ — see RAID 1

indecency *n* **1** the quality or state of being obscene ⟨parents complained about the *indecency* of the song's lyrics⟩ — see OBSCENITY 1

2 the quality or state of not being socially proper ⟨the *indecency* of the remark at a meeting of the school board made everyone gasp⟩ — see IMPROPRIETY 1

indecent *adj* depicting or referring to sexual matters in a way that is unacceptable in polite society ⟨paintings of nude figures are artistic, not *indecent*⟩ — see OBSCENE 1

indecision *n* the act or an instance of pausing because of uncertainty about the right course of action ⟨her *indecision* about where to go for dinner, while everyone was getting hungrier, was frustrating⟩ — see HESITATION

indecorous *adj* not appropriate for a particular occasion or situation ⟨an *indecorous* joke for a solemn moment in the marriage ceremony⟩ — see INAPPROPRIATE

indeed *interj* how surprising, doubtful, or unbelievable ⟨*indeed,* you really dyed your hair sixteen different colors!⟩ — see NO

indeed *adv* **1** without any question ⟨I know that you can *indeed* do better than that⟩

synonyms assuredly, certainly, definitely, doubtless, forsooth, incontestably, incontrovertibly, indisputably, really, surely, truly, undeniably, undoubtedly, unquestionably

related words conceivably, likely, perhaps, possibly; probably; clearly, obviously, unmistakably

phrases by all means, for sure

2 not merely this but also ⟨that is not merely a reason, but is *indeed* the entire point⟩ — see EVEN

indefatigable *adj* showing no signs of weariness even after long hard effort ⟨an *indefatigable* laborer who can work from sunrise to sunset⟩ — see TIRELESS

indefatigably *adv* with great effort or determination ⟨worked *indefatigably* for six days straight to get the project done⟩ — see HARD 1

indefensible *adj* too bad to be excused or justified ⟨getting your sister into trouble with the school authorities is *indefensible*⟩ — see INEXCUSABLE

indefinable *adj* beyond the power to describe ⟨some *indefinable* quality makes that movie star very appealing⟩ — see INDESCRIBABLE

indefinite *adj* **1** being or seeming to be without limits ⟨the *indefinite* vastness of the frozen tundra⟩ — see INFINITE

2 not clearly expressed ⟨an *indefinite* longing for something new and exciting in her life⟩ — see VAGUE 1

3 not seen or understood clearly ⟨through the dense fog we could just barely discern the *indefinite* form of another boat⟩ — see FAINT 1

indelicacy *n* the quality or state of lacking refinement or good taste ⟨the *indelicacy* of their dinner conversation made the other guests wince in embarrassment⟩ — see VULGARITY 1

indelicateness *n* the quality or state of lacking refinement or good taste ⟨the well-known *indelicateness* of the comedian's humor made him a poor choice for master of ceremonies⟩ — see VULGARITY 1

indemnification *n* payment to another for a loss or injury ⟨that insurance company is known to be slow for making *indemnifications* to their clients⟩ — see COMPENSATION 1

indemnify *vb* to provide (someone) with a just payment for loss or injury ⟨the company *indemnifies* workers who are injured on the job⟩ — see COMPENSATE 1

indemnity *n* payment to another for a loss or injury ⟨she now lives on a pension and an *indemnity* from her late husband's company⟩ — see COMPENSATION 1

indentation *n* **1** a sunken area forming a separate space ⟨the previous occupant's furniture had left some fairly noticeable *indentations* in the carpet⟩ — see HOLE 2

2 a V-shaped cut usually on an edge or a surface ⟨deep *indentations* along the edge of the leaf⟩ — see NOTCH 1

indented *adj* curved inward ⟨that *indented* area of the mountainside is prone to avalanches⟩ — see HOLLOW

independence *n* **1** the ability to care for one's self ⟨children are supposed to achieve some measure of *independence* by the time they are 18⟩ — see SELF-SUFFICIENCY

2 the state of being free from the control or power of another ⟨college freshmen often revel in their new-found *independence*⟩ — see FREEDOM 1

independent *adj* **1** able to take care of oneself without outside help ⟨an *independent* boy who moved out of his parents' house while still quite young⟩ — see SELF-SUFFICIENT

2 not being under the rule or control of another ⟨finally an *independent* people, after centuries of domination by their more powerful neighbors⟩ — see FREE 1

independently *adv* without aid or support ⟨*independently* came to the same conclusion⟩ — see ALONE 1

in–depth *adj* covering everything or all important points ⟨an *in-depth* report on the issue of violence in popular entertainment⟩ — see ENCYCLOPEDIC

indescribable *adj* beyond the power to describe ⟨the *indescribable* immensity of Mount Everest⟩

synonyms incommunicable, indefinable, ineffable, inexpressible, nameless, unspeakable, unutterable

related words inconceivable, incredible, unbelievable, unimaginable, unthinkable; characterless, featureless, nondescript

near antonyms conceivable, imaginable, thinkable

antonyms communicable, definable, expressible, speakable

indestructible *adj* impossible to destroy ⟨diamonds are widely considered to be *indestructible*, because they are one of the hardest known substances⟩

synonyms imperishable, inextinguishable

related words incorruptible; deathless, immortal, perpetual, undying; indelible; durable, enduring, lasting, permanent, unbreakable; strong, sturdy, tough

near antonyms mortal; impermanent, transient, transitory; breakable, delicate, flimsy, fragile, frail

antonyms destructible, extinguishable, perishable

index *n* an arrow-shaped piece on a dial or scale for registering information ⟨the *index* on the thermometer dropped below zero⟩ — see POINTER 1

index *vb* to put (someone or something) on a list ⟨*indexed* all the books in the library by category⟩ — see ¹LIST 2

Indian *n* a member of any of the native peoples of the western hemisphere usually not including the Eskimos ⟨a look at how *Indians* lived before the coming of the Europeans⟩ — see AMERICAN INDIAN

indicate *vb* to convey an idea indirectly ⟨her expression *indicated* that she was unhappy, but she was too polite to say so⟩ — see HINT

indication *n* a slight or indirect pointing to something (as a solution or explanation) ⟨there are *indications* that the medical breakthrough is imminent⟩ — see HINT 1

indicative *adj* indicating something 〈a wide-eyed look that is *indicative* of his constant curiosity〉

synonyms denotative, denoting, significant, signifying, telltale

related words alluding, allusive, referring; characteristic, symptomatic; demonstrative, exhibiting, expressive; symbolic (*also* symbolical); connoting, hinting, implying, insinuating, suggestive

indicator *n* an arrow-shaped piece on a dial or scale for registering information 〈you should refill when the *indicator* on the gas gauge shows that there's only a quarter of a tank〉 — see POINTER 1

indict *vb* to make a claim of wrongdoing against 〈the grand jury could *indict* the mayor for fraud and embezzlement〉 — see ACCUSE

indictment *n* a formal claim of criminal wrongdoing against a person 〈that prosecutor gets an *indictment* for 90% of his cases〉 — see CHARGE 1

indifference *n* lack of interest or concern 〈he felt only *indifference* towards his schoolwork〉

synonyms apathy, casualness, disinterestedness, disregard, insouciance, nonchalance, unconcern

related words halfheartedness, lukewarmness; carelessness, heedlessness, recklessness, unawareness; lethargy, listlessness; calmness, detachment, dispassion; callousness, hardheartedness, hardness, insensitivity; impassivity, phlegm; aloofness, coldness

near antonyms attentiveness, awareness, conscientiousness, heedfulness; sensitivity, warmheartedness; bias, partiality, prejudice; ardor, fervency, passion, warmth, zeal

antonyms concern, interest, regard

indifferent *adj* **1** having or showing a lack of interest or concern 〈*indifferent* about the result of the football game〉

synonyms apathetic, casual, disinterested, incurious, insouciant, nonchalant, perfunctory, unconcerned, uncurious, uninterested

related words halfhearted, lukewarm; aloof, cold, numb, remote, unemotional; calm, detached, dispassionate; careless, heedless, mindless; impassive, phlegmatic, stoic (*or* stoical), stolid; lethargic, listless; unawed, undazzled, unimpressed

near antonyms attentive, aware, conscientious, heedful, mindful; caring, sensitive, warmhearted; ardent, fervent, passionate, warm, zealous

antonyms concerned, interested

2 of average to below average quality 〈an *indifferent* but drinkable cup of coffee〉 — see MEDIOCRE 1

indigence *n* the state of lacking sufficient money or material possessions 〈there are various state and federal programs to help people in *indigence*〉 — see POVERTY 1

indigenous *adj* belonging to a particular place by birth or origin 〈the culture of the *indigenous* people of that country〉 — see NATIVE 1

indigent *adj* lacking money or material possessions 〈*indigent* people who require some outside assistance〉 — see POOR 1

indignant *adj* feeling or showing anger 〈the card player became *indignant* at the accusation of cheating〉 — see ANGRY

indignation *n* an intense emotional state of displeasure with someone or something 〈her *indignation* at the offensive television show led her to start a protest campaign〉 — see ANGER

indignity *n* an act or expression showing scorn and usually intended to hurt another's feelings 〈minor *indigni-*

ties such as intentionally mispronouncing a person's name〉 — see INSULT

indirect *adj* not straightforward or direct 〈the cab driver took a very *indirect* route to the hotel〉 〈a long-winded, *indirect* answer to a very simple question〉

synonyms circuitous, circular, roundabout

related words crooked, serpentine, sinuous, tortuous, twisting, winding; meandering, rambling, wandering; circumlocutory, long-winded, prolix, verbose; deceitful, deceptive, devious, dishonest, duplicitous, insidious, misleading, sneaky, underhand, underhanded; calculating, crafty, cunning, subtle, tricky

near antonyms candid, forthright, frank, honest, open, plain, unconcealed, undisguised

antonyms direct, straight, straightforward

indiscreet *adj* showing poor judgment especially in personal relationships or social situations 〈telling a friend's secrets is *indiscreet,* and unkind as well〉

synonyms ill-advised, imprudent, inadvisable, injudicious, tactless, unadvisable, unwise

related words dumb, idiotic, moronic, stupid; inconsiderate, thoughtless; ill-mannered, improper, inappropriate, indecorous, unbecoming, uncivil, unseemly; foolish, harebrained, nonsensical, preposterous, senseless, silly

near antonyms intelligent, logical, rational, sensible, smart, sound; appropriate, becoming, civil, decorous, proper, seemly; sage, sane, sapient

antonyms advisable, discreet, judicious, prudent, tactful, wise

indiscretion *n* a socially improper or unsuitable act or remark 〈a single *indiscretion* can get someone kicked out of that exclusive club〉 — see IMPROPRIETY 2

indispensable *adj* impossible to do without 〈you're my *indispensable* helper〉 — see ESSENTIAL 1

indisposed *adj* **1** having doubts about the wisdom of doing something 〈one person in the reading group is *indisposed* to choosing a racy book〉 — see HESITANT

2 temporarily suffering from a disorder of the body 〈stays home from school whenever he feels the least *indisposed*〉 — see SICK 1

indisposition *n* the condition of not being in good health 〈a brief *indisposition* made her miss the test〉 — see SICKNESS 1

indisputable *adj* not capable of being challenged or proved wrong 〈an *indisputable* fact is not a good debate topic〉 — see IRREFUTABLE

indisputably *adv* without any question 〈you are *indisputably* correct〉 — see INDEED 1

indistinct *adj* not seen or understood clearly 〈managed to discern a blurry, *indistinct* shadow through the rain〉 — see FAINT 1

indistinguishable *adj* **1** not perceptible by a sense or by the mind 〈*indistinguishable* differences that can be measured only electronically〉 — see IMPERCEPTIBLE

2 not seen or understood clearly 〈*indistinguishable* shapes in the fog〉 — see FAINT 1

3 resembling another in every respect 〈a synthetic fabric that supposedly is *indistinguishable* from real silk〉 — see SAME 1

individual *adj* **1** of, relating to, or belonging to a single person 〈everyone has his or her own *individual* opinion about the subject, but you will have to work together〉

synonyms individualized, particular, peculiar, personal, personalized, private, privy, separate, singular, unique

related words characteristic, distinctive, intimate; identifying, idiosyncratic; special, specific; indepen-

dent, nonconformist, self-directed, self-sufficient; custom, customized, specialized
near antonyms broad, prevailing, prevalent, widespread; common, normal, regular, typical
antonyms general, generic, popular, public, shared, universal
2 not the same or shared ⟨guest rooms at the inn have *individual* bathrooms⟩ — see SEPARATE 1
3 serving to identify as belonging to an individual or group ⟨he's got a highly *individual* laugh that I would know anywhere⟩ — see CHARACTERISTIC 1
individual *n* **1** a member of the human race ⟨every *individual* has value⟩ — see HUMAN
2 one that has a real and independent existence ⟨our general concept of what constitutes a chair is based on our experience with many *individuals* that were called chairs⟩ — see ENTITY
individualist *n* a person who does not conform to generally accepted standards or customs ⟨an *individualist* who steadfastly refuses to do what everyone else is doing⟩ — see NONCONFORMIST 1
individuality *n* the set of qualities that make a person different from other people ⟨her *individuality* showed through in everything she did⟩
synonyms character, identity, personality, selfhood, self-identity
related words distinctiveness, oneness, peculiarity, separateness, singleness, singularity, uniqueness; disposition, humor, nature, temper, temperament; independence
near antonyms conformity, conventionality
individualized *adj* of, relating to, or belonging to a single person ⟨an *individualized* plan of study for a gifted student⟩ — see INDIVIDUAL 1
indoctrinate *vb* to cause to acquire knowledge or skill in some field ⟨*indoctrinated* children in proper safety procedures⟩ — see TEACH
indolence *n* an inclination not to do work or engage in activities ⟨a general feeling of *indolence* overtook them during summer vacation⟩ — see LAZINESS
indolent *adj* not easily aroused to action or work ⟨an *indolent* boy who had to be forced to help out with the chores⟩ — see LAZY
indomitable *adj* incapable of being defeated, overcome, or subdued ⟨an *indomitable* spirit was needed to endure the rigors of pioneer life⟩ — see INVINCIBLE
indubitable *adj* not capable of being challenged or proved wrong ⟨the *indubitable* fact that there are no more woolly mammoths or saber-toothed tigers around⟩ — see IRREFUTABLE
induce *vb* **1** to be the cause of (a situation, action, or state of mind) ⟨the medication *induced* labor⟩ — see EFFECT
2 to cause (someone) to agree with a belief or course of action by using arguments or earnest requests ⟨finally *induced* her to cooperate with the police⟩ — see PERSUADE
inducement *n* the act of reasoning or pleading with someone to accept a belief or course of action ⟨gave up smoking only after a prolonged *inducement* by all the other family members⟩ — see PERSUASION 1
inducing *n* the act of reasoning or pleading with someone to accept a belief or course of action ⟨after the intense *inducing* of his friends, he went on a diet and joined a health club⟩ — see PERSUASION 1
induct *vb* to put into an office or welcome into an organization with special ceremonies ⟨*inducted* the

pitcher into the Baseball Hall of Fame⟩ — see INSTALL 1
inductee *n* a person forced or required to enroll in military service ⟨a new crop of *inductees* produced by the draft⟩ — see CONSCRIPT
induction *n* the process or an instance of being formally placed in an office or organization ⟨the formal *induction* will be tomorrow, but the college president has already started work⟩ — see INSTALLATION 1
indulge *vb* to give in to (a desire) ⟨the grandparents generally *indulged* the child's wishes⟩
synonyms cater (to), gratify, humor
related words bask, luxuriate, revel, wallow; coddle, mollycoddle, pamper, spoil; delight, please, pleasure; sate, satiate, satisfy
near antonyms bridle, check, constrain, curb, inhibit, restrain, stifle
indulgence *n* **1** an act of kind assistance ⟨as an only child, she was used to getting every kind of *indulgence* from her parents⟩ — see FAVOR 1
2 something adding to pleasure or comfort but not absolutely necessary ⟨bubble baths were her one *indulgence*⟩ — see LUXURY 1
industrious *adj* involved in often constant activity ⟨an *industrious* worker who never seemed to sleep⟩ — see BUSY 1
industriously *adv* with great effort or determination ⟨worked *industriously* to complete the project ahead of schedule⟩ — see HARD 1
industriousness *n* attentive and persistent effort ⟨she did twice as much work as anyone else through sheer *industriousness*⟩ — see DILIGENCE
industry *n* attentive and persistent effort ⟨he isn't the smartest kid in class, but he gets the best grades by determined *industry*⟩ — see DILIGENCE
inebriate *adj* being under the influence of alcohol ⟨those *inebriate* sports fans who yell and scream throughout the game⟩ — see DRUNK 1
inebriate *n* a person who makes a habit of getting drunk ⟨a clinic to help *inebriates* cope with their addiction⟩ — see DRUNK
inebriated *adj* being under the influence of alcohol ⟨after a whole night spent partying, the fraternity brothers were all severely *inebriated*⟩ — see DRUNK
ineffable *adj* beyond the power to describe ⟨an *ineffable* beauty descends on the canyon as the sun begins to set⟩ — see INDESCRIBABLE
ineffective *adj* **1** not producing the desired result ⟨an *ineffective* effort to move the bookcase⟩
synonyms ineffectual, inefficient, inexpedient
related words abortive, bootless, fruitless, futile, nonproductive, pointless, unavailing, unproductive, unprofitable, unsuccessful, useless, worthless
near antonyms availing, beneficial, helpful, productive, profitable, successful, useful, worthwhile
antonyms effective, effectual, efficacious, efficient, expedient
2 producing no results ⟨an *ineffective* medication that will be denied FDA approval⟩ — see FUTILE
ineffectual *adj* **1** not producing the desired result ⟨an *ineffectual* effort to reach their destination did at least lead them to another lovely spot⟩ — see INEFFECTIVE 1
2 producing no results ⟨an *ineffectual* plan to lose weight without dieting or exercising⟩ — see FUTILE
inefficient *adj* not producing the desired result ⟨*inefficient* measures to solve the problem of teenage smoking⟩ — see INEFFECTIVE 1

inelegant *adj* **1** lacking social grace and assurance 〈*inelegant* teens still learning how to act at formal events〉 — see AWKWARD 1

2 marked by an obvious lack of style or good taste 〈*inelegant* furniture that looked like it belonged in a budget motel〉 — see TACKY 1

inept *adj* **1** lacking qualities (as knowledge, skill, or ability) required to do a job 〈a well-meaning but *inept* secretary〉 — see INCOMPETENT

2 not appropriate for a particular occasion or situation 〈an *inept* comparison between nursing-home residents and day-care children〉 — see INAPPROPRIATE

3 showing or marked by a lack of skill and tact (as in dealing with a situation) 〈an *inept* effort to be friends with their future son-in-law〉 — see AWKWARD 2

ineptitude *n* the lack of sufficient ability, power, or means 〈her *ineptitude* made it clear that she would be happier in a different line of work〉 — see INABILITY

inequity *n* the state of being unfair or unjust 〈the *inequity* of the punishment upset him〉 — see INJUSTICE 1

inert *adj* **1** not being in a state of use, activity, or employment 〈the *inert*, abandoned factories that are scattered all over that dying city〉 — see INACTIVE 2

2 slow to move or act 〈a sleepy, *inert* reptile〉 — see INACTIVE 1

inertia *n* an inclination not to do work or engage in activities 〈*inertia* that grips so many of the club's members is the reason why nothing ever gets done〉 — see LAZINESS

inertness *n* lack of action or activity 〈the *inertness* of the campus on weekends, when most of the students go home〉 — see INACTION

inescapable *adj* impossible to avoid or evade 〈some people believe that your fate is determined at birth and thus *inescapable*〉 — see INEVITABLE

inescapably *adv* because of necessity 〈*inescapably*, we must take some drastic measures〉 — see NEEDS

inevitable *adj* impossible to avoid or evade 〈getting wet is *inevitable* if you are going to try to give your dog a bath〉

synonyms certain, inescapable, necessary, sure, unavoidable

related words decided, definite, settled; likely, possible, probable; destined, fated, foreordained, predestined, predetermined, preordained; inexorable, relentless, unremitting

phrases in the bag

near antonyms preventable (*also* preventible); doubtful, dubious, questionable, shaky, unclear; undecided, unsettled; undependable, unreliable; improbable, unlikely

antonyms avoidable, escapable, uncertain, unsure

inevitably *adv* because of necessity 〈we must *inevitably* make some sacrifices if we are going to save money〉 — see NEEDS

inexact *adj* **1** not precisely correct 〈a thousand is an *inexact* figure for the number of islands in the St. Lawrence River〉

synonyms imprecise, inaccurate, loose

related words approximate; erroneous, false, incorrect, off, wrong; general, indefinable, indefinite, indeterminate, indistinct, undefined, undetermined, unsettled; vague; faulty, flawed, mistaken; specious; distorted, fallacious, misleading; doubtful, dubious, questionable, uncertain; inconclusive, indecisive; debatable, disputable; invalidated, unconfirmed, unsubstantiated, unsupported

near antonyms certain, incontestable, indubitable, positive, sure, undeniable, unquestionable; correct, errorless, factual, right, sound, true, valid; clear-cut, decisive, definable, defined, definite; incontrovertible, indisputable, irrefutable; absolute, unqualified; confirmed, corroborated, determined, established, substantiated, supported, validated

antonyms accurate, dead, exact, precise

2 not being in agreement with what is true 〈an *inexact* and misleading statement〉 — see FALSE 1

inexcusable *adj* too bad to be excused or justified 〈spitting at a teacher is *inexcusable* behavior and will be severely punished〉

synonyms indefensible, unforgivable, unjustifiable, unpardonable, unwarrantable

related words insufferable, insupportable, intolerable, unbearable, unendurable; abominable, atrocious, heinous, monstrous, outrageous, scandalous, shocking; egregious, flagrant, glaring, gross, rank; unacceptable, untenable; black, evil, iniquitous, vicious, wicked; base, contemptible, deplorable, despicable, dirty, execrable, ignoble, reprobate, vile, wretched; cruel, nasty; blamable, blameworthy, censurable, reprehensible; banned, barred, condemned, disallowed, forbidden, interdicted, outlawed, prohibited, proscribed

near antonyms acceptable, tolerable; authorized, legal, permissible; allowed, permitted, tolerated; approved, endorsed, sanctioned; abetted, encouraged, promoted, supported; ethical, good, moral, virtuous

antonyms defensible, excusable, forgivable, justifiable, pardonable

inexhaustible *adj* showing no signs of weariness even after long hard effort 〈*inexhaustible* horses that pulled heavy wagons across the wide prairies〉 — see TIRELESS

inexpedient *adj* not producing the desired result 〈an *inexpedient* method for losing weight〉 — see INEFFECTIVE 1

inexpensive *adj* costing little 〈*inexpensive* but pretty jewelry〉 — see CHEAP 1

inexperienced *adj* **1** lacking in adult experience or maturity 〈*inexperienced* teenagers who still thought they knew everything〉 — see CALLOW

2 lacking or showing a lack of expert skill 〈an *inexperienced* carpenter had obviously built the roughhewn cabin〉 — see AMATEURISH

inexpert *adj* **1** lacking or showing a lack of expert skill 〈an *inexpert* attempt at putting on an outdoor concert〉 — see AMATEURISH

2 lacking qualities (as knowledge, skill, or ability) required to do a job 〈the *inexpert* mechanic only made the problem worse—and charged me a fortune for doing it〉 — see INCOMPETENT

3 showing or marked by a lack of skill and tact (as in dealing with a situation) 〈well-meaning but *inexpert* expressions of sympathy from friends after the funeral〉 — see AWKWARD 2

inexplicable *adj* impossible to explain 〈an *inexplicable* desire for ice cream at two in the morning〉

synonyms unaccountable, unexplainable

related words indefinable, indescribable, inexpressible; enigmatic (*also* enigmatical), impenetrable, incomprehensible, inscrutable, mysterious, unfathomable, unknowable; irrational, unreasonable, unsound; foolish, mindless, senseless; absurd, odd, peculiar, strange, unusual, weird

near antonyms logical, rational, reasonable, understandable; sane, sensible, wise; compelling, convincing, persuasive, plausible, satisfying; confirmed, corroborated, determined, established, explained, substantiated, validated

antonyms accountable, explainable, explicable

inexpressible *adj* beyond the power to describe ⟨overcome by an *inexpressible* awe at the sight of the thunderous waterfall⟩ — see INDESCRIBABLE

inexpressive *adj* not expressing any emotion ⟨kept an *inexpressive* face throughout the poker game⟩ — see BLANK 1

inextinguishable *adj* impossible to destroy ⟨freedom is an *inextinguishable* idea for people around the world⟩ — see INDESTRUCTIBLE

infallible *adj* **1** not being or likely to be wrong ⟨a teacher with an *infallible* memory for names⟩

synonyms unerring, unfailing

related words errorless, faultless, flawless, impeccable; certain, foolproof, perfect, sure; dependable, reliable

near antonyms defective, faulty, flawed, imperfect; undependable, unreliable

antonyms fallible

2 not likely to fail ⟨an *infallible* cure for hiccups⟩

synonyms certain, sure, unfailing

related words dependable, reliable, surefire; deadly, unerring

near antonyms doubtful, questionable, uncertain

antonyms fallible

infamous *adj* not respectable ⟨an *infamous* criminal⟩ — see DISREPUTABLE

infamy *n* the state of having lost the esteem of others ⟨the *infamy* of a war criminal⟩ — see DISGRACE 1

infant *n* a recently born person ⟨*infants* should be kept warm at all times⟩ — see BABY

infantile *adj* having or showing the annoying qualities (as silliness) associated with children ⟨the *infantile* humor that teenage boys are justly famous for⟩ — see CHILDISH

infatuated (with) *adj* filled with an intense or excessive love for ⟨*infatuated with* the rock band's lead singer⟩ — see ENAMORED (OF)

infatuation *n* a strong but often short-lived liking for another person ⟨had a brief *infatuation* with the captain of the ski team⟩ — see CRUSH 1

infectious *adj* exciting a similar feeling or reaction in others ⟨an *infectious* giggle that got the whole class laughing⟩ — see CONTAGIOUS 2

infelicitous *adj* not appropriate for a particular occasion or situation ⟨an *infelicitous* comment on the weight of the guest of honor at the banquet⟩ — see INAPPROPRIATE

infelicity *n* the quality or state of being unsuitable or unfitting ⟨the *infelicity* of holiday decorations at a funeral home⟩ — see INAPPROPRIATENESS 1

infer *vb* **1** to form an opinion through reasoning and information ⟨he *inferred* that she had left because her coat was gone⟩

synonyms conclude, deduce, extrapolate, gather, judge, reason, understand

related words conjecture, guess, speculate, surmise; construe, interpret; contemplate, rationalize, think; ascertain, dope (out), find out

phrases draw a conclusion

2 to convey an idea indirectly ⟨the results *infer* that there might be a problem with one piece of the equipment⟩ — see HINT

inferable *adj* being or provable by reasoning in which the conclusion follows necessarily from given information

⟨the *inferable* but unstated conclusion of the report on this social problem⟩ — see DEDUCTIVE

inference *n* an opinion arrived at through a process of reasoning ⟨that seems like a reasonable *inference,* but in this case it happens to be incorrect⟩ — see CONCLUSION 1

inferior *adj* **1** situated lower down ⟨creatures that inhabit the dark, *inferior* depths of the ocean⟩

synonyms lower, nether

related words lowest, nethermost; underlying

near antonyms highest, uppermost; overhanging, overhead

antonyms higher, superior, upper

2 of little or less value or merit ⟨a girl who has always felt *inferior* to her older sister⟩

synonyms mean, minor, secondary, second-class, second-rate

related words junior, lesser, lower, petty, smaller, subordinate, under; average, common, fair, middling, ordinary; amiss, bad, defective, unsatisfactory, wrong; deficient, inadequate, insufficient, unacceptable; littler, slighter, smaller; jerkwater, one-horse, two-bit

near antonyms major, more, primary, senior; choice, exceptional, first-class, first-rate, high-grade, premium, prime; acceptable, adequate, sufficient

antonyms greater, higher, superior

3 belonging to the class of people of low social or economic rank ⟨at one time, the upper crust liked to believe that *inferior* people were fit only to be servants⟩ — see IGNOBLE 1

4 falling short of a standard ⟨an *inferior* science textbook that was out-of-date the day that it was published⟩ — see BAD 1

5 having not so great importance or rank as another ⟨an *inferior* officer cannot strike a superior under any circumstances⟩ — see LESSER

6 of low quality ⟨*inferior* chocolate candy that no serious chocolate lover would think of eating⟩ — see CHEAP 2

inferior *n* one who is of lower rank and typically under the authority of another ⟨she is nice to her *inferiors* as well as to her superiors⟩ — see UNDERLING

inferno *n* a destructive burning ⟨firefighters rushed into the *inferno* to save the cat⟩ — see FIRE

infertile *adj* **1** not able to produce fruit or offspring ⟨an *infertile* cow is of limited use to a farmer⟩ — see STERILE 1

2 producing inferior or only a small amount of vegetation ⟨only parched, *infertile* fields after months of drought⟩ — see BARREN 1

infest *vb* to spread or swarm over in a troublesome manner ⟨called in an exterminator because the house was *infested* with ants⟩

synonyms overrun

related words beset, overspread, overwhelm; abound, crawl, teem; annoy, pester, plague; contaminate, infect

infidelity *n* **1** lack of faithfulness especially to one's husband or wife ⟨*infidelity* can lead to divorce⟩

synonyms disloyalty, faithlessness, falseness, falsity, inconstancy, perfidiousness, perfidy, unfaithfulness

related words adultery; betrayal, double-cross, double-dealing, duplicity, sellout, treachery, treason; deceit, deception, lying

near antonyms staunchness, steadfastness; dependability, reliability; honesty, trustworthiness

antonyms allegiance, constancy, devotedness, devotion, faith, faithfulness, fealty, fidelity, loyalty

2 the act or fact of violating the trust or confidence of another ⟨the one thing that the political boss will not forgive is *infidelity*⟩ — see BETRAYAL

infiltrate *vb* to introduce in a gradual, secret, or clever way ⟨undercover agents *infiltrated* the crime ring and eventually busted their gambling racket⟩ — see INSINUATE

infinite *adj* being or seeming to be without limits ⟨the *infinite* expanse of outer space⟩
synonyms boundless, endless, illimitable, immeasurable, indefinite, limitless, measureless, unbounded, unfathomable, unlimited
related words abysmal, bottomless; countless, incalculable, inestimable, innumerable, unmeasured; inexhaustible; far-flung, immense, vast
near antonyms fathomable, measurable; depthless, shallow, superficial
antonyms bounded, circumscribed, confined, definite, finite, limited, restricted

infinitesimal *adj* very small in size ⟨a soft drink with only an *infinitesimal* amount of caffeine⟩ — see TINY

infinity *n* endless time ⟨it seemed as though that meeting might extend into *infinity*⟩ — see ETERNITY 1

infirm *adj* lacking bodily strength ⟨the elderly and *infirm* have to be careful in winter⟩ — see WEAK 1

infirmity *n* **1** an abnormal state that disrupts a plant's or animal's normal bodily functioning ⟨suffered from a genetic *infirmity*⟩ — see DISEASE
2 the quality or state of lacking physical strength or vigor ⟨a period of *infirmity* left the athlete completely out of shape⟩ — see WEAKNESS 1

inflame *vb* **1** to make angry ⟨the newspaper editorial *inflamed* her enough to inspire her to write a letter to the editor⟩ — see ANGER
2 to set (something) on fire ⟨a carelessly tossed cigarette *inflamed* the papers in the garbage⟩ — see BURN 2

inflamed *adj* **1** being on fire ⟨the *inflamed* hillsides in one of the largest wildfires in the state's history⟩ — see ABLAZE 1
2 feeling or showing anger ⟨he gets red-faced when he's *inflamed* enough⟩ — see ANGRY

inflammable *adj* capable of catching or being set on fire ⟨some pajamas are made of *inflammable* material, so be careful⟩ — see COMBUSTIBLE

inflexibility *n* the quality or state of being demanding or unyielding (as in discipline or criticism) ⟨the principal's *inflexibility* in matters of discipline is the stuff of school legend⟩ — see SEVERITY

inflexible *adj* **1** not capable of changing or being changed ⟨the *inflexible* law of gravity⟩
synonyms fixed, hard-and-fast, immutable, invariable, unalterable, unchangeable
related words changeless, constant, determinate, established, set, settled, stable, steadfast, steady, unaltered, unchanging, unvarying; immovable, unmovable
near antonyms adaptable, adjustable; fickle, fluctuating, inconstant, uncertain, unstable, varying
antonyms alterable, changeable, flexible, mutable, variable
2 incapable of or highly resistant to bending ⟨shoes made of *inflexible* plastic hurt my feet⟩ — see STIFF 1
3 not allowing for any exceptions or loosening of standards ⟨*inflexible* entry rules for the contest ban anyone who works for the company as well as any of their relatives⟩ — see RIGID 1
4 sticking to an opinion, purpose, or course of action in spite of reason, arguments, or persuasion ⟨her *inflexi-*

ble father was unmoved by tears and pleading, and he grounded her anyway⟩ — see OBSTINATE

inflow *n* a flowing or coming in ⟨the *inflow* of new students every September means that there will always be new blood for student organizations⟩ — see INFLUX

influence *n* **1** the power to direct the thinking or behavior of others usually indirectly ⟨a mayor who doesn't hesitate to use her *influence* to get business leaders behind civic improvements⟩
synonyms authority, clout, pull, sway, weight
related words command, dominance, dominion, mastery, predominance, scepter, sovereignty, supremacy; consequence, eminence, importance, moment; impact, impression, mark
near antonyms helplessness, impotence, powerlessness, weakness
2 the power to bring about a result on another ⟨the basic premise of astrology is that the position of the stars has an *influence* on human affairs⟩ — see EFFECT 2

influence *vb* to act upon (a person or a person's feelings) so as to cause a response ⟨the news reports of the devastating flood *influenced* a great many people to make contributions for food and supplies⟩ — see ¹AFFECT 1

influential *adj* **1** having power over the minds or behavior of others ⟨in light of the effect that they have had, religious leaders such as Jesus and Muḥammad must be regarded as among the most *influential* people ever⟩
synonyms authoritative, forceful, weighty
related words controlling, dominating, masterful; dominant, predominant, sovereign, supreme; eminent, important, momentous
near antonyms helpless, impotent, powerless, weak; incapable, unable
2 having great power or influence ⟨a particularly *influential* politician got the team a new ballpark⟩ — see IMPORTANT 2

influx *n* a flowing or coming in ⟨a sudden *influx* of people⟩
synonyms flux, inflow, inrush
related words deluge, flood, flow, inundation, overflow, spate, torrent; rush, stampede; flow, river, stream, tide
near antonyms emigration, exodus, flight
antonyms outflow, outpouring

inform *vb* **1** to give information (as to the authorities) about another's improper or unlawful activities ⟨the police only caught the mastermind of the burglary because his partner *informed*⟩ — see SQUEAL 1
2 to give information to ⟨chose teaching as a career because it affords the opportunity to *inform* a whole generation of young minds⟩ — see ENLIGHTEN 1

informal *adj* **1** not rigidly following established form, custom, or rules ⟨an *informal* meeting allowed everyone to get acquainted⟩
synonyms irregular, unceremonious, unconventional, unorthodox
related words unauthorized, unofficial; casual, easygoing, lax, loose, relaxed
near antonyms correct, decorous, proper; constrained, inhibited, restrained, rigid, stiff, stuffy, uptight
antonyms ceremonial, ceremonious, conventional, formal, orthodox, regular, routine
2 not designed for special occasions ⟨chose an *informal* flowery dress⟩ — see CASUAL 1
3 used in or suitable for speech and not formal writing ⟨please don't use *informal* language in a serious essay⟩ — see COLLOQUIAL 1

informant *n* a person who provides secret information about another's wrongdoing ⟨the FBI is working with *informants* to find out about the subversive group⟩ — see INFORMER

information *n* a report of recent events or facts not previously known ⟨the news story had some more *information* about the wildfires out in the West⟩ — see NEWS

informational *adj* providing useful information or knowledge ⟨an *informational* presentation from the company's health care provider⟩ — see INFORMATIVE

informative *adj* providing useful information or knowledge ⟨some Web sites for family vacation resorts are very *informative* and some are practically useless⟩
synonyms educational, educative, informational, instructional, instructive
related words comprehensive, detailed, full; edifying, elucidative, enlightening, explanatory, illuminating; chatty, gossipy, newsy; availing, beneficial, constructive, helpful, profitable; practical, serviceable, usable, useful, worthwhile
near antonyms impractical, unhelpful, unusable, useless
antonyms uninstructive

informed *adj* 1 based on sound reasoning or information ⟨the expert's *informed* opinion⟩ — see GOOD 1
2 having information especially as a result of study or experience ⟨people who are *informed* about nutrition have misgivings about this new diet⟩ — see FAMILIAR 2

informer *n* a person who provides secret information about another's wrongdoing ⟨the *informer* who told the police about that conspiracy angered a lot of dangerous people⟩
synonyms betrayer, informant, snitcher, squealer, stool pigeon, talebearer, tattler, tattletale, telltale
related words collaborator; blabbermouth, gossip, gossiper; snoop, snooper, spy; notifier

infraction *n* a failure to uphold the requirements of law, duty, or obligation ⟨speeding is only a minor *infraction*, but murder is a serious felony⟩ — see BREACH 1

infrequent *adj* not often occurring or repeated ⟨a shut-in who made *infrequent* trips to the store⟩
synonyms occasional, rare, sporadic
related words scarce, scattered, uncommon, unique, unusual; choppy, discontinuous, erratic, fitful, intermittent, irregular, spasmodic, spotty, unsteady
near antonyms common, ordinary, routine
antonyms frequent

infrequently *adv* not often ⟨their grandparents were disappointed that they visited so *infrequently*⟩ — see SELDOM

infringe *vb* to fail to keep ⟨a law that was struck down by the court for *infringing* the fifth amendment to the U.S. Constitution⟩ — see VIOLATE 1

infringement *n* a failure to uphold the requirements of law, duty, or obligation ⟨any government action limiting freedom of speech is an *infringement* of the U.S. Constitution⟩ — see BREACH 1

infuriate *vb* to make angry ⟨the quarterback's mistake *infuriated* the coach⟩ — see ANGER

infuriated *adj* feeling or showing anger ⟨an *infuriated* correspondent who keeps sending increasingly vicious letters⟩ — see ANGRY

infuse *vb* to cause (as a person) to become filled or saturated with a certain quality or principle ⟨parents who *infuse* their children with strong moral values⟩
synonyms imbue, inculcate, ingrain, inoculate, invest, steep, suffuse

related words animate, enliven, invigorate; implant, instill, plant; impregnate, permeate, pervade, saturate; deluge, drown, fill, flood, inundate, overwhelm, submerge
near antonyms deprive, divest, strip; clear, empty; eliminate, remove, take away

ingenious *adj* 1 having the skill and imagination to create new things ⟨an *ingenious* but eccentric inventor⟩ — see CREATIVE 1
2 showing a use of the imagination and creativity especially in inventing ⟨a chair that can't tip over is quite *ingenious*⟩ — see CLEVER 1

ingeniousness *n* the skill and imagination to create new things ⟨hired a new designer with real *ingeniousness*⟩ — see CREATIVITY 1

ingenuity *n* the skill and imagination to create new things ⟨the mystery writer's exceptional *ingenuity* enabled her to devise plots that always had readers guessing to the very end⟩ — see CREATIVITY 1

ingenuous *adj* 1 free from any intent to deceive or impress others ⟨photographs that capture the *ingenuous* smiles of young children at play⟩ — see GUILELESS
2 lacking in worldly wisdom or informed judgment ⟨an *ingenuous* newcomer to the big city who outwits the slickers at their own game⟩ — see NAIVE 1

ingenuously *adv* without any attempt to impress by deception or exaggeration ⟨*ingenuously* admitted that the idea had been hers⟩ — see NATURALLY 3

ingenuousness *n* the quality or state of being simple and sincere ⟨his *ingenuousness* endeared him to his sophisticated new friends⟩ — see NAÏVETÉ 1

ingest *vb* 1 to take in as food ⟨*ingested* too much ice cream and ended up with a stomachache⟩ — see EAT 1
2 to take into the stomach through the mouth and throat ⟨*ingested* the foul-tasting medicine with only the greatest difficulty⟩ — see SWALLOW 1

ingrain *vb* 1 to cause (as a person) to become filled or saturated with a certain quality or principle ⟨the journalism professor *ingrained* his students with a deep respect for their chosen profession⟩ — see INFUSE
2 to produce a vivid impression of ⟨the third-world privation he witnessed forever *ingrained* itself upon the young doctor's memory⟩ — see ENGRAVE 2
3 to set solidly in or as if in surrounding matter ⟨tried to *ingrain* traditional values in their children⟩ — see ENTRENCH

ingrained *adj* being a part of the innermost nature of a person or thing ⟨her deeply *ingrained* distrust of all authority⟩ — see INHERENT

ingratiating *adj* likely to win one's affection ⟨one of the orphans had a most *ingratiating* smile⟩
synonyms disarming, endearing, winning, winsome
related words adorable, charming, likable, lovable; affecting, poignant, touching; adulatory, deferential, groveling (*or* grovelling), kowtowing, obsequious, servile, sycophantic; drooling, slavering, slobbering; soapy, sugary, unctuous
near antonyms alienating, disaffecting, displeasing; repugnant, repulsive; arrogant, disdainful, haughty, insolent, proud, scornful

ingredient *n* one of the parts that make up a whole ⟨one of the *ingredients* is sugar⟩ — see ELEMENT 1

inhabitable *adj* suitable for living in ⟨an *inhabitable* planet⟩ — see LIVABLE

inhabitant *n* one who lives permanently in a place ⟨the *inhabitants* of the town don't like the tourists⟩
synonyms denizen, dweller, habitant, occupant, resident, resider

related words aborigine, native; citizen, national, subject; colonist, émigré (*also* emigre), migrant, newcomer, settler; burgher, townie, villager

near antonyms alien, foreigner; guest, tourist, visitor; defector, escaper, evacuee, exile, expatriate, refugee

antonyms transient

inharmonious *adj* **1** not being in agreement or harmony ⟨the inn bans young children because the owners believe that they are *inharmonious* with the quiet atmosphere other guests desire⟩ — see INCONSISTENT

2 marked by or producing a harsh combination of sounds ⟨a deliberately *inharmonious* piece of music⟩ — see DISSONANT

inherent *adj* being a part of the innermost nature of a person or thing ⟨an *inherent* concept of justice⟩

synonyms essential, inborn, inbred, ingrained, innate, integral, intrinsic, natural

related words basic, constitutional, elemental, fundamental; congenital, hereditary, inherited, inmost, inner, interior; internal; characteristic, distinctive, peculiar; normal, regular, typical

near antonyms alien, foreign; accidental, coincidental, incidental; acquired; superficial, surface; exterior, external

antonyms adventitious, extraneous, extrinsic

inherently *adv* by natural character or ability ⟨girls are not *inherently* better at language skills than boys⟩ — see NATURALLY 1

inheritable *adj* genetically passed or capable of being passed from parent to offspring ⟨blue eye color is an *inheritable* trait⟩ — see HEREDITARY

inheritance *n* something that is or may be inherited ⟨a sense of humor was her *inheritance* from her mother⟩

synonyms bequest, birthright, heritage, legacy, patrimony

related words heirloom; bestowal, gift, offering, present

inherited *adj* genetically passed or capable of being passed from parent to offspring ⟨hair color is *inherited*⟩ — see HEREDITARY

inheritor *n* a person who has the right to inherit property ⟨hired a detective to find the millionaire's *inheritor*⟩ — see HEIR

inhibit *vb* **1** to create difficulty for the work or activity of ⟨the cold *inhibited* her from getting much work done that morning⟩ — see HAMPER

2 to keep from exceeding a desirable degree or level (as of expression) ⟨laws designed to *inhibit* the powers of the intelligence organizations⟩ — see CONTROL 1

3 to steer (a person) from an activity or course of action ⟨the people were *inhibited* from asking too many questions of the candidate⟩ — see DISCOURAGE 2

inhibition *n* **1** the checking of one's true feelings and impulses when dealing with others ⟨an innate *inhibition* made it difficult for him to tell his girlfriend what he was really feeling⟩ — see CONSTRAINT 1

2 something that makes movement or progress more difficult ⟨without the *inhibition* of their jackets, the boys were able to wrestle more vigorously⟩ — see ENCUMBRANCE

inhospitable *adj* marked by opposition or ill will ⟨the proposal received an unexpectedly *inhospitable* response⟩ — see HOSTILE 1

inhuman *adj* **1** difficult to endure ⟨kept the prisoners in *inhuman* conditions⟩ — see HARSH 1

2 having or showing a lack of sympathy or tender feelings ⟨an *inhuman* indifference to the sufferings of other human beings⟩ — see HARD 1

inhumane *adj* **1** having or showing a lack of sympathy or tender feelings ⟨*inhumane* wardens who regularly ignored the crying children in their care⟩ — see HARD 1

2 having or showing the desire to inflict severe pain and suffering on others ⟨an *inhumane* dictator who tortured and murdered thousands of his own people⟩ — see CRUEL 1

inhumanity *n* the willful infliction of pain and suffering on others ⟨man's *inhumanity* to man has been a recurring theme in human history⟩ — see CRUELTY

inimical *adj* **1** marked by opposition or ill will ⟨received an *inimical* response rather than the anticipated support⟩ — see HOSTILE 1

2 opposed to one's interests ⟨laws designed to enhance national security that some regard as *inimical* to cherished freedoms⟩ — see ADVERSE 1

inimitable *adj* having no equal or rival for excellence or desirability ⟨an *inimitable* performer of violin solos⟩ — see ONLY 1

iniquitous *adj* not conforming to a high moral standard; morally unacceptable ⟨*iniquitous* behavior such as cheating and lying⟩ — see BAD 2

iniquity *n* **1** immoral conduct or practices harmful or offensive to society ⟨drug use is not only a destroyer of personal health but also an *iniquity* that undermines our society⟩ — see VICE 1

2 that which is morally unacceptable ⟨a nation still struggling with the aftereffects of the *iniquity* of slavery⟩ — see EVIL

initial *adj* coming before all others in time or order ⟨you've resolved my *initial* complaint, but now I have a new question⟩ — see FIRST 1

initially *adv* in the beginning ⟨we *initially* intended to rebuild the school from the ground up⟩ — see ORIGINALLY

initiate *vb* **1** to be responsible for the creation and early operation or use of ⟨no one knows who *initiated* written language⟩ — see FOUND

2 to impart knowledge of a new thing or situation to ⟨*initiated* the new recruits in the unspoken laws of military conduct⟩ — see ACQUAINT 1

3 to put into an office or welcome into an organization with special ceremonies ⟨*initiated* her as Surgeon General before an army of reporters and photographers⟩ — see INSTALL 1

initiation *n* the process or an instance of being formally placed in an office or organization ⟨the *initiation* of the new members of the Scout troop⟩ — see INSTALLATION 1

initiative *n* readiness to engage in daring or difficult activity ⟨the soldier showed great *initiative* and bravery in foiling the terrorist attack⟩ — see ENTERPRISE 2

initiator *n* a person who establishes a whole new field of endeavor ⟨as the *initiator* of printing from movable type, Gutenberg revolutionized people's access to written language⟩ — see FATHER 2

inject *vb* to put among or between others ⟨*injected* one more comment into the body of the text⟩ — see INSERT

injudicious *adj* showing poor judgment especially in personal relationships or social situations ⟨lost a job because of an *injudicious* comment on the boss's toupee⟩ — see INDISCREET

injure *vb* **1** to cause bodily damage to ⟨*injured* himself while skiing⟩

synonyms damage, harm, hurt, wound

related words batter, bruise, contuse, gash, gore, lacerate, scald, scar, scathe, tear; cripple, lame, maim, mangle, mutilate; afflict, torment, torture; lay up; blemish, impair, mar, scrape, spoil

near antonyms cure, fix, heal, mend, remedy

2 to reduce the soundness, effectiveness, or perfection of ⟨the agent's treachery has *injured* our national security for years to come⟩ — see DAMAGE 1

injurious *adj* causing or capable of causing harm ⟨inaccurate news reports are *injurious* to the public's faith in the media⟩ — see HARMFUL

injury *n* **1** something that causes loss or pain ⟨the harsh words were the worst *injury*⟩

synonyms damage, detriment, harm, hurt

related words disservice, injustice, outrage, wrong; affront, dart, indignity, insult, offense (*or* offence); crippling, mayhem, mutilation; defacement, disablement, disability, disfigurement; abrasion, bruise, bump, contusion, scald, scar, scathe, scrape, scratch, sear

near antonyms healing, recovery; cure, fix, remedy

2 unfair or inadequate treatment of someone or something or an instance of this ⟨the state did him an *injury* when it destroyed his herd of cattle without adequate proof it was diseased⟩ — see DISSERVICE

injustice *n* **1** the state of being unfair or unjust ⟨the *injustice* of the coach's accusation that I'd been lazy frustrated and angered me⟩

synonyms inequity, unfairness, unjustness

related words dirtiness, foulness

antonyms equity, fairness, justice

2 unfair or inadequate treatment of someone or something or an instance of this ⟨suffered *injustice* and even insults at the hands of the court system⟩ — see DISSERVICE

inkling *n* a slight or indirect pointing to something (as a solution or explanation) ⟨did not give the slightest *inkling* that he was planning to quit⟩ — see HINT 1

inlet *n* a part of a body of water that extends beyond the general shoreline ⟨went fishing in the quiet *inlets* of the coast⟩ — see GULF 1

inn *n* a place that provides rooms and usually a public dining room for overnight guests ⟨we stayed at an *inn* rather than keep driving all night⟩ — see HOTEL

innards *n pl* the internal organs of the body ⟨carefully examined the *innards* of a frog for science class⟩ — see GUT 1

innate *adj* being a part of the innermost nature of a person or thing ⟨an *innate* athletic ability that allowed him to excel at just about any sport⟩ — see INHERENT

innately *adv* by natural character or ability ⟨some people are *innately* good at math⟩ — see NATURALLY 1

inner *adj* **1** situated farther in ⟨an *inner* area of the national park that is some distance from the nearest road⟩

synonyms inside, interior, internal, inward

related words inmost, innermost; central, mid, middle

near antonyms outermost, outmost

antonyms exterior, external, outer, outside, outward

2 of or relating to the mind ⟨kept his *inner* life private⟩ — see MENTAL 1

innocence *n* **1** the quality or state of being free from guilt or blame ⟨the accused criminal eventually proved her *innocence* and was released⟩

synonyms blamelessness, faultlessness, guiltlessness, impeccability

related words decency, goodness, honesty, incorruptibility, integrity, righteousness, uprightness, virtuousness; morality, virtue; chastity, purity; harmlessness, inoffensiveness

near antonyms blame, fault, responsibility; corruption, criminality, depravity, evil, immorality, reprehensibleness, sinfulness, wickedness; harmfulness, offensiveness

antonyms blameworthiness, culpability, guilt, guiltiness

2 the quality or state of being simple and sincere ⟨the *innocence* of the child's question touched everyone⟩ — see NAÏVETÉ 1

innocent *adj* **1** free from sin ⟨an *innocent* baby⟩

synonyms pure

related words chaste, moral, virtuous; immaculate, spotless, unblemished, unstained, unsullied; decent, ethical, good, honest, honorable, righteous, upright, virtuous; blameless, guiltless

near antonyms lascivious, lewd, lustful, unchaste; evil, immoral, iniquitous, reprobate, unrighteous, wicked; corrupt, debased, debauched, degenerate, depraved, dissolute, erring, fallen, lost, perverted; condemned, damned

antonyms impure, sinful

2 free from guilt or blame ⟨the robbery suspect was found to be *innocent*⟩

synonyms blameless, clear, faultless, guiltless, impeccable, irreproachable

related words absolved, acquitted, cleared, exonerated, vindicated; ethical, law-abiding, moral, righteous, upright, virtuous

phrases in the clear

near antonyms blamable, blameworthy, censurable, culpable, impeachable, indictable, punishable; accused, impeached, indicted; condemned, convicted; hangdog, shamed, shamefaced

antonyms guilty

3 free from any intent to deceive or impress others ⟨an *innocent* offer to sing before the gathering⟩ — see GUILELESS

4 lacking in worldly wisdom or informed judgment ⟨an *innocent* young woman who felt a little out of place among her more sophisticated roommates⟩ — see NAIVE 1

5 not causing injury or hurt ⟨good-natured teasing that is just *innocent* fun⟩ — see HARMLESS

innocent *n* an innocent or gentle person ⟨an *innocent* who is often puzzled by and prey to the evils of the world⟩ — see LAMB

innocently *adv* **1** without any attempt to impress by deception or exaggeration ⟨"you look nice," she commented *innocently*⟩ — see NATURALLY 3

2 with purity of thought and deed ⟨very young children approach the world so *innocently*⟩ — see PURELY

innocuous *adj* not causing injury or hurt ⟨those *innocuous* lies we must tell every day if society is to remain civil⟩ — see HARMLESS

innovate *vb* to be responsible for the creation and early operation or use of ⟨*innovated* a new system for filing books that dramatically improved efficiency⟩ — see FOUND

innovation *n* something (as a device) created for the first time through the use of the imagination ⟨the computer is one *innovation* that revolutionized the business world⟩ — see INVENTION 1

innovative *adj* having the skill and imagination to create new things ⟨an award for the most *innovative* designer of consumer electronics⟩ — see CREATIVE 1

innovator *n* one who creates or introduces something new ⟨thank goodness for the *innovator* who thought up the remote control⟩ — see INVENTOR

innumerable *adj* too many to be counted ⟨our reasons to give thanks are as *innumerable* as the stars⟩ — see COUNTLESS

inoculate *vb* to cause (as a person) to become filled or saturated with a certain quality or principle ⟨*inoculated* them with the idea that the individual can always make a difference⟩ — see INFUSE

inoffensive *adj* not causing injury or hurt ⟨an *inoffensive* little joke⟩ — see HARMLESS

inoperable *adj* **1** not being in working order ⟨we have several *inoperable* cars on the property⟩

synonyms inoperative, malfunctioning, nonfunctional, nonfunctioning, nonoperating

related words broken; off; deactivated, deadlocked, ineffective, ineffectual, nonproductive, unproductive, unusable, unworkable, useless

phrases on the blink, out of commission

near antonyms effective, effectual, employable, performing, producing, productive, serving, usable, useful, viable, workable

antonyms functional, functioning, operable, operating, operational, operative, running, working

2 not capable of being put to use or account ⟨a delightfully creative but *inoperable* plan⟩ — see IMPRACTICAL

inoperative *adj* **1** not being in a state of use, activity, or employment ⟨be careful when putting your hands in even an *inoperative* garbage disposal⟩ — see INACTIVE 2

2 not being in working order ⟨fixed the *inoperative* grandfather clock⟩ — see INOPERABLE 1

inopportune *adj* occurring before the usual or expected time ⟨their *inopportune* arrival before the house was cleaned⟩ — see EARLY 2

inopportunely *adv* before the usual or expected time ⟨dropped in *inopportunely*, before dinner was ready⟩ — see EARLY

inordinate *adj* going beyond a normal or acceptable limit in degree or amount ⟨an *inordinate* number of complaints⟩ — see EXCESSIVE

inordinately *adv* beyond a normal or acceptable limit ⟨taking an *inordinately* long time to finish⟩ — see TOO 1

inquest *n* a systematic search for the truth or facts about something ⟨the police conducted an *inquest* into the case⟩ — see INQUIRY 1

inquire (into) *vb* to search through or into ⟨the principal *inquired into* the possibility of holding graduation at a larger hall⟩ — see EXPLORE 1

inquire (of) *vb* to put a question or questions to ⟨the interrogator *inquired of* the prisoners the movements of their military unit before they were captured⟩ — see ASK 1

inquiry *n* **1** a systematic search for the truth or facts about something ⟨an *inquiry* into the origins of the universe⟩

synonyms delving, examination, exploration, inquest, inquisition, investigation, probe, probing, research, study

related words quest; audit, check; checkup, diagnosis, inspection; hearing, interrogation, trial; feeler, query, question; poll, questionnaire; challenge, cross-examination, grilling, quiz

2 an act or instance of asking for information ⟨one student made a hesitant *inquiry* about the assignment⟩ — see QUESTION 2

inquisition *n* a systematic search for the truth or facts about something ⟨there's no need to conduct an *inqui-*

sition to find out who ate the last cupcake⟩ — see INQUIRY 1

inquisitive *adj* interested in what is not one's own business ⟨an *inquisitive* woman who tends to everybody's business but her own⟩ — see CURIOUS 1

inquisitiveness *n* an eager desire to find out about things that are often none of one's business ⟨his *inquisitiveness* made people reluctant to socialize with him⟩ — see CURIOSITY 1

inroad *n* a sudden attack on and entrance into hostile territory ⟨the army is finally making *inroads* into the hostile country⟩ — see RAID 1

inrush *n* a flowing or coming in ⟨a sudden *inrush* of air blew my hair back⟩ — see INFLUX

insane *adj* **1** having or showing a very abnormal or sick state of mind ⟨only an *insane* person would jump off a skyscraper⟩

synonyms balmy, bananas, batty, crackbrained, cracked, crazed, crazy, cuckoo, daffy, daft, demented, deranged, loco, loony (*also* looney), lunatic, mad, maniacal (*also* maniac), mental, moonstruck, nuts, nutty, screwy, unbalanced, unsound, wacky

related words dotty, off; aberrant, delusional, disordered; eccentric, odd, queer, strange; foolish, senseless, witless; irrational, unreasonable; berserk, delirious; depressed; distraught, frantic, frenzied, hysterical

phrases around the bend, off one's rocker, out of one's head (*or* mind)

near antonyms clear, lucid, rational, reasonable; judicious, sensible, wise; healthy, normal

antonyms balanced, sane, sound

2 conceived or made without regard for reason or reality ⟨a completely *insane* plan to fly to the moon on a homemade rocket⟩ — see FANTASTIC 1

3 showing or marked by a lack of good sense or judgment ⟨an *insane* urge to jump off a cliff⟩ — see FOOLISH 1

insanity *n* **1** a serious mental disorder that prevents one from living a safe and normal life ⟨his *insanity* requires that he spend the rest of his life in a mental hospital⟩

synonyms aberration, dementia, derangement, lunacy, madness, mania

related words irrationality, unreasonableness; delirium, frenzy, hysteria; neurosis, psychosis, schizophrenia; delusion, hallucination, obsession, phobia; abnormality, unsoundness

near antonyms lucidity, rationality, reasonableness; normality, soundness

antonyms mind, saneness, sanity

2 a foolish act or idea ⟨everyone laughed at the latest *insanity* from the town eccentric⟩ — see FOLLY 1

3 lack of good sense or judgment ⟨had the *insanity* to think that taking over a government building in protest of our foreign policy was a good idea⟩ — see FOOLISHNESS 1

inscribe *vb* **1** to cut (as letters or designs) on a hard surface ⟨paid a jeweler to *inscribe* their names and wedding date on their wedding rings⟩ — see ENGRAVE 1

2 to enter in a list or roll ⟨*inscribed* him on the class list⟩ — see ENROLL 1

3 to put (someone or something) on a list ⟨*inscribed* his name on the list of the school's valedictorians⟩ — see ¹LIST 2

inscrutable *adj* **1** being beyond one's powers to know, understand, or explain ⟨the *inscrutable* mysteries of that ancient religion⟩ — see MYSTERIOUS 1

2 having an often intentionally veiled or uncertain meaning ⟨ancient oracles typically uttered *inscrutable* prophecies that could be interpreted almost any way one chose〉 — see OBSCURE 1

insecure *adj* not tightly fastened, tied, or stretched 〈*insecure* twine allowed the bundle of newspapers to break open as soon as it was tossed to the ground〉 — see LOOSE 1

insecurity *n* the quality or state of not being firmly fixed in position 〈the *insecurity* of the bookcase made it dangerous for a household with small children who like to climb〉 — see INSTABILITY

insensate *adj* having or showing a lack of sympathy or tender feelings 〈an *insensate* boss who refuses to allow time off for funerals〉 — see HARD 1

insensibility *n* 1 a lack of emotion or emotional expressiveness 〈the husband's general *insensibility* is creating great tension in the marriage〉 — see APATHY 1
2 a temporary or permanent state of unconsciousness 〈knocked into *insensibility* by the blow to the head〉 — see FAINT

insensible *adj* 1 having lost consciousness 〈if a choking person is *insensible,* you should lay them down before performing the Heimlich maneuver〉 — see UNCONSCIOUS 1
2 not perceptible by a sense or by the mind 〈the fragile glass flowers can be damaged by even the most *insensible* tremors〉 — see IMPERCEPTIBLE

insensitive *adj* 1 having or showing a lack of sympathy or tender feelings 〈an *insensitive* remark about his dead turtle that made him cry〉 — see HARD 1
2 lacking in sensation or feeling 〈fingers rendered *insensitive* by the cold〉 — see NUMB

inseparability *n* the state of being in a very personal or private relationship 〈never seen apart, the two boys had an *inseparability* that was legendary among their friends〉 — see FAMILIARITY 1

insert *vb* to put among or between others 〈*inserted* a book in its proper place on the shelf〉
synonyms fit (in *or* into), inject, insinuate, interject, interpolate, interpose, introduce
related words inlay, inset, install, weave, work (in); cram, sandwich, shove, thrust, wedge; add, append, attach
near antonyms eject, eliminate, exclude, expel, extract, withdraw; deduct, detach, subtract; reject

inside *adj* 1 not known or meant to be known by the general populace 〈made a stock trade based on *inside* information〉 — see PRIVATE 1
2 situated farther in 〈chose the *inside* lane to run around the track〉 — see INNER 1

inside *n* 1 an interior or internal part 〈the *inside* of the clock features an amazingly complex mechanism〉
synonyms interior, within
related words bowels, guts, innards; stuffing; recesses; center, core, heart
near antonyms border, boundary, brim, brink, edge, end, extremity, fringe, limit, lip, margin, perimeter, periphery, rim
antonyms exterior, outside
2 *usually* **insides** *pl* the internal organs of the body 〈medical students eager to see what people's *insides* look like〉 — see GUT 1

insight *n* the ability to understand inner qualities or relationships 〈a therapist with real *insight* into people's personalities〉 — see WISDOM 1

insightful *adj* having or showing deep understanding and intelligent application of knowledge 〈a book report with an *insightful* analysis of the lead character〉 — see WISE 1

insignificant *adj* 1 lacking importance 〈an *insignificant* detail that we can safely ignore〉 — see UNIMPORTANT
2 so small or unimportant as to warrant little or no attention 〈the *insignificant* wear on the doll's face does nothing to diminish its considerable value as an antique〉 — see NEGLIGIBLE 1

insincere *adj* not being or expressing what one appears to be or express 〈the *insincere* compliments of a spiteful gossip〉
synonyms artificial, backhanded, double-dealing, feigned, hypocritical, left-handed, mealy, mealy-mouthed, two-faced, unctuous
related words empty, hollow, meaningless; deceitful, devious, dishonest, untruthful; facile, glib, superficial; bogus, counterfeit, fake, false, phony (*also* phoney), sham; facetious, jocular
near antonyms candid, direct, forthright, frank, open, plain, straightforward
antonyms genuine, heartfelt, honest, sincere, unfeigned

insincerity *n* the pretending of having virtues, principles, or beliefs that one in fact does not have 〈the *insincerity* of the family's professed concern for the environment is pretty much exposed by the gas-guzzler parked in the driveway〉 — see HYPOCRISY

insinuate *vb* 1 to introduce in a gradual, secret, or clever way 〈the spy *insinuated* himself into the terrorist organization〉
synonyms infiltrate, slip, sneak, work (in), worm
related words creep, edge, wiggle; insert, interpolate, interpose, introduce
2 to convey an idea indirectly 〈are you *insinuating* that I cheated?〉 — see HINT
3 to put among or between others 〈carefully *insinuated* herself among the equipment crew for the rock band〉 — see INSERT

insipid *adj* 1 lacking in taste or flavor 〈an apple pie with a mushy, *insipid* filling that strongly resembled soggy cardboard〉
synonyms flat, flavorless, savorless, tasteless
related words bland, dilute, thin, watery, weak; plain, unflavored
near antonyms disgusting, distasteful, loathsome, sickening, unappetizing, unpalatable; appetizing, delectable, delicious, palatable, toothsome; piquant, seasoned, spicy; flavored; heavy, rich
antonyms flavorful, savory, tasty
2 lacking in qualities that make for spirit and character 〈an *insipid* and somewhat boring movie about teenagers in love〉 — see WISHY-WASHY 1

insist *vb* to state as a fact usually forcefully 〈she continued to *insist* that she was right, even in the face of all the evidence〉 — see CLAIM 1

insist (on) *vb* to ask for (something) earnestly or with authority 〈the teacher *insisted on* assignments being completed in pen〉 — see DEMAND 1

insistence *n* a solemn and often public declaring of the truth or existence of something 〈a continued *insistence* that there was a massive cover-up by the government〉 — see PROTESTATION

insistent *adj* continuing despite difficulties, opposition, or discouragement 〈Margaret Sanger is remembered as an *insistent* crusader for birth control〉 — see PERSISTENT

insolence *n* 1 disrespectful or argumentative talk given in response to a command or request 〈I will not tolerate such *insolence* when I tell you what to do〉 — see BACK TALK

2 rude behavior ⟨you can convey your disagreement with the visiting speaker's views without resorting to *insolence*⟩ — see DISCOURTESY

insolent *adj* displaying or marked by rude boldness ⟨an *insolent* reply to a reasonable request⟩ — see NERVY 1

insouciance *n* lack of interest or concern ⟨wandered into class with complete *insouciance* to the fact that she was late⟩ — see INDIFFERENCE

insouciant *adj* **1** having or showing a lack of concern or seriousness ⟨she's so *insouciant* when it comes to schoolwork and anything else that might interfere with her social life⟩ — see CAREFREE

2 having or showing a lack of interest or concern ⟨an *insouciant* attitude about punctuality⟩ — see INDIFFERENT 1

inspect *vb* to look over closely (as for judging quality or condition) ⟨*inspected* the animal before the show⟩
synonyms audit, check (out), examine, review, scan, scrutinize, survey
related words notice, observe, watch; peruse, pore (over); analyze, dissect; delve (into), explore, investigate, probe, research, study; categorize, classify
phrases go over
near antonyms skim; glance (at *or* over); miss, overlook

inspection *n* a close look at or over someone or something in order to judge condition ⟨a room *inspection* should include looking under the bed⟩
synonyms audit, check, checkup, examination, review, scan, scrutiny, survey
related words analysis, dissection; exploration, investigation, probe, research, study; inquisition, interrogation; perusal; observation, surveillance, watch

inspire *vb* to fill with courage or strength of purpose ⟨the rousing speech *inspired* everyone to go out and sell that candy for the school band⟩ — see ENCOURAGE 1

inspiring *adj* causing great emotional or mental stimulation ⟨an *inspiring* idea for a national program involving young people in community service⟩ — see EXCITING 1

instability *n* the quality or state of not being firmly fixed in position ⟨the *instability* of the bridge became apparent when it suddenly collapsed⟩
synonyms insecurity, precariousness, shakiness, unsteadiness
related words insubstantiality, unsoundness; changeability, inconstancy, mutability
near antonyms firmness, soundness, substantiality
antonyms fixedness, security, stability, steadiness

install *vb* **1** to put into an office or welcome into an organization with special ceremonies ⟨*installed* her as the new principal⟩
synonyms baptize, inaugurate, induct, initiate, instate, invest
related words swear in; accept, admit, receive, take in; enlist, enroll (*also* enrol)
near antonyms can, discharge, fire, terminate; muster out

2 to establish or place comfortably or snugly ⟨*installed* herself in an easy chair by the fireplace and remained there for the rest of the afternoon⟩ — see ENSCONCE 1

installation *n* **1** the process or an instance of being formally placed in an office or organization ⟨the *installation* of a new president takes place once every four years⟩
synonyms baptism, inaugural, inauguration, induction, initiation, installment, investiture
related words enlistment, enrollment; promotion

near antonyms discharge, removal

2 a structure that is designed and built for a particular purpose ⟨a military *installation* used as a hangar⟩ — see FACILITY

installment *n* the process or an instance of being formally placed in an office or organization ⟨attended the *installment* of the new university president⟩ — see INSTALLATION 1

instance *n* one of a group or collection that shows what the whole is like ⟨this is just one *instance* of his repeated failure to do his chores⟩ — see EXAMPLE

instance *vb* **1** to give as an example ⟨*instanced* one particular incident as an illustration of their penchant for practical jokes⟩ — see QUOTE 1

2 to make reference to or speak about briefly but specifically ⟨*instanced* the latest astronomical research in her presentation on measuring star magnitude⟩ — see MENTION 1

3 to show or make clear by using examples ⟨*instanced* the hero's moral courage with several examples from the novel⟩ — see ILLUSTRATE 1

instant *adj* **1** done or occurring without any noticeable lapse in time ⟨an *instant* response to the cry for help⟩ — see INSTANTANEOUS

2 needing immediate attention ⟨an *instant* need for food supplies in the famine-stricken country⟩ — see ACUTE 2

instant *n* a very small space of time ⟨it all happened in an *instant*⟩
synonyms flash, jiffy, minute, moment, second, shake, split second, trice, twinkle, twinkling, wink
related words microsecond, nanosecond; snatch, spurt
near antonyms aeon (*or* eon), age, eternity; infinity, lifetime

instantaneous *adj* done or occurring without any noticeable lapse in time ⟨the thunder following the lightning was nearly *instantaneous*⟩
synonyms immediate, instant, straightaway
related words summary; fast, hit-and-run, prompt, quick, rapid, speedy, swift
near antonyms dilatory, tardy; slow, sluggish; prolonged, protracted; deferred, delayed

instantly *adv* without delay ⟨reacted *instantly* to the crisis⟩ — see IMMEDIATELY

instate *vb* to put into an office or welcome into an organization with special ceremonies ⟨the new secretary of the treasury was *instated* on Monday⟩ — see INSTALL 1

instead *adv* as a substitute ⟨I was offered a ride, but I chose to walk *instead*⟩
synonyms first, rather
related words alternately, alternatively

instigate *vb* **1** to cause or encourage the development of ⟨the medical breakthrough *instigated* a whole new field of therapy⟩ — see INCITE 1

2 to rouse to strong feeling or action ⟨stop *instigating* your sister to anger, and she'll stop smacking you⟩ — see PROVOKE 1

instigating *adj* serving or likely to arouse a strong reaction ⟨an artist who deliberately creates *instigating* works of art that are sure to arouse controversy⟩ — see PROVOCATIVE

instigation *n* **1** something that arouses a strong response from another ⟨you'll both be punished: you for fighting, and your brother for *instigation*⟩ — see PROVOCATION 1

2 something that arouses action or activity ⟨the threat of punishment was all the *instigation* they needed⟩ — see IMPULSE

instigator *n* a person who stirs up public feelings especially of discontent ⟨an *instigator* who always managed to be innocently standing by once the fighting began⟩ — see AGITATOR

instinctive *adj* done instantly and without conscious thought or decision ⟨the *instinctive* reaction of a mother is to protect her children⟩ — see AUTOMATIC 1

instinctual *adj* done instantly and without conscious thought or decision ⟨the birds' *instinctual* response is to fly away when startled⟩ — see AUTOMATIC 1

institute *n* **1** a group of persons formally joined together for some common interest ⟨founded an *institute* to combat the cruel treatment of animals⟩ — see ASSOCIATION 2
2 a public organization with a particular purpose or function ⟨a scientific *institute* researching a cure for cancer⟩ — see INSTITUTION 1

institute *vb* to be responsible for the creation and early operation or use of ⟨Elizabeth Cady Stanton is generally credited with *instituting* the women's-rights movement in 1848⟩ — see FOUND

instituter *or* **institutor** *n* a person who establishes a whole new field of endeavor ⟨Eli Whitney is known as the *instituter* of the American system of manufacture for his pioneering concept of the mass production of interchangeable parts⟩ — see FATHER 2

institution *n* **1** a public organization with a particular purpose or function ⟨a charitable *institution* devoted to raising funds to feed the hungry⟩
synonyms establishment, foundation, institute
related words body, collective, group; corporation, enterprise; charity, philanthropy; think tank
2 a group of persons formally joined together for some common interest ⟨an *institution* devoted to studying social problems and proposing solutions for them⟩ — see ASSOCIATION 2

instruct *vb* **1** to cause to acquire knowledge or skill in some field ⟨spent his military career *instructing* young pilots⟩ — see TEACH
2 to give information to ⟨*instructed* everyone in the use of the new system⟩ — see ENLIGHTEN 1
3 to issue orders to (someone) by right of authority ⟨the proctors *instructed* everyone to put their pencils down and hand in their tests⟩ — see COMMAND 1

instruction *n* **1** a statement of what to do that must be obeyed by those concerned ⟨she's good at following *instructions*⟩ — see COMMAND 1
2 the act or process of imparting knowledge or skills to another ⟨the view that the *instruction* of our nation's youth should be our highest priority⟩ — see EDUCATION 1

instructional *adj* providing useful information or knowledge ⟨an *instructional* video on home repair for do-it-yourselfers⟩ — see INFORMATIVE

instructive *adj* providing useful information or knowledge ⟨an *instructive* demonstration of the proper way to pack a suitcase so your clothes don't arrive in a mess⟩ — see INFORMATIVE

instructor *n* a person whose occupation is to give formal instruction in a school ⟨you're all expected to listen to the *instructor*⟩ — see TEACHER

instrument *n* **1** a written or printed paper giving information about or proof of something ⟨a valid will is a legal *instrument*⟩ — see CERTIFICATE

2 an article intended for use in work ⟨always choose the right *instrument* for any woodworking job⟩ — see IMPLEMENT
3 something used to achieve an end ⟨he sees scouting as an *instrument* for building character in young people⟩ — see AGENT 1

instrumentalist *n* a person who plays a musical instrument ⟨he excels as a conductor, a composer, and as an *instrumentalist*⟩ — see MUSICIAN 1

instrumentality *n* something used to achieve an end ⟨computer literacy is only an *instrumentality* for acquiring an education, and not an end in itself⟩ — see AGENT 1

insubordinate *adj* given to resisting authority or another's control ⟨the junior officer was court-martialed for being *insubordinate*⟩ — see DISOBEDIENT

insubordination *n* refusal to obey ⟨was fired for chronic *insubordination*⟩ — see DISOBEDIENCE

insubstantial *adj* **1** being of a material lacking in sturdiness or substance ⟨an *insubstantial* carton that could not possibly stand up during long-dsitance shipping⟩ — see FLIMSY 1
2 not composed of matter ⟨energy is *insubstantial*⟩ — see IMMATERIAL 1

insufferable *adj* more than can be put up with ⟨an *insufferable* bore whose only topic of conversation is himself⟩ — see UNBEARABLE

insufficiency *n* a falling short of an essential or desirable amount or number ⟨dealt with the school's *insufficiency* of art supplies by buying materials out of her own pocket⟩ — see DEFICIENCY

insufficient *adj* not coming up to a usual standard or meeting a particular need ⟨an *insufficient* number of volunteers for the job, so I'll have to select someone⟩ — see SHORT 3

insular *adj* not broad or open in views or opinions ⟨an *insular* community that is not receptive of new ideas, especially from outsiders⟩ — see NARROW 2

insulate *vb* to set or keep apart from others ⟨tried to *insulate* their children from the often disturbing news in the mass media⟩ — see ISOLATE

insulation *n* the state of being alone or kept apart from others ⟨she grew up in such *insulation* that she'd never met anyone of a different race⟩ — see ISOLATION

insult *n* an act or expression showing scorn and usually intended to hurt another's feelings ⟨yelling an *insult* at the bully was not a very smart thing to do⟩
synonyms affront, barb, dart, dig, epithet, indignity, name, offense (*or* offence), outrage, put-down, sarcasm, slight, slur
related words gibe (*or* jibe), jeer, sneer, taunt; abuse, invective, vituperation; disapproval, opprobrium; disgrace, dishonor, shame; attack, criticism, slam; torment, torture
near antonyms accolade, commendation, compliment; acclaim, applause, praise; adulation, flattery

insult *vb* to cause hurt feelings or deep resentment in ⟨*insulted* the people by saying their home was ugly⟩
synonyms affront, dis [*slang*], offend, outrage, slight, wound
related words cut, snub; displease, distress, disturb, hurt, pain, trouble, upset; jeer, mock, ridicule, sneer (at), taunt; defame, disparage, libel, malign, revile, slander, slur, smear; oppress, persecute, torment, torture
near antonyms acclaim, applaud, approve, hail; commend, compliment, eulogize, praise; adulate, flatter; exalt, glorify, honor; delight, gratify, please, satisfy

insupportable *adj* more than can be put up with ⟨the *insupportable* arrogance of that jerk is more than anyone should have to bear⟩ — see UNBEARABLE

insure *vb* to make sure, certain, or safe ⟨*insured* the proper completion of the project⟩ — see ENSURE

insurgency *n* open fighting against authority (as one's own government) ⟨there always seems to be *insurgency* of some type in that troubled country⟩ — see REBELLION

insurgent *adj* taking part in a rebellion ⟨*insurgent* soldiers will be dealt with harshly⟩ — see REBELLIOUS 1

insurgent *n* a person who rises up against authority ⟨the government subjected the *insurgents* to the most inhuman torture imaginable⟩ — see REBEL

insurmountable *adj* incapable of being defeated, overcome, or subdued ⟨the familiar story of the underdog who ultimately triumphs despite *insurmountable* odds⟩ — see INVINCIBLE

insurrection *n* open fighting against authority (as one's own government) ⟨the famous *insurrection* of the slaves in ancient Rome under Spartacus⟩ — see REBELLION

insurrectionary *adj* taking part in a rebellion ⟨a small *insurrectionary* force that was soundly defeated by the loyalists⟩ — see REBELLIOUS 1

insurrectionary *n* a person who rises up against authority ⟨brave *insurrectionaries* who were willing to stand up to the dictator⟩ — see REBEL

insurrectionist *n* a person who rises up against authority ⟨an *insurrectionist* bombed the capitol⟩ — see REBEL

intact *adj* not lacking any part or member that properly belongs to it ⟨it's rare to find such an old chess set that is *intact*⟩ — see COMPLETE 1

intangible *adj* not capable of being perceived by the sense of touch ⟨electrical energy is completely *intangible*⟩
synonyms impalpable
related words bodiless, immaterial, incorporeal, insubstantial, unsubstantial; ethereal, spiritual, unreal
near antonyms tactile; corporeal, physical; embodied, material, real, solid, substantial
antonyms palpable, tangible, touchable

integer *n* a character used to represent a mathematical value ⟨three is a positive *integer*⟩ — see NUMBER

integral *adj* **1** being a part of the innermost nature of a person or thing ⟨a car dealer respected for his *integral* honesty and straightforwardness⟩ — see INHERENT
2 impossible to do without ⟨she's an *integral* member of the basketball team⟩ — see ESSENTIAL 1
3 not lacking any part or member that properly belongs to it ⟨a prep school that adheres to the belief that athletics are essential to an *integral* life⟩ — see COMPLETE 1

integrate *vb* **1** to make a part of a body or system ⟨*integrate* the new developments into our understanding of cancer⟩ — see EMBODY 1
2 to turn into a single mass that is more or less the same throughout ⟨*integrate* the powders thoroughly before adding them to the liquid⟩ — see BLEND 1

integrity *n* **1** conduct that conforms to an accepted standard of right and wrong ⟨demonstrated his *integrity* by taking responsibility for his actions⟩ — see MORALITY 1
2 devotion to telling the truth ⟨her *integrity* is such that she tells the truth even when people least want to hear it⟩ — see HONESTY 1
3 faithfulness to high moral standards ⟨a politician of great honesty and *integrity*⟩ — see HONOR 1

intellect *n* **1** a very smart person ⟨one of the finest *intellects* of our time⟩ — see GENIUS 1
2 the ability to learn and understand or to deal with problems ⟨a child of great *intellect* as well as artistic talent⟩ — see INTELLIGENCE 1

intellectual *adj* **1** much given to learning and thinking ⟨as the daughter of college professors, she's used to being around *intellectual* people⟩
synonyms cerebral, highbrow
related words cultivated, cultured; erudite, learned, literate, scholarly, well-read; academic, bookish, professorial; didactic, pedantic; high-hat, snobbish, snobby, snooty; educated, schooled; brainy, bright, brilliant, clever, intelligent, quick-witted, smart
near antonyms uncultivated, uncultured; ignorant, illiterate, uneducated, unlettered, unread; dumb, foolish, idiotic, moronic, slow, stupid, unintelligent
antonyms lowbrow, nonintellectual
2 of or relating to the mind ⟨*intellectual* pursuits such as reading and studying⟩ — see MENTAL 1

intelligence *n* **1** the ability to learn and understand or to deal with problems ⟨high scores on this test supposedly demonstrate great *intelligence*⟩
synonyms brain(s), gray matter, intellect, reason, sense
related words acumen, alertness, astuteness, discernment, insight, judgment (*or* judgement), mentality, perception, perspicacity; sagacity, sapience, wisdom, wit; head, mind, skull
near antonyms denseness, density, doltishness, dopiness, dullness (*also* dulness), dumbness, fatuity, feeblemindedness, foolishness, idiocy, imbecility, senselessness, simpleness, slowness, stupidity
2 a report of recent events or facts not previously known ⟨received the latest *intelligence* about how the war was going⟩ — see NEWS

intelligent *adj* **1** having or showing quickness of mind ⟨the dolphin is considered one of the most *intelligent* animals⟩ ⟨running for help was an *intelligent* response to the emergency⟩
synonyms alert, brainy, bright, brilliant, clever, keen, nimble, quick, quick-witted, sharp, sharp-witted, smart
related words apt, ingenious, resourceful; acute, astute, discerning, insightful, knowing, perceptive, perspicacious, sagacious, sapient, savvy, wise; cerebral, erudite, highbrow, knowledgeable, learned, literate, scholarly, well-read; educated, informed, schooled, skilled, trained; creative, inventive, judicious, prudent, sage, sane, sapient, sensible, sound, wise; crafty, cunning, foxy, shrewd, wily; logical, rational, reasonable
near antonyms retarded; foolish, idiotic, imbecile, imbecilic, moronic, silly, witless; ignorant, illiterate, lowbrow, nonintellectual, unacademic, uneducated, uninformed
antonyms brainless, dense, doltish, dorky, dull, dumb, mindless, obtuse, simple, slow, stupid, thick, unintelligent
2 having the ability to reason ⟨there is some debate over whether dolphins are *intelligent* animals⟩ — see RATIONAL 1

intemperate *adj* showing no signs of being under control ⟨*intemperate* anger that is so extreme that he should be in therapy⟩ — see RAMPANT 1

intend *vb* to have in mind as a purpose or goal ⟨he *intends* to be the president of a large corporation someday⟩
synonyms aim, aspire, contemplate, design, mean, meditate, plan, propose

related words dream, hope, wish; consider, debate, mull (over), ponder; attempt, endeavor, strive, struggle, try; plot, scheme; accomplish, achieve, effect, execute, perform

phrases figure on

intended *n* the person to whom one is engaged to be married ⟨she and her *intended* have finally picked out a wedding site⟩ — see BETROTHED

intense *adj* extreme in degree, power, or effect ⟨the *intense* cold of the polar regions⟩

synonyms deep, explosive, exquisite, fearful, ferocious, fierce, furious, hard, heavy, intensive, profound, terrible, vehement, vicious, violent

related words accentuated, aggravated, concentrated, deepened; emphasized, enhanced, heightened, intensified, magnified; stressed; exhaustive, thorough; harsh, rigorous, severe

near antonyms feeble, weak; shallow, superficial; moderated, qualified; alleviated, eased, lightened, toned (down); abated, decreased, diminished, lessened, reduced, subdued

antonyms light, moderate, soft

intensely *adv* with great effort or determination ⟨struggled *intensely* to master the foreign language⟩ — see HARD 1

intensify *vb* to make markedly greater in measure or degree ⟨*intensified* her efforts to move that bookcase by herself⟩

synonyms amplify, beef (up), boost, consolidate, deepen, enhance, heighten, magnify, redouble, step up, strengthen

related words broaden, enlarge, expand, extend, lengthen; accelerate, hasten, quicken; accentuate, emphasize, stress; augment, reinforce, supplement; maximize; enliven, jazz (up); aggravate, exacerbate

near antonyms decrease, diminish, lessen, let up (on), reduce, subdue, tone (down), weaken; dwindle, recede, subside, taper (off), wane; alleviate, ease, lighten

antonyms abate, moderate

intensity *n* 1 depth of feeling ⟨spoke with great *intensity* and eloquence on the need to combat racism⟩ — see ARDOR 1

2 the quality or state of being forceful (as in expression) ⟨the *intensity* of the actor's performance captured everyone's attention⟩ — see VEHEMENCE 1

intensive *adj* extreme in degree, power, or effect ⟨an *intensive* windstorm blew down the power lines⟩ — see INTENSE

intensively *adv* with great effort or determination ⟨labored *intensively* over the parade float⟩ — see HARD 1

intent *adj* 1 fully committed to achieving a goal ⟨*intent* on finishing her homework before the start of the game⟩ — see DETERMINED 1

2 having the mind fixed on something ⟨he was so *intent* on his work that he didn't hear the dog bark⟩ — see ATTENTIVE

intent *n* 1 something that one hopes or intends to accomplish ⟨I'm sorry that I hurt you; that wasn't my *intent*⟩ — see GOAL

2 the idea that is conveyed or intended to be conveyed to the mind by language, symbol, or action ⟨the wording was a little unclear, but I think I grasped the *intent*⟩ — see MEANING 1

intention *n* something that one hopes or intends to accomplish ⟨her *intention* is to be President someday⟩ — see GOAL

intentional *adj* made, given, or done with full awareness of what one is doing ⟨I'm fairly sure that your "accidental" attack on your sister with a water balloon was really *intentional*⟩

synonyms deliberate, purposeful, willful (*or* wilful)

related words knowing, witting; designed, intended, planned; conscious; advised, calculated, considered, measured, reasoned, studied, thoughtful, weighed; premeditated; discretionary, elective, optional, volunteer

near antonyms inadvertent, unwitting; accidental, chance, haphazard, hit-or-miss, incidental, random; aimless, desultory, purposeless; abrupt, impetuous, sudden; coerced, forced, involuntary; compulsory, mandatory, necessary, nonelective, obligatory, ordered, required; casual; extemporaneous, impromptu, impulsive, instinctive, spontaneous, unforced, unpremeditated

antonyms unintentional

intentionally *adv* with full awareness of what one is doing ⟨the witness *intentionally* gave misleading answers to the questions⟩

synonyms consciously, deliberately, designedly, knowingly, purposefully, purposely, willfully, wittingly

related words calculatingly, studiedly; voluntarily, willingly

phrases on purpose

near antonyms accidentally, incidentally, randomly; involuntarily, unwillingly; impulsively, instinctively, spontaneously

antonyms inadvertently, unconsciously, unintentionally, unknowingly, unwittingly

intently *adv* with great effort or determination ⟨*intently* studied his notes just before the test⟩ — see HARD 1

intentness *n* a mental state free of jesting or trifling ⟨studied the dance steps with great *intentness*⟩ — see EARNESTNESS

inter *vb* to place (a dead body) in the earth, a tomb, or the sea ⟨the soldier was *interred* at Arlington National Cemetery⟩ — see BURY 1

interaction *n* doings between individuals or groups ⟨she guessed from the friendly *interaction* that he was close to the other children⟩ — see RELATION 1

intercede *vb* to act as a go-between for opposing sides ⟨asked his mother to *intercede* with the teacher⟩ — see INTERVENE

intercessor *n* one who works with opposing sides in order to bring about an agreement ⟨eventually, they hired an *intercessor*, because they were getting nowhere⟩ — see MEDIATOR

intercommunicate *vb* to engage in an exchange of information or ideas ⟨you people will need to *intercommunicate* better if you're going to do the group assignment well⟩ — see COMMUNICATE 2

intercourse *n* 1 doings between individuals or groups ⟨the niceties of social *intercourse* are lost on that nerd⟩ — see RELATION 1

2 sexual union involving penetration of the vagina by the penis ⟨*intercourse* can lead to pregnancy if no precautions are taken⟩ — see SEXUAL INTERCOURSE

interdict *n* an order that something not be done or used ⟨the church issued an *interdict* on the use of birth control devices⟩ — see PROHIBITION 2

interdict *vb* to order not to do or use or to be done or used ⟨the school *interdicts* the use of calculators on math tests⟩ — see FORBID

interdicted *adj* that may not be permitted ⟨an *interdicted* hold in wrestling⟩ — see IMPERMISSIBLE

interdicting *n* the act of ordering that something not be done or used ⟨the *interdicting* against bullying at school, along with stiff penalties, was long overdue⟩ — see PROHIBITION 1

interdiction *n* **1** an order that something not be done or used ⟨a written *interdiction* against the wearing of clothing incorporating gang colors⟩ — see PROHIBITION 2

2 the act of ordering that something not be done or used ⟨the recent *interdiction* against open fires on the beach has riled summer revelers⟩ — see PROHIBITION 1

interest *n* **1** a legal right to participation in the advantages, profits, and responsibility of something ⟨all of the workers at the food cooperative have an *interest* in it⟩

synonyms claim, share, stake

related words ownership, part, partnership, possession, title

2 the state of doing well especially in relation to one's happiness or success ⟨she was determined to act in her own *interest* in the business deal⟩ — see WELFARE

interest *vb* to hold the attention of ⟨the book didn't *interest* me, so I ended up daydreaming instead of reading⟩ — see ENGAGE 1

interesting *adj* holding the attention or provoking interest ⟨the history lecture was so *interesting* that I didn't fall asleep after all⟩

synonyms absorbing, arresting, engaging, engrossing, enthralling, fascinating, gripping, immersing, intriguing, involving, riveting

related words breathtaking, electric, electrifying, exciting, exhilarating, galvanizing, inspiring, rousing, stimulating, stirring, thrilling; provocative, tantalizing; emphatic, showy, splashy, striking; alluring, attractive, bewitching, captivating, charming, enchanting, spellbinding; hypnotizing, mesmerizing; curious, odd, unusual, weird; amazing, astonishing, astounding, eye-opening, fabulous, marvelous (*or* marvellous), surprising, wonderful, wondrous; amusing, entertaining

near antonyms tiresome, tiring, wearisome, wearying; unexciting; dreary, humdrum, pedestrian; demoralizing, discouraging, disheartening, dispiriting

antonyms boring, drab, dry, dull, heavy, monotonous, tedious, uninteresting

interfere *vb* to interest oneself in what is not one's concern ⟨a strong resentment of outsiders who *interfered* with their traditional ways of doing things⟩

synonyms butt in, intrude, meddle, mess, nose, obtrude, poke, pry, snoop

related words intercede, interpose, intervene; encroach, infringe, invade, trespass; fiddle, fool, monkey, play, tamper

near antonyms avoid, eschew, shun; disregard, ignore, neglect, overlook

interfere (with) *vb* to create difficulty for the work or activity of ⟨his little sister was always *interfering with* his chores, trying to "help"⟩ — see HAMPER

interference *n* something that makes movement or progress more difficult ⟨without the *interference* of the rain, we could have made good time on that road trip⟩ — see ENCUMBRANCE

interferer *n* a person who meddles in the affairs of others ⟨an incurable *interferer*, she couldn't mind her own business to save her life⟩ — see BUSYBODY

interfering *adj* thrusting oneself where one is not welcome or invited ⟨an *interfering* woman who showed up for every party, even when she wasn't invited⟩ — see INTRUSIVE

interim *adj* intended to last, continue, or serve for a limited time ⟨only an *interim* president until a permanent replacement can be found⟩ — see TEMPORARY 1

interim *n* a break in continuity ⟨there was a brief *interim* in the proceedings while everyone got organized⟩ — see GAP 2

interior *adj* situated farther in ⟨was given an *interior* office⟩ — see INNER 1

interior *n* an interior or internal part ⟨the *interior* of the computer was clogged with dust⟩ — see INSIDE 1

interject *vb* to put among or between others ⟨she occasionally *interjected* comments into the conversation⟩ — see INSERT

interlace *vb* **1** to cause to twine about one another ⟨*interlaced* braids about her head⟩ — see INTERTWINE 1

2 to scatter or set here and there among other things ⟨*interlaced* jokes between the serious passages in the speech⟩ — see THREAD 1

3 to twist together into a usually confused mass ⟨I've *interlaced* the cables on my audio-video system so confusingly that I've no idea what connects what⟩ — see ENTANGLE 1

interloper *n* a person who meddles in the affairs of others ⟨they stopped talking until the *interloper* wandered away⟩ — see BUSYBODY

interlude *n* a break in continuity ⟨there was a brief *interlude* in the performance while the stagehands shifted scenery⟩ — see GAP 2

intermediary *adj* occupying a position equally distant from the ends or extremes ⟨the bridal couple were ensconced in *intermediary* seats at the head table⟩ — see MIDDLE 1

intermediary *n* one who works with opposing sides in order to bring about an agreement ⟨an *intermediary* resolved the labor dispute⟩ — see MEDIATOR

intermediate *adj* **1** being about midway between extremes of amount or size ⟨with a compact being too small and a van too large, we settled on an *intermediate*-sized sedan⟩ — see MIDDLE 2

2 occupying a position equally distant from the ends or extremes ⟨although the party activists tend to back candidates with somewhat extreme views, ordinary voters generally prefer the *intermediate* aspirant⟩ — see MIDDLE 1

interment *n* the act or ceremony of putting a dead body in its final resting place ⟨a respectful but nonreligious *interment* in a private cemetery⟩ — see BURIAL

intermingle *vb* to turn into a single mass that is more or less the same throughout ⟨thoroughly *intermingle* the different kinds of candy so that each bag will get a good assortment⟩ — see BLEND 1

intermission *n* a break in continuity ⟨an awkward *intermission* between speeches⟩ — see GAP 2

intermittent *adj* **1** occurring or appearing at intervals ⟨*intermittent* showers had me opening and closing my umbrella all day long⟩

synonyms continual, periodic, periodical, recurrent, recurring

related words alternate, alternating, cyclic (*or* cyclical), rhythmic (*or* rhythmical), seasonal, serial; erratic, fitful, irregular, occasional, spasmodic, sporadic, spotty, unsteady

near antonyms eternal, everlasting, interminable, perpetual

antonyms constant, continuous, incessant, unceasing

2 lacking in steadiness or regularity of occurrence ⟨the breadwinner's *intermittent* employment put the family in a difficult position financially⟩ — see FITFUL

intermix *vb* to turn into a single mass that is more or less the same throughout ⟨*intermixed* the ingredients until there were no lumps in the batter⟩ — see BLEND 1

intermixture *n* a distinct entity formed by the combining of two or more different things ⟨the building was a beautiful *intermixture* of classical and modern elements⟩ — see BLEND

intern *vb* to put in or as if in prison ⟨some Polish citizens were *interned* in Russian camps during World War II⟩ — see IMPRISON

internal *adj* situated farther in ⟨grave robbers hadn't managed to locate and enter the *internal* chambers of the Egyptian tomb⟩ — see INNER 1

interned *adj* taken and held prisoner ⟨the soldiers daringly rescued their *interned* comrades⟩ — see CAPTIVE

internee *n* one that has been taken and held in confinement ⟨all *internees* were finally released when the war was over⟩ — see CAPTIVE

internment *n* the act of confining or the state of being confined ⟨the *internment* of Americans of Japanese descent during World War II is one of the more shameful chapters in United States history⟩
synonyms captivity, confinement, immurement, imprisonment, incarceration
related words bondage, enslavement, servitude; restraint, restriction; arrest, capture, entrapment; custody, detainment, detention
near antonyms emancipation, liberation, manumission, redemption, release; freedom, independence, liberty

interpenetrate *vb* to spread throughout ⟨the dye *interpenetrated* the entire fabric⟩ — see PERMEATE

interpolate *vb* to put among or between others ⟨*interpolated* a new paragraph into the essay⟩ — see INSERT

interpose *vb* 1 to act as a go-between for opposing sides ⟨an elder statesman who *interposed* a number of times in international conflicts⟩ — see INTERVENE
2 to cause a disruption in a conversation or discussion ⟨I hate to *interpose*, but could you tell me what you meant by that last remark⟩ — see INTERRUPT
3 to put among or between others ⟨a solid line of police in riot gear *interposed* itself between the trade ministers and the crowd of protesters⟩ — see INSERT

interposer *n* one who works with opposing sides in order to bring about an agreement ⟨I think that we can resolve this dispute ourselves, without the help of some outside *interposer*⟩ — see MEDIATOR

interpret *vb* to make plain or understandable ⟨a biblical passage that scholars haven't been able to *interpret* to everyone's satisfaction⟩ — see EXPLAIN 1

interpretation *n* a statement that makes something clear ⟨that's one possible *interpretation* of that scene⟩ — see EXPLANATION 1

interpretive *adj* serving to explain ⟨an edition of Shakespeare's plays with many *interpretive* footnotes that students should find very helpful⟩ — see EXPLANATORY

interring *n* the act or ceremony of putting a dead body in its final resting place ⟨fittingly, the *interring* took place on a gloomy, rainy day⟩ — see BURIAL

interrogate *vb* 1 to put a question or questions to ⟨*interrogated* him about where he'd gone last night⟩ — see ASK 1
2 to put a series of questions to ⟨the police *interrogated* a murder suspect for hours⟩ — see EXAMINE 1

interrupt *vb* to cause a disruption in a conversation or discussion ⟨it's rude to *interrupt* when someone is making an important point⟩

synonyms break (in), chime in, cut in, interpose, intrude
related words barge (in), bother; add, chip in, contribute, put in

interruption *n* 1 a break in continuity ⟨an *interruption* in cable service during the lightning storm⟩ — see GAP 2
2 a momentary halt in an activity ⟨a brief *interruption* in the discussion while we all got coffee⟩ — see PAUSE

intersect *vb* to divide by passing through or across ⟨the highway *intersects* that road⟩
synonyms bisect, cross
related words crisscross

intersection *n* a place where roads meet ⟨take a left turn at the next *intersection*⟩ — see CROSSROAD 1

intersperse *vb* to scatter or set here and there among other things ⟨*intersperse* some photos among the other decorations on the wall⟩ — see THREAD 1

intertwine *vb* 1 to cause to twine about one another ⟨*intertwined* two different colors of yarn⟩
synonyms interlace, interweave, lace
related words blend, fuse, join, link, mix
near antonyms disentangle, uncoil, untangle, untwine, unwind
2 to twist together into a usually confused mass ⟨*intertwining* yarn is usually a bad idea, because you'll never get it all sorted out again⟩ — see ENTANGLE

interval *n* 1 a break in continuity ⟨there were *intervals* of thousands of years between ice ages⟩ — see GAP 2
2 an open space in a barrier (as a wall or hedge) ⟨unable to find my way out of the maze, I cheated and squeezed through an *interval* in the hedge⟩ — see GAP 1

intervene *vb* to act as a go-between for opposing sides ⟨*intervened* in the argument before any real harm was done⟩
synonyms intercede, interpose, mediate
related words butt in, interfere, intrude, meddle, obtrude, pry, snoop; arbitrate, moderate, negotiate; barge (in), bother; break (in), chime in, cut in; infringe, invade, trespass
near antonyms stand by; avoid, eschew, shun; disregard, ignore, overlook

interweave *vb* 1 to cause to twine about one another ⟨*interweaved* garlands of red and gold beads and wrapped them around the Christmas tree⟩ — see INTERTWINE 1
2 to scatter or set here and there among other things ⟨the author *interweaves* excerpts from soldiers' letters in his history of the Vietnam War⟩ — see THREAD 1
3 to twist together into a usually confused mass ⟨in our play the kitten and I managed to *interweave* the skeins of yarn into a hopeless tangle⟩ — see ENTANGLE 1

intimacy *n* the state of being in a very personal or private relationship ⟨there can be both rewards and regrets from *intimacy* with another person⟩ — see FAMILIARITY 1

intimate *adj* 1 closely acquainted ⟨*intimate* friends who can practically finish each other's sentences⟩ — see FAMILIAR 1
2 not known or meant to be known by the general populace ⟨they broke up after she shared *intimate* information with all 500 of her closest friends⟩ — see PRIVATE 1

intimate *n* a person who has a strong liking for and trust in another ⟨he's actually quite relaxed with his *intimates*⟩ — see FRIEND 1

intimate *vb* to convey an idea indirectly ⟨trying to *intimate* that there was more going on than anyone knew⟩ — see HINT

intimation *n* a slight or indirect pointing to something (as a solution or explanation) ⟨the newscaster could not resist giving a slight *intimation* that the voting results might be unexpected⟩ — see HINT 1

intimidate *vb* to make timid or fearful by or as if by threats ⟨refusing to be *intimidated* by the manager's harsh stare, I demanded my money back⟩
synonyms browbeat, bully, cow, hector
related words affright, alarm, frighten, horrify, scare, shock, spook, startle, terrify; menace, terrorize, threaten; badger, harass, hound; bulldoze, coerce, compel, constrain, dragoon, force, make, oblige, press, pressure; demoralize, unman, unnerve; discompose, disconcert, disquiet, distress, disturb, perturb, upset
near antonyms cheer, comfort, console, reassure, solace, soothe; embolden, encourage, hearten, steel; convince, persuade

intimidating *adj* **1** causing fear ⟨the *intimidating* prospect of the college entrance exams⟩ — see FEARFUL 1
2 harsh and threatening in manner or appearance ⟨an *intimidating* bodyguard keeping the fans away from the rock star⟩ — see GRIM 1

intimidator *n* a person who teases, threatens, or hurts smaller or weaker persons ⟨the loan shark hired an *intimidator* to make sure that he got all that was owed him⟩ — see BULLY 1

intolerable *adj* more than can be put up with ⟨this stifling heat is *intolerable*⟩ — see UNBEARABLE

intolerant *adj* **1** unable or unwilling to endure ⟨*intolerant* of pain⟩
synonyms impatient
related words uncompromising, unforgiving, unyielding; complaining, fussing, griping, grumbling, protesting, squawking, whining
near antonyms accepting, forgiving, long-suffering, resigned, uncomplaining, willing; indulgent
antonyms abiding, enduring, forbearing, patient, tolerant
2 unwilling to grant other people social rights or to accept other viewpoints ⟨*intolerant* people supported racism⟩
synonyms bigoted, narrow, narrow-minded, prejudiced, small-minded
related words conservative, hidebound, old-fashioned, reactionary; insular, parochial, provincial; biased, one-sided, partial, partisan
near antonyms extreme, progressive, radical; impartial, objective, unbiased
antonyms broad-minded, liberal, open-minded, tolerant, unprejudiced

intone *vb* to utter in musical or drawn out tones ⟨"The day is begun," the narrator *intoned*⟩ — see CHANT 1

intoxicant *n* a fermented or distilled beverage that can make a person drunk ⟨rubbing alcohol is not an *intoxicant*, despite the "alcohol" in the name⟩ — see ALCOHOL

intoxicate *vb* to cause a pleasurable stimulation of the feelings ⟨the stunning spectacle is sure to *intoxicate* spectators⟩ — see THRILL

intoxicated *adj* **1** being under the influence of alcohol ⟨driving while *intoxicated* is illegal⟩ — see DRUNK
2 experiencing or marked by overwhelming usually pleasurable emotion ⟨the *intoxicated* moment when she found out that she'd won the award⟩ — see ECSTATIC

intoxication *n* a state of overwhelming usually pleasurable emotion ⟨the *intoxication* felt by two people who have just fallen in love⟩ — see ECSTASY

intractability *n* refusal to obey ⟨the *intractability* of the dog forced the family to try obedience training by a professional⟩ — see DISOBEDIENCE

intractable *adj* **1** given to resisting authority or another's control ⟨an *intractable* child who deliberately did the opposite of whatever he was told⟩ — see DISOBEDIENT
2 given to resisting control or discipline by others ⟨cats are by nature fairly *intractable* animals⟩ — see UNCONTROLLABLE

intrepid *adj* feeling or displaying no fear by temperament ⟨an *intrepid* explorer who probed parts of the rain forest never previously attempted⟩ — see BRAVE

intrepidity *n* strength of mind to carry on in spite of danger ⟨he managed to get back to camp, despite the bears, through sheer *intrepidity*⟩ — see COURAGE

intrepidness *n* strength of mind to carry on in spite of danger ⟨a girl of great *intrepidness* who never flinches from any challenge life has to offer⟩ — see COURAGE

intricacy *n* **1** something that makes a situation more complicated or difficult ⟨just now learning the *intricacies* of owning one's own business⟩ — see COMPLICATION 1
2 the state or quality of having many interrelated parts or aspects ⟨the *intricacy* of the puzzle required close concentration⟩ — see COMPLEXITY 1

intricate *adj* **1** having many parts or aspects that are usually interrelated ⟨an *intricate* machine that requires some training to use it properly⟩ — see COMPLEX 1
2 made or done with great care or with much detail ⟨an *intricate* hairstyle⟩ — see ELABORATE 1

intrigue *n* a secret plan for accomplishing evil or unlawful ends ⟨the *intrigue* was discovered, and the would-be assassins were arrested⟩ — see PLOT 1

intrigue *vb* **1** to engage in a secret plan to accomplish evil or unlawful ends ⟨he *intrigued* to kill the queen⟩ — see PLOT
2 to hold the attention of ⟨the mystery story *intrigued* me so that I read it in one sitting⟩ — see ENGAGE 1

intriguing *adj* holding the attention or provoking interest ⟨an *intriguing* concept that should engender much debate⟩ — see INTERESTING

intrinsic *adj* being a part of the innermost nature of a person or thing ⟨the question of whether people have an *intrinsic* sense of right and wrong⟩ — see INHERENT

intrinsically *adv* by natural character or ability ⟨he's worked hard to be good at baseball, as he's not *intrinsically* athletic⟩ — see NATURALLY 1

introduce *vb* **1** to make (one person) known (to another) socially ⟨a friend *introduced* him to the woman who later became his wife⟩
synonyms acquaint, present
related words address, greet, hail, meet
2 to present or bring forward for discussion ⟨the moderator *introduced* a new topic for the debate⟩
synonyms bring up, broach, moot, raise
related words allude (to), cite, mention, name, refer (to); offer, propose, suggest; air, express, speak (of), talk (about), vent, ventilate; interject, interrupt; debate, discuss, thrash (out *or* over)
near antonyms censor, hush (up), quiet, silence, suppress
3 to be responsible for the creation and early operation or use of ⟨Luther Burbank *introduced* the idea of plant breeding, developing over 800 new varieties of fruits, vegetables, grains, and grasses⟩ — see FOUND

4 to impart knowledge of a new thing or situation to ⟨*introduced* everyone to the new phone system⟩ — see ACQUAINT 1

5 to put among or between others ⟨*introduce* a new variable to the equation⟩ — see INSERT

introducer *n* one who creates or introduces something new ⟨the *introducer* of the ballpoint pen was a man by the name of John Loud⟩ — see INVENTOR

introduction *n* a short section (as of a book) that leads to or explains the main part ⟨a famous person wrote the *introduction* to that new textbook⟩

synonyms foreword, preamble, preface, prelude, prologue

related words beginning, commencement, initiation, opening, origin, origination, outset, start

near antonyms postscript; aftermath; cessation, close, closing, conclusion, end, finale, finish, stop, termination

antonyms epilogue

introductory *adj* coming before the main part or item usually to introduce or prepare for what follows ⟨an *introductory* paragraph to the chapter on evolution⟩ — see PRELIMINARY

introverted *adj* not comfortable around people ⟨a quiet, *introverted* child who likes to sit at home and read books⟩ — see SHY 2

intrude *vb* **1** to cause a disruption in a conversation or discussion ⟨forgive me for *intruding*, but I think I know where that restaurant is⟩ — see INTERRUPT

2 to interest oneself in what is not one's concern ⟨the story of a would-be matchmaker who *intrudes* into the lives of her friends⟩ — see INTERFERE

intrude (upon) *vb* to thrust oneself upon (another) without invitation ⟨a man with an opinion on everything, he doesn't hesitate to *intrude upon* whoever happens to be standing by⟩ — see BOTHER 1

intruder *n* a person who meddles in the affairs of others ⟨an inveterate *intruder*, he needs to get a life⟩ — see BUSYBODY

intruding *adj* thrusting oneself where one is not welcome or invited ⟨an *intruding* child who likes to interrupt adult conversations simply to get attention⟩ — see INTRUSIVE

intrusive *adj* thrusting oneself where one is not welcome or invited ⟨that *intrusive* neighbor never knocks before coming in⟩

synonyms interfering, intruding, meddlesome, meddling, nosy (*or* nosey), obtrusive, officious, presumptuous, prying, snoopy

related words bold, brazen, impertinent, impudent, insolent, rude; invading, trespassing; curious, inquisitive; annoying, harassing, pestiferous

near antonyms quiet, reserved, reticent, retiring, silent, taciturn, withdrawn; inhibited, restrained, subdued

antonyms unobtrusive

inundate *vb* to cover or become filled with a flood ⟨the bathtub overflowed and *inundated* the bathroom floor⟩ — see FLOOD

inundation *n* a great flow of water or of something that overwhelms ⟨the shed was washed away in the last *inundation*⟩ — see FLOOD

inure *vb* to make able to withstand physical hardship, strain, or exposure ⟨the hardship of army training *inured* her to the rigors of desert warfare⟩ — see HARDEN 2

inured *adj* able to withstand hardship, strain, or exposure ⟨the weather-beaten *inured* faces of farmers⟩ — see HARDY 1

invade *vb* to enter for conquest or plunder ⟨a superpower that had a tendency to *invade* and take over smaller and weaker countries⟩

synonyms foray (into), overrun, raid

related words despoil, loot, maraud, pillage, plunder, ravage, sack; conquer, crush, overcome, overpower, overwhelm, subdue, subjugate; assail, assault, attack; battle, combat, fight, war (with); encroach, infringe, trespass; besiege, blockade; occupy

near antonyms defend, guard, protect, shield; oppose, resist, withstand; capitulate (to), cede (to), submit (to), succumb (to), surrender (to), yield (to)

invader *n* one that starts armed conflict against another especially without reasonable cause ⟨defenders at the border were able to repel the *invaders*⟩ — see AGGRESSOR

¹invalid *adj* chronically or repeatedly suffering from poor health ⟨an old and now *invalid* woman who rarely gets out anymore⟩ — see SICKLY 1

²invalid *adj* **1** having no legal or binding force ⟨the treaty is *invalid* once one side violates it⟩ — see NULL 1

2 not being in agreement with what is true ⟨that's an *invalid* assumption on your part⟩ — see FALSE 1

3 not using or following good reasoning ⟨an argument which has one untrue premise is *invalid*⟩ — see ILLOGICAL

4 having no basis in reason or fact ⟨an *invalid* claim that can be easily disproved by the facts⟩ — see GROUNDLESS

invalidate *vb* to put an end to by formal action ⟨those nations eventually *invalidated* their trade agreement⟩ — see ABOLISH

invariability *n* the state of continuing without change ⟨the *invariability* of the weather gets boring sometimes⟩ — see CONSTANCY 1

invariable *adj* not capable of changing or being changed ⟨an *invariable* interest rate⟩ — see INFLEXIBLE 1

invariably *adv* on every relevant occasion ⟨he *invariably* gives the same response to the questions about his career plans⟩ — see ALWAYS 1

invariant *adj* not varying ⟨an *invariant* value⟩ — see UNIFORM

invasion *n* a sudden attack on and entrance into hostile territory ⟨the *invasion* of the Soviet Union by Germany during World War II⟩ — see RAID 1

invective *n* harsh insulting language ⟨hurled curses and *invective* at the person who cut them off in traffic⟩ — see ABUSE 1

invent *vb* to create or think of by clever use of the imagination ⟨they *invented* an explanation for the broken vase that would satisfy their grandmother⟩

synonyms concoct, contrive, cook (up), devise, fabricate, make up, manufacture, think (up)

related words coin, contrive, create, design, hatch, produce; daydream, dream, fantasize; conceive, envisage, imagine, picture, visualize

near antonyms copy, duplicate, imitate, mimic, replicate

invented *adj* not real and existing only in the imagination ⟨a daydreamer who lives mostly in her *invented* magic kingdom⟩ — see IMAGINARY

invention *n* **1** something (as a device) created for the first time through the use of the imagination ⟨his clever *invention* made people's lives easier⟩

synonyms coinage, concoction, contrivance, creation, innovation, wrinkle

related words contraption, device, gadget, gizmo (*or* gismo), novelty; design, product, work; dream, fantasy (*also* phantasy), picture, vision; conception, imagining, origination

near antonyms copy, duplicate, imitation

2 something that is the product of the imagination ⟨the story about being kidnapped by aliens was pure *invention*⟩ — see FICTION

3 the ability to form mental images of things that either are not physically present or have never been conceived or created by others ⟨a writer with *invention*, she is able to create on the page worlds that don't exist but certainly seem like they could⟩ — see IMAGINATION

4 the skill and imagination to create new things ⟨a person of seemingly endless *invention*, Thomas Edison held a world-record 1,093 patents⟩ — see CREATIVITY 1

inventive *adj* having the skill and imagination to create new things ⟨an *inventive* little boy⟩ — see CREATIVE 1

inventiveness *n* **1** the ability to form mental images of things that either are not physically present or have never been conceived or created by others ⟨the artist's fertile *inventiveness* allows her to put on canvas landscapes that have never been trod by mortal feet⟩ — see IMAGINATION

2 the skill and imagination to create new things ⟨the contention that, in order to prosper, cities must attract young, well-educated people of great *inventiveness* in both the arts and high technology⟩ — see CREATIVITY 1

inventor *n* one who creates or introduces something new ⟨the *inventor* of the electric light bulb⟩

synonyms contriver, designer, developer, deviser, formulator, innovator, introducer, originator

related words author, creator, establisher, father, founder, inaugurator, originator; pioneer, researcher; builder, maker, producer; dreamer

near antonyms copier, duplicator, imitator

inventory *vb* to make a list of ⟨*inventory* the supplies in the back room⟩ — see ¹LIST 1

invert *vb* to change the position of (an object) so that the opposite side or end is showing ⟨if you *invert* the coin, there's a picture of a buffalo on the back⟩ — see REVERSE 2

invertebrate *adj* lacking strength of will or character ⟨an *invertebrate* man who did whatever anyone wanted⟩ — see WEAK 2

invest *vb* **1** to cause (as a person) to become filled or saturated with a certain quality or principle ⟨*invested* the film with his own enthusiasm for the wonders of flight⟩ — see INFUSE

2 to furnish with something freely or naturally ⟨a woman *invested* with the strong desire to make the world a better place⟩ — see ENDOW 1

3 to give official or legal power to ⟨*invested* him with power of attorney⟩ — see AUTHORIZE 1

4 to outfit with clothes and especially fine or special clothes ⟨a fashion designer who has *invested* a number of the winners of the best actress award⟩ — see CLOTHE 1

5 to put into an office or welcome into an organization with special ceremonies ⟨the beloved actor was finally *invested* as a knight by the queen⟩ — see INSTALL 1

6 to surround (as a fortified place) with armed forces for the purpose of capturing or preventing commerce and communication ⟨the city was *invested* for an entire year, but never fell⟩ — see BESIEGE

7 to surround or cover closely ⟨nightfall *invested* the land⟩ — see ENFOLD 1

investigate *vb* to search through or into ⟨experts *investigating* new ways of dealing with the problem⟩ — see EXPLORE 1

investigation *n* a systematic search for the truth or facts about something ⟨officials launched an *investigation* of the plane crash to find out what caused it⟩ — see INQUIRY 1

investigator *n* a person whose business is solving crimes and catching criminals or gathering information that is not easy to get ⟨the *investigator* in charge of the case was an expert at tracing stolen art⟩ — see DETECTIVE

investiture *n* the process or an instance of being formally placed in an office or organization ⟨the *investiture* of a new member of parliament⟩ — see INSTALLATION 1

investment *n* the cutting off of an area by military means to stop the flow of people or supplies ⟨the *investment* of Cuba was one of the decisive moments in the Cuban Missile Crisis⟩ — see BLOCKADE

inveterate *adj* **1** firmly established over time ⟨he has an *inveterate* tendency to tell tall tales that began when he was just a little boy⟩

synonyms confirmed, deep-rooted, deep-seated, entrenched (*also* intrenched), hard-core, rooted, settled

related words fixed, immutable, set; implanted, inculcated, instilled; inborn, inbred, inherent, innate, natural; accustomed, chronic, customary, habitual, regular, typical, usual; abiding, enduring, lifelong, persistent, persisting

near antonyms brief, ephemeral, fleeting, impermanent, momentary, short-lived, temporary, transient

2 being such by habit and not likely to change ⟨the man is an *inveterate* liar who only rarely tells the truth⟩ — see HABITUAL 1

invidious *adj* having or showing mean resentment of another's possessions or advantages ⟨the *invidious* attention of the less successful sales representatives⟩ — see ENVIOUS

invidiousness *n* a painful awareness of another's possessions or advantages and a desire to have them too ⟨blinded by *invidiousness* into dealing drugs on the side in order to make some easy money⟩ — see ENVY

invigorate *vb* to give life, vigor, or spirit to ⟨the fresh air and sunshine *invigorated* the children after a long day indoors⟩ — see ANIMATE

invigorated *adj* made or become fresh in spirits or vigor ⟨an *invigorated* worker returning from a relaxing vacation⟩ — see NEW 4

invigorating *adj* having a renewing effect on the state of the body or mind ⟨an *invigorating* breeze made our sail all the more enjoyable⟩ — see TONIC

invincible *adj* incapable of being defeated, overcome, or subdued ⟨an *invincible* wrestler who has never lost a match⟩

synonyms impregnable, indomitable, insurmountable, invulnerable, unbeatable, unconquerable

related words inviolable, unassailable, untouchable; armored, defended, guarded, protected, safe, safeguarded, secure, shielded; unbeaten, unconquered, undefeated, unsubdued

near antonyms exposed, imperiled, insecure, liable, open, susceptible, unguarded, unprotected, unsafe, unshielded; defenseless, helpless, powerless, weak

antonyms surmountable, vulnerable

inviolable *adj* not to be violated, criticized, or tampered with ⟨*inviolable* moral standards⟩ ⟨an *inviolable* trust between lawyer and client⟩ — see SACRED 1

invite *vb* to act so as to make (something) more likely ⟨you're just *inviting* ridicule by making such outrageous claims⟩ — see COURT 1

invoice *n* a record of goods sold or services performed together with the costs due ⟨the *invoice* stated that we owed $1500⟩ — see ¹BILL 1

involuntary *adj* **1** not made or done willingly or by choice ⟨my long stays on the sidelines during our football games were strictly *involuntary*⟩
synonyms coerced, forced, unintended, unintentional, unwilling
related words accidental, unplanned, unpremeditated; automatic, impulsive, instinctive, spontaneous, unprompted; inadvertent, unconscious, unknowing, unwitting
near antonyms advised, conscious, considered, knowing, planned, premeditated, purposeful; volitional
antonyms deliberate, intentional, unforced, voluntary, willful (*or* wilful), willing
2 done instantly and without conscious thought or decision ⟨breathing is *involuntary*⟩ — see AUTOMATIC 1
3 forcing one's compliance or participation by or as if by law ⟨*involuntary* servitude⟩ — see MANDATORY

involution *n* the state or quality of having many interrelated parts or aspects ⟨the *involution* of the thriller's plot made it hard to follow⟩ — see COMPLEXITY 1

involve *vb* **1** to be the business or affair of ⟨this isn't something that *involves* you, so don't worry about it⟩ — see CONCERN 2
2 to have as part of a whole ⟨a tragic play usually *involves* a number of plot devices, including the hero's fatal flaw⟩ — see INCLUDE
3 to hold the attention of ⟨her daydream so completely *involved* her that she never heard the knock on the door⟩ — see ENGAGE 1

involved *adj* **1** having many parts or aspects that are usually interrelated ⟨a remarkably *involved* story for a writer so young⟩ — see COMPLEX 1
2 made or done with great care or with much detail ⟨very *involved* descriptions of every last detail of the lavish wedding⟩ — see ELABORATE 1

involving *adj* holding the attention or provoking interest ⟨an *involving* book you won't be able to put down⟩ — see INTERESTING

invulnerable *adj* incapable of being defeated, overcome, or subdued ⟨Superman is supposed to be *invulnerable*⟩ — see INVINCIBLE

inward *adj* situated farther in ⟨moved towards the *inward* room for more privacy⟩ — see INNER 1

in–your–face *adj* having or showing a bold forcefulness in the pursuit of a goal ⟨an *in-your-face* attitude that sometimes puts people off⟩ — see AGGRESSIVE 1

iota *n* the smallest amount or part imaginable ⟨there's not an *iota* of doubt regarding the defendant's guilt⟩ — see JOT

irascibility *n* readiness to show annoyance or impatience ⟨his natural *irascibility* tends to make people leave him alone⟩ — see PETULANCE

irascible *adj* easily irritated or annoyed ⟨an *irascible* teacher who handed out a lot of detentions⟩ — see IRRITABLE

irate *adj* feeling or showing anger ⟨the big increase in cable rates prompted a flood of *irate* calls and letters⟩ — see ANGRY

irateness *n* an intense emotional state of displeasure with someone or something ⟨his *irateness* was such that we feared he might have a heart attack or stroke⟩ — see ANGER

ire *n* an intense emotional state of displeasure with someone or something ⟨the patronizing comment roused her *ire*⟩ — see ANGER

ireful *adj* feeling or showing anger ⟨*ireful* expressions on the faces of the protesters⟩ — see ANGRY

irk *vb* to disturb the peace of mind of (someone) especially by repeated disagreeable acts ⟨she *irked* her friend by chewing her gum loudly during the movie⟩ — see IRRITATE 1

irksome *adj* causing annoyance ⟨the *irksome* habit of leaving all the cabinet doors open⟩ — see ANNOYING

iron *adj* not showing weakness or uncertainty ⟨he had an *iron* determination to succeed in business⟩ — see FIRM 1

irons *n pl* something that physically prevents free movement ⟨guards put the prisoner in *irons* so that he couldn't escape⟩ — see BOND 1

irradiate *vb* to supply with light ⟨the light from a galaxy of flashing signs *irradiates* the center of Las Vegas⟩ — see ILLUMINATE 1

irrational *adj* not using or following good reasoning ⟨it's *irrational* to think that you can continue to consume an excess of calories and not gain weight⟩ — see ILLOGICAL

irrecoverable *adj* **1** not capable of being cured or reformed ⟨an *irrecoverable* criminal⟩ — see HOPELESS 1
2 not capable of being repaired, regained, or undone ⟨one computer file was *irrecoverable* after the crash⟩ — see IRREPARABLE

irredeemable *adj* **1** not capable of being cured or reformed ⟨*irredeemable* practical jokers⟩ — see HOPELESS 1
2 not capable of being repaired, regained, or undone ⟨the *irredeemable* loss of innocence that the war brought about⟩ — see IRREPARABLE

irrefutable *adj* not capable of being challenged or proved wrong ⟨the *irrefutable* reply of "Because I like it!"⟩
synonyms incontestable, incontrovertible, indisputable, indubitable, unanswerable, undeniable, unquestionable
related words certain, definite, positive, sure; unambiguous, unequivocal; absolute, clear, conclusive, decisive; uncontested, undisputed
near antonyms controversial, debated, disputed; doubtful, dubious, inconclusive, indecisive, uncertain; ambiguous, equivocal
antonyms answerable, debatable, disputable, questionable

irregular *adj* **1** departing from some accepted standard of what is normal ⟨slightly *irregular* behavior that made people suspicious⟩ — see DEVIANT
2 lacking in steadiness or regularity of occurrence ⟨*irregular* mail delivery to the island⟩ — see FITFUL
3 not having a level or smooth surface ⟨although the moon looks smooth from here, it actually has a very bumpy and *irregular* surface⟩ — see UNEVEN 1
4 not rigidly following established form, custom, or rules ⟨the request is *irregular*, but I'll allow it⟩ — see INFORMAL 1
5 not staying constant ⟨*irregular* gusts of wind⟩ — see UNEVEN 2

irregularly *adv* without definite aim, direction, rule, or method ⟨attended class only *irregularly*⟩ — see HIT OR MISS

irrelevance *n* the quality or state of not having anything to do with the matter at hand ⟨the *irrelevance* of the comment brought conversation to a standstill⟩

synonyms extraneousness, inapplicability

related words inappropriateness, inaptness, unfitness, unsuitability; insignificance, unimportance; pointlessness, uselessness

near antonyms bearing, connection; appropriateness, aptness, fitness, suitability; importance, significance; usefulness

antonyms applicability, materiality, pertinence, relevance

irrelevant *adj* not having anything to do with the matter at hand ⟨*irrelevant* questions that merely disrupted the classroom lesson⟩

synonyms extraneous, immaterial, inapplicable

related words inconsequential, insignificant, unimportant; meaningless, pointless, senseless, useless; inappropriate, inapt, unsuitable

phrases beside the point

near antonyms important, meaningful, significant; sensible, useful; appropriate, apt, fit, suitable

antonyms applicable, apposite, apropos, germane, material, pertinent, relevant

irreligious *adj* lacking religious emotions, principles, or practices ⟨raised in an *irreligious* family where the subject of God was never even discussed⟩

synonyms godless, nonreligious

related words ungodly, unholy; blasphemous, impious, irreverent, sacrilegious; agnostic, atheistic; unconsecrated, unhallowed; profane, secular, worldly

near antonyms devout, godly, holy, pious, prayerful, reverent, worshipful, worshipping (*also* worshiping); sanctimonious

antonyms religious

irremediable *adj* **1** not capable of being cured or reformed ⟨no juvenile delinquent is *irremediable*⟩ — see HOPELESS 1

2 not capable of being repaired, regained, or undone ⟨it turned out that the flood damage was not *irremediable*⟩ — see IRREPARABLE

irremovable *adj* incapable of moving or being moved ⟨the driveway had to be built to curve around an *irremovable* tree⟩ — see IMMOVABLE 1

irreparable *adj* not capable of being repaired, regained, or undone ⟨*irreparable* damage to the car⟩

synonyms irrecoverable, irredeemable, irremediable, irretrievable, irreversible, unrecoverable, unredeemable

related words irreplaceable, irrevocable; unredeemed, unrepaired

near antonyms corrected, fixed, recovered, remedied, repaired

antonyms fixable, redeemable, remediable, retrievable

irreproachable *adj* **1** free from guilt or blame ⟨the captain of the force is a police officer of absolutely *irreproachable* character⟩ — see INNOCENT 2

2 being entirely without fault ⟨an *irreproachable* solution to the problem that should satisfy everyone⟩ — see PERFECT 1

irresolution *n* the act or an instance of pausing because of uncertainty about the right course of action ⟨after a moment of anguished *irresolution*, I raised my rifle and fired at the charging animal⟩ — see HESITATION

irresponsible *adj* having or showing a lack of concern for the consequences of one's actions ⟨it was *irresponsible* to go off and leave your little brother alone⟩ — see RECKLESS 1

irretrievable *adj* **1** not capable of being cured or reformed ⟨an *irretrievable* drug addict who had wasted a once-promising life⟩ — see HOPELESS 1

2 not capable of being repaired, regained, or undone ⟨this is just an *irretrievable* mess, so let's start all over again⟩ — see IRREPARABLE

irreverence *n* an act of great disrespect shown to God or to sacred ideas, people, or things ⟨certain sects of Islam consider a woman showing her face in public to be a gross *irreverence*⟩ — see BLASPHEMY

irreverent *adj* not showing proper reverence for the holy or sacred ⟨*irreverent* behavior during church services⟩

synonyms blasphemous, impious, profane, sacrilegious

related words agnostic, atheistic; godless, irreligious, nonreligious, secular; ungodly, unholy; unconsecrated, unhallowed, unsanctified

near antonyms devout, godly, holy, prayerful, religious, worshipful, worshipping (*also* worshiping); consecrated, hallowed, sanctified

antonyms pious, reverent

irreversible *adj* not capable of being repaired, regained, or undone ⟨fortunately, it wasn't an *irreversible* error since it was discovered early⟩ — see IRREPARABLE

irrigate *vb* to pour liquid over or through in order to cleanse ⟨if you get the chemical in your eye, *irrigate* the eye thoroughly with water⟩ — see FLUSH 1

irritability *n* readiness to show annoyance or impatience ⟨the librarian's well-known *irritability* makes students hesitant to ask questions⟩ — see PETULANCE

irritable *adj* easily irritated or annoyed ⟨that *irritable* old man always yells at people to stay off of his lawn⟩

synonyms choleric, crabby, cranky, cross, crotchety, grouchy, grumpy, irascible, peevish, perverse, pettish, petulant, quick-tempered, short-tempered, snappish, snappy, snippy, testy, waspish

related words bearish, bilious, cantankerous, disagreeable, dyspeptic, ill-humored, ill-natured, ill-tempered, ornery, surly; sensitive, sulky, thin-skinned, touchy; hot-blooded, passionate

phrases out of sorts

near antonyms affable, cordial, friendly, genial, sociable; amiable, good-natured, good-tempered, well-disposed; carefree, easygoing, relaxed; obliging, patient, tolerant, uncomplaining, understanding

irritableness *n* readiness to show annoyance or impatience ⟨the old man's chronic *irritableness* makes him the terror of the nursing home⟩ — see PETULANCE

irritant *n* something that is a source of irritation ⟨the whining child was a constant *irritant* to his long-suffering parents⟩ — see ANNOYANCE 3

irritate *vb* **1** to disturb the peace of mind of (someone) especially by repeated disagreeable acts ⟨constant chatter *irritated* the student, who was trying to concentrate on a hard assignment⟩

synonyms aggravate, annoy, bother, bug, chafe, exasperate, gall, get, grate, irk, nettle, peeve, persecute, pique, put out, rasp, rile, vex

related words hassle, heckle; nag; inflame, provoke, rouse; bait, harass, harry, pester; anger, enrage, incense, infuriate, madden; agitate, disturb, fret, perturb, upset; affront, insult, offend, outrage

phrases rub the wrong way

near antonyms appease, conciliate, mollify, oblige, pacify, placate, propitiate; delight, gladden, gratify, please, satisfy; comfort, console, content, quiet, soothe

2 to make sore by continued rubbing ⟨new shoes usually *irritate* my feet⟩ — see CHAFE 1

irritating *adj* causing annoyance ⟨his particularly *irritat-*

ing habit of leaving his dirty clothes on the floor⟩ — see ANNOYING

irritation *n* the feeling of impatience or anger caused by another's repeated disagreeable acts ⟨Dad's general *irritation* at the incessant complaining coming from the back seat of the car⟩ — see ANNOYANCE 2

irruption *n* a sudden attack on and entrance into hostile territory ⟨the *irruptions* of the Goths into Italy in the 5th century⟩ — see RAID 1

island *n* a fairly small area of land completely surrounded by water ⟨they're taking a trip to an *island* in Hawaii for vacation⟩
synonyms isle, islet
related words barrier reef, cay, coral reef, key; archipelago, atoll; cape, headland, peninsula, promontory
near antonyms continent, main, mainland

isle *n* a fairly small area of land completely surrounded by water ⟨the Australian seas are full of uninhabited *isles*⟩ — see ISLAND

islet *n* a fairly small area of land completely surrounded by water ⟨landed the boat on a tiny *islet* that we had all to ourselves⟩ — see ISLAND

isolate *vb* to set or keep apart from others ⟨*isolated* her in a corner for a five-minute punishment after she threw a book at her friend⟩
synonyms cut off, insulate, seclude, segregate, separate, sequester
related words quarantine; confine, immure, incarcerate, intern, jail, lock (up), restrain, restrict; detach, disengage, remove; detain, hold, keep
near antonyms associate, connect, join, link, unite; discharge, free, liberate, loose, release
antonyms desegregate, integrate

isolated *adj* hidden from view ⟨the hikers unexpectedly came upon an *isolated* mountain cabin⟩ — see SECLUDED

isolation *n* the state of being alone or kept apart from others ⟨*isolation* always made the sociable child lonely⟩
synonyms insulation, secludedness, seclusion, segregation, separateness, sequestration, solitariness, solitude
related words loneliness, lonesomeness; confinement, incarceration, internment, quarantine; retirement, withdrawal
near antonyms companionship, company

issuance *n* the act or process of giving out something to each member of a group ⟨the *issuance* of an instruction sheet to each member of the class⟩ — see DISTRIBUTION 1

issue *n* 1 a condition or occurrence traceable to a cause ⟨one of the *issues* of the Civil War was the resolution to the question of states' rights⟩ — see EFFECT 1
2 a place or means of going out ⟨since the lake is the *issue* of the polluted river, it is becoming polluted as well⟩ — see EXIT 1
3 the descendants of a person, animal, or plant ⟨someone who dies without *issue* might have their estate turned over to the state⟩ — see OFFSPRING

issue *vb* 1 to produce and release for distribution in printed form ⟨plans to *issue* a monthly newsletter⟩ — see PUBLISH 1
2 to throw or give off ⟨a volcano *issuing* vast clouds of hot ash⟩ — see EMIT 1

Italian sandwich *n* a large sandwich on a long split roll ⟨that restaurant makes a great *Italian sandwich*⟩ — see SUBMARINE

itch *n* a strong wish for something ⟨has an *itch* to travel to far-off and exciting places⟩ — see DESIRE

itch (for) *vb* to have an earnest wish to own or enjoy ⟨a bully who's just *itching for* a fight⟩ — see DESIRE

item *n* 1 a separate part in a list, account, or series ⟨she got all the *items* on her grocery list except cereal⟩
synonyms detail, particular, point
related words article, belonging, object, stuff, thing; characteristic, constituent, element, feature; ingredient; division, particle, piece, portion, section, segment
near antonyms aggregate, composite, compound, conglomerate; entirety, sum, total, totality, whole
2 a report of recent events or facts not previously known ⟨our next *item* is about the blizzard blanketing the East Coast⟩ — see NEWS

itemize *vb* 1 to make a list of ⟨*itemized* the various expenses⟩ — see ¹LIST 1
2 to specify one after another ⟨*itemized* the potential problems if the plan goes through⟩ — see ENUMERATE 1

itinerant *adj* traveling from place to place ⟨an *itinerant* musician can see a lot of the world⟩
synonyms errant, gallivanting (*also* galavanting), nomad (*or* nomadic), peripatetic, ranging, roaming, roving, vagabond, vagrant, wandering, wayfaring
related words drifting, footloose, meandering, rambling; sauntering, strolling, traipsing, walking
near antonyms immobile, settled, stationary

J

jab *n* a quick thrust ⟨gave the jellyfish on the beach a cautious *jab* with my stick⟩ — see ¹POKE

jabber *n* unintelligible or meaningless talk ⟨to me the baby's speech was simply *jabber*, but his mother seemed to know exactly what he was saying⟩ — see GIBBERISH

jabber *vb* **1** to engage in casual or rambling conversation ⟨please do not *jabber* during the quiz⟩ — see CHAT

2 to speak rapidly, inarticulately, and usually unintelligibly ⟨monkeys *jabbering* at each other in their cages⟩ — see BABBLE 1

jabberer *n* a person who talks constantly ⟨our teacher's policy is to seat classroom *jabberers* as far away from each other as possible⟩ — see CHATTERBOX

jabberwocky *n* unintelligible or meaningless talk ⟨when he talks in a sort of agitated *jabberwocky*⟩ — see GIBBERISH

jack *n* **1** *slang* something (as pieces of stamped metal or printed paper) customarily and legally used as a medium of exchange, a measure of value, or a means of payment ⟨I'd buy that watch, but I don't have the *jack*⟩ — see MONEY

2 a piece of cloth with a special design that is used as an emblem or for signaling ⟨a Portuguese ship flying the national *jack*⟩ — see FLAG 1

3 an adult male human being ⟨hey, *jack*, can you spare some change?⟩ — see MAN 1

4 one who operates or navigates a seagoing vessel ⟨the streets of the old seaport were once full of *jacks*, harlots, and other dockside denizens⟩ — see SAILOR

jack (up) *vb* **1** to lift with effort ⟨*jack up* the car so we can change that tire⟩ — see HEAVE 1

2 to move from a lower to a higher place or position ⟨*jacked up* prices for the summer tourist season⟩ — see RAISE 1

jackass *n* **1** a person who lacks good sense or judgment ⟨only a *jackass* would dive into a lake without checking to see how deep the water is⟩ — see FOOL 1

2 a stupid person ⟨you don't have to act like a *jackass* just to get a girl to notice you⟩ — see IDIOT

3 a sturdy and patient domestic mammal that is used especially to carry things ⟨with our *jackasses* loaded with supplies, we slowly made our way down to the floor of the canyon⟩ — see DONKEY 1

jacked (up) *adj* being at a higher level than average ⟨the convenience store had the item I needed but at a *jacked up* price⟩ — see HIGH 2

jacket *n* something that encloses another thing especially to protect it ⟨slip the art book into its *jacket* so it won't get dirty⟩ — see ¹CASE 1

jackpot *n* the total of the bets at stake at one time ⟨once the *jackpot* hit $100 million, everybody and his cousin was buying lottery tickets⟩ — see POT 1

jack–tar *n* one who operates or navigates a seagoing vessel ⟨a *jack-tar* swabbing the deck under the critical eye of the first mate⟩ — see SAILOR

jade *vb* to make weary and restless by being dull or monotonous ⟨the movie's long opening credits were really starting to *jade* me⟩ — see ²BORE

jaded *adj* **1** depleted in strength, energy, or freshness ⟨after that long test, I'm too *jaded* for anything but a nap⟩ — see WEARY 1

2 having one's patience, interest, or pleasure exhausted ⟨even *jaded* sci-fi fans are finding this new space adventure fresh and exciting⟩ — see WEARY 2

jading *adj* causing weariness, restlessness, or lack of interest ⟨the *jading* task of sorting and counting change⟩ — see BORING

jagged *adj* **1** having an uneven edge or outline ⟨it's going to be hard to repair the *jagged* tear so that it doesn't show⟩ — see RAGGED 1

2 not having a level or smooth surface ⟨rode our mountain bikes down *jagged* terrain, which for made for a bumpy ride⟩ — see UNEVEN 1

jail *n* a place of confinement for persons held in lawful custody ⟨sentenced to three years in *jail* for his crime⟩
synonyms brig, gaol [*chiefly British*], guardroom, hoosegow, jug, lockup, pen, penitentiary, prison, stockade
related words bull pen; concentration camp, prison camp; dungeon, keep; reformatory, reform school
near antonyms freedom

jail *vb* to put in or as if in prison ⟨threatened to *jail* the punks if they so much as jaywalked⟩ — see IMPRISON

jailbird *n* a person convicted as a criminal and serving a prison sentence ⟨had spent most of his sorry life as a *jailbird* in hoosegows across the South⟩ — see CONVICT

jailed *adj* taken and held prisoner ⟨the *jailed* protestors were demanding to see their lawyers⟩ — see CAPTIVE

jam *n* a difficult, puzzling, or embarrassing situation from which there is no easy escape ⟨the heavy rain puts us in a real *jam*: all of the preparations are for a garden wedding⟩ — see PREDICAMENT

jam *vb* **1** to fit (something) into a tight space ⟨*jammed* his clothes into the already bulging hamper⟩ — see CROWD 1

2 to prevent passage through ⟨firefighters found the nightclub's doorways *jammed* with trapped patrons⟩ — see CLOG 1

3 to put into (something) as much as can be held or contained ⟨the inn will *jam* a guest's picnic basket with an array of tempting foods⟩ — see FILL 1

jammed *adj* **1** containing or seeming to contain the greatest quantity or number possible ⟨the bus is *jammed* with eager sightseers⟩ — see FULL 1

2 firmly positioned in place and difficult to dislodge ⟨the *jammed* door just won't budge⟩ — see TIGHT 2

jam–pack *vb* to put into (something) as much as can be held or contained ⟨we *jam-packed* the box with goodies for our sick friend⟩ — see FILL 1

jam–packed *adj* **1** containing or seeming to contain the greatest quantity or number possible ⟨a film *jam-packed* with spectacular action sequences⟩ — see FULL 1

2 having little space between items or parts ⟨the *jam-packed* placement of the chicken pieces in the frying pan prevented them from browning properly⟩ — see CLOSE 1

janitor *n* **1** a person who takes care of a property sometimes for an absent owner ⟨got a job as the night *janitor* at the elementary school⟩ — see CUSTODIAN 1

2 a person who tends a door ⟨according to popular Christian tradition, St. Peter acts as *janitor* at Heaven's pearly gates⟩ — see DOORKEEPER

jar *n* **1** a forceful coming together of two things ⟨this padded case should protect your instrument from the *jars* normally experienced while traveling⟩ — see IMPACT 1

2 something that makes a strong impression because it is so unexpected ⟨the flow of her day was interrupted with the *jar* of an unexpected crisis⟩ — see SURPRISE 1

jar *vb* to be out of harmony or agreement usually noticeably ⟨the bright orange of the walls *jars* with the light pastels of the furnishings⟩ — see CLASH

jargon *n* the special terms or expressions of a particular group or field ⟨I don't understand a lot of computer *jargon*⟩ — see TERMINOLOGY

jarring *adj* disagreeable to one's aesthetic or artistic sense ⟨the final chord of that song is too *jarring* for me⟩ — see HARSH 2

jaundice *n* a deep-seated ill will ⟨the *jaundice* in the eyes of the two feuding neighbors was enough to kill crabgrass⟩ — see ENMITY

jaundiced *adj* **1** having or showing mean resentment of another's possessions or advantages ⟨took a *jaundiced* view of his opponent's triumphs on the tennis court⟩ — see ENVIOUS

2 marked by opposition or ill will ⟨environmentalists tend to cast a *jaundiced* eye on the oversized, gasguzzling vehicles⟩ — see HOSTILE 1

jaunt *n* a short trip for pleasure ⟨took a *jaunt* up to the mountains for the day⟩ — see EXCURSION 1

jauntily *adv* **1** in a bright and showy way ⟨*jauntily* wore an enormous feathered hat to the garden party⟩ — see GAILY 3

2 in a quick and spirited manner ⟨the devil-may-care couple waltzed *jauntily* around the ballroom⟩ — see GAILY 2

jaunty *adj* having much high-spirited energy and movement ⟨oozing charm, the *jaunty* dance instructor literally swept the women off their feet⟩ — see LIVELY 1

javelin *n* a weapon with a long straight handle and sharp head or blade ⟨in track and field events, his specialty is throwing the discus and the *javelin*⟩ — see SPEAR

jaw *vb* **1** to criticize (someone) severely or angrily especially for personal failings ⟨you don't have to *jaw* me to death just because I bite my nails⟩ — see SCOLD

2 to engage in casual or rambling conversation ⟨just a group of girls sitting around the locker room and *jawing* about the usual stuff⟩ — see CHAT

jazz *n* unintelligible or meaningless talk ⟨started spewing some *jazz* about how much his collection of baseball cards would be worth someday⟩ — see GIBBERISH

jazz (up) *vb* to give life, vigor, or spirit to ⟨your assignment is to *jazz up* the design of that Web page⟩ — see ANIMATE

jazziness *n* the quality or state of having abundant or intense activity ⟨the surprising *jazziness* of the city's art scene⟩ — see VITALITY 1

jazzy *adj* **1** attractively eye-catching in style ⟨that's a *jazzy* bathing suit, with all those spangles⟩

synonyms flashy, snazzy, splashy

related words cool, hip, neat; à la mode (*also* a la mode), chic, dashing; faddish, fashionable, in, modish, posh, ritzy, sharp, smart, snappy, spruce, stylish; custom, designer; garish, gaudy, loud, rakish, wild

near antonyms classic, elegant, genteel, polished, refined, sophisticated, stately, swank; plain, quiet, restrained, simple, understated

2 having much high-spirited energy and movement ⟨a *jazzy* little dance routine that the aerobics instructor created⟩ — see LIVELY 1

jealous *adj* **1** intolerant of rivalry or unfaithfulness ⟨became *jealous* whenever she paid attention to anyone but him⟩

synonyms possessive

related words controlling, demanding, grasping; covetous, envious, invidious, jaundiced; distrustful, mistrustful, suspicious

phrases green with envy

near antonyms undemanding; tolerant, trustful, trusting, understanding

2 having or showing mean resentment of another's possessions or advantages ⟨was *jealous* of his friend's great popularity with the girls⟩ — see ENVIOUS

jealousy *n* a painful awareness of another's possessions or advantages and a desire to have them too ⟨her *jealousy* over her sister's singing career drove the two of them apart⟩ — see ENVY

jeer *n* a vocal sound made to express scorn or disapproval ⟨ignored the *jeers* of the other team's fans and just focused on his free throw shot⟩ — see CATCALL

jeer *vb* to make (someone or something) the object of unkind laughter ⟨bullies *jeering* at the kids waiting to board the bus to music camp⟩ — see RIDICULE

Jehovah *n* the being worshipped as the creator and ruler of the universe ⟨in the Lord *Jehovah* is everlasting strength⟩ — see DEITY 2

jell *vb* **1** to take on a definite form ⟨my idea for a science project is just beginning to *jell*⟩ — see FORM 1

2 to turn from a liquid into a substance resembling jelly ⟨the sauce will *jell* once it cools down⟩ — see COAGULATE

jelly *vb* to turn from a liquid into a substance resembling jelly ⟨this fruit juice is taking longer to *jelly* than I expected⟩ — see COAGULATE

jeopardize *vb* to place in danger ⟨don't do anything that will *jeopardize* your place on the ski team⟩ — see ENDANGER

jeopardizing *adj* involving potential loss or injury ⟨that stupid prank could turn out to be a *jeopardizing* event in your academic career⟩ — see DANGEROUS

jeopardy *n* the state of not being protected from injury, harm, or evil ⟨don't place your life in *jeopardy* just because somebody dared you to do something⟩ — see DANGER 1

jerk *n* **1** a person whose behavior is offensive to others ⟨his constant rudeness and insensitivity made everyone think he was a real *jerk*⟩

synonyms beast, boor, cad, churl, clown, creep, cretin, cur, heel, joker, louse, lout, skunk, slob, snake, stinker

related words brute, Neanderthal, savage; rascal, rogue, scamp, villain; fool, jackass, nincompoop, nitwit; blockhead, dolt, goon, idiot

near antonyms hero, idol, role model

2 the act or an instance of applying force on something so that it moves in the direction of the force ⟨guided the rowboat with a *jerk* of the rope⟩ — see PULL 1

jerk *vb* **1** to move or cause to move with a sharp quick motion ⟨I *jerked* to one side to avoid getting hit⟩ ⟨*jerked* the leash to get the dog's attention⟩

synonyms buck, hitch, jolt, twitch, yank

related words bump, jounce, lurch, stagger; jiggle, shake; lug, pull, tug; pluck, tweak; grab, snap, snatch, wrench, wrest, wring

2 to make jerky or restless movements ⟨you've got to quit *jerking*, or the barber will nick you by accident⟩ — see FIDGET

jerky *adj* **1** marked by a series of sharp quick motions ⟨made *jerky* progress walking with the new crutches⟩

synonyms bumpy, rough

related words choppy, erratic, fitful, irregular, spasmodic, spastic, unsteady

near antonyms calm, placid, smooth, steady, still

2 showing or marked by a lack of good sense or judgment ⟨he's acting *jerky* just to get people's attention⟩ — see FOOLISH 1

jest *n* **1** an attitude or manner not to be taken seriously ⟨you should know that our teasing was done in *jest*⟩ — see FUN 2

2 something said or done to cause laughter ⟨laughed at his *jest* about his pet mosquito⟩ — see JOKE 1

jest *vb* to make jokes ⟨when I asked my sister for a loan, she laughingly replied, "Surely you *jest!*"⟩ — see JOKE

jester *n* **1** a person (as a writer) noted for or specializing in humor ⟨a gentle *jester*, the cartoonist more often tries to evoke a broad smile than a hearty guffaw⟩ — see HUMORIST

2 a person formerly kept in a royal or noble household to amuse with jests and pranks ⟨the king called for some much-needed entertainment from his *jester*⟩ — see FOOL 2

jesting *adj* marked by or expressive of mild or good-natured teasing ⟨made *jesting* comments about my need for serious fashion advice⟩ — see QUIZZICAL

jesting *n* good-natured teasing or exchanging of clever remarks ⟨lots of laughter and elbow-nudging *jesting* at family reunions⟩ — see BANTER

jet *vb* **1** to flow out in great quantities or with force ⟨water *jetting* out of opened fire hydrants at a dangerous rate⟩ — see GUSH 1

2 to throw out or off (something from within) often violently ⟨the volcano has been *jetting* out fiery lava in life-threatening amounts⟩ — see ERUPT 1

jettison *n* the getting rid of whatever is unwanted or useless ⟨the ship was rapidly sinking, so the captain ordered a *jettison* of much of its cargo⟩ — see DISPOSAL 1

jettison *vb* to get rid of as useless or unwanted ⟨just *jettison* that plan, because we know it won't work⟩ — see DISCARD

jetty *n* a structure used by boats and ships for taking on or landing cargo and passengers ⟨didn't see any passengers waiting for the ferry, so the captain sailed past the *jetty*⟩ — see DOCK

jewel *n* **1** a usually valuable stone cut and polished for ornament ⟨a necklace set with priceless *jewels*⟩ — see GEM 1

2 an asset that brings praise or renown ⟨an illuminated medieval manuscript that is the *jewel* of the library's collection of rare books⟩ — see GLORY 2

3 someone or something unusually desirable ⟨a star athlete who would be a *jewel* for any team⟩ — see PRIZE 1

jibe *vb* to be in agreement on every point ⟨that doesn't *jibe* with what I know⟩ — see CHECK 1

jiffy *n* a very small space of time ⟨I'll be there in a *jiffy*⟩ — see INSTANT

jig *n* a clever often underhanded means to achieve an end ⟨okay, buster, the *jig* is up⟩ — see TRICK 1

jigger *n* an interesting and often novel device with a practical use ⟨a kitchen store filled with neat little *jiggers* that you didn't know you needed⟩ — see GADGET

jiggling *n* a series of slight movements by a body back and forth or from side to side ⟨the *jiggling* we got when we drove over the railroad tracks⟩ — see VIBRATION

jim–dandy *adj* of the very best kind ⟨a jim-dandy guitarist who would be an asset to any band⟩ — see EXCELLENT

jim–dandy *n* something very good of its kind ⟨the brand new car was a *jim-dandy*⟩

synonyms beauty, corker, crackerjack, dandy, knockout, nifty, pip

related words marvel, wonder; gem, jewel, treasure

near antonyms disappointment, failure, lemon, loser

jimmy *vb* to raise, move, or pull apart with or as if with a lever ⟨try to *jimmy* the door with my credit card⟩ — see ¹PRY 1

jingle *n* **1** a series of short high ringing sounds ⟨the *jingle* of change in my pocket⟩ — see TINKLE

2 a short musical composition for the human voice often with instrumental accompaniment ⟨loved that *jingle* on the commercial for the fast-food place⟩ — see SONG 1

jingle *vb* to make a repeated sharp light ringing sound ⟨the bell on the kitten's collar *jingled* as she walked⟩

synonyms chink, clink, tinkle

related words clack, clang, clank; clatter, rattle; ding, jangle, ping, ring

jingo *n* **1** one who shows excessive favoritism towards his or her country ⟨a *jingo* who thought other countries should automatically follow his country's policies⟩ — see NATIONALIST

2 one who urges or attempts to cause a war ⟨the often bitter rhetoric between the *jingoes* and pacifists⟩ — see WARMONGER

jingoism *n* excessive favoritism towards one's own country ⟨his loudmouthed *jingoism* will not win us any foreign allies⟩ — see CHAUVINISM

jinx *n* something that brings bad luck ⟨believed the broken mirror was a *jinx*⟩

synonyms hex, hoodoo

related words curse, evil eye, spell; augury, omen, portent

near antonyms amulet, charm, talisman

jitters *n pl* a sense of panic or extreme nervousness ⟨always got the *jitters* right before a test⟩

synonyms dither, nerves, shakes, shivers, willies

related words cold sweat, creeps; anxiety, fear, hysteria; frazzle, nervous breakdown

near antonyms aplomb, composure, coolheadedness, equanimity, imperturbability, self-possession

jittery *adj* **1** easily excited by nature ⟨a *jittery* person who shouldn't even consider a career as an air traffic controller⟩ — see EXCITABLE

2 feeling or showing uncomfortable feelings of uncertainty ⟨a little *jittery* before the flight⟩ — see NERVOUS 1

jive *vb* **1** to make fun of in a good-natured way ⟨don't be upset—we're just *jiving* you⟩ — see TEASE 1

2 to make jokes ⟨the team was laughing and *jiving* after our win⟩ — see JOKE

job *n* **1** an assignment at which one regularly works for pay ⟨a high-paying *job* as a banker⟩

synonyms appointment, berth, billet, capacity, function, place, position, post, situation

related words business, employment, occupation, profession; work; office, spot; calling, pursuit, vocation; line, racket; engagement; livelihood, living; assignment, mission, task

near antonyms avocation; joblessness, unemployment

2 a piece of work that needs to be done regularly ⟨taking the trash out is one of my *jobs*⟩ — see CHORE 1

3 a specific task with which a person or group is charged ⟨your *job* on this committee is to review the curriculum and suggest changes⟩ — see MISSION

4 the action for which a person or thing is specially fitted or used or for which a thing exists ⟨a coffeemaker's *job* is to make coffee⟩ — see ROLE

jobholder *n* one who works for another for wages or a salary ⟨more *jobholders* than the company has ever had in the past⟩ — see EMPLOYEE

jocose *adj* indicative of or marked by high spirits or good humor ⟨the comedian's *jocose* introductions kept the awards ceremony from becoming a stodgy affair⟩ — see MERRY

jocosely *adv* in a cheerful or happy manner ⟨a group of friends sitting around and commenting *jocosely* on the other wedding guests⟩ — see GAILY 1

jocular *adj* given to or marked by mature intelligent humor ⟨people in the business like to make the *jocular* observation that best way to make a small fortune with wine is to start off with a large fortune⟩ — see WITTY

jocund *adj* indicative of or marked by high spirits or good humor ⟨old friends engaged in *jocund* teasing⟩ — see MERRY

jog *vb* **1** to go at a pace faster than a walk ⟨had to *jog* to catch up to them⟩ — see RUN 1

2 to make short up-and-down movements ⟨her purse *jogging* against her hip as she walked⟩ — see NOD

joggle *vb* to make a series of small irregular or violent movements ⟨the old bus *joggled* as it barreled down the dirt road⟩ — see SHAKE 1

join *vb* **1** to be adjacent to ⟨our classroom *joins* the gym⟩ — see ADJOIN 1

2 to become a member of ⟨we're looking for new people to *join* the club⟩ — see ENTER 2

3 to come together to form a single unit ⟨one oxygen atom and two hydrogen atoms *join* to make one water molecule⟩ — see UNITE 1

4 to participate or assist in a joint effort to accomplish an end ⟨nations *joining* to bring aid to the earthquake-devastated region⟩ — see COOPERATE 1

5 to put or bring together so as to form a new and longer whole ⟨the plan is to *join* the various bike paths so that cyclists can travel from one end of the cape to the other⟩ — see CONNECT 1

joining *adj* having a border in common ⟨friends sitting in *joining* cubicles in the library⟩ — see ADJACENT

joint *adj* used or done by a number of people as a group ⟨a *joint* effort by residents of the neighborhood to help reduce crime⟩ — see COLLECTIVE

joint *n* **1** a place where two or more things are united ⟨the leak was found at a *joint* in the pipe⟩
synonyms connection, coupling, junction, juncture
related words crux, link, tie; interconnection, intersection; abutment, articulation; seam, suture; concourse, confluence, meeting; union
near antonyms crack, separation

2 a building, room, or suite of rooms occupied by a service business ⟨let's go to the local burger *joint*⟩ — see PLACE 2

jointly *adv* in or by combined action or effort ⟨bought our mother's present *jointly*⟩ — see TOGETHER 2

joke *n* **1** something said or done to cause laughter ⟨he was known for his hilarious *jokes*⟩
synonyms crack, gag, jest, laugh, pleasantry, quip, sally, waggery, wisecrack, witticism
related words funning, joking, wisecracking; antic, buffoonery, caper, monkeyshine(s), prank; caricature, lampoon, parody, put-on; banter, persiflage, raillery, repartee; facetiousness, funniness, hilariousness, humorousness; barb, humor, wit, wordplay

2 a poor, insincere, or insulting imitation of something ⟨her rendition of the national anthem is a *joke*⟩ — see MOCKERY 1

joke *vb* to make jokes ⟨he was known for his ability to *joke*⟩
synonyms banter, fool, fun, jest, jive, josh, kid, quip, wisecrack
related words chaff, mock, rally, razz, rib, ridicule, tease; caricature, lampoon, parody, satirize; amuse, divert, entertain

joker *n* **1** a person (as a writer) noted for or specializing in humor ⟨he's the *joker* of the family, always making us laugh⟩ — see HUMORIST

2 a person whose behavior is offensive to others ⟨just ignore that *joker* and his rude comments⟩ — see JERK 1
3 an adult male human being ⟨sat at the table next to some poor *joker* who just lost his job⟩ — see MAN 1

jokester *n* a person (as a writer) noted for or specializing in humor ⟨hired the hot new Hollywood *jokester* to write the sitcom script⟩ — see HUMORIST

joking *adj* marked by or expressive of mild or good-natured teasing ⟨grinned and gave him a *joking* nudge with my elbow⟩ — see QUIZZICAL

jollification *n* joyful or festive activity ⟨the *jollification* will begin after the parade⟩ — see MERRYMAKING

jollity *n* joyful or festive activity ⟨I love all of the *jollity* of the holiday season⟩ — see MERRYMAKING

jolly *adj* indicative of or marked by high spirits or good humor ⟨an especially *jolly* crowd of well-wishers at their wedding reception⟩ — see MERRY

jolly *adv* to a great degree ⟨I *jolly* well agree that that's the right thing to do⟩ — see VERY 1

jolt *n* **1** a forceful coming together of two things ⟨pack the glass vase so that it won't fall victim to any hard *jolts* in transit⟩ — see IMPACT 1

2 something that makes a strong impression because it is so unexpected ⟨the news of the principal's retirement was a *jolt* to us all⟩ — see SURPRISE 1

jolt *vb* **1** to make a series of small irregular or violent movements ⟨the roller coaster car jerked and *jolted* as it coursed along the old wooden tracks⟩ — see SHAKE 1

2 to move or cause to move with a sharp quick motion ⟨she *jolted* the door open with her elbow⟩ — see JERK 1

3 to cause an often unpleasant surprise for ⟨the sneak terrorist attack *jolted* the country out of its indolence and indifference⟩ — see SHOCK 1

josh *vb* **1** to make fun of in a good-natured way ⟨don't cry! I'm just *joshing* you⟩ — see TEASE 1

2 to make jokes ⟨a very outgoing man who *joshes* with everyone he meets⟩ — see JOKE

joshing *adj* marked by or expressive of mild or good-natured teasing ⟨a *joshing* response to my earnest question⟩ — see QUIZZICAL

joshing *n* good-natured teasing or exchanging of clever remarks ⟨for all his *joshing*, he can be very serious when he needs to be⟩ — see BANTER

jot *n* the smallest amount or part imaginable ⟨it's obvious that he doesn't have a *jot* of interest in history⟩
synonyms hoot, iota, lick, modicum, rap, tittle, whit
related words ace, bit, crumb, dab, driblet, glimmer, hint, little, mite, nip, ounce, peanuts, ray, scruple, shade, shadow, shred, smidgen, snap, speck, spot, sprinkling, strain, streak, suspicion, touch, trace

jot (down) *vb* to make a written note of ⟨I'll *jot down* the message⟩ — see RECORD 1

jounce *vb* **1** to make a series of small irregular or violent movements ⟨a rickety cart *jouncing* as it was being pulled over the cobblestoned streets⟩ — see SHAKE 1
2 to make short up-and-down movements ⟨her head *jounced* as the horse began to gallop⟩ — see NOD

journal *n* a publication that appears at regular intervals ⟨a monthly scientific *journal*⟩
synonyms gazette, magazine, newspaper, organ, paper, periodical, review
related words annual, bimonthly, biweekly, daily, monthly, quarterly, semimonthly, semiweekly, weekly, yearbook; broadside, extra, sheet, tabloid

journalist *n* a person employed by a newspaper, magazine, or radio or television station to gather, write, or report news ⟨a *journalist* who has won awards for two of her feature stories⟩ — see REPORTER

journey *n* a going from one place to another usually of some distance ⟨they were hungry and tired after their long *journey*⟩
synonyms expedition, passage, peregrination, travel(s), trek, trip
related words errand, excursion, flight, hop, jaunt, junket, outing, sally, tour; cruise, sail, voyage; drive, ride, spin; odyssey, pilgrimage, progress, quest, safari

journey *vb* to take a trip especially of some distance ⟨a yearning to *journey* to distant lands⟩ — see TRAVEL 1

jovial *adj* indicative of or marked by high spirits or good humor ⟨the trip to the amusement park put everyone in a *jovial* mood⟩ — see MERRY

joviality *n* a mood characterized by high spirits and amusement and often accompanied by laughter ⟨the last day of school is always filled with *joviality*⟩ — see MIRTH

jovially *adv* in a cheerful or happy manner ⟨*jovially* waved good morning to us⟩ — see GAILY 1

joy *n* **1** a feeling or state of well-being and contentment ⟨the inexpressible *joy* that the couple are feeling upon the birth of their first child⟩ — see HAPPINESS 1
2 a source of great satisfaction ⟨my car is my pride and *joy*⟩ — see DELIGHT 1

joy *vb* to feel or express joy or triumph ⟨the whole town is *joying* in the fact that its oldest church has been restored to its Victorian splendor⟩ — see EXULT

joyful *adj* experiencing pleasure, satisfaction, or delight ⟨the news of the child's safe return made us all *joyful*⟩ — see GLAD 1

joyless *adj* feeling unhappiness ⟨was *joyless* after her dog died⟩ — see SAD 1

joylessness *n* a state or spell of low spirits ⟨you'll overcome this *joylessness* and once again be your usual smiling self⟩ — see SADNESS

joyous *adj* experiencing pleasure, satisfaction, or delight ⟨a *joyous* crowd eagerly awaiting the countdown to midnight on New Year's Eve⟩ — see GLAD 1

jubilant *adj* having or expressing feelings of joy or triumph ⟨the nominee's *jubilant* acceptance speech before the cheering crowd⟩ — see EXULTANT

jubilee *n* a time or program of special events and entertainment in honor of something ⟨the town is planning a year-long *jubilee* in celebration of its founding 200 years ago⟩ — see FESTIVAL

judge *n* **1** a person who impartially decides or resolves a dispute or controversy ⟨their father always played the role of *judge* when there was a disagreement⟩
synonyms arbiter, arbitrator, referee, umpire
related words justice, magistrate; intermediary, mediator, negotiator; conciliator, go-between, peacemaker, reconciler; decider

2 a public official having authority to decide questions of law ⟨the *judge* gave the defendant a suspended sentence⟩
synonyms bench, court, justice, magistrate
related words justice of the peace
near antonyms claimant, plaintiff; defendant

judge *vb* **1** to give an opinion about (something at issue or in dispute) ⟨the committee will *judge* the case based on the evidence⟩
synonyms adjudge, adjudicate, arbitrate, decide, determine, referee, rule (on), settle, umpire
related words consider, hear, ponder, weigh; size (up); mediate, moderate, negotiate; prosecute, try; find (for *or* against)
near antonyms equivocate, skirt
2 to decide the size, amount, number, or distance of (something) without actual measurement ⟨considering the amount of dough we have, I *judge* we'll get about six dozen cookies out of it⟩ — see ESTIMATE 2
3 to form an opinion through reasoning and information ⟨I *judge* that the girl has a troubled relationship with her mother⟩ — see INFER 1

judgment *or* **judgement** *n* **1** a decision made by a court or tribunal regarding a case it has heard ⟨the court will give its *judgment* in this case tomorrow morning⟩ — see SENTENCE
2 a position arrived at after consideration ⟨eventually came to the *judgment* that the lawsuit wasn't worth their time⟩ — see DECISION 1
3 an idea that is believed to be true or valid without positive knowledge ⟨your *judgment* of the situation isn't a very good one⟩ — see OPINION 1
4 an opinion on the nature, character, or quality of something ⟨critical *judgment* on that new comedy has been overwhelmingly negative⟩ — see ESTIMATION 1

judicious *adj* **1** having or showing good judgment and restraint especially in conduct or speech ⟨a good teacher who knows how to give *judicious* criticism as well as praise⟩ — see DISCREET
2 suitable for bringing about a desired result under the circumstances ⟨I'll ask for the raise at a time I deem most *judicious*⟩ — see EXPEDIENT

jug *n* **1** a place of confinement for persons held in lawful custody ⟨some no-good fellow who had spent most of his life in and out of the county *jug*⟩ — see JAIL
2 a handled container for holding and pouring liquids that usually has a lip or a spout ⟨put a *jug* of milk on the table⟩ — see PITCHER

jug *vb* to put in or as if in prison ⟨the luckless crooks got *jugged* before they knew what hit them⟩ — see IMPRISON

jugglery *n* the use of clever underhanded actions to achieve an end ⟨the *jugglery* of offering to get me a cookie and sneaking one yourself while you're reaching in the cookie jar⟩ — see TRICKERY

juiciness *n* the quality or state of being full of juice ⟨the *juiciness* of ripe pears⟩ — see SUCCULENCE

juicy *adj* full of juice ⟨she bit into the *juicy* orange⟩
synonyms fleshy, pulpy, succulent
related words sappy, watery
near antonyms dehydrated, dry, withered

jumble *n* **1** a state in which everything is out of order ⟨the house is always in a *jumble* before and after vacation trips⟩ — see CHAOS
2 an unorganized collection or mixture of various things ⟨a *jumble* of rubber bands, batteries, and pencil stubs all stuffed into that drawer⟩ — see MISCELLANY 1

jumble *vb* to undo the proper order or arrangement of ⟨the contest editor has *jumbled* the letters in common words⟩ — see DISORDER

jumbled *adj* lacking in order, neatness, and often cleanliness ⟨a *jumbled* closet⟩ — see MESSY

jumbo *adj* unusually large ⟨a *jumbo* jet⟩ — see HUGE

jumbo *n* something that is unusually large and powerful ⟨the winner in the contest for biggest pumpkin was a *jumbo* that weighed in at over a thousand pounds⟩ — see GIANT

jump *n* **1** an act of leaping into the air ⟨her first *jump* from an airplane at the age of 12⟩
  synonyms bound, hop, leap, spring, vault
  related words bounce, lope, skip; caper, gambol; attack, pounce; dive, pitch, plunge
  2 the more favorable condition or position in a competition ⟨get a *jump* on the competition by starting early⟩ — see ADVANTAGE 1

jump *vb* **1** to propel oneself upward or forward into the air ⟨*jumped* across the ditch⟩
  synonyms bound, hop, leap, spring, vault
  related words bounce, hurdle, lope, skip; buck; caper, cavort, frolic, gambol, romp; attack, pounce; shoot, skyrocket
  2 to move suddenly and sharply (as in surprise) ⟨the mouse scurrying across the floor made me *jump*⟩ — see START 1

jump (on) *vb* **1** to take sudden, violent action against ⟨the robbers waited until he passed by them and then *jumped on* him⟩ — see ATTACK 1
  2 to criticize harshly and usually publicly ⟨no need to *jump on* him just because he locked the keys in the car⟩ — see ATTACK 2

jumpiness *n* a state of nervousness marked by sudden jerky movements ⟨the police detective interpreted the suspect's *jumpiness* as a sign of guilt⟩
  synonyms edginess, fidgets, flightiness, restiveness, skittishness
  related words agitation, anxiety, anxiousness, apprehension, apprehensiveness, disquiet, feverishness, nervousness, perturbation, uneasiness, upset, worry; nerves, tenseness, tension; dither, jitters, shakes, shivers, willies
  near antonyms confidence, self-assurance, self-confidence, sureness; control, self-control; aplomb, calm, calmness, collectedness, composure, coolheadedness, coolness, ease, easiness, equanimity, imperturbability, self-possession

jumpy *adj* **1** easily excited by nature ⟨a *jumpy* little terrier⟩ — see EXCITABLE
  2 feeling or showing uncomfortable feelings of uncertainty ⟨being alone in the house at night makes me *jumpy*⟩ — see NERVOUS 1

junction *n* **1** a place where two or more things are united ⟨turn left at the *junction* of those two roads⟩ — see JOINT 1
  2 the act or an instance of joining two or more things into one ⟨the *junction* of our two military forces has not been without problems⟩ — see UNION 1

juncture *n* **1** a particular and often important moment in time ⟨at the present *juncture*, I think the country is looking for a strong president⟩ — see POINT 1
  2 a place where two or more things are united ⟨the water is leaking at the *juncture* of those two pipes⟩ — see JOINT 1
  3 a time or state of affairs requiring prompt or decisive action ⟨we have now arrived at a *juncture* where something must be done to avert war⟩ — see EMERGENCY

junior *adj* having not so great importance or rank as another ⟨*junior* advisers to the governor⟩ — see LESSER

junior *n* one who is of lower rank and typically under the authority of another ⟨she's his *junior* in the company⟩ — see UNDERLING

junk *n* discarded or useless material ⟨*junk* on the side of the road waiting for the trash collection⟩ — see GARBAGE

junk *vb* to get rid of as useless or unwanted ⟨will have to *junk* this old car⟩ — see DISCARD

junket *n* a short trip for pleasure ⟨took a *junket* to the city for some sightseeing and shopping⟩ — see EXCURSION 1

junket *vb* to entertain with a fancy meal ⟨a lobbyist who regularly *junkets* politicians who are friendly toward the oil industry⟩ — see FEAST

junkie *also* **junky** *n* a person who regularly uses drugs especially illegally ⟨heroin *junkies* wasting their lives⟩ — see DOPER

junking *n* the getting rid of whatever is unwanted or useless ⟨that old chair needs *junking*⟩ — see DISPOSAL 1

junky *adj* **1** having no usefulness ⟨that broken basket is *junky*⟩ — see WORTHLESS
  2 of low quality ⟨a *junky* coat that is sure to fall apart after one winter⟩ — see CHEAP 2

junto *n* a group of persons formally joined together for some common interest ⟨a secret *junto* planning to overthrow the government⟩ — see ASSOCIATION 2

jurisdiction *n* lawful control over the affairs of a political unit (as a nation) ⟨the United States has no *jurisdiction* over Cuba⟩ — see RULE 2

just *adj* **1** being what is called for by accepted standards of right and wrong ⟨a *just* punishment should fit the crime⟩
  synonyms deserved, due, merited, right, rightful, warranted
  related words applicable, appropriate, apt, fit, fitting, meet, proper, requisite, suitable; lawful, legal; accurate, correct
  near antonyms incoherent, irrelevant; improper, inapplicable, inappropriate, inapt, inequitable; arbitrary, despotic
  antonyms undeserved, undue, unjust, unwarranted
  2 based on sound reasoning or information ⟨there are *just* reasons for the state's ban of the private use of fireworks⟩ — see GOOD 1
  3 conforming to a high standard of morality or virtue ⟨they are a *just* people who are guided by a firm belief in God and a love of traditional values⟩ — see GOOD 2
  4 following the accepted rules of moral conduct ⟨the sort of *just* conduct that we expect of every Scout⟩ — see HONORABLE 1
  5 guided by or in accordance with one's sense of right and wrong ⟨stopping to help a stranded motorist is simply the *just* thing to do⟩ — see CONSCIENTIOUS 1
  6 marked by justice, honesty, and freedom from bias ⟨a *just* decision that benefits everyone⟩ — see FAIR 2

just *adv* **1** in a like manner ⟨you can do it *just* the way they do⟩
  synonyms exactly, precisely
  related words as well, dead, even, expressly, perfectly
  phrases to a T
  near antonyms slightly, somewhat, vaguely
  2 by a very small margin ⟨I was *just* over the minimum height requirement for admittance to the amusement park ride⟩

synonyms barely, hardly, marginally, scarcely, slightly
related words minimally, minutely; approximately, more or less, roughly, somewhat
near antonyms definitely, easily, plainly, positively, quite, unquestionably; abundantly, completely, copiously, generously, greatly
antonyms considerably, significantly, substantially, well

3 nothing more than ⟨I was *just* kidding⟩
synonyms but, merely, only, simply

4 as stated or indicated without the slightest difference ⟨the length of the curtain is *just* right⟩ — see EXACTLY 1

5 for nothing other than ⟨got this present *just* for you⟩ — see SOLELY 1

6 not long ago ⟨I *just* bought this dress⟩ — see NEWLY

justice *n* **1** the act or practice of giving to others what is their due ⟨they felt that *justice* had been done in the case⟩
synonyms equity, right
related words fairness, impartiality; goodness, virtue; honor; decorum
near antonyms bias, partiality, prejudice; corruption, foul play; crime
antonyms inequity, injustice, wrong

2 a public official having authority to decide questions of law ⟨a *justice* of the U.S. Supreme Court⟩ — see JUDGE 2

justifiable *adj* capable of being defended with good reasoning against verbal attack ⟨had *justifiable* reasons for leaving early⟩ — see TENABLE 1

justification *n* an explanation that frees one from fault or blame ⟨offered a weak *justification* for why he had to cheat on the test⟩ — see EXCUSE

justified *adj* based on sound reasoning or information ⟨in a well-*justified* ruling the court voted unanimously to overturn the law⟩ — see GOOD 1

justify *vb* **1** to be an acceptable reason for ⟨you seem to think that losing a basketball game *justifies* a temper tantrum⟩
synonyms excuse
related words account (for), explain, rationalize; brush (aside *or* off), condone, disregard, forgive, gloss (over), ignore, pardon, pass over, remit, shrug off, wink (at)

2 to continue to declare to be true or proper despite opposition or objections ⟨failed to *justify* the need for a war at this time⟩ — see MAINTAIN 2

jut *n* a part that sticks out from the general mass of something ⟨Cape Fear is one of the more colorfully named *juts* along the North Carolina coast⟩ — see BULGE

jut *vb* to extend outward beyond a usual point ⟨the sandbar *juts* out into the ocean⟩ — see BULGE

juvenile *adj* **1** being in the early stage of life, growth, or development ⟨a *juvenile* alligator just hatched from its egg⟩ — see YOUNG

2 having or showing the annoying qualities (as silliness) associated with children ⟨throwing a tantrum is *juvenile* behavior for a person your age⟩ — see CHILDISH

3 lacking in adult experience or maturity ⟨a spoiled, *juvenile* golfer who does not know how to win gracefully⟩ — see CALLOW

juvenile *n* a young person who is between infancy and adulthood ⟨a medical study that followed *juveniles* through adolescence and into adulthood⟩ — see CHILD 1

juxtaposed *adj* having a border in common ⟨the *juxtaposed* photographs of the country's richest and poorest areas are a telling commentary on inequality⟩ — see ADJACENT

K

keelhaul *vb* to criticize (someone) severely or angrily especially for personal failings ⟨no need to *keelhaul* him just because you don't like his hair⟩ — see SCOLD

keen *adj* **1** able to sense slight impressions or differences ⟨pilots with especially *keen* eyesight⟩ — see ²ACUTE 1

2 causing intense discomfort to one's skin ⟨the *keen* wind gave me chapped lips⟩ — see CUTTING 1

3 having an edge thin enough to cut or pierce something ⟨lanced open the boil with a *keen* scalpel⟩ — see SHARP 1

4 having or showing quickness of mind ⟨a *keen* student used to getting nothing but straight A's⟩ — see INTELLIGENT 1

5 of the very best kind ⟨that new skateboard is *keen*⟩ — see EXCELLENT

6 showing urgent desire or interest ⟨a *keen* hunger for fame and fortune⟩ — see EAGER

keen *n* a crying out in grief ⟨the loud *keens* of the widows were heard throughout the city⟩ — see LAMENT 1

keen *vb* to make a long loud mournful sound ⟨mourners *keening* for the victims of the bombing⟩ — see HOWL 1

keenness *n* **1** a harsh or sharp quality ⟨the *keenness* of the ax should tell you that it is not a toy⟩ ⟨that writer was famed for the *keenness* of her wit⟩ — see EDGE 1

2 urgent desire or interest ⟨was looking forward to his gala party with particular *keenness*⟩ — see EAGERNESS

keep *vb* **1** to act properly in relation to ⟨*keep* the Sabbath by not working⟩

synonyms celebrate, commemorate, observe

related words bless, consecrate, sanctify, solemnize; honor, laud, praise; obey, respect, revere, reverence, venerate; remember

phrases live up to

near antonyms disregard, forget, ignore, neglect, overlook

antonyms break, transgress, violate

2 to continue to have in one's possession or power ⟨the money is yours to *keep*⟩ ⟨*keep* my secret and don't tell it to anyone⟩

synonyms hang on (to), hold, reserve, retain, withhold

related words conserve, preserve, save; enjoy, have, own, possess; conduct, control, detain, direct; bear, harbor

near antonyms abandon, cede, yield; contribute, donate, give; discard, dump; decline, reject, repudiate, spurn

antonyms hand over, relinquish, surrender

3 to do what is required by the terms of ⟨make sure you *keep* your promise to help out at the homeless shelter⟩ — see FULFILL 1

4 to place somewhere for safekeeping or ready availability ⟨I *keep* extra toothbrushes for unexpected overnight guests⟩ — see STORE 1

keep (from) *vb* to resist the temptation of ⟨try to *keep from* eating all the chocolate in one day!⟩ — see FORBEAR

keep (to) *vb* to give steadfast support to ⟨always *keeps to* his positions even when they are unpopular⟩ — see ADHERE

keeper *n* **1** a person or group that watches over someone or something ⟨how should I know where she is? I'm not her *keeper*⟩ — see GUARD 1

2 a person who takes care of a property sometimes for an absent owner ⟨during the winter the *keeper* of the family's beach house is a local resident who looks after the place⟩ — see CUSTODIAN 1

keeping *n* **1** responsibility for the safety and well-being of someone or something ⟨put the house keys into a neighbor's secure *keeping* while they were on vacation⟩ — see CUSTODY

2 the fact or state of having (something) at one's disposal ⟨the principal has a bunch of confiscated squirt guns in his *keeping*⟩ — see POSSESSION 1

keepsake *n* something that serves to keep alive the memory of a person or event ⟨bought a *keepsake* of their Niagara Falls trip at the gift shop⟩ — see MEMORIAL

keep up *vb* **1** to continue to operate or to meet one's needs ⟨let's hope the air conditioner *keeps up* through this heat wave⟩ — see HOLD OUT

2 to keep in good condition ⟨*kept* the house *up* while the owners were gone⟩ — see MAINTAIN 1

3 to remain indefinitely in existence or in the same state ⟨let's hope the beautiful weather *keeps up* during our vacation⟩ — see CONTINUE 1

keg *n* an enclosed wooden vessel for holding beverages ⟨a *keg* of beer⟩ — see CASK

kerchief *n* a scarf worn on the head ⟨tied the *kerchief* around her head to keep her hair out of her face⟩ — see BANDANNA

kerf *n* a V-shaped cut usually on an edge or a surface ⟨with a handsaw made a *kerf* in the board to mark where I needed to cut⟩ — see NOTCH 1

key *adj* **1** coming before all others in importance ⟨maintains that Sir Isaac Newton remains the *key* figure in physical science⟩ — see FOREMOST 1

2 of the greatest possible importance ⟨first—and this is *key*—I wasn't even there that evening⟩ — see CRUCIAL

key *n* **1** an explanatory list of the symbols on a map or chart ⟨in order to know what those dotted lines represent, you'll need to look at the *key*⟩ — see LEGEND 1

2 something that allows someone to achieve a desired goal ⟨a good education is the *key* to success⟩ — see PASSPORT

key *vb* to bring to a state free of conflicts, inconsistencies, or differences ⟨her reaction was perfectly *keyed* to the situation⟩ — see HARMONIZE 2

keystone *n* an immaterial thing upon which something else rests ⟨complete honesty is the *keystone* of our friendship⟩ — see BASE 1

kibitzer *n* a person who meddles in the affairs of others ⟨a nosy *kibitzer* who always knows who is dating whom⟩ — see BUSYBODY

kick *n* **1** a pleasurably intense stimulation of the feelings ⟨I get a *kick* out of downhill skiing⟩ — see THRILL

2 a source of great satisfaction ⟨I love that TV show—it's such a *kick*⟩ — see DELIGHT 1

3 a feeling or declaration of disapproval or dissent ⟨nowadays there seem to be few words in the dictionary that do not raise a *kick* from one person or another⟩ — see OBJECTION

kick *vb* **1** to express dissatisfaction, pain, or resentment usually tiresomely ⟨he's been *kicking* all week about not making the varsity team⟩ — see COMPLAIN

2 to present an opposing opinion or argument ⟨students have already started to *kick* about the big increase in homework, claiming that it leaves no time for after-school activities〉 — see OBJECT

kick in *vb* to make a donation as part of a group effort 〈if everyone *kicks in*, we can get our grandparents a nice present〉 — see CONTRIBUTE 1

kick off *vb* to take the first step in (a process or course of action) 〈I'll *kick off* the discussion with this question〉 — see BEGIN 1

kid *n* a young person who is between infancy and adulthood 〈the fire was accidentally started by a couple of *kids* fooling around〉 — see CHILD 1

kid *vb* **1** to make fun of in a good-natured way 〈everybody's *kidding* me about my braces〉 — see TEASE 1
2 to make jokes 〈a group of girls *kidding* and giggling in the corner booth〉 — see JOKE

kidding *adj* marked by or expressive of mild or good-natured teasing 〈made *kidding* remarks about her lack of skills in the kitchen〉 — see QUIZZICAL

kiddish *adj* having or showing the annoying qualities (as silliness) associated with children 〈*kiddish* behavior is not appropriate when the doctor is trying to examine you〉 — see CHILDISH

kidnap *vb* to carry a person away by unlawful force or against his or her will 〈the child was *kidnapped* and held for ransom〉
   synonyms abduct
   related words impress, shanghai, waylay; snatch, spirit
   phrases make away with
   near antonyms deliver, ransom, redeem, rescue; restore, return

kill *vb* **1** to deprive of life 〈the soldier was *killed* in battle〉
   synonyms croak [*slang*], destroy, dispatch, do in, fell, slay
   related words annihilate, blot out, butcher, decimate, massacre, slaughter, wipe out; cut down, finish, nip, snuff; assassinate, execute, murder, smite
   phrases do away with
   near antonyms restore, resurrect, resuscitate, revive; nurture
   antonyms animate
2 to reject by or as if by a vote 〈the senate *killed* the bill〉 — see NEGATIVE 1
3 to show (something written) to be no longer valid by drawing a cross over or a line through it 〈I don't like that paragraph, so *kill* it〉 — see X (OUT)

killer *adj* **1** likely to cause or capable of causing death 〈*killer* viruses that claimed millions of lives〉 — see DEADLY
2 requiring considerable physical or mental effort 〈a *killer* calculus exam that few students expected to pass〉 — see HARD 2

killer *n* a person who kills another person 〈gunned down by hired *killers*〉 — see ASSASSIN

killjoy *n* a person who spoils the pleasure of others 〈his constant negative attitude made him a real *killjoy* when others were trying to have fun〉
   synonyms party pooper, spoilsport
   related words fuddy-duddy, goody-goody, old maid, stick-in-the-mud; defeatist, pessimist; complainer, grouch, sorehead, whiner
   near antonyms cutup, live wire; carouser, celebrant, celebrator, merrymaker, reveler (*or* reveller), roisterer; libertine, playboy, rake

kilter *n* a state of being or fitness 〈since I dropped my CD player, it's been all out of *kilter*〉 — see CONDITION 1

kin *n* **1** a group of persons who come from the same ancestor 〈invited all of his kith and *kin* to his graduation party〉 — see FAMILY 1

2 a person connected with another by blood or marriage 〈since she did not appear to be *kin* to either side, we've no idea what she was doing at the wedding〉 — see RELATIVE

kind *adj* **1** given to or made with heedful anticipation of the needs and happiness of others 〈providing the grieving widow with a homemade meal was a *kind* deed〉 — see THOUGHTFUL 1
2 having or marked by sympathy and consideration for others 〈a *kind* person who volunteers at the homeless shelter〉 — see HUMANE 1

kind *n* **1** a number of persons or things that are grouped together because they have something in common 〈I like that *kind* of candy〉 — see SORT 1
2 one of the units into which a whole is divided on the basis of a common characteristic 〈we looked at just about every *kind* of flooring before deciding which to use in the kitchen〉 — see CLASS 2

kindhearted *adj* having or marked by sympathy and consideration for others 〈*kindhearted* donations to the local animal shelter〉 — see HUMANE 1

kindheartedness *n* the capacity for feeling for another's unhappiness or misfortune 〈your *kindheartedness* is one reason why you're thinking about becoming a medical missionary〉 — see HEART 1

kindle *vb* to set (something) on fire 〈*kindle* some twigs for the campfire〉 — see BURN 2

kindled *adj* being on fire 〈*kindled* straw was responsible for the blaze that destroyed the barn〉 — see ABLAZE 1

kindliness *n* **1** kindly concern, interest, or support 〈has always depended upon the *kindliness* of strangers〉 — see GOODWILL 1
2 the capacity for feeling for another's unhappiness or misfortune 〈as a result of her *kindliness*, several poor families have the makings for a Thanksgiving feast〉 — see HEART 1

kindly *adj* having or marked by sympathy and consideration for others 〈brought homemade chicken soup out of *kindly* concern for my health〉 — see HUMANE 1

kindly *adv* with good reason or courtesy 〈would you *kindly* hand me the scissors〉 — see WELL 4

kindness *n* **1** an act of kind assistance 〈what a *kindness* to allow us to use your car〉 — see FAVOR 1
2 the capacity for feeling for another's unhappiness or misfortune 〈out of the *kindness* of your heart, would you at least consider adopting this stray cat〉 — see HEART 1

kind of *adv* to some degree or extent 〈those sheets are *kind of* new, so use something else to cover the floor while painting〉 — see FAIRLY

kindred *adj* **1** having a close connection like that between family members 〈archaeology and the *kindred* science of anthropology〉 — see RELATED
2 having or marked by agreement in feeling or action 〈finally found people who were *kindred* spirits when she joined the hiking club〉 — see HARMONIOUS 3

kindred *n* a group of persons who come from the same ancestor 〈the kingdom's royal *kindred* actually numbers in the thousands〉 — see FAMILY 1

kinfolk *n pl* a group of persons who come from the same ancestor 〈let's invite all our *kinfolk* for the holidays〉 — see FAMILY 1

king *n* a person of rank, power, or influence in a particular field 〈the *king* of automobile sales for the entire metropolitan area〉 — see MAGNATE

kingdom come *n* a dwelling place of perfect bliss for the soul after death 〈be careful with that thing, or you'll send us all to *kingdom come*〉 — see HEAVEN 1

kingly *adj* fit for or worthy of a royal ruler ⟨a *kingly* gift of 50 million dollars to his old alma mater⟩ — see MONARCHICAL

kingpin *n* the person (as an employer or supervisor) who tells people and especially workers what to do ⟨caught the mob *kingpin* who had been controlling all the gambling rackets⟩ — see BOSS

king–size *or* **king–sized** *adj* **1** unusually large ⟨built a *king-size* mansion with the money he had made in the stock market⟩ — see HUGE
2 of great extent from end to end ⟨the *king-size* snake known as the anaconda⟩ — see LONG 1

king's ransom *n* a very large amount of money ⟨that enormous diamond ring must have cost a *king's ransom*⟩ — see FORTUNE 2

kinky *adj* different from the ordinary in a way that causes curiosity or suspicion ⟨while passing through the airport, don't wear any *kinky* clothing that is likely to pique the interest of security⟩ — see ODD 2

kinsfolk *n pl* a group of persons who come from the same ancestor ⟨my *kinsfolk* all live in the East⟩ — see FAMILY 1

kinship *n* the fact or state of having something in common ⟨she and I have a special *kinship* since we both grew up in England⟩ — see CONNECTION 1

kinsman *n* a person connected with another by blood or marriage ⟨visited my brothers, cousins, and other *kinsmen*⟩ — see RELATIVE

kirk *n, chiefly Scottish* a building for public worship and especially Christian worship ⟨left Edinburgh early in the morning for St. John's *Kirk* in Perth⟩ — see CHURCH 1

kiss *vb* **1** to touch one another with the lips as a sign of love ⟨it's traditional for couples to *kiss* under the mistletoe at Christmastime⟩
synonyms make out, pet, smooch
related words smack; caress, fondle, hug; bill, cuddle, nestle, snuggle
2 to pass lightly across or touch gently especially in passing ⟨a gentle breeze *kissing* the water's surface⟩ — see BRUSH

kisser *n, slang* **1** the front part of the head ⟨angrily threw his unwanted valentine back in his *kisser*⟩ — see FACE 1
2 the opening through which food passes into the body of an animal ⟨how'd you like a punch right in the *kisser*?⟩ — see MOUTH 1

kittenish *adj* affecting shyness or modesty in order to attract masculine interest ⟨the days when young ladies at a dance were supposed to be *kittenish* around young men⟩ — see COY 1

¹kitty *n* a small domestic animal known for catching mice ⟨delighted to receive a stray *kitty* from the pound⟩ — see CAT 1

²kitty *n* a sum of money set aside for a particular purpose ⟨why don't you get us all sodas and just take the money from the party *kitty*⟩ — see FUND 1

knack *n* a special and usually inborn ability ⟨a rap artist with an incredible *knack* for rhymes⟩ — see TALENT

knapsack *n* a soft-sided case designed for carrying belongings especially on the back ⟨grabbed my *knapsack* from the hook and ran to meet the bus⟩ — see PACK 1

knave *n* a mean, evil, or unprincipled person ⟨in the school play he got the part of the *knave* who tries to foil the hero⟩ — see VILLAIN

knavery *n* playful, reckless behavior that is not intended to cause serious harm ⟨quit that *knavery*, or you're going to end up hurting someone⟩ — see MISCHIEF 1

knavish *adj* tending to or exhibiting reckless playfulness ⟨a *knavish* group of kids roughhousing in the yard⟩ — see MISCHIEVOUS 1

knell *vb* to make the clear sound heard when metal vibrates ⟨the church bells *knelled* to mark the death of the nation's beloved leader⟩ — see RING 1

knickknack *n* a small object displayed for its attractiveness or interest ⟨a variety of pretty porcelain *knickknacks* adorned the mantel⟩
synonyms bauble, curio, curiosity, gaud, gewgaw, novelty, ornamental, trinket
related words bric-a-brac, trumpery; trifle; figurine, objet d'art, ornament; souvenir

knife *n* an instrument with a sharp edge for cutting ⟨be careful in using the *knife* to split open the cardboard box⟩
synonyms blade, cutter
related words bayonet, bolo, bowie knife, dagger, dirk, machete, pocketknife, poniard, stiletto, switchblade; saber, steel, sword; scalpel

knob *n* a small uneven mass ⟨toss a *knob* of butter into the frying pan⟩ — see LUMP 1

knock *n* **1** a hard strike with a part of the body or an instrument ⟨gave the door a good *knock*⟩ — see ¹BLOW
2 bad luck or an example of this ⟨the school of hard *knocks*⟩ — see MISFORTUNE

knock *vb* **1** to come into usually forceful contact with something ⟨my knee *knocked* against the table leg⟩ — see HIT 2
2 to deliver a blow to (someone or something) usually in a strong vigorous manner ⟨*knocked* the young man on the shoulder with his cane⟩ — see HIT 1
3 to express one's unfavorable opinion of the worth or quality of ⟨hey, don't *knock* it until you try it⟩ — see CRITICIZE

knock (about) *vb* to move about from place to place aimlessly ⟨we *knocked about* from town to town⟩ — see WANDER

knock (down *or* over) *vb* to strike (someone) so forcefully as to cause a fall ⟨*knocked* me *over* trying to get out the door⟩ — see FELL 1

knockabout *adj* being rough or noisy in a high-spirited way ⟨a *knockabout* game of football in the mud⟩ — see BOISTEROUS

knock down *vb* to take apart ⟨right after the holidays the stores start to *knock down* the window displays⟩ — see DISASSEMBLE

knock off *vb* **1** to bring (as an action or operation) to an immediate end ⟨*knock* it *off*⟩ — see STOP 1
2 to stop doing (something) permanently ⟨decided it was time to *knock off* telling fantastic fibs⟩ — see QUIT 2

knockout *adj* very pleasing to look at ⟨a *knockout* sports car that's the talk of the neighborhood⟩ — see BEAUTIFUL

knockout *n* **1** a lovely woman ⟨the cosmetics company wants a model who's a real *knockout*⟩ — see BEAUTY 2
2 a temporary or permanent state of unconsciousness ⟨a splash of cold water brought the boxer out of his *knockout*⟩ — see FAINT
3 something very good of its kind ⟨the band's new CD is a *knockout*⟩ — see JIM-DANDY

knot *n* **1** a number of things considered as a unit ⟨from the summit we could see *knots* of houses up and down the river⟩ — see GROUP 1
2 a small rounded mass of swollen tissue ⟨felt a small *knot* on the back of his head⟩ — see BUMP 1

3 a uniting or binding force or influence ⟨their business partnership is strengthened by the *knot* of personal friendship⟩ — see BOND 2

4 a usually small number of persons considered as a unit ⟨*knots* of people were quietly chatting around the meeting hall⟩ — see GROUP 2

5 something that requires thought and skill for resolution ⟨mercy killing is generally seen as a matter fraught with legal and medical *knots*⟩ — see PROBLEM 1

knot *vb* to twist together into a usually confused mass ⟨the extension cords were hopelessly *knotted* together⟩ — see ENTANGLE 1

knothead *n* a stupid person ⟨an obnoxious *knothead*⟩ — see IDIOT

knotty *adj* **1** having many parts or aspects that are usually interrelated ⟨the *knotty* problems that arise when every nation is part of the global marketplace⟩ — see COMPLEX 1

2 requiring exceptional skill or caution in performance or handling ⟨the candidates cautiously gave their views on an array of *knotty* issues⟩ — see TRICKY

know *vb* **1** to have a practical understanding of ⟨he *knows* several languages⟩

synonyms comprehend, grasp, understand

related words appreciate, apprehend, fathom, perceive; have, possess

near antonyms misapprehend, misconceive, misinterpret, misunderstand

2 to come to a knowledge of (something) by living through it ⟨a gripping story on orphans who have come to *know* war⟩ — see EXPERIENCE

know–how *n* knowledge gained by actually doing or living through something ⟨you'll gain some practical *know-how* in this auto mechanics class⟩ — see EXPERIENCE 1

knowing *adj* **1** having inside information ⟨exchanged a *knowing* look with her business partner⟩ — see WISE 2

2 having or showing a practical cleverness or judgment ⟨*knowing* movie producers do not invest their own money in their risky ventures⟩ — see SHREWD

knowingly *adv* with full awareness of what one is doing ⟨cannot convict unless the defendant *knowingly* committed perjury⟩ — see INTENTIONALLY

knowledge *n* **1** a body of facts learned by study or experience ⟨the forest ranger shared some of his vast *knowledge* of the woods with us⟩

synonyms lore, science, wisdom

related words information, intelligence, lowdown, news; data, evidence, facts; acquaintance, awareness, familiarity, literacy

near antonyms ignorance, inexperience, unfamiliarity

2 the understanding and information gained from being educated ⟨tests evaluate how much *knowledge* you have gained in a particular subject⟩ — see EDUCATION 2

knowledgeable *adj* **1** having information especially as a result of study or experience ⟨I'm *knowledgeable* about cars⟩ — see FAMILIAR 2

2 having or displaying advanced knowledge or education ⟨*knowledgeable* historians regard that story as pure fiction⟩ ⟨a *knowledgeable* report on the latest advances in cancer research⟩ — see EDUCATED

knuckle under *vb* **1** to cease resistance (as to another's arguments, demands, or control) ⟨encouraged her to stand firm and not *knuckle under* to political pressure⟩ — see YIELD 3

2 to yield to the control or power of enemy forces ⟨the remote outpost was overrun and forced to *knuckle under*⟩ — see FALL 2

kook *n* a person of odd or whimsical habits ⟨if you insist on using that old water can as a hat, everyone will assume you are a *kook*⟩ — see ECCENTRIC

kooky *adj* showing or marked by a lack of good sense or judgment ⟨a *kooky* bicyclist who refuses to wear helmets⟩ ⟨that was a *kooky* thing to do⟩ — see FOOLISH 1

kowtow *vb* to use flattery or the doing of favors in order to win approval especially from a superior ⟨you can try *kowtowing* to the principal, but he'll see right through you⟩ — see FAWN

L

label *n* a slip (as of paper or cloth) that is attached to something to identify or describe it ⟨on its frame the painting had a *label* with its title and the name of the artist⟩

synonyms marker, tag, ticket

related words caption, legend; brand, emblem, logo, mark, symbol; badge, decal, plaque, seal, stamp, sticker

label *vb* **1** to attach an identifying slip to ⟨he *labeled* all of the poisonous materials with the familiar skull and crossbones⟩

synonyms mark, tag, ticket

related words caption, earmark, stamp; call, designate, identify, name, tab; brand, stigmatize

2 to give a name to ⟨teachers had a tendency to *label* the students "slow learners" when in fact they had treatable learning disabilities⟩ — see NAME 1

labor *n* **1** a dull, unpleasant, or difficult piece of work ⟨one of the *labors* of Hercules in classical mythology was to clean out the stables of King Augeas⟩ — see CHORE 2

2 the active use of energy in producing a result ⟨much *labor* went into designing and building the pyramids of Egypt⟩ — see EFFORT

3 very hard or unpleasant work ⟨he was forced to do six months of hard *labor* in the mines as punishment⟩ — see TOIL

4 the act or process of giving birth to children ⟨the mother's *labor* lasted for six hours⟩ — see CHILDBIRTH

labor *vb* to devote serious and sustained effort ⟨he *labored* most of the evening over the difficult homework assignment⟩

synonyms drudge, endeavor, fag, grub, hump, hustle, moil, peg (away), plod, plow, plug, slave, slog, strain, strive, struggle, sweat, toil, travail, work

related words apply (oneself), attempt, buckle (down), hammer (away), pitch in; attack, drive; essay, try; exercise, exert, overexert, overwork; eke out, grind (out), put out, scratch; trudge, wade; employ, ply, use, utilize, wield

near antonyms break, ease (up), let up, slacken; bum, goldbrick, idle, loaf, lounge, shirk, slack (off); dawdle, poke, tarry; relax, rest; disport, frolic, gambol, play, recreate, rollick, romp, sport

antonyms dabble, fiddle (around), fool (around), mess (around), putter (around)

laborer *n* a person who does very hard or dull work ⟨the *laborers* worked all day carrying supplies back and forth to the camp⟩ — see SLAVE 2

laborious *adj* **1** involved in often constant activity ⟨the volunteers have been commendably *laborious* in their cleanup of the playground⟩ — see BUSY 1

2 requiring considerable physical or mental effort ⟨the workers soon wearied of their *laborious* tasks⟩ — see HARD 2

3 requiring much time, effort, or careful attention ⟨the students spent hours researching and writing the *laborious* report⟩ — see DEMANDING 1

laboriously *adv* with great effort or determination ⟨the farmer *laboriously* pruned all season long to produce the finest crop of grapes possible⟩ — see HARD 1

laborsaving *adj* designed to replace or decrease human labor and especially physical labor ⟨a new *laborsaving* device let us clean the house in half the time⟩

synonyms automated, automatic, robotic, self-acting

related words mechanical, motorized; computerized; aiding, helping; easing, relieving; timesaving

labyrinth *n* a confusing and complicated arrangement of passages ⟨we discovered that we were lost in the *labyrinth* of hallways in the museum⟩ — see MAZE

labyrinthine *adj* having many parts or aspects that are usually interrelated ⟨the *labyrinthine* politics of central Europe left us totally befuddled⟩ — see COMPLEX 1

lace *n* **1** a length of braided, flexible material that is used for tying or connecting things ⟨I had to replace the *lace* of my shoe because it kept breaking whenever I pulled the knot too tight⟩ — see CORD

2 a length of something formed of three or more strands woven together ⟨there was gold *lace* decorating both sleeves of the new uniform⟩ — see BRAID

lace *vb* **1** to cause to twine about one another ⟨the gardener *laced* the shoots of ivy around the trellis to direct their growth⟩ — see INTERTWINE 1

2 to scatter or set here and there among other things ⟨the decorator *laced* small mirrors among the knickknacks for added effect⟩ — see THREAD 1

3 to strike repeatedly ⟨energetically *laced* the seaman's back with the cat-o'-nine-tails⟩ — see BEAT 1

laceration *n* a long deep cut ⟨the fall from the bike left him with several *lacerations* from the sharp rocks⟩ — see GASH

lachrymose *adj* given to expressing strong emotion (as sorrow) by readily shedding tears ⟨the *lachrymose* mourners at the funeral required a steady supply of tissues⟩ — see TEARFUL 1

lacing *n* **1** a length of braided, flexible material that is used for tying or connecting things ⟨the soccer player stopped briefly to tighten the *lacing* on his shoes, and was off and running again⟩ — see CORD

2 a length of something formed of three or more strands woven together ⟨the *lacing* on the uniform looks nice⟩ — see BRAID

lack *n* **1** the fact or state of being absent ⟨the *lack* of news about the fate of the soldiers was frustrating⟩

synonyms absence, dearth, want

related words deficiency, deficit, inadequacy, insufficiency, meagerness, paucity, poverty, scantiness, scarceness, scarcity, shortage, skimpiness; deprivation, loss, necessity, need, needfulness, omission; privation; vacuum, void

near antonyms abundance, amplitude, bounty, plenitude, plenty, wealth; adequacy, sufficiency; excess, overabundance, oversupply, surfeit, surplus; deluge, flood; heap, mountain, peck, pile, pot, quantity, raft, stack, volume, wad; fund, pool, stock, supply; hoard, stockpile

antonyms presence

2 a falling short of an essential or desirable amount or number ⟨the *lack* of eligible candidates for the jury kept the trial from getting started⟩ — see DEFICIENCY

3 a state of being without something necessary, desirable, or useful ⟨the *lack* of fresh water at the campsite was a problem, but fortunately we had thought to bring enough bottled water from home⟩ — see NEED 1

lackadaisical *adj* lacking bodily energy or motivation ⟨the *lackadaisical* children lazily tossed a ball back and forth⟩ — see LISTLESS

lackey *n* a person hired to perform household or personal services ⟨the office manager sent her *lackey* to fetch some more coffee⟩ — see SERVANT

lacking *adj* **1** not coming up to a usual standard or meeting a particular need ⟨we felt the afternoon television offerings were somewhat *lacking* in entertainment value⟩ — see SHORT 3

2 not present or in evidence ⟨for the moment anyway, wood for the fireplace is *lacking*⟩ — see ABSENT 2

laconic *adj* **1** marked by the use of few words to convey much information or meaning ⟨the sportscaster's color commentary tends to be *laconic* but very much to the point⟩ — see CONCISE

2 tending not to speak frequently (as by habit or inclination) ⟨the *laconic* man found the monastery's vow of silence was very much to his liking⟩ — see SILENT 2

laconically *adv* in a few words ⟨she answered the prosecutor's questions *laconically* and had to be coaxed into giving more details⟩ — see SHORTLY 1

lad *n* **1** a male person who has not yet reached adulthood ⟨George Washington supposedly cut down a cherry tree when he was just a *lad*⟩ — see BOY

2 an adult male human being ⟨pass me another beer—will you, *lad*?⟩ — see MAN 1

ladder *n* a scheme of rank or order ⟨their team placed third on the tournament *ladder*⟩ — see ³SCALE 1

laddie *n* a male person who has not yet reached adulthood ⟨not all the *laddies* in Scotland wear kilts, you know!⟩ — see BOY

lade *vb* **1** to lift out with something that holds liquid ⟨the cook *laded* the stew into small bowls⟩ — see DIP 2

2 to place a weight or burden on ⟨the trucks were heavily *laden* with cargo for the market⟩ — see LOAD 1

lading *n* a mass or quantity of something taken up and carried, conveyed, or transported ⟨a bill of *lading* is a document issued by a carrier that lists goods being shipped and specifies the terms of their transport⟩ — see LOAD 1

ladle *n* a utensil with a bowl and a handle that is used especially in cooking and serving food ⟨the chef hunted for a *ladle* to add the chicken broth to the pot⟩ — see SPOON

ladle *vb* to lift out with something that holds liquid ⟨the server *ladled* out the soup from a large tureen⟩ — see DIP 2

lady *n* **1** an adult female human being ⟨"*ladies* and gentlemen, please observe closely," said the magician⟩ — see WOMAN

2 the female partner in a marriage ⟨the husband was frequently seen holding hands with his *lady* in the grocery store⟩ — see WIFE

3 a woman of high birth or social position ⟨the *ladies* of the royal court were all dressed extravagantly⟩ — see GENTLEWOMAN

ladylove *n* a woman with whom one is in love ⟨He bought an enormous bouquet of flowers for his *ladylove*⟩ — see GIRLFRIEND

lag *vb* **1** to lose bodily strength or vigor ⟨in the fourth quarter the whole team seemed to *lag*⟩ — see WEAKEN 2

2 to move or act slowly ⟨the tired puppy was *lagging* behind the pack⟩ — see DELAY 1

laggard *adj* moving or proceeding at less than the normal, desirable, or required speed ⟨I hate having to honk my horn at *laggard* motorists on the freeway⟩ — see SLOW 1

laggard *n* someone who moves slowly or more slowly than others ⟨the camp counselor tried to encourage the *laggards* at the back of the line during the hike⟩ — see SLOWPOKE

laggardly *adv* at a pace that is less than usual, desirable, or expected ⟨some students *laggardly* wandered in to class, obviously dreading the upcoming quiz⟩ — see SLOW

lagger *n* someone who moves slowly or more slowly than others ⟨after ten hours, there wasn't anyone left to cheer the *laggers* as they finished the marathon⟩ — see SLOWPOKE

lagging *adj* moving or proceeding at less than the normal, desirable, or required speed ⟨the *lagging* pace of work on the project was worrisome⟩ — see SLOW

lagniappe *n* **1** something given in addition to what is ordinarily expected or owed ⟨the meal was served with a *lagniappe* of freshly made cornbread⟩ — see BONUS

2 something given to someone without expectation of a return ⟨the hotel threw in some free shampoo as a *lagniappe*⟩ — see GIFT 1

laid–back *adj* having a relaxed, casual manner ⟨the *laid-back* fisherman didn't really care if he caught anything, as long as he was able to relax and enjoy the sunshine⟩ — see EASYGOING 1

lair *n* **1** a place where a person goes to hide ⟨the detectives tracked the thieves to their *lair* and made immediate arrests⟩ — see HIDEOUT

2 the shelter or resting place of a wild animal ⟨we found an abandoned fox's *lair* in the woods behind the barn⟩ — see DEN 1

lam *n* the act or an instance of getting free from danger or confinement ⟨the prisoners were recaptured after only three days on the *lam*⟩ — see ESCAPE 1

lam *vb* to get free from a dangerous or confining situation ⟨we had to *lam* out from our old hiding spot so that the enemy wouldn't find us⟩ — see ESCAPE 1

lamb *n* an innocent or gentle person ⟨the new guys at football camp were *lambs* who hardly knew what awaited them⟩

synonyms angel, dove, innocent, sheep

related words fledgling, greenhorn, ingenue (*or* ingénue); cherub, saint; mollycoddle, sissy, softy (*or* softie), weakling, wimp; dupe, pigeon, sap, sucker

near antonyms bully, roughneck, rowdy, tough; beast, boor, cad, churl, clown, creep, cretin, cur, heel, jerk; shark, skunk, snake, stinker; rascal, rogue, scamp, villain

antonyms wolf

lambaste *or* **lambast** *vb* **1** to criticize (someone) severely or angrily especially for personal failings ⟨the director *lambasted* them for forgetting their lines during the final dress rehearsal⟩ — see SCOLD

2 to criticize harshly and usually publicly ⟨critics across the country *lambasted* the new film for its uncalled-for violence⟩ — see ATTACK 2

3 to strike repeatedly ⟨stern schoolmasters who *lambasted* the boys for the smallest violation of the rules⟩ — see BEAT 1

lambent *adj* giving off or reflecting much light ⟨the *lambent* flames from our campfire cast a comforting glow⟩ — see BRIGHT 1

lame *vb* to cause severe or permanent injury to ⟨we were afraid that the horse would be *lamed* from its horrible fall⟩ — see MAIM

lamella *n* a small thin piece of material that resembles an animal scale ⟨the gemstone's distinctive iridescence is caused by light passing from one *lamella* of crystal to another⟩ — see ²SCALE

lament *n* **1** a crying out in grief ⟨the national *lament* that was heard when President Kennedy was assassinated⟩
synonyms groan, howl, keen, lamentation, moan, plaint, wail
related words grieving, mourning, weeping; regret; complaint, outcry, protest
near antonyms cheering, laughing, smiling
antonyms exultation, rejoicing
2 a composition expressing one's grief over a loss ⟨a poem that is her *lament* for her late grandmother⟩
synonyms dirge, elegy, requiem, threnody
related words taps
near antonyms encomium, eulogy, paean, panegyric
lament *vb* **1** to feel or express sorrow for ⟨she *lamented* the loss of her beloved pet⟩
synonyms bemoan, bewail, deplore, grieve (for), mourn, wail (for)
related words elegize; complain (about), cry (for), groan (about), keen, moan, weep; regret, rue; deprecate, disapprove (of)
near antonyms beam, cheer, laugh, smile; boast, brag, crow
antonyms exult (in), glory (in), rejoice (in)
2 to feel sorry or dissatisfied about ⟨he *lamented* not having spent more time with his late grandfather⟩ — see REGRET
lamentable *adj* **1** expressing or suggesting mourning ⟨the *lamentable* cries of the women for their slain sons lasted until dawn⟩ — see MOURNFUL 1
2 of a kind to cause great distress ⟨it's a *lamentable* situation, but I don't see how it can be fixed⟩ — see REGRETTABLE
lamentation *n* a crying out in grief ⟨there was a great *lamentation* on Wall Street when the government's unemployment figures were published⟩ — see LAMENT 1
lamina *n* a small thin piece of material that resembles an animal scale ⟨each *lamina* of stratified rock was deposited separately, building upwards as time passed⟩ — see ²SCALE
lamp *n* something that provides illumination ⟨I didn't realize it had gotten so dark in the room until my mom came in and turned on the *lamp*, momentarily blinding me⟩ — see LIGHT 2
lampoon *n* a creative work that uses sharp humor to point up the foolishness of a person, institution, or human nature in general ⟨this classic musical is a *lampoon* of the movie business when sound was introduced⟩ — see SATIRE
lance *n* a weapon with a long straight handle and sharp head or blade ⟨the *lance* struck squarely on the knight's shield, knocking him from his horse⟩ — see SPEAR
lance *vb* to penetrate or hold (something) with a pointed object ⟨doctors used to *lance* infected sores, so that they could drain clean⟩ — see IMPALE
land *n* **1** a body of people composed of one or more nationalities usually with its own territory and government ⟨the whole *land* rose up in outrage over the tyrant's unconscionable cruelties⟩ — see NATION
2 a broad geographical area ⟨the *land* to the west was said to have incredibly rich soil and plentiful water⟩ — see REGION 2
3 the solid part of our planet's surface as distinguished from the sea and air ⟨it's always good to be back on dry *land* after a long boat ride⟩ — see EARTH 2
land *vb* **1** to stop at or near a place along the shore ⟨the Pilgrims *landed* at Plymouth after exploring Cape Cod Bay⟩
synonyms anchor, dock
related words moor, tie up; beach, ground; harbor; arrive, reach; debark, disembark
phrases drop anchor, make port
near antonyms embark, launch, sail
2 to get to a destination ⟨we *landed* at the hotel just before midnight⟩ — see COME 2
3 to go ashore from a ship ⟨the passengers on the cruise *landed* at St. George in Bermuda⟩ — see DISEMBARK
4 to come to rest after descending from the air ⟨our plane is *landing* in 15 minutes, so we need to put all of our things away⟩ — see ALIGHT
5 to receive as return for effort ⟨because of his work on the boss's pet project, he *landed* a promotion as well as a raise⟩ — see EARN 1
6 to take physical control or possession of (something) suddenly or forcibly ⟨after struggling for half an hour, the fisherman finally *landed* a ten-pound bass⟩ — see CATCH 1
landfill *n* a place where discarded materials (as trash) are dumped ⟨we took all of our old, broken furniture to the *landfill*⟩ — see DUMP 1
landing *n* a structure used by boats and ships for taking on or landing cargo and passengers ⟨our families waved good-bye to us from the *landing* as we left on our honeymoon cruise⟩ — see DOCK
landlord *n* the owner of land or housing that is rented to another ⟨agreed to pay the *landlord* the rent on the first Monday of each month⟩
synonyms lessor, renter
related words landlady; laird, landholder, landowner; host, proprietor; slumlord
antonyms lessee, lodger, tenant
landmark *n* a point in a chain of events at which an important change (as in one's fortunes) occurs ⟨some people feel that turning 21 is a *landmark* in one's life⟩ — see TURNING POINT
language *n* **1** the stock of words, pronunciation, and grammar used by a people as their basic means of communication ⟨Great Britain, the United States, Australia, and other countries where English is the dominant *language*⟩
synonyms lingo, mother tongue, speech, tongue, vocabulary
related words argot, cant, dialect, idiom, jargon, parlance, patois, patter, pidgin, slang, vernacular; colloquialism, localism, regionalism; terminology
2 the special terms or expressions of a particular group or field ⟨"love" means "nothing" in the *language* of tennis⟩ — see TERMINOLOGY
3 the way in which something is put into words ⟨finding the *language* of the legal documents to be difficult to understand⟩ — see WORDING
languid *adj* **1** lacking bodily energy or motivation ⟨a few *languid* dancers swayed about on the dance floor without much enthusiasm⟩ — see LISTLESS
2 lacking bodily strength ⟨the tired athlete's *languid* movements on the tennis court⟩ — see WEAK 1
3 moving or proceeding at less than the normal, desirable, or required speed ⟨the ballerina proceeded in slow, *languid* steps across the stage⟩ — see SLOW 1
languish *vb* to lose bodily strength or vigor ⟨older people, especially, were *languishing* during the prolonged heat wave⟩ — see WEAKEN 2
languishing *adj* lacking bodily energy or motivation ⟨his lingering sickness left him *languishing* and uninterested in his usual activities⟩ — see LISTLESS

languor *n* the quality or state of lacking physical strength or vigor ⟨the tropical heat sapped our strength, leaving us in a state of unaccustomed *languor*⟩ — see WEAKNESS 1

languorous *adj* lacking bodily energy or motivation ⟨the drummer's *languorous* playing caused the rest of the band to keep missing the beat⟩ — see LISTLESS

lank *adj* not stiff in structure ⟨right after a shower, her *lank* hair hung down to her shoulders⟩ — see LIMP 1

lanky *adj* being tall, thin and usually loose-jointed ⟨the *lanky* basketball star was great at slam-dunking⟩
synonyms gangling, gangly, rangy, spindling, spindly
related words angular, bony, gaunt, lank, rawboned, scrawny, skinny; lean, slender, slim, spare, thin; racy, reedy, spidery, stringy, twiggy, wiry; spindle-shanked
near antonyms chubby, chunky, heavyset, pudgy, squat, stocky, stout, stubby, stumpy, sturdy, thick-bodied, thickset; muscle-bound

lap *n* a portion of a trip ⟨we were on the last *lap* of the journey, eagerly heading for home⟩ — see LEG 2

¹lap *vb* **1** to flow along or against ⟨the waves gently *lapped* the shore⟩ — see WASH 1
2 to flow in a broken irregular stream ⟨the creek *lapped* along through the ravine before collecting in the pond⟩ — see GURGLE
3 to move with a splashing motion ⟨a stiff breeze that was causing the lake waters to *lap* against the hull with some force⟩ — see SLOSH

²lap *vb* **1** to lie over parts of one another ⟨the armadillo's plates *lap* tightly so as to form a protective shield⟩ — see OVERLAP
2 to surround or cover closely ⟨this recording of the symphony is sure to *lap* the listeners in stereophonic bliss⟩ — see ENFOLD 1

lapping *n* a partial covering of one thing by an adjoining thing ⟨the *lapping* of the roofing shingles should be several inches in order to avoid leaks⟩ — see OVERLAP

lapse *n* **1** a change in status for the worse usually temporarily ⟨the scandal caused the president to suffer a *lapse* in popularity⟩ — see REVERSE 1
2 an unintentional departure from truth or accuracy ⟨his slip of the tongue about the mayor's name was an unfortunate *lapse*⟩ — see ERROR 1
3 the stopping of a process or activity ⟨wasn't bothered by the *lapse* of her membership at the health club⟩ — see END 1

lapse *vb* to come to an end ⟨the contract will *lapse* at the end of the year unless we renew⟩ — see CEASE 1

larceny *n* the unlawful taking and carrying away of property without the consent of its owner ⟨breaking into someone's house and taking their stereo is an act of *larceny*⟩ — see THEFT 1

large *adj* of a size greater than average of its kind ⟨he was hungry, so he ordered the *large* pizza⟩
synonyms big, bulky, considerable, goodly, good-sized, grand, great, handsome, hefty, hulking, largish, outsize (*also* outsized), oversize (*or* oversized), sizable (*or* sizeable), substantial, tidy, voluminous
related words astronomical (*also* astronomic), bumper, cavernous, colossal, enormous, gigantic, gross, heroic, huge, immense, jumbo, king-size (*or* king-sized), major, mammoth, massive, monolithic, monstrous, monumental, prodigious, staggering, stupendous, super, tremendous, vast, vasty, whacking, whopping; excessive, exorbitant, extravagant, extreme, immoderate, inordinate; abundant, ample, appreciable, copious, plentiful; fat, thick; capacious, commodious, roomy, spacious

near antonyms diminutive, microscopic (*or* microscopical), midget, miniature, minute, pint-size (*or* pint-sized), pocket-size (*also* pocket-sized), pygmy, smallish, teeny, teeny-weeny, tiny, wee; petite, slender, slight, slim, thin
antonyms little, puny, small, undersized

largely *adv* **1** for the most part ⟨the earth's surface is *largely* composed of water⟩ — see CHIEFLY
2 to a large extent or degree ⟨with this land purchase, the corporation *largely* increases its holdings in the area⟩ — see GREATLY 2

largeness *n* the quality or state of being large in size ⟨I was impressed by the *largeness* of the portions at the new restaurant⟩
synonyms bigness, bulkiness, grandness, greatness, heftiness, substantiality, voluminousness
related words enormity, enormousness, extensiveness, grossness, healthiness, hugeness, immenseness, immensity, magnitude, massiveness, stupendousness, vastness; excessiveness, extravagance, extremeness, immoderacy; abundance, ampleness, bountifulness, copiousness, liberality; adequacy, sufficiency; weightiness
near antonyms diminutiveness, minuteness, tininess; slightness; meagerness, poorness, scantiness, scarceness, scarcity, skimpiness, slenderness, slimness, spareness, sparseness, stinginess; deficiency, inadequacy
antonyms fineness, littleness, puniness, smallness

largess *or* **largesse** *n* **1** something given to someone without expectation of a return ⟨the alumna's huge bequest was an unexpected *largess*⟩ — see GIFT 1
2 the quality or state of being generous ⟨the philanthropist was known for his *largess* to all of the city's cultural institutions⟩ — see LIBERALITY

largish *adj* **1** of a size greater than average of its kind ⟨she was hungry, so she took a somewhat *largish* portion of food from the buffet⟩ — see LARGE
2 sufficiently large in size, amount, or number to merit attention ⟨a *largish* amount of attention was paid to the politician's latest speech⟩ — see CONSIDERABLE 1

lariat *n* a rope or long leather thong with a noose used especially for catching livestock ⟨the cowboy could throw a *lariat* around a running steer's head from 20 yards away⟩ — see LASSO

lark *n* a time or instance of carefree fun ⟨the kids had a grand *lark* at the carnival⟩ — see FLING 1

lark *vb* to play and run about happily ⟨we preferred to *lark* about in the summer rather than get part-time jobs⟩ — see FROLIC 1

larva *n* a young wingless often wormlike form (as a grub or caterpillar) that hatches from the egg of many insects ⟨the *larva* looked ugly, but it was destined to hatch into a beautiful butterfly⟩
synonyms naiad, nymph

lascivious *adj* **1** depicting or referring to sexual matters in a way that is unacceptable in polite society ⟨the author's *lascivious* comments were enough to cause the editors of the magazine to reject the article⟩ — see OBSCENE 1
2 having a strong sexual desire ⟨all of the debutantes were warned about the *lascivious* playboy⟩ — see LUSTFUL

lasciviousness *n* the quality or state of being obscene ⟨the minister preached a sermon against the *lasciviousness* of much of popular culture⟩ — see OBSCENITY 1

lash *n* a long thin or flexible tool for striking ⟨the rider repeatedly struck the horse with the *lash* to force it to go faster⟩ — see WHIP

lash *vb* to strike repeatedly with something long and thin or flexible ⟨the cat's tail *lashed* the table leg⟩ — see WHIP 1

lass *n* a young usually unmarried woman ⟨she's only a gawky *lass* now, but she'll be a beautiful woman some day⟩ — see GIRL 1

lassie *n* a young usually unmarried woman ⟨a pretty young *lassie* of sixteen years⟩ — see GIRL 1

lassitude *n* a complete depletion of energy or strength ⟨our *lassitude* was such that we couldn't even be bothered to get more soda from the fridge⟩ — see FATIGUE

lasso *n* a rope or long leather thong with a noose used especially for catching livestock ⟨the cowpuncher skillfully tossed the *lasso* around the calf's neck⟩
synonyms lariat, reata, riata

last *adj* following all others of the same kind in order or time ⟨*last* one in the pool is a rotten egg⟩
synonyms closing, concluding, final, hindmost, latest, latter, rearmost, terminal, terminating, ultimate
related words consequent, ensuing, eventual, following, succeeding; conclusive, crowning, decisive, definitive; farthest, furthest, remotest; lowermost, lowest, nethermost; endmost, extreme, outermost, outmost; penultimate
near antonyms eminent, premier, superior
antonyms beginning, earliest, first, inaugural, initial, maiden, opening, original, primary, starting

last *vb* **1** to continue to operate or to meet one's needs ⟨we were lucky that the batteries *lasted* until we could get to the store to buy more⟩ — see HOLD OUT
2 to remain indefinitely in existence or in the same state ⟨this heavy drought has *lasted* all summer⟩ — see CONTINUE 1

last word *n* a practice or interest that is very popular for a short time ⟨an outfit that is the *last word* in sportswear⟩ — see FAD

late *adj* **1** not arriving, occurring, or settled at the due, usual, or proper time ⟨I ran as fast as I could, but was still *late* for class⟩
synonyms behind, behindhand, belated, delinquent, latish, overdue, tardy
related words delayed, detained, postponed; dilatory, laggard, slow, sluggish
near antonyms opportune, seasonable, timely; prompt, punctual
antonyms early, premature
2 having been such at some previous time ⟨the *late* councilman said he would never have allowed such behavior while he was in charge⟩ — see FORMER
3 no longer living ⟨our *late* granduncle remembered us in his will⟩ — see DEAD 1

late *adv* not long ago ⟨the actress, *late* of New York but now of Los Angeles, is being eagerly sought for film roles⟩ — see NEWLY

lately *adv* not long ago ⟨have you been listening to the radio much *lately*?⟩ — see NEWLY

latency *n* a state of temporary inactivity ⟨the flower bulbs went from *latency* to full bloom in a matter of days⟩ — see ABEYANCE

lateness *n* the quality or state of being late ⟨we were unable to get into the movie due to our *lateness* in arriving⟩
synonyms belatedness, delinquency, tardiness
related words dilatoriness, sluggishness
near antonyms promptness, punctuality
antonyms earliness

latent *adj* not being in a state of use, activity, or employment ⟨he has a *latent* talent for acting that he hasn't had a chance to express yet⟩ — see INACTIVE 2

later *adj* being, occurring, or carried out at a time after something else ⟨the details of the plan will be filled in at a *later* date⟩ — see SUBSEQUENT

later *adv* following in time or place ⟨we're going to go to the mall *later* on, but first we have to finish our homework⟩ — see AFTER

lateral *adj* of, relating to, or located on one side ⟨the surgeon made a *lateral* incision above the inflamed appendix⟩ — see SIDE

latest *adj* following all others of the same kind in order or time ⟨the *latest* news reveals many details we didn't know before⟩ — see LAST

lather *n* **1** a light mass of fine bubbles formed in or on a liquid ⟨she worked the shampoo into a *lather* before rubbing it into her pet dog's coat⟩ — see FOAM
2 a state of nervous or irritated concern ⟨he worked himself into a *lather* waiting for the results of the test⟩ — see FRET

lathery *adj* covered with, consisting of, or resembling foam ⟨the *lathery* crests of the waves washed up and down the sandy beach⟩ — see FOAMY

latish *adj* not arriving, occurring, or settled at the due, usual, or proper time ⟨the school bus was often a little *latish*, but never more than by a few minutes⟩ — see LATE 1

latitude *n* the right to act or move freely ⟨the new laws gave the police more *latitude* in dealing with suspected criminals⟩ — see FREEDOM 2

latrine *n* a room furnished with a fixture for flushing body waste ⟨where's the nearest *latrine*, soldier?⟩ — see TOILET

latter *adj* following all others of the same kind in order or time ⟨the multiplex was showing a comedy and a horror film, and we thought that the *latter* would be more fun to watch⟩ — see LAST

laud *vb* **1** to declare enthusiastic approval of ⟨the critics *lauded* the new book by the best-selling author⟩ — see ACCLAIM
2 to proclaim the glory of ⟨the oppressed people were expected to *laud* the dictator at every opportunity⟩ — see PRAISE 1

laudable *adj* deserving of high regard or great approval ⟨his actions in rescuing the kitten were highly *laudable*⟩ — see ADMIRABLE

laugh *n* **1** an explosive sound that is a sign of amusement ⟨the child's frown turned into a *laugh* when he saw the clown⟩
synonyms cackle, chortle, chuckle, giggle, guffaw, laughter, snicker, snigger, titter
related words crow, whoop; grin, simper, smile, smirk
near antonyms cry, groan, moan, sob, wail
2 someone or something that is very funny ⟨that new sitcom is a *laugh*⟩ — see SCREAM
3 something said or done to cause laughter ⟨the film comedy had a good *laugh* in just about every scene⟩ — see JOKE 1

laugh *vb* to express scornful amusement by means of facial contortions ⟨you're going to try out for the football team? Don't make me *laugh*!⟩ — see SNEER

laugh (at) *vb* to make (someone or something) the object of unkind laughter ⟨the mean kids all *laughed at* Tommy when he ripped his shirt in gym class⟩ — see RIDICULE

laughable *adj* **1** causing or intended to cause laughter ⟨the *laughable*, boisterous antics of the circus clowns⟩ — see FUNNY 1

2 so foolish or pointless as to be worthy of scornful laughter ⟨the student's *laughable* mistakes on the chalkboard caused quite a few chuckles in the back of the classroom⟩ — see RIDICULOUS 1

laughing *adj* indicative of or marked by high spirits or good humor ⟨the satisfying comedy put us in a *laughing* mood for the rest of the evening⟩ — see MERRY

laughingstock *n* a person or thing that is made fun of ⟨his nerdy clothes made him the *laughingstock* of the schoolyard⟩
synonyms butt, mark, mock, mockery, target
related words chump, dupe, fall guy, fool, gull, monkey, pigeon, sap, sucker, victim
near antonyms favorite, darling, pet

laughter *n* an explosive sound that is a sign of amusement ⟨the nervous producers were reassured by the sounds of *laughter* coming from the theater⟩ — see LAUGH 1

launch *n* **1** a rising from a surface at the start of a flight (as of a rocket) ⟨the reporters all held their breath as they watched the space shuttle's *launch*⟩ — see LIFT-OFF

2 the point at which something begins ⟨we are at the *launch* of a new age of space exploration⟩ — see BEGINNING

launch *vb* **1** to be responsible for the creation and early operation or use of ⟨after retiring, he *launched* a small company devoted to making medical devices⟩ — see FOUND

2 to take the first step in (a process or course of action) ⟨she *launched* a career in journalism after quitting acting school⟩ — see BEGIN 1

3 to send through the air especially with a quick forward motion of the arm ⟨soldiers *launching* grenades at the nest of machine gunners⟩ — see THROW

laurels *n pl* public acknowledgment or admiration for an achievement ⟨the medics received many *laurels* for their heroic actions during the disaster⟩ — see GLORY 1

lavaliere *also* **lavalliere** *n* an ornament worn on a chain around the neck or wrist ⟨gave his girlfriend a golden *lavaliere* engraved with his name⟩ — see PENDANT

lavatory *n* a room furnished with a fixture for flushing body waste ⟨the teacher allowed each student a five-minute break during the test for use of the *lavatory*⟩ — see TOILET

lave *vb* to flow along or against ⟨the cold water from the stream gently *laved* her burned fingers⟩ — see WASH 1

lavish *adj* **1** going beyond a normal or acceptable limit in degree or amount ⟨big-spending guests are provided with a *lavish* free meal by the gambling resort⟩ — see EXCESSIVE

2 pouring forth in great amounts ⟨the spring provided *lavish* amounts of water to the village⟩ — see PROFUSE

3 showing obvious signs of wealth and comfort ⟨the *lavish* apartment even boasted a marble bathroom with gold-plated fixtures⟩ — see LUXURIOUS

lavish *vb* **1** to give readily and in large quantities ⟨doting parents *lavishing* lots of attention on their children⟩ — see RAIN 2

2 to use up carelessly ⟨a great actor who *lavished* his talent in lousy movies⟩ — see WASTE 1

lavishly *adv* in a luxurious manner ⟨Hollywood celebrities are known for living *lavishly*⟩ — see HIGH

lavishness *n* the quality or fact of being free or wasteful in the expenditure of money ⟨the lottery winner's friends were struck by the *lavishness* of his new lifestyle⟩ — see EXTRAVAGANCE 1

law *n* **1** a rule of conduct or action laid down by a governing authority and especially a legislator ⟨a record number of *laws* were passed in that legislative session⟩
synonyms act, enactment, ordinance, statute
related words decree, directive, edict, fiat, ruling; bylaw, regulation, rule; amendment, bill, legislation; common law, martial law; prohibition, restriction; canon, encyclical

2 a collection or system of rules of conduct ⟨it's important to obey the *law* at all times, or else you might end up in jail⟩ — see CODE

3 the department of government that keeps order, fights crime, and enforces statutes ⟨a petty thief who had somehow managed to avoid the *law* for most of his life⟩ — see POLICE 1

law-abiding *adj* readily giving in to the command or authority of another ⟨the *law-abiding* citizens of the neighborhood did everything they could to help reduce street crime⟩ — see OBEDIENT

lawbreaker *n* a person who has committed a crime ⟨the chronic *lawbreaker* was sentenced to jail by the judge for his crimes⟩ — see CRIMINAL

lawbreaking *adj* not restrained by or under the control of legal authority ⟨some sociologists specialize in studying the *lawbreaking* elements of society⟩ — see LAWLESS

lawbreaking *n* **1** a breaking of a moral or legal code ⟨even something as simple as littering is considered an example of *lawbreaking*⟩ — see OFFENSE 1

2 activities that are in violation of the laws of the state ⟨an outbreak of *lawbreaking* plagued the city in the months following the end of the war⟩ — see CRIME 1

lawful *adj* permitted by law ⟨hunting is a *lawful* activity if you have the proper license⟩ — see LEGAL 1

lawfulness *n* the quality or state of being legal ⟨the lawyers had to work for weeks to determine the *lawfulness* of the proposed contract⟩ — see LEGALITY

lawgiver *n* a member of an organized body of persons having the authority to make laws ⟨political activists lobbied the state's *lawgivers* to expand the scope of the civil rights legislation⟩ — see LEGISLATOR

lawless *adj* not restrained by or under the control of legal authority ⟨the *lawless* rioters were destroying everything in sight⟩
synonyms anarchic, disorderly, lawbreaking, unruly
related words defiant, insubordinate, mutinous, rebellious, refractory, riotous; undisciplined; criminal, illegal, illegitimate, illicit, unlawful, wrongful
near antonyms lawful, legal, legalized, legitimate
antonyms law-abiding, orderly

lawlessness *n* **1** a state in which there is widespread wrongdoing and disregard for rules and authority ⟨the frontier was known for its *lawlessness*⟩ — see ANARCHY

2 activities that are in violation of the laws of the state ⟨the teenagers' *lawlessness* quickly attracted the attention of the police⟩ — see CRIME 1

lawmaker *n* a member of an organized body of persons having the authority to make laws ⟨the *lawmakers* worked long into the night drafting a bill that would be acceptable to everyone⟩ — see LEGISLATOR

lawsuit *n* a court case for enforcing a right or claim ⟨she filed a *lawsuit* against the moving company that was responsible for breaking her furniture⟩

synonyms action, proceeding, suit
related words litigation; case, cause, complaint

lawyer *n* a person whose profession is to conduct lawsuits for clients or to advise about legal rights and obligations ⟨their *lawyers* told them that they couldn't use the park for the concert without permission from the city⟩
synonyms advocate, attorney, counsel, counselor (*or* counsellor)
related words pettifogger, shyster; district attorney, prosecutor; solicitor; jurist; lawgiver, lawmaker, legislator, solon

lax *adj* **1** failing to give proper care and attention ⟨*lax* parents who let their kids stay out as late as they want⟩ — see NEGLIGENT
2 not bound by rigid standards ⟨the guidelines for the essay contest were fairly *lax*, permitting a wide variety of topics⟩ — see EASYGOING 2
3 not tightly fastened, tied, or stretched ⟨the sheet on the foresail was *lax*, and so the sail was flapping wildly in the stiff wind⟩ — see LOOSE 1

laxness *n* failure to take the care that a cautious person usually takes ⟨the mountain climber's uncharacteristic *laxness* almost caused an accident⟩ — see NEGLIGENCE 1

lay *n* **1** a rhythmic series of musical tones arranged to give a pleasing effect ⟨the minstrel strummed a cheerful *lay* on his lute⟩ — see MELODY
2 a short musical composition for the human voice often with instrumental accompaniment ⟨she sang a short *lay* dedicated to her husband⟩ — see SONG 1

lay *vb* **1** to arrange something in a certain spot or position ⟨just *lay* the book over there on the table for now⟩ — see PLACE 1
2 to cause to come to rest at the bottom (as of a liquid) ⟨the rain was just hard enough to *lay* the dust in the air⟩ — see SETTLE 1
3 to establish or apply as a charge or penalty ⟨the officials tried to *lay* a tax on merchandise sold over the Internet⟩ — see IMPOSE
4 to make ready in advance ⟨she's *laying* plans for the prom months ahead of time⟩ — see PREPARE 1
5 to put a layer of on a surface ⟨the worker *laid* mortar over the first row of bricks before starting the second⟩ — see SPREAD 2
6 to risk (something) on the outcome of an uncertain event ⟨I'll *lay* five dollars that you can't do it⟩ — see BET

lay away *vb* to put (something of future use or value) in a safe or secret place ⟨the weather forecast warned of a severe storm, so my family *laid away* several bottles of water and cans of food just in case⟩ — see HOARD

lay down *vb* **1** to put into effect through legislative or authoritative action ⟨the city council promises to *lay down* new ordinances that will force dog walkers to clean up after their animals⟩ — see ENACT
2 to state clearly and strongly ⟨our parents *laid down* the rules for the party and wouldn't accept any arguments⟩ — see ASSERT 1
3 to give the rules about (something) clearly and exactly ⟨the supervisor *laid down* the procedure for a complaint of sexual harassment⟩ — see PRESCRIBE

layoff *n* the termination of the employment of an employee or a work force often temporarily ⟨many people lost their jobs in the *layoff*⟩
synonyms discharge, dismissal, furlough
related words closing, shutdown; downsizing

lay off *vb* to bring (as an action or operation) to an immediate end ⟨you need to *lay off* eating those jelly doughnuts, or you'll end up gaining too much weight⟩ — see STOP 1

lay off (of) *vb* to stop doing (something) permanently ⟨we warned him to *lay off of* the cigarette smoking⟩ — see QUIT 2

layout *n* **1** the way in which something is sized, arranged, or organized ⟨the decorator changed the *layout* of the living room three times before declaring it finished⟩ — see FORMAT 1
2 the way in which the elements of something (as a work of art) are arranged ⟨the *layout* of his portraits typically consists of a finely drawn subject against a roughly sketched background⟩ — see COMPOSITION 3

lay out *vb* **1** to hand over or use up in payment ⟨my dad *laid out* $500 for a new lawnmower that runs by itself⟩ — see SPEND 1
2 to work out the details of (something) in advance ⟨they *laid out* a backup plan in case of an emergency⟩ — see PLAN 1

layover *n* a brief halt in a journey ⟨our flight from New York to San Francisco made a *layover* in Chicago⟩ — see STOP 1

lay up *vb* to put (something of future use or value) in a safe or secret place ⟨an eating disorder that would impel her to *lay up* candy bars in her closet for all-night food binges⟩ — see HOARD

laziness *n* an inclination not to do work or engage in activities ⟨although she often talks about ambitious household projects, nothing even gets started because of her *laziness*⟩
synonyms idleness, indolence, inertia, shiftlessness, sloth
related words apathy, languor, lassitude, lethargy, listlessness, sluggishness; goldbricking, loafing
near antonyms enterprise, initiative; assiduity, diligence, perseverance; energy, pep, vigor, vim, vitality
antonyms drive, industriousness, industry

lazy *adj* not easily aroused to action or work ⟨the *lazy* dog just wanted to lie on the couch all day and sleep⟩
synonyms idle, indolent, shiftless, slothful
related words apathetic, languorous, lazyish, lethargic, listless, sluggish, torpid
near antonyms ambitious, diligent, enterprising, zealous; dynamic, energetic, exuberant, lively, vigorous
antonyms industrious

lazybones *n pl* a lazy person ⟨he's a *lazybones* who is never willing to do any work⟩
synonyms drone, idler, loafer, slouch, slug, sluggard
related words bum, ne'er-do-well; sleepyhead; dawdler, laggard, putterer, slowpoke, stick-in-the-mud, trifler; goldbrick, malingerer, shirker, slacker; dallier, lingerer, loiterer, lounger, saunterer; delayer, procrastinator; dropout, quitter
near antonyms live wire, powerhouse
antonyms doer, go-getter, hummer, hustler, rustler, self-starter

lea *n* open land over which livestock may roam and feed ⟨the cattle were free to range over the *lea*⟩ — see RANGE 1

lead *adj* highest in rank or authority ⟨the *lead* diplomat was responsible for making policy for the entire embassy⟩ — see HEAD

lead *n* **1** the person who has the most important role in a play, movie, or TV show ⟨my cousin is excited because he was picked to be the *lead* in the school play⟩ — see STAR 2

2 the space or amount of space between two points, lines, surfaces, or objects ⟨the athlete maintained a *lead* of several meters all the way down the track⟩ — see DISTANCE

3 a piece of advice or useful information especially from an expert ⟨the police finally got a *lead* in the case when they received an anonymous phone call⟩ — see ¹TIP 1

4 a slight or indirect pointing to something (as a solution or explanation) ⟨we were glad to get a *lead* on the answer to the brainteaser⟩ — see HINT 1

lead *vb* **1** to point out the way for (someone) especially from a position in front ⟨the tour guide *led* the group through the museum⟩

synonyms conduct, direct, guide, marshal, pilot, route, show, steer, usher

related words precede; accompany, attend, chaperone (or chaperon), convoy, escort, see; control, manage

near antonyms dog, hound, shadow, tail, tailgate

antonyms follow, trail

2 to serve as leader of ⟨the honor of *leading* the soccer squad⟩

synonyms boss, captain, command, dominate, head, spearhead

related words control, direct, govern, handle, manage, oversee, regulate, superintend, supervise

near antonyms bow (to), comply (with), defer (to), follow, obey, serve, submit (to), yield (to)

3 to be at the front of ⟨the marching band *led* the parade⟩

synonyms head

related words precede; announce, herald; accompany, attend, escort, usher

near antonyms conclude, end, finish, stop, terminate; tail, tailgate; dog, follow, trail

4 to be positioned along a certain course or in a certain direction ⟨this old road *leads* to an abandoned quarry⟩ — see RUN 3

5 to give advice and instruction to (someone) regarding the course or process to be followed ⟨the salesclerk *led* us through the maze of options now available to television buyers⟩ — see GUIDE 1

leaden *adj* **1** causing weariness, restlessness, or lack of interest ⟨the *leaden* performance of the classic play nearly put us to sleep⟩ — see BORING

2 of the color gray ⟨the *leaden* sky made everything seem dark and depressing⟩ — see GRAY 1

leader *n* **1** a long hollow cylinder for carrying a substance (as a liquid or gas) ⟨the *leader* funneled water off of the roof down into the cistern⟩ — see PIPE 1

2 the person (as an employer or supervisor) who tells people and especially workers what to do ⟨the team *leader* was good at making sure that everyone kept busy at their assigned tasks⟩ — see BOSS

leading *adj* **1** coming before all others in importance ⟨they are the *leading* suppliers of processed meat in the country⟩ — see FOREMOST 1

2 highest in rank or authority ⟨a professor known as the *leading* authority on astronomical matters⟩ — see HEAD

lead on *vb* to lead away from a usual or proper course by offering some pleasure or advantage ⟨although I tried to be good, I was frequently *led on* by my mischievous little brother⟩ — see LURE

leafage *n* green leaves or plants ⟨the springtime *leafage* enveloping the park made it seem much more private⟩ — see GREENERY 1

leaflet *n* a short printed publication with no cover or with a paper cover ⟨the school nurse has a bunch of *leaflets* about common allergies in the infirmary⟩ — see PAMPHLET

leafy *adj* covered with a thick, healthy natural growth ⟨the backyard's *leafy* bushes looked nice, but had a tendency to attract deer⟩ — see LUSH 1

league *n* **1** a group of persons formally joined together for some common interest ⟨a *league* of concerned parishioners who are seeking a greater voice in church affairs⟩ — see ASSOCIATION 2

2 an association of persons, parties, or states for mutual assistance and protection ⟨created to prevent war, the *League* of Nations was a forerunner of the United Nations⟩ — see CONFEDERACY

league *vb* to form or enter into an association that furthers the interests of its members ⟨the whole block *leagued* together to keep a liquor store from opening in their neighborhood⟩ — see ALLY

leak (out) *vb* to become known ⟨they didn't want the information about the surprise party to *leak out* early⟩ — see GET OUT 1

lean *adj* having a noticeably small amount of body fat ⟨all of the marathoners were extremely *lean*⟩ — see THIN 1

lean *n* the degree to which something rises up from a position level with the horizon ⟨the floor of the tree house has a noticeable *lean*, but we don't really care⟩ — see SLANT

lean *vb* **1** to set or cause to be at an angle ⟨just *lean* the ladder against the tree and climb up it⟩

synonyms angle, cant, cock, heel, incline, list, slant, slope, tilt, tip

related words bank; bend, deviate, swerve, veer; decline, descend, recline, retreat

near antonyms even, flatten, level, straighten

2 to show a liking or proneness (for something) ⟨his diet *leans* toward greasy food⟩

synonyms incline, run, tend, trend

related words go, gravitate; indicate, point, suggest

near antonyms avoid, shun, shy (from *or* away from)

3 to place reliance or trust ⟨you can always *lean* on me if you need help⟩ — see DEPEND 2

lean (toward) *vb* to show partiality toward ⟨I'm *leaning toward* sausage on my pizza tonight—we got pepperoni the last three times⟩ — see PREFER 1

leaning *adj* running in a slanting direction ⟨the *leaning* tower of Pisa is a popular tourist attraction in Italy⟩ — see DIAGONAL

leaning *n* **1** a prevailing or general movement or inclination ⟨the media is often accused of having liberal *leanings*⟩ — see TREND 1

2 a habitual attraction to some activity or thing ⟨despite what his athletic *leanings* might suggest, he was actually a very lazy kid⟩ — see INCLINATION 1

leap *n* an act of leaping into the air ⟨the horse cleared the hurdle with a tremendous *leap*⟩ — see JUMP 1

leap *vb* to propel oneself upward or forward into the air ⟨the baseball player *leaped* into the air to catch the ball before it went over the fence⟩ — see JUMP 1

leaping *adj* passing from one topic to another ⟨we had trouble following his *leaping* look at archaeological discoveries around the world⟩ — see DISCURSIVE

learn *vb* **1** to acquire complete knowledge, understanding, or skill in ⟨after months of trying, he finally *learned* the dance steps⟩

synonyms get, master, pick up

related words apprehend, comprehend, grasp, know, understand; absorb, assimilate, digest, imbibe; ascertain, descry, detect, determine, dig up, discern, discover, examine, find out, hear, hit (on *or* upon), run down, scare up, search (for), see, track (down), tumble (to), unearth; major (in), study; memorize
phrases get the hang (*or* knack) of
near antonyms forget, misunderstand; miss, overlook; disregard, ignore, neglect
antonyms unlearn
2 to come to an awareness ⟨I *learned* that honesty really is the best policy⟩ — see DISCOVER 1
3 to come upon after searching, study, or effort ⟨the police were astonished when they *learned* the identity of the students who had vandalized the school⟩ — see FIND 1
4 to commit to memory ⟨it's going to take us a long time to *learn* our lines for the school play⟩ — see MEMORIZE
learned *adj* **1** having or displaying advanced knowledge or education ⟨the *learned* professor can speak knowledgeably on a wide array of subjects⟩ — see EDUCATED
2 suggestive of the vocabulary used in books ⟨he tried to impress us with all of his *learned* words⟩ — see BOOKISH
learnedness *n* the understanding and information gained from being educated ⟨the librarian exuded an aura of *learnedness*⟩ — see EDUCATION 2
learning *n* the understanding and information gained from being educated ⟨the *learning* that you get from books is just as important as the experience you get from life⟩ — see EDUCATION 2
lease *vb* **1** to give the possession and use of (something) in return for periodic payment ⟨the landlord was willing to *lease* the apartment for less than we had expected⟩ — see RENT 1
2 to take or get the temporary use of (something) for a set sum ⟨I couldn't afford to buy a car outright, so I decided to *lease* one instead⟩ — see HIRE 1
least *adj* being the least in amount, number, or size possible ⟨ten is the *least* number of people needed to get the discount⟩ — see MINIMAL
leather *n* **1** the hairless natural covering of an animal prepared for use ⟨the company claims to use only the finest *leathers* for its shoes and handbags⟩
synonyms hide, skin
related words coat, fleece, fur, pelt; alligator, buckskin, calfskin, chamois, cordovan, cowhide, deerskin, doeskin, goatskin, horsehide, kid, kidskin, lambskin, morocco, pigskin, seal, sharkskin, sheepskin, snakeskin, suede
2 the outer covering of an animal removed for its commercial value ⟨this jacket was made from real *leather*⟩ — see HIDE 1
leathery *adj* not easily chewed ⟨the *leathery* meat served in the cafeteria drove many of us to start bringing our own lunches⟩ — see TOUGH 1
leave *n* **1** a period during which the usual routine of school or work is suspended ⟨the soldier was on *leave* for three days before having to report back to base⟩ — see VACATION
2 the approval by someone in authority for the doing of something ⟨the principal gave us *leave* to organize a new school newspaper⟩ — see PERMISSION
leave *vb* **1** to cause to remain behind ⟨you can *leave* your lunch in the refrigerator while we're outside⟩ ⟨lovers who promise never to *leave* one another⟩

synonyms abandon, desert, forsake, maroon, quit
related words discard, ditch, dump, fling, jettison, junk, scrap, shed, shuck (off), throw away, throw out; deliver, give up, hand over, relinquish, surrender, yield; retreat (from), take off (from), vacate, withdraw (from); abjure, cut off, disown, reject, renounce, repudiate, separate (from); sacrifice; distance; disregard, forget, ignore, neglect
phrases walk out on
near antonyms harbor, have, hold, keep, own, possess, reserve, retain, withhold; redeem, rescue, save
antonyms reclaim
2 to give by means of a will ⟨I'm going to *leave* all of my possessions to my children⟩
synonyms bequeath, will
related words deed; hand down, pass (down); devise
3 to give up (a job or office) ⟨he *left* his job in the city and moved out into the country⟩ — see QUIT 1
4 to put (something) into the possession or safekeeping of another ⟨why don't you *leave* your watch with me while you swim?⟩ — see GIVE 2
leave off *vb* **1** to bring (as an action or operation) to an immediate end ⟨we usually *leave off* working as soon as the bell rings⟩ — see STOP 1
2 to come to an end ⟨the snow should *leave off* around midnight⟩ — see CEASE 1
leave–taking *n* **1** the act of leaving a place ⟨the *leave-taking* of the guest of honor was scheduled for 11 o'clock⟩ — see DEPARTURE
2 the act or process of two or more persons going off in different directions ⟨the sweethearts' *leave-taking* was filled with pauses and promises to meet again⟩ — see PARTING 1
leavings *n pl* a remaining group or portion ⟨the *leavings* of the banquet were packed up and delivered to a shelter for the homeless⟩ — see REMAINDER 1
lecture *vb* **1** to criticize (someone) severely or angrily especially for personal failings ⟨my folks *lectured* me for an hour after seeing the F on my report card⟩ — see SCOLD
2 to give a formal often extended talk on a subject ⟨the professor gave a fascinating *lecture* about the history of Spain⟩ — see TALK 1
leech *n* a person who is supported or seeks support from another without making an adequate return ⟨whenever the gang went out for pizza, the *leech* in the group always had an excuse for not paying his fair share⟩
synonyms hanger-on, parasite, sponge, sponger
related words dependent; deadbeat, idler; flunky (*also* flunkey), henchman, lackey, satellite, stooge, sycophant, toady, yes-man; cheapskate, miser, niggard, piker, scrooge, skinflint, tightwad
near antonyms benefactor, philanthropist, supporter
leer (at) *vb* to look at in a flirtatious or desiring way ⟨the boys would always *leer at* the girls in the swimming pool⟩ — see OGLE
leery *adj* inclined to doubt or question claims ⟨I'm *leery* of his story about seeing Bigfoot last summer at camp⟩ — see SKEPTICAL 1
leeward *adj* being in the direction that the wind is blowing ⟨we moved to the *leeward* side of the ship so that we wouldn't have the wind in our faces⟩ — see DOWNWIND
left *n* a political belief stressing progress, the essential goodness of humankind, and individual freedom ⟨the campaign featured one conservative candidate and one candidate representing the *left*⟩ — see LIBERALISM

left–handed *adj* not being or expressing what one appears to be or express ⟨failed to realize that he had received a *left-handed* compliment⟩ — see INSINCERE

leftover *n* an unused or unwanted piece or item typically of small size or value ⟨that doormat is just a *leftover* from when the new carpet was installed⟩ — see ¹SCRAP 1

leftovers *n* a remaining group or portion ⟨take as many of these calendars as you want, and put the *leftovers* back on the shelf⟩ — see REMAINDER 1

leg *n* **1** a lower limb of an animal ⟨he broke his *leg* when he accidentally stepped in that gopher hole⟩
synonyms pin
related words member; foreleg, forelimb; calf, drumstick, shank, shin, thigh
2 a portion of a trip ⟨on the first *leg* of the cruise they went south to the Caribbean⟩
synonyms lap, stage
related words layover, stopover

leg (it) *vb* to go on foot ⟨the car was in the shop so we had to *leg it* to the library for a couple of days⟩ — see WALK

legacy *n* something that is or may be inherited ⟨the old locket was part of a *legacy* from my great-great-grandmother⟩ — see INHERITANCE

legal *adj* **1** permitted by law ⟨drinking is only *legal* if you are 21 years old⟩
synonyms lawful, legitimate
related words allowable, authorized, noncriminal, permissible; justifiable, warrantable; regulation, statutory; good, innocent, proper, right
near antonyms bad, corrupt, evil, immoral, iniquitous, reprobate, sinful, wicked, wrong; banned, criminal, forbidden, guilty, outlawed, prohibited, unauthorized, unjust; nonconstitutional, unconstitutional
antonyms illegal, illegitimate, illicit, unlawful, wrongful
2 following or according to the rules ⟨the referee declared it a *legal* play⟩ — see FAIR 3

legality *n* the quality or state of being legal ⟨the senator questioned the *legality* of the proposed program⟩
synonyms lawfulness, legitimacy
related words rightfulness, rightness; permissibility, permissibleness
near antonyms badness, immorality, iniquity, sinfulness, unjustness, wickedness, wrongness; criminality, unconstitutionality
antonyms illegality, illegitimacy, unlawfulness, wrongfulness

legal tender *n* something (as pieces of stamped metal or printed paper) customarily and legally used as a medium of exchange, a measure of value, or a means of payment ⟨coins and bills are considered *legal tender*, but postage stamps are not⟩ — see MONEY

legate *n* a person sent on a mission to represent another ⟨the *legate* was charged with a list of objectives to accomplish on behalf of his country⟩ — see AMBASSADOR

legatee *n* a person who has the right to inherit property ⟨they had no children, so they declared their nephew their only *legatee*⟩ — see HEIR

legend *n* **1** an explanatory list of the symbols on a map or chart ⟨the *legend* indicated that a large circle represented each city, while a small circle stood for a small town⟩
synonyms key
related words scale; caption; guide, table

2 an explanation or description accompanying a pictorial illustration ⟨the *legend* in the science textbook indicated that the accompanying picture had been enlarged by 1000%⟩ — see CAPTION 1
3 a traditional but unfounded story that gives the reason for a current custom, belief, or fact of nature ⟨some ancient civilizations had *legends* about spirits that lived in the trees and rocks⟩ — see MYTH 1
4 the body of customs, beliefs, stories, and sayings associated with a people, thing, or place ⟨that story of how the world came to be has long been part of Native American *legend*⟩ — see FOLKLORE

legendary *adj* based on, described in, or being a myth ⟨the unicorn is a *legendary* creature⟩ — see MYTHICAL 1

legerdemain *n* **1** the art or skill of performing tricks or illusions for entertainment ⟨we were all impressed by the *legerdemain* of the stage magician when he pulled a rabbit out of a baseball cap⟩ — see MAGIC 2
2 the use of clever underhanded actions to achieve an end ⟨we nearly fell for the *legerdemain* of the unscrupulous car dealer⟩ — see TRICKERY

legion *n* **1** a large body of men and women organized for land warfare ⟨joined the French Foreign *Legion*⟩ — see ARMY 1
2 a great number of persons or things gathered together ⟨there were *legions* of teenagers crowding the stadium at the rock concert⟩ — see CROWD 1

legionary *n* a person engaged in military service ⟨many stories have been written about the exploits of the French *legionaries*⟩ — see SOLDIER

legionnaire *n* a person engaged in military service ⟨the *legionnaires* are well respected for their fighting prowess⟩ — see SOLDIER

legislate *vb* to put into effect through legislative or authoritative action ⟨wants the congress to *legislate* new laws banning the use of these types of weapons⟩ — see ENACT

legislator *n* a member of an organized body of persons having the authority to make laws ⟨the *legislators* met in an all-night session to hammer out the details of the bill⟩
synonyms lawgiver, lawmaker, solon
related words assemblyman, assemblywoman; congressman, congresswoman; senator

legitimacy *n* the quality or state of being legal ⟨the *legitimacy* of the military dictatorship was not recognized by most other nations⟩ — see LEGALITY

legitimate *adj* permitted by law ⟨a good businessman always follows *legitimate* business practices⟩ — see LEGAL 1

lei *n* an ornamental chain or string (as of beads) worn around the neck ⟨we were presented with flowery *leis* as soon as we stepped off the plane in Hawaii⟩ — see NECKLACE

leisure *n* freedom from activity or labor ⟨upon retiring, the old couple looked forward to a life of *leisure*⟩ — see ¹REST 1

leisurely *adj* moving or proceeding at less than the normal, desirable, or required speed ⟨after buying our stuff, we just wandered around the mall at a *leisurely* pace⟩ — see SLOW 1

leisurely *adv* at a pace that is less than usual, desirable, or expected ⟨the old hound dog moved *leisurely* over to his water bowl to take a drink⟩ — see SLOW

lemon *n* something that has failed ⟨the used car he bought turned out to be a *lemon* and soon had trouble starting⟩ — see FAILURE 3

lend *vb* to give to another for temporary use with the understanding that it or a like thing will be returned ⟨I can *lend* you my copy of the textbook until the weekend⟩ ⟨can you *lend* me five dollars?⟩

synonyms advance, loan

related words furnish, give, grant; lease, let [*chiefly British*], rent

near antonyms receive, take

antonyms borrow

length *n* the space or amount of space between two points, lines, surfaces, or objects ⟨the *length* of a professional tennis court is 78 feet from baseline to baseline⟩ — see DISTANCE

lengthen *vb* to make longer ⟨I had to *lengthen* the handle of the paint roller in order to reach the top of the wall⟩ — see EXTEND 1

lengthening *n* the act of making longer ⟨the *lengthening* of the concert was a direct response to all the people who felt shortchanged⟩ — see EXTENSION 1

lengthy *adj* **1** of great extent from end to end ⟨she used a *lengthy* piece of rope to tie her dog to a tree⟩ — see LONG 1

2 lasting for a considerable time ⟨we had to listen to a *lengthy* sermon on the evils of shoplifting⟩ — see LONG 2

lenience *n* kind, gentle, or compassionate treatment especially towards someone who is undeserving of it ⟨a judge's reputation for *lenience* towards the criminals⟩ — see MERCY 1

leniency *n* kind, gentle, or compassionate treatment especially towards someone who is undeserving of it ⟨when we were caught, all we could do was wait and hope for *leniency* on the part of our parents⟩ — see MERCY 1

lenity *n* kind, gentle, or compassionate treatment especially towards someone who is undeserving of it ⟨the gentle king's *lenity* is well documented by historians⟩ — see MERCY 1

leprechaun *n* an imaginary being usually having a small human form and magical powers ⟨the story that if you follow a rainbow to its end, you'll find a *leprechaun's* pot of gold⟩ — see FAIRY

less *adj* having not so great importance or rank as another ⟨no *less* a person than the governor himself declared our project a winner⟩ — see LESSER

lessen *vb* **1** to make smaller in amount, volume, or extent ⟨we *lessened* our efforts as it became clear they weren't having an effect⟩ — see DECREASE 1

2 to grow less in scope or intensity especially gradually ⟨the sound of the plane slowly *lessened* as it flew out of sight⟩ — see DECREASE 2

lesser *adj* having not so great importance or rank as another ⟨it was the *lesser* evil of the two choices⟩

synonyms inferior, junior, less, lower, minor, smaller, subordinate, under

related words little, mean, small; minute, petty; jerkwater, one-horse, second-class, second-rate, two-bit; secondary, subsidiary

near antonyms exceptional, first-class, first-rate

antonyms greater, higher, major, more, primary, prime, senior, superior

lesson *n* something assigned to be read or studied ⟨your *lesson* for tonight will be the chapter on chemical reactions⟩

synonyms assignment, reading

related words homework, schoolwork; lecture; drill, exercise, practice (*also* practise); etude, study

lessor *n* the owner of land or housing that is rented to another ⟨the *lessor* is entitled to charge as much as he or she wants for a house⟩ — see LANDLORD

let *n* something that makes movement or progress more difficult ⟨a private resort that allows vacationers to shed without *let* their clothing⟩ — see ENCUMBRANCE

let *vb* **1** to give permission to ⟨the teacher *let* us stay late to do some extra studying for tomorrow's test⟩ — see ALLOW

2 *chiefly British* to give the possession and use of (something) in return for periodic payment ⟨she has begun *letting* rooms in her house to earn some extra money⟩ — see RENT 1

3 to make able or possible ⟨the low gravity on the moon *lets* you make enormous leaps and jumps⟩ — see ENABLE 1

letdown *n* **1** the emotion felt when one's expectations are not met ⟨the museum exhibit was just so-so, and we returned home with a vague sense of *letdown*⟩ — see DISAPPOINTMENT 1

2 something that disappoints ⟨the eagerly anticipated new movie by our favorite actor turned out to be a big *letdown*⟩ — see DISAPPOINTMENT 2

let down *vb* to fall short in satisfying the expectation or hope of ⟨I thought that she might lend me the money to go to the movies, but she *let* me *down*⟩ — see DISAPPOINT

lethal *adj* likely to cause or capable of causing death ⟨we were lucky that the snake's venom wasn't *lethal*, and our friend turned out to be all right⟩ — see DEADLY

lethargic *adj* slow to move or act ⟨a big meal always makes me feel *lethargic* and sleepy⟩ — see INACTIVE 1

let on *vb* to take on a false or deceptive appearance ⟨she's not half as innocent as she likes to *let on*⟩ — see PRETEND 1

letter *n* a message on paper from one person or group to another ⟨he wrote her a *letter* every week she was away⟩

synonyms dispatch, epistle, memo, memorandum, missive, note

related words airmail, card, electronic mail, e-mail, junk mail, mail, postal card, postcard; communication, report; encyclical

letter carrier *n* a person who delivers mail ⟨we like to leave a little gift in the mailbox around Christmas for our *letter carrier*⟩ — see POSTMAN

letter–perfect *adj* being entirely without fault or flaw ⟨the actress's recitation was *letter-perfect*⟩ — see PERFECT 1

letup *n* a usually gradual decrease in the pace or level of activity of something ⟨the downpour continued for hours without *letup*⟩ — see SLOWDOWN

let up *vb* **1** to come to an end ⟨the rain *let up* just as we reached the house⟩ — see CEASE 1

2 to grow less in scope or intensity especially gradually ⟨the windmill slowed down as the wind *let up*⟩ — see DECREASE 2

levee *n* **1** a bank of earth constructed to control water ⟨the raging floodwaters were too much for the *levee* to handle⟩ — see DAM

2 a structure used by boats and ships for taking on or landing cargo and passengers ⟨we tied the boat up at the *levee* and started unloading the fish we had caught⟩ — see DOCK

level *adj* having a surface without bends, breaks, or irregularities ⟨looked for a *level* place to land the plane⟩

synonyms even, flat, flush, plane, smooth

related words exact, uniform; aligned, regular, true; horizontal, tabular; plumb, straight, vertical

near antonyms inexact, irregular, unaligned; undulating, wavy

antonyms bumpy, coarse, lumpy, rough, uneven

level *n* the placement of someone or something in relation to others in a vertical arrangement ⟨a young karate student ready to rise to the next *level* in his chosen art of self-defense⟩ — see RANK 1

level *vb* **1** to make equal in amount, degree, or status ⟨we'll give both teams the same equipment so as to *level* the playing field⟩ — see EQUALIZE

2 to make free from breaks, curves, or bumps ⟨the construction workers *leveled* the ground before laying a foundation for the new house⟩ — see EVEN 1

3 to point or turn (something) toward a target or goal ⟨he *leveled* his gun at the target and fired⟩ — see AIM 1

4 to strike (someone) so forcefully as to cause a fall ⟨the boxer *leveled* his outclassed opponent with a single blow⟩ — see FELL 1

levelheaded *adj* based on sound reasoning or information ⟨I've always appreciated my father's *levelheaded* advice⟩ — see GOOD 1

levelheadedness *n* the ability to make intelligent decisions especially in everyday matters ⟨the judge had developed a reputation for his *levelheadedness* in deciding cases⟩ — see COMMON SENSE

lever *vb* to raise, move, or pull apart with or as if with a lever ⟨we had to *lever* the rusty gate open so that we could get into the playground⟩ — see ¹PRY 1

leviathan *n* something that is unusually large and powerful ⟨a *leviathan* of the seas, that cruise ship is said to be the largest one in the world⟩ — see GIANT

levity *n* a lack of seriousness often at an improper time ⟨the teachers disapprove of any displays of *levity* during school assemblies⟩ — see FRIVOLITY 1

levy *n* a charge usually of money collected by the government from people or businesses for public use ⟨the legislators approved a new *levy* on imported cattle to help protect American ranchers⟩ — see TAX

levy *vb* to establish or apply as a charge or penalty ⟨the baseball commissioner is *levying* on each player a fine of $10,000 for fighting⟩ — see IMPOSE

lewd *adj* **1** depicting or referring to sexual matters in a way that is unacceptable in polite society ⟨bystanders were shocked by the *lewd* behavior of the couple in the park⟩ — see OBSCENE 1

2 having a strong sexual desire ⟨with his unwelcome advances, the *lewd* executive had alienated all of the women in the office⟩ — see LUSTFUL

3 hinting at or intended to call to mind matters regarded as indecent ⟨he kept telling *lewd* jokes until we told him to shut up⟩ — see SUGGESTIVE 1

lewdness *n* the quality or state of being obscene ⟨the *lewdness* of the material on that Web site makes it inappropriate for children⟩ — see OBSCENITY 1

lexical *adj* of or relating to words or language ⟨since a dictionary gives *lexical* information, it tells you what the word "cat" means—not all there is to know about cats⟩ — see VERBAL 1

lexicon *n* a reference book giving information about the meanings, pronunciations, uses, and origins of words listed in alphabetical order ⟨one writer who considers an unabridged *lexicon* of the English language to be the most important reference on her bookshelf⟩ — see DICTIONARY

liability *n* **1** a feature of someone or something that creates difficulty for achieving success ⟨his allergy to eggs turned out to be a big *liability* when he tried to learn how to bake cookies⟩ — see DISADVANTAGE

2 the state of being held as the cause of something that needs to be set right ⟨the *liability* for the accident is held by the person who was driving too fast⟩ — see RESPONSIBILITY 1

3 the state of being left without shelter or protection against something harmful ⟨if you don't clean that cut right away, you'll have a *liability* to infection⟩ — see EXPOSURE 1

liable *adj* **1** being in a situation where one is likely to meet with harm ⟨because of his frail constitution, he's *liable* to diseases⟩

synonyms endangered, exposed, open, sensitive, subject (to), susceptible, vulnerable

related words likely, prone; uncovered, undefended, unguarded, unprotected, unscreened, unsecured, unsheltered, unshielded

phrases in jeopardy

near antonyms covered, guarded, protected, safeguarded, screened, secured, sheltered, shielded, warded

antonyms invulnerable, unexposed

2 being the one who must meet an obligation or suffer the consequences for failing to do so ⟨the owner of a pet is *liable* for any damage that that pet might do⟩ — see RESPONSIBLE 1

liaison *n* **1** the fact or state of having something in common ⟨a variety of political factions are attracted to that presidential contender, and there doesn't appear to be much of a *liaison* between them and the candidate⟩ — see CONNECTION 1

2 the state of having shared interests or efforts (as in social or business matters) ⟨the strong *liaison* between the parents and teachers is based on the fact that both have the students' best interests at heart⟩ — see ASSOCIATION 1

liar *n* a person who tells lies ⟨she knew he was a *liar* when he started claiming that he was an astronaut⟩

synonyms fabricator, fibber, prevaricator, storyteller

related words defamer, libeler (*or* libeller), slanderer; perjurer; distorter, falsifier; equivocator, palterer; gossip, gossiper, talebearer; charlatan, cheat, cheater, confidence man, counterfeiter, cozener, deceiver, defrauder, dissembler, dissimulator, double-dealer, fraud, hustler, mountebank, pretender

near antonyms square shooter

libation *n* a liquid suitable for drinking ⟨a variety of *libations,* appropriate for all ages, will be available at the wedding reception⟩ — see DRINK 1

libel *n* the making of false statements that damage another's reputation ⟨the governor's office issued a statement accusing the state's largest newspaper of *libel*⟩ — see SLANDER

libel *vb* to make untrue and harmful statements about ⟨newspaper and magazine reporters should always get their facts straight so that they don't end up *libeling* someone⟩ — see SLANDER

libeling *n* the making of false statements that damage another's reputation ⟨the underhanded politician resorted to *libeling* when it became clear that that was the only way he was going to win the election⟩ — see SLANDER

libelous *or* **libellous** *adj* causing or intended to cause unjust injury to a person's good name ⟨*libelous* statements about a celebrity for which the tabloid was sued⟩

synonyms defamatory, scandalous, slanderous

related words erroneous, false, inaccurate, incorrect, inexact, invalid, off, unsound, untrue, wrong; depreciative, depreciatory, derogatory, detractive, disparaging, uncomplimentary, unfavorable; invidious, objectionable; maligning, traducing, vilifying; hateful, malevolent, malicious, spiteful

near antonyms appreciative, complimentary, favorable; adulatory, commendatory, eulogistic, laudatory; accurate, correct, errorless, factual, right, sound, true, valid

liberal *adj* **1** not bound by traditional ways or beliefs ⟨parents who take a very *liberal* attitude toward letting their children stay out late⟩
synonyms broad-minded, nonconventional, nonorthodox, nontraditional, open-minded, progressive, radical, unconventional, unorthodox
related words advanced, contemporary, modern; forbearing, indulgent, lenient, permissive, tolerant; extreme; impartial, objective, unbiased
near antonyms hard, rigid, strict; doctrinal, dogmatic; bigoted, intolerant, narrow-minded; reactionary
antonyms conservative, conventional, nonprogressive, old-fashioned, orthodox, traditional
2 being more than enough without being excessive ⟨he always puts *liberal* amounts of grated cheese on his pizza⟩ — see PLENTIFUL
3 giving or sharing in abundance and without hesitation ⟨the woman who lives next door is known to be a *liberal* dispenser of Halloween candy⟩ — see GENEROUS 1

liberalism *n* a political belief stressing progress, the essential goodness of humankind, and individual freedom ⟨*liberalism* had always claimed to stand for the greatest social good⟩
synonyms left
related words radicalism, socialism
antonyms conservatism, right

liberality *n* the quality or state of being generous ⟨already known for his *liberality*, the billionaire continued to give away record amounts of money⟩
synonyms bountifulness, bounty, generosity, largess (*or* largesse), openhandedness, openheartedness, philanthropy, unselfishness
related words beneficence, charity; kindness; gift, gratuity, lagniappe; tribute; extravagance, improvidence, lavishness, prodigality, wastefulness; spendthrift; dissipating, squandering
near antonyms conserving, economizing, economy, frugality, husbandry, providence, scrimping, skimping, thrift; conservation, saving; husbanding, managing; scraping; cutting back
antonyms cheapness, closeness, meanness, miserliness, parsimony, penuriousness, pinching, stinginess, tightness

liberally *adv* in a generous manner ⟨she spread frosting *liberally* over the cake until it oozed over the edges⟩ — see WELL 2

liberate *vb* **1** to set free (as from slavery or confinement) ⟨the college kids snuck into the laboratory in the middle of the night to *liberate* all of the animals⟩ — see FREE 1
2 to set free from entanglement or difficulty ⟨we were *liberated* from our financial woes when we hit the grand prize in the lottery⟩ — see EXTRICATE

liberation *n* the act of setting free from slavery ⟨the *liberation* of the slaves was one of the key results of the Civil War⟩

synonyms emancipation, enfranchisement, freeing, manumission
related words deliverance, redemption, salvation; autonomy, freedom, independence, liberty, self-government, sovereignty
near antonyms bondage, serfdom, servitude, thralldom (*or* thraldom), yoke; captivity, enchainment, imprisonment, incarceration; conquest, subjugation
antonyms enslavement

libertine *n* a person who has sunk below the normal moral standard ⟨the legend of Don Juan depicts him as a playboy and *libertine*⟩ — see DEGENERATE

liberty *n* the state of being free from the control or power of another ⟨with the end of the school year, we celebrated our new-found *liberty* by hanging out at the mall all day⟩ — see FREEDOM 1

library *n* **1** a place where books, periodicals, and records are kept for use but not for sale ⟨I went to the *library* to do some research for my report⟩
synonyms archive
related words stacks
2 an organized group of objects acquired and maintained for study, exhibition, or personal pleasure ⟨his *library* of comic books is the envy of the entire neighborhood⟩ — see COLLECTION 1

licensable *adj* that may be permitted ⟨only drugs that have the approval of the FDA are *licensable*⟩ — see PERMISSIBLE

license *also* **licence** *vb* to give official or legal power to ⟨a state statute *licenses* county sheriffs to choose their own deputies⟩ — see AUTHORIZE 1

license *or* **licence** *n* **1** the approval by someone in authority for the doing of something ⟨during school hours students may not leave the grounds without *license*⟩ — see PERMISSION
2 the granting of power to perform various acts or duties ⟨a restaurant owner has to get a *license* to serve food and drink⟩ — see COMMISSION 1
3 the right to act or move freely ⟨he wanted full *license* to stay out all night, but we knew he'd never get it⟩ — see FREEDOM 2

licentious *adj* having a strong sexual desire ⟨*licentious* soldiers were given illustrated lectures on the consequences of sexual promiscuity⟩ — see LUSTFUL

licentiousness *n* immoral conduct or practices harmful or offensive to society ⟨our minister often condemns the *licentiousness* he sees portrayed in modern media⟩ — see VICE 1

lick *n* **1** a hard strike with a part of the body or an instrument ⟨gave the ball a hard *lick* with the bat⟩ — see ¹BLOW
2 a very small amount ⟨the soup needs just a *lick* more of salt⟩ — see PARTICLE 1
3 the smallest amount or part imaginable ⟨you haven't done a *lick* of work all day⟩ — see JOT

lick *vb* **1** to strike repeatedly ⟨your father will *lick* you good if he hears you using swear words⟩ — see BEAT 1
2 to achieve a victory over ⟨we can *lick* this test if we study enough⟩ — see BEAT 2

licking *n* failure to win a contest ⟨our team took a *licking* last night, but we'll get them next time⟩ — see DEFEAT 1

lid *n* **1** a piece placed over an open container to hold in, protect, or conceal its contents ⟨I had to get a screwdriver to pry the *lid* off of the paint can⟩ — see COVER 1

2 *slang* a covering for the head usually having a shaped crown ⟨the rules require students to take their *lids* off in school⟩ — see HAT

lie *n* a statement known by its maker to be untrue and made in order to deceive ⟨he wanted to deny the accusation, but he couldn't tell a *lie*⟩

synonyms fabrication, fairy tale, falsehood, falsity, fib, mendacity, prevarication, story, tale, untruth, whopper

related words distortion, exaggeration, half-truth; ambiguity, equivocation; defamation, libel, slander; perjury; bluff, pose, pretense (*or* pretence); humbug, jive, nonsense; fallacy, misconception, myth; misinformation, misrepresentation, misstatement; deceit, deceitfulness, dishonesty, duplicity, fraudulence

near antonyms fact, truism, verity; honesty, truthfulness, veracity; authentication, confirmation, substantiation, validation, verification

antonyms truth

lie *vb* **1** to make a statement one knows to be untrue ⟨would I *lie* to you about that?⟩

synonyms fabricate, fib, prevaricate

related words forswear, perjure; equivocate, fudge, palter; beguile, cozen, deceive, delude, dupe, fool, gull, hoax, hoodwink, kid, snow, take in, trick; defame, libel, slander, traduce; falsify, misrepresent, misstate; distort, garble; dissemble, dissimulate; misguide, misinform, mislead

phrases tell stories (*or* tales)

near antonyms assert, swear, testify; authenticate, confirm, substantiate, validate, verify

2 to be positioned along a certain course or in a certain direction ⟨the train tracks *lie* just over that hill⟩ — see RUN 3

3 to occupy a place or location ⟨I left the book *lying* on the counter⟩ — see STAND 1

lie detector *n* an instrument for detecting physical signs of the tension that goes with lying ⟨hooked the suspect up to a *lie detector* before interrogating him about the robbery⟩

synonyms polygraph

life *n* **1** a history of a person's life ⟨our assignment is to write a short *life* of an author of our own choosing⟩ — see BIOGRAPHY

2 a member of the human race ⟨an appalling number of *lives* were lost in the war⟩ — see HUMAN

3 active strength of body or mind ⟨even though he's 86 years old, he still shows a lot of *life*⟩ — see VIGOR 1

4 the period during which something exists, lasts, or is in progress ⟨the Egyptian civilization had an extremely long *life*⟩ — see DURATION 1

5 the way people live at a particular time and place ⟨frontier *life* must have been rugged, exciting, challenging, and not a little dangerous⟩ — see CIVILIZATION 1

lifeless *adj* no longer living ⟨seeing the *lifeless* body of the squirrel by the side of the road made us feel ill⟩ — see DEAD 1

lifelessness *n* the state of being dead ⟨the sight of her husband's corpse, in all of its embalmed *lifelessness*, was heartbreaking⟩ — see DEATH 2

lifelike *adj* closely resembling the object imitated ⟨the eyes of the *lifelike* portrait seemed to follow you around the room⟩ — see NATURAL 2

life span *n* the period during which something exists, lasts, or is in progress ⟨some exotic substances created in laboratories have *life spans* of only a fraction of a second⟩ — see DURATION 1

lifestyle *n* the way people live at a particular time and place ⟨we enjoy a more casual, stress-free *lifestyle*⟩ — see CIVILIZATION 1

lifetime *n* the period during which something exists, lasts, or is in progress ⟨we play so many games that the *lifetime* of the batteries typically is reduced to hours instead of weeks⟩ — see DURATION 1

lift *n* **1** an act or instance of helping ⟨the vice president gave his son a *lift* up the corporate ladder⟩ — see HELP 1

2 a means of getting to a destination in a vehicle driven by another ⟨my mom gave me a *lift* to the library, but I'm going to have to ride the bus to get home⟩ — see RIDE

lift *vb* **1** to move from a lower to a higher place or position ⟨I needed help *lifting* the heavy globe back up to the top shelf⟩ — see RAISE 1

2 to move or extend upward ⟨with wide eyes, we watched the space shuttle majestically *lift* off⟩ — see ASCEND

lifted *adj* being positioned above a surface ⟨with *lifted* heels and bent knees, the runners tensely waited for the gun to go off⟩ — see ELEVATED 1

lift–off *n* a rising from a surface at the start of a flight (as of a rocket) ⟨everyone was quiet in the control room as they waited for *lift-off*⟩

synonyms launch, takeoff

near antonyms crash; splashdown

antonyms landing

ligature *n* **1** something that physically prevents free movement ⟨the surgeon tied a *ligature* around the tube to keep it in place⟩ — see BOND 1

2 a uniting or binding force or influence ⟨a common language is often the *ligature* that unites the people of a nation⟩ — see BOND 2

¹light *adj* **1** having little weight ⟨the suitcase was as *light* as a feather after all the clothes fell out⟩

synonyms airy, feathery, lightweight, underweight, weightless

related words bantam, diminutive, little, minute, small, smallish, puny, tiny, undersized, wee; flimsy, fragile, insubstantial; petite, slender, slight, slim, thin

near antonyms big, considerable, extensive, goodly, good-sized, great, handsome, huge, hulking, jumbo, king-size (*or* king-sized), large, largish, massive, oversize (*or* oversized), sizable (*or* sizeable), substantial, super, voluminous, whacking; bulky, cumbersome, unwieldy

antonyms heavy, hefty, leaden, overweight, ponderous, weighty

2 involving minimal difficulty or effort ⟨a little *light* work was all it took to straighten up the room⟩ — see EASY 1

3 less plentiful than what is normal, necessary, or desirable ⟨traffic on the highway seems to be very *light* today⟩ — see MEAGER

4 moving easily ⟨the dancer was *light* on her feet⟩ — see GRACEFUL 1

5 not harsh or stern especially in manner, nature, or effect ⟨*light* punishment to fit a minor offense⟩ — see GENTLE 1

6 resembling air in lightness ⟨the waves had an especially *light* foam at their crests because of the strong breeze⟩ — see AIRY 1

²light *adj* **1** filled with much light ⟨the *light*, airy room is exceptionally cheerful⟩ — see BRIGHT 2

2 lacking intensity of color ⟨we painted the walls a *light* sky blue⟩ — see PALE 1

3 of light complexion ⟨her *light* skin tends to freckle easily in the sun⟩ — see FAIR 4

light *n* **1** the steady giving off of the form of radiation that makes vision possible ⟨he read poetry by the *light* of the moon⟩

synonyms blaze, flare, fluorescence, glare, gleam, glow, illumination, incandescence, luminescence, radiance, shine

related words flash, glimmer, glint, glitter, scintillation, shimmer, sparkle, twinkle; daylight, moonlight, sunlight; afterglow, aureole, aurora, beam, ray, shaft, streak, stream; glisten, gloss, luster (*or* lustre), polish, reflection, sheen

near antonyms blackness, dark, darkness, dimness, dusk, duskiness, gloom, night, shadow

2 something that provides illumination ⟨turn off the *light* when you go to bed⟩

synonyms beacon, lamp

related words arc lamp (*also* arc light), candelabra, candelabrum, candle, chandelier, dark lantern, electric, flare, flash, flashbulb, flashcube, flashlight, floodlight, fluorescent lamp, gaslight, headlight, incandescent lamp, klieg light (*or* kleig light), lantern, light bulb, lighthouse, lighting, sconce, spotlight, streetlight

3 a person who is widely known and usually much talked about ⟨a leading *light* in the acting profession⟩ — see CELEBRITY 1

¹**light** *vb* to come to rest after descending from the air ⟨the bird *lit* on the branch and began to sing⟩ — see ALIGHT

²**light** *vb* **1** to set (something) on fire ⟨we *lit* the kindling before adding the heavier logs⟩ — see BURN 2

2 to supply with light ⟨the lights from the TV cameras will *light* this room as though it were high noon⟩ — see ILLUMINATE 1

lighted *or* **lit** *adj* **1** filled with much light ⟨the coat room was just *lit* well enough for us to identify our jackets⟩ — see BRIGHT 2

2 being on fire ⟨some *lighted* torches lined the path to the shrine⟩ — see ABLAZE 1

lighten *vb* to supply with light ⟨the room was gradually *lightened* by the rising sun⟩ — see ILLUMINATE 1

light–footed *adj* moving easily ⟨the *light-footed* cat crept silently through the house⟩ — see GRACEFUL 1

light–headed *adj* **1** having a feeling of being whirled about and in danger of falling down ⟨I always get *light-headed* after riding roller coasters, even when I'm standing still again⟩ — see DIZZY 1

2 lacking in seriousness or maturity ⟨we couldn't concentrate on our work because we were feeling so *light-headed*⟩ — see GIDDY 1

light–headedness *n* a lack of seriousness often at an improper time ⟨teenagers, with all of their usual *light-headedness*, are not the best audience for this serious play⟩ — see FRIVOLITY 1

lighthearted *adj* having or showing a lack of concern or seriousness ⟨his *lighthearted* attitude in the face of danger was the source of some concern⟩ — see CAREFREE

lightheartedness *n* carefree freedom from constraint ⟨he approaches his medical duties with a *lighthearted-ness* that some patients find disturbing⟩ — see ABANDON

lighting out *n* the act of leaving a place ⟨your *lighting out* of church before the end of services did not go unnoticed⟩ — see DEPARTURE

lightly *adv* without difficulty ⟨you're not going to get off *lightly* if they catch you!⟩ — see EASILY

¹**lightness** *n* **1** the state or quality of having little weight ⟨the first thing I noticed about the little bird was its *lightness*; I could hardly tell I was holding it in my hand⟩

synonyms slightness, weightlessness

related words airiness, delicacy, etherealness; flimsi-ness, fluffiness, insubstantiality

near antonyms solidity, solidness, substantiality

antonyms heaviness, heftiness, massiveness, ponderousness, weightiness

2 a lack of seriousness often at an improper time ⟨the inappropriate *lightness* of the anchorman's tone while he was reading the story of the freak accident in which people died⟩ — see FRIVOLITY 1

²**lightness** *n* the quality or state of having or giving off light ⟨the photographer was concerned that the *lightness* of the background would cast the main subject into shadow⟩ — see BRILLIANCE 1

lightning *adj* moving, proceeding, or acting with great speed ⟨he made a *lightning* dash for the goal⟩ — see FAST 1

lightsome *adj* having or showing a good mood or disposition ⟨she skipped along with a *lightsome* gait⟩ — see CHEERFUL 1

lightweight *adj* having little weight ⟨it's going to be hot, so wear mostly *lightweight* clothing⟩ — see ¹LIGHT 1

lightweight *n* a person of no importance or influence ⟨among astronomers she's considered a *lightweight*⟩ — see NOBODY

like *adj* having qualities in common ⟨you're not talking about *like* things when you compare football and golf⟩ — see ALIKE

like *adv* to some degree or extent ⟨the cat would curl up *like* and just go to sleep⟩ — see FAIRLY

like *conj* the way it would be or one would do if ⟨it looks *like* it's going to rain at any moment⟩ — see AS IF

¹**like** *n* **1** a number of persons or things that are grouped together because they have something in common ⟨you can never trust his *like*, because they'll always let you down⟩ — see SORT 1

2 one that is equal to another in status, achievement, or value ⟨we'd never seen its *like* in any other shop in town⟩ — see EQUAL

²**like** *n* positive regard for something ⟨she thought he was unusually interested in her *likes* and dislikes⟩ — see LIKING

like *vb* **1** to wish to have ⟨I'd *like* another slice of pizza, but I've already eaten more than I should have⟩

synonyms care (for), want

related words adore, delight (in), dig, enjoy, fancy, groove (on), like, love, relish, revel (in); covet, crave, die (for), wish (for), yearn (for)

2 to show partiality toward ⟨I *like* romantic comedies more than action movies⟩ — see PREFER 1

3 to take pleasure in ⟨an adventuresome young woman who *likes* skydiving⟩ — see ENJOY 1

4 to see fit ⟨feel free to order whatever you *like* from the menu⟩ — see CHOOSE 2

likelihood *n* the quality or state of being likely to occur ⟨the weatherman on TV said that the *likelihood* of rain today was fairly high⟩ — see PROBABILITY 1

likeliness *n* the quality or state of being likely to occur ⟨there's no reasonable *likeliness* that the party will be cancelled⟩ — see PROBABILITY 1

likely *adj* **1** having a high chance of occurring ⟨if you don't do well in school, your *likely* fate is a low-paying job⟩

synonyms probable

related words conceivable, earthly, imaginable, possible, potential; apt, bound, certain, doubtless, inescapable, inevitable, necessary, sure, unavoidable

near antonyms inconceivable, unimaginable

antonyms doubtful, dubious, improbable, questionable, unlikely

2 having qualities which inspire hope ⟨this looks like a *likely* spot for good trout fishing⟩ — see HOPEFUL 1

3 worthy of being accepted as true or reasonable ⟨we didn't find her excuse a very *likely* story⟩ — see BELIEVABLE

likely *adv* without much doubt ⟨the picnic will *likely* be cancelled if the storm continues⟩ — see PROBABLY

liken *vb* **1** to describe as similar ⟨he generally *likened* the math tests to some horrible form of torture⟩ — see COMPARE 1

2 to regard or represent as equal or comparable ⟨I think that we can *liken* the two pianists, at least in terms of natural talent⟩ — see EQUATE 1

likeness *n* **1** a two-dimensional design intended to look like a person or thing ⟨the wealthy businessman hired a leading artist to paint his *likeness*⟩ — see PICTURE 1

2 something or someone that strongly resembles another ⟨why, you're the very *likeness* of your mother!⟩ — see IMAGE 1

3 the quality or state of having many qualities in common ⟨the forgery was difficult to detect due to the pinpoint *likeness* it bore to the original⟩ — see SIMILARITY 1

likewise *adv* **1** in addition to what has been said ⟨the owner of the arcade is *likewise* the owner of the deli next door⟩ — see MORE 1

2 in like manner ⟨I mind my own business, and you should do *likewise*⟩ — see ALSO 1

liking *n* positive regard for something ⟨I have a *liking* for dark chocolate⟩

synonyms appetite, fancy, favor, fondness, like, love, partiality, preference, relish, shine, taste, use

related words craving, desire, longing, thirst, yen; enthusiasm, interest, passion; bias, prejudice; bent, inclination, leaning, propensity, tendency; weakness

near antonyms apathy, indifference, unconcern

antonyms aversion, disfavor, dislike, distaste, hatred, loathing

lily–livered *adj* having or showing a shameful lack of courage ⟨the pacifist was mistakenly accused of being a *lily-livered* coward⟩ — see COWARDLY

limb *n* a major outgrowth from the main stem of a woody plant ⟨we hung the swing from the highest *limb* of the tree that we could reach⟩ — see BRANCH 1

limber *adj* able to bend easily without breaking ⟨he shaped the basket out of *limber* branches that could bend easily around a frame⟩ — see WILLOWY

limit *n* **1** a real or imaginary point beyond which a person or thing cannot go ⟨there was no *limit* to the number of challenges they faced⟩

synonyms bound, boundary, ceiling, confines, end, extent, limitation, line, termination

related words border, brim, edge, margin, rim, verge; bar, barrier, fence, hedge, restraint, stop, wall

2 the most extreme or advanced point ⟨those bratty kids have pushed my patience to the *limit*⟩ — see HEIGHT 2

limit *vb* **1** to set bounds or an upper limit for ⟨*limit* the note to a few words⟩

synonyms circumscribe, confine, restrict

related words bar, block, hinder, impede, obstruct; constrict, contract, lessen, narrow, pinch, squeeze, tighten; quell, repress, suppress; number; modify, qualify

near antonyms broaden, expand, widen; overextend, overreach

antonyms exceed

2 to mark the limits of ⟨adjectives *limit* the meanings of nouns⟩

synonyms bound, circumscribe, define, delimit, demarcate, mark (out), terminate

related words control, determine, govern; delineate, describe

limitation *n* **1** a real or imaginary point beyond which a person or thing cannot go ⟨the bridge had a weight *limitation* that prevented heavy trucks from crossing⟩ — see LIMIT

2 something that limits one's freedom of action or choice ⟨my parents put strict *limitations* on my after-school activities⟩ — see RESTRICTION 1

3 the act or practice of keeping something (as an activity) within certain boundaries ⟨the *limitation* of the city library's hours made it hard to get there before it closed for the night⟩ — see RESTRICTION 2

limited *adj* **1** having distinct or certain limits ⟨to avoid overcrowding, the number of tickets to the outdoor concerts is *limited*⟩

synonyms bounded, circumscribed, defined, definite, determinate, finite, measured, narrow, restricted

related words modified, qualified; detailed, exact, precise, specific; confined, constricted, moderate, modest; minute, puny, small, tiny; determined, fixed, settled

near antonyms bottomless, countless, incalculable, inestimable, inexhaustible, innumerable, unfathomable; general, indeterminate, nebulous, vague; enlarged, escalated, expanded; copious, plentiful; big, bulky, bumper, considerable, extensive, goodly, good-sized, great, handsome, hefty, hulking, jumbo, king-size (*or* king-sized), large, largish, oversize (*or* oversized), respectable, sizable (*or* sizeable), substantial, super, vast, voluminous, whacking; epic, grandiose, major; ample, broad, comprehensive, cosmopolitan, expansive, global, inclusive, universal, whole

antonyms boundless, dimensionless, endless, illimitable, immeasurable, indefinite, infinite, limitless, measureless, unbounded, undefined, unlimited, unmeasured

2 having a limit ⟨the *limited* number of answers for multiple-choice questions means that there'll be a good deal of guessing⟩ — see FINITE 1

limitless *adj* being or seeming to be without limits ⟨the *limitless* nature of the universe is awe-inspiring⟩ — see INFINITE

limp *adj* **1** not stiff in structure ⟨his broken arm was *limp* as he held it against his side⟩

synonyms droopy, flaccid, floppy, lank, yielding

related words flabby, mushy, semisoft, soft, squashy, squishy; delicate, flimsy, insubstantial; elastic, flexible, lax, loose, pliant, relaxed, resilient, springy, stretchy, supple

near antonyms firm, hard, indurated, solid, sound, strong; brittle, crisp; compact, dense, substantial

antonyms inflexible, resilient, rigid, stiff, sturdy, tense; firm, hard, indurated, solid, sound, strong

2 depleted in strength, energy, or freshness ⟨the *limp* runners just dropped to the ground after crossing the finish line⟩ — see WEARY 1

3 lacking bodily energy or motivation ⟨he made a *limp* motion with his hand when his name was called, but didn't look up from his book⟩ — see LISTLESS

limp *vb* **1** to walk while favoring one leg ⟨she *limped* all day after stubbing her toe on the lawn sprinkler⟩
synonyms halt, hobble
related words hitch; blunder, falter, lurch, shuffle, stagger, stumble, teeter, totter, waver, wobble; dodder
near antonyms breeze, glide, sail
antonyms stride
2 to make progress in a clumsy, struggling manner ⟨the damaged boat *limped* back into port⟩ — see FLOUNDER 1

limpid *adj* easily seen through ⟨her eyes were the blue of a *limpid* stream of water⟩ — see CLEAR 1

limpidity *n* the state or quality of being easily seen through ⟨Crystal Lake was obviously named for the *limpidity* of its water⟩ — see CLARITY 1

limpidness *n* the state or quality of being easily seen through ⟨the *limpidness* of the water allowed us to actually see fish swimming along the bottom⟩ — see CLARITY 1

line *n* **1** a series of persons or things arranged one behind another ⟨we waited in the *line* for lunch for what seemed like hours⟩
synonyms column, cue, file, queue, range, string, train
related words echelon, rank, row, tier; progression, sequence, succession; array
2 a way of acting or proceeding ⟨since the election, the president has taken a very conservative *line*⟩ — see COURSE 1
3 the activity by which one regularly makes a living ⟨my *line* of business is used cars, and have I got a deal for you!⟩ — see OCCUPATION
4 a region of activity, knowledge, or influence ⟨advanced mathematics is a little outside of my *line*, but I'll see what I can do to help⟩ — see FIELD 2
5 a real or imaginary point beyond which a person or thing cannot go ⟨you really crossed the *line* with that outrageous display of bad behavior⟩ — see LIMIT
6 a long hollow cylinder for carrying a substance (as a liquid or gas) ⟨the workers rushed to fix the leak in the gas *line*⟩ — see PIPE 1
7 a length of braided, flexible material that is used for tying or connecting things ⟨he made sure to bring extra fishing *line* in case a fish broke free⟩ — see CORD
8 a group of vehicles traveling together or under one management ⟨she owns a *line* of limousines⟩ — see FLEET
9 the direction along which something or someone moves ⟨the airplane took a southerly *line* toward the capital⟩ — see PATH 1
10 a group of persons who come from the same ancestor ⟨a tenth of all island residents are members of the *line* of this early settler⟩ — see FAMILY 1
11 the line of ancestors from whom a person is descended ⟨he comes from a noble *line* that goes back several centuries⟩ — see ANCESTRY

lineage *n* **1** the line of ancestors from whom a person is descended ⟨his Italian *lineage* was very important to him⟩ — see ANCESTRY
2 a group of persons who come from the same ancestor ⟨it is now generally accepted that the *lineage* of Thomas Jefferson includes black as well as white members⟩ — see FAMILY 1

linear *adj* free from irregularities (as curves, bends, or angles) in course ⟨the bullets from early firearms were notorious for not following a strictly *linear* path through the air⟩ — see STRAIGHT 1

linger *vb* to move or act slowly ⟨since they were charging by the hour, the house painters *lingered* in finishing up their work⟩ — see DELAY 1

lingerer *n* someone who moves slowly or more slowly than others ⟨he was known as a *lingerer*, always the last to arrive and the last to leave⟩ — see SLOWPOKE

lingo *n* **1** the stock of words, pronunciation, and grammar used by a people as their basic means of communication ⟨the missionaries struggling to learn the *lingo* of the African tribes⟩ — see LANGUAGE 1
2 the special terms or expressions of a particular group or field ⟨the shorthand medical *lingo* that the hospital staffers use with one another⟩ — see TERMINOLOGY

linguistic *adj* of or relating to words or language ⟨the age that which children begin to acquire *linguistic* skills⟩ — see VERBAL 1

link *n* **1** a rod-shaped portion of seasoned ground meat in a casing ⟨I like to put maple syrup on my breakfast *links*⟩ — see SAUSAGE
2 a uniting or binding force or influence ⟨those old love letters were her only remaining *link* with her late grandparents⟩ — see BOND 2

link *vb* **1** to put or bring together so as to form a new and longer whole ⟨she *linked* the flowers together to form a long chain⟩ — see CONNECT 1
2 to think of (something) in combination ⟨since the accident, I tend to *link* in my mind skiing and broken legs⟩ — see ASSOCIATE 2

link (up) *vb* to come together to form a single unit ⟨carbon atoms *link up* to form a diamond crystal⟩ — see UNITE 1

linkage *n* the fact or state of having something in common ⟨the accountants noticed a *linkage* between the two supposedly independent companies⟩ — see CONNECTION 1

linking *n* the act or an instance of joining two or more things into one ⟨the *linking* of state roads and highways into one interstate highway system⟩ — see UNION 1

linkup *n* the state of having shared interests or efforts (as in social or business matters) ⟨the *linkup* of the two art museums has proved beneficial to both institutions⟩ — see ASSOCIATION 1

lint *n* a soft airy substance or covering ⟨it's important to clean the *lint* out of the dryer every time you use it⟩ — see FUZZ

lionhearted *adj* feeling or displaying no fear by temperament ⟨the *lionhearted* soldiers marched into battle even though they were greatly outnumbered⟩ — see BRAVE

liquefy *vb* to go from a solid to a liquid state ⟨the steel *liquefied* in the intense heat of the forge⟩
synonyms deliquesce, flux, fuse, melt, run, thaw
related words found, gutter, smelt, try; dissolve, render; soften, thin
near antonyms clot, coagulate, congeal, gel, jell, jelly, thicken
antonyms harden, set, solidify

liquid *adj* **1** capable of moving like a liquid ⟨always have in the kitchen a dispenser of *liquid* soap available for hand washing⟩ — see FLUID 1
2 easily seen through ⟨the *liquid* air of the remote mountains⟩ — see CLEAR 1

liquidate *vb* **1** to destroy all traces of ⟨a decisive act that *liquidated* all doubts and fears about his governing abilities⟩ — see ANNIHILATE 1

2 to put to death deliberately ⟨his first act as absolute ruler was to *liquidate* all opponents⟩ — see MURDER 1

3 to give what is owed for ⟨used our lottery winnings to *liquidate* all debts⟩ — see PAY 2

liquor *n* a fermented or distilled beverage that can make a person drunk ⟨you can't order *liquor* in a bar until you're 21 years old⟩ — see ALCOHOL

lissome *also* **lissom** *adj* **1** moving easily ⟨the *lissome* actress's dance training is apparent in the way she moves on stage⟩ — see GRACEFUL 1

2 able to bend easily without breaking ⟨rattan is such a *lissome* material that it can be used for all manner of furniture and baskets⟩ — see WILLOWY

¹list *n* a record of a series of items (as names or titles) usually arranged according to some system ⟨we put eggs, sour cream, tomatoes, roast beef, and cheddar cheese on the shopping *list*⟩

synonyms canon, catalog (*or* catalogue), checklist, listing, menu, register, registry, roll, roster, schedule, table

related words agenda, bibliography, compilation, directory, docket, glossary, index, inventory, manifest, payroll; calendar, chronology, timetable

²list *n* the act of positioning or an instance of being positioned at an angle ⟨the extreme *list* of the racing yacht made it hard for the crew to keep their balance⟩ — see TILT

³list *n* a long narrow piece of material ⟨shave a thin *list* from the side of board⟩ — see STRIP

¹list *vb* **1** to make a list of ⟨he *listed* the people on the team⟩

synonyms enumerate, inventory, itemize, numerate

related words count, mark, number; check (off), tick (off)

2 to put (someone or something) on a list ⟨her number isn't *listed* in the phone book⟩

synonyms catalog (*or* catalogue), enroll (*also* enrol), enter, index, inscribe, put down, record, register, schedule, slate

related words book, file, note; classify, compile, tabulate; reschedule

near antonyms delete

3 to enter in a list or roll ⟨that runner was never *listed* in the official list of marathon participants⟩ — see ENROLL 1

4 to specify one after another ⟨do I need to *list* all of the reasons why your idea won't work?⟩ — see ENUMERATE 1

²list *vb* to set or cause to be at an angle ⟨the sudden shift of the load in the hull *listed* the ship badly⟩ — see LEAN 1

listen *vb* to pay attention especially through the act of hearing ⟨would you *listen* to what I have to say?⟩

synonyms attend, hark, hear, hearken, heed, mind

phrases prick up one's ears

near antonyms discount, disregard

antonyms ignore, tune out

listen (to) *vb* to take notice of and be guided by ⟨you'd better *listen to* my advice!⟩ — see HEED 1

listen in (on) *vb* to listen to (another in private conversation) ⟨it's not polite to *listen in on* other people's private conversations⟩ — see EAVESDROP (ON)

listing *adj* **1** inclined or twisted to one side ⟨we hurried to straighten the *listing* bird feeder before all of the seed fell out⟩ — see AWRY

2 running in a slanting direction ⟨the *listing* lines of a poem scrawled on a chalkboard⟩ — see DIAGONAL

listing *n* a record of a series of items (as names or titles) usually arranged according to some system ⟨an alphabetical *listing* of all of the students currently enrolled in the school⟩ — see ¹LIST

listless *adj* lacking bodily energy or motivation ⟨when I had the flu, I felt *listless* and worn-out⟩

synonyms enervated, lackadaisical, languid, languishing, languorous, limp, spiritless

related words indolent, lazy, slothful; lethargic, logy, sleepy, sluggish, torpid; exhausted, tired, weary; feeble, frail, weak; apathetic, impassive, phlegmatic, stolid; careless, heedless, thoughtless, unwary; inactive, inert

near antonyms active, dynamic, industrious; avid, eager, enthusiastic, keen, lively, vivacious; cheerful, chipper, perky, up; agog, alert, awake, dapper, open-eyed, sleepless, vigilant, watchful, wide-awake

antonyms ambitious, animated, energetic, enterprising, motivated

listlessness *n* the state of being bored ⟨we searched desperately for something to jar us out of our *listlessness*⟩ — see BOREDOM

literal *adj* restricted to or based on fact ⟨a *literal* account of the explorer's adventures is actually a lot less interesting than his own exaggerated stories⟩ — see FACTUAL 1

literary *adj* suggestive of the vocabulary used in books ⟨the teacher was impressed with the *literary* prose that the student used in her report⟩ — see BOOKISH

literate *adj* having or displaying advanced knowledge or education ⟨the columnist's witty and *literate* comments on current events make her a popular guest on political talk shows⟩ — see EDUCATED

lithe *adj* **1** able to bend easily without breaking ⟨the *lithe* blade of a fencing foil⟩ — see WILLOWY

2 moving easily ⟨*lithe* dancers glided across the stage⟩ — see GRACEFUL 1

lithesome *adj* moving easily ⟨the *lithesome* panther moved effortlessly and noiselessly through the rain forest⟩ — see GRACEFUL 1

litter *n* **1** an unorganized collection or mixture of various things ⟨a *litter* of magazines covered the bedroom floor⟩ — see MISCELLANY 1

2 discarded or useless material ⟨if you get caught throwing your *litter* on the ground, you will have to pay a fine⟩ — see GARBAGE

littered *adj* lacking in order, neatness, and often cleanliness ⟨is that any wonder that you can never find anything in your *littered* desk?⟩ — see MESSY

little *adj* **1** having relatively little height ⟨there was a *little* hedge separating the two lawns⟩ — see SHORT 1

2 lacking importance ⟨there were just a few *little* details left to take care of⟩ — see UNIMPORTANT

3 not broad or open in views or opinions ⟨*little*-minded people who dislike the fact that human society is always progressing⟩ — see NARROW 2

4 not lasting for a considerable time ⟨let's take a *little* pause to relax⟩ — see SHORT 2

5 of a size that is less than average ⟨the petting zoo had a *little* horse in addition to all of the goats and sheep⟩ — see SMALL 1

little *adv* **1** in a very small quantity or degree ⟨we had *little* more than we needed to survive in the wilderness⟩

synonyms negligibly, nominally, slightly

related words meagerly, scantily; barely, hardly, just, marginally, minimally, scarcely

phrases a bit

near antonyms completely, entirely, purely, thoroughly, totally, utterly; eminently, exceptionally; appreciably, discernibly, noticeably, palpably; abundantly, plentifully; generously, handsomely, liberally; astronomically, grandly, hugely, monstrously, monumentally

antonyms awful, awfully, beastly, considerably, deadly, especially, exceedingly (*also* exceeding), extensively, extra, extremely, far, frightfully, full, greatly, heavily, highly, jolly, mightily, mighty, mortally, most, much, particularly, rattling, real, right, significantly, so, something, substantially, super, terribly, too, very, whacking

2 not often ⟨he's been studying very *little*⟩ — see SELDOM

little *n* a very small amount ⟨there's just a *little* of the pie left⟩ — see PARTICLE 1

little by little *adv* by small steps or amounts ⟨*little by little*, we pieced together the jigsaw puzzle⟩ — see GRADUALLY

littleness *n* the quality or state of being little in size ⟨the *littleness* of the painting hardly gives any indication of its price—which is a fortune⟩ — see SMALLNESS

littlest *adj* being the least in amount, number, or size possible ⟨the *littlest* kitten in the litter was also the cutest⟩ — see MINIMAL

livable *also* **liveable** *adj* suitable for living in ⟨after adding some furniture and painting the walls, the apartment was *livable*⟩

synonyms habitable, inhabitable

related words comfortable, cozy, homelike, homey, intimate, snug; deluxe, lavish, luxuriant, luxurious, plush, sumptuous; opulent, palatial, rich; acceptable, bearable, endurable, sufferable, supportable, sustainable, tolerable

near antonyms uncomfortable; humble, Spartan; economical, frugal, spare, thrifty; intolerable, unacceptable, unbearable, unendurable, insupportable

antonyms uninhabitable, unlivable

live *adj* having or showing life ⟨there was a tank of *live* lobsters sitting at the front of the restaurant⟩ — see ALIVE 1

live *vb* **1** to have a home ⟨he *lived* next door to the hospital⟩

synonyms abide, dwell, reside

related words lodge, settle, stay; frequent, hang out (at), haunt; inhabit, occupy; people, populate; lease, rent, sublet, tenant

2 to have life ⟨Socrates was a philosopher who *lived* in ancient Greece⟩ — see BE 1

liveliness *n* the quality or state of having abundant or intense activity ⟨we were surprised by the *liveliness* of the crowd at the nightclub despite the early hour⟩ — see VITALITY 1

lively *adj* **1** having much high-spirited energy and movement ⟨the *lively* puppy was racing around the dining room floor chasing after people's shoelaces⟩

synonyms active, animate, animated, bouncing, brisk, energetic, frisky, gay, jaunty, jazzy, peppy, perky, pert, racy, snappy, spanking, sparky, spirited, sprightly, springy, vital, vivacious, zippy

related words dapper, dashing, spiffy; agog, alert, awake, open-eyed, up, wide-awake; agile, nimble, spry; bright, buoyant, cheerful, chipper, effervescent, upbeat; eager, enthusiastic, keen; frolicsome, impish, playful; bubbly, exuberant, high-spirited; high-strung, nervous, skittish

phrases on the go

near antonyms indolent, lazy, unambitious; inert, lethargic, sleepy, sluggish, tired, torpid, weary; apa-

thetic, impassive, phlegmatic, stolid; boring, dull, irksome, tedious

antonyms dead, inactive, inanimate, lackadaisical, languid, languishing, languorous, lifeless, limp, listless, spiritless, unanimated

2 marked by much life, movement, or activity ⟨the band played music with a *lively* tempo⟩ — see ALIVE 2

liven (up) *vb* to give life, vigor, or spirit to ⟨the bandleader tried to *liven up* the party by playing more energetic music so people would dance⟩ — see ANIMATE

livery *n* the distinctive clothing worn by members of a particular group ⟨the limousine chauffeur was easily distinguished from the cab drivers by his *livery*⟩ — see UNIFORM

live wire *n* an ambitious person who eagerly goes after what is desired ⟨that new reporter on the police beat is a real *live wire*⟩ — see GO-GETTER

livid *adj* lacking a healthy skin color ⟨her face was *livid* with fear⟩ — see PALE 2

living *adj* **1** being in effective operation ⟨a *living* tradition of the holiday season⟩ ⟨a *living* culture that has survived a number of foreign invasions⟩ — see ACTIVE 1

2 having being at the present time ⟨there are fewer than a dozen *living* former presidents⟩ — see EXTANT 1

3 having or showing life ⟨is your hamster still *living*?⟩ — see ALIVE 1

load *n* **1** a mass or quantity of something taken up and carried, conveyed, or transported ⟨they placed a *load* of grain on the truck going to Florida⟩

synonyms burden, cargo, draft, freight, haul, lading, loading, payload, weight

related words consignment, boatload, carload, shipload, truckload; ballast, deadweight; overload, surcharge; bale, bundle, pack, package, packet, parcel; shipment; manifest; body, bulk, mass

2 loads *pl* a considerable amount ⟨there's no rush, since we've got *loads* of time left⟩ — see LOT 2

load *vb* **1** to place a weight or burden on ⟨students complaining that their teachers were *loading* them with work⟩

synonyms burden, encumber, lade, lumber, saddle, weight

related words clog, clutter, fill, heap; press, weigh; strain, tax; overburden, overload, overtax, surcharge; handicap; afflict, oppress

near antonyms alleviate, ease, lighten, relieve

antonyms disencumber, unburden, unload

2 to put into (something) as much as can be held or contained ⟨she *loaded* her plate at the buffet with as much food as she could carry and with more than any sane person should eat⟩ — see FILL 1

loaded *adj* **1** containing or seeming to contain the greatest quantity or number possible ⟨the sign said to park the *loaded* trucks closest to the building and the unloaded ones at the other end of the lot⟩ — see FULL 1

2 having goods, property, or money in abundance ⟨the guy in the fancy foreign sports car obviously was *loaded*⟩ — see RICH 1

3 *slang* being under the influence of alcohol ⟨the departing party guest was *loaded*, so we held his car keys until he had sobered up⟩ — see DRUNK

loading *n* a mass or quantity of something taken up and carried, conveyed, or transported ⟨the accident was caused by a truck with a *loading* in excess of the legal limit⟩ — see LOAD 1

loaf *vb* to spend time doing nothing ⟨the kind of hot August afternoon that makes you just want to *loaf*⟩ — see IDLE

loafer *n* a lazy person ⟨an idle *loafer* who never accomplished anything⟩ — see LAZYBONES

loamy *adj* consisting or suggestive of earth ⟨the *loamy* ground in the backyard is perfect for growing a garden⟩ — see EARTHY 1

loan *vb* to give to another for temporary use with the understanding that it or a like thing will be returned ⟨can you *loan* me your bike this weekend?⟩ — see LEND

loath *or* **loth** *adj* having doubts about the wisdom of doing something ⟨I was *loath* to accept his claim of having climbed that mountain⟩ — see HESITANT

loathe *vb* to dislike strongly ⟨I simply *loathe* tapioca pudding⟩ — see HATE

loathing *n* **1** a dislike so strong as to cause stomach upset or queasiness ⟨the sight of his mortal enemy filled him with *loathing*⟩ — see DISGUST

2 a very strong dislike ⟨I have an uncompromising *loathing* for anyone who would deliberately harm an animal⟩ — see HATE 1

loathsome *adj* causing intense displeasure, disgust, or resentment ⟨we traced the foul smell to a pile of *loathsome* garbage by the back wall⟩ — see OFFENSIVE 1

lob *vb* to send through the air especially with a quick forward motion of the arm ⟨he lightly *lobbed* the ball over the fence to his friend⟩ — see THROW

lobby *n* **1** a centrally located room in a building that serves as a gathering or waiting area or as a passageway into the interior ⟨we met downstairs in the *lobby* of the hotel before going out to dinner⟩ — see FOYER 1

2 the entrance room of a building ⟨the ticket booth is located in the theater's outer *lobby*⟩ — see HALL 1

local *n* a local unit of an organization ⟨the truck drivers are members of *Local* 349 of the Teamsters' Union⟩ — see CHAPTER

locale *n* the area or space occupied by or intended for something ⟨we found an ideal *locale* for our annual picnic⟩ — see PLACE 1

locality *n* the area or space occupied by or intended for something ⟨a *locality* filled with exotic plants⟩ — see PLACE 1

locate *vb* to come upon after searching, study, or effort ⟨we were finally able to *locate* the missing cat, who had been sleeping in the closet the whole time⟩ — see FIND 1

location *n* the area or space occupied by or intended for something ⟨we chose the old church on Main Street as the *location* for the ceremony⟩ — see PLACE 1

loch *n, Scottish* a part of a body of water that extends beyond the general shoreline ⟨in his biography of Samuel Johnson, James Boswell tells of being conducted by a Scottish boatman "across one of the *lochs*, as they call them, or arms of the sea"⟩ — see GULF 1

lock (up) *vb* to put in or as if in prison ⟨if they catch you, they're going to *lock* you *up* and throw away the key!⟩ — see IMPRISON

locker *n* **1** a covered rectangular container for storing or transporting things ⟨the soldier stored his uniform in his *locker* at the foot of his bed⟩ — see CHEST

2 a storage case typically having doors and shelves ⟨leave your books in your *locker* between classes so you don't have to carry them around all day⟩ — see CABINET

lockup *n* a place of confinement for persons held in lawful custody ⟨the sheriff threw the cattle rustlers into the county *lockup*⟩ — see JAIL

loco *adj* having or showing a very abnormal or sick state of mind ⟨that dog's plumb *loco*, just running around in circles all day long⟩ — see INSANE 1

locus *n* the area or space occupied by or intended for something ⟨the *locus* of brightness occurs where the rays of sunlight converge in front of the lens⟩ — see PLACE 1

locution *n* a distinctive way of putting ideas into words ⟨in the poet's somewhat affected *locution*, word order is often reversed and so we have "the sea serene"⟩ — see STYLE 1

lodestone *n* something that attracts interest ⟨the young woman's wealth unfortunately made her a *lodestone* for fortune hunters⟩ — see MAGNET

lodge *n* **1** a place that provides rooms and usually a public dining room for overnight guests ⟨when we go on country vacation, we always stay at this little *lodge* in the middle of nowhere⟩ — see HOTEL

2 an often small house for recreational or seasonal use ⟨every summer my family rents a small *lodge* by the lake⟩ — see COTTAGE

3 the meeting place of an organization ⟨the Masons meet at the *lodge* every Thursday evening⟩ — see CLUB 2

4 the shelter or resting place of a wild animal ⟨the family of beavers built a *lodge* near the narrow point of the river⟩ — see DEN 1

lodge *vb* to provide with living quarters or shelter ⟨the landlord can legally *lodge* up to 20 people in his apartment building at one time⟩ — see HOUSE 1

2 to establish or place comfortably or snugly ⟨our pet guinea pig *lodged* himself in the far corner of his cage and wouldn't come out⟩ — see ENSCONCE 1

3 to set solidly in or as if in surrounding matter ⟨the gunman had managed to *lodge* a bullet in my back, just inches from my spine⟩ — see ENTRENCH

lodged *adj* firmly positioned in place and difficult to dislodge ⟨we had to use pliers to extract the *lodged* screws from the board⟩ — see TIGHT 2

lodger *n* one who rents a room or apartment in another's house ⟨the mysterious *lodger* slept all day and only went out at night⟩ — see TENANT

lodging *n* **1** the place where one lives ⟨food and *lodging* are two of the largest expenses of living in the city⟩ — see HOME 1

2 lodgings *pl* a room or set of rooms in a private house or a block used as a separate dwelling place ⟨I've rented *lodgings* in the old boardinghouse downtown⟩ — see APARTMENT 1

loft *vb* to send through the air especially with a quick forward motion of the arm ⟨he *lofted* the ball down the center of the field toward a receiver⟩ — see THROW

loftiest *adj* being at a point or level higher than all others ⟨from the *loftiest* part of the mountain ridge you could see all the way to the next state⟩ — see TOP 1

loftiness *n* an exaggerated sense of one's importance that shows itself in the making of excessive or unjustified claims ⟨we were offended by the new club member's air of *loftiness*⟩ — see ARROGANCE

lofty *adj* **1** extending to a great distance upward ⟨the ever-increasing *lofty* heights of the world's skyscrapers⟩ — see HIGH 1

2 having a feeling of superiority that shows itself in an overbearing attitude ⟨she acts all *lofty* and superior just because she gets straight A's⟩ — see ARROGANT

3 having or displaying feelings of scorn for what is regarded as beneath oneself ⟨his *lofty* attitude toward menial chores really rankles the other camp counselors⟩ — see PROUD 1

4 having, characterized by, or arising from a dignified and generous nature ⟨remained true to the cause's *lofty*

ideals, regardless of the changing winds of popular opinion⟩ — see NOBLE 2

5 very dignified in form, tone, or style ⟨the *lofty* nature of the coronation ceremony⟩ — see ELEVATED 2

log *vb* to make a written note of ⟨the policeman *logged* the arrest and left the station⟩ — see RECORD 1

logger *n* a person whose job is to cut down trees ⟨the *loggers* were obliged to plant as many trees as they cut down⟩ — see LUMBERJACK

logic *n* the thought processes that have been established as leading to valid solutions to problems ⟨I tried to use *logic* to figure out the solution to the puzzle⟩
  synonyms reason, reasoning, sense
  related words cogency, coherence, rationality, thought; analysis; deduction, induction
  near antonyms incoherence, insanity, irrationality

logical *adj* **1** according to the rules of logic ⟨the lawyer won the case with a *logical* argument about the motives of the suspect⟩
  synonyms analytic (*or* analytical), coherent, good, rational, reasonable, sensible, sound, valid
  related words sane; thoughtful; scientific
  near antonyms specious; crazy; insane; senseless, thoughtless
  antonyms illogical, incoherent, invalid, irrational, unreasonable, unsound

2 based on sound reasoning or information ⟨that's the *logical* choice under the circumstances⟩ — see GOOD 1

logo *n* a device, design, or figure used as an identifying mark ⟨the company's *logo* is instantly recognizable all over the world⟩ — see EMBLEM

logy *adj* depleted in strength, energy, or freshness ⟨the next morning I was feeling *logy* after staying up half the night⟩ — see WEARY 1

loiter *vb* to move or act slowly ⟨don't *loiter* on your way home from the grocery store⟩ — see DELAY 1

loiterer *n* someone who moves slowly or more slowly than others ⟨she yelled at the *loiterers* at the end of the line to hurry up⟩ — see SLOWPOKE

loll *vb* **1** to be limp from lack of water or vigor ⟨the heads of the flowers *lolled* on their stems in the blistering heat⟩ — see DROOP 1

2 to refrain from labor or exertion ⟨farmhands *lolling* about in the shade and taking a break from the midday sun⟩ — see REST 1

3 to spend time doing nothing ⟨some members of the decorating committee were hard at work, and some were just *lolling* about⟩ — see IDLE

lone *adj* **1** being the one or ones of a class with no other members ⟨the *lone* ripe apple in the entire bag⟩ — see ONLY 2

2 not being in the company of others ⟨just one *lone* cow in the middle of the field⟩ — see ALONE 1

lonely *adj* **1** not being in the company of others ⟨a single *lonely* cactus in the desert⟩ — see ALONE 1

2 sad from lack of companionship or separation from others ⟨I was *lonely* when I first got to summer camp, but I soon made friends⟩ — see LONESOME 1

loner *n* a person who does not conform to generally accepted standards or customs ⟨that guy is a *loner*, and never wants to hang out with the rest of us⟩ — see NONCONFORMIST 1

lonesome *adj* **1** sad from lack of companionship or separation from others ⟨a *lonesome* kitten left at the pound by its owners⟩
  synonyms desolate, forlorn, lonely, lorn
  related words friendless; abandoned, deserted, forgotten, forsaken, neglected; alone, lone, solitary; only, sole

near antonyms accompanied, attended, escorted

2 not being in the company of others ⟨a *lonesome* cypress tree on a rocky, windswept point⟩ — see ALONE 1

lone wolf *n* a person who does not conform to generally accepted standards or customs ⟨a *lone wolf* in the art world, he has his own style and paints to please himself⟩ — see NONCONFORMIST 1

long *adj* **1** of great extent from end to end ⟨giraffes have *long* necks to help them reach leaves on tall trees⟩
  synonyms elongated, extended, king-size (*or* king-sized), lengthy
  related words extensive, far-reaching, longish, outstretched; oblong, rectangular; big, considerable, good-sized, hefty, hulking, large, largish, oversize (*or* oversized), sizable (*or* sizeable), substantial, super
  near antonyms abbreviated, abridged, curtailed, diminished, shortened; diminutive, little, minute, puny, small, smallish, tiny, undersized, wee
  antonyms brief, short

2 lasting for a considerable time ⟨summer vacation seemed *long*, but we had to go back to school soon enough⟩
  synonyms extended, far, great, lengthy, long-lived, long-range, long-term, marathon
  related words endless, everlasting, interminable, persistent; longish, overlong, prolonged, protracted; permanent
  near antonyms abrupt, sudden; abbreviated, condensed, curtailed; ephemeral, fleeting, momentary, transient, transitory; impermanent
  antonyms brief, short, short-lived, short-range, short-term

long (for) *vb* to have an earnest wish to own or enjoy ⟨I *long for* the day my parents let me have a room of my own⟩ — see DESIRE

longhand *n* writing done by hand ⟨my computer was broken so I wrote out my report in *longhand*⟩ — see HANDWRITING 2

longing *n* a strong wish for something ⟨by four o'clock in the afternoon, I usually experience a strong *longing* for chocolate⟩ — see DESIRE

long–lived *adj* **1** being of advanced years and especially past middle age ⟨that sequoia tree is especially *long-lived,* having an age generally estimated to be at least 3,000 years⟩ — see ELDERLY

2 lasting for a considerable time ⟨much to the relief of his parents, his interest in the piano proved to be *long-lived*⟩ — see LONG 2

long–range *adj* lasting for a considerable time ⟨it's important to consider *long-range* planning as well as your short-term goals⟩ — see LONG 2

longshoreman *n* one who loads and unloads ships at a port ⟨the *longshoremen* moved all of the fish into cold storage for shipment to the market⟩ — see DOCKWORKER

long–suffering *adj* accepting pains or hardships calmly or without complaint ⟨the *long-suffering* parents calmly waited until the tantrum had passed⟩ — see PATIENT 1

long–suffering *n* the capacity to endure what is difficult or disagreeable without complaining ⟨you will need infinite *long-suffering* to put up with that arrogant upstart⟩ — see PATIENCE

long–term *adj* lasting for a considerable time ⟨before approving a new drug, the government insists on some *long-term* research to determine any possible side effects⟩ — see LONG 2

long–winded *adj* using or containing more words than necessary to express an idea ⟨his *long-winded* explanation could have been boiled down to two sentences⟩ — see WORDY

long-windedness *n* the use of too many words to express an idea ⟨the professor's *long-windedness* is legendary on campus⟩ — see VERBIAGE

look *n* **1** facial appearance regarded as an indication of mood or feeling ⟨you should have seen the *look* on your face when we yelled "Surprise!"⟩

synonyms cast, countenance, expression, face, visage

related words frown, grimace, mouth, scowl; air, appearance, aspect, bearing, demeanor, manner, mien

2 an instance of looking especially briefly ⟨she gave the junk mail a quick *look* before throwing it in the garbage pail⟩

synonyms cast, eye, gander, glance, glimpse, peek, peep, regard, sight, view

related words gape, gaze, glare, leer, ogle, stare; squint

3 the outward form of someone or something especially as indicative of a quality ⟨he has the *look* of a prosperous businessman⟩ — see APPEARANCE 1

4 looks *pl* the qualities in a person or thing that as a whole give pleasure to the senses ⟨a supermodel's career tends to be entirely based on her exceptional good *looks*⟩ — see BEAUTY 1

look *vb* **1** to give the impression of being ⟨it *looks* like it might rain⟩ — see SEEM

2 to make known (as an idea, emotion, or opinion) ⟨the teacher *looked* her displeasure with a fierce frown⟩ — see EXPRESS 1

look (at) *vb* to make note of (something) through the use of one's eyes ⟨I found her at the mall *looking at* the new outfits on the mannequins⟩ — see SEE 1

look (into) *vb* to search through or into ⟨the owner is being forced to *look into* new options for promoting his declining business⟩ — see EXPLORE 1

look (toward) *vb* to stand or sit with the face or front toward ⟨the bay window *looks toward* the park⟩ — see FACE 1

looking glass *n* a smooth or polished surface (as of glass) that forms images by reflection ⟨always remember that the image is reversed in the *looking glass*⟩ — see MIRROR

lookout *n* **1** a high place or structure from which a wide view is possible ⟨we went up to the *lookout* on the top of the hill to watch the fireworks⟩

synonyms observatory, outlook

related words aerie, crow's nest, tower, watchtower

2 all that can be seen from a certain point ⟨we were struck by the amazing beauty of the *lookout* from the top of the tower⟩ — see VIEW 1

3 the act or state of being constantly attentive and responsive to signs of opportunity, activity, or danger ⟨keep a sharp *lookout* for oncoming traffic as you cross the street⟩ — see VIGILANCE

4 a person or group that watches over someone or something ⟨make sure to post a *lookout* so that no one can sneak up on us⟩ — see GUARD 1

look up *vb* to go in search of ⟨be sure to *look* me *up* if you're ever in town⟩ — see SEEK 1

loom *vb* to be about to happen ⟨he could tell that trouble was *looming* when the bullies swaggered into the park⟩

synonyms brew, impend

related words advance, approach, close in, draw on, gather, near; lower (*also* lour), menace, threaten

near antonyms die down, diminish, disappear, dwindle, fade, vanish, wane; fall back, pass, recede, retreat, withdraw

loony *n* a person judged to be legally or medically insane ⟨his insistence that aliens from outer space were monitoring his thoughts forced doctors to conclude that he was in fact a *loony*⟩ — see LUNATIC 1

loony *also* **looney** *adj* **1** showing or marked by a lack of good sense or judgment ⟨that's got to be the *looniest* idea I've ever heard⟩ — see FOOLISH 1

2 having or showing a very abnormal or sick state of mind ⟨that guy talking to himself on the street is indeed *loony*⟩ — see INSANE 1

loop *n* a circular strip ⟨cut the paper into narrow strips, and then paste those into *loops*⟩ — see RING 2

loop *vb* to pass completely around ⟨to tie a knot, first *loop* the string around itself⟩ — see ENCIRCLE 1

loose *adj* **1** not tightly fastened, tied, or stretched ⟨secure your neckerchief with a *loose* knot⟩

synonyms insecure, lax, loosened, relaxed, slack, slackened, unsecured

related words detached, free, unattached, unbound, undone, unfastened, untied; baggy; nonrestrictive

near antonyms constrained, restrained; attached, bound, fastened, tied

antonyms taut, tense, tight

2 consisting of particles that do not stick together ⟨the car wheels slipped on the *loose* gravel in the driveway⟩

synonyms incoherent, unconsolidated

related words nonadhesive; disconnected, disjointed, separate, unconnected; coarse, granular, rough

near antonyms connected, solid; compacted, compressed; adhesive, gluey, sticky

antonyms coherent, compact, dense, packed

3 not bound by rigid standards ⟨we were given some *loose* guidelines for our science projects⟩ — see EASYGOING 2

4 not bound, confined, or detained by force ⟨there was a brief panic when the lion got *loose* from its cage at the zoo⟩ — see FREE 3

5 not precisely correct ⟨a *loose* guess about the size of the crowd⟩ — see INEXACT 1

loose *vb* **1** to cause (a projectile) to be driven forward with force ⟨the archers *loosed* a great volley of arrows at the enemy soldiers charging towards them⟩ — see SHOOT 1

2 to find emotional release for ⟨do not *loose* your pent-up frustrations on the next person who happens by⟩ — see TAKE OUT 1

3 to set free (as from slavery or confinement) ⟨animal-rights activists *loosed* the monkeys from their laboratory cages⟩ — see FREE 1

4 to set free (from a state of being held in check) ⟨the storm *loosed* its full fury when it hit the coastline at high tide⟩ — see RELEASE 1

loosen *vb* **1** to make less taut ⟨he *loosened* the climbing rope so that the other climber could have more room to maneuver⟩ — see SLACKEN

2 to set free (as from slavery or confinement) ⟨the secret police have ways of *loosening* your tongue⟩ — see FREE 1

3 to set free (from a state of being held in check) ⟨the well-known fact that alcohol tends to *loosen* a person's inhibitions⟩ — see RELEASE 1

loosen (up) *vb* to free from obstruction or difficulty ⟨asked the school administration to *loosen up* the rules on what can be printed on T-shirts⟩ — see EASE 1

loosened *adj* not tightly fastened, tied, or stretched ⟨the *loosened* nuts finally dropped off of the screws⟩ — see LOOSE 1

loot *n* valuables stolen or taken by force ⟨the burglar was caught when he stopped to examine the *loot* from the robbery⟩
synonyms booty, plunder, spoil, swag
related words prize; catch, haul, take; pilferage; windfall

loot *vb* to search through with the intent of committing robbery ⟨the bandits *looted* the archaeological dig before riding off into the night⟩ — see RANSACK 1

lop (off) *vb* to make (as hair) shorter with or as if with the use of shears ⟨the hair stylist started by *lopping off* several inches from her long tresses, before beginning to shape what was left⟩ — see CLIP

lope *vb* to move with a light bouncing step ⟨the jogger *loped* along, just enjoying the fresh morning air⟩ — see SKIP 1

lopsided *adj* inclined or twisted to one side ⟨the portrait in the foyer was *lopsided*, so I straightened it while I was waiting⟩ — see AWRY

loquacious *adj* fond of talking or conversation ⟨the *loquacious* television host introduced the celebrity by rattling off some little-known facts about her⟩ — see TALKATIVE

Lord *n* the being worshipped as the creator and ruler of the universe ⟨at this point all that we can do is put our fate in the hands of the *Lord*⟩ — see DEITY 2

lord (it over) *vb* to assume or treat with an air of superiority ⟨waiters at that fancy restaurant like to *lord it over* the customers, acting like they're doing them a favor just being there⟩ — see CONDESCEND 2

lordliness *n* an exaggerated sense of one's importance that shows itself in the making of excessive or unjustified claims ⟨the *lordliness* of his manner got on his colleagues' nerves since he had no real authority over them⟩ — see ARROGANCE

lordly *adj* **1** having a feeling of superiority that shows itself in an overbearing attitude ⟨one dinner guest was a little *lordly* about her status as a vegetarian, even asking the other diners how they could bear to eat dead animals⟩ — see ARROGANT
2 having or displaying feelings of scorn for what is regarded as beneath oneself ⟨his *lordly* attitude toward people who enjoy popular music⟩ — see PROUD 1
3 having, characterized by, or arising from a dignified and generous nature ⟨born to great wealth, he has always displayed a *lordly* generosity toward the less fortunate⟩ — see NOBLE 2

lore *n* **1** a body of facts learned by study or experience ⟨the home gardener had acquired her herbal *lore* from many years of trial and error⟩ — see KNOWLEDGE 1
2 the body of customs, beliefs, stories, and sayings associated with a people, thing, or place ⟨set out to study the rich *lore* of the Cajun people of Louisiana before it all vanished⟩ — see FOLKLORE

lorn *adj* sad from lack of companionship or separation from others ⟨the *lorn* widow missed her husband greatly⟩ — see LONESOME 1

lose *vb* **1** to be unable to find or have at hand ⟨I always *lose* my keys⟩
synonyms mislay, misplace
near antonyms have
antonyms find, locate
2 to get rid of as useless or unwanted ⟨we told him to *lose* the flashy shirts and dress conservatively for the job interview⟩ — see DISCARD

loser *n* something that has failed ⟨the first movie in the series was good, but all the sequels were *losers*⟩ — see FAILURE 3

loss *n* **1** the act or an instance of not having or being able to find ⟨he was upset over the *loss* of his bike⟩
synonyms mislaying, misplacement
related words deprivation, dispossession; forfeit, forfeiture, penalty; sacrifice; bereavement
antonyms acquisition, gain
2 a person or thing harmed, lost, or destroyed ⟨the platoon was able to accomplish its mission without any *losses*⟩ — see CASUALTY 1
3 failure to win a contest ⟨we're discouraged by our *loss* on Friday, but we're training hard for next week's game anyway⟩ — see DEFEAT 1
4 the amount by which something is lessened ⟨was determined to stay on the diet until he showed a *loss* of ten pounds⟩ — see DECREASE
5 the state of being robbed of something normally enjoyed ⟨her *loss* of sleep meant that she had trouble concentrating in class⟩ — see PRIVATION
6 the state or fact of being rendered nonexistent, physically unsound, or useless ⟨the *loss* of the ship was more significant than the *loss* of its cargo⟩ — see DESTRUCTION

lost *adj* no longer possessed ⟨they searched all over the house for the *lost* keys⟩
synonyms gone, mislaid, misplaced, missing
related words absent, castaway; irrecoverable, irretrievable; forgotten, unknown
near antonyms cherished, protected, treasured
antonyms owned, possessed, retained

lot *n* **1** a small piece of land that is developed or available for development ⟨we often played in the vacant *lot* down at the end of the street⟩
synonyms parcel, plat, plot, property, tract
related words patch; frontage; lease; development; real estate
2 a considerable amount ⟨they needed to do a *lot* of studying for the test⟩
synonyms abundance, barrel, bucket, bushel, deal, gobs, heap, loads, mass, mountain, much, oodles, peck, pile, plenitude, plenty, pot, profusion, quantity, raft, reams, scads, stack, volume, wad, wealth
related words embarrassment, excess, overabundance, overage, overkill, overmuch, oversupply, superabundance, superfluity, surfeit, surplus; deluge, flood, overflow
near antonyms atom, crumb, fragment, grain, iota, jot, modicum, molecule, particle, scrap, shred, tittle, whit; scattering, smattering; drop, morsel, shot; piece, portion, section; absence, dearth, lack, paucity, poverty, scarceness, scarcity, shortage, want; deficiency, deficit, inadequacy, insufficiency, meagerness, scantiness, skimpiness
antonyms ace, bit, dab, driblet, glimmer, hint, lick, little, mite, mouthful, ounce, peanuts, pinch, scruple, smidgen, speck, spot, sprinkling, suspicion, taste, touch, trace
3 a small area of usually open land ⟨we set up a picnic in the *lot* by the stream⟩ — see FIELD 1
4 a number of things considered as a unit ⟨the auctioneer next introduced a *lot* containing several pieces of fine china⟩ — see GROUP 1
5 a state or end that seemingly has been decided beforehand ⟨will it always be my *lot* to be picked last in gym class?⟩ — see FATE 1
6 a group of people sharing a common interest and relating together socially ⟨you should stop hanging out with that *lot*, or you'll end up in trouble⟩ — see GANG 2

7 a usually small number of persons considered as a unit ⟨the school is indeed fortunate in its science teachers, because there's not a bad one in the *lot*⟩ — see GROUP 2

loud *adj* **1** marked by a high volume of sound ⟨*loud* music that could be heard all over the neighborhood⟩
synonyms blaring, blasting, booming, clamorous, clangorous, deafening, earsplitting, piercing, resounding, ringing, roaring, sonorous, stentorian, thunderous
related words brazen, dinning, discordant, noisy, obstreperous, raucous, rip-roaring, vociferous; grating, harsh, shrill, strident
near antonyms dead, quiet, silent, still; dreamy, peaceful, restful, soothing, tranquil; softened, toned (down)
antonyms gentle, low, soft
2 excessively showy ⟨his *loud* Hawaiian shirt made his face look especially pale⟩ — see GAUDY

lounge *n* a long upholstered piece of furniture designed for several sitters ⟨the tired youth stretched out on the *lounge* and breathed a huge sigh of relief⟩ — see COUCH

lounge *vb* **1** to refrain from labor or exertion ⟨police found him *lounging* in the shade behind the building⟩ — see REST 1
2 to spend time doing nothing ⟨when summer vacation first started, all we wanted to do was *lounge* around all day and relax⟩ — see IDLE

louse *n* a person whose behavior is offensive to others ⟨I can't believe you're willing to spend time with that lying *louse*⟩ — see JERK 1

louse up *vb* to make or do (something) in a clumsy or unskillful way ⟨I *loused up* my term paper when I mistakenly researched the wrong King Louis⟩ — see BOTCH

lousy *adj* **1** arousing or deserving of one's loathing and disgust ⟨why, you *lousy* cheater!⟩ — see CONTEMPTIBLE 1
2 falling short of a standard ⟨I actually play a pretty *lousy* game of tennis⟩ — see BAD 1
3 extremely unsatisfactory ⟨a *lousy* meal that we shouldn't have had to pay for⟩ — see WRETCHED 1
4 of low quality ⟨a tacky store selling *lousy* souvenirs that were made in some foreign sweatshop⟩ — see CHEAP 2

lout *n* **1** a big clumsy often slow-witted person ⟨watch where you're going, you big *lout*!⟩ — see OAF
2 a person whose behavior is offensive to others ⟨Howard's rude behavior at dances earned him a reputation as a *lout*⟩ — see JERK 1

loutish *adj* having or showing crudely insensitive or impolite manners ⟨the *loutish* bully didn't have a whole lot of friends⟩ — see CLOWNISH

lovable *adj* having qualities that tend to make one loved ⟨she was a *lovable* child, always helpful and kind⟩
synonyms adorable, darling, dear, disarming, endearing, precious, sweet, winning
related words embraceable, kissable; beloved, cherished, treasured; attractive, beautiful, desirable, lovely; captivating, charming, fascinating; admirable, likable (*or* likeable), reputable, respectable; affable, agreeable, cheerful, cordial, friendly, genial, gracious, kind, pleasant; delightful, pleasing
near antonyms unloved; contemptible, disagreeable, disgusting, distasteful, heinous, horrible, offensive, unlikable, unpleasant; frightful, grotesque, hideous, illfavored, monstrous, ogreish, repellent (*also* repellant), repugnant, repulsive; ugly, unattractive, unsightly, vile

antonyms abhorrent, abominable, detestable, hateful, odious, unlovable

love *n* **1** a feeling of strong or constant regard for and dedication to someone ⟨her *love* for her children was truly selfless⟩
synonyms affection, attachment, devotedness, devotion, fondness, passion
related words appetite, favor, like, liking, partiality, preference, taste; craving, crush, desire, infatuation, longing, lust, yearning; ardor, eagerness, enthusiasm, fervor, zeal; esteem, regard, respect; adoration, idolatry, worship; allegiance, fealty, fidelity, loyalty
near antonyms allergy, animosity, antipathy, aversion, disfavor, dislike; abhorrence, disgust, repugnance, repulsion, revulsion; misanthropy
antonyms abomination, hate, hatred, loathing, rancor
2 a person with whom one is in love ⟨she is the *love* of my life⟩ — see SWEETHEART
3 positive regard for something ⟨a *love* of chocolate that I will pay anything to indulge⟩ — see LIKING

love *vb* **1** to hold dear ⟨patriots who *loved* their country well enough to die for it⟩
synonyms appreciate, cherish, prize, treasure, value
related words delight (in), dig, enjoy, fancy, groove (on), like, relish, revel (in); admire, esteem, regard, respect, revere, reverence, venerate; enshrine, memorialize; adore, dote (on), idolize, worship
phrases set store (by *or* on)
near antonyms undervalue; abhor, abominate, despise, detest, execrate, hate, loathe; disdain, scorn, scout; belittle, decry, deprecate, depreciate, disparage; abandon, forget, neglect
2 to feel passion, devotion, or tenderness for ⟨a husband who *loves* his wife more than anything⟩
synonyms adore, cherish, worship
related words idealize, idolize; revere, reverence, venerate; delight (in), dote (on)
phrases fall for, lose one's heart (to)
near antonyms antagonize, displease; disapprove (of), disfavor, dislike; disgust, repulse, turn off
antonyms abhor, abominate, despise, detest, execrate, hate, loathe
3 to take pleasure in ⟨I *love* playing Frisbee in the summer rain⟩ — see ENJOY 1
4 to touch or handle in a tender or loving manner ⟨the baby responded to my caresses and kisses by *loving* me right back⟩ — see FONDLE

love affair *n* a brief romantic relationship ⟨the tabloids feel obliged to keep us informed of the *love affairs* of celebrities, whether we care to know or not⟩ — see AFFAIR 1

loved *adj* granted special treatment or attention ⟨her grandparents' constant doting made her feel especially *loved*⟩ — see DARLING 1

loveliness *n* the qualities in a person or thing that as a whole give pleasure to the senses ⟨our daughter was a vision of *loveliness* in her prom dress⟩ — see BEAUTY 1

lovely *adj* very pleasing to look at ⟨a *lovely* painting that deserved to win first prize⟩ — see BEAUTIFUL

lover *n* a person with a strong and habitual liking for something ⟨a *lover* of all kinds of team sports⟩ — see FAN

loving *adj* feeling or showing love ⟨they were a *loving* family, supporting each other when times were bad⟩
synonyms adoring, affectionate, devoted, fond, tender, tenderhearted
related words caring, compassionate, considerate, cordial, doting, forgiving, friendly, kind, warmhearted; ar-

dent, fervent, impassioned, passionate, warm; amatory, amorous, erotic; enamored, infatuated, lovesick; mushy, romantic, sentimental; brotherly, fatherly, motherly, sisterly

near antonyms aloof, detached, hardhearted, indifferent, pitiless, reserved, uncaring, unfeeling; disaffected, unconcerned, uninvolved; cold, frigid, unfriendly; hard-boiled, unromantic, unsentimental

antonyms unloving

low *adj* **1** being near the equator ⟨we took a cruise to the *low* northern latitudes⟩

synonyms equatorial, tropical

near antonyms temperate

antonyms polar

2 belonging to or characteristic of an early level of skill or development ⟨once considered the latest thing, electric typewriters now look like *low* technology indeed⟩ — see PRIMITIVE 1

3 belonging to the class of people of low social or economic rank ⟨people, both high and *low*, have been worshipping in this cathedral for centuries⟩ — see IGNOBLE 1

4 feeling unhappiness ⟨I was feeling *low*, and wanted to do something exciting to cheer myself up⟩ — see SAD 1

5 having a low musical pitch or range ⟨the tuba's *low* notes made the floor vibrate⟩ — see DEEP 2

6 having relatively little height ⟨the *low* hedge surrounding the garden wasn't meant to keep anything out, just to look pretty⟩ — see SHORT 1

7 lacking bodily strength ⟨the week-long bout of chicken pox laid her *low*⟩ — see WEAK 1

8 lacking in refinement or good taste ⟨jokes about toilets are generally considered *low* humor⟩ — see COARSE 2

9 not following or in accordance with standards of honor and decency ⟨*low* tactics of that sort will not be tolerated on this hockey team⟩ — see IGNOBLE 2

10 not loud in pitch or volume ⟨turned the music down *low* so as not to disturb the neighbors⟩ — see SOFT 1

11 costing little ⟨gas is *low* right now, but prices will inevitably rise this summer, when people start driving more⟩ — see CHEAP 1

lowbred *adj* lacking in refinement or good taste ⟨having been brought up in a genteel family, she began to resent her fiancé's *lowbred* ways⟩ — see COARSE 2

lowbrow *adj* lacking in refinement or good taste ⟨his *lowbrow* humor distressed his teacher as much as it entertained the other kids⟩ — see COARSE 2

lowbrow *n* a person who is chiefly interested in material comfort and is hostile or indifferent to art and culture ⟨the town's *lowbrows* think that the school's music program is a complete waste of taxpayers' money⟩ — see PHILISTINE

lowdown *n* information not generally available to the public ⟨have you heard the *lowdown* on the new student?⟩ — see DOPE 1

lower *adj* **1** having or not so great importance or rank as another ⟨a *lower* position in the company⟩ — see LESSER

2 situated lower down ⟨this book goes on the *lower* shelf⟩ — see INFERIOR 1

¹lower *vb* **1** to cause to fall intentionally or unintentionally ⟨workmen slowly *lowered* the heavy statue into place⟩ — see DROP 1

2 to go to a lower level ⟨prices of the new type of televisions *lowered* considerably as competition and sales increased⟩ — see DROP 2

3 to make smaller in amount, volume, or extent ⟨decided to *lower* his career ambitions to something more achievable⟩ — see DECREASE 1

4 to grow less in scope or intensity especially gradually ⟨the noise of the jet engine *lowered* as the plane disappeared in the distance⟩ — see DECREASE 2

5 to reduce to a lower standing in one's own eyes or in others' eyes ⟨how could you *lower* yourself by passing off someone else's work as your own?⟩ — see HUMBLE

²lower *also* **lour** *vb* **1** to take on a gloomy or forbidding look ⟨the sky *lowered* overhead, threatening a fierce thunderstorm⟩ — see DARKEN 1

2 to look with anger or disapproval ⟨the motorist *lowered* at the guy who had cut in front of her⟩ — see FROWN

lower *also* **lour** *n* a twisting of the facial features in disgust or disapproval ⟨he turned to see the scornful *lower* on her face⟩ — see GRIMACE

lower–class *adj* belonging to the class of people of low social or economic rank ⟨they were finally earning enough to get out of the *lower-class* tax bracket⟩ — see IGNOBLE 1

lowered *adj* directed down ⟨she wouldn't look at me, preferring instead to just sit there with *lowered* eyes⟩ — see DOWNCAST 1

lowering *also* **louring** *adj* **1** covered over by clouds ⟨the *lowering* sky made us think twice about going to the park⟩ — see OVERCAST

2 harsh and threatening in manner or appearance ⟨we chose our next words carefully due to the *lowering* expression on his face⟩ — see GRIM 1

lowest *adj* being the least in amount, number, or size possible ⟨I play my radio at the *lowest* volume, but the neighbors still complain about the noise⟩ — see MINIMAL

low–grade *adj* of low quality ⟨plumbing fixtures that were made out of *low-grade* materials⟩ — see CHEAP 2

lowliness *n* the absence of any feelings of being better than others ⟨that saint is often held up as a role model for her piety and unaffected *lowliness*⟩ — see HUMILITY

lowly *adj* **1** belonging to the class of people of low social or economic rank ⟨a tycoon who struggled all his life to overcome his *lowly* origins⟩ — see IGNOBLE 1

2 not having or showing any feelings of superiority, self-assertiveness, or showiness ⟨the nuns at the convent strive to be *lowly* servants of the Lord⟩ — see HUMBLE 1

lowly *adv* in a manner showing no signs of pride or self-assertion ⟨the courtier bowed *lowly* before his king during the ceremony⟩

synonyms deferentially, humbly, meekly, modestly, sheepishly, submissively

related words fearfully, timidly; bashfully, diffidently, shyly; civilly, courteously, politely, respectfully

near antonyms fearlessly; discourteously, disdainfully, disrespectfully, impertinently, rashly, recklessly, saucily; impolitely, impudently, rudely, ungraciously

antonyms arrogantly, audaciously, boldly, brashly, brazenly, contemptuously, haughtily, pridefully, proudly, scornfully, swaggeringly

low–lying *adj* having relatively little height ⟨the *low-lying* hills only blocked our view of the sea a little bit⟩ — see SHORT 1

lowness *n* **1** the quality or state of lacking refinement or good taste ⟨the *lowness* of the comedian's humor is something movie fans either love or hate⟩ — see VULGARITY 1

2 the quality or state of lacking physical strength or vigor ⟨her lingering illness reduced her to a state of *lowness* she had never known before⟩ — see WEAKNESS 1

low–pressure *adj* having a relaxed, casual manner ⟨a *low-pressure* boss who lets employees do their work without looking over their shoulders⟩ — see EASYGOING 1

low–spirited *adj* feeling unhappiness ⟨the captain tried to cheer up her *low-spirited* teammates after their big loss⟩ — see SAD 1

loyal *adj* firm in one's allegiance to someone or something ⟨we remain *loyal* to the ideals for which this organization stands⟩ — see FAITHFUL 1

loyalist *n* a person who loves his or her country and supports its interests and policies ⟨*loyalists* engaging in espionage against the revolutionaries⟩ — see PATRIOT

loyalty *n* adherence to something to which one is bound by a pledge or duty ⟨there was no denying the dog's *loyalty* to his master⟩ — see FIDELITY

lozenge *n* a small mass containing medicine to be taken orally ⟨take one of these *lozenges* for your cold⟩ — see PILL

lubber *n* a big clumsy often slow-witted person ⟨although he's something of a *lubber*, everyone agrees that he has a kind heart⟩ — see OAF

lubberly *adj* lacking in physical ease and grace in movement or in the use of the hands ⟨a *lubberly* worker who is not allowed to do any of the fine work in the shop⟩ — see CLUMSY 1

lubricate *vb* to coat (something) with a slippery substance in order to reduce friction ⟨it's not a good idea to use olive oil to *lubricate* the gears in an appliance⟩
synonyms grease, oil, slick, wax
near antonyms coarsen, rough, roughen

lubricated *adj* having or being a surface so smooth as to make sliding or falling likely ⟨the *lubricated* parts of the machine were whirring smoothly without friction⟩ — see SLICK 1

lucent *adj* **1** easily seen through ⟨the pristine waters of *lucent* mountain seas⟩ — see CLEAR 1
2 giving off or reflecting much light ⟨the moon was a *lucent* orb in the autumn sky⟩ — see BRIGHT 1

lucid *adj* **1** giving off or reflecting much light ⟨the *lucid* bands that spread across the arctic sky and are known as the northern lights⟩ — see BRIGHT 1
2 having full use of one's mind and control over one's actions ⟨decided to make out her will while she was still *lucid*⟩ — see SANE
3 not subject to misinterpretation or more than one interpretation ⟨tried to make his instructions as *lucid* as possible so that everyone would understand what to do⟩ — see CLEAR 2

lucidity *n* **1** clearness of expression ⟨the *lucidity* of the recipe should ensure a minimum of confusion⟩ — see SIMPLICITY 2
2 the quality or state of having or giving off light ⟨the exceptional *lucidity* of the moon on a clear winter's night⟩ — see BRILLIANCE 1

lucidness *n* clearness of expression ⟨she was impressed by the *lucidness* of his explanation⟩ — see SIMPLICITY 2

Lucifer *n* the supreme personification of evil often represented as the ruler of Hell ⟨*Lucifer* was a powerful but proud angel before rebelling against Heaven⟩ — see DEVIL 1

luck *n* **1** success that is partly the result of chance ⟨some people have all the *luck*⟩

synonyms fortunateness, fortune, luckiness
related words break, fluke, godsend, hit, serendipity, strike, windfall; chance, opportunity; coup, stroke
near antonyms knock, misadventure, mishap; adversity, curse, sorrow, tragedy, trouble; calamity, cataclysm, catastrophe, disaster; defeat, failure, fizzle, nonsuccess; accident, casualty; disappointment, letdown, setback; circumstance, destiny, doom, fate, lot, portion
antonyms mischance, misfortune, unluckiness
2 the uncertain course of events ⟨let's plan our vacation rather than leave everything to *luck*⟩ — see CHANCE 1

luckiness *n* success that is partly the result of chance ⟨a rabbit's foot is said to bring you *luckiness*, but we have always wondered if the rabbit would agree⟩ — see LUCK 1

luckless *adj* having, prone to, or marked by bad luck ⟨the *luckless* gambler quickly lost of all of his money⟩ — see UNLUCKY

lucky *adj* **1** having good luck ⟨the *lucky* gambler walked out of the casino with $10,000⟩
synonyms fortunate, happy
related words blessed, favored, gifted, privileged; fair, golden, promising
near antonyms cursed, disadvantaged
antonyms hapless, ill-fated, ill-starred, luckless, starcrossed, unfortunate, unhappy, unlucky
2 coming or happening by good luck especially unexpectedly ⟨finding this twenty-dollar bill on the way to the candy store was a *lucky* break⟩ — see FORTUNATE 1

lucrative *adj* yielding a profit ⟨the skillful businessman quickly turned the failing store into a *lucrative* operation⟩ — see PROFITABLE 1

lucre *n* **1** something (as pieces of stamped metal or printed paper) customarily and legally used as a medium of exchange, a measure of value, or a means of payment ⟨foreign coins are not acceptable *lucre* in most vending machines in this country⟩ — see MONEY
2 the amount of money left when expenses are subtracted from the total amount received ⟨she runs her antiques store more for personal satisfaction than for *lucre*⟩ — see PROFIT 1

ludicrous *adj* **1** causing or intended to cause laughter ⟨the *ludicrous* sight of their teacher in a Halloween costume⟩ — see FUNNY 1
2 so foolish or pointless as to be worthy of scornful laughter ⟨a *ludicrous* and easily detected attempt to forge his father's signature on a note to school⟩ — see RIDICULOUS 1

lug *n* a big clumsy often slow-witted person ⟨get off of my feet, you big *lug*!⟩ — see OAF

lug *vb* **1** to cause to follow by applying steady force on ⟨*lugged* the lawn mower out into the backyard⟩ — see PULL 1
2 to support and take from one place to another ⟨I don't understand why he's always *lugging* all of his books around when his locker is right over there⟩ — see CARRY 1

lugubrious *adj* expressing or suggesting mourning ⟨the *lugubrious* expression on the kid who had missed his ride home⟩ — see MOURNFUL 1

lukewarm *adj* **1** having or giving off heat to a moderate degree ⟨I left the bowl of soup sitting on the counter too long, and now it's *lukewarm*⟩ — see WARM 1

2 showing little or no interest or enthusiasm ⟨the dentist's lecture on the merits of flossing got only a *lukewarm* response⟩ — see TEPID 1

lukewarmness *n* the quality or state of being moderate in temperature ⟨the *lukewarmness* of the soda pop did nothing for its taste⟩ — see WARMTH 1

lull *n* a momentary halt in an activity ⟨we took the opportunity of a *lull* in the conversation to make our announcement⟩ — see PAUSE

lulling *adj* tending to calm the emotions and relieve stress ⟨the *lulling* sound of a gently flowing stream⟩ — see SOOTHING 1

lumber *n* tree logs as prepared for human use ⟨a huge amount of *lumber* will be needed to build the house⟩ — see WOOD

lumber *vb* **1** to move heavily or clumsily ⟨the elephant *lumbered* through the jungle⟩
synonyms barge, clump, flounder, lump, pound, scuff, scuffle, shamble, shuffle, stamp, stomp, stumble, stump, tramp, tromp
related words drag, flop, haul; labor, plod, trudge; careen, lurch, stagger, sway, teeter, totter, waddle, weave, wobble
near antonyms float, hover, waft
antonyms breeze, coast, glide, slide, waltz, whisk
2 to make progress in a clumsy, struggling manner ⟨the parade *lumbered* to its destination in a somewhat disorganized fashion⟩ — see FLOUNDER 1
3 to make a low heavy rolling sound ⟨the horse-drawn wagon *lumbered* along the trail⟩ — see RUMBLE
4 to place a weight or burden on ⟨preparations that will *lumber* the expedition with unnecessary equipment and supplies⟩ — see LOAD 1

lumbering *adj* lacking in physical ease and grace in movement or in the use of the hands ⟨the *lumbering* giant was no match for the quick-witted hero⟩ — see CLUMSY 1

lumberjack *n* a person whose job is to cut down trees ⟨the sawmill gets most of its business from the *lumberjacks* up north⟩
synonyms logger
related words sawyer; forester

luminary *n* **1** a ball-shaped gaseous celestial body that shines by its own light ⟨awed by the vast number of *luminaries* in the night sky⟩ — see STAR 1
2 a person who is widely known and usually much talked about ⟨*luminaries* from the worlds of sports, entertainment, and politics were at the gala⟩ — see CELEBRITY 1

luminescence *n* the steady giving off of the form of radiation that makes vision possible ⟨we could see in the cave even without a flashlight because of the *luminescence* coming from some of the fungus on the walls⟩ — see LIGHT 1

luminosity *n* the quality or state of having or giving off light ⟨the *luminosity* of the fireflies made for an enchanting nighttime show⟩ — see BRILLIANCE 1

luminous *adj* giving off or reflecting much light ⟨the *luminous* moon bathed the snow-covered fields with a pearly glow⟩ — see BRIGHT 1

lump *n* **1** a small uneven mass ⟨she dumped a *lump* of clay on the table and started to sculpt⟩
synonyms blob, chunk, clod, clump, glob, gob, gobbet, hunk, knob, nub, nubble, nugget, wad
related words bead, drop, globule; block, body, bulk; particle, piece, portion; bit, chip, crumb, morsel, scrap
2 a small rounded mass of swollen tissue ⟨I got a good-sized *lump* on my head from that fall⟩ — see BUMP 1

3 an abnormal mass of tissue ⟨advised by her doctor to examine her breasts regularly for unusual *lumps*⟩ — see GROWTH 1

lump *vb* **1** to bring together in one body or place ⟨when we *lumped* all of our pocket change together, we found that we had just enough a buy a carton of ice cream⟩ — see GATHER 1
2 to move heavily or clumsily ⟨while I was on crutches, I was *lumping* about the house like an elephant⟩ — see LUMBER 1

lumpish *adj* lacking in physical ease and grace in movement or in the use of the hands ⟨the *lumpish* waiter spilled water on us even before we got a chance to open the menus⟩ — see CLUMSY 1

lumpy *adj* **1** having small pieces or lumps spread throughout ⟨the *lumpy* mashed potatoes were cold as well⟩ — see CHUNKY 1
2 not having a level or smooth surface ⟨before painting, we had to sand the *lumpy* surface to make it smooth⟩ — see UNEVEN 1

lunacy *n* **1** a foolish act or idea ⟨you want to sneak into school after dark? That's *lunacy!*⟩ — see FOLLY 1
2 a serious mental disorder that prevents one from living a safe and normal life ⟨the judge ruled that the *lunacy* of the accused made him incompetent to stand trial⟩ — see INSANITY 1
3 lack of good sense or judgment ⟨our friend's *lunacy* makes him of no use in an emergency but very entertaining companion nevertheless⟩ — see FOOLISHNESS 1

lunatic *adj* **1** having or showing a very abnormal or sick state of mind ⟨his *lunatic* obsession with personal hygiene drove all of his friends away⟩ — see INSANE 1
2 showing or marked by a lack of good sense or judgment ⟨his *lunatic* clowning was completely inappropriate for the church service⟩ — see FOOLISH 1

lunatic *n* **1** a person judged to be legally or medically insane ⟨the *lunatic* was committed to an institution after running naked through the department store⟩
synonyms crackbrain, loony (*also* looney), maniac, neurotic, nut, psychopath, psychotic
related words madman, madwoman; deviant; paranoid, schizophrenic; character, crackpot, crank, eccentric, kook, oddball, screwball; case, patient
2 a person who lacks good sense or judgment ⟨we all knew she was a *lunatic*, but we never expected her to try to jump off of the roof of the school with a hang glider⟩ — see FOOL 1

lurch *vb* **1** to make a series of unsteady side-to-side motions ⟨the room *lurched* with every jolt of the earthquake⟩ — see ROCK 1
2 to move forward while swaying from side to side ⟨dressed in my zombie costume, I *lurched* down the street in my quest for Halloween candy⟩ — see STAGGER 1

lure *n* **1** something that persuades one to perform an action for pleasure or gain ⟨the promise of easy money is always the *lure* for some people to take up a life of crime⟩
synonyms allurement, bait, enticement, temptation, turn-on
related words appeal, call; attraction, goad, incentive, inducement, persuasion, seduction, spur; decoy, snare, trap
near antonyms caution, warning
2 something used to attract animals to a hook or into a trap ⟨the fish simply didn't seem to like the *lure* I was using, and I didn't catch a thing⟩ — see BAIT 1

3 the act or pressure of giving in to a desire especially when ill-advised ⟨the *lure* of the carnival was distracting me from my studies⟩ — see TEMPTATION 1

lure *vb* to lead away from a usual or proper course by offering some pleasure or advantage ⟨the hunter *lured* the lion into the open with the antelope carcass⟩

synonyms allure, beguile, decoy, entice, lead on, seduce, tempt

related words inveigle, persuade, rope (in), snow; catch, ensnare, entrap, snare; captivate, charm, enchant

near antonyms caution, ward (off), warn; drive (away *or* off), repulse, turn away

lurid *adj* **1** extremely disturbing or repellent ⟨we quickly drove past the *lurid* scene of the accident⟩ — see HORRIBLE 1

2 lacking a healthy skin color ⟨the doctor was alarmed by the patient's *lurid* complexion⟩ — see PALE 2

3 arousing a strong and usually superficial interest or emotional reaction ⟨the *lurid* news reports about the romance between the two Hollywood stars⟩ — see SENSATIONAL 1

luring *adj* having an often mysterious or magical power to attract ⟨the *luring* sight of sparkling gemstones in a jewelry-store window⟩ — see FASCINATING 1

lurk *vb* to move about in a sly or secret manner ⟨we caught a glimpse of someone *lurking* around the corner⟩ — see SNEAK 1

lurker *n* someone who acts in a sly and secret manner ⟨suddenly, the mysterious *lurker* leapt out into the light!⟩ — see SNEAK

luscious *adj* **1** very pleasing to the sense of taste ⟨a *luscious* strawberry bursting with juice⟩ — see DELICIOUS 1

2 pleasing to the physical senses ⟨*luscious* silk fabric that slid across her hands⟩ — see SENSUAL

3 giving pleasure or contentment to the mind or senses ⟨the *luscious* thought that while she was basking on the beach, her coworkers were slaving away at the office⟩ — see PLEASANT

lusciousness *n* the quality of being delicious ⟨it was hard to resist the *lusciousness* of the three-layer chocolate cake⟩ — see DELICIOUSNESS

lush *adj* **1** covered with a thick healthy natural growth ⟨they loved to go for picnics in the *lush* woodlands⟩

synonyms green, leafy, luxuriant, overgrown, verdant

related words fat, fecund, fertile, fruitful, productive, rich; dense, tangled

near antonyms bleak, depleted, infertile, poor, unproductive; arid, dead, desert, dry, parched

antonyms barren, leafless

2 growing thickly and vigorously ⟨*lush* dandelions had turned the meadow into a sea of yellow⟩ — see RANK 1

lust (for *or* after) *vb* to have an earnest wish to own or enjoy ⟨I'm *lusting after* that new mountain bike⟩ — see DESIRE

lust *n* a strong wish for something ⟨the belief that most politicians have a *lust* for power⟩ — see DESIRE

luster *or* **lustre** *n* brightness created by light reflected from a surface ⟨the Hope diamond is famous for its brilliant *luster*⟩ — see SHINE 1

lusterless *adj* lacking a surface luster or gloss ⟨a small tombstone of *lusterless* granite marks his grave⟩ — see MATTE

lustful *adj* having a strong sexual desire ⟨the *lustful* student was always chasing after girls⟩

synonyms lascivious, lewd, licentious, passionate, wanton

related words prurient; dissipated, dissolute, libertine; corrupt, debauched, depraved, immoral, indecent

near antonyms celibate, chaste, decent, modest, moral, pure, virtuous; monastic, monkish; maidenly, virginal; innocent, lily-white

lustiness *n* the quality or state of having abundant or intense activity ⟨campaign volunteers working for their candidate with a *lustiness* that is inspiring⟩ — see VITALITY 1

lustrous *adj* **1** giving off or reflecting much light ⟨the *lustrous* finish on the satin bedspread adds to the feeling of luxury⟩ — see BRIGHT 1

2 having a shiny surface or finish ⟨*lustrous* silver jewelry adorned her neck⟩ — see GLOSSY

lusty *adj* **1** having active strength of body or mind ⟨the *lusty* young rowers on the college crew team⟩ — see VIGOROUS 1

2 not showing weakness or uncertainty ⟨a *lusty* spirit of adventure⟩ — see FIRM 1

luxuriant *adj* **1** covered with a thick, healthy natural growth ⟨an older man who still has a *luxuriant* head of hair⟩ — see LUSH 1

2 growing thickly and vigorously ⟨a *luxuriant* coat of fur⟩ — see RANK 1

3 producing abundantly ⟨*luxuriant* soil that yields endless fields of grain⟩ — see FERTILE

4 showing obvious signs of wealth and comfort ⟨the fashion model always wore the most *luxuriant* outfits⟩ — see LUXURIOUS

luxurious *adj* showing obvious signs of wealth and comfort ⟨the *luxurious* apartment was filled with the latest electronic gadgets and fine works of art⟩

synonyms deluxe, lavish, luxuriant, opulent, palatial, plush, sumptuous

related words costly, expensive; rich; extravagant, grandiose, ostentatious, pretentious, showy; awesome, awful, beautiful, gorgeous, grand, imposing, impressive, magnificent, majestic, splendid, stately; comfortable, cozy, homelike, homey, snug

near antonyms economical, frugal, meager (*or* meagre), spare, thrifty

antonyms ascetic, austere, humble, Spartan

luxuriously *adv* in a luxurious manner ⟨we welcomed the opportunity to live *luxuriously* while on the ocean liner⟩ — see HIGH

luxury *n* something adding to pleasure or comfort but not absolutely necessary ⟨a private yacht is a *luxury*⟩

synonyms amenity, comfort, extra, frill, indulgence, superfluity

related words extravagance; dainty, delicacy, treat; accessory, option

antonyms basic, essential, fundamental, necessity, requirement

2 something that adds to one's ease ⟨having one's own bathroom is one of life's greatest *luxuries*⟩ — see COMFORT 2

lying *adj* telling or containing lies ⟨the *lying* reporter was fired for making up details in his stories⟩ — see DISHONEST 1

lynx–eyed *adj* having unusually keen vision ⟨the *lynx-eyed* teacher never seemed to miss an error in her students' work⟩ — see SHARP-EYED

lyric *adj* **1** having a pleasantly flowing quality suggestive of music ⟨they performed a slow, *lyric* dance for the audience⟩

synonyms euphonious, lyrical, mellifluous, mellow, melodic, melodious, musical *related words* dulcet, golden, sweet

near antonyms disconnected, staccato; discordant, grating, harsh, jarring, strident

2 having qualities suggestive of poetry ⟨the film's *lyric* photography really enhanced the mood of romantic drama⟩ — see POETIC

lyric *n* **1** a composition using rhythm and often rhyme to create a lyrical effect ⟨would you care to read your short *lyric* to the class?⟩ — see POEM

2 a short musical composition for the human voice often with instrumental accompaniment ⟨the guitarist sang a gentle *lyric* while playing⟩ — see SONG 1

lyrical *adj* **1** having a pleasantly flowing quality suggestive of music ⟨the *lyrical* cadences of voice-over narration give the film a very poignant quality⟩ — see LYRIC 1

2 having qualities suggestive of poetry ⟨the photographer achieves a very *lyrical* effect with her intentionally blurred images of flowers growing in the wild⟩ — see POETIC

M

ma *n* a female human parent ⟨I told my *ma* I'd be late for dinner tonight⟩ — see MOTHER

macabre *adj* extremely disturbing or repellent ⟨a *macabre* movie about animated corpses⟩ — see HORRIBLE 1

Machiavellian *adj* not guided by or showing a concern for what is right ⟨a power-mad dictator with a *Machiavellian* plan to take over the world⟩ — see UNPRINCIPLED

machinate *vb* 1 to engage in a secret plan to accomplish evil or unlawful ends ⟨a trio of courtiers who were discovered to be *machinating* against the queen⟩ — see PLOT

2 to plan out usually with subtle skill or care ⟨the hackers *machinated* a way to cheat on the test⟩ — see ENGINEER

machination *n* a secret plan for accomplishing evil or unlawful ends ⟨incredibly complicated *machinations* to assassinate the president that inevitably failed⟩ — see PLOT 1

machine *n* 1 a device that changes energy into mechanical motion ⟨a *machine* that washes dishes for you⟩ — see ENGINE

2 a self-propelled passenger vehicle on wheels ⟨that Corvette is a *machine* that any guy would love to own⟩ — see CAR

machinery *n* something used to achieve an end ⟨believes that the *machinery* of government can be used to better people's lives⟩ — see AGENT 1

mackintosh *or* **macintosh** *n, chiefly British* a coat made of water-resistant material ⟨be sure to wear a *mackintosh* while hiking over the misty mountains of England's Lake District⟩ — see RAINCOAT

macrocosm *n* the whole body of things observed or assumed ⟨your personal problems are small indeed from the perspective of the whole *macrocosm*⟩ — see UNIVERSE

mad *adj* 1 feeling or showing anger ⟨the constant harassment finally made her good and *mad*⟩ — see ANGRY

2 having or showing a very abnormal or sick state of mind ⟨the man who thinks he's turned into a bug is clearly *mad*⟩ — see INSANE 1

3 marked by great and often stressful excitement or activity ⟨a *mad* rush to finish the shopping before Christmas⟩ — see FURIOUS 1

4 showing or marked by a lack of good sense or judgment ⟨the *mad* decision to quit a good job and run off to the big city⟩ — see FOOLISH 1

mad (about) *adj* filled with an intense or excessive love for ⟨I'm just *mad about* the girl that just moved into our neighborhood⟩ — see ENAMORED (OF)

madcap *adj* foolishly adventurous or bold ⟨a *madcap* scheme to go over Niagara Falls in a barrel⟩ — see FOOLHARDY 1

madden *vb* 1 to cause to go insane or as if insane ⟨the endless swarms of mosquitoes all but *maddened* the explorers⟩ — see CRAZE

2 to make angry ⟨their disrespectful attitude *maddened* their teachers to no end⟩ — see ANGER

maddening *adj* causing annoyance ⟨after a few days, she found the boring work to be absolutely *maddening*⟩ — see ANNOYING

mademoiselle *n* a young usually unmarried woman ⟨a pretty young *mademoiselle* enjoying the spring sunshine⟩ — see GIRL 1

made-up *adj* not real and existing only in the imagination ⟨a *made-up* story about a bright blue dragon⟩ — see IMAGINARY

madhouse *n* 1 a place where insane people are cared for ⟨it was hard to believe that this place with the bright cheery walls was really a *madhouse*⟩

synonyms asylum

related words institution; hospice, hospital, sanatorium, sanitarium; home

2 a place of uproar or confusion ⟨our house is always a *madhouse* on school mornings, with five kids and two dogs running around⟩

synonyms babel, bedlam, circus, hell

related words commotion, havoc, pandemonium, racket, ruckus, tumult, turmoil; clamor, clatter, din, hubbub, noise; chaos, confusion, disarrangement, disarray, disorder, maelstrom, mess, muss

near antonyms heaven, paradise, utopia; order, orderliness, organization; calm, peace; hush, quiet, silence, soundlessness, stillness

madly *adv* 1 in a confused and reckless manner ⟨dashed *madly* around the house during last-minute preparations for the party⟩ — see HELTER-SKELTER 1

2 in an enthusiastic manner ⟨the young singer has been so *madly* praised by the critics you'd think she had invented singing itself⟩ — see SKY-HIGH

madness *n* 1 a serious mental disorder that prevents one from living a safe and normal life ⟨nowadays certain forms of *madness* are quite treatable⟩ — see INSANITY 1

2 lack of good sense or judgment ⟨to do something so reckless would be sheer *madness*⟩ — see FOOLISHNESS 1

maelstrom *n* water moving rapidly in a circle with a hollow in the center ⟨our rubber raft got caught in a *maelstrom* in a particularly rough section of white water⟩ — see WHIRLPOOL

maestro *n* a person with a high level of knowledge or skill in a field ⟨a *maestro* with the violin⟩ — see EXPERT

Mafia *n* a group involved in secret or criminal activities ⟨an informant telling the police how the local *Mafia* of drug dealers operated⟩ — see RING 1

magazine *n* 1 a building for storing goods ⟨the village kept a *magazine* where people left common supplies⟩ — see STOREHOUSE

2 a place where military arms are stored ⟨the *magazine* is heavily guarded to prevent theft⟩ — see ARMORY

3 a publication that appears at regular intervals ⟨a weekly sports *magazine*⟩ — see JOURNAL

magic *adj* 1 being or appearing to be under a magic spell ⟨a *magic* castle in which even the furniture comes to life⟩ — see ENCHANTED

2 having seemingly supernatural qualities or powers ⟨truth seekers of all sorts seem to be attracted to this *magic* spot in the desert⟩ — see MYSTIC 1

magic *n* 1 the power to control natural forces through supernatural means ⟨he claimed that he could summon a storm through *magic*⟩

synonyms bewitchment, black art, black magic, conjuring, enchantment, mojo, necromancy, sorcery, voodooism, witchcraft, witchery, wizardry

related words abracadabra, amulet, charm, fetish (*also* fetich), mascot, phylactery, talisman; curse, hex, incantation, jinx, spell; augury, divining, forecasting, foreknowing, foreseeing, foretelling, fortune-telling, predicting, presaging, prognosticating, prophesying, soothsaying; hoodoo, occultism, spiritualism; augur, omen; exorcism; alchemy

near antonyms science

2 the art or skill of performing tricks or illusions for entertainment ⟨they hired someone to do *magic* for their child's tenth birthday party⟩

synonyms conjuring, legerdemain

related words deception, trickery

phrases sleight of hand

3 the power of irresistible attraction ⟨a leader so charismatic that his appeal was like *magic*⟩ — see CHARM 2

magical *adj* **1** being or appearing to be under a magic spell ⟨the gym was decorated to resemble a *magical* wonderland for the party⟩ — see ENCHANTED

2 being so extraordinary or abnormal as to suggest powers which violate the laws of nature ⟨modern aviation must seem *magical* to someone who doesn't understand how airplanes work⟩ — see SUPERNATURAL 2

3 having seemingly supernatural qualities or powers ⟨his musical talent is so spectacular that it seems *magical*⟩ — see MYSTIC 1

magician *n* **1** a person skilled in using supernatural forces ⟨the *magician* was able to turn birds purple with a simple spell⟩

synonyms charmer, conjurer (*or* conjuror), enchanter, necromancer, sorcerer, voodoo, witch, wizard

related words enchantress, hag, hex, sorceress, warlock; medicine man; foreseer, fortune-teller, prognosticator, prophesier, prophet, soothsayer; medium; exorcist

2 one who practices tricks and illusions for entertainment ⟨the famous *magician's* best trick was always pulling a rabbit out of a hat⟩

synonyms conjurer (*or* conjuror), prestidigitator, trickster

related words charmer, enchanter, enchantress

magistrate *n* a public official having authority to decide questions of law ⟨chose to take their case before the local *magistrate*⟩ — see JUDGE 2

magnanimous *adj* having, characterized by, or arising from a dignified and generous nature ⟨a *magnanimous* donation to the town's animal shelter⟩ — see NOBLE 2

magnanimously *adv* in a manner befitting a person of the highest character and ideals ⟨*magnanimously* decided to forgive the classmates who had treated her so badly⟩ — see GREATLY 1

magnate *n* a person of rank, power, or influence in a particular field ⟨the film studio *magnate* had movie stars at his beck and call⟩

synonyms baron, czar (*also* tsar *or* tzar), king, mogul, prince, tycoon

related words big shot, bigwig, figure, nabob, notable, personage, VIP; celebrity, personality, star; moneybags, plutocrat

magnet *n* something that attracts interest ⟨the giant theme park is a *magnet* for tourists to the area⟩

synonyms attraction, draw, lodestone

related words capital, cynosure, mecca; allure, allurement, bait, enticement, fascination, lure, temptation,

turn-on; appeal, call; incentive, inducement, persuasion, spur

magnetic *adj* having an often mysterious or magical power to attract ⟨a cult leader who attracted followers with his *magnetic* gaze⟩ — see FASCINATING 1

magnetism *n* the power of irresistible attraction ⟨she managed to win the election by sheer *magnetism*⟩ — see CHARM 2

magnetize *vb* to attract or delight as if by magic ⟨the store's gorgeous window displays never fail to *magnetize* shoppers and sightseers⟩ — see CHARM 1

magnification *n* the representation of something in terms that go beyond the facts ⟨most movies don't deal in reality but in a *magnification* of reality where everything is more intense⟩ — see EXAGGERATION

magnificence *n* impressiveness of beauty on a large scale ⟨the *magnificence* of the great castle hallway is beyond description⟩

synonyms augustness, brilliance, gloriousness, glory, grandeur, grandness, majesty, nobility, nobleness, resplendence, splendor, stateliness, stupendousness, sublimeness, superbness

related words awesomeness, marvelousness, wondrousness; lavishness, luxuriance, luxury, opulence, sumptuousness; grandiosity, ostentation, pretentiousness; flashiness, gaudiness, ornateness, showiness; extraordinariness, remarkableness

magnificent *adj* large and impressive in size, grandeur, extent, or conception ⟨a *magnificent* mansion that still takes away the breath of visitors⟩ — see GRAND 1

magnify *vb* **1** to add to the interest of by including made-up details ⟨there's no need to *magnify* the events of your trip in order to make it seem impressive⟩ — see EMBROIDER

2 to enhance the status of ⟨his new-found fame as an actor has finally *magnified* him in the eyes of his perennially doubting family⟩ — see EXALT

3 to make markedly greater in measure or degree ⟨the movie's sound effects *magnify* every crash and boom in the action scenes⟩ — see INTENSIFY

4 to proclaim the glory of ⟨imposing cathedrals that were built to *magnify* the Lord and to inspire awe in worshippers⟩ — see PRAISE 1

magnitude *n* **1** the quality or state of being important ⟨the *magnitude* of the issue can scarcely be overstated⟩ — see IMPORTANCE

2 the quality or state of being very large ⟨the mountain's sheer *magnitude* usually leaves tourists speechless⟩ — see IMMENSITY

3 the total amount of measurable space or surface occupied by something ⟨the *magnitude* of the planned skyscraper is totally disproportionate with that of the other buildings on the block⟩ — see ¹SIZE

magnum opus *n* something (as a work of art) that is a great achievement and often its creator's greatest achievement ⟨this symphony is usually considered Beethoven's *magnum opus*⟩ — see MASTERPIECE

magpie *n* a person who talks constantly ⟨my lab partner is such a *magpie* that sometimes she gives me a headache⟩ — see CHATTERBOX

maid *n* **1** a female domestic servant ⟨they hired a *maid* to do the housework after the baby was born⟩

synonyms charwoman, domestic, housekeeper, housemaid, maidservant

related words attendant, chambermaid, handmaiden (*also* handmaid), lady-in-waiting; nursemaid

2 a young usually unmarried woman ⟨a dance where the fair *maids* and handsome bucks of the village hoped to meet one another⟩ — see GIRL 1

maiden *adj* **1** coming before all others in time or order ⟨the Titanic sank on its *maiden* voyage⟩ — see FIRST 1

2 never having had sexual relations ⟨only *maiden* girls were allowed to serve as priestesses in that temple in ancient Roman times⟩ — see VIRGIN 1

maiden *n* a young usually unmarried woman ⟨a story about a beautiful *maiden* and her mysterious father⟩ — see GIRL 1

maidservant *n* a female domestic servant ⟨a large estate that once had many *maidservants*⟩ — see MAID 1

mail *n* communications or parcels sent or carried through the postal system ⟨whenever they were separated, the lovers always sent each other lots of *mail*⟩

  synonyms matter, parcel post, post [*chiefly British*]

  related words electronic mail, e-mail; dispatch, epistle, message, missive, note, postcard; airmail, rural free delivery, special delivery; junk mail

mail *vb* to send through the postal system ⟨if you don't *mail* that letter soon, it's going to arrive late⟩

  synonyms post

  related words airmail; address, consign; direct, dispatch, forward, remit, route, ship, transmit, transport; register

  near antonyms receive

mail carrier *n* a person who delivers mail ⟨we give the *mail carrier* a card for Christmas⟩ — see POSTMAN

mailman *n* a person who delivers mail ⟨the *mailman* usually leaves packages outside the mailbox⟩ — see POSTMAN

maim *vb* to cause severe or permanent injury to ⟨on-the-job accidents *maim* far too many workers every year⟩

  synonyms cripple, disable, lame, mutilate

  related words dismember, hamstring, hobble; batter, bruise, bung (up), mangle, maul, rough (up); gore, lacerate, wound; disfigure, scar; break, damage, harm, hurt, impair, injure; bash, beat, belt, bludgeon, buffet, drub, hammer, lace, lambaste (*or* lambast), lick, paste, pelt, pound, pummel, thump; bang, box, hit, punch, slap, smack, smash, sock, spank, swat, swipe, thrash, thwack, whack; flog, lash, wallop, whip; kill, murder; torment, torture

  near antonyms cure, heal, remedy; doctor, fix, mend, patch; rebuild, recondition, reconstruct, rejuvenate, renew, renovate, repair, restore

main *adj* coming before all others in importance ⟨this is the *main* point of the study⟩ — see FOREMOST 1

main *n* **1** muscular strength ⟨all their might and *main* could not budge the stalled car⟩ — see MUSCLE 1

2 one of the great divisions of land on the globe or the main part of such a division ⟨traveled back to the *main* for supplies⟩ — see MAINLAND

3 the main or greater part of something as distinguished from its appendages ⟨the *main* of the tree is still healthy⟩ — see BODY 1

mainland *n* one of the great divisions of land on the globe or the main part of such a division ⟨the boat back to the *mainland* leaves once every two days⟩

  synonyms continent, main

  related words subcontinent, supercontinent

  near antonyms island, isle, islet; atoll, barrier reef, cay, coral reef, key; cape, headland, peninsula, promontory

mainly *adv* for the most part ⟨you *mainly* need to focus on improving your spelling⟩ — see CHIEFLY

mainstay *n* something or someone to which one looks for support ⟨Mom has been our *mainstay* in this crisis⟩ — see DEPENDENCE 2

maintain *vb* **1** to keep in good condition ⟨he repairs and *maintains* antique cars as a hobby⟩

  synonyms conserve, keep up, preserve, save

  related words support, sustain; care (for), husband, manage; defend, guard, protect, safeguard, screen, shield; cure, fix, heal, remedy; mend, patch, rebuild, reconstruct

  near antonyms disregard, ignore, neglect; break, damage, destroy, harm, hurt, impair, injure, ruin, wreck

2 to continue to declare to be true or proper despite opposition or objections ⟨part of debating is learning to *maintain* your position in the face of harsh challenges⟩

  synonyms defend, justify, support, uphold

  related words advocate, champion, espouse; confirm, vindicate, warrant; affirm, assert, avow, claim, contend, declare, insist, proclaim, profess, state; argue, debate, discuss; emphasize, stress, underline, underscore

  near antonyms abandon, forsake, recant, retract, take back, withdraw; controvert, disprove, rebut, refute

3 to pay the living expenses of ⟨we simply cannot afford to *maintain* a horse⟩ — see SUPPORT 2

4 to state (something) as a reason in support of or against something under consideration ⟨she continued to *maintain* that a sewing machine would end up paying for itself since she could make her own clothes⟩ — see ARGUE 1

5 to state as a fact usually forcefully ⟨he *maintains* that there is indeed hard evidence for extraterrestrial visitors⟩ — see CLAIM 1

maintainable *adj* capable of being defended with good reasoning against verbal attack ⟨it is important to choose a *maintainable* position for your thesis⟩ — see TENABLE 1

maintenance *n* the act or activity of keeping something in an existing and usually satisfactory condition ⟨I was hired to perform basic *maintenance* until the property could be sold⟩

  synonyms conservation, conserving, preservation, preserving, upkeep

  related words support, sustaining; care, guardianship; defense, guarding, protection, safeguarding, safekeeping

  near antonyms dereliction, ignoring, neglect; damage, destruction, harm, hurt, injury, ruin

majestic *adj* **1** having or showing elegance ⟨a *majestic* pillar of society who continues to entertain in grand style⟩ — see ELEGANT 1

2 large and impressive in size, grandeur, extent, or conception ⟨a *majestic* Egyptian pyramid that has enthralled travelers for aeons⟩ — see GRAND 1

3 very dignified in form, tone, or style ⟨the *majestic* language and beautiful cadences of the King James Version of the Bible⟩ — see ELEVATED 2

majesty *n* **1** a dignified bearing or appearance befitting royalty ⟨even as a child, the princess possessed a certain *majesty* that would later serve her well⟩

  synonyms augustness, stateliness

  related words high-mindedness, magnanimity, nobility; haughtiness, lordliness, pompousness; dignity, poise; grandeur, grandness, greatness, impressiveness, magnificence, resplendence, splendor

2 dignified or restrained beauty of form, appearance, or style ⟨the bishop carries himself with an impressive *majesty*⟩ — see ELEGANCE

3 impressiveness of beauty on a large scale ⟨the *majesty* of the Roman Colosseum is breathtaking⟩ — see MAGNIFICENCE

major *adj* having great meaning or lasting effect ⟨a *major* change in how science is taught in our high schools⟩ — see IMPORTANT 1

majority *n* the state of being fully grown or developed ⟨she will inherit a fortune upon her *majority*⟩ — see MATURITY

make *vb* **1** to bring into being by combining, shaping, or transforming materials ⟨will you help me *make* the dough for the cookies?⟩

synonyms fabricate, fashion, form, frame, manufacture, produce

related words assemble, build, construct, erect, make up, put up, raise, rear, structure, throw up; craft, handcraft; forge, mold, shape; prefabricate; create, invent, originate; establish, father, institute, organize; concoct, contrive, cook up, design, devise, imagine, think (up); conceive, envisage, picture, visualize; refashion, remake, remanufacture

phrases put together

near antonyms disassemble, dismantle, take apart; break up, dismember; abolish, annihilate, demolish, destroy, devastate, eradicate, exterminate, extinguish, flatten, pulverize, raze, ruin, shatter, smash, wreck; break, damage, harm, hurt, impair; blow up, explode

2 to obtain (as a goal) through effort ⟨we finally *made* it!⟩ — see ACHIEVE 1

3 to be the cause of (a situation, action, or state of mind) ⟨the sudden collapse of the woman *made* a disturbance in the theater⟩ — see EFFECT

4 to carry through (as a process) to completion ⟨one student will be asked to *make* a speech at the commencement ceremonies⟩ — see PERFORM 1

5 to cause (a person) to give in to pressure ⟨*made* him do all the work while everyone else just lounged around⟩ — see FORCE

6 to decide the size, amount, number, or distance of (something) without actual measurement ⟨I *make* that to be about six feet⟩ — see ESTIMATE 2

7 to form by putting together parts or materials ⟨*make* a model airplane⟩ — see BUILD

8 to give the impression of being ⟨the family *made* merry despite the worries⟩ — see SEEM

9 to go on a specified course or in a certain direction ⟨the baby *made* straight for the toy lying on the rug⟩ — see HEAD 1

10 to put into effect through legislative or authoritative action ⟨the legislature failed to *make* any new laws last session⟩ — see ENACT

11 to receive as return for effort ⟨I *made* almost $20 mowing lawns today⟩ — see EARN 1

12 to recognize the meaning of ⟨what do you *make* of the latest information?⟩ — see COMPREHEND 1

make–believe *adj* not real and existing only in the imagination ⟨zoomed around the house in a *make-believe* car⟩ — see IMAGINARY

make out *vb* **1** to meet one's day-to-day needs ⟨we're not rich, but we're *making out* all right⟩ — see GET ALONG 1

2 to recognize the meaning of ⟨I can't quite *make out* that phrase⟩ — see COMPREHEND 1

3 to touch one another with the lips as a sign of love ⟨a young couple *making out* on the couch⟩ — see KISS 1

make over *vb* **1** to change in form, appearance, or use ⟨*make over* the room into a nursery⟩ — see CONVERT 2

2 to give over the legal possession or ownership of ⟨*made* the deed *over* to his daughter⟩ — see TRANSFER 1

3 to make different in some way ⟨just got up one day and decided to *make over* her hairstyle and her appearance in general⟩ — see CHANGE 1

Maker *n* the being worshipped as the creator and ruler of the universe ⟨let us give thanks to our *Maker* for this meal⟩ — see DEITY 2

makeshift *adj* taking the place of one that came before ⟨turned a towel into a *makeshift* skirt⟩ — see NEW 1

makeshift *n* a temporary replacement ⟨when his belt broke, he used string as a *makeshift* until he could get home to replace it⟩

synonyms expedient, stopgap

related words recourse, refuge, resort; alternate, backup, standby, stand-in, substitute, understudy

near antonyms archetype, original, prototype

makeup *n* **1** preparations intended to beautify the face or hair ⟨she never left the house without applying her *makeup* and arranging her jewelry⟩

synonyms cosmetics, paint

related words greasepaint; camouflage; cold cream, cream, eye shadow, kohl, lipstick, lotion, mascara, oil, powder, rouge, vanishing cream

2 the way in which the elements of something (as a work of art) are arranged ⟨the *makeup* of the memorial is strikingly simple: a single massive globe signifying world unity⟩ — see COMPOSITION 3

make up *vb* **1** to be all the substance of ⟨the book is *made up* of 20 chapters⟩ — see CONSTITUTE 1

2 to create or think of by clever use of the imagination ⟨your assignment is to *make up* a new society that would not repeat the mistakes of our own⟩ — see INVENT

3 to form by putting together parts or materials ⟨we'll have to *make up* the bookcase, which came in a box marked "some assembly required"⟩ — see BUILD

make up (for) *vb* to balance with an equal force so as to make ineffective ⟨the lavish present almost *made up for* forgetting his birthday⟩ — see OFFSET

making *n* the basic elements from which something can be developed ⟨she had all the *makings* of an excellent leader, but she needed some experience first⟩

synonyms material, raw material, stuff, substance

related words possibility, potential, potentiality; matter

maladroit *adj* showing or marked by a lack of skill and tact (as in dealing with a situation) ⟨a *maladroit* effort to cheer him up that backfired⟩ — see AWKWARD 2

malady *n* an abnormal state that disrupts a plant's or animal's normal bodily functioning ⟨in the olden days people were always suffering from some unknown *malady*⟩ — see DISEASE

malcontent *adj* having a feeling that one has been wronged or thwarted in one's ambitions ⟨she seems like a very *malcontent* person, always acting as if the entire world were out to get her⟩ — see DISCONTENTED

male *adj* considered characteristic of or appropriate for men ⟨the *male* attitude toward housekeeping that irks so many women⟩ — see MASCULINE

male *n* an adult male human being ⟨she sometimes felt vaguely threatened by large *males* that she passed on the street⟩ — see MAN 1

malediction *n* a prayer that harm will come to someone ⟨*maledictions* have been known to bring misfortune to their supplicants rather than to their intended targets⟩ — see CURSE 1

malefaction *n* a breaking of a moral or legal code ⟨*malefactions* in this school will not go unpunished⟩ — see OFFENSE 1

malefactor *n* **1** a person who commits moral wrongs ⟨she regards anyone who would cause the breakup of a family as a *malefactor* of the worst sort⟩ — see EVILDOER 1
2 a person who has committed a crime ⟨the victim was able to give a clear description of the *malefactor* to the police⟩ — see CRIMINAL

malevolence *n* the desire to cause pain for the satisfaction of doing harm ⟨only mindless *malevolence* would explain this cruel vandalism⟩ — see MALICE

malevolent *adj* having or showing a desire to cause someone pain or suffering for the sheer enjoyment of it ⟨a bully with a *malevolent* urge to torment anyone younger or weaker⟩ — see HATEFUL

malevolently *adv* in a mean or spiteful manner ⟨"I'll get you yet!" she hissed *malevolently*⟩ — see NASTILY

malfeasance *n* improper or illegal behavior ⟨a campaign to impeach the governor for *malfeasance* in office⟩ — see MISCONDUCT

malformed *adj* badly or imperfectly formed ⟨a clay sculpture of an eagle that was so *malformed* that it looked more like a feathered football⟩
synonyms deformed, distorted, misshapen, monstrous, shapeless
related words defaced, disfigured; aberrant, abnormal, freakish, mutant; asymmetrical (*or* asymmetric), crooked, disproportionate, irregular, lopsided, nonsymmetrical, overbalanced, unbalanced, unequal; horrible, horrific, terrible; ugly, unattractive
near antonyms flawless, perfect
antonyms shapely

malfunctioning *adj* not being in working order ⟨a *malfunctioning* computer cost us days of work⟩ — see INOPERABLE 1

malice *n* the desire to cause pain for the satisfaction of doing harm ⟨there was no reason other than pure *malice* to spread such disgusting lies all over school⟩
synonyms cattiness, despite, hatefulness, malevolence, maliciousness, malignancy, malignity, meanness, nastiness, spite, spitefulness, spleen, venom, viciousness
related words abusiveness, cruelty; abhorrence, abomination, execration, hate, hatred, loathing; animosity, antagonism, antipathy, bitterness, enmity, grudge, hostility, ill will, jaundice, rancor, resentment; despicableness, invidiousness, vengefulness, vindictiveness; aversion, disgust, distaste, horror, repugnance, repulsion, revulsion; contempt, disdain; jealousy, pique, resentment, scorn; bile, rancor, virulence, vitriol
near antonyms devotion, love, passion; amiability, amicability, amity, civility, cordiality, friendliness, hospitality; adoration, ardor, infatuation, veneration, worship; affection, charity, kindliness; comity, empathy, friendship, goodwill, sympathy, understanding

malicious *adj* having or showing a desire to cause someone pain or suffering for the sheer enjoyment of it ⟨there was the class chatterbox once again spreading *malicious* gossip⟩ — see HATEFUL

maliciously *adv* in a mean or spiteful manner ⟨*maliciously* tried to ruin her reputation⟩ — see NASTILY

maliciousness *n* the desire to cause pain for the satisfaction of doing harm ⟨the older boy knocked down the toddler out of sheer *maliciousness*⟩ — see MALICE

malign *adj* having or showing a desire to cause someone pain or suffering for the sheer enjoyment of it ⟨the pair of bullies had a *malign* desire to hurt anyone who even looked at them the wrong way⟩ — see HATEFUL

malign *vb* to make untrue and harmful statements about ⟨a candidate who believes that it is possible to win an election without *maligning* anyone⟩ — see SLANDER

malignancy *n* the desire to cause pain for the satisfaction of doing harm ⟨her *malignancy* was such that she even attacked her friends behind their backs⟩ — see MALICE

malignant *adj* having or showing a desire to cause someone pain or suffering for the sheer enjoyment of it ⟨a *malignant* wish to lash out at everyone who was smarter, richer, or better looking than he was⟩ — see HATEFUL

malignantly *adv* in a mean or spiteful manner ⟨*malignantly* planned to destroy his chief rival's art project⟩ — see NASTILY

maligning *n* the making of false statements that damage another's reputation ⟨public *maligning* of a person can actually be grounds for a lawsuit⟩ — see SLANDER

malignity *n* the desire to cause pain for the satisfaction of doing harm ⟨one of the characters in the novel is a slave driver of such *malignity* that he came to be one of the most famous villains in all of literature⟩ — see MALICE

malleability *n* the quality or state of being easily molded ⟨work with the clay until it reaches the right level of *malleability*⟩ — see PLASTICITY

malleable *adj* **1** capable of being easily molded or modeled ⟨*malleable* cookie dough⟩ — see PLASTIC
2 capable of being readily changed ⟨the cult leader took advantage of the *malleable*, cooperative personalities of his followers⟩ — see FLEXIBLE 1

malodorous *adj* having an unpleasant smell ⟨the garbage became quite *malodorous* after it sat there for two weeks⟩
synonyms fetid, foul, fusty, musty, noisome, rank, reeking, reeky, smelly, stinking, stinky, strong
related words putrid, rancid, stale; bad, disgusting, offensive, repulsive, revolting, vile; decayed, decaying, decomposed, decomposing, rotted, rotten, rotting, spoiled, spoiling; dirty, filthy, nasty, noxious; odoriferous, odorous
near antonyms flowery, fruity, spicy, woodsy
antonyms ambrosial, aromatic, fragrant, perfumed, redolent, savory, scented, sweet

maltreat *vb* **1** to inflict physical or emotional harm upon ⟨it's possible to *maltreat* someone severely using only words⟩ — see ABUSE 1
2 to abuse physically ⟨if you *maltreat* the puppy, we will take it away immediately⟩ — see MANHANDLE 1

mama *n* a female human parent ⟨your *mama* will feed you in just a moment⟩ — see MOTHER

mammoth *adj* unusually large ⟨a *mammoth* book with color plates of birds native to North America⟩ — see HUGE

mammoth *n* something that is unusually large and powerful ⟨even as sport-utility vehicles go, that one is a *mammoth*⟩ — see GIANT

mammy *n* a female human parent ⟨the toddler clung to her *mammy* and eyed the strangers fearfully⟩ — see MOTHER

man *n* **1** an adult male human being ⟨the children always feel better when there's a *man* or a woman around⟩
synonyms bloke [*chiefly British*], buck, cat [*slang*], chap [*chiefly British*], dude, fellow, gent, gentleman, guy, hombre, jack, joker, lad, male
related words master, mister, sir
2 a male romantic companion ⟨I'm going to see my *man* again tonight⟩ — see BOYFRIEND

3 a member of the human race ⟨every *man* has a responsibility to safeguard the planet⟩ — see HUMAN

4 the human race ⟨*man* is always coming up with new advances in science and technology⟩ — see MANKIND

5 the male partner in a marriage ⟨I now pronounce you *man* and wife⟩ — see HUSBAND

manacle *n* **1** something that physically prevents free movement ⟨a *manacle* kept the bear within the cage⟩ — see BOND 1

2 something that makes movement or progress more difficult ⟨views bigotry of any kind as a *manacle* on human society that must be broken⟩ — see ENCUMBRANCE

manacle *vb* **1** to confine or restrain with or as if with chains ⟨*manacled* the prisoner to the wall⟩ — see BIND 1

2 to create difficulty for the work or activity of ⟨in this situation, the police are *manacled* by unnecessary regulations⟩ — see HAMPER

manage *vb* **1** to deal with (something) usually skillfully or efficiently ⟨as usual, she *managed* the crisis with a minimum of fuss⟩ — see HANDLE 1

2 to look after and make decisions about ⟨*managed* a household and a business simultaneously⟩ — see CONDUCT 1

3 to meet one's day-to-day needs ⟨it'll be hard for a few weeks, but we'll *manage*⟩ — see GET ALONG 1

management *n* the act or activity of looking after and making decisions about something ⟨*management* of the sports facility can be challenging⟩ — see CONDUCT 1

manager *n* a person who manages or directs ⟨we wanted to change the policy regarding refunds, but the store *manager* refused⟩ — see EXECUTIVE

managerial *adj* suited for or relating to the directing of things ⟨her *managerial* style is very direct and detail-oriented⟩ — see EXECUTIVE

managing *adj* highest in rank or authority ⟨the *managing* editor has the ultimate say on what goes in the student newspaper⟩ — see HEAD

man-at-arms *n* a person engaged in military service ⟨nowadays standard equipment for a *man-at-arms* may include a bullet-proof vest and special goggles for nighttime vision⟩ — see SOLDIER

mandate *n* the granting of power to perform various acts or duties ⟨gave his second-in-command a *mandate* to run things in his absence⟩ — see COMMISSION 1

mandatory *adj* forcing one's compliance or participation by or as if by law ⟨the tests are *mandatory* for all students wishing to graduate⟩

synonyms compulsory, forced, imperative, incumbent, involuntary, necessary, nonelective, obligatory, peremptory, required

related words all-important, essential, indispensable, needed, requisite; insistent, persistent, pressing, urgent; demanded, enforced; coercive

near antonyms chosen, discretionary; dispensable, unnecessary, unneeded, unwanted; inconsequential, insignificant, nonessential, unimportant

antonyms elective, optional, voluntary

maneuver *vb* **1** to deal with (something) usually skillfully or efficiently ⟨*maneuvered* the conversation so that touchy subjects were avoided⟩ — see HANDLE 1

2 to plan out usually with subtle skill or care ⟨successfully *maneuvered* a way to get him to ask her to the dance⟩ — see ENGINEER

manful *adj* feeling or displaying no fear by temperament ⟨a *manful* effort to protect the remaining herds of African elephants⟩ — see BRAVE

mangle *vb* to make or do (something) in a clumsy or unskillful way ⟨you've *mangled* this so badly that we'll have to do it over⟩ — see BOTCH

mangy *adj* showing signs of advanced wear and tear and neglect ⟨a *mangy* old car that was covered in rust⟩ — see SHABBY 1

manhandle *vb* **1** to abuse physically ⟨charges that the police *manhandled* peaceful protesters⟩

synonyms maltreat, maul, mishandle, rough (up)

related words abuse, ill-treat, ill-use, mistreat, misuse; roughhouse, wrestle; bash, batter, beat, buffet, drub, lambaste (*or* lambast), lick, pound, pummel, slap, thrash; harm, hurt, injure, wound; oppress, persecute, wrong; ambush, assail, attack; clobber, fight, gang up (on), hit, jump, knock; torment, torture

near antonyms caress, fondle, pet; coddle, mollycoddle, pamper; care (for), foster, nurture

2 to inflict physical or emotional harm upon ⟨if you see anyone *manhandling* a child, you should call the authorities⟩ — see ABUSE 1

manhood *n* the set of qualities considered appropriate for or characteristic of men ⟨a society that highly values *manhood* and courage⟩ — see VIRILITY

mania *n* **1** a serious mental disorder that prevents one from living a safe and normal life ⟨that form of *mania* often manifests itself in excessive and often incoherent talkativeness⟩ — see INSANITY 1

2 something about which one is constantly thinking or concerned ⟨a shopping *mania* that resulted in her buying things for which she had no conceivable need⟩ — see FIXATION

maniac *n* **1** a person judged to be legally or medically insane ⟨they locked up the *maniac* who was responsible for the kidnappings⟩ — see LUNATIC 1

2 a person with a strong and habitual liking for something ⟨I'm a *maniac* for anything flavored with peppermint⟩ — see FAN

maniacal *also* **maniac** *adj* having or showing a very abnormal or sick state of mind ⟨a *maniacal* glint in his eye as he secretly observed his next victim⟩ — see INSANE 1

manifest *adj* not subject to misinterpretation or more than one interpretation ⟨your lack of interest in this topic is quite *manifest*, so you can stop staring at the clock⟩ — see CLEAR 2

manifest *vb* **1** to make known (something abstract) through outward signs ⟨a frustration that is often *manifested* by a minor tic⟩ — see SHOW 2

2 to represent in visible form ⟨graduates of the military academies *manifest*, we hope, the best that this country has to offer⟩ — see EMBODY 2

manifestation *n* a visible representation of something abstract (as a quality) ⟨a portrait of a mother and child that is regarded as the very *manifestation* of maternal love⟩ — see EMBODIMENT

manifold *adj* being of many and various kinds ⟨the *manifold* attractions of that state make it an ideal destination for a family vacation⟩

synonyms divers, multifarious, myriad

related words multiform, multiple, multiplex, multitudinous; heterogeneous, miscellaneous, mixed, sundry, various; different, diverse, unlike, varied

near antonyms homogeneous, monolithic, unmixed, unvaried; alike, identical, same; distinct, distinctive, individual, separate; alone, lone, only, sole, solitary; singular, unique

manikin *or* **mannikin** *n* **1** a three-dimensional representation of the human body used especially for displaying clothes ⟨the store had *manikins* so lifelike that they startled me several times⟩ — see MANNEQUIN 1
2 a person who poses with or wears merchandise (as clothes) often for pictorial advertising ⟨undulating movements of the *manikins* as they strutted down the catwalk⟩ — see MODEL 2

manipulate *vb* **1** to control or take advantage of by artful, unfair, or insidious means ⟨*manipulated* their parents into agreeing to let them stay out later by telling their mother that their father agreed, and vice versa⟩
synonyms exploit, play (upon)
related words engineer, finagle, jockey, maneuver; beguile, bluff, cozen, deceive, delude, dupe, fool, gull, hoax, hoodwink, kid, snow, take in, trick; intrigue, machinate, plot, scheme; arrange, contrive, devise, finesse, mastermind; cheat, chisel, defraud, fleece, gyp, hustle, swindle
2 to deal with (something) usually skillfully or efficiently ⟨a scientist effortlessly *manipulating* a slew of statistics while testifying before congress⟩ — see HANDLE 1
3 to plan out usually with subtle skill or care ⟨*manipulated* the schedule of presidential primaries so that the choice of the party elders would win the nomination⟩ — see ENGINEER

mankind *n* the human race ⟨all of *mankind* stands to gain if world peace is finally achieved⟩
synonyms Homo sapiens, humanity, humankind, man
related words being, body, creature, fellowman, human, individual, mortal, party, person

manlike *adj* **1** considered characteristic of or appropriate for men ⟨people used to believe that military service was strictly a *manlike* occupation⟩ — see MASCULINE
2 having qualities or traits that are traditionally considered inappropriate for a girl or woman ⟨having grown up with four brothers, she had developed a *manlike* disregard for how her hair looked while playing sports⟩ — see UNFEMININE

manliness *n* the set of qualities considered appropriate for or characteristic of men ⟨studio executives wondered if the actor possessed the *manliness* expected in an action hero⟩ — see VIRILITY

manly *adj* considered characteristic of or appropriate for men ⟨a *manly* deep voice⟩ — see MASCULINE

man–made *adj* being such in appearance only and made with or manufactured from usually cheaper materials ⟨*man-made* diamonds that were really just glass⟩ — see IMITATION

manna *n* **1** a source of great satisfaction ⟨the announcement that there would be a sequel was *manna* to the many fans of the original movie⟩ — see DELIGHT 1
2 something that provides happiness or does good for a person or thing ⟨the company's Christmas bonus was especially welcome *manna* this year⟩ — see BLESSING 2

mannequin *n* **1** a three-dimensional representation of the human body used especially for displaying clothes ⟨the *mannequin* over there looks so real⟩
synonyms dummy, figure, form, manikin (*or* mannikin)
related words doll
2 a person who poses with or wears merchandise (as clothes) often for pictorial advertising ⟨several *man-*

nequins posing for this year's catalogue look especially emaciated⟩ — see MODEL 2

manner *n* **1** **manners** *pl* personal conduct or behavior as evaluated by an accepted standard of appropriateness for a social or professional setting ⟨her table *manners* were so impeccable that she even knew how to use all five forks⟩
synonyms etiquette, form, mores, proprieties
related words amenities, civilities, pleasantries; bearing, demeanor, deportment; courtesy, decorum, mannerliness, politeness; formalities, protocol, rules; air, attitude, carriage, poise, polish, pose, posture, presence; custom, habit, pattern, practice (*also* practise), trick, way, wont; convention, fashion, mode, style
2 a distinctive way of putting ideas into words ⟨the former doctor writes her novels very much in the *manner* of someone who is used to observing the smallest detail⟩ — see STYLE 1
3 a number of persons or things that are grouped together because they have something in common ⟨fish and all *manner* of sea life on view at the aquarium⟩ — see SORT 1
4 the means or procedure for doing something ⟨you happened to reach the correct answer, but your *manner* of solving the problem was all wrong⟩ — see METHOD

mannerism *n* an odd or peculiar habit ⟨quirky *mannerisms* such as toying with her hair and tapping her toes⟩ — see IDIOSYNCRASY

mannerliness *n* speech or behavior that is a sign of good breeding ⟨*mannerliness* consists of not only saying the right words but also acting considerately⟩ — see POLITENESS

mannerly *adj* showing consideration, courtesy, and good manners ⟨a *mannerly* child is welcome everywhere⟩ — see POLITE 1

mannish *adj* **1** considered characteristic of or appropriate for men ⟨a *mannish* fondness for coarse and suggestive jokes⟩ — see MASCULINE
2 having qualities or traits that are traditionally considered inappropriate for a girl or woman ⟨for her first outing as a spelunker she wore the same *mannish* jeans as the guys⟩ — see UNFEMININE

manor *n* a large impressive residence ⟨the old family *manor* has 117 rooms⟩ — see MANSION

manor house *n* a large impressive residence ⟨entertained everyone at their *manor house* after the wedding⟩ — see MANSION

manpower *n* a body of persons at work or available for work ⟨we're a little short on *manpower* today, so we'll need you to do some extra tasks⟩ — see FORCE 1

mansion *n* a large impressive residence ⟨if I ever win the lottery, I'm going to buy a *mansion* in the mountains⟩
synonyms castle, château, countryseat, estate, hacienda, hall, manor, manor house, palace, villa
related words showplace; abode, domicile, dwelling, habitation, hearth, home, house, lodging(s), pad, place; housing, nest, quarter(s), residency, roof; aerie, penthouse; salon, suite, townhouse

man–size *or* **man–sized** *adj* considered characteristic of or appropriate for men ⟨worked up a *man-size* appetite playing soccer⟩ — see MASCULINE

manta *n* any of several extremely large rays ⟨a *manta* glided by along the sea bottom⟩ — see DEVILFISH

manta ray *n* any of several extremely large rays ⟨the *manta ray* blended in beautifully with the sandy ocean floor⟩ — see DEVILFISH

mantilla *n* a scarf worn on the head ⟨a beautiful Spanish lady with a lace *mantilla*⟩ — see BANDANNA

mantle *n* **1** a sleeveless garment worn so as to hang over the shoulders, arms, and back ⟨a long black velvet *mantle*⟩ — see ¹CAPE
2 something that covers or conceals like a piece of cloth ⟨the *mantle* of secrecy that surrounds the operations of the organization's hierarchy⟩ — see CLOAK 1

mantle *vb* to surround or cover closely ⟨early-morning fog *mantled* the fields along the river⟩ — see ENFOLD 1

manual *n* a book used for instruction in a subject ⟨an owner's *manual* comes with the camera⟩ — see TEXTBOOK

manufactory *n* a building or set of buildings for the manufacturing of goods ⟨a *manufactory* for light bulbs⟩ — see FACTORY

manufacture *vb* **1** to bring into being by combining, shaping, or transforming materials ⟨the company *manufactures* appliances and electronics⟩ — see MAKE 1
2 to create or think of by clever use of the imagination ⟨*manufacture* a creative excuse to get out of gym class⟩ — see INVENT

manumission *n* the act of setting free from slavery ⟨the official *manumission* of the slaves came after the Civil War⟩ — see LIBERATION

manumit *vb* to set free (as from slavery or confinement) ⟨several servants were *manumitted* when the soldiers liberated the town⟩ — see FREE 1

manuscript *n* writing done by hand ⟨beautiful, careful *manuscript* on the school's diplomas⟩ — see HANDWRITING 2

many *adj* being of a large but indefinite number ⟨a journey of *many* miles begins with a single step⟩
synonyms multiple, multiplex, multitudinous, numerous
related words countless, innumerable, numberless, uncountable, unnumbered, untold; several, some; miscellaneous, mixed, sundry, various; divers, manifold, multifarious, myriad
near antonyms countable, limited
antonyms few

map *n* an illustration of certain features of a geographical area ⟨there is a *map* of the United States on the wall over there⟩
synonyms chart
related words graph, graphic; relief map

map (out) *vb* to work out the details of (something) in advance ⟨*mapped out* several alternate routes⟩ — see PLAN 1

mar *vb* **1** to affect slightly with something morally bad or undesirable ⟨*mar* a politician's reputation with scurrilous rumors⟩ — see TAINT 1
2 to reduce the soundness, effectiveness, or perfection of ⟨a slight scratch *marred* the baby's cheek at the time of the photograph⟩ — see DAMAGE 1

marathon *adj* lasting for a considerable time ⟨a *marathon* study session the night before the exam⟩ — see LONG 2

maraud *vb* to search through with the intent of committing robbery ⟨just for kicks, teenagers *marauded* neighborhood houses while their owners were away⟩ — see RANSACK 1

marble *vb* to mark with small spots especially unevenly ⟨*marble* the paper with several different dyes to get a striking effect⟩ — see SPOT 1

marbled *adj* having blotches of two or more colors ⟨a *marbled* chocolate and white cake⟩ — see PIED

march *n* **1** a region along the dividing line between two countries ⟨the sheriff of the *march* is charged with guarding against border incursions⟩ — see FRONTIER 1
2 forward movement in time or place ⟨the *march* of time⟩ — see ADVANCE 1

march *vb* **1** to move along with a steady regular step especially in a group ⟨the band had to practice for hours to be able to *march* in perfect step⟩
synonyms file, pace, parade, stride
related words goose-step; perambulate, step, traipse, tread; hike, tramp; lumber, plod, stamp, stomp, stride, trudge
near antonyms amble, meander, ramble, stroll, wander
2 to move forward along a course ⟨students *marching* off to class⟩ — see GO 1

margin *n* the line or relatively narrow space that marks the outer limit of something ⟨the *margins* of the paper are to be only an inch wide⟩ — see BORDER 1

margin *vb* to serve as a border for ⟨rocks *margining* the shoreline⟩ — see BORDER

marginally *adv* by a very small margin ⟨that's a *marginally* better idea, but not much⟩ — see JUST 2

marine *adj* **1** of or relating to the sea ⟨he loves collecting little *marine* creatures while at the beach⟩
synonyms maritime, oceanic, pelagic
related words abyssal, deep-sea, deepwater, saltwater; admiralty, nautical, naval; undersea, underwater; hydrographic, oceanographic
2 of or relating to navigation of the sea ⟨a collection of *marine* instruments, including a sextant⟩
synonyms maritime, nautical, navigational
related words admiralty, naval; oceangoing, seafaring, seagoing; hydrographic, oceanographic

mariner *n* one who operates or navigates a seagoing vessel ⟨the ancient Phoenicians were outstanding *mariners* who explored and colonized much of the eastern Mediterranean⟩ — see SAILOR

marital *adj* of or relating to marriage ⟨neither of them ever forgot their *marital* vows, no matter how hard things sometimes were⟩
synonyms conjugal, connubial, married, matrimonial, nuptial, wedded
related words espoused, matched, mated; bridal; wifely; affianced, betrothed, committed, engaged, pledged, promised

maritime *adj* **1** of or relating to navigation of the sea ⟨a rare *maritime* chart from the 17th century⟩ — see MARINE 2
2 of or relating to the sea ⟨the *maritime* occupation of fishing⟩ — see MARINE 1

mark *n* **1** a person or thing that is made fun of ⟨the comedian liked to use politicians as a *mark*⟩ — see LAUGHINGSTOCK
2 a person or thing that is the object of abuse, criticism, or ridicule ⟨it's cruel to use any child who is somehow different as the easy *mark* for bullying⟩ — see TARGET 1
3 overall quality as seen or judged by people in general ⟨a brand of crystal that bears the *mark* of excellence⟩ — see REPUTATION
4 something set up as an example against which others of the same type are compared ⟨your scholastic achievement has exceeded the *mark* by a wide standard⟩ — see STANDARD 1
5 something that one hopes or intends to accomplish ⟨set *marks* for expected daily output⟩ — see GOAL

6 something that sets apart an individual from others of the same kind ⟨a sensitive expression that is the *mark* of a poet⟩ — see CHARACTERISTIC

7 something that spoils the appearance or completeness of a thing ⟨a small *mark* where the car had scraped a wall⟩ — see BLEMISH

8 the power to bring about a result on another ⟨a person of some *mark*⟩ — see EFFECT 2

mark *vb* **1** to attach an identifying slip to ⟨*marked* each application with a numbered sticker⟩ — see LABEL 1

2 to be an important feature of ⟨an annual event *marked* mostly by noise and confusion⟩ — see CHARACTERIZE 2

3 to make a written note of ⟨*mark* down the names of everyone who is late⟩ — see RECORD 1

mark (out) *vb* to mark the limits of ⟨*marked* out the outline of the mural first⟩ — see LIMIT 2

mark down *vb* to lower the price or value of ⟨*marked down* the seasonal goods after the holidays⟩ — see DEPRECIATE 1

marked *adj* likely to attract attention ⟨walked with a *marked* limp⟩ — see NOTICEABLE

marker *n* a slip (as of paper or cloth) that is attached to something to identify or describe it ⟨the *markers* on the rock and mineral specimens were old and faded⟩ — see LABEL

market *vb* to offer for sale to the public ⟨local farmers *market* their garden-fresh produce in roadside stands all over the valley⟩
  synonyms deal (in), merchandise, put up, retail, sell, vend
  related words wholesale; hawk, peddle; barter, distribute, exchange, export, handle, trade, traffic (in); advertise, ballyhoo, boost, plug, promote, tout; bargain, chaffer, dicker, haggle, horse-trade, palter; auction; provide, supply; keep, stock
  antonyms buy, purchase

marketable *adj* **1** fit to be offered for sale ⟨you'll need to clean that car up a bit before it's *marketable*⟩
  synonyms salable (*or* saleable)
  related words commercial, profitable; costly, fancy, fine, high-grade, precious, premium, prime, valuable; dear, expensive, extravagant
  near antonyms damaged, shopworn; cheap, useless, worthless; bad, inferior, low-grade, substandard, unsatisfactory
  antonyms nonsalable, unmarketable, unsalable

2 fit or likely to be sold especially on a large scale ⟨trying to turn their invention into a *marketable* product⟩ — see COMMERCIAL

marketplace *n* the buying and selling of goods especially on a large scale and between different places ⟨nations struggling to compete in the global *marketplace*⟩ — see COMMERCE

market value *n* the amount of money for which something will find a buyer ⟨a classic car with a *market value* of tens of thousands of dollars⟩ — see VALUE 1

marksman *n* a person skilled in shooting at a target ⟨only the best *marksmen* can hit the bull's-eye at 500 feet⟩
  synonyms sharpshooter, shooter, shot
  related words rifleman, trapshooter; gunman, gunner, sniper

maroon *vb* to cause to remain behind ⟨pets that had been *marooned* by their owners at the end of the summer⟩ — see LEAVE 1

marriage *n* **1** a union representing a special kind of social and legal partnership between two people ⟨some religions consider *marriage* a sacrament⟩
  synonyms match, matrimony, wedlock
  related words bigamy, monogamy, polygamy; intermarriage, miscegenation, remarriage; attachment, commitment, relationship; betrothal, engagement, espousal, hand, pledge, promise, proposal, troth
  near antonyms annulment, divorce, separation

2 a ceremony in which two people are united in matrimony ⟨we've been invited to a *marriage* next month⟩ — see WEDDING

married *adj* of or relating to marriage ⟨a sermon on the joys and responsibilities of *married* love⟩ — see MARITAL

marry *vb* **1** to perform the ceremony of marriage for ⟨they chose a very nice priest to *marry* them⟩
  synonyms wed
  related words match, mate; conjoin, connect, unite; affiance

2 to give in marriage ⟨they worried about the cost of *marrying* off five daughters⟩
  synonyms espouse, match, wed
  related words commit, engage; affiance, betroth, pledge, promise

3 to take as a spouse ⟨he *married* his girlfriend three years ago, and they've been happy ever since⟩
  synonyms espouse, wed
  related words affiance, betroth, commit, engage, pledge, promise, propose; remarry
  near antonyms separate (from)
  antonyms divorce

4 to take a spouse ⟨she had always believed she would never *marry*, but fate proved her wrong⟩
  synonyms wed
  related words couple, mate; pair off, remarry
  phrases tie the knot
  near antonyms divorce, separate

5 to come together to form a single unit ⟨white wine and chicken *marry* especially well⟩ — see UNITE 1

marsh *n* spongy land saturated or partially covered with water ⟨the *marshes* along the coast support a remarkable variety of plants and animals⟩ — see SWAMP

marshal *vb* **1** to assemble and make ready for action ⟨*marshaled* their forces for battle⟩ — see MOBILIZE

2 to point out the way for (someone) especially from a position in front ⟨*marshaling* a small group of children on a tour of the science museum⟩ — see LEAD 1

3 to put into a particular arrangement ⟨*marshal* your arguments before you stand up to speak⟩ — see ORDER 1

marshaling *or* **marshalling** *n* an act of gathering forces together to renew or attempt an effort ⟨the last-minute *marshaling* of the troops failed to repel the onslaught⟩ — see RALLY 1

marshland *n* spongy land saturated or partially covered with water ⟨grasses, sedges, and rushes are the plant species most commonly found on *marshland*⟩ — see SWAMP

martial *adj* **1** of, relating to, or suitable for war or a warrior ⟨the young recruit looked all grown up in his new *martial* uniform⟩
  synonyms military, soldierly
  related words aggressive, bellicose, combative, contentious, guerrilla, pugnacious, quarrelsome, scrappy, truculent, warlike; belligerent, militant, warring; antagonistic, argumentative, fierce, gladiatorial, hot-tempered; mercenary

near antonyms civil, civilian, nonmilitary; conciliatory, nonviolent, pacific, peaceable, peaceful; affable, amiable, amicable, benevolent, complaisant, cordial, easygoing, friendly, genial, good-natured, gracious, ingratiating, obliging
antonyms unsoldierly
2 of or relating to the armed services ⟨one of the basic tenets of *martial* law⟩ — see MILITARY 1
martyr *vb* to cause persistent suffering to ⟨stop pretending that your homework load is *martyring* you⟩ — see AFFLICT
marvel *n* something extraordinary or surprising ⟨that new electric car really is a *marvel*⟩ — see WONDER 1
marveling *or* **marvelling** *adj* filled with amazement or wonder ⟨with *marveling* stares onlookers gathered round the remarkable invention⟩ — see OPENMOUTHED
marvelous *or* **marvellous** *adj* **1** causing wonder or astonishment ⟨the sheer immensity of the ancient ruin known as Stonehenge is *marvelous* to behold⟩
synonyms amazing, astonishing, astounding, awesome, awful, eye-opening, fabulous, miraculous, portentous, prodigious, staggering, stunning, stupendous, sublime, surprising, wonderful, wondrous
related words incomprehensible, inconceivable, incredible, unbelievable, unimaginable, unthinkable; extraordinary, phenomenal, rare, sensational, spectacular; singular, uncommon, unique, unusual, unwonted; conspicuous, notable, noticeable, outstanding, remarkable; impressive, striking; animating, energizing, enlightening, enlivening, exciting, galvanizing, invigorating, stimulating; alluring, attracting, attractive, beguiling, bewitching, captivating, charming, enchanting, entertaining, enthralling, fascinating, interesting
near antonyms unimpressive, uninspiring, unremarkable; boring, dull, jading, monotonous, tedious, tiring, uninspired, uninteresting, wearisome, weary, wearying; common, customary, mundane, normal, ordinary, typical, unexceptional, usual; draining, enervating, exhausting, fatiguing, wearing; debilitating, enfeebling; demoralizing, discouraging, disheartening, dispiriting
2 excitingly or mysteriously unusual ⟨old seafarers' tales of *marvelous* lands and their strange inhabitants⟩ — see EXOTIC
3 of the very best kind ⟨that mystery novel is just *marvelous*⟩ — see EXCELLENT
mascot *n* something worn or kept to bring good luck or keep away evil ⟨wears a *mascot* made of ebony and silver on a chain around her neck⟩ — see CHARM 1
masculine *adj* considered characteristic of or appropriate for men ⟨some people consider chest hair to be a particularly appealing *masculine* trait⟩
synonyms male, manlike, manly, mannish, man-size (*or* man-sized), virile
related words boyish, tomboyish
near antonyms girlish, sissy; feminine, womanish, womanlike, womanly; emasculated, impotent, weakened
antonyms effeminate, unmanly, unmasculine
masculinity *n* the set of qualities considered appropriate for or characteristic of men ⟨some men believe that wearing pink would undermine their *masculinity*⟩ — see VIRILITY
mash *vb* **1** to apply external pressure on so as to force out the juice or contents of ⟨this press can *mash* ten bushels of apples at a time⟩ — see PRESS 2
2 to cause to become a pulpy mass ⟨the baby *mashed* the banana on the floor⟩ — see CRUSH 1

mask *n* **1** a cover or partial cover for the face used to disguise oneself ⟨he loved his gorilla *mask* so much that he even tried to sleep with it on⟩
synonyms vizard
related words camouflage, disguise; bill, cloak, domino, hood, veil, visor (*also* vizor)
2 something that covers or conceals like a piece of cloth ⟨his friendliness is just a *mask*, for he always has an ulterior motive⟩ — see CLOAK 1
mask *vb* **1** to change the dress or looks of so as to conceal true identity ⟨the federal agents *masked* their surveillance vehicle so that it looked like an ordinary moving van⟩ — see DISGUISE
2 to keep secret or shut off from view ⟨*masked* his real motives for wanting to see the house that was for sale⟩ — see ¹HIDE 2
masquerade *n* a display of emotion or behavior that is insincere or intended to deceive ⟨although she was deeply bored, she maintained a *masquerade* of polite interest as her guest droned on⟩
synonyms act, airs, charade, facade (*also* façade), front, guise, pose, pretense (*or* pretence), put-on, semblance, show
related words appearance, color, gloss; camouflage, cloak, disguise; affectation, deceit, deception, doubledealing, duplicity, fraud, guile; betrayal, double cross, faithlessness, falseness, falsity, infidelity, perfidy, treachery, treason, unfaithfulness; excuse, pretext
near antonyms candor, frankness, openheartedness, sincerity
masquerade (as) *vb* to pretend to be (what one is not) in appearance or behavior ⟨she was arrested for *masquerading as* a doctor and trying to steal another woman's baby⟩ — see IMPERSONATE 1
mass *n* **1** masses *pl* the body of the community as contrasted with the elite ⟨the *masses* demanded the elimination of tax breaks for the rich⟩
synonyms commoners, herd, mob, people, plebeians, populace, rank and file
related words proletariat, rabble, riffraff, scum, trash; bourgeoisie, middle class; public
near antonyms aristocracy, gentry, nobility, upper class, upper crust
antonyms elite
2 a considerable amount ⟨I have a *mass* of work to do tonight⟩ — see LOT 2
3 a distinct and separate portion of matter ⟨a *mass* of leaves in a corner of the yard⟩ — see BODY 2
4 the main or greater part of something as distinguished from its appendages ⟨when taking pictures, focus your attention on the *mass* of the main subject⟩ — see BODY 1
massacre *n* the killing of a large number of people ⟨the infamous *massacre* of more than 200 Sioux at Wounded Knee, South Dakota⟩
synonyms butchery, carnage, slaughter
related words bloodshed, foul play, homicide, killing, manslaughter, murder, slaying; mortality; annihilation, decimation, demolishing, destruction, devastation, eradication, extermination; genocide; assassination, execution
massacre *vb* to kill on a large scale ⟨the country's rival ethnic groups began *massacring* one another⟩
synonyms butcher, mow (down), slaughter
related words assassinate, execute, murder, slay; annihilate, decimate, demolish, destroy, devastate, eradicate, exterminate, waste, wipe out

massive *adj* **1** having great weight ⟨a *massive* piece of furniture that was nearly impossible to move⟩ — see HEAVY 1

2 unusually large ⟨the *massive* statue took up most of the small yard⟩ — see HUGE

massively *adv* to a large extent or degree ⟨I am *massively* irritated by this new development⟩ — see GREATLY 2

massiveness *n* **1** the quality or state of being very large ⟨the *massiveness* of the puppy's paws suggested that this would be a very large dog⟩ — see IMMENSITY

2 the state or quality of being heavy ⟨I need something with sufficient *massiveness* to block the wheels so this car won't roll down the ramp⟩ — see WEIGHTINESS 1

mass–produced *adj* made beforehand in large numbers ⟨a cheap *mass-produced* plastic toy⟩ — see READY-MADE

master *adj* having or showing exceptional knowledge, experience, or skill in a field of endeavor ⟨a *master* craftsman who makes fine wood furniture of his own designs⟩ — see PROFICIENT

master *n* **1** a person with a high level of knowledge or skill in a field ⟨a *master* at chess⟩ — see EXPERT

2 one that defeats an enemy or opponent ⟨little did the tennis pro know that his new student would someday become his *master*⟩ — see VICTOR 1

3 the person (as an employer or supervisor) who tells people and especially workers what to do ⟨I'm the *master* of this operation, and you'll do what I say⟩ — see BOSS

master *vb* **1** to achieve a victory over ⟨finally *mastered* her opponent at chess⟩ — see BEAT 2

2 to acquire complete knowledge, understanding, or skill in ⟨I think I've *mastered* algebra at last⟩ — see LEARN 1

masterful *adj* **1** accomplished with trained ability ⟨a *masterful* performance of a difficult piece for the violin⟩ — see SKILLFUL 1

2 fond of ordering people around ⟨a *masterful* coworker who liked to tell other people how to do their jobs⟩ — see BOSSY

3 having a feeling of superiority that shows itself in an overbearing attitude ⟨a *masterful* businesswoman who didn't hesitate to step on a lot of people as she climbed the ladder of success⟩ — see ARROGANT

4 having or showing exceptional knowledge, experience, or skill in a field of endeavor ⟨a president who was celebrated as a *masterful* communicator of his administration's policies⟩ — see PROFICIENT

masterfully *adv* in a skillful or expert manner ⟨plays the violin *masterfully*, especially for a performer of her age⟩ — see WELL 3

masterfulness *n* **1** subtle or imaginative ability in inventing, devising, or executing something ⟨the sheer *masterfulness* of the thieves' plan could not be denied, even by the police⟩ — see SKILL 1

2 an exaggerated sense of one's importance that shows itself in the making of excessive or unjustified claims ⟨the shameless *masterfulness* that invested his every move was positively galling to his colleagues⟩ — see ARROGANCE

masterly *adj* **1** accomplished with trained ability ⟨a *masterly* performance of one of the most difficult ballets in the repertory⟩ — see SKILLFUL 1

2 having or showing exceptional knowledge, experience, or skill in a field of endeavor ⟨a *masterly* handling of a complex topic in philosophy⟩ — see PROFICIENT

mastermind *vb* to plan out usually with subtle skill or care ⟨charged with *masterminding* a plan to redecorate the suite of offices without seriously disrupting business operations⟩ — see ENGINEER

masterpiece *n* something (as a work of art) that is a great achievement and often its creator's greatest achievement ⟨Michelangelo's frescoes in the Sistine Chapel are often considered to be his *masterpieces*⟩

synonyms classic, magnum opus

related words pièce de résistance, showpiece; blockbuster, success; gem, jewel, prize, treasure

near antonyms debacle (*also* débâcle), disaster, failure, fiasco, fizzle, turkey

mastership *n* a highly developed skill in or knowledge of something ⟨we're still working on *mastership* of the new computer system⟩ — see COMMAND 2

mastery *n* **1** a highly developed skill in or knowledge of something ⟨returned from her year in Spain with a complete *mastery* of the language⟩ — see COMMAND 2

2 the right or means to command or control others ⟨the British monarch has only token *mastery* over the citizens of the United Kingdom⟩ — see POWER 1

masticate *vb* to crush or grind with the teeth ⟨mindlessly *masticated* peanuts while watching the baseball game on TV⟩ — see BITE (ON)

match *n* **1** a competitive encounter between individuals or groups carried on for amusement, exercise, or in pursuit of a prize ⟨a chess *match*⟩ — see GAME 1

2 a union representing a special kind of social and legal partnership between two people ⟨from all appearances the young couple have got a good *match* there⟩ — see MARRIAGE 1

3 either of a pair matched in one or more qualities ⟨I can't find the *match* to this sock⟩ — see MATE 1

4 one that is equal to another in status, achievement, or value ⟨for a wife he wants a woman who will be his *match* in every aspect of their lives⟩ — see EQUAL

5 something or someone that strongly resembles another ⟨Erin is so nearly my exact *match* you'd think she must be my twin and not just my cousin⟩ — see IMAGE 1

match *vb* **1** to be the exact counterpart of ⟨does this handbag's shade of blue *match* my navy blue pants?⟩ ⟨the rare blood type that exactly *matched* that of the transplant recipient⟩

synonyms correspond (to), equal, parallel

related words blend (with), coordinate (with), go (with), harmonize (with); complement, supplement; counterbalance, counterpoise; echo, mirror, repeat; amount (to), approach, near; measure (up), partake (of), rival, suggest

2 to give in marriage ⟨they were happy to *match* their daughter to a man from a good family⟩ — see MARRY 2

3 to produce something equal to (as in quality or value) ⟨no one has ever been able to *match* that novel for its portrayal of the horrors of war⟩ — see EQUAL 1

matching *adj* having qualities in common ⟨*matching* barrettes⟩ — see ALIKE

matchless *adj* having no equal or rival for excellence or desirability ⟨the *matchless* beauty of Yosemite Valley⟩ — see ONLY 1

mate *n* **1** either of a pair matched in one or more qualities ⟨have you seen the *mate* to this glove anywhere?⟩

synonyms companion, fellow, half, match, twin

related words coordinate; counterpart, equal, equivalent, like, parallel, peer, rival; carbon copy, double, duplicate, identical twin, ringer; analogue (*or* analog), similarity

near antonyms antithesis, converse, opposite, reverse
2 a person frequently seen in the company of another ⟨Matthew and his *mates* were known troublemakers in the neighborhood⟩ — see ASSOCIATE 1
3 *chiefly British* a person who helps a more skilled person ⟨a plumber and his *mate* showed up to fix the sink in our London hotel room⟩ — see HELPER
4 the person to whom another is married ⟨they vowed to each other that they would remain *mates* for life⟩ — see SPOUSE
mate *vb* to engage in sexual intercourse ⟨cats conceive almost every time they *mate*⟩ — see COPULATE
material *adj* **1** relating to or composed of matter ⟨there's no *material* evidence, such as a dead body, that a murder has been committed⟩
synonyms concrete, physical, substantial
related words bodily, carnal, corporal, corporeal, fleshly; appreciable, detectable, discernible, noticeable, observable, palpable, perceptible, sensible, tangible; objective, phenomenal; bulky, heavy, massive, solid, weighty
near antonyms bodiless, disembodied, incorporeal; ethereal, insubstantial, unsubstantial; impalpable, imperceptible, insensible, intangible, invisible, unnoticeable; airy, diaphanous, tenuous, thin, vaporous; metaphysical, spiritual
antonyms immaterial, nonmaterial, nonphysical
2 having great meaning or lasting effect ⟨there's no *material* difference between the two designs for the skyscraper: one's as bad as the other⟩ — see IMPORTANT 1
3 having to do with life on earth especially as opposed to that in heaven ⟨people who worry more about *material* concerns than about spiritual ones⟩ — see EARTHLY
4 having to do with the matter at hand ⟨that information, while fascinating, is not *material* to our discussion⟩ — see PERTINENT
5 of or relating to the human body ⟨*material* needs such as food and warmth⟩ — see PHYSICAL 1
material *n* **1** the basic elements from which something can be developed ⟨she's clearly star *material*⟩ — see MAKING
2 *usually* **materials** *pl* items needed for the performance of a task or activity ⟨I have all the *materials* to build the mobile⟩ — see EQUIPMENT
materialist *n* a person who is chiefly interested in material comfort and is hostile or indifferent to art and culture ⟨a *materialist* who knows the price of everything and the value of nothing⟩ — see PHILISTINE
materiality *n* **1** something that actually exists ⟨preferred a single *materiality* to a slew of theories⟩ — see FACT 2
2 the fact or state of being pertinent ⟨the *materiality* of that fact is not in dispute⟩ — see PERTINENCE
3 the quality of being actual ⟨seems to question the very *materiality* of the universe⟩ — see FACT 1
materialize *vb* **1** to come into existence ⟨the business speculator promised profits that never seemed to *materialize*⟩ — see BEGIN 2
2 to come into view ⟨the train station *materialized* through the fog⟩ — see APPEAR 1
3 to come to one's attention especially gradually or unexpectedly ⟨an unforeseen problem with this project seems to have *materialized*⟩ — see ARISE 2
4 to represent in visible form ⟨a statue of a grieving woman that seems to *materialize* the very concept of grief⟩ — see EMBODY 2

matériel *or* **materiel** *n* items needed for the performance of a task or activity ⟨the army is running short of clothing and other *matériel*⟩ — see EQUIPMENT
maternal *adj* of, relating to, or characteristic of a mother ⟨her *maternal* instincts told her that something was wrong⟩ — see MOTHERLY
maternity *n* motherly character or qualities ⟨she had such *maternity* at such a young age that all her classmates went to her for comfort⟩
synonyms motherliness
related words nurturance; fertility, fruitfulness, productivity, richness
mathematical *adj* meeting the highest standard of accuracy ⟨produced an answer of *mathematical* precision⟩ — see PRECISE 1
mating *n* sexual union involving penetration of the vagina by the penis ⟨if the mare doesn't get pregnant from this *mating*, you don't have to pay for the second try⟩ — see SEXUAL INTERCOURSE
matriarch *n* a dignified usually elderly woman of some rank or authority ⟨even though she was 87, the *matriarch* of the family knew everything that was going on⟩
synonyms dame, dowager, matron
related words grandam (*or* grandame); headmistress, mistress; ma, mama, mammy, mom, momma
matriculate *vb* to enter in a list or roll ⟨the college *matriculated* 1000 students for the fall⟩ — see ENROLL 1
matrimonial *adj* of or relating to marriage ⟨plans to focus on *matrimonial* concerns after she's established in her career⟩ — see MARITAL
matrimony *n* a union representing a special kind of social and legal partnership between two people ⟨we intend to be joined in *matrimony* until "death do us part"⟩ — see MARRIAGE 1
matron *n* a dignified usually elderly woman of some rank or authority ⟨the *matron* firmly ordered the rowdy little boys back to their seats⟩ — see MATRIARCH
matte *also* **mat** *or* **matt** *adj* lacking a surface luster or gloss ⟨I chose a paint with a *matte* finish so the walls wouldn't be too shiny⟩
synonyms dim, dull, dulled, flat, lusterless
related words tarnished, unpolished; cloudy, dingy, dirty, drab, mousy (*or* mousey), muddy; gray (*also* grey), leaden, pale; dark, darkened, dimmed, dusky, gloomy, murky, obscure, obscured, somber (*or* sombre)
near antonyms buffed, burnished, glazed, lacquered, polished, shellacked, varnished; satin, satiny; silken, silky; slick, slippery; gleaming, glimmering, glinting, glistening, glittering, scintillating, shimmering, shining, sparkling, twinkling; beaming, bedazzling, bright, brightened, brilliant, dazzling, effulgent, lucent, lucid, luminous, radiant, shining
antonyms glossy, lustrous, shiny, sleek
matter *n* **1** a major object of interest or concern (as in a discussion or artistic composition) ⟨that is not relevant to the *matter* under discussion⟩
synonyms content, motif, motive, question, subject, theme, topic
related words idea, point, purpose; issue, problem; body, bulk, burden, core, crux, fundamental, generality, gist, heart, kernel, keynote, main, marrow, mass, nub, nucleus, pith, purport, quick, staple, substance, sum; basis; bottom, essential, essentiality; affair, argument, debate
near antonyms aside, digression, interjection, parenthesis, tangent

2 something to be dealt with ⟨we must take care of this *matter* before it becomes a real problem⟩
synonyms affair, business, thing
related words problem; crisis, crossroad, emergency, exigency, juncture, strait, zero hour; concern, trouble, worry; care, lookout, responsibility; deadlock, impasse, stalemate; corner, fix, hole, hot water, pinch, predicament, scrape, spot
3 communications or parcels sent or carried through the postal system ⟨first-class *matter*⟩ — see MAIL
4 something that requires thought and skill for resolution ⟨I've been thinking about the *matter* all night, and I believe I have a solution⟩ — see PROBLEM 1
matter *vb* to be of importance ⟨she believes that doing well in school really does *matter*⟩
synonyms count, import, mean, signify, weigh
related words affect, influence, sway; add up (to), amount (to)
phrases carry weight, cut ice
matter–of–fact *adj* **1** restricted to or based on fact ⟨a *matter-of-fact* recitation of events⟩ — see FACTUAL 1
2 willing to see things as they really are and deal with them sensibly ⟨a *matter-of-fact* woman who didn't worry about "what ifs"⟩ — see REALISTIC 1
maturation *n* the process of becoming mature ⟨a flower's *maturation* from bud to full bloom can take weeks⟩
synonyms development, growth, maturing, ripening
related words blossoming, flourishing, flowering; mellowing, softening
near antonyms decadence, decline, declining, deterioration; fading, shriveling, waning, wilting, withering; death, dying, expiring, perishing; regression, retrogression, reversion
mature *adj* **1** fully grown or developed ⟨I like pears when they're still hard, before they're *mature*⟩
synonyms adult, full-blown, full-fledged, full-grown, matured, ripe, ripened
related words aged, aging (*or* ageing), old; golden, mellow
near antonyms blooming, blossoming, burgeoning, flourishing, flowering; undeveloped, unfinished, unformed
antonyms green, immature, juvenile, unripened, young, youthful
2 having reached the date at which payment is required ⟨*mature* bonds⟩ — see DUE 1
mature *vb* to become mature ⟨a young figure skater whose talent is still *maturing*⟩
synonyms age, develop, grow, grow up, progress, ripen
related words mellow, soften; bloom, blossom, burgeon, flourish, flower; open, unfold; advance, evolve
near antonyms decline, deteriorate; dry, fade, shrivel, wane, wilt, wither; regress, retrogress, revert; backslide, lapse, return
matured *adj* fully grown or developed ⟨a *matured* plant in full bloom⟩ — see MATURE 1
maturing *n* the process of becoming mature ⟨the *maturing* of young horses can take several years⟩ — see MATURATION
maturity *n* the state of being fully grown or developed ⟨people are legally considered to have reached *maturity* at eighteen years old in the United States⟩
synonyms adulthood, majority
related words manhood, womanhood; bloom, flush, heyday, prime; middle age, seniority
maudlin *adj* appealing to the emotions in an obvious and tiresome way ⟨a *maudlin* movie about a lovable tramp⟩ — see CORNY

maul *vb* **1** to abuse physically ⟨demonstrators who claimed that they had been *mauled* by the police⟩ — see MANHANDLE 1
2 to strike repeatedly ⟨the irate store owner was *mauling* the shoplifter when the police showed up⟩ — see BEAT 1
maunder *vb* **1** to move about from place to place aimlessly ⟨*maundered* all over town on his day off⟩ — see WANDER
2 to talk at length without sticking to a topic or getting to a point ⟨ask her a question and she'll *maunder* for half an hour⟩ — see RAMBLE 1
maundering *adj* passing from one topic to another ⟨a long, *maundering* conversation about what was wrong with the world and how he could fix it⟩ — see DISCURSIVE
maverick *n* a person who does not conform to generally accepted standards or customs ⟨there's always one *maverick* who has to go his own way⟩ — see NONCONFORMIST 1
mawkish *adj* appealing to the emotions in an obvious and tiresome way ⟨a *mawkish* plea for donations to the charity⟩ — see CORNY
mawkishness *n* the state or quality of having an excess of tender feelings (as of love, nostalgia, or compassion) ⟨the *mawkishness* of her poetry makes me want to stamp on wildflowers⟩ — see SENTIMENTALITY
maxim *n* **1** an idea or statement about all of the members of a group or all the instances of a situation ⟨very few *maxims* are true for every single possible case, but they're reasonably good predictors⟩ — see GENERALIZATION
2 an often stated observation regarding something from common experience ⟨it's a common *maxim* that "a watched pot never boils," but that's not literally true⟩ — see SAYING
maximum *adj* **1** of the greatest or highest degree or quantity ⟨the *maximum* amount of time⟩ — see ULTIMATE 1
2 of the highest degree ⟨put out *maximum* effort⟩ — see FULL 2
maximum *n* the greatest amount, number, or part ⟨achieved the *maximum*⟩ — see MOST
maybe *adv* it is possible ⟨*maybe* we can make it to the library, if we hurry⟩ — see PERHAPS
mayhap *adv* it is possible ⟨*mayhap* I could see you again next week, depending on my schedule⟩ — see PERHAPS
maze *n* a confusing and complicated arrangement of passages ⟨the mansion had a beautifully landscaped *maze* constructed of tall cypresses⟩
synonyms labyrinth
related words meander; jungle, quagmire; knot, snarl, tangle, web; entanglement, entrapment, snare, trap
meager *or* **meagre** *adj* less plentiful than what is normal, necessary, or desirable ⟨ever since he started the diet, his dinners have been more *meager* than he would like⟩
synonyms hand-to-mouth, light, niggardly, poor, scant, scanty, scarce, skimpy, slender, slim, spare, sparse, stingy
related words deficient, inadequate, insufficient, lacking, wanting; bare, mere, minimum; slight, small; barren, infertile, sterile, unfruitful, unproductive
near antonyms adequate, enough, sufficient; fat, fecund, fertile, fruitful, prolific, rich; lavish, luxuriant; blooming, bursting, flourishing, swarming, teeming, thriving
antonyms abundant, ample, bountiful, copious, generous, liberal, plenteous, plentiful

meal *n* food eaten or prepared for eating at one time ⟨all she wants to do is sit quietly after the large Thanksgiving *meal*⟩

synonyms chow, feed, mess, repast, table

related words board; breakfast, buffet, dinner, lunch, luncheon, refreshments, smorgasbord, snack, supper, tea; bite, gulp, morsel, serving, taste; banquet, feast, spread; bake, barbecue, clambake, cookout, fry, luau, picnic, potluck, roast

mealy *adj* not being or expressing what one appears to be or express ⟨a *mealy* apology that was really no apology at all⟩ — see INSINCERE

mealymouthed *adj* not being or expressing what one appears to be or express ⟨a *mealymouthed* compliment from a jealous competitor⟩ — see INSINCERE

mean *adj* **1** belonging to the class of people of low social or economic rank ⟨Alexander Hamilton seems to have had feelings of inferiority because of his *mean* origins⟩ — see IGNOBLE 1

2 giving or sharing as little as possible ⟨a *mean* child who hoarded all his toys⟩ — see STINGY 1

3 having or showing a desire to cause someone pain or suffering for the sheer enjoyment of it ⟨a *mean*, embittered old woman who wanted company for her misery⟩ — see HATEFUL

4 not following or in accordance with standards of honor and decency ⟨a *mean* trick to play on a trusting person⟩ — see IGNOBLE 2

5 of little or less value or merit ⟨it's no *mean* feat to memorize that long poem⟩ — see INFERIOR 2

6 of the very best kind ⟨I'm a *mean* dancer, so you could do worse than go to the prom with me⟩ — see EXCELLENT

7 showing signs of advanced wear and tear and neglect ⟨a *mean* little car that was almost 20 years old⟩ — see SHABBY 1

mean *n* **1** a middle point between extremes ⟨that candidate's moderate views were seen as the *mean* that voters were looking for⟩

synonyms golden mean, medium, middle, midpoint

related words arithmetic mean, average; median, norm, par, standard

near antonyms maximum, minimum

2 means *pl* an action planned or taken to achieve a desired result ⟨won by fair and honest *means*⟩ — see MEASURE 1

3 means *pl* something used to achieve an end ⟨the ends don't justify the *means*⟩ — see AGENT 1

4 means *pl* the total of one's money and property ⟨a woman of considerable *means*⟩ — see WEALTH 1

mean *vb* **1** to communicate or convey (as an idea) to the mind ⟨the national anthem *means* various things to various people⟩

synonyms denote, express, import, signify, spell

related words connote, imply, suggest; add up (to), amount (to); hint, insinuate, intimate; embody, epitomize, personify, represent, symbolize; advert, allude (to), mention, refer (to); indicate, point (to), signal; announce, declare; elucidate, explain

2 to be of importance ⟨your presence at my graduation would *mean* a lot to me⟩ — see MATTER

3 to have in mind as a purpose or goal ⟨I *mean* to win this race⟩ — see INTEND

meander *vb* to move about from place to place aimlessly ⟨*meandering* around the schoolyard waiting for classes to start⟩ — see WANDER

meaning *adj* clearly conveying a special meaning (as one's mood) ⟨gave me a *meaning* look after I said that⟩ — see EXPRESSIVE

meaning *n* **1** the idea that is conveyed or intended to be conveyed to the mind by language, symbol, or action ⟨the unmistakable *meaning* of the skier's upraised arms as he finished his spectacular run⟩

synonyms denotation, drift, import, intent, purport, sense, significance, signification

related words connotation; hint, implication, intimation, suggestion; message, tenor, theme; bottom, essence, essentiality, nature, soul, stuff; acceptance, definition; burden, crux, gist; core, heart, kernel, marrow, nub, nucleus, pith, point, quick; matter, motif, motive, subject, topic

2 something that one hopes or intends to accomplish ⟨the people have a right to know what the president's *meaning* is in getting the nation involved in this war⟩ — see GOAL

meaningful *adj* **1** clearly conveying a special meaning (as one's mood) ⟨gave a *meaningful* sigh when I asked her how things were going⟩ — see EXPRESSIVE

2 having great meaning or lasting effect ⟨that was a very *meaningful* ceremony⟩ — see IMPORTANT 1

meaningless *adj* having no meaning ⟨this is an utterly *meaningless* bit of nonsense⟩

synonyms empty, inane, pointless, senseless

related words insignificant, trivial, unimportant; absurd, asinine, balmy, brainless, crazy, daffy, daft, dotty, fatuous, foolish, half-witted, harebrained, insane, jerky, kooky, loony (*also* looney); lunatic, mad, mindless, nonsensical, nutty, preposterous, sappy, silly, unintelligent, unwise, wacky, weak-minded, witless, zany; irrational, unreasonable; aimless, haphazard, purposeless

near antonyms eloquent, expressive, pregnant, revealing, suggestive, telling; logical, rational, reasonable, valid

antonyms meaningful

meanly *adv* in a mean or spiteful manner ⟨in a *meanly* worded letter she told me that she never wanted to see me again⟩ — see NASTILY

meanness *n* the desire to cause pain for the satisfaction of doing harm ⟨unprovoked *meanness* drove him to smash the child's toy⟩ — see MALICE

measly *adj* so small or unimportant as to warrant little or no attention ⟨offered them only one *measly* cookie⟩ — see NEGLIGIBLE 1

measure *n* **1** an action planned or taken to achieve a desired result ⟨such new security *measures* as metal detectors at all the entrances⟩

synonyms expedient, means, move, shift, step

related words act, deed, doing, feat, thing; procedure, proceeding, process; accomplishment, achievement, exploit; activity, affair, business, dealing, enterprise, event; attempt, endeavor, essay, initiative, operation, undertaking; effort, exertion, labor, pains, trouble, work; project, proposal, proposition; makeshift, resort, resource, stopgap

2 a given or particular mass or aggregate of matter ⟨each day prisoners were given only a small *measure* of rice to live on⟩ — see AMOUNT

3 something set up as an example against which others of the same type are compared ⟨during the Renaissance, man came to be viewed as the *measure* of all things⟩ — see STANDARD 1

4 the recurrent pattern formed by a series of sounds having a regular rise and fall in intensity ⟨the song's soft, soothing *measures* make it a good lullaby⟩ — see RHYTHM

5 the total amount of measurable space or surface occupied by something ⟨a slipcover for the couch made to *measure*⟩ — see ¹SIZE

measure *vb* to find out the size, extent, or amount of ⟨for this experiment, you need to carefully *measure* all the chemicals before you mix them together⟩

synonyms gauge (*also* gage), scale, span

related words weigh; calibrate; lay off, mark (off); calculate, compute, figure, reckon, work out; conjecture, estimate, guess, judge, suppose; add up, sum, tally, total; ascertain, discover, dope (out), figure out, find out

measured *adj* **1** decided on as a result of careful thought ⟨a *measured* response to the terrorist attack⟩ — see DELIBERATE 1

2 having distinct or certain limits ⟨the *measured* authority of the mayor in running the town's affairs⟩ — see LIMITED 1

3 marked by or occurring with a noticeable regularity in the rise and fall of sound ⟨the soldier's funeral procession moved along to the *measured* beating of a drum⟩ — see RHYTHMIC

measureless *adj* being or seeming to be without limits ⟨the bodies of the fallen sailors were consigned to the *measureless* depths of the sea⟩ — see INFINITE

measurement *n* the total amount of measurable space or surface occupied by something ⟨the *measurement* of the average house lot is half an acre⟩ — see ¹SIZE

measure up (to) *vb* to come near or nearer to in character or quality ⟨he always worried about *measuring up to* his brother⟩ — see APPROXIMATE

meat *n* **1** animal and especially mammal tissue used as food ⟨we need to go shopping; there's only enough *meat* in the freezer for one more dinner⟩

synonyms flesh

related words game, poultry, variety meat

2 substances intended to be eaten ⟨offered his guests *meat* and drink⟩ — see FOOD

mecca *n* a thing or place that is of greatest importance to an activity or interest ⟨that region of Connecticut is a *mecca* for antique hunters⟩ — see CENTER 1

mechanical *adj* **1** done instantly and without conscious thought or decision ⟨the waiter's *mechanical* reply of "Everything on the menu is good"⟩ — see AUTOMATIC 1

2 lacking in natural or spontaneous quality ⟨a somewhat *mechanical* vocal performance⟩ — see ARTIFICIAL 1

medal *n* a piece of metal given in honor of a special event, a person, or an achievement ⟨the display case held an impressive array of military *medals* from World War II⟩

synonyms medallion, order

related words decoration, honor; crown, insignia, laurel, ribbon, title; badge, button, chevron, cockade, color, ensign, rosette; distinction; award, prize, trophy; citation, commendation

medallion *n* a piece of metal given in honor of a special event, a person, or an achievement ⟨received a gold *medallion* at the Olympics⟩ — see MEDAL

meddle *vb* to interest oneself in what is not one's concern ⟨please stop *meddling* in your sister's studying, even though you mean well⟩ — see INTERFERE

meddler *n* a person who meddles in the affairs of others ⟨a *meddler* who stayed up all night watching the neighbors⟩ — see BUSYBODY

meddlesome *adj* thrusting oneself where one is not welcome or invited ⟨*meddlesome* neighbors kept asking the couple when they were going to have children⟩ — see INTRUSIVE

meddling *adj* thrusting oneself where one is not welcome or invited ⟨the bride's parents promised that they would never become the kind of *meddling* in-laws that every husband fears⟩ — see INTRUSIVE

medial *adj* occupying a position equally distant from the ends or extremes ⟨two is the *medial* number between one and three⟩ — see MIDDLE 1

median *adj* **1** being situated midway between extremes of amount or size ⟨the *median* price of a home in the area⟩ — see MIDDLE 2

2 occupying a position equally distant from the ends or extremes ⟨determine the *median* point between your two speakers, and test your stereo system from there⟩ — see MIDDLE 1

mediate *vb* to act as a go-between for opposing sides ⟨the middle child is often ask to *mediate* between the oldest and the youngest⟩ — see INTERVENE

mediator *n* one who works with opposing sides in order to bring about an agreement ⟨if you two cannot resolve this argument on your own, we'll have to bring in a *mediator*⟩

synonyms conciliator, go-between, intercessor, intermediary, interposer, middleman, peacemaker

related words moderator; bargainer, negotiator; appeaser, pacifier, reconciler; broker; agent, attorney, deputy, factor, procurator, proxy; liaison; ambassador, emissary, envoy, messenger; delegate, representative; busybody, interferer, meddler; arbiter, arbitrator, judge, referee, umpire; adviser (*or* advisor), counselor

medic *n* a person specially trained in healing human medical disorders ⟨the wounded soldier called for a *medic*⟩ — see DOCTOR

medication *n* a substance or preparation used to treat disease ⟨the doctor prescribed two different *medications* for the infection⟩ — see MEDICINE

medicine *n* a substance or preparation used to treat disease ⟨if you don't take all the doses of your *medicine*, you might get sick again⟩

synonyms cure, drug, medication, pharmaceutical, physic, remedy, specific

related words botanical, patent medicine, prescription; cordial, tonic; miracle drug, wonder drug; capsule, pill, tablet; injection, shot; liniment, lotion, ointment, potion, poultice, salve; syrup, tincture; antibiotic, antiseptic, serum

mediocre *adj* **1** of average to below average quality ⟨your grades are *mediocre* and barely acceptable⟩

synonyms common, fair, indifferent, medium, middling, ordinary, passable, run-of-the-mill, second-rate, so-so

related words acceptable, adequate, all right, alright, decent, OK (*or* okay), reasonable, satisfactory, sufficient, sufficing, tolerable; moderate, modest; presentable, respectable; minimal, unexceptional; fine, good, nice

near antonyms distinguished, excellent, exceptional, exquisite, first-class, first-rate, matchless, maximum, optimal, optimum, outstanding, peerless, preeminent, special, superior, supreme, top-notch; unmatched, unparalleled, unsurpassed; deficient, inadequate, insufficient, lacking, unacceptable, unsatisfactory, wanting

2 of low quality ⟨*mediocre* carvings in a pseudo-African style that are sold to tourists⟩ — see CHEAP 2

meditate *vb* **1** to give serious and careful thought to ⟨I've been *meditating* a career change for months⟩ — see PONDER

2 to have in mind as a purpose or goal ⟨*meditated* a quick return to work after having the baby⟩ — see INTEND

meditation *n* long or deep thinking about spiritual matters ⟨devotes an hour a day to quiet *meditation*⟩ — see CONTEMPLATION

meditative *adj* given to or marked by long, quiet thinking ⟨I've been in a *meditative* mood all day⟩ — see CONTEMPLATIVE

medium *adj* **1** being about midway between extremes of amount or size ⟨taxpayers of *medium* income⟩ — see MIDDLE 2

2 occupying a position equally distant from the ends or extremes ⟨a politician who first reads the polls and then inevitably takes the *medium* stance on every issue⟩ — see MIDDLE 1

3 of average to below average quality ⟨another *medium* effort from a movie director who can do better⟩ — see MEDIOCRE 1

medium *n* **1** a middle point between extremes ⟨trying to achieve a happy *medium*⟩ — see MEAN 1

2 something used to achieve an end ⟨worked through the *medium* of someone else⟩ — see AGENT 1

3 the circumstances, conditions, or objects by which one is surrounded ⟨an artist who enjoys the cultural *medium* of the big city⟩ — see ENVIRONMENT

medley *n* an unorganized collection or mixture of various things ⟨a *medley* of snack foods available on the buffet table⟩ — see MISCELLANY 1

meek *adj* not having or showing any feelings of superiority, self-assertiveness, or showiness ⟨a *meek* girl who quietly went along with whatever her circle of friends wanted⟩ — see HUMBLE 1

meekly *adv* in a manner showing no signs of pride or self-assertion ⟨Justin is always taking advantage of his so-called best friend, who just *meekly* accepts it⟩ — see LOWLY

meekness *n* the absence of any feelings of being better than others ⟨like most other things, *meekness* is best practiced in moderation⟩ — see HUMILITY

meet *adj* meeting the requirements of a purpose or situation ⟨in this case, splitting the winnings of the contested lottery ticket seems like a *meet* solution⟩ — see FIT 1

meet *n* a competitive encounter between individuals or groups carried on for amusement, exercise, or in pursuit of a prize ⟨a swim *meet*⟩ — see GAME 1

meet *vb* **1** to come upon face-to-face or as if face-to-face ⟨we never once *met* another car on that lonely country road⟩

synonyms chance (upon), encounter, happen (upon), stumble (upon)

related words accost, confront; face, greet, salute; collide (with), crash (into); crisscross, cross, pass; hit (upon), light (upon), tumble (to)

phrases bump into

near antonyms avoid, elude, escape, evade, shun

2 to come together into one body or place ⟨we'll *meet* for dinner, with a discussion to follow, next week⟩ — see ASSEMBLE 1

3 to come upon unexpectedly or by chance ⟨*met* her future husband at a party⟩ — see HAPPEN (ON *or* UPON)

4 to do what is required by the terms of ⟨a financially struggling city trying to *meet* its loans⟩ — see FULFILL 1

5 to enter into contest or conflict with ⟨the up and coming boxer will *meet* the reigning champ for the first time tomorrow⟩ — see ENGAGE 2

6 to produce something equal to (as in quality or value) ⟨I'll *meet* your bet, nay, I'll even raise it⟩ — see EQUAL 1

7 to put up with (something painful or difficult) ⟨trying to *meet* the challenge of going to college while working at a full-time job⟩ — see BEAR 2

meeting *n* **1** a coming together of a number of persons for a specified purpose ⟨there will be another committee *meeting* next week to discuss the parish fair⟩

synonyms assembly, conference, congress, convention, convocation, council, gathering, get-together, huddle, powwow, roundtable, seminar

related words caucus, conclave, synod; demonstration, rally; conversation, dialogue (*also* dialog), discourse, discussion, palaver, talk; negotiation, parley; audience, interview, session

2 a body of people come together in one place ⟨a *meeting* marked by no consensus of what needs to be done⟩ — see GATHERING 1

3 the coming together of two or more things to the same point ⟨a *meeting* of two railroad lines⟩ — see CONVERGENCE

meetly *adv* in a manner suitable for the occasion or purpose ⟨replied *meetly* and reasonably to the interviewer's questions⟩ — see PROPERLY

megahit *n* a person or thing that is successful ⟨the band's latest album is a *megahit*⟩ — see HIT 1

megalopolis *n* a thickly settled, highly populated area ⟨what was once a series of discrete towns interspersed with countryside is now one vast *megalopolis*⟩ — see CITY

melancholy *adj* **1** causing unhappiness ⟨the *melancholy* thought of having to say good-bye to all the friends he had made over the summer⟩ — see SAD 2

2 feeling unhappiness ⟨she was a bit *melancholy* after school ended for the year⟩ — see SAD 1

3 given to or marked by long, quiet thinking ⟨a *melancholy* period in the artist's life that is reflected in his work⟩ — see CONTEMPLATIVE

melancholy *n* a state or spell of low spirits ⟨the bleakness of winter sometimes gives me cause for *melancholy*⟩ — see SADNESS

mélange *n* an unorganized collection or mixture of various things ⟨a *mélange* of outfits for her workouts at the gym⟩ — see MISCELLANY 1

melee *n* a rough and often noisy fight usually involving several people ⟨a verbal disagreement at the football game soon turned into a general *melee* involving scores of spectators⟩ — see BRAWL 1

meliorate *vb* to make better ⟨regulations intended to *meliorate* the working conditions of migrant farm laborers⟩ — see IMPROVE

mellifluous *adj* having a pleasantly flowing quality suggestive of music ⟨a rich, *mellifluous* voice that gets her a lot of work in radio and TV commercials⟩ — see LYRIC 1

mellow *adj* **1** having a pleasantly flowing quality suggestive of music ⟨the *mellow* tones of an old violin⟩ — see LYRIC 1

2 not harsh or stern especially in manner, nature, or effect ⟨a teacher with a *mellow* approach to classroom discipline⟩ — see GENTLE 1

melodic *adj* having a pleasantly flowing quality suggestive of music ⟨a sweetly *melodic* chant⟩ — see LYRIC 1

melodious *adj* **1** having a pleasantly flowing quality suggestive of music ⟨preferred the *melodious* sounds of the woodlands to anything produced in a concert hall⟩ — see LYRIC 1

2 having a pleasing mixture of notes ⟨a particularly *melodious* fanfare for the president⟩ — see HARMONIOUS 1

melodramatic *adj* **1** given to or marked by attention-getting behavior suggestive of stage acting ⟨made the *melodramatic* declaration that she might as well be dead⟩ — see THEATRICAL 1

2 having the general quality or effect of a stage performance ⟨he gave his usual *melodramatic* speech that he had learned his lesson and thereafter would always remain faithful to his wife⟩ — see DRAMATIC 1

melody *n* a rhythmic series of musical tones arranged to give a pleasing effect ⟨this week, we'll learn to play a more complicated *melody* on the saxophone⟩

  synonyms air, lay, song, strain, tune, warble

  related words descant; cadence, measure, meter, rhythm; ballad, ditty, hymn, lyric, madrigal

melt *vb* **1** to cease to be visible ⟨the fog soon *melted* away after the sun rose⟩ — see DISAPPEAR

2 to go from a solid to a liquid state ⟨left a carton of ice cream *melting* on the counter⟩ — see LIQUEFY

member *n* **1** one of the parts that make up a whole ⟨you're only one *member* of this group effort⟩ — see ELEMENT 1

2 one of the pieces from which something is designed to be assembled ⟨lost an indispensable *member* of the kit⟩ — see PART 1

memento *n* something that serves to keep alive the memory of a person or event ⟨kept a seashell as a *memento* of their first meeting, which happened to be at the beach⟩ — see MEMORIAL

memo *n* **1** a message on paper from one person or group to another ⟨a long series of *memos* between the two authors collaborating on the book⟩ — see LETTER

2 a usually brief written reminder ⟨taped a *memo* to her computer about the upcoming meeting⟩ — see NOTE 1

3 a written communication giving information or directions ⟨*memos* were the standard means of office communication before the arrival of e-mail⟩ — see MEMORANDUM 1

memoir *n* a history of a person's life ⟨the ex-president has a contract to write his *memoirs*, in which he will supposedly set the record straight⟩ — see BIOGRAPHY

memorandum *n* **1** a written communication giving information or directions ⟨I'm waiting for the *memorandum* that will explain the new vacation policy⟩

  synonyms directive, memo, notice

  related words announcement, declaration, proclamation, pronouncement; charge, command, dictate; directions, instructions, orders, word; encyclical, epistle, letter, mail, message, missive, note

2 a message on paper from one person or group to another ⟨the studio executives depend on endless *memoranda* to keep track of what's going on at a movie shot on location⟩ — see LETTER

3 a usually brief written reminder ⟨dispatched a *memorandum* to her secretary about the assignment⟩ — see NOTE 1

memorial *adj* serving to preserve the memory of a person, thing, or an event ⟨a *memorial* plaque on the bridge for a diver who died in the line of duty⟩ — see COMMEMORATIVE

memorial *n* something that serves to keep alive the memory of a person or event ⟨the Vietnam War *Memorial* is a starkly beautiful testimonial to the bravery of the soldiers who served in Vietnam⟩

  synonyms commemorative, keepsake, memento, monument, remembrance, reminder, souvenir, token

  related words memorabilia; relic, vestige; cairn, landmark, marker; testimonial, tribute

memorialize *vb* to be a memorial of ⟨at the entrance to the park stands a statue *memorializing* the novelist Sir Walter Scott⟩ — see COMMEMORATE 1

memorializing *adj* serving to preserve the memory of a person, thing, or an event ⟨a *memorializing* book on the sinking of the Titanic⟩ — see COMMEMORATIVE

memorize *vb* to commit to memory ⟨everyone has to *memorize* a poem for next week⟩

  synonyms con, learn, study

  related words recall, recollect, relive, remember, reminisce, retain; accept, apprehend, comprehend, get, grasp, understand; absorb, digest

  near antonyms forget; ignore, neglect, overlook

  antonyms unlearn

memory *n* **1** the power or process of recalling what has been previously learned or experienced ⟨a photographic *memory* makes taking tests entirely too easy⟩

  synonyms mind, recollection, remembrance, reminiscence

  related words contemplation, musing, reflection, retrospection, thinking; awareness, cognizance, consciousness; apprehension, comprehension, understanding

  near antonyms forgetfulness

2 a particular act or instance of recalling or the thing remembered ⟨I have only the vaguest *memory* of the family vacation we took the year I turned three⟩

  synonyms recall, recollection, remembrance, reminiscence

  related words flashback; memento, memorial, reminder, souvenir, token; association

3 the body of knowledge that has been retained in one's mind or the use of it ⟨a blow to the head made her temporarily lose her *memory*⟩ — see HEART 2

menace *n* something that may cause injury or harm ⟨a loaded gun is a *menace* that this household doesn't need⟩ — see DANGER 2

menace *vb* **1** to place in danger ⟨*menaced* the children by leaving them in the car unattended⟩ — see ENDANGER

2 to remain poised to inflict harm, danger, or distress on ⟨stockpiles of nuclear weapons that continue to *menace* the inhabitants of this planet⟩ — see THREATEN

menacing *adj* **1** being or showing a sign of evil or calamity to come ⟨warns that the emergence of new viruses is one of the most *menacing* developments we face⟩ — see OMINOUS

2 involving potential loss or injury ⟨fears that the unemployment rate may be reaching *menacing* proportions⟩ — see DANGEROUS

ménage *n* those who live as a family in one house ⟨getting the whole *ménage* ready for an outing takes quite a while⟩ — see HOUSEHOLD

mend *vb* **1** to put into good shape or working order again ⟨that shirt will be as good as new when I'm finished *mending* it⟩

  synonyms doctor, fix, patch, recondition, renovate, repair, revamp

related words overhaul, rebuild, reconstruct, refurbish; aid, cure, heal, help; condition, prepare, ready; care (for), maintain, service; rejuvenate, renew, restore; adjust, correct, modify, rectify, redress, reform, right; ameliorate, better, improve, meliorate
near antonyms break, damage, harm, hurt, impair, injure, mar, ruin, spoil, wreck; cripple, disable
2 to become healthy and strong again after illness or weakness ⟨she's *mending* after a particularly nasty bout of the flu⟩ — see CONVALESCE
3 to restore to a healthy condition ⟨*mended* the broken plant so that it was soon thriving again⟩ — see HEAL 1
mendacious *adj* telling or containing lies ⟨that tabloid routinely publishes *mendacious* stories about celebrities⟩ — see DISHONEST 1
mendacity *n* **1** a statement known by its maker to be untrue and made in order to deceive ⟨that politician will tell any *mendacity* to get elected⟩ — see LIE
2 the tendency to tell lies ⟨you need to overcome this deplorable *mendacity*, or no one will ever believe anything you say⟩ — see DISHONESTY 1
mendicant *n* a person who lives by public begging ⟨those wretched *mendicants* on the streets of Calcutta⟩ — see BEGGAR
mending *n* the process or period of gradually regaining one's health and strength ⟨it was a long slow *mending* of his injuries from the car crash, but he's fine now⟩ — see CONVALESCENCE
menial *n* a person hired to perform household or personal services ⟨immigrants to that country faced fierce prejudice and could expect to find work only as *menials*⟩ — see SERVANT
menstruation *n* an occurrence of menstruating ⟨a first *menstruation* can be somewhat scary for girls who are unprepared⟩ — see PERIOD 1
mental *adj* **1** of or relating to the mind ⟨a funny *mental* image made him laugh out loud⟩
synonyms cerebral, inner, intellectual, psychological (*also* psychologic)
related words cognitive, conscious; psychic (*also* psychical), telepathic; spiritual; alert, brainy, bright, clever, intelligent, quick-witted, rational, reasoning, smart, thinking
near antonyms bodily, carnal, corporal, corporeal, fleshly, physical, somatic
2 having or showing a very abnormal or sick state of mind ⟨humane treatment of *mental* patients⟩ — see INSANE 1
mention *vb* **1** to make reference to or speak about briefly but specifically ⟨you only *mentioned* in passing some of your accomplishments⟩
synonyms advert (to), cite, instance, name, note, notice, quote, refer (to), specify, touch (on *or* upon)
related words allude (to), hint (at), imply, infer, intimate, suggest; point (out), signal, signify; denominate, designate; indicate; bring up, broach, interject, interpolate, interpose, introduce; infiltrate, insinuate, worm; announce, declare, pronounce; elucidate, explain
near antonyms disregard, ignore, neglect, overlook, pass over, slight
2 to give as an example ⟨*mentioned* several legal precedents in support of her argument⟩ — see QUOTE 1
mentor *vb* to give advice and instruction to (someone) regarding the course or process to be followed ⟨we're looking for volunteers to *mentor* students in the theater arts⟩ — see GUIDE 1

menu *n* **1** a list of foods served at or available for a meal ⟨the *menu* at the fancy restaurant listed many dishes that I had never heard of⟩
synonyms bill of fare
related words chow, cuisine, fare, grub
2 a record of a series of items (as names or titles) usually arranged according to some system ⟨checked the *menu* of available books⟩ — see ¹LIST
mercenary *adj* having or marked by an eager and often selfish desire especially for material possessions ⟨a *mercenary* urge to own the latest and most expensive item in home electronics⟩ — see GREEDY 1
merchandise *n* products that are bought and sold in business ⟨we stock only the finest-quality *merchandise* in this store⟩
synonyms commodities, goods, wares
related words line; export, import; inventory, staples, stock, stuff
merchandise *vb* to offer for sale to the public ⟨the now-familiar practice of stores *merchandising* goods at dramatically lower prices on the day after Thanksgiving⟩ — see MARKET
merchandiser *n* **1** a buyer and seller of goods for profit ⟨the *merchandiser* makes a 15% profit on those toys⟩ — see MERCHANT
2 the person in a business deal who hands over an item in exchange for money ⟨a scattering of small *merchandisers* selling souvenirs around the fairgrounds⟩ — see VENDOR
merchant *n* a buyer and seller of goods for profit ⟨free trade agreements that are favored by *merchants* on both sides of the border⟩
synonyms dealer, merchandiser, trader, tradesman, trafficker
related words businessman; buyer, purchaser; hawker, peddler (*also* pedlar); retailer, seller, shopkeeper, storekeeper, vendor (*also* vender); jobber, middleman, wholesaler; distributor, provider, supplier
mercifulness *n* kind, gentle, or compassionate treatment especially towards someone who is undeserving of it ⟨preached that the *mercifulness* of the Lord is without limit⟩ — see MERCY 1
merciless *adj* having or showing a lack of sympathy or tender feelings ⟨she is a *merciless* competitor at board games of any kind⟩ — see HARD 1
mercurial *adj* likely to change frequently, suddenly, or unexpectedly ⟨his mood is so *mercurial* that we never know how he's going to react to anything⟩ — see FICKLE 1
mercy *n* **1** kind, gentle, or compassionate treatment especially towards someone who is undeserving of it ⟨always show your enemies *mercy*, because it makes you a better person⟩
synonyms charity, clemency, lenience, leniency, lenity, mercifulness, quarter
related words humanitarianism, philanthropy; empathy, pity, sympathy, understanding; commiseration, favor, grace; benevolence, care, compassion, gentleness, goodness, goodwill, kindliness, kindness, meekness, mildness, niceness, softness, tenderness; altruism, generosity, magnanimity, nobility; affection, devotion, love, worship
near antonyms reprisal, retaliation, retribution, revenge, vengeance; venom, vindictiveness, virulence, vitriol; brutality, cruelty, savagery, violence; castigation, chastisement, punishment, scolding; abhorrence, abomination, execration, hate, hatred, loathing; cattiness, malevolence, malice, malignity, meanness, spite,

spitefulness, spleen; animosity, antagonism, antipathy, bitterness, enmity, grudge, hostility, jealousy, pique, resentment; bile, jaundice, rancor; hatefulness, invidiousness; coarseness, grimness, hardness, harshness, roughness

2 an act of kind assistance ⟨did a *mercy* for the stranded motorist and was richly rewarded⟩ — see FAVOR 1

3 the capacity for feeling for another's unhappiness or misfortune ⟨a woman of such *mercy* that she's been known to cry over dead rodents⟩ — see HEART 1

mere *n, chiefly British* a small often deep body of water ⟨one of the most scenic *meres* in England's Lake District⟩ — see ¹POOL

mere *adj* being this and no more ⟨the *mere* idea of your traveling alone to Europe is ridiculous⟩

synonyms bare, very

related words absolute, sheer, simple, stark, utter; alone, only, singular, sole, solitary, solo, unique

merely *adv* nothing more than ⟨the noise was *merely* a raccoon knocking over the garbage can⟩ — see JUST 3

merge *vb* to turn into a single mass that is more or less the same throughout ⟨years of living side by side failed to *merge* the various ethnic groups into one community, and the city remained more of a mosaic than a melting pot⟩ — see BLEND 1

merging *n* the act or an instance of joining two or more things into one ⟨the *merging* of the two companies resulted in a corporation with a totally different configuration⟩ — see UNION 1

meridian *n* the highest part or point ⟨a lawyer at the *meridian* of his career arguing a case before the U.S. Supreme Court⟩ — see HEIGHT 1

merit *n* **1** a quality that gives something special worth ⟨this mystery novel at least has the *merit* of an original plot⟩ — see EXCELLENCE 2

2 the relative usefulness or importance of something as judged by specific qualities ⟨that idea has some *merit*, so let's explore it⟩ — see WORTH 1

merit *vb* to be or make worthy of (as a reward or punishment) ⟨that selfless act of heroism *merited* a public ceremony to honor the young swimmer⟩ — see EARN 2

merited *adj* being what is called for by accepted standards of right and wrong ⟨the punishment was *merited*⟩ — see JUST 1

meritorious *adj* **1** deserving of high regard or great approval ⟨worked all night with *meritorious* determination to get the project done on time⟩ — see ADMIRABLE

2 having sufficient worth or merit to receive one's honor, esteem, or reward ⟨all agreed that the most *meritorious* science project had won the competition⟩ — see WORTHY

merrily *adv* in a cheerful or happy manner ⟨she *merrily* announced that it was her birthday⟩ — see GAILY 1

merriment *n* **1** a mood characterized by high spirits and amusement and often accompanied by laughter ⟨their unexpected *merriment* made him nervously inquire as to the reason for it⟩ — see MIRTH

2 joyful or festive activity ⟨the *merriment* lasted long into the night⟩ — see MERRYMAKING

merriness *n* a mood characterized by high spirits and amusement and often accompanied by laughter ⟨I hate the forced *merriness* of so many New Year's Eve parties⟩ — see MIRTH

merry *adj* indicative of or marked by high spirits or good humor ⟨Santa Claus has *merry*, twinkling blue eyes⟩

synonyms blithesome, festive, gay, gleeful, jocose, jocund, jolly, jovial, laughing, mirthful, sunny

related words amused, beaming, chuckling, giggling, smiling; bright, buoyant, carefree, cheerful, cheery, chipper, lighthearted, lightsome, upbeat; animated, jaunty, lively, perky, sprightly, vivacious; blessed, blissful, delighted, ecstatic, elated, enraptured, entranced, euphoric, exhilarated, exuberant, exultant, gladsome, happy, high, joyful, joyous, jubilant, overjoyed, radiant, rapturous, ravished, thrilled; amusing, facetious, flippant, funny, hilarious, jesting, joking, joshing, playful, witty; careless, cavalier, devil-may-care, easygoing, happy-go-lucky, insouciant, unconcerned; hopeful, optimistic, rosy, sanguine

near antonyms abject, aggrieved, anguished, blue, brokenhearted, dejected, depressed, despondent, disconsolate, disheartened, dispirited, downcast, downhearted, forlorn, heartbroken, heartsick, melancholy, sad, sorrowful, unhappy; crying, groaning, moaning, sobbing, wailing; discontented, disgruntled, moody; doleful, dolorous, joyless, lachrymose, mournful, plaintive, sorry, woeful; black, dark, desolate, gloomy, glum, gray (*also* grey); miserable, woebegone, wretched; dull, lethargic, listless, sluggish, torpid

merrymaker *n* one who engages in merrymaking especially in honor of a special occasion ⟨*merrymakers* gathered to celebrate New Year's Eve in grand style⟩ — see CELEBRANT

merrymaking *n* joyful or festive activity ⟨Christmas Eve is always an occasion of much *merrymaking* at our home⟩

synonyms conviviality, festivity, gaiety (*also* gayety), jollification, jollity, merriment, reveling, revelry

related words carousal, carouse; delight, diversion, entertainment, fun, pleasure, recreation, riot; glee, gleefulness, joviality, merriness, mirth, mirthfulness; carnival, celebration, party, revel; frolicking, gamboling, rollicking, romping; enjoyment, happiness, joy; binge, fling, frolic, gambol, lark, rollick, romp, spree; buffoonery, clownishness, flippancy, frivolity, funning, jesting, jocularity, joking, joshing, levity, lightheartedness, playfulness; zaniness

near antonyms blackness, darkness, gloominess, glumness, grief, grieving, heartbreak, miserableness, misery, mournfulness, mourning, wretchedness; anguish, dejection, depression, despondence, forlornness, melancholy, sorrow, unhappiness

mesa *n* a broad flat area of elevated land ⟨a *mesa* in the Arizona desert⟩ — see PLATEAU

mesh *n* a fabric made of strands loosely twisted, knotted, or woven together at regular intervals ⟨spread a *mesh* across the doorway to keep out insects⟩ — see ¹NET 1

mesh *vb* to catch or hold as if in a net ⟨dolphins sometimes become *meshed* in fishnets⟩ — see ENTANGLE 2

mesmerism *n* the art or act of inducing in a person a sleep-like state during which he or she readily follows suggestions ⟨made a living at *mesmerism* and the selling of medical remedies of dubious value⟩ — see HYPNOSIS

mesmerize *vb* to hold the attention of as if by a spell ⟨discovered that the children were *mesmerized* by a television show⟩ — see ENTHRALL 1

mess *n* **1** a state in which everything is out of order ⟨the party left the house a total *mess*⟩ — see CHAOS

2 food eaten or prepared for eating at one time ⟨a *mess* of oatmeal⟩ — see MEAL

3 something unpleasant to look at ⟨the car was a *mess* after the accident⟩ — see EYESORE

mess *vb* to interest oneself in what is not one's concern ⟨please don't *mess* with me while I'm trying to concentrate⟩ — see INTERFERE

mess (around) *vb* to spend time in aimless activity ⟨spent the vacation day just *messing around*⟩ — see FIDDLE (AROUND)

mess (up) *vb* **1** to make or do (something) in a clumsy or unskillful way ⟨*messed up* the drawing and had to start over⟩ — see BOTCH
2 to undo the proper order or arrangement of ⟨a nap had *messed up* her hair and she looked a sight⟩ — see DISORDER

mess (with) *vb* to handle thoughtlessly, ignorantly, or mischievously ⟨please don't *mess with* the buttons on the camera⟩ — see TAMPER

message *n* a piece of conveyed information ⟨answered the phone and took a *message*⟩ — see COMMUNICATION

messed *adj* lacking in order, neatness, and often cleanliness ⟨came home to find a *messed* basement with his tools scattered about⟩ — see MESSY

messenger *n* one that carries a message or does an errand ⟨the *messenger* comes by twice a day to pick up packages⟩
synonyms courier, go-between, page, runner
related words forerunner, harbinger, herald; agent, ambassador, delegate, deputy, emissary, envoy, representative; bearer, carrier, deliveryman, letter carrier, mail carrier, mailman

messy *adj* lacking in order, neatness, and often cleanliness ⟨you cannot go out to play until you clean up this *messy* room and put away all your toys⟩
synonyms chaotic, cluttered, confused, disarranged, disarrayed, disheveled (*or* dishevelled), disordered, disorderly, higgledy-piggledy, hugger-mugger, jumbled, littered, messed, muddled, mussed, mussy, pell-mell, rumpled, sloppy, topsy-turvy, tousled, tumbled, unkempt, untidy, upside-down
related words besmirched, blackened, dingy, dirty, filthy, foul, grimy, grubby, grungy, mucky, nasty, soiled, spotted, squalid, stained, sullied, unclean, uncleanly; dowdy, frowsy (*or* frowzy), slatternly, slovenly, uncombed; wrinkled; contaminated, defiled, polluted, tainted; knotted, snarled, tangled; seedy, shabby, sleazy, sordid; neglected, neglectful, negligent
phrases at sixes and sevens
near antonyms clean, cleaned, cleanly, hygienic, immaculate, sparkling, spick-and-span (*or* spic-and-span), spotless, stainless, unsoiled, unsullied; methodical, systematic; careful, fastidious, fussy, meticulous; combed, groomed, manicured; taintless, undefiled, unpolluted, untainted, wholesome
antonyms neat, ordered, orderly, organized, shipshape, snug, tidied, tidy, trim

metamorphose *vb* to change in form, appearance, or use ⟨a science fiction story in which radiation *metamorphoses* people into giant bugs⟩ — see CONVERT 2

metamorphosis *n* a change in form, appearance, or use ⟨the *metamorphosis* of caterpillars into butterflies⟩ — see CONVERSION

metaphor *n* an elaborate or fanciful way of expressing something ⟨"it's raining cats and dogs" is just a colorful *metaphor* and not a meteorological announcement⟩ — see CONCEIT 1

metaphorical *adj* expressing one thing in terms normally used for another ⟨an author fond of such *metaphorical* phrases as "the desert was a fiery furnace"⟩ — see FIGURATIVE

metaphysical *adj* of, relating to, or being part of a reality beyond the observable physical universe ⟨belief in a *metaphysical* world⟩ — see SUPERNATURAL 1

mete (out) *vb* to give out (something) in appropriate amounts or to appropriate individuals ⟨determined to *mete out* an appropriate punishment for the student guilty of plagiarism⟩ — see ADMINISTER 1

meter *n* the recurrent pattern formed by a series of sounds having a regular rise and fall in intensity ⟨the poem's *meter* is meant to reinforce the atmosphere of gloom⟩ — see RHYTHM

method *n* the means or procedure for doing something ⟨all experiments must be conducted using the proper scientific *method*⟩
synonyms approach, fashion, form, manner, strategy, style, system, tack, tactics, technique, way
related words mode; blueprint, design, game, ground plan, intrigue, layout, line, plan, plot, program, route, scheme; expedient, move, shift, step; practice (*also* practise), process, routine; project, proposal, proposition; policy

methodical *adj* following a set method, arrangement, or pattern ⟨a *methodical* study plan that included lists of points to memorize⟩
synonyms orderly, organized, regular, systematic, systematized
related words regularized, standardized; accurate, correct, exact, precise; detailed, specific; businesslike
near antonyms chaotic, disordered, disorderly, unordered
antonyms disorganized, haphazard, irregular, unsystematic

meticulous *adj* taking great care and effort ⟨did a *meticulous* job of cleaning up⟩ — see PAINSTAKING

metric *adj* marked by or occurring with a noticeable regularity in the rise and fall of sound ⟨the *metric* chugging of the machinery had a hypnotic effect⟩ — see RHYTHMIC

metrical *adj* marked by or occurring with a noticeable regularity in the rise and fall of sound ⟨a *metrical* accent that was pleasant to listen to⟩ — see RHYTHMIC

metropolis *n* a thickly settled, highly populated area ⟨a big, teeming *metropolis* where ambitious people from all over come to make their mark⟩ — see CITY

metropolitan *n* a person with the outlook, experience, and manners thought to be typical of big city dwellers ⟨a TV series about the lives and loves of a group of young, attractive *metropolitans*⟩ — see COSMOPOLITAN

mettlesome *adj* marked by a lively display of strong feeling ⟨a *mettlesome* debate on the teaching of evolution in the schools⟩ — see SPIRITED 1

mewl *vb* to utter feeble plaintive cries ⟨the tiny kitten *mewled* for its mother⟩ — see WHIMPER

microminiature *adj* very small in size ⟨a *microminiature* model of the city to be used for the movie's special effects⟩ — see TINY

microscopic *also* **microscopical** *adj* very small in size ⟨even a *microscopic* speck of dust in the eye will cause pain⟩ — see TINY

mid *adj* occupying a position equally distant from the ends or extremes ⟨inserted her *mid* finger into the opening⟩ — see MIDDLE 1

mid *prep* in or into the middle of ⟨ran excitedly *mid* the crowd⟩ — see AMONG

midday *n* the middle of the day ⟨by *midday* the sun and heat were unbearable⟩ — see NOON

middle *adj* **1** occupying a position equally distant from the ends or extremes ⟨you must mark the exact *middle* point of each of these lines in order to solve the problem〉

synonyms halfway, intermediary, intermediate, medial, median, medium, mid, middlemost, midmost, midway

related words equidistant; central, inmost, inner, innermost, nearest

near antonyms outer, peripheral

antonyms extreme, farthest, farthermost, furthermost, furthest, outermost, outmost, remotest, utmost

2 being about midway between extremes of amount or size 〈a house that is *middle*-sized for that neighborhood〉 〈a man of *middle* height〉

synonyms average, intermediate, median, medium, moderate, modest

related words reasonable; common, commonplace, conventional, normal, popular, regular, routine, standard, typical, usual; passable, tolerable

near antonyms excessive, extreme; rare, strange, uncommon, unusual; distinctive, idiosyncratic, special, unique; individual, peculiar, private

middle *n* **1** a middle point between extremes 〈his salary is exactly at the *middle* of the company's pay scale〉 — see MEAN 1

2 an area or point that is an equal distance from all points along an edge or outer surface 〈put the dish in the *middle* of the table〉 — see CENTER 2

3 the middle region of the human body 〈clutched the football tightly against her *middle*〉 — see MIDRIFF

4 the most intense or characteristic phase of something 〈I'm right in the *middle* of this, so can you come back later?〉 — see THICK

middleman *n* one who works with opposing sides in order to bring about an agreement 〈the retired statesman is often asked to be a *middleman* in international disputes〉 — see MEDIATOR

middlemost *adj* occupying a position equally distant from the ends or extremes 〈took the *middlemost* seat in the auditorium〉 — see MIDDLE 1

middle–of–the–road *adj* avoiding major social change or extreme political ideas 〈a candidate with *middle-of-the-road* views on most issues〉 — see MODERATE 2

middling *adj* of average to below average quality 〈the historian's latest book is only *middling*〉 — see MEDIOCRE 1

midget *n* a living thing much smaller than others of its kind 〈a breed that is the *midget* of the horse world〉 — see DWARF 1

midmost *adj* occupying a position equally distant from the ends or extremes 〈take the *midmost* door〉 — see MIDDLE 1

midpoint *n* **1** a middle point between extremes 〈always choose a wine that is at the *midpoint* of the range of prices on the list〉 — see MEAN 1

2 an area or point that is an equal distance from all points along an edge or outer surface 〈that house is the precise *midpoint* of the school district〉 — see CENTER 2

midriff *n* the middle region of the human body 〈*midriff*-baring tops are popular this summer〉

synonyms middle, waist, waistline

related words abdomen, torso, trunk

midst *n* **1** an area or point that is an equal distance from all points along an edge or outer surface 〈stood in the *midst* of the crowd〉 — see CENTER 2

2 the most intense or characteristic phase of something 〈in the *midst* of illustrating a new book〉 — see THICK

midst *prep* in or into the middle of 〈gave a victory speech *midst* cheering supporters〉 — see AMONG

midway *adj* occupying a position equally distant from the ends or extremes 〈the restaurant is *midway* between the two gas stations〉 — see MIDDLE 1

mien *n* the outward form of someone or something especially as indicative of a quality 〈the stern *mien* of the librarian suggested that she was not one to put up with any nonsense〉 — see APPEARANCE 1

might *n* the ability to exert effort for the accomplishment of a task 〈currently the president lacks the *might* to push his programs through the congress〉 — see POWER 2

mightily *adv* **1** to a great degree 〈every volunteer contributed *mightily* to the cause〉 — see VERY 1

2 with great effort or determination 〈struggled *mightily* to climb up the steep cliff〉 — see HARD 1

3 in a vigorous and forceful manner 〈it is a foregone conclusion that the president's supporters will *mightily* applaud virtually every line of his speech〉 — see HARD 3

mighty *adj* having great power or influence 〈one of the *mighty* leaders of the financial world〉 — see IMPORTANT 2

mighty *adv* to a great degree 〈he was *mighty* hungry after raking leaves all afternoon〉 — see VERY 1

migrant *adj* having a way of life that involves moving from one region to another typically on a seasonal basis 〈a *migrant* laborer living in substandard housing〉 — see MIGRATORY

migrant *n* one that leaves one place to settle in another 〈the city will have to expand and upgrade its social services in order to handle the latest influx of *migrants*〉 — see EMIGRANT

migratory *adj* having a way of life that involves moving from one region to another typically on a seasonal basis 〈most of the apple crop is picked by *migratory* workers〉 〈*migratory* birds heading south for the winter〉

synonyms migrant, mobile

related words errant, itinerant, nomadic, peripatetic, ranging, roaming, roving, traveling (*or* travelling), vagabond, vagrant, wandering, wayfaring; ambulatory, drifting, footloose, gallivanting (*also* galavanting), lingering, meandering, rambling, sauntering, strolling, traipsing, walking

near antonyms immobile, stationary; established, fast, fixed, rooted, set, settled

antonyms nonmigratory, resident

mild *adj* **1** marked by temperatures that are neither too high nor too low 〈the *mild* weather that makes springtime such a delight〉 — see CLEMENT

2 not harsh or stern especially in manner, nature, or effect 〈a quiet gentleman with a kindly soul and a *mild* disposition〉 — see GENTLE 1

milestone *n* a point in a chain of events at which an important change (as in one's fortunes) occurs 〈the new drug was regarded as a *milestone* in the treatment of heart disease〉 — see TURNING POINT

milieu *n* the circumstances, conditions, or objects by which one is surrounded 〈young, innovative artists thrive in the freewheeling *milieu* that a big city offers〉 — see ENVIRONMENT

militancy *n* an inclination to fight or quarrel 〈the *militancy* of the radical organization made the authorities a little nervous〉 — see BELLIGERENCE

militant *adj* **1** feeling or displaying eagerness to fight ⟨political radicals with a *militant* unwillingness to compromise on any issue⟩ — see BELLIGERENT

2 having or showing a bold forcefulness in the pursuit of a goal ⟨after a campaign by *militant* feminists lasting more than 70 years, American women received the right to vote in 1919⟩ — see AGGRESSIVE 1

militant *n* one who is intensely or excessively devoted to a cause ⟨*militants* within the movement insisted that there could be no compromise on the abolition of slavery⟩ — see ZEALOT

militarist *n* one who urges or attempts to cause a war ⟨the *militarists* who dominated the Japanese government in the first half of the 20th century⟩ — see WARMONGER

military *adj* **1** of or relating to the armed services ⟨the colonel testified that revealing any more information would have required giving away *military* secrets⟩
synonyms martial, service
related words naval; GI, gladiatorial, mercenary, soldierly; aggressive, bellicose, combative, contentious, militant, militaristic, pugnacious, quarrelsome, scrappy, truculent, warlike
near antonyms civilian
antonyms nonmilitary

2 of, relating to, or suitable for war or a warrior ⟨after returning from the war, the college president very unsuccessfully tried to impose *military* discipline on the students⟩ — see MARTIAL 1

military *n* the combined army, air force, and navy of a nation ⟨some would insist that the *military's* budget is still inadequate⟩ — see ARMED FORCES

mill *n* a building or set of buildings for the manufacturing of goods ⟨a steel *mill* that remains the town's principal employer⟩ — see FACTORY

mime *n* an actor in a story performed silently and entirely by body movements ⟨that annoying *mime* on the sidewalk is pretending to be in an invisible box again⟩
synonyms mimic, mummer, pantomime, pantomimist
related words entertainer, performer, player, trouper; imitator, impersonator, impressionist

mime *vb* to use (someone or something) as the model for one's speech, mannerisms, or behavior ⟨as a joke, Eric knelt by the dinner table and began *miming* a dog begging for food⟩ — see IMITATE 1

mimetic *adj* using or marked by the use of something else as a basis or model ⟨boys have a tendency toward *mimetic* behavior, often imitating their fathers at a fairly early age⟩ — see IMITATIVE

mimic *adj* **1** being such in appearance only and made with or manufactured from usually cheaper materials ⟨police were concerned that the *mimic* gun, although intended only as a toy, might be confused with the real thing in certain situations⟩ — see IMITATION

2 using or marked by the use of something else as a basis or model ⟨a *mimic* battle fought by kids playing around in the schoolyard⟩ — see IMITATIVE

mimic *n* **1** a person who imitates another's voice and mannerisms for comic effect ⟨a gifted *mimic* who can do a terrific imitation of anyone's voice⟩
synonyms imitator, impersonator, impressionist
related words caricaturist, lampooner, mocker, parodist, satirist; mime, mummer, pantomimist; entertainer, performer, player, trouper; parrot

2 an actor in a story performed silently and entirely by body movements ⟨a *mimic* in black clothes and white facial makeup⟩ — see MIME

mimic *vb* **1** to copy or exaggerate (someone or something) in order to make fun of ⟨the comedian was famous for *mimicking* the President's distinctive lisp⟩
synonyms burlesque, caricature, imitate, mock, parody, take off (on), travesty
related words lampoon, satirize; deride, ridicule; ape, parrot; duplicate, emulate, replicate, reproduce; act, counterfeit, dissemble, fake, feign, pretend, sham, simulate; elaborate, embellish, embroider, exaggerate, magnify, pad, stretch; amplify, enhance, enlarge (upon), expand, flesh (out), overdraw, overstate; mime, pantomime; impersonate, perform, play

2 to use (someone or something) as the model for one's speech, mannerisms, or behavior ⟨began to learn their language by *mimicking* the sounds they made⟩ — see IMITATE 1

mince *vb* to cut into small pieces ⟨*minced* some garlic and added it to the stew⟩ — see CHOP

mind *vb* **1** to pay attention especially through the act of hearing ⟨I'll assign you extra homework if you don't straighten up and *mind*⟩ — see LISTEN

2 *chiefly dialect* to bring back to mind ⟨I seemed to *mind* such a tale from way back⟩ — see REMEMBER

3 to act according to the commands of ⟨*mind* your teachers and you just may turn out all right⟩ — see OBEY

4 to be cautious of or on guard against ⟨*mind* the slippery steps⟩ — see BEWARE (OF)

5 to have an interest or concern for ⟨he didn't *mind* the cold weather⟩ — see CARE

6 to take charge of especially on behalf of another ⟨the babysitter will *mind* the children while the parents are away⟩ — see ²TEND 1

7 to take notice of and be guided by ⟨*mind* the instructions that appear at the top of the first page of the exam⟩ — see HEED 1

mind *n* **1** the part of a person that feels, thinks, perceives, wills, and especially reasons ⟨scientists still disagree about exactly where the *mind* is located⟩
synonyms cerebrum, head
related words brain, gray matter, intellect, intelligence, reason; acumen, alertness, astuteness, brilliance, insight, judgment (*or* judgement), mentality, perception, perspicacity, sagacity, sapience, wisdom, wit; awareness, cognizance, consciousness, self-awareness, self-consciousness

2 the normal or healthy condition of the mental abilities ⟨everyone used to tease him and tell him he was out of his *mind* when he swore he'd seen a flying saucer⟩
synonyms head, reason, saneness, sanity, wit
related words rationality, reasonableness, sense; health, healthfulness, healthiness, wholesomeness; lucidity, lucidness, normality, soundness; wisdom
near antonyms delusion, hallucination; delirium, frenzy, hysteria
antonyms derangement, insanity, lunacy, madness, mania

3 an idea that is believed to be true or valid without positive knowledge ⟨please speak your *mind* on the matter⟩ — see OPINION 1

4 the power or process of recalling what has been previously learned or experienced ⟨call to *mind* the events of last year⟩ — see MEMORY 1

mindful *adj* having specified facts or feelings actively impressed on the mind ⟨a truly considerate person, always *mindful* of the needs of others⟩ — see CONSCIOUS

mindless *adj* **1** not having or showing an ability to absorb ideas readily ⟨a dead-end job fit only for *mindless* drones⟩ — see STUPID 1
2 not paying or showing close attention especially for the purpose of avoiding trouble ⟨*mindless* of danger as always, the skiers ignored the avalanche warnings⟩ — see CARELESS 1

mindlessness *n* the quality or state of lacking intelligence or quickness of mind ⟨despised the sheer *mindlessness* of the movie's violence⟩ — see STUPIDITY 1

mine *n* a usually concealed explosive device designed to go off when disturbed ⟨the soldiers were careful to disarm any *mines* they found in their path⟩ — see BOOBY TRAP 1

mine *vb* to place hidden explosive devices in or under ⟨the troops *mined* the field before they gave it up to the enemy⟩
synonyms boobytrap
related words blow up, bomb; ambush, snare, trap; attack

mingle *vb* **1** to turn into a single mass that is more or less the same throughout ⟨the site where the river and the ocean *mingle* their waters to form a broad estuary⟩ — see BLEND 1
2 to take part in social activities ⟨*mingling* at a cocktail party⟩ — see SOCIALIZE

miniature *adj* very small in size ⟨a dollhouse with *miniature* furnishings⟩ — see TINY

miniature *n* an exact representation of something in greatly reduced size ⟨a diorama filled with *miniatures* of town buildings as they looked in the 19th century⟩ — see MODEL 1

minimal *adj* being the least in amount, number, or size possible ⟨the beached whales were returned to the sea with only *minimal* loss of life⟩
synonyms least, littlest, lowest, minimum, slightest
related words fewer, lesser, low, slight, small, smaller
near antonyms highest
antonyms full, greatest, largest, maximum, top, topmost, utmost

minimize *vb* to express scornfully one's low opinion of ⟨sore losers trying to *minimize* the other team's victory⟩ — see DECRY 1

minimum *adj* being the least in amount, number, or size possible ⟨spent the *minimum* amount necessary to acquire the party decorations⟩ — see MINIMAL

minion *n* a person or thing that is preferred over others ⟨most of the top appointments went to the new governor's personal *minions* and political cronies⟩ — see FAVORITE

minister *n* **1** a person sent on a mission to represent another ⟨the British *ministers* at the international peace conference⟩ — see AMBASSADOR
2 a person specially trained and authorized to conduct religious services in a Christian church ⟨our *minister* gives an interesting sermon every week⟩ — see CLERGYMAN

minister (to) *vb* to attend to the needs and comforts of ⟨volunteered to help *minister* to the sick at the local hospice⟩ — see NURSE 1

ministerial *adj* of, relating to, or characteristic of the clergy ⟨a priest conscientiously tending to his *ministerial* duties⟩ — see CLERICAL

minor *adj* **1** having not so great importance or rank as another ⟨some *minor* official with an exaggerated sense of his own importance⟩ — see LESSER
2 of little or less value or merit ⟨a *minor* poet who is little read nowadays⟩ — see INFERIOR 2

3 lacking importance ⟨only a *minor* detail, which we can easily disregard for the moment⟩ — see UNIMPORTANT

minstrel *n* a person who writes poetry ⟨Edna St. Vincent Millay was unofficially the *minstrel* of Maine, as her poetry celebrates its coast and countryside⟩ — see POET

minstrelsy *n* writing that uses rhythm, vivid language, and often rhyme to provoke an emotional response ⟨the traditional forms of German *minstrelsy*⟩ — see POETRY 1

mint *n* a very large amount of money ⟨she's making a *mint* selling her homemade cookies⟩ — see FORTUNE 2

minus *n* a feature of someone or something that creates difficulty for achieving success ⟨a plan with lots of pluses and only a few *minuses*⟩ — see DISADVANTAGE

minus *prep* not having ⟨the contraption was like a giant carousel *minus* the horses⟩ — see WITHOUT 1

minute *adj* **1** including many small descriptive features ⟨a *minute* description of the setting of the story⟩ — see DETAILED 1
2 lacking importance ⟨a person who wastes her time on the most *minute* aspects of everyday life⟩ — see UNIMPORTANT
3 so small or unimportant as to warrant little or no attention ⟨only *minute* flaws remained in the material⟩ — see NEGLIGIBLE 1
4 made or done with extreme care and accuracy ⟨a *minute* examination of the marine specimen⟩ — see FINE 2
5 very small in size ⟨made some *minute* adjustments to the controls⟩ — see TINY

minute *n* a very small space of time ⟨I'll be with you in just a *minute*⟩ — see INSTANT

minutely *adv* with attention to all aspects or details ⟨a *minutely* detailed analysis of the series of glitches that resulted in the blackout⟩ — see THOROUGHLY 1

miracle *n* something extraordinary or surprising ⟨it's a *miracle* that you weren't hurt in the accident⟩ — see WONDER 1

miraculous *adj* **1** being so extraordinary or abnormal as to suggest powers which violate the laws of nature ⟨the *miraculous* nature of the revelation⟩ — see SUPERNATURAL 2
2 causing wonder or astonishment ⟨his *miraculous* escape from the burning building⟩ — see MARVELOUS 1

mire *n* **1** soft wet earth ⟨played on a football field that was thick with *mire*⟩ — see MUD
2 spongy land saturated or partially covered with water ⟨much of the land in that area is *mire* that cannot be developed⟩ — see SWAMP

mire *vb* **1** to make dirty ⟨the returning hunters *mired* the floor of the garage⟩ — see DIRTY
2 to place in conflict or difficulties ⟨the case has been *mired* in the courts for years⟩ — see EMBROIL

mirror *n* a smooth or polished surface (as of glass) that forms images by reflection ⟨breaking a *mirror* is supposed to bring seven years of bad luck⟩
synonyms looking glass
related words pier glass; reflector

mirror *vb* to reproduce or show (an exact likeness) as a mirror would ⟨the still waters of the pond *mirroring* the cloudless sky above⟩ — see REFLECT

mirth *n* a mood characterized by high spirits and amusement and often accompanied by laughter ⟨as charming as your mutual *mirth* is, could you refrain from nudging each other and giggling during class?⟩

synonyms cheer, cheerfulness, cheeriness, festivity, glee, gleefulness, hilarity, joviality, merriment, merriness, mirthfulness

related words frivolity, levity; carnival, gaiety (*also* gayety), jollification, jollity, reveling, revelry; brightness, buoyancy, good-humoredness, good-naturedness, humor, sunniness; insouciance, lightheartedness, playfulness, buffoonery, clownishness, flippancy, funning, jesting, jocularity, joking, joshing; animation, jauntiness, liveliness, perkiness, vivacity; joyfulness, joyousness, jubilance, rejoicing; frolicking, gamboling (*or* gambolling), rollicking, romping

near antonyms blues, dejection, depression, despondence, forlornness, sadness, sorrow, unhappiness; bile, gloom, melancholy, sourness, spleen; earnestness, graveness, gravity, grimness, seriousness, soberness, solemnity; discontent, disgruntlement, moodiness; dolefulness, dolorousness, joylessness, mournfulness, plaintiveness, woe, woefulness; blackness, darkness, gloominess, glumness; desolateness, desolation; heartbreak, miserableness, misery, mourning, wretchedness

mirthful *adj* indicative of or marked by high spirits or good humor ⟨*mirthful* laughter of old teammates telling silly jokes and ribald stories⟩ — see MERRY

mirthfully *adv* in a cheerful or happy manner ⟨singing *mirthfully* as we sat around the campfire⟩ — see GAILY 1

mirthfulness *n* a mood characterized by high spirits and amusement and often accompanied by laughter ⟨their *mirthfulness* was contagious, and pretty soon we were all laughing⟩ — see MIRTH

miry *adj* full of or covered with soft wet earth ⟨*miry* fields that required a good pair of boots⟩ — see MUDDY 1

misadventure *n* bad luck or an example of this ⟨a string of financial *misadventures* eventually left him broke⟩ — see MISFORTUNE

misanthrope *n* a person who distrusts other people and believes that everything is done for selfish reasons ⟨a former *misanthrope* who now rejoices in a new love of mankind⟩ — see CYNIC

misanthropic *adj* having or showing a deep distrust of human beings and their motives ⟨a *misanthropic* outlook on life that is probably due to his miserable childhood⟩ — see CYNICAL

misapplication *n* incorrect or improper use ⟨this silly gossiping is a serious *misapplication* of your time⟩ — see MISUSE

misapply *vb* to put to a bad or improper use ⟨you've *misapplied* the theorem to certain problems that require a different formula⟩ ⟨kids who *misapply* their boundless energy and get into trouble⟩

synonyms abuse, misuse, pervert, profane, prostitute

related words degrade, twist; mismanage; corrupt, debase, desecrate

near antonyms apply, employ, use, utilize; respect

misapprehend *vb* to fail to understand the true or actual meaning of ⟨unfortunately, the message that the artist was trying to convey has been *misapprehended* by many museum patrons⟩ — see MISUNDERSTAND

misapprehension *n* 1 a failure to understand correctly ⟨tried to eliminate all *misapprehensions* about the planned real estate development⟩ — see MISUNDERSTANDING 1

2 a wrong judgment ⟨a common *misapprehension* about how our language functions⟩ — see MISTAKE 1

misappropriate *vb* to take (something) without right and with an intent to keep ⟨*misappropriating* funds from her clients' accounts⟩ — see STEAL 1

misbegotten *adj* born to a father and mother who are not married ⟨a *misbegotten* child who never knew his father⟩ — see ILLEGITIMATE 1

misbehave *vb* to behave badly ⟨if the two of you *misbehave* in public like that again, you'll have to go to bed early for a week⟩

synonyms act up, carry on

related words misconduct; disobey; clown (around), cut up, fool (around), horse (around); show off; roughhouse

phrases raise Cain, run riot

near antonyms obey; acquit, act, bear, comport, demean, deport, quit; comply, conform; check, collect, compose, constrain, contain, control, curb, handle, inhibit, move, quiet, repress, restrain

misbehaving *adj* engaging in or marked by childish misbehavior ⟨a new approach for disciplining a chronically *misbehaving* child⟩ — see NAUGHTY

misbehavior *n* improper or illegal behavior ⟨would not tolerate any *misbehavior* from her students⟩ — see MISCONDUCT

miscalculate *vb* to make an incorrect judgment regarding ⟨they *miscalculated* how difficult the long trip would be⟩

synonyms misconceive, misjudge, mistake

related words misconstrue, misinterpret, misunderstand; overestimate, overrate, overvalue; underestimate, underrate, undervalue; miscount

miscarry *vb* to go wrong ⟨the scheme to save the dolphins *miscarried*, and all were lost⟩

synonyms misfire

related words miss; break down, conk (out), crash, die, fail, stall; fizzle, flop, flunk, fold, wash out; flounder, struggle; decline, slip, slump, wane

phrases fall flat, fall short

near antonyms prevail, succeed; flourish, prosper, thrive

miscellaneous *adj* consisting of many things of different sorts ⟨the bottom of the drawer was always a *miscellaneous* accumulation of odds and ends⟩

synonyms assorted, heterogeneous, mixed, motley, patchwork, promiscuous, varied

related words manifold, multifarious; multiple, multiplex, myriad; disparate, divergent, diverse, sundry, various; chaotic, cluttered, confused, disarranged, disarrayed, disheveled (*or* dishevelled), disordered, jumbled, littered, messed, messy, muddled; amalgamated, blended, combined, conglomerated, fused, incorporated, intermingled, intermixed, merged, mingled; unclassified, unsorted

near antonyms monolithic, uniform; alike, identical, like, same; distinct, distinctive, individual, separate

antonyms homogeneous

miscellaneousness *n* the quality or state of being composed of many different elements or types ⟨the *miscellaneousness* of the store's merchandise makes it a browser's delight⟩ — see VARIETY 1

miscellany *n* 1 an unorganized collection or mixture of various things ⟨the box from the attic contained a *miscellany* of old records, family photo albums, and long-forgotten love letters⟩

synonyms assortment, clutter, hash, hodgepodge, hotchpotch, jumble, litter, medley, mélange, mishmash, motley, muddle, potpourri, rummage, scramble, shuffle, tumble, variety, welter *related words* notions, odds and ends, sundries; accumulation, aggregation, conglomeration; catchall, patchwork; admixture, amalgam, blend, combination, composite, compound, fusion, intermixture, mix, mixture; chaos, confusion, disarrangement, disarray, disorder, mess, muddle, shambles; knot, snarl, tangle

phrases odds and ends

2 a collection of writings ⟨the volume is a *miscellany* of tales and legends of the New England coast⟩ — see ANTHOLOGY

mischance *n* **1** a chance and usually sudden event bringing loss or injury ⟨the smallest *mischance* could spell disaster for our plan⟩ — see ACCIDENT 1

2 bad luck or an example of this ⟨by *mischance* she took a wrong turn and became hopelessly lost in the city⟩ — see MISFORTUNE

mischief *n* **1** playful, reckless behavior that is not intended to cause serious harm ⟨the children claimed that setting off a firecracker was harmless *mischief*, but they got a lecture anyway⟩

synonyms devilishness, devilment, devilry (*or* deviltry), hob, impishness, knavery, mischievousness, rascality, roguishness, shenanigans, waggery, wickedness

related words diabolicalness, naughtiness; friskiness, playfulness, sportiveness; chicanery, hanky-panky, trickery; high jinks, monkeyshines, skylarking, tomfoolery; antic, caper, practical joke; aggravation, annoyance, exasperation, irritation

near antonyms gravity, seriousness, solemnity

2 a natural disposition for playful behavior ⟨your mother was full of *mischief* as a child, believe it or not⟩ — see PLAYFULNESS

3 an appealingly mischievous person ⟨he's a little *mischief* who means no harm⟩ — see SCAMP 1

mischievous *adj* **1** tending to or exhibiting reckless playfulness ⟨the children had been so *mischievous* that we had to pay the babysitter extra and then clean up the mess⟩

synonyms devilish, elvish, impish, knavish, pixieish, prankish, rascally, roguish, sly, waggish, wicked

related words antic, coltish, frisky, kittenish, playful, sportive; gay, happy, lighthearted, whimsical; energetic, lively, spirited, sprightly; artful, cunning, tricky; misbehaving, naughty; pestering, riling, teasing

near antonyms grave, grim, sober, solemn, stern

2 engaging in or marked by childish misbehavior ⟨punished for their *mischievous* tricks on the neighbors⟩ — see NAUGHTY

3 causing or capable of causing harm ⟨*mischievous* gossip that ruined a good woman's reputation⟩ — see HARMFUL

mischievousness *n* **1** a natural disposition for playful behavior ⟨as they grew older, they lost much of their youthful *mischievousness*⟩ — see PLAYFULNESS

2 playful, reckless behavior that is not intended to cause serious harm ⟨bored kids often engage in a certain amount of *mischievousness* during the long summer vacation⟩ — see MISCHIEF 1

misconceive *vb* to make an incorrect judgment regarding ⟨*misconceived* the distance still to be traveled on the trip⟩ — see MISCALCULATE

misconception *n* a false idea or belief ⟨it is a popular *misconception* that toilets flush in the opposite direction in the Southern Hemisphere⟩ — see FALLACY 1

misconduct *n* improper or illegal behavior ⟨some rough play got the hockey player fined for *misconduct* on the ice⟩

synonyms malfeasance, misbehavior, misdoing, wrongdoing

related words crime, malefaction, misdeed, sin, wrong; malpractice; familiarity, gaffe, impropriety, indiscretion; blunder, error, fault, flub, fumble, goof, lapse, miscue, misstep, mistake, slip, slipup, stumble

misconduct *vb* to manage badly ⟨*misconducted* the polar expedition and paid for his mistakes with his life⟩ — see MISMANAGE

misconstruction *n* a failure to understand correctly ⟨his *misconstruction* of the blueprints led to some costly and time-consuming repairs⟩ — see MISUNDERSTANDING 1

misconstrue *vb* to fail to understand the true or actual meaning of ⟨listen carefully so you do not *misconstrue* my instructions⟩ — see MISUNDERSTAND

misconstruing *n* a failure to understand correctly ⟨there are several words in English that are the result of the common *misconstruing* of singular forms as plurals⟩ — see MISUNDERSTANDING 1

miscreant *n* a mean, evil, or unprincipled person ⟨halt, vile *miscreant*, and face justice!⟩ — see VILLAIN

miscue *n* an unintentional departure from truth or accuracy ⟨the slightest *miscue* could make the trapeze artist lose his grip and fall to the mat below⟩ — see ERROR 1

misdeed *n* a breaking of a moral or legal code ⟨punished for her *misdeeds* by the church elders⟩ — see OFFENSE 1

misdoing *n* **1** a breaking of a moral or legal code ⟨the *misdoings* of the city councilman were exposed as a result of an intense investigation by the local newspaper⟩ — see OFFENSE 1

2 improper or illegal behavior ⟨kept a watchful eye for any *misdoing* by the members of the clergy⟩ — see MISCONDUCT

miser *n* a mean grasping person who is usually stingy with money ⟨the *miser* liked to sit and play with his money⟩

synonyms cheapskate, niggard, piker, scrooge, skinflint, tightwad

related words hoarder, saver

near antonyms prodigal, profligate, spender, spendthrift, squanderer, waster, wastrel

miserable *adj* **1** causing or marked by an atmosphere lacking in cheer ⟨a *miserable* jail cell in which the political prisoner was left to rot⟩ — see GLOOMY 1

2 feeling unhappiness ⟨the awful news made us *miserable*⟩ — see SAD 1

3 of low quality ⟨a *miserable* meal that I wouldn't feed to a dog⟩ — see CHEAP 2

4 showing signs of advanced wear and tear and neglect ⟨a *miserable* little apartment⟩ — see SHABBY 1

5 deserving of one's pity ⟨*miserable* refugees from the war-torn country⟩ — see PATHETIC 1

miserliness *n* the quality of being overly sparing with money ⟨some kids like to grouse about the *miserliness* of their parents as far as allowances are concerned⟩ — see PARSIMONY

misery *n* **1** a situation or state that causes great suffering and unhappiness ⟨the flood brought *misery* to the many hundreds whom it had made homeless⟩ — see HELL 2

2 a state of great suffering of body or mind ⟨a medication that promises to provide greater relief to those living in *misery* because of arthritis⟩ — see DISTRESS 1

misfire *vb* to go wrong ⟨their scheme to rob the bank *misfired* disastrously and landed them all in jail⟩ — see MISCARRY

misfortune *n* bad luck or an example of this ⟨through sheer *misfortune* our car got a flat tire and we were late⟩ ⟨our *misfortunes* of the last year included the loss of a beloved pet⟩

synonyms adversity, knock, misadventure, mischance, mishap

related words calamity, cataclysm, catastrophe, disaster; tragedy; affliction, hardship, trial, tribulation; distress, misery, suffering, unhappiness; defeat, failure, fizzle, nonsuccess; curse, sorrow, trouble; accident, casualty; disappointment, letdown, setback; circumstance, destiny, doom, fate, lot, portion

near antonyms break, chance, fluke, godsend, hit, opportunity, stroke, windfall; accomplishment, achievement, success

antonyms fortune, luck

misgiving *n* **1** a feeling or attitude that one does not know the truth, truthfulness, or trustworthiness of someone or something ⟨I had *misgivings* about her idea for a science project, but I didn't want to be discouraging⟩ — see DOUBT

2 an uneasy feeling about the rightness of what one is doing or going to do ⟨he was filled with *misgivings* about skipping school that day⟩ — see QUALM

3 suspicion or fear of future harm or misfortune ⟨overcome by a sudden *misgiving* upon seeing the creepy old mansion⟩ — see APPREHENSION 1

misgovern *vb* to manage badly ⟨the ruling party was soundly defeated at the polls for having disastrously *misgoverned* the country⟩ — see MISMANAGE

misguide *vb* to cause to believe what is untrue ⟨we were *misguided* by the flashy advertisements for what turned out to be pretty lousy pizza⟩ — see DECEIVE

mishandle *vb* **1** to inflict physical or emotional harm upon ⟨having been shuffled from foster home to foster home, the orphaned girl felt she had been *mishandled* by an uncaring society⟩ — see ABUSE 1

2 to abuse physically ⟨adopted a sadly *mishandled* puppy from the pound⟩ — see MANHANDLE 1

3 to manage badly ⟨we took over as soon as we realized that she had been *mishandling* the situation⟩ — see MISMANAGE

mishap *n* **1** a chance and usually sudden event bringing loss or injury ⟨the usual *mishaps* of a family vacation⟩ — see ACCIDENT 1

2 bad luck or an example of this ⟨*mishap* followed wherever he went⟩ — see MISFORTUNE

mishmash *n* an unorganized collection or mixture of various things ⟨the painting was just a *mishmash* of colors and abstract shapes as far as we could tell⟩ — see MISCELLANY 1

misinform *vb* to cause to believe what is untrue ⟨had been *misinformed* about the purpose of the meeting and walked in on what was a surprise birthday party⟩ — see DECEIVE

misinterpret *vb* **1** to change so much as to create a wrong impression or alter the meaning of ⟨his note on this passage in the novel *misinterprets* the author's meaning⟩ — see GARBLE

2 to fail to understand the true or actual meaning of ⟨we *misinterpreted* the directions and ended up on the wrong side of town⟩ — see MISUNDERSTAND

misinterpretation *n* a failure to understand correctly ⟨his *misinterpretation* of the vague instructions was hardly his fault⟩ — see MISUNDERSTANDING 1

misjudge *vb* to make an incorrect judgment regarding ⟨the gymnast *misjudged* her landing and sprained her ankle⟩ — see MISCALCULATE

misjudging *n* a wrong judgment ⟨a series of small *misjudgings* along the way eventually amounted to a colossal mistake⟩ — see MISTAKE 1

misjudgment *n* a wrong judgment ⟨one serious *misjudgment* at this point could cost the candidate the election⟩ — see MISTAKE 1

mislaid *adj* no longer possessed ⟨looking for his *mislaid* papers⟩ — see LOST

mislay *vb* to be unable to find or have at hand ⟨I'm always *mislaying* my bus pass⟩ — see LOSE 1

mislaying *n* the act or an instance of not having or being able to find ⟨your *mislaying* of the car keys caused us to be late for work once again⟩ — see LOSS 1

mislead *vb* to cause to believe what is untrue ⟨the coral snake's attractive colors can *mislead* you into thinking that it is harmless⟩ — see DECEIVE

misleading *adj* tending or having power to deceive ⟨the *misleading* text of the advertisement would like you to believe that you're getting something for nothing⟩ — see DECEPTIVE 1

mismanage *vb* to manage badly ⟨the business was *mismanaged* so seriously that it had to declare bankruptcy⟩

synonyms misconduct, misgovern, mishandle, misrule

related words abuse, ill-treat, ill-use, maltreat, mistreat, misuse; damage, harm, hurt, violate

near antonyms govern, handle, manage, rule; care (for), nurture; aid, help, protect, rescue

misplace *vb* to be unable to find or have at hand ⟨I seem to have *misplaced* my keys⟩ — see LOSE 1

misplaced *adj* no longer possessed ⟨we eventually found the *misplaced* tickets in his coat pocket⟩ — see LOST

misplacement *n* the act or an instance of not having or being able to find ⟨they worried that his *misplacement* of the invitation would keep them from getting in, but fortunately their names were on the list⟩ — see LOSS 1

misread *vb* to fail to understand the true or actual meaning of ⟨I *misread* her body language and thought she was angry⟩ — see MISUNDERSTAND

misreading *n* a failure to understand correctly ⟨your *misreading* of the definition of the word is what got you into trouble⟩ — see MISUNDERSTANDING 1

misrepresent *vb* **1** to change so much as to create a wrong impression or alter the meaning of ⟨this summary seriously *misrepresents* the general tone and substance of the speech⟩ — see GARBLE

2 to give a false idea of ⟨deliberately *misrepresented* the facts of the case⟩ — see BELIE 1

misrule *n* a state in which there is widespread wrongdoing and disregard for rules and authority ⟨the country's long period of *misrule* had made it a hotbed for terrorist organizations⟩ — see ANARCHY

misrule *vb* to manage badly ⟨accused of *misruling* his island nation to the point of economic collapse⟩ — see MISMANAGE

miss *n* a young usually unmarried woman ⟨you should ask that young *miss* if she would like to dance⟩ — see GIRL 1

miss *vb* **1** to fail to attend ⟨had to *miss* school for a week because of the flu⟩ — see CUT 2

2 to fail to understand the true or actual meaning of ⟨I think you're *missing* the point⟩ — see MISUNDERSTAND

misshapen *adj* badly or imperfectly formed ⟨the returning camper presented his mother with a *misshapen* clay bowl that he had made in crafts class⟩ — see MALFORMED

missing *adj* **1** no longer possessed ⟨the *missing* socks turned up in the dog's special hiding place⟩ — see LOST
2 not present or in evidence ⟨any sense of how real people talk and act is *missing* from this novel⟩ — see ABSENT 2
3 not at a certain place ⟨our church organist is *missing* this morning, so we'll have to sing without her accompaniment⟩ — see ABSENT 1

mission *n* a specific task with which a person or group is charged ⟨your *mission* is to clean up the house before company arrives⟩
synonyms assignment, charge, job, operation, post
related words burden, chore, duty, need, obligation, requirement, responsibility; labor, work; commitment, pledge, promise; appointment, designation, nomination; compulsion, constraint, restraint

missive *n* a message on paper from one person or group to another ⟨the two old friends like to fire off *missives* filled with good-natured teasing and mock insults⟩ — see LETTER

misspend *vb* to use up carelessly ⟨warned that a childhood spent playing video games was a *misspent* youth indeed⟩ — see WASTE 1

misstate *vb* to change so much as to create a wrong impression or alter the meaning of ⟨a person who can be counted on to *misstate* even the simplest telephone message⟩ — see GARBLE

misstep *n* an unintentional departure from truth or accuracy ⟨a *misstep* that could lead to disaster⟩ — see ERROR 1

mist *n* **1** a light or fine rain ⟨a *mist* was falling on the streets as we drove home⟩ — see DRIZZLE
2 an atmospheric condition in which suspended particles in the air rob it of its transparency ⟨a heavy *mist* obscured our view of the city from the observatory⟩ — see HAZE 1

mist *vb* to make dark, dim, or indistinct ⟨the damp air *misted* the window pane⟩ — see CLOUD 1

mistake *n* **1** a wrong judgment ⟨I made a *mistake* when I assumed that you were the one who broke the window⟩
synonyms misapprehension, misjudging, misjudgment
related words blunder, error, fault, flub, fumble, goof, inaccuracy, lapse, miscue, misstep, slipup, stumble; foul-up, muff; miscalculation, misstatement; misconception, misconstruction, misconstruing, misinterpretation
2 an unintentional departure from truth or accuracy ⟨made a *mistake* on the exam that almost cost her a passing grade⟩ — see ERROR 1

mistake *vb* **1** to fail to understand the true or actual meaning of ⟨the auctioneer *mistook* my nod for a bid, and I ended up buying a painting I don't even like⟩ — see MISUNDERSTAND
2 to make an incorrect judgment regarding ⟨you seriously *mistake* me if you think I scare so easily⟩ — see MISCALCULATE

mistaken *adj* having an opinion that does not agree with truth or the facts ⟨meat loaf is on the cafeteria's menu today if I'm not *mistaken*⟩ — see INCORRECT 1

mistakenly *adv* in a mistaken or inappropriate way ⟨we *mistakenly* thought that this was our classroom⟩ — see WRONGLY

mistreat *vb* to inflict physical or emotional harm upon ⟨the foster parent who had been *mistreating* his charges was sent to jail⟩ — see ABUSE 1

mistrust *n* a feeling or attitude that one does not know the truth, truthfulness, or trustworthiness of someone or something ⟨had an unfortunate *mistrust* of doctors⟩ — see DOUBT

mistrust *vb* to have no trust or confidence in ⟨a recluse who *mistrusts* her neighbors and stays in her house all day⟩ — see DISTRUST

mistrustful *adj* **1** inclined to doubt or question claims ⟨we were *mistrustful* of the so-called "miracle cure"⟩ — see SKEPTICAL 1
2 not feeling sure about the truth, wisdom, or trustworthiness of someone or something ⟨inhabitants of that remote community tend to be *mistrustful* of outsiders⟩ — see DOUBTFUL 1

mistrustfully *adv* with distrust ⟨our cat tends to view strangers *mistrustfully*⟩ — see ASKANCE

mistrustfulness *n* a feeling or attitude that one does not know the truth, truthfulness, or trustworthiness of someone or something ⟨eyed the strange invention with his usual *mistrustfulness*⟩ — see DOUBT

misty *adj* filled with or dimmed by fine particles (as of dust or water) in suspension ⟨enjoyed the *misty* view of the thunderous falls from the deck of the sight-seeing boat⟩ — see HAZY 1

misunderstand *vb* to fail to understand the true or actual meaning of ⟨you *misunderstood* that poem because you didn't look up the words you didn't know⟩
synonyms misapprehend, misconstrue, misinterpret, misread, miss, mistake
related words misconceive
antonyms apprehend, catch, comprehend, conceive, fathom, grasp, know, make out, penetrate, perceive, savvy, see, seize, take in, understand

misunderstanding *n* **1** a failure to understand correctly ⟨people once thought that there were canals on Mars because of a common *misunderstanding* of a report by an Italian astronomer⟩
synonyms misapprehension, misconstruction, misconstruing, misinterpretation, misreading
related words misconception, mistake
near antonyms appreciation, apprehension, comprehension, conception, grasp, knowledge, perception, understanding; awareness, consciousness, realization
2 an often noisy or angry expression of differing opinions ⟨tried to resolve their *misunderstandings* peacefully⟩ — see ARGUMENT 1

misusage *n* incorrect or improper use ⟨the teacher was appalled by his *misusage* of some basic scientific terms⟩ — see MISUSE

misuse *n* incorrect or improper use ⟨the warranty for this dryer is null and void if you subject the product to deliberate *misuse*⟩
synonyms abuse, misapplication, misusage, perversion
related words mishandling, mismanagement, mismanaging; maltreatment, mistreatment; damage, destruction, ruin, spoiling, wrecking; corruption, debasement, desecration, profanation, prostitution
near antonyms application, employment, use, utilization

misuse *vb* **1** to put to a bad or improper use ⟨an actor who *misused* his considerable talent by appearing in too many lousy movies⟩ — see MISAPPLY
2 to inflict physical or emotional harm upon ⟨sadly *misused* by the people he had trusted⟩ — see ABUSE 1

mite *n* **1** a very small sum of money ⟨I have only a *mite* left to buy lunch for the rest of the week⟩
synonyms peanuts, pittance, shoestring, song
related words petty cash, pin money, pocket money, spending money

near antonyms capital, means, wherewithal; opulence, riches, treasure, wealth; heap, pile, pot; bonanza, mine, treasure trove, treasury
antonyms fortune, king's ransom, mint, wad
2 a living thing much smaller than others of its kind ⟨the kitten was just a *mite*, hardly the size of my palm⟩ — see DWARF 1
3 a very small amount ⟨that speech didn't make a *mite* of sense⟩ — see PARTICLE 1
mitigate *vb* to make more bearable or less severe ⟨this medicine should *mitigate* the pain until the strained muscle heals itself⟩ — see HELP 2
mix *n* a distinct entity formed by the combining of two or more different things ⟨guacamole is usually a *mix* of avocado, tomato, onion, and spices⟩ — see BLEND
mix *vb* **1** to turn into a single mass that is more or less the same throughout ⟨those ingredients should not be *mixed* until the last stage of the recipe⟩ — see BLEND 1
2 to take part in social activities ⟨*mixing* with the other guests at the party⟩ — see SOCIALIZE
mix (up) *vb* to undo the proper order or arrangement of ⟨*mixed up* student records and had to sort them out later⟩ — see DISORDER
mixed *adj* **1** being offspring produced by parents of different races, breeds, species, or genera ⟨our *mixed* dog has a greyhound's body but the features of a collie⟩
synonyms crossbred, hybrid, mongrel
related words dihybrid, trihybrid; crossbred, crossed, hybridized, interbred, outcrossed
near antonyms pedigreed; inbred
antonyms full-blooded, purebred, thoroughbred
2 consisting of many things of different sorts ⟨the summer school offers a very *mixed* selection of courses⟩ — see MISCELLANEOUS
mixture *n* a distinct entity formed by the combining of two or more different things ⟨add eggs to the *mixture* of dry ingredients⟩ — see BLEND
mix–up *n* an instance of confusion ⟨there was a *mix-up* at the airport and our luggage was accidentally sent to Ohio⟩ — see FOUL-UP
moan *n* **1** a long low sound indicating pain or grief ⟨she uttered an agonized *moan* and clutched her stomach⟩
synonyms groan, wail
related words blubbering, crying, sniveling, sobbing, weeping, whimpering, whining, yammering; keen, lament; bawl, cry, howl, shriek, squall, whimper, whine, yelp, yowl
near antonyms cackle, chuckle, chortle, giggle, guffaw, laugh, snicker, titter
2 a crying out in grief ⟨a great *moan* arose from the crowd when the awful news was announced⟩ — see LAMENT 1
moan *vb* **1** to utter a moan ⟨he *moaned* and cried for days after his dog died⟩
synonyms groan, wail
related words cry, blubber, sob, weep; sniff, snivel, whimper, whine; bemoan, bewail, deplore, keen, lament, rue; bleed, grieve, mourn, sorrow, suffer; bawl, howl, shriek, squall, yammer, yelp, yowl
near antonyms cackle, chuckle, chortle, giggle, guffaw, laugh, snicker, titter
2 to express dissatisfaction, pain, or resentment usually tiresomely ⟨*moaned* whenever anyone asked him to do some work⟩ — see COMPLAIN
mob *n* **1** a great number of persons or things gathered together ⟨a *mob* of pigeons flocked around us when we took out the bread crumbs⟩ — see CROWD 1

2 a group involved in secret or criminal activities ⟨he was accused of having connections with a *mob* of racketeers⟩ — see RING 1
3 the body of the community as contrasted with the elite ⟨political speeches designed to appeal to the *mob*⟩ — see MASS 1
mob *vb* to move upon or fill (something) in great numbers ⟨the snack bar was *mobbed* as soon as the lunch bell rang⟩ — see CROWD 2
mobile *adj* **1** capable of being moved especially with ease ⟨a *mobile* electric generator⟩ — see MOVABLE
2 having a way of life that involves moving from one region to another typically on a seasonal basis ⟨*mobile* workers who work the New England resorts in the summer and the ones in Florida during the winter⟩ — see MIGRATORY
mobile home *n* a motor vehicle that is specially equipped for living while traveling ⟨a *mobile home* for traveling around the country⟩ — see CAMPER
mobilization *n* an act of gathering forces together to renew or attempt an effort ⟨called for the prompt *mobilization* of all national resources to combat the threat⟩ — see RALLY 1
mobilize *vb* to assemble and make ready for action ⟨we are prepared to *mobilize* the troops on very short notice⟩
synonyms marshal, muster, rally
related words arrange, line up, order, organize; call (up), convene, summon; activate
near antonyms disarrange, disorder, disorganize; deactivate, dismiss
antonyms demobilize
mobster *n* a violent, brutal person who is often a member of an organized gang ⟨the *mobster* threatened to break his legs if he didn't pay up⟩ — see HOODLUM
mock *adj* **1** being such in appearance only and made with or manufactured from usually cheaper materials ⟨*mock* turtle soup⟩ — see IMITATION
2 lacking in natural or spontaneous quality ⟨since I had inadvertently learned what I was getting, I opened the present with *mock* surprise⟩ — see ARTIFICIAL 1
mock *n* a person or thing that is made fun of ⟨made a *mock* of him in front of the whole school⟩ — see LAUGHINGSTOCK
mock *vb* **1** to copy or exaggerate (someone or something) in order to make fun of ⟨*mocked* the bully's swaggering walk behind his back⟩ — see MIMIC 1
2 to make (someone or something) the object of unkind laughter ⟨the smart alecks thought it was funny to *mock* the teacher—until they were caught and punished⟩ — see RIDICULE
mocker *n* a person who causes repeated emotional pain, distress, or annoyance to another ⟨someday, she swore, she'd get back at the *mockers* who were making her life miserable⟩ — see TORMENTOR
mockery *n* **1** a poor, insincere, or insulting imitation of something ⟨the resort's Old West show for tourists is a *mockery* of Native American culture⟩
synonyms caricature, farce, joke, parody, sham, travesty
related words burlesque, comedy; lampoon, takeoff; counterfeit, fake, feigning, pretense (*or* pretence), simulation
near antonyms homage, tribute
2 a person or thing that is made fun of ⟨you won't make a *mockery* of me!⟩ — see LAUGHINGSTOCK

3 the making of unkind jokes as a way of showing one's scorn for someone or something ⟨insulted by their *mockery* of his Southern mannerisms⟩ — see RIDICULE

mod *adj* being or involving the latest methods, concepts, information, or styles ⟨the young artist's converted loft is decorated in a self-consciously *mod* style⟩ — see MODERN

¹mode *n* **1** a distinctive way of putting ideas into words ⟨a colloquial *mode* of expression for his informal essays⟩ — see STYLE 1

2 a state of mind dominated by a particular emotion ⟨when I'm in my cooking *mode*, I just have to go into the kitchen and make something⟩ — see MOOD 1

²mode *n* a practice or interest that is very popular for a short time ⟨slim, tanned bodies are definitely the *mode* at this beach resort⟩ — see FAD

model *adj* constituting, serving as, or worthy of being a pattern to be imitated ⟨why can't you be like your sister, who is such a well-behaved *model* child?⟩

synonyms archetypal, classic, exemplary, paradigmatic, quintessential

related words ideal, nonpareil, special, unique; absolute, flawless, impeccable, perfect; bang-up, banner, capital, dandy, fine, first-class, first-rate, grand, great, groovy, jim-dandy, par excellence, prime, superb, superior, superlative, terrific, tip-top, top, top-notch, unsurpassed, wonderful; exceptional, fancy, high-grade

near antonyms bad, poor, substandard, unsatisfactory; atrocious, execrable, wretched; deficient, disappointing, failed, inadequate, inferior, poor; average, normal, ordinary, representative, typical; mediocre, second-class, second-rate

model *n* **1** an exact representation of something in greatly reduced size ⟨the dollhouse was a tiny, perfect *model* of the family's actual house⟩

synonyms miniature

related words copy, duplicate, duplication, imitation, replica, replication, reproduction; dwarf, midget, mini, pygmy

near antonyms archetype, original, prototype; blowup, enlargement

2 a person who poses with or wears merchandise (as clothes) often for pictorial advertising ⟨the most famous *models* can earn thousands of dollars an hour⟩

synonyms manikin, mannequin

related words figure, form; doll, dummy

3 someone of such unequaled perfection as to deserve imitation ⟨she's the very *model* of the dedicated teacher⟩ — see IDEAL 1

moderate *adj* **1** avoiding extremes in behavior or expression ⟨he was only a *moderate* drinker, stopping after a couple of glasses of wine⟩

synonyms temperate

related words controlled, curbed, disciplined, restrained, self-controlled; calculated, deliberate, measured; rational, reasonable; average, mediocre, medium, modest, ordinary, run-of-the-mill, so-so; normal, ordinary, regular, routine, typical, usual

near antonyms excessive, extreme, inordinate, radical; irrational, unreasonable; extremist, fanatic (*or* fanatical), rabid, radical

antonyms immoderate, intemperate

2 avoiding major social change or extreme political ideas ⟨the principal's *moderate* position on cell phones is that students can use them at school but only for emergencies⟩

synonyms middle-of-the-road

related words conventional, orthodox, traditional, rational, reasonable; neutral

near antonyms excessive; conservative, reactionary, rightist; leftist, liberal, progressive; fanatic (*or* fanatical), revolutionary, revolutionist, subversive, violent; agitating, fomenting, incendiary, inciting, instigating, provocative, provoking; rabble-rousing; dissenting

antonyms extremist, radical

3 being about midway between extremes of amount or size ⟨a *moderate* snowfall was forecast for the region⟩ — see MIDDLE 2

4 marked by temperatures that are neither too high nor too low ⟨a city that is celebrated for its *moderate* climate⟩ — see CLEMENT

moderate *vb* to grow less in scope or intensity especially gradually ⟨the wind began to *moderate* as the night wore on⟩ — see DECREASE 2

moderately *adv* to some degree or extent ⟨it was raining *moderately* hard outside⟩ — see FAIRLY

moderateness *n* an avoidance of extremes in one's actions, beliefs, or habits ⟨the *moderateness* of their enthusiasm for my proposed outing suggested that they would rather do something else⟩ — see TEMPERANCE

moderation *n* an avoidance of extremes in one's actions, beliefs, or habits ⟨does everything in *moderation*⟩ — see TEMPERANCE

moderator *n* a person in charge of a meeting ⟨the *moderator* should make sure that everyone gets a chance to speak⟩ — see CHAIR 1

modern *adj* being or involving the latest methods, concepts, information, or styles ⟨this hairstyle is absolutely the most *modern* fashion out there⟩

synonyms contemporary, current, hot, mod, modernistic, new, newfangled, new-fashioned, present-day, red-hot, space-age, ultramodern, up-to-date

related words fashionable, in, modish, stylish; last, latest; modernized, updated; futuristic, nontraditional

near antonyms anachronistic; aged, age-old, ancient, antediluvian, hoary, old, venerable; bygone, former, late, olden, past; antique, historic, historical; obsolete, outmoded, outworn; old-world; discarded, disused, moth-eaten; forgotten, remote; ageless, dateless, timeless

antonyms antiquated, archaic, dated, fusty, musty, noncontemporary, oldfangled, old-fashioned, old-time, out-of-date, passé

modern *n* a person with very modern ideas ⟨the leaders of the American suffragists were originally regarded by many people as uppity *moderns* who should have stayed in their place⟩

synonyms ultramodernist

related words leftist, liberal, progressive; extremist, radical; bohemian

near antonyms conservative, rightist, Tory; old hand, old-timer, veteran

antonyms antediluvian, dodo, fogy (*also* fogey), fossil, fuddy-duddy, reactionary, stick-in-the-mud

modernistic *adj* being or involving the latest methods, concepts, information, or styles ⟨bought a *modernistic* lamp for the side table⟩ — see MODERN

modest *adj* **1** being about midway between extremes of amount or size ⟨was awarded a *modest* pension when he retired⟩ — see MIDDLE 2

2 free from any trace of the coarse or indecent ⟨tended to wear more *modest* swimsuits⟩ — see CHASTE

3 not comfortable around people ⟨a *modest* winner who said a quick thank-you and promptly left the stage⟩ — see SHY 2

4 not having or showing any feelings of superiority, self-assertiveness, or showiness ⟨*modest* about her success in the fashion industry⟩ — see HUMBLE 1

modestly *adv* **1** in a manner showing no signs of pride or self-assertion ⟨spoke *modestly* about his accomplishments⟩ — see LOWLY

2 with purity of thought and deed ⟨dressed *modestly* to go to church⟩ — see PURELY

modesty *n* **1** the absence of any feelings of being better than others ⟨his natural *modesty* makes him reluctant to run for class officer⟩ — see HUMILITY

2 the quality or state of being morally pure ⟨very becoming *modesty* in a teenager for this day and age⟩ — see CHASTITY

modicum *n* the smallest amount or part imaginable ⟨only a *modicum* of skill is necessary to put the kit together⟩ — see JOT

modifiable *adj* capable of being readily changed ⟨architects designed the arena to be easily *modifiable* for staging a variety of events⟩ — see FLEXIBLE 1

modification *n* the act, process, or result of making different ⟨the rough draft needed only a few *modifications*⟩ — see CHANGE

modify *vb* **1** to limit the meaning of (as a noun) ⟨adjectives are words that *modify* nouns, while adverbs can *modify* adjectives and verbs⟩ — see QUALIFY 1

2 to make different in some way ⟨he *modified* the appliance so that it would run more quietly⟩ — see CHANGE 1

modish *adj* **1** being in the latest or current fashion ⟨the *modish* gowns that actresses wear to award shows⟩ — see STYLISH

2 enjoying widespread favor or approval ⟨a *modish* chef who is currently the darling of the restaurant reviewers⟩ — see POPULAR 1

modishness *n* the state of enjoying widespread approval ⟨the *modishness* of that hairstyle is now so intense that the really hip people have moved on to something else⟩ — see POPULARITY

mogul *n* a person of rank, power, or influence in a particular field ⟨movie *moguls* promising to turn young actresses into stars⟩ — see MAGNATE

moiety *n* one of two equal or nearly equal parts ⟨the lot was sold in two separate *moieties*⟩ — see HALF 1

moil *vb* to devote serious and sustained effort ⟨miners *moiling* all day in the sunless recesses of the earth⟩ — see LABOR

moist *adj* slightly or moderately wet ⟨luckily, my new suede shoes are only a bit *moist* after I accidentally wore them in the rain⟩

synonyms damp, dank

related words dewy; clammy; humid, muggy, sticky; sultry, summery, sweltering, torrid, tropical; dripping, drenched, saturated, soaked, soaking, sodden, soggy, sopping, soppy, steeped, water-logged

near antonyms arid, dry, waterless; baked, burned, burnt, dehydrated, desert, droughty, dusty, parched, scorched, seared, sere

moisten *vb* to make or become slightly or moderately wet ⟨*moisten* the cloth before cleaning with it⟩

synonyms dampen

related words drench, saturate, soak, steep; humidify; dip, immerge, immerse

near antonyms dehumidify, dehydrate, parch, scorch, sear

antonyms dry

moisture *n* the amount of water suspended in the air in tiny droplets ⟨dew is really just *moisture* from the air

that condenses and collects when the temperature drops at night⟩

synonyms dampness, humidity

related words mugginess, stickiness, stuffiness; sultriness; clamminess, dankness, sogginess, wetness

near antonyms aridity, dehydration, dryness

mojo *n* **1** something worn or kept to bring good luck or keep away evil ⟨a *mojo* is a type of voodoo charm⟩ — see CHARM 1

2 the power to control natural forces through supernatural means ⟨joked that he had worked his *mojo* to assure a sunny day for the picnic⟩ — see MAGIC 1

molder *vb* to go through decomposition ⟨leaves *moldering* in the compost pile⟩ — see DECAY 1

molecule *n* a very small piece ⟨not a *molecule* of sense in that girl⟩ — see BIT 1

mollify *vb* **1** to lessen the anger or agitation of ⟨an apology would probably *mollify* your friend⟩ — see PACIFY

2 to make more bearable or less severe ⟨a friendly gesture that did a lot to *mollify* their suspicions about the new neighbor⟩ — see HELP 2

mollifying *adj* tending to lessen or avoid conflict or hostility ⟨using *mollifying* flattery to overcome a bad first impression⟩ — see PACIFIC 1

mollycoddle *n* a person without strength of character ⟨accused him of being a *mollycoddle* when he wouldn't stand up to his wife⟩ — see WEAKLING 2

mollycoddle *vb* to treat with great or excessive care ⟨refused to *mollycoddle* her malingering son and sent him off to school⟩ — see BABY

molt *vb* to cast (a natural bodily covering or appendage) aside ⟨a crab *molts* its shell as it grows larger⟩ — see SHED 1

mom *n* a female human parent ⟨be sure to tell your *mom* and dad that you'll be home late for supper⟩ — see MOTHER

moment *n* **1** a particular point at which an event takes place ⟨at that *moment* he suddenly turned around and headed toward me⟩ — see OCCASION 1

2 the quality or state of being important ⟨an event of great *moment*⟩ — see IMPORTANCE

3 a very small space of time ⟨I'll be there in just a *moment*⟩ — see INSTANT

4 the time currently existing or in progress ⟨I'm not doing anything at the *moment*⟩ — see PRESENT 1

momentarily *adv* at or within a short time ⟨we'll be finished *momentarily*⟩ — see SHORTLY 2

momentary *adj* lasting only for a short time ⟨the pain of the flu shot was only *momentary*⟩

synonyms ephemeral, evanescent, flash, fleeting, fugitive, impermanent, passing, short-lived, temporary, transient, transitory

related words brief, short; acting, interim

near antonyms lifelong

antonyms enduring, eternal, everlasting, lasting, long-lived, permanent, perpetual

momentous *adj* having great meaning or lasting effect ⟨a *momentous* occasion that will go down in the history books⟩ — see IMPORTANT 1

momentum *n* something that arouses action or activity ⟨the former president's endorsement was all the *momentum* the campaign needed⟩ — see IMPULSE

momma *n* a female human parent ⟨she always does what her *momma* tells her to do⟩ — see MOTHER

monarch *n* one who rules over a people with a sole, supreme, and usually hereditary authority ⟨the ruling *monarch* of Britain at that time was Queen Elizabeth I⟩

synonyms autocrat, ruler, sovereign
related words czar (*also* tsar *or* tzar), emperor, empress, kaiser, king, lord, mogul, prince, queen, satrap, sultan; authoritarian, despot, dictator, overlord, potentate, tyrant; royalty

monarchal *or* **monarchial** *adj* fit for or worthy of a royal ruler 〈a singing superstar with a *monarchal* haughtiness that drives her assistants crazy〉 — see MONARCHICAL

monarchical *also* **monarchic** *adj* fit for or worthy of a royal ruler 〈guests who stay in the hotel's most expensive suite live in *monarchical* splendor〉
synonyms kingly, monarchal (*or* monarchial), princely, queenly, regal, royal
related words aristocratic, baronial, imperial, lordly, noble, patrician

monastery *n* a residence for men under religious vows 〈Gregory Mendel worked out his concepts of genetics by doing breeding experiments using pea plants in the *monastery's* garden〉
synonyms abbey, cloister, friary, priory
related words house; convent, nunnery; lamasery

monetary *adj* of or relating to money, banking, or investments 〈critical of this administration's *monetary* policies〉 — see FINANCIAL

money *n* something (as pieces of stamped metal or printed paper) customarily and legally used as a medium of exchange, a measure of value, or a means of payment 〈are you sure you have enough *money* to buy all that?〉
synonyms bread [*slang*], cash, chips, currency, dough, gold, jack [*slang*], legal tender, lucre, pelf, tender, wampum [*slang*]
related words change, coinage, specie; paper money, scrip; banknote, cashier's check, check, draft, money order, note; bill, buck, dollar, greenback; bankroll, capital, finances, funds; mite, pittance; bundle, fortune, king's ransom, mint, wad; abundance, means, opulence, riches, treasure, wealth; resources, wherewithal; pin money, pocket money, spending money

moneyed *or* **monied** *adj* having goods, property, or money in abundance 〈the *moneyed* tourist traveling the world〉 — see RICH 1

mongrel *adj* being offspring produced by parents of different races, breeds, species, or genera 〈a *mongrel* dog〉 — see MIXED 1

mongrel *n* an offspring of parents with different genes especially when of different races, breeds, species, or genera 〈*mongrels* often suffer fewer health problems than purebreds〉 — see HYBRID

monitor *vb* to pay continued close attention to (something) for a particular purpose 〈police regularly *monitor* that road to record traffic density and catch speeders〉
synonyms cover, watch
related words eye; behold, look, regard, see; gape, gawk, gaze, glare, goggle, peer, stare; glance, glimpse, peek, peep
phrases keep an eye on

monkey *n* an appealingly mischievous person 〈come back here, you little *monkey!*〉 — see SCAMP 1

monkey (around) *vb* **1** to engage in attention-getting playful or boisterous behavior 〈stop *monkeying around* in the house or you'll break something〉 — see CUT UP
2 to spend time in aimless activity 〈would rather just *monkey around* instead of doing work〉 — see FIDDLE (AROUND)

monkey (with) *vb* to handle thoughtlessly, ignorantly, or mischievously 〈don't *monkey with* that broken lawnmower〉 — see TAMPER

monkeying *n* wildly playful or mischievous behavior 〈all that *monkeying* was sure to end in someone or something getting hurt〉 — see HORSEPLAY

monkeyshines *n pl* wildly playful or mischievous behavior 〈hockey players who are known for their *monkeyshines* on and off the ice〉 — see HORSEPLAY

monochromatic *adj* having or consisting of a single color 〈although marble and bronze sculptures are *monochromatic*, they can be amazingly lifelike〉
synonyms solid
related words colored, colorful, pigmented; chromatic
near antonyms dappled (*also* dapple), marbled, shaded; mottled, piebald, pied, pinto; barred, brindled (*or* brindle); checkered, patterned, plaid, striped
antonyms motley, multicolored, polychromatic, varicolored, variegated

monopolize *vb* to have complete control over 〈it is illegal in the United States to *monopolize* an entire industry or product〉 〈you shouldn't *monopolize* that toy while your friends are waiting to play with it〉
synonyms sew up
related words corner, hog; absorb, consume, engross; have, hold, own, possess; control, direct, govern, manage, reign (over), rule

monotonous *adj* causing weariness, restlessness, or lack of interest 〈the lecturer's *monotonous* delivery threatened to put us to sleep〉 — see BORING

monotonousness *n* a tedious lack of variety 〈detested the *monotonousness* of the task but knew that it had to be done〉 — see MONOTONY

monotony *n* a tedious lack of variety 〈the *monotony* of the cafeteria's selections was almost as bad as the quality〉
synonyms monotonousness, sameness
related words uniformity; boredom, dullness (*also* dulness), ennui, restlessness, tediousness, tedium, tiresomeness, weariness, wearisomeness
near antonyms diversity, multiplicity, variety; variability, variation; absorption, engagement, engrossment, enthrallment, fascination, grip, interest, intrigue; animation, excitement, invigoration, stimulation

monster *adj* unusually large 〈a *monster* truck competition〉 — see HUGE

monster *n* **1** a strange or horrible and often frightening creature 〈both children insisted that their parents check under the bed for *monsters* every night〉
synonyms monstrosity, ogre
related words ogre; bête noire, bogey (*also* bogy *or* bogie), bugaboo, bugbear; banshee, bogeyman, demon (*or* daemon), devil, fiend, fright, imp, incubus; horror, terror; abomination, anathema; abnormality, freak; mutant, mutation
2 a person, thing, or event that is not normal 〈the gardener destroyed all of the *monsters* that mutated from his tomato plants〉 — see FREAK 1
3 a mean, evil, or unprincipled person 〈the guards at the concentration camps were *monsters* who enjoyed seeing their victims suffer〉 — see VILLAIN 1
4 something that is unusually large and powerful 〈a *monster* of a sandwich that could easily feed two hearty eaters〉 — see GIANT

monstrosity *n* **1** a person, thing, or event that is not normal 〈any *monstrosities* born to the farm animals were sent to the agricultural college for study〉 — see FREAK 1

2 a strange or horrible and often frightening creature ⟨filled the haunted house with all sorts of spooks and mechanical *monstrosities*⟩ — see MONSTER 1
3 something unpleasant to look at ⟨we were glad when the city tore down that *monstrosity* that used to stand across from the park⟩ — see EYESORE
4 the quality of inspiring intense dread or dismay ⟨the *monstrosity* of the famine can scarcely be conveyed to those who have not witnessed it in person⟩ — see HORROR 1
5 the state or quality of being utterly evil ⟨the *monstrosity* of the terrorists' actions shocked the entire civilized world⟩ — see ENORMITY 1
monstrous *adj* **1** badly or imperfectly formed ⟨a *monstrous* melon that was clearly not fit to eat⟩ — see MALFORMED
2 extremely disturbing or repellent ⟨the *monstrous* measures taken by the dictator against anyone who opposed his regime⟩ — see HORRIBLE 1
3 unusually large ⟨a *monstrous* tomato as big as a basketball⟩ — see HUGE
monstrously *adv* **1** beyond a normal or acceptable limit ⟨our team wasn't merely bad—we were *monstrously* inept⟩ — see TOO 1
2 to a large extent or degree ⟨a *monstrously* expensive movie⟩ — see GREATLY 2
monthlies *n pl* an occurrence of menstruating ⟨she couldn't go swimming because of her *monthlies*⟩ — see PERIOD 1
monument *n* **1** a shaped stone laid over or erected near a grave and usually bearing an inscription to identify and preserve the memory of the deceased ⟨the dates of her birth and death were inscribed on the *monument*⟩ — see TOMBSTONE
2 something that serves to keep alive the memory of a person or event ⟨a moving *monument* to the great war and a tribute to the untold millions who died in it⟩ — see MEMORIAL
monumental *adj* **1** large and impressive in size, grandeur, extent, or conception ⟨a *monumental* misunderstanding that had far-reaching consequences⟩ — see GRAND 1
2 unusually large ⟨serves a *monumental* sundae that usually requires three people to finish⟩ — see HUGE
mooch *vb* to move about from place to place aimlessly ⟨kids on vacation *mooching* about the house looking for something to do⟩ — see WANDER
mood *n* **1** a state of mind dominated by a particular emotion ⟨losing my favorite sweater left me in a bad *mood* for the rest of the day⟩
synonyms cheer, frame, humor, mode, spirit, temper
related words attitude, outlook, perspective, standpoint, viewpoint; emotion, feeling, heart, passion, sentiment; strain; belief, conviction, mind, opinion; expression, tone, vein; character, disposition, individuality, personality, temperament; responsiveness, sensibility, sensitiveness, sensitivity
2 a special quality or impression associated with something ⟨there's a haunting *mood* of melancholy about the ruined old castle⟩ — see AURA
moody *adj* frequently influenced by moods and especially bad moods ⟨teenagers are often both *moody* and changeable⟩
synonyms temperamental
related words capricious, changeable, changeful, fickle, fluctuating, fluid, inconstant, mercurial, mutable, uncertain, unsettled, unstable, unsteady, variable, volatile, whimsical

near antonyms equable, even; changeless, constant, settled, stable, steady, unchanging
moonshine *n* **1** illegally produced liquor ⟨during Prohibition, *moonshine* and "bathtub gin" were made secretly⟩
synonyms bootleg
related words alcohol, booze, drink, grog, spirits
2 a fermented or distilled beverage that can make a person drunk ⟨serving all sorts of *moonshine* at the bar⟩ — see ALCOHOL
3 unintelligible or meaningless talk ⟨a couple of ne'er-do-wells talking nothing but *moonshine*⟩ — see GIBBERISH
moonstruck *adj* having or showing a very abnormal or sick state of mind ⟨police asked psychiatrists to put together a portrait of the *moonstruck* marksman who was responsible for the shootings⟩ — see INSANE 1
moor *vb* to put securely in place or in a desired position ⟨*moored* the boat to the dock⟩ — see FASTEN 2
moot *adj* open to question or dispute ⟨it's a *moot* question what might have happened if the American colonies had not broken away from Great Britain⟩ — see DEBATABLE 1
moot *vb* **1** to present or bring forward for discussion ⟨conservatives had shouted down the proposal when it was first *mooted*⟩ — see INTRODUCE 2
2 to talk about (an issue) usually from various points of view and for the purpose of arriving at a decision or opinion ⟨the issue of whether a person's nature or upbringing is more important continues to be *mooted* by experts and laymen alike⟩ — see DISCUSS
mope *vb* **1** to move about from place to place aimlessly ⟨*moping* about the school grounds after classes had ended⟩ — see WANDER
2 to silently go about in a bad mood ⟨she's *moping* because her parents won't let her go to the party⟩ — see SULK
mopes *n pl* a state or spell of low spirits ⟨he's got the *mopes* because his girlfriend is mad at him⟩ — see SADNESS
moral *adj* **1** conforming to a high standard of morality or virtue ⟨the kind of *moral* behavior that is expected of everyone in the parish's youth organization⟩ — see GOOD 2
2 guided by or in accordance with one's sense of right and wrong ⟨a *moral* decision to refrain from sexual relations until after marriage⟩ — see CONSCIENTIOUS 1
moralist *n* a person who is greatly concerned with seemly behavior and morality especially regarding sexual matters ⟨a smattering of *moralists* around the country tried to get the songs banned from the radio⟩ — see PRUDE
morality *n* **1** conduct that conforms to an accepted standard of right and wrong ⟨the candidate claimed to be the best choice because of his unswerving *morality*⟩
synonyms character, decency, goodness, honesty, integrity, probity, rectitude, righteousness, uprightness, virtue, virtuousness
related words high-mindedness, honor, incorruptibility; appropriateness, correctness, decorousness, decorum, etiquette, fitness, propriety, seemliness; ethics, morals
near antonyms impropriety, indecency, indiscretion; debauchery, degeneracy, degradation, depravity, perversion; crookedness, dishonesty, underhandedness, unscrupulousness; lowness, meanness, viciousness, vileness; corruption, sin

antonyms badness, evil, immorality, wickedness

2 the code of good conduct for an individual or group ⟨the *morality* that members of the Mafia are expected to adhere to—or suffer the consequences⟩ — see ETHICS

morally *adv* with purity of thought and deed ⟨a politician who is in the habit of acting legally without behaving *morally*⟩ — see PURELY

morals *n pl* the code of good conduct for an individual or group ⟨at issue were the doctor's professional ethics, not her private *morals*⟩ — see ETHICS

morass *n* spongy land saturated or partially covered with water ⟨the distracted driver had driven his car off the road and into a *morass*⟩ — see SWAMP

morbid *adj* causing or marked by an atmosphere lacking in cheer ⟨a pessimist who is given to *morbid* introspection and thoughts of death⟩ — see GLOOMY 1

mordant *adj* marked by the use of wit that is intended to cause hurt feelings ⟨a *mordant* review of the movie that compared it to having one's teeth pulled for two hours⟩ — see SARCASTIC

more *adj* resulting in an increase in amount or number ⟨bought *more* apples⟩ — see ADDITIONAL

more *adv* **1** in addition to what has been said ⟨the sci-fi movie was totally unbelievable and, what's *more*, it was boring⟩

synonyms additionally, again, also, besides, further, furthermore, likewise, moreover, then, too, withal, yet

phrases as well, in addition to, to boot

2 to a greater or higher extent ⟨the boxers for this bout are *more* evenly matched than the last two were⟩

synonyms better

more or less *adv* **1** very close to but not completely ⟨the lot is 16 acres *more or less*⟩ — see ALMOST

2 to some degree or extent ⟨most couples in the survey said that they were *more or less* happy in their marriage⟩ — see FAIRLY

moreover *adv* in addition to what has been said ⟨it's against the rules and, *moreover*, it's dangerous⟩ — see MORE 1

mores *n pl* personal conduct or behavior as evaluated by an accepted standard of appropriateness for a social or professional setting ⟨the *mores* of academic life as opposed to those of the business world⟩ — see MANNER 1

moribund *adj* nearly dead ⟨with its run-down look and empty aisles, the business appeared *moribund*⟩

synonyms dying

related words expiring, fading, passing away, sinking; decadent, declining, deteriorating; dead, deceased, defunct, departed, gone, passed away; terminal

near antonyms alive, animate, living; being, breathing, existing, subsisting, surviving; flourishing, prospering, thriving

morn *n* **1** the first appearance of light in the morning or the time of its appearance ⟨my herald of the *morn* is my cat, sticking his paw in my face to wake me up⟩ — see DAWN 1

2 the time from sunrise until noon ⟨we've been working on this project from *morn* till night to get it done on time⟩ — see MORNING 1

morning *n* **1** the time from sunrise until noon ⟨I hate getting up in the *morning* to go to school⟩

synonyms forenoon, morn

related words aurora, dawn, dawning, daybreak, daylight; cockcrow, sunrise, sunup; day, daytime, light

near antonyms dark, darkness, night, nighttime, twilight; dusk, evening, nightfall, sundown, sunset; afternoon

2 the first appearance of light in the morning or the time of its appearance ⟨*morning* has broken⟩ — see DAWN 1

3 the point at which something begins ⟨the period when people in ancient Mesopotamia began living in cities is usually regarded as the *morning* of civilization⟩ — see BEGINNING

moron *n* a stupid person ⟨some *moron* forgot to lock the doors before going home⟩ — see IDIOT

morose *adj* causing or marked by an atmosphere lacking in cheer ⟨those *morose* job seekers who have grown accustomed to rejection⟩ — see GLOOMY 1

morsel *n* **1** a small piece or quantity of food ⟨I suppose you can have dessert, since you only left a couple *morsels* on your plate⟩

synonyms bite, mouthful, nibble, taste, tidbit (*also* titbit)

related words snack; appetizer, hors d'oeuvre; bit, chew, crumb, dab, driblet, hint, lick, nubbin, nugget, pinch, scrap, shred, smidgen (*also* smidgeon *or* smidgin), speck, spot, sprinkling, suspicion, touch, trace; dash, drop; gulp, swallow, swig

2 a very small piece ⟨searching for any *morsel* of useful information⟩ — see BIT 1

mortal *adj* **1** likely to cause or capable of causing death ⟨a *mortal* wound⟩ — see DEADLY

2 of, relating to, or suggestive of death ⟨a wounded soldier writhing in *mortal* agony⟩ — see DEATHLY 1

3 relating to or characteristic of human beings ⟨just an ordinary guy with all the usual *mortal* limitations⟩ — see HUMAN

mortal *n* a member of the human race ⟨just an ordinary *mortal* living an ordinary life⟩ — see HUMAN

mortally *adv* to a great degree ⟨I'm *mortally* certain that I've seen that guy before⟩ — see VERY 1

mortician *n* a person who manages funerals and prepares the dead for burial or cremation ⟨the *mortician* will take care of all of the arrangements for the funeral⟩ — see FUNERAL DIRECTOR

mortification *n* the emotional state of being made self-consciously uncomfortable ⟨the *mortification* of being dumped the night before the prom⟩ — see EMBARRASSMENT 1

mortify *vb* to throw into a state of self-conscious distress ⟨was *mortified* by the teenagers' atrocious manners⟩ — see EMBARRASS 1

¹most *adv* to a great degree ⟨a *most* careful driver⟩ — see VERY 1

²most *adv* very close to but not completely ⟨the cost of *most* everything is higher nowadays⟩ — see ALMOST

most *adj* of the greatest or highest degree or quantity ⟨the player with the *most* ability on the tennis team⟩ — see ULTIMATE 1

most *n* the greatest amount, number, or part ⟨this room will accommodate 50 people at the *most*⟩

synonyms maximum, outside

related words best, utmost

antonyms least, minimum

mostly *adv* for the most part ⟨the weather this month has been *mostly* mild⟩ — see CHIEFLY

mote *n* a very small piece ⟨there's not a *mote* of dirt in that woman's house⟩ — see BIT 1

moth–eaten *adj* **1** having passed its time of use or usefulness ⟨*moth-eaten* scientific theories no one's believed in ages⟩ — see OBSOLETE

2 showing signs of advanced wear and tear and neglect ⟨a man who's been wearing the same *moth-eaten* clothes for decades⟩ — see SHABBY 1

3 used or heard so often as to be dull ⟨an uncle who tells the same *moth-eaten* stories every Thanksgiving⟩ — see STALE

mother *n* a female human parent ⟨he dreaded telling his *mother* that her favorite figurine had gotten broken⟩
synonyms ma, mama, mammy, mom, momma, mum [*chiefly British*]
related words matriarch, matron

mother *vb* to attend to the needs and comforts of ⟨*mothered* the patients with chicken soup⟩ — see NURSE 1

motherland *n* the land of one's birth, residence, or citizenship ⟨all his life he longed to return to his *motherland*⟩ — see COUNTRY 1

motherliness *n* motherly character or qualities ⟨he cherished his foster parent for her *motherliness*⟩ — see MATERNITY

motherly *adj* of, relating to, or characteristic of a mother ⟨she showed a sweet *motherly* tenderness toward the tiny kitten she was taking care of⟩
synonyms maternal
related words parental; female, feminine, womanish, womanlike, womanly; matriarchal, matronly; caring, giving, nurturing

mother tongue *n* the stock of words, pronunciation, and grammar used by a people as their basic means of communication ⟨although the anthropologist could speak the local language fairly well, she was always glad to find someone who spoke her *mother tongue*⟩ — see LANGUAGE 1

motif *n* **1** a major object of interest or concern (as in a discussion or artistic composition) ⟨the *motif* of mute figures standing in lonely isolation is a recurrent one in the artist's works⟩ — see MATTER 1
2 a unit of decoration that is repeated all over something (as a fabric) ⟨the fabric for the upholstery features a scallop shell *motif*⟩ — see PATTERN 1

motion *n* the act or an instance of changing position ⟨we were instructed not to make any sudden *motions* or we might scare away the deer⟩ — see MOVEMENT 1

motion *vb* to direct or notify by a movement or gesture ⟨the referee *motioned* the team captains to confer with him on the sideline⟩
synonyms beckon, flag, gesture, signal, wave
related words gesticulate, pantomime, sign; signalize; acquaint, advise, inform, relate, tell; flourish, shrug

motionlessly *adv* without motion ⟨could sit *motionlessly* for hours⟩ — see STILL 1

motion picture *n* **1** a story told by means of a series of continuously projected pictures and a sound track ⟨went to see a *motion picture* festival downtown⟩ — see MOVIE 1
2 motion pictures *pl* the art or business of making a movie ⟨I want to be in *motion pictures* when I grow up⟩ — see MOVIE 2

motivation *n* something that arouses action or activity ⟨fear of failing should be plenty of *motivation* to study for the test⟩ — see IMPULSE

motive *n* **1** a major object of interest or concern (as in a discussion or artistic composition) ⟨the principal *motive* of the piece was introduced in the flute section⟩ — see MATTER 1
2 a unit of decoration that is repeated all over something (as a fabric) ⟨decorated with a paisley *motive*⟩ — see PATTERN 1
3 something (as a belief) that serves as the basis for another thing ⟨the detective felt that the first suspect didn't have any *motive* for committing the crime⟩ — see REASON 2

motley *adj* **1** consisting of many things of different sorts ⟨a ship with a *motley* crew of old salts, young adventurers, and shifty characters of all ages⟩ — see MISCELLANEOUS
2 marked by a variety of usually vivid colors ⟨a tropical bird with *motley* plumage⟩ — see COLORFUL

motley *n* **1** a person formerly kept in a royal or noble household to amuse with jests and pranks ⟨the *motleys* with their colorful outfits⟩ — see FOOL 2
2 an unorganized collection or mixture of various things ⟨a *motley* of old junk stored in the attic⟩ — see MISCELLANY 1

motor *n* **1** a device that changes energy into mechanical motion ⟨the device was equipped with a small electrical *motor* to make the gears spin⟩ — see ENGINE
2 a self-propelled passenger vehicle on wheels ⟨went shopping for a new automobile at Valley *Motors*⟩ — see CAR

motor *vb* to travel by a motorized vehicle ⟨*motoring* along the highway at the speed limit⟩ — see DRIVE 2

motorboat *n* a boat equipped with a motor ⟨*motorboats* are banned on the lake because they are a hazard to swimmers⟩
synonyms powerboat, speedboat
related words cabin cruiser, cruiser, runabout

motorcade *n* a group of vehicles traveling together or under one management ⟨the next part of the parade was a *motorcade* of fire engines⟩ — see FLEET

motorcar *n* a self-propelled passenger vehicle on wheels ⟨a convention for those who love antique *motorcars*⟩ — see CAR

motor home *n* a motor vehicle that is specially equipped for living while traveling ⟨they lived out of their *motor home* until they found a suitable house⟩ — see CAMPER

motorist *n* a person who travels by automobile ⟨environmental organizations suggest that *motorists* get together and carpool to avoid using several cars and adding to pollution⟩
synonyms automobilist, driver
related words operator; chauffeur; carpooler

motor vehicle *n* a self-propelled passenger vehicle on wheels ⟨got a license to drive a *motor vehicle* the minute she turned 16⟩ — see CAR

mottle *n* a small area that is different (as in color) from the main part ⟨canvases covered with streaks and *mottles*⟩ — see SPOT 1

mottle *vb* to mark with small spots especially unevenly ⟨old papers that were *mottled* by mold⟩ — see SPOT

mottled *adj* **1** having blotches of two or more colors ⟨a *mottled* complexion⟩ — see PIED
2 marked with spots ⟨*mottled* leather upholstery that isn't supposed to look perfect⟩ — see SPOTTED 1

mound *n* **1** a pile or ridge of granular matter (as sand or snow) ⟨*mounds* of snow after the plow had passed⟩ — see ²BANK
2 a quantity of things thrown or stacked on one another ⟨an ever-growing *mound* of dirty laundry on the floor⟩ — see ¹PILE 1
3 an area of high ground ⟨a pitcher's *mound*⟩ — see HEIGHT 4

mound *vb* **1** to form into a pile or ridge of earth ⟨he likes to sit on the beach and *mound* sand into sand castles⟩
synonyms bank, hill
related words heap, pile, pyramid, stack; embank; bunch, bundle, clump, lump, mass, wad; accumulate, amass, assemble, collect, gather, group

2 to lay or throw on top of one another ⟨*mounding* slices of cheese on top of her sandwich meat⟩ — see PILE

¹**mount** *n* an elevation of land higher than a hill ⟨*Mount* Everest⟩ — see MOUNTAIN 1

²**mount** *n* something that holds up or serves as a foundation for something else ⟨hammered together a *mount* for the cameras⟩ — see SUPPORT 1

mount *vb* **1** to become greater in extent, volume, amount, or number ⟨medical expenses began to *mount*⟩ — see INCREASE 2

2 to bring before the public in performance or exhibition ⟨the huge amount of money needed to *mount* an opera⟩ — see PRESENT 1

3 to move or extend upward ⟨the cable car continues to *mount* to ever higher terrain until the moment when the entire valley comes into view⟩ — see ASCEND

mountain *n* **1** an elevation of land higher than a hill ⟨my cousin likes to climb *mountains* just because she can⟩
synonyms alp, mount, peak
related words mountain range, seamount; mountaintop, pinnacle, precipice, summit
near antonyms basin, bowl, depression, hollow, vale, valley

2 a considerable amount ⟨sends a *mountain* of mail every year for the holidays⟩ — see LOT 2

3 a quantity of things thrown or stacked on one another ⟨piled a *mountain* of mashed potatoes on his plate⟩ — see ¹PILE 1

mountain lion *n* a large tawny cat of the wild ⟨the problem of *mountain lions* coming into contact with humans in suburban developments⟩ — see COUGAR

mountainous *adj* unusually large ⟨the seemingly *mountainous* obstacles he had to overcome⟩ — see HUGE

mountebank *n* one who makes false claims of identity or expertise ⟨felt that many doctors were frauds and *mountebanks*⟩ — see IMPOSTOR

mounting *n* something that holds up or serves as a foundation for something else ⟨built a new *mounting* for the engine⟩ — see SUPPORT 1

mourn *vb* **1** to feel deep sadness or mental pain ⟨we *mourned* for weeks after our pet's death⟩ — see GRIEVE

2 to feel or express sorrow for ⟨an editorial that *mourns* the loss of the town's last movie theater⟩ — see LAMENT 1

mournful *adj* **1** expressing or suggesting mourning ⟨she had such a *mournful* expression that someone teasingly asked if her dog had died⟩
synonyms anguished, bemoaning, bewailing, deploring, doleful, dolorous, funeral, grieving, heartbroken, lamentable, lugubrious, plaintive, regretful, rueful, sorrowful, sorry, wailing, weeping, woeful
related words elegiac, melancholy; dejected, depressed, despondent, disconsolate, dispirited, downcast, downhearted, heartsick, inconsolable; careworn, sad, unhappy, woebegone; bawling, crying, groaning, howling, keening, moaning, yammering; bleeding, suffering; black, bleak, cheerless, comfortless, dark, darkening, desolate, dismal, dreary, funereal, gloomy, glum, gray (*also* grey), joyless, low, miserable, moody, morbid, morose, pathetic, pessimistic, piteous, saturnine, somber (*or* sombre), sullen, wretched
near antonyms delighted, exulting, glorying, happy, joyful, rejoicing, triumphant; bright, cheerful, cheering, cheery; laughing, smiling; blithe, blithesome, buoyant, gay, jocund, jolly, joyous, lighthearted, merry, mirthful; encouraging, hopeful, optimistic

2 feeling unhappiness ⟨the *mournful* survivors of the disaster⟩ — see SAD 1

mournfully *adv* with feelings of bitterness or grief ⟨cried out *mournfully* for the son who would never return from the war⟩ — see HARD 2

mouse *vb* to move about in a sly or secret manner ⟨a cat *mousing* along in the shadows of the garden⟩ — see SNEAK 1

mousy *or* **mousey** *adj* easily frightened ⟨a *mousy* little girl who hid behind her mother the entire time we were there⟩ — see SHY 1

mouth *n* **1** the opening through which food passes into the body of an animal ⟨the baby chicks opened their *mouths* very wide and chirped piteously when their mother came back with worms⟩
synonyms kisser [*slang*], mug
related words countenance, face, puss [*slang*], visage; muzzle; jaws, mandible, maxilla; gullet, maw

2 a twisting of the facial features in disgust or disapproval ⟨the boy usually makes a *mouth* when he gets a shot⟩ — see GRIMACE

mouth *vb* to speak softly and unclearly ⟨*mouthed* the words under his breath⟩ — see MUMBLE

mouth (off) *vb* to talk as if giving an important and formal speech ⟨some crank *mouthing off* in the center of town to anyone who would listen⟩ — see ORATE 1

mouthful *n* a small piece or quantity of food ⟨took a small *mouthful* of the soup to see if she liked it⟩ — see MORSEL 1

mouthpiece *n* a person who speaks for another or for a group ⟨a statement read by the official *mouthpiece* of the company⟩ — see SPOKESPERSON

movable *or* **moveable** *adj* capable of being moved especially with ease ⟨any furniture that is not *movable* will be covered with protective cloths by the painters⟩
synonyms mobile, portable
related words adjustable, flexible, modular; removable, transferable, transportable; motile, moving; unsteady, unstable; manageable
near antonyms motionless, moveless, static, stationary, still, stuck, unmoving, wedged; fast, fixed, rooted, steadfast
antonyms immobile, immovable, irremovable, unmovable

movables *or* **moveables** *n pl* **1** the movable articles in a room ⟨when painting a room, you should first cover or remove all of the *movables*⟩ — see FURNITURE

2 transportable items that one owns ⟨packed our *movables* into the van and headed off to our new home⟩ — see POSSESSION 2

move *n* **1** an action planned or taken to achieve a desired result ⟨retiring early was a smart *move*⟩ — see MEASURE 1

2 the act or an instance of changing position ⟨don't make a *move*⟩ — see MOVEMENT 1

move *vb* **1** to change the place or position of ⟨I need you to *move* all your books off the chair before company gets here⟩
synonyms budge, dislocate, displace, disturb, remove, shift, transfer, transpose
related words bear, carry, convey, drive, haul, transmit, transport; transplant; replace, supersede, supplant; alter, make over, modify, redo, refashion, remake, remodel, revamp, revise, rework, vary
near antonyms fix, freeze, set, stabilize

2 to set or keep in motion ⟨the hands of the wall clock are *moved* by battery⟩

synonyms actuate, drive, impel, propel, work

related words activate, motivate, provoke; abet, ferment, foment, incite, raise, stir (up), whip (up); set off, trigger; excite, galvanize, inflame, inspire, motivate, rouse

near antonyms check, curb, inhibit, restrain

3 to change one's position ⟨don't *move* while I'm trying to draw your portrait⟩

synonyms budge, shift, stir

related words fidget, jiggle, squirm, twitch, wiggle, writhe; rouse

near antonyms remain, stay; stabilize

antonyms freeze

4 to act upon (a person or a person's feelings) so as to cause a response ⟨we were deeply *moved* by the patriotic music⟩ — see ¹AFFECT 1

5 to rouse to strong feeling or action ⟨the speech *moved* the people to reach into their pockets and donate generously⟩ — see PROVOKE 1

6 to cause (someone) to agree with a belief or course of action by using arguments or earnest requests ⟨the report *moved* me to change my mind⟩ — see PERSUADE

7 to cause to function ⟨this one button *moves* the whole machine⟩ — see ACTIVATE

8 to leave a place often for another ⟨the police officer told the loiterers to *move* along⟩ — see GO 2

movement *n* **1** the act or an instance of changing position ⟨a sudden *movement* in the far corner of the room made her turn in that direction⟩

synonyms motion, move, shift, shifting, stir, stirring

related words dislocation, migration, relocation; locomotion, mobility, motility; fiddling, fidgeting, squirming, twitching, wriggling, writhing; flailing, flapping, waving

near antonyms immobility; inertia, inertness, stillness; ending, finish, halt, pause, stop, termination

antonyms motionlessness

2 a series of activities undertaken to achieve a goal ⟨a *movement* for political reform in the city⟩ — see CAMPAIGN

movie *n* **1** a story told by means of a series of continuously projected pictures and a sound track ⟨there was much excitement when it was announced that the popular children's book would be turned into a *movie*⟩

synonyms film, motion picture, moving picture, picture

related words animated cartoon, cartoon, docudrama, documentary, feature

2 movies *pl* the art or business of making a movie ⟨many a small-town girl has gone to Hollywood, dreaming of making it big in the *movies*⟩

synonyms cinema, film, motion pictures, pictures, screen

related words show business

moving *adj* having the power to affect the feelings or sympathies ⟨he gave a truly *moving* graduation speech that had some graduates in tears⟩

synonyms affecting, emotional, impressive, poignant, stirring, touching

related words eloquent, expressive, meaningful, significant; demonstrative, excitable, feeling, passionate, responsive, sensitive; exciting, provoking, rousing, stimulating; dramatic, histrionic, melodramatic, theatrical

near antonyms cold, cool, detached, dispassionate; deadpan

antonyms unemotional, unimpressive

moving picture *n* a story told by means of a series of continuously projected pictures and a sound track ⟨in the 20th century *moving pictures* became an important form of artistic expression⟩ — see MOVIE 1

mow *vb* **1** to shorten the standing leafy plant cover of ⟨you really should *mow* the lawn before it gets much higher⟩

synonyms cut

related words clip, crop, dock, lop, manicure, pare, prune, trim; shave, shear

2 to bring down by cutting ⟨an afternoon spent *mowing* hay⟩ — see FELL 2

mow (down) *vb* to kill on a large scale ⟨machine guns *mowed down* the advancing troops without mercy⟩ — see MASSACRE

much *adv* **1** to a great degree ⟨*much* gratified by the favorable response to her novel⟩ — see VERY 1

2 to a large extent or degree ⟨the new decorations made me *much* happier⟩ — see GREATLY 2

3 very close to but not completely ⟨today the old neighborhood looks *much* as it did years ago⟩ — see ALMOST

much *n* a considerable amount ⟨*much* of what people think they know about words is inaccurate or downright false⟩ — see LOT 2

muck *n* **1** foul matter that mars the purity or cleanliness of something ⟨spattered with *muck* from the pigpen⟩ — see FILTH 1

2 soft wet earth ⟨her shoes were covered with *muck* by the end of the soccer game⟩ — see MUD

mucky *adj* **1** full of or covered with soft wet earth ⟨the ground was very *mucky* after a night of pouring rain⟩ — see MUDDY 1

2 not clean ⟨only too happy to remove those old *mucky* clothes⟩ — see DIRTY 1

mud *n* soft wet earth ⟨we cannot play softball today because the field turned to *mud* after last night's heavy rain⟩

synonyms mire, muck, ooze, slime, slop, sludge, slush

related words gumbo, silt; clay, dirt, gravel, humus, loam, sand, soil

muddle *n* **1** a state in which everything is out of order ⟨the newly built school was all in a *muddle* on opening day⟩ — see CHAOS

2 a state of mental confusion ⟨I was in such a *muddle* after the accident that I didn't know where I was⟩ — see HAZE 2

3 a state of mental uncertainty ⟨the new, supposedly improved forms simply put taxpayers in a bigger *muddle*⟩ — see CONFUSION 1

4 an unorganized collection or mixture of various things ⟨a *muddle* of old magazines piled on the shelves⟩ — see MISCELLANY 1

muddle *vb* **1** to throw into a state of mental uncertainty ⟨a car shopper thoroughly *muddled* by too much well-meaning advice⟩ — see CONFUSE 1

2 to undo the proper order or arrangement of ⟨some mischievous brat had *muddled* the household accounts⟩ — see DISORDER

muddled *adj* lacking in order, neatness, and often cleanliness ⟨a *muddled* arrangement of trophies in the display case⟩ — see MESSY

muddy *adj* **1** full of or covered with soft wet earth ⟨please do not walk in the house with *muddy* boots on, as you will get the carpet dirty⟩

synonyms miry, mucky, oozy, slimy, sludgy, slushy

related words clayey, loamy, silty; bedraggled; dirty, filthy, foul, grimy, grubby, grungy, impure, squalid, unclean, uncleanly

near antonyms clean, cleanly, immaculate, spotless, unsoiled, unsullied

2 having visible particles in liquid suspension ⟨whether *muddy* or not, water taken from lakes and streams should be boiled by campers⟩ — see CLOUDY 1

3 not clean ⟨we were all *muddy* after playing outside⟩ — see DIRTY 1

muddy *vb* **1** to throw into a state of mental uncertainty ⟨my mind had been thoroughly *muddied* by the long hours of exacting work⟩ — see CONFUSE 1

2 to make (something) unclear to the understanding ⟨that argument is irrelevant and will just *muddy* the issue we're trying to resolve⟩ — see CONFUSE 2

3 to make dirty ⟨forgot to take off our shoes and accidentally *muddied* the kitchen floor⟩ — see DIRTY

muff *vb* to make or do (something) in a clumsy or unskillful way ⟨*muffed* the repair job and had to do it again⟩ — see BOTCH

muffle *vb* to deaden the sound of ⟨the walls *muffled* their conversation so that only a low murmur was heard⟩

synonyms mute

related words insulate, soundproof; dampen, mellow, soften, subdue, tone (down); baffle; smother

near antonyms amplify, enhance, heighten, increase, magnify, strengthen

mug *n* **1** a round vessel equipped with a handle and designed for drinking ⟨a coffee *mug*⟩ — see CUP

2 a violent, brutal person who is often a member of an organized gang ⟨just a bunch of *mugs* with no respect for anyone, not even themselves⟩ — see HOODLUM

3 the front part of the head ⟨she joked about not having to see his ugly *mug* anymore⟩ — see FACE 1

4 an opening through which food passes into the body of an animal ⟨keep your *mug* shut and listen up⟩ — see MOUTH 1

mug *vb* **1** to distort one's face ⟨every time their picture was snapped, both children *mugged* by sticking out their tongues or scrunching up their faces⟩

synonyms grimace

related words pout; contort, deform, twist, warp; frown, glare, gloom, glower, lower (*also* lour), scowl; gape, gaze, ogle, stare; growl, snarl, sneer; simper, smirk

phrases make faces

near antonyms beam, grin, smile

2 to take a photograph of ⟨*mugging* captured criminals for the police records⟩ — see PHOTOGRAPH

muggy *adj* containing or characterized by an uncomfortable amount of moisture ⟨the air was so *muggy* we felt we just had to go for a swim⟩ — see HUMID

mulct *n* a sum of money to be paid as a punishment ⟨the loan shark usually imposed a *mulct* of an additional 20% on overdue payments⟩ — see FINE

mulct *vb* to rob by the use of trickery or threats ⟨trying to *mulct* the insurance company for an accident that never happened⟩ — see FLEECE

mulish *adj* sticking to an opinion, purpose, or course of action in spite of reason, arguments, or persuasion ⟨a *mulish* determination to have his own way⟩ — see OBSTINATE

mulishness *n* a steadfast adherence to an opinion, purpose, or course of action ⟨cursed their *mulishness* for failing to own up to what seemed like an obvious mistake to him⟩ — see OBSTINACY

mull (over) *vb* to give serious and careful thought to ⟨*mull over* the idea for a while and then let me know⟩ — see PONDER

multicolored *adj* marked by a variety of usually vivid colors ⟨displays of *multicolored* pottery from her native Mexico⟩ — see COLORFUL

multifarious *adj* being of many and various kinds ⟨the *multifarious* interests and activities in which Benjamin Franklin immersed himself⟩ — see MANIFOLD

multiple *adj* being of a large but indefinite number ⟨the *multiple* achievements of her long career in public education⟩ — see MANY

multiplex *adj* being of a large but indefinite number ⟨would sometimes experience *multiplex* moods in the course of a single day⟩ — see MANY

multiplication *n* the act or process of becoming greater in number ⟨there's been a steady *multiplication* in our attic of old video equipment since the revolution in consumer electronics⟩

synonyms accumulating, accumulation, addition, increase, proliferation

related words doubling, quadrupling, tripling; growth, rise, spread; enlargement, escalation, expansion; amplification, distention, inflation; accretion, accrual, augmentation; extension, lengthening

near antonyms compressing, compression, condensation, condensing, constricting, constriction, contracting, contraction, diminishing, diminishment, lessening, lowering, shrinking; retrenching, retrenchment, shortening

antonyms decrease

multiply *vb* **1** to bring forth offspring ⟨rabbits *multiply* rapidly⟩ — see PROCREATE

2 to make greater in size, amount, or number ⟨the booming economy *multiplied* the wealth of investors⟩ — see INCREASE 1

3 to become greater in extent, volume, amount, or number ⟨with each attempt the problems *multiplied*⟩ — see INCREASE 2

multitude *n* a great number of persons or things gathered together ⟨awed by the *multitude* of stars in the night sky⟩ — see CROWD 1

multitudinous *adj* being of a large but indefinite number ⟨the *multitudinous* questions that seem to be an inevitable part of opening day at school⟩ — see MANY

mum *n, chiefly British* a female human parent ⟨have you met my *mum*?⟩ — see MOTHER

mum *adj* deliberately refraining from speech ⟨kept *mum* about the surprise⟩ — see SILENT 1

mumble *n* speech that is not clear enough to be understood ⟨please answer the question without your usual *mumble* and try to use complete sentences⟩

synonyms grunt, grunting, murmur, murmuring, mutter, muttering

related words undertone, whisper; babble, babbling, blab, blabbing, chatter, chattering, drivel, driveling (*or* drivelling), gabble, gabbling, jabber, jabbering, maundering, prattle, prattling, rambling

mumble *vb* to speak softly and unclearly ⟨I can't understand you if you *mumble*⟩

synonyms grunt, mouth, murmur, mutter

related words babble, blab, chatter, drivel, gabble, gibber, jabber, maunder, prattle, ramble; breathe, gasp, pant, whisper

near antonyms articulate, enunciate

antonyms speak out, speak up

mumbo jumbo *n* unintelligible or meaningless talk ⟨the soothsayer's predictions were nothing but *mumbo jumbo*⟩ — see GIBBERISH

mummer *n* **1** an actor in a story performed silently and entirely by body movements ⟨a street festival featuring *mummers* in a pantomime⟩ — see MIME

2 one who acts professionally (as in a play, movie, or television show) ⟨those moonstruck *mummers* on TV soap operas who have more hair than talent⟩ — see ACTOR

mundane *adj* **1** having to do with the practical details of regular life ⟨they didn't want to be bothered with *mundane* concerns like doing the dishes while on vacation⟩
synonyms everyday, prosaic, workaday
related words earthly, temporal, worldly; average, common, commonplace, customary, familiar, garden, normal, ordinary, plain, popular, routine, run-of-the-mill, typical, unexceptional, unremarkable, usual; frequent, habitual, regular; expected, predictable
near antonyms high-minded, lofty, noble, sublime; aberrant, abnormal, atypical; exceptional, extraordinary, odd, peculiar, phenomenal, rare, singular, special, uncommon, uncustomary, unique, unusual, unwonted; bizarre, curious, funny, odd, outlandish, quaint, remarkable, strange, weird

2 having to do with life on earth especially as opposed to that in heaven ⟨a period for reflection and penitence, when spiritual concerns should take precedence over those that are *mundane*⟩ — see EARTHLY

municipality *n* a thickly settled, highly populated area ⟨a *municipality* with an excellent police department⟩ — see CITY

munificent *adj* giving or sharing in abundance and without hesitation ⟨a *munificent* host who has presided over many charitable events at his mansion⟩ — see GENEROUS 1

munificently *adv* in a generous manner ⟨has shared her wealth *munificently* on countless occasions⟩ — see WELL 2

murder *n* **1** a situation or state that causes great suffering and unhappiness ⟨this weather is *murder* on my sinuses⟩ — see HELL 2

2 the intentional and unlawful taking of another person's life ⟨arrested for attempting to commit *murder*⟩ — see HOMICIDE

murder *vb* **1** to put to death deliberately ⟨those people made me so mad I felt like I wanted to *murder* them⟩
synonyms dispatch, do in, execute, liquidate, slay
related words blot out, destroy, fell, kill, smite, zap; assassinate; butcher, massacre, mow (down), slaughter; annihilate, eliminate, eradicate, exterminate, wipe out
phrases do away with

2 to make or do (something) in a clumsy or unskillful way ⟨we listened in horror as she *murdered* our favorite song on stage⟩ — see BOTCH

murderer *n* a person who kills another person ⟨the *murderer* was sentenced to life in prison without the possibility of parole⟩ — see ASSASSIN

murdering *adj* eager for or marked by the shedding of blood, extreme violence, or killing ⟨a vow to bring down the *murdering* fiend who had destroyed his family⟩ — see BLOODTHIRSTY

murderous *adj* **1** difficult to endure ⟨the *murderous* heat of the desert⟩ — see HARSH 1

2 requiring considerable physical or mental effort ⟨those exams were *murderous*⟩ — see HARD 2

3 likely to cause or capable of causing death ⟨braved *murderous* machine-gun fire to capture the hill from the enemy⟩ — see DEADLY

4 eager for or marked by the shedding of blood, extreme violence, or killing ⟨Viking warriors became legendary for the *murderous* fury they displayed in battle⟩ — see BLOODTHIRSTY

murk *n* **1** a time or place of little or no light ⟨a robber lying unseen in the *murk*⟩ — see DARK 1

2 an atmospheric condition in which suspended particles in the air rob it of its transparency ⟨stuck outside in the *murk* and the rain⟩ — see HAZE 1

murkiness *n* the quality or state of having a veiled or uncertain meaning ⟨we had trouble understanding the passage because of its *murkiness*⟩ — see OBSCURITY 1

murky *adj* **1** being without light or without much light ⟨I didn't like walking around the *murky* campground without a flashlight⟩ — see DARK 1

2 causing or marked by an atmosphere lacking in cheer ⟨the *murky* shadows of the cemetery⟩ — see GLOOMY 1

3 filled with or dimmed by fine particles (as of dust or water) in suspension ⟨skies made *murky* from the smoke of forest fires that were many miles to the west⟩ — see HAZY 1

4 having an often intentionally veiled or uncertain meaning ⟨a *murky* reply to a question about his intentions⟩ — see OBSCURE 1

5 not seen or understood clearly ⟨a gubernatorial candidate with a *murky* position on capital punishment⟩ — see FAINT 1

murmur *n* **1** an expression of dissatisfaction, pain, or resentment ⟨finished the job without a *murmur*⟩ — see COMPLAINT 1

2 speech that is not clear enough to be understood ⟨could just barely hear the *murmurs* of the audience⟩ — see MUMBLE

murmur *vb* **1** to express dissatisfaction, pain, or resentment usually tiresomely ⟨no prisoner dared *murmur* out loud⟩ — see COMPLAIN

2 to speak softly and unclearly ⟨a college professor who tends to *murmur*⟩ — see MUMBLE

murmurer *n* an irritable and complaining person ⟨the *murmurers* among the patients usually got fed last⟩ — see GROUCH

murmuring *n* speech that is not clear enough to be understood ⟨his surprising announcement brought *murmurings* from the crowd⟩ — see MUMBLE

muscle *n* **1** muscular strength ⟨I'm going to need someone with real *muscle* to help me move all this furniture⟩
synonyms brawn, main
related words force, might, potency, power, puissance, sinew
near antonyms impotence, weakness

2 the ability to exert effort for the accomplishment of a task ⟨at the time the military lacked the *muscle* to fight two wars at once⟩ — see POWER 2

muscle *vb* **1** to cause (a person) to give in to pressure ⟨was *muscled* out of command by his opponents at military headquarters⟩ — see FORCE

2 to force one's way ⟨*muscling* straight through the packed crowd of people waiting to board the ship⟩ — see PRESS 4

muscular *adj* **1** marked by a well-developed musculature ⟨Olympic runners tend to have very *muscular* legs⟩
synonyms brawny, sinewy

related words wiry; powerful, strong; beefy, burly, hefty, hulking, husky; able-bodied, athletic, herculean, mighty, robust, rugged, stalwart, strapping, sturdy

near antonyms nonathletic; delicate, feeble, fragile, frail, weak, weakly, wimpy; light, lightweight, slight; lean, slender, slim, svelte, sylphlike, thin, willowy; emaciated, gaunt, lank, rawboned, spare

antonyms scrawny, skinny

2 having muscles capable of exerting great physical force ⟨a *muscular* superhero who can easily lift a ton or more⟩ — see STRONG 1

museum *n* a building or part of a building in which objects of interest are displayed ⟨we're taking a trip to the *Museum* of Natural History as a special treat for science class⟩

synonyms gallery, salon

related words archives, collection, library; display, exhibition; studio

mush *n* **1** something (as a work of literature or music) that is too sentimental ⟨an opera that is pure *mush*⟩ — see CORN

2 the state or quality of having an excess of tender feelings (as of love, nostalgia, or compassion) ⟨couldn't stand all the *mush* in the movie's romantic scenes⟩ — see SENTIMENTALITY

mushroom *vb* to become greater in extent, volume, amount, or number ⟨the suburb's population has *mushroomed* tremendously in the last decade⟩ — see INCREASE 2

mushy *adj* **1** appealing to the emotions in an obvious and tiresome way ⟨a *mushy* love story⟩ — see CORNY

2 giving easily to the touch ⟨*mushy* fruit that was obviously overripe⟩ — see SOFT 3

musical *adj* **1** having a pleasantly flowing quality suggestive of music ⟨the *musical* sounds of the babbling brook⟩ — see LYRIC 1

2 having a pleasing mixture of notes ⟨the song of the skylark has been celebrated for being especially *musical*⟩ — see HARMONIOUS 1

musicale *n* an entertainment featuring singing or the playing of musical instruments ⟨gathered every month in someone's home for an informal *musicale*⟩ — see CONCERT

musician *n* **1** a person who plays a musical instrument ⟨the violinist was a famous and exquisitely talented *musician*⟩

synonyms instrumentalist, player

related words artist, performer; maestro, virtuoso; accompanist, recitalist, soloist; accordionist, bassoonist, clarinetist (*or* clarinettist), cornetist (*or* cornettist), drummer, fiddler, flautist, flutist, guitarist, harpist, oboist, organ-grinder, organist, percussionist, pianist, piper, saxophonist, trombonist, trumpeter, violinist

2 a person who writes musical compositions ⟨that *musician* is known for having written music that is very difficult to perform⟩ — see COMPOSER

muskeg *n* spongy land saturated or partially covered with water ⟨local farmers can make extra money by digging peat out of the nearby *muskeg*⟩ — see SWAMP

muss *vb* to undo the proper order or arrangement of ⟨the wind *mussed* up my hair⟩ — see DISORDER

mussed *adj* lacking in order, neatness, and often cleanliness ⟨the charmingly *mussed* look of a rock star in full rebel regalia⟩ — see MESSY

mussy *adj* lacking in order, neatness, and often cleanliness ⟨a *mussy* pile of papers and books⟩ — see MESSY

must *n* something necessary, indispensable, or unavoidable ⟨exercise is a *must* if you want to stay healthy⟩ — see ESSENTIAL 1

must *vb* to be under necessity or obligation to ⟨we *must* be quiet during the performance⟩ — see NEED 2

muster *n* a body of people come together in one place ⟨a *muster* of concerned citizens⟩ — see GATHERING 1

muster *vb* **1** to assemble and make ready for action ⟨a command to *muster* the troops⟩ — see MOBILIZE

2 to bring together in assembly by or as if by command ⟨all the supporters that I could *muster* for the fundraising campaign⟩ — see CONVOKE

muster out *vb* to let go from office, service, or employment ⟨*mustered out* of the army at the end of the war⟩ — see DISMISS 1

musty *adj* **1** having an unpleasant smell ⟨*musty* old gym socks⟩ — see MALODOROUS

2 used or heard so often as to be dull ⟨the *musty* prose of writers who use the same expressions over and over⟩ — see STALE

mutable *adj* likely to change frequently, suddenly, or unexpectedly ⟨a politician with very *mutable* positions on all the issues⟩ — see FICKLE 1

mutate *vb* to pass from one form, state, or level to another ⟨colored lights that slowly *mutate* from green to blue and on across the color spectrum⟩ — see CHANGE 2

mute *adj* **1** unable to speak ⟨the child is both deaf and *mute* because her hearing was lost at birth⟩

synonyms inarticulate, speechless, voiceless

related words tongue-tied; incoherent, incomprehensible; closemouthed, laconic, taciturn, tight-lipped, uncommunicative; mum, nonspeaking, quiet, silent, wordless

near antonyms communicative, gabby, garrulous, loquacious, talkative, talky, vocal; expatiating, speaking out, speaking up; articulating, speaking, talking; articulate, eloquent, fluent, voluble

2 deliberately refraining from speech ⟨remained *mute* no matter how much we pleaded for an answer⟩ — see SILENT 1

mute *n* a device on a musical instrument that deadens or softens its tone ⟨I got in trouble for practicing my trumpet at three in the morning when the *mute* fell out, and I woke everyone up⟩

synonyms damper

related words muffler, quieter, softener

mute *vb* **1** to stop the noise or speech of ⟨*muted* the television while she was on the phone⟩ — see SILENCE 1

2 to deaden the sound of ⟨closing the windows *muted* the traffic noise so we could get to sleep⟩ — see MUFFLE

muted *adj* **1** mostly or entirely without sound ⟨the *muted* cry of a frightened witness to a murder⟩ — see SILENT 3

2 not excessively showy ⟨painted with *muted* colors⟩ — see QUIET 2

muteness *n* incapacity for or restraint from speaking ⟨we were baffled by his uncharacteristic *muteness*⟩ — see SILENCE 1

mutilate *vb* to cause severe or permanent injury to ⟨was lucky not to be *mutilated* in the car crash⟩ — see MAIM

mutineer *n* a person who rises up against authority ⟨the *mutineers* were captured after they turned to piracy on the open seas⟩ — see REBEL

mutinous *adj* taking part in a rebellion ⟨vowed that he would someday see the *mutinous* crew hang⟩ — see REBELLIOUS 1

mutiny *n* open fighting against authority (as one's own government) ⟨a *mutiny* led by the ship's cook⟩ — see REBELLION

mutiny *vb* to rise up against established authority ⟨the party's conservative faction *mutinied* just before the election⟩ — see REBEL

mutter *n* speech that is not clear enough to be understood ⟨the distracting *mutter* of some member of the audience⟩ — see MUMBLE

mutter *vb* **1** to express dissatisfaction, pain, or resentment usually tiresomely ⟨a *muttering* group of workers⟩ — see COMPLAIN
2 to speak softly and unclearly ⟨*muttering* to himself under his breath⟩ — see MUMBLE

mutterer *n* an irritable and complaining person ⟨the usual *mutterers* about the food in the cafeteria⟩ — see GROUCH

muttering *n* speech that is not clear enough to be understood ⟨barely heard *mutterings* of discontent⟩ — see MUMBLE

mutual *adj* used or done by a number of people as a group ⟨every film is a *mutual* effort by the director, writer, actors, and a host of others⟩ — see COLLECTIVE

myopic *adj* **1** able to see near things more clearly than distant ones ⟨he became so *myopic* that he finally broke down and got contact lenses⟩ — see NEARSIGHTED
2 not thinking about and providing for the future ⟨the *myopic* city designers who did not plan for growth⟩ — see IMPROVIDENT

myriad *adj* being of many and various kinds ⟨the *myriad* problems that today's cities face⟩ — see MANIFOLD

mysterious *adj* **1** being beyond one's powers to know, understand, or explain ⟨the huge stone statues on Easter Island are ancient, *mysterious*, and haunting⟩
synonyms cryptic, darkling, deep, enigmatic (*also* enigmatical), impenetrable, inscrutable, mystic, occult, uncanny
related words dark, murky, obscure, shadowy, vague; ambiguous, equivocal; incomprehensible, unfathomable, unintelligible; inexplicable, unaccountable, unexplainable; unanswerable, unknowable; metaphysical, mystical, supernatural; abstruse, esoteric, recondite; baffling, bewildering, confounding, confusing, mystifying, perplexing, puzzling
near antonyms fathomable, intelligible, understandable; clear, obvious, open-and-shut, plain, straightforward, transparent
2 having an often intentionally veiled or uncertain meaning ⟨the stranger's *mysterious* words⟩ — see OBSCURE 1

mystery *n* something hard to understand or explain ⟨why my sister dyed her hair blue is a *mystery*⟩
synonyms conundrum, enigma, mystification, puzzle, puzzlement, riddle, secret
related words brainteaser, challenge, perplexity, poser, problem, stumper

mystic *adj* **1** having seemingly supernatural qualities or powers ⟨the notion that a cat has nine lives is based upon the belief that nine is a *mystic* number⟩
synonyms magic, magical, occult, weird
related words bewitched, enchanted, spellbound; bewitching, charming, conjuring, enchanting, wiling; awesome, extraordinary, marvelous (*or* marvellous), wondrous; divining, forecasting, foreknowing, foreseeing, foretelling, fortune-telling, predicting, presaging, prognosticating, prophesying, soothsaying
near antonyms commonplace, ordinary, unremarkable
2 being beyond one's powers to know, understand, or explain ⟨the belief that there are *mystic* forces at work here⟩ — see MYSTERIOUS 1
3 having an often intentionally veiled or uncertain meaning ⟨*mystic* prophesies that are never understood until it is too late⟩ — see OBSCURE 1

mystification *n* **1** a state of mental uncertainty ⟨the new information did little to ease our *mystification*⟩ — see CONFUSION 1
2 something hard to understand or explain ⟨an event that is one of the great *mystifications* in all of maritime history⟩ — see MYSTERY

mystify *vb* to throw into a state of mental uncertainty ⟨we were *mystified* by the sudden changes at school⟩ — see CONFUSE 1

myth *n* **1** a traditional but unfounded story that gives the reason for a current custom, belief, or fact of nature ⟨according to an ancient Greek *myth*, humans acquired fire from a giant who had stolen it from heaven⟩
synonyms fable, legend
related words allegory, parable; fabrication, fantasy (*also* phantasy), fiction, figment, invention; narrative, saga, story, tale, yarn
2 the body of customs, beliefs, stories, and sayings associated with a people, thing, or place ⟨over the years Davy Crockett evolved from an actual person to one of the great figures of American *myth*⟩ — see FOLKLORE
3 a false idea or belief ⟨the idea that alligators can live in the sewers of New York is just a *myth*⟩ — see FALLACY 1

mythical *or* **mythic** *adj* **1** based on, described in, or being a myth ⟨for years the Spanish conquistadors searched for the *mythical* El Dorado, a place of unimaginable riches⟩
synonyms fabled, fabulous, legendary
related words famed, romanticized, storied; fabricated, fantastic, fantastical, fictional, fictitious; fanciful; allegorical, mythological
near antonyms actual, real; historical; factual, true
2 not real and existing only in the imagination ⟨the *mythical* unicorn⟩ — see IMAGINARY

mythology *n* the body of customs, beliefs, stories, and sayings associated with a people, thing, or place ⟨Ares is the god of war in Greek *mythology*⟩ — see FOLKLORE

N

nab *vb* **1** to take or keep under one's control by authority of law ⟨the officer *nabbed* the purse snatcher before he could escape⟩ — see ARREST 1
2 to take physical control or possession of (something) suddenly or forcibly ⟨a pickpocket *nabbed* my wallet⟩ — see CATCH 1

nag *n* a large hoofed domestic animal that is used for carrying or drawing loads and for riding ⟨a poor farmer who could only afford one old *nag*⟩ — see HORSE

nag *vb* to subject (someone) to constant scoldings and sharp reminders ⟨she kept *nagging* him to fix the furnace before the weather got any colder⟩
synonyms henpeck, hound, needle
related words carp (at), fuss (about *or* over), nitpick; annoy, badger, bait, bother, bug, chivy, harass, harry, hassle, irk, pester, plague, ride, vex, yap (at); egg, goad, incite, prod, prompt, spur, urge; exhort, insist, press, pressure, push; blandish, cajole, coax, wheedle; beg, importune, plead
near antonyms compliment; commend, laud, praise, recommend, tout; acclaim, applaud, eulogize, extol (*also* extoll)

naiad *n* **1** a mythical goddess represented as a young girl and said to live outdoors ⟨in Greek mythology, *naiads* supposedly drowned the young men with whom they became enamored⟩ — see NYMPH 1
2 a young wingless often wormlike form (as a grub or caterpillar) that hatches from the egg of many insects ⟨in science class we learned how to distinguish a dragonfly *naiad* from an earthworm⟩ — see LARVA

nail *vb* to take physical control or possession of (something) suddenly or forcibly ⟨the running back saw the pass coming in and *nailed* it⟩ — see CATCH 1

naive *or* **naïve** *adj* **1** lacking in worldly wisdom or informed judgment ⟨a first-time buyer who was so *naive* that he believed the salesman and paid good money for the rusty and broken-down car⟩
synonyms green, ingenuous, innocent, simple, simpleminded, uncritical, unknowing, unsophisticated, unsuspecting, unsuspicious, unwary, unworldly, wide-eyed
related words callow, dewy, inexperienced, raw; childlike, idealistic, impractical; believing, credulous, gullible, susceptible, trustful, trusting, unguarded; beguiled, duped, gulled, tricked; careless, heedless
near antonyms critical, doubting, incredulous, skeptical, suspecting, suspicious, unconvinced; careful, cautious, guarded, leery, wary, watchful; down-to-earth, hardheaded, pragmatic (*also* pragmatical), realistic, sober
antonyms cynical, experienced, knowing, sophisticated, worldly, worldly-wise
2 free from any intent to deceive or impress others ⟨the young girl gave honest and *naive* answers to the social worker's questions⟩ — see GUILELESS
3 readily taken advantage of ⟨we continue to get junk mail because you are *naive* enough to keep entering these dumb contests⟩ — see EASY 2

naively *adv* without any attempt to impress by deception or exaggeration ⟨she *naively* admitted to the job interviewer that she actually had little work experience⟩ — see NATURALLY 3

naïveté *also* **naivete** *n* **1** the quality or state of being simple and sincere ⟨her *naïveté* led her to leave her new bike outside the mall unchained while she shopped⟩
synonyms artlessness, greenness, guilelessness, ingenuousness, innocence, naturalness, simpleness, simplicity, unsophistication, unworldliness
related words candor, frankness, genuineness, honesty, openness, sincerity, straightforwardness; callowness, childishness, inexperience, rawness; carelessness, heedlessness; ignorance, obliviousness, unawareness; credulity, credulousness, gullibility; idealism, impracticality, optimism
near antonyms affectedness, artificiality, pretentiousness; deviousness, dishonesty, insincerity; disbelief, doubtfulness, incredulity, suspiciousness; carefulness, caution, wariness; pessimism, skepticism; maturity
antonyms artfulness, cynicism, sophistication, worldliness
2 readiness to believe the claims of others without sufficient evidence ⟨though he was streetwise, the investigative reporter assumed an air of *naïveté* when he was interviewing confidence men, charlatans, counterfeiters, and other assorted swindlers of the general public⟩ — see CREDULITY

naked *adj* **1** lacking or shed of clothing ⟨had recurrent nightmares about being *naked* in public⟩
synonyms bare, disrobed, nude, stripped, unclad, unclothed, undressed
related words denuded, peeled; raw, stark; unveiled
near antonyms covered, veiled; arrayed, caparisoned, decked (out), rigged (out), tricked (out); vested; decent
antonyms appareled (*or* apparelled), attired, clad, clothed, dressed, garbed, invested, robed, suited
2 lacking a usual or natural covering ⟨the winter trees were *naked* without their colorful fall leaves⟩
synonyms bald, bare, denuded, exposed, open, peeled, stripped, uncovered
related words displayed, revealed; hairless, shaven; disrobed, unclad, unclothed, undressed; skinned; divested; unprotected, unsheltered
near antonyms mantled; overgrown, overrun, overspread; bearded, hairy
antonyms covered
3 free from all additions or embellishment ⟨a *naked* room waiting for an interior decorator's inspired touch⟩ — see PLAIN 1

name *adj* having a good reputation especially in a field of knowledge ⟨the university's physics department boasts a number of *name* physicists⟩ — see RESPECTABLE 1

name *n* **1** a word or combination of words by which a person or thing is regularly known ⟨introduced himself and then asked what my *name* was⟩
synonyms appellation, cognomen, denomination, denotation, designation, handle, title
related words christian name, forename, given name; family name, maiden name, surname; epithet, nickname, sobriquet (*also* soubriquet); alias, nom de plume, pen name, pseudonym; binomial, vernacular; misnomer; label, trademark
2 an act or expression showing scorn and usually intended to hurt another's feelings ⟨quit calling her *names*⟩ — see INSULT

3 outward and often deceptive indication ⟨the head of the charitable organization in *name* only⟩ — see APPEARANCE 2

4 overall quality as seen or judged by people in general ⟨has a good *name* among fellow marine biologists⟩ — see REPUTATION

name *vb* **1** to give a name to ⟨decided to *name* her new puppy "Bubbles"⟩
synonyms baptize, call, christen, denominate, designate, dub, entitle, label, style, term, title
related words denote, specify; miscall, misname; nickname; rename

2 to make reference to or speak about briefly but specifically ⟨I don't want to *name* anyone in particular, but someone in this room fiddled with my car's radio⟩ — see MENTION 1

3 to pick (someone) by one's authority for a specific position or duty ⟨was *named* the provost of the university⟩ — see APPOINT 2

4 to decide to accept (someone or something) from a group of possibilities ⟨you don't like my offer? Just *name* your price⟩ — see CHOOSE 1

5 to decide upon (the time or date for an event) usually from a position of authority ⟨you *name* the date and I'll make sure I'm there⟩ — see APPOINT 1

nameless *adj* **1** not named or identified by a name ⟨the victim of the crime will remain *nameless* to protect his privacy⟩ ⟨*nameless* editors who write TV listings in the newspaper⟩
synonyms anonymous, incognito, unbaptized, unchristened, unidentified, unnamed, untitled
related words unspecified; obscure, uncelebrated, unheard-of, unknown, unnoted, unremarkable
near antonyms denominated, designated, specified; labeled (*or* labelled), tabbed, titled; celebrated, famed, famous, known, notable, noted, noteworthy, remarkable, renowned, well-known
antonyms baptized, christened, dubbed, named, termed

2 beyond the power to describe ⟨was seized with a *nameless,* vague fear that made her seek the companionship of another person⟩ — see INDESCRIBABLE

3 not widely known ⟨a *nameless* poet who has just been rediscovered by readers of love poems⟩ — see OBSCURE 2

namer *n* someone with the right or responsibility for making a selection ⟨we can't start the ceremony until the *namer* of the scholarship winners shows up⟩ — see SELECTOR

¹nap *n* a short sleep ⟨so tired that she needed to take a refreshing *nap* before soccer practice⟩
synonyms catnap, doze, drowse, forty winks, siesta, snooze, wink
related words repose, rest; slumber; bed

²nap *n* a soft airy substance or covering ⟨high-quality suede has a good, even *nap*⟩ — see FUZZ

nap *vb* **1** to sleep lightly or briefly ⟨decided to let the kids *nap* for a few more minutes before waking them⟩
synonyms catnap, doze, drowse, slumber, snooze
related words relax, repose, rest; couch, lay, lie, roost; lull
near antonyms arise, arouse, awake, awaken, get up, rise, rouse, uprise, wake (up), waken

2 be in a state of sleep ⟨I'm just going to *nap* the entire afternoon⟩ — see SLEEP 1

napping *adj* being in a state of suspended consciousness ⟨the *napping* children looked so peaceful⟩ — see ASLEEP 1

napping *n* a natural periodic loss of consciousness during which the body restores itself ⟨some people think that *napping* in the afternoon will keep you from sleeping well at night⟩ — see SLEEP 1

narcotic *adj* **1** tending to calm the emotions and relieve stress ⟨some therapists believe that certain scents can have a *narcotic* effect on people⟩ — see SOOTHING 1

2 tending to cause sleep ⟨the lecturer spoke in a *narcotic* monotone that soon had the entire class struggling to stay awake⟩ — see HYPNOTIC

narrate *vb* to give an oral or written account of in some detail ⟨got a CD of this children's story that happens to be *narrated* by the author herself⟩ — see TELL 1

narrative *n* **1** a relating of events usually in the order in which they happened ⟨wrote a witty, chatty *narrative* of all the happenings at the party⟩ — see ACCOUNT 1

2 a work with imaginary characters and events that is shorter and usually less complex than a novel ⟨in such *narratives* as "The Murders in the Rue Morgue" and "The Purloined Letter," Edgar Allan Poe created the modern detective story⟩ — see STORY 1

narrow *adj* **1** being of less than usual width ⟨found a *narrow* opening in the fence that he was able to squeeze through⟩
synonyms fine, hairline, needlelike, skinny, slender, slim, thin
related words attenuated, elongated, linear; close, compressed, condensed, constricted, contracted, squeezed, tight, tightened; reedy, stalky, stringy, twiggy, wispy; spare
near antonyms chunky, squat, stocky, stumpy, thick, thickset; bulky, massive
antonyms broad, fat, wide

2 not broad or open in views or opinions ⟨a *narrow* person who thought that anyone who owned a television was morally corrupt⟩
synonyms insular, little, parochial, petty, provincial, sectarian, small, small-minded
related words inflexible, obdurate, obstinate, rigid, set, stubborn, unyielding, wrongheaded; bigoted, intolerant, narrow-minded; biased, discriminating, discriminatory, jaundiced, one-sided, partial, partisan, prejudiced; old-fashioned, reactionary, stodgy, straitlaced (*or* straightlaced); dogmatic, opinionated; limited
near antonyms impartial, nonpartisan, objective, unbiased, unprejudiced
antonyms broad-minded, catholic, cosmopolitan, liberal, open, open-minded, receptive, tolerant

3 having distinct or certain limits ⟨a play about human suffering, but in a *narrower* sense, also about the modern struggles of the working-class poor⟩ — see LIMITED 1

4 showing little difference in the standing of the competitors ⟨a *narrow* contest, the outcome of which may depend upon a handful of votes⟩ — see CLOSE 3

5 unwilling to grant other people social rights or to accept other viewpoints ⟨a *narrow* man who wouldn't work for a woman because he refused to believe women had the proper temperament for management⟩ — see INTOLERANT 2

narrow-minded *adj* unwilling to grant other people social rights or to accept other viewpoints ⟨integration of the public schools was vigorously opposed by *narrow-minded* people⟩ — see INTOLERANT 2

narrows *n pl* a narrow body of water between two land masses ⟨we had to row our dinghy through the *narrows* before reaching the open water of the bay⟩ — see CHANNEL 2

nastily *adv* in a mean or spiteful manner ⟨he *nastily* stuck his foot out and tripped the front runner because he couldn't stand to see her win⟩

synonyms cattily, despitefully, hatefully, malevolently, maliciously, malignantly, meanly, spitefully, viciously, villainously, virulently, wickedly

related words contemptuously, deprecatingly, disdainfully, scornfully; acrimoniously, antagonistically, caustically, hostilely, invidiously, obnoxiously, rancorously, venomously; bitterly, enviously, jealously, resentfully; balefully, callously, cruelly, hardheartedly, heartlessly, inhumanely, mercilessly, pitilessly, ruthlessly, soullessly, unfeelingly; disagreeably, ill, ungraciously, unkindly; ill-naturedly, inconsiderately, insensitively, thoughtlessly; diabolically, fiendishly; misanthropically

near antonyms affably, agreeably, amiably, cordially, genially, good-humoredly, good-naturedly, graciously, nicely, pleasantly; altruistically, humanely; considerately, feelingly, lovingly, mercifully, sensitively, softheartedly, solicitously, soulfully, thoughtfully; compassionately, sympathetically; angelically, divinely, sweetly, tenderly

antonyms benevolently, benignantly, good-heartedly, kindheartedly, kindly

nastiness *n* **1** the desire to cause pain for the satisfaction of doing harm ⟨there was a natural *nastiness* about him that was evident from the time he was a small child⟩ — see MALICE

2 the quality or state of being obscene ⟨the *nastiness* of the graffiti required that the school remove it immediately⟩ — see OBSCENITY 1

3 the state or quality of being dirty ⟨the piles of rotting food in the kitchen contributed in a big way to the apartment's general *nastiness*⟩ — see DIRTINESS 1

nasty *adj* **1** arousing or deserving of one's loathing and disgust ⟨fortunately, the story's *nasty* characters are balanced by some truly good people⟩ — see CONTEMPTIBLE 1

2 causing intense displeasure, disgust, or resentment ⟨a *nasty* video game that was so violent that I could hardly watch the opening scenes⟩ — see OFFENSIVE 1

3 causing or feeling bodily pain ⟨a *nasty* cut on my lip⟩ — see PAINFUL 1

4 depicting or referring to sexual matters in a way that is unacceptable in polite society ⟨*nasty* magazines that are not sold to minors⟩ — see OBSCENE 1

5 having or showing a desire to cause someone pain or suffering for the sheer enjoyment of it ⟨made *nasty* comments about how ugly she was⟩ — see HATEFUL

6 marked by wet and windy conditions ⟨bring your raincoat, as the weather's supposed to be *nasty*⟩ — see FOUL 1

7 not clean ⟨it's incredibly *nasty* inside that garbage bin, so stay away from there⟩ — see DIRTY 1

8 not giving pleasure to the mind or senses ⟨the smell of those old leftovers is downright *nasty*⟩ — see UNPLEASANT

nation *n* a body of people composed of one or more nationalities usually with its own territory and government ⟨the American people became one *nation* when they adopted the Constitution in 1789⟩

synonyms commonwealth, country, land, sovereignty, state

related words city-state; domain, dominion, empire, kingdom, realm, republic; duchy, dukedom, principality, seigniory (*or* seignory), sultanate; democracy, dictatorship, monarchy, oligarchy, sovereign, theocracy;

colony, dependency, province, settlement, soil; fatherland, homeland, motherland; power, superpower

national *adj* of or relating to a nation ⟨played the home team's *national* anthem before the start of the soccer game⟩

synonyms civil, public, state

related words civic, federal, municipal; government, governmental; domestic, internal; democratic, republican; nationwide

near antonyms global, international; alien, external, foreign

antonyms nonnational

national *n* a person who owes allegiance to a government and is protected by it ⟨recommended that foreign *nationals* living in the region evacuate immediately⟩ — see CITIZEN 1

nationalism *n* **1** excessive favoritism towards one's own country ⟨Nazism's almost epic *nationalism* appealed to downtrodden Germans still suffering the humiliation of being defeated in World War I⟩ — see CHAUVINISM

2 love and support for one's country ⟨American *nationalism* is often most visible during Fourth of July celebrations⟩ — see PATRIOTISM

nationalist *adj* having or showing love and support for one's country ⟨*nationalist* fervor is often at its highest when a country is at war⟩ — see PATRIOTIC

nationalist *n* one who shows excessive favoritism towards his or her country ⟨a staunch *nationalist* who favored any policy that would give the country more power in the international arena⟩

synonyms chauvinist, jingo

related words loyalist, patriot; hawk, warmonger

near antonyms internationalist; neutralist

nationalistic *adj* having or showing love and support for one's country ⟨a *nationalistic* display of the country's flag at all civic events⟩ — see PATRIOTIC

native *adj* **1** belonging to a particular place by birth or origin ⟨though she now lived in the Northeast, she was a *native* Midwesterner⟩

synonyms aboriginal, born, endemic, indigenous

related words domestic, local; original

near antonyms imported, introduced, transplanted; alien, exotic, foreign, strange; expatriate, immigrant

antonyms nonnative

2 being such as found in nature and not altered by processing or refining ⟨diamonds in their *native* state are not the bright, flashy gems that one might imagine⟩ — see CRUDE 1

Native American *n* a member of any of the native peoples of the western hemisphere usually not including the Eskimos ⟨his grandfather was a *Native American* from the Choctaw nation⟩ — see AMERICAN INDIAN

nativity *n* the act or instance of being born ⟨my father and grandparents were present at my *nativity*⟩ — see BIRTH 1

nattily *adv* in a strikingly neat and trim manner ⟨he's very *nattily* dressed in a new tailored suit⟩ — see SMARTLY

natty *adj* being strikingly neat and trim in style or appearance ⟨a *natty* woman, she's usually impeccably dressed in tailored clothing from Europe⟩ — see SMART 1

natural *adj* **1** being such from birth or by nature ⟨from his first visits to the wading pool, we could tell he loved water and was a *natural* swimmer⟩

synonyms born, congenital

related words chronic, confirmed, habitual, ingrained, inveterate, proper, regular; constitutional, consum-

mate; elemental, elementary, essential, hereditary, in-born, inherent, innate, intimate, intrinsic, native; in-stinctual, intuitive
near antonyms cultivated, developed, trained; alien, foreign, unnatural
antonyms nonnatural
2 closely resembling the object imitated ⟨the display of stuffed birds and plastic plants actually looked very *natural*⟩
synonyms lifelike, near, realistic
related words alike, like, living, matching; akin, analogous, approximate, comparable, resembling; accurate, close, faithful, true; convincing
near antonyms dissimilar, off, unalike, unlike; incomparable, unmatched; contrasted, contrasting, different, disparate; fake, mock, phony (*also* phoney), sham
antonyms nonnatural, nonrealistic, unrealistic
3 being a part of the innermost nature of a person or thing ⟨her *natural* talent for music first became apparent when she started banging on a toy piano⟩ — see IN-HERENT
4 being such as found in nature and not altered by processing or refining ⟨*natural* salts are not edible until they are washed and processed⟩ — see CRUDE 1
5 existing without human habitation or cultivation ⟨photographs of animals in their *natural* habitat⟩ — see WILD 2
6 free from any intent to deceive or impress others ⟨she was completely *natural* in expressing her feelings for him, unafraid of how they would be received⟩ — see GUILELESS
7 relating to or characteristic of human beings ⟨it's only *natural* to make mistakes—it's part of being human⟩ — see HUMAN
naturally *adv* **1** by natural character or ability ⟨tour guides who are *naturally* outgoing and can easily approach and converse with strangers⟩
synonyms constitutionally, inherently, innately, intrinsically
related words elementally, essentially, fundamentally; instinctively, intuitively; intimately
near antonyms artificially, unnaturally
2 according to the usual course of things ⟨we *naturally* like to be as comfortable as possible⟩
synonyms commonly, generally, normally, ordinarily, typically, usually
related words customarily, habitually, regularly, routinely; familiarly; conventionally, traditionally
phrases of course
near antonyms oddly, peculiarly, queerly, strangely; anomalously, irregularly; radically
antonyms abnormally, atypically, extraordinarily, uncommonly, unusually
3 without any attempt to impress by deception or exaggeration ⟨he tried to act *naturally* around the girl he had a crush on⟩
synonyms artlessly, guilelessly, ingenuously, innocently, naively, sincerely, unaffectedly, unfeignedly, unpretentiously
related words genuinely, honestly, simply, truly; freely, openheartedly, openly; candidly, frankly, matter-of-factly; informally, relaxedly, unceremoniously
near antonyms artfully, cannily, deceitfully, deceptively, deviously, dishonestly, falsely; archly, calculatingly, craftily, cunningly, furtively, insidiously, sharply, shiftily, slickly, slyly, underhand, underhanded, underhandedly; flatteringly, sycophantically, unctuously

antonyms affectedly, artificially, hypocritically, insincerely, pretentiously, unnaturally
naturalness *n* **1** carefree freedom from constraint ⟨the children danced with a *naturalness* born of the sheer enjoyment of music and movement⟩ — see ABANDON
2 the quality or state of being simple and sincere ⟨admired the very *naturalness* of the Amish lifestyle⟩ — see NAÏVETÉ 1
nature *n* **1** the set of qualities that makes a person, a group of people, or a thing different from others ⟨it was the violent *nature* of his stories that got them banned from school libraries⟩ ⟨her *nature* was such that lying was never an option for her⟩ ⟨the stoic *nature* of these people enables them to endure one calamity after another⟩
synonyms character, complexion, constitution, genius, personality, tone
related words distinctiveness, distinctness, individuality, singularity, uniqueness; attribute, characteristic, earmark, feature, flavor, hallmark, mark, point, property, savor, stamp, trait; disposition, grain, sort, temper, temperament; composition, makeup; essence, essentiality, soul, spirit, stuff, substance; habit, way
2 that part of the physical world that is removed from human habitation ⟨needed to get out of the office and be out in *nature* to clear his head⟩
synonyms open, open air, outdoors, out-of-doors, wild, wilderness
related words backwoods, bush, country, frontier, hinterland, sticks, up-country; outside, without; badland, barren, desert, waste, wasteland
3 a number of persons or things that are grouped together because they have something in common ⟨group together anything round: buttons, lids, coins, and things of that *nature*⟩ — see SORT 1
4 one's characteristic attitude or mood ⟨a boy of a quiet and shy *nature*⟩ — see DISPOSITION 1
5 the quality or qualities that make a thing what it is ⟨some artists say that color, light, and shadow are the very *nature* of painting⟩ — see ESSENCE
6 the whole body of things observed or assumed ⟨the belief that all of *nature* is controlled by an unseen Supreme Being⟩ — see UNIVERSE
naught *also* **nought** *n* the numerical symbol 0 or the absence of number or quantity represented by it ⟨my locker number is *naught*-seven-two⟩ — see ZERO 1
naughty *adj* engaging in or marked by childish misbehavior ⟨told her to act her age and stop throwing temper tantrums like a *naughty* little girl⟩
synonyms bad, contrary, errant, froward, misbehaving, mischievous
related words defiant, disrespectful, ill-mannered, ill-natured, impolite, improper, impudent, indecorous, insolent, rude, uncouth, unmannerly; disobedient, headstrong, intractable, obstreperous, recalcitrant, refractory, transgressing, unruly, untoward, willful (*or* wilful); balky, restive, uncontrollable, ungovernable, wayward, wild; arch, elfish, impish, monkeying, monkeyish, ornery, pixieish, prankish, rascally, roguish, waggish; dissolute, perverse, wrongheaded; disorderly, rowdy, ruffianly; corrupt, evil, wicked; insurgent, mutinous, rebellious; disobliging, inconsiderate, selfish, thoughtless, unkind, unkindly; babyish, childish, immature, infantile, puerile
near antonyms acquiescent, compliant, complying, dutiful, obedient, submissive; clean, correct, decent, decorous, moral, proper, respectable; considerate, courteous, kindly, mannerly, polite, thoughtful; an-

gelic, divine, heavenly; amenable, docile, governable, tractable; amiable, complaisant, good-natured, obliging, pleasant; discreet, modest; grown-up, mature
antonyms behaved, behaving, nice, orderly

nausea *n* **1** a disturbed condition of the stomach in which one feels like vomiting ⟨symptoms include fever accompanied by a loss of appetite and *nausea*⟩
synonyms qualmishness, queasiness, queerness, sickness, squeamishness
related words qualm; airsickness, morning sickness, motion sickness, seasickness
2 a dislike so strong as to cause stomach upset or queasiness ⟨such graphic scenes of senseless violence fill me with *nausea*⟩ — see DISGUST

nauseate *vb* to cause to feel disgust ⟨such hateful graffiti would *nauseate* anyone with an ounce of human decency⟩ — see DISGUST

nauseated *adj* **1** affected with nausea ⟨being aboard ship during that storm would make anyone but the most experienced sailor *nauseated*⟩ — see NAUSEOUS
2 filled with disgust ⟨*nauseated* critics panned the movie comedy for its celebration of gross behavior⟩ — see SICK 2

nauseating *adj* causing intense displeasure, disgust, or resentment ⟨her vicious gossiping is absolutely *nauseating*⟩ — see OFFENSIVE 1

nauseous *adj* affected with nausea ⟨after eating the last four pieces of the two-week-old pizza, he was feeling a little *nauseous*⟩
synonyms ill, nauseated, qualmish, queasy (*also* queazy), queer, queerish, sick, sickish, squeamish
related words green, peaked, sickly; unsettled, upset, woozy
near antonyms settled; healthy, well

nautical *adj* of or relating to navigation of the sea ⟨collected sextants and other antique *nautical* equipment⟩ — see MARINE 2

navigable *adj* capable of being traveled on ⟨this map shows which rivers are *navigable* and which aren't⟩ — see PASSABLE 1

navigate *vb* to travel on water in a vessel ⟨the months that were once required to *navigate* around South America in the days before the Panama Canal⟩ — see SAIL 1

navigational *adj* of or relating to navigation of the sea ⟨the folly of trying to sail with outdated *navigational* maps⟩ — see MARINE 2

navigator *n* one who operates or navigates a seagoing vessel ⟨our crew comprised a captain, a *navigator*, and a few deckhands⟩ — see SAILOR

nay *adv* not merely this but also ⟨I was angry—*nay*, furious—at the way they were treating that poor dog⟩ — see EVEN

nay *n* **1** a vote or decision against something ⟨when the votes were tallied, it was 241 yeas and 54 *nays*⟩ — see NO 1
2 an unwillingness to grant something asked for ⟨gave a resounding *nay* to the request for a mixed-company camping trip⟩ — see DENIAL 1

Neanderthal *adj* not civilized ⟨her boyfriend's *Neanderthal* tastes and manners⟩ — see SAVAGE 1

near *adj* **1** being the less far of two ⟨grab the comforter from the *near* side of the bed⟩
synonyms closer, hither, nigher, this
related words fore, forward, front, inside
near antonyms distant, remote, remoter; back, outside
antonyms far, farther, further, opposite, other, that

2 being such only when compared to something else ⟨the perpetual busyness of the family next-door makes us look like we live in *near* retirement⟩ — see COMPARATIVE
3 closely resembling the object imitated ⟨the dress is made from a *near* silk that would fool anyone but an expert⟩ — see NATURAL 2
4 not being distant in time, space, or significance ⟨the famous prediction that in the *near* future everyone will be famous for 15 minutes⟩ — see CLOSE 2

near *adv* **1** at, within, or to a short distance or time ⟨the campers were cold, so they moved *nearer* to the campfire⟩ ⟨as summer draws *near*, we usually start planning our annual vacation⟩
synonyms around, by, close, hard, in, nearby, nigh
related words hereabouts (*or* hereabout), thereabouts (*or* thereabout); along, alongside
phrases at close quarters, at hand
2 to a close degree ⟨copy the artist's drawing into your own sketchbook as *near* as you can⟩
synonyms closely, nearly
near antonyms distantly, remotely
3 very close to but not completely ⟨it's *near* six o'clock, so go wash up for dinner⟩ — see ALMOST

near *prep* close to ⟨don't cough *near* me⟩ — see AROUND 1

near *vb* **1** to come near or nearer ⟨as the procession *nears*, you'll be able to take a better picture of the graduates⟩ — see APPROACH 1
2 to move closer to ⟨as we *near* the church, you'll be able to see the intricate carvings better⟩ — see COME 1

nearby *adj* not being distant in time, space, or significance ⟨grabbed the *nearby* quilt and threw it over the sleeping child⟩ — see CLOSE 2

nearby *adv* at, within, or to a short distance or time ⟨I'll be *nearby* if you need anything⟩ — see NEAR 1

nearing *adj* being soon to appear or take place ⟨teachers preparing for the fast-*nearing* school year⟩ — see FORTHCOMING

nearly *adv* **1** to a close degree ⟨copy that design as *nearly* as you can⟩ — see NEAR 2
2 very close to but not completely ⟨I *nearly* fell down the stairs⟩ — see ALMOST

nearness *n* **1** the state of being in a very personal or private relationship ⟨my cousin and I have lost that *nearness* we had when we were kids⟩ — see FAMILIARITY 1
2 the state or condition of being near ⟨our *nearness* to the amusement park has endeared us to relatives from all over the country⟩ — see PROXIMITY

nearsighted *adj* able to see near things more clearly than distant ones ⟨I am a little *nearsighted* and need to wear glasses to drive⟩
synonyms myopic, shortsighted
related words astigmatic
antonyms farsighted

neat *adj* **1** being clean and in good order ⟨keep the kitchen *neat* so the cook doesn't have to work around piles of dirty dishes⟩
synonyms crisp, groomed, orderly, picked up, shipshape, snug, tidied, tidy, trim, uncluttered
related words dapper, natty, prim, saucy, smart, spiffy, spruce; immaculate, spick-and-span (*or* spic-and-span), spotless; rakish, sleek, streamlined, taut; organized, straight, systematic
near antonyms seedy, shabby, slipshod, sloppy; dirty, filthy, foul, nasty, sordid, squalid; frowzy, rumpled, tousled, tumbled; disorganized, unsystematic

antonyms disheveled (*or* dishevelled), disordered, disorderly, messy, mussed, mussy, slovenly, unkempt, untidy

2 free from added matter ⟨I like my soda *neat,* so skip the ice cubes⟩ — see PURE 1

3 of the very best kind ⟨that new skateboard park is *neat*⟩ — see EXCELLENT

nebulous *adj* **1** having an often intentionally veiled or uncertain meaning ⟨made *nebulous* references to some changes the future may hold⟩ — see OBSCURE 1

2 not seen or understood clearly ⟨could just make out the *nebulous* outline of a fishing shack in the dense fog⟩ — see FAINT 1

nebulousness *n* the quality or state of having a veiled or uncertain meaning ⟨the *nebulousness* of the imagery in his poetry seems to be part of its attraction to some readers⟩ — see OBSCURITY 1

necessarily *adv* because of necessity ⟨the argument that the existence of the universe *necessarily* implies the existence of an all-powerful being responsible for creating it⟩ — see NEEDS

necessary *adj* **1** forcing one's compliance or participation by or as if by law ⟨an emissions test is *necessary* before you can renew the registration for your car⟩ — see MANDATORY

2 impossible to avoid or evade ⟨taxes will always be a *necessary* evil⟩ — see INEVITABLE

3 impossible to do without ⟨food and water are *necessary* for survival⟩ — see ESSENTIAL 1

necessitate *vb* to have as a requirement ⟨getting new shoes would *necessitate* another trip to the mall⟩ — see NEED 1

necessity *n* something necessary, indispensable, or unavoidable ⟨on any road trip, accurate maps are a *necessity*⟩ — see ESSENTIAL 1

necklace *n* an ornamental chain or string (as of beads) worn around the neck ⟨found a lovely *necklace* to match the bracelet and ring her mother had given her⟩

synonyms choker, lei

related words rope, strand; bangle, lavaliere (*also* lavalliere), locket, pendant (*also* pendent)

necromancer *n* a person skilled in using supernatural forces ⟨in ancient times any kind of disaster was apt to be regarded as the work of some evil-minded *necromancer*⟩ — see MAGICIAN 1

necromancy *n* the power to control natural forces through supernatural means ⟨in the conjuring of the souls of the dead, *necromancy* seemed to offer a means of exerting some control over an uncertain world⟩ — see MAGIC 1

need *n* **1** a state of being without something necessary, desirable, or useful ⟨when it came time to wrap the presents, he found he was in *need* of adhesive tape⟩

synonyms absence, lack, needfulness, want

related words deficiency, deficit, inadequacy, insufficiency; dearth, meagerness, paucity, poverty, scantiness, scarceness, scarcity, shortage, skimpiness; defect, minus; deprivation, famishment, privation; demand, essential, necessity, requirement, requisite

near antonyms adequacy, enough, sufficiency; fund, pool, stock, supply; excess, fill, overabundance, oversupply, plenty, surfeit, surplus; hoard, stockpile

2 something necessary, indispensable, or unavoidable ⟨got a job that provided for his basic *needs*⟩ — see ESSENTIAL 1

3 something one must do because of prior agreement ⟨no *need* to apologize⟩ — see OBLIGATION

4 the state of lacking sufficient money or material possessions ⟨donating money to help those in *need*⟩ — see POVERTY 1

need *vb* **1** to have as a requirement ⟨a national crisis that *needs* a strong leader to solve it⟩

synonyms demand, necessitate, require, take, want, warrant

related words entail, involve; ask, beg, claim, clamor (for), cry (for); lack; command, enjoin, exact, insist, press, quest, stipulate

phrases call for

near antonyms own, possess

antonyms have, hold

2 to be under necessity or obligation to ⟨you *need* not stand when she enters the room⟩

synonyms have (to), must, ought (to), shall, should

related words will

needed *adj* impossible to do without ⟨pack only what will be *needed*⟩ — see ESSENTIAL 1

needful *adj* impossible to do without ⟨purchase *needful* provisions⟩ — see ESSENTIAL 1

needfulness *n* a state of being without something necessary, desirable, or useful ⟨I can scarcely describe my *needfulness* for a hot shower after a hard-fought game of racquetball⟩ — see NEED 1

neediness *n* the state of lacking sufficient money or material possessions ⟨a family's general level of *neediness* is the determining factor in the allocation of charitable donations⟩ — see POVERTY 1

needle *n* **1** a slender hollow instrument by which material is put into or taken from the body through the skin ⟨the nurse inserted the *needle* into his vein and collected some blood for testing⟩

synonyms hypodermic, hypodermic needle, hypodermic syringe, syringe

2 an arrow-shaped piece on a dial or scale for registering information ⟨simply by reading the compass *needle* you should be able to figure out in which direction we're heading⟩ — see POINTER 1

needle *vb* **1** to attack repeatedly with mean put-downs or insults ⟨we *needled* him mercilessly for thinking that he had any chance of being the prom date for the school's most popular girl⟩ — see TEASE 2

2 to subject (someone) to constant scoldings and sharp reminders ⟨quit *needling* me! I'll take out the trash in a minute!⟩ — see NAG

needlelike *adj* being of less than usual width ⟨I need a *needlelike* piece of wire to finish making this wreath⟩ — see NARROW 1

needler *n* a person who causes repeated emotional pain, distress, or annoyance to another ⟨those merciless *needlers* who had her in tears almost every day at school⟩ — see TORMENTOR

needless *adj* not needed by the circumstances or to accomplish an end ⟨*needless* expenditures that pushed the project way over budget⟩ — see UNNECESSARY

needlework *n* decorative stitching done on cloth with the use of a needle ⟨a school outing to the museum to see an exhibition of 18th century *needlework*⟩

synonyms embroidery

related words crewel, cross-stitch, needlepoint; hemstitch, fagoting (*or* faggoting), smocking; fancywork

needs *adv* because of necessity ⟨the dangers of global warming must *needs* be recognized—and recognized soon—by the industrialized nations of the world⟩

synonyms inescapably, inevitably, necessarily, perforce, unavoidably

related words involuntarily
antonyms unnecessarily

needy *adj* lacking money or material possessions ⟨regularly give money and donate clothes to help the *needy*⟩ — see POOR 1

ne'er *adv* at no time ⟨fare thee well, for *ne'er* shall I return⟩ — see NEVER 1

nefarious *adj* not conforming to a high moral standard; morally unacceptable ⟨the tragic heroines and *nefarious* villains of old-time melodramas⟩ — see BAD 2

nefariousness *n* the state or quality of being utterly evil ⟨the *nefariousness* of Jack the Ripper's crimes⟩ — see ENORMITY 1

negate *vb* **1** to declare not to be true ⟨this evidence *negates* his claim that he was not at the scene of the accident⟩ — see DENY 1
2 to put an end to by formal action ⟨Prohibition was established by the 18th amendment to the U.S. Constitution, only to be *negated* by the 21st amendment 13 years later⟩ — see ABOLISH
3 to think not to be true or real ⟨you can't *negate* your feelings for someone, even if they don't feel the same way about you⟩ — see DISBELIEVE

negation *n* a refusal to confirm the truth of a statement ⟨issued specific *negations* of all of the charges against her⟩ — see DENIAL 2

negative *adj* **1** marked by opposition or ill will ⟨classes that hopefully will change the *negative* attitude that some students have toward the recent immigrants⟩ — see HOSTILE 1
2 opposed to one's interests ⟨an almost universally *negative* reaction to the book⟩ — see ADVERSE 1

negative *n* **1** a vote or decision against something ⟨in the absence of a firm *negative* from the commander, we decided to continue on the mission⟩ — see NO 1
2 something that is as different as possible from something else ⟨happiness is the *negative* of misery⟩ — see OPPOSITE

negative *vb* **1** to reject by or as if by a vote ⟨though the rebuttal was very eloquent, he *negatived* it in favor of the first argument⟩ ⟨she *negatived* pizza for dinner, noting that they had already had it for three nights that week⟩
synonyms blackball, kill, veto
related words decline, disallow, disapprove, dismiss, refuse; blacklist
near antonyms admit, allow, approve, assent (to), pass, sanction; elect, support
antonyms confirm, ratify
2 to declare not to be true ⟨the governor's press secretary promptly *negatived* the rumor that he was not running for reelection⟩ — see DENY 1
3 to show unwillingness to accept, do, engage in, or agree to ⟨even though I had *negatived* the invitation, Mom thought I should go anyway⟩ — see DECLINE 1

neglect *n* **1** the state of being unattended to or not cared for ⟨the barn sat in *neglect* until it finally fell down⟩
synonyms desolation, dilapidation, disrepair, seediness
related words inattention, negligence; abandonment, desertion; decay, decrepitude, dereliction, deterioration, disintegration, ruin, ruination
near antonyms conservation, preservation
antonyms repair
2 the nonperformance of an assigned or expected action ⟨your ongoing *neglect* of your health is going to land you in the hospital someday⟩ — see FAILURE 1

neglect *vb* **1** to fail to give proper attention to ⟨the news media *neglected* the real issues of the campaign and focused on personalities⟩
synonyms disregard, forget, ignore, overlook, overpass, pass over, slight, slur (over)
related words fail; miss, omit; brush (aside *or* off), reject, shrug off, slough (off); disdain, pooh-pooh, scorn; scant, skimp
near antonyms appreciate, cherish, prize, treasure, value; cultivate, foster, nurse, nurture; pamper; remember; listen (to), watch; follow, mark, note, notice, observe, remark
antonyms attend (to), heed, mind, regard, tend (to)
2 to leave undone or unattended to especially through carelessness ⟨she plays too much and *neglects* her homework⟩ ⟨I've *neglected* my garden, and now it's overgrown with weeds⟩
synonyms forget, shirk
related words slack (off)
near antonyms carry out, do, execute, perform; accomplish, achieve
antonyms attend (to), remember
3 to miss the opportunity or obligation ⟨the job applicant *neglected* to mention his criminal record⟩
synonyms fail, forget, omit
related words disregard, ignore, overlook, overpass, pass over, slight; slide, slip; default; skip
near antonyms heed, mind, remember; keep, observe; carry out, do, execute, perform, practice (*or* practise); discharge, fulfill (*or* fulfil), meet, satisfy; comply (with)

neglected *adj* showing signs of advanced wear and tear and neglect ⟨a *neglected* teddy bear, missing one eye and both ears, shoved into the closet⟩ — see SHABBY 1

neglectful *adj* failing to give proper care and attention ⟨he's certainly not a *neglectful* father as he takes very good care of his children⟩ — see NEGLIGENT

neglecting *adj* failing to give proper care and attention ⟨a chronically *neglecting* custodian has let trash accumulate around the warehouse⟩ — see NEGLIGENT

negligence *n* **1** failure to take the care that a cautious person usually takes ⟨exhibiting his usual *negligence*, he failed to set the emergency brake, and the car rolled down the steep hill and crashed into the telephone pole⟩
synonyms carelessness, dereliction, heedlessness, incautiousness, laxness, remissness, slackness
related words foolhardiness, rashness, recklessness, wildness; neglect, omission; delinquency, irresponsibility, malfeasance, malpractice, misconduct; misdirection, mishandling, mismanagement; forgetfulness, inattention, inattentiveness, obliviousness, shortsightedness, unwariness
near antonyms alertness, attention, attentiveness, awareness; circumspection, observance, vigilance, watchfulness; responsibility, responsibleness
antonyms care, carefulness, caution, cautiousness, heedfulness
2 the nonperformance of an assigned or expected action ⟨the factory's owners are being charged with criminal *negligence* for the fire that killed a dozen workers⟩ — see FAILURE 1

negligent *adj* failing to give proper care and attention ⟨has been *negligent* in taking care of the neighbor's dog, repeatedly forgetting to feed the poor animal⟩
synonyms careless, derelict, lax, neglectful, neglecting, remiss, slack
related words heedless, incautious, irresponsible, reckless, wild; unguarded, unwary; forgetful; disregardful,

disregarding, inattentive, oblivious, thoughtless, un-heeding, unmindful, unthinking; apathetic, disinterested, indifferent, unconcerned, uninterested; delinquent; loose

near antonyms meticulous, painstaking, punctilious; cautious, chary, circumspect, gingerly, guarded; alert, heedful, heeding, mindful, observant, regardful, regarding, vigilant, wary, watchful; foresighted, fore-thoughtful, provident, responsible; thinking, thoughtful; concerned, interested

antonyms attentive, careful, conscientious

negligible *adj* **1** so small or unimportant as to warrant little or no attention ⟨the two cents in change was such a *negligible* sum that she left the store without collecting the pennies from the cashier⟩

synonyms inconsequential, inconsiderable, insignificant, measly, minute, nominal, paltry, petty, picayune, piddling, slight, trifling, trivial

related words inferior, mean; imperceptible, inappreciable; little, puny, tiny; hairsplitting, nitpicking, pettifogging; one-horse, small-fry, two-bit

near antonyms serious, substantial, weighty; eventful, momentous; conspicuous, noteworthy, prominent, outstanding, remarkable, striking; appreciable, discernible, measurable

antonyms big, consequential, considerable, important, material, significant

2 lacking importance ⟨the results from that small study of coffee drinkers are *negligible* and can be ignored⟩ — see UNIMPORTANT

3 small in degree ⟨there's a *negligible* chance I may make it to the picnic, but don't count on it⟩ — see REMOTE 1

negligibly *adv* in a very small quantity or degree ⟨this box is *negligibly* bigger than the other one, but it's such a slight difference I don't think it matters⟩ — see LITTLE 1

negotiable *adj* capable of being traveled on ⟨waited until winter when the glacier would be *negotiable*⟩ — see PASSABLE 1

negotiate *vb* **1** to bring about through discussion and compromise ⟨wanted to *negotiate* a higher salary before she accepted the job offer⟩

synonyms arrange, concert, conclude

related words settle (on *or* upon); bargain, chaffer, deal, dicker, haggle, horse-trade, palter; agree; contract, covenant; argue, debate, discuss, hammer (out), hash (over), reason, talk, talk over, work out

2 to deal with (something) usually skillfully or efficiently ⟨she's good at *negotiating* conflicts between coworkers⟩ — see HANDLE 1

3 to plan out usually with subtle skill or care ⟨the prisoners *negotiated* their escape by using Morse code to tap messages to each other through the walls⟩ — see ENGINEER

4 to talk over or dispute the terms of a purchase ⟨told them I'd take $8,000 for the car and wasn't in the mood to *negotiate*⟩ — see BARGAIN

negotiation *n* the act or practice of each side giving up something in order to reach an agreement ⟨it will take some *negotiation*, but I think we can get each side to agree to a cease-fire⟩ — see CONCESSION 1

neigh *vb* to make the cry typical of a horse ⟨the horses *neighed* when the rider came into the barn⟩

synonyms nicker, whinny

neighborhood *n* **1** an area (as of a city) set apart for some purpose or having some special feature ⟨are you familiar with the city's Latino *neighborhood*?⟩ — see DISTRICT

2 the people living in a particular area ⟨invited practically the whole *neighborhood* over for a big party⟩ — see COMMUNITY 1

neighboring *adj* not being distant in time, space, or significance ⟨the statehouse and its *neighboring* buildings⟩ — see CLOSE 2

neighborly *adj* having or showing kindly feeling and sincere interest ⟨they were *neighborly* folks, always ready to lend a helping hand whenever necessary⟩ — see FRIENDLY 1

nemesis *n* **1** one who inflicts punishment in return for an injury or offense ⟨Batman is the Joker's main *nemesis* and always foils his wicked plots⟩

synonyms avenger, castigator, chastiser, punisher, scourge, vigilante

related words revenger; redresser, righter; requiter

near antonyms ransomer, redeemer, vindicator

2 suffering, loss, or hardship imposed in response to a crime or offense ⟨social ostracism was once society's *nemesis* for those who defied its sexual mores⟩ — see PUNISHMENT

neophyte *n* a person who is just starting out in a field of activity ⟨a *neophyte* in snowboarding⟩ — see BEGINNER

neoplasm *n* an abnormal mass of tissue ⟨removed a *neoplasm* from the patient's abdomen⟩ — see GROWTH 1

nerd *n* a person slavishly devoted to intellectual or academic pursuits ⟨was such a *nerd* she stayed home from the party to study for the exam on Monday⟩

synonyms bookworm, grind

related words egghead, highbrow, intellectual; brain, genius; scholar

near antonyms slacker, underachiever; lowbrow

nerve *n* **1** shameless boldness ⟨you've got a lot of *nerve* showing up here⟩ — see EFFRONTERY

2 strength of mind to carry on in spite of danger ⟨that daring rescue took some *nerve*⟩ — see COURAGE

3 nerves *pl* a sense of panic or extreme nervousness ⟨a veteran performer who still gets a case of the *nerves* before performances⟩ — see JITTERS

nerve *vb* to prepare (oneself) mentally or emotionally ⟨needs to *nerve* himself for the big game tomorrow⟩ — see FORTIFY 1

nerved *adj* inclined or willing to take risks ⟨a *nerved* and fearless driver of race cars⟩ — see BOLD 1

nerveless *adj* **1** lacking strength of will or character ⟨he's a *nerveless* pushover⟩ — see WEAK 2

2 not easily panicked or upset ⟨to be a paramedic, you need to be calm, clearheaded, and *nerveless* in emergencies⟩ — see UNFLAPPABLE

nerviness *n* shameless boldness ⟨didn't appreciate her *nerviness* in asking my boyfriend on a date⟩ — see EFFRONTERY

nervous *adj* **1** feeling or showing uncomfortable feelings of uncertainty ⟨he was *nervous* about how he would do at the varsity basketball tryouts⟩

synonyms aflutter, anxious, dithery, edgy, het up, hung up, jittery, jumpy, nervy, perturbed, tense, troubled, uneasy, unquiet, upset, uptight, worried

related words aggrieved, bothered, concerned, disquieted, distraught, distressed, disturbed; apprehensive, foreboding, hesitant, misgiving; fretful, fretting, stewing, vexed; qualmish, qualmy; flustered, twittered, undone, unnerved, unstrung; obsessed, preoccupied, restless; fidgety, flighty, fluttery, high-strung, skittish, spooky

phrases keyed up, on edge, on pins and needles
near antonyms confident, self-assured, self-confident, sure; controlled, self-controlled
antonyms calm, collected, cool, easy, nerveless, relaxed
2 marked by or causing agitation or uncomfortable feelings ⟨a *nervous* silence filled the room as the teacher handed out the graded exams⟩
synonyms agitating, anxious, disquieting, distressful, distressing, disturbing, restless, tense, unnerving, unsettling, worrisome
related words bothersome, troublesome; foreboding, misgiving; discouraging, disheartening, strained; restive, restless, unrestful; awkward, embarrassing
near antonyms restful; pacific
antonyms calming, comfortable, easy, peaceful, quiet, quieting, tranquil
3 easily excited by nature ⟨a *nervous* sort of person, she's completely thrown by anything unexpected⟩ — see EXCITABLE
nervousness *n* an uneasy state of mind usually over the possibility of an anticipated misfortune or trouble ⟨your *nervousness* over your son's safety is only natural⟩ — see ANXIETY 1
nervy *adj* **1** displaying or marked by rude boldness ⟨the *nervy* waiter held up the small tip and called out to the departing customers, "Hope it doesn't break the bank!"⟩
synonyms arch, bold, bold-faced, brash, brassy, brazen, cheeky, cocky, fresh, impertinent, impudent, insolent, sassy, saucy
related words assertive, forward, obtrusive; audacious, defiant, disrespectful; shameless, unabashed, unblushing; bluff, blunt, curt; facetious, flip, flippant, pert, smart, smart-alecky (*or* smart-aleck)
near antonyms demure, humble, modest; courteous, genteel, mannerly, polite, proper; deferential, respectful; abashed, ashamed, blushing, embarrassed; gentle, mild; inconspicuous, unobtrusive
antonyms meek, mousy (*or* mousey), retiring, shy, timid
2 feeling or showing uncomfortable feelings of uncertainty ⟨I'm a little *nervy* about my first job interview⟩ — see NERVOUS 1
3 inclined or willing to take risks ⟨*nervy* rock climbers wanting to make gravity-defying ascents⟩ — see BOLD 1
nest *n* a place where a person goes to hide ⟨headed back to her *nest* for a little rest and relaxation⟩ — see HIDE-OUT
nest egg *n* a sum of money set aside for a particular purpose ⟨paid for the computer out of his *nest egg*⟩ — see FUND 1
nestle *vb* **1** to lie close ⟨*nestled* in next to the other kittens in the box⟩ — see NUZZLE
2 to sit or recline comfortably or cozily ⟨*nestling* with her children on the couch⟩ — see SNUGGLE 1
¹net *n* **1** a fabric made of strands loosely twisted, knotted, or woven together at regular intervals ⟨the basketball didn't go into the basket, it just hit the *net*⟩
synonyms mesh, netting, network
related words web, webbing; grille (*also* grill), lattice, screen, screening; filigree, lace
2 a device or scheme for capturing another by surprise ⟨a fish caught in the *net*⟩ — see TRAP 1
3 something that catches and holds ⟨caught in a *net* of intrigues⟩ — see WEB 1

²net *n* the amount of money left when expenses are subtracted from the total amount received ⟨his *net* for the year was about 60% of his total income⟩ — see PROFIT 1
nether *adj* situated lower down ⟨skied the *nether* slope of the mountain⟩ — see INFERIOR 1
netting *n* a fabric made of strands loosely twisted, knotted, or woven together at regular intervals ⟨wore a veil of *netting*⟩ — see ¹NET 1
nettle *vb* to disturb the peace of mind of (someone) especially by repeated disagreeable acts ⟨don't *nettle* your brother while he's trying to do his homework⟩ — see IRRITATE 1
nettling *adj* causing annoyance ⟨you constant sniffling is extremely *nettling*⟩ — see ANNOYING
network *n* **1** a fabric made of strands loosely twisted, knotted, or woven together at regular intervals ⟨didn't like to embroider *network* as it tore so easily⟩ — see ¹NET 1
2 something made up of many interdependent or related parts ⟨a computer *network*⟩ — see SYSTEM 1
neurotic *n* a person judged to be legally or medically insane ⟨a fidgety *neurotic* constantly picking at her lip⟩ — see LUNATIC 1
neuter *vb* to remove the sex organs of ⟨Dad agreed to buy us the dog on the condition that we have her *neutered* so she couldn't have puppies⟩
synonyms alter, desex
related words castrate, emasculate, geld; spay; sterilize
neutral *adj* not favoring or joined to either side in a quarrel, contest, or war ⟨Sweden remained *neutral* during World War II, refusing to join either side of the conflict⟩
synonyms nonpartisan, unallied
related words autonomous, independent, sovereign, unaffiliated; nonbelligerent; individualistic; disinterested, evenhanded, fair, impartial, unbiased, uninfluenced, unprejudiced; bipartisan
near antonyms biased, partial, partisan, prejudiced, unfair; affiliated, associated, federated; belligerent
antonyms allied, confederate
neutrality *n* lack of favoritism toward one side or another ⟨his *neutrality* makes him a great person to judge which of us is right⟩ — see DETACHMENT 1
neutralize *vb* to balance with an equal force so as to make ineffective ⟨alkalies will *neutralize* acids⟩ — see OFFSET
neutralizer *n* a force or influence that makes an opposing force ineffective or less effective ⟨stricter laws acting as a *neutralizer* on violence⟩ — see COUNTERBALANCE
never *adv* **1** at no time ⟨I have *never* been out of the country⟩
synonyms ne'er
related words nevermore; not; infrequently, little, rarely, seldom
near antonyms eternally, everlastingly, evermore, invariably; frequently, often, recurrently, repeatedly
antonyms always, constantly, continuously, endlessly, ever, forever, perpetually
2 not in any degree, way, or under any condition ⟨though she turned down his offer of marriage twice, he was *never* convinced that she did not love him⟩
synonyms no, none, nothing, noway (*or* noways), nowise
related words nowhere near
phrases by no means, in no wise, nothing doing, on no account

near antonyms completely, extremely, full, fully, par excellence, right, very; altogether, exactly; somehow, someway (*also* someways); out

antonyms anyhow, anyway, anywise, at all, ever, half, however

nevertheless *adv* in spite of that ⟨I don't want to; *nevertheless*, I will do it because you asked me to⟩ — see HOWEVER

new *adj* **1** taking the place of one that came before ⟨after my bike was stolen, my scooter became my *new* mode of transportation⟩

synonyms backup, makeshift, substitute

related words alternate, alternative; different, other, separate; extra, spare; another, second; utility; successive; equivalent

near antonyms first, former; equal, identical, same; lasting, permanent

antonyms original

2 not known or experienced before ⟨Spanish was a *new* course of study for her⟩ ⟨the Americas were *new* lands for the European explorers⟩

synonyms fresh, novel, original, strange, unaccustomed, unfamiliar, unheard-of, unknown, unprecedented

related words innovative, unique; nontraditional, unconventional, untried, unused, unworn

near antonyms conventional, established, traditional, tried, tried-and-true; derivative, imitative

antonyms familiar, old, time-honored, tired

3 recently made and never used before ⟨that unique scent that is the telltale sign of a *new* car⟩

synonyms brand-new, spick-and-span (*or* spic-and-span), unused

related words clean, fresh, pristine, unspoiled; untouched; newfangled, new-fashioned; natural, raw, virgin, unprocessed, untreated, unworked

near antonyms dirty, soiled, spoiled, stale; aged, beat-up, old, worn

antonyms hand-me-down, second hand, used

4 made or become fresh in spirits or vigor ⟨a little rest made him a *new* man after the exhausting basketball game⟩

synonyms energized, freshened, invigorated, reanimated, recreated, reenergized, refreshed, regenerated, renewed, resuscitated, revived

related words animated, enlivened, exhilarated, jazzed (up); resurrected; rested, untired, unwearied

near antonyms tired, weary; dampened, deadened; emasculated, unmanned; demoralized, disheartened, dispirited

antonyms drained, enervated, exhausted, weakened

5 being or involving the latest methods, concepts, information, or styles ⟨*new* techniques in surgery⟩ — see MODERN

new *adv* not long ago ⟨*new*-mown grass⟩ — see NEWLY

newborn *n* a recently born person ⟨bought clothes that were too big for her *newborn* but would fit him in a few months⟩ — see BABY

newcomer *n* a person who is just starting out in a field of activity ⟨he's a *newcomer* to ice hockey⟩ — see BEGINNER

newfangled *adj* being or involving the latest methods, concepts, information, or styles ⟨got one of those *newfangled* espresso makers⟩ — see MODERN

new–fashioned *adj* being or involving the latest methods, concepts, information, or styles ⟨husbands staying at home with a family's children is a fairly *new-fashioned* idea⟩ — see MODERN

newly *adv* not long ago ⟨as soon as he left the room, his dog jumped on the *newly* made bed and rumpled it again⟩

synonyms freshly, just, late, lately, new, now, only, recently

related words latterly

phrases of late

near antonyms ago, before, earlier, early, erstwhile, formerly, previously; heretofore, hitherto

antonyms anciently

newness *n* the quality or appeal of being new ⟨the *newness* of having a driver's license was outlived by the frustration of having to pay auto insurance⟩ — see NOVELTY 1

news *n pl* a report of recent events or facts not previously known ⟨dropped by to give me the latest *news* about her daughter⟩

synonyms information, intelligence, item, story, tidings, word

related words announcement, communication, message; dope, lowdown, scoop, tidbit (*also* titbit), tip; gossip, rumor, tale, tattle; feedback

newspaper *n* a publication that appears at regular intervals ⟨liked to read the *newspaper* every morning⟩ — see JOURNAL

newsy *adj* having the style and content of everyday conversation ⟨a *newsy* local TV program⟩ — see CHATTY 1

next *adj* being the one that comes immediately after another ⟨my house is the *next* one⟩ ⟨turn at the *next* street, not this one⟩ ⟨she was *next* in line for concert tickets⟩

synonyms coming, ensuing, following, succeeding

related words consecutive, sequential, successive; posterior, subsequent; immediate; second

phrases on deck

near antonyms anterior, former; past; last

antonyms antecedent, foregoing, precedent, preceding, previous, prior

next–door *adj* not being distant in time, space, or significance ⟨a *next-door* neighbor⟩ — see CLOSE 2

next to *adv* very close to but not completely ⟨bought it for *next to* nothing⟩ — see ALMOST

next to *prep* close to ⟨enjoys living *next to* the ocean⟩ — see AROUND 1

nib *n* the jaws of a bird together with their hornlike covering ⟨a finch cracking seeds in its *nib*⟩ — see BEAK

nibble *n* a small piece or quantity of food ⟨I don't want a whole dessert, so can I just have a *nibble* of yours?⟩ — see MORSEL 1

nibble *vb* to crush or grind with the teeth ⟨*nibbling* crackers⟩ — see BITE (ON)

nice *adj* **1** following the established traditions of refined society and good taste ⟨had *nice* manners⟩ — see PROPER 1

2 giving pleasure or contentment to the mind or senses ⟨a cool glass of lemonade sure would be *nice*⟩ — see PLEASANT

3 hard to please ⟨she's far too *nice* to entertain⟩ — see FINICKY

4 having an easygoing and pleasing manner especially in social situations ⟨such a *nice* person⟩ — see AMIABLE

5 made or done with extreme care and accuracy ⟨folded the clothes in a very *nice* way⟩ — see FINE 2

nicely *adv* **1** in a pleasing way ⟨he's a *nicely* helpful child⟩ — see WELL 5

2 in a satisfactory way ⟨I'm doing *nicely*, and thanks for asking⟩ — see WELL 1

3 with good reason or courtesy ⟨excuse yourself *nicely* and you should be fine⟩ — see WELL 4

niceness *n* the state or quality of having a pleasant or agreeable manner in socializing with others ⟨his *niceness* makes him a great student to have in class⟩ — see AMIABILITY 1

nicety *n* a single piece of information ⟨knows all the *niceties* of octopus anatomy⟩ — see FACT 3

niche *n* **1** a hollowed-out space in a wall ⟨statues of various saints occupy the *niches* lining the abbey's many corridors⟩
synonyms alcove, nook, recess
related words corner, cranny, cubbyhole; cubicle; dent, indentation
2 the place where a plant or animal is usually or naturally found ⟨the platypus's *niche* is the waters of eastern Australia and Tasmania⟩ — see HOME 2

nick *n* a V-shaped cut usually on an edge or a surface ⟨I made a *nick* in the frame when I accidentally dropped it⟩ — see NOTCH 1

nicker *vb* to make the cry typical of a horse ⟨horses *nickering* in the barn⟩ — see NEIGH

nickname *n* a descriptive or familiar name given instead of or in addition to the one belonging to an individual ⟨his wavy hair earned him the *nickname* "Curly" early in life⟩
synonyms alias, cognomen, epithet, sobriquet (*also* soubriquet)
related words appellation, denomination, denotation, designation, handle, label, title; nom de plume, pen name, pseudonym

nifty *adj* of the very best kind ⟨that popcorn popper is *nifty*⟩ — see EXCELLENT

nifty *n* something very good of its kind ⟨that joke was a *nifty*⟩ — see JIM-DANDY

niggard *adj* giving or sharing as little as possible ⟨in Shakespeare's sonnet, the narrator begs his love to give him more praise "than *niggard* truth would willingly impart"⟩ — see STINGY 1

niggard *n* a mean grasping person who is usually stingy with money ⟨such a *niggard* that he refused to hand out candy at Halloween, saying it would cost too much money⟩ — see MISER

niggardly *adj* **1** giving or sharing as little as possible ⟨she's a *niggardly* woman, so don't expect a handout from her⟩ — see STINGY 1
2 less plentiful than what is normal, necessary, or desirable ⟨*niggardly* portions for dinner⟩ — see MEAGER

nigh *adj* not being distant in time, space, or significance ⟨the end is *nigh*⟩ — see CLOSE 2

nigh *adv* **1** at, within, or to a short distance or time ⟨have worked for them for *nigh* on ten years⟩ — see NEAR 1
2 very close to but not completely ⟨he has *nigh* completed his degree⟩ — see ALMOST

nigher *adj* being the less far of two ⟨the town has only two motels, and the one *nigher* to the train station is actually the better one⟩ — see NEAR 1

night *adj* of, relating to, or occurring in the night ⟨took a *night* flight out to the coast⟩ — see NOCTURNAL

night *n* **1** the time from sunset to sunrise when there is no visible sunlight ⟨loved to sit outside at *night* and watch the stars⟩
synonyms dark, darkness, nighttime
related words dusk, evening, gloaming, nightfall, twilight; midnight
near antonyms dawn, daybreak, forenoon, morning; high noon, midday, noon, noonday, noontide, noontime; afternoon

antonyms day, daytime
2 a time or place of little or no light ⟨snuck out of town under the cover of *night*⟩ — see DARK 1

nightclub *n* a bar or restaurant offering special nighttime entertainment (as music, dancing, or comedy acts) ⟨decided to go dancing at a local *nightclub* after the long dinner and movie⟩
synonyms cabaret, café (*also* cafe), disco, discotheque, roadhouse
related words barroom, pub [*chiefly British*], public house [*chiefly British*], saloon, tavern; dive, speakeasy; canteen

nightdress *n* a loose pullover garment worn in bed ⟨bought a long *nightdress* for the cold winter months⟩ — see NIGHTGOWN

nightfall *n* the time from when the sun begins to set to the onset of total darkness ⟨since you aren't taking a flashlight, make sure you're back at camp by *nightfall*⟩ — see DUSK 1

nightgown *n* a loose pullover garment worn in bed ⟨decided to buy a flannel *nightgown* instead of pajamas⟩
synonyms nightdress, nightshirt
related words nightclothes; pajamas, pj's, pyjamas [*chiefly British*]; nightcap; lingerie

nightly *adj* of, relating to, or occurring in the night ⟨the elderly couple's *nightly* walk around the neighborhood⟩ — see NOCTURNAL

nightmare *n* **1** a series of often striking pictures created by the imagination during sleep ⟨the child woke up from the terrible *nightmare* sweating and crying⟩ — see DREAM 1
2 a situation or state that causes great suffering and unhappiness ⟨that 20-page exam was a *nightmare*⟩ — see HELL 2

nightmarish *adj* extremely disturbing or repellent ⟨a photographic exhibit of *nightmarish* images from the wars of the 20th century⟩ — see HORRIBLE 1

nightshirt *n* a loose pullover garment worn in bed ⟨preferred *nightshirts* over pajama sets⟩ — see NIGHTGOWN

nightstick *n* a heavy rigid stick used as a weapon or for punishment ⟨police officers fitted out with *nightsticks* and handcuffs⟩ — see CLUB 1

nighttime *adj* of, relating to, or occurring in the night ⟨warnings about protecting household pets from *nighttime* predators in the outer reaches of suburbia⟩ — see NOCTURNAL

nighttime *n* the time from sunset to sunrise when there is no visible sunlight ⟨before electricity, gas lamps were used for illumination during the *nighttime*⟩ — see NIGHT 1

nil *n* the numerical symbol 0 or the absence of number or quantity represented by it ⟨the difference in the audio performance of those two CD players is *nil*⟩ — see ZERO 1

nimble *adj* **1** having or showing quickness of mind ⟨possessing a *nimble* wit, he always has a cutting comeback for any intended insult thrown his way⟩ — see INTELLIGENT 1
2 moving easily ⟨her *nimble* fingers make knitting look so easy⟩ — see GRACEFUL 1

nimbleness *n* ease and grace in physical activity ⟨that dance routine requires a certain amount of *nimbleness* and flexibility⟩ — see DEXTERITY 2

nincompoop *n* **1** a person who lacks good sense or judgment ⟨quit acting like a *nincompoop*, because I know you're smarter than that⟩ — see FOOL 1
2 a stupid person ⟨who wants a *nincompoop* as a lab partner?⟩ — see IDIOT

ninny *n* **1** a person who lacks good sense or judgment ⟨only a *ninny* would try to cross a swollen, raging river⟩ — see FOOL 1

2 a stupid person ⟨was such a *ninny* that he kept forgetting my name, even though I was wearing a name tag⟩ — see IDIOT

¹nip *n* **1** a very small amount ⟨I'll have just a *nip* of your sandwich⟩ — see PARTICLE 1

2 an uncomfortable degree of coolness ⟨there's a *nip* in the air today⟩ — see CHILL

²nip *n* the portion of a serving of a beverage that is swallowed at one time ⟨give me just a *nip* of milk to help me swallow this pill⟩ — see DRINK 2

nip *vb* **1** to make (as hair) shorter with or as if with the use of shears ⟨I'm just going to *nip* these hedges, and then I'll be done with the work outside⟩ — see CLIP

2 to squeeze tightly between two surfaces, edges, or points ⟨the puppy *nipped* her hand while playing⟩ — see PINCH 1

3 to take (something) without right and with an intent to keep ⟨that guy *nipped* my wallet from the restaurant table when I turned away⟩ — see STEAL 1

nip and tuck *adj* showing little difference in the standing of the competitors ⟨the race was *nip and tuck* to the very end, with the judges needing to look at photos of the finish three times⟩ — see CLOSE 3

nipper *n* a male person who has not yet reached adulthood ⟨the little *nipper* can't quite reach the cabinet⟩ — see BOY

nipping *adj* having a low or subnormal temperature ⟨a *nipping* and numbing wind coming off the lake⟩ — see COLD 1

nippy *adj* **1** having a low or subnormal temperature ⟨bring a jacket, as it's a little *nippy* outside⟩ — see COLD 1

2 having a powerfully stimulating odor or flavor ⟨blue cheese is a little too *nippy* for my taste⟩ — see SHARP 3

3 moving, proceeding, or acting with great speed ⟨racing around the neighborhood on a *nippy* scooter⟩ — see FAST 1

4 uncomfortably cool ⟨a *nippy* wind that chilled parade watchers to the bone⟩ — see CHILLY 1

nitpick *vb* to make often peevish criticisms or objections about matters that are minor, unimportant, or irrelevant ⟨he *nitpicks* about everything: from how she puts the plates away to how she files the bills⟩ — see QUIBBLE

nitpicker *n* a person given to harsh judgments and to finding faults ⟨a tiresome *nitpicker* who seems to think that I can't do anything right⟩ — see CRITIC 1

nitwit *n* **1** a person who lacks good sense or judgment ⟨don't let a *nitwit*—wear a seatbelt!⟩ — see FOOL 1

2 a stupid person ⟨an absolute *nitwit* as far as geography is concerned⟩ — see IDIOT

no *interj* how surprising, doubtful, or unbelievable ⟨*no* —you can't possibly mean that I failed that test! I studied for days!⟩

synonyms ah, aha, fie, indeed, pshaw, well, what, why

related words gee, ha, hello, hey, lo, oh; fiddlesticks, phooey, pooh; there; oops, ugh; egad, gad, the deuce, the devil, the dickens, zounds

no *adv* **1** not in any degree, way, or under any condition ⟨this cake is *no* better than the last one we made⟩ — see NEVER 2

2 certainly not ⟨in *no* uncertain terms we were told to leave⟩ — see HARDLY 2

no *n* **1** a vote or decision against something ⟨though I wanted spaghetti for dinner, the consensus was a decisive *no*⟩

synonyms nay, negative

related words con; blackball, veto; denial, negation, refusal

near antonyms pro; acceptance, approval, grace

antonyms positive, yea, yes

2 an unwillingness to grant something asked for ⟨gave him a *no* when he asked her to dance⟩ — see DENIAL 1

nobility *n* impressiveness of beauty on a large scale ⟨was struck by the *nobility* of such an old, distinguished castle⟩ — see MAGNIFICENCE

noble *adj* **1** of high birth, rank, or station ⟨despite his *noble* background, the prince is known for his unpretentious way with common people⟩

synonyms aristocratic, genteel, gentle, grand, highborn, patrician, upper-class, wellborn

related words high, lofty, superior; elevated, ennobled, exalted; gentlemanly, kingly, knightly, ladylike, lordly, princely, queenly, regal, royal; high-level, senior

near antonyms inferior, knavish; bastard, illegitimate; ordinary, plain; abased, degraded; junior, subordinate

antonyms baseborn, common, humble, ignoble, low, lower-class, lowly, mean, plebeian

2 having, characterized by, or arising from a dignified and generous nature ⟨the factory owner had a kind, *noble* disposition that showed in his unstinting generosity toward the poor⟩ ⟨our country was founded on the *noble* ideas that are put forth in the founding fathers' writings⟩

synonyms chivalrous, elevated, gallant, great, greathearted, high, high-minded, lofty, lordly, magnanimous, sublime

related words ennobled, exalted, glorified; heroic, honorable, venerable, worthy; knightly, princely, regal; moving, inspiring, uplifting; august, magnificent, majestic

near antonyms sordid, squalid, vile, wretched; abominable, contemptible, despicable, detestable, hateful, offensive, repulsive, ugly; dastardly, dirty, lousy, sorry; little, mean, narrow, small-minded; degrading, discreditable, humiliating, ignominious; coarse, crude, vulgar

antonyms base, debased, degenerate, degraded, ignoble, low

3 following the accepted rules of moral conduct ⟨his *noble* behavior when he was being unjustly attacked by his political opponents⟩ — see HONORABLE 1

4 large and impressive in size, grandeur, extent, or conception ⟨Peter the Great's plan to build for Russia a capital city as *noble* as any in Europe⟩ — see GRAND 1

5 of the very best kind ⟨a *noble* racehorse⟩ — see EXCELLENT

6 standing above others in rank, importance, or achievement ⟨a *noble* professor known internationally for his medical research⟩ — see EMINENT

noble *n* a man of high birth or social position ⟨men like Jefferson and Washington were the *nobles* of colonial Virginia⟩ — see GENTLEMAN 1

nobleman *n* a man of high birth or social position ⟨his impeccable manners immediately marked him as a *nobleman*⟩ — see GENTLEMAN 1

nobleness *n* impressiveness of beauty on a large scale ⟨the pictures just don't convey the breathtaking *nobleness* of St. Peter's basilica in Rome⟩ — see MAGNIFICENCE

noblewoman *n* a woman of high birth or social position ⟨traditionally, *noblewomen*—whether they are titled or not—have served as great patronesses of the arts⟩ — see GENTLEWOMAN

nobly *adv* in a manner befitting a person of the highest character and ideals ⟨civil rights activists *nobly* striving for justice and equality⟩ — see GREATLY 1

nobody *n* a person of no importance or influence ⟨she felt like a *nobody* until she won the National Spelling Bee⟩

  synonyms lightweight, nonentity, nothing, shrimp, twerp, whippersnapper, zero, zilch

  related words least; inferior, mediocrity, obscurity; figurehead, puppet

  near antonyms chief, head, lead, leader; celebrity, luminary, notable, personality, star, superstar; authority, superior; great power, party, power

  antonyms big shot, bigwig, eminence, figure, magnate, nabob, personage, somebody, VIP

nobody *pron* no person ⟨there is *nobody* home⟩ ⟨*nobody* wants to clean up that mess⟩

  synonyms none, no one

  near antonyms anybody, anyone; somebody, someone

  antonyms everybody, everyone

nocturnal *adj* of, relating to, or occurring in the night ⟨he bought a new telescope so he could pursue his favorite *nocturnal* hobby of astronomy⟩

  synonyms night, nightly, nighttime

  related words late; midnight, overnight

  near antonyms noon

  antonyms daily, diurnal

nod *vb* to make short up-and-down movements ⟨though she couldn't see the rain, she knew it had started because she could see the flowers *nod* as raindrops hit them⟩

  synonyms bob, bobble, jog, jounce, pump, seesaw

  related words jerk, jiggle, shake, wiggle, wobble; oscillate, rock, sway, swing, undulate; drop, duck

nodding *adj* bending downward or forward ⟨some students, with *nodding* heads, were falling asleep during the boring lecture⟩

  synonyms bowed, bowing, declined, declining, descendant (*or* descendent), descending, drooping, droopy, hanging, hung (*also* hanged), inclining, pendulous, sagging, stooping

  related words floppy, limp; dangling, falling, pendent (*or* pendant); suspended; dipping, sinking, slumping

  near antonyms erect, inflexible, rigid, stiff; elevated, raised, upraised

  antonyms unbending, upright

noddle *n* the upper or front part of the body that contains the brain, the major sense organs, and the mouth ⟨tapped his *noddle* to indicate he was thinking⟩ — see HEAD 1

node *n* a small rounded mass of swollen tissue ⟨examined the *node* on my knee before deciding it was the result of arthritis⟩ — see BUMP 1

nodule *n* a small rounded mass of swollen tissue ⟨a *nodule* on the leaf indicated that a worm had laid eggs there⟩ — see BUMP 1

Noel *n* the season celebrating Christmas ⟨for *Noel* the town puts on a festival of indoor and outdoor events, including strolling carolers in Victorian dress⟩ — see YULETIDE

noggin *n* the upper or front part of the body that contains the brain, the major sense organs, and the mouth ⟨watch the lintel above the door, unless you want to bang your *noggin*⟩ — see HEAD 1

no-good *adj* having no usefulness ⟨that *no-good* chair should be thrown away⟩ — see WORTHLESS

no-good *n* a mean, evil, or unprincipled person ⟨neighbors remembered the killer as having been an utter *no-good* since childhood⟩ — see VILLAIN

noise *n* **1** loud, confused, and usually unharmonious sound ⟨the blaring *noise* of traffic on Fifth Avenue made casual conversation impossible⟩

  synonyms bluster, cacophony, clamor, clangor, din, discordance, racket, roar

  related words discord, dissonance; commotion, furor, hubbub, hullabaloo, hurly-burly, rumpus, tumult, uproar; babel; clatter, jangle; bang, blast, boom, clap, crack, crash

  near antonyms calm, hush, lull; quietude, serenity, tranquillity (*or* tranquility)

  antonyms quiet, silence, still, stillness

2 a violent shouting ⟨keep the *noise* down, you kids!⟩ — see CLAMOR 1

noise (about) *vb* to make (as a piece of information) the subject of common talk without any authority or confirmation of accuracy ⟨we *noised about* her expulsion until a teacher set the record straight and informed us that the girl had been suspended⟩ — see RUMOR

noiseless *adj* mostly or entirely without sound ⟨tried to remain *noiseless* as he crept up the stairs⟩ — see SILENT 3

noisome *adj* **1** bad for the well-being of the body ⟨it's no fun having asthma and living in an area with *noisome* smog⟩ — see UNHEALTHY 1

2 causing intense displeasure, disgust, or resentment ⟨a *noisome* remark about my weight that stuck with me for days⟩ — see OFFENSIVE 1

3 having an unpleasant smell ⟨the *noisome* air of the area that was downwind of the dog food factory⟩ — see MALODOROUS

noisy *adj* **1** making loud, confused, and usually unharmonious sounds ⟨the *noisy* crowd moved up the street, shouting louder as they went along⟩

  synonyms clangorous, dinning, discordant

  related words cacophonous, dissonant; resounding, sonorous; clamorous, uproarious; blatant, obstreperous, strident, vociferous; blaring, booming, brassy, brazen, clanging, earsplitting

  near antonyms calm, hushed

  antonyms noiseless, quiet, silent, soundless, still

2 full of or characterized by the presence of noise ⟨the crowded auditorium was *noisy*, packed with excited theatergoers eager for the show to start⟩ ⟨the manufacturing company was a *noisy* place, so we wore ear protection while we toured⟩

  synonyms clamorous, clangorous, clattering, clattery, resounding

  related words resonant, sonorous; buzzing, humming, murmuring; blustery, boisterous, raucous, rip-roaring, roaring, roistering, romping, rowdy; tumultuous, uproarious, woolly (*also* wooly); obstreperous, vociferous

  near antonyms calm, peaceful, serene, tranquil

  antonyms hushed, noiseless, quiet, silent, soundless, stilled, stilly

nomad *or* **nomadic** *adj* traveling from place to place ⟨*nomad* caravans of Bedouins⟩ ⟨a *nomadic* people⟩ — see ITINERANT

nomad *n* a person who roams about without a fixed route or destination ⟨after college she became quite the *nomad*, backpacking through Europe with no particular destination⟩

  synonyms drifter, gadabout, rambler, roamer, rover, stroller, vagabond, wanderer, wayfarer *related words* laggard, straggler; lingerer, loiterer, sojourner; bum, hobo, tramp; sightseer, traveler (*or* traveller); transient, vagrant; ambler, saunterer

near antonyms homebody; denizen, dweller, habitant, inhabitant, resident, settler

nominal *adj* **1** being something in name or form only ⟨he was the *nominal* head of state—everyone knew the country was actually run by one of his advisers⟩

synonyms formal, paper, titular

related words so-called; phantom, virtual

near antonyms actual, real, true

2 so small or unimportant as to warrant little or no attention ⟨when you pay $400 for an airline ticket, a ticketing fee of five dollars seems *nominal*⟩ — see NEGLIGIBLE 1

nominally *adv* in a very small quantity or degree ⟨although the more expensive TV set is *nominally* better than the other, it's not worth the big difference in price⟩ — see LITTLE 1

nonaction *n* lack of action or activity ⟨your *nonaction* on this matter will result in an arrest warrant⟩ — see INACTION

nonbinding *adj* having no legal or binding force ⟨a verbal agreement is considered *nonbinding* in this state⟩ — see NULL 1

nonchalance *n* lack of interest or concern ⟨with their usual *nonchalance* they arrived at the wedding ceremony half an hour late⟩ — see INDIFFERENCE

nonchalant *adj* having or showing a lack of interest or concern ⟨you shouldn't be so *nonchalant* about something that is so important to your parents⟩ — see INDIFFERENT 1

noncombustible *adj* incapable of being burned ⟨firefighting gear is made of *noncombustible* material⟩ — see INCOMBUSTIBLE

nonconflicting *adj* not having or showing any apparent conflict ⟨there are several *nonconflicting* reports on the effectiveness of the new drug⟩ — see CONSISTENT

nonconformist *adj* deviating from commonly accepted beliefs or practices ⟨a cattle-ranching family that took some time in getting used to their daughter's *nonconformist* adoption of vegetarianism⟩ — see HERETICAL

nonconformist *n* **1** a person who does not conform to generally accepted standards or customs ⟨always the *nonconformist*, she insisted on wearing red on St. Patrick's Day and not green like everyone else⟩

synonyms bohemian, deviant, individualist, loner, lone wolf, maverick

related words character, codger, crackbrain, crackpot, crank, eccentric, freak, kook, nut, oddball, screwball, weirdo; misfit, outsider; anomaly

near antonyms adherent, follower, supporter; sheep

antonyms conformer, conformist

2 a person who believes or teaches something opposed to accepted beliefs ⟨a *nonconformist* who was excommunicated from her church for her teachings⟩ — see HERETIC

nonconformity *n* departure from a generally accepted theory, opinion, or practice ⟨an artistic movement that doesn't tolerate *nonconformity*⟩ — see HERESY

nonconventional *adj* not bound by traditional ways or beliefs ⟨his *nonconventional* cures were the subject of some controversy⟩ — see LIBERAL 1

none *adv* **1** certainly not ⟨your help comes *none* too soon⟩ — see HARDLY 2

2 not in any degree, way, or under any condition ⟨I'll switch his mug with mine, and he'll be *none* the wiser⟩ — see NEVER 2

none *pron* no person ⟨*none* will come to the party⟩ — see NOBODY

nonelective *adj* forcing one's compliance or participation by or as if by law ⟨language arts, math, and science are *nonelective* subjects taken by all students at the school⟩ — see MANDATORY

nonentity *n* a person of no importance or influence ⟨was so quiet he was almost a *nonentity* at the meeting⟩ — see NOBODY

nonessential *adj* not needed by the circumstances or to accomplish an end ⟨money's tight, so we'll have to skip *nonessential* purchases⟩ — see UNNECESSARY

nonetheless *adv* in spite of that ⟨sometimes you can be a real jerk, but I like you *nonetheless*⟩ — see HOWEVER

nonexistent *adj* not present or in evidence ⟨our perennially *nonexistent* principal is, once again, not here today⟩ — see ABSENT 2

nonfictional *adj* restricted to or based on fact ⟨a *nonfictional* account of a disastrous ascent of Mount Everest⟩ — see FACTUAL 1

nonflammable *adj* incapable of being burned ⟨children's pajamas made of *nonflammable* fabric⟩ — see INCOMBUSTIBLE

nonfunctional *adj* not being in working order ⟨that gas pump is *nonfunctional*, which is the reason for the plastic bag over the nozzle⟩ — see INOPERABLE 1

nonfunctioning *adj* not being in working order ⟨the Ferris wheel is *nonfunctioning* at the moment⟩ — see INOPERABLE 1

noninflammable *adj* incapable of being burned ⟨*noninflammable* materials used for construction of the interior of the nightclub⟩ — see INCOMBUSTIBLE

nonliterary *adj* used in or suitable for speech and not formal writing ⟨slang words are usually considered *nonliterary*⟩ — see COLLOQUIAL 1

nonliterate *adj* lacking in education or the knowledge gained from books ⟨an organization helping *nonliterate* adults improve their reading skills⟩ — see IGNORANT 1

nonmaterial *adj* not composed of matter ⟨Newton's laws explain the effects of *nonmaterial* forces on bodies⟩ — see IMMATERIAL 1

nonmotile *adj* incapable of moving or being moved ⟨an examination of the slides of *nonmotile* cells⟩ — see IMMOVABLE 1

nonmoving *adj* **1** fixed in a place or position ⟨the casino is actually in a *nonmoving* vessel permanently docked on the city's waterfront⟩ — see STATIONARY 1

2 incapable of moving or being moved ⟨all of the machine's *nonmoving* parts⟩ — see IMMOVABLE 1

nonnative *adj* being, relating to, or characteristic of a country other than one's own ⟨*nonnative* customs that made the recent immigrants stand out in their new country⟩ — see FOREIGN 1

nonnative *n* a person who is not native to or known to a community ⟨the problems encountered by a *nonnative* after moving into a close-knit community⟩ — see STRANGER

no–nonsense *adj* not joking or playful in mood or manner ⟨a *no-nonsense* gymnastics coach⟩ — see SERIOUS 1

nonoperating *adj* not being in working order ⟨fixed all *nonoperating* parts⟩ — see INOPERABLE 1

nonorthodox *adj* **1** deviating from commonly accepted beliefs or practices ⟨one of the few colonies to tolerate *nonorthodox* religious beliefs⟩ — see HERETICAL

2 not bound by traditional ways or beliefs ⟨a *nonorthodox* approach to teaching music⟩ — see LIBERAL 1

nonpareil *adj* having no equal or rival for excellence or desirability ⟨the *nonpareil* beauty of Helen of Troy⟩ — see ONLY 1

nonpareil *n* someone of such unequaled perfection as to deserve imitation ⟨among the knights of the Round Table, Galahad stood alone as the *nonpareil* of nobility and selflessness⟩ — see IDEAL 1

nonpartisan *adj* 1 marked by justice, honesty, and freedom from bias ⟨made a *nonpartisan* decision⟩ — see FAIR 2

2 not favoring or joined to either side in a quarrel, contest, or war ⟨*nonpartisan* observers who were there to ensure a fair election⟩ — see NEUTRAL

nonphysical *adj* not composed of matter ⟨ghosts are generally thought to be *nonphysical* in nature⟩ — see IMMATERIAL 1

nonplus *vb* to throw into a state of self-conscious distress ⟨I was *nonplussed* by his openly expressed admiration of me⟩ — see EMBARRASS 1

nonpractical *adj* not capable of being put to use or account ⟨an inventor who seemed to be able to create only *nonpractical* gadgets⟩ — see IMPRACTICAL

nonprofessional *adj* lacking or showing a lack of expert skill ⟨didn't like the *nonprofessional* photos they did for her⟩ — see AMATEURISH

nonpublic *adj* not known or meant to be known by the general populace ⟨school records are regarded as *nonpublic* information⟩ — see PRIVATE 1

nonrational *adj* not using or following good reasoning ⟨was so upset that he was completely *nonrational* for a moment⟩ — see ILLOGICAL

nonrealistic *adj* using elements of form (as color, line, or texture) with little or no attempt at creating a realistic picture ⟨*nonrealistic* paintings⟩ — see ABSTRACT 2

nonreligious *adj* 1 lacking religious emotions, principles, or practices ⟨grew up in a *nonreligious* family⟩ — see IRRELIGIOUS

2 not involving religion or religious matters ⟨*nonreligious* cards expressing good wishes for the holiday season⟩ — see PROFANE 1

nonresistant *adj* receiving or enduring without offering resistance ⟨the *nonresistant* arrest of most of the demonstrators⟩ — see PASSIVE

nonsense *n* 1 language, behavior, or ideas that are absurd and contrary to good sense ⟨told him to stop his mischievous *nonsense* and start behaving properly⟩ ⟨the discussion about building a time machine was complete *nonsense*⟩ ⟨a hundred years ago, the idea that man could walk on the moon was regarded as impractical *nonsense*⟩

synonyms bunk, claptrap, drivel, fiddlesticks, folly, foolishness, fudge, hogwash, humbug, humbuggery, piffle, rot, senselessness, silliness, slush, stupidity, trash

related words absurdity, asininity, fatuity, foolery, idiocy, imbecility, inanity, insanity, lunacy; absurdness, craziness, foolishness, madness, senselessness, witlessness; monkeyshines, shenanigans, tomfoolery; gas, hot air, jazz, moonshine, rigmarole, twaddle; double-talk

near antonyms levelheadedness, rationality, reasonability, reasonableness, sensibleness; common sense, horse sense, sense; discernment, judgment (*or* judgement), wisdom

2 unintelligible or meaningless talk ⟨when you talk with your mouth full of food, everything just comes out as *nonsense*⟩ — see GIBBERISH

nonsensical *adj* 1 conceived or made without regard for reason or reality ⟨the idea that we can stop global warming by opening all of the world's refrigerators at once is *nonsensical* at best⟩ — see FANTASTIC 1

2 showing or marked by a lack of good sense or judgment ⟨your plan to lose weight through total starvation is completely *nonsensical*⟩ — see FOOLISH 1

nonsensicalness *n* lack of good sense or judgment ⟨the *nonsensicalness* of your attempt to swim across the river is beyond words⟩ — see FOOLISHNESS 1

nonspecific *adj* relating to the main elements and not to specific details ⟨his criticism of the picture is fairly *nonspecific*⟩ — see GENERAL 2

nonsuccess *n* a falling short of one's goals ⟨although not a total dud, the movie is regarded by the studio as a *nonsuccess*, to say the least⟩ — see FAILURE 2

nontraditional *adj* not bound by traditional ways or beliefs ⟨a *nontraditional* wedding⟩ — see LIBERAL 1

nonvalid *adj* 1 having no legal or binding force ⟨failure to inform the suspect of his rights rendered his confession *nonvalid*⟩ — see NULL 1

2 having no basis in reason or fact ⟨a *nonvalid* theory that most scientists rejected long ago⟩ — see GROUNDLESS

nonviolent *adj* not involving violence or force ⟨*nonviolent* protests⟩ — see PEACEFUL 2

nook *n* a hollowed-out space in a wall ⟨books filled every *nook* in the house⟩ — see NICHE 1

noon *n* the middle of the day ⟨we eat a big lunch around *noon* then have dinner in the evening⟩

synonyms high noon, midday, noonday, noontide, noontime

related words forenoon, morning; afternoon, evening

noonday *n* the middle of the day ⟨in the tropics the *noonday* heat can be overwhelming⟩ — see NOON

no one *pron* no person ⟨*no one* is home⟩ — see NOBODY

noontide *n* the middle of the day ⟨we like to work off lunch with a *noontide* ramble⟩ — see NOON

noontime *n* the middle of the day ⟨listening to the radio at *noontime* for news updates⟩ — see NOON

norm *n* what is typical of a group, class, or series ⟨sales figures that are within the *norm* of a store of that size⟩ — see AVERAGE

normal *adj* 1 being of the type that is encountered in the normal course of events ⟨just had a *normal* school day⟩ — see ORDINARY 1

2 having full use of one's mind and control over one's actions ⟨if you run around screaming like that, no one will think you are *normal*⟩ — see SANE

3 having or showing the qualities associated with the members of a particular group or kind ⟨she has *normal* reading abilities for a child her age⟩ — see TYPICAL 1

normal *n* what is typical of a group, class, or series ⟨a temperature chart showing the *normals* and extremes for various regions⟩ — see AVERAGE

normalcy *n* the state or fact of being the way things usually are ⟨a soldier longing for the *normalcy* of peacetime life⟩ — see NORMALITY

normality *n* the state or fact of being the way things usually are ⟨the county slowly has returned to *normality* after a week of flash flooding⟩

synonyms normalcy, status quo

related words groove, routine, rut; currency, prevalence; conventionality; orderliness, peace

near antonyms irregularity, uncommonness, unusualness; disorderliness, disruptiveness; disruption, disturbance; anomalousness, deviance; exceptionalness, extraordinariness, noteworthiness, remarkableness; unconventionality *antonyms* abnormality

normalize *vb* to make agree with a single established standard or model ⟨English spelling wasn't *normalized* until printed books became common⟩ — see STANDARDIZE

normally *adv* according to the usual course of things ⟨*normally* I go home after school, but today I'll take the bus to Molly's house⟩ — see NATURALLY 2

nose *vb* **1** to become aware of by means of the sense organs in the nose ⟨could *nose* the garbage from across the street⟩ — see SMELL 1
2 to interest oneself in what is not one's concern ⟨a neighbor who likes to *nose* around and discover everyone's secrets⟩ — see INTERFERE

nosedive *n* the act or process of going to a lower level or altitude ⟨the pilot struggled to pull his plane out of a *nosedive*⟩ — see DESCENT 1

nose–dive *vb* to go to a lower level ⟨prices on just about everything *nose-dived* right after the holidays⟩ — see DROP 2

nosegay *n* a bunch of flowers ⟨a procession of bridesmaids holding small *nosegays*⟩ — see BOUQUET 1

nosiness *n* an eager desire to find out about things that are often none of one's business ⟨your annoying *nosiness* isn't going to win you any friends⟩ — see CURIOSITY 1

nosy *or* **nosey** *adj* **1** interested in what is not one's own business ⟨a *nosy* raccoon rummaging through the garbage⟩ — see CURIOUS 1
2 thrusting oneself where one is not welcome or invited ⟨a *nosy* coworker sat down right next to us as we were having an unmistakably private conversation⟩ — see INTRUSIVE

notable *adj* standing above others in rank, importance, or achievement ⟨a panel made up of *notable* authorities on the viral research⟩ — see EMINENT

notable *n* a person who is widely known and usually much talked about ⟨directors, actors, and other *notables* at the annual gathering for the Academy Awards⟩ — see CELEBRITY 1

notation *n* a usually brief written reminder ⟨he had scribbled his *notation* so quickly I couldn't read it⟩ — see NOTE 1

notch *n* **1** a V-shaped cut usually on an edge or a surface ⟨lifted up the fence rail and put it in the *notch* cut into the post⟩
synonyms chip, hack, indentation, kerf, nick
related words punch; groove, score; slit, slot
2 a narrow opening between hillsides or mountains that can be used for passage ⟨try to get through the *notch* before the storm blows in⟩ — see CANYON
3 an individual part of a process, series, or ranking ⟨sales for the album increased, and it moved up another *notch* on the music charts⟩ — see DEGREE 1

note *n* **1** a usually brief written reminder ⟨I'll make a *note* to myself so I don't forget to pick up some milk on the way home⟩
synonyms memo, memorandum, notation
related words memoir, minutes, report; line; document, writing
2 a message on paper from one person or group to another ⟨write a friendly *note* to the neighbors asking them to keep the noise down⟩ — see LETTER
3 a natural vocal sound made by an animal ⟨can you distinguish between the *notes* of the whippoorwill and the mockingbird?⟩ — see CALL 1
4 a piece of printed paper used as money ⟨will you be paying in coins or *notes*?⟩ — see ¹BILL 2

5 a special quality or impression associated with something ⟨spoke with a *note* of irritation in her voice⟩ — see AURA
6 overall quality as seen or judged by people in general ⟨a writer of *note* among readers of modern poetry⟩ — see REPUTATION
7 a briefly expressed opinion ⟨let me read a few *notes* I jotted down while you were auditioning⟩ — see REMARK

note *vb* **1** to make a statement of one's opinion ⟨I'd like to *note* that I don't care for that tone of voice⟩ — see REMARK 1
2 to make a written note of ⟨a waitress *noting* our orders⟩ — see RECORD 1
3 to make note of (something) through the use of one's eyes ⟨*note* the artist's rendering of the trees, how their leaves seem to dance in the wind⟩ — see SEE 1
4 to make reference to or speak about briefly but specifically ⟨the lecturer *noted* several sources where listeners could go for further information⟩ — see MENTION 1
5 to take notice of and be guided by ⟨please *note* that the office will be closed tomorrow⟩ — see HEED 1

noted *adj* widely known ⟨a *noted* Broadway actor⟩ — see FAMOUS

notepad *n* a number of sheets of writing paper glued together at one edge ⟨grabbed a new *notepad* for each class's notes⟩ — see PAD 1

noteworthiness *n* the fact or state of being above others in rank or importance ⟨her *noteworthiness* as a neurosurgeon gets her many referrals from doctors around the country⟩ — see EMINENCE 1

noteworthy *adj* standing above others in rank, importance, or achievement ⟨*noteworthy* contributions to the field of genetics⟩ — see EMINENT

nothing *adv* not in any degree, way, or under any condition ⟨*nothing* daunted by the poor reception his first novel received, he proceeded to write another one⟩ — see NEVER 2

nothing *n* **1** a person of no importance or influence ⟨his friends couldn't understand why he'd want to marry a girl who was an obvious *nothing*⟩ — see NOBODY
2 something of little importance ⟨you're always worrying about *nothing*⟩ — see TRIFLE
3 the numerical symbol 0 or the absence of number or quantity represented by it ⟨two minus two equals *nothing*⟩ — see ZERO 1

notice *n* **1** a published statement informing the public of a matter of general interest ⟨a public safety *notice* regarding the need for a smoke detector in the home⟩ — see ANNOUNCEMENT
2 a state of being aware ⟨this malicious note will be brought to the *notice* of the principal⟩ — see ATTENTION 2
3 a written communication giving information or directions ⟨received a *notice* of promotion from the head of the company⟩ — see MEMORANDUM 1
4 an essay evaluating or analyzing something ⟨avidly reads the latest theater *notices* in the paper⟩ — see CRITICISM
5 the act or an instance of telling beforehand of danger or risk ⟨in the event of a terrorist threat, the building will be evacuated with little *notice* beforehand⟩ — see WARNING 1

notice *vb* **1** to make note of (something) through the use of one's eyes ⟨did you *notice* what she was wearing?⟩ — see SEE 1

2 to make reference to or speak about briefly but specifically ⟨briefly *noticed* in his lecture the author's first published work⟩ — see MENTION 1

noticeable *adj* likely to attract attention ⟨the stain on the new carpet was quite *noticeable,* and nothing we did made it any lighter⟩

synonyms arresting, bold, catchy, conspicuous, dramatic, emphatic, eye-catching, flamboyant, marked, prominent, pronounced, remarkable, showy, splashy, striking

related words detectable, discernible, observable, perceptible, visible; outstanding, salient; distinguished, eminent, impressive, notable, noteworthy; highlighted, spotlighted; flagrant, glaring, screaming; flashy, garish, gaudy, glitzy, jazzy, loud, meretricious, swank (*or* swanky), tawdry; high-falutin, ostentatious, pretentious; extravagant, fancy, florid, glittery, spectacular; opulent, ornate, overdone, overwrought; absorbing, engrossing, enthralling, fascinating, interesting, riveting

near antonyms subtle; concealed, hidden, shrouded; dim, faint, obscure; insignificant, undistinguished, unimportant; modest, unaffected, unassuming, unpretentious; conservative, plain, quiet, simple, unaffected, understated; muted, restrained, subdued, subtle, toned-down

antonyms inconspicuous, unemphatic, unnoticeable, unobtrusive, unremarkable

notification *n* a published statement informing the public of a matter of general interest ⟨a *notification* posted by the health board that its inspectors had cited the restaurant for several violations⟩ — see ANNOUNCEMENT

notion *n* **1 notions** *pl* small useful items ⟨the fabric store had a wide variety of thread, pins, buttons, and other *notions*⟩

synonyms novelties, odds and ends, sundries

related words bauble(s), bric-a-brac, gewgaw(s), knick-knack(s), trinket(s); hodgepodge, miscellany, variety

2 a sudden impulsive and apparently unmotivated idea or action ⟨I have a *notion* to go roller-skating this afternoon⟩ — see WHIM

3 an idea that is believed to be true or valid without positive knowledge ⟨has this naive *notion* that most people are basically honest⟩ — see OPINION 1

4 something imagined or pictured in the mind ⟨that modernistic building does not match my *notion* of what a country cottage should look like⟩ — see IDEA

notoriety *n* the fact or state of being known to the public ⟨a lawyer of *notoriety* for the huge awards he's won in medical malpractice cases⟩ — see FAME

notorious *adj* **1** not respectable ⟨a *notorious* criminal mastermind⟩ — see DISREPUTABLE

2 widely known ⟨a book signing for a *notorious* author of mystery novels⟩ — see FAMOUS

notwithstanding *adv* in spite of that ⟨you're rather late getting here, but you're welcome to join us for dinner *notwithstanding*⟩ — see HOWEVER

notwithstanding *prep* without being prevented by ⟨we went to see the show, my objections *notwithstanding*⟩ — see DESPITE

nourish *vb* **1** to help the growth or development of ⟨wanted to *nourish* her students' love of art⟩ — see FOSTER 1

2 to supply with nourishment ⟨we've always been *nourished* by such good food when staying at their house⟩ — see SUSTAIN 1

nourishing *adj* providing the substances necessary for health and bodily growth ⟨milk should be part of a *nourishing* breakfast⟩ — see NUTRITIOUS

novel *adj* not known or experienced before ⟨that's a *novel* idea for a TV series⟩ — see NEW 2

novelette *n* a work with imaginary characters and events that is shorter and usually less complex than a novel ⟨bought a collection of his novels and *novelettes*⟩ — see STORY 1

novella *n* a work with imaginary characters and events that is shorter and usually less complex than a novel ⟨pressed for time, many English teachers have their students read the one *novella* among the novelist's works⟩ — see STORY 1

novelty *n* **1** the quality or appeal of being new ⟨the *novelty* of having a cat wore off after the first time I had to change the litter box⟩

synonyms freshness, newness, originality

related words strangeness, unfamiliarity, unusualness; progressiveness; up-to-dateness; departure, divergence, innovation, offshoot, shoot

near antonyms banality, commonness, familiarity, staleness

2 novelties *pl* small useful items ⟨travel kits filled with small bars of soap, a folding toothbrush, and other *novelties*⟩ — see NOTION 1

3 a small object displayed for its attractiveness or interest ⟨a shop selling souvenirs, T-shirts, and assorted *novelties* for tourists passing through⟩ — see KNICK-KNACK

novice *n* a person who is just starting out in a field of activity ⟨a *novice* chess player⟩ — see BEGINNER

now *adv* **1** at the present time ⟨that company doesn't make those toys *now* because they are unsafe⟩

synonyms anymore, currently, nowadays, presently, right now, today

related words here

near antonyms away, far, farthest, remotest; heretofore, hitherto, since; ago, previously

antonyms before, formerly, long, once, then

2 not long ago ⟨I was just *now* wondering what to do⟩ — see NEWLY

3 on some occasions ⟨goes *now* here, *now* there⟩ — see SOMETIMES

4 without delay ⟨come here right *now*⟩ — see IMMEDIATELY

now *conj* for the reason that ⟨I'll repeat my question *now* that you are paying attention⟩ — see SINCE

now *n* the time currently existing or in progress ⟨I know I said you could go, but that was then and this is *now*⟩ — see PRESENT 1

nowadays *adv* at the present time ⟨*nowadays* wives are just as likely to work outside the home as their husbands are⟩ — see NOW 1

noway *or* **noways** *adv* not in any degree, way, or under any condition ⟨that will *noway* hurt your chances of getting on the team⟩ — see NEVER 2

no way *adv* certainly not ⟨*no way* will I go with you to the dance⟩ — see HARDLY 2

nowise *adv* not in any degree, way, or under any condition ⟨her romance novels are *nowise* different from those of scores of other writers⟩ — see NEVER 2

noxious *adj* **1** bad for the well-being of the body ⟨mixing bleach and ammonia can cause *noxious* fumes that can seriously harm you⟩ — see UNHEALTHY 1

2 causing or capable of causing harm ⟨*noxious* smog that for years has been encrusting the historic cathedral with soot⟩ — see HARMFUL

nth *adj* of the greatest or highest degree or quantity ⟨exaggerates to the *nth* degree about everything she ever did⟩ — see ULTIMATE 1

nub *n* **1** a small uneven mass ⟨throw a *nub* of butter into the pan⟩ — see LUMP 1

2 the central part or aspect of something under consideration ⟨the *nub* of the argument is that the intelligence agencies failed the country⟩ — see CRUX

nubbin *n* a very small piece ⟨had only a *nubbin* of crayon left⟩ — see BIT 1

nubble *n* a small uneven mass ⟨dropped a *nubble* of mud on the floor⟩ — see LUMP 1

nubbly *adj* having small pieces or lumps spread throughout ⟨the walls were painted with a *nubbly* paint that was supposed to give them an interesting texture⟩ — see CHUNKY 1

nubby *adj* having small pieces or lumps spread throughout ⟨a *nubby* yarn that produces bumpy fabrics when woven⟩ — see CHUNKY 1

nucleus *n* a thing or place that is of greatest importance to an activity or interest ⟨a college campus that was a *nucleus* of opposition to the war⟩ — see CENTER 1

nude *adj* lacking or shed of clothing ⟨Picasso's paintings of *nude* art models⟩ — see NAKED 1

nudge *vb* to pass lightly across or touch gently especially in passing ⟨accidentally *nudged* me as they squeezed past⟩ — see BRUSH

nugget *n* a small uneven mass ⟨a *nugget* of gold⟩ — see LUMP 1

nuisance *n* **1** one who is obnoxiously annoying ⟨my little brother was being a *nuisance* by poking and prodding me throughout the long car trip⟩

synonyms annoyance, annoyer, bother, gadfly, gnawer, persecutor, pest, tease, teaser

related words headache; harrier, heckler; hassle, plague; molester, tormentor, torturer

near antonyms charmer, smoothy (*or* smoothie)

2 something that is a source of irritation ⟨folding up this map correctly is such a *nuisance*⟩ — see ANNOYANCE 3

null *adj* **1** having no legal or binding force ⟨the contract was *null* because the other person forgot to sign it⟩

synonyms invalid, nonbinding, nonvalid, null and void, void

related words illegal; useless, worthless; ineffective, ineffectual

near antonyms legal; working

antonyms binding, good, valid

2 having no usefulness ⟨that information is as *null* as no information at all⟩ — see WORTHLESS

null and void *adj* having no legal or binding force ⟨public disclosure of the terms of the settlement renders it *null and void*⟩ — see NULL 1

nullify *vb* to put an end to by formal action ⟨the constitutional amendment that *nullified* Prohibition⟩ — see ABOLISH

numb *adj* lacking in sensation or feeling ⟨I sat in one position too long and now my feet are *numb*⟩

synonyms asleep, benumbed, dead, insensitive, numbed, unfeeling

related words chilled, nipped; anesthetized, deadened, drugged, stupefied; insensible, senseless, unconscious; inanimate, insensate

near antonyms awake

antonyms sensitive, sensitive

numb *vb* to reduce or weaken in strength or feeling ⟨wait for the medication to *numb* your mouth⟩ — see DULL 1

numbed *adj* lacking in sensation or feeling ⟨*numbed* fingers that needed warming by the fire⟩ — see NUMB

number *n* a character used to represent a mathematical value ⟨asked him to write out the equation in *numbers*, not letters⟩

synonyms digit, figure, integer, numeral, whole number

related words decimal, fraction; cipher; symbol

number *vb* **1** to find the sum of (a collection of things) by noting each one as it is being added ⟨*number* those apples and tell me how many you have⟩ — see COUNT 1

2 to have a total of ⟨the average size of the classes *numbers* 20 students⟩ — see AMOUNT (TO) 1

3 to have as part of a whole ⟨is *numbered* among the great minds of our times⟩ — see INCLUDE

numberless *adj* too many to be counted ⟨the *numberless* stars in the universe⟩ — see COUNTLESS

numbing *adj* having a low or subnormal temperature ⟨the *numbing* air of that wintry morning⟩ — see COLD 1

numbness *n* a lack of emotion or emotional expressiveness ⟨the prisoner exhibited the *numbness* of someone who had spent more years behind bars than he could remember⟩ — see APATHY 1

numeral *n* a character used to represent a mathematical value ⟨write the answer in Roman *numerals*⟩ — see NUMBER

numerate *vb* **1** to make a list of ⟨*numerate* the dish's ingredients for me⟩ — see ¹LIST 1

2 to specify one after another ⟨I don't have the time to *numerate* all the reasons, so I'll offer just a few⟩ — see ENUMERATE 1

numerous *adj* being of a large but indefinite number ⟨received *numerous* complaints about that product⟩ — see MANY

numskull *or* **numbskull** *n* a stupid person ⟨don't be such a *numbskull*—we can't fly to Mars!⟩ — see IDIOT

nuptial *adj* of or relating to marriage ⟨newlyweds still in a state of *nuptial* bliss⟩ — see MARITAL

nuptial *n, usually* **nuptials** *pl* a ceremony in which two people are united in matrimony ⟨their *nuptials* will take place at the university chapel⟩ — see WEDDING

nurse *n* a girl or woman employed to care for a young child or children ⟨sent his little son back to his *nurse* so that he could return to his study to work⟩

synonyms babysitter, nursemaid, nurser, sitter

related words mammy; governess

nurse *vb* **1** to attend to the needs and comforts of ⟨took some time to *nurse* his grandmother, helping her get from one room to the other and making sure she was warm⟩

synonyms care (for), minister (to), mother

related words cure, heal, remedy; doctor, treat; aid, conserve, preserve, provide (for), support; baby, coddle, mollycoddle, pamper, spoil; cater (to), humor; indulge

phrases look after, look out for, look to, see to, take care of

near antonyms brush (aside *or* off), forget, ignore, neglect, overlook, slight

2 to keep in one's mind or heart ⟨he continues to *nurse* a tender affection for his first girlfriend⟩ — see HARBOR 1

3 to treat with great or excessive care ⟨*nursed* his scraped knee for the rest of the week⟩ — see BABY

nursemaid *n* a girl or woman employed to care for a young child or children ⟨sent the children to their *nursemaid*⟩ — see NURSE

nurser *n* a girl or woman employed to care for a young child or children ⟨volunteered at the hospital as a *nurser* to hold premature babies⟩ — see NURSE

nurture *vb* 1 to help the growth or development of ⟨wanted to find the art school that would best *nurture* his artistic talent⟩ — see FOSTER 1

2 to provide (someone) with moral or spiritual understanding ⟨she feels that her lifelong practice of reading the Bible daily has *nurtured* her in ways she cannot describe⟩ — see ENLIGHTEN 2

3 to supply with nourishment ⟨*nurtured* her children with home-cooked soup⟩ — see SUSTAIN 1

nut *n* 1 a person of odd or whimsical habits ⟨a show devoted to those lovable *nuts* who collect the weirdest things just for fun⟩ — see ECCENTRIC

2 a person who lacks good sense or judgment ⟨anyone who drives like that sure is a *nut*⟩ — see FOOL 1

3 a person with a strong and habitual liking for something ⟨a baseball *nut* who's still waiting for the Boston Red Sox to win the World Series⟩ — see FAN

4 a person judged to be legally or medically insane ⟨the man walking down the street talking to himself looked like a *nut* until we realized he was talking into his cell phone⟩ — see LUNATIC 1

nutrient *adj* providing the substances necessary for health and bodily growth ⟨enriched with *nutrient* proteins and vitamins⟩ — see NUTRITIOUS

nutritional *adj* providing the substances necessary for health and bodily growth ⟨the doctor recommended *nutritional* supplements⟩ — see NUTRITIOUS

nutritious *adj* providing the substances necessary for health and bodily growth ⟨opted for a *nutritious* snack and bought an apple instead of a candy bar⟩

synonyms nourishing, nutrient, nutritional, nutritive

related words dietary, dietetic; beneficial, healthful, healthy, restorative, salubrious, salutary, wholesome

near antonyms insalubrious, unhealthful, unhealthy, unwholesome

antonyms nonnutritious

nutritive *adj* providing the substances necessary for health and bodily growth ⟨some people believe whole wheat bread is more *nutritive* than white bread⟩ — see NUTRITIOUS

nuts *adj* 1 having or showing a very abnormal or sick state of mind ⟨in olden times people suffering from a variety of neurological disorders were just classified as *nuts*⟩ — see INSANE 1

2 showing urgent desire or interest ⟨I'm *nuts* for the homecoming game⟩ — see EAGER

nuts (about) *adj* filled with an intense or excessive love for ⟨I'm not exactly *nuts about* the idea of you camping overnight by yourself⟩ — see ENAMORED (OF)

nuttiness *n* lack of good sense or judgment ⟨her incurable *nuttiness* makes her an easy target for swindlers⟩ — see FOOLISHNESS 1

nutty *adj* 1 having or showing a very abnormal or sick state of mind ⟨the only other prisoner in the dungeon was a *nutty* soul who feasted on bugs⟩ — see INSANE 1

2 showing or marked by a lack of good sense or judgment ⟨that's a *nutty* idea that won't work at all⟩ — see FOOLISH 1

nuzzle *vb* to lie close ⟨newborn puppies *nuzzling* against their mother to stay warm⟩

synonyms cuddle, nestle, snuggle

related words curl up; crouch, huddle

near antonyms blench, flinch, quail, recoil, shrink, shy, start, wince

nymph *n* 1 a mythical goddess represented as a young girl and said to live outdoors ⟨she bought the book of fairy tales for the beautiful engravings of *nymphs* and fairies featured between the stories⟩

synonyms dryad, naiad, oread

related words mermaid, siren

2 a young wingless often wormlike form (as a grub or caterpillar) that hatches from the egg of many insects ⟨mayfly *nymphs*⟩ — see LARVA

O

oaf *n* a big clumsy often slow-witted person ⟨it is not polite to call your brother a stupid *oaf*⟩
synonyms clod, gawk, hulk, lout, lubber, lug
related words chump, loser, schlemiel, turkey; ass, blockhead, dolt, donkey, dope, dumbbell, dummy, goon, half-wit, idiot, ignoramus, imbecile, jackass, moron, nincompoop, ninny, nitwit, simpleton; beast, boor, brute, cad, churl, clown, creep, cretin, cur, heel, louse, skunk, snake, stinker, villain; booby, fool, goose, loony (*also* looney), lunatic, madman, nut; featherbrain, scatterbrain; rascal, rogue, scamp
near antonyms brain, genius; egghead, intellectual, sage, thinker

oafish *adj* not having or showing an ability to absorb ideas readily ⟨far from being *oafish*, the professional wrestler was in fact a college graduate⟩ — see STUPID 1

oafishness *n* the quality or state of lacking intelligence or quickness of mind ⟨the *oafishness* of the investigators, who missed clues and mishandled physical evidence, is the reason why that crime was never solved⟩ — see STUPIDITY 1

oar *vb* to move a boat by means of oars ⟨since the wind had completely died, they had to *oar* the sailboat back to shore⟩ — see ¹ROW

oarsman *n* a person who drives a boat forward by means of oars ⟨the only *oarsman* in a rowboat designed for two⟩
synonyms rower, sculler
related words coxswain, crewman; puller, sailor

oath *n* a person's solemn declaration that he or she will do or not do something ⟨I need your *oath* that you won't do anything until I have had time make a decision⟩ — see PROMISE

obduracy *n* a steadfast adherence to an opinion, purpose, or course of action ⟨the administrator was known for her unyielding *obduracy* even in the face of proof that she was wrong⟩ — see OBSTINACY

obdurate *adj* 1 having or showing a lack of sympathy or tender feelings ⟨the *obdurate* refusal of her parents to let her go on the trip despite tears and pleading⟩ — see HARD 1
2 sticking to an opinion, purpose, or course of action in spite of reason, arguments, or persuasion ⟨an *obdurate* farmer who could never be convinced to try a different method of fertilization⟩ — see OBSTINATE

obedience *n* 1 a bending to the authority or control of another ⟨the drill sergeant demanded complete and unquestioning *obedience* from the recruits⟩
synonyms compliance, conformity, observance, submission, subordination
related words acquiescence, agreeability, amenability; docility, submissiveness; capitulation, surrender, yielding; servility, slavishness, subservience; inhibition, repression, restraint, suppression; control, discipline, order
near antonyms contrariness, frowardness, intractability, rebelliousness, recalcitrance, refractoriness; disrespect, impudence, insolence, rudeness; insurgency, insurrection, mutiny, revolt; hardheadedness, mulishness, obstinacy, perversity, stubbornness, willfulness; misbehavior, mischievousness, naughtiness; dissent, dissidence

antonyms disobedience, insubordination, noncompliance, rebelling, rebellion
2 a readiness or willingness to yield to the wishes of others ⟨the cowardly *obedience* with which the dictator's henchmen followed his every command⟩ — see COMPLIANCE 1

obedient *adj* readily giving in to the command or authority of another ⟨that boy is so *obedient* that he does everything the first time he is asked⟩
synonyms amenable, compliant, conformable, docile, law-abiding, submissive, tractable
related words acquiescent, agreeable, amiable, obliging; surrendering, yielding; obsequious, servile, slavish, subservient; decorous, disciplined, mannerly, orderly; constrained, curbed, inhibited, repressed, restrained; controllable, governable, manageable; gentle, meek, mild
near antonyms insurgent, mutinous; dogged, hardheaded, headstrong, mulish, obdurate, obstinate, peevish, pigheaded, self-willed, stubborn, unyielding, willful (*or* wilful); obstreperous, restive, uncontrollable, ungovernable, unmanageable, wild; balky, defiant, perverse, resistant, wayward; bad, disorderly, errant, misbehaving, mischievous, naughty; ill-bred, undisciplined; dissident, nonconformist; disrespectful, ill-mannered, impolite, impudent, insolent, rude
antonyms contrary, disobedient, froward, insubordinate, intractable, rebellious, recalcitrant, refractory, unruly

obese *adj* having an excess of body fat ⟨the basset was so *obese* that its stomach touched the floor⟩ — see FAT 1

obesity *n* the condition of having an excess of body fat ⟨*obesity* has been linked to a number of health risks, such as heart disease⟩ — see CORPULENCE

obey *vb* to act according to the commands of ⟨it is important to *obey* your teachers immediately in the case of an emergency⟩ ⟨most people *obey* the law and wear their seat belts⟩
synonyms comply (with), conform (to), follow, mind, observe
related words defer (to), submit (to), surrender (to), yield (to); accede (to), acquiesce (to), agree (to), assent (to); attend, hear, heed, listen (to), mark, note, notice, regard, watch
phrases abide by
near antonyms challenge, dare; rebel (against); defy; direct, lead; brush off, disregard, ignore, overlook, overpass, pass over, tune out, wink (at); dismiss, pooh-pooh, shrug off; break, transgress, violate; deride, flout, scorn
antonyms disobey

object *n* 1 something material that can be perceived by the senses ⟨I kept tripping over countless little *objects* scattered about the darkened room⟩
synonyms thing
related words article, item, piece; being, entity, substance; commodity, good, ware; accessory, accompaniment, bauble, curio; knickknack, spangle, token, trinket
2 one that has a real and independent existence ⟨trying to determine whether communication with the dead is an *object* for study, a hoax, or a figment of the imagination⟩ — see ENTITY

3 something that one hopes or intends to accomplish ⟨the *object* of this course is to teach you algebra⟩ — see GOAL

object *vb* to present an opposing opinion or argument ⟨they *objected* to the conductor's insistence that their train tickets were not valid⟩

synonyms demur, expostulate (with), kick, protest, remonstrate (with)

related words cavil, quibble; challenge, dare, defy; conflict (with), debate, dispute, hassle, quarrel, squabble, wrangle; complain, inveigh (against); balk (at), stick (at); censure, criticize, denounce; disobey, rebel (against); demonstrate (against)

phrases take exception

near antonyms approve, sanction; accept; accede (to), acquiesce (to), agree (with), assent (to); comply (with), obey; advocate, champion, defend, maintain, support, sustain, uphold

objection *n* a feeling or declaration of disapproval or dissent ⟨pardon me, but I have an *objection* to any plan that requires staying out all night⟩

synonyms challenge, complaint, demur, expostulation, fuss, protest, question, remonstrance

related words compunction, doubt, misgiving, qualm, scruple; difficulty, misunderstanding; cavil, quibble; argument, conflict, debate, dispute, dissent, hassle, quarrel, squabble; censure, criticism; defiance, disobedience, rebellion

near antonyms willingness; approval, sanction; acceptance, acquiescence, agreement, assent; compliance, obedience

objectionable *adj* provoking or likely to provoke protest ⟨that T-shirt displays *objectionable* images which are not appropriate for school⟩

synonyms censurable, exceptionable, obnoxious, offensive, reprehensible

related words bawdy, coarse, crude, dirty, filthy, foul, gross, indecent, lewd, nasty, obscene, smutty, vulgar; blamable, blameworthy, lascivious, pornographic, ribald, scurrilous; debasing, perverted, profane; racy, salty, suggestive; unacceptable, undesirable, unwanted, unwelcome; abhorrent, disgusting, loathsome, repellent (*also* repellant), repugnant, repulsive, revolting; disagreeable, displeasing, distasteful, unpleasant; bad, execrable, lousy, miserable; atrocious, infamous; indecent, indecorous, unbecoming; earthy, unprintable; naughty, wicked

near antonyms acceptable, agreeable, pleasant, pleasing, welcome; good; approved, endorsed, sanctioned; abetted, encouraged, promoted, supported; becoming, correct, decent, decorous, exemplary, seemly; blameless, commendable, creditable; immaculate, perfect, pure, spotless

antonyms inoffensive, unobjectionable

objective *adj* **1** based on observation or experience ⟨an *objective* judgment based solely upon the results of the experiment⟩ — see EMPIRICAL

2 marked by justice, honesty, and freedom from bias ⟨the judge removed herself from the case because she doubted her own ability to be *objective*, given her friendship with one of the attorneys⟩ — see FAIR 2

3 restricted to or based on fact ⟨the paper's news stories strive to be scrupulously *objective*, with opinions clearly labeled as commentary⟩ — see FACTUAL 1

objective *n* something that one hopes or intends to accomplish ⟨the *objective* of your training at tennis camp is to become tournament-level players⟩ — see GOAL

objectivity *n* lack of favoritism toward one side or another ⟨the teacher's *objectivity* would be seriously compromised if his own child were placed in the class⟩ — see DETACHMENT 1

obligate *vb* to cause (a person) to give in to pressure ⟨just because you created a problem, don't think that you can *obligate* me to help⟩ — see FORCE

obligation *n* something one must do because of prior agreement ⟨their financial *obligations* keep them from giving to charities as much as they would like⟩

synonyms burden, charge, commitment, duty, need, responsibility

related words pledge, promise; arrangement, prearrangement, setup; compact, contract, covenant, pact; payment, tribute; compulsion, constraint, restraint; must, requirement; coercion, duress, force; appointment, engagement, reservation

near antonyms grace, postponement, stay; discharge, exemption, release, waiver; alternative, choice, option, pick, preference, selection

obligatory *adj* forcing one's compliance or participation by or as if by law ⟨in this state, school attendance is *obligatory* until the age of 16⟩ — see MANDATORY

oblige *vb* **1** to do a service or favor for ⟨I would appreciate it greatly if you could *oblige* me by bringing a dessert to the party⟩

synonyms accommodate, favor

related words humor, indulge; coddle, mollycoddle, pamper; appease, conciliate, mollify, pacify, placate; delight, gladden, gratify, please, satisfy; abet, aid, assist, help, support; attend, care (for), minister (to), relieve, succor

near antonyms bother, discommode, disturb, incommode, inconvenience, trouble; burden, encumber, saddle, weigh; desert, disappoint, fail, let down; constrain, hamper, hamstring, hinder, hobble, hold back, impede, obstruct, restrain; frustrate, oppose, sabotage, thwart

antonyms disoblige

2 to cause (a person) to give in to pressure ⟨I know you're in a hurry, but you can't *oblige* me to drive any faster than the speed limit⟩ — see FORCE

obliged *adj* feeling or expressing gratitude ⟨I'd be much *obliged* if you could do me this favor⟩ — see GRATEFUL 1

oblique *adj* **1** inclined or twisted to one side ⟨gave him an *oblique* glance out of the corner of her eye⟩ — see AWRY

2 running in a slanting direction ⟨in the painting the artist repeats the *oblique* line of the path with the *oblique* line of the outstretched arm⟩ — see DIAGONAL

obliquely *adv* in a line or direction running from corner to corner ⟨the photographer has framed the shot so that the river runs *obliquely* through it, creating a great sense of depth for the viewer⟩ — see CROSSWISE

obliterate *vb* to destroy all traces of ⟨in a stroke, the March snowstorm *obliterated* our hopes for an early spring⟩ — see ANNIHILATE 1

obliteration *n* the state or fact of being rendered nonexistent, physically unsound, or useless ⟨the ill-advised *obliteration* of the town's historic district in order to make way for a shopping center⟩ — see DESTRUCTION

oblivion *n* a state of being disregardful or unconscious of one's surroundings, concerns, or obligations ⟨for two weeks each year the stressed-out couple enjoy the blissful *oblivion* that comes with a vacation at the beach⟩

synonyms forgetfulness, obliviousness

related words ignorance, unawareness, unconsciousness, unfamiliarity *near antonyms* memory, recall, recollection, remembrance; alertness, awareness, cognizance, consciousness

oblivious *adj* not informed about or aware of something ⟨the out-of-state motorist claimed to be *oblivious* of the local speed limit, even though the signs must have been hard to miss⟩ — see IGNORANT 2

obliviousness *n* **1** a state of being disregardful or unconscious of one's surroundings, concerns, or obligations ⟨her chronic *obliviousness* often results in her walking into walls and other hard-to-miss objects⟩ — see OBLIVION

2 the state of being unaware or uninformed ⟨traditionally, one's *obliviousness* regarding the existence of a law is not an acceptable excuse for breaking it⟩ — see IGNORANCE 1

obnoxious *adj* **1** causing intense displeasure, disgust, or resentment ⟨an *obnoxious* law that was widely flouted and engendered a whole new level of criminal activity⟩ — see OFFENSIVE 1

2 provoking or likely to provoke protest ⟨an *obnoxious* comment for which there should be an immediate apology⟩ — see OBJECTIONABLE

obscene *adj* **1** depicting or referring to sexual matters in a way that is unacceptable in polite society ⟨*obscene* language and artwork is forbidden in this school⟩

synonyms bawdy, coarse, crude, dirty, filthy, foul, gross, indecent, lascivious, lewd, nasty, pornographic, ribald, smutty, unprintable, vulgar, wanton

related words earthy, racy, salty, suggestive; indecorous, unbecoming; debasing, perverted, profane; naughty, wicked; exceptionable, objectionable, unacceptable, undesirable, unwanted, unwelcome; abhorrent, disgusting, loathsome, offensive, repellent (*also* repellant), repugnant, repulsive, revolting; distasteful, obnoxious, unpleasant; blamable, blameworthy, censurable, reprehensible; atrocious, infamous; abusive, scurrilous

near antonyms priggish, prim, prudish, puritanical, straitlaced (*or* straightlaced), Victorian; correct, decorous, genteel, polite, proper, seemly; innocuous, inoffensive; acceptable, agreeable, desirable, pleasant, pleasing, welcome; appropriate, becoming, fit, meet, suitable; immaculate, perfect, pure, spotless; approved, endorsed, sanctioned

antonyms clean, decent

2 causing intense displeasure, disgust, or resentment ⟨that ugly new store is really an *obscene* bit of architecture⟩ — see OFFENSIVE 1

obscenity *n* **1** the quality or state of being obscene ⟨the issue of whether *obscenity* is a fundamental part of rap music⟩

synonyms bawdiness, coarseness, crudeness, dirt, dirtiness, filth, filthiness, foulness, grossness, indecency, lasciviousness, lewdness, nastiness, ribaldry, smuttiness, vulgarity

related words raciness, saltiness, suggestiveness; perversion, profanity; naughtiness, wickedness; loathsomeness, offensiveness, repulsiveness; distastefulness, obnoxiousness, unpleasantness

near antonyms priggishness, primness, prudery, prudishness, puritanism; correctness, decency, decorousness, decorum, seemliness; appropriateness, fitness, suitability, suitableness; immaculateness, perfection, purity, spotlessness

2 a disrespectful or indecent word or expression ⟨Dad uttered a loud *obscenity* when he dropped the hammer on his toe⟩ — see SWEARWORD

obscure *adj* **1** having an often intentionally veiled or uncertain meaning ⟨a fantasy writer who likes to put lots of *obscure* references and images in her tales of wizards and warlocks⟩

synonyms ambiguous, cryptic, dark, darkling, deep, enigmatic (*also* enigmatical), equivocal, inscrutable, murky, mysterious, mystic, nebulous, occult

related words abstruse, esoteric, recondite; bleary, cloudy, dim, faint, foggy, fuzzy, hazy, indefinite, indistinct, indistinguishable, shadowy, unclear, uncertain, undefined, undetermined, vague; impenetrable, incomprehensible; inexplicable; eerie, uncanny, weird; impalpable, inappreciable, intangible, invisible; unanswerable, unknowable; baffling, bewildering, confounding, confusing, mystifying, perplexing, puzzling, unfathomable; difficult, complex, complicated, obtuse

near antonyms comprehensible, fathomable, intelligible, knowable, understandable; bright, distinct, evident; certain, firm, strong, sure; defined, determined; direct, straightforward; definite, exact, explicit; appreciable, palpable, tangible, visible; blatant, patent, unmistakable

antonyms clear, obvious, plain, unambiguous, unequivocal

2 not widely known ⟨he's an *obscure* artist now, but he's sure to be famous someday⟩

synonyms anonymous, nameless, uncelebrated, unknown, unnoted, unsung

related words insignificant, minor, unimportant; undistinguished, unexceptional; unpopular; faceless

near antonyms fabled, fabulous, legendary; infamous; distinguished, eminent, exceptional, great, illustrious, leading, notable, outstanding, prestigious, remarkable; important, significant; favorite, popular, preferred; estimable, honorable, reputable, respectable; influential, major

antonyms celebrated, famed, famous, noted, notorious, prominent, renowned, well-known

3 being without light or without much light ⟨hid in an *obscure* spot among the trees⟩ — see DARK 1

4 not seen or understood clearly ⟨a distinction so *obscure* that only the experts can really see it⟩ — see FAINT 1

obscure *vb* **1** to keep secret or shut off from view ⟨the investigative reporters *obscured* their real motives for visiting the company by pretending the story was about something else⟩ — see ¹HIDE 2

2 to make dark, dim, or indistinct ⟨when it isn't *obscured* by smog, the view of the city from the observatory can be spectacular⟩ — see CLOUD 1

obscured *adj* being without light or without much light ⟨an *obscured* area of the prison yard that was the perfect escape route⟩ — see DARK 1

obscurity *n* **1** the quality or state of having a veiled or uncertain meaning ⟨the 16th-century astrologer's predictions are so filled with *obscurity* that people can interpret them any way they want⟩

synonyms ambiguity, ambiguousness, darkness, equivocalness, equivocation, murkiness, nebulousness, opacity

related words cloudiness, dimness, faintness, fogginess, fuzziness, haziness, indefiniteness, indistinctness, uncertainty, vagueness; impenetrability, incomprehensibility; deepness, profoundness; intangibility, invisibility; abstruseness; complexity, complication, difficulty, obtuseness

near antonyms comprehensibility, intelligibility; brightness, distinctness; certainty, surety; definiteness, exactness, explicitness; directness, straightforwardness; palpability, tangibility, visibility

antonyms clarity, clearness, obviousness, plainness

2 the quality or state of being mostly or completely unknown ⟨the singer languished in relative *obscurity* for years before becoming famous⟩

synonyms anonymity

related words oblivion; inconspicuousness, invisibility; insignificance, unimportance; unpopularity

near antonyms name, report, reputation, repute; popularity; importance, significance; distinction, eminence, glory, greatness, honor, illustriousness, note, preeminence, prominence; cachet, position, prestige, rank, standing, stature; acclaim, acknowledgment (*also* acknowledgement), praise, recognition; adoration, idolization

antonyms celebrity, fame, notoriety, renown

observable *adj* capable of being seen ⟨scientists often work with phenomena that are not directly *observable*⟩ — see VISIBLE

observance *n* **1** an act of following a custom, rule, or law ⟨the *observance* of this family tradition would make your grandmother very happy⟩

synonyms observation

related words attention, heed, notice; respecting, upholding

near antonyms infraction, offense (*or* offence), sin, trespass, wrong; disregard, forgetting, ignoring, neglect, overlooking; delinquency, dereliction

antonyms breach, infringement, nonobservance, transgression, violation

2 an oft-repeated action or series of actions performed in accordance with tradition or a set of rules ⟨some religions require very specific *observances* on holy days⟩ — see RITE

3 a bending to the authority or control of another ⟨a lot of motorists in this state seem to think that *observance* of the posted speed limit is strictly optional⟩ — see OBEDIENCE 1

4 a state of being aware ⟨if you've been doing any significant studying, it has escaped my *observance*⟩ — see ATTENTION 2

observation *n* **1** a state of being aware ⟨it has come to my *observation* that you've been missing a lot of school lately⟩ — see ATTENTION 2

2 an act of following a custom, rule, or law ⟨a society in which a strict *observation* of business etiquette is expected of visiting foreigners⟩ — see OBSERVANCE 1

observational *adj* based on observation or experience ⟨her reports on the great apes were based on firsthand *observational* evidence⟩ — see EMPIRICAL

observatory *n* a high place or structure from which a wide view is possible ⟨the *observatory* is located on a mountaintop⟩ — see LOOKOUT 1

observe *vb* **1** to act according to the commands of ⟨you must *observe* all the rules of this school, not simply the ones that meet with your personal approval⟩ — see OBEY

2 to act properly in relation to ⟨a time when few people in New England *observed* Christmas⟩ — see KEEP 1

3 to keep one's eyes on ⟨happily spent many hours *observing* the birds at the backyard feeder⟩ — see WATCH 1

4 to make a statement of one's opinion ⟨"I think you might be mistaken," he *observed*⟩ — see REMARK 1

5 to make note of (something) through the use of one's eyes ⟨she *observed* that the weather had changed again⟩ — see SEE 1

6 to take notice of and be guided by ⟨generally *observes* the suggestions of the experts regarding baby care⟩ — see HEED 1

obsessed *adj* having extreme or relentless concern ⟨the boy was so *obsessed* with video games that he refused to go outside and play⟩ — see HUNG UP 1

obsession *n* something about which one is constantly thinking or concerned ⟨her latest *obsession* is a movie star who she thinks is very handsome⟩ — see FIXATION

obsessive *adj* caused by or suggestive of an irresistible urge ⟨the man's *obsessive* counting of everyday objects⟩ — see COMPULSIVE

obsolete *adj* having passed its time of use or usefulness ⟨the abacus was considered *obsolete* once the electronic calculator was invented⟩

synonyms antiquated, archaic, dated, moth-eaten, outdated, outmoded, out-of-date, outworn, passé

related words aging, obsolescent; discarded, disused, superannuated, worn-out; inoperable, unusable, unworkable, useless; dead, defunct, extinct; dormant, fallow, free, idle, inactive, inert, inoperative, latent; ancient, antediluvian, antique, fusty, musty, old, old-fangled, old-fashioned, old-time, old-world; aged, age-old, hoary, venerable; bygone, erstwhile, former, late, past; historic, historical

near antonyms contemporary, current, mod, modern, new, newfangled, new-fashioned, present-day, recent, ultramodern, up-to-date; fresh; modernized, refurbished, remodeled, renewed; functional, operable, operational, workable; active, alive, busy, employed, functioning, operating, operative

obstacle *n* something that makes movement or progress more difficult ⟨the number of *obstacles* along the path made it impossible to travel on without stumbling⟩ — see ENCUMBRANCE

obstinacy *n* a steadfast adherence to an opinion, purpose, or course of action ⟨the mindless *obstinacy* of those people who continue to insist that the earth is flat⟩

synonyms doggedness, hardheadedness, mulishness, obduracy, peevishness, persistence, pertinaciousness, pertinacity, self-will, stubbornness, tenaciousness, tenacity, willfulness

related words perverseness, perversity, resistance, waywardness, wrongheadedness; hardness, inflexibility, relentlessness, sternness, strictness; certainty, determination, firmness; inexorability, resolve, rigidity, rigidness, steadfastness; contrariness, defiance, disobedience, insubordination, recalcitrance

near antonyms broad-mindedness, open-mindedness, reasonableness, receptivity; acceptance, acquiescence, flexibility, pliability; compliance, docility, obedience; submission, surrender, willingness, yielding; slavishness, subservience

obstinate *adj* sticking to an opinion, purpose, or course of action in spite of reason, arguments, or persuasion ⟨the child was *obstinate* about wanting that specific toy, despite being offered several others⟩

synonyms adamant, adamantine, dogged, hard, hardened, hardheaded, hardhearted, headstrong, immovable, implacable, inflexible, mulish, obdurate, opinionated, ossified, pat, peevish, pertinacious, perverse, pigheaded, rigid, self-willed, stubborn, unbending, uncompromising, unrelenting, unyielding, willful (*or* wilful)

related words hidebound, narrow-minded; resistant, wayward, wrongheaded; persistent, tenacious; iron, relentless; grim, severe, stern, strict; determined, firm, inexorable, resolved, single-minded, steadfast, sure, unflinching; contrary, disobedient, froward, insubordinate, intractable, recalcitrant, refractory, uncooperative, ungovernable, unmanageable, unruly; defiant, insurgent, mutinous; indomitable, invincible, unconquerable; confirmed, inveterate, unregenerate; demanding, exacting

near antonyms docile, law-abiding, obedient, submissive, tractable; accepting, receptive, responsive, willing; governable, manageable, reasonable, temperate; slavish, subservient

antonyms acquiescent, agreeable, amenable, compliant, complying, flexible, pliable, pliant, relenting, yielding

obstreperous *adj* engaging in or marked by loud and insistent cries especially of protest ⟨an *obstreperous* crowd protesting the government's foreign policy⟩ — see VOCIFEROUS

obstruct *vb* **1** to create difficulty for the work or activity of ⟨this would go much faster if you would stop *obstructing* me⟩ — see HAMPER

2 to prevent passage through ⟨at the moment the city's only tunnel between downtown and the airport is *obstructed* by an overturned tanker truck⟩ — see CLOG 1

obstruction *n* something that makes movement or progress more difficult ⟨an *obstruction* in the drain has the water all backed up⟩ — see ENCUMBRANCE

obtain *vb* to receive as return for effort ⟨after a lot of hard work, she *obtained* a medical degree⟩ — see EARN 1

obtainable *adj* possible to get ⟨gas was in such short supply that it was just not *obtainable* at any price⟩ — see AVAILABLE 1

obtrude *vb* to interest oneself in what is not one's concern ⟨please stop *obtruding* in your brother's affairs⟩ — see INTERFERE

obtrusive *adj* thrusting oneself where one is not welcome or invited ⟨meddling in other people's romantic lives is both *obtrusive* and rude⟩ — see INTRUSIVE

obtuse *adj* **1** lacking sharpness of edge or point ⟨*obtuse* scissors designed so that young users will not cut themselves⟩ — see DULL 1

2 not having or showing an ability to absorb ideas readily ⟨"I know you're not *obtuse*," the teacher said, "so it's clear that you simply don't want to learn long division"⟩ — see STUPID 1

obtuseness *n* the quality or state of lacking intelligence or quickness of mind ⟨our guest's *obtuseness* was such that he failed to take even the broadest hint that it was time to leave⟩ — see STUPIDITY 1

obviate *vb* to keep from happening by taking action in advance ⟨regular tooth-brushing should *obviate* the need for frequent trips to the dentist⟩ — see PREVENT

obviating *n* the act or practice of keeping something from happening ⟨the *obviating* of expensive auto repairs is best accomplished by regular maintenance⟩ — see PREVENTION

obvious *adj* **1** not subject to misinterpretation or more than one interpretation ⟨that remark was an *obvious* joke⟩ — see CLEAR 2

2 very noticeable especially for being incorrect or bad ⟨*obvious* errors in the book that the editor or proofreader should have caught⟩ — see EGREGIOUS

occasion *n* **1** a particular point at which an event takes place ⟨the *occasion* of our last meeting with our old friend was several years ago, unfortunately⟩

synonyms moment, time

related words flash, instant, jiffy, minute, second, shake, split second, trice, twinkle, wink; while

2 a favorable combination of circumstances, time, and place ⟨the substitute violinist rose to the *occasion* and performed the piece beautifully⟩ — see OPPORTUNITY

3 someone or something responsible for a result ⟨your graduation will be an *occasion* for celebration⟩ — see CAUSE 1

4 something that happens ⟨weddings are generally happy *occasions*⟩ — see EVENT 1

occasional *adj* **1** lacking in steadiness or regularity of occurrence ⟨the area should be experiencing *occasional* rain this weekend⟩ — see FITFUL

2 not often occurring or repeated ⟨an *occasional* mechanical problem with our car, but nothing serious⟩ — see INFREQUENT

occasionally *adv* on some occasions ⟨we *occasionally* stop for ice cream on the way home⟩ — see SOMETIMES

occult *adj* **1** being beyond one's powers to know, understand, or explain ⟨the *occult* ways in which the human mind works⟩ — see MYSTERIOUS 1

2 having an often intentionally veiled or uncertain meaning ⟨an *occult* reference in the text that has puzzled scholars ever since⟩ — see OBSCURE 1

3 having seemingly supernatural qualities or powers ⟨Great Britain's Stonehenge is one of those *occult* places people expect something of cosmic significance to happen⟩ — see MYSTIC 1

occult *vb* to keep secret or shut off from view ⟨*occulted* their house from prying eyes by planting large trees around it⟩ — see ¹HIDE 2

occupant *n* one who lives permanently in a place ⟨the only *occupants* of that house are an old lady and her cat, although her grandchildren often visit⟩ — see INHABITANT

occupation *n* the activity by which one regularly makes a living ⟨my primary *occupation* is as a stockbroker, but I'm a drummer in a rock band on the weekends⟩

synonyms calling, employment, line, profession, trade, vocation, work

related words racket; art, craft, handicraft; appointment, assignment, berth, billet, duty, function, job, office, place, position, post, situation; business, engagement, livelihood, living

near antonyms avocation, hobby, pursuit

occupied *adj* involved in often constant activity ⟨the boy is constantly *occupied*, usually with sports or schoolwork⟩ — see BUSY 1

occupy *vb* **1** to hold the attention of ⟨a puzzle will *occupy* that child for hours⟩ — see ENGAGE 1

2 to keep, control, or experience as one's own ⟨while that nation is *occupied* by another country its people will never feel free⟩ — see HAVE 1

occur *vb* to take place ⟨let me know when the lunar eclipse is scheduled to *occur*⟩ — see HAPPEN

occur (to) *vb* to come into the mind of ⟨it didn't *occur to* me to ask until much later⟩

synonyms dawn (on), strike

related words appear, arrive, come, emerge, materialize; con, learn, memorize; recall, recollect, remember, reminisce

near antonyms forget, unlearn; disregard, neglect, overlook

occurrence *n* something that happens ⟨life is full of random *occurrences*⟩ — see EVENT 1

ocean *n* the whole body of salt water that covers nearly three-fourths of the earth ⟨the Vikings explored the

ocean in small open boats, beginning in the eighth century⟩
synonyms blue, brine, deep, sea, seven seas
related words high seas, main, waters; basin; Davy Jones's locker
oceanic *adj* of or relating to the sea ⟨the theory that ancient mariners took advantage of *oceanic* currents to roam the seas on primitive rafts⟩ — see MARINE 1
ocular *adj* of, relating to, or used in vision ⟨recommends regular eye examinations for the early detection of such *ocular* diseases as glaucoma⟩ — see VISUAL 1
odd *adj* 1 being one of a pair or set without a corresponding mate ⟨somehow, there's always at least one *odd* sock that comes out of the dryer⟩
synonyms unmatched, unpaired
related words alone, lone, only, single, singular, sole, solitary
antonyms matched, paired
2 different from the ordinary in a way that causes curiosity or suspicion ⟨one girl dyed her hair purple with pink polka dots, which was a rather *odd* effect⟩
synonyms bizarre, curious, far-out, funny, kinky, outlandish, out-of-the-way, outré, peculiar, quaint, queer, queerish, quirky, remarkable, screwy, strange, wacky, way-out, weird, wild
related words aberrant, abnormal, atypical, extraordinary, fantastic, flaky, freak, freakish, idiosyncratic, phenomenal, singular, unique, unusual, unwonted; conspicuous, notable, noticeable, outstanding, prominent, salient, striking; atrocious, outrageous, shocking; nonconformist, unconventional, unorthodox; eccentric, idiosyncratic; rare, uncommon, uncustomary; baffling, bewildering, confounding, mystifying, perplexing, puzzling
near antonyms average, commonplace, everyday, garden, ordinary, prosaic, routine, run-of-the-mill, typical, unexceptional, unremarkable, usual, workaday; conformist, conservative, conventional; expected, familiar, predictable; common, customary, frequent, habitual, regular, wonted
3 being out of the ordinary ⟨the only *odd* grade for the exam was the one perfect score⟩ — see EXCEPTIONAL
4 noticeably different from what is generally found or experienced ⟨the *odd* occurrences in the area attracted the attention of people interested in psychic phenomena⟩ — see UNUSUAL 1
oddball *n* a person of odd or whimsical habits ⟨she's known as an *oddball* for wearing mismatched sneakers to class⟩ — see ECCENTRIC
oddity *n* 1 an odd or peculiar habit ⟨his one *oddity* is collecting used pencil leads⟩ — see IDIOSYNCRASY
2 something strange or unusual that is an object of interest ⟨years ago circus sideshows used to display people with unusual physical features as *oddities*⟩ — see CURIOSITY 1
oddment *n* an unused or unwanted piece or item typically of small size or value ⟨the fabric store sells *oddments* left over from cutting⟩ — see ¹SCRAP 1
odds *n pl* a measure of how often an event will occur instead of another ⟨the *odds* of winning the lottery are currently 200 million to one⟩ — see PROBABILITY 2
odds and ends *n pl* 1 small useful items ⟨she's always searching among the *odds and ends* in the drawer for the tool she needs⟩ — see NOTION 1
2 a remaining group or portion ⟨almost all of the piece of leather will be needed for upholstering the chair, so just throw away any *odds and ends*⟩ — see REMAINDER 1

odious *adj* causing intense displeasure, disgust, or resentment ⟨an *odious* and unforgivable insult⟩ — see OFFENSIVE 1
odium *n* the state of having lost the esteem of others ⟨time did nothing to diminish the *odium* in which the traitor lived out his days⟩ — see DISGRACE 1
odor *n* the quality of a thing that makes it perceptible to the sense organs in the nose ⟨some people find the *odor* of skunk rather pleasant⟩ — see SMELL
of *prep* 1 earlier than ⟨it's ten minutes *of* two right now⟩ — see BEFORE 1
2 having to do with ⟨the librarian read stories *of* kings and princesses to the group⟩ — see ABOUT 1
off *adv* from this or that place ⟨move *off* a few yards before I throw the football⟩ — see AWAY
off *adj* 1 falling short of a standard ⟨the milk tasted *off*⟩ — see BAD 1
2 not being in a state of use, activity, or employment ⟨the computer is *off*, so you'll have to turn it on in order to use it⟩ — see INACTIVE 2
3 not being in agreement with what is true ⟨that claim that everyone is actually related to everyone else seems a bit *off*⟩ — see FALSE 1
4 small in degree ⟨on the *off* chance that you do get straight A's, you can skip a grade⟩ — see REMOTE 1
offbeat *adj* noticeably different from what is generally found or experienced ⟨this writer has an enjoyably *offbeat* sense of humor⟩ — see UNUSUAL 1
offend *vb* 1 to commit an offense ⟨since this is the first time you've *offended*, we'll let you off lightly⟩
synonyms err, sin, transgress, trespass
related words breach, break, infringe, violate; backslide, lapse
phrases break the law, fall from grace
near antonyms forgive, justify; repent
2 to cause hurt feelings or deep resentment in ⟨the visitor unintentionally *offended* his hosts terribly by failing to compliment them on the meal⟩ — see INSULT
offender *n* a person who has committed a crime ⟨juvenile *offenders* have their criminal records sealed when they turn 18⟩ — see CRIMINAL
offense *or* **offence** *n* 1 a breaking of a moral or legal code ⟨wartime *offenses* that are crimes against all of humanity⟩
synonyms breach, crime, debt, error, lawbreaking, malefaction, misdeed, misdoing, sin, transgression, trespass, violation, wrongdoing
related words felony, misdemeanor; fault, foible, peccadillo; break, infringement; immorality, iniquity, sinfulness, vice, wickedness; criminality, illegality, lawlessness, unlawfulness
near antonyms blamelessness, faultlessness, guiltlessness, innocence; goodness, morality, righteousness, virtue, virtuousness
2 the act or action of setting upon with force or violence ⟨combat casualties grew enormously as the weapons of *offense* became far more technologically advanced than defensive armor⟩ — see ATTACK 1
3 an act or expression showing scorn and usually intended to hurt another's feelings ⟨a diplomat never deliberately gives *offense*⟩ — see INSULT
4 the feeling of being offended or resentful after a slight or indignity ⟨my mother was prone to take *offense* even at the most innocent remark⟩ — see PIQUE
offensive *adj* 1 causing intense displeasure, disgust, or resentment ⟨I find your disrespectful attitude toward religion very *offensive*⟩ ⟨the smell of rotting food is quite *offensive*⟩

synonyms abhorrent, abominable, appalling, awful, distasteful, dreadful, foul, hideous, horrendous, horrible, horrid, loathsome, nasty, nauseating, noisome, obnoxious, obscene, odious, repellent (*also* repellant), repugnant, repulsive, revolting, scandalous, shocking, sickening, ugly

related words exceptionable, objectionable; disagreeable, unpleasant; contemptible, despicable, detestable, hateful; unhealthy, unwholesome; execrable, lousy, miserable; atrocious, heinous, unspeakable; barbarous, unchristian, uncivilized, ungodly, unholy

near antonyms acceptable, agreeable, attractive, delectable, delightful, desirable, likable (*or* likeable), pleasant, pleasing, welcome; unobjectionable; healthy, wholesome

antonyms inoffensive

2 provoking or likely to provoke protest 〈insensitive, *offensive* remarks about the plight of the homeless〉 — see OBJECTIONABLE

offensive *n* the act or action of setting upon with force or violence 〈the primary *offensive* by the ground forces will commence at dawn tomorrow〉 — see ATTACK 1

offer *n* something which is presented for consideration 〈a job *offer* that I couldn't refuse〉 — see PROPOSAL

offer *vb* **1** to put before another for acceptance or consideration 〈I *offered* my boss an alternative to the plan that required me to work overtime〉

synonyms extend, give, proffer, tender

related words pose, propose

near antonyms accept, receive, take; decline, refuse, reject; retract, withdraw; consider, contemplate, mull (over), ponder, study, think (over)

2 to set before the mind for consideration 〈*offered* the idea of a vacation to a beach resort in the Caribbean〉 — see PROPOSE 1

3 to bring before the public in performance or exhibition 〈a summer theater *offering* a full schedule of musicals to the vacationing public〉 — see PRESENT 1

4 to give up as an offering to a god 〈when fruits, flowers, or crops are *offered*, the offering is known as a bloodless sacrifice〉 — see SACRIFICE

offering *n* something offered to a god 〈some ancient gods were thought to demand burnt *offerings*〉 — see SACRIFICE

offhand *adj* made or done without previous thought or preparation 〈an *offhand* comment that later caused the politician much embarrassment〉 — see EXTEMPORANEOUS

offhanded *adj* made or done without previous thought or preparation 〈a quick, *offhanded* suggestion that was actually much better than any of the prepared proposals〉 — see EXTEMPORANEOUS

office *n* a large unit of a governmental, business, or educational organization 〈the company's main *office* is in Atlanta〉 — see DIVISION 2

officeholder *n* a person who holds a public office 〈the last *officeholder* was extremely conscientious about not using public funds for his personal gain〉 — see OFFICIAL

officer *n* **1** a member of a force charged with law enforcement at the local level 〈if you are ever lost, find the nearest *officer* and ask for help〉

synonyms bobby [*British*], bull [*slang*], constable, cop, policeman, police officer

related words patrolman, policewoman; detective, inspector, plainclothesman; marshal, sheriff, trooper; captain, lieutenant, sergeant

2 a person who holds a public office 〈an *officer* of the court〉 — see OFFICIAL

official *adj* ordered or allowed by those in authority 〈the *official* languages for those Olympic Games were French and English〉

synonyms authorized, sanctioned

related words legal, permissible; approved, endorsed; abetted, encouraged, promoted, suggested, supported; certified, licensed (*also* licenced); authoritative, canonical, ex officio; semiofficial

near antonyms illegal, illicit, unlawful; unapproved, unendorsed, unlicensed

antonyms unauthorized, unofficial, unsanctioned

official *n* a person who holds a public office 〈some of our best public *officials* do their jobs quietly and are never in the news〉

synonyms functionary, officeholder, officer, public servant

related words bureaucrat; administrator, commissioner, director, executive, manager, superintendent, supervisor; chair, chairman

officious *adj* thrusting oneself where one is not welcome or invited 〈an *officious* little man who was always telling everyone else how to do their jobs〉 — see INTRUSIVE

offing *n* time that is to come 〈major changes are in the *offing* for the company〉 — see FUTURE 1

offset *n* a force or influence that makes an opposing force ineffective or less effective 〈a better performance this time will be an *offset* to last year's dismal showing〉 — see COUNTERBALANCE

offset *vb* to balance with an equal force so as to make ineffective 〈if you get a high grade on this quiz, it will *offset* the D from your last one〉

synonyms annul, cancel (out), compensate (for), correct, counteract, counterbalance, counterpoise, make up (for), neutralize

related words invalidate, negate, nullify; atone (for); outweigh, redeem; redress, relieve, remedy; override, overrule

offshoot *n* **1** a branch of a main stem especially of a plant 〈we knew the rose bush had survived the winter when it began producing *offshoots* and turning green again〉

synonyms outgrowth, shoot

related words excrescence, growth; bough, limb, twig; bud, floret; spray, sprig

2 something that naturally develops or is developed from something else 〈opened a shop selling fancy foods as an *offshoot* of their very successful restaurant〉 — see DERIVATIVE

offspring *n* the descendants of a person, animal, or plant 〈the racehorse's *offspring* all proved to be very good racers as well〉 〈the couple celebrated their 50th wedding anniversary surrounded by three generations of *offspring*〉

synonyms issue, posterity, progeny, seed, spawn

related words brood, hatch, litter, young; child, scion (*also* cion)

near antonyms ancestor, antecedent, forebear (*also* forbear), forefather, parent

offstage *adj or adv* off or away from the part of the stage visible to the audience 〈please wait until you are *offstage* to start changing costumes〉

synonyms backstage

related words upstage

phrases behind the scenes

oft *adv* many times 〈as I have *oft* said, you need to look before you leap〉 — see OFTEN

often *adv* many times ⟨I seem to stumble *often* when I try to walk in high heels⟩

synonyms constantly, continually, frequently, oft, oftentimes (*or* ofttimes), repeatedly

related words always, consistently, continuously, perpetually; afresh, again, anew; commonly, ordinarily, regularly, routinely; intermittently, periodically, recurrently; generally, usually

phrases again and again, over and over, time after time, time and again

near antonyms occasionally, sometimes, sporadically, never; once

antonyms infrequently, rarely, seldom

oftentimes *or* **ofttimes** *adv* many times ⟨children *oftentimes* don't realize how quickly time passes⟩ — see OFTEN

ogle *vb* to look at in a flirtatious or desiring way ⟨I do wish you two would stop *ogling* each other during class⟩

synonyms leer (at)

related words eye, gape, gawk, gaze, glare, goggle, peer, rubberneck, stare

ogre *n* **1** a strange or horrible and often frightening creature ⟨a horror movie filled with *ogres* and demons of every description⟩ — see MONSTER 1

2 something or someone that causes fear or dread especially without reason ⟨the *ogre* of the standardized test keeps recurring⟩ — see BOGEY 1

oh *n* the numerical symbol 0 or the absence of number or quantity represented by it ⟨the number is one-*oh*-two-four⟩ — see ZERO 1

oil *n* a picture created with usually oil paint ⟨that artist is known to have created only *oils* and charcoal sketches⟩ — see PAINTING

oil *vb* to coat (something) with a slippery substance in order to reduce friction ⟨if you *oil* the machinery on a regular basis, it will operate more efficiently⟩ — see LUBRICATE

oiled *adj* having or being a surface so smooth as to make sliding or falling likely ⟨following the fuel spill, the resulting *oiled* stretch of roadway had to be closed to traffic⟩ — see SLICK 1

oil painting *n* a picture created with usually oil paint ⟨hung a beautiful *oil painting* of the bay on the living room wall⟩ — see PAINTING

oilskin *n* a coat made of water-resistant material ⟨the *oilskins* worn by the fishing boat's crew gave them scant protection from the cold, driving rain⟩ — see RAINCOAT

OK *or* **okay** *adj* **1** being to one's liking ⟨that dinner was *OK*, but I liked yesterday's better⟩ — see SATISFACTORY 1

2 of a level of quality that meets one's needs or standards ⟨this latest draft of the essay is *OK* but could be better⟩ — see ADEQUATE

OK *or* **okay** *adv* **1** in a satisfactory way ⟨you did *OK* on that last test⟩ — see WELL 1

2 used to express agreement ⟨*OK*, fine, I'll go to the party⟩ — see YES

OK *or* **okay** *n* an acceptance of something as satisfactory ⟨our teacher gave his *OK* on the project, so we can go ahead with it⟩ — see APPROVAL 1

OK *or* **okay** *vb* **1** to give official acceptance of something as satisfactory ⟨a judge will have to *OK* the search warrant⟩ — see APPROVE

2 to have a favorable opinion of ⟨I'm glad that my friends *OK'd* my choice of girlfriend⟩ — see APPROVE (OF)

old *adj* **1** being of advanced years and especially past middle age ⟨every day the *old* fisherman set out in his small boat to brave the dangers of the sea⟩ — see ELDERLY

2 dating or surviving from the distant past ⟨an extremely *old* piece of jewelry was discovered in the Egyptian ruins⟩ — see ANCIENT 1

3 having been such at some previous time ⟨I ran into my *old* fourth-grade teacher yesterday⟩ — see FORMER

older *adj* being of advanced years and especially past middle age ⟨an *older* woman was the chief librarian for the town⟩ — see ELDERLY

oldfangled *adj* pleasantly reminiscent of an earlier time ⟨those big solid-iron phones are an *oldfangled* reminder of the time when you had to rent a phone from the telephone company⟩ — see OLD-FASHIONED 1

old–fashioned *adj* **1** pleasantly reminiscent of an earlier time ⟨an elegant, *old-fashioned* bun that was held in place with pearl hairpins⟩

synonyms antique, oldfangled, old-time, old-world, quaint

related words antiquated, obsolete; historic, historical, olden, traditional; outdated, outmoded, out-of-date, outworn, passé; dated, fusty, moth-eaten, musty; aged, age-old, ancient, antediluvian, fossilized, hoary, venerable; bygone, erstwhile, former, late, past; forgotten, remote; ageless, dateless; timeless

near antonyms fresh, new, up-to-date; chic, fashionable, smart, stylish; modernized, refurbished, remodeled, renewed

antonyms contemporary, hot, mod, modern, newfangled, new-fashioned, ultramodern

2 tending to favor established ideas, conditions, or institutions ⟨Mom, expecting me to never be alone with a boy until I'm 18 is so *old-fashioned*!⟩ — see CONSERVATIVE 1

old hand *n* a person with long experience in a specified area ⟨with 25 years on the job, Vinnie was the *old hand* everyone went to with their problems⟩ — see VETERAN

old–maidish *adj* hard to please ⟨an *old-maidish* teacher who required that every essay be written in very formal English⟩ — see FINICKY

old man *n* **1** a male human parent ⟨I'll ask my *old man* if I can go to the movies tonight⟩ — see FATHER 1

2 the male partner in a marriage ⟨my *old man* and I have been together for 10 years now⟩ — see HUSBAND

oldster *n* a person of advanced years ⟨a family film that will appeal to youngsters and *oldsters* alike⟩ — see SENIOR CITIZEN

old–time *adj* pleasantly reminiscent of an earlier time ⟨an *old-time* song that took the long-married couple back to when they were first dating⟩ — see OLD-FASHIONED 1

old–timer *n* **1** a person of advanced years ⟨a group of *old-timers* playing shuffleboard⟩ — see SENIOR CITIZEN

2 a person with long experience in a specified area ⟨the *old-timer* at the company will be retiring at the end of the year⟩ — see VETERAN

old wives' tale *n* a false idea or belief ⟨the belief that going outside with wet hair will cause you to catch cold is just an *old wives' tale*⟩ — see FALLACY 1

old–world *adj* pleasantly reminiscent of an earlier time ⟨the theater has been painstakingly restored to its *old-world* elegance⟩ — see OLD-FASHIONED 1

omen *n* something believed to be a sign or warning of a future event ⟨some people believe that a black cat

crossing your path is an *omen* that something bad is about to happen to you⟩
synonyms augury, auspice, boding, foreboding, foreshadowing, portent, prefiguring, presage
related words forerunner, harbinger, herald, precursor; foretaste, hint, inkling, intimation, suggestion; forewarning, forecast, foretelling, prediction, prognostication, prophecy; badge, mark, note, token
ominous *adj* being or showing a sign of evil or calamity to come ⟨that comment about downsizing from the company president sounded *ominous*⟩
synonyms baleful, dire, foreboding, inauspicious, menacing, portentous, sinister, threatening
related words black, dark, gloomy; unfavorable, unpromising; ill-fated, ill-starred, star-crossed, unfortunate, unlucky; evil, malign, malignant
near antonyms auspicious, benign, favorable, promising, propitious
omission *n* something left out ⟨the disk contains a selection of deleted scenes, and a couple of the *omissions* greatly add to the intelligibility of the movie's plot⟩
synonyms deletion
related words elimination; blank, skip; lapse, slip; deduction, reduction, subtraction
near antonyms inclusion; accretion, accrual, addendum, addition, augmentation, boost, gain, increase, increment, raise, rise, supplement
omit *vb* to miss the opportunity or obligation ⟨you must not *omit* mentioning the sources you used in researching your paper⟩ — see NEGLECT 3
omnibus *adj* covering everything or all important points ⟨the president's state of the union speech is usually an *omnibus* look at the issues that the country is confronting⟩ — see ENCYCLOPEDIC
omnipotent *adj* having unlimited power or authority ⟨the nearly universal religious belief that God is *omnipotent* and can do anything⟩
synonyms all-powerful, almighty
related words great, sovereign, supreme, towering, transcendent; authoritative, chief, majestic, masterful; mighty, potent, powerful, strong; divine, godlike
near antonyms helpless, impotent, powerless; limited, restricted
omnipresent *adj* present in all places and at all times ⟨seeking some much-needed relief from the *omnipresent* noise of the big city⟩
synonyms ubiquitous, universal
related words boundless, endless, illimitable, immeasurable, indefinite, infinite, limitless, measureless, unbounded, unfathomable, unlimited
near antonyms bounded, circumscribed, confined, finite, limited, restricted
on *adj* being in effective operation ⟨please don't leave the sanding machine *on* if you're not going to be near it⟩ — see ACTIVE 1
on *adv* 1 toward a point ahead in space or time ⟨we really must move *on* now if we're going to end this meeting before midnight⟩ — see ONWARD 1
2 toward or at a point lying in advance in space or time ⟨he's getting *on* in years and doesn't see or hear as well as he used to⟩ — see ALONG
on *prep* 1 having to do with ⟨books *on* sports heroes are my favorite reading matter⟩ — see ABOUT 1
2 in or into contact with ⟨place your test *on* the teacher's desk when you're finished⟩ — see AGAINST
oncoming *adj* being soon to appear or take place ⟨we're looking forward to your *oncoming* visit⟩ — see FORTHCOMING

one *adj* known but not named ⟨*one* person that I know said that it was the best movie he had ever seen⟩ — see CERTAIN 1
one–dimensional *adj* having or showing a lack of depth of understanding or character ⟨a *one-dimensional* analysis of a novel that has a lot to say about personal courage⟩ — see SUPERFICIAL 2
onerous *adj* 1 difficult to endure ⟨had the *onerous* and stressful job of notifying the families of soldiers killed in action⟩ — see HARSH 1
2 requiring much time, effort, or careful attention ⟨building the scale model was an *onerous* task⟩ — see DEMANDING 1
one–sided *adj* inclined to favor one side over another ⟨my brother's account of how the lamp got broken was somewhat *one-sided*⟩ — see PARTIAL 1
one–sidedness *n* an attitude that always favors one way of feeling or acting especially without considering any other possibilities ⟨the obvious *one-sidedness* of the host means that his radio talk show isn't the open forum that he pretends it is⟩ — see BIAS
onetime *adj* having been such at some previous time ⟨the *onetime* English teacher now works for a newspaper⟩ — see FORMER
ongoing *adj* 1 being in progress or development ⟨we do seem to be making some headway on that *ongoing* project⟩ ⟨the ever *ongoing* quest for knowledge by men and women of science⟩
synonyms afoot, proceeding, under way
related words functioning, happening, operating, working; afloat, alive, going; advancing, gaining
near antonyms receding, regressing, retrogressing
antonyms arrested, halted, stalled, stopped
2 existing or in progress right now ⟨the *ongoing* presidential campaign⟩ — see PRESENT 1
only *adj* 1 having no equal or rival for excellence or desirability ⟨the *only* way to really appreciate the beauty of the forest is to walk through it⟩
synonyms incomparable, inimitable, matchless, nonpareil, peerless, unequaled (*or* unequalled), unexampled, unmatched, unparalleled, unrivaled (*or* unrivalled), unsurpassable, unsurpassed
related words singular, unique; exceptional, extraordinary, rare, uncommon, unusual; A1, bang-up, banner, boss [*slang*], capital, classic, dandy, excellent, fabulous, fine, first-class, first-rate, grand, great, groovy, jim-dandy, keen, marvelous (*or* marvellous), mean, neat, par excellence, prime, superb, superior, superlative, terrific, tip-top, top-notch; better, preferred; exceptional, fancy, high-grade, special
near antonyms common, everyday, normal, ordinary, usual; inferior, lesser, worse, worst; bad, low, lower; low-grade, substandard, unsatisfactory; mediocre, second-class, second-rate; atrocious, execrable, wretched
2 being the one or ones of a class with no other members ⟨that is the *only* possible right answer⟩ ⟨we were the *only* passengers on the tour bus⟩
synonyms alone, lone, singular, sole, solitary, special, unique
related words solo, unaccompanied, unattended; incomparable, inimitable, matchless, peerless, unequaled (*or* unequalled), unmatched, unparalleled, unrivaled (*or* unrivalled), unsurpassable, unsurpassed; distinct, distinctive, individual, separate
near antonyms manifold, multifarious, myriad; assorted, heterogenous, miscellaneous, mixed, motley
only *adv* 1 for nothing other than ⟨you're doing that *only* to annoy me⟩ — see SOLELY 1

2 not long ago ⟨we won the election *only* six days ago⟩ — see NEWLY

3 nothing more than ⟨I was *only* fooling when I said I saw a shark in the water⟩ — see JUST 3

only *conj* if it were not for the fact that ⟨that's a very nice idea, *only* it won't help⟩ — see EXCEPT

onrush *n* forward movement in time or place ⟨a sudden *onrush* of development in an area that was rural until very recently⟩ — see ADVANCE 1

onset *n* **1** the act or action of setting upon with force or violence ⟨the walls withstood the *onset* of the first battalion⟩ — see ATTACK 1

2 the point at which something begins ⟨the claim that if you take enough vitamin C at the *onset* of a cold, you'll often recover faster⟩ — see BEGINNING

onslaught *n* the act or action of setting upon with force or violence ⟨the massive *onslaught* of enemy troops caught the country by surprise⟩ — see ATTACK 1

onward *also* **onwards** *adv* **1** toward a point ahead in space or time ⟨we must continue to move *onward*, or we will die in this desert⟩
synonyms ahead, forth, forward, on
near antonyms backward

2 toward or at a point lying in advance in space or time ⟨work on the project has been continuing *onward* at a steady pace⟩ — see ALONG

oodles *n* a considerable amount ⟨the neighbors let us know that they bought *oodles* of candy for Halloween this year⟩ — see LOT 2

ooze *n* soft wet earth ⟨our car tires sank deep in the *ooze*⟩ — see MUD

ooze *vb* to flow forth slowly through small openings ⟨maple sap *oozed* slowly from the cut in the tree and into the bucket⟩ — see EXUDE 1

oozy *adj* full of or covered with soft wet earth ⟨lost a shoe in the *oozy* field⟩ — see MUDDY 1

opacity *n* the quality or state of having a veiled or uncertain meaning ⟨the *opacity* of the abstract painter's works simply baffles many gallery visitors⟩ — see OBSCURITY 1

opaque *adj* not seen or understood clearly ⟨an *opaque* remark that seemed to hint that there would be future retaliation⟩ — see FAINT 1

open *adj* **1** allowing passage without obstruction ⟨thank you for clearing out the hallway so that it's *open* again⟩
synonyms clear, cleared, free, unclogged, unclosed, unobstructed, unstopped
related words emptied, unoccupied, vacant; exposed, revealed; gaping, wide, yawning; unbarred, unbolted, unclasped, unfastened, unlatched, unlocked, unsealed; unbuttoned, unclenched, unfolded, unfurled, unzipped
near antonyms constricted, cramped, encumbered, hampered, hindered, impeded, interfered (with), trammeled; barricaded, blockaded, dammed
antonyms blocked, clogged, closed, jammed, obstructed, plugged, shut, stopped, stuffed, uncleared

2 freely available for use or participation by all ⟨the beach's *open* sand castle-building contest that every year attracts competitors of all ages and abilities⟩
synonyms free-for-all, public, unrestricted
related words collective, common, communal, shared; accessible, available, free; unregulated
near antonyms limited; inaccessible, unavailable
antonyms closed, exclusive, off-limits, private, restricted

3 being in a situation where one is likely to meet with harm ⟨the country's *open* to invasion if its borders remain unguarded⟩ — see LIABLE 1

4 free in expressing one's true feelings and opinions ⟨a talkative and *open* child who tells people more than they want to know⟩ — see FRANK

5 lacking a usual or natural covering ⟨*open* wounds in his legs⟩ — see NAKED 2

6 not known by only a select few ⟨the two boxers have an *open* dislike for each other⟩ — see PUBLIC 1

7 not yet settled or decided ⟨that issue will have to remain *open* until the supervisor can decide⟩ — see PENDING 1

8 willing to consider new or different ideas ⟨she is always *open* and ready to listen to anyone's suggestions⟩ — see OPEN-MINDED 1

open *n* that part of the physical world that is removed from human habitation ⟨backpacking in the *open*⟩ — see NATURE 2

open *vb* **1** to change from a closed to an open position ⟨please *open* the door to let the cat out⟩
synonyms unclose
related words unbar, unbolt, unclasp, unfasten, unlatch, unlock; unbutton, unclench, unfold, unfurl, unzip; disengage, release, slip
near antonyms bar, bolt, clasp, fasten, latch, lock; button (up), zip (up)
antonyms close, shut

2 to arrange clear passage of (something) by removing obstructions ⟨we need to *open* this drain that's clogged with hair⟩
synonyms clear, free, unclog, unstop
related words ease, facilitate, loosen (up), smooth
near antonyms constrict, encumber, hamper, hinder, impede, interfere (with), obstruct, trammel; barricade, blockade
antonyms block, clog (up), close, dam (up), plug (up), stop

3 to arrange the parts of (something) over a wider area ⟨when we got too close, the cardinal *opened* its wings and flew to a higher branch⟩
synonyms expand, extend, fan (out), flare (out), spread (out), stretch (out), outspread, outstretch, unfold
related words overspread
near antonyms compact, compress, condense, reduce
antonyms close, contract, fold

4 to rid the surface of (an area) from things in the way ⟨snowplows *opened* the runway without much trouble⟩ — see CLEAR 1

5 to take the first step in (a process or course of action) ⟨we will *open* the proceedings tomorrow with a short ceremony⟩ — see BEGIN 1

open–air *adj* of, relating to, or held in the open air ⟨an *open-air* concert under the stars⟩ — see OUTDOORS

open air *n* that part of the physical world that is removed from human habitation ⟨a family of city dwellers who can't wait to go camping in the *open air*⟩ — see NATURE 2

open–and–shut *adj* not subject to misinterpretation or more than one interpretation ⟨an *open-and-shut* case of robbery⟩ — see CLEAR 2

open–eyed *adj* paying close attention usually for the purpose of anticipating approaching danger or opportunity ⟨an *open-eyed* deer cautiously grazed in the backyard⟩ — see ALERT 1

openhanded *adj* giving or sharing in abundance and without hesitation ⟨the surprisingly *openhanded* toddler offered to share his toys with each newcomer at the day-care center⟩ — see GENEROUS 1

openhandedness *n* the quality or state of being generous ⟨the *openhandedness* of the queen in bestowing honors was legendary⟩ — see LIBERALITY

openhearted *adj* free in expressing one's true feelings and opinions ⟨many therapists believe that it is better to be *openhearted* than to repress one's feelings, however hostile⟩ — see FRANK

openheartedness *n* **1** the free expression of one's true feelings and opinions ⟨his *openheartedness* about his private life often startled new acquaintances⟩ — see CANDOR

2 the quality or state of being generous ⟨their natural *openheartedness* made them easy prey for every trickster with a sad story⟩ — see LIBERALITY

opening *n* **1** a favorable combination of circumstances, time, and place ⟨she saw an *opening* for her remarks and seized it⟩ — see OPPORTUNITY

2 a place in a surface allowing passage into or through a thing ⟨an *opening* in the roof is letting rain drip inside⟩ — see HOLE 1

3 an open space in a barrier (as a wall or hedge) ⟨the rabbit found a little *opening* in the bushes and darted through⟩ — see GAP 1

open–minded *adj* **1** willing to consider new or different ideas ⟨all I ask is that you try to be *open-minded* when we present our suggestions⟩

synonyms broad-minded, open, receptive

related words impartial, neutral, objective, unbiased, unprejudiced; easygoing, tolerant; calm, detached, dispassionate; amenable, compliant; impressionable, suggestible, susceptible; persuadable, persuasible

near antonyms biased, one-sided, partial, partisan, prejudiced; bigoted, intolerant

antonyms narrow-minded

2 not bound by traditional ways or beliefs ⟨younger people are often more *open-minded* on social and political issues⟩ — see LIBERAL 1

openmouthed *adj* filled with amazement or wonder ⟨I was *openmouthed* at the stunning view from the mountaintop⟩

synonyms amazed, astonished, astounded, awed, awestruck, dumbfounded (*or* dumfounded), flabbergasted, marveling (*or* marvelling), wondering

related words startled, surprised; bemused, bewildered, puzzled; overwhelmed, staggered, stunned, stupefied

near antonyms unimpressed; disinterested, incurious, indifferent, unconcerned, uninterested; dispassionate, emotionless, impassive, unemotional; bored, jaded

openness *n* **1** the free expression of one's true feelings and opinions ⟨her *openness* was refreshing after the tiresome coyness of her friends⟩ — see CANDOR

2 the state of being left without shelter or protection against something harmful ⟨doctors concerned about the population's *openness* to the new strain of the flu virus⟩ — see EXPOSURE 1

open sesame *n* something that allows someone to achieve a desired goal ⟨it turned out that a simple "please" was the *open sesame* for charming the lunch lady into giving extra dessert⟩ — see PASSPORT

operable *adj* capable of or suitable for being used for a particular purpose ⟨that machine is only *operable* for sewing⟩ — see USABLE 1

operate *vb* **1** to control the mechanical operation of ⟨do not *operate* heavy machinery, including cars, after taking this medication⟩

synonyms handle, run, work

related words use; maneuver, manipulate, ply, wield; command, control, direct, drive, guide, pilot, steer

2 to look after and make decisions about ⟨it takes years to learn how to *operate* that business so that it makes money⟩ — see CONDUCT 1

3 to produce a desired effect ⟨the medicine will take an hour or so to *operate* the first time you use it⟩ — see ACT 2

4 to put into action or service ⟨wouldn't dream of *operating* a vehicle under the influence of alcohol⟩ — see USE 1

operating *adj* being in effective operation ⟨the only *operating* nuclear power plant in the state⟩ — see ACTIVE 1

operation *n* **1** a specific task with which a person or group is charged ⟨a secret *operation* which, if it is discovered, the government will deny any knowledge of⟩ — see MISSION

2 a usually fixed or ordered series of actions or events leading to a result ⟨a specific mathematical *operation* is required in order to get the correct answer⟩ — see PROCESS 1

3 the act or activity of looking after and making decisions about something ⟨the *operation* of a convenience store can be quite stressful⟩ — see CONDUCT 1

4 the act or practice of employing something for a particular purpose ⟨that's the only *operation* for which anyone would ever need this weapon⟩ — see USE 1

operational *adj* being in effective operation ⟨a fully *operational* oil refinery⟩ — see ACTIVE 1

operative *adj* being in effective operation ⟨the last *operative* bookbinder of its kind in the business⟩ — see ACTIVE 1

operative *n* **1** a person who tries secretly to obtain information for one country in the territory of another usually unfriendly country ⟨CIA *operatives* take terrible risks to find out the secrets of foreign countries⟩ — see SPY

2 a person whose business is solving crimes and catching criminals or gathering information that is not easy to get ⟨hired a private *operative* to find out what kind of activity his wife was engaged in⟩ — see DETECTIVE

opiate *adj* tending to cause sleep ⟨morphine is an *opiate* drug⟩ — see HYPNOTIC

opine *vb* to make a statement of one's opinion ⟨"I really like your shirt!" he *opined*⟩ — see REMARK 1

opinion *n* **1** an idea that is believed to be true or valid without positive knowledge ⟨my *opinion* is that such interference was unnecessary⟩

synonyms belief, conviction, eye, feeling, judgment (*or* judgement), mind, notion, persuasion, sentiment, verdict, view

related words say; impression, perception, take; attitude; assumption, presumption, presupposition; conclusion, decision, determination; deliverance, esteem, estimate, estimation; credence, credit, faith; concept, conception, idea, thought; position, stand; comment, observation, reflection, remark; conjecture, guess, hunch, hypothesis, surmise, theory; advice, recommendation, suggestion; angle, outlook, perspective, point of view, shoes, slant, standpoint, viewpoint

near antonyms fact, truth

2 a position arrived at after consideration ⟨my *opinion* is that we should refuse to do business with that company⟩ — see DECISION 1

opinionated *adj* sticking to an opinion, purpose, or course of action in spite of reason, arguments, or persuasion ⟨she's so *opinionated* and completely unwilling to entertain the notion that she might be wrong⟩ — see OBSTINATE

opponent *n* **1** one that takes a position opposite another in a competition or conflict ⟨in martial arts, before the match begins, always bow to your *opponent*⟩
synonyms adversary, antagonist, rival
related words equal, match; enemy, foe; archenemy, nemesis; competitor, contestant; bane, bête noire, curse; assailant, attacker, combatant, invader
near antonyms accomplice, ally, confederate, partner; advocate, champion, exponent, proponent, supporter
2 one that is hostile toward another ⟨the senator has many political *opponents* who would love to ruin his career⟩ — see ENEMY

opportune *adj* especially suitable for a certain time ⟨an *opportune* rain shower gave them an excuse to leave the outdoor concert early⟩ — see TIMELY 1

opportunist *n* one who does things only for his own benefit and with little regard for right and wrong ⟨an *opportunist* who makes friends and then drops them as soon as they aren't useful anymore⟩ — see SELF-SEEKER

opportunity *n* a favorable combination of circumstances, time, and place ⟨this art school could be a wonderful *opportunity* for you to finally develop your talent for painting⟩
synonyms chance, occasion, opening, room
related words break; play, way; juncture, pass

oppose *vb* **1** to refuse to give in to ⟨I will continue to *oppose* any attempts to infringe upon our civil liberties⟩ — see RESIST
2 to strive to reduce or eliminate ⟨we must *oppose* ignorance and prejudice wherever and whenever they arise⟩ — see FIGHT 2

opposite *adj* being as different as possible ⟨your suggestion that we hold the meeting at night is precisely *opposite* to our original plan for a nice breakfast⟩
synonyms antipodal, antipodean, antithetical, contradictory, contrary, diametric (*or* diametrical), polar
related words adverse, negative, unfavorable; antagonistic, antipathetic, counter, hostile; converse, inverse, reverse; disparate, dissimilar, divergent, unalike, unlike
near antonyms alike, analogous, like, similar; equivalent, identical, same; synonymous
antonyms noncontradictory

opposite *n* something that is as different as possible from something else ⟨no matter what I say, you insist on the *opposite*⟩
synonyms antipode, antithesis, contrary, negative, reverse
related words negation; antonym; converse, inverse
near antonyms synonym; analogue, counterpart; carbon copy, copy, duplicate, replica

opposition *n* the inclination to resist ⟨your stubborn *opposition* to wearing boots in the snow is going to leave you with very cold feet⟩ — see RESISTANCE 1

oppress *vb* **1** to make sad ⟨this gloomy weather is *oppressing* all of us⟩ — see DEPRESS 1
2 to subject to incapacitating emotional or mental stress ⟨I'm simply *oppressed* by the demands of my job and schoolwork⟩ — see OVERWHELM 1

oppression *n* a state or spell of low spirits ⟨suffered a lingering *oppression* in the weeks after his dog died⟩ — see SADNESS

oppressive *adj* difficult to endure ⟨an *oppressive* regime that ruled through terror⟩ — see HARSH 1

oppressively *adv* in a manner so as to cause loss or suffering ⟨forced to live under an *oppressively* cruel government⟩ — see HARDLY 1

oppressor *n* **1** a person who causes repeated emotional pain, distress, or annoyance to another ⟨I finally stood up to my schoolyard *oppressor* and made the bullying stop⟩ — see TORMENTOR
2 a person who uses power or authority in a cruel, unjust, or harmful way ⟨the people eventually rebelled against their odious *oppressor*⟩ — see DESPOT

opprobrium *n* the state of having lost the esteem of others ⟨the *opprobrium* that was long attached to the convicted embezzler's name⟩ — see DISGRACE 1

opt *vb* to come to a judgment after discussion or consideration ⟨they *opted* to reinstate the telephone service⟩ — see DECIDE 1

opt (for) *vb* to decide to accept (someone or something) from a group of possibilities ⟨I think I'll *opt for* the mashed potatoes instead of the french fries or cole slaw⟩ — see CHOOSE 1

optic *adj* of, relating to, or used in vision ⟨the *optic* nerve⟩ — see VISUAL 1

optical *adj* of, relating to, or used in vision ⟨an *optical* illusion that fools most people⟩ — see VISUAL 1

optimism *n* an inclination to believe in the most favorable outcome ⟨your perpetual *optimism* even when things look bleak⟩
synonyms sanguinity
related words brightness, cheerfulness, perkiness, sunniness; hope, hopefulness, rosiness; idealism
near antonyms pessimism, skepticism; cynicism; desperation, discouragement, disheartenment, hopelessness; bleakness, cheerlessness, dreariness, gloom, gloominess; pragmatism, realism

optimistic *adj* having qualities which inspire hope ⟨the latest economic prediction is actually quite *optimistic*⟩ — see HOPEFUL 1

option *n* **1** the act or power of making one's own choices or decisions ⟨you always have the *option* to learn as much or as little as you want in this class⟩ — see FREE WILL
2 the power, right, or opportunity to choose ⟨you will have the *option* to select one of several very different projects⟩ — see CHOICE 1

optional *adj* subject to one's freedom of choice ⟨certain activities are *optional*, and you may choose not to participate if you wish⟩
synonyms discretionary, elective, voluntary
related words alternative, chosen; dispensable, unnecessary, unneeded, unwanted
near antonyms essential, indispensable, necessary, requisite
antonyms compulsory, mandatory, nonelective, obligatory, required

opulence *n* the total of one's money and property ⟨the movie star's *opulence* amazed visitors to her estate⟩ — see WEALTH 1

opulent *adj* **1** having goods, property, or money in abundance ⟨an *opulent* businessman who liked to show off his possessions⟩ — see RICH 1
2 showing obvious signs of wealth and comfort ⟨an *opulent* mansion filled with priceless art and antiques⟩ — see LUXURIOUS

opulently *adv* in a luxurious manner ⟨an *opulently* furnished palace⟩ — see HIGH

opus *n* a literary, musical, or artistic production ⟨the composer's final *opus* was performed posthumously to great acclaim⟩ — see COMPOSITION 1

oral *adj* **1** created by the body's organs of sound ⟨a baby's crying is usually interpreted as an *oral* expression of distress⟩ — see VOCAL

2 made or carried on through speaking rather than in writing ⟨you will all have to give *oral* reports on Monday⟩ — see VERBAL 2

orate *vb* **1** to talk as if giving an important and formal speech ⟨politicians will *orate* lengthily at any opportunity⟩

synonyms declaim, discourse, harangue, mouth (off)

related words rant, rave; lecture, preach; advertise, announce, broadcast, declare, proclaim, pronounce; speak, talk

2 to give a formal often extended talk on a subject ⟨the famous anthropologist will *orate* about her latest research findings⟩ — see TALK 1

oration *n* a usually formal discourse delivered to an audience ⟨the celebrated *orations* of Daniel Webster in unwavering support of the federal union⟩ — see SPEECH 1

oratorical *adj* marked by the use of impressive-sounding but mostly meaningless words and phrases ⟨a speech that was an *oratorical* endorsement of the value of education but one that refused to call for greater spending on education⟩ — see RHETORICAL

oratory *n* **1** the art of speaking in public eloquently and effectively ⟨this debate class will teach you all to be skilled at *oratory*⟩

synonyms elocution

related words bombast, grandiloquence; rhetoric; discourse, speech, talk

2 language that is impressive-sounding but not meaningful or sincere ⟨the politician's *oratory* sounded good only to people who didn't bother to think⟩ — see RHETORIC 1

orb *n* a more or less round body or mass ⟨out of the countless celestial *orbs* twirling in space, the planet Earth remains the only one we can call home⟩ — see ¹BALL 1

orbit *vb* to pass completely around ⟨the moon *orbits* the Earth⟩ — see ENCIRCLE 1

orchestra *n* a usually large group of musicians playing together ⟨the *orchestra* will be performing a selection of Beethoven pieces tomorrow night⟩ — see ²BAND 1

ordain *vb* **1** to determine the fate of in advance ⟨some religions believe that a person is *ordained* at birth to be saved or not⟩ — see DESTINE

2 to give an order ⟨Mother always *ordained* that we be properly dressed for church⟩ — see COMMAND 2

ordeal *n* a test of faith, patience, or strength ⟨the hikers were finally rescued after an *ordeal* of three days in the wilderness⟩ — see TRIAL 1

order *n* **1** the way objects in space or events in time are arranged or follow one another ⟨you always keep your books in perfect alphabetical *order*⟩ ⟨we haven't found out the *order* of the speeches yet⟩

synonyms arrangement, array, disposal, disposition, distribution, ordering, sequence, setup

related words continuity; precedence, priority; chain, progression, succession; series; aligning, alignment, lining up; design, layout, pattern, structure, system

near antonyms confusion, disorder, disorganization, disruption, upset; disconnection, disjointedness

2 a group of persons formally joined together for some common interest ⟨a religious *order*⟩ — see ASSOCIATION 2

3 a number of persons or things that are grouped together because they have something in common ⟨col-lects movie posters, photographs and autographs of the stars, and other memorabilia of that *order*⟩ — see SORT 1

4 a piece of metal given in honor of a special event, a person, or an achievement ⟨wore the *order* of the Freemasons⟩ — see MEDAL

5 a state of being or fitness ⟨finally got the car back in working *order*⟩ — see CONDITION 1

6 a statement of what to do that must be obeyed by those concerned ⟨the commander issued an *order* that the number of guards for the prisoner be doubled⟩ — see COMMAND 1

7 one of the segments of society into which people are grouped ⟨the lower *orders* were once expected to be content living out their lives as servants to the upper classes⟩ — see CLASS 1

8 one of the units into which a whole is divided on the basis of a common characteristic ⟨zoologists had problems deciding to which *order* the platypus belongs⟩ — see CLASS 2

order *vb* **1** to put into a particular arrangement ⟨I've *ordered* all of my CDs according to type of music⟩ ⟨he likes to *order* his life so that there are few surprises⟩

synonyms arrange, array, classify, codify, dispose, draw up, marshal, organize, range, systematize

related words groom, make up, spruce (up), straighten (up), tidy (up); unscramble; align, line, line up, queue; alphabetize, file; emplace, place, set; display, lay out, map (out)

antonyms derange, disarrange, disarray, disorder, mess (up), muss (up), rumple, upset

2 to give a request or demand for ⟨they *ordered* hamburgers for lunch⟩

synonyms ask (for), request, requisition

related words commission, solicit; charter, hire, license (*also* licence)

phrases call for

3 to give an order ⟨the teacher *ordered* that everyone sit down immediately and be quiet⟩ — see COMMAND 2

4 to issue orders to (someone) by right of authority ⟨the police officer *ordered* the crowd to back away from the suspect⟩ — see COMMAND 1

ordering *n* **1** a scheme of rank or order ⟨in the *ordering* of crimes, ripping the tags off upholstered furniture should rank fairly low⟩ — see ³SCALE 1

2 the way objects in space or events in time are arranged or follow one another ⟨the *ordering* of the children in the procession was according to height⟩ — see ORDER 1

orderly *adj* **1** being clean and in good order ⟨a small, unpretentious inn offering pleasant, *orderly* rooms⟩ — see NEAT 1

2 following a set method, arrangement, or pattern ⟨the Dewey decimal system is an *orderly* filing system for books⟩ — see METHODICAL

ordinance *n* a rule of conduct or action laid down by a governing authority and especially by a legislator ⟨a local *ordinance* forbids all street parking during snowstorms⟩ — see LAW 1

ordinarily *adv* according to the usual course of things ⟨*ordinarily*, we'd have a quiz today, but the fire drill means it will be postponed⟩ — see NATURALLY 2

ordinary *adj* **1** being of the type that is encountered in the normal course of events ⟨it was a perfectly *ordinary* and undistinguished shirt⟩

synonyms average, common, commonplace, everyday, garden, normal, prosaic, routine, run-of-the-mill, standard, unexceptional, unremarkable, usual, workaday

related words regular, typical; familiar, homely, plain, popular, vulgar; natural; customary, wonted; insignificant, trivial, unimportant; customary, frequent, habitual; expected, predictable

near antonyms curious, funny, peculiar, quaint, queer; aberrant, atypical, irregular; rare, scarce; fantastic, phenomenal; bizarre, far-out, outrageous, outré, weird, wild; eccentric, idiosyncratic, nonconformist, unconventional, unorthodox; freak, freakish; conspicuous, notable, outstanding, prominent, salient, signal, striking; singular, unique

antonyms abnormal, exceptional, extraordinary, odd, out-of-the-way, strange, unusual

2 of average to below average quality ⟨the pizza at that restaurant is just *ordinary*⟩ — see MEDIOCRE 1

3 often observed or encountered ⟨an *ordinary* hairstyle for boys of that age⟩ — see COMMON 1

ordnance *n* large firearms (as cannon or rockets) ⟨the army is waiting for the heavy *ordnance* to be brought in⟩ — see ARTILLERY

oread *n* a mythical goddess represented as a young girl and said to live outdoors ⟨*oreads* supposedly prefer to live in hills and mountains⟩ — see NYMPH 1

organ *n* **1** a publication that appears at regular intervals ⟨that newspaper is an *organ* for the whole university community⟩ — see JOURNAL

2 something used to achieve an end ⟨used the business as an *organ* to fund a variety of political and social causes⟩ — see AGENT 1

organization *n* a group of persons formally joined together for some common interest ⟨an *organization* of people devoted to promoting world peace⟩ — see ASSOCIATION 2

organize *vb* to put into a particular arrangement ⟨carefully *organized* the hotel's silverware by pattern⟩ — see ORDER 1

organized *adj* following a set method, arrangement, or pattern ⟨an *organized* approach to the job⟩ — see METHODICAL

orient *vb* to impart knowledge of a new thing or situation to ⟨*oriented* the new employees to the job requirements⟩ — see ACQUAINT 1

orientate *vb* to impart knowledge of a new thing or situation to ⟨will *orientate* all incoming freshmen to the layout of the high school⟩ — see ACQUAINT 1

orifice *n* a place in a surface allowing passage into or through a thing ⟨the mouth is a bodily *orifice*⟩ — see HOLE 1

origin *n* the line of ancestors from whom a person is descended ⟨they could trace their *origins* back 15 generations⟩ — see ANCESTRY

original *adj* **1** coming before all others in time or order ⟨the *original* plan had to be discarded when the situation changed drastically⟩ — see FIRST 1

2 having the skill and imagination to create new things ⟨an *original* artist who wanted his paintings to convey his emotional responses to the people, objects, and landscapes he painted⟩ — see CREATIVE 1

3 not known or experienced before ⟨separate categories for *original* and adapted screenplays⟩ — see NEW 2

original *n* something from which copies are made ⟨please make copies to hand out, but keep the *original*⟩

synonyms archetype, prototype

related words example, paradigm, pattern; beau ideal, exemplar, classic, ideal, model, nonpareil, paragon; blueprint, draft

near antonyms copy, imitation, replica, reproduction; counterfeit, fake, forgery, sham

originality *n* **1** the quality or appeal of being new ⟨the *originality* of the sculpture sparked a heated controversy in the art world⟩ — see NOVELTY 1

2 the skill and imagination to create new things ⟨a poet of great *originality*, she brought a whole new range of subject matter and imagery to poetry⟩ — see CREATIVITY 1

originally *adv* in the beginning ⟨we *originally* planned to go out tonight, but we changed our minds⟩

synonyms firstly, initially, primarily

related words incipiently; primitively

phrases at first

near antonyms finally, lastly, ultimately

originate *vb* to come into existence ⟨the theory of relativity *originated* with Albert Einstein⟩ — see BEGIN 2

originator *n* **1** one who creates or introduces something new ⟨Thomas Edison was the *originator* of the light bulb⟩ — see INVENTOR

2 a person who establishes a whole new field of endeavor ⟨Copernicus is sometimes hailed as the *originator* of modern astronomy, for he overturned the notion of an earth-centered universe⟩ — see FATHER 2

orison *n* an address to God or a deity ⟨a fervent *orison* asking for divine inspiration in the course of taking the math test⟩ — see PRAYER 1

ornament *n* something that decorates or beautifies ⟨bought the wreath as an *ornament* for the door⟩ — see DECORATION 1

ornament *vb* to make more attractive by adding something that is beautiful or becoming ⟨*ornamented* the Christmas tree with tinsel and lights⟩ — see DECORATE

ornamental *adj* serving to add beauty ⟨the trim on Victorian houses is sometimes elaborately *ornamental*⟩ — see DECORATIVE

ornamental *n* a small object displayed for its attractiveness or interest ⟨a collection of fragile *ornamentals* kept in a glass cabinet⟩ — see KNICKKNACK

ornate *adj* elaborately and often excessively decorated ⟨an *ornate* gambling casino that is designed to look like an Italian palace⟩

synonyms bedizened, florid, gingerbread, overdecorated, overwrought

related words arabesque, baroque, rococo; extravagant, flamboyant, spectacular, splashy; flashy, garish, gaudy, glitzy, loud, ostentatious, pretentious, showy, swank, tawdry; elaborate, extreme; adorned, arrayed, beautified, bedecked, decked, decorated, dressed, embellished, enriched, garnished, ornamented, trimmed; flowery, frilly, lacy; enhanced, heightened, intensified; bossed, chased, emblazoned, embossed, embroidered, flounced, fringed, garlanded, gilded, laced, wreathed

near antonyms bare, denuded, exposed, naked, stripped, uncovered; modest, simple, unassuming, unpretentious; conservative, muted, quiet, restrained, subdued, tasteful, toned-down, understated, unobtrusive

antonyms austere, plain, severe, stark, unadorned

ornery *adj* having or showing a habitually bad temper ⟨an *ornery* old man who always yelled at kids to keep off his lawn⟩ — see ILL-TEMPERED

orthodox *adj* **1** following or agreeing with established form, custom, or rules ⟨teachers tended to favor poets who followed a very *orthodox* style of poetry⟩ — see FORMAL 1

2 tending to favor established ideas, conditions, or institutions ⟨*orthodox* in their view of the world, the

Founding Fathers subscribed to the 18th-century notion that only men with property should be allowed to vote⟩ — see CONSERVATIVE 1

oscillation *n* a series of slight movements by a body back and forth or from side to side ⟨the *oscillation* of a pendulum⟩ — see VIBRATION

ossified *adj* sticking to an opinion, purpose, or course of action in spite of reason, arguments, or persuasion ⟨the company's *ossified* management team failed to see the technological revolution that was sweeping their own industry⟩ — see OBSTINATE

ostensible *adj* appearing to be true on the basis of evidence that may or may not be confirmed ⟨the *ostensible* reason for the meeting turned out to be a trick to get him to the surprise party⟩ — see APPARENT 1

ostensibly *adv* to all outward appearances ⟨*ostensibly* a university student studying abroad, he was actually an espionage agent⟩ — see APPARENTLY

ostentation *n* excessive or unnecessary display ⟨the sheer *ostentation* of the rock star's mansion was overwhelming⟩

synonyms flamboyance, flashiness, garishness, gaudiness, glitz, ostentatiousness, pretentiousness, showiness, swank

related words extravaganza, pageant, parade, show; dazzle, pageantry, spectacle; adornment, decoration, dressing, embellishment, garnishment, ornamentation, trimming; extravagance, fanciness, luxuriousness, opulence, richness, sumptuousness; loudness, luridness, meretriciousness, tawdriness, vulgarity

near antonyms conservativeness, moderation, modesty, restraint, simplicity, understatement; elegance, gracefulness, tastefulness

antonyms austerity, plainness, severity

ostentatious *adj* **1** excessively showy ⟨wore an *ostentatious* diamond ring on his little finger⟩ — see GAUDY

2 self-consciously trying to present an appearance of grandeur or importance ⟨an *ostentatious* man who desperately wanted to impress people with his newly acquired wealth⟩ — see PRETENTIOUS 1

ostentatiousness *n* excessive or unnecessary display ⟨the *ostentatiousness* of the wedding banquet was overwhelming⟩ — see OSTENTATION

other *adj* **1** being not of the same kind ⟨no, I need the *other* pen, the blue one⟩ — see DIFFERENT 1

2 resulting in an increase in amount or number ⟨we'll be taking one *other* person on the trip⟩ — see ADDITIONAL

other *adv* in a different way ⟨we cannot make it to the party *other* than by canceling the previous engagement⟩ — see OTHERWISE

otherwise *adv* in a different way ⟨a serious student who always does his best, for his conscience will not let him do *otherwise*⟩

synonyms differently, else, other

related words diversely, variously

near antonyms similarly

antonyms likewise

ought (to) *vb* to be under necessity or obligation to ⟨you *ought to* do your homework before going out to play⟩ — see NEED 2

ounce *n* a very small amount ⟨an *ounce* of prevention is worth a pound of cure⟩ — see PARTICLE 1

oust *vb* **1** to drive or force out ⟨she was *ousted* from her job after it was proven she'd been pilfering company supplies⟩ — see EJECT 1

2 to remove from a position of prominence or power (as a throne) ⟨the people finally rose up and *ousted* the dictator⟩ — see DEPOSE 1

out *adv* **1** in or into the open air ⟨you really should get *out* more⟩ — see OUTDOORS

2 with one's normal voice speaking the words ⟨read *out* what the note says so that the rest of the class will know⟩ — see ALOUD

out *adj* not at a certain place ⟨half the staff is *out* with the flu⟩ — see ABSENT 1

out *n* the act or a means of getting or keeping away from something undesirable ⟨I really don't want to go to the party, and I've been searching for an *out*⟩ — see ESCAPE 2

out *vb* to become known ⟨the truth will *out* eventually⟩ — see GET OUT 1

out–and–out *adj* **1** having no exceptions or restrictions ⟨an *out-and-out* cheater at every game she plays⟩ — see ABSOLUTE 2

2 trying all possibilities ⟨an *out-and-out* effort to find the lost child⟩ — see EXHAUSTIVE

outbrave *vb* to oppose (something hostile or dangerous) with firmness or courage ⟨the boy *outbraved* his fear of heights and successfully climbed to the top of the cliff⟩ — see FACE 2

outbreak *n* a sudden and usually temporary growth of activity ⟨there was an immediate *outbreak* of paper shuffling and a pretense of work when the teacher re-entered the room⟩

synonyms burst, flare, flare-up, flash, flicker, flurry, flutter, outburst, spurt

related words binge, jag, spree; boost, increase, pickup, upswing, upturn; epidemic, eruption, explosion, paroxysm; deluge, flood, rush, spate, surge; commotion, furor, uproar

near antonyms calm, doldrums, slump

outburst *n* **1** a sudden intense expression of strong feeling ⟨when the coach suddenly started crying hysterically, everyone was shocked by the unexpected *outburst*⟩

synonyms agony, burst, eruption, explosion, fit, flare, flare-up, flash, flush, gale, gush, gust, paroxysm, spasm, storm

related words blowup, grouch, rage, tantrum; ecstasy, rapture, transport; delirium, frenzy, furor

2 a sudden and usually temporary growth of activity ⟨there was a remarkable *outburst* of work in the classroom the moment the teacher returned⟩ — see OUTBREAK

outcast *n* one who is cast out or rejected by society ⟨they were convinced that they would become total *outcasts* if they didn't buy the newest fashions⟩

synonyms castaway, castoff, pariah, reject

related words untouchable; outsider; deportee, exile

near antonyms insider

outcome *n* a condition or occurrence traceable to a cause ⟨one expected *outcome* of hard work is greater success⟩ — see EFFECT 1

outcry *n* a violent shouting ⟨when the dancing was abruptly ended, there was an *outcry* from the students⟩ — see CLAMOR 1

outdated *adj* having passed its time of use or usefulness ⟨an *outdated* rotary telephone⟩ — see OBSOLETE

outdistance *vb* to be greater, better, or stronger than ⟨the new student rapidly *outdistanced* the rest of the class in math⟩ — see SURPASS 1

outdo *vb* to be greater, better, or stronger than ⟨the little girl tried to *outdo* her older brother at games⟩ — see SURPASS 1

outdoor *also* **outdoors** *adj* of, relating to, or held in the open air ⟨an *outdoor* picnic is always at the mercy of the weather, of course⟩
synonyms open-air, out-of-door (*or* out-of-doors)
related words airy; exterior, external, outer, outside, outward; outermost, outmost
near antonyms inner, inside, interior, internal, inward; inmost, innermost
antonyms indoor

outdoors *adv* in or into the open air ⟨please wait until you're *outdoors* to run around and scream⟩
synonyms out, outside
related words without
near antonyms in, inside, within
antonyms indoors

outdoors *n* that part of the physical world that is removed from human habitation ⟨our family loves to hike and camp in the great *outdoors*⟩ — see NATURE 2

outer *adj* situated on the outside or farther out ⟨the *outer* edge of the blade of your figure skate always wears out faster than the inner because you use it more⟩
synonyms exterior, external, outside, outward
related words outermost, outlying, outmost; superficial, surface
near antonyms inmost, innermost
antonyms inner, inside, interior, internal, inward

outermost *adj* most distant from a center ⟨the *outermost* ring of listeners had trouble hearing the concert⟩ — see EXTREME 1

outfit *n* 1 clothing chosen as appropriate for a specific situation ⟨you'll need a special *outfit* for the scout troop⟩ ⟨do you want to buy a new *outfit* for the Halloween party?⟩
synonyms costume, dress, garb, getup, guise, togs
related words apparel, attire, clothes, duds, raiment; fashion, mode, style; array, caparison, vestments
2 a commercial or industrial activity or organization ⟨they're an *outfit* specializing in travel tours for senior citizens⟩ — see ENTERPRISE 1
3 a group of people working together on a task ⟨the whole *outfit* quit early for lunch⟩ — see GANG 1
4 items needed for the performance of a task or activity ⟨you'll need to requisition the full hiking *outfit* from the supply⟩ — see EQUIPMENT
5 the distinctive clothing worn by members of a particular group ⟨the highway patrol *outfit* includes jackboots and a high-crowned hat⟩ — see UNIFORM

outfit *vb* to provide (someone) with what is needed for a task or activity ⟨*outfitted* the scuba instructors handsomely with all new gear⟩ — see FURNISH 1

outflow *n* a flowing or going out ⟨there was an immediate *outflow* of students from the door when the bell rang⟩
synonyms exodus, gush, outpouring
related words drain, flow; ebb, reflux; rush, stampede; emigration, flight; discharge, emanation, emission
near antonyms deluge, flood, inundation, overflow, spate, torrent; flow, river, stream, tide
antonyms flux, inflow, influx, inrush

outfox *vb* to get the better of through cleverness ⟨the prisoners *outfoxed* the guards by tunneling beneath the prison walls⟩ — see OUTWIT

outgo *n* a payment made in the course of achieving a result ⟨last year the company's *outgoes* exceeded its revenues by a wide margin⟩ — see EXPENSE

outgoing *adj* likely to seek or enjoy the company of others ⟨a sweet, *outgoing* toddler who said "hi" to everyone⟩ — see CONVIVIAL

outgrowth *n* 1 a branch of a main stem especially of a plant ⟨trimmed back some of the tree's *outgrowths* so they wouldn't interfere with power lines⟩ — see OFFSHOOT 1
2 a condition or occurrence traceable to a cause ⟨a predictable *outgrowth* of the suburb's ever growing population will be the need for more schools⟩ — see EFFECT 1
3 something that naturally develops or is developed from something else ⟨an industry that is an *outgrowth* of the technology first developed for the U.S. space program⟩ — see DERIVATIVE

outing *n* a short trip for pleasure ⟨an *outing* to the zoo⟩ — see EXCURSION 1

outlander *n* a person who is not native to or known to a community ⟨although we had lived in the village for years, to the natives whose families had been there for generations, we were still *outlanders*⟩ — see STRANGER

outlandish *adj* 1 different from the ordinary in a way that causes curiosity or suspicion ⟨an *outlandish* outfit made entirely out of bottle caps⟩ — see ODD 2
2 excitingly or mysteriously unusual ⟨the *outlandish* tribal rituals that astonished early explorers of that land⟩ — see EXOTIC

outlast *vb* to last longer than ⟨I truly hope this car will *outlast* our previous one⟩ ⟨your work will probably *outlast* you⟩
synonyms outlive, outwear
related words survive; outstay; abide (beyond), endure (past), hold (past), hold out (past), last (beyond), persist (beyond); draw out, perpetuate; succeed

outlaw *vb* to order not to do or use or to be done or used ⟨the federal government *outlawed* the sale of alcohol for a while in the 1920s⟩ — see FORBID

outlawed *adj* that may not be permitted ⟨the *outlawed* drug was found to cause malformations of infants born to mothers who used it during pregnancy⟩ — see IMPERMISSIBLE

outlawing *n* the act of ordering that something not be done or used ⟨the *outlawing* of open containers of beer in moving vehicles is intended to reduce drunk driving⟩ — see PROHIBITION 1

outlay *n* a payment made in the course of achieving a result ⟨the *outlays* for the upcoming wedding seem to be multiplying at an incredible rate⟩ — see EXPENSE

outlet *n* a place or means of going out ⟨this road is the only *outlet* for traffic coming from the racetrack⟩ — see EXIT 1

outline *n* 1 a line that traces the outer limits of an object or surface ⟨place your hand on the paper and draw an *outline* around it⟩
synonyms contour, figure, silhouette
related words delineation, sketch; profile, skyline; form, cast, configuration, conformation, geometry, shape; framework, skeleton
2 a short statement of the main points ⟨each chapter in the textbook is preceded by an *outline*⟩ — see SUMMARY

outline *vb* 1 to draw or make apparent the outline of ⟨she carefully *outlined* the tree before she started drawing in the leaves⟩
synonyms define, delineate, silhouette, sketch, trace
related words line; bound, fringe, margin, skirt; edge, hem, rim, trim; frame; circle, compass, encircle, girdle,

girth, loop, ring, round, surround; chart, diagram, draw, map (out)

2 to make into a short statement of the main points (as of a report) ⟨*outlined* the important points in the introduction⟩ — see SUMMARIZE

outlive *vb* to last longer than ⟨tortoises will *outlive* most people, as they live to be over 100 years old⟩ — see OUTLAST

outlook *n* **1** a high place or structure from which a wide view is possible ⟨a remote *outlook* used for keeping watch for forest fires⟩ — see LOOKOUT 1

2 a way of looking at or thinking about something ⟨tried to keep a cheerful *outlook* on life⟩ — see POINT OF VIEW

3 all that can be seen from a certain point ⟨the *outlook* from the tower is spectacular in all directions⟩ — see VIEW 1

out loud *adv* with one's normal voice speaking the words ⟨registered their dissatisfaction with the meal *out loud* to the waiter⟩ — see ALOUD

outmaneuver *vb* to get the better of through cleverness ⟨*outmaneuvered* the larger army by marching his troops around it⟩ — see OUTWIT

outmoded *adj* having passed its time of use or usefulness ⟨*outmoded* computers that can be recycled⟩ — see OBSOLETE

outmost *adj* most distant from a center ⟨the *outmost* areas of the park are still wilderness⟩ — see EXTREME 1

out–of–date *adj* having passed its time of use or usefulness ⟨the *out-of-date* information that one finds fairly frequently online⟩ — see OBSOLETE

out–of–door *or* **out-of-doors** *adj* of, relating to, or held in the open air ⟨an *out-of-door* performance under the stars⟩ — see OUTDOORS

out–of–doors *n* that part of the physical world that is removed from human habitation ⟨hiking in the *out-of-doors* can be a tremendous appetite builder⟩ — see NATURE 2

out–of–the–way *adj* different from the ordinary in a way that causes curiosity or suspicion ⟨an *out-of-the-way* tavern that worried the locals⟩ — see ODD 2

outpouring *n* a flowing or going out ⟨an *outpouring* of affection and support for the high school athlete in need of an organ transplant⟩ — see OUTFLOW

output *n* something produced by physical or intellectual effort ⟨your *output* at this job has always been above average⟩ — see PRODUCT 1

outrage *n* **1** an act or expression showing scorn and usually intended to hurt another's feelings ⟨the booing during the graduation speech was an *outrage*⟩ — see INSULT

2 an intense emotional state of displeasure with someone or something ⟨Mom's *outrage* over the smashed picture was justifiable⟩ — see ANGER

outrage *vb* **1** to cause hurt feelings or deep resentment in ⟨the spiteful comment *outraged* her so much that she's still holding a grudge⟩ — see INSULT

2 to make angry ⟨the vandalism in the cemetery *outraged* the entire community⟩ — see ANGER

outraged *adj* feeling or showing anger ⟨the principal is *outraged* over the vandalism to the school's computers⟩ — see ANGRY

outrank *vb* to be greater in importance than ⟨one hard fact *outranks* a mountain of speculation anytime⟩ — see OUTWEIGH

outré *adj* different from the ordinary in a way that causes curiosity or suspicion ⟨*outré* behavior that

raised some eyebrows among the townspeople⟩ — see ODD 2

outright *adj* having no exceptions or restrictions ⟨that's an *outright* lie!⟩ — see ABSOLUTE 2

outset *n* the point at which something begins ⟨I wish you'd mentioned this problem at the *outset*⟩ — see BEGINNING

outshine *vb* to be greater, better, or stronger than ⟨the trumpeter *outshined* all of his fellow band members⟩ — see SURPASS 1

outside *adj* **1** situated on the outside or farther out ⟨the *outside* ring of seats⟩ — see OUTER

2 small in degree ⟨there's only an *outside* chance of winning this game⟩ — see REMOTE 1

outside *adv* in or into the open air ⟨go *outside* and play⟩ — see OUTDOORS

outside *n* **1** an outer part or layer ⟨painted the *outside* of the house⟩ — see EXTERIOR

2 the greatest amount, number, or part ⟨there were 300 people at the *outside* who attended the softball game⟩ — see MOST

outside *prep* **1** not including ⟨*outside* that one suggestion, I haven't heard any better ideas⟩ — see EXCEPT

2 out of the reach or sphere of ⟨honors work is *outside* your grasp unless you manage better grades⟩ — see BEYOND 2

outside of *prep* **1** not including ⟨*outside of* that project you don't like, I don't think you have many choices⟩ — see EXCEPT

2 out of the reach or sphere of ⟨that math class appears to be *outside of* your abilities this year⟩ — see BEYOND 2

outsider *n* a person who is not native to or known to a community ⟨everyone in that small town always stared suspiciously at *outsiders*⟩ — see STRANGER

outsize *also* **outsized** *adj* **1** unusually large ⟨an *outsize* cat who weighed 25 pounds⟩ — see HUGE

2 of a size greater than average of its kind ⟨she likes to make dramatic appearances wearing her trademark *outsize* sunglasses⟩ — see LARGE

outskirts *n pl* the area around a city ⟨some people prefer to live on the *outskirts* and work inside the city⟩ — see ENVIRONS 1

outsmart *vb* to get the better of through cleverness ⟨the kitten *outsmarted* the dog and scampered up a tree⟩ — see OUTWIT

outspoken *adj* free in expressing one's true feelings and opinions ⟨an *outspoken* young man who was running for class president⟩ — see FRANK

outspread *vb* to arrange the parts of (something) over a wider area ⟨*outspread* the blanket over the sand⟩ — see OPEN 3

outstanding *adj* **1** not yet paid ⟨there are several *outstanding* bills left, but at least we paid the rest⟩

synonyms overdue, owed, owing, payable, unpaid, unsettled

related words due, mature

near antonyms prepaid

antonyms cleared, liquidated, paid (off *or* up), repaid, settled

2 standing above others in rank, importance, or achievement ⟨the award goes to the most *outstanding* student in science⟩ — see EMINENT

outstretch *vb* to arrange the parts of (something) over a wider area ⟨*outstretched* the canvas over the frame before starting to paint⟩ — see OPEN 3

outstrip *vb* to be greater, better, or stronger than ⟨before she had reached her teens, the child prodigy had *outstripped* her music teacher's abilities⟩ — see SURPASS 1

outward *adj* situated on the outside or farther out ⟨the *outward* side of the door was blue, but the inside was painted white⟩ — see OUTER

outwear *vb* to last longer than ⟨these running shoes are *outwearing* any others that I have bought⟩ — see OUTLAST

outweigh *vb* to be greater in importance than ⟨the need to finish your homework *outweighs* your desire to see your favorite TV show⟩

synonyms outrank, overbalance, overshadow, overweigh

related words count, import, matter, mean, signify, weigh; dwarf; exceed, outstrip, surpass, transcend

outwit *vb* to get the better of through cleverness ⟨a plan to *outwit* their opponents at their own game⟩

synonyms fox, outfox, outsmart, outmaneuver, overreach

related words outguess, second-guess; baffle, balk, circumvent, foil, frustrate, thwart; cozen, deceive, dupe, fool, gull, trick; conquer, defeat, lick, overcome; bar, block, hinder, impede, obstruct

outworn *adj* having passed its time of use or usefulness ⟨*outworn* clothes with holes in them⟩ — see OBSOLETE

oval *adj* having the shape of an egg ⟨the *Oval* Office in the White House⟩

synonyms elliptic (*or* elliptical), ovate, ovoid

ovate *adj* having the shape of an egg ⟨a bald, *ovate* head⟩ — see OVAL

ovation *n* enthusiastic and usually public expression of approval ⟨received a standing *ovation* for the performance⟩ — see APPLAUSE

over *adj* brought or having come to an end ⟨the play is *over* now⟩ — see COMPLETE 2

over *adv* **1** from one side to the other of an intervening space ⟨let's swim *over* to that island⟩

synonyms across, through

related words clear

2 yet another time ⟨you'll need to do that assignment *over*, this time without help⟩ — see AGAIN 1

3 to or in a higher place ⟨I heard the noise and was startled to discover that the plane was directly *over*⟩ — see ABOVE

4 from beginning to end ⟨read it *over* until you understand it thoroughly⟩ — see THROUGH 1

5 toward or in a lower position ⟨the baby toddled two steps and then fell *over*⟩ — see DOWN

over *prep* **1** higher than ⟨the boy towered *over* his siblings⟩ — see ABOVE

2 in the course of ⟨the students learned a lot *over* the summer⟩ — see DURING

3 on or to the farther side of ⟨stared *over* the wall⟩ — see BEYOND 1

4 to the opposite side of ⟨hopped *over* the dropped ball⟩ — see ACROSS

5 in random positions within the boundaries of ⟨marbles scattered all *over* the room⟩ — see AROUND 2

overabundance *n* the state or an instance of going beyond what is usual, proper, or needed ⟨an *overabundance* of pencils was provided⟩ — see EXCESS

overactive *adj* being in a state of increased activity or agitation ⟨the boy manages to panic himself by his own *overactive* imagination⟩ — see FEVERISH 1

overage *n* the state or an instance of going beyond what is usual, proper, or needed ⟨the *overage* of food that is traditionally consumed on Thanksgiving⟩ — see EXCESS

overall *adj* **1** belonging or relating to the whole ⟨the *overall* view seems to be that we're doing fine⟩ — see GENERAL 1

2 relating to the main elements and not to specific details ⟨there's an *overall* similarity in the looks of the models for that chain of clothing stores⟩ — see GENERAL 2

overall *adv* for the most part ⟨*overall*, this is a good essay, but you need to work on punctuation⟩ — see CHIEFLY

over and above *prep* in addition to ⟨we'll need another gallon of milk *over and above* what we already have⟩ — see BESIDES 1

overbalance *vb* to be greater in importance than ⟨my determination to finish the job *overbalanced* my exhaustion⟩ — see OUTWEIGH

overbear *vb* to achieve a victory over ⟨that year the football team simply *overbore* opponent after opponent⟩ — see BEAT 2

overbearing *adj* fond of ordering people around ⟨an *overbearing* classroom monitor who abused her position⟩ — see BOSSY

overbold *adj* foolishly adventurous or bold ⟨one *overbold* tourist almost tumbled over the rocks and into the sea⟩ — see FOOLHARDY 1

overburden *vb* to fill or load to excess ⟨if you *overburden* the cart, the wheels may break under the weight⟩ — see OVERLOAD

overcast *adj* covered over by clouds ⟨the dark, *overcast* sky made the whole day seem depressing⟩

synonyms beclouded, clouded, cloudy, dull, hazed, hazy, heavy, lowering (*also* louring), overclouded

related words bedimmed, befogged, blackened, darkened, darksome, dim, dimmed, dulled, dusky, misty, murky, obscure, obscured, overshadowed; sunless; black, bleak, cheerless, dark, desolate, dismal, drear, dreary, funereal, gloomy, glum, gray (*also* grey), somber (*or* sombre), sullen

near antonyms sunny, sunshiny; brightened, brilliant, dazzling, illuminated, illumined, lighted (*or* lit), lightened, radiant, shiny

antonyms clear, cloudless

overcast *vb* to make dark, dim, or indistinct ⟨an impenetrable fog *overcast* our view of the harbor⟩ — see CLOUD 1

overcharge *vb* **1** to charge (someone) too much for goods or services ⟨I think that store may have *overcharged* us for the shoes, which were supposed to be on sale⟩

synonyms gouge, soak, sting, surcharge

related words cheat, defraud, stick; clip, fleece, skin

antonyms undercharge

2 to fill or load to excess ⟨*overcharged* his thesis with long, fancy words⟩ — see OVERLOAD

overcloud *vb* to make dark, dim, or indistinct ⟨they had trouble seeing once dusk *overclouded* the playing field⟩ — see CLOUD 1

overclouded *adj* covered over by clouds ⟨*overclouded* skies are a common feature in that artist's landscape paintings⟩ — see OVERCAST

overcoat *n* a warm outdoor coat ⟨put your *overcoat* on — it's freezing out there!⟩

synonyms greatcoat, surcoat, topcoat

related words chesterfield, frock coat, mackinaw, ulster; jacket, parka; oilskin, raincoat, sou'wester; wrap

near antonyms undercoat

overcome *vb* **1** to achieve a victory over ⟨the baseball team finally *overcame* their opponents in the 13th inning⟩ — see BEAT 2
2 to subject to incapacitating emotional or mental stress ⟨already under stress, she was *overcome* by news of a death in the family⟩ — see OVERWHELM 1

overconfident *adj* foolishly adventurous or bold ⟨an *overconfident* parachutist had to be forced to check his equipment⟩ — see FOOLHARDY 1

overcritical *adj* given to making or expressing unfavorable judgments about things ⟨an *overcritical* teacher can discourage even the most dedicated of students⟩ — see CRITICAL 1

overdecorated *adj* elaborately and often excessively decorated ⟨the room was so *overdecorated* that no one thing was shown to its best advantage⟩ — see ORNATE

overdo *vb* to describe or express in too strong terms ⟨I think you might be *overdoing* it a bit by claiming that your life will be over if you don't get those sneakers⟩ — see OVERSTATE

overdraw *vb* to describe or express in too strong terms ⟨the family tends to *overdraw* its supposed misery in order to win sympathy⟩ — see OVERSTATE

overdue *adj* **1** not arriving, or occurring, or settled at the due, usual, or proper time ⟨an *overdue* library book will be subject to daily fines⟩ — see LATE 1
2 not yet paid ⟨an *overdue* bill that's started incurring interest charges⟩ — see OUTSTANDING 1

overeat *vb* to eat greedily or to excess ⟨if you *overeat* tonight, you're going to get a stomachache⟩ — see GORGE 2

overeater *n* one who eats greedily or too much ⟨not every fat person is actually an *overeater*⟩ — see GLUTTON

overestimate *vb* to place too high a value on ⟨they *overestimated* their ability to do the work on such short notice⟩
synonyms overrate, overvalue
related words appreciate, cherish, prize, treasure, value; admire, esteem, regard, respect; adore, idolize, revere, reverence, venerate, worship
near antonyms belittle, decry, depreciate, disparage; despise, disdain, scorn; abhor, abominate, detest, loathe
antonyms underestimate, underrate, undervalue

overfamiliar *adj* showing a lack of proper social reserve or modesty ⟨calling your teacher "Shortie" is a bit *overfamiliar*⟩ — see PRESUMPTUOUS 1

overfill *vb* **1** to fill or load to excess ⟨*overfilled* the wheelbarrow until finally no one could push it⟩ — see OVERLOAD
2 to flow over the brim or top of ⟨water *overfilled* the tub and ran onto the floor⟩ — see OVERFLOW 1

overflow *n* **1** a great flow of water or of something that overwhelms ⟨an *overflow* of juice ran all over the table⟩ — see FLOOD
2 the state or an instance of going beyond what is usual, proper, or needed ⟨an *overflow* of help actually made the job more complicated⟩ — see EXCESS

overflow *vb* **1** to flow over the brim or top of ⟨the tea in the cup *overflowed* onto the saucer⟩
synonyms overfill, run over
related words boil over, spill, well (up); flow, flush, gush, pour, sluice, spout, spurt, stream; deluge, drown, engulf, flood, inundate, overwhelm, submerge, submerse, swamp; wash (over); brim, cascade, slop, slosh
near antonyms recede

2 to cover or become filled with a flood ⟨the swollen river *overflowed* the surrounding land and washed houses away⟩ — see FLOOD

overgrown *adj* covered with a thick, healthy natural growth ⟨a field allowed to become *overgrown* with weeds again⟩ — see LUSH 1

overhang *n* a part that sticks out from the general mass of something ⟨huge icicles extended from the house's *overhang*⟩ — see BULGE

overhang *vb* **1** to extend outward beyond a usual point ⟨the narrow streets of the old European city are lined with row houses often having *overhanging* second stories⟩ — see BULGE
2 to remain poised to inflict harm, danger, or distress on ⟨a cancer patient who refuses to put his life on hold even though the constant threat of death has been *overhanging* him for several years⟩ — see THREATEN

overhaul *vb* to move fast enough to get even with ⟨in the final moments of the race, the horse in the rear sped forwards at a furious pace and *overhauled* the horse that had been leading⟩ — see OVERTAKE

overhead *adv* to or in a higher place ⟨the majestic sight of eagles soaring *overhead*⟩ — see ABOVE

overhear *vb* to listen to (another in private conversation) ⟨it's not polite to try to *overhear* intimate friends telling secrets⟩ — see EAVESDROP (ON)

overjoy *vb* **1** to fill with overwhelming emotion (as wonder or delight) ⟨I was *overjoyed* to finally see in person art masterpieces that I had previously known only through books⟩ — see ENTRANCE
2 to fill with great joy ⟨she was *overjoyed* by the unexpected promotion⟩ — see ELATE

overkill *n* the state or an instance of going beyond what is usual, proper, or needed ⟨by then you had made your point—the additional five pages of argument is *overkill*⟩ — see EXCESS

overlap *n* a partial covering of one thing by an adjoining thing ⟨the orthodontist will try to fix that *overlap* of two of your upper incisors⟩
synonyms lapping, overlaying, overlying, overspreading
related words shingling

overlap *vb* to lie over parts of one another ⟨there were so many papers on the desk that many of them *overlapped*⟩
synonyms lap, overlay, overlie, overspread
related words shingle

overlay *vb* **1** to form a layer over ⟨snow *overlaid* the roads to a sufficient depth to make driving treacherous⟩ — see COVER 2
2 to lie over parts of one another ⟨cedar shingles *overlaying* each other on the roof⟩ — see OVERLAP

overlaying *n* a partial covering of one thing by an adjoining thing ⟨an *overlaying* of a bedspread with a throw or comforter is very fashionable with interior decorators these days⟩ — see OVERLAP

overlie *vb* **1** to lie over parts of one another ⟨the puzzle pieces *overlay* one another in complete disarray on the floor⟩ — see OVERLAP
2 to form a layer over ⟨there will be freezing rain tonight, so we can expect to find a thick layer of ice *overlying* the car windshield in the morning⟩ — see COVER 2

overload *vb* to fill or load to excess ⟨try not to *overload* your backpack, or you could end up with back problems⟩
synonyms overburden, overcharge, overfill

related words stuff; burden, charge, encumber, lade, load, lumber, saddle, weight

near antonyms lighten, unburden, unload

overlook *vb* **1** to look down on ⟨the fortress *overlooks* the city⟩

synonyms command, dominate

related words face, front

2 to fail to give proper attention to ⟨you've *overlooked* your chores again this week⟩ — see NEGLECT 1

overly *adv* beyond a normal or acceptable limit ⟨there's no need to be *overly* careful about the rough draft, since we'll polish it afterwards⟩ — see TOO 1

overlying *n* a partial covering of one thing by an adjoining thing ⟨the *overlying* of the two trees' branches results in a very inviting garden bower⟩ — see OVERLAP

overmaster *vb* to subject to incapacitating emotional or mental stress ⟨the student was *overmastered* by the stress of taking the test and broke down crying⟩ — see OVERWHELM 1

overmatch *vb* to achieve a victory over ⟨our school's tennis team *overmatched* their traditional rivals in the championship⟩ — see BEAT 2

overmuch *adj* going beyond a normal or acceptable limit in degree or amount ⟨I think you put *overmuch* care into your personal appearance⟩ — see EXCESSIVE

overmuch *adv* beyond a normal or acceptable limit ⟨you worry *overmuch* about what other people think⟩ — see TOO 1

overmuch *n* the state or an instance of going beyond what is usual, proper, or needed ⟨Ralph Waldo Emerson's world-weary observation that "the world hath *overmuch* of pain"⟩ — see EXCESS

overpass *vb* to fail to give proper attention to ⟨army officers who had been unjustly *overpassed* for promotion⟩ — see NEGLECT 1

overpower *vb* **1** to bring under one's control by force of arms ⟨the invading army *overpowered* the countryside with lightning speed⟩ — see CONQUER 1

2 to subject to incapacitating emotional or mental stress ⟨*overpowered* by fear of the unknown⟩ — see OVERWHELM 1

overpowering *n* the act or process of bringing someone or something under one's control ⟨the *overpowering* of much of Europe by the Nazis during World War II⟩ — see CONQUEST

overpraise *n* excessive praise ⟨there's no need to offer *overpraise* for such a simple task⟩ — see FLATTERY

overpraise *vb* to praise too much ⟨proud parents are likely to *overpraise* their children for their earnest efforts at making handicrafts⟩ — see FLATTER 1

overrate *vb* to place too high a value on ⟨I think the critics *overrated* that movie⟩ — see OVERESTIMATE

overreach *vb* **1** to get the better of through cleverness ⟨a real estate developer who is always trying to *overreach* his competitors⟩ — see OUTWIT

2 to go beyond the limit of ⟨the mountain climbers *overreached* their abilities and paid for it dearly⟩ — see EXCEED

overripe *adj* having lost forcefulness, courage, or spirit ⟨an *overripe* artist whose abstract paintings are no longer considered fresh or new⟩ — see EFFETE 1

overrun *vb* **1** to enter for conquest or plunder ⟨waves of barbarians *overran* the Roman Empire during its long decline⟩ — see INVADE

2 to go beyond the limit of ⟨he must not *overrun* his authority as governor⟩ — see EXCEED

3 to spread or swarm over in a troublesome manner ⟨ants *overran* the garden⟩ — see INFEST

oversee *vb* **1** to look after and make decisions about ⟨will *oversee* the new manufacturing division⟩ — see CONDUCT 1

2 to be in charge of ⟨looking for someone to *oversee* the project from start to finish⟩ — see BOSS 1

3 to take charge of especially on behalf of another ⟨*oversee* the household until Dad gets home⟩ — see ²TEND 1

overshadow *vb* **1** to make dark, dim, or indistinct ⟨great swarms of bugs *overshadowed* the area under the streetlight⟩ — see CLOUD 1

2 to be greater in importance than ⟨later you'll find that verbal skills *overshadow* any skills you have at video games⟩ — see OUTWEIGH

overshoot *vb* to go beyond the limit of ⟨don't worry if you *overshoot* the length requirement by three pages⟩ — see EXCEED

oversight *n* **1** the act or activity of looking after and making decisions about something ⟨*oversight* of the club's fund-raising activities⟩ — see CONDUCT 1

2 an unintentional departure from truth or accuracy ⟨claiming "three billion" instead of "three million" was just an *oversight*⟩ — see ERROR 1

3 the duty or function of watching or guarding for the sake of proper direction or control ⟨you'll have *oversight* of the group for this lesson⟩ — see SUPERVISION 1

4 the nonperformance of an assigned or expected action ⟨failing to lock the car can be an expensive *oversight*, if it gets stolen⟩ — see FAILURE 1

oversize *or* **oversized** *adj* **1** unusually large ⟨the woman's *oversize* hat was blocking my view of the minister⟩ — see HUGE

2 of a size greater than average of its kind ⟨a softball is an *oversize* and less densely stuffed baseball⟩ — see LARGE

overspread *vb* **1** to form a layer over ⟨the butter should evenly *overspread* the baking pan⟩ — see COVER 2

2 to lie over parts of one another ⟨autumn leaves *overspreading* one another on the lawn to form a colorful mosaic⟩ — see OVERLAP

overspreading *n* a partial covering of one thing by an adjoining thing ⟨the *overspreading* of one notice by another made it difficult to find the one thing I was looking for on the bulletin board⟩ — see OVERLAP

overstate *vb* to describe or express in too strong terms ⟨it appears you've somewhat *overstated* your computer skills, if you can't find the "on" button!⟩

synonyms exaggerate, overdo, overdraw, put on

related words color, elaborate, embellish, embroider, magnify, pad, stretch; fudge, hedge; overemphasize, overplay

near antonyms belittle, minimize, play down

antonyms understate

overstatement *n* the representation of something in terms that go beyond the facts ⟨a claim to worldwide fame is a bit of an *overstatement* on the part of that nightclub⟩ — see EXAGGERATION

overstep *vb* to go beyond the limit of ⟨the principal *overstepped* her authority in ordering everyone to remain in the unheated school⟩ — see EXCEED

oversupply *n* the state or an instance of going beyond what is usual, proper, or needed ⟨an *oversupply* of volunteers for the parade this year⟩ — see EXCESS

overtake *vb* to move fast enough to get even with ⟨she had to hurry to *overtake* her friends, who had forgotten their umbrellas⟩ ⟨the thunderstorm *overtook* them⟩

synonyms catch up (with), overhaul

related words chase, pursue; gain, reach; pass, surpass

near antonyms fall short

overthrow *n* failure to win a contest ⟨the surprising *overthrow* of the world's top-ranked chess player⟩ — see DEFEAT 1

overtop *vb* to be greater, better, or stronger than ⟨the oldest athlete easily *overtopped* the younger ones in his dedication to practicing⟩ — see SURPASS 1

overturn *vb* to turn on one's side or upside down ⟨afraid that my kayak would *overturn*⟩ — see CAPSIZE

overvalue *vb* to place too high a value on ⟨some people *overvalue* material things⟩ — see OVERESTIMATE

overweening *adj* **1** having too high an opinion of oneself ⟨an *overweening* little girl who thought that her looks made her better than other people⟩ — see CONCEITED

2 going beyond a normal or acceptable limit in degree or amount ⟨*overweening* desire to have more money than anyone else⟩ — see EXCESSIVE

3 having a feeling of superiority that shows itself in an overbearing attitude ⟨an *overweening* administrator⟩ — see ARROGANT

overweigh *vb* to be greater in importance than ⟨proper food and sleep should *overweigh* all-night partying in your priorities⟩ — see OUTWEIGH

overweight *adj* having an excess of body fat ⟨an *overweight* person who had difficulty running⟩ — see FAT 1

overwhelm *vb* **1** to subject to incapacitating emotional or mental stress ⟨just the thought of how much work there is to do *overwhelms* me⟩

synonyms carry away, crush, devastate, floor, oppress, overcome, overmaster, overpower, prostrate, snow under, swamp, whelm

related words deluge, drown; confute, defeat, refute; demoralize, distress, disturb, rock, shatter, stagger, unman, unnerve, upset

2 to cover or become filled with a flood ⟨that spring the massive runoff from melting snows *overwhelmed* the valley⟩ — see FLOOD

overwrought *adj* **1** being in a state of increased activity or agitation ⟨became *overwrought* when she heard that her child was missing⟩ — see FEVERISH 1

2 elaborately and often excessively decorated ⟨an *overwrought* iron fence⟩ — see ORNATE

ovoid *adj* having the shape of an egg ⟨an *ovoid* toy that the baby couldn't tip over⟩ — see OVAL

owed *adj* not yet paid ⟨finally paid the *owed* amount⟩ — see OUTSTANDING 1

owing *adj* not yet paid ⟨there's one bill still *owing*⟩ — see OUTSTANDING 1

owing to *prep* as the result of ⟨*owing to* the extra snow days this year, we'll have to run an additional two days into June⟩ — see BECAUSE OF

own *vb* to keep, control, or experience as one's own ⟨*owned* a house and a car⟩ — see HAVE 1

own (up) *vb* to accept the truth or existence of (something) usually reluctantly ⟨*owned up* to damaging the car⟩ — see ADMIT

owner *n* one who has a legal or rightful claim to ownership ⟨the *owner* of the building will have to decide whether or not to sell⟩ — see PROPRIETOR

P

pa *n* a male human parent 〈I'll see if my *pa* would like to come along〉 — see FATHER 1

pace *vb* to move along with a steady regular step especially in a group 〈six horses *paced* neatly alongside one another in the parade〉 — see MARCH 1

pacific *adj* **1** tending to lessen or avoid conflict or hostility 〈as a *pacific* gesture, we invited our feuding neighbors to our backyard barbecue〉

synonyms appeasing, conciliating, conciliatory, disarming, mollifying, pacifying, peacemaking, placating, propitiatory

related words endearing, ingratiating; peaceable, peaceful; nonbelligerent, unaggressive, unassertive; calming, comforting, quieting, soothing; obliging, satisfying; affable, amiable, amicable, benevolent, gentle, kind, kindly; submissive, surrendering, yielding

near antonyms aggravating, annoying, exasperating, inflammatory, irritating, nettling, offensive, provocative, provoking, vexing; engaging, incensing, infuriating, maddening; antagonistic, hostile; aggressive, assertive, bellicose, belligerent, combative, contentious, pugnacious, quarrelsome, scrappy, truculent; martial, militant, military, warlike

antonyms antagonizing

2 inclined to live in peace and to avoid war 〈a *pacific* nation that has managed to remain neutral even during times of world conflict〉 — see PEACEFUL 1

pacifist *n* a person who opposes war or warlike policies 〈Gandhi was a famous *pacifist* who succeeded in bringing about Indian independence using only nonviolence〉 — see DOVE 1

pacify *vb* to lessen the anger or agitation of 〈the only thing that would *pacify* the child and end the tantrum was a new toy〉

synonyms appease, conciliate, disarm, mollify, placate, propitiate

related words calm, comfort, console, content, quiet, soothe; endear (to), ingratiate; delight, gladden, gratify, please; blarney, flatter, overpraise, soft-soap; assuage, quench, sate, satiate, satisfy; cater (to), humor, indulge; blandish, cajole, coax, wheedle; coddle, mollycoddle, pamper, spoil

near antonyms aggravate, annoy, bother, bug, chafe, cross, exasperate, gall, get, grate, irk, irritate, nettle, peeve, pique, put out, rankle, rile, roil, ruffle, vex; provoke, rouse; harass, harry, pester; agitate, distress, disturb, fret, perturb, upset; affront, insult, offend

antonyms anger, enrage, incense, infuriate, madden, outrage

pacifying *adj* **1** tending to calm the emotions and relieve stress 〈a *pacifying* treat of warm milk and toast〉 — see SOOTHING 1

2 tending to lessen or avoid conflict or hostility 〈adopted a *pacifying* tone to try to calm everyone down〉 — see PACIFIC 1

pack *n* **1** a soft-sided case designed for carrying belongings especially on the back 〈part of basic training is becoming accustomed to taking very long hikes with an eighty-pound *pack*〉

synonyms backpack, knapsack, rucksack

related words haversack; grip, luggage, suitcase, traveling bag

2 a wrapped or sealed case containing an item or set of items 〈tucked a small *pack* of lozenges into her bag〉 — see PACKAGE 1

pack *vb* **1** to close up so that no empty spaces remain 〈carefully *pack* the container with food so we'll have as much as possible for the picnic〉 — see FILL 2

2 to put into (something) as much as can be held or contained 〈*packed* the suitcase so tightly that it wouldn't close〉 — see FILL 1

3 to support and take from one place to another 〈remember to *pack* several changes of clothing〉 — see CARRY 1

4 to wear or have on one's person 〈a private detective *packing* a weapon〉 — see CARRY 2

pack (off) *vb* to cause to go or be taken from one place to another 〈*packed* the child *off* to a good boarding school〉 — see SEND

package *n* **1** a wrapped or sealed case containing an item or set of items 〈Mom needed our help carrying all the *packages* and bags home from the store〉

synonyms bundle, pack, packet, parcel

related words bag, poke [*chiefly Southern and Midland*], pouch, sack; box, container, crate

2 a number of things considered as a unit 〈ate a whole *package* of cookies at once〉 — see GROUP 1

packed *adj* **1** containing or seeming to contain the greatest quantity or number possible 〈the auditorium was *packed*〉 — see FULL 1

2 having little space between items or parts 〈a *packed* jar of pickles〉 — see CLOSE 1

packet *n* a wrapped or sealed case containing an item or set of items 〈a *packet* of letters that her husband wrote while he was in the army〉 — see PACKAGE 1

pact *n* **1** a formal agreement between two or more nations or peoples 〈a *pact* between the two small nations to defend one another in case of attack〉 — see TREATY

2 an arrangement about action to be taken 〈they made a *pact* to meet every week at the same time〉 — see AGREEMENT 2

pad *n* **1** a number of sheets of writing paper glued together at one edge 〈we'll need to buy a new *pad* for telephone messages soon〉

synonyms notepad, tablet

related words album, notebook, scrapbook; booklet, pamphlet

2 a place set aside for sleeping 〈went back to my *pad* to get some rest〉 — see BED 1

3 something that serves as a protective barrier 〈a *pad* on the chair to keep it from getting scratched〉 — see CUSHION

4 the place where one lives 〈welcome to my *pad*〉 — see HOME 1

pad *vb* **1** to add to the interest of by including made-up details 〈the journalist was fired for *padding* certain stories to make them more interesting〉 — see EMBROIDER

2 to go on foot 〈a cat *padded* silently by〉 — see WALK

padding *n* **1** soft material that is used to fill the hollow parts of something 〈the *padding* is leaking out of that pillow〉 — see FILLING

2 the representation of something in terms that go beyond the facts 〈that feature writer is sometimes guilty of *padding*, but he keeps it from getting out of hand⟩ — see EXAGGERATION

paddle *vb* to move a boat by means of oars ⟨I like to *paddle* on the river for exercise and relaxation⟩ — see ¹ROW

padre *n* a person specially trained and authorized to conduct religious services in a Christian church ⟨the local *padre* is a beloved figure in the village⟩ — see CLERGYMAN

paean *n* a formal expression of praise ⟨the retirement party included many *paeans* for his long years of service to the company⟩ — see ENCOMIUM

pagan *n* a person who does not worship the God of the Bible ⟨regarded the native peoples of the lands that they conquered as *pagans* who were uncivilized and inherently inferior⟩ — see HEATHEN 1

page *n* one that carries a message or does an errand ⟨dispatch a *page* to bring coffee to the senator⟩ — see MESSENGER

pageant *n* a staged presentation often with music that consists of a procession of narrated or enacted scenes ⟨we always put on a Christmas *pageant* every year⟩
synonyms cavalcade
related words tableau; kaleidoscope, montage, panorama; drama, play; demonstration, performance, presentation, production; exhibition, extravaganza, show, spectacle; parade

pail *n* a round container that is open at the top and outfitted with a handle ⟨fetch me a *pail* full of water, please⟩
synonyms bucket
related words cauldron, kettle, pot; canteen, flagon, jar, jug, pitcher; bail, hod; tank, tub, vat

pain *n* **1** a sharp unpleasant sensation usually felt in some specific part of the body ⟨the child was crying because of a *pain* in her knee⟩
synonyms ache, pang, prick, smart, sting, stitch, throe, tingle, twinge
related words discomfort, distress, soreness, tenderness; agony, anguish, misery, suffering, torment, torture; inflammation, swelling; damage, harm, hurt, injury; backache, bellyache, charley horse, colic, earache, gripe, headache, stomachache, toothache
near antonyms comfort, ease
2 a state of great suffering of body or mind ⟨a sprained ankle caused him great *pain* for a week⟩ — see DISTRESS 1
3 pains *pl* strict attentiveness to what one is doing ⟨take *pains* to be sure that you don't damage anything⟩ — see CARE 1
4 pains *pl* the active use of energy in producing a result ⟨she was at *pains* to reassure us that everything would be fine⟩ — see EFFORT

pain *vb* to feel or cause physical pain ⟨my poor head was *paining* so from all that racket⟩ — see HURT 1

painful *adj* **1** causing or feeling bodily pain ⟨her broken arm was too *painful* for her to go on the trip⟩
synonyms aching, hurting, nasty, sore
related words damaging, harmful, hurtful, injurious; raw, tender; bleeding, burning, chafing, cramping, festering; itching, nagging, pinching, pricking, prickling, smarting, stinging; inflamed, swollen; threatening, wounding
near antonyms curative, healing, helping, remedial
antonyms painless
2 hard to accept or bear especially emotionally ⟨it's been very *painful* to accept that my father is gone⟩ — see BITTER 2

painfully *adv* with feelings of bitterness or grief ⟨*painfully* she recounted the years of physical abuse she had received at his hands⟩ — see HARD 2

painkiller *n* something (as a drug) that relieves pain ⟨a lot of *painkillers* have turned out to be addictive substances for patients⟩
synonyms analgesic, anesthetic
related words sedative, tranquilizer (*also* tranquillizer); narcotic , opiate

painless *adj* involving minimal difficulty or effort ⟨watching the movie version of the book should be a *painless* assignment⟩ — see EASY 1

painlessly *adv* without difficulty ⟨the move to our new house was accomplished rather *painlessly*⟩ — see EASILY

painstaking *adj* taking great care and effort ⟨she was always *painstaking* about her homework⟩
synonyms careful, conscientious, fussy, meticulous
related words assiduous, diligent, indefatigable, persevering, sedulous; exhaustive, thorough, thoroughgoing; attentive, observant, vigilant, watchful; accurate, precise; critical, demanding, discriminating, exacting, finicky, particular; cautious, chary, circumspect, gingerly, guarded, heedful, wary; deliberate, plodding, slow; studied, thoughtful; all-out, determined, dogged, intensive, tenacious, tireless, zealous
near antonyms cursory; heedless, inattentive, incautious, mindless, unguarded, unwary; lax, neglectful, negligent, slipshod, sloppy, slovenly; imprecise, inaccurate, uncritical, undemanding, undiscriminating; bold, impetuous, rash, reckless; apathetic, indifferent, lackadaisical, lazy
antonyms careless

paint *n* preparations intended to beautify the face or hair ⟨Mom refuses to be seen in public without her *paint*⟩ — see MAKEUP 1

paint *vb* **1** to give a representation or account of in words ⟨the description *painted* a perfect image of the sun setting over the ocean⟩ — see DESCRIBE 1
2 to give color or a different color to ⟨I've decided to *paint* the bathroom walls purple⟩ — see COLOR 1

painting *n* a picture created with usually oil paint ⟨the Mona Lisa is a beautiful *painting* of a woman with a most mysterious smile⟩
synonyms canvas, oil, oil painting
related words fresco, mural, panorama; cartoon, drawing, etching, pastel, sketch, watercolor, work; masterpiece; pièce de résistance, showpiece
phrases work of art

pair *n* two things of the same or similar kind that match or are considered together ⟨a *pair* of blue socks⟩ ⟨the cheerleader and the computer nerd make quite a *pair* together⟩
synonyms brace, couple, duo, twain, twosome
related words span, yoke; partnership, team; companion, complement, doublet, fellow, half, match, mate, twin; counterpart, equal, equivalent, like, parallel, peer

pal *n* a person who has a strong liking for and trust in another ⟨I always choose my best *pal* for my softball team first⟩ — see FRIEND 1

pal (around) *vb* to come or be together as friends ⟨they began to *pal around* on the first day of school⟩ — see ASSOCIATE 1

palace *n* **1** a large impressive residence ⟨the billionaire's "summer cottage" turned out to be a huge *palace*⟩ — see MANSION
2 a large, magnificent, or massive building ⟨the governor's opponents accused him of building *palaces* to house the state government⟩ — see EDIFICE 1

3 the residence of a ruler ⟨Buckingham *Palace* flies a special flag to indicate when the monarch is in residence⟩ — see COURT 1

palatable *adj* **1** being to one's liking ⟨I did not find the idea of moving again very *palatable*⟩ — see SATISFACTORY 1

2 giving pleasure or contentment to the mind or senses ⟨I always associate the *palatable* odor of roasting turkey with Thanksgiving⟩ — see PLEASANT

3 very pleasing to the sense of taste ⟨the new vegetable dish turned out to be surprisingly *palatable*⟩ — see DELICIOUS 1

palatial *adj* showing obvious signs of wealth and comfort ⟨a *palatial* new apartment⟩ — see LUXURIOUS

palaver *n* friendly, informal conversation or an instance of this ⟨we should get together and have a nice *palaver* sometime⟩ — see CHAT

palaver *vb* to engage in casual or rambling conversation ⟨mothers *palavering* and drinking coffee while watching their children play⟩ — see CHAT

pale *adj* **1** lacking intensity of color ⟨we chose a very *pale* pink for the walls of the room⟩
synonyms dull, dulled, faded, light, pastel, washed-out
related words flat, lackluster, lusterless, matte (*also* mat *or* matt); dim, faint; dirty, muddy; achromatic, colorless, uncolored, undyed, unpainted, unstained; blanched, bleached, washed, white, whitened; gray (*also* grey), indistinct, neutral
near antonyms bright, brilliant, vibrant, vivid; chromatic, colored, dyed, painted, stained, tinged, tinted; colorful, multicolored, polychromatic, polychrome, varicolored, variegated; flashy, garish, gaudy, loud, showy, splashy
antonyms dark, deep, gay, rich
2 lacking a healthy skin color ⟨after a week with the flu, she was deathly *pale* and noticeably thinner⟩
synonyms ashen, ashy, blanched, cadaverous, livid, lurid, paled, pallid, pasty, peaked, wan
related words sallow, sick, sickly, waxen, waxy; white, whitened; deathlike; anemic, bloodless; untanned
near antonyms blooming, blushing, flushed, glowing, pink
antonyms florid, flush, rubicund, ruddy, sanguine

pale *vb* to make white or whiter by removing color ⟨the sun eventually *paled* my bright blue shirt⟩ — see WHITEN

paled *adj* lacking a healthy skin color ⟨the shock of the news left him *paled* and shaking⟩ — see PALE 2

palisade *n* a steep wall of rock, earth, or ice ⟨the *palisades* that line the west bank of the Hudson River for about 15 miles⟩ — see CLIFF

palliate *vb* **1** to make (something) seem less bad by offering excuses ⟨don't try to *palliate* your constant lying by claiming that everybody lies⟩
synonyms excuse, extenuate, gloss (over), gloze (over), whitewash
related words sugarcoat, varnish; apologize, atone, confess; explain, justify, rationalize; alleviate, lessen, lighten, mitigate, moderate, soften, temper; absolve, acquit, clear, exculpate, exonerate, vindicate
2 to make more bearable or less severe ⟨this medicine should *palliate* your cough at least a little⟩ — see HELP 2

pallid *adj* lacking a healthy skin color ⟨a *pallid* child who looked as though he'd never seen the sun⟩ — see PALE 2

palm off *vb* to offer (something fake, useless, or inferior) as genuine, useful, or valuable ⟨please stop trying to *palm off* your broken toys on me⟩ — see FOIST

palmy *adj* **1** having attained a desired end or state of good fortune ⟨knew her in her *palmy* days when she was living high⟩ — see SUCCESSFUL 1

2 marked by vigorous growth and well-being especially economically ⟨a *palmy* suburb with lots of new homes and shopping malls⟩ — see PROSPEROUS 1

palpable *adj* **1** able to be perceived by a sense or by the mind ⟨the tension in the negotiating room was *palpable*⟩ — see PERCEPTIBLE

2 capable of being perceived by the sense of touch ⟨a small but *palpable* lump in my neck⟩ — see TANGIBLE

3 not subject to misinterpretation or more than one interpretation ⟨a *palpable* case of lying under oath⟩ — see CLEAR 2

palpitate *vb* to expand and contract in a rhythmic manner ⟨the man's heart began to *palpitate,* and he feared another attack was coming on⟩ — see PULSATE

palpitation *n* a rhythmic expanding and contracting ⟨a *palpitation* of the blood vessels⟩ — see PULSATION

palsy *n* complete or partial loss of physical function (as motion or sensation) in a part of the body ⟨*palsy* can sometimes be caused by a brain injury⟩ — see PARALYSIS

palter *vb* to talk over or dispute the terms of a purchase ⟨unwilling to *palter* over the price of the car⟩ — see BARGAIN

paltry *adj* so small or unimportant as to warrant little or no attention ⟨wanted me to sell him my bike for a *paltry* sum⟩ — see NEGLIGIBLE 1

pamper *vb* to treat with great or excessive care ⟨*pamper* a sick child⟩ — see BABY

pamphlet *n* a short printed publication with no cover or with a paper cover ⟨*pamphlets* about common safety precautions that we all can put into use⟩
synonyms booklet, brochure, circular, flier (*or* flyer), folder, leaflet
related words advertisement, catalog (*or* catalogue); tract; paperback, pocket book; guidebook, handbook, instructions, manual

pan *vb* to express one's unfavorable opinion of the worth or quality of ⟨all the movie critics *panned* the latest sequel⟩ — see CRITICIZE

panacea *n* something that cures all ills or problems ⟨Mom seems to believe that aspirin is a *panacea* for nearly everything⟩ — see CURE-ALL

pancake *n* a flat cake made from thin batter and cooked on both sides (as on a griddle) ⟨every Sunday morning, we have *pancakes* and bacon for breakfast⟩
synonyms flapjack, griddle cake, hotcake, slapjack
related words crepe (*or* crêpe); waffle

pandemonium *n* a state of noisy, confused activity ⟨Christmas morning is always marked by *pandemonium*⟩ — see COMMOTION

panegyric *n* a formal expression of praise ⟨wrote a *panegyric* on the centennial of the Nobel laureate's birth⟩ — see ENCOMIUM

panel *n* **1** a meeting featuring a group discussion ⟨there will be a discussion *panel* on Tuesday⟩ — see FORUM

2 a select group of persons assigned to consider or take action on some matter ⟨assembled a prestigious *panel* to investigate ways to stem the rising cost of health care⟩ — see COMMITTEE

pang *n* a sharp unpleasant sensation usually felt in some specific part of the body ⟨those hunger *pangs* that strike you in the middle of the afternoon⟩ — see PAIN 1

panhandler *n* a person who lives by public begging ⟨a *panhandler* asking for money to buy food⟩ — see BEGGAR

panic *n* the emotion experienced in the presence or threat of danger ⟨the sight of the bear filled her with *panic*⟩ — see FEAR

panic *vb* to strike with fear ⟨for some reason, the feeding animals at the zoo *panicked* him⟩ — see FRIGHTEN

panorama *n* all that can be seen from a certain point ⟨admired the *panorama* from the top of the mountain⟩ — see VIEW 1

panoramic *adj* covering everything or all important points ⟨a *panoramic* look at America's fascination with the automobile⟩ — see ENCYCLOPEDIC

pan out *vb* 1 to come to be ⟨the eagerly anticipated trip never *panned out*⟩ — see COME OUT 1

2 to turn out as planned or desired ⟨the plan didn't quite *pan out*⟩ — see SUCCEED 1

pant *vb* to breathe hard, quickly, or with difficulty ⟨the dog *panted* after running across the field⟩ — see GASP

pant (after) *vb* to have an earnest wish to own or enjoy ⟨*panting after* the latest video game⟩ — see DESIRE

pantaloons *n pl* an outer garment covering each leg separately from waist to ankle ⟨a man in snug velvet *pantaloons*⟩ — see PANTS

panther *n* a large tawny cat of the wild ⟨the *panther* is surprisingly difficult to spot⟩ — see COUGAR

pantomime *n* 1 a movement of the body or limbs that expresses or emphasizes an idea or feeling ⟨the game requires that you use *pantomime* to communicate an idea⟩ — see GESTURE 1

2 an actor in a story performed silently and entirely by body movements ⟨in ancient Rome *pantomimes* performed tragic love stories⟩ — see MIME

pantomimist *n* an actor in a story performed silently and entirely by body movements ⟨an exquisitely graceful *pantomimist*⟩ — see MIME

pants *n pl* an outer garment covering each leg separately from waist to ankle ⟨you'll need a nice pair of *pants* for the job interview⟩

synonyms breeches, pantaloons, slacks, trousers

related words corduroys, denims, jeans; hose, legging (*or* leggin), pantsuit

papa *n* a male human parent ⟨a proud *papa* of newborn twins⟩ — see FATHER 1

paper *adj* being something in name or form only ⟨there's a *paper* boycott of that company's products that nobody seems to be honoring⟩ — see NOMINAL 1

paper *n* 1 a piece of paper with information written or to be written on it ⟨handed in the correct *papers*⟩ — see FORM 2

2 a publication that appears at regular intervals ⟨we get the *paper* every morning⟩ — see JOURNAL

3 a short piece of writing done as a school exercise ⟨write a *paper* about your favorite author⟩ — see COMPOSITION 2

4 a short piece of writing typically expressing a point of view ⟨the *papers* written by the Founding Fathers urging adoption of the federal constitution⟩ — see ESSAY 1

par *n* 1 something set up as an example against which others of the same type are compared ⟨that last dining experience was not quite up to *par*⟩ — see STANDARD 1

2 the state or fact of being exactly the same in number, amount, status, or quality ⟨victories on *par* with his sporting ambitions⟩ — see EQUIVALENCE

3 what is typical of a group, class, or series ⟨a pulse of 70 is *par* for people of that age group⟩ — see AVERAGE

parable *n* a story intended to teach a basic truth or moral about life ⟨the *parable* in which the repentant sinner is compared to the returning prodigal son who is welcomed home⟩ — see ALLEGORY

parade *n* a body of individuals moving along in an orderly and often ceremonial way ⟨a Fourth of July *parade*⟩ — see CORTEGE 2

parade *vb* 1 to move along with a steady regular step especially in a group ⟨the marching band *paraded* past jubilant crowds⟩ — see MARCH 1

2 to present so as to invite notice or attention ⟨*parade* her expensive new dress at the party⟩ — see SHOW 1

paradigmatic *adj* constituting, serving as, or worthy of being a pattern to be imitated ⟨a *paradigmatic* essay in which the writer presents his point of view clearly and engagingly⟩ — see MODEL

paradise *n* 1 a place or state of great happiness ⟨Susan's idea of *paradise* was a world where no one had to go to work⟩

synonyms Eden, Elysium, heaven, utopia

related words dreamland, fairyland, promised land, wonderland; bliss, euphoria, gladness, joy

antonyms hell

2 a dwelling place of perfect bliss for the soul after death ⟨a firm belief that good people will be rewarded in *paradise*⟩ — see HEAVEN 1

3 a state of overwhelming usually pleasurable emotion ⟨that early stage of a romance when lovers are in *paradise*⟩ — see ECSTASY

paradox *n* someone or something with qualities or features that seem to conflict with one another ⟨the *paradox* of fighting a war for peace⟩ — see CONTRADICTION 1

paragon *n* someone of such unequaled perfection as to deserve imitation ⟨in Arthurian legend, Sir Galahad is depicted as the one knight who is a *paragon* of virtue⟩ — see IDEAL 1

parallel *adj* having qualities in common ⟨*parallel* lives of two friends who first met in college⟩ — see ALIKE

parallel *n* 1 a point which two or more things share in common ⟨pointed out some *parallels* between the two novels⟩ — see SIMILARITY 2

2 one that is equal to another in status, achievement, or value ⟨an advance that is without *parallel* in the history of virology⟩ — see EQUAL

parallel *vb* to be the exact counterpart of ⟨developments in the television show *paralleled* those in the lead actor's real life⟩ — see MATCH 1

parallelism *n* the quality or state of having many qualities in common ⟨the striking *parallelism* between the two crimes got police to thinking that they were committed by the same mastermind⟩ — see SIMILARITY 1

paralysis *n* complete or partial loss of physical function (as motion or sensation) in a part of the body ⟨the car accident left one athlete with *paralysis* from the waist down⟩

synonyms palsy

related words cerebral palsy, multiple sclerosis, poliomyelitis; debilitation, debility, decrepitude, enfeeblement, feebleness, frailness, weakness; infirmity, lameness; disability, impairment

near antonyms mobility, motility, sensation

paralytic *adj* affected with paralysis ⟨at first, he would not accept that he was now *paralytic* and needed help⟩

synonyms paralyzed

related words challenged, crippled, disabled, handicapped, maimed, mutilated; hobbled, lame, lamed; im-

paired, incapacitated; hamstrung; debilitated, decrepit, enfeebled, feeble, infirm, weak, weakened
near antonyms able-bodied

paralyze *vb* to render powerless, ineffective, or unable to move ⟨a blizzard *paralyzed* the city for two days⟩
synonyms cripple, disable, hamstring, immobilize, incapacitate, prostrate
related words attenuate, debilitate, enfeeble, sap, undermine, weaken; hobble, lame; maim, mutilate
near antonyms energize, galvanize, vitalize; fortify, strengthen; empower; refresh, rejuvenate, restore

paralyzed *adj* affected with paralysis ⟨special ramps for *paralyzed* people in wheelchairs⟩ — see PARALYTIC

paramount *adj* **1** coming before all others in importance ⟨the *paramount* goal is to complete the renovations of the house with complete historical accuracy⟩ — see FOREMOST 1
2 of the greatest or highest degree or quantity ⟨maintaining the secrecy of the agreement is of *paramount* importance⟩ — see ULTIMATE 1

paraphernalia *n* **1** items needed for the performance of a task or activity ⟨mountain-climbing *paraphernalia*⟩ — see EQUIPMENT
2 transportable items that one owns ⟨packed up all of their *paraphernalia* for the move across the country⟩ — see POSSESSION 2

paraphrase *n* an instance of expressing something in different words ⟨your essays on human rights should have some original thought and not be simply a *paraphrase* of what's in the textbook⟩
synonyms rephrasing, restatement, restating, rewording, translating, translation
related words rehash; summary
near antonyms copy, transcript, transcription
antonyms quotation, quote

paraphrase *vb* to express something (as a text or statement) in different words ⟨could you *paraphrase* your diagnosis of my medical condition, using simpler language?⟩
synonyms rephrase, restate, reword, translate
related words summarize
near antonyms repeat; copy, reproduce, transcribe
antonyms quote

parasite *n* a person who is supported or seeks support from another without making an adequate return ⟨a *parasite* who lived in the family's basement and refused to get a job or pay rent⟩ — see LEECH

parboil *vb* to cook in a liquid heated to the point that it gives off steam ⟨*parboil* a lobster⟩ — see BOIL 2

parcel *n* **1** a number of things considered as a unit ⟨her absurd explanation for the collision was a *parcel* of lies⟩ — see GROUP 1
2 a small area of usually open land ⟨wandered around the little *parcel* out back⟩ — see FIELD 1
3 a small piece of land that is developed or available for development ⟨subdivided the huge farm into smaller *parcels* for sale⟩ — see LOT 1
4 a usually small number of persons considered as a unit ⟨a *parcel* of kids trailing at their heels⟩ — see GROUP 2
5 a wrapped or sealed case containing an item or set of items ⟨received a mysterious *parcel* in the mail⟩ — see PACKAGE 1

parcel (out) *vb* to give out (something) in appropriate amounts or to appropriate individuals ⟨*parceled out* the assignments for work on the parish fair⟩ — see ADMINISTER 1

parcel post *n* communications or parcels sent or carried through the postal system ⟨only *parcel post* bearing a return address and not exceeding size and weight limits will be accepted⟩ — see MAIL

parch *vb* to make dry ⟨the heat has really *parched* my throat⟩ — see DRY 1

pardon *n* release from the guilt or penalty of an offense ⟨the criminal is hoping for a Presidential *pardon*⟩
synonyms absolution, amnesty, forgiveness, remission, remittal
related words parole; acquittal, exculpation, exoneration, vindication; exemption, immunity, impunity, indemnity; commutation, commuting, reprieve
near antonyms conviction, sentence; assessment, charge, fine, imposition, levying; castigation, chastening, chastisement, condemnation
antonyms penalty, punishment, retribution

pardon *vb* **1** to cease to have feelings of anger or bitterness toward ⟨eventually *pardoned* his sister for destroying his toy⟩ — see FORGIVE 1
2 to overlook or dismiss as of little importance ⟨I'm willing to *pardon* a little sloppiness of dress in such a kind and loving person⟩ — see EXCUSE 1

pardonable *adj* worthy of forgiveness ⟨the new parents' gushing pride was *pardonable*⟩ — see VENIAL

pare *vb* to make (as hair) shorter with or as if with the use of shears ⟨*pared* the stray branches on the tree⟩ — see CLIP

parentage *n* the line of ancestors from whom a person is descended ⟨pleased that their son's girlfriend was of good *parentage*⟩ — see ANCESTRY

parenthood *n* the caring for a child by its parents ⟨*parenthood* is a difficult task requiring great commitment⟩ — see PARENTING

parenting *n* the caring for a child by its parents ⟨as the big day approaches, the expectant couple are starting to get worried about their fitness for *parenting*⟩
synonyms parenthood
related words raising, rearing, upbringing; fatherhood, fathering, paternity; maternity, motherhood, mothering

par excellence *adj* of the very best kind ⟨a chef *par excellence*⟩ — see EXCELLENT

pariah *n* one who is cast out or rejected by society ⟨I felt like a *pariah* when I wore the wrong outfit to school⟩ — see OUTCAST

parity *n* the state or fact of being exactly the same in number, amount, status, or quality ⟨rules requiring that there be *parity* in what schools spend on men's and women's sports⟩ — see EQUIVALENCE

park *n* the area around and belonging to a building ⟨the tycoon's country estate is surrounded by a 500-acre *park*⟩ — see GROUND 1

parley *n* **1** a meeting featuring a group discussion ⟨held a *parley* to debate the issue⟩ — see FORUM
2 an exchange of views for the purpose of exploring a subject or deciding an issue ⟨can we meet for a *parley* and see if we produce a compromise?⟩ — see DISCUSSION 1

parley *vb* to exchange viewpoints or seek advice for the purpose of finding a solution to a problem ⟨*parleyed* for weeks over the question of where to build the new school⟩ — see CONFER 2

parliament *n* the highest lawmaking body of a political unit ⟨the treaty was referred to the nation's *parliament* for ratification⟩ — see CONGRESS 1

parlor *n* a building, room, or suite of rooms occupied by a service business ⟨an ice cream *parlor*⟩ — see PLACE 2

parlous *adj* involving potential loss or injury ⟨window washing can be a *parlous* occupation on a skyscraper⟩ — see DANGEROUS

parochial *adj* not broad or open in views or opinions ⟨the *parochial* outlook of the people in that rural backwater⟩ — see NARROW 2

parody *n* **1** a work that imitates and exaggerates another work for comic effect ⟨the musical was a *parody* of *Romeo and Juliet*, with silly songs during the sad scenes⟩
   synonyms burlesque, caricature, spoof, takeoff
   related words lampoon, mockery, satire, travesty; comedy, farce, sketch, slapstick, squib; distortion, exaggeration; imitation, impersonation, mimicking
   near antonyms archetype, original, prototype
   2 a poor, insincere, or insulting imitation of something ⟨the young man sported a feeble *parody* of a mustache in a vain attempt to make himself look older⟩ — see MOCKERY 1

parody *vb* to copy or exaggerate (someone or something) in order to make fun of ⟨*parodying* a public figure's distinctive mannerisms takes particular talent⟩ — see MIMIC 1

paroxysm *n* **1** a sudden intense expression of strong feeling ⟨a *paroxysm* of laughter greeted the pratfall⟩ — see OUTBURST 1
   2 a violent disturbance (as of the political or social order) ⟨Darwin's introduction of the theory of evolution created *paroxysms* in both religion and science that are still being felt today⟩ — see CONVULSION 1

parrot *vb* to say after another ⟨the toddler *parroted* everything her father said, often to his embarrassment⟩ — see REPEAT 3

parsimonious *adj* giving or sharing as little as possible ⟨a *parsimonious* woman who insists that charity begins—and ends—at home⟩ — see STINGY 1

parsimony *n* the quality of being overly sparing with money ⟨her *parsimony* was so extreme that she'd walk five miles to the store to save a few cents on gas⟩
   synonyms cheapness, closeness, miserliness, penuriousness, pinching, stinginess, tightness
   related words conserving, economizing, economy, frugality, husbandry, providence, scrimping, skimping, thrift; conservation, saving; husbanding, managing
   near antonyms extravagance, lavishness; dissipation, improvidence, prodigality, squandering, wastefulness
   antonyms generosity, liberality, openhandedness, openheartedness, philanthropy

parson *n* a person specially trained and authorized to conduct religious services in a Christian church ⟨found a *parson* to conduct the marriage ceremony on the spot⟩ — see CLERGYMAN

part *adv* in some measure or degree ⟨well, you're at least *part* right⟩ — see PARTLY

part *n* **1** one of the pieces from which something is designed to be assembled ⟨the model car came in several small *parts* that had to be assembled⟩
   synonyms member, partition, portion, section, segment
   related words component, constituent, element, factor, ingredient, moiety, parcel; cut, length; bit, fragment, particle, scrap
   near antonyms whole; aggregate, composite, compound, sum, total, totality
   2 something belonging to, due to, or contributed by an individual member of a group ⟨wanted no *part* of the profits⟩ — see SHARE 1
   3 the action for which a person or thing is specially fit-

ted or used or for which a thing exists ⟨I'll do my *part*, so don't worry⟩ — see ROLE
   4 *usually* **parts** *pl* a broad geographical area ⟨I'm not from around these *parts*⟩ — see REGION 2

part *vb* to set or force apart ⟨*parted* the prongs with pliers⟩ — see SEPARATE 1

partake *vb* to take a share or part ⟨we should all *partake* of this fine meal together⟩
   synonyms participate, share
   related words endure, experience, feel, see, taste, undergo; encounter, meet; accept, receive

partaker *n* one who takes part in something ⟨any *partaker* in forbidden activities will be punished⟩ — see PARTICIPANT

partial *adj* **1** inclined to favor one side over another ⟨that judge is always *partial* to the defense, so be careful⟩
   synonyms biased, one-sided, partisan, prejudiced
   related words jaundiced, unfriendly, unsympathetic; colored, distorted, misrepresented, warped; convinced, influenced, persuaded, predisposed, prepossessed, swayed; affected, concerned, interested
   near antonyms open, open-minded, persuasible, receptive; fair, honest, just, reasonable; bipartisan; autonomous, independent, unallied; aloof, detached, dispassionate, hardheaded, impersonal, objective, unemotional; apathetic, indifferent, unenthusiastic, uninterested
   antonyms evenhanded, impartial, neutral, nonpartisan, unbiased, unprejudiced
   2 having a liking or affection ⟨*partial* to chocolate cake⟩ — see FOND 1
   3 lacking some necessary part ⟨a *partial* answer to the problem⟩ — see INCOMPLETE

partiality *n* **1** an attitude that always favors one way of feeling or acting especially without considering any other possibilities ⟨*partiality* blinded the administrator to the benefits of the proposed system for distributing work⟩ — see BIAS
   2 a habitual attraction to some activity or thing ⟨a person with an unfortunate *partiality* for jumping to conclusions⟩ — see INCLINATION 1
   3 positive regard for something ⟨a *partiality* toward outdoor sports of all kinds⟩ — see LIKING

partially *adv* in some measure or degree ⟨the project is only *partially* complete⟩ — see PARTLY

participant *n* one who takes part in something ⟨he seemed to be a willing *participant* in the prank⟩
   synonyms partaker, participator, party, sharer
   related words actor; accessory, aide, assistant, helper; colleague, partner
   near antonyms bystander, looker-on, observer, onlooker, spectator, watcher
   antonyms nonparticipant

participate *vb* to take a share or part ⟨eager to *participate* in after-school activities⟩ — see PARTAKE

participator *n* one who takes part in something ⟨a willing *participator* in any game anyone suggested⟩ — see PARTICIPANT

particle *n* **1** a very small amount ⟨I did all but a *particle* of my work⟩
   synonyms ace, bit, crumb, dab, driblet, glimmer, hint, lick, little, mite, nip, ounce, peanuts, ray, scruple, shade, shadow, shred, smidgen (*also* smidgeon *or* smidgin), snap, spark, speck, spot, sprinkling, strain, streak, suspicion, touch, trace
   related words iota, jot, modicum, tittle, whit; atom, dot, fleck, flyspeck, grain, granule, molecule, morsel, mote, nubbin, patch, scrap; dash, drop, pinch; part,

portion, section; bite, nibble, taste; handful, scattering, smattering; dose, shot; chip, flake, fragment, shard, shiver, sliver, smithereens, splinter; shred, tatter; clipping, paring, shaving

near antonyms abundance, barrel, bucket, bushel, deal, gobs, heaps, loads, mass, mountain, much, peck, pile, plenty, profusion, quantity, raft, scads, stack, wad, wealth; volume; embarrassment, excess, overabundance, overage, overflow, overkill, overmuch, oversupply, superabundance, superfluity, surfeit, surplus; chunk, hunk, lump, slab

2 a very small piece ⟨a *particle* of cookie fell on the carpet⟩ — see BIT 1

particular *adj* **1** hard to please ⟨she's very *particular* about the cleanliness of her car⟩ — see FINICKY

2 of, relating to, or belonging to a single person ⟨that *particular* mug is Mike's⟩ — see INDIVIDUAL 1

3 tending to select carefully ⟨he's *particular* about the corn he buys⟩ — see SELECTIVE

particular *n* **1** a separate part in a list, account, or series ⟨requested a bill of *particulars* for the care he received in the hospital⟩ — see ITEM 1

2 a single piece of information ⟨everyone wanted to know all the *particulars* about the situation⟩ — see FACT 3

particularity *n* **1** careful thoroughness of detail ⟨with great *particularity* she described the qualities she's looking for in a boyfriend⟩

synonyms explicitness, specificity

related words attentiveness, care, carefulness, conscientiousness, finickiness, fussiness, meticulousness; alertness, cautiousness, circumspection, heedfulness, safeness; discrimination; accuracy, exactitude, exactness, precision

near antonyms imprecision, inaccuracy, inexactness; indistinctness, vagueness

antonyms generality

2 a single piece of information ⟨I can't comment without knowing the *particularities* of the case before the court⟩ — see FACT 3

particularized *adj* including many small descriptive features ⟨the hope is that from their *particularized* descriptions of the landscape we can retrace the explorers' route⟩ — see DETAILED 1

particularly *adv* to a great degree ⟨a *particularly* good explanation⟩ — see VERY 1

parting *adj* given, taken, or performed at parting ⟨she gave him a *parting* gift to remember her by⟩

synonyms farewell, valedictory

related words final, last, ultimate; departing, leaving

parting *n* **1** the act or process of two or more persons going off in different directions ⟨although their *parting* was sad, they knew they would see each other again⟩

synonyms farewell, leave-taking, separation

related words departure, egress, exit, exiting, exodus, going, leaving, quitting, running away; decampment, flight, withdrawal; abandonment, desertion, forsaking

near antonyms reunion; arrival, greeting, welcome; gathering, joining, meeting

2 the act of leaving a place ⟨everyone waved goodbye at his *parting*⟩ — see DEPARTURE

partisan *adj* inclined to favor one side over another ⟨a *partisan* teacher who tends to let the class favorites get away with things⟩ — see PARTIAL 1

partisan *n* **1** one who follows the opinions or teachings of another ⟨*partisans* of the charismatic leader refuse to tolerate any criticism of him at all⟩ — see FOLLOWER

2 one who is intensely or excessively devoted to a cause ⟨a *partisan* of the revolution who was even willing to give her life for it⟩ — see ZEALOT

partisanship *n* an attitude that always favors one way of feeling or acting especially without considering any other possibilities ⟨*partisanship* can discourage any serious search for the truth⟩ — see BIAS

partition *n* **1** one of the pieces from which something is designed to be assembled ⟨one of the *partitions* of a prefabricated house⟩ — see PART 1

2 something that divides, separates, or marks off ⟨put up a *partition* to divide the room into two⟩ — see DIVISION 1

3 the act or process of a whole separating into two or more parts or pieces ⟨the *partition* of Czechoslovakia into the Czech Republic and Slovakia⟩ — see SEPARATION 1

partly *adv* in some measure or degree ⟨you're only *partly* right⟩

synonyms incompletely, part, partially

related words in part

near antonyms absolutely, dead, downright, plain, plumb, utterly

antonyms completely, entirely, totally, wholly

partner *n* the person to whom another is married ⟨takes marriage very seriously and wants a man who will be her *partner* for life⟩ — see SPOUSE

partnership *n* the state of having shared interests or efforts (as in social or business matters) ⟨the symphony orchestra is presenting the choral piece in *partnership* with the city's leading choral society⟩ — see ASSOCIATION 1

parturition *n* the act or process of giving birth to children ⟨*parturition* can sometimes proceed more quickly than anticipated⟩ — see CHILDBIRTH

party *n* **1** a social gathering ⟨we're all invited to the big *party* to celebrate the end of the term⟩

synonyms affair, blowout, event, fete (*or* fête), function, get-together, reception, shindig

related words ball, formal, prom; celebration, gala, occasion; orgy, saturnalia; benefit, clambake, hen party, housewarming, masquerade, mixer, shower, salon, soiree (*or* soirée), stag, tea

2 a group of people acting together within a larger group ⟨a small *party* got together to protest the new chairman's decision⟩ — see FACTION

3 a group of people working together on a task ⟨a search *party*⟩ — see GANG 1

4 a member of the human race ⟨my grandfather's a determined old *party*⟩ — see HUMAN

5 a usually small number of persons considered as a unit ⟨for *parties* of more than six people the restaurant automatically adds a 15% service charge to the bill⟩ — see GROUP 2

6 one who takes part in something ⟨a *party* to the agreement⟩ — see PARTICIPANT

party pooper *n* a person who spoils the pleasure of others ⟨a *party pooper* who insisted they turn the music down⟩ — see KILLJOY

pass *n* **1** a narrow opening between hillsides or mountains that can be used for passage ⟨a mountain *pass* that was impassable during the winter⟩ — see CANYON

2 a passage cleared for public vehicular travel ⟨take the second *pass* on the right⟩ — see WAY 1

3 a small sheet of plastic, paper, or paperboard showing that the bearer has a claim to something (as admittance) ⟨a bathroom *pass*⟩ — see TICKET 1

4 an effort to do or accomplish something ⟨a final *pass* at the assignment⟩ — see ATTEMPT

pass *vb* **1** to shift possession of (something) from one person to another ⟨could you please *pass* me the phone?⟩

synonyms hand, hand over, reach, transfer

related words relay; bear, carry; finger, handle, paw; cede, give, give up, release, relinquish, surrender

2 to come to an end ⟨eventually, the storm *passed*⟩ — see CEASE 1

3 to put (something) into the possession or safekeeping of another ⟨*pass* your papers to the teacher⟩ — see GIVE 2

4 to put into effect through legislative or authoritative action ⟨Congress cannot *pass* any law restricting free speech⟩ — see ENACT

5 to take place ⟨and the destruction of the town came to *pass,* just as the seer had predicted⟩ — see HAPPEN

pass (on) *vb* to stop living ⟨my grandfather *passed on* at the age of 92⟩ — see DIE 1

pass (over) *vb* to make one's way through, across, or over ⟨*passed over* two bridges⟩ — see TRAVERSE

passable *adj* **1** capable of being traveled on ⟨after the snowstorm, the roads might not be *passable* for the morning ride to school⟩

synonyms navigable, negotiable

related words clear, cleared, open, unclogged, unobstructed

near antonyms blocked, choked, clogged, closed, congested, dammed, jammed, obstructed; barricaded, blockaded

antonyms impassable

2 capable of being passed into or through ⟨the jungle is not *passable* without a machete⟩ — see PENETRABLE

3 of a level of quality that meets one's needs or standards ⟨that's a *passable* paper⟩ — see ADEQUATE

4 of average or below average quality ⟨the actor's Scottish accent is *passable* at best⟩ — see MEDIOCRE 1

passably *adv* in a satisfactory way ⟨looking for a husband who is rich as well as *passably* handsome⟩ — see WELL 1

passage *n* **1** an established course for traveling from one place to another ⟨the long *passage* down the Atlantic seaboard, around Cape Horn, and up the Pacific Coast to California⟩

synonyms approach, avenue, path, route, way

related words bypath, byway, lane; bypass, drive, freeway, highway, road, street, thoroughfare; trace, track, trail; airway; channel, watercourse, waterway; door, doorway, gate, gateway, portal

2 a going from one place to another usually of some distance ⟨an arduous *passage* across the country⟩ — see JOURNEY

3 a journey over water in a vessel ⟨the *passage* to Britain requires several days⟩ — see SAIL

4 a part taken from a longer work ⟨quoted a *passage* from the novel⟩ — see EXCERPT

5 forward movement in time or place ⟨a swift *passage* from mere liking to actual love⟩ — see ADVANCE 1

passageway *n* **1** a passage cleared for public vehicular travel ⟨turned down a narrow *passageway* in a seedy section of the city⟩ — see WAY 1

2 a typically long narrow way connecting parts of a building ⟨the *passageway* to the other side of the school⟩ — see HALL 2

pass away *vb* to stop living ⟨the old woman *passed away* quietly⟩ — see DIE 1

passé *adj* having passed its time of use or usefulness ⟨that tactic is a bit *passé* now⟩ — see OBSOLETE

passel *n* **1** a number of things considered as a unit ⟨a whole *passel* of questions for the new basketball coach⟩ — see GROUP 1

2 a usually small number of persons considered as a unit ⟨had a *passel* of babies in the span of a few years⟩ — see GROUP 2

passing *adj* lasting only for a short time ⟨his parents were willing to buy him a piano as long as his interest in music was more than a *passing* fancy⟩ — see MOMENTARY

passing *n* the permanent stopping of all the vital bodily activities ⟨the precise moment of his *passing* was recorded by the machines at his bedside⟩ — see DEATH 1

passion *n* **1** a feeling of strong or constant regard for and dedication to someone ⟨they shared such *passion* that they were married at 18 and have been together for half a century⟩ — see LOVE 1

2 a strong but often short-lived liking for another person ⟨her *passion* passed when the next movie star arrived on the scene⟩ — see CRUSH 1

3 a strong wish for something ⟨a *passion* to become a doctor⟩ — see DESIRE

4 a subjective response to a person, thing, or situation ⟨people are sometimes slaves to their own *passions*⟩ — see FEELING 1

5 depth of feeling ⟨your *passion* for your cause is admirable, but you still can't insult people who disagree⟩ — see ARDOR 1

6 passions *pl* general emotional condition ⟨people who are swayed by their *passions* and not by reason⟩ — see FEELING 2

passionate *adj* **1** having a strong sexual desire ⟨a *passionate* couple having an affair⟩ — see LUSTFUL

2 having or expressing great depth of feeling ⟨a *passionate* defense of the play⟩ — see FERVENT

passive *adj* receiving or enduring without offering resistance ⟨the student body was surprisingly *passive* about having recess shortened⟩

synonyms acquiescent, nonresistant, resigned, tolerant, tolerating, unresistant, unresisting, yielding

related words forbearing, long-suffering, patient, uncomplaining; agreeable, amenable, compliant, complying, conformist, docile, guidable, law-abiding, obedient, subordinate, tractable, willing; submissive, surrendering; amiable, obliging; slavish, subservient; disciplined, governable, manageable; apathetic, uncaring, unresponsive

near antonyms defiant; contrary, disobedient, insubordinate, insurgent, intractable, mutinous, rebellious, recalcitrant, refractory, uncontrollable, ungovernable, unruly; balky, perverse, wayward, wrongheaded; headstrong, willful (*or* wilful); indomitable; undisciplined, unmanageable; dissident, nonconformist

antonyms protesting, resistant, resisting, unyielding

pass off *vb* to offer (something fake, useless, or inferior) as genuine, useful, or valuable ⟨tried to *pass off* a piece of blue glass as a sapphire⟩ — see FOIST

pass out *vb* to lose consciousness ⟨*pass out* from the flu⟩ — see FAINT

pass over *vb* **1** to fail to give proper attention to ⟨*passed over* an important notice⟩ — see NEGLECT 1

2 to overlook or dismiss as of little importance ⟨I'd be willing to *pass over* this latest episode of tardiness if there hadn't been so many before⟩ — see EXCUSE 1

passport *n* something that allows someone to achieve a desired goal ⟨meeting that movie director could be your *passport* to a big acting career⟩

synonyms gateway, key, open sesame

related words password; accomplishment, achievement, success; manner, means, method, system, technique, way; blueprint, design, plan, scheme, strategy

password *n* a word or phrase that must be spoken by a person in order to pass a guard ⟨the *password* for the dance party will be changed next week⟩

synonyms countersign, watchword

related words shibboleth, sign; signal; hint, indication

past *adj* having been such at some previous time ⟨a *past* editor of the newspaper⟩ — see FORMER

past *n* the events or experience of former times ⟨we spent a pleasant evening recalling the *past* together⟩

synonyms auld lang syne, history, yesterday, yesteryear, yore

related words bygone; flashback; annals, chronicle, record; memoir; antiquity

near antonyms future, tomorrow; present

past *prep* on or to the farther side of ⟨drive *past* the school⟩ — see BEYOND 1

paste *vb* to deliver a blow to (someone or something) usually in a strong vigorous manner ⟨*pasted* the soccer ball halfway across the field⟩ — see HIT 1

pastel *adj* lacking intensity of color ⟨a *pastel* blue to go with the pale pink walls⟩ — see PALE 1

past master *n* a person with a high level of knowledge or skill in a field ⟨a movie director who was widely regarded as the *past master* of suspense⟩ — see EXPERT

pastoral *adj* 1 of, relating to, associated with, or typical of open areas with few buildings or people ⟨painted a *pastoral* scene of a flower-filled meadow⟩ — see RURAL

2 of, relating to, or characteristic of the clergy ⟨*pastoral* advice to a young couple preparing to marry⟩ — see CLERICAL

pasturage *n* open land over which livestock may roam and feed ⟨put the cows out on the back *pasturage*⟩ — see RANGE 1

pasture *n* open land over which livestock may roam and feed ⟨horses grazing in a fenced *pasture*⟩ — see RANGE 1

pasture *vb* to feed on grass or herbs ⟨*pasturing* sheep on town lands was actually a cheaper alternative to mowing⟩ — see ¹GRAZE

pasty *adj* lacking a healthy skin color ⟨she's *pasty* after a whole winter spent indoors⟩ — see PALE 2

pat *adj* sticking to an opinion, purpose, or course of action in spite of reason, arguments, or persuasion ⟨on the issue of raising taxes the governor stands *pat*⟩ — see OBSTINATE

pat *vb* to touch or handle in a tender or loving manner ⟨*patted* the baby on the head⟩ — see FONDLE

patch *n* 1 a small area that is different (as in color) from the main part ⟨a black cat with a small *patch* of white next to her nose⟩ — see SPOT 1

2 a very small piece ⟨a *patch* of land hardly big enough for a garden⟩ — see BIT 1

patch *vb* to put into good shape or working order again ⟨*patch* the tire and it'll be as good as new⟩ — see MEND 1

patch (together) *vb* to make or assemble roughly or hastily ⟨the stranded hikers *patched together* a shelter that gave some protection from the wind⟩ — see COBBLE (TOGETHER)

patchwork *adj* consisting of many things of different sorts ⟨a *patchwork* collection of antiques⟩ — see MISCELLANEOUS

pate *n* the upper or front part of the body that contains the brain, the major sense organs, and the mouth ⟨plopped a cap on his bald *pate*⟩ — see HEAD 1

patent *adj* 1 not subject to misinterpretation or more than one interpretation ⟨a *patent* attempt to cheat on the exam⟩ — see CLEAR 2

2 very noticeable especially for being incorrect or bad ⟨a *patent* error that should have been caught before the book was published⟩ — see EGREGIOUS

path *n* 1 the direction along which something or someone moves ⟨try to stay out of the *path* of the golf balls while playing⟩ ⟨I tripped over a rock directly in my *path*⟩

synonyms course, line, pathway, route, steps, track, way

related words circle, circuit, loop, orbit; flight path, trajectory; ascent, descent

2 a rough course or way formed by or as if by repeated footsteps ⟨a *path* worn through the library lawn by too many people walking over it⟩ — see TRAIL 1

3 an established course for traveling from one place to another ⟨the *path* along which ancient traders traveled from Europe to China was known as the Silk Road⟩ — see PASSAGE 1

pathetic *adj* 1 deserving of one's pity ⟨the plight of the homeless family was quite *pathetic*⟩

synonyms heartbreaking, heartrending, miserable, piteous, pitiable, pitiful, poor, rueful, sorry, wretched

related words deplorable, lamentable, regrettable; emotional, impressive, inspiring; affecting, moving, poignant, stirring, touching; awful, horrible, terrible; distressing, disturbing, upsetting; grievous, sad, sorrowful, woeful

near antonyms unimpressive, uninspiring

2 causing unhappiness ⟨a *pathetic* story that made her cry⟩ — see SAD 2

pathway *n* 1 a rough course or way formed by or as if by repeated footsteps ⟨a gravel *pathway* laid down where people liked to walk⟩ — see TRAIL 1

2 the direction along which something or someone moves ⟨the long, winding *pathway* of the river⟩ — see PATH 1

patience *n* the capacity to endure what is difficult or disagreeable without complaining ⟨my mother is endowed with nearly endless *patience*⟩

synonyms forbearance, long-suffering, sufferance, tolerance

related words acquiescence, resignation; passiveness, passivity; amenability, compliance, conformism, docility, obedience, subordination, tractability, willingness; discipline, self-control; submission, submissiveness

near antonyms defiance; contrariness, disobedience, insubordination, intractability, recalcitrance, resistance, willfulness

antonyms impatience

patient *adj* 1 accepting pains or hardships calmly or without complaint ⟨you were very *patient* about having to wait for me for so long⟩

synonyms forbearing, long-suffering, stoic (*or* stoical), tolerant, uncomplaining

related words lenient; acquiescent, passive, resigned, unresistant, unresisting, yielding; agreeable, amenable, compliant, complying, conformist, docile, law-abiding, obedient, submissive, subordinate, tractable, willing; slavish, subservient; amiable, obliging; collected, composed; constrained, contained, curbed, inhibited, repressed, restrained; disciplined, self-contained, self-controlled; apathetic, uncaring, unresponsive

near antonyms bored, tired, weary; defiant, resistant; contrary, disobedient, insubordinate, intractable, rebellious, recalcitrant, refractory, ungovernable, unmanageable, unruly

antonyms complaining, fed up, impatient, protesting

2 continuing despite difficulties, opposition, or discouragement ⟨a *patient* effort to finish college⟩ — see PERSISTENT

patient *n* an individual awaiting or under medical care and treatment ⟨the nurse asked the *patient* to change into a paper gown⟩

synonyms case

related words inpatient, outpatient; sufferer, victim; convalescent, nursling

patio *n* an open space wholly or partly enclosed (as by buildings or walls) ⟨there's a *patio* in the center of the apartment complex⟩ — see COURT 2

patois *n* the special terms or expressions of a particular group or field ⟨the medical *patois* that the hospital staffers used among themselves was incomprehensible to me⟩ — see TERMINOLOGY

patrician *adj* of high birth, rank, or station ⟨came from a *patrician* family⟩ — see NOBLE 1

patrician *n* a man of high birth or social position ⟨a congressman with the air and manners of a *patrician*⟩ — see GENTLEMAN 1

patrimony *n* something that is or may be inherited ⟨her *patrimony* was the family business⟩ — see INHERITANCE

patriot *n* a person who loves his or her country and supports its interests and policies ⟨the contention that true *patriots* would be willing to do anything for their country⟩

synonyms loyalist

related words chauvinist; jingoist, nationalist; compatriot, countryman

near antonyms collaborator, quisling, spy, traitor; betrayer, deserter, recreant; renegade

patriotic *adj* having or showing love and support for one's country ⟨hanging a flag outside is a *patriotic* gesture⟩

synonyms nationalist, nationalistic

related words chauvinist; jingoistic; constant, devoted, faithful, loyal, staunch (*or* stanch), steadfast, steady, true; ardent, fervent, fervid, impassioned, passionate

near antonyms traitorous, treasonous; disaffected, disloyal, faithless, false, fickle, inconstant, perfidious, recreant, treacherous, unfaithful

antonyms unpatriotic

patriotism *n* love and support for one's country ⟨her *patriotism* was so great that she quit her job to work for the war effort⟩

synonyms nationalism

related words chauvinism; jingoism; allegiance, constancy, devotion, faithfulness, fealty, loyalty, staunchness, steadfastness; fervency, fervidness, passion

near antonyms desertion, treason; disaffection, disloyalty, faithlessness, falseness, fickleness, inconstancy, perfidiousness, treachery, unfaithfulness

patron *n* **1** a person who buys a product or uses a service from a business ⟨a restaurant *patron*⟩ — see CUSTOMER 1

2 a person who takes the responsibility for some other person or thing ⟨the *patron* for the art exhibit is the city's biggest banking institution⟩ — see SPONSOR

3 one that helps another with gifts or money ⟨he's now a famous writer because he had a *patron* who paid for his college education⟩ — see BENEFACTOR

patronize *vb* **1** to assume or treat with an air of superiority ⟨*patronize* a child with an overly simple explanation⟩ — see CONDESCEND 2

2 to promote the interests or cause of ⟨a company that loyally *patronizes* the arts⟩ — see SUPPORT 1

patter *vb* to engage in casual or rambling conversation ⟨the toddler *pattered* on for what seemed like hours⟩ — see CHAT

patter *n* the special terms or expressions of a particular group or field ⟨the *patter* that one hears in fasionable art galleries⟩ — see TERMINOLOGY

pattern *n* **1** a unit of decoration that is repeated all over something (as a fabric) ⟨a quilt with tiny pink roses as the *pattern*⟩

synonyms design, figure, motif, motive

related words device; adornment, caparison, decoration, embellishment, frill, garnish, ornament, trim

2 a usual manner of behaving or doing ⟨it was her *pattern* to have coffee and a bagel every morning for breakfast⟩ — see HABIT

3 an established and often automatic or monotonous series of actions followed when engaging in some activity ⟨with her, everything must be done strictly according to *pattern*⟩ — see ROUTINE 1

4 the way in which the elements of something (as a work of art) are arranged ⟨many of the artist's paintings use the same *pattern* of a lone figure surrounded by a vast landscape⟩ — see COMPOSITION 3

patty *also* **pattie** *n* a small usually rounded mass of minced food that has been fried ⟨a fish *patty*⟩ — see CAKE

paucity *n* a falling short of an essential or desirable amount or number ⟨a *paucity* of useful answers to the traffic congestion⟩ — see DEFICIENCY

paunch *n* an enlarged or bulging abdomen ⟨Santa is depicted as a white-bearded man with a big *paunch*⟩ — see POTBELLY

pauperism *n* the state of lacking sufficient money or material possessions ⟨*pauperism* forced the family to briefly go on welfare⟩ — see POVERTY 1

pause *n* a momentary halt in an activity ⟨there was a brief *pause* for applause in her speech⟩

synonyms break, breath, breather, interruption, lull, recess

related words time-out; interim, interlude, intermission, interval, respite, rest; cessation, discontinuance, ending, expiration, finishing, lapse, stopping, termination; abeyance, moratorium, surcease, suspension; discontinuity, gap, hiatus

near antonyms continuation, endurance, persistence, progress, progression; extension, prolongation

pause *vb* to come to a temporary halt in one's activity ⟨he *paused* for a moment to tie his shoe⟩

synonyms break

related words break in, interrupt; cease, discontinue, end, finish, stop, terminate; knock off, lay off, quit; lapse, let up

near antonyms continue, persist; advance, progress; extend, prolong, stretch

pawn *n* **1** one that is or can be used to further the purposes of another ⟨she disliked being a *pawn* in her friends' power games⟩

synonyms puppet, tool

related words chump, dupe, foil, gull, sucker, victim; minion, stooge; yes-man

2 something given or held to assure that the giver will keep a promise ⟨offered her license as a *pawn* that she would bring back the rental canoe⟩ — see PLEDGE 1

pawn *vb* to leave as a guarantee of repayment of a loan ⟨he *pawned* his watch in order to pay off his gambling debt⟩
synonyms hock, pledge
related words deposit, mortgage; bond
near antonyms buy (back), redeem, win (back)

pay *n* **1** the money paid regularly to a person for labor or services ⟨it's difficult to support two children on her *pay*⟩ — see WAGE
2 something (as money) that is given or received in return for goods or services ⟨we should demand *pay* for all the overtime we're putting in⟩ — see PAYMENT 2

pay *vb* **1** to give (someone) the sum of money owed for goods or services received ⟨we need to *pay* the cashier and then we can leave⟩
synonyms compensate, recompense, remunerate
related words reimburse, repay, requite; pay off, pay up, prepay
2 to give what is owed for ⟨you ought to *pay* that bill before it's overdue⟩
synonyms clear, discharge, foot, liquidate, pay off, pay up, quit, recompense, settle, spring (for), stand
antonyms repudiate
3 to hand over or use up in payment ⟨*paid* seven dollars to get into the movie⟩ — see SPEND 1
4 to produce as revenue ⟨an investment *paying* six percent⟩ — see YIELD 2

payable *adj* not yet paid ⟨keep the bills *payable* separate from the receipts⟩ — see OUTSTANDING 1

paying *adj* yielding a profit ⟨finally found a *paying* job⟩ — see PROFITABLE 1

paying *n* the act of offering money in exchange for goods or services ⟨the actual shopping was quick, but with the long lines, *paying* for the stuff seemed to take forever⟩ — see PAYMENT 1

payload *n* a mass or quantity of something taken up and carried, conveyed, or transported ⟨the space shuttle can carry a *payload* of almost a million pounds⟩ — see LOAD 1

payment *n* **1** the act of offering money in exchange for goods or services ⟨they are very prompt in the *payment* of their credit card bills⟩
synonyms compensation, disbursement, giving, paying, remittance, remuneration
related words rendering, tendering; reimbursement, repayment; paying off, paying up, prepayment; overpayment
near antonyms underpayment
antonyms nonpayment, repudiation
2 something (as money) that is given or received in return for goods or services ⟨their *payment* for mowing the lawn was $20⟩ ⟨we finally mailed our last car *payment* last week⟩
synonyms compensation, consideration, pay, recompense, remittance, remuneration, requital
related words salary, stipend, wage(s); disbursement, expenditure, outlay; rebate, refund; indemnity, recoupment, redress, reparation, restitution; adjustment, settlement; deposit; reimbursement, repayment; prepayment; overpayment; rent, rental
3 the money paid regularly to a person for labor or services ⟨your *payment* will be issued as a weekly check⟩ — see WAGE

payoff *n* the amount of money left when expenses are subtracted from the total amount received ⟨the *payoff* on the investment was only about $500⟩ — see PROFIT 1

pay off *vb* to give what is owed for ⟨I finally *paid off* the loan⟩ — see PAY 2

pay up *vb* to give what is owed for ⟨for once our bills are all *paid up*⟩ — see PAY 2

peace *n* **1** a state without war ⟨after a long and bitter war, the troubled region finally achieved *peace*⟩
synonyms peacefulness
related words accord, amity, concord, harmony; calm, quiet, serenity, tranquillity (*or* tranquility); order, stability; pacification
near antonyms conflict, contention, discord, dissidence, strife, trouble; tumult, turmoil, unrest, upheaval; fighting, warfare; action, battle, combat
antonyms war
2 a state of freedom from storm or disturbance ⟨the eerie *peace* after a tornado⟩ — see CALM
3 peaceful coexistence ⟨can't we all just live in *peace*?⟩ — see HARMONY 2

peaceable *adj* **1** inclined to live in peace and to avoid war ⟨a *peaceable* nation that has never had any interest in conquest⟩ — see PEACEFUL 1
2 not involving violence or force ⟨trying to find a *peaceable* resolution⟩ — see PEACEFUL 2

peaceful *adj* **1** inclined to live in peace and to avoid war ⟨a *peaceful* tribe that had quietly inhabited these shores for centuries before the arrival of the Europeans⟩
synonyms pacific, peaceable
related words calm, mild, neutral, quiet, relaxed, serene, tranquil; affable, amiable, amicable, benevolent, gentle, kind, kindly; nonbelligerent, unaggressive; submissive, yielding
near antonyms militaristic; aggressive, bellicose, belligerent, combative, contentious, discordant, pugnacious, quarrelsome, scrappy, truculent; antagonistic, argumentative, fierce, gladiatorial, hostile, hot-tempered
antonyms warlike
2 not involving violence or force ⟨UN officials struggled to find a *peaceful* solution to the troublesome conflict⟩
synonyms nonviolent, peaceable
related words conciliatory, pacific, peacemaking; nonbelligerent, unaggressive, unassertive; appeasing, conciliating, mollifying, pacifying, placating; calming, quieting, soothing
near antonyms armed, martial, militant, military, warlike; aggressive, assertive, bellicose, belligerent, combative, contentious, quarrelsome; antagonistic, argumentative, fierce, gladiatorial, hostile; tempestuous, volcanic
antonyms forced, violent
3 free from disturbing noise or uproar ⟨a *peaceful* house, now that the kids are all grown and departed⟩ — see QUIET 1
4 free from storms or physical disturbance ⟨a *peaceful* lake⟩ — see CALM 1

peacefulness *n* **1** a state of freedom from storm or disturbance ⟨the *peacefulness* of the beach was refreshing⟩ — see CALM
2 a state without war ⟨a period of *peacefulness* that remained unbroken until World War I⟩ — see PEACE 1

peacemaker *n* one who works with opposing sides in order to bring about an agreement ⟨a child who often assumes the role of *peacemaker* when his siblings are fighting⟩ — see MEDIATOR

peacemaking *adj* tending to lessen or avoid conflict or hostility ⟨although still smarting from our argument, I accepted my brother's *peacemaking* gesture of help on my science project⟩ — see PACIFIC 1

peak *n* **1** an elevation of land higher than a hill ⟨the nearest *peak* worth climbing is hundreds of miles away⟩ — see MOUNTAIN 1

2 the highest part or point ⟨a pop singer at the *peak* of her career⟩ — see HEIGHT 1

3 the projecting front part of a hat or cap ⟨accidentally stepped on the hat and crushed the *peak*⟩ — see VISOR

peaked *adj* **1** lacking a healthy skin color ⟨you probably should go home, as you're looking awfully *peaked*⟩ — see PALE 2

2 tapering to a thin tip ⟨the church's *peaked* spire is a prominent feature of the town's skyline⟩ — see POINTED 1

3 temporarily suffering from a disorder of the body ⟨I'm feeling a little *peaked*, so I'm going to lie down⟩ — see SICK 1

peal *vb* to make the clear sound heard when metal vibrates ⟨the village bells *pealed* every hour in commemoration⟩ — see RING 1

peanuts *n pl* **1** a very small amount ⟨that's *peanuts* compared to what I had to deal with yesterday⟩ — see PARTICLE 1

2 a very small sum of money ⟨employees griping that they were working for *peanuts*⟩ — see MITE 1

pearl *n* someone or something unusually desirable ⟨friends who agree that his new bride is a real *pearl*⟩ — see PRIZE 1

pebbly *adj* not having a level or smooth surface ⟨a jerky ride on a *pebbly* road⟩ — see UNEVEN 1

peck *n* a considerable amount ⟨now you're in a *peck* of trouble⟩ — see LOT 2

peculiar *adj* **1** being out of the ordinary ⟨a writer with a *peculiar* talent for capturing the qualities of everyday conversation⟩ — see EXCEPTIONAL

2 different from the ordinary in a way that causes curiosity or suspicion ⟨a *peculiar* and catlike way of walking⟩ — see ODD 2

3 noticeably different from what is generally found or experienced ⟨a *peculiar* response to a polite query about his health⟩ — see UNUSUAL 1

4 of, relating to, or belonging to a single person ⟨his *peculiar* way of talking⟩ — see INDIVIDUAL 1

5 serving to identify as belonging to an individual or group ⟨the koala is *peculiar* to Australia⟩ — see CHARACTERISTIC 1

peculiarity *n* **1** an odd or peculiar habit ⟨had the *peculiarity* of constantly fussing with his hair⟩ — see IDIOSYNCRASY

2 something that sets apart an individual from others of the same kind ⟨as its name indicates, the red-winged blackbird has the distinctive *peculiarity* of a red patch on its wings⟩ — see CHARACTERISTIC

pecuniary *adj* of or relating to money, banking, or investments ⟨that makes good *pecuniary* sense⟩ — see FINANCIAL

pedagogue *n* a person whose occupation is to give formal instruction in a school ⟨a *pedagogue* whose classroom lessons consisted entirely of reading directly from the textbook in a monotone⟩ — see TEACHER

peddle *vb* to sell from place to place usually in small quantities ⟨he traveled around the country *peddling* Bibles⟩
synonyms hawk

related words retail, wholesale; deal (in), distribute, high-pressure, hustle, market, merchandise, trade (in), vend

peddler *also* **pedlar** *n* one who sells things outdoors ⟨the *peddler* on the street corner selling baseball caps⟩
synonyms hawker, huckster
related words dealer, merchandiser, seller, vendor (*also* vender); concessionaire; black marketer, bootlegger, fence, fencer, hustler, smuggler, trader
near antonyms buyer, purchaser; consumer, end user, user

pedestrian *adj* causing weariness, restlessness, or lack of interest ⟨a TV detective show filled with *pedestrian* plots stolen from older and better series⟩ — see BORING

pedigree *n* the line of ancestors from whom a person is descended ⟨a woman of good *pedigree*⟩ — see ANCESTRY

pedigreed *adj* of unmixed ancestry ⟨a *pedigreed* puppy is expensive⟩ — see PUREBRED

peek *n* an instance of looking especially briefly ⟨took a *peek* at her Christmas gift hidden in the closet⟩ — see LOOK 2

peek *vb* to take a quick or hasty look ⟨*peek* out the window⟩ — see GLANCE 2

peel *vb* to remove the natural covering of ⟨she *peeled* an apple with great care⟩
synonyms bark, flay, hull, husk, shell, shuck, skin
related words bare, denude, expose, scale, strip; pare

peel (off) *vb* to rid oneself of (a garment) ⟨*peeled off* the wet clothes and tossed them over the shower rod⟩ — see REMOVE 1

peeled *adj* lacking a usual or natural covering ⟨a *peeled* banana⟩ — see NAKED 2

peep *n* an instance of looking especially briefly ⟨stole a *peep* at our neighbor's new pool⟩ — see LOOK 2

peep *vb* to make a short sharp sound like a small bird ⟨the baby *peeped* when she was picked up⟩ — see CHIRP

peer *n* one that is equal to another in status, achievement, or value ⟨a jury of one's *peers*⟩ — see EQUAL

peer *vb* to look long and hard in wonder or surprise ⟨*peered* at the variety of marine life in the aquarium's huge tank⟩ — see GAPE

peerless *adj* having no equal or rival for excellence or desirability ⟨travelers raved about the *peerless* beauty of that tropical isle⟩ — see ONLY 1

peeve *n* **1** something that is a source of irritation ⟨my pet *peeve* is people who don't use proper grammar⟩ — see ANNOYANCE 3

2 the feeling of being offended or resentful after a slight or indignity ⟨he holds on to a *peeve* until the offending person apologizes⟩ — see PIQUE

peeve *vb* to disturb the peace of mind of (someone) especially by repeated disagreeable acts ⟨*peeved* her by humming tunes while she was trying to concentrate⟩ — see IRRITATE 1

peeving *adj* causing annoyance ⟨a *peeving* insistence that everyone drop their work just to help him⟩ — see ANNOYING

peevish *adj* **1** easily irritated or annoyed ⟨I prefer to figure things out on my own rather than ask that *peevish* librarian for help⟩ — see IRRITABLE

2 sticking to an opinion, purpose, or course of action in spite of reason, arguments, or persuasion ⟨a *peevish* man engaged in a perpetual struggle against progress⟩ — see OBSTINATE

peevishness *n* **1** a steadfast adherence to an opinion, purpose, or course of action ⟨facts, no matter how indisputable, were no match for their *peevishness*⟩ — see OBSTINACY

2 readiness to show annoyance or impatience ⟨his constant *peevishness* made everyone around him cranky as well⟩ — see PETULANCE

peewee *n* a living thing much smaller than others of its kind ⟨that particular species is the *peewee* of the salmon world⟩ — see DWARF 1

peg *n* an individual part of a process, series, or ranking ⟨took the arrogant student down a *peg*⟩ — see DEGREE 1

peg *vb* **1** to arrange or assign according to type ⟨*pegged* him as a smart boy right from the beginning⟩ — see CLASSIFY 1

2 to send through the air especially with a quick forward motion of the arm ⟨*pegged* the ball to the second baseman⟩ — see THROW

peg (away) *vb* to devote serious and sustained effort ⟨he usually *pegs away* at his essays until he gets things exactly right⟩ — see LABOR

pelage *n* the hairy covering of a mammal especially when fine, soft, and thick ⟨color variation in the snow leopard's *pelage*⟩ — see FUR 1

pelagic *adj* of or relating to the sea ⟨among *pelagic* animals the undisputed king is the blue whale, the largest creature currently roaming the face of the earth⟩ — see MARINE 1

pelf *n* something (as pieces of stamped metal or printed paper) customarily and legally used as a medium of exchange, a measure of value, or a means of payment ⟨seemed perpetually short of *pelf*⟩ — see MONEY

pellet *n* a usually round or cone-shaped little piece of lead made to be fired from a firearm ⟨a supply of shotgun *pellets*⟩ — see BULLET

pell–mell *adj* **1** acting or done with excessive or careless speed ⟨a *pell-mell* dash for safety after bullets started flying around⟩ — see HASTY 1

2 lacking in order, neatness, and often cleanliness ⟨*pell-mell* piles of books everywhere in the library⟩ — see MESSY

pell–mell *adv* **1** in a confused and reckless manner ⟨tossed stuff *pell-mell* into the room⟩ — see HELTER-SKELTER 1

2 with excessive or careless speed ⟨ran *pell-mell* down the road to get help⟩ — see HASTILY 1

pellucid *adj* easily seen through ⟨the *pellucid* waters that lap upon that island's beaches⟩ — see CLEAR 1

pelt *n* the outer covering of an animal removed for its commercial value ⟨caught beavers and sold the *pelts* to fur traders⟩ — see HIDE 1

pelt *vb* **1** to proceed or move quickly ⟨*pelted* away when the cops arrived⟩ — see HURRY 2

2 to send through the air especially with a quick forward motion of the arm ⟨*pelted* snowballs at each other while waiting for the bus⟩ — see THROW

3 to strike repeatedly ⟨*pelted* the other kids with pebbles⟩ — see BEAT 1

pen *n* **1** a place of confinement for persons held in lawful custody ⟨earned six years in a federal *pen*⟩ — see JAIL

2 an enclosure with an open framework for keeping animals ⟨a goat *pen*⟩ — see CAGE

pen *vb* **1** to close or shut in by or as if by barriers ⟨remember to *pen* up the dogs when visitors come over⟩ — see ENCLOSE 1

2 to compose and set down on paper the words of ⟨I wish that I could *pen* a love song to show her how much I love her⟩ — see WRITE 1

penal *adj* inflicting, involving, or serving as punishment ⟨Australia was once a *penal* colony⟩ — see PUNITIVE

penalize *vb* to inflict a penalty on for a fault or crime ⟨you will be *penalized* by a letter grade for every day an assignment is late⟩ — see PUNISH

penalizing *adj* inflicting, involving, or serving as punishment ⟨forced to listen to a *penalizing* lecture on the consequences of lying⟩ — see PUNITIVE

penalty *n* **1** a feature of someone or something that creates difficulty for achieving success ⟨a one-stroke *penalty* at golf⟩ — see DISADVANTAGE

2 a sum of money to be paid as a punishment ⟨the *penalty* for speeding is $10 for every mile over the speed limit⟩ — see FINE

3 suffering, loss, or hardship imposed in response to a crime or offense ⟨the *penalty* for being mean to your sister is missing that party you were planning to attend⟩ — see PUNISHMENT

penchant *n* a habitual attraction to some activity or thing ⟨a *penchant* for sitting by the window and staring moodily off into space⟩ — see INCLINATION 1

pencil (in) *vb* to compose and set down on paper the words of ⟨*penciled in* notes all over the manuscript⟩ — see WRITE 1

pendant *also* **pendent** *n* an ornament worn on a chain around the neck or wrist ⟨Navajo necklaces with *pendants* finely studded in genuine sky-blue turquoise⟩
synonyms bangle, charm, lavalier (*also* lavalliere)
related words locket, teardrop

pendent *or* **pendant** *adj* extending freely from a support from above ⟨a *pendent* bucket hung in the well⟩ — see DEPENDENT 1

pending *adj* **1** not yet settled or decided ⟨a decision is *pending* about whether to buy computers or sports equipment with this money⟩
synonyms open, undecided, undetermined, unresolved, unsettled
related words hanging; arguable, debatable, disputable, moot, uncertain, unsure
near antonyms confirmed, established; certain, sure
antonyms decided, determined, resolved, settled

2 being soon to appear or take place ⟨a *pending* review of your work so far this term⟩ — see FORTHCOMING

3 giving signs of immediate occurrence ⟨the sky darkened with a *pending* storm⟩ — see IMMINENT 1

pendulous *adj* **1** bending downward or forward ⟨a cow with a *pendulous* udder⟩ — see NODDING

2 extending freely from a support from above ⟨a *pendulous* crystal chandelier dominated the ballroom⟩ — see DEPENDENT 1

penetrable *adj* capable of being passed into or through ⟨unfortunately, our netting proved to be a rather *penetrable* barrier that allowed in our cabin a steady stream of mosquitoes⟩
synonyms passable, permeable, porous
related words absorbent
near antonyms airtight, watertight; close, compact, dense, thick
antonyms impassable, impenetrable, impermeable, impervious, nonporous

penetrate *vb* to go or come in or into ⟨a needle *penetrated* the heavy cloth only with great effort⟩ — see ENTER 1

penetrating *adj* causing intense discomfort to one's skin ⟨an icy, *penetrating* rain that made you feel really miserable⟩ — see CUTTING 1

peninsula *n* an area of land that juts out into a body of water ⟨the *peninsula* is constantly buffeted by storms⟩ — see ²CAPE

penitence *n* a feeling of responsibility for wrongdoing ⟨he's never been one to feel *penitence* for anything he's done⟩ — see GUILT 1

penitent *adj* **1** feeling sorrow for a wrong that one has done ⟨a *penitent* gossip who had come to ask for forgiveness⟩ — see CONTRITE 1
2 suffering from or expressive of a feeling of responsibility for wrongdoing ⟨a *penitent* attempt to make restitution to the store where she had shoplifted⟩ — see GUILTY 2

penitentiary *n* a place of confinement for persons held in lawful custody ⟨a sentence in the state *penitentiary* for robbery⟩ — see JAIL

penman *n* a person who creates a written work ⟨the prolific *penman* of dozens of horror stories⟩ — see AUTHOR 1

penmanship *n* **1** the form or style of a particular person's writing ⟨doctors are famous for their illegible *penmanship*⟩ — see HANDWRITING 1
2 writing done by hand ⟨essays must be typed, not in *penmanship*⟩ — see HANDWRITING 2

pennant *n* a piece of cloth with a special design that is used as an emblem or for signaling ⟨a knight's individual *pennant*⟩ — see FLAG 1

penniless *adj* lacking money or material possessions ⟨went from being a *penniless* girl to owner of her own restaurant⟩ — see POOR 1

pennon *n* a piece of cloth with a special design that is used as an emblem or for signaling ⟨*pennons* flew from the yachts gathered in the harbor for festival⟩ — see FLAG 1

pensive *adj* given to or marked by long, quiet thinking ⟨spent a *pensive* day in preparation for taking religious vows⟩ — see CONTEMPLATIVE

penstock *n* a long hollow cylinder for carrying a substance (as a liquid or gas) ⟨a *penstock* carried water for the waterwheel⟩ — see PIPE 1

penthouse *n* a smaller structure added to a main building ⟨had a small *penthouse* built to serve as a toolshed⟩ — see ANNEX

penumbra *n* partial darkness due to the obstruction of light rays ⟨occasionally, the moon will cast a *penumbra* over the Earth⟩ — see SHADE 1

penurious *adj* **1** giving or sharing as little as possible ⟨the *penurious* couple brought only a cheap, tacky gift to the wedding⟩ — see STINGY 1
2 lacking money or material possessions ⟨although we were a *penurious* family, we never lacked for love or happiness⟩ — see POOR 1

penuriousness *n* **1** the quality of being overly sparing with money ⟨he daily practiced such *penuriousness* that few would have guessed that he was one of the state's wealthiest residents⟩ — see PARSIMONY
2 the state of lacking sufficient money or material possessions ⟨the abject *penuriousness* of so many of the city's inhabitants should be a cause for concern⟩ — see POVERTY 1

penury *n* the state of lacking sufficient money or material possessions ⟨lived in a time when single women like herself faced a lifetime of genteel *penury*⟩ — see POVERTY 1

peon *n* a person who does very hard or dull work ⟨the company had plenty of low-paying positions for people who were content to be *peons* all their lives⟩ — see SLAVE 2

people *n pl* **1** human beings in general ⟨despite the horrors she witnessed, Anne Frank never lost her faith in *people*⟩
synonyms folks, humanity, humankind, public, society, world
related words crowd, masses, mob, populace, proletariat, rabble, riffraff
2 the body of the community as contrasted with the elite ⟨tensions mounted until the *people* rose up in rebellion⟩ — see MASS 1
3 a group of persons who come from the same ancestor ⟨introduced my new boyfriend to my *people*⟩ — see FAMILY 1

pep *n* active strength of body or mind ⟨a baseball team full of *pep*⟩ — see VIGOR 1

pep (up) *vb* to give life, vigor, or spirit to ⟨the music at the party *pepped* everyone *up*⟩ — see ANIMATE

pepper *vb* **1** to cover by or as if by scattering something over or on ⟨*pepper* the costume with flecks of glitter⟩ — see SCATTER 2
2 to mark with small spots especially unevenly ⟨spilled flour *peppered* the kitchen floor⟩ — see SPOT

peppery *adj* marked by a lively display of strong feeling ⟨a *peppery* discussion on whether cheating can ever be justified⟩ — see SPIRITED 1

peppiness *n* the quality or state of having abundant or intense activity ⟨the *peppiness* of the city's music scene in the last year has been encouraging⟩ — see VITALITY 1

peppy *adj* **1** having active strength of body or mind ⟨a *peppy* and entertaining group of young musicians⟩ — see VIGOROUS 1
2 having much high-spirited energy and movement ⟨a *peppy* dance performance⟩ — see LIVELY 1

per *prep* using the means or agency of ⟨the infection is spread to the rest of the body *per* the bloodstream⟩ — see BY 2

perambulation *n* a relaxed journey on foot for exercise or pleasure ⟨took a invigorating *perambulation* around the lake to get some fresh air⟩ — see WALK

per capita *adv* for each one ⟨the town charges resident families five dollars *per capita* for use of the town beach⟩ — see APIECE

perceive *vb* **1** to have a vague awareness of ⟨I thought I *perceived* a problem, but I wasn't sure⟩ — see FEEL 1
2 to make note of (something) through the use of one's eyes ⟨*perceived* that it was going to be a nice day⟩ — see SEE 1
3 to recognize the meaning of ⟨I *perceive* your point, but I still disagree⟩ — see COMPREHEND 1

percentage *n* a measure of how often an event will occur instead of another ⟨since most car thefts are never solved, there will always be greedy people ready to take advantage of this *percentage*⟩ — see PROBABILITY 2

perceptible *adj* able to be perceived by a sense or by the mind ⟨you should note a *perceptible* temperature change when you add the second element⟩
synonyms appreciable, detectable, discernible, distinguishable, palpable, sensible
related words audible, observable, tangible, visible; clear, conspicuous, evident, eye-catching, manifest, noticeable, obvious, plain, prominent, striking; apparent, distinct, significant, straightforward

near antonyms inaudible, intangible, invisible; inconspicuous, indistinct, unnoticeable; faint, insignificant, slight, trivial; buried, concealed, covert, disguised, hidden, obscure, shrouded, vague

antonyms impalpable, imperceptible, inappreciable, indistinguishable, insensible

perception *n* **1** the ability to understand inner qualities or relationships ⟨a writer of considerable *perception*, she remembers how it feels to be confused and insecure⟩ — see WISDOM 1

2 the knowledge gained from the process of coming to know or understand something ⟨a growing *perception* of the enormity of the problem⟩ — see COMPREHENSION

perceptive *adj* **1** able to sense slight impressions or differences ⟨a *perceptive* princess would notice a pea under her mattress⟩ — see ACUTE 1

2 having or showing deep understanding and intelligent application of knowledge ⟨a *perceptive* therapist was able to discover what was really troubling the youth⟩ — see WISE 1

perceptiveness *n* the ability to understand inner qualities or relationships ⟨with great *perceptiveness*, the therapist suggested that maybe I was upset with myself more than anything⟩ — see WISDOM 1

perch *vb* **1** to come to rest after descending from the air ⟨pigeons *perching* on the roof⟩ — see ALIGHT

2 to establish or place comfortably or snugly ⟨*perched* the baby in a basket⟩ — see ENSCONCE 1

perchance *adv* it is possible ⟨could we go shopping later, *perchance*?⟩ — see PERHAPS

percolate *vb* to flow forth slowly through small openings ⟨water *percolating* through the coffee filter⟩ — see EXUDE

percolate (into) *vb* to spread throughout ⟨open that window and allow some fresh air to *percolate into* this room⟩ — see PERMEATE

perdition *n* the place of punishment for the wicked after death ⟨simple stupidity is not enough to doom one to *perdition*⟩ — see HELL 1

peregrinate *vb* to take a trip especially of some distance ⟨a couple of backpacking college students who decided to spend the summer *peregrinating* around Ireland⟩ — see TRAVEL 1

peregrination *n* a going from one place to another usually of some distance ⟨planning a leisurely *peregrination* across Europe for our honeymoon⟩ — see JOURNEY

peremptoriness *n* an exaggerated sense of one's importance that shows itself in the making of excessive or unjustified claims ⟨the *peremptoriness* that was apparent in his voice irritated everyone⟩ — see ARROGANCE

peremptory *adj* **1** fond of ordering people around ⟨the governor's *peremptory* personal assistant began telling the crowd of reporters and photographers exactly where they had to stand⟩ — see BOSSY

2 forcing one's compliance or participation by or as if by law ⟨a *peremptory* summons to appear before the committee⟩ — see MANDATORY

3 having a feeling of superiority that shows itself in an overbearing attitude ⟨she had such a *peremptory* approach to running the club that people started to avoid her⟩ — see ARROGANT

4 having or showing a tendency to force one's will on others without any regard to fairness or necessity ⟨a *peremptory* insistence that the staff wait on them first⟩ — see ARBITRARY 1

perfect *adj* **1** being entirely without fault or flaw ⟨a stunningly *perfect* performance—not the slightest mistake—won her the gold medal in women's figure skating⟩

synonyms absolute, faultless, flawless, ideal, impeccable, irreproachable, letter-perfect, unblemished

related words consummate, expert, masterly; classic, dandy, excellent, fabulous, fine, first-class, first-rate, grand, great, marvelous (*or* marvellous), prime, superb, superior, superlative, terrific, top, top-notch, unsurpassed; completed, finished, perfected, polished; complete, entire, intact, whole; immaculate, unbruised, undamaged, unimpaired, uninjured, unmarred, unspoiled; exceptional, fancy, high-grade, special; accurate, correct, exact, precise; infallible, unerring, unfailing

near antonyms deficient, inadequate, incomplete, insufficient, wanting; unfinished, unpolished; fallible; blemished, blighted, broken, damaged, defaced, disfigured, impaired, injured, marred, spoiled, vitiated; atrocious, execrable, wretched; imprecise, inaccurate, incorrect, inexact, wrong

antonyms bad, censurable, defective, faulty, flawed, imperfect, reproachable

2 having no exceptions or restrictions ⟨living in *perfect* happiness in the country⟩ — see ABSOLUTE 2

3 not lacking any part or member that properly belongs to it ⟨I have a *perfect* recollection of that conversation⟩ — see COMPLETE 1

perfect *vb* **1** to bring (something) to a state where nothing remains to be done ⟨*perfected* the arrangements for their long-awaited European vacation⟩ — see FINISH 1

2 to make better ⟨an art teacher who seems to believe that you can always *perfect* a painting with some additional brush strokes⟩ — see IMPROVE

perfection *n* the most perfect type or example ⟨Rembrandt's portraits are the *perfection* of the art of using facial expression, pose, and gesture to reveal the subject's interior life⟩ — see QUINTESSENCE 1

perfectly *adv* **1** without any flaws or errors ⟨you did that handspring *perfectly* on your first try⟩

synonyms faultlessly, flawlessly, ideally, impeccably

related words excellently, fabulously, finely, grandly, greatly, marvelously, superbly, superiorly, superlatively, terrifically; exceptionally, fancily, specially

phrases to a nicety, to a T, to a turn

near antonyms deficiently, inadequately, incompletely, insufficiently; fallibly; atrociously, execrably, wretchedly

antonyms badly, defectively, faultily, imperfectly

2 to a full extent or degree ⟨you know *perfectly* well what I'm talking about, so don't pretend⟩ — see FULLY 1

perfidious *adj* not true in one's allegiance to someone or something ⟨a *perfidious* campaign worker revealed his strategy to his leading rival for the nomination⟩ — see FAITHLESS

perfidiousness *n* lack of faithfulness especially to one's husband or wife ⟨their mutual *perfidiousness* led to a quick divorce⟩ — see INFIDELITY 1

perfidy *n* **1** lack of faithfulness especially to one's husband or wife ⟨before their marriage she had told him that *perfidy* was the one thing she would never tolerate in a spouse⟩ — see INFIDELITY 1

2 the act or fact of violating the trust or confidence of another ⟨the unspeakable *perfidy* of her telling the practically whole school my secret⟩ — see BETRAYAL

perforate *vb* to make a hole or series of holes in ⟨he *perforated* the sheet with his pencil and put it in his binder⟩

  synonyms bore, drill, hole, pierce, punch, puncture

  related words broach, tap; poke, prick; penetrate; burrow (into), excavate, gouge, groove, hollow; break, cut, gash, notch, rend, rupture, slash, slit, split

  near antonyms fill, patch, plug, seal

perforation *n* **1** a mark or small hole made by a pointed instrument ⟨absentmindedly made *perforations* in his paper with his pencil⟩ — see PRICK 1

  2 a place in a surface allowing passage into or through a thing ⟨poked the button through a *perforation* in the fabric⟩ — see HOLE 1

perforce *adv* because of necessity ⟨we must, *perforce*, deal with this issue immediately⟩ — see NEEDS

perform *vb* **1** to carry through (as a process) to completion ⟨she *performed* the task quickly and expertly⟩

  synonyms accomplish, achieve, carry out, commit, compass, do, execute, follow through, fulfill (*or* fulfil), make

  related words bring about, effect, effectuate, implement; engage (in), practice (*or* practise); work (at); reduplicate, reenact, repeat; actualize, attain, realize; complete, end, finish, wind up

  phrases go through

  near antonyms fail; skimp, slight, slur

  2 to have a certain purpose ⟨the kidneys *perform* as a kind of filtering system for the blood⟩ — see FUNCTION

  3 to present a portrayal or performance of ⟨has always dreamed of *performing* Hamlet on stage⟩ — see ACT 1

  4 to produce a desired effect ⟨the new medication *performed* surprisingly well⟩ — see ACT 2

performance *n* the doing of an action ⟨the *performance* of her nightly ritual, the taking of a warm bath, calmed her⟩ — see COMMISSION 2

perfume *n* a sweet or pleasant smell ⟨the *perfume* of fresh flowers filled the room⟩ — see FRAGRANCE

perfume *vb* to fill or infuse with a pleasant odor or odor-releasing substance ⟨roses *perfumed* the wedding chapel⟩ — see SCENT 1

perfumed *adj* having a pleasant smell ⟨delicately *perfumed* stationery⟩ — see FRAGRANT

perfunctory *adj* having or showing a lack of interest or concern ⟨made a *perfunctory* inquiry after his health⟩ — see INDIFFERENT 1

perhaps *adv* it is possible ⟨*perhaps* we will not have to take this exam, but I doubt it⟩

  synonyms conceivably, maybe, mayhap, perchance, possibly

  related words likely, probably; certainly, doubtless, surely, undoubtedly; presumably

peril *n* **1** something that may cause injury or harm ⟨life is full of unexpected *perils*⟩ — see DANGER 2

  2 the state of not being protected from injury, harm, or evil ⟨they were unhappy about sending their son into *peril* overseas⟩ — see DANGER 1

perilous *adj* involving potential loss or injury ⟨a *perilous* journey through hostile territory⟩ — see DANGEROUS

perimeter *n* the line or relatively narrow space that marks the outer limit of something ⟨soldiers guarding the *perimeter* of the camp⟩ — see BORDER 1

period *n* **1** an occurrence of menstruating ⟨girls having their *period* will be excused from gym class⟩

  synonyms menstruation, monthlies

  related words menses

  2 an extent of time associated with a particular person or thing ⟨the *period* of the dinosaurs⟩ — see AGE 1

periodic *adj* **1** appearing in parts or numbers that follow regularly ⟨a *periodic* novel in the newspaper⟩ — see SERIAL

  2 appearing or occurring repeatedly from time to time ⟨sent out *periodic* reminders⟩ — see REGULAR 1

  3 occurring or appearing at intervals ⟨*periodic* snow showers that might leave up to an inch⟩ — see INTERMITTENT 1

periodical *adj* **1** appearing in parts or numbers that follow regularly ⟨read the *periodical* transcripts of the trial in the newspaper⟩ — see SERIAL

  2 occurring or appearing at intervals ⟨*periodical* announcements from airline personnel concerning the delay⟩ — see INTERMITTENT 1

periodical *n* a publication that appears at regular intervals ⟨subscribed to three new *periodicals*⟩ — see JOURNAL

peripatetic *adj* traveling from place to place ⟨a *peripatetic* vegetable seller⟩ — see ITINERANT

peripheral *adj* available to supply something extra when needed ⟨*peripheral* computer equipment⟩ — see AUXILIARY

periphery *n* the line or relatively narrow space that marks the outer limit of something ⟨wander around the *periphery* of the mansion's flower garden⟩ — see BORDER 1

perish *vb* to stop living ⟨twelve people *perished* in the plane crash⟩ — see DIE 1

perk (up) *vb* **1** to become glad or hopeful ⟨we *perked up* once the sun came out⟩ — see CHEER (UP) 1

  2 to move from a lower to a higher place or position ⟨the cat *perked up* her tail in greeting⟩ — see RAISE 1

perky *adj* having much high-spirited energy and movement ⟨a *perky* cheerleader⟩ — see LIVELY 1

permanent *adj* lasting forever ⟨no trial or problem is *permanent*⟩ — see EVERLASTING

permanently *adv* for all time ⟨planned to stay there *permanently*⟩ — see EVER 1

permeable *adj* capable of being passed into or through ⟨a *permeable* fabric that allows your body heat to escape will be much more comfortable in the summertime⟩ — see PENETRABLE

permeate *vb* to spread throughout ⟨the smell of freshly baked bread *permeated* the house⟩

  synonyms interpenetrate, percolate (into), pervade, suffuse, transfuse

  related words diffuse (through), impregnate, pass (into), penetrate; fill (up); drench, infuse, saturate, soak, steep; flood, glut

permissible *adj* that may be permitted ⟨fortunately, that is a *permissible* shortcut to the answer⟩

  synonyms admissible, allowable, licensable

  related words acceptable, bearable, endurable, tolerable; accredited, allowed, authorized, certified, endorsed, licensed (*also* licenced), OK (*or* okay), permitted, sanctioned, warranted; mandatory, ordered, required

  near antonyms intolerable, unacceptable, unbearable, unendurable; objectionable; denied, disallowed, refused, rejected, vetoed; repressed, suppressed; outlawed

  antonyms banned, barred, forbidden, impermissible, inadmissible, interdicted, prohibited, proscribed

permission *n* the approval by someone in authority for the doing of something ⟨she asked for *permission* to have a piece of candy⟩ ⟨the President granted *permission* for the foreign diplomats to have special quarters⟩

synonyms allowance, authorization, clearance, concurrence, consent, granting, leave, license (*or* licence), sanction, sufferance
related words imprimatur, seal, signature, stamp; accreditation, certification; liberty, pass; concession, patent, permit; acceptance, acquiescence, agreement, assent, OK (*or* okay); accord, grant
near antonyms denial, refusal, rejection, revocation; taboo; injunction, veto; deterrence, discouragement, repression, suppression; ban, embargo, exclusion
antonyms interdiction, prohibition, proscription
permit *vb* **1** to give permission for or to approve of ⟨the school won't *permit* such an activity on its grounds⟩ — see ALLOW 1
2 to give permission to ⟨I can't *permit* you to go out on a school night⟩ — see ALLOW 2
3 to make able or possible ⟨we'll have our picnic on Thursday, weather *permitting*⟩ — see ENABLE 1
pernicious *adj* causing or capable of causing harm ⟨the *pernicious* effect that illegal narcotics have on a society⟩ — see HARMFUL
perpendicular *adj* rising straight up ⟨rivers rafters staring awestruck at the canyon's nearly *perpendicular* cliffs⟩ — see ERECT
perpetration *n* the doing of an action ⟨the *perpetration* of a series of pranks that resulted in an expulsion from school⟩ — see COMMISSION 2
perpetual *adj* lasting forever ⟨a *perpetual* love that even death could not end⟩ — see EVERLASTING
perpetually *adv* **1** for all time ⟨even our sun will not exist *perpetually*⟩ — see EVER 1
2 on every relevant occasion ⟨was *perpetually* asking me to cut my hair⟩ — see ALWAYS 1
perpetuate *vb* to give eternal or lasting existence to ⟨we hope to *perpetuate* this holiday tradition⟩
synonyms immortalize
related words commemorate, memorialize; celebrate, enshrine, honor; conserve, keep up, maintain, preserve, support, sustain; defend, guard, protect, safeguard
near antonyms extinguish, put out, snuff (out); annihilate, crush, decimate, demolish, destroy, devastate; eradicate, erase, expunge, extirpate, obliterate, wipe out
perpetuity *n* endless time ⟨lands that should remain in their wild state for *perpetuity*⟩ — see ETERNITY 1
perplex *vb* **1** to make complex or difficult ⟨let's not *perplex* the issue further with irrelevant concerns⟩ — see COMPLICATE
2 to throw into a state of mental uncertainty ⟨the question *perplexed* me⟩ — see CONFUSE 1
perplexity *n* a state of mental uncertainty ⟨seeing her *perplexity*, the teacher stepped in with a helpful hint⟩ — see CONFUSION 1
perquisite *n* **1** a small sum of money given for a service over and above what is due ⟨give the movers a *perquisite* if they do a good job⟩ — see ²TIP 1
2 something given in addition to what is ordinarily expected or owed ⟨the use of a company car is one *perquisite* of the job⟩ — see BONUS
persecute *vb* **1** to cause persistent suffering to ⟨people who were *persecuted* simply for practicing their religious faith⟩ — see AFFLICT
2 to disturb the peace of mind of (someone) especially by repeated disagreeable acts ⟨she likes to *persecute* her sister with pointless, annoying questions at inopportune times⟩ — see IRRITATE 1
persecutor *n* **1** a person who causes repeated emotional pain, distress, or annoyance to another ⟨years later his

schoolyard *persecutor* would end up being one of his low-paid employees⟩ — see TORMENTOR
2 one who is obnoxiously annoying ⟨on this flight my airline-appointed *persecutor* was a chattering nitwit who could not stop talking about himself⟩ — see NUISANCE 1
persevere *vb* to continue despite difficulties, opposition, or discouragement ⟨although he was frustrated by the lack of financial resources and support, he *persevered* in his scientific research⟩
synonyms carry on, persist
related words hang on; follow through; knuckle down
phrases hang in there
near antonyms give up, quit, surrender, yield; falter, hesitate, vacillate, waver
persevering *adj* continuing despite difficulties, opposition, or discouragement ⟨at the end of the long, winding trail, *persevering* hikers will be rewarded with an inviting, secluded lake⟩ — see PERSISTENT
persiflage *n* good-natured teasing or exchanging of clever remarks ⟨their tongue-in-cheek *persiflage* is sometimes mistaken for an exchange of insults by people who don't know them⟩ — see BANTER
persist *vb* **1** to continue despite difficulties, opposition, or discouragement ⟨she *persisted* in her efforts and eventually got the job she wanted⟩ — see PERSEVERE
2 to remain indefinitely in existence or in the same state ⟨my headache *persisted* for almost the entire day⟩ — see CONTINUE 1
persistence *n* **1** continuing existence ⟨the *persistence* of the child's fever made us start to worry⟩
synonyms continuance, durability, endurance
related words longevity, staying power, tenacity; permanence; survival; continuation
near antonyms discontinuance; cessation, desisting, ending, finish, quitting, stop
2 uninterrupted or lasting existence ⟨the *persistence* of the fever for a week caused me great worry⟩ — see CONTINUATION
3 a steadfast adherence to an opinion, purpose, or course of action ⟨she found the *persistence* of her would-be boyfriend anything but endearing⟩ — see OBSTINACY
persistent *adj* continuing despite difficulties, opposition, or discouragement ⟨although his first attempts were unsuccessful, he was *persistent* in his pursuit of a career in rock music⟩
synonyms dogged, insistent, patient, persevering, pertinacious, tenacious
related words assured, certain, dedicated, determined, firm, intent, positive, resolute, resolved, single-minded, sure; hardheaded, headstrong, mulish, obdurate, obstinate, opinionated, peevish, perverse, pigheaded, self-willed, stubborn, unyielding; unfaltering, unhesitating, unwavering; resistant, wayward, wrongheaded; constant, devoted, faithful, good, loyal, staunch (*or* stanch), steadfast, steady, true; indomitable, unconquerable; hard, inflexible, relentless, stern, unbending, unrelenting, unyielding
near antonyms quitting, surrendering, yielding; faltering, hesitant, hesitating, irresolute, vacillating, wavering; disloyal, faithless, false, fickle, inconstant, perfidious, traitorous, treacherous
person *n* a member of the human race ⟨is there any *person* here who knows how to speak Spanish?⟩ — see HUMAN
personage *n* a person who is widely known and usually much talked about ⟨*personages* from the fields of sport

and entertainment will be special guests at the political convention⟩ — see CELEBRITY 1

personal *adj* of, relating to, or belonging to a single person ⟨kept *personal* items in a separate drawer⟩ — see INDIVIDUAL 1

personality *n* **1** a person who is widely known and usually much talked about ⟨a local television *personality* who is beloved by area residents⟩ — see CELEBRITY 1
2 the set of qualities that make a person different from other people ⟨she's got a great *personality*⟩ — see INDIVIDUALITY
3 the set of qualities that makes a person, a group of people, or a thing different from others ⟨it has never been in the nation's *personality* to adhere to a rigid class system⟩ — see NATURE 1

personalize *vb* to represent in visible form ⟨in the character of the good-hearted, virtuous seaman, the author has *personalized* the concept of perfect innocence⟩ — see EMBODY 2

personalized *adj* of, relating to, or belonging to a single person ⟨a *personalized* jewelry box that had been engraved with her initials⟩ — see INDIVIDUAL 1

personally *adv* in person and usually privately ⟨told me *personally* that I was invited⟩ — see TÊTE-À-TÊTE

personalty *n* transportable items that one owns ⟨and I will my *personalty* to my children⟩ — see POSSESSION 2

personification *n* a visible representation of something abstract (as a quality) ⟨he's the *personification* of kindness⟩ — see EMBODIMENT

personify *vb* to represent in visible form ⟨she just *personifies* the spirit of charity⟩ — see EMBODY 2

personnel *n* a body of persons at work or available for work ⟨we finally have enough *personnel* to start that big project⟩ — see FORCE 1

perspective *n* a way of looking at or thinking about something ⟨whether she was being rude or candid is all a matter of *perspective*⟩ — see POINT OF VIEW

perspicuity *n* clearness of expression ⟨the *perspicuity* of this author's prose is one of the reasons why her novels are still read and those of her contemporaries are gathering dust⟩ — see SIMPLICITY 2

perspicuous *adj* not subject to misinterpretation or more than one interpretation ⟨believing that poetry need not be as *perspicuous* as prose, he writes poems that are intentionally ambiguous⟩ — see CLEAR 2

perspicuousness *n* clearness of expression ⟨the *perspicuousness* of the prosecutor's closing argument⟩ — see SIMPLICITY 2

persuade *vb* to cause (someone) to agree with a belief or course of action by using arguments or earnest request ⟨she *persuaded* us that she can indeed communicate with the dead⟩ ⟨he *persuaded* his teachers to grant an extension⟩
synonyms argue, convince, get, induce, move, prevail (on *or* upon), satisfy, talk (into), win (over)
related words cajole, coax, exhort, urge; lead on, seduce, snow, tempt; incline, influence, move, prompt, sell, sway; attract, bring, draw, entice, interest; chew over, converse, debate, discuss, dispute, hash (over), moot; reason (with)
near antonyms dissuade

persuading *n* the act of reasoning or pleading with someone to accept a belief or course of action ⟨no amount of *persuading* could make Mom change her mind⟩ — see PERSUASION 1

persuasion *n* **1** the act of reasoning or pleading with someone to accept a belief or course of action ⟨the suffragists' gradual *persuasion* of the American people that voting rights had to be extended to women⟩
synonyms convincing, inducement, inducing, persuading, suasion
related words cajolery, coaxing, exhortation, urging; seduction, tempting; influencing, prompting, swaying; lobbying, pressuring
2 a body of beliefs and practices regarding the supernatural and the worship of one or more deities ⟨debating theology with someone of a different *persuasion*⟩ — see RELIGION 1
3 an idea that is believed to be true or valid without positive knowledge ⟨he's of the *persuasion* that everything that happens in this world is part of a divine plan⟩ — see OPINION 1

persuasive *adj* having the power to persuade ⟨a *persuasive* argument for increasing funding for the city's library system⟩ — see COGENT

persuasiveness *n* the capacity to persuade ⟨the *persuasiveness* of her closing statement changed the minds of several jurors who had been leaning toward conviction⟩ — see COGENCY 1

pert *adj* **1** having much high-spirited energy and movement ⟨a *pert* girl who is a member of the cheerleading squad⟩ — see LIVELY 1
2 making light of something usually regarded as serious or sacred ⟨a *pert* retort that irritated the teacher⟩ — see FLIPPANT

pertain *vb* **1** to be the property of a person or group of persons ⟨the belief that quality medical care is a right that *pertains* to everyone⟩ — see BELONG 2
2 to have a relation or connection ⟨a person who is an expert in anything *pertaining* to the theater⟩ — see APPLY 1

pertain (to) *vb* to have (something) as a subject matter ⟨where would I find books *pertaining* to birds?⟩ — see CONCERN 1

pertinacious *adj* **1** continuing despite difficulties, opposition, or discouragement ⟨a *pertinacious* little boy who was determined to catch and collect reptiles⟩ — see PERSISTENT
2 sticking to an opinion, purpose, or course of action in spite of reason, arguments, or persuasion ⟨a *pertinacious* salesman who would simply not take "No!" for an answer⟩ — see OBSTINATE

pertinaciousness *n* a steadfast adherence to an opinion, purpose, or course of action ⟨thanks to his *pertinaciousness*, he eventually succeeded where all others had failed⟩ — see OBSTINACY

pertinacity *n* a steadfast adherence to an opinion, purpose, or course of action ⟨without the *pertinacity* of the suffragists, voting rights for women would never have become a reality⟩ — see OBSTINACY

pertinence *n* the fact or state of being pertinent ⟨job applicants should question the *pertinence* of any questions about their personal lives⟩
synonyms applicability, bearing, connection, materiality, relevance, relevancy
related words appropriateness, aptness, fitness, suitability; importance, significance; usefulness
near antonyms inappropriateness, inaptness, unfitness, unsuitability; insignificance, unimportance; pointlessness, uselessness
antonyms extraneousness, inapplicability, irrelevance

pertinent *adj* having to do with the matter at hand ⟨he impressed the jury with his concise, *pertinent* answers to the attorney's questions⟩

synonyms applicable, apposite, apropos, germane, material, pointed, relative, relevant

related words appropriate, apt, fit, fitting, suitable; important, meaningful, significant; sensible, useful; admissible, allowable

phrases in point, to the point

near antonyms inconsequential, insignificant, unimportant; meaningless, purposeless, senseless, useless; inappropriate, inapt, unsuitable; inadmissible

antonyms extraneous, immaterial, inapplicable, irrelevant, pointless

pertly *adv* in a quick and spirited manner ⟨the young girl *pertly* informed him that he was her favorite uncle⟩ — see GAILY 2

pertness *n* shameless boldness ⟨the startling *pertness* with which the waitress responded to our request to make a substitution⟩ — see EFFRONTERY

perturb *vb* to trouble the mind of; to make uneasy ⟨his strange remark *perturbed* me enough to keep me awake⟩ — see DISTURB 1

perturbation *n* an uneasy state of mind usually over the possibility of an anticipated misfortune or trouble ⟨in her *perturbation* she kept calling her son, a freshman, to see if everything was all right at college⟩ — see ANXIETY 1

perturbed *adj* feeling or showing uncomfortable feelings of uncertainty ⟨a *perturbed* look betrayed her nervousness at her first job interview⟩ — see NERVOUS 1

perturbing *adj* causing worry or anxiety ⟨the *perturbing* news meant that we'd have to go home early⟩ — see TROUBLESOME

peruse *vb* to go over and mentally take in the content of ⟨*perused* the manuscript, checking for errors⟩ — see READ

pervade *vb* to spread throughout ⟨the delicious scent of roasting turkey *pervaded* the house⟩ — see PERMEATE

perverse *adj* 1 easily irritated or annoyed ⟨how can you be so cheerful one day, and so *perverse* the next?⟩ — see IRRITABLE

2 having or showing lowered moral character or standards ⟨social conservatives who believe that Hollywood is a *perverse* world that exerts an unhealthy influence on the young⟩ — see CORRUPT

3 sticking to an opinion, purpose, or course of action in spite of reason, arguments, or persuasion ⟨a fact so self-evident that not even the most *perverse* of opponents could deny it⟩ — see OBSTINATE

perverseness *n* readiness to show annoyance or impatience ⟨her *perverseness* caused her to snap at everyone who made the mistake of greeting her⟩ — see PETULANCE

perversion *n* 1 a sinking to a state of low moral standards and behavior ⟨claimed rap and rock music were responsible for the *perversion* of the nation's young people⟩ — see CORRUPTION 2

2 incorrect or improper use ⟨a *perversion* of the word⟩ — see MISUSE

perversity *n* readiness to show annoyance or impatience ⟨his habitual *perversity* makes him unpleasant to be around⟩ — see PETULANCE

pervert *n* a person who has sunk below the normal moral standard ⟨warned not to go near the neighborhood *pervert*⟩ — see DEGENERATE

pervert *vb* 1 to change so much as to create a wrong impression or alter the meaning of ⟨that summary really *perverts* the other candidate's views on taxes⟩ — see GARBLE

2 to lower in character or dignity ⟨*perverted* the Bible story by reveling in the sinners' lewd behavior before the moment of divine retribution⟩ — see DEBASE 1

3 to put to a bad or improper use ⟨accused of *perverting* the Internal Revenue Service by using it to harass political opponents⟩ — see MISAPPLY

perverted *adj* having or showing lowered moral character or standards ⟨the *perverted* values of a society that had taken permissiveness to the extreme⟩ — see CORRUPT

pessimist *n* 1 one who emphasizes bad aspects or conditions and expects the worst ⟨she's such a *pessimist* that she's convinced she'll fail every test⟩

synonyms defeatist

related words cynic, fatalist; pragmatist, realist

near antonyms dreamer, idealist, romantic, utopian, visionary; sentimentalist

antonyms optimist

2 a person who distrusts other people and believes that everything is done for selfish reasons ⟨a true *pessimist*, he's convinced that there will be wars as long as there are people to wage them⟩ — see CYNIC

pessimistic *adj* 1 emphasizing or expecting the worst ⟨with that *pessimistic* attitude, it's no wonder you're depressed⟩

synonyms defeatist, despairing, hopeless

related words cynical, fatalistic; desperate, discouraging, disheartening, inauspicious, unlikely, unpromising; bleak, cheerless, comfortless, dismal, dreary, gloomy; grim; contrary, hostile, negative

near antonyms auspicious, encouraging, fair, heartening, likely, promising, propitious; cheering, comforting, reassuring; favorable, good, positive; idealist, romantic, utopian, visionary

antonyms hopeful, optimistic, rose-colored, rosy, upbeat

2 having or showing a deep distrust of human beings and their motives ⟨*pessimistic* about the prospects for a lasting peace in the area⟩ — see CYNICAL

pest *n* 1 a widespread disease resulting in a high rate of death ⟨one of the great *pests* of the 20th century was the influenza epidemic of 1918, which killed millions across the globe⟩ — see PLAGUE

2 one who is obnoxiously annoying ⟨stop being a *pest* to your sister and go find something else to do⟩ — see NUISANCE 1

3 something that is a source of irritation ⟨a never-ending construction project that continues to be a *pest* for motorists⟩ — see ANNOYANCE 3

pester *vb* to thrust oneself upon (another) without invitation ⟨*pestered* his brother by incessantly asking him for help with his homework⟩ — see BOTHER 1

pestering *n* the act of making unwelcome intrusions upon another ⟨the endless *pestering* finally drove me to study at the library⟩ — see ANNOYANCE 1

pestilence *n* a widespread disease resulting in a high rate of death ⟨the fear that terrorists could unleash a *pestilence* that would wreak unspeakable havoc⟩ — see PLAGUE

pestilent *adj* likely to cause or capable of causing death ⟨*pestilent* diseases such as bubonic plague and smallpox⟩ — see DEADLY

pesty *adj* causing annoyance ⟨a *pesty* toddler who followed me everywhere⟩ — see ANNOYING

pet *adj* granted special treatment or attention ⟨spent my free time on my *pet* project⟩ — see DARLING 1

pet *n* **1** a person or thing that is preferred over others ⟨the teacher's *pet* was always getting special privileges⟩ — see FAVORITE

2 a state of resentful silence or irritability ⟨stalked off in a *pet* after being refused permission to go to the movies⟩ — see SULK

pet *vb* **1** to touch or handle in a tender or loving manner ⟨a cat who loves to be *petted*⟩ — see FONDLE

2 to touch one another with the lips as a sign of love ⟨teenagers who are just starting to *pet*⟩ — see KISS 1

petition *n* an earnest request ⟨a *petition* to be allowed extra time for the test⟩ — see PLEA 1

petition *vb* to make a request to (someone) in an earnest or urgent manner ⟨*petitioned* my parents to let me go to the party⟩ — see BEG

petitioner *n* one who asks earnestly for a favor or gift ⟨the lottery winner was beset by a horde of *petitioners*, all of whom thought that they were most deserving of his charity⟩ — see SUPPLICANT

pettish *adj* easily irritated or annoyed ⟨a *pettish* baby who always seemed to be crying⟩ — see IRRITABLE

pettishness *n* readiness to show annoyance or impatience ⟨his self-indulgent *pettishness* is more than his coworkers should endure⟩ — see PETULANCE

petty *adj* **1** not broad or open in views or opinions ⟨a *petty* little town that was not ethnically diverse and very happy about the situation⟩ — see NARROW 2

2 so small or unimportant as to warrant little or no attention ⟨obsessed over even *petty* problems⟩ — see NEGLIGIBLE 1

petulance *n* readiness to show annoyance or impatience ⟨I do not appreciate your *petulance* and eagerness to argue⟩

synonyms biliousness, crankiness, crossness, crotchetiness, grouchiness, grumpiness, huffiness, irascibility, irritability, irritableness, peevishness, perverseness, perversity, pettishness, testiness, waspishness

related words cantankerousness, disagreeableness, dyspepsia, fretfulness, orneriness, sulkiness, surliness; aggression, aggressiveness, bellicosity, belligerence, combativeness, contentiousness, contrariness, disputatiousness, fight, pugnacity, scrappiness, truculence; fussiness, querulousness, rudeness; oversensitiveness, sensitivity; antagonism, fierceness, hostility, unfriendliness; anger, exasperation, rage, wrath; hot-bloodedness, passion

near antonyms forbearance, patience, tolerance, understanding; affability, amicability, cordiality, friendliness, sociability; amiability, good-humoredness, good-naturedness, good-temperedness; coolness, serenity, tranquility; easygoingness, gentleness, kindliness, mildness

petulant *adj* easily irritated or annoyed ⟨a *petulant* and fussy man who blamed everyone for his problems⟩ — see IRRITABLE

pewter *adj* of the color gray ⟨a *pewter* car that's almost invisible in fog⟩ — see GRAY 1

phantasm *n* **1** a conception or image created by the imagination and having no objective reality ⟨frightened by the *phantasms* of his own making⟩ — see FANTASY 1

2 the soul of a dead person thought of especially as appearing to living people ⟨believed that she'd seen the *phantasm* of her father on the anniversary of his death⟩ — see GHOST

phantasmal *adj* not real and existing only in the imagination ⟨*phantasmal* fears that prevented her from living a normal life⟩ — see IMAGINARY

phantom *adj* not real and existing only in the imagination ⟨the company claimed that the only hazards involving its product were the *phantom* dangers created by consumer groups⟩ — see IMAGINARY

phantom *n* the soul of a dead person thought of especially as appearing to living people ⟨Halloween is supposed to be a time when *phantoms* return to walk among us⟩ — see GHOST

pharmaceutical *n* a substance or preparation used to treat disease ⟨some *pharmaceuticals* can be risky unless taken correctly⟩ — see MEDICINE

pharmacist *n* a person who prepares drugs according to a doctor's prescription ⟨the *pharmacist* caught an error in the prescription⟩ — see DRUGGIST

pharmacy *n* a retail store where medicines and miscellaneous articles are sold ⟨stopped at the *pharmacy* for tissues and cold medicine⟩ — see DRUGSTORE

phase *n* **1** a certain way in which something appears or may be regarded ⟨the moral *phase* of the problem has yet to be considered⟩ — see ASPECT 1

2 an individual part of a process, series, or ranking ⟨in the final *phase* of production⟩ — see DEGREE 1

phased *adj* proceeding or changing by steps or degrees ⟨a *phased* construction of the tunnel through the heart of the city⟩ — see GRADUAL

phenomenal *adj* **1** being out of the ordinary ⟨the *phenomenal* growth that the suburb has experienced over the last decade⟩ — see EXCEPTIONAL

2 being so extraordinary or abnormal as to suggest powers which violate the laws of nature ⟨the *phenomenal* ability to remember the names of thousands of people⟩ — see SUPERNATURAL 2

phenomenon *n* something extraordinary or surprising ⟨our jaws dropped when we saw this basketball *phenomenon* play for the first time⟩ — see WONDER 1

philanthropic *adj* having or showing a concern for the welfare of others ⟨a *philanthropic* society that has been doing good for over a century⟩ — see CHARITABLE 1

philanthropy *n* **1** a gift of money or its equivalent to a charity, humanitarian cause, or public institution ⟨among the industrialist's *philanthropies* was a college scholarship fund for deserving students from the inner city⟩ — see CONTRIBUTION

2 the giving of necessities and especially money to the needy ⟨he was so dedicated to *philanthropy* that he had little money left for himself⟩ — see CHARITY 1

3 the quality or state of being generous ⟨a society dowager renowned for her *philanthropy*⟩ — see LIBERALITY

philharmonic *n* a usually large group of musicians playing together ⟨served as a conductor for the *philharmonic*⟩ — see ²BAND 1

philistine *n* a person who is chiefly interested in material comfort and is hostile or indifferent to art and culture ⟨the town's *philistines* who think that spending on the arts is a waste of taxpayers' money⟩

synonyms lowbrow, materialist

related words capitalist, plutocrat; boor, cad, churl, clown, creep, cur, jerk, lout

near antonyms highbrow; egghead, intellectual, sage, thinker; brain, genius

philosophy *n* the basic beliefs or guiding principles of a person or group ⟨our *philosophy* is to do no harm to anyone⟩ — see CREED 1

phlegm *n* a lack of emotion or emotional expressiveness ⟨a man of remarkable *phlegm,* never showing enthusiasm nor displeasure⟩ — see APATHY 1

phlegmatic *adj* not feeling or showing emotion ⟨a *phlegmatic* response to what should have been happy news⟩ — see IMPASSIVE 1

phone *vb* to make a telephone call to ⟨*phoned* her friend to invite her over for dinner⟩ — see CALL 2

phony *also* **phoney** *adj* **1** being such in appearance only and made or manufactured with the intention of committing fraud ⟨a *phony* watch with a designer logo⟩ — see COUNTERFEIT

2 lacking in natural or spontaneous quality ⟨always has this *phony* smile just before she betrays you⟩ — see ARTIFICIAL 1

phony *also* **phoney** *n* **1** an imitation that is passed off as genuine ⟨the fancy "emerald" ring turned out to be a *phony*⟩ — see FAKE 1

2 one who makes false claims of identity or expertise ⟨the person who performed the operation was later discovered to be a *phony*⟩ — see IMPOSTOR

photo *n* a picture created from an image recorded on a light-sensitive surface by a camera ⟨an album of wedding *photos*⟩ — see PHOTOGRAPH

photo *vb* to take a photograph of ⟨*photoed* the historic mansion for a decorating magazine⟩ — see PHOTOGRAPH

photograph *n* a picture created from an image recorded on a light-sensitive surface by a camera ⟨the old *photograph* was faded but still clear enough to make out⟩

synonyms photo, print, shot, snap, snapshot

related words blowup, close-up, enlargement, still; daguerreotype, monochrome, tintype

photograph *vb* to take a photograph of ⟨we *photographed* the baby birds frequently⟩

synonyms mug, photo, shoot, snap

related words image, picture, retake; film, videotape

phrases capture on film

photographer *n* one who takes photographs ⟨we'll need to choose a *photographer* for the wedding⟩

synonyms shooter, shutterbug

related words cinematographer

phrase *n* a sequence of words having a specific meaning ⟨draw a literal representation of the *phrase* "to rain cats and dogs"⟩

synonyms expression, idiom

related words cliché; locution, term; epithet, expletive, name; byword, cry, motto, shibboleth, slogan, watchword; archaism, colloquialism, euphemism, modernism, neologism, provincialism, vulgarism

phrases figure of speech

phrase *vb* to convey in appropriate or telling terms ⟨he had trouble thinking of how to *phrase* his question for the visiting dignitary⟩

synonyms articulate, clothe, couch, express, formulate, put, say, state, word

related words craft, frame; hint, imply, insinuate, intimate, suggest; paraphrase, rephrase, restate, reword, summarize, translate; communicate, disclose, speak, tell; describe, render, write up

phraseology *n* **1** a distinctive way of putting ideas into words ⟨I recognized the writer's distinctive *phraseology* even before I saw the name⟩ — see STYLE 1

2 the way in which something is put into words ⟨the unique *phraseology* of the suspect's answer stuck in my mind⟩ — see WORDING

phrasing *n* the way in which something is put into words ⟨the particularly delicate and careful *phrasing* of the statement regarding their relationship⟩ — see WORDING

phylactery *n* something worn or kept to bring good luck or keep away evil ⟨wore a small *phylactery* on a cord around his neck⟩ — see CHARM 1

physic *n* a substance or preparation used to treat disease ⟨the museum has an exhibit on some of the strange *physics* that were once used to cure disease⟩ — see MEDICINE

physical *adj* **1** of or relating to the human body ⟨*physical* sensations such as heat and pain⟩

synonyms animal, bodily, carnal, corporal, corporeal, fleshly, material, somatic

related words anatomic (*or* anatomical), physiological; sensual, sensuous; hand-to-hand

near antonyms intellectual, mental, psychological (*also* psychologic); bodiless, immaterial, incorporeal, spiritual; ethereal, metaphysical, psychic (*also* psychical)

antonyms nonmaterial, nonphysical

2 relating to or composed of matter ⟨couldn't tell the difference between a *physical* object and a shadow in the dim light⟩ — see MATERIAL 1

physician *n* a person specially trained in healing human medical disorders ⟨you should always consult a *physician* if you develop a high fever⟩ — see DOCTOR

physique *n* the type of body that a person has ⟨she had a well-toned *physique*⟩

synonyms build, constitution, figure, form, frame, shape

related words anatomy, structure

picayune *adj* so small or unimportant as to warrant little or no attention ⟨irritatingly *picayune* complaints⟩ — see NEGLIGIBLE 1

pick *n* **1** a person or thing that is chosen ⟨that team is my *pick* to win the Super Bowl⟩ — see CHOICE 2

2 individuals carefully selected as being the best of a class ⟨the *pick* of the contestants will go on to the next competition⟩ — see ELITE

3 the power, right, or opportunity to choose ⟨you have first *pick* of your classmates for the team⟩ — see CHOICE 1

pick *vb* **1** to catch or collect (a crop or natural resource) for human use ⟨*pick* peas and beans from the garden for dinner⟩ — see HARVEST

2 to decide to accept (someone or something) from a group of possibilities ⟨I *pick* you as my partner⟩ — see CHOOSE 1

picked *adj* singled out from a number or group as more to one's liking ⟨a *picked* group of people for the project⟩ — see SELECT 1

picked up *adj* being clean and in good order ⟨if your room is all *picked up*, you can go to the party⟩ — see NEAT 1

picker *n* someone with the right or responsibility for making a selection ⟨a book reviewer who is one of the *pickers* of the Pulitzer Prize for fiction⟩ — see SELECTOR

picket *n* a person or group that watches over someone or something ⟨set out a *picket* to watch the camp⟩ — see GUARD 1

picking *n* the act or process of selecting ⟨the *picking* of new recruits went on for three days⟩ — see SELECTION 1

pickle *n* a difficult, puzzling, or embarrassing situation from which there is no easy escape ⟨well, this is a bit of a *pickle* we've gotten ourselves into⟩ — see PREDICAMENT

pick up *vb* **1** to acquire complete knowledge, understanding, or skill in ⟨has a knack for *picking up* a language in a few weeks⟩ — see LEARN 1

2 to bring together in one body or place ⟨*pick up* all of your things because we have to be off this beach before dark⟩ — see GATHER 1

3 to get possession of (something) by giving money in exchange for ⟨could you *pick up* some milk at the store?⟩ — see BUY

4 to increase in ⟨the boat was just *picking up* speed when it was rammed by another boat⟩ — see GAIN 1

5 to move from a lower to a higher place or position ⟨*pick up* your feet while I vacuum in front of the sofa⟩ — see RAISE 1

6 to take or keep under one's control by authority of law ⟨*picked up* the fugitive when she went out to buy food⟩ — see ARREST 1

picky *adj* **1** hard to please ⟨a *picky* cat who would only eat one particular kind of food, and only if it was served in his special dish⟩ — see FINICKY

2 tending to select carefully ⟨she's *picky*, but she always finds the best quality in fresh meat and fish⟩ — see SELECTIVE

picnic *n* something that is easy to do ⟨this class is no *picnic*, but I've really been learning a lot⟩ — see CINCH

pictorial *adj* **1** consisting of or relating to pictures ⟨he's planning to do a primarily *pictorial* report on Africa⟩

synonyms graphic (*also* graphical), visual

related words photographic, video; drawn, painted, represented; illustrative; pictographic

2 producing a mental picture through clear and impressive description ⟨she writes a very *pictorial* kind of poetry, using words the way a painter applies strokes of color⟩ — see GRAPHIC 1

picture *n* **1** a two-dimensional design intended to look like a person or thing ⟨she produced a beautiful *picture* of her mother using watercolors⟩

synonyms illustration, image, likeness

related words delineation, depiction, representation; portrait; drawing, finger painting; etching, silhouette, sketch, watercolor; caricature, cartoon, doodle; collage, montage, photograph; hieroglyphic, ideogram; pictograph

2 a story told by means of a series of continuously projected pictures and a sound track ⟨the actor's latest *picture* is another thriller⟩ — see MOVIE 1

3 a vivid representation in words of someone or something ⟨the newspaper report gives a detailed *picture* of the current situation in that troubled country⟩ — see DESCRIPTION 1

4 position with regard to conditions and circumstances ⟨when personal opinion becomes part of the *picture*, the journalist isn't just reporting the news⟩ — see SITUATION 1

5 something or someone that strongly resembles another ⟨the young teen is the very *picture* of her mother⟩ — see IMAGE 1

6 something imagined or pictured in the mind ⟨I think I get the *picture*: you want me to leave⟩ — see IDEA

7 **pictures** *pl* the art or business of making a movie ⟨hoping for a career in *pictures*⟩ — see MOVIE 2

picture *vb* **1** to present a picture of ⟨the famous painting that *pictures* the Founding Fathers signing the Declaration of Independence⟩

synonyms depict, image, portray, represent

related words delineate, describe, render; outline, sketch; illustrate, show; caricature

2 to form a mental picture of ⟨*pictured* the town from the description of it in the author's memoirs⟩ — see IMAGINE 1

3 to give a representation or account of in words ⟨*pictured* the sailing ship in vivid language⟩ — see DESCRIBE 1

picturesque *adj* producing a mental picture through clear and impressive description ⟨wrote a *picturesque* tale of their journey across the country⟩ — see GRAPHIC 1

piddling *adj* so small or unimportant as to warrant little or no attention ⟨raised one final, *piddling* objection⟩ — see NEGLIGIBLE 1

piebald *adj* having blotches of two or more colors ⟨a *piebald* horse that looked like it had been splashed with black and white paint⟩ — see PIED

piece *n* **1** a broken or irregular part of something that often remains incomplete ⟨a *piece* of stone fell from the wall⟩ — see FRAGMENT

2 a literary, musical, or artistic production ⟨presented a new interpretation of the *piece* by Mozart⟩ — see COMPOSITION 1

3 a portable weapon from which a shot is discharged by gunpowder ⟨carrying a *piece* under his coat⟩ — see GUN 1

piece *vb* to form by putting together parts or materials ⟨*piece* together a quilt from odd patches of cloth⟩ — see BUILD

piece by piece *adv* by small steps or amounts ⟨worked out the solution *piece by piece*⟩ — see GRADUALLY

piecemeal *adj* proceeding or changing by steps or degrees ⟨a *piecemeal* attempt to remedy the traffic congestion⟩ — see GRADUAL

piecemeal *adv* **1** by small steps or amounts ⟨remodeled the house *piecemeal*⟩ — see GRADUALLY

2 into parts or to pieces ⟨one well-aimed blow ripped the piñata *piecemeal*⟩ — see APART

pied *adj* having blotches of two or more colors ⟨although the mother's was pure black, the foal's coat was *pied*⟩

synonyms blotched, dappled (*also* dapple), marbled, mottled, piebald, pinto, splotched, spotted

related words shaded; checkered, motley, multicolored, polychromatic, polychrome, varicolored, variegated; blotted, brindled (*or* brindle), specked, speckled, streaked; colored, colorful, pigmented; dotted, peppered, sprinkled; stippled; discolored, dyed, marked, stained; flecked, streaked; bespattered, spattered

near antonyms monochromatic, solid

pier *n* **1** a structure used by boats and ships for taking on or landing cargo and passengers ⟨tied the boat up at the *pier*⟩ — see DOCK

2 an upright shaft that supports an overhead structure ⟨a bridge *pier*⟩ — see PILLAR 1

pierce *vb* **1** to go or come in or into ⟨thoughts of revenge *pierced* her mind⟩ — see ENTER 1

2 to make a hole or series of holes in ⟨*pierced* his ears with a needle⟩ — see PERFORATE

3 to penetrate or hold (something) with a pointed object ⟨the saber *pierced* his chest, releasing a spurt of blood⟩ — see IMPALE

piercing *adj* **1** causing intense discomfort to one's skin ⟨that light sweater will be no match for the *piercing* wind outside⟩ — see CUTTING 1

2 marked by a high volume of sound ⟨the baby emitted a *piercing* shriek that could be heard all over the house⟩ — see LOUD 1

piety *n* **1** belief and trust in and loyalty to God ⟨her *piety* is quiet but profound⟩ — see FAITH 1

2 the quality or state of being spiritually pure or virtuous ⟨among fellow clerics he is respected and admired for his *piety*⟩ — see HOLINESS

piffle *n* **1** language, behavior, or ideas that are absurd and contrary to good sense ⟨the belief that soda is made out of acid is just *piffle*⟩ — see NONSENSE 1
2 unintelligible or meaningless talk ⟨she may think that she's writing poetry, but it's pure *piffle*⟩ — see GIBBERISH

pigeon *n* one who is easily deceived or cheated ⟨a confidence man in search of a new *pigeon*⟩ — see DUPE

piggish *adj* having a huge appetite ⟨a *piggish* dog who ate anything left within reach⟩ — see VORACIOUS 1

pigheaded *adj* sticking to an opinion, purpose, or course of action in spite of reason, arguments, or persuasion ⟨a *pigheaded* child who insisted that a monster really was living under his bed⟩ — see OBSTINATE

pigment *n* a substance used to color other materials ⟨I'm running out of the black *pigment*⟩
synonyms color, coloring, dye, dyestuff, stain, tincture
related words cast, hue, shade, tinge, tint, tone

pig out *vb* to eat greedily or to excess ⟨one holiday when you're expected to *pig out* on junk food⟩ — see GORGE 2

pigpen *n* a dirty or messy place ⟨your room is a *pigpen*—so clean it up!⟩
synonyms hole, pigsty, shambles
related words chaos, confusion, disarrangement, disarray, disorder, jumble, mess, muddle; dump; clutter, litter, mishmash

pigsty *n* a dirty or messy place ⟨the kitchen is a *pigsty* after cooking that big dinner⟩ — see PIGPEN

¹pike *n* a passage cleared for public vehicular travel ⟨take the *pike* in to the city⟩ — see WAY 1

²pike *n* a weapon with a long straight handle and sharp head or blade ⟨a foot soldier armed with a *pike*⟩ — see SPEAR

³pike *n* the last and usually sharp or tapering part of something long and narrow ⟨the spear's metal *pike* was designed to cause a gaping wound when it was pulled out of the victim⟩ — see POINT 2

piker *n* a mean grasping person who is usually stingy with money ⟨don't be such a *piker*—live it up a little while you're on vacation!⟩ — see MISER

pikestaff *n* a weapon with a long straight handle and sharp head or blade ⟨*pikestaffs* were in use from the Middle Ages to the 18th century⟩ — see SPEAR

pilaster *n* an upright shaft that supports an overhead structure ⟨the rectangular *pilasters* spaced along the building's facade lend an air of classical grandeur⟩ — see PILLAR 1

¹pile *n* **1** a quantity of things thrown or stacked on one another ⟨a large *pile* of newspapers that needed to be disposed of⟩
synonyms cock, heap, hill, mound, mountain, rick, stack
related words bank, bar, drift, embankment; pyramid; barrow, cairn, pyre; accumulation, aggregate, assemblage, collection, conglomeration, gathering, grouping, hoard, jumble
2 a considerable amount ⟨a job that paid *piles* of money⟩ — see LOT 2

²pile *n* **1** a soft airy substance or covering ⟨the lush *pile* of the carpeting⟩ — see FUZZ
2 the hairy covering of a mammal especially when fine, soft, and thick ⟨a dog with such a dense *pile* that it never minded the cold⟩ — see FUR 1

pile *vb* to lay or throw on top of one another ⟨*piled* all the clothes on the chair before putting them away⟩
synonyms heap, mound, stack
related words bank; layer, pyramid; accumulate, amass, assemble, collect, gather, group, mass; bunch, clump, lump
antonyms unpile

pile (up) *vb* to gradually form into a layer, pile, or mass ⟨snow *piling up* in the driveway at a rapid pace⟩ — see COLLECT 2

pilfer *vb* to take (something) without right and with an intent to keep ⟨would *pilfer* pencils from other students' desks⟩ — see STEAL 1

pilgrimage *vb* to take a trip especially of some distance ⟨tourists *pilgrimaging* to all of the traditional destinations across Europe⟩ — see TRAVEL 1

pill *n* a small mass containing medicine to be taken orally ⟨you'll have to take one of these *pills* every six hours for your flu⟩
synonyms capsule, lozenge, tablet
related words drug, medication, pharmaceutical, specific; miracle drug, wonder drug; potion, preparation; dosage, dose, drop, sleeping pill, tranquilizer (*also* tranquillizer)

pillage *vb* to search through with the intent of committing robbery ⟨soldiers *pillaging* the countryside for anything of value⟩ — see RANSACK 1

pillar *n* **1** an upright shaft that supports an overhead structure ⟨the ancient Greek temple boasted graceful marble *pillars* with richly ornamented tops⟩
synonyms column, pier, pilaster, post, stanchion
related words caryatid, pedestal; buttress, flying buttress; needle, obelisk
2 something or someone to which one looks for support ⟨my father has been my *pillar* throughout this crisis⟩ — see DEPENDENCE 2

pilot *adj* made or done as an experiment ⟨a new *pilot* program⟩ — see EXPERIMENTAL 1

pilot *n* one who flies or is qualified to fly an aircraft or spacecraft ⟨the airline is seeking experienced *pilots* to fly the new airplane⟩
synonyms airman, aviator, birdman, flier (*or* flyer)
related words ace, bush pilot, copilot, test pilot

pilot *vb* **1** to give advice and instruction to (someone) regarding the course or process to be followed ⟨*piloted* the athlete through the championships⟩ — see GUIDE 1
2 to point out the way for (someone) especially from a position in front ⟨the lead rider *piloted* the rest of the team⟩ — see LEAD 1

pin *n* a lower limb of an animal ⟨a cat that was still a little unsteady on its *pins* after anesthesia⟩ — see LEG 1

pinch *n* an instance of theft ⟨the *pinch* of my favorite sweater really bugged me!⟩ — see THEFT 2
2 the act of taking or holding under one's control by authority of law ⟨an innocent person caught up in a city-wide *pinch* of drug dealers⟩ — see ARREST

pinch *vb* **1** to squeeze tightly between two surfaces, edges, or points ⟨the zipper on those jeans always *pinches* me⟩
synonyms nip
related words clasp, clutch, grasp, grip
near antonyms drop, free, loose, loosen, release
2 to take (something) without right and with an intent to keep ⟨*pinched* her sister's earrings⟩ — see STEAL 1
3 to take or keep under one's control by authority of law ⟨*pinched* the criminal just two blocks from where he had robbed the old lady⟩ — see ARREST 1

pincher *n* one who steals ⟨the police caught the *pincher* trying to sell the stolen goods⟩ — see THIEF

pinch–hit *vb* to serve as a replacement usually for a time only ⟨assigned to *pinch-hit* as a math teacher⟩ — see COVER 1

pinch hitter *n* a person or thing that takes the place of another ⟨the business brought in a *pinch hitter* until a permanent manager could be hired⟩ — see SUBSTITUTE

pinching *adj* giving or sharing as little as possible ⟨kids who were trick-or-treating knew better than to bother to knock on that *pinching* couple's door⟩ — see STINGY 1

pinching *n* the quality of being overly sparing with money ⟨this *pinching* is getting ridiculous—we can afford to turn on one or two lights!⟩ — see PARSIMONY

pine (for) *vb* to have an earnest wish to own or enjoy ⟨*pining for* a house in the mountains⟩ — see DESIRE

pinhead *n* a stupid person ⟨what *pinhead* put this together backwards?⟩ — see IDIOT

pinhole *n* a mark or small hole made by a pointed instrument ⟨*pinholes* in a bedsheet will look like stars if you shine a light from behind it⟩ — see PRICK 1

pining *n* a strong wish for something ⟨a sudden *pining* to have steak for dinner⟩ — see DESIRE

pinnacle *n* the highest part or point ⟨a singer who has reached the *pinnacle* of success⟩ — see HEIGHT 1

pinpoint *adj* meeting the highest standard of accuracy ⟨the *pinpoint* measurement of brain tumors is critically important⟩ — see PRECISE 1

pinpoint *vb* to find out or establish the identity of ⟨*pinpointed* the culprit by checking everyone's backpack⟩ — see IDENTIFY 1

pinprick *n* a mark or small hole made by a pointed instrument ⟨the nurse kindly put a decorated bandage over the *pinprick* from the injection⟩ — see PRICK 1

pinto *adj* having blotches of two or more colors ⟨somehow, the pure white mother had a *pinto* foal⟩ — see PIED

pint–size *or* **pint–sized** *adj* of a size that is less than average ⟨a *pint-size* wrestler who could defeat people twice his size⟩ — see SMALL 1

pioneer *adj* coming before all others in time or order ⟨the nation's *pioneer* institution for the education of African-Americans⟩ — see FIRST 1

pioneer *n* a person who settles in a new region ⟨the hardships that the *pioneers* endured while taming the wilderness⟩ — see FRONTIERSMAN

pioneer *vb* to be responsible for the creation and early operation or use of ⟨he *pioneered* the university's institute of medical research⟩ — see FOUND

pious *adj* **1** firm in one's allegiance to someone or something ⟨a *pious* supporter of his school's athletic teams, during winning and losing seasons alike⟩ — see FAITHFUL 1
2 showing a devotion to God and to a life of virtue ⟨a *pious* woman who decided to become a nun⟩ — see HOLY 1

piousness *n* **1** the pretending of having virtues, principles, or beliefs that one in fact does not have ⟨an outward *piousness* that was just a ploy to get him the support of religious-minded voters⟩ — see HYPOCRISY
2 the quality or state of being spiritually pure or virtuous ⟨the *piousness* with which he lived every aspect of his life was an inspiration to the other monks at the abbey⟩ — see HOLINESS

pip *n* something very good of its kind ⟨that new sports car is a real *pip*⟩ — see JIM-DANDY

pipe *n* **1** a long hollow cylinder for carrying a substance (as a liquid or gas) ⟨the plumber came and fixed the water *pipe* that was leaking⟩
synonyms channel, conduit, duct, leader, line, penstock, trough, tube
related words drain, drainpipe, funnel, hydrant, main, smokestack, spout, stovepipe, tile, waterspout; pipeline, piping
2 an enclosed wooden vessel for holding beverages ⟨a full *pipe* of wine⟩ — see CASK

pipe *vb* **1** to cause to move to a central point or along a restricted pathway ⟨*piped* water into every house⟩ — see CHANNEL
2 to make a short sharp sound like a small bird ⟨the baby *piped* shrilly in his bed⟩ — see CHIRP

pipe dream *n* a conception or image created by the imagination and having no objective reality ⟨opening our own restaurant has long been a *pipe dream*⟩ — see FANTASY 1

pipeline *n* a direct way of passing along information or supplies ⟨an equipment hauler serves as the columnist's *pipeline* for gossip about the rock band⟩ ⟨the battle was ultimately lost because the enemy had destroyed our *pipeline* for resupply⟩
synonyms channel
related words conduit; grapevine, outlet; fountainhead, origin, source, wellspring; supplier; connection, contact

piping *adj* having a high musical pitch or range ⟨the *piping* sound of the teakettle caught my attention⟩ — see SHRILL

piping hot *adj* having a notably high temperature ⟨the appeal of *piping hot* cocoa after an afternoon of shoveling snow⟩ — see HOT 1

piquancy *n* the quality or state of being stimulating to the mind or senses ⟨a talk show host known for the quickness and *piquancy* of his wit⟩ ⟨I appreciated the *piquancy* of the peppers in the sauce⟩
synonyms pungency, zest
related words raciness, spiciness; fieriness, hotness; acuteness, keenness, sharpness; provocativeness; excitement, invigoration, stimulation, thrill; flavor, savor, tastiness
near antonyms flatness, tastelessness; dullness (*also* dulness), monotonousness, predictability, tediousness; blandness, thinness, weakness
antonyms insipidity

piquant *adj* sharp and pleasantly stimulating to the mind or senses ⟨a *piquant* tidbit of information about the new neighbors⟩ ⟨the *piquant* cuisine of India boasts some highly spiced dishes⟩
synonyms pungent, zesty
related words racy, spicy; fiery, hot; acute, keen; biting, bitter, cutting, mordant, trenchant; animating, energizing, enlightening, exciting, galvanizing, invigorating, provocative; appetizing, delectable, delicious, palatable, toothsome; flavorful, savory, tasty; absorbing, engaging, engrossing, enthralling, fascinating, gripping, interesting, intriguing
near antonyms flat, flavorless, savorless, tasteless; banal, boring, dull, monotonous, pedestrian, predictable, tedious, tiring, uninteresting, wearisome, wearying; bland, dilute, thin, watery, weak
antonyms insipid

pique *n* the feeling of being offended or resentful after a slight or indignity ⟨she's still in a *pique* over being snubbed by a so-called friend at the party⟩

synonyms dudgeon, huff, offense (*or* offence), peeve, resentment, umbrage

related words aggravation, anger, annoyance, bother, discomfort, exasperation, frustration, irritation, vexation; agitation, angriness, displeasure, distress, disturbance, indignation, irateness, ire, outrage, perturbation, upset; dander, temper; fit, pet, sulk(s), tantrum, tizzy; affront, insult

near antonyms satisfaction; appeasement, mollification, pacification; delight, pleasure

pique *vb* **1** to disturb the peace of mind of (someone) especially by repeated disagreeable acts ⟨*piqued* her by repeatedly poking her with a pencil⟩ — see IRRITATE 1

2 to rouse to strong feeling or action ⟨the comment *piqued* him to respond sharply⟩ — see PROVOKE 1

piquing *adj* serving or likely to arouse a strong reaction ⟨*piquing* remarks that were said mainly to get a rise out of the other guests at the party⟩ — see PROVOCATIVE

piracy *n* the act or pursuit of robbing ships at sea ⟨many countries have harsh penalties for *piracy* now⟩

synonyms pirating

related words depredation, despoilment, despoliation, looting, marauding, pillaging, plunder, plundering, raiding, robbery; privateering; burglary, housebreaking, stealing, thieving; hijacking (*also* highjacking), rustling

pirate *n* someone who engages in robbery of ships at sea ⟨Sir Francis Drake was a British *pirate* who preyed on Spanish ships with the permission of the British queen⟩

synonyms buccaneer, corsair, freebooter, rover

related words looter, marauder, pillager, plunderer, raider, robber; privateer; burglar, housebreaker, stealer, thief; hijacker, rustler

pirating *n* the act or pursuit of robbing ships at sea ⟨officially sanctioned *pirating* used to be common among warring nations⟩ — see PIRACY

pirouette *n* a rapid turning about on an axis or central point ⟨the ballerina's perfectly executed *pirouette*⟩ — see SPIN 1

pirouette *vb* to move in circles around an axis or center ⟨the ballerina *pirouetted* across the stage⟩ — see SPIN 1

pit *n* a sunken area forming a separate space ⟨removal of the tree stump left a gaping *pit* in the yard⟩ — see HOLE 2

pit–a–pat *vb* to expand and contract in a rhythmic manner ⟨her heart *pit-a-patted* with surprise⟩ — see PULSATE

pitch *n* **1** an act or instance of diving ⟨the daring *pitch* of the escaped prisoner into the swirling ocean waters at the base of the cliff⟩ — see DIVE 1

2 the degree to which something rises up from a position level with the horizon ⟨the steep *pitch* of the roof makes it too dangerous to walk on⟩ — see SLANT

pitch *vb* **1** to fix in an upright position ⟨*pitch* a tent⟩ — see ERECT 1

2 to cast oneself head first into deep water ⟨the intense heat prompted me to *pitch* into the water the instant we arrived at the beach⟩ — see DIVE

3 to make a series of unsteady side-to-side motions ⟨the ship *pitched* in the choppy sea⟩ — see ROCK 1

4 to send through the air especially with a quick forward motion of the arm ⟨*pitched* the baseball almost 50 feet⟩ — see THROW

pitch–black *adj* **1** being without light or without much light ⟨finding anything in a *pitch-black* room is almost impossible⟩ — see DARK 1

2 having the color of soot or coal ⟨a *pitch-black* cat with green eyes⟩ — see BLACK 1

pitch–dark *adj* **1** being without light or without much light ⟨with its only light burned out, the closet was *pitch-dark*⟩ — see DARK 1

2 having the color of soot or coal ⟨dyed her *pitch-dark* hair bright blond⟩ — see BLACK 1

pitched *adj* running in a slanting direction ⟨a sharply *pitched* rooftop⟩ — see DIAGONAL

pitcher *n* a handled container for holding and pouring liquids that usually has a lip or a spout ⟨please bring me the *pitcher* full of lemonade from the table⟩

synonyms flagon, jug

related words carafe, decanter; bucket, pail, pot; canteen, cup, flask, mug, stein; barrel, cask, hogshead, pipe, puncheon

pitch in *vb* to make a donation as part of a group effort ⟨everyone *pitched in* to buy a gift for the soon-to-be-wed couple⟩ — see CONTRIBUTE 1

pitchy *adj* having the color of soot or coal ⟨a white-haired woman with strikingly *pitchy* eyes⟩ — see BLACK 1

piteous *adj* deserving of one's pity ⟨a *piteous* beggar⟩ — see PATHETIC 1

pitfall *n* **1** a danger or difficulty that is hidden or not easily recognized ⟨buying a house can be full of *pitfalls* for the unwary⟩

synonyms booby trap, catch, snag

related words snare, trap, web; hazard, peril, risk; bombshell, surprise; bait, lure

2 something that may cause injury or harm ⟨one of the *pitfalls* of ignorance is that people will also assume you're stupid⟩ — see DANGER 2

pith *n* the central part or aspect of something under consideration ⟨finally got to the *pith* of the discussion⟩ — see CRUX

pithily *adv* in a few words ⟨the observation that "War is hell" is how General Sherman *pithily* summed up his experiences in combat⟩ — see SHORTLY 1

pithiness *n* the quality or state of being marked by or using only few words to convey much meaning ⟨the *pithiness* of Calvin Coolidge's campaign announcement: "I do not choose to run for President in 1928"⟩ — see SUCCINCTNESS

pithy *adj* marked by the use of few words to convey much information or meaning ⟨a fairly *pithy* criticism about the excessive length of the book⟩ — see CONCISE

pitiable *adj* **1** arousing or deserving of one's loathing and disgust ⟨a *pitiable* excuse for a chemistry experiment⟩ — see CONTEMPTIBLE 1

2 deserving pitying scorn (as for inadequacy) ⟨a *pitiable* attempt at singing⟩ — see PITIFUL 1

3 deserving of one's pity ⟨a *pitiable,* starving old dog⟩ — see PATHETIC 1

pitiful *adj* **1** deserving pitying scorn (as for inadequacy) ⟨that is a *pitiful* attempt at an essay on patriotism; you'll have to do it over⟩

synonyms contemptible, despicable, pitiable, sorry

related words deplorable, discreditable, disgraceful, disreputable, infamous, notorious; abhorrent, abominable, detestable, hateful, odious; bad, inferior, poor; disgusting, dishonorable, shameful; unworthy, worthless; scandalous, shocking, sordid, unsavory

near antonyms admirable, creditable, laudable, meritorious, praiseworthy; notable, noteworthy, noticeable, outstanding, reputable, worthy; excellent; flawless, perfect; honorable, noble; honest, straight

antonyms decent, presentable, respectable

2 arousing or deserving of one's loathing and disgust ⟨a *pitiful* coward⟩ — see CONTEMPTIBLE 1

3 deserving of one's pity ⟨*pitiful* orphans who had lost everything in the war⟩ — see PATHETIC 1

pitiless *adj* having or showing a lack of sympathy or tender feelings ⟨gave the beggar in the street a *pitiless* look and kept on walking⟩ — see HARD 1

pittance *n* a very small sum of money ⟨the summer job offers only a *pittance* for a salary, but there's the promise of adventure on the high seas⟩ — see MITE 1

pitter–patter *vb* to expand and contract in a rhythmic manner ⟨his heart *pitter-pattered* with excitement⟩ — see PULSATE

pity *n* **1** a regrettable or blameworthy act ⟨it's a *pity* you had to hit your sister, because you'll be grounded for it⟩ — see CRIME 2

2 the capacity for feeling for another's unhappiness or misfortune ⟨a woman of boundless *pity* who tried to care for every abandoned animal she found⟩ — see HEART 1

pity *vb* to have sympathy for ⟨I always *pity* the people who have to work in this freezing weather⟩

synonyms bleed (for), commiserate (with), condole (with), feel (for), sympathize (with)

related words care (for); grieve (for), sorrow (for); love; tolerate, understand

near antonyms disregard, ignore, neglect, overlook; dislike, hate, scorn

pivot *n* the central part or aspect of something under consideration ⟨an issue that is the real *pivot* of the controversy⟩ — see CRUX

pivot *vb* to move (something) in a curved or circular path on or as if on an axis ⟨the telescope is mounted on a tripod so you can easily *pivot* it for viewing in any direction⟩ — see TURN 1

pivotal *adj* of the greatest possible importance ⟨the report was missing a *pivotal* piece of information⟩ — see CRUCIAL

pixie *also* **pixy** *n* an imaginary being usually having a small human form and magical powers ⟨leave a dish of milk and some bread out for the *pixies*⟩ — see FAIRY

pixieish *adj* tending to or exhibiting reckless playfulness ⟨a *pixieish* group of children enjoying a day off from school⟩ — see MISCHIEVOUS 1

placard *n* a sheet bearing an announcement for posting in a public place ⟨a *placard* announcing a campaign rally at the downtown plaza⟩ — see POSTER

placard *vb* **1** to affix (as a notice) to or on a suitable place ⟨*placarded* the poster about the upcoming play to the bulletin board⟩ — see ¹POST 1

2 to make known openly or publicly ⟨*placarded* the news about the party all over school⟩ — see ANNOUNCE

placate *vb* to lessen the anger or agitation of ⟨attempted to *placate* her mother by reassuring her that nothing improper had happened at the party⟩ — see PACIFY

placating *adj* tending to lessen or avoid conflict or hostility ⟨a *placating* comment that seemed to calm everyone down a bit⟩ — see PACIFIC 1

place *n* **1** the area or space occupied by or intended for something ⟨the *place* chosen for the picnic⟩ ⟨there's the *place* where I left my umbrella⟩

synonyms locale, locality, location, locus, point, position, site, spot

related words scene; region, section, sector

2 a building, room, or suite of rooms occupied by a service business ⟨we're going to our favorite *place* to eat⟩

synonyms establishment, joint, parlor, salon

related words spot, station; facility, installation; studio; den, dive, hole

3 an assignment at which one regularly works for pay ⟨a friend got her a *place* in a department store's clothing department⟩ — see JOB 1

4 an extent or area available for or used up by some activity or thing ⟨let's make a *place* around our campfire for the newest member of our group⟩ — see ROOM 1

5 the action for which a person or thing is specially fitted or used or for which a thing exists ⟨knew his *place* in the organization⟩ — see ROLE

6 the place where one lives ⟨they have a nice little *place* in the country⟩ — see HOME 1

7 the placement of someone or something in relation to others in a vertical arrangement ⟨came in fourth *place* in the marathon⟩ — see RANK 1

place *vb* **1** to arrange something in a certain spot or position ⟨he carefully *placed* the flowers in a vase⟩

synonyms deposit, dispose, fix, lay, position, put, set, set up, situate, stick

related words rearrange, reorder; orient; establish, locate, settle; assemble, collect; carry; berth, park; affix, anchor, wedge; lay out, line up, queue, rank; set down

near antonyms relocate, remove, take; banish; displace, replace, supplant

2 to arrange or assign according to type ⟨I'd *place* them in the middle reading group⟩ — see CLASSIFY 1

3 to decide the size, amount, number, or distance of (something) without actual measurement ⟨I'd *place* that as roughly the third largest house in the neighborhood⟩ — see ESTIMATE 2

4 to take or have a certain position within a group arranged in vertical classes ⟨*placed* second in the competition⟩ — see RANK 1

placid *adj* **1** free from emotional or mental agitation ⟨an exceptionally *placid* mother who was rarely upset by her six children⟩ — see CALM 2

2 free from storms or physical disturbance ⟨a *placid* lake⟩ — see CALM 1

placidity *n* **1** a state of freedom from storm or disturbance ⟨the *placidity* of the area makes it a perfect vacation spot for people who just want to relax⟩ — see CALM

2 evenness of emotions or temper ⟨his evident lack of *placidity* makes him poorly suited for such an important position⟩ — see EQUANIMITY

plague *n* a widespread disease resulting in a high rate of death ⟨the Black Death was a *plague* that killed about one third of Europe's population in the Middle Ages⟩

synonyms pest, pestilence

related words epidemic, pandemic; affection, affliction, contagion, contagious disease, infection, infectious disease, infirmity, malady; curse, scourge

plague *vb* to cause persistent suffering to ⟨*plagued* by a cough for all of last week⟩ — see AFFLICT

plain *adj* **1** free from all additions or embellishment ⟨I like my hamburgers *plain*, with no ketchup or relish⟩ ⟨just give us the *plain* facts and none of your snide comments⟩

synonyms bald, bare, naked, simple, unadorned, undecorated, unvarnished

related words chaste, modest; unexaggerated, unsophisticated; denuded, divested, stripped; dry, laconic, terse; unpretentious; austere, bleak, severe, spartan, stark; inconspicuous, muted, restrained, subdued, toned (down), unobtrusive; conservative, quiet, understated *near antonyms* flamboyant, flashy, garish, gaudy, glittery, glitzy, loud, ostentatious, showy, splashy, swank (*or* swanky), tawdry; bedizened, florid, lurid, ornate; exaggerated, overdecorated, overdone, overwrought; baroque, extravagant, rococo; arrayed, bedecked, decked-out, dressed, garnished, trimmed

antonyms adorned, decorated, embellished, fancy, ornamented

2 free from added matter ⟨I'd prefer my pasta *plain*, not flavored with tomato or spinach or anything else⟩ — see PURE 1

3 free in expressing one's true feelings and opinions ⟨the piano teacher is honest and *plain*, if not always tactful⟩ — see FRANK

4 going straight to the point clearly and firmly ⟨a *plain* report on the current situation⟩ — see STRAIGHTFOR-WARD 1

5 not subject to misinterpretation or more than one interpretation ⟨let me make my meaning *plain*⟩ — see CLEAR 2

plain *adv* in an honest and direct manner ⟨told her *plain* that he loved her⟩ — see STRAIGHTFORWARD

plain *n* a broad area of level or rolling treeless country ⟨the first settlers in that area lived on the vast *plains* in lonely log cabins⟩

synonyms down, grassland, prairie, savanna (*also* savannah), steppe, tundra, veld (*or* veldt)

related words pampas; floodplain; bottom, bottomland, flat, lowland; plateau, table, tableland, upland

plainclothesman *n* a person whose business is solving crimes and catching criminals or gathering information that is not easy to get ⟨a *plainclothesman* posing as a fence succeeded in breaking up a ring of jewelry thieves⟩ — see DETECTIVE

plainly *adv* in an honest and direct manner ⟨you'll have to tell your relatives very *plainly* that you don't like perfume, or they'll keep giving it to you⟩ — see STRAIGHTFORWARD

plainness *n* **1** the free expression of one's true feelings and opinions ⟨his *plainness* in telling people exactly what he thought of them was often offensive⟩ — see CANDOR

2 the quality or state of having a form or structure of few parts or elements ⟨the *plainness* and clean lines of that coffeemaker make it a piece of modern sculpture as well as a kitchen appliance⟩ — see SIMPLICITY 1

plainspoken *adj* free in expressing one's true feelings and opinions ⟨a *plainspoken* woman who never hesitated to answer any question put to her⟩ — see FRANK

plaint *n* **1** a crying out in grief ⟨the day after the massacre the *plaints* of bereaved mothers and wives could be heard throughout the village⟩ — see LAMENT 1

2 an expression of dissatisfaction, pain, or resentment ⟨there's always an accumulation of *plaints* in the "suggestions" box⟩ — see COMPLAINT 1

plaintiff *n* the person in a legal proceeding who makes a charge of wrongdoing against another ⟨the judge ruled that the *plaintiff's* lawsuit was groundless, and he dismissed it⟩ — see COMPLAINANT

plaintive *adj* expressing or suggesting mourning ⟨the puppy's *plaintive* expression after we put the toy away was rather amusing⟩ — see MOURNFUL 1

plait *n* a length of something formed of three or more strands woven together ⟨she wore a *plait* down her back that reached her waist⟩ — see BRAID

plait *vb* to form into a braid ⟨*plaited* the doll's hair so it wouldn't tangle⟩ — see BRAID

plan *n* **1** a method worked out in advance for achieving some objective ⟨there is a contingency *plan* in the office for handling almost any emergency⟩

synonyms arrangement, blueprint, design, game, ground plan, program, project, scheme, strategy, system

related words collusion, conspiracy, plot; maneuver, ruse, stratagem, subterfuge, trick; means, method, tactic, technique, way; conception, idea, proposal; aim, intention, purpose; diagram, formula, layout, map, policy, recipe, setup

2 something that one hopes or intends to accomplish ⟨our *plan* is to finish up by next Friday⟩ — see GOAL

plan *vb* **1** to work out the details of (something) in advance ⟨we *planned* the school dance down to the smallest detail⟩

synonyms arrange, blueprint, calculate, chart, design, frame, lay out, map (out), project, schematize, scheme (out)

related words conspire, intrigue, machinate; draft, outline, sketch; aim, figure, intend, mean; contemplate, meditate, premeditate

2 to have in mind as a purpose or goal ⟨I *plan* to have a party for my birthday, even if I have to throw it myself⟩ — see INTEND

plane *adj* having a surface without bends, breaks, or irregularities ⟨you can do these tracings on any *plane* surface⟩ — see LEVEL

plane *vb* **1** to make free from breaks, curves, or bumps ⟨*planed* the wood for the picnic table perfectly smooth so that no one would get splinters⟩ — see EVEN 1

2 to move through the air with or as if with outstretched wings ⟨an eagle *planed* effortlessly overhead, gliding on an air current⟩ — see FLY 1

planet *n* the celestial body on which we live ⟨we need to be careful not to destroy the *planet*⟩ — see EARTH 1

plant *n* a building or set of buildings for the manufacturing of goods ⟨a furniture *plant* that employs hundreds of people⟩ — see FACTORY

plant *vb* to put or set into the ground to grow ⟨I'll *plant* the marigold seeds in the spring⟩

synonyms drill, put in, seed, sow

related words bed; replant, transplant; scatter; pot

near antonyms gather, harvest, reap

plantation *n* a settlement in a new country or region ⟨the struggling *plantation* almost failed during the first winter⟩ — see COLONY 1

planter *n* a person who cultivates the land and grows crops on it ⟨the *planters* are too busy around harvest time to pay the tourists much mind⟩ — see FARMER

plash *vb* **1** to flow in a broken irregular stream ⟨water *plashed* down the drain⟩ — see GURGLE

2 to move with a splashing motion ⟨a child happily *plashing* in the tub⟩ — see SLOSH

3 to wet or soil by striking with something liquid or mushy ⟨passing cars *plashed* us with roadside slush as we walked to school⟩ — see SPLASH 2

plaster *n* a medicated covering used to heal an injury ⟨put a *plaster* on the burn and don't touch it⟩ — see DRESSING 1

plastic *adj* capable of being easily molded or modeled ⟨Silly Putty is famous for being very *plastic*⟩

synonyms malleable

related words adaptable; ductile, pliable, pliant, supple, willowy; elastic, flexible, resilient, workable; bending, giving, tractable, yielding

near antonyms inflexible, rigid, stiff

plasticity *n* the quality or state of being easily molded ⟨we chose that type of clay for its greater *plasticity*⟩
synonyms malleability
related words adaptability; pliability, suppleness; elasticity, flexibility, resilience
near antonyms inflexibility, rigidity, stiffness

plat *n* **1** a small area of usually open land ⟨each settler was granted a *plat* to farm⟩ — see FIELD 1
2 a small piece of land that is developed or available for development ⟨plans to build a shopping center on the last undeveloped *plat* in town⟩ — see LOT 1

plate *n* **1** a small thin piece of material that resembles an animal scale ⟨the tiny silver *plates* on the brooch are arranged to look like fish scales⟩ — see ²SCALE
2 something that visually explains or decorates a text ⟨a *plate* illustrating the internal organs of the human body⟩ — see ILLUSTRATION 1

plateau *n* a broad flat area of elevated land ⟨Native Americans have inhabited the *plateau* for centuries⟩
synonyms mesa, table, tableland
related words butte, dome, height, highland, upland

platform *n* a level usually raised surface ⟨you'll have to stand up there on the *platform* for your speech⟩
synonyms dais, podium, rostrum, stage, stand
related words altar, pulpit; balcony

platitude *n* an idea or expression that has been used by many people ⟨"blondes have more fun" is a silly *platitude*⟩ — see COMMONPLACE

plaudit *n, usually* **plaudits** *pl* enthusiastic and usually public expression of approval ⟨the student received many *plaudits* for her essay on civic responsibility⟩ — see APPLAUSE

plausible *adj* worthy of being accepted as true or reasonable ⟨it's a *plausible* explanation for the demise of that prehistoric species⟩ — see BELIEVABLE

play *n* **1** activity engaged in to amuse oneself ⟨it's such a delight to watch the children in their *play*⟩
synonyms dalliance, frolic, frolicking, fun, recreation, relaxation, rollicking, sport
related words gamboling, romping; amusement, diversion, entertainment; delight, enjoyment, pleasure; friskiness, playfulness, sportiveness, wantonness; devilment, devilry (*or* deviltry), hob, impishness, mischief, mischievousness, rascality, roguishness, waggery; binge, fling, lark, revel, spree; hilarity, merrymaking, revelry; buffoonery, horseplay, tomfoolery
near antonyms drudgery, labor, work; duty, obligation, responsibility
2 a written work in which the story is told through speech and action that is intended to be acted out on stage ⟨we'll be putting on a school *play* using that stage⟩
synonyms drama, dramatization
related words comedy, melodrama, musical, musical comedy, tragedy, tragicomedy; magnum opus, opus, work; adaptation
3 an attitude or manner not to be taken seriously ⟨I didn't mean to insult anyone, for it was all just *play*⟩ — see FUN 2
4 the act or practice of employing something for a particular purpose ⟨the host's sense of humor was obviously in *play* during the awards ceremony⟩ — see USE 1

play *vb* **1** to engage in activity for amusement ⟨you need some time to run and *play* in the yard after that hard work⟩
synonyms dally, disport, frolic, recreate, rollick, sport

related words gambol, romp; dabble, trifle; amuse, divert, entertain; delight, please; dabble, mess (around), putter; bum (around), dawdle, goldbrick, idle, loaf, lounge (around *or* about), relax, rest, slack (off); jest, joke, tease
near antonyms drudge, labor, plod, plug (away), slave, strain, strive, struggle, sweat, toil, work
2 to present a portrayal or performance of ⟨*played* Hamlet in the school production of the classic⟩ — see ACT 1
3 to pretend to be (what one is not) in appearance or behavior ⟨stop *playing* the innocent, because I know that you were behind that prank⟩ — see IMPERSONATE 1
4 to spend time in aimless activity ⟨just *played* around while we waited for the bus to arrive⟩ — see FIDDLE (AROUND)

play (on *or* upon) *vb* to take unfair advantage of ⟨*played on* his father's sympathies to get an extra dessert⟩ — see EXPLOIT 1

play (up) *vb* to indicate the importance of by giving prominent display ⟨that TV station *plays up* sensational stories just to get higher ratings⟩ — see EMPHASIZE

play (upon) *vb* to control or take advantage of by artful, unfair, or insidious means ⟨*played upon* the customer's vanity to convince her to buy the expensive makeup kit⟩ — see MANIPULATE 1

play (with) *vb* to handle thoughtlessly, ignorantly, or mischievously ⟨please don't *play with* the telephone⟩ — see TAMPER

played out *adj* depleted in strength, energy, or freshness ⟨I'm just *played out* after the week I've had⟩ — see WEARY 1

player *n* **1** a person who plays a musical instrument ⟨a horn *player*⟩ — see MUSICIAN 1
2 one who acts professionally (as in a play, movie, or television show) ⟨hired one of the best *players* in the world for the part⟩ — see ACTOR

playful *adj* given to good-natured joking or teasing ⟨the little girl was lighthearted and *playful*⟩
synonyms antic, coltish, elfish, fay, frisky, frolicsome, rollicking, sportive
related words kittenish; gay, happy, lighthearted, whimsical; energetic, lively, spirited, sprightly; devilish, knavish, rascally; amusing, diverting, enjoyable, entertaining, fun, pleasurable; dabbling, frivolous, trifling; delightful, pleasant, pleasing; jesting, joking, teasing
near antonyms dutiful, responsible; grave, grim, serious, solemn, somber (*or* sombre), stern, stolid; nononsense, priggish, starchy, stuffy; decorous, formal, proper, sedate, staid; guarded, inhibited, restrained
antonyms earnest, serious-minded, sober

playfulness *n* a natural disposition for playful behavior ⟨the *playfulness* of the kitten can be quite amusing⟩
synonyms friskiness, impishness, mischief, mischievousness, prankishness, sportiveness
related words devilment, devilry (*or* deviltry), hob, rascality, waggery; devilishness, diabolicalness, knavery; frivolousness; energy, liveliness, sprightliness; gaiety (*also* gayety), lightheartedness, whimsicality
near antonyms graveness, grimness, seriousness, solemnity, sternness; priggishness, starchiness, stuffiness; constraint, restraint, self-control
antonyms earnestness, soberness

playhouse *n* a building or part of a building where movies are shown ⟨they're renovating the old *playhouse* and adding extra screens⟩ — see THEATER 1

plea *n* **1** an earnest request ⟨the student made an impassioned *plea* for more time to finish the test⟩
synonyms appeal, cry, entreaty, petition, prayer, solicitation, suit, supplication
related words application; call, demand, insistence
2 an explanation that frees one from fault or blame ⟨my only *plea* is that I've been overworked lately⟩ — see EXCUSE

plead *vb* to state (something) as a reason in support of or against something under consideration ⟨can I *plead* temporary insanity for having made that foolish decision?⟩ — see ARGUE 1

plead (for) *vb* to make a request for ⟨we *pleaded for* a kitten for Christmas⟩ — see ASK (FOR) 1

plead (to) *vb* to make a request to (someone) in an earnest or urgent manner ⟨those students who are always *pleading to* the teacher to be allowed extra time for their projects⟩ — see BEG

pleader *n* one who asks earnestly for a favor or gift ⟨the parents finally granted the persistent *pleader* his wish: a puppy⟩ — see SUPPLICANT

pleading *adj* asking humbly ⟨a *pleading* husband seeking forgiveness once again from his long-suffering wife⟩ — see SUPPLIANT

pleasant *adj* giving pleasure or contentment to the mind or senses ⟨the massage was extremely *pleasant* and relaxing⟩
synonyms agreeable, congenial, darling, delectable, delicious, delightful, dreamy, enjoyable, felicitous, good, grateful, gratifying, heavenly, luscious, nice, palatable, pleasing, pleasurable, satisfying, welcome
related words alluring, attractive, desirable, inviting, tempting; charming, enchanting, fascinating; calming, comforting, soothing; affable, amiable, amusing, cheerful, cheery, genial, goodly, good-natured, gracious, hospitable, kindly, personable; blissful, glad, happy, joyous; elating, exhilarating, intoxicating; ecstatic, euphoric, rapturous
near antonyms abominable, horrid, miserable, wretched; disgusting, distasteful, obnoxious, offensive, repellent (*also* repellant), repugnant, repulsive; abhorrent, detestable, hateful, odious; boring, commonplace, dull, flat, insipid, irksome, stale, tedious; displeasing, dissatisfying; depressing, disheartening, dismal, dreary, gloomy; black, blue, dejected, depressed, despondent, disconsolate, down, downcast, downhearted, forlorn, hangdog, heartbreaking, heartrending, heartsick, heartsore, inconsolable, joyless, lachrymose, lowspirited, sad, unhappy; bemoaning, bewailing, deploring, doleful, dolorous, grieving, lugubrious, mournful, plaintive, regretful, rueful, sorrowful, wailing, weeping; aggravating, annoying, exasperating, irritating, peeving, perturbing, vexing; forbidding; hostile, intimidating; angering, enraging, incensing, inflaming, infuriating, maddening, outraging, rankling, riling; distressing, disturbing, upsetting
antonyms disagreeable, unpalatable, unpleasant, unwelcome

pleasantly *adv* in a pleasing way ⟨we were *pleasantly* surprised by their offer to put us up for the night⟩ — see WELL 5

pleasantness *n* the state or quality of having a pleasant or agreeable manner in socializing with others ⟨his habitual *pleasantness* makes him everyone's first choice for a party guest⟩ — see AMIABILITY 1

pleasantry *n* something said or done to cause laughter ⟨his after-dinner speeches usually include a gentle *pleasantry* that raises a chuckle⟩ — see JOKE 1

please *vb* to give satisfaction to ⟨fresh flowers *please* me greatly⟩
synonyms content, delight, gladden, gratify, rejoice, satisfy, suit, warm
related words appease, mollify, pacify, placate, soothe; assuage, quench, sate, satiate; excite, tickle, titillate; overjoy, thrill; calm, comfort; cater (to), humor, indulge; coddle, mollycoddle, pamper, spoil
near antonyms aggravate, annoy, bother, bug, chafe, cross, exasperate, gall, get, grate, irk, irritate, nettle, peeve, perturb, pique, put out, ruffle, vex; anger, enrage, incense, inflame, infuriate, madden, outrage, rankle, rile, roil; provoke, rouse; agitate, distress, disturb, fret, upset; harass, harry, pester; affront, insult, offend
antonyms displease

pleased *adj* **1** experiencing pleasure, satisfaction, or delight ⟨she looked *pleased* at the gift⟩ — see GLAD 1
2 feeling that one's needs or desires have been met ⟨a sleepy, *pleased* cat⟩ — see CONTENT

pleasing *adj* giving pleasure or contentment to the mind or senses ⟨*pleasing* music in the background⟩ — see PLEASANT

pleasingly *adv* in a pleasing way ⟨the dining room at the inn has a *pleasingly* old-fashioned look to it⟩ — see WELL 5

pleasurable *adj* **1** giving pleasure or contentment to the mind or senses ⟨a *pleasurable* hot bath after a tiring day⟩ — see PLEASANT
2 providing amusement or enjoyment ⟨a number of *pleasurable* additions to the state fair this year⟩ — see FUN

pleasure *n* **1** the feeling experienced when one's wishes are met ⟨nothing gives me more *pleasure* than a hot meal after a long day⟩
synonyms content, contentedness, contentment, delectation, delight, enjoyment, gladness, gratification, happiness, relish, satisfaction
related words bliss, felicity, glee, gleefulness, joy; amusement, diversion, entertainment; elatedness, elation, exhilaration, exultation, intoxication; ecstasy, euphoria, heaven, rapture; cheer, cheerfulness, exuberance, gaiety (*also* gayety), jollity, joyfulness, jubilation; comfort, ease, restfulness
near antonyms misery, sadness, unhappiness, wretchedness; anguish, desolation, joylessness, sorrow, woe; dejection, depression, despondency, dispiritedness, gloom, melancholy; aggravation, annoyance, exasperation, irritation, pique, vexation; anger, fury, rage; agitation, distress, disturbance, upset; discomfort, restlessness, uneasiness
antonyms discontent, discontentedness, discontentment, displeasure, dissatisfaction, unhappiness
2 a source of great satisfaction ⟨the new car is a real *pleasure* to drive⟩ — see DELIGHT 1
3 someone or something that provides amusement or enjoyment ⟨a good-humored girl who's a *pleasure* to be around⟩ — see FUN 1

pleat *vb* to form into a braid ⟨*pleat* ribbons⟩ — see BRAID

plebeian *adj* belonging to the class of people of low social or economic rank ⟨wondered what the people at the prepatory school would think of his *plebeian* origins⟩ — see IGNOBLE 1

plebeians *n pl* the body of the community as contrasted with the elite ⟨the current administration evidently believes that we *plebeians* cannot withstand a dose of harsh reality⟩ — see MASS 1

pledge *n* **1** something given or held to assure that the giver will keep a promise ⟨I was required to leave my keys as a *pledge* that I would bring the car back⟩
synonyms gage, guarantee, guaranty, pawn, security
related words bail, bond; deposit, down payment; surety, warranty; oath, promise, word; commitment, compact, contract, covenant; recognizance
2 a person's solemn declaration that he or she will do or not do something ⟨I give you my *pledge* that I won't interfere with your marriage⟩ — see PROMISE

pledge *vb* **1** to obligate by prior agreement ⟨I would love to go to dinner with you, but I've *pledged* myself to a play with my parents that night⟩
synonyms commit, engage, troth
related words affiance, betroth, plight, promise, swear, vow; contract, enlist, enroll (*also* enrol), sign on, sign up
near antonyms renege
2 to leave as a guarantee of repayment of a loan ⟨*pledged* the house against the loan⟩ — see PAWN
3 to make a solemn declaration of intent ⟨I *pledge* that I will abide by all of the rules of this organization⟩ — see PROMISE 1

plenary *adj* not lacking any part or member that properly belongs to it ⟨the delegation to the international convention was given *plenary* authority to negotiate a treaty in the nation's best interest⟩ — see COMPLETE 1

plenitude *n* **1** a considerable amount ⟨there's a *plenitude* of natural beauty in the state⟩ — see LOT 2
2 an amount or supply more than sufficient to meet one's needs ⟨a *plenitude* of food for the dinner party⟩ — see PLENTY 1

plenteous *adj* being more than enough without being excessive ⟨a *plenteous* supply of napkins for the backyard barbecue⟩ — see PLENTIFUL

plentiful *adj* being more than enough without being excessive ⟨a *plentiful* amount of strawberries that will be more than enough for a couple of pies⟩
synonyms abundant, ample, bountiful, comfortable, generous, liberal, plenteous
related words abounding, overflowing, replete, rich, rife, teeming, wealthy; adequate, enough, sufficient; fat, fecund, fertile, fruitful, prolific; copious, galore, lavish, profuse; luxuriant
near antonyms deficient, inadequate, insufficient, lacking, wanting; meager (*or* meagre), niggardly, stingy; skimpy; least, minimum; light, slight, small; barren, infertile, sterile, unfruitful, unproductive
antonyms bare, minimal, scant

plentitude *n* an amount or supply more than sufficient to meet one's needs ⟨a *plentitude* of lumber for the current housing market⟩ — see PLENTY 1

plenty *n* **1** an amount or supply more than sufficient to meet one's needs ⟨you'll have *plenty* of time to do your science project⟩
synonyms abundance, plenitude, plentitude, superabundance, wealth
related words adequacy, competence, competency, enough, sufficiency; amplitude, liberality; excess, overflow, overkill, oversupply, superfluity, surfeit, surplus; fecundity, fertility, fruitfulness, richness; lavishness, luxuriance
near antonyms paucity, poverty, scarcity; barrenness, infertility, sterility
antonyms deficiency, inadequacy, insufficiency
2 a considerable amount ⟨*plenty* of people showed up⟩ — see LOT 2

pliable *adj* able to bend easily without breaking ⟨the wooden strips become more *pliable* if they are first soaked in water⟩ — see WILLOWY

pliant *adj* able to bend easily without breaking ⟨a *pliant* branch bent low with the weight of ripe fruit⟩ — see WILLOWY

plod *vb* **1** to devote serious and sustained effort ⟨*plodded* night and day to get the assignment done⟩ — see LABOR
2 to make progress in a clumsy, struggling manner ⟨oxen *plodding* through deep mud⟩ — see FLOUNDER 1
3 to move slowly ⟨*plodded* reluctantly off to school⟩ — see CRAWL 2

plop *vb* to throw or set down clumsily or casually ⟨*plopped* his backpack down on a chair⟩ — see FLOP 1

plot *n* **1** a secret plan for accomplishing evil or unlawful ends ⟨they uncovered a *plot* to assassinate the President just in time⟩
synonyms conspiracy, design, intrigue, machination, scheme
related words frame-up; manipulation, subterfuge, trickery; artifice, contrivance, maneuver, stratagem, trick; cabal, confederacy, ring; game, gimmick, racket; ground plan, program, strategy, system; collusion, complicity, connivance, conniving
2 a small area of usually open land ⟨grew vegetables in a little *plot*⟩ — see FIELD 1
3 a small piece of land that is developed or available for development ⟨subdivided the old farm into *plots* for tract houses⟩ — see LOT 1

plot *vb* to engage in a secret plan to accomplish evil or unlawful ends ⟨mobsters were caught *plotting* to take over the company⟩
synonyms conspire, contrive, intrigue, machinate, scheme
related words brew, concoct, cook (up), hatch; connive; engineer, jockey, maneuver, manipulate; design, frame, lay out, map, plan, shape

plow *vb* **1** to cut into and turn over the sod of (a piece of land) using a bladed implement ⟨we'll have to get out there and *plow* and plant both fields before it rains⟩
synonyms break, furrow
related words cultivate, till; fallow; harrow, hoe, rake
2 to devote serious and sustained effort ⟨*plowed* determinedly through the book⟩ — see LABOR

ploy *n* a clever often underhanded means to achieve an end ⟨asking me to go shopping turned out to be a *ploy* to get me to the surprise party⟩ — see TRICK 1

pluck *n* **1** the act or an instance of applying force on something so that it moves in the direction of the force ⟨a quick *pluck* pulled the hair right out⟩ — see PULL 1
2 the strength of mind that enables a person to endure pain or hardship ⟨it takes *pluck* to survive a crippling car accident and still go on to become successful⟩ — see FORTITUDE

plug *vb* **1** to close up so that no empty spaces remain ⟨*plugged* the hole in the wall with putty⟩ — see FILL 2
2 to devote serious and sustained effort ⟨*plugged* away at solving the math problem⟩ — see LABOR
3 to provide publicity for ⟨the actress is giving lots of interviews to *plug* her latest movie⟩ — see PUBLICIZE 1
4 to strike with a missile from a gun ⟨the gangster *plugged* the stool pigeon as a lesson for any others who were tempted to talk⟩ — see SHOOT 3

plug (up) *vb* to prevent passage through ⟨hair *plugged up* the drain⟩ — see CLOG 1

plugger *n* a person who does very hard or dull work ⟨the *pluggers* are the ones who really keep this company going⟩ — see SLAVE 2

plum *n* someone or something unusually desirable ⟨that job is considered a real *plum* in the broadcasting business⟩ — see PRIZE 1

plumb *adj* rising straight up ⟨a *plumb* line⟩ — see ERECT

plumb *adv* **1** in a direct line or course ⟨walk *plumb* ahead to the next room and wait for the museum guide⟩ — see DIRECTLY 1

2 *chiefly dialect* to a full extent or degree ⟨I'm *plumb* tuckered out⟩ — see FULLY 1

plumb *vb* to measure the depth of (as a body of water) typically with a weighted line ⟨*plumbed* the bay to make sure it was deep enough for the ship⟩ — see ²SOUND 1

plume *n* something given in recognition of achievement ⟨the Nobel Prize for Literature is the *plume* that all authors covet⟩ — see AWARD

plume *vb* to think highly of (oneself) ⟨that jerk *plumes* himself on his supposed athletic skills⟩ — see PRIDE

plummet *vb* to go to a lower level ⟨a week in which stock prices *plummeted*⟩ — see DROP 2

plump *adj* having an excess of body fat ⟨a *plump* cat who could barely walk⟩ — see FAT 1

plump *adv* in a direct line or course ⟨there was a squirrel on the sidewalk *plump* in front of us⟩ — see DIRECTLY 1

plump *vb* to throw or set down clumsily or casually ⟨*plumped* herself down on the couch and turned on the TV⟩ — see FLOP 1

plumpness *n* the condition of having an excess of body fat ⟨a woman of considerable *plumpness* sat down next to me and proceeded to take up most of the bench⟩ — see CORPULENCE

plunder *n* valuables stolen or taken by force ⟨the thieves were arrested when they tried to sell their *plunder*⟩ — see LOOT

plunder *vb* to search through with the intent of committing robbery ⟨the escaped convict *plundered* the house in search of valuables⟩ — see RANSACK 1

plunge *n* **1** an act or instance of diving ⟨a *plunge* off a diving board⟩ — see DIVE 1

2 the act or process of going to a lower level or altitude ⟨an overnight *plunge* in temperature sent the thermometer to below the freezing mark⟩ — see DESCENT 1

plunge *vb* **1** to cast oneself head first into deep water ⟨she took a deep breath and *plunged* from the side of the pool⟩ — see DIVE

2 to go to a lower level ⟨prices for those televisions have really *plunged* since they were first introduced⟩ — see DROP 2

3 to lead or extend downward ⟨a stairway *plunging* into darkness⟩ — see DESCEND 1

plunk *vb* to throw or set down clumsily or casually ⟨*plunked* a battered hat on his head⟩ — see FLOP 1

plus *n* something added (as by growth) ⟨a recalculation of the year's income that resulted in a *plus* in the company's profits⟩ — see INCREASE 1

plush *adj* showing obvious signs of wealth and comfort ⟨a *plush* estate filled with priceless art and antiques⟩ — see LUXURIOUS

ply *vb* to bring to bear especially forcefully or effectively ⟨she *plied* all of her charm and intelligence to convince everyone to volunteer as tutors⟩ — see EXERT

poach *vb* to cook in a liquid heated to the point that it gives off steam ⟨*poaching* fish in a stock flavored with white wine⟩ — see BOIL 2

po'boy *also* **poor boy** *n* a large sandwich on a long split roll ⟨ordered a fried catfish *po'boy*⟩ — see SUBMARINE

pocket *adj* of a size that is less than average ⟨a *pocket* dictionary⟩ — see SMALL 1

pocket *n* available money ⟨the ring I wanted to buy for her was beyond my *pocket*⟩ — see FUND 2

pocket *vb* **1** to refrain from openly showing or uttering ⟨*pocketed* my anger and just let the insult pass⟩ — see SUPPRESS 2

2 to take (something) without right and with an intent to keep ⟨she casually *pocketed* the note from his desk to read later⟩ — see STEAL 1

pocketbook *n* a container for carrying money and small personal items ⟨she pulled some lip balm out of her *pocketbook*⟩ — see PURSE

pocket–size *also* **pocket–sized** *adj* of a size that is less than average ⟨a *pocket-size* country in the Pyrenees⟩ — see SMALL 1

pockmark *n* something that spoils the appearance or completeness of a thing ⟨the explosion left little *pockmarks* all over the face of the adjacent building⟩ — see BLEMISH

pod *n* something that encloses another thing especially to protect it ⟨a seed *pod*⟩ ⟨a fuel *pod*⟩ — see ¹CASE 1

podium *n* a level usually raised surface ⟨the conductor on the *podium* tonight is one of the leading figures of classical music⟩ — see PLATFORM

poem *n* a composition using rhythm and often rhyme to create a lyrical effect ⟨your assignment is to write two *poems* about springtime⟩

synonyms lyric, song, verse

related words rhyme (*also* rime); ballad, lay; elegy, English sonnet, epic, epigram, haiku, jingle, lament, limerick, ode, psalm, sonnet; blank verse, free verse, minstrelsy, poesy, poetry

poesy *n* writing that uses rhythm, vivid language, and often rhyme to provoke an emotional response ⟨in olden days young gentlemen were expected to be skilled at the art of *poesy*⟩ — see POETRY 1

poet *n* a person who writes poetry ⟨Emily Dickinson is famous as the *poet* who rarely left the house but often journeyed to the depths of the human heart⟩

synonyms bard, minstrel, versifier

related words poetess; poet laureate; troubadour; epigrammatist, rhymer, sonneteer

poetic *adj* having qualities suggestive of poetry ⟨your description of the sun setting over the Grand Canyon was a particularly *poetic* piece of writing⟩

synonyms lyric, lyrical, poetical

related words metric, metrical, rhyming, rhythmic (*or* rhythmical); rhapsodic (*also* rhapsodical); florid, flowery, grandiloquent, highfalutin, high-flown, ornate; figurative, metaphorical, symbolic (*also* symbolical)

near antonyms factual, literal, matter-of-fact

antonyms prosaic, prose, unpoetic

poetical *adj* having qualities suggestive of poetry ⟨love letters that were filled with *poetical* phrases⟩ — see POETIC

poetry *n* **1** writing that uses rhythm, vivid language, and often rhyme to provoke an emotional response ⟨not all *poetry* has to rhyme⟩

synonyms minstrelsy, poesy, song, verse

related words rhyme (*also* rime); blank verse, free verse

antonyms prose

2 the art or power of speaking or writing in a forceful and convincing way ⟨the speeches of Dr. Martin Luther King were filled with the kind of *poetry* that touches people of all races⟩ — see ELOQUENCE

poignancy *n* a harsh or sharp quality ⟨there was a *poignancy* to his wit that often left his targets smarting⟩ — see EDGE 1

poignant *adj* having the power to affect the feelings or sympathies ⟨a *poignant* story of a love affair that ends in tragedy⟩ — see MOVING

point *n* **1** a particular and often important moment in time ⟨it was at that *point* that I had to stop and check on the experiment⟩

synonyms juncture

related words flash, instant, jiffy, minute, moment, second, shake, split second, trice, twinkle, wink; bit, spell, stretch, while; brink, threshold, verge

2 the last and usually sharp or tapering part of something long and narrow ⟨be careful with the *point* on that umbrella, or you could hurt someone⟩

synonyms apex, cusp, end, pike, tip

related words prong, tine; barb, jag, prickle, snag, spike, sticker

3 a separate part in a list, account, or series ⟨went down the list *point* by *point*⟩ — see ITEM 1

4 a single piece of information ⟨two *points* that are important to remember⟩ — see FACT 3

5 a small area that is different (as in color) from the main part ⟨the little *points* of gold in the blue ceiling are supposed to represent stars⟩ — see SPOT 1

6 an area of high ground jutting out into a body of water beyond the line of the coast ⟨the racing yacht rounded the *point* far ahead of its closest rival⟩ — see HEADLAND 1

7 an area of land that juts out into a body of water ⟨*Point* Reyes, California⟩ — see ²CAPE

8 an individual part of a process, series, or ranking ⟨the melting *point* of ice⟩ — see DEGREE 1

9 something that sets apart an individual from others of the same kind ⟨impeccable politeness has always been her strong *point*⟩ — see CHARACTERISTIC

10 the area or space occupied by or intended for something ⟨runners began lining up by the starting *point*⟩ — see PLACE 1

11 the quality of an utterance that provokes interest and produces an effect ⟨her jokes are often long, rambling stories that have no *point* whatsoever⟩ — see ¹PUNCH 1

point (toward) *vb* to stand or sit with the face or front toward ⟨the town's monument to its lost fishermen *points toward* the sea, the source of its wealth as well as its sorrow⟩ — see FACE 1

point (up) *vb* to indicate the importance of by giving prominent display ⟨I'd like to *point up* an earlier observation that may have been overlooked⟩ — see EMPHASIZE

pointed *adj* **1** tapering to a thin tip ⟨the snake plant's long *pointed* leaves make it an easily recognized houseplant⟩

synonyms peaked, sharp, tipped

related words barbed, jagged, pronged, spiky

near antonyms dull, rounded

antonyms blunt

2 having to do with the matter at hand ⟨he made a number of *pointed* remarks on the crisis abroad⟩ — see PERTINENT

pointer *n* **1** an arrow-shaped piece on a dial or scale for registering information ⟨the *pointer* on my bathroom scale must be stuck—I know I lost weight⟩

synonyms hand, index, indicator, needle

related words dial, face, gauge (*also* gage)

2 a piece of advice or useful information especially from an expert ⟨my mom gave me a few *pointers* but otherwise let me do the cooking all by myself⟩ — see ¹TIP 1

pointless *adj* having no meaning ⟨a *pointless* remark that left everyone scratching their heads in confusion⟩ — see MEANINGLESS

point of view *n* a way of looking at or thinking about something ⟨who actually has the right to possession of that wilderness area depends on your *point of view*⟩

synonyms angle, outlook, perspective, shoes, slant, standpoint, viewpoint

related words interpretation, spin; belief, conviction, eye, feeling, judgment (*or* judgement), mind, notion, opinion, perception, persuasion, sentiment, verdict, view; impression, take; wavelength; side; attitude, position, posture, stand

poise *n* a condition in which opposing forces are equal to one another ⟨there must be a *poise* between the rights of the individual and the rights of society⟩ — see BALANCE 1

poise *vb* to rest or move along the surface of a liquid or in the air ⟨the falcon *poised* in the air for an instant before zeroing in on its prey⟩ — see FLOAT

poison *adj* containing or contaminated with a substance capable of injuring or killing a living thing ⟨the witch gave Snow White a *poison* apple⟩ — see POISONOUS

poison *n* a substance that by chemical action can kill or injure a living thing ⟨the only way to get rid of rats is to leave out *poison*⟩

synonyms bane, toxin, venom

related words cancer, contagion, disease, virus; fungicide, germicide, herbicide, insecticide

near antonyms antidote, antivenin; cure; cure-all, elixir, panacea

poison *vb* **1** to affect slightly with something morally bad or undesirable ⟨*poisoning* the minds of impressionable children with ethnic hatred⟩ — see TAINT 1

2 to make unfit for use by the addition of something harmful or undesirable ⟨exhaust fumes *poisoning* the air⟩ — see CONTAMINATE

3 to lower in character or dignity ⟨this party partisanship *poisons* the national debate we should be having about this urgent problem⟩ — see DEBASE 1

poisoned *adj* containing or contaminated with a substance capable of injuring or killing a living thing ⟨leaving *poisoned* food to try to kill the roaches⟩ — see POISONOUS

poisonous *adj* containing or contaminated with a substance capable of injuring or killing a living thing ⟨some evil person was leaving out *poisonous* meat for neighborhood dogs to eat⟩

synonyms envenomed, poison, poisoned, toxic, venomous

related words contagious, infectious; deleterious, harmful, hurtful, injurious, malignant, noxious, virulent; unhealthful, unhealthy, unwholesome; calamitous, deadly, fatal, lethal, murderous

near antonyms beneficial, curative, healthful, healthy, helpful, palliative, remedial, salubrious, salutary, wholesome; benign, harmless, innocuous, inoffensive; nonfatal, nonlethal

antonyms nonpoisonous, nontoxic, nonvenomous

¹**poke** n a quick thrust ⟨please stop giving the cat *pokes* while it's trying to sleep⟩
synonyms dab, dig, jab
related words punch; stab, stick; push, shove; jam, jerk, jog, nudge

²**poke** n, *chiefly Southern & Midland* a container made of a flexible material (as paper or plastic) ⟨the old warning against buying a pig in a *poke*⟩ — see BAG 1

poke vb 1 to extend outward beyond a usual point ⟨saw his head *poking* through the window⟩ — see BULGE
2 to interest oneself in what is not one's concern ⟨told him to stop *poking* into other people's business⟩ — see INTERFERE
3 to move or act slowly ⟨just *poked* around all morning and didn't accomplish much⟩ — see DELAY 1
4 to move slowly ⟨they were just *poking* along home⟩ — see CRAWL 2

poking adj moving or proceeding at less than the normal, desirable, or required speed ⟨the *poking* pace of the repair work has put everything way behind schedule⟩ — see SLOW 1

poky or **pokey** adj moving or proceeding at less than the normal, desirable, or required speed ⟨frustrated with the *poky* traffic during rush hour⟩ — see SLOW 1

polar adj 1 being as different as possible ⟨they're friends despite their *polar* positions on a number of issues⟩ — see OPPOSITE
2 having a low or subnormal temperature ⟨a *polar* air mass seemed to have settled over our area in January⟩ — see COLD 1

police n 1 the department of government that keeps order, fights crime, and enforces statutes ⟨the appearance of a ransom note meant that the teenager's disappearance was now a matter for the *police*⟩
synonyms law
related words judiciary, jurisprudence, justice
2 a body of officers of the law ⟨the National Guard will serve as backup for the metropolitan *police* in the event of violent protests⟩
synonyms constabulary, police force
related words constable, cop, gendarme, officer, policeman, police officer, policewoman, trooper

police force n a body of officers of the law ⟨mobilized practically the entire *police force* to track down the escaped criminal⟩ — see POLICE 2

policeman n a member of a force charged with law enforcement at the local level ⟨reported the crime to the nearest *policeman*⟩ — see OFFICER 1

police officer n a member of a force charged with law enforcement at the local level ⟨there were *police officers* directing traffic around the scene of the accident⟩ — see OFFICER 1

policy n a way of acting or proceeding ⟨it's always been my *policy* not to spread rumors⟩ — see COURSE 1

polish n 1 a high level of taste and enlightenment as a result of extensive intellectual training and exposure to the arts ⟨acquired a great deal of *polish* during his year abroad⟩ — see CULTURE 1
2 brightness created by light reflected from a surface ⟨buffed the silver plate to a high *polish*⟩ — see SHINE 1

polish vb to make smooth or glossy usually by repeatedly applying surface pressure ⟨you'll need to *polish* your shoes with a clean rag before the performance⟩
synonyms buff, burnish, dress, gloss, grind, rub, shine, smooth

related words sleek, slick; coat, glaze; finish, veneer; brighten; rasp, sand, sandblast, sandpaper, scour, scrape, scrub
near antonyms rough (up), roughen, scuff (up)

polished adj 1 having a shiny surface or finish ⟨she could see her face reflected in the *polished* hood of the car⟩ — see GLOSSY
2 having or showing a taste for the fine arts and gracious living ⟨showing the *polished* manners of a cosmopolitan woman⟩ — see CULTIVATED

polite adj 1 showing consideration, courtesy, and good manners ⟨it's only *polite* to hold the door for the person behind you⟩
synonyms civil, courteous, genteel, gracious, mannerly, well-bred
related words attentive, considerate, thoughtful; chivalrous, courtly, gallant; ceremonial, ceremonious; formal, suave, unctuous, urbane; elegant, refined; deferential, dutiful, respectful, submissive, yielding; acceptable, appropriate, becoming, befitting, correct, decent, decorous, fit, fitting, good, meet, proper, respectable, right, seemly, suitable; affable, cordial, friendly, genial, hospitable, sociable; felicitous, graceful; humble, meek, modest, unassertive
near antonyms heedless, inconsiderate, thoughtless; audacious, bold, bold-faced, brash, brassy, disrespectful, impertinent, impudent, insolent, saucy, shameless; boorish, churlish, clownish, loutish, uncouth, vulgar; casual, informal, unceremonious; improper, inappropriate, incorrect, indecent, indecorous, uncalled-for, unrespectable, unseemly; arrogant, conceited, presumptuous, pretentious
antonyms discourteous, ill-bred, ill-mannered, impolite, inconsiderate, rude, thoughtless, uncivil, ungracious, unmannerly
2 following the established traditions of refined society and good taste ⟨such matters are never mentioned in *polite* conversation⟩ — see PROPER 1

politeness n speech or behavior that is a sign of good breeding ⟨the little girl's *politeness* greatly impressed her teacher⟩
synonyms civility, courteousness, courtesy, gentility, graciousness, mannerliness
related words attentiveness, consideration, thoughtfulness; ceremonialness, ceremoniousness, ceremony, formality; chivalrousness, chivalry, courtliness, gallantry; breeding, manners; suaveness, unctuousness, urbanity; elegance, refinement; deference, respect; decency, decorousness, decorum, propriety, respectability, seemliness; affability, cordiality, friendliness, geniality, hospitality, sociability; felicitousness, gracefulness; humility, meekness, modesty, shyness
near antonyms audaciousness, audacity, boldness, brashness, brassiness, disrespect, impertinence, impudence, insolence, sauciness, shamelessness; boorishness, churlishness, clownishness, loutishness, vulgarity; casualness, informality; impropriety, inappropriateness, incorrectness, indecency; inconsideration, thoughtlessness; arrogance, conceit, presumption, pretentiousness
antonyms discourteousness, discourtesy, impoliteness, incivility, rudeness, ungraciousness

politic adj suitable for bringing about a desired result under the circumstances ⟨it probably would not be *politic* to tell your boss that his latest idea is the worst thing you've ever heard⟩ — see EXPEDIENT

poll n the upper or front part of the body that contains the brain, the major sense organs, and the mouth ⟨his bizarre behavior had us shaking our *polls* in amazement⟩ — see HEAD 1

poll *vb* to go around and approach (people) with a request for opinions or information ⟨assigned to *poll* residents on their feelings about a program for recycling⟩ — see CANVASS

pollutant *n* something that is or that makes impure ⟨filtered the *pollutants* out of the water⟩ — see IMPURITY

pollute *vb* to make unfit for use by the addition of something harmful or undesirable ⟨outmoded factories *polluting* the air⟩ — see CONTAMINATE

polluted *adj* containing foreign or lower-grade substances ⟨called in to clean up the *polluted* stream⟩ — see IMPURE

poltergeist *n* the soul of a dead person thought of especially as appearing to living people ⟨we thought a *poltergeist* was knocking dishes off the shelves, but it turned out to just be vibrations from passing trains⟩ — see GHOST

poltroon *n* a person who shows a shameful lack of courage in the face of danger ⟨those *poltroons* in the state legislature who have caved in to bigotry on this important issue of basic civil rights⟩ — see COWARD

polychromatic *adj* marked by a variety of usually vivid colors ⟨a *polychromatic* tropical bird⟩ — see COLORFUL

polychrome *adj* marked by a variety of usually vivid colors ⟨*polychrome* pottery featuring designs from the American Southwest⟩ — see COLORFUL

polygraph *n* an instrument for detecting physical signs of the tension that goes with lying ⟨intelligence agents were trained to fool the *polygraph*⟩ — see LIE DETECTOR

pommel *vb* to strike repeatedly ⟨the elderly woman *pommeled* the would-be thief with her handbag until he begged for mercy⟩ — see BEAT 1

pompous *adj* **1** having a feeling of superiority that shows itself in an overbearing attitude ⟨the *pompous* waiter served us in the manner of a person doing some poor soul a great favor⟩ — see ARROGANT

2 having too high an opinion of oneself ⟨a *pompous* music teacher who thought that music was lucky to have her⟩ — see CONCEITED

3 self-consciously trying to present an appearance of grandeur or importance ⟨a *pompous* gambling casino decorated to look like a palace in ancient Rome⟩ — see PRETENTIOUS 1

pompousness *n* **1** an exaggerated sense of one's importance that shows itself in the making of excessive or unjustified claims ⟨offended by the *pompousness* of the minor official⟩ — see ARROGANCE

2 an often unjustified feeling of being pleased with oneself or with one's situation or achievements ⟨the *pompousness* of the self-made billionaire was evident in the gaudy mansion he built for himself⟩ — see COMPLACENCE

ponder *vb* to give serious and careful thought to ⟨I'm *pondering* whether or not I should join another club⟩
 synonyms chew over, cogitate, consider, contemplate, debate, deliberate, entertain, meditate, mull (over), question, ruminate, study, think (about *or* over), weigh
 related words muse (upon), reflect (on *or* upon), reminisce; conclude, reason; second-guess, speculate; brood (about *or* over), fret (about *or* over), obsess (about *or* over); believe, conceive, opine; absorb, assimilate, digest, drink (in)
 phrases cudgel one's brains

near antonyms disregard, ignore, overlook, slight; dismiss, pooh-pooh (*also* pooh), reject

ponderous *adj* **1** causing weariness, restlessness, or lack of interest ⟨fell asleep during the *ponderous* speech⟩ — see BORING

2 having great weight ⟨those *ponderous* pachyderms more commonly known as elephants⟩ — see HEAVY 1

ponderousness *n* the state or quality of being heavy ⟨the sheer *ponderousness* of each stone of the huge pyramid makes its construction all the more remarkable⟩ — see WEIGHTINESS 1

pooch *n* a domestic mammal that is related to the wolves and foxes ⟨walking down the street with several *pooches* on leashes⟩ — see DOG

¹pool *n* a small often deep body of water ⟨when it rains, that small *pool* grows to almost the size of a lake⟩
 synonyms mere [*chiefly British*], puddle
 related words basin, hole, sinkhole; swimming pool; lake

²pool *n* **1** a body of persons at work or available for work ⟨a large *pool* of applicants⟩ — see FORCE 1

2 the number of individuals or amount of something available at any given time ⟨a *pool* of ideas ready to use⟩ — see SUPPLY

3 a sum of money set aside for a particular purpose ⟨office workers setting up a *pool* for the collective purchase of lottery tickets⟩ — see FUND 1

4 the total of the bets at stake at one time ⟨two coworkers split last week's football *pool*⟩ — see POT 1

poor *adj* **1** lacking money or material possessions ⟨every year, we make up a basket of food at Thanksgiving for a *poor* family in the neighborhood⟩
 synonyms beggared, broke, destitute, impecunious, impoverished, indigent, needy, penniless, penurious, poverty-stricken, stone-broke
 related words deprived, disadvantaged, underprivileged; bankrupt, bankrupted, insolvent; depressed, pinched, reduced, straitened; low, short
 phrases hard up
 near antonyms comfortable, prosperous
 antonyms affluent, flush, moneyed (*or* monied), opulent, rich, wealthy, well-heeled, well-off, well-to-do

2 producing inferior or only a small amount of vegetation ⟨land that is too *poor* for farming⟩ — see BARREN 1

3 less plentiful than what is normal, necessary, or desirable ⟨a *poor* crop because of the drought this year⟩ — see MEAGER

4 falling short of a standard ⟨a pretty *poor* musician⟩ — see BAD 1

5 of low quality ⟨the *poor* workmanship of the goods from that country⟩ — see CHEAP 2

6 deserving of one's pity ⟨the *poor* kitten hurt its paw⟩ — see PATHETIC 1

poorly *adj* temporarily suffering from a disorder of the body ⟨she stayed home because she was feeling *poorly*⟩ — see SICK 1

poorly *adv* in an unsatisfactory way ⟨he tends to perform *poorly* on standardized tests⟩ — see BADLY

poorness *n* the state of lacking sufficient money or material possessions ⟨each country has its own standard of *poorness*, and one nation's needy inhabitant can be another's fairly well-off citizen⟩ — see POVERTY 1

¹pop *n* a loud explosive sound ⟨the soda can opened with a sharp *pop*⟩ — see CLAP 1

²pop *n* a male human parent ⟨ask your *pop* if he knows where the keys to the shed are⟩ — see FATHER 1

pop *vb* **1** to break open or into pieces usually because of internal pressure ⟨a balloon *popped* suddenly and startled us all⟩ — see EXPLODE 1

2 to break suddenly with an explosive sound ⟨the last strand *popped*, causing the chandelier to drop to the floor with a great crash⟩ — see CRACK 1

3 to cause to break open or into pieces by or as if by an explosive ⟨*popping* popcorn over a campfire⟩ — see BLAST 1

4 to strike with a missile from a gun ⟨went into the woods hoping to *pop* the rabbit that was eating our vegetables⟩ — see SHOOT 3

pop (in) *vb* to make a brief visit ⟨I just *popped in* to say hello⟩ — see CALL 3

populace *n* the body of the community as contrasted with the elite ⟨high officials mingling with the general *populace*⟩ — see MASS 1

popular *adj* **1** enjoying widespread favor or approval ⟨bell-bottom jeans were *popular* in the seventies⟩

synonyms fashionable, hot, in, modish, popularized, vogue

related words favorite, preferred; desirable, liked, wanted; celebrated, famed, famous, noted, notorious, prominent, renowned, well-known; fabled, fabulous, legendary; leading, notable, outstanding, remarkable; important, significant

near antonyms washed-up; despised, detested, disliked, hated, rejected; insignificant, unimportant; indistinguished, unexceptional; anonymous, nameless, obscure, unknown; inconspicuous

antonyms out, unpopular

2 accepted, used, or practiced by most people ⟨the *popular* custom of exchanging greeting cards during the holiday season⟩ — see CURRENT 1

3 held by or applicable to a majority of the people ⟨*popular* opinion on that issue has changed over the years⟩ — see GENERAL 3

4 of, relating to, or favoring political democracy ⟨a truly *popular* revolution, not one that replaced one dictatorship with another⟩ — see DEMOCRATIC

popularity *n* the state of enjoying widespread approval ⟨the sudden *popularity* of low-cut blouses horrified my mother⟩

synonyms fashionableness, favor, hotness, modishness, vogue

related words craze, fad, mode, rage, style, trend; bandwagon; fame, notoriety, prominence, renown; enthusiasm, fervor, passion

near antonyms oblivion, obscurity

antonyms disfavor, unpopularity

popularized *adj* enjoying widespread favor or approval ⟨a recently *popularized* hobby among kids⟩ — see POPULAR 1

pore (over) *vb* to go over and mentally take in the content of ⟨he *pored over* the textbook for hours preparing for the test⟩ — see READ

pornographic *adj* depicting or referring to sexual matters in a way that is unacceptable in polite society ⟨the store kept all of its *pornographic* videos locked up and would only let adults purchase them⟩ — see OBSCENE 1

porous *adj* capable of being passed into or through ⟨a cleaner that should not be used on *porous* surfaces⟩ — see PENETRABLE

port *n* a part of a body of water protected and deep enough to be a place of safety for ships ⟨the cruise ship stops at each *port* for one night only⟩ — see HARBOR 1

portable *adj* capable of being moved especially with ease ⟨a *portable* stereo system⟩ — see MOVABLE

portal *n* a barrier by which an entry is closed and opened ⟨the main *portal* to the estate is an elaborate wrought iron gate on the side facing the road⟩ — see DOOR 1

portent *n* **1** something believed to be a sign or warning of a future event ⟨a red sky in the morning can be a *portent* of a coming storm⟩ — see OMEN

2 something extraordinary or surprising ⟨a scout was sent to have a look at this teenage pitcher who was supposed to be the latest *portent* of the baseball world⟩ — see WONDER 1

portentous *adj* **1** being or showing a sign of evil or calamity to come ⟨an eerie and *portentous* stillness hung over the camp the night before the battle⟩ — see OMINOUS

2 causing wonder or astonishment ⟨in 1969 people regarded the first landing on the moon as a truly *portentous* event⟩ — see MARVELOUS 1

porter *n*, *chiefly British* a person who tends a door ⟨he tipped the *porter* for hailing a taxi⟩ — see DOORKEEPER

portion *n* **1** a state or end that seemingly has been decided beforehand ⟨he had always just assumed that lifelong bachelorhood would be his *portion*⟩ — see FATE 1

2 one of the pieces from which something is designed to be assembled ⟨equal *portions* of the students' day are devoted to study, recreation, and sleep⟩ — see PART 1

3 something belonging to, due to, or contributed by an individual member of a group ⟨each student gets an equal *portion* of the food⟩ — see SHARE 1

portion *vb* to give out (something) in appropriate amounts or to appropriate individuals ⟨*portioned* out the medical supplies equally⟩ — see ADMINISTER 1

portliness *n* the condition of having an excess of body fat ⟨the whole family was known for its *portliness*⟩ — see CORPULENCE

portly *adj* having an excess of body fat ⟨a *portly* gentleman who clearly didn't get enough exercise⟩ — see FAT 1

portmanteau *n* a bag carried by hand and designed to hold a traveler's clothing and personal articles ⟨carried her possessions with her in an old *portmanteau*⟩ — see TRAVELING BAG

portrait *n* a vivid representation in words of someone or something ⟨his account created in the juror's heads a detailed *portrait* of a lonely old man⟩ — see DESCRIPTION 1

portray *vb* **1** to give a representation or account of in words ⟨the author *portrays* her characters in vivid detail⟩ — see DESCRIBE 1

2 to point out the chief quality or qualities of an individual or group ⟨*portrayed* the natives as wise and noble⟩ — see CHARACTERIZE 1

3 to present a picture of ⟨a landscape that *portrays* the scenery near the house where the painter grew up⟩ — see PICTURE 1

4 to present a portrayal or performance of ⟨*portraying* Susan B. Anthony in the class play⟩ — see ACT 1

portrayal *n* a vivid representation in words of someone or something ⟨his novel presents a moving *portrayal* of a woman searching for happiness⟩ — see DESCRIPTION 1

pose *n* a display of emotion or behavior that is insincere or intended to deceive ⟨my cheerfulness was just a *pose*, for I was feeling miserable⟩ — see MASQUERADE

pose *vb* to set before the mind for consideration ⟨*posed* an interesting question for the teacher⟩ — see PROPOSE 1

pose (as) *vb* to pretend to be (what one is not) in appearance or behavior ⟨the spy decided to *pose as* a soldier in order to sneak onto the base⟩ — see IMPERSONATE 1

position *n* 1 an assignment at which one regularly works for pay ⟨he holds the *position* of manager at the store⟩ — see JOB 1
2 the action for which a person or thing is specially fitted or used or for which a thing exists ⟨man's *position* in nature⟩ — see ROLE
3 the area or space occupied by or intended for something ⟨took her *position* at the head of the line⟩ — see PLACE 1
4 the place where someone is assigned to stand or remain ⟨the soldiers were commanded to hold their *position* on the hill⟩ — see STATION 1
5 the placement of someone or something in relation to others in a vertical arrangement ⟨holds the lead *position* in the standings⟩ — see RANK 1

position *vb* to arrange something in a certain spot or position ⟨*positioned* the chairs around the room⟩ — see PLACE 1

positive *adj* 1 expressing approval ⟨hoped for a *positive* reaction from the audience⟩ — see FAVORABLE 1
2 having or showing a mind free from doubt ⟨I'm *positive* that this is the right direction⟩ — see CERTAIN 2

positiveness *n* a state of mind in which one is free from doubt ⟨I can't state with any *positiveness* that I know what really happened⟩ — see CONFIDENCE 2

possess *vb* to keep, control, or experience as one's own ⟨she *possesses* a keen insight into people⟩ — see HAVE 1

possession *n* 1 the fact or state of having (something) at one's disposal ⟨a student who was found to have several overdue library books in his *possession*⟩
synonyms control, hands, keeping
related words ownership, proprietorship; authority, command, dominion, mastery, power; enjoyment, repossession, retention; claiming, collaring, commandeering, confiscation, procurement
near antonyms dispossession, relinquishment, surrendering, transferal
antonyms nonpossession
2 **possessions** *pl* transportable items that one owns ⟨we packed up all of our *possessions* and moved to a new house⟩
synonyms belongings, chattels, effects, holdings, movables (*or* moveables), paraphernalia, personalty, things
related words treasures, valuables; junk, stuff; appointments, fixtures, furnishings; property, tangibles; collateral
near antonyms real estate

possessive *adj* intolerant of rivalry or unfaithfulness ⟨he was very *possessive* of his girlfriend's attention, and it was really starting to annoy her⟩ — see JEALOUS 1

possessor *n* one who has a legal or rightful claim to ownership ⟨she was the *possessor* of several acres of land in the country⟩ — see PROPRIETOR

possibility *n* 1 something that can develop or become actual ⟨there's a *possibility* for violence in the situation⟩ — see POTENTIAL
2 something that might happen ⟨winning the championship is a real *possibility* for us⟩ — see EVENT 2

possible *adj* 1 capable of being done or carried out ⟨I think that building the entire set in two days is *possible*, if difficult⟩

synonyms achievable, attainable, doable, feasible, practicable, realizable, viable, workable
related words practical, reasonable, sensible; likely, probable; acceptable, believable, conceivable, creditable, plausible; available, usable
near antonyms impractical, unrealistic; doubtful, dubious, far-fetched, improbable, unlikely; implausible, inconceivable, incredible, unbelievable; futile, useless, vain; absurd, fantastic, outlandish, preposterous, ridiculous; unthinkable
antonyms hopeless, impossible, impracticable, unachievable, unattainable, unworkable
2 existing only as a possibility and not in fact ⟨only one of several *possible* outcomes⟩ — see POTENTIAL

possibly *adv* it is possible ⟨he may *possibly* recover after such a serious mistake, but it doesn't seem likely⟩ — see PERHAPS

¹post *n, chiefly British* communications or parcels sent or carried through the postal system ⟨the *post* always comes at tea time⟩ — see MAIL

²post *n* 1 a specific task with which a person or group is charged ⟨selling lemonade was my *post* at the church fair⟩ — see MISSION
2 the place where someone is assigned to stand or remain ⟨he stayed at his *post* during the emergency⟩ — see STATION 1
3 an assignment at which one regularly works for pay ⟨she's held a number of teaching *posts* at local colleges⟩ — see JOB 1

³post *n* an upright shaft that supports an overhead structure ⟨hung the hammock between a tree and a *post* in the fence⟩ — see PILLAR 1

¹post *vb* 1 to affix (as a notice) to or on a suitable place ⟨the student organizations always *post* their announcements on the cafeteria walls⟩
synonyms placard
related words nail, plaster, tack (up); advertise, announce, blaze, broadcast, call, declare, proclaim, promulgate, publicize, publish
near antonyms remove, take down
2 to make known openly or publicly ⟨*posted* the students' grades⟩ — see ANNOUNCE

²post *vb* to assign to a place or position ⟨the police are planning to *post* an officer outside the hospital room of the witness⟩
synonyms detail, station
related words set; appoint; place, position

³post *vb* to send through the postal system ⟨*post* the letter this afternoon⟩ — see MAIL

postdate *vb* to come after in time ⟨the inscription at the base actually *postdates* the statue itself by a number of years⟩ — see FOLLOW 1

poster *n* a sheet bearing an announcement for posting in a public place ⟨we put up a hundred *posters* announcing the concert⟩
synonyms bill, placard
related words billboard, sign, signboard; broadside, flier (*or* flyer), handbill, handout, playbill; ad, advertisement, announcement, bulletin, dispatch, release

posterior *adj* 1 being at or in the part of something opposite the front part ⟨the chapel's *posterior* location in the church serves to make it a quiet retreat⟩ — see BACK
2 being, occurring, or carried out at a time after something else ⟨artifacts dating from a *posterior* historical period⟩ — see SUBSEQUENT

posterior *n* the part of the body upon which someone sits ⟨the baseball players were always slapping one another on the *posterior*⟩ — see BUTTOCKS

posterity *n* the descendants of a person, animal, or plant ⟨an association for people who have claims for being the *posterity* of Thomas Jefferson⟩ — see OFFSPRING

posthaste *adv* with great speed ⟨sent *posthaste* for the doctor⟩ — see FAST 1

posthumous *adj* occurring after one's death ⟨the soldier was awarded a *posthumous* medal for valor⟩
synonyms postmortem
related words belated, delayed, late

posting *n* a published statement informing the public of a matter of general interest ⟨a *posting* in the local newspaper of the public auction of a house on which a bank had foreclosed⟩ — see ANNOUNCEMENT

postman *n* a person who delivers mail ⟨the *postman* comes at around nine every morning⟩
synonyms letter carrier, mail carrier, mailman
related words messenger; postmaster

postmortem *adj* occurring after one's death ⟨a *postmortem* examination of the cancerous tissue⟩ — see POSTHUMOUS

postmortem *n* examination of a dead body especially to find out the cause of death ⟨the *postmortem* revealed that the cause of death was an undetected heart defect⟩ — see AUTOPSY

postmortem examination *n* examination of a dead body especially to find out the cause of death ⟨a coroner performed the *postmortem examination* with painstaking thoroughness⟩ — see AUTOPSY

postpone *vb* to assign to a later time ⟨we'll have to *postpone* the decision until we have all the information⟩
synonyms defer, delay, hold off (on), hold up, put off, shelve
related words suspend; hesitate, pause, stay; detain, retard, slow; extend, lengthen, prolong, protract, stretch (out); wait
near antonyms act, deal (with), decide (upon), do, work (on)

postulate *n* something taken as being true or factual and used as a starting point for a course of action or reasoning ⟨one of the *postulates* that the true agnostic rejects is the assumption that it is even possible for us to know whether God exists⟩ — see ASSUMPTION

postulate *vb* to take as true or as a fact without actual proof ⟨*postulates* that all people are born with certain rights that can never be taken away from them⟩ — see ASSUME 2

posture *n* 1 a general way of holding the body ⟨a good upright *posture* will prevent backaches⟩
synonyms carriage, stance
related words attention; body language; pose, seat; bearing, behavior, conduct, demeanor, deportment; air, poise, presence; aspect, look, mien
2 position with regard to conditions and circumstances ⟨claims that the country's defense *posture* is weak⟩ — see SITUATION 1

posy *n* a bunch of flowers ⟨gathered a *posy* of wildflowers to present to his girlfriend⟩ — see BOUQUET 1

pot *n* 1 the total of the bets at stake at one time ⟨everyone got a bit nervous when the *pot* was more than a hundred dollars⟩
synonyms jackpot, pool
related words fund, kitty; bet, stake, wager
2 a considerable amount ⟨made a *pot* of money in the real estate market⟩ — see LOT 2

potable *adj* suitable for drinking ⟨around here, the only *potable* water comes from wells⟩
synonyms drinkable
related words clean, fresh, pure, uncontaminated, unpolluted; nonpoisonous
near antonyms contaminated, dirty, foul, polluted; poison, poisonous, toxic; unhealthful, unhealthy, unwholesome
antonyms undrinkable

potbelly *n* an enlarged or bulging abdomen ⟨he began exercising to get rid of his growing *potbelly* and tighten up his stomach⟩
synonyms paunch
related words belly, breadbasket [*slang*], gut, stomach, tummy; chubbiness, corpulence, fat, fatness, fleshiness, obesity, overweight, paunchiness, plumpness, portliness, pudginess; chunkiness, heaviness, stoutness

potency *n* the ability to exert effort for the accomplishment of a task ⟨vitamins of high *potency* that should be taken only in the proper dosage⟩ — see POWER 2

potent *adj* 1 having an abundance of some characteristic quality (as flavor) ⟨a *potent* tea that is the perfect morning pick-me-up⟩ — see FULL-BODIED
2 having great power or influence ⟨a *potent* argument for expanding our program of space exploration⟩ — see IMPORTANT 2
3 producing or capable of producing a desired result ⟨*potent* medicine that can be obtained through a doctor's prescription⟩ — see EFFECTIVE 1

potentate *n* a person who uses power or authority in a cruel, unjust, or harmful way ⟨those *potentates* who ruled the coastal states of North Africa and exacted tribute from American vessels in the early 19th century⟩ — see DESPOT

potential *adj* existing only as a possibility and not in fact ⟨I can see a few *potential* problems with getting a puppy, but we'll wait and see if they come up⟩
synonyms possible
related words conceivable, imaginable, plausible, thinkable; likely, probable; conjectural, hypothetical, suppositional, theoretical (*also* theoretic); alleged, assumed, purported, reputed, supposed; achievable, attainable, doable, feasible, practicable, viable, workable
near antonyms authenticated, confirmed, demonstrated, established, proven, substantiated; authentic, bona fide, genuine, true
antonyms actual, existent, factual, real

potential *n* something that can develop or become actual ⟨a time when cloning was merely a *potential* and the stuff of science fiction⟩
synonyms eventuality, possibility, potentiality
related words likelihood, probability; latency
near antonyms actuality, reality; certainty

potentiality *n* something that can develop or become actual ⟨would like to see a colony on the moon an actuality and not merely a *potentiality*⟩ — see POTENTIAL

pother *n* 1 a state of nervous or irritated concern ⟨always in a *pother* over the state of her garden⟩ — see FRET
2 a state of noisy, confused activity ⟨the *pother* of city traffic that commuters face every day⟩ — see COMMOTION

potpourri *n* an unorganized collection or mixture of various things ⟨a *potpourri* of hit songs from the last ten years⟩ — see MISCELLANY 1

potter (around) *vb* to spend time in aimless activity ⟨*pottering around* indoors on a rainy day⟩ — see FIDDLE (AROUND)

potterer *n* a person who regularly or occasionally engages in an activity without being or becoming an expert at it ⟨a camera designed for people who don't pretend to be anything more than *potterers* at photography⟩ — see AMATEUR

potter's field *n* a piece of land used for burying the dead ⟨criminals and unidentified people are sometimes buried in a *potter's field*⟩ — see CEMETERY

pottery *n* articles made of baked clay ⟨we picked up some ceramic vases in a *pottery* store⟩ — see CROCKERY

pouch *n* a container made of a flexible material (as paper or plastic) ⟨we sealed the catnip in a cloth *pouch* and tossed it to the cat⟩ — see BAG 1

poultice *n* a medicated covering used to heal an injury ⟨placed a *poultice* over the infected cut⟩ — see DRESSING 1

pounce (on *or* upon) *vb* to take sudden, violent action against ⟨the muggers *pounced on* the unsuspecting tourists as soon as they rounded the corner⟩ — see ATTACK 1

pound *n* **1** a hard strike with a part of the body or an instrument ⟨give the nail a final *pound* with the hammer⟩ — see ¹BLOW
2 an enclosure with an open framework for keeping animals ⟨stray dogs wearing tags are kept in that *pound* until their owners can be notified⟩ — see CAGE

pound *vb* **1** to move heavily or clumsily ⟨*pounding* down the road as fast as he could run⟩ — see LUMBER 1
2 to deliver a blow to (someone or something) usually in a strong vigorous manner ⟨*pounding* nails into boards all day long⟩ — see HIT 1
3 to strike repeatedly ⟨during the storm the waves furiously *pounded* the beach⟩ — see BEAT 1
4 to shape with a hammer ⟨*pounding* out a depression in the metal⟩ — see HAMMER 1

pour *vb* **1** to cause to flow in a stream ⟨she lifted the teakettle and *poured* some hot water through the spout⟩
synonyms stream
related words ladle, spoon; cascade, trickle; deluge, flood, inundate, overflow
2 to move in a stream ⟨water *pouring* down the canal toward the dam⟩ — see FLOW 1
3 to flow out in great quantities or with force ⟨tears *pouring* down his cheeks⟩ — see GUSH 1
4 to fall as water in a continuous stream of drops from the clouds ⟨it's *pouring* outside, so you'd better take an umbrella⟩ — see RAIN 1
5 to give readily and in large quantities ⟨*poured* money into the project⟩ — see RAIN 2

pouring *adj* marked by or abounding with rain ⟨a *pouring*, miserable day⟩ — see RAINY

pout *n* **1** a twisting of the facial features in disgust or disapproval ⟨that storekeeper's face seems to be in a permanent *pout*⟩ — see GRIMACE
2 pouts *pl* a state of resentful silence or irritability ⟨she stayed in the *pouts* all day⟩ — see SULK

pout *vb* to silently go about in a bad mood ⟨*pouted* and didn't say a word to anyone all morning⟩ — see SULK

pouting *adj* given to or displaying a resentful silence and often irritability ⟨stayed in a *pouting* mood until they apologized⟩ — see SULKY

poverty *n* **1** the state of lacking sufficient money or material possessions ⟨he dreamed of finding a good job and working his way out of *poverty* and debt⟩

synonyms beggary, destitution, impecuniousness, impoverishment, indigence, need, neediness, pauperism, penuriousness, penury, poorness, want
related words misery, woe, wretchedness; exigency, necessity; austerity, deprivation, privation; bankruptcy, insolvency; belt-tightening, pinching, straitening
near antonyms luxury, prosperity
antonyms affluence, opulence, richness, wealthiness
2 a falling short of an essential or desirable amount or number ⟨a *poverty* of information about the new policies⟩ — see DEFICIENCY

poverty–stricken *adj* lacking money or material possessions ⟨*poverty-stricken* immigrants struggling to make ends meet⟩ — see POOR 1

powder *vb* to reduce to fine particles ⟨you have to *powder* the antibiotic tablet and mix it with food⟩
synonyms atomize, crush, grind, pulverize
related words grate; crumble, crunch; break, bust, dash, fracture, fragment; shatter, smash, splinter; mill

powdery *adj* consisting of very small particles ⟨the kind of *powdery* snow that is perfect for skiing⟩ — see FINE 1

power *n* **1** the right or means to command or control others ⟨the principal has nearly complete *power* over this school⟩
synonyms arm, authority, clutch, command, control, dominion, grip, hold, mastery, sway
related words clout, influence, pull, weight; jurisdiction; direction, management; dominance, predominance, sovereignty, supremacy; prerogative, privilege, right; eminence, importance, moment
near antonyms helplessness, weakness
antonyms impotence, powerlessness
2 the ability to exert effort for the accomplishment of a task ⟨the corporation has the *power* to accomplish almost anything⟩ ⟨you'll need to build a bit more *power* in order to be a star pitcher⟩
synonyms energy, force, might, muscle, potency, puissance, sinew, strength, vigor
related words aptitude, capability, capacity, competence, competency; adequacy, effectiveness, effectualness, usefulness
near antonyms disability, inability, inaptitude, incapability, incapacity, incompetence, incompetency; ineffectiveness, ineffectualness, uselessness; helplessness, paralysis
antonyms impotence, powerlessness, weakness
3 a natural ability of the mind or body ⟨dogs have a very highly developed *power* of smell⟩
synonyms faculty
related words function; capability, capacity; aptitude, endowment, flair, genius, gift, instinct, knack, talent
near antonyms inability, incapability, incapacity; inaptitude, inaptness, ineptness
4 something with a usable capacity for doing work ⟨nuclear *power*⟩ — see FUEL

powerboat *n* a boat equipped with a motor ⟨his friend had a *powerboat* and took them out water-skiing⟩ — see MOTORBOAT

powerful *adj* having great power or influence ⟨a *powerful* producer in the music business who is considered responsible for the careers of several superstars⟩ — see IMPORTANT 2

powerfully *adv* in a vigorous and forceful manner ⟨began to row *powerfully* toward the shore⟩ — see HARD 3

powerhouse *n* an ambitious person who eagerly goes after what is desired ⟨from the very start of her singing career, she had a reputation for being a very determined *powerhouse*⟩ — see GO-GETTER

powerless *adj* unable to act or achieve one's purpose ⟨I wish I could help you, but I am *powerless* in this situation⟩
  synonyms helpless, impotent, weak
  related words incapable, incompetent, ineffective, ineffectual, inept, unfit, useless; feeble, frail, infirm, passive, spineless, supine, unaggressive
  near antonyms able, capable, competent, effective, efficient; authoritarian, autocratic, despotic, dictatorial, magisterial, tyrannical (*also* tyrranic); dominant, dynamic, energetic, forceful, robust, sturdy, tough, vigorous; important, major, significant; high-level, senior, top
  antonyms mighty, potent, powerful, puissant, strong

powerlessness *n* the lack of sufficient ability, power, or means ⟨cursed his *powerlessness* to affect the outcome of his friend's life-threatening illness⟩ — see INABILITY

powwow *n* **1** a coming together of a number of persons for a specified purpose ⟨all the departments met for a brief *powwow* after lunch⟩ — see MEETING 1
  2 a meeting featuring a group discussion ⟨the mayor's *powwow* with local business leaders to discuss downtown development⟩ — see FORUM

powwow *vb* to exchange viewpoints or seek advice for the purpose of finding a solution to a problem ⟨civic leaders *powwowed* for hours trying to resolve the issue⟩ — see CONFER 2

practicable *adj* **1** capable of being done or carried out ⟨a solution that is not *practicable* in the time available⟩ — see POSSIBLE 1
  2 capable of being put to use or account ⟨a *practicable* knowledge of carpentry that came in handy when he volunteered to build houses for underprivileged families⟩ — see PRACTICAL 1
  3 capable of or suitable for being used for a particular purpose ⟨that flimsy little saw is not a very *practicable* tool for cutting tree trunks⟩ — see USABLE 1

practical *adj* **1** capable of being put to use or account ⟨a *practical* and simple solution for the town's waste disposal⟩ ⟨she has some *practical* information on sightseeing in San Francisco⟩
  synonyms applicable, functional, practicable, serviceable, usable, useful, workable, working
  related words down-to-earth, pragmatic (*also* pragmatical), utilitarian; accessible, available, obtainable, reachable; all-around (*also* all-round), handy; active, alive, busy, employed, functioning, operating, operative
  near antonyms abstract, academic, theoretical (*also* theoretic); inaccessible, unattainable, unavailable, unobtainable, unreachable; unsuitable
  antonyms impracticable, impractical, unusable, unworkable, useless
  2 willing to see things as they really are and deal with them sensibly ⟨a *practical* caseworker who doesn't spend a lot of time philosophizing while doing social work in the inner city⟩ — see REALISTIC 1

practical joke *n* a playful or mischievous act intended as a joke ⟨friends had left the slippery banana peel in his path as a *practical joke*⟩ — see PRANK

practically *adv* very close to but not completely ⟨*practically* everyone agreed to help⟩ — see ALMOST

practice *also* **practise** *n* **1** a private performance or session in preparation for a public appearance ⟨we held one last *practice* before the big concert⟩ — see REHEARSAL

2 a usual manner of behaving or doing ⟨the store's *practice* has always been to honor all major credit cards⟩ — see HABIT
  3 something done over and over in order to develop skill ⟨*practice* makes perfect⟩ — see EXERCISE 2

practice *or* **practise** *vb* to do over and over so as to become skilled ⟨in order to play the guitar well, you need to *practice* fingering every single day⟩
  synonyms exercise, rehearse
  related words prepare (for), train (with); drill, repeat; work (at *or* on); review, study

practiced *or* **practised** *adj* **1** having or showing exceptional knowledge, experience, or skill in a field of endeavor ⟨a simple dish that any *practiced* chef should be able to produce even blindfolded⟩ — see PROFICIENT
  2 accomplished with trained ability ⟨a *practiced* performance of a classic ballet⟩ — see SKILLFUL

pragmatic *also* **pragmatical** *adj* willing to see things as they really are and deal with them sensibly ⟨a *pragmatic* man, not given to flights of fancy⟩ — see REALISTIC 1

prairie *n* a broad area of level or rolling treeless country ⟨you can see for miles in every direction on the *prairie*⟩ — see PLAIN

praise *vb* **1** to proclaim the glory of ⟨hymns that *praise* God⟩
  synonyms bless, extol (*also* extoll), glorify, laud, magnify
  related words adore, deify, idolize, worship; acclaim, applaud, commend, compliment, hail, salute; celebrate, cheer, eulogize, rhapsodize; cite; flatter; crack up, recommend, tout
  near antonyms blame, censure, reprehend, reprobate; criticize, reprove; admonish, chide, rebuke, reprimand, reproach; castigate, lambaste (*or* lambast)
  2 to declare enthusiastic approval of ⟨we were *praised* for our excellent work⟩ — see ACCLAIM

praiseworthy *adj* deserving of high regard or great approval ⟨a *praiseworthy* effort to introduce inner-city youths to the visual arts⟩ — see ADMIRABLE

prance *vb* to walk with exaggerated arm and leg movements ⟨*pranced* across the room dressed in an outrageous costume⟩ — see STRUT 1

prank *n* a playful or mischievous act intended as a joke ⟨as a *prank*, several students managed to change all the classroom clocks to different times⟩
  synonyms antic, caper, escapade, frolic, practical joke, trick
  related words skylarking; adventure, experience, game, lark, time; high jinks, horseplay, play, roughhousing, rowdiness; shenanigans, tomfoolery; joking, kidding, teasing; gambit, hoax, maneuver, ploy; deed, feat, mission, performance, stunt; caprice, conceit, fancy, vagary, whim, whimsy; deceit, deception, delusion, fooling, fraud, hoodwinking, ruse, sham, stratagem, subterfuge, trickery, wile

prankish *adj* tending to or exhibiting reckless playfulness ⟨told the *prankish* lad that someone would eventually get hurt if he kept it up⟩ — see MISCHIEVOUS 1

prankishness *n* a natural disposition for playful behavior ⟨her irrepressible *prankishness* sometimes got her into trouble⟩ — see PLAYFULNESS

prate *vb* to engage in casual or rambling conversation ⟨the young executive *prated* on about his weekend hobnobbing with the rich⟩ — see CHAT

prattle *n* unintelligible or meaningless talk ⟨parents often claim to understand the *prattle* of their infant offspring⟩ — see GIBBERISH

prattle *vb* **1** to engage in casual or rambling conversation ⟨spent an hour on the phone *prattling* on about nothing in particular⟩ — see CHAT

2 to speak rapidly, inarticulately, and usually unintelligibly ⟨stop *prattling* and calmly tell us the news⟩ — see BABBLE 1

prattler *n* a person who talks constantly ⟨stuck next to a *prattler* in the doctor's waiting room, she found the wait interminable⟩ — see CHATTERBOX

pray *vb* to make a request to (someone) in an earnest or urgent manner ⟨I *pray* you: tell me where they went⟩ — see BEG

prayer *n* **1** an address to God or a deity ⟨he always directed a bedside *prayer* to God before going to sleep⟩

synonyms orison

related words collect, grace, invocation, litany, thanksgiving; evensong, matins, vespers; appeal, begging, beseeching, entreaty, imploring, petition, pleading, request, soliciting, suit, supplication

2 an earnest request ⟨we hope that the governor will hear our *prayer* and do something about this pressing problem⟩ — see PLEA 1

prayerful *adj* asking humbly ⟨impressed by such *prayerful* petitioners, the governor promised that he'd see what he could do⟩ — see SUPPLIANT

preacher *n* a person specially trained and authorized to conduct religious services in a Christian church ⟨the marriage will be performed by our usual *preacher*⟩ — see CLERGYMAN

preamble *n* a short section (as of a book) that leads to or explains the main part ⟨we spent the whole class discussing the *preamble* to the Constitution of the United States⟩ — see INTRODUCTION

precariousness *n* the quality or state of not being firmly fixed in position ⟨she quickly moved the china teapot after noticing its *precariousness* on the shelf⟩ — see INSTABILITY

precautionary *adj* concerned with or serving to keep something from happening ⟨moved the furniture out of the way as a *precautionary* measure⟩ — see PREVENTIVE

precede *vb* to go or come before in time ⟨there are two speeches which will *precede* yours⟩

synonyms antedate, forego, predate

antonyms follow, succeed

precedence *n* the right to one's attention before other things considered less important ⟨his merchandise order takes *precedence* because we received it first⟩ — see PRIORITY

precedent *adj* going before another in time or order ⟨behavior that may be explained by a *precedent* event in her life⟩ — see PREVIOUS

preceding *adj* going before another in time or order ⟨had not eaten since the *preceding* day⟩ — see PREVIOUS

preceptor *n* a person whose occupation is to give formal instruction in a school ⟨a *preceptor* at a small English boarding school⟩ — see TEACHER

precious *adj* **1** commanding a large price ⟨diamonds and other *precious* stones⟩ — see COSTLY

2 granted special treatment or attention ⟨parents who refuse to hear the slightest criticism of their *precious* children⟩ — see DARLING 1

3 having qualities that tend to make one loved ⟨a *precious* friend⟩ — see LOVABLE

precipice *n* a steep wall of rock, earth, or ice ⟨climbed up the steep *precipice*⟩ — see CLIFF

precipitate *adj* acting or done with excessive or careless speed ⟨the army's *precipitate* withdrawal from the field of battle⟩ — see HASTY 1

precipitate *n* matter that settles to the bottom of a body of liquid ⟨the chemist filtered out the *precipitate* from the solution⟩ — see DEPOSIT 1

precipitate *vb* to fall as water in a continuous stream of drops from the clouds ⟨the air mass was dry, as much of the moisture had *precipitated* out on the other side of the mountains⟩ — see RAIN 1

precipitately *adv* with excessive or careless speed ⟨acted *precipitately* when faced with the unexpected turn of events⟩ — see HASTILY 1

precipitating *adj* marked by or abounding with rain ⟨thick, *precipitating* clouds that just stayed in our region for days⟩ — see RAINY

precipitation *n* excited and often showy or disorderly speed ⟨I fear that I may have acted with *precipitation* on this matter, so I would like to reconsider⟩ — see HURRY 1

precipitous *adj* **1** acting or done with excessive or careless speed ⟨soon regretted our *precipitous* actions⟩ — see HASTY 1

2 having an incline approaching the perpendicular ⟨a *precipitous* slope⟩ — see STEEP 1

precipitously *adv* with excessive or careless speed ⟨the sight of swimmers exiting the water *precipitously* when some joker shouted "Shark!"⟩ — see HASTILY 1

precipitousness *n* excited and often showy or disorderly speed ⟨the *precipitousness* with which he acted would soon be a cause for regret⟩ — see HURRY 1

précis *n* a short statement of the main points ⟨a *précis* of the bill that the legislature is currently considering⟩ — see SUMMARY

precise *adj* **1** meeting the highest standard of accuracy ⟨a machine which takes very *precise* measurements⟩

synonyms accurate, close, delicate, exact, fine, hairline, mathematical, pinpoint, rigorous

related words correct, right, strict, true; definite, definitive; nice, subtle; careful, fastidious, finicky

near antonyms approximate, round; false, incorrect, untrue, wrong; careless, loose; indefinite, unclear, vague; doubtful, dubious, questionable, unreliable, untrustworthy

antonyms coarse, imprecise, inaccurate, inexact, rough

2 being in agreement with the truth or a fact or a standard ⟨gave very *precise* answers to the members of the investigative committee⟩ — see CORRECT 1

3 being neither more nor less than a certain amount, number, or extent ⟨gave him the *precise* amount that he owed him⟩ — see EVEN 1

4 following an original exactly ⟨a *precise* translation of the original Greek⟩ — see FAITHFUL 2

5 of a particular or exact sort ⟨at that *precise* moment the lights went out⟩ — see EXPRESS 1

precisely *adv* **1** as stated or indicated without the slightest difference ⟨arrived *precisely* at noon⟩ — see EXACTLY 1

2 in a like manner ⟨I feel *precisely* the same way⟩ — see JUST 1

3 without any relaxation of standards or precision ⟨measured the length of the wood *precisely*⟩ — see STRICTLY

preciseness *n* the quality or state of being very accurate ⟨the final result will be determined by the *preciseness* of the measurements⟩ — see PRECISION

precision *n* the quality or state of being very accurate ⟨the company that measures TV ratings prides itself on the *precision* of its calculations⟩
  synonyms accuracy, closeness, delicacy, exactitude, exactness, fineness, preciseness, rigorousness, veracity
  related words correctness, rightness, strictness, truth; definiteness, definitiveness; nicety, subtlety; care, carefulness, fastidiousness
  near antonyms approximation, roundness; falseness, falsity, incorrectness, wrongness; carelessness, guesswork, looseness; indefiniteness, unclearness, vagueness
  antonyms coarseness, impreciseness, imprecision, inaccuracy, inexactness, roughness

preclude *vb* to keep from happening by taking action in advance ⟨issued a strict schedule for doing household chores so as to *preclude* any arguments⟩ — see PREVENT

precluding *n* the act or practice of keeping something from happening ⟨the *precluding* of any misunderstanding seemed to be her top priority⟩ — see PREVENTION

precocious *adj* occurring before the usual or expected time ⟨a *precocious* baldness makes him look older than he really is⟩ — see EARLY 2

precociously *adv* before the usual or expected time ⟨*precociously* turning gray at the age of 30, she decided to color her hair⟩ — see EARLY

preconception *n* an attitude, belief, or impression formed in advance of actual experience of something ⟨tried to go into the training sessions without any *preconceptions*⟩ — see PREPOSSESSION 1

precursor *n* **1** one that announces or indicates the later arrival of another ⟨18th century poets like Robert Burns were *precursors* of the Romantics⟩ — see FORERUNNER 1
  2 something belonging to an earlier time from which something else was later developed ⟨a *precursor* of the modern eggplant⟩ — see ANCESTOR 2

predaceous *or* **predacious** *adj* living by killing and eating other animals ⟨a *predaceous* animal of the jungle⟩ — see PREDATORY

predate *vb* to go or come before in time ⟨gunpowder *predated* the invention of the gun by several centuries⟩ — see PRECEDE

predatory *adj* living by killing and eating other animals ⟨hawks are *predatory* and pose a danger to rabbits and other pets⟩
  synonyms predaceous (*or* predacious), rapacious
  related words carnivorous; aggressive, deadly, ferocious, fierce, savage, violent; untamed, wild
  near antonyms herbivorous, vegetarian; gentle, submissive, tame

predecessor *n* something belonging to an earlier time from which something else was later developed ⟨the typewriter was the *predecessor* of today's electronic keyboard⟩ — see ANCESTOR 2

predestine *vb* to determine the fate of in advance ⟨our victory was seemingly *predestined*⟩ — see DESTINE

predetermine *vb* to determine the fate of in advance ⟨religious sects that believe that an individual's salvation has been *predetermined* by God⟩ — see DESTINE

predicament *n* a difficult, puzzling, or embarrassing situation from which there is no easy escape ⟨if you had told the truth in the first place, we wouldn't be in this *predicament*⟩
  synonyms corner, fix, hole, jam, pickle, spot
  related words difficulty, dilemma, hot water, pinch, plight, quagmire, quandary, scrape, trouble; deadlock,

halt, impasse, stalemate, standstill; clutch, crisis, crossroad, emergency, exigency, juncture, strait

predicate *vb* to find a basis ⟨she has *predicated* her theory on recent findings by other astronomers⟩ — see BASE

predict *vb* to tell of or describe beforehand ⟨I *predict* that you will meet a tall, dark stranger⟩ — see FORETELL

predicting *n* a declaration that something will happen in the future ⟨those annual *predictings* by self-styled psychics⟩ — see PREDICTION

prediction *n* a declaration that something will happen in the future ⟨we were all amazed when the fortuneteller's *predictions* turned out to be true⟩
  synonyms auguring, cast, forecast, forecasting, foretelling, predicting, presaging, prognosis, prognosticating, prognostication, prophecy, soothsaying
  related words augury, omen, portent, sign; anticipation, foreknowledge; foresight; conjecture, guess, surmise

predictive *adj* being a sign of a later course of events ⟨unfortunately, the stock market crash of 1929 turned out to be a *predictive* event, for the next decade was consumed by the Great Depression⟩ — see PROPHETIC

predilection *n* a habitual attraction to some activity or thing ⟨a *predilection* for telling tall tales⟩ — see INCLINATION 1

predisposition *n* a habitual attraction to some activity or thing ⟨the young woman's *predisposition* to date men who are very much like her father⟩ — see INCLINATION 1

predominance *n* controlling power or influence over others ⟨the *predominance* of the Dutch in international trade during the 17th century⟩ — see SUPREMACY 1

predominant *adj* coming before all others in importance ⟨parental involvement has been found to be the *predominant* factor in a child's success in school⟩ — see FOREMOST 1

predominantly *adv* for the most part ⟨a *predominantly* middle-class neighborhood⟩ — see CHIEFLY

preeminence *n* **1** exceptionally high quality ⟨the restaurant is known for the *preeminence* of its seafood dishes⟩ — see EXCELLENCE 1
  2 controlling power or influence over others ⟨some historians contended that no nation had attained such undisputed *preeminence* since the glory days of the Roman Empire⟩ — see SUPREMACY 1
  3 the fact or state of being above others in rank or importance ⟨his *preeminence* in the field of medicine⟩ — see EMINENCE 1

preeminent *adj* **1** coming before all others in importance ⟨the *preeminent* reason for the booming economy⟩ — see FOREMOST 1
  2 highest in rank or authority ⟨the *preeminent* golfer of his generation⟩ — see HEAD
  3 standing above others in rank, importance, or achievement ⟨a meeting of *preeminent* scientists from around the world⟩ — see EMINENT

preempt *vb* to take or make use of without authority or right ⟨the thoughtless teenagers had *preempted* frontrow seats that were reserved for the guests of honor⟩ — see APPROPRIATE 1

preface *n* a short section (as of a book) that leads to or explains the main part ⟨a noted critic has written a short *preface* to her story to explain some of the historical background⟩ — see INTRODUCTION

prefer *vb* **1** to show partiality toward ⟨I generally *prefer* chocolate ice cream over vanilla⟩

synonyms favor, lean (toward), like

related words adore, cotton (to), delight (in), dig, enjoy, fancy, groove (on), relish, revel (in); choose, cull, handpick, name, pick, select, single (out), take; covet, crave, desire, want, wish (for); bias, prejudice; incline (towards), tend (to); admire, appreciate, cherish, prize, treasure, value

phrases be partial to

near antonyms disfavor, dislike; abhor, abominate, detest, hate, loathe; decline, refuse, reject, turn down; discard, jettison, throw away, throw out

2 to decide to accept (someone or something) from a group of possibilities ⟨most buyers of that vehicle have *preferred* the model with four-wheel drive⟩ — see CHOOSE 1

preferably *adv* by choice or preference ⟨I like football, but *preferably* watching from the stands rather than being down on the field⟩ — see RATHER 1

preference *n* **1** a person or thing that is preferred over others ⟨my *preference* is soul music⟩ — see FAVORITE

2 positive regard for something ⟨a *preference* for cool weather⟩ — see LIKING

3 the power, right, or opportunity to choose ⟨he was promised his *preference* when the time came to repaint his bedroom⟩ — see CHOICE 1

preferment *n* a raising or a state of being raised to a higher rank or position ⟨anticipated her *preferment* to a better-paying position within the company⟩ — see ADVANCEMENT 1

preferred *adj* singled out from a number or group as more to one's liking ⟨my *preferred* flavor of ice cream⟩ — see SELECT 1

prefigure *vb* to give a slight indication of beforehand ⟨the first crocus traditionally *prefigures* the arrival of spring⟩ — see FORESHADOW

prefiguring *n* something believed to be a sign or warning of a future event ⟨the preaching of John the Baptist is generally regarded by Christians as a *prefiguring* of the ministry of Jesus⟩ — see OMEN

pregnancy *n* the state of containing unborn young within the body ⟨an elephant's *pregnancy* can last almost a year⟩

synonyms gestation

related words conception; begetting, breeding, generation, siring, spawning

near antonyms barrenness, infertility

pregnant *adj* **1** containing unborn young within the body ⟨we only realized that our cat had been *pregnant* when she unexpectedly delivered three kittens⟩

synonyms expectant, gravid

related words childbearing; brooding; conceiving, impregnated

phrases with child, with young

near antonyms barren, infertile; aborting, miscarrying; delivered

antonyms nonpregnant

2 clearly conveying a special meaning (as one's mood) ⟨a *pregnant* silence followed the ill-advised attempt at humor⟩ — see EXPRESSIVE

prejudgment *n* an attitude, belief, or impression formed in advance of actual experience of something ⟨the general public's *prejudgment* of the accused long before the trial had even started⟩ — see PREPOSSESSION 1

prejudice *n* **1** an attitude that always favors one way of feeling or acting especially without considering any other possibilities ⟨her lifelong *prejudice* against doing "dirty" jobs⟩ — see BIAS

2 hatred of or discrimination against a person or persons based on their race ⟨fought racial *prejudice* through the use of the court system⟩ — see RACISM 2

prejudice *vb* to cause to have often negative opinions formed without sufficient knowledge ⟨all the bad stories I had heard about that teacher *prejudiced* me against him even before the first class⟩

synonyms bias

related words dispose, incline, predispose; influence, prepossess; convince, persuade, suggest

prejudiced *adj* **1** inclined to favor one side over another ⟨an employer who is known to be *prejudiced* toward his own kind⟩ — see PARTIAL 1

2 unwilling to grant other people social rights or to accept other viewpoints ⟨many people after the Civil War were still *prejudiced* against African-Americans⟩ — see INTOLERANT 2

prejudicial *adj* **1** causing or capable of causing harm ⟨pretrial publicity that may be extremely *prejudicial* to a defendant's right to a fair trial⟩ — see HARMFUL

2 opposed to one's interests ⟨the defense will try to counterbalance the mass of *prejudicial* evidence presented by the prosecution⟩ — see ADVERSE 1

preliminary *adj* coming before the main part or item usually to introduce or prepare for what follows ⟨we need to do some *preliminary* research in order to properly focus the experiment⟩

synonyms introductory, preparatory

related words introducing, prefacing, preparing, readying; premonitory, warning; basic, fundamental; ahead, early, former, preceding, previous, prior

near antonyms after, behind, following, subsequent

prelude *n* a short section (as of a book) that leads to or explains the main part ⟨the musical had a brief *prelude* to get the audience in the proper mood⟩ — see INTRODUCTION

premature *adj* occurring before the usual or expected time ⟨his *premature* arrival at his own surprise party almost ruined everything⟩ — see EARLY 2

prematurely *adv* before the usual or expected time ⟨a baby born three weeks *prematurely*⟩ — see EARLY

premier *adj* **1** coming before all others in time or order ⟨a space shuttle on its *premier* voyage⟩ — see FIRST 1

2 highest in rank or authority ⟨the *premier* authority on butterflies⟩ — see HEAD

3 coming before all others in importance ⟨the *premier* social occasion of the season⟩ — see FOREMOST 1

premise *n* **1** something taken as being true or factual and used as a starting point for a course of action or reasoning ⟨your reasoning is all wrong because you started out with a false *premise*⟩ — see ASSUMPTION

2 premises *pl* the area around and belonging to a building ⟨detectives painstakingly searched the *premises* for clues⟩ — see GROUND 1

premise *vb* to take as true or as a fact without actual proof ⟨let us *premise* certain things, such as every person's need for love, before beginning our line of reasoning⟩ — see ASSUME 2

premium *adj* commanding a large price ⟨lavish feasts at which *premium* wines flowed freely⟩ — see COSTLY

premium *n* something given in recognition of achievement ⟨encouraging Girl Scouts to sell more cookies by offering *premiums*⟩ — see AWARD

premonition *n* a feeling that something bad will happen ⟨she had a *premonition* that her cat would somehow get hurt that day⟩

synonyms foreboding, presage, presentiment

related words anticipation, foreknowledge; insight, intuition; augury, omen, portent, sign; impression, suspicion; anxiety, apprehension, care, concern, disquiet, doubt, dread, fear, misgiving, unease, worry; foresight

preoccupation *n* something about which one is constantly thinking or concerned ⟨the future entomologist's *preoccupation* with insects from a very early age⟩ — see FIXATION

preoccupied *adj* lost in thought and unaware of one's surroundings or actions ⟨too *preoccupied* with her worries to enjoy the meal⟩ — see ABSENTMINDED 1

preparatory *adj* coming before the main part or item usually to introduce or prepare for what follows ⟨a *preparatory* investigation to see if there is enough evidence to warrant bringing charges⟩ — see PRELIMINARY

prepare *vb* **1** to make ready in advance ⟨I think I *prepared* myself well for this test⟩ ⟨we *prepared* the classroom for the important visitors by getting rid of some unsightly clutter⟩
synonyms fit, fix, lay, ready
related words brace, fortify, steel; batten, gather, gear (up), mount, train; boot (up), prime; arrange, set, spread; arm, equip, furnish, outfit, provide, supply; incline, predispose; draft, draw (up), frame; warm (up)
2 to make competent (as by training, skill, or ability) for a particular office or function ⟨basic training is intended to *prepare* raw recruits for active duty in the military⟩ — see QUALIFY 2
3 to put (something) into proper and usually carefully worked out written form ⟨asked his assistant to *prepare* a statement for the press⟩ — see COMPOSE 1

prepared *adj* being in a state of fitness for some experience or action ⟨a marathoner completely *prepared* for the grueling race⟩ — see READY 1

prepossession *n* **1** an attitude, belief, or impression formed in advance of actual experience of something ⟨the foreign tourists' *prepossessions* about life in the U.S. had been formed by many hours of American TV shows⟩
synonyms preconception, prejudgment
related words bias, prejudice; conjecture, hypothesis, imagining, predetermination, presumption, presupposition, speculation, supposition, theorizing, theory; concept, thought
2 something about which one is constantly thinking or concerned ⟨tried to cure him of his *prepossession* with money⟩ — see FIXATION

preposterous *adj* **1** conceived or made without regard for reason or reality ⟨the idea that pigs could fly is *preposterous*⟩ — see FANTASTIC 1
2 showing or marked by a lack of good sense or judgment ⟨a *preposterous* suggestion to go swimming in freezing weather⟩ — see FOOLISH 1
3 so foolish or pointless as to be worthy of scornful laughter ⟨the movie thriller had such a *preposterous* plot that we were on the edge of our seats snickering⟩ — see RIDICULOUS 1

preposterousness *n* lack of good sense or judgment ⟨laughed at the sheer *preposterousness* of the idea⟩ — see FOOLISHNESS 1

prerogative *n* something to which one has a just claim ⟨it's your *prerogative* to refuse to attend religious services⟩ — see RIGHT 1

presage *n* **1** a feeling that something bad will happen ⟨I had a nagging *presage* that the results of my medical tests would not be good⟩ — see PREMONITION

2 something believed to be a sign or warning of a future event ⟨the sight of the first robin is always a welcome *presage* of spring⟩ — see OMEN

presage *vb* to tell of or describe beforehand ⟨people used to believe that a comet *presaged* a major event, such as the death of a king⟩ — see FORETELL

presaging *n* a declaration that something will happen in the future ⟨the *presagings* of self-styled seers about current celebrities⟩ — see PREDICTION

prescience *n* **1** the special ability to see or know about events before they actually occur ⟨most believers would probably agree that complete *prescience* is one of God's attributes⟩ — see FORESIGHT 1
2 concern or preparation for the future ⟨parents who had the *prescience* to make everything in their house childproof before the arrival of their first baby⟩ — see FORESIGHT 2

prescient *adj* having or showing awareness of and preparation for the future ⟨*prescient* environmentalists and politicians who long ago made sure that these beautiful areas would forever be spared from development⟩ — see FORESIGHTED

prescribe *vb* to give the rules about (something) clearly and exactly ⟨in chess, you can move the various pieces only in certain *prescribed* ways⟩
synonyms define, lay down, specify
related words decree, dictate, ordain; assign, direct, fix, set, settle; arrange, order; choose, select; adjure, bid, charge, command, enjoin, instruct, tell; conduct, control, lead, manage; coerce, constrain, force; oblige, require

presence *n* **1** a position within view ⟨men should watch their language when in the *presence* of ladies⟩
synonyms sight
related words nearness, proximity
2 the outward form of someone or something especially as indicative of a quality ⟨the orchestra's musical director has a very stately *presence*⟩ — see APPEARANCE 1

present *adj* **1** existing or in progress right now ⟨I am very busy at the *present* moment⟩
synonyms current, extant, ongoing, present-day
related words contemporary, mod, modern, new, new-fangled, new-fashioned, now, recent, red-hot, space-age, ultramodern, up-to-date; being, breathing, existing, living
near antonyms done, ended, finished, over; ancient, antediluvian, antiquated, antique, archaic, dated, fusty, musty, noncontemporary, obsolete, old, oldfangled, old-fashioned, old-time, out-of-date, outworn, passé; bygone, erstwhile, formerly
antonyms ago, past; future
2 being within the confines of a specified place ⟨all of you are required to be *present* for every class⟩
synonyms attending
related words accompanying, observing, participating; available; abounding; latent; breathing, existing, existent, extant, live
phrases in attendance, on hand
near antonyms departed, gone, retired; nonexistent; AWOL, truant; dead, departed, lost, vanished; delayed, late, overdue, tardy
antonyms absent, away, missing, out

present *n* **1** the time currently existing or in progress ⟨I cannot talk to you at *present*, but perhaps in a few minutes⟩
synonyms moment, now, today

related words phase, stage, state; tonight, tomorrow
near antonyms yesterday, yesteryear
antonyms past; future
2 something given to someone without expectation of a return ⟨opened lots of *presents* every Christmas morning⟩ — see GIFT 1

present *vb* **1** to bring before the public in performance or exhibition ⟨we will *present* a performance of *Our Town* this week⟩
synonyms carry, give, mount, offer, stage
related words display, exhibit, show; preview; act, impersonate, perform, play, portray; depict, dramatize, enact, render, represent; extend, proffer, tender
2 to make (one person) known (to another) socially ⟨may I *present* my niece Sarah?⟩ — see INTRODUCE 1
3 to make a present of ⟨*presented* a gold watch to him on the occasion of his retirement⟩ — see GIVE 1

presentation *n* something given to someone without expectation of a return ⟨a *presentation* of much-needed money to the children's charity⟩ — see GIFT 1

present–day *adj* **1** being or involving the latest methods, concepts, information, or styles ⟨*present-day* technology constantly replacing yesterday's methods⟩ — see MODERN
2 existing or in progress right now ⟨the *present-day* administration in Washington⟩ — see PRESENT 1

presentiment *n* a feeling that something bad will happen ⟨a *presentiment* of danger⟩ — see PREMONITION

presently *adv* **1** at or within a short time ⟨I cannot attend to the matter this instant, but I will *presently*⟩ — see SHORTLY 2
2 at the present time ⟨we are *presently* waiting in line for our turn⟩ — see NOW 1

preservation *n* **1** the act or activity of keeping something in an existing and usually satisfactory condition ⟨each curator is responsible for the *preservation* of the works of art within his or her department⟩ — see MAINTENANCE
2 the careful maintaining and protection of something valuable especially in its natural or original state ⟨the *preservation* of the tropical rainforests is a global responsibility⟩ — see CONSERVATION 1

preserve *vb* to keep in good condition ⟨vigilantly *preserving* the ancient statue for future generations to enjoy⟩ — see MAINTAIN 1

preserving *n* the act or activity of keeping something in an existing and usually satisfactory condition ⟨the *preserving* of our rights and civil liberties⟩ — see MAINTENANCE

president *n* a person in charge of a meeting ⟨the *president* of the teachers' conference⟩ — see CHAIR 1

preside (over) *vb* to exercise authority or power over ⟨this former small-town grocer now *presides over* a supermarket empire with hundreds of stores⟩ — see GOVERN 1

presiding *adj* highest in rank or authority ⟨a senator who is the *presiding* member of the armed services committee⟩ — see HEAD

press *n* a great number of persons or things gathered together ⟨he pushed his way through the *press* of people outside the courthouse⟩ — see CROWD 1

press *vb* **1** to push steadily against with some force ⟨an old doorbell that requires you to *press* the button hard⟩
synonyms bear (down on), depress, shove, weigh (on or upon)
related words compress, squash, squeeze; compel, force, pressure; lean (on *or* against), muscle; drive, propel, thrust; compact, constrict, contract, crush,

scrunch, wring; cram, jam, jam-pack, pack, stuff, wedge
2 to apply external pressure on so as to force out the juice or contents of ⟨my family will only drink juice from freshly *pressed* oranges⟩
synonyms crush, express, mash, squeeze
related words pulp, puree; extract, extrude
3 to gather into a closely packed group ⟨everyone *pressed* around me to see the pictures⟩
synonyms bunch, cluster, crowd, huddle
related words assemble, collect, congregate, flock, gather, herd, swarm, throng; encircle, mob, surround; embrace, hug
4 to force one's way ⟨we continued to *press* deeper and deeper into the tangled rain forest⟩
synonyms bulldoze, elbow, muscle, push
related words jostle; ram, shove, thrust
5 to cause (a person) to give in to pressure ⟨a manager *pressed* by a business crisis to return from his vacation ahead of schedule⟩ — see FORCE
6 to try to persuade (someone) through earnest appeals to follow a course of action ⟨*pressed* us to go with them to the meeting⟩ — see URGE

press (for) *vb* to ask for (something) earnestly or with authority ⟨workers *pressing for* higher wages and better working conditions⟩ — see DEMAND 1

pressing *adj* needing immediate attention ⟨she had *pressing* business on the other side of town⟩ — see ACUTE 2

pressure *n* **1** the burden on one's emotional or mental well-being created by demands on one's time ⟨a business executive who works well under *pressure*⟩ — see STRESS 1
2 the use of power to impose one's will on another ⟨*pressure* from their peers can often cause teens to do things that they normally wouldn't consider⟩ — see FORCE 2

pressure *vb* to cause (a person) to give in to pressure ⟨his father *pressured* him to go out for the swim team⟩ — see FORCE

prestidigitator *n* one who practices tricks and illusions for entertainment ⟨a skilled *prestidigitator* can make entire buildings seem to disappear⟩ — see MAGICIAN 2

prestigious *adj* **1** having a good reputation especially in a field of knowledge ⟨a nutritional study that has been published by a *prestigious* medical school⟩ — see RESPECTABLE 1
2 standing above others in rank, importance, or achievement ⟨the most *prestigious* social club in town⟩ — see EMINENT

presto *adv* with great speed ⟨the hungry men dived into the food and, *presto*, it was gone⟩ — see FAST 1

presumably *adv* **1** to all outward appearances ⟨*presumably* he's going on the trip for business reasons, but we have our doubts⟩ — see APPARENTLY
2 without much doubt ⟨*presumably* he'll come later⟩ — see PROBABLY

presume *vb* **1** to form an opinion from little or no evidence ⟨I *presume* you'll fly if you do go⟩ — see GUESS 1
2 to take as true or as a fact without actual proof ⟨we should *presume* that a person is innocent until proven guilty⟩ — see ASSUME 2

presumed *adj* appearing to be true on the basis of evidence that may or may not be confirmed ⟨the *presumed* culprit⟩ — see APPARENT 1

presuming *adj* showing a lack of proper social reserve or modesty ⟨thought it *presuming* of him to think that we would invite him along⟩ — see PRESUMPTUOUS 1

presumption *n* **1** shameless boldness ⟨shocked by his *presumption* in insisting that we buy his raffle tickets⟩ — see EFFRONTERY

2 something taken as being true or factual and used as a starting point for a course of action or reasoning ⟨the *presumption* of innocence⟩ — see ASSUMPTION

presumptuous *adj* **1** showing a lack of proper social reserve or modesty ⟨it's a little *presumptuous* of you to assume that I'm your new best friend just because I invited you along⟩

synonyms bold, familiar, forward, free, immodest, overfamiliar, presuming

related words arrogant, complacent, conceited, egoistic, egotistic (*or* egotistical), important, overweening, pompous, prideful, proud, self-assertive, self-conceited, self-important, self-satisfied, smug, uppity, vain, vainglorious; cavalier, disdainful, haughty, lordly, pretentious, snobbish, stuck-up, supercilious, superior; audacious, brash, brassy, brazen, fresh, impertinent, impudent, pert, saucy; confident, self-assured, self-confident, sure; boastful, braggart, bragging; domineering, high-handed, imperious; self-centered, selfish

near antonyms humble, meek, unassertive; bashful, retiring, shy; diffident, self-doubting

antonyms modest, unassuming

2 having a feeling of superiority that shows itself in an overbearing attitude ⟨the *presumptuous* doctor didn't even bother to tell me about the treatment that I would be receiving⟩ — see ARROGANT

3 thrusting oneself where one is not welcome or invited ⟨the *presumptuous* salesclerk started picking out some very expensive accessories for the outfit I had just chosen⟩ — see INTRUSIVE

presumptuousness *n* **1** an exaggerated sense of one's importance that shows itself in the making of excessive or unjustified claims ⟨offended by the *presumptuousness* of his assertion that he was an expert on the subject⟩ — see ARROGANCE

2 shameless boldness ⟨he found that a certain amount of *presumptuousness* could get you in trouble, but it could also get you into places where you normally weren't allowed⟩ — see EFFRONTERY

presuppose *vb* to take as true or as a fact without actual proof ⟨the book *presupposes* its readers will already know something about the subject⟩ — see ASSUME 2

presupposition *n* something taken as being true or factual and used as a starting point for a course of action or reasoning ⟨the cynic's *presupposition* that everyone acts out of purely selfish motives⟩ — see ASSUMPTION

pretend *adj* not real and existing only in the imagination ⟨it's just a *pretend* gun, so please pretend that I got you and play dead⟩ — see IMAGINARY

pretend *vb* **1** to take on a false or deceptive appearance ⟨I *pretended* that I was scared of the vacuum cleaner⟩

synonyms dissemble, let on

related words act, impersonate, masquerade, play, pose; affect, assume, counterfeit, fake, feign, profess, put on, simulate; camouflage, conceal, disguise, mask; bluff, feint

phrases make a pretense, make a show, make believe, put on an act, put up a front

2 to present a false appearance of ⟨as if I would ever *pretend* illness just to get out of going to school⟩ — see FEIGN

pretended *adj* lacking in natural or spontaneous quality ⟨shows a *pretended* affection for his girlfriend's cat⟩ — see ARTIFICIAL 1

pretender *n* one who makes false claims of identity or expertise ⟨it turns out that the guy who claimed to work for a modeling agency was just a *pretender*⟩ — see IMPOSTOR

pretense *or* **pretence** *n* **1** the quality or state of appearing or trying to appear more important or more valuable than is the case ⟨she seemed to be a very down-to-earth woman who was completely free of *pretense*⟩

synonyms affectation, affectedness, grandiosity, pretension, pretentiousness

related words arrogance, complacency, conceit, egotism, pride, self-assertion, self-conceit, self-importance, self-satisfaction, smugness, vaingloriousness, vainglory, vainness, vanity; disdain, haughtiness, lordliness, snobbery, snobbishness, superciliousness, superiority; confidence, presumption, self-assurance, self-confidence, sureness; boastfulness, braggadocio; aggressiveness, assertiveness, audaciousness, boldness, brassiness, cheekiness, cockiness, forwardness, impudence, insolence, rudeness; grandiloquence; flashiness, gaudiness, ostentation, show, showiness

near antonyms demureness, humbleness, humility, meekness, modesty; bashfulness, diffidence, shyness, timidity; naturalness, sincerity

2 a display of emotion or behavior that is insincere or intended to deceive ⟨her display of bravado was just a *pretense*⟩ — see MASQUERADE

3 an entitlement to something ⟨the book on gardening makes no *pretense* at completeness⟩ — see CLAIM 1

4 an exaggerated sense of one's importance that shows itself in the making of excessive or unjustified claims ⟨the *pretense* of that woman in thinking that the other hotel guests should be inconvenienced just for her⟩ — see ARROGANCE

pretension *n* **1** an entitlement to something ⟨a *pretension* of long standing to the throne of Hungary⟩ — see CLAIM 1

2 an exaggerated sense of one's importance that shows itself in the making of excessive or unjustified claims ⟨a woman full of *pretension* and pompousness⟩ — see ARROGANCE

3 the quality or state of appearing or trying to appear more important or more valuable than is the case ⟨the *pretension* of that French restaurant is more than I can bear⟩ — see PRETENSE 1

4 something that one hopes or intends to accomplish ⟨has serious *pretensions* of becoming a writer⟩ — see GOAL

pretentious *adj* **1** self-consciously trying to present an appearance of grandeur or importance ⟨the *pretentious* hosts served caviar at their party, even though they themselves dislike it⟩

synonyms affected, grandiose, highfalutin, ostentatious, pompous

related words grandiloquent, high-sounding, sententious; arrogant, complacent, conceited, egoistic, egotistic (*or* egotistical), important, overweening, prideful, proud, self-assertive, self-conceited, self-important, self-satisfied, smug, uppity, vain, vainglorious; cavalier, disdainful, haughty, lordly, snobbish, snobby, stuck-up, supercilious, superior; confident, self-assured, self-confident, sure; boastful, braggart, bragging; aggressive, assertive, audacious, bold, brassy, cheeky, cocky, forward, impudent, insolent, rude; flashy, flaunting, gaudy, showy

near antonyms demure, homely, humble, lowly, meek, retiring, unassertive, unassuming; bashful, diffident,

mousy (*or* mousey), overmodest, passive, quiet, reserved, shy, timid
antonyms modest, unpretentious
2 having a feeling of superiority that shows itself in an overbearing attitude ⟨a *pretentious* author whose books only appeal to equally *pretentious* readers⟩ — see ARROGANT

pretentiousness *n* **1** an exaggerated sense of one's importance that shows itself in the making of excessive or unjustified claims ⟨everyone took her ingrained *pretentiousness* into account when considering her statements⟩ — see ARROGANCE
2 excessive or unnecessary display ⟨the sheer *pretentiousness* of the debutante's wedding⟩ — see OSTENTATION
3 the quality or state of appearing or trying to appear more important or more valuable than is the case ⟨the utter *pretentiousness* of the movie is matched only by the incomprehensibility of its story⟩ — see PRETENSE 1

preternatural *adj* of, relating to, or being part of a reality beyond the observable physical universe ⟨an investigator of *preternatural* phenomena⟩ — see SUPERNATURAL 1

prettiness *n* the qualities in a person or thing that as a whole give pleasure to the senses ⟨the *prettiness* of the knickknacks is sure to appeal to a certain type of collector⟩ — see BEAUTY 1

pretty *adj* very pleasing to look at ⟨a *pretty* young girl⟩ — see BEAUTIFUL

pretty *adv* to some degree or extent ⟨we've had some *pretty* cold weather lately⟩ — see FAIRLY

prevail *vb* **1** to achieve victory (as in a contest) ⟨we shall *prevail* despite the overwhelming odds⟩ — see WIN 1
2 to continue to operate or to meet one's needs ⟨a custom that still *prevails* in many areas⟩ — see HOLD OUT

prevail (on *or* upon) *vb* to cause (someone) to agree with a belief or course of action by using arguments or earnest requests ⟨we *prevailed on* him to sing in front of all his friends⟩ — see PERSUADE

prevail (over) *vb* to achieve a victory over ⟨*prevailed over* their traditional rivals for the first time in years⟩ — see BEAT 2

prevailing *adj* **1** accepted, used, or practiced by most people ⟨disagrees with the *prevailing* attitude toward corporal punishment⟩ — see CURRENT 1
2 held by or applicable to a majority of the people ⟨the *prevailing* custom here is to leave one's doors unlocked⟩ — see GENERAL 3

prevalence *n* the fact or state of happening often ⟨the *prevalence* of rumors in the small office⟩ — see FREQUENCY

prevalent *adj* accepted, used, or practiced by most people ⟨the kinds of accidents seen in places where snowmobiles are *prevalent*⟩ — see CURRENT 1

prevaricate *vb* to make a statement one knows to be untrue ⟨during the hearings the witness was willing to *prevaricate* in order to protect his friend⟩ — see LIE 1

prevarication *n* a statement known by its maker to be untrue and made in order to deceive ⟨she knew that his account was a pure *prevarication*⟩ — see LIE

prevaricator *n* a person who tells lies ⟨she was clearly one of the more practiced *prevaricators* ever to come before the congressional committee⟩ — see LIAR

prevent *vb* to keep from happening by taking action in advance ⟨a lot of problems would have been *prevented* if we'd just prepared better⟩
synonyms avert, forestall, help, obviate, preclude

related words anticipate, provide; negate, neutralize, nullify; avoid, save; baffle, balk, checkmate, deter, foil, frustrate, thwart; bar, block, hamper, hinder, impede, interfere (with), retard, stall; deflect, fend (off), head (off), stave off, stop, ward (off); avoid, circumvent, dodge, elude, escape, evade; forbid, inhibit, prohibit; arrest, check, halt, stop; counteract, offset
near antonyms abet, aid, assist; ease, facilitate, smooth; advance, cultivate, encourage, forward, foster, further, nurture, promote; allow, leave, let, permit

preventative *adj* concerned with or serving to keep something from happening ⟨took *preventative* measures against international terrorism⟩ — see PREVENTIVE

prevention *n* the act or practice of keeping something from happening ⟨good crowd control is crucial to the *prevention* of riots⟩
synonyms averting, forestallment, obviating, precluding
related words avoidance, circumvention; negation, neutralization, nullification; baffling, balking, checkmate, debarment, determent, deterrence, foiling, frustration, thwarting; bar, block, hindrance, interference; interdiction, prohibition
near antonyms aid, assistance; facilitation; advancement, cultivation, encouragement, nurture, promotion

preventive *adj* concerned with or serving to keep something from happening ⟨if you start taking this *preventive* medicine now, you may not get sick after all⟩
synonyms precautionary, preventative
related words deterrent, deterring; negating, neutralizing, nullifying; baffling, balking, foiling, frustrating, thwarting; blocking, hampering, hindering, impeding, retardant, stalling
near antonyms abetting, aiding, assisting; easing, facilitating, smoothing; encouraging, forwarding, fostering, furthering, nurturing, promoting

previous *adj* going before another in time or order ⟨the new instructor should consult with the *previous* teacher about the lesson plans⟩ ⟨the *previous* math problem also included a reference to store discounts⟩
synonyms antecedent, anterior, foregoing, precedent, preceding, prior
related words advance, early, premature; earliest, first, inaugural, initial, maiden, original, pioneer; preexisting; introductory, preliminary; erstwhile, former, whilom
near antonyms advanced, late; final, last, terminal, ultimate
antonyms after, ensuing, following, subsequent, succeeding

previously *adv* so as to precede something in order of time ⟨he had prepared the meat stocks *previously* so as to make things easier on the day of the big dinner⟩ — see AHEAD 1

previous to *prep* earlier than ⟨his passport arrived just *previous to* his trip⟩ — see BEFORE 1

prey *n* an animal that is hunted or killed ⟨rabbits are common *prey* for owls and hawks⟩
synonyms chase, quarry
related words game; kill, victim; creature, critter, beast, brute; target
near antonyms carnivore; chaser, hunter, pursuer; killer, murderer
antonyms predator

prey (on *or* upon) *vb* to seize and eat (something) as prey ⟨a fox has been *preying on* the chickens⟩

synonyms feed (on, upon, *or* off)
related words chase, hunt, pursue; destroy, dispatch, do in, fell, kill, slay

price *n* **1** the amount of money that is demanded as payment for something ⟨I really wanted to buy that shirt, but the *price* was more money than I had⟩
synonyms charge, cost, fee, figure
related words list price, market value, rate, tariff, unit price; carrying charge, overcharge, surcharge; deduction, discount, markdown, reduction, sale; deposit; down payment; account, bill, check, invoice, tab
2 the loss or penalty involved in achieving a goal ⟨I finished the essay, but the *price* was losing a night's sleep⟩
synonyms cost
related words expense, toll; forfeit, penalty, sacrifice
3 something offered or given in return for a service performed ⟨there was a *price* on the criminal's head⟩ — see REWARD

prick *n* **1** a mark or small hole made by a pointed instrument ⟨the immunization shot left a *prick* on my arm that turned into a bruise⟩
synonyms perforation, pinhole, pinprick, punch, puncture, stab
related words gouge, groove, hollow; break, cut, gash, notch, rupture, slash, slit
2 a sharp unpleasant sensation usually felt in some specific part of the body ⟨she felt a sharp *prick* when the nurse gave her the shot⟩ — see PAIN 1

prickly *adj* likely to cause a scratch ⟨waded carefully through the *prickly* bushes⟩ — see SCRATCHY 1

pride *n* **1** a reasonable or justifiable sense of one's worth or importance ⟨finishing that survival course gave me a real sense of *pride* and confidence in my abilities⟩
synonyms ego, pridefulness, self-esteem, self-regard, self-respect
related words confidence, self-assurance, self-confidence; dignity, face, honor, prestige
near antonyms disgrace, humiliation, shame; demureness, humbleness, humility, modesty; diffidence, meekness, shyness, timidity, timidness
2 an asset that brings praise or renown ⟨the football championship was the *pride* of the whole school⟩ — see GLORY 2
3 an often unjustified feeling of being pleased with oneself or with one's situation or achievements ⟨so full of *pride* that they were ripe for a big comedown⟩ — see COMPLACENCE

pride *vb* to think highly of (oneself) ⟨he *prides* himself on the quality of his writing⟩
synonyms flatter, plume
related words boast, brag, vaunt; congratulate, felicitate

prideful *adj* **1** having or displaying feelings of scorn for what is regarded as beneath oneself ⟨*prideful* intellectuals long considered rock music unworthy of serious study⟩ — see PROUD 1
2 having too high an opinion of oneself ⟨at the wedding the *prideful* snobs ignored their poor relations⟩ — see CONCEITED

pridefulness *n* **1** a reasonable or justifiable sense of one's worth or importance ⟨beaming with understandable *pridefulness*, the physically challenged graduate accepted his college diploma⟩ — see PRIDE 1
2 an often unjustified feeling of being pleased with oneself or with one's situation or achievements ⟨an inordinate amount of *pridefulness* for someone who has much to be modest about⟩ — see COMPLACENCE

priest *n* a person specially trained and authorized to conduct religious services in a Christian church ⟨searched for a *priest* who could perform an exorcism⟩ — see CLERGYMAN

priestly *adj* of, relating to, or characteristic of the clergy ⟨majestically robed in *priestly* garments⟩ — see CLERICAL

prim *adj* given to or marked by very conservative standards regarding personal behavior or morals ⟨a *prim* and proper matron was in charge of the girls' dorm⟩ — see STRAITLACED

primal *adj* relating to or occurring near the beginning of a process, series, or time period ⟨there was a period of *primal* idealism after the founding of the republic and before the rise of partisan politics⟩ — see EARLY 1

primarily *adv* **1** in the beginning ⟨the university was *primarily* an agricultural college when it was founded over two centuries ago⟩ — see ORIGINALLY
2 for the most part ⟨ketchup is *primarily* made from tomatoes⟩ — see CHIEFLY

primary *adj* **1** coming before all others in importance ⟨the *primary* concern for the house hunters was the price⟩ — see FOREMOST 1
2 done or working without something else coming in between ⟨a crop failure that was the *primary* cause of the famine⟩ — see DIRECT 1
3 highest in rank or authority ⟨the movie's *primary* screenwriter⟩ — see HEAD

prime *adj* **1** highest in rank or authority ⟨the *prime* strategist in the senator's presidential campaign⟩ — see HEAD
2 of the very best kind ⟨owns a thousand acres of *prime* farmland⟩ — see EXCELLENT

prime *n* **1** a state or time of great activity, thriving, or achievement ⟨in the *prime* of her life⟩ — see BLOOM 1
2 individuals carefully selected as being the best of a class ⟨chose the *prime* of the flock of sheep⟩ — see ELITE

primer *n* a book used for instruction in a subject ⟨a *primer* of human anatomy⟩ — see TEXTBOOK

primeval *adj* relating to or occurring near the beginning of a process, series, or time period ⟨*primeval* forests slowly disappearing as the climate changed⟩ — see EARLY 1

primitive *adj* **1** belonging to or characteristic of an early level of skill or development ⟨*primitive* wooden tools were used before the Iron Age⟩
synonyms crude, low, rude, rudimentary
related words basic, simple, uncomplicated; homely, homespun, unsophisticated; early, primeval, primordial; backward, underdeveloped, undeveloped; aged, ancient, antediluvian, antiquated, antique, dated, fusty, hoary, musty, obsolete, old, oldfangled, old-fashioned, old-time, out-of-date, outworn, passé, past
near antonyms complex, complicated, intricate, involved, sophisticated; full-blown, full-grown, grown, mature, matured, perfected, ripe, ripened; civilized, cultivated, enlightened, refined; contemporary, current, latest, mod, modern, new, newfangled, new-fashioned, novel, now, present-day, space-age, ultramodern, up-to-date
antonyms advanced, developed, evolved, higher
2 relating to or occurring near the beginning of a process, series, or time period ⟨a *primitive* period in church history when members still lived in communes⟩ — see EARLY 1

primordial *adj* relating to or occurring near the beginning of a process, series, or time period ⟨all life on

Earth supposedly came from a *primordial* ooze in existence many millions of years ago⟩ — see EARLY 1

prince *n* a person of rank, power, or influence in a particular field ⟨a neighborhood in which the city's merchant *princes* built palaces that shamelessly celebrated their wealth⟩ — see MAGNATE

princely *adj* fit for or worthy of a royal ruler ⟨set a *princely* meal before their guests⟩ — see MONARCHICAL

principal *adj* **1** coming before all others in importance ⟨our *principal* reason for coming here today⟩ — see FOREMOST 1

2 highest in rank or authority ⟨the *principal* researcher in the company's chemical division⟩ — see HEAD

principal *n* the person who has the most important role in a play, movie, or TV show ⟨my cousin is one of the *principals* in a new sitcom this fall⟩ — see STAR 2

principally *adv* for the most part ⟨we were *principally* concerned with the quantity of the food, and only secondarily with the quality⟩ — see CHIEFLY

principled *adj* **1** following the accepted rules of moral conduct ⟨a high-*principled* art expert who always told clients what he honestly thought their items were worth⟩ — see HONORABLE 1

2 guided by or in accordance with one's sense of right and wrong ⟨a politician widely respected for her *principled* behavior in every office she ever held⟩ — see CONSCIENTIOUS 1

principles *n pl* **1** general or basic truths on which other truths or theories can be based ⟨if you don't learn the *principles* of algebra now, you won't understand much later on⟩

synonyms basics, elements, essentials, fundamentals, rudiments

related words basis, foundation, groundwork; nitty-gritty; belief, canon, doctrine, dogma, faith, philosophy; axiom, law, precept, tenet; rule, standard; theorem

near antonyms details, trivia

2 the code of good conduct for an individual or group ⟨stuck to his *principles* even in the face of extreme pressure⟩ — see ETHICS

print *n* **1** a perceptible trace left by pressure ⟨one telltale sign that I had been napping was the *print* left by the chenille bedspread on my cheek⟩

synonyms impress, impression, imprint, stamp

related words dent, hollow, indentation; mark, sign

2 a picture created from an image recorded on a light-sensitive surface by a camera ⟨we still get our *prints* developed at the local drugstore⟩ — see PHOTOGRAPH

print *vb* to produce and release for distribution in printed form ⟨the publisher has been *printing* the town newspaper for over a century⟩ — see PUBLISH 1

prior *adj* going before another in time or order ⟨we made *prior* arrangements⟩ — see PREVIOUS

priority *n* the right to one's attention before other things considered less important ⟨the principal has decided to give your request *priority*, so you'll have a meeting early tomorrow morning⟩

synonyms precedence, right-of-way

related words preference; urgency; ascendancy, preeminence, primacy, supremacy; transcendence; order, progression, sequence, succession

prior to *prep* earlier than ⟨make sure all revisions are approved by the author *prior to* publication⟩ — see BEFORE 1

priory *n* a residence for men under religious vows ⟨you can hear the bells from the *priory* from the other side of the village⟩ — see MONASTERY

prison *n* a place of confinement for persons held in lawful custody ⟨the ongoing debate whether drug users should go to *prison*⟩ — see JAIL

prisoner *n* one that has been taken and held in confinement ⟨the *prisoners* were fed only bread and water twice a day⟩ — see CAPTIVE

pristine *adj* being in an original and unused or unspoiled state ⟨a *pristine* forest that has never been subjected to logging or development⟩ — see FRESH 1

private *adj* **1** not known or meant to be known by the general populace ⟨that he is planning to retire is *private* information until he makes a public announcement⟩

synonyms confidential, hushed, inside, intimate, nonpublic, privy, secret

related words classified, top secret; unadvertised, unannounced, undisclosed, unmentioned; clandestine, collusive, conspiratorial, covert; surreptitious, undercover, underhand, underhanded; personal; closeted, concealed, hidden; repressed, silenced, stifled, suppressed

near antonyms well-known; advertised, aired, announced, blazed, broadcast, declared, disclosed, divulged, enunciated, heralded, proclaimed, professed, promulgated, publicized, published, reported, spotlighted; general, popular, prevailing, vulgar; prevalent, rife, widespread; communal, shared

antonyms common, open, public

2 undertaken or done so as to escape being observed or known by others ⟨a *private* investigation of the organization's activities⟩ — see SECRET 1

3 of, relating to, or belonging to a single person ⟨club lockers in which *private* property may be stored⟩ — see INDIVIDUAL 1

privation *n* the state of being robbed of something normally enjoyed ⟨the constant *privation* of sleep was starting to affect my schoolwork⟩

synonyms deprivation, loss

related words lack, need, want; dispossession; denial, forfeit, forfeiture, penalty, sacrifice; bereavement

near antonyms ownership, possession; accumulation, acquiring, gain

privilege *n* something granted as a special favor ⟨you will have the *privilege* of leading the line today⟩

synonyms appanage, boon, concession, honor

related words courtesy; claim, entitlement, right; birthright; perquisite, prerogative; charter, grant, patent; exemption, immunity, waiver

near antonyms duty, obligation, responsibility

privy *adj* **1** not known or meant to be known by the general populace ⟨*privy* information on the state of peace negotiations⟩ — see PRIVATE 1

2 undertaken or done so as to escape being observed or known by others ⟨*privy* meetings between high-level representatives from both sides for the purpose of bringing about an armistice⟩ — see SECRET 1

3 of, relating to, or belonging to a single person ⟨a *privy* seal that can be used only by the British monarch⟩ — see INDIVIDUAL 1

prize *n* **1** someone or something unusually desirable ⟨in her parents' view, her current boyfriend is certainly no *prize*⟩

synonyms catch, gem, jewel, pearl, plum, treasure

related words find, godsend, goody, valuable, windfall; booty, loot, spoil; glory, pride; jackpot, treasure trove *near antonyms* lemon, loser

2 something given in recognition of achievement ⟨won a *prize* for finishing first in the essay contest⟩ — see AWARD

¹**prize** *vb* **1** to draw out by force or with effort ⟨*prizing* the stubborn nails out of the board⟩ — see EXTRACT

2 to raise, move, or pull apart with or as if with a lever ⟨trying to *prize* apart the jammed gears⟩ — see ¹PRY 1

²**prize** *vb* to hold dear ⟨veterinarians know that pets are highly *prized* by their owners⟩ — see LOVE 1

prizefighter *n* one that engages in the sport of fighting with the fists ⟨a *prizefighter* who is generally acknowledged to be one of the ring's most dangerous men⟩ — see BOXER

probability *n* **1** the quality or state of being likely to occur ⟨the plot of the movie thriller was exciting and surprising but woefully lacking in *probability*⟩

synonyms likelihood, likeliness

related words credibility, plausibility; liability; feasibility, feasibleness, possibility, potentiality, reasonability, viability

near antonyms doubtfulness, dubiousness; impracticability, impracticality; implausibility, incredibility

antonyms improbability, unlikelihood, unlikeliness

2 a measure of how often an event will occur instead of another ⟨the *probability* of flipping a coin and getting heads fifty times in a row is not good⟩

synonyms chance, odds, percentage

related words outlook, prospect; possibility, potential, potentiality

probable *adj* **1** worthy of being accepted as true or reasonable ⟨the counselor could find no *probable* reason for the girl's actions⟩ — see BELIEVABLE

2 having a high chance of occurring ⟨a *probable* outcome of the price increase will be lower consumption⟩ — see LIKELY 1

probably *adv* without much doubt ⟨we would *probably* win that bet⟩

synonyms doubtless, likely, presumably

related words mayhap, perchance, perhaps, possibly; conceivably, imaginably, plausibly, practically, reasonably; potentially; assuredly, certainly, clearly, conclusively, decisively, definitely, definitively, indubitably, positively, surely

near antonyms implausibly, inconceivably, incredibly, unbelievably

antonyms improbably

probe *n* a systematic search for the truth or facts about something ⟨a congressional *probe* into the accusations⟩ — see INQUIRY 1

probe *vb* **1** to search through or into ⟨*probe* every detail of the singer's private life⟩ — see EXPLORE 1

2 to go into or range over for purposes of discovery ⟨*probing* the depths of the undersea trench⟩ — see EXPLORE 2

probing *n* a systematic search for the truth or facts about something ⟨questionings and *probings* by several committees into the affair⟩ — see INQUIRY 1

probity *n* **1** conduct that conforms to an accepted standard of right and wrong ⟨a person of indisputable *probity* must head the disciplinary panel⟩ — see MORALITY 1

2 devotion to telling the truth ⟨questioned the *probity* of the witness⟩ — see HONESTY 1

3 faithfulness to high moral standards ⟨ideals of fairness and *probity* in journalism⟩ — see HONOR 1

problem *n* **1** something that requires thought and skill for resolution ⟨the *problem* of world hunger⟩

synonyms case, knot, matter, trouble

related words issue, question; challenge; corner, fix, hole, hot water, jam, pickle, predicament, situation; glitch, hitch, snag; conundrum, enigma, mystery, puzzle, puzzlement, riddle; brainteaser, perplexer, poser, stumper

antonyms answer, solution

2 an interrogative expression often used to test knowledge ⟨there were only ten *problems* on the exam, but they were all challenging⟩ — see QUESTION 1

3 something that is a source of irritation ⟨the mosquitoes are only a *problem* in the evenings⟩ — see ANNOYANCE 3

problematic *also* **problematical** *adj* **1** requiring exceptional skill or caution in performance or handling ⟨the *problematic* situation of somehow having two dates for the same party⟩ — see TRICKY

2 giving good reason for being doubted, questioned, or challenged ⟨whether we should even bother finishing the project at this point is *problematic*⟩ — see DOUBTFUL 2

procedure *n* **1** a usually fixed or ordered series of actions or events leading to a result ⟨followed the *procedure* for replacing the broken part exactly as the owner's manual said⟩ — see PROCESS 1

2 a way of acting or proceeding ⟨followed standard *procedure* for dealing with a consumer complaint⟩ — see COURSE 1

proceed *vb* to move forward along a course ⟨you may *proceed* with your plan⟩ — see GO 1

proceed (along) *vb* to make one's way through, across, or over ⟨the hikers *proceeded along* the ridge for several hundred feet⟩ — see TRAVERSE

proceeding *adj* being in progress or development ⟨currently *proceeding* projects include construction of a new school gym⟩ — see ONGOING 1

proceeding *n* **1** a court case for enforcing a right or claim ⟨a divorce *proceeding*⟩ — see LAWSUIT

2 a usually fixed or ordered series of actions or events leading to a result ⟨this is not the haphazard *proceeding* that it may seem to the casual observer⟩ — see PROCESS 1

proceeds *n pl* **1** an increase usually measured in money that comes from labor, business, or property ⟨the *proceeds* of a sale of used furniture⟩ — see INCOME

2 the amount of money left when expenses are subtracted from the total amount received ⟨all *proceeds* from the special promotion will go to charity⟩ — see PROFIT 1

process *n* **1** a usually fixed or ordered series of actions or events leading to a result ⟨the *process* by which the elastic fibers spun by silkworms is turned into soft, lustrous cloth⟩

synonyms course, operation, procedure, proceeding

related words fashion, manner, method, mode, style, system, technique, way; approach, blueprint, design, game plan, layout, plan, plot, program, scheme, strategy; accomplishment, achievement, attainment, enterprise, performance, undertaking, work; activity, functioning, movement

2 forward movement in time or place ⟨in the *process* of doing this project we all learned a lot⟩ — see ADVANCE 1

procession *n* **1** a body of individuals moving along in an orderly and often ceremonial way ⟨a *procession* of mourners leaving the cemetery⟩ — see CORTEGE 2

2 forward movement in time or place ⟨watched the constant *procession* of cars headed out of the city at the start of the weekend⟩ — see ADVANCE 1

proclaim *vb* to make known openly or publicly ⟨loudly *proclaimed* her innocence⟩ — see ANNOUNCE

proclivity *n* a habitual attraction to some activity or thing ⟨showed artistic *proclivities* at an early age⟩ — see INCLINATION 1

procreate *vb* to bring forth offspring ⟨in life science class we learned how animals *procreate*⟩
synonyms breed, multiply, propagate, reproduce
related words bear, beget, engender, generate, get, mother, parent, produce, sire; hatch, spawn

procurable *adj* possible to get ⟨the necessary ingredients should be *procurable* at almost any grocery store⟩ — see AVAILABLE 1

procurator *n* a person who acts or does business for another ⟨he was appointed *procurator* of the church and was responsible for all of the financial arrangements⟩ — see AGENT 2

procure *vb* to receive as return for effort ⟨*procured* new desks for her students⟩ — see EARN 1

prod *vb* **1** to urge or push forward with or as if with a pointed object ⟨my sister keeps *prodding* me with her pencil to move along faster⟩
synonyms goad, spur
related words chuck, jab, jog, nudge, poke; bore, drill, pierce, prick, punch, puncture, stab, stick; drive, propel
2 to try to persuade (someone) through earnest appeals to follow a course of action ⟨a public outcry *prodded* the politicians into action⟩ — see URGE

prodigal *adj* given to spending money freely or foolishly ⟨the *prodigal* child always spent her allowance the minute she got it⟩
synonyms extravagant, profligate, spendthrift, squandering, thriftless, unthrifty, wasteful
related words improvident, myopic, shortsighted; bountiful, generous, lavish, liberal, openhanded, openhearted, philanthropic; careless, heedless, imprudent, incautious, injudicious, unwise; indulgent, reckless, self-indulgent, splurging, wanton
near antonyms cheap, close, mean, miserly, niggardly, parsimonious, penurious, pinching, spare, sparing, stingy, tight, tightfisted; careful, judicious, prudent, sensible, wise; farsighted, forehanded, foresighted, forethoughtful, provident
antonyms conserving, economical, economizing, frugal, scrimping, skimping, thrifty

prodigal *n* someone who carelessly spends money ⟨the million-dollar lottery winner was such a *prodigal* that there was no money left after a few years⟩
synonyms profligate, spender, spendthrift, squanderer, waster, wastrel
near antonyms miser, skinflint, tightwad; conserver, saver
antonyms economizer

prodigality *n* **1** an instance of spending money or resources without care or restraint ⟨his purchase of a new yacht was only one of a series of reckless *prodigalities*⟩ — see WASTE 1
2 the quality or fact of being free or wasteful in the expenditure of money ⟨his *prodigality* eventually turned him into a pauper⟩ — see EXTRAVAGANCE 1

prodigious *adj* **1** causing wonder or astonishment ⟨stage magicians performing *prodigious* feats for audiences⟩ — see MARVELOUS 1

2 unusually large ⟨a *prodigious* supply of food kept in the basement for emergencies⟩ — see HUGE

prodigy *n* something extraordinary or surprising ⟨a new drug that is being hailed as the latest *prodigy* of the medical world⟩ — see WONDER 1

produce *n* something produced by physical or intellectual effort ⟨a book that was the *produce* of a lifetime of study on the subject⟩ — see PRODUCT 1

produce *vb* **1** to be the cause of (a situation, action, or state of mind) ⟨hopefully, the new approach will *produce* results⟩ — see EFFECT
2 to bring forth from the womb ⟨fish can potentially *produce* many offspring at once⟩ — see BEAR 1
3 to bring into being by combining, shaping, or transforming materials ⟨a factory *producing* steel⟩ — see MAKE 1

product *n* **1** something produced by physical or intellectual effort ⟨that book is the *product* of years of work⟩ ⟨a rebuilt car which is the *product* of several people's labor⟩
synonyms affair, fruit, handiwork, output, produce, production, thing, work, yield
related words article, commodity, object; goods, line, merchandise, wares; handcraft, handicraft; aftereffect, aftermath, conclusion, consequence, development, effect, issue, outcome, result, upshot; by-product, derivative, offshoot, outgrowth, residual, side effect, spin-off
2 a condition or occurrence traceable to a cause ⟨her relentless ambition is a *product* of her home environment⟩ — see EFFECT 1

production *n* something produced by physical or intellectual effort ⟨the total *production* of one week's intensive labor⟩ — see PRODUCT 1

productive *adj* **1** having a role in deciding something's final form ⟨contributed several *productive* ideas to the project⟩ — see FORMATIVE
2 producing abundantly ⟨*productive* farmland⟩ — see FERTILE
3 producing or capable of producing a desired result ⟨panicking during a crisis is not *productive* behavior⟩ — see EFFECTIVE 1

productiveness *n* the power to produce a desired result ⟨the prodigious *productiveness* of the nation's shipyards during World War II⟩ — see EFFICACY

profane *adj* **1** not involving religion or religious matters ⟨it was hard to juggle the requirements of church and our more *profane* duties⟩
synonyms secular, temporal
related words atheistic, godless, irreligious, pagan; lay, nonclerical; nondenominational, nonsectarian; earthly, mundane, terrestrial, worldly; material, physical, substantial; bodily, carnal, corporal, fleshly; blasphemous, impious, irreverent, sacrilegious; unconsecrated, unhallowed, unsanctified
near antonyms divine, spiritual; consecrated, hallowed, holy, sanctified; churchly, devout, godly, pious, prayerful, reverent, worshipful; ethereal, insubstantial, metaphysical, unsubstantial; bodiless, immaterial, incorporeal, nonphysical
antonyms religious, sacred
2 not showing proper reverence for the holy or sacred ⟨offended by the *profane* language that her coworkers used so casually⟩ — see IRREVERENT

profane *vb* **1** to lower in character or dignity ⟨the once-lovely landscape had been *profaned* by ugly factories⟩ — see DEBASE 1

2 to put to a bad or improper use ⟨*profaned* his considerable acting talents by appearing in some wretched movies⟩ — see MISAPPLY

3 to treat (a sacred place or object) shamefully or with great disrespect ⟨invading troops *profaned* the altar by playing poker on it⟩ — see DESECRATE

profess *vb* **1** to present a false appearance of ⟨*professed* friendship while secretly plotting revenge⟩ — see FEIGN

2 to state clearly and strongly ⟨*professed* her love in a series of letters to the soldier⟩ — see ASSERT 1

3 to state as a fact usually forcefully ⟨*professed* his innocence to anyone who would listen⟩ — see CLAIM 1

profession *n* **1** a solemn and often public declaring of the truth or existence of something ⟨the weekly *profession* of faith by the members of the congregation⟩ — see PROTESTATION

2 the activity by which one regularly makes a living ⟨he was very good at his chosen *profession*⟩ — see OCCUPATION

proffer *n* something which is presented for consideration ⟨a generous *proffer* of his estate for the charity gala⟩ — see PROPOSAL

proffer *vb* **1** to put before another for acceptance or consideration ⟨*proffered* his assistance in helping them reach a compromise⟩ — see OFFER 1

2 to set before the mind for consideration ⟨*proffered* a novel solution for getting themselves out of debt⟩ — see PROPOSE 1

proficiency *n* **1** a highly developed skill in or knowledge of something ⟨surprised by his *proficiency* at the game after only the briefest explanation of the rules⟩ — see COMMAND 2

2 knowledge gained by actually doing or living through something ⟨acquired *proficiency* at golf through long hours of practice⟩ — see EXPERIENCE 1

proficient *adj* having or showing exceptional knowledge, experience, or skill in a field of endeavor ⟨she is quite *proficient* at computer repair⟩ ⟨a *proficient* rendition of a difficult piano piece⟩

synonyms accomplished, ace, adept, consummate, crack, crackerjack, experienced, expert, good, great, master, masterful, masterly, practiced (*or* practised), skilled, skillful, versed, veteran, virtuoso

related words adroit, clever, deft, dexterous (*also* dextrous), handy; gifted, talented; experienced, polished, refined; effective, effectual, efficient, workmanlike; able, capable, competent, fit, qualified; educated, knowledgeable, schooled, taught, trained, tutored; all-around (*also* all-round), well-rounded; long-term, old

near antonyms incapable, incompetent, inept, unable, unfit, unqualified; artless, crude, rude; ineffective, ineffectual, inefficient; ungifted, untalented; ignorant, unschooled, untaught, untrained, untutored; beginning, green, inexperienced, new, raw, untested, untried; rough, unpolished

antonyms amateur, amateurish, inexperienced, inexpert, unexperienced, unpracticed, unprofessional, unseasoned, unskilled, unskillful

proficiently *adv* in a skillful or expert manner ⟨an administrator who can deal with the problems quickly and *proficiently*⟩ — see WELL 3

profit *n* **1** the amount of money left when expenses are subtracted from the total amount received ⟨after we deducted the cost of sugar, lemons, and paper cups, the *profit* from a day of lemonade sales was about $20⟩

synonyms earnings, gain, lucre, net, payoff, proceeds, return

related words killing, windfall; gross; compensation, emolument, income, pay, payment, remittal, requital, salary, wages; interest, return, yield; (the) black; royalty

near antonyms cost, expenditure, expense, loss, outgo, outlay

2 an increase usually measured in money that comes from labor, business, or property ⟨found that there was a *profit* in training dogs for rich people⟩ — see INCOME

profit *vb* to provide with something useful or desirable ⟨an agreement that *profited* us all⟩ — see BENEFIT

profitable *adj* **1** yielding a profit ⟨selling lemonade turned out to be a *profitable* venture⟩

synonyms fat, gainful, lucrative, paying, remunerative

related words advantageous, beneficial, rewarding, useful, worthwhile

antonyms unprofitable

2 conferring benefits; promoting or contributing to personal or social well-being ⟨I have always found honesty to be a *profitable* course of action⟩ — see BENEFICIAL

profligate *adj* given to spending money freely or foolishly ⟨*profligate* movie producers hoping to create the next blockbuster⟩ — see PRODIGAL

profligate *n* **1** someone who carelessly spends money ⟨cautioned the *profligate* to pay more attention to prices when buying things⟩ — see PRODIGAL

2 a person who has sunk below the normal moral standard ⟨a drunken *profligate*, he was given to wretched excess in every aspect of his life⟩ — see DEGENERATE

profound *adj* **1** difficult for one of ordinary knowledge or intelligence to understand ⟨a *profound* observation about good and evil that few listeners fully grasped⟩

synonyms abstruse, deep, esoteric, recondite

related words erudite, learned, scholarly; academic, pedantic; complex, complicated, hard; darkling, enigmatic (*also* enigmatical), inscrutable, mysterious, mystic, uncanny; impenetrable, incomprehensible, unfathomable, unintelligible; ambiguous, cryptic; unanswerable, unknowable; baffling, bewildering, confounding, confusing, mystifying, perplexing, puzzling

near antonyms easy, facile, simple, straightforward; comprehensible, fathomable, intelligible, understandable; clear, obvious, plain

antonyms shallow

2 extreme in degree, power, or effect ⟨a *profound* silence fell over the audience after the last note had sounded⟩ — see INTENSE

3 having no exceptions or restrictions ⟨a *profound* dislike of raw vegetables⟩ — see ABSOLUTE 2

profoundness *n* the quality of being great in extent (as of insight) ⟨we were struck by the *profoundness* of his observation⟩ — see DEPTH 2

profundity *n* the quality of being great in extent (as of insight) ⟨a philosopher who is widely respected for the *profundity* of her thinking⟩ — see DEPTH 2

profuse *adj* pouring forth in great amounts ⟨we received *profuse* thanks for our efforts⟩ ⟨a *profuse* rush of water from the collapsing dike⟩

synonyms copious, galore, gushing, lavish, riotous

related words abounding, abundant, ample, bounteous, bountiful, liberal, plenteous, plentiful; extravagant, luxuriant; fat, fecund, fertile; free, liberal, munificent, openhanded, unsparing, unstinting; excessive, immoderate; adequate, complete, enough, sufficient

near antonyms meager, niggardly, poor, scant, scanty, spare, sparse, stingy; deficient, inadequate, incomplete,

insufficient, lacking, unsatisfactory, wanting; bare, mere, minimal; slight, small
  antonyms dribbling, trickling

profusion *n* a considerable amount ⟨apples grow in *profusion* in this valley⟩ — see LOT 2

progeny *n* the descendants of a person, animal, or plant ⟨carefully examined the *progeny* of the new breed of cattle⟩ — see OFFSPRING

prognosis *n* a declaration that something will happen in the future ⟨the analyst's *prognosis* for the stock market in the new year⟩ — see PREDICTION

prognosticate *vb* to tell of or describe beforehand ⟨using current trends to *prognosticate* what the workplace of the future will be like⟩ — see FORETELL

prognosticating *n* a declaration that something will happen in the future ⟨because there are always unforeseen breakthroughs in every field, in the past most *prognosticatings* have fallen short⟩ — see PREDICTION

prognostication *n* a declaration that something will happen in the future ⟨the complete fulfillment of his *prognostication* surprised even him⟩ — see PREDICTION

prognosticator *n* one who predicts future events or developments ⟨one of the best *prognosticators* in the weather business⟩ — see PROPHET

program *n* **1** a listing of things to be presented or considered (as at a concert or play) ⟨the *program* will tell us the scheduled order of musical numbers⟩
  synonyms agenda, calendar, docket, schedule, timetable
  related words card, exercises; arrangement, order, organization
  2 a method worked out in advance for achieving some objective ⟨we need to come up with a *program* to deal with kids skipping school⟩ — see PLAN 1
  3 a way of acting or proceeding ⟨recommends a *program* of regular dental checkups⟩ — see COURSE 1

progress *n* **1** forward movement in time or place ⟨we're making slow *progress* against the stiff head wind⟩ — see ADVANCE 1
  2 the act or process of going from the simple or basic to the complex or advanced ⟨the rapid *progress* of medical science in the last century⟩ — see DEVELOPMENT 1

progress *vb* **1** to become mature ⟨generally a species *progresses* from simple forms to more specialized forms⟩ — see MATURE
  2 to move forward along a course ⟨our plans are *progressing* nicely⟩ — see GO 1

progression *n* **1** a series of things linked together ⟨a *progression* of events that ended in utter disaster⟩ — see CHAIN 1
  2 forward movement in time or place ⟨our *progression* was slow but steady⟩ — see ADVANCE 1
  3 the act or process of going from the simple or basic to the complex or advanced ⟨that civilization's gradual *progression* from simple bartering to a complex economy and monetary system⟩ — see DEVELOPMENT 1

progressive *adj* **1** being far along in development ⟨*progressive* forms of animal life⟩ — see ADVANCED 1
  2 not bound by traditional ways or beliefs ⟨a *progressive* community, it was the first to provide for the public education of girls⟩ — see LIBERAL 1

prohibit *vb* to order not to do or use or to be done or used ⟨the city *prohibits* swimming in the lake after dark⟩ — see FORBID

prohibited *adj* that may not be permitted ⟨there will be no toleration for smoking and other *prohibited* activities⟩ — see IMPERMISSIBLE

prohibiting *n* the act of ordering that something not be done or used ⟨not surprisingly, the *prohibiting* of the use of cell phones proved to be unpopular⟩ — see PROHIBITION 1

prohibition *n* **1** the act of ordering that something not be done or used ⟨the principal's *prohibition* against the use of cell phones in the school building met with unanimous approval by the teachers⟩
  synonyms banning, barring, enjoining, forbidding, interdicting, interdiction, outlawing, prohibiting, proscribing, proscription
  related words bidding, charging, decreeing, dictation, direction, instruction; deterrence, discouragement, dissuading; repression, suppression; coercion, compulsion, constraint, force
  near antonyms allowance, permission, sufferance, toleration; approval, endorsement; encouragement, promotion, support; compliance, obedience
  2 an order that something not be done or used ⟨the school issued a *prohibition* against wearing clothing with obscene and provocative slogans⟩
  synonyms ban, embargo, interdict, interdiction, proscription, veto
  related words taboo (*also* tabu); injunction; constraint, inhibition, limitation, restraint, restriction; deterrent, discouragement; repression, suppression; prevention; denial, disallowance, negation, refusal, rejection; objection, protest
  near antonyms sufferance, tolerance, toleration; allowance, allowing, authorization, consent, granting, leave, letting, license (*or* licence), licensing, permission, permitting, sanctioning; approval, endorsement; enabling, encouragement, facilitation, promotion, support; compliance, obedience; accession, acquiescence, agreement, assent
  antonyms prescription

project *n* a method worked out in advance for achieving some objective ⟨a *project* to develop the city's waterfront⟩ — see PLAN 1

project *vb* **1** to extend outward beyond a usual point ⟨some boulders *projected* dangerously out above the trail⟩ — see BULGE
  2 to work out the details of (something) in advance ⟨we must *project* next year's budget now⟩ — see PLAN 1

projection *n* a part that sticks out from the general mass of something ⟨filed down all the *projections* until the surface was smooth⟩ — see BULGE

proletarian *adj* belonging to the class of people of low social or economic rank ⟨a self-made Internet magnate who is not at all ashamed of his *proletarian* background⟩ — see IGNOBLE 1

proletariat *n* people looked down upon as ignorant and of the lowest class ⟨the Bolsheviks believed that Russia's discontented *proletariat* made that nation ripe for revolution⟩ — see RABBLE

proliferate *vb* to become greater in extent, volume, amount, or number ⟨rumors about the incident *proliferated* on the Internet⟩ — see INCREASE 2

proliferation *n* **1** something added (as by growth) ⟨a large *proliferation* in the number of electrical appliances was placing enormous demands upon the region's power supply⟩ — see INCREASE 1
  2 the act or process of becoming greater in number ⟨the *proliferation* of mistakes as the students became more and more tired⟩ — see MULTIPLICATION

prolific *adj* producing abundantly ⟨a famously *prolific* author who could produce several works of fiction and nonfiction a year⟩ — see FERTILE

prolix *adj* using or containing more words than necessary to express an idea ⟨a person known for habitually transforming brief anecdotes into *prolix* sagas that exhaust their listeners⟩ — see WORDY

prolixity *n* the use of too many words to express an idea ⟨*prolixity* is one of the worst offenses that a writer of any age can commit⟩ — see VERBIAGE

prologue *n* a short section (as of a book) that leads to or explains the main part ⟨a brief *prologue* sets the scene for the story that follows⟩ — see INTRODUCTION

prolong *vb* to make longer ⟨would like to *prolong* our vacation by any means possible⟩ — see EXTEND 1

prolongation *n* the act of making longer ⟨the indefinite *prolongation* of the cease-fire⟩ — see EXTENSION 1

prolonging *n* the act of making longer ⟨his habitual *prolonging* of any task so that it fills up an entire afternoon⟩ — see EXTENSION 1

prom *n* a social gathering for dancing ⟨he resolved to ask her to the school *prom* at the first opportunity⟩ — see DANCE

prominence *n* an area of high ground ⟨a rocky *prominence* that commands a stunning view of the surrounding area⟩ — see HEIGHT 4

prominent *adj* **1** likely to attract attention ⟨an attorney who occupies a *prominent* position in the town's social hierarchy⟩ — see NOTICEABLE
2 widely known ⟨*prominent* figures in the history of sports⟩ — see FAMOUS

promiscuous *adj* consisting of many things of different sorts ⟨since I just collect stamps that I happen to like, my collection is pretty *promiscuous*⟩ — see MISCELLANEOUS

promise *n* a person's solemn declaration that he or she will do or not do something ⟨he gave a *promise* that he would arrive on time⟩
synonyms oath, pledge, troth, vow, word
related words appointment, arrangement, commitment, engagement; compact, contract, covenant; assurance, guarantee, guaranty; bail, bond, deposit, gage, pawn, security, token, warranty

promise *vb* **1** to make a solemn declaration of intent ⟨I *promised* not to fight with my sister⟩
synonyms covenant, pledge, swear, vow
related words affiance, betroth, plight, troth; accede, agree, assent, consent; contract, engage, guarantee, undertake; affirm, assert, aver, avouch, avow, declare, insist, warrant
phrases give one's word
2 to show signs of a favorable or successful outcome ⟨the new sitcom *promises* to be an excellent show⟩ — see BODE

promising *adj* **1** having qualities which inspire hope ⟨a *promising* writer who just may write the great American novel someday⟩ — see HOPEFUL 1
2 pointing toward a happy outcome ⟨all the signs for the new business are *promising*⟩ — see FAVORABLE 2

promontory *n* **1** an area of high ground jutting out into a body of water beyond the line of the coast ⟨stood on the windswept *promontory* overlooking the bay⟩ — see HEADLAND 1
2 an area of land that juts out into a body of water ⟨Cape May is by far Delaware Bay's largest *promontory*⟩ — see ²CAPE

promote *vb* **1** to move higher in rank or position ⟨the Navy *promoted* her to captain for her record of outstanding performance⟩
synonyms advance, elevate, raise, upgrade

related words forward, further; aggrandize, boost, heighten, improve, lift, uplift; commission, ennoble, knight; acclaim, applaud, celebrate, cite, commend, compliment, congratulate, decorate; eulogize, extol (*also* extoll), glorify, hail, honor, laud, praise, salute
near antonyms depose, dethrone, dismiss, expel, impeach, oust, overthrow, remove, unmake, unseat; demean, disgrace, dishonor, humble, humiliate, mortify, shame, take down; censure, condemn, damn, denounce, reprobate
antonyms abase, degrade, demote, downgrade, lower, reduce
2 to help the growth or development of ⟨a campaign *promoting* good dental hygiene⟩ — see FOSTER 1
3 to look after or assist the growth of by labor and care ⟨spends all her time now *promoting* her new business⟩ — see GROW 1
4 to provide publicity for ⟨*promoting* a new line of toys based on the popular movie⟩ — see PUBLICIZE 1

promoter *n* a person who actively supports or favors a cause ⟨a *promoter* of greater understanding and cooperation among churches⟩ — see EXPONENT

promotion *n* a raising or a state of being raised to a higher rank or position ⟨after ten years at the company she was rewarded with a *promotion* to vice president⟩ — see ADVANCEMENT 1

prompt *adj* **1** done, carried out, or given without delay ⟨*prompt* treatment of snakebites is always advisable⟩
synonyms immediate, punctual, timely
related words apt, quick, ready, willing; opportune, seasonable; early
near antonyms delinquent, latish, overdue; behind, behindhand, delayed, detained; dilatory, laggard, slow
antonyms belated, late, tardy
2 having or showing the ability to respond without delay or hesitation ⟨*prompt* to answer when called upon by the teacher⟩ — see QUICK 1

prompt *vb* **1** to be the cause of (a situation, action, or state of mind) ⟨pride *prompted* the family to refuse all offers of help⟩ — see EFFECT
2 to try to persuade (someone) through earnest appeals to follow a course of action ⟨*prompted* the reluctant performer onto the stage with loud cheers and whistles⟩ — see URGE

promptitude *n* the quality or habit of arriving on time ⟨the teacher's *promptitude* was such that you could set your watch by his morning arrival⟩
synonyms promptness, punctuality, timeliness
related words aptness, quickness, readiness, willingness; earliness
near antonyms belatedness, lateness; slowness
antonyms tardiness

promptly *adv* without delay ⟨shipped the package *promptly* so that it would arrive on time⟩ — see IMMEDIATELY

promptness *n* the quality or habit of arriving on time ⟨the *promptness* of the local bus line has always been reassuring⟩ — see PROMPTITUDE

promulgate *vb* to make known openly or publicly ⟨the encyclical that *promulgated* the church's position on artificial birth control⟩ — see ANNOUNCE

prone *adj* **1** having a tendency to be or act in a certain way ⟨he was *prone* to emotional outbursts under stress⟩
synonyms apt, given, inclined, tending
related words choosing, preferring; disposed, likely, predisposed, willing

near antonyms averse, disinclined, indisposed, loath (*or* loth), unwilling

2 lying with the face downwards ⟨stretched out *prone* on the bed for a backrub⟩

synonyms prostrate

related words flat, recumbent; reclining, reposing; horizontal

near antonyms erect, raised, standing, upright, upstanding, vertical

antonyms supine

proneness *n* an established pattern of behavior ⟨the child's unfortunate *proneness* to infection⟩ — see TENDENCY 1

pronounced *adj* **1** likely to attract attention ⟨a *pronounced* tendency to slurp her soup⟩ — see NOTICEABLE

2 very noticeable especially for being incorrect or bad ⟨walking with a *pronounced* limp⟩ — see EGREGIOUS

pronto *adv* **1** with great speed ⟨you'd better finish that assignment *pronto* or it'll be too late⟩ — see FAST 1

2 without delay ⟨the kind of boss who wants everything *pronto*⟩ — see IMMEDIATELY

proof *n* something presented in support of the truth or accuracy of a claim ⟨she presented *proof* that she had not cheated⟩

synonyms attestation, confirmation, corroboration, documentation, evidence, substantiation, testament, testimony, validation, witness

related words (the) goods; certificate, document, exhibit; demonstration, illustration; authentication, identification, manifestation, verification

near antonyms rebuttal, refutation; accusation, allegation, charge; assumption, conjecture, guess, presumption, surmise, suspicion

antonyms disproof

prop (up) *vb* **1** to hold up or serve as a foundation for ⟨these beams are *propping up* the entire roof⟩ — see SUPPORT 3

2 to provide (someone) with what is useful or necessary to achieve an end ⟨invariably his strong religious faith *props* him *up* in times of crisis⟩ — see HELP 1

propagate *vb* **1** to bring forth offspring ⟨an apple tree can *propagate* by grafting⟩ — see PROCREATE

2 to cause to be known over a considerable area or by many people ⟨the various ways in which churches can *propagate* the faith⟩ — see SPREAD 1

propel *vb* **1** to apply force to (someone or something) so that it moves in front of one ⟨playfully he *propelled* his rambunctious friend into the swimming pool to cool off⟩ — see PUSH 1

2 to cause to function ⟨the use of steam to *propel* ships⟩ — see ACTIVATE

3 to set or keep in motion ⟨a bicycle is *propelled* by pedals⟩ — see MOVE 2

propensity *n* **1** an established pattern of behavior ⟨the criminal *propensities* of the family extended over several generations⟩ — see TENDENCY 1

2 a habitual attraction to some activity or thing ⟨a neighbor who has an unfortunate *propensity* for snooping⟩ — see INCLINATION 1

proper *adj* **1** following the established traditions of refined society and good taste ⟨the formal ball called for *proper* attire—tuxedos and full-length gowns only⟩

synonyms correct, decent, decorous, genteel, nice, polite, respectable, seemly

related words acceptable, adequate, satisfactory, tolerable; dress, dressy, formal; dignified, elegant, gracious; priggish, prim, stuffy; apt, material, relevant; compati-

ble, congenial, harmonious; allowed, authorized, kosher, permitted

near antonyms intolerable, unacceptable, unsatisfactory; casual, grungy, informal; seedy, shabby, tacky; banned, barred, disallowed; forbidden, interdicted, outlawed, prohibited, proscribed; awkward, gauche, ungraceful

antonyms improper, incorrect, indecent, indecorous, unbecoming, unseemly

2 being in agreement with the truth or a fact or a standard ⟨there is really more than one *proper* way to pronounce that word in English⟩ — see CORRECT 1

3 marked by or showing careful attention to set forms and details ⟨we had nodded and said hello to one another but had never had a *proper* introduction⟩ — see CEREMONIOUS 1

4 meeting the requirements of a purpose or situation ⟨you'll need to have a *proper* diet if you want to lose weight⟩ — see FIT 1

5 serving to identify as belonging to an individual or group ⟨malaria and other diseases that are *proper* to the tropics⟩ — see CHARACTERISTIC 1

properly *adv* in a manner suitable for the occasion or purpose ⟨the scouts were *properly* dressed for a week of camping⟩

synonyms appropriately, congruously, correctly, fittingly, happily, meetly, rightly, suitably

related words well; acceptably, adequately, passably, satisfactorily, tolerably; decently, decorously

near antonyms unacceptably, unsatisfactorily; inopportunely, unfortunately, unseasonably; inaptly, irrelevantly; awkwardly, ungracefully

antonyms improperly, inappropriately, incongruously, incorrectly, unsuitably, wrongly

property *n* **1** a small piece of land that is developed or available for development ⟨bought a secluded *property* in the mountains⟩ — see LOT 1

2 something that sets apart an individual from others of the same kind ⟨the ability to be magnetized is a common *property* of metals⟩ — see CHARACTERISTIC

prophecy *n* a declaration that something will happen in the future ⟨a *prophecy* of doom for the adventurers⟩ — see PREDICTION

prophesier *n* one who predicts future events or developments ⟨a *prophesier* of good things for the team in the coming season⟩ — see PROPHET

prophesy *vb* to tell of or describe beforehand ⟨holy men were *prophesying* the coming of a new messiah⟩ — see FORETELL

prophet *n* one who predicts future events or developments ⟨a *prophet* who swore he could see wars before they happened⟩

synonyms augur, diviner, forecaster, foreseer, foreteller, fortune-teller, futurist, prognosticator, prophesier, seer, soothsayer

related words prophetess; mystic, oracle; astrologer

prophetic *or* **prophetical** *adj* being a sign of a later course of events ⟨the breaking of the cereal bowl was a *prophetic* start to a day filled with accidents and foul-ups⟩

synonyms predictive

related words baleful, dire, foreboding, menacing, portentous, sinister, threatening; inauspicious, unpromising; oracular; revelatory, telling

near antonyms auspicious, promising, propitious, rosy

propitiate *vb* to lessen the anger or agitation of ⟨*propitiated* his parents by agreeing to dress up for the dinner guests⟩ — see PACIFY

propitiatory *adj* tending to lessen or avoid conflict or hostility ⟨sent his girlfriend flowers as a *propitiatory* gesture for a date gone sour⟩ — see PACIFIC 1

propitious *adj* 1 having qualities which inspire hope ⟨the success of the first big movie in May was a *propitious* start for the summer season of blockbusters⟩ — see HOPEFUL 1

2 pointing toward a happy outcome ⟨a *propitious* time for starting a business⟩ — see FAVORABLE 2

proponent *n* a person who actively supports or favors a cause ⟨a vocal *proponent* of the use of electric-powered cars⟩ — see EXPONENT

proportion *n* 1 a balanced, pleasing, or suitable arrangement of parts ⟨the head was drawn too large, being way out of *proportion* with the body⟩ — see HARMONY 1

2 something belonging to, due to, or contributed by an individual member of a group ⟨we all did our *proportion* of the work⟩ — see SHARE 1

3 the relationship in quantity, amount, or size between two or more things ⟨the *proportion* of length to width for those screens was usually three to two⟩ — see RATIO

4 the total amount of measurable space or surface occupied by something ⟨the exact *proportions* of the room were critical⟩ — see ¹SIZE

proportional *adj* corresponding in size, amount, extent, or degree ⟨each child receives an allowance *proportional* to his or her age and needs⟩

synonyms commensurate, proportionate

related words balanced, symmetrical; correlative, reciprocal; contingent, dependent, relative; akin, comparable, similar

phrases in proportion

near antonyms asymmetrical (*or* asymmetric), distorted, irregular, lopsided, nonsymmetrical, twisted, unsymmetrical; unbalanced

antonyms disproportionate

proportionate *adj* corresponding in size, amount, extent, or degree ⟨financial returns *proportionate* to your efforts⟩ — see PROPORTIONAL

proposal *n* something which is presented for consideration ⟨the city council is accepting *proposals* for ways to use that land⟩

synonyms offer, proffer, proposition, suggestion

related words feeler, overture; motion; advancement, nomination, recommendation; presentation, submission, tender; arrangement, game, ground plan, layout, line, plan, plot, project, strategy, system; conception, idea, notion, thought

propose *vb* 1 to set before the mind for consideration ⟨he *proposed* that we go for a walk this afternoon⟩

synonyms advance, offer, pose, proffer, propound, suggest, vote

related words move; nominate, recommend; present, submit, tender; file, lay, lodge; arrange, calculate, chart, contrive, cover, frame, map, plan, plot, shape

phrases put forward

2 to have in mind as a purpose or goal ⟨we *propose* to buy a new house within the next year⟩ — see INTEND

proposition *n* 1 an idea that is the starting point for making a case or conducting an investigation ⟨started the discussion with the simple *proposition* that no one ever does anything out of pure altruism⟩ — see THEORY

2 something which is presented for consideration ⟨a neighbor with a business *proposition* to tell us about⟩ — see PROPOSAL

propound *vb* to set before the mind for consideration ⟨let us *propound* the question whether mercy killing should ever be an option⟩ — see PROPOSE 1

proprieties *n pl* personal conduct or behavior as evaluated by an accepted standard of appropriateness for a social or professional setting ⟨observed all of the appropriate *proprieties* for a formal dance⟩ — see MANNER 1

proprietor *n* one who has a legal or rightful claim to ownership ⟨I am the sole *proprietor* of my car⟩

synonyms holder, owner, possessor

related words homeowner, landowner

near antonyms squatter; lessee, renter, tenant

propriety *n* socially acceptable behavior ⟨some people miss the straitlaced *propriety* that was largely abandoned in the 1960s⟩ — see DECENCY 1

prorate *vb* to give out (something) in appropriate amounts or to appropriate individuals ⟨shares in the company's profits were *prorated* according to the workers' length of service⟩ — see ADMINISTER 1

prosaic *adj* 1 being of the type that is encountered in the normal course of events ⟨my job at the TV station dealt with the much more *prosaic* business of cleaning the floors⟩ — see ORDINARY 1

2 having to do with the practical details of regular life ⟨*prosaic* advice on how to remove common stains from clothing⟩ — see MUNDANE 1

proscribe *vb* to order not to do or use or to be done or used ⟨regulations *proscribe* the use of electronic devices on board a plane while it is landing⟩ — see FORBID

proscribed *adj* that may not be permitted ⟨the following is a list of *proscribed* actions during the field trip⟩ — see IMPERMISSIBLE

proscribing *n* the act of ordering that something not be done or used ⟨the *proscribing* of the use of alcohol was to be expected⟩ — see PROHIBITION 1

proscription *n* 1 the act of ordering that something not be done or used ⟨the *proscription* of the use of skateboards on the sidewalks outraged the local teenagers⟩ — see PROHIBITION 1

2 an order that something not be done or used ⟨a strongly worded *proscription* against smoking indoors⟩ — see PROHIBITION 2

proselyte *n* a person who has recently been persuaded to join a religious sect ⟨an adult *proselyte* who had only recently been baptized⟩ — see CONVERT 1

proselytize *vb* to persuade to change to one's religious faith ⟨the efforts of early missionaries to *proselytize* the Native Americans of Minnesota were largely unproductive⟩ — see CONVERT 1

prospect *n* 1 all that can be seen from a certain point ⟨gazing at the wide *prospect* spread out before me⟩ — see VIEW 1

2 one who seeks an office, honor, position, or award ⟨a good *prospect* for the position of auditor⟩ — see CANDIDATE

prospect *vb* to go into or range over for purposes of discovery ⟨*prospecting* the mountain streams for gold⟩ — see EXPLORE 2

prosper *vb* 1 to grow vigorously ⟨the plants seem to be *prospering* on the new fertilizers⟩ — see THRIVE 1

2 to reach a desired level of accomplishment ⟨began to *prosper* after years of crushing setbacks⟩ — see SUCCEED 2

prospering *adj* marked by vigorous growth and well-being especially economically ⟨selling a whole range of new products to the *prospering* middle class⟩ — see PROSPEROUS 1

prosperous *adj* 1 marked by vigorous growth and well-being especially economically ⟨a *prosperous* business that will soon be expanding⟩
synonyms booming, flourishing, golden, palmy, prospering, roaring, successful, thriving
related words affluent, moneyed (*or* monied), opulent, rich, substantial, wealthy, well-heeled, well-off, well-to-do; comfortable
near antonyms declining, dying, failing, floundering, languishing, struggling; bankrupt, bankrupted, insolvent
antonyms unsuccessful
2 having attained a desired end or state of good fortune ⟨one of the most *prosperous* families in the community⟩ — see SUCCESSFUL 1
3 growing thickly and vigorously ⟨at the nursery look for plants with green and *prosperous* leaves⟩ — see RANK 1

prostitute *n* a woman who engages in sexual activities for money ⟨the town was horrified to discover that she had once been a *prostitute*⟩
synonyms harlot, whore
related words coquette, flirt, libertine, siren, tempter, temptress, wench

prostitute *vb* 1 to lower in character or dignity ⟨*prostituting* himself by writing pulp novels for money⟩ — see DEBASE 1
2 to put to a bad or improper use ⟨urged not to *prostitute* her musical talents by writing jingles for TV commercials⟩ — see MISAPPLY

prostitution *n* the practice of engaging in sexual activities for money ⟨*prostitution* is illegal in most states⟩
synonyms harlotry

prostrate *adj* 1 depleted in strength, energy, or freshness ⟨*prostrate* marathoners typically spend the day after the race recovering⟩ — see WEARY 1
2 lacking bodily strength ⟨*prostrate* with fear⟩ — see WEAK 1
3 lying with the face downwards ⟨a runner fell *prostrate* at the finish line⟩ — see PRONE 2

prostrate *vb* 1 to diminish the physical strength of ⟨an athlete *prostrated* for weeks by a bout of pneumonia⟩ — see WEAKEN 1
2 to render powerless, ineffective, or unable to move ⟨the huge increase in gas prices really *prostrated* the economy⟩ — see PARALYZE
3 to subject to incapacitating emotional or mental stress ⟨a widow *prostrated* by grief⟩ — see OVERWHELM 1

prostrated *adj* lacking bodily strength ⟨patients should expect to feel very *prostrated* after the surgery⟩ — see WEAK 1

prostration *n* a complete depletion of energy or strength ⟨experiencing *prostration* after the intense workout⟩ — see FATIGUE

protean *adj* able to do many different kinds of things ⟨a *protean* actor who is equally comfortable with light comedy and serious drama⟩ — see VERSATILE

protect *vb* to drive danger or attack away from ⟨the mother bear was just trying to *protect* her cubs⟩ — see DEFEND 1

protection *n* 1 means or method of defending ⟨this small umbrella is adequate *protection* in a sudden shower⟩ — see DEFENSE 1
2 someone that protects ⟨he was her *protection* from bullies on the playground⟩ — see PROTECTOR

3 the state of not being exposed to danger ⟨the open boat offered no *protection* from the weather⟩ — see SAFETY 1

protective *adj* intended to resist or prevent attack or aggression ⟨we took *protective* measures in case the animals attacked⟩ — see DEFENSIVE

protector *n* someone that protects ⟨a bigger girl served as her *protector* against bullies at school⟩
synonyms custodian, defender, guard, protection
related words bodyguard, champion; keeper, lookout, sentinel, sentry, warden, warder, watch, watchdog, watchman; conserver, keeper, preserver, saver

protest *n* a feeling or declaration of disapproval or dissent ⟨submitted an official *protest* about her treatment⟩ — see OBJECTION

protest *vb* 1 to state as a fact usually forcefully ⟨he *protested* that he usually was very good at baseball, and all the strikeouts were just bad luck⟩ — see CLAIM 1
2 to present an opposing opinion or argument ⟨*protest* against a judge's ruling⟩ — see OBJECT

protestation *n* a solemn and often public declaring of the truth or existence of something ⟨the governor went on television to make a passionate *protestation* of his innocence in the bribery scandal⟩
synonyms affirmation, assertion, avouchment, avowal, claim, declaration, insistence, profession
related words announcement, proclamation, pronouncement; argument, justification, rationalization, reason; confirmation, vindication
near antonyms disclaimer; challenge, dispute, question; confutation, disproof, rebuttal, refutation; contradiction, denial, negation
antonyms disavowal

prototype *n* something from which copies are made ⟨the manufacturer exhaustively tested the *prototype* of the vehicle before approving production⟩ — see ORIGINAL

protract *vb* to make longer ⟨a *protracted* lawsuit against the corporation⟩ — see EXTEND 1

protrude *vb* to extend outward beyond a usual point ⟨we spotted the kitten's tail *protruding* from beneath the dresser⟩ — see BULGE

protrusion *n* a part that sticks out from the general mass of something ⟨the bizarrely shaped *protrusions* of a coral reef⟩ — see BULGE

protuberance *n* a part that sticks out from the general mass of something ⟨rounded *protuberances* marring the surface of the paint where the wall wasn't completely smooth⟩ — see BULGE

proud *adj* 1 having or displaying feelings of scorn for what is regarded as beneath oneself ⟨the unemployed woman was too *proud* to take a job as a maid⟩
synonyms disdainful, haughty, highfalutin, lofty, lordly, prideful, superior
related words complacent, conceited, egoistic, egotistic (*or* egotistical), important, self-assertive, self-conceited, self-important, self-satisfied, smug, uppity, vain, vainglorious; arrogant, pretentious, snobbish, stuck-up, supercilious; cavalier, overbearing, overweening, peremptory, swaggering; high-sounding, pompous; condescending, patronizing; cocky, overconfident, presumptuous; bloated, boastful, bombastic; audacious, bold, brash, brassy, cheeky, cocksure, forward, impertinent, impudent, saucy; confident, presuming, self-assured, self-confident, sure; domineering, high-handed, imperious; self-centered, selfish; dominating, magisterial, masterful
near antonyms demure, homely, meek, unassuming, unpretentious; bashful, retiring, shy, timid; diffident,

self-doubting; acquiescent, compliant, deferential, resigned, submissive, unassertive, yielding; apologetic, cowering, cringing, shrinking; passive, quiet, reserved, subdued, unobtrusive

antonyms humble, lowly, modest

2 having too high an opinion of oneself ⟨a *proud* cheerleader who thought she should be treated like royalty⟩ — see CONCEITED

3 large and impressive in size, grandeur, extent, or conception ⟨*proud* old castles⟩ — see GRAND 1

provable *adj* capable of being proven as true or real ⟨his guilt was easily *provable* with all of the evidence that the police had gathered⟩ — see VERIFIABLE

prove *vb* **1** to show the existence or truth of by evidence ⟨the prosecutor used DNA evidence to *prove* the defendant's guilt⟩

synonyms demonstrate, document, establish, substantiate, validate

related words back (up), buttress, corroborate; evidence, evince, record, support, witness; adduce, attest, authenticate, certify, identify; confirm, sustain, verify; clinch, nail, settle; depose, testify

near antonyms challenge, dispute, object; allege, assume, conjecture, guess, presume, surmise, suspect

antonyms disprove, rebut, refute

2 to come to be ⟨the new automobile engine design *proved* impractical⟩ — see COME OUT 1

3 to gain full recognition or acceptance of ⟨*proved* herself a great actress on the Broadway stage⟩ — see ESTABLISH 1

provender *n* substances intended to be eaten ⟨for two centuries wayfarers have stopped at the inn for shelter and *provender*⟩ — see FOOD

proverb *n* an often stated observation regarding something from common experience ⟨her grandfather has a *proverb* for every occasion⟩ — see SAYING

provide *vb* **1** to put (something) into the possession of someone for use or consumption ⟨this luxury hotel *provides* all the comforts of home to well-heeled vacationers⟩ — see FURNISH 2

provide (for) *vb* to pay the living expenses of ⟨sufficient income to *provide for* a large family⟩ — see SUPPORT 2

providence *n* **1** careful management of material resources ⟨practicing its customary *providence*, the snowbound family was able to make the meager stores last until help arrived⟩ — see ECONOMY

2 concern or preparation for the future ⟨had the *providence* to lay in supplies before the storm hit⟩ — see FORESIGHT 2

3 *cap* the being worshipped as the creator and ruler of the universe ⟨she trusted in *Providence* to see her through the crisis⟩ — see DEITY 2

provident *adj* **1** careful in the management of money or resources ⟨it is possible to be *provident* without being miserly⟩ — see FRUGAL

2 having or showing awareness of and preparation for the future ⟨her *provident* measures kept us safe while we waited out the hurricane⟩ — see FORESIGHTED

providential *adj* coming or happening by good luck especially unexpectedly ⟨winning the lottery could not have come at a more *providential* time for the recently laid-off worker⟩ — see FORTUNATE 1

province *n* a region of activity, knowledge, or influence ⟨a legal question outside the doctor's *province*⟩ — see FIELD 2

provincial *adj* not broad or open in views or opinions ⟨some people regard a fear of new things as an unmistakable sign of a *provincial* attitude⟩ — see NARROW 2

provincial *n* an awkward or simple person especially from a small town or the country ⟨the confidence man figured that fleecing these *provincials* would be easy⟩ — see HICK

provision *n* **1** something upon which the carrying out of an agreement or offer depends ⟨loaned them the car with the *provision* that they refill the gas tank before returning it⟩ — see CONDITION 2

2 *provisions pl* substances intended to be eaten ⟨gave them ample *provisions* so they would not get hungry on the trip⟩ — see FOOD

provision *vb* to provide food or meals for ⟨hunting trips to help *provision* the settlers for the winter ahead⟩ — see FEED 1

provisional *adj* intended to last, continue, or serve for a limited time ⟨formed a *provisional* government until a new leader could be elected⟩ — see TEMPORARY 1

proviso *n* something upon which the carrying out of an agreement or offer depends ⟨released the drunken revelers with the *proviso* that they behave⟩ — see CONDITION 2

provocation *n* **1** something that arouses a strong response from another ⟨Dad only gets angry from the greatest of *provocations*⟩

synonyms excitement, incitement, instigation, stimulant, stimulation, stimulus

related words encouragement, goad, incentive, inducement, jog, prod, spur; induction, inspiration, motivation; aggravation, annoyance, bother, exasperation, frustration, hassle, headache, irritant, nuisance, peeve, pest

near antonyms subduing

2 something that arouses action or activity ⟨ready to retaliate at the slightest *provocation*⟩ — see IMPULSE

provocative *adj* serving or likely to arouse a strong reaction ⟨a *provocative* editorial that sparked a heated discussion⟩

synonyms exciting, inciting, instigating, piquing, provoking, stimulating

related words explosive, fiery, incendiary, inflammatory, triggering; inducing, inspirational, inspiring, motivating; jeering, taunting, teasing; activating, energizing, galvanizing, quickening, vitalizing; angering, enraging, maddening, upsetting; aggravating, annoying, bothersome, exasperating, galling, irksome, irritating, pesky, vexatious, vexing

near antonyms subduing

provoke *vb* **1** to rouse to strong feeling or action ⟨his teasing finally *provoked* her to anger⟩ ⟨a strong chilling breeze *provoked* the picnickers to move inside⟩

synonyms arouse, encourage, excite, fire (up), incite, instigate, move, pique, stimulate, stir

related words fan, inflame, kindle, trigger; activate, energize, galvanize, induce, inspire, motivate, quicken, vitalize; abet, ferment, foment, raise, whip (up); anger, enrage, madden, upset; jeer, taunt, tease; aggravate, annoy, bother, exasperate, gall, get, irritate, vex

near antonyms calm, soothe, subdue, tranquilize (*also* tranquillize)

2 to cause or encourage the development of ⟨comments that are sure to *provoke* an argument⟩ — see INCITE 1

provoking *adj* serving or likely to arouse a strong reaction ⟨the host's *provoking* opinions are what get people to listen to his radio talk show⟩ — see PROVOCATIVE

proximity *n* the state or condition of being near ⟨the *proximity* of the curtains to the fireplace was a cause of concern to the safety inspector⟩

synonyms closeness, contiguity, immediacy, nearness
related words abutment, juxtaposition
antonyms distance, remoteness

proxy *n* a person who acts or does business for another ⟨sent a *proxy* to the meeting to cast his vote for him⟩ — see AGENT 2

prude *n* a person who is greatly concerned with seemly behavior and morality especially regarding sexual matters ⟨it's not true that only a *prude* would object to being pressured for physical intimacy⟩
synonyms moralist, puritan
related words goody-goody; fuddy-duddy, old maid, prig, spoilsport
near antonyms libertarian, libertine

prudence *n* the ability to make intelligent decisions especially in everyday matters ⟨in the long run, *prudence* will pay off more often than taking wild risks⟩ — see COMMON SENSE

prudent *adj* **1** having or showing good judgment and restraint especially in conduct or speech ⟨her calm response was very *prudent* under the circumstances⟩ — see DISCREET
2 suitable for bringing about a desired result under the circumstances ⟨it wouldn't be *prudent* to ask for a raise while the company is having financial troubles⟩ — see EXPEDIENT

prudery *n* a tendency to care a great deal about seemly behavior and morals especially in sexual matters ⟨such *prudery* regarding artistic depictions of the nude has no place on a college campus⟩
synonyms prudishness, puritanism
related words priggishness, primness; morality, virtue
near antonyms libertarianism

prudish *adj* given to or marked by very conservative standards regarding personal behavior or morals ⟨by the *prudish* standards of the 19th century, any depiction of the nude was scandalous⟩ — see STRAITLACED

prudishness *n* a tendency to care a great deal about seemly behavior and morals especially in sexual matters ⟨the *prudishness* of the people of the Victorian era was a hindrance to the dissemination of some basic information on human health and hygiene⟩ — see PRUDERY

prune *vb* to make (as hair) shorter with or as if with the use of shears ⟨*pruned* the dead branches from the old apple tree⟩ — see CLIP

¹pry *vb* **1** to raise, move, or pull apart with or as if with a lever ⟨it took some effort to *pry* up the trap door⟩
synonyms jimmy, lever, prize
related words elevate, hoist, lift, uplift; break, break up, detach, disengage, disjoin, divide, part, pull, separate; shift
near antonyms connect, join
2 to draw out by force or with effort ⟨*prying* the toys from the clutches of my sleeping brother⟩ — see EXTRACT

²pry *vb* to interest oneself in what is not one's concern ⟨don't go *prying* into other people's business⟩ — see INTERFERE

prying *adj* **1** interested in what is not one's own business ⟨as we moved into our new home, we could sense that there were *prying* eyes watching us⟩ — see CURIOUS 1
2 thrusting oneself where one is not welcome or invited ⟨*prying* neighbors who refuse to mind their own business⟩ — see INTRUSIVE

psalm *n* a religious song ⟨after the sermon we sang a brief *psalm*⟩ — see HYMN

psalmody *n* a book of hymns ⟨a *psalmody* containing many beloved hymns⟩ — see HYMNAL

pseudo *adj* lacking in natural or spontaneous quality ⟨the *pseudo* friendliness of a salesperson trying to sell you something⟩ — see ARTIFICIAL 1

pseudonym *n* a fictitious or assumed name ⟨the most notorious serial killer of the 19th century remains known only by the *pseudonym* of Jack the Ripper⟩
synonyms alias
related words nom de plume, pen name; appellation, designation; misnomer; epithet, nickname, sobriquet (*also* soubriquet)

pshaw *interj* how surprising, doubtful, or unbelievable ⟨*pshaw*! anyone else could have done that job in half the time that it took her⟩ — see NO

psyche *n* an immaterial force within a human being thought to give the body life, energy, and power ⟨a biography that attempts to understand the *psyche* of this brilliant but troubled artist⟩ — see SOUL 1

psychological *also* **psychologic** *adj* of or relating to the mind ⟨suffered from *psychological* disorders all of his life⟩ — see MENTAL 1

psychopath *n* a person judged to be legally or medically insane ⟨declared that he was a dangerous *psychopath* who needed to be locked up⟩ — see LUNATIC 1

psychotic *n* a person judged to be legally or medically insane ⟨the *psychotic* seemed to have difficulty distinguishing reality from fantasy⟩ — see LUNATIC 1

pub *n* a place of business where alcoholic beverages are sold to be consumed on the premises ⟨coworkers enjoying the convivial atmosphere of the Irish *pub*⟩ — see BARROOM

public *adj* **1** not known by only a select few ⟨it was *public* knowledge that they were expecting a baby⟩
synonyms open
related words general, popular, unclassified, wellknown; advertised, aired, announced, broadcast, declared, disclosed, divulged, heralded, posted, proclaimed, promulgated, publicized, published, spotlighted; current, prevalent, rife, widespread; communal, shared; reported, reputed, rumored
near antonyms classified; unadvertised, unannounced, undisclosed; clandestine, collusive, conspiratorial, covert; surreptitious, undercover, underhand, underhanded; intimate, personal; concealed, repressed, reserved, silenced, stifled, suppressed, withheld; recanted, retracted, revoked
antonyms confidential, private, privy, secret
2 freely available for use or participation by all ⟨a *public* swimming pool⟩ — see OPEN 2
3 of or relating to a nation ⟨a trade agreement in the *public* interest⟩ — see NATIONAL
4 held by or applicable to a majority of the people ⟨*public* sentiment was against the war⟩ — see GENERAL 3
5 used or done by a number of people as a group ⟨*public* transportation⟩ — see COLLECTIVE

public *n* human beings in general ⟨a lecture open to the *public*⟩ — see PEOPLE 1

public house *n* **1** a place that provides rooms and usually a public dining room for overnight guests ⟨took lodging at a cheap *public house* in a seedy part of town⟩ — see HOTEL
2 *chiefly British* a place of business where alcoholic beverages are sold to be consumed on the premises ⟨visited a *public house* in London that has been welcoming customers since the time of Charles Dickens⟩ — see BARROOM

publicity *n* newsworthy information released to the media that is designed to gain public attention or support for a person, business, or cause ⟨an endless flow of *publicity* for our charity event resulted in a great turnout⟩

synonyms ballyhoo

related words ad, advertisement, commercial, message, plug, promotion, spot, word; banner, bill, billboard, placard, poster, sign; advertising, marketing, propaganda; pronouncement, publication, release; broadcast, bulletin, dispatch, newscast, report, story; testimonial, write-up

publicize *vb* **1** to provide publicity for ⟨the movie studios widely *publicized* their summer blockbusters⟩

synonyms ballyhoo, plug, promote, tout

related words advertise; push; acclaim, hail, laud, praise; recommend, review; announce, broadcast, publish

2 to make known openly or publicly ⟨the city hasn't done a good job of *publicizing* the new regulations in its recycling operation⟩ — see ANNOUNCE

public servant *n* **1** a person who holds a public office ⟨the new governor vowed that he would always remember why he was called a *public servant* and not the people's master⟩ — see OFFICIAL

2 a worker in a government agency ⟨concerned that the new federal agency would just add another slew of *public servants* to the government payroll⟩ — see BUREAUCRAT

publish *vb* **1** to produce and release for distribution in printed form ⟨our local animal shelter *publishes* a newsletter⟩

synonyms get out, issue, print

related words serialize; contribute, edit, syndicate; manufacture, produce; distribute, market

near antonyms censor, suppress

2 to make known openly or publicly ⟨will *publish* the exam scores as soon as they are available⟩ — see ANNOUNCE

puck *n* an imaginary being usually having a small human form and magical powers ⟨dreamed that her garden was the secret meeting place of *pucks* and sprites⟩ — see FAIRY

puddle *n* a small often deep body of water ⟨splashing in the shallow *puddles* on the way home from the bus stop⟩ — see ¹POOL

pudginess *n* the condition of having an excess of body fat ⟨started to notice a little *pudginess* around his middle⟩ — see CORPULENCE

pudgy *adj* having an excess of body fat ⟨at this point the *pudgy* toddler is still cute, but she will have health problems if she continues to be overweight⟩ — see FAT 1

puerile *adj* **1** having or showing the annoying qualities (as silliness) associated with children ⟨told him that such *puerile* behavior would not be tolerated during the ceremony⟩ — see CHILDISH

2 lacking in adult experience or maturity ⟨allowed the company to be taken over by a bunch of *puerile* whippersnappers fresh out of business school⟩ — see CALLOW

3 lacking in seriousness or maturity ⟨the kind of *puerile* jokes that teenage moviegoers apparently love⟩ — see GIDDY 1

puff *n* a slight or gentle movement of air ⟨felt a *puff* of wind on his face⟩ — see BREEZE 1

puff *vb* to breathe hard, quickly, or with difficulty ⟨he came running up the stairs *puffing* and wheezing⟩ — see GASP

pugilist *n* one that engages in the sport of fighting with the fists ⟨a *pugilist* with the trademark of the boxing ring: a nose that showed signs of having been broken on more than one occasion⟩ — see BOXER

pugnacious *adj* feeling or displaying eagerness to fight ⟨I was already feeling *pugnacious,* and his nasty remarks just made me feel like fighting even more⟩ — see BELLIGERENT

pugnacity *n* an inclination to fight or quarrel ⟨the coach felt that the boy would be better off if his natural *pugnacity* were channeled toward sports⟩ — see BELLIGERENCE

puissance *n* the ability to exert effort for the accomplishment of a task ⟨the president pledged to put the full *puissance* of the nation into the war effort⟩ — see POWER 2

puissant *adj* having great power or influence ⟨one of the nation's most respected and *puissant* advocates for the rights of minorities⟩ — see IMPORTANT 2

pule *vb* to utter feeble plaintive cries ⟨a distressed baby *puling* for its mother⟩ — see WHIMPER

pull *n* **1** the act or an instance of applying force on something so that it moves in the direction of the force ⟨I gave the door such a *pull* that when it suddenly opened, I nearly fell backwards⟩

synonyms draw, haul, jerk, pluck, tug, wrench, yank

related words drag, tow; hitch, jerk, twitch; grab, snatch

near antonyms heave, shove, thrust

antonyms push

2 the power to direct the thinking or behavior of others usually indirectly ⟨the lawyer supposedly has a lot of *pull* with the administration in Washington⟩ — see INFLUENCE 1

pull *vb* **1** to cause to follow by applying steady force on ⟨a team of horses *pulling* a heavy wagon⟩

synonyms drag, draw, hale, haul, lug, tow, tug

related words attract; jerk, yank; carry, convey, ferry, move, transport

near antonyms shove, thrust

antonyms drive, propel, push

2 to draw out by force or with effort ⟨the dentist had to struggle to *pull* the tooth⟩ — see EXTRACT

3 to injure by overuse, misuse, or pressure ⟨lift the crate carefully, or you'll *pull* a muscle⟩ — see STRAIN 1

pull (out) *vb* to leave a place often for another ⟨the party's been fun, but it's time to *pull out*⟩ — see GO 2

pulp *vb* to cause to become a pulpy mass ⟨*pulped* three oranges to get their juice⟩ — see CRUSH 1

pulpiness *n* the quality or state of being full of juice ⟨select ripe peaches of sufficient *pulpiness* to readily yield the amount of juice required by the recipe⟩ — see SUCCULENCE

pulpy *adj* **1** full of juice ⟨good, ripe peaches will be *pulpy* and not mealy⟩ — see JUICY

2 giving easily to the touch ⟨the *pulpy* flesh of ripe fruit⟩ — see SOFT 3

pulsate *vb* to expand and contract in a rhythmic manner ⟨the heart muscle *pulsates* regularly to pump blood⟩

synonyms beat, palpitate, pit-a-pat, pitter-patter, pulse, throb

related words fluctuate, oscillate, vibrate; quiver, tremble

pulsation *n* a rhythmic expanding and contracting ⟨you should press against the artery in your wrist and count the *pulsations* to calculate your heart rate⟩
synonyms beat, palpitation, pulse, throb
related words fluctuation, oscillation, vibration; quiver, tremble, tremor

pulse *n* a rhythmic expanding and contracting ⟨when he was at rest, the patient's heart rate was showing 70 *pulses* a minute⟩ — see PULSATION

pulse *vb* to expand and contract in a rhythmic manner ⟨blood vessels *pulsing* in time with the heartbeat⟩ — see PULSATE

pulverize *vb* **1** to bring to a complete end the physical soundness, existence, or usefulness of ⟨buildings *pulverized* by a killer tornado⟩ — see DESTROY 1
2 to reduce to fine particles ⟨*pulverize* the cement into dust for reuse⟩ — see POWDER

puma *n* a large tawny cat of the wild ⟨adult *pumas* can weigh as much as 220 pounds or more⟩ — see COUGAR

pummel *vb* to strike repeatedly ⟨*pummeled* the mugger with her fists until help arrived⟩ — see BEAT 1

pump *vb* **1** to make short up-and-down movements ⟨the knees of the bicyclists were *pumping* furiously as they neared the finish line⟩ — see NOD
2 to put a series of questions to ⟨prying neighbors *pumped* the guileless child for information about the family's new pool⟩ — see EXAMINE 1
3 to remove (liquid) gradually or completely ⟨*pumped* water from the well⟩ — see DRAIN 1

¹punch *n* **1** the quality of an utterance that provokes interest and produces an effect ⟨the real *punch* of the speech came in its closing lines⟩
synonyms cogency, effectiveness, force, forcefulness, impact, point
related words payoff; importance, significance; appeal, attraction, charm, fascination
2 active strength of body or mind ⟨we're going to need a candidate with real *punch* if voters are ever going to get excited about this election⟩ — see VIGOR 1
3 a hard strike with a part of the body or an instrument ⟨the poor boxer wasn't able to land a single *punch* on his opponent⟩ — see ¹BLOW

²punch *n* a mark or small hole made by a pointed instrument ⟨old computers used to get information by reading the *punches* on a series of cards⟩ — see PRICK 1

punch *vb* **1** to deliver a blow to (someone or something) usually in a strong vigorous manner ⟨his mother told him to stop *punching* his little brother⟩ — see HIT 1
2 to make a hole or series of holes in ⟨*punch* a ticket⟩ — see PERFORATE
3 to urge, push, or force onward ⟨cowboys *punching* cattle⟩ — see DRIVE 1

puncheon *n* an enclosed wooden vessel for holding beverages ⟨stored the *puncheons* of rum in the cellar⟩ — see CASK

punctual *adj* done, carried out, or given without delay ⟨the *punctual* delivery of the daily mail⟩ — see PROMPT 1

punctuality *n* the quality or habit of arriving on time ⟨the teacher appreciates *punctuality* in her students⟩ — see PROMPTITUDE

puncture *n* a mark or small hole made by a pointed instrument ⟨a leak caused by several small *punctures* in the rubber gasket⟩ — see PRICK 1

puncture *vb* **1** to make a hole or series of holes in ⟨a nail *punctured* the tire⟩ — see PERFORATE

2 to penetrate or hold (something) with a pointed object ⟨I could never *puncture* my own skin with a hypodermic needle⟩ — see IMPALE

pungency *n* **1** a harsh or sharp quality ⟨that salad dressing needs the *pungency* of vinegar⟩ — see EDGE 1
2 the quality or state of being stimulating to the mind or senses ⟨theatergoers have long delighted in the *pungency* of the play's dialogue⟩ — see PIQUANCY

pungent *adj* **1** having a powerfully stimulating odor or flavor ⟨a *pungent* chili⟩ — see SHARP 3
2 marked by the use of wit that is intended to cause hurt feelings ⟨a *pungent* put-down that she will not soon forget⟩ — see SARCASTIC
3 sharp and pleasantly stimulating to the mind or senses ⟨a newspaper columnist known for his *pungent* observations on everyday life⟩ — see PIQUANT

puniness *n* the quality or state of being little in size ⟨she remarked on the *puniness* of the samples that the bakery was handing out⟩ — see SMALLNESS

punish *vb* to inflict a penalty on for a fault or crime ⟨the child was *punished* for breaking dishes on purpose⟩ ⟨if caught, the thief will be severely *punished*⟩
synonyms castigate, chasten, chastise, correct, discipline, penalize
related words assess, charge, dock, fine, impose, levy, mulct; convict, sentence; condemn, damn, denounce; criticize, reprove; wreak
near antonyms forfeit; get off, ransom, release; commute, reprieve; absolve, acquit, exculpate, exonerate, vindicate
antonyms excuse, pardon, spare

punisher *n* one who inflicts punishment in return for an injury or offense ⟨a father who regrets the fact that he always ends up being the household's disciplinarian and resident *punisher*⟩ — see NEMESIS 1

punishment *n* suffering, loss, or hardship imposed in response to a crime or offense ⟨the child's *punishment* was confiscation of his toys for a day⟩
synonyms castigation, chastisement, correction, desert, discipline, nemesis, penalty, wrath
related words reprisal, retaliation, retribution, revenge, vengeance; assessment, charge, fine, mulct; example, sentence; confinement, imprisonment, incarceration; condemnation, damnation, denouncement; criticism, reproof
near antonyms amnesty, indemnity, pardon, parole; acquittal, exculpation, exoneration, vindication; exemption, immunity, impunity; release; commutation, reprieve; absolution, forgiveness, remission, remitment; condonation, disregard, overlooking

punitive *adj* inflicting, involving, or serving as punishment ⟨any misbehavior was immediately met with a *punitive* response⟩ ⟨the company had to pay a million dollars in *punitive* damages⟩
synonyms castigating, chastening, chastising, correcting, correctional, corrective, disciplinary, disciplining, penal, penalizing
related words retaliatory, retributive, retributory, revengeful; vengeful, wrathful
near antonyms compensatory; acquitting, exculpating, exculpatory, exonerating, vindicating; absolving, condoning, pardoning, remitting; commuting, reprieving

punk *adj* **1** falling short of a standard ⟨she plays a *punk* game of tennis, so you won't have any trouble beating her⟩ — see BAD 1
2 extremely unsatisfactory ⟨the acting in the movie ranged all the way from poor to *punk*⟩ — see WRETCHED 1

3 temporarily suffering from a disorder of the body ⟨I've been feeling *punk* today⟩ — see SICK 1

punk *n* a violent, brutal person who is often a member of an organized gang ⟨warned that he'd never be anything more than a cheap *punk* if he didn't reform⟩ — see HOODLUM

puny *adj* of a size that is less than average ⟨a *puny*, wrinkled apple⟩ — see SMALL 1

pupil *n* **1** one who attends a school ⟨the teacher had twenty *pupils* in each class⟩ — see STUDENT
2 one who follows the opinions or teachings of another ⟨to *pupils* of the philosopher Henry David Thoreau, the shores of Walden Pond are hallowed ground⟩ — see FOLLOWER

puppet *n* **1** a small figure often of a human being used especially as a child's plaything ⟨gave her a *puppet* with strings for a gift⟩ — see DOLL 1
2 one that is or can be used to further the purposes of another ⟨accused the newspaper editor of being just a *puppet* for the moneyed people of the town⟩ — see PAWN 1

purchasable *adj* open to improper influence and especially bribery ⟨*purchasable* members of the state legislature whose votes could be bought⟩ — see VENAL

purchase *vb* to get possession of (something) by giving money in exchange for ⟨I need to *purchase* a new heavy coat⟩ — see BUY

pure *adj* **1** free from added matter ⟨I'm allergic to any jewelry that isn't *pure* silver⟩ ⟨the solution must be kept *pure* for the experiment to work⟩
synonyms absolute, fine, neat, plain, purified, refined, straight, unadulterated, unalloyed, undiluted, unmixed
related words clarified, filtered, refined; clean, uncontaminated, uncorrupted, undefiled, unpolluted, untainted; rendered, tried; concentrated, full-bodied, strong; uncombined
near antonyms befouled, besmirched, contaminated, corrupted, debased, defiled, fouled, polluted, soiled, spoiled, sullied, tainted; amalgamated, blended, coalesced, combined, commingled, compounded, incorporated, intermingled, intermixed, merged, mingled; conjoined, fused, joined, linked, united; cheapened, doctored, watered (down)
antonyms adulterated, alloyed, diluted, impure, mixed
2 free from any trace of the coarse or indecent ⟨the humor in the movie is as *pure* and wholesome as any parent could wish⟩ — see CHASTE
3 free from sin ⟨in one beatitude those who are *pure* in heart are promised the sight of God⟩ — see INNOCENT 1
4 having no exceptions or restrictions ⟨that story is *pure* nonsense⟩ — see ABSOLUTE 2

purebred *adj* of unmixed ancestry ⟨that horse is a *purebred* Arabian⟩
synonyms full-blooded, pedigreed, thoroughbred
related words inbred
near antonyms crossbred, crossed, hybridized, interbred, outcrossed
antonyms hybrid, mixed, mongrel

purely *adv* with purity of thought and deed ⟨the devout girl vowed to live her life *purely* and in the service of God⟩
synonyms chastely, innocently, modestly, morally, righteously, virtuously
related words decently, decorously, properly; priggishly, primly, prudishly
near antonyms indecently, obscenely, vulgarly; lasciviously, lewdly, lustfully

antonyms evilly, immorally, impurely, sinfully, wickedly

purge *vb* to free from moral guilt or blemish especially ceremonially ⟨a day on which the faithful are expected to *purge* themselves of their sins through prayer and fasting⟩ — see PURIFY 1

purification *n* the act or fact of freeing from sin or moral guilt ⟨some people must undergo a ritual *purification* after certain activities⟩
synonyms cleansing, sanctification
related words rebirth, regeneration, restoration; grace, redemption, salvation; absolution, forgiveness, remission; acquittal, clearance, clearing, exoneration, vindication; atonement, expiation
near antonyms blasphemy, defilement, desecration, profanation, violation; corruption, debasement, perversion; contamination, pollution, sullying, tarnishing

purified *adj* free from added matter ⟨*purified* water⟩ — see PURE 1

purify *vb* **1** to free from moral guilt or blemish especially ceremonially ⟨Catholics go to confession to be *purified*⟩
synonyms cleanse, purge, sanctify
related words amend, improve, refine; heal, regenerate, restore; elevate, ennoble, uplift; absolve, acquit, clear, exonerate, vindicate
near antonyms corrupt, debase, debauch, defile, degrade, demean, deprave, pervert, stain, warp; poison, profane, prostitute; sully, tarnish
2 to remove usually visible impurities from ⟨*purify* the water by distillation⟩ — see CLARIFY 1

puritan *n* a person who is greatly concerned with seemly behavior and morality especially regarding sexual matters ⟨some of the town's *puritans* maintained that sex education had no place in the schools⟩ — see PRUDE

puritanical *adj* given to or marked by very conservative standards regarding personal behavior or morals ⟨some older campers regarded the summer camp's rules regarding mixed company as rather *puritanical*⟩ — see STRAITLACED

puritanism *n* a tendency to care a great deal about seemly behavior and morals especially in sexual matters ⟨the Victorian era was often characterized by a hypocritical *puritanism*⟩ — see PRUDERY

purity *n* the quality or state of being morally pure ⟨struggling to live a life of *purity* while surrounded by wickedness⟩ — see CHASTITY

purlieus *n pl* the area around a city ⟨the peaceful *purlieus* of the suburbs⟩ — see ENVIRONS 1

purloin *vb* to take (something) without right and with an intent to keep ⟨printed a document *purloined* from their rival's offices⟩ — see STEAL 1

purloiner *n* one who steals ⟨she demanded that the pusillanimous *purloiner* of her chocolates step forward⟩ — see THIEF

purport *n* the idea that is conveyed or intended to be conveyed to the mind by language, symbol, or action ⟨was able to give the *purport* of the governor's speech in a few words⟩ — see MEANING 1

purpose *n* **1** something that one hopes or intends to accomplish ⟨the *purpose* of the research is to discover how the virus is transmitted⟩ — see GOAL
2 the action for which a person or thing is specially fitted or used or for which a thing exists ⟨still trying to discover her *purpose* in life⟩ — see ROLE

purposeful *adj* **1** fully committed to achieving a goal ⟨soft-spoken but *purposeful* criminal investigator⟩ — see DETERMINED 1

2 made, given, or done with full awareness of what one is doing ⟨there's a difference between a *purposeful* lie rather than an accidental untruth⟩ — see INTENTIONAL

purposefully *adv* with full awareness of what one is doing ⟨he *purposefully* chose the more difficult problem to try to solve⟩ — see INTENTIONALLY

purposefulness *n* firm or unwavering adherence to one's purpose ⟨approached the challenge with grim *purposefulness*⟩ — see DETERMINATION 1

purposely *adv* with full awareness of what one is doing ⟨he *purposely* stayed late at school so that he wouldn't have to ride the bus home⟩ — see INTENTIONALLY

purr *n* a monotonous sound like that of an insect in motion ⟨listened to the reassuring *purr* of the car engine⟩ — see HUM

purse *n* a container for carrying money and small personal items ⟨I left my *purse* at home, so I can't buy anything after all⟩
synonyms bag, handbag, pocketbook
related words billfold, wallet; compact, vanity; poke, pouch, sack; backpack, haversack, knapsack, rucksack

pursue *vb* **1** to go after or on the track of ⟨the policeman *pursued* the pickpocket through the crowded subway station⟩ — see FOLLOW 2
2 to go in search of ⟨urged the graduates to *pursue* happiness instead of financial success⟩ — see SEEK 1

pursuing *n* the act of going after or in the tracks of another ⟨the controversy concerning the *pursuing* of criminals in speeding vehicles along busy highways⟩ — see PURSUIT

pursuit *n* the act of going after or in the tracks of another ⟨the constant *pursuit* of the rock band by a horde of screaming fans as they roamed about the city⟩
synonyms chase, chasing, dogging, following, hounding, pursuing, shadowing, tagging, tailing, tracing, tracking, trailing
related words tagging along; path, track, trail; search, seeking

push *vb* **1** to apply force to (someone or something) so that it moves in front of one ⟨I had to *push* my damaged bike all the way home⟩
synonyms drive, propel, shove, thrust
related words impel, move; bear (down), compress, depress, jam, pressure, squash, squeeze, weigh (upon); bulldoze, compel, force, lean (on *or* against), muscle, ram
2 to force one's way ⟨*pushing* through the crowd to the window so we could see the arriving planes⟩ — see PRESS 4

pushover *n* something that is easy to do ⟨I've studied so much that this test is going to be a *pushover*⟩ — see CINCH

pusillanimous *adj* having or showing a shameful lack of courage ⟨a college graduate suffering from the *pusillanimous* fear of a future full of possibility⟩ — see COWARDLY

¹puss *n, slang* the front part of the head ⟨the snowball smacked him right in the *puss*⟩ — see FACE 1

²puss *n* a small domestic animal known for catching mice ⟨I don't want a purebred cat, just some playful *puss* in need of a good home⟩ — see CAT 1

pussy *n* a small domestic animal known for catching mice ⟨fed his *pussy* only the finest fish for its supper⟩ — see CAT 1

pussyfoot *vb* **1** to avoid giving a definite answer or position ⟨politicians who try to *pussyfoot* around controversial topics⟩ — see EQUIVOCATE

2 to move about in a sly or secret manner ⟨*pussyfooting* through the hallways in the middle of the night⟩ — see SNEAK 1

put *vb* **1** to arrange something in a certain spot or position ⟨just *put* the books on the table for now⟩ — see PLACE 1
2 to convey in appropriate or telling terms ⟨tried to think of a good way of *putting* the news⟩ — see PHRASE
3 to decide the size, amount, number, or distance of (something) without actual measurement ⟨*put* the time of the photograph at about noon⟩ — see ESTIMATE 2
4 to establish or apply as a charge or penalty ⟨a proposal to *put* a special tax on luxuries⟩ — see IMPOSE

put by *vb* to put (something of future use or value) in a safe or secret place ⟨have money *put by* for an emergency⟩ — see HOARD

put–down *n* **1** an act or expression showing scorn and usually intended to hurt another's feelings ⟨the *put-downs* of the other kids hurt him a great deal until he learned to ignore them⟩ — see INSULT
2 the act of making a person or a thing seem little or unimportant ⟨your never-ending *put-down* of my musical talents is really starting to annoy me⟩ — see DEPRECIATION

put down *vb* **1** to express scornfully one's low opinion of ⟨always being *put down* by the school snobs for the way she dresses⟩ — see DECRY 1
2 to make a written note of ⟨*put down* the rules so that we wouldn't forget them⟩ — see RECORD 1
3 to put (someone or something) on a list ⟨*put her down* as one of the chaperones for the field trip⟩ — see ¹LIST 2
4 to put a stop to (something) by the use of force ⟨a tyrant who ruthlessly *put down* uprisings⟩ — see QUELL 1

put in *vb* to put or set into the ground to grow ⟨*put in* a crop⟩ — see PLANT

put off *vb* **1** to assign to a later time ⟨never *put off* until tomorrow what you can do today⟩ — see POSTPONE
2 to rid oneself of (a garment) ⟨*put off* your coat⟩ — see REMOVE 1

put–on *adj* lacking in natural or spontaneous quality ⟨a *put-on* goofy voice⟩ — see ARTIFICIAL 1

put–on *n* a display of emotion or behavior that is insincere or intended to deceive ⟨my bravery was all a *put-on*⟩ — see MASQUERADE

put on *vb* **1** to place on one's person ⟨I *put on* a coat and shoes to go outside⟩
synonyms don, slip (on *or* into), throw (on)
related words apparel, array, attire, bedeck, bedizen, bundle up, caparison, clothe, doll up, dress, garb, rig, robe, suit, trick, uniform; overdress
near antonyms disrobe, strip, undress
antonyms doff, remove, take off
2 to describe or express in too strong terms ⟨some critics are *putting* it *on* when they say it's the best comedy ever made⟩ — see OVERSTATE
3 to present a false appearance of ⟨*put on* a show of anger just for fun⟩ — see FEIGN

put out *vb* **1** to bring to bear especially forcefully or effectively ⟨*put out* all my strength to move the piano⟩ — see EXERT
2 to cause to cease burning ⟨*put out* the campfire before leaving⟩ — see EXTINGUISH 1
3 to disturb the peace of mind of (someone) especially by repeated disagreeable acts ⟨my father was *put out* by all the noise outside our house⟩ — see IRRITATE 1

putrefaction *n* the process by which dead organic matter separates into simpler substances ⟨we studied the *putrefaction* of vegetables in biology class⟩ — see CORRUPTION 1

putrefied *adj* having undergone organic breakdown ⟨we had to throw out the *putrefied* tomatoes that had been sitting on the counter all week⟩ — see ROTTEN 1

putrefy *vb* to go through decomposition ⟨we traced the bad smell to a dead skunk *putrefying* under the house⟩ — see DECAY 1

putrid *adj* having undergone organic breakdown ⟨the *putrid* remains of a dead raccoon on the side of the highway⟩ — see ROTTEN 1

putter (around) *vb* to spend time in aimless activity ⟨I spent all weekend at home just *puttering around*⟩ — see FIDDLE (AROUND)

putterer *n* a person who regularly or occasionally engages in an activity without being or becoming an expert at it ⟨we want only experts on this project: no dilettantes or *putterers* allowed⟩ — see AMATEUR

put up *vb* **1** to fix in an upright position ⟨the builders *put up* the walls before starting on the roof⟩ — see ERECT 1
2 to form by putting together parts or materials ⟨plans to *put up* a pavilion in the public gardens⟩ — see BUILD
3 to offer for sale to the public ⟨*put* their possessions up for auction⟩ — see MARKET
4 to provide with living quarters or shelter ⟨the university *puts up* students in a variety of buildings⟩ — see HOUSE 1

puzzle *n* something hard to understand or explain ⟨it's a *puzzle* as to who took the chairs from the room and why⟩ — see MYSTERY

puzzle *vb* to throw into a state of mental uncertainty ⟨it is the cause of the disease that *puzzles* doctors⟩ — see CONFUSE 1

puzzle (out) *vb* to find an answer for through reasoning ⟨I was able to *puzzle out* the riddle in a fairly short time⟩ — see SOLVE

puzzlement *n* **1** a state of mental uncertainty ⟨her explanation did little to relieve his *puzzlement*⟩ — see CONFUSION 1
2 something hard to understand or explain ⟨the whole situation remains a *puzzlement* to everyone who was there⟩ — see MYSTERY

pygmy *adj* of a size that is less than average ⟨a *pygmy* elephant⟩ — see SMALL 1

pygmy *n* a living thing much smaller than others of its kind ⟨hummingbirds may be the *pygmies* of the avian world, but what they lack in size they make up for in beauty⟩ — see DWARF 1

quack *n* one who makes false claims of identity or expertise ⟨don't bother to see that doctor, as I've heard he's a *quack*⟩ — see IMPOSTOR

quadrangle *n* an open space wholly or partly enclosed (as by buildings or walls) ⟨since the weather was sunny, the convocation was held outside in the college's *quadrangle*⟩ — see COURT 2

quaff *n* the portion of a serving of a beverage that is swallowed at one time ⟨so thirsty that she drank her iced tea in one long *quaff*⟩ — see DRINK 2

quaff *vb* to swallow in liquid form ⟨after digging our car out of the snow, we were ready to *quaff* some hot chocolate⟩ — see DRINK 1

quail *vb* **1** to draw back in fear, pain, or disgust ⟨we *quailed* when the waiter unexpectedly presented us with a hindquarter of frog's legs⟩ — see FLINCH

2 to draw back or crouch down in fearful submission ⟨brave resisters who did not *quail* before the tyrant's wrath⟩ — see COWER

quaint *adj* **1** different from the ordinary in a way that causes curiosity or suspicion ⟨the sudden appearance of a man dressed in *quaint* clothes immediately drew the notice of passersby⟩ — see ODD 2

2 pleasantly reminiscent of an earlier time ⟨passed by a *quaint* general store on the side of the road⟩ — see OLD-FASHIONED 1

quake *n* a shaking of the earth ⟨the *quake* registered 6.5 on the Richter scale, causing widespread damage⟩ — see EARTHQUAKE

quake *vb* to make a series of small irregular or violent movements ⟨the horror film was so scary it left us *quaking* with fear for hours afterwards⟩ — see SHAKE 1

quaking *adj* marked by or given to small uncontrollable bodily movements ⟨found the *quaking* stray dog wandering outside in the rain⟩ — see SHAKY 1

qualification *n* **1** a skill, an ability, or knowledge that makes a person able to do a particular job ⟨the fashion firm was looking for an applicant who could list superior sewing skills among his or her *qualifications*⟩

synonyms capability, credentials, stuff

related words command, expertise, mastery, proficiency; ability, capacity, competence, competency, facility, faculty; flair, genius, gift, talent; forte, specialty; fitness, suitability, suitableness; makings, potentiality

2 something upon which the carrying out of an agreement or offer depends ⟨will give us his permission to go on the trip with the *qualification* that we find a suitable chaperon⟩ — see CONDITION 2

qualified *adj* having the required skills for an acceptable level of performance ⟨the candidate has demonstrated that he is *qualified* for the position⟩ — see COMPETENT

qualify *vb* **1** to limit the meaning of (as a noun) ⟨*qualifying* the noun "adventure" in the title of your story with a descriptive adjective would make it more attention-grabbing⟩

synonyms modify, restrict

related words alter, distort, twist; narrow; compare, conjugate, decline, inflect

near antonyms broaden, expand, widen

2 to make competent (as by training, skill, or ability) for a particular office or function ⟨raising five children has *qualified* her to be an advice columnist on parenting⟩

synonyms equip, fit, prepare, ready, season

related words accustom, adapt, adjust, condition, groom, habituate, shape, tailor, train; authorize, entitle; empower, enable

3 to give a right to ⟨this coupon *qualifies* the bearer for an extra 15% off the discounted price⟩ — see ENTITLE 1

4 to give official or legal power to ⟨passing the state bar exam will *qualify* you to practice law⟩ — see AUTHORIZE 1

quality *n* **1** degree of excellence ⟨we expect a high *quality* of service in such a fancy restaurant⟩

synonyms caliber (*or* calibre), class, grade, rate

related words hallmark, standard; mark; footing, place, position, rank, standing, stature, status

2 high position within society ⟨a glamorous invitation-only party for all the people of *quality* in the summer resort⟩ — see RANK 2

3 something that sets apart an individual from others of the same kind ⟨unfailing kindness is one of her many fine *qualities*⟩ — see CHARACTERISTIC

qualm *n* an uneasy feeling about the rightness of what one is doing or going to do ⟨she had no *qualms* about selling her old term papers to other students, even though it was against the academic honor code⟩

synonyms compunction, misgiving, scruple

related words conscience; distrust, doubt, mistrust, suspicion, uncertainty; qualmishness, unease, uneasiness; reluctance, unwillingness; demur, objection, protest; guilt, regret, remorse, self-reproach, shame; contrition, penitence, repentance

near antonyms aplomb, assurance, certainty, certitude, confidence, conviction, self-assurance, self-confidence, sureness

qualmish *adj* affected with nausea ⟨felt a little *qualmish* after the bumpy landing on the airstrip⟩ — see NAUSEOUS

qualmishness *n* **1** a disturbed condition of the stomach in which one feels like vomiting ⟨her *qualmishness* subsided after she had sipped a little ginger ale⟩ — see NAUSEA 1

2 the tendency to be or state of being squeamish ⟨I can't explain my *qualmishness* about spiders, but for some reason they really bother me⟩ — see DELICACY 3

quandary *n* a situation in which one has to choose between two or more equally unsatisfactory choices ⟨I'm in a *quandary* about whether I should try to repair my stereo or buy a new one, even though I don't have the money to do either⟩ — see DILEMMA

quantity *n* **1** a considerable amount ⟨I wish you *quantities* of happiness in the New Year⟩ — see LOT 2

2 a given or particular mass or aggregate of matter ⟨prepared a huge *quantity* of mashed potatoes for the feast⟩ — see AMOUNT

quarrel *n* an often noisy or angry expression of differing opinions ⟨a loud *quarrel* erupted at the next table over⟩ — see ARGUMENT 1

quarrel *vb* to express different opinions about something often angrily ⟨the coach and the referee *quarreled* about whether the ball was in bounds⟩ — see ARGUE 2

quarreler *or* **quarreller** *n* a person who takes part in a dispute ⟨known as the *quarreler* in the family, she never dropped an argument, no matter how pointless⟩ — see DISPUTANT

quarrelsome *adj* **1** feeling or displaying eagerness to fight ⟨a *quarrelsome* student who was always being sent to the principal's office for starting fights in the halls⟩ — see BELLIGERENT

2 given to arguing ⟨you're so *quarrelsome*: you can never do anything without a fuss⟩ — see ARGUMENTATIVE 1

quarry *n* an animal that is hunted or killed ⟨a hunter relentlessly tracking his *quarry*⟩ — see PREY

quarter *n* **1** an area (as of a city) set apart for some purpose or having some special feature ⟨lived on the edge of the central business *quarter*⟩ — see DISTRICT

2 kind, gentle, or compassionate treatment especially towards someone who is undeserving of it ⟨told the team to show their opponents no *quarter* during the championship game⟩ — see MERCY 1

3 the place where someone is assigned to stand or remain ⟨call the crew to their *quarters* on deck to await further instruction⟩ — see STATION 1

4 quarters *pl* the place where one lives ⟨the innkeeper showed us to our *quarters* so we could rest for the evening⟩ — see HOME 1

quarter *vb* to provide with living quarters or shelter ⟨the militia is being *quartered* just outside the city⟩ — see HOUSE 1

¹**quash** *vb* to put a stop to (something) by the use of force ⟨the dictator commanded the army to *quash* the uprising without mercy⟩ — see QUELL 1

²**quash** *vb* to put an end to by formal action ⟨attorneys asked the court to *quash* the indictment⟩ — see ABOLISH

quaver *vb* to sing with the alternation of two musical tones ⟨know-it-alls snickered as the opera singer *quavered* on the high note⟩ — see WARBLE

quavery *adj* marked by or given to small uncontrollable bodily movements ⟨a *quavery* foal trying to stand for the first time⟩ — see SHAKY 1

quay *n* a structure used by boats and ships for taking on or landing cargo and passengers ⟨docked the ferry at the *quay* to let the passengers off⟩ — see DOCK

queasiness *n* **1** a disturbed condition of the stomach in which one feels like vomiting ⟨still battled *queasiness* even on large cruise ships⟩ — see NAUSEA 1

2 the tendency to be or state of being squeamish ⟨a girl who has no *queasiness* about bugs at all⟩ — see DELICACY 3

queasy *also* **queazy** *adj* affected with nausea ⟨felt a little *queasy* after eating too much Easter candy⟩ — see NAUSEOUS

queenly *adj* fit for or worthy of a royal ruler ⟨a richly appointed, *queenly* bedroom, complete with a massive four-poster bed⟩ — see MONARCHICAL

queer *adj* **1** affected with nausea ⟨the combination of ice cream and deep-fried shrimp would make most people feel a little *queer*⟩ — see NAUSEOUS

2 different from the ordinary in a way that causes curiosity or suspicion ⟨had a *queer* way of running that attracted a lot of attention from the spectators⟩ — see ODD 2

3 noticeably different from what is generally found or experienced ⟨a lot of *queer* things started happening almost from the day that we moved into the house⟩ — see UNUSUAL 1

queerish *adj* **1** affected with nausea ⟨if you don't take that antibiotic with food, you might feel a little *queerish* at first⟩ — see NAUSEOUS

2 different from the ordinary in a way that causes curiosity or suspicion ⟨that candy I found on the street left a *queerish* taste in my mouth⟩ — see ODD 2

queerness *n* a disturbed condition of the stomach in which one feels like vomiting ⟨after the roller coaster ride, I had to rest to overcome the dizziness and *queerness* that I was feeling⟩ — see NAUSEA 1

quell *vb* **1** to put a stop to (something) by the use of force ⟨the National Guard was called in to help *quell* the late-night disturbances downtown⟩

synonyms clamp down (on), crack down (on), crush, put down, quash, repress, silence, snuff (out), squash, squelch, subdue, suppress

related words douse, extinguish, put out, quench; smother, stifle, strangle; annihilate, destroy, smash; exterminate, obliterate, wipe out; conquer, overcome, overwhelm, subjugate, vanquish

near antonyms abet, aid, assist, help, support; incite, instigate, provoke, stir; advance, encourage, foster, further, promote

2 to stop the noise or speech of ⟨the principal held up her hand to *quell* the students so they could hear the announcement⟩ — see SILENCE 1

quench *vb* **1** to cause to cease burning ⟨we thoroughly *quenched* the campfire before we headed to bed⟩ — see EXTINGUISH 1

2 to put a complete end to (a physical need or desire) ⟨this lemonade really *quenches* my thirst⟩ — see SATISFY 1

quencher *n* a liquid suitable for drinking ⟨marathon runners often find that plain water is the best *quencher* of all⟩ — see DRINK 1

querulous *adj* given to complaining a lot ⟨car trips that were frequently spoiled by a couple of *querulous* passengers in the back⟩ — see FUSSY 1

query *n* an act or instance of asking for information ⟨please respond to my *query* at your earliest convenience⟩ — see QUESTION 2

query *vb* **1** to demand proof of the truth or rightness of ⟨it seems odd that someone would want two stoves, so you'd better *query* that order⟩ — see CHALLENGE 1

2 to put a question or questions to ⟨*queried* the teacher about the assignment⟩ — see ASK 1

3 to put a series of questions to ⟨once the statement was given, the press secretary allowed reporters to *query* the President⟩ — see EXAMINE 1

quest *n* an act or process of looking carefully or thoroughly for someone or something ⟨the Holy Grail was the object of a mystical *quest* by the knights of the Round Table⟩ — see SEARCH

quest *vb* **1** to ask for (something) earnestly or with authority ⟨I respectfully *quest* your assistance in this matter⟩ — see DEMAND 1

2 to go in search of ⟨many daydreamers trekked to California *questing* riches during the great gold rush of 1849⟩ — see SEEK 1

3 to make a request for ⟨please wait until the lecturer specifically *quests* comments from the audience before chiming in⟩ — see ASK (FOR) 1

question *n* **1** an interrogative expression often used to test knowledge ⟨because I have missed so many classes, I had a hard time answering every *question* on today's surprise quiz⟩

synonyms problem

related words brainteaser, conundrum, poser, puzzle, quiz, riddle, stickler, stumper

near antonyms answer, response, solution

2 an act or instance of asking for information ⟨after reading the brief statement to the reporters, the lawyer ended the press conference by saying, "No more *questions*, please"⟩ ⟨the dozens of *questions* researched by the reference librarians⟩
synonyms call, inquiry, request, query
related words questionnaire, survey; inquisition, interrogating, interrogation, questioning
3 a feeling or declaration of disapproval or dissent ⟨that these measurements are accurate is beyond *question*⟩ — see OBJECTION
4 a major object of interest or concern (as in a discussion or artistic composition) ⟨the *question* at hand is whether allowing students in the cafeteria during their free periods would be a good idea⟩ — see MATTER 1

question *vb* **1** to demand proof of the truth or rightness of ⟨he openly *questioned* the authority of the town's police force to impose a curfew on residents under the age of 18⟩ — see CHALLENGE 1
2 to give serious and careful thought to ⟨*question* your motives before you join the team: are you doing it because you really enjoy soccer, or are you doing it just to impress your friends?⟩ — see PONDER
3 to have no trust or confidence in ⟨it was apparent that voters were *questioning* the President's ability to manage the economy⟩ — see DISTRUST
4 to put a question or questions to ⟨the press should be allowed to *question* public officials about any matter of general interest⟩ — see ASK 1
5 to put a series of questions to ⟨the police *questioned* the suspect before deciding that there was insufficient evidence to hold him⟩ — see EXAMINE 1

questionable *adj* **1** giving good reason for being doubted, questioned, or challenged ⟨the runner's unexpected first-place finish is *questionable*, so a drug test has been ordered⟩ — see DOUBTFUL 2
2 not likely to be true or to occur ⟨it's *questionable* that he will show up tonight considering all the bad weather we're having⟩ — see IMPROBABLE
3 open to question or dispute ⟨whether it will rain today or not is *questionable*⟩ — see DEBATABLE 1

questioner *n* a person who is always ready to doubt or question the truth or existence of something ⟨Father Henry is always happy to talk with any *questioner* of the faith⟩ — see SKEPTIC

questioning *adj* inclined to doubt or question claims ⟨a naturally *questioning* person, she demands rock-solid proof before she believes anything⟩ — see SKEPTICAL 1

queue *n* a series of persons or things arranged one behind another ⟨join the *queue* to my left if you need to return merchandise⟩ — see LINE 1

quibble *vb* to make often peevish criticisms or objections about matters that are minor, unimportant, or irrelevant ⟨he spent the entire evening *quibbling* about the historical inaccuracies in the television series on World War II⟩
synonyms carp, cavil, fuss, nitpick
related words criticize, fault; beef, bellyache, complain, crab, croak, gripe, grouse, growl, grumble, moan, squawk, wail, whine, yammer; murmur, mutter
phrases split hairs
near antonyms applaud, commend, compliment, praise, recommend; approve, back, endorse (*also* indorse), support

quick *adj* **1** having or showing the ability to respond without delay or hesitation ⟨she was a *quick* wit, always ready with a pun or joke when the moment called for one⟩
synonyms alacritous, alert, expeditious, prompt, ready, willing
related words receptive, responsive; immediate, instant, instantaneous, summary; fast, hit-and-run, rapid, speedy, swift; eager, keen, sharp; apt, clever, smart
near antonyms unresponsive; dull, indolent, laggard, lazy, logy, slothful, slow, sluggish, tardy; dormant, idle, inactive, inert
2 having or showing quickness of mind ⟨a *quick* lad, he caught on right away how to operate the machinery⟩ — see INTELLIGENT 1
3 moving, proceeding, or acting with great speed ⟨a *quick* run through the car wash, and your vehicle will look as good as new⟩ — see FAST 1

quick *adv* with great speed ⟨watch out, as the cars pass by here pretty *quick*⟩ — see FAST 1

quick *n* the seat of one's deepest thoughts and emotions ⟨that nasty comment cut me to the *quick*⟩ — see CORE 1

quicken *vb* **1** to cause to move or proceed fast or faster ⟨she eventually *quickened* her pace so she could keep up with the others⟩ — see HURRY 1
2 to give life, vigor, or spirit to ⟨the news that we'd head to Florida for Christmas *quickened* the children, who instantly began jumping for joy⟩ — see ANIMATE

quickly *adv* with great speed ⟨*quickly* moved to block the goal⟩ — see FAST 1

quickness *n* a high rate of movement or performance ⟨his agility and overall *quickness* made him the football coach's top choice for receiver⟩ — see SPEED

quick–tempered *adj* easily irritated or annoyed ⟨a *quicktempered* man who invariably utters threats at any kids who wander into his yard⟩ — see IRRITABLE

quick–witted *adj* having or showing quickness of mind ⟨the *quick-witted* child easily figured out the trick to making the toy work⟩ — see INTELLIGENT 1

quiescence *n* **1** a state of temporary inactivity ⟨the resort community's social scene is lively during the summer but undergoes a deep *quiescence* during the long winter⟩ — see ABEYANCE
2 lack of action or activity ⟨was struck by the elk's *quiescence* as it just stood there in the clearing⟩ — see INACTION

quiescent *adj* slow to move or act ⟨a group of *quiescent* loungers recovering from the Thanksgiving feast⟩ — see INACTIVE 1

quiet *adj* **1** free from disturbing noise or uproar ⟨left the din of the rock concert and went to a *quiet* restaurant where we could hear one another talk⟩
synonyms calm, hushed, peaceful, restful, serene, still, stilly, tranquil
related words noiseless, silent, soundless; speechless, wordless; dead, motionless, quiescent; muffled, muted, quieted
near antonyms crazy, tempestuous, wild
antonyms boisterous, clamorous, clattery, deafening, loud, noisy, raucous, rip-roaring, roistering, romping, rowdy, tumultuous, uproarious, woolly (*also* wooly)
2 not excessively showy ⟨she decided to wear a *quiet* business suit to the interview instead of her blue satin party dress⟩
synonyms conservative, muted, restrained, subdued, toned-down, understated, unpretentious
related words appropriate, fit, fitting, proper, suitable; modest, plain, simple, unadorned; inconspicuous, unobtrusive; tasteful; drab, mousy (*or* mousey); practical, sensible

near antonyms meretricious; graceless, inelegant, tacky, tasteless, vulgar; baroque, fancy, frilly, gilded, ornate, rococo; overdecorated, overdone, overwrought
antonyms flamboyant, flashy, garish, gaudy, glitzy, loud, ostentatious, splashy, swank (*or* swanky), tawdry
3 free from storms or physical disturbance ⟨a *quiet* interlude as the eye of the storm passed over us⟩ — see CALM 1
4 hidden from view ⟨a *quiet* little house set far back from the street⟩ — see SECLUDED
5 mostly or entirely without sound ⟨a diver who loves to retreat to the *quiet* world beneath the surface of the sea⟩ — see SILENT 3
6 not loud in pitch or volume ⟨*quiet* music is generally more relaxing⟩ — see SOFT 1
quiet *n* **1** a state of freedom from storm or disturbance ⟨sailors enjoying the *quiet* of a clear evening⟩ — see CALM
2 the near or complete absence of sound ⟨new parents appreciating the blessed *quiet* that comes when their baby finally falls asleep⟩ — see SILENCE 2
quiet *adv* without motion ⟨lie *quiet* and no one will guess you're hiding under the bed⟩ — see STILL 1
quiet *vb* **1** to become still and orderly ⟨told his rowdy class to *quiet* down during the lesson⟩
synonyms calm (down), cool, hush, settle (down)
related words relax, tranquilize (*also* tranquillize), unwind
near antonyms agitate, discompose, disrupt, disturb, provoke, rile, ruffle, stir; annoy, irritate
antonyms act up, carry on, cut up
2 to free from distress or disturbance ⟨*quiet* a crying toddler with candy⟩ — see CALM 1
quiet (down) *vb* to stop talking ⟨the kids *quieted down* when they realized I was about to ask them if they wanted ice cream⟩ — see SHUT UP
quieted *adj* mostly or entirely without sound ⟨one could hear a pin drop in the *quieted* concert hall as conductor raised his baton⟩ — see SILENT 3
quieting *adj* tending to calm the emotions and relieve stress ⟨a nice *quieting* cup of tea after a hard day at work⟩ — see SOOTHING 1
quietly *adv* without motion ⟨stood *quietly* behind the curtains, hoping to scare her sister when she came into the room⟩ — see STILL 1
quietness *n* **1** a state of freedom from storm or disturbance ⟨preferred the *quietness* of the mall in the early morning, before the frenzy of shopping began later in the day⟩ — see CALM
2 the near or complete absence of sound ⟨the tense *quietness* of the crowd as it anxiously awaited the announcement of the winner⟩ — see SILENCE 2
quietude *n* **1** a state of freedom from storm or disturbance ⟨after his tantrum, the toddler lapsed into an exhausted *quietude* and fell asleep⟩ — see CALM
2 the near or complete absence of sound ⟨the *quietude* of the early morning was broken only by the occasional chirping of birds⟩ — see SILENCE 2
quietus *n* **1** a freeing from an obligation or responsibility ⟨was granted a *quietus* on the remainder of the debt in the old man's will⟩ — see RELEASE 1
2 the permanent stopping of all the vital bodily activities ⟨her unshakable belief in a blissful afterlife allowed her to meet her *quietus* without the slightest tinge of fear or regret⟩ — see DEATH 1
quintessence *n* **1** the most perfect type or example ⟨the Parthenon in Greece was considered the *quintessence* of the perfectly proportioned building⟩

synonyms beau ideal, classic, epitome, exemplar, ideal, perfection
related words archetype, model, prototype; paradigm, standard; nonpareil, paragon; embodiment, incarnation, personification; acme, height, last word, ultimate, zenith
2 the quality or qualities that make a thing what it is ⟨a selfless desire to help others is the *quintessence* of the virtue of charity⟩ — see ESSENCE
quintessential *adj* constituting, serving as, or worthy of being a pattern to be imitated ⟨Helen of Troy was supposedly the *quintessential* beauty of the ancient world⟩ — see MODEL
quip *n* something said or done to cause laughter ⟨laughed aloud at the author's witty *quip*⟩ — see JOKE 1
quip *vb* to make jokes ⟨she rolled her eyes at her brother's bragging and *quipped*, "Here's a quarter to call someone who cares"⟩ — see JOKE
quirk *n* an odd or peculiar habit ⟨wearing red shoes every day is just one of her *quirks*⟩ — see IDIOSYNCRASY
quirky *adj* different from the ordinary in a way that causes curiosity or suspicion ⟨the waitress styles her hair in a *quirky* way that always gets her remembered by customers⟩ — see ODD 2
quisling *n* one who betrays a trust or an allegiance ⟨warned that all *quislings* would be punished without mercy⟩ — see TRAITOR
quit *adj* no longer burdened with something unpleasant or painful ⟨I am finally *quit* of that terrible task⟩ — see FREE 2
quit *vb* **1** to give up (a job or office) ⟨decided to *quit* his job at the fast-food restaurant⟩
synonyms leave, resign (from), retire (from), step down (from)
related words abandon, vacate; drop out (of), throw up
phrases give notice
near antonyms hire (out *or* on)
antonyms stay (at)
2 to stop doing (something) permanently ⟨told her it was high time she *quit* smoking⟩
synonyms discontinue, drop, give up, knock off, lay off (of)
related words break off, break up, close, conclude, end, expire, finish; pause, taper off; throw up; cease, desist, leave off
phrases have done (with)
near antonyms go, run on; hang on, hold on, persevere, persist; follow through, see out; resume; preserve, stay
antonyms carry on, continue, keep, keep up, maintain
3 to bring (as an action or operation) to an immediate end ⟨*quit* pestering your sister⟩ — see STOP 1
4 to cause to remain behind ⟨he *quit* the house sometime around nine this morning⟩ — see LEAVE 1
5 to cease resistance (as to another's arguments, demands, or control) ⟨tried to persuade his daughter to remain at home, but eventually he just *quit* and let her go out on her own⟩ — see YIELD 3
6 to come to an end ⟨will this teasing ever *quit*?⟩ — see CEASE 1
7 to give what is owed for ⟨eager to *quit* all debts before starting married life⟩ — see PAY 2
8 to leave a place often for another ⟨we plan to *quit* the amusement park around seven tonight and then head to the diner for some food⟩ — see GO 2

9 to manage the actions of (oneself) in a particular way ⟨I thought the kids *quitted* themselves quite well at the concert tonight⟩ — see BEHAVE

quite *adv* **1** to a full extent or degree ⟨are you *quite* sure you have permission to go?⟩ — see FULLY 1

2 to some degree or extent ⟨we camped *quite* near Mount Rushmore⟩ — see FAIRLY

quittance *n* **1** a freeing from an obligation or responsibility ⟨the indentured servant obtained a *quittance* from his master stating he was free to leave and was no longer required to work⟩ — see RELEASE 1

2 payment to another for a loss or injury ⟨the court awarded the plaintiff a substantial *quittance* for bodily injury and emotional distress⟩ — see COMPENSATION 1

quitting *n* the act of leaving a place ⟨we simply didn't know what to make of their sudden *quitting* of the party⟩ — see DEPARTURE

quiver *n* an instance of shaking involuntarily with fear or cold ⟨a *quiver* ran through the audience when the monster cornered the movie's hero⟩ — see SHIVER 1

quiver *vb* to make a series of small irregular or violent movements ⟨aspen leaves *quivering* in the breeze⟩ — see SHAKE 1

quivering *n* a series of slight movements by a body back and forth or from side to side ⟨the kids were fascinated by the *quivering* of the jellyfish and kept poking it to see it wiggle⟩ — see VIBRATION

quiz *vb* **1** to put a question or questions to ⟨quickly *quizzed* her about the assignment before heading off to class⟩ — see ASK 1

2 to put a series of questions to ⟨hated the way those relatives would *quiz* me about my mother and new stepfather⟩ — see EXAMINE 1

quiz *n* **1** a person who causes repeated emotional pain, distress, or annoyance to another ⟨always eager to put everything down, my sister had to be a *quiz* and make fun of the actors and costumes in the school play⟩ — see TORMENTOR

2 a set of questions or problems designed to assess knowledge, skills, or intelligence ⟨did well on the surprise *quiz* in history⟩ — see EXAMINATION 1

quizzer *n* a person who causes repeated emotional pain, distress, or annoyance to another ⟨some *quizzer* in the front row was getting more laughs than the comedian on stage⟩ — see TORMENTOR

quizzical *adj* marked by or expressive of mild or good-natured teasing ⟨my puns are usually greeted with loud *quizzical* groans by my so-called friends⟩

synonyms bantering, chaffing, fooling, funning, jesting, joking, joshing, kidding, rallying, razzing, ribbing

related words bandying, quipping; deriding, derisive, derisory, jeering, mocking, ridiculing, taunting; contemptuous, sarcastic, scornful

quota *n* something belonging to, due to, or contributed by an individual member of a group ⟨you need to meet your sales *quota*, or you'll be put on probation⟩ — see SHARE 1

quotation *n* a passage referred to, repeated, or offered as an example ⟨the beautiful autumn day brought to mind this *quotation* from Thoreau: "So live in each season as it passes; breathe the air, drink the drink, taste the fruit, and resign yourself to the influences of each"⟩

synonyms citation, quote

related words allusion, reference; excerpt, extract; line, part, section

quote *n* a passage referred to, repeated, or offered as an example ⟨got a book of *quotes* from his favorite author for his birthday⟩ — see QUOTATION

quote *vb* **1** to give as an example ⟨I could *quote* to you a hundred instances in the past when you've shamelessly lied to me⟩

synonyms adduce, cite, instance, mention

related words exemplify, represent; illustrate, refer (to); document, substantiate

2 to make reference to or speak about briefly but specifically ⟨*quoted* Thomas Jefferson's views on liberty in her paper on the American Revolution⟩ — see MENTION 1

3 to say after another ⟨don't *quote* this to anyone, but I think we're going to Veracruz for winter vacation⟩ — see REPEAT 3

R

rabble *n* people looked down upon as ignorant and of the lowest class ⟨the crown prince was reminded that even the *rabble* of the realm deserved his attention and compassion⟩
synonyms proletariat, riffraff, scum, trash
related words dregs; herd, masses, mob, people, populace, public, rank and file; bourgeoisie, middle class, working class
near antonyms elect, establishment; gentlefolk, nobility
antonyms aristocracy, elite, gentry, society, upper class, upper crust

rabble–rouser *n* a person who stirs up public feelings especially of discontent ⟨*rabble-rousers* inciting hungry people in breadlines to demand social justice⟩ — see AGITATOR

rabid *adj* **1** being very far from the center of public opinion ⟨soccer fans whose *rabid* enthusiasm makes them go berserk when their team wins⟩ — see EXTREME 2
2 feeling or showing anger ⟨became *rabid* when the bank manager told him he would lose the family farm if he didn't pay the mortgage⟩ — see ANGRY
3 marked by bursts of destructive force or intense activity ⟨a *rabid* nationalism that leads people to attack immigrants and anyone else they perceive as being different⟩ — see VIOLENT 1
4 marked by great and often stressful excitement or activity ⟨the *rabid* witch hunts that occurred in Salem in 1692, when 150 people were accused of witchcraft and imprisoned⟩ — see FURIOUS 1

race *n* a group of persons who come from the same ancestor ⟨a man, born of noble *race*, who was now living in impoverished circumstances⟩ — see FAMILY 1

race *vb* **1** to engage in a contest ⟨just how many candidates are *racing* for the senatorial seat this year?⟩ — see COMPETE
2 to proceed or move quickly ⟨*racing* around trying to get everything done before her trip⟩ — see HURRY 2

raceway *n* an open man-made passageway for water ⟨the child who fell through the ice was helplessly swept along the *raceway*, still trapped under the ice, by the current⟩ — see CHANNEL 1

racial *adj* of, relating to, or reflecting the traits exhibited by a group of people with a common ancestry and culture ⟨humanitarian aid workers are often given special training to help them understand the *racial* differences between them and the people they will be serving⟩
synonyms ethnic, tribal
related words familial; folk; kin, kindred; cultural, multicultural, national

racialism *n* **1** the belief that certain races of people are by birth and nature superior to others ⟨the *racialism* of some of the nation's founders seems to contradict their professed belief that "all men are created equal"⟩ — see RACISM 1
2 hatred of or discrimination against a person or persons based on their race ⟨ugly incidents of *racialism* at the school have decreased since the introduction of multiracial rap sessions⟩ — see RACISM 2

racialist *n* a person who believes that one race should control all others ⟨unfortunately, there are still *racialists* who adhere to the belief that there is one superior race⟩ — see SUPREMACIST

racism *n* **1** the belief that certain races of people are by birth and nature superior to others ⟨Hitler's declaration of his belief in a "master race" was the first indication of the inherent *racism* of the Nazi movement⟩
synonyms racialism
related words apartheid, segregation; eugenics
near antonyms desegregation, integration
2 hatred of or discrimination against a person or persons based on their race ⟨the 1963 bombing of the Sixteenth Street Baptist Church in Birmingham, Alabama, was one of the most notorious incidents of *racism* that occurred during the civil rights movement of the 1960s⟩
synonyms prejudice, racialism
related words apartheid, jim crow, segregation; bigotry, intolerance, narrow-mindedness, narrowness

racist *n* a person who believes that one race should control all others ⟨after the passage of the 13th Amendment to the Constitution, *racists* still used violence and intimidation to prevent African-Americans from enjoying their new constitutional rights⟩ — see SUPREMACIST

rack *vb* **1** to cause persistent suffering to ⟨*racked* with guilt over the lie he had told to his parents⟩ — see AFFLICT
2 to injure by overuse, misuse, or pressure ⟨*racked* her brain trying to remember where she'd put the money⟩ — see STRAIN 1

racket *n* **1** a scheme in which the victim is cheated out of his money after first gaining his trust ⟨the *racket* of selling "insurance policies" that are worth no more than the paper on which they are printed⟩ — see CONFIDENCE GAME
2 loud, confused, and usually unharmonious sound ⟨if all the *racket* on the stairs is any indication, someone must be moving into apartment 3B⟩ — see NOISE 1

racketeer *n* a person who gets money from another by using force or threats ⟨the *racketeer* threatened to have his thugs vandalize the shop if the shopkeeper didn't pay him a monthly bribe⟩
synonyms blackmailer, extortioner, extortionist
related words crook, gangster, hoodlum, mafioso, mobster; bully, ruffian, thug; cheat, cheater, chiseler, confidence man, defrauder, double-dealer, gouger, gyp, hustler, profiteer, shark, sharper, swindler

racking *adj* intensely or unbearably painful ⟨a *racking* cough kept him awake all night⟩ — see EXCRUCIATING 1

rack up *vb* to gain (as points or runs in a game) as credit towards one's total number of points ⟨the team *racked up* its fourth straight victory of the season last night⟩ — see SCORE 2

racy *adj* **1** having much high-spirited energy and movement ⟨vivid writing and a *racy* plot that keeps readers turning the pages⟩ — see LIVELY 1
2 hinting at or intended to call to mind matters regarded as indecent ⟨the father wouldn't let his son watch that movie because he felt that the language was a little *racy* for an 8-year-old⟩ — see SUGGESTIVE 1

radiance *n* **1** the quality or state of having or giving off light ⟨the *radiance* of the midday sun created a harsh glare for the skiers⟩ — see BRILLIANCE 1

2 the steady giving off of the form of radiation that makes vision possible ⟨had a dream in which she was steadily moving down a dark tunnel toward a *radiance* at the far end⟩ — see LIGHT 1

radiant *adj* **1** having or being an outward sign of good feelings (as of love, confidence, or happiness) ⟨left the interview with a *radiant* smile on her face, confident she had gotten the job⟩ ⟨a *radiant* bride⟩
synonyms aglow, beaming, glowing, sunny
related words brilliant, dazzling, effulgent, gleaming, luminous, refulgent, shining, starry; blithe, blithesome, bright, cheerful, cheery, chipper, gay, gladsome, lightsome, merry, mirthful, optimistic, upbeat; jocund, jovial, laughing, smiling; blooming, rosy
near antonyms flat, listless, stoic (*or* stoical), unemotional; dark, darkening, depressing, dismal, gloomy, glum, gray (*also* grey), melancholy, sullen; frowning, glaring, glowering, lowering (*also* louring), scowling
2 giving off or reflecting much light ⟨from the plane we could see the statehouse's *radiant* gold dome⟩ — see BRIGHT 1

radiate *vb* **1** to extend outwards from or as if from a central point ⟨the heat *radiating* from the fire⟩ ⟨the spokes of a bicycle wheel *radiate* from the hub towards the rim⟩
synonyms branch, diverge, fan (out)
related words diffuse, dispel, disperse, dissipate; fork, stem; divide, separate, split; scatter, splay, spread; arise, derive, emanate, flow, issue, proceed, spring
near antonyms approach, close in (on), near; center (on), centralize
antonyms concentrate, converge, focus, funnel, meet
2 to emit rays of light ⟨fireflies give off their light by means of a chemical reaction that causes their abdomens to *radiate*⟩ — see SHINE 1

radical *adj* **1** being very far from the center of public opinion ⟨the baggy trousers that Amelia Bloomer introduced in the 1850s were considered a *radical* form of dress for women at the time⟩ — see EXTREME 2
2 not bound by traditional ways or beliefs ⟨*radical* proponents of spelling reform would have every word spelled "just the way it sounds"⟩ — see LIBERAL 1

radical *n* a person who favors rapid and sweeping changes especially in laws and methods of government ⟨*radicals* staged large, violent protests in the hopes of toppling the government⟩
synonyms extremist, revolutionary, revolutionist
related words leftist, red; progressive, reformer; anarchist, subversive; agitator, insurgent, insurrectionist, rebel; secessionist, separatist
near antonyms conservative, reactionary, rightist, Tory
antonyms moderate

raffish *adj* lacking in refinement or good taste ⟨the dowager cringed at the thought of *raffish* peasants in rough boots tromping all over her Persian rugs⟩ — see COARSE 2

raffishness *n* the quality or state of lacking refinement or good taste ⟨the *raffishness* of the crowd in the pub offended the courtly gentleman, and so he elected instead to dine at the hotel⟩ — see VULGARITY 1

raft *n* a considerable amount ⟨the babysitter had to listen to a whole *raft* of rules before she was allowed to even pick up the baby⟩ — see LOT 2

rage *n* **1** a state of wildly excited activity or emotion ⟨found her at home in a *rage* of scrubbing and cleaning in preparation for the rabbi's visit⟩ — see FRENZY

2 an intense emotional state of displeasure with someone or something ⟨boiling with *rage* at the bank teller's insult, he demanded to see the manager⟩ — see ANGER
3 a practice or interest that is very popular for a short time ⟨there was time when playing with Frisbees was all the *rage*⟩ — see FAD

rage *vb* **1** to express one's anger usually violently ⟨the bad call prompted the coach to *rage* about the refereeing, even throwing his clipboard at one referee⟩
synonyms bristle, fume, storm
related words blow up, flare (up), flip; bluster, carry on, fulminate, rampage, rant, rave, take on; burn, foam, seethe, smolder, steam; chafe, fret, stew
near antonyms allay, appease, pacify, soothe; check, collect, compose, contain, curb, hold in, rein, repress, restrain, smother, subdue, suppress; moderate, tone (down), temper; ease, let up, relax; calm, cool, hush, quell, quiet, settle, still
2 to be excited or emotionally stirred up with anger ⟨still *raging* about his assistant's burnt pies, the pastry cook forgot to add the egg whites to his cake batter⟩ — see BOIL 1

ragged *adj* **1** having an uneven edge or outline ⟨the Rocky Mountains cut an angular, *ragged* profile against the sky, in contrast to the rounded silhouette of the rolling, green Adirondack Mountains⟩
synonyms broken, craggy, jagged, scraggly, scraggy
related words saw-toothed, serrate, serrated; harsh, rough, rugged; irregular, nonuniform
near antonyms regular, uniform; flat, level, plane
antonyms clean, even, smooth, unbroken
2 worn or torn into or as if into rags ⟨finally convinced her to throw away her favorite pair of jeans, *ragged* from decades of yard work⟩
synonyms frayed, raggedy, ratty, seedy, shabby, tattered, threadbare, worn-out
related words dowdy, scruffy; dingy, faded; shredded; holey, patchy
3 not having a level or smooth surface ⟨cut herself on the *ragged* edge of the tin can's lid⟩ — see UNEVEN 1
4 wearing torn or worn out clothes ⟨*ragged* and hungry refugees emerging from the jungle where they had been in hiding for weeks⟩ — see TATTERED 1

raggedy *adj* **1** wearing torn or worn out clothes ⟨*raggedy* urchins playing in the village streets⟩ — see TATTERED 1
2 worn or torn into or as if into rags ⟨wears *raggedy* old T-shirts and jeans around the house⟩ — see RAGGED 2

rags *n pl* covering for the human body ⟨the girls showed up at the party wearing their most elegant *rags*⟩ — see CLOTHING

ragtag *adj* wearing torn or worn out clothes ⟨a *ragtag* and weary regiment arrived back at headquarters with the latest news from the front⟩ — see TATTERED 1

raid *n* **1** a sudden attack on and entrance into hostile territory ⟨repeated Viking *raids* wore down the defenses of the seaside village⟩
synonyms descent, foray, incursion, inroad, invasion, irruption
related words pillage, plunder; aggression, assault, offense (*or* offence), offensive, onset, onslaught, siege, storm, strike; charge, sally, sortie; ambuscade, ambush, surprise; air raid, blitz, blitzkrieg, bombardment
2 the act or action of setting upon with force or violence ⟨an early morning *raid* by Federal agents took the smugglers in their hideout by surprise⟩ — see ATTACK 1

raid *vb* **1** to enter for conquest or plunder ⟨a fox has been *raiding* the chicken coop, and now we're down to eight hens⟩ — see INVADE

2 to take sudden, violent action against ⟨the enemy tribe *raided* the village just before dawn, taking everyone by surprise⟩ — see ATTACK 1

raider *n* one that starts armed conflict against another especially without reasonable cause ⟨villagers lived in constant fear of the *raiders* who captured their women and children and sold them into slavery⟩ — see AGGRESSOR

rail *n* **1** a protective barrier consisting of a horizontal bar and its supports ⟨the stairs are icy, so hold onto the *rail*⟩ — see RAILING

2 a roadway overlaid with parallel steel rails over which trains travel ⟨an abandoned stretch of *rail* overgrown with brush⟩ — see RAILROAD

rail (at *or* against) *vb* to criticize (someone) severely or angrily especially for personal failings ⟨we could hear the cook in the kitchen *railing against* his assistant and wondered if we'd ever get our food⟩ — see SCOLD

railer *n* a person given to harsh judgments and to finding faults ⟨a radio show host who knows how to tactfully cut off *railers* who want to vent their personal grievances⟩ — see CRITIC 1

railing *n* a protective barrier consisting of a horizontal bar and its supports ⟨had to put a *railing* on the balcony when the baby started walking⟩

synonyms balustrade, banister, guardrail, rail

related words handrail; taffrail; bar; fender

raillery *n* good-natured teasing or exchanging of clever remarks ⟨Luke had to put up with a lot of *raillery* from his sister the first time he asked a girl for a date⟩ — see BANTER

railroad *n* a roadway overlaid with parallel steel rails over which trains travel ⟨Grandpa used to walk along the main *railroad* in town to get to school⟩

synonyms rail, railway, road

related words el, elevated, elevated railroad; monorail

railway *n* a roadway overlaid with parallel steel rails over which trains travel ⟨a system of *railways* that crisscrosses the whole nation⟩ — see RAILROAD

raiment *n* covering for the human body ⟨the prince exchanged his silken *raiment* for the pauper's humble homespun⟩ — see CLOTHING

rain *n* **1** a steady falling of water from the sky in significant quantity ⟨Mom yelled at us to come in out of the *rain* before we caught cold⟩

synonyms cloudburst, deluge, downpour, rainfall, rainstorm, storm, wet

related words precipitation, shower; thunderstorm

near antonyms drizzle, mist, sprinkle

2 a heavy fall of objects ⟨the Norman invaders fled when the castle's defenders threw a *rain* of stones down upon them⟩

synonyms hail, shower, storm

related words barrage, broadside, cannonade, fusillade, salvo, volley; flood, gush, rush, spate, torrent; eruption, outbreak, outburst

rain *vb* **1** to fall as water in a continuous stream of drops from the clouds ⟨it started *raining* this morning and hasn't let up since⟩

synonyms pour, precipitate, storm

related words shower; hail, squall; deluge, flood

phrases rain cats and dogs

near antonyms drizzle, mist, spit, sprinkle

2 to give readily and in large quantities ⟨she *rained* praise upon her graduating students⟩ ⟨the squadron *rained* bombs on the enemy's fortifications⟩

synonyms heap, lavish, pour, shower

related words gush, stream; flood, inundate, overflow; bombard, hail

near antonyms hold back, keep, reserve, retain, withhold

raincoat *n* a coat made of water-resistant material ⟨grabbed my umbrella and *raincoat* before going out in the thunderstorm⟩

synonyms mackintosh (*or* macintosh) [*chiefly British*], oilskin, slicker, waterproof [*chiefly British*]

related words rainwear; poncho, sou'wester, trench coat

rainfall *n* a steady falling of water from the sky in significant quantity ⟨a torrential *rainfall* washed away most of the little sprouts in our vegetable garden⟩ — see RAIN 1

rainstorm *n* a steady falling of water from the sky in significant quantity ⟨we ran into a big *rainstorm* on Highway 6, and the visibility was so poor we had to pull over⟩ — see RAIN 1

rainy *adj* marked by or abounding with rain ⟨found that the cold, *rainy* weather made his joints swell and ache⟩

synonyms pouring, precipitating, stormy, wet

related words drizzling, drizzly, misty, spitting, sprinkling

near antonyms dry

raise *n* something added (as by growth) ⟨the school board approved a *raise* in the maximum family income for students qualifying for reduced-price lunches⟩ — see INCREASE 1

raise *vb* **1** to move from a lower to a higher place or position ⟨asked the students to *raise* their hands if they knew the answer⟩

synonyms boost, crane, elevate, heave, heft, heighten, hike, hoist, jack (up), lift, perk (up), pick up, up, uphold, uplift, upraise

related words ascend, mount, rise; rear, upend

near antonyms descend, fall, pitch, plunge, slip; bear, depress, press, push; sink, submerge

antonyms drop, lower

2 to bring to maturity through care and education ⟨since her mother died when she was two, the girl was *raised* mainly by her aunt⟩ — see BRING UP 1

3 to cause or encourage the development of ⟨a proposal to cover the library's red brick with vinyl siding *raised* a mighty ruckus with those favoring historical preservation⟩ — see INCITE 1

4 to draw out (something hidden, latent, or reserved) ⟨the lawsuit *raised* old hatreds that had never been completely extinguished⟩ — see EDUCE

5 to fix in an upright position ⟨the mattress will fit into the moving truck only if we *raise* it on its side⟩ — see ERECT 1

6 to form by putting together parts or materials ⟨*raised* a memorial on the site of the accident in memory of those who had been killed⟩ — see BUILD

7 to look after or assist the growth of by labor and care ⟨*raises* ducks, geese, and other exotic fowl ultimately destined for the dinner table⟩ — see GROW 1

8 to make greater in size, amount, or number ⟨the multiplex *raised* the minimum age for paid admissions from four to six⟩ — see INCREASE 1

9 to move higher in rank or position ⟨his dad was recently *raised* to lieutenant in the fire department⟩ — see PROMOTE 1

10 to present or bring forward for discussion ⟨Sheila *raised* the subject of appropriate attire for the trip to sacred sites in the Holy Land⟩ — see INTRODUCE 2

raised *adj* **1** being at a higher level than average ⟨due to *raised* levels of mercury in the water, there is a warning against eating the local shrimp⟩ — see HIGH 2

2 being positioned above a surface ⟨directed the filming of the movie's battle scene from a *raised* platform⟩ — see ELEVATED 1

3 rising straight up ⟨the 63 Braille characters are made up of one to six *raised* dots arranged in a matrix⟩ — see ERECT

rake *vb* to look through (as a place) carefully or thoroughly in an effort to find or discover something ⟨the pathetic sight of hungry children *raking* the garbage for food⟩ — see SEARCH 1

rakishly *adv* in a bright and showy way ⟨*rakishly* balancing on the wall and trying to tap dance, he fell off⟩ — see GAILY 3

rally *n* **1** an act of gathering forces together to renew or attempt an effort ⟨in a last-minute *rally* the Confederates at Bull Run were able to turn a near defeat into an upset victory⟩

synonyms marshaling (*or* marshalling), mobilization, rallying

related words call-up, summons; convening, muster, mustering

2 a mass meeting for the purpose of displaying or arousing support for a cause or person ⟨a huge *rally* for the candidate on the eve of the election⟩

synonyms demonstration

related words assembly, convention, gathering; march; protest, sit-down, sit-down strike, sit-in, strike

3 the process or period of gradually regaining one's health and strength ⟨the doctors were amazed at the sick child's unexpected *rally,* which was apparently due to the new drug⟩ — see CONVALESCENCE

¹rally *vb* **1** to assemble and make ready for action ⟨*rallied* the Red Cross workers to deal with the devastating earthquake⟩ — see MOBILIZE

2 to become healthy and strong again after illness or weakness ⟨despite the best care that medicine could provide, Grandma never *rallied* after she broke her hip⟩ — see CONVALESCE

3 to regain a former or normal state ⟨after wavering a moment on the balance beam, she quickly *rallied* and finished with a fine dismount⟩ — see RECOVER 2

²rally *vb* to make fun of in a good-natured way ⟨his friends *rallied* him for walking to school with the new girl⟩ — see TEASE 1

rallying *n* an act of gathering forces together to renew or attempt an effort ⟨the *rallying* of students to support our petition for better bus service was made a lot easier by this morning's subzero temperatures⟩ — see RALLY 1

rallying *adj* marked by or expressive of mild or good-natured teasing ⟨took his friends' *rallying* remarks about his girlfriend good-naturedly⟩ — see QUIZZICAL

ram *vb* **1** to come into usually forceful contact with something ⟨the truck suddenly swerved and *rammed* into the side of a building⟩ — see HIT 2

2 to fit (something) into a tight space ⟨*rammed* as many candies into his mouth as he could fit⟩ — see CROWD 1

ramble *n* a relaxed journey on foot for exercise or pleasure ⟨our usual practice is to take a *ramble* around the neighborhood after dinner⟩ — see WALK

ramble *vb* **1** to talk at length without sticking to a topic or getting to a point ⟨the teenagers sat around the pizza parlor, *rambling* on about dating, homework, movies, and the local football team⟩

synonyms maunder, rattle, run on

related words deviate, digress, stray, wander; sidetrack; blab, chatter, gab, gabble, jabber, patter, prate, prattle

2 to move about from place to place aimlessly ⟨tirelessly *rambling* around San Francisco for a week we probably saw more of it than many residents ever have⟩ — see WANDER

rambler *n* a person who roams about without a fixed route or destination ⟨a *rambler* her whole life, my aunt is likely to send me a postcard from just about any corner of the world⟩ — see NOMAD

rambling *adj* **1** passing from one topic to another ⟨I listened patiently to Mrs. Parsifal's *rambling* reminiscences, though I had no idea who "Dorothy" and "the stepson" were⟩ — see DISCURSIVE

2 using or containing more words than necessary to express an idea ⟨the new minister gives *rambling* sermons that, if they have a point, are lost on the congregation, which invariably falls asleep⟩ — see WORDY

rambunctious *adj* being rough or noisy in a high-spirited way ⟨Jared often takes his younger siblings to the playground when they are feeling *rambunctious*⟩ — see BOISTEROUS

ramify *vb* to set or force apart ⟨the rise of cable television *ramified* the audience, creating ever smaller segments for an ever growing array of programming choices⟩ — see SEPARATE 1

rampage *n* a state of wildly excited activity or emotion ⟨some crazy guy went on a *rampage* in the public library and started grabbing books off the shelves and tossing them around⟩ — see FRENZY

rampant *adj* **1** showing no signs of being under control ⟨the mayor promised to put a stop to the *rampant* crime that plagued the city⟩

synonyms intemperate, unbridled, unchecked, uncontrolled, uncurbed, ungoverned, unhampered, unhindered, unrestrained

related words uncontrollable, ungovernable; immoderate; riotous, uninhibited, wild

near antonyms moderate, tempered

antonyms checked, controlled, curbed, hampered, hindered, restrained, temperate

2 growing thickly and vigorously ⟨try to avoid the patch of *rampant* poison ivy near the resting spot on the trail⟩ — see RANK 1

ramrod *adj* given to exacting standards of discipline and self-restraint ⟨a *ramrod* camp director who's been known to send kids home for a minor infraction of the rules⟩ — see SEVERE 1

ranch *n* a piece of land and its buildings used to grow crops or raise livestock ⟨lives on a cattle *ranch* in Texas that's as big as the whole state of Rhode Island⟩ — see FARM

rancor *n* a deep-seated ill will ⟨controversy over use of pesticides has caused a lot of *rancor* in this agricultural community⟩ — see ENMITY

rancorous *adj* having or showing deep-seated resentment ⟨a *rancorous* autobiography in which the author heaps blame on just about everyone who had the misfortune of knowing him⟩ — see BITTER 1

random *adj* lacking a definite plan, purpose, or pattern ⟨since we were new in town, our choice of a vet for our dog was entirely *random*⟩

synonyms aimless, arbitrary, desultory, erratic, haphazard, hit-or-miss, scattered, slapdash, stray *related words* accidental, casual, chance, fluky, fortuitous, inadvertent, incidental, lucky, unconsidered, unintended, unintentional, unplanned, unpremeditated; irregular, sporadic, spot; objectless, purposeless; indiscriminate, unsystematic; unaimed, undirected

near antonyms established, fixed, regular, set, stable, steady; constant, continuous, even; arranged, managed, orchestrated, ordered, planned; aware, conscious, deliberate, purposeful, thoughtful

antonyms methodical, nonrandom, orderly, systematic

randomly *adv* without definite aim, direction, rule, or method ⟨the winner will be *randomly* chosen from among all of the entries⟩ — see HIT OR MISS

range *n* **1** open land over which livestock may roam and feed ⟨knew exactly how many head of cattle were turned out on the *range* that morning to graze⟩
synonyms lea, pasturage, pasture
related words ranch, station; feedlot, stockyard, yard; grassland, pampas, prairie, savanna (*also* savannah), steppe

2 an area over which activity, capacity, or influence extends ⟨didn't know she had such a wide *range* of knowledge until I talked to her⟩
synonyms amplitude, breadth, compass, dimension(s), extent, reach, realm, scope, sweep, width
related words gamut, spectrum, spread; domain, field, sphere; horizon, panorama

3 the distance or extent between possible extremes ⟨an actor who can go through the full *range* of emotion, from joy to sorrow, in mere minutes⟩
synonyms gamut, scale, spectrum, spread, stretch
related words measure, pitch, scale; amplitude, compass, dimension(s), extent, reach, realm, scope, sweep, width

4 a relaxed journey on foot for exercise or pleasure ⟨stopped by security personnel while taking an innocent *range* through the palace grounds⟩ — see WALK

5 a series of persons or things arranged one behind another ⟨from the air, the mountain *range* stretched as far as we could see in both directions⟩ — see LINE 1

6 an appliance that prepares food for consumption by heating it ⟨the soup was already heating on the *range* when we arrived at Grandma's⟩ — see COOKER 1

7 the place where a plant or animal is usually or naturally found ⟨the American robin's winter *range* has steadily extended farther and farther north⟩ — see HOME 2

range *vb* **1** to arrange or assign according to type ⟨the campers were *ranged* in patrols, each patrol consisting of girls in a certain age group⟩ — see CLASSIFY 1

2 to move about from place to place aimlessly ⟨she let her dog off the leash and whistled for him every now and then to make sure he didn't *range* out of hearing⟩ — see WANDER

3 to occur within a continuous range of variation ⟨the color of Florida grapefruit can *range* anywhere from pale pink to ruby red⟩ — see RUN 4

4 to put into a particular arrangement ⟨chairs were *ranged* round the perimeter of the room⟩ — see ORDER 1

ranging *adj* traveling from place to place ⟨a *ranging* bear has been spotted at bird feeders in different parts of town⟩ — see ITINERANT

rangy *adj* being tall, thin and usually loose-jointed ⟨we could use a *rangy* girl like you on our basketball team⟩ — see LANKY

rank *adj* **1** growing thickly and vigorously ⟨covered with trumpet vines so *rank* you couldn't see the trellis beneath them⟩
synonyms lush, luxuriant, prosperous, rampant, weedy
related words lavish, profuse; overgrown, overrun; close, dense, thick
near antonyms dormant; blighted, stunted
antonyms sparse

2 having an unpleasant smell ⟨Mr. Pinfold and his *rank* cigars usually send me running for fresh air⟩ — see MALODOROUS

3 very noticeable especially for being incorrect or bad ⟨the article about fairy tales was full of *rank* errors, such as a reference to "Cinderella biting into the poisoned apple"⟩ — see EGREGIOUS

rank *n* **1** the placement of someone or something in relation to others in a vertical arrangement ⟨attained the highest *rank* in Boy Scouting⟩
synonyms degree, footing, level, place, position, ranking, situation, standing, station, status
related words condition, echelon, estate, order, walk; capacity, function; rating

2 high position within society ⟨was born a woman of *rank* who socialized only with other members of the elite⟩
synonyms class, dignity, quality, standing
related words gentility, gentleness, nobility, nobleness; grandness, highness, loftiness; distinction, precedence, preeminence, primacy; caste, position, station, status; preferment
near antonyms debasement, degradation; subordinateness, subordination; baseness, commonness, inferiority, lowliness, lowness

3 a series of people or things arranged side by side ⟨*rank* upon *rank* of cavalry came thundering down the hill⟩ — see ROW 1

4 *usually* **ranks** *pl* one of the units into which a whole is divided on the basis of a common characteristic ⟨this book will someday join the *ranks* of the world's great novels⟩ — see CLASS 2

rank *vb* **1** to take or have a certain position within a group arranged in vertical classes ⟨my favorite pitcher *ranks* first in the league for number of consecutive outs⟩
synonyms be, grade, place, rate
related words seed; count; class, classify, set, sort; install, instate

2 to arrange or assign according to type ⟨most critics would *rank* him among our best actors⟩ — see CLASSIFY 1

rank and file *n* the body of the community as contrasted with the elite ⟨the chosen few might have the opportunity for a trip in the space shuttle, but it will be a while before the *rank and file* are taking space trips⟩ — see MASS 1

ranking *n* **1** a scheme of rank or order ⟨in one *ranking* of the best places to live, San Francisco surpassed all the other cities in the U.S.⟩ — see ³SCALE 1

2 the placement of someone or something in relation to others in a vertical arrangement ⟨the President's *ranking* in the polls is at its highest level since he took office⟩ — see RANK 1

rankle *vb* to make angry ⟨it *rankles* me when some schools can't even afford paper and pencils for the students⟩ — see ANGER

rankling *adj* causing annoyance ⟨to Tristan and his friends, the most *rankling* aspect of the new security measures was the closing of the gym at the end of the regular school day⟩ — see ANNOYING

ransack *vb* **1** to search through with the intent of committing robbery ⟨it was clear that the thieves who had *ransacked* the museum were professionals—they bypassed most of the exhibits and went straight for the vaults⟩
synonyms despoil, loot, maraud, pillage, plunder, sack, strip
related words burglarize; comb, hunt, rake, rifle, rummage; harry, raid; ravish
2 to look through (as a place) carefully or thoroughly in an effort to find or discover something ⟨I've *ransacked* the whole house for that bracelet you lent me and it's not anywhere⟩ — see SEARCH 1

ransom *vb* to free from captivity or punishment by paying a price ⟨the prince emptied the treasury to *ransom* his son from the kidnappers⟩
synonyms redeem
related words bail; deliver, rescue, save; emancipate, liberate; recover, regain, retrieve; release; buy; salvage

rant *n* **1** a long angry speech or scolding ⟨after complaining about the hotel's lousy service, the woman went off on another *rant* about the condition of her room⟩ — see TIRADE
2 boastful speech or writing ⟨instead of addressing the current crisis, the mayor's speech was a lot of *rant* emphasizing his accomplishments⟩ — see BOMBAST 1

rant *vb* to talk loudly and wildly ⟨when the salesclerk gave him incorrect change, he began *ranting* about the sorry state of math education today⟩
synonyms bluster, fulminate, rave, spout
related words sound off, speak out, speak up; blare, blurt out, bolt; declaim, harangue, mouth, orate, pontificate; carry on, rage, storm, take on
near antonyms grunt, murmur, mutter, slur; breathe, whisper

¹rap *n* **1** a formal claim of criminal wrongdoing against a person ⟨the headlines in the paper today are all about the mayor facing an embezzlement *rap*⟩ — see CHARGE 1
2 a hard strike with a part of the body or an instrument ⟨the doctor used a little hammer to give me a *rap* on the knee to test my reflexes⟩ — see ¹BLOW
3 responsibility for wrongdoing or failure ⟨would sooner take the *rap* for the missing money than tell on his friend⟩ — see BLAME 1

²rap *n* friendly, informal conversation or an instance of this ⟨likes staying after school for a friendly *rap* with Mr. Easton, the science teacher⟩ — see CHAT

³rap *n* the smallest amount or part imaginable ⟨I don't care a *rap* about losing that old jacket⟩ — see JOT

¹rap *vb* to deliver a blow to (someone or something) usually in a strong vigorous manner ⟨Tom Sawyer got his knuckles *rapped* for trying to steal sugar under his aunt's very nose⟩ — see HIT 1
2 to strike or cause to strike lightly and usually rhythmically ⟨the impatient man was *rapping* his pipe on the door⟩ — see ¹TAP

²rap *vb* to engage in casual or rambling conversation ⟨my dad's new friend likes to *rap* with him about basketball⟩ — see CHAT

rapacious *adj* **1** having a huge appetite ⟨nothing livens things up like a whole team of *rapacious* basketball players descending upon the pizza parlor⟩ — see VORACIOUS 1
2 living by killing and eating other animals ⟨*rapacious* mammals, such as coyotes, foxes, and bobcats⟩ — see PREDATORY

3 having or marked by an eager and often selfish desire especially for material possessions ⟨*rapacious* plunderers who despoiled the ancient pyramids⟩ — see GREEDY 1

rapaciousness *n* an intense selfish desire for wealth or possessions ⟨the land developer's *rapaciousness* knew no bounds, and if what she wanted wasn't for sale, she would force the owner into selling it⟩ — see GREED

rapacity *n* an intense selfish desire for wealth or possessions ⟨accused his daughter of *rapacity*, claiming that she was only being nice because she wanted to inherit his money⟩ — see GREED

rapid *adj* moving, proceeding, or acting with great speed ⟨the *rapid* descent of the roller coaster made me feel very queasy⟩ — see FAST 1

rapid–fire *adj* moving, proceeding, or acting with great speed ⟨the witness stayed unruffled all through the prosecutor's *rapid-fire* questioning⟩ — see FAST 1

rapidity *n* a high rate of movement or performance ⟨the *rapidity* with which she can do mental math calculations is amazing⟩ — see SPEED

rapidly *adv* with great speed ⟨summer vacation has gone by way too *rapidly*⟩ — see FAST 1

rapidness *n* a high rate of movement or performance ⟨the *rapidness* of the response to a call for assistance is critical in saving a person suffering a heart attack⟩ — see SPEED

rapport *n* a friendly relationship marked by ready communication and mutual understanding ⟨his good *rapport* with his students was one of the reasons why the school board named him Teacher of the Year⟩
synonyms communion, fellowship, rapprochement
related words accord, agreement, concord, harmony; oneness, solidarity, togetherness, unity; affinity, empathy, sympathy, understanding; amity, chumminess, companionship, friendship; reciprocity, symbiosis
near antonyms alienation, disaffection, estrangement; coldness, cold shoulder, distance, iciness; animosity, antagonism, enmity, hostility, rancor, spite

rapprochement *n* a friendly relationship marked by ready communication and mutual understanding ⟨an era of *rapprochement* between Mexico and the U.S. that was highlighted by a new trade agreement⟩ — see RAPPORT

rapscallion *n* **1** a mean, evil, or unprincipled person ⟨the city's run-down waterfront was occupied mostly by disreputable places frequented by drunkards and *rapscallions*⟩ — see VILLAIN
2 an appealingly mischievous person ⟨that little *rapscallion* kept hiding my shoes and making me go look for them⟩ — see SCAMP 1

rapt *adj* having the mind fixed on something ⟨with a mixture of delight and awe, the *rapt* children stared at the chick in the incubator breaking out of its shell⟩ — see ATTENTIVE

rapture *n* a state of overwhelming usually pleasurable emotion ⟨in *The Nutcracker* Clara gazes in *rapture* as the Christmas tree grows before her very eyes⟩ — see ECSTASY

rapturous *adj* experiencing or marked by overwhelming usually pleasurable emotion ⟨heard the whoops of the *rapturous* fan whose quest for an autograph had met with success⟩ — see ECSTATIC

rare *adj* **1** being out of the ordinary ⟨even among the prize roses, this one is a *rare* beauty⟩ — see EXCEPTIONAL

2 having qualities that appeal to a refined taste ⟨*rare* specialty wools, such as cashmere, prized for their fineness, lightness and exceptional warmth⟩ — see CHOICE

3 not often occurring or repeated ⟨the French pronunciation of the family's name is *rare,* except in Louisiana⟩ — see INFREQUENT

4 noticeably different from what is generally found or experienced ⟨"Such good manners are *rare* these days," remarked Mrs. Denby, as the young man let her go ahead of him in line⟩ — see UNUSUAL 1

rarely *adv* not often ⟨summer thunderstorms occur only *rarely* along the Oregon coast⟩ — see SELDOM

raring *adj* showing urgent desire or interest ⟨we'd gotten up so early that by the time eight o'clock rolled around, we were *raring* to get started on the hike⟩ — see EAGER

rarity *n* something strange or unusual that is an object of interest ⟨an American visitor in the remote Chinese village is a *rarity*⟩ — see CURIOSITY 2

rascal *n* **1** a mean, evil, or unprincipled person ⟨some cold-blooded *rascal* had set the barn afire, killing all of the horses⟩ — see VILLAIN

2 an appealingly mischievous person ⟨you little *rascal,* I saw you snitching some hors d'oeuvres even though our guests haven't even arrived yet⟩ — see SCAMP 1

rascality *n* playful, reckless behavior that is not intended to cause serious harm ⟨switching the entrance and exits signs in the school parking lot may seem like harmless *rascality,* if you're not the one involved in an accident⟩ — see MISCHIEF 1

rascally *adj* tending to or exhibiting reckless playfulness ⟨those *rascally* boys have removed the numbers from our lockers again⟩ — see MISCHIEVOUS 1

rash *adj* acting or done with excessive or careless speed ⟨that was too *rash* a move, for now I've lost my bishop and probably the whole chess game⟩ — see HASTY 1

rashly *adv* with excessive or careless speed ⟨I *rashly* agreed to babysit for the Franklin family, completely forgetting that the last time had been torture⟩ — see HASTILY 1

rasp *n* a harsh grating sound ⟨the rusted lock opened with a *rasp*⟩

synonyms creak, grind, scrape, scratch

related words clash, jangle, jar; croak; blast, bleat, bray, screech

rasp *vb* **1** to make smooth by friction ⟨after sawing the board in half, *rasp* the ends to remove any splinters⟩ — see GRIND 1

2 to pass roughly and noisily over or against a surface ⟨the sound of chalk *rasping* on the blackboard makes me cringe⟩ — see SCRAPE 1

3 to disturb the peace of mind of (someone) especially by repeated disagreeable acts ⟨the two siblings seemed intent on *rasping* each other for the entire car trip⟩ — see IRRITATE 1

raspberry *n* a vocal sound made to express scorn or disapproval ⟨there were *raspberries* from the audience when the actress kept forgetting her lines⟩ — see CATCALL

rasping *adj* harsh and dry in sound ⟨a patient beset by a *rasping* cough from years of smoking⟩ — see HOARSE

raspy *adj* harsh and dry in sound ⟨the dying man spoke in a barely audible, *raspy* voice⟩ — see HOARSE

rat (on) *vb* to leave (a cause or party) often in order to take up another ⟨Julia has *ratted on* our circle of hospital volunteers and has started hanging out with that new, hip crowd⟩ — see DEFECT

rate *n* **1** degree of excellence ⟨not being of the first *rate,* these apples are usually sold as food for livestock⟩ — see QUALITY 1

2 the relationship in quantity, amount, or size between two or more things ⟨the exchange *rate* was ten pesos to the dollar when we visited Mexico⟩ — see RATIO

¹rate *vb* **1** to be or make worthy of (as a reward or punishment) ⟨how does my brother *rate* being allowed to go to the movies when he hasn't even finished his homework?⟩ — see EARN 2

2 to make an approximate or tentative judgment regarding ⟨most students would probably *rate* their cell phone as an "essential" piece of electronic equipment⟩ — see ESTIMATE 1

3 to take or have a certain position within a group arranged in vertical classes ⟨a restaurant that consistently *rates* high in all the standard categories⟩ — see RANK 1

4 to think of in a particular way ⟨I would *rate* her my best friend; after all, she's always been there when I needed her⟩ — see CONSIDER 1

²rate *vb* to criticize (someone) severely or angrily especially for personal failings ⟨a tyrannical father who usually spent most of dinnertime *rating* his children on their multitude of failings⟩ — see SCOLD

rather *adv* **1** by choice or preference ⟨I would *rather* go to the movies than stay at home⟩

synonyms first, preferably, readily, soon, willingly

related words alternately, alternatively, either, instead; electively, optionally; desirably, gladly, wishfully; voluntarily

near antonyms reluctantly; forcibly, willy-nilly

antonyms involuntarily, unwillingly

2 as a substitute ⟨don't think of the test as torture but *rather* as a chance to show off how much you know⟩ — see INSTEAD

3 to some degree or extent ⟨I say, don't you think that's *rather* expensive for a hamburger?⟩ — see FAIRLY

ratify *vb* to give official acceptance of as satisfactory ⟨Lincoln's home state of Illinois was the first to *ratify* the 13th Amendment to the U.S. Constitution, which provided for the abolition of slavery⟩ — see APPROVE

ratio *n* the relationship in quantity, amount, or size between two or more things ⟨the *ratio* of students to teachers in my school is nine to one⟩

synonyms proportion, rate

related words average; frequency; correspondence; percentage

near antonyms disproportion

ration *vb* to give as a share or portion ⟨the region has to *ration* water during times of drought⟩ — see ALLOT

rational *adj* **1** having the ability to reason ⟨human beings are *rational* creatures⟩

synonyms intelligent, reasonable, reasoning, thinking

related words analytic (*or* analytical), logical; brainy, cerebral, highbrow, intellectual; cognitive, mental; practical, sane, sensible

near antonyms brainless, mindless, stupid; illogical

antonyms irrational, nonrational, unintelligent, unreasonable, unreasoning, unthinking

2 according to the rules of logic ⟨insisted there was a *rational* explanation for the strange creaking noises and that there were no such things as ghosts⟩ — see LOGICAL 1

3 based on sound reasoning or information ⟨taking all your money out of your savings account and hiding it in a sock is not a *rational* move⟩ — see GOOD 1

rationale *n* a statement given to explain a belief or act ⟨the *rationale* for starting the school day an hour later is that kids will supposedly get an extra hour of sleep⟩ — see REASON 1

rationalize *vb* to give the reason for or cause of ⟨*rationalized* putting off his homework until Sunday night by convincing himself that the long rest would do his mind good⟩ — see EXPLAIN 2

rattle *vb* **1** to make a series of short sharp noises ⟨the children tromped through the kitchen, making the plates on the shelf *rattle*⟩
synonyms clack, clatter
related words chink, chirp, clank, click, clink; clang, clash, crash; spatter, sputter
2 to engage in casual or rambling conversation ⟨one minute Adam was *rattling* away about his day at kindergarten, and the next minute he was sound asleep⟩ — see CHAT
3 to talk at length without sticking to a topic or getting to a point ⟨she *rattled* on and on about various vacations and all her shopping trips, but I wasn't listening⟩ — see RAMBLE 1
4 to throw into a state of self-conscious distress ⟨don't let a little mistake *rattle* you while you're playing during the piano recital⟩ — see EMBARRASS 1

rattling *adj* moving, proceeding, or acting with great speed ⟨we drove off at a *rattling* pace⟩ — see FAST 1

rattling *adv* to a great degree ⟨a *rattling* good storyteller⟩ — see VERY 1

ratty *adj* **1** showing signs of advanced wear and tear and neglect ⟨some *ratty* old magazines were the only reading material in the mountaintop cabin⟩ — see SHABBY 1
2 worn or torn into or as if into rags ⟨can I use this *ratty* old T-shirt to wipe up some paint?⟩ — see RAGGED 2

raucous *adj* being rough or noisy in a high-spirited way ⟨the partying neighbors kept up their *raucous* laughter half the night⟩ — see BOISTEROUS

ravage *vb* to bring destruction to (something) through violent action ⟨Hurricane Andrew *ravaged* Louisiana and Florida in 1992, causing $19 billion in damage⟩
synonyms destroy, devastate, ruin, scourge
related words despoil, foray, harry, loot, maraud, pillage, plunder, sack, strip; annihilate, desolate, extirpate, obliterate, smash, waste, wipe out, wreck; decimate, mow; demolish, raze; crush, overpower, overrun, overthrow, overwhelm
near antonyms recondition, recover, redeem, rehabilitate, restore

rave *vb* to make an exaggerated display of affection or enthusiasm ⟨to break the awkward silence after my parents' argument, our guest *raved* about the canned beans and franks we'd set before him⟩ — see GUSH 2
2 to talk loudly and wildly ⟨a man stood outside city hall *raving* like a lunatic about his tax bill⟩ — see RANT

rave *n, often* **raves** *pl* enthusiastic and usually public expression of approval ⟨the books have received even more *raves* from parents than from the kids they were written for⟩ — see APPLAUSE

ravel (out) *vb* to separate the various strands of ⟨since the sweater is too small you could *ravel* the yarn *out* and make something else with it⟩ — see UNRAVEL 1

raven *adj* having the color of soot or coal ⟨a black satin dress that matches her silky, *raven* hair⟩ — see BLACK 1

ravenous *adj* having a huge appetite ⟨we were *ravenous* after our canoe paddling, and the chili bubbling on the campfire smelled heavenly⟩ — see VORACIOUS 1

ravine *n* a narrow opening between hillsides or mountains that can be used for passage ⟨he urged his horse down into the *ravine* where there was a thin stream of water flowing⟩ — see CANYON

ravish *vb* to fill with overwhelming emotion (as wonder or delight) ⟨travelers have long been *ravished* with wonder and awe by the immensity of the Great Pyramid at Giza⟩ — see ENTRANCE

ravishing *adj* very pleasing to look at ⟨with her red curls falling around her shoulders, she looked *ravishing* in her green dress⟩ — see BEAUTIFUL

raw *adj* **1** not cooked ⟨you should wash your hands after handling *raw* chicken⟩
synonyms uncooked
related words unbaked, unheated; rare; underdone
near antonyms well-done; overdone; baked, boiled, braised, broiled, fried, grilled, heated, roasted, sautéed
antonyms cooked
2 being such as found in nature and not altered by processing or refining ⟨*raw* sugar is honey-colored because the crystals retain cane juices, minerals, and other impurities that haven't been refined out⟩ — see CRUDE 1
3 lacking in adult experience or maturity ⟨recruiters like to say the military turns *raw* youths into responsible men and women⟩ — see CALLOW
4 marked by wet and windy conditions ⟨the day of the funeral was one of those bleak, blustery, *raw* winter days that was as gloomy as our spirits⟩ — see FOUL 1
5 uncomfortably cool ⟨evenings in those mountains, even during the summer, tend to be a little *raw*⟩ — see CHILLY 1
6 causing intense discomfort to one's skin ⟨bundle up if you're going sailing, as there's a *raw* wind out there in the bay⟩ — see CUTTING 1

raw deal *n* unfair or inadequate treatment of someone or something or an instance of this ⟨these mice are really getting a *raw deal*: after we're through using them for our science experiment, they get fed to our snake⟩ — see DISSERVICE

rawhide *vb* to strike repeatedly with something long and thin or flexible ⟨a strict disciplinarian, the rancher would *rawhide* his disobedient sons until they were black and blue⟩ — see WHIP 1

raw material *n* the basic elements from which something can be developed ⟨Canada now converts most of its *raw materials* into manufactured goods such as automobiles and auto parts⟩ — see MAKING

rawness *n* an uncomfortable degree of coolness ⟨lit a fire in the hearth to combat the *rawness* of that blustery March morning⟩ — see CHILL

ray *n* **1** a narrow sharply defined line of light radiating from an object ⟨two red eyes reflected in the *ray* of light from the flashlight⟩ — see SHAFT 1
2 a very small amount ⟨the tapping sound ceased, extinguishing the last *ray* of hope that the trapped miners were still alive⟩ — see PARTICLE 1

raze *vb* **1** to bring to a complete end the physical soundness, existence, or usefulness of ⟨an entire city block *razed* by a terrible fire⟩ — see DESTROY 1
2 to destroy (as a building) completely by knocking down or breaking to pieces ⟨the developer *razed* the old school building and built a high-rise condominium complex⟩ — see DEMOLISH 1

razz *vb* to make fun of in a good-natured way ⟨got *razzed* all day for wearing mismatched sneakers⟩ — see TEASE 1

razzing *adj* marked by or expressive of mild or good-natured teasing ⟨his little sister made *razzing* kissing noises whenever he was on the phone with his girlfriend⟩ — see QUIZZICAL

reach *n* **1** a wide space or area ⟨a wide *reach* of woods⟩ — see EXPANSE

2 an area over which activity, capacity, or influence extends ⟨joining the cheerleading team was out of her *reach* this year, but she decided to try out when she became a sophomore⟩ — see RANGE 2

reach *vb* **1** to shift possession of (something) from one person to another ⟨would you *reach* me the potatoes, please?⟩ — see PASS 1

2 to transmit information or requests to ⟨you can *reach* me by phone after 3:00 p.m. most days⟩ — see CONTACT

reachable *adj* situated within easy reach ⟨placed the book at a *reachable* distance from the bed⟩ — see CONVENIENT

reacquire *vb* to get again in one's possession ⟨the hockey team is hoping to *reacquire* the Stanley Cup this year⟩ — see RECOVER 1

react *vb* to act or behave in response (as to a stimulus or influence) ⟨it was my first touchdown, and I didn't know how to *react* to the cheers of the crowd⟩
synonyms reply, respond
related words answer, return; retaliate; construe, interpret, read, take, understand
near antonyms act, behave; affect, cause, draw, effect

reaction *n* action or behavior that is done in return to other action or behavior ⟨we were startled by her extreme *reaction* to the bad grade⟩
synonyms reply, response, take
related words answer, return; backlash; rebound; revulsion, rise; jerk, start, twitch
near antonyms action, behavior; cause, effect

reactionary *adj* tending to favor established ideas, conditions, or institutions ⟨my *reactionary* grandparents don't like the idea of teens doing serious dating⟩ — see CONSERVATIVE

reactionary *n* **1** a person whose political beliefs are centered on tradition and keeping things the way they are ⟨*reactionaries* tried to stop the passage of the legislation extending civil rights⟩ — see CONSERVATIVE 1

2 a person with old-fashioned ideas ⟨a *reactionary* who thinks that watching any TV at all will rot your brain⟩ — see FOGY

read *vb* to go over and mentally take in the content of ⟨he always *reads* the newspaper in the morning as he eats breakfast⟩
synonyms peruse, pore (over)
related words browse, dip (into), leaf (through), scan, skim, thumb (through); slog (through), wade (through); reread; proofread; decipher; review, study; apprehend, comprehend, get, grasp, make, make out, perceive, see, understand

readdress *vb* to consider again especially with the possibility of change or reversal ⟨the senate will *readdress* pending gun control legislation in their next session⟩ — see RECONSIDER

readily *adv* **1** by choice or preference ⟨she would *readily* give up piano lessons for a season ticket to go skiing⟩ — see RATHER 1

2 without difficulty ⟨always gives directions that are *readily* understood⟩ — see EASILY

reading *n* something assigned to be read or studied ⟨make sure you do the assigned *reading* for tonight⟩ — see LESSON

ready *adj* **1** being in a state of fitness for some experience or action ⟨after studying for a whole month, she felt *ready* for the final exam⟩
synonyms fit, go, prepared, set
related words conditioned, primed; braced, fortified, steeled; qualified, trained
near antonyms unqualified, untrained
antonyms half-cocked, unprepared, unready

2 having a desire or inclination (as for a specified course of action) ⟨I'm *ready* to help, if I can⟩ — see WILLING 1

3 having or showing the ability to respond without delay or hesitation ⟨had a *ready* response to her objections⟩ — see QUICK 1

4 involving minimal difficulty or effort ⟨we're hoping you have a *ready* solution to our problem⟩ — see EASY 1

ready *vb* **1** to make competent (as by training, skill, or ability) for a particular office or function ⟨this advanced course should *ready* him for college⟩ — see QUALIFY 2

2 to make ready in advance ⟨*ready* the desserts for the party tomorrow⟩ — see PREPARE 1

3 to prepare (oneself) mentally or emotionally ⟨the basketball players sat quietly in the locker room, *readying* themselves for the final game of the season⟩ — see FORTIFY 1

ready–made *adj* made beforehand in large numbers ⟨the store was full of inexpensive *ready-made* clothing⟩
synonyms mass-produced, store
related words ready-to-wear; commercial; prefabricated
near antonyms handcrafted, handmade, homemade; tailored, tailor-made
antonyms custom, custom-made

real *adj* **1** being exactly as appears or as claimed ⟨this shirt is *real* silk, not polyester⟩ — see AUTHENTIC 1

2 existing in fact and not merely as a possibility ⟨asked her parents if the Tooth Fairy was *real*⟩ — see ACTUAL

3 free from any intent to deceive or impress others ⟨*real* folk who don't put on airs⟩ — see GUILELESS

real *adv* to a great degree ⟨this fish tastes *real* good⟩ — see VERY 1

realistic *adj* **1** willing to see things as they really are and deal with them sensibly ⟨our guidance counselor encouraged us to be more *realistic* in our job choices, so we reluctantly gave up the idea of becoming professional snake charmers⟩
synonyms down-to-earth, earthy, hardheaded, matter-of-fact, practical, pragmatic (*also* pragmatical)
related words philistine, utilitarian; logical, no-nonsense, rational, reasonable, sane, sensible, sound; hard-boiled, unromantic, unsentimental; cynical, disillusioned
near antonyms fanciful, fantastic, imaginative; romantic, sentimental; illogical, insane, irrational, unreasonable; theoretical (*also* theoretic)
antonyms idealistic, impractical, unrealistic, utopian, visionary

2 closely resembling the object imitated ⟨those special effects look really *realistic*—I'd never guess they were all computer-generated⟩ — see NATURAL 2

reality *n* **1** something that actually exists ⟨the ambition to make his dreams a *reality*⟩ — see FACT 2

2 the fact of being or of being real ⟨no one denies the *reality* of electricity though few people understand it fully⟩ — see EXISTENCE

3 the quality of being actual ⟨the *reality* of the situation finally dawned on her and she sat down in stunned silence⟩ — see FACT 1

realizable *adj* capable of being done or carried out ⟨waited until their goal was *realizable* and then acted⟩ — see POSSIBLE 1

realization *n* the state of being actual or complete ⟨this research paper is the *realization* of an entire year's work⟩ — see FRUITION

realize *vb* **1** to come to an awareness ⟨I just *realized* that I can't go out to dinner tonight because I'm supposed to babysit for our neighbor⟩ — see DISCOVER 1

2 to receive as return for effort ⟨if you deposit your paycheck in a savings account, you'll *realize* a little interest on it⟩ — see EARN 1

really *adv* **1** in actual fact ⟨I'm *really* sorry I upset you⟩ — see VERY 2

2 to tell the truth ⟨well, *really*, I'd rather go to the movies than go to dinner⟩ — see ACTUALLY 1

3 without any question ⟨that was *really* a sweet gesture on your part⟩ — see INDEED 1

realm *n* **1** a region of activity, knowledge, or influence ⟨medieval history is really Professor Clinton's *realm*, so I'll let her answer your question⟩ — see FIELD 2

2 an area over which activity, capacity, or influence extends ⟨a medical breakthrough that is within the *realm* of possibility⟩ — see RANGE 2

reams *n pl* a considerable amount ⟨I have *reams* of paperwork to do before I can leave today⟩ — see LOT 2

reanalyze *vb* to consider again especially with the possibility of change or reversal ⟨your team needs to *reanalyze* the data because the numbers don't tally⟩ — see RECONSIDER

reanimate *vb* to bring back to life, practice, or activity ⟨the new multiplex has begun to *reanimate* the shabby neighborhood⟩ — see REVIVE 1

reanimated *adj* made or become fresh in spirits or vigor ⟨the hikers were *reanimated* and ready to go after their brief rest along the side of the trail⟩ — see NEW 4

reanimation *n* the act or an instance of bringing something back to life, public attention, or vigorous activity ⟨a call for the *reanimation* of curfew ordinances that were discarded decades ago⟩ — see REVIVAL

reap *vb* to catch or collect (a crop or natural resource) for human use ⟨my great-grandfather had to *reap* the wheat on his family farm with a hand scythe⟩ — see HARVEST

reappraisal *n* a usually critical look at a past event ⟨teachers are undertaking a *reappraisal* of the current grading system, as the consensus is that A's have been given out too easily of late⟩ — see REVIEW 1

rear *adj* being at or in the part of something opposite the front part ⟨go to the back of the building and look out the *rear* window and you'll see the eagle⟩ — see BACK

rear *n* the part of the body upon which someone sits ⟨fell off her skates onto her *rear*⟩ — see BUTTOCKS

rear *vb* **1** to bring to maturity through care and education ⟨watched a documentary on how wolves *rear* their young⟩ — see BRING UP 1

2 to fix in an upright position ⟨it took all the men in the village to *rear* the frame for the barn, pulling hard at the ropes until all the sides were standing⟩ — see ERECT 1

3 to form by putting together parts or materials ⟨the city has plans for *rearing* a new convention center over the next two years⟩ — see BUILD

4 to look after or assist the growth of by labor and care ⟨an amateur who *rears* rare orchids in a professional-grade greenhouse⟩ — see GROW 1

rearmost *adj* following all others of the same kind in order or time ⟨the *rearmost* kids in the cafeteria line often get the dregs that nobody wanted and for good reason⟩ — see LAST

rearward *adj* **1** being at or in the part of something opposite the front part ⟨got *rearward* quarters aboard the ship⟩ — see BACK

2 directed, turned, or done toward the back ⟨the tearful girl gave a *rearward* glance to her younger brother as she was being led down the street for her first day at school⟩ — see BACKWARD

reason *n* **1** a statement given to explain a belief or act ⟨gave a good *reason* for her seemingly suspicious behavior⟩

synonyms argument, case, explanation, rationale

related words alibi, defense, excuse, justification; appeal, plea; guise, pretense (*or* pretence), pretext, rationalization

2 something (as a belief) that serves as the basis for another thing ⟨a firm belief that we are here on earth to help others is the *reason* for her tireless volunteer work⟩

synonyms grounds, motive, wherefore, why

related words antecedent, cause, occasion

3 an explanation that frees one from fault or blame ⟨what *reason* do you have for being in such a bad mood?⟩ — see EXCUSE

4 someone or something responsible for a result ⟨what's the meteorological *reason* for tornadoes?⟩ — see CAUSE 1

5 the ability to learn and understand or to deal with problems ⟨you'll need to use all of your *reason* to get out of this tight spot⟩ — see INTELLIGENCE 1

6 the normal or healthy condition of the mental abilities ⟨was afraid that with all the stress he was under, he'd lose all *reason*⟩ — see MIND 2

7 the thought processes that have been established as leading to valid solutions to problems ⟨in a time of national crisis we need to listen to the voice of *reason*⟩ — see LOGIC

reason *vb* **1** to form an opinion through reasoning and information ⟨she *reasoned* that since all of the cakes were on sale for the same price, she might as well pick the biggest one⟩ — see INFER 1

2 to state (something) as a reason in support of or against something under consideration ⟨he tried to *reason* that no one in their right mind would buy his brother's old video games, but they were put on the online auction anyway⟩ — see ARGUE 1

reasonable *adj* **1** according to the rules of logic ⟨his answer is perfectly *reasonable*⟩ — see LOGICAL 1

2 based on sound reasoning or information ⟨those playing rules sound *reasonable* to me⟩ — see GOOD 1

3 costing little ⟨desperately trying to find *reasonable* hotel rates for the holiday weekend⟩ — see CHEAP 1

4 having the ability to reason ⟨some people once believed that women were not by nature *reasonable* beings, but generations of female scholars have proved those people wrong⟩ — see RATIONAL 1

reasonably *adv* with good reason or courtesy ⟨I expect to be treated *reasonably* by the clerks when I shop at a store⟩ — see WELL 4

reasoned *adj* **1** based on sound reasoning or information ⟨a candidate with a *reasoned* stance on this important issue⟩ — see GOOD 1

2 being or provable by reasoning in which the conclusion follows necessarily from given information ⟨given the information you have, that is the only *reasoned* solution to the problem⟩ — see DEDUCTIVE

3 decided on as a result of careful thought ⟨arrived at a well-*reasoned* position on the issue that took both sides into account⟩ — see DELIBERATE 1

reasoning *adj* having the ability to reason ⟨judged by the courts not to be a *reasoning* being who could be held accountable for his crimes⟩ — see RATIONAL 1

reasoning *n* the thought processes that have been established as leading to valid solutions to problems ⟨your *reasoning* here is faulty, for although all wives are spouses, not all spouses are wives⟩ — see LOGIC

reassure *vb* to ease the grief or distress of ⟨tried to *reassure* her that the dog would come back home by nightfall⟩ — see COMFORT 1

reata *n* a rope or long leather thong with a noose used especially for catching livestock ⟨the gauchos tied their *reatas* and rode out onto the pampas to rope calves⟩ — see LASSO

rebel *n* a person who rises up against authority ⟨the *rebel* would not submit peacefully, even after he was captured⟩
synonyms insurgent, insurrectionary, insurrectionist, mutineer, red, revolter, revolutionary, revolutionist, revolutionizer
related words challenger, defier, resister; anarchist; extremist, malcontent, radical
near antonyms loyalist, supporter; counterrevolutionary, counterrevolutionist

rebel *vb* to rise up against established authority ⟨the colonists *rebelled* when the unfair tax was imposed⟩
synonyms mutiny, revolt
related words defy, disobey; revolutionize
near antonyms obey, submit; attend, serve

rebel (against) *vb* to go against the commands, prohibitions, or rules of ⟨experts tell parents that if their once-compliant children *rebel against* them, then they should take it as a sign the kids are growing up and becoming their own persons⟩ — see DISOBEY

rebellion *n* open fighting against authority (as one's own government) ⟨the *rebellion* would have failed if not for the aid sent by other countries⟩
synonyms insurgency, insurrection, mutiny, revolt, revolution, uprising
related words coup, coup d'état, overthrow; sedition, treachery, treason; sabotage, subversion
near antonyms counterrevolution

rebellious *adj* **1** taking part in a rebellion ⟨the *rebellious* troops fought a pitched battle with divisions still loyal to the government⟩
synonyms insurgent, insurrectionary, mutinous, revolutionary
related words seditious, traitorous, treacherous, treasonous
near antonyms loyal; obedient
2 given to resisting authority or another's control ⟨expected her son to grow a little more *rebellious* as he got older, but she knew he understood when to kick and when to obey⟩ — see DISOBEDIENT

rebelliousness *n* refusal to obey ⟨her habitual *rebelliousness* eventually landed her in the principal's office⟩ — see DISOBEDIENCE

rebirth *n* the act or an instance of bringing something back to life, public attention, or vigorous activity ⟨a renewed interest in long-playing records led to the *rebirth* of the turntable⟩ — see REVIVAL

rebound *vb* **1** to regain a former or normal state ⟨the economy will *rebound* after this latest slump⟩ — see RECOVER 2

2 to strike and fly off at an angle ⟨the ball *rebounded* off the rim⟩ — see GLANCE 1

rebuff *n* treatment that is deliberately unfriendly ⟨took her *rebuff* in stride, and still greeted her cousin with a friendly smile the next time they met⟩ — see COLD SHOULDER

rebuke *n* an often public or formal expression of disapproval ⟨delivered a stinging *rebuke* to the congress, calling for an end to backstabbing and arguing⟩ — see CENSURE

rebuke *vb* **1** to criticize (someone) usually gently so as to correct a fault ⟨*rebuked* the toddler for his habit of telling fibs⟩
synonyms admonish, chide, reprimand, reproach, reprove
related words berate, castigate, chew out, dress down, flay, jaw, keelhaul, lambaste (*or* lambast), lecture, rail (at *or* against), scold, score, upbraid; abuse, assail, attack, bad-mouth, blame, blast, censure, condemn, criticize, crucify, denounce, dis [*slang*], excoriate, fault, knock, lash, pan, reprehend, slam; belittle, disparage, mock, put down; ridicule, scoff, scorn
near antonyms approve, endorse (*also* indorse), sanction; extol (*also* extoll), laud, praise
2 to criticize (someone) severely or angrily especially for personal failings ⟨strongly *rebuked* the girl for playing with matches⟩ — see SCOLD
3 to express public or formal disapproval of ⟨in a rare move, the state's supreme court *rebuked* the governor for trying to circumvent one of its recent rulings⟩ — see CENSURE 1

rebut *vb* to prove to be false ⟨Magellan's circumnavigation of the globe effectively *rebutted* any lingering notions that the earth is flat⟩ — see DISPROVE

recalcitrance *n* refusal to obey ⟨punished her *recalcitrance* by taking away her driving privileges⟩ — see DISOBEDIENCE

recalcitrant *adj* **1** given to resisting authority or another's control ⟨warned the children against becoming *recalcitrant* while they were in the babysitter's care⟩ — see DISOBEDIENT
2 given to resisting control or discipline by others ⟨a heart-to-heart talk with the *recalcitrant* youth revealed that he had a troubled life at home⟩ — see UNCONTROLLABLE

recall *n* **1** a particular act or instance of recalling or the thing remembered ⟨his *recall* of the events of that turbulent time is significantly different from the accounts of other eyewitnesses⟩ — see MEMORY 2
2 the act of putting an end to something planned or previously agreed to ⟨we can't get a refund on the plane tickets, so the trip is beyond *recall*⟩ — see CANCELLATION

recall *vb* **1** to bring back to mind ⟨I don't *recall* meeting you before⟩ — see REMEMBER
2 to put an end to (something planned or previously agreed to) ⟨I'll *recall* my purchase order if the company refuses to guarantee that it'll arrive before Christmas⟩ — see CANCEL 1

recant *vb* to solemnly or formally reject or go back on (as something formerly adhered to) ⟨the Inquisition forced Galileo to *recant* his support of the Copernican observation that the earth revolves around the sun⟩ — see ABJURE

recap *n* a short statement of the main points ⟨after a *recap* of this morning's meeting, we can discuss the issues that were raised⟩ — see SUMMARY

recap *vb* to make into a short statement of the main points (as of a report) ⟨please *recap* the highlights of the game for me⟩ — see SUMMARIZE

recapitulate *vb* to make into a short statement of the main points (as of a report) ⟨I don't want your essay to *recapitulate* the whole story for me, but to discuss in detail one particular incident that you thought was interesting⟩ — see SUMMARIZE

recapitulation *n* a short statement of the main points ⟨will begin his presentation with a *recapitulation* of the research done on the disease up to this point⟩ — see SUMMARY

recapture *vb* to get again in one's possession ⟨our team managed to *recapture* the ball after the fumble⟩ — see RECOVER 1

recast *vb* to make different in some way ⟨I don't understand what you're asking—can you *recast* the question for me?⟩ — see CHANGE 1

recede *vb* **1** to grow less in scope or intensity especially gradually ⟨the sound of sirens *receded* as the fire engines roared off into the distance⟩ — see DECREASE 2
2 to move back or away (as from something difficult, dangerous, or disagreeable) ⟨after the rain stops, the floodwaters should gradually *recede*⟩ — see RETREAT 1

recently *adv* not long ago ⟨I *recently* purchased a car⟩ ⟨have you seen her *recently*?⟩ — see NEWLY

receptacle *n* something into which a liquid or smaller objects can be put for storage or transportation ⟨place all wrappers in the trash *receptacles* at the entrances of the theater⟩ — see CONTAINER

reception *n* a social gathering ⟨a wedding *reception*⟩ — see PARTY 1

receptive *adj* willing to consider new or different ideas ⟨needed a partner who was *receptive* to new ways of managing the business⟩ — see OPEN-MINDED 1

recess *n* **1** a hollowed-out space in a wall ⟨in that video game, you'll find the secret treasure in one of the *recesses* of the tomb wall⟩ — see NICHE 1
2 a period during which the usual routine of school or work is suspended ⟨the couple goes to Florida every January for a month-long *recess* from the rigors of winter⟩ — see VACATION
3 a momentary halt in an activity ⟨the class took an extra *recess* after the math lesson⟩ — see PAUSE
4 a sunken area forming a separate space ⟨decided to camp in a sandy *recess* where the beach met the forest⟩ — see HOLE 2

recess *vb* to bring to a formal close for a period of time ⟨the judge *recessed* the court for lunch⟩ — see ADJOURN

recessed *adj* curved inward ⟨placed the vase on a *recessed* shelf in the wall⟩ — see HOLLOW

recession *n* **1** a period of decreased economic activity ⟨the country is just coming out of a *recession*, so expect to see fewer layoffs and more new jobs in the coming year⟩ — see DEPRESSION 1
2 an act of moving away especially from something difficult, dangerous, or disagreeable ⟨she made a slow *recession* away from the snake in the grass⟩ — see RETREAT 1

reciprocal *adj* related to each other in such a way that one completes the other ⟨the two nations agreed to give *reciprocal* work rights to each other's citizens, thus facilitating the daily border crossings of workers from both countries⟩ — see COMPLEMENTARY

recite *vb* **1** to give an oral or written account of in some detail ⟨*recited* the funny story of how he and his girlfriend met⟩ — see TELL 1
2 to give from memory ⟨asked her to *recite* the Gettysburg Address for the Memorial Day service⟩ — see REPEAT 2

reckless *adj* **1** having or showing a lack of concern for the consequences of one's actions ⟨the *reckless* skiers were making everyone nervous by schussing down the mountainside at lightning speed⟩
synonyms daredevil, devil-may-care, foolhardy, irresponsible
related words adventurous, bold, daring, venturesome; hasty, headlong, hotheaded, impetuous, precipitate, rash, wild; nonchalant, unconcerned, unworried; careless, heedless, inattentive, incautious, unheeding; inconsiderate, thoughtless, unthinking
near antonyms careful, cautious, circumspect, heedful; overcareful, overcautious, timid
antonyms responsible
2 foolishly adventurous or bold ⟨a *reckless* man who jumped into an icy river to save his dog from drowning, only to end up drowned himself⟩ — see FOOLHARDY 1

reckon *vb* **1** to decide the size, amount, number, or distance of (something) without actual measurement ⟨tried to *reckon* the size of the crowd at the stadium⟩ — see ESTIMATE 2
2 *chiefly dialect* to have as an opinion ⟨I *reckon* you must be new to these parts⟩ — see BELIEVE 2
3 to determine (a value) by doing the necessary mathematical operations ⟨asked the class to assume it was 2:00 pm. on March 4 and *reckon* the number of seconds left in the calendar year⟩ — see CALCULATE 1
4 to place reliance or trust ⟨don't *reckon* on being provided with low-cost housing if you take a summer job there⟩ — see DEPEND 2
5 to think of in a particular way ⟨he was *reckoned* among the great heroes of his time⟩ — see CONSIDER 1

reckoning *n* **1** the act of placing a value on the nature, character, or quality of something ⟨by my *reckoning*, that old chest isn't worth much, but an antiques dealer might think otherwise⟩ — see ESTIMATE 1
2 the act or process of performing mathematical operations to find a value ⟨you forgot about the decimal point, so your *reckoning* was way off⟩ — see CALCULATION

reclaim *vb* **1** to get again in one's possession ⟨she *reclaimed* the championship title after losing it last year⟩ — see RECOVER 1
2 to make better in behavior or character ⟨a program to *reclaim* juvenile offenders by requiring them to do community service⟩ — see REFORM 1
3 to obtain (a raw material) by separating it from a byproduct or waste product ⟨after *reclaiming* the glycerin from used vegetable oil, you can use the oil to create a fuel that burns cleaner than regular gasoline⟩ — see RECYCLE

reclamation *n* the act or process of getting something back ⟨pumped water out of the field as part of the land *reclamation* program designed to provide farmers with more farmland⟩ — see RECOVERY 1

recluse *n* a person who lives away from others ⟨he was sick of cities and crowds, so he decided to go live by himself in the woods as a *recluse*⟩
synonyms anchorite, hermit, solitary
related words homebody, shut-in; monk
near antonyms socialite

recognize *vb* to show appreciation, respect, or affection for (someone) with a public celebration ⟨we've gathered together to *recognize* our school custodians and kitchen workers, without whose hard work the school could not function⟩ — see HONOR

recoil *vb* to draw back in fear, pain, or disgust ⟨tried not to *recoil* from the sight of the cockroach in the bathtub⟩ — see FLINCH

recollect *vb* to bring back to mind ⟨I can't *recollect* if I turned the stove off or not before leaving the house⟩ — see REMEMBER

re-collect *vb* **1** to gain emotional or mental control of ⟨she had to calm down and *re-collect* herself after being told she had won the lottery⟩ — see COLLECT 1

2 to get again in one's possession ⟨*re-collect* the papers the wind tore from my hands⟩ — see RECOVER 1

recollection *n* **1** a particular act or instance of recalling or the thing remembered ⟨I have no *recollection* of ever saying that⟩ — see MEMORY 2

2 the power or process of recalling what has been previously learned or experienced ⟨the gradual *recollection* of that long-ago romance brought back both happy and painful feelings⟩ — see MEMORY 1

recommend *vb* to put forward as one's choice for a wise or proper course of action ⟨I would *recommend* you look into that option a little more closely because I don't think it will work nearly as well as you think⟩ — see ADVISE 2

recompense *n* **1** payment to another for a loss or injury ⟨the jury awarded an additional $5,000 in *recompense* for physical pain and suffering⟩ — see COMPENSATION 1

2 something (as money) that is given or received in return for goods or services ⟨as *recompense* for fixing my car, I'll let you use it for a week⟩ — see PAYMENT 2

recompense *vb* **1** to give (someone) the sum of money owed for goods or services received ⟨promised to *recompense* them well for waxing his car if they did a good job⟩ — see PAY 1

2 to give what is owed for ⟨that company still needs to *recompense* the delivery we made to them last week⟩ — see PAY 2

3 to provide (someone) with a just payment for loss or injury ⟨decided to *recompense* them with new plants for the garden after he accidentally mowed down the old plants⟩ — see COMPENSATE 1

reconceive *vb* to consider again especially with the possibility of change or reversal ⟨will have to *reconceive* my earlier opinion about him in light of his recent behavior⟩ — see RECONSIDER

reconcile *vb* to bring to a state free of conflicts, inconsistencies, or differences ⟨historians have never been able to *reconcile* the two eyewitness accounts of the battle⟩ — see HARMONIZE 2

recondite *adj* difficult for one of ordinary knowledge or intelligence to understand ⟨geochemistry is a *recondite* subject⟩ — see PROFOUND 1

recondition *vb* to put into good shape or working order again ⟨asked my dad to help me *recondition* the old tractor for use on the family farm⟩ — see MEND 1

reconsider *vb* to consider again especially with the possibility of change or reversal ⟨the new information forced the general to *reconsider* his plan of attack⟩

synonyms readdress, reanalyze, reconceive, reevaluate, reexamine, rethink, review, reweigh

related words reappraise, reassess; amend, correct, emend, rectify, reform, remedy, revise

phrases change one's mind (about), go over, think better of, view in a new light

near antonyms assert, defend, maintain, uphold

reconsideration *n* a usually critical look at a past event ⟨the discovery of new evidence calls for a *reconsideration* of the case⟩ — see REVIEW 1

record *n* **1** a relating of events usually in the order in which they happened ⟨the town paper published a *record* of the debate, as well as a synopsis of each candidate's stance on the major questions⟩ — see ACCOUNT 1

2 an account of important events in the order in which they happened ⟨historical *records* on the rise of the Roman Empire are plentiful⟩ — see HISTORY 1

record *vb* **1** to make a written note of ⟨the reporter *recorded* the events of the evening in her notebook for later reference⟩

synonyms jot (down), log, mark, note, put down, register, set down

related words chronicle; chalk (up), score; rerecord

2 to put (someone or something) on a list ⟨he was *recorded* as having been a passenger on that ill-fated ship, but his body was never recovered⟩ — see ¹LIST 2

recount *vb* to give an oral or written account of in some detail ⟨a novel that *recounted* an American soldier's adventures among the samurai warriors of 19th-century Japan⟩ — see TELL 1

recoup *vb* **1** to get again in one's possession ⟨tried to *recoup* the $1,000 he had when he walked into the casino by risking his last dollar on a slot machine⟩ — see RECOVER 1

2 to provide (someone) with a just payment for loss or injury ⟨I'll pay for the movie as a way of *recouping* you for the pizza⟩ — see COMPENSATE 1

recoupment *n* **1** payment to another for a loss or injury ⟨the jury's award included a *recoupment* for emotional distress⟩ — see COMPENSATION 1

2 the act or process of getting something back ⟨immediately after the ending of the strike, the company began the *recoupment* of lost business⟩ — see RECOVERY 1

recourse *n* something that one uses to accomplish an end especially when the usual means is not available ⟨a toddler quickly learns that a tantrum is a surefire *recourse* when a polite request for something is met with parental indifference⟩ — see RESOURCE 1

recover *vb* **1** to get again in one's possession ⟨after fishing around in the garbage for ten minutes, I was able to *recover* my lost keys⟩

synonyms reacquire, recapture, reclaim, re-collect, recoup, regain, retake, retrieve

related words recruit, replenish; redeem, repurchase; rescue

phrases get back

near antonyms lose, mislay, misplace

2 to regain a former or normal state ⟨after a disastrous first half, the team was able to *recover* toward the end of the game and manage a win⟩

synonyms rally, rebound, snap back

related words reanimate, revitalize, revive

phrases make a comeback

near antonyms decline, fail, worsen

3 to become healthy and strong again after illness or weakness ⟨I see you're *recovering* well from the accident⟩ — see CONVALESCE

4 to obtain (a raw material) by separating it from a byproduct or waste product ⟨can *recover* aluminum from old cans⟩ — see RECYCLE

recovery *n* **1** the act or process of getting something back ⟨the *recovery* of the sunken boat took over a week⟩

synonyms reclamation, recoupment, repossession, retrieval

related words recruitment, replenishment; redemption, rescue

near antonyms loss, misplacement

2 the process or period of gradually regaining one's health and strength ⟨his *recovery* from the flu was remarkably quick⟩ — see CONVALESCENCE

recreant *adj* **1** having or showing a shameful lack of courage ⟨the victors had only contempt for the *recreant* enemy soldiers who surrendered without firing a shot⟩ — see COWARDLY

2 not true in one's allegiance to someone or something ⟨*recreant* campaign workers who walked out as soon as their candidate began dropping in the polls⟩ — see FAITHLESS

recreant *n* **1** a person who abandons a cause or organization usually without right ⟨traditionally armies have dealt harshly with *recreants*, with execution being a common punishment for desertion during wartime⟩ — see RENEGADE

2 a person who shows a shameful lack of courage in the face of danger ⟨the historian reserved his greatest contempt for those *recreants* who opposed the witch hunt but lacked the courage to speak out against it⟩ — see COWARD

3 one who betrays a trust or an allegiance ⟨a spy and *recreant* to his country⟩ — see TRAITOR

recreate *vb* **1** to bring back to a former condition or vigor ⟨supporters of preservation hope to *recreate* the architectural splendor that the old movie theater had when it first opened⟩ — see RENEW 1

2 to engage in activity for amusement ⟨an old summer resort where families have been *recreating* for over a century⟩ — see PLAY 1

recreated *adj* made or become fresh in spirits or vigor ⟨the club finally got some new, enthusiastic members, and the *recreated* organization actually began contributing to the community⟩ — see NEW 4

recreation *n* **1** activity engaged in to amuse oneself ⟨decided to take a bike tour of the island for *recreation* and relaxation⟩ — see PLAY 1

2 someone or something that provides amusement or enjoyment ⟨roller-skating is great *recreation* on a rainy afternoon⟩ — see FUN 1

3 the act or activity of providing pleasure or amusement especially for the public ⟨water parks have become a significant part of the *recreation* business⟩ — see ENTERTAINMENT 1

recruit *n* a person who is just starting out in a field of activity ⟨the skydiving instructor and other experienced jumpers tried to encourage the new *recruits* on their first jump⟩ — see BEGINNER

rectifiable *adj* capable of being corrected ⟨the mistake is *rectifiable* because you wrote it in pencil⟩ — see REMEDIABLE

rectify *vb* to remove errors, defects, deficiencies, or deviations from ⟨let me get the store manager, and he'll *rectify* the invoice for your order⟩ — see CORRECT 1

rectifying *adj* serving to raise or adjust something to some standard or proper condition ⟨the golf coach gave her stance a *rectifying* adjustment before letting her tee off⟩ — see CORRECTIVE 1

rectitude *n* **1** conduct that conforms to an accepted standard of right and wrong ⟨encouraged the graduates to go on to live lives of unimpeachable *rectitude* and integrity⟩ — see MORALITY 1

2 faithfulness to high moral standards ⟨has a finely honed sense of *rectitude* that keeps him from cheating on exams⟩ — see HONOR 1

recuperate *vb* to become healthy and strong again after illness or weakness ⟨half the class was out, many students being sick or *recuperating* from the flu⟩ — see CONVALESCE

recuperation *n* the process or period of gradually regaining one's health and strength ⟨the older you get, the longer *recuperation* takes⟩ — see CONVALESCENCE

recurrent *adj* occurring or appearing at intervals ⟨had *recurrent* problems with the computer for months and finally junked it⟩ — see INTERMITTENT 1

recurring *adj* occurring or appearing at intervals ⟨death and spirituality are *recurring* themes throughout the whole of this author's work⟩ — see INTERMITTENT 1

recycle *vb* to obtain (a raw material) by separating it from a by-product or waste product ⟨*recycling* the aluminum from pop cans is environmentally sound⟩

synonyms reclaim, recover

related words reuse; process

red *n* a person who rises up against authority ⟨the *reds* demanded a violent overthrow of the government⟩ — see REBEL

red–blooded *adj* having active strength of body or mind ⟨a *red-blooded* rugby player who always plays to win⟩ — see VIGOROUS 1

redden *vb* to develop a rosy facial color (as from excitement or embarrassment) ⟨his face *reddened* when she flashed him a dazzling smile⟩ — see BLUSH

redeem *vb* **1** to do what is required by the terms of ⟨our dad *redeemed* his pledge to take us out for pizza if we aced the exam⟩ — see FULFILL 1

2 to free from captivity or punishment by paying a price ⟨the government has consistently refused to *redeem* hostages captured by terrorists⟩ — see RANSOM

3 to free from the penalties or consequences of sin ⟨the belief that sinners are *redeemed* by their faith in God⟩ — see SAVE 1

4 to make better in behavior or character ⟨made a determined effort to *redeem* himself in his neighbors' eyes⟩ — see REFORM 1

redeemer *n* one that saves from danger or destruction ⟨the rescued hostages profusely thanked their camouflage-clad *redeemers*⟩ — see SAVIOR

red–hot *adj* **1** being or involving the latest methods, concepts, information, or styles ⟨this *red-hot* automobile uses the latest technology for its engine design⟩ — see MODERN

2 having a notably high temperature ⟨don't touch the stove—it's *red-hot*⟩ — see HOT 1

3 having or expressing great depth of feeling ⟨*red-hot* calls to action for and against the war⟩ — see FERVENT

redo *vb* **1** to make different in some way ⟨desperately wanted to *redo* the red living room in shades of green⟩ — see CHANGE 1

2 to make or do again ⟨the conductor kept asking the violinist to *redo* that passage until he was completely satisfied⟩ — see REPEAT 4

redoing *n* the act, process, or result of making different ⟨her hair looked no better for all the *redoing* she did to it⟩ — see CHANGE

redolence *n* **1** a sweet or pleasant smell ⟨breathed in the *redolence* of the apple orchard⟩ — see FRAGRANCE

2 the quality of a thing that makes it perceptible to the sense organs in the nose ⟨the *redolence* of oranges always reminds me of Christmas⟩ — see SMELL

redolent *adj* having a pleasant smell ⟨my grandmother's house always seemed to be *redolent* with the aroma of baking bread⟩ — see FRAGRANT

redouble *vb* **1** to make markedly greater in measure or degree ⟨rescuers *redoubled* their efforts to reach the people buried in the rubble after unexpectedly hearing someone call for help⟩ — see INTENSIFY
2 to make twice as great or as many ⟨if we *redouble* the recipe, we'll have enough cookies for the whole class⟩ — see DOUBLE 1

redoubtable *adj* causing fear ⟨his next opponent, the reigning champion, would be by far the most *redoubtable* adversary the young boxer had ever faced⟩ — see FEARFUL 1

redraft *vb* to prepare for publication by correcting, rewriting, or updating ⟨if you *redraft* that paper and include more recent data, I think we could publish it⟩ — see EDIT

redress *n* payment to another for a loss or injury ⟨the skis were certainly an adequate *redress* for the lost snowboard⟩ — see COMPENSATION 1

reduce *vb* **1** to bring to a lower grade or rank ⟨was *reduced* from team captain to team member as punishment for his misbehavior on the court⟩ — see DEMOTE
2 to make smaller in amount, volume, or extent ⟨you'll have to *reduce* the amount of money you spend on CDs if you want to have any money left for college⟩ — see DECREASE 1

reduction *n* **1** something that is or may be subtracted ⟨there was a sizable *reduction* in her weekly pay when she decided to buy health insurance⟩ — see DEDUCTION 1
2 the amount by which something is lessened ⟨saw a ten percent *reduction* in the number of students applying to the school⟩ — see DECREASE

redundancy *n* the use of too many words to express an idea ⟨even though the phrase "free gift" is a *redundancy*, many retailers still use it to assure customers that an item is really free⟩ — see VERBIAGE

reduplicate *vb* **1** to make an exact likeness of ⟨*reduplicate* a tape of the concert for my friend⟩ — see COPY 1
2 to make or do again ⟨found out halfway through the project that I was *reduplicating* another team member's efforts, so we had to figure out who was going to do what⟩ — see REPEAT 4

reduplication *n* **1** something that is made to look exactly like something else ⟨that old-looking colonial mansion is actually a 20th-century *reduplication* of the original, which was destroyed many years ago⟩ — see COPY
2 the act of saying or doing over again ⟨what you just said is a verbatim *reduplication* of what I told you earlier⟩ — see REPEAT

reecho *vb* to continue or be repeated in a series of reflected sound waves ⟨thunder *reechoing* though the canyon⟩ — see REVERBERATE

reek *n* **1** a strong unpleasant smell ⟨a terrible *reek* coming from the garbage can⟩ — see STINK
2 an atmospheric condition in which suspended particles in the air rob it of its transparency ⟨couldn't see through the *reek* of smog and smoke surrounding the steel plant⟩ — see HAZE 1

reek *vb* to give off an extremely unpleasant smell ⟨those old sneakers *reek* something awful⟩ — see STINK

reeking *adj* having an unpleasant smell ⟨I would rather not be the one to wash your *reeking* gym clothes⟩ — see MALODOROUS

reeky *adj* having an unpleasant smell ⟨a *reeky* riverbank smelling of rotting fish⟩ — see MALODOROUS

reel *n* a rapid turning about on an axis or central point ⟨she slipped and, after an out-of-control *reel*, fell on her backside⟩ — see SPIN 1

reel *vb* **1** to be in a confused state as if from being twirled around ⟨his mind *reeled* upon hearing the news that he had made the varsity team⟩ — see SPIN 2
2 to move forward while swaying from side to side ⟨got off the amusement park ride *reeling* and barely able to stand⟩ — see STAGGER 1

reeling *adj* having a feeling of being whirled about and in danger of falling down ⟨the blood donor was *reeling* after standing up too quickly⟩ — see DIZZY 1

reenergized *adj* made or become fresh in spirits or vigor ⟨was *reenergized* after a short nap⟩ — see NEW 4

reevaluate *vb* to consider again especially with the possibility of change or reversal ⟨I'll have to *reevaluate* your final grade in the class⟩ — see RECONSIDER

reexamination *n* a usually critical look at a past event ⟨a congressional *reexamination* of the incident to see if it could have been prevented⟩ — see REVIEW 1

reexamine *vb* to consider again especially with the possibility of change or reversal ⟨in light of your broken leg, we should *reexamine* our decision to go on a hiking vacation this summer⟩ — see RECONSIDER

refashion *vb* to make different in some way ⟨*refashioned* my old pair of jeans into a cover for my math book⟩ — see CHANGE 1

refashioning *n* the act, process, or result of making different ⟨the *refashioning* of the school auditorium will make it more up-to-date⟩ — see CHANGE

refer *vb* to have a relation or connection ⟨I don't think that playing rule *refers* to this particular situation⟩ — see APPLY 1

refer (to) *vb* **1** to make reference to or speak about briefly but specifically ⟨try not to *refer to* the recent death of her aunt⟩ — see MENTION 1
2 to use or seek out as a source of aid, relief, or advantage ⟨she studied so she wouldn't have to *refer to* the book during the exam⟩ — see RESORT (TO) 1

referee *n* a person who impartially decides or resolves a dispute or controversy ⟨served as the unofficial *referee* in disputes over the family business⟩ — see JUDGE 1

referee *vb* to give an opinion about (something at issue or in dispute) ⟨Dad is usually the one who has to *referee* any disputes concerning use of the big TV⟩ — see JUDGE 1

reference *n* relation to or concern with something specified ⟨this reply is in *reference* to your last question⟩ — see RESPECT 1

refine *vb* to make better ⟨worked on *refining* her backhand before the big tennis match⟩ — see IMPROVE

refined *adj* **1** being far along in development ⟨a *refined* analysis of the factors that produce economic wealth⟩ — see ADVANCED 1
2 free from added matter ⟨*refined* gold⟩ — see PURE 1
3 having or showing a taste for the fine arts and gracious living ⟨a *refined* couple who have hosted many elegant benefits for organizations promoting the arts⟩ — see CULTIVATED
4 having or showing elegance ⟨a *refined* woman with gracious manners⟩ — see ELEGANT 1
5 made or done with extreme care and accuracy ⟨the dressmaker took a set of quite *refined* measurements before actually starting work⟩ — see FINE 2

6 satisfying or pleasing because of fineness or mildness ⟨the chef's *refined* cuisine is one that true gourmets will appreciate⟩ — see DELICATE 1

refinement *n* **1** an instance of notable progress in the development of knowledge, technology, or skill ⟨the recent *refinements* in this area of medical technology⟩ — see ADVANCE 2

2 a high level of taste and enlightenment as a result of extensive intellectual training and exposure to the arts ⟨had a sense of *refinement* that her small hometown couldn't satisfy, so she moved to New York City to be closer to great museums and concert halls⟩ — see CULTURE 1

3 dignified or restrained beauty of form, appearance, or style ⟨although she can afford all the jewelry that money can buy, she dresses with the gentle *refinement* that only taste can bestow⟩ — see ELEGANCE

reflect *vb* to reproduce or show (an exact likeness) as a mirror would ⟨her face was *reflected* in the waters of the still pond⟩

synonyms image, mirror

related words copy, duplicate, imitate, reduplicate, repeat, replicate, reproduce

reflection *n* **1** a briefly expressed opinion ⟨does anyone want to share their *reflections* on the passage we just read?⟩ — see REMARK

2 a cause of shame ⟨your constant lying is a serious *reflection* on your character⟩ — see DISGRACE 2

reflective *adj* given to or marked by long, quiet thinking ⟨one of the twins was outgoing and talkative while the other was withdrawn and *reflective*⟩ — see CONTEMPLATIVE

reform *vb* **1** to make better in behavior or character ⟨a *reformed* criminal who is now a productive member of society⟩

synonyms reclaim, redeem, rehabilitate

related words amend, improve; cleanse, purify, restore

near antonyms abase, corrupt, debauch, degrade, demean, demoralize, deprave, pervert, poison, profane, prostitute, subvert, warp

2 to remove errors, defects, deficiencies, or deviations from ⟨he had better *reform* his ways if he wants any of us to trust him⟩ — see CORRECT 1

reformative *adj* serving to raise or adjust something to some standard or proper condition ⟨took *reformative* measures to curb abuses in the state's welfare system⟩ — see CORRECTIVE 1

reformatory *adj* serving to raise or adjust something to some standard or proper condition ⟨the belief that manual labor was a *reformatory* experience for convicted felons, who would learn the value of hard work⟩ — see CORRECTIVE 1

refractoriness *n* refusal to obey ⟨if your *refractoriness* continues, you will not be allowed to go on the upcoming field trip⟩ — see DISOBEDIENCE

refractory *adj* **1** given to resisting authority or another's control ⟨*refractory* players will be ejected from the game⟩ — see DISOBEDIENT

2 given to resisting control or discipline by others ⟨believing that rules are only for other people, he's been *refractory* virtually his entire life⟩ — see UNCONTROLLABLE

refrain *n* a part of a song or hymn that is repeated every so often ⟨I didn't know the verses of the song, so I only sang on the *refrain*⟩ — see CHORUS 2

refrain (from) *vb* to resist the temptation of ⟨couldn't *refrain from* ruffling her nephew's neatly combed hair when she saw him⟩ — see FORBEAR

refresh *vb* to bring back to a former condition or vigor ⟨brought out some iced tea to *refresh* the spirits of the folks working out in the sun⟩ — see RENEW 1

refreshed *adj* made or become fresh in spirits or vigor ⟨woke the next morning *refreshed* and ready for the day⟩ — see NEW 4

refreshen *vb* to bring back to a former condition or vigor ⟨*refreshened* the wilting flowers by cutting the stems again and putting them in a vase with water⟩ — see RENEW 1

refreshing *adj* having a renewing effect on the state of the body or mind ⟨the cool wind off the ocean is *refreshing* on such a hot day⟩ — see TONIC

refrigerate *vb* to cause to lose heat ⟨*refrigerate* the cake after you frost it so the frosting doesn't melt⟩ — see COOL 1

refuge *n* something (as a building) that offers cover from the weather or protection from danger ⟨hunting is strictly forbidden in the wildlife *refuge*⟩ — see SHELTER

refugee *n* a person forced to emigrate for political reasons ⟨*refugees* began returning to their homeland after years of political unrest and war⟩ — see ÉMIGRÉ 1

refulgence *n* the quality or state of having or giving off light ⟨the *refulgence* of a full moon on a clear autumn night⟩ — see BRILLIANCE 1

refulgent *adj* giving off or reflecting much light ⟨*refulgent* sunlight broke through the clouds, creating huge swaths of light in the valley below us⟩ — see BRIGHT 1

refund *vb* to make a return payment to ⟨will *refund* you your money⟩ — see REPAY

refusal *n* an unwillingness to grant something asked for ⟨his flat *refusal* of our reasonable request upset us all⟩ — see DENIAL 1

refuse *n* discarded or useless material ⟨*refuse* had littered the playground until our volunteer group cleaned it up⟩ — see GARBAGE

refuse *vb* **1** to be unwilling to grant ⟨the reclusive movie star usually *refuses* requests for interviews⟩ — see DENY 2

2 to show unwillingness to accept, do, engage in, or agree to ⟨she *refused* the award, citing the hard work of others who deserved the award more than she did⟩ — see DECLINE 1

refute *vb* to prove to be false ⟨the victories of African-American athlete Jesse Owens in the 1936 Olympics effectively *refuted* the racial view of the Nazis⟩ — see DISPROVE

regain *vb* to get again in one's possession ⟨our team *regained* the ball with just two minutes left on the clock⟩ — see RECOVER 1

regal *adj* **1** fit for or worthy of a royal ruler ⟨the actress's *regal* bearing makes her a perfect choice to play royalty on the screen⟩ — see MONARCHICAL

2 large and impressive in size, grandeur, extent, or conception ⟨envisioned a *regal* wedding with hundreds of guests, a full choir, and a reception at the fanciest hotel in town⟩ — see GRAND 1

regale *vb* **1** to cause (someone) to pass the time agreeably occupied ⟨*regaled* his grandchildren with stories of his time in Morocco⟩ — see AMUSE

2 to entertain with a fancy meal ⟨an inn that nightly *regales* its guests with five-course meals prepared by a master chef⟩ — see FEAST

regalia *n* dressy clothing ⟨was impressed with the *regalia* of the women at the ball⟩ — see FINERY

regard *n* **1** a feeling of great approval and liking ⟨I have a deep *regard* for humanitarian aid workers who risk everything to help the poor⟩ — see ADMIRATION 1

2 an instance of looking especially briefly ⟨flashed the young man an imperial *regard* that clearly indicated such behavior was out of line⟩ — see LOOK 2

3 relation to or concern with something specified ⟨with *regard* to your request for time off, go ahead and take the whole week for vacation⟩ — see RESPECT 1

4 **regards** *pl* best wishes ⟨give your parents my *regards*⟩ — see COMPLIMENT

regard *vb* **1** to make note of (something) through the use of one's eyes ⟨she *regarded* him with astonishment when he announced he had gotten engaged⟩ — see SEE 1

2 to take notice of and be guided by ⟨if you *regard* the rules of the pool, you can swim⟩ — see HEED 1

3 to think of in a particular way ⟨I wouldn't *regard* that off-hand comment as a serious threat to your personal safety⟩ — see CONSIDER 1

4 to think very highly or favorably of ⟨an astronomer who is highly *regarded* by his peers⟩ — see ADMIRE

regardful *adj* marked by or showing proper regard for another's higher status ⟨his *regardful* willingness to let his elderly father carve the turkey this year⟩ — see RESPECTFUL

regarding *prep* having to do with ⟨wanted to talk to my teacher *regarding* my grade in her class⟩ — see ABOUT 1

regardless *adv* in spite of everything ⟨the weather looked bad, but they were resolved to go on with their picnic *regardless*⟩
synonyms anyhow, anyway
related words nevertheless
phrases in any case, no matter

regenerate *vb* **1** to bring back to a former condition or vigor ⟨the neighborhood was *regenerated* by a government grant for restoring all the old buildings and creating studio spaces for artists⟩ — see RENEW 1

2 to bring back to life, practice, or activity ⟨dairy farming in the area was *regenerated* when new arrivals bought the old creamery⟩ — see REVIVE 1

regenerated *adj* made or become fresh in spirits or vigor ⟨after a cool dip in the river, the *regenerated* hikers continued on their way⟩ — see NEW 4

regeneration *n* the act or an instance of bringing something back to life, public attention, or vigorous activity ⟨the *regeneration* of knitting and crocheting is in full bloom, with Hollywood stars admitting they knit and crochet on movie sets⟩ — see REVIVAL

regime *also* **régime** *n* lawful control over the affairs of a political unit (as a nation) ⟨the *regime* of the dictator collapsed very abruptly⟩ — see RULE 2

regimen *n* lawful control over the affairs of a political unit (as a nation) ⟨a new party will have *regimen* over the nation after the start of the new year⟩ — see RULE 2

region *n* **1** a part or portion having no fixed boundaries ⟨if you look in the upper left *region* of the sky, you can see the constellation Orion⟩
synonyms area, demesne, field, zone
related words section; locale, locality, location, locus, place, point, position, site, spot

2 a broad geographical area ⟨corn is mostly grown in the central *regions* of the country⟩
synonyms belt, land, part(s), tract, zone
related words district, territory

¹register *n* a person whose job is to keep records ⟨ask the county *register* for a copy of your birth certificate⟩ — see CLERK 1

²register *n* a record of a series of items (as names or titles) usually arranged according to some system ⟨check the student *register* to see if I am enrolled for that class⟩ — see ¹LIST

register *vb* **1** to enter in a list or roll ⟨I have to *register* my new car when I get my driver's license⟩ — see ENROLL 1

2 to make a written note of ⟨the management *registered* her complaint in their log and promised to get back to her in a week⟩ — see RECORD 1

3 to put (someone or something) on a list ⟨please *register* me for the Spanish 101 class⟩ — see ¹LIST 2

registrar *n* a person whose job is to keep records ⟨got a copy of his transcript from the school's *registrar*⟩ — see CLERK 1

registration *n* the number of individuals registered ⟨there was a large *registration* for the popular swim classes at the community center⟩
synonyms enrollment, registry
related words class

registry *n* **1** a record of a series of items (as names or titles) usually arranged according to some system ⟨got a copy of the couple's bridal *registry* from the store's computer and scanned it for items we could afford⟩ — see ¹LIST

2 the number of individuals registered ⟨has the *registry* for the senior seminar reached its limit yet?⟩ — see REGISTRATION

regress *vb* to go back to a previous and usually lower state or level ⟨in extreme circumstances, people sometimes *regress* to the behavior they exhibited in childhood⟩
synonyms retrogress, revert
related words backslide, lapse, relapse; return
near antonyms grow, mature, ripen
antonyms advance, develop, evolve, progress

regression *n* the act or an instance of going back to an earlier and lower level especially of intelligence or behavior ⟨the *regression* to really childish behavior that boys often undergo when put in large groups⟩
synonyms retrogression, reversion
related words backslide, lapse, relapse; return; nondevelopment
near antonyms growth, maturation, ripening
antonyms advancement, development, evolution, progression

regret *n* a feeling of responsibility for wrongdoing ⟨she was consumed with *regret* for belittling him in public and felt much better once she had apologized⟩ — see GUILT 1

regret *vb* to feel sorry or dissatisfied about ⟨we *regret* any inconvenience that we may have caused you⟩
synonyms bemoan, deplore, lament, repent, rue
related words bewail, grieve (for), mourn, sorrow (for)

regretful *adj* **1** expressing or suggesting mourning ⟨gave me a *regretful* look when I told him my dog had run away⟩ — see MOURNFUL 1

2 feeling sorrow for a wrong that one has done ⟨was truly *regretful* that she had yelled at him⟩ — see CONTRITE 1

regretfully *adv* with feelings of bitterness or grief ⟨I must *regretfully* inform you that you are not among those who have been accepted for our summer program⟩ — see HARD 2

regrettable *adj* of a kind to cause great distress ⟨the explorers forged ahead despite the *regrettable* loss of some of their companions⟩

synonyms deplorable, distressful, distressing, grievous, heartbreaking, heartrending, lamentable, unfortunate, woeful

related words affecting, moving, poignant, touching; awful, dire, dreadful, fearful, terrible; horrible, horrifying, intolerable, overwhelming, shocking, sickening, unbearable; miserable, pitiful, wretched; calamitous, disastrous

near antonyms gratifying, pleasing, rewarding, satisfying; comforting, encouraging, heartening; cheering, heartwarming, inspiring; fortunate, happy, lucky

regular *adj* **1** appearing or occurring repeatedly from time to time ⟨what with one or another of our pets having problems, we've been *regular* visitors at the animal hospital⟩

synonyms constant, frequent, habitual, periodic, repeated, steady

related words chronic, confirmed, inveterate; expected, usual

near antonyms unexpected, unusual

antonyms inconstant, infrequent, irregular

2 following a set method, arrangement, or pattern ⟨planned out the trip in a very *regular* way⟩ — see METHODICAL

3 following or agreeing with established form, custom, or rules ⟨thought about having a nontraditional wedding but in the end went with a *regular* ceremony instead⟩ — see FORMAL 1

4 having no exceptions or restrictions ⟨your room is a *regular* sty, and you need to clean it before you can go to the movies⟩ — see ABSOLUTE 2

5 having or showing the qualities associated with the members of a particular group or kind ⟨tantrums aren't his *regular* behavior⟩ ⟨was just a *regular* teenager who preferred hanging out with friends⟩ — see TYPICAL 1

regular *n* a person engaged in military service ⟨throughout the war, the *regulars* were supplemented by corps of volunteers and militiamen⟩ — see SOLDIER

regularize *vb* to make agree with a single established standard or model ⟨the fashion industry agreed to *regularize* women's clothing sizes so one company's size six wasn't another company's size ten⟩ — see STANDARDIZE

regulate *vb* **1** to keep from exceeding a desirable degree or level (as of expression) ⟨the candidate assured voters that he wanted to better *regulate* the percentage of their income that people pay in taxes⟩ — see CONTROL 1

2 to look after and make decisions about ⟨the government agency that *regulates* the nuclear power industry in this country⟩ — see CONDUCT 1

regulation *n* **1** a statement spelling out the proper procedure or conduct for an activity ⟨it's against camp *regulations* to leave your cabin after 11:00 p.m.⟩ — see RULE 1

2 the act or activity of looking after and making decisions about something ⟨the owner seldom visited the plant and did not take an active part in the *regulation* of the company⟩ — see CONDUCT 1

3 the duty or function of watching or guarding for the sake of proper direction or control ⟨the *regulation* of the soccer team was left entirely to the head coach and the assistant coaches⟩ — see SUPERVISION 1

regulator *n* a mechanism for adjusting the operation of a device, machine, or system ⟨the voltage *regulator* will make sure your car's alternator gets the right amount of electricity⟩ — see CONTROL 1

rehabilitate *vb* **1** to make better in behavior or character ⟨an organization that *rehabilitates* criminals so they can reenter society⟩ — see REFORM 1

2 to restore to a healthy condition ⟨went to physical therapy to help *rehabilitate* her broken elbow⟩ — see HEAL 1

rehabilitation *n* the process or period of gradually regaining one's health and strength ⟨his *rehabilitation* from the flu was brief, and he was up and running around within a few days⟩ — see CONVALESCENCE

rehearsal *n* a private performance or session in preparation for a public appearance ⟨we made a few mistakes in *rehearsal*, but we were pretty sure that we'd be okay on opening night⟩

synonyms dry run, practice (*also* practise), trial

related words dress rehearsal; preview; drill, exercise

rehearse *vb* **1** to do over and over so as to become skilled ⟨the orchestra *rehearsed* the symphony until they finally got it to the conductor's satisfaction⟩ — see PRACTICE

2 to give an oral or written account of in some detail ⟨wrote a letter to the management *rehearsing* in lurid detail our terrible stay at their hotel⟩ — see TELL 1

3 to say or state again ⟨*rehearsed* her story about why she was late as she walked into class⟩ — see REPEAT 1

4 to specify one after another ⟨*rehearsed* the list of things he wanted for his birthday so that there would be no doubt in my mind⟩ — see ENUMERATE 1

reimburse *vb* to make a return payment to ⟨make sure you let the school know how much the copies cost so we can *reimburse* you for your expenses⟩ — see REPAY

rein *n* the place of leadership or command ⟨after the president resigned, the vice-president stepped in and took the *reins* of the company⟩ — see HEAD 2

rein (in) *vb* to keep from exceeding a desirable degree or level (as of expression) ⟨try to *rein in* your spending, so you have some money left for saving⟩ — see CONTROL 1

reiterate *vb* **1** to make or do again ⟨*reiterated* the throw and this time made the basket⟩ — see REPEAT 4

2 to say or state again ⟨I want to *reiterate* that under no circumstances are you to leave the house⟩ — see REPEAT 1

reiteration *n* the act of saying or doing over again ⟨there's no need for the *reiteration* of the rules, as I know them already⟩ — see REPEAT

reiterative *adj* marked by repetition ⟨the novelist's *reiterative* style really bores some readers⟩ — see REPETITIVE

reject *n* **1** one who is cast out or rejected by society ⟨felt sorry for the class *reject* and sat with him at lunch⟩ — see OUTCAST

2 something separated from a group or lot for not being as good as the others ⟨that apple has a mushy spot on it, so it's a *reject*⟩ — see CULL

reject *vb* **1** to be unwilling to grant ⟨*rejected* his request for time off⟩ — see DENY 2

2 to declare not to be true ⟨I *reject* the claim that I have ever lied about that⟩ — see DENY 1

3 to get rid of as useless or unwanted ⟨sorted through the nuts and *rejected* any that had cracked shells or were shattered⟩ — see DISCARD

4 to show unwillingness to accept, do, engage in, or agree to ⟨*rejected* his marriage proposal⟩ — see DECLINE 1

rejected *adj* left unoccupied or unused ⟨picked up the *rejected* toy to see what was wrong with it⟩ — see ABANDONED

rejection *n* **1** a refusal to confirm the truth of a statement ⟨made a flat *rejection* of the charges against him⟩ — see DENIAL 2

2 an unwillingness to grant something asked for ⟨the principal's swift *rejection* of our request for a classroom in which to hold our club meetings⟩ — see DENIAL 1

3 something separated from a group or lot for not being as good as the others ⟨that pile is for *rejections,* and this one is for applications we'll be accepting⟩ — see CULL

rejoice *vb* **1** to feel or express joy or triumph ⟨*rejoiced* over our unexpected victory on the soccer field⟩ — see EXULT

2 to give satisfaction to ⟨your thoughtful present *rejoiced* me greatly⟩ — see PLEASE

rejoicing *adj* having or expressing feelings of joy or triumph ⟨the *rejoicing* winner of the lottery⟩ — see EXULTANT

rejoin *vb* to speak or write in reaction to a question or to another reaction ⟨when I asked if she wouldn't mind picking up dinner on her way home from soccer practice, she *rejoined,* "Only if you wouldn't mind me taking out the pickup later tonight!"⟩ — see ANSWER 1

rejoinder *n* something spoken or written in reaction especially to a question ⟨he always has a smart-aleck *rejoinder* to everything⟩ — see ANSWER 1

rejuvenate *vb* **1** to bring back to a former condition or vigor ⟨the shower *rejuvenated* me after a long day of cleaning out the horse stalls⟩ — see RENEW 1

2 to bring back to life, practice, or activity ⟨that rock star has *rejuvenated* '80s fashion for a whole new generation⟩ — see REVIVE 1

rejuvenation *n* the act or an instance of bringing something back to life, public attention, or vigorous activity ⟨Hollywood was seeing the *rejuvenation* of kung fu movies⟩ — see REVIVAL

rekindle *vb* to bring back to life, practice, or activity ⟨the trip to Ireland *rekindled* her interest in learning Gaelic⟩ — see REVIVE 1

relate *vb* **1** to form a close personal relationship ⟨she and I *relate* so well it's almost like we're siblings⟩ — see COMMUNE

2 to give an oral or written account of in some detail ⟨asked our uncle to *relate* the story of his visit to communist Russia many years ago⟩ — see TELL 1

3 to have a relation or connection ⟨your college essay should *relate* to your experiences in high school⟩ — see APPLY 1

4 to think of (something) in combination ⟨most Americans *relate* tea to the United Kingdom and coffee to the U.S.⟩ — see ASSOCIATE 2

related *adj* having a close connection like that between family members ⟨the *related* fields of anthropology and archaeology⟩

synonyms affiliated, akin, allied, kindred

related words associated, connected; alike, analogous, comparable, correspondent, corresponding, like, matching, parallel, resembling, similar, such, suchlike; identical, same; germane, pertinent, relevant

near antonyms different, disparate, dissimilar, distinct, distinctive, distinguishable, diverse, other, unalike, unlike

antonyms unrelated

relation *n* **1 relations** *pl* doings between individuals or groups ⟨*relations* between the rival newspapers remained friendly despite their competition for the same stories⟩

synonyms dealings, interaction, intercourse

related words interrelationship

2 a person connected with another by blood or marriage ⟨he and I are *relations* on our mother's side⟩ — see RELATIVE

3 the fact or state of having something in common ⟨there's no *relation* between you losing your favorite baseball hat and your team losing the game⟩ — see CONNECTION 1

4 the state of having shared interests or efforts (as in social or business matters) ⟨our intramural baseball team had a *relation* with the other baseball teams in the area⟩ — see ASSOCIATION 1

relationship *n* **1** the fact or state of having something in common ⟨studied the *relationship* between the phases of the moon and ocean tides⟩ — see CONNECTION 1

2 the state of having shared interests or efforts (as in social or business matters) ⟨the street's shopkeepers have a good business *relationship*⟩ — see ASSOCIATION 1

relative *adj* **1** being such only when compared to something else ⟨after being crammed into a one-bedroom apartment, they lived in *relative* comfort in a two-bedroom house⟩ — see COMPARATIVE

2 having to do with the matter at hand ⟨I don't need the whole story, just the details that are *relative* to the case⟩ — see PERTINENT

relative *n* a person connected with another by blood or marriage ⟨it's always fun to see all your *relatives* at a big family gathering⟩

synonyms kin, kinsman, relation

related words in-law; kinswoman; blood, clan, family, folk, house, kindred, kinfolk, kinsfolk, line, lineage, people, race, stock, tribe

relatively *adv* to some degree or extent ⟨the in-laws felt *relatively* comfortable at our family reunion⟩ — see FAIRLY

relax *vb* **1** to get rid of nervous tension or anxiety ⟨she took deep breaths to *relax* before going on stage⟩

synonyms unwind

related words loosen (up), unbend; repose, rest; alleviate, comfort, ease, relieve; calm, compose, cool, quiet, settle

antonyms tense (up)

2 to make less taut ⟨*relax* the rope a bit so I can pick up the slack and tie this knot⟩ — see SLACKEN

3 to refrain from labor or exertion ⟨I just want to kick back and *relax* after mowing that huge lawn⟩ — see REST 1

relaxation *n* **1** activity engaged in to amuse oneself ⟨rode my bike along the canal for *relaxation* and exercise⟩ — see PLAY 1

2 freedom from activity or labor ⟨meditating in a state of total *relaxation*⟩ — see ¹REST 1

relaxed *adj* **1** enjoying physical comfort ⟨was totally *relaxed* after the warm bath⟩ — see COMFORTABLE 2

2 not bound by rigid standards ⟨we've having a *relaxed* study hall since today is the last day before school break⟩ — see EASYGOING 2

3 not tightly fastened, tied, or stretched ⟨the fishing line was *relaxed* and looped lazily into the pond⟩ — see LOOSE 1

relaxing *adj* tending to calm the emotions and relieve stress ⟨a *relaxing* cup of chamomile tea⟩ — see SOOTHING 1

release *n* **1** a freeing from an obligation or responsibility ⟨after they declared bankruptcy, the bank agreed to a *release* from their debt⟩

synonyms delivery, discharge, quietus, quittance
related words exemption, immunity, waiver
2 a document containing a declaration of an intentional giving up of a right, claim, or privilege ⟨had to sign a liability *release* before they'd let us go rock climbing on their property⟩ — see WAIVER
3 a published statement informing the public of a matter of general interest ⟨a press *release* announcing that the governor would not run for a second term⟩ — see ANNOUNCEMENT
release *vb* **1** to set free (from a state of being held in check) ⟨he *released* his anger with a great yell of frustration⟩
synonyms loose, loosen, uncork, unleash, unlock, unloose, unloosen
related words discharge, emancipate, enfranchise, free, liberate, manumit, spring, unbind, uncage, unchain, unfetter; air, express, vent
near antonyms manacle, shackle, trammel; bind, confine, enchain, fetter
antonyms bridle, check, constrain, contain, control, curb, govern, hold in, inhibit, regulate, rein (in), restrain, tame
2 to find emotional release for ⟨tried to find other ways of *releasing* tension than by chewing her fingernails⟩ — see TAKE OUT 1
3 to set free (as from slavery or confinement) ⟨*release* the prisoners immediately⟩ — see FREE 1
4 to set free from entanglement or difficulty ⟨finally managed to *release* himself from his rash promise⟩ — see EXTRICATE
5 to throw or give off ⟨an air freshener that *releases* a pleasing scent into the room⟩ — see EMIT 1
relent *vb* to grow less in scope or intensity especially gradually ⟨the fury of the storm *relented*, and the next day the sun finally broke through the clouds⟩ — see DECREASE 2
relentless *adj* showing no signs of slackening or yielding in one's purpose ⟨the team's offense was *relentless* in trying to score a touchdown⟩ — see UNYIELDING 1
relevance *n* the fact or state of being pertinent ⟨I appreciate that you did the dishes tonight, but that has no *relevance* to my enforcement of the punishment you got earlier this week⟩ — see PERTINENCE
relevancy *n* the fact or state of being pertinent ⟨that extra information has no *relevancy* to the case⟩ — see PERTINENCE
relevant *adj* having to do with the matter at hand ⟨make sure your comments during the class discussion are short and *relevant*⟩ — see PERTINENT
reliability *n* worthiness as the recipient of another's trust or confidence ⟨we never had to question the *reliability* of the park rangers in an emergency⟩
synonyms dependability, reliableness, solidity, solidness, sureness, trustworthiness
related words infallibility
near antonyms doubtfulness, dubiousness
reliable *adj* worthy of one's trust ⟨I need a *reliable* car that's not going to break down constantly⟩ — see DEPENDABLE
reliableness *n* worthiness as the recipient of another's trust or confidence ⟨the proven *reliableness* of that brand of house appliances⟩ — see RELIABILITY
reliance *n* **1** something or someone to which one looks for support ⟨he's been the family's foremost *reliance* in times of trouble many times⟩ — see DEPENDENCE 2

2 the quality or state of needing something or someone ⟨a baby's *reliance* on her parents⟩ ⟨his *reliance* on his neighbor for all the local gossip⟩ — see DEPENDENCE 1
relic *n* **1** a tiny often physical indication of something lost or vanished ⟨a crude stone ax and other *relics* of the Neanderthals⟩ — see VESTIGE
2 something belonging to or surviving from an earlier period ⟨in my grandparents' attic are many *relics* from the 1960s⟩ — see ANTIQUE
relief *n* **1** a feeling of ease from grief or trouble ⟨my classmates' kind words offered gave me some *relief* from the harsh criticism I had received from the teacher⟩ — see COMFORT 1
2 a person or thing that takes the place of another ⟨I can't go home from my shift until my *relief* shows up to take over⟩ — see SUBSTITUTE
3 reduction of or freedom from pain ⟨the aspirin gave him some *relief* from the headache⟩ — see EASE 1
relieve *vb* **1** to make more bearable or less severe ⟨an ice pack will *relieve* the swelling⟩ — see HELP 2
2 to set (a person or thing) free of something that encumbers ⟨the bellhop *relieved* him of his luggage and led him to the elevator⟩ — see RID
religion *n* **1** a body of beliefs and practices regarding the supernatural and the worship of one or more deities ⟨the Jewish *religion* has followers in many parts of the globe⟩
synonyms credo, creed, cult, faith, persuasion
related words church, communion, denomination, sect; belief, doctrine, dogma, theology; monotheism, polytheism, theism
near antonyms agnosticism, atheism, secularism
2 belief and trust in and loyalty to God ⟨without his *religion*, he would not have been able to survive all the difficulties he has faced over the years⟩ — see FAITH 1
religious *adj* **1** of, relating to, or used in the practice or worship services of a religion ⟨J.S. Bach wrote some of the most beautiful *religious* music in the world⟩
synonyms devotional, sacred, spiritual
related words blessed, consecrated, hallowed, holy, sacrosanct, sanctified; liturgical, ritual, sacramental
near antonyms earthly, mundane, worldly; irreligious, semireligious
antonyms nonreligious, profane, secular
2 showing a devotion to God and to a life of virtue ⟨a deeply *religious* woman who eventually decided to quit her job and to become a nun⟩ — see HOLY 1
relinquish *vb* **1** to give (something) over to the control or possession of another usually under duress ⟨the boy reluctantly *relinquished* the illegal fireworks to the police officer⟩ — see SURRENDER 1
2 to give up (as a position of authority) formally ⟨the retiring CEO *relinquished* his position to the company's vice president with very mixed feelings⟩ — see ABDICATE
relinquishment *n* the usually forced yielding of one's person or possessions to the control of another ⟨miraculously, the *relinquishment* of the hostages was accomplished without bloodshed⟩ — see SURRENDER
relish *n* **1** positive regard for something ⟨she has great *relish* for early morning walks, which she takes nearly every day⟩ — see LIKING
2 the feeling experienced when one's wishes are met ⟨ate the bowl of ice cream with *relish*⟩ — see PLEASURE 1
relish *vb* to take pleasure in ⟨visit again soon, for I *relish* your company⟩ — see ENJOY 1

reluctance *n* a lack of willingness or desire to do or accept something ⟨the mice showed an odd *reluctance* to eat the cheese we had put out for them⟩
synonyms disinclination, hesitance, hesitancy, unwillingness
related words faltering, hesitation, indecision, irresolution, shilly-shallying, staggering, vacillation, wavering, wobbling; distrust, distrustfulness, doubt, incertitude, misgiving, mistrust, mistrustfulness, skepticism, suspicion, uncertainty
near antonyms certainty, certitude, sureness, surety
antonyms inclination, willingness

reluctant *adj* having doubts about the wisdom of doing something ⟨I'm *reluctant* to let you borrow my new CD since you never give back anything I lend you⟩ — see HESITANT

rely *vb* to place reliance or trust ⟨rigorously tested the rope before starting out, for the rock climbers would be *relying* on it with their very lives⟩ — see DEPEND 2

remain *vb* to continue to be in a place for a significant amount of time ⟨one of the three bridges known as "the London Bridge," it was moved in the late 1960s to Lake Havasu City, Arizona, where it *remains* today⟩ — see STAY 1

remainder *n* **1** a remaining group or portion ⟨the *remainder* of the pills were saved in case they were needed later⟩
synonyms balance, leavings, leftovers, odds and ends, remains, remnant, residue, rest
related words fragment, scrap; oddment, scraping(s), stub, stump; excess, surplus
near antonyms bulk, most
2 an unused or unwanted piece or item typically of small size or value ⟨Grandma let me play with the *remainder* of the dough while she finished putting the crust on the pie⟩ — see ¹SCRAP 1

remains *n pl* **1** the portion or bits of something left over or behind after it has been destroyed ⟨the *remains* of the house ripped apart by the tornado littered the block for weeks afterward⟩
synonyms ashes, debris, residue, rubble, ruins, wreck, wreckage
related words detritus, flotsam, jetsam; garbage, refuse, trash
2 a dead body ⟨archaeologists discovered the *remains* of an Incan woman and carefully excavated her burial site, which promised to yield important clues about her status⟩ — see CORPSE
3 a remaining group or portion ⟨gathered up the *remains* of the buffet and delivered them to a local homeless shelter⟩ — see REMAINDER 1

remake *vb* **1** to make different in some way ⟨one of those people who left the security and conformity of a small town to *remake* their lives in the big city⟩ — see CHANGE 1
2 to make or do again ⟨yesterday's soup was so good we begged Mom to *remake* it⟩ — see REPEAT 4

remaking *n* the act, process, or result of making different ⟨thought that the room looked no better for all the *remaking* and rearranging we did⟩ — see CHANGE

remark *n* a briefly expressed opinion ⟨the speaker made some short *remarks* about the new museum before officially opening the doors to visitors⟩
synonyms comment, note, observation, reflection
related words analysis, commentary, exposition; annotation; belief, conviction, eye, feeling, judgment (*or* judgement), mind, notion, opinion, persuasion, sentiment, verdict, view

remark *vb* **1** to make a statement of one's opinion ⟨he *remarked* on the attractiveness of the background music in the restaurant⟩
synonyms comment, note, observe, opine
related words articulate, express, say, speak, state, talk, tell, utter, verbalize, vocalize
2 to make note of (something) through the use of one's eyes ⟨I *remarked* the change in her hair color but didn't think it would be polite to say anything other than she was looking good⟩ — see SEE 1

remarkable *adj* **1** different from the ordinary in a way that causes curiosity or suspicion ⟨one participant in the race had a *remarkable* walk that was half-run, half-skip⟩ — see ODD 2
2 likely to attract attention ⟨there's a *remarkable* fixation with vanity of earthly pleasures in this author's poetry⟩ — see NOTICEABLE

remediable *adj* capable of being corrected ⟨the problems with the local transportation system were severe but still *remediable*⟩
synonyms correctable, fixable, rectifiable, repairable, reparable
related words amendable, improvable, resolvable; redeemable
near antonyms irredeemable, irretrievable, unrecoverable
antonyms incorrigible, irremediable, irreparable

remedial *adj* serving to raise or adjust something to some standard or proper condition ⟨took a *remedial* math course over the summer so he'd be ready for algebra the following school year⟩ — see CORRECTIVE 1

remedy *n* **1** a substance or preparation used to treat disease ⟨preferred to treat colds with a homemade *remedy* made from garlic⟩ — see MEDICINE
2 something that corrects or counteracts something undesirable ⟨the mayor was desperately searching for a *remedy* to the recent surge in crime the city had been experiencing⟩ — see CURE 1

remedy *vb* **1** to bring about recovery from ⟨a little extra studying should *remedy* your poor performance in history thus far this year⟩ — see CURE 1
2 to remove errors, defects, deficiencies, or deviations from ⟨needed to wear glasses to *remedy* her bad vision⟩ — see CORRECT 1

remedying *adj* serving to raise or adjust something to some standard or proper condition ⟨I've given the engine a *remedying* tune-up that should put an end to that knocking⟩ — see CORRECTIVE 1

remember *vb* to bring back to mind ⟨I *remember* the fun we had last summer very clearly, but I can't *remember* anything I learned in school yesterday⟩
synonyms hark back (to), mind [*chiefly dialect*], recall, recollect, reminisce (about), think (of)
related words recapture, recur; educe, elicit, evoke, extract, remind; relive
phrases look back (on *or* upon)
near antonyms disregard, ignore, neglect, overlook; lose, miss; blank (out)
antonyms forget, unlearn

remembrance *n* **1** a particular act or instance of recalling or the thing remembered ⟨a happy couple with many fond *remembrances* of when they were dating in college⟩ — see MEMORY 2
2 something that serves to keep alive the memory of a person or event ⟨gave her boyfriend on the eve of his military service one of her lockets as a *remembrance* of their abiding affection⟩ — see MEMORIAL

3 the power or process of recalling what has been previously learned or experienced ⟨*remembrance* will wane with age⟩ — see MEMORY 1

reminder *n* something that serves to keep alive the memory of a person or event ⟨the peach tree in our front yard is a living *reminder* of my late grandfather, who owned an orchard⟩ — see MEMORIAL

reminisce (about) *vb* to bring back to mind ⟨friends *reminiscing about* the good old days⟩ — see REMEMBER

reminiscence *n* **1** a particular act or instance of recalling or the thing remembered ⟨his *reminiscences* about the war were painful to hear⟩ — see MEMORY 2
2 the power or process of recalling what has been previously learned or experienced ⟨wondered whether she could trust her *reminiscence* of events that happened so long ago⟩ — see MEMORY 1

reminiscent *adj* provoking a memory or mental association ⟨a sparkling winter day that was oddly *reminiscent* of summer in its cheering sunniness⟩ — see SUGGESTIVE 2

remiss *adj* failing to give proper care and attention ⟨I would be *remiss* if I didn't tell you how much I appreciated the lovely gift⟩ — see NEGLIGENT

remission *n* release from the guilt or penalty of an offense ⟨the *remission* of sins⟩ — see PARDON

remissness *n* failure to take the care that a cautious person usually takes ⟨it took an incredible amount of reckless *remissness* on your part to leave the house with the front door wide open⟩ — see NEGLIGENCE 1

remit *vb* **1** to grow less in scope or intensity especially gradually ⟨waited until the rain *remitted* a little and ran to the car⟩ — see DECREASE 2
2 to overlook or dismiss as of little importance ⟨the judge refused to *remit* the young man's cavalier disregard for his pile of unpaid speeding tickets and summarily revoked his driver's license⟩ — see EXCUSE 1

remitment *n* the act of offering money in exchange for goods or services ⟨the charge account will be closed upon the *remitment* of the outstanding balance⟩ — see PAYMENT 1

remittable *adj* worthy of forgiveness ⟨forgetting a doctor's appointment that was made months in advance is a *remittable* offense⟩ — see VENIAL

remittal *n* release from the guilt or penalty of an offense ⟨a king who was once obliged to do public penance for the *remittal* of his sins⟩ — see PARDON

remittance *n* **1** something (as money) that is given or received in return for goods or services ⟨always mails in her *remittance* on time so she won't ever be charged a late fee on her electric bill⟩ — see PAYMENT 2
2 the act of offering money in exchange for goods or services ⟨the *remittance* of your outstanding balance is required before you can make more purchases⟩ — see PAYMENT 1

remnant *n* **1** a remaining group or portion ⟨sailed home with just a *remnant* of the colony's original population aboard⟩ — see REMAINDER 1
2 an unused or unwanted piece or item typically of small size or value ⟨gathered together her fabric *remnants* to see if she had enough of them to sew a doll blanket for her niece⟩ — see ¹SCRAP 1

remodel *vb* to make different in some way ⟨*remodeled* the house right after we moved in⟩ — see CHANGE 1

remodeling *n* the act, process, or result of making different ⟨moved out of the apartment and into a motel during the *remodeling*⟩ — see CHANGE

remonstrance *n* a feeling or declaration of disapproval or dissent ⟨over the vociferous *remonstrances* of my parents I decided to drop my music lessons⟩ — see OBJECTION

remonstrate (with) *vb* to present an opposing opinion or argument ⟨discouraged her from *remonstrating with* her father, whose mind was obviously made up⟩ — see OBJECT

remorse *n* a feeling of responsibility for wrongdoing ⟨felt a deep *remorse* for having cheated on the test⟩ — see GUILT 1

remorseful *adj* **1** feeling sorrow for a wrong that one has done ⟨was *remorseful* about all the trouble that he had caused in the family⟩ — see CONTRITE 1
2 suffering from or expressive of a feeling of responsibility for wrongdoing ⟨sent us a *remorseful* letter of apology⟩ ⟨a *remorseful* criminal for whom there is a real possibility of rehabilitation⟩ — see GUILTY 2

remorsefulness *n* a feeling of responsibility for wrongdoing ⟨was gnawed by a unrelenting *remorsefulness* for the pain that he had caused people⟩ — see GUILT 1

remorseless *adj* not sorry for having done wrong ⟨the *remorseless* killer was sentenced to life in prison without chance of parole⟩
synonyms impenitent, unrepentant
related words compassionless, cruel, merciless, pitiless, ruthless, unmerciful; shameless, unashamed
near antonyms ashamed, hangdog, shamed, shamefaced
antonyms contrite, guilty, penitent, regretful, remorseful, repentant, sorry

remote *adj* **1** small in degree ⟨there's a *remote* chance that it'll rain today, so I brought an umbrella⟩
synonyms negligible, off, outside, slight, slim, small
near antonyms great, large; distinct, significant
antonyms good
2 having or showing a lack of friendliness or interest in others ⟨his grandfather had been a somewhat *remote* figure, at least until they got to spend a summer together⟩ — see COOL 1
3 hidden from view ⟨a *remote* cottage on the far side of the mountain⟩ — see SECLUDED
4 not close in time or space ⟨a permanent base on Mars is likely to happen only in the *remote* future⟩ — see DISTANT 1

remotest *adj* most distant from a center ⟨news of the emperor's death had spread even to the *remotest* corners of the empire⟩ — see EXTREME 1

removal *n* the getting rid of whatever is unwanted or useless ⟨a product for the *removal* of warts⟩ — see DISPOSAL 1

remove *n* the space or amount of space between two points, lines, surfaces, or objects ⟨their farm is just a *remove* of two miles from the town center⟩ — see DISTANCE

remove *vb* **1** to rid oneself of (a garment) ⟨I *removed* my coat as soon as I got inside⟩
synonyms doff, peel (off), put off, take off
related words husk, shed
near antonyms wear
antonyms don, put on, slip (into)
2 to take away from a place or position ⟨he carefully *removed* the old manuscript from the shelf⟩
synonyms clear, draw, withdraw
related words demount, dislodge; abstract, cut, extract, pull; move, shift, transfer
near antonyms mount
antonyms place, put
3 to change the place or position of ⟨please *remove* that chair to the other room⟩ — see MOVE 1

4 to let go from office, service, or employment ⟨voters *removed* the racist selectman from office the first chance they got⟩ — see DISMISS 1

removed *adj* not close in time or space ⟨an island far *removed* from the mainland⟩ — see DISTANT 1

remunerate *vb* **1** to give (someone) the sum of money owed for goods or services received ⟨promptly *remunerated* the repair company for fixing the dryer⟩ — see PAY 1

2 to provide (someone) with a just payment for loss or injury ⟨the negligent landlord must *remunerate* those made homeless by the fire by finding new housing for them at his own expense⟩ — see COMPENSATE 1

remuneration *n* **1** the act of offering money in exchange for goods or services ⟨customers who are tardy in their *remuneration* will be subject to extra charges⟩ — see PAYMENT 1

2 payment to another for a loss or injury ⟨the vandals were ordered to pay the property owners thousands of dollars in *remuneration*⟩ — see COMPENSATION 1

3 something (as money) that is given or received in return for goods or services ⟨we can't accept your *remuneration* for services provided until we officially bill you⟩ — see PAYMENT 2

remunerative *adj* yielding a profit ⟨made a highly *remunerative* investment that will end up paying my college tuition⟩ — see PROFITABLE 1

rend *vb* to cause (something) to separate into jagged pieces by violently pulling at it ⟨the prophecy that the disaster would cause people to *rend* their garments in mourning⟩ — see TEAR 1

render *vb* to give (something) over to the control or possession of another usually under duress ⟨a gentleman bandit who graciously asked his victims to *render* their wallets to his safe possession⟩ — see SURRENDER 1

rendezvous *vb* to come together into one body or place ⟨we'll *rendezvous* at the corner market at 6:00 p.m.⟩ — see ASSEMBLE 1

rendezvous *n* **1** a place for spending time or for socializing ⟨the arcade was the *rendezvous* of choice for most of the teenagers in town⟩ — see HANGOUT

2 an agreement to be present at a specified time and place ⟨I have a *rendezvous* with him at lunchtime⟩ — see ENGAGEMENT 2

renegade *n* a person who abandons a cause or organization usually without right ⟨a band of *renegades* who had deserted their infantry units and were making their way to Mexico⟩

synonyms defector, deserter, recreant

related words betrayer, double-crosser, quisling, traitor, turncoat; chicken, coward, craven, dastard, poltroon; defier, insurgent, insurrectionary, insurrectionist, mutineer, rebel, red, revolter, revolutionary, revolutionist, revolutionizer

near antonyms adherent, disciple, follower, zealot

antonyms loyalist

renege *vb* to break a promise or agreement ⟨Dad promised to take me out for ice cream on the weekend, only to *renege* on Saturday morning⟩

synonyms back down, back off, cop out

related words chicken (out); disavow, recall, recant, retract, take back, withdraw

phrases go back on

near antonyms follow through; fulfill (*or* fulfil), honor

renew *vb* **1** to bring back to a former condition or vigor ⟨the trip to New York *renewed* our enthusiasm for travel⟩

synonyms freshen, recreate, refresh, refreshen, regenerate, rejuvenate, restore, revitalize, revive

related words make over, refurbish, rehabilitate, remake, remodel, renovate; refill, replenish, resupply

2 to begin again or return to after an interruption ⟨with daybreak, the rescue team will *renew* its efforts to reach the stranded hikers⟩ — see RESUME

3 to bring back to life, practice, or activity ⟨the spate of recent movies based on classic comic book characters has *renewed* interest in the comics themselves⟩ — see REVIVE 1

renewal *n* the act or an instance of bringing something back to life, public attention, or vigorous activity ⟨roller-skating experienced a major *renewal* after the introduction of in-line skates⟩ — see REVIVAL

renewed *adj* made or become fresh in spirits or vigor ⟨I was a *renewed* reader after that short nap⟩ — see NEW 4

renounce *vb* **1** to give up (as a position of authority) formally ⟨in wake of the corruption scandal, the politician was forced to *renounce* his position in the senate⟩ — see ABDICATE

2 to solemnly or formally reject or go back on (as something formerly adhered to) ⟨after another failed romance he decided to *renounce* the world and become a monk⟩ — see ABJURE

renouncement *n* the act or practice of giving up or rejecting something once enjoyed or desired ⟨her *renouncement* of chocolate had a lot to do with the fact that it was causing her skin to break out⟩ — see RENUNCIATION

renovate *vb* to put into good shape or working order again ⟨will have to *renovate* the house extensively before we can move in⟩ — see MEND 1

renown *n* the fact or state of being known to the public ⟨a basketball player whose *renown* is truly international⟩ — see FAME

renowned *adj* widely known ⟨the *renowned* painter and inventor, Leonardo da Vinci⟩ — see FAMOUS

rent *n* **1** a long deep cut ⟨getting her skirt caught on a nail resulted in a four-inch *rent* that she couldn't possibly repair⟩ — see GASH

2 an open space in a barrier (as a wall or hedge) ⟨peered through the *rent* in the old garden wall for a glimpse of her mysterious new neighbor⟩ — see GAP 1

rent *vb* **1** to give the possession and use of (something) in return for periodic payment ⟨we *rented* the apartment to a college student for $500 a month⟩

synonyms lease, let [*chiefly British*]

related words charter, hire; lodge; sublease, sublet

2 to take or get the temporary use of (something) for a set sum ⟨will need to *rent* a car while we're in Europe⟩ — see HIRE 1

renter *n* **1** one who rents a room or apartment in another's house ⟨one of the *renters* of our condo called to tell us the hot water heater was broken⟩ — see TENANT

2 the owner of land or housing that is rented to another ⟨left our apartment keys at the *renter's* office just before leaving in the moving truck⟩ — see LANDLORD

renunciation *n* the act or practice of giving up or rejecting something once enjoyed or desired ⟨his *renunciation* of his smoking habit pleased his whole family⟩

synonyms abnegation, renouncement, repudiation, self-denial

related words denial, refusal; relinquishment, resignation, surrender

near antonyms acceptance; adoption, embrace, espousal

antonyms indulgence, self-indulgence

reopen *vb* to begin again or return to after an interruption ⟨court will *reopen* after a brief recess⟩ — see RESUME

repair *n* a state of being or fitness ⟨the table is in good *repair*, so you won't need to refinish it⟩ — see CONDITION 1

repair *vb* to put into good shape or working order again ⟨*repair* the broken stereo⟩ — see MEND 1

repairable *adj* capable of being corrected ⟨the damage to her career from this scandal may not be *repairable*⟩ — see REMEDIABLE

reparable *adj* capable of being corrected ⟨whether the harm your lying has done to our friendship is *reparable* or irreparable depends a lot on you⟩ — see REMEDIABLE

reparation *n* payment to another for a loss or injury ⟨the government instituted a program of *reparations* to the descendants of Native Americans who were driven from their land⟩ — see COMPENSATION 1

repartee *n* 1 a quick witty response ⟨that *repartee* to his question drew laughs from the bystanders⟩ — see RETORT 1
2 good-natured teasing or exchanging of clever remarks ⟨I wish we weren't apart, as *repartee* is harder to do in letters⟩ — see BANTER

repast *n* food eaten or prepared for eating at one time ⟨monks taking their evening *repast* in silence⟩ — see MEAL

repay *vb* to make a return payment to ⟨I *repaid* my friend the twenty dollars he had lent me⟩
synonyms refund, reimburse
related words quit, satisfy, settle
phrases pay back

repeal *n* the act of putting an end to something planned or previously agreed to ⟨the long overdue *repeal* of laws prohibiting interracial marriage⟩ — see CANCELLATION

repeal *vb* 1 to put an end to (something planned or previously agreed to) ⟨the company called the furniture store to *repeal* the order for six new desks⟩ — see CANCEL 1
2 to put an end to by formal action ⟨in 1933, Congress passed the 21st Amendment which *repealed* the Prohibition Amendment of 1919, thus making the sale, distribution, and use of alcohol legal once again⟩ — see ABOLISH

repeat *n* the act of saying or doing over again ⟨the news story will be broadcast on the six o'clock show, with a *repeat* on the 11 o'clock newscast⟩
synonyms duplication, reduplication, reiteration, repetition, replication
related words rerun

repeat *vb* 1 to say or state again ⟨I *repeated* the address over and over until I had it memorized⟩
synonyms din, rehearse, reiterate
related words echo, parrot; mouth
2 to give from memory ⟨*repeated* correctly all the verses she had memorized⟩
synonyms recite, say
related words declaim, mouth, orate, speak
near antonyms read
3 to say after another ⟨now *repeat* the oath after me⟩
synonyms echo, parrot, quote
related words mouth; copy, imitate, mimic
4 to make or do again ⟨try not to *repeat* your mistakes⟩
synonyms duplicate, redo, reduplicate, reiterate, remake, replicate

related words renew

repeated *adj* appearing or occurring repeatedly from time to time ⟨made *repeated* attempts to get in touch with her⟩ — see REGULAR 1

repeatedly *adv* many times ⟨I've told him *repeatedly* not to do that⟩ — see OFTEN

repel *vb* 1 to drive back ⟨the defenders *repelled* the attacking army after several hours of fierce fighting⟩
synonyms fend (off), repulse, stave off
related words hold off, resist, withstand; deflect, ward (off); rebuff, snub, spurn
near antonyms welcome
2 to cause to feel disgust ⟨the idea of chocolate-covered grasshoppers *repels* me⟩ — see DISGUST
3 to refuse to give in to ⟨*repelled* the temptation to stay out late and call in sick the next day⟩ — see RESIST

repelled *adj* filled with disgust ⟨*repelled* reviewers couldn't believe how violent the movie was⟩ — see SICK 2

repellent *also* **repellant** *adj* causing intense displeasure, disgust, or resentment ⟨your behavior towards my friends is so *repellent* I can't stand to be around you anymore⟩ — see OFFENSIVE 1

repent *vb* to feel sorry or dissatisfied about ⟨after hearing what a great time you guys had at the party, I am *repenting* my decision to stay home⟩ — see REGRET

repentance *n* a feeling of responsibility for wrongdoing ⟨preached that *repentance* was the first step on the path of redemption⟩ — see GUILT 1

repentant *adj* 1 feeling sorrow for a wrong that one has done ⟨*repentant* sinners⟩ — see CONTRITE 1
2 suffering from or expressive of a feeling of responsibility for wrongdoing ⟨wrote a *repentant* letter to his wife asking her for one last chance to make amends⟩ — see GUILTY 2

repercussion *n* the power to bring about a result on another ⟨your decision not to go to college will have *repercussions* you'll feel for years to come⟩ — see EFFECT 2

repetition *n* the act of saying or doing over again ⟨the *repetition* of the honor society's oath at the initiation ceremonies got old really quickly⟩ — see REPEAT

repetitious *adj* marked by repetition ⟨at a real trial, *repetitious* questioning by the attorneys makes the whole affair less than thrilling⟩ — see REPETITIVE

repetitive *adj* marked by repetition ⟨the *repetitive* lyrics of so many rock songs⟩
synonyms reiterative, repetitious

rephrase *vb* to express something (as a text or statement) in different words ⟨I don't understand what you're asking—could you *rephrase* your question?⟩ — see PARAPHRASE

rephrasing *n* an instance of expressing something in different words ⟨a more polite *rephrasing* of your request might get better results⟩ — see PARAPHRASE

repine *vb* to express dissatisfaction, pain, or resentment usually tiresomely ⟨there was no use *repining* over a love that's been long lost⟩ — see COMPLAIN

repine (for) *vb* to have an earnest wish to own or enjoy ⟨during the deep cold of winter, I *repine for* warm tropical beaches⟩ — see DESIRE

replace *vb* 1 to take the place of ⟨the old street lights were *replaced* with more energy-efficient models⟩
synonyms displace, substitute, supersede, supplant
related words preempt, usurp
2 to bring, send, or put back to a former or proper place ⟨took the fragile vase down to look at it and then gently *replaced* it on the shelf⟩ — see RETURN 1

replacement *n* a person or thing that takes the place of another ⟨seeing that the quarterback was unable to play, the coach immediately called in his *replacement*⟩ — see SUBSTITUTE

replete *adj* possessing or covered with great numbers or amounts of something specified ⟨a gym that is *replete* with the very latest in home exercise equipment⟩ — see RIFE

replica *n* **1** something or someone that strongly resembles another ⟨filled with the usual chain stores, the new mall is a too-familiar *replica* of hundreds of other malls⟩ — see IMAGE 1
2 something that is made to look exactly like something else ⟨assembled a small-scale *replica* of the Queen Mary ocean liner⟩ — see COPY

replicate *vb* **1** to make an exact likeness of ⟨*replicated* the famous painting in our art class⟩ — see COPY 1
2 to make or do again ⟨I can't *replicate* your results when I do the experiment⟩ — see REPEAT 4

replication *n* **1** something that is made to look exactly like something else ⟨bought a smaller and cheaper *replication* of the marble statue for his garden⟩ — see COPY
2 the act of saying or doing over again ⟨we'll need to do a *replication* of that experiment so we can collect more data⟩ — see REPEAT

reply *n* **1** action or behavior that is done in return to other action or behavior ⟨decided the best *reply* to a wrongful discharge from employment was a lawsuit claiming discrimination⟩ — see REACTION
2 something spoken or written in reaction especially to a question ⟨I look forward to your *reply* to my request⟩ — see ANSWER 1

reply *vb* **1** to act or behave in response (as to a stimulus or influence) ⟨*replied* to the news that she had won the scholarship by jumping around the room and cheering⟩ — see REACT
2 to speak or write in reaction to a question or to another reaction ⟨please *reply* to my question at your earliest convenience⟩ — see ANSWER 1

report *n* **1** a loud explosive sound ⟨heard the *report* of a gun⟩ — see CLAP 1
2 a relating of events usually in the order in which they happened ⟨gave a full *report* of their trip to London⟩ — see ACCOUNT 1
3 overall quality as seen or judged by people in general ⟨he's a player of good *report* in golfing circles⟩ — see REPUTATION

report *vb* to give an oral or written account of in some detail ⟨the substitute teacher was forced to *report* his misbehavior to the principal⟩ — see TELL 1

reporter *n* a person employed by a newspaper, magazine, or radio or television station to gather, write, or report news ⟨the *reporter* was careful to ask as many questions as possible without annoying anyone⟩
synonyms correspondent, journalist
related words announcer, broadcaster, newscaster, newsman, newspaperman; anchor, anchorman, anchorperson, anchorwoman, legman; columnist, commentator, copyreader, editor, sportswriter, staffer

repose *n* **1** a natural periodic loss of consciousness during which the body restores itself ⟨typically the wealthy socialite spends most of the morning in *repose,* is served lunch, and then embarks on an exhaustive afternoon of shopping⟩ — see SLEEP 1
2 a state of freedom from storm or disturbance ⟨enjoyed the *repose* of a serene summer evening⟩ — see CALM

3 freedom from activity or labor ⟨the doctor ordered a period of *repose* for the patient recovering from pneumonia⟩ — see ¹REST 1

repose *vb* to refrain from labor or exertion ⟨*reposed* in the Caribbean sun, enjoying her break from the world of work⟩ — see REST 1

repository *n* a building for storing goods ⟨nurses going back and forth to the medication *repository*⟩ — see STOREHOUSE

repossess *vb* to get again in one's possession ⟨if you don't pay off the loan, the bank will come and *repossess* your car⟩ — see RECOVER 1

repossession *n* the act or process of getting something back ⟨an account of France's loss of the Louisiana Territory to Spain and its brief *repossession* of the area before selling it to the U.S. in 1803⟩ — see RECOVERY 1

reprehend *vb* **1** to declare to be morally wrong or evil ⟨that denomination *reprehends* murder in any form, contending that the taking of life is never justified⟩ — see CONDEMN 1
2 to express one's unfavorable opinion of the worth or quality of ⟨without exception, book reviewers *reprehended* the novel's tired plot⟩ — see CRITICIZE

reprehensible *adj* **1** deserving reproach or blame ⟨a *reprehensible* tyrant, who oppressed his country for decades, has finally been brought to justice⟩ — see BLAMEWORTHY
2 provoking or likely to provoke protest ⟨your behavior towards the other team was truly *reprehensible*, so you're being suspended from the next three games⟩ — see OBJECTIONABLE

represent *vb* **1** to point out the chief quality or qualities of an individual or group ⟨the writer of the magazine article *represented* the students at the academy as a bunch of spoiled brats⟩ — see CHARACTERIZE 1
2 to present a picture of ⟨a painting *representing* the ocean at sunrise⟩ — see PICTURE 1
3 to serve as a material counterpart of ⟨this orange *represents* the sun and this pea *represents* the Earth⟩ — see SYMBOLIZE 1

representative *n* **1** a person who acts or does business for another ⟨a *representative* from the car dealership called to ask how we were enjoying the new car⟩ — see AGENT 2
2 a person sent on a mission to represent another ⟨I speak as a *representative* of the people of the United States⟩ — see AMBASSADOR
3 one of a group or collection that shows what the whole is like ⟨this song is a fairly good *representative* of the other songs on the album⟩ — see EXAMPLE

representative *adj* **1** having or showing the qualities associated with the members of a particular group or kind ⟨a *representative* example of what that talented chef can do with food⟩ — see TYPICAL 1
2 having the function or meaning of a symbol ⟨a red cross on this map is *representative* of a hospital or other medical facility⟩ — see SYMBOLIC

repress *vb* **1** to put a stop to (something) by the use of force ⟨quickly *repressed* the rebellion in the city and restored order⟩ — see QUELL 1
2 to refrain from openly showing or uttering ⟨you can't *repress* your feelings forever, so tell her how you feel about her⟩ — see SUPPRESS 2

repression *n* the checking of one's true feelings and impulses when dealing with others ⟨psychologists talking about the *repression* of anger and how it affects one's health⟩ — see CONSTRAINT 1

reprimand *n* an often public or formal expression of disapproval ⟨while reviewing the troops, the officer delivered a curt *reprimand* to one of the soldiers⟩ — see CENSURE

reprimand *vb* **1** to criticize (someone) severely or angrily especially for personal failings ⟨*reprimanded* the girl for her constant tardiness to class⟩ — see SCOLD
2 to criticize (someone) usually gently so as to correct a fault ⟨quietly *reprimanded* the toddler for not being quiet during nap time⟩ — see REBUKE 1
3 to express public or formal disapproval of ⟨the president was forced to *reprimand* the general for publicly voicing his disagreements with the nation's foreign policy⟩ — see CENSURE 1

reprisal *n* the act or an instance of paying back an injury with an injury ⟨after defeating them last year in the finals, our team awaited the *reprisal* of our rival team in this year's tournament⟩ — see REVENGE

reproach *n* **1** a cause of shame ⟨your public display of boorish behavior is a *reproach* to this entire school⟩ — see DISGRACE 2
2 an often public or formal expression of disapproval ⟨a letter of *reproach* was added to her student file⟩ — see CENSURE
3 the state of having lost the esteem of others ⟨nothing the traitor did in later life lessened the *reproach* in which he was universally held⟩ — see DISGRACE 1

reproach *vb* **1** to criticize (someone) severely or angrily especially for personal failings ⟨our neighbor loudly *reproached* us for tromping through his yard⟩ — see SCOLD
2 to criticize (someone) usually gently so as to correct a fault ⟨she cleared her throat as a way of *reproaching* us for having our elbows on the table⟩ — see REBUKE 1
3 to express public or formal disapproval of ⟨the governor *reproached* the legislature for failing to pass the budget on time and once again throwing the state into fiscal chaos⟩ — see CENSURE 1

reproachable *adj* deserving reproach or blame ⟨yelling at one's teacher is the kind of *reproachable* behavior that won't be tolerated in this school⟩ — see BLAMEWORTHY

reprobate *adj* having or showing lowered moral character or standards ⟨a *reprobate* judge who could be bribed, and often with astonishing ease⟩ — see CORRUPT

reprobate *n* a mean, evil, or unprincipled person ⟨a program for rehabilitating hard-core *reprobates* and turning them into hard-working, law-abiding citizens⟩ — see VILLAIN

reprobate *vb* to declare to be morally wrong or evil ⟨spent much of her talk *reprobating* the callous indifference of a materialistic society to the suffering of people in need⟩ — see CONDEMN 1

reproduce *vb* **1** to bring forth offspring ⟨mice *reproduce* at a much faster rate than humans do⟩ — see PROCREATE
2 to make an exact likeness of ⟨you'll have to *reproduce* that design on every tile in the bathroom⟩ — see COPY 1

reproduction *n* something that is made to look exactly like something else ⟨walked through a *reproduction* of the interior of the Parthenon as it must have looked when it was first built⟩ — see COPY

reproof *n* an often public or formal expression of disapproval ⟨even in church we were not free from Mother's familiar *reproof* of our ingrained tendency to fidget in our seats⟩ — see CENSURE

reprove *vb* **1** to criticize (someone) usually gently so as to correct a fault ⟨my piano teacher often *reproves* me for slouching while playing, observing that good posture helps one play better⟩ — see REBUKE 1
2 to express public or formal disapproval of ⟨the principal *reproved* the hockey team for their display of poor sportsmanship on the ice and ordered that a letter of apology be sent to the other school⟩ — see CENSURE 1
3 to hold an unfavorable opinion of ⟨my parents *reprove* my taste in music⟩ — see DISAPPROVE (OF)

republic *n* government in which the supreme power is held by the people and used by them directly or indirectly through representation ⟨when asked by a passerby what sort of government the constitutional convention had formulated for the new nation, Benjamin Franklin memorably replied, "A *republic*, if you can keep it"⟩ — see DEMOCRACY

republican *adj* of, relating to, or favoring political democracy ⟨a small but well-organized *republican* movement working quietly to overthrow the military dictatorship⟩ — see DEMOCRATIC

repudiate *vb* **1** to declare not to be true ⟨vigorously *repudiated* the charge that she had lied on her résumé⟩ — see DENY 1
2 to refuse to acknowledge as one's own or as one's responsibility ⟨the angry mother bitterly *repudiated* her daughter, telling her that she never wanted to see or hear from her again⟩ — see DISCLAIM 1
3 to show unwillingness to accept, do, engage in, or agree to ⟨we didn't like the terms, so we *repudiated* the contract⟩ — see DECLINE 1

repudiation *n* **1** a refusal to confirm the truth of a statement ⟨voters seemed satisfied by the candidate's public *repudiation* of the beliefs of an organization to which he had briefly belonged as a youth⟩ — see DENIAL 2
2 the act or practice of giving up or rejecting something once enjoyed or desired ⟨New Year's resolutions typically include the *repudiation* of chocolate and other sugary sweets and the promise to resume working out at the gym⟩ — see RENUNCIATION

repugnance *n* a dislike so strong as to cause stomach upset or queasiness ⟨could barely contain her *repugnance* of frogs and nearly threw up when she found out we'd have to dissect one in science class⟩ — see DISGUST

repugnant *adj* causing intense displeasure, disgust, or resentment ⟨called his teacher an absolutely *repugnant* name and immediately got suspended for it⟩ — see OFFENSIVE 1

repulse *n* treatment that is deliberately unfriendly ⟨the waiter's incredibly rude *repulse* of our polite request for a better table—one that wasn't right next to the kitchen—prompted us to walk out⟩ — see COLD SHOULDER

repulse *vb* **1** to cause to feel disgust ⟨the smell of that paper mill totally *repulses* me⟩ — see DISGUST
2 to drive back ⟨the defense repeatedly *repulsed* all of the offense's attempts to move the ball forward, keeping them firmly planted on the 20-yard line⟩ — see REPEL 1

repulsed *adj* filled with disgust ⟨I am *repulsed* that you think it's okay to lie your way into college, whereas the rest of us have to work hard to get there honestly⟩ — see SICK 2

repulsion *n* a dislike so strong as to cause stomach upset or queasiness ⟨we giggled at my father, who was overcome with *repulsion* when he realized he was eating octopus⟩ — see DISGUST

repulsive *adj* causing intense displeasure, disgust, or resentment 〈a *repulsive* display of shameless flattery that made the actor wrinkle his nose in disgust〉 — see OFFENSIVE 1

repulsiveness *n* the quality of inspiring intense dread or dismay 〈horror films that seem to be trying to outdo one another in the *repulsiveness* of their monsters〉 — see HORROR 1

reputable *adj* having a good reputation especially in a field of knowledge 〈make sure you buy your car from a *reputable* dealer〉 — see RESPECTABLE 1

reputation *n* overall quality as seen or judged by people in general 〈the college's athletic department has a good *reputation*, but the school's science facilities are a bit lacking〉
  synonyms character, mark, name, note, report, repute
  related words credit, honor; celebrity, fame, notoriety, renown
  near antonyms infamy

repute *n* overall quality as seen or judged by people in general 〈that's a repair shop of good *repute*〉 — see REPUTATION

reputed *adj* **1** appearing to be true on the basis of evidence that may or may not be confirmed 〈this treatment is a *reputed* cure for colon cancer, but studies haven't confirmed that claim〉 — see APPARENT 1
2 having a good reputation especially in a field of knowledge 〈a *reputed* oceanographer whose excellent work is known internationally〉 — see RESPECTABLE 1

request *n* an act or instance of asking for information 〈the medical columnist is unable to answer individual *requests* for specific information on various disorders〉 — see QUESTION 2

request *vb* **1** to give a request or demand for 〈the teachers *requested* silence during the exam〉 — see ORDER 2
2 to make a request for 〈*request* extra ketchup for my fries〉 — see ASK (FOR) 1
3 to make a request of 〈I'm *requesting* you to turn down the music〉 — see ASK 2

requiem *n* a composition expressing one's grief over a loss 〈the choir will sing Mozart's *Requiem*〉 — see LAMENT 1

require *vb* to have as a requirement 〈the toy *requires* four batteries, which are not included〉 — see NEED 1

required *adj* **1** forcing one's compliance or participation by or as if by law 〈formal instruction in driving is *required* in this state before you can get your driver's license〉 — see MANDATORY
2 impossible to do without 〈with these frigid winds, hats, scarves, and good mittens are *required* equipment for heading outside〉 — see ESSENTIAL 1

requirement *n* something necessary, indispensable, or unavoidable 〈this course is a *requirement* for graduation〉 — see ESSENTIAL 1

requisite *adj* impossible to do without 〈this new CD is the *requisite* album of the year〉 — see ESSENTIAL 1

requisite *n* something necessary, indispensable, or unavoidable 〈Art 101 is a *requisite* for Art 201〉 — see ESSENTIAL 1

requisition *n* something that someone insists upon having 〈a brand-new, top-notch computer was the new science teacher's first *requisition*〉 — see DEMAND 1

requisition *vb* to give a request or demand for 〈the invading soldiers *requisitioned* food and gasoline from the townspeople〉 — see ORDER 2

requital *n* **1** payment to another for a loss or injury 〈the judge ordered the landlord to pay his former tenants $100,000 each as *requital* for goods lost or damaged in the apartment fire〉 — see COMPENSATION 1
2 something (as money) that is given or received in return for goods or services 〈the electrician's *requital* for the used car was in the form of work on the dealer's house〉 — see PAYMENT 2
3 the act or an instance of paying back an injury with an injury 〈"an eye for an eye" is a form of *requital* that is still legal in some countries〉 — see REVENGE

requite *vb* **1** to provide (someone) with a just payment for loss or injury 〈the company *requited* the employee who had fallen on the ice while leaving work by promptly paying all his medical bills, hoping that would stave off a lawsuit〉 — see COMPENSATE 1
2 to punish in kind the wrongdoer responsible for 〈the future writer would later *requite* the abuse he suffered at the hands of his classmates by creating scathing portraits of them in his novels〉 — see AVENGE

rescind *vb* **1** to put an end to (something planned or previously agreed to) 〈*rescinded* our travel plans when a freak blizzard closed the major highways〉 — see CANCEL 1
2 to put an end to by formal action 〈the new mayor vowed not to seek to *rescind* existing laws prohibiting smoking in the city's public places〉 — see ABOLISH

rescission *n* the act of putting an end to something planned or previously agreed to 〈the school board promised to reconsider its *rescission* of the junior prom〉 — see CANCELLATION

rescue *vb* to remove from danger or harm 〈*rescue* a beached whale〉 — see SAVE 2

rescuer *n* one that saves from danger or destruction 〈*rescuers* went out immediately in search of the lost child〉 — see SAVIOR

research *n* a systematic search for the truth or facts about something 〈I'll have to do some *research* for this project〉 — see INQUIRY 1

research *vb* to search through or into 〈*researched* the public record for more information about her great-grandparents〉 — see EXPLORE 1

resemblance *n* **1** a point which two or more things share in common 〈I see a family *resemblance* between you and your brother〉 — see SIMILARITY 2
2 the quality or state of having many qualities in common 〈the look of the director's latest film bears a strong *resemblance* to the look of his last film〉 — see SIMILARITY 1

resembling *adj* having qualities in common 〈*resembling* Impressionist landscapes were hung side by side so that visitors could compare how fellow artists treated the same subject matter〉 — see ALIKE

resentful *adj* **1** having or showing deep-seated resentment 〈was *resentful* that my brother got invited to the party but I didn't〉 — see BITTER 1
2 having or showing mean resentment of another's possessions or advantages 〈*resentful* of her cousin's wealth〉 — see ENVIOUS

resentfully *adv* with feelings of bitterness or grief 〈she apologized later, but it was clear she did so *resentfully*〉 — see HARD 2

resentment *n* **1** a lingering ill will towards a person for a real or imagined wrong 〈her *resentment* over not winning the spelling bee last year has nearly ruined her friendship with the eventual winner〉 — see GRUDGE 1
2 a painful awareness of another's possessions or advantages and a desire to have them too 〈I don't have any *resentment* over my friend's luxurious house〉 — see ENVY

3 the feeling of being offended or resentful after a slight or indignity ⟨my *resentment* at being spoken to like I'm stupid⟩ — see PIQUE

reservation *n* something upon which the carrying out of an agreement or offer depends ⟨gave us his approval without any *reservations*⟩ — see CONDITION 2

reserve *n* **1** the checking of one's true feelings and impulses when dealing with others ⟨the salesclerk showed great *reserve* in dealing with the unreasonable demands of the angry customer⟩ — see CONSTRAINT 1

2 a collection of things kept available for future use or need ⟨our fuel *reserves* are low⟩ — see STORE

3 a person or thing that takes the place of another ⟨when the first platoon fell back in retreat, the commander sent out the *reserves* to try to hold the line of battle⟩ — see SUBSTITUTE

4 an interchangeable part or piece of equipment that is kept on hand for replacement of an original ⟨don't throw that extra bike chain away, as I want to keep it as a *reserve* in case the current one breaks⟩ — see SPARE

reserve *vb* **1** to arrange to have something (as a hotel room) held for one's future use ⟨we made sure to *reserve* a kennel for our dog several months before the start of the family vacation⟩

synonyms bespeak, book

related words earmark; contract, engage, retain

2 to continue to have in one's possession or power ⟨I'm *reserving* the right to work by myself if you don't do your share of the project⟩ — see KEEP 2

3 to keep or intend for a special purpose ⟨we must *reserve* this cup for ceremonial use only⟩ — see DEVOTE 1

reserved *adj* tending not to speak frequently (as by habit or inclination) ⟨a *reserved* and shy person who was wrongly thought to be stuck-up until someone finally got into a conversation with her⟩ — see SILENT 2

reside *vb* to have a home ⟨he's a free-lance writer who *resides* in the Midwest⟩ — see LIVE 1

residence *n* the place where one lives ⟨police stopped by his *residence* to question him⟩ — see HOME 1

resident *n* one who lives permanently in a place ⟨a *resident* of Atlanta⟩ — see INHABITANT

resider *n* one who lives permanently in a place ⟨was born in the U.S. but is now a *resider* of Dresden, Germany⟩ — see INHABITANT

residue *n* **1** the portion or bits of something left over or behind after it has been destroyed ⟨the detective noticed an ashy *residue* in the sink and deduced that a piece of paper had been burned there⟩ — see REMAINS 1

2 a remaining group or portion ⟨most of the audience had gone home, but there was a *residue* of theatergoers still milling about the lobby⟩ — see REMAINDER 1

resign *vb* to give up (as a position of authority) formally ⟨following the election, the incumbent cabinet members *resigned* their positions so the president could feel free to pick a new administration⟩ — see ABDICATE

resign (from) *vb* to give up (a job or office) ⟨*resigned from* the company after the news broke that he had been falsifying financial statements for years⟩ — see QUIT 1

resigned *adj* receiving or enduring without offering resistance ⟨I am *resigned* to the fact that I'll never make the cheerleading squad⟩ — see PASSIVE

resilient *adj* able to revert to original size and shape after being stretched, squeezed, or twisted ⟨made the soles of these tennis shoes out of a *resilient* new rubber that wouldn't tear with heavy use⟩ — see ELASTIC 1

resist *vb* to refuse to give in to ⟨it is important to *resist* the temptation to run away from your problems⟩

synonyms buck, defy, fight, oppose, repel, withstand

related words battle, combat, contend (with), counter; contest, dispute; baffle, balk, foil, frustrate, thwart; check, counter, hinder, obstruct, stem

antonyms bow (to), capitulate (to), give in (to), submit (to), succumb (to), surrender (to), yield (to)

resistance *n* **1** the inclination to resist ⟨there was much *resistance* to the idea of removing our baseball caps while eating⟩

synonyms defiance, opposition

related words demur, objection, protest, remonstrance; compunction, misgiving, reservation; disobedience, noncompliance

near antonyms compliance, obedience; acceptance, approval

antonyms acquiescence

2 a secret organization in a conquered country fighting against enemy forces ⟨soldiers from the *resistance* were captured after a short battle outside the foreign ministry⟩

synonyms underground

related words cabal, conspiracy

resolute *adj* fully committed to achieving a goal ⟨I was *resolute* in my decision to go abroad for my junior year, and nothing my parents said could convince me not to go⟩ — see DETERMINED 1

resoluteness *n* firm or unwavering adherence to one's purpose ⟨with a *resoluteness* that was admirable, the losing team continued to play hard until the bitter end⟩ — see DETERMINATION 1

resolution *n* **1** a position arrived at after consideration ⟨her *resolution* to become a vegetarian is based on what she recently learned about modern farming practices⟩ — see DECISION 1

2 firm or unwavering adherence to one's purpose ⟨that athlete's *resolution* to win is amazing⟩ — see DETERMINATION 1

resolvable *adj* capable of having the reason for or cause of determined ⟨the conflict in the two totals is *resolvable*, but it will take some work to figure it out⟩ — see SOLVABLE

resolve *n* firm or unwavering adherence to one's purpose ⟨I admire your *resolve* to get that science project done in three days, but you may not be going about it in the wisest way⟩ — see DETERMINATION 1

resolve *vb* **1** to come to a judgment after discussion or consideration ⟨after talking with my friends, I *resolved* to try out for the play⟩ — see DECIDE 1

2 to find an answer for through reasoning ⟨*resolve* the apparent contradictions in the collected data⟩ — see SOLVE

3 to set or force apart ⟨a prism will *resolve* a beam of light into an array of colors⟩ — see SEPARATE 1

resolved *adj* fully committed to achieving a goal ⟨only the most *resolved* of explorers had any chance of finding the source of the Nile⟩ — see DETERMINED 1

resonant *adj* marked by conspicuously full and rich sounds or tones ⟨the orator's *resonant* voice filled the hall⟩

synonyms golden, resounding, reverberant, reverberating, ringing, round, sonorous, vibrant

related words deep, full, mellifluous, mellow, rich; loud, powerful, stentorian, thundering, thunderous

near antonyms cavernous, hollow; faint, low, murmurous, muted, smothered, soft, weak; thin, tinny

resonate *vb* to continue or be repeated in a series of reflected sound waves ⟨the deep note from the bass *resonated* through the concert hall⟩ — see REVERBERATE

resort (to) *vb* **1** to use or seek out as a source of aid, relief, or advantage ⟨we were so desperate for better grades on our homework that we were forced to *resort to* spending all our evenings at the library⟩
synonyms go (to), refer (to), turn (to)
related words employ, use, utilize; depend (on), rely (on)
phrases fall back on
2 to go to or spend time in often ⟨*resorted to* the library for a little peace and quiet⟩ — see FREQUENT

resort *n* **1** a place for spending time or for socializing ⟨the local pizza place was our favorite *resort* after jazz concerts⟩ — see HANGOUT
2 something that one uses to accomplish an end especially when the usual means is not available ⟨use this only as a last *resort*⟩ — see RESOURCE 1

resound *vb* to continue or be repeated in a series of reflected sound waves ⟨thunder *resounded* across the plain⟩ — see REVERBERATE

resounding *adj* **1** full of or characterized by the presence of noise ⟨the *resounding* streets of New York City⟩ — see NOISY 2
2 marked by a high volume of sound ⟨the emcee announced the winner in a *resounding* voice that could be heard at the back of the hall⟩ — see LOUD 1
3 marked by conspicuously full and rich sounds or tones ⟨a *resounding* chord⟩ — see RESONANT
4 marked by or uttered with forcefulness ⟨a *resounding* defeat⟩ — see EMPHATIC 1

resource *n* **1** something that one uses to accomplish an end especially when the usual means is not available ⟨we used every possible *resource* to raise the funds needed to save our town's oldest house⟩
synonyms expedient, recourse, resort
related words hope, opportunity, possibility, relief; makeshift, replacement, stopgap, substitute
2 resources *pl* available money ⟨do you have the *resources* to buy a new car or even a used car?⟩ — see FUND 2

respect *n* **1** relation to or concern with something specified ⟨with *respect* to your application⟩
synonyms reference, regard
2 a feeling of great approval and liking ⟨I have a lot of *respect* for Martin Luther King, Jr.'s steadfast courage⟩ — see ADMIRATION 1
3 respects *pl* best wishes ⟨give your mother my *respects*⟩ — see COMPLIMENT

respect *vb* to think very highly or favorably of ⟨I *respect* your decision to do volunteer work this summer instead of getting a paying job⟩ — see ADMIRE

respectable *adj* **1** having a good reputation especially in a field of knowledge ⟨no *respectable* dietician would advise people to eat just one kind of food⟩
synonyms esteemed, name, prestigious, reputable, reputed, respected
related words honorable, worthy; creditable, good, praiseworthy; celebrated, distinguished, famed, famous, honored, illustrious, notable, prominent, renowned, well-known
antonyms disreputable, loose
2 following the accepted rules of moral conduct ⟨cheating is not a *respectable* thing to do under any circumstances⟩ — see HONORABLE 1

3 following the established traditions of refined society and good taste ⟨has the *respectable* manners of someone who was well brought up⟩ — see PROPER 1
4 of a level of quality that meets one's needs or standards ⟨hopefully the roast beef will be a little more *respectable* this time around, as it was far too tough the last time⟩ — see ADEQUATE
5 sufficiently large in size, amount, or number to merit attention ⟨got paid a *respectable* sum for speaking at our graduation⟩ — see CONSIDERABLE 1

respected *adj* having a good reputation especially in a field of knowledge ⟨a *respected* doctor whose reputation brought her patients from all over the world⟩ — see RESPECTABLE 1

respectful *adj* marked by or showing proper regard for another's higher status ⟨the children were remarkably *respectful* while in the President's office⟩
synonyms deferential, dutiful, regardful
related words reverent, reverential, venerating, worshipful; fawning, groveling (*or* grovelling), obsequious, servile, subservient, sycophantic, toadying; civil, courteous, gracious, polite
near antonyms abusive, insulting, offensive; contemptuous, impudent, irreverent; discourteous, insolent, rude, uncivil
antonyms disrespectful

respecting *prep* having to do with ⟨*respecting* your earlier question I'd like to make an additional comment⟩ — see ABOUT 1

respective *adj* not the same or shared ⟨the kids went to their *respective* bedrooms⟩ — see SEPARATE 1

respire *vb* to inhale and exhale air ⟨though unconscious, the patient is still *respiring*⟩ — see BREATHE 1

resplendence *n* impressiveness of beauty on a large scale ⟨the fabled *resplendence* of the Taj Mahal⟩ — see MAGNIFICENCE

respond *vb* **1** to act or behave in response (as to a stimulus or influence) ⟨doctors studying how the brain *responds* to pain⟩ — see REACT
2 to speak or write in reaction to a question or to another reaction ⟨please *respond* as soon as you can⟩ — see ANSWER 1

response *n* **1** action or behavior that is done in return to other action or behavior ⟨my *response* to my first boxing defeat was to train even harder⟩ — see REACTION
2 something spoken or written in reaction especially to a question ⟨the real estate office's *response* to my question about what houses in the area are renting for⟩ — see ANSWER 1

responsibility *n* **1** the state of being held as the cause of something that needs to be set right ⟨*responsibility* for the accident lies with the driver who was speeding⟩
synonyms blame, fault, liability
related words accountability
2 something one must do because of prior agreement ⟨feeding the dog is my *responsibility*⟩ — see OBLIGATION

responsible *adj* **1** being the one who must meet an obligation or suffer the consequences for failing to do so ⟨each student is *responsible* for getting his or her own homework done on time⟩
synonyms accountable, answerable, liable
related words beholden, indebted, obligated, obliged
near antonyms exempt, immune
antonyms irresponsible, unaccountable
2 worthy of one's trust ⟨our regular babysitter is very *responsible*⟩ — see DEPENDABLE

¹**rest** *n* **1** freedom from activity or labor ⟨I'm looking forward to enjoying some *rest* at the end of the school term⟩

synonyms ease, leisure, relaxation, repose

related words catnapping, dozing, napping, resting, sleep, slumber, slumbering, snoozing; quiet, silence, stillness; calm, peace, peacefulness, placidity, restfulness, serenity, tranquillity (*or* tranquility)

near antonyms pressure, strain, stress, tension

antonyms exertion, labor, toil, work

2 a natural periodic loss of consciousness during which the body restores itself ⟨after a long day, I lay down on the couch for a little *rest* before dinner⟩ — see SLEEP 1

²**rest** *n* a remaining group or portion ⟨can you hand me the *rest* of those papers?⟩ — see REMAINDER 1

rest *vb* **1** to refrain from labor or exertion ⟨a beach resort that caters to gung ho exercisers and athletes as well as vacationers who just want to *rest*⟩

synonyms bask, loll, lounge, relax, repose

related words bum, goldbrick, idle, loaf, slack (off)

near antonyms drudge, grub, hump, hustle, labor, moil, peg (away), plod, plow, plug, slave, slog, strain, strive, struggle, sweat, toil, travail, work; exercise, work out

2 be in a state of sleep ⟨just close your eyes and *rest*, and in the morning we'll keep looking for your missing earring⟩ — see SLEEP 1

3 to find a basis ⟨you're *resting* your argument on a faulty premise⟩ — see BASE

restart *vb* to begin again or return to after an interruption ⟨after answering the door, I *restarted* packing for my trip⟩ — see RESUME

restate *vb* to express something (as a text or statement) in different words ⟨though I couldn't remember the exact words he used, I *restated* his message as accurately as I could⟩ — see PARAPHRASE

restatement *n* an instance of expressing something in different words ⟨I need a *restatement* of the contract, as I don't understand what half the words mean⟩ — see PARAPHRASE

restating *n* an instance of expressing something in different words ⟨I think the intent of the passage comes through better in the editor's *restating*⟩ — see PARAPHRASE

restaurant *n* a public establishment where meals are served to paying customers for consumption on the premises ⟨when we get sick of cooking dinner at home, we like to go out to eat at a nice *restaurant*⟩

synonyms café (*also* cafe), diner, grill

related words cafeteria, coffeehouse, garden, luncheonette, lunchroom, snack bar, tearoom; bar, barroom, inn, tavern

restful *adj* free from disturbing noise or uproar ⟨I hope you had a relaxing and *restful* weekend⟩ — see QUIET 1

restfulness *n* a state of freedom from storm or disturbance ⟨enjoyed the bucolic *restfulness* of the retreat center⟩ — see CALM

resting *adj* being in a state of suspended consciousness ⟨quiet, your father is *resting*⟩ — see ASLEEP 1

resting *n* a natural periodic loss of consciousness during which the body restores itself ⟨the hyena is ready to scavenge again after its brief *resting*⟩ — see SLEEP 1

restitution *n* payment to another for a loss or injury ⟨sought *restitution* from the other driver's insurance company for lost wages⟩ — see COMPENSATION 1

restive *adj* **1** given to resisting authority or another's control ⟨the *restive* horse threw its head and refused to

move when the rider urged it forward⟩ — see DISOBEDIENT

2 lacking or denying rest ⟨spent a *restive* night worrying about the next day's exam⟩ — see RESTLESS 1

restiveness *n* **1** a disturbed or uneasy state ⟨the nighttime tornado warnings were the source of our neighborhood's *restiveness*⟩ — see UNREST

2 a state of nervousness marked by sudden jerky movements ⟨I sensed that his *restiveness* at breakfast probably had something to do with that big test at school today⟩ — see JUMPINESS

restless *adj* **1** lacking or denying rest ⟨the worried mother spent a *restless* night, tossing and turning in bed for hours⟩

synonyms restive, uneasy, unquiet, unrestful

related words agitated, distressed, disturbed, perturbed, troubled, unsettled; aflutter, anxious, dithery, edgy, fidgety, het up, hung up, jittery, jumpy, nervous, nervy, tense, upset, uptight, worried

near antonyms calm, easy, peaceful, quiet, relaxing, tranquil

antonyms restful

2 marked by or causing agitation or uncomfortable feelings ⟨the *restless* fidgeting of the kids waiting to get their flu shots⟩ — see NERVOUS 2

restlessness *n* **1** a disturbed or uneasy state ⟨the *restlessness* of the crowd was apparent as it waited to learn whether the football player was seriously injured⟩ — see UNREST

2 the state of being bored ⟨she began to pick at the grass near her hammock out of sheer *restlessness*⟩ — see BOREDOM

restorative *adj* **1** good for the health ⟨took a *restorative* vitamin mix to improve his immune system⟩ — see HEALTHFUL

2 having a renewing effect on the state of the body or mind ⟨was in need of a long, *restorative* vacation⟩ — see TONIC

restore *vb* **1** to bring back to a former condition or vigor ⟨*restore* an old car⟩ — see RENEW 1

2 to bring, send, or put back to a former or proper place ⟨*restored* the delicate teacup to its shelf⟩ — see RETURN 1

restrain *vb* **1** to keep from exceeding a desirable degree or level (as of expression) ⟨try to *restrain* your usual boisterousness while we're at the fancy restaurant⟩ — see CONTROL 1

2 to take or keep under one's control by authority of law ⟨the suspect is currently being *restrained* in an undisclosed location⟩ — see ARREST 1

restrained *adj* not excessively showy ⟨a *restrained* but elegant black purse⟩ — see QUIET 2

restraint *n* **1** the checking of one's true feelings and impulses when dealing with others ⟨it will take a great deal of *restraint* to keep from telling her how ugly that dress is⟩ — see CONSTRAINT 1

2 something that limits one's freedom of action or choice ⟨will have to place *restraints* on who can and can't go to the basketball game Thursday⟩ — see RESTRICTION 1

3 the power to control one's actions, impulses, or emotions ⟨very young children don't seem to have any *restraint* and will say anything that pops into their heads⟩ — see WILL 1

restrict *vb* **1** to set bounds or an upper limit for ⟨will *restrict* access to the laboratory⟩ — see LIMIT 1

2 to limit the meaning of (as a noun) ⟨if you want to suggest a sense of foreboding, maybe you should *re-*

strict the word "darkness" with an adjective like "vast" or "eerie"⟩ — see QUALIFY 1

restricted *adj* having distinct or certain limits ⟨dogs are allowed only on a *restricted* area of the beach⟩ — see LIMITED 1

restriction *n* 1 something that limits one's freedom of action or choice ⟨my parents placed several *restrictions* on the party we were planning⟩
synonyms check, condition, constraint, curb, fetter, limitation, restraint
related words exception, proviso, qualification, reservation, stipulation, strings
near antonyms freedom, latitude
2 the act or practice of keeping something (as an activity) within certain boundaries ⟨the *restriction* of surfing to the southern end of the beach rankled some surfers⟩
synonyms confinement, limitation
related words constraint, restraint; isolation, segregation

rest room *n* a room furnished with a fixture for flushing body waste ⟨wasn't feeling well and during the flight made a number of trips to the *rest room*⟩ — see TOILET

result *n* 1 a condition or occurrence traceable to a cause ⟨please share the *results* of your experiment with the class⟩ — see EFFECT 1
2 something attained by mental effort and especially by computation ⟨40 times 40 yields 1,600 as a *result*⟩ — see ANSWER 2

result (in) *vb* to be the cause of (a situation, action, or state of mind) ⟨the mix of icy conditions and rush-hour traffic *resulted in* a number of accidents on the interstate⟩ — see EFFECT

resultant *adj* coming as a result ⟨frequent trips to the ice cream parlor and the *resultant* gain in weight were starting to affect my tennis game⟩
synonyms attendant, consequent, consequential, due (to)
related words accompanying, coincident, concomitant
near antonyms causal

resultant *n* a condition or occurrence traceable to a cause ⟨a person's decision to purchase a certain automobile is often the *resultant* of an array of factors, ranging from the actual performance of the vehicle to the buyer's self-image⟩ — see EFFECT 1

resume *vb* to begin again or return to after an interruption ⟨we *resumed* the game as soon as the rain had passed⟩
synonyms continue, renew, reopen, restart
related words resuscitate, revive
near antonyms complete, conclude, consummate, end, finalize, finish; belay, break, can, cease, check, cut, desist, discontinue, drop, halt, knock off, leave off, quit, scuttle, shut off, stay, stop, terminate

résumé *or* **resume** *also* **resumé** *n* a short statement of the main points ⟨a book on the assassination that is in effect a *résumé* of all of the evidence that points to a conspiracy⟩ — see SUMMARY

resurgence *n* the act or an instance of bringing something back to life, public attention, or vigorous activity ⟨a *resurgence* of nightlife after the neighborhood was rehabilitated⟩ — see REVIVAL

resurrect *vb* to bring back to life, practice, or activity ⟨a few regional groups tried to *resurrect* square dancing but it really took off after hip college students started doing it⟩ — see REVIVE 1

resurrection *n* the act or an instance of bringing something back to life, public attention, or vigorous activity

⟨a general *resurrection* of patriotism after the war began⟩ — see REVIVAL

resuscitate *vb* to bring back to life, practice, or activity ⟨people trying to *resuscitate* some old theories that the assassination was really a conspiracy⟩ — see REVIVE 1

resuscitated *adj* made or become fresh in spirits or vigor ⟨after the gloom of winter, I felt *resuscitated* by the unexpected gift of a bouquet of tulips⟩ — see NEW 4

resuscitation *n* the act or an instance of bringing something back to life, public attention, or vigorous activity ⟨this top-notch *resuscitation* of a beloved Broadway show has been greeted with universal applause by the theater community⟩ — see REVIVAL

retail *vb* to offer for sale to the public ⟨the textile manufacturer doesn't *retail* its fabrics to consumers, offering them only to wholesalers and garment makers⟩ — see MARKET

retain *vb* 1 to continue to have in one's possession or power ⟨I plan to *retain* the family heirlooms until my own children are mature enough to appreciate them, and then I will lovingly pass them on⟩ — see KEEP 2
2 to keep, control, or experience as one's own ⟨that author *retains* the right to veto any changes in his books suggested by his publisher's editor⟩ — see HAVE 1
3 to provide with a paying job ⟨her neighbor *retained* her as a nanny for the summer, thus giving her something to do until school started again⟩ — see EMPLOY 1

retainer *n* a person hired to perform household or personal services ⟨knights being dressed for battle by their *retainers*⟩ — see SERVANT

retake *vb* to get again in one's possession ⟨still crying because her playmate had taken her doll, the little girl angrily *retook* it and refused to play⟩ — see RECOVER 1

retaliate *vb* to punish in kind the wrongdoer responsible for ⟨*retaliated* his neighbor's malicious destruction of his flower garden by cutting down the man's prize apple tree⟩ — see AVENGE

retaliation *n* the act or an instance of paying back an injury with an injury ⟨even though she had tripped him accidentally, he tripped her in *retaliation* anyway⟩ — see REVENGE

retard *vb* to cause to move or proceed at a less rapid pace ⟨an herbicide to *retard* the growth of weeds⟩ — see SLOW 1

retardation *n* a usually gradual decrease in the pace or level of activity of something ⟨scientists discovered that they could achieve the *retardation* of light if they shined it through a variety of different substances⟩ — see SLOWDOWN

retarding *n* a usually gradual decrease in the pace or level of activity of something ⟨the *retarding* of mildew is one thing that this cleaner claims to be good for⟩ — see SLOWDOWN

retch *vb* to discharge the contents of the stomach through the mouth ⟨the smell of rotten cabbage makes me *retch*⟩ — see VOMIT

rethink *vb* to consider again especially with the possibility of change or reversal ⟨since my efforts to solve this problem aren't working, I need to *rethink* my approach⟩ — see RECONSIDER

reticent *adj* 1 given to keeping one's activities hidden from public observation or knowledge ⟨the panel decided to investigate the company, which has always been *reticent* about its internal operations, for fraud⟩ — see SECRETIVE
2 tending not to speak frequently (as by habit or inclination) ⟨her husband is by nature a *reticent* person, and

she resigned herself to that fact long ago⟩ — see SILENT 2

retinue *n* a body of employees or servants who accompany and wait on a person ⟨the quarterback and his *retinue* of friends and admirers filled the hallway leading to the locker room⟩ — see CORTEGE 1

retire *vb* **1** to go to one's bed in order to sleep ⟨I'm exhausted, so I think I'll *retire* for the evening⟩ — see BED

2 to let go from office, service, or employment ⟨the school immediately *retired* the coach upon discovering that he had been fixing games⟩ — see DISMISS 1

3 to move back or away (as from something difficult, dangerous, or disagreeable) ⟨upon spotting the snake, she *retired* slowly, edging her way back towards the house⟩ — see RETREAT 1

retire (from) *vb* to give up (a job or office) ⟨at the age of 72, she finally *retired from* the job she had held at the shoe factory for over 50 years⟩ — see QUIT 1

retired *adj* hidden from view ⟨hiked out to a *retired* beach and fished in the surf⟩ — see SECLUDED

retirement *n* an act of moving away especially from something difficult, dangerous, or disagreeable ⟨military historians have blamed the defeat on that battalion's *retirement* from the front lines⟩ — see RETREAT 1

retiring *adj* **1** not comfortable around people ⟨one *retiring* young girl was sitting alone quietly in a corner during the party⟩ — see SHY 2

2 not having or showing any feelings of superiority, self-assertiveness, or showiness ⟨a gentle and *retiring* woman who generously credits all that she's accomplished in her life to the support of others⟩ — see HUMBLE 1

retiringness *n* the absence of any feelings of being better than others ⟨he's a man of such deep-rooted *retiringness* and reserve that casual acquaintances never guess that he's chief executive of a major corporation⟩ — see HUMILITY

retort *n* **1** a quick witty response ⟨the clever boy responded to the bully's threat with a rude *retort*⟩
synonyms comeback, repartee, riposte
related words back talk; crack, quip, sally, wisecrack, witticism; cut, insult, put-down
2 something spoken or written in reaction especially to a question ⟨I didn't appreciate your nasty *retort* to my question about whether you had finished your homework⟩ — see ANSWER 1

retort *vb* to speak or write in reaction to a question or to another reaction ⟨when told she couldn't have it, she *retorted*, "Fine, I didn't want it anyway!"⟩ — see ANSWER 1

retract *vb* to solemnly or formally reject or go back on (as something formerly adhered to) ⟨the newspaper was forced to *retract* the story, which turned out to be based on fabricated reporting⟩ — see ABJURE

retreat *n* **1** an act of moving away especially from something difficult, dangerous, or disagreeable ⟨we made a strategic *retreat* when we realized that we were outnumbered⟩
synonyms recession, retirement, retreat, revulsion, withdrawal
related words flinch, recoil, shrinking
antonyms advancement
2 something (as a building) that offers cover from the weather or protection from danger ⟨her bedroom served as a *retreat* from the frequent arguing between her parents⟩ — see SHELTER

retreat *vb* **1** to move back or away (as from something difficult, dangerous, or disagreeable) ⟨we *retreated* to the safety of the cellar at the first sign of the tornado⟩
synonyms back (away), fall back, recede, retire, withdraw
related words flinch, recoil, shrink; chicken (out); back down, backtrack; abandon, depart, evacuate, go, leave, quit, vacate
phrases give way, lose ground
near antonyms beard, brave, brazen, breast, confront, dare, defy, face, outbrave
antonyms advance
2 to hasten away from something dangerous or frightening ⟨the untried soldiers *retreated* in humiliating disarray almost as soon as the enemy's onslaught began⟩ — see RUN 2

retribution *n* the act or an instance of paying back an injury with an injury ⟨the villain kidnapped the superhero's girlfriend in *retribution* for overthrowing his plans to destroy the city⟩ — see REVENGE

retrieval *n* the act or process of getting something back ⟨waited at the clerk's desk for the *retrieval* of my birth certificate from the files⟩ — see RECOVERY 1

retrieve *vb* to get again in one's possession ⟨needed to *retrieve* the book from my friend so I could return it to the library⟩ — see RECOVER 1

retrograde *adj* directed, turned, or done toward the back ⟨*retrograde* pedaling will engage the brakes on that bike⟩ — see BACKWARD

retrogress *vb* to go back to a previous and usually lower state or level ⟨needed to *retrogress* the design for the space shuttle when testing showed that some of the experimental materials wouldn't survive reentry⟩ — see REGRESS

retrogression *n* the act or an instance of going back to an earlier and lower level especially of intelligence or behavior ⟨I can't tell if these new work groups are an improvement or a *retrogression* when it comes to class organization⟩ — see REGRESSION

retrospect *n* a usually critical look at a past event ⟨in *retrospect*, we should have saved more money for college⟩ — see REVIEW 1

retrospection *n* a usually critical look at a past event ⟨the president is confident that future *retrospections* will decide that he did the right thing⟩ — see REVIEW 1

return *n* **1** something spoken or written in reaction especially to a question ⟨I was moved by my grandfather's lengthy *return* to my casual question about his experiences in the Vietnam War⟩ — see ANSWER 1

2 an increase usually measured in money that comes from labor, business, or property ⟨if we buy better equipment, we'll be able to make the product faster, thus getting a better *return* on our investment⟩ — see INCOME

3 the amount of money left when expenses are subtracted from the total amount received ⟨I made a 1000% *return* on those old baseball cards that I had originally bought for a few dollars⟩ — see PROFIT 1

return *vb* **1** to bring, send, or put back to a former or proper place ⟨when I'm done reading a book, I always *return* it to the very shelf I got it from⟩
synonyms replace, restore
near antonyms remove, take
2 to produce as revenue ⟨my dad says this technology stock will *return* a 40% profit⟩ — see YIELD 2
3 to speak or write in reaction to a question or to another reaction ⟨when I asked him to sit down to dinner,

he *returned* that he would come when he was good and ready⟩ — see ANSWER 1

revamp *vb* **1** to make different in some way ⟨come into our salon today and *revamp* your image with a new haircut⟩ — see CHANGE 1
2 to prepare for publication by correcting, rewriting, or updating ⟨*revamped* the short story so that it would fit better with the magazine's other offerings⟩ — see EDIT
3 to put into good shape or working order again ⟨you'll need to *revamp* that old washing machine before installing it⟩ — see MEND 1

revamping *n* the act, process, or result of making different ⟨the room looks much better for the *revamping*⟩ — see CHANGE

reveal *vb* **1** to make known (as information previously kept secret) ⟨at the end of the book, the detective *reveals* the identity of the mysterious stranger⟩
synonyms bare, disclose, discover, divulge, expose, spill, tell, unbosom, uncloak, uncover, unmask, unveil
related words debunk, show up; unclothe, undrape; advertise, announce, blaze, broadcast, declare, placard, post, proclaim, promulgate, publicize, publish, sound; betray, blab, give away, leak, let on; inform, squeal, talk; communicate, impart, relate; acknowledge, admit, avow, concede, confess, own; disinter, unearth
phrases spill the beans (about)
near antonyms camouflage, disguise; gild, gloss (over), varnish, whitewash; becloud, bedim, befog, cloud, darken, eclipse, obscure, overcast, overshadow, shade
antonyms cloak, conceal, cover (up), enshroud, hide, mask, shroud, veil
2 to make known (something abstract) through outward signs ⟨a habitual smirk that *reveals* his contempt for other people⟩ — see SHOW 2

revealing *adj* clearly conveying a special meaning (as one's mood) ⟨gave my friend a *revealing* wink as our teacher opened the desk drawer we had filled with frogs⟩ — see EXPRESSIVE

revel *n* a time or instance of carefree fun ⟨in Finland, Midsummer Day ushers in a nationwide *revel* as the Finns celebrate the endless hours of sunlight with bonfires and parties⟩ — see FLING 1

revel (in) *vb* to take pleasure in ⟨winter-weary residents *reveling in* the warm spring weather⟩ — see ENJOY 1

revelation *n* the act or an instance of making known something previously unknown or concealed ⟨the *revelation* of the movie star's secret marriage by the tabloids⟩ ⟨a new biography of the former president that contains several shocking *revelations*⟩
synonyms disclosure, divulgence, exposure
related words bombshell, surprise; acknowledgment (*also* acknowledgement), admission, avowal, concession, confession
near antonyms concealment, cover-up

reveler *or* **reveller** *n* one who engages in merrymaking especially in honor of a special occasion ⟨wedding *revelers* whooping it up until dawn⟩ — see CELEBRANT

reveling *n* joyful or festive activity ⟨the *reveling* was too much for her, so she went to bed early even though the party was still going strong⟩ — see MERRYMAKING

revelry *n* joyful or festive activity ⟨the *revelry* that always accompanies the last day of school⟩ — see MERRYMAKING

revenge *n* the act or an instance of paying back an injury with an injury ⟨my *revenge* on the bully who stole my lunch money was the talk of the whole school⟩
synonyms reprisal, requital, retaliation, retribution, vengeance

related words counter, counterattack, counteroffensive; castigation, chastisement, correction; desert(s), discipline, nemesis, penalty, punishment, wrath; amends, compensation, indemnification, indemnity, quittance, recompense, recoupment, redress, remuneration, reparation(s), restitution
near antonyms clemency, grace, leniency, lenity, mercy; forgiveness, pardon, remission

revenge *vb* to punish in kind the wrongdoer responsible for ⟨a TV movie about a man who took maters into his own hands and *revenged* the death of his brother⟩ — see AVENGE

revengeful *adj* likely to seek revenge ⟨after losing on their own turf, our football team was feeling especially *revengeful*⟩ — see VINDICTIVE

revenue *n* an increase usually measured in money that comes from labor, business, or property ⟨the struggling business didn't create much *revenue* during its first year of operation⟩ — see INCOME

reverberant *adj* marked by conspicuously full and rich sounds or tones ⟨the pastor's *reverberant* voice could be heard all over the cemetery as he read the final prayers for the deceased⟩ — see RESONANT

reverberate *vb* to continue or be repeated in a series of reflected sound waves ⟨a room with nothing but hard surfaces will cause the music from your audio system to *reverberate*⟩
synonyms echo, reecho, resonate, resound, sound
near antonyms damp, dampen, deaden, dull, quiet

reverberating *adj* marked by conspicuously full and rich sounds or tones ⟨the temple was filled with the *reverberating* sound of the gong⟩ — see RESONANT

revere *vb* to offer honor or respect to (someone) as a divine power ⟨in some cultures people *revere* their ancestors, even leaving food offerings for them⟩ — see WORSHIP 1

revered *adj* deserving honor and respect especially by reason of age ⟨a professor who is highly *revered* at the college where she has taught for the last four decades⟩ — see VENERABLE 1

reverence *vb* to offer honor or respect to (someone) as a divine power ⟨devotees coming to *reverence* their god⟩ — see WORSHIP 1

reverend *adj* deserving honor and respect especially by reason of age ⟨our *reverend* elders should be accorded a place of honor at the ceremonies⟩ — see VENERABLE 1

reverend *n* a person specially trained and authorized to conduct religious services in a Christian church ⟨called their *reverend* and asked if he could marry them next June⟩ — see CLERGYMAN

reverie *also* **revery** *n* the state of being lost in thought ⟨unfortunately, I was deep in *reverie* when the teacher called my name⟩
synonyms daydreaming, study, trance, woolgathering
related words contemplation, meditation, musing; absentmindedness, absorption, abstraction, preoccupation; chimera, conceit, daydream, delusion, dream, fancy, fantasy (*also* phantasy), figment, hallucination, illusion, phantasm, pipe dream, unreality, vision

reversal *n* a change in status for the worse usually temporarily ⟨fortunately, they are a loving family and can weather the *reversal* of fortune that the stock market crash brought on⟩ — see REVERSE 1

reverse *n* **1** a change in status for the worse usually temporarily ⟨the loss of my paper route was just the first of my financial *reverses* since the start of the new year⟩

synonyms lapse, reversal, setback

related words disappointment, frustration, letdown; comedown, decline, descent, down, downfall, fall; turnabout, turnaround; recession, regression, retrogression, reversion; relapse; breakdown, collapse, crash, meltdown, ruin, undoing

near antonyms status quo

2 something that is as different as possible from something else ⟨how could you think I don't like pizza, when it's just the *reverse*: I love pizza⟩ — see OPPOSITE

reverse *vb* **1** to change (as an opinion) to the contrary ⟨the principal refused to *reverse* his decision regarding the use of cellular phones⟩

synonyms switch

related words abrogate, overturn, repeal, rescind, revoke, strike (down); countermand, about-face, backtrack, revert

near antonyms maintain, support, uphold

2 to change the position of (an object) so that the opposite side or end is showing ⟨when one side of the cleaning cloth gets dirty, just *reverse* it⟩ ⟨you can *reverse* the jacket for a whole new look⟩

synonyms flip, invert, turn (over)

related words transpose; exchange, interchange, shift, switch; overturn, upset

reversion *n* the act or an instance of going back to an earlier and lower level especially of intelligence or behavior ⟨after the birth of his baby brother, the toddler temporarily underwent a kind of *reversion,* acting like a baby himself⟩ — see REGRESSION

revert *vb* to go back to a previous and usually lower state or level ⟨after the national emergency had passed, the political parties abandoned their unity and *reverted* to their partisan squabbling⟩ — see REGRESS

review *n* **1** a usually critical look at a past event ⟨a *review* of yesterday's football game gave us a lot of good ideas on how to improve for the next one⟩

synonyms reappraisal, reconsideration, reexamination, retrospect, retrospection

related words recap, recapitulation, rehash

near antonyms preview

2 a close look at or over someone or something in order to judge condition ⟨took the car to her mechanic for a complete mechanical *review* before she decided to sell it⟩ — see INSPECTION

3 a publication that appears at regular intervals ⟨had his poetry published in a literary *review*⟩ — see JOURNAL

4 an essay evaluating or analyzing something ⟨a harsh movie *review* of an expected summer blockbuster⟩ — see CRITICISM

review *vb* **1** to consider again especially with the possibility of change or reversal ⟨since we can't follow that plan, we'll have to *review* our options and decide on something else⟩ — see RECONSIDER

2 to look over closely (as for judging quality or condition) ⟨*reviewed* her theme for misspellings and made the necessary corrections⟩ — see INSPECT

reviewer *n* a person who makes or expresses a judgment on the quality of offerings in some field of endeavor ⟨loves music so much and is so knowledgeable about it that she wants to be a music *reviewer* when she grows up⟩ — see CRITIC 2

revise *n* the act, process, or result of making different ⟨that paper needs one more *revise,* and then I think it's ready to turn in⟩ — see CHANGE

revise *vb* **1** to make different in some way ⟨with the snow, we'll need to *revise* our travel plans⟩ — see CHANGE 1

2 to prepare for publication by correcting, rewriting, or updating ⟨*revise* the article and add more up-to-date information so we can reprint it⟩ — see EDIT

revision *n* the act, process, or result of making different ⟨the director didn't like the scene's dialogue at first, but after a *revision* he was satisfied that it fit the characters⟩ — see CHANGE

revitalization *n* the act or an instance of bringing something back to life, public attention, or vigorous activity ⟨the mayor was present at the ceremony marking the *revitalization* of the old industrial neighborhood as a new center for art galleries and lofts⟩ — see REVIVAL

revitalize *vb* **1** to bring back to a former condition or vigor ⟨a new cream that claims to *revitalize* sun-damaged skin⟩ — see RENEW 1

2 to bring back to life, practice, or activity ⟨the bowling alley, eager to *revitalize* the sport for a younger crowd, started offering "disco bowling" every Friday night with disco lights, loud pop music, and free soda⟩ — see REVIVE 1

revival *n* the act or an instance of bringing something back to life, public attention, or vigorous activity ⟨there was a *revival* of interest in the author's classic horror stories after a film version of his best-known story was released⟩

synonyms reanimation, rebirth, regeneration, rejuvenation, renewal, resurgence, resurrection, resuscitation, revitalization

related words renaissance, renascence; reactivation; rally, recovery, recuperation

near antonyms death, expiration, extinction

revive *vb* **1** to bring back to life, practice, or activity ⟨an effort to *revive* the once-common custom of celebrating May 1 as a springtime festival of games and dances⟩

synonyms reanimate, regenerate, rejuvenate, rekindle, renew, resurrect, resuscitate, revitalize

related words reactivate, restart

near antonyms extinguish, quench, suppress

2 to bring back to a former condition or vigor ⟨running through the sprinkler always *revives* us on hot August afternoons⟩ — see RENEW 1

3 to gain consciousness again ⟨the patient eventually *revived* and was able to give us her name and address⟩ — see COME TO

revived *adj* made or become fresh in spirits or vigor ⟨*revived* farmers heading back out to the fields after a hearty lunch⟩ — see NEW 4

reviving *adj* having a renewing effect on the state of the body or mind ⟨took a *reviving* vacation in the Caribbean⟩ — see TONIC

revocation *n* the act of putting an end to something planned or previously agreed to ⟨threatened the *revocation* of his driving privileges⟩ — see CANCELLATION

revoke *vb* to put an end to (something planned or previously agreed to) ⟨the judge *revoked* the jail sentence when the defendant promised to do community service instead⟩ — see CANCEL 1

revolt *n* open fighting against authority (as one's own government) ⟨soon the *revolt* had spread to every corner of the country⟩ — see REBELLION

revolt *vb* **1** to cause to feel disgust ⟨the very idea of eating snails *revolts* me⟩ — see DISGUST

2 to rise up against established authority ⟨the students practically *revolted* when the school cancelled the championship football game⟩ — see REBEL

revolted *adj* filled with disgust ⟨we were *revolted* when we learned about the prevalence of child labor in the Third World⟩ — see SICK 2

revolter *n* a person who rises up against authority ⟨Spartacus, who led a slave revolt in ancient Rome, has served as an inspiration for a number of other *revolters* over the centuries⟩ — see REBEL

revolting *adj* causing intense displeasure, disgust, or resentment ⟨he thinks that sushi is *revolting*, but I love it⟩ — see OFFENSIVE 1

revolution *n* **1** a rapid turning about on an axis or central point ⟨revved the engine to 3000 *revolutions* per minute⟩ — see SPIN 1
2 open fighting against authority (as one's own government) ⟨the *revolution* by which the American colonies gained their independence from Great Britain necessitated going up against the world's most powerful army⟩ — see REBELLION

revolutionary *adj* **1** being very far from the center of public opinion ⟨a candidate with a lot of crazy, *revolutionary* ideas that no one would go for⟩ — see EXTREME 2
2 taking part in a rebellion ⟨*revolutionary* forces that were defeated before reaching the capital⟩ — see REBELLIOUS 1

revolutionary *n* **1** a person who favors rapid and sweeping changes especially in laws and methods of government ⟨after the collapse of the Russian monarchy, the moderate socialists governed until being overthrown by the communist *revolutionaries* known as the Bolsheviks⟩ — see RADICAL
2 a person who rises up against authority ⟨at first government was not worried about a small band of unarmed *revolutionaries*⟩ — see REBEL

revolutionist *adj* being very far from the center of public opinion ⟨his *revolutionist* ideas won't get him elected⟩ — see EXTREME 2

revolutionist *n* **1** a person who favors rapid and sweeping changes especially in laws and methods of government ⟨after a long series of weak leaders, the people were ready for a *revolutionist* who promised to bring sweeping change to the nation⟩ — see RADICAL
2 a person who rises up against authority ⟨historically, *revolutionists* have generally been young men willing to risk everything, even their lives, in the pursuit of their cause⟩ — see REBEL

revolutionizer *n* a person who rises up against authority ⟨one of the great *revolutionizers* in astronomy and in all science was Copernicus, who overthrew the ancient and established belief that the Earth was the center of the universe⟩ — see REBEL

revolve *vb* **1** to move (something) in a curved or circular path on or as if on an axis ⟨*revolved* the display case so I could see the CDs on the other side of it⟩ — see TURN 1
2 to move in circles around an axis or center ⟨the Earth *revolves* around the sun⟩ — see SPIN 1

revulsion *n* **1** a dislike so strong as to cause stomach upset or queasiness ⟨managed to overcome his initial *revulsion* of lizards and eventually bought one as a pet⟩ — see DISGUST
2 an act of moving away especially from something difficult, dangerous, or disagreeable ⟨society's eventual *revulsion* from racial segregation⟩ — see RETREAT 1

reward *n* something offered or given in return for a service performed ⟨there was a *reward* of twenty dollars for the return of her missing cat⟩

synonyms bounty, price
related words bonus, lagniappe, premium; bonanza, jackpot, treasure trove; award, decoration, distinction, honor, plume, premium, prize; gratuity, tip; desert(s), wages

reward *vb* to give something as a token of gratitude or admiration for a service or achievement ⟨the firefighters were *rewarded* by the city for their heroic actions with vacations⟩
synonyms award
related words cite, decorate, honor, remember; compensate, pay, recompense, requite; reimburse, repay; acclaim, applaud, commend, compliment, hail, praise, salute

rewarding *adj* making one feel good inside ⟨pursued a *rewarding* career helping poor children in rural areas get adequate medical care as well as an education⟩ — see HEARTWARMING

reweigh *vb* to consider again especially with the possibility of change or reversal ⟨*reweighed* her statement that a pound of feathers is lighter than a pound of lead⟩ — see RECONSIDER

reword *vb* to express something (as a text or statement) in different words ⟨I'll *reword* the question for you so you can completely understand it⟩ — see PARAPHRASE

rewording *n* an instance of expressing something in different words ⟨I like your *rewording* of that paragraph better than the original⟩ — see PARAPHRASE

rework *vb* **1** to make different in some way ⟨the sculptor *reworked* the clay into another shape⟩ — see CHANGE 1
2 to prepare for publication by correcting, rewriting, or updating ⟨the magazine will publish your poem if you *rework* it so that it's a little shorter⟩ — see EDIT

reworking *n* the act, process, or result of making different ⟨the painting looked significantly different after the artist's *reworking* of the composition⟩ — see CHANGE

rhapsodic *also* **rhapsodical** *adj* experiencing or marked by overwhelming usually pleasurable emotion ⟨a *rhapsodic* welcome for the military personnel returning from service overseas⟩ — see ECSTATIC

rhapsodically *adv* in an enthusiastic manner ⟨*rhapsodically* described the glittering party at the mansion⟩ — see SKY-HIGH

rhapsodize *vb* to make an exaggerated display of affection or enthusiasm ⟨*rhapsodized* about the food so as not to hurt their host's feelings⟩ — see GUSH 2

rhapsody *n* a state of overwhelming usually pleasurable emotion ⟨listening to Mozart always left him in a *rhapsody* that lingered for the remainder of the evening⟩ — see ECSTASY

rhetoric *n* **1** language that is impressive-sounding but not meaningful or sincere ⟨the mayor's promise to fight drugs was just *rhetoric*, since there was no money in the city budget for a drug program⟩
synonyms bombast, gas, grandiloquence, hot air, oratory, wind
related words claptrap, drivel, gibberish, hogwash, humbug, jabberwocky, jazz, moonshine, nonsense; affectedness, floweriness, grandiosity, loftiness, pomposity, pretension, pretentiousness; verboseness, verbosity, windiness, wordiness
2 the art or power of speaking or writing in a forceful and convincing way ⟨great leaders have often been masters of *rhetoric*, which they have used for both good and ill⟩ — see ELOQUENCE

rhetorical *adj* marked by the use of impressive-sounding but mostly meaningless words and phrases ⟨an essay on civic duty that was mostly *rhetorical*, full of flowery quotations but providing nothing helpful⟩

synonyms bombastic, gaseous, gassy, grandiloquent, oratorical, windy

related words elevated, florid, flowery, grandiose, highfalutin, high-flown, high-sounding, inflated, lofty, pompous, pretentious, stilted; overdone, verbose, wordy

near antonyms eloquent, well-spoken; bald, direct, matter-of-fact, plain, plainspoken, simple, stark, straightforward, unadorned, unaffected, unpretentious

rhythm *n* the recurrent pattern formed by a series of sounds having a regular rise and fall in intensity ⟨the steady *rhythm* of the rain falling on the roof⟩

synonyms beat, cadence, measure, meter

related words accent, accentuation, emphasis, stress; drum, throb; lilt, movement, sway; hexameter, pentameter, tetrameter, trimeter

rhythmic *or* **rhythmical** *adj* marked by or occurring with a noticeable regularity in the rise and fall of sound ⟨lulled to sleep by the *rhythmic* sound of her mother's voice reading the Bible⟩

synonyms cadenced, measured, metric, metrical

related words even, regular, steady, uniform; lilting, musical, swaying

antonyms unmeasured, unrhythmic

riata *n* a rope or long leather thong with a noose used especially for catching livestock ⟨the cowboy neatly tossed a *riata* over the head of the escaping cow⟩ — see LASSO

rib *vb* to make fun of in a good-natured way ⟨*ribbed* him a bit about the fumbling the easy play⟩ — see TEASE 1

ribald *adj* 1 depicting or referring to sexual matters in a way that is unacceptable in polite society ⟨the mischievous classmate whispered a *ribald* suggestion just to make her blush⟩ — see OBSCENE 1

2 hinting at or intended to call to mind matters regarded as indecent ⟨a *ribald* tale filled with words having double meanings⟩ — see SUGGESTIVE 1

ribaldry *n* the quality or state of being obscene ⟨there's a *ribaldry* in the works of Chaucer that generations of English students have heartily enjoyed⟩ — see OBSCENITY 1

ribbing *adj* marked by or expressive of mild or good-natured teasing ⟨the lightly *ribbing* tone tipped me off that this wasn't a serious reprimand⟩ — see QUIZZICAL

ribbon *n* a long narrow piece of material ⟨tied a silk *ribbon* in her hair⟩ — see STRIP

rich *adj* 1 having goods, property, or money in abundance ⟨Tanya's dad works as chauffeur for the *richest* man in town, a big oil baron⟩

synonyms affluent, flush, loaded, moneyed (*or* monied), opulent, wealthy, well-heeled, well-off, well-to-do

related words comfortable, propertied, prosperous, successful; flourishing, prospering, thriving; advantaged, blessed, privileged

near antonyms deprived, disadvantaged, underprivileged; bankrupt, bankrupted, beggared, broke, indebted, insolvent, pauperized, ruined, stone-broke; depressed, pinched, reduced, straitened; low, short

antonyms destitute, impecunious, impoverished, indigent, needy, penniless, penurious, poor, poverty-stricken

2 containing much seasoning, fat, or sugar ⟨stay away from *rich* foods before you sing tonight⟩

synonyms heavy

related words buttery, fat, fatty, greasy, oily; caloric, calorific, fattening; cloying, filling, overfilling, satiating, sating; spicy, sugary; creamy, sauced

near antonyms natural, plain, simple; unseasoned; diet, nonfattening, slimming; nonfat

antonyms light

3 having an abundance of some characteristic quality (as flavor) ⟨*rich* wines complemented the meal⟩ — see FULL-BODIED

4 producing abundantly ⟨*rich* farmland⟩ — see FERTILE

riches *n* the total of one's money and property ⟨industrialists who had amassed *riches* of a magnitude that few had dreamed possible⟩ — see WEALTH 1

richly *adv* in a luxurious manner ⟨a *richly* decorated penthouse that showed off the owner's art collection to its best advantage⟩ — see HIGH

richness *n* the amusing quality or element in something ⟨the *richness* of the irony—I had just contributed to the political campaign of a multimillionaire—was too much for me to ignore⟩ — see HUMOR 1

rick *n* a quantity of things thrown or stacked on one another ⟨*ricks* of hay dotting the fields⟩ — see ¹PILE 1

ricochet *vb* to strike and fly off at an angle ⟨a ball *ricocheted* off the wall and struck me in the knee⟩ — see GLANCE 1

rid *vb* to set (a person or thing) free of something that encumbers ⟨worked two jobs to *rid* himself of debt⟩

synonyms clear, disburden, disencumber, free, relieve, unburden

related words discharge, emancipate, enfranchise, liberate, loose, loosen, manumit, release, spring, unbind, uncage, unchain, unfetter; bail (out), deliver, redeem, rescue; disengage, disentangle, extricate

near antonyms bog (down), fetter, restrain, shackle, subject, weigh (down), weight (down)

antonyms burden, encumber, saddle

riddance *n* the getting rid of whatever is unwanted or useless ⟨the *riddance* of all fleas from the house was a relief to everyone concerned⟩ — see DISPOSAL 1

riddle *n* something hard to understand or explain ⟨his motives for starting an argument with the coach were a complete *riddle*⟩ — see MYSTERY

riddle *vb* to find an answer for through reasoning ⟨at long last archaeologists were able to *riddle* the mystery of Egyptian hieroglyphics with the discovery of the Rosetta stone⟩ — see SOLVE

ride *n* a means of getting to a destination in a vehicle driven by another ⟨Laurie sometimes gets a *ride* to school from her neighbor⟩

synonyms lift, transportation

related words drive, spin, turn; joyride; conveyance, passage, transit, transport

ride *vb* 1 to attack repeatedly with mean put-downs or insults ⟨that supervisor is always *riding* everyone for every little thing⟩ — see TEASE 2

2 to make fun of in a good-natured way ⟨if you don't quit *riding* me about my silly socks, I'm going to throw one at you!⟩ — see TEASE 1

3 to rest or move along the surface of a liquid or in the air ⟨a condor *riding* high in the sky⟩ — see FLOAT

ride (out) *vb* to come safely through ⟨just as we always have in the past, we'll *ride out* this latest crisis⟩ — see SURVIVE 1

ridge *n* the line formed when two sloping surfaces come together along their topmost edge ⟨pigeons roosting along the *ridge* of the roof⟩

synonyms crest

related words divide; backbone, chine, ridgepole, spine; eminence, peak, prominence, promontory, rise

ridicule *n* the making of unkind jokes as a way of showing one's scorn for someone or something ⟨the early efforts by the suffragists to obtain voting rights for women were met with *ridicule*⟩

synonyms derision, mockery

related words contempt, disdain, scorn; belittlement, deprecation, disparagement; insult, put-down; laughter, snickering; burlesque, caricature, mimicry, satire

near antonyms applause, approval, commendation, praise

ridicule *vb* to make (someone or something) the object of unkind laughter ⟨the term "big bang theory" was originally coined to *ridicule* the belief that the universe was created by a giant explosion⟩

synonyms deride, gibe (*or* jibe), jeer, laugh (at), mock, scout

related words scoff (at), scorn, sneer (at); bad-mouth, belittle, decry, disparage, pooh-pooh (*also* pooh), put down; chaff, jive, josh, kid, quiz, rally, razz, rib, ride, tease; bait, bug, harass, harry, hassle, heckle, needle, pester, target, taunt, torment; ape, burlesque, caricature, imitate, lampoon, mimic, parody, parrot, satirize, take off (on), travesty

phrases make fun of, poke fun at

near antonyms applaud, approve, commend, endorse (*also* indorse), sanction

ridiculer *n* a person who causes repeated emotional pain, distress, or annoyance to another ⟨any person of great vision has his or her *ridiculers*, who inevitably fail to appreciate genius and originality⟩ — see TORMENTOR

ridiculous *adj* 1 so foolish or pointless as to be worthy of scornful laughter ⟨a movie thriller with such a *ridiculous* plot that it gets only guffaws from audiences⟩

synonyms absurd, comical, derisive, derisory, farcical, laughable, ludicrous, preposterous, risible, silly

related words asinine, brainless, dumb, fatuous, foolish, half-witted, harebrained, idiotic, imbecilic, inane, jerky, moronic, nonsensical, simpleminded, stupid, unwise, weak-minded, witless; balmy, cockeyed, crazy, cuckoo, daffy, daft, dotty, insane, kooky, loony (*also* looney), lunatic, mad, nutty, screwball, senseless, wacky; fantastic, far-fetched, inconceivable, incredible, unbelievable, unreal, unreasonable

near antonyms earnest, serious, solemn; believable, conceivable, credible, logical, rational, realistic, reasonable, sensible

2 causing or intended to cause laughter ⟨a movie comedian who has perfected the *ridiculous* pratfall⟩ — see FUNNY 1

rife *adj* possessing or covered with great numbers or amounts of something specified ⟨our school is *rife* with rumors about the incoming principal⟩

synonyms abounding, flush, fraught, replete, swarming, teeming, thick, thronging

related words brimming, bulging, bursting, chock-full (*or* chockful), crammed, crowded, fat, filled, full, jammed, jam-packed, loaded, packed, saturated, stuffed; clogged, congested, overcrowded, overfilled, overflowing, overfull, overloaded, overstuffed, surfeited; alive, animated, astir, bustling, busy, buzzing, humming, lively

near antonyms bare, barren, blank, devoid, empty, stark, vacant, void; depleted, drained, exhausted; deficient, incomplete, insufficient, short

riffraff *n* 1 discarded or useless material ⟨the sight of piles and piles of *riffraff* at the town dump was a sobering reminder that we are indeed a society of consumers⟩ — see GARBAGE

2 people looked down upon as ignorant and of the lowest class ⟨local ordinances that are intended to keep the *riffraff* out of the town⟩ — see RABBLE

rifle *vb* to look through (as a place) carefully or thoroughly in an effort to find or discover something ⟨*rifled* the desk drawer in search of the insurance policy⟩ — see SEARCH 1

rift *n* 1 an irregular usually narrow break in a surface created by pressure ⟨a small *rift* opened in the earth's crust⟩ — see CRACK 1

2 an open space in a barrier (as a wall or hedge) ⟨it was possible to peek through the *rift* in the fence and see the ball game⟩ — see GAP 1

rig *n* a horse-drawn wheeled vehicle for carrying passengers ⟨romantic couples enjoy being driven in the old-fashioned *rig* through the park⟩ — see CARRIAGE 1

rig *vb* to provide (someone) with what is needed for a task or activity ⟨carefully *rigged* each diver with the required equipment before starting out⟩ — see FURNISH 1

rig (out) *vb* to outfit with clothes and especially fine or special clothes ⟨everyone was *rigged out* for a fancy party⟩ — see CLOTHE 1

right *adj* 1 following an original exactly ⟨a modern replica of an 18th-century British warship that is *right* in all of its details⟩ — see FAITHFUL 2

2 being exactly as appears or as claimed ⟨despite the name, New York's East River is a strait and not a *right* river⟩ — see AUTHENTIC 1

3 being in agreement with the truth or a fact or a standard ⟨the obvious answer is not always the *right* one⟩ — see CORRECT 1

4 being what is called for by accepted standards of right and wrong ⟨trying to do what is *right*⟩ — see JUST 1

5 conforming to a high standard of morality or virtue ⟨a *right* woman who did not hang around waterfront bars⟩ — see GOOD 3

6 free from irregularities (as curves, bends, or angles) in course ⟨the first city in America laid out with broad, *right* avenues⟩ — see STRAIGHT 1

7 having full use of one's mind and control over one's actions ⟨he hasn't been *right* since he suffered serious brain injury in the accident⟩ — see SANE

8 meeting the requirements of a purpose or situation ⟨the *right* tool for the job⟩ — see FIT 1

right *adv* 1 as stated or indicated without the slightest difference ⟨stay *right* where you are⟩ — see EXACTLY 1

2 in a direct line or course ⟨walk *right* over here now⟩ — see DIRECTLY 1

3 to a great degree ⟨a *right* beautiful day we're having!⟩ — see VERY 1

right *n* 1 something to which one has a just claim ⟨everyone has the *right* to life, liberty, and the pursuit of happiness⟩

synonyms appanage, birthright, prerogative

related words due, entitlement, perquisite, privilege

2 an entitlement to something ⟨what *right* do you have to tell us what to do?⟩ — see CLAIM 1

3 the act or practice of giving to others what is their due ⟨activists who have fought all their lives for *right*⟩ — see JUSTICE 1

right away *adv* without delay ⟨you need to have this fixed *right away*⟩ — see IMMEDIATELY

righteous *adj* **1** conforming to a high standard of morality or virtue ⟨a *righteous* man can be trusted to act honorably regardless of the circumstances⟩ — see GOOD 2
2 following the accepted rules of moral conduct ⟨*righteous* behavior is its own reward⟩ — see HONORABLE 1

righteously *adv* with purity of thought and deed ⟨if you have acted *righteously*, you have nothing to fear⟩ — see PURELY

righteousness *n* **1** conduct that conforms to an accepted standard of right and wrong ⟨the laws do not always dictate *righteousness,* for what is legal is not always moral⟩ — see MORALITY 1
2 faithfulness to high moral standards ⟨a life lived with *righteousness* guarantees that you will always respect yourself⟩ — see HONOR 1

rightful *adj* being what is called for by accepted standards of right and wrong ⟨in light of her admission of having lied, the only *rightful* course of action for the governor would be to resign⟩ — see JUST 1

rightist *n* a person whose political beliefs are centered on tradition and keeping things the way they are ⟨*rightists* opposed the new social programs⟩ — see CONSERVATIVE

rightly *adv* in a manner suitable for the occasion or purpose ⟨marveling at the sight, we had to agree that the Grand Canyon was *rightly* named⟩ — see PROPERLY

right–minded *adj* conforming to a high standard of morality or virtue ⟨a group of *right-minded* people working for change⟩ — see GOOD 2

rightness *n* the quality or state of being especially suitable or fitting ⟨the *rightness* of the criticism didn't make it any more pleasant to hear⟩ — see APPROPRIATENESS

right now *adv* **1** at the present time ⟨*right now* we are in the middle of a major home renovation⟩ — see NOW 1
2 without delay ⟨answer my question *right now*⟩ — see IMMEDIATELY

right–of–way *n* the right to one's attention before other things considered less important ⟨the bill for emergency aid was immediately granted *right-of-way*⟩ — see PRIORITY

rigid *adj* **1** not allowing for any exceptions or loosening of standards ⟨*rigid* enforcement of drug laws⟩
synonyms exacting, inflexible, rigorous, strict, stringent, uncompromising
related words close, conscientious, scrupulous, undeviating; adamant, adamantine, determined, dogged, firm, relentless, resolved, single-minded, steadfast, stubborn, tenacious, unbending, unflinching; immovable, implacable, unrelenting, unyielding; austere, demanding, flinty, grim, hard, hardened, hardhearted, harsh, ironbound, severe, stern, tough
near antonyms acquiescent, compliant, compromising, pliable, pliant, relenting, yielding; easy, easygoing, gentle, indulgent, kindly, lenient, merciful, mild, pampering, soft, spoiling, tolerant
antonyms flexible, lax, loose, relaxed
2 given to exacting standards of discipline and self-restraint ⟨a *rigid* man who cannot seem to relax⟩ — see SEVERE 1
3 having a consistency that does not easily yield to pressure ⟨*rigid* steel bars that should be able to hold the weight⟩ — see FIRM 2
4 incapable of or highly resistant to bending ⟨corsets, those *rigid* undergarments for women, must have been murder to wear⟩ — see STIFF 1
5 sticking to an opinion, purpose, or course of action in spite of reason, arguments, or persuasion ⟨a *rigid*

mother who never yielded to pleading⟩ — see OBSTINATE
6 stretched with little or no give ⟨make sure that the clothesline is *rigid* so that the longer garments don't drag on the ground⟩ — see TAUT

rigidity *n* the quality or state of being demanding or unyielding (as in discipline or criticism) ⟨sometimes the *rigidity* of the headmaster's discipline was deemed excessive by even much of the faculty⟩ — see SEVERITY

rigidly *adv* without any relaxation of standards or precision ⟨stuck *rigidly* to the letter of the law⟩ — see STRICTLY

rigidness *n* the quality or state of being demanding or unyielding (as in discipline or criticism) ⟨no one even asked anymore, as their father's *rigidness* regarding bedtime was legendary⟩ — see SEVERITY

rigmarole *n* unintelligible or meaningless talk ⟨listened patiently as the student gave the usual *rigmarole*, then asked for the real reason why he hadn't done the assignment⟩ — see GIBBERISH

rigor *n* something that is a cause for suffering or special effort especially in the attainment of a goal ⟨survived many *rigors* on the way to the promised land⟩ — see DIFFICULTY 1

rigorous *adj* **1** given to exacting standards of discipline and self-restraint ⟨a *rigorous* football coach who pushed his players to the limit⟩ — see SEVERE 1
2 meeting the highest standard of accuracy ⟨a *rigorous* analysis of the data⟩ — see PRECISE 1
3 not allowing for any exceptions or loosening of standards ⟨a *rigorous* diet and exercise regimen⟩ — see RIGID 1

rigorously *adv* without any relaxation of standards or precision ⟨a *rigorously* accurate accounting of the war casualties⟩ — see STRICTLY

rigorousness *n* **1** the quality or state of being demanding or unyielding (as in discipline or criticism) ⟨the *rigorousness* of the training paid off when the dance students performed brilliantly at the recital⟩ — see SEVERITY
2 the quality or state of being very accurate ⟨these days the *rigorousness* of electronic timing is necessary to measure the minute differences in the performances of Olympic athletes⟩ — see PRECISION

rile *vb* to disturb the peace of mind of (someone) especially by repeated disagreeable acts ⟨one sure way to *rile* me is to keep yelling for me⟩ — see IRRITATE 1

rile *vb* to make angry ⟨Dad isn't easily *riled*, but once he is, he stays that way for days⟩ — see ANGER

riled *adj* feeling or showing anger ⟨the woman was obviously *riled*, as she kept throwing things⟩ — see ANGRY

riling *adj* causing annoyance ⟨a *riling* habit that drives his wife crazy⟩ — see ANNOYING

rill *n* a natural body of running water smaller than a river ⟨there are a few tiny fish in the *rill*⟩ — see CREEK 1

rim *n* the line or relatively narrow space that marks the outer limit of something ⟨the *rim* of a glass⟩ — see BORDER 1

rim *vb* to serve as a border for ⟨long lashes *rimmed* his eyes⟩ — see BORDER

rime *n* a covering of tiny ice crystals on a cold surface ⟨*rime* on the bedroom window after a bitterly cold night⟩ — see FROST

rime *vb* to cover with a hardened layer ⟨frost *riming* the doorknob⟩ — see ENCRUST

ring *n* **1** a group involved in secret or criminal activities ⟨a *ring* of counterfeiters passing phony $20 bills⟩

synonyms cabal, conspiracy, gang, Mafia, mob, syndicate

related words circle, clan, clique, coterie, crowd; junta, oligarchy

2 a circular strip ⟨a metal *ring* encircled the barrel⟩

synonyms band, circle, eye, hoop, loop, round

related words belt, cincture, collar, girdle; wreath; coil, spiral

3 a communication by telephone ⟨give me a *ring* when you're ready to go⟩ — see CALL 3

4 a group of people sharing a common interest and relating together socially ⟨a gaming *ring* that meets once a week to play⟩ — see GANG 2

5 something with a perfectly round circumference ⟨the coffee cup left a *ring* on the table⟩ — see CIRCLE 1

ring *vb* **1** to make the clear sound heard when metal vibrates ⟨I didn't hear the doorbell *ring*⟩

synonyms chime, knell, peal, toll

related words clang, clank, ding, jangle, jingle, ping, tinkle; resound, reverberate

2 to form a circle around ⟨trees *ringing* the park⟩ — see SURROUND

3 to pass completely around ⟨the line of ticket buyers *ringed* the block⟩ — see ENCIRCLE 1

ring (up) *vb, chiefly British* to make a telephone call to ⟨our friend *rang* us *up* to see if we wanted to go to a cricket match⟩ — see CALL 2

ringer *n* something or someone that strongly resembles another ⟨he's a dead *ringer* for his grandfather⟩ — see IMAGE 1

ringing *adj* **1** marked by a high volume of sound ⟨an angry, *ringing* denial of the charges⟩ — see LOUD 1

2 marked by conspicuously full and rich sounds or tones ⟨sings in a *ringing* baritone that can be heard throughout the hall⟩ — see RESONANT

ringlet *n* a length of hair that forms a loop or series of loops ⟨a little girl with perfect, golden *ringlets*⟩ — see CURL

rinse *vb* to pour liquid over or through in order to cleanse ⟨*rinse* that shirt immediately, or the paint will set⟩ — see FLUSH 1

riot *n* someone or something that is very funny ⟨she's such a *riot* at parties⟩ — see SCREAM

riotous *adj* **1** causing or intended to cause laughter ⟨his *riotous* mugging always has everyone in hysterics⟩ — see FUNNY 1

2 pouring forth in great amounts ⟨a painting by that artist is usually a *riotous* display of color⟩ — see PROFUSE

rip *n* a long deep cut ⟨the hoe left *rips* in the lawn⟩ — see GASH

rip *vb* **1** to cause (something) to separate into jagged pieces by violently pulling at it ⟨the dog *ripped* the sleeve of my shirt by grabbing it with his teeth⟩ — see TEAR 1

2 to penetrate with a sharp edge (as a knife) ⟨you can see where someone *ripped* the painting with a penknife⟩ — see CUT 1

3 to proceed or move quickly ⟨the car went *ripping* down the road⟩ — see HURRY 2

4 to separate or remove by forceful pulling ⟨*rip* a sheet off the pad of paper⟩ — see TEAR 2

ripe *adj* fully grown or developed ⟨a *ripe* tomato⟩ — see MATURE 1

ripen *vb* to become mature ⟨pears *ripening* on the tree⟩ — see MATURE

ripened *adj* fully grown or developed ⟨a fully *ripened* musical talent⟩ — see MATURE 1

ripening *n* the process of becoming mature ⟨the *ripening* of a pumpkin can take a whole season⟩ — see MATURATION

rip–off *n* an instance of theft ⟨a daring burglary of the art museum that resulted in one of the greatest *rip-offs* in history⟩ — see THEFT 2

rip off *vb* **1** to remove valuables from (a place) unlawfully ⟨the teens *ripped off* the store where they worked⟩ — see ROB

2 to take (something) without right and with an intent to keep ⟨*ripped off* some jewelry as soon as no one was looking⟩ — see STEAL 1

riposte *n* a quick witty response ⟨he's known for having a brilliant *riposte* to nearly any insult⟩ — see RETORT 1

ripple *vb* to flow in a broken irregular stream ⟨water *rippling* gently over the tiers of the fountain⟩ — see GURGLE

rip–roaring *adj* causing great emotional or mental stimulation ⟨a *rip-roaring* party that lasted all night⟩ — see EXCITING 1

rise *n* **1** a raising or a state of being raised to a higher rank or position ⟨his rapid *rise* to president of the company⟩ — see ADVANCEMENT 1

2 an area of high ground ⟨if we can get to the top of that *rise*, we'll be able to see for miles⟩ — see HEIGHT 4

3 an upward slope ⟨the *rise* of the hill was relatively gentle⟩ — see ASCENT 2

4 something added (as by growth) ⟨an unexpected *rise* in prices⟩ — see INCREASE 1

5 the act or an instance of rising or climbing up ⟨unfortunately, the descent of the balloon was just as swift as its *rise*⟩ — see ASCENT 1

rise *vb* **1** to become greater in extent, volume, amount, or number ⟨the snow accumulation is *rising* at an alarming rate⟩ — see INCREASE 2

2 to leave one's bed ⟨I generally *rise* around six and leave for work by seven⟩ — see ARISE 1

3 to move or extend upward ⟨mountains majestically *rising* towards the sky⟩ — see ASCEND

risible *adj* **1** causing or intended to cause laughter ⟨a *risible* comment that made the whole class laugh⟩ — see FUNNY 1

2 so foolish or pointless as to be worthy of scornful laughter ⟨the idea that people are meant to have wings is *risible*⟩ — see RIDICULOUS 1

rising *n* the act or an instance of rising or climbing up ⟨the *rising* of the sun⟩ — see ASCENT 1

risk *n* **1** something that may cause injury or harm ⟨mountain climbing is a *risk*, but the thrill and challenge are worth it⟩ — see DANGER 2

2 the state of not being protected from injury, harm, or evil ⟨children living in poverty are considered at *risk* for a number of medical and developmental problems⟩ — see DANGER 1

risk *vb* **1** to take a chance on ⟨Colette didn't want to *risk* running out of film on her trip, so she brought along a dozen rolls⟩

synonyms chance, gamble (on), hazard, venture

related words brave, challenge, dare, defy, face; compromise, endanger, imperil, jeopardize, menace; expose, subject; bet (on), wager

2 to place in danger ⟨we refuse to *risk* our life savings on this project⟩ — see ENDANGER

risky *adj* involving potential loss or injury ⟨a *risky* new adventure⟩ — see DANGEROUS

rite *n* an oft-repeated action or series of actions performed in accordance with tradition or a set of rules

⟨the annual summer *rite* of loading up the car for the big family vacation⟩
synonyms ceremonial, ceremony, form, formality, observance, ritual, solemnity
related words amenities, civility, decorum, etiquette, graces, proprieties; convention, custom, habit, manners, mores, practice (*also* practise), standard, tradition, way; celebration, service

ritual *n* an oft-repeated action or series of actions performed in accordance with tradition or a set of rules ⟨a *ritual* that the natives of that country believe will bring rain⟩ — see RITE

rival *n* **1** one that is equal to another in status, achievement, or value ⟨a design that is a *rival* to any produced by a professional graphic artist⟩ — see EQUAL
2 one that takes a position opposite another in a competition or conflict ⟨the boxer's toughest *rival* thus far⟩ — see OPPONENT 1
3 one who strives for the same thing as another ⟨the four cities that are the top *rivals* for the site of the next Olympic Games⟩ — see COMPETITOR

rivalry *n* an earnest effort for superiority or victory over another ⟨a healthy *rivalry* between the two schools⟩ — see CONTEST 1

rive *vb* to cause (something) to separate into jagged pieces by violently pulling at it ⟨the bitter disappointment threatened to *rive* my heart in two⟩ — see TEAR 1

rivet *vb* to fix (as one's attention) steadily toward a central objective ⟨everyone *riveted* their eyes on the magician's trick⟩ — see CONCENTRATE 2

riveting *adj* holding the attention or provoking interest ⟨a *riveting* explanation of light waves that fascinated the class⟩ — see INTERESTING

rivulet *n* a natural body of running water smaller than a river ⟨small *rivulets* trickled down the side of the cliff⟩ — see CREEK 1

road *n* **1** a passage cleared for public vehicular travel ⟨I think we should take one of the less congested *roads*⟩ — see WAY 1
2 a roadway overlaid with parallel steel rails over which trains travel ⟨the railway companies are perpetually repairing their *roads*⟩ — see RAILROAD

roadhouse *n* a bar or restaurant offering special nighttime entertainment (as music, dancing, or comedy acts) ⟨stopped at a *roadhouse* for dinner and dancing⟩ — see NIGHTCLUB

roadway *n* a passage cleared for public vehicular travel ⟨a cow wandered into the *roadway*⟩ — see WAY 1

roam *vb* to move about from place to place aimlessly ⟨he took a year off and *roamed* over Europe before going on to college⟩ — see WANDER

roamer *n* a person who roams about without a fixed route or destination ⟨the couple retired, sold their house, and became carefree *roamers* in an RV⟩ — see NOMAD

roaming *adj* traveling from place to place ⟨a *roaming* circus that plays small towns across the country⟩ — see ITINERANT

roar *n* **1** a violent shouting ⟨a *roar* went up from the crowd⟩ — see CLAMOR 1
2 loud, confused, and usually unharmonious sound ⟨the *roar* of the machinery in the factory⟩ — see NOISE 1

roar *vb* to make a long loud deep noise or cry ⟨its engine *roared* as the car sped away⟩
synonyms bellow, boom, growl, thunder

related words grumble, roll, rumble; blare, blast, peal, scream, screech, shriek, squall; cry, holler, hoot, shout, whoop, yell; caterwaul, howl, wail, yowl
near antonyms mumble, murmur, mutter, whisper; squeak, whimper

roaring *adj* **1** marked by a high volume of sound ⟨a *roaring* party that annoyed the neighbors⟩ — see LOUD 1
2 marked by vigorous growth and well-being especially economically ⟨the *roaring* mining town attracted job seekers eager to share in the boom⟩ — see PROSPEROUS 1

roast *vb* to make fun of in a good-natured way ⟨playfully *roasting* their mother for her choice of hat⟩ — see TEASE 1

roasting *adj* having a notably high temperature ⟨turn on the air conditioner—the house is *roasting* today!⟩ — see HOT 1

rob *vb* to remove valuables from (a place) unlawfully ⟨in jail for *robbing* a bank⟩
synonyms burglarize, rip off, steal (from)
related words despoil, loot, pillage, plunder, sack, spoil, strip; bleed, break in, cheat, chisel, cozen, defraud, exploit, fleece, gyp, mulct, rook, squeeze, stick, swindle; hold up, mug, stick up

robber *n* one who steals ⟨the *robber* wore a ski mask while holding up the bank⟩ — see THIEF

robbery *n* the unlawful taking and carrying away of property without the consent of its owner ⟨the first sign that there had been a *robbery* was the broken door lock⟩ — see THEFT 1

robe *vb* to outfit with clothes and especially fine or special clothes ⟨*robed* the queen in her ceremonial garments⟩ — see CLOTHE 1

robotic *adj* designed to replace or decrease human labor and especially physical labor ⟨the dishwasher is one of the greatest *robotic* devices ever invented⟩ — see LABORSAVING

robust *adj* **1** enjoying health and vigor ⟨a *robust* and sturdy toddler⟩ — see HEALTHY 1
2 having active strength of body or mind ⟨a *robust* older man who still bicycles ten miles a day⟩ — see VIGOROUS 1
3 having an abundance of some characteristic quality (as flavor) ⟨beef and other red meats should be accompanied by *robust* wines⟩ — see FULL-BODIED
4 not showing weakness or uncertainty ⟨a *robust* slap on the back welcoming me to the company⟩ — see FIRM 1

robustness *n* **1** the condition of being sound in body ⟨her *robustness* saved her from a serious bout of illness when the flu was going around⟩ — see HEALTH
2 the quality or state of having abundant or intense activity ⟨the *robustness* of the city has always inspired writers and artists⟩ — see VITALITY 1

rock *vb* **1** to make a series of unsteady side-to-side motions ⟨the boat was *rocking* so much that Rosa felt seasick⟩
synonyms careen, lurch, pitch, roll, seesaw, sway, toss, wobble
related words blunder, dodder, falter, flounder, halt, hitch, hobble, jerk, reel, stagger, stumble, teeter, toddle, totter, tumble, waddle, weave; oscillate, undulate, wag, waggle
2 to swing unsteadily back and forth or from side to side ⟨the drunk *rocked* on his heels for a moment and then fell flat on his back⟩ — see TEETER 1

rock bottom *n* the lowest part, place, or point ⟨once you've hit *rock bottom*, there's nowhere to go but up⟩ — see BOTTOM 3

rocket *vb* **1** to proceed or move quickly ⟨the startled cat *rocketed* out of the room⟩ — see HURRY 2

2 to rise abruptly and rapidly ⟨the child actor *rocketed* to stardom at the age of eight⟩ — see SKYROCKET

rod *n* **1** a heavy rigid stick used as a weapon or for punishment ⟨arrested for using a *rod* on his dogs in violation of the state's animal cruelty laws⟩ — see CLUB 1

2 a straight piece (as of wood or metal) that is longer than it is wide ⟨a curtain *rod*⟩ — see BAR 1

rogue *n* **1** a mean, evil, or unprincipled person ⟨a *rogue* who had nothing but contempt for people who made their living honestly⟩ — see VILLAIN

2 an appealingly mischievous person ⟨the little *rogue* always seems to end up being forgiven for his pranks⟩ — see SCAMP 1

roguish *adj* tending to or exhibiting reckless playfulness ⟨a *roguish* grin was the only sign of her plan to pull a prank that the school would never forget⟩ — see MISCHIEVOUS 1

roguishness *n* playful, reckless behavior that is not intended to cause serious harm ⟨a bit of childish *roguishness* that ended up with a window being broken⟩ — see MISCHIEF 1

roil *vb* **1** to be in a state of violent rolling motion ⟨the waters of the gulf tossed and *roiled* as the hurricane surged toward the shore⟩ — see SEETHE 1

2 to make angry ⟨the clerk's refusal *roiled* her enough to prompt a complaint to his supervisor⟩ — see ANGER

roiled *adj* **1** feeling or showing anger ⟨he waited until he wasn't so obviously *roiled* before voicing a complaint to the manager⟩ — see ANGRY

2 having visible particles in liquid suspension ⟨the *roiled* water made more difficult the work of the divers searching the river for the missing canoeists⟩ — see CLOUDY 1

roisterer *n* one who engages in merrymaking especially in honor of a special occasion ⟨the rowdy *roisterers* who fill the streets of New Orleans during Mardi Gras⟩ — see CELEBRANT

role *also* **rôle** *n* the action for which a person or thing is specially fitted or used or for which a thing exists ⟨in science class we're studying the *role* of sunlight in the body's production of vitamin D⟩

synonyms capacity, function, job, part, place, position, purpose, task, work

related words affair, business, concern, involvement, participation; niche, office, post, situation; calling, occupation, pursuit, vocation; activity, assignment, charge, commission, duty, mission, responsibility, service, use

roll *n* **1** a rapid turning about on an axis or central point ⟨the squirrel did a quick *roll* and vanished up a tree⟩ — see SPIN 1

2 a record of a series of items (as names or titles) usually arranged according to some system ⟨called the *roll* of people supposed to be in the class⟩ — see ¹LIST

roll *vb* **1** to form into a round compact mass ⟨*rolled* up the wrapper from the straw and threw it⟩ — see WAD

2 to make a low heavy rolling sound ⟨thunder *rolling* in the distance⟩ — see RUMBLE

3 to make a series of unsteady side-to-side motions ⟨the car suddenly was *rolling* somewhat in the high winds⟩ — see ROCK 1

4 to move (something) in a curved or circular path on or as if on an axis ⟨in order to knock your opponent off balance, you have to *roll* the log when he least expects it⟩ — see TURN 1

5 to move in a stream ⟨just laying on the beach, watching the clouds *roll* by⟩ — see FLOW 1

6 to move in circles around an axis or center ⟨*rolled* her head around her shoulders to loosen herself up⟩ — see SPIN 1

7 to move or proceed smoothly and readily ⟨once we started *rolling*, everything went perfectly⟩ — see FLOW 2

rollick *n* a time or instance of carefree fun ⟨the class trip turned out to be a complete *rollick*⟩ — see FLING 1

rollick *vb* **1** to engage in activity for amusement ⟨an educator who realized that children need to *rollick* as well as to study and learn⟩ — see PLAY 1

2 to play and run about happily ⟨children *rollicking* during recess⟩ — see FROLIC 1

rollicking *adj* given to good-natured joking or teasing ⟨a *rollicking* boy who quickly charms everyone he meets⟩ — see PLAYFUL

rollicking *n* activity engaged in to amuse oneself ⟨likes to indulge in mindless *rollicking* after work in order to relax⟩ — see PLAY 1

roly–poly *adj* having an excess of body fat ⟨a *roly-poly* baby who grew into a slender child⟩ — see FAT 1

romance *n* a brief romantic relationship ⟨a high school *romance* that fizzled when the two left for separate colleges⟩ — see AFFAIR 1

romantic *adj* excitingly or mysteriously unusual ⟨dreamed of meeting a tall, *romantic* stranger who would introduce her to a life of adventure⟩ — see EXOTIC

romantic *n* one whose conduct is guided more by the image of perfection than by the real world ⟨she's a *romantic* who believes that her one true love is somewhere waiting to be found⟩ — see IDEALIST

romanticist *n* one whose conduct is guided more by the image of perfection than by the real world ⟨*romanticists* who are perpetually surprised by mean or criminal behavior⟩ — see IDEALIST

romanticize *vb* to represent or think of as better than reality ⟨*romanticized* what life in a small town would be like, only to be later disappointed when reality intruded⟩ — see IDEALIZE

romp *n* a time or instance of carefree fun ⟨one last *romp* before starting school again⟩ — see FLING 1

romp *vb* to play and run about happily ⟨*romped* on the lawn until dinner was ready⟩ — see FROLIC 1

roof *n* **1** a raised covering over something for decoration or protection ⟨the *roof* of the pavilion leaks when it rains⟩ — see CANOPY

2 the place where one lives ⟨as long as you're living under my *roof*, you'll obey my rules⟩ — see HOME 1

roof *vb* to provide with living quarters or shelter ⟨fed and *roofed* them for a week⟩ — see HOUSE 1

rook *vb* to rob by the use of trickery or threats ⟨once you learn to recognize these swindler's tricks, no one will be able to use them to *rook* you⟩ — see FLEECE

rookie *n* a person who is just starting out in a field of activity ⟨although a star in his old sport of basketball, he was still just a *rookie* as far as baseball was concerned⟩ — see BEGINNER

room *n* **1** an extent or area available for or used up by some activity or thing ⟨need more *room* to do a cartwheel⟩ ⟨made *room* for him on the bench⟩

synonyms elbowroom, place, space, way

related words capacity, range, scope; clearance, freedom, latitude, leeway, play

2 an area within a building that has been set apart from surrounding space by a wall ⟨finally had a *room* to himself when his brother went off to college⟩
synonyms apartment, cell, chamber, closet
related words accommodation, berth, booth, cabin, compartment, cubicle
3 a favorable combination of circumstances, time, and place ⟨there's still *room* for improvement⟩ — see OPPORTUNITY

roomer *n* one who rents a room or apartment in another's house ⟨the new owners took in *roomers* to help pay for the house⟩ — see TENANT

roomy *adj* more than adequate or average in capacity ⟨a small car that's surprisingly *roomy* inside⟩ — see SPACIOUS

roost *vb* **1** to come to rest after descending from the air ⟨pigeons flying home to *roost* on the roof⟩ — see ALIGHT
2 to establish or place comfortably or snugly ⟨a gang of friends had *roosted* themselves around the ski lodge's massive fireplace⟩ — see ENSCONCE 1

root *vb* to set solidly in or as if in surrounding matter ⟨*rooted* the post securely in the dirt⟩ — see ENTRENCH

root (out) *vb* **1** to destroy all traces of ⟨*root out* and eliminate prejudice in the educational system⟩ — see ANNIHILATE 1
2 to draw out by force or with effort ⟨a dog *rooting out* a buried toy⟩ — see EXTRACT

rooted *adj* firmly established over time ⟨a popular, *rooted* misconception that has proved very resistant to correction⟩ — see INVETERATE 1

rope *n* a length of braided, flexible material that is used for tying or connecting things ⟨used a *rope* to tie the boat to the dock⟩ — see CORD

ropy *adj* being of a consistency that resists flow ⟨because the paint was so old, it was *ropy* and couldn't be smoothly applied to the wood⟩ — see THICK 2

roquelaure *n* a sleeveless garment worn so as to hang over the shoulders, arms, and back ⟨the dark, brooding hero of the romance novel often wears a *roquelaure*⟩ — see ¹CAPE

rose–colored *adj* having qualities which inspire hope ⟨an incurable optimist sees the world through a *rose-colored* perspective⟩ — see HOPEFUL 1

roster *n* a record of a series of items (as names or titles) usually arranged according to some system ⟨the *roster* of subscribers to the journal⟩ — see ¹LIST

rostrum *n* a level usually raised surface ⟨stood on a *rostrum* to give the speech⟩ — see PLATFORM

rosy *adj* **1** having a healthy reddish skin tone ⟨*rosy* and cheerful after a day outside in the snow⟩ — see RUDDY
2 having qualities which inspire hope ⟨that's a particularly *rosy* view of the situation, and one that may not be justified⟩ — see HOPEFUL 1

rot *n* **1** language, behavior, or ideas that are absurd and contrary to good sense ⟨I won't stand here and listen to such *rot*⟩ — see NONSENSE 1
2 the process by which dead organic matter separates into simpler substances ⟨the *rot* begins shortly after the fish are killed⟩ — see CORRUPTION 1
3 unintelligible or meaningless talk ⟨the drunkard was spouting his usual *rot* about his battlefield heroics⟩ — see GIBBERISH

rot *vb* **1** to become worse or of less value ⟨the house slowly fell into disrepair and *rotted*⟩ — see DETERIORATE
2 to go through decomposition ⟨*rotting* vegetation on the bank of the river⟩ — see DECAY 1

rotate *vb* **1** to move (something) in a curved or circular path on or as if on an axis ⟨*rotate* the mirror 180 degrees⟩ — see TURN 1
2 to move in circles around an axis or center ⟨with mirrors on three sides, she *rotated* all around to see how the dress looked on her⟩ — see SPIN 1

rotation *n* a rapid turning about on an axis or central point ⟨the Earth completes a single *rotation* around its axis in approximately 24 hours⟩ — see SPIN 1

rote *n* **1** an established and often automatic or monotonous series of actions followed when engaging in some activity ⟨learned the *rote* for the exercise warm-up but not the reasoning behind it⟩ — see ROUTINE 1
2 the body of knowledge that has been retained in one's mind or the use of it ⟨children who can recite the pledge by *rote* but have little understanding of what they are saying⟩ — see HEART 2

rotten *adj* **1** having undergone organic breakdown ⟨*rotten*, smelly meat that should have been refrigerated⟩
synonyms addled, bad, corrupted, decayed, decomposed, putrefied, putrid, spoiled
related words curdled, fermented, rancid, sour, soured, turned; contaminated, defiled, fouled, polluted, tainted; corroded, crumbled, degenerated, deteriorated, disintegrated; decaying, decomposing, moldering, moldy, putrefying, rotting
near antonyms fresh, good, preserved; pristine, uncontaminated, undefiled, unpolluted, unspoiled, untainted, untouched
2 falling short of a standard ⟨that was a truly *rotten* attempt; so you'll have to do it over⟩ — see BAD 1
3 not conforming to a high moral standard; morally unacceptable ⟨played a *rotten* trick and then lied about it⟩ — see BAD 2
4 not giving pleasure to the mind or senses ⟨had a *rotten* time while on vacation⟩ — see UNPLEASANT
5 extremely unsatisfactory ⟨*rotten* housing that no one should be forced to tolerate⟩ — see WRETCHED 1
6 of low quality ⟨I can't do anything with these *rotten* tools⟩ — see CHEAP 2

rotund *adj* having an excess of body fat ⟨a *rotund* little man who was asked to play Santa every year⟩ — see FAT 1

rotundity *n* the condition of having an excess of body fat ⟨finally a diet that really worked, allowing her to leave behind a lifetime of *rotundity* and ridicule⟩ — see CORPULENCE

rough *adj* **1** covered with or as if with hair ⟨a face *rough* with a couple days' worth of beard⟩ — see HAIRY 1
2 marked by bursts of destructive force or intense activity ⟨*rough* waters that made sailing risky⟩ — see VIOLENT 1
3 marked by wet and windy conditions ⟨at least wear a raincoat if you're going out into that *rough* weather⟩ — see FOUL 1
4 not having a level or smooth surface ⟨a *rough* board can give you splinters⟩ — see UNEVEN 1
5 requiring considerable physical or mental effort ⟨a *rough* assignment⟩ — see HARD 2
6 difficult to endure ⟨I've had a *rough* time of it since I lost my job⟩ — see HARSH 1
7 harsh and threatening in manner or appearance ⟨the *rough* faces of hardened criminals who had spent most of their lives behind bars⟩ — see GRIM 1
8 hastily or roughly constructed ⟨made a *rough* camp as darkness fell⟩ — see RUDE 1

9 lacking in refinement or good taste ⟨learned polite words to replace the *rough* language he had known in the slums⟩ — see COARSE 2

10 made of or resembling hair ⟨a *rough*-coated dog who was always shedding his fur⟩ — see HAIRY 2

11 marked by a series of sharp quick motions ⟨a *rough* flight that made some people nauseated⟩ — see JERKY 1

rough (up) *vb* to abuse physically ⟨the bigger boys won't be allowed to *rough up* the little ones⟩ — see MANHANDLE 1

roughened *adj* not having a level or smooth surface ⟨*roughened* hands from hard work⟩ — see UNEVEN 1

roughhewn *adj* **1** hastily or roughly constructed ⟨a *roughhewn* shelter in the wilderness⟩ — see RUDE 1

2 lacking in refinement or good taste ⟨a *roughhewn* girl who had to learn to behave properly in polite company⟩ — see COARSE 2

3 lacking social grace and assurance ⟨*roughhewn* military cadets feeling a little self-conscious at their first formal dance⟩ — see AWKWARD 1

roughhouse *n* wildly playful or mischievous behavior ⟨wouldn't tolerate any *roughhouse* in the living room⟩ — see HORSEPLAY

roughhousing *n* wildly playful or mischievous behavior ⟨*roughhousing* was simply part of growing up in a family with four boys⟩ — see HORSEPLAY

roughly *adv* in a manner so as to cause loss or suffering ⟨if you treat the toy *roughly*, it will break⟩ — see HARDLY 1

roughneck *n* a violent, brutal person who is often a member of an organized gang ⟨a group of *roughnecks* like to hang out there and harass people⟩ — see HOODLUM

roughness *n* **1** a harsh or sharp quality ⟨a *roughness* to the wine that should decrease with age⟩ — see EDGE 1

2 the quality or state of lacking refinement or good taste ⟨the *roughness* of pioneer life is mentioned in the documentary⟩ — see VULGARITY 1

round *adj* **1** having every part of the surface the same distance from the center ⟨*round* golf balls⟩ ⟨the earth is not perfectly *round*⟩

synonyms global, spherical

related words annular, circular, disklike (*or* disclike), ringlike; curved, looped, spiral; balled, rotund, rounded, roundish; elliptic (*or* elliptical), oval, ovate, ovoid

2 having an excess of body fat ⟨a *round* little grandmother who was a natural to play Mrs. Claus⟩ — see FAT 1

3 marked by conspicuously full and rich sounds or tones ⟨an organ with a beautifully *round* sound⟩ — see RESONANT

4 being neither more nor less than a certain amount, number, or extent ⟨a *round* dozen eggs⟩ — see EVEN 1

round *adv* **1** from beginning to end ⟨people working there year *round*⟩ — see THROUGH 1

2 on all sides or in every direction ⟨gather *round* and listen to my story⟩ — see AROUND 1

3 toward the opposite direction ⟨turned *round* to see who was calling out⟩ — see AROUND 2

round *n* **1** a circular strip ⟨a *round* of steel to reinforce the wooden beam⟩ — see RING 2

2 a series of events or actions that repeat themselves regularly and in the same order ⟨a busy *round* of parties during the holiday season⟩ — see CYCLE 1

3 something with a perfectly round circumference ⟨use a cookie cutter to make the *rounds* of dough⟩ — see CIRCLE 1

round *prep* in random positions within the boundaries of ⟨talked to voters *round* the city⟩ — see AROUND 2

round *vb* **1** to form into a round compact mass ⟨carefully *rounded* the dough and placed it on a cookie tray⟩ — see WAD

2 to pass completely around ⟨a monorail for visitors that *rounds* the park⟩ — see ENCIRCLE 1

3 to turn away from a straight line or course ⟨*rounded* on the track and headed for the finish line⟩ — see CURVE 1

round (off *or* out) *vb* **1** to bring (an event) to a natural or appropriate stopping point ⟨I'll *round off* the lesson here and let everyone go a little early⟩ — see CLOSE 3

2 to serve as a completing element to ⟨coffee and dessert *rounded out* the meal⟩ — see COMPLEMENT

roundabout *adj* not straightforward or direct ⟨took a *roundabout* route to the beach⟩ — see INDIRECT

roundly *adv* with attention to all aspects or details ⟨few sitcoms were as *roundly* disliked as that one⟩ — see THOROUGHLY 1

roundtable *n* **1** a coming together of a number of persons for a specified purpose ⟨we'll have a *roundtable* to decide what to do about the issue⟩ — see MEETING 1

2 a meeting featuring a group discussion ⟨an international *roundtable* of medical experts on the disease⟩ — see FORUM

roundup *n* a short statement of the main points ⟨I can't read 500 pages by tomorrow, so just give me the *roundup*⟩ — see SUMMARY

round up *vb* to bring together in one body or place ⟨*rounded* everyone *up* for one final training session⟩ — see GATHER 1

rouse *vb* **1** to cause to stop sleeping ⟨the honking horns *roused* her from a deep sleep⟩ — see WAKE 1

2 to cease to be asleep ⟨I finally *roused* around noon, after going to bed very late⟩ — see WAKE 2

rousing *adj* causing great emotional or mental stimulation ⟨a *rousing* rendition of our national anthem⟩ — see EXCITING 1

rout *n* failure to win a contest ⟨the championship game was a humiliating *rout* for the team that had been favored to win⟩ — see DEFEAT 1

rout *vb* **1** to achieve a victory over ⟨we must *rout* this deadly new virus before it raises havoc among our people⟩ — see BEAT 2

2 to defeat by a large margin ⟨as expected, the professional team had no trouble *routing* the amateurs⟩ — see WHIP 2

3 to drive or force out ⟨the nation's ground and air forces quickly *routed* the would-be invaders⟩ — see EJECT 1

route *n* **1** a passage cleared for public vehicular travel ⟨take *Route* 190 for six miles, then get off⟩ — see WAY 1

2 an established course for traveling from one place to another ⟨we're going to get stuck in traffic if we take the usual *route*⟩ — see PASSAGE 1

3 the direction along which something or someone moves ⟨hurricanes generally take a northerly *route* up the Atlantic seaboard⟩ — see PATH 1

route *vb* to point out the way for (someone) especially from a position in front ⟨the guide *routed* us smoothly through the jungle⟩ — see LEAD 1

routine *adj* **1** being of the type that is encountered in the normal course of events ⟨this is just a *routine* inspection⟩ — see ORDINARY 1

2 following or agreeing with established form, custom, or rules ⟨the *routine* procedure for filing a complaint with the board⟩ — see FORMAL 1

3 often observed or encountered ⟨the movie is a *routine* thriller that has little to recommend it⟩ — see COMMON 1

routine *n* **1** an established and often automatic or monotonous series of actions followed when engaging in some activity ⟨part of my morning *routine* is drinking a cup of hot chocolate while waiting for the bus⟩

synonyms groove, pattern, rote, rut, treadmill

related words custom, fashion, habit, practice (*also* practise), trick, wont; approach, manner, method, procedure, strategy, style, tack, way; design, plan, program, scheme; convention, policy, tradition

2 something done over and over in order to develop skill ⟨a weapons training *routine*⟩ — see EXERCISE 2

rove *vb* to move about from place to place aimlessly ⟨buffalo *roving* over the vast plains⟩ — see WANDER

rover *n* **1** a person who roams about without a fixed route or destination ⟨ever since he developed a strong case of wanderlust in college, he's been a *rover*⟩ — see NOMAD

2 someone who engages in robbery of ships at sea ⟨a story of the days when sea *rovers* plied the Caribbean⟩ — see PIRATE

roving *adj* traveling from place to place ⟨a *roving* substitute teacher who works in a different district every day⟩ — see ITINERANT

row *n* **1** a series of people or things arranged side by side ⟨stood in a *row* to have their picture taken⟩ ⟨three *rows* of eight jelly beans equals 24 jelly beans⟩

synonyms bank, rank

related words chain, column, cue, file, line, procession, queue, string, train; echelon, tier; array, sequence

2 a passage cleared for public vehicular travel ⟨drive up Market *Row* and turn left⟩ — see WAY 1

3 a rough and often noisy fight usually involving several people ⟨a county fair that had a long history of bloody *rows*⟩ — see BRAWL 1

4 a state of noisy, confused activity ⟨the combination of drums and shouting contributed to the awful *row*⟩ — see COMMOTION

5 an often noisy or angry expression of differing opinions ⟨he had a *row* with his girlfriend yesterday, and now they aren't speaking⟩ — see ARGUMENT 1

¹row *vb* to move a boat by means of oars ⟨*rowed* around the lake⟩

synonyms oar, paddle, scull

related words canoe; pole, punt

²row *vb* to express different opinions about something often angrily ⟨the couple *rows* all the time, and yet they seem happy together⟩ — see ARGUE 2

rowdy *adj* being rough or noisy in a high-spirited way ⟨a *rowdy* but good-natured group of teenagers⟩ — see BOISTEROUS

rowdy *n* a violent, brutal person who is often a member of an organized gang ⟨*rowdies* had overtaken the neighborhood and were threatening people on the street⟩ — see HOODLUM

rower *n* a person who drives a boat forward by means of oars ⟨the racing shell carries four *rowers* and a coxswain⟩ — see OARSMAN

royal *adj* **1** fit for or worthy of a royal ruler ⟨the school superintendent received a *royal* welcome⟩ — see MONARCHICAL

2 large and impressive in size, grandeur, extent, or conception ⟨had a *royal* argument⟩ — see GRAND 1

rub *vb* **1** to damage or diminish by continued friction ⟨the brake pads were *rubbed* away as a result of years of use⟩ — see ABRADE 1

2 to make smooth by friction ⟨*rubbed* the board perfectly smooth with sandpaper⟩ — see GRIND 1

3 to make smooth or glossy usually by repeatedly applying surface pressure ⟨*rubbed* the silver tea set until it gleamed⟩ — see POLISH

rubbed *adj* having a shiny surface or finish ⟨*rubbed* brass that showed my reflection⟩ — see GLOSSY

rubberlike *adj* able to revert to original size and shape after being stretched, squeezed, or twisted ⟨a *rubberlike* material that is used for household products⟩ — see ELASTIC 1

rubberneck *vb* to look long and hard in wonder or surprise ⟨drivers pausing on the highway to *rubberneck* at the accident⟩ — see GAPE

rubbery *adj* able to revert to original size and shape after being stretched, squeezed, or twisted ⟨mozzarella is a *rubbery* cheese known to every pizza lover⟩ — see ELASTIC 1

rubbish *n* discarded or useless material ⟨it's illegal to throw *rubbish* out of your car on the highway⟩ — see GARBAGE

rubbishy *adj* of low quality ⟨*rubbishy* merchandise that is mainly bought by tourists⟩ — see CHEAP 2

rubble *n* the portion or bits of something left over or behind after it has been destroyed ⟨clearing the *rubble* after the earthquake⟩ — see REMAINS 1

rubicund *adj* having a healthy reddish skin tone ⟨the *rubicund* face of a man who clearly got a lot of fresh air and exercise⟩ — see RUDDY

rub out *vb* to destroy all traces of ⟨a promise to *rub out* the city's drug trade⟩ — see ANNIHILATE 1

rubric *n* a word or series of words often in larger letters placed at the beginning of a passage or at the top of a page in order to introduce or categorize ⟨the *rubrics* at the beginning of the chapters are intended to be humorous⟩ — see HEADING

rucksack *n* a soft-sided case designed for carrying belongings especially on the back ⟨scouts carrying their food and water in *rucksacks*⟩ — see PACK 1

ruckus *n* **1** a rough and often noisy fight usually involving several people ⟨the *ruckus* left one person with a sprained wrist⟩ — see BRAWL 1

2 a state of noisy, confused activity ⟨quit creating such a *ruckus*—I'm trying to sleep!⟩ — see COMMOTION

ruction *n* **1** a rough and often noisy fight usually involving several people ⟨the *ruction* ended with everyone involved getting arrested⟩ — see BRAWL 1

2 a state of noisy, confused activity ⟨the *ruction* outside the door prompted me to investigate what was going on⟩ — see COMMOTION

ruddy *adj* having a healthy reddish skin tone ⟨his *ruddy* complexion runs in the family⟩

synonyms blooming, florid, flush, glowing, rosy, rubicund, sanguine

related words bronzed, brown, suntanned, tanned; flushed, pink, pinkish, warm; cherubic

near antonyms ashen, ashy, pale, pallid, pasty, sallow, wan, waxen, waxy; blanched, white, whitened; anemic, peaked, sick, sickly; bloodless, cadaverous, deathlike

rude *adj* **1** hastily or roughly constructed ⟨a *rude* shelter built from unfinished logs by some forgotten pioneer⟩
synonyms artless, clumsy, crude, rough, roughhewn, unrefined
related words defective, faulty, flawed, imperfect; imprecise, inexact; inartistic, undressed, unfinished, unpolished, unworked; amateur, amateurish, inexpert, unprofessional, unskilled, unskillful; primitive, rudimentary
near antonyms faultless, finished, meticulous, perfected, polished, well-done; adept, adroit, dexterous (*also* dextrous), expert, masterful, masterly, neat, practiced (*or* practised), skillful, workmanlike; artful, artistic, sophisticated; exact, precise
antonyms refined
2 belonging to or characteristic of an early level of skill or development ⟨*rude* stone tools⟩ — see PRIMITIVE 1
3 lacking in refinement or good taste ⟨a comedian who uses a lot of *rude* language in his nightclub act⟩ — see COARSE 2
4 not civilized ⟨missionaries who believed that it was their duty to convert the *rude* peoples of the world⟩ — see SAVAGE 1
5 showing a lack of manners or consideration for others ⟨it's *rude* to call someone "ugly"⟩ — see IMPOLITE
rudeness *n* **1** rude behavior ⟨such *rudeness* will not be tolerated⟩ — see DISCOURTESY
2 the quality or state of lacking refinement or good taste ⟨the *rudeness* of frontier life gradually diminished with time⟩ — see VULGARITY 1
rudimentary *adj* **1** belonging to or characteristic of an early level of skill or development ⟨*rudimentary* shelters built by prehistoric peoples⟩ — see PRIMITIVE 1
2 of or relating to the simplest facts or theories of a subject ⟨had only a *rudimentary* knowledge of science⟩ — see ELEMENTARY
rudiments *n pl* general or basic truths on which other truths or theories can be based ⟨learned the *rudiments* of mathematics⟩ — see PRINCIPLES 1
rue *n* a feeling of responsibility for wrongdoing ⟨a soul filled with pain and *rue*⟩ — see GUILT 1
rue *vb* to feel sorry or dissatisfied about ⟨I *rue* the day I agreed to this stupid plan⟩ — see REGRET
rueful *adj* **1** expressing or suggesting mourning ⟨the *rueful* faces of friends and family who had gathered to pay their last respects⟩ — see MOURNFUL 1
2 feeling sorrow for a wrong that one has done ⟨a *rueful* youth who had come to ask for forgiveness⟩ — see CONTRITE 1
3 deserving of one's pity ⟨the *rueful*, desperate poverty of people in parts of the Third World⟩ — see PATHETIC 1
ruefully *adv* with feelings of bitterness or grief ⟨*ruefully* accepted the fact that the drunk driver would never adequately pay for his crime⟩ — see HARD 2
ruffian *n* a violent, brutal person who is often a member of an organized gang ⟨a gang of *ruffians* preying upon people who ventured into that section of town⟩ — see HOODLUM
ruffle *n* a strip of fabric gathered or pleated on one edge and used as trimming ⟨likes lace curtains without *ruffles* and chintz curtains with *ruffles*⟩
synonyms flounce, frill, furbelow
related words border, edging, fringe, trim; pleat, ruff; bunting, skirting
rugged *adj* **1** able to withstand hardship, strain, or exposure ⟨a *rugged* construction that survived for hundreds of years⟩ — see HARDY 1

2 difficult to endure ⟨*rugged* conditions that every polar explorer had to endure⟩ — see HARSH 1
3 harsh and threatening in manner or appearance ⟨the warrior's *rugged* features frightened the child⟩ — see GRIM 1
4 having muscles capable of exerting great physical force ⟨a *rugged* athlete who's competing in weight lifting in the Olympics⟩ — see STRONG 1
5 not having a level or smooth surface ⟨*rugged* terrain⟩ — see UNEVEN 1
ruin *n* **1** the state or fact of being rendered nonexistent, physically unsound, or useless ⟨the building was left in *ruins*⟩ — see DESTRUCTION
2 ruins *pl* the portion or bits of something left over or behind after it has been destroyed ⟨the *ruins* of an abandoned abbey⟩ — see REMAINS 1
ruin *vb* **1** to cause to lose one's fortune and become unable to pay one's debts ⟨*ruined* by the Great Chicago Fire of 1871, the industrialist was forced to sell his mansion and start all over again⟩
synonyms bankrupt, bust
related words beggar, impoverish, pauperize; break, reduce, straiten; clean (out), wipe out
near antonyms enrich, richen
2 to bring destruction to (something) through violent action ⟨tornadoes *ruined* a wide swath of the county⟩ — see RAVAGE
3 to bring to a complete end the physical soundness, existence, or usefulness of ⟨a huge fire that *ruined* an entire city block⟩ — see DESTROY 1
ruination *n* the state or fact of being rendered nonexistent, physically unsound, or useless ⟨although this is a setback, it isn't complete *ruination*⟩ — see DESTRUCTION
ruinous *adj* **1** bringing about ruin or misfortune ⟨a *ruinous* miscalculation left them bankrupt⟩ — see FATAL 1
2 causing or tending to cause destruction ⟨a *ruinous* windstorm destroyed the crops⟩ — see DESTRUCTIVE 1
rule *n* **1** a statement spelling out the proper procedure or conduct for an activity ⟨read the *rules* that are posted before you use the pool⟩
synonyms bylaw, ground rule, regulation
related words code, constitution, decalogue; act, law, ordinance, statute; command, decree, dictate, directive, edict, fiat, order; axiom, fundamental, maxim, precept; moral, principle, value; prohibition, restriction; convention, custom, habit, manners, mores, practice (*also* practise), tradition, way; blueprint, canon, formula, guide, guideline, recipe, standard
2 lawful control over the affairs of a political unit (as a nation) ⟨the years during which Russia was under Communist *rule*⟩
synonyms administration, authority, governance, government, jurisdiction, regime (*also* régime), regimen
related words reign; dominion, power, sovereignty, supremacy, sway; command, leadership; direction, management, regulation, superintendence, supervision; dictatorship, domination, mastery, oppression, subjugation, tyranny
rule *vb* to exercise authority or power over ⟨a sea captain who *ruled* sternly but justly⟩ — see GOVERN
rule (on) *vb* to give an opinion about (something at issue or in dispute) ⟨the coach *ruled on* the question of whether a schoolyard fight ought to disqualify someone from the team⟩ — see JUDGE 1

rule out *vb* to prevent the participation or inclusion of ⟨another loss would *rule* them *out* of the tournament⟩ — see EXCLUDE

ruler *n* one who rules over a people with a sole, supreme, and usually hereditary authority ⟨the *ruler* agonized over the choice of an heir⟩ — see MONARCH

ruling *n* **1** a decision made by a court or tribunal regarding a case it has heard ⟨the controversial *ruling* by the state's supreme court caused an uproar⟩ — see SENTENCE

2 an order publicly issued by an authority ⟨the school board's *ruling* against the wearing of colored T-shirts drew some complaints⟩ — see EDICT 1

rumble *vb* to make a low heavy rolling sound ⟨when thunder *rumbled* in the distant sky, we wisely began packing up our stuff⟩
synonyms growl, grumble, lumber, roll
related words boom, drum, thunder

ruminant *adj* given to or marked by long, quiet thinking ⟨wandered around campus in a *ruminative* mood⟩ — see CONTEMPLATIVE

ruminate *vb* to give serious and careful thought to ⟨the minister hoped that the congregation would spend the remainder of the week *ruminating* the message of his sermon⟩ — see PONDER

rummage *n* an unorganized collection or mixture of various things ⟨a *rummage* of textbooks, notebooks, and old school papers all over the desk⟩ — see MISCELLANY 1

rummage *vb* to look through (as a place) carefully or thoroughly in an effort to find or discover something ⟨*rummaged* the desk drawer trying to find the spare keys⟩ — see SEARCH 1

rumor *vb* to make (as a piece of information) the subject of common talk without any authority or confirmation of accuracy ⟨for years people have been *rumoring* the principal's imminent retirement⟩
synonyms bruit (about), circulate, noise (about), whisper
related words bandy (about), blab, gossip; disclose, divulge, report, reveal, tell; hint, imply, insinuate, intimate, let on, suggest; broadcast, promulgate, propagate, spread

rump *n* the part of the body upon which someone sits ⟨plopped down on her *rump* to listen to the campfire story⟩ — see BUTTOCKS

rumple *vb* **1** to create (as by crushing) an irregular mass of creases in ⟨*rumpled* the bedspread by lying down on it⟩ — see CRUMPLE 1

2 to develop creases or folds ⟨the linen skirt *rumpled* as soon as she started wearing it⟩ — see WRINKLE 1

3 to undo the proper order or arrangement of ⟨the aunt would invariably *rumple* the little boy's hair whenever she came to visit⟩ — see DISORDER

rumpled *adj* lacking in order, neatness, and often cleanliness ⟨a *rumpled* room that suited its teenage occupant just fine⟩ — see MESSY

rumpus *n* a state of noisy, confused activity ⟨the kids made such a *rumpus* that they woke up everyone else in the house⟩ — see COMMOTION

run *n* **1** a prevailing or general movement or inclination ⟨the company's stock has remained consistent with the overall *run* of the market⟩ — see TREND 1

2 *chiefly Midland* a natural body of running water smaller than a river ⟨a *run* full of catfish⟩ — see CREEK 1

3 the period during which something exists, lasts, or is in progress ⟨the actor has been assigned the part for the *run* of the show⟩ — see DURATION 1

4 the right to act or move freely ⟨gave the dogs the *run* of the place⟩ — see FREEDOM 2

run *vb* **1** to go at a pace faster than a walk ⟨*ran* all the way to the bus stop, but still missed the bus⟩
synonyms dash, gallop, jog, scamper, sprint, trip, trot
related words bound, canter, leap, lope, skip, spring; foot (it), hoof (it), hotfoot (it), leg (it); nip, race, scuttle, step (along)
near antonyms amble, lumber, plod, saunter, shamble, shuffle, stroll; crawl, creep, poke; plod, trudge; hobble, limp

2 to hasten away from something dangerous or frightening ⟨rather than *run* from a black bear, it's better to hold your ground and make lots of noise⟩
synonyms bolt, break, flee, fly, retreat, run away, run off
related words abscond, clear out, decamp, elope, escape, light out, retreat, scat, scram, skip (out)
phrases beat it, turn tail
near antonyms beard, brave, confront, dare, defy, face

3 to be positioned along a certain course or in a certain direction ⟨the road *runs* along the river for a while⟩
synonyms extend, go, head, lead, lie
related words cross, cut, pass; follow, span, traverse

4 to occur within a continuous range of variation ⟨the electric bill *runs* between 30 and 50 dollars a month⟩
synonyms go, range, vary
related words alternate, move, shift; change, mutate; extend, reach, stretch, sweep

5 to move in a stream ⟨water *running* down the window⟩ — see FLOW 1

6 to proceed or move quickly ⟨*run* and get the teacher⟩ — see HURRY 2

7 to show a liking or proneness (for something) ⟨unfortunately, members of his family *run* to fatness⟩ — see LEAN 2

8 to urge, push, or force onward ⟨*ran* the horses in order to get to the ranch quickly⟩ — see DRIVE 1

9 to control the mechanical operation of ⟨I know how to *run* that machine⟩ — see OPERATE 1

10 to eventually have as a state or quality ⟨through wasteful spending the family *ran* into debt⟩ — see BECOME

11 to go from a solid to a liquid state ⟨her makeup started to *run* when she got in the pool⟩ — see LIQUEFY

12 to look after and make decisions about ⟨learning to *run* the family business⟩ — see CONDUCT 1

13 to cause to function ⟨in olden days mills were *run* by flowing water⟩ — see ACTIVATE

run away *vb* **1** to get free from a dangerous or confining situation ⟨*ran away* from the reform school⟩ — see ESCAPE 1

2 to hasten away from something dangerous or frightening ⟨the child *runs away* from dogs⟩ — see RUN 2

run–down *adj* **1** showing signs of advanced wear and tear and neglect ⟨a *run-down* old house that really should be torn down⟩ — see SHABBY 1

2 temporarily suffering from a disorder of the body ⟨I'm afraid I'll be staying home today as I'm feeling *run-down*⟩ — see SICK 1

run down *vb* to come upon after searching, study, or effort ⟨finally *ran down* the answer after hours of research⟩ — see FIND 1

run–in *n* a brief clash between enemies or rivals ⟨the rival gangs had a bit of a *run-in* last night⟩ — see ENCOUNTER

runner *n* one that carries a message or does an errand ⟨sent a *runner* to tell them that all was ready for the feast⟩ — see MESSENGER

running *adj* being in effective operation ⟨the car has been *running* for almost an entire day⟩ — see ACTIVE 1

running *n* the act or activity of looking after and making decisions about something ⟨left the *running* of the corporation to his subordinates⟩ — see CONDUCT 1

runny *adj* having an overly soft liquid consistency ⟨*runny* scrambled eggs⟩

synonyms soupy, watery

related words flowing, fluid, liquefied; dilute, diluted, thin, thinned, watered (down), weak; slushy, soggy, wet

near antonyms syrupy, viscid, viscous; creamy, heavy, thick, thickened, thickish; gelatinous, gluey, glutinous, gooey, gummy, sticky

run off *vb* **1** to drive or force out ⟨the dog often ran *off* cats and other animals that intruded upon his owner's property⟩ — see EJECT 1

2 to get free from a dangerous or confining situation ⟨their daughter's *run off* because she was disciplined again⟩ — see ESCAPE 1

3 to hasten away from something dangerous or frightening ⟨the mouse *ran off* as soon as it saw us⟩ — see RUN 2

run–of–the–mill *adj* **1** being of the type that is encountered in the normal course of events ⟨just another *run-of-the-mill* suburb with its shopping malls and fast-food restaurants⟩ — see ORDINARY 1

2 of average or below average quality ⟨his latest offering is rather *run-of-the-mill* for this usually excellent novelist⟩ — see MEDIOCRE 1

run on *vb* **1** to engage in casual or rambling conversation ⟨we were just *running on* about how neither of us has aged a bit after all these years⟩ — see CHAT

2 to remain indefinitely in existence or in the same state ⟨allow the savings account to *run on* for now⟩ — see CONTINUE 1

3 to talk at length without sticking to a topic or getting to a point ⟨she's very sweet, but she does tend to *run on*⟩ — see RAMBLE 1

run over *vb* to flow over the brim or top of ⟨got distracted while pouring the juice, and it *ran over* the glass⟩ — see OVERFLOW 1

runt *n* a living thing much smaller than others of its kind ⟨one kitten was definitely the *runt*, weighing only six ounces at birth⟩ — see DWARF 1

run through *vb* to use up carelessly ⟨how did you manage to *run through* $300 in one day?⟩ — see WASTE 1

rural *adj* of, relating to, associated with, or typical of open areas with few buildings or people ⟨grew up in a *rural* community where more than half the people were farmers⟩ ⟨a painter noted for his *rural* landscapes⟩

synonyms bucolic, country, pastoral, rustic

related words countrified (*also* countryfied), provincial; agrarian, agricultural

near antonyms citified, urbanized; metropolitan, municipal; nonagricultural, nonfarm

antonyms urban

rush *n* **1** excited and often showy or disorderly speed ⟨what's the reason for all this *rush*?⟩ — see HURRY 1

2 the act or action of setting upon with force or violence ⟨the regiment recaptured the hill with a single *rush*⟩ — see ATTACK 1

rush *vb* **1** to cause to move or proceed fast or faster ⟨I wouldn't make so many mistakes if you'd stop *rushing* me⟩ — see HURRY 1

2 to flow out in great quantities or with force ⟨in the spring the stream's *rushing* waters make crossing treacherous⟩ — see GUSH 1

3 to proceed or move quickly ⟨*rushing* is a good way to slip and fall⟩ — see HURRY 2

4 to take sudden, violent action against ⟨one goat suddenly *rushed* the other and knocked it down⟩ — see ATTACK 1

rushed *adj* acting or done with excessive or careless speed ⟨a *rushed* job with a number of errors⟩ — see HASTY 1

rustic *adj* of, relating to, associated with, or typical of open areas with few buildings or people ⟨a *rustic* area doesn't even have electricity⟩ — see RURAL

rustic *n* an awkward or simple person especially from a small town or the country ⟨a *rustic* who was awed by the price of everything in the city⟩ — see HICK

rustle *vb* to proceed or move quickly ⟨*rustled* around enthusiastically on the morning of the big trip⟩ — see HURRY 2

rustler *n* an ambitious person who eagerly goes after what is desired ⟨the job requires a *rustler* who doesn't always need to be told what to do⟩ — see GO-GETTER

rut *n* an established and often automatic or monotonous series of actions followed when engaging in some activity ⟨I've fallen into a *rut*, watching television and then going to bed every night⟩ — see ROUTINE 1

ruthless *adj* having or showing a lack of sympathy or tender feelings ⟨an office supervisor a *ruthless* disregard for others' feelings⟩ — see HARD 1

S

sable *adj* having the color of soot or coal ⟨a beautiful *sable* cat⟩ — see BLACK 1

saccharine *adj* appealing to the emotions in an obvious and tiresome way ⟨the movie was funny, but it had a *saccharine* ending in which everyone lives happily ever after⟩ — see CORNY

sacerdotal *adj* of, relating to, or characteristic of the clergy ⟨*sacerdotal* garments such as a cassock and miter⟩ — see CLERICAL

sack *n* **1** a container made of a flexible material (as paper or plastic) ⟨please put all the loaves of bread in the same *sack*⟩ — see BAG 1

2 a place set aside for sleeping ⟨I think I'm ready to hit the *sack*⟩ — see BED 1

sack *vb* **1** to let go from office, service, or employment ⟨he was *sacked* for showing up late once too often⟩ — see DISMISS 1

2 to search through with the intent of committing robbery ⟨thieves *sacked* the house in search of the diamond necklace⟩ — see RANSACK 1

sacred *adj* **1** not to be violated, criticized, or tampered with ⟨we took a *sacred* oath not to let anyone find our hideout⟩
synonyms holy, inviolable, sacrosanct, unassailable, untouchable
related words inviolate, pure; privileged, protected, shielded; exempt, immune
near antonyms blasphemous, irreverent, profane

2 of, relating to, or being God ⟨a *sacred* name that must not be uttered in vain⟩ — see HOLY 3

3 of, relating to, or used in the practice or worship services of a religion ⟨a *sacred* chalice⟩ — see RELIGIOUS 1

4 set apart or worthy of veneration by association with God ⟨the *sacred* bones of a saint⟩ — see HOLY 2

sacrifice *n* something offered to a god ⟨the herders selected their best lamb as a *sacrifice* in order to receive blessings from their god⟩
synonyms immolation, offering, victim
related words holocaust; contribution, donation

sacrifice *vb* to give up as an offering to a god ⟨in the Old Testament Abraham was willing to *sacrifice* even his son to God⟩
synonyms immolate, offer
related words consecrate, dedicate, devote; give, surrender, yield

sacrilege *n* an act of great disrespect shown to God or to sacred ideas, people, or things ⟨spitting on the temple floor is a great *sacrilege*⟩ — see BLASPHEMY

sacrilegious *adj* not showing proper reverence for the holy or sacred ⟨a *sacrilegious*, obscene joke—and told in church at that!⟩ — see IRREVERENT

sacristy *n* a room in a church building for sacred furnishings (as vestments) ⟨our choir robes were stored in the *sacristy*⟩
synonyms vestry
related words cloakroom

sacrosanct *adj* **1** not to be violated, criticized, or tampered with ⟨the teacher's book of grades is *sacrosanct*, and someone could be expelled for changing anything in it⟩ — see SACRED 1

2 set apart or worthy of veneration by association with God ⟨believers eventually built a chapel on the *sacro-*

sanct spot where the miracle was thought to have taken place⟩ — see HOLY 2

sad *adj* **1** feeling unhappiness ⟨movies in which the hero dies always make us feel *sad*⟩
synonyms bad, blue, brokenhearted, crestfallen, dejected, depressed, despondent, disconsolate, doleful, down, downcast, downhearted, droopy, forlorn, gloomy, glum, heartbroken, heartsick, heartsore, inconsolable, joyless, low, low-spirited, melancholy, miserable, mournful, saddened, sorrowful, sorry, unhappy, woebegone, woeful, wretched
related words aggrieved, distressed, troubled; despairing, hopeless; disappointed, discouraged, disheartened, dispirited; suicidal; dolorous, lugubrious, plaintive, tearful; regretful, rueful; grieving, wailing, weeping; black, bleak, cheerless, comfortless, dark, darkening, depressing, desolate, dismal, drear, dreary, funereal, gray (*also* grey), morbid, morose, murky, saturnine, somber (*or* sombre), sullen
near antonyms ecstatic, elated, enraptured, entranced, euphoric, exhilarated, exuberant, exultant; blithe, blithesome, gay, jocund, jolly, jovial, lightsome, merry, mirthful; excited, thrilled; hopeful, optimistic; encouraged, heartened; animated, jaunty, lively, perky, sprightly, vivacious; content, gratified, pleased, satisfied; beaming, grinning, laughing, smiling; boon, carefree, careless, cavalier, devil-may-care, easygoing, happy-go-lucky, insouciant, lighthearted, unconcerned
antonyms blissful, buoyant, buoyed, cheerful, cheery, chipper, delighted, glad, gladdened, gladsome, gleeful, happy, joyful, joyous, jubilant, sunny, upbeat

2 causing unhappiness ⟨the *sad* news about our uncle's death made my father cry⟩
synonyms depressing, dismal, drear, dreary, heartbreaking, heartrending, melancholy, pathetic, saddening, sorry, tearful, teary
related words discomforting, discomposing, disquieting, distressing, disturbing, perturbing; affecting, moving, poignant, touching; discouraging, disheartening, dispiriting
near antonyms heartening, heartwarming, inspiring, stimulating, stirring, uplifting; agreeable, pleasant, pleasurable; exhilarating, thrilling
antonyms cheering, cheery, glad, happy

sadden *vb* to make sad ⟨the arrival of winter always *saddens* me⟩ — see DEPRESS 1

saddened *adj* feeling unhappiness ⟨we were all *saddened* when our minister retired⟩ — see SAD 1

saddening *adj* causing unhappiness ⟨the *saddening* discovery that something is threatening the birds in the area⟩ — see SAD 2

saddle *vb* to place a weight or burden on ⟨my teachers have *saddled* me with too many assignments⟩ — see LOAD 1

sadism *n* the willful infliction of pain and suffering on others ⟨a troubled youth with a streak of *sadism* in him⟩ — see CRUELTY

sadistic *adj* having or showing the desire to inflict severe pain and suffering on others ⟨the troubled youth is being treated by a psychotherapist for his *sadistic* urges to hurt animals⟩ — see CRUEL 1

sadly *adv* with feelings of bitterness or grief ⟨*sadly* she told us how her dog died⟩ — see HARD 2

sadness *n* a state or spell of low spirits ⟨she was filled with *sadness* at the thought of having to leave her family⟩

synonyms blues, dejection, depression, desolation, despondency, disconsolateness, dispiritedness, doldrums, downheartedness, dreariness, dumps, forlornness, gloom, gloominess, heartsickness, joylessness, melancholy, mopes, oppression, unhappiness

related words melancholia, self-pity; anguish, dolor, grief, sorrow; dolefulness, mournfulness, somberness, sorrowfulness, woefulness; agony, distress, pain; misery, woe, wretchedness; discouragement, disheartenment; moodiness; despair, desperation, hopelessness; boredom, ennui, tedium

near antonyms gaiety (*also* gayety), gayness, glee, gleefulness, humor, jollity, joviality, lightheartedness, merriment, mirth, mirthfulness; cheer, cheerfulness, hopefulness, optimism, sunniness; content, contentedness, contentment, satisfaction; delight, gratification

antonyms bliss, blissfulness, ecstasy, elatedness, elation, euphoria, exhilaration, exuberance, exultation, felicity, gladness, gladsomeness, happiness, heaven, intoxication, joy, joyfulness, joyousness, jubilation, rapture, rapturousness

safe *adj* 1 not exposed to the threat of loss or injury ⟨the minute the rain started, we ran to a place where we were *safe* from getting wet⟩

synonyms all right, alright, secure

related words hale, healthy, intact, sound, well, whole; scatheless, unharmed, unhurt, uninjured, unscathed

near antonyms damaged, harmed, hurt, injured, scathed, wounded

antonyms endangered, imperiled, insecure, liable, threatened, unsafe, vulnerable

2 providing safety ⟨we tried to find a *safe* place to hide the candy⟩

synonyms secure, snug

related words guarding, protecting, safeguarding, sheltering, shielding; defended, guarded, protected, sheltered, shielded; impregnable, inviolable, invulnerable, unassailable, unconquerable

near antonyms undefended, unguarded, unprotected, vulnerable

antonyms dangerous, hazardous, insecure, risky, unsafe

3 having or showing a close attentiveness to avoiding danger or trouble ⟨rewarded *safe* drivers with lower insurance rates⟩ — see CAREFUL 1

4 not causing injury or hurt ⟨that pain reliever is *safe* for most people to take⟩ — see HARMLESS

5 worthy of one's trust ⟨she always offers *safe* advice⟩ — see DEPENDABLE

safe *n* a specially reinforced container to keep valuables safe ⟨the hotel recommended that we keep all our valuables in its *safe* during our stay⟩

synonyms coffer, safe-deposit box, strongbox

related words vault; locker, storeroom, treasury; footlocker, trunk

safe–deposit box *n* a specially reinforced container to keep valuables safe ⟨kept the deed to the house in a *safe-deposit box* at the bank⟩ — see SAFE

safeguard *n* means or method of defending ⟨with these *safeguards* in place, no one should be able to break into our computers⟩ — see DEFENSE 1

safeguard *vb* to drive danger or attack away from ⟨sheepdogs *safeguard* the flock from attacks by wolves⟩ — see DEFEND 1

safekeeping *n* responsibility for the safety and well-being of someone or something ⟨entrusted her daughter into his *safekeeping* while she was away on business⟩ — see CUSTODY

safeness *n* the state of not being exposed to danger ⟨the *safeness* of her children was something that she worried about constantly⟩ — see SAFETY 1

safety *n* 1 the state of not being exposed to danger ⟨we were lucky to make it to *safety* just as the lions broke loose from their cage at the zoo⟩

synonyms protection, safeness, security

related words aegis, defense, guardianship, ward; guard, safeguard, screen, shield; asylum, harbor, haven, refuge, retreat, shelter; inviolability, invulnerability

near antonyms hazard, risk, threat; instability, precariousness

antonyms danger, distress, endangerment, imperilment, jeopardy, peril, trouble

2 a protective device (as on a weapon) to prevent accidental operation ⟨the gun couldn't be fired as long as the *safety* was on⟩

synonyms guard

related words lock

sag *n* the extent to which something hangs or dips below a straight line ⟨if there's too much *sag* in the rod, the curtains will drag on the floor⟩

synonyms droop, slack, slackness

related words laxity, laxness, looseness

near antonyms tautness, tenseness, tension, tightness

sag *vb* 1 to be limp from lack of water or vigor ⟨the plant's leaves were *sagging* feebly after I forgot to water it for three days⟩ — see DROOP 1

2 to decline gradually from a standard level ⟨sales figures have *sagged* slightly over the past six months⟩ — see SLIP 1

3 to lose bodily strength or vigor ⟨after a whole day of working in the hot sun, he began to *sag*⟩ — see WEAKEN 2

sagacious *adj* having or showing deep understanding and intelligent application of knowledge ⟨a *sagacious* critique of the current social climate⟩ — see WISE 1

sagaciousness *n* the ability to understand inner qualities or relationships ⟨a woman of such down-to-earth *sagaciousness* that she ought be writing an advice column for the newspaper⟩ — see WISDOM 1

sagacity *n* the ability to understand inner qualities or relationships ⟨a novelist of surprising *sagacity* considering his youthfulness⟩ — see WISDOM 1

sage *adj* having or showing deep understanding and intelligent application of knowledge ⟨a *sage* suggestion that she think long and hard before deciding to marry at such a young age⟩ — see WISE 1

sage *n* a person of deep wisdom or learning ⟨the young prince visited the *sage* to learn the meaning of life⟩

synonyms savant, scholar

related words brain, egghead, genius, highbrow, intellectual, thinker; guru, mahatma; rabbi; master, mentor, teacher

near antonyms blockhead, dodo, dolt, donkey, dope, dumbbell, dummy, dunce, fathead, fool, goon, half-wit, idiot, ignoramus, imbecile, jackass, knothead, know-nothing, moron, nincompoop, ninny, nitwit, numskull (*or* numbskull), pinhead, simpleton, stock, turkey

sageness *n* the ability to understand inner qualities or relationships ⟨Mom has always shown an unpretentious *sageness* about the practicalities of life⟩ — see WISDOM 1

sagging *adj* bending downward or forward ⟨*sagging* branches that were weighted down with snow⟩ — see NODDING

sail *n* a journey over water in a vessel ⟨we went for a brief *sail* on the bay to relax⟩
synonyms crossing, cruise, passage, voyage
sail *vb* **1** to travel on water in a vessel ⟨I can't *sail* when there's any breeze at all because I get seasick easily⟩
synonyms boat, cruise, navigate, voyage
related words yacht; coast; log
phrases make sail
2 to move or proceed smoothly and readily ⟨*sailed* through the latest assignment⟩ — see FLOW 2
3 to rest or move along the surface of a liquid or in the air ⟨a leaf *sailed* by, carried by the breeze⟩ — see FLOAT
sailboat *n* a boat equipped with one or more sails ⟨we were stuck in the *sailboat* for an hour until the wind came up and we could move again⟩
synonyms bark, dinghy, windjammer
related words brigantine, caravel, catboat, clipper, corvette, cutter, frigate, galleon, galley, junk, ketch, lugger, outrigger, pinnace, schooner, shallop, ship, sloop, square-rigger, xebec, yacht, yawl; bottom, craft, vessel
sailor *n* one who operates or navigates a seagoing vessel ⟨the *sailors* were glad to be arriving in port after their long voyage⟩
synonyms gob, jack, jack-tar, mariner, navigator, salt, sea dog, seafarer, seaman, swab, tar
related words crewman, deckhand
saint *vb* to declare to be a saint and worthy of public respect ⟨Brigid of Sweden was *sainted* in October of 1391⟩
synonyms canonize
related words deify, worship; consecrate, hallow, sanctify; beatify, venerate
sainted *adj* showing a devotion to God and to a life of virtue ⟨renowned as theologian as well as for his work as medical missionary in Africa, Dr. Albert Schweitzer was widely regarded as one of the most *sainted* individuals of his time⟩ — see HOLY 1
sainthood *n* the quality or state of being spiritually pure or virtuous ⟨while you're a perfectly nice person, you're not exactly an example of *sainthood*⟩ — see HOLINESS
saintliness *n* the quality or state of being spiritually pure or virtuous ⟨true *saintliness* requires utter selflessness and devotion to others⟩ — see HOLINESS
saintly *adj* showing a devotion to God and to a life of virtue ⟨a *saintly* man who devoted his life to caring for the dying⟩ — see HOLY 1
saintship *n* the quality or state of being spiritually pure or virtuous ⟨a man who always maintained that his mother's *saintship* was beyond question⟩ — see HOLINESS
salable *or* **saleable** *adj* **1** fit or likely to be sold especially on a large scale ⟨an item that would be expensive to produce and attractive to too few people to ever be considered a *salable* commodity⟩ — see COMMERCIAL
2 fit to be offered for sale ⟨the car has to be put in better condition before it will be *salable*⟩ — see MARKETABLE 1
salary *n* the money paid regularly to a person for labor or services ⟨signed a contract for a new job with a *salary* of $40,000 per year⟩ — see WAGE
sale *n* the transfer of ownership of something from one person to another for a price ⟨my neighbor tried to make a *sale*, but no one was interested in buying his old car⟩

synonyms deal, trade, transaction
related words auction; haggle, negotiation; bargain, buy; purchase; clearance; fair; garage sale, rummage sale, yard sale
salesclerk *n* a person employed to sell goods or services especially in a store ⟨the *salesclerk* told us where to find the jewelry department⟩ — see SALESPERSON
salesman *n* a person employed to sell goods or services especially in a store ⟨a furniture *salesman* followed us around the whole time we looked for a new couch⟩ — see SALESPERSON
salesperson *n* a person employed to sell goods or services especially in a store ⟨we asked a *salesperson* to see if they had any shoes in the stockroom in our size⟩
synonyms clerk, salesclerk, salesman
related words salespeople; saleswoman
saline *adj* of, relating to, or containing salt ⟨tears are *saline*⟩ — see SALTY 1
salinity *n* the quality or state of being salty ⟨distilling will eliminate the *salinity* of seawater⟩ — see SALTINESS
saliva *n* the fluid that is secreted into the mouth by certain glands ⟨our mouths filled with *saliva* when we smelled the delicious dinner⟩
synonyms slobber, spit, spittle
related words foam, froth; expectoration, sputum
salivate *vb* to let saliva or some other substance flow from the mouth ⟨the dog *salivated* at the sight of the raw meat⟩ — see DROOL
sallow *adj* lacking the warm skin color indicative of or associated with good health ⟨he was still a bit *sallow* after a week spent in bed with the flu⟩ — see SICKLY 2
sally *n* **1** a short trip for pleasure ⟨a morning *sally* out to see the historic monuments around the city⟩ — see EXCURSION 1
2 something said or done to cause laughter ⟨the final *sally* made her laugh, and that ended the argument⟩ — see JOKE 1
sally (forth) *vb* to leave a place often for another ⟨he eagerly *sallied forth* from his small town to seek a new life in the bustling city⟩ — see GO 2
salon *n* **1** a building or part of a building in which objects of interest are displayed ⟨a fashionable *salon* filled with works of modern art⟩ — see MUSEUM
2 a building, room, or suite of rooms occupied by a service business ⟨a hair *salon*⟩ — see PLACE 2
saloon *n* a place of business where alcoholic beverages are sold to be consumed on the premises ⟨cowboys drinking in the *saloon* after their work was done for the day⟩ — see BARROOM
salt *adj* of, relating to, or containing salt ⟨the oceans are *salt* water⟩ — see SALTY 1
salt *n* one who operates or navigates a seagoing vessel ⟨an old *salt* who taught me a lot about sailing and the sea⟩ — see SAILOR
salt away *vb* to put (something of future use or value) in a safe or secret place ⟨*salted away* some jewels in a safe-deposit box for the lean times⟩ — see HOARD
saltiness *n* the quality or state of being salty ⟨the *saltiness* of the pretzels went well with the soda pop we were drinking⟩
synonyms brininess, salinity, saltness
near antonyms purity; sweetness
saltness *n* the quality or state of being salty ⟨the excessive *saltness* of the soup made it inedible⟩ — see SALTINESS
salty *adj* **1** of, relating to, or containing salt ⟨*salty* sea water is safe to swim in, but you really shouldn't swallow it⟩

synonyms briny, saline, salt
related words brackish
near antonyms sweet; clear, pure
2 hinting at or intended to call to mind matters regarded as indecent ⟨*salty* language that made all the boys snicker⟩ — see SUGGESTIVE 1

salubrious *adj* good for the health ⟨fresh air and exercise are always *salubrious*⟩ — see HEALTHFUL

salutary *adj* **1** conferring benefits; promoting or contributing to personal or social well-being ⟨the low interest rates should have a *salutary* effect on business⟩ — see BENEFICIAL
2 good for the health ⟨some people believe that a glass of wine a day is quite *salutary*⟩ — see HEALTHFUL

salutation *n* **1** a formal expression of praise ⟨the speaker introduced the evening's honored guest with a lavish *salutation*⟩ — see ENCOMIUM
2 an expression of goodwill upon meeting ⟨began the discussion with a pleasant *salutation* to the distinguished assembly⟩ — see HELLO

salute *n* an expression of goodwill upon meeting ⟨offered a cheery *salute* as they passed on the street⟩ — see HELLO

salute *vb* to declare enthusiastic approval of ⟨I *salute* the idea of better lunch options in our schools⟩ — see ACCLAIM

salvation *n* the saving from danger or evil ⟨we spent the night in the jungle praying for *salvation* from the dangerous animals⟩
synonyms deliverance
related words ransom, recovery, redemption, rescue; extrication; defense, protection, safeguarding; conservation, preservation

salvo *n* a rapid or overwhelming outpouring of many things at once ⟨attacked the manager with a *salvo* of complaints before she even managed to say "hello"⟩ — see BARRAGE

same *adj* **1** resembling another in every respect ⟨I bought the *same* shirt at the mall for five dollars less⟩
synonyms coequal, duplicate, equal, even, identical, indistinguishable
related words akin, alike, analogous, comparable, correspondent, corresponding, equivalent, like, matching, parallel, similar, such, suchlike, tantamount
near antonyms disparate, diverse, varied, various; distinct, distinctive
antonyms different, dissimilar, distinguishable, other, unalike, unlike
2 being one and not another ⟨that's the *same* guy I saw down at the beach yesterday⟩
synonyms identical, selfsame, very
near antonyms disparate, dissimilar, distinct, distinctive, distinguishable, diverse, unalike, unlike, varied, various
antonyms another, different, other

sameness *n* **1** a tedious lack of variety ⟨the endless *sameness* of what we keep having for dinner is starting to bore me⟩ — see MONOTONY
2 the state of being exactly alike ⟨the *sameness* of the two essays made the teacher immediately suspect plagiarism⟩ — see IDENTITY 1
3 the state or fact of being exactly the same in number, amount, status, or quality ⟨the striking *sameness* of the results for both experiments suggests that this is a real discovery⟩ — see EQUIVALENCE

sample *n* **1** a number of things selected from a group to stand for the whole ⟨based on a *sample* of the menu items, we decided that this was the best restaurant in town⟩
synonyms cross section
related words case, example, exemplar, illustration, instance, representative, specimen; selection
2 one of a group or collection that shows what the whole is like ⟨this vase is a *sample* of the high-quality glassware that the glassblowers can produce⟩ — see EXAMPLE

sample *vb* to put (something) to a test ⟨*sampled* the soup to see if it tasted good⟩ — see TRY (OUT) 1

sanctification *n* **1** the act of making something holy through religious ritual ⟨the sacred site required another *sanctification* after it had been defiled⟩ — see CONSECRATION
2 the act or fact of freeing from sin or moral guilt ⟨the Christian belief that the suffering and death of Jesus was responsible for the *sanctification* of all humankind⟩ — see PURIFICATION

sanctified *adj* set apart or worthy of veneration by association with God ⟨a *sanctified* site where the faithful believe that a young girl had visions of the Virgin Mary⟩ — see HOLY 2

sanctify *vb* **1** to free from moral guilt or blemish especially ceremonially ⟨received the sacrament of penance, whereby they were *sanctified* and restored to divine grace⟩ — see PURIFY 1
2 to make holy through prayers or ritual ⟨*sanctify* the bread for Communion⟩ — see BLESS 1

sanctimoniousness *n* the pretending of having virtues, principles, or beliefs that one in fact does not have ⟨the *sanctimoniousness* of the television evangelist became apparent when the lavishness of his lifestyle was exposed⟩ — see HYPOCRISY

sanction *n* the approval by someone in authority for the doing of something ⟨you cannot make a student video without the principal's *sanction* of its subject matter prior to shooting⟩ — see PERMISSION

sanction *vb* to give official acceptance of something as satisfactory ⟨the administration will *sanction* almost any field trip with educational value⟩ — see APPROVE

sanctioned *adj* ordered or allowed by those in authority ⟨I won't believe this was *sanctioned* until I've seen the signed permission form⟩ — see OFFICIAL

sanctity *n* the quality or state of being spiritually pure or virtuous ⟨the *sanctity* of the elderly nun shone through in her every word and gesture⟩ — see HOLINESS

sanctuary *n* **1** a place that is considered sacred (as within a religion) ⟨by law, anyone who sought refuge in a religious *sanctuary* was safe from arrest by the civil authorities⟩ — see SHRINE
2 something (as a building) that offers cover from the weather or protection from danger ⟨the marshland has been set aside as a *sanctuary* for shorebirds along that section of the coast⟩ — see SHELTER

sanctum *n* **1** a place that is considered sacred (as within a religion) ⟨the city of Jerusalem is a *sanctum* for Christians, Jews, and Muslims alike⟩ — see SHRINE
2 something (as a building) that offers cover from the weather or protection from danger ⟨used the cabin in the woods as a *sanctum* from the commotion and interference of his family⟩ — see SHELTER

sand *vb* to make smooth by friction ⟨carefully *sanded* down the wooden floors of the old house⟩ — see GRIND 1

sandwich *vb* to fit (something) into a tight space ⟨*sandwiched* six kids into the backseat somehow⟩ — see CROWD 1

sandy *adj* of a pale yellow or yellowish brown color ⟨the child with *sandy* hair really stood out among the brunettes⟩ — see BLOND

sane *adj* having full use of one's mind and control over one's actions ⟨the court ruled that the woman was indeed *sane* when she made out her will⟩
synonyms balanced, clearheaded, lucid, normal, right, stable
related words clear, logical, rational, reasonable; judicious, levelheaded, sensible, wise; healthy, sound
near antonyms balmy, bananas, batty, crackbrained, cracked, cuckoo, daffy, daft, dotty, loco [*slang*], loony (*also* looney), moonstruck, nuts, nutty, off, screwy, wacky; aberrant, disordered; delusional, neurotic, paranoid, psychotic, schizophrenic; eccentric, odd, queer, strange; foolish, senseless, witless; irrational, unreasonable; berserk, delirious; depressed, despondent; distraught, frantic, frenzied, hysterical
antonyms crazed, crazy, demented, deranged, insane, lunatic, mad, maniacal (*also* maniac), mental, unbalanced, unsound

saneness *n* the normal or healthy condition of the mental abilities ⟨a woman of remarkable *saneness*, considering the fact that she had just spent a rainy week in a cabin with four kids⟩ — see MIND 2

sanguinary *adj* eager for or marked by the shedding of blood, extreme violence, or killing ⟨a movie so *sanguinary* that I covered my eyes during at least half of it⟩ — see BLOODTHIRSTY

sanguine *adj* **1** eager for or marked by the shedding of blood, extreme violence, or killing ⟨the Civil War remains the nation's most *sanguine* conflict⟩ — see BLOODTHIRSTY
2 having a healthy reddish skin tone ⟨a baby with a *sanguine* complexion is more likely to leave the hospital early than a sickly-looking one⟩ — see RUDDY
3 having or showing a mind free from doubt ⟨I'm reasonably *sanguine* about the adoption of the latest proposal⟩ — see CERTAIN 2

sanguinity *n* an inclination to believe in the most favorable outcome ⟨Pollyanna had so great a tendency to look for the good in everyone and everything that her name has become a synonym for someone of irrepressible *sanguinity*⟩ — see OPTIMISM

sanitary *adj* free from filth, infection, or dangers to health ⟨the nurse made sure that everything in the room was *sanitary* so that the baby wouldn't get sick⟩
synonyms aseptic, germfree, hygienic, sterile
related words antibacterial, antibiotic, antiseptic, germicidal; clean, immaculate, spick-and-span (*or* spic-and-span), spotless, stainless, unsoiled, unsullied; beneficial, healthful, healthy, restorative, salubrious, salutary, wholesome
near antonyms pathogenic; bedraggled, besmirched, dingy, dirty, draggled, dusty, filthy, foul, grimy, grubby, grungy, mucky, muddy, nasty, soiled, sordid, stained, sullied, unclean, uncleanly; insalubrious, noxious, unhealthful, unhealthy, unwholesome
antonyms insanitary, unhygienic, unsanitary

sanitary landfill *n* a place where discarded materials (as trash) are dumped ⟨even after many years in *sanitary landfills*, disposable diapers have proven to be resistant to decomposition⟩ — see DUMP 1

sanity *n* the normal or healthy condition of the mental abilities ⟨these working conditions are threatening my *sanity!*⟩ — see MIND 2

sans *prep* not having ⟨anyone *sans* shirt will not be allowed in the restaurant⟩ — see WITHOUT 1

sap *n* **1** active strength of body or mind ⟨a child full of *sap* and vivacity⟩ — see VIGOR 1
2 one who is easily deceived or cheated ⟨some other poor *sap* will probably fall for that scam⟩ — see DUPE

sap *vb* to diminish the physical strength of ⟨weeks of hard work had *sapped* her and left her exhausted⟩ — see WEAKEN 1

sapience *n* the ability to understand inner qualities or relationships ⟨the kind of *sapience* that comes from fifty years of experience as an educator⟩ — see WISDOM 1

sapient *adj* having or showing deep understanding and intelligent application of knowledge ⟨an uncle who is always good for valuable insights and some *sapient* advice⟩ — see WISE 1

sapped *adj* lacking bodily strength ⟨I was completely *sapped* after the first day hauling logs⟩ — see WEAK 1

sappiness *n* the state or quality of having an excess of tender feelings (as of love, nostalgia, or compassion) ⟨the *sappiness* of the verse on the greeting card⟩ — see SENTIMENTALITY

sappy *adj* **1** appealing to the emotions in an obvious and tiresome way ⟨a *sappy* letter filled with silly romantic clichés⟩ — see CORNY
2 showing or marked by a lack of good sense or judgment ⟨a *sappy* plan to try to get her divorced parents back together again⟩ — see FOOLISH 1

sarcasm *n* an act or expression showing scorn and usually intended to hurt another's feelings ⟨I know you're not happy, but there's no need to resort to petty *sarcasms* to make your point⟩ — see INSULT

sarcastic *adj* marked by the use of wit that is intended to cause hurt feelings ⟨her *sarcastic* comments that my singing reminded her of the time her dog was sick⟩
synonyms acrid, biting, caustic, cutting, mordant, pungent, sardonic, satiric (*or* satirical), scalding, scathing, sharp, smart-alecky (*or* smart-aleck), tart
related words acid, acidic, cross, sour; incisive, trenchant; cynical, dry, ironic, wry; facetious, flippant, tongue-in-cheek; acrimonious, bitter, resentful; harsh, rough, severe, stringent; concise, crisp, curt, pithy, succinct, terse; backhanded, insincere
near antonyms amusing, droll, merry, playful, sportive, waggish; gentle, mild; bland; good-humored, good-natured; diplomatic, polite, smooth, suave, urbane; affable, cordial, genial, gracious

sardonic *adj* marked by the use of wit that is intended to cause hurt feelings ⟨a *sardonic* little jab that made her visitor quiet and subdued for the rest of the night⟩ — see SARCASTIC

sash *n* a strip of flexible material (as leather) worn around the waist ⟨a dress with a flowered silk *sash*⟩ — see ²BELT

sass *n* disrespectful or argumentative talk given in response to a command or request ⟨Mom greeted any *sass* with a quick smack on the bottom⟩ — see BACK TALK

sassy *adj* displaying or marked by rude boldness ⟨*sassy* kids shouting, "Out of our way, you old bag!"⟩ — see NERVY 1

Satan *n* the supreme personification of evil often represented as the ruler of Hell ⟨some people believe that *Satan* can successfully tempt almost anyone with lies and flattery⟩ — see DEVIL 1

satanic *adj* of, relating to, or worthy of an evil spirit ⟨the cat's eyes reflected a *satanic* red in the dark⟩ — see FIENDISH

sate *vb* **1** to fill with food to capacity ⟨I *sated* myself with an array of offerings from the dessert table⟩ — see GORGE 1

2 to put a complete end to (a physical need or desire) ⟨a huge meal that should have *sated* everyone's hunger⟩ — see SATISFY 1

sated *adj* having one's appetite completely satisfied ⟨the *sated* baby fell instantly to sleep⟩ — see FULL 3

satiate *adj* having one's appetite completely satisfied ⟨a couple of *satiate* dinner guests had ensconced themselves on the living room sofa⟩ — see FULL 3

satiate *vb* to put a complete end to (a physical need or desire) ⟨a long drink of water at last *satiated* my thirst⟩ — see SATISFY 1

satiated *adj* having one's appetite completely satisfied ⟨he was too *satiated* even to have a cookie⟩ — see FULL 3

satin *adj* **1** having a shiny surface or finish ⟨*satin* paint⟩ — see GLOSSY

2 smooth or delicate in appearance or feel ⟨the *satin* petals of a rose⟩ — see SOFT 2

satiny *adj* **1** having a shiny surface or finish ⟨the *satiny* short coat of an Arabian horse⟩ — see GLOSSY

2 smooth or delicate in appearance or feel ⟨a lovely *satiny* fabric that feels so good next to the skin⟩ — see SOFT 2

satire *n* a creative work that uses sharp humor to point up the foolishness of a person, institution, or human nature in general ⟨a *satire* about the music industry in which a handsome but untalented youth is turned into a rock star⟩

synonyms lampoon

related words burlesque, caricature, parody, spoof, takeoff; comedy, farce, sketch, slapstick, squib; derision, ridicule; mockery, travesty

satiric *or* **satirical** *adj* marked by the use of wit that is intended to cause hurt feelings ⟨a *satiric* story about the movie business⟩ — see SARCASTIC

satisfaction *n* **1** the feeling experienced when one's wishes are met ⟨readers will close the covers of this mystery novel with complete *satisfaction*⟩ — see PLEASURE 1

2 payment to another for a loss or injury ⟨he's demanding *satisfaction* from his neighbor for running over his prize tulips⟩ — see COMPENSATION 1

satisfactorily *adv* **1** in a satisfactory way ⟨the matter has been resolved *satisfactorily*⟩ — see WELL 1

2 in or to a degree or quantity that meets one's requirements or satisfaction ⟨supplied us *satisfactorily*, if not lavishly, with meals during our stay⟩ — see ENOUGH 1

satisfactoriness *n* the quality or state of meeting one's needs adequately ⟨the overall *satisfactoriness* of the service led us to leave a reasonable tip⟩ — see SUFFICIENCY

satisfactory *adj* **1** being to one's liking ⟨we found the meal most *satisfactory*⟩

synonyms agreeable, all right, alright, copacetic (*also* copasetic *or* copesetic), fine, good, OK (*or* okay), palatable

related words delectable, delicious, delightful, dreamy, felicitous, gratifying, nice, pleasant, pleasing, scrumptious, welcome; acceptable, adequate, decent, passable, tolerable

antonyms disagreeable, unsatisfactory

2 of a level of quality that meets one's needs or standards ⟨his first attempt at cooking dinner was actually quite *satisfactory*⟩ — see ADEQUATE

satisfied *adj* **1** experiencing pleasure, satisfaction, or delight ⟨*satisfied* customers tend to come back over and over⟩ — see GLAD 1

2 feeling that one's needs or desires have been met ⟨a *satisfied* vacationer is one who has spent the time doing exactly what he or she wanted⟩ — see CONTENT

satisfy *vb* **1** to put a complete end to (a physical need or desire) ⟨they *satisfied* their hunger after the game with a big pasta dinner⟩

synonyms assuage, quench, sate, satiate

related words cater (to), gratify, indulge; alleviate, lighten, relieve

near antonyms arouse, excite, pique, stimulate; tantalize, tease

2 to cause (someone) to agree with a belief or course of action by using arguments or earnest requests ⟨it took me a while to *satisfy* my teacher that I had a good excuse for being late⟩ — see PERSUADE

3 to do what is required by the terms of ⟨had failed to *satisfy* the terms of the agreement⟩ — see FULFILL 1

4 to give satisfaction to ⟨a hot dinner and a relaxing massage never fails to *satisfy* her husband⟩ — see PLEASE

satisfying *adj* **1** giving pleasure or contentment to the mind or senses ⟨a *satisfying* and relaxing bubble bath after a long day⟩ — see PLEASANT

2 having the power to persuade ⟨"I don't feel like it" is not a *satisfying* reason for skipping your chores⟩ — see COGENT

3 making one feel good inside ⟨a *satisfying* compliment on her gardening efforts⟩ — see HEARTWARMING

satisfyingly *adv* in a pleasing way ⟨the story with a *satisfyingly* happy ending⟩ — see WELL 5

saturate *vb* to wet thoroughly with liquid ⟨*saturate* your hair with water before applying the dye⟩ — see SOAK 1

saturated *adj* containing, covered with, or thoroughly penetrated by water ⟨the carpet should be damp but not entirely *saturated*⟩ — see WET

saturnine *adj* causing or marked by an atmosphere lacking in cheer ⟨the men awaiting interrogation by the police shared a *saturnine* silence⟩ — see GLOOMY 1

sauce *n* **1** a savory fluid food used as a topping or accompaniment to a main dish ⟨the chef poured *sauce* over the meat just before he served it⟩

synonyms dressing, gravy

related words condiment, relish, seasoning; fixing(s), garnish, topping; dip, marinade

2 disrespectful or argumentative talk given in response to a command or request ⟨if you put up with any *sauce* from them, they'll only get worse⟩ — see BACK TALK

3 shameless boldness ⟨the woman was shocked by the *sauce* of the child who ran right up to her and called her a "witch"⟩ — see EFFRONTERY

sauciness *n* shameless boldness ⟨had the *sauciness* to ask a total stranger what her age was⟩ — see EFFRONTERY

saucy *adj* displaying or marked by rude boldness ⟨irritated his fellow travelers with *saucy* questions and comments⟩ — see NERVY 1

saunter *n* a relaxed journey on foot for exercise or pleasure ⟨tourists on a morning *saunter* around the old section of the city⟩ — see WALK

sausage *n* a rod-shaped portion of seasoned ground meat in a casing ⟨a couple of *sausages* and eggs make a good breakfast⟩

synonyms link

related words bologna, frankfurter, hot dog, knockwurst, liverwurst, pepperoni, salami, wiener

savage *adj* **1** not civilized ⟨Tarzan is usually portrayed as a noble but *savage* warrior of the jungle⟩
synonyms barbarous, heathen, heathenish, Neanderthal, rude, uncivil, uncivilized, uncultivated, wild
related words coarse, crude, primitive, rough; uncouth, uncultured
near antonyms cultured, enlightened, humane, sophisticated; genteel, polite, refined, urbane, well-bred
antonyms civilized
2 having or showing the desire to inflict severe pain and suffering on others ⟨a *savage* attack on a helpless person⟩ — see CRUEL 1
3 living outdoors without taming or domestication by humans ⟨*savage* beasts that seemed threatening to the tourists⟩ — see WILD 1
4 violently unfriendly or aggressive in disposition ⟨early explorers avoided those areas that were rumored to be inhabited by *savage* natives⟩ — see FIERCE 1
savage *n* **1** a mean, evil, or unprincipled person ⟨what kind of *savage* would hurt a baby?⟩ — see VILLAIN 1
2 an uncivilized person ⟨inhabitants of exotic lands were invariably portrayed as *savages*⟩ — see HEATHEN 2
savageness *n* the willful infliction of pain and suffering on others ⟨the unthinkable *savageness* that must be required to torture a prisoner⟩ — see CRUELTY
savagery *n* the willful infliction of pain and suffering on others ⟨a study of the *savagery* shown by soldiers in wartime⟩ — see CRUELTY
savanna *also* **savannah** *n* a broad area of level or rolling treeless country ⟨lions roaming the *savanna*⟩ — see PLAIN
savant *n* a person of deep wisdom or learning ⟨a *savant* in the field of medical ethics⟩ — see SAGE
save *prep* not including ⟨everyone *save* me is going to the party⟩ — see EXCEPT
save *vb* **1** to free from the penalties or consequences of sin ⟨the Christian belief that Jesus lived and died to *save* humanity⟩
synonyms deliver, redeem
related words reclaim, reform; forgive, pardon, remit; bless, hallow; consecrate, purify, sanctify
2 to remove from danger or harm ⟨the fire fighter *saved* my brother from the burning building⟩
synonyms bail out, deliver, rescue
related words salvage; emancipate, free, liberate, manumit, release; disentangle, extricate; recover
antonyms compromise, endanger, imperil, jeopardize
3 to avoid unnecessary waste or expense ⟨we'll have to scrimp and *save* to be able to afford college⟩ — see ECONOMIZE
4 to keep in good condition ⟨lovingly *saved* the classic car and even upgraded its engine⟩ — see MAINTAIN 1
5 to keep or intend for a special purpose ⟨I'm *saving* this dress for a formal occasion⟩ — see DEVOTE 1
saver *n* one that saves from danger or destruction ⟨of all the *savers* of Jews during the Holocaust, none was more heroic than the Swedish diplomat Raoul Wallenberg⟩ — see SAVIOR
saving *conj* if it were not for the fact that ⟨I would be ready, *saving* the fact that I can't find my missing shoe⟩ — see EXCEPT
saving *prep* not including ⟨*saving* three members, the club is now fully committed to the project⟩ — see EXCEPT
savior *or* **saviour** *n* one that saves from danger or destruction ⟨the policeman proved to be our *savior*, ar-

riving on the scene just as we were about to be mugged⟩
synonyms deliverer, redeemer, rescuer, saver
related words custodian, defender, guard, guardian, keeper, lookout, protector, sentinel, sentry, warden, warder, watch, watchman
savor *n* **1** the property of a substance that can be identified by the sense of taste ⟨a gourmet who can identify the ingredients in any dish solely by their *savor*⟩ — see TASTE 1
2 the quality of being delicious ⟨the wonderful *savor* of Mom's apple pie⟩ — see DELICIOUSNESS
savor *vb* to make more pleasant to the taste by adding something intensely flavored ⟨*savored* the chicken with cloves of garlic⟩ — see SEASON 1
savoriness *n* the quality of being delicious ⟨the *savoriness* of freshly baked bread simply cannot be overrated⟩ — see DELICIOUSNESS
savorless *adj* lacking in taste or flavor ⟨the white rice was filling, but rather *savorless*⟩ — see INSIPID 1
savory *adj* **1** having a pleasant smell ⟨a *savory* bakery filled with the aromas of pastry and breads⟩ — see FRAGRANT
2 very pleasing to the sense of taste ⟨a *savory* beef stew⟩ — see DELICIOUS 1
savvy *n* knowledge gained by actually doing or living through something ⟨she's an excellent scholar of political science, but lacks the kind of *savvy* needed to run for public office⟩ — see EXPERIENCE 1
saw *n* an often stated observation regarding something from common experience ⟨the old *saw* that a red sunset presages fair skies the next day⟩ — see SAYING
saw-toothed *adj* notched or toothed along the edge ⟨a *saw-toothed* barrette⟩ — see SERRATED
say *vb* **1** to express (a thought or emotion) in words ⟨why don't you just *say* what's on your mind?⟩
synonyms articulate, speak, state, talk, tell, utter, verbalize, vocalize
related words air, discuss, express, give, look, sound, state, vent, ventilate, voice; advertise, announce, blaze, broadcast, declare, enunciate, proclaim, publicize, publish; affirm, allege, assert, aver, avouch, avow; breathe, drawl, gasp, mouth, murmur, shout, splutter, spout, whisper; couch, formulate, phrase, put, word; comment, remark
phrases put into words
near antonyms stifle, suppress
2 to convey in appropriate or telling terms ⟨I'm not quite sure how to *say* this, but that's the worst essay I've ever read⟩ — see PHRASE
3 to give from memory ⟨*say* your prayers⟩ — see REPEAT 2
say *n* the right to express a wish, choice, or opinion ⟨even if they decide otherwise, at least I had my *say*⟩ — see VOICE 1
saying *n* an often stated observation regarding something from common experience ⟨there's an old *saying* that you should let sleeping dogs lie⟩
synonyms adage, aphorism, byword, epigram, maxim, proverb, saw
related words cliché, commonplace, platitude; expression, felicity; axiom, motto, precept, truism, truth; observation, reflection, remark
scabby *adj* arousing or deserving of one's loathing and disgust ⟨that's a *scabby* trick to play on someone trying to help⟩ — see CONTEMPTIBLE 1
scads *n pl* a considerable amount ⟨*scads* of people showed up for the party⟩ — see LOT 2

scalawag *or* **scallywag** *n* a mean, evil, or unprincipled person ⟨a *scalawag* who had taken to begging on street corners while posing as a blind person⟩ — see VILLAIN

scalding *adj* **1** having a notably high temperature ⟨the *scalding* water of a geyser⟩ — see HOT 1

2 marked by the use of wit that is intended to cause hurt feelings ⟨*scalding* reviews for the overproduced horror movie⟩ — see SARCASTIC

¹**scale** *n* a device for measuring weight ⟨I hate getting on the bathroom *scale*⟩
synonyms balance
related words gravimeter

²**scale** *n* a small thin piece of material that resembles an animal scale ⟨*scales* of mica were embedded in the granite⟩
synonyms lamella, lamina, plate
related words chip, flake, sliver, splinter

³**scale** *n* **1** a scheme of rank or order ⟨a student who scored very highly on a standard intelligence *scale*⟩
synonyms graduation, ladder, ordering, ranking
related words arrangement, array, disposal, disposition, distribution, order, sequence, series

2 the distance or extent between possible extremes ⟨with the *scale* going from one to ten, what did you think of the movie?⟩ — see RANGE 3

scale *vb* to find out the size, extent, or amount of ⟨*scaled* the logs to get a rough idea of the amount of usable lumber they were likely to yield⟩ — see MEASURE

scaly *adj* composed of or covered with scales ⟨the snake's *scaly* skin was dry to the touch⟩
synonyms squamous
related words scalelike
near antonyms smooth
antonyms scaleless

scamp *n* **1** an appealingly mischievous person ⟨those little *scamps* are always getting into trouble, but no one has the heart to punish them⟩
synonyms devil, hellion, imp, mischief, monkey, rapscallion, rascal, rogue, urchin
related words cutup, madcap, skylarker; ragamuffin; brat, disrupter, nuisance; juvenile delinquent; gamin, gamine
near antonyms beast, boor, cad, churl, clown, creep, cretin, cur, heel, joker, louse, lout, skunk, snake, stinker; knave, scalawag (*or* scallywag), scoundrel, villain

2 a mean, evil, or unprincipled person ⟨an insincere and ruthlessly ambitious *scamp* who was willing to do anything to win the TV show's grand prize⟩ — see VILLAIN

scamper *vb* to go at a pace faster than a walk ⟨the child *scampered* off to play⟩ — see RUN 1

scan *n* a close look at or over someone or something in order to judge condition ⟨gave the car a good *scan* to see if it was worth buying⟩ — see INSPECTION

scan *vb* to look over closely (as for judging quality or condition) ⟨*scanned* the manuscript carefully for any overlooked errors⟩ — see INSPECT

scandal *n* a cause of shame ⟨a *scandal* that for many years haunted the family of the banker convicted of embezzlement⟩ — see DISGRACE 2

scandalous *adj* **1** causing intense displeasure, disgust, or resentment ⟨the *scandalous* news that a police officer beat someone up⟩ — see OFFENSIVE 1

2 causing or intended to cause unjust injury to a person's good name ⟨spread a *scandalous* rumor about him that almost cost him his job⟩ — see LIBELOUS

scant *adj* less plentiful than what is normal, necessary, or desirable ⟨a baby born with *scant* hair⟩ — see MEAGER

scant *vb* to use or give out in stingy amounts ⟨don't *scant* the peanut butter on those sandwiches!⟩ — see SPARE

scantiness *n* a falling short of an essential or desirable amount or number ⟨the *scantiness* of grass meant that we had to feed the cows extra hay⟩ — see DEFICIENCY

scanty *adj* less plentiful than what is normal, necessary, or desirable ⟨the camera's *scanty* instructions left me somewhat confused⟩ — see MEAGER

scapegoat *n* a person or thing taking the blame for others ⟨companies often use the economy as a *scapegoat* to avoid taking responsibility for dropping sales⟩
synonyms fall guy, goat, whipping boy
related words victim; butt, dupe, fool, laughingstock, mockery, monkey; excuse

scar *n* something that spoils the appearance or completeness of a thing ⟨the *scars* left by carelessly scratching the car door with one's keys⟩ — see BLEMISH

scarce *adj* **1** less plentiful than what is normal, necessary, or desirable ⟨food was a bit *scarce* last winter⟩ — see MEAGER

2 not coming up to a usual standard or meeting a particular need ⟨help is always *scarce* in the resort town during the busy summer season⟩ — see SHORT 3

scarcely *adv* **1** by a very small margin ⟨was *scarcely* able to walk after the near-fatal accident⟩ — see JUST 2

2 certainly not ⟨I *scarcely* think that one person sick is an "epidemic"⟩ — see HARDLY 2

scarceness *n* a falling short of an essential or desirable amount or number ⟨the continuing *scarceness* of supplies means that we will have to ration ourselves⟩ — see DEFICIENCY

scarcity *n* a falling short of an essential or desirable amount or number ⟨the *scarcity* of good restaurants around here is surprising⟩ — see DEFICIENCY

scare *vb* to strike with fear ⟨thunderstorms *scare* her⟩ — see FRIGHTEN

scared *adj* filled with fear or dread ⟨at the sight of the monster he froze, being too *scared* to even run away⟩ — see AFRAID 1

scare up *vb* to come upon after searching, study, or effort ⟨I can probably *scare up* my old textbooks if you need them⟩ — see FIND 1

scarp *n* a steep wall of rock, earth, or ice ⟨years of violent ocean storms had heavily eroded the beach, creating a *scarp* along one end of it⟩ — see CLIFF

scary *adj* **1** causing fear ⟨a *scary* movie that gave the child nightmares for weeks⟩ — see FEARFUL 1

2 easily frightened ⟨a *scary* horse who spooked and kicked at its own shadow⟩ — see SHY 1

scathe *vb* to criticize harshly and usually publicly ⟨newspaper cartoonists *scathed* the dishonest politician with a series of cruel caricatures⟩ — see ATTACK 2

scathing *adj* marked by the use of wit that is intended to cause hurt feelings ⟨*scathing* commentary on the latest theory concerning the assassination⟩ — see SARCASTIC

scatter *vb* **1** to cause (members of a group) to move widely apart ⟨the noise of the backfiring car *scattered* the pigeons⟩
synonyms clear out, disband, dispel, disperse, dissipate
related words break up, isolate, part, segregate, separate, split up; diffuse, disseminate, diverge, spread
near antonyms agglutinate, conglomerate; unify, unite
antonyms assemble, cluster, collect, concentrate, congregate, gather

2 to cover by or as if by scattering something over or on ⟨the hillside was *scattered* with wildflowers⟩

synonyms bestrew, dot, pepper, sow, spray, sprinkle, strew

related words blanket, dust; stud; dapple, fleck, speckle, spot, stipple

scatterbrained *adj* lacking in seriousness or maturity ⟨a *scatterbrained* child who couldn't seem to pay attention or stop fooling around⟩ — see GIDDY 1

scattered *adj* lacking a definite plan, purpose, or pattern ⟨a hodgepodge of *scattered* ideas that didn't add up to a clear hypothesis⟩ — see RANDOM

scattering *n* **1** an act or process in which something scatters or is scattered ⟨the *scattering* of the protesters suddenly turned violent and chaotic⟩

synonyms disbandment, dispersal, dispersion, dissipation

near antonyms assembly, collection, concentration, gathering

2 a small number ⟨a *scattering* of people in the mostly empty theater⟩ — see FEW

scenario *n* the written form of a story prepared for film production ⟨submitted a *scenario* to the producers⟩ — see SCREENPLAY

scene *n* **1** the place and time in which the action for a portion of a dramatic work (as a movie) is set ⟨the first *scene* was the kitchen of a fancy restaurant during dinner⟩

synonyms background, setting

related words backdrop, scenery, set; tableau

2 an outburst or display of excited anger ⟨please don't make a *scene* while we're at the restaurant⟩ — see TANTRUM

3 position with regard to conditions and circumstances ⟨the current political *scene*⟩ — see SITUATION 1

4 the array of painted backgrounds and furnishings used for a scene in a stage production ⟨helped build and paint *scenes* for the school play⟩ — see SCENERY

scenery *n* the array of painted backgrounds and furnishings used for a scene in a stage production ⟨the *scenery* in the high school production was all handmade⟩

synonyms scene, set

related words backdrop, drop; background, setting; prop, property

scent *n* **1** a sweet or pleasant smell ⟨the delightful *scent* of her perfume⟩ — see FRAGRANCE

2 the quality of a thing that makes it perceptible to the sense organs in the nose ⟨couldn't detect the *scent* of anything because I had a cold⟩ — see SMELL 1

scent *vb* **1** to fill or infuse with a pleasant odor or odor-releasing substance ⟨fancy bars of soap *scented* with lavender⟩

synonyms perfume

near antonyms deodorize

2 to become aware of by means of the sense organs in the nose ⟨the dog *scented* a rabbit and suddenly took off⟩ — see SMELL

3 to have a vague awareness of ⟨he *scented* danger⟩ — see FEEL 1

scented *adj* having a pleasant smell ⟨a bowl of *scented* petals used to perfume a room⟩ — see FRAGRANT

schedule *n* **1** a listing of things to be presented or considered (as at a concert or play) ⟨the *schedule* of events for the conference⟩ — see PROGRAM 1

2 a record of a series of items (as names or titles) usually arranged according to some system ⟨a *schedule* of arrivals and departures⟩ — see ¹LIST

schedule *vb* to put (someone or something) on a list ⟨I've *scheduled* you for an appointment tomorrow⟩ — see ¹LIST 2

scheduled *adj* being in accordance with the prescribed, normal, or logical course of events ⟨a *scheduled* stop for the train⟩ — see DUE 2

schematize *vb* to work out the details of (something) in advance ⟨*schematized* the plan for evacuating the building in an emergency⟩ — see PLAN 1

scheme *n* **1** a clever often underhanded means to achieve an end ⟨a *scheme* to fool people into volunteering for the cleanup of the park⟩ — see TRICK 1

2 a secret plan for accomplishing evil or unlawful ends ⟨a *scheme* to kidnap the President's daughter⟩ — see PLOT 1

3 a method worked out in advance for achieving some objective ⟨a *scheme* to upgrade the city's mass transit system⟩ — see PLAN 1

scheme *vb* to engage in a secret plan to accomplish evil or unlawful ends ⟨*scheming* to cheat on the test in a way that no one had ever thought of before⟩ — see PLOT

scheme (out) *vb* to work out the details of (something) in advance ⟨*schemed out* a way to make it to both parties being held on the same night⟩ — see PLAN 1

schism *n* **1** a lack of agreement or harmony ⟨*schism* within the charitable organization was preventing it from achieving its goals⟩ — see DISCORD

2 the act or process of a whole separating into two or more parts or pieces ⟨the *schism* of the Christian church into the Roman Catholic and Eastern Orthodox churches⟩ — see SEPARATION 1

schmaltz *also* **schmalz** *n* something (as a work of literature or music) that is too sentimental ⟨the love song was a piece of *schmaltz*⟩ — see CORN

schmaltzy *adj* appealing to the emotions in an obvious and tiresome way ⟨a *schmaltzy* television commercial featuring a photogenic, perfect family⟩ — see CORNY

scholar *n* **1** a person of deep wisdom or learning ⟨*scholars* have long debated whether there is ever such a thing as a truly selfless act⟩ — see SAGE

2 a person with a high level of knowledge or skill in a field ⟨a *scholar* who is a specialist in the history of ancient Greece⟩ — see EXPERT

3 one who attends a school ⟨the college graduated 300 *scholars* last year⟩ — see STUDENT

scholarly *adj* **1** having or displaying advanced knowledge or education ⟨a *scholarly* analysis of the historical document⟩ — see EDUCATED

2 of or relating to schooling or learning especially at an advanced level ⟨a *scholarly* essay making comparisons between 18th-century French authors and their Germanic counterparts⟩ — see ACADEMIC

scholarship *n* the understanding and information gained from being educated ⟨a woman possessing both native intelligence and great *scholarship*⟩ — see EDUCATION 2

scholastic *adj* of or relating to schooling or learning especially at an advanced level ⟨*scholastic* endeavors⟩ — see ACADEMIC

school *n* a place or establishment for teaching and learning ⟨one of the first *schools* in the country to admit girls as students⟩

synonyms academy, seminary

related words elementary school, grammar school, high school, junior high school, middle school, preparatory school, public school, secondary school, trade school; Sunday school, yeshiva (*also* yeshivah)

school *vb* to cause to acquire knowledge or skill in some field ⟨*schooled* him in proper etiquette for formal occasions⟩ — see TEACH

schooling *n* the act or process of imparting knowledge or skills to another ⟨the extended *schooling* needed for a horse to be able to make those precision movements⟩ — see EDUCATION 1

schoolteacher *n* a person whose occupation is to give formal instruction in a school ⟨*schoolteachers* don't always get the summers off, for some teach during that period as well⟩ — see TEACHER

science *n* 1 a body of facts learned by study or experience ⟨the *science* of medicine grew tremendously in the course of the 19th century⟩ — see KNOWLEDGE 1

2 the understanding and information gained from being educated ⟨I speak from *science*, not merely personal opinion⟩ — see EDUCATION 2

scintillate *vb* 1 to give off sparks ⟨we watched contentedly as our campfire *scintillated* in the darkness⟩ — see SPARK 1

2 to shoot forth bursts of light ⟨the diamond ring *scintillated* in the sunlight⟩ — see FLASH 1

scoffer *n* a person who causes repeated emotional pain, distress, or annoyance to another ⟨the movie actress proved the *scoffers* wrong when she succeeded brilliantly on stage⟩ — see TORMENTOR

scold *n* a person given to harsh judgments and to finding faults ⟨the supervisor was something of a *scold*, complaining whenever anything wasn't done perfectly⟩ — see CRITIC 1

scold *vb* to criticize (someone) severely or angrily especially for personal failings ⟨he *scolded* the kids for not cleaning up the mess they had made in the kitchen⟩

synonyms berate, castigate, chew out, dress down, flay, jaw, keelhaul, lambaste (*or* lambast), lecture, rail (at *or* against), rate, rebuke, reprimand, reproach, score, upbraid

related words admonish, chide, remonstrate (with), reprove; abuse, assail, attack, bad-mouth, blame, blast, censure, condemn, criticize, crucify, denounce, dis [*slang*], excoriate, fault, knock, lash, pan, reprehend, slam; belittle, disparage, mock, put down; ridicule, scoff, scorn

phrases read the riot act (to), take to task

near antonyms approve, endorse (*also* indorse), sanction; extol (*also* extoll), laud, praise

scoop *n* 1 a utensil with a bowl and a handle that is used especially in cooking and serving food ⟨an ice cream *scoop*⟩ — see SPOON

2 information not generally available to the public ⟨come on, I know you know the *scoop* on their breakup⟩ — see DOPE 1

scoop *vb* to lift out with something that holds liquid ⟨*scooped* broth out of the pan with a spoon⟩ — see DIP 2

scoot *vb* to proceed or move quickly ⟨now we've got to *scoot*, or we'll be late⟩ — see HURRY 2

scope *n* an area over which activity, capacity, or influence extends ⟨the *scope* of the rescue effort is quite impressive⟩ — see RANGE 2

scorch *vb* to burn on the surface ⟨the picnickers kept *scorching* their marshmallows, deliberately sticking their skewers into the licking flames of the campfire⟩

synonyms char, sear, singe

related words fire, ignite, inflame, kindle, light; bake, cremate, incinerate; scald, scathe

scorching *adj* having a notably high temperature ⟨wore only a bathing suit around the yard on *scorching* summer days⟩ — see HOT 1

score *n* a lingering ill will towards a person for a real or imagined wrong ⟨I've got a *score* to settle with that bully⟩ — see GRUDGE 1

score *vb* 1 to mark with or as if with a line or groove ⟨the glassblower *scored* the glass rod first so that it would break cleanly⟩

synonyms groove, scribe, seam

related words abrade, file, graze, rasp, scarify, scratch

2 to gain (as points or runs in a game) as credit towards one's total number of points ⟨he *scored* the winning goal in the final minute of play⟩

synonyms rack up, tally

related words triumph, win; best, defeat

near antonyms lose

3 to obtain (as a goal) through effort ⟨finally *scored* a good job after years of hard work⟩ — see ACHIEVE 1

4 to criticize (someone) severely or angrily especially for personal failings ⟨*scored* her for failing to report the incident immediately⟩ — see SCOLD

scorn *n* open dislike for someone or something considered unworthy of one's concern or respect ⟨has nothing but *scorn* for newfangled ideas of any kind⟩ — see CONTEMPT

scorn *vb* 1 to show contempt for ⟨*scorned* the religious traditions of their ancestors⟩

synonyms disdain, high-hat, slight, sniff (at), snub

related words scout; abhor, despise, detest, hate, loathe; disapprove (of), discountenance, disfavor, frown (on *or* upon)

phrases look down on, sneeze at

near antonyms cherish, prize, treasure, value; admire, esteem; revere, venerate, worship; accept, appreciate, approve (of), care (for), countenance, favor, OK (*or* okay), subscribe (to)

antonyms honor, respect

2 to ignore in a disrespectful manner ⟨she *scorned* the suggestions of her classmates for the parade float⟩

synonyms despise, disregard, flout

related words dismiss, forget, ignore, neglect, overlook, overpass, pass over, slight, slur (over)

near antonyms accept, approve; use

scorner *n* a person who causes repeated emotional pain, distress, or annoyance to another ⟨his many *scorners* looked silly when he succeeded in getting himself elected governor⟩ — see TORMENTOR

scornful *adj* 1 feeling or showing open dislike for someone or something regarded as undeserving of respect or concern ⟨gave the other science projects a *scornful* look and stalked off⟩ — see CONTEMPTUOUS 1

2 intended to make a person or thing seem of little importance or value ⟨in response to my complaint of a sprained ankle, came the *scornful* reply, "You should experience a broken leg sometime"⟩ — see DEROGATORY

Scot *n* a person born or living in Scotland ⟨my grandfather was a *Scot*, but my grandmother was Welsh⟩

synonyms Scotchman, Scotsman, Scottie

Scotch *adj* of, relating to, or characteristic of the people of Scotland ⟨the wearing of kilts is a *Scotch* custom⟩ — see SCOTTISH

Scotchman *n* a person born or living in Scotland ⟨*Scotchmen* are quite content to let tourists look for the Loch Ness monster⟩ — see SCOT

Scots *adj* of, relating to, or characteristic of the people of Scotland ⟨a thick *Scots* burr⟩ — see SCOTTISH

Scotsman *n* a person born or living in Scotland ⟨a *Scotsman* enjoying a traditional Scottish meal⟩ — see SCOT

Scottie *n* a person born or living in Scotland ⟨*Scotties* cheering for their country at the Olympics⟩ — see SCOT

Scottish *adj* of, relating to, or characteristic of the people of Scotland ⟨golf was originally a *Scottish* game⟩
synonyms Scotch, Scots

scoundrel *n* a mean, evil, or unprincipled person ⟨some *scoundrel* stole my wallet⟩ — see VILLAIN

scour *vb* to look through (as a place) carefully or thoroughly in an effort to find or discover something ⟨Prince Charming *scoured* the kingdom in hopes of finding the woman who fit the glass slipper⟩ — see SEARCH 1

scourge *n* 1 a long thin or flexible tool for striking ⟨brutally struck the donkey with a *scourge*⟩ — see WHIP 1
2 one who inflicts punishment in return for an injury or offense ⟨a superhero who is the *scourge* of evildoers everywhere⟩ — see NEMESIS 1

scourge *vb* 1 to bring destruction to (something) through violent action ⟨barbarians *scourged* the countryside, leaving village after village burned to the ground⟩ — see RAVAGE
2 to strike repeatedly with something long and thin or flexible ⟨*scourge* the tree with a whip to loosen the bark⟩ — see WHIP 1

scout *n* a member of the human race ⟨you're a good *scout*⟩ — see HUMAN

scout *vb* to make (someone or something) the object of unkind laughter ⟨*scouted* the child's claim of dragons living under his bed⟩ — see RIDICULE

scout (up) *vb* to come upon after searching, study, or effort ⟨I think I've *scouted up* a way for us to manage this⟩ — see FIND 1

scowl *n* a twisting of the facial features in disgust or disapproval ⟨the man across the street never seems to wear anything but a *scowl*⟩ — see GRIMACE

scowl *vb* to look with anger or disapproval ⟨*scowled* down at the misbehaving child⟩ — see FROWN

scrabble *n* a forceful effort to reach a goal or objective ⟨it'll be a long *scrabble* to pull ourselves out of poverty⟩ — see STRUGGLE 1

scraggly *adj* having an uneven edge or outline ⟨a *scraggly* little tree⟩ — see RAGGED 1

scraggy *adj* 1 having an uneven edge or outline ⟨a *scraggy* beard⟩ — see RAGGED 1
2 not having a level or smooth surface ⟨climbers scraped their limbs on the *scraggy* cliffs⟩ — see UNEVEN 1

scramble *n* an unorganized collection or mixture of various things ⟨a *scramble* of pens and pencils in the desk drawer⟩ — see MISCELLANY 1

scramble *vb* 1 to move (as up or over something) often with the help of the hands in holding or pulling ⟨the toddler *scrambled* up the stairs⟩ — see CLIMB 1
2 to undo the proper order or arrangement of ⟨*scrambled* the letters of the word⟩ — see DISORDER

¹**scrap** *n* 1 an unused or unwanted piece or item typically of small size or value ⟨only a *scrap* of silk was left on the sewing table after they had finished the project⟩
synonyms end, fag end, leftover, oddment, remainder, remnant, stub
related words leavings, odds and ends, remains, residual, residue, scraping(s), stump; balance, rest; chip, flake, fragment, piece, sliver, splinter; ribbon(s), shred, tatter

near antonyms whole
2 a broken or irregular part of something that often remains incomplete ⟨a *scrap* of paper fluttered to the floor⟩ — see FRAGMENT
3 a physical dispute between opposing individuals or groups ⟨the sisters got into a *scrap* over their favorite toy, both tugging at it until it broke⟩ — see FIGHT 1
4 a very small piece ⟨brushed away a *scrap* of lint⟩ — see BIT 1
5 discarded or useless material ⟨the rest of this stuff is just *scrap*, so sweep it up and throw it away⟩ — see GARBAGE

²**scrap** *n* an often noisy or angry expression of differing opinions ⟨the state legislature's annual *scrap* over the budget⟩ — see ARGUMENT 1

¹**scrap** *vb* to express different opinions about something often angrily ⟨the couple often *scrapped* about money and their spending habits⟩ — see ARGUE 2

²**scrap** *vb* to get rid of as useless or unwanted ⟨we've decided to *scrap* the second car⟩ — see DISCARD

scrape *n* 1 a brief clash between enemies or rivals ⟨got into a *scrape* that almost led to violence⟩ — see ENCOUNTER
2 a harsh grating sound ⟨the *scrape* of a shovel on concrete⟩ — see RASP

scrape *vb* 1 to pass roughly and noisily over or against a surface ⟨the rusty old gate *scraped* whenever anyone managed to open it⟩
synonyms grate, grind, rasp, scratch
related words rub; groan, whine
near antonyms glide, skate, slide
2 to damage by rubbing against a sharp or rough surface ⟨she *scraped* her knee when she fell down⟩
synonyms abrade, graze, scratch, scuff
related words bark, skin; chafe, fret, gall; claw, cut, lacerate; bruise, contuse
near antonyms polish, smooth, soften, wax
3 to get with great difficulty ⟨we're *scraping* out a living on the farm⟩ — see EKE OUT
4 to press or strike against or together so as to make a scraping sound ⟨*scraped* a rock along the fence as he walked⟩ — see GRIND 2

scrape (together) *vb* to bring together in one body or place ⟨I think I can *scrape together* enough people for a decent party⟩ — see GATHER 1

scrappiness *n* an inclination to fight or quarrel ⟨his ingrained *scrappiness* is always getting him into trouble at school⟩ — see BELLIGERENCE

scrapping *n* the getting rid of whatever is unwanted or useless ⟨the *scrapping* of the park's last horse-drawn carriage marks the end of an era⟩ — see DISPOSAL 1

scrappy *adj* 1 feeling or displaying eagerness to fight ⟨she was a *scrappy* girl despite—or, perhaps, because of—her small size⟩ — see BELLIGERENT
2 given to arguing ⟨a pair of *scrappy* movie critics who can never agree on anything⟩ — see ARGUMENTATIVE 1

scratch *n* a harsh grating sound ⟨the *scratch* of metal on metal is not a good sound for a car to make⟩ — see RASP

scratch *vb* 1 to damage by rubbing against a sharp or rough surface ⟨*scratched* his arm on a branch⟩ — see SCRAPE 2
2 to pass roughly and noisily over or against a surface ⟨*scratched* the chalk down the blackboard⟩ — see SCRAPE 1
3 to write or draw hastily or carelessly ⟨*scratched* a quick doodle in the margins⟩ — see SCRIBBLE

scratch (out) *vb* **1** to compose and set down on paper the words of ⟨*scratched out* a poem for his beloved⟩ — see WRITE 1
2 to show (something written) to be no longer valid by drawing a cross over or a line through it ⟨*scratched out* the old phone number and wrote in the new one⟩ — see X (OUT)

scratchy *adj* **1** likely to cause a scratch ⟨*scratchy* shrubbery that's intended to keep kids and pets off the old man's property⟩
synonyms brambly, prickly, thistly, thorny
related words burred; coarse, jagged, rough; irritating, itchy, stinging
near antonyms polished, smooth, soft, soothing; gentle
2 harsh and dry in sound ⟨her voice was *scratchy* from a cold⟩ — see HOARSE

scrawl *vb* to write or draw hastily or carelessly ⟨*scrawled* a quick note, stuck it in their mailbox, and hurried off⟩ — see SCRIBBLE

scream *n* someone or something that is very funny ⟨that new comedy is a *scream*⟩
synonyms laugh, riot
related words howler; crack, gag, jest, joke, pleasantry, quip, sally, waggery, wisecrack, witticism; caution, sight
near antonyms bummer, downer

scream *vb* to cry out loudly and emotionally ⟨we *screamed* when the roller coaster began its thirty foot plunge⟩
synonyms howl, screech, shriek, shrill, squall, squeal, yelp, yell
related words bay, caterwaul, keen, squawk, wail, yawp (*or* yaup), yowl; bawl, call, cry, holler, shout, vociferate
near antonyms murmur, mutter, whisper

screaming *adj* **1** arousing a strong and usually superficial interest or emotional reaction ⟨*screaming* headlines about the war overseas⟩ — see SENSATIONAL 1
2 causing or intended to cause laughter ⟨a *screaming* picture of everyone making silly faces⟩ — see FUNNY 1

screech *vb* to cry out loudly and emotionally ⟨the little girl *screeched* in pain upon stubbing her toe⟩ — see SCREAM

screeching *adj* having a high musical pitch or range ⟨the *screeching* blast of the factory whistle hurt my ears⟩ — see SHRILL

screen *n* **1** the art or business of making a movie ⟨he was a star of both the stage and the *screen*⟩ — see MOVIE 2
2 means or method of defending ⟨many animals use mimicry as a *screen* against predators⟩ — see DEFENSE 1

screen *vb* **1** to drive danger or attack away from ⟨the whole class was in a conspiracy to *screen* the student responsible for pulling the prank⟩ — see DEFEND 1
2 to keep secret or shut off from view ⟨bushes *screened* the swimming pool from passersby on the street⟩ — see ¹HIDE 2
3 to pass through a filter ⟨*screened* the cooking oil to remove impurities⟩ — see STRAIN 2
4 to place a protective layer over ⟨*screened* his eyes with his hand to block the sun⟩ — see COVER 3

screenplay *n* the written form of a story prepared for film production ⟨each actor was given a copy of the *screenplay* to study⟩
synonyms scenario, script
related words story, text

screw *vb* to twist (something) out of a natural or normal shape or condition ⟨*screwed* up his face at the taste of the medicine⟩ — see CONTORT

screwball *adj* showing or marked by a lack of good sense or judgment ⟨she's always off on some *screwball* plan⟩ — see FOOLISH 1

screwball *n* a person of odd or whimsical habits ⟨a *screwball* who liked to save lint and bits of string⟩ — see ECCENTRIC

screwing *n* the twisting of something out of its natural or normal shape or condition ⟨you'll regret the constant *screwing* of your face—someday it's going to freeze in that position!⟩ — see CONTORTION

screwlike *adj* turning around an axis like the thread of a screw ⟨performed a *screwlike* dive into the pool⟩ — see SPIRAL

screwy *adj* **1** different from the ordinary in a way that causes curiosity or suspicion ⟨a *screwy* comment that made everyone else in the audience turn and stare⟩ — see ODD 2
2 having or showing a very abnormal or sick state of mind ⟨some *screwy* delusion that the attendants wanted to eat him⟩ — see INSANE 1

scribble *vb* to write or draw hastily or carelessly ⟨she *scribbled* a quick note on the pad by the door before leaving⟩
synonyms scratch, scrawl
related words doodle; jot (down); ink, inscribe, letter, pen, pencil, print, write

scribe *n* a person whose job is to keep records ⟨the *scribe* keeps the minutes of the club's meetings⟩ — see CLERK 1

scribe *vb* to mark with or as if with a line or groove ⟨carefully *scribed* two lines into the wood⟩ — see SCORE 1

scrimmage *n* a physical dispute between opposing individuals or groups ⟨the two players got into a *scrimmage* off the court and got suspended⟩ — see FIGHT 1

scrimmage (with) *vb* to oppose (someone) in physical conflict ⟨*scrimmaged with* the bully and retrieved his books⟩ — see FIGHT 1

scrimp *vb* to avoid unnecessary waste or expense ⟨had to *scrimp* and save for years in order to be able to afford a house⟩ — see ECONOMIZE

scrimping *adj* careful in the management of money or resources ⟨a *scrimping* homemaker⟩ — see FRUGAL

scrimping *n* careful management of material resources ⟨dedicated *scrimping* enabled him to buy a new car⟩ — see ECONOMY

script *n* **1** the form or style of a particular person's writing ⟨has a neat, careful *script* with delicate loops⟩ — see HANDWRITING 1
2 the written form of a story prepared for film production ⟨sold two *scripts* to the movie studio⟩ — see SCREENPLAY
3 writing done by hand ⟨sending a thank-you note in *script*—and not just an e-mail—is the only proper way to express one's gratitude⟩ — see HANDWRITING 2

Scripture *n* a book made up of the writings accepted by Christians as coming from God ⟨one of the greatest commands from *Scripture* is "Love thy neighbor"⟩ — see BIBLE

scrooge *n* a mean grasping person who is usually stingy with money ⟨don't be such a *scrooge*—you can afford an ice cream cone!⟩ — see MISER

scrounge *vb* to get with great difficulty ⟨*scrounged* up an extra textbook from the school basement⟩ — see EKE OUT

scrub *n* a living thing much smaller than others of its kind 〈the little tree out front is a *scrub*〉 — see DWARF 1

scruffy *adj* showing signs of advanced wear and tear and neglect 〈dressed in *scruffy* old clothes to clean out the garage〉 — see SHABBY 1

scrumptious *adj* very pleasing to the sense of taste 〈baked a *scrumptious* chocolate cake〉 — see DELICIOUS 1

scrunch *vb* **1** to create (as by crushing) an irregular mass of creases in 〈*scrunched* up the shirt and tossed it in the laundry〉 — see CRUMPLE 1

2 to lie low with the limbs close to the body 〈*scrunched* down in her chair and hoped the teacher wouldn't notice her〉 — see CROUCH

3 to press or strike against or together so as to make a scraping sound 〈*scrunched* loose gravel with every footstep〉 — see GRIND 2

scruple *n* **1** a very small amount 〈went about her business without even a *scruple* of suspicion〉 — see PARTICLE 1

2 a very small piece 〈left just a *scruple* of asparagus on the plate〉 — see BIT 1

3 an uneasy feeling about the rightness of what one is doing or going to do 〈having some *scruples* about accepting help on his science project〉 — see QUALM

scrupulous *adj* guided by or in accordance with one's sense of right and wrong 〈made a *scrupulous* decision never to cheat〉 — see CONSCIENTIOUS 1

scrupulousness *n* strict attentiveness to what one is doing 〈the admirable *scrupulousness* with which they performed every step of the experiment〉 — see CARE 1

scrutinize *vb* to look over closely (as for judging quality or condition) 〈*scrutinized* every last science project before awarding the prizes〉 — see INSPECT

scrutiny *n* a close look at or over someone or something in order to judge condition 〈the students squirmed under the intense *scrutiny* of the judges〉 — see INSPECTION

scuff *vb* **1** to damage by rubbing against a sharp or rough surface 〈*scuffed* up her shoes by rubbing her feet under the rung of the chair〉 — see SCRAPE 2

2 to move heavily or clumsily 〈he *scuffed* past in heavy boots〉 — see LUMBER 1

scuffle *n* a physical dispute between opposing individuals or groups 〈several chairs were knocked over in the *scuffle*〉 — see FIGHT 1

scuffle *vb* **1** to move heavily or clumsily 〈she *scuffled* along in too-large shoes〉 — see LUMBER 1

2 to seize and attempt to unbalance one another for the purpose of achieving physical mastery 〈the burglar and the homeowner briefly *scuffled* together in the dark〉 — see WRESTLE

scull *vb* to move a boat by means of oars 〈a couple *sculled* past in a racing shell〉 — see ¹ROW

sculler *n* a person who drives a boat forward by means of oars 〈*scullers* tend to have well-developed arm muscles〉 — see OARSMAN

sculpt *vb* to create a three-dimensional representation of (something) using solid material 〈I *sculpted* a figure of a giraffe out of clay in art class today〉

synonyms carve, sculpture

related words chisel, engrave, etch, grave, incise, inscribe; cast, form, model, mold, shape

sculpture *vb* to create a three-dimensional representation of (something) using solid material 〈*sculptured* a horse out of ice〉 — see SCULPT

scum *n* people looked down upon as ignorant and of the lowest class 〈claimed that only *scum* lived in that part of town〉 — see RABBLE

scummy *adj* arousing or deserving of one's loathing and disgust 〈a *scummy* attempt to steal a younger child's lunch money〉 — see CONTEMPTIBLE 1

scurry *vb* to proceed or move quickly 〈everyone *scurried* off to the next class as soon as the bell rang〉 — see HURRY 2

scurvy *adj* arousing or deserving of one's loathing and disgust 〈for a *scurvy* trick like that you deserve to be severely punished〉 — see CONTEMPTIBLE 1

scuttle *vb* to proceed or move quickly 〈mice *scuttling* across the floor to escape the cats〉 — see HURRY 2

sea *n* the whole body of salt water that covers nearly three-fourths of the earth 〈millions of plants and animals live in the *sea*〉 — see OCEAN

sea devil *n* any of several extremely large rays 〈a *sea devil* glided along the ocean floor〉 — see DEVILFISH

sea dog *n* one who operates or navigates a seagoing vessel 〈a couple of *sea dogs* sharing a drink and talking about their seafaring adventures〉 — see SAILOR

seafarer *n* one who operates or navigates a seagoing vessel 〈an old *seafarer* who always walked with an oddly rolling gait whenever he was on land〉 — see SAILOR

seam *vb* to mark with or as if with a line or groove 〈in fencing circles it is a mark of honor to have one's face *seamed* with saber cuts〉 — see SCORE 1

seaman *n* one who operates or navigates a seagoing vessel 〈a weathered old *seaman* who now captains a tour boat〉 — see SAILOR

sear *vb* **1** to burn on the surface 〈lightly *seared* the steaks, but didn't cook them all the way through〉 — see SCORCH

2 to make dry 〈the hot wind was *searing* my eyes, constantly making me blink〉 — see DRY 1

search *n* an act or process of looking carefully or thoroughly for someone or something 〈the *search* for the lost puppy took hours〉

synonyms hunt, quest

related words chase, pursuit; reconnaissance, scout; canvas, survey; exploration, probe, forage

search *vb* **1** to look through (as a place) carefully or thoroughly in an effort to find or discover something 〈we *searched* the closet for half an hour until we found the missing shoe〉

synonyms comb, dig (through), dredge, hunt (through), rake, ransack, rifle, rummage, scour

related words audit, check (out), examine, inspect, investigate, review, scan, scrutinize, survey; ascertain, descry, detect, determine, discover, ferret (out), find, find out, get, hit (on *or* upon), learn, locate, run down, scare up, track (down); explore, probe, prospect, skirmish, snoop; browse, glance (over), look over; peruse, study

near antonyms hide; abandon, lose; ignore, neglect

2 to go into or range over for purposes of discovery 〈the Spanish conquistadors *searched* vast areas of the Southwest in their quest for the fabled cities of gold〉 — see EXPLORE 2

search (for *or* out) *vb* to go in search of 〈the knight set off to *search for* the princess being held captive by a dragon〉 — see SEEK 1

searing *adj* having a notably high temperature 〈the baby usually wore only a diaper on *searing* days〉 — see HOT 1

season *vb* **1** to make more pleasant to the taste by adding something intensely flavored ⟨the chef *seasoned* the vegetables as soon as they came out of the oven⟩
synonyms flavor, savor, spice
related words enhance, enrich, sauce; salt, pepper
2 to bring to a proper or desired state of fitness ⟨carefully *seasoned* the frying pan with vegetable oil before using it for the first time⟩ — see CONDITION 1
3 to make able to withstand physical hardship, strain, or exposure ⟨troops that had been *seasoned* by months of heavy fighting⟩ — see HARDEN 2
4 to make competent (as by training, skill, or ability) for a particular office or function ⟨her campaign manager is a *seasoned* veteran of several gubernatorial campaigns⟩ — see QUALIFY 2

seasonable *adj* especially suitable for a certain time ⟨*seasonable* advice is more likely to be listened to⟩ — see TIMELY 1

seasoning *n* **1** something (as a spice or herb) that adds an agreeable or interesting taste to food ⟨the stew was too bland before they added the *seasoning*⟩
synonyms flavor, flavoring, spice
related words sauce
2 something used to enhance the flavor of cooked or prepared food ⟨she thinks salt is the ideal *seasoning* for nearly everything⟩ — see CONDIMENT

seat *n* **1** a place from which authority is exercised ⟨all applications had to be submitted at the county *seat* for proper processing⟩
synonyms command, headquarters
related words center, home; capital
2 the part of the body upon which someone sits ⟨fell down on his well-padded *seat*⟩ — see BUTTOCKS
3 a thing or place that is of greatest importance to an activity or interest ⟨a capital that is the *seat* of culture for the whole nation⟩ — see CENTER 1

seat *vb* to cause to sit down ⟨the usher *seated* them in the third row⟩
synonyms set down, sit
related words ensconce, settle; lay, lie, rest; place, put; recline, repose

seclude *vb* to set or keep apart from others ⟨*secluded* the patients until they were no longer contagious⟩ — see ISOLATE

secluded *adj* hidden from view ⟨we stayed in a *secluded* resort, far away from the regular tourist crowds⟩
synonyms cloistered, covert, isolated, quiet, remote, retired, secret, sheltered
related words lonely, reclusive, solitary; private
near antonyms obvious, visible; exposed

secludedness *n* the state of being alone or kept apart from others ⟨the inn's greatest appeal for guests was its woodland *secludedness*⟩ — see ISOLATION

seclusion *n* the state of being alone or kept apart from others ⟨she went into *seclusion* in order to focus entirely on writing her book⟩ — see ISOLATION

second *n* a very small space of time ⟨I'll be ready in a *second*⟩ — see INSTANT

secondary *adj* **1** taken or created from something original or basic ⟨history textbooks are *secondary* sources for historical information and do not represent original research⟩
synonyms derivative, secondhand
related words unoriginal; consequent, resultant
near antonyms fundamental, nonderivative; first, primary
antonyms basic, original

2 of little or less value or merit ⟨while we were rushing to the hospital, I was worried about the car breaking down, but that was a *secondary* concern⟩ — see INFERIOR 2

second–class *adj* of little or less value or merit ⟨produced only *second-class* work⟩ — see INFERIOR 2

secondhand *adj* taken or created from something original or basic ⟨memoirs filled with *secondhand* stories about show-business celebrities⟩ — see SECONDARY 1

second–rate *adj* **1** of average to below average quality ⟨a *second-rate* song from a songwriter who has done much better⟩ — see MEDIOCRE 1
2 of little or less value or merit ⟨a *second-rate* company that was never considered among the top manufacturers of televisions⟩ — see INFERIOR 2
3 of low quality ⟨*second-rate* goods specifically manufactured for the low end of the market⟩ — see CHEAP 2

secrecy *n* the practice or habit of keeping secrets or keeping one's affairs secret ⟨in picking helpers for a surprise party, you'd very much want to choose people known for their *secrecy*⟩
synonyms closeness, secretiveness
related words discreetness, discretion, prudence; circumspection, wariness; reserve, reticence, silence, taciturnity; furtiveness, shiftiness, slyness, sneakiness, underhandedness; concealment, stealth, subterfuge
near antonyms candor, frankness, honesty, openness; imprudence, indiscretion

secret *adj* **1** undertaken or done so as to escape being observed or known by others ⟨a *secret* operation to rescue captive soldiers behind enemy lines⟩
synonyms clandestine, covert, furtive, hugger-mugger, private, privy, sneak, sneaking, sneaky, stealthy, surreptitious, undercover, underground, underhand, underhanded
related words classified, confidential, restricted, top secret, undisclosed; concealed, hidden, secreted, subterranean, unadvertised, unexposed
near antonyms acknowledged, avowed; aboveboard, straightforward, unconcealed, undisguised; unclassified, unrestricted; clear, evident, manifest, obvious, patent, plain
antonyms open, overt, public
2 working on missions in which one's objectives, activities, or true identity are not publicly revealed ⟨*secret* agents whose wartime exploits were known only by top government officials⟩
synonyms undercover
related words covert, private, secretive, subterranean
near antonyms overt
3 hidden from view ⟨a *secret* cave that is screened by trees⟩ — see SECLUDED
4 not known or meant to be known by the general populace ⟨*secret* information that its business rivals would love to have⟩ — see PRIVATE 1

secret *n* **1** information shared only with another or with a select few ⟨they're best friends and are constantly sharing *secrets*⟩
synonyms confidence
related words dope, lowdown
near antonyms open secret
2 something hard to understand or explain ⟨the *secrets* of the Egyptian pyramids include the construction methods used to lift the huge blocks of stone in place⟩ — see MYSTERY

secrete *vb* to put into a hiding place ⟨*secreted* jewels in the mattress⟩ — see ¹HIDE 1

secretion *n* the placing of something out of sight ⟨the *secretion* of their money in the backyard turned out to be a huge mistake⟩ — see CONCEALMENT 1

secretive *adj* given to keeping one's activities hidden from public observation or knowledge ⟨the intelligence agency remained *secretive* despite the media's demands for more openness in government⟩

synonyms close, closemouthed, dark, reticent, uncommunicative

related words quiet, reserved, silent, taciturn, tight-lipped; discreet, prudent; clandestine, covert, furtive, hugger-mugger, secret, sneak, sneaky, stealthy, surreptitious, undercover, underhand, underhanded

near antonyms candid, frank, honest; blunt, outspoken, tactless

antonyms communicative, open

secretiveness *n* the practice or habit of keeping secrets or keeping one's affairs secret ⟨his *secretiveness* always made some people suspicious of what he might be hiding⟩ — see SECRECY

sect *n* a group of people acting together within a larger group ⟨one *sect* of medical researchers holds the minority view that the disease is not caused by that virus⟩ — see FACTION

sectarian *adj* not broad or open in views or opinions ⟨a man with a *sectarian* mind that would not allow him to see that society is always evolving⟩ — see NARROW 2

section *n* **1** an area (as of a city) set apart for some purpose or having some special feature ⟨the cultural *section* of the city is home to several museums⟩ — see DISTRICT

2 one of the pieces from which something is designed to be assembled ⟨had trouble fitting the *sections* of the bookcase together⟩ — see PART 1

secular *adj* not involving religion or religious matters ⟨that's an issue for the *secular* authorities, not the church⟩ — see PROFANE 1

secure *adj* **1** firmly positioned in place and difficult to dislodge ⟨tried to pry the rock out of the pipe, but it was *secure*⟩ — see TIGHT 2

2 having or showing great faith in oneself or one's abilities ⟨he's so *secure* about winning the marathon that he's practically spent the prize money⟩ — see CONFIDENT 1

3 not exposed to the threat of loss or injury ⟨the fortress was *secure* against attack⟩ — see SAFE 1

4 providing safety ⟨escaped to a *secure* location⟩ — see SAFE 2

secure *vb* **1** to drive danger or attack away from ⟨sent troops to *secure* the city⟩ — see DEFEND 1

2 to make sure, certain, or safe ⟨believed that we'd *secured* our future⟩ — see ENSURE

3 to put securely in place or in a desired position ⟨candidates for admission are asked to *secure* a recent photo to their application forms⟩ — see FASTEN 2

4 to receive as return for effort ⟨*secured* a job after sending out dozens of applications⟩ — see EARN 1

security *n* **1** means or method of defending ⟨measures taken to beef up our national *security*⟩ — see DEFENSE 1

2 something given or held to assure that the giver will keep a promise ⟨he left his credit card as a *security* that he'd return the car⟩ — see PLEDGE 1

3 the state of not being exposed to danger ⟨only a search of the entire room for monsters would reassure the child of her *security*⟩ — see SAFETY 1

sedate *adj* not joking or playful in mood or manner ⟨a *sedate*, older woman who didn't enjoy pranks⟩ — see SERIOUS 1

sedative *adj* tending to calm the emotions and relieve stress ⟨some people find a glass of wine to be a civilized and *sedative* addition to an evening meal⟩ — see SOOTHING 1

sediment *n* matter that settles to the bottom of a body of liquid ⟨the thick layer of *sediment* at the bottom of a cup of hot chocolate⟩ — see DEPOSIT 1

sediment *vb* to cause to come to rest at the bottom (as of a liquid) ⟨shaking the bottle of lemonade kept it from *sedimenting* the pulp before I could drink it⟩ — see SETTLE 1

seduce *vb* to lead away from a usual or proper course by offering some pleasure or advantage ⟨the pleasant spring day *seduced* me away from my work⟩ — see LURE

seducer *n* one that tries to get a person to give in to a desire ⟨my playful sister was always the *seducer*, tempting me to fool around when I should have been cleaning up my room⟩ — see TEMPTER

seduction *n* the act or pressure of giving in to a desire especially when ill-advised ⟨the *seduction* of the college freshman into a life of drinking and partying⟩ — see TEMPTATION 1

seductive *adj* having an often mysterious or magical power to attract ⟨people always remarked on the cult leader's *seductive* eyes⟩ — see FASCINATING 1

seductiveness *n* the power of irresistible attraction ⟨her sexy *seductiveness* enabled her to attract—and eventually marry—a succession of six men⟩ — see CHARM 2

seductress *n* a woman whom men find irresistibly attractive ⟨in the movie she played Cleopatra, one of history's most famous *seductresses*⟩ — see SIREN

sedulous *adj* involved in often constant activity ⟨an impressively *sedulous* suitor, he was constantly sending her flowers and other tokens of his affection⟩ — see BUSY 1

sedulously *adv* with great effort or determination ⟨*sedulously* devoted herself to completing the project on time⟩ — see HARD 1

see *vb* **1** to make note of (something) through the use of one's eyes ⟨out of the corner of my eye I *saw* the deer run into the woods⟩

synonyms behold, descry, discern, distinguish, espy, eye, look (at), note, notice, observe, perceive, regard, remark, sight, spy, view, witness

related words identify, make out, pick out; attend (to), consider, heed, mark, mind; study, watch; examine, inspect, scan, scrutinize, survey; glance (at), glimpse, peer (at)

phrases get a load of [*slang*], lay eyes on, set eyes on

near antonyms disregard, ignore, neglect, overpass, pass over; miss, overlook

2 to come to a knowledge of (something) by living through it ⟨a writer who *saw* World War II through the eyes of a common soldier⟩ — see EXPERIENCE

3 to come to an awareness ⟨their parents would eventually *see* that they were meant for each other⟩ — see DISCOVER 1

4 to have a vague awareness of ⟨I *see* a certain sadness in his letters to his relatives back home⟩ — see FEEL 1

5 to make a social call upon ⟨plans to *see* the new mother and of course admire the cute baby⟩ — see VISIT 1

6 to recognize the meaning of ⟨I *see* your point⟩ — see COMPREHEND 1

seeable *adj* capable of being seen ⟨a *seeable* flaw in the windowpane⟩ — see VISIBLE

seed *n* the descendants of a person, animal, or plant ⟨the famous stallion's *seed* can be found on racetracks all over the world⟩ — see OFFSPRING

seed *vb* to put or set into the ground to grow ⟨*seeded* grass in the backyard⟩ — see PLANT

seediness *n* the state of being unattended to or not cared for ⟨the general *seediness* of the neighborhood suggested that its residents had no pride⟩ — see NEGLECT 1

seedy *adj* 1 showing signs of advanced wear and tear and neglect ⟨a *seedy* neighborhood that's just waiting for some new homeowners to come in and rehabilitate it⟩ — see SHABBY 1

2 worn or torn into or as if into rags ⟨chose old, *seedy* clothes to wear while painting the bathroom⟩ — see RAGGED 2

seeing *conj* for the reason that ⟨*seeing* as we're already running late, there's no reason to waste any more time⟩ — see SINCE

seek *vb* 1 to go in search of ⟨the knights of the Round Table fervently *sought* the Holy Grail⟩

synonyms cast about (for), cast around (for), forage (for), hunt, look up, pursue, quest, search (for *or* out)

related words ferret (out), root (out)

phrases look for

near antonyms hide, lose; ignore, neglect

2 to make a request for ⟨came *seeking* advice⟩ — see ASK (FOR) 1

3 to make an effort to do ⟨*seek* to find the best solution⟩ — see ATTEMPT

seeker *n* one who seeks an office, honor, position, or award ⟨predicted a tough year for summer job *seekers*⟩ — see CANDIDATE

seem *vb* to give the impression of being ⟨I tried to cheer them up because they *seemed* depressed⟩

synonyms act, appear, look, make, sound

related words dissemble, pretend; resemble, suggest; hint, imply, insinuate

seeming *adj* appearing to be true on the basis of evidence that may or may not be confirmed ⟨a *seeming* contradiction that disappeared upon closer analysis⟩ — see APPARENT 1

seemingly *adv* to all outward appearances ⟨a *seemingly* contented baby who was fast asleep in his crib⟩ — see APPARENTLY

seemliness *n* the quality or state of being especially suitable or fitting ⟨the *seemliness* of that outfit for church is debatable⟩ — see APPROPRIATENESS

seemly *adj* following the established traditions of refined society and good taste ⟨a *seemly* choice of china and place settings for the formal dinner party⟩ — see PROPER 1

seep *vb* to flow forth slowly through small openings ⟨water *seeping* through the basement walls⟩ — see EXUDE

seer *n* one who predicts future events or developments ⟨religiously follows the suggestions of a Wall Street *seer* who claims to know what the stock market will do⟩ — see PROPHET

seesaw *vb* 1 to make a series of unsteady side-to-side motions ⟨as their boat *seesawed* in the rough water, the rescue team tried to get the passengers off the sinking ship⟩ — see ROCK 1

2 to make short up-and-down movements ⟨the price of the stock has been *seesawing* all week⟩ — see NOD

seethe *vb* 1 to be in a state of violent rolling motion ⟨the water *seethed* with schools of feeding piranha⟩

synonyms boil, churn, roil

related words reel, spin, swirl, whirl; agitate, stir

near antonyms abate, calm, subside

2 to be excited or emotionally stirred up with anger ⟨she *seethed* at the very thought of the staff's staggering incompetence⟩ — see BOIL 1

segment *n* one of the pieces from which something is designed to be assembled ⟨I think I lost one *segment* of this model kit⟩ — see PART 1

segregate *vb* to set or keep apart from others ⟨*segregated* the misbehaving child for five minutes⟩ — see ISOLATE

segregation *n* the state of being alone or kept apart from others ⟨the forced *segregation* of racial minorities was once widely accepted as a fact of life⟩ — see ISOLATION

seize *vb* 1 to recognize the meaning of ⟨an artist who *seizes* everyday reality and captures it on canvas⟩ — see COMPREHEND 1

2 to take or keep under one's control by authority of law ⟨*seized* the leaders of one of the city's major drug rings⟩ — see ARREST 1

3 to take physical control or possession of (something) suddenly or forcibly ⟨*seized* the escaping balloon⟩ — see CATCH 1

seizure *n* a sudden experiencing of a physical or mental disorder ⟨an epileptic *seizure*⟩ — see ATTACK 2

seldom *adv* not often ⟨we *seldom* go to the theater downtown because its prices are so high⟩

synonyms infrequently, little, rarely

related words ne'er, never

phrases hardly ever

near antonyms generally, usually; always, constantly, continuously, endlessly, eternally, ever, everlastingly, evermore, forever, invariably; recurrently, repeatedly

antonyms frequently, often

select *adj* 1 singled out from a number or group as more to one's liking ⟨they use only *select* beans to make their coffee⟩

synonyms chosen, elect, favored, picked, preferred, selected

related words fashionable; exclusive; culled, screened, weeded (out), winnowed (out)

near antonyms average, common, commonplace, ordinary, run-of-the-mill

2 having qualities that appeal to a refined taste ⟨*select* fabrics that the shop makes into expensive suits for its well-heeled clientele⟩ — see CHOICE

select *vb* to decide to accept (someone or something) from a group of possibilities ⟨*select* two people out of sixteen applicants⟩ — see CHOOSE 1

selected *adj* singled out from a number or group as more to one's liking ⟨a *selected* brand of ice cream⟩ — see SELECT 1

selecting *n* the act or process of selecting ⟨the *selecting* of the party's nominee took three days and a half dozen votes⟩ — see SELECTION 1

selection *n* 1 the act or process of selecting ⟨his *selection* of a running mate was a long, tedious affair⟩

synonyms choice, choosing, election, picking, selecting

related words option; appointment, assignment, designation, naming, nomination

2 a person or thing that is chosen ⟨our *selection* is the third entrant in the contest⟩ — see CHOICE 2

selective *adj* tending to select carefully ⟨we were highly *selective* about the music we listened to while trying out loudspeakers⟩

synonyms choosy (*or* choosey), particular, picky
related words fastidious, finicky, fussy; discerning, discriminating, judicious
near antonyms indiscriminate
antonyms nonselective

selector *n* someone with the right or responsibility for making a selection ⟨the librarians who are the *selectors* of the annual award for best children's book⟩
synonyms chooser, namer, picker
related words elector, voter

self–acting *adj* designed to replace or decrease human labor and ,especially physical labor ⟨*self-acting* machines that were ushered in with the industrial revolution⟩ — see LABORSAVING

self–admiration *n* an often unjustified feeling of being pleased with oneself or with one's situation or achievements ⟨his *self-admiration* blinded him to constructive criticism of any kind⟩ — see COMPLACENCE

self–assertive *adj* having or showing a bold forcefulness in the pursuit of a goal ⟨we need to hire *self-assertive* salespeople who don't require constant supervision⟩ — see AGGRESSIVE 1

self–assurance *n* great faith in oneself or one's abilities ⟨her *self-assurance* led her to quit her dead-end job and start her own company⟩ — see CONFIDENCE 1

self–assured *adj* having or showing great faith in oneself or one's abilities ⟨he's a *self-assured* and competent yachtsman⟩ — see CONFIDENT 1

self–centered *adj* overly concerned with one's own desires, needs, or interests ⟨a group of *self-centered* friends with no interest or involvement in their community⟩ — see EGOCENTRIC

self–centeredness *n* excessive interest in oneself ⟨in her extreme *self-centeredness* she hadn't even noticed that her friend was emotionally troubled⟩ — see EGOISM

self–conceit *n* an often unjustified feeling of being pleased with oneself or with one's situation or achievements ⟨the movie star became a victim of her own *self-conceit*, having deluded herself into believing that she was as great as her press agent said she was⟩ — see COMPLACENCE

self–conceited *adj* having too high an opinion of oneself ⟨a clique of *self-conceited* girls who thought that they ruled the school⟩ — see CONCEITED

self–confidence *n* great faith in oneself or one's abilities ⟨for so young an equestrian, she has remarkable composure and *self-confidence*⟩ — see CONFIDENCE 1

self–confident *adj* having or showing great faith in oneself or one's abilities ⟨only a *self-confident* person can win the trust of others and serve as an effective leader⟩ — see CONFIDENT 1

self–containment *n* the power to control one's actions, impulses, or emotions ⟨a man of extraordinary *self-containment*, he refused to lose his temper even in the most trying of circumstances⟩ — see WILL 1

self–control *n* 1 the power to control one's actions, impulses, or emotions ⟨toddlers have very little *self-control*⟩ — see WILL 1
2 the checking of one's true feelings and impulses when dealing with others ⟨she could be passionate and intense, but generally exercised *self-control* in the company of strangers⟩ — see CONSTRAINT 1

self–denial *n* the act or practice of giving up or rejecting something once enjoyed or desired ⟨dieting is an endless exercise in *self-denial*⟩ — see RENUNCIATION

self–destruction *n* the act of deliberately killing oneself ⟨the controversy over *self-destruction* accomplished with the assistance of a physician or other person⟩ — see SUICIDE

self–determination *n* the act or power of making one's own choices or decisions ⟨the United States officially recognizes 18 as the age at which someone is entitled to *self-determination*⟩ — see FREE WILL

self–discipline *n* the power to control one's actions, impulses, or emotions ⟨it takes *self-discipline* not to yell when someone makes you angry⟩ — see WILL 1

self–esteem *n* 1 a reasonable or justifiable sense of one's worth or importance ⟨friends and family have tried to help the shy child develop some *self-esteem*⟩ — see PRIDE 1
2 an often unjustified feeling of being pleased with oneself or with one's situation or achievements ⟨his towering *self-esteem* made praise from other people entirely unnecessary⟩ — see COMPLACENCE
3 great faith in oneself or one's abilities ⟨the kind of *self-esteem* that an actor needs to keep going in the face of constant discouragement and rejection⟩ — see CONFIDENCE 1

self–governing *adj* 1 not being under the rule or control of another ⟨she left home and became entirely *self-governing* and financially independent at the age of 18⟩ — see FREE 1
2 of, relating to, or favoring political democracy ⟨a *self-governing* nation⟩ — see DEMOCRATIC

self–government *n* 1 government in which the supreme power is held by the people and used by them directly or indirectly through representation ⟨the people revolted and overturned their ruler in favor of *self-government*⟩ — see DEMOCRACY
2 the power to control one's actions, impulses, or emotions ⟨*self-government* was all that kept her from lashing out⟩ — see WILL 1
3 the state of being free from the control or power of another ⟨children dream of *self-government*, but with that privilege comes responsibility⟩ — see FREEDOM 1

selfhood *n* the set of qualities that make a person different from other people ⟨he spent a year in a monastery determining the core of his *selfhood*⟩ — see INDIVIDUALITY

self–identity *n* the set of qualities that make a person different from other people ⟨twins making an effort to establish their separate *self-identities*⟩ — see INDIVIDUALITY

self–importance *n* 1 an exaggerated sense of one's importance that shows itself in the making of excessive or unjustified claims ⟨*self-importance* led to constant announcements that he was capable of doing impossible things⟩ — see ARROGANCE
2 an often unjustified feeling of being pleased with oneself or with one's situation or achievements ⟨her *self-importance* shone through her haughty bearing⟩ — see COMPLACENCE

self–important *adj* having too high an opinion of oneself ⟨a *self-important* businessman who believed his plans mattered more than anyone else's⟩ — see CONCEITED

self–interest *n* excessive interest in oneself ⟨her *self-interest* was reflected in her endless conversation about herself⟩ — see EGOISM

selfish *adj* overly concerned with one's own desires, needs, or interests ⟨a *selfish* desire to succeed at the expense of others⟩ — see EGOCENTRIC

selfishness *n* excessive interest in oneself ⟨the only reason for constantly ignoring everyone else's problems is *selfishness*⟩ — see EGOISM

self-possessed *adj* free from emotional or mental agitation ⟨a calm, *self-possessed* teacher who could handle any crisis⟩ — see CALM 2

self-possession *n* **1** evenness of emotions or temper ⟨his *self-possession* in the face of problems is legendary⟩ — see EQUANIMITY

2 the power to control one's actions, impulses, or emotions ⟨the little girl's *self-possession* very occasionally gave way to crying fits⟩ — see WILL 1

self-protective *adj* intended to resist or prevent attack or aggression ⟨a *self-protective* gesture to ward off the blow⟩ — see DEFENSIVE

self-regard *n* **1** excessive interest in oneself ⟨her *self-regard* meant that she assumed everyone wanted to hear about every tiny detail of her life⟩ — see EGOISM

2 a reasonable or justifiable sense of one's worth or importance ⟨people with enough *self-regard* to keep their modest home in spotless condition⟩ — see PRIDE 1

self-reliance *n* the ability to care for one's self ⟨some people don't achieve *self-reliance* until they're over 30 years old⟩ — see SELF-SUFFICIENCY

self-reliant *adj* able to take care of oneself without outside help ⟨a surprisingly calm and *self-reliant* child⟩ — see SELF-SUFFICIENT

self-reproach *n* a feeling of responsibility for wrongdoing ⟨he never got over his *self-reproach* for causing the accident⟩ — see GUILT 1

self-respect *n* a reasonable or justifiable sense of one's worth or importance ⟨getting a job and moving out did a lot to increase his *self-respect*⟩ — see PRIDE 1

self-restraint *n* **1** the power to control one's actions, impulses, or emotions ⟨she demonstrated a near-unnatural *self-restraint* during the fight⟩ — see WILL 1

2 the checking of one's true feelings and impulses when dealing with others ⟨we must practice *self-restraint* even with people who are deliberately rude⟩ — see CONSTRAINT 1

self-rule *n* government in which the supreme power is held by the people and used by them directly or indirectly through representation ⟨the newly created United States opted for *self-rule* rather than monarchy⟩ — see DEMOCRACY

self-ruling *adj* of, relating to, or favoring political democracy ⟨chose to be a *self-ruling* state⟩ — see DEMOCRATIC

selfsame *adj* being one and not another ⟨that's the *selfsame* man who once helped me⟩ — see SAME 2

self-satisfaction *n* an often unjustified feeling of being pleased with oneself or with one's situation or achievements ⟨radiated *self-satisfaction*⟩ — see COMPLACENCE

self-satisfied *adj* having too high an opinion of oneself ⟨a *self-satisfied* woman who thought that if she could balance two careers, everyone should⟩ — see CONCEITED

self-seeker *n* one who does things only for his own benefit and with little regard for right and wrong ⟨he was accused of being a *self-seeker*, of being nice only to people who could do him favors⟩

synonyms opportunist, temporizer

related words egoist, egotist; conniver, machinator, plotter, schemer

self-seeking *adj* **1** having a strong desire for personal advancement ⟨a *self-seeking* worker who claimed others' ideas and achievements as his own⟩ — see AMBITIOUS 1

2 overly concerned with one's own desires, needs, or interests ⟨a *self-seeking* woman who sidetracked all conversation into discussion of her problems⟩ — see EGOCENTRIC

self-starter *n* an ambitious person who eagerly goes after what is desired ⟨hired a *self-starter* who knew what needed to be done, and did it⟩ — see GO-GETTER

self-sufficiency *n* the ability to care for one's self ⟨*self-sufficiency* is a goal that all teenagers should work towards⟩

synonyms independence, self-reliance, self-support

related words autonomy, self-determination; potency, power, resilience, strength

near antonyms helplessness, impotence, inadequacy, weakness

antonyms dependence, reliance

self-sufficient *adj* able to take care of oneself without outside help ⟨the college student worked nights so that he would be *self-sufficient*⟩

synonyms independent, self-reliant, self-supporting

related words potent, powerful, resilient, strong

near antonyms helpless, inadequate, insufficient; impotent, weak

antonyms dependent, reliant

self-support *n* the ability to care for one's self ⟨the child with fifteen siblings learned *self-support* early⟩ — see SELF-SUFFICIENCY

self-supporting *adj* able to take care of oneself without outside help ⟨she had to take a higher-paying job in order to be *self-supporting*⟩ — see SELF-SUFFICIENT

self-will *n* a steadfast adherence to an opinion, purpose, or course of action ⟨a streak of *self-will* and rebellion⟩ — see OBSTINACY

self-willed *adj* sticking to an opinion, purpose, or course of action in spite of reason, arguments, or persuasion ⟨a *self-willed* toddler who refused to take her shoes off⟩ — see OBSTINATE

sell *vb* to offer for sale to the public ⟨*sell* groceries in a small market⟩ — see MARKET

sell (for) *vb* to have a price of ⟨the house finally *sold for* $100,000⟩ — see COST

sell (out) *vb* to be unfaithful or disloyal to ⟨the band *sold out* its faithful followers⟩ — see BETRAY 1

seller *n* the person in a business deal who hands over an item in exchange for money ⟨the *seller* ceremoniously gave me the title to the car when I handed him my check⟩ — see VENDOR

sellout *n* the act or fact of violating the trust or confidence of another ⟨the *sellout* makes it much harder for me to trust you again⟩ — see BETRAYAL

semblance *n* **1** a display of emotion or behavior that is insincere or intended to deceive ⟨some *semblance* of calm hid an inner turmoil⟩ — see MASQUERADE

2 outward and often deceptive indication ⟨a *semblance* of beauty⟩ — see APPEARANCE 2

semidarkness *n* a time or place of little or no light ⟨fumbling around in the *semidarkness*⟩ — see DARK 1

seminar *n* **1** a coming together of a number of persons for a specified purpose ⟨a *seminar* on financial management⟩ — see MEETING 1

2 a meeting featuring a group discussion ⟨a *seminar* to discuss the future of the group⟩ — see FORUM

seminary *n* a place or establishment for teaching and learning ⟨a *seminary* exclusively for women⟩ — see SCHOOL

send *vb* to cause to go or be taken from one place to another ⟨they promised to *send* the package in the morning⟩

synonyms consign, pack (off), ship, transfer, transmit, transport *related words* convey, deliver, hand over; advance, drop, launch, remit; address, forward; bestow, contribute, donate, give, present

near antonyms acquire, draw, earn, gain, garner, get, obtain, procure, secure

antonyms accept, receive

senior *adj* being of advanced years and especially past middle age ⟨bought special food intended for *senior* dogs⟩ — see ELDERLY

senior *n* **1** one who is older than another ⟨since the man next door is my *senior* by a number of years, I always address him as "Mr. Barton"⟩

synonyms elder

related words ancestor, forerunner, predecessor

near antonyms contemporary, peer; descendant (*or* descendent), successor

antonyms junior

2 one who is above another in rank, station, or office ⟨asked my *senior* frequent questions until I got the hang of it⟩ — see SUPERIOR

3 the senior member of a group ⟨when he retires, she will be the *senior*⟩ — see DEAN

senior citizen *n* a person of advanced years ⟨more and more *senior citizens* are living active, rewarding lives⟩

synonyms ancient, elder, golden-ager, oldster, old-timer

related words senior; graybeard, patriarch; beldam (*or* beldame), grandam (*or* grandame); adult, grown-up

near antonyms adolescent, minor; child, cub, juvenile, kid

antonyms youngster, youth

sensation *n* **1** an indefinite physical response to a stimulus ⟨we felt just the barest *sensation* of warmth when we leaned against the radiator⟩

synonyms feel, feeling, sense

related words impression, perception; hint, suggestion

2 a practice or interest that is very popular for a short time ⟨the band was a short-lived media *sensation*⟩ — see FAD

3 something extraordinary or surprising ⟨the first clone was considered a *sensation*⟩ — see WONDER 1

sensational *adj* **1** arousing a strong and usually superficial interest or emotional reaction ⟨the *sensational* news story caused a stir, but after a few days everyone forgot about it⟩

synonyms lurid, screaming

related words colorful, juicy, racy; dramatic, histrionic, melodramatic, theatrical; coarse, vulgar

near antonyms innocuous, inoffensive; dignified, formal, proper, restrained

2 of or relating to physical sensation or the senses ⟨*sensational* hallucinations⟩ — see SENSORY

3 of the very best kind ⟨this ice cream is *sensational*⟩ — see EXCELLENT

sense *n* **1** an indefinite physical response to a stimulus ⟨a strange *sense* of discomfort⟩ — see SENSATION 1

2 the ability to learn and understand or to deal with problems ⟨although he has little formal education, he is a man of considerable practical *sense*⟩ — see INTELLIGENCE 1

3 the ability to make intelligent decisions especially in everyday matters ⟨you have the *sense* to handle anything that comes up⟩ — see COMMON SENSE

4 the idea that is conveyed or intended to be conveyed to the mind by language, symbol, or action ⟨got the *sense* of the passage⟩ — see MEANING 1

5 the thought processes that have been established as leading to valid solutions to problems ⟨your argument simply shows no *sense*⟩ — see LOGIC

sense *vb* to have a vague awareness of ⟨the deer seemed to *sense* danger⟩ — see FEEL 1

senseless *adj* **1** having lost consciousness ⟨she collapsed, *senseless*, after hitting her head⟩ — see UNCONSCIOUS 1

2 having no meaning ⟨a pretty but *senseless* phrase⟩ — see MEANINGLESS

3 not having or showing an ability to absorb ideas readily ⟨a *senseless* student who required a lot of extra tutoring⟩ — see STUPID 1

4 showing or marked by a lack of good sense or judgment ⟨a *senseless* decision to risk his life on a joke⟩ — see FOOLISH 1

senselessness *n* **1** lack of good sense or judgment ⟨who had the *senselessness* to mix these dangerous chemicals together?⟩ — see FOOLISHNESS 1

2 language, behavior, or ideas that are absurd and contrary to good sense ⟨babbled some *senselessness* about being eaten by horses⟩ — see NONSENSE 1

3 the quality or state of lacking intelligence or quickness of mind ⟨the *senselessness* of a tiny baby⟩ — see STUPIDITY 1

sensibilities *n* general emotional condition ⟨the violent movie upset their *sensibilities*⟩ — see FEELING 2

sensible *adj* **1** able to be perceived by a sense or by the mind ⟨a *sensible* change in the weather⟩ — see PERCEPTIBLE

2 according to the rules of logic ⟨this is the only *sensible* conclusion⟩ — see LOGICAL 1

3 based on sound reasoning or information ⟨a *sensible* decision⟩ — see GOOD 1

4 having specified facts or feelings actively impressed on the mind ⟨*sensible* of the shift in attitude⟩ — see CONSCIOUS

sensibleness *n* the ability to make intelligent decisions especially in everyday matters ⟨her *sensibleness* is the reason her parents trusted her to stay home alone all weekend⟩ — see COMMON SENSE

sensitive *adj* **1** able to sense slight impressions or differences ⟨a scale that is *sensitive* to the smallest change in weight⟩ — see ACUTE 1

2 being in a situation where one is likely to meet with harm ⟨she's very *sensitive* to sunburn if she's out in the sun for any length of time⟩ — see LIABLE 1

3 easily injured without careful handling ⟨the *sensitive* skin of a newborn mouse⟩ — see TENDER 1

4 of or relating to physical sensation or the senses ⟨*sensitive* data⟩ — see SENSORY

sensor *n* a device that detects some physical quantity and responds usually with a transmitted signal ⟨the thief accidentally triggered the motion *sensor*, which alerted the police⟩

synonyms detector

related words eye; electric eye, photoelectric cell; alarm, trigger

sensory *adj* of or relating to physical sensation or the senses ⟨trying to listen to music while watching the TV and eating dinner caused a sort of *sensory* overload⟩

synonyms sensational, sensitive, sensuous

related words afferent, receptive; sensual

near antonyms extrasensory, intuitional

sensual *adj* pleasing to the physical senses ⟨the *sensual* feel of a velvet shirt against the skin⟩

synonyms carnal, fleshly, luscious, sensuous, voluptuous

related words bodily, corporeal; agreeable, delectable, delicious, delightful, dreamy, gratifying, palatable, pleasant, pleasing, pleasurable, scrumptious; epicurean, luxurious, self-indulgent
near antonyms harsh, painful, uncomfortable

sensuous *adj* **1** of or relating to physical sensation or the senses ⟨the *sensuous* pleasure of a massage⟩ — see SENSORY
2 pleasing to the physical senses ⟨a gentle, *sensuous* breeze⟩ — see SENSUAL

sentence *n* a decision made by a court or tribunal regarding a case it has heard ⟨the court-martial pronounced a *sentence* of not guilty on all counts of cowardice⟩
synonyms doom, finding, holding, judgment (*or* judgement), ruling
related words verdict; injunction; decree, edict, order; declaration, deliverance, dictum, pronouncement; conclusion, decision, determination, opinion, resolution; discipline, penalty, punishment

sentence *vb* to impose a judicial punishment on ⟨the judge *sentenced* him to a fine of fifty dollars and time served⟩
synonyms condemn, damn, doom
related words adjudge, judge; castigate, chasten, chastise, correct, discipline, penalize, punish; conclude, decide, determine, find, opine, resolve

sentient *adj* having specified facts or feelings actively impressed on the mind ⟨*sentient* of the danger⟩ — see CONSCIOUS

sentiment *n* **1** a subjective response to a person, thing, or situation ⟨a *sentiment* of happiness and good will⟩ — see FEELING 1
2 an idea that is believed to be true or valid without positive knowledge ⟨anti-slavery *sentiments*⟩ — see OPINION 1

sentimental *adj* appealing to the emotions in an obvious and tiresome way ⟨a *sentimental* plea to help the orphans⟩ — see CORNY

sentimentalism *n* the state or quality of having an excess of tender feelings (as of love, nostalgia, or compassion) ⟨the book's *sentimentalism* bored me⟩ — see SENTIMENTALITY

sentimentality *n* the state or quality of having an excess of tender feelings (as of love, nostalgia, or compassion) ⟨the *sentimentality* of the story of star-crossed lovers only made it even more popular with moviegoers⟩
synonyms mawkishness, mush, sappiness, sentimentalism, sloppiness
related words emotion; sentiment; corn, schmaltz (*also* schmalz)
near antonyms cynicism, hardheadedness, hardheartedness

sentinel *n* a person or group that watches over someone or something ⟨a *sentinel* kept watch over the fort⟩ — see GUARD 1

sentry *n* a person or group that watches over someone or something ⟨a *sentry* posted to watch for intruders⟩ — see GUARD 1

separable *adj* capable of being split into two or more parts or pieces ⟨the outdated belief that the atom is the smallest particle of matter and is not *separable*⟩
synonyms divisible
related words detachable
near antonyms combinable, joinable
antonyms indivisible, inseparable

separate *adj* **1** not the same or shared ⟨we stayed in *separate* apartments on our vacation⟩

synonyms different, individual, respective
related words disparate, dissimilar, distinct, distinctive, distinguishable, diverse, unalike, varied
near antonyms identical, selfsame, very
antonyms same
2 not physically attached to another unit ⟨the housing development has 200 *separate* homes, each with its own enclosed yard⟩
synonyms detached, disconnected, discrete, freestanding, single, unattached, unconnected
related words independent, self-contained; individual, private
antonyms attached, connected, joined
3 not being under the rule or control of another ⟨a *separate* country⟩ — see FREE 1
4 of, relating to, or belonging to a single person ⟨*separate* interests⟩ — see INDIVIDUAL 1

separate *vb* **1** to set or force apart ⟨we tried to *separate* the gluey pages, but they were stuck tight⟩
synonyms break up, disconnect, disjoin, disjoint, dissever, dissociate, disunite, divide, divorce, part, ramify, resolve, sever, split, sunder, uncouple, unlink, unyoke
related words decompose, disassemble, dissolve; bisect, fractionate, halve, quarter, segment, subdivide; break, rend, rip, rupture, tear; cut off, insulate, isolate, seclude, segregate, sequester; detach, disengage, disentangle, untie
near antonyms assemble, associate, blend, combine, mingle, mix; connect, couple; unify; accumulate, agglutinate, attach, bind, cement, close, fasten, fuse, stick, weld
antonyms join, link, unify, unite
2 to go or move in different directions from a central point ⟨the searchers *separated* in order to cover more ground⟩
synonyms branch (out), diverge, divide, fork
related words bestrew, broadcast, clear out, disband, dispel, disperse, dissipate, distribute, scatter, sow; distance, recede, retreat
near antonyms assemble, gather, meet
antonyms converge, join
3 to arrange or assign according to type ⟨*separate* the students by reading ability⟩ — see CLASSIFY 1
4 to set or keep apart from others ⟨*separated* her from the rest of the children until she calmed down⟩ — see ISOLATE
5 to understand or point out the difference ⟨trying to *separate* science from religion on one specific point⟩ — see DISTINGUISH 1

separateness *n* the state of being alone or kept apart from others ⟨*separateness* didn't make him lonely⟩ — see ISOLATION

separation *n* **1** the act or process of a whole separating into two or more parts or pieces ⟨the *separation* of Czechoslovakia into the Czech Republic and Slovakia⟩
synonyms breakup, dissolution, disunion, division, fractionation, partition, schism, split
related words breach, rupture; decomposition, disassembly, segmentation, subdivision; dispersal, scattering; administration, apportionment, distribution; isolation, seclusion, segregation, sequestration
near antonyms assemblage, association; attachment, connection, link, linkage, linkup; combination, fusion
antonyms unification, union
2 the state of being kept distinct ⟨the *separation* of church and state is an important concept in the United States⟩

synonyms demarcation, discreteness, discrimination, distinction

related words differentiation

near antonyms blurring, confusion

3 a movement in different directions away from a common point ⟨a sudden *separation* of the herd of deer when they were startled⟩ — see DIVERGENCE

4 an open space in a barrier (as a wall or hedge) ⟨the *separation* between posts in the fence⟩ — see GAP 1

5 the act or process of two or more persons going off in different directions ⟨*separations* always made her sad⟩ — see PARTING 1

sepulcher *or* **sepulchre** *n* a final resting place for a dead person ⟨Grandfather had his *sepulcher* built while he was still alive⟩ — see GRAVE

sepulchral *adj* causing or marked by an atmosphere lacking in cheer ⟨a *sepulchral* tone that gave everyone a chill⟩ — see GLOOMY 1

sepulture *n* **1** a final resting place for a dead person ⟨opened the *sepulture* and examined the mummy⟩ — see GRAVE

2 the act or ceremony of putting a dead body in its final resting place ⟨the final *sepulture* of the body had to wait until the ground wasn't frozen⟩ — see BURIAL

sequel *n* a condition or occurrence traceable to a cause ⟨higher prices are a logical *sequel* to higher costs for manufacturers⟩ — see EFFECT 1

sequence *n* **1** a condition or occurrence traceable to a cause ⟨the attempt to help was a natural *sequence* to her charitable nature⟩ — see EFFECT 1

2 a series of things linked together ⟨a *sequence* of events that no one predicted⟩ — see CHAIN 1

3 the way objects in space or events in time are arranged or follow one another ⟨the *sequence* of the holidays⟩ — see ORDER 1

sequential *adj* following one after another without others coming in between ⟨the two required algebra semesters have to be *sequential*, or you could forget the material⟩ — see CONSECUTIVE

sequester *vb* **1** to set or keep apart from others ⟨*sequestered* the woman until she had her baby⟩ — see ISOLATE

2 to take ownership or control of (something) by right of one's authority ⟨police found and *sequestered* several illegal weapons⟩ — see CONFISCATE

sequestration *n* the state of being alone or kept apart from others ⟨what would you bring for *sequestration* on a desert island?⟩ — see ISOLATION

sere *adj* marked by little or no precipitation or humidity ⟨remember to drink a lot of water on *sere* days⟩ — see DRY 1

serene *adj* **1** free from disturbing noise or uproar ⟨a *serene* vacation spot⟩ — see QUIET 1

2 free from emotional or mental agitation ⟨a *serene* woman who was everyone's source of support⟩ — see CALM 2

3 free from storms or physical disturbance ⟨a *serene* lake⟩ — see CALM 1

sereneness *n* a state of freedom from storm or disturbance ⟨the *sereneness* of the weather made our vacation perfect⟩ — see CALM

serenity *n* **1** a state of freedom from storm or disturbance ⟨the *serenity* after the tornado was remarkable⟩ — see CALM

2 evenness of emotions or temper ⟨his *serenity* calmed those around him⟩ — see EQUANIMITY

serial *adj* appearing in parts or numbers that follow regularly ⟨"Uncle Tom's Cabin" first appeared as a *serial* novel from 1851 to 1852⟩

synonyms episodic, periodic, periodical

related words sequential; recurrent, regular

serious *adj* **1** not joking or playful in mood or manner ⟨our parents were quite *serious* when they told us not to stay out too late⟩

synonyms earnest, grave, humorless, no-nonsense, sedate, severe, sober, solemn, staid, uncomic, unfunny, unsmiling, weighty

related words harsh, stern, strict; dignified, distinguished, elevated, serious-minded

near antonyms antic, comic, comical, droll, farcical, funny, hilarious, hysterical, laughable, light, lightheaded, ludicrous, ridiculous, risible, riotous, screaming, side-splitting, uproarious; featherbrained, flighty, frivolous, goofy, harebrained, lighthearted, puerile, scatterbrained; absurd, asinine, balmy, brainless, cockeyed, crazy, cuckoo, daffy, daft, dotty, fatuous, foolish, half-witted, insane, jerky, kooky, loony (*also* looney), lunatic, mad, nonsensical, nutty, preposterous, sappy, screwball, senseless, silly, unwise, wacky, weak-minded, witless, zany

antonyms facetious, flip, flippant, humorous, jesting, jocular, joking, playful

2 having a matter of importance as its topic ⟨a very *serious* film that dealt with the aftermath of the Gulf War⟩

synonyms grave, heavy, weighty

related words big, consequential, eventful, important, major, material, meaningful, momentous, significant, substantial

near antonyms insignificant, little, minor, slight, small, trivial, unimportant

antonyms light

3 involving potential loss or injury ⟨a *serious* accident⟩ — see DANGEROUS

seriousness *n* a mental state free of jesting or trifling ⟨please try to summon up some *seriousness* just for this test⟩ — see EARNESTNESS

sermon *n* a public speech usually by a member of the clergy for the purpose of giving moral guidance or uplift ⟨a *sermon* whose message was that we should love our neighbors as much as we love ourselves⟩

synonyms homily

related words lecture, speech; lesson

serpent *n* a limbless reptile with a long body ⟨an apparent stick in the grass turned out to be a *serpent*⟩ — see SNAKE 1

serpentine *adj* marked by a long series of irregular curves ⟨drove carefully on the *serpentine* road⟩ — see CROOKED 1

serrate *adj* notched or toothed along the edge ⟨a *serrate* saw⟩ — see SERRATED

serrated *adj* notched or toothed along the edge ⟨you should use a *serrated* knife when cutting bread, so you don't squash the loaf⟩

synonyms saw-toothed, serrate

related words wavy

near antonyms flat, smooth

serried *adj* having little space between items or parts ⟨a *serried* collection of little houses⟩ — see CLOSE 1

servant *n* a person hired to perform household or personal services ⟨the wealthy family had *servants* to clean and cook for them⟩

synonyms domestic, flunky (*also* flunkey), lackey, menial, retainer, steward *related words* butler, footman, groom, houseboy, man, majordomo, manservant, servitor, valet; handmaiden (*also* handmaid), housekeeper, housemaid, lady-in-waiting, maid, maidservant, wench, woman; attendant, follower

near antonyms boss, captain, chief, foreman, head, headman, helmsman, kingpin, leader, taskmaster

antonyms master

serve *vb* **1** to be a servant for ⟨he *served* his master faithfully for twenty years⟩

synonyms slave (for), work (for)

phrases wait on, wait upon

2 to be enough ⟨they made the pasta *serve* for eight guests⟩

synonyms do, suffice

related words answer, suit; assuage, content, quench, sate, satiate, satisfy

3 to be fitting or proper ⟨that tea set will *serve* for the dinner⟩ — see DO 1

4 to behave toward in a stated way ⟨my parents *served* me well in preparing me for life⟩ — see TREAT 1

5 to have a certain purpose ⟨the example *served* to teach everyone a lesson⟩ — see FUNCTION

6 to provide with something useful or desirable ⟨an excellent college *served* her in terms of getting a good education⟩ — see BENEFIT

server *n* a person who serves food or drink ⟨we had barely finished ordering when the *server* brought our salads⟩

synonyms waiter

related words waitress; bartender; steward, stewardess

service *adj* of or relating to the armed services ⟨spent his time in the army as a correspondent for *service* newspapers⟩ — see MILITARY 1

service *n* **1** an act of kind assistance ⟨performed many *services* for the charitable organization⟩ — see FAVOR 1

2 the capacity for being useful for some purpose ⟨that broom is worn out beyond all *service*⟩ — see USE 2

3 the combined army, air force, and navy of a nation ⟨at the time the country had about a million men and women in the *service*⟩ — see ARMED FORCES

serviceability *n* the capacity for being useful for some purpose ⟨I have doubts about the *serviceability* of some of the junk we've accumulated⟩ — see USE 2

serviceable *adj* **1** capable of being put to use or account ⟨be sure to wear *serviceable* shoes if you're going to be walking on the rocks along the shore⟩ — see PRACTICAL 1

2 capable of or suitable for being used for a particular purpose ⟨a perfectly *serviceable*, if old, set of screwdrivers worked fine for repairing the door⟩ — see USABLE 1

serviceableness *n* the capacity for being useful for some purpose ⟨the *serviceableness* of a lot of the junk that my grandfather had been hoarding was very doubtful⟩ — see USE 2

serviceman *n* a person engaged in military service ⟨wishing our *servicemen* overseas the best of luck⟩ — see SOLDIER

servility *n* the state of being a slave ⟨the joy that emancipation must have brought to people who had known only *servility* since birth⟩ — see SLAVERY 1

servitude *n* the state of being a slave ⟨the Fugitive Slave Act had the effect of returning slaves who had made it to freedom in the North to a brutal life of *servitude* in the South⟩ — see SLAVERY 1

set *adj* **1** being in a state of fitness for some experience or action ⟨we're all *set* to go⟩ — see READY 1

2 firmly positioned in place and difficult to dislodge ⟨that rock is really *set* in the hillside⟩ — see TIGHT 2

3 fully committed to achieving a goal ⟨*set* on being the first in her family to graduate from college⟩ — see DETERMINED 1

4 having been established and usually not subject to change ⟨the library is only open during *set* hours⟩ — see FIXED 1

5 of a particular or exact sort ⟨international law has *set* rules for the treatment of prisoners of war⟩ — see EXPRESS 1

set *n* **1** a group of people acting together within a larger group ⟨the rebellious *set* among the students at the high school⟩ — see FACTION

2 a group of people sharing a common interest and relating together socially ⟨met up with their social *set* at the mall⟩ — see GANG 2

3 a number of things considered as a unit ⟨a *set* of tools⟩ — see GROUP 1

4 one of the units into which a whole is divided on the basis of a common characteristic ⟨the next *set* of job applicants had far more education and practical experience⟩ — see CLASS 2

5 the array of painted backgrounds and furnishings used for a scene in a stage production ⟨built *sets* for the play⟩ — see SCENERY

set *vb* **1** to cover and warm eggs to hatch them ⟨the hen *set* for days⟩

synonyms brood, hatch, incubate, sit

related words lay, spawn; pip

2 to decide upon (the time or date for an event) usually from a position of authority ⟨*set* a date for the wedding⟩ — see APPOINT 2

3 to make an approximate or tentative judgment regarding ⟨fire losses were *set* at a million dollars⟩ — see ESTIMATE 1

4 *chiefly dialect* to rest on the buttocks or haunches ⟨come over and *set* for a spell⟩ — see SIT 1

5 to point or turn (something) toward a target or goal ⟨determined to see the West, she *set* her car towards the sun and drove off⟩ — see AIM 1

6 to come to an agreement or decision concerning the details of ⟨finally *set* some plans for the luncheon⟩ — see ARRANGE 1

7 to put securely in place or in a desired position ⟨*set* a diamond into the ring mount⟩ — see FASTEN 2

8 to turn from a liquid into a substance resembling jelly ⟨the gelatin is just starting to *set* now⟩ — see COAGULATE

9 to arrange something in a certain spot or position ⟨*set* a book on the table⟩ — see PLACE 1

10 to become physically firm or solid ⟨the concrete must *set* completely before anyone will be allowed to walk on it⟩ — see HARDEN 1

setback *n* a change in status for the worse usually temporarily ⟨the colonists persevered despite suffering *setbacks* that would have discouraged lesser souls⟩ — see REVERSE 1

set down *vb* **1** to cause to sit down ⟨*set* all the toddlers *down* in their seats⟩ — see SEAT

2 to make a written note of ⟨*set down* the names of those in attendance⟩ — see RECORD 1

set in *vb* to come into existence ⟨a cold spell *set in* sometime last week⟩ — see BEGIN 2

set off *vb* to cause to function ⟨*set off* a bomb⟩ — see ACTIVATE

settee *n* a long upholstered piece of furniture designed for several sitters ⟨the young couple snuggled on the *settee*⟩ — see COUCH

setting *n* **1** the circumstances, conditions, or objects by which one is surrounded ⟨the novice camper felt lost outside of his familiar urban *setting*⟩ — see ENVIRONMENT

2 the place and time in which the action for a portion of a dramatic work (as a movie) is set ⟨the *setting* for the novel is Victorian England⟩ — see SCENE 1

settle *vb* **1** to cause to come to rest at the bottom (as of a liquid) ⟨the light rain will *settle* the dust in the air⟩ ⟨careful handling will *settle* the lees in the bottom of the wine bottle⟩

synonyms lay, sediment

related words filter, screen, sieve, sift, strain; resettle

near antonyms disturb, mix, stir

antonyms raise

2 to give an opinion about (something at issue or in dispute) ⟨*settled* the lawsuit in favor of the defendant⟩ — see JUDGE 1

3 to come to an agreement or decision concerning the details of ⟨*settled* their wedding plans without any major disagreements⟩ — see ARRANGE 1

4 to come to rest after descending from the air ⟨birds *settling* on the branches of the maple tree⟩ — see ALIGHT

5 to establish or place comfortably or snugly ⟨*settled* the sleeping baby into her crib⟩ — see ENSCONCE 1

6 to free from distress or disturbance ⟨a hot meal *settled* the children down⟩ — see CALM 1

7 to gain emotional or mental control of ⟨*settled* himself only with visible effort after the angry outburst⟩ — see COLLECT 1

8 to give what is owed for ⟨*settle* a debt⟩ — see PAY 2

9 to make final, definite, or beyond dispute ⟨this information should *settle* the question of who is right⟩ — see CLINCH

10 to stop the noise or speech of ⟨*settled* the class with a firm "quiet!"⟩ — see SILENCE 1

settle (down) *vb* to become still and orderly ⟨*settle down* and get to work, please⟩ — see QUIET 1

settled *adj* **1** firmly established over time ⟨a remote village with a *settled* distrust of outsiders⟩ — see INVETERATE 1

2 having been established and usually not subject to change ⟨*settled* rules that cannot be disregarded when it is convenient to do so⟩ — see FIXED 1

settlement *n* an arrangement about action to be taken ⟨eventually reached a peace *settlement*⟩ — see AGREEMENT 2

settler *n* **1** a person who settles in a new region ⟨*settlers* learning to live in peace with the natives⟩ — see FRONTIERSMAN

2 one that leaves one place to settle in another ⟨in 1889 Jane Addams, in an effort to provide Chicago's latest wave of *settlers* with much-needed services, founded the city's first settlement house⟩ — see EMIGRANT

setup *n* **1** the way in which something is sized, arranged, or organized ⟨the textbook's *setup* calls for a list of questions at the end of each chapter⟩ — see FORMAT 1

2 the way objects in space or events in time are arranged or follow one another ⟨changed the *setup* of the living room furniture several times before being satisfied⟩ — see ORDER 1

set up *vb* **1** to arrange something in a certain spot or position ⟨*set up* tables in the living room for the party⟩ — see PLACE 1

2 to be responsible for the creation and early operation or use of ⟨*set up* a scholarship fund for deserving students from the inner city⟩ — see FOUND

3 to fix in an upright position ⟨*set up* a post from which to hang the sign⟩ — see ERECT 1

4 to form by putting together parts or materials ⟨*set up* the prefabricated shed by following the instructions⟩ — see BUILD

seven seas *n pl* the whole body of salt water that covers nearly three-fourths of the earth ⟨sailing the *seven seas* in search of adventure⟩ — see OCEAN

sever *vb* to set or force apart ⟨disapproving parents who were willing to do anything to *sever* the young lovers⟩ — see SEPARATE 1

severe *adj* **1** given to exacting standards of discipline and self-restraint ⟨a *severe*, uncompromising teacher who locked the classroom door precisely when the bell rang and let no one in afterward⟩

synonyms austere, authoritarian, flinty, hard, harsh, heavy-handed, ramrod, rigid, rigorous, stern, strict

related words demanding, exacting; uncharitable, unforgiving; adamant, adamantine, hardened, hardhearted, immovable, implacable, inflexible, ossified, unbending, uncompromising, unyielding; dour, gruff; ascetic, monastic; browbeating, bullying; determined, firm, resolved, single-minded, steadfast, unflinching; dogged, intractable, obstinate, relentless

near antonyms easy, easygoing, laid-back, undemanding; charitable, kind, merciful, patient, soft, softhearted; accepting, compromising, yielding; responsive, willing; acquiescent, agreeable, amenable, compliant, flexible, pliable, pliant

antonyms forbearing, indulgent, lax, lenient, tolerant

2 harsh and threatening in manner or appearance ⟨clergymen who dressed in *severe* clothing⟩ — see GRIM 1

3 not joking or playful in mood or manner ⟨the judge maintained a *severe* expression throughout the trial⟩ — see SERIOUS 1

4 difficult to endure ⟨a *severe* winter that was among the coldest on record⟩ — see HARSH 1

5 requiring considerable physical or mental effort ⟨a *severe* test of courage⟩ — see HARD 2

severely *adv* in a manner so as to cause loss or suffering ⟨the building was *severely* damaged by the explosion⟩ — see HARDLY 1

severity *n* the quality or state of being demanding or unyielding (as in discipline or criticism) ⟨Jane's parents were legendary for the *severity* of their discipline — she never got away with so much as a white lie⟩

synonyms hardness, harshness, inflexibility, rigidity, rigidness, rigorousness, sternness, strictness

related words hardheartedness, implacability, obduracy; dourness, gruffness; asceticism, austerity, monasticism; determination, firmness, resolve, steadfastness; obstinacy, stubbornness

near antonyms forbearance, indulgence, kindness, lenience, patience, softness, tenderness, tolerance; responsiveness, willingness; compliance, pliability

antonyms flexibility, gentleness, laxness, mildness

sew *vb* to close up with a series of interlacing stitches ⟨luckily, Mom was able to *sew* the tear in my pants so skillfully that they looked as good as new⟩

synonyms darn, stitch

related words mend, patch, repair; baste, ease, fell, finish, overcast; crochet, knit, quilt

sew up *vb* to have complete control over ⟨*sewed up* the available openings so that no one else had a chance to play golf⟩ — see MONOPOLIZE

sex *n* sexual union involving penetration of the vagina by the penis ⟨the students learned about the mechanics of *sex* and reproduction in health class⟩ — see SEXUAL INTERCOURSE

sexual intercourse *n* sexual union involving penetration of the vagina by the penis ⟨many people believe that it's best to wait to experience *sexual intercourse* until you're mature enough to handle it⟩

synonyms coitus, copulating, copulation, intercourse, mating, sex, sexual relations

related words fornication; safe sex; sexuality

phrases making love

sexual relations *n pl* sexual union involving penetration of the vagina by the penis ⟨adultery is defined as a married person engaging in *sexual relations* with someone other than their spouse⟩ — see SEXUAL INTERCOURSE

sexy *adj* of, relating to, or expressing sexual attraction ⟨he found her new dress very *sexy* while still being tasteful⟩ — see EROTIC

shabby *adj* **1** showing signs of advanced wear and tear and neglect ⟨*shabby* wallpaper that was peeling from the walls⟩

synonyms dilapidated, dog-eared, grungy, mangy, mean, miserable, moth-eaten, neglected, ratty, run-down, scruffy, seedy, tacky, threadbare

related words abandoned, desolate, forlorn; broken-down, decrepit, worn-out; bedraggled, dingy, ragged, tattered; decaying, deteriorated, deteriorating, ramshackle; broken, damaged, destroyed, harmed, hurt, impaired, injured, ruined, wrecked

phrases gone to seed

near antonyms brand-new, fresh, new; cared-for, kept-up, maintained; mended, patched, rebuilt, reconstructed; smart, spiffy, spruce

2 worn or torn into or as if into rags ⟨*shabby*, stained clothes that are barely better than rags⟩ — see RAGGED 2

shack *n* a small, simply constructed, and often temporary dwelling ⟨a farmer's *shack* out in the fields that's used for lambing and as a shelter from storms⟩

synonyms cabin, camp, hovel, hut, hutch, shanty

related words lean-to, shed; cot, cottage, lodge; cabana; bungalow, chalet; hogan, wickiup, wigwam

shackle *n* **1** something that physically prevents free movement ⟨placed *shackles* on the legs of the prisoners⟩ — see BOND 1

2 shackles *pl* something that makes movement or progress more difficult ⟨the *shackles* of illiteracy can be just as confining as leg irons⟩ — see ENCUMBRANCE

shackle *vb* **1** to confine or restrain with or as if with chains ⟨unwilling to *shackle* the dogs to the wall of the house⟩ — see BIND 1

2 to create difficulty for the work or activity of ⟨*shackled* by poverty and ignorance⟩ — see HAMPER

shade *n* **1** partial darkness due to the obstruction of light rays ⟨it was hard to see in the *shade* after being in the brilliant sunlight⟩ ⟨the trees cast *shade*⟩

synonyms penumbra, shadiness, shadow, umbra

related words blackness, dimness, duskiness, gloominess, murkiness, obscurity, somberness; cloudiness, dullness (*also* dulness)

near antonyms brightness, brilliance, effulgence, illumination, incandescence, light, lightness, lucidity, lucidness, luminosity, radiance

2 a time or place of little or no light ⟨enjoying the cool *shade* of the evening⟩ — see DARK 1

3 a property that becomes apparent when light falls on an object and by which things that are identical in form can be distinguished ⟨a lovely *shade* of blue⟩ — see COLOR 1

4 a very small amount ⟨just a *shade* taller than his dance partner⟩ — see PARTICLE 1

5 the soul of a dead person thought of especially as appearing to living people ⟨spirits and *shades* haunting the night⟩ — see GHOST

shade *vb* to shelter (something) from light and heat ⟨the trees *shaded* us quite nicely from the noonday sun⟩

synonyms shadow

related words cloud, darken, dim, dull; canopy, cover, protect, screen

near antonyms illuminate, light, lighten; expose

shaded *adj* protected from the sun's rays ⟨walking along the park's *shaded* pathway⟩ — see SHADY 1

shadiness *n* partial darkness due to the obstruction of light rays ⟨the inviting *shadiness* of a woodland grove⟩ — see SHADE 1

shadow *n* **1** a person whose business is solving crimes and catching criminals or gathering information that is not easy to get ⟨having noticed that someone was following him, he ducked into an alley in an attempt to lose this unwanted *shadow*⟩ — see DETECTIVE

2 partial darkness due to the obstruction of light rays ⟨the valley was in *shadow*⟩ — see SHADE 1

3 shadows *pl* a time or place of little or no light ⟨lurking in the *shadows*⟩ — see DARK 1

4 a tiny often physical indication of something lost or vanished ⟨a run-down mansion that is only a *shadow* of its former glory⟩ — see VESTIGE

5 a very small amount ⟨not even a *shadow* of a doubt about the defendant's guilt⟩ — see PARTICLE 1

6 the soul of a dead person thought of especially as appearing to living people ⟨rumors of a *shadow* haunting the castle⟩ — see GHOST

shadow *vb* **1** to go after or on the track of ⟨*shadowing* the suspect to see what he was up to⟩ — see FOLLOW 2

2 to make dark, dim, or indistinct ⟨thickening clouds *shadowed* the countryside⟩ — see CLOUD 1

3 to shelter (something) from light and heat ⟨a pathway *shadowed* by a canopy of arching branches⟩ — see SHADE

shadowed *adj* protected from the sun's rays ⟨sat in a *shadowed* corner of the garden⟩ — see SHADY 1

shadowing *n* the act of going after or in the tracks of another ⟨the relentless *shadowing* of the destroyer by the submarine⟩ — see PURSUIT

shadowy *adj* **1** not seen or understood clearly ⟨the *shadowy* area between tough interrogation and torture⟩ — see FAINT 1

2 protected from the sun's rays ⟨a *shadowy* lane that is a mosaic of colors during the autumn foliage season⟩ — see SHADY 1

shady *adj* **1** protected from the sun's rays ⟨a lovely *shady* spot in the park that was pleasantly cool⟩

synonyms shaded, shadowed, shadowy

related words canopied, covered, sheltered; cloudy; dark, darkened, darkish, darkling, darksome, dim, dimmed, dusky, gloomy, moonless, murky, obscure, obscured, pitch-black, pitch-dark, somber (*or* sombre), sunless

near antonyms bedazzling, bright, brightened, brilliant, dazzling, effulgent, illuminated, illumined, incan-

descent, light, lighted (*or* lit), lucent, lucid, luminous; beaming, lambent, radiant, shining; lustrous
antonyms sunny
2 given to or marked by cheating and deception ⟨a *shady* business deal⟩ — see DISHONEST 2
3 giving good reason for being doubted, questioned, or challenged ⟨cited some *shady* statistics to back up his argument⟩ — see DOUBTFUL 2
4 given to acting in secret and to concealing one's intentions ⟨*shady* characters hanging out in the park after nightfall⟩ — see SNEAKY 1
shaft *n* **1** a narrow sharply defined line of light radiating from an object ⟨*shafts* of late-afternoon sunlight pierced the blinds and streaked the floor⟩
synonyms beam, ray
related words moonbeam, sunbeam; laser, spotlight
2 a weapon with a long straight handle and sharp head or blade ⟨the footmen set their *shafts* so as to form a bank of steel against the enemy's charging cavalry⟩ — see SPEAR
shaggy *adj* **1** covered with or as if with hair ⟨a big, *shaggy* dog kept trying to lick my face⟩ — see HAIRY 1
2 made of or resembling hair ⟨a *shaggy* carpet⟩ — see HAIRY 2
shake *vb* **1** to make a series of small irregular or violent movements ⟨the bus rattled and *shook* as it barreled down a rutted road⟩
synonyms agitate, convulse, joggle, jolt, jounce, quake, quiver, shudder, vibrate, wobble
related words rock, sway; quaver, shiver, tremble; dodder, waver; flicker, fluctuate, flutter, oscillate, wave; beat, palpitate, pit-a-pat, pitter-patter, pulsate, pulse, throb
2 to get or keep away from (as a responsibility) through cleverness or trickery ⟨we *shook* our pursuers by cutting through the abandoned lot⟩ — see ESCAPE 2
shake *n* **1** a very small space of time ⟨I'll be there in two *shakes*⟩ — see INSTANT
2 shakes *pl* a sense of panic or extreme nervousness ⟨I get the *shakes* every time I hear her voice⟩ — see JITTERS
shake up *vb* to cause an often unpleasant surprise for ⟨the news that we had failed the test *shook* us *up*⟩ — see SHOCK 1
shakiness *n* the quality or state of not being firmly fixed in position ⟨we added a couple more ropes to help reduce the *shakiness* of the footbridge⟩ — see INSTABILITY
shaking *adj* marked by or given to small uncontrollable bodily movements ⟨suffered a *shaking* chill during his bout with the flu⟩ — see SHAKY 1
shaking *n* **1** a series of slight movements by a body back and forth or from side to side ⟨gave the jar a good *shaking*⟩ — see VIBRATION
2 the act or a means of getting or keeping away from something undesirable ⟨condemned the government's *shaking* of its overseas responsibilities⟩ — see ESCAPE 2
shaky *adj* **1** marked by or given to small uncontrollable bodily movements ⟨the old man's hands were so *shaky* that I was afraid he'd drop the glass⟩
synonyms quaking, quavery, shaking, shuddering, shuddery, tottery, trembling, tremulous, wobbling, wobbly
related words shivering, shivery
near antonyms controlled, firm, settled, stable, steady
2 giving good reason for being doubted, questioned, or challenged ⟨results that were arrived at using some *shaky* experimental procedures⟩ — see DOUBTFUL 2

shall *vb* to be under necessity or obligation to ⟨you *shall* do as I say⟩ — see NEED 2
shallow *adj* **1** lacking significant physical depth ⟨the dog quickly dug a *shallow* hole that was barely deep enough to accommodate his bone⟩
synonyms depthless, shoal
related words skin-deep, superficial, surface; fathomable, measurable; finite, limited, measured, restricted; even, flat, flush, horizontal, level, plane, smooth
near antonyms abysmal, abyssal, bottomless, boundless, endless, immeasurable, inestimable, infinite, limitless, measureless, unfathomable, unlimited, vast; navigable
antonyms deep
2 having or showing a lack of depth of understanding or character ⟨we felt it was pretty *shallow* of him to be worrying about his car while the pedestrian was in need of medical attention⟩ — see SUPERFICIAL 2
shallow *n*, *usually* **shallows** *pl* a place where a body of water (as a sea or river) is shallow ⟨we waded through the *shallows* looking for tadpoles⟩ — see SHOAL
sham *adj* **1** being such in appearance only and made with or manufactured from usually cheaper materials ⟨a sofa upholstered in *sham* leather⟩ — see IMITATION
2 being such in appearance only and made or manufactured with the intention of committing fraud ⟨street vendors selling *sham* pearl necklaces to gullible tourists⟩ — see COUNTERFEIT
3 lacking in natural or spontaneous quality ⟨the *sham* friendliness of a salesman trying to sell you something⟩ — see ARTIFICIAL 1
sham *n* **1** a poor, insincere, or insulting imitation of something ⟨condemned the rigged election as a total *sham*⟩ — see MOCKERY 1
2 an imitation that is passed off as genuine ⟨the bank robber's "gun" turned out to be a *sham*⟩ — see FAKE 1
sham *vb* to present a false appearance of ⟨*shammed* a most unconvincing limp just to get sympathy⟩ — see FEIGN
shamble *vb* to move heavily or clumsily ⟨the bear *shambled* across the clearing toward the abandoned campsite⟩ — see LUMBER 1
shambles *n pl* **1** a dirty or messy place ⟨this room is a *shambles*—clean it up right now!⟩ — see PIGPEN
2 a state in which everything is out of order ⟨the earthquake left the whole town in a *shambles*⟩ — see CHAOS
shame *n* **1** a feeling of responsibility for wrongdoing ⟨racked with *shame* over her actions of the previous week⟩ — see GUILT 1
2 a regrettable or blameworthy act ⟨it's a *shame* you won't be able to come to the party⟩ — see CRIME 2
3 the state of having lost the esteem of others ⟨left the room in *shame* after his angry outburst⟩ — see DISGRACE 1
shame *vb* to reduce to a lower standing in one's own eyes or in others' eyes ⟨*shamed* the family name with his conviction for embezzlement⟩ — see HUMBLE
shamed *adj* suffering from or expressive of a feeling of responsibility for wrongdoing ⟨the *shamed* look of someone who knows that he is being given credit he doesn't deserve⟩ — see GUILTY 2
shamefaced *adj* suffering from or expressive of a feeling of responsibility for wrongdoing ⟨the newspaper offered a *shamefaced* apology for having published photographs that were later exposed as fakes⟩ — see GUILTY 2

shameful *adj* not respectable ⟨*shameful* behavior by a bunch of drunken boors⟩ — see DISREPUTABLE

shanty *n* a small, simply constructed, and often temporary dwelling ⟨lived just off the beach in a crude *shanty*⟩ — see SHACK

shape *n* **1** a state of being or fitness ⟨she was in good *shape* after having worked outdoors all summer long⟩ — see CONDITION 1

2 the outward appearance of something as distinguished from its substance ⟨that part of the state is known as the panhandle because of its *shape*⟩ — see FORM 1

3 the type of body that a person has ⟨most fashion models have the kind of *shape* that shows elegant clothes to their best advantage⟩ — see PHYSIQUE

shape *vb* to change (something) so as to make it suitable for a new use or situation ⟨a dress *shaped* to the customer's particular figure⟩ — see ADAPT

shape (up) *vb* to take on a definite form ⟨the summer is *shaping up* as one of the hottest on record⟩ — see FORM 1

shapeless *adj* **1** badly or imperfectly formed ⟨a *shapeless* old hat⟩ — see MALFORMED

2 having no definite or recognizable form ⟨right now this clay is just a *shapeless* lump, but wait until I'm done sculpting it⟩ — see FORMLESS

share *n* **1** something belonging to, due to, or contributed by an individual member of a group ⟨my *share* of the lottery winnings is over a million dollars⟩ ⟨Sue's *share* of the bill comes to $13.44⟩

synonyms allotment, allowance, cut, part, portion, proportion, quota

related words lot, ration; commission, percentage; member, partition, section, segment

near antonyms aggregate, composite, compound, sum, total, totality; whole

2 a legal right to participation in the advantages, profits, and responsibility of something ⟨she sold her *share* in the business to her partner⟩ — see INTEREST 1

share *vb* to take a share or part ⟨everyone in the enterprise will *share* in the profits⟩ — see PARTAKE

shared *adj* used or done by a number of people as a group ⟨*shared* resources⟩ — see COLLECTIVE

sharer *n* one who takes part in something ⟨all pilots are *sharers* of the same air space⟩ — see PARTICIPANT

shark *n* **1** a dishonest person who uses clever means to cheat others out of something of value ⟨a card *shark*⟩ — see TRICKSTER 1

2 a person with a high level of knowledge or skill in a field ⟨a *shark* at arithmetic⟩ — see EXPERT

sharp *adj* **1** having an edge thin enough to cut or pierce something ⟨be careful, as that knife is *sharp* enough to slice off a finger⟩

synonyms cutting, edged, edgy, ground, honed, keen, sharpened, stropped, trenchant, whetted

related words clawlike; jabbing, jagged, lacerating, piercing, scratching, stabbing

near antonyms rounded, seamless, smooth; soft; even, flat, level, slick

antonyms blunt, blunted, dull, dulled, obtuse

2 causing intense mental or physical distress ⟨sudden *sharp* pains in your right lower belly can be a sign of appendicitis⟩

synonyms acute, agonizing, biting, excruciating, smart, smarting

related words bitter, cutting, keen, penetrating, piercing, raw, stinging; afflicting, distressing, disturbing, upsetting; cruel, grievous, harsh, heartrending, hurtful,

lacerating, painful, paralyzing, severe, tormenting, torturous; insufferable, insupportable, intolerable, unacceptable, unbearable, unsupportable; appalling, awful, bad, dire, dreadful, ghastly, horrible, miserable, nasty, rotten, terrible, vile, wretched

near antonyms painless; acceptable, bearable, endurable, supportable, sustainable, tolerable; livable (*also* liveable), sufferable

antonyms dull

3 having a powerfully stimulating odor or flavor ⟨the cheese is so *sharp* that its rank aroma can practically clear a room⟩

synonyms nippy, pungent, strong

related words acid, acidic; acrid, bitter, harsh; piquant, spicy, tart, zesty; putrid, rancid, rank; acute, keen; animating, energizing, exciting, galvanizing, invigorating, provocative; appetizing, delectable, delicious, palatable, toothsome; flavorful, savory, tasty

near antonyms aged, mellow; gentle, soft; flat, flavorless, insipid; savorless, tasteless; dilute, thin, watery, weak

antonyms bland, mild, smooth

4 tapering to a thin tip ⟨tipped with a *sharp* arrowhead⟩ — see POINTED 1

5 being in the latest or current fashion ⟨wore a *sharp* suit to his first big job interview⟩ — see STYLISH

6 being strikingly neat and trim in style or appearance ⟨a television personality who's known as a *sharp* dresser⟩ — see SMART 1

7 causing intense discomfort to one's skin ⟨I got chapped lips from sailing all day in that *sharp* wind⟩ — see CUTTING 1

8 given to or marked by cheating and deception ⟨*sharp* business practices that are being investigated by the state's consumer protection agency⟩ — see DISHONEST 2

9 having or showing a practical cleverness or judgment ⟨a *sharp* customer who wasn't about to be taken in by that smooth-tongued salesman⟩ — see SHREWD

10 having or showing quickness of mind ⟨any *sharp* student would have noticed the error immediately⟩ — see INTELLIGENT 1

11 marked by the use of wit that is intended to cause hurt feelings ⟨an unnecessarily *sharp* retort to a perfectly civil question⟩ — see SARCASTIC

12 able to sense slight impressions or differences ⟨you have *sharp* eyes⟩ — see ACUTE 1

13 uncomfortably cool ⟨a spell of unusually *sharp* weather for this time of year⟩ — see CHILLY 1

sharp *adv* as stated or indicated without the slightest difference ⟨be there at four o'clock *sharp*⟩ — see EXACTLY 1

sharpen *vb* to make sharp or sharper ⟨you need to *sharpen* your penknife's blade frequently in order to be able to whittle properly⟩

synonyms edge, grind, hone, strop, whet

related words file

near antonyms buff, burnish, gloss, polish, round, smooth

antonyms blunt, dull

sharpened *adj* having an edge thin enough to cut or pierce something ⟨the *sharpened* blade of a lawn mower⟩ — see SHARP 1

sharper *n* a dishonest person who uses clever means to cheat others out of something of value ⟨carnival *sharpers* eager to relieve the yokels of their money⟩ — see TRICKSTER 1

sharp–eyed *adj* having unusually keen vision ⟨a very *sharp-eyed* child found the last Easter egg, which was hidden in the flower arrangement⟩
synonyms clear-sighted, lynx-eyed
related words sighted; alert, attentive, aware, observant, observing, vigilant, watchful
near antonyms blind, eyeless, sightless, stone-blind, unseeing; astigmatic, myopic, nearsighted, short-sighted; unobservant, unobserving; purblind

sharply *adv* in a strikingly neat and trim manner ⟨*sharply* dressed groomsmen at a formal wedding⟩ — see SMARTLY

sharpness *n* **1** a harsh or sharp quality ⟨he found that the bland crackers helped cut the *sharpness* of the cheese⟩ — see EDGE 1
2 an uncomfortable degree of coolness ⟨dress warmly; there's a bit of *sharpness* in the air today⟩ — see CHILL

sharpshooter *n* a person skilled in shooting at a target ⟨the police stationed *sharpshooters* on rooftops all along the route of the presidential motorcade⟩ — see MARKSMAN

sharp–witted *adj* **1** having or showing a practical cleverness or judgment ⟨her *sharp-witted* questions always cut right to the core of the issue⟩ — see SHREWD
2 having or showing quickness of mind ⟨a TV game show that allows *sharp-witted* contestants to show their stuff⟩ — see INTELLIGENT 1

shatter *vb* **1** to bring to a complete end the physical soundness, existence, or usefulness of ⟨tried to restore their *shattered* hopes⟩ — see DESTROY 1
2 to cause to break open or into pieces by or as if by an explosive ⟨*shattered* the sealed clay pot to find out what was inside⟩ — see BLAST 1
3 to cause to break with violence and much noise ⟨*shattered* the glass vase in one clumsy fall⟩ — see SMASH 1

shave *vb* **1** to make (as hair) shorter with or as if with the use of shears ⟨he always *shaves* most of his hair off when the weather starts getting warmer⟩ — see CLIP
2 to pass lightly across or touch gently especially in passing ⟨just *shaved* the concrete post as the car turned the corner⟩ — see BRUSH

shaver *n* a male person who has not yet reached adulthood ⟨back in the old days when my dad was just a little *shaver*⟩ — see BOY

shear *vb* to make (as hair) shorter with or as if with the use of shears ⟨it took almost a week to *shear* all the wool off the flock of sheep⟩ — see CLIP

sheath *n* something that encloses another thing especially to protect it ⟨he removed his knife from its *sheath* and started to whittle⟩ — see ¹CASE 1

sheathe *vb* to cover with something that protects ⟨sometimes shipbuilders *sheathe* a ship's bottom with copper for extra protection from barnacles and other threats⟩
synonyms face
related words apparel, array, clothe, dress, garb, robe; side, skin; embosom, embower, embrace, encase, enclose (*also* inclose), encompass, enshroud, envelop, enwrap, invest, lap, mantle, shroud, surround, swathe, veil, wrap; blanket, overlay, overspread
near antonyms bare, denude, expose, strip

shed *vb* **1** to cast (a natural bodily covering or appendage) aside ⟨a snake's skin doesn't grow as the snake does, so every so often the snake will *shed* its old skin⟩
synonyms exfoliate, molt, slough (*also* sluff)
related words flake, peel, scale; discard

2 to get rid of as useless or unwanted ⟨you need to *shed* your old notions of propriety and have some fun for a change⟩ — see DISCARD

sheen *n* brightness created by light reflected from a surface ⟨polished the metal until it had an even *sheen*⟩ — see SHINE 1

sheep *n* an innocent or gentle person ⟨he felt that the members of the cult were *sheep* who naively went along with whatever their leader said⟩ — see LAMB

sheepish *adj* not comfortable around people ⟨a *sheepish* scholar who is most comfortable when surrounded by books⟩ — see SHY 2

sheepishly *adv* in a manner showing no signs of pride or self-assertion ⟨the younger boy, who idolized the older one, would *sheepishly* follow him around and be at his beck and call⟩ — see LOWLY

sheer *adj* **1** very thin and easy to see through ⟨we had to get window shades because passersby could see right through our *sheer* curtains⟩
synonyms filmy, gauzy, gossamer, gossamery, transparent
related words clear, limpid, liquid, lucent, pellucid; lucid, translucent; dainty, delicate, flimsy, fragile, frail; colorless, uncolored
near antonyms opaque; cloudy, foggy, hazy, misty, murky, smoky (*also* smokey); drab, dull, lackluster, lusterless
2 having no exceptions or restrictions ⟨survivors of the earthquake told of experiencing *sheer* terror⟩ — see ABSOLUTE 2
3 having an incline approaching the perpendicular ⟨the *sheer* slopes of the ravine⟩ — see STEEP 1

sheer *vb* **1** to change one's course or direction ⟨the cruise ship *sheered* to the northwest, putting it safely out of the path of the hurricane⟩ — see TURN 3
2 to depart abruptly from a straight line or course ⟨the car *sheered* to avoid hitting the dog⟩ — see SWERVE 1

sheet *vb* to form a layer over ⟨dust *sheeted* the floors of the old, abandoned house⟩ — see COVER 2

shell *n* **1** something that encloses another thing especially to protect it ⟨eating oysters straight out of their *shells*⟩ — see ¹CASE 1
2 the arrangement of parts that gives something its basic form ⟨workers at the shipyard have thus far erected the *shell* of the ship⟩ — see FRAME 1

shell *vb* **1** to remove the natural covering of ⟨*shelling* peanuts⟩ — see PEEL
2 to use bombs or artillery against ⟨the enemy *shelled* the city for days without letup⟩ — see BOMBARD

shellacking *n* failure to win a contest ⟨suffered a *shellacking* at the hands of a vastly superior opposition⟩ — see DEFEAT 1

shell–shocked *adj* suffering from high levels of physical and especially psychological stress ⟨even after the long furlough, the returning soldiers still felt a little *shell-shocked*⟩ — see STRESSED-OUT

shelter *n* something (as a building) that offers cover from the weather or protection from danger ⟨the sudden fierce storm forced us to run to the nearest *shelter*⟩
synonyms asylum, harbor, harborage, haven, refuge, retreat, sanctuary, sanctum
related words anchorage, mooring, port; cover, screen; abode, diggings, domicile, dwelling, habitation, house, housing, lodging, lodgment (*or* lodgement), pad, place, quarters, residence, rest, roof; den, lair, hermitage, hideaway, hideout; fastness, fort, fortress, palisade, stronghold; lean-to, shed, windbreak

shelter *vb* **1** to be or provide a shelter for ⟨the abandoned barn *shelters* a colony of stray cats⟩
synonyms harbor
related words cover, defend, protect, safeguard, screen, shield, ward; domicile, house, place; shade, shadow
near antonyms expose
2 to provide with living quarters or shelter ⟨*sheltered* the troops in tents until permanent barracks could be built⟩ — see HOUSE 1
sheltered *adj* hidden from view ⟨moored the sailboat in a *sheltered* cove⟩ — see SECLUDED
shelve *vb* to assign to a later time ⟨let's *shelve* the project for now⟩ — see POSTPONE
shenanigans *n pl* **1** playful, reckless behavior that is not intended to cause serious harm ⟨students engaging in youthful *shenanigans* on the last day of school⟩ — see MISCHIEF 1
2 wildly playful or mischievous behavior ⟨an act of vandalism that went way beyond the usual *shenanigans* at summer camp⟩ — see HORSEPLAY
shepherd *vb* to give advice and instruction to (someone) regarding the course or process to be followed ⟨*shepherding* her through the procedure of taking out a loan⟩ — see GUIDE 1
shibboleth *n* **1** an attention-getting word or phrase used to publicize something (as a campaign or product) ⟨we knew that their claim of giving "the best deal in town" was just a *shibboleth*⟩ — see SLOGAN
2 an idea or expression that has been used by many people ⟨there's a lot of truth in the *shibboleth* that crime does not pay⟩ — see COMMONPLACE
shield *n* means or method of defending ⟨the slightly built boy used his sharp wit as a *shield* against the school's bullies⟩ — see DEFENSE 1
shield *vb* **1** to drive danger or attack away from ⟨celebrities who are *shielded* by a cluster of bodyguards whenever they appear in public⟩ — see DEFEND 1
2 to place a protective layer over ⟨*shielded* her eyes from the sun with her hand⟩ — see COVER 3
shift *n* **1** an action planned or taken to achieve a desired result ⟨desperate *shifts* to stave off disaster⟩ — see MEASURE 1
2 the act or an instance of changing position ⟨made a small *shift* to the left to make more room on the bench⟩ — see MOVEMENT 1
shift *vb* **1** to change the place or position of ⟨he *shifted* the vase closer to the wall so that it wouldn't get knocked over⟩ — see MOVE 1
2 to change one's position ⟨she *shifted* uncomfortably in her seat throughout the interview⟩ — see MOVE 3
3 to pass from one form, state, or level to another ⟨she watched the aurora in fascination as its colors *shifted* from green to blue⟩ — see CHANGE 2
4 to give up (something) and take something else in return ⟨my brother and I *shifted* seats just before takeoff so that he could sit by the window⟩ — see CHANGE 3
5 to meet one's day-to-day needs ⟨left the others to *shift* for themselves⟩ — see GET ALONG 1
shifting *n* the act or an instance of changing position ⟨the *shifting* of the toys to the front of the display was a direct result of their sudden popularity⟩ — see MOVEMENT 1
shiftless *adj* not easily aroused to action or work ⟨*shiftless* spongers who never thought to do anything for themselves⟩ — see LAZY
shiftlessness *n* an inclination not to do work or engage in activities ⟨with the start of the warm weather, com-

bating the students' *shiftlessness* was a constant ordeal⟩ — see LAZINESS
shifty *adj* **1** given to acting in secret and to concealing one's intentions ⟨*shifty* politicians making deals to channel federal funds into their districts⟩ — see SNEAKY 1
2 given to or marked by cheating and deception ⟨*shifty* deals made in back lots⟩ — see DISHONEST 2
shillelagh *n* a heavy rigid stick used as a weapon or for punishment ⟨the bartender in the Irish pub keeps a *shillelagh* behind the bar just in case there's trouble⟩ — see CLUB 1
shilly-shally *vb* to show uncertainty about the right course of action ⟨I didn't *shilly-shally* but instead raced to the hospital as soon as I heard the news⟩ — see HESITATE
shilly-shallying *n* the act or an instance of pausing because of uncertainty about the right course of action ⟨fortunately, during the crisis there was no *shilly-shallying* on the part of the president⟩ — see HESITATION
shimmer *vb* to shoot forth bursts of light ⟨a sequined dress *shimmering* under the studio lights⟩ — see FLASH 1
shindig *n* a social gathering ⟨we're hosting a little *shindig* this weekend for some friends⟩ — see PARTY 1
shindy *n* a state of noisy, confused activity ⟨created a brief *shindy* with his unexpected appearance⟩ — see COMMOTION
shine *n* **1** brightness created by light reflected from a surface ⟨the troop inspector insisted on nothing less than a dazzling *shine* from every pair of shoes in the line of review⟩
synonyms gloss, luster (or lustre), polish, sheen
related words glare, gleam, glimmer, glint, glisten, glow, shimmer; flicker, sparkle, twinkle; illumination, irradiation; iridescence, luminescence; brightness, brilliance, luminosity, radiance; finish, glaze
near antonyms dimness, dinginess, dirtiness, drabness, dullness (*also* dulness), flatness; grayness, paleness; cloudiness, gloom, murkiness, obscurity, somberness
2 the steady giving off of the form of radiation that makes vision possible ⟨by the *shine* of the full moon we could see the rabbit helping himself to our garden vegetables⟩ — see LIGHT 1
3 positive regard for something ⟨took quite a *shine* to the new neighbors⟩ — see LIKING
shine *vb* **1** to emit rays of light ⟨the sun appears to *shine* particularly brightly in summer because that is when it's closest to the Earth⟩
synonyms beam, radiate
related words blaze, burn, fire, flame, gleam, glimmer, glint, glisten, glitter, glow, shimmer; blink, flare, flash, flicker, scintillate, sparkle, twinkle, wink; beat (down), glare; brighten, illuminate, illumine, irradiate, light, lighten; bedazzle, blind, daze, dazzle
near antonyms blacken, darken; lower (*also* lour)
2 to make smooth or glossy usually by repeatedly applying surface pressure ⟨the salesman *shined* his shoes every morning before leaving the house⟩ — see POLISH
shining *adj* giving off or reflecting much light ⟨the *shining* moon formed a nice backdrop for our outdoor concert⟩ — see BRIGHT 1
shiny *adj* giving off or reflecting much light ⟨we could see our reflections in the *shiny* surface of the marble walls⟩ — see BRIGHT 1

ship *n* a large craft for travel by water ⟨we chose to spend our vacation on a cruise *ship* traveling through the Caribbean⟩
synonyms boat, vessel
related words argosy, containership, corvette, cruiser, cutter, destroyer, ferryboat, flagship, freighter, icebreaker, ironclad, lightship, liner, man-of-war, merchantman, merchant ship, packet, steamer, supertanker, tanker, trader, tramp, transport, warship

ship *vb* to cause to go or be taken from one place to another ⟨we *shipped* those books out yesterday⟩ — see SEND

shippable *adj* capable of being taken from one place to another by public carrier ⟨only boxes of five pounds and under are *shippable* by the postal service⟩
synonyms transferable, transmittable, transportable
related words addressable
antonyms nontransferable, receivable

shipshape *adj* being clean and in good order ⟨made everything *shipshape* for the inspection⟩ — see NEAT 1

shipwreck *n* the destruction or loss of a ship ⟨the *shipwreck* of much of the Spanish Armada ended Spain's plans for invading England⟩
synonyms shipwrecking, wreck, wreckage, wrecking
related words beaching, grounding, stranding; foundering, sinking
near antonyms salvage, salvaging

shipwreck *vb* to cause irreparable damage to (a ship) by running aground or sinking ⟨the helmsman fell asleep at the wheel and *shipwrecked* his yacht on the rocks⟩
synonyms strand, wreck
related words beach; founder, sink
near antonyms salvage

shipwrecking *n* the destruction or loss of a ship ⟨the *shipwrecking* of the Titanic by an iceberg ranks as one of the greatest disasters in the annals of the sea⟩ — see SHIPWRECK

shirk *vb* **1** to get or keep away from (as a responsibility) through cleverness or trickery ⟨you always try to *shirk* paying your fair share of the bill by claiming you "forgot" your wallet⟩ — see ESCAPE 2
2 to leave undone or unattended to especially through carelessness ⟨a deadbeat who has been *shirking* his duty to his family for years⟩ — see NEGLECT 2

shirker *n* one who deliberately avoids work or duty ⟨even before we weighed anchor, the captain forcefully asserted that there would be no *shirkers* on his ship⟩ — see SLACKER

shirty *adj, chiefly British* feeling or showing anger ⟨felt as though he had encountered every *shirty* bloke in London while he was there on a business trip⟩ — see ANGRY

shiver *n* **1** an instance of shaking involuntarily with fear or cold ⟨Joe experienced a sudden *shiver* when confronted with the sight of the dark basement⟩
synonyms quiver, shudder, tremble
related words agitation, convulsing, jolt, quake, shake, tremor, vibration, wobble; fluctuation, flutter, oscillation, wave; beat, palpitation, pulsation, pulse, throb
2 shivers *pl* a sense of panic or extreme nervousness ⟨looking down from the window ledge sent *shivers* up my spine⟩ — see JITTERS

shivery *adj* having a low or subnormal temperature ⟨those *shivery* days of January⟩ — see COLD 1

shoal *adj* lacking significant physical depth ⟨*shoal* waters of the bay meant that our ship had to be moored a considerable distance from shore⟩ — see SHALLOW 1

shoal *n* a place where a body of water (as a sea or river) is shallow ⟨the *shoals* off Nantucket Island are famous as the final resting places of many ill-fated ships⟩
synonyms ford, shallows
related words bank, bar, sandbank, sandbar
near antonyms trench; abyss, deep, depth

shock *n* **1** a forceful coming together of two things ⟨the whole railway platform shook from the *shock* of the two trains colliding⟩ — see IMPACT 1
2 the state of being strongly impressed by something unexpected or unusual ⟨were in *shock* after they heard the news of the death of the president⟩ — see SURPRISE 2

shock *vb* **1** to cause an often unpleasant surprise for ⟨Mom was *shocked* by the terrible news that her cousin had died in an accident⟩ ⟨Jack was *shocked* to find out that his grades were much lower than he realized⟩
synonyms appall, bowl (over), floor, jolt, shake up
related words affright, alarm, dismay, frighten, horrify, panic, scare, spook, startle, terrify, terrorize; disgust, nauseate, repel, revolt, sicken, turn off; displease, offend, outrage, scandalize; amaze, astound, awe; chill, daunt, demoralize, dispirit, unman, unnerve; discompose, disconcert, disquiet, disturb, perturb, unsettle, upset; crush, overpower, overwhelm
phrases knock for a loop
near antonyms cushion; delight, gratify, please, rejoice, tickle; charm, entice, tempt; cheer, comfort, console, solace, soothe; reassure
2 to make a strong impression on (someone) with something unexpected ⟨were *shocked* by the way the law was constantly being broken⟩ — see SURPRISE 1
3 to strike with fear ⟨the sudden appearance of the ghost *shocked* us to the core⟩ — see FRIGHTEN

shocked *adj* **1** affected with sudden and great wonder or surprise ⟨the escaping bridegroom greeted the *shocked* churchgoers with a cheerful wave as he ran out the door⟩ — see THUNDERSTRUCK
2 filled with disgust ⟨we were *shocked* at the appalling conditions in the prison⟩ — see SICK 2

shocking *adj* **1** causing a strong emotional reaction because unexpected ⟨we all clustered around to hear the *shocking* news of our school's poor showing⟩ — see SURPRISING 1
2 causing fear ⟨the *shocking* appearance of a shark just a few yards off shore⟩ — see FEARFUL 1
3 causing intense displeasure, disgust, or resentment ⟨the *shocking* behavior of some rowdies at the dance⟩ — see OFFENSIVE 1
4 extremely disturbing or repellent ⟨a soldier who had witnessed the *shocking* sight of his best friend being killed⟩ — see HORRIBLE 1

shoddy *adj* of low quality ⟨*shoddy* merchandise that soon fell to pieces⟩ — see CHEAP 2

shoes *n pl* a way of looking at or thinking about something ⟨suppose you were in your friend's *shoes*?⟩ — see POINT OF VIEW

shoestring *n* a very small sum of money ⟨trying to start a business on a *shoestring*⟩ — see MITE 1

shoot *n* a branch of a main stem especially of a plant ⟨collected the most tender *shoots* for the vegetable dish he was making⟩ — see OFFSHOOT 1

shoot *vb* **1** to cause (a projectile) to be driven forward with force ⟨BB guns *shoot* small round metal pellets⟩
synonyms blast, discharge, fire, loose
related words launch, project; blaze (at), snipe (at); cast, catapult, fling, heave, hurl, pelt, pitch, sling, throw, toss

2 to cause a weapon to release a missile with great force ⟨soldiers train extensively to learn to *shoot* accurately and quickly⟩
synonyms blast, discharge, fire
related words blaze, pepper, snipe
3 to strike with a missile from a gun ⟨hunters can *shoot* deer only during the legally specified open season⟩
synonyms drill, gun, plug, pop
related words blaze, pepper; blast (at), fire (at); pick off; overshoot; snipe (at); croak [*slang*], destroy, dispatch, do in, fell, kill, slay; annihilate, blot out, butcher, decimate, massacre, slaughter, wipe out
4 to proceed or move quickly ⟨some show-off *shot* past on all the other skiers on the slope⟩ — see HURRY 2
5 to take a photograph of ⟨*shooting* the scene while the light lasted⟩ — see PHOTOGRAPH
6 to throw or give off ⟨suddenly the old, broken-down toaster began *shooting* out sparks⟩ — see EMIT 1
shoot (up) *vb* to rise abruptly and rapidly ⟨gas prices *shot up* seemingly overnight⟩ — see SKYROCKET
shooter *n* **1** a person skilled in shooting at a target ⟨there were eight *shooters* taking turns at the same target in the final competition⟩ — see MARKSMAN
2 one who takes photographs ⟨he's one of the best *shooters* of wildlife in all of professional photography⟩ — see PHOTOGRAPHER
shop *n* **1** *also* **shoppe** an establishment where goods are sold to consumers ⟨the only *shop* which carries that game is halfway across the state⟩
synonyms bazaar, emporium, store
related words market, marketplace, outlet, showroom; boutique, department store, dime store, five-and-ten, thrift shop, variety store
2 a building or set of buildings for the manufacturing of goods ⟨a machine *shop*⟩ — see FACTORY
¹shore *n* something that holds up or serves as a foundation for something else ⟨the carpenter placed a *shore* underneath the sagging roof of the porch⟩ — see SUPPORT 1
²shore *n* the usually sandy or gravelly land bordering a body of water ⟨a vacation home just a few yards from the *shore* of the lake⟩ — see BEACH
shore (up) *vb* to hold up or serve as a foundation for ⟨a highway tunnel *shored up* by massive columns of concrete⟩ — see SUPPORT 3
short *adj* **1** having relatively little height ⟨a lot of boys are *shorter* than the girls in middle school, but they quickly catch up by high school⟩
synonyms little, low, low-lying
related words dwarf, dwarfish; petite, slight; diminutive, little, pint-size (*or* pint-sized), small, smallish; bantam, bitty, dinky, miniature, minimized, minute, puny, teeny, teeny-weeny, tiny, undersized, wee; dumpy, flat, scrubby, squat, squatty, stubby, stumpy, stunted
near antonyms elevated, lifted, raised, uplifted, upswept; high-rise, statuesque; gangling, gangly, lanky, rangy
antonyms high, lofty, tall, towering
2 not lasting for a considerable time ⟨fortunately for those of us in the hot sun, the graduation speech was *short* and to the point⟩
synonyms brief, condensed, little
related words abbreviated, abridged, curtailed, cutback, shortened; compact, condensed; abrupt, sudden; ephemeral, fleeting, momentary, short-lived, transient, transitory; impermanent; compendious, concise, crisp, epigrammatic, laconic, pithy, succinct, summary, terse; short-range, short-term

near antonyms endless, everlasting, interminable, persistent, unending; longish, overlong, prolonged, protracted; permanent; enlarged, expanded, supplemented; long-range, long-term
antonyms extended, great, lengthy, long, long-lived, marathon
3 not coming up to a usual standard or meeting a particular need ⟨regrettably, the art supplies are *short* this year, so you'll have to share⟩
synonyms deficient, inadequate, insufficient, lacking, scarce, shy, wanting
related words hand-to-mouth, light, meager, niggardly, poor, scant, scanty, skimpy, slender, slim, spare, sparse, stingy; bare, mere, minimum; slight, small
near antonyms abundant, ample, bounteous, bountiful, copious, generous, liberal, plenteous, plentiful; enlarged, expanded, supplemented; abounding, overflowing, teeming; lavish, luxuriant, rich; big, considerable, hefty, jumbo, large, largish, oversize (*or* oversized), sizable (*or* sizeable), substantial, super
antonyms adequate, enough, sufficient
4 having a texture that readily breaks into little pieces under pressure ⟨*short* pastry⟩ — see CRISP 1
short *adv* with great suddenness ⟨the bicyclist ahead of me unexpectedly pulled up *short* and I plowed into him⟩
synonyms abruptly, suddenly
related words quickly; surprisingly, unexpectedly
near antonyms gradually, slowly; hesitantly
shortage *n* a falling short of an essential or desirable amount or number ⟨there was a troubling *shortage* of school supplies this year⟩ — see DEFICIENCY
shortchange *vb* to rob by the use of trickery or threats ⟨was *shortchanged* out of a promotion⟩ — see FLEECE
shortcoming *n* a defect in character ⟨a wife who never tires of listing her husband's *shortcomings*⟩ — see FAULT 1
shorten *vb* to make less in extent or duration ⟨we decided to *shorten* the distance we had to walk home by cutting across the neighbor's lawn⟩ ⟨if Grandma has to go shopping today, you'll need to *shorten* your visit⟩
synonyms abbreviate, abridge, curtail, cut back
related words digest, summarize; abate, compress, constrict, contract, cut, cut down, pare, prune, trim; decrease, de-escalate, deflate, diminish, dock, dwindle, lessen, lower, moderate, modify, reduce, retrench, shrink, slash, taper
near antonyms enlarge, expand, supplement; add, aggrandize, amplify, augment, balloon, boost, dilate, escalate, heighten, increase, maximize, raise; blow up, distend, inflate, swell
antonyms elongate, extend, lengthen, prolong, protract
short-lived *adj* lasting only for a short time ⟨the skier's triumph turned out to be *short-lived*, as the next competitor bested her time⟩ — see MOMENTARY
shortly *adv* **1** in a few words ⟨the sudden closing of the restaurant was announced only with a *shortly* worded sign: "Out of Business"⟩
synonyms briefly, compactly, concisely, crisply, laconically, pithily, succinctly, summarily, tersely
related words aphoristically; exactly, precisely; abruptly, bluntly, brusquely, curtly
phrases in a nutshell
near antonyms redundantly, repetitiously
antonyms diffusely, long-windedly, verbosely, wordily
2 at or within a short time ⟨the test will begin *shortly*, so don't go too far away to find a bathroom⟩

synonyms anon, momentarily, presently, soon
related words directly, forthwith, immediately, instantly, now, promptly, pronto, right away, right now, straightaway
phrases by and by

shortness *n* the condition of being short ⟨the *shortness* of the commencement speech was much appreciated by the impatient graduates⟩ — see BREVITY 1

shortsighted *adj* **1** able to see near things more clearly than distant ones ⟨because she's so *shortsighted*, she's forced to wear her glasses every waking moment⟩ — see NEARSIGHTED
2 not thinking about and providing for the future ⟨*shortsighted* investors who failed to see that the boom couldn't last⟩ — see IMPROVIDENT

short story *n* a work with imaginary characters and events that is shorter and usually less complex than a novel ⟨her very first *short story* was accepted for publication in a local journal⟩ — see STORY 1

short–tempered *adj* easily irritated or annoyed ⟨shop customers learned not to bother the *short-tempered* dog on their way out⟩ — see IRRITABLE

short–term *adj* intended to last, continue, or serve for a limited time ⟨this is only a *short-term* solution to a long-term problem⟩ — see TEMPORARY 1

shot *n* **1** a directed propelling of a missile by a firearm or artillery piece ⟨cannon operators often had to use several *shots* to figure out the range of their targets⟩
synonyms blasting, discharge, firing
related words potshot; barrage, bombardment, broadside, burst, cannonade, fusillade, hail, salvo, storm, volley
2 an effort to do or accomplish something ⟨take another *shot* at the puzzle⟩ — see ATTEMPT
3 a picture created from an image recorded on a light-sensitive surface by a camera ⟨took a *shot* of his family for the scrapbook⟩ — see PHOTOGRAPH
4 a person skilled in shooting at a target ⟨a soldier who's an excellent *shot* with a rifle⟩ — see MARKSMAN
5 the portion of a serving of a beverage that is swallowed at one time ⟨drank a *shot* of whisky⟩ — see DRINK 2

should *vb* to be under necessity or obligation to ⟨you *should* study harder⟩ — see NEED 2

shoulder *vb* to take to or upon oneself ⟨agreed to *shoulder* the burden⟩ — see ASSUME 1

shout *n* a loud vocal expression of strong emotion ⟨Jason gave a sudden *shout* of surprise when the shower abruptly turned ice-cold⟩
synonyms cry, holler, hoot, howl, yell, yowl, whoop
related words scream, screech, shriek, squall, squeak, squeal, yelp; bellow, clamor, roar; caterwaul, wail
near antonyms mumble, murmur, mutter; gasp, whimper, whisper

shout *vb* to speak so as to be heard at a distance ⟨he *shouted* to passengers from the dock⟩ — see CALL 1

shove *vb* **1** to apply force to (someone or something) so that it moves in front of one ⟨I had to keep *shoving* my heavy suitcase as I slowly made my way to the head of the line⟩ — see PUSH 1
2 to push steadily against with some force ⟨quit *shoving* your hand in my face⟩ — see PRESS 1

shove (off) *vb* to leave a place often for another ⟨time to *shove off* for home⟩ — see GO 2

shovel *vb* to hollow out or form (something) by removing earth ⟨the troops quickly *shoveled* a trench⟩ — see DIG 1

show *n* **1** an outward and often exaggerated indication of something abstract (as a feeling) for effect ⟨the children made a *show* of disgust when confronted with asparagus⟩
synonyms demonstration, display, exhibition, flaunting
related words act, pretense (*or* pretence), simulation; affectation, pose, sham; betrayal, disclosure
2 a display of emotion or behavior that is insincere or intended to deceive ⟨her "concern" for the less fortunate is all just a big *show*⟩ — see MASQUERADE
3 outward and often deceptive indication ⟨a false *show* of strength that fooled the enemy⟩ — see APPEARANCE 2
4 a public showing of objects of interest ⟨a boat *show* at the convention center⟩ — see EXHIBITION 1

show *vb* **1** to present so as to invite notice or attention ⟨Julie made sure she *showed* the test paper with a big A on it to everyone in her family⟩
synonyms display, disport, exhibit, expose, flash, flaunt, parade, show off, sport, strut, unveil
related words brandish, flourish; advertise, air, broadcast, proclaim, publicize; divulge, talk (about), tell (of); bare, discover, reveal, uncloak, uncover
near antonyms camouflage, disguise, mask; conceal, cover, curtain, enshroud, hide, obscure, occult, shroud, veil
2 to make known (something abstract) through outward signs ⟨John's expressive face *shows* his every thought and emotion clearly⟩
synonyms bespeak, betray, demonstrate, display, expose, evince, give away, manifest, reveal
related words bare, disclose, unbosom, uncloak, uncover; advertise, air, broadcast, proclaim, publicize
near antonyms belie, misrepresent; distort, falsify, garble, twist; camouflage, disguise; gild, gloss (over), varnish, whitewash; conceal, counterfeit, cover, hide, mask, obscure, veil
3 to gain full recognition or acceptance of ⟨that *shows* we're right⟩ — see ESTABLISH 1
4 to give advice and instruction to (someone) regarding the course or process to be followed ⟨*showed* me how to play the guitar⟩ — see GUIDE 1
5 to point out the way for (someone) especially from a position in front ⟨*showed* them the way to get home⟩ — see LEAD 1

shower *n* **1** a heavy fall of objects ⟨a *shower* of books fell from the collapsing shelves⟩ — see RAIN 2
2 a rapid or overwhelming outpouring of many things at once ⟨a *shower* of insults and curses rained down on the criminal as he was led through the crowd⟩ — see BARRAGE

shower *vb* to give readily and in large quantities ⟨*showered* gifts on the guests of honor⟩ — see RAIN 2

showiness *n* excessive or unnecessary display ⟨we were somewhat put off by the *showiness* of the military parade⟩ — see OSTENTATION

show off *vb* **1** to engage in attention-getting playful or boisterous behavior ⟨the athletes warmed up, happily *showing off* for the crowd before the match officially started⟩ — see CUT UP
2 to present so as to invite notice or attention ⟨she just wants to *show off* her new jewelry⟩ — see SHOW 1

show up *vb* **1** to come into view ⟨they *showed up* just as we were about to leave⟩ — see APPEAR 1
2 to get to a destination ⟨*showed up* an hour late⟩ — see COME 2

3 to reveal the true nature of ⟨were *shown up* for what they really are⟩ — see EXPOSE 1

showy *adj* likely to attract attention ⟨orchid plants are known for their huge *showy* flowers⟩ — see NOTICEABLE

shred *n* a very small amount ⟨the vandals showed not a *shred* of decency⟩ — see PARTICLE 1

shred *vb* to cause (something) to separate into jagged pieces by violently pulling at it ⟨*shredded* some cooked chicken for the soup⟩ — see TEAR 1

shrew *n* a bad-tempered scolding woman ⟨Rip Van Winkle went off into mountains to escape his wife, a *shrew* who made his life miserable⟩

   synonyms fury, harpy, termagant, virago

   related words carper, castigator, censurer, caviler (*or* caviller), critic, faultfinder, nitpicker, railer, scold; belittler, derider, detractor; pettifogger, quibbler

shrewd *adj* having or showing a practical cleverness or judgment ⟨a *shrewd* used car dealer who knew how to make the best possible deal⟩ ⟨*shrewd* investments that paid off big⟩

   synonyms astute, canny, clear-sighted, hardheaded, knowing, sharp, sharp-witted, smart

   related words artful, cagey (*also* cagy), crafty, cunning, devious, foxy, guileful, slick, sly, subtle, wily; discerning, insightful, perceptive, perspicacious, sagacious, sage, sapient, wise; experienced, veteran; discriminating, discriminative; agile, alert, brainy, bright, brilliant, clever, intelligent, keen, quick, quick-witted; apt, ingenious, resourceful; informed, knowledgeable, well-read

   near antonyms artless, guileless, ingenuous, innocent, naive (*or* naïve); exploitable, gullible; undiscerning, unperceptive, unwise; dense, dull, obtuse; brainless, dumb, feebleminded, simple, slow, stupid, unintelligent, weak-minded; foolish, idiotic, imbecilic, moronic, silly, simple, thoughtless, witless; ignorant, uninformed

   antonyms unknowing

shriek *vb* to cry out loudly and emotionally ⟨the children *shrieked* with excitement⟩ — see SCREAM

shrieking *adj* having a high musical pitch or range ⟨*shrieking* horns of impatient drivers stuck in a traffic jam⟩ — see SHRILL

shrill *adj* having a high musical pitch or range ⟨the *shrill* sound of a policeman's whistle⟩

   synonyms acute, high-pitched, piping, screeching, shrieking, squeaking, squeaky, treble, whistling

   related words peeping, thin, tinny; piercing, earsplitting, piercing, penetrating, strident; squealing, whining, yelping

   near antonyms gruff

   antonyms bass, deep, low, throaty

shrill *vb* to cry out loudly and emotionally ⟨the splattered bystanders were *shrilling* with outrage at the inconsiderate motorist⟩ — see SCREAM

shrimp *n* **1** a living thing much smaller than others of its kind ⟨the boy was just a *shrimp* until he had a growth spurt⟩ — see DWARF 1

   2 a person of no importance or influence ⟨you have no business telling me what to do, you little *shrimp!*⟩ — see NOBODY

shrine *n* a place that is considered sacred (as within a religion) ⟨for centuries pilgrims have traveled to the *shrine* of Saint Thomas à Becket in Canterbury, England⟩

   synonyms sanctuary, sanctum

   related words reliquary

shrink *vb* **1** to become smaller in size or volume through the drawing together of particles of matter ⟨the sweater will *shrink* when washed⟩ — see CONTRACT 2

   2 to draw back in fear, pain, or disgust ⟨*shrinking* back from the approaching flames⟩ — see FLINCH

   3 to grow less in scope or intensity especially gradually ⟨his crush on her is likely to *shrink* over the course of the summer⟩ — see DECREASE 1

shrinkage *n* the amount by which something is lessened ⟨she knew that her diet was working by the striking *shrinkage* of her waist⟩ — see DECREASE

shroud *n* something that covers or conceals like a piece of cloth ⟨the truth of the affair will always be hidden under a *shroud* of secrecy⟩ — see CLOAK 1

shroud *vb* **1** to keep secret or shut off from view ⟨*shrouded* the fact that the child had been adopted⟩ — see ¹HIDE 2

   2 to make dark, dim, or indistinct ⟨the smog *shrouded* our aerial view of the city⟩ — see CLOUD 1

   3 to surround or cover closely ⟨during rainy season the summit of the mountain is *shrouded* in mist⟩ — see ENFOLD 1

shrug off *vb* to overlook or dismiss as of little importance ⟨an administration willing to *shrug off* the problem⟩ — see EXCUSE 1

shuck *vb* to remove the natural covering of ⟨*shucking* peas⟩ — see PEEL

shuck (off) *vb* to get rid of as useless or unwanted ⟨bad habits are hard to *shuck off*⟩ — see DISCARD

shudder *n* an instance of shaking involuntarily with fear or cold ⟨a *shudder* ran through him as he stepped outside into the snow⟩ — see SHIVER 1

shudder *vb* to make a series of small irregular or violent movements ⟨we *shuddered* with fear as the ghost story built to a climax⟩ — see SHAKE 1

shuddering *adj* marked by or given to small uncontrollable bodily movements ⟨with a *shuddering* extension of his hand, the poor beggar asked for a little charity⟩ — see SHAKY 1

shuddering *n* a series of slight movements by a body back and forth or from side to side ⟨tried to control the *shuddering* of his hand⟩ — see VIBRATION

shuddery *adj* marked by or given to small uncontrollable bodily movements ⟨with a few *shuddery* strokes of a pen, she signed her last will and testament⟩ — see SHAKY 1

shuffle *n* an unorganized collection or mixture of various things ⟨the paper got lost in the *shuffle* on his desk⟩ — see MISCELLANY 1

shuffle *vb* **1** to move heavily or clumsily ⟨*shuffled* across the floor in his slippers⟩ — see LUMBER 1

   2 to undo the proper order or arrangement of ⟨*shuffle* the cards and deal five to each player⟩ — see DISORDER

shun *vb* to get or keep away from (as a responsibility) through cleverness or trickery ⟨just a ruse to *shun* the debt collectors⟩ — see ESCAPE 2

shunning *n* the act or a means of getting or keeping away from something undesirable ⟨this *shunning* of your financial responsibilities cannot continue indefinitely⟩ — see ESCAPE 2

shush *vb* to stop the noise or speech of ⟨*shushed* the crying baby⟩ — see SILENCE 1

shut *vb* **1** to position (something) so as to prevent passage through an opening ⟨please *shut* the door⟩ — see CLOSE 1

   2 to stop the operations of ⟨*shut* both stores for a week⟩ — see CLOSE 2

shutdown *n* the stopping of a process or activity ⟨resumed operation after a brief *shutdown* for repairs⟩ — see END 1

shutoff *n* the stopping of a process or activity ⟨threatened the *shutoff* of electricity if the bills weren't paid⟩ — see END 1

shut off *vb* to bring (as an action or operation) to an immediate end ⟨threatened to *shut off* peace talks if the other side kept making unreasonable demands⟩ — see STOP 1

shutterbug *n* one who takes photographs ⟨an avid *shutterbug* who takes her camera with her everywhere⟩ — see PHOTOGRAPHER

shut up *vb* to stop talking ⟨it's not polite to tell your classmates to *shut up*, even if you disagree with them⟩
synonyms clam up, hush, quiet (down)
related words calm (down), cool (down), settle (down); haw, hem
antonyms speak, talk

shy *adj* **1** easily frightened ⟨a *shy* cat who hid under the bed every time she heard any loud noise⟩
synonyms fainthearted, fearful, mousy (*or* mousey), scary, skittish, timid, timorous
related words chicken, chickenhearted, cowardly, craven, dastardly, lily-livered, jittery, jumpy, pusillanimous, spineless, unheroic, yellow; anxious, apprehensive, nervous; afraid, alarmed, horrified, panicked, panicky, scared, shocked, spooked, startled, terrified, terrorized
near antonyms brave, courageous, dauntless, doughty, fearless, gallant, greathearted, heroic, intrepid, lionhearted, stalwart, stout, stouthearted, valiant, valorous; assured, confident, self-assured, self-confident; determined, firm, game, plucky, resolute, unflinching, unswerving; mettlesome, spirited, spunky
antonyms adventuresome, adventurous, audacious, bold, daring, dashing, gutsy, hardy, venturous, venturesome
2 not comfortable around people ⟨a *shy* person who finds talking to anyone but a close friend to be an awkward and unpleasant experience⟩
synonyms bashful, coy, demure, diffident, introverted, modest, retiring, sheepish
related words antisocial, unsociable, unsocial; awkward, embarrassed, self-conscious, unadventurous, unassertive, unenterprising; inhibited, reserved, uneasy, uptight
near antonyms convivial, sociable, social; bold, dashing, forceful; brash, forward, uninhibited, unreserved
antonyms extroverted (*also* extraverted), immodest, outgoing
3 not coming up to a usual standard or meeting a particular need ⟨the team is *shy* a couple of players because of illness⟩ — see SHORT 3

sick *adj* **1** temporarily suffering from a disorder of the body ⟨Jessie was *sick* with a cold on Monday and had to stay home from school⟩
synonyms ailing, bad, down, ill, indisposed, peaked, poorly, punk, run-down, sickened, unhealthy, unsound, unwell
related words nauseated, nauseous, qualmish, queasy (*also* queazy), sickish, squeamish; airsick, carsick, seasick, dizzy, light-hearted, woozy; achy, feverish; diseased, disordered; feeble, frail, infirm, sickly, weak, weakly; afflicted, troubled; challenged, crippled, debilitated, disabled, incapacitated, lame
phrases out of sorts, under the weather

near antonyms cured; better, convalescing, improved, mending, recovering, recuperating, rehabilitated; hardy, hearty, lusty, robust, rugged, stalwart, strong, tough; blooming, bouncing, flourishing, flush, thriving
antonyms chipper, hale, healthful, healthy, sound, well, whole, wholesome
2 filled with disgust ⟨it makes me *sick* to think of someone hurting a helpless animal⟩
synonyms disgusted, nauseated, repelled, repulsed, revolted, shocked, sickened, squeamish
related words angry, displeased, mad, upset
near antonyms delighted, pleased, thrilled; beguiled, bewitched, captivated, charmed, enchanted, enthralled, fascinated, mesmerized
3 affected with nausea ⟨the bumpy ride made her *sick* to her stomach⟩ — see NAUSEOUS
4 having one's patience, interest, or pleasure exhausted ⟨I'm *sick* of listening to this radio station⟩ — see WEARY 2

sicken *vb* to cause to feel disgust ⟨*sickened* by the awful sight of abused animals⟩ — see DISGUST

sicken (with) *vb* to become affected with (a disease or disorder) ⟨a number of the passengers on the cruise ship had *sickened with* food poisoning⟩ — see CONTRACT 1

sickened *adj* **1** temporarily suffering from a disorder of the body ⟨the *sickened* passengers were rushed to the emergency room for treatment⟩ — see SICK 1
2 filled with disgust ⟨many audience members, *sickened* by the movie's violence, stormed out of the theater⟩ — see SICK 2

sickening *adj* causing intense displeasure, disgust, or resentment ⟨a *sickening* display of emotion⟩ — see OFFENSIVE 1

sickish *adj* affected with nausea ⟨the fumes from the freshly applied paint made her feel *sickish*⟩ — see NAUSEOUS

sickly *adj* chronically or repeatedly suffering from poor health ⟨a *sickly* foal that seemed to catch everything that the other horses had⟩
synonyms ailing, invalid, weakly
related words bedridden; delicate, fragile, frail; dying, fading, incurable, moribund; challenged, crippled, debilitated, incapacitated, lame; decrepit, enfeebled, feeble, infirm, weak, weakened, worn-out
near antonyms able-bodied, nondisabled; hardy, lusty, rugged, stalwart, strong
antonyms healthy, well

sickness *n* **1** the condition of not being in good health ⟨Jamie pleaded *sickness* and tried to stay home from school every single time there was a spelling test scheduled⟩
synonyms illness, indisposition, unhealthiness, unsoundness
related words malaise; ailment, condition, disease, disorder, malady, trouble, upset; debility, decrepitude, feebleness, frailness, infirmity, lameness
near antonyms fettle, fitness, shape; hardiness, heartiness, lustiness, robustness, ruggedness, stamina, strength, toughness, vigor, vigorousness, vitality; bloom, flush, flushness; weal, welfare, well-being
antonyms health, healthiness, soundness, wellness, wholeness, wholesomeness
2 an abnormal state that disrupts a plant or animal's normal bodily functioning ⟨a *sickness* that resulted in the death of millions of the nation's elm trees⟩ — see DISEASE 1

3 a disturbed condition of the stomach in which one feels like vomiting ⟨the *sickness* that women typically feel upon rising during the early months of a pregnancy⟩ — see NAUSEA 1

side *adj* of, relating to, or located on one side ⟨please bring all deliveries to the *side* door⟩
synonyms lateral
related words left, right; one-sided

side *n* **1** a place, space, or direction away from or beyond a central point or line ⟨will everyone who wants to sign up for volleyball please stand off to this *side* of the gym?⟩
synonyms flank, hand
related words direction, face, outside, underpart, underside; lee, leeward, windward; left, right
2 a certain way in which something appears or may be regarded ⟨examined the problem from all *sides*⟩ — see ASPECT 1
3 a group of people acting together within a larger group ⟨our *side* won, and the club will have a holiday party after all⟩ — see FACTION

sideboard *n* a storage case typically having doors and shelves ⟨all of the silverware was kept in the *sideboard*⟩ — see CABINET

sidekick *n* a person who helps a more skilled person ⟨the hero relied on his *sidekick* to help him catch the crooks⟩ — see HELPER

side–splitting *adj* causing or intended to cause laughter ⟨his *side-splitting* jokes usually have audiences helpless with laughter⟩ — see FUNNY 1

sidestep *vb* **1** to avoid having to comply with (something) especially through cleverness ⟨*sidestepped* the regulations by lying about his age⟩ — see CIRCUMVENT 1
2 to move suddenly aside or to and fro ⟨*sidestepped* away from the oncoming ball⟩ — see DODGE 1

sideways *adv* with one side faced forward ⟨I had to walk *sideways* to get between the two towering piles of boxes⟩
synonyms broadside, edgewise, sidewise
related words aslant, obliquely, indirectly; laterally, sideward (*or* sidewards)
near antonyms dead, direct, right, straight

sidewise *adv* with one side faced forward ⟨standing *sidewise* in the doorway⟩ — see SIDEWAYS

siege *n* **1** a sudden experiencing of a physical or mental disorder ⟨a *siege* of typhoid fever hit the city⟩ — see ATTACK 2
2 the cutting off of an area by military means to stop the flow of people or supplies ⟨after a *siege* of six weeks, the city of Vicksburg surrendered to General Grant and his Union forces⟩ — see BLOCKADE

siesta *n* a short sleep ⟨took a *siesta* after lunch until it grew a little cooler outside⟩ — see ¹NAP

sigh *vb* to take in and let out a deep audible breath or to make a similar sound ⟨Mom always used to *sigh* loudly whenever she found a mess on the floor⟩ ⟨a breeze *sighed* through the leaves⟩
synonyms sough
related words gasp, huff, pant, puff, wheeze; breathe, respire; exhale, expire, inhale, inspire; yawn

sigh (for) *vb* to have an earnest wish to own or enjoy ⟨people have always been *sighing for* the "good old days"⟩ — see DESIRE

sight *n* **1** a position within view ⟨get out of my *sight*!⟩ — see PRESENCE 1
2 an instance of looking especially briefly ⟨he always fainted at the merest *sight* of blood⟩ — see LOOK 2

3 something unpleasant to look at ⟨the house was a *sight* the morning after the party⟩ — see EYESORE
4 the ability to see ⟨lost his *sight* in an accident when he was young⟩ — see EYESIGHT

sight *vb* to make note of (something) through the use of one's eyes ⟨the crew was overwhelmed with excitement upon hearing that the lookout had *sighted* land⟩ — see SEE 1

sightless *adj* lacking the power of sight ⟨bats are often thought to be completely *sightless*, but this is not really true⟩ — see BLIND

sightly *adj* very pleasing to look at ⟨*sightly* handwriting would be desirable on the diplomas⟩ — see BEAUTIFUL

sightseer *n* a person who travels for pleasure ⟨we shared the bus with a group of *sightseers* from out of town⟩ — see TOURIST

sign *n* **1** a movement of the body or limbs that expresses or emphasizes an idea or feeling ⟨made a *sign* for them to be quiet⟩ — see GESTURE 1
2 a written or printed mark that is meant to convey information to the reader ⟨a plus *sign*⟩ — see CHARACTER 1

sign *vb* to write one's name on (as a document) ⟨you'll have to *sign* the contract for it to be legal⟩
synonyms autograph
related words countersign, endorse (*also* indorse), register, sign on; author, pen, pencil (in), scratch (out), scrawl, scribble, write

signal *adj* standing above others in rank, importance, or achievement ⟨the Louisiana Purchase is cited by many historians as one of the most *signal* events in American history⟩ — see EMINENT

signal *n* **1** an object intended to give public notice or warning ⟨stop signs are *signals* for vehicles to come to a full stop — not suggestions for slowing down, as some drivers seem to think⟩
synonyms flag, tocsin
2 a movement of the body or limbs that expresses or emphasizes an idea or feeling ⟨quietly waiting for the *signal* to advance⟩ — see GESTURE 1

signal *vb* to direct or notify by a movement or gesture ⟨*signaled* the oncoming traffic to stop while the wrecked car was being towed away⟩ — see MOTION

significance *n* **1** the idea that is conveyed or intended to be conveyed to the mind by language, symbol, or action ⟨the *significance* of that word is much debated by biblical scholars⟩ — see MEANING 1
2 the quality or state of being important ⟨the political *significance* of the special commission's report⟩ — see IMPORTANCE

significant *adj* **1** clearly conveying a special meaning (as one's mood) ⟨after remarking that tardiness was on the rise, our teacher cast a *significant* glance my way⟩ — see EXPRESSIVE
2 indicating something ⟨the town's generous library budget is *significant* of the value its residents place on learning⟩ — see INDICATIVE
3 having great meaning or lasting effect ⟨made a *significant* change in the procedure⟩ — see IMPORTANT 1
4 having great power or influence ⟨a producer who is playing a *significant* role in the creation of the new film⟩ — see IMPORTANT 2
5 sufficiently large in size, amount, or number to merit attention ⟨paid a *significant* amount of money for the movie rights to the book⟩ — see CONSIDERABLE 1

signification *n* the idea that is conveyed or intended to be conveyed to the mind by language, symbol, or action ⟨we should assume that the author is using the word in its ordinary *signification*⟩ — see MEANING 1

signify *vb* **1** to be of importance ⟨never mind, as the color of the room doesn't *signify* in the least⟩ — see MATTER

2 to communicate or convey (as an idea) to the mind ⟨the symbol failed to *signify* anything to me—until I realized that it was upside down⟩ — see MEAN 1

signifying *adj* indicating something ⟨his tendency to use weasel words is seen as a signifying character trait⟩ — see INDICATIVE

sign on (for) *vb* to become a member of ⟨I *signed on for* the crew team simply as a lark⟩ — see ENTER 2

sign up (for) *vb* to become a member of ⟨*signed up for* Spanish class⟩ — see ENTER 2

silence *n* **1** incapacity for or restraint from speaking ⟨the teacher expects complete *silence* from everyone during all tests⟩
synonyms dumbness, muteness, speechlessness, stillness
related words inarticulateness, voicelessness; reserve, reticence, reticency, taciturnity
near antonyms communication, speaking, talking; eloquence, fluency, volubility; chattiness, garrulousness, loquaciousness, loquacity, talkativeness; verboseness, verbosity, windiness, wordiness

2 the near or complete absence of sound ⟨the *silence* of the garden was refreshing after the din of the party inside⟩
synonyms hush, quiet, quietness, quietude, still, stillness
related words calm, lull, peacefulness, tranquility
near antonyms din, clamor, hubbub, racket, tumult, uproar
antonyms noise, sound

silence *vb* **1** to stop the noise or speech of ⟨the instructor quickly *silenced* anyone who tried to interrupt⟩ ⟨we need to have a repairman come and *silence* that door alarm⟩
synonyms hush, mute, quell, settle, shush, still
near antonyms agitate, stir

2 to put a stop to (something) by the use of force ⟨*silenced* all political dissent in the country⟩ — see QUELL 1

silent *adj* **1** deliberately refraining from speech ⟨the suddenly *silent* child had to be prompted to say hello⟩
synonyms dumb, mum, mute, speechless, uncommunicative
related words inarticulate, tongue-tied; nonvocal, voiceless
near antonyms articulate, eloquent, fluent, voluble; gabby, garrulous, loquacious, talkative, talky; outspoken, unreserved, vocal
antonyms communicative, speaking, talking

2 tending not to speak frequently (as by habit or inclination) ⟨a naturally *silent* boy, he was often overshadowed by his louder siblings⟩
synonyms closemouthed, laconic, reserved, reticent, taciturn, tight-lipped, uncommunicative
related words inhibited, introverted, restrained; sedate, self-contained, sober, staid
near antonyms free-spoken, outspoken, vocal; blabby, gossipy, talebearing; long-winded, verbose, windy, wordy
antonyms chatty, communicative, conversational, gabby, garrulous, loquacious, talkative, talky, unreserved

3 mostly or entirely without sound ⟨the room was so *silent* that you could have heard a pin drop⟩
synonyms hushed, muted, noiseless, quiet, quieted, soundless, still
related words peaceful, tranquil
antonyms noisy, unquiet

silhouette *n* a line that traces the outer limits of an object or surface ⟨cartoonists often try to give their characters recognizable *silhouettes*⟩ — see OUTLINE 1

silhouette *vb* to draw or make apparent the outline of ⟨in the photograph the majestic mountain is strikingly *silhouetted* against the setting sun⟩ — see OUTLINE 1

silken *adj* smooth or delicate in appearance or feel ⟨the *silken* texture of the synthetic fabric⟩ — see SOFT 2

silky *adj* smooth or delicate in appearance or feel ⟨the plant's fibers feel *silky* to the touch⟩ — see SOFT 2

silliness *n* **1** lack of good sense or judgment ⟨she was both amused and irritated by the *silliness* of his comments⟩ — see FOOLISHNESS 1

2 language, behavior, or ideas that are absurd and contrary to good sense ⟨stop this *silliness* at once!⟩ — see NONSENSE 1

silly *adj* **1** lacking in seriousness or maturity ⟨the theater was filled with a bunch of *silly* children making noise⟩ — see GIDDY 1

2 showing or marked by a lack of good sense or judgment ⟨dismissed the *silly* ideas immediately⟩ — see FOOLISH 1

3 so foolish or pointless as to be worthy of scornful laughter ⟨had the *silly* notion that the world was shaped like a giant burrito⟩ — see RIDICULOUS 1

silver *adj* of the color gray ⟨a distinguished-looking gentleman with *silver* hair⟩ — see GRAY 1

silver *n* eating and serving utensils ⟨laid out the *silver* for the dinner guests⟩ — see TABLEWARE 1

silverware *n* eating and serving utensils ⟨kept the *silverware* in a separate drawer⟩ — see TABLEWARE 1

silvery *adj* of the color gray ⟨a *silvery* metal of some kind⟩ — see GRAY 1

similar *adj* having qualities in common ⟨accidentally wore *similar* outfits to the dance⟩ — see ALIKE

similarity *n* **1** the quality or state of having many qualities in common ⟨the *similarity* between the two essays is too great to be coincidental — one student virtually copied the other⟩
synonyms alikeness, community, correspondence, likeness, parallelism, resemblance, similitude
related words analogousness; equivalence, equivalency, parity; identicalness, identity, sameness; correlation, relationship; exchangeability, interchangeability; accordance, agreement, compatibility, conformity, congruity
near antonyms inequality; conflict, disagreement, discrepancy, disparity, variance; incompatibility, incongruity, incongruousness
antonyms dissimilarity, unlikeness

2 a point which two or more things share in common ⟨the only *similarity* between this project and the last one is that both will involve some lab work⟩
synonyms correspondence, parallel, resemblance, similitude
related words counterpart, equal, equivalent
near antonyms difference, discrepancy; deviance, divergence; change, modification, variation
antonyms dissimilarity

similarly *adv* in like manner ⟨all the other men were removing their ties, so I did *similarly*⟩ — see ALSO 1

similitude *n* **1** the quality or state of having many qualities in common ⟨the striking *similitude* between that modern city and the Rome of ancient times⟩ — see SIMILARITY 1

2 a point which two or more things share in common ⟨the two robberies, committed on opposite ends of the country, show some curious *similitudes*⟩ — see SIMILARITY 2

simmer *vb* to cook in a liquid heated to the point that it gives off steam ⟨I gently *simmered* the chili for an hour⟩ — see BOIL 2

simple *adj* **1** free from all additions or embellishment ⟨a *simple* design, and one that never goes out of fashion⟩ — see PLAIN 1

2 free from any intent to deceive or impress others ⟨growing up in *simple* innocence⟩ — see GUILELESS

3 having no exceptions or restrictions ⟨that's the *simple* truth⟩ — see ABSOLUTE 2

4 involving minimal difficulty or effort ⟨got all of the answers right because it was such a *simple* test⟩ — see EASY 1

5 lacking in worldly wisdom or informed judgment ⟨developers mistakenly thought that the local residents were *simple* people who would sell their land for practically nothing⟩ — see NAIVE 1

6 lacking in education or the knowledge gained from books ⟨the fact that he didn't go to college doesn't mean he's *simple*⟩ — see IGNORANT 1

7 not having or showing an ability to absorb ideas readily ⟨don't be so quick to characterize people who have trouble with computers as *simple*⟩ — see STUPID 1

simpleminded *adj* **1** lacking in worldly wisdom or informed judgment ⟨a *simpleminded* view of a complex problem⟩ — see NAIVE 1

2 showing or marked by a lack of good sense or judgment ⟨scornful of their *simpleminded* belief that their parents would always be there to take care of them⟩ — see FOOLISH 1

simpleness *n* **1** the quality or state of being simple and sincere ⟨the *simpleness* of the villagers was so disarming that she temporarily abandoned her natural cynicism⟩ — see NAÏVETÉ 1

2 the quality or state of lacking intelligence or quickness of mind ⟨we must always remember that the often frustrating *simpleness* of the mentally challenged does not alter the fact that they are still children of God⟩ — see STUPIDITY 1

simpleton *n* **1** a person who lacks good sense or judgment ⟨his silly antics have earned him a reputation as a *simpleton*⟩ — see FOOL 1

2 a stupid person ⟨she felt like such a *simpleton* for missing the easy questions on the quiz⟩ — see IDIOT 1

simplicity *n* **1** the quality or state of having a form or structure of few parts or elements ⟨the *simplicity* of this machine should enable everyone to learn how to use it⟩

synonyms plainness, unsophistication

related words homogeneity, unity

antonyms complexity, complication, elaborateness, intricacy, sophistication

2 clearness of expression ⟨the *simplicity* of this poem is beautiful⟩

synonyms clarity, explicitness, lucidity, lucidness, perspicuity, perspicuousness

related words incisiveness, directness, forthrightness, openness, straightforwardness

near antonyms ambiguity, equivocalness; incomprehensibility, unintelligibility; circuitousness, deviousness, indirectness, indistinctness; dimness, disjointedness, incoherence; faintness, fuzziness, muddiness, nebulousness, vagueness

antonyms obscurity

3 lack of good sense or judgment ⟨the stupefying *simplicity* of the generals who thought that war would be over in a month!⟩ — see FOOLISHNESS 1

4 the quality or state of being simple and sincere ⟨answered the judge's questions with childlike *simplicity*⟩ — see NAÏVETÉ 1

simplify *vb* to make less complex ⟨you need to *simplify* this process somewhat or you'll never finish it today⟩

synonyms streamline

related words oversimplify; prune, strip (down), trim; purify, refine

near antonyms elaborate

antonyms complicate, perplex, sophisticate

simply *adv* **1** for nothing other than ⟨uninterested in food, she eats *simply* to keep alive⟩ — see SOLELY 1

2 nothing more than ⟨it's *simply* smart to shop around before buying an item⟩ — see JUST 3

simulate *vb* to present a false appearance of ⟨cosmetics that *simulate* a suntan⟩ — see FEIGN

simulated *adj* **1** being such in appearance only and made with or manufactured from usually cheaper materials ⟨a *simulated* leopard skin rug⟩ — see IMITATION

2 lacking in natural or spontaneous quality ⟨the *simulated* friendliness in public of two politicians who can't stand each other in private⟩ — see ARTIFICIAL 1

simultaneous *adj* existing or occurring at the same period of time ⟨a *simultaneous* release of the movie and its soundtrack on CD⟩ — see CONTEMPORARY 1

simultaneously *adv* at one and the same time ⟨fires broke out *simultaneously* in several parts of town⟩ — see TOGETHER 1

sin *n* **1** a breaking of a moral or legal code ⟨she knows that lying is a *sin*⟩ — see OFFENSE 1

2 that which is morally unacceptable ⟨a minister who worries that modern society has abandoned the concept of *sin*⟩ — see EVIL

3 immoral conduct or practices harmful or offensive to society ⟨a sordid section of the city that is mainly known for *sin* and degradation⟩ — see VICE 1

4 a regrettable or blameworthy act ⟨it's a *sin* to waste food when people are starving⟩ — see CRIME 2

sin *vb* to commit an offense ⟨bless me, Father, for I have *sinned*⟩ — see OFFEND 1

since *conj* for the reason that ⟨*since* I've done all my chores today, I should be allowed to go out and play⟩

synonyms as, because, for, inasmuch as, now, seeing, whereas

phrases as long as (*or* so long as), in view (*or* light) of the fact

sincere *adj* free from any intent to deceive or impress others ⟨done out of a *sincere* desire to help others⟩ — see GUILELESS

sincerely *adv* without any attempt to impress by deception or exaggeration ⟨thanked them *sincerely* for their help⟩ — see NATURALLY 3

sinew *n* the ability to exert effort for the accomplishment of a task ⟨the justices displayed great intellectual *sinew* in writing their opinion on this case⟩ — see POWER 2

sinewy *adj* **1** having muscles capable of exerting great physical force ⟨the lithe, *sinewy* body of the ballet company's leading male dancer⟩ — see STRONG 1

2 marked by a well-developed musculature ⟨the *sinewy* arms of the weight lifter⟩ — see MUSCULAR 1

sinful *adj* not conforming to a high moral standard; morally unacceptable ⟨chastised by his minister for his *sinful* behavior⟩ — see BAD 2

sinfulness *n* the state or quality of being utterly evil ⟨regretted the *sinfulness* of her actions⟩ — see ENORMITY 1

sing *vb* **1** to produce musical sounds with the voice ⟨it's relatively rare to find actors who can also *sing* well⟩
synonyms carol, chant, descant, vocalize
related words belt, croon, harmonize, hum, lilt, quaver, scat, sharp, slur, trill, troll, warble, yodel; serenade
2 to utter in musical or drawn out tones ⟨the cantor *sang* the prayers before the entire congregation⟩ — see CHANT 1
3 to utter one's distinctive animal sound ⟨I can hear a bird *singing* in the distance⟩ — see CRY 2

singe *vb* to burn on the surface ⟨the marshmallows got a bit *singed* over the campfire, but we like them that way⟩ — see SCORCH

singer *n* one who sings ⟨a famous opera *singer* will be performing tomorrow⟩
synonyms caroler (*or* caroller), songster, vocalist, vocalizer, voice
related words harmonizer, hummer, warbler, yodeler; serenader; cantor, chorist; songstress

single *adj* **1** not married ⟨there was such a shortage of *single* men in the neighborhood that he had his pick of girlfriends⟩
synonyms unattached, unmarried, unwed
related words fancy-free, footloose; marriageable, unmated, unpaired; divorced, separated
near antonyms mated, paired; affianced, betrothed, committed, engaged, pledged, promised; remarried
antonyms attached, espoused, married, wed
2 belonging only to the one person, unit, or group named ⟨any view expressed on the newspaper's editorial pages is the *single* opinion of the writer of the column⟩ — see SOLE 1
3 not physically attached to another unit ⟨the average price of *single* homes in the area⟩ — see SEPARATE 2

single (out) *vb* **1** to decide to accept (someone or something) from a group of possibilities ⟨she *singled out* the most qualified candidate from the pool of the applicants⟩ — see CHOOSE 1
2 to find out or establish the identity of ⟨through careful reasoning and the process of elimination, neighbors *singled* her *out* as the writer of the anonymous letter⟩ — see IDENTIFY 1

single–handedly *adv* without aid or support ⟨typically the superhero defeats the monster *single-handedly*⟩ — see ALONE 1

singly *adv* without aid or support ⟨either *singly* or with the cooperation of other nations, we must do something about this pressing environmental issue⟩ — see ALONE 1

singular *adj* **1** being out of the ordinary ⟨a contemporary artist of *singular* attainments⟩ — see EXCEPTIONAL
2 noticeably different from what is generally found or experienced ⟨on the way home we had a *singular* adventure that we must tell you about⟩ — see UNUSUAL 1
3 of, relating to, or belonging to a single person ⟨preserving our national heritage is not a *singular* responsibility but our collective duty⟩ — see INDIVIDUAL 1
4 being the one or ones of a class with no other members ⟨this crime was a *singular* case, and using it as a reason for revising the criminal code would be ill-advised⟩ — see ONLY 2

singularity *n* an odd or peculiar habit ⟨a college professor with *singularities* of dress and speech that endeared him to his students⟩ — see IDIOSYNCRASY

sinister *adj* being or showing a sign of evil or calamity to come ⟨*sinister* rumblings from the island's volcano⟩ — see OMINOUS

sink *vb* **1** to become worse or of less value ⟨his fortunes have steadily *sunk* since the breakup of his marriage⟩ — see DETERIORATE
2 to go to a lower level ⟨that evening we sat on the beautiful beach, dreamily watching the sun *sink* beneath the horizon⟩ — see DROP 2

sinner *n* a person who commits moral wrongs ⟨even the worst *sinner* can be redeemed⟩ — see EVILDOER 1

sinuous *adj* marked by a long series of irregular curves ⟨the river flowed in a *sinuous* path through the lush valley⟩ — see CROOKED 1

sip *n* the portion of a serving of a beverage that is swallowed at one time ⟨there's only a single *sip* left in the glass⟩ — see DRINK 2

sip *vb* to swallow in liquid form ⟨slowly *sipping* the hot soup⟩ — see DRINK 1

siphon *vb* **1** to remove (liquid) gradually or completely ⟨I let the stranded motorist *siphon* some of my gas so he could be on his way⟩ — see DRAIN 1
2 to cause to move to a central point or along a restricted pathway ⟨investigators discovered that the so-called charitable organization was *siphoning* funds to a terrorist organization⟩ — see CHANNEL

sire *vb* to become the father of ⟨the champion race horse went on to *sire* a long line of winners⟩ — see FATHER

siren *n* a woman whom men find irresistibly attractive ⟨one of history's most famous *sirens*, Cleopatra charmed both Julius Caesar and Mark Antony⟩
synonyms enchantress, seductress, temptress
related words charmer, seducer

sissy *adj* having or displaying qualities more suitable for women than for men ⟨thought it was *sissy* for a boy to like flowers⟩ — see EFFEMINATE

sissy *n* a person who shows a shameful lack of courage in the face of danger ⟨called him a *sissy* when he refused to play dodgeball⟩ — see COWARD

sit *vb* **1** to rest on the buttocks or haunches ⟨everybody needs to *sit* down, or no one will be able to see the movie⟩
synonyms set [*chiefly dialect*]
related words perch; lounge, slouch, sprawl, squat, straddle
near antonyms arise, get up, rise, stand
2 to cause to sit down ⟨the host had to *sit* some of the guests on the porch⟩ — see SEAT
3 to cover and warm eggs to hatch them ⟨we didn't want to disturb the hens, as they were *sitting*⟩ — see SET 1
4 to occupy a place or location ⟨the monument that *sits* at the entrance to the battlefield⟩ — see STAND 1

site *n* the area or space occupied by or intended for something ⟨the *site* of the signing of the treaty⟩ — see PLACE 1

sitter *n* a girl or woman employed to care for a young child or children ⟨the woman who is the Martins' usual *sitter* when they go out for the evening⟩ — see NURSE

sitting duck *n* a person or thing that is the object of abuse, criticism, or ridicule ⟨those stupid comments just made him a *sitting duck* for comedians⟩ — see TARGET 1

situate *vb* to arrange something in a certain spot or position ⟨city planners *situated* the new building close to the highway⟩ — see PLACE 1

situation *n* **1** position with regard to conditions and circumstances ⟨the school's *situation* is improving with additional financial help⟩
synonyms footing, picture, posture, scene, status
related words rank, standing; place, spot, state; score, status quo
2 an assignment at which one regularly works for pay ⟨there were the usual "*situation* wanted" postings in the local newspaper⟩ — see JOB 1
3 the placement of someone or something in relation to others in a vertical arrangement ⟨in earlier times people were unable to alter their *situation* in life, so if you were born a servant, you stayed a servant⟩ — see RANK 1

sixth sense *n* the power of seeing or knowing about things that are not present to the senses ⟨she seems to have a *sixth sense* about how members of her widely scattered family are faring⟩ — see CLAIRVOYANCE

sizable *or* **sizeable** *adj* **1** of a size greater than average of its kind ⟨a *sizable* sum of money⟩ — see LARGE
2 sufficiently large in size, amount, or number to merit attention ⟨a *sizable* increase in attendance since the team began its winning streak⟩ — see CONSIDERABLE 1

sizably *adv* to a large extent or degree ⟨the spill grew *sizably* larger as they helplessly watched⟩ — see GREATLY 2

size *n* the total amount of measurable space or surface occupied by something ⟨we worried that the immense *size* of the sofa would make getting it through the doorway impossible⟩
synonyms dimension, extent, magnitude, measure, measurement, proportion
related words area; capaciousness, commodiousness, roominess, spaciousness; ampleness, amplitude, bigness, bulk, bulkiness, enormousness, grandness, greatness, grossness, heftiness, hugeness, immenseness, immensity, largeness, mass, massiveness, monstrousness, stupendousness, tremendousness, vastness, volume, voluminousness

size *n* a substance used to stick things together ⟨coated the fabric with *size* before applying it to the wall⟩ — see GLUE

sizzle *n* a sound similar to the speech sound \s\ stretched out ⟨there was a brief *sizzle* as the moth flew into the flame⟩ — see HISS 1

sizzle *vb* to make a sound like that of stretching out the speech sound \s\ ⟨from my bed I could hear the bacon *sizzling* in the frying pan⟩ — see HISS

skeletal *adj* suffering extreme weight loss as a result of hunger or disease ⟨the stray kitten's *skeletal* body was pitiful to look at⟩ — see EMACIATED

skeleton *n* the arrangement of parts that gives something its basic form ⟨Native Americans covered the *skeletons* of their wigwams with bark, rush mats, or hides⟩ — see FRAME 1

skeptic *n* a person who is always ready to doubt or question the truth or existence of something ⟨the demand by *skeptics* that believers in Bigfoot produce some hard evidence of that hairy humanoid⟩
synonyms disbeliever, doubter, questioner, unbeliever
related words cynic, misanthrope, pessimist; derider, ridiculer, scoffer
near antonyms chump, dupe, gull, pigeon, sucker

skeptical *adj* **1** inclined to doubt or question claims ⟨it's good to be *skeptical* about what you see on TV⟩
synonyms disbelieving, distrustful, doubting, incredulous, leery, mistrustful, questioning, suspecting, suspicious, unbelieving
related words paranoid; critical, puzzled, quizzical; careful, cautious, guarded, leery, wary, watchful; cynical, experienced, knowing, sophisticated, worldly, worldly-wise; curious, inquiring, inquisitive, nosy (*or* nosey); snoopy; uncertain, unconvinced, undecided, undetermined, unsettled, unsure; hesitant
near antonyms green, ingenuous, innocent, naive (*or* naïve), simple, simpleminded, unknowing, unsophisticated, unworldly, wide-eyed; certain, confident, positive, sure; callow, inexperienced, raw; childlike, idealistic, impractical; beguiled, deceived, duped, gulled, tricked; careless, heedless, unsuspecting, unsuspicious, unwary
antonyms credulous, gullible, trustful, trusting, uncritical, unquestioning
2 not feeling sure about the truth, wisdom, or trustworthiness of someone or something ⟨I'm a little *skeptical* of this low bid, since it's way below what the other contractors said that they would charge⟩ — see DOUBTFUL 1

skeptically *adv* with distrust ⟨we looked at the cafeteria's new nutritional offerings somewhat *skeptically*⟩ — see ASKANCE

skepticism *n* a feeling or attitude that one does not know the truth, truthfulness, or trustworthiness of someone or something ⟨our alibi was met with *skepticism* at first, but we gradually convinced them of the truth⟩ — see DOUBT

sketch *n* **1** a picture using lines to represent the chief features of an object or scene ⟨made a quick *sketch* so that she could paint it in oil later⟩ — see DRAWING
2 a vivid representation in words of someone or something ⟨gave his boss quick *sketches* of the personalities of the clients she was about to meet⟩ — see DESCRIPTION 1

sketch *vb* **1** to draw or make apparent the outline of ⟨*sketched* the garden pavilion on a pad of paper so the homeowners would have a rough idea of how it was going to look⟩ — see OUTLINE 1
2 to give a representation or account of in words ⟨briefly *sketched* the intent of the plan⟩ — see DESCRIBE 1

skewed *adj* inclined or twisted to one side ⟨he could see that the ropes had gotten all *skewed* in the collision⟩ — see AWRY

skewer *vb* to penetrate or hold (something) with a pointed object ⟨let's *skewer* our marshmallows on these sticks and start toasting⟩ — see IMPALE

skill *n* **1** subtle or imaginative ability in inventing, devising, or executing something ⟨with unbelievable *skill*, the expert in origami transformed a few sheets of paper into a menagerie of exotic animals⟩
synonyms adeptness, adroitness, art, artfulness, artifice, artistry, cleverness, craft, cunning, deftness, masterfulness, skillfulness
related words dexterity, ease, finesse, handiness; experience, expertise, expertness, know-how, proficiency; creativity, ingenuity, inventiveness, knowledge, learning; aptitude, bent, flair, gift, knack, talent
near antonyms amateurishness, awkwardness, clumsiness, crudeness, rudeness; inability, inadequacy, incapability, incapacity, incompetence, ineffectiveness, ineffectualness, inefficiency
antonyms artlessness, ineptitude, ineptness, maladroitness

2 skills *pl* knowledge gained by actually doing or living through something ⟨he had acquired valuable *skills* during his life at sea⟩ — see EXPERIENCE 1

skilled *adj* having or showing exceptional knowledge, experience, or skill in a field of endeavor ⟨a delicate brain operation requiring the services of a highly *skilled* surgeon⟩ — see PROFICIENT

skillful *adj* **1** accomplished with trained ability ⟨the ice skater performed a *skillful* and graceful series of jumps⟩

synonyms adroit, artful, delicate, dexterous (*also* dextrous), expert, masterful, masterly, practiced (*or* practised), virtuoso, workmanlike

related words facile, smooth; artistic, creative, fancy, ingenious, neat; adept, clever, cunning; able, adequate, capable, competent

near antonyms awkward, clumsy, crude; ineffective, ineffectual; incompetent, inept

antonyms amateur, amateurish, artless, rude, unprofessional, unskillful

2 having or showing exceptional knowledge, experience, or skill in a field of endeavor ⟨performance testing of automobiles that should be done only by *skillful* drivers on a closed course⟩ — see PROFICIENT

skillfully *adv* in a skillful or expert manner ⟨*skillfully* guided the powerboat around the obstacles⟩ — see WELL 3

skillfulness *n* subtle or imaginative ability in inventing, devising, or executing something ⟨the *skillfulness* with which she handled that touchy situation is indeed admirable⟩ — see SKILL 1

skim *vb* **1** to move or proceed smoothly and readily ⟨a lone hang glider *skimming* along just slightly above the treetops⟩ — see FLOW 2

2 to pass lightly across or touch gently especially in passing ⟨her hand just barely *skimmed* the wall as she ran down the hallway⟩ — see BRUSH

3 to strike and fly off at an angle ⟨the rock just *skimmed* the surface of the water⟩ — see GLANCE 1

4 to take a quick or hasty look ⟨he impatiently *skimmed* through the book, looking for the specific passage he remembered seeing⟩ — see GLANCE 2

skimp *vb* to avoid unnecessary waste or expense ⟨we must *skimp* and save if we are going to afford a vacation this summer⟩ — see ECONOMIZE

skimp (on) *vb* to use or give out in stingy amounts ⟨I'd like a baked potato, and don't *skimp on* the sour cream⟩ — see SPARE

skimping *n* careful management of material resources ⟨after years of *skimping* and saving, he was finally able to afford the sports car he always wanted⟩ — see ECONOMY

skimpy *adj* less plentiful than what is normal, necessary, or desirable ⟨*skimpy* portions that would barely satisfy a small child⟩ — see MEAGER

skin *n* **1** an outer part or layer ⟨space-age materials used on the *skin* of the aircraft⟩ — see EXTERIOR

2 the outer covering of an animal removed for its commercial value ⟨hats made from beaver *skins* were once fashionable⟩ — see HIDE 1

3 the hairless natural covering of an animal prepared for use ⟨calf*skin* gloves⟩ — see LEATHER 1

skin *vb* **1** to remove the natural covering of ⟨*skinned* an onion and sliced it thin⟩ — see PEEL

2 to rob by the use of trickery or threats ⟨got his revenge on the dirty swindler who had *skinned* him⟩ — see FLEECE

skin–deep *adj* **1** lying on or affecting only the outer layer of something ⟨fortunately, the cut was only *skin-deep*⟩ — see SUPERFICIAL 1

2 having or showing a lack of depth of understanding or character ⟨this movie is a *skin-deep* interpretation of one of the world's greatest novels⟩ — see SUPERFICIAL 2

skinflint *n* a mean grasping person who is usually stingy with money ⟨the youth accused his parents of being *skinflints* for refusing to raise his allowance⟩ — see MISER

skinny *adj* **1** being of less than usual width ⟨the tree swing was supported only by a couple of *skinny* branches⟩ — see NARROW 1

2 having a noticeably small amount of body fat ⟨her grandmother was always insisting that she was too *skinny* and never tired of trying to force more food on her⟩ — see THIN 1

skip *vb* **1** to move with a light bouncing step ⟨children *skipping* across the playground⟩

synonyms bound, hop, lope, trip

related words caper, frisk, gambol, romp; skim, skitter; jump, leap, vault

near antonyms lumber, plod, trudge

2 to fail to attend ⟨*skipping* class on a nice spring day⟩ — see CUT 2

3 to strike and fly off at an angle ⟨the stone went *skipping* across the water⟩ — see GLANCE 1

skipper *n* a person in overall command of a ship ⟨we asked the *skipper* how long it would be before we reached port⟩ — see CAPTAIN 1

skirmish *n* **1** a brief clash between enemies or rivals ⟨the candidate's first debate was only a *skirmish* in a very long campaign⟩ — see ENCOUNTER

2 a physical dispute between opposing individuals or groups ⟨the troops had just begun a *skirmish* when they received the order to withdraw⟩ — see FIGHT

skirmish (with) *vb* to oppose (someone) in physical conflict ⟨for years the Apache leader had been *skirmishing with* the Mexicans, who were responsible for his nickname, Geronimo⟩ — see FIGHT 1

skirt *n* the line or relatively narrow space that marks the outer limit of something ⟨an old shack on the *skirts* of the town⟩ — see BORDER 1

skirt *vb* **1** to avoid by going around ⟨*skirted* the construction zone⟩ — see DETOUR 1

2 to avoid having to comply with (something) especially through cleverness ⟨the ever-inventive ways in which students at boarding schools try to *skirt* the rules⟩ — see CIRCUMVENT 1

3 to be adjacent to ⟨the commercial district *skirts* the river's edge⟩ — see ADJOIN 1

4 to serve as a border for ⟨the wooden fence that *skirts* the encampment⟩ — see BORDER

skirting *adj* having a border in common ⟨she loved the property, but she was a bit leery of the *skirting* swamp⟩ — see ADJACENT

skittish *adj* **1** easily excited by nature ⟨the *skittish* colt leapt up when we approached⟩ — see EXCITABLE

2 easily frightened ⟨the *skittish* moviegoers probably should shield their eyes during some of the scenes⟩ — see SHY 1

skittishness *n* a state of nervousness marked by sudden jerky movements ⟨we did our best to advance slowly and make allowances for the kitten's *skittishness*⟩ — see JUMPINESS

skulk *vb* to move about in a sly or secret manner ⟨I thought I saw someone *skulking* about in the shadows⟩ — see SNEAK 1

skulker *n* someone who acts in a sly and secret manner ⟨she surprised the *skulker* eavesdropping beneath her window⟩ — see SNEAK

skull *n* the case of bone that encloses the brain and supports the jaws of vertebrates ⟨anthropologists just found the *skull* of a prehistoric man in the desert⟩
synonyms cranium
related words braincase; death's-head; head, noddle, noggin, pate, poll; crown, scalp

skunk *n* a person whose behavior is offensive to others ⟨he's nothing but a dirty, rotten *skunk*⟩ — see JERK 1

skunk *vb* **1** to defeat by a large margin ⟨we ended up *skunking* them, as our goalie was able to prevent the other team from scoring a single goal⟩ — see WHIP 2
2 to achieve a victory over ⟨our football team consistently *skunks* our traditional rivals Thanksgiving after Thanksgiving⟩ — see BEAT 2

sky *n* the expanse of air surrounding the earth ⟨the *sky* usually looks deep blue on a bright clear day⟩
synonyms blue, firmament, heaven(s), high
related words horizon, skyline

sky–high *adv* in an enthusiastic manner ⟨some reviewers had praised the movie *sky-high*, but we thought that it was just a so-so comedy⟩
synonyms enthusiastically, exuberantly, madly, rhapsodically
related words avidly, eagerly, excitedly, impatiently, keenly; fanatically, rabidly, zealously
near antonyms aloofly, disinterestedly, impassively, incuriously; hesitantly, reluctantly, unwillingly
antonyms apathetically, indifferently, lukewarmly, perfunctorily

skylark *vb* to engage in attention-getting playful or boisterous behavior ⟨some members of the band were *skylarking* in the back of the bus⟩ — see CUT UP

skylarking *n* wildly playful or mischievous behavior ⟨it wouldn't be summer camp if there weren't a good deal of *skylarking*⟩ — see HORSEPLAY

skyrocket *vb* to rise abruptly and rapidly ⟨the price of candy bars in the vending machine has *skyrocketed* over the past few months⟩
synonyms rocket, shoot (up), soar, zoom
related words accumulate, appreciate, balloon, build (up), burgeon, enlarge, escalate, expand, increase, mount, multiply, mushroom, proliferate, snowball, swell, wax; crest, peak, surge; heighten, intensify
near antonyms collapse, fall; contract, decrease, diminish, drop, lessen, wane
antonyms nose-dive, plummet, plunge, slump, tumble

skyward *adv* to or in a higher place ⟨home prices were soaring *skyward*⟩ — see ABOVE

slack *adj* **1** failing to give proper care and attention ⟨a building contractor known mainly for his firm's *slack* workmanship and slipshod construction⟩ — see NEGLIGENT
2 not bound by rigid standards ⟨*slack* supervision on the project⟩ — see EASYGOING 2
3 not tightly fastened, tied, or stretched ⟨left the ropes *slack*⟩ — see LOOSE 1

slack *n* **1** the extent to which something hangs or dips below a straight line ⟨take up the *slack* of a rope⟩ — see SAG
2 slacks *pl* an outer garment covering each leg separately from waist to ankle ⟨she prefers wearing *slacks* instead of a dress⟩ — see PANTS

slack *vb* to make less taut ⟨the skipper ordered the crew to *slack* off the sheets on the mainsail⟩ — see SLACKEN

slacken *vb* to make less taut ⟨you'll need to *slacken* the rope a bit to get it free of that post⟩
synonyms ease, loosen, relax, slack
related words detach, free, unbind, undo, unfasten, untie
near antonyms attach, bind, fasten, tie; constrain, restrain
antonyms strain, stretch, tense, tighten

slackened *adj* not tightly fastened, tied, or stretched ⟨*slackened* lines⟩ — see LOOSE 1

slacker *n* one who deliberately avoids work or duty ⟨there will be no *slackers* tolerated in this group—anyone who doesn't do their share will get booted out⟩
synonyms goldbrick, shirker
related words malingerer; dropout, quitter; drone, idler, lazybones, loafer, slouch, slug, sluggard; dallier, lingerer, loiterer, lounger, saunterer; dawdler, laggard, putterer, slowpoke
near antonyms live wire, powerhouse; doer, go-getter, hummer, hustler, rustler, self-starter

slackness *n* **1** failure to take the care that a cautious person usually takes ⟨considering the chemical company's *slackness* when it comes to safety, it's a wonder there hasn't been a catastrophe⟩ — see NEGLIGENCE 1
2 the extent to which something hangs or dips below a straight line ⟨there's simply too much *slackness* in this clothesline⟩ — see SAG

slam *n* **1** a hard strike with a part of the body or an instrument ⟨gave the stubborn nail one last *slam* with the hammer⟩ — see BLOW 1
2 a loud explosive sound ⟨shut the door with a loud *slam*⟩ — see CLAP 1

slam *vb* **1** to shove into a closed position with force and noise ⟨the sulky child ran into her room and *slammed* the door loudly⟩
synonyms bang
related words close, shut, stop; bar, batten (down), bolt, chain, fasten, latch, lock, seal, secure
near antonyms open; unbar, unbolt, unfasten, unlatch, unlock, unseal
2 to deliver a blow to (someone or something) usually in a strong vigorous manner ⟨she *slammed* the ball deep into center field⟩ — see HIT 1
3 to come into usually forceful contact with something ⟨the car *slammed* into the wall with a fearful crunch⟩ — see HIT 2
4 to criticize harshly and usually publicly ⟨*slammed* the cast members for forgetting their lines on opening night⟩ — see ATTACK 2

slander *n* the making of false statements that damage another's reputation ⟨unhappy that she hadn't won, the girl resorted to *slander* and claimed that the winner's science project had actually been done by his father⟩
synonyms aspersing, blackening, defamation, defaming, libel, libeling, maligning, smearing, traducing, vilification, vilifying
related words aspersion, innuendo, smear; backbiting, detraction; abuse, invective, vituperation; attack, criticism, censure, denunciation; contempt, disdain, scorn; belittlement, disparagement; cattiness, despite, hatefulness, malevolence, malice, maliciousness, malignancy, malignity, meanness, nastiness, spite, spitefulness, spleen, venom, viciousness
near antonyms acclaim, accolade, applause, commendation, praise; esteem, honor, respect; adulation, flattery; adoration, reverence, veneration, worship

slander *vb* to make untrue and harmful statements about ⟨for some reason, that newspaper seems determined to *slander* one particular celebrity⟩

synonyms asperse, blacken, defame, libel, malign, smear, traduce, vilify

related words belittle, detract, disparage; discredit, disgrace, dishonor, shame; abase, debase, degrade, humble, humiliate; disdain, scorn

near antonyms exalt, glorify, honor; acclaim, applaud, commend, praise; esteem, respect; admire, regard; adore, revere, venerate, worship

slanderous *adj* causing or intended to cause unjust injury to a person's good name ⟨made *slanderous* comments about his opponent's military record⟩ — see LIBELOUS

slang *n* the special terms or expressions of a particular group or field ⟨tends to use too much hacker's *slang* when talking to coworkers about their computer problems⟩ — see TERMINOLOGY

slant *n* **1** the degree to which something rises up from a position level with the horizon ⟨the road has just enough of a *slant* to make bicycling up it a little strenuous⟩

synonyms cant, diagonal, grade, gradient, inclination, incline, lean, pitch, slope, tilt, upgrade

related words ascent, bank, climb, rise

near antonyms declension, declination, decline, declivity, descent, dip, downgrade, fall, receding

2 a way of looking at or thinking about something ⟨an interesting *slant* on the problem of underage drinking⟩ — see POINT OF VIEW

slant *vb* to set or cause to be at an angle ⟨a ramp *slanted* at a 20 degree angle⟩ — see LEAN 1

slanted *adj* **1** inclined or twisted to one side ⟨a *slanted* fence post⟩ — see AWRY

2 running in a slanting direction ⟨*slanted* stripes⟩ — see DIAGONAL

slanting *adj* inclined or twisted to one side ⟨an old, torn flag hanging from a *slanting* flagpole⟩ — see AWRY

slantways *adv* so as to slant ⟨the temporary supports were placed *slantways* against the side of the sagging wall⟩ — see SLANTWISE

slantwise *adj* **1** inclined or twisted to one side ⟨a hodgepodge of *slantwise* postcards tacked to the wall of his cubicle⟩ — see AWRY

2 running in a slanting direction ⟨the *slantwise* cables that run between the roadway and the towers give the bridge a cathedral-like appearance⟩ — see DIAGONAL

slantwise *adv* so as to slant ⟨be careful not to lay the first boards *slantwise*, or the whole bookcase won't be straight⟩

synonyms slantways

related words down, downward (*or* downwards), up, upward (*or* upwards)

slap *n* a hard strike with a part of the body or an instrument ⟨doctors used to give newborns a light *slap* to get them to start breathing⟩ — see ¹BLOW

slap *vb* to deliver a blow to (someone or something) usually in a strong vigorous manner ⟨she was so mad that she *slapped* him right across the face⟩ — see HIT 1

slapdash *adj* lacking a definite plan, purpose, or pattern ⟨a *slapdash* tour of Europe that ended in disaster⟩ — see RANDOM

slapjack *n* a flat cake made from thin batter and cooked on both sides (as on a griddle) ⟨had a big plate of *slapjacks* with syrup for breakfast⟩ — see PANCAKE

slapstick *n* humorous entertainment ⟨an actor whose roles range from *slapstick* to serious drama⟩ — see COMEDY

slash *n* a long deep cut ⟨made a *slash* in the fabric with a knife⟩ — see GASH

slash *vb* **1** to penetrate with a sharp edge (as a knife) ⟨she *slashed* the tape binding the package and eagerly opened it⟩ — see CUT 1

2 to strike repeatedly with something long and thin or flexible ⟨wildly *slashing* the ground with his club and never once hitting the golf ball he was aiming at⟩ — see WHIP 1

slate *adj* of the color gray ⟨he felt that the *slate* sky was a sure sign of rain⟩ — see GRAY 1

slate *vb* to put (someone or something) on a list ⟨I've *slated* all the people who have promised to give blood⟩ — see ¹LIST 2

slated *adj* being in accordance with the prescribed, normal, or logical course of events ⟨*slated* to arrive at five o'clock⟩ — see DUE 2

slaty *adj* of the color gray ⟨*slaty* stones in the riverbed⟩ — see GRAY 1

slaughter *n* the killing of a large number of people ⟨all civilized nations should protest this senseless *slaughter*⟩ — see MASSACRE

slaughter *vb* to kill on a large scale ⟨modern poultry farms *slaughter* a vast number of chickens every day⟩ — see MASSACRE

slave *n* **1** a person who is considered the property of another person ⟨many American *slaves* reached freedom in the North through the network known as the Underground Railroad⟩

synonyms bondman, bondsman, chattel, thrall

related words helot, serf; attendant, domestic, drudge, lackey, menial, servant

near antonyms freedman; enslaver, slave driver, slaveholder, slaver; master, taskmaster

antonyms freeman

2 a person who does very hard or dull work ⟨unappreciated office *slaves* who perform the necessary but tedious task of filing paperwork⟩

synonyms drudge, drudger, fag, grubber, laborer, peon, plugger, slogger, toiler, worker

related words workhorse; coolie, serf

near antonyms goldbrick, shirker; drone, idler, lazybones, loafer, slouch, slug, sluggard

slave *vb* to devote serious and sustained effort ⟨*slaving* over a hot stove⟩ — see LABOR

slave (for) *vb* to be a servant for ⟨had been *slaving for* the head of the household for most of his life⟩ — see SERVE 1

slave driver *n* a boss who assigns much work ⟨a real *slave driver*, my math teacher seems intent on assigning more and more pages of homework⟩ — see TASKMASTER 1

slaver *vb* to let saliva or some other substance flow from the mouth ⟨a dog *slavering* over a bone⟩ — see DROOL

slavery *n* **1** the state of being a slave ⟨a child born into *slavery* was considered simply another addition to the master's wealth and property⟩

synonyms bondage, enslavement, servility, servitude, thrall, thralldom (*or* thraldom), yoke

related words peonage, serfdom; dependence, subjection, subjugation; captivity, enchainment, imprisonment, incarceration

near antonyms emancipation, enfranchisement, liberation, manumission; autonomy, independence, self-government, sovereignty slavish • slide**   **720

antonyms freedom, liberty

2 very hard or unpleasant work ⟨*slavery* of working in the coal mines every day of his adult life⟩ — see TOIL

slavish *adj* using or marked by the use of something else as a basis or model ⟨*slavish* copying of the great masters will never make you a painter in your own right⟩ — see IMITATIVE

slavishly *adv* with great effort or determination ⟨detectives on the case *slavishly* pursued every lead and relentlessly tracked down every suspect⟩ — see HARD 1

slay *vb* **1** to deprive of life ⟨millions have been *slain* worldwide by this dreadful disease⟩ — see KILL 1

2 to put to death deliberately ⟨vowed to *slay* without mercy whoever was responsible for murdering his family⟩ — see MURDER 1

slaying *n* the intentional and unlawful taking of another person's life ⟨a despicable criminal wanted for the *slaying* of women across the state⟩ — see HOMICIDE

sleazy *adj* of low quality ⟨a *sleazy* yellow coat that was marked down to practically nothing and not worth even that⟩ — see CHEAP 2

sleek *adj* having a shiny surface or finish ⟨a striking beauty with *sleek* raven hair⟩ — see GLOSSY

sleep *n* **1** a natural periodic loss of consciousness during which the body restores itself ⟨eight hours of *sleep* or more are necessary for children and teenagers to function⟩

synonyms catnapping, dozing, napping, repose, rest, resting, slumber, slumbering, snoozing

related words catnap, doze, drowse, forty winks, nap, siesta, snooze, wink; oversleeping; dreaming, rapid eye movement

near antonyms insomnia, sleeplessness

antonyms consciousness, wakefulness

2 the state of being dead ⟨had to put their pet to *sleep*⟩ — see DEATH 2

sleep *vb* **1** be in a state of sleep ⟨the baby *slept* for the entire length of the car trip⟩

synonyms catnap, doze, nap, rest, slumber, snooze

related words drowse (off), nod (off); oversleep; dream, hibernate

near antonyms arise, arouse, awake, rise

2 to engage in sexual intercourse ⟨her mother told her never to *sleep* with anyone she didn't intend to marry⟩ — see COPULATE

sleeper *n* one who sleeps ⟨Joe is a restless *sleeper* who always wakes up with the covers kicked off⟩

synonyms dozer, slumberer

related words nodder

near antonyms insomniac; riser, waker

sleepiness *n* the quality or state of desiring or needing sleep ⟨Sarah suffered such *sleepiness* in class that there were days when she could hardly keep her eyes open⟩

synonyms drowsiness, somnolence

related words lassitude, lethargy, sluggishness, torpor; dozing, resting, sleeping, slumbering; oversleeping

near antonyms awareness, consciousness

antonyms insomnia, sleeplessness, wakefulness

sleeping *adj* being in a state of suspended consciousness ⟨let *sleeping* dogs lie⟩ — see ASLEEP 1

sleepless *adj* not sleeping or able to sleep ⟨lay *sleepless* with worry⟩ — see WAKEFUL

sleepy *adj* **1** desiring or needing sleep ⟨the *sleepy* children were carried up to bed⟩

synonyms drowsy, slumberous (*or* slumbrous), somnolent

related words asleep, dormant, dozing, resting, sleeping, slumbering; nodding, yawning

near antonyms restive, restless, sleepless

antonyms alert, awake, conscious, wakeful, wide-awake

2 slow to move or act ⟨a *sleepy* little town on the coast⟩ — see INACTIVE 1

sleight *n* **1** a clever often underhanded means to achieve an end ⟨must have employed some *sleight* to con the couple out of their money⟩ — see TRICK 1

2 mental skill or quickness ⟨a brilliant new solution that pays tribute to his remarkable *sleight* of mind⟩ — see DEXTERITY 1

3 ease and grace in physical activity ⟨a muscle-bound weight lifter known more for his might than his *sleight*⟩ — see DEXTERITY 2

slender *adj* **1** being of less than usual width ⟨graceful, *slender* table legs⟩ — see NARROW 1

2 having a noticeably small amount of body fat ⟨the diet left her noticeably more *slender*⟩ — see THIN 1

3 less plentiful than what is normal, necessary, or desirable ⟨people of *slender* means simply can't afford those prices⟩ — see MEAGER

sleuth *n* a person whose business is solving crimes and catching criminals or gathering information that is not easy to get ⟨the expert *sleuth* was able to crack the case with ease⟩ — see DETECTIVE

slice *n* a piece that has been separated from the whole by cutting ⟨took a *slice* from the cake before passing it down the table⟩ — see CUT 1

slice *vb* **1** to cut into long slender pieces ⟨*slice* the carrot into tiny strips⟩ — see SLIVER

2 to penetrate with a sharp edge (as a knife) ⟨the shard of glass *sliced* my hand, and I started bleeding profusely⟩ — see CUT 1

slick *adj* **1** having or being a surface so smooth as to make sliding or falling likely ⟨roads are often *slick* during the first hour of a rainstorm⟩

synonyms greased, greasy, lubricated, oiled, slicked, slippery, slithery

related words brushed, buffed, burnished, glossed, ground, polished, rubbed, shined; coated, glazed, waxed; soapy, waxy; rasped, sandblasted, sanded, sandpapered, scoured, scraped, scrubbed

near antonyms coarsened, rough, roughened, scuffed, uneven

2 clever at attaining one's ends by indirect and often deceptive means ⟨a *slick* ad campaign that made smoking seem healthful⟩ — see ARTFUL 1

slick *vb* to coat (something) with a slippery substance in order to reduce friction ⟨*slicking* the bottom of their skis with wax⟩ — see LUBRICATE

slicked *adj* having or being a surface so smooth as to make sliding or falling likely ⟨area roadways, *slicked* with ice, were absolutely treacherous for driving⟩ — see SLICK 1

slicker *n* a coat made of water-resistant material ⟨he forgot to put on his *slicker* and arrived at school soaking wet⟩ — see RAINCOAT

slickness *n* skill in achieving one's ends through indirect, subtle, or underhanded means ⟨we were both impressed and outraged by the *slickness* with which the swindler fooled us⟩ — see CUNNING 1

slide *vb* **1** to move about in a sly or secret manner ⟨*slid* gently into his seat without anyone else in church noticing⟩ — see SNEAK 1

2 to move or proceed smoothly and readily ⟨at this point the river *slides* past its banks with barely a ripple⟩ — see FLOW 2

slight *adj* **1** lacking bodily strength ⟨a small lad with a *slight* build⟩ — see WEAK 1
2 lacking importance ⟨a *slight* comedy that did nothing to further her career⟩ — see UNIMPORTANT
3 of a size that is less than average ⟨the rewards were *slight*⟩ — see SMALL 1
4 so small or unimportant as to warrant little or no attention ⟨apart from a *slight* fishy taste, the dish was fine⟩ — see NEGLIGIBLE 1
5 small in degree ⟨only a *slight* chance of success⟩ — see REMOTE 1
slight *n* an act or expression showing scorn and usually intended to hurt another's feelings ⟨refused to respond to the petty *slights*⟩ — see INSULT
slight *vb* **1** to cause hurt feelings or deep resentment in ⟨he felt *slighted* by the harsh comments of the judges⟩ — see INSULT
2 to deliberately ignore or treat rudely ⟨*slighted* by the usual cliques at the school dance⟩ — see SNUB 1
3 to show contempt for ⟨music critics who *slight* any style of music that doesn't fit their personal taste⟩ — see SCORN 1
4 to fail to give proper attention to ⟨*slighted* several major authors in her survey⟩ — see NEGLECT 1
slightest *adj* being the least in amount, number, or size possible ⟨there's not the *slightest* chance that your plan will work⟩ — see MINIMAL
slighting *adj* intended to make a person or thing seem of little importance or value ⟨*slighting* remarks about the general lack of musical talent among the contestants⟩ — see DEROGATORY
slightly *adv* **1** by a very small margin ⟨I thought the first one was *slightly* better⟩ — see JUST 2
2 in a very small quantity or degree ⟨he was *slightly* curious about it, but not enough to bother asking⟩ — see LITTLE 1
slightness *n* **1** the quality or state of being little in size ⟨the *slightness* of the charge is not the issue—the restaurant shouldn't be charging anything for a glass of water⟩ — see SMALLNESS
2 the state or quality of having little weight ⟨his *slightness* will serve him well if he ever decides to become a jockey⟩ — see ¹LIGHTNESS 1
slim *adj* **1** being of less than usual width ⟨a *slim* volume of poetry⟩ — see NARROW 1
2 having a noticeably small amount of body fat ⟨the pressure on ballet dancers to remain gracefully *slim*⟩ — see THIN 1
3 less plentiful than what is normal, necessary, or desirable ⟨*slim* pickings at the garage sale⟩ — see MEAGER
4 small in degree ⟨a *slim* chance is still better than none⟩ — see REMOTE 1
slime *n* soft wet earth ⟨she picked her steps carefully so as not to get any *slime* on her new shoes⟩ — see MUD
slimy *adj* full of or covered with soft wet earth ⟨please remove your *slimy* boots before coming into the house⟩ — see MUDDY 1
¹sling *vb* to place on an elevated point without support from below ⟨*sling* a hammock between the trees⟩ — see HANG 1
²sling *vb* to send through the air especially with a quick forward motion of the arm ⟨*slinging* stones at the fence post⟩ — see THROW
slink *vb* to move about in a sly or secret manner ⟨like a thief *slinking* about in the middle of the night⟩ — see SNEAK 1

¹slip *n* a long narrow piece of material ⟨baskets woven from *slips* of wicker⟩ — see STRIP
²slip *n* **1** an unintentional departure from truth or accuracy ⟨a careless *slip* of the tongue⟩ — see ERROR 1
2 the act of going down from an upright position suddenly and involuntarily ⟨had a nasty *slip* on the ice⟩ — see FALL 1
3 the act or an instance of getting free from danger or confinement ⟨gave her pursuers the *slip*⟩ — see ESCAPE 1
slip *vb* **1** to decline gradually from a standard level ⟨Susie's grades *slipped* somewhat after she joined five after-school activities⟩
synonyms sag
related words drop, fall, slump; flag, sink, slacken, slow (down), weaken; abate, contract, decrease, de-escalate, die (down), diminish, dwindle, ebb, lessen, let up, lower, moderate, recede, relent, shrink, subside, taper, taper off, wane
near antonyms rocket, shoot (up), soar; balloon, burgeon, enlarge, escalate, expand, increase, mount, multiply, mushroom, proliferate, snowball, swell, wax; crest, peak, surge
2 to go down from an upright position suddenly and involuntarily ⟨be careful not to *slip* on the spilled oil⟩ — see FALL 1
3 to introduce in a gradual, secret, or clever way ⟨casually *slipped* it into the conversation⟩ — see INSINUATE
4 to move about in a sly or secret manner ⟨*slipped* behind the cover of the trees⟩ — see SNEAK 1
5 to move or proceed smoothly and readily ⟨jumped into the car and *slipped* behind the wheel⟩ — see FLOW 2
slip (on *or* into) *vb* to place on one's person ⟨wait here while I *slip into* something more comfortable⟩ — see PUT ON 1
slippery *adj* **1** given to acting in secret and to concealing one's intentions ⟨a bar where a lot of *slippery* characters were known to hang out⟩ — see SNEAKY 1
2 hard to find, capture, or isolate ⟨a *slippery* concept that we had trouble understanding⟩ — see ELUSIVE
3 having or being a surface so smooth as to make sliding or falling likely ⟨had trouble keeping upright on the *slippery* ice⟩ — see SLICK 1
slipup *n* an unintentional departure from truth or accuracy ⟨he made sure there were no *slipups* for the important presentation⟩ — see ERROR 1
slit *n* a long deep cut ⟨made a *slit* in the fabric about nine inches long⟩ — see GASH
slit *vb* to penetrate with a sharp edge (as a knife) ⟨the robber threatened to *slit* my throat⟩ — see CUT 1
slither *vb* to move slowly with the body close to the ground ⟨a snake *slithering* through the garden⟩ — see CRAWL 1
slithery *adj* having or being a surface so smooth as to make sliding or falling likely ⟨the rocks along the beach are covered with seaweed and are quite *slithery*⟩ — see SLICK 1
sliver *n* a small flat piece separated from a whole ⟨I got a *sliver* of wood stuck in my finger⟩ — see CHIP 1
sliver *vb* to cut into long slender pieces ⟨carefully *slivered* the rattan stems into strips for basketry⟩
synonyms slice, splinter
related words chip, chop, dice, hash, mince; saw, scissor; cleave, rive, split; gash, incise, rip, slash, slit

slob *n* **1** a dirty or sloppy person ⟨only a *slob* would let his bedroom get so messy that his own mother couldn't remember what the floor looked like⟩
synonyms sloven
related words slattern, slut
near antonyms cleaner
antonyms old maid
2 a person whose behavior is offensive to others ⟨he's my friend, but sometimes he can be a real *slob*⟩ — see JERK 1

slobber *n* the fluid that is secreted into the mouth by certain glands ⟨the dog got *slobber* all over our tennis ball⟩ — see SALIVA

slobber *vb* **1** to let saliva or some other substance flow from the mouth ⟨our dog always starts to *slobber* whenever we open a can of food⟩ — see DROOL
2 to make an exaggerated display of affection or enthusiasm ⟨*slobbering* over relatives that she hadn't seen in years⟩ — see GUSH 2

slog *vb* **1** to deliver a blow to (someone or something) usually in a strong vigorous manner ⟨the two boxers were so exhausted they just *slogged* each other indiscriminately⟩ — see HIT 1
2 to devote serious and sustained effort ⟨*slogging* through the difficult assignment⟩ — see LABOR

slogan *n* an attention-getting word or phrase used to publicize something (as a campaign or product) ⟨within days, virtually everyone was familiar with the newest advertising *slogan* for that brand of soda⟩
synonyms cry, shibboleth, watchword
related words tag line; expression, idiom; cliché; maxim, motto

slogger *n* a person who does very hard or dull work ⟨nothing but respect for the *sloggers* who work in the basement archives⟩ — see SLAVE 2

slop *n* **1** soft wet earth ⟨slipped and fell in the *slop* behind the shed⟩ — see MUD
2 slops *pl* solid matter discharged from an animal's alimentary canal ⟨cleaned the *slops* out of the cow barn⟩ — see DROPPING 1

slope *n* the degree to which something rises up from a position level with the horizon ⟨the next stretch of the trail had a gentle *slope* which made it easier to climb⟩ — see SLANT

slope *vb* to set or cause to be at an angle ⟨we'll *slope* the kid's slide so that the ride down will be very gentle⟩ — see LEAN 1

sloped *adj* running in a slanting direction ⟨the *sloped* arrangement of the pictures along the staircase wall should follow the line of the banister⟩ — see DIAGONAL

sloping *adj* running in a slanting direction ⟨a *sloping* ray of light that illuminates the painting's central figure is symbolic of heavenly inspiration⟩ — see DIAGONAL

sloppily *adv* in a careless or unfashionable manner ⟨everyone dressed *sloppily* for the task of cleaning out the garage⟩
synonyms dowdily, slovenly, unstylishly
related words slatternly; chaotically, messily, untidily; shabbily, sleazily; dingily, dirtily, filthily, foully, grubbily, nastily
near antonyms neatly, orderly, tidily; fashionably, modishly; carefully, fastidiously, fussily, meticulously; cleanly, immaculately, spotlessly
antonyms nattily, sharply, smartly, sprucely

sloppiness *n* the state or quality of having an excess of tender feelings (as of love, nostalgia, or compassion) ⟨that song practically drips with tearful *sloppiness*⟩ — see SENTIMENTALITY

sloppy *adj* **1** lacking neatness in dress or person ⟨a *sloppy* child who always seems to have spilled something on his clothes⟩
synonyms dowdy, frowsy (*or* frowzy), slovenly, unkempt, untidy
related words slatternly, sluttish; chaotic, cluttered, confused, disarranged, disheveled (*or* dishevelled), disordered, messed, messy, muddled, mussed, mussy, rumpled, uncombed, wrinkled; shabby, sleazy; besmirched, blackened, dingy, dirty, filthy, foul, grimy, grubby, grungy, mucky, nasty, soiled, spotted, squalid, stained, sullied, unclean, uncleanly
near antonyms chic, fashionable, modish, stylish; combed, groomed; neat, ordered, orderly, tidy; careful, fastidious, fussy, meticulous; clean, cleaned, cleanly, immaculate, sparkling, spotless, stainless, unsoiled, unsullied
antonyms dapper, dashing, dolled up, sharp, smart, spruce
2 lacking in order, neatness, and often cleanliness ⟨dumped the papers in a *sloppy* pile on the desk⟩ — see MESSY
3 appealing to the emotions in an obvious and tiresome way ⟨a cinematic romance with a *sloppy* musical score that will have audiences reaching for their handkerchiefs⟩ — see CORNY

slosh *vb* to move with a splashing motion ⟨the baby gurgled contentedly as the water *sloshed* gently around him in the bathtub⟩
synonyms lap, plash, splash, swash
related words babble, bubble, gurgle, ripple

sloth *n* an inclination not to do work or engage in activities ⟨a youth inclined more toward *sloth* than athletics⟩ — see LAZINESS

slothful *adj* not easily aroused to action or work ⟨the *slothful* teenagers just sat around the house all weekend⟩ — see LAZY

slouch *n* a lazy person ⟨was no *slouch* when it came to cooking⟩ — see LAZYBONES

slough *also* **slue** *n* spongy land saturated or partially covered with water ⟨alligators living in the *sloughs* of the Everglades⟩ — see SWAMP

slough *also* **sluff** *vb* **1** to cast (a natural bodily covering or appendage) aside ⟨the means by which the animal can *slough* dead tissue⟩ — see SHED 1
2 to get rid of as useless or unwanted ⟨finally *sloughed* off the depression that had been weighing him down for months⟩ — see DISCARD

sloven *n* a dirty or sloppy person ⟨for his first job interview, the new college graduate instantly went from *sloven* to dandy⟩ — see SLOB 1

slovenly *adj* lacking neatness in dress or person ⟨for the sake of their image, the band members transformed themselves from clean-cut lads to *slovenly* rockers⟩ — see SLOPPY 1

slovenly *adv* in a careless or unfashionable manner ⟨scolded for dressing *slovenly*⟩ — see SLOPPILY

slow *adj* **1** moving or proceeding at less than the normal, desirable, or required speed ⟨because of the holiday, traffic to the beach was particularly *slow*⟩ ⟨*slow* readers⟩
synonyms crawling, creeping, dallying, dawdling, dilatory, dillydallying, dragging, laggard, lagging, languid, leisurely, poking, poky (*or* pokey), sluggish, tardy, unhurried

related words deliberate, measured; inactive, inert, lethargic, loafing, lounging; lingering, loitering, tarrying; ambling, inching, plodding, shuffling, strolling; decelerating, slowing; filibustering, procrastinating, stalling

near antonyms expeditious, prompt, ready; accelerated, hastened, quickened; hurried, rushed

antonyms barreling, bolting, breakneck, breathless, brisk, careering, dizzy, fast, fleet, flying, hasty, hurrying, lightning, quick, racing, rapid, rocketing, running, rushing, scooting, scudding, scurrying, snappy, speeding, speedy, swift, whirling, whirlwind, whisking, zipping

2 not having or showing an ability to absorb ideas readily ⟨the *slower* students worked together in a separate group⟩ — see STUPID 1

slow *adv* at a pace that is less than usual, desirable, or expected ⟨you need to go *slow* with this experiment, or you'll make mistakes⟩

synonyms laggardly, leisurely, slowly, sluggishly, tardily

related words carefully, cautiously, deliberately, purposefully; ploddingly

near antonyms immediately, posthaste, presto, promptly, pronto, readily, soon; impetuously, impulsively, rashly, recklessly; abruptly, suddenly

antonyms apace, briskly, fast, fleetly, full tilt, hastily, quick, quickly, rapidly, snappily, speedily, swift, swiftly

slow *vb* to cause to move or proceed at a less rapid pace ⟨if you don't *slow* your delivery down a bit, your speech will be over too soon⟩

synonyms brake, decelerate, retard

related words halt, stop; encumber, hamper, handicap, hinder, hobble, hold back, hold up, impede, inhibit, obstruct, tie up; arrest, check, constrain, curb, rein, restrain; baffle, foil, frustrate, sabotage, thwart

near antonyms drive, encourage, goad, propel, push, spur, stir, urge; advance, aid, dispatch, ease, expedite, facilitate, forward, further, help

antonyms accelerate, hasten, hurry, quicken, rush, speed (up), step up

slowdown *n* a usually gradual decrease in the pace or level of activity of something ⟨disease experts are encouraged by the recent *slowdown* in the spread of the virus⟩

synonyms braking, deceleration, letup, retardation, retarding

related words decline, drop, slump; ebb, remission, retreat, wane; flagging, weakening; arrest, check, halt, stoppage; collapse, crash, fall, plunge

antonyms acceleration, hastening, quickening

slowly *adv* at a pace that is less than usual, desirable, or expected ⟨walked *slowly* toward the ringing phone⟩ — see SLOW

slowness *n* the quality or state of lacking intelligence or quickness of mind ⟨her natural shyness was sometimes mistaken for *slowness* by people who did not know her well⟩ — see STUPIDITY 1

slowpoke *n* someone who moves slowly or more slowly than others ⟨quit being such a *slowpoke* this morning, or you'll be late⟩

synonyms crawler, creeper, dallier, dawdler, dragger, laggard, lagger, lingerer, loiterer, snail, stick-in-the-mud, straggler

related words latecomer; drone, idler, lazybones, loafer, lounger, slouch, slug, sluggard; delayer, procrastinator

near antonyms go-getter, hustler, scrambler; hurrier, rusher, speeder

antonyms speedster

sludge *n* soft wet earth ⟨after a day of heavy rain, the fairgrounds had turned into pure *sludge*⟩ — see MUD

sludgy *adj* full of or covered with soft wet earth ⟨a *sludgy* riverbed⟩ — see MUDDY 1

¹slug *n* a hard strike with a part of the body or an instrument ⟨one well aimed *slug* on the head knocked him out⟩ — see ¹BLOW

²slug *n* **1** a lazy person ⟨he's always a *slug* in the morning, which is why he prefers to sleep late⟩ — see LAZYBONES

2 the portion of a serving of a beverage that is swallowed at one time ⟨poured himself a *slug* of whiskey⟩ — see DRINK 2

slug *vb* to deliver a blow to (someone or something) usually in a strong vigorous manner ⟨she got so angry that she *slugged* the back of the chair and nearly knocked it over⟩ — see HIT 1

sluggard *n* a lazy person ⟨tried to wake up the *sluggards* who were still sleeping⟩ — see LAZYBONES

sluggish *adj* **1** moving or proceeding at less than the normal, desirable, or required speed ⟨the *sluggish* pace of the project is worrisome⟩ — see SLOW 1

2 slow to move or act ⟨reptiles are naturally *sluggish* at low temperatures⟩ — see INACTIVE 1

sluggishly *adv* at a pace that is less than usual, desirable, or expected ⟨the car responded *sluggishly* until it warmed up⟩ — see SLOW

sluice *vb* to pour liquid over or through in order to cleanse ⟨he *sluiced* the gutters with lots of water in order to make sure they were clear⟩ — see FLUSH 1

slumber *n* a natural periodic loss of consciousness during which the body restores itself ⟨a toddler looking so peaceful in *slumber*⟩ — see SLEEP 1

slumber *vb* **1** be in a state of sleep ⟨she *slumbered* for hours while the train rolled on⟩ — see SLEEP 1

2 to sleep lightly or briefly ⟨*slumbering* restlessly in the heat⟩ — see NAP 1

slumberer *n* one who sleeps ⟨Rip Van Winkle is one of literature's most famous *slumberers*⟩ — see SLEEPER

slumbering *adj* being in a state of suspended consciousness ⟨made a comparison between the inattentive nation and a *slumbering* giant⟩ — see ASLEEP 1

slumbering *n* a natural periodic loss of consciousness during which the body restores itself ⟨after my extended *slumbering* I was more than ready for a hearty breakfast⟩ — see SLEEP 1

slumberous or **slumbrous** *adj* **1** desiring or needing sleep ⟨putting her *slumberous* child to bed⟩ — see SLEEPY 1

2 tending to cause sleep ⟨a *slumberous* sound⟩ — see HYPNOTIC

slump *n* a period of decreased economic activity ⟨the stock market was in a bit of a *slump*, but analysts expected things to pick up in the next fiscal quarter⟩ — see DEPRESSION 1

slur *n* an act or expression showing scorn and usually intended to hurt another's feelings ⟨she brushed off the *slurs* and proceeded to go about her business⟩ — see INSULT

slur (over) *vb* to fail to give proper attention to ⟨a documentary that *slurs over* certain important facts as it offers a very biased case for a conspiracy theory⟩ — see NEGLECT 1

slurp *vb* to swallow in liquid form ⟨kids sitting on the curb *slurping* their drinks⟩ — see DRINK 1

slush *n* **1** language, behavior, or ideas that are absurd and contrary to good sense ⟨how can you stand to read that *slush* in the tabloids?⟩ — see NONSENSE 1
2 soft wet earth ⟨he paused in front of the doorway to wipe the *slush* off of his boots⟩ — see MUD

slushy *adj* full of or covered with soft wet earth ⟨the *slushy* racetrack resulted in a significantly slower time for the winning horse⟩ — see MUDDY 1

sly *adj* **1** clever at attaining one's ends by indirect and often deceptive means ⟨even his rivals concede that he's one *sly* maker of business deals⟩ — see ARTFUL 1
2 given to acting in secret and to concealing one's intentions ⟨why, you *sly* fellow! I had no idea you were planning my birthday party⟩ — see SNEAKY 1
3 tending to or exhibiting reckless playfulness ⟨a *sly* joke that backfired⟩ — see MISCHIEVOUS 1

slyness *n* skill in achieving one's ends through indirect, subtle, or underhanded means ⟨the *slyness* with which the FBI agent infiltrated the subversive organization was indeed impressive⟩ — see CUNNING 1

smack *n* a hard strike with a part of the body or an instrument ⟨gave him a *smack* on the wrist when he tried to sneak an early taste of the sauce⟩ — see ¹BLOW

smack *vb* to deliver a blow to (someone or something) usually in a strong vigorous manner ⟨*smacked* the punching bag one final time before heading to the showers⟩ — see HIT 1

smack–dab *adv* as stated or indicated without the slightest difference ⟨a restaurant that's *smack-dab* in the center of town⟩ — see EXACTLY 1

small *adj* **1** of a size that is less than average ⟨a *small* cat who never weighed more than five pounds⟩
synonyms bantam, diminutive, dinky, dwarf, dwarfish, fine, little, pint-size (*or* pint-sized), pocket, pocket-size (*also* pocket-sized), puny, pygmy, slight, smallish, undersized
related words petite; scrubby, stunted; bitty, inappreciable, infinitesimal, micro, microscopic (*also* microscopical), midget, miniature, miniaturized, minute, teeny, teeny-weeny, tiny, wee; underweight; meager (*or* meagre); niggardly, poor, scant, scanty, scarce, skimpy, slender, slim, spare, sparse, stingy; deficient, inadequate, insufficient, lacking, wanting
near antonyms bulky, hefty, hulking, massive, voluminous; cavernous, colossal, elephantine, enormous, giant, gigantic, gross, Herculean, heroic, huge, immense, jumbo, mammoth, monolithic, monstrous, monumental, prodigious, staggering, stupendous, tremendous, vast; abundant, ample, appreciable, bountiful, copious, generous, healthy, liberal, plenteous, plentiful; fat, thick; broad, wide; boundless, cosmic, immeasurable, infinite; adequate, enough, sufficient ⦁
antonyms big, bumper, considerable, goodly, good-sized, grand, great, handsome, king-size (*or* king-sized), large, largish, outsize (*also* outsized), oversize (*or* oversized), sizable (*or* sizeable), substantial, super, whacking, whopping
2 small in degree ⟨your chances of winning the lottery are so *small* that it's best not to count on it⟩ — see REMOTE 1
3 lacking importance ⟨reluctant to bring such a *small* matter to his attention⟩ — see UNIMPORTANT
4 not broad or open in views or opinions ⟨townspeople who were helpful to one another but who also could be *small* and intolerant⟩ — see NARROW 2

small arm *n* a portable weapon from which a shot is discharged by gunpowder ⟨the soldiers keep their *small arms* securely in their holsters when not on patrol⟩ — see GUN 1

smaller *adj* having not so great importance or rank as another ⟨a *smaller* task but one that needs to be done nevertheless⟩ — see LESSER

small–fry *adj* lacking importance ⟨a *small-fry* official in state government⟩ — see UNIMPORTANT

smallish *adj* of a size that is less than average ⟨a *smallish* row of bushes lining the yard⟩ — see SMALL 1

small–minded *adj* **1** unwilling to grant other people social rights or to accept other viewpoints ⟨a *small-minded* man only concerned with his own well-being⟩ — see INTOLERANT 1
2 not broad or open in views or opinions ⟨resented the *small-minded* people who automatically opposed every new idea⟩ — see NARROW 2

smallness *n* the quality or state of being little in size ⟨my grandmother was surprised by the *smallness* of the latest electronic devices⟩
synonyms diminutiveness, fineness, littleness, puniness, slightness
related words minuteness, tininess; meagerness, poorness, scantiness, scarceness, scarcity, skimpiness, slenderness, slimness, spareness, sparseness, stinginess; deficiency, inadequacy
near antonyms enormity, enormousness, grossness, hugeness, immenseness, immensity, stupendousness; extensiveness, vastness; excessiveness, extravagance, extremeness, immoderacy; abundance, ampleness, bountifulness, copiousness, healthiness, liberality; adequacy, sufficiency; heaviness, heftiness, weightiness; bulkiness, massiveness, voluminousness
antonyms bigness, grandness, greatness, largeness, magnitude

small talk *n* friendly, informal conversation or an instance of this ⟨made *small talk* with some new friends at the party⟩ — see CHAT

smart *adj* **1** being strikingly neat and trim in style or appearance ⟨dressed in their *smart* new uniforms, the cadets proudly paraded around the grounds of the military school⟩
synonyms dapper, natty, sharp, spruce
related words dressy, elegant, formal; neat, orderly, tidy; fashionable, modish, stylish; careful, fastidious, fussy, meticulous; clean, immaculate, spotless
near antonyms messy, untidy; shabby, sleazy; dingy, dirty, filthy, foul, grimy, grubby, nasty; dowdy, inelegant, unfashionable, unstylish
antonyms sloppy, slovenly
2 being in the latest or current fashion ⟨boutiques specializing in *smart* clothes for cosmopolitan women⟩ — see STYLISH
3 causing intense mental or physical distress ⟨administered a *smart* reproof⟩ — see SHARP 2
4 given to or marked by mature intelligent humor ⟨something one sees so rarely on TV: a *smart* sitcom⟩ — see WITTY
5 making light of something usually regarded as serious or sacred ⟨just joked and made *smart* comments during the ceremony⟩ — see FLIPPANT
6 having or showing a practical cleverness or judgment ⟨a *smart* investment that has really paid off⟩ — see SHREWD
7 having or showing quickness of mind ⟨a *smart* child who will do well in school⟩ — see INTELLIGENT 1
8 having a wide and refined knowledge of the world especially from personal experience ⟨a novelist who got

much of the material for his works by hanging out with the *smart* set⟩ — see WORLDLY-WISE

smart *n* a sharp unpleasant sensation usually felt in some specific part of the body ⟨whining over the *smart* from the cut⟩ — see PAIN 1

smart *vb* to feel or cause physical pain ⟨the injection only *smarted* for a moment⟩ — see HURT 1

smart aleck *n* a person who likes to show off in a clever but annoying way ⟨some *smart aleck* in the audience kept shouting clever insults at the speaker⟩

  synonyms smarty (*or* smartie), wiseacre, wise guy

  related words know-it-all; wisecracker; hotshot, show-off

smart–alecky *or* **smart–aleck** *adj* **1** making light of something usually regarded as serious or sacred ⟨you wouldn't be so *smart-alecky* if you were the one having the surgery⟩ — see FLIPPANT

2 marked by the use of wit that is intended to cause hurt feelings ⟨*smart-alecky* comments about her new clothes⟩ — see SARCASTIC

smarting *adj* **1** causing intense discomfort to one's skin ⟨we had to press on, despite the *smarting* sleet that was blowing in our faces⟩ — see CUTTING 1

2 causing intense mental or physical distress ⟨the *smarting* pain of having been jilted by one's girlfriend⟩ — see SHARP 2

smartly *adv* in a strikingly neat and trim manner ⟨the *smartly* dressed scouts marched at the head of the Memorial Day parade⟩

  synonyms dashingly, nattily, sharply, sprucely

  related words neatly, orderly, tidily, trimly; elegantly, fashionably, modishly, stylishly, swankily; carefully, fastidiously, fussily, meticulously; cleanly, immaculately, spotlessly

  near antonyms dowdily, inelegantly, unstylishly; slatternly; messily, untidily; shabbily, sleazily; dingily, dirtily, filthily, foully, grubbily, nastily

  antonyms sloppily, slovenly

smarty *or* **smartie** *n* a person who likes to show off in a clever but annoying way ⟨think so, *smarty*? Well, you're wrong, and I can prove it!⟩ — see SMART ALECK

smash *n* **1** a forceful coming together of two things ⟨the awful *smash* when his dreams got hit by reality⟩ — see IMPACT 1

2 the violent coming together of two bodies into destructive contact ⟨the sound of the *smash* made all of the bystanders immediately whip their heads around⟩ — see CRASH 1

3 a hard strike with a part of the body or an instrument ⟨gave the tennis ball a *smash* and sent it flying over the other side of the net⟩ — see ¹BLOW

4 a loud explosive sound ⟨the bikes collided with a huge *smash*⟩ — see CLAP 1

5 a person or thing that is successful ⟨the new show is a *smash*⟩ — see HIT 1

smash *vb* **1** to cause to break with violence and much noise ⟨deliberately *smashed* a glass against the brick fireplace⟩

  synonyms crash, shatter

  related words bust, fracture, fragment; bash, demolish, destroy, pulverize, ruin, wreck; shiver, splinter, split; crack, crunch, crush, snap

2 to cause to break open or into pieces by or as if by an explosive ⟨the firecracker *smashed* the clay pot⟩ — see BLAST 1

3 to bring to a complete end the physical soundness, existence, or usefulness of ⟨*smashed* the resistance and went on to conquer the country⟩ — see DESTROY 1

4 to come into usually forceful contact with something ⟨we nearly *smashed* into each other on the skating rink⟩ — see HIT 2

smashup *n* the violent coming together of two bodies into destructive contact ⟨three cars were involved in a *smashup* on my street last night⟩ — see CRASH 1

smattering *n* a small number ⟨a *smattering* of guests at the art exhibit⟩ — see FEW

smear *vb* **1** to rub an oily or sticky substance over ⟨the toddler gleefully *smeared* her hair and face with maple syrup⟩

  synonyms anoint, bedaub, besmear, daub

  related words coat, paint, plaster; grease, oil; gum, lard, pitch, tar; begrime, besmirch, blacken, dirty, foul, grime, mire, muddy, smirch, smudge, soil, stain, sully

2 to make untrue and harmful statements about ⟨willing to *smear* his opponent if doing so would win the election⟩ — see SLANDER

smearing *n* the making of false statements that damage another's reputation ⟨this *smearing* has got to stop, or the voters will conclude that there's absolutely no one worth voting for⟩ — see SLANDER

smell *n* the quality of a thing that makes it perceptible to the sense organs in the nose ⟨the *smell* of vanilla is supposed to be very soothing⟩

  synonyms odor, redolence, scent, sniff

  related words whiff; aroma, bouquet, fragrance, perfume; ambrosia, lusciousness, savor, savoriness, spice, tang; acridness, fetidness, foulness, noisomeness, rancidity, rankness, stench, stink; incense, musk

smell *vb* **1** to become aware of by means of the sense organs in the nose ⟨we *smelled* the aroma of freshly baked cookies as soon as we walked in the house⟩

  synonyms nose, scent, sniff, whiff

  related words breathe, drink (in), inhale

2 to have a vague awareness of ⟨I *smell* something fishy about this situation⟩ — see FEEL 1

smelly *adj* having an unpleasant smell ⟨your *smelly* sneakers are enough to raise the dead⟩ — see MALODOROUS

smidgen *also* **smidgeon** *or* **smidgin** *n* a very small amount ⟨cleaned the house until there wasn't even a *smidgen* of dust left⟩ — see PARTICLE 1

smile *vb* **1** to express an emotion (as amusement) by curving the lips upward ⟨he *smiled* in pleasure when he saw the giant sign welcoming him home⟩

  synonyms beam, grin

  related words laugh, simper; smirk, sneer

  near antonyms grimace; frown, glare, glower, scowl

2 to express scornful amusement by means of facial contortions ⟨*smiled* at their ridiculous antics and walked away in disgust⟩ — see SNEER

smirch *n* a mark of guilt or disgrace ⟨a *smirch* on her reputation⟩ — see STAIN 1

smirch *vb* **1** to make dirty ⟨their clothes were *smirched* by dust from the trail⟩ — see DIRTY

2 to reduce to a lower standing in one's own eyes or in others' eyes ⟨this scandal will forever *smirch* the name of a once-great family⟩ — see HUMBLE

smite *vb* to deliver a blow to (someone or something) usually in a strong vigorous manner ⟨he shall *smite* his enemies with a mighty fist⟩ — see HIT 1

smog *n* an atmospheric condition in which suspended particles in the air rob it of its transparency ⟨the city's *smog* was once so bad that darkness often prevailed, even at noon⟩ — see HAZE 1

smoggy *adj* filled with or dimmed by fine particles (as of dust or water) in suspension ⟨it was hard to see through the *smoggy* afternoon sky⟩ — see HAZY 1

smooch *vb* to touch one another with the lips as a sign of love ⟨came across the couple *smooching* in a dark corner⟩ — see KISS 1

smooth *adj* **1** having or showing very polished and worldly manners ⟨a *smooth* salesman⟩ — see SUAVE
2 involving minimal difficulty or effort ⟨it should be *smooth* going from this point on⟩ — see EASY 1
3 having a surface without bends, breaks, or irregularities ⟨a *smooth* skating rink⟩ — see LEVEL

smooth *vb* **1** to free from obstruction or difficulty ⟨a willingness to compromise will *smooth* the way to an early agreement⟩ — see EASE 1
2 to make free from breaks, curves, or bumps ⟨the workers *smoothed* the surface of the concrete before letting it dry⟩ — see EVEN 1
3 to make smooth or glossy usually by repeatedly applying surface pressure ⟨used fine sandpaper to *smooth* the face of the wood⟩ — see POLISH

smoothly *adv* without difficulty ⟨proceeded *smoothly* to the next stage of the project⟩ — see EASILY

smother *vb* **1** to be or cause to be killed by lack of breathable air ⟨you should never play inside discarded appliances because you could become trapped and *smother*⟩
synonyms choke, stifle, strangle, suffocate
related words garrote (*or* garotte), throttle; asphyxiate; drown
near antonyms breathe, exhale, expire, inhale, inspire
2 to refrain from openly showing or uttering ⟨he quickly *smothered* his inappropriate laughter at the ceremony⟩ — see SUPPRESS 2

smudge *vb* to make dirty ⟨she accidentally *smudged* her collar with the lipstick⟩ — see DIRTY

smug *adj* having too high an opinion of oneself ⟨a winner who was so *smug* that he lost the goodwill of the crowd⟩ — see CONCEITED

smugness *n* an often unjustified feeling of being pleased with oneself or with one's situation or achievements ⟨the sense of *smugness* that can come with too many easy victories⟩ — see COMPLACENCE

smut *n* foul matter that mars the purity or cleanliness of something ⟨once a year they cleaned all of the *smut* out of the chimney⟩ — see FILTH 1

smuttiness *n* the quality or state of being obscene ⟨we were offended by the *smuttiness* of the jokes that the comedian was telling⟩ — see OBSCENITY 1

smutty *adj* **1** depicting or referring to sexual matters in a way that is unacceptable in polite society ⟨the movie was rated R because of some nude scenes and *smutty* dialogue⟩ — see OBSCENE 1
2 not clean ⟨a street urchin with a *smutty* face⟩ — see DIRTY 1

snag *n* a danger or difficulty that is hidden or not easily recognized ⟨we ran into a slight *snag* the night before the show⟩ — see PITFALL 1

snail *n* someone who moves slowly or more slowly than others ⟨go and tell the *snails* in the back to hurry up⟩ — see SLOWPOKE

snake *n* **1** a limbless reptile with a long body ⟨*snakes* are cold-blooded, so they regulate their body temperature by alternately basking in sunlight and seeking shade⟩
synonyms serpent, viper
related words adder, anaconda, asp, blacksnake, boa, bull snake, bushmaster, cobra, constrictor, copperhead, coral snake, cottonmouth moccasin, diamond-back rattlesnake, fer-de-lance, garter snake, glass snake, gopher snake, green snake, hognose snake, indigo snake, king cobra, king snake, krait, mamba, milk snake, pit viper, puff adder, python, racer, rat snake, rattlesnake, sea serpent, sidewinder, water moccasin, water snake
2 a person whose behavior is offensive to others ⟨why, that dirty, rotten *snake*!⟩ — see JERK 1

snake *vb* **1** to move about in a sly or secret manner ⟨*snaking* softly through the brush⟩ — see SNEAK 1
2 to move slowly with the body close to the ground ⟨commandos *snaking* through the grass toward the house⟩ — see CRAWL 1

snap *adj* **1** involving minimal difficulty or effort ⟨a *snap* course that even an idiot could pass⟩ — see EASY 1
2 made or done without previous thought or preparation ⟨made a *snap* decision⟩ — see EXTEMPORANEOUS

snap *n* **1** a loud explosive sound ⟨the plastic coat hook broke off with a loud *snap* when he tried to hang the heavy bag on it⟩ — see CLAP 1
2 a picture created from an image recorded on a light-sensitive surface by a camera ⟨took several *snaps* of his family for the scrapbook⟩ — see PHOTOGRAPH
3 active strength of body or mind ⟨the team is showing a lot of *snap* tonight⟩ — see VIGOR 1
4 a weather condition marked by low temperatures ⟨a prolonged cold *snap*⟩ — see COLD
5 a very small amount ⟨I don't care a *snap* about gossip⟩ — see PARTICLE 1
6 something that is easy to do ⟨this test will be a *snap*⟩ — see CINCH

snap *vb* **1** to speak sharply or irritably ⟨the shopkeeper finally *snapped* at one customer who couldn't seem to make up his mind⟩
synonyms bark, snarl
related words shout, yell; blow up, explode
2 to break suddenly with an explosive sound ⟨the fragile twig *snapped* in her hands⟩ — see CRACK 1
3 to take a photograph of ⟨be sure to *snap* everything you see on your vacation, and then you can show us⟩ — see PHOTOGRAPH

snap (**up**) *vb* to take physical control or possession of (something) suddenly or forcibly ⟨*snapped up* the last remaining cupcake⟩ — see CATCH 1

snapback *n* the process or period of gradually regaining one's health and strength ⟨predicted a quick *snapback* for the rugged young soldier⟩ — see CONVALESCENCE

snap back *vb* **1** to become healthy and strong again after illness or weakness ⟨teenagers will often *snap back* remarkably quickly⟩ — see CONVALESCE
2 to regain a former or normal state ⟨analysts hoped that the economy would *snap back* over the next few months⟩ — see RECOVER 2

snappily *adv* with great speed ⟨she *snappily* completed the test and put down her pencil⟩ — see FAST 1

snappish *adj* easily irritated or annoyed ⟨I always start feeling *snappish* whenever I get really hungry⟩ — see IRRITABLE

snappy *adj* **1** being in the latest or current fashion ⟨that *snappy* outfit really should impress your date⟩ — see STYLISH
2 easily irritated or annoyed ⟨we tried to avoid her when she was acting *snappy*⟩ — see IRRITABLE
3 having a low or subnormal temperature ⟨typically *snappy* weather for March⟩ — see COLD 1
4 having much high-spirited energy and movement ⟨much *snappy* repartee at the party⟩ — see LIVELY 1

5 moving, proceeding, or acting with great speed ⟨bring us some more french fries, and make it *snappy*⟩ — see FAST 1

snapshot *n* a picture created from an image recorded on a light-sensitive surface by a camera ⟨took a *snapshot* of the falling star⟩ — see PHOTOGRAPH

snare *n* **1** a device or scheme for capturing another by surprise ⟨you fell for my clever *snare*, you fool!⟩ — see TRAP 1

2 something that catches and holds ⟨someday you'll find that your lies are a *snare* from which you can't escape⟩ — see WEB 1

snare *vb* **1** to catch or hold as if in a net ⟨easily distracted by any bright object that *snared* his eye⟩ — see ENTANGLE 2

2 to take physical control or possession of (something) suddenly or forcibly ⟨campers trying to *snare* fish for supper⟩ — see CATCH 1

¹snarl *vb* to speak sharply or irritably ⟨she *snarled* at me after I kept badgering her with questions⟩ — see SNAP 1

²snarl *vb* to twist together into a usually confused mass ⟨you'll be awfully sorry if you *snarl* your fishing line⟩ — see ENTANGLE 1

snatch *vb* to take physical control or possession of (something) suddenly or forcibly ⟨the seagull *snatched* the french fry right from my hand⟩ — see CATCH 1

snatching *n* an instance of theft ⟨an industry in which the *snatching* of trade secrets is greatly feared⟩ — see THEFT 2

snazzy *adj* attractively eye-catching in style ⟨a *snazzy* car⟩ — see JAZZY 1

sneak *adj* undertaken or done so as to escape being observed or known by others ⟨a *sneak* attack⟩ — see SECRET 1

sneak *n* someone who acts in a sly and secret manner ⟨"Why, you little *sneak*," Mom exclaimed, "you made my birthday present right under my nose!"⟩

synonyms lurker, skulker

related words skunk, snake; sharper, slicker, swindler; stalker

sneak *vb* **1** to move about in a sly or secret manner ⟨the little kids *sneak* around upstairs when they're supposed to be in bed⟩

synonyms lurk, mouse, pussyfoot, skulk, slide, slink, slip, snake, steal

related words crawl, creep, edge, inch, worm; pad, tiptoe

2 to introduce in a gradual, secret, or clever way ⟨*sneak* the topic into the conversation any way you can⟩ — see INSINUATE

sneakiness *n* skill in achieving one's ends through indirect, subtle, or underhanded means ⟨she was impressed by the *sneakiness* with which they had planned the surprise party⟩ — see CUNNING 1

sneaking *adj* **1** given to or acting in secret and to concealing one's intentions ⟨never let one of those *sneaking* salespeople into your house⟩ — see SNEAKY 1

2 undertaken or done so as to escape being observed or known by others ⟨a *sneaking* admiration for an opponent⟩ — see SECRET 1

sneaky *adj* **1** given to acting in secret and to concealing one's intentions ⟨the *sneaky* little girl was clearly up to something⟩

synonyms furtive, shady, shifty, slippery, sly, sneaking, stealthy

related words devious, guileful; close, closemouthed, reticent, secretive; clandestine, covert, dark; deceitful,

deceiving, deceptive, tricky, underhand, underhanded; crooked, dishonest, double-dealing, two-faced; lying, mendacious, untrustworthy, untruthful; insidious, perfidious, treacherous

near antonyms aboveboard, forthright, straightforward; candid, frank, open, plain; honest, trustworthy, truthful

2 undertaken or done so as to escape being observed or known by others ⟨a *sneaky* plan to replace the priceless painting with a copy⟩ — see SECRET 1

sneer *vb* to express scornful amusement by means of facial contortions ⟨the most popular girl in school *sneered* every time she saw the "nerds"⟩

synonyms laugh, smile, snicker, snigger

related words sniff, snort; catcall, hoot, insult, jeer, mock, ridicule; decry, despise, disdain; scorn

snicker *n* an explosive sound that is a sign of amusement ⟨a *snicker* of derision⟩ — see LAUGH 1

snicker *vb* to express scornful amusement by means of facial contortions ⟨he *snickered* at the puzzled look on her face⟩ — see SNEER

snide *adj* not following or in accordance with standards of honor and decency ⟨a *snide* trick⟩ — see IGNOBLE 2

sniff *n* the quality of a thing that makes it perceptible to the sense organs in the nose ⟨took a *sniff* to try to identify the ingredients of the sauce⟩ — see SMELL

sniff *vb* to become aware of by means of the sense organs in the nose ⟨*sniffing* the flowers in the garden⟩ — see SMELL 1

sniff (at) *vb* to show contempt for ⟨her skills are nothing to *sniff at*⟩ — see SCORN 1

snigger *n* an explosive sound that is a sign of amusement ⟨the teacher tried to find the source of the *sniggers*⟩ — see LAUGH 1

snigger *vb* to express scornful amusement by means of facial contortions ⟨we *sniggered* as the actor kept forgetting his lines⟩ — see SNEER

snip *vb* to make (as hair) shorter with or as if with the use of shears ⟨*snipped* the loose ends⟩ — see CLIP

snippet *n* a very small piece ⟨read them a *snippet* of his latest poem⟩ — see BIT 1

snippy *adj* **1** being or characterized by direct, brief, and potentially rude speech or manner ⟨*snippy* remarks about the quality of the food⟩ — see BLUNT 1

2 easily irritated or annoyed ⟨feeling *snippy* after a long day of work⟩ — see IRRITABLE

¹snitch *vb* to give information (as to the authorities) about another's improper or unlawful activities ⟨always *snitching* on someone⟩ — see SQUEAL 1

²snitch *vb* to take (something) without right and with an intent to keep ⟨*snitched* a dollar from a classmate but was promptly caught and punished⟩ — see STEAL 1

snitcher *n* a person who provides secret information about another's wrongdoing ⟨he swore that he'd get revenge if he ever found out who the *snitcher* was⟩ — see INFORMER

snoop *vb* to interest oneself in what is not one's concern ⟨*snooping* around the abandoned warehouse⟩ — see INTERFERE

snoopy *adj* **1** interested in what is not one's own business ⟨she feels that being *snoopy* is a desirable trait in a reporter⟩ — see CURIOUS 1

2 thrusting oneself where one is not welcome or invited ⟨put a fence around the yard to keep out *snoopy* neighbors⟩ — see INTRUSIVE

snooze *n* a short sleep ⟨took a *snooze* after lunch to refresh himself⟩ — see NAP

snooze *vb* **1** be in a state of sleep ⟨*snooze* through those long winter nights⟩ — see SLEEP 1

2 to sleep lightly or briefly ⟨she was just *snoozing* when she heard the knock at the door⟩ — see ¹NAP 1

snoozing *n* a natural periodic loss of consciousness during which the body restores itself ⟨all that *snoozing* should have you well rested and ready for some hard work⟩ — see SLEEP 1

snort *n* **1** a vocal sound made to express scorn or disapproval ⟨made a *snort* of derision⟩ — see CATCALL

2 the portion of a serving of a beverage that is swallowed at one time ⟨the old cowpoke asked for a *snort* of whiskey⟩ — see DRINK 2

snow *vb* to cause to believe what is untrue ⟨easily *snowed* by her glib talk⟩ — see DECEIVE

snowball *vb* to become greater in extent, volume, amount, or number ⟨the little problems we ignored began to *snowball* into huge headaches⟩ — see INCREASE 2

snow under *vb* **1** to defeat by a large margin ⟨the challenger *snowed* the incumbent *under* in a big upset⟩ — see WHIP 1

2 to subject to incapacitating emotional or mental stress ⟨*snowed under* by the huge pile of homework⟩ — see OVERWHELM 1

snub *n* treatment that is deliberately unfriendly ⟨he accepted the *snubs* as well deserved for his awful behavior the previous weekend⟩ — see COLD SHOULDER

snub *vb* **1** to deliberately ignore or treat rudely ⟨the snob in town always *snubbed* anyone she thought was beneath her⟩

synonyms cold-shoulder, cut, slight

related words ostracize; brush (aside *or* off), disdain, rebuff, reject, repulse; disregard, forget, neglect, overlook, overpass, pass over, shrug off

2 to show contempt for ⟨a social set that *snubs* anyone below their income bracket⟩ — see SCORN 1

snuff (out) *vb* **1** to cause to cease burning ⟨*snuff out* the candle⟩ — see EXTINGUISH 1

2 to destroy all traces of ⟨the forest fire *snuffed out* all of the animal life in the immediate area⟩ — see ANNIHILATE 1

3 to put a stop to (something) by the use of force ⟨*snuffed out* the movement for democratic rule⟩ — see QUELL 1

snug *adj* **1** being clean and in good order ⟨a *snug* military cadet⟩ — see NEAT 1

2 providing physical comfort ⟨a *snug* cottage that's the perfect retreat for a rustic vacation⟩ — see COMFORTABLE 1

3 enjoying physical comfort ⟨while *snug* in our warm beds, we listened to the winter storm raging outside⟩ — see COMFORTABLE 2

4 firmly positioned in place and difficult to dislodge ⟨make sure that all screw and nuts in the shelving unit are *snug*⟩ — see TIGHT 2

5 providing safety ⟨yachtsmen looking for a *snug* harbor in which to anchor for the night⟩ — see SAFE 2

snug *vb* to sit or recline comfortably or cozily ⟨the farm hand *snugged* down in the hay and proceeded to go to sleep⟩ — see SNUGGLE 1

snuggle *vb* **1** to sit or recline comfortably or cozily ⟨it's particularly nice to *snuggle* next to the fire on a snowy day⟩

synonyms cuddle, curl up, nestle, snug

related words huddle

2 to lie close ⟨*snuggle* up to a friendly cat⟩ — see NUZZLE

so *adj* being in agreement with the truth or a fact or a standard ⟨I'm afraid that some of what you've said just isn't *so*⟩ — see CORRECT 1

so *adv* **1** for this or that reason ⟨it was raining, *so* we stayed inside⟩ — see THEREFORE

2 in like manner ⟨the boss works very hard, and *so* does everyone else⟩ — see ALSO 1

3 to a great degree ⟨*so* cold outside⟩ — see VERY 1

soak *n* a person who makes a habit of getting drunk ⟨felt sorry for the town *soak*⟩ — see DRUNK 1

soak *vb* **1** to wet thoroughly with liquid ⟨we ran for home as soon as the rain started, but our clothes still ended up *soaked*⟩

synonyms drench, drown, impregnate, saturate, sop, souse, steep

related words marinate; presoak; dip, immerse, inundate, submerge; bathe, douse, wash, water, wet; infiltrate, penetrate, permeate

near antonyms dehydrate, dry; drain, empty, void

antonyms wring (out)

2 to charge (someone) too much for goods or services ⟨a merchant who *soaks* the tourists every summer⟩ — see OVERCHARGE 1

3 to make wet ⟨that downpour *soaked* my hair, and now I look like a sight⟩ — see WET

soak (up) *vb* to take in (something liquid) through small openings ⟨this sponge should *soak up* the spilled juice very nicely⟩ — see ABSORB 1

soaked *adj* containing, covered with, or thoroughly penetrated by water ⟨a miserable, *soaked* cat who looked like a drowned rat⟩ — see WET

soaking *adj* containing, covered with, or thoroughly penetrated by water ⟨couldn't wait to take off his *soaking* socks⟩ — see WET

soap *n* a substance used for cleaning ⟨a little *soap* and water should clean this in no time⟩ — see CLEANER

soar *n* the act or an instance of rising or climbing up ⟨the *soar* of the space shuttle never fails to inspire⟩ — see ASCENT 1

soar *vb* **1** to move or extend upward ⟨the Eiffel Tower *soaring* into the skies above Paris⟩ — see ASCEND

2 to move through the air with or as if with outstretched wings ⟨bats *soaring* and swooping through the night air⟩ — see FLY 1

3 to rise abruptly and rapidly ⟨prices *soared* overnight because of the shortage⟩ — see SKYROCKET

sob *vb* to shed tears often while making meaningless sounds as a sign of pain or distress ⟨the child *sobbed* when she found the dead frog⟩ — see CRY 1

sober *adj* **1** not having one's mind affected by alcohol ⟨it's important to stay *sober* if you're going to be driving a car⟩

synonyms clearheaded, straight

related words abstemious, abstinent, dry, temperate

near antonyms alcoholic

antonyms befuddled, dissipated, drunk, drunken, high, inebriate, inebriated, intoxicated, loaded [*slang*], soused, tipsy

2 based on sound reasoning or information ⟨a *sober* assessment of the situation⟩ — see GOOD 1

3 not joking or playful in mood or manner ⟨a *sober* reply to the teasing comment⟩ — see SERIOUS 1

soberness *n* a mental state free of jesting or trifling ⟨the unexpected *soberness* of the class clown at the memorial service was startling⟩ — see EARNESTNESS

sobriety *n* a mental state free of jesting or trifling ⟨an abrupt *sobriety* fell over the group when they heard the news⟩ — see EARNESTNESS

sobriquet *also* **soubriquet** *n* a descriptive or familiar name given instead of or in addition to the one belonging to an individual ⟨tagged her with the *sobriquet* "peanut" because of her diminutive size⟩ — see NICKNAME

sociability *n* the quality or state of being social ⟨her *sociability* was called into question when she said she hated parties⟩

synonyms conviviality, gregariousness

related words amiability, friendliness, neighborliness; camaraderie, companionship, fellowship; boldness, brashness, extroversion (*or* extraversion), forwardness, immodesty

near antonyms bashfulness, coyness, diffidence, shyness, timidity, timidness; introversion; modesty

sociable *adj* **1** likely to seek or enjoy the company of others ⟨he's an intensely *sociable* child, even prone to fits of depression when he's left alone⟩ — see CONVIVIAL

2 showing a natural kindness and courtesy especially in social situations ⟨a pleasant and *sociable* hostess who puts everyone instantly at ease⟩ — see GRACIOUS 1

social *adj* likely to seek or enjoy the company of others ⟨dogs are *social* animals, preferring by nature to be part of a pack⟩ — see CONVIVIAL

socialize *vb* to take part in social activities ⟨he likes to *socialize* with his coworkers after work ends⟩

synonyms associate, fraternize, hobnob, mingle, mix

phrases rub elbows, rub shoulders

near antonyms avoid, eschew, shun; slight, snub

society *n* **1** a group of persons formally joined together for some common interest ⟨a debate *society*⟩ — see ASSOCIATION 2

2 human beings in general ⟨*society* benefits as a whole by the practice of good manners⟩ — see PEOPLE 1

3 the feeling of closeness and friendship that exists between companions ⟨an evening marked by a lovely dinner and the *society* of our closest friends⟩ — see COMPANIONSHIP

4 the way people live at a particular time and place ⟨a pre-automobile *society* in which ordinary people rarely strayed far from home⟩ — see CIVILIZATION 1

sock *n* **1** a close-fitting covering for the foot and leg ⟨black *socks* to go with black pants and shoes⟩ — see STOCKING

2 a hard strike with a part of the body or an instrument ⟨a wiseacre who deserves a good *sock* in the face⟩ — see ¹BLOW

sock *vb* to deliver a blow to (someone or something) usually in a strong vigorous manner ⟨kept *socking* the punching bag until he was exhausted⟩ — see HIT 1

sod *n* the land of one's birth, residence, or citizenship ⟨a sentimental journey back to the old *sod*⟩ — see COUNTRY 1

sodality *n* a group of persons formally joined together for some common interest ⟨a 19th-century observer of American society noted that Americans had a fondness for forming *sodalities*⟩ — see ASSOCIATION 2

sodden *adj* containing, covered with, or thoroughly penetrated by water ⟨eyes peering out between strands of *sodden* hair⟩ — see WET

sofa *n* a long upholstered piece of furniture designed for several sitters ⟨curled up on the *sofa* with a book⟩ — see COUCH

soft *adj* **1** not loud in pitch or volume ⟨*soft* music played in the background while we ate⟩

synonyms dull, low, quiet

related words dead, silent, still; dreamy, peaceful, restful, soothing, tranquil; muffled, muted, softened, toned (down)

near antonyms brazen, dinning, discordant, noisy, obstreperous, raucous, rip-roaring, vociferous; grating, harsh, shrill, strident

antonyms blaring, blasting, booming, clamorous, clangorous, deafening, earsplitting, loud, piercing, resounding, ringing, roaring, sonorous, stentorian, thunderous

2 smooth or delicate in appearance or feel ⟨I like this sweater the best because it is so *soft* and comfortable⟩

synonyms cottony, downy, satin, satiny, silken, silky, velvety

related words creamy; delicate, fine, slick, smooth

near antonyms bumpy, lumpy, pebbly; broken, jagged, ragged, rugged; grainy, granular, gritty

antonyms coarse, harsh, rough, scratchy

3 giving easily to the touch ⟨*soft* mattresses make it very easy to fall asleep, but they have a tendency to get lumpy⟩

synonyms flabby, mushy, pulpy, spongy, squashy, squishy

related words unhardened; doughy, fleshy; droopy, flaccid, floppy, lank, limp, slack, yielding; compressible, malleable, pliable, pliant, workable

near antonyms inflexible, resilient, rigid, stiff, tense; resistant, sound, strong, sturdy, tough, unyielding; hardened, indurated, tempered

antonyms firm, hard, solid

4 involving minimal difficulty or effort ⟨looking for a *soft* job in local government⟩ — see EASY 1

5 lacking bodily strength ⟨*soft* recruits who will get toughened up in the army⟩ — see WEAK 1

6 lacking strength of will or character ⟨a *soft* woman who tends to yield to stronger personalities⟩ — see WEAK 2

7 not harsh or stern especially in manner, nature, or effect ⟨a *soft* breeze coming off the lake⟩ — see GENTLE 1

8 providing physical comfort ⟨a warm, *soft* bed to rest my weary bones⟩ — see COMFORTABLE 1

soften *vb* **1** to diminish the physical strength of ⟨three weeks of being sick in bed had noticeably *softened* her⟩ — see WEAKEN 1

2 to lessen the shock of ⟨had tried to *soften* the blow of the rejection⟩ — see CUSHION

softened *adj* lacking bodily strength ⟨the athlete, *softened* by the long period of convalescence, had to begin his training program almost from scratch⟩ — see WEAK 1

softhearted *adj* having or marked by sympathy and consideration for others ⟨a *softhearted* woman who never hesitates to help anyone in trouble⟩ — see HUMANE 1

softheartedness *n* the capacity for feeling for another's unhappiness or misfortune ⟨the kind of *softheartedness* that makes him an easy target for anyone with a tale of woe⟩ — see HEART 1

softness *n* the quality or state of lacking strength of will or character ⟨*softness* is the one quality that the public will not tolerate in a leader⟩ — see WEAKNESS 2

soft–soap *vb* **1** to get (someone) to do something by gentle urging, special attention, or flattery ⟨*soft-soaped* her parents into letting her go on the trip⟩ — see COAX

2 to praise too much ⟨shrewd voters who know when a politician is trying to *soft-soap* them⟩ — see FLATTER 1

soft soap *n* excessive praise ⟨a salesman who knows the value of *soft soap* in making a sale⟩ — see FLATTERY

softy *or* **softie** *n* a person lacking in physical strength ⟨a *softy* who usually needs someone else's strong hands to open bottles and jars⟩ — see WEAKLING 1

soggy *adj* containing, covered with, or thoroughly penetrated by water ⟨spread the *soggy* papers out to dry⟩ — see WET

soil *n* **1** foul matter that mars the purity or cleanliness of something ⟨got some sort of *soil* on my white pants⟩ — see FILTH 1

2 the loose surface material in which plants naturally grow ⟨bought rich *soil* to plant flowers in⟩ — see DIRT 1

3 the solid part of our planet's surface as distinguished from the sea and air ⟨happy to have reached *soil* after that long sea voyage⟩ — see EARTH 2

soil *vb* to make dirty ⟨oil and grease *soiled* the mechanic's shirt⟩ — see DIRTY

soiled *adj* not clean ⟨a *soiled* carpet in need of a good shampooing⟩ — see DIRTY 1

sojourn *n* a temporary residing as another's guest ⟨spent a relaxing *sojourn* in her friend's summer home⟩ — see VISIT 1

sojourn *vb* to reside as a temporary guest ⟨began their retirement by leisurely *sojourning* with friends and relatives across the country⟩ — see VISIT 2

solace *n* **1** a feeling of ease from grief or trouble ⟨the kind words brought a little *solace*⟩ — see COMFORT 1
2 the giving of hope and strength in times of grief, distress, or suffering ⟨the selfless *solace* of the sick by the workers at the hospice⟩ — see CONSOLATION 1

solace *vb* to ease the grief or distress of ⟨counselors did their best to *solace* the bereaved children⟩ — see COMFORT 1

solacing *n* the giving of hope and strength in times of grief, distress, or suffering ⟨I will be forever grateful for my friend's *solacing* of me when my mother died⟩ — see CONSOLATION 1

solar plexus *n* the part of the body between the chest and the pelvis ⟨a punch in the *solar plexus* knocked the air out of him⟩ — see STOMACH

soldier *n* a person engaged in military service ⟨one of the goals of war is to keep as many *soldiers* as possible from being killed⟩
synonyms fighter, legionary, legionnaire, man-at-arms, regular, serviceman, warrior
related words servicewoman; cavalier, cuirassier, dragoon, trooper; dogface, doughboy, footman, foot soldier, infantryman; commando, marine, ranger; artilleryman, musketeer, rifleman; archer, lancer, spearman; Confederate, Continental, Federal, GI, guardsman, Rough Rider; guerilla, irregular, partisan; combatant, noncombatant; mercenary, soldier of fortune; veteran, war-horse; conscript, draftee, recruit; reservist
antonyms civilian

soldierly *adj* of, relating to, or suitable for war or a warrior ⟨Noah Webster's brief contribution to the Revolutionary cause suggests that his *soldierly* skills were few⟩ — see MARTIAL 1

sole *adj* **1** belonging only to the one person, unit, or group named ⟨the landowner has *sole* rights to the property, so he can do whatever he wants to with it⟩
synonyms exclusive, single, unshared
related words proprietary
near antonyms joint, mutual, shared
antonyms nonexclusive

2 being the one or ones of a class with no other members ⟨the eldest son became the family's *sole* support⟩ — see ONLY 1

solecism *n* a socially improper or unsuitable act or remark ⟨the *solecism* of asking one's hosts how much something in their house cost them⟩ — see IMPROPRIETY 2

solely *adv* **1** for nothing other than ⟨I fight *solely* for my country, not for money!⟩
synonyms alone, exclusively, just, only, simply
related words mainly, mostly, primarily
near antonyms additionally, also, likewise
2 without aid or support ⟨you undertook that project *solely* on your own, and you will finish it likewise⟩ — see ALONE 1

solemn *adj* **1** having or showing a serious and reserved manner ⟨the director of the funeral home has a fittingly *solemn* demeanor⟩ — see DIGNIFIED
2 not joking or playful in mood or manner ⟨*solemn* as a judge⟩ — see SERIOUS 1

solemnity *n* **1** a mental state free of jesting or trifling ⟨the coronation ceremony requires absolute *solemnity*⟩ — see EARNESTNESS
2 an oft-repeated action or series of actions performed in accordance with tradition or a set of rules ⟨the *solemnities* of the Easter vigil service⟩ — see RITE

solicit *vb* **1** to go around and approach (people) with a request for opinions or information ⟨*solicited* several opinions about which job he should accept⟩ — see CANVASS
2 to make a request for ⟨*solicit* donations for a charity⟩ — see ASK (FOR) 1
3 to make a request of ⟨*solicited* him to join the team⟩ — see ASK 2
4 to make a request to (someone) in an earnest or urgent manner ⟨*solicit* the President for relief funds⟩ — see BEG

solicitation *n* an earnest request ⟨the mail is always full of *solicitations* from worthy causes⟩ — see PLEA 1

soliciting *adj* asking humbly ⟨a *soliciting* tone is better when asking for lenient treatment you don't deserve⟩ — see SUPPLIANT

solicitor *n* **1** one that tries to get a person to give in to a desire ⟨money, that great *solicitor* that has often succeeded in persuading people to sell their very souls⟩ — see TEMPTER
2 one who asks earnestly for a favor or gift ⟨even a billionaire doesn't have the wherewithal to grant the wish of every deserving *solicitor* who comes his way⟩ — see SUPPLICANT

solicitous *adj* **1** given to or made with heedful anticipation of the needs and happiness of others ⟨a most *solicitous* husband, he had already cleaned the house and cooked dinner by the time his wife returned home from work⟩ — see THOUGHTFUL 1
2 showing urgent desire or interest ⟨a family that is *solicitous* to put this whole unfortunate affair behind them and to move on with their lives⟩ — see EAGER

solicitude *n* an uneasy state of mind usually over the possibility of an anticipated misfortune or trouble ⟨a growing *solicitude* over the possible results of the criminal investigation⟩ — see ANXIETY 1

solid *adj* **1** based on sound reasoning or information ⟨the only *solid* conclusion that the jury could have reached⟩ — see GOOD 1
2 having a consistency that does not easily yield to pressure ⟨the ice cream is too *solid* to scoop right now⟩ — see FIRM 2

3 having or consisting of a single color ⟨both kittens are black, but one has a *solid* coat and the other has a few white patches⟩ — see MONOCHROMATIC

4 not showing weakness or uncertainty ⟨some people see a *solid* handshake as a sign of strong character⟩ — see FIRM 1

5 worthy of one's trust ⟨a *solid* source of information to reporters⟩ — see DEPENDABLE

solidify *vb* **1** to become physically firm or solid ⟨water *solidifying* into ice⟩ — see HARDEN 1

2 to take on a definite form ⟨my ideas on this topic are just starting to *solidify*⟩ — see FORM 1

solidity *n* worthiness as the recipient of another's trust or confidence ⟨the *solidity* of his word is such that I don't need a written contract—or anything else⟩ — see RELIABILITY

solidness *n* worthiness as the recipient of another's trust or confidence ⟨her proven *solidness* as a friend is something that I can't even begin to describe⟩ — see RELIABILITY

solitariness *n* the state of being alone or kept apart from others ⟨it was the overwhelming *solitariness* of his existence that caused the marooned sailor to go mad⟩ — see ISOLATION

solitary *adj* **1** being the one or ones of a class with no other members ⟨a *solitary* example⟩ — see ONLY 2

2 not being in the company of others ⟨a *solitary* sailboat was the only object on the horizon⟩ — see ALONE 1

solitary *n* a person who lives away from others ⟨weary of European civilization, the painter Paul Gauguin famously abandoned France to become a *solitary* in the South Seas⟩ — see RECLUSE

solitude *n* the state of being alone or kept apart from others ⟨sought the kind of *solitude* where his thoughts would be his only companions⟩ — see ISOLATION

solo *adj* not being in the company of others ⟨a *solo* flight⟩ — see ALONE 1

solon *n* a member of an organized body of persons having the authority to make laws ⟨one of the most politically adept *solons* in the state legislature⟩ — see LEGISLATOR

soluble *adj* capable of having the reason for or cause of determined ⟨one murder case that proved to be *soluble* after all⟩ — see SOLVABLE

solution *n* something attained by mental effort and especially by computation ⟨the *solution* to a math problem⟩ — see ANSWER 2

solvable *adj* capable of having the reason for or cause of determined ⟨I'm sure that the mystery of what happened to the missing pizza is *solvable*⟩

synonyms answerable, explainable, explicable, resolvable, soluble

related words analyzable, decipherable; feasible, workable

near antonyms impossible

antonyms inexplicable, insoluble, unexplainable, unsolvable

solve *vb* to find an answer for through reasoning ⟨it took me half an hour to *solve* the logic puzzle⟩

synonyms answer, break, crack, dope (out), figure out, puzzle (out), resolve, riddle, unravel, work, work out

related words clear (up), iron out, straighten (out), unscramble, untangle, untie; divine, guess; decipher, decode

somatic *adj* of or relating to the human body ⟨a *somatic* disorder that was once thought to be "all in the patient's head"⟩ — see PHYSICAL 1

somber *or* **sombre** *adj* **1** being without light or without much light ⟨the prison's *somber* interrogation room has the desired effect of striking fear and despair into the prisoner⟩ — see DARK 1

2 causing or marked by an atmosphere lacking in cheer ⟨the *somber* occasion of a friend's funeral⟩ — see GLOOMY 1

some *adj* known but not named ⟨*some* people won't be able to come⟩ — see CERTAIN 1

some *adv* very close to but not completely ⟨*some* 400 people may have perished in that fire⟩ — see ALMOST

somebody *n* a person who is widely known and usually much talked about ⟨hopes to become a *somebody* someday⟩ — see CELEBRITY 1

someday *adv* at a later time ⟨we'll get to the other planets *someday*⟩ — see YET 1

something *adv* **1** to a great degree ⟨smells *something* awful⟩ — see VERY 1

2 to some degree or extent ⟨a person of *something* less than total honesty⟩ — see FAIRLY

something *n* one that has a real and independent existence ⟨I heard *something* fall off the counter⟩ — see ENTITY

sometime *adj* having been such at some previous time ⟨a *sometime* athlete who's gotten awfully fat⟩ — see FORMER

sometime *adv* at a later time ⟨we'll get around to it *sometime*⟩ — see YET 1

sometimes *adv* on some occasions ⟨*sometimes* I like to go skiing, and *sometimes* I prefer to stay inside where it's warm⟩

synonyms now, occasionally

related words intermittently, periodically; infrequently, rarely, seldom; irregularly, sporadically

phrases at times, from time to time, now and then, once in a while

near antonyms frequently, often, oftentimes (*or* ofttimes); commonly, ordinarily, regularly, usually; always, constantly, invariably; continually, continuously, incessantly, perpetually, unceasingly, uninterruptedly; endlessly, ever, interminably

somewhat *adv* to some degree or extent ⟨*somewhat* chilly today⟩ — see FAIRLY

somnolence *n* the quality or state of desiring or needing sleep ⟨*somnolence* is likely to be the most typical and telling reaction to this novel⟩ — see SLEEPINESS

somnolent *adj* desiring or needing sleep ⟨trying to teach *somnolent* students on a very hot day⟩ — see SLEEPY 1

song *n* **1** a short musical composition for the human voice often with instrumental accompaniment ⟨she sang a short *song* for the talent show⟩

synonyms ballad, ditty, jingle, lay, lyric, vocal

related words anthem, canticle, carol, chorale, hymn, noel, psalm, spiritual; dirge, lament, requiem, threnody; hallelujah, paean; aria, barcarole (*or* barcarolle), blues, cantata, chantey (*or* chanty), chorus, croon, descant, glee, lullaby, madrigal, motet, part-song, pop, rocker, round, roundelay, serenade, troll

2 a composition using rhythm and often rhyme to create a lyrical effect ⟨the *songs* of Shakespeare⟩ — see POEM

3 a rhythmic series of musical tones arranged to give a pleasing effect ⟨whistle a *song* as accompaniment to your work⟩ — see MELODY

4 a very small sum of money ⟨bought the land for a *song*⟩ — see MITE 1

5 writing that uses rhythm, vivid language, and often rhyme to provoke an emotional response ⟨a hero honored in *song* and story⟩ — see POETRY 1

songster *n* one who sings ⟨one of the most popular *songsters* during the World War II era⟩ — see SINGER

songwriter *n* a person who writes musical compositions ⟨he's both a singer and a *songwriter*⟩ — see COMPOSER

sonny *n* a male person who has not yet reached adulthood ⟨come over here, *sonny*, and help me clean up⟩ — see BOY

sonorous *adj* **1** marked by a high volume of sound ⟨a *sonorous* waterfall⟩ — see LOUD 1
2 marked by conspicuously full and rich sounds or tones ⟨a baritone with a particularly *sonorous* voice⟩ — see RESONANT

soon *adv* **1** at or within a short time ⟨we'll be done *soon*⟩ — see SHORTLY 2
2 by choice or preference ⟨I'd *sooner* have a cavity filled than suffer through that⟩ — see RATHER 1
3 with great speed ⟨as *soon* as possible⟩ — see FAST 1

soothe *vb* **1** to ease the grief or distress of ⟨there seemed no words sufficient to *soothe* the bereaved parents⟩ — see COMFORT 1
2 to free from distress or disturbance ⟨*soothed* the baby with a bottle⟩ — see CALM 1
3 to make more bearable or less severe ⟨hot tea with honey will *soothe* a sore throat⟩ — see HELP 2

soothing *adj* **1** tending to calm the emotions and relieve stress ⟨the *soothing* music eventually put the entire yoga class in the proper mood⟩
synonyms calming, comforting, dreamy, lulling, narcotic, pacifying, quieting, relaxing, sedative, tranquilizing (*also* tranquillizing)
related words hypnotic, opiate; anesthetic, deadening, depressant, numbing
near antonyms energizing, invigorating, stimulant, stimulating; aggravating, annoying, bothersome, exasperating, galling, grating, irksome, irritating, troublesome, vexing
2 not harsh or stern especially in manner, nature, or effect ⟨spoke to the boy in a *soothing* voice⟩ — see GENTLE 1

soothsayer *n* one who predicts future events or developments ⟨a *soothsayer* predicted that I would meet the man who would become my husband on a blind date⟩ — see PROPHET

soothsaying *n* a declaration that something will happen in the future ⟨took the *soothsayings* published in the tabloids with a grain of salt⟩ — see PREDICTION

sop *n* something given or promised in order to improperly influence a person's conduct or decision ⟨as a *sop* to the teachers' union for supporting his reelection campaign, the mayor promised to push for the abolition of the residency requirement⟩ — see BRIBE

sop *vb* to wet thoroughly with liquid ⟨*sopped* the bread in milk⟩ — see SOAK 1

sophisticate *n* a person with the outlook, experience, and manners thought to be typical of big city dwellers ⟨*sophisticates* laughing at people they thought of as hicks⟩ — see COSMOPOLITAN

sophisticate *vb* to make complex or difficult ⟨there's no need to *sophisticate* something that is beautiful in its simplicity⟩ — see COMPLICATE

sophisticated *adj* **1** having a wide and refined knowledge of the world especially from personal experience ⟨a surprisingly *sophisticated* and widely traveled child⟩ — see WORLDLY-WISE

2 having many parts or aspects that are usually interrelated ⟨a very *sophisticated* machine that is a marvel of modern design⟩ — see COMPLEX 1
3 having or showing very polished and worldly manners ⟨a *sophisticated* gentleman, he is a welcomed guest at dinner parties all over town⟩ — see SUAVE
4 made or done with great care or with much detail ⟨a *sophisticated* plan for totally redesigning the city's complicated traffic patterns⟩ — see ELABORATE 1

sophistication *n* the state or quality of having many interrelated parts or aspects ⟨the engine's *sophistication* requires that all repairs be done by an experienced mechanic⟩ — see COMPLEXITY 1

soppy *adj* containing, covered with, or thoroughly penetrated by water ⟨trudging through *soppy* ground⟩ — see WET

sorcerer *n* a person skilled in using supernatural forces ⟨a *sorcerer* who used his power for evil ends⟩ — see MAGICIAN 1

sorceress *n* a woman believed to have often harmful supernatural powers ⟨asked the *sorceress* to cast an evil spell over the village⟩ — see WITCH 1

sorcery *n* the power to control natural forces through supernatural means ⟨in olden times people suspected of *sorcery* were often put to death⟩ — see MAGIC 1

sordid *adj* **1** not clean ⟨managed to rise above the *sordid* streets upon which he grew up⟩ — see DIRTY 1
2 not following or in accordance with standards of honor and decency ⟨a *sordid* affair involving bribery and corruption in high places⟩ — see IGNOBLE 2

sore *adj* **1** causing or feeling bodily pain ⟨my legs are *sore* after that long walk yesterday⟩ — see PAINFUL 1
2 feeling or showing anger ⟨promise not to get *sore* if I tell you what I really think of your new hairstyle?⟩ — see ANGRY
3 having or showing deep-seated resentment ⟨he's been *sore* ever since she insulted him⟩ — see BITTER 1

sorely *adv* with feelings of bitterness or grief ⟨our principal, who is retiring at the end of the year, will be *sorely* missed⟩ — see HARD 2

sorriness *n* deep sadness especially for the loss of someone or something loved ⟨the *sorriness* she felt upon the untimely death of her father can scarcely be described or even imagined⟩ — see SORROW

sorrow *n* deep sadness especially for the loss of someone or something loved ⟨he felt great *sorrow* at the loss of his beloved pet⟩
synonyms affliction, anguish, dolefulness, dolor, grief, heartache, heartbreak, sorriness, woe
related words agony, distress, pain, suffering, torment; blues, dejection, depression, desolateness, desolation, despondency, disconsolateness, dispiritedness, distress, doldrums, downheartedness, dreariness, dumps, forlornness, gloom, gloominess, heartsickness, joylessness, melancholy, miserableness, misery, mopes, oppression, sadness, unhappiness, wretchedness; regret, remorse, rue
near antonyms gaiety (*also* gayety), gayness, humor, jollity, joviality, lightheartedness, merriment, merrymaking, mirth, mirthfulness; hopefulness, optimism; enjoyment; content, contentedness
antonyms blessedness, bliss, blissfulness, cheer, cheerfulness, cheeriness, delight, ecstasy, elatedness, elation, euphoria, exhilaration, exuberance, exultation, gladness, gladsomeness, glee, gleefulness, happiness, joy, joyfulness, joyousness, jubilation, pleasure, rapture, rapturousness

sorrow *vb* to feel deep sadness or mental pain ⟨the soldier's widow continued to *sorrow* long after her husband's last letter had turned yellow with age⟩ — see GRIEVE

sorrowful *adj* **1** expressing or suggesting mourning ⟨adopted a *sorrowful* tone of voice to read the news story about the former governor's death⟩ — see MOURNFUL 1

2 feeling unhappiness ⟨she was *sorrowful* for a whole day after breaking up with her boyfriend⟩ — see SAD 1

sorrowfully *adv* with feelings of bitterness or grief ⟨in a *sorrowfully* worded statement she announced that she was dropping out of the race for governor⟩ — see HARD 2

sorry *adj* **1** arousing or deserving of one's loathing and disgust ⟨one more *sorry* stunt like that and you'll be expelled⟩ — see CONTEMPTIBLE 1

2 causing unhappiness ⟨we have *sorry* news to report tonight⟩ — see SAD 2

3 deserving pitying scorn (as for inadequacy) ⟨a *sorry* spectacle⟩ — see PITIFUL 1

4 feeling sorrow for a wrong that one has done ⟨she's genuinely *sorry* for hurting his feelings⟩ — see CONTRITE 1

5 feeling unhappiness ⟨I'm *sorry* you feel that way, but you still have to pay the bill⟩ — see SAD 1

6 expressing or suggesting mourning ⟨was *sorry* to see the family farm being sold⟩ — see MOURNING 1

7 deserving of one's pity ⟨some *sorry* wretch had the task of putting all of those files back in order⟩ — see PATHETIC 1

sort *n* **1** a number of persons or things that are grouped together because they have something in common ⟨I prefer jackets with zippers to the *sort* that close with buttons⟩

synonyms breed, class, description, feather, ilk, kind, like, manner, nature, order, type

related words model; sample, specimen; bracket, category, division, family, grade, group, lot, persuasion, rank(s), set

2 a member of the human race ⟨he's a decent *sort*⟩ — see HUMAN

sort *vb* to arrange or assign according to type ⟨*sorted* the mail into bills to be paid and junk to be thrown out⟩ — see CLASSIFY 1

sort of *adv* to some degree or extent ⟨you've been acting *sort of* funny all week⟩ — see FAIRLY

so–so *adj* of average to below average quality ⟨a *so-so* production of a great play⟩ — see MEDIOCRE 1

so–so *adv* in a satisfactory way ⟨I think I did *so-so* on the test⟩ — see WELL 1

sot *n* a person who makes a habit of getting drunk ⟨a *sot* who was arrested after a bar fight⟩ — see DRUNK 1

sough *vb* to take in and let out a deep audible breath or to make a similar sound ⟨all night long the patient was *soughing* in her sleep⟩ — see SIGH

soul *n* **1** an immaterial force within a human being thought to give the body life, energy, and power ⟨many religions teach that the *soul* is immortal⟩

synonyms psyche, spirit

related words life, vitality

near antonyms body, flesh

2 a member of the human race ⟨I promise I won't tell another *soul*⟩ — see HUMAN

3 the quality or qualities that make a thing what it is ⟨a kind act that was the very *soul* of charity⟩ — see ESSENCE

4 the seat of one's deepest thoughts and emotions ⟨knew in her *soul* that it was true⟩ — see CORE 1

soulless *adj* having or showing a lack of sympathy or tender feelings ⟨the public's *soulless* response to the news about the famine overseas⟩ — see HARD 1

sound *adj* **1** according to the rules of logic ⟨*sound* reasoning⟩ — see LOGICAL 1

2 enjoying health and vigor ⟨the horse is getting along in years, but still perfectly *sound*⟩ — see HEALTHY 1

3 marked by the ability to withstand stress without structural damage or distortion ⟨the shed looks flimsy, but it's actually surprisingly *sound*⟩ — see STABLE 1

sound *n* **1** a narrow body of water between two land masses ⟨Long Island *Sound* is between Long Island, New York, and Connecticut⟩ — see CHANNEL 2

2 range of hearing ⟨wandered off, out of her parents' sight and *sound*⟩ — see EARSHOT

¹sound *vb* **1** to continue or be repeated in a series of reflected sound waves ⟨the stranded hiker's cries *sounded* throughout the canyon⟩ — see REVERBERATE

2 to give the impression of being ⟨the idea at least *sounds* plausible⟩ — see SEEM

3 to make known (as an idea, emotion, or opinion) ⟨a person who certainly isn't shy about *sounding* her opinions⟩ — see EXPRESS 1

4 to make known openly or publicly ⟨the grand opening of the region's newest and largest mall has been loudly *sounded* for months⟩ — see ANNOUNCE

²sound *vb* **1** to measure the depth of (as a body of water) typically with a weighted line ⟨the pilot *sounded* the river to make sure we weren't in any danger of running aground⟩

synonyms fathom, plumb

related words gauge (*also* gage), measure, scale

2 to cast oneself head first into deep water ⟨a whale surfaced and then suddenly *sounded*⟩ — see DIVE

soundless *adj* mostly or entirely without sound ⟨crept in on *soundless* little feet⟩ — see SILENT 3

soundness *n* **1** the ability to withstand force or stress without being distorted, dislodged, or damaged ⟨the car manufacturer tested the *soundness* of the new model in various types of collisions⟩ — see STABILITY 1

2 the condition of being sound in body ⟨his athletic *soundness* is open to question since he's been away from the sport for so long⟩ — see HEALTH

sound off *vb* to voice one's opinions freely with force ⟨never missed a chance to *sound off* about the latest "stupid" political decisions⟩ — see SPEAK UP

soup *n* an atmospheric condition in which suspended particles in the air rob it of its transparency ⟨in *soup* like this, amateur pilots can easily become disoriented⟩ — see HAZE 1

soupy *adj* **1** filled with or dimmed by fine particles (as of dust or water) in suspension ⟨the *soupy* skies over the island make a nighttime landing a very risky business⟩ — see HAZY 1

2 having an overly soft liquid consistency ⟨*soupy* ice cream that had been left out on the counter⟩ — see RUNNY

sour *adj* **1** causing or characterized by the one of the four basic taste sensations that is produced chiefly by acids ⟨the *sour* candy made our mouths all wrinkly inside⟩

synonyms acid, acidic, tart, vinegary

related words dry, soured, unsweetened; pungent, sharp, tangy; astringent, puckery; acetic; hyperacid

near antonyms sweet; bland, smooth

2 not giving pleasure to the mind or senses ⟨you'll have to face up to the *sour* truth of the matter⟩ — see UNPLEASANT

sour *vb* to cause to change from friendly or loving to unfriendly or uncaring ⟨a misunderstanding that *soured* their relationship for a long time⟩ — see ESTRANGE

source *n* the beginning part of a stream ⟨19th-century explorers who sought the *source* of the Nile⟩ — see HEADWATER

souring *n* the loss of friendship or affection ⟨the *souring* of the partnership led to an ugly legal battle⟩ — see ESTRANGEMENT

souse *n* a person who makes a habit of getting drunk ⟨an old *souse* who went home with a full bottle of gin every night⟩ — see DRUNK 1

souse *vb* **1** to make wet ⟨a passing car barreled through the puddle and *soused* us good⟩ — see WET

2 to sink or push (something) briefly into or as if into a liquid ⟨repeatedly *soused* the tools in the tub to get the dirt off⟩ — see DIP 1

3 to wet thoroughly with liquid ⟨firefighters *soused* the neighboring houses so that they wouldn't catch fire as well⟩ — see SOAK 1

soused *adj* **1** being under the influence of alcohol ⟨stumbled off to bed completely *soused*⟩ — see DRUNK

2 containing, covered with, or thoroughly penetrated by water ⟨peeled off his *soused* socks and instantly felt much more comfortable⟩ — see WET

souvenir *n* something that serves to keep alive the memory of a person or event ⟨kept their love letters as *souvenirs* of their courtship⟩ — see MEMORIAL

sovereign *adj* **1** coming before all others in importance ⟨the *sovereign* issue for voters is what to do about the schools⟩ — see FOREMOST 1

2 not being under the rule or control of another ⟨a *sovereign* state⟩ — see FREE 1

sovereign *n* one who rules over a people with a sole, supreme, and usually hereditary authority ⟨after the current *sovereign* dies, the monarchy may be abolished⟩ — see MONARCH

sovereignty *n* **1** the state of being free from the control or power of another ⟨upon leaving home she felt that she had achieved *sovereignty* for the first time in her life⟩ — see FREEDOM 1

2 a body of people composed of one or more nationalities usually with its own territory and government ⟨as parts of the same *sovereignty*, the states should not enact laws intended to harm one another economically⟩ — see NATION

sow *vb* **1** to cover by or as if by scattering something over or on ⟨*sow* the fields with maize in early spring, and the crop should be ready by late summer⟩ — see SCATTER 2

2 to put or set into the ground to grow ⟨first *sow* the seeds in potting soil⟩ — see PLANT

spa *n* a building or room used for sports activities and exercising ⟨a six-month membership in a health *spa* with the specific purpose of losing weight⟩ — see GYM

space *n* **1** an extent or area available for or used up by some activity or thing ⟨how much *space* will you need for the art project?⟩ — see ROOM 1

2 an indefinite but usually short period of time ⟨in the *space* of a few minutes the room had filled up⟩ — see WHILE 1

space–age *adj* being or involving the latest methods, concepts, information, or styles ⟨*space-age* technology⟩ — see MODERN

spacing *n* the space or amount of space between two points, lines, surfaces, or objects ⟨the *spacing* of the houses was a little tight⟩ — see DISTANCE

spacious *adj* more than adequate or average in capacity ⟨almost all of the guests were able to fit into the *spacious* living room⟩

synonyms ample, capacious, commodious, roomy

related words broad, wide; big, bulky, considerable, generous, goodly, good-sized, grand, great, handsome, hefty, hulking, king-size (*or* king-sized), large, largish, outsize (*also* outsized), oversize (*or* oversized), sizable (*or* sizeable), substantial, super, voluminous; enormous, immense, vast; expansive, extended, extensive; boundless, limitless, unbounded

near antonyms confined, cramped, limited, narrow, restricted; small, snug, tight, tiny

span *vb* to find out the size, extent, or amount of ⟨tried to *span* the distance between the two trees by eye⟩ — see MEASURE

spank *n* a hard strike with a part of the body or an instrument ⟨delivered a quick *spank* to the child's bottom for disobedience⟩ — see ¹BLOW

spanking *adj* having much high-spirited energy and movement ⟨a *spanking* and speedy little horse⟩ — see LIVELY 1

spare *adj* **1** being over what is needed ⟨I had some *spare* time to kill, so I cleaned up my room a bit⟩

synonyms excess, extra, superfluous, supernumerary, surplus

related words accessory, additional, supplemental, supplementary; dispensable, extraneous, gratuitous, needless, nonessential, unessential, unnecessary, unneeded, unwanted

near antonyms inadequate, insufficient, meager, scant, scanty, scarce, short, sparse

2 giving or sharing as little as possible ⟨a man who is kind and gentle but definitely *spare* of speech⟩ — see STINGY 1

3 having a noticeably small amount of body fat ⟨a tall, *spare* man⟩ — see THIN 1

4 less plentiful than what is normal, necessary, or desirable ⟨*spare* vegetation that made foraging very difficult⟩ — see MEAGER

spare *n* an interchangeable part or piece of equipment that is kept on hand for replacement of an original ⟨first we took the burnt light bulb out, and then we replaced it with the *spare*⟩

synonyms extra, reserve

related words backup, substitute; stock; copy, double, duplicate, replacement

near antonyms archetype, original

spare *vb* to use or give out in stingy amounts ⟨I'll have a banana split and don't *spare* the whipped cream⟩

synonyms scant, skimp (on), stint (on)

related words dole (out), mete (out), portion (out), ration (out); pinch, shortchange

near antonyms lavish, rain

sparing *adj* **1** careful in the management of money or resources ⟨a *sparing* couple who are trying to save up enough for a house⟩ — see FRUGAL

2 giving or sharing as little as possible ⟨a government agency that has always been *sparing* of public information⟩ — see STINGY 1

spark *n* a very small amount ⟨not a *spark* of interest in the actress's memoirs⟩ — see PARTICLE 1

spark *vb* **1** to give off sparks ⟨the broken radio *sparked* and smoked the instant it was plugged in⟩

synonyms scintillate, sparkle
related words flash; burn
2 to cause to function ⟨interesting questions that are designed to *spark* the reader's brain⟩ — see ACTIVATE

sparkle *vb* **1** to give off sparks ⟨while fireworks that *sparkle* may be entertaining to look at, they can be highly dangerous when used indoors⟩ — see SPARK 1
2 to shoot forth bursts of light ⟨the crystal *sparkled* in the sunlight⟩ — see FLASH 1

sparky *adj* having much high-spirited energy and movement ⟨that *sparky* little kid tires me out just looking at him⟩ — see LIVELY 1

sparse *adj* less plentiful than what is normal, necessary, or desirable ⟨open land is *sparse* around here⟩ — see MEAGER

spasm *n* **1** a painful sudden tightening of a muscle ⟨suffers from back *spasms*⟩ — see CRAMP
2 a sudden intense expression of strong feeling ⟨a *spasm* of love that he had never experienced before⟩ — see OUTBURST 1

spasmodic *adj* lacking in steadiness or regularity of occurrence ⟨*spasmodic* problems that we will have to deal with as they crop up⟩ — see FITFUL

spat *n* an often noisy or angry expression of differing opinions ⟨like any couple, they have their *spats*⟩ — see ARGUMENT 1

spat *vb* to express different opinions about something often angrily ⟨we tend to *spat* over money more than anything else⟩ — see ARGUE 2

spate *n* a great flow of water or of something that overwhelms ⟨a *spate* of words has been published on this controversial topic⟩ — see FLOOD

spatter *vb* **1** to cause (something liquid or mushy) to move along in sheets ⟨*spattered* mud on her clothes⟩ — see SPLASH 1
2 to wet or soil by striking with something liquid or mushy ⟨the dog vigorously shook himself, *spattering* the carpet and walls with water⟩ — see SPLASH 2

spawn *n* the descendants of a person, animal, or plant ⟨sometimes I think those little brats are the *spawn* of Satan himself⟩ — see OFFSPRING

spawn *vb* to be the cause of (a situation, action, or state of mind) ⟨these artists *spawned* a whole new movement in painting⟩ — see EFFECT

speak *vb* **1** to express (a thought or emotion) in words ⟨finally *spoke* her fears⟩ — see SAY 1
2 to give a formal often extended talk on a subject ⟨they've been invited to *speak* about their latest archaeological discoveries⟩ — see TALK 1

speak (to *or* with) *vb* to communicate with by means of spoken words ⟨*spoke to* him about opening a shop⟩ — see TALK 1

speaker *n* **1** a person in charge of a meeting ⟨the *speaker* announced that it was time for the club to move on to another matter⟩ — see CHAIR 1
2 a person who speaks for another or for a group ⟨unofficially chose a *speaker* to broach the subject with the teacher⟩ — see SPOKESPERSON

speak out *vb* to voice one's opinions freely with force ⟨it's a free country, so anyone can *speak out*⟩ — see SPEAK UP

speak up *vb* to voice one's opinions freely with force ⟨she's never been afraid to *speak up* in class⟩
synonyms sound off, speak out, spout (off)
related words bawl, call, cry, holler, shout, sing (out), vociferate, yell; articulate, enunciate
phrases speak one's mind

near antonyms hush, suppress; quiet

spear *n* a weapon with a long straight handle and sharp head or blade ⟨the Roman gladiator thrust his *spear* triumphantly into the lion's side⟩
synonyms javelin, lance, pike, pikestaff, shaft
related words dart, spike; gaff, halberd, harpoon, trident

spear *vb* to penetrate or hold (something) with a pointed object ⟨*speared* a pea with her fork⟩ — see IMPALE

spearhead *vb* to serve as leader of ⟨unofficially at least, Martin Luther King *spearheaded* the civil rights movement⟩ — see LEAD 2

special *adj* **1** being the one or ones of a class with no other members ⟨claimed that international terrorism was a *special* threat that required a *special* way of dealing with it⟩ — see ONLY 2
2 granted special treatment or attention ⟨one student who was treated as *special* by the teacher⟩ — see DARLING 1
3 of a particular or exact sort ⟨you'll need *special* permission from the principal to do that⟩ — see EXPRESS 1

speciality *n* something for which a person shows a special talent ⟨my *speciality* is linguistics⟩ — see FORTE

specialized *adj* used by or intended for experts in a particular field of knowledge ⟨highly *specialized* terms that have very specific meanings in legal documents⟩ — see TECHNICAL

specialty *n* **1** a region of activity, knowledge, or influence ⟨a doctor with a *specialty* in internal medicine⟩ — see FIELD 2
2 something for which a person shows a special talent ⟨singing is my *specialty*⟩ — see FORTE

species *n* one of the units into which a whole is divided on the basis of a common characteristic ⟨a music that is now generally regarded as a distinct *species* of rap⟩ — see CLASS 2

specific *adj* **1** of a particular or exact sort ⟨we need a *specific* type of pen⟩ — see EXPRESS 1
2 so clearly expressed as to leave no doubt about the meaning ⟨*specific* instructions regarding the interrogation of prisoners⟩ — see EXPLICIT

specific *n* a substance or preparation used to treat disease ⟨quinine is a *specific* for malaria⟩ — see MEDICINE

specificity *n* careful thoroughness of detail ⟨the *specificity* of that explanation was a bit more than I needed⟩ — see PARTICULARITY 1

specify *vb* **1** to give the rules about (something) clearly and exactly ⟨the document *specifies* precisely how you may use the information it contains⟩ — see PRESCRIBE
2 to make reference to or speak about briefly but specifically ⟨they didn't *specify* the model of car the robbers were driving⟩ — see MENTION 1

specimen *n* **1** a member of the human race ⟨he's a particularly handsome *specimen*⟩ — see HUMAN
2 one of a group or collection that shows what the whole is like ⟨chose one frog as a good *specimen* of the breed⟩ — see EXAMPLE

specious *adj* tending or having power to deceive ⟨a *specious* argument that really does not stand up under close examination⟩ — see DECEPTIVE 1

speck *n* **1** a small area that is different (as in color) from the main part ⟨a lizard with *specks* of white against a green body⟩ — see SPOT 1
2 a very small amount ⟨not a *speck* of explanation to accompany the book's pictures⟩ — see PARTICLE 1

3 a very small piece ⟨a *speck* of dust⟩ — see BIT 1

speck *vb* to mark with small spots especially unevenly ⟨dirt that had *specked* the windows for ages⟩ — see SPOT

speckle *n* a small area that is different (as in color) from the main part ⟨the cat has a *speckle* of orange right at her whiskers⟩ — see SPOT 1

speckle *vb* to mark with small spots especially unevenly ⟨*speckled* the cookies with colored sugar⟩ — see SPOT

speckled *adj* marked with spots ⟨a *speckled* dog⟩ — see SPOTTED 1

specs *n pl* a pair of lenses set in a frame that is held in place with ear supports and which are usually worn to correct vision ⟨I wear *specs* to read⟩ — see GLASSES 1

spectacles *n pl* a pair of lenses set in a frame that is held in place with ear supports and which are usually worn to correct vision ⟨bought a pair of *spectacles* with clear lenses simply to look more intelligent⟩ — see GLASSES 1

specter *or* **spectre** *n* the soul of a dead person thought of especially as appearing to living people ⟨feeling so terrified that every shadow became a *specter*⟩ — see GHOST

spectrum *n* the distance or extent between possible extremes ⟨the complete *spectrum* of opinions on this hotly debated subject⟩ — see RANGE 3

speculate *vb* to form an opinion from little or no evidence ⟨I *speculate* that someone lost this on their way to class⟩ — see GUESS 1

speculation *n* a risky undertaking ⟨lost all their money in real estate *speculations*⟩ — see GAMBLE

speculative *adj* existing only as an assumption or speculation ⟨a *speculative* explanation of why this ancient pottery was found hundreds of miles from where it was made⟩ — see THEORETICAL 1

speech *n* **1** a usually formal discourse delivered to an audience ⟨the guest of honor gave a short *speech* in appreciation of the award⟩
synonyms address, declamation, harangue, oration, talk
related words diatribe, rant, tirade; eulogy, panegyric, tribute; keynote address, lecture; homily, sermon; monologue, soliloquy; pitch, presentation, spiel
2 the stock of words, pronunciation, and grammar used by a people as their basic means of communication ⟨wanting to develop a writing system for his people, Sequoya created a system of 86 symbols representing all the syllables of Cherokee *speech*⟩ — see LANGUAGE 1

speechless *adj* **1** deliberately refraining from speech ⟨he remained *speechless*, even in the face of outrageous accusations⟩ — see SILENT 1
2 unable to speak ⟨if only this poor, *speechless* animal could tell us what's wrong with it⟩ — see MUTE 1

speechlessness *n* incapacity for or restraint from speaking ⟨the *speechlessness* of our cat never seemed so frustrating as the time that it was sick⟩ — see SILENCE 1

speed *n* a high rate of movement or performance ⟨we did our homework with as much *speed* as possible so we could go to the movies⟩
synonyms celerity, fastness, fleetness, haste, hurry, quickness, rapidity, rapidness, speediness, swiftness, velocity
related words clip, pace, rate, tempo; drive, hustle; acceleration, rush; dispatch, expedition, expeditiousness, promptness

near antonyms languidness, languor, leisureliness, lethargy, torpor; reluctance; deliberateness, deliberation
antonyms slowness, sluggishness

speed *vb* to proceed or move quickly ⟨a train *speeding* across the lush countryside⟩ — see HURRY 2

speed (up) *vb* to cause to move or proceed fast or faster ⟨we have to *speed up* production⟩ — see HURRY 1

speedboat *n* a boat equipped with a motor ⟨*speedboats* leaving wakes that cause damage to docked vessels and the shoreline⟩ — see MOTORBOAT

speedily *adv* with great speed ⟨*speedily* finished his homework and left to play ball⟩ — see FAST 1

speediness *n* a high rate of movement or performance ⟨the *speediness* with which she types is simply amazing⟩ — see SPEED

speedy *adj* moving, proceeding, or acting with great speed ⟨a *speedy* worker but not a very careful one⟩ — see FAST 1

spell *n* **1** a spoken word or set of words believed to have magic power ⟨the witch cast a *spell* that turned the prince into a toad⟩
synonyms bewitchment, charm, conjuration, enchantment, incantation
related words curse, hex, jinx; black magic, conjuring, magic, mojo, necromancy, sorcery, voodooism, witchcraft, witchery, wizardry
2 a sudden experiencing of a physical or mental disorder ⟨a dizzy *spell* that caused me to fall⟩ — see ATTACK 2
3 an indefinite but usually short period of time ⟨come rest a *spell*⟩ — see WHILE 1

spell *vb* **1** to cast a spell on ⟨it was as if he had *spelled* the public into believing his ridiculous claims⟩ — see BEWITCH 1
2 to communicate or convey (as an idea) to the mind ⟨that summertime combination of hot temperatures and hot tempers can *spell* trouble⟩ — see MEAN 1

spellbind *vb* to hold the attention of as if by a spell ⟨the tale about pirates and their buried treasure *spellbound* him for hours⟩ — see ENTHRALL 1

spellbound *adj* being or appearing to be under a magic spell ⟨*spellbound* audiences never tire of this annual Christmas favorite⟩ — see ENCHANTED

spell out *vb* to make plain or understandable ⟨*spelled out* what she wanted⟩ — see EXPLAIN 1

spend *vb* **1** to hand over or use up in payment ⟨I always end up *spending* too much money at the mall⟩
synonyms disburse, expend, give, lay out, pay
related words lavish, rain; blow; squander, waste
near antonyms cache, hoard, save; acquire, earn, make
2 to make complete use of ⟨the town has already *spent* its budget for snow removal, and it's only January⟩ — see DEPLETE
3 to use up carelessly ⟨*spent* all his energy on impractical schemes⟩ — see WASTE 1

spender *n* someone who carelessly spends money ⟨he's a *spender* and she's a tightwad, so naturally they quarrel about money a lot⟩ — see PRODIGAL

spendthrift *adj* given to spending money freely or foolishly ⟨*spendthrift* consumers had amassed a mountain of debt on their credit cards⟩ — see PRODIGAL

spendthrift *n* someone who carelessly spends money ⟨the *spendthrift* managed to blow all of his inheritance in a single year⟩ — see PRODIGAL

spent *adj* depleted in strength, energy, or freshness ⟨he sagged in his chair, completely *spent*, and fell asleep⟩ — see WEARY 1

spew *vb* **1** to flow out in great quantities or with force ⟨water *spewing* violently from the broken pipe⟩ — see GUSH 1

2 to throw out or off (something from within) often violently ⟨a volcano *spewing* out lava⟩ — see ERUPT 1

sphere *n* **1** a more or less round body or mass ⟨this *sphere* that we live on is just a tiny speck in the universe⟩ — see ¹BALL 1

2 a region of activity, knowledge, or influence ⟨mathematics is a little outside my *sphere*⟩ — see FIELD 2

spherical *adj* having every part of the surface the same distance from the center ⟨the planet Earth is not, in fact, perfectly *spherical*⟩ — see ROUND 1

spice *n* **1** a sweet or pleasant smell ⟨a cologne for men that captures all of the *spice* of the sea⟩ — see FRAGRANCE

2 something (as a spice or herb) that adds an agreeable or interesting taste to food ⟨Europe in Columbus's time imported rare and valuable *spices* from the Indies⟩ — see SEASONING 1

spice *vb* to make more pleasant to the taste by adding something intensely flavored ⟨*spice* the stew with more pepper⟩ — see SEASON 1

spick-and-span *or* **spic-and-span** *adj* **1** free from dirt or stain ⟨let's make the house *spick-and-span* for our visitors⟩ — see CLEAN 1

2 recently made and never used before ⟨a *spick-and-span* waffle iron that our host was obviously using for the first time⟩ — see NEW 3

spicy *adj* hinting at or intended to call to mind matters regarded as indecent ⟨a *spicy* suggestion that earned him a slap in the face⟩ — see SUGGESTIVE 1

spigot *n* a fixture for controlling the flow of a liquid ⟨the plumber has installed a new *spigot* over the kitchen sink⟩ — see FAUCET

spike *vb* to penetrate or hold (something) with a pointed object ⟨scorpions use their stinger-equipped tails to *spike* their prey⟩ — see IMPALE

spill *n* the act of going down from an upright position suddenly and involuntarily ⟨tripped over the toy and had a *spill* on the stairs⟩ — see FALL 1

spill *vb* to make known (as information previously kept secret) ⟨*spilled* the secret to a tabloid for $40,000⟩ — see REVEAL 1

spin *n* **1** a rapid turning about on an axis or central point ⟨the ice skater moved into a tight *spin* at the end of her routine⟩

synonyms gyration, pirouette, reel, revolution, roll, rotation, twirl, wheel, whirl

related words circuit, circulation; coil, curl, curve, spiral, twist; circle, orbit; eddy, swirl

2 a state of mental confusion ⟨the news left me all in a *spin*⟩ — see HAZE 2

spin *vb* **1** to move in circles around an axis or center ⟨after *spinning* around three times blindfolded, I tried to pin the tail on the donkey and almost fell over⟩

synonyms gyrate, pirouette, revolve, roll, rotate, turn, twirl, wheel, whirl

related words coil, curl, curve, round, spiral, twine, twist, wind; circle, orbit

2 to be in a confused state as if from being twirled around ⟨my head *spun* as I contemplated all the possible problems this could cause⟩

synonyms reel, swim, whirl

near antonyms calm, collect; settle, steady

3 to move (something) in a curved or circular path on or as if on an axis ⟨*spun* the child around until he was hopelessly dizzy⟩ — see TURN 1

spinal column *n* a column of bones supporting the trunk of a vertebrate animal ⟨a diagram of the *spinal column*⟩ — see SPINE

spindling *adj* being tall, thin and usually loose-jointed ⟨a sickly, *spindling* child who spent most of his time indoors⟩ — see LANKY

spindly *adj* being tall, thin and usually loose-jointed ⟨*spindly*, underfed dogs roamed the poverty-stricken village⟩ — see LANKY

spine *n* a column of bones supporting the trunk of a vertebrate animal ⟨he hurt his *spine* in the accident, but the doctor says he'll be walking again in no time⟩

synonyms backbone, chine, spinal column, vertebral column

related words back, spinal cord, vertebra

spineless *adj* **1** lacking strength of will or character ⟨a *spineless* man who let his wife make all the decisions⟩ — see WEAK 2

2 having or showing a shameful lack of courage ⟨*spineless* seamen who trembled at the first roar of the cannon⟩ — see COWARDLY

spinelessness *n* **1** the quality or state of lacking strength of will or character ⟨the *spinelessness* that the grown woman has shown in dealing with her overbearing mother⟩ — see WEAKNESS 2

2 a shameful lack of courage in the face of danger ⟨charged the midshipman with sickening *spinelessness* under fire⟩ — see COWARDICE

spin-off *n* something that naturally develops or is developed from something else ⟨a *spin-off* of the popular television series⟩ — see DERIVATIVE

spiny *adj* requiring exceptional skill or caution in performance or handling ⟨this promises to be a *spiny* problem to negotiate⟩ — see TRICKY

spiral *adj* turning around an axis like the thread of a screw ⟨a *spiral* staircase takes visitors up into the Statue of Liberty⟩

synonyms coiling, corkscrew, helical, screwlike, winding

related words curving, curling, twisting

near antonyms lineal, linear, straight

spiral *vb* to follow a circular or spiral course ⟨a narrow road *spiraling* up the mountain to the summit⟩ — see WIND

spirit *n* **1** an immaterial force within a human being thought to give the body life, energy, and power ⟨the theological and philosophical belief that the *spirit* is superior to the body⟩ — see SOUL 1

2 a state of mind dominated by a particular emotion ⟨had been in a combative *spirit* all week⟩ — see MOOD 1

3 the soul of a dead person thought of especially as appearing to living people ⟨Hamlet's late father appears to him in the form of a *spirit* and with the revelation that he was in fact murdered⟩ — see GHOST

4 **spirits** *pl* a fermented or distilled beverage that can make a person drunk ⟨a hotel bar that's well stocked with *spirits*⟩ — see ALCOHOL

spirited *adj* **1** marked by a lively display of strong feeling ⟨the town meeting featured a *spirited* debate about the proposed ban on skateboarding in the plaza downtown⟩

synonyms fiery, gingery, high-spirited, mettlesome, peppery, spunky

related words animate, animated, bouncing, bouncy, brisk, energetic, frisky, jaunty, jazzy, peppy, perky, pert, racy, snappy, spanking, sparky, sprightly, springy, vital, vivacious, zippy; ardent, fervent, impassioned, passionate

near antonyms boring, dull, lifeless

antonyms spiritless

2 having much high-spirited energy and movement ⟨a team known for its *spirited* and in-your-face basketball⟩ — see LIVELY 1

spiritless *adj* lacking bodily energy or motivation ⟨he was *spiritless* and depressed for weeks after being fired⟩ — see LISTLESS

spiritual *adj* **1** not composed of matter ⟨a staunch skeptic and realist, he scoffs at the very notion of ghosts and other *spiritual* entities⟩ — see IMMATERIAL 1

2 of, relating to, or used in the practice or worship services of a religion ⟨*spiritual* songs that have been sung by generations of worshippers⟩ — see RELIGIOUS 1

spiritual *n* a religious song ⟨sang a *spiritual* at the funeral⟩ — see HYMN

¹spit *n* an area of land that juts out into a body of water ⟨at the northeast end of the island is a long *spit* whose terminal is crowned by a towering lighthouse⟩ — see ²CAPE

²spit *n* **1** something or someone that strongly resembles another ⟨the *spit* and image of his father⟩ — see IMAGE 1

2 the fluid that is secreted into the mouth by certain glands ⟨so dry that he felt as if he had no *spit* left in his mouth⟩ — see SALIVA

spite *n* the desire to cause pain for the satisfaction of doing harm ⟨spread cruel lies out of pure *spite*⟩ — see MALICE

spiteful *adj* having or showing a desire to cause someone pain or suffering for the sheer enjoyment of it ⟨said vicious things with a *spiteful* smile⟩ — see HATEFUL

spitefully *adv* in a mean or spiteful manner ⟨*spitefully* told the orphans that they'd never amount to anything⟩ — see NASTILY

spitefulness *n* the desire to cause pain for the satisfaction of doing harm ⟨cut down their neighbors' tree out of sheer *spitefulness*⟩ — see MALICE

spittle *n* the fluid that is secreted into the mouth by certain glands ⟨unaware that *spittle* was leaking out of his mouth while he slept⟩ — see SALIVA

spit up *vb* to discharge the contents of the stomach through the mouth ⟨the baby finished nursing and promptly *spit up*⟩ — see VOMIT

splash *vb* **1** to cause (something liquid or mushy) to move along in sheets ⟨I always *splash* water at my sister when we go to the pool⟩

synonyms spatter

related words dabble, lap, plash, wash

2 to wet or soil by striking with something liquid or mushy ⟨the bus *splashed* us as it passed⟩

synonyms bespatter, dash, plash, spatter, splatter

related words drench, drown, impregnate, saturate, soak, sop, souse, steep; bathe, douse, wash, water, wet; throw; spray; slop, sprinkle; squirt

3 to flow along or against ⟨water constantly *splashing* the wooden pilings eventually weakened them⟩ — see WASH 1

4 to flow in a broken irregular stream ⟨the spilled juice *splashed* over the counter and onto the floor⟩ — see GURGLE

5 to move with a splashing motion ⟨a baby *splashing* about in the tub⟩ — see SLOSH

splashy *adj* **1** likely to attract attention ⟨a *splashy* new restaurant that's currently the in place to go⟩ — see NOTICEABLE

2 attractively eye-catching in style ⟨a *splashy* ad for the new brand of blue jeans⟩ — see JAZZY 1

3 excessively showy ⟨a *splashy* outfit that was definitely out of place in church⟩ — see GAUDY

splatter *vb* to wet or soil by striking with something liquid or mushy ⟨the house painters accidentally *splattered* my car with paint⟩ — see SPLASH 2

spleen *n* **1** an intense emotional state of displeasure with someone or something ⟨vented her *spleen* and felt much better⟩ — see ANGER

2 the desire to cause pain for the satisfaction of doing harm ⟨the bill's failure to pass in the legislature was due to nothing more than partisan *spleen*⟩ — see MALICE

splendid *adj* **1** large and impressive in size, grandeur, extent, or conception ⟨a *splendid* mansion⟩ — see GRAND 1

2 of the very best kind ⟨the chef can always be relied upon to prepare a *splendid* dinner⟩ — see EXCELLENT

splendidly *adv* in a pleasing way ⟨the party went *splendidly*⟩ — see WELL 5

splendor *n* **1** impressiveness of beauty on a large scale ⟨the *splendor* of the ancient monument awed us into silence⟩ — see MAGNIFICENCE

2 the quality or state of having or giving off light ⟨the *splendor* of the huge diamond can scarcely be described⟩ — see BRILLIANCE 1

splenetic *adj* having or showing a habitually bad temper ⟨the newspaper publisher's *splenetic* editorials often struck fear into local politicians⟩ — see ILL-TEMPERED

splint *n* a small flat piece separated from a whole ⟨a *splint* off the board⟩ — see CHIP 1

splinter *n* a small flat piece separated from a whole ⟨got a *splinter* from the unfinished wall⟩ — see CHIP 1

splinter *vb* to cut into long slender pieces ⟨*splintered* the carrots into little sticks⟩ — see SLIVER

split *adj* disagreeing with each other ⟨opinions are *split* on the subject⟩ — see DIVIDED

split *n* **1** an irregular usually narrow break in a surface created by pressure ⟨an earthquake left a *split* in the ground⟩ — see CRACK 1

2 the act or process of a whole separating into two or more parts or pieces ⟨the *split* of the group into two factions marked the beginning of the end of the organization⟩ — see SEPARATION 1

split *vb* to set or force apart ⟨*split* logs for the winter's supply of wood⟩ — see SEPARATE 1

split second *n* a very small space of time ⟨a devastating accident can cause everything in your life to change in a *split second*⟩ — see INSTANT

splotch *n* a small area that is different (as in color) from the main part ⟨the bleach left a small white *splotch* on my shirt⟩ — see SPOT 1

splotch *vb* to mark with small spots especially unevenly ⟨ink from a leaking pen had badly *splotched* his shirt pocket⟩ — see SPOT

splotched *adj* having blotches of two or more colors ⟨a *splotched* tan and white puppy⟩ — see PIED

splotchy *adj* marked with spots ⟨a country road *splotchy* with patches of snow⟩ — see SPOTTED 1

spoil *n* valuables stolen or taken by force ⟨the bandits escaped with their lives but not with the *spoils*⟩ — see LOOT

spoil *vb* **1** to affect slightly with something morally bad or undesirable ⟨too much coddling will *spoil* the child⟩ — see TAINT 1

2 to go through decomposition ⟨the meat has *spoiled*⟩ — see DECAY 1

3 to reduce the soundness, effectiveness, or perfection of ⟨know when to stop, for an unnecessary brushstroke can *spoil* a painted portrait⟩ — see DAMAGE 1

4 to treat with great or excessive care ⟨when they were newlyweds, the wife tended to *spoil* her husband, but she soon got over that⟩ — see BABY

spoilage *n* the process by which dead organic matter separates into simpler substances ⟨studying *spoilage* in science class⟩ — see CORRUPTION 1

spoiled *adj* having undergone organic breakdown ⟨*spoiled* milk⟩ — see ROTTEN 1

spoilsport *n* a person who spoils the pleasure of others ⟨if you don't want to play, at least don't be a *spoilsport*⟩ — see KILLJOY

spoken *adj* made or carried on through speaking rather than in writing ⟨a *spoken* agreement is too easily broken⟩ — see VERBAL 2

spokesman *n* a person who speaks for another or for a group ⟨a *spokesman* for the cattle industry⟩ — see SPOKESPERSON

spokesperson *n* a person who speaks for another or for a group ⟨the *spokesperson* for the protesting students presented their demands to the principal⟩
synonyms mouthpiece, speaker, spokesman
related words spokeswoman; sayer, talker; agent, delegate, deputy, representative

sponge *n* a person who is supported or seeks support from another without making an adequate return ⟨finally told the *sponge* to move out of their house and to get a job⟩ — see LEECH

sponge *vb* to take in (something liquid) through small openings ⟨the ground quickly *sponged* up the much-needed rain⟩ — see ABSORB 1

sponger *n* a person who is supported or seeks support from another without making an adequate return ⟨a spoiled *sponger* who, after college, moved back in with her parents and seems to be in no hurry to get a job⟩ — see LEECH

spongy *adj* giving easily to the touch ⟨*spongy* moss covered the ground⟩ — see SOFT 3

sponsor *n* a person who takes the responsibility for some other person or thing ⟨you need a *sponsor* to recommend you in order to get into the exclusive country club⟩
synonyms backer, guarantor, patron, surety
related words chaperone (*or* chaperon); advocate, champion, supporter; benefactor; coach, mentor, teacher

spontaneity *n* carefree freedom from constraint ⟨sacrificed some of the *spontaneity* in their lives when they had a baby⟩ — see ABANDON

spontaneous *adj* done instantly and without conscious thought or decision ⟨hugging the crying child is simply a *spontaneous* reaction⟩ — see AUTOMATIC 1

spoof *n* a work that imitates and exaggerates another work for comic effect ⟨many viewers thought that the *spoof* of a television newscast was the real thing⟩ — see PARODY 1

spook *n* **1** a person who tries secretly to obtain information for one country in the territory of another usually unfriendly country ⟨Russia recalled its *spooks* after the collapse of the Soviet Union⟩ — see SPY

2 the soul of a dead person thought of especially as appearing to living people ⟨Halloween is the night when *spooks* and goblins are said to roam abroad⟩ — see GHOST

spook *vb* to strike with fear ⟨the sudden noise *spooked* her out of her skin⟩ — see FRIGHTEN

spooked *adj* filled with fear or dread ⟨Ichabod Crane was so *spooked* that he left Sleepy Hollow for good⟩ — see AFRAID 1

spooky *adj* **1** easily excited by nature ⟨a *spooky* horse shying at shadows⟩ — see EXCITABLE

2 fearfully and mysteriously strange or fantastic ⟨a *spooky* tale of strange hauntings and mysterious reincarnations⟩ — see EERIE

spoon *n* a utensil with a bowl and a handle that is used especially in cooking and serving food ⟨it's easier to eat soup with a *spoon* than with a fork⟩
synonyms dipper, ladle, scoop
related words skimmer

spoon *vb* to lift out with something that holds liquid ⟨lovingly *spooned* the homemade stew out of the pot⟩ — see DIP 2

sporadic *adj* **1** lacking in steadiness or regularity of occurrence ⟨*sporadic* loud noises kept startling everyone⟩ — see FITFUL

2 not often occurring or repeated ⟨so long as the complaints remain *sporadic*, we're doing fine⟩ — see INFREQUENT

sport *n* **1** activity engaged in to amuse oneself ⟨I don't care terribly whether I actually catch any fish, as I'm just doing this for *sport*⟩ — see PLAY 1

2 an attitude or manner not to be taken seriously ⟨teasing that began in *sport* ended with some hateful words being exchanged⟩ — see FUN 2

sport *vb* **1** to engage in activity for amusement ⟨from sailing to snorkeling, each day we *sported* at a different activity offered by the beach resort⟩ — see PLAY 1

2 to play and run about happily ⟨children *sporting* on the estate's spacious grounds⟩ — see FROLIC 1

3 to present so as to invite notice or attention ⟨*sported* his new car by driving it all over town⟩ — see SHOW 1

sportive *adj* given to good-natured joking or teasing ⟨a *sportive* teacher who could get everyone laughing⟩ — see PLAYFUL

sportiveness *n* a natural disposition for playful behavior ⟨her high-spirited *sportiveness* can sometimes distract her and others from serious work⟩ — see PLAYFULNESS

sportsmanlike *adj* following or according to the rules ⟨admired by the fans for his *sportsmanlike* conduct on the ice⟩ — see FAIR 3

sportsmanly *adj* following or according to the rules ⟨in wrestling, biting is not *sportsmanly*, and will result in a forfeit⟩ — see FAIR 3

spot *n* **1** a small area that is different (as in color) from the main part ⟨in summer the white coat of the snow leopard is studded with brownish black *spots*⟩
synonyms blotch, dapple, dot, eyespot, fleck, mottle, patch, point, speck, speckle, splotch
related words birthmark, freckle, mole; blot, mark, smear, smudge, stain; spatter, splash

2 a difficult, puzzling, or embarrassing situation from which there is no easy escape ⟨we're in a bit of a *spot* right now⟩ — see PREDICAMENT

3 a mark of guilt or disgrace ⟨scandalous conduct that will forever be a *spot* upon the family name⟩ — see STAIN 1

4 a very small amount ⟨had only a *spot* of stew for dinner, as he wasn't very hungry⟩ — see PARTICLE 1

5 the area or space occupied by or intended for something ⟨the cat took my *spot* on the couch as soon as I stood up⟩ — see PLACE 1

spot *vb* to mark with small spots especially unevenly ⟨to give the effect of sunlight on water, the artist *spotted* the lake in his painting with flecks of gold paint⟩
synonyms blotch, dapple, dot, fleck, freckle, marble, mottle, pepper, speck, speckle, splotch, sprinkle, stipple
related words blot, dye, stain; streak, stripe; intersperse, stud; bespatter, spatter
spotless *adj* free from dirt or stain ⟨a *spotless* white dress⟩ — see CLEAN 1
spotted *adj* **1** marked with spots ⟨the *spotted* tablecloth clashed with the stripes on the wallpaper⟩
synonyms dappled (*also* dapple), dotted, flecked, freckled, mottled, speckled, splotchy, spotty, stippled, variegated
related words spangled; marbled, moiré (*or* moire), veined; motley, multicolored; piebald, roan
near antonyms solid
2 having blotches of two or more colors ⟨not surprisingly, the white cow and black bull had a *spotted* calf⟩ — see PIED
spotting *n* the act or process of sighting or learning the existence of something for the first time ⟨the *spotting* of a new bird is always a thrill for an avid birdwatcher⟩ — see DISCOVERY 1
spotty *adj* **1** lacking in steadiness or regularity of occurrence ⟨only *spotty* business failures marred the economic boom⟩ — see FITFUL
2 marked with spots ⟨Dalmatians are *spotty* dogs⟩ — see SPOTTED 1
spouse *n* the person to whom another is married ⟨employees and their *spouses* are covered by the health plan⟩
synonyms consort, mate, partner
related words husband, man, old man; lady, wife
near antonyms single; bachelor; maid, maiden, spinster
spout *n* a pipe or channel for carrying off water from a roof ⟨during the winter, runoff from the *spout* tends to freeze over and form a dangerous patch of ice on the walkway⟩ — see GUTTER 1
spout *vb* **1** to flow out in great quantities or with force ⟨water *spouting* from the hose⟩ — see GUSH 1
2 to talk loudly and wildly ⟨a self-important loudmouth who is always *spouting* about the mess that politicians have made of everything⟩ — see RANT
3 to throw out or off (something from within) often violently ⟨the drain suddenly *spouted* water and debris⟩ — see ERUPT 1
spout (off) *vb* to voice one's opinions freely with force ⟨got in trouble for *spouting off* in class in a disrespectful way⟩ — see SPEAK UP
spray *vb* to cover by or as if by scattering something over or on ⟨*sprayed* the lawn with pesticides⟩ — see SCATTER 2
spread *n* **1** a decorative cloth used as a top covering for a bed ⟨bought a brightly colored *spread* for summer⟩ — see COUNTERPANE
2 a large fancy meal often accompanied by ceremony or entertainment ⟨they really know how to put out a good *spread*⟩ — see FEAST
3 a wide space or area ⟨a vast *spread* of land just waiting to be settled⟩ — see EXPANSE
4 the distance or extent between possible extremes ⟨the *spread* of grades was from 15 to 79 on that quiz⟩ — see RANGE 3
5 the space or amount of space between two points, lines, surfaces, or objects ⟨a *spread* of nearly 100 miles between farms⟩ — see DISTANCE

spread *vb* **1** to cause to be known over a considerable area or by many people ⟨*spread* the news!⟩
synonyms broadcast, circulate, disseminate, propagate
related words radiate, sprawl; diffuse, dispense, disperse, dissipate, scatter, sow; communicate, pass (on), transmit
near antonyms conceal, hide, hold (in), secrete; contain, limit, restrict
2 to put a layer of on a surface ⟨we *spread* the fertilizer over the lawn evenly until it was fully covered⟩
synonyms apply, lay
related words dab, daub, plaster, smear; blanket, carpet, coat, cover, layer, overlay, overlie, overspread, sheet, surface
near antonyms peel, strip, uncover
3 to become known ⟨once the news that the war was over *spread*, spontaneous celebrations broke out all over⟩ — see GET OUT 1
4 to cause (something) to pass from one to another ⟨living conditions that help to *spread* chicken pox⟩ — see COMMUNICATE 1
spread (out) *vb* to arrange the parts of (something) over a wider area ⟨let's *spread* the puzzle *out* on the floor and see what we've got⟩ — see OPEN 3
spreading *adj* exciting a similar feeling or reaction in others ⟨*spreading* enthusiasm that got our club rolling again⟩ — see CONTAGIOUS 2
spree *n* a time or instance of carefree fun ⟨went on a spending *spree*⟩ — see FLING 1
sprightliness *n* the quality or state of having abundant or intense activity ⟨the *sprightliness* of the young girl made us tired just watching her⟩ — see VITALITY 1
sprightly *adv* in a quick and spirited manner ⟨every morning the elderly couple *sprightly* sets out on a walk⟩ — see GAILY 2
sprightly *adj* having much high-spirited energy and movement ⟨a *sprightly* child who often claims to be too tired to move when it's time to do chores⟩ — see LIVELY 1
spring *n* an act of leaping into the air ⟨the deer gave a sudden *spring* and disappeared into the woods⟩ — see JUMP 1
spring *vb* **1** to come into existence ⟨when it comes to love and romance, hope *springs* eternally⟩ — see BEGIN 2
2 to propel oneself upward or forward into the air ⟨the cat *sprang* and pounced on the mouse⟩ — see JUMP 1
3 to set free (as from slavery or confinement) ⟨had to spend a night in jail until their lawyer could come to *spring* them⟩ — see FREE 1
spring (for) *vb* to give what is owed for ⟨offered to *spring for* dinner for the whole gang⟩ — see PAY 2
spring (up) *vb* to come to one's attention especially gradually or unexpectedly ⟨a new issue *sprang up* at yesterday's meeting of the school board⟩ — see ARISE 2
springy *adj* **1** able to revert to original size and shape after being stretched, squeezed, or twisted ⟨pillows made with *springy* foam that bounces right back⟩ — see ELASTIC 1
2 having much high-spirited energy and movement ⟨walks with a *springy* step⟩ — see LIVELY 1
sprinkle *n* **1** a light or fine rain ⟨decided it was not worth carrying an umbrella for just a *sprinkle*⟩ — see DRIZZLE
2 a small number ⟨received only a *sprinkle* of suggestions for the name of the school mascot⟩ — see FEW

sprinkle *vb* **1** to cover by or as if by scattering something over or on ⟨*sprinkle* the newly seeded lawn with water⟩ — see SCATTER 2

2 to mark with small spots especially unevenly ⟨*sprinkled* the cake with bits of coconut⟩ — see SPOT

sprinkling *n* **1** a small number ⟨a *sprinkling* of fans showed up at the airport⟩ — see FEW

2 a very small amount ⟨just a *sprinkling* of experience with the computer program⟩ — see PARTICLE 1

sprint *vb* to go at a pace faster than a walk ⟨*sprinted* off to class so as to avoid being late⟩ — see RUN 1

sprite *n* an imaginary being usually having a small human form and magical powers ⟨the child insisted that he'd seen a *sprite* hiding behind the sofa⟩ — see FAIRY

spruce *adj* being strikingly neat and trim in style or appearance ⟨a slim, *spruce* man in a tailor-made business suit⟩ — see SMART 1

sprucely *adv* in a strikingly neat and trim manner ⟨*sprucely* dressed, I set out for my first job interview⟩ — see SMARTLY

spry *adj* moving easily ⟨an older woman who's still surprisingly *spry*⟩ — see GRACEFUL 1

spryness *n* ease and grace in physical activity ⟨the *spryness* and flexibility of a professional athlete⟩ — see DEXTERITY 2

spume *n* a light mass of fine bubbles formed in or on a liquid ⟨*spume* floating on the ocean⟩ — see FOAM

spunk *n* the strength of mind that enables a person to endure pain or hardship ⟨had the *spunk* to overcome a severe physical disability⟩ — see FORTITUDE

spunky *adj* marked by a lively display of strong feeling ⟨a *spunky* protest against the new rules⟩ — see SPIRITED 1

spur *n* something that arouses action or activity ⟨the threat of losing television privileges was the *spur* she needed to do her homework⟩ — see IMPULSE

spur *vb* to urge or push forward with or as if with a pointed object ⟨gently *spurred* the horse with his heels⟩ — see PROD 1

spurious *adj* **1** being such in appearance only and made or manufactured with the intention of committing fraud ⟨a *spurious* Picasso painting that wouldn't have fooled an art expert for a second⟩ — see COUNTERFEIT

2 lacking in natural or spontaneous quality ⟨claimed that the governor's election-year enthusiasm for conservation was *spurious*, since he had cut funding for state parks⟩ — see ARTIFICIAL 1

spurn *vb* to show unwillingness to accept, do, engage in, or agree to ⟨*spurned* all offers of help⟩ — see DECLINE 1

spur-of-the-moment *adj* made or done without previous thought or preparation ⟨a *spur-of-the-moment* trip to the zoo⟩ — see EXTEMPORANEOUS

spurt *n* a sudden and usually temporary growth of activity ⟨a *spurt* of economic growth for the first quarter of the year⟩ — see OUTBREAK

spurt *vb* **1** to flow out in great quantities or with force ⟨water *spurted* from the garden hose just as I was checking the nozzle⟩ — see GUSH 1

2 to throw out or off (something from within) often violently ⟨the pipe suddenly cracked and began *spurting* water⟩ — see ERUPT 1

sputter *vb* to speak rapidly, inarticulately, and usually unintelligibly ⟨she was so shocked that, for a moment, all she could do was *sputter*⟩ — see BABBLE 1

spy *n* a person who tries secretly to obtain information for one country in the territory of another usually unfriendly country ⟨the government *spy* risked his life every day to get vital information back to his country⟩

synonyms operative, spook

related words counterspy, shadow

phrases secret agent, undercover agent

spy *vb* to make note of (something) through the use of one's eyes ⟨I *spy* a motel off in the distance, so let's spend the night there⟩ — see SEE 1

spying *n* the secret gathering of information on others ⟨traditionally, anyone caught engaging in *spying* during wartime was shot or hanged⟩ — see ESPIONAGE

squabble *n* an often noisy or angry expression of differing opinions ⟨frightened by noise of the *squabble*, the cat hid under the couch⟩ — see ARGUMENT 1

squabble *vb* to express different opinions about something often angrily ⟨the children *squabbled* loudly over who got to play with the toy first⟩ — see ARGUE 2

squabbler *n* a person who takes part in a dispute ⟨the *squabblers* finally agreed to compromise⟩ — see DISPUTANT

squad *n* a group of people working together on a task ⟨the cleaning *squad* usually arrives after regular business hours⟩ — see GANG 1

squalidness *n* the state or quality of being dirty ⟨the *squalidness* of the shack made my stomach turn⟩ — see DIRTINESS 1

squall *n* **1** a disturbance of the atmosphere accompanied by wind and often by precipitation (as rain or snow) ⟨a snow *squall* is expected tonight⟩ — see STORM 1

2 a state of noisy, confused activity ⟨the annual *squall* created when the store holds its biggest sale of the year⟩ — see COMMOTION

squall *vb* to cry out loudly and emotionally ⟨the baby *squalled* in pain⟩ — see SCREAM

squally *adj* marked by wet and windy conditions ⟨be careful driving in this *squally* weather⟩ — see FOUL 1

squamous *adj* composed of or covered with scales ⟨a *squamous* plant bulb⟩ — see SCALY

squander *vb* to use up carelessly ⟨*squandered* all her money gambling in casinos⟩ — see WASTE 1

squanderer *n* someone who carelessly spends money ⟨the elderly woman refused to leave any money to the family's most notorious *squanderer*⟩ — see PRODIGAL

squandering *adj* given to spending money freely or foolishly ⟨the nightclub's ridiculous prices seem geared to *squandering* revelers with more money than sense⟩ — see PRODIGAL

square *adj* marked by justice, honesty, and freedom from bias ⟨received a *square* hearing from the disciplinary panel⟩ — see FAIR 2

square *vb* **1** to be in agreement on every point ⟨that explanation *squares* entirely with the evidence that we've seen⟩ — see CHECK 1

2 to influence someone with a bribe ⟨tried to *square* the police officer into ignoring the illegal operation⟩ — see BRIBE

squarely *adv* as stated or indicated without the slightest difference ⟨a line that is *squarely* in the middle⟩ — see EXACTLY 1

squash *vb* **1** to cause to become a pulpy mass ⟨the sort of person who couldn't even *squash* a bug⟩ — see CRUSH 1

2 to put a stop to (something) by the use of force ⟨*squashed* any effort to reform the country's power structure⟩ — see QUELL 1

squashy *adj* giving easily to the touch ⟨a bed covered in big *squashy* pillows⟩ — see SOFT 3

squat *adj* being compact and broad in build and often short in stature ⟨a short, *squat* woman⟩ — see STOCKY

squat *vb* to lie low with the limbs close to the body ⟨a detective *squatting* to examine something on the ground⟩ — see CROUCH

squatty *adj* being compact and broad in build and often short in stature ⟨a *squatty* little wrestler⟩ — see STOCKY

squawk *n* an expression of dissatisfaction, pain, or resentment ⟨if we don't receive any *squawks*, we can assume the change was acceptable⟩ — see COMPLAINT 1

squawk *vb* to express dissatisfaction, pain, or resentment usually tiresomely ⟨she *squawked* on for hours about how salespeople were always rude to her⟩ — see COMPLAIN

squeak *vb* to make a short shrill noise ⟨a loose board that *squeaked* every time we walked on the floor⟩
   synonyms creak
   related words cheep, peep; scream, screech, shriek, shrill, sing, squeal, yelp, yip

squeaking *adj* having a high musical pitch or range ⟨a baby bird making little *squeaking* cries⟩ — see SHRILL

squeaky *adj* having a high musical pitch or range ⟨a child with a *squeaky* voice⟩ — see SHRILL

squeal *vb* **1** to give information (as to the authorities) about another's improper or unlawful activities ⟨as soon as the stool pigeon got to the police station, he *squealed* to the police about the whole smuggling operation⟩
   synonyms inform, snitch, talk, tell
   related words betray, give away, rat (on), turn in; blab, tattle; tip (off)
   2 to cry out loudly and emotionally ⟨the child *squealed* with frustration⟩ — see SCREAM

squealer *n* a person who provides secret information about another's wrongdoing ⟨after finding out who told on them, the hoodlums proceeded to give the *squealer* the beating of his life⟩ — see INFORMER

squeamish *adj* **1** affected with nausea ⟨the rolling of the ship made her *squeamish*⟩ — see NAUSEOUS
   2 filled with disgust ⟨a dirty diaper makes me *squeamish*⟩ — see SICK 2

squeamishness *n* **1** a disturbed condition of the stomach in which one feels like vomiting ⟨an ever-rising *squeamishness* suddenly overwhelmed her, and she ran for the bathroom⟩ — see NAUSEA 1
   2 the tendency to be or state of being squeamish ⟨his general *squeamishness* makes him a terrible choice as a lab partner for a dissection⟩ — see DELICACY 3

squeeze *vb* **1** to apply external pressure on so as to force out the juice or contents of ⟨kept *squeezing* the bottle until the ketchup squirted all over the table⟩ — see PRESS 2
   2 to fit (something) into a tight space ⟨I think we can *squeeze* a bit more into the washing machine⟩ — see CROWD 1
   3 to get with great difficulty ⟨managed to *squeeze* a living by cleaning houses⟩ — see EKE OUT
   4 to reduce in size or volume by or as if by pressing parts or members together ⟨*squeezed* the blanket until it fit into the box⟩ — see COMPRESS 1
   5 to rob by the use of trickery or threats ⟨the mob *squeezes* all the local merchants by threatening violence⟩ — see FLEECE

squeezing *n* the act or process of reducing the size or volume of something by or as if by pressing ⟨the tight *squeezing* of his hands made her face turn red⟩ — see COMPRESSION

squelch *vb* to put a stop to (something) by the use of force ⟨immediately *squelched* any signs of rebellion⟩ — see QUELL 1

squinch *vb* **1** to lie low with the limbs close to the body ⟨*squinched* down to fit under the table⟩ — see CROUCH
   2 to twist (something) out of a natural or normal shape or condition ⟨*squinched* up her eyes in disgust⟩ — see CONTORT

squinching *n* the twisting of something out of its natural or normal shape or condition ⟨warned him that the constant *squinching* of his face would someday leave him with a permanently deformed look⟩ — see CONTORTION

squire *vb* to go along with in order to provide assistance, protection, or companionship ⟨her father *squired* her to the dance to make sure she got there all right⟩ — see ACCOMPANY

squirm *vb* to make jerky or restless movements ⟨the toddler *squirmed* the whole time we were in the waiting room⟩ — see FIDGET

squirrel (away) *vb* to put (something of future use or value) in a safe or secret place ⟨*squirreled* the information *away* for future reference⟩ — see HOARD

squirt *vb* to flow out in great quantities or with force ⟨water *squirting* out of the faucet⟩ — see GUSH 1

squishy *adj* giving easily to the touch ⟨a *squishy* beanbag chair⟩ — see SOFT 3

stab *n* **1** a mark or small hole made by a pointed instrument ⟨the injection left a small *stab* on her upper arm⟩ — see PRICK 1
   2 an effort to do or accomplish something ⟨everybody will get a *stab* at solving the problem⟩ — see ATTEMPT

stab *vb* to penetrate or hold (something) with a pointed object ⟨*stabbed* the pesky leaf with the tines of the rake⟩ — see IMPALE

stability *n* **1** the ability to withstand force or stress without being distorted, dislodged, or damaged ⟨the bridge was designed with such great *stability* that it supposedly will not collapse even under the harshest weather conditions⟩
   synonyms firmness, soundness, steadiness, strength, sturdiness
   related words dependability, durability, reliability; solidity, solidness; cohesion, toughness
   near antonyms insecurity, weakness
   antonyms instability, unsoundness, unsteadiness
   2 the state of continuing without change ⟨the *stability* of the regime is in jeopardy⟩ — see CONSTANCY 1

stable *adj* **1** marked by the ability to withstand stress without structural damage or distortion ⟨the tower was *stable* enough to withstand the strongest winds without collapsing⟩
   synonyms fast, firm, sound, stalwart, strong, sturdy
   related words dependable, durable, reliable; solid; cohesive, tough
   near antonyms insecure, weak
   antonyms unsound, unstable, unsteady
   2 having been established and usually not subject to change ⟨a nation badly in need of a *stable* government⟩ — see FIXED 1
   3 having full use of one's mind and control over one's actions ⟨she made some strange decisions back when she wasn't entirely *stable*⟩ — see SANE
   4 not undergoing a change in condition ⟨a *stable* economic climate is best for business⟩ — see CONSTANT 1

stack *n* **1** a considerable amount ⟨won a *stack* of money⟩ — see LOT 2

2 a quantity of things thrown or stacked on one another ⟨a *stack* of playing cards⟩ — see ¹PILE 1

stack *vb* to lay or throw on top of one another ⟨*stacked* the split logs by the house⟩ — see PILE

stack up (against *or* with) *vb* to come near or nearer to in character or quality ⟨how does the new school *stack up against* your old one?⟩ — see APPROXIMATE

stadium *n* a large usually roofless building for sporting events with tiers of seats for spectators ⟨the football game will be held at the new *stadium*, which seats 100,000 people⟩

synonyms bowl, circus, coliseum, colosseum

related words gym, gymnasium, spa; arena, hippodrome

staff *n* **1** a body of persons at work or available for work ⟨working with a short *staff* today⟩ — see FORCE 1

2 a heavy rigid stick used as a weapon or for punishment ⟨carried a *staff* for self-defense⟩ — see CLUB 1

stage *n* **1** a level usually raised surface ⟨spoke to the audience from a small *stage* in front⟩ — see PLATFORM

2 a portion of a trip ⟨this is only the first *stage* of the journey⟩ — see LEG 2

3 an individual part of a process, series, or ranking ⟨in the last *stage* of the project⟩ — see DEGREE 1

4 the public performance of plays ⟨drawn to the *stage* as a career⟩ — see DRAMA 1

stage *vb* to bring before the public in performance or exhibition ⟨*staged* the full body of Shakespeare's plays in the course of a year⟩ — see PRESENT 1

stagger *vb* **1** to move forward while swaying from side to side ⟨I was so tired last night that I just *staggered* upstairs to bed without eating dinner⟩

synonyms careen, dodder, lurch, reel, teeter, totter, waddle

related words rock, sway, weave, wobble; clump, flounder, lumber, lump, pound, scuff, scuffle, shamble, shuffle, stamp, stomp, stumble, tramp, tromp

2 to show uncertainty about the right course of action ⟨a daunting problem that would make even the most decisive person *stagger*⟩ — see HESITATE

staggering *adj* causing wonder or astonishment ⟨the *staggering* scope of the new construction on campus⟩ — see MARVELOUS 1

staid *adj* **1** not joking or playful in mood or manner ⟨everyone was surprised by the joke from the usually *staid* teacher⟩ — see SERIOUS 1

2 having or showing a serious and reserved manner ⟨*staid* colors that would be good for business attire⟩ — see DIGNIFIED

stain *n* **1** a mark of guilt or disgrace ⟨the *stain* of this cowardly act would haunt him for the rest of his career⟩

synonyms blot, brand, smirch, spot, stigma, taint

related words discredit, disgrace, dishonor, disrepute, guilt, ignominy, infamy, odium, opprobrium, reproach, shame

near antonyms award, credit, honor

2 a substance used to color other materials ⟨applied several coats of *stain* to the wood⟩ — see PIGMENT

stain *vb* **1** to affect slightly with something morally bad or undesirable ⟨her poor choice of companions *stained* her reputation somewhat⟩ — see TAINT 1

2 to give color or a different color to ⟨*stained* the table to look like cherry⟩ — see COLOR 1

3 to make dirty ⟨oil *stained* his pants⟩ — see DIRTY 1

stained *adj* not clean ⟨always seen wearing *stained* clothes⟩ — see DIRTY 1

stainless *adj* free from dirt or stain ⟨bleach got the sheets perfectly *stainless* again⟩ — see CLEAN 1

stake *n* **1** a legal right to participation in the advantages, profits, and responsibility of something ⟨if I invest in your business, I expect a *stake* in it in return⟩ — see INTEREST 1

2 the money or thing risked on the outcome of an uncertain event ⟨lost his entire *stake* with a single roll of the dice⟩ — see BET

stake *vb* **1** to provide money for ⟨the actor *staked* the production of the film with his own money⟩ — see FINANCE 1

2 to risk (something) on the outcome of an uncertain event ⟨I'd *stake* a year's salary that she'll win⟩ — see BET

stale *adj* used or heard so often as to be dull ⟨viewers were bored by the *stale* story lines of the new crop of sitcoms⟩

synonyms banal, commonplace, hackney, hackneyed, moth-eaten, musty, stereotyped, threadbare, tired, trite

related words canned, unimaginative, uninspired, unoriginal; normal, ordinary, rote, routine, standard, stock, typical, usual; boring, drab, dreary, dry, dull, flat, heavy, humdrum, jading, leaden, monotonous, pedestrian, ponderous, prosaic, tame, tedious, tiresome, tiring, unanimated, undramatic, uninteresting, vapid, wearisome, weary, wearying; corny, maudlin, mawkish, mushy, saccharine, sappy, schmaltzy, sentimental, sloppy, sugarcoated, sugary

near antonyms animating, energizing, enlivening, exciting, galvanizing, invigorating, stimulating; absorbing, engaging, engrossing, gripping, interesting, intriguing, involving; atypical, extraordinary, uncommon, unusual

antonyms fresh, new, original

stalemate *n* **1** a point in a struggle where neither side is capable of winning or willing to give in ⟨a new negotiator finally got both sides past the *stalemate*⟩ — see IMPASSE

2 a situation in which neither participant in a contest, competition, or struggle comes out ahead of the other ⟨after playing chess for 16 hours, we ended the game in a *stalemate*⟩ — see TIE 1

stalk *vb* **1** to seek out (game) for food or sport ⟨lions *stalking* gazelles on the plains⟩ — see HUNT 1

2 to walk with exaggerated arm and leg movements ⟨he *stalked* off in a huff⟩ — see STRUT 1

stall *vb* **1** to bring (something) to a standstill ⟨endless complaints *stalled* the process⟩ — see ¹HALT 1

2 to stop functioning ⟨the engine *stalls* sometimes when it's very cold outside⟩ — see FAIL 1

stalwart *adj* **1** feeling or displaying no fear by temperament ⟨*stalwart* soldiers⟩ — see BRAVE

2 having muscles capable of exerting great physical force ⟨a *stalwart* yet lithe athlete⟩ — see STRONG 1

3 marked by the ability to withstand stress without structural damage or distortion ⟨the *stalwart* walls of the castle⟩ — see STABLE 1

stamp *n* a perceptible trace left by pressure ⟨a *stamp* left in the mud⟩ — see PRINT 1

stamp *vb* **1** to move heavily or clumsily ⟨*stamping* around in oversized boots⟩ — see LUMBER 1

2 to tread on heavily so as to crush or injure ⟨*stamped* the grass down in a circle⟩ — see TRAMPLE

stamp (out) *vb* to destroy all traces of ⟨working to *stamp out* racism in this country⟩ — see ANNIHILATE 1

stance *n* a general way of holding the body ⟨a slightly aggressive *stance*⟩ — see POSTURE 1

stanchion *n* an upright shaft that supports an overhead structure ⟨the *stanchion* of an arch⟩ — see PILLAR 1

stand *n* a level usually raised surface ⟨marchers passed by the reviewing *stand*⟩ — see PLATFORM

stand *vb* 1 to occupy a place or location ⟨the monument *stands* in the middle of the town plaza⟩
synonyms be, lie, sit
related words command, overlook; remain, rest, stay; await, wait; post, station
2 to put up with (something painful or difficult) ⟨I don't know how you can *stand* that job⟩ — see BEAR 2
3 to give what is owed for ⟨I'll *stand* lunch, and you can pay me back later⟩ — see PAY 2

standard *adj* 1 accepted, used, or practiced by most people ⟨*standard* procedure⟩ — see CURRENT 1
2 being of the type that is encountered in the normal course of events ⟨a *standard* bandage is all that that wound needs⟩ — see ORDINARY 1
3 having or showing the qualities associated with the members of a particular group or kind ⟨he's pretty much your *standard* high-school jock⟩ — see TYPICAL 1

standard *n* 1 something set up as an example against which others of the same type are compared ⟨the animation in that movie set the *standard* against which all later animated cartoons were judged⟩
synonyms benchmark, criterion, grade, mark, measure, par, touchstone, yardstick
related words rule; case, example, instance; acme, apex, meridian, peak, pinnacle, summit, zenith
near antonyms aberration, abnormality, deviation
2 a piece of cloth with a special design that is used as an emblem or for signaling ⟨a ship flying the queen's *standard*⟩ — see FLAG 1
3 what is typical of a group, class, or series ⟨somewhat shorter than the *standard* for boys that age⟩ — see AVERAGE
4 standards *pl* the code of good conduct for an individual or group ⟨a life guided by high *standards*⟩ — see ETHICS

standardize *vb* to make agree with a single established standard or model ⟨the plan is to *standardize* the test for reading comprehension so that we can see how students across the state compare⟩
synonyms formalize, homogenize, normalize, regularize
related words codify, organize, systematize; average, equalize, even; accredit, certify; control, govern, regulate; coordinate, harmonize, integrate, reconcile, synthesize
near antonyms customize, individualize, tailor

standby *n* something or someone to which one looks for support ⟨our old *standby*⟩ — see DEPENDENCE 2

stand–in *n* a person or thing that takes the place of another ⟨hired him as a *stand-in* for the person who quit⟩ — see SUBSTITUTE

stand in *vb* to serve as a replacement usually for a time only ⟨she will be *standing in* for the regular teacher for a week⟩ — see COVER 1

standing *adj* 1 fixed in a place or position ⟨bought the house and all *standing* appliances and fixtures⟩ — see STATIONARY 1
2 rising straight up ⟨all *standing* timbers are in sound condition⟩ — see ERECT

standing *n* 1 high position within society ⟨a man of *standing* in his community⟩ — see RANK 2

2 the period during which something exists, lasts, or is in progress ⟨a tradition of long *standing*⟩ — see DURATION 1
3 the placement of someone or something in relation to others in a vertical arrangement ⟨my *standing* in the class at the time of graduation⟩ — see RANK 1

standoff *n* a situation in which neither participant in a contest, competition, or struggle comes out ahead of the other ⟨we feared no one could resolve the *standoff*⟩ — see TIE 1

standoffish *adj* having or showing a lack of friendliness or interest in others ⟨she proved to be simply shy, not *standoffish*⟩ — see COOL 1

standout *n* a person who is widely known and usually much talked about ⟨several *standouts* from show biz were at the gala⟩ — see CELEBRITY 1

stand out *vb* to extend outward beyond a usual point ⟨the carvings *stand out* from the wall quite strikingly⟩ — see BULGE

standpoint *n* a way of looking at or thinking about something ⟨I never thought about it from that *standpoint* before⟩ — see POINT OF VIEW

standstill *n* a point in a struggle where neither side is capable of winning or willing to give in ⟨battled each other to a *standstill*⟩ — see IMPASSE

staple *n* the main or greater part of something as distinguished from its appendages ⟨reading is the very *staple* of a person's education⟩ — see BODY 1

star *adj* 1 of or relating to the stars ⟨*star* observations⟩ — see STELLAR 1
2 standing above others in rank, importance, or achievement ⟨the teacher's *star* pupil⟩ — see EMINENT
3 widely known ⟨looking for *star* actors to play the leads⟩ — see FAMOUS

star *n* 1 a ball-shaped gaseous celestial body that shines by its own light ⟨it's difficult to see the *stars* at night in the middle of the city because of all the streetlights⟩
synonyms luminary, sun
related words constellation; dwarf, fixed star, giant star, lodestar (*also* loadstar), neutron star, nova, red giant, supernova, variable star, white dwarf
2 the person who has the most important role in a play, movie, or TV show ⟨when the *star* of the school play came down with the flu on opening night, her understudy got to go on⟩
synonyms lead, principal
related words leading lady, leading man; superstar; ingenue (*or* ingénue), starlet
near antonyms extra, supernumerary
3 a person who is widely known and usually much talked about ⟨the public's endless fascination with *stars*⟩ — see CELEBRITY 1

starch *n* active strength of body or mind ⟨a middle-aged woman who has retained the *starch* of youth⟩ — see VIGOR 1

starchy *adj* marked by or showing careful attention to set forms and details ⟨a *starchy* and demanding teacher⟩ — see CEREMONIOUS 1

star–crossed *adj* having, prone to, or marked by bad luck ⟨Romeo and Juliet are famous *star-crossed* lovers⟩ — see UNLUCKY

stare *vb* to look long and hard in wonder or surprise ⟨her friends *stared* in disbelief upon seeing that she had dyed her hair purple⟩ — see GAPE

stark *adj* 1 harsh and threatening in manner or appearance ⟨*stark* and forbidding mountains that the settlers knew that they would have to cross⟩ — see GRIM 1

2 having no exceptions or restrictions ⟨the school's *stark* prohibition against obscene slogans on clothing⟩ — see ABSOLUTE 2

3 lacking contents that could or should be present ⟨house buyers trying to imagine what those *stark* rooms would look like when filled with furniture⟩ — see EMPTY 1

4 producing inferior or only a small amount of vegetation ⟨a once-lush landscape rendered depressingly *stark* by strip-mining and deforestation⟩ — see BARREN 1

starry *adj* of or relating to the stars ⟨the *starry* light of the firmament on a clear night⟩ — see STELLAR 1

start *n* the point at which something begins ⟨knew from the *start* of the game that he would win easily⟩ — see BEGINNING

start *vb* **1** to move suddenly and sharply (as in surprise) ⟨I *started* from my chair when I heard the sudden scream⟩

synonyms bolt, jump, startle

related words jerk, twitch; flinch, recoil; bound, leap, spring; react, respond

2 to be responsible for the creation and early operation or use of ⟨*started* the impressionist movement in art⟩ — see FOUND

3 to cause to function ⟨trying to *start* the car on a frigid morning⟩ — see ACTIVATE

4 to come into existence ⟨the argument *started* when one child tripped the other⟩ — see BEGIN 2

5 to extend outward beyond a usual point ⟨frightened horses with *starting* eyes⟩ — see BULGE

6 to take the first step in (a process or course of action) ⟨we'll be ready to *start* the concert in a moment⟩ — see BEGIN 1

startle *vb* **1** to make a strong impression on (someone) with something unexpected ⟨the lightning *startled* the children and sent them seeking cover⟩ — see SURPRISE 1

2 to move suddenly and sharply (as in surprise) ⟨the cat *startled* when the door opened with a bang⟩ — see START 1

3 to strike with fear ⟨loud noises always *startled* her⟩ — see FRIGHTEN

startling *adj* causing a strong emotional reaction because unexpected ⟨the *startling* news that my sister will be having a baby⟩ — see SURPRISING 1

starved *adj* feeling a desire or need for food ⟨after that long soccer practice, the children were really *starved*⟩ — see HUNGRY 1

starving *adj* feeling a desire or need for food ⟨I missed lunch, and now I'm *starving*⟩ — see HUNGRY 1

stash *n* a supply stored up and often hidden away ⟨keeps a *stash* of tissues in her desk in case anyone needs one⟩ — see HOARD 1

stash *vb* to put (something of future use or value) in a safe or secret place ⟨*stashed* the extra antifreeze in the trunk of the car⟩ — see HOARD

stashing *n* the placing of something out of sight ⟨the *stashing* of the title to the house in a strongbox that wasn't fireproof was foolish⟩ — see CONCEALMENT 1

state *adj* of or relating to a nation ⟨claimed that the envoy was revealing *state* secrets⟩ — see NATIONAL

state *n* a body of people composed of one or more nationalities usually with its own territory and government ⟨the British monarch is the head of *state*, while the prime minister is the head of the government⟩ — see NATION

state *vb* **1** to convey in appropriate or telling terms ⟨please *state* the problem as clearly and briefly as possible⟩ — see PHRASE

2 to express (a thought or emotion) in words ⟨"I believe this theory is wrong," she *stated*⟩ — see SAY 1

3 to make known (as an idea, emotion, or opinion) ⟨everyone has a right to *state* his or her opinion, no matter how unpopular it may be⟩ — see EXPRESS 1

state house *n* the building in which a state legislature meets ⟨a field trip to the *state house* to see the legislature in session⟩ — see CAPITOL

stateliness *n* **1** a dignified bearing or appearance befitting royalty ⟨the princess has a *stateliness* that will serve her well when she becomes queen⟩ — see MAJESTY 1

2 dignified or restrained beauty of form, appearance, or style ⟨the *stateliness* of the mansion that has served as the official home of the state's governors since the 18th century⟩ — see ELEGANCE

3 impressiveness of beauty on a large scale ⟨the *stateliness* of this mountain range is best appreciated from one of its summits⟩ — see MAGNIFICENCE

stately *adj* **1** having or showing a serious and reserved manner ⟨the governor watched with *stately* aloofness as his wife charmed the party guests⟩ — see DIGNIFIED

2 having or showing elegance ⟨a *stately* dowager in an evening gown⟩ — see ELEGANT 1

3 large and impressive in size, grandeur, extent, or conception ⟨*stately* homes that are now open to the public as museums⟩ — see GRAND 1

4 very dignified in form, tone, or style ⟨a *stately* composition that has served as the musical accompaniment for countless graduations and other ceremonial occasions⟩ — see ELEVATED 2

statement *n* **1** a record of goods sold or services performed together with the costs due ⟨received a *statement* from the plumber in the mail⟩ — see ¹BILL 1

2 an act, process, or means of putting something into words ⟨a careful *statement* of the legal case before the court⟩ — see EXPRESSION 1

3 something that is said ⟨her *statement* was met with considerable skepticism⟩ — see WORD 2

static *adj* fixed in a place or position ⟨the *static* installation of the statue in that niche means that no one will ever see its back, which is also of interest⟩ — see STATIONARY 1

station *n* **1** the place where someone is assigned to stand or remain ⟨the soldiers remained at their *station* even though a huge enemy force was approaching⟩

synonyms position, post, quarter

related words assignment, detail

2 a regular stopping place ⟨the historic house was once a *station* on the Underground Railroad, the network that helped slaves reach freedom in the North⟩

synonyms stop, way station

related words depot, terminal; layover, stopover

3 the placement of someone or something in relation to others in a vertical arrangement ⟨in colonial America, women occupied the lowest *station* in society and were not allowed to take part in public life⟩ — see RANK 1

station *vb* to assign to a place or position ⟨*stationed* guards around the perimeter of the encampment⟩ — see ²POST

stationary *adj* **1** fixed in a place or position ⟨a *stationary* bicycle is good for exercise, but you won't enjoy the scenery very much⟩

synonyms immobile, nonmoving, standing, static

related words immovable, irremovable, nonmotile, unmovable; frozen, motionless, stagnant, still, unbudging
near antonyms motile
antonyms mobile, movable (*or* moveable), moving, nonstationary
2 not undergoing a change in condition ⟨auction prices for that artist's works have been *stationary* for some time⟩ — see CONSTANT 1

statuette *n* a small statue ⟨won a gold-plated *statuette* as the prize⟩ — see FIGURINE

stature *n* the distance of something or someone from bottom to top ⟨a man of surprisingly great *stature*⟩ — see HEIGHT 3

status *n* **1** position with regard to conditions and circumstances ⟨let me know if your *status* changes and you're available to work⟩ — see SITUATION 1
2 the placement of someone or something in relation to others in a vertical arrangement ⟨resented her lowly *status* in the organization⟩ — see RANK 1

status quo *n* the state or fact of being the way things usually are ⟨civic leaders who are afraid to do anything that might change the town's *status quo*⟩ — see NORMALITY

statute *n* a rule of conduct or action laid down by a governing authority and especially a legislator ⟨a new anti-littering *statute*⟩ — see LAW 1

staunch *or* **stanch** *adj* firm in one's allegiance to someone or something ⟨a *staunch* believer in the democratic system⟩ — see FAITHFUL 1

stave off *vb* to drive back ⟨managed to *stave off* the invaders⟩ — see REPEL 1

¹**stay** *n* a temporary residing as another's guest ⟨my mother-in-law is coming for a brief *stay* next week⟩ — see VISIT 1

²**stay** *n* something that holds up or serves as a foundation for something else ⟨a free press is one of the principal *stays* of a democratic society⟩ — see SUPPORT 1

stay *vb* **1** to continue to be in a place for a significant amount of time ⟨let's *stay* inside this pavilion until it stops raining⟩
synonyms abide, dwell, hang around, remain, stick around, tarry
related words await, hang on, hold on, wait; dally, linger, loiter; keep
antonyms go, leave, quit
2 to bring (something) to a standstill ⟨*stay* the trial until this new evidence has been processed⟩ — see ¹HALT 1
3 to hold up or serve as a foundation for ⟨beams being used to *stay* the bridge while it is undergoing repairs⟩ — see SUPPORT 3
4 to remain in place in readiness or expectation of something ⟨we'll *stay* for a while longer and see if anyone shows up⟩ — see WAIT
5 to reside as a temporary guest ⟨let's *stay* at a quaint inn rather than at a motel⟩ — see VISIT 2

steadfast *adj* firm in one's allegiance to someone or something ⟨a *steadfast* supporter of women's rights⟩ — see FAITHFUL 1

steadfastness *n* adherence to something to which one is bound by a pledge or duty ⟨his *steadfastness* to his beliefs is admirable, even if one does not agree with them⟩ — see FIDELITY

steadiness *n* **1** the ability to withstand force or stress without being distorted, dislodged, or damaged ⟨I have my doubts about the *steadiness* of that little shed⟩ — see STABILITY 1

2 the state of continuing without change ⟨the *steadiness* of the weather is something that every New Englander knows not to trust⟩ — see CONSTANCY 1

steady *adj* **1** firm in one's allegiance to someone or something ⟨even as wild accusations were circulating, she remained *steady* in her support for the candidate⟩ — see FAITHFUL 1
2 appearing or occurring repeatedly from time to time ⟨a popular author who produced a *steady* output of best sellers over the years⟩ — see REGULAR 1
3 not undergoing a change in condition ⟨a *steady* breeze from the west⟩ — see CONSTANT 1
4 not varying ⟨support for her presidential bid has been *steady*⟩ — see UNIFORM
5 worthy of one's trust ⟨a quiet but *steady* man who is one of the pillars of the community⟩ — see DEPENDABLE

steal *n* something bought or offered for sale at a desirable price ⟨that shirt at 50% off is a real *steal*⟩ — see BARGAIN 1

steal *vb* **1** to take (something) without right and with an intent to keep ⟨the guy who tried to *steal* my car was sentenced to a year in jail⟩
synonyms appropriate, filch, hook, misappropriate, nip, pilfer, pinch, pocket, purloin, rip off, snitch, swipe, thieve
related words burglarize, fleece, rob; loot, pillage, plunder, sack; hijack (*or* highjack); pick, rifle; poach, rustle, shoplift; collar, grab, grasp, nail, seize, snatch, take; mooch, sponge; abduct, kidnap, shanghai, spirit
phrases make away with, run off with, walk off with
near antonyms buy, purchase; bestow, contribute, donate, give, present
2 to move about in a sly or secret manner ⟨children *stealing* into the kitchen to swipe some cookies⟩ — see SNEAK 1

steal (from) *vb* to remove valuables from (a place) unlawfully ⟨little wonder that the store went out of business, as employees had been *stealing from* it for years⟩ — see ROB

stealer *n* one who steals ⟨you're a habitual *stealer*—you've done nothing but steal your whole life⟩ — see THIEF

stealing *n* the unlawful taking and carrying away of property without the consent of its owner ⟨in those days the *stealing* of a horse was a very serious crime⟩ — see THEFT 1

stealthy *adj* **1** given to acting in secret and to concealing one's intentions ⟨cats are among the *stealthiest* of stalkers⟩ — see SNEAKY 1
2 undertaken or done so as to escape being observed or known by others ⟨constantly harassed the enemy with *stealthy* raids⟩ — see SECRET 1

steam *vb* to be excited or emotionally stirred up with anger ⟨cruel lies that make him *steam*⟩ — see BOIL 1

steaming *adj* feeling or showing anger ⟨she was *steaming* after hearing that she was being slandered by someone who had once been her best friend⟩ — see ANGRY

steed *n* a large hoofed domestic animal that is used for carrying or drawing loads and for riding ⟨the knight mounted his trusty *steed*⟩ — see HORSE

steel *n* a hand weapon with a length of metal sharpened on one or both sides and usually tapered to a sharp point ⟨drew *steel* on the bandits, who immediately fled for their lives⟩ — see SWORD

steel *vb* **1** to fill with courage or strength of purpose ⟨hoped that his talk would *steel* the youths in their pursuit of their dreams⟩ — see ENCOURAGE 1

2 to make able to withstand physical hardship, strain, or exposure ⟨years of running a farm had *steeled* the hard-bitten woman⟩ — see HARDEN 2

3 to prepare (oneself) mentally or emotionally ⟨he had spent the night before *steeling* himself for the moment when he would demand a raise⟩ — see FORTIFY 1

steely *adj* **1** harsh and threatening in manner or appearance ⟨pinned them with a *steely* gaze and demanded to know what they were doing⟩ — see GRIM 1

2 of the color gray ⟨*steely* eyes that were the color of a stormy sky⟩ — see GRAY 1

steep *adj* **1** having an incline approaching the perpendicular ⟨a very *steep* rock face that was nearly impossible to climb⟩

synonyms abrupt, bold, precipitous, sheer

related words perpendicular, plumb, straight, vertical; craggy, hilly, mountainous, scarped; angled, canted, cocked, heeled, inclined, listed, slanted, sloped, tilted, tipped

near antonyms gentle, gradual, moderate; even, flat, flush, horizontal, level, plane, smooth, unruffled, unwrinkled

antonyms easy

2 going beyond a normal or acceptable limit in degree or amount ⟨that price is a bit *steep* for an ice cream cone⟩ — see EXCESSIVE

steep *vb* **1** to cause (as a person) to become filled or saturated with a certain quality or principle ⟨grew up *steeped* in the ways of his ancestors⟩ ⟨a town *steeped* in history⟩ — see INFUSE

2 to wet thoroughly with liquid ⟨chew fresh ginger that has been *steeped* in hot water to aid digestion⟩ — see SOAK 1

steer *vb* to point out the way for (someone) especially from a position in front ⟨the man in the train station *steered* us back in the direction we'd just come from⟩ — see LEAD 1

stellar *adj* **1** of or relating to the stars ⟨humankind's dream of *stellar* navigation is hampered by the vast distances between the stars, even in our own galaxy⟩

synonyms astral, star, starry

related words celestial, empyrean, heavenly; astronomical (*also* astronomic), astrophysical; astronautic (*or* astronautical); starlike, star-spangled

2 of the very best kind ⟨this miniature palm tree is a *stellar* example of the art of bonsai⟩ — see EXCELLENT

stench *n* a strong unpleasant smell ⟨we finally discovered the dead rat that was causing the *stench* in the basement⟩ — see STINK

stentorian *adj* marked by a high volume of sound ⟨we could hear Mr. Parkhurst's *stentorian* voice from across the hall⟩ — see LOUD 1

step *n* **1** an action planned or taken to achieve a desired result ⟨took *steps* to ensure that there would be no more incidences of food poisoning⟩ — see MEASURE 1

2 an individual part of a process, series, or ranking ⟨we'll go through the math problem one *step* at a time⟩ — see DEGREE 1

3 the mark or impression made by a foot ⟨*steps* in the sand leading into the water and back out again⟩ — see FOOTPRINT

4 **steps** *pl* the direction along which something or someone moves ⟨their *steps* led them through a long corridor⟩ — see PATH 1

step *vb* **1** to go on foot ⟨*stepping* along lightly, feeling free as a bird on the first day of summer vacation⟩ — see WALK

2 to perform a series of usually rhythmic bodily movements to music ⟨she was in her element, happily *stepping* around the dance floor⟩ — see DANCE 1

step (along) *vb* to proceed or move quickly ⟨we wanted to see what all the fuss was about, but a cop made us *step along*⟩ — see HURRY 2

step–by–step *adj* proceeding or changing by steps or degrees ⟨a *step-by-step* improvement in his medical condition⟩ — see GRADUAL

step down (from) *vb* **1** to give up (a job or office) ⟨he agreed to *step down from* the mayor's office, though he continued to insist that the accusations against him were false⟩ — see QUIT 1

2 to give up (as a position of authority) formally ⟨even in the face of a palace revolt, Queen Elizabeth I refused to *step down from* the throne⟩ — see ABDICATE

steppe *n* a broad area of level or rolling treeless country ⟨nomads graze yaks on the *steppes* of Tibet⟩ — see PLAIN

step up *vb* to make markedly greater in measure or degree ⟨candidates *stepping up* their campaigns as election day draws near⟩ ⟨*stepped up* the pace to catch up with the others⟩ — see INTENSIFY

stereotype *n* an idea or statement about all of the members of a group or all the instances of a situation ⟨meeting kids of other races and cultures erases *stereotypes*⟩ — see GENERALIZATION

stereotyped *adj* used or heard so often as to be dull ⟨the *stereotyped* characters seen on TV sitcoms⟩ — see STALE

sterile *adj* **1** not able to produce fruit or offspring ⟨*sterile* couples sometimes choose to adopt needy children⟩ ⟨the apple tree turned out to be *sterile*, never yielding a crop of apples⟩

synonyms barren, impotent, infertile, unfruitful

related words altered, desexed, neutered, sterilized; castrated, emasculated, gelded; spayed; fruitless, unproductive

near antonyms fecund, luxuriant, productive, prolific; enriched, fertilized, rich; impregnated, pregnant; potent; bearing, producing, yielding; blooming, bursting, flourishing, swarming, teeming

antonyms fat, fertile, fruitful

2 free from filth, infection, or dangers to health ⟨the surgeon dropped his scalpel on the floor, and the nurse replaced it with a *sterile* one⟩ — see SANITARY

sterling *adj* of the very best kind ⟨the pitcher's *sterling* performance on the mound⟩ — see EXCELLENT

stern *adj* **1** given to exacting standards of discipline and self-restraint ⟨my dad claims that when he was in school the teachers were much *sterner* and you couldn't get away with anything⟩ — see SEVERE 1

2 harsh and threatening in manner or appearance ⟨a *stern* receptionist who took our names without even looking up⟩ — see GRIM 1

sternly *adv* in a manner so as to cause loss or suffering ⟨*sternly* reprimanded us for sticking our heads out the bus windows⟩ — see HARDLY 1

sternness *n* the quality or state of being demanding or unyielding (as in discipline or criticism) ⟨with exceptional *sternness* he threatened to punish anyone who cheated on the test⟩ — see SEVERITY

stevedore *n* one who loads and unloads ships at a port ⟨on the wharves, *stevedores* were unloading cargo from around the world⟩ — see DOCKWORKER

stew *n* **1** a state of nervous or irritated concern ⟨our club president was all in a *stew* because over half the members weren't at the meeting⟩ — see FRET

2 a state of noisy, confused activity ⟨there was a big *stew* when the poison was discovered missing⟩ — see COMMOTION

stew *vb* **1** to cook in a liquid heated to the point that it gives off steam ⟨*stew* the chicken till tender, and then remove the meat from the bones⟩ — see BOIL 2

2 to experience concern or anxiety ⟨stop *stewing* over that game and just try to do better next time⟩ — see WORRY 1

steward *n* a person hired to perform household or personal services ⟨the earl couldn't imagine how he'd manage without his *steward*⟩ — see SERVANT

stick *vb* **1** to hold to something firmly as if by adhesion ⟨those magnets are strong enough to *stick* well to the refrigerator⟩

synonyms adhere, cleave, cling, hew

related words bind, cohere, fasten, fuse, glue, unite

near antonyms loosen; drop, fall

2 to arrange something in a certain spot or position ⟨you can *stick* that box in the corner until I figure out where to put everything⟩ — see PLACE 1

3 to penetrate or hold (something) with a pointed object ⟨could hardly feel the needle when the nurse *stuck* me with it⟩ — see IMPALE

4 to rob by the use of trickery or threats ⟨keeps getting *stuck* by guys who promise to pay him for the yard work and never do⟩ — see FLEECE

stick (to *or* with) *vb* to give steadfast support to ⟨thanks for *sticking with* me when all my other so-called friends have turned their backs⟩ — see ADHERE

stick around *vb* to continue to be in a place for a significant amount of time ⟨we *stuck around* afterwards to help clean up⟩ — see STAY 1

stick–in–the–mud *n* **1** a person with old-fashioned ideas ⟨too much of a *stick-in-the-mud* to want a personal computer⟩ — see FOGY

2 someone who moves slowly or more slowly than others ⟨our oldest dog is becoming a *stick-in-the-mud* and stays behind when the other dogs go running off⟩ — see SLOWPOKE

stick out *vb* **1** to extend outward beyond a usual point ⟨no feet *sticking out* in the aisles, please⟩ — see BULGE

2 to put up with (something painful or difficult) ⟨managed to *stick out* the whole race despite her bad knee⟩ — see BEAR 2

sticks *n pl* the open rural area outside of big towns and cities ⟨grew up in the *sticks* and is used to traveling miles just to get a loaf of bread⟩ — see COUNTRY 2

sticky *adj* **1** being of such a thick consistency as to readily cling to objects upon contact ⟨the *sticky* maple syrup was a mess to clean up⟩

synonyms adhesive, gelatinous, gluey, glutinous, gooey, gummy, viscid, viscous

related words ropy, tacky; adherent, tenacious

antonyms nonadhesive, nonviscous

2 containing or characterized by an uncomfortable amount of moisture ⟨a warm *sticky* day when all we wanted to do was sit somewhere with air-conditioning⟩ — see HUMID

stiff *adj* **1** incapable of or highly resistant to bending ⟨use a *stiff* piece of paper for the project⟩

synonyms inflexible, rigid, stiffened, unyielding

related words inelastic; firm, hard, solid, sound, strong; brittle, crisp; compact, dense, substantial; arthritic, rheumatic; nonelastic, nonmalleable

near antonyms elastic, resilient, springy, stretchy, workable; malleable; droopy, flabby, flaccid, mushy,

semisoft, soft, squashy, squishy; lank, limber, limp, lissome (*also* lissom), lithe, willowy

antonyms flexible, floppy, pliable, pliant, supple, yielding

2 difficult to endure ⟨*stiff* winds⟩ — see HARSH 1

3 going beyond a normal or acceptable limit in degree or amount ⟨don't you think taking away his bike for three months is rather *stiff* punishment?⟩ — see EXCESSIVE

4 having a consistency that does not easily yield to pressure ⟨stir two cups of flour with the remaining ingredients to make a *stiff* dough⟩ — see FIRM 2

5 lacking social grace and assurance ⟨felt *stiff* and ill-at-ease whenever she was introduced to her father's friends⟩ — see AWKWARD 1

6 requiring considerable physical or mental effort ⟨getting this couch up to the third floor is going to be a *stiff* job⟩ — see HARD 2

stiffened *adj* incapable of or highly resistant to bending ⟨*stiffened* corpses⟩ ⟨an old-fashioned dress with a *stiffened* lace collar⟩ — see STIFF 1

stiffly *adv* **1** in a manner so as to cause loss or suffering ⟨*stiffly* criticized for saying such things in public⟩ — see HARDLY 1

2 in a vigorous and forceful manner ⟨a *stiffly* fought battle⟩ — see HARD 3

stifle *vb* **1** to be or cause to be killed by lack of breathable air ⟨unfortunately, the robbers were *stifled* when they got trapped in the airless bank vault⟩ — see SMOTHER 1

2 to refrain from openly showing or uttering ⟨*stifled* a yawn⟩ — see SUPPRESS 2

stifling *adj* lacking fresh air ⟨the room was *stifling*, so we quickly opened windows⟩ — see STUFFY 1

stigma *n* a mark of guilt or disgrace ⟨the *stigma* of slavery remained long after it had been abolished⟩ — see STAIN 1

still *adj* **1** free from disturbing noise or uproar ⟨for a few seconds after the music had ended, the audience remained *still* before bursting into thunderous applause⟩ — see QUIET 1

2 free from storms or physical disturbance ⟨the air seemed almost too *still*, and the effect was ominous somehow⟩ — see CALM 1

3 mostly or entirely without sound ⟨in his paintings Paul Gauguin depicts a *still* tropical paradise inhabited by mute and motionless natives⟩ — see SILENT 3

still *adv* **1** without motion ⟨now, you have to sit very *still* while the hairdresser cuts your hair⟩

synonyms motionlessly, quiet, quietly

related words immovably; inactively

near antonyms movably

2 in spite of that ⟨Mrs. Archer's a good teacher; *still*, I'd rather have Mr. Grove because he lets us work in groups⟩ — see HOWEVER

still *n* **1** a state of freedom from storm or disturbance ⟨in the *still* of the forest he could relax and forget his worries⟩ — see CALM

2 the near or complete absence of sound ⟨a loud noise shattered the *still* of the night⟩ — see SILENCE 2

still *vb* **1** to bring (something) to a standstill ⟨it seemed as though nothing could *still* the fighting⟩ — see ¹HALT 1

2 to free from distress or disturbance ⟨maybe this warm drink will *still* and comfort you⟩ — see CALM 1

3 to stop the noise or speech of ⟨was *stilled* in midsentence by the reproving look of the teacher⟩ — see SILENCE 1

stillness *n* **1** a state of freedom from storm or disturbance ⟨dozing in the warm *stillness* of a summer afternoon⟩ — see CALM

2 incapacity for or restraint from speaking ⟨from the couple's tense *stillness* I sensed that they had been quarreling just before I arrived⟩ — see SILENCE 1

3 the near or complete absence of sound ⟨the only thing that broke the *stillness* of the garden was the droning of a bee⟩ — see SILENCE 2

stilly *adj* **1** free from disturbing noise or uproar ⟨bats taking flight in the *stilly* night⟩ — see QUIET 1

2 free from storms or physical disturbance ⟨dipping my paddle into the *stilly* water, I began canoeing across the pond⟩ — see CALM 1

stilted *adj* lacking social grace and assurance ⟨a *stilted* welcome was the best we could expect when we showed up in the midst of a big family argument⟩ — see AWKWARD 1

stimulant *n* **1** something that arouses a strong response from another ⟨one sarcastic remark is all the *stimulant* that is needed for a full-blown fight between those two⟩ — see PROVOCATION 1

2 something that arouses action or activity ⟨a D minus might serve as a *stimulant* to spend more time doing math homework⟩ — see IMPULSE

stimulate *vb* **1** to give life, vigor, or spirit to ⟨nothing like a day at the pool to *stimulate* appetites⟩ — see ANIMATE

2 to rouse to strong feeling or action ⟨*stimulated* by all the controversy to write a letter to her state representative⟩ — see PROVOKE 1

stimulating *adj* **1** causing great emotional or mental stimulation ⟨enjoys the good food and *stimulating* conversation at his best friend's house⟩ — see EXCITING 1

2 having a renewing effect on the state of the body or mind ⟨a brisk, *stimulating* walk on a bright, clear wintry day⟩ — see TONIC

3 serving or likely to arouse a strong reaction ⟨an article containing a *stimulating* argument for raising the tax on gasoline⟩ — see PROVOCATIVE

stimulation *n* something that arouses a strong response from another ⟨a bone didn't offer sufficient *stimulation* to lure the dog away from the mailman⟩ — see PROVOCATION 1

stimulative *adj* having a renewing effect on the state of the body or mind ⟨the supposed *stimulative* power of herbal teas⟩ — see TONIC

stimulus *n* **1** something that arouses a strong response from another ⟨Nora's suspension for cheating was the *stimulus* for a heated debate among his friends on the issue⟩ — see PROVOCATION 1

2 something that arouses action or activity ⟨seeing a Broadway play for the first time was the *stimulus* for her career in the theater⟩ — see IMPULSE

sting *n* a sharp unpleasant sensation usually felt in some specific part of the body ⟨the *sting* of the injection brought tears to her eyes⟩ — see PAIN 1

sting *vb* **1** to charge (someone) too much for goods or services ⟨a nightclub that's been *stinging* patrons for years⟩ — see OVERCHARGE 1

2 to rob by the use of trickery or threats ⟨swindlers who *sting* unwary tourists by posing as officials demanding money⟩ — see FLEECE

stinginess *n* the quality of being overly sparing with money ⟨Mr. Franklin's *stinginess*—he never tips—is legendary among the waitresses at the diner⟩ — see PARSIMONY

stinging *adj* causing intense discomfort to one's skin ⟨protective clothing designed to help firefighters withstand the *stinging* heat of fires⟩ — see CUTTING 1

stingy *adj* **1** giving or sharing as little as possible ⟨until his redemption, Ebenezer Scrooge is the classic example of a very *stingy*, heartless miser⟩

synonyms cheap, close, closefisted, mean, niggard, niggardly, parsimonious, penurious, pinching, spare, sparing, stinting, tight, tightfisted, uncharitable

related words careful, chary, conserving, economical, economizing, frugal, saving, scrimping, skimping, thrifty; acquisitive, avaricious, avid, coveting, covetous, desirous, grasping, greedy, hoggish, itchy, mercenary, rapacious, selfish, shabby, small, sordid; begrudging, envious, grudging, resentful; inhospitable

near antonyms altruistic, selfless, unselfish; extravagant, free, handsome, lavish, profuse; beneficent, benevolent, hospitable, humanitarian, philanthropic; compassionate, good-hearted, greathearted, kindly, magnanimous, openhearted; thriftless, unthrifty; dissipating, frittering, prodigal, profligate, spendthrift, splurging, squandering, wasteful, wasting

antonyms bounteous, bountiful, charitable, freehanded, generous, liberal, munificent, openhanded, unsparing, unstinting

2 less plentiful than what is normal, necessary, or desirable ⟨a *stingy* serving of mashed potatoes⟩ — see MEAGER

stink *n* a strong unpleasant smell ⟨the *stink* of burned plastic lingered in the kitchen for days after we accidentally melted a spatula on the stove⟩

synonyms reek, stench

related words acridness, fetidness, foulness, fustiness, malodorousness, mustiness, rancidity, rankness, staleness; badness, vileness; dirt, dirtiness, filth, filthiness, nastiness; odor, redolence, scent, sniff

near antonyms floweriness, lusciousness, savoriness, spiciness, sweetness; bouquet; ambrosia

antonyms aroma, fragrance, perfume

stink *vb* to give off an extremely unpleasant smell ⟨the dog *stinks* because she tangled with a skunk again⟩

synonyms reek

related words exhale, savor, smell; decay, decompose, rot, spoil; disgust, offend, repulse, revolt

stinker *n* a person whose behavior is offensive to others ⟨some *stinker* scribbled on the library tables with a permanent ink⟩ — see JERK 1

stinking *adj* having an unpleasant smell ⟨came home from their trip to find *stinking* garbage that had been left in the kitchen⟩ — see MALODOROUS

stinky *adj* having an unpleasant smell ⟨a *stinky* plant that attracts certain insects and then devours them⟩ — see MALODOROUS

stint *n* **1** a fixed period of time during which a person holds a job or position ⟨signed up for a three-year *stint* in the army⟩ — see TERM 1

2 a piece of work that needs to be done regularly ⟨my regular *stint* is changing the cat's litter⟩ — see CHORE 1

stint (on) *vb* to use or give out in stingy amounts ⟨a hostess who doesn't *stint on* food and drink and even sends guests home with leftovers⟩ — see SPARE

stinting *adj* giving or sharing as little as possible ⟨a *stinting* boss who doesn't give paid sick leave no matter how long you've worked for him⟩ — see STINGY 1

stipend *n* the money paid regularly to a person for labor or services ⟨camp counselors are considered volunteers, though they do receive a modest *stipend*⟩ — see WAGE

stipple vb to mark with small spots especially unevenly ⟨the sunlight falling through the lace curtain *stippled* her face⟩ — see SPOT

stippled adj marked with spots ⟨create a *stippled* effect by dabbing a contrasting color of paint over an undercoat with a rag or sponge⟩ — see SPOTTED 1

stipulate (for) vb to ask for (something) earnestly or with authority ⟨for the field trip we expressly *stipulated for* an air-conditioned bus⟩ — see DEMAND 1

stipulation n something upon which the carrying out of an agreement or offer depends ⟨my only *stipulation* is that you be home from the concert before midnight⟩ — see CONDITION 2

stir n 1 a state of noisy, confused activity ⟨the plane's first jolt caused a *stir* among the passengers, and by the third one they were in a panic⟩ — see COMMOTION
2 the act or an instance of changing position ⟨we were warned that the slightest *stir* would scare the mother bird so we hardly dared to breathe⟩ — see MOVEMENT 1

stir vb 1 to cause (as a liquid) to move about in a circle especially repeatedly ⟨the recipe says to *stir* the mixture carefully until it's properly blended⟩
synonyms agitate, churn, swirl, whirl
related words beat, paddle, whip, whisk; reel, shake, wheel
2 to change one's position ⟨no one *stirred* when the teacher asked for volunteers⟩ — see MOVE 3
3 to rouse to strong feeling or action ⟨I was *stirred* by the talk to donate my lunch money to the fire victims⟩ — see PROVOKE 1

stir (up) vb to cause or encourage the development of ⟨couldn't *stir up* any interest in a Saturday morning outing to the art museum⟩ — see INCITE 1

stirring adj 1 causing great emotional or mental stimulation ⟨the message of brotherhood in Martin Luther King's *stirring* "I Have a Dream" speech still resonates today⟩ — see EXCITING 1
2 having the power to affect the feelings or sympathies ⟨a *stirring* rendition of the national anthem⟩ — see MOVING

stirring n the act or an instance of changing position ⟨I thought I detected a slight *stirring* of the leaves, and yet there wasn't a breath of wind⟩ — see MOVEMENT 1

stitch n a sharp unpleasant sensation usually felt in some specific part of the body ⟨had to drop out of the race when the *stitch* in his side became too painful⟩ — see PAIN 1

stitch vb to close up with a series of interlacing stitches ⟨the doctor *stitched* the wound so adroitly that the scar was barely visible after the stitches were removed⟩ — see SEW

stock adj accepted, used, or practiced by most people ⟨the *stock* send-off of "Have a nice day!"⟩ — see CURRENT 1

stock n 1 a group of persons who come from the same ancestor ⟨the bride comes of good *stock*⟩ — see FAMILY 1
2 a stupid person ⟨just sat there like a *stock*, staring at me blankly when I asked him a question⟩ — see IDIOT
3 firm belief in the integrity, ability, effectiveness, or genuineness of someone or something ⟨put no *stock* in her promises, for she just tells you what she thinks you want to hear⟩ — see TRUST 1
4 the line of ancestors from whom a person is descended ⟨despite their poverty, they were of noble *stock*, tracing their line back to Charlemagne⟩ — see ANCESTRY

stockade n a place of confinement for persons held in lawful custody ⟨prisoners of war confined in a *stockade*⟩ — see JAIL

stocking n a close-fitting covering for the foot and leg ⟨be sure to wear your thick wool *stockings* if it's cold today⟩
synonyms hose, sock
related words hosiery; anklet, bobby socks, bootee

stockpile n a supply stored up and often hidden away ⟨his *stockpile* of candy bars was severely depleted the night his friends stayed over⟩ — see HOARD 1

stockpile vb to put (something of future use or value) in a safe or secret place ⟨*stockpiles* all his old sneakers because he can't bear to part with them⟩ — see HOARD

stocky adj being compact and broad in build and often short in stature ⟨he was a tough, *stocky* little boy, muscular and solid⟩
synonyms chunky, dumpy, heavyset, squat, squatty, stout, stubby, stumpy, thickset
related words beefy, brawny, bulky, burly, husky, sturdy, thick, thickish, weighty; chubby, corpulent, fat, fleshy, full, gross, heavy, obese, overweight, plump, portly, pudgy, roly-poly, rotund, round, tubby; paunchy, potbellied; flabby, soft
near antonyms delicate, fragile, frail, puny; lean, skinny, slender, slim, spare, thin; angular, bony, gaunt, lank, lanky, rawboned, sinewy; scraggy, scrawny, slight; anorexic, cadaverous, emaciated, haggard, skeletal, wasted; spindly, twiggy, waspish, weedy, willowy, wiry

stodgy adj causing weariness, restlessness, or lack of interest ⟨spent the holidays with a bunch of *stodgy* relatives whose idea of fun is playing card games⟩ — see BORING

stoic or **stoical** adj 1 accepting pains or hardships calmly or without complaint ⟨after waiting six years for permission to immigrate to the U.S., the family is *stoic* about a six-month postponement⟩ — see PATIENT 1
2 not feeling or showing emotion ⟨at her husband's funeral she remained *stoic*, and only a few imagined the depth of her grief⟩ — see IMPASSIVE 1

stolid adj 1 not expressing any emotion ⟨the butler responded to the duchess's constant demands with *stolid* indifference⟩ — see BLANK 1
2 not feeling or showing emotion ⟨his spouse was a *stolid* creature who had long ceased to have any feelings for him at all⟩ — see IMPASSIVE 1

stomach n the part of the body between the chest and the pelvis ⟨please don't lean on my *stomach*—I just had a big meal⟩
synonyms abdomen, belly, breadbasket [*slang*], gut, solar plexus, tummy
related words middle, midriff, waist; paunch, potbelly; thorax

stomach vb to put up with (something painful or difficult) ⟨cannot *stomach* the gossip going around about the new girl, because it's just being spread for spite⟩ — see BEAR 2

stomachache n abdominal pain especially when focused in the digestive organs ⟨you can stay home from school tomorrow if you still have a *stomachache*⟩
synonyms bellyache
related words colic, cramps

stomp vb 1 to move heavily or clumsily ⟨came *stomping* up the stairs and tossed her backpack on the bed⟩ — see LUMBER 1

2 to tread on heavily so as to crush or injure ⟨*stomping* the burning leaves in a vain attempt to put out the fire⟩ — see TRAMPLE

stone blind *adj* lacking the power of sight ⟨being inside the pitch-black cave was like being *stone blind*⟩ — see BLIND

stone–broke *adj* lacking money or material possessions ⟨claimed that he was *stone-broke*⟩ — see POOR 1

stoneware *n* articles made of baked clay ⟨collects 19th-century English *stoneware*, especially soup tureens⟩ — see CROCKERY

stony *also* **stoney** *adj* having or showing a lack of sympathy or tender feelings ⟨Jane's heart sank at the sight of the judge's *stony* expression as he prepared to pronounce sentence⟩ — see HARD 1

stool pigeon *n* a person who provides secret information about another's wrongdoing ⟨Joe wondered who the *stool pigeon* was who'd turned him in to the police⟩ — see INFORMER

stoop *vb* to descend to a level that is beneath one's dignity ⟨I won't *stoop* to copying, even if it means I'll flunk⟩ — see CONDESCEND 1

stooping *adj* bending downward or forward ⟨rested under the *stooping* branches of the willow tree⟩ — see NODDING

stop *n* **1** a brief halt in a journey ⟨our guide called for a *stop* at the trail hut to eat and rest a bit⟩
synonyms layover, stopover
related words break, pause, rest
2 a regular stopping place ⟨had lunch on a picnic table at a shady rest *stop* along the highway⟩ — see STATION 2
3 something that makes movement or progress more difficult ⟨pulled out all the *stops* and presented the most spectacular show ever⟩ — see ENCUMBRANCE
4 the stopping of a process or activity ⟨put a *stop* to this nonsense⟩ — see END 1

stop *vb* **1** to bring (as an action or operation) to an immediate end ⟨please *stop* that running in the library⟩
synonyms break, break off, can [*slang*], cease, cut (out), desist (from), discontinue, drop, end, halt, knock off, lay off, leave off, quit, shut off
related words complete, conclude, finish; close (down); deactivate; block, blockade, dam, delay, detain, hinder, hold, hold back, impede, obstruct, stem; call, suspend; arrest, brake, check, clamp down, rein (in), squash, squelch, stamp, stanch (*also* staunch), stunt, suppress, turn back; pause, stay, suspend; abolish, abort, annul, demolish, destroy, dissolve, kill, ruin, scuttle, snuff
phrases have done with, put the kibosh on
near antonyms carry on, continue, follow through, keep up, run on; advance, proceed, progress; actuate, drive, impel, propel, stir
2 to bring (something) to a standstill ⟨the highway traffic was *stopped* for over an hour by the overturned truck⟩ — see ¹HALT 1
3 to close up so that no empty spaces remain ⟨a crude log cabin with the spaces between the logs *stopped* with mud⟩ — see FILL 2
4 to come to an end ⟨the music *stopped* but we kept on dancing⟩ — see CEASE 1

stop (by *or* **in)** *vb* to make a brief visit ⟨*stop by* on your way to the game so we can go there together⟩ — see CALL 3

stop (up) *vb* to prevent passage through ⟨something must be *stopping up* this trumpet, for I can't get it to make a sound⟩ — see CLOG 1

stopcock *n* a fixture for controlling the flow of a liquid ⟨when the pipe broke, we had to find the main *stopcock* that would turn off all the water in the house⟩ — see FAUCET

stopgap *n* a temporary replacement ⟨the coach we have now was only hired as a *stopgap* until someone with more experience is found⟩ — see MAKESHIFT

stopover *n* a brief halt in a journey ⟨I've been to Belgium—if you count a *stopover* in Brussels on my way to Istanbul⟩ — see STOP 1

stoppage *n* the stopping of a process or activity ⟨yet another *stoppage* in play for some unexplained reason⟩ — see END 1

storage *n* a building for storing goods ⟨in Colonial times the granary was one of the community's most important *storages*⟩ — see STOREHOUSE

store *adj* made beforehand in large numbers ⟨preferred homemade bread to *store* brands⟩ — see READY-MADE

store *n* **1** a collection of things kept available for future use or need ⟨Dad has a *store* of funny stories for when conversation lags at company parties⟩
synonyms cache, deposit, hoard, reserve
related words budget, fund, nest egg, pool, reservoir, stock, stockpile, supply; accumulation, assemblage, collection, gathering
2 a supply stored up and often hidden away ⟨keeps a *store* of quarters in the glove compartment for the parking meters⟩ — see HOARD 1
3 an establishment where goods are sold to consumers ⟨go to the grocery *store* for orange juice and eggs⟩ — see SHOP 1

store *vb* **1** to place somewhere for safekeeping or ready availability ⟨we decided to *store* the lawn mower in the shed instead of the garage⟩
synonyms keep, stow
related words garage, house; file, pack, shelve
2 to put (something of future use or value) in a safe or secret place ⟨squirrels commonly *store* nuts in the hollows of trees and other places to prepare for the winter⟩ — see HOARD

storehouse *n* a building for storing goods ⟨the company has a large *storehouse* filled with lumber for manufacturing its line of furniture⟩
synonyms depository, depot, magazine, repository, storage, stowage, warehouse
related words cache, stockroom, storeroom; bank, bin, container, locker, safe-deposit box, strongbox; arsenal, dump

storm *n* **1** a disturbance of the atmosphere accompanied by wind and often by precipitation (as rain or snow) ⟨a winter *storm* bringing about six inches of snow⟩
synonyms squall, tempest
related words blizzard, hail storm, ice storm, northeaster, norther, rainstorm, sandstorm, snowstorm, southeaster, southwester, thunderstorm, windstorm; cyclone, hurricane, typhoon
2 a heavy fall of objects ⟨the Indians' arrows were no match for the *storm* of bullets⟩ — see RAIN 2
3 a rapid or overwhelming outpouring of many things at once ⟨the army's spokesperson faced a *storm* of questions from reporters⟩ — see BARRAGE
4 a state of noisy, confused activity ⟨a few minutes of calm before the *storm*, when the store would open its doors on the busiest day of the year⟩ — see COMMOTION
5 a steady falling of water from the sky in significant quantity ⟨the *storm* caused major damage to our barn⟩ — see RAIN 1

6 a sudden intense expression of strong feeling ⟨a *storm* of indignation and demands for his resignation arose when the mayor's dishonesty was exposed⟩ — see OUTBURST 1

7 a violent disturbance (as of the political or social order) ⟨civil wars and other *storms* of unrest swept through the African continent⟩ — see CONVULSION

storm *vb* **1** to express one's anger usually violently ⟨brandishing his knife at his assistant, the chef began *storming* on about the ruined sauces⟩ — see RAGE 1

2 to fall as water in a continuous stream of drops from the clouds ⟨it *storms* so frequently up in the mountains that the peaks are rarely visible from the valley below⟩ — see RAIN 1

3 to take sudden, violent action against ⟨the pirates *stormed* the ship, easily taking the whole crew as their prisoners⟩ — see ATTACK 1

stormy *adj* **1** marked by bursts of destructive force or intense activity ⟨a small nation but one with a long and *stormy* history⟩ — see VIOLENT 1

2 marked by or abounding with rain ⟨*stormy* weather was forecast for the next three days, so we cancelled our camping trip⟩ — see RAINY

3 marked by sudden or violent disturbance ⟨the chef's *stormy* temper has made it difficult to get kitchen help⟩ — see CONVULSIVE

4 marked by turmoil or disturbance especially of natural elements ⟨Neptune has the *stormiest* atmosphere of any planet, with winds of up to 900 miles per hour⟩ — see WILD 3

5 marked by wet and windy conditions ⟨*stormy* seas forced the schooner far away from its intended course⟩ — see FOUL 1

story *n* **1** a work with imaginary characters and events that is shorter and usually less complex than a novel ⟨if you go right to bed, Daddy will read a *story* to you⟩
synonyms narrative, novelette, novella, short story, tale, yarn
related words exemplum, fable, parable; anecdote, joke; fairy tale, folktale, legend, myth, romance; account, annals, chronicle, history, record, report

2 a brief account of something interesting that happened especially to one personally ⟨Grandpa is always telling *stories* about what it was like growing up on a farm⟩
synonyms anecdote, tale, yarn
related words episode, event, happening, incident, occurrence; recital, recitation

3 a report of recent events or facts not previously known ⟨a *story* in the morning paper about plans for a new library⟩ — see NEWS

4 a relating of events usually in the order in which they happened ⟨gave us the whole *story* of the accident⟩ — see ACCOUNT 1

5 a rumor or report of a personal or sensational nature ⟨*stories* going around that the old man had died with thousands of dollars hidden under his mattress⟩ — see TALE 1

6 a statement known by its maker to be untrue and made in order to deceive ⟨she tells *stories* just to get attention, so don't believe that stuff about her father being somebody important⟩ — see LIE

storyteller *n* a person who tells lies ⟨she's the biggest *storyteller* I know, so I don't believe for a minute that she knows how to fly a plane⟩ — see LIAR

stout *adj* **1** able to withstand hardship, strain, or exposure ⟨erected a *stout* wooden fence to keep the wild animals out⟩ — see HARDY 1

2 being compact and broad in build and often short in stature ⟨the wrestler is *stout* in build, so he is frequently underestimated by his opponents⟩ — see STOCKY

3 feeling or displaying no fear by temperament ⟨*stout* souls who boldly ventured forward, not knowing what kinds of danger they faced⟩ — see BRAVE

4 having muscles capable of exerting great physical force ⟨covered wagons drawn by *stout* oxen⟩ — see STRONG 1

5 not showing weakness or uncertainty ⟨a *stout* defender of women's rights in the third world⟩ — see FIRM 1

stouthearted *adj* feeling or displaying no fear by temperament ⟨*stouthearted* men and women who served in the army medical corps⟩ — see BRAVE

stoutly *adv* in a vigorous and forceful manner ⟨a settler *stoutly* defending his right to be on the land⟩ — see HARD 3

stoutness *n* strength of mind to carry on in spite of danger ⟨the *stoutness* shown by the nation's soldiers was never doubted, even by those who opposed the war⟩ — see COURAGE

stow *vb* **1** to place somewhere for safekeeping or ready availability ⟨*stow* the extra life jackets in the chest⟩ — see STORE 1

2 to put (something of future use or value) in a safe or secret place ⟨*stowed* candy bars, which were forbidden at the summer camp, under a board in the cabin's floor⟩ — see HOARD

stowage *n* a building for storing goods ⟨the *stowage* for oats is behind the corn crib⟩ — see STOREHOUSE

straggler *n* someone who moves slowly or more slowly than others ⟨by three o'clock, only a few *stragglers* were still making their painful way to the marathon's finish⟩ — see SLOWPOKE

straight *adj* **1** free from irregularities (as curves, bends, or angles) in course ⟨in the wide, open spaces of the West some rural roads are incredibly *straight*⟩
synonyms linear, right, straightaway, straightforward
related words unbent, uncurled, untwisted; direct, undeviating, unswerving
near antonyms bowed, rounded; entwined, kinked, swirled, turned, turning, twined, twining, twisted, twisting, veering, warped; bending, coiled, coiling, corkscrew, curled, curling, curved, curving, looped, looping, spiral, spiraling (*or* spiralling), winding; meandering, weaving; devious, serpentine, sinuous, zigzag, zigzagging
antonyms crooked

2 conforming to a high standard of morality or virtue ⟨a store owner known and trusted for his *straight* dealings⟩ — see GOOD 2

3 free from added matter ⟨Grandma can't stand prune juice *straight* and usually mixes it with orange juice⟩ — see PURE 1

4 free in expressing one's true feelings and opinions ⟨it's easier to be *straight* with your peers⟩ — see FRANK

5 going straight to the point clearly and firmly ⟨a politician who can never give a *straight* answer to questions about his positions⟩ — see STRAIGHTFORWARD 1

6 not having one's mind affected by alcohol ⟨an alcoholic who's been *straight* for almost eight months now⟩ — see SOBER 1

straight *adv* **1** in a direct line or course ⟨when we got to the airport, we went *straight* to the baggage claim area⟩ — see DIRECTLY 1

2 in an honest and direct manner ⟨just tell it to me *straight*—did I flunk?⟩ — see STRAIGHTFORWARD

straightaway *adj* **1** done or occurring without any noticeable lapse in time ⟨her first novel was a *straightaway* success⟩ — see INSTANTANEOUS

2 free from irregularities (as curves, bends, or angles) in course ⟨the doomed ship was headed on a *straightaway* course in the path of the iceberg⟩ — see STRAIGHT 1

straightaway *adv* without delay ⟨he got to the hospital, and *straightaway* he was admitted and given intravenous fluids⟩ — see IMMEDIATELY

straighten *vb* to cause to follow a line that is without bends or curls ⟨*straighten* that extension cord—it should be just long enough to reach the wall outlet⟩
synonyms unbend, uncurl
related words uncoil, unwind; disentangle, untangle, untwine, untwist
near antonyms arc, bend, bow, hook, round; entwine, kink, swirl, turn, twine, twist; coil, loop, spiral, wind
antonyms bend, crook, curl, curve

straightforward *also* **straightforwards** *adv* in an honest and direct manner ⟨she finally told him *straightforward* that she wasn't interested in a date⟩
synonyms directly, forthrightly, foursquare, plain, plainly, straight, straightforwardly
related words candidly, frankly, honestly, openheartedly, openly, unguardedly, unreservedly; artlessly, earnestly, sincerely; abruptly, bluntly, brusquely, curtly, gruffly, sharply; impolitely, inconsiderately, rudely, tactlessly; truthfully, veraciously
near antonyms long-windedly, verbosely, wordily; civilly, courteously, diplomatically, politely, tactfully; deceitfully, mendaciously, untruthfully; erroneously, fallaciously, falsely, hypocritically, insincerely; ambiguously, circuitously, equivocally, evasively, indirectly

straightforward *adj* **1** going straight to the point clearly and firmly ⟨a *straightforward* account of the football game with no digressions or personal comments⟩
synonyms direct, forthright, foursquare, plain, straight
related words aboveboard, candid, frank, free-spoken, honest, open, openhearted, outspoken, plainspoken, unguarded, unreserved; artless, earnest, sincere; uninhibited, unrestrained; abrupt, bluff, blunt, brusque, curt, gruff, sharp; impolite, inconsiderate, rude, tactless, undiplomatic; true, truthful, veracious
near antonyms circumlocutory, long-winded, prolix, verbose, wordy; inhibited, reserved, restrained; civil, courteous, polite, tactful; deceitful, lying, mendacious, untruthful; erroneous, fallacious, false; ambiguous, equivocal, evasive, misleading; double-dealing, hypocritical, two-faced
antonyms circuitous, indirect, roundabout

2 free from irregularities (as curves, bends, or angles) in course ⟨the missile continued on its *straightforward* path toward the enemy's command post⟩ — see STRAIGHT 1

3 free in expressing one's true feelings and opinions ⟨I want you to be *straightforward* with me and tell me if this dress looks awful⟩ — see FRANK

straightforwardly *adv* in an honest and direct manner ⟨*straightforwardly* yet compassionately, the doctor tells his cancer patients what their odds for survival are⟩ — see STRAIGHTFORWARD

straightforwardness *n* the free expression of one's true feelings and opinions ⟨not all of her voice students appreciate the *straightforwardness* with which she tells

them that they're not going to make it as professional singers⟩ — see CANDOR

straightway *adv* without delay ⟨*straightway*, the decorator told us that the old couch had to go⟩ — see IMMEDIATELY

¹**strain** *n* **1** the line of ancestors from whom a person is descended ⟨descended from a *strain* of Irish seafarers⟩ — see ANCESTRY

2 a rhythmic series of musical tones arranged to give a pleasing effect ⟨the *strain* of an old Irish tune rose up from the revelers downstairs⟩ — see MELODY

3 a very small amount ⟨detected a *strain* of panic in her voice when she asked if the substance was poisonous⟩ — see PARTICLE 1

²**strain** *n* the burden on one's emotional or mental well-being created by demands on one's time ⟨the family's constant moving is putting a real *strain* on the children⟩ — see STRESS 1

strain *vb* **1** to injure by overuse, misuse, or pressure ⟨in order to lift something heavy, squat down and lift with your legs, or you'll *strain* your back⟩
synonyms pull, rack, stretch, wrench
related words fray, tax, weaken; damage, harm, hurt, impair, wound; batter, bruise, tear; cripple, lame, mangle, mutilate

2 to pass through a filter ⟨better *strain* that coffee carefully to get all the grounds out⟩
synonyms filter, screen
related words percolate; refilter

3 to devote serious and sustained effort ⟨I have to *strain* to see your tiny little pimple even in good light⟩ — see LABOR

4 to flow forth slowly through small openings ⟨put the cooked fruit in a cheesecloth bag and let the juice *strain* into a pan⟩ — see EXUDE

5 to subject (a personal quality or faculty) to often excessive stress ⟨*strained* her memory but the name just wouldn't come to her⟩ — see TRY (OUT) 2

strained *adj* lacking in natural or spontaneous quality ⟨I took the complaint manager's *strained* smile to mean I wasn't a welcome sight⟩ — see ARTIFICIAL 1

strait *n* **1** a narrow body of water between two land masses ⟨as the ship headed east through the *Strait* of Gibraltar, Spain was on our left and Africa on our right⟩ — see CHANNEL 2

2 *often* **straits** *pl* a state of great suffering of body or mind ⟨in great *straits* over the loss of her mother's cherished necklace⟩ — see DISTRESS 1

straitlaced *or* **straightlaced** *adj* given to or marked by very conservative standards regarding personal behavior or morals ⟨a very *straitlaced* old lady who believed women shouldn't even show a bare ankle in public⟩
synonyms prim, prudish, puritanical
related words priggish, staid, stuffy; genteel, proper, refined; decent, honest, moral, right, righteous, upright, virtuous
near antonyms liberated, permissive; bad, immoral, improper, indecent, lax, loose, wicked; debauched, degenerate, degraded, depraved, perverted

strand *n* the usually sandy or gravelly land bordering a body of water ⟨the dim lights dotting the *strand* turned out to be the campfires of the shipwreck survivors⟩ — see BEACH

strand *vb* to cause irreparable damage to (a ship) by running aground or sinking ⟨the remains of ships that had been *stranded* by the reef⟩ — see SHIPWRECK

stranded *adj* resting on the shore or bottom of a body of water ⟨*stranded* whales often die because their bodies overheat on the hot beach⟩ — see AGROUND

strange *adj* **1** different from the ordinary in a way that causes curiosity or suspicion ⟨the *strange* smell we'd noticed turned out, unhappily, to be from the dinner our host was making⟩ — see ODD 2

2 excitingly or mysteriously unusual ⟨*strange* fruits from faraway lands⟩ — see EXOTIC

3 not known or experienced before ⟨using public transportation was all very *strange* to a rural girl like her⟩ — see NEW 2

4 noticeably different from what is generally found or experienced ⟨a rather *strange* story about a garden filled with poisonous plants⟩ — see UNUSUAL 1

stranger *n* a person who is not native to or known to a community ⟨the people of the island are quick to make *strangers* feel at home⟩

synonyms foreigner, nonnative, outlander, outsider

related words alien; outcast, pariah; drifter, transient, wanderer

near antonyms buddy, chum, comrade, confidant, crony, familiar, friend, intimate, pal; acquaintance, associate, cohort, colleague, companion, fellow, hearty, hobnobber, mate, partner, peer; adversary, antagonist, enemy, foe, opponent, rival; archenemy, nemesis; citizen, inhabitant, resident

antonyms native

strangle *vb* **1** to be or cause to be killed by lack of breathable air ⟨the gull got tangled in a piece of fishing line on the beach and was *strangled*⟩ — see SMOTHER 1

2 to keep (someone) from breathing by exerting pressure on the windpipe ⟨the boy felt like he was being *strangled* by his tie⟩ — see CHOKE 1

3 to refrain from openly showing or uttering ⟨*strangled* a gasp of surprise upon hearing the news⟩ — see SUPPRESS 2

stratagem *n* a clever often underhanded means to achieve an end ⟨tried various *stratagems* to get the cat into the carrier, but the feisty feline was wise to them all⟩ — see TRICK 1

strategy *n* **1** a method worked out in advance for achieving some objective ⟨a state-wide *strategy* to raise students' achievement test scores over the next three years⟩ — see PLAN 1

2 the means or procedure for doing something ⟨you'll need a better *strategy* than just knocking on doors if you want to sell that many magazines⟩ — see METHOD

stratum *n* one of the segments of society into which people are grouped ⟨in the upper *strata* of London society, no one had even heard of the tragic death of the homeless woman⟩ — see CLASS 1

straw *adj* of a pale yellow or yellowish brown color ⟨the cheese maker told us that the best Parmesan cheeses are *straw*, not white, in color⟩ — see BLOND

stray *adj* lacking a definite plan, purpose, or pattern ⟨*stray* sightings of UFO's, none of which have been rigorously analyzed by scientists⟩ — see RANDOM

streak *n* **1** a line or long narrow section differing in color from the background ⟨the flower has white petals with red *streaks*⟩ — see STRIPE

2 a very small amount ⟨there's just a *streak* of stubbornness in that child⟩ — see PARTICLE 1

streak *vb* to make stripes on ⟨*streaked* his face and body with paint, just as the Native Americans did in preparation for war⟩ — see STRIPE

streaked *adj* having stripes ⟨hair *streaked* with gray⟩ — see STRIPED

stream *vb* **1** to cause to flow in a stream ⟨his eyes were *streaming* tears⟩ — see POUR 1

2 to move in a stream ⟨blood *streaming* out of a wound⟩ — see FLOW 1

3 to move or proceed smoothly and readily ⟨cars *streaming* along the freeway⟩ — see FLOW 2

streamer *n* a piece of cloth with a special design that is used as an emblem or for signaling ⟨knights in armor with *streamers* on their lances⟩ — see FLAG 1

streamlet *n* a natural body of running water smaller than a river ⟨the raging brook of last spring is a mere *streamlet* now that it's July⟩ — see CREEK 1

streamline *vb* to make less complex ⟨*streamline* the work of mailing out fliers by using computer-generated labels⟩ — see SIMPLIFY

street *n* a passage cleared for public vehicular travel ⟨going the wrong way on a one-way *street*⟩ — see WAY 1

strength *n* **1** the ability to exert effort for the accomplishment of a task ⟨the murdered man's wife didn't have the emotional *strength* to face reporters⟩ — see POWER 2

2 the ability to withstand force or stress without being distorted, dislodged, or damaged ⟨I don't think that little stool has the *strength* to hold you⟩ — see STABILITY 1

strengthen *vb* **1** to increase the ability of (as a muscle) to exert physical force ⟨lifting weights every day will eventually *strengthen* your muscles⟩ ⟨the Army makes new recruits run for miles in order to *strengthen* them⟩

synonyms beef (up), fortify, harden, toughen

related words anneal, temper; firm (up), tone (up); energize, invigorate, vitalize; restrengthen

near antonyms cripple, incapacitate, paralyze; damage, harm, hurt, impair, injure; break down, wear out; sap, undermine

antonyms debilitate, enervate, enfeeble, weaken

2 to make able to withstand physical hardship, strain, or exposure ⟨required weeks of physical therapy to *strengthen* his arm enough to pitch for the team again⟩ — see HARDEN 2

3 to make markedly greater in measure or degree ⟨encouraged the boarding school students to *strengthen* their ties with the community by doing public service⟩ — see INTENSIFY

4 to prepare (oneself) mentally or emotionally ⟨*strengthened* herself for the moment she'd have to tell her friend that she had lost the borrowed necklace⟩ — see FORTIFY

strenuous *adj* **1** marked by or uttered with forcefulness ⟨parents who voiced *strenuous* objections to the new textbooks⟩ — see EMPHATIC 1

2 requiring considerable physical or mental effort ⟨a *strenuous* workout on the obstacle course⟩ — see HARD 2

strenuously *adv* **1** in a vigorous and forceful manner ⟨argued *strenuously* in favor of easing the academic requirements for participation in school sports⟩ — see HARD 3

2 with great effort or determination ⟨*strenuously* resisted all efforts to interest him in reading until he discovered science fiction⟩ — see HARD 1

stress *n* **1** the burden on one's emotional or mental well-being created by demands on one's time ⟨with a full-time job and her college courses, the young woman is under a lot of *stress* right now⟩

synonyms pressure, strain, tension

related words load, weight; anxiety, concern, uneasiness, worry; aggravation, anger, annoyance, exasperation, irritation, persecution, trouble

near antonyms comfort, consolation

2 a special notice or importance given to something ⟨our English teacher places great *stress* on learning grammar⟩ — see EMPHASIS 1

stress *vb* to indicate the importance of by giving prominent display ⟨his bad performance only *stressed* what I'd been saying all along⟩ — see EMPHASIZE

stressed–out *adj* suffering from high levels of physical and especially psychological stress ⟨I'm becoming *stressed-out* from trying to keep up with the demands of my school work and the grueling workouts for the football team⟩

synonyms shell-shocked

related words burned-out (*or* burnt-out), exhausted, tired, worn-out; undone, unmanned, unnerved, unstrung; edgy, nervous, tense, uneasy; agitated, disturbed, perturbed, troubled, upset; aggravated, angry, annoyed, exasperated, irritated

near antonyms relaxed, rested

stretch *adj* able to revert to original size and shape after being stretched, squeezed, or twisted ⟨*stretch* fabrics that don't wrinkle or sag⟩ — see ELASTIC 1

stretch *n* **1** a wide space or area ⟨a narrow *stretch* of beach below the cliffs⟩ — see EXPANSE

2 an indefinite but usually short period of time ⟨there was a cardinal at our bird feeder for a short *stretch* last spring⟩ — see WHILE 1

3 the distance or extent between possible extremes ⟨though all the stories take place in 1981–1982, they were written over a *stretch* of years⟩ — see RANGE 3

4 the space or amount of space between two points, lines, surfaces, or objects ⟨the longest *stretch* of the drive without any place to get gas⟩ — see DISTANCE

stretch *vb* **1** to add to the interest of by including made-up details ⟨it was *stretching* the truth to say she'd been in the movies: she was once an extra whose scene was cut in the final version⟩ — see EMBROIDER

2 to injure by overuse, misuse, or pressure ⟨I *stretched* a back muscle, and the pain is killing me⟩ — see STRAIN 1

3 to make longer ⟨the time it would take to fix the car got *stretched* from three hours to two days when the part we needed had to be ordered⟩ — see EXTEND 1

4 to subject (a personal quality or faculty) to often excessive stress ⟨your whining is *stretching* my patience to the limit⟩ — see TRY (OUT) 2

stretch (out) *vb* to arrange the parts of (something) over a wider area ⟨you can't *stretch out* your legs to the point where you're blocking the aisle⟩ — see OPEN 3

stretchable *adj* able to revert to original size and shape after being stretched, squeezed, or twisted ⟨*stretchable* gloves⟩ ⟨*stretchable* bandages⟩ — see ELASTIC 1

stretching *n* **1** the act of making longer ⟨no amount of *stretching* and straining was going to get that tiny shoe on her big foot⟩ — see EXTENSION 1

2 the representation of something in terms that go beyond the facts ⟨your constant *stretching* of the truth is going to get you in trouble someday⟩ — see EXAGGERATION

strew *vb* to cover by or as if by scattering something over or on ⟨sidewalks *strewed* with trash left by the parade watchers⟩ — see SCATTER 2

strict *adj* **1** following an original exactly ⟨not a *strict* translation, because a lot of the humor is in the word-play⟩ — see FAITHFUL 2

2 given to exacting standards of discipline and self-restraint ⟨Mrs. Banfield is *strict* and doesn't let us fool around in gym⟩ — see SEVERE 1

3 not allowing for any exceptions or loosening of standards ⟨on a *strict* diet⟩ ⟨*strict* adherence to the letter of the law⟩ — see RIGID 1

strictly *adv* without any relaxation of standards or precision ⟨*strictly* speaking, Columbus did not discover America—the people living there had long known about it⟩ ⟨the rules must be *strictly* obeyed⟩

synonyms exactly, precisely, rigidly, rigorously

related words carefully, conscientiously, meticulously, scrupulously

antonyms imprecisely, inexactly, loosely

strictness *n* the quality or state of being demanding or unyielding (as in discipline or criticism) ⟨some of the guys are complaining about the coach's *strictness* because if you're late for practice twice, you're off the team⟩ — see SEVERITY

stricture *n* an often public or formal expression of disapproval ⟨the church's *strictures* on the morals and mores of contemporary society⟩ — see CENSURE

stride *vb* to move along with a steady regular step especially in a group ⟨one of the robbers, clutching an empty sack, *strode* into the bank and approached the teller⟩ — see MARCH 1

strife *n* a lack of agreement or harmony ⟨in order to avoid family *strife*, the children spend equal time during the holidays with both of their grandmothers⟩ — see DISCORD

strike *n* **1** a work stoppage by a body of workers intended to force an employer to meet their demands ⟨the nurses will go on *strike* tomorrow unless they're finally given a pay raise⟩

synonyms walkout

related words shutdown, shutoff, sit-down, slowdown; lockout

2 the act or action of setting upon with force or violence ⟨the first *strike* was directed at a munitions warehouse⟩ — see ATTACK 1

3 a feature of someone or something that creates difficulty for achieving success ⟨kids born into poverty already have a *strike* against them⟩ — see DISADVANTAGE

4 a forceful coming together of two things ⟨the *strike* of a hammer against a nail always has a satisfying sound when you're building something yourself⟩ — see IMPACT 1

strike *vb* **1** to refuse to work in order to force an employer to meet demands ⟨the union is calling for its members to *strike* until the mining company agrees to meet safety standards⟩

synonyms walk out

related words knock off, lay off; leave, quit, resign; decamp, depart, exit, go, leave, light out, part

2 to act upon (a person or a person's feelings) so as to cause a response ⟨we were *struck* by the willingness of total strangers to go out of their way to help us⟩ — see ¹AFFECT 1

3 to come into the mind of ⟨it *struck* her later that no one had asked for identification⟩ — see OCCUR (TO)

4 to come into usually forceful contact with something ⟨almost as soon as the lightning *struck*, we heard a loud crack⟩ — see HIT 2

5 to deliver a blow to (someone or something) usually in a strong vigorous manner ⟨the driver of the car behind me applied his brakes too late and *struck* my car from the rear⟩ — see HIT 1

6 to take apart ⟨the stagehands *struck* the sets the morning after the play closed⟩ — see DISASSEMBLE

7 to take sudden, violent action against ⟨a rattlesnake *strikes* its prey with lightning speed⟩ — see ATTACK 1

strike (into) *vb* to take the first step in (a process or course of action) ⟨before you actually *strike into* your speech, you should introduce yourself⟩ — see BEGIN 1

strike (out) *vb* to show (something written) to be no longer valid by drawing a cross over or a line through it ⟨*struck out* all references to indecent matters⟩ — see X (OUT)

striking *adj* **1** likely to attract attention ⟨you'd be amazed what a *striking* difference new wallpaper can make in a room⟩ — see NOTICEABLE

2 very noticeable especially for being incorrect or bad ⟨several *striking* contradictions in her argument⟩ — see EGREGIOUS

string *n* **1** a length of braided, flexible material that is used for tying or connecting things ⟨a piece of *string* won't hold that gate shut if a big wind comes along⟩ — see CORD

2 a series of persons or things arranged one behind another ⟨a *string* of cars stretching as far as we could see⟩ — see LINE 1

3 a series of things linked together ⟨recounted the *string* of events that led to the murder⟩ — see CHAIN 1

string *vb* to put together into a series by means of or as if by means of a thread ⟨the prosecuting attorney *strung* the evidence together so that the accused man really did look guilty⟩ — see THREAD 2

string along *vb* to cause to believe what is untrue ⟨the student succeeded in *stringing* even his teachers *along* with his tales of family hardships⟩ — see DECEIVE

stringent *adj* not allowing for any exceptions or loosening of standards ⟨*stringent* rules against unauthorized persons being in the building⟩ — see RIGID 1

stringy *adj* resembling or having the texture of a mass of strings ⟨*stringy* hair that clearly needed a good washing⟩

synonyms fibrous

related words knotty, ropy, thready; sinewy, wiry

strip *n* a long narrow piece of material ⟨now tear the paper into *strips* and fold them up carefully⟩

synonyms list, ribbon, slip

related words band, bandage, belt, binding, strap, swath, tape

strip *vb* **1** to remove clothing from ⟨the nurse was telling the nervous mother to *strip* her screaming baby down to his diaper for the exam⟩ — see UNDRESS

2 to search through with the intent of committing robbery ⟨the burglars *stripped* the apartment, taking all the electronic equipment⟩ — see RANSACK 1

stripe *n* a line or long narrow section differing in color from the background ⟨the United States flag has seven red *stripes*⟩

synonyms band, bar, streak

related words blaze, crossbar, pinstripe

stripe *vb* to make stripes on ⟨the children carefully *striped* the paper with red and blue paint⟩

synonyms band, bar, streak

related words blaze

striped *adj* having stripes ⟨the zebra is a black-and-white *striped* animal⟩

synonyms barred, streaked

related words corded, tabby

stripling *n* a male person who has not yet reached adulthood ⟨my great grandfather often spoke of those innocent times when he was a *stripling*⟩ — see BOY

stripped *adj* **1** lacking a usual or natural covering ⟨Jack removed the paint, and then Jill sanded the *stripped* furniture and shellacked it⟩ — see NAKED 2

2 lacking or shed of clothing ⟨highway construction workers, *stripped* to the waist, toiled away in the sweltering heat⟩ — see NAKED 1

strive *vb* **1** to devote serious and sustained effort ⟨not only must we *strive* for peace in time of war, we must *strive* mightily to maintain that peace⟩ — see LABOR

2 to make an effort to do ⟨*strove* to bring her D-plus up to at least a B-minus⟩ — see ATTEMPT

stroke *n* a hard strike with a part of the body or an instrument ⟨all it took was one hard *stroke* to knock the ball out of the tree⟩ — see ¹BLOW

stroke *vb* to touch or handle in a tender or loving manner ⟨the young mother gently *stroked* the sleeping child's brow and then leaned over and kissed him⟩ — see FONDLE

stroke (out) *vb* to show (something written) to be no longer valid by drawing a cross over or a line through it ⟨if you make a mistake on the form, just *stroke* it *out*⟩ — see X (OUT)

stroll *n* a relaxed journey on foot for exercise or pleasure ⟨we arrived early and took a *stroll* through the park before dinner⟩ — see WALK

stroller *n* a person who roams about without a fixed route or destination ⟨back in olden days when *strollers* and vagabonds wandered the Scottish countryside⟩ — see NOMAD

strong *adj* **1** having muscles capable of exerting great physical force ⟨I need some *strong* people to help me move furniture⟩

synonyms brawny, muscular, rugged, sinewy, stalwart, stout

related words forceful, mighty, potent, powerful, puissant; able-bodied, athletic, fit, trim; beefy, burly, husky, strapping; masculine, virile; hard, inured, strengthened, sturdy, tough, toughened; energetic, energized, invigorated, lusty, red-blooded, robust, vigorous, vitalized; hale, healthy, hearty, sound

near antonyms challenged, disabled, incapacitated, paralyzed; impotent, powerless; puny, slight, small, unfit, unhealthy

antonyms delicate, feeble, frail, weak, wimpy

2 able to withstand hardship, strain, or exposure ⟨the doctor soon declared her *strong* enough to go home from the hospital⟩ — see HARDY 1

3 having a powerfully stimulating odor or flavor ⟨you don't want to use a *strong* cheese on pizza, so use something mild like mozzarella⟩ — see SHARP 3

4 having an abundance of some characteristic quality (as flavor) ⟨*strong* coffee⟩ ⟨that's mighty *strong* perfume you're wearing⟩ — see FULL-BODIED

5 having an unpleasant smell ⟨the dog's *strong* breath nearly bowled me over⟩ — see MALODOROUS

6 having great power or influence ⟨a time when the country needed a *strong* leader⟩ — see IMPORTANT 2

7 having the power to persuade ⟨made a *strong* argument for starting school an hour later each day⟩ — see COGENT

8 marked by the ability to withstand stress without structural damage or distortion ⟨buildings *strong* enough to withstand an earthquake⟩ — see STABLE 1

9 not showing weakness or uncertainty ⟨a *strong* belief in the value of hard work⟩ — see FIRM 1

strongbox *n* a specially reinforced container to keep valuables safe ⟨keeps her jewelry in a *strongbox*⟩ — see SAFE

stronghold *n* a structure or place from which one can resist attack ⟨the island was the pirates' last *stronghold* in the West Indies⟩ — see FORT

strongly *adv* in a vigorous and forceful manner ⟨argued *strongly* in favor of shortening the length of the students' summer vacation⟩ — see HARD 3

strop *vb* to make sharp or sharper ⟨at the museum they showed us how men used to *strop* razors with leather bands before the days of disposable blades⟩ — see SHARPEN

stropped *adj* having an edge thin enough to cut or pierce something ⟨I was surprised at how sharp the *stropped* razor was⟩ — see SHARP 1

structure *n* **1** something built as a dwelling, shelter, or place for human activity ⟨the only *structure* on the island is an old Spanish fort—or what's left of it⟩ — see BUILDING
2 something put together by arranging or connecting an array of parts ⟨the Egyptian pyramids are among the most remarkable *structures* ever built⟩ — see CONSTRUCTION 1
3 the arrangement of parts that gives something its basic form ⟨the basic *structure* of all those tract houses is the same: basically, a box⟩ — see FRAME 1

struggle *n* **1** a forceful effort to reach a goal or objective ⟨a physically challenged child's determined *struggle* to make straight A's in school⟩
synonyms battle, fight, fray, scrabble
related words effort, exertion, labor, pains, trouble, work; drudgery, grind, sweat, toil, travail; combat, conflict, contest, strife, tussle, war, warfare; attempt, endeavor, essay, try
2 a physical dispute between opposing individuals or groups ⟨there was a *struggle* between the armed robber and the shopkeeper, and the gun went off⟩ — see FIGHT 1
3 an earnest effort for superiority or victory over another ⟨her staunchest supporters in her *struggle* for the office⟩ — see CONTEST 1

struggle *vb* to devote serious and sustained effort ⟨*struggled* to make ends meet⟩ — see LABOR

strut *vb* **1** to walk with exaggerated arm and leg movements ⟨the toy soldiers in the Christmas pageant *strutted* stiffly across the stage⟩
synonyms prance, stalk, swagger
related words flounce, mince, traipse; pussyfoot, tiptoe; parade, promenade; pad, step, tread; pace, stride; lumber, lurch, pound, shamble, shuffle, stagger
2 to present so as to invite notice or attention ⟨*strutting* his blue ribbon for all to see⟩ — see SHOW 1

stub *n* an unused or unwanted piece or item typically of small size or value ⟨an ashtray full of cigarette *stubs*⟩ ⟨ticket *stubs*⟩ — see ¹SCRAP 1

stubborn *adj* sticking to an opinion, purpose, or course of action in spite of reason, arguments, or persuasion ⟨he's just being *stubborn*, refusing even to try the new toothpaste⟩ — see OBSTINATE

stubbornness *n* a steadfast adherence to an opinion, purpose, or course of action ⟨between my *stubbornness* and my brother's, it's amazing when we come to an agreement⟩ — see OBSTINACY

stubby *adj* being compact and broad in build and often short in stature ⟨seven *stubby* little fellows carried the sleeping Snow White back to their home in a cave⟩ — see STOCKY

stuck *adj* firmly positioned in place and difficult to dislodge ⟨the car was hopelessly *stuck* in the mud⟩ — see TIGHT 2

stuck–up *adj* having too high an opinion of oneself ⟨thought that the kids at his new school were snobbish and *stuck-up*⟩ — see CONCEITED

student *n* one who attends a school ⟨a straight-A *student* at the local high school⟩
synonyms pupil, scholar
related words schoolboy, schoolchild, schoolgirl; schoolfellow, schoolmate; collegian, postgraduate, undergraduate; freshman, junior, senior, sophomore; underclassman, upperclassman

studied *adj* decided on as a result of careful thought ⟨a *studied* move by the company that was designed to put the competition out of business⟩ — see DELIBERATE 1

study *n* **1** a systematic search for the truth or facts about something ⟨conducted a *study* to determine the sleep needs of adolescents⟩ — see INQUIRY 1
2 the state of being lost in thought ⟨found her staring at the fire in a deep *study*⟩ — see REVERIE

study *vb* **1** to use the mind to acquire knowledge ⟨you'll have to *study* hard and learn all about the Revolutionary War in order to pass the history test⟩
synonyms bone (up)
related words cram; analyze, deduce, find out; learn, read; research, restudy
phrases go over, go through
2 to commit to memory ⟨having carefully *studied* the document, he could repeat what it said exactly⟩ — see MEMORIZE
3 to give serious and careful thought to ⟨scientists who *study* the origin of the universe⟩ — see PONDER

stuff *n* **1** a skill, an ability, or knowledge that makes a person able to do a particular job ⟨a guy who has the *stuff* it takes to be team captain⟩ — see QUALIFICATION 1
2 the basic elements from which something can be developed ⟨reading, writing, and arithmetic—the *stuff* of an education⟩ — see MAKING
3 the quality or qualities that make a thing what it is ⟨the real *stuff* of nobility of character isn't riches or a title, but honor and integrity⟩ — see ESSENCE

stuff *vb* **1** to close up so that no empty spaces remain ⟨*stuffed* the box with tissue paper so the contents wouldn't rattle around⟩ — see FILL 2
2 to fill with food to capacity ⟨kids who *stuff* themselves with junk food after school and then don't have any room for supper⟩ — see GORGE 1
3 to fit (something) into a tight space ⟨*stuffed* all the kids into the back of the car⟩ — see CROWD 1
4 to prevent passage through ⟨I can't smell anything, as my nose is all *stuffed*⟩ — see CLOG 1
5 to put into (something) as much as can be held or contained ⟨*stuffed* a whole suitcase with gifts for her relatives in Mexico⟩ — see FILL 1

stuffed *adj* **1** containing or seeming to contain the greatest quantity or number possible ⟨had never seen shelves so *stuffed* with books⟩ — see FULL 1
2 having one's appetite completely satisfied ⟨we were still *stuffed* from our huge breakfast and didn't want lunch⟩ — see FULL 3

stuffer *n* one who eats greedily or too much ⟨the different kinds of hot dog eaters: the *stuffer* who downs it in two bites; the nibbler; the mustard loader⟩ — see GLUTTON

stuffing *n* soft material that is used to fill the hollow parts of something ⟨never heard of using goose down as *stuffing* for comforters until she moved to a cold climate⟩ — see FILLING

stuffy *adj* **1** lacking fresh air ⟨the house was so *stuffy* after being closed up for a month⟩
synonyms breathless, close, stifling, suffocating
related words airless, unventilated; heavy, oppressive, thick
near antonyms bracing, brisk, invigorating, refreshed, sweet; ventilated
antonyms airy, breezy
2 causing weariness, restlessness, or lack of interest ⟨nothing *stuffy* about this science museum—it's all interactive and fun⟩ — see BORING

stumble *n* **1** an unintentional departure from truth or accuracy ⟨was his remark a regrettable *stumble*, or was it made with artful intention?⟩ — see ERROR 1
2 the act of going down from an upright position suddenly and involuntarily ⟨has bones so brittle that a minor *stumble* could result in a serious break⟩ — see FALL 1

stumble *vb* **1** to go down from an upright position suddenly and involuntarily ⟨the bride *stumbled* on the altar steps and landed smack in the arms of the minister⟩ — see FALL 1
2 to make progress in a clumsy, struggling manner ⟨*stumbled* twice while she was reciting the "Gettysburg Address"⟩ — see FLOUNDER 1
3 to move heavily or clumsily ⟨they left the path and wearily *stumbled* through the tangled undergrowth⟩ — see LUMBER 1

stumble (on *or* onto) *vb* to come upon unexpectedly or by chance ⟨*stumbled on* some old family photos when she was cleaning out a drawer⟩ — see HAPPEN (ON *or* UPON)

stumble (upon) *vb* to come upon face-to-face or as if face-to-face ⟨*stumbled upon* an old acquaintance at the airport⟩ — see MEET 1

stumbling block *n* something that makes progress or movement more difficult ⟨the only *stumbling block* to our move across the country was finding someone to take our cats⟩ — see ENCUMBRANCE

stump *vb* **1** to move heavily or clumsily ⟨the seemingly endless parade finally ended, and the drummers and tuba players *stumped* wearily to their buses⟩ — see LUMBER 1
2 to invite (someone) to take part in a contest or to perform a feat ⟨when my grandfather was a kid, he and his friends would *stump* each other to dive into the local quarry⟩ — see CHALLENGE 2

stumpy *adj* being compact and broad in build and often short in stature ⟨*stumpy* penguins become agile swimmers the moment they hit the water⟩ — see STOCKY

stun *vb* **1** to make senseless or dizzy by a blow ⟨a powerful uppercut to the jaw *stunned* the boxer and sent him crashing to the canvas⟩
synonyms daze
related words deaden, knock out, paralyze; benumb, numb, stupefy; bowl (over), knock (down)
phrases knock for a loop
2 to make a strong impression on (someone) with something unexpected ⟨the news of President Kennedy's assassination *stunned* the nation⟩ — see SURPRISE 1

stunned *adj* **1** affected with sudden and great wonder or surprise ⟨the billionaire's relatives sat there, *stunned*, after the lawyer had finished reading the will⟩ — see THUNDERSTRUCK
2 suffering from mental confusion ⟨the loud blast left her momentarily *stunned*⟩ — see DIZZY 2

stunner *n* **1** a lovely woman ⟨not only is she smart, she's a real *stunner*⟩ — see BEAUTY 2
2 something that makes a strong impression because it is so unexpected ⟨Jason's grades are vastly better than last year's, but the real *stunner* is the jump from 62 to 92 in his math grade⟩ — see SURPRISE 1

stunning *adj* **1** causing a strong emotional reaction because unexpected ⟨we suffered a *stunning* defeat at the hands of the bottom-ranked team in the division⟩ — see SURPRISING 1
2 causing wonder or astonishment ⟨the *stunning* beauty of the star-filled sky on a cloudless night⟩ — see MARVELOUS 1
3 very pleasing to look at ⟨how *stunning* the performers look in their costumes⟩ — see BEAUTIFUL

stunt *n* an act of notable skill, strength, or cleverness ⟨performs mental *stunts*, such as pronouncing words backwards as soon as you say them⟩ — see FEAT 1

stunt *vb* to hold back the normal growth of ⟨unfortunately, an unusually dry summer seems to have permanently *stunted* the tree⟩
synonyms dwarf, suppress
related words arrest, catch, check, halt, hold up, stall, stay, still, stop; balk, block, hold back, impede, obstruct, stem
near antonyms advance, boost, encourage, forward, promote

stupefied *adj* **1** affected with sudden and great wonder or surprise ⟨gazed, *stupefied*, as humanoids with large heads emerged from the hovering UFO⟩ — see THUNDERSTRUCK
2 suffering from mental confusion ⟨when the plane began to nose-dive, the *stupefied* passengers were unsure how to act⟩ — see DIZZY 2

stupefy *vb* to make a strong impression on (someone) with something unexpected ⟨*stupefied* by the ruling that he could not compete because his missed the qualifying age by two days⟩ — see SURPRISE 1

stupefying *adj* causing a strong emotional reaction because unexpected ⟨the *stupefying* figures for poverty and starvation in some parts of the third world⟩ — see SURPRISING 1

stupendous *adj* causing wonder or astonishment ⟨the *stupendous* engineering feats of the ancient Romans⟩ — see MARVELOUS 1

stupendously *adv* to a large extent or degree ⟨a *stupendously* successful Broadway debut⟩ — see GREATLY 2

stupendousness *n* impressiveness of beauty on a large scale ⟨nothing matched the Palace of Versailles for stunning *stupendousness* when it was built⟩ — see MAGNIFICENCE

stupid *adj* **1** not having or showing an ability to absorb ideas readily ⟨it's not nice to constantly call your brother *stupid* and ugly⟩ ⟨don't ask *stupid* questions⟩
synonyms brainless, dense, doltish, dopey, dorky [*slang*], dull, dumb, fatuous, half-witted, mindless, oafish, obtuse, senseless, simple, slow, thick, thickheaded, unintelligent, vacuous, weak-minded, witless
related words feebleminded, retarded, simpleminded; foolish, idiotic, imbecile, imbecilic, moronic; ignorant, illiterate, lowbrow, uneducated, uninformed, untaught, unthinking; absurd, asinine, balmy, cockeyed, crazy, cuckoo, daffy, daft, dotty, harebrained, insane, kooky, loony (*also* looney), lunatic, mad, nonsensical, nutty, preposterous, sappy, screwball, silly, unwise, wacky, zany; fallacious, illogical, invalid, irrational, unreasonable

near antonyms ingenious, resourceful; acute, astute, discerning, insightful, keen, knowing, perceptive, perspicacious, sagacious, sage, sapient, savvy, wise; cerebral, erudite, highbrow, intellectual, knowledgeable, learned, literate, scholarly, thinking, well-read; educated, informed, schooled, skilled, trained; crafty, cunning, foxy, shrewd, wily; judicious, prudent, sane, sensible, sound; logical, rational, reasonable, valid
antonyms apt, brainy, bright, brilliant, clever, intelligent, keen, nimble, quick, quick-witted, sharp, sharp-witted, smart
2 causing weariness, restlessness, or lack of interest ⟨I can't believe we sat through the whole *stupid* movie⟩ — see BORING
3 showing or marked by a lack of good sense or judgment ⟨not liking the captain is a *stupid* reason to quit the team⟩ — see FOOLISH 1
stupidity *n* **1** the quality or state of lacking intelligence or quickness of mind ⟨the *stupidity* of the dialogue between the two romantic leads had movie audiences giggling uncontrollably⟩
synonyms brainlessness, denseness, density, doltishness, dopiness, dullness (*also* dulness), dumbness, fatuity, foolishness, mindlessness, oafishness, obtuseness, senselessness, simpleness, slowness, stupidness, vacuity, witlessness
related words absurdity, asininity, balminess, craziness, daftness, folly, idiocy, inanity, insanity, lunacy, madness, nonsensicalness, nuttiness, preposterousness, silliness, simplicity, wackiness, zaniness; fallacy, irrationality, unreasonableness
near antonyms acumen, alertness, astuteness, discernment, insight, judgment (*or* judgement), perception, perspicacity; sagacity, sageness, sapience, wisdom, wit; logicalness, rationality, reasonableness, soundness, validity
antonyms braininess, brightness, brilliance, cleverness, intelligence, keenness, quickness, quick-wittedness, sharpness, smartness
2 a foolish act or idea ⟨the various *stupidities* of the company's owners were bound to result in bankruptcy⟩ — see FOLLY 1
3 language, behavior, or ideas that are absurd and contrary to good sense ⟨leaving her bags unguarded inside the airport terminal was nothing but *stupidity* on her part⟩ — see NONSENSE 1
stupidness *n* the quality or state of lacking intelligence or quickness of mind ⟨I'm not sure if he leaves his front door unlocked from carelessness or just plain *stupidness*⟩ — see STUPIDITY 1
sturdily *adv* in a vigorous and forceful manner ⟨no longer so *sturdily* maintained his innocence when his alibi proved false⟩ — see HARD 3
sturdiness *n* the ability to withstand force or stress without being distorted, dislodged, or damaged ⟨demonstrated the suitcase's *sturdiness* by dropping it from a third-floor window⟩ — see STABILITY 1
sturdy *adj* **1** able to withstand hardship, strain, or exposure ⟨it took a *sturdy* person to endure the life of a pioneer⟩ — see HARDY 1
2 marked by the ability to withstand stress without structural damage or distortion ⟨wear *sturdy* boots because we will be going over sharp rocks and uneven terrain⟩ — see STABLE 1
3 not showing weakness or uncertainty ⟨you'll need a *sturdy* grasp of the concepts of algebra before you can take calculus⟩ — see FIRM 1

style *n* **1** a distinctive way of putting ideas into words ⟨I correctly identified the quotation because I recognized Mark Twain's inimitable *style*⟩
synonyms fashion, locution, manner, mode, phraseology, tone, vein
related words delivery, elocution; archaism, colloquialism, regionalism; acceptation, connotation, denotation, idiom
2 the means or procedure for doing something ⟨unfortunately, the club president's usual *style* was to make plans without asking anyone's advice or approval⟩ — see METHOD
3 a practice or interest that is very popular for a short time ⟨parents who were very relieved when the *style* for having one's nose pierced faded⟩ — see FAD
style *vb* to give a name to ⟨although nowadays he's often *styled* a biologist, he's probably better thought of as a classic 19th-century naturalist⟩ — see NAME 1
styleless *adj* marked by an obvious lack of style or good taste ⟨forced to wear a *styleless* uniform for her restaurant job, she loves to dress up on weekends⟩ — see TACKY 1
stylish *adj* being in the latest or current fashion ⟨a pretty, *stylish* dress⟩
synonyms à la mode (*also* a la mode), chic, fashionable, in, modish, sharp, smart, snappy
related words dapper, dashing, natty, rakish, spiffy, spruce; posh, ritzy, swank (*or* swanky); elegant, graceful, handsome, majestic, refined, sophisticated, stately, tasteful, understated; dandyish, dudish, foppish; classic, exquisite, quiet, restrained, simple; affected, grandiose, pretentious
near antonyms tacky, unattractive, unbecoming; graceless, inelegant, tasteless, unhandsome; frowsy (*or* frowzy), sloppy, slovenly, unkempt, untidy; disheveled (*or* dishevelled), messy, mussy, rumpled, wrinkled; shabby, sleazy
antonyms dowdy, outmoded, styleless, unfashionable, unstylish
suasion *n* the act of reasoning or pleading with someone to accept a belief or course of action ⟨a defense lawyer uses not only legal arguments but also moral *suasion* to appeal to a jury's sense of right and wrong⟩ — see PERSUASION 1
suave *adj* having or showing very polished and worldly manners ⟨the *suave* gentleman was a great favorite of the elegant ladies who attended parties at the embassy⟩
synonyms debonair, smooth, sophisticated, urbane
related words glib, slick, unctuous; civilized, cultivated, cultured, graceful, poised, polished, refined; cosmopolitan, smart, worldly-wise; experienced, knowing, practiced (*or* practised), schooled, seasoned; amiable, appealing, attractive; assured, calm, collected, composed, confident, cool, placid, secure, self-assured, self-confident, self-possessed, serene, tranquil, undisturbed, unperturbed
near antonyms awkward, clumsy, gauche, graceless, stiff, stilted, uncomfortable, uneasy, ungraceful, wooden; callow, green, inexperienced, raw; parochial, provincial, roughhewn, rustic; inelegant, philistine, uncivilized, uncultured, unrefined; unsophisticated, unworldly; gawky, lubberly, stodgy, ungainly; diffident, insecure
antonyms boorish, churlish, clownish, loutish, uncouth
¹sub *n* a large sandwich on a long split roll ⟨we shared a tuna *sub* at lunch⟩ — see SUBMARINE

²**sub** *n* a person or thing that takes the place of another ⟨we had a *sub* in English today, so we didn't get our test results back⟩ — see SUBSTITUTE

sub *vb* to serve as a replacement usually for a time only ⟨Mrs. Andrews is *subbing* today for Mr. O'Rourke, but he's expected to be back in the classroom tomorrow⟩ — see COVER 1

subdue *vb* **1** to achieve a victory over ⟨*subdued* her fear of the dark by joining a club for spelunkers⟩ — see BEAT 2
2 to bring under one's control by force of arms ⟨*subdued* the rebels and sent their leaders to the gallows⟩ — see CONQUER 1
3 to put a stop to (something) by the use of force ⟨labored through the night to *subdue* the river's rising waters by building a wall of sandbags around their property⟩ — see QUELL 1

subdued *adj* not excessively showy ⟨the wedding was a *subdued* affair, with only close family and friends attending⟩ — see QUIET 2

subduer *n* one that defeats an enemy or opponent ⟨time and again Native Americans made treaties with the whites, only to see their *subduers* break those treaties⟩ — see VICTOR 1

subduing *n* the act or process of bringing someone or something under one's control ⟨the *subduing* of the nomadic tribes was accomplished, not by force of arms, but by a drought that eventually destroyed their grazing lands⟩ — see CONQUEST

subject *n* **1** a major object of interest or concern (as in a discussion or artistic composition) ⟨the *subject* of our discussion switched from who would be the next president to who was the greatest president in the nation's history⟩ — see MATTER 1
2 a person who owes allegiance to a government and is protected by it ⟨because of the tense situation in that country, British *subjects* were advised to return home as soon as possible⟩ — see CITIZEN 1

subject *vb* to bring under one's control by force of arms ⟨Attila the Hun *subjected* most of Europe to his barbaric pillage⟩ — see CONQUER 1

subject (to) *adj* **1** determined by something else ⟨your extra piano lesson on Tuesdays is *subject to* the availability of the music room⟩ — see DEPENDENT 2
2 being in a situation where one is likely to meet with harm ⟨this type of wound is highly *subject to* infection⟩ — see LIABLE 1

subjecting *n* the act or process of bringing someone or something under one's control ⟨a time when the *subjecting* of Asian and African peoples to European rule was regarded as acceptable⟩ — see CONQUEST

subjection *n* the act or process of bringing someone or something under one's control ⟨a holy man for whom the *subjection* of earthly desires is the path to spiritual perfection⟩ — see CONQUEST

subjugate *vb* to bring under one's control by force of arms ⟨explorers who *subjugated* the natives in the name of religion⟩ — see CONQUER 1

subjugating *n* the act or process of bringing someone or something under one's control ⟨a military occupation that was seen by the people as just another *subjugating* by an outside power⟩ — see CONQUEST

subjugation *n* the act or process of bringing someone or something under one's control ⟨the *subjugation* of much of Europe by Napoleon⟩ — see CONQUEST

sublime *adj* **1** causing wonder or astonishment ⟨the *sublime* beauty of the firmament⟩ — see MARVELOUS 1
2 having, characterized by, or arising from a dignified and generous nature ⟨the *sublime* virtue of having given all one's worldly goods to the poor⟩ — see NOBLE 2

sublimeness *n* impressiveness of beauty on a large scale ⟨the awe-inspiring *sublimeness* of Yosemite Valley⟩ — see MAGNIFICENCE

submarine *adj* living, lying, or occurring below the surface of the water ⟨the *submarine* fossils that are to be found in coral reefs⟩ — see UNDERWATER

submarine *n* a large sandwich on a long split roll ⟨always orders a roast beef *submarine* with the works⟩
synonyms grinder, hero, hoagie, Italian sandwich, po'boy (*also* poor boy), sub

submerge *vb* **1** to cover or become filled with a flood ⟨*submerged* by requests to babysit after she received a write-up in the local newspaper⟩ — see FLOOD
2 to sink or push (something) briefly into or as if into a liquid ⟨*submerge* the tomatoes in boiling hot water for a few seconds and they will be easier to peel⟩ — see DIP 1

submerged *adj* living, lying, or occurring below the surface of the water ⟨*submerged* local roadways made for hazardous driving⟩ — see UNDERWATER

submerse *vb* **1** to cover or become filled with a flood ⟨a week of nonstop rain that *submersed* the corn fields and delayed planting⟩ — see FLOOD
2 to sink or push (something) briefly into or as if into a liquid ⟨those hardy souls who daily *submerse* themselves in icy cold water for its invigorating effect⟩ — see DIP 1

submission *n* **1** a bending to the authority or control of another ⟨not given to unquestioning *submission*, he often came in conflict with his superiors⟩ — see OBEDIENCE 1
2 the usually forced yielding of one's person or possessions to the control of another ⟨the judge ordered the *submission* of all the company's records to the prosecutors⟩ — see SURRENDER

submissive *adj* readily giving in to the command or authority of another ⟨it's not in her nature to be *submissive*⟩ — see OBEDIENT

submissively *adv* in a manner showing no signs of pride or self-assertion ⟨all of the extended family was expected to be *submissively* amenable to the matriarch's wishes⟩ — see LOWLY

submissiveness *n* a readiness or willingness to yield to the wishes of others ⟨his uncharacteristic *submissiveness* to the doctor's advice must mean he's really sick⟩ — see COMPLIANCE 1

submit *vb* **1** to cease resistance (as to another's arguments, demands, or control) ⟨in the end he *submitted* and agreed to take that awful-tasting medicine⟩ — see YIELD 3
2 to give up and cease resistance (as to a liking, temptation, or habit) ⟨refusing to *submit* to sleep, she stayed by her son's hospital bed the whole night⟩ — see YIELD 1
3 to yield to the control or power of enemy forces ⟨the fort's commander received orders not to *submit* under any circumstances, as reinforcements were on the way⟩ — see FALL 2

submitting *n* the usually forced yielding of one's person or possessions to the control of another ⟨his *submitting* of his own desires to the will of God⟩ — see SURRENDER

subordinate *adj* having not so great importance or rank as another ⟨his contention is that environment plays a *subordinate* role to heredity in determining what we become⟩ — see LESSER

subordinate *n* one who is of lower rank and typically under the authority of another ⟨*subordinates* do most of the actual creation of the famous designer's clothing designs⟩ — see UNDERLING

subordination *n* a bending to the authority or control of another ⟨an oligarchy requires *subordination* by the masses to the will of a tiny elite⟩ — see OBEDIENCE 1

subpoena *n* a written notice ordering a person to appear in court ⟨received a *subpoena* to appear as a witness for the prosecution⟩ — see SUMMONS

subscribe (to) *vb* to have a favorable opinion of ⟨I don't *subscribe to* the belief that some people are predestined to eternal happiness and others to eternal punishment⟩ — see APPROVE (OF)

subsequent *adj* being, occurring, or carried out at a time after something else ⟨I'll do the first problem as an example, but all *subsequent* efforts must be done on your own⟩
synonyms after, ensuing, later, posterior
related words behind, belated, delayed, late, slow; eventual, last, ultimate; following
near antonyms advance, early, premature
antonyms antecedent, anterior, fore, precedent, preceding, previous, prior

subsequently *adv* following in time or place ⟨*subsequently* found the missing glove⟩ — see AFTER

subside *vb* to grow less in scope or intensity especially gradually ⟨as the noise of the siren *subsided*, I was able to fall back to sleep⟩ — see DECREASE 2

subsidize *vb* 1 to furnish (as an institution) with a regular source of income ⟨the museum is annually *subsidized* by funds from several major corporations⟩ — see ENDOW 2
2 to provide money for ⟨housing for the elderly that was *subsidized* by the federal government⟩ — see FINANCE 1

subsidy *n* a sum of money allotted for a specific use by official or formal action ⟨government *subsidies* for farmers in case of crop failure⟩ — see APPROPRIATION

subsist *vb* to have life ⟨a love that was as great as any that ever did *subsist*⟩ — see BE 1

subsistence *n* 1 the fact of being or of being real ⟨believes in the *subsistence* of a soul as a separate entity from the body⟩ — see EXISTENCE
2 uninterrupted or lasting existence ⟨the *subsistence* of the patient's infection, even after the use of antibiotics, had the doctors puzzled⟩ — see CONTINUATION

substance *n* 1 the basic elements from which something can be developed ⟨many thought that the mayor's speech lacked *substance* because specific proposals for solving the city's problems were few⟩ — see MAKING
2 the quality or qualities that make a thing what it is ⟨tireless caring and nurturing that was the very *substance* of maternal love⟩ — see ESSENCE
3 the total of one's money and property ⟨measure the worth of a person not by his earthly *substance* but by his good deeds⟩ — see WEALTH 1
4 one that has a real and independent existence ⟨the question of whether the soul is a *substance* entirely independent of the body⟩ — see ENTITY

substance abuser *n* a person who regularly uses drugs especially illegally ⟨arranges for former *substance abusers* to give talks to school groups⟩ — see DOPER

substandard *adj* falling short of a standard ⟨a teacher who rejects *substandard* work without hesitation⟩ — see BAD 1

substantial *adj* 1 having great meaning or lasting effect ⟨*substantial* changes to the school dress code that made a lot of people unhappy⟩ — see IMPORTANT 1
2 of a size greater than average of its kind ⟨the amount he inherited was quite *substantial*, so he quit his job and set out to see the world⟩ — see LARGE
3 relating to or composed of matter ⟨the Land of Oz turned out to be a world of dreams, even less *substantial* than a rainbow⟩ — see MATERIAL 1
4 sufficiently large in size, amount, or number to merit attention ⟨there's been a *substantial* increase in attendance at girls' volleyball games ever since the start of their winning streak⟩ — see CONSIDERABLE 1

substantiality *n* the quality or state of being large in size ⟨their donation may not be impressive in its *substantiality*, but it did come from the heart, and that is what is really important⟩ — see LARGENESS

substantially *adv* for the most part ⟨the *Little House* books are *substantially* based on the memories of Laura Ingalls Wilder⟩ — see CHIEFLY

substantiate *vb* 1 to gain full recognition or acceptance of ⟨*substantiated* his claim to local mountaineering fame with a photo of himself on the summit of Mount McKinley⟩ — see ESTABLISH 1
2 to give evidence or testimony to the truth or factualness of ⟨Mr. MacGregor couldn't *substantiate* that it was Peter, and not some other rabbit, in the cabbage patch⟩ — see CONFIRM
3 to represent in visible form ⟨the artist's intense feelings are *substantiated* by his paintings' bold colors and broad brush strokes⟩ — see EMBODY 2
4 to show the existence or truth of by evidence ⟨*substantiate* the need for a tuition increase with some concrete figures⟩ — see PROVE 1

substantiating *adj* serving to give support to the truth or factualness of something ⟨without some *substantiating* evidence, such as a stub from a bus ticket, who's going to believe you went to New York last weekend?⟩ — see CORROBORATIVE

substantiation *n* something presented in support of the truth or accuracy of a claim ⟨the signature of a witness provides *substantiation* that a person's will is genuine⟩ — see PROOF

substitute *adj* 1 being such in appearance only and made with or manufactured from usually cheaper materials ⟨*substitute* wools that supposedly have the look and feel of cashmere⟩ — see IMITATION
2 taking the place of one that came before ⟨had to find *substitute* transportation during the bus strike⟩ — see NEW 1

substitute *n* a person or thing that takes the place of another ⟨you'll be getting a *substitute* until your regular teacher is feeling better⟩ ⟨if you like, you can use nuts as a *substitute* for coconut in that recipe⟩
synonyms backup, pinch hitter, relief, replacement, reserve, stand-in, sub
related words alternate, understudy; apology, makeshift, stopgap; agent, attorney, commissary, delegate, deputy, envoy, factor, procurator, proxy, representative, surrogate; assistant, second

substitute *vb* 1 to give up (something) and take something else in return ⟨can I *substitute* coleslaw for potato salad if I order the chicken plate?⟩ — see CHANGE 3
2 to serve as a replacement usually for a time only ⟨*substituting* for the talk show host while she is on vacation⟩ — see COVER 1

3 to take the place of ⟨"John Doe," "Jane Doe," and "Baby Doe" *substituted* the real names of the parties involved to preserve their privacy⟩ — see REPLACE 1

subterfuge *n* the use of clever underhanded actions to achieve an end ⟨propagandists who use a kind of photographic *subterfuge*, superimposing one image on another to create a false "reality"⟩ — see TRICKERY

subtle *adj* **1** clever at attaining one's ends by indirect and often deceptive means ⟨used *subtle* methods of persuasion⟩ — see ARTFUL 1

2 made or done with extreme care and accuracy ⟨the *subtle* strokes of the painter's brush⟩ — see FINE 2

3 satisfying or pleasing because of fineness or mildness ⟨a *subtle* suggestion of the Near East in the soup's flavoring⟩ — see DELICATE 1

subtleness *n* skill in achieving one's ends through indirect, subtle, or underhanded means ⟨the *subtleness* with which the boutique owner convinces you that you have to have that outrageously priced article of clothing⟩ — see CUNNING 1

subtlety *n* skill in achieving one's ends through indirect, subtle, or underhanded means ⟨we appreciated the *subtlety* with which our host indicated that it was time to leave: he volunteered to pack us a little lunch for the road⟩ — see CUNNING 1

subtract *vb* to take away (an amount or number) from a total ⟨if you *subtract* 10 from 23, you get 13⟩ ⟨you can *subtract* the time you spent daydreaming from your total homework time⟩

synonyms deduct, take off

related words decrease, diminish, discount, downsize, lessen, lower, reduce; abbreviate, abridge, clip, crop, curtail, cut, cut back, cut down, dock, pare, prune, retrench, shorten, slash, trim, truncate, whittle

near antonyms adjoin, annex, append, tack (on); add (to), complement, supplement; enhance, heighten, intensify; aggrandize, amplify, augment, boost, enlarge, escalate, expand, increase, raise

antonyms add

subtraction *n* the act or an instance of taking away from a total ⟨the dog was responsible for the unexplained *subtraction* in the number of potato chips on my sister's plate⟩

synonyms deduction

related words discount; abatement, decline, decrement, diminishment, diminution, drop, fall, loss, reduction, shrinkage; curtailment, cut, cutback

near antonyms boost, enlargement, gain, increase, increment, raise, rise; accretion, accrual, accumulation, addendum, appendix, supplement

antonyms addition

suburbia *n* the area around a city ⟨the migration of families to *suburbia* and the resulting disintegration of inner-city neighborhoods⟩ — see ENVIRONS 1

subvert *vb* to lower in character or dignity ⟨by insisting that she pay me for helping her, she *subverted* my noble desire to do a good deed without reward⟩ — see DEBASE 1

succeed *vb* **1** to turn out as planned or desired ⟨the advertising campaign that finally *succeeded* used humor to sell the product⟩

synonyms click, deliver, go over, pan out, work out

related words catch on; flourish, prosper, thrive

phrases catch fire

near antonyms languish; flounder, struggle; decline, slip, slump, wane

antonyms collapse, fail, flop, flunk, fold, wash out

2 to reach a desired level of accomplishment ⟨if you want to *succeed* in show business, you have to feel comfortable in front of an audience⟩

synonyms flourish, prosper, thrive

related words prevail, triumph, win

phrases get ahead, make good, make it

near antonyms flounder, struggle

antonyms fail

3 to come after in time ⟨only the results on election day will tell who will *succeed* the current president⟩ — see FOLLOW 1

succeeding *adj* **1** being the one that comes immediately after another ⟨the couple purchased some land, and in the course of the *succeeding* year built a house on it⟩ — see NEXT

2 following one after another without others coming in between ⟨that land remained in the family for five *succeeding* generations⟩ — see CONSECUTIVE

success *n* **1** a person or thing that is successful ⟨their homemade jellies have been such a *success* that they are now distributed nationwide⟩ — see HIT 1

2 a successful result brought about by hard work ⟨a long list of *successes* that the retiring president of the college can point to with pride⟩ — see ACCOMPLISHMENT 1

successful *adj* **1** having attained a desired end or state of good fortune ⟨the family runs several *successful* restaurants⟩

synonyms flourishing, going, palmy, prosperous, thriving, triumphant

related words coming, promising; booming, growing, roaring, robust

near antonyms futureless, hopeless, inauspicious, nogood; collapsing, failing, flopping, flunking, folding, washing-out; declining, slipping, slumping, waning; bankrupt, destroyed, ruined, wrecked

antonyms failed, unsuccessful

2 marked by vigorous growth and well-being especially economically ⟨sold their *successful* dry-cleaning business and retired to Hawaii⟩ — see PROSPEROUS 1

successional *adj* following one after another without others coming in between ⟨the *successional* stages that an area goes through following a devastating forest fire⟩ — see CONSECUTIVE

successive *adj* following one after another without others coming in between ⟨made the honor roll for three *successive* school terms⟩ — see CONSECUTIVE

succinct *adj* marked by the use of few words to convey much information or meaning ⟨a pocket guide that provides *succinct* explanations for rules of grammar and punctuation⟩ — see CONCISE

succinctly *adv* in a few words ⟨found it difficult to explain *succinctly* to the technician the nature of the problems she was having with her computer⟩ — see SHORTLY 1

succinctness *n* the quality or state of being marked by or using only few words to convey much meaning ⟨Caesar's observation, "I came, I saw, I conquered," is famous for its *succinctness*⟩

synonyms brevity, briefness, compactness, conciseness, crispness, pithiness, terseness

related words abruptness, bluntness, brusqueness, curtness, shortness

near antonyms redundancy, repetitiousness

antonyms diffuseness, long-windedness, prolixity, verbosity, wordiness

succulence *n* the quality or state of being full of juice ⟨the *succulence* of the apple was such that the first bite sent juice running down my chin⟩
synonyms fleshiness, juiciness, pulpiness
related words sap, sappiness

succulent *adj* full of juice ⟨vines weighted down with plump, *succulent* grapes⟩ — see JUICY

succumb *vb* **1** to cease resistance (as to another's arguments, demands, or control) ⟨Mom finally *succumbed* and let us go to the movies⟩ — see YIELD 3
2 to give up and cease resistance (as to a liking, temptation, or habit) ⟨refused to *succumb* to her fears and defiantly walked through the dark cemetery⟩ — see YIELD 1
3 to stop living ⟨the patient lay so still and pale that everyone thought he had *succumbed*, and then he opened his eyes⟩ — see DIE 1
4 to yield to the control or power of enemy forces ⟨the doctor worked tirelessly until finally he, too, *succumbed* to the fever⟩ — see FALL 2

such *adj* having qualities in common ⟨all *such* questions should be saved until the end of the class⟩ — see ALIKE

suchlike *adj* having qualities in common ⟨kept asking me how long I'd lived here, and how I liked it, and *suchlike* questions⟩ — see ALIKE

suck (up) *vb* to take in (something liquid) through small openings ⟨these lilacs *sucked up* all the water I added to the vase yesterday⟩ — see ABSORB 1

sucker *n* one who is easily deceived or cheated ⟨I was a *sucker* and believed them when they said the only tickets they could get were double the price⟩ — see DUPE

suddenly *adv* **1** with great suddenness ⟨the bus stopped *suddenly*, and somebody's lunch landed in the aisle⟩ — see SHORT
2 without warning ⟨*suddenly*, something fell out of the sky and landed in the field a few feet away⟩ — see UNAWARES

suds *n* a light mass of fine bubbles formed in or on a liquid ⟨I can't seem to get any *suds* to form with this cheap dish detergent⟩ — see FOAM

sudsy *adj* covered with, consisting of, or resembling foam ⟨came out of the bathroom with her hair all *sudsy* because someone had turned off the water⟩ — see FOAMY

sue (for) *vb* to make a request for ⟨after another devastating attack, the nation *sued for* peace⟩ — see ASK (FOR) 1

suer *n* the person in a legal proceeding who makes a charge of wrongdoing against another ⟨the landlord was suing his *suers* in return, with each side alleging wrongdoing on the other's part⟩ — see COMPLAINANT

suffer *vb* **1** to give permission to ⟨the elderly woman *suffered* her relatives to make a big fuss over her 90th birthday, although that was the last thing she wanted⟩ — see ALLOW 2
2 to come to a knowledge of (something) by living through it ⟨willingly *suffered* hardships so that their children would have a better life⟩ — see EXPERIENCE
3 to feel deep sadness or mental pain ⟨the husband *suffered* deeply at the mere suggestion that he had been unfaithful⟩ — see GRIEVE
4 to give permission for or to approve of ⟨contends that the death penalty is something that no civilized society should *suffer*⟩ — see ALLOW 1

sufferable *adj* capable of being endured ⟨the only thing that makes visiting my cousins *sufferable* is their gigantic TV⟩ — see BEARABLE

sufferance *n* **1** the approval by someone in authority for the doing of something ⟨was pointedly reminded that he was at the private beach on *sufferance* and could be kicked out at any time⟩ — see PERMISSION
2 the capacity to endure what is difficult or disagreeable without complaining ⟨spending a whole day with my bratty cousins is beyond *sufferance*⟩ — see PATIENCE

suffice *vb* to be enough ⟨I was told I have to wear shoes—will thong sandals *suffice*?⟩ — see SERVE 2

sufficiency *n* the quality or state of meeting one's needs adequately ⟨the *sufficiency* of the portions is such that you will leave the restaurant with a full stomach but without doggie bags⟩
synonyms acceptability, adequacy, satisfactoriness
related words appropriateness, correctness, fitness, goodness, properness, rightness, seemliness, suitability, suitableness; bountifulness, copiousness; excess, overabundance, oversupply, surfeit, surplus; abundance, amplitude, plenitude, plenty
near antonyms lack, want; dearth, shortage; meagerness, paucity, poorness, poverty, rareness, rarity, scantiness, scarceness, scarcity, skimpiness; necessity, need, privation
antonyms inadequacy, insufficiency

sufficiently *adv* in or to a degree or quantity that meets one's requirements or satisfaction ⟨after eight afterschool tutoring sessions, I felt *sufficiently* prepared for the test⟩ — see ENOUGH 1

suffocate *vb* to be or cause to be killed by lack of breathable air ⟨the law requires the owner of a discarded refrigerator to remove its door so that a child won't get trapped inside and *suffocate*⟩ — see SMOTHER 1

suffocating *adj* lacking fresh air ⟨inside the bunker it was *suffocating*, and some of the men passed out⟩ — see STUFFY 1

suffrage *n* the right to formally express one's position or will in an election ⟨even as the world entered the 21st century, some nations still did not permit women's *suffrage*⟩ — see VOTE 1

suffuse *vb* **1** to cause (as a person) to become filled or saturated with a certain quality or principle ⟨she was *suffused* with an overwhelming feeling of liberation as her horse broke into a gallop⟩ — see INFUSE
2 to spread throughout ⟨a living room *suffused* with warm sunlight⟩ — see PERMEATE

sugarcoated *adj* appealing to the emotions in an obvious and tiresome way ⟨those *sugarcoated* versions of family life that old TV sitcoms portrayed⟩ — see CORNY

sugary *adj* appealing to the emotions in an obvious and tiresome way ⟨writes *sugary* lyrics for singers of country music⟩ — see CORNY

suggest *vb* **1** to convey an idea indirectly ⟨this letter *suggests* that there's more going on than she's telling us⟩ — see HINT
2 to put forward as one's choice for a wise or proper course of action ⟨I *suggested* that he talk to the school counselor about his problems at home⟩ — see ADVISE 2
3 to set before the mind for consideration ⟨might I *suggest*, for an appetizer, our jumbo shrimp cocktail?⟩ — see PROPOSE 1

suggestion *n* **1** a slight or indirect pointing to something (as a solution or explanation) ⟨if you don't want to give the *suggestion* that you're evading the truth, you must look your questioner in the eye⟩ — see HINT 1

2 something which is presented for consideration ⟨no one had any better *suggestions*, so as usual we spent the afternoon at the basketball court⟩ — see PROPOSAL

suggestive *adj* **1** hinting at or intended to call to mind matters regarded as indecent ⟨making *suggestive* remarks to one's classmates will not be tolerated⟩

synonyms bawdy, lewd, racy, ribald, salty, spicy

related words leering; coarse, crude, earthy, foul, gross; dirty, filthy, lascivious, nasty, obscene, pornographic, smutty, unprintable, vulgar; indecorous, unbecoming; naughty, wicked; exceptionable, objectionable, unacceptable, undesirable, unwanted, unwelcome

near antonyms clean, decent; innocuous, inoffensive; priggish, prim, prudish, puritanical, straitlaced (*or* straightlaced), Victorian; correct, decorous, genteel, polite, proper, seemly; acceptable, agreeable, desirable, pleasant, pleasing, welcome; appropriate, becoming, fit, meet, suitable; immaculate, pure, spotless

2 provoking a memory or mental association ⟨a haunting and *suggestive* song about a long-lost love⟩

synonyms evocative, reminiscent

related words eloquent, expressive, meaningful, significant; affecting, emotional, moving, poignant, stirring, touching; exciting, provocative, provoking, rousing, stimulating

3 clearly conveying a special meaning (as one's mood) ⟨the dog's aggressive behavior is *suggestive* of some past mistreatment⟩ — see EXPRESSIVE

suicide *n* the act of deliberately killing oneself ⟨teenagers are more prone to *suicide* because they mistakenly believe their troubles are insurmountable⟩

synonyms self-destruction

related words martyrdom; foul play, homicide, murder, slaying; killing, manslaughter; assassination, execution; euthanasia, mercy killing

suit *n* **1** a court case for enforcing a right or claim ⟨filed a *suit* against the company that had manufactured the faulty heater, claiming they were responsible for the fire⟩ — see LAWSUIT

2 an earnest request ⟨the days when a gentleman made *suit* to marry his lady love⟩ — see PLEA 1

suit *vb* **1** to be fitting or proper ⟨no, a second-floor room won't *suit* if there's no elevator, since one of us has a disability⟩ — see DO 1

2 to give satisfaction to ⟨the location of our hotel *suited* us just fine⟩ — see PLEASE

3 to outfit with clothes and especially fine or special clothes ⟨went to the party *suited* in a strange getup that he'd picked out himself⟩ — see CLOTHE 1

suitability *n* the quality or state of being especially suitable or fitting ⟨the *suitability* of the accommodations will ultimately depend on whether they're accessible for someone in a wheelchair⟩ — see APPROPRIATENESS

suitable *adj* **1** having the required skills for an acceptable level of performance ⟨with only one *suitable* candidate it's not difficult to decide for whom to vote⟩ — see COMPETENT

2 meeting the requirements of a purpose or situation ⟨I don't have anything *suitable* to wear to a bar mitzvah⟩ — see FIT 1

suitableness *n* the quality or state of being especially suitable or fitting ⟨questioned the *suitableness* of bringing a dog to a wedding⟩ — see APPROPRIATENESS

suitably *adv* in a manner suitable for the occasion or purpose ⟨tried to appear *suitably* amused by his anecdote⟩ — see PROPERLY

suitcase *n* a bag carried by hand and designed to hold a traveler's clothing and personal articles ⟨it'll be much easier to carry a backpack than to lug that *suitcase* all over the place⟩ — see TRAVELING BAG

suite *n* **1** a body of employees or servants who accompany and wait on a person ⟨an athlete accompanied everywhere by a *suite* of attendants, including his personal trainer, a dietician, and a massage therapist⟩ — see CORTEGE 1

2 a number of things considered as a unit ⟨replaced the mismatched bed and chests of drawers with a handsome new bedroom *suite*⟩ — see GROUP 1

3 a room or set of rooms in a private house or a block used as a separate dwelling place ⟨whenever he visits the city, he stays in his uncle's 10th-floor *suite*⟩ — see APARTMENT 1

suitor *n* **1** a man who courts a woman usually with the goal of marrying her ⟨my sister finally married her *suitor* of six years on Sunday⟩

synonyms gallant, swain, wooer

related words beau, boyfriend, fellow, man; admirer, crush, steady; beloved, darling, dear, favorite, flame, honey, love, lover, sweet, sweetheart, valentine; date, escort; fiancé, intended

2 one who asks earnestly for a favor or gift ⟨the inventor had several *suitors* for his patent, but he wasn't interested in dealing with a big company⟩ — see SUPPLICANT

sulk *n* a state of resentful silence or irritability ⟨a child sitting in a *sulk* over a minor disagreement⟩

synonyms pet, pouts, sulkiness, sullenness

related words blues, dumps, mopes; surliness; biliousness, crankiness, crossness, crotchetiness, grouchiness, grumpiness, irascibility, irritability, peevishness, perverseness, perversity, pettishness, petulance, testiness, waspishness; cantankerousness, disagreeableness, orneriness

near antonyms sociability; cheerfulness, gaiety (*also* gayety), gladsomeness, good-humoredness, high-spiritedness, lightheartedness, perkiness

sulk *vb* to silently go about in a bad mood ⟨the toddler *sulked* all day whenever he didn't get his way⟩

synonyms mope, pout

related words brood, dwell (on), mull (over), muse (over), ponder; frown, glower, lower (*also* lour), scowl; carry on, take on

sulkiness *n* a state of resentful silence or irritability ⟨turned into a very pleasant adult when she finally outgrew her adolescent *sulkiness*⟩ — see SULK

sulky *adj* given to or displaying a resentful silence and often irritability ⟨your teenage daughter turns *sulky* if we refuse to let her borrow the car⟩

synonyms glum, pouting, sullen, surly

related words dour, gloomy, morose; choleric, crabby, cranky, cross, crotchety, grouchy, grumpy, irascible, irritable, peevish, perverse, pettish, petulant, quick-tempered, short-tempered, snappy, snippy, testy, waspish; brooding, moping; bearish, bilious, cantankerous, disagreeable, dyspeptic, ill-humored, ill-natured, ill-tempered, ornery; sensitive, temperamental, thin-skinned, touchy

near antonyms sociable; cheerful, cheery, gladsome, good-humored, good-natured, perky

sullen *adj* **1** causing or marked by an atmosphere lacking in cheer ⟨*sullen* skies that matched our mood on the day of the funeral⟩ — see GLOOMY 1

2 given to or displaying a resentful silence and often irritability ⟨Ben was *sullen* and bored at his aunt's house because he'd wanted to spend the day with his best friend⟩ — see SULKY

sullenness *n* a state of resentful silence or irritability ⟨Ben's aunt managed to dispel his *sullenness* by placing a plate of homemade chocolate chip cookies in front of him⟩ — see SULK

sullied *adj* not clean ⟨lying in *sullied* bed linens that had not seen the inside of a washing machine for some time⟩ — see DIRTY 1

sully *vb* to make dirty ⟨people that *sully* our state parks with their trash⟩ ⟨a once-gleaming marble interior *sullied* by decades of exposure to cigarette smoke⟩ — see DIRTY

sultry *adj* **1** containing or characterized by an uncomfortable amount of moisture ⟨on really *sultry* days we go to the mall to hang out and cool off⟩ — see HUMID
2 having a notably high temperature ⟨the incredibly dry, *sultry* desert air⟩ — see HOT 1

sum *n* **1** a complete amount of something ⟨the *sum* of human knowledge on that subject⟩ — see WHOLE
2 a short statement of the main points ⟨the district attorney delivered a *sum* of the evidence against the accused that was simply staggering⟩ — see SUMMARY

sum *vb* to combine (numbers) into a single sum ⟨can *sum* figures in his head faster than I can punch them into a calculator⟩ — see ADD 2

sum (to *or* into) *vb* to have a total of ⟨a lifetime of charitable contributions that *sum into* the millions⟩ — see AMOUNT (TO) 1

summarily *adv* in a few words ⟨*summarily* informed us that our help was not welcome⟩ — see SHORTLY 1

summarization *n* a short statement of the main points ⟨what you wrote goes way beyond a *summarization* of the speech⟩ — see SUMMARY

summarize *vb* to make into a short statement of the main points (as of a report) ⟨the closing minute of the newscast *summarizes* the main story of the day⟩
synonyms abstract, digest, encapsulate, epitomize, outline, recap, recapitulate, sum up, wrap up
related words abridge, condense, curtail, shorten; downsize, shrink; concentrate, consolidate; simplify, streamline
near antonyms amplify, elaborate (on *or* upon), enlarge (on *or* upon), expand

summary *adj* marked by the use of few words to convey much information or meaning ⟨obviously a one-volume encyclopedia can offer only a very *summary* account of the American Civil War⟩ — see CONCISE

summary *n* a short statement of the main points ⟨many book reports choose to begin with a *summary* of the book⟩
synonyms abstract, digest, encapsulation, epitome, outline, précis, recap, recapitulation, résumé (*or* resume *also* resumé), roundup, sum, summarization, synopsis
related words abbreviation, abridgment (*or* abridgement), condensation, curtailment, shortening; brief; rundown; simplification, streamlining
near antonyms amplification, enlargement, expansion

summation *n* a complete amount of something ⟨the *summation* of climatic conditions that affect plant growth⟩ — see WHOLE

summit *n* the highest part or point ⟨a new movie that some enthusiastic reviewers are already calling the *summit* of cinematic achievement⟩ — see HEIGHT 1

summon *vb* **1** to demand or request the presence or service of ⟨without explanation, the principal *summoned* me to his office⟩
synonyms call, hail

related words cite, subpoena; assemble, convene, convoke, muster; ask, bid, invite; command, order, request, requisition; beckon, demand, invoke
phrases send for
near antonyms dismiss, send (away), turn away
2 to call into being through the use of one's inner resources or powers ⟨managed to *summon* a bright smile despite the gloomy day⟩
synonyms conjure (up), gather (up)
related words educe, elicit, evoke, raise
3 to bring together in assembly by or as if by command ⟨*summoned* a special session of parliament⟩ — see CONVOKE

summons *n* a written notice ordering a person to appear in court ⟨if you ignore a court *summons*, you will be fined⟩
synonyms subpoena
related words warrant, writ

sumptuous *adj* showing obvious signs of wealth and comfort ⟨the cruise ship claims to offer *sumptuous* furnishings, exquisitely prepared cuisine, and stellar entertainment⟩ — see LUXURIOUS

sumptuously *adv* in a luxurious manner ⟨a history book *sumptuously* illustrated with maps, drawings, and photographs⟩ — see HIGH

sum up *vb* to make into a short statement of the main points (as of a report) ⟨in *summing up* the evidence against the defendant, the district attorney presented fact after damning fact⟩ — see SUMMARIZE

sun *n* **1** the light given off by the star around which the planet Earth revolves ⟨be sure to wear sunscreen if you plan to spend more than a few minutes in the *sun*⟩
synonyms sunlight, sunshine
related words sunburst; daylight
near antonyms cloudiness; penumbra, shade, shadiness, shadow, umbra
2 a ball-shaped gaseous celestial body that shines by its own light ⟨the incomprehensible vastness of a universe filled with billions of *suns*⟩ — see STAR 1

sunder *vb* to set or force apart ⟨during the cold war East and West Berlin were *sundered* by an impenetrable wall⟩ — see SEPARATE 1

sundown *n* the time from when the sun begins to set to the onset of total darkness ⟨we were told that the best time to see elk is at *sundown*⟩ — see DUSK 1

sundowner *n, Australian* a homeless wanderer who may beg or steal for a living ⟨*sundowners* showing up at a sheep station looking for work⟩ — see TRAMP

sundries *n pl* small useful items ⟨the only things she needed for her overnight stay were her carryall and a small bag for *sundries*⟩ — see NOTION 1

sunken *adj* **1** curved inward ⟨our convalescing guest's *sunken* cheeks soon filled out on a diet of my mother's cooking⟩ — see HOLLOW
2 living, lying, or occurring below the surface of the water ⟨diving for *sunken* treasure⟩ — see UNDERWATER

sunlight *n* the light given off by the star around which the planet Earth revolves ⟨raise the shades and let in some *sunlight*⟩ — see SUN 1

sunny *adj* **1** having or being an outward sign of good feelings (as of love, confidence, or happiness) ⟨her *sunny* laughter filled the house with joy⟩ — see RADIANT 1
2 having or showing a good mood or disposition ⟨momentarily forgot their worries at the sight of baby Alice's *sunny* smile⟩ — see CHEERFUL 1

3 indicative of or marked by high spirits or good humor ⟨the good-natured waitresses enhance the restaurant's *sunny* and cheery atmosphere⟩ — see MERRY

4 not stormy or cloudy ⟨we were hoping for a *sunny* weekend so we could spend it at the beach⟩ — see FAIR 1

sunrise *n* the first appearance of light in the morning or the time of its appearance ⟨a job that requires him to get up before *sunrise*⟩ — see DAWN 1

sunset *n* the time from when the sun begins to set to the onset of total darkness ⟨the glow of the western sky at *sunset*⟩ — see DUSK 1

sunshine *n* the light given off by the star around which the planet Earth revolves ⟨spent a week at the shore soaking up the *sunshine* and the salt air⟩ — see SUN 1

sunshiny *adj* not stormy or cloudy ⟨we're due for a *sunshiny* weekend, as it has rained for the last three⟩ — see FAIR 1

sunup *n* the first appearance of light in the morning or the time of its appearance ⟨have you ever actually heard a rooster crow at *sunup*?⟩ — see DAWN 1

sup *n* the portion of a serving of a beverage that is swallowed at one time ⟨the old mariner took a *sup* of grog and began his tale⟩ — see DRINK 2

sup *vb* to swallow in liquid form ⟨*supped* the broth slowly⟩ — see DRINK 1

super *adj* unusually large ⟨drinks come in three sizes: medium, large, or *super*⟩ — see HUGE

super *adv* to a great degree ⟨my computer is *super* slow this morning⟩ — see VERY 1

superabundance *n* **1** an amount or supply more than sufficient to meet one's needs ⟨a *superabundance* of donations flowed in after the family's plight was seen on national TV⟩ — see PLENTY 1

2 the state or an instance of going beyond what is usual, proper, or needed ⟨a *superabundance* of applicants for a limited number of jobs⟩ — see EXCESS

superb *adj* of the very best kind ⟨he makes a *superb* chocolate cake⟩ — see EXCELLENT

superbness *n* **1** exceptionally high quality ⟨the *superbness* of the orchestra's performance was such that the music critics were straining for superlatives⟩ — see EXCELLENCE 1

2 impressiveness of beauty on a large scale ⟨climbers rave about the *superbness* of the view from the mountain's summit⟩ — see MAGNIFICENCE

supercilious *adj* having a feeling of superiority that shows itself in an overbearing attitude ⟨the *supercilious* bus driver made Laura feel like an idiot because she'd lost her bus pass⟩ — see ARROGANT

superciliousness *n* an exaggerated sense of one's importance that shows itself in the making of excessive or unjustified claims ⟨can't bear the *superciliousness* of her cousin who lives in New York City and thinks everybody in Tennessee is a hick⟩ — see ARROGANCE

superficial *adj* **1** lying on or affecting only the outer layer of something ⟨a *superficial* scratch that barely even broke the skin⟩

synonyms skin-deep, surface

related words depthless, shallow, shoal; two-dimensional

near antonyms deep, deep-rooted, deep-seated; subcutaneous, subterranean

2 having or showing a lack of depth of understanding or character ⟨a *superficial* analysis of how movie and video violence affects young people⟩

synonyms facile, one-dimensional, shallow, skin-deep

related words cursory, hasty, sketchy; aimless, desultory, haphazard, hit-or-miss, random; limited, narrow, restricted

near antonyms discerning, penetrating; definitive, hard; broad, complete, comprehensive, exhaustive, extensive, far-reaching, wide; general, global, inclusive; detailed, in-depth; critical

antonyms deep, profound

superfluity *n* **1** something adding to pleasure or comfort but not absolutely necessary ⟨spent her travel money on souvenirs and other *superfluities* and didn't have enough to pay her share for lodging⟩ — see LUXURY 1

2 the state or an instance of going beyond what is usual, proper, or needed ⟨a *superfluity* of wire coat hangers from all of those trips to the dry cleaners⟩ — see EXCESS

superfluous *adj* being over what is needed ⟨cleared off all the *superfluous* stuff on his desk to make room for the computer⟩ — see SPARE 1

superheated *adj* having a notably high temperature ⟨certain *superheated* liquids change to gas with almost explosive violence⟩ — see HOT 1

superhuman *adj* **1** being so extraordinary or abnormal as to suggest powers which violate the laws of nature ⟨in his dreams the boy can always perform *superhuman* feats⟩ — see SUPERNATURAL 2

2 of, relating to, or being part of a reality beyond the observable physical universe ⟨myths that represent natural phenomena as *superhuman* beings⟩ — see SUPERNATURAL 1

superintend *vb* **1** to be in charge of ⟨*superintends* the construction of all scenery at the summer theater⟩ — see BOSS 1

2 to look after and make decisions about ⟨homeschooling parents who *superintend* their children's education⟩ — see CONDUCT 1

3 to take charge of especially on behalf of another ⟨whoever's *superintending* the warehouse will know what's been delivered today⟩ — see ²TEND 1

superintendence *n* **1** the act or activity of looking after and making decisions about something ⟨under her lax *superintendence* the company eventually went bankrupt⟩ — see CONDUCT 1

2 the duty or function of watching or guarding for the sake of proper direction or control ⟨the *superintendence* of the local music festival is handled jointly by the city and the county⟩ — see SUPERVISION 1

superintendency *n* the duty or function of watching or guarding for the sake of proper direction or control ⟨*superintendency* of the polling places is largely carried out by retired citizens⟩ — see SUPERVISION 1

superintendent *n* a person who manages or directs ⟨the office of the *superintendent* of parks issues camping permits⟩ — see EXECUTIVE

superior *adj* **1** having a feeling of superiority that shows itself in an overbearing attitude ⟨that *superior* sportscaster lets it be known that he thinks all foreign baseball teams are second-rate⟩ — see ARROGANT

2 having or displaying feelings of scorn for what is regarded as beneath oneself ⟨the *superior* attitude of the store owner's son drove the other employees crazy⟩ — see PROUD 1

3 of the very best kind ⟨if you want a really *superior* mango, try one picked ripe from the tree⟩ — see EXCELLENT

4 standing above others in rank, importance, or achievement ⟨a university known for attracting *superior* scientists and mathematicians⟩ — see EMINENT

superior *n* one who is above another in rank, station, or office 〈if a customer is rude to you, report it to your *superior* and they'll handle it〉
synonyms better, elder, senior
related words boss, chief, head, leader, master
near antonyms assistant, deputy
antonyms inferior, subordinate, underling

superiority *n* **1** an exaggerated sense of one's importance that shows itself in the making of excessive or unjustified claims 〈the *superiority* of some of the customers at the exclusive beauty salon is enough to curl your hair〉 — see ARROGANCE

2 exceptionally high quality 〈the *superiority* of tree-ripened mangoes might make you want to spend the rest of your life in a tropical climate〉 — see EXCELLENCE 1

3 the fact or state of being above others in rank or importance 〈the *superiority* of the nation in military might〉 — see EMINENCE 1

superlative *adj* of the very best kind 〈the New England town meeting is a *superlative* example of grass-roots democracy〉 — see EXCELLENT

supernal *adj* **1** of the very best kind 〈an absolutely *supernal* performance of the concerto by a 16-year old prodigy〉 — see EXCELLENT

2 of, relating to, or suggesting heaven 〈a couple enjoying the *supernal* joys of parenthood for the first time〉 — see CELESTIAL

supernatural *adj* **1** of, relating to, or being part of a reality beyond the observable physical universe 〈Susie believes in ghosts, guardian angels, and other *supernatural* beings〉
synonyms metaphysical, preternatural, superhuman, unearthly
related words occult; extrasensory; celestial, divine, heavenly
antonyms natural

2 being so extraordinary or abnormal as to suggest powers which violate the laws of nature 〈he seems to read books with *supernatural* speed〉
synonyms magical, miraculous, phenomenal, superhuman, uncanny, unearthly
related words bizarre, curious, far-out, funny, kinky, outlandish, out-of-the-way, outrageous, outré, peculiar, quaint, queer, queerish, quirky, remarkable, screwy, strange, wacky, way-out, weird, wild; baffling, bewildering, confounding, mystifying, perplexing, puzzling, shocking; aberrant, abnormal, atypical, extraordinary, fantastic, flaky, freak, freakish, idiosyncratic, rare, singular, uncommon, unique, unusual, unwonted; unconventional, uncustomary, unorthodox; conspicuous, notable, noticeable, outstanding, prominent, salient, striking
near antonyms average, commonplace, everyday, garden, ordinary, prosaic, routine, run-of-the-mill, typical, unexceptional, unremarkable, usual, workaday; expected, familiar, predictable; common, customary, frequent, habitual, regular, wonted

3 of, relating to, or being God 〈believed he had a *supernatural* calling to join the ministry〉 — see HOLY 3

supernumerary *adj* being over what is needed 〈a third, *supernumerary* witness to the signing of the will〉 — see SPARE 1

supersede *vb* to take the place of 〈that edition of the dictionary that you have has been *superseded* by a more recent one〉 — see REPLACE 1

superstar *n* a person who is widely known and usually much talked about 〈a basketball *superstar*〉 — see CELEBRITY 1

supervene *vb* to come after in time 〈it was not the slow-spreading cancer that caused his death but a *supervening* heart attack〉 — see FOLLOW 1

supervise *vb* **1** to be in charge of 〈for each sailboat an experienced hand is assigned to *supervise* a novice seaman〉 — see BOSS 1

2 to look after and make decisions about 〈*supervises* all the affairs of the sailing club, including hiring someone to run the summer sailing camp〉 — see CONDUCT 1

3 to take charge of especially on behalf of another 〈we need someone to *supervise* the rigging of the vessels by the novices〉 — see ²TEND 1

supervision *n* **1** the duty or function of watching or guarding for the sake of proper direction or control 〈our French teacher has *supervision* of all activities of the French Club〉
synonyms care, charge, guidance, headship, oversight, regulation, superintendence, superintendency
related words monitoring, observing; administration, control, direction, management, running; leadership, piloting, shepherding, steering; government, reign, rule; aegis, guardianship, protection, tutelage

2 the act or activity of looking after and making decisions about something 〈one of the senior cheerleaders took over *supervision* of the squad's practices while their coach was on maternity leave〉 — see CONDUCT 1

supervisor *n* a person who manages or directs 〈the salesclerk said she would have to ask her *supervisor* if I could return the defective CD without a receipt〉 — see EXECUTIVE

supervisory *adj* suited for or relating to the directing of things 〈was promoted to a *supervisory* position with several assistants working under him〉 — see EXECUTIVE

supplant *vb* to take the place of 〈old traditions that were fading away and being *supplanted* by modern ways〉 — see REPLACE 1

supple *adj* **1** able to bend easily without breaking 〈a dome tent outfitted with *supple* fiberglass tent poles〉 — see WILLOWY

2 able to revert to original size and shape after being stretched, squeezed, or twisted 〈shoes made from really *supple* leather〉 — see ELASTIC 1

supplement *n* **1** something added (as by growth) 〈this new rule against wearing caps is only a *supplement* to the preexisting policy regarding the wearing of distracting clothing in class〉 — see INCREASE 1

2 something that serves to complete or make up for a deficiency in something else 〈recommends taking a vitamin C *supplement* to prevent colds〉 — see COMPLEMENT 1

supplemental *adj* available to supply something extra when needed 〈works at the store only during those busy times when *supplemental* help is needed〉 — see AUXILIARY

supplementary *adj* **1** available to supply something extra when needed 〈the teacher's edition of the textbook comes with a lot of *supplementary* material〉 — see AUXILIARY

2 related to each other in such a way that one completes the other 〈regards theology and philosophy as *supplementary* fields of study〉 — see COMPLEMENTARY

suppliant *adj* asking humbly 〈the *suppliant* student pleaded for a second chance〉

synonyms beseeching, entreating, imploring, pleading, prayerful, soliciting, supplicant, supplicating
related words importunate, insistent, persistent

suppliant *n* one who asks earnestly for a favor or gift 〈didn't like being in the position of a *suppliant*, having to ask her parents to help her pay the rent on her apartment〉 — see SUPPLICANT

supplicant *adj* asking humbly 〈hated having to go before his boss like a *supplicant* beggar whenever he needed some time off to attend to personal matters〉 — see SUPPLIANT

supplicant *n* one who asks earnestly for a favor or gift 〈the new governor soon had to deal with a long line of *supplicants* asking for jobs and other political favors〉
synonyms petitioner, pleader, solicitor, suitor, suppliant
related words beggar, mendicant, panhandler; asker, requester, suer

supplicate *vb* to make a request to (someone) in an earnest or urgent manner 〈the minister reminded his flock that God is a being to be obeyed and worshiped always and not just someone to be *supplicated* in times of trouble〉 — see BEG

supplicating *adj* asking humbly 〈in a *supplicating* gesture, he got down on his knees and asked, "Will you marry me?"〉 — see SUPPLIANT

supplication *n* an earnest request 〈the Red Cross made an urgent *supplication* for donations of food and blankets for the earthquake victims〉 — see PLEA 1

supply *n* the number of individuals or amount of something available at any given time 〈the *supply* of grownups willing to coach soccer seems to be shrinking〉
synonyms budget, fund, pool
related words reserve, reservoir, resource; cache, hoard, stockpile; refill, renewal, replacement; kitty, nest egg, pot, purse; source, well, wellspring

supply *vb* 1 to provide (someone) with what is needed for a task or activity 〈you should bring your own pencils for the test, in case they don't *supply* you with any〉 — see FURNISH 1
2 to put (something) into the possession of someone for use or consumption 〈the teacher said she'd *supply* the pencils and paper we'd need for the test〉 — see FURNISH 2

support *n* 1 something that holds up or serves as a foundation for something else 〈if you don't add a couple more *supports* to that tower of blocks, it's going to fall down〉
synonyms brace, bulwark, buttress, mount, mounting, shore, stay, underpinning
related words column, pedestal, pilaster, pillar; arch, bracket, cantilever; crutch, mainstay, peg, post, stake, stanchion, stand, stilt, truss; base, foundation, frame
2 an act or instance of helping 〈the team's victory owes a lot to Joe's strong *support* in left field〉 — see HELP 1
3 something or someone to which one looks for support 〈Grandfather has long been the extended family's emotional and financial *support* in times of trouble〉 — see DEPENDENCE 2

support *vb* 1 to promote the interests or cause of 〈my parents *support* the local schools both by volunteering and by fiercely opposing funding cuts at town meetings〉
synonyms advocate, back, champion, endorse (*also* indorse), patronize
related words adopt, embrace, espouse; abet, aid, assist, prop (up), second; bolster, boost, buttress, reinforce; bail out, deliver, rescue, save

phrases stand up for
near antonyms baffle, foil, frustrate, interfere, oppose, sabotage, thwart; desert, disappoint, fail, let down
2 to pay the living expenses of 〈a young widow *supporting* a sick mother as well as two small children on a teacher's salary〉
synonyms maintain, provide (for)
related words finance, fund, stake
phrases foot the bills for, take care of
3 to hold up or serve as a foundation for 〈pillars *supporting* the bridge〉
synonyms bear, bolster, brace, buttress, carry, prop (up), shore (up), stay, underpin, uphold
related words steady, truss, underlie
4 to continue to declare to be true or proper despite opposition or objections 〈we *support* the students' right to speak out on local issues that affect them〉 — see MAINTAIN 2
5 to give evidence or testimony to the truth or factualness of 〈her grades don't *support* her claim that her after-school job isn't affecting her grades〉 — see CONFIRM
6 to provide (someone) with what is useful or necessary to achieve an end 〈sent reinforcements to *support* the troops already in the thick of battle〉 — see HELP 1
7 to put up with (something painful or difficult) 〈he could never *support* the thought of having to go on living without his beloved wife at his side〉 — see BEAR 2

supportable *adj* 1 capable of being defended with good reasoning against verbal attack 〈are there ever circumstances where laws that restrict a person's freedom of speech are *supportable*?〉 — see TENABLE 1
2 capable of being endured 〈her cat had been rescued from the burning house, making her other losses at least *supportable*〉 — see BEARABLE
3 capable of being proven as true or real 〈the news editor simply assumed the facts of the story were *supportable* and did not assign it to a fact checker〉 — see VERIFIABLE

supporter *n* 1 a person who actively supports or favors a cause 〈President Lyndon B. Johnson was a strong *supporter* of civil rights〉 — see EXPONENT
2 someone associated with another to give assistance or moral support 〈both blacks and whites were among Martin Luther King Jr.'s *supporters* in the movement for civil rights〉 — see ALLY

supporting *adj* serving to give support to the truth or factualness of something 〈scientists looking for direct *supporting* evidence of microscopic black holes, the existence of which is theoretical〉 — see CORROBORATIVE

supportive *adj* serving to give support to the truth or factualness of something 〈the jimmied window latch is *supportive* of the theory that there was forced entry into the house〉 — see CORROBORATIVE

suppose *vb* 1 to decide the size, amount, number, or distance of (something) without actual measurement 〈if we *suppose* a minimum profit of $100 from the car wash, we should be able to pay for the bus trip〉 — see ESTIMATE 2
2 to form an opinion from little or no evidence 〈what do you *suppose* he's going to do with the prize money he won?〉 — see GUESS 1
3 to have as an opinion 〈voters wrongly *supposed* that the new mayor would be opposed to letting hazardous waste be transported through the city〉 — see BELIEVE 2

4 to take as true or as a fact without actual proof ⟨never *supposed* that her father would leave the family farm to anyone but her in his will⟩ — see ASSUME 2

supposed *adj* appearing to be true on the basis of evidence that may or may not be confirmed ⟨this new computer program is a *supposed* improvement over the old one⟩ — see APPARENT 1

supposedly *adv* to all outward appearances ⟨*supposedly*, she's too sick to come—or so she says⟩ — see APPARENTLY

supposition *n* **1** an idea that is the starting point for making a case or conducting an investigation ⟨my *supposition* is that this grape variety, which flourishes in southern France, should do equally well here, given the similar climate⟩ — see THEORY

2 an opinion or judgment based on little or no evidence ⟨it's pure *supposition* that there's something illegal going on next door⟩ — see CONJECTURE

3 something taken as being true or factual and used as a starting point for a course of action or reasoning ⟨worthless genetic research that was based on the erroneous *supposition* that acquired characteristics can be passed on to offspring⟩ — see ASSUMPTION

suppositional *adj* existing only as an assumption or speculation ⟨concepts regarding the origin and structure of the universe must perforce be *suppositional*⟩ — see THEORETICAL 1

suppress *vb* **1** to keep from being publicly known ⟨the government tried to *suppress* the truth about that incident⟩
synonyms cover (up), hush (up)
related words censor, silence; repress, smother, squash, squelch, stifle
phrases keep a lid on
near antonyms debunk, expose, reveal, show up, uncloak, uncover, unmask; disclose, divulge, tell, unveil; broadcast, circulate, publish, spread; describe, narrate, recite, recount, rehearse, relate, report

2 to refrain from openly showing or uttering ⟨he managed to *suppress* a scream at the sight of the dead body⟩ ⟨*suppressed* her anger⟩
synonyms choke (back), pocket, repress, smother, stifle, strangle, swallow
related words control, govern, handle, manage; bridle, check, curb, hold back, quell; bottle up, contain, hold in; muffle, squelch
near antonyms loose, release, take out, unleash, vent

3 to hold back the normal growth of ⟨pruning helps *suppress* buds at the ends of developed branches and encourages new growth elsewhere⟩ — see STUNT

4 to put a stop to (something) by the use of force ⟨nothing could *suppress* the rising tide of protest against the dictator's latest injustices⟩ — see QUELL 1

suppression *n* the checking of one's true feelings and impulses when dealing with others ⟨learned that *suppression* of her angry feelings didn't necessarily make them go away⟩ — see CONSTRAINT 1

supremacist *n* a person who believes that one race should control all others ⟨white *supremacists* were arrested for painting racial slurs on a church⟩
synonyms racialist, racist
related words segregationist; bigot

supremacy *n* **1** controlling power or influence over others ⟨the Roman empire had *supremacy* over the entire Mediterranean world⟩
synonyms ascendancy, dominance, dominion, predominance, preeminence

related words primacy, superiority; lordship, scepter, sovereignty; arm, authority, clutch, command, control, grip, hold, mastery, sway; takeover; direction, jurisdiction, management; clout, pull, weight; eminence, importance, moment; prerogative, privilege, right
near antonyms helplessness, weakness; impotence, powerlessness

2 exceptionally high quality ⟨the *supremacy* of cashmere among wools accounts for its high price⟩ — see EXCELLENCE 1

supreme *adj* **1** highest in rank or authority ⟨the *supreme* commander of the multinational force⟩ — see HEAD

2 coming before all others in importance ⟨in our neighborhood, skateboarding reigns *supreme* as the after-school activity of choice⟩ — see FOREMOST 1

3 of the greatest or highest degree or quantity ⟨considers a letter of gratitude from a former student the *supreme* reward for his years of teaching⟩ — see ULTIMATE 1

Supreme Being *n* the being worshipped as the creator and ruler of the universe ⟨anthropologists have found that most cultures around the world believe in a *Supreme Being*⟩ — see DEITY 2

surcease *n* the stopping of a process or activity ⟨hoping the new medicine would bring *surcease* to his pain⟩ — see END 1

surcharge *vb* to charge (someone) too much for goods or services ⟨contends that with the present tax structure, the state's lower-income residents are being *surcharged* and the wealthiest residents are getting off too lightly⟩ — see OVERCHARGE 1

surcoat *n* a warm outdoor coat ⟨a knight in a fur-lined and hooded *surcoat* over a long tunic stood in the forest clearing⟩ — see OVERCOAT

sure *adj* **1** having or showing a mind free from doubt ⟨are you absolutely *sure* that she said she was coming today?⟩ — see CERTAIN 2

2 impossible to avoid or evade ⟨the joke's a *sure* dud if you don't pause in the right places⟩ — see INEVITABLE

3 not likely to fail ⟨a *sure* cure for the winter blues—a week in the Bahamas⟩ — see INFALLIBLE 1

4 worthy of one's trust ⟨a sister is a *sure* friend for life⟩ — see DEPENDABLE

surely *adv* without any question ⟨*surely* there's something I can do to help⟩ — see INDEED 1

sureness *n* **1** a state of mind in which one is free from doubt ⟨unfortunately, he lacked the *sureness* of his opponent in the tennis match⟩ — see CONFIDENCE 2

2 worthiness as the recipient of another's trust or confidence ⟨investors in those risky foreign enterprises were gambling on the *sureness* of their instincts⟩ — see RELIABILITY

surety *n* **1** a formal agreement to fulfill an obligation ⟨Christy's brother gave his *surety* that he would pay back the loan if she was unable to for any reason⟩ — see GUARANTEE 1

2 a person who takes the responsibility for some other person or thing ⟨Tony agreed to act as *surety* if I lent Christy some money, since I wasn't certain that she'd be able to pay it back⟩ — see SPONSOR

surf *n* a light mass of fine bubbles formed in or on a liquid ⟨Aimee laughed with glee as the ocean *surf* filled the holes she'd dug in the sand⟩ — see FOAM

surface *adj* lying on or affecting only the outer layer of something ⟨a *surface* stain on the wood that can easily be removed with a mild detergent⟩ — see SUPERFICIAL 1

surface *n* an outer part or layer ⟨the *surface* of just about everything in the kitchen was covered with soot after we put the grease fire out⟩ — see EXTERIOR

surface *vb* **1** to come to one's attention especially gradually or unexpectedly ⟨no information regarding the stolen car has *surfaced* since the police found it abandoned on a country road⟩ — see ARISE 2
2 to penetrate the surface (as of water) from below ⟨a submarine *surfaced* on the starboard side of the aircraft carrier⟩ — see BROACH 1

surfeit *n* the state or an instance of going beyond what is usual, proper, or needed ⟨ended up with a *surfeit* of volunteers who simply got in each other's way⟩ — see EXCESS

surfeit *vb* to fill with food to capacity ⟨having *surfeited* ourselves on raw oysters, we had to decline the rest of the restaurant's offerings⟩ — see GORGE 1

surfeited *adj* having one's appetite completely satisfied ⟨*surfeited* by the Thanksgiving repast, the grown-ups dozed off in front of the TV while the children raised Cain around the house⟩ — see FULL 3

surge *n* a moving ridge on the surface of water ⟨a huge *surge* nearly capsized the boat and drenched the hapless fishermen⟩ — see WAVE

surly *adj* **1** given to or displaying a resentful silence and often irritability ⟨went about his chores in a *surly* huff, totally annoyed that he was stuck at home on this beautiful Saturday⟩ — see SULKY
2 having or showing a habitually bad temper ⟨the *surly* receptionist told us we'd have to wait outside in the rain⟩ — see ILL-TEMPERED

surmise *n* an opinion or judgment based on little or no evidence ⟨my *surmise* is that the couple's "good news" is the announcement that they are going to have a baby⟩ — see CONJECTURE

surmise *vb* to form an opinion from little or no evidence ⟨we *surmised* that she had purchased the apple pie since there was a bakery box on the kitchen counter⟩ — see GUESS 1

surmount *vb* to achieve a victory over ⟨an Olympic swimmer who *surmounted* endless obstacles to achieve her goals⟩ — see BEAT 2

surpass *vb* **1** to be greater, better, or stronger than ⟨she always tried to *surpass* her older brother at anything he did⟩
synonyms beat, better, eclipse, excel, outdistance, outdo, outshine, outstrip, overtop, top, transcend
related words exceed, outpace, outrun, overpass; best, clobber, conquer, crush, defeat, drub, lick, master, overcome, overmatch, prevail (over), rout, skunk, subdue, surmount, thrash, trim, triumph (over), trounce, wallop, whip, win (against), worst; outweigh, overbear, overshadow
phrases go one better
near antonyms lose (to)
2 to go beyond the limit of ⟨the sales of the band's newest CD have *surpassed* the combined sales of its two earlier discs⟩ — see EXCEED

surplus *adj* being over what is needed ⟨*surplus* stock gets shipped to the warehouse and is eventually sold at auction⟩ — see SPARE 1

surplus *n* the state or an instance of going beyond what is usual, proper, or needed ⟨we have a *surplus* of plastic knives, but we're short on forks and spoons for the picnic⟩ — see EXCESS

surprise *also* **surprize** *vb* **1** to make a strong impression on (someone) with something unexpected ⟨I was very surprised when my parents offered to pay for guitar lessons⟩
synonyms amaze, astonish, astound, bowl (over), dumbfound (*also* dumfound), flabbergast, floor, shock, startle, stun, stupefy
related words befuddle, bewilder, confound, confuse, discomfit, disconcert, dismay, muddle, nonplus, perplex
phrases knock for a loop, take aback, take by surprise
2 to lie in wait for and attack by surprise ⟨FBI agents *surprised* the counterfeiters in their own base of operations⟩ — see AMBUSH

surprise *n* **1** something that makes a strong impression because it is so unexpected ⟨the birthday party was such a complete *surprise* that Jane was speechless for a moment⟩
synonyms bolt, bombshell, jar, jolt, stunner
related words shock, thunderclap; revelation, shocker
2 the state of being strongly impressed by something unexpected or unusual ⟨Danny stared in utter *surprise* at the deer in his living room⟩
synonyms amazement, astonishment, shock
related words awe, wonder, wonderment; startle; bewilderment, confusion, discomfiture, dismay
3 a scheme in which hidden persons wait to attack by surprise ⟨waited under cover of darkness and took the enemy encampment by *surprise* at dawn⟩ — see AMBUSH 1

surprising *adj* **1** causing a strong emotional reaction because unexpected ⟨the *surprising* news that they were going to have a baby had them rushing to buy nursery furniture⟩
synonyms amazing, astonishing, astounding, dumbfounding (*or* dumfounding), eye-opening, flabbergasting, shocking, startling, stunning, stupefying
related words unannounced, unanticipated, unexpected, unforeseen; awesome, awful, breathtaking, fabulous, marvelous (*or* marvellous), miraculous, portentous, prodigious, staggering, stupendous, sublime, wonderful, wondrous; extraordinary, phenomenal, rare, sensational, spectacular; befuddling, bewildering, confounding, confusing, discomfiting, disconcerting, dismaying, muddling, nonplussing, perplexing; incomprehensible, inconceivable, incredible, unbelievable, unimaginable, unthinkable; singular, uncommon, unique, unusual, unwonted; conspicuous, notable, noticeable, outstanding, remarkable; impressive, striking
near antonyms common, customary, mundane, normal, ordinary, typical, unexceptional, unremarkable, usual
2 causing wonder or astonishment ⟨it's *surprising* how much knowledge of physics the architects of those immense medieval cathedrals must have had⟩ — see MARVELOUS 1

surrender *n* the usually forced yielding of one's person or possessions to the control of another ⟨the police demanded the *surrender* of all hostages as a condition for allowing the hijackers safe passage out of the country⟩
synonyms capitulating, capitulation, relinquishment, submission, submitting
related words acceptance, acquiescence, concession; compromise; appeasement, conciliation; capture, fall
near antonyms resistance

surrender *vb* **1** to give (something) over to the control or possession of another usually under duress ⟨Annie *surrendered* the doll to her mother after a brief struggle⟩

⟨the commander *surrendered* the garrison without having fired a single shot⟩
synonyms cede, deliver, give up, hand over, relinquish, render, turn over, yield
related words commit, consign, entrust; waive; renounce, resign; abandon, desert, discard, forsake, shed
near antonyms keep, retain, withhold
2 to cease resistance (as to another's arguments, demands, or control) ⟨the father refused to *surrender* to his son's constant begging for a BB gun⟩ — see YIELD 3
3 to give up (as a position of authority) formally ⟨the aging queen refused to *surrender* the throne to her increasingly impatient heir⟩ — see ABDICATE
4 to give up and cease resistance (as to a liking, temptation, or habit) ⟨determined to give up smoking, she so far has not *surrendered* to her continuing desire to have a cigarette⟩ — see YIELD 1
5 to yield to the control or power of enemy forces ⟨General Robert E. Lee *surrendered* to General Ulysses S. Grant on April 9, 1865, thus ending the Civil War⟩ — see FALL 2
surreptitious *adj* undertaken or done so as to escape being observed or known by others ⟨Eileen made a *surreptitious* signal to Kory that the teacher was coming up behind her⟩ — see SECRET 1
surround *vb* to form a circle around ⟨she was *surrounded* by cheering fans within moments of scoring the winning goal⟩
synonyms circle, encircle, enclose (*also* inclose), encompass, ring
related words fence (in), hem (in), wall; besiege, entrench (*also* intrench), invest
surroundings *n pl* the circumstances, conditions, or objects by which one is surrounded ⟨we relaxed and forgot our worries for a while in the plush *surroundings* of the hotel⟩ — see ENVIRONMENT
surveillance *n* the act or state of being constantly attentive and responsive to signs of opportunity, activity, or danger ⟨the police are maintaining a strict *surveillance* of the suspect⟩ — see VIGILANCE
survey *n* a close look at or over someone or something in order to judge condition ⟨a *survey* of the premises revealed that four of the exit doors were locked⟩ — see INSPECTION
survey *vb* **1** to go around and approach (people) with a request for opinions or information ⟨*surveyed* the students and found out that 60% of them don't think they get enough sleep⟩ — see CANVASS
2 to look over closely (as for judging quality or condition) ⟨*surveyed* the puny weaklings and wondered how he could ever make a football team out of them⟩ — see INSPECT
survive *vb* **1** to come safely through ⟨the cat miraculously *survived* a two-story fall⟩
synonyms ride (out), weather
related words outlast, outlive; pull through; abide, continue, endure, hang on, last, lead, persist; be, breathe, exist, live, subsist; flourish, prosper, thrive
near antonyms croak [*slang*], decease, depart, die, expire, pass (on), pass away, perish, succumb; disappear, evaporate, fade, vanish; cease, end, stop
2 to continue to operate or to meet one's needs ⟨some old-world customs still *survive* in modern-day America⟩ — see HOLD OUT
susceptibility *n* the quality or state of having little resistance to some outside agent ⟨Carol's unfortunate *susceptibility* to viruses meant she was nearly always sick⟩

⟨Stephen had a well-known *susceptibility* to anyone with a pathetic story⟩
synonyms defenselessness, vulnerability, weakness
related words helplessness, powerlessness; passiveness, passivity; feebleness, frailness; exposure, liability, openness, sensitivity; receptiveness, receptivity; easiness, gullibility, näiveté (*also* naivete); credulity, credulousness
near antonyms immunity; impenetrability, indomitability, indomitableness, invincibility
antonyms invulnerability
susceptible *adj* **1** being in a situation where one is likely to meet with harm ⟨some people are more *susceptible* to depression during the winter because of reduced amounts of sunlight⟩ — see LIABLE 1
2 lacking protection from danger or resistance against attack ⟨completely *susceptible* and totally defenseless against the imploring eyes of the puppy in the pet store⟩ — see HELPLESS 1
3 readily taken advantage of ⟨having recently lost his job, he was more *susceptible* to the illusory promises of get-rich-quick schemes⟩ — see EASY 2
suspect *adj* giving good reason for being doubted, questioned, or challenged ⟨her claim to the store's detectives that she had intended to pay for the items was *suspect*, since she was carrying no cash or credit cards⟩ — see DOUBTFUL 2
suspect *vb* **1** to form an opinion from little or no evidence ⟨we *suspected* that the runaway was a little younger than the 16 she claimed to be—more like 13⟩ — see GUESS 1
2 to have no trust or confidence in ⟨I *suspected* him from the moment he said he was an old friend of my sister's, since I probably would have heard about him⟩ — see DISTRUST
suspecting *adj* inclined to doubt or question claims ⟨*suspecting* dieters probably wouldn't fall for a weight-loss plan that claims you can eat as much as you want⟩ — see SKEPTICAL 1
suspend *vb* **1** to bring to a formal close for a period of time ⟨the judge *suspended* the hearing to give the district attorney more time to process evidence⟩ — see ADJOURN
2 to place on an elevated point without support from below ⟨*suspended* a banner proclaiming the town's "Heritage Days" from the archway⟩ — see HANG 1
suspense *n* a state of temporary inactivity ⟨the lawsuit is in *suspense* until the court makes a decision concerning a related lawsuit⟩ — see ABEYANCE
suspension *n* a state of temporary inactivity ⟨trading with that nation is in *suspension* until it improves its record on human rights⟩ — see ABEYANCE
suspicion *vb, chiefly dialect* to form an opinion from little or no evidence ⟨I'm going to pull a prank, and I'm going to do it so no one will ever *suspicion* that I'm the one who did it⟩ — see GUESS 1
suspicion *n* **1** a feeling or attitude that one does not know the truth, truthfulness, or trustworthiness of someone or something ⟨all his promises were received with *suspicion*⟩ — see DOUBT
2 a very small amount ⟨new parents who were alarmed by just a *suspicion* of a rash on their baby's chest⟩ — see PARTICLE 1
suspicious *adj* **1** giving good reason for being doubted, questioned, or challenged ⟨*suspicious* claims of being the rightful owner of the property⟩ — see DOUBTFUL 2

2 inclined to doubt or question claims ⟨*suspicious* of any menu dish having a name she can't pronounce⟩ — see SKEPTICAL 1

3 not feeling sure about the truth, wisdom, or trustworthiness of someone or something ⟨you should be very *suspicious* of those telephone calls from people telling you that you're the winner of a contest you never entered⟩ — see DOUBTFUL 1

suspiciously *adv* with distrust ⟨eyed me *suspiciously* when she saw me cover my paper with a book⟩ — see ASKANCE

sustain *vb* **1** to supply with nourishment ⟨a granola bar will *sustain* you long enough to last until lunch⟩
synonyms nourish, nurture
related words sate, satiate, satisfy; cloy, fill, surfeit; fortify, strengthen; feed; board, cater, provision
2 to come to a knowledge of (something) by living through it ⟨*sustained* heavy losses in the flood⟩ — see EXPERIENCE
3 to put up with (something painful or difficult) ⟨I won't *sustain* such insolence!⟩ — see BEAR 2

sustainable *adj* **1** capable of being defended with good reasoning against verbal attack ⟨a line of argument probably not *sustainable* in a public debate against tough opponents⟩ — see TENABLE 1
2 capable of being proven as true or real ⟨has no *sustainable* claim to the property without a deed or some other document⟩ — see VERIFIABLE
3 capable of being endured ⟨the general didn't think that such heavy casualties could be *sustainable* for much longer⟩ — see BEARABLE

swab *n* one who operates or navigates a seagoing vessel ⟨old *swabs* swapping sea stories as they spend their last days in the veterans' home⟩ — see SAILOR

swag *n* valuables stolen or taken by force ⟨robbed a bank and hid the *swag* under the floorboards⟩ — see LOOT

swagger *vb* **1** to praise or express pride in one's own possessions, qualities, or accomplishments often to excess ⟨I, too, would *swagger* if I'd won first place in the bowling tournament⟩ — see BOAST
2 to walk with exaggerated arm and leg movements ⟨imitating a fashion model, she *swaggered* across the bedroom in her new pajamas⟩ — see STRUT 1

swain *n* **1** a male romantic companion ⟨she was such a coquette, always surrounded by *swains* that she enjoyed toying with⟩ — see BOYFRIEND
2 a man who courts a woman usually with the goal of marrying her ⟨Grandma claims that she had several *swains* pursuing her, but it was only Grandpa who won her heart⟩ — see SUITOR 1

swallow *n* the portion of a serving of a beverage that is swallowed at one time ⟨drank the cool refreshing water in two *swallows* and held out her cup for more⟩ — see DRINK 2

swallow *vb* **1** to take into the stomach through the mouth and throat ⟨try not to *swallow* the toothpaste, because it's not good for you⟩
synonyms down, ingest
related words drink, imbibe, sip; bolt, devour, gobble (up *or* down), gulp; consume, eat, mouth (down); gorge, scarf, scoff, wolf; chew, gnaw (at *or* on), lap, lick, nibble (on); dispatch, polish off
2 to refrain from openly showing or uttering ⟨*swallowed* his pride and asked for help⟩ — see SUPPRESS 2
3 to regard as right or true ⟨my little sister *swallows* everything I tell her⟩ — see BELIEVE 1

swamp *n* spongy land saturated or partially covered with water ⟨be careful in the *swamp*, because alligators sometimes lurk there⟩
synonyms bog, fen, marsh, marshland, mire, morass, muskeg, slough (*also* slue), swampland
related words quagmire; muck, mud, ooze, slime, slop, sludge, slush

swamp *vb* **1** to cover or become filled with a flood ⟨the boat was *swamped* by the huge wave⟩ ⟨*swamped* with homework ever since the first week of school⟩ — see FLOOD
2 to subject to incapacitating emotional or mental stress ⟨parents feeling *swamped* by work and family obligations⟩ — see OVERWHELM 1

swampland *n* spongy land saturated or partially covered with water ⟨much of the county's *swampland* was drained for agriculture⟩ — see SWAMP

swank *or* **swanky** *adj* excessively showy ⟨drove up in a red sports car, the *swank* interior of which was decorated in silver and black⟩ — see GAUDY

swank *n* excessive or unnecessary display ⟨service that is the essence of *swank*: the waiters pull out your chair for you and even place your napkin on your lap⟩ — see OSTENTATION

swankily *adv* in a bright and showy way ⟨an old waiter who remembered when *swankily* dressed mobsters would tip him with a hundred-dollar bill⟩ — see GAILY 3

swap *n* a giving or taking of one thing of value in return for another ⟨we made a *swap*: I'll do the dishes tonight and she'll do them for me tomorrow⟩ — see EXCHANGE 1

swap *vb* to give up (something) and take something else in return ⟨Bobby wasn't willing to *swap* his Yankee's cap for four candy bars⟩ — see CHANGE 3

swarm *n* a great number of persons or things gathered together ⟨a *swarm* of tourists descends upon the island every summer⟩ — see CROWD 1

swarm *vb* to move upon or fill (something) in great numbers ⟨the pirates *swarmed* the decks of the merchant ship⟩ — see CROWD 2

swarming *adj* possessing or covered with great numbers or amounts of something specified ⟨the museum was *swarming* with schoolchildren, since it caters to school groups on Tuesdays⟩ — see RIFE

swash *vb* to move with a splashing motion ⟨waves *swashing* against the shore⟩ — see SLOSH

swat *n* a hard strike with a part of the body or an instrument ⟨Timmy got a *swat* on his wrist for stepping into the street by himself⟩ — see ¹BLOW

swat *vb* to deliver a blow to (someone or something) usually in a strong vigorous manner ⟨didn't sleep a wink all night because she was too busy *swatting* mosquitoes⟩ — see HIT 1

swathe *vb* to surround or cover closely ⟨handed me an odd-shaped package *swathed* in bright pink tissue paper⟩ — see ENFOLD 1

sway *n* **1** the power to bring about a result on another ⟨after the last day of school, under the *sway* of euphoria, I offered to take my little sister to the park⟩ — see EFFECT 2
2 the power to direct the thinking or behavior of others usually indirectly ⟨outdated attitudes that still hold *sway* in some communities⟩ — see INFLUENCE 1
3 the right or means to command or control others ⟨a time when Rome held *sway* over a vast empire that stretched from Britain to the Near East⟩ — see POWER 1

sway *vb* **1** to act upon (a person or a person's feelings) so as to cause a response 〈how can you not be *swayed* by that precious kitten, meowing as if to say, "Please take me home with you?"〉 — see ¹AFFECT 1

2 to make a series of unsteady side-to-side motions 〈the way the ski lift was *swaying* in the wind made me nervous〉 — see ROCK 1

swear *vb* **1** to use offensive or indecent language 〈you're not allowed to *swear* in this house〉

synonyms blaspheme, curse, cuss

related words confound, damn, execrate, imprecate; fulminate, rail, rant

2 to make a solemn declaration of intent 〈*swear* to tell the truth, the whole truth, and nothing but the truth〉 — see PROMISE 1

3 to make a solemn declaration under oath for the purpose of establishing a fact 〈the *sworn* statement of the witness was presented as evidence〉 — see TESTIFY

swearword *n* a disrespectful or indecent word or expression 〈this is a list of *swearwords* that will not be permitted in my classroom〉

synonyms curse, cuss, expletive, obscenity, vulgarism

related words profanity; execration, imprecation, malediction; epithet, name; oath

sweat *n* **1** the active use of energy in producing a result 〈save your *sweat*: no one will appreciate your efforts anyway〉 — see EFFORT

2 very hard or unpleasant work 〈it took years of *sweat* to bring the farm to the point where it is now〉 — see TOIL

sweat *vb* **1** to devote serious and sustained effort 〈spent the afternoon *sweating* over those six math problems〉 — see LABOR

2 to experience concern or anxiety 〈don't *sweat* over getting the application in a day late, as it probably doesn't matter〉 — see WORRY 1

3 to work hard and long 〈after *sweating* so hard to build the business out of nothing, we lost everything〉 — see TOIL

4 to flow forth slowly through small openings 〈the oil coat may *sweat* through this varnish〉 — see EXUDE

sweep *n* an area over which activity, capacity, or influence extends 〈Mrs. Griswold has been a teacher so long, the *sweep* of her influence extends across three generations of the townspeople〉 — see RANGE 2

sweep *vb* **1** to move or proceed smoothly and readily 〈the wind *swept* across the plain〉 — see FLOW 1

2 to turn away from a straight line or course 〈from this point the mountain range *sweeps* to the northeast and extends into the next state〉 — see CURVE 1

sweepstakes *n pl* a competitive encounter between individuals or groups carried on for amusement, exercise, or in pursuit of a prize 〈bought a ticket in a *sweepstakes*, where the chance of winning the grand prize was one in three million〉 — see GAME 1

sweet *adj* **1** granted special treatment or attention 〈promised that he would always take care of his *sweet* sister〉 — see DARLING 1

2 having a pleasant smell 〈breathed in the *sweet* air of the azalea garden〉 — see FRAGRANT

3 having an easygoing and pleasing manner especially in social situations 〈a very *sweet* man directed us to the lost and found〉 — see AMIABLE

4 having qualities that tend to make one loved 〈a *sweet* little kitten〉 — see LOVABLE

sweet *n* **1** a food having a high sugar content 〈remember to brush your teeth after eating *sweets*〉

synonyms confection, sweetmeat

related words confectionery; candy, dessert, pastry

2 a person with whom one is in love 〈Anna, my darling, my *sweet*, won't you be mine?〉 — see SWEETHEART

sweetheart *n* a person with whom one is in love 〈I married my high-school *sweetheart* as soon as we both finished college〉

synonyms beloved, darling, dear, flame, honey, love, sweet

related words beau, boyfriend, fellow, lover, man, swain; gal, girl, girlfriend, ladylove, mistress; date, escort; gallant, suitor, wooer; groom, husband; fiancé, intended; admirer, crush, steady

sweetmeat *n* a food having a high sugar content 〈16th-century Naples carried on a vast export trade in silks and *sweetmeats*〉 — see SWEET 1

sweetness *n* the state or quality of having a pleasant or agreeable manner in socializing with others 〈one sister's *sweetness* was offset by the other's crotchetiness〉 — see AMIABILITY 1

swell *adj* of the very best kind 〈his uncle always talks about what a *swell* time he had when he was in the army〉 — see EXCELLENT

swell *n* a moving ridge on the surface of water 〈huge *swells* overwhelmed the tiny craft〉 — see WAVE

swell *vb* **1** to become greater in extent, volume, amount, or number 〈the club membership has really *swelled* in recent months〉 — see INCREASE 2

2 to make greater in size, amount, or number 〈more layoffs will *swell* the ranks of the unemployed to unprecedented levels〉 — see INCREASE 1

swelling *n* a small rounded mass of swollen tissue 〈was worried that the *swelling* on her neck was cancer〉 — see BUMP 1

sweltering *adj* having a notably high temperature 〈the air conditioning was broken, and it was *sweltering* in the office〉 — see HOT 1

swerve *vb* **1** to depart abruptly from a straight line or course 〈the car *swerved* sharply to avoid the squirrel in the road〉

synonyms sheer, veer, yaw

related words skew, slew (*also* slue); arc, arch, bend, bow, crook, curve, hook, round, sweep, wheel; circle, coil, curl, loop, spiral; turn, twist, wind; deviate, stray, wander, waver

antonyms straighten

2 to turn away from a straight line or course 〈the bike path gently *swerves* to the right〉 — see CURVE 1

3 to cause to turn away from a straight line 〈a dog dashed out in front of me and made me *swerve* my bike into the path of an oncoming car〉 — see BEND 1

swift *adj* moving, proceeding, or acting with great speed 〈the sleekest, *swiftest* boat ever to have sailed in the regatta〉 — see FAST 1

swift *adv* with great speed 〈tried to cross the *swift*-flowing river〉 — see FAST 1

swiftly *adv* with great speed 〈*swiftly* established himself as a star in Hollywood〉 — see FAST 1

swiftness *n* a high rate of movement or performance 〈with amazing *swiftness*, the airline agent got our ticket changed, and we boarded the plane just as it was about to leave〉 — see SPEED

swig *n* the portion of a serving of a beverage that is swallowed at one time 〈can I have just a *swig* of your lemonade to wash down those french fries?〉 — see DRINK 2

swig *vb* to swallow in liquid form ⟨the only way he can stay awake at his night job is by constantly *swigging* drinks containing caffeine⟩ — see DRINK 1

swill *n* the portion of a serving of a beverage that is swallowed at one time ⟨took his daily *swill* of the foul-tasting medicine⟩ — see DRINK 2

swill *vb* **1** to eat greedily or to excess ⟨you spend your time *swilling* in fast-food restaurants, and then you wonder why you're fat⟩ — see GORGE 2

2 to swallow in liquid form ⟨the way she *swills* carbonated drinks, she ought to own stock in a soda company⟩ — see DRINK 1

swiller *n* one who eats greedily or too much ⟨after the swinish *swiller* had finally had his fill, he belched loudly⟩ — see GLUTTON

swim *vb* to be in a confused state as if from being twirled around ⟨once they were in the elevator, the scent of the woman's perfume was so overpowering that it made his head *swim*⟩ — see SPIN 2

swimmingly *adv* in a pleasing way ⟨the rehearsals were going *swimmingly* until half the cast came down with the flu⟩ — see WELL 5

swindle *n* a scheme in which the victim is cheated out of his money after first gaining his trust ⟨a *swindle* that involved selling a lot of land that really didn't exist⟩ — see CONFIDENCE GAME

swindle *vb* to rob by the use of trickery or threats ⟨hundreds of people were *swindled* out of their savings, and all they had to show for it were fake land deeds⟩ — see FLEECE

swindler *n* a dishonest person who uses clever means to cheat others out of something of value ⟨the *swindlers*, representing themselves as land developers, produced a glossy brochure showing beaches, palm trees, and golf links⟩ — see TRICKSTER 1

swing *vb* **1** to change one's course or direction ⟨thinking that we were being followed, we abruptly *swung* to the left at the next intersection⟩ — see TURN 3

2 to change the course or direction of (something) ⟨at the sound of gunfire, the cavalry officer *swung* his horse around and galloped rapidly back to the fort⟩ — see TURN 2

3 to deal with (something) usually skillfully or efficiently ⟨a man who's able to *swing* two full-time jobs⟩ — see HANDLE 1

4 to move (something) in a curved or circular path on or as if on an axis ⟨*swung* the bat and missed the ball⟩ ⟨don't let the wind *swing* that gate shut⟩ — see TURN 1

5 to place on an elevated point without support from below ⟨beach towels *swung* up to dry on the lifeguard's high chair⟩ — see HANG 1

swipe *n* a hard strike with a part of the body or an instrument ⟨one *swipe* of a grizzly's paw can do a person in⟩ — see ¹BLOW

swipe *vb* **1** to come into usually forceful contact with something ⟨an odd personage *swiping* at windmills with his sword⟩ — see HIT 2

2 to deliver a blow to (someone or something) usually in a strong vigorous manner ⟨that car just *swiped* the fender of our car⟩ — see HIT 1

3 to take (something) without right and with an intent to keep ⟨somebody *swiped* the stop sign that used to be on the corner⟩ — see STEAL 1

swiping *n* an instance of theft ⟨when the cheese *swipings* abruptly stopped, we wondered if the mouse had met his end elsewhere⟩ — see THEFT 2

swirl *vb* **1** to cause (as a liquid) to move about in a circle especially repeatedly ⟨kept *swirling* her lemonade until

I thought the sound of clinking ice would drive me insane⟩ — see STIR 1

2 to move (something) in a curved or circular path on or as if on an axis ⟨*swirled* her skirts as she danced the tango⟩ — see TURN 1

swish *n* a sound similar to the speech sound \s\ stretched out ⟨the steady *swish* of the windshield wipers⟩ — see HISS 1

swish *vb* to make a sound like that of stretching out the speech sound \s\ ⟨with their satin costumes *swishing*, the little ballerinas pirouetted onto the stage⟩ — see HISS

switch *n* **1** a long thin or flexible tool for striking ⟨struck the horse's hide with a leather *switch*, and it took off at a gallop⟩ — see WHIP

2 a quick jerky movement from side to side or up and down ⟨that telltale *switch* of the cat's tail meant there was a mouse under the piano⟩ — see WAG 1

switch *vb* **1** to give up (something) and take something else in return ⟨*switched* the real grapes for fake ones⟩ ⟨*switched* the day of his flight from Thursday to Friday⟩ — see CHANGE 3

2 to move from side to side or up and down with quick jerky motions ⟨cows lazily *switching* their tails and chewing their cud⟩ — see WAG

3 to strike repeatedly with something long and thin or flexible ⟨kept *switching* his horse to make it go faster⟩ — see WHIP 1

4 to change (as an opinion) to the contrary ⟨a politician who has *switched* his position on a number of issues⟩ — see REVERSE 1

swoon *n* a temporary or permanent state of unconsciousness ⟨fell into a *swoon* at the sight of the handsome movie star⟩ — see FAINT

swoon *vb* to lose consciousness ⟨whenever the young woman *swooned*, she always seemed to manage falling into the arms of a good-looking man⟩ — see FAINT

sword *n* a hand weapon with a length of metal sharpened on one or both sides and usually tapered to a sharp point ⟨once upon a time dueling with *swords* was the gentlemanly way to settle a point of honor⟩

synonyms blade, steel

related words broadsword, cutlass, rapier, saber (*or* sabre), scimitar

sycophant *n* a person who flatters another in order to get ahead ⟨my teacher isn't fooled by the class *sycophants*, who are always telling her what a wonderful teacher she is⟩

synonyms fawner, flunky (*also* flunkey), toady

related words yes-man; hanger-on, leech, parasite, sponge, sponger; henchman, lackey, minion, satellite, slave, stooge; admirer, cultist, devotee, enthusiast, fan, groveler (*or* groveller), idolater (*or* idolator), worshipper (*or* worshiper), zealot; adherent, convert, disciple, follower, partisan, pupil, votary

symbol *n* **1** a device, design, or figure used as an identifying mark ⟨we immediately recognized the physician's *symbol* on the door—a staff entwined with a snake⟩ — see EMBLEM

2 a written or printed mark that is meant to convey information to the reader ⟨the *symbol* ¶ indicates where a new paragraph should begin⟩ — see CHARACTER 1

symbolic *also* **symbolical** *adj* having the function or meaning of a symbol ⟨the teddy bear in the story was intended to be *symbolic* of a mother's love⟩

synonyms emblematic (*also* emblematical), representative

related words figurative, metaphorical; allegorical

antonyms nonsymbolic

symbolize *vb* to serve as a material counterpart of ⟨the flag *symbolizes* our country⟩
synonyms represent
related words embody, epitomize, incarnate, manifest, materialize, personalize, personify; exemplify, illustrate
phrases stand for

symmetry *n* a balanced, pleasing, or suitable arrangement of parts ⟨planted an azalea bush on either side of the steps for *symmetry*⟩ — see HARMONY 1

sympathetic *adj* **1** having or showing the capacity for sharing the feelings of another ⟨a *sympathetic* smile⟩ ⟨Jane was always a *sympathetic* listener⟩
synonyms compassionate, humane, understanding
related words gentle, sensitive, softhearted, tender, tenderhearted, warm, warmhearted; benevolent, benignant, charitable, kind, clement, lenient, merciful; cordial, friendly, good-natured, good-tempered, gracious; affectionate, loving
near antonyms inconsiderate, insensitive, thoughtless, unthinking; uncaring, unloving; merciless, pitiless, ruthless; grim, hard-bitten, hard-boiled, harsh, oppressive, rough, severe, stern, tough, ungentle; abusive, acrimonious, disagreeable, hateful, ill-natured, ill-tempered, malevolent, malicious, mean, rancorous, spiteful, surly, virulent
antonyms callous, cold-blooded, hardhearted, heartless, inhuman, inhumane, unfeeling, unsympathetic
2 having or marked by sympathy and consideration for others ⟨a *sympathetic* store manager who let us use the employee restrooms⟩ ⟨*sympathetic* letters from supporters after the disappointing election results⟩ — see HUMANE 1

sympathize (with) *vb* to have sympathy for ⟨don't expect me to *sympathize with* you—you should have started your homework yesterday instead of waiting till Sunday evening⟩ — see PITY

sympathizer *n* someone associated with another to give assistance or moral support ⟨doesn't have many *sympathizers* since everyone knows he brought his troubles on himself⟩ — see ALLY

sympathy *n* **1** sorrow or the capacity to feel sorrow for another's suffering or misfortune ⟨although I'd never lost a relative, I felt great *sympathy* for the classmate whose grandfather died⟩
synonyms commiseration, compassion, feeling
related words condolence, regret; humanity, kindheartedness, kindliness, kindness, mercy, pity, softheartedness; affinity, empathy, rapport, sensitivity; altruism, benevolence, benignity, charity, generosity, goodwill, humanitarianism, philanthropy
near antonyms indifference, insensitivity, unconcern; cruelty, harshness; animosity, antipathy, dislike, hatred, hostility
antonyms callousness, hardheartedness, heartlessness
2 the capacity for feeling for another's unhappiness or misfortune ⟨the least you could do is have some *sympathy* for me if I have to stay home⟩ — see HEART 1

symphonic *adj* having a pleasing mixture of notes ⟨a *symphonic* chorus of frogs⟩ — see HARMONIOUS 1

symphony *n* **1** a balanced, pleasing, or suitable arrangement of parts ⟨the satisfying *symphony* of color in Renoir's canvases⟩ — see HARMONY 1

2 a usually large group of musicians playing together ⟨a performance of a Bach concerto by the San Antonio *Symphony*⟩ — see ²BAND 1

symphony orchestra *n* a usually large group of musicians playing together ⟨plays oboe in the local *symphony orchestra*⟩ — see ²BAND 1

symposium *n* a meeting featuring a group discussion ⟨recently attended a day-long *symposium* on new methods of chromatography⟩ — see FORUM

symptomatic *adj* serving to identify as belonging to an individual or group ⟨a fever's refusal to respond to antibiotics is *symptomatic* of a viral infection⟩ — see CHARACTERISTIC 1

synchronous *adj* existing or occurring at the same period of time ⟨the *synchronous* arrival of a baby sister and loss of a beloved grandmother strongly affected the child⟩ — see CONTEMPORARY 1

syndicate *n* **1** a group involved in secret or criminal activities ⟨a *syndicate* of counterfeiters⟩ — see RING 1
2 a number of businesses or enterprises united for commercial advantage ⟨a powerful banking *syndicate* that controls loans in the small country⟩ — see CARTEL

synopsis *n* a short statement of the main points ⟨I don't need to know every little plot twist; just give me a *synopsis* of the movie⟩ — see SUMMARY

synthetic *adj* being such in appearance only and made with or manufactured from usually cheaper materials ⟨*synthetic* fur collars⟩ ⟨boots of waterproof *synthetic* leather⟩ — see IMITATION

syringe *n* a slender hollow instrument by which material is put into or taken from the body through the skin ⟨the *syringe* the nurse was leveling at my arm looked to me to be at least ten inches long⟩ — see NEEDLE 1

syrupy *adj* being of a consistency that resists flow ⟨instead of neat squares of fudge we had *syrupy* goo⟩ — see THICK 2

system *n* **1** something made up of many interdependent or related parts ⟨the national highway *system* allows travel from one end of the country to the other⟩ ⟨the constitutional *system* of checks and balances in government⟩
synonyms complex, network
related words interlacement, Internet, net, web; aggregate, conglomerate, totality, whole
2 a method worked out in advance for achieving some objective ⟨if you're going to wrap all these presents in one afternoon, you'll need a *system*⟩ — see PLAN 1
3 the means or procedure for doing something ⟨not the best *system* perhaps, but it gets the job done⟩ — see METHOD

systematic *adj* following a set method, arrangement, or pattern ⟨the first *systematic* effort to find witnesses to the crime⟩ ⟨*systematic* elimination and reintroduction of certain foods to determine what he's allergic to⟩ — see METHODICAL

systematize *vb* to put into a particular arrangement ⟨Carl Linnaeus was the first to *systematize* the plant and animal kingdoms by creating a uniform system for naming genera and species of organisms⟩ — see ORDER 1

systematized *adj* following a set method, arrangement, or pattern ⟨a *systematized* arrangement of books⟩ — see METHODICAL

T

tab *n* **1** a record of goods sold or services performed together with the costs due ⟨I don't have any cash on me, so can you put this on my *tab*?⟩ — see ¹BILL 1

2 the amount owed at a bar or restaurant or the slip of paper stating the amount ⟨asked the server to put our dinners on separate *tabs* so we could each pay for our own meal⟩ — see CHECK 1

tabernacle *n* a building for public worship and especially Christian worship ⟨worshippers gathering at the *tabernacle* on a bright Sunday morning⟩ — see CHURCH 1

table *n* **1** a leg-mounted piece of furniture with a broad flat top designed for the serving of food ⟨we sat at the kitchen *table*, playing cards for hours on end⟩
synonyms board
related words coffee table, refectory table; bar, counter; buffet, sideboard

2 food eaten or prepared for eating at one time ⟨offers a well-prepared *table* for his guests⟩ — see MEAL

3 a broad flat area of elevated land ⟨the area between the two canyons forms one broad *table*⟩ — see PLATEAU

4 a record of a series of items (as names or titles) usually arranged according to some system ⟨the periodic *table* of chemical elements⟩ — see ¹LIST

5 substances intended to be eaten ⟨the *table* that the innkeeper set out each morning made for a bountiful breakfast indeed⟩ — see FOOD

tableland *n* a broad flat area of elevated land ⟨to the east of the valley lies a vast, fertile *tableland*⟩ — see PLATEAU

tablet *n* **1** a number of sheets of writing paper glued together at one edge ⟨please take out your writing *tablet* and flip to a clean page for your spelling test⟩ — see PAD 1

2 a small mass containing medicine to be taken orally ⟨take two *tablets* of the medication every eight hours⟩ — see PILL

table talk *n* friendly, informal conversation or an instance of this ⟨he thought he weathered the *table talk* over dinner with his future in-laws rather well⟩ — see CHAT

tableware *n* **1** eating and serving utensils ⟨we ran short of *tableware*, so Emily went next door and borrowed some forks and knives⟩
synonyms flatware, silver, silverware
related words place setting, setting; silver plate; cutlery; chopstick, fork, knife, spoon, tablespoon, teaspoon

2 dishes used for eating or serving food or drink ⟨Betty would take out her good *tableware* only on special occasions, as when the mayor came to dinner⟩
synonyms dinnerware
related words setting; china, chinaware, crockery, earthenware, porcelain, pottery, stoneware, ware; crystal, glassware; plate, saucer; cup, glass, goblet, mug, teacup; bowl, casserole, charger, platter, tureen

taboo *also* **tabu** *adj* that may not be permitted ⟨asking a guest how much money he or she makes is strictly *taboo* because it's a rude question to ask a stranger⟩ — see IMPERMISSIBLE

tacit *adj* understood although not put into words ⟨we have a *tacit* agreement that if I wash the dishes, she dries them and puts them away⟩ — see IMPLICIT

taciturn *adj* tending not to speak frequently (as by habit or inclination) ⟨a *taciturn* man, he almost never starts a conversation with someone⟩ — see SILENT 2

tack *n* the means or procedure for doing something ⟨this clearly isn't working, so let's take a different *tack* in trying to solve the problem⟩ — see METHOD

tack (on) *vb* to join (something) to a mass, quantity, or number so as to bring about an overall increase ⟨the teacher *tacked on* extra assignments just before the start of winter break⟩ — see ADD 1

tackle *n* items needed for the performance of a task or activity ⟨grabbed my fishing *tackle* and headed out early one morning⟩ — see EQUIPMENT

tackle *vb* to start work on energetically ⟨once I clean the kitchen, I think I'll *tackle* the bathroom⟩ — see ATTACK 3

tacky *adj* **1** marked by an obvious lack of style or good taste ⟨it was *tacky* to wear sneakers, but Tracey's dress shoes hurt her feet⟩ ⟨*tacky* plastic flowers⟩
synonyms cheesy, dowdy, inelegant, styleless, tasteless, trashy, unfashionable, unstylish
related words inappropriate, incorrect, unbecoming, unseemly, unsuitable, wrong; outmoded, out-of-date, passé; coarse, crude, unrefined, vulgar; cheap, common, inferior, junky, lousy, low-grade, second-rate, shoddy, sleazy, tawdry; gaudy, loud, ostentatious, overdone, showy, splashy
near antonyms appropriate, becoming, correct, fitting, proper, right, seemly, suitable; genteel, handsome, neat, quiet, refined, understated; contemporary, modern, up-to-date
antonyms elegant, fashionable, modish, ritzy, smart, stylish, tasteful

2 showing signs of advanced wear and tear and neglect ⟨a *tacky* old couch that needed new upholstery⟩ — see SHABBY 1

tact *n* the ability to deal with others in touchy situations without offending them ⟨with supreme *tact*, Isabel suggested to her neighbor that her flower garden was probably not the best place for his dog to use as a bathroom⟩
synonyms diplomacy, tactfulness
related words considerateness, consideration, courtesy, delicacy, graciousness, thoughtfulness; civility, etiquette, mannerliness, manners, politeness; charm, gallantry, gentility, grace, gracefulness, suaveness, suavity; adroitness, deftness, dexterity, finesse; deference, regard, respect
near antonyms discourteousness, discourtesy, inconsiderateness, inconsideration, indelicacy, thoughtlessness, ungraciousness, unthoughtfulness; impoliteness, incivility; boorishness, brashness, brassiness, loutishness; awkwardness, gaucheness, gracelessness, maladroitness; disregard, disrespect, impertinence, impudence, insolence, rudeness
antonyms tactlessness

tactful *adj* having or showing tact ⟨Allie tried to be *tactful* when asked to comment on the short story that a classmate had written⟩
synonyms diplomatic
related words considerate, courteous, delicate, gracious, thoughtful; civil, mannerly, polite; charming,

gallant, genteel, suave; deferential, regardful, respectful

near antonyms discourteous, inconsiderate, indelicate, thoughtless, ungracious, unthoughtful; ill-bred, ill-mannered, impolite, uncivil, unmannerly; boorish, brash, brassy, loutish; disregardful, disrespectful, impertinent, impudent, insolent, rude

antonyms tactless, undiplomatic

tactfulness *n* the ability to deal with others in touchy situations without offending them ⟨the *tactfulness* with which the secretary of state handled that diplomatic crisis is commendable⟩ — see TACT

tactical *adj* suitable for bringing about a desired result under the circumstances ⟨made the *tactical* move of becoming friendly with the journalism teacher, hoping that this would get him appointed editor of the school newspaper⟩ — see EXPEDIENT

tactics *n pl* the means or procedure for doing something ⟨used dishonest *tactics* to win the school council elections⟩ — see METHOD

tactless *adj* showing poor judgment especially in personal relationships or social situations ⟨made a *tactless* remark about how the girl's dress had that "homemade" look⟩ — see INDISCREET

tad *n* a male person who has not yet reached adulthood ⟨grandfather never tires of telling us about the days when he was just a *tad*⟩ — see BOY

tag *n* a slip (as of paper or cloth) that is attached to something to identify or describe it ⟨read the *tag* on the shirt to find out if I could wash it or if it had to be dry cleaned⟩ — see LABEL

tag *vb* **1** to attach an identifying slip to ⟨*tagged* all the dresses with sale stickers before putting them on the rack⟩ — see LABEL 1

2 to go after or on the track of ⟨wildlife experts surreptitiously *tagged* the timber wolf, carefully keeping a safe distance so the wolf wouldn't catch their scent and run⟩ — see FOLLOW 2

tagging *n* the act of going after or in the tracks of another ⟨after a week-long *tagging* of the suspect, the detective had the all the evidence he needed that there was a smuggling operation going on⟩ — see PURSUIT

tail *n* a person whose business is solving crimes and catching criminals or gathering information that is not easy to get ⟨the robber sped away in the getaway car, hoping to shake the *tail* that was following him⟩ — see DETECTIVE

tail *vb* to go after or on the track of ⟨*tailed* my older brother to see where he was going at that time of the evening⟩ — see FOLLOW 2

tailing *n* the act of going after or in the tracks of another ⟨my attempt at secretly *tailing* the girls was ruined by my loud and uncontrollable hiccups⟩ — see PURSUIT

tailored *adj* made or fitted to the needs or preferences of a specific customer ⟨pants bought off the rack never fit me so I have to buy *tailored* pants instead⟩ — see CUSTOM-MADE

tailor–made *adj* made or fitted to the needs or preferences of a specific customer ⟨took my measurements for the *tailor-made* bridal gown⟩ — see CUSTOM-MADE

taint *n* a mark of guilt or disgrace ⟨that rare political campaign that wasn't marred by the *taint* of false accusations⟩ — see STAIN 1

taint *vb* **1** to affect slightly with something morally bad or undesirable ⟨criticism of her sister's singing that was *tainted* by envy⟩ ⟨a tendency toward conceitedness *taints* that athlete's status as a role model⟩

synonyms blemish, mar, poison, spoil, stain, tarnish, touch, vitiate

related words besmear, besmirch, blacken, cloud, dirty, discolor, smear, smirch, smudge, smut, soil, sully, tar; color, distort, twist; damage, deface, flaw, harm, hurt, impair; destroy, ruin, wreck

near antonyms cleanse, purify; elevate, ennoble, uplift

2 to make unfit for use by the addition of something harmful or undesirable ⟨smog has long *tainted* the air of that city, making it difficult to breathe⟩ — see CONTAMINATE

tainted *adj* containing foreign or lower-grade substances ⟨*tainted* groundwater that is unfit to drink⟩ — see IMPURE

take *n* **1** action or behavior that is done in return to other action or behavior ⟨what's your *take* on the announcement that the principal is retiring?⟩ — see REACTION

2 the total amount collected or obtained especially at one time ⟨who will win the card game and collect the whole *take*?⟩ — see HAUL 1

take *vb* **1** to reach for and take hold of by embracing with the fingers or arms ⟨*take* my hand, or we'll get separated in this crowd⟩

synonyms clasp, grasp, grip, hold

related words clench, cling (to), clutch, hang on (to), hold on (to); catch, nab, seize, snatch

phrases lay hold of

near antonyms discharge, drop, free, liberate, release; give, hand, relinquish, unhand

2 to agree to receive whether willingly or reluctantly ⟨will you *take* that call?⟩ ⟨*took* a cut in pay⟩

synonyms accept, have

related words accede (to), assent (to), concede (to), consent (to), OK (*or* okay); acquiesce (to), bow (to), capitulate (to), give in (to), submit (to), succumb (to), surrender (to), yield (to); bear, endure, shoulder, tolerate, swallow; adopt, embrace, welcome

near antonyms dissent (to), object (to), oppose, protest; hold off, resist, withstand

antonyms decline, refuse, reject, spurn, turn down

3 to become affected with (a disease or disorder) ⟨if you don't cover your head in this weather, you'll *take* cold and be stuck inside all weekend⟩ — see CONTRACT 1

4 to decide to accept (someone or something) from a group of possibilities ⟨you can *take* the white side this time, since I got to be white for our last chess game⟩ — see CHOOSE 1

5 to get possession of (something) by giving money in exchange for ⟨I'll *take* two cheeseburgers to go, please⟩ — see BUY

6 to have as a requirement ⟨it will *take* a lot of courage to stand up to the bully⟩ — see NEED 1

7 to make or have room for ⟨I think we can *take* two more in this elevator⟩ — see ACCOMMODATE 1

8 to produce a desired effect ⟨it will be a few hours before this medication *takes*⟩ — see ACT 2

9 to put up with (something painful or difficult) ⟨I can't *take* your whining about your former boyfriend anymore⟩ — see BEAR 2

take (for) *vb* to think of in a particular way ⟨what do you *take* me *for*, a fool?⟩ — see CONSIDER 1

take back *vb* to solemnly or formally reject or go back on (as something formerly adhered to) ⟨I *take back* what I said about her: she's not the brat I thought she was⟩ — see ABJURE

take down *vb* **1** to reduce to a lower standing in one's own eyes or in others' eyes ⟨there's no need to *take* us *down* by making fun of our clothes⟩ — see HUMBLE

2 to take apart ⟨electricians will *take down* all the lights for the set after the play has finished its run⟩ — see DISASSEMBLE

take in *vb* **1** to cause to believe what is untrue ⟨that new kid completely *took* me *in* when he told me that his father owned a major software company⟩ — see DECEIVE

2 to have as part of a whole ⟨this report *takes in* all the latest information on the subject⟩ — see INCLUDE

3 to provide with living quarters or shelter ⟨*took in* the stray dog⟩ — see HOUSE 1

takeoff *n* **1** a rising from a surface at the start of a flight (as of a rocket) ⟨make sure your tray table is safely put away during *takeoff*⟩ — see LIFT-OFF

2 a work that imitates and exaggerates another work for comic effect ⟨a sitcom that's a *takeoff* of an old TV show from the 1960s⟩ — see PARODY 1

take off *vb* **1** to leave a place often for another ⟨I can only stay for a few minutes, and then I'll need to *take off* again⟩ — see GO 2

2 to rid oneself of (a garment) ⟨*take off* your coat⟩ — see REMOVE 1

3 to take away (an amount or number) from a total ⟨the store will *take* an additional 20% *off* if you bring in this coupon⟩ — see SUBTRACT

take off (on) *vb* to copy or exaggerate (someone or something) in order to make fun of ⟨I didn't know I bounced when I walked until I saw the little kids in my neighborhood *taking off on* my walk⟩ — see MIMIC 1

take on *vb* **1** to enter into contest or conflict with ⟨will *take on* his chief opponent in the next debate⟩ — see ENGAGE 2

2 to provide with a paying job ⟨decided to *take* her *on* as store manager⟩ — see EMPLOY 1

take out *vb* **1** to find emotional release for ⟨*took out* his frustrations by splitting a cord of firewood⟩

synonyms loose, release, unleash, vent

phrases give way (to)

near antonyms control, govern, handle, manage; bridle, check, contain, curb, hold back, hold in, quell, restrain, smother; allay, lull, quiet, soothe, still; choke, inhibit, muffle, pocket, repress, stifle, strangle, swallow

antonyms bottle (up), repress, suppress

2 to go on a social engagement with ⟨she'd like to *take* the new boy *out* to the movies sometime⟩ — see DATE 1

take over *vb* **1** to serve as a replacement usually for a time only ⟨I'll *take over* for her until she gets back from her morning break⟩ — see COVER 1

2 to take to or upon oneself ⟨*took over* the responsibility of caring for the animals⟩ — see ASSUME 1

take up *vb* to take for one's own use (something originated by another) ⟨the emcee of the sports awards program started chanting the team name of the champions, and the crowd quickly *took up* the cry⟩ — see ADOPT

taking *adj* very pleasing to look at ⟨had never seen such a *taking* city as Venice⟩ — see BEAUTIFUL

tale *n* **1** a rumor or report of a personal or sensational nature ⟨don't believe the *tales* you hear about our neighbor's kid⟩

synonyms story, whisper

related words dirt, gossip, scuttlebutt, talebearing, talk, tattle; defamation, libel, slander; hearsay; fabrication, fairy tale, falsehood, falsity, fib, lie

2 a brief account of something interesting that happened especially to one personally ⟨asked Dad to tell the *tale* of how, as a kid, he broke his arm jumping out of a tree⟩ — see STORY 2

3 a statement known by its maker to be untrue and made in order to deceive ⟨told tall *tales* in an attempt to impress me with her British background⟩ — see LIE

4 a work with imaginary characters and events that is shorter and usually less complex than a novel ⟨when we asked for a bedtime story, Dad read us the *tale* of Sleeping Beauty⟩ — see STORY 1

talebearer *n* a person who provides secret information about another's wrongdoing ⟨the teacher told him not to be such a *talebearer*, as she was quite capable of detecting student misbehavior on her own⟩ — see INFORMER

talent *n* a special and usually inborn ability ⟨Liza's musical *talent* was already apparent by the time she was five⟩ ⟨Jim's *talent* for coming up with really funny answers⟩

synonyms aptitude, endowment, faculty, flair, genius, gift, knack

related words bent, inclination, leaning, partiality, penchant, predilection, predisposition, proclivity, propensity, turn; ear, eye, head, mind, nose; feel, hang, instinct, touch, way; capability, competence, facility, proficiency, skill; capacity, potential, power

near antonyms disability, handicap, inability, incapacity; shortcoming, weakness

talisman *n* something worn or kept to bring good luck or keep away evil ⟨asked the witch for a *talisman* that was sure to make the prince fall in love with her⟩ — see CHARM 1

talk *n* **1** a usually formal discourse delivered to an audience ⟨went to the auditorium to hear the author's *talk* on the modern novel⟩ — see SPEECH 1

2 an exchange of views for the purpose of exploring a subject or deciding an issue ⟨what good will all this *talk* do when we need to take action now?⟩ — see DISCUSSION 1

3 friendly, informal conversation or an instance of this ⟨sat down by the fire and had a nice little *talk* about what was new in the village⟩ — see CHAT

talk *vb* **1** to give a formal often extended talk on a subject ⟨detective Connolly often *talks* at school assemblies about safety⟩

synonyms declaim, descant, discourse, expatiate, harangue, lecture, orate, speak

related words recite, soliloquize; mouth, spout; filibuster; stump; eulogize

phrases hold forth, take the floor

2 to engage in casual or rambling conversation ⟨*talked* with our neighbor as we unloaded the groceries from the car⟩ — see CHAT

3 to express (a thought or emotion) in words ⟨you're *talking* nonsense: take a minute and think about what you are trying to say, and then start speaking⟩ — see SAY 1

4 to give information (as to the authorities) about another's improper or unlawful activities ⟨after being threatened, the man started *talking* at length about what he had seen in the alley⟩ — see SQUEAL 1

5 to relate sometimes questionable or secret information of a personal nature ⟨you're a fine one to *talk* about your sister's boy problems when you have had plenty of your own⟩ — see GOSSIP

talk (into) *vb* to cause (someone) to agree with a belief or course of action by using arguments or earnest request

⟨the salesman *talked* us *into* buying a new vacuum⟩ — see PERSUADE 1

talk (to) *vb* to communicate with by means of spoken words ⟨Patty had never *talked to* a real live cowboy before⟩
synonyms chat (with), converse (with), speak (to *or* with)
related words accost, address, greet, hail, herald; inform, notify, tell
phrases engage in conversation

talkative *adj* fond of talking or conversation ⟨a *talkative* outgoing tour guide showed our school group around the city⟩
synonyms chatty, conversational, gabby, garrulous, loquacious, talky
related words communicative, expansive; demonstrative, effusive, gushing; outspoken, unreserved, vocal; articulate, fluent, glib, voluble; blabby, gossipy, talebearing; long-winded, prolix, verbose, windy, wordy; extroverted (*also* extraverted), gregarious, outgoing, sociable
near antonyms quiet, shy; mum, mute, silent, speechless, tongue-tied, wordless; evasive, nonvocal, secretive, self-contained, uncommunicative; aloof, introverted, unsociable, withdrawn
antonyms closemouthed, laconic, reserved, reticent, taciturn, tight-lipped

talker *n* a person who talks constantly ⟨your brother is quite a *talker*—he wouldn't let me get a word in edgewise⟩ — see CHATTERBOX

talk over *vb* to talk about (an issue) usually from various points of view and for the purpose of arriving at a decision or opinion ⟨your father and I will have to *talk* it *over* before we'll agree to let you go on the class trip⟩ — see DISCUSS

talky *adj* fond of talking or conversation ⟨a *talky* person who will keep you at his desk for hours with stories about his vacation⟩ — see TALKATIVE

tall *adj* **1** extending to a great distance upward ⟨*tall* skyscrapers that cast long shadows over the park⟩ — see HIGH 1
2 requiring considerable physical or mental effort ⟨that's a pretty *tall* order⟩ — see HARD 2

tally *n* a total number obtained or recorded by noting each thing as it was being added ⟨the final *tally* for worshippers at Sunday services was 126⟩ — see COUNT 1

tally *vb* **1** to be in agreement on every point ⟨our lists for best movies of the year *tally* perfectly⟩ — see CHECK 1
2 to gain (as points or runs in a game) as credit towards one's total number of points ⟨our team *tallied* four touchdowns and gained a total of 435 yards last game⟩ — see SCORE 2

tame *adj* **1** changed from the wild state so as to become useful and obedient to humans ⟨every evening, a Canada goose is at the food trough with our *tame* geese⟩
synonyms domestic, domesticated, tamed
related words broken, housebroken, trained; docile, gentle
near antonyms unbroken, untrained
antonyms feral, nondomesticated, undomesticated, untamed, wild
2 causing weariness, restlessness, or lack of interest ⟨that action movie was so *tame* I fell asleep about 20 minutes into it⟩ — see BORING

tame *vb* to keep from exceeding a desirable degree or level (as of expression) ⟨try to *tame* your language when you're in front of the kids⟩ — see CONTROL 1

tamed *adj* changed from the wild state so as to become useful and obedient to humans ⟨circus trainers work with *tamed* tigers and elephants⟩ — see TAME 1

tamper (with) *vb* to handle thoughtlessly, ignorantly, or mischievously ⟨someone has *tampered with* my computer files⟩
synonyms fiddle (with), fool (with), mess (with), monkey (with), play (with), tinker (with)
related words alter, doctor, manhandle, manipulate, misuse; butt in, interfere, intrude, meddle

tan *vb* to strike repeatedly with something long and thin or flexible ⟨Grandpa told us that when he was a kid, if he misbehaved at all, his father would *tan* his backside⟩ — see WHIP 1

tangent *n* a departure from the subject under consideration ⟨in the middle of her description of her dog's symptoms, she went off on a *tangent* about its cute behavior⟩
synonyms digression, excursion
related words aside, parenthesis; rambling; circuitousness, circularity, circumlocution

tangible *adj* capable of being perceived by the sense of touch ⟨a firm belief in the existence of the soul, even though it is not at all *tangible*⟩
synonyms palpable, touchable
related words tactile; corporeal, physical; actual, concrete, embodied, existent, material, real, substantial; discernible, observable, perceptible, sensible
near antonyms bodiless, immaterial, incorporeal, insubstantial, nonmaterial, nonphysical, unsubstantial; abstract, ethereal, spiritual, unreal
antonyms impalpable, intangible

tangle *vb* **1** to catch or hold as if in a net ⟨was *tangled* in the web of lies that he had told to everyone⟩ — see ENTANGLE 2
2 to twist together into a usually confused mass ⟨the kitten *tangled* the yarn I was trying to knit with and now I have to pull out all the knots out before I can continue⟩ — see ENTANGLE 1

tantrum *n* an outburst or display of excited anger ⟨had a *tantrum* when he found his little sister using his model paints⟩
synonyms blowup, explosion, fireworks, fit, huff, scene
related words eruption, flare-up, outburst, storm; agitation, delirium, distraction, frenzy, furor, furore, fury, hysteria, rage, rampage, uproar; convulsion(s), paroxysm, seizure, spasm, upheaval; reaction, rise; dander, temper; pet, pouts, sulk(s)

tap *n* a fixture for controlling the flow of a liquid ⟨turn the *tap* to the right for cold water and to the left for hot water⟩ — see FAUCET

¹tap *vb* to strike or cause to strike lightly and usually rhythmically ⟨*tapped* her foot in time to the music⟩ ⟨kept *tapping* the desk with his pencil⟩
synonyms beat, drum, rap, thrum
related words bang, hammer, hit, knock, pound, thud, thump, thwack, whack; chink, clatter, clink, ping; pat; chuck, clap, flick, tip

²tap *vb* to remove (liquid) gradually or completely ⟨the oil company *tapped* that first oil well dry⟩ — see DRAIN 1

taper *vb* to grow less in scope or intensity especially gradually ⟨you'll find the symptoms begin *tapering* gradually about 24 hours after you take the medicine⟩ — see DECREASE 2

taper off *vb* to grow less in scope or intensity especially gradually ⟨at this time of the year, light begins to *taper off* a little earlier each day⟩ — see DECREASE 2

tar *n* one who operates or navigates a seagoing vessel ⟨got a book from the library about the adventurous lives of *tars*, skippers, and pirates of the 18th century⟩ — see SAILOR

tardily *adv* at a pace that is less than usual, desirable, or expected ⟨the money that I had lent him for the CDs came *tardily* and only after I told him that if he didn't repay me, I was taking the CDs back⟩ — see SLOW

tardiness *n* the quality or state of being late ⟨habitual *tardiness* will lower your grade in my class⟩ — see LATENESS

tardy *adj* **1** moving or proceeding at less than the normal, desirable, or required speed ⟨thus far progress on the project has been *tardy*⟩ — see SLOW 1
2 not arriving, occurring, or settled at the due, usual, or proper time ⟨explained that I was *tardy* because our car broke down on the way to school⟩ — see LATE 1

target *n* **1** a person or thing that is the object of abuse, criticism, or ridicule ⟨Cinderella became the *target* of her stepsisters' envy⟩
synonyms butt, mark, sitting duck, victim
related words laughingstock, mockery; fall guy, goat, scapegoat, whipping boy
near antonyms gossip, gossiper, talebearer, tattler, tattletale, troublemaker; defamer, libeler (*or* libeller), traducer; baiter, heckler, needler, ribber, taunter, teaser, tormentor; derider, insulter, mocker, ridiculer, scoffer, scorner; caricaturist, lampooner, parodist, satirist
2 a person or thing that is made fun of ⟨after my botched haircut, I became the *target* of lots of jokes at school⟩ — see LAUGHINGSTOCK
3 something that one hopes or intends to accomplish ⟨our *target* is to raise $100,000 for a new playground by August⟩ — see GOAL

tarnish *vb* to affect slightly with something morally bad or undesirable ⟨an arrest for shoplifting *tarnished* her reputation for many years afterwards⟩ — see TAINT 1

tarry *vb* **1** to continue to be in a place for a significant amount of time ⟨upon seeing the sun beginning to sink in the sky, we realized we had *tarried* too long on the summit of the mountain⟩ — see STAY 1
2 to move or act slowly ⟨the principal *tarried* in making his decision, still not sure if he should suspend the student or not⟩ — see DELAY 1
3 to reside as a temporary guest ⟨he *tarried* with us all summer, sleeping on the screened-in porch most nights⟩ — see VISIT 2

tart *adj* **1** causing or characterized by the one of the four basic taste sensations that is produced chiefly by acids ⟨I didn't add enough sugar to the lemonade, and now it's way too *tart*⟩ — see SOUR 1
2 marked by the use of wit that is intended to cause hurt feelings ⟨stood ready with a *tart* comeback in case the lout asked her if she wanted to dance⟩ — see SARCASTIC

tartness *n* **1** a harsh or sharp quality ⟨there's a *tartness* to this movie critic's reviews that a little tiresome⟩ — see EDGE 1
2 biting sharpness of feeling or expression ⟨there's a telltale *tartness* between these two teams that nobody could miss⟩ — see ACRIMONY 1

task *n* **1** a piece of work that needs to be done regularly ⟨one of my *tasks* in the morning is to make lunches for everyone in the family⟩ — see CHORE 1
2 the action for which a person or thing is specially fitted or used or for which a thing exists ⟨the forklift's *task* is to stack pallets of goods in the warehouse⟩ — see ROLE

taskmaster *n* **1** a boss who assigns much work ⟨pitiless *taskmaster* that he was, Ebenezer Scrooge only reluctantly let his ill-paid clerk have Christmas day off⟩
synonyms slave driver
related words enslaver; authoritarian, disciplinarian, discipliner, martinet, stickler; despot, dictator, oppressor, tyrant; dominator, overlord
2 the person (as an employer or supervisor) who tells people and especially workers what to do ⟨known as a tough but fair *taskmaster*⟩ — see BOSS

taste *n* **1** the property of a substance that can be identified by the sense of taste ⟨Nora can't stand the *taste* of cherry-flavored cough syrup⟩
synonyms flavor, savor
related words relish, smack, tang; savoriness, tastiness; aftertaste
2 a small piece or quantity of food ⟨I'll just have a *taste* of your dessert⟩ — see MORSEL 1
3 positive regard for something ⟨trying to develop a *taste* for classical music⟩ — see LIKING

taste *vb* **1** to come to a knowledge of (something) by living through it ⟨an adventurer who has *tasted* danger and lived to tell the tale⟩ — see EXPERIENCE
2 to have a vague awareness of ⟨by your language I can *taste* that something is wrong⟩ — see FEEL 1

tasteful *adj* having or showing elegance ⟨a *tasteful* arrangement of white flowers and dark greenery⟩ — see ELEGANT 1

tasteless *adj* **1** lacking in refinement or good taste ⟨a completely *tasteless* comment about her slight amount of facial hair⟩ — see COARSE 2
2 lacking in taste or flavor ⟨breakfast was usually plain, *tasteless* oatmeal⟩ — see INSIPID 1
3 marked by an obvious lack of style or good taste ⟨a *tasteless* suit that he wore to the party as a joke⟩ — see TACKY 1

tastelessness *n* the quality or state of lacking refinement or good taste ⟨the *tastelessness* of his comments about some of the prom dresses was appalling⟩ — see VULGARITY 1

tastiness *n* the quality of being delicious ⟨the *tastiness* of homemade bread⟩ — see DELICIOUSNESS

tasty *adj* very pleasing to the sense of taste ⟨a selection of *tasty* donuts from the corner bakery⟩ — see DELICIOUS 1

tatter *vb* to cause (something) to separate into jagged pieces by violently pulling at it ⟨the kids will *tatter* that doll beyond repair if they don't quit yanking on it⟩ — see TEAR 1

tattered *adj* **1** wearing torn or worn out clothes ⟨arrived at the refugee camp *tattered* and exhausted⟩
synonyms ragged, raggedy, ragtag
related words bedraggled, scruffy, shabby, threadbare
near antonyms decked (out), dolled up, dressed up; spiffy
2 worn or torn into or as if into rags ⟨a hobo in *tattered* old clothes and worn-down shoes⟩ — see RAGGED 2

tattle *vb* to relate sometimes questionable or secret information of a personal nature ⟨those neighborhood busybodies, constantly *tattling* and whispering over their backyard fences⟩ — see GOSSIP

tattler *n* a person who provides secret information about another's wrongdoing ⟨if the class *tattler* sees that I'm late, he'll tell Mrs. Smith first thing⟩ — see INFORMER

tattletale *n* a person who provides secret information about another's wrongdoing ⟨don't be such a *tattletale* and tell me every little thing you think your sister is doing wrong⟩ — see INFORMER

taunt *vb* to attack repeatedly with mean put-downs or insults ⟨*taunted* the new girl about her unusual name⟩ — see TEASE 2

taunter *n* a person who causes repeated emotional pain, distress, or annoyance to another ⟨tired of always being the butt of their jokes, he decided to get back at his *taunters*⟩ — see TORMENTOR

taut *adj* stretched with little or no give ⟨a *taut* clothesline⟩
synonyms drawn, rigid, tense, tight
related words firm, inflexible, stiff, tightened, unrelaxed, unyielding
near antonyms drooping, droopy, flaccid, floppy, hanging, lank, limp, loosened, relaxed, slackened, yielding
antonyms lax, loose, slack

tavern *n* **1** a place of business where alcoholic beverages are sold to be consumed on the premises ⟨the gunslinger swaggered into the *tavern*, put his six-shooter on the bar, and challenged the sheriff to a gunfight⟩ — see BARROOM
2 a place that provides rooms and usually a public dining room for overnight guests ⟨a colonial-era *tavern* that has been serving weary travelers for two and a half centuries⟩ — see HOTEL

tawdry *adj* excessively showy ⟨wore huge, *tawdry* necklaces and bracelets that looked like they were made of plastic⟩ — see GAUDY

tawny *adj* of a pale yellow or yellowish brown color ⟨the *tawny* coat of a lion⟩ — see BLOND

tax *n* a charge usually of money collected by the government from people or businesses for public use ⟨the state sales *tax* boosted the final cost of my new computer⟩
synonyms assessment, duty, imposition, impost, levy
related words custom(s), excise, income tax, poll tax, sales tax, tariff, toll, tribute, withholding tax; surcharge, surtax; revenue

tax *vb* to subject (a personal quality or faculty) to often excessive stress ⟨your constant arguing is starting to *tax* my patience⟩ — see TRY (OUT) 2

taxi *n* an automobile that carries passengers for a fare usually determined by the distance traveled ⟨couldn't hail a *taxi* so I had to run in the rain to make my appointment⟩ — see TAXICAB

taxicab *n* an automobile that carries passengers for a fare usually determined by the distance traveled ⟨took a *taxicab* to the airport⟩
synonyms cab, hack, taxi
related words hackney; limousine; rickshaw (*also* ricksha)

taxing *adj* requiring much time, effort, or careful attention ⟨a very *taxing* workload that is taking a lot of time to finish⟩ — see DEMANDING 1

teach *vb* to cause to acquire knowledge or skill in some field ⟨*taught* us about the basics of organic gardening⟩
synonyms educate, indoctrinate, instruct, school, train, tutor
related words coach, mentor, drill, fit, ground, prepare, prime, qualify; direct, guide, lead, rear; catechize, lecture, moralize, preach; implant, inculcate, instill; homeschool; edify, enlighten; brief, familiarize, impart (to), inform, verse; initiate, introduce, show; reeducate, retrain

teacher *n* a person whose occupation is to give formal instruction in a school ⟨a young man who ardently wants to become a *teacher* and teach first grade⟩
synonyms educator, instructor, pedagogue, preceptor, schoolteacher
related words headmaster, master, schoolmaster; headmistress, schoolmarm (*or* schoolma'am), schoolmistress; coach, guide, guru, trainer; mentor, tutor; drillmaster; dean, don, professor; pedant; governess, homeschooler; catechist, lecturer, moralizer, preacher

teaching *n* the act or process of imparting knowledge or skills to another ⟨a chemist who has devoted his career to *teaching*, even though he could have made a lot more money in an industrial job⟩ — see EDUCATION 1

team *n* a group of people working together on a task ⟨asked the Boy Scout troop to split into *teams* and begin pitching their tents⟩ — see GANG 1

team (up) *vb* to participate or assist in a joint effort to accomplish an end ⟨our class will be *teaming up* with the class next door for this special experiment in physics lab⟩ — see COOPERATE 1

teamwork *n* the work and activity of a number of persons who individually contribute toward the efficiency of the whole ⟨it takes *teamwork* to pull off a successful fund-raiser⟩
synonyms collaboration, cooperation, coordination
related words fellowship, partnership; community, mutualism, symbiosis; synergism; communion, oneness, solidarity, togetherness, unity

tear *n* a long deep cut ⟨repaired a *tear* in the theater curtain just before the start of the show⟩ — see GASH

tear *vb* **1** to cause (something) to separate into jagged pieces by violently pulling at it ⟨angrily *tore* the letter to shreds⟩
synonyms rend, rip, rive, shred, tatter
related words break, cleave, rupture, split; cut, gash, incise, lacerate, slash; butcher, dismember, dissect, hack, mangle
2 to separate or remove by forceful pulling ⟨*tore* the book from his hand⟩
synonyms rip, wrench, wrest, yank
related words grab, nab, seize, snap (up), snatch; lop (off), nip, jerk; amputate, cut (off), dissever, sever; force, pry
near antonyms reattach
3 to proceed or move quickly ⟨she *tore* out of the room as soon as the phone started to ring⟩ — see HURRY 2

tear (out) *vb* to draw out by force or with effort ⟨you'll never *tear* that secret *out* of me⟩ — see EXTRACT

tear down *vb* **1** to bring to a complete end the physical soundness, existence, or usefulness of ⟨vandals *tore down* the wooden fence blocking the entrance to the beach⟩ — see DESTROY 1
2 to destroy (as a building) completely by knocking down or breaking to pieces ⟨with the end of the cold war, officials triumphantly *tore down* the Berlin Wall⟩ — see DEMOLISH 1

tearful *adj* **1** given to expressing strong emotion (as sorrow) by readily shedding tears ⟨a *tearful* woman who can be counted on to cry at every wedding, anniversary, and funeral⟩
synonyms lachrymose, teary
related words emotional; maudlin, mawkish, sentimental; bawling, blubbering, crying, keening, sniffling, sniveling, sobbing, wailing, weeping, whimpering; bemoaning, bewailing; doleful, dolorous, grieving,

mournful, plaintive; funereal, gloomy, lugubrious; brokenhearted, sad, sorrowful, woeful
near antonyms grinning, laughing, smiling; blithe, blithesome, cheerful, cheery, gay, happy, lighthearted, lightsome, merry, mirthful, sunny
2 causing unhappiness ⟨the *tearful* end to what had once been a close friendship⟩ — see SAD 2

teary *adj* **1** causing unhappiness ⟨a *teary* ending to what had been up to that point a lighthearted movie⟩ — see SAD 2
2 given to expressing strong emotion (as sorrow) by readily shedding tears ⟨my *teary* aunt cries at funerals, at weddings, and even at the drop of a hat⟩ — see TEARFUL 1

tease *n* **1** a person who causes repeated emotional pain, distress, or annoyance to another ⟨she can be a very cruel *tease* when she happens upon an unpopular girl who is easily hurt⟩ — see TORMENTOR
2 one who is obnoxiously annoying ⟨my youngest brother is a complete *tease*, following me around everywhere and aping my every move⟩ — see NUISANCE 1

tease *vb* **1** to make fun of in a good-natured way ⟨Hilary liked to *tease* her twin brother about his girlfriend⟩
synonyms chaff, jive, josh, kid, rally, razz, rib, ride, roast
related words banter, joke; fool, fun, string along; jest, quip, wisecrack
2 to attack repeatedly with mean put-downs or insults ⟨some of the boys *teased* Michael because his parents were hog farmers⟩
synonyms bait, bug, hassle, heckle, needle, ride, taunt
related words haze; gibe (*or* jibe), mock, ridicule; annoy, bother, chafe, fret, nag, nettle, irritate, gall, get, gnaw (at), pester, trouble, vex; aggravate, exasperate, goad, test, try; aggrieve, agitate, bedevil, beleaguer, discomfort, disturb, perturb; badger, dog, hound; browbeat, bully, hector; harass, harry, persecute, plague, terrorize, torment, torture
phrases pick on

teaser *n* **1** a person who causes repeated emotional pain, distress, or annoyance to another ⟨asked the teacher to move me to a different desk, as far as possible away from that group of *teasers*⟩ — see TORMENTOR
2 one who is obnoxiously annoying ⟨he was by a nature a *teaser*, someone who kept testing people to see if they could calmly bear his put-downs⟩ — see NUISANCE 1

teasing *n* the act of making unwelcome intrusions upon another ⟨stop that *teasing* before you make the baby cry⟩ — see ANNOYANCE 1

technical *adj* used by or intended for experts in a particular field of knowledge ⟨although the owner's manual for the receiver was supposedly written for the average consumer, it's filled with *technical* language⟩
synonyms specialized
related words esoteric, especial, exclusive, limited, narrow, peculiar, restricted, special, specific, unique; authoritative, expert, professional, specialist (*or* specialistic)
near antonyms common, generalized, generic, nonexclusive, nonspecific, ordinary, universal; inexpert, lay, nonprofessional, unprofessional
antonyms general, nonspecialized, nontechnical

technique *n* the means or procedure for doing something ⟨showed me a different knitting *technique*⟩ — see METHOD

tedious *adj* causing weariness, restlessness, or lack of interest ⟨a long and *tedious* staff meeting⟩ — see BORING

tedium *n* the state of being bored ⟨the *tedium* of spending a hot afternoon trapped inside the house⟩ — see BOREDOM

teeming *adj* possessing or covered with great numbers or amounts of something specified ⟨oceans *teeming* with life⟩ — see RIFE

teeny *adj* very small in size ⟨had to look hard to see the *teeny* splinter in her foot⟩ — see TINY

teeny–weeny *adj* very small in size ⟨kept losing the *teeny-weeny* coffee mugs for the kitchen in her dollhouse⟩ — see TINY

teeter *vb* **1** to swing unsteadily back and forth or from side to side ⟨*teetered* at the edge of the pool⟩
synonyms falter, rock, totter, waver, wobble
related words flounder, lurch, stumble, toddle; quaver, tremble; careen, reel, stagger, weave
2 to move forward while swaying from side to side ⟨*teetered* down the stairs on her mother's high heels⟩ — see STAGGER 1
3 to show uncertainty about the right course of action ⟨was *teetering* on the brink of making a decision about college⟩ — see HESITATE

telephone *vb* to make a telephone call to ⟨I'll try to *telephone* the office and make an appointment today⟩ — see CALL 2

tell *vb* **1** to give an oral or written account of in some detail ⟨*told* the story of how they had met⟩
synonyms describe, narrate, recite, recount, rehearse, relate, report
related words deliver, give, state, utter, voice; detail, enumerate, itemize, particularize; disclose, divulge, reveal; delineate, depict, express, render, sketch
2 to express (a thought or emotion) in words ⟨just *tell* us what is in your heart⟩ — see SAY 1
3 to find the sum of (a collection of things) by noting each one as it is being added ⟨who can *tell* the number of grains of sand in the world?⟩ — see COUNT 1
4 to give information (as to the authorities) about another's improper or unlawful activities ⟨if you do that, I'll *tell* on you to Grandma⟩ — see SQUEAL 1
5 to give information to ⟨*tell* me, when did you begin playing the violin?⟩ — see ENLIGHTEN 1
6 to issue orders to (someone) by right of authority ⟨*told* us to sit still and wait⟩ — see COMMAND 1
7 to make known (as information previously kept secret) ⟨I won't *tell* your secret to anyone⟩ — see REVEAL 1

tell (on) *vb* to act upon (a person or a person's feelings) so as to cause a response ⟨the pressure of final exams is beginning to *tell on* the students in the dorm⟩ — see ¹AFFECT 1

telling *adj* having the power to persuade ⟨presented us with *telling* evidence that convinced us he was right⟩ — see COGENT

telltale *adj* indicating something ⟨I know you've been eating chocolate because of the *telltale* smudges on your face⟩ — see INDICATIVE

telltale *n* a person who provides secret information about another's wrongdoing ⟨the department *telltale* told the boss that his coworkers were taking extra long breaks⟩ — see INFORMER

temerity *n* shameless boldness ⟨she had the *temerity* to ask my boyfriend if she could go out with him should he and I ever break up⟩ — see EFFRONTERY

temperance *n* an avoidance of extremes in one's actions, beliefs, or habits ⟨Mr. Grindell attributes his ripe old age to *temperance* in all things, especially eating and drinking⟩

synonyms moderateness, moderation, temperateness
related words constraint, control, discipline, restraint, self-control, self-discipline; asceticism, austerity, frugality, mortification, sacrifice, self-denial, self-deprivation; abnegation, abstention, avoidance, eschewal, forbearance; modesty, rationality, reasonableness; abstinence, soberness, sobriety
near antonyms excess, superfluity; extremeness, extremity; unconstraint, unrestraint; extremism, radicalness; irrationality, unreasonableness
antonyms excessiveness, immoderacy, intemperance, intemperateness

temper *n* **1** a special quality or impression associated with something ⟨there's a *temper* of tranquility about the retreat that visitors find very inviting⟩ — see AURA
2 a state of mind dominated by a particular emotion ⟨was in quite a bad *temper* after spilling his juice all over his new shirt⟩ — see MOOD 1
3 one's characteristic attitude or mood ⟨she has an even *temper* and a calm manner that sets everyone all at ease⟩ — see DISPOSITION 1

temperament *n* one's characteristic attitude or mood ⟨looking for a dog with a sweet *temperament*⟩ — see DISPOSITION 1

temperamental *adj* **1** frequently influenced by moods and especially bad moods ⟨one of those *temperamental* actresses who can make life difficult for everyone around her⟩ — see MOODY
2 likely to change frequently, suddenly, or unexpectedly ⟨stock prices have been pretty *temperamental* lately, often fluctuating wildly⟩ — see FICKLE 1

temperate *adj* **1** avoiding extremes in behavior or expression ⟨rather *temperate* in his appraisal of the movie, calling it good but not great⟩ — see MODERATE 1
2 marked by temperatures that are neither too high nor too low ⟨escaped a cold Midwestern winter by vacationing in a more *temperate* climate down south⟩ — see CLEMENT

temperateness *n* an avoidance of extremes in one's actions, beliefs, or habits ⟨there was a steadfast *temperateness* about every aspect of his life⟩ — see TEMPERANCE

tempest *n* **1** a disturbance of the atmosphere accompanied by wind and often by precipitation (as rain or snow) ⟨the sudden summertime *tempest* drove us off the golf course and into the clubhouse⟩ — see STORM 1
2 a violent disturbance (as of the political or social order) ⟨the town council handled the *tempest* over cuts to the school budget as well as could be expected⟩ — see CONVULSION

tempestuous *adj* **1** marked by bursts of destructive force or intense activity ⟨order was restored to the court after the judge put a stop to the defendant's *tempestuous* outburst⟩ — see VIOLENT 1
2 marked by sudden or violent disturbance ⟨in terms of social change, the 1960s are generally considered the most *tempestuous* decade in recent American history⟩ — see CONVULSIVE
3 marked by turmoil or disturbance especially of natural elements ⟨we spent a *tempestuous* night stranded on the summit of the mountain⟩ — see WILD 3
4 marked by wet and windy conditions ⟨stay indoors this weekend as the weather promises to be *tempestuous*⟩ — see FOUL 1

temple *n* a building for public worship and especially Christian worship ⟨the largest *temple* in the Gothic style in the country⟩ — see CHURCH 1

temporal *adj* **1** having to do with life on earth especially as opposed to that in heaven ⟨do not worry about *temporal* concerns, but instead focus on spiritual matters⟩ — see EARTHLY
2 not involving religion or religious matters ⟨administrators on campus are in place to deal with students' *temporal* needs, and spiritual advisors are available to help students with their nontemporal needs⟩ — see PROFANE 1

temporary *adj* **1** intended to last, continue, or serve for a limited time ⟨summer workers look for *temporary* accommodations in private homes⟩ ⟨a *temporary* cook until a permanent replacement can be found⟩
synonyms impermanent, interim, provisional, short-term
related words acting; alternate, proxy, substitute; expedient, improvised, makeshift; intermediary, intermediate, transitional; ephemeral, short-lived, transitory; conditional, contingent, limited, qualified, short-range, tentative; replaceable, terminable
near antonyms final, fixed, set, settled; unconditional, unlimited, unqualified; extended, lasting, long-range, standing; dateless, endless, enduring, eternal, everlasting, perpetual, timeless, unending
antonyms long-term, permanent
2 lasting only for a short time ⟨a *temporary* lapse of memory⟩ — see MOMENTARY

temporizer *n* one who does things only for his own benefit and with little regard for right and wrong ⟨a lifelong *temporizer*, he was for the war as long as it was popular and against it the minute the tide of public opinion went the other way⟩ — see SELF-SEEKER

tempt *vb* to lead away from a usual or proper course by offering some pleasure or advantage ⟨that chocolate dessert sure *tempts* me, but I should stick with my diet⟩ — see LURE

temptation *n* **1** the act or pressure of giving in to a desire especially when ill-advised ⟨resisted the *temptation* to go sailing and did his chores instead⟩
synonyms allurement, enticement, lure, seduction
related words appeal, attraction; beckoning, invitation; inducement, influence, persuasion, power, sway
2 something that persuades one to perform an action for pleasure or gain ⟨money, power, and other overwhelming *temptations* can cause a person to commit crimes⟩ — see LURE 1

tempter *n* one that tries to get a person to give in to a desire ⟨there is no greater *tempter* to put off studying than my dog when he wants to play⟩
synonyms baiter, seducer, solicitor
related words enchantress, siren, temptress; briber, inducer, persuader; corrupter (*or* corruptor), debaucher, undoer

temptress *n* a woman whom men find irresistibly attractive ⟨Greta Garbo, one of the most famous *temptresses* ever to appear on screen, died in 1990⟩ — see SIREN

tenable *adj* **1** capable of being defended against physical attack ⟨the soldiers' encampment on the open plain was not *tenable*, so they retreated to higher ground⟩
synonyms defensible
related words defended, guarded, protected, safeguarded, secure, secured, shielded; impregnable, indomitable, invincible, inviolable, invulnerable, unassailable, unbeatable, unconquerable, untouchable
near antonyms assailable, exposed, insecure, liable, open, susceptible, undefended, unguarded, unprotected, unsecured, unshielded; defenseless, helpless, powerless, vulnerable, weak

antonyms indefensible, untenable

2 capable of being defended with good reasoning against verbal attack ⟨the *tenable* theory that a giant meteor strike set off a chain of events resulting in the demise of the dinosaurs⟩

synonyms defendable, defensible, justifiable, maintainable, supportable, sustainable

related words rational, reasonable, sensible; acceptable, admissible, allowable, exceptional, legitimate, passable, unobjectionable, viable, warrantable; confirmable, provable, verifiable; explainable, explicable

near antonyms absurd, irrational, ridiculous; extreme, outrageous, unreasonable; groundless, objectionable, unacceptable, unfounded; inexplicable, unexplainable

antonyms indefensible, insupportable, unjustifiable, untenable

tenacious *adj* continuing despite difficulties, opposition, or discouragement ⟨a *tenacious* trainer, she adheres to her grueling swimming schedule no matter what⟩ — see PERSISTENT

tenaciousness *n* a steadfast adherence to an opinion, purpose, or course of action ⟨the mountain climber's *tenaciousness* in training paid off when the day for the big climb arrived⟩ — see OBSTINACY

tenacity *n* a steadfast adherence to an opinion, purpose, or course of action ⟨his *tenacity* in always maintaining that he's right, regardless of any evidence to the contrary, makes it difficult to have a worthwhile discussion with him⟩ — see OBSTINACY

tenant *n* one who rents a room or apartment in another's house ⟨the laundry in the basement is for *tenants* only⟩

synonyms boarder, lodger, renter, roomer

related words roommate; guest, visitor; occupant, resident, resider

near antonyms landholder, landowner, proprietor; landlady; slumlord; host, innkeeper

antonyms landlord

¹tend *vb* to show a liking or proneness (for something) ⟨her wardrobe *tends* towards dark colors and heavy fabrics⟩ — see LEAN 2

²tend *vb* **1** to take charge of especially on behalf of another ⟨*tend* the store while I run an errand⟩

synonyms attend, care (for), mind, oversee, superintend, supervise

related words direct, manage; guard, patrol, protect, safeguard; baby, baby-sit, chaperone (*or* chaperon), mother, shepherd

phrases look after, see to

near antonyms abandon, disregard, forget, ignore, neglect

2 to look after or assist the growth of by labor and care ⟨our class *tended* the baby chicks for several weeks⟩ — see GROW 1

3 to work by plowing, sowing, and raising crops on ⟨*tends* a garden in her backyard⟩ — see FARM

tendency *n* **1** an established pattern of behavior ⟨a *tendency* to drop things⟩ ⟨a *tendency* to make snap judgements⟩

synonyms aptness, proneness, propensity, way

related words bent, disposition, inclination, leaning, penchant, predilection, predisposition, proclivity; custom, habit, pattern, practice (*also* practise), routine, wont; oddity, peculiarity, quirk, singularity, trick

near antonyms averseness, disinclination, indisposition

2 a prevailing or general movement or inclination ⟨we'll be seeing a *tendency* for skirt lengths to get shorter this coming season⟩ — see TREND 1

3 a habitual attraction to some activity or thing ⟨a youth with a natural *tendency* towards crafts instead of sports⟩ — see INCLINATION 1

tender *adj* **1** easily injured without careful handling ⟨a *tender* wound⟩ ⟨*tender* plants that cannot take the cold⟩ ⟨*tender* pride that got bruised when his girlfriend dumped him⟩

synonyms delicate, fragile, frail, sensitive

related words breakable, brittle; flimsy, puny, soft, weak; nonhardy, perishable, resistless, susceptible, unresistant, vulnerable, yielding

near antonyms durable, firm, flinty, hard, hardy, resistant, robust, rugged, solid, sound, stiff, stout, strong, sturdy, substantial; nonbreakable, unbreakable; hardened, inured, strengthened, tempered, toughened

antonyms tough

2 feeling or showing love ⟨a *tender* embrace between father and daughter⟩ — see LOVING

3 having or marked by sympathy and consideration for others ⟨a *tender* teacher who loves having kids with special educational needs in her class⟩ — see HUMANE 1

4 lacking bodily strength ⟨a very *tender* child who always seems to be sick⟩ — see WEAK 1

5 not harsh or stern especially in manner, nature, or effect ⟨his *tender* comments on how to improve her writing were gratefully received⟩ — see GENTLE 1

tender *n* something (as pieces of stamped metal or printed paper) customarily and legally used as a medium of exchange, a measure of value, or a means of payment ⟨money from that board game is not legal *tender* and can't be exchanged for goods or services⟩ — see MONEY

tender *vb* to put before another for acceptance or consideration ⟨the coach *tendered* his resignation and started a new job as a physical therapist⟩ — see OFFER 1

tenderfoot *n* a person who is just starting out in a field of activity ⟨skateboarders who are *tenderfeet* will inevitably fall as they learn their first moves⟩ — see BEGINNER

tenderhearted *adj* **1** feeling or showing love ⟨a *tenderhearted* new mother⟩ — see LOVING

2 having or marked by sympathy and consideration for others ⟨a *tenderhearted* offer of help for the victims of the earthquake⟩ — see HUMANE 1

tending *adj* having a tendency to be or act in a certain way ⟨men *tending* towards daily exercise will cut their risk of cardiac arrest⟩ — see PRONE 1

tenement *n* a room or set of rooms in a private house or a block used as a separate dwelling place ⟨an exhibit of pictures showing the *tenements* of the New York City neighborhood of Hell's Kitchen during the 1920s⟩ — see APARTMENT 1

tense *adj* **1** feeling or showing uncomfortable feelings of uncertainty ⟨was *tense* about the upcoming exam⟩ — see NERVOUS 1

2 marked by or causing agitation or uncomfortable feelings ⟨a *tense* relationship existed between the two teachers⟩ — see NERVOUS 2

3 stretched with little or no give ⟨a *tense* rope⟩ — see TAUT

tension *n* the burden on one's emotional or mental well-being created by demands on one's time ⟨under a lot of *tension* right now about her decision not to go to college⟩ — see STRESS 1

tent *n* a raised covering over something for decoration or protection ⟨a huge *tent* was erected for the outdoor wedding reception⟩ — see CANOPY

tentative *adj* determined by something else ⟨our plans are only *tentative* at this point and will depend on whether you can come⟩ — see DEPENDENT 2

tenure *n* a fixed period of time during which a person holds a job or position ⟨during his *tenure* as president the college experienced steady growth⟩ — see TERM 1

tepid *adj* **1** showing little or no interest or enthusiasm ⟨the proposed table tennis club met with only a *tepid* response⟩

synonyms halfhearted, lukewarm, uneager, unenthusiastic

related words apathetic, disinterested, dispassionate, indifferent, neutral, uncaring, uninterested; lackadaisical, languid, listless, perfunctory, undemonstrative, unemotional, unresponsive; unfeeling, unsympathetic; chill, chilly, cold, cool, frigid, frosty, glacial, icy, unfriendly, wintry

near antonyms agog, ardent, avid, exuberant, gung ho, impassioned, raring; engaged, engrossed, interested; ready, willing; cordial, friendly, genial, warmhearted

antonyms eager, enthusiastic, hearty, keen, passionate, warm, wholehearted

2 having or giving off heat to a moderate degree ⟨make sure the water is just *tepid* or you'll burn yourself⟩ — see WARM 1

term *n* **1** a fixed period of time during which a person holds a job or position ⟨elected for a two-year *term* as mayor⟩

synonyms hitch, stint, tenure, tour

related words shift, watch; go, turn; duration, standing, time; cycle, span, spell, stretch; life, life span, lifetime

2 a pronounceable series of letters having a distinct meaning especially in a particular field ⟨what's the *term* for the odd feeling that you've experienced an event before?⟩ — see WORD 1

term *vb* to give a name to ⟨the armed forces began a rescue mission *termed* Operation In and Out⟩ — see NAME 1

termagant *n* a bad-tempered scolding woman ⟨living with that *termagant* was almost as bad as living with a rabid dog⟩ — see SHREW

terminal *adj* following all others of the same kind in order or time ⟨took me to the *terminal* point of that bus route⟩ — see LAST

terminate *vb* **1** to bring (an event) to a natural or appropriate stopping point ⟨we need to *terminate* the discussion for this evening, but we'll resume tomorrow morning⟩ — see CLOSE 3

2 to come to an end ⟨this class will *terminate* with the arrival of Memorial Day⟩ — see CEASE 1

3 to mark the limits of ⟨*terminated* the area set aside for the runners to change their clothes with a series of folding screens⟩ — see LIMIT 2

terminated *adj* brought or having come to an end ⟨peace talks have now been *terminated*⟩ — see COMPLETE 2

terminating *adj* following all others of the same kind in order or time ⟨the *terminating* speech of the convention turned out to be the most inspiring⟩ — see LAST

termination *n* **1** a real or imaginary point beyond which a person or thing cannot go ⟨I've reached the *termination* of my patience with you bratty kids⟩ — see LIMIT

2 the act of ceasing to exist ⟨feels that the voluntary *termination* of one's life should be left entirely up to the patient⟩ — see DEATH 3

3 the stopping of a process or activity ⟨at the *termination* of the movie, please throw away any empty food containers in the appropriate bins⟩ — see END 1

terminology *n* the special terms or expressions of a particular group or field ⟨the *terminology* favored by sportscasters⟩ ⟨medical *terminology* that can be hard for the patient to understand⟩

synonyms argot, cant, dialect, jargon, language, lingo, patois, patter, slang, vocabulary

related words colloquialism, idiom, localism, parlance, pidgin, provincialism, regionalism, speech, vernacular; journalese

terrestrial *adj* having to do with life on earth especially as opposed to that in heaven ⟨scientists haven't even found all the *terrestrial* life on our planet⟩ — see EARTHLY

terrible *adj* **1** causing fear ⟨a *terrible* nightmare⟩ — see FEARFUL 1

2 extreme in degree, power, or effect ⟨I have a *terrible* headache⟩ — see INTENSE

3 extremely disturbing or repellent ⟨that is a *terrible* movie to let your six-year-old watch⟩ — see HORRIBLE 1

4 extremely unsatisfactory ⟨this ice cream is *terrible*⟩ — see WRETCHED 1

5 of low quality ⟨manufactures *terrible* clothes that often tear after a single wash⟩ — see CHEAP 2

terribly *adv* to a great degree ⟨I'm *terribly* sorry to bother you⟩ — see VERY 1

terrific *adj* of the very best kind ⟨you've done a *terrific* job on this report⟩ — see EXCELLENT

terrified *adj* filled with fear or dread ⟨*terrified* dogs hiding under the couch⟩ — see AFRAID 1

terrify *vb* to strike with fear ⟨the prospect of speaking in front of a huge crowd of people absolutely *terrifies* me⟩ — see FRIGHTEN

terrifying *adj* causing fear ⟨heard a *terrifying* noise coming from the next room⟩ — see FEARFUL 1

territory *n* the place where a plant or animal is usually or naturally found ⟨that plant's *territory* extends from Georgia all the way north to Maine⟩ — see HOME 2

terror *n* the emotion experienced in the presence or threat of danger ⟨the haunted house at the carnival struck *terror* into our hearts, and we were jumpy the rest of the night⟩ — see FEAR

terrorize *vb* to strike with fear ⟨thunderstorms *terrorize* our cats, who all scamper downstairs when it rains⟩ — see FRIGHTEN

terrorized *adj* filled with fear or dread ⟨the *terrorized* residents didn't know where to run during the bombing raid⟩ — see AFRAID 1

terse *adj* marked by the use of few words to convey much information or meaning ⟨could tell from his *terse* replies to my questions that he was in no mood to talk⟩ — see CONCISE

tersely *adv* in a few words ⟨she stated her dissatisfaction rather *tersely* with a simple "I don't approve"⟩ — see SHORTLY 1

terseness *n* the quality or state of being marked by or using only few words to convey much meaning ⟨the *terseness* of my replies simply meant that I was too busy to talk at that time⟩ — see SUCCINCTNESS

test *n* **1** a procedure or operation carried out to resolve an uncertainty ⟨will need to run some *tests* on the blood sample to rule out blood poisoning⟩ — see EXPERIMENT

2 a set of questions or problems designed to assess knowledge, skills, or intelligence ⟨hadn't studied for the *test* this morning⟩ — see EXAMINATION 1

test *vb* **1** to put (something) to a test ⟨please *test* this sample for the presence of lead⟩ — see TRY (OUT) 1

2 to subject (a personal quality or faculty) to often excessive stress ⟨all these question are *testing* my patience⟩ — see TRY (OUT) 2

testament *n* something presented in support of the truth or accuracy of a claim ⟨the "before" and "after" pictures are a *testament* to the effectiveness of the weight loss program⟩ — see PROOF

testify *vb* to make a solemn declaration under oath for the purpose of establishing a fact ⟨Mrs. Pattle was called to *testify* against the man whom she saw stealing her neighbor's car⟩
synonyms attest, depose, swear, witness
related words vouch; vow, promise
phrases bear witness

testify (to) *vb* to declare (something) to be true or genuine ⟨that auction house will always *testify to* a painting's authenticity⟩ — see CERTIFY 1

testimony *n* something presented in support of the truth or accuracy of a claim ⟨will review the witness's *testimony* when we return from the recess⟩ — see PROOF

testiness *n* readiness to show annoyance or impatience ⟨attributed his unusual *testiness* this morning to being hungry⟩ — see PETULANCE

testy *adj* easily irritated or annoyed ⟨are you feeling a little *testy* after Mom refused to let you go to the mall?⟩ — see IRRITABLE

tête-à-tête *adv* in person and usually privately ⟨met *tête-à-tête* with the student's parents to discuss his disciplinary problems in class⟩
synonyms face-to-face, personally
related words familiarly, intimately; confidentially, secretly; directly, immediately
phrases in private
near antonyms distantly, indirectly; openly, publicly

tête-à-tête *n* friendly, informal conversation or an instance of this ⟨had a quick *tête-à-tête* with my neighbor before heading off to school⟩ — see CHAT

text *n* a book used for instruction in a subject ⟨go to the bookstore and pick up the *text* for this class⟩ — see TEXTBOOK

textbook *n* a book used for instruction in a subject ⟨new, up-to-date middle school science *textbooks*⟩
synonyms handbook, manual, primer, text
related words schoolbook; grammar, reader, speller; tract, treatise; dictionary, lexicon, vocabulary, wordbook; encyclopedia, reference; bible, guide, guidebook

textile *n* a woven or knitted material (as of cotton or nylon) ⟨brought back a whole suitcase of beautiful *textiles* from India⟩ — see CLOTH

thankful *adj* feeling or expressing gratitude ⟨I am *thankful* for all your help⟩ — see GRATEFUL 1

thankfulness *n* acknowledgment of having received something good from another ⟨expressed her *thankfulness* for helping her move by taking us all out for dinner⟩ — see THANKS

thankless *adj* not showing gratitude ⟨a *thankless* guest who complained that my home cooking was not to her liking⟩
synonyms unappreciative, ungrateful
related words rude, thoughtless, ungracious
near antonyms beholden, indebted; gratified, pleased; courteous, gracious, thoughtful

antonyms appreciative, grateful, obliged, thankful

2 not likely to be appreciated by those who benefit ⟨the *thankless* job of cleaning up after a party⟩
synonyms unappreciated
related words uncredited, underrated, undervalued, unnoticed, unrecognized, unrewarded, unsung, unvalued
near antonyms credited, esteemed, honored, prized, recognized, regarded, rewarded, valued; creditable, meritorious, praiseworthy
antonyms appreciated, thanked

thanks *n pl* acknowledgment of having received something good from another ⟨to express our *thanks*, we'd like to present you with this plaque⟩
synonyms appreciation, appreciativeness, gratefulness, gratitude, thankfulness
related words thanksgiving; gratification, indebtedness, satisfaction; acknowledgment (*also* acknowledgement), recognition, tribute
antonyms ingratitude, thanklessness, ungratefulness

thaw *vb* to go from a solid to a liquid state ⟨will have to *thaw* the apple juice concentrate before you can mix it with water⟩ — see LIQUEFY

thawed *adj* freed from a frozen state by exposure to warmth ⟨recommends cooking *thawed* fish within 24 hours⟩
synonyms defrosted, unfrozen
related words liquefied, melted, molten; deiced; heated, warmed
near antonyms chilled, iced, refrigerated; quick-frozen, refrozen, supercooled; congealed, glaciated, semisolid; frostbitten, frosty, icy
antonyms frozen, unthawed

theater *or* **theatre** *n* **1** a building or part of a building where movies are shown ⟨there's still one *theater* in town that shows movies for two dollars⟩
synonyms cinema, playhouse
related words nickelodeon; multiplex; drive-in

2 the public performance of plays ⟨have been fascinated by the *theater* ever since I was a child⟩ — see DRAMA 1

3 a large room or building for enclosed public gatherings ⟨the lecturer waited until the *theater* was full before beginning⟩ — see HALL 3

theatrical *adj* **1** given to or marked by attention-getting behavior suggestive of stage acting ⟨after stepping out of their hired limousine, the prom couple made a *theatrical* entrance in their evening clothes⟩
synonyms dramatic, histrionic, melodramatic
related words overacted, overdone, sensational, staged; conspicuous, elaborate, flamboyant, grandiose, ostentatious, showy; affected, artificial, exaggerated, formal, mannered, pretentious, self-conscious, studied, unnatural
near antonyms nondramatic, nontheatrical, unaffected, underplayed, unpretentious; muted, restrained, subdued, toned (down); conservative, discreet, inconspicuous; modest, quiet, plain, simple
antonyms undramatic, untheatrical

2 having the general quality or effect of a stage performance ⟨in a very *theatrical* voice the actress announced that she did not sign autographs⟩ — see DRAMATIC 1

theatricals *n pl* the public performance of plays ⟨has been involved in amateur *theatricals* for most of his adult life⟩ — see DRAMA 1

theft *n* **1** the unlawful taking and carrying away of property without the consent of its owner ⟨*theft* has never been a big problem at our school⟩
synonyms larceny, robbery, stealing, thievery
related words burglary, housebreaking; embezzlement, embezzling, graft, misappropriation; filching, pilfering, purloining, shoplifting; abduction, hijacking, kidnapping, shanghaiing; despoilment, despoliation, looting, pillage, plundering, rapine; poaching, rustling, smuggling; banditry, piracy
2 an instance of theft ⟨the police found the stolen car an hour after the *theft* was reported⟩
synonyms grab, pinch, rip-off, snatching, swiping
related words burglary, holdup, mugging, stickup; confidence game, con game

theme *n* **1** a major object of interest or concern (as in a discussion or artistic composition) ⟨this dance piece deals with the timeless *themes* of birth and death⟩ — see MATTER 1
2 a short piece of writing done as a school exercise ⟨please write a one page *theme* on the main character of this book⟩ — see COMPOSITION 2
3 a short piece of writing typically expressing a point of view ⟨in her weekly *themes* on modern American life, the columnist tackles a wide range of issues, both trivial and serious⟩ — see ESSAY 1

then *adv* in addition to what has been said ⟨there's the cost of the car itself, and *then* there's the cost of insurance and maintenance⟩ — see MORE 1

theoretical *also* **theoretic** *adj* **1** existing only as an assumption or speculation ⟨the merits of the new testing procedures are purely *theoretical*, since no one has ever used them before⟩
synonyms conjectural, hypothetical, speculative, suppositional
related words alleged, assumed, presumed, presupposed, proposed, supposed, unproved, unproven, untested; academic, debatable, moot; abstract, conceptual, intellectual; nonclinical, nonpractical; nonempirical
near antonyms clinical, practical; concrete, defined, definite, distinct; attested, authenticated, confirmed, demonstrated, established, proven, substantiated, tested, time-tested, validated, verified; empirical (*also* empiric), observational
antonyms actual, factual, real
2 dealing with or expressing a quality or idea ⟨that's just *theoretical* thinking and hasn't much to do with real life⟩ — see ABSTRACT 1

theory *n* an idea that is the starting point for making a case or conducting an investigation ⟨set out to prove her *theory* that people can't really taste any difference between colas, so they buy according to the product's image⟩
synonyms hypothesis, proposition, supposition
related words assumption, concession, premise, presumption, presupposition; generalization, guess, guesswork, inference, speculation, surmise; proffer, proposal, suggestion; feeling, hunch, impression, inkling, notion, suspicion; abstraction, concept, conception
near antonyms assurance, certainty, fact, knowledge

thereafter *adv* following in time or place ⟨gave his speech and left the room shortly *thereafter*⟩ — see AFTER

therefore *adv* for this or that reason ⟨it's snowing hard; *therefore* I think we should stay home⟩
synonyms accordingly, consequently, ergo, hence, so, thereupon, thus, wherefore

theretofore *adv* up to this or that time ⟨*theretofore* the couple hadn't given much thought to marriage⟩ — see HITHERTO

thereupon *adv* for this or that reason ⟨she didn't get into the college of her choice and *thereupon* decided to study for a year before taking the college entrance exams⟩ — see THEREFORE

thesis *n* an idea or opinion that is put forth in a discussion or debate ⟨you'll need to state your *thesis* clearly in the first paragraph so I'll know what your paper is trying to prove⟩ — see CONTENTION

thick *adj* **1** having or being of relatively great depth or extent from one surface to its opposite ⟨a *thick* board was laid across the pit⟩
synonyms chunky, fat
related words bulky, dense, hefty, thickish; broad, deep, wide
near antonyms narrow, shallow
antonyms skinny, slender, slim, thin
2 being of a consistency that resists flow ⟨*thick* maple syrup for pancakes⟩
synonyms ropy, syrupy, viscid, viscous
related words creamy, heavy, slushy, thickened, thickish, turbid, undiluted; gluey, glutinous, sticky; gelatinous, gooey, gummy, jellylike; concentrated, condensed
near antonyms flowing, fluid; dilute, diluted, liquid, watered (down), weak
antonyms runny, soupy, thin, watery
3 closely acquainted ⟨those two have been *thick* since grade school⟩ — see FAMILIAR 1
4 having a greater than usual measure across ⟨cross your name off the list with a really *thick* line so I can see it⟩ — see WIDE 1
5 having little space between items or parts ⟨a hedge *thick* with gorse bushes⟩ — see CLOSE 1
6 not having or showing an ability to absorb ideas readily ⟨couldn't believe that his guests were so *thick* that they were missing his hints that it was time to leave⟩ — see STUPID 1
7 possessing or covered with great numbers or amounts of something specified ⟨a meadow *thick* with flowers⟩ — see RIFE

thick *n* the most intense or characteristic phase of something ⟨in the *thick* of winter many Northerners are dreaming of tropical islands⟩
synonyms deep, depth, height, middle, midst
related words center, heart

thicket *n* a thick patch of shrubbery, small trees, or underbrush ⟨flushed a pheasant from a *thicket* of willows⟩
synonyms brake, brushwood, chaparral, coppice, copse, covert
related words canebrake; brush, bush, scrub, scrubland; bramble, jungle, tangle; grove, hedge, stand, woodlot; forest, greenwood, wildwood, wood, woodland

thickheaded *adj* not having or showing an ability to absorb ideas readily ⟨don't think that he's *thickheaded* just because he doesn't understand English very well⟩ — see STUPID 1

thickness *n* the degree to which a fluid can resist flowing ⟨beat the eggs and sugar until the mixture has the *thickness* of heavy cream⟩ — see CONSISTENCY

thickset *adj* being compact and broad in build and often short in stature ⟨a short, *thickset* bulldog⟩ — see STOCKY

thief *n* one who steals ⟨sentenced the *thief* who stole Mrs. Stuckey's rosebushes to 30 hours of community service in the municipal rose garden⟩
synonyms pincher, purloiner, robber, stealer
related words burglar, housebreaker; embezzler, grafter; kleptomaniac; pickpocket, pilferer, rifler, shoplifter; abductor, hijacker, kidnapper, skyjacker; despoiler, looter, plunderer, ransacker, ravisher; poacher, rustler, smuggler; bandit, highwayman, pirate; grabber, mugger

thieve *vb* to take (something) without right and with an intent to keep ⟨someone's been *thieving* my cookies!⟩ — see STEAL 1

thievery *n* the unlawful taking and carrying away of property without the consent of its owner ⟨our neighborhood had been unaffected by *thievery* until recently⟩ — see THEFT 1

thin *adj* 1 having a noticeably small amount of body fat ⟨after her bout with pneumonia, she looked *thinner*⟩
synonyms lean, skinny, slender, slim, spare
related words angular, bony, rawboned, scraggy, scrawny, sinewy; lank, lanky, rangy, reedy, spindling, spindly, twiggy, waspish, weedy, willowy, wiry; anorexic, cadaverous, emaciated, gaunt, haggard, pinched, skeletal, wasted, wizened; puny, meager (or meagre), slight
near antonyms beefy, bulky, chunky, fleshy, heavy, heavyset, stocky, stout, thick, thickset, weighty; brawny, burly, husky; dumpy, pudgy, roly-poly, squat, stubby; paunchy, potbellied; flabby, soft; buxom; fleshed-out, full, round
antonyms chubby, corpulent, fat, gross, obese, overweight, plump, portly, rotund, tubby
2 being of less than usual width ⟨the *thin* threads of a cobweb⟩ — see NARROW 1
3 not containing very much of some important element ⟨the evidence for that oddball theory is pretty *thin*⟩ — see WEAK 3

thin *vb* to alter (something) for the worse with the addition of foreign or lower-grade substances ⟨*thinned* the cream with milk but didn't tell anyone⟩ — see ADULTERATE

thing *n* 1 a member of the human race ⟨you poor *thing*, you must be exhausted⟩ — see HUMAN
2 one that has a real and independent existence ⟨because she was allergic to so much, she avoided *things* that had a strong fragrance⟩ — see ENTITY
3 something done by someone ⟨one of the *things* you can do is to help me clean up⟩ — see ACTION 1
4 something material that can be perceived by the senses ⟨can you hand me that *thing* over there?⟩ — see OBJECT 1
5 something produced by physical or intellectual effort ⟨just the latest *thing* from her fertile imagination⟩ — see PRODUCT 1
6 something that happens ⟨the burglary was just one of those *things* that can happen anywhere⟩ — see EVENT 1
7 something that one hopes or intends to accomplish ⟨the *thing* is to get this project done on time⟩ — see GOAL
8 something to be dealt with ⟨I have lots of *things* to do this afternoon⟩ — see MATTER 2
9 things *pl* transportable items that one owns ⟨gather your *things* and get out⟩ — see POSSESSION 2

think *vb* to have as an opinion ⟨I *think* banning CD players from school is a dumb idea⟩ — see BELIEVE 2

think (about *or* over) *vb* to give serious and careful thought to ⟨I'll have to *think over* everything you've said before deciding what to do⟩ — see PONDER

think (of) *vb* to bring back to mind ⟨that postcard from Florida makes me *think of* all the fun we used to have there as kids⟩ — see REMEMBER

think (up) *vb* to create or think of by clever use of the imagination ⟨did you *think up* that story all by yourself?⟩ — see INVENT

thinker *n* a very smart person ⟨she's a very nice person, but she's no great *thinker*⟩ — see GENIUS 1

thinking *adj* having the ability to reason ⟨*thinking* human beings don't believe such nonsense⟩ — see RATIONAL 1

thinned *adj* 1 containing foreign or lower-grade substances ⟨genuine maple syrup *thinned* with corn syrup⟩ — see IMPURE
2 not containing very much of some important element ⟨the *thinned* iced tea that the restaurant serves is barely distinguishable from water⟩ — see WEAK 3

thirst *n* 1 a strong wish for something ⟨his *thirst* for knowledge is evident in his book-filled house⟩ — see DESIRE
2 urgent desire or interest ⟨an unquenchable *thirst* for travel that has led her to the far corners of the globe⟩ — see EAGERNESS

thirst (for) *vb* to have an earnest wish to own or enjoy ⟨blessed are those who hunger and *thirst for* righteousness⟩ — see DESIRE

thirsty *adj* 1 marked by little or no precipitation or humidity ⟨struggling to survive in that hot and *thirsty* climate⟩ — see DRY 1
2 showing urgent desire or interest ⟨young athletes *thirsty* for a chance to prove themselves⟩ — see EAGER

this *adj* being the less far of two ⟨it's on *this* side of the car⟩ — see NEAR 1

thistly *adj* likely to cause a scratch ⟨caught her sleeve on a *thistly* bush⟩ — see SCRATCHY 1

thorn *n* something that is a source of irritation ⟨your constant questions are a *thorn* in my side⟩ — see ANNOYANCE 3

thorny *adj* 1 likely to cause a scratch ⟨stay out of that *thorny* bramble unless you want a ton of scratches⟩ — see SCRATCHY 1
2 requiring exceptional skill or caution in performance or handling ⟨the candidate tried to avoid discussing his views on the *thorny* issue of abortion⟩ — see TRICKY

thorough *adj* 1 having no exceptions or restrictions ⟨had *thorough* access to the files for her research⟩ — see ABSOLUTE 2
2 including many small descriptive features ⟨gave me a *thorough* description of her new prom dress⟩ — see DETAILED 1
3 trying all possibilities ⟨a *thorough* search of the building that turned up no evidence of a bomb⟩ — see EXHAUSTIVE

thoroughbred *adj* of unmixed ancestry ⟨a *thoroughbred* dog⟩ — see PUREBRED

thoroughfare *n* a passage cleared for public vehicular travel ⟨one of the city's main *thoroughfares*⟩ — see WAY 1

thoroughgoing *adj* 1 having no exceptions or restrictions ⟨graduates with every right to a *thoroughgoing* sense of accomplishment⟩ — see ABSOLUTE 2
2 trying all possibilities ⟨a *thoroughgoing* attempt to solve the puzzle and still no luck⟩ — see EXHAUSTIVE

thoroughly *adv* **1** with attention to all aspects or details ⟨they searched the grounds *thoroughly* for any sign of the intruder⟩
synonyms completely, comprehensively, detailedly, exhaustively, fully, minutely, roundly, totally
related words all-out, full blast, intensively; broadly, extensively, generally, globally, widely; conclusively, consummately, definitely, perfectly
phrases in detail
near antonyms aimlessly, desultorily, haphazardly, hit-or-miss, randomly; cursorily, imperfectly, inadequately, narrowly, shallowly, sketchily, summarily, superficially; indeterminately, nebulously, vaguely
2 to a full extent or degree ⟨Mom is *thoroughly* disgusted with your behavior⟩ — see FULLY 1

though *conj* in spite of the fact that ⟨*though* Dad was really upset with us, he managed to hide it until we got home⟩ — see ALTHOUGH

though *adv* in spite of that ⟨I know we didn't win, but I was happy with how we played, *though*⟩ — see HOWEVER

thought *n* **1** a careful weighing of the reasons for or against something ⟨I'll give your request some *thought* and then let you know what my decision is⟩ — see CONSIDERATION 1
2 something imagined or pictured in the mind ⟨I just had a *thought*: what if we both pitched in and bought him one big present instead of two smaller presents for his birthday?⟩ — see IDEA

thoughtful *adj* **1** given to or made with heedful anticipation of the needs and happiness of others ⟨a *thoughtful* offer to watch the neighbors' children on moving day⟩ ⟨a *thoughtful* aunt who never forgets the birthday of a niece or nephew⟩
synonyms attentive, considerate, kind, solicitous
related words brotherly, good, good-hearted, helpful, hospitable, kindhearted, kindly, neighborly, nice; caring, compassionate, sympathetic, tender; chivalrous, courteous, courtly, gallant, gracious, polite; diplomatic, tactful; deferential, dutiful, obliging, regardful, respectful; altruistic, beneficent, benevolent, benignant, humane, selfless, unselfish; charitable, generous, magnanimous
near antonyms inattentive, uncaring, unheeding; inhospitable, unkind, unkindly, unneighborly; ill-bred, ill-mannered, impolite, rude, uncivil, uncourteous, unmannerly; unhelpful, unobliging; malevolent, malicious, mean, spiteful
antonyms heedless, inconsiderate, thoughtless, unthinking
2 decided on as a result of careful thought ⟨a *thoughtful* argument for military action⟩ — see DELIBERATE 1
3 given to or marked by long, quiet thinking ⟨was a quiet and *thoughtful* child who rarely spoke but when he did, he almost always had something worthwhile to say⟩ — see CONTEMPLATIVE

thoughtfully *adv* with good reason or courtesy ⟨very *thoughtfully* sent a present for my birthday⟩ — see WELL 4

thoughtless *adj* showing a lack of manners or consideration for others ⟨always making *thoughtless* comments that hurt other people's feelings⟩ — see IMPOLITE

thrall *n* **1** a person who is considered the property of another person ⟨I'm not your *thrall*, so you'll have to pick up after yourself⟩ — see SLAVE 1
2 the state of being a slave ⟨a people who still bear the scars of having been in *thrall* for so many years⟩ — see SLAVERY 1

thralldom *or* **thraldom** *n* the state of being a slave ⟨having known only *thralldom*, the newly emancipated had little idea how to live as freedmen⟩ — see SLAVERY 1

thrash *vb* **1** to achieve a victory over ⟨our team handily *thrashed* our opponents and went on to the championships⟩ — see BEAT 2
2 to defeat by a large margin ⟨the incumbent has been *thrashing* his opponents for so long that there's never any real contest for the senate seat⟩ — see WHIP 2
3 to strike repeatedly with something long and thin or flexible ⟨*thrashed* the horse with the riding crop⟩ — see WHIP 1
4 to strike repeatedly ⟨the tree branches *thrashed* the sides of the house as the storm continued to rage⟩ — see BEAT 1

thread *vb* **1** to scatter or set here and there among other things ⟨this history book *threads* excerpts from the diaries of pioneer women into its account of the settlement of the West⟩
synonyms interlace, intersperse, interweave, lace, weave, wreathe
related words insert, intermingle, mingle, mix; alternate, juxtapose; amalgamate, assimilate, blend, combine, commingle, embody, fuse, incorporate, integrate, merge
2 to put together into a series by means of or as if by means of a thread ⟨the reporter *threaded* his newspaper articles about the basketball team into a book that was essentially a chronicle of their championship season⟩
synonyms concatenate, string
related words chain, connect, join, link, unite; interlace, intersperse, intertwine, interweave, lace, weave, wreathe

threadbare *adj* **1** showing signs of advanced wear and tear and neglect ⟨bought a *threadbare* couch at a garage sale⟩ — see SHABBY 1
2 used or heard so often as to be dull ⟨a novel filled with nothing but *threadbare* clichés⟩ — see STALE
3 worn or torn into or as if into rags ⟨I loved that *threadbare* shirt, but after 10 years of wear, it was time to throw it away⟩ — see RAGGED 2

threat *n* something that may cause injury or harm ⟨terrorism is a *threat* to the safety of people everywhere⟩ — see DANGER 2

threaten *vb* to remain poised to inflict harm, danger, or distress on ⟨unless the home fans' unacceptable behavior and name-calling stops, the possibility of expulsion from the league *threatens* the school's basketball team⟩
synonyms hang (over), hover (over), impend (over), menace, overhang
related words endanger, hazard, imperil, jeopardize

threatening *adj* **1** giving signs of immediate occurrence ⟨economists warning of a *threatening* recession⟩ — see IMMINENT 1
2 being or showing a sign of evil or calamity to come ⟨a *threatening* silence followed the loud thump in the adjoining motel room⟩ — see OMINOUS
3 involving potential loss or injury ⟨*threatening* rocks lined that narrow stretch of the river through which we would be rafting⟩ — see DANGEROUS

threefold *adj* having three units or parts ⟨a *threefold* approach to solving the problem⟩ — see TRIPLE

threesome *n* a group of three ⟨the *threesome* from Crystal Falls—Jocelyn, Katie, and Lynn—missed their plane and joined up with the rest of the group the next day⟩

synonyms triad, trinity, trio, triple, triplet, triumvirate
related words trilogy; triplicate; triplex

threnody *n* a composition expressing one's grief over a loss ⟨the composer's cello concerto was composed as a moving *threnody* for his late wife⟩ — see LAMENT 2

threshold *n* the point at which something begins ⟨at the *threshold* of the new year, it's time to look back and make resolutions for the future⟩ — see BEGINNING

thrift *n* careful management of material resources ⟨years of living on a relatively small income has sharpened her *thrift*⟩ — see ECONOMY

thriftless *adj* given to spending money freely or foolishly ⟨a *thriftless* girl who didn't keep track of her finances and overspent constantly⟩ — see PRODIGAL

thrifty *adj* careful in the management of money or resources ⟨if you are *thrifty*, you can find ways to decorate your room stylishly yet inexpensively⟩ — see FRUGAL

thrill *n* a pleasurably intense stimulation of the feelings ⟨everyone gets a real *thrill* out of the Independence Day fireworks⟩
synonyms bang, exhilaration, kick, titillation
related words arousal, electrification, intoxication, stimulation; jolt, shock, surprise; delectation, delight, enjoyment, joy, lift, pleasure; amusement, diversion, entertainment, fun, treat

thrill *vb* to cause a pleasurable stimulation of the feelings ⟨was *thrilled* by the news of Betsy's promotion⟩
synonyms electrify, excite, exhilarate, galvanize, intoxicate, titillate, turn on
related words arouse, incite, inspire, provoke, stimulate; bewitch, captivate, charm, delight, enchant, enthrall (*or* enthral), hypnotize, mesmerize, rivet, spellbind; interest, intrigue, tantalize
near antonyms bore, jade, pall, tire, weary; deject, demoralize, discourage, dishearten, dispirit

thrilling *adj* causing great emotional or mental stimulation ⟨a *thrilling* adventure movie⟩ — see EXCITING 1

thrive *vb* 1 to grow vigorously ⟨these plants *thrive* with relatively little sunlight⟩
synonyms burgeon, flourish, prosper
related words luxuriate, overgrow, proliferate, shoot up; germinate, root, sprout; bloom, flower, fruit, produce, propagate, regenerate, seed
2 to reach a desired level of accomplishment ⟨going to a school for gifted students will help him *thrive* as a musical prodigy⟩ — see SUCCEED 2

thriving *adj* 1 having attained a desired end or state of good fortune ⟨our new business is *thriving*⟩ — see SUCCESSFUL 1
2 marked by much life, movement, or activity ⟨the fine arts are *thriving* at that school⟩ — see ALIVE 2
3 marked by vigorous growth and well-being especially economically ⟨a *thriving* manufacturing community that is experiencing a tremendous growth in new jobs⟩ — see PROSPEROUS 1

throaty *adj* 1 harsh and dry in sound ⟨had a bad cold and a *throaty* cough to go with it⟩ — see HOARSE
2 having a low musical pitch or range ⟨a *throaty* alto⟩ — see DEEP 2

throb *n* a rhythmic expanding and contracting ⟨I seemed to feel anew the pain of her death with each *throb* of my heart⟩ — see PULSATION

throb *vb* to expand and contract in a rhythmic manner ⟨the car's stereo speakers *throbbing* with the song's bass line⟩ — see PULSATE

throe *n* a sharp unpleasant sensation usually felt in some specific part of the body ⟨collapsed in the *throes* of agony⟩ — see PAIN 1

throng *n* a great number of persons or things gathered together ⟨grabbed a megaphone and addressed the vast *throng*⟩ — see CROWD 1

throng *vb* to move upon or fill (something) in great numbers ⟨fans *thronged* the field to celebrate the win⟩ — see CROWD 2

thronging *adj* possessing or covered with great numbers or amounts of something specified ⟨a field of ripe corn *thronging* with hundreds of crows⟩ — see RIFE

throttle *vb* to keep (someone) from breathing by exerting pressure on the windpipe ⟨we all squealed and covered our eyes when the villain of the movie wrapped his hands around the hero's neck and tried to *throttle* him⟩ — see CHOKE 1

through *adv* 1 from beginning to end ⟨read the letter *through* twice⟩ ⟨never once missed class the whole year *through*⟩
synonyms around, over, round, throughout
2 from one side to the other of an intervening space ⟨the bullet struck the door and went right *through*⟩ — see OVER 1

through *prep* 1 in or into the middle of ⟨lost control of the car and drove *through* the crowd⟩ — see AMONG
2 in random positions within the boundaries of ⟨you'll find horse farms *through* the whole valley⟩ — see AROUND 2
3 in the course of ⟨thoughtless people talking *through* the whole movie⟩ — see DURING
4 to the opposite side of ⟨walked *through* the room⟩ — see ACROSS
5 along the way of ⟨got to the concert *through* the bus system⟩ — see BY 1
6 as the result of ⟨won the tournament *through* practice and hard work⟩ — see BECAUSE OF
7 using the means or agency of ⟨apparently got his money *through* stealing it⟩ — see BY 2

through *adj* brought or having come to an end ⟨a standing ovation for the cast when the play was *through*⟩ — see COMPLETE 2

throughout *prep* 1 in random positions within the boundaries of ⟨saw red-tailed hawks *throughout* the game preserve⟩ — see AROUND 2
2 in the course of ⟨a soloist plays guitar *throughout* Sunday brunch⟩ — see DURING

throughout *adv* 1 from beginning to end ⟨while some fans deserted the singer during her troubled years, others remained loyal *throughout*⟩ — see THROUGH 1
2 in every place or in all places ⟨a cake studded *throughout* with raisins⟩ — see EVERYWHERE

throw *vb* to send through the air especially with a quick forward motion of the arm ⟨*threw* a life preserver to the drowning man⟩
synonyms cast, catapult, chuck, dash, fire, fling, heave, hurl, hurtle, launch, lob, loft, peg, pelt, pitch, sling, toss
related words bowl, flip, hook, pass, roll, shoot; buck, eject, impel, precipitate, project, propel, rifle, thrust

throw (on) *vb* to place on one's person ⟨*threw* a sweater on and headed outside⟩ — see PUT ON 1

throw away *vb* 1 to get rid of as useless or unwanted ⟨I should *throw away* that torn shirt⟩ — see DISCARD
2 to use up carelessly ⟨he's just *throwing away* money on soda and chips⟩ — see WASTE 1

throwing away *n* the getting rid of whatever is unwanted or useless ⟨the *throwing away* of her old stuffed animals marked the beginning of her mental preparation for an independent life as a college student⟩ — see DISPOSAL 1

throw out *vb* **1** to drive or force out ⟨the player was *thrown out* of the game after assaulting the ref⟩ — see EJECT 1

2 to get rid of as useless or unwanted ⟨would you mind if I *threw out* that leftover pizza that's been in the fridge for two weeks?⟩ — see DISCARD

throw up *vb* **1** to discharge the contents of the stomach through the mouth ⟨she must have eaten something that didn't agree with her because she *threw up* right after dinner⟩ — see VOMIT

2 to make or assemble roughly or hastily ⟨when the townspeople realized that the President's motorcade would be coming through on its way to the conference, they *threw up* a hasty "Welcome" sign⟩ — see COBBLE (TOGETHER)

thrum *n* a monotonous sound like that of an insect in motion ⟨the steady *thrum* of turbines in a power plant⟩ — see HUM

thrum *vb* to strike or cause to strike lightly and usually rhythmically ⟨*thrummed* his fingers on the table to show he was exasperated by having to wait so long for his dinner⟩ — see ¹TAP

thrust *vb* to apply force to (someone or something) so that it moves in front of one ⟨*thrust* his head into the room to see if Mom was around, and then tiptoed in⟩ — see PUSH 1

thud *n* a hard strike with a part of the body or an instrument ⟨felt a *thud* on his head before losing consciousness⟩ — see ¹BLOW

thud *vb* to come into usually forceful contact with something ⟨the snowball *thudded* against the side of my car⟩ — see HIT 2

thug *n* a violent, brutal person who is often a member of an organized gang ⟨the mob boss regularly sent his *thugs* after people who were slow to pay their debts⟩ — see HOODLUM

thumb *vb* to travel by securing free rides ⟨thought I'd *thumb* into town instead of paying for a cab⟩ — see HITCHHIKE

thump *n* a hard strike with a part of the body or an instrument ⟨gave him a *thump* against the side of his head whenever he said something obnoxious⟩ — see ¹BLOW

thump *vb* **1** to deliver a blow to (someone or something) usually in a strong vigorous manner ⟨*thumped* the desk with his hand as he delivered his speech⟩ — see HIT 1

2 to strike repeatedly ⟨a bass player *thumping* the strings⟩ — see BEAT 1

thunder *vb* to make a long loud deep noise or cry ⟨as we got closer, the waterfall *thundered* louder and louder⟩ — see ROAR

thunderous *adj* marked by a high volume of sound ⟨the last *thunderous* chord of the symphony rang throughout the hall⟩ — see LOUD 1

thunderstruck *adj* affected with sudden and great wonder or surprise ⟨Colin was *thunderstruck* when his parents told him he was adopted⟩

synonyms amazed, astonished, astounded, awestruck, bowled over, dumbfounded (*or* dumfounded), flabbergasted, shocked, stunned, stupefied

related words startled, surprised; aghast, appalled, dismayed, horrified; bewildered, confused, dazed, overwhelmed; agape, awed, awesome, openmouthed, wide-eyed, widemouthed

near antonyms casual, nonchalant, unruffled

antonyms unawed

thus *adv* for this or that reason ⟨we didn't have room for all seven of us in my car and *thus* took two cars to go to the movies⟩ — see THEREFORE

thus far *adv* up to this or that time ⟨we haven't heard any news about the school board's decision *thus far*⟩ — see HITHERTO

thwack *n* **1** a hard strike with a part of the body or an instrument ⟨disciplined the toddler for giving his older sister a *thwack* with his toy⟩ — see ¹BLOW

2 a loud explosive sound ⟨even from the top of the bleachers we could hear the loud *thwack* of the ball being hit⟩ — see CLAP 1

thwack *vb* to deliver a blow to (someone or something) usually in a strong vigorous manner ⟨*thwacked* the growling dog on the nose with a rolled-up newspaper⟩ — see HIT 1

thwart *vb* to prevent from achieving a goal ⟨the rain *thwarted* us from holding our picnic this afternoon⟩ — see FRUSTRATE

tick (off) *vb* to specify one after another ⟨*ticked off* everything she would need to buy while her daughter wrote the items down on a list⟩ — see ENUMERATE 1

ticket *n* **1** a small sheet of plastic, paper, or paperboard showing that the bearer has a claim to something (as admittance) ⟨only people with *tickets* will be allowed past the front gates⟩

synonyms check, coupon, pass

related words certificate, note, token, voucher

2 a slip (as of paper or cloth) that is attached to something to identify or describe it ⟨the price on the *ticket* is $20 more than the advertised price⟩ — see LABEL

ticket *vb* to attach an identifying slip to ⟨quickly the attendant *ticketed* my coat and handed the claim stub back to me⟩ — see LABEL 1

tickled *adj* experiencing pleasure, satisfaction, or delight ⟨I'm *tickled* that you like the present so much⟩ — see GLAD 1

ticklish *adj* requiring exceptional skill or caution in performance or handling ⟨trying to tell him that his zipper is down without embarrassing him will be a *ticklish* task⟩ — see TRICKY

tidbit *also* **titbit** *n* **1** something that is pleasing to eat because it is rare or a luxury ⟨gave her an expensive box of chocolate *tidbits*⟩ — see DELICACY 1

2 a small piece or quantity of food ⟨I'll just have a *tidbit* of the dessert, nothing too big⟩ — see MORSEL 1

tide *n* a prevailing or general movement or inclination ⟨the *tide* of the battle turned suddenly, and the would-be invaders were forced to retreat⟩ — see TREND 1

tidied *adj* being clean and in good order ⟨that rare teenager who keeps a nicely-*tidied* room⟩ — see NEAT 1

tidings *n pl* a report of recent events or facts not previously known ⟨any *tidings* from the front, soldier?⟩ — see NEWS

tidy *adj* **1** being clean and in good order ⟨could easily find everything on her *tidy* desk⟩ — see NEAT 1

2 of a size greater than average of its kind ⟨paid a *tidy* sum for that painting⟩ — see LARGE

3 sufficiently large in size, amount, or number to merit attention ⟨signed a contract for a *tidy* amount of time and money⟩ — see CONSIDERABLE 1

tie *n* **1** a situation in which neither participant in a contest, competition, or struggle comes out ahead of the other ⟨the competition for first place in the dessert di-

vision ended in a *tie* between the chocolate pecan pie and the walnut fudge tart⟩
synonyms dead heat, draw, stalemate, standoff
related words deadlock, impasse; photo finish; toss-up
2 a uniting or binding force or influence ⟨their marriage will serve to form a very strong *tie* between our families⟩ — see BOND 2

tie *vb* **1** to gather into a tight mass by means of a line or cord ⟨*tied* the newspapers into a bundle⟩
synonyms band, bind, gird, truss
related words cinch, cord, rope, strap, thread, wire; lash, leash, tether; interlace, intertwine, interweave, lace; entangle, knot, snarl, tangle, twist; coil, wind
near antonyms undo, unfasten, unlace, unlash, unloose, unloosen, unthread; unleash, untether; disentangle, uncoil, untangle, untwine, untwist, unwind
antonyms unbind, untie
2 to produce something equal to (as in quality or value) ⟨no one has yet *tied* that composer for his contributions to American music⟩ — see EQUAL 1

tie–up *n* the state of having shared interests or efforts (as in social or business matters) ⟨in a *tie-up* with the film studio, the toy company is producing a whole line of figures featuring characters from the animated movie⟩ — see ASSOCIATION 1

tie up *vb* to create difficulty for the work or activity of ⟨an accident is *tying up* traffic at 5th and Broadway⟩ — see HAMPER

tiff *n* an often noisy or angry expression of differing opinions ⟨got into a little *tiff* about what color sheets to buy for their bed⟩ — see ARGUMENT 1

tight *adj* **1** not allowing penetration (as by gas, liquid, or light) ⟨a *tight* hull that was no match for an iceberg⟩
synonyms impenetrable, impermeable, impervious
related words close, compact, dense, snug, thick; airtight, hermetic, watertight; lightproof, soundproof, waterproof
near antonyms absorbent, leaky, porous, unsealed
antonyms penetrable, permeable
2 firmly positioned in place and difficult to dislodge ⟨a *tight* screw that won't come loose⟩ ⟨a jar with a *tight* lid⟩
synonyms fast, firm, frozen, jammed, lodged, secure, set, snug, stuck, wedged
related words bonded, cemented, glued; anchored, clamped; embedded, entrenched (*also* intrenched), implanted; attached, bound, fastened, secured; immovable, unyielding
near antonyms detached, dislodged, freed, loosened, unattached, unbound, undone, unfastened, unsecured; movable (*or* moveable), yielding
antonyms insecure, loose
3 giving or sharing as little as possible ⟨is fairly *tight* with his money⟩ — see STINGY 1
4 having little space between items or parts ⟨it's *tight* in that packed nightclub⟩ — see CLOSE 1
5 showing little difference in the standing of the competitors ⟨a *tight* race for governor⟩ — see CLOSE 3
6 stretched with little or no give ⟨the rope was pulled *tight*⟩ — see TAUT

tightfisted *adj* giving or sharing as little as possible ⟨your younger brother is pretty *tightfisted* about lending his video games to others⟩ — see STINGY 1

tight–lipped *adj* tending not to speak frequently (as by habit or inclination) ⟨she's usually *tight-lipped* about her private life⟩ — see SILENT 2

tightness *n* the quality of being overly sparing with money ⟨a man of legendary *tightness*, he has plenty of money in his savings account⟩ — see PARSIMONY

tightwad *n* a mean grasping person who is usually stingy with money ⟨you're always such a *tightwad* when charity comes calling⟩ — see MISER

till *vb* to work by plowing, sowing, and raising crops on ⟨farmers *tilling* the soil from sunup to sunset⟩ — see FARM

tiller *n* a person who cultivates the land and grows crops on it ⟨the Morgan have been *tillers* of that plot of land for five generations⟩ — see FARMER

tilt *n* the act of positioning or an instance of being positioned at an angle ⟨indicated her approval with a slight forward *tilt* of her head⟩
synonyms angling, bend, cock, inclination, list, tip
related words turn, twist, veer; bow, dip, nod

tilt *vb* to set or cause to be at an angle ⟨a robin *tilting* its head and eyeing the wriggling worm⟩ — see LEAN 1

tilted *adj* **1** inclined or twisted to one side ⟨stared at me with a *tilted* head and a quizzical look⟩ — see AWRY
2 running in a slanting direction ⟨the floors of the old house were *tilted* slightly⟩ — see DIAGONAL

tilting *adj* running in a slanting direction ⟨a rickety, *tilting* staircase that did not look safe⟩ — see DIAGONAL

timber *n* **1** a dense growth of trees and shrubs covering a large area ⟨upon our approach the deer disappeared back into the *timber* from whence it had come⟩ — see FOREST
2 tree logs as prepared for human use ⟨needed a new load of *timber* to finish building the house⟩ — see WOOD

timberland *n* a dense growth of trees and shrubs covering a large area ⟨make sure you cover up when hiking through the *timberland* because we have lots of poison ivy around here⟩ — see FOREST

time *n* **1** a particular point at which an event takes place ⟨remember that one *time* you tried to wash the dog in the sink⟩ — see OCCASION 1
2 an exciting or noteworthy event that one experiences firsthand ⟨enjoys telling us about the *times* he had while he was in the army⟩ — see ADVENTURE
3 an extent of time associated with a particular person or thing ⟨back in my parents' *time*, families usually had only one car⟩ — see AGE 1
4 the period during which something exists, lasts, or is in progress ⟨how much *time* will the project take?⟩ — see DURATION 1

timeliness *n* the quality or habit of arriving on time ⟨your *timeliness* will make a good impression on the person interviewing you for the job⟩ — see PROMPTITUDE

timely *adj* **1** especially suitable for a certain time ⟨a *timely* invitation to lunch that came just as I was starting to feel hungry⟩
synonyms opportune, seasonable
related words appropriate, apt, fit, fitting, meet, pat, proper, relevant, suitable; fortunate, lucky, propitious; anticipated, expected; prompt, punctual, undelayed
near antonyms improper, inappropriate, irrelevant, unfit, unsuitable; unfortunate, unlucky; behind, behindhand, belated, delayed, delinquent, late, latish, overdue, postponed, slow, tardy; anticipatory, early, precocious, premature; abrupt, sudden, unanticipated, unexpected
antonyms inopportune, unseasonable, untimely
2 done, carried out, or given without delay ⟨when I order a pizza, I expect it to be delivered in a *timely* manner⟩ — see PROMPT 1

timepiece *n* a device to measure time ⟨the only *timepiece* she used at the cabin was a garden sundial⟩

synonyms chronometer, clock, timer

related words alarm clock, atomic clock, cuckoo clock, grandfather clock, time clock; hourglass, sandglass, sundial, water clock; chronograph, stopwatch, watch

timer *n* a device to measure time ⟨set the kitchen *timer* to 30 minutes⟩ — see TIMEPIECE

timetable *n* a listing of things to be presented or considered (as at a concert or play) ⟨checked the *timetable* of events to see if I'd be able to get something to eat beforehand⟩ — see PROGRAM 1

timid *adj* easily frightened ⟨a *timid* rabbit hopping cautiously out of the hedge⟩ — see SHY 1

timidity *n* lack of willingness to assert oneself and take risks ⟨none of the scouts showed the least *timidity* about rappeling down the cliff⟩

synonyms faintheartedness, timidness, timorousness

related words bashfulness, constraint, embarrassment, inhibition, restraint, shyness, skittishness; hesitation, indecision, indecisiveness, irresoluteness, irresolution; alarm, anxiety, apprehension, concern, discomposure, dismay, fear, panic, upset, worry; cowardice, cowardliness, cravenness, spinelessness, yellowness

near antonyms assurance, confidence, self-assurance, self-confidence; composure, coolness, insouciance, nonchalance, unconcern; backbone, decisiveness, determination, fiber, firmness, fortitude, gameness, grit, gumption, mettle, resoluteness, resolution, spunk; bravery, courage, courageousness, daring, dauntlessness, doughtiness, fearlessness, intrepidity, intrepidness

antonyms audaciousness, audacity, boldness, guts, nerve

timidness *n* lack of willingness to assert oneself and take risks ⟨because of his natural *timidness*, he never once asked a girl on a date throughout high school⟩ — see TIMIDITY

timorous *adj* easily frightened ⟨wild animals are *timorous*, so make sure you don't make any sudden moves around them⟩ — see SHY 1

timorousness *n* lack of willingness to assert oneself and take risks ⟨her innate *timorousness* puts her at a disadvantage in job interviews⟩ — see TIMIDITY

tincture *n* a substance used to color other materials ⟨added a few drops of dark green *tincture* to the white paint to make a pleasing shade of light green⟩ — see PIGMENT

tinge *n* a property that becomes apparent when light falls on an object and by which things that are identical in form can be distinguished ⟨there's a bluish *tinge* to your lips—you must be freezing!⟩ — see COLOR 1

tinge *vb* to give color or a different color to ⟨just slightly *tinge* the frosting with yellow food coloring to give it a lemon look⟩ — see COLOR 1

tingle *n* a sharp unpleasant sensation usually felt in some specific part of the body ⟨can't stand those funny *tingles* I get when my foot falls asleep⟩ — see PAIN 1

tinker (with) *vb* to handle thoughtlessly, ignorantly, or mischievously ⟨don't ever *tinker with* the power tools in the workshop because you could seriously hurt yourself⟩ — see TAMPER

tinkle *n* a series of short high ringing sounds ⟨Mrs. Mouse ignored the warning *tinkle* of the cat's bell, and now her children are orphans⟩

synonyms chime(s), jingle, tintinnabulation

related words clatter, jangle, rattle; chink, clang, clank, clink, dingdong, ping, ring, toll; chirr, ripple, trill, warble

tinkle *vb* to make a repeated sharp light ringing sound ⟨the chimes *tinkled* in the breeze⟩ — see JINGLE

tint *vb* to give color or a different color to ⟨if you *tint* that blue paint with this yellow paint, you'll get green paint⟩ — see COLOR 1

tint *n* a property that becomes apparent when light falls on an object and by which things that are identical in form can be distinguished ⟨painted the seascape in yellow, blue, and brown *tints*⟩ — see COLOR 1

tintinnabulation *n* a series of short high ringing sounds ⟨the merry *tintinnabulation* of church bells⟩ — see TINKLE

tiny *adj* very small in size ⟨the forest ranger showed us how every square foot of forest is alive with *tiny* creatures⟩

synonyms atomic, bitty, infinitesimal, microminiature, microscopic (*also* microscopical), miniature, minute, teeny, teeny-weeny, wee

related words diminutive, dwarf, little, midget, model, petite, pocket, pocket-size (*also* pocket-sized), pygmy, small, smallish; dinky, dwarfish, insignificant, pint-size (*or* pint-sized), puny, scrubby, undersized

near antonyms big, bulky, bumper, considerable, extensive, good, goodly, good-sized, grand, great, gross, handsome, hefty, hulking, jumbo, king-size (*or* king-sized), large, largish, major, outsize (*also* outsized), oversize (*or* oversized), sizable (*or* sizeable), substantial, super, whacking, whopping; formidable, grandiose, imposing, lofty, majestic, monolithic, staggering, stupendous, towering; boundless, cavernous, immeasurable, infinite, vast, vasty, voluminous

antonyms astronomical (*also* astronomic), colossal, cosmic, elephantine, enormous, giant, gigantic, herculean, heroic, huge, immense, mammoth, massive, monster, monstrous, monumental, mountainous, prodigious, titanic, tremendous

¹**tip** *n* **1** a piece of advice or useful information especially from an expert ⟨got some *tips* from a horticulturist on how to get my violets to bloom⟩

synonyms hint, lead, pointer

related words advice, advisement, assistance, counsel, guidance, recommendation, suggestion; caution, cautioning, sign, signal, telltale, tip-off, warning; brief, direction, feedback, instruction, observation; prompt, reminder, urging; answer, clue, solution

2 information not generally available to the public ⟨I'll give you a little *tip*: if you hit the soda pop machine just above the company logo, you'll get a free bottle of pop⟩ — see DOPE 1

²**tip** *n* **1** a small sum of money given for a service over and above what is due ⟨gave our waiter an extra large *tip* for such fantastic service⟩

synonyms gratuity, perquisite

related words donation, gift, lagniappe, largess (*or* largesse), present; bonus, favor, reward; contribution, offering

2 something given in addition to what is ordinarily expected or owed ⟨a customer who always gives his paper carrier a very generous *tip* at Christmastime⟩ — see BONUS

³**tip** *n* the act of positioning or an instance of being positioned at an angle ⟨the speedboat had run aground and was now perched on the sandbar at a precarious *tip*⟩ — see TILT

⁴**tip** *n* the last and usually sharp or tapering part of something long and narrow ⟨the *tip* of a knitting needle⟩ — see POINT 2

tip *vb* to set or cause to be at an angle ⟨be careful because if you *tip* your cup any more, you'll spill your tea⟩ — see LEAN 1

tipped *adj* tapering to a thin tip ⟨a round-*tipped* needle⟩ — see POINTED 1

tipping *adj* inclined or twisted to one side ⟨a boat *tipping* under the weight of a lopsided load⟩ — see AWRY

tippler *n* a person who makes a habit of getting drunk ⟨her husband was a *tippler* who had hidden small stashes of liquor all over the house⟩ — see DRUNK 1

tipsy *adj* being under the influence of alcohol ⟨our uncle had too much to drink and was a little *tipsy*⟩ — see DRUNK

tip–top *adj* of the very best kind ⟨the doctor told me I was in *tip-top* shape⟩ — see EXCELLENT

tip–top *n* the highest part or point ⟨could just barely reach the *tip-top* of the bookcase⟩ — see HEIGHT 1

tirade *n* a long angry speech or scolding ⟨after the inspection by the health department, Jay had to listen to his boss's *tirade* about keeping the restaurant's kitchen cleaner⟩

synonyms diatribe, harangue, rant

related words assault, attack, invective, lambasting, lashing, tongue-lashing, vituperation; berating, chewing out, rebuke, reprimand, reproach, reproof; abuse, castigation, censure, condemnation, criticism, denunciation; belittlement, deprecation, depreciation, disparagement, dissing; excoriation, execration, revilement; admonishment, admonition, lecture, sermon

near antonyms encomium, eulogy, panegyric, rhapsody, tribute; acclaim, acclamation, accolade, citation, homage, honor, praise; approval, blessing, commendation, endorsement, sanction; ovation, plaudit, rave

tire *vb* 1 to diminish the physical strength of ⟨a pentathlon would *tire* all but the hardiest athletes⟩ — see WEAKEN 1

2 to make weary and restless by being dull or monotonous ⟨this long dry lecture will *tire* the audience if you don't insert some jokes into it⟩ — see ²BORE

3 to use up all the physical energy of ⟨I don't want our walk to *tire* you too much⟩ — see EXHAUST 1

tired *adj* 1 depleted in strength, energy, or freshness ⟨I'm *tired* after a long night of studying⟩ — see WEARY 1

2 having one's patience, interest, or pleasure exhausted ⟨I'm sick and *tired* of your antics⟩ — see WEARY 2

3 used or heard so often as to be dull ⟨*tired* phrases won't hold your reader's interest⟩ — see STALE

tiredness *n* 1 a complete depletion of energy or strength ⟨your *tiredness* will go away after a good rest⟩ — see FATIGUE

2 the state of being bored ⟨keeping the kids inside on such a sunny day will only lead to whining and *tiredness* on their part⟩ — see BOREDOM

tireless *adj* showing no signs of weariness even after long hard effort ⟨a *tireless* advocate for human rights⟩

synonyms indefatigable, inexhaustible, unflagging, untiring, unwearying, weariless

related words assiduous, conscientious, diligent, meticulous, painstaking, sedulous; determined, dogged, patient, persevering, persistent, pertinacious, plodding, relentless, steadfast, steady, stubborn, tenacious, unabating, unfailing, unfaltering, unflinching, unrelenting, unremitting, unwavering; active, busy, dynamic, energetic, feverish, spirited, vigorous; hard, industrious, intense, laborious, slavish, strenuous

near antonyms indolent, lackadaisical, laggard, lazy, listless, shiftless, slothful, sluggish; apathetic, casual, desultory, languid, spiritless; beat, broken, burned-out

(or burnt-out), done in, drained, enervated, jaded, overtaxed, overworked, played out, sapped, spent, tuckered (out), wearied, worn-out

tirelessly *adv* with great effort or determination ⟨will work *tirelessly* to ensure that justice is done in this case⟩ — see HARD 1

tiresome *adj* causing weariness, restlessness, or lack of interest ⟨what a *tiresome* church service that turned out to be⟩ — see BORING

tiring *adj* causing weariness, restlessness, or lack of interest ⟨a dull, *tiring* lecture that had the students falling asleep⟩ — see BORING

titan *n* something that is unusually large and powerful ⟨this newest ocean liner is a true *titan* of the sea⟩ — see GIANT

titanic *adj* unusually large ⟨that baseball player signed a contract for a *titanic* amount of money⟩ — see HUGE

titillate *vb* to cause a pleasurable stimulation of the feelings ⟨the world's newest and highest roller coaster promises to *titillate* as none has ever before⟩ — see THRILL

titillation *n* a pleasurably intense stimulation of the feelings ⟨the final minutes of the football game gave us all the *titillation* that the highly anticipated game had promised⟩ — see THRILL

title *n* 1 a word or combination of words by which a person or thing is regularly known ⟨asked the clerk to help him find a movie recommended by a friend, even though he couldn't remember the *title* or who was in it⟩ — see NAME 1

2 a word or series of words often in larger letters placed at the beginning of a passage or at the top of a page in order to introduce or categorize ⟨the *title* of this chapter is "Women and Power in *Jane Eyre*"⟩ — see HEADING

3 the position occupied by the one who comes in first in a competition ⟨won the singles *title* three years in a row⟩ — see CROWN 2

title *vb* to give a name to ⟨what do you plan on *titling* your latest album?⟩ — see NAME 1

titter *n* an explosive sound that is a sign of amusement ⟨a *titter* swept through the crowd at his verbal slip⟩ — see LAUGH 1

tittle *n* 1 a very small piece ⟨just a *tittle* of dessert, as I'm on a diet⟩ — see BIT 1

2 the smallest amount or part imaginable ⟨there's not a *tittle* of sense in that book⟩ — see JOT

titular *adj* being something in name or form only ⟨he's the *titular* headmaster of the school, though we all know the assistant headmaster is really the one who runs things around here⟩ — see NOMINAL 1

tizzy *n* a state of nervous or irritated concern ⟨all in a *tizzy* because she left her lunch at home⟩ — see FRET

to *prep* earlier than ⟨right now it's 25 minutes *to* 10:00⟩ — see BEFORE 1

toady *n* a person who flatters another in order to get ahead ⟨no one liked the office *toady*, who spent most of her time complimenting the boss on what a great job he was doing⟩ — see SYCOPHANT

toady *vb* to use flattery or the doing of favors in order to win approval especially from a superior ⟨*toadying* will get you nowhere in this class—you'll have to earn your grades by actually doing the work⟩ — see FAWN

toast *vb* to cause to have or give off heat to a moderate degree ⟨come over and *toast* your toes by the fire⟩ — see WARM 1

toasty *adj* having or giving off heat to a moderate degree ⟨I'm nice and *toasty* in front of the fire⟩ — see WARM 1

tocsin *n* **1** an object intended to give public notice or warning ⟨the *tocsin* rang out, warning us of the approaching tornado⟩ — see SIGNAL 1
2 something that tells of approaching danger or risk ⟨noted that a sudden drop in a student's grades may be a *tocsin* of a serious personal problem⟩ — see WARNING 2

today *adv* at the present time ⟨even *today*, arranged marriages remain a common practice in some parts of the world⟩ — see NOW 1

today *n* the time currently existing or in progress ⟨live for *today* and let tomorrow worry about itself⟩ — see PRESENT 1

to–do *n* a state of noisy, confused activity ⟨there was such a *to-do* when the mice got loose from the science room that I thought the principal was going to close the school⟩ — see COMMOTION

together *adv* **1** at one and the same time ⟨the two packages, although sent on different days, arrived *together*⟩
synonyms coincidentally, coincidently, concurrently, contemporaneously, simultaneously
related words close, immediately, narrowly, near
phrases at once
near antonyms apart, independently, individually, singly; consecutively, successively
antonyms separately
2 in or by combined action or effort ⟨working *together*, we can get this project done on time⟩
synonyms conjointly, jointly
related words collectively, mutually, reciprocally, unanimously, unitedly; cooperatively, symbiotically
phrases in concert
antonyms apart, independently, individually, separately, severally, singly, unilaterally

togs *n pl* **1** clothing chosen as appropriate for a specific situation ⟨put on your party *togs* and come over to our place for an all-night dance party⟩ — see OUTFIT 1
2 covering for the human body ⟨hey, snazzy *togs* you're wearing⟩ — see CLOTHING

toil *n* very hard or unpleasant work ⟨after years of *toil* in a sweatshop, Kim was finally able to start her own dressmaking business⟩
synonyms drudgery, grind, labor, slavery, sweat, travail
related words effort, exertion, pains, struggle, trouble; chore, duty, job, obligation, responsibility; routine, tedium, treadmill
near antonyms ease, leisure, relaxation, repose, rest; amusement, diversion, entertainment, recreation, sport; idleness, inactivity, inertia, inertness
antonyms fun, play

toil *vb* to devote serious and sustained effort ⟨*toiled* for many years on the mammoth sculpture⟩ — see LABOR

toiler *n* a person who does very hard or dull work ⟨on Labor Day we should give a thought to those *toilers* who work long hours at low-paying jobs⟩ — see SLAVE 2

toilet *n* a room furnished with a fixture for flushing body waste ⟨we were directed to the *toilets* in the church basement⟩
synonyms bath, bathroom, latrine, lavatory, rest room, washroom, water closet
related words commode; outhouse, privy

toilsome *adj* **1** requiring considerable physical or mental effort ⟨learning how to snowboard is a *toilsome* task when you don't have much coordination⟩ — see HARD 2

2 requiring much time, effort, or careful attention ⟨this is the most *toilsome* part of the construction, so we'll go slowly to make sure we're doing it right⟩ — see DEMANDING 1

token *n* something that serves to keep alive the memory of a person or event ⟨please accept this parting gift as a *token* of our lasting affection⟩ — see MEMORIAL

tolerable *adj* **1** capable of being endured ⟨stubbing your toe is at least a more *tolerable* pain than breaking your foot⟩ — see BEARABLE
2 of a level of quality that meets one's needs or standards ⟨the accommodations are *tolerable* though not exactly luxurious⟩ — see ADEQUATE

tolerably *adv* in a satisfactory way ⟨I'm doing *tolerably*, thanks for asking⟩ — see WELL 1

tolerance *n* the capacity to endure what is difficult or disagreeable without complaining ⟨showed great *tolerance* in dealing with the angry and tired toddler's tantrums⟩ — see PATIENCE

tolerant *adj* **1** accepting pains or hardships calmly or without complaint ⟨this job requires a *tolerant* person who is used to dealing with complaints and angry customers⟩ — see PATIENT 1
2 receiving or enduring without offering resistance ⟨a *tolerant* acceptance of the terrible way that his wife always treated him⟩ — see PASSIVE

tolerate *vb* to put up with (something painful or difficult) ⟨with her headache Mom couldn't *tolerate* all the noise we were making⟩ — see BEAR 2

tolerating *adj* receiving or enduring without offering resistance ⟨old pictures of a graciously *tolerating* father letting his young children climb all over him⟩ — see PASSIVE

toll *vb* to make the clear sound heard when metal vibrates ⟨let the church bells joyously *toll* on this most happy occasion⟩ — see RING 1

tomb *n* a final resting place for a dead person ⟨explored the old graveyard and saw *tombs* dating back for two centuries⟩ — see GRAVE

tomboyish *adj* having qualities or traits that are traditionally considered inappropriate for a girl or woman ⟨her father thought that ice hockey was a little too *tomboyish* for her, but her mother and older brother encouraged her to take it up⟩ — see UNFEMININE

tombstone *n* a shaped stone laid over or erected near a grave and usually bearing an inscription to identify and preserve the memory of the deceased ⟨the many *tombstones* marking the graves of children in the old cemetery reveal the harshness of pioneer life⟩
synonyms gravestone, headstone, monument
related words cross, marker, plaque, stone, table, tablet; monolith, obelisk, pillar; memorial, shrine

tome *n* a set of printed sheets of paper bound together between covers and forming a work of fiction or nonfiction ⟨picked up a thick *tome* on the Roman Empire at a used book store⟩ — see BOOK 1

tomfoolery *n* wildly playful or mischievous behavior ⟨we were so excited that school was cancelled we were jumping on the bed until Mom told us to stop all the *tomfoolery*⟩ — see HORSEPLAY

tone *n* **1** a distinctive way of putting ideas into words ⟨the angry *tone* of his letter makes it clear he doesn't want to speak to me ever again⟩ — see STYLE 1
2 a property that becomes apparent when light falls on an object and by which things that are identical in form can be distinguished ⟨fall fashions in deep jewel *tones*⟩ — see COLOR 1

3 the set of qualities that makes a person, a group of people, or a thing different from others ⟨all that show-biz glitz is out of keeping with the *tone* of the college⟩ — see NATURE 1

toned–down *adj* not excessively showy ⟨after such a heated argument, it was a relief to hear someone use *toned-down* language to state their position⟩ — see QUIET 2

tongue *n* the stock of words, pronunciation, and grammar used by a people as their basic means of communication ⟨he spoke in a *tongue* that I didn't understand⟩ — see LANGUAGE 1

tonic *adj* having a renewing effect on the state of the body or mind ⟨breathe in clear *tonic* mountain air⟩ ⟨never underestimate the *tonic* power of humor on a sick person⟩
synonyms bracing, invigorating, refreshing, restorative, reviving, stimulating, stimulative, vitalizing
related words conditioning, strengthening; animating, exhilarating, exhilarative, quickening, sharp; corrective, curative, curing, medicinal, rectifying, reformative, reformatory, remedial, remedying, reparative, therapeutic; beneficial, healthful, healthy, helpful, salubrious, salutary, wholesome
near antonyms deadening, debilitating, enervating, enfeebling, exhausting, numbing, sapping, weakening

too *adv* **1** beyond a normal or acceptable limit ⟨Ryan thought the test was *too* hard, but, on the other hand, he hadn't studied for it⟩
synonyms devilishly, excessively, exorbitantly, inordinately, monstrously, overly, overmuch, unacceptably, unduly
related words extravagantly, immoderately, intemperately; extortionately, inexcusably, intolerably, unbearably, unconscionably, unreasonably; improperly, inappropriately; abnormally, extraordinarily, freakishly, singularly, uncommonly, uncustomarily, unusually; astronomically, considerably, eminently, especially, exceedingly, exceptionally, extensively, extra, extremely, incredibly, remarkably, significantly, substantially, super, very, whacking
phrases to a fault
near antonyms acceptably, moderately, modestly, reasonably, temperately; barely, hardly, just, marginally, minimally, scarcely
antonyms deficiently, inadequately, insufficiently
2 in addition to what has been said ⟨I want to buy this sweater—and that sweater *too*!⟩ — see MORE 1
3 to a great degree ⟨the audience didn't seem *too* interested in what the speaker had to say⟩ — see VERY 1

tool *n* **1** an article intended for use in work ⟨needed a special *tool* to open the case of the CD player⟩ — see IMPLEMENT
2 one that is or can be used to further the purposes of another ⟨a ruthless leader using his trusting followers as *tools* in his quest for power⟩ — see PAWN 1
3 one who is easily deceived or cheated ⟨if you believe that you can break the school rules because your best friend said so, then you're just a pathetic *tool*⟩ — see DUPE

tooth and nail *adv* with all power or resources being used ⟨I'll fight *tooth and nail* to win the finals⟩ — see FULL BLAST

toothsome *adj* very pleasing to the sense of taste ⟨a *toothsome* chocolate dessert⟩ — see DELICIOUS 1

top *adj* **1** being at a point or level higher than all others ⟨an office in the *top* story of the building⟩ ⟨the *top* student in our graduating class⟩

synonyms highest, loftiest, topmost, upmost, uppermost
related words higher, loftier, upper; maximized, maximum, peaked, utmost; chief, first, foremost, head, leading, predominant, preeminent, premier, principal; dominant, dominating, eminent, prominent, towering; elevated, escalated, heightened, jacked (up), lifted, raised, uplifted, upraised
near antonyms below, lower, under; low, lowered, low-lying, sunken
antonyms lowermost, lowest, nethermost, undermost
2 of the greatest or highest degree or quantity ⟨your safety is our *top* priority⟩ — see ULTIMATE 1
3 of the highest degree ⟨going at *top* speed⟩ — see FULL 2
4 of the very best kind ⟨he's one of the tennis club's *top* players⟩ — see EXCELLENT

top *n* **1** a piece placed over an open container to hold in, protect, or conceal its contents ⟨make sure the *top* is on the juice blender before you turn it on⟩ — see COVER 1
2 the highest part or point ⟨a hawk's nest at the very *top* of the tree⟩ — see HEIGHT 1

top *vb* to be greater, better, or stronger than ⟨the next contender's javelin throw *topped* the reigning champion's and set a new world record⟩ — see SURPASS 1

topcoat *n* a warm outdoor coat ⟨threw on a wool *topcoat* and headed out into the snow⟩ — see OVERCOAT

topic *n* a major object of interest or concern (as in a discussion or artistic composition) ⟨the *topic* of his poem is the bitter conflict in Northern Ireland⟩ — see MATTER 1

topmost *adj* **1** being at a point or level higher than all others ⟨his kite got tangled in the *topmost* branches of the tree⟩ — see TOP 1
2 of the highest degree ⟨our *topmost* goal is to help students learn foreign languages in an easy and natural way⟩ — see FULL 2

top–notch *adj* of the very best kind ⟨a *top-notch* violinist who had no trouble getting a position with the symphony⟩ — see EXCELLENT

topper *n* something (as a fact or argument) that is decisive or overwhelming ⟨there are lots of good reasons we can't go to the concert, but the fact that the tickets are all sold out is the *topper*⟩ — see CLINCHER

topple *vb* to go down from an upright position suddenly and involuntarily ⟨the tower of blocks *toppled* even though I bumped into it ever so slightly⟩ — see FALL 1

topsy–turvy *adj* lacking in order, neatness, and often cleanliness ⟨the office is still *topsy-turvy* even though we moved in months ago⟩ — see MESSY

torment *n* **1** a situation or state that causes great suffering and unhappiness ⟨the released soldiers gave interviews trying to explain to civilians the *torment* that prisoners of war experience⟩ — see HELL 2
2 a state of great suffering of body or mind ⟨was in *torment* for weeks after he broke up with his girlfriend⟩ — see DISTRESS 1

torment *vb* to cause persistent suffering to ⟨he was *tormented* by nightmares about the accident⟩ — see AFFLICT

tormenting *adj* **1** hard to accept or bear especially emotionally ⟨it was a *tormenting* moment as they helplessly watched the other team score in the final seconds of the game⟩ — see BITTER 2
2 intensely or unbearably painful ⟨a *tormenting* injury⟩ — see EXCRUCIATING 1

tormentor *n* a person who causes repeated emotional pain, distress, or annoyance to another ⟨Phillip was relieved when his *tormentor* moved away, and he no longer had to take pains to avoid the bully⟩
synonyms baiter, heckler, mocker, needler, oppressor, persecutor, quiz, quizzer, ridiculer, scoffer, scorner, taunter, tease, teaser, torturer
related words belittler, derider, detractor, insulter; lampooner, satirist; accuser, blamer, troublemaker; assailant, attacker, molester; bother, disturber, pest
near antonyms defender, deliverer, protector, rescuer, saviour; comforter, consoler, solace, soother, succorer

torpid *adj* **1** lacking bodily strength ⟨the settlers were *torpid* after a long winter with little food⟩ — see WEAK 1
2 slow to move or act ⟨a *torpid* sloth that refused to budge off its tree branch⟩ — see INACTIVE 1

torrent *n* a great flow of water or of something that overwhelms ⟨the dam broke and unleashed a *torrent* down the dry riverbed⟩ — see FLOOD

torrid *adj* having a notably high temperature ⟨the dry, *torrid* summers in southern Arizona⟩ — see HOT 1

tortuous *adj* marked by a long series of irregular curves ⟨a *tortuous* mountain road marked by numerous hairpin turns⟩ — see CROOKED 1

torture *n* **1** a situation or state that causes great suffering and unhappiness ⟨it's *torture* to see you so unhappy⟩ — see HELL 2
2 a state of great suffering of body or mind ⟨spent an afternoon in *torture* waiting for news on whether her brother had made it home safely⟩ — see DISTRESS 1

torture *vb* to cause persistent suffering to ⟨the neighbor's dog constantly *tortures* our cat, barking at him and chasing him down the street⟩ — see AFFLICT

torturer *n* a person who causes repeated emotional pain, distress, or annoyance to another ⟨finally summoned up the courage to tell her *torturer* that she wouldn't take it anymore⟩ — see TORMENTOR

torturing *adj* intensely or unbearably painful ⟨watched the final *torturing* moments of the game as the lead constantly shifted between the two teams⟩ — see EXCRUCIATING 1

torturous *adj* **1** intensely or unbearably painful ⟨in order to remain close to her family, she made the *torturous* decision to turn down the scholarship to study overseas⟩ — see EXCRUCIATING 1
2 hard to accept or bear especially emotionally ⟨a *torturous* period of waiting to see if the test result was positive⟩ — see BITTER 2

toss *vb* **1** to make a series of unsteady side-to-side motions ⟨the boat *tossed* to and fro in the heavy seas⟩ — see ROCK 1
2 to make jerky or restless movements ⟨*tossed* and turned in bed all night, unable to sleep in the heat⟩ — see FIDGET
3 to send through the air especially with a quick forward motion of the arm ⟨*toss* that football over here⟩ — see THROW

toss (down *or* off) *vb* to swallow in liquid form ⟨*tossed* off the last of the medicine⟩ — see DRINK 1

total *adj* **1** having no exceptions or restrictions ⟨had *total* power over the people of that country⟩ — see ABSOLUTE 2
2 not lacking any part or member that properly belongs to it ⟨gave us a *total* rundown of the events⟩ — see COMPLETE 1
3 trying all possibilities ⟨a *total* effort to rid the city of gangs⟩ — see EXHAUSTIVE

total *n* a complete amount of something ⟨that's the *total* for our wheat harvest this year⟩ — see WHOLE

total *vb* **1** to have a total of ⟨two and two *total* four⟩ — see AMOUNT (TO) 1
2 to combine (numbers) into a single sum ⟨*total* all the receipts and tell me how much I owe you⟩ — see ADD 2

totalitarianism *n* a system of government in which the ruler has unlimited power ⟨in times of crisis, when a nation's people are frightened, there are often calls for *totalitarianism*⟩ — see DESPOTISM

totality *n* a complete amount of something ⟨the *totality* of the stars in the universe can only be loosely guessed at⟩ — see WHOLE

totally *adv* **1** to a full extent or degree ⟨I am *totally* upset you can't make it⟩ — see FULLY 1
2 with attention to all aspects or details ⟨he made *totally* sure the door was locked when he left the house⟩ — see THOROUGHLY 1

tote *vb* to support and take from one place to another ⟨*toted* his dog from the muddy backyard to the bathtub for a thorough washing⟩ — see CARRY 1

totter *vb* **1** to move forward while swaying from side to side ⟨*tottered* around the house as she practiced walking in high heels⟩ — see STAGGER 1
2 to swing unsteadily back and forth or from side to side ⟨the figurine *tottered* precariously for a moment before falling off the shelf⟩ — see TEETER 1

tottery *adj* marked by or given to small uncontrollable bodily movements ⟨with a *tottery* gait the frail, elderly woman slowly climbed the steps of the church⟩ — see SHAKY 1

touch *n* a very small amount ⟨added just a *touch* of parsley to the dish⟩ — see PARTICLE 1

touch *vb* **1** to come into bodily contact with (something) so as to perceive a slight pressure on the skin ⟨be careful not to *touch* this pan—it's still hot⟩
synonyms feel
related words caress, embrace, finger, fondle, hug, paw, rub, stroke; brush, graze; clasp, clench, cling (to), clutch, grasp, grip, handle, hold, palm; chuck, clap, dab, flick, pat, tag, tap, tip; hit, knock, pound, rap, whack
2 to act upon (a person or a person's feelings) so as to cause a response ⟨your speech on the meaning of patriotism *touched* me deeply⟩ — see ¹AFFECT 1
3 to affect slightly with something morally bad or undesirable ⟨unfortunately, his insufferable arrogance tends to *touch* even the good deeds that he does⟩ — see TAINT 1
4 to be adjacent to ⟨our property *touches* theirs right where that big elm tree is⟩ — see ADJOIN 1
5 to be the business or affair of ⟨I don't think this decision *touches* you, so butt out⟩ — see CONCERN 2

touch (on *or* upon) *vb* to make reference to or speak about briefly but specifically ⟨I do want to briefly *touch* upon the medieval view of the world before talking about Gothic architecture⟩ — see MENTION 1

touchable *adj* capable of being perceived by the sense of touch ⟨not very comfortable with abstractions, I usually relate better to *touchable* things⟩ — see TANGIBLE

touch down *vb* to come to rest after descending from the air ⟨the plane will *touch down* in about 30 minutes⟩ — see ALIGHT

touching *adj* **1** having a border in common ⟨*touching* lots in the housing development will eventually be separated by hedges for privacy⟩ — see ADJACENT

2 having the power to affect the feelings or sympathies ⟨a *touching* movie about two lost animals who try to find their way home⟩ — see MOVING

touch off *vb* to cause to function ⟨his obscene comment *touched off* a heated debate about the need for censorship on live broadcasts⟩ — see ACTIVATE

touchstone *n* something set up as an example against which others of the same type are compared ⟨his book has long been a *touchstone* for travel writing that aspires to be literature⟩ — see STANDARD 1

touchy *adj* requiring exceptional skill or caution in performance or handling ⟨money is a *touchy* subject for many people and shouldn't be discussed casually⟩ — see TRICKY

tough *adj* **1** not easily chewed ⟨her steak was so *tough* that she suggested the waiter use it as a hockey puck⟩
synonyms chewy, leathery
related words fibrous, gristly, sinewy, stringy; brittle, crunchy, hard
near antonyms mushy, soft
antonyms tender
2 able to withstand hardship, strain, or exposure ⟨this is a *tough* plant that easily withstands harsh winters⟩ — see HARDY 1
3 difficult to endure ⟨*tough* weather conditions on the top of the mountain all year long⟩ — see HARSH 1
4 requiring considerable physical or mental effort ⟨even though I studied for it, it's still a *tough* exam⟩ — see HARD 2
5 requiring exceptional skill or caution in performance or handling ⟨handled a *tough* situation with the aplomb and tact of a true diplomat⟩ — see TRICKY

tough *n* a violent, brutal person who is often a member of an organized gang ⟨didn't want her brother hanging out with the neighborhood *toughs*⟩ — see HOODLUM

toughen *vb* **1** to increase the ability of (as a muscle) to exert physical force ⟨weight lifting will help *toughen* those flabby muscles of yours⟩ — see STRENGTHEN 1
2 to make able to withstand physical hardship, strain, or exposure ⟨hiking every morning through snow and ice *toughened* him considerably⟩ — see HARDEN 2

toughened *adj* able to withstand hardship, strain, or exposure ⟨a group of *toughened* mountain bikers barreling up the hill⟩ — see HARDY 1

toughie *n* a violent, brutal person who is often a member of an organized gang ⟨after numerous suspensions, the school *toughies* were finally expelled for gang activities on campus⟩ — see HOODLUM

tour *n* a fixed period of time during which a person holds a job or position ⟨asked the soldiers to consider signing up for a second *tour* of duty⟩ — see TERM 1

tour *vb* to take a trip especially of some distance ⟨thought it would be lots of fun to *tour* all over Europe this summer⟩ — see TRAVEL 1

tourist *n* a person who travels for pleasure ⟨*tourists* from all over like to take pictures of the alligators in the bayou⟩
synonyms excursionist, sightseer, traveler (*or* traveller), tripper [*chiefly British*]
related words holidayer, vacationer, vacationist; guest, visitor; transient; journeyer, pilgrim, wayfarer

tournament *n* a competitive encounter between individuals or groups carried on for amusement, exercise, or in pursuit of a prize ⟨a golf *tournament* in which professionals compete against amateurs⟩ — see GAME 1

tourney *n* a competitive encounter between individuals or groups carried on for amusement, exercise, or in pursuit of a prize ⟨progressed to the final round of the tennis *tourney*⟩ — see GAME 1

tousle *vb* to undo the proper order or arrangement of ⟨my grandfather always *tousles* my neatly combed hair when he sees me⟩ — see DISORDER

tousled *adj* lacking in order, neatness, and often cleanliness ⟨a *tousled* pile of yarn and material scraps at the bottom of her craft box⟩ — see MESSY

tout *vb* **1** to praise or publicize lavishly and often excessively ⟨a new cleaning agent *touted* as the only product a homeowner needs for all his or her cleaning chores⟩
synonyms ballyhoo, crack up, glorify, trumpet
related words advance, advertise, announce, boost, herald, offer, plug, promote, publicize; assert, aver, claim, declare, lay down, make out, proclaim, pronounce
2 to declare enthusiastic approval of ⟨statements from several former patients *touting* the doctor's alleged cancer cure⟩ — see ACCLAIM
3 to provide publicity for ⟨an avalanche of ads *touting* the new movie⟩ — see PUBLICIZE 1

tow *vb* to cause to follow by applying steady force on ⟨*towed* the car into the shop for repair⟩ — see PULL 1

toward *or* **towards** *prep* having to do with ⟨didn't know what his attitude *toward* women in the military was⟩ — see ABOUT 1

tower *n* a large, magnificent, or massive building ⟨a hill from which one can gaze upon the *towers* of that great and historic city⟩ — see EDIFICE 1

towering *adj* **1** extending to a great distance upward ⟨the *towering* mountain peaks of the Rockies⟩ — see HIGH 1
2 going beyond a normal or acceptable limit in degree or amount ⟨parents who tend to give their children *towering* praise for very minor accomplishments⟩ — see EXCESSIVE
3 very dignified in form, tone, or style ⟨an article that in *towering* language decries the evils of modern society⟩ — see ELEVATED 2

town *n* a thickly settled, highly populated area ⟨after driving for miles with nothing but corn and wheat fields to look at, we were relieved to roll into a small *town* and have a bite to eat at the local diner⟩ — see CITY

townie *n* a person who lives in a town on a permanent basis ⟨the university board met with an association representing the *townies* to figure out a solution to the problems created by off-campus parties⟩ — see BURGHER

toxic *adj* containing or contaminated with a substance capable of injuring or killing a living thing ⟨certain plants are *toxic* if eaten⟩ — see POISONOUS

toxin *n* a substance that by chemical action can kill or injure a living thing ⟨read a pamphlet on the *toxin* responsible for botulism, a food poisoning that can cause paralysis and death in some cases⟩ — see POISON

trace *n* **1** a mark or series of marks left on a surface by something that has passed along it ⟨the wolf came and went without leaving a *trace* on the hard, dry ground⟩ — see TRACK 1
2 a passage cleared for public vehicular travel ⟨an old *trace* that dates back to the days of the covered wagon⟩ — see WAY 1
3 a rough course or way formed by or as if by repeated footsteps ⟨stay on the *trace*, or you'll get lost in these thick woods⟩ — see TRAIL 1
4 a tiny often physical indication of something lost or vanished ⟨a ship that appears to have vanished without a *trace* on the high seas⟩ — see VESTIGE

5 a very small amount ⟨doctors detected only a *trace* of bacteria in the blood sample but put the patient on antibiotics just in case⟩ — see PARTICLE 1

trace *vb* **1** to draw or make apparent the outline of ⟨*trace* your hand onto this piece of paper⟩ — see OUTLINE 1
2 to go after or on the track of ⟨police *traced* the burglar back to his apartment, where they discovered a ton of stolen loot⟩ — see FOLLOW 2

tracing *n* the act of going after or in the tracks of another ⟨the *tracing* of this mountain lion is going to be difficult if the rain washes away all the tracks⟩ — see PURSUIT

track *n* **1** a mark or series of marks left on a surface by something that has passed along it ⟨a muddy *track* across the kitchen floor⟩
synonyms imprint, trace, trail
related words footprint, footstep, path, print, step, tread; artifact, evidence, leavings, mark, relic, remainder, remain(s), reminder, remnant, residual, residue, sign, spoor, telltale, token, vestige; clue, cue, hint, indication, inkling, intimation, suggestion; scent, shadow, whiff
2 a rough course or way formed by or as if by repeated footsteps ⟨there was still a faint *track* through the underbrush that indicated where the path used to be⟩ — see TRAIL 1
3 the direction along which something or someone moves ⟨I saw the *track* of the thief's eyes as he watched me put the money in my purse⟩ — see PATH 1

track *vb* to go after or on the track of ⟨predators stealthily *tracking* their prey⟩ — see FOLLOW 2

track (down) *vb* to come upon after searching, study, or effort ⟨I'll try to *track down* his last known address⟩ — see FIND 1

tracking *n* the act of going after or in the tracks of another ⟨took a class in the *tracking* of game that the hunters' association offers⟩ — see PURSUIT

tract *n* **1** a broad geographical area ⟨a vast and fertile *tract* of farmland⟩ — see REGION 2
2 a small area of usually open land ⟨the town had planned on turning that *tract* of meadow into a park⟩ — see FIELD 1
3 a small piece of land that is developed or available for development ⟨had a number of small *tracts* for sale, but we couldn't afford to buy land and then build a house⟩ — see LOT 1

tractable *adj* readily giving in to the command or authority of another ⟨put the dog in obedience classes, with the hopes of making her a little more *tractable*⟩ — see OBEDIENT

trade *n* **1** a giving or taking of one thing of value in return for another ⟨when the other team finally offered to hand over its top pitcher for our star shortstop, our coach agreed to the *trade*⟩ — see EXCHANGE 1
2 an occupation requiring skillful use of the hands ⟨a youth eager to learn the *trade* of cabinetmaking⟩ — see CRAFT 1
3 the activity by which one regularly makes a living ⟨writing is my *trade*⟩ — see OCCUPATION
4 the buying and selling of goods especially on a large scale and between different places ⟨a bill regulating *trade* with that country⟩ — see COMMERCE
5 the transfer of ownership of something from one person to another for a price ⟨the *trade* of all of her holdings in the company just before the stock plunged in value immediately aroused suspicions⟩ — see SALE

trade *vb* **1** to carry on the business of buying and selling goods or other property ⟨the U.S. agreed to *trade* with China⟩
synonyms deal, traffic
related words bargain, barter, horse-trade, negotiate, transact; auction, exchange, merchandise, rebuy, resell, swap; buy, purchase; distribute, market, peddle, retail, sell, supply, vend, wholesale; bootleg, fence, smuggle; corner, monopolize, undersell; invest, speculate
near antonyms boycott
2 to give up (something) and take something else in return ⟨I'll *trade* my chocolate chip cookie for your bag of chips⟩ — see CHANGE 3

trademark *n* **1** a device (as a word) identifying the maker of a piece of merchandise and legally reserved for the exclusive use of that person or company ⟨*Kleenex* is a *trademark* for a cleansing tissue⟩
synonyms brand
related words hallmark, imprint, label, logo, mark, name, service mark, stamp; copyright, patent
2 a device, design, or figure used as an identifying mark ⟨the golden arches are a *trademark* of McDonald's⟩ — see EMBLEM

trader *n* a buyer and seller of goods for profit ⟨a coffee *trader*⟩ — see MERCHANT

tradesman *n* **1** a buyer and seller of goods for profit ⟨an antique dealer who's known as a good *tradesman*, buying his items cheaply and selling them for a hefty profit⟩ — see MERCHANT
2 a person whose occupation requires skill with the hands ⟨carpenters joining the *tradesmen's* union⟩ — see ARTISAN

tradition *n* **1** an inherited or established way of thinking, feeling, or doing ⟨the town *tradition* of having the oldest resident ride at the head of the parade⟩
synonyms convention, custom
related words ethic, form, mode, mores, norm, values; birthright, inheritance, legacy; folklore, lore, superstition; culture, heritage, lifestyle
2 the body of customs, beliefs, stories, and sayings associated with a people, thing, or place ⟨according to *tradition*, this field was the site of a skirmish between the first settlers and the Native Americans living in the area⟩ — see FOLKLORE

traditional *adj* **1** based on customs usually handed down from a previous generation ⟨Ruben had a *traditional* Passover meal at his grandparents' house⟩
synonyms classical, conventional, customary
related words authentic, established, fixed, historical; common, habitual, orthodox, usual; ancestral, historic, old-time, old-world; aged, age-old, ancient, hoary, old, venerable; ageless, dateless, immemorial, timeless
near antonyms contemporary, current, modern, modernized, new, present-day, updated, up-to-date; futuristic, hot, latest, mod, modernistic, newfangled, new-fashioned, red-hot, space-age, ultramodern; nonconformist, nonorthodox, original, progressive, revolutionary, unorthodox, unusual
antonyms nontraditional, unconventional, uncustomary
2 tending to favor established ideas, conditions, or institutions ⟨a family that is very *traditional* when it comes to institutions like marriage⟩ — see CONSERVATIVE 1

traduce *vb* to make untrue and harmful statements about ⟨my opponent in this campaign may *traduce* me, but I will not stoop to his level⟩ — see SLANDER

traducing *n* the making of false statements that damage another's reputation ⟨this endless *traducing* of candidates has got to stop, or the public will lose all faith in the electoral process⟩ — see SLANDER

traffic *n* the buying and selling of goods especially on a large scale and between different places ⟨the United Nations released a report on countries that still condone the *traffic* of women and children⟩ — see COMMERCE

traffic *vb* to carry on the business of buying and selling goods or other property ⟨arrested him for *trafficking* in drugs⟩ — see TRADE 1

trafficker *n* a buyer and seller of goods for profit ⟨a *trafficker* who sold pirated DVDs from the back of his car⟩ — see MERCHANT

tragedy *n* a sudden violent event that brings about great loss or destruction ⟨the earthquake was only the latest in a series of *tragedies* for the city⟩ — see DISASTER

trail *n* **1** a rough course or way formed by or as if by repeated footsteps ⟨took a *trail* through the woods to get to the main road⟩
synonyms footpath, path, pathway, trace, track
related words bridle path; towpath; bypath, byroad, byway, passageway, walkway; detour, shortcut; course, passage, road, route, run, runway, way
2 a mark or series of marks left on a surface by something that has passed along it ⟨the slugs left a slimy *trail* on the sidewalk⟩ — see TRACK 1

trail *vb* to go after or on the track of ⟨we *trailed* our brother into the woods, spoiling his plans for a solitary hike⟩ — see FOLLOW 2

trailer *n* a motor vehicle that is specially equipped for living while traveling ⟨the band packed their equipment back into their *trailer* and headed off to their next gig⟩ — see CAMPER

trailing *n* the act of going after or in the tracks of another ⟨did you think I didn't know about your constant *trailing* of me?⟩ — see PURSUIT

train *n* **1** a body of employees or servants who accompany and wait on a person ⟨a movie star who never goes anywhere without a *train* of personal assistants to cater to his every whim and need⟩ — see CORTEGE 1
2 a group of vehicles traveling together or under one management ⟨a *train* of coal cars delivering coal to the Midwest⟩ — see FLEET
3 a series of persons or things arranged one behind another ⟨already a long *train* of ticket buyers waiting outside the stadium⟩ — see LINE 1
4 a series of things linked together ⟨you've broken my *train* of thought—now what were we talking about?⟩ — see CHAIN 1

train *vb* **1** to bring to a proper or desired state of fitness ⟨has been *training* track and field athletes at the school for years⟩ — see CONDITION 1
2 to cause to acquire knowledge or skill in some field ⟨will *train* the students in good study habits⟩ — see TEACH
3 to fix (as one's attention) steadily toward a central objective ⟨*train* all your thoughts on imagining how you'd score the winning goal in the game⟩ — see CONCENTRATE 2
4 to point or turn (something) toward a target or goal ⟨*trained* his eyes on the distant bull's-eye⟩ — see AIM 1

trainer *n* a person who trains performers or athletes ⟨hired a personal *trainer* to help her get in shape⟩ — see COACH

training *n* **1** something done over and over in order to develop skill ⟨a boxer who's been doing a lot of *training* with his footwork⟩ — see EXERCISE 2
2 the act or process of imparting knowledge or skills to another ⟨entered a convent for religious *training*⟩ — see EDUCATION 1

traipse *vb* **1** to go on foot ⟨*traipsed* down the hall to get her paper from the computer room⟩ — see WALK
2 to move about from place to place aimlessly ⟨a group of friends *traipsing* around the country the summer after graduation⟩ — see WANDER

trait *n* something that sets apart an individual from others of the same kind ⟨honesty is one of her defining *traits*⟩ — see CHARACTERISTIC

traitor *n* one who betrays a trust or an allegiance ⟨accused by her family of being a *traitor* when she sold their traditionally animal-friendly business to a competitor known to use animals for testing its products⟩
synonyms apostate, betrayer, double-crosser, quisling, recreant, turncoat
related words collaborationist, collaborator, subversive; conspirator, intriguer, plotter, schemer; defector, deserter, renegade; blabbermouth, gossip, gossiper, informant, informer, rat, snitcher, talebearer, talker, tattler, tattletale

traitorous *adj* not true in one's allegiance to someone or something ⟨when our coach took a job at a rival school, a few *traitorous* players went right along with him⟩ — see FAITHLESS

trammel *n* something that makes movement or progress more difficult ⟨students and parents who want to throw off the *trammels* of outdated school policies⟩ — see ENCUMBRANCE

trammel *vb* **1** to confine or restrain with or as if with chains ⟨years after his death, she was still *trammeled* by inconsolable grief for her deceased husband⟩ — see BIND 1
2 to create difficulty for the work or activity of ⟨the new paperwork requirements will only *trammel* us and lower our productivity⟩ — see HAMPER

tramp *n* a homeless wanderer who may beg or steal for a living ⟨the police encouraged the *tramps* who were sleeping in the park to spend the bitterly cold night in the homeless shelter⟩
synonyms bum, hobo, sundowner [*Australian*], vagabond, vagrant
related words drifter, roamer, transient; beggar, derelict; dodger, malingerer, shirker, slacker; gamine, ragamuffin, urchin, waif

tramp *vb* **1** to move heavily or clumsily ⟨*tramped* wearily up the stairs after a long day at work⟩ — see LUMBER 1
2 to tread on heavily so as to crush or injure ⟨didn't mean to *tramp* your toes as I was running past you⟩ — see TRAMPLE

trample *vb* to tread on heavily so as to crush or injure ⟨Isabel looked out her window and beheld the neighbor's Labrador retriever *trampling* her begonias⟩
synonyms stamp, stomp, tramp, tromp
related words override, run down, run over, step (on); mash, smash, squash; boot, kick

trance *n* the state of being lost in thought ⟨lulled by the sound of the train, she stared out the window in a *trance*, unaware of the porter taking tickets⟩ — see REVERIE

tranquil *adj* **1** free from disturbing noise or uproar ⟨the house was once again *tranquil* after the kids moved outside to play⟩ — see QUIET 1

2 free from emotional or mental agitation ⟨though she should have been upset, she felt oddly *tranquil* upon learning that she would not be receiving the scholarship⟩ — see CALM 2

3 free from storms or physical disturbance ⟨drifting dreamily through *tranquil* seas⟩ — see CALM 1

tranquilize *also* **tranquillize** *vb* to free from distress or disturbance ⟨at long last the crying baby was *tranquilized* by the steady rocking of her cradle⟩ — see CALM 1

tranquilizing *also* **tranquillizing** *adj* tending to calm the emotions and relieve stress ⟨a woman who put a lot of faith in the *tranquilizing* effects of a cup of tea⟩ — see SOOTHING 1

tranquillity *or* **tranquility** *n* **1** a state of freedom from storm or disturbance ⟨enjoyed the *tranquillity* of the snow-covered field at dusk⟩ — see CALM

2 evenness of emotions or temper ⟨a psychotherapist valued for her *tranquillity* and ability to listen⟩ — see EQUANIMITY

transaction *n* the transfer of ownership of something from one person to another for a price ⟨if you want to return any merchandise, make sure you keep the receipt for the initial sales *transaction*⟩ — see SALE

transcend *vb* to be greater, better, or stronger than ⟨a man whose practical knowledge of botany *transcends* that of his more educated colleagues⟩ — see SURPASS 1

transfer *vb* **1** to give over the legal possession or ownership of ⟨Claire's grandfather agreed to *transfer* certain stocks to her when she turned 18⟩

synonyms alienate, assign, cede, deed, make over

related words bequeath, hand down, leave, pass down, will; bestow, confer, contribute, deliver, donate, grant, hand over, move, pass, present, release, relinquish, surrender, turn in, turn over, transmit, vest, yield; consign, entrust, trust; lease, lend, loan, rent

2 to cause (something) to pass from one to another ⟨they used Morse Code to *transfer* the message from one room to another⟩ — see COMMUNICATE 1

3 to cause to go or be taken from one place to another ⟨will have to *transfer* you from our San Francisco office to our New York office⟩ — see SEND

4 to change the place or position of ⟨*transferred* the car keys from my pocket to my purse⟩ — see MOVE 1

5 to put (something) into the possession or safekeeping of another ⟨before she left the country, she *transferred* all her record books and important papers to her mother⟩ — see GIVE 2

6 to shift possession of (something) from one person to another ⟨*transferred* the ball to the running back⟩ — see PASS 1

transferable *adj* capable of being taken from one place to another by public carrier ⟨supplemental charges for oversized *transferable* goods like pianos⟩ — see SHIPPABLE

transfiguration *n* a change in form, appearance, or use ⟨after his *transfiguration* into a Buddhist monk, all his family and friends were amazed by his newly found patience and tranquility⟩ — see CONVERSION

transfigure *vb* to change in form, appearance, or use ⟨married life had seemingly *transfigured* his formerly aimless existence⟩ — see CONVERT 2

transfix *vb* to penetrate or hold (something) with a pointed object ⟨*transfixed* the inanimate butterfly specimens to the collection board⟩ — see IMPALE

transform *vb* to change in form, appearance, or use ⟨by clicking a few buttons, this toy car can be *transformed* into a robot⟩ — see CONVERT 2

transformation *n* a change in form, appearance, or use ⟨a raven-haired starlet who underwent an attention-getting *transformation* and showed up at the awards ceremony as a blonde⟩ — see CONVERSION

transfuse *vb* **1** to cause (something) to pass from one to another ⟨a teacher who is able to *transfuse* his enthusiasm and passion for history to his students⟩ — see COMMUNICATE 1

2 to spread throughout ⟨light *transfused* the room as the sun rose⟩ — see PERMEATE

transgress *vb* **1** to commit an offense ⟨I didn't realize I was *transgressing* when I told your sister she looked like she had lost weight⟩ — see OFFEND 1

2 to fail to keep ⟨don't even think about *transgressing* the laws of that Asian country, for punishments are severe and there's nothing that our government can do to intervene⟩ — see VIOLATE 1

transgression *n* **1** a breaking of a moral or legal code ⟨acts that are *transgressions* against the laws of civilized societies everywhere⟩ — see OFFENSE 1

2 a failure to uphold the requirements of law, duty, or obligation ⟨a dying woman asking for divine forgiveness for a lifetime of *transgressions*⟩ — see BREACH 1

transient *adj* lasting only for a short time ⟨had *transient* thoughts of running away but never acted upon them⟩ — see MOMENTARY

transitory *adj* lasting only for a short time ⟨a *transitory* panic struck me until I saw my brother, safe and sound, inside the house⟩ — see MOMENTARY

translate *vb* to express something (as a text or statement) in different words ⟨would you mind *translating* this German article for me?⟩ — see PARAPHRASE

translating *n* an instance of expressing something in different words ⟨his *translating* of that passage really captured the tone of the original⟩ — see PARAPHRASE

translation *n* an instance of expressing something in different words ⟨had to read Dante's *Divine Comedy* in *translation* since I don't speak Italian⟩ — see PARAPHRASE

transmit *vb* **1** to cause (something) to pass from one to another ⟨sneezing and coughing can *transmit* disease⟩ — see COMMUNICATE 1

2 to cause to go or be taken from one place to another ⟨I'll *transmit* this information over the airwaves⟩ — see SEND

3 to put (something) into the possession or safekeeping of another ⟨*transmitted* the deed of his house to his lawyer⟩ — see GIVE 2

transmittable *adj* **1** capable of being passed by physical contact from one person to another ⟨that disease is only *transmittable* through direct contact with an infected person, not through contact with something the infected person has touched⟩ — see CONTAGIOUS 1

2 capable of being taken from one place to another by public carrier ⟨I doubt that animals are *transmittable* through the mail⟩ — see SHIPPABLE

transparency *n* the state or quality of being easily seen through ⟨because of the *transparency* of the Caribbean waters, we could see sharks and tropical fish swimming 20 or 30 feet below the surface⟩ — see CLARITY 1

transparent *adj* **1** easily seen through ⟨bottles of blue *transparent* glass⟩ — see CLEAR 1

2 not subject to misinterpretation or more than one interpretation ⟨his meaning in leaving the conversation is *transparent*: he doesn't want to talk about his combat experiences⟩ — see CLEAR 2

3 very thin and easy to see through ⟨told her she had to wear a slip under that nearly *transparent* skirt⟩ — see SHEER 1

transpire *vb* to take place ⟨please tell me what *transpired* on the night of October 1⟩ — see HAPPEN

transport *n* **1** a state of overwhelming usually pleasurable emotion ⟨was in *transports* of joy after winning the championship⟩ — see ECSTASY
2 something used to carry goods or passengers ⟨took public *transport* into the city⟩ — see CONVEYANCE

transport *vb* **1** to cause to go or be taken from one place to another ⟨I'll have to *transport* the car to our new home overseas by public carrier⟩ — see SEND
2 to fill with great joy ⟨was absolutely *transported* when she heard that her brother was getting married⟩ — see ELATE
3 to fill with overwhelming emotion (as wonder or delight) ⟨was *transported* with wonder when she saw the Matterhorn for the first time⟩ — see ENTRANCE
4 to force to leave a country ⟨the journalist was *transported* out of the country and ordered to never return⟩ — see BANISH 1
5 to support and take from one place to another ⟨will you *transport* this heavy casserole dish to the dining room for me?⟩ — see CARRY 1

transportable *adj* capable of being taken from one place to another by public carrier ⟨you'll need to see if that food is *transportable* overseas before you send boxes of it to your relatives in the military⟩ — see SHIPPABLE

transportation *n* **1** a means of getting to a destination in a vehicle driven by another ⟨I'm without *transportation* tonight, so I can't meet you at the movies⟩ — see RIDE
2 something used to carry goods or passengers ⟨right now my bike is my only *transportation*⟩ — see CONVEYANCE

transpose *vb* to change the place or position of ⟨*transposed* the two pieces of music so the violinist was playing the viola part and vice versa⟩ — see MOVE 1

transversely *adv* in a line or direction running from corner to corner ⟨the coat of arms had a line of white horses running *transversely* from one corner to another on a blue background⟩ — see CROSSWISE

trap *n* **1** a device or scheme for capturing another by surprise ⟨undercover agents devised a *trap* to catch the counterfeiters⟩ ⟨a bear *trap*⟩
synonyms ambush, net, snare, web
related words entanglement, entrapment; booby trap, catch, hazard, pitfall, snag; deception, ploy, ruse, subterfuge, trick
2 a scheme in which hidden persons wait to attack by surprise ⟨an overland route to the Far East that was once notorious for the many robbers who laid *traps* for unsuspecting wayfarers⟩ — see AMBUSH 1

trap *vb* **1** to catch or hold as if in a net ⟨an ambitious young man who was now *trapped* in a series of shady business deals⟩ — see ENTANGLE 2
2 to take physical control or possession of (something) suddenly or forcibly ⟨finally *trapped* the annoying fly in his hand⟩ — see CATCH 1

trash *n* **1** discarded or useless material ⟨the neighbor's dog was rooting around in our *trash* this morning⟩ — see GARBAGE
2 language, behavior, or ideas that are absurd and contrary to good sense ⟨don't talk *trash* to me!⟩ — see NONSENSE 1
3 people looked down upon as ignorant and of the lowest class ⟨snooty people who thought that we were

trash because we were in the cleaning business⟩ — see RABBLE

trashy *adj* **1** marked by an obvious lack of style or good taste ⟨I know that sequined shirt cost a lot of money, but I still think it looks kind of *trashy*⟩ — see TACKY 1
2 of low quality ⟨*trashy* furniture that fell apart after a few weeks⟩ — see CHEAP 2

travail *n* very hard or unpleasant work ⟨these villagers now have decent housing, so our *travail* has not been in vain⟩ — see TOIL

travail *vb* to devote serious and sustained effort ⟨Labor Day is the day on which we recognize those men and women who daily *travail* with little appreciation or compensation⟩ — see LABOR

travel *vb* **1** to take a trip especially of some distance ⟨loves to *travel* and has been to 34 countries⟩
synonyms journey, peregrinate, pilgrimage, tour, trek, voyage
related words gallivant (*also* galavant), hop, jaunt, knock (about), ramble, roam, rove, traipse, wander; cruise, drive, fly, jet, motor, navigate, sail
2 to make one's way through, across, or over ⟨will *travel* the river for a while and then continue on land⟩ — see TRAVERSE

travel *n, often* **travels** *pl* a going from one place to another usually of some distance ⟨in all his *travels* he'd never met pleasanter people than he had in that village⟩ — see JOURNEY

traveler *or* **traveller** *n* a person who travels for pleasure ⟨a company that offers guidebooks and maps for *travelers*⟩ — see TOURIST

traveling bag *n* a bag carried by hand and designed to hold a traveler's clothing and personal articles ⟨*traveling bags* made of lightweight but tough fabrics⟩
synonyms carryall, grip, handbag, portmanteau, suitcase
related words carpetbag, duffel bag, kit; backpack, haversack, knapsack, rucksack; attaché case, valise; baggage, bags, luggage

traverse *vb* to make one's way through, across, or over ⟨Julie watched the spider *traverse* the entire wall from floor to ceiling⟩
synonyms cover, crisscross, cross, cut (across), follow, go, pass (over), proceed (along), travel
related words hike, tread, walk; ride

travesty *n* a poor, insincere, or insulting imitation of something ⟨rigged from the start, his trial was a *travesty* of justice⟩ — see MOCKERY 1

travesty *vb* to copy or exaggerate (someone or something) in order to make fun of ⟨this comedy sketch mindlessly *travesties* the hard work of relief workers around the world⟩ — see MIMIC 1

treacherous *adj* not true in one's allegiance to someone or something ⟨a *treacherous* friend, she's been known to turn against people in the blink of an eye⟩ — see FAITHLESS

treachery *n* the act or fact of violating the trust or confidence of another ⟨was upset she revealed his secret and never forgave her for the *treachery*⟩ — see BETRAYAL

tread *vb* to go on foot ⟨to protect the fragile environment of the beach dunes, we must *tread* cautiously and lightly⟩ — see WALK

treadmill *n* an established and often automatic or monotonous series of actions followed when engaging in some activity ⟨the *treadmill* of the morning commute to work⟩ — see ROUTINE 1

treason *n* the act or fact of violating the trust or confidence of another ⟨reading a friend's diary without permission would have to be regarded as the ultimate act of *treason*⟩ — see BETRAYAL

treasure *n* **1** an asset that brings praise or renown ⟨ancient archaeological *treasures* that today would never be allowed out of the country of origin⟩ — see GLORY 2
2 someone or something unusually desirable ⟨in thanking them for their contributions, the mayor referred to the volunteers at the homeless shelter as the city's greatest *treasures*⟩ — see PRIZE 1

treasure *vb* to hold dear ⟨I'll always *treasure* the time my friend and I spent together this past summer⟩ — see LOVE 1

treat *n* **1** a source of great satisfaction ⟨getting to go to the amusement park is a real *treat*⟩ — see DELIGHT 1
2 something that is pleasing to eat because it is rare or a luxury ⟨for us sushi is a real *treat* since no restaurant around here makes it⟩ — see DELICACY 1

treat *vb* **1** to behave toward in a stated way ⟨she tries to *treat* all of her students fairly and equally, regardless of her personal feelings toward them⟩
 synonyms act (toward), be (to), deal (with), handle, serve, use
 related words consider, regard; react (to), respond (to)
2 to deal with (something) usually skillfully or efficiently ⟨the school *treated* the vandalism of the students' artwork as a very serious matter⟩ — see HANDLE 1
3 to exchange viewpoints or seek advice for the purpose of finding a solution to a problem ⟨I will *treat* with my lawyer and let you know what we decide⟩ — see CONFER 2
4 to give medical treatment to ⟨a nurse *treating* a patient⟩ — see DOCTOR 1

treat (of) *vb* to have (something) as a subject matter ⟨his paper *treats of* the problems that doctors face every day in the emergency rooms of urban hospitals⟩ — see CONCERN 1

treaty *n* a formal agreement between two or more nations or peoples ⟨in accordance with a *treaty* between the United States and the tribes of the Pacific Northwest, commercial fishing of certain kinds of salmon is limited to Native Americans⟩
 synonyms accord, alliance, compact, convention, covenant, pact
 related words bargain, charter, contract, deal, settlement, understanding

treble *adj* **1** having a high musical pitch or range ⟨the *treble* shrieks of children playing on the playground⟩ — see SHRILL
2 having three units or parts ⟨a *treble* painting, with each panel telling a different part of the Nativity story⟩ — see TRIPLE

trek *n* a going from one place to another usually of some distance ⟨started on our *trek* up the mountain before the sun rose⟩ — see JOURNEY

trek *vb* to take a trip especially of some distance ⟨adventurers *trekking* across the desert in search of a fabled city of gold⟩ — see TRAVEL 1

tremble *n* an instance of shaking involuntarily with fear or cold ⟨with a *tremble*, she ventured out into the snow⟩ — see SHIVER 1

trembling *adj* marked by or given to small uncontrollable bodily movements ⟨*trembling* from the cold⟩ — see SHAKY 1

trembling *n* a series of slight movements by a body back and forth or from side to side ⟨at the first sign of the room's *trembling*, I ducked for cover, for I was certain that it was the start of the big quake⟩ — see VIBRATION

tremendous *adj* unusually large ⟨that's a *tremendous* amount of work⟩ — see HUGE

tremendously *adv* to a large extent or degree ⟨I'm *tremendously* upset I didn't get into that school⟩ — see GREATLY 2

tremor *n* a shaking of the earth ⟨smaller *tremors* continued for days after the major earthquake⟩ — see EARTHQUAKE

tremulous *adj* marked by or given to small uncontrollable bodily movements ⟨the frail woman extended a *tremulous* hand in welcome⟩ — see SHAKY 1

trench *n* a long narrow channel dug in the earth ⟨dug a *trench* filled with water in an attempt to keep the forest fire off her property⟩ — see DITCH

trenchant *adj* having an edge thin enough to cut or pierce something ⟨even the most *trenchant* sword could not sever the bonds of loyalty between them⟩ — see SHARP 1

trend *n* **1** a prevailing or general movement or inclination ⟨according to the survey, there's a growing *trend* for companies to run their own day-care centers for the benefit of employees⟩
 synonyms current, drift, leaning, run, tendency, tide, wind
 related words curve, shift, swing, turn; custom, habit, propensity, tenor, way
2 a practice or interest that is very popular for a short time ⟨still had a coat from the last *trend* for fake fur, when the material lined everything from boots to coats to bracelets⟩ — see FAD

trend *vb* to show a liking or proneness (for something) ⟨our school system *trends* towards canceling school at the drop of a hat—or at least a snowflake⟩ — see LEAN 2

trepidation *n* the emotion experienced in the presence or threat of danger ⟨shaking with *trepidation*, I stepped into the old abandoned house⟩ — see FEAR

trespass *n* **1** a breaking of a moral or legal code ⟨forgive us our *trespasses* as we forgive those who trespass against us⟩ — see OFFENSE 1
2 a failure to uphold the requirements of law, duty, or obligation ⟨plagiarism is a serious *trespass* of academic integrity⟩ — see BREACH 1

trespass *vb* to commit an offense ⟨I consider him to be *trespassing* against all of us when he *trespasses* against any one of us⟩ — see OFFEND 1

triad *n* a group of three ⟨a *triad* of candlesticks on the mantle⟩ — see THREESOME

triadic *adj* having three units or parts ⟨the application to this music school is *triadic* in structure: there's the written application, then the audition, and finally an interview with the admissions board⟩ — see TRIPLE

trial *adj* made or done as an experiment ⟨a *trial* medical procedure⟩ — see EXPERIMENTAL 1

trial *n* **1** a test of faith, patience, or strength ⟨Nancy found living with her cousin a real *trial* and couldn't wait for the summer to end⟩
 synonyms cross, crucible, gauntlet (*also* gantlet), ordeal
 related words adversity, affliction, asperity, misfortune, mishap, privation, tragedy, tribulation, trouble, vicissitude, woe; challenge, complication, difficulty, grief, hardship, rigor; annoyance, discomfort, inconvenience, nuisance

2 a private performance or session in preparation for a public appearance ⟨ran another *trial* of the aerial performance before opening night⟩ — see REHEARSAL

3 a procedure or operation carried out to resolve an uncertainty ⟨*trials* by medical researchers haven't determined whether the medication is safe or not⟩ — see EXPERIMENT

4 an effort to do or accomplish something ⟨will rest and make another *trial* at climbing the mountain⟩ — see ATTEMPT

tribal *adj* of, relating to, or reflecting the traits exhibited by a group of people with a common ancestry and culture ⟨a *tribal* solidarity that transcends all other loyalties or bonds⟩ — see RACIAL

tribe *n* a group of persons who come from the same ancestor ⟨the wedding joined the two *tribes* together⟩ — see FAMILY 1

tribulation *n* a state of great suffering of body or mind ⟨a documentary chronicling the lasting *tribulation* of Holocaust survivors⟩ — see DISTRESS 1

tribunal *n* an assembly of persons for the administration of justice ⟨was tried before a military *tribunal* and found not guilty of the charges⟩ — see COURT 3

tribute *n* a formal expression of praise ⟨*tributes* were received from all over the world at the opera singer's farewell concert⟩ — see ENCOMIUM

trice *n* a very small space of time ⟨it's just a scrape on the knee—we'll have you fixed up in a *trice*⟩ — see INSTANT

trick *n* **1** a clever often underhanded means to achieve an end ⟨used every *trick* in the book to get out of appearing in the fashion show featuring clothes for teens⟩
synonyms artifice, device, dodge, gimmick, jig, ploy, scheme, sleight, stratagem, wile
related words bluff, deception, feint; fraud, hoax, swindle

2 a playful or mischievous act intended as a joke ⟨thought that gluing the silver dollar to the floor and watching him struggle to pick it up would be a good *trick*⟩ — see PRANK

3 a usual manner of behaving or doing ⟨he's up to his usual *tricks*⟩ — see HABIT

4 an act of notable skill, strength, or cleverness ⟨it'd be quite a *trick* to hit that target from here⟩ — see FEAT 1

5 an odd or peculiar habit ⟨a dog with the *trick* of eating cabbage⟩ — see IDIOSYNCRASY

trick *vb* to cause to believe what is untrue ⟨you *tricked* me into thinking she wasn't coming tonight⟩ — see DECEIVE

trickery *n* the use of clever underhanded actions to achieve an end ⟨Delia resorted to *trickery*—even loading up the fishing equipment—to induce her dog into the car for his vet appointment⟩
synonyms artifice, chicanery, hanky-panky, jugglery, legerdemain, subterfuge, wile
related words artfulness, caginess, craftiness, cunning, deviousness, foxiness, shadiness, sharpness, shiftiness, slickness, slipperiness, slyness, sneakiness, treachery, underhandedness, wiliness; deceit, deceitfulness, deception, deceptiveness, dishonesty, dissimulation, double-dealing, duplicity, guile, hypocrisy, insincerity; fakery, humbuggery, imposture, quackery; design, plotting, scheming, secrecy, stealth

trickle *vb* **1** to fall or let fall in or as if in drops ⟨*trickled* a little honey into her tea⟩ — see DRIP

2 to flow in a broken irregular stream ⟨the brook *trickled* along the glade⟩ — see GURGLE

trickster *n* **1** a dishonest person who uses clever means to cheat others out of something of value ⟨a heartless *trickster* swindled the elderly woman out of her life savings⟩
synonyms cheat, cheater, confidence man, cozener, defrauder, dodger, hoaxer, shark, sharper, swindler
related words double-crosser, double-dealer; bluffer, charlatan, fake, faker, humbug, imposter, mountebank, pretender, quack; adventurer, fox, knave, prankster, rascal, rogue; slicker, smoothy (*or* smoothie); plotter, schemer, sneak

2 one who practices tricks and illusions for entertainment ⟨a very adept *trickster* who used mirrors to make huge items—even buildings—seem to disappear⟩ — see MAGICIAN 2

tricky *adj* requiring exceptional skill or caution in performance or handling ⟨a *tricky* musical passage for the woodwind section⟩
synonyms catchy, delicate, difficult, knotty, problematic (*also* problematical), spiny, thorny, ticklish, touchy, tough
related words abstract, abstruse, complex, complicated, hard, intricate, involved, recondite; stubborn, troublesome, vexatious, vexing; burdensome, demanding, discommoding, exacting, importunate, inconvenient, onerous, oppressive, painful
near antonyms easy, manageable, painless, straightforward, uncomplicated, undemanding, untroublesome

tried *adj* worthy of one's trust ⟨a *tried* method for catching fish⟩ — see DEPENDABLE

tried–and–true *adj* worthy of one's trust ⟨a *tried-and-true* friend⟩ — see DEPENDABLE

trifle *n* something of little importance ⟨let us not speak of *trifles* when our nation may be going to war⟩
synonyms child's play, frippery, nothing, triviality
related words naught, nothingness, smoke, zero; molehill, peanuts, pittance, song, straw, two bits; nonsense, trivia

trifle *vb* **1** to show a liking for someone of the opposite sex just for fun ⟨do not *trifle* with me unless you mean to ask me to marry you⟩ — see FLIRT

2 to spend time in aimless activity ⟨spent a lazy afternoon *trifling* on the front porch⟩ — see FIDDLE (AROUND)

trifling *adj* **1** lacking importance ⟨deciding what you want to do for a living is no *trifling* matter⟩ — see UNIMPORTANT

2 so small or unimportant as to warrant little or no attention ⟨*trifling* differences between the theatrical and DVD versions of the movie⟩ — see NEGLIGIBLE 1

trigger *vb* to cause to function ⟨mold *triggers* my allergies⟩ — see ACTIVATE

trill *vb* to sing with the alternation of two musical tones ⟨the bluebird *trilled* outside our window⟩ — see WARBLE

trim *adj* being clean and in good order ⟨kept his journal entries *trim*, never crossing out words or scribbling, but printing exactly and nicely⟩ — see NEAT 1

trim *n* **1** a state of being or fitness ⟨the doctor declared her to be in good *trim* for the race⟩ — see CONDITION 1

2 something that decorates or beautifies ⟨added a little *trim* to her dress to make it a little fancier⟩ — see DECORATION 1

trim *vb* **1** to achieve a victory over ⟨a speed skater who consistently *trimmed* all his competition⟩ — see BEAT 2

2 to defeat by a large margin ⟨they *trimmed* our team by 40 points⟩ — see WHIP 2

3 to make (as hair) shorter with or as if with the use of shears ⟨*trimmed* her bangs⟩ — see CLIP
4 to make more attractive by adding something that is beautiful or becoming ⟨*trim* a tree for Christmas⟩ — see DECORATE

trimmer *n* one that defeats an enemy or opponent ⟨last year's winner of the tournament was unexpectedly trimmed in the first round, and the *trimmer* was a young player that no one had ever heard of⟩ — see VICTOR 1

trimming *n* failure to win a contest ⟨our football team suffered a pretty severe *trimming*⟩ — see DEFEAT 1

trinity *n* a group of three ⟨read novels and poetry produced by that sisterly *trinity* of English literature: Charlotte, Anne, and Emily Brontë⟩ — see THREESOME

trinket *n* a small object displayed for its attractiveness or interest ⟨the top of his desk was littered with *trinkets* that were collected as souvenirs from various vacations⟩ — see KNICKKNACK

trio *n* a group of three ⟨the band was just a *trio* of musicians on piano, drums, and saxophone⟩ — see THREESOME

trip *n* a going from one place to another usually of some distance ⟨I'd like to book a *trip* to Greece with your travel agency⟩ — see JOURNEY

trip *vb* **1** to go at a pace faster than a walk ⟨went *tripping* up the steps of city hall in their eagerness to get married⟩ — see RUN 1
2 to go down from an upright position suddenly and involuntarily ⟨*tripped* over a chair and landed on her face⟩ — see FALL 1
3 to move with a light bouncing step ⟨dancers *tripping* lightly across the stage⟩ — see SKIP 1

tripartite *adj* having three units or parts ⟨negotiated a *tripartite* agreement with its trading partner, with the first and second parts coming into effect immediately and the last part in five years later⟩ — see TRIPLE

triple *adj* having three units or parts ⟨a *triple* scoop of chocolate ice cream⟩
  synonyms threefold, treble, triadic, tripartite, triplex
  related words triplicate

triple *n* a group of three ⟨that *triple* of terrors for the wintertime driver: snow, ice, and sleet⟩ — see THREESOME

triplet *n* a group of three ⟨the theater piece is actually a *triplet* of comedy sketches, all of them having romantic love as their theme⟩ — see THREESOME

triplex *adj* having three units or parts ⟨a *triplex* house that features a separate apartment on each floor⟩ — see TRIPLE

tripper *n*, *chiefly British* a person who travels for pleasure ⟨day *trippers* who come to spend a few hours on the island⟩ — see TOURIST

trippingly *adv* in a quick and spirited manner ⟨loves words that roll *trippingly* off the tongue⟩ — see GAILY 2

trite *adj* used or heard so often as to be dull ⟨by the time the receiving line had ended, the bride and groom's thanks sounded *trite* and tired⟩ — see STALE

triumph *n* **1** a successful result brought about by hard work ⟨getting into Harvard is quite a *triumph*⟩ — see ACCOMPLISHMENT 1
2 an instance of defeating an enemy or opponent ⟨our stunning *triumph* on the field won us the title of regional champs⟩ — see VICTORY

triumph *vb* **1** to achieve victory (as in a contest) ⟨despite an accident early on, the runner persevered and ultimately *triumphed*⟩ — see WIN 1
2 to feel or express joy or triumph ⟨in that part of the world it's customary for people to *triumph* by firing guns into the air⟩ — see EXULT

triumph (over) *vb* to achieve a victory over ⟨with teamwork, we can *triumph over* anything⟩ — see BEAT 2

triumphant *adj* **1** having attained a desired end or state of good fortune ⟨the *triumphant* bidder on the house⟩ — see SUCCESSFUL 1
2 having or expressing feelings of joy or triumph ⟨he was positively *triumphant* when the school troublemaker finally got expelled⟩ — see EXULTANT

triumvirate *n* a group of three ⟨among the city's cultural institutions, the art museum, the symphony orchestra, and the opera company reign as the supreme *triumvirate*⟩ — see THREESOME

trivial *adj* **1** lacking importance ⟨why spend so much time on *trivial* decisions, like whether the soda should be regular or diet?⟩ — see UNIMPORTANT
2 so small or unimportant as to warrant little or no attention ⟨figured that customers wouldn't notice such a *trivial* surcharge on their bill⟩ — see NEGLIGIBLE 1

triviality *n* something of little importance ⟨overlooked such *trivialities* as haphazardly folded napkins when rating the quality of restaurants⟩ — see TRIFLE

troll *n* an imaginary being usually having a small human form and magical powers ⟨"The Three Billy Goats Gruff," is the story of three goats trying to cross a bridge guarded by a nasty *troll* living beneath it⟩ — see FAIRY

tromp *vb* **1** to move heavily or clumsily ⟨sleepily *tromped* into the kitchen to answer the ringing phone, tripping over an array of clothes and books along the way⟩ — see LUMBER 1
2 to tread on heavily so as to crush or injure ⟨the kids *tromped* my flowers to smithereens⟩ — see TRAMPLE

troop *n* **1** an organized group of stage performers ⟨a celebrating acting *troop* will be coming to town next month to perform one of Shakespeare's plays⟩ — see COMPANY 1
2 **troops** *pl* the combined army, air force, and navy of a nation ⟨the *troops* overseas are grateful for the support of so many at home⟩ — see ARMED FORCES

tropical *adj* being near the equator ⟨wanted to escape winter and visit some *tropical* location where freezing to death would not be a possibility⟩ — see LOW 1

trot *vb* **1** to go at a pace faster than a walk ⟨had to *trot* to keep up with Mom and Dad's quick pace⟩ — see RUN 1
2 to proceed or move quickly ⟨now *trot* along and get washed up for supper⟩ — see HURRY 2

troth *n* **1** a person's solemn declaration that he or she will do or not do something ⟨by my *troth*, I will not trespass on your property⟩ — see PROMISE
2 the act or state of being engaged to be married ⟨solemnly announced their *troth* before the church's congregation⟩ — see ENGAGEMENT 1

troth *vb* to obligate by prior agreement ⟨I *troth* myself eternally to your service⟩ — see PLEDGE 1

trouble *n* **1** an abnormal state that disrupts a plant's or animal's normal bodily functioning ⟨hoping that the doctor will be able to accurately diagnose my *trouble*⟩ — see DISEASE
2 something that may cause injury or harm ⟨that wild dog is *trouble*, so stay away⟩ — see DANGER 2
3 something that requires thought and skill for resolution ⟨the police officers first broke up the fight and then asked what the *trouble* was⟩ — see PROBLEM 1
4 the active use of energy in producing a result ⟨please, don't go to all that *trouble* just for me⟩ — see EFFORT

5 the state of not being protected from injury, harm, or evil ⟨if you think your brother might be in *trouble*, then let's go check up on him⟩ — see DANGER 1

trouble *vb* **1** to experience concern or anxiety ⟨don't *trouble* about me—I'll be fine⟩ — see WORRY 1

2 to cause discomfort to or trouble for ⟨I hate to *trouble* you, but would you mind moving for a minute to I can sweep under your chair?⟩ — see INCONVENIENCE

troubled *adj* feeling or showing uncomfortable feelings of uncertainty ⟨the *troubled* looks on their faces showed that they were still waiting for news about the accident⟩ — see NERVOUS 1

troublesome *adj* causing worry or anxiety ⟨the *troublesome* news that there will be more cuts in the school budget⟩

synonyms discomforting, discomposing, disquieting, distressing, disturbing, perturbing, troubling, troublous, unsettling, upsetting, worrisome

related words daunting, demoralizing, discomfiting, disconcerting, discouraging, disheartening, dismaying, dispiriting

near antonyms calming, quieting, settling, soothing

antonyms reassuring, untroublesome

troubling *adj* causing worry or anxiety ⟨the most *troubling* sign of all is that he's stopped returning my phone calls⟩ — see TROUBLESOME

troublous *adj* causing worry or anxiety ⟨a *troublous* teen whose law-breaking antics had us all on edge⟩ — see TROUBLESOME

trough *n* **1** a long hollow cylinder for carrying a substance (as a liquid or gas) ⟨all of the wiring for the converted residential loft is concealed in a vertical *trough*⟩ — see PIPE 1

2 a long narrow channel dug in the earth ⟨I slid and fell into the *trough* by the side of the road, scraping my leg⟩ — see DITCH

3 a pipe or channel for carrying off water from a roof ⟨the *troughs* on the eaves of the house were clogged with leaves⟩ — see GUTTER 1

trounce *vb* **1** to achieve a victory over ⟨unfortunately, our football rivals *trounced* us in the division finals⟩ — see BEAT 2

2 to defeat by a large margin ⟨our candidate *trounced* her opponent in the election, winning with 76% of the vote⟩ — see WHIP 2

trouncing *n* failure to win a contest ⟨took a serious *trouncing* during the last three minutes of the game⟩ — see DEFEAT 1

troupe *n* an organized group of stage performers ⟨desperately want to join our school's acting *troupe* and get a lead role⟩ — see COMPANY 1

trouper *n* one who acts professionally (as in a play, movie, or television show) ⟨had been a well-known Broadway *trouper* before making his screen debut⟩ — see ACTOR

trousers *n pl* an outer garment covering each leg separately from waist to ankle ⟨picked up his *trousers* from the dry cleaners⟩ — see PANTS

truce *n* a temporary stopping of fighting ⟨both sides agreed to a 24-hour *truce* beginning at midnight on Christmas Eve⟩

synonyms armistice, cease-fire

related words accord, reconciliation; peace, peacetime

truck *n* a giving or taking of one thing of value in return for another ⟨a *truck* in which she traded her old roller skates for brand new ice skates⟩ — see EXCHANGE 1

truculence *n* an inclination to fight or quarrel ⟨a *truculence* that resulted in her spending most of the school

year either suspended or in the principal's office⟩ — see BELLIGERENCE

truculent *adj* feeling or displaying eagerness to fight ⟨fans who became *truculent* and violent after their team's loss⟩ — see BELLIGERENT

trudge *vb* to make progress in a clumsy, struggling manner ⟨*trudged* up the hill, visibly straining under the weight of his backpack⟩ — see FLOUNDER 1

true *adj* **1** being exactly as appears or as claimed ⟨his claim that he's the heir to the throne can't be *true*⟩ — see AUTHENTIC 1

2 being in agreement with the truth or a fact or a standard ⟨if that is *true*, then we can't get in without a key⟩ — see CORRECT 1

3 existing in fact and not merely as a possibility ⟨the *true* scope of this environmental problem is far greater than anyone imagined⟩ — see ACTUAL

4 firm in one's allegiance to someone or something ⟨he will be *true* to his word⟩ — see FAITHFUL 1

5 following an original exactly ⟨it's not a *true* reproduction of the painting because the original is much larger⟩ — see FAITHFUL 2

6 free from any intent to deceive or impress others ⟨may our love for one another always be *true*⟩ — see GUILELESS

7 restricted to or based on fact ⟨that news story is completely *true*, for the station released a list of its sources to back it up⟩ — see FACTUAL 1

8 worthy of one's trust ⟨a *true* friend when you need one⟩ — see DEPENDABLE

true–blue *adj* firm in one's allegiance to someone or something ⟨a *true-blue* patriot⟩ — see FAITHFUL 1

truism *n* an idea or expression that has been used by many people ⟨ended his letter with the *truism*, "You can't win them all!"⟩ — see COMMONPLACE

truly *adv* **1** not merely this but also ⟨he is a kind, *truly* generous man⟩ — see EVEN

2 to tell the truth ⟨*truly*, I had no idea you were throwing me a party⟩ — see ACTUALLY 1

3 without any question ⟨I very much appreciate your gift—*truly*, I can't thank you enough!⟩ — see INDEED 1

trumpery *adj* of low quality ⟨*trumpery* knick-knacks from some souvenir shop⟩ — see CHEAP 2

trumpet *vb* to praise or publicize lavishly and often excessively ⟨critics *trumpeted* the band's latest album as the best of the decade⟩ — see TOUT 1

truncheon *n* a heavy rigid stick used as a weapon or for punishment ⟨the thug threatened the hero with a *truncheon*⟩ — see CLUB 1

trunk *n* a covered rectangular container for storing or transporting things ⟨threw the rest of her books and tapes in the *trunk* and closed the lid⟩ — see CHEST

truss *vb* to gather into a tight mass by means of a line or cord ⟨after stuffing the turkey, the chef quickly *trussed* it so the stuffing wouldn't fall out and the meat would all cook evenly⟩ — see TIE 1

trust *n* **1** firm belief in the integrity, ability, effectiveness, or genuineness of someone or something ⟨a relationship of mutual *trust* between lawyer and client⟩

synonyms confidence, credence, faith, stock

related words acceptance, assurance, assuredness, certainty, certitude, conviction, positiveness, sureness; credit, dependence, hope, reliance

near antonyms disbelief, incredulity, unbelief; doubt, dubiousness, incertitude, nonconfidence, skepticism, suspicion, uncertainty

antonyms distrust, mistrust

2 a number of businesses or enterprises united for commercial advantage ⟨government lawyers argued against allowing the telephone companies to merge, arguing that such a merger would result in a *trust* that would stifle competition⟩ — see CARTEL

3 responsibility for the safety and well-being of someone or something ⟨left her cat in the *trust* of her neighbors while she was on vacation⟩ — see CUSTODY

4 the right to take possession of goods before paying for them ⟨as his inner-city customers are often short on money, the neighborhood grocer has to frequently sell on *trust*⟩ — see CREDIT 1

trust *vb* **1** to give a task, duty, or responsibility to ⟨*trusted* him with walking the dog every morning⟩ — see ENTRUST 1

2 to put (something) into the possession or safekeeping of another ⟨I wouldn't *trust* my wallet with that guy if I were you⟩ — see GIVE 2

3 to regard as right or true ⟨don't *trust* everything you read in the newspaper⟩ — see BELIEVE 1

trustful *adj* having or showing trust in another ⟨a *trustful* child quietly sleeping, sure in the knowledge that his parents would be there when he woke⟩ — see TRUSTING 1

trusting *adj* **1** having or showing trust in another ⟨Delia couldn't look into her dog's *trusting* eyes as she drove him to the vet⟩

synonyms confiding, trustful

related words artless, childlike, credulous, guileless, gullible, innocent, naive (*also* naïve), simple, unsophisticated; dependent, hopeful, reliant; accepting, believing, certain, confident, convinced, overconfident, secure, sure, unquestioning, unsuspecting, unsuspicious, unwary

near antonyms disbelieving, incredulous, unbelieving, unconvinced, unpersuaded; hesitant, leery, oversuspicious, skeptical, suspicious, uncertain, unsure, wary

antonyms distrustful, doubtful, doubting, mistrustful

2 readily taken advantage of ⟨a corrupt stockbroker who preyed upon *trusting* customers⟩ — see EASY 2

trustworthiness *n* worthiness as the recipient of another's trust or confidence ⟨you have to prove your *trustworthiness* before I will tell you my secrets⟩ — see RELIABILITY

trustworthy *adj* worthy of one's trust ⟨a *trustworthy* bodyguard⟩ — see DEPENDABLE

trusty *adj* worthy of one's trust ⟨movie cowboys always get on their *trusty* horses and ride off into the sunset⟩ — see DEPENDABLE

truth *n* agreement with fact or reality ⟨there is no *truth* to her accusation that Emory cheated on the test⟩

synonyms factuality, verity

related words accuracy, actuality, authenticity, correctness; credibility, honesty, trustworthiness, truthfulness, veracity; dependability, reliability

near antonyms erroneousness, fallaciousness, fallacy; falsehood, fiction, inaccuracy, incorrectness; deceit, dishonesty, mendacity, untruthfulness

antonyms falseness, falsity, untruth

truthful *adj* being in the habit of telling the truth ⟨a *truthful* youngster who wouldn't just make up a story like that⟩

synonyms honest, veracious

related words candid, frank, open, plainspoken; believable, credible, veritable, true; conscientious, moral, principled, scrupulous; dependable, reliable, trustworthy, trusty

near antonyms fallacious, false, untrue; unbelievable, undependable, unreliable, untrustworthy; bluffing, dissembling, dissimulating, duplicitous, equivocating, hypocritical, insincere, posing, pretending; artful, deceitful, deceptive, devious, slick, slippery, sly, sneaky, treacherous, tricky, underhanded, wily

antonyms dishonest, fibbing, lying, mendacious, prevaricating, untruthful

truthfully *adv* to tell the truth ⟨*truthfully*, I'd rather go to the amusement park than the museum, but I'll go along with the rest of the group⟩ — see ACTUALLY 1

truthfulness *n* devotion to telling the truth ⟨the principal was impressed by her *truthfulness* in admitting she had started the fight⟩ — see HONESTY 1

try *n* an effort to do or accomplish something ⟨was granted another *try* at the field goal⟩ — see ATTEMPT

try *vb* to make an effort to do ⟨*try* to unlock the door⟩ ⟨will *try* to call later tonight⟩ — see ATTEMPT

try (out) *vb* **1** to put (something) to a test ⟨want to *try out* my new skateboard?⟩ ⟨*tried* his skill at archery⟩

synonyms sample, test

related words check out, examine, experiment (with), explore, feel (out), research

2 to subject (a personal quality or faculty) to often excessive stress ⟨you're *trying* my patience⟩

synonyms strain, stretch, tax, test

related words demand, exact, importune, press, pressure, push; aggravate, agitate, exasperate, get (to), gnaw (at), grate, harass, harry, hassle, irk, irritate, pain, pester

trying *adj* difficult to endure ⟨an account of the *trying* conditions experienced by the hostages prior to their release⟩ — see HARSH 1

tryst *n* an agreement to be present at a specified time and place ⟨both lovers had to hurry to keep their noontime *tryst* in the park⟩ — see ENGAGEMENT 2

tubby *adj* having an excess of body fat ⟨in America, Santa Claus is portrayed as a jolly but *tubby* older gentleman⟩ — see FAT 1

tube *n* a long hollow cylinder for carrying a substance (as a liquid or gas) ⟨watched the liquid move through the *tube* between the flasks and recorded the movement in his chemistry notebook⟩ — see PIPE 1

tucker (out) *vb* to use up all the physical energy of ⟨we're hoping that the mountain bike ride will *tucker* the kids *out* so they'll sleep well tonight⟩ — see EXHAUST 1

tuckered (out) *adj* depleted in strength, energy, or freshness ⟨*tuckered out* after a long day of playing tennis⟩ — see WEARY 1

tug *n* the act or an instance of applying force on something so that it moves in the direction of the force ⟨gave the man in front a *tug* on his shirt sleeve as a sign that he was supposed to step aside⟩ — see PULL 1

tug *vb* to cause to follow by applying steady force on ⟨*tugged* on the door until it opened⟩ — see PULL 1

tug–of–war *n* an earnest effort for superiority or victory over another ⟨the effort to get their teenage son to keep his room clean is a constant *tug-of-war*⟩ — see CONTEST 1

tumble *n* **1** an unorganized collection or mixture of various things ⟨cleaned a crazy *tumble* of buttons, hair bands, loose change, and old candy wrappers out from the couch cushions⟩ — see MISCELLANY 1

2 the act of going down from an upright position suddenly and involuntarily ⟨took a little *tumble* on the ice⟩ — see FALL 1

tumble *vb* **1** to go down from an upright position suddenly and involuntarily ⟨the infant stood for a moment and then *tumbled* on the carpet⟩ — see FALL 1

2 to go to a lower level ⟨prices for those stocks have really *tumbled*⟩ — see DROP 2

3 to undo the proper order or arrangement of ⟨*tumbled* all the clothes in her closet as she furiously searched for her favorite pair of jeans⟩ — see DISORDER

tumble (to) *vb* to recognize the meaning of ⟨I finally *tumbled to* the fact that I had been duped into getting involved in a phony investment scheme⟩ — see COMPREHEND 1

tumbled *adj* lacking in order, neatness, and often cleanliness ⟨a *tumbled* entryway filled with the usual jumble of sports equipment, backpacks, papers, and shoes⟩ — see MESSY

tummy *n* the part of the body between the chest and the pelvis ⟨tickled the toddler's *tummy*⟩ — see STOMACH

tumor *n* an abnormal mass of tissue ⟨the scan showed a small *tumor* in her abdomen that was easily removed⟩ — see GROWTH 1

tumult *n* **1** a state of noisy, confused activity ⟨in the *tumult* of the evacuation from the coast, we accidentally left on the television, which was of course tuned to the local newscast breathlessly reporting on the hurricane we were fleeing⟩ — see COMMOTION

2 a violent disturbance (as of the political or social order) ⟨the political *tumult* that swept the American colonies in the late 1700s⟩ — see CONVULSION

3 a violent shouting ⟨went to the window to see what the great *tumult* was and discovered a crowd of demonstrators marching down the street⟩ — see CLAMOR 1

tumultuous *adj* **1** marked by sudden or violent disturbance ⟨one of the most *tumultuous* periods in the history of the region⟩ — see CONVULSIVE

2 marked by turmoil or disturbance especially of natural elements ⟨watched the *tumultuous* weather from the dry safety of our house⟩ — see WILD 3

tundra *n* a broad area of level or rolling treeless country ⟨a report on the arctic *tundra* of Alaska and the polar bears that inhabit that vast, frozen plain⟩ — see PLAIN

tune *n* **1** a rhythmic series of musical tones arranged to give a pleasing effect ⟨hummed a little *tune* while I sorted the laundry⟩ — see MELODY

2 a state of consistency ⟨your negative comments on the short story seem to be in *tune* with the opinions of the rest of the class⟩ — see CONFORMITY 1

tuneful *adj* having a pleasing mixture of notes ⟨some especially *tuneful* songs have been written for this new animated film⟩ — see HARMONIOUS 1

turbid *adj* having visible particles in liquid suspension ⟨the pond water became *turbid* from our swimming and splashing⟩ — see CLOUDY 1

turbulent *adj* **1** marked by bursts of destructive force or intense activity ⟨the *turbulent* struggle for civil rights that shook up American society in the 1960s⟩ — see VIOLENT 1

2 marked by turmoil or disturbance especially of natural elements ⟨the *turbulent* rapids of the river were certainly daunting to those of us who were new to river rafting⟩ — see WILD 3

3 marked by wet and windy conditions ⟨expect *turbulent* weather as the cold front brings rain and sleet⟩ — see FOUL 1

turkey *n* **1** a person who lacks good sense or judgment ⟨only a *turkey* would think it's a good idea to go for a jog when the weather drops below zero⟩ — see FOOL 1

2 a stupid person ⟨you *turkey*, that wasn't my boyfriend—it was my brother!⟩ — see IDIOT

3 something that has failed ⟨his business venture ended up being a *turkey*, and he lost quite a bit of money on it⟩ — see FAILURE 3

turmoil *n* **1** a disturbed or uneasy state ⟨was in *turmoil* most of the night, trying to convince himself he had made the right decision⟩ — see UNREST

2 a state of noisy, confused activity ⟨avoided the *turmoil* of the mall during the holiday season⟩ — see COMMOTION

turn *n* **1** a relaxed journey on foot for exercise or pleasure ⟨would you care to take a *turn* around the garden?⟩ — see WALK

2 an act of kind assistance ⟨one good *turn* deserves another⟩ — see FAVOR 1

3 a habitual attraction to some activity or thing ⟨an adventurous *turn* of mind that led him towards more physical activities like biking and skateboarding⟩ — see INCLINATION 1

4 something that curves or is curved ⟨right after this *turn* in the road and you'll find the antique shop on the right⟩ — see BEND 1

turn *vb* **1** to move (something) in a curved or circular path on or as if on an axis ⟨*turned* the doorknob as quietly as possible⟩

synonyms pivot, revolve, roll, rotate, spin, swing, swirl, twirl, twist, wheel, whirl

related words screw, unscrew; twiddle; crank, reel, wind; circulate

2 to change the course or direction of (something) ⟨the dog *turned* the stampeding flock of sheep around⟩ ⟨he *turned* his cart uphill⟩

synonyms deflect, divert, swing, veer, wheel, whip

related words avert, move, rechannel, shift, shunt, sidetrack, switch, transfer; swivel, twist, whirl, zigzag; bend, curve, sway; reverse, turn back

3 to change one's course or direction ⟨we *turned* left at the light⟩ ⟨the storm unexpectedly *turned* south and missed our area⟩

synonyms detour, deviate, sheer, swing, turn off, veer

related words tack, zigzag; double (back), turn back

4 to eventually have as a state or quality ⟨will *turn* 12 in six months⟩ — see BECOME

5 to move in circles around an axis or center ⟨the wheels *turned*, but the car was hopelessly stuck and wasn't moving⟩ — see SPIN 1

turn (over) *vb* to change the position of (an object) so that the opposite side or end is showing ⟨would you mind *turning* the picture *over* so I can see if the backing needs to be replaced⟩ — see REVERSE 2

turn (to) *vb* to use or seek out as a source of aid, relief, or advantage ⟨no need to *turn to* violence when we can talk things out peacefully⟩ — see RESORT (TO) 1

turncoat *n* one who betrays a trust or an allegiance ⟨the plot of the story revolved around the gangster's relentless attempts to learn the identity of the *turncoat*⟩ — see TRAITOR

turn down *vb* to show unwillingness to accept, do, engage in, or agree to ⟨I'm afraid that I will have to *turn down* your invitation⟩ — see DECLINE 1

turn in *vb* to go to one's bed in order to sleep ⟨it's almost midnight, so it's time to *turn in*⟩ — see BED

turning point *n* a point in a chain of events at which an important change (as in one's fortunes) occurs ⟨the *turning point* came when Victor finally admitted he was a werewolf⟩

synonyms climax, landmark, milestone

related words break, clincher, highlight; conversion, metamorphosis, transfiguration, transformation, turnabout, turnaround; clutch, crisis, crossroad(s), crunch, emergency, exigency, head, juncture, zero hour

turn off *vb* **1** to cause to feel disgust ⟨that bad meal *turned* me *off* about restaurant food for a while⟩ — see DISGUST

2 to change one's course or direction ⟨*turn off* at the third exit and follow the ramp to your left⟩ — see TURN 3

turn–on *n* something that persuades one to perform an action for pleasure or gain ⟨knew the offer of free pizza would be a major *turn-on* to the pair of teenagers she had just asked to help her move⟩ — see LURE 1

turn on *vb* **1** to cause a pleasurable stimulation of the feelings ⟨the crowd was *turned on* by the movie's amazing special effects and the exciting plot⟩ — see THRILL

2 to cause to function ⟨would you *turn on* the TV?⟩ — see ACTIVATE

turn out *vb* to come to be ⟨everything will *turn out* fine in the end⟩ — see COME OUT 1

turn over *vb* **1** to give (something) over to the control or possession of another usually under duress ⟨reluctantly *turned* the ship *over* to the first mate while he went below to try to stop the leak⟩ — see SURRENDER 1

2 to put (something) into the possession or safekeeping of another ⟨*turned* the evidence *over* to the police⟩ — see GIVE 2

turnpike *n* a passage cleared for public vehicular travel ⟨the *turnpike* was jammed with people heading south for the long weekend⟩ — see WAY 1

turn up *vb* **1** to come into view ⟨my missing car keys *turned up* just in time⟩ — see APPEAR 1

2 to get to a destination ⟨when do you think our guests will *turn up*?⟩ — see COME 2

tussle *n* a physical dispute between opposing individuals or groups ⟨a small *tussle* on the playground that was broken up by the teachers⟩ — see FIGHT 1

tussle *vb* to seize and attempt to unbalance one another for the purpose of achieving physical mastery ⟨puppies *tussling* with one another, rolling over and over on the carpet⟩ — see WRESTLE

tutelage *n* the act or process of imparting knowledge or skills to another ⟨a governess overseeing the *tutelage* of the family's children⟩ — see EDUCATION 1

tutor *vb* **1** to cause to acquire knowledge or skill in some field ⟨*tutored* me in Spanish⟩ — see TEACH

2 to give advice and instruction to (someone) regarding the course or process to be followed ⟨bought a video series designed to *tutor* a person in the fine art of decorating cakes⟩ — see GUIDE 1

tutoring *n* the act or process of imparting knowledge or skills to another ⟨found his calling in the *tutoring* of children with special educational needs⟩ — see EDUCATION 1

twain *n* two things of the same or similar kind that match or are considered together ⟨I like rap and my parents like country music, and never the *twain* shall meet in our house⟩ — see PAIR

tweet *vb* to make a short sharp sound like a small bird ⟨the computer *tweeted* again, signaling another error⟩ — see CHIRP

twerp *n* a person of no importance or influence ⟨kids thought he was just a little *twerp* until he won the National Spelling Bee⟩ — see NOBODY

twice *adv* to two times the amount or degree ⟨after being turned down, he is *twice* shy about asking a girl out⟩ — see DOUBLY

twilight *n* **1** a time or place of little or no light ⟨stumbled around the *twilight* of the shuttered room, unable to see where she was going⟩ — see DARK 1

2 the time from when the sun begins to set to the onset of total darkness ⟨watched as *twilight* descended and the woods fell silent⟩ — see DUSK 1

twin *adj* consisting of two members or parts that are usually joined ⟨a *twin*-cylinder engine⟩ — see DOUBLE 1

twin *n* either of a pair matched in one or more qualities ⟨I've found one sock but can't find its *twin*⟩ — see MATE 1

twine *vb* to follow a circular or spiral course ⟨the snake silently *twined* around the tree trunk⟩ — see WIND

twinge *n* a sharp unpleasant sensation usually felt in some specific part of the body ⟨felt a *twinge* in her knee on that cold, rainy morning⟩ — see PAIN 1

twinkle *n* a very small space of time ⟨in just a *twinkle*, the shooting star was gone⟩ — see INSTANT

twinkle *vb* **1** to shine with light at regular intervals ⟨her eyes *twinkled*⟩ — see BLINK 1

2 to shoot forth bursts of light ⟨stars *twinkling* on a crisp September night⟩ — see FLASH 1

twinkling *n* a very small space of time ⟨in a *twinkling*, the rabbit had disappeared⟩ — see INSTANT

twirl *n* a rapid turning about on an axis or central point ⟨the *twirl* of the dancer's skirt mesmerized me⟩ — see SPIN 1

twirl *vb* **1** to move (something) in a curved or circular path on or as if on an axis ⟨absentmindedly *twirled* a lock of her hair around her finger⟩ — see TURN 1

2 to move in circles around an axis or center ⟨an ice-skater *twirling* in place⟩ — see SPIN 1

twist *n* a forceful rotating or pulling motion for the purpose of dislodging something ⟨with a forceful *twist* she loosened the bolt⟩ — see WRENCH 1

twist *vb* **1** to change so much as to create a wrong impression or alter the meaning of ⟨my enemies will *twist* my words, but you'll only hear the truth out of me⟩ — see GARBLE

2 to follow a circular or spiral course ⟨the path gently *twisted* down the hill⟩ — see WIND

3 to move (something) in a curved or circular path on or as if on an axis ⟨*twisted* my wrist around to stretch it⟩ — see TURN 1

4 to move by or as if by a forceful rotation ⟨kept *twisting* the cap until it came free⟩ — see WRENCH 1

twisted *adj* marked by a long series of irregular curves ⟨a *twisted* walking stick⟩ — see CROOKED 1

twisting *adj* marked by a long series of irregular curves ⟨a *twisting* mountain road that requires careful driving⟩ — see CROOKED 1

twisting *n* a forceful rotating or pulling motion for the purpose of dislodging something ⟨it took some *twisting*, but I finally got the top off the jar⟩ — see WRENCH 1

twitch *vb* **1** to make jerky or restless movements ⟨the dog *twitched* in her sleep⟩ — see FIDGET

2 to move or cause to move with a sharp quick motion ⟨the rabbit *twitched* its nose⟩ — see JERK 1

twitching *n* a series of slight movements by a body back and forth or from side to side ⟨the *twitching* of my cat's ears was a signal that I should stop petting her before she got any angrier⟩ — see VIBRATION

twitter *n* a state of nervous or irritated concern ⟨our teacher was all in a *twitter* because a crawfish had gotten free from the fish tank⟩ — see FRET

twitter *vb* **1** to engage in casual or rambling conversation ⟨a local diner where the town gossips like to *twitter*⟩ — see CHAT

2 to make a short sharp sound like a small bird ⟨his two-way radio *twittered* as he answered it⟩ — see CHIRP

two–faced *adj* not being or expressing what one appears to be or express ⟨a *two-faced* friend⟩ — see INSINCERE

twofold *adj* being twice as great or as many ⟨my reasons for keeping you home are *twofold*: first, you need to clean your room, and second, you have piano practice this afternoon⟩ — see DOUBLE 2

twosome *n* two things of the same or similar kind that match or are considered together ⟨those sisters are a constant *twosome*, going everywhere together⟩ — see PAIR

tycoon *n* a person of rank, power, or influence in a particular field ⟨an oil *tycoon* who's widely considered the most powerful man in the county⟩ — see MAGNATE

type *n* **1** a number of persons or things that are grouped together because they have something in common ⟨what *type* of people do you generally hang out with?⟩ — see SORT 1

2 one of the units into which a whole is divided on the basis of a common characteristic ⟨a music store that has a good selection of all *types* of music, not just pop, rock, and rap⟩ — see CLASS 2

typical *adj* **1** having or showing the qualities associated with the members of a particular group or kind ⟨*typical* behavior for a two-year-old⟩

synonyms archetypal, average, characteristic, normal, regular, representative, standard

related words common, conventional, customary, ordinary, usual, wonted; expected, familiar, habitual, predictable, routine, unexceptional, unremarkable; predominant, preponderant

near antonyms uncommon, unconventional, uncustomary, unusual, unwonted; distinctive, especial, exceptional, extraordinary, infrequent, noteworthy, rare, remarkable, singular, special, unexpected, unfamiliar,

unique, unpredictable; eccentric, idiosyncratic, nonconformist, peculiar, unknown, unorthodox; curious, funny, odd, queer, strange; bizarre, fantastic, far-out, freak, freakish, out-of-the-way, outrageous, outré, unnatural, weird, wild

antonyms aberrant, abnormal, anomalous, atypical, deviant, irregular, nonrepresentative, nontypical

2 serving to identify as belonging to an individual or group ⟨when I asked what he had learned in school that day, he gave me the *typical* answer of teenagers: "I don't know"⟩ — see CHARACTERISTIC 1

typically *adv* according to the usual course of things ⟨prairie dogs *typically* live in open spaces⟩ — see NATURALLY 2

tyrannical *also* **tyrannic** *adj* **1** exercising power or authority without interference by others ⟨a *tyrannical* ruler whose terrible reign was marked by unceasing violence⟩ — see ABSOLUTE 1

2 fond of ordering people around ⟨even when he was still a toddler, he tended to be a *tyrannical* playmate⟩ — see BOSSY

tyrannous *adj* **1** exercising power or authority without interference by others ⟨studied the *tyrannous* rule of Stalin, communist dictator of the Soviet Union⟩ — see ABSOLUTE 1

2 fond of ordering people around ⟨my older sister is a *tyrannous* bore who isn't happy unless she's in charge⟩ — see BOSSY

tyranny *n* a system of government in which the ruler has unlimited power ⟨a popular uprising replaced that nation's *tyranny* with freedom and democracy⟩ — see DESPOTISM

tyrant *n* a person who uses power or authority in a cruel, unjust, or harmful way ⟨the people universally feared the *tyrant*, who was notorious for his frequent use of torture⟩ — see DESPOT

tyro *n* a person who is just starting out in a field of activity ⟨he's a good musician, but at 14, he's still a *tyro* and has a lot to learn⟩ — see BEGINNER

U

ubiquitous *adj* **1** often observed or encountered ⟨by that time cell phones had become *ubiquitous*, and people had long ceased to be impressed by the sight of one⟩ — see COMMON 1
2 present in all places and at all times ⟨was weary of the *ubiquitous* noise of the big city and longed for the quiet of the country⟩ — see OMNIPRESENT

ugly *adj* **1** unpleasant to look at ⟨her first attempt at painting was pretty *ugly*—a portrait of her sister that was not at all flattering⟩
synonyms grotesque, hideous, homely, ill-favored, unappealing, unattractive, unbeautiful, unhandsome, unlovely, unpleasing, unpretty, unsightly, vile
related words disgusting, repugnant, repulsive, revolting; unimposing, unimpressive, unprepossessing; plain, unaesthetic, unbecoming, unshapely
near antonyms becoming, bonny [*chiefly British*], cute, shapely; imposing, impressive, prepossessing
antonyms attractive, beauteous, beautiful, comely, cute, fair, gorgeous, handsome, lovely, pretty, stunning, taking
2 causing intense displeasure, disgust, or resentment ⟨an *ugly* suggestion for controlling the overpopulation of deer in the area⟩ — see OFFENSIVE 1

ultimate *adj* **1** of the greatest or highest degree or quantity ⟨the *ultimate* speed yet attained by a land-based vehicle⟩
synonyms consummate, maximum, most, nth, paramount, supreme, top, utmost, uttermost
related words unequaled (*or* unequalled), unmatched, unparalleled, unrivaled (*or* unrivalled), unsurpassed; topmost, upmost, uppermost
near antonyms littlest, smallest; lowest
antonyms least, minimal, minimum
2 following all others of the same kind in order or time ⟨the *ultimate* speaker at today's meeting⟩ — see LAST
3 most distant from a center ⟨the *ultimate* edges of the universe⟩ — see EXTREME 1

ultimately *adv* at a later time ⟨we'll *ultimately* renovate this section of the house, but for now it will stay as it is⟩ — see YET 1

ultimatum *n* something that someone insists upon having ⟨issued the *ultimatum* that the project be finished by the following week, or it would be terminated⟩ — see DEMAND 1

ultra *adj* being very far from the center of public opinion ⟨espouses a kind of *ultra* conservatism that even some members of his own party cannot support⟩ — see EXTREME 2

ultramodern *adj* being or involving the latest methods, concepts, information, or styles ⟨an *ultramodern* design for the company's new line of automobiles⟩ — see MODERN

ultramodernist *n* a person with very modern ideas ⟨an *ultramodernist* in interior decoration, she freely uses man-made materials to achieve a look that enthusiastically embraces the 21st century⟩ — see MODERN

umbra *n* **1** a time or place of little or no light ⟨strange noises were coming from the *umbra* beyond our campfire⟩ — see DARK 1
2 partial darkness due to the obstruction of light rays ⟨during a solar eclipse observers located within the

umbra experience a complete blocking of the sun by the moon⟩ — see SHADE 1

umbrage *n* the feeling of being offended or resentful after a slight or indignity ⟨took *umbrage* at the slightest suggestion of disrespect⟩ — see PIQUE

umpire *n* a person who impartially decides or resolves a dispute or controversy ⟨Mom usually acts as *umpire* in our frequent squabbles over the sailboat⟩ — see JUDGE 1

umpire *vb* to give an opinion about (something at issue or in dispute) ⟨in our family, disputes regarding the use of the pool are *umpired* by Dad⟩ — see JUDGE 1

unabashed *adj* not embarrassed or ashamed ⟨*unabashed* by their booing, he continued with his performance⟩
synonyms unashamed, unblushing, unembarrassed
related words prideful, proud; bold, brassy, brazen, impudent, insolent, saucy, shameless; unapologetic, undaunted, undeterred, undismayed; unblinking, unflinching, unshrinking
near antonyms discomfited, disconcerted, nonplussed (*also* nonplused)
antonyms abashed, ashamed, embarrassed, shamefaced, sheepish

unacceptable *adj* falling short of a standard ⟨this work is entirely *unacceptable*⟩ — see BAD 1

unacceptably *adv* **1** beyond a normal or acceptable limit ⟨*unacceptably* cold in the house⟩ — see TOO 1
2 in an unsatisfactory way ⟨she does her chores quickly but usually *unacceptably*⟩ — see BADLY

unacclimated *adj* not having acquired a habit or tolerance ⟨*unacclimated* to the intense heat of the tropics⟩ — see UNUSED 1

unaccompanied *adj* not being in the company of others ⟨an *unaccompanied* child on the airplane flight⟩ — see ALONE 1

unaccountable *adj* impossible to explain ⟨has an *unaccountable* dislike for that color⟩ — see INEXPLICABLE

unaccustomed *adj* **1** not having acquired a habit or tolerance ⟨pampered youngsters who were *unaccustomed* to such hard work⟩ — see UNUSED 1
2 not known or experienced before ⟨the *unaccustomed* friendliness of my relatives after I won the lottery⟩ — see NEW 2
3 noticeably different from what is generally found or experienced ⟨*unaccustomed* styles of cooking that the tourists had to be persuaded to try⟩ — see UNUSUAL 1

unachievable *adj* incapable of being solved or accomplished ⟨if you set *unachievable* goals, you will always feel like a failure⟩ — see IMPOSSIBLE

unacquainted *adj* not informed about or aware of something ⟨*unacquainted* with the latest developments in the field of astronomy⟩ — see IGNORANT 2

unadapted *adj* not having acquired a habit or tolerance ⟨the animals which were *unadapted* to harsh cold quickly died out during the Ice Age⟩ — see UNUSED 1

unadjusted *adj* not having acquired a habit or tolerance ⟨*unadjusted* to the lifestyle of a boarding school student⟩ — see UNUSED 1

unadorned *adj* free from all additions or embellishment ⟨the completely *unadorned* clothing favored by members of that religious sect⟩ — see PLAIN 1

unadulterated *adj* **1** free from added matter ⟨*unadulterated* cranberry juice is sour⟩ — see PURE 1

2 having no exceptions or restrictions ⟨the *unadulterated* nonsense that you sometimes hear⟩ — see ABSOLUTE 2

unadvisable *adj* showing poor judgment especially in personal relationships or social situations ⟨it's *unadvisable* to try to take six classes in a single semester⟩ — see INDISCREET

unaesthetic *adj* disagreeable to one's aesthetic or artistic sense ⟨believes that the design of even industrial buildings need not be *unaesthetic*⟩ — see HARSH 2

unaffected *adj* free from any intent to deceive or impress others ⟨a relaxed and *unaffected* style of public speaking⟩ — see GUILELESS

unaffectedly *adv* without any attempt to impress by deception or exaggeration ⟨writes *unaffectedly* simple love poems⟩ — see NATURALLY 3

unaided *adv* without aid or support ⟨took pictures of the first time that the baby was able to walk *unaided*⟩ — see ALONE 1

unalike *adj* being not of the same kind ⟨our opinions of the movie couldn't have been more *unalike*⟩ — see DIFFERENT 1

unallied *adj* not favoring or joined to either side in a quarrel, contest, or war ⟨preferred to stay *unallied* in the sibling rivalry⟩ — see NEUTRAL

unalloyed *adj* **1** free from added matter ⟨*unalloyed* chemicals⟩ — see PURE 1
2 having no exceptions or restrictions ⟨the *unalloyed* happiness that marriage has brought them⟩ — see ABSOLUTE 2

unalterable *adj* not capable of changing or being changed ⟨the rules of the game are *unalterable*, regardless of who is playing⟩ — see INFLEXIBLE 1

unambiguous *adj* **1** not subject to misinterpretation or more than one interpretation ⟨looked at his neighbor's new car with *unambiguous* envy⟩ — see CLEAR 2
2 so clearly expressed as to leave no doubt about the meaning ⟨an *unambiguous* declaration of his love for her⟩ — see EXPLICIT

unanimated *adj* causing weariness, restlessness, or lack of interest ⟨an *unanimated* discussion of a topic that no one was much interested in anyway⟩ — see BORING

unanimity *n* the act or fact of being of one opinion about something ⟨in a rare moment of *unanimity* the club members decided to throw a party for themselves⟩ — see AGREEMENT 1

unanimous *adj* having or marked by agreement in feeling or action ⟨a *unanimous* vote to upgrade the school's facilities⟩ — see HARMONIOUS 3

unanswerable *adj* not capable of being challenged or proved wrong ⟨the *unanswerable* assertion that she didn't know much about art but she knew what she liked⟩ — see IRREFUTABLE

unanticipated *adj* not expected ⟨ran into some *unanticipated* difficulties with the computer program⟩ — see UNEXPECTED

unappealing *adj* unpleasant to look at ⟨an *unappealing* mess of dirt and trash in the corner of the room⟩ — see UGLY 1

unappeasable *adj* showing no signs of slackening or yielding in one's purpose ⟨warned that the nation was dealing with an *unappeasable* enemy⟩ — see UNYIELDING 1

unappetizing *adj* disagreeable or disgusting to the sense of taste ⟨the array of *unappetizing* foods that we encountered at that cheap roadside restaurant⟩ — see DISTASTEFUL 1

unappreciated *adj* not likely to be appreciated by those who benefit ⟨a number of *unappreciated* little favors that we did for the neighbors⟩ — see THANKLESS 2

unappreciative *adj* not showing gratitude ⟨vowed that his *unappreciative* niece would never receive another birthday present from him⟩ — see THANKLESS 1

unapproachable *adj* hard or impossible to get to or get at ⟨a nearly *unapproachable* fortress in the mountains⟩ — see INACCESSIBLE

unapt *adj* **1** not appropriate for a particular occasion or situation ⟨has a knack for saying the most *unapt* things at the worst possible moments⟩ — see INAPPROPRIATE
2 not likely to be true or to occur ⟨at this point an admission of guilt from him would be most *unapt*⟩ — see IMPROBABLE

unashamed *adj* not embarrassed or ashamed ⟨*unashamed* of her religious beliefs and values⟩ — see UNABASHED

unasked *adj* not searched or asked for ⟨received a lot of *unasked* advice on the project⟩ — see UNSOUGHT

unassailable *adj* not to be violated, criticized, or tampered with ⟨one of the *unassailable* beliefs of that political party⟩ — see SACRED 1

unassisted *adv* without aid or support ⟨managed to do the group project *unassisted* after his partners got sick⟩ — see ALONE 1

unassuming *adj* not having or showing any feelings of superiority, self-assertiveness, or showiness ⟨a talented but surprisingly *unassuming* musician⟩ — see HUMBLE 1

unattached *adj* **1** not married ⟨everyone was surprised when the *unattached* woman finally fell in love⟩ — see SINGLE 1
2 not physically attached to another unit ⟨preferred an *unattached* house⟩ — see SEPARATE 2

unattainable *adj* **1** hard or impossible to get to or get at ⟨an eagle's nest in an *unattainable* location⟩ — see INACCESSIBLE
2 incapable of being solved or accomplished ⟨unfortunately, world peace is probably an *unattainable* ideal⟩ — see IMPOSSIBLE

unattractive *adj* unpleasant to look at ⟨an *unattractive*, awkward baby bird⟩ — see UGLY 1

unauthentic *adj* being such in appearance only and made or manufactured with the intention of committing fraud ⟨trying to sell *unauthentic* autographs of American presidents⟩ — see COUNTERFEIT

unavailable *adj* hard or impossible to get to or get at ⟨the commander is *unavailable* right now⟩ — see INACCESSIBLE

unavailing *adj* producing no results ⟨an *unavailing* effort to avert a war⟩ — see FUTILE

unavoidable *adj* impossible to avoid or evade ⟨unfortunately, kitchen duty will be *unavoidable* tonight⟩ — see INEVITABLE

unavoidably *adv* because of necessity ⟨we'll be *unavoidably* late this evening⟩ — see NEEDS

unaware *adj* not informed about or aware of something ⟨she was *unaware* of the change in plans⟩ — see IGNORANT 2

unaware *adv* without warning ⟨the attack took airmen completely *unaware*⟩ — see UNAWARES

unawareness *n* the state of being unaware or uninformed ⟨the couple's *unawareness* of current events was surprising and sad⟩ — see IGNORANCE 1

unawares *adv* without warning ⟨the thunderstorm caught us *unawares*, and we scrambled to get off the ridge as lightning started to flash⟩

synonyms aback, suddenly, unaware, unexpectedly
related words abruptly, short
phrases all of a sudden
near antonyms slowly; obviously

unbalance *vb* to cause to go insane or as if insane ⟨the shock of the loss of his wife and children completely *unbalanced* him⟩ — see CRAZE

unbalanced *adj* **1** having or showing a very abnormal or sick state of mind ⟨crimes that obviously were committed by a very *unbalanced* person⟩ — see INSANE 1
2 not being in or able to maintain a state of balance ⟨in such an *unbalanced* political situation, the probability of war increases⟩ — see UNSTABLE 1

unbaptized *adj* not named or identified by a name ⟨thus far the novel I've been working on remains *unbaptized*⟩ — see NAMELESS 1

unbearable *adj* more than can be put up with ⟨this heat is *unbearable*—when are we going to get air-conditioning?⟩
synonyms insufferable, insupportable, intolerable, unendurable, unsupportable
related words unacceptable; crushing, overwhelming; comfortless, harsh, painful, uncomfortable
near antonyms acceptable; adequate
antonyms endurable, sufferable, supportable, tolerable

unbeatable *adj* incapable of being defeated, overcome, or subdued ⟨a seemingly *unbeatable* baseball team⟩ — see INVINCIBLE

unbeautiful *adj* unpleasant to look at ⟨a makeshift shelter that was *unbeautiful* perhaps, but it kept us out of the rain⟩ — see UGLY 1

unbecoming *adj* not appropriate for a particular occasion or situation ⟨behavior *unbecoming* an officer⟩ — see INAPPROPRIATE

unbeknownst *also* **unbeknown** *adj* happening or existing without one's knowledge ⟨*unbeknownst* to me, my mother was planning a party⟩ — see UNKNOWN 1

unbelief *n* refusal to accept as true ⟨a natural-born skeptic, she typically greets the latest conspiracy theory with head-shaking *unbelief*⟩ — see DISBELIEF

unbelievable *adj* too extraordinary or improbable to believe ⟨a completely *unbelievable* story about why he was late for school⟩ — see INCREDIBLE

unbeliever *n* a person who is always ready to doubt or question the truth or existence of something ⟨a hardheaded *unbeliever* who demanded to see concrete evidence of any alleged UFO activity⟩ — see SKEPTIC

unbelieving *adj* inclined to doubt or question claims ⟨*unbelieving* scientists who demand that all phenomena be subjected to rigorous scientific scrutiny⟩ — see SKEPTICAL 1

unbend *vb* to cause to follow a line that is without bends or curls ⟨the new highway will largely *unbend* that twisting path that the old road used to follow⟩ — see STRAIGHTEN

unbending *adj* sticking to an opinion, purpose, or course of action in spite of reason, arguments, or persuasion ⟨the school's new headmaster is reputed to be an *unbending* disciplinarian⟩ — see OBSTINATE

unbiased *adj* marked by justice, honesty, and freedom from bias ⟨offered an *unbiased* judgment of the dancer's performance⟩ — see FAIR 2

unbidden *also* **unbid** *adj* not searched or asked for ⟨she arrived, *unbidden*, to help out at the Red Cross center⟩ — see UNSOUGHT

unbind *vb* **1** to disengage the knotted parts of ⟨*unbind* a rope⟩ — see UNTIE

2 to set free (as from slavery or confinement) ⟨a newly elected democratic government whose first act was to *unbind* the nation's political prisoners⟩ — see FREE 1

unblemished *adj* being entirely without fault or flaw ⟨a modeling agency looking for people with *unblemished* complexions⟩ — see PERFECT 1

unblock *vb* to rid the surface of (as an area) from things in the way ⟨*unblock* the road so that the convoy can proceed⟩ — see CLEAR 1

unblushing *adj* not embarrassed or ashamed ⟨an *unblushing* patriotism that is manifested in the family's public display of the flag⟩ — see UNABASHED

unborn *adj* of a time after the present ⟨a home entertainment system that can be adapted for products as yet *unborn*⟩ — see FUTURE

unbosom *vb* to make known (as information previously kept secret) ⟨*unbosomed* his fear of dying only to his closest friends⟩ — see REVEAL 1

unbound *adj* not bound, confined, or detained by force ⟨a dog left *unbound* in the yard⟩ — see FREE 3

unbounded *adj* being or seeming to be without limits ⟨the *unbounded* enthusiasm shown by the new club members⟩ — see INFINITE

unbraid *vb* to separate the various strands of ⟨*unbraided* the line⟩ — see UNRAVEL 1

unbridled *adj* showing no signs of being under control ⟨a case that was solved only because of one detective's *unbridled* determination to bring the killer to justice⟩ — see RAMPANT 1

unbroken *adj* **1** going on and on without any interruptions ⟨just mile after mile of *unbroken* woodland⟩ — see CONTINUOUS
2 living outdoors without taming or domestication by humans ⟨a young, *unbroken* horse⟩ — see WILD 1

unbudging *adj* incapable of moving or being moved ⟨the massive old bed was simply *unbudging*, despite our best efforts⟩ — see IMMOVABLE 1

unburden *vb* **1** to empty or rid of cargo ⟨the crew was frantically *unburdening* the ship in an attempt to save it⟩ — see UNLOAD 1
2 to set (a person or thing) free of something that encumbers ⟨*unburdened* her of that particular worry⟩ — see RID

unburdened *adj* no longer burdened with something unpleasant or painful ⟨now *unburdened* of his painful secret, he felt free for the first time in years⟩ — see FREE 2

uncage *vb* to set free (as from slavery or confinement) ⟨*uncaged* the bird and let it fly away⟩ — see FREE 1

uncalled–for *adj* **1** not needed by the circumstances or to accomplish an end ⟨*uncalled-for* restrictions on freedom of the press during the national emergency⟩ — see UNNECESSARY
2 showing a lack of manners or consideration for others ⟨hurtful remarks about a person's looks that are simply *uncalled-for*⟩ — see IMPOLITE

uncanny *adj* **1** being beyond one's powers to know, understand, or explain ⟨a number of *uncanny* parallels in the lives of the two women⟩ — see MYSTERIOUS 1
2 being so extraordinary or abnormal as to suggest powers which violate the laws of nature ⟨an *uncanny* gift for knowing when someone, no matter how distant, needed help⟩ — see SUPERNATURAL 2
3 fearfully and mysteriously strange or fantastic ⟨*uncanny* and unexpected shadows along the mountainsides⟩ — see EERIE

uncataloged *adj* not appearing on a list ⟨hundreds of *uncataloged* runners ran in the marathon⟩ — see UNLISTED

unceasing *adj* going on and on without any interruptions ⟨this *unceasing* rain will turn me into a mushroom!⟩ — see CONTINUOUS

uncelebrated *adj* not widely known ⟨a gifted but *uncelebrated* poet⟩ — see OBSCURE 2

unceremonious *adj* not rigidly following established form, custom, or rules ⟨her *unceremonious* approach to her hosting duties puts party guests immediately at ease⟩ — see INFORMAL 1

uncertain *adj* 1 likely to change frequently, suddenly, or unexpectedly ⟨the stifling heat would occasionally be relieved by an *uncertain* breeze⟩ — see FICKLE 1
2 not feeling sure about the truth, wisdom, or trustworthiness of someone or something ⟨never *uncertain* of her political beliefs or judgment, she was a decisive and fearless leader⟩ — see DOUBTFUL 1

uncertainty *n* a feeling or attitude that one does not know the truth, truthfulness, or trustworthiness of someone or something ⟨*uncertainty* about her job prospects has her worried⟩ — see DOUBT

unchain *vb* to set free (as from slavery or confinement) ⟨activists for animal rights who would like to *unchain* zoo animals and return them to the wild⟩ — see FREE 1

unchangeable *adj* not capable of changing or being changed ⟨I'm afraid that my opinion on this matter is *unchangeable*⟩ — see INFLEXIBLE 1

unchangeableness *n* the state of continuing without change ⟨the endless days of sunshine were certainly pleasant, but the *unchangeableness* of the weather got to be boring after a while⟩ — see CONSTANCY 1

unchanging *adj* 1 not undergoing a change in condition ⟨took comfort in *unchanging* family traditions⟩ — see CONSTANT 1
2 not varying ⟨an *unchanging* expression of boredom throughout the entire lecture⟩ — see UNIFORM

uncharitable *adj* 1 giving or sharing as little as possible ⟨an *uncharitable* couple who wouldn't even donate food to needy families at Thanksgiving⟩ — see STINGY 1
2 having or showing a lack of sympathy or tender feelings ⟨an *uncharitable* attitude towards people who give in to alcohol or other temptations⟩ — see HARD 1

unchecked *adj* showing no signs of being under control ⟨*unchecked* corruption in the prison system⟩ — see RAMPANT 1

unchristened *adj* not named or identified by a name ⟨some *unchristened* dog that we just adopted from the local pound⟩ — see NAMELESS 1

uncivil *adj* 1 not civilized ⟨the *uncivil* and wild land that the pioneers tamed and settled⟩ — see SAVAGE 1
2 showing a lack of manners or consideration for others ⟨such *uncivil* behavior will not be tolerated⟩ — see IMPOLITE

uncivilized *adj* not civilized ⟨unfairly branded as *uncivilized* by European explorers, they have a culture that was actually quite advanced⟩ — see SAVAGE

unclad *adj* lacking or shed of clothing ⟨drawings and sculptures of the *unclad* human figure⟩ — see NAKED 1

unclean *adj* not clean ⟨a lackadaisical waiter who tried to set my table with smudged glasses and *unclean* silverware⟩ — see DIRTY 1

uncleanliness *n* the state or quality of being dirty ⟨the *uncleanliness* of the restaurant's windows wasn't very appetizing either⟩ — see DIRTINESS 1

uncleanly *adj* not clean ⟨the *uncleanly* uniforms of the restaurant's staff⟩ — see DIRTY 1

uncleanness *n* the state or quality of being dirty ⟨the general *uncleanness* of the restaurant turned my stomach⟩ — see DIRTINESS 1

unclear *adj* 1 not clearly expressed ⟨their suggestion for correcting the problem is a bit *unclear*⟩ — see VAGUE 1
2 not seen or understood clearly ⟨obtained at best an *unclear* glimpse of the bird from across the road⟩ — see FAINT 1

uncloak *vb* 1 to make known (as information previously kept secret) ⟨*uncloaked* the latest plan for improvements to the state capitol⟩ — see REVEAL 1
2 to reveal the true nature of ⟨investigative reporters *uncloaked* the real estate tycoon, revealing him to be nothing more than a slumlord⟩ — see EXPOSE 1

unclog *vb* 1 to arrange clear passage of (something) by removing obstructions ⟨*unclog* a drain with a cleaner⟩ — see OPEN 2
2 to free from obstruction or difficulty ⟨*unclog* the way for more people to take advantage of the government program⟩ — see EASE 1

unclogged *adj* allowing passage without obstruction ⟨an *unclogged* pipe works much more efficiently⟩ — see OPEN 1

unclose *vb* to change from a closed to an open position ⟨one nurse closed the window in my room, and a minute later another nurse *unclosed* it⟩ — see OPEN 1

unclosed *adj* allowing passage without obstruction ⟨escaped through the one remaining *unclosed* passageway⟩ — see OPEN 1

unclothe *vb* to remove clothing from ⟨partially *unclothed* the patient for treatment⟩ — see UNDRESS

unclothed *adj* lacking or shed of clothing ⟨wandering around *unclothed* is illegal in most states⟩ — see NAKED 1

unclouded *adj* not stormy or cloudy ⟨campers awaking to the sight of a completely *unclouded* blue sky⟩ — see FAIR 1

uncluttered *adj* being clean and in good order ⟨I work better with an *uncluttered* desk⟩ — see NEAT 1

uncolored *adj* lacking an addition of color ⟨the walls will be left *uncolored*, so you can choose your own color scheme⟩ — see COLORLESS

uncomfortable *adj* 1 causing discomfort ⟨unfortunately, dressing up for the dance meant wearing an *uncomfortable* shirt⟩
synonyms comfortless, discomforting, harsh
related words aching, hurting, nasty, painful, sore; distressing, disturbing, upsetting; awkward, cumbersome, inconvenient, ungainly; uneasy
near antonyms easy, soothing; cozy, snug
antonyms comfortable
2 causing embarrassment ⟨the *uncomfortable* situation of running into an ex-friend at a social gathering⟩ — see AWKWARD 3
3 lacking social grace and assurance ⟨a person who is *uncomfortable* at parties with lots of strangers⟩ — see AWKWARD 1

uncomic *adj* not joking or playful in mood or manner ⟨the movie takes a very *uncomic* approach to underage drinking, finding nothing funny about drunken teens⟩ — see SERIOUS 1

uncommon *adj* 1 being out of the ordinary ⟨a landscape of *uncommon* beauty⟩ — see EXCEPTIONAL
2 noticeably different from what is generally found or experienced ⟨backyard swimming pools are not an *un*-

common sight in that neighborhood⟩ — see UNUSUAL 1

uncommunicative *adj* **1** deliberately refraining from speech ⟨the child was *uncommunicative* and unhelpful to school investigators⟩ — see SILENT 1
2 given to keeping one's activities hidden from public observation or knowledge ⟨intelligence agencies must be *uncommunicative* about their operations if they are to be at all effective⟩ — see SECRETIVE
3 tending not to speak frequently (as by habit or inclination) ⟨resigned to the fact that her husband was always going to be an *uncommunicative* partner⟩ — see SILENT 2

uncomplaining *adj* accepting pains or hardships calmly or without complaint ⟨an *uncomplaining* single mother of five⟩ — see PATIENT 1

uncomplimentary *adj* intended to make a person or thing seem of little importance or value ⟨an *uncomplimentary* description of the town in which the writer grew up⟩ — see DEROGATORY

uncompromising *adj* **1** not allowing for any exceptions or loosening of standards ⟨an *uncompromising* adherence to the rules⟩ — see RIGID 1
2 sticking to an opinion, purpose, or course of action in spite of reason, arguments, or persuasion ⟨the teacher is generally an *uncompromising* stickler for deadlines, but he will make exceptions for genuine need⟩ — see OBSTINATE

unconcern *n* lack of interest or concern ⟨wore an expression of general *unconcern* throughout the trial⟩ — see INDIFFERENCE

unconcerned *adj* **1** having or showing a lack of concern or seriousness ⟨playful and *unconcerned* despite his medical emergency⟩ — see CAREFREE
2 having or showing a lack of interest or concern ⟨a featherbrain completely *unconcerned* about the important issues of the day⟩ — see INDIFFERENT 1

unconditional *adj* having no exceptions or restrictions ⟨demanded an *unconditional* surrender⟩ — see ABSOLUTE 2

unconfined *adj* not bound, confined, or detained by force ⟨residents of the camp for drug rehabilitation are completely *unconfined*—no one is there unless they want to be⟩ — see FREE 3

uncongenial *adj* not giving pleasure to the mind or senses ⟨a dank and *uncongenial* castle⟩ — see UNPLEASANT

unconnected *adj* **1** not clearly or logically connected ⟨a delirious inmate whose *unconnected* ramblings frustrated the staff⟩ — see INCOHERENT 1
2 not physically attached to another unit ⟨the *unconnected* houses in the private development have common areas and share certain facilities⟩ — see SEPARATE 2

unconquerable *adj* incapable of being defeated, overcome, or subdued ⟨an *unconquerable* spirit that got the family through some hard times⟩ — see INVINCIBLE

unconscionable *adj* **1** going beyond a normal or acceptable limit in degree or amount ⟨an *unconscionable* number of errors for an important government report⟩ — see EXCESSIVE
2 not guided by or showing a concern for what is right ⟨a politician with an *unconscionable* disregard for the truth⟩ — see UNPRINCIPLED

unconscious *adj* **1** having lost consciousness ⟨the guard was knocked *unconscious* by a blow to the head⟩
synonyms cold, insensible, senseless

related words semiconscious; anesthetized
near antonyms alert, awake, aware, up
antonyms conscious
2 not informed about or aware of something ⟨*unconscious* of the somber expression she wore⟩ — see IGNORANT 2

unconsidered *adj* made or done without previous thought or preparation ⟨regretted some *unconsidered* comments that she made during a live TV interview⟩ — see EXTEMPORANEOUS

unconsolidated *adj* consisting of particles that do not stick together ⟨*unconsolidated* soil⟩ — see LOOSE 2

uncontrollable *adj* given to resisting control or discipline by others ⟨the *uncontrollable* child kept throwing tantrums in public and creating scenes⟩
synonyms froward, headstrong, intractable, recalcitrant, refractory, ungovernable, unmanageable, unruly, untoward, wayward, willful (*or* wilful)
related words contrary, incorrigible, obstinate, perverse, self-willed, stubborn; undisciplined, unpunished; uncontrolled, ungoverned, wild; boisterous, rambunctious, rowdy; disobedient, insubordinate, rebellious; misbehaving, naughty
phrases out of hand
near antonyms docile, obedient, well-behaved; compliant, submissive, yielding
antonyms controllable, governable, tractable

uncontrolled *adj* showing no signs of being under control ⟨a tirade filled with *uncontrolled* anger about what the government was doing⟩ — see RAMPANT 1

unconventional *adj* **1** deviating from commonly accepted beliefs or practices ⟨the Shakers acquired their name because of their *unconventional* practice of dancing with shaking movements during worship⟩ — see HERETICAL
2 not bound by traditional ways or beliefs ⟨had *unconventional* opinions on the raising of children⟩ — see LIBERAL 1
3 not rigidly following established form, custom, or rules ⟨young, creative people who lead *unconventional* but happy lifestyles⟩ — see INFORMAL 1

unconvinced *adj* not feeling sure about the truth, wisdom, or trustworthiness of someone or something ⟨*unconvinced* that the prosecution had proven guilt beyond a reasonable doubt⟩ — see DOUBTFUL 1

unconvincing *adj* too extraordinary or improbable to believe ⟨the excuse was too *unconvincing* to be accepted⟩ — see INCREDIBLE

uncooked *adj* not cooked ⟨crunching on *uncooked* rice⟩ — see RAW 1

uncordial *adj* lacking in friendliness or warmth of feeling ⟨extended a correct but decidedly *uncordial* welcome to the other nation's diplomats at the peace negotiations⟩ — see COLD 2

uncork *vb* to set free (from a state of being held in check) ⟨*uncorked* her emotions once she was alone in her room⟩ — see RELEASE 1

uncountable *adj* too many to be counted ⟨an *uncountable* number of mosquitoes in the yard⟩ — see COUNTLESS

uncounted *adj* too many to be counted ⟨gazed in wonder at the *uncounted* stars of the sky⟩ — see COUNTLESS

uncouple *vb* to set or force apart ⟨*uncoupled* the two railroad cars⟩ — see SEPARATE 1

uncouth *adj* **1** having or showing crudely insensitive or impolite manners ⟨will not tolerate any *uncouth* behavior, such as eating with one's mouth open⟩ — see CLOWNISH

2 lacking in refinement or good taste ⟨the movie's *uncouth* humor seemed to be purposely offensive⟩ — see COARSE 2

uncover *vb* **1** to make known (as information previously kept secret) ⟨*uncovered* the location of the secret documents⟩ — see REVEAL 1

2 to reveal the true nature of ⟨a magazine article that purports to *uncover* the inner operations of what many regard as a religious cult⟩ — see EXPOSE 1

uncovered *adj* lacking a usual or natural covering ⟨trees *uncovered* in the wintertime⟩ — see NAKED 2

uncritical *adj* lacking in worldly wisdom or informed judgment ⟨had an *uncritical* trust in the nation's leaders⟩ — see NAIVE 1

uncrown *vb* to remove from a position of prominence or power (as a throne) ⟨*uncrowned* the king when he married a commoner⟩ — see DEPOSE 1

unctuous *adj* **1** not being or expressing what one appears to be or express ⟨an *unctuous* effort to appear religious to the voters⟩ — see INSINCERE

2 overly or insincerely flattering ⟨an *unctuous* appraisal of the musical talent shown by the boss's daughter⟩ — see FULSOME

uncultivated *adj* **1** existing without human habitation or cultivation ⟨miles of *uncultivated* land that had never been touched by a plow or an ax⟩ — see WILD 2

2 lacking in refinement or good taste ⟨an *uncultivated* and ignorant philistine who cared only about money⟩ — see COARSE 2

3 not civilized ⟨an *uncultivated* age when people lived just to meet their day-to-day needs⟩ — see SAVAGE 1

uncultured *adj* lacking in refinement or good taste ⟨a dreadful and *uncultured* society that still had the manners of the frontier⟩ — see COARSE 2

uncurbed *adj* showing no signs of being under control ⟨the *uncurbed* energy of the teenage years⟩ — see RAMPANT 1

uncurious *adj* having or showing a lack of interest or concern ⟨how can you be so *uncurious* about the world around you?⟩ — see INDIFFERENT 1

uncurl *vb* to cause to follow a line that is without bends or curls ⟨*uncurled* the ribbon and flattened it out⟩ — see STRAIGHTEN

uncustomary *adj* **1** being out of the ordinary ⟨has *uncustomary* grace and poise for a girl of her age⟩ — see EXCEPTIONAL

2 noticeably different from what is generally found or experienced ⟨anger that was very *uncustomary* for such an even-tempered man⟩ — see UNUSUAL 1

undaunted *adj* feeling or displaying no fear by temperament ⟨*undaunted* despite their repeated failures at starting a business⟩ — see BRAVE

undeceive *vb* to free from mistaken beliefs or foolish hopes ⟨*undeceived* the young woman about the sincerity of the man's intentions⟩ — see DISILLUSION

undecided *adj* **1** not yet settled or decided ⟨a number of *undecided* matters still before the committee⟩ — see PENDING 1

2 not feeling sure about the truth, wisdom, or trustworthiness of someone or something ⟨voters still seem to be *undecided* about that candidate's fitness for the office of president⟩ — see DOUBTFUL 1

undecorated *adj* free from all additions or embellishment ⟨left the room simple and *undecorated* so that she'd be able to concentrate when she studied there⟩ — see PLAIN 1

undefended *adj* lacking protection from danger or resistance against attack ⟨the soldiers marched off, leaving the palace *undefended*⟩ — see HELPLESS 1

undefined *adj* not seen or understood clearly ⟨plagued by *undefined* worries that kept her awake at night⟩ — see FAINT 1

undemonstrative *adj* not feeling or showing emotion ⟨an *undemonstrative* person by nature, he nevertheless loved her very much⟩ — see IMPASSIVE 1

undeniable *adj* not capable of being challenged or proved wrong ⟨*undeniable* evidence of guilt⟩ — see IRREFUTABLE

undeniably *adv* without any question ⟨*undeniably* handsome, he's never been conceited about his looks⟩ — see INDEED 1

under *adj* having not so great importance or rank as another ⟨called for one of the *under* cooks⟩ — see LESSER

under *adv* in or to a lower place ⟨crouch down *under* where they won't see you⟩ — see BELOW 1

under *prep* in a lower position than ⟨found the cat *under* the bed⟩ — see BELOW

underbelly *n* the side or part facing downward from something ⟨the *underbelly* of the old submarine is in bad shape⟩ — see BOTTOM 1

underbody *n* the side or part facing downward from something ⟨the *underbody* of the car was starting to rust⟩ — see BOTTOM 1

underclothes *n pl* clothing intended to be worn underneath other clothing ⟨kept her *underclothes* in a separate drawer⟩ — see UNDERWEAR

underclothing *n* clothing intended to be worn underneath other clothing ⟨he changed his *underclothing* every day⟩ — see UNDERWEAR

undercover *adj* **1** undertaken or done so as to escape being observed or known by others ⟨an *undercover* operation to infiltrate the terrorist operation⟩ — see SECRET 1

2 working on missions in which one's objectives, activities, or true identity are not publicly revealed ⟨for months she's been an *undercover* agent pretending to be a drug dealer⟩ — see SECRET 2

undergarments *n pl* clothing intended to be worn underneath other clothing ⟨pack plenty of warm *undergarments* for the ski vacation⟩ — see UNDERWEAR

undergo *vb* to come to a knowledge of (something) by living through it ⟨students in this program must *undergo* two years of rigorous training⟩ — see EXPERIENCE

underground *adj* undertaken or done so as to escape being observed or known by others ⟨an *underground* operation to smuggle ancient artifacts out of the country⟩ — see SECRET 1

underground *n* a secret organization in a conquered country fighting against enemy forces ⟨joined the *underground* while still a teenager⟩ — see RESISTANCE 2

underhand *adj* **1** given to or marked by cheating and deception ⟨willing to stoop to *underhand* methods in order to win⟩ — see DISHONEST 2

2 undertaken or done so as to escape being observed or known by others ⟨a quick, *underhand* move to swap the cards⟩ — see SECRET 1

underhanded *adj* **1** given to or marked by cheating and deception ⟨I wouldn't have anything to do with that *underhanded* car dealer⟩ — see DISHONEST 2

2 undertaken or done so as to escape being observed or known by others ⟨an *underhanded* attempt at infiltrating the other party's headquarters⟩ — see SECRET 1

underline *vb* to indicate the importance of by giving prominent display ⟨a report that *underlines* the contributions of fathers to successful, happy families⟩ — see EMPHASIZE

underling *n* one who is of lower rank and typically under the authority of another ⟨he instructed his *underlings* to carry out the order immediately⟩
synonyms inferior, junior, subordinate
related words attendant, follower, retainer; domestic, menial, steward; flunky (*also* flunkey), henchman, lackey, minion; adjutant, aid, aide, assistant, coadjutor, deputy, second; helpmate, helpmeet, mate, sidekick
near antonyms boss, captain, chief, foreman, head, headman, helmsman, kingpin, leader, master, taskmaster
antonyms senior, superior

underlying *adj* of or relating to the simplest facts or theories of a subject ⟨the *underlying* differences between democracy and dictatorship⟩ — see ELEMENTARY

underneath *adv* in or to a lower place ⟨the ball rolled under the porch, so you'll have to crawl *underneath* to get it⟩ — see BELOW 1

underpin *vb* to hold up or serve as a foundation for ⟨the central beliefs that *underpin* a free society⟩ — see SUPPORT 3

underpinning *n* **1** an immaterial thing upon which something else rests ⟨the *underpinnings* of the theory have recently been called into question⟩ — see BASE 1
2 something that holds up or serves as a foundation for something else ⟨the bridge's *underpinnings* are sagging⟩ — see SUPPORT 1

underprivileged *adj* kept from having the necessities of life or a healthful environment ⟨*underprivileged* children often don't do as well on standardized tests as more privileged students⟩ — see DEPRIVED

underscore *vb* to indicate the importance of by giving prominent display ⟨a history of the Old West that *underscores* the role that pioneer women had in bringing order and stability to the frontier⟩ — see EMPHASIZE

underside *n* the side or part facing downward from something ⟨the *underside* of the cat's coat is pure white⟩ — see BOTTOM 1

undersized *adj* of a size that is less than average ⟨an *undersized* puppy⟩ — see SMALL 1

understand *vb* **1** to form an opinion through reasoning and information ⟨as I *understand* it, this is the best plan that we have⟩ — see INFER 1
2 to have a practical understanding of ⟨I think I *understand* how an engine works now⟩ — see KNOW 1
3 to recognize the meaning of ⟨after a few weeks in Russia I began to *understand* the language a little bit⟩ — see COMPREHEND 1

understanding *adj* having or showing the capacity for sharing the feelings of another ⟨a kind and *understanding* teacher who often helps troubled students⟩ — see SYMPATHETIC 1

understanding *n* **1** an arrangement about action to be taken ⟨they finally came to an *understanding* about what to do about the money that was owed⟩ — see AGREEMENT 2
2 the knowledge gained from the process of coming to know or understand something ⟨a social observer with a deep *understanding* of the problems that the nation's cities face in the 21st century⟩ — see COMPREHENSION

understated *adj* not excessively showy ⟨an *understated* dress that would be appropriate for a business meeting⟩ — see QUIET 2

undersurface *n* the side or part facing downward from something ⟨painted the *undersurface* of the plane blue⟩ — see BOTTOM 1

undertake *vb* to take to or upon oneself ⟨*undertook* the responsibility of raising the orphaned children as their own⟩ — see ASSUME 1

undertaker *n* a person who manages funerals and prepares the dead for burial or cremation ⟨the *undertaker* wore black clothes and a solemn expression⟩ — see FUNERAL DIRECTOR

underwater *adj* living, lying, or occurring below the surface of the water ⟨*underwater* plants don't require as much light to grow as surface plants⟩ ⟨*underwater* exploring takes a long time because you can't move quickly⟩
synonyms aquatic, submarine, submerged, sunken
related words oceanic; abysmal, abyssal, deep, deepsea, deepwater

under way *adj* being in progress or development ⟨the repainting of the massive bridge is one maintenance job that is always *under way*⟩ — see ONGOING 1

underwear *n* clothing intended to be worn underneath other clothing ⟨*underwear* has got to be the most boring thing that one could ever receive as a birthday present!⟩
synonyms underclothes, underclothing, undergarments, undies
related words lingerie; pantie (*or* panty), petticoat, slip, underskirt; briefs, drawers, long johns, pants, shorts, underdrawers, underpants, undershirt, union suit; nightdress, nightgown, nightshirt, pajamas, pj's
near antonyms outerwear

underweight *adj* having little weight ⟨the long illness left him frail and *underweight*⟩ — see ¹LIGHT 1

underwrite *vb* to provide money for ⟨a university willing to *underwrite* an archaeological expedition⟩ — see FINANCE 1

undesired *adj* not searched or asked for ⟨an *undesired* suggestion that I promptly ignored⟩ — see UNSOUGHT

undetermined *adj* **1** not seen or understood clearly ⟨an *undetermined* form seen only from a distance⟩ — see FAINT 1
2 not yet settled or decided ⟨the fate of the prisoners is still *undetermined*⟩ — see PENDING 1

undeviating *adj* not varying ⟨an *undeviating* dedication to duty⟩ — see UNIFORM

undies *n pl* clothing intended to be worn underneath other clothing ⟨likes to wear silk *undies*⟩ — see UNDERWEAR

undiluted *adj* free from added matter ⟨*undiluted* cranberry juice would be too strong for anyone to drink⟩ — see PURE 1

undisturbed *adj* free from emotional or mental agitation ⟨didn't tell him the sad news until after the test, so he would remain *undisturbed*⟩ — see CALM 2

undivided *adj* not divided or scattered among several areas of interest or concern ⟨a teacher who insists on the *undivided* attention of her students⟩ — see WHOLE 1

undo *vb* **1** to deprive of courage or confidence ⟨the sudden shriek *undid* the campers⟩ — see UNNERVE 1
2 to disengage the knotted parts of ⟨*undo* a tangled shoelace⟩ — see UNTIE
3 to trouble the mind of; to make uneasy ⟨the mere mention of the incident still had the power to *undo* her⟩ — see DISTURB 1

undomesticated *adj* living outdoors without taming or domestication by humans ⟨*undomesticated* cattle can actually be dangerous to people⟩ — see WILD 1

undoubtedly *adv* without any question 〈we will *undoubtedly* have to do some editing of our home video〉 — see INDEED 1

undress *vb* to remove clothing from 〈Mom *undressed* the mud-covered little toddler and plopped her in the bath〉
synonyms disrobe, strip, unclothe
related words bare, denude, divest, expose, uncover, undrape, unveil; bark, flay, peel, skin
near antonyms apparel, array, attire, caparison, clothe, costume, cover, deck, feather, garb, garment, invest, rig (out), vest; cloak, mantle; drape, swaddle, swathe; accoutre (*or* accouter), equip, furnish, outfit
antonyms dress, gown, robe

undressed *adj* **1** being such as found in nature and not altered by processing or refining 〈*undressed* animal hides〉 — see CRUDE 1
2 lacking or shed of clothing 〈an *undressed* patient waiting to be examined by the doctor〉 — see NAKED 1

undue *adj* going beyond a normal or acceptable limit in degree or amount 〈try to avoid *undue* delay〉 — see EXCESSIVE

unduly *adv* beyond a normal or acceptable limit 〈*unduly* upset by the slight delay of our departure〉 — see TOO 1

undyed *adj* lacking an addition of color 〈pieces of *undyed* leather〉 — see COLORLESS

undying *adj* lasting forever 〈a duet in which the singers swear *undying* love for one another〉 — see EVERLASTING

uneager *adj* showing little or no interest or enthusiasm 〈received the usual *uneager* response when she asked for volunteers to help clean up〉 — see TEPID 1

unearth *vb* to remove from place of burial 〈*unearthed* a hoard of treasures from the Egyptian tomb〉 — see EXHUME

unearthing *n* the act or process of sighting or learning the existence of something for the first time 〈the *unearthing* of a prehistoric man who had been preserved in an Alpine glacier proved to be a great boon to science〉 — see DISCOVERY 1

unearthly *adj* **1** being so extraordinary or abnormal as to suggest powers which violate the laws of nature 〈an *unearthly* knack for picking winning lottery numbers〉 — see SUPERNATURAL 2
2 fearfully and mysteriously strange or fantastic 〈an *unearthly* wail came from the darkness〉 — see EERIE
3 of, relating to, or being part of a reality beyond the observable physical universe 〈*unearthly* messages that she believed were coming from her deceased father〉 — see SUPERNATURAL 1

uneasiness *n* **1** a disturbed or uneasy state 〈a general *uneasiness* descended over the city in the wake of a series of unsolved murders〉 — see UNREST
2 an uneasy state of mind usually over the possibility of an anticipated misfortune or trouble 〈her *uneasiness* ended once she heard the perfectly rational explanation〉 — see ANXIETY 1

uneasy *adj* **1** feeling or showing uncomfortable feelings of uncertainty 〈I'm a bit *uneasy* about taking a baby on such a long trip〉 — see NERVOUS 1
2 lacking or denying rest 〈an *uneasy* night sleeping in his car〉 — see RESTLESS 1
3 lacking social grace and assurance 〈a shy lad, he's always a bit *uneasy* at parties〉 — see AWKWARD 1

uneducated *adj* lacking in education or the knowledge gained from books 〈a literary reference that could not be grasped by an *uneducated* person〉 — see IGNORANT 1

unembarrassed *adj* not embarrassed or ashamed 〈an *unembarrassed* gaze of an autograph seeker at a movie premiere〉 — see UNABASHED

unemotional *adj* not feeling or showing emotion 〈a surprisingly *unemotional* expression for someone who was just informed that his wife was missing〉 — see IMPASSIVE 1

unending *adj* lasting forever 〈the pain you will experience from the procedure will not be *unending*, although it may seem so at the time〉 — see EVERLASTING

unendurable *adj* more than can be put up with 〈this heat is *unendurable*〉 — see UNBEARABLE

unenjoyable *adj* not giving pleasure to the mind or senses 〈an *unenjoyable* evening spent working〉 — see UNPLEASANT

unenthusiastic *adj* showing little or no interest or enthusiasm 〈an *unenthusiastic* response to the suggestion that they take in another stray dog〉 — see TEPID 1

unequal *adj* not staying constant 〈*unequal* pulsations of the heart that might be a sign of trouble〉 — see UNEVEN 2

unequaled *or* **unequalled** *adj* having no equal or rival for excellence or desirability 〈a horse of *unequaled* beauty〉 — see ONLY 1

unequivocal *adj* **1** having no exceptions or restrictions 〈received *unequivocal* authorization to proceed with the project〉 — see ABSOLUTE 2
2 not subject to misinterpretation or more than one interpretation 〈an *unequivocal* frown showed that he was not happy with the situation〉 — see CLEAR 2
3 so clearly expressed as to leave no doubt about the meaning 〈the *unequivocal* directions on the vial state that the drug should not be taken by pregnant women〉 — see EXPLICIT

unerring *adj* not being or likely to be wrong 〈an *unerring* taste in interior decoration〉 — see INFALLIBLE 1

unessential *adj* not needed by the circumstances or to accomplish an end 〈fancy clothes, while fun to wear, are *unessential* to the enjoyment of classical music〉 — see UNNECESSARY

unethical *adj* **1** not conforming to a high moral standard; morally unacceptable 〈*unethical* treatment of prisoners of war that was a clear violation of international law〉 — see BAD 2
2 not guided by or showing a concern for what is right 〈an *unethical* attorney, he had no qualms about getting off clients who he knew were guilty〉 — see UNPRINCIPLED

uneven *adj* **1** not having a level or smooth surface 〈we had to plane and sand down the *uneven* wooden board before we could paint it〉
synonyms broken, bumpy, coarse, irregular, jagged, lumpy, pebbly, ragged, rough, roughened, rugged, scraggy
related words lopsided, unbalanced; inexact, irregular, unaligned; rutted, rutty, undulating, wavy; burred, harsh, nubbly, nubby, scraggly, scratchy; nonuniform
near antonyms exact, uniform; aligned, regular, true; horizontal, tabular; plumb, straight, vertical; flush
antonyms even, flat, level, plane, smooth
2 not staying constant 〈the level of attendance at the ball park has been very *uneven* this season〉
synonyms changing, erratic, fluctuating, irregular, unequal, unstable, unsteady, varying
related words capricious, changeable, changeful, choppy, fickle, fluid, inconsistent, inconstant, mercurial, mutable, uncertain, unsettled, variable, volatile

antonyms changeless, constant, stable, steady, unchanging, unvarying

3 inclined or twisted to one side ⟨an *uneven* grin⟩ — see AWRY

unexampled *adj* having no equal or rival for excellence or desirability ⟨a period of *unexampled* success for the company⟩ — see ONLY 1

unexceptional *adj* being of the type that is encountered in the normal course of events ⟨an *unexceptional* design that no one could recall later on⟩ — see ORDINARY 1

unexpected *adj* not expected ⟨the pop quiz was *unexpected*, but fortunately I was prepared⟩

   synonyms unanticipated, unforeseen, unlooked-for

   related words unintended, unplanned; improbable, unlikely; startling, surprising

   near antonyms predicted, prophesied

   antonyms anticipated, expected, foreseen

unexpectedly *adv* without warning ⟨the snow started *unexpectedly*⟩ — see UNAWARES

unexplainable *adj* impossible to explain ⟨a series of *unexplainable* weather events⟩ — see INEXPLICABLE

unexpressed *adj* understood although not put into words ⟨they shared an *unexpressed* but nevertheless deep affection⟩ — see IMPLICIT

unfailing *adj* **1** not being or likely to be wrong ⟨an *unfailing* judge of personal character⟩ — see INFALLIBLE 1

2 not likely to fail ⟨something that I found to be an *unfailing* remedy for a cold⟩ — see INFALLIBLE 2

unfailingly *adv* on every relevant occasion ⟨he *unfailingly* cooks dinner for the family⟩ — see ALWAYS 1

unfair *adj* not being in accordance with the rules or standards of what is fair in sport ⟨a team that is notorious throughout the league for its record of *unfair* play⟩ — see FOUL 2

unfairness *n* the state of being unfair or unjust ⟨the *unfairness* of the referee's decision made her furious⟩ — see INJUSTICE 1

unfaithful *adj* not true in one's allegiance to someone or something ⟨colonists who later proved to be *unfaithful* to the cause of independence⟩ — see FAITHLESS

unfaithfulness *n* **1** lack of faithfulness especially to one's husband or wife ⟨he eventually forgave his wife's *unfaithfulness*⟩ — see INFIDELITY 1

2 the act or fact of violating the trust or confidence of another ⟨the *unfaithfulness* of the person she had considered her best friend was deeply hurtful⟩ — see BETRAYAL

unfamiliar *adj* not known or experienced before ⟨ordered an *unfamiliar* wine and was surprised to find that it was much drier than what they were used to⟩ — see NEW 2

unfamiliarity *n* the state of being unaware or uninformed ⟨some intense studying rapidly remedied my *unfamiliarity* with the subject⟩ — see IGNORANCE 1

unfashionable *adj* marked by an obvious lack of style or good taste ⟨an old and *unfashionable* jacket that someone had donated to charity⟩ — see TACKY 1

unfasten *vb* to disengage the knotted parts of ⟨gently *unfastened* the strings of the baby's hood⟩ — see UNTIE

unfathomable *adj* **1** being or seeming to be without limits ⟨the *unfathomable* wilderness that greeted the first inhabitants of the continent⟩ — see INFINITE

2 impossible to understand ⟨for some *unfathomable* reason the family decided to venture out into the blizzard⟩ — see INCOMPREHENSIBLE

unfavorable *adj* opposed to one's interests ⟨appealed the *unfavorable* judgment of the lower court⟩ — see ADVERSE 1

unfeeling *adj* **1** having or showing a lack of sympathy or tender feelings ⟨gave the homeless people on the street only an *unfeeling* glance⟩ — see HARD 1

2 lacking in sensation or feeling ⟨her heart was as cold and hard as the *unfeeling* marble statue in her garden⟩ — see NUMB

unfeignedly *adv* without any attempt to impress by deception or exaggeration ⟨parents who are *unfeignedly* enthusiastic about the man their daughter has chosen to marry⟩ — see NATURALLY 3

unfeminine *adj* having qualities or traits that are traditionally considered inappropriate for a girl or woman ⟨in bygone days pants were considered *unfeminine*, and even women bicycling were expected to wear skirts⟩

   synonyms hoydenish, manlike, mannish, tomboyish, unladylike, unwomanly

   related words gentlemanly, male, manly, masculine

   near antonyms effeminate, girlish, sissy, unmanly, unmasculine, womanish, womanlike; distaff, petticoat

   antonyms female, feminine, ladylike, womanly

unfetter *vb* to set free (as from slavery or confinement) ⟨authorities eventually *unfettered* the menagerie of wild animals that had been kept illegally as pets⟩ — see FREE 1

unfit *adj* **1** lacking qualities (as knowledge, skill, or ability) required to do a job ⟨just because I don't have actual work experience doesn't mean I'm *unfit* for the job⟩ — see INCOMPETENT

2 not appropriate for a particular occasion or situation ⟨casual china that was rather *unfit* for such a formal dinner⟩ — see INAPPROPRIATE

unfitness *n* **1** the quality or state of being unsuitable or unfitting ⟨the obvious *unfitness* of my little handsaw for the task of cutting down the large tree⟩ — see INAPPROPRIATENESS 1

2 the quality or state of not being socially proper ⟨the manifest *unfitness* of such a coarse gesture at an elegant party⟩ — see IMPROPRIETY 1

unflagging *adj* showing no signs of weariness even after long hard effort ⟨being rewarded for the *unflagging* zeal with which she led the fund-raising campaign⟩ — see TIRELESS

unflappable *adj* not easily panicked or upset ⟨the *unflappable* teacher never even blinked when the wall map came crashing down⟩

   synonyms imperturbable, nerveless, unshakable

   related words calm, collected, composed, cool, coolheaded, nonchalant, placid, self-possessed, serene, tranquil, undisturbed, unperturbed, unruffled, unshaken, untroubled, unworried

   near antonyms panicky; aflutter, anxious, dithery, edgy, het up, hung up, jittery, jumpy, nervous, nervy, perturbed, shaky, tense, troubled, uneasy, upset, uptight, worried

   antonyms perturbable, shakable

unfledged *adj* lacking in adult experience or maturity ⟨the kind of mistake in judgment that an *unfledged* youth could be expected to make⟩ — see CALLOW

unflinching *adj* showing no signs of slackening or yielding in one's purpose ⟨he was *unflinching* in his determination to see that justice was done⟩ — see UNYIELDING 1

unfold *vb* **1** to arrange the parts of (something) over a wider area ⟨carefully *unfold* that antique map so that it doesn't tear⟩ — see OPEN 3

2 to gradually become clearer or more detailed ⟨as the situation *unfolded,* it became clear that more help would be needed⟩ — see DEVELOP 1

3 to produce flowers ⟨the rosebud *unfolded* literally overnight⟩ — see BLOOM

unforced *adj* done, made, or given with one's own free will ⟨the participation of the people on the project must be *unforced,* or it really isn't a volunteer effort⟩ — see VOLUNTARY 1

unforeseen *adj* not expected ⟨there are almost always *unforeseen* consequences for any major endeavor⟩ — see UNEXPECTED

unforgivable *adj* too bad to be excused or justified ⟨an *unforgivable* crime that society must seek just punishment for⟩ — see INEXCUSABLE

unformed *adj* having no definite or recognizable form ⟨what was once an *unformed* lump of clay is now an attractive, useful bowl⟩ — see FORMLESS

unfortunate *adj* **1** bringing about ruin or misfortune ⟨an *unfortunate* chain of events destroyed the business⟩ — see FATAL 1

2 having, prone to, or marked by bad luck ⟨up to that point in her life she had been *unfortunate* in love⟩ — see UNLUCKY

3 of a kind to cause great distress ⟨an *unfortunate* choice of words that would later prove to be embarrassing for the talk show host⟩ — see REGRETTABLE

unfounded *adj* having no basis in reason or fact ⟨the accusation proved to be *unfounded*⟩ — see GROUNDLESS

unfriendly *adj* **1** lacking in friendliness or warmth of feeling ⟨the *unfriendly* looks quickly warmed when we were recognized as long-unseen relatives⟩ — see COLD 2

2 marked by opposition or ill will ⟨an *unfriendly* nation⟩ — see HOSTILE 1

3 opposed to one's interests ⟨the claim that the state's numerous regulations create a climate *unfriendly* to small businesses⟩ — see ADVERSE 1

unfrozen *adj* freed from a frozen state by exposure to warmth ⟨a recently *unfrozen* section of land⟩ — see THAWED

unfruitful *adj* not able to produce fruit or offspring ⟨disappointed to discover that the mare was *unfruitful*⟩ — see STERILE 1

unfunny *adj* not joking or playful in mood or manner ⟨the documentary takes an *unfunny* look at the excessive drinking often found at college parties⟩ — see SERIOUS 1

ungainly *adj* **1** difficult to use or operate especially because of size, weight, or design ⟨an *ungainly* machine for one person to try to operate⟩ — see CUMBERSOME

2 lacking in physical ease and grace in movement or in the use of the hands ⟨she had become a somewhat *ungainly* exerciser by her eighth month of pregnancy⟩ — see CLUMSY 1

ungentle *adj* harsh and threatening in manner or appearance ⟨a demanding and *ungentle* land that was not for the fainthearted⟩ — see GRIM 1

ungodly *adj* falling short of a standard ⟨the *ungodly* performances of some of the contestants at the talent show⟩ — see BAD 1

ungovernable *adj* given to resisting authority or another's control ⟨a troubled youth who was deemed by his parents to be hopelessly *ungovernable*⟩ — see DISOBEDIENT

2 given to resisting control or discipline by others ⟨resigned to the fact that my cat is basically an *ungovern*-

able beast with a will of his own⟩ — see UNCONTROLLABLE

ungoverned *adj* showing no signs of being under control ⟨an *ungoverned* rage that quickly turned violent⟩ — see RAMPANT 1

ungraceful *adj* lacking social grace and assurance ⟨an *ungraceful* but well-meaning hostess⟩ — see AWKWARD 1

ungracious *adj* showing a lack of manners or consideration for others ⟨an *ungracious* demand for a second serving when other people were still waiting to be served⟩ — see IMPOLITE

ungraciousness *n* rude behavior ⟨the *ungraciousness* shown by some of the guests at the school dance⟩ — see DISCOURTESY

ungrateful *adj* not showing gratitude ⟨although the food was being provided for free, the *ungrateful* recipients could not refrain from complaining that it was not to their liking⟩ — see THANKLESS 1

ungrounded *adj* **1** having no basis in reason or fact ⟨an *ungrounded* suspicion that his neighbors were spying on him⟩ — see GROUNDLESS

2 not informed about or aware of something ⟨dismayed that some of the students were *ungrounded* in even the basics of English grammar⟩ — see IGNORANT 2

unguarded *adj* **1** free in expressing one's true feelings and opinions ⟨the swimming coach was completely *unguarded* in his appraisal of the boy's chances of ever making it to the Olympics⟩ — see FRANK

2 lacking protection from danger or resistance against attack ⟨an *unguarded* gate that would later prove to be the fatal weakness in the city's defenses⟩ — see HELPLESS 1

3 not paying or showing close attention especially for the purpose of avoiding trouble ⟨in an *unguarded* moment I let my mind wander and smashed my car into a tree⟩ — see CARELESS 1

unhampered *adj* showing no signs of being under control ⟨has an *unhampered* enthusiasm for just about every kind of sporting activity⟩ — see RAMPANT 1

unhandsome *adj* unpleasant to look at ⟨a boy who is perhaps *unhandsome* but very kind and good-natured⟩ — see UGLY 1

unhandy *adj* **1** difficult to use or operate especially because of size, weight, or design ⟨a large and *unhandy* boat to use on such a narrow body of water⟩ — see CUMBERSOME

2 lacking in physical ease and grace in movement or in the use of the hands ⟨an *unhandy* person should be kept away from knives and other sharp objects⟩ — see CLUMSY 1

unhappily *adv* with feelings of bitterness or grief ⟨an *unhappily* married couple being counseled by a professional⟩ — see HARD 2

unhappiness *n* a state or spell of low spirits ⟨with time the young woman got over her *unhappiness*⟩ — see SADNESS

unhappy *adj* **1** feeling unhappiness ⟨he's been *unhappy* ever since his family's move, which took him away from all his friends⟩ — see SAD 1

2 having, prone to, or marked by bad luck ⟨an *unhappy* effort to start a business⟩ — see UNLUCKY

3 not appropriate for a particular occasion or situation ⟨a guest unintentionally made *unhappy* reference to what is a painful situation for the family⟩ — see INAPPROPRIATE

unhealthful *adj* bad for the well-being of the body ⟨too much junk food is *unhealthful*⟩ — see UNHEALTHY 1

unhealthiness *n* the condition of not being in good health ⟨remedied his general *unhealthiness* with a change to a healthy diet and exercise⟩ — see SICKNESS 1

unhealthy *adj* 1 bad for the well-being of the body ⟨we knew that the junk food at the carnival was *unhealthy*, but it tasted so good!⟩
synonyms noisome, noxious, unhealthful, unwholesome
related words insanitary, unhygienic, unsanitary; nonnutritious; poisonous, toxic; fatal, lethal, mortal
near antonyms hygienic, sanitary; nutritious
antonyms healthful, healthy
2 involving potential loss or injury ⟨an *unhealthy* sport⟩ — see DANGEROUS
3 temporarily suffering from a disorder of the body ⟨she's been *unhealthy* for almost a week now⟩ — see SICK 1

unheard–of *adj* not known or experienced before ⟨houses selling at *unheard-of* prices⟩ — see NEW 2

unheroic *adj* having or showing a shameful lack of courage ⟨has the rather *unheroic* policy of simply not getting involved when there's a cry for help⟩ — see COWARDLY

unhindered *adj* showing no signs of being under control ⟨with *unhindered* anger she told him just what she thought of him⟩ — see RAMPANT 1

unhinge *vb* 1 to cause to go insane or as if insane ⟨the endless harassment by the guards completely *unhinged* the prisoners of war⟩ — see CRAZE
2 to trouble the mind of; to make uneasy ⟨I was momentarily *unhinged* by the unexpected question⟩ — see DISTURB 1

unhurried *adj* moving or proceeding at less than the normal, desirable, or required speed ⟨the *unhurried* pace of the people ahead of me was frustrating, as I was already late⟩ — see SLOW 1

unidentified *adj* 1 known but not named ⟨an *unidentified* worker reported the problem⟩ — see CERTAIN 1
2 not named or identified by a name ⟨some *unidentified* person helped them and then left quietly⟩ — see NAMELESS 1

unification *n* the act or an instance of joining two or more things into one ⟨the *unification* of East and West Germany⟩ — see UNION 1

uniform *adj* not varying ⟨with flat-screen TVs, picture sharpness is *uniform* over the entire screen, even in the corners⟩
synonyms invariant, steady, unchanging, undeviating, unvarying, unwavering
related words immutable, invariable, unalterable, unchangeable
antonyms changing, deviating, varying

uniform *n* the distinctive clothing worn by members of a particular group ⟨the band *uniform* was brown with red and white stripes⟩
synonyms livery, outfit
related words fatigues, full dress, regimentals; costume, finery, regalia

unify *vb* 1 to bring (something) to a central point or under a single control ⟨will *unify* the several departments into a single operation⟩ — see CENTRALIZE
2 to come together to form a single unit ⟨the two labor unions *unified* in order to strengthen their bargaining position with the manufacturers⟩ — see UNITE 1

unimaginable *adj* too extraordinary or improbable to believe ⟨a nearly *unimaginable* string of coincidences⟩ — see INCREDIBLE

unimportant *adj* lacking importance ⟨we figured that the details were *unimportant* as long as we got the basic design correct⟩
synonyms frivolous, inconsequential, inconsiderable, insignificant, little, minor, minute, negligible, slight, small, small-fry, trifling, trivial
related words jerkwater, one-horse; paltry, petty, worthless; anonymous, nameless, obscure, uncelebrated, unknown
near antonyms decisive, fatal, fateful; distinctive, exceptional, impressive, outstanding, prominent, remarkable; valuable, worthwhile, worthy; distinguished, eminent, great, illustrious, preeminent, prestigious; famous, notorious, renowned; all-important, basic, essential, fundamental
antonyms big, consequential, eventful, important, major, material, meaningful, momentous, significant, substantial, weighty

uninflammable *adj* incapable of being burned ⟨an *uninflammable* stage curtain⟩ — see INCOMBUSTIBLE

uninformed *adj* not informed about or aware of something ⟨I was *uninformed* of the change in plans⟩ — see IGNORANT 2

uninhibited *adj* showing feeling freely ⟨an *uninhibited* child who laughed and cried with equal abandon⟩ — see DEMONSTRATIVE

uninstructed *adj* lacking in education or the knowledge gained from books ⟨gathered the village's children, who were *uninstructed* for the most part, and formed a school⟩ — see IGNORANT 1

unintelligent *adj* not having or showing an ability to absorb ideas readily ⟨you're not *unintelligent*, so you must just be stubbornly resisting all attempts to teach you something⟩ — see STUPID 1

unintelligible *adj* impossible to understand ⟨uttered only a string of *unintelligible* murmurs⟩ — see INCOMPREHENSIBLE

unintended *adj* 1 happening by chance ⟨backyard digging that resulted in *unintended* damage to buried phone wires⟩ — see ACCIDENTAL
2 not made or done willingly or by choice ⟨a response that yielded an *unintended* insight into her personal character⟩ — see INVOLUNTARY 1

unintentional *adj* 1 happening by chance ⟨an *unintentional* injury⟩ — see ACCIDENTAL
2 not made or done willingly or by choice ⟨an *unintentional* insult that nevertheless was very hurtful⟩ — see INVOLUNTARY 1

uninterested *adj* having or showing a lack of interest or concern ⟨a surprisingly *uninterested* group of sixth graders being led through the museum of natural history⟩ — see INDIFFERENT 1

uninteresting *adj* causing weariness, restlessness, or lack of interest ⟨a particularly *uninteresting* lesson that had many students yawning⟩ — see BORING

uninterrupted *adj* going on and on without any interruptions ⟨a movie comedy that is 90 minutes of *uninterrupted* hilarity⟩ — see CONTINUOUS

uninvited *adj* not searched or asked for ⟨I always ignore *uninvited* advice⟩ — see UNSOUGHT

union *n* 1 the act or an instance of joining two or more things into one ⟨the *union* of nonstop action, many plot twists, and pulsating music make this a thrilling movie⟩
synonyms combination, combining, connecting, con-

nection, consolidation, coupling, junction, linking, merging, unification

related words amalgamation, blend, commingling, compounding, fusion, intermingling, intermixture, mingling, mix, mixture; reunification, reunion

near antonyms detachment, divorcement, separation, severance

antonyms breakup, disconnection, dissociation, dissolution, disunion, division, parting, partition, schism, split

2 an association of persons, parties, or states for mutual assistance and protection 〈in 1949 the U.S. and Canada joined their European allies in a transatlantic *union* to defend Western Europe from aggression by the Soviet Union〉 — see CONFEDERACY

3 the state of having shared interests or efforts (as in social or business matters) 〈the movie studio is producing the film in *union* with another studio because of the tremendous cost involved〉 — see ASSOCIATION 1

unique *adj* **1** of, relating to, or belonging to a single person 〈a *unique* characteristic〉 — see INDIVIDUAL 1

2 being out of the ordinary 〈a *unique* hairstyle that people often commented about and always remembered〉 — see EXCEPTIONAL

3 being the one or ones of a class with no other members 〈the huge glass globe that visitors can walk through is *unique*—there's not another one like it anywhere〉 — see ONLY 2

4 noticeably different from what is generally found or experienced 〈a *unique* ability to add large sums in his head〉 — see UNUSUAL 1

unison *n* the act or fact of being of one opinion about something 〈the entire committee is in *unison* on this point〉 — see AGREEMENT 1

unite *vb* **1** to come together to form a single unit 〈using the microscope, we watched the water droplets *unite* into a single pool〉

synonyms associate, coalesce, combine, conjoin, conjugate, connect, couple, fuse, join, link (up), marry, unify

related words mate, yoke; ally, confederate, league; chain, compound, hitch, hook; congregate, gather, meet; recombine, rejoin, reunify, reunite

near antonyms detach, disconnect, disjoin, disjoint, dissociate, disunite, divide, divorce, fractionate, isolate, resolve, uncouple, unyoke; disband, disperse, scatter

antonyms break up, dissever, part, section, separate, sever, split, sunder, unlink

2 to bring (something) to a central point or under a single control 〈*united* several teams under the new management〉 — see CENTRALIZE

3 to form or enter into an association that furthers the interests of its members 〈parents *united* to reform the school's curriculum〉 — see ALLY

united *adj* **1** having or marked by agreement in feeling or action 〈the party must present a *united* front if it hopes to win the election〉 — see HARMONIOUS 3

2 used or done by a number of people as a group 〈when a campaign to raise funds is this successful, it's only because of the *united* effort of all concerned〉 — see COLLECTIVE

unity *n* a balanced, pleasing, or suitable arrangement of parts 〈there's a *unity* to the sculpture garden that makes it an ideal spot for quiet relaxing〉 — see HARMONY 1

universal *adj* **1** able to do many different kinds of things 〈a *universal* wrench〉 — see VERSATILE

2 belonging or relating to the whole 〈the human race's *universal* need for affection〉 — see GENERAL 1

3 covering everything or all important points 〈the genius of Leonardo da Vinci was *universal*: he was an artist, an architect, an engineer, and a scientist, among other things〉 — see ENCYCLOPEDIC

4 present in all places and at all times 〈after the home team won the national championship, a sense of civic pride was as *universal* as the air〉 — see OMNIPRESENT

universe *n* the whole body of things observed or assumed 〈the theory that the *universe* is constantly expanding〉

synonyms cosmos, creation, macrocosm, nature, world

related words existence, reality

near antonyms nothingness, void

unjustifiable *adj* too bad to be excused or justified 〈an *unjustifiable* attack that must be avenged〉 — see INEXCUSABLE

unjustness *n* the state of being unfair or unjust 〈the sheer *unjustness* of the accusation infuriated her〉 — see INJUSTICE 1

unkempt *adj* **1** lacking in order, neatness, and often cleanliness 〈an *unkempt* and cluttered room〉 — see MESSY

2 lacking neatness in dress or person 〈the stereotype of the *unkempt* but brilliant scientist〉 — see SLOPPY 1

unknowing *adj* **1** lacking in worldly wisdom or informed judgment 〈those *unknowing* people who think that the world is a kindly place are in for a rude awakening〉 — see NAIVE 1

2 not informed about or aware of something 〈the *unknowing* recipient of a surprise party, Linda thought that she was actually going to a meeting〉 — see IGNORANT 2

unknown *adj* **1** happening or existing without one's knowledge 〈*unknown* to me was the fact that while I was out, my family was hurriedly preparing a surprise birthday party〉

synonyms unbeknownst (*also* unbeknown)

related words unperceived, unrecognized, unsuspected; unaware, unconscious, unmindful; unknowing, unsuspecting, unwitting; ignorant, unacquainted, unfamiliar

2 not known or experienced before 〈becoming a father brought *unknown* joy to his life〉 — see NEW 2

3 not widely known 〈looking for a relatively *unknown* singer to record the song〉 — see OBSCURE 2

unlade *vb* to empty or rid of cargo 〈*unlade* the truck as soon as possible〉 — see UNLOAD 1

unladylike *adj* having qualities or traits that are traditionally considered inappropriate for a girl or woman 〈riding a horse astride was once considered an *unladylike* position for a woman〉 — see UNFEMININE

unlash *vb* to disengage the knotted parts of 〈*unlashed* the tied leather belt〉 — see UNTIE

unlawful *adj* contrary to or forbidden by law 〈it is *unlawful* to litter in this state〉 — see ILLEGAL 1

unlearn *vb* to be unable to recall or think of 〈let's hope that over the summer I don't *unlearn* everything I learned over the course of this past year〉 — see FORGET 1

unlearned *adj* lacking in education or the knowledge gained from books 〈although the people of the farming community were largely an *unlearned* lot, they wanted an advanced education for their children〉 — see IGNORANT 1

unleash *vb* **1** to set free (from a state of being held in check) ⟨*unleashed* all of his unspoken love for her in a long letter that he hoped he would have the courage to mail⟩ — see RELEASE 1

2 to find emotional release for ⟨lifting weights is a way for me to *unleash* all the frustrations of the workday⟩ — see TAKE OUT 1

unlettered *adj* lacking in education or the knowledge gained from books ⟨*unlettered* moviegoers could scarcely imagine how little resemblance the film bore to the novel on which it was supposedly based⟩ — see IGNORANT 1

unlike *adj* being not of the same kind ⟨you're trying to compare very *unlike* things—like those proverbial apples and oranges⟩ — see DIFFERENT 1

unlikely *adj* not likely to be true or to occur ⟨it is *unlikely* that he will fail the driving test⟩ — see IMPROBABLE

unlikeness *n* the quality or state of being different ⟨because of the general *unlikeness* of their features, most new acquaintances are surprised to learn that they are brothers⟩ — see DIFFERENCE 1

unlimited *adj* **1** being or seeming to be without limits ⟨no ruler should ever be given *unlimited* power⟩ — see INFINITE

2 not limited or specialized in application or purpose ⟨an insurance policy that offers *unlimited* coverage in case of loss⟩ — see GENERAL 4

unlink *vb* to set or force apart ⟨*unlinked* the railroad cars⟩ — see SEPARATE 1

unlisted *adj* not appearing on a list ⟨she kept her phone number *unlisted* so as to reduce the number of unwanted calls⟩

synonyms uncataloged, unrecorded, unregistered

related words unwritten; unidentified, unspecified; undisclosed, unknown, unrevealed

antonyms cataloged (*or* catalogued), listed, recorded, registered

unliterary *adj* used in or suitable for speech and not formal writing ⟨wrote very *unliterary* but entertaining memoirs⟩ — see COLLOQUIAL 1

unload *vb* **1** to empty or rid of cargo ⟨the dockworkers *unloaded* the ship⟩

synonyms disburden, discharge, disencumber, unburden, unlade, unpack

related words free, lighten, relieve; clear, empty, evacuate, vacate, void

near antonyms charge, cram, fill, heap, jam, jam-pack, stuff

antonyms load, pack

2 to get rid of as useless or unwanted ⟨I can't seem to *unload* this old car—even the charities won't take it!⟩ — see DISCARD

unlock *vb* to set free (from a state of being held in check) ⟨that last insult *unlocked* her tongue, and she finally said what she really thought⟩ — see RELEASE 1

unlooked–for *adj* not expected ⟨the interesting stuff found in the attic was an *unlooked-for* bonus for the new homeowners⟩ — see UNEXPECTED

unloose *vb* to set free (from a state of being held in check) ⟨the familiar scent *unloosed* a flood of pleasant memories from her childhood⟩ — see RELEASE 1

unloosen *vb* to set free (from a state of being held in check) ⟨a relaxing bath *unloosened* all the mental and physical tension that had been building throughout the day⟩ — see RELEASE 1

unlovely *adj* **1** not giving pleasure to the mind or senses ⟨Sunday night is often spoiled by the *unlovely* thought of having to go back to school or work the next morning⟩ — see UNPLEASANT

2 unpleasant to look at ⟨an *unlovely* but efficient little machine⟩ — see UGLY 1

unlucky *adj* having, prone to, or marked by bad luck ⟨the *unlucky* campers had rain all week⟩ ⟨an *unlucky* throw of the dice⟩

synonyms hapless, ill-fated, ill-starred, luckless, starcrossed, unfortunate, unhappy

related words adverse, ill, inauspicious, unfavorable, unpromising, untoward; calamitous, catastrophic, disastrous; damned, doomed, tragic

near antonyms blessed, favored, gifted, privileged; auspicious, fair, favorable, golden, promising, propitious

antonyms fortunate, happy, lucky

unmake *vb* to remove from a position of prominence or power (as a throne) ⟨a movie studio chief who likes to boast that he can *unmake* any star in Hollywood if he wishes⟩ — see DEPOSE 1

unman *vb* **1** to deprive of courage or confidence ⟨the near crash of their airplane was a completely *unmanning* experience⟩ — see UNNERVE 1

2 to lessen the courage or confidence of ⟨players refusing to be *unmanned* by the loss of a single game⟩ — see DISCOURAGE 1

unmanageable *adj* given to resisting control or discipline by others ⟨an *unmanageable* dog who had to be returned to the pound⟩ — see UNCONTROLLABLE

unmanly *adj* having or displaying qualities more suitable for women than for men ⟨an *unmanly* shedding of tears that may have cost the candidate his bid for the White House⟩ — see EFFEMINATE

unmannerly *adj* showing a lack of manners or consideration for others ⟨in an *unmannerly* disregard for anyone else's comfort, she turned up the heat without saying a word⟩ — see IMPOLITE

unmarried *adj* not married ⟨a girl who swore she'd remain *unmarried* for her whole life⟩ — see SINGLE 1

unmask *vb* **1** to make known (as information previously kept secret) ⟨*unmasked* the corporation's plans to merge with its chief rival⟩ — see REVEAL 1

2 to reveal the true nature of ⟨*unmasked* the motives of the people advocating the sale of the publicly owned land⟩ — see EXPOSE 1

unmatched *adj* **1** being one of a pair or set without a corresponding mate ⟨a drawer full of *unmatched* socks⟩ — see ODD 1

2 having no equal or rival for excellence or desirability ⟨the house cat is a mouse-hunting machine of *unmatched* efficiency⟩ — see ONLY 1

unmelodious *adj* marked by or producing a harsh combination of sounds ⟨the *unmelodious* clatter of children running around the kitchen during breakfast⟩ — see DISSONANT

unmerciful *adj* having or showing a lack of sympathy or tender feelings ⟨an *unmerciful* insistence that all the kids earn their allowances⟩ — see HARD 1

unmindful *adj* not informed about or aware of something ⟨*unmindful* of the consequences of such a rash decision⟩ — see IGNORANT 2

unmistakable *adj* not subject to misinterpretation or more than one interpretation ⟨a glint in his eye that was an *unmistakable* expression of greed⟩ — see CLEAR 2

unmitigated *adj* having no exceptions or restrictions ⟨two political rivals who have an *unmitigated* contempt for one another⟩ — see ABSOLUTE 2

unmixed *adj* free from added matter ⟨chocolate has a great taste, but I prefer my milk *unmixed*⟩ — see PURE 1

unmoral *adj* not guided by or showing a concern for what is right ⟨an *unmoral* desire to succeed at any cost⟩ — see UNPRINCIPLED

unmovable *adj* incapable of moving or being moved ⟨the tree was *unmovable*, so we designed the garden pond around it⟩ — see IMMOVABLE 1

unmusical *adj* marked by or producing a harsh combination of sounds ⟨a very *unmusical* chorus of squawks from the ravens, who were upset⟩ — see DISSONANT

unnamed *adj* **1** known but not named ⟨used some *unnamed* procedure for testing the accuracy of the device⟩ — see CERTAIN 1
2 not named or identified by a name ⟨the battlefield grave of an *unnamed* soldier⟩ — see NAMELESS 1

unnatural *adj* **1** departing from some accepted standard of what is normal ⟨a baby with a very *unnatural* taste for sour foods⟩ — see DEVIANT
2 lacking in natural or spontaneous quality ⟨just before the debate, the candidates flashed *unnatural* smiles for the cameras⟩ — see ARTIFICIAL 1

unnecessary *adj* not needed by the circumstances or to accomplish an end ⟨a hair dryer was an *unnecessary* item on a trip to the desert⟩
synonyms dispensable, gratuitous, needless, nonessential, uncalled-for, unessential, unwarranted
related words discretionary, elective, optional; extra, extraneous, irrelevant, redundant, superfluous
near antonyms all-important, crucial, important, vital; imperative, pressing, urgent
antonyms essential, indispensable, necessary, needed, needful, required

unnerve *vb* **1** to deprive of courage or confidence ⟨the riding accident so *unnerved* me that for a while I was afraid to get back on a horse⟩
synonyms demoralize, emasculate, undo, unman, unstring
related words debilitate, enervate, enfeeble, weaken; prostrate, sap, soften, tire, waste; frighten, scare, terrify, terrorize; daunt, discourage, dishearten, dismay, dispirit; craze, derange, madden, unbalance, unhinge; discompose, disquiet, disturb, faze, perturb, unsettle, upset
near antonyms fortify, strengthen; embolden, encourage, hearten
antonyms nerve
2 to lessen the courage or confidence of ⟨a figure skater can't afford to be *unnerved* by an occasional slipup⟩ — see DISCOURAGE 1

unnerving *adj* marked by or causing agitation or uncomfortable feelings ⟨quite an *unnerving* storm for youngsters just learning to sail⟩ — see NERVOUS 3

unnoted *adj* not widely known ⟨a collection of paintings by relatively *unnoted* artists⟩ — see OBSCURE 2

unnoticeable *adj* not readily seen or noticed ⟨a nearly *unnoticeable* change in the color⟩ — see UNOBTRUSIVE

unnumbered *adj* too many to be counted ⟨fields with *unnumbered* sheep⟩ — see COUNTLESS

unobstructed *adj* allowing passage without obstruction ⟨only one *unobstructed* road was available⟩ — see OPEN 1

unobtainable *adj* hard or impossible to get to or get at ⟨that information is *unobtainable* as long as my computer is down⟩ — see INACCESSIBLE

unobtrusive *adj* not readily seen or noticed ⟨the notice that an 18% tip would be automatically added was so *unobtrusive* we almost didn't see it at the bottom of the menu⟩
synonyms inconspicuous, unnoticeable
related words unnoticed; impalpable, imperceptible, inappreciable, indistinguishable, insensible; faint, indistinct, obscure; concealed, hidden
near antonyms arresting, eye-catching, showy, striking; apparent, blatant, clear, distinct, evident, manifest, obvious, plain, unmistakable
antonyms conspicuous, noticeable

unoriginal *adj* using or marked by the use of something else as a basis or model ⟨*unoriginal* essays will be graded harshly⟩ — see IMITATIVE

unorthodox *adj* **1** deviating from commonly accepted beliefs or practices ⟨a time when people with *unorthodox* religious views were banished from the colony⟩ — see HERETICAL
2 not bound by traditional ways or beliefs ⟨raised by an aunt, whose *unorthodox* parenting practices made for a strange but fun childhood⟩ — see LIBERAL 1
3 not rigidly following established form, custom, or rules ⟨an *unorthodox* but effective procedure for opening a wine bottle without a corkscrew⟩ — see INFORMAL 1

unpack *vb* to empty or rid of cargo ⟨*unpacked* the car the minute they got back from vacation⟩ — see UNLOAD 1

unpaid *adj* not yet paid ⟨my goal is to have no *unpaid* balances on my credit cards⟩ — see OUTSTANDING 1

unpainted *adj* lacking an addition of color ⟨the wooden shingles on the island's houses are usually left *unpainted*, and over time the salt air turns them a soft gray⟩ — see COLORLESS

unpaired *adj* being one of a pair or set without a corresponding mate ⟨found an *unpaired* shoe in the back of the closet⟩ — see ODD 1

unpalatable *adj* disagreeable or disgusting to the sense of taste ⟨pasta and honey is an *unpalatable* combination⟩ — see DISTASTEFUL 1

unparalleled *adj* having no equal or rival for excellence or desirability ⟨on the table was a vase of *unparalleled* beauty⟩ — see ONLY 1

unpardonable *adj* too bad to be excused or justified ⟨regards cruelty to animals as an *unpardonable* sin⟩ — see INEXCUSABLE

unperturbed *adj* free from emotional or mental agitation ⟨remained *unperturbed* despite the latest problems in the construction of their new house⟩ — see CALM 2

unplanned *adj* **1** happening by chance ⟨an *unplanned* change in our itinerary—we got lost!⟩ — see ACCIDENTAL
2 made or done without previous thought or preparation ⟨stumbled through a completely *unplanned* acceptance speech⟩ — see EXTEMPORANEOUS

unpleasant *adj* not giving pleasure to the mind or senses ⟨the burnt pot roast had a very *unpleasant* odor⟩
synonyms bad, disagreeable, displeasing, distasteful, nasty, rotten, sour, uncongenial, unlovely, unpleasing, unsatisfying, unwelcome
related words abhorrent, abominable, appalling, awful, beastly, disgusting, dreadful, foul, hideous, horrendous, horrible, horrid, invidious, loathsome, nauseating, noisome, obnoxious, obscene, odious, repellent (*also* repellant), repugnant, repulsive, revolting, scandalous, shocking, sickening, ugly, villainous; annoying, galling, irritating, vexing
near antonyms delectable, delicious, delightful, dreamy, felicitous; affable, amiable, friendly, genial,

good-natured, good-tempered, gracious, sweet, well-disposed
antonyms agreeable, congenial, good, grateful, gratifying, nice, palatable, pleasant, pleasing, pleasurable, satisfying, welcome

unpleasing *adj* **1** not giving pleasure to the mind or senses ⟨an *unpleasing* combination of flavors in the dish⟩ — see UNPLEASANT
2 unpleasant to look at ⟨an *unpleasing* combination of fuchsia and green⟩ — see UGLY 1

unpolished *adj* lacking in refinement or good taste ⟨an *unpolished* but well-meaning young man⟩ — see COARSE 2

unprecedented *adj* not known or experienced before ⟨this is an *unprecedented* request for the reference desk⟩ — see NEW 2

unpredictable *adj* likely to change frequently, suddenly, or unexpectedly ⟨*unpredictable* spring weather that makes it really hard to know what to wear⟩ — see FICKLE 1

unprejudiced *adj* marked by justice, honesty, and freedom from bias ⟨an *unprejudiced* judicial opinion⟩ — see FAIR 2

unpremeditated *adj* **1** happening by chance ⟨an *unpremeditated* encounter with an old classmate⟩ — see ACCIDENTAL
2 made or done without previous thought or preparation ⟨an *unpremeditated* verbal attack that was prompted by an unexpected question at the press conference⟩ — see EXTEMPORANEOUS

unprepared *adj* made or done without previous thought or preparation ⟨an obviously *unprepared* acceptance speech by the surprise winner⟩ — see EXTEMPORANEOUS

unpretending *adj* free from any intent to deceive or impress others ⟨an *unpretending* manner that makes her quite a winning performer⟩ — see GUILELESS

unpretentious *adj* **1** free from any intent to deceive or impress others ⟨a simple and *unpretentious* speech⟩ — see GUILELESS
2 not excessively showy ⟨lives in a rather *unpretentious* house for someone so wealthy⟩ — see QUIET 2
3 not having or showing any feelings of superiority, self-assertiveness, or showiness ⟨the *unpretentious* disposition of an award-winning scientist who has nothing to prove to anyone⟩ — see HUMBLE 1

unpretentiously *adv* without any attempt to impress by deception or exaggeration ⟨a restaurant reviewer who writes engagingly but *unpretentiously* about food⟩ — see NATURALLY 3

unpretty *adj* unpleasant to look at ⟨an *unpretty* accumulation of trash right next to the entrance to the restaurant⟩ — see UGLY 1

unprincipled *adj* not guided by or showing a concern for what is right ⟨the *unprincipled* businessman made a lot of money—and didn't care how he made it⟩
synonyms cutthroat, immoral, Machiavellian, unconscionable, unethical, unmoral, unscrupulous
related words calculating, intriguing, opportunistic, scheming; merciless, pitiless, remorseless, ruthless; crooked, deceitful, dishonest; corrupt, debased, debauched, decadent, degenerate, degraded, demoralized, depraved, dissipated
near antonyms good, just, noble, righteous, virtuous
antonyms ethical, moral, principled, scrupulous

unprintable *adj* depicting or referring to sexual matters in a way that is unacceptable in polite society ⟨uttered an *unprintable* oath⟩ — see OBSCENE 1

unprocessed *adj* being such as found in nature and not altered by processing or refining ⟨*unprocessed* foods that still have much of their original flavor⟩ — see CRUDE 1

unproductive *adj* **1** producing inferior or only a small amount of vegetation ⟨crop rotation had prevented the farmland from becoming *unproductive*⟩ — see BARREN 1
2 producing no results ⟨weeks of *unproductive* effort at trying to write a novel⟩ — see FUTILE

unprofessional *adj* lacking or showing a lack of expert skill ⟨an *unprofessional* carelessness about the accuracy of the news story⟩ — see AMATEURISH

unprofitable *adj* producing no results ⟨an *unprofitable* effort to find the information⟩ — see FUTILE

unprogressive *adj* tending to favor established ideas, conditions, or institutions ⟨a candidate with *unprogressive* ideas about public education⟩ — see CONSERVATIVE 1

unprotected *adj* lacking protection from danger or resistance against attack ⟨I was uncomfortable about leaving my house *unprotected*, so I bought a dog⟩ — see HELPLESS 1

unqualified *adj* **1** having no exceptions or restrictions ⟨the new play is an *unqualified* success⟩ — see ABSOLUTE 2
2 lacking qualities (as knowledge, skill, or ability) required to do a job ⟨if we hire an *unqualified* candidate, we'll just be wasting our time⟩ — see INCOMPETENT
3 not limited or specialized in application or purpose ⟨an *unqualified* denial of the charges⟩ — see GENERAL 4

unquestionable *adj* not capable of being challenged or proved wrong ⟨a person of *unquestionable* integrity⟩ — see IRREFUTABLE

unquestionably *adv* without any question ⟨we are *unquestionably* early for this party, since there's not another soul in sight⟩ — see INDEED 1

unquiet *adj* **1** feeling or showing uncomfortable feelings of uncertainty ⟨plagued with an *unquiet* mind the whole time her son was stationed overseas⟩ — see NERVOUS 1
2 lacking or denying rest ⟨an *unquiet* curiosity that impelled him to study the world about him relentlessly⟩ — see RESTLESS 1

unravel *vb* **1** to separate the various strands of ⟨it took us forever to *unravel* the jumbled mass of Christmas tree lights⟩
synonyms disentangle, ravel (out), unbraid, unsnarl, untangle, untwine, untwist
related words smooth, straighten (out); undo, unlace, unstring, unthread, untie, unwind
near antonyms braid, knot, lace, tie, wind
antonyms entangle, snarl, tangle
2 to find an answer for through reasoning ⟨*unraveled* the mystery⟩ — see SOLVE

unreachable *adj* hard or impossible to get to or get at ⟨my pen fell behind my desk into an *unreachable* spot⟩ — see INACCESSIBLE

unread *adj* lacking in education or the knowledge gained from books ⟨an officer who seemed to be completely *unread* in military theory⟩ — see IGNORANT 1

unreal *adj* **1** conceived or made without regard for reason or reality ⟨a claim that is *unreal* and very distant from the slightest hint of truth⟩ — see FANTASTIC 1
2 not real and existing only in the imagination ⟨the *unreal* world of TV sitcoms⟩ — see IMAGINARY

unreality *n* a conception or image created by the imagination and having no objective reality ⟨a sci-fi author who seems to have preferred the *unrealities* of his own fiction to the realities of the world about him⟩ — see FANTASY 1

unreasonable *adj* **1** having no basis in reason or fact ⟨an *unreasonable* assumption⟩ — see GROUNDLESS

2 not using or following good reasoning ⟨an *unreasonable* worship for a man who did not deserve it⟩ — see ILLOGICAL

unreasoning *adj* not using or following good reasoning ⟨an *unreasoning* argument based on some false assumptions⟩ — see ILLOGICAL

unrecorded *adj* not appearing on a list ⟨an *unrecorded* contribution⟩ — see UNLISTED

unrecoverable *adj* **1** not capable of being cured or reformed ⟨believed that there was no such thing as an *unrecoverable* criminal⟩ — see HOPELESS 1

2 not capable of being repaired, regained, or undone ⟨made an *unrecoverable* mess of it⟩ — see IRREPARABLE

unredeemable *adj* **1** not capable of being cured or reformed ⟨*unredeemable* sinners⟩ — see HOPELESS 1

2 not capable of being repaired, regained, or undone ⟨assured the senior citizens that there was no such thing as an *unredeemable* error when operating a computer⟩ — see IRREPARABLE

unrefined *adj* **1** being such as found in nature and not altered by processing or refining ⟨*unrefined* sugar⟩ — see CRUDE 1

2 hastily or roughly constructed ⟨an *unrefined* mountaineer's hut⟩ — see RUDE 1

3 lacking in refinement or good taste ⟨guilty of such *unrefined* behavior as eating with their mouths open⟩ — see COARSE 2

unregistered *adj* not appearing on a list ⟨an *unregistered* car⟩ — see UNLISTED

unrehearsed *adj* made or done without previous thought or preparation ⟨an *unrehearsed* speech of thanks⟩ — see EXTEMPORANEOUS

unrelenting *adj* **1** sticking to an opinion, purpose, or course of action in spite of reason, arguments, or persuasion ⟨that teacher tends to be *unrelenting* about deadlines⟩ — see OBSTINATE

2 showing no signs of slackening or yielding in one's purpose ⟨*unrelenting* in the pursuit of equality for all races⟩ — see UNYIELDING 1

unremarkable *adj* being of the type that is encountered in the normal course of events ⟨a quiet and *unremarkable* child⟩ — see ORDINARY 1

unremitting *adj* going on and on without any interruptions ⟨*unremitting* rain that lasted for six days⟩ — see CONTINUOUS

unrepentant *adj* not sorry for having done wrong ⟨she was *unrepentant* about punching the bully in the nose⟩ — see REMORSELESS

unreserved *adj* **1** free in expressing one's true feelings and opinions ⟨the politician was criticized for being too *unreserved* in his pronouncements on touchy subjects⟩ — see FRANK

2 showing feeling freely ⟨people in that part of the world tend to be *unreserved* mourners, and funerals are marked by loud wailing⟩ — see DEMONSTRATIVE

unresistant *adj* **1** lacking protection from danger or resistance against attack ⟨a weakened immune system that rendered him *unresistant* to pneumonia⟩ — see HELPLESS 1

2 receiving or enduring without offering resistance ⟨the baby became limp and *unresistant* when picked up⟩ — see PASSIVE

unresisting *adj* receiving or enduring without offering resistance ⟨protestors who were *unresisting* when arrested⟩ — see PASSIVE

unresolved *adj* not yet settled or decided ⟨we have to deal with several *unresolved* issues⟩ — see PENDING 1

unrest *n* a disturbed or uneasy state ⟨*unrest* gripped the city as the people nervously awaited the expected bombardment⟩ ⟨his stomach *unrest* was just a sign of stage fright⟩

synonyms disquiet, ferment, restiveness, restlessness, turmoil, uneasiness

related words fidgets; agitation, commotion, confusion, tumult, turbulence, upheaval; anarchy, chaos, disorder

near antonyms order, orderliness

antonyms calm, ease, peace, quiet

unrestful *adj* lacking or denying rest ⟨spent an *unrestful* night worrying about her children⟩ — see RESTLESS 1

unrestrained *adj* **1** not bound by rigid standards ⟨a playful and *unrestrained* teacher⟩ — see EASYGOING 2

2 not bound, confined, or detained by force ⟨*unrestrained* dogs⟩ — see FREE 3

3 showing feeling freely ⟨acting happy and *unrestrained* at the celebration⟩ — see DEMONSTRATIVE

4 showing no signs of being under control ⟨*unrestrained* laughter⟩ — see RAMPANT 1

unrestraint *n* carefree freedom from constraint ⟨the cheerful *unrestraint* of children⟩ — see ABANDON

unrestricted *adj* **1** freely available for use or participation by all ⟨it's an *unrestricted* marathon—anyone can run in it⟩ — see OPEN 2

2 not bound by rigid standards ⟨the author of the book has an *unrestricted* view of what qualifies as "art"⟩ — see EASYGOING 2

3 not limited or specialized in application or purpose ⟨an *unrestricted* license to operate a motor vehicle⟩ — see GENERAL 4

unrighteous *adj* not conforming to a high moral standard; morally unacceptable ⟨an *unrighteous* act that cannot go unpunished⟩ — see BAD 2

unripe *adj* lacking in adult experience or maturity ⟨*unripe* and inexperienced recruits that are not ready for combat⟩ — see CALLOW

unripened *adj* lacking in adult experience or maturity ⟨the *unripened* thoughts of a young writer with limited life experiences⟩ — see CALLOW

unrivaled *or* **unrivalled** *adj* having no equal or rival for excellence or desirability ⟨a violinist who is hailed for his *unrivaled* musicianship⟩ — see ONLY 1

unruliness *n* refusal to obey ⟨any *unruliness* will be cause for ejection from this class⟩ — see DISOBEDIENCE

unruly *adj* **1** given to resisting authority or another's control ⟨*unruly* pupils were given detention as a matter of course⟩ — see DISOBEDIENT

2 given to resisting control or discipline by others ⟨a camp that was known as a place where *unruly* youths were given their last chance to shape up⟩ — see UNCONTROLLABLE

3 not restrained by or under the control of legal authority ⟨*unruly* mobs roamed the streets of the capital after the government leaders had fled⟩ — see LAWLESS

unsafe *adj* **1** involving potential loss or injury ⟨workers are forbidden from engaging in *unsafe* activities on company time⟩ — see DANGEROUS

2 not paying or showing close attention especially for the purpose of avoiding trouble ⟨people who have a record of being *unsafe* drivers usually have to pay higher insurance premiums⟩ — see CARELESS 1

unsatisfactorily *adv* in an unsatisfactory way ⟨finished the project on time, but did it *unsatisfactorily*⟩ — see BADLY

unsatisfactory *adj* falling short of a standard ⟨an *unsatisfactory* first attempt at building a birdhouse⟩ — see BAD 1

unsatisfying *adj* not giving pleasure to the mind or senses ⟨although the play certainly has some interesting moments, ultimately it was *unsatisfying*⟩ — see UNPLEASANT

unsavory *adj* **1** disagreeable or disgusting to the sense of taste ⟨an *unsavory* blend of spices that simply overwhelmed the fish's delicate flavor⟩ — see DISTASTEFUL 1

2 not conforming to a high moral standard; morally unacceptable ⟨*unsavory* doings that ruined the couple's good name in the community⟩ — see BAD 2

unsay *vb* to solemnly or formally reject or go back on (as something formerly adhered to) ⟨the witness tried to *unsay* the very testimony that he had given a few days earlier⟩ — see ABJURE

unschooled *adj* lacking in education or the knowledge gained from books ⟨an *unschooled* woman who desperately wanted to learn how to read⟩ — see IGNORANT 1

unscrupulous *adj* not guided by or showing a concern for what is right ⟨an *unscrupulous* businessman manipulated them into selling their land for practically nothing⟩ — see UNPRINCIPLED

unseasonable *adj* occurring before the usual or expected time ⟨an *unseasonable* snowstorm in early November⟩ — see EARLY 2

unseasonably *adv* before the usual or expected time ⟨it's been *unseasonably* hot this spring⟩ — see EARLY

unseat *vb* to remove from a position of prominence or power (as a throne) ⟨a governor who was *unseated* by the first successful recall in the state's history⟩ — see DEPOSE 1

unsecured *adj* not tightly fastened, tied, or stretched ⟨an *unsecured* luggage rack on top of the car that was a hazard to other vehicles on the road⟩ — see LOOSE 1

unseemly *adj* not appropriate for a particular occasion or situation ⟨an *unseemly* interest in their host's income and expenses⟩ — see INAPPROPRIATE

unselfish *adj* giving or sharing in abundance and without hesitation ⟨an *unselfish* man who spends much of his time helping his community⟩ — see GENEROUS 1

unselfishness *n* the quality or state of being generous ⟨her natural *unselfishness* sometimes attracts those who would take advantage⟩ — see LIBERALITY

unsettle *vb* to trouble the mind of; to make uneasy ⟨the funny noise that the car is making really *unsettles* me⟩ — see DISTURB 1

unsettled *adj* **1** likely to change frequently, suddenly, or unexpectedly ⟨we've been having a lot of *unsettled* weather lately⟩ — see FICKLE 1

2 not yet paid ⟨I keep *unsettled* bills next to the checkbook⟩ — see OUTSTANDING 1

3 not yet settled or decided ⟨we can't move on as long as this important question remains *unsettled*⟩ — see PENDING 1

4 not feeling sure about the truth, wisdom, or trustworthiness of someone or something ⟨I'm still *unsettled* about whether I should take that job⟩ — see DOUBTFUL 1

unsettling *adj* **1** causing worry or anxiety ⟨*unsettling* new developments in the effort to bring peace and stability to that region⟩ — see TROUBLESOME

2 marked by or causing agitation or uncomfortable feelings ⟨had the *unsettling* task of picking out a coffin and making the other funeral arrangements for his father⟩ — see NERVOUS 2

unshakable *adj* not easily panicked or upset ⟨we need the kind of leader who will be *unshakable* in a national crisis⟩ — see UNFLAPPABLE

unshaken *adj* free from emotional or mental agitation ⟨she remained *unshaken* throughout the ordeal⟩ — see CALM 1

unshaped *adj* having no definite or recognizable form ⟨an *unshaped* mass of clay that was just in need of some inspiration from the modeler⟩ — see FORMLESS

unshared *adj* belonging only to the one person, unit, or group named ⟨with her older sister off to college, she was thrilled to have an *unshared* bedroom for the first time in her life⟩ — see SOLE 1

unshielded *adj* lacking protection from danger or resistance against attack ⟨a warship attacking an *unshielded* merchantman⟩ — see HELPLESS 1

unshorn *adj* covered with or as if with hair ⟨the sight of their *unshorn* heads is something that these male recruits will not see during their basic training⟩ — see HAIRY 1

unsightly *adj* unpleasant to look at ⟨strip-mining leaves an *unsightly* gash in the landscape⟩ — see UGLY 1

unskilled *adj* **1** lacking or showing a lack of expert skill ⟨an *unskilled* handling of the facial features in the painted portrait⟩ — see AMATEURISH

2 lacking qualities (as knowledge, skill, or ability) required to do a job ⟨hired *unskilled* workers because they would work for lower wages⟩ — see INCOMPETENT

unskillful *adj* **1** lacking qualities (as knowledge, skill, or ability) required to do a job ⟨an *unskillful* editor can be worse than none at all⟩ — see INCOMPETENT

2 lacking or showing a lack of expert skill ⟨some painfully *unskillful* playing by the band's guitarist⟩ — see AMATEURISH

unsmiling *adj* not joking or playful in mood or manner ⟨delivered the lecture with a harsh and *unsmiling* face⟩ — see SERIOUS 1

unsnarl *vb* to separate the various strands of ⟨*unsnarled* the fishing lines⟩ — see UNRAVEL 1

unsociable *adj* having or showing a lack of friendliness or interest in others ⟨an *unsociable* but not an overtly rude child⟩ — see COOL 1

unsoiled *adj* free from dirt or stain ⟨never managed to make it through the day with *unsoiled* shoes⟩ — see CLEAN 1

unsolicited *adj* not searched or asked for ⟨tired of the *unsolicited* advice from friends and family⟩ — see UNSOUGHT

unsolvable *adj* incapable of being solved or accomplished ⟨an apparently *unsolvable* problem⟩ — see IMPOSSIBLE

unsophisticated *adj* lacking in worldly wisdom or informed judgment ⟨mistakenly believed that the tribe was *unsophisticated* and would sell their land for a fraction of its worth⟩ — see NAIVE 1

unsophistication *n* **1** the quality or state of being simple and sincere ⟨the *unsophistication* of the plea touched his heart⟩ — see NAÏVETÉ 1

2 the quality or state of having a form or structure of few parts or elements ⟨the *unsophistication* of the cof-

feemaker's design is part of its appeal⟩ — see SIMPLIC-
ITY 1

unsought *adj* not searched or asked for ⟨the meddling
neighbor insisted on giving us *unsought* advice⟩
synonyms unasked, unbidden (*also* unbid), undesired,
uninvited, unsolicited, unwanted, unwelcome
related words objectionable, offensive, unacceptable,
undesirable; uncalled-for, unnecessary
near antonyms necessary, needed, required
antonyms desired, solicited, wanted, welcome

unsound *adj* **1** having or showing a very abnormal or
sick state of mind ⟨disgruntled relatives had to prove
that the woman was of *unsound* mind when she made
her will⟩ — see INSANE 1
2 not being in agreement with what is true ⟨an *unsound*
and dangerous assumption⟩ — see FALSE 1
3 not using or following good reasoning ⟨it is clearly
unsound to argue that just because it's raining right
now, it will rain for the rest of our vacation⟩ — see IL-
LOGICAL
4 temporarily suffering from a disorder of the body ⟨an
unsound horse that will have to be disqualified from
the race⟩ — see SICK 1

unsoundness *n* the condition of not being in good
health ⟨the overall *unsoundness* of her health in her
last years greatly limited what she could do⟩ — see
SICKNESS 1

unsparing *adj* **1** giving or sharing in abundance and
without hesitation ⟨neighbors were *unsparing* in their
charity when a local family was rendered homeless by
a fire⟩ — see GENEROUS 1
2 having or showing a lack of sympathy or tender feelings ⟨*unsparing* in his criticism of the welfare state⟩ —
see HARD 1

unspeakable *adj* beyond the power to describe ⟨beheld
unspeakable beauty in their travels through the Alps⟩
— see INDESCRIBABLE

unspecialized *adj* not limited or specialized in application or purpose ⟨preferred to have one *unspecialized*
tool rather than buy 16 specialized ones⟩ — see GEN-
ERAL 4

unspecified *adj* known but not named ⟨some *unspecified*
person is expected to replace him⟩ — see CERTAIN 1

unspoken *adj* understood although not put into words
⟨an *unspoken* promise to remain faithful to one an-
other⟩ — see IMPLICIT

unsportsmanlike *adj* not being in accordance with the
rules or standards of what is fair in sport ⟨was suspended for *unsportsmanlike* conduct⟩ — see FOUL 2

unstable *adj* **1** not being in or able to maintain a state of
balance ⟨when we put the books down on the *unstable*
desk, the whole stack went crashing to the floor⟩
synonyms unbalanced, unsteady
related words rickety, shaky, tottery, wobbly; cockeyed, lopsided, uneven
near antonyms even, level, straight; sound, sturdy, substantial
antonyms balanced, stable, steady
2 likely to change frequently, suddenly, or unexpectedly ⟨financial investors don't like an *unstable* econ-
omy⟩ — see FICKLE 1
3 not staying constant ⟨*unstable* temperatures are not
ideal storage conditions for wine⟩ — see UNEVEN 2

unstained *adj* lacking an addition of color ⟨bought an
unstained picnic table they planned to finish them-
selves⟩ — see COLORLESS

unsteadiness *n* the quality or state of not being firmly
fixed in position ⟨the *unsteadiness* of the candle would
seem to constitute a fire hazard⟩ — see INSTABILITY

unsteady *adj* **1** lacking in steadiness or regularity of occurrence ⟨a year of *unsteady* economic growth⟩ — see
FITFUL
2 likely to change frequently, suddenly, or unexpectedly ⟨in the days of sailing ships, mariners were constantly at the mercy of *unsteady* winds⟩ — see
FICKLE 1
3 not being in or able to maintain a state of balance
⟨cautiously climbed up the *unsteady* ladder⟩ — see
UNSTABLE 1
4 not staying constant ⟨*unsteady* business conditions
that rattled investors⟩ — see UNEVEN 2

unstop *vb* to arrange clear passage of (something) by removing obstructions ⟨the plumber *unstopped* the
drain⟩ — see OPEN 2

unstopped *adj* allowing passage without obstruction ⟨an
unstopped hole⟩ — see OPEN 1

unstring *vb* **1** to cause to go insane or as if insane ⟨the
kind of fierce combat that can *unstring* even hardened
soldiers⟩ — see CRAZE
2 to deprive of courage or confidence ⟨a little *unstrung*
by the fact that he was competing in the National
Spelling Bee for the first time⟩ — see UNNERVE 1

unstructured *adj* having no definite or recognizable
form ⟨writes *unstructured* compositions that some people might not even regard as poems⟩ — see FORMLESS

unstylish *adj* marked by an obvious lack of style or good
taste ⟨chose a bizarrely *unstylish* hairstyle for the Halloween party⟩ — see TACKY 1

unstylishly *adv* in a careless or unfashionable manner
⟨tends to dress *unstylishly* because she prefers to worry
about other things⟩ — see SLOPPILY

unsubstantial *adj* **1** not composed of matter ⟨as thin and
unsubstantial as the wind⟩ — see IMMATERIAL 1
2 being of a material lacking in sturdiness or substance
⟨*unsubstantial* wisps of lace⟩ — see FLIMSY 1
3 lacking bodily strength ⟨an *unsubstantial* child who
was unfit to play sports of any kind⟩ — see WEAK 1

unsubstantiated *adj* having no basis in reason or fact
⟨an *unsubstantiated* claim that was thrown out of
court⟩ — see GROUNDLESS

unsuccessful *adj* producing no results ⟨an *unsuccessful*
attempt to fix the faucet ourselves⟩ — see FUTILE

unsuitable *adj* not appropriate for a particular occasion
or situation ⟨an *unsuitable* effort to drum up business
for his insurance agency at a friend's funeral⟩ — see
INAPPROPRIATE

unsuitably *adv* in a mistaken or inappropriate way
⟨dressed *unsuitably* for the weather⟩ — see WRONGLY

unsullied *adj* free from dirt or stain ⟨only *unsullied* vestments are ever appropriate for church services⟩ — see
CLEAN 1

unsung *adj* not widely known ⟨an *unsung* hero of the
Holocaust⟩ — see OBSCURE 2

unsupportable *adj* more than can be put up with ⟨these
high taxes are just *unsupportable*⟩ — see UNBEARABLE

unsupported *adj* having no basis in reason or fact ⟨an
unsupported claim that the structure was built by
Vikings⟩ — see GROUNDLESS

unsure *adj* not feeling sure about the truth, wisdom, or
trustworthiness of someone or something ⟨*unsure* of
her ability to handle the pressure of competing in the
Olympic Games⟩ — see DOUBTFUL 1

unsurpassable *adj* having no equal or rival for excellence or desirability ⟨the *unsurpassable* splendor of the palace⟩ — see ONLY 1

unsurpassed *adj* **1** having no equal or rival for excellence or desirability ⟨an artist who is *unsurpassed* at painting portraits⟩ — see ONLY 1
2 of the very best kind ⟨a French restaurant known for its *unsurpassed* cuisine⟩ — see EXCELLENT

unsuspecting *adj* lacking in worldly wisdom or informed judgment ⟨sidewalk vendors selling bogus gems to *unsuspecting* tourists⟩ — see NAIVE 1

unsuspicious *adj* lacking in worldly wisdom or informed judgment ⟨a happy-go-lucky, *unsuspicious* fellow who was easy prey for confidence men⟩ — see NAIVE 1

unsympathetic *adj* **1** having or showing a lack of sympathy or tender feelings ⟨gave them an *unsympathetic* look and pointed out that they'd brought the problem on themselves⟩ — see HARD 1
2 lacking in friendliness or warmth of feeling ⟨an aloof and *unsympathetic* man⟩ — see COLD 2
3 marked by opposition or ill will ⟨a bohemian artist who found the *unsympathetic* environment of the small town too much to bear⟩ — see HOSTILE 1
4 opposed to one's interests ⟨an *unsympathetic* reaction to the proposal⟩ — see ADVERSE 1

untamed *adj* **1** existing without human habitation or cultivation ⟨a dangerous and *untamed* land⟩ — see WILD 2
2 living outdoors without taming or domestication by humans ⟨tried to capture the *untamed* horse⟩ — see WILD 1

untangle *vb* **1** to separate the various strands of ⟨gently *untangled* the baby's hair⟩ — see UNRAVEL 1
2 to set free from entanglement or difficulty ⟨I'll *untangle* you from your financial troubles, but I'm not going to fix all your problems⟩ — see EXTRICATE

untaught *adj* lacking in education or the knowledge gained from books ⟨an *untaught* artist whose primitive paintings are now prized by collectors⟩ — see IGNORANT 1

unthinkable *adj* too extraordinary or improbable to believe ⟨to most people it seemed *unthinkable* that such a gentle man could be guilty of such awful crimes⟩ — see INCREDIBLE

unthrifty *adj* given to spending money freely or foolishly ⟨the *unthrifty* couple ended up having to declare bankruptcy⟩ — see PRODIGAL

unthrone *vb* to remove from a position of prominence or power (as a throne) ⟨a rebellion that eventually *unthroned* a king⟩ — see DEPOSE 1

untidy *adj* **1** lacking in order, neatness, and often cleanliness ⟨could never seem to find anything in the *untidy* office⟩ — see MESSY
2 lacking neatness in dress or person ⟨neighbors gossiped about the woman's rumpled and *untidy* children⟩ — see SLOPPY 1

untie *vb* to disengage the knotted parts of ⟨she always made sure to *untie* her shoelaces before removing her shoes⟩
  synonyms unbind, undo, unfasten, unlash
  related words unbraid, unlace; disentangle, ravel, unravel, unsnarl, untangle, unwind; loose, loosen
  near antonyms braid, interlace, interweave, lace, wind; entangle, snarl, tangle
  antonyms bind, fasten, knot, lash, tie

untimely *adj* occurring before the usual or expected time ⟨the *untimely* arrival of our guests caught us by surprise⟩ — see EARLY 2

untiring *adj* showing no signs of weariness even after long hard effort ⟨the camel's reputation as an *untiring* beast of burden⟩ — see TIRELESS

untitled *adj* not named or identified by a name ⟨working on a book that remains *untitled*⟩ — see NAMELESS 1

untold *adj* too many to be counted ⟨*untold* millions have lived and died in this ancient land⟩ — see COUNTLESS

untouchable *adj* **1** hard or impossible to get to or get at ⟨*untouchable* oil lying deep within the earth⟩ — see INACCESSIBLE
2 not to be violated, criticized, or tampered with ⟨an *untouchable* target for criticism as far as the local newspaper was concerned⟩ — see SACRED 1

untoward *adj* **1** given to resisting authority or another's control ⟨tried to reason with the *untoward* child⟩ — see DISOBEDIENT
2 given to resisting control or discipline by others ⟨a program for *untoward* teenagers that is designed to give them the kind of discipline that their parents were unable or unwilling to administer⟩ — see UNCONTROLLABLE

untreated *adj* being such as found in nature and not altered by processing or refining ⟨*untreated* wool⟩ — see CRUDE 1

untroubled *adj* **1** free from emotional or mental agitation ⟨*untroubled* by household chaos around her⟩ — see CALM 2
2 free from storms or physical disturbance ⟨quietly canoeing on an *untroubled* lake⟩ — see CALM 1

untrue *adj* **1** not being in agreement with what is true ⟨"the sky is purple" is an *untrue* statement⟩ — see FALSE 1
2 not true in one's allegiance to someone or something ⟨*untrue* to his country in its time of need⟩ — see FAITHLESS

untruth *n* **1** a false idea or belief ⟨an argument which relies on an *untruth* is invalid⟩ — see FALLACY 1
2 a statement known by its maker to be untrue and made in order to deceive ⟨used an innocent *untruth* to mislead them into agreeing to help⟩ — see LIE
3 the quality or state of being false ⟨there is an element of *untruth* in all forms of art: works of art provide only a semblance of reality⟩ — see FALLACY 2

untruthful *adj* **1** not being in agreement with what is true ⟨an unintentionally *untruthful* statement⟩ — see FALSE 1
2 telling or containing lies ⟨an *untruthful* excuse won't get you out of doing the work but it will get you into trouble⟩ — see DISHONEST 1

untruthfulness *n* the tendency to tell lies ⟨consistent *untruthfulness* on your part will result in consistent distrustfulness on other people's part⟩ — see DISHONESTY 1

untutored *adj* lacking in education or the knowledge gained from books ⟨to the *untutored* observer these works of art must seem strange indeed⟩ — see IGNORANT 1

untwine *vb* to separate the various strands of ⟨*untwined* his shoelaces⟩ — see UNRAVEL 1

untwist *vb* to separate the various strands of ⟨*untwisted* the ball of thread⟩ — see UNRAVEL 1

unusable *adj* not capable of being put to use or account ⟨a completely *unusable* gadget that's just taking up space in the drawer⟩ — see IMPRACTICAL

unused *adj* **1** not having acquired a habit or tolerance ⟨while in Mexico we tried to stay out of the sun because we were simply *unused* to the tropical heat⟩
synonyms unacclimated, unaccustomed, unadapted, unadjusted
related words unhardened, unseasoned
near antonyms unaffected, uninfluenced
antonyms acclimated, accustomed, adapted, adjusted, habituated, used
2 recently made and never used before ⟨preferred to start with *unused* pencils⟩ — see NEW 3

unusual *adj* **1** noticeably different from what is generally found or experienced ⟨finding some *unusual* shells by the high-tide mark, we brought them home for our collection⟩
synonyms curious, extraordinary, funny, odd, offbeat, peculiar, queer, rare, singular, strange, unaccustomed, uncommon, uncustomary, unique, weird
related words bizarre, eccentric, far-out, outlandish, outré, way-out; aberrant, abnormal, atypical, exceptional, irregular; newsworthy, notable, noteworthy, noticeable, particular, remarkable, special
near antonyms unexceptional; expected, predictable; familiar, normal, regular, typical
antonyms common, ordinary, usual
2 being out of the ordinary ⟨accepted the award with *unusual* grace and humility⟩ — see EXCEPTIONAL

unutterable *adj* beyond the power to describe ⟨*unutterable* joy that a baby can bring to a household⟩ — see INDESCRIBABLE

unvarnished *adj* free from all additions or embellishment ⟨I'm telling the *unvarnished* truth⟩ — see PLAIN 1

unvarying *adj* **1** not undergoing a change in condition ⟨an *unvarying* dedication to the welfare of her community⟩ — see CONSTANT 1
2 not varying ⟨*unvarying* temperatures and humidity are best for the preservation of ancient artifacts⟩ — see UNIFORM

unveil *vb* **1** to make known (as information previously kept secret) ⟨*unveiled* the techniques that the self-styled clairvoyant used to trick her clients⟩ — see REVEAL 1
2 to present so as to invite notice or attention ⟨*unveiled* the new sculpture before a gathering of dignitaries⟩ — see SHOW 1

unvoiced *adj* understood although not put into words ⟨an *unvoiced* promise to be waiting for him when he returned from the war⟩ — see IMPLICIT

unwanted *adj* not searched or asked for ⟨always doing *unwanted* favors for people⟩ — see UNSOUGHT

unwarrantable *adj* too bad to be excused or justified ⟨the *unwarrantable* arrogance of that man⟩ — see INEXCUSABLE

unwarranted *adj* **1** not needed by the circumstances or to accomplish an end ⟨*unwarranted* investigations by the committee⟩ — see UNNECESSARY
2 having no basis in reason or fact ⟨don't leap to *unwarranted* conclusions⟩ — see GROUNDLESS

unwary *adj* **1** lacking in worldly wisdom or informed judgment ⟨mail-order companies that take advantage of *unwary* buyers⟩ — see NAIVE 1
2 not paying or showing close attention especially for the purpose of avoiding trouble ⟨a dangerous stretch of desert that has claimed many *unwary* travelers⟩ — see CARELESS 1

unwavering *adj* not varying ⟨an *unwavering* commitment to justice⟩ — see UNIFORM

unwearying *adj* showing no signs of weariness even after long hard effort ⟨buildings that were saved only because of the *unwearying* efforts of firefighters⟩ — see TIRELESS

unwed *adj* not married ⟨two *unwed* sisters living together⟩ — see SINGLE 1

unwelcome *adj* **1** not giving pleasure to the mind or senses ⟨the *unwelcome* heat of the city⟩ — see UNPLEASANT
2 not searched or asked for ⟨*unwelcome* advances from a coworker⟩ — see UNSOUGHT

unwell *adj* temporarily suffering from a disorder of the body ⟨she missed work because she was *unwell*⟩ — see SICK 1

unwholesome *adj* bad for the well-being of the body ⟨some people claim that fast food is very *unwholesome*⟩ — see UNHEALTHY 1

unwieldy *adj* difficult to use or operate especially because of size, weight, or design ⟨an *unwieldy* machine that requires two people to operate it⟩ — see CUMBERSOME

unwilling *adj* not made or done willingly or by choice ⟨*unwilling* contributions from city employees who felt pressured to make them⟩ — see INVOLUNTARY 1

unwillingness *n* a lack of willingness or desire to do or accept something ⟨your *unwillingness* to help with the cooking means that you don't get to share in the eating⟩ — see RELUCTANCE

unwind *vb* to get rid of nervous tension or anxiety ⟨soft music and a good book help me *unwind*⟩ — see RELAX 1

unwise *adj* **1** showing or marked by a lack of good sense or judgment ⟨made the *unwise* decision to invest in a brand-new company⟩ — see FOOLISH 1
2 showing poor judgment especially in personal relationships or social situations ⟨an *unwise* urge to confide in total strangers⟩ — see INDISCREET

unwitting *adj* **1** happening by chance ⟨an *unwitting* mistake made in copying the material⟩ — see ACCIDENTAL
2 not informed about or aware of something ⟨an *unwitting* accomplice to the crime⟩ — see IGNORANT 2

unwomanly *adj* having qualities or traits that are traditionally considered inappropriate for a girl or woman ⟨aggression and assertiveness were once considered *unwomanly*⟩ — see UNFEMININE

unwonted *adj* being out of the ordinary ⟨honored for the *unwonted* bravery he showed in battle⟩ — see EXCEPTIONAL

unworkable *adj* not capable of being put to use or account ⟨an *unworkable* scheme⟩ — see IMPRACTICAL

unworldliness *n* the quality or state of being simple and sincere ⟨there's a sweet *unworldliness* about her that makes men want to be her protector⟩ — see NAÏVETÉ 1

unworldly *adj* lacking in worldly wisdom or informed judgment ⟨the guy's *unworldly* enough to think that any stranger who would approach him on a city street is simply trying to help him⟩ — see NAIVE 1

unworried *adj* free from emotional or mental agitation ⟨remained *unworried* despite the panic all around her⟩ — see CALM 2

unwritten *adj* made or carried on through speaking rather than in writing ⟨an *unwritten* contract may not be enforceable⟩ — see VERBAL 2

unyielding *adj* **1** showing no signs of slackening or yielding in one's purpose ⟨the pioneers faced the challenge of settling the frontier with *unyielding* courage⟩
synonyms determined, dogged, grim, implacable, relentless, unappeasable, unflinching, unrelenting

related words hardheaded, headstrong, mulish, obdurate, opinionated, peevish, pertinacious, perverse, pigheaded, self-willed, stubborn, uncooperative, willful (*or* wilful); merciless, ruthless, unforgiving

near antonyms slackening, softening, yielding; impotent, invertebrate, slack, spineless, weak

2 having a consistency that does not easily yield to pressure ⟨knead the dough until it feels reasonably *unyielding*⟩ — see FIRM 2

3 incapable of or highly resistant to bending ⟨an *unyielding* steel bar⟩ — see STIFF 1

4 sticking to an opinion, purpose, or course of action in spite of reason, arguments, or persuasion ⟨my parents remained *unyielding* to my pleas for clemency, and I remained at home for the entire weekend⟩ — see OBSTINATE

unyoke *vb* to set or force apart ⟨*unyoke* these two boats and tie them to the dock separately⟩ — see SEPARATE 1

up *adj* **1** being at a higher level than average ⟨the level of the lake is *up* this spring⟩ — see HIGH 2

2 brought or having come to an end ⟨okay, time is *up*⟩ — see COMPLETE 2

3 having information especially as a result of study or experience ⟨she's always *up* on the latest developments⟩ — see FAMILIAR 2

up *vb* **1** to make greater in size, amount, or number ⟨*upped* our allowance⟩ — see INCREASE 1

2 to move from a lower to a higher place or position ⟨*upped* the boat's sail⟩ — see RAISE 1

3 to move or extend upward ⟨the road constantly *ups* and downs as it makes its way over the hills⟩ — see ASCEND

upbeat *adj* **1** having or showing a good mood or disposition ⟨an *upbeat* attitude about life⟩ — see CHEERFUL 1

2 having qualities which inspire hope ⟨several *upbeat* signs that the economy is improving⟩ — see HOPEFUL 1

upbraid *vb* to criticize (someone) severely or angrily especially for personal failings ⟨*upbraided* them for making such a careless mistake⟩ — see SCOLD

upcoming *adj* being soon to appear or take place ⟨an *upcoming* election⟩ — see FORTHCOMING

up–country *n* a rural region that forms the edge of the settled or developed part of a country ⟨built a cabin in the *up-country*⟩ — see FRONTIER 2

upend *vb* to fix in an upright position ⟨we had to *upend* the sofa in order to fit it into the elevator⟩ — see ERECT 1

upgrade *n* **1** an upward slope ⟨had to walk our bicycles on the *upgrades* on our ride through the hills⟩ — see ASCENT 2

2 a raising or a state of being raised to a higher rank or position ⟨received an *upgrade* to lieutenant⟩ — see ADVANCEMENT 1

3 the degree to which something rises up from a position level with the horizon ⟨there's a steep *upgrade* to some of the hills on that route⟩ — see SLANT

upgrade *vb* to move higher in rank or position ⟨*upgraded* them to first class⟩ — see PROMOTE 1

upheaval *n* a violent disturbance (as of the political or social order) ⟨the civil rights movement caused *upheavals* all over the country⟩ — see CONVULSION

uphold *vb* **1** to continue to declare to be true or proper despite opposition or objections ⟨determined to *uphold* her views in the face of all challenges⟩ — see MAINTAIN 2

2 to hold up or serve as a foundation for ⟨an official who is pledged to *uphold* the laws of the land⟩ — see SUPPORT 3

3 to move from a lower to a higher place or position ⟨worshipers *upheld* their joined hands and sang the praises of the Lord⟩ — see RAISE 1

upkeep *n* the act or activity of keeping something in an existing and usually satisfactory condition ⟨the *upkeep* of the old place was costing a fortune⟩ — see MAINTENANCE

upland *n* an area of high ground ⟨the animals huddled on the *upland* as the floodwater rose⟩ — see HEIGHT 4

uplift *vb* to move from a lower to a higher place or position ⟨*uplifted* his head⟩ — see RAISE 1

uplifted *adj* being positioned above a surface ⟨an *uplifted* area of ground⟩ — see ELEVATED 1

upmost *adj* being at a point or level higher than all others ⟨the *upmost* floor of the building⟩ — see TOP 1

upon *prep* in or into contact with ⟨leaned *upon* the desk⟩ — see AGAINST

upper–class *adj* of high birth, rank, or station ⟨*upper-class* boys who believed they were better than everyone else⟩ — see NOBLE 1

upper class *n* the highest class in a society ⟨a school founded to educate the children of the *upper class*⟩ — see ARISTROCRACY

upper crust *n* **1** individuals carefully selected as being the best of a class ⟨the *upper crust* of the fifth-grade class⟩ — see ELITE

2 the highest class in a society ⟨a specialty clothing store for the *upper crust*⟩ — see ARISTROCRACY

upper hand *n* the more favorable condition or position in a competition ⟨finally gained the *upper hand* in the argument⟩ — see ADVANTAGE 1

uppermost *adj* being at a point or level higher than all others ⟨the *uppermost* floor of the house gets very hot in the summer⟩ — see TOP 1

uppish *adj* having a feeling of superiority that shows itself in an overbearing attitude ⟨they were *uppish* and full of themselves⟩ — see ARROGANT

uppity *adj* having a feeling of superiority that shows itself in an overbearing attitude ⟨*uppity* social climbers who were the biggest snobs in town⟩ — see ARROGANT

upraise *vb* **1** to move from a lower to a higher place or position ⟨an earthquake *upraised* an area on one side of the fault⟩ — see RAISE 1

2 to fix in an upright position ⟨archaeologists are still not sure how the mysterious statues on Easter Island were *upraised*⟩ — see ERECT 1

upraised *adj* being positioned above a surface ⟨these *upraised* earthworks are believed to have been built by Native Americans hundreds of years ago and used for enclosure, burial, religious rites, or defense⟩ — see ELEVATED 1

upright *adj* **1** conforming to a high standard of morality or virtue ⟨an honest and *upright* people⟩ — see GOOD 2

2 following the accepted rules of moral conduct ⟨informing the clerk that he had just given me back too much in change was the only *upright* thing to do⟩ — see HONORABLE 1

3 rising straight up ⟨only one pillar of the ruined temple remained *upright*⟩ — see ERECT

uprightness *n* **1** conduct that conforms to an accepted standard of right and wrong ⟨the *uprightness* of our cause is not what is being called into question here⟩ — see MORALITY 1

2 faithfulness to high moral standards ⟨the members of this special investigative committee must be personages of unquestionable *uprightness*⟩ — see HONOR 1

uprise *vb* **1** to leave one's bed ⟨*uprise!* we have lots of work to do today!⟩ — see ARISE 1

2 to move or extend upward ⟨as we went from the coast into the state's interior, the land gradually began *uprising* and eventually we were on mountainous terrain⟩ — see ASCEND

uprising *n* open fighting against authority (as one's own government) ⟨the *uprising* was quickly and brutally suppressed⟩ — see REBELLION

uproar *n* **1** a state of noisy, confused activity ⟨the house is always in a jubilant *uproar* during the holidays⟩ — see COMMOTION

2 a state of wildly excited activity or emotion ⟨the ref's controversial call put the crowd into an *uproar*⟩ — see FRENZY

3 a violent disturbance (as of the political or social order) ⟨the *uproar* created by the institution of a new statewide system of mandatory testing⟩ — see CONVULSION

4 a violent shouting ⟨an *uproar* arose from the crowd when it was announced that the concert was cancelled and refunds might not be available⟩ — see CLAMOR 1

uproarious *adj* causing or intended to cause laughter ⟨an *uproarious* movie⟩ — see FUNNY 1

uproot *vb* to draw out by force or with effort ⟨*uprooted* the old bridge's pilings upon the completion of its replacement⟩ — see EXTRACT

upset *adj* feeling or showing uncomfortable feelings of uncertainty ⟨she was *upset* by the unexplained change in plans⟩ — see NERVOUS 1

upset *n* an act or instance of the order of things being disturbed ⟨the move to a new town is just the latest in a series of *upsets* for my family over the last year⟩
synonyms derangement, dislocation, disruption, disturbance
related words convulsion, revolution, upheaval

upset *vb* **1** to trouble the mind of; to make uneasy ⟨the smallest things can *upset* us if we're already stressed⟩ — see DISTURB 1

2 to turn on one's side or upside down ⟨a wave out of nowhere *upset* our canoe, and suddenly we were in the water⟩ — see CAPSIZE

3 to undo the proper order or arrangement of ⟨the change in the bus schedule *upset* our daily routine⟩ — see DISORDER

upsetting *adj* causing worry or anxiety ⟨the constant arguing is *upsetting* to a sensitive person like your grandmother⟩ — see TROUBLESOME

upshot *n* a condition or occurrence traceable to a cause ⟨the *upshot* of that unexpected kindness has been some thawing of the chilly relations between the two neighbors⟩ — see EFFECT 1

upside–down *adj* lacking in order, neatness, and often cleanliness ⟨the frantic search left the room *upside-down*⟩ — see MESSY

upstanding *adj* **1** following the accepted rules of moral conduct ⟨a fine, *upstanding* woman who deserves to be nominated to the state's highest court⟩ — see HONORABLE 1

2 rising straight up ⟨not a single wall remained *upstanding* after the tornado had passed⟩ — see ERECT

upsweep *vb* to move or extend upward ⟨a tidal wave *upswept* from the sea, virtually destroying the low-lying village⟩ — see ASCEND

uptight *adj* feeling or showing uncomfortable feelings of uncertainty ⟨don't be so *uptight*—it'll work out fine⟩ — see NERVOUS 1

up–to–date *adj* **1** being or involving the latest methods, concepts, information, or styles ⟨demanded the most *up-to-date* computer system available⟩ — see MODERN

2 having information especially as a result of study or experience ⟨I'm afraid that I'm not *up-to-date* on that issue⟩ — see FAMILIAR 2

upturn *vb* to move or extend upward ⟨at this point the road *upturns* steeply, the trees become scarcer, and the valley unfolds before you⟩ — see ASCEND

urbane *adj* having or showing very polished and worldly manners ⟨a gentlemanly and *urbane* host of elegant dinner parties⟩ — see SUAVE

urbanize *vb* to accustom to the ways of the city ⟨every September the city of Boston *urbanizes* a new crop of college students from small towns across the country⟩ — see CITIFY

urchin *n* an appealingly mischievous person ⟨we could never resist the little *urchin's* pleas for candy⟩ — see SCAMP 1

urge *n* a strong wish for something ⟨a sudden *urge* to see the night sky without interference from the bright lights of the city⟩ — see DESIRE

urge *vb* to try to persuade (someone) through earnest appeals to follow a course of action ⟨our teacher *urged* us to do a good job on the assignment⟩
synonyms egg (on), encourage, exhort, goad, press, prod, prompt
related words drive, propel, spur, stimulate; hurry, hustle, push, rush; beseech, implore, importune; blandish, cajole, coax, soft-soap, wheedle; high-pressure, nag, needle, pressure; foment, incite, instigate, provoke, stir (up)
near antonyms deter, discourage, dissuade; brake, check, constrain, curb, hold back, inhibit, restrain

urgent *adj* needing immediate attention ⟨I'll put off until tomorrow everything but the *urgent* issues⟩ — see ACUTE 2

usable *adj* **1** capable of or suitable for being used for a particular purpose ⟨although the spade was *usable* as a snow shovel, it didn't do a very good job⟩
synonyms available, employable, exploitable, fit, functional, operable, practicable, serviceable, useful
related words applicable, relevant; doable, feasible; reusable
near antonyms outdated, outmoded
antonyms impracticable, inoperable, nonfunctional, unavailable, unemployable, unusable

2 capable of being put to use or account ⟨there's a scrap of *usable* information in that article on finding the right pet for one's family⟩ — see PRACTICAL 1

usage *n* the act or practice of employing something for a particular purpose ⟨the now-standard *usage* of computers to search for all manner of information on the Internet⟩ — see USE 1

use *n* **1** the act or practice of employing something for a particular purpose ⟨the *use* of boom boxes was strictly prohibited in the park⟩
synonyms application, employment, exercise, operation, play, usage
related words exertion; reuse
near antonyms disuse

2 the capacity for being useful for some purpose ⟨the broken grill wasn't going to be of much *use* in cooking the hamburgers⟩

synonyms account, avail, service, serviceability, serviceableness, usefulness, utility
related words advantage, benefit, gain; aid, assistance, help; applicability, appropriateness, fitness, relevance; profit, value, worth
near antonyms inapplicability, inappropriateness
antonyms uselessness, worthlessness
3 positive regard for something ⟨I have no *use* for slackers⟩ — see LIKING
use *vb* **1** to put into action or service ⟨I think I'm going to need to *use* the large hammer for this project⟩
synonyms apply, employ, exercise, exploit, harness, operate, utilize
related words handle, manipulate, wield; direct, run, work; recycle, reuse
phrases draw on (*or* upon), make use of
near antonyms ignore, neglect; misapply, misuse
2 to behave toward in a stated way ⟨*used* the new employee with some harshness simply because he was unfamiliar with the way that things were done around there⟩ — see TREAT 1
3 to take unfair advantage of ⟨*used* her friend's secret to make herself more popular with the other girls⟩ — see EXPLOIT 1
used *adj* being in the habit or custom ⟨I'm *used* to getting up early⟩ — see ACCUSTOMED
useful *adj* **1** capable of being put to use or account ⟨*useful* suggestions for limiting the amount of food we eat⟩ — see PRACTICAL 1
2 capable of or suitable for being used for a particular purpose ⟨I've found this tool really *useful* for making sure all my pictures are hung straight⟩ — see USABLE 1
usefulness *n* the capacity for being useful for some purpose ⟨the well-known *usefulness* of thick phone books as seat boosters for short diners⟩ — see USE 2
useless *adj* **1** not capable of being put to use or account ⟨a garage full of *useless* junk⟩ — see IMPRACTICAL
2 producing no results ⟨a *useless* search for my keys⟩ — see FUTILE
user *n* a person who regularly uses drugs especially illegally ⟨a person who started out as a *user* and is now a drug dealer as well⟩ — see DOPER
use up *vb* to make complete use of ⟨*used up* the last of the flour making waffles⟩ — see DEPLETE
usher *vb* to point out the way for (someone) especially from a position in front ⟨*ushered* the job applicant into the room and then left⟩ — see LEAD 1
usual *adj* **1** accepted, used, or practiced by most people ⟨that's not the *usual* method, but it works⟩ — see CURRENT 1
2 being of the type that is encountered in the normal course of events ⟨the characters in this novel are drawn with greater depth than is *usual* for a work of science fiction⟩ — see ORDINARY 1
3 often observed or encountered ⟨the *usual* reaction to the sight of the falls is one of absolute awe⟩ — see COMMON 1

usually *adv* according to the usual course of things ⟨we *usually* go out to eat on Fridays⟩ — see NATURALLY 2
usurp *vb* to take or make use of without authority or right ⟨*usurped* his challenger's right to speak first in the debate⟩ — see APPROPRIATE 1
utensil *n* an article intended for use in work ⟨participants in the class must supply their own writing *utensils*⟩ — see IMPLEMENT
utility *n* the capacity for being useful for some purpose ⟨the measuring cup's *utility* was greatly reduced when the handle broke off⟩ — see USE 2
utilize *vb* to put into action or service ⟨we must *utilize* all the tools at our disposal⟩ — see USE 1
utmost *adj* **1** most distant from a center ⟨supreme power that extended to the *utmost* points of the empire⟩ — see EXTREME 1
2 of the greatest or highest degree or quantity ⟨inhabitants of the war-ravaged region experience the *utmost* misery imaginable⟩ — see ULTIMATE 1
3 of the highest degree ⟨an intelligence operation that must be conducted with the *utmost* secrecy⟩ — see FULL 2
utopia *n* a place or state of great happiness ⟨dreamed of one day retiring to a tropical *utopia*⟩ — see PARADISE 1
utopian *n* one whose conduct is guided more by the image of perfection than by the real world ⟨in the 19th century *utopians* founded a number of short-lived socialist communities⟩ — see IDEALIST
utter *adj* having no exceptions or restrictions ⟨the parish fair was an *utter* success⟩ — see ABSOLUTE 2
utter *vb* **1** to send forth using the vocal chords ⟨she tried not to *utter* a sound as the doctor gave her a flu shot⟩
synonyms emit
related words blurt (out), ejaculate, exclaim; gasp, groan, heave, hoot, moan, pant, quaver, snarl, sob, sputter, squawk, squeak, squeal, stammer, stutter, whimper, yowl; mouth, whisper
2 to express (a thought or emotion) in words ⟨*uttered* a single comment⟩ — see SAY 1
utterance *n* **1** an act, process, or means of putting something into words ⟨many writers have used poetry as a means to give *utterance* to their deepest thoughts⟩ — see EXPRESSION 1
2 something that is said ⟨celebrities whose every *utterance* is treated as though it were newsworthy⟩ — see WORD 2
uttered *adj* created by the body's organs of sound ⟨her first *uttered* cry for help since the start of the ordeal⟩ — see VOCAL
utterly *adv* **1** to a full extent or degree ⟨we are in fact *utterly* out of food⟩ — see FULLY 1
2 to a large extent or degree ⟨as a teacher she was *utterly* overwhelmed by the demands on her time⟩ — see GREATLY 2
uttermost *adj* of the greatest or highest degree or quantity ⟨I have the *uttermost* faith in your abilities⟩ — see ULTIMATE 1

V

vacancy *n* **1** empty space ⟨the vast *vacancy* that exists between our solar system and the nearest star having its own orbiting planets⟩
  synonyms blank, blankness, emptiness, vacuity, void
  related words nothingness; vacuum; bareness, barrenness, bleakness, desolateness, hollowness
  near antonyms fullness, repleteness
  2 the quality or state of being empty ⟨the *vacancy* of the cavernous gymnasium was eerily apparent to me as I shot baskets alone⟩
  synonyms bareness, emptiness, vacuity
  related words hollowness; blankness, vacuum, void; barrenness, bleakness, desolateness; availability, clearness, openness; depletion, dryness, exhaustion
  near antonyms completeness; abundance, fatness, repleteness
  antonyms fullness

vacant *adj* **1** lacking contents that could or should be present ⟨a *vacant* room that could be converted into a classroom⟩ — see EMPTY 1
  2 not being in a state of use, activity, or employment ⟨looking for *vacant* land on which to build a house⟩ — see INACTIVE 2
  3 not expressing any emotion ⟨the prisoner's *vacant* and distracted expression⟩ — see BLANK 1

vacate *vb* to remove the contents of ⟨*vacated* the house⟩ — see EMPTY

vacated *adj* left unoccupied or unused ⟨*vacated* cottages that are easy targets for burglars during the winter⟩ — see ABANDONED

vacation *n* a period during which the usual routine of school or work is suspended ⟨we take a *vacation* at the beach for a week every year⟩
  synonyms break, holiday [*chiefly British*], leave, recess
  related words furlough, liberty; breather, relaxation, respite, rest; interim, intermission, interval; feast, holy day, legal holiday; honeymoon; idling, loafing, lounging, slacking off
  near antonyms routine, work

vacation *vb* to take or spend a vacation ⟨Sue is hoping to *vacation* in Spain this summer⟩
  synonyms holiday
  related words escape, get away; break, ease up, let up, relax, rest; bum, goldbrick, idle, loaf, lounge, slack off
  near antonyms drudge, endeavor, grub, hump, hustle, labor, moil, peg (away), plod, plow, plug, slave, slog, strain, strive, struggle, sweat, toil, travail, work

vacillate *vb* to show uncertainty about the right course of action ⟨*vacillated* for so long that someone else stepped in and made the decision⟩ — see HESITATE

vacillation *n* the act or an instance of pausing because of uncertainty about the right course of action ⟨the President must always be decisive, never showing public *vacillation*⟩ — see HESITATION

vacuity *n* **1** empty space ⟨the seemingly endless *vacuity* between settlements in the desert⟩ — see VACANCY 1
  2 the quality or state of being empty ⟨the *vacuity* of the house after everyone had moved out was striking and depressing⟩ — see VACANCY 2
  3 the quality or state of lacking intelligence or quickness of mind ⟨the *vacuity* of the starlet's comments on the important issues of the day⟩ — see STUPIDITY 1

vacuous *adj* not having or showing an ability to absorb ideas readily ⟨a movie that was derided for its *vacuous* dialogue⟩ — see STUPID 1

vagabond *adj* traveling from place to place ⟨a *vagabond* group of entertainers⟩ — see ITINERANT

vagabond *n* **1** a homeless wanderer who may beg or steal for a living ⟨be wary of the *vagabonds* in that corner of the city⟩ — see TRAMP
  2 a person who roams about without a fixed route or destination ⟨the couple became *vagabonds* after they retired⟩ — see NOMAD

vagary *n* a sudden impulsive and apparently unmotivated idea or action ⟨the *vagaries* of a rather eccentric, elderly lady⟩ — see WHIM

vagrant *adj* traveling from place to place ⟨bands of *vagrant* children in the streets of the city⟩ — see ITINERANT

vagrant *n* a homeless wanderer who may beg or steal for a living ⟨*vagrants* sleeping in cardboard boxes on the sidewalk⟩ — see TRAMP

vague *adj* **1** not clearly expressed ⟨Johnny gave as *vague* a reply to the test question as he could, hoping for partial credit⟩
  synonyms fuzzy, indefinite, unclear
  related words ambiguous, cryptic, dark, enigmatic (*also* enigmatical), equivocal, murky, nebulous, obscure, unintelligible; bleary, dim, faint, foggy, hazy, indeterminate, indistinguishable, uncertain, undefinable, undefined, undetermined; inexplicable, inscrutable, mysterious; baffling, bewildering, confounding, confusing, mystifying, perplexing, puzzling, unfathomable
  near antonyms candid, direct, forthright, foursquare, frank, honest, open, openhearted, outspoken, plainspoken, straight, straightforward, unguarded; obvious, plain, unambiguous, understandable, unequivocal; comprehensible, fathomable, intelligible; defined, distinct; blatant, patent, unmistakable
  antonyms clear, definite, explicit, specific
  2 not seen or understood clearly ⟨I have only a *vague* idea of what you're talking about⟩ — see FAINT 1

vain *adj* **1** having too high an opinion of oneself ⟨a man so *vain* that he spent hours admiring himself in the mirror⟩ — see CONCEITED
  2 producing no results ⟨all their efforts to escape proved *vain*⟩ — see FUTILE

vainglorious *adj* having too high an opinion of oneself ⟨a *vainglorious* woman who always insists on being the center of attention⟩ — see CONCEITED

vaingloriousness *n* an often unjustified feeling of being pleased with oneself or with one's situation or achievements ⟨a tiresome *vaingloriousness* that manifested itself in the old general's incessant boasting about his battlefield victories⟩ — see COMPLACENCE

vainglory *n* an often unjustified feeling of being pleased with oneself or with one's situation or achievements ⟨the *vainglory* that nations have historically shown after they have achieved military supremacy⟩ — see COMPLACENCE

vainness *n* an often unjustified feeling of being pleased with oneself or with one's situation or achievements ⟨the vexing *vainness* that seemed to fill every page of his memoirs⟩ — see COMPLACENCE

vale *n* an area of lowland between hills or mountains ⟨settled in a lush *vale* in the shadow of the mountains⟩ — see VALLEY

valedictory *adj* given, taken, or performed at parting ⟨a *valedictory* gift to the school upon his retirement as principal⟩ — see PARTING

valiant *adj* feeling or displaying no fear by temperament ⟨*valiant* soldiers marching off to war⟩ — see BRAVE

valid *adj* **1** according to the rules of logic ⟨you make a *valid* argument against censorship⟩ — see LOGICAL 1

2 based on sound reasoning or information ⟨only further investigation will show whether your theory is *valid*⟩ — see GOOD 1

validate *vb* **1** to give evidence or testimony to the truth or factualness of ⟨a witness independently *validated* the policeman's version of events⟩ — see CONFIRM

2 to show the existence or truth of by evidence ⟨the booming economy in and of itself *validated* the soundness of the government's economic policies⟩ — see PROVE 1

validation *n* something presented in support of the truth or accuracy of a claim ⟨I'm afraid we cannot act on your claim without *validation*⟩ — see PROOF

valley *n* an area of lowland between hills or mountains ⟨the *valley* will be the first to flood if the river rises⟩
synonyms dale, hollow, vale
related words canyon, dell, depression, dingle, glen, ravine, rift valley; basin, bowl
near antonyms alp, mount, peak; mountain range; mountaintop, pinnacle, precipice, summit

valor *n* strength of mind to carry on in spite of danger ⟨the absence of indecision even in the face of death is the true mark of *valor*⟩ — see COURAGE

valorous *adj* feeling or displaying no fear by temperament ⟨*valorous* deeds that will be long remembered⟩ — see BRAVE

valuable *adj* commanding a large price ⟨an extremely *valuable* diamond necklace⟩ — see COSTLY

valuation *n* **1** the act of placing a value on the nature, character, or quality of something ⟨my *valuation* of your musical talent has nothing to do with our friendship⟩ — see ESTIMATE 1

2 the amount of money for which something will find a buyer ⟨the final auction bid was still less than the minimum *valuation* that we had specified as acceptable, so the painting was withdrawn⟩ — see VALUE 1

3 the relative usefulness or importance of something as judged by specific qualities ⟨the low *valuation* that society places on knowledge for the sake of knowledge⟩ — see WORTH 1

value *n* **1** the amount of money for which something will find a buyer ⟨the real *value* of that house is close to a million dollars⟩
synonyms market value, valuation, worth
related words charge, cost, fee, figure, price; appraisal, assessment, estimate, estimation, evaluation; face value, list price, unit price

2 a quality that gives something special worth ⟨defending the democratic system's intrinsic *values*⟩ — see EXCELLENCE 2

3 the relative usefulness or importance of something as judged by specific qualities ⟨guessed the *value* of the thing based on the way it was being jealously guarded by the courier⟩ — see WORTH 1

value *vb* **1** to hold dear ⟨a nation that *values* individualism and self-reliance⟩ — see LOVE 1

2 to make an approximate or tentative judgment regarding ⟨*values* his stocks at $50,000 or thereabouts⟩ — see ESTIMATE 1

valueless *adj* having no usefulness ⟨a fish that was once regarded as *valueless* and routinely thrown away by fishermen⟩ — see WORTHLESS

valve *n* a fixture for controlling the flow of a liquid ⟨a hot water *valve*⟩ — see FAUCET

vandal *n* a person who damages or destroys property on purpose ⟨a group of *vandals* broke into school and painted graffiti on the walls⟩
synonyms defacer
related words demolisher, desecrater (*or* desecrator), despoiler, destroyer, dynamiter, ravager, ruiner, saboteur, wrecker; looter, pillager, plunderer, spoiler
near antonyms conserver, preserver, protector, saver

vandalism *n* deliberate damaging or destroying of another's property ⟨anyone guilty of *vandalism* to school property will be expelled⟩
synonyms defacement
related words demolishing, demolition, desecrating, desecration, despoiling, despoilment, destruction, ravaging, ruin, ruination, wrecking; sabotage; looting, pillaging, plunder, plundering, sacking
near antonyms conservation, preservation, protection, saving

vandalize *vb* to deliberately cause the damage or destruction of another's property ⟨he decided to *vandalize* the store because the owner had kicked him out⟩
synonyms deface
related words desecrate, violate; break, damage, despoil, harm, hurt, impair, mar, shatter, spoil; demolish, destroy, devastate, ravage, raze, ruin, scourge, smash, tear down, waste, wipe out, wreck; sabotage; loot, pillage, plunder, sack
near antonyms conserve, preserve, protect, save; build, rebuild

vanguard *n* the leading or most important part of a movement ⟨in the *vanguard* of the conservative movement⟩ — see FOREFRONT

vanish *vb* to cease to be visible ⟨the house *vanished* into the fog behind us⟩ — see DISAPPEAR

vanished *adj* no longer existing ⟨the *vanished* tradition of the maypole as the center for May Day festivities⟩ — see EXTINCT

vanity *n* an often unjustified feeling of being pleased with oneself or with one's situation or achievements ⟨an all-consuming *vanity* that made him hunger for constant praise from others⟩ — see COMPLACENCE

vanquish *vb* to bring under one's control by force of arms ⟨*vanquished* nation after nation in his conquest of Europe⟩ — see CONQUER 1

vanquisher *n* one that defeats an enemy or opponent ⟨held a parade for the return of the nation's most celebrated *vanquisher*⟩ — see VICTOR 1

vanquishing *n* the act or process of bringing someone or something under one's control ⟨a movie about the *vanquishing* of Egypt by Rome⟩ — see CONQUEST

vantage *n* the more favorable condition or position in a competition ⟨the *vantage* had been entirely ours for the first half of the contest⟩ — see ADVANTAGE 1

variable *adj* **1** capable of being readily changed ⟨a *variable* expense that we could reduce if we needed to⟩ — see FLEXIBLE 1

2 likely to change frequently, suddenly, or unexpectedly ⟨*variable* income from his job as a real estate agent⟩ — see FICKLE 1

variance *n* a lack of agreement or harmony ⟨persistent *variance* within the rock band eventually caused it to break up⟩ — see DISCORD

variation *n* the act, process, or result of making different ⟨the latest in a long line of *variations* in her hair color⟩ — see CHANGE

varicolored *adj* marked by a variety of usually vivid colors ⟨a brilliantly *varicolored* blanket⟩ — see COLORFUL

varied *adj* consisting of many things of different sorts ⟨a highly *varied* collection of junk⟩ — see MISCELLANEOUS

variegated *adj* **1** marked by a variety of usually vivid colors ⟨the *variegated* costumes of the dancers in the nightclub⟩ — see COLORFUL
2 marked with spots ⟨a variety of *variegated* tulip that is highly prized by gardeners⟩ — see SPOTTED 1

variety *n* **1** the quality or state of being composed of many different elements or types ⟨the sheer *variety* of the city's ethnic restaurants was dazzling⟩
synonyms assortment, diverseness, diversity, miscellaneousness, variousness
related words heterogeneousness; disparateness, disparity, dissimilarity, distinction, distinctiveness, distinctness, unlikeness
near antonyms homogeneity, likeness, sameness, similarity; fewness, paucity
2 an unorganized collection or mixture of various things ⟨every kitchen has a drawer crammed with a *variety* of things for which there just doesn't seem to be any other place⟩ — see MISCELLANY 1

variousness *n* the quality or state of being composed of many different elements or types ⟨the outfits that he wears to work are always interesting for their *variousness* and unpredictability⟩ — see VARIETY 1

varlet *n* a mean, evil, or unprincipled person ⟨challenged the dastardly *varlet* to a duel⟩ — see VILLAIN

vary *vb* **1** to be unlike; to not be the same ⟨opinions by experts on the subject *vary*⟩ — see DIFFER 1
2 to make different in some way ⟨*varied* the method occasionally for the sake of experimentation⟩ — see CHANGE 1
3 to occur within a continuous range of variation ⟨the appliance store is offering discounts that *vary* from 10 to 40 percent, depending upon the brand⟩ — see RUN 4
4 to pass from one form, state, or level to another ⟨terrain that constantly *varied* as we traveled from the coast to the interior⟩ — see CHANGE 2

varying *adj* not staying constant ⟨a *varying* commitment to the cause that meant that one could never be sure if the volunteers would show up⟩ — see UNEVEN 2

vast *adj* unusually large ⟨a *vast* expanse of land just waiting to be settled⟩ — see HUGE

vastly *adv* to a large extent or degree ⟨*vastly* disturbed by the way that the war was going⟩ — see GREATLY 2

vastness *n* the quality or state of being very large ⟨the *vastness* of the underground chamber created an interesting echo⟩ — see IMMENSITY

vasty *adj* unusually large ⟨the days when intrepid explorers sailed the *vasty* deep in small vessels⟩ — see HUGE

¹vault *n* an underground burial chamber ⟨archaeologists were thrilled to discover an ancient *vault* that hadn't been looted by grave robbers⟩ — see CRYPT

²vault *n* an act of leaping into the air ⟨a *vault* over the car's hood by the frightened deer⟩ — see JUMP 1

vault *vb* to propel oneself upward or forward into the air ⟨*vaulted* over the obstacle with ease⟩ — see JUMP 1

veer *vb* **1** to change one's course or direction ⟨at this point the river *veers* to the southwest before finally emptying into the Atlantic Ocean⟩ — see TURN 3
2 to change the course or direction of (something) ⟨*veered* the ship abruptly to the right to avoid a collision⟩ — see TURN 2
3 to depart abruptly from a straight line or course ⟨without warning the car *veered* to the left and into an oncoming truck⟩ — see SWERVE 1

vegetation *n* green leaves or plants ⟨all the local *vegetation* is flourishing as a result of the recent rains⟩ — see GREENERY 1

vehemence *n* **1** the quality or state of being forceful (as in expression) ⟨the *vehemence* in her voice when she said that she never gossiped surprised me⟩
synonyms aggressiveness, assertiveness, emphasis, fierceness, forcefulness, intensity, vigorousness
related words potency, power, strength; eloquence; fervency, insistence, passion, warmth; absoluteness, clearness, incisiveness, plainness
near antonyms ambiguity, equivocation
antonyms feebleness, mildness, weakness
2 depth of feeling ⟨every cause that she pursues is pursued with great *vehemence*⟩ — see ARDOR 1

vehement *adj* **1** marked by or uttered with forcefulness ⟨*vehement* complaints about the restaurant's poor service⟩ — see EMPHATIC 1
2 extreme in degree, power, or effect ⟨despite the *vehement* opposition of the club's treasurer, the motion was passed⟩ — see INTENSE
3 having or expressing great depth of feeling ⟨a *vehement* defender of the rights of minorities⟩ — see FERVENT

vehicle *n* **1** something used to achieve an end ⟨used organized protests as a *vehicle* for change⟩ — see AGENT 1
2 something used to carry goods or passengers ⟨bought a larger *vehicle* after they had a third baby⟩ — see CONVEYANCE

veil *n* something that covers or conceals like a piece of cloth ⟨under the *veil* of descending darkness the thieves began their operation⟩ — see CLOAK 1

veil *vb* **1** to keep secret or shut off from view ⟨a thicket of bushes *veils* the private beach from the road⟩ — see ¹HIDE 2
2 to surround or cover closely ⟨morning fog *veiled* the fields⟩ — see ENFOLD 1

vein *n* a distinctive way of putting ideas into words ⟨the author goes on in that sarcastic *vein* for a while⟩ — see STYLE 1

veld *or* **veldt** *n* a broad area of level or rolling treeless country ⟨lions prowling the African *veld*⟩ — see PLAIN

velocity *n* a high rate of movement or performance ⟨the *velocity* of light is about 186,000 miles per second⟩ — see SPEED

velvety *adj* smooth or delicate in appearance or feel ⟨a horse's *velvety* nose⟩ — see SOFT 2

venal *adj* open to improper influence and especially bribery ⟨that judge is known for being *venal* and easily bought⟩
synonyms bribable, corruptible, purchasable
related words hack, mercenary; crooked, cutthroat, dishonest, unethical, unprincipled, unscrupulous; corrupt, debased, debauched, degenerate, degraded, demoralized, depraved, dissipated, dissolute, perverse, perverted, warped; bad, evil, immoral, iniquitous, nefarious, sinful, vicious, wicked

near antonyms ethical, honest, principled; good, moral, righteous, virtuous
antonyms incorruptible, uncorruptible
vend *vb* to offer for sale to the public 〈*vends* food and novelties at fairs〉 — see MARKET
vendor *also* **vender** *n* the person in a business deal who hands over an item in exchange for money 〈we're thinking of making a deal with that other software *vendor*〉
synonyms dealer, merchandiser, seller
related words auctioneer, concessionaire; black marketer, bootlegger, fence, fencer, hustler, smuggler, trader; distributor, retailer; sacrificer; wholesaler; hawker, huckster, peddler (*also* pedlar); salesclerk, salesman, salesperson, saleswoman; exporter, handler; bargainer, haggler, horse trader, palterer
near antonyms consumer, end user, user
antonyms buyer, purchaser
veneer *n* an outer part or layer 〈the top and sides of the desk are overlaid with cherry *veneers*, while the interior wood is white pine〉 — see EXTERIOR
venerable *adj* **1** deserving honor and respect especially by reason of age 〈the *venerable* old man was a cherished source of advice and wisdom for the villagers〉
synonyms hallowed, revered, reverend, venerated
related words honorable, reputable, respectable; honored, respected, reverenced; admirable, estimable, redoubtable; good, moral, righteous
near antonyms bad, discreditable, disgraceful, dishonorable, disreputable, ignominious, infamous, loose, notorious, shameful; immoral, seamy, shady, sordid, unsavory, vile, wicked; base, contemptible, despicable, detestable, dirty, low, mean, wretched
2 dating or surviving from the distant past 〈a *venerable* tradition that colleges have been maintaining for centuries〉 — see ANCIENT 1
venerate *vb* to offer honor or respect to (someone) as a divine power 〈a proper setting in which to *venerate* God〉 — see WORSHIP 1
venerated *adj* deserving honor and respect especially by reason of age 〈a beloved and *venerated* professor who has been a fixture on campus for decades〉 — see VENERABLE 1
vengeance *n* the act or an instance of paying back an injury with an injury 〈sought *vengeance* after his sister was murdered〉 — see REVENGE
vengeful *adj* likely to seek revenge 〈a *vengeful* person never lets go of a grudge〉 — see VINDICTIVE
venial *adj* worthy of forgiveness 〈stealing pencils is a *venial* offense〉
synonyms excusable, forgivable, pardonable, remittable
related words justifiable, redeemable; allowable; insignificant, minor, trifling, trivial; harmless, tolerable
near antonyms abominable, criminal, damning, evil, heinous; sinful, vile, wicked
antonyms inexcusable, mortal, unforgivable, unpardonable
venom *n* **1** a substance that by chemical action can kill or injure a living thing 〈an antidote to snake *venom*〉 — see POISON
2 the desire to cause pain for the satisfaction of doing harm 〈a neighborhood gossip of such *venom* that she was feared by all and genuinely liked by no one〉 — see MALICE
venomous *adj* containing or contaminated with a substance capable of injuring or killing a living thing 〈a *venomous* arrow〉 — see POISONOUS

vent *vb* **1** to find emotional release for 〈*vented* her anger and then calmed down〉 — see TAKE OUT 1
2 to make known (as an idea, emotion, or opinion) 〈*vented* his opinions freely and loudly at town meetings〉 — see EXPRESS 1
3 to throw or give off 〈the dryer *venting* steam〉 — see EMIT 1
ventilate *vb* to make known (as an idea, emotion, or opinion) 〈a person who tends to *ventilate* opinions without first thinking them through〉 — see EXPRESS 1
venture *n* a risky undertaking 〈their latest business *venture* failed〉 — see GAMBLE
venture *vb* **1** to place in danger 〈don't *venture* more money than you can afford to lose〉 — see ENDANGER
2 to take a chance on 〈*ventured* to speak plainly at the meeting〉 — see RISK 1
venturesome *adj* **1** inclined or willing to take risks 〈a *venturesome* child tried to climb the huge tree〉 — see BOLD 1
2 involving potential loss or injury 〈the first solo pilot to undertake the *venturesome* crossing of the Atlantic Ocean by air〉 — see DANGEROUS
venturous *adj* inclined or willing to take risks 〈at the time, any woman *venturous* enough to want to be an astronaut faced ridicule〉 — see BOLD 1
veracious *adj* **1** being in the habit of telling the truth 〈he has a reputation for being *veracious*, so people generally take his word for things〉 — see TRUTHFUL
2 following an original exactly 〈a television sitcom is rarely a *veracious* depiction of reality〉 — see FAITHFUL 2
veracity *n* **1** devotion to telling the truth 〈her innate *veracity* is beyond question〉 — see HONESTY 1
2 the quality or state of being very accurate 〈I challenge the *veracity* of many of the quotations in his memoirs, for he recreates conversations that occurred decades ago〉 — see PRECISION
verbal *adj* **1** of or relating to words or language 〈the child didn't yet have the *verbal* skills needed to tell the doctor about the pain he was experiencing〉
synonyms lexical, linguistic
related words communicative, conversational
2 made or carried on through speaking rather than in writing 〈a *verbal* agreement carries less force than a written contract〉
synonyms oral, spoken, unwritten
related words implicit, informal; articulated, verbalized; given, pronounced, said, sounded, stated, told, voiced
near antonyms explicit, formal
antonyms written
verbalize *vb* to express (a thought or emotion) in words 〈couldn't quite *verbalize* the cause of his mental distress〉 — see SAY 1
verbatim *adv* in the same words 〈you can't just copy the encyclopedia article *verbatim* for your report—that's plagiarism〉
synonyms directly, exactly
related words accurately, precisely; identically; literally
phrases word for word
near antonyms basically, essentially; carelessly, freely, imprecisely, inaccurately, loosely
antonyms inexactly
verbiage *n* the use of too many words to express an idea 〈teachers loathe the *verbiage* that students resort to in order to pad a paper〉

synonyms circumlocution, diffuseness, long-windedness, prolixity, redundancy, verboseness, verbosity, windiness, wordiness

related words circuitousness, circularity; tautology; reiteration, repetition, repetitiousness; embellishment, embroidering, exaggeration, hyperbole

near antonyms brevity, briefness, compactness, conciseness, crispness, pithiness, succinctness, terseness

verbose *adj* using or containing more words than necessary to express an idea ⟨had to wade through a *verbose* letter of complaint⟩ — see WORDY

verboseness *n* the use of too many words to express an idea ⟨the *verboseness* of the essay is obviously the result of being forced to meet a minimum-page requirement⟩ — see VERBIAGE

verbosity *n* the use of too many words to express an idea ⟨your ideas are good, but your penchant for *verbosity* is unfortunate⟩ — see VERBIAGE

verdant *adj* covered with a thick, healthy natural growth ⟨a beautiful, *verdant* field⟩ — see LUSH 1

verdict *n* **1** a position arrived at after consideration ⟨the consultant's *verdict* was that we were doing fine⟩ — see DECISION 1
2 an idea that is believed to be true or valid without positive knowledge ⟨the general *verdict* among her friends on her boyfriend's looks was positive⟩ — see OPINION 1

verdure *n* green leaves or plants ⟨a good time to tour the wine country is when it is clothed with the *verdure* of midsummer⟩ — see GREENERY 1

verge (on) *vb* **1** to be adjacent to ⟨our land *verges on* a wildlife refuge⟩ — see ADJOIN 1
2 to come very close to being ⟨a comment that *verged on* insulting⟩ — see BORDER (ON)

verge *n* the line or relatively narrow space that marks the outer limit of something ⟨the southern *verge* of the national park⟩ — see BORDER 1

verging *adj* having a border in common ⟨the two brothers bought *verging* properties⟩ — see ADJACENT

verifiable *adj* capable of being proven as true or real ⟨we're not sure whether that's a *verifiable* hypothesis⟩ ⟨you need a *verifiable* note from your doctor to be excused from gym class⟩

synonyms confirmable, demonstrable, provable, supportable, sustainable

related words certifiable, documentable, warrantable; excusable, justifiable; alleged, assumed, conjectured, guessed, presumed, surmised, suspected

near antonyms debatable, disputable, refutable

antonyms insupportable, unsupportable

verify *vb* to give evidence or testimony to the truth or factualness of ⟨the dispatcher was able to *verify* the content of the phone call⟩ — see CONFIRM

verifying *adj* serving to give support to the truth or factualness of something ⟨failed to produce any *verifying* evidence⟩ — see CORROBORATIVE

verily *adv* **1** to tell the truth ⟨*verily*, I don't remember a single thing about that course⟩ — see ACTUALLY 1
2 not merely this but also ⟨I shall pay back your loan and *verily* do so with considerable interest⟩ — see EVEN

veritably *adv* in actual fact ⟨the view from the summit of the mountain is *veritably* breathtaking⟩ — see VERY 2

verity *n* **1** agreement with fact or reality ⟨the local tourist bureau is less concerned with the *verity* of the legend than the fact that it attracts visitors to the area⟩ — see TRUTH

2 devotion to telling the truth ⟨no one is questioning your *verity*—just your memory of events that happened long ago⟩ — see HONESTY 1

vernacular *adj* used in or suitable for speech and not formal writing ⟨writes essays in a very easy-to-read, *vernacular* style⟩ — see COLLOQUIAL 1

versatile *adj* able to do many different kinds of things ⟨a *versatile* baseball player can play any position⟩ ⟨this tool is *versatile* enough to serve as a wrench or pliers⟩

synonyms adaptable, all-around (*also* all-round), protean, universal

related words multipurpose; well-rounded; able, ace, adept, experienced, expert, masterful, skilled, skillful; adjustable, alterable, changeable, elastic, flexible, fluid, malleable, modifiable, variable

near antonyms limited; amateur, inexperienced

verse *n* **1** a composition using rhythm and often rhyme to create a lyrical effect ⟨your assignment is to write a fourteen-line *verse*⟩ — see POEM
2 writing that uses rhythm, vivid language, and often rhyme to provoke an emotional response ⟨skilled at *verse*⟩ — see POETRY 1

versed *adj* **1** having information especially as a result of study or experience ⟨*versed* in the latest developments in aeronautics⟩ — see FAMILIAR 2
2 having or showing exceptional knowledge, experience, or skill in a field of endeavor ⟨well *versed* in the techniques of laser surgery⟩ — see PROFICIENT

versifier *n* a person who writes poetry ⟨I may not be a great poet, but I'm as good as those *versifiers* hired by the greeting card companies⟩ — see POET

vertebral column *n* a column of bones supporting the trunk of a vertebrate animal ⟨carefully reconstructed the *vertebral column* of the dinosaur⟩ — see SPINE

vertical *adj* rising straight up ⟨a *vertical* cliff face⟩ — see ERECT

verve *adj* active strength of body or mind ⟨the actor plays the part of the superhero with tremendous *verve* and obvious enjoyment⟩ — see VIGOR 1

very *adj* **1** being one and not another ⟨I ran into Sam today—the *very* one you went to school with⟩ — see SAME 2
2 being this and no more ⟨the *very* thought of having to go through that again is scary⟩ — see MERE
3 existing in fact and not merely as a possibility ⟨tourism is the *very* lifeblood of this community—the town would surely die without it⟩ — see ACTUAL

very *adv* **1** to a great degree ⟨that was a *very* brave thing to do⟩

synonyms awful, awfully, beastly, deadly, especially, exceedingly (*also* exceeding), extra, extremely, far, frightfully, full, greatly, heavily, highly, hugely, jolly, mightily, mighty, mortally, most, much, particularly, rattling, real, right, so, something, super, terribly, too, whacking

related words completely, entirely, purely, thoroughly, totally, utterly; eminently, exceptionally; considerably, extensively, significantly, substantially; appreciably, discernibly, noticeably, palpably; abundantly, plentifully; astronomically, grandly, monstrously, monumentally

phrases by far, far and away, good and, in particular

near antonyms meagerly, scantily; barely, hardly, just, marginally, minimally, scarcely

antonyms little, negligibly, nominally, slightly

2 in actual fact ⟨the *very* same thing happened to me⟩

synonyms actually, authentically, genuinely, really, veritably *related words* accurately, exactly, just, precisely, right, sharp, smack-dab, squarely; almost, nearly, practically; literally, truly

phrases in truth

near antonyms apparently, ostensibly, outwardly, seemingly

antonyms professedly, supposedly

vessel *n* **1** a large craft for travel by water ⟨a new ocean liner that claims to be the largest commercial *vessel* afloat⟩ — see SHIP

2 a small buoyant structure for travel on water ⟨any *vessel* that is buoyant and steerable can be entered in the annual race down the river⟩ — see BOAT 1

3 a usually circular utensil for holding something (as food) ⟨uses a large copper *vessel* for beating egg whites⟩ — see DISH

4 something into which a liquid or smaller objects can be put for storage or transportation ⟨any watertight *vessel* can be used for mixing the paints⟩ — see CONTAINER

vest *vb* to put (something) into the possession or safekeeping of another ⟨*vested* the power to access their retirement accounts with their attorney⟩ — see GIVE 2

vestibule *n* the entrance room of a building ⟨please leave your wet boots in the *vestibule*⟩ — see HALL 1

vestige *n* a tiny often physical indication of something lost or vanished ⟨a few strange words carved on a tree were the only *vestige* of the lost colony of Roanoke⟩

synonyms relic, shadow, trace

related words memento, remembrance, reminder; artifact; afterimage, aftertaste; balance, oddment, remainder, remnant, scrap, scraping(s); leavings, remains, residual, residue, rest

vestry *n* a room in a church building for sacred furnishings (as vestments) ⟨the priest returned the chalice to the *vestry*⟩ — see SACRISTY

vet *n* a person with long experience in a specified area ⟨he's a *vet* of many political campaigns⟩ — see VETERAN

veteran *adj* having or showing exceptional knowledge, experience, or skill in a field of endeavor ⟨a *veteran* teacher who is quick to help new teachers⟩ — see PROFICIENT

veteran *n* a person with long experience in a specified area ⟨as a *veteran* of politics, she is often consulted by eager young hopefuls⟩

synonyms old hand, old-timer, vet

related words war-horse; expert, master, pro, professional

near antonyms apprentice, cub; boot, novitiate; amateur, dilettante; learner, student, trainee; candidate, entrant, probationer

antonyms beginner, colt, fledgling, freshman, greenhorn, neophyte, newcomer, novice, recruit, rookie, tenderfoot, tyro

veto *n* an order that something not be done or used ⟨the administration's *veto* of our suggestion for vending machines in the cafeteria⟩ — see PROHIBITION 2

veto *vb* to reject by or as if by a vote ⟨Mom *vetoed* my suggestion that we adopt the stray dog⟩ — see NEGATIVE 1

vex *vb* to disturb the peace of mind of (someone) especially by repeated disagreeable acts ⟨the constantly ringing phone *vexed* me⟩ — see IRRITATE 1

vexation *n* **1** the act of making unwelcome intrusions upon another ⟨the repeated *vexations* guaranteed that she wouldn't get any work done⟩ — see ANNOYANCE 1

2 the feeling of impatience or anger caused by another's repeated disagreeable acts ⟨he suppressed his rising *vexation* and answered politely⟩ — see ANNOYANCE 2

vexatious *adj* causing annoyance ⟨those *vexatious* phone calls from salespeople during the dinner hour⟩ — see ANNOYING

vexing *adj* causing annoyance ⟨the repeated schedule changes were somewhat *vexing*, but I coped⟩ — see ANNOYING

via *prep* along the way of ⟨we're going to their house *via* the back roads⟩ — see BY 1

viable *adj* capable of being done or carried out ⟨more research will be required to see if this is a *viable* solution⟩ — see POSSIBLE 1

viands *n pl* substances intended to be eaten ⟨the inn serves its choice *viands* on delicate china and its selection of vintage wines in the finest crystal available⟩ — see FOOD

vibrancy *n* the quality or state of having abundant or intense activity ⟨the addition of several new stores enhances the *vibrancy* of the town⟩ — see VITALITY 1

vibrant *adj* **1** marked by much life, movement, or activity ⟨was sometimes rather tired by the *vibrant* environment of the big city⟩ — see ALIVE 2

2 marked by conspicuously full and rich sounds or tones ⟨a throaty, *vibrant* singing voice⟩ — see RESONANT

vibrate *vb* to make a series of small irregular or violent movements ⟨glasses and knickknacks *vibrated* on the shelves during the slight earthquake⟩ — see SHAKE 1

vibration *n* a series of slight movements by a body back and forth or from side to side ⟨the *vibration* of the floor caused by thundering feet in the hallway⟩

synonyms jiggling, oscillation, quivering, shaking, shuddering, trembling, twitching

related words jiggle, palpitation, shake, shudder, tremor, twitch

vice *n* **1** immoral conduct or practices harmful or offensive to society ⟨that section of the city is legendary for crime and *vice*⟩

synonyms corruption, debauchery, depravity, immorality, iniquity, licentiousness, sin

related words bad, badness, blackness, evil, evildoing, ill, wickedness, wrong, villainy; atrociousness, evilness, heinousness, nefariousness, sinfulness, unscrupulousness, viciousness, vileness; devilry (*or* deviltry), fiendishness; corruptness, debasement, degeneracy, degeneration, depravedness, dissolution; indecency, lasciviousness, lewdness, looseness, perversion; abomination, anathema, taboo (*also* tabu); criminality, reprehensibleness; baseness, despicableness, dirtiness, lowness, meanness; lousiness, miserableness, wretchedness

near antonyms good, right; honesty, honor, integrity, legitimacy, probity, rectitude, scrupulousness, uprightness; goodness, righteousness, virtuousness; blamelessness; chastity, innocence, perfection, pureness, purity, spotlessness; cleanness, correctness, decency, decorousness, propriety, rightness, seemliness

antonyms morality, virtue

2 a defect in character ⟨curiosity in children is not a *vice*, but something to be encouraged⟩ — see FAULT 1

vicious *adj* **1** extreme in degree, power, or effect ⟨a *vicious* winter storm ripped through the region⟩ — see INTENSE

2 having or showing the desire to inflict severe pain and suffering on others ⟨she made a *vicious* effort to destroy the lives of the people who had wronged her⟩ — see CRUEL 1

3 not conforming to a high moral standard; morally unacceptable ⟨the truly *vicious* philosophy of that racist organization⟩ — see BAD 2

4 violently unfriendly or aggressive in disposition ⟨a *vicious* dog that has already bitten several people⟩ — see FIERCE 1

viciously *adv* in a mean or spiteful manner ⟨the administrator *viciously* denied me time off so that I could attend a dear aunt's funeral⟩ — see NASTILY

viciousness *n* **1** the desire to cause pain for the satisfaction of doing harm ⟨simple *viciousness* can be the only reason for spreading such vile, unfounded rumors⟩ — see MALICE

2 the willful infliction of pain and suffering on others ⟨the unspeakable *viciousness* of the medical experiments carried out at the concentration camps⟩ — see CRUELTY

victim *n* **1** a person or thing harmed, lost, or destroyed ⟨helped the *victims* of the fire⟩ — see CASUALTY 1

2 a person or thing that is the object of abuse, criticism, or ridicule ⟨the *victim* of teasing in the schoolyard⟩ — see TARGET 1

3 something offered to a god ⟨the Aztecs are believed to have sacrificed thousands of *victims* annually to the sun⟩ — see SACRIFICE

victimize *vb* to rob by the use of trickery or threats ⟨*victimized* by a confidence man with a slick story⟩ — see FLEECE

victor *n* **1** one that defeats an enemy or opponent ⟨the computer is usually the *victor* in a chess match against a human opponent⟩

synonyms beater, conqueror, master, subduer, trimmer, vanquisher, whipper, winner

related words champion, finalist; ruler, subjugator

near antonyms pushover, quitter; failure, flop, washout

antonyms loser

2 the person who comes in first in a competition ⟨the *victor* in the science fair had constructed a functioning telescope⟩ — see CHAMPION 1

victory *n* an instance of defeating an enemy or opponent ⟨with great effort, our team managed an upset *victory* in the final moments⟩

synonyms triumph, win

related words conquest, mastery, subjugation, vanquishing; landslide, shutout, sweep; success; takeover

near antonyms upset; collapse, debacle (*also* débâcle), failure, fizzle, flop, folding, nonsuccess, washout; decline, slip, slump, wane; lurch, setback

antonyms beating, defeat, licking, loss, overthrow, rout, shellacking, trimming, whipping

victuals *n pl* substances intended to be eaten ⟨sat down with a plate of hearty *victuals* and a mug of ale⟩ — see FOOD

vie *vb* to engage in a contest ⟨*vied* with them to see who was better at basketball⟩ — see COMPETE

view *n* **1** all that can be seen from a certain point ⟨the *view* of the mountains from the inn's porch is spectacular⟩

synonyms lookout, outlook, panorama, prospect, vista

related words landscape, scene, scenery; ken, sight

2 an idea that is believed to be true or valid without positive knowledge ⟨that's one *view*, but I happen to disagree⟩ — see OPINION 1

3 an instance of looking especially briefly ⟨took a quick *view* of the Web page and decided that it didn't have what he was looking for⟩ — see LOOK 2

view *vb* to make note of (something) through the use of one's eyes ⟨*viewed* the latest changes and approved them⟩ — see SEE 1

viewpoint *n* a way of looking at or thinking about something ⟨from my *viewpoint* the rules against slogans on T-shirts infringe on my right to free speech⟩ — see POINT OF VIEW

vigilance *n* the act or state of being constantly attentive and responsive to signs of opportunity, activity, or danger ⟨eternal *vigilance* is the price of freedom⟩

synonyms alertness, attentiveness, lookout, surveillance, watch, watchfulness

related words aliveness, awareness, consciousness, sensitivity; heedfulness, observance, observation; sleeplessness, wakefulness; care, carefulness, caution, chariness, wariness; preparation, readiness

near antonyms absentmindedness, absorption, abstraction, daydreaming, daze, distraction; engrossment, obliviousness, preoccupation; unawareness, unconsciousness; carelessness, heedlessness, inattention, inattentiveness; unwariness

vigilant *adj* paying close attention usually for the purpose of anticipating approaching danger or opportunity ⟨you must stay *vigilant* all night, or you'll miss the lunar eclipse⟩ — see ALERT 1

vigilante *n* one who inflicts punishment in return for an injury or offense ⟨the danger of these self-appointed *vigilantes* is that they sometimes go after innocent people⟩ — see NEMESIS 1

vigor *n* **1** active strength of body or mind ⟨she was picked for the soccer team because of her *vigor* and enthusiasm⟩

synonyms bounce, dash, drive, energy, esprit, ginger, go, hardihood, life, pep, punch, sap, snap, starch, verve, vim, vitality, zing, zip

related words animation, briskness, jauntiness, liveliness, spiritedness, sprightliness, vivaciousness, vivacity; ardor, fervor, fire, passion, zeal; main, might, muscle, potency, power, puissance, strength; brawniness, fitness, hardiness, huskiness, virility; haleness, health, healthiness, soundness, wellness

near antonyms indolence, laziness; debilitation, debility, delicacy, delicateness, disablement, enfeeblement, faintness, feebleness, frailness, frailty, impotence, infirmity, powerlessness, puniness, slightness, softness, tenderness, weakness; enervation, exhaustion, prostration

antonyms lethargy, listlessness, sluggishness

2 the ability to exert effort for the accomplishment of a task ⟨a drug for lowering cholesterol that acts with proven *vigor*⟩ — see POWER 2

vigorous *adj* **1** having active strength of body or mind ⟨he remains healthy and *vigorous* despite being over eighty years old⟩

synonyms dynamic, energetic, flush, gingery, lusty, peppy, red-blooded, robust, vital

related words animated, lively, spirited, sprightly, vivacious; energized, enlivened, invigorated, vitalized; firm, fortified, mettlesome, mighty, powerful, puissant, strong; refreshed, rejuvenated, revitalized; able-bodied, beefy, brawny, fit, fortified, hardy, husky, rugged, stalwart, stout, strapping, sturdy, tough; hale, healthy, sound; capable, competent

near antonyms delicate, effete, enervated, faint, feeble, frail, infirm, weak, weakened; impotent, powerless, prostrate, prostrated, sapped, tired; indolent, lackadaisical, languid, lazy; invertebrate, nerveless, soft, spineless, wimpy; ill, unhealthy, unsound, unwell; broken-down, debilitated, decrepit, disabled, wasted, worn-out

antonyms lethargic, listless, sluggish, torpid

2 able to withstand hardship, strain, or exposure ⟨*vigorous* and sturdy little sheep bred to live in mountainous regions⟩ — see HARDY 1

3 marked by or uttered with forcefulness ⟨offered a *vigorous* dissent⟩ — see EMPHATIC 1

4 not showing weakness or uncertainty ⟨gave the bottle of sauce a *vigorous* shaking⟩ — see FIRM 1

vigorously *adv* in a vigorous and forceful manner ⟨*vigorously* shook my hand and told me how happy he was to be there⟩ — see HARD 3

vigorousness *n* the quality or state of being forceful (as in expression) ⟨the *vigorousness* of the ideas in the essay was surpassed only by the vibrancy of its language⟩ — see VEHEMENCE 1

vile *adj* **1** not conforming to a high moral standard; morally unacceptable ⟨a *vile* plot to murder their political enemies⟩ — see BAD 2

2 not following or in accordance with standards of honor and decency ⟨a *vile* trick to play on someone⟩ — see IGNOBLE 2

3 unpleasant to look at ⟨an outfit with a truly *vile* combination of colors⟩ — see UGLY 1

vileness *n* the state or quality of being utterly evil ⟨no one can question the sheer *vileness* of this act of terrorism⟩ — see ENORMITY 1

vilification *n* the making of false statements that damage another's reputation ⟨warned that the constant *vilification* of candidates for public office was undermining the people's faith in the political system⟩ — see SLANDER

vilify *vb* to make untrue and harmful statements about ⟨claimed that she had been *vilified* by the press because of her conservative views⟩ — see SLANDER

vilifying *n* the making of false statements that damage another's reputation ⟨the nonstop *vilifying* had the effect of making some people sympathetic to the victim⟩ — see SLANDER

villa *n* a large impressive residence ⟨a millionaire with a luxurious *villa* in Mexico⟩ — see MANSION

villager *n* a person who lives in a town on a permanent basis ⟨the *villagers* have a reputation for being polite and helpful to the tourists⟩ — see BURGHER

villain *n* a mean, evil, or unprincipled person ⟨only a heartless *villain* would kidnap a baby for ransom⟩

synonyms beast, brute, devil, evildoer, fiend, heavy, knave, miscreant, monster, no-good, rapscallion, rascal, reprobate, rogue, savage, scalawag (*or* scallywag), scamp, scoundrel, varlet, wretch

related words blackguard; criminal, crook, culprit, felon, lawbreaker, malefactor, offender, transgressor; perpetrator, sinner, trespasser, wrongdoer; cad, heel; bravo, desperado, outlaw; convict, jailbird; assassin, cutthroat, gangster, gunman, hoodlum, racketeer, ruffian, thug; ne'er-do-well, trash

near antonyms angel, saint; hero

villainous *adj* not conforming to a high moral standard; morally unacceptable ⟨*villainous* behavior that made him one of the most notorious figures in history and gave rise to the legend of Dracula⟩ — see BAD 2

villainously *adv* in a mean or spiteful manner ⟨the bully *villainously* stole my clothes and shoes⟩ — see NASTILY

villainy *n* that which is morally unacceptable ⟨psychologists and sociologists have tried to discover the roots of such unspeakable *villainy*⟩ — see EVIL

vim *n* active strength of body or mind ⟨some food and a little rest should give me back some of my *vim*⟩ — see VIGOR 1

vindicate *vb* **1** to free from a charge of wrongdoing ⟨vowed that the evidence would completely *vindicate* him⟩ — see EXCULPATE

2 to give evidence or testimony to the truth or factualness of ⟨recent discoveries have generally *vindicated* the physicist's theories⟩ — see CONFIRM

vindicating *adj* serving to give support to the truth or factualness of something ⟨*vindicating* documents have turned up only recently⟩ — see CORROBORATIVE

vindictive *adj* likely to seek revenge ⟨be careful not to annoy the *vindictive* old woman who lives down the street⟩

synonyms revengeful, vengeful

related words avenging; resentful, uncharitable, unforgiving; catty, cruel, despiteful, hateful, malevolent, malicious, malign, malignant, mean, nasty, sadistic, spiteful, vicious, virulent; grim, implacable, merciless, relentless, unrelenting; baleful, baneful, evil; harsh, hostile, inimical

near antonyms charitable, forgiving, merciful, relenting; benevolent, benign, benignant, loving; brotherly, compassionate, good, good-hearted, kind, kindhearted, kindly, sympathetic, warm, warmhearted; altruistic, humane, humanitarian, philanthropic; sweet, tender, tenderhearted; high-minded, magnanimous, noble

vinegary *adj* causing or characterized by the one of the four basic taste sensations that is produced chiefly by acids ⟨*vinegary* potato chips⟩ — see SOUR 1

violate *vb* **1** to fail to keep ⟨you *violated* the school rule against swearing at sporting events⟩

synonyms breach, break, infringe, transgress

related words disobey, rebel; brush off, disregard, ignore, overlook, overpass, pass over, tune out, wink (at); dismiss, pooh-pooh (*also* pooh), scorn, shrug off; defy, resist, withstand

near antonyms defer (to), serve, submit (to), surrender (to), yield (to); attend, hear, heed, listen (to), mark, note, notice, regard, watch

antonyms comply (with), conform (to), follow, mind, obey, observe

2 to treat (a sacred place or object) shamefully or with great disrespect ⟨the invaders *violated* the temple by using it to stable their horses⟩ — see DESECRATE

violation *n* **1** a breaking of a moral or legal code ⟨in Colonial times blasphemy was considered a serious civil *violation* that merited harsh punishment⟩ — see OFFENSE 1

2 a failure to uphold the requirements of law, duty, or obligation ⟨a military action that must be regarded as a *violation* of the treaty⟩ — see BREACH 1

violence *n* the use of brute strength to cause harm to a person or property ⟨the police believe that the woman died of natural causes rather than as a result of *violence*⟩

synonyms force, foul play

related words coercion, compulsion, constraint, duress, pressure; damage, detriment, harm, hurt, impairment, injury; crippling, maiming, mayhem, mutilation; assault, attack, bashing, battering, battery, batting, beating, belting, bludgeoning, buffeting, clubbing, drubbing, flogging, hammering, lacing, licking, mauling, pelting, pommeling, pounding, pummeling, thrashing, thumping, walloping, whaling, whipping; onslaught, outbreak, outrage, paroxysm, rampage, revolt, riot, shock, terror, threat, turbulence, upheaval, uproar; browbeating, bulldozing, bullying

near antonyms pacifism

antonyms nonviolence

violent *adj* **1** marked by bursts of destructive force or intense activity ⟨a *violent* fight that left several people badly hurt⟩

synonyms explosive, ferocious, fierce, furious, hot, rabid, rough, stormy, tempestuous, turbulent, volcanic

related words brutal, savage, vicious; antagonistic, hostile; aggressive, assertive, bellicose, belligerent, combative, contentious, gladiatorial, quarrelsome; frantic, frenzied, mad; destructive, ruinous

near antonyms calm, pacific, serene, tranquil; nonbelligerent, unaggressive, unassertive

antonyms nonviolent, peaceable, peaceful

2 extreme in degree, power, or effect ⟨a *violent* thunderstorm⟩ — see INTENSE

3 marked by great and often stressful excitement or activity ⟨my grandmother's imminent arrival provoked a *violent* effort to get the place cleaned up⟩ — see FURIOUS 1

VIP *n* a person who is widely known and usually much talked about ⟨the *VIPs* insisted on being seated in the restaurant's private dining room⟩ — see CELEBRITY 1

viper *n* a limbless reptile with a long body ⟨a *viper* sliding silently through the field⟩ — see SNAKE 1

virago *n* a bad-tempered scolding woman ⟨fairy tales that typically portray stepmothers as *viragoes*⟩ — see SHREW

virgin *adj* **1** never having had sexual relations ⟨*virgin* boys are sometimes unfairly teased⟩

synonyms maiden, virginal

related words chaste, modest, pure; innocent, untouched; abstinent, celibate; unmarried, unwed

2 being in an original and unused or unspoiled state ⟨a vast expanse of *virgin* land⟩ — see FRESH 1

virginal *adj* never having had sexual relations ⟨a *virginal* girl who would not permit any liberties to be taken with her body⟩ — see VIRGIN 1

virile *adj* considered characteristic of or appropriate for men ⟨men were once expected to be interested only in such *virile* activities as hunting⟩ — see MASCULINE

virility *n* the set of qualities considered appropriate for or characteristic of men ⟨many cultures value *virility* as a sign of power⟩

synonyms manhood, manliness, masculinity

related words maleness; boyishness, mannishness, tomboyishness

near antonyms girlishness; femaleness; girlhood, maidenhood

antonyms femininity

virtually *adv* very close to but not completely ⟨fell in love with a man who was *virtually* penniless⟩ — see ALMOST

virtue *n* **1** a quality that gives something special worth ⟨the *virtue* of wool as a clothing material is that it will provide insulation from the cold even when wet⟩ — see EXCELLENCE 2

2 conduct that conforms to an accepted standard of right and wrong ⟨a lady of honor and *virtue*⟩ — see MORALITY 1

virtuoso *adj* **1** accomplished with trained ability ⟨a *virtuoso* performance of a piano concerto⟩ — see SKILLFUL

2 having or showing exceptional knowledge, experience, or skill in a field of endeavor ⟨a *virtuoso* director,

he is known for using every resource and technique known to film to tell a story⟩ — see PROFICIENT

virtuoso *n* a person with a high level of knowledge or skill in a field ⟨a violin *virtuoso*⟩ — see EXPERT

virtuous *adj* conforming to a high standard of morality or virtue ⟨*virtuous* behavior is its own reward⟩ — see GOOD 2

virtuously *adv* with purity of thought and deed ⟨lived simply and *virtuously*⟩ — see PURELY

virtuousness *n* conduct that conforms to an accepted standard of right and wrong ⟨once a cleric's *virtuousness* is seriously called into doubt, he loses his authority as a moral leader⟩ — see MORALITY 1

virulence *n* biting sharpness of feeling or expression ⟨I was surprised by the *virulence* of the criticism⟩ — see ACRIMONY 1

virulent *adj* having or showing a desire to cause someone pain or suffering for the sheer enjoyment of it ⟨the *virulent* look on her face warned me that she was about to be unkind⟩ — see HATEFUL

virulently *adv* in a mean or spiteful manner ⟨an organization that is even more *virulently* bigoted than others of its kind⟩ — see NASTILY

visage *n* **1** facial appearance regarded as an indication of mood or feeling ⟨an old man with a noticeably happy *visage*⟩ — see LOOK 1

2 the front part of the head ⟨visitors to the mountain range had long noted that the natural rock formation bore a striking resemblance to the *visage* of a man⟩ — see FACE 1

viscera *n pl* the internal organs of the body ⟨examined the *viscera* of a frog for biology class⟩ — see GUT 1

viscid *adj* **1** being of a consistency that resists flow ⟨honey that turned even more *viscid* in the cold⟩ — see THICK 2

2 being of such a thick consistency as to readily cling to objects upon contact ⟨*viscid* tree resin⟩ — see STICKY 1

viscosity *n* the degree to which a fluid can resist flowing ⟨conducted an experiment to determine the *viscosity* of motor oil⟩ — see CONSISTENCY

viscous *adj* **1** being of a consistency that resists flow ⟨*viscous* syrup that takes forever to pour from a narrow-neck bottle⟩ — see THICK 2

2 being of such a thick consistency as to readily cling to objects upon contact ⟨the *viscous* glue on this packing tape means that once the tape is on, it doesn't come off⟩ — see STICKY 1

visible *adj* capable of being seen ⟨the *visible* light spectrum runs from red to violet⟩

synonyms apparent, observable, seeable, visual

related words external, outer, outward; detectable, discernible, noticeable, perceptible; clear, conspicuous, evident, eye-catching, manifest, obvious, plain, prominent, striking

near antonyms disappeared, dissolved, evanesced, evaporated, melted, vanished; imperceptible, inconspicuous, indistinct, unnoticeable; faint, insignificant, slight, vague; buried, concealed, covert, disguised, hidden, latent, obscure, shrouded

antonyms invisible, unseeable

vision *n* **1** a conception or image created by the imagination and having no objective reality ⟨a *vision* of the future that no other film director had ever created⟩ — see FANTASY 1

2 a series of often striking pictures created by the imagination during sleep ⟨haunted by *visions* of natural catastrophes⟩ — see DREAM 1

3 the ability to see ⟨the bright light temporarily robbed me of *vision*⟩ — see EYESIGHT

4 the soul of a dead person thought of especially as appearing to living people ⟨believed he'd seen a *vision* of his mother⟩ — see GHOST

vision *vb* to form a mental picture of ⟨*visioned* her idea of the perfect meal⟩ — see IMAGINE 1

visionary *n* one whose conduct is guided more by the image of perfection than by the real world ⟨19th-century *visionaries* who founded short-lived communities in which everyone was supposed to live in perfect peace and harmony⟩ — see IDEALIST

visit *n* **1** a temporary residing as another's guest ⟨my aunt always looks forward to her week-long annual *visit* with her mother⟩
synonyms sojourn, stay
related words field trip; layover, stopover
2 a coming to see another briefly for social or business reasons ⟨came by for a quick *visit*⟩ — see CALL 2

visit *vb* **1** to make a social call upon ⟨the club ladies make a point of *visiting* everyone who moves into the neighborhood⟩
synonyms call (on *or* upon), see
related words look up, seek (out); frequent, hang out (at), haunt
phrases drop in on
near antonyms brush (off), cold-shoulder, ignore, snub
2 to reside as a temporary guest ⟨Johnny loves it when his friend Susie comes to *visit* for a month every summer⟩
synonyms sojourn, stay, tarry
related words frequent, hang out (at), haunt; inhabit, occupy
near antonyms abide, dwell, live, reside
3 to engage in casual or rambling conversation ⟨tries to *visit* with her best friend on the phone at least once a week⟩ — see CHAT
4 to go to or spend time in often ⟨*visit* Ireland for a few weeks every year⟩ — see FREQUENT
5 to make a brief visit ⟨stopped to *visit* with my father on the way out of town⟩ — see CALL 3

visitant *n* a person who visits another ⟨the four ghostly *visitants* who pay calls on Ebenezer Scrooge⟩ — see GUEST

visitation *n* a coming to see another briefly for social or business reasons ⟨the pastor and curate could hardly express how honored they were to receive this *visitation* from the bishop⟩ — see CALL 2

visitor *n* a person who visits another ⟨please put nicer clothes on, as we have *visitors* coming⟩ — see GUEST 1

visor *also* **vizor** *n* the projecting front part of a hat or cap ⟨the *visor* of her baseball cap shades her eyes nicely⟩
synonyms bill, brim, peak
related words shade

vista *n* all that can be seen from a certain point ⟨a gorgeous *vista* of the mountains from the front window⟩ — see VIEW 1

visual *adj* **1** of, relating to, or used in vision ⟨the eyes are the primary *visual* organs in humans⟩
synonyms ocular, optic, optical
related words seeing, sighted; focusing
antonyms nonvisual
2 capable of being seen ⟨the funny face was a *visual* hint that she was getting bored⟩ — see VISIBLE
3 consisting of or relating to pictures ⟨*visual* evidence that could be presented in court⟩ — see PICTORIAL 1

visualize *vb* to form a mental picture of ⟨I can *visualize* how silly they must have looked⟩ — see IMAGINE 1

vital *adj* **1** having active strength of body or mind ⟨a man who remained *vital* well into his 90s⟩ — see VIGOROUS 1
2 having much high-spirited energy and movement ⟨the child is *vital* and active again after being sick⟩ — see LIVELY 1
3 impossible to do without ⟨I forgot one *vital* ingredient, and now the biscuits taste very strange⟩ — see ESSENTIAL 1
4 likely to cause or capable of causing death ⟨received a *vital* wound in the abdomen⟩ — see DEADLY
5 of the greatest possible importance ⟨a matter that is *vital* to our national security⟩ — see CRUCIAL

vitality *n* **1** the quality or state of having abundant or intense activity ⟨a city known for the *vitality* of its entertainment and sports scenes⟩
synonyms animation, briskness, exuberance, jazziness, liveliness, lustiness, peppiness, robustness, sprightliness, vibrancy
related words buoyancy, jauntiness, springiness; brightness, cheer, cheerfulness, effervescence, vivaciousness, vivacity; eagerness, enthusiasm, keenness, spiritedness; friskiness, impishness, pertness, playfulness
near antonyms indolence, laziness; languor, lethargy, limpness, listlessness, sleepiness, sluggishness, torpor, weariness; apathy, impassivity; dullness (*also* dulness), tediousness, tedium
antonyms inactivity, lifelessness
2 active strength of body or mind ⟨her *vitality* seemed to spread to everyone around her⟩ — see VIGOR 1

vitalize *vb* to give life, vigor, or spirit to ⟨a hearty lunch and a long nap afterwards *vitalized* him again⟩ — see ANIMATE

vitalizing *adj* having a renewing effect on the state of the body or mind ⟨a *vitalizing* steam bath⟩ — see TONIC

vitals *n pl* the internal organs of the body ⟨remember to wear a full vest to protect your *vitals* while sparring⟩ — see GUT 1

vitiate *vb* **1** to affect slightly with something morally bad or undesirable ⟨believed that luxury *vitiates* even the most principled person⟩ — see TAINT 1
2 to reduce the soundness, effectiveness, or perfection of ⟨numerous grammatical errors *vitiate* the effectiveness of your writing⟩ — see DAMAGE 1

vitriol *n* **1** biting sharpness of feeling or expression ⟨a film critic noted for the *vitriol* and sometimes outright cruelty of his pronouncements⟩ — see ACRIMONY 1
2 harsh insulting language ⟨the review was more than just unfavorable—it was loaded with *vitriol*⟩ — see ABUSE 1

vittles *n pl* substances intended to be eaten ⟨pack a big bag of *vittles* for the hike⟩ — see FOOD

vituperate *vb* to criticize harshly and usually publicly ⟨the teacher *vituperated* the little snobs for being cruel to other students⟩ — see ATTACK 2

vituperation *n* harsh insulting language ⟨such *vituperation* has no place in a review of a student's work⟩ — see ABUSE 1

vivacious *adj* **1** having much high-spirited energy and movement ⟨a *vivacious* girl who became a cheerleader⟩ — see LIVELY 1
2 joyously unrestrained ⟨the poem is a *vivacious* expression of his love for her⟩ — see EXUBERANT

vivid *adj* producing a mental picture through clear and impressive description ⟨*vivid* language that made the scene come alive in my mind⟩ — see GRAPHIC 1

vivify *vb* to give life, vigor, or spirit to ⟨this re-creation of a town in the Old West really *vivifies* the history that visitors learned in school⟩ — see ANIMATE

vizard *n* a cover or partial cover for the face used to disguise oneself ⟨the knight donned a *vizard* for the combat⟩ — see MASK 1

vocabulary *n* 1 the special terms or expressions of a particular group or field ⟨scientific *vocabulary*⟩ — see TERMINOLOGY
2 the stock of words, pronunciation, and grammar used by a people as their basic means of communication ⟨children learn enough of the common *vocabulary* to make themselves understood by around the age of two⟩ — see LANGUAGE 1

vocal *adj* created by the body's organs of sound ⟨our cat is given to making strange *vocal* noises in the dead of night⟩
synonyms oral, uttered, voiced
related words articulate, articulated, spoken; breathed, drawled, gasped, mouthed, mumbled, murmured, muttered, shouted, spluttered, sputtered, whispered
near antonyms inarticulate; mute, quiet, silent; unexpressed, unspoken, unuttered, unvoiced
antonyms nonvocal

vocal *n* a short musical composition for the human voice often with instrumental accompaniment ⟨a recording artist who arranges his own *vocals*⟩ — see SONG 1

vocalist *n* one who sings ⟨hired a *vocalist* for their jazz band⟩ — see SINGER

vocalize *vb* 1 to express (a thought or emotion) in words ⟨she's not one to *vocalize* her worries⟩ — see SAY 1
2 to produce musical sounds with the voice ⟨spent some time *vocalizing* before the concert⟩ — see SING 1

vocalizer *n* one who sings ⟨a critic who disdains many of today's pop singers as mere *vocalizers* with little artistry⟩ — see SINGER

vocation *n* the activity by which one regularly makes a living ⟨finally made sculpting her *vocation* instead of just a hobby⟩ — see OCCUPATION

vociferate *vb* to speak so as to be heard at a distance ⟨he can never seem to voice his opinions at a decent decibel level; he has to *vociferate*⟩ — see CALL 1

vociferous *adj* engaging in or marked by loud and insistent cries especially of protest ⟨*vociferous* opponents of the bill protested angrily outside the chambers of the legislature⟩
synonyms blatant, clamorous, obstreperous
related words clangorous, dinning, discordant, noisy; loudmouthed, outspoken, vocal; boisterous, rowdy, uproarious; cacophonous, dissonant, shrill, strident; blaring, booming, brassy, brazen
near antonyms noiseless, quiet, silent, soundless, still; calm, hushed, subdued

vogue *adj* enjoying widespread favor or approval ⟨always tries to use the *vogue* words of the moment so as to appear cool⟩ — see POPULAR 1

vogue *n* 1 a practice or interest that is very popular for a short time ⟨it was then the *vogue* to curl one's hair and wear dark lipstick⟩ — see FAD
2 the state of enjoying widespread approval ⟨she's the sort of person who does whatever is in *vogue*⟩ — see POPULARITY

voice *n* 1 the right to express a wish, choice, or opinion ⟨everyone will have a *voice* in the decision of where to go for our field trip⟩
synonyms say, vote

related words part, role, share; enfranchisement, franchise, suffrage; judgment (*or* judgement), say-so; belief, conviction, opinion, sentiment, view
2 an act, process, or means of putting something into words ⟨a publisher who used his newspaper as a *voice* for his extreme conservatism⟩ — see EXPRESSION 1
3 one who sings ⟨one of the great *voices* of her generation⟩ — see SINGER

voice *vb* to make known (as an idea, emotion, or opinion) ⟨*voiced* a suggestion about where to go⟩ — see EXPRESS 1

voiced *adj* created by the body's organs of sound ⟨a loudly *voiced* expression of pain⟩ — see VOCAL

voiceless *adj* unable to speak ⟨an advocate for the rights of *voiceless* animals⟩ — see MUTE 1

void *vb* to put an end to by formal action ⟨the court's decision *voided* the will⟩ — see ABOLISH

void *adj* 1 having no legal or binding force ⟨an agreement is null and *void* if obtained by force⟩ — see NULL 1
2 lacking contents that could or should be present ⟨a nuclear explosion that would leave the landscape as *void* and lifeless as one could imagine⟩ — see EMPTY 1
3 utterly lacking in something needed, wanted, or expected ⟨entirely *void* of common sense⟩ — see DEVOID 1

void *n* empty space ⟨those ancient travelers who traversed those vast watery *voids* between the islands of Oceania⟩ — see VACANCY 1

void *vb* to remove the contents of ⟨*void* the room of all furniture⟩ — see EMPTY

volatile *adj* likely to change frequently, suddenly, or unexpectedly ⟨a boss of *volatile* moods is frustrating to work for⟩ — see FICKLE 1

volcanic *adj* marked by bursts of destructive force or intense activity ⟨a man with a *volcanic* temper that could go off at any moment⟩ — see VIOLENT 1

volition *n* the act or power of making one's own choices or decisions ⟨left the church of her own *volition*⟩ — see FREE WILL

volley *n* a rapid or overwhelming outpouring of many things at once ⟨surprised by the *volley* of complaints⟩ — see BARRAGE

volume *n* 1 a considerable amount ⟨we can only make money if we sell our goods in *volume*⟩ — see LOT 2
2 a given or particular mass or aggregate of matter ⟨produces great *volumes* of work each day⟩ — see AMOUNT
3 a set of printed sheets of paper bound together between covers and forming a work of fiction or nonfiction ⟨reissued the trilogy in a single *volume*⟩ — see BOOK 1

voluminous *adj* of a size greater than average of its kind ⟨a *voluminous* storm cloud hovered over us⟩ — see LARGE

voluminousness *n* the quality or state of being large in size ⟨the awesome *voluminousness* of the garment made it look more like a tent than a dress⟩ — see LARGENESS

voluntarily *adv* of one's own free will ⟨you took part in this *voluntarily*, so you have no cause to complain⟩
synonyms freely, willingly
related words consciously, knowingly, wittingly
phrases of one's own accord
near antonyms unconsciously, unknowingly, unwittingly
antonyms involuntarily, unwillingly

voluntary *adj* **1** done, made, or given with one's own free will ⟨a *voluntary* contribution to the school's fundraising drive⟩
synonyms freewill, unforced, volunteer, willing
related words discretionary, elective, nonobligatory, optional; impulsive, instinctive, spontaneous, unforced, unpremeditated; conscious, deliberate, intentional, knowing, willful (*or* wilful)
near antonyms compulsory, mandatory, necessary, nonelective, obligatory, ordered, required
antonyms coerced, forced, involuntary
2 subject to one's freedom of choice ⟨participation in the resort's recreational activities is strictly *voluntary*⟩ — see OPTIONAL

volunteer *adj* done, made, or given with one's own free will ⟨*volunteer* work at the hospital⟩ — see VOLUNTARY 1

voluptuous *adj* pleasing to the physical senses ⟨the *voluptuous* richness of the music⟩ — see SENSUAL

vomit *vb* to discharge the contents of the stomach through the mouth ⟨the children with the flu *vomited* every time they tried to eat something⟩
synonyms gag, heave, retch, spit up, throw up
related words disgorge, regurgitate; eject, expel, spew

voodoo *n* a person skilled in using supernatural forces ⟨found a *voodoo* who was willing to put a hex on the man who had jilted her⟩ — see MAGICIAN 1

voodooism *n* the power to control natural forces through supernatural means ⟨*voodooism* is condemned by several religions⟩ — see MAGIC 1

voracious *adj* **1** having a huge appetite ⟨it seemed like the *voracious* kitten was eating all the time⟩
synonyms gluttonous, greedy, hoggish, piggish, rapacious, ravenous
related words hearty, wolfish; devouring, gobbling, gorging, gormandizing, insatiable, unquenchable; empty, famished, hungry, starved, starving; malnourished, underfed, undernourished
near antonyms full, content, sated, satisfied
2 showing urgent desire or interest ⟨a *voracious* reader⟩ — see EAGER

vortex *n* water moving rapidly in a circle with a hollow in the center ⟨a boat sucked down into the *vortex*⟩ — see WHIRLPOOL

votary *n* one who follows the opinions or teachings of another ⟨a *votary* of the religious leader⟩ — see FOLLOWER

vote *n* **1** the right to formally express one's position or will in an election ⟨in the United States, women were granted the *vote* by the Nineteenth Amendment in 1920⟩
synonyms enfranchisement, franchise, suffrage
related words say, voice
antonyms disenfranchisement
2 a piece of paper indicating a person's preferences in an election ⟨dropped her *vote* into the ballot box⟩ — see BALLOT
3 the right to express a wish, choice, or opinion ⟨he argued for a *vote* in the matter, since he was going to be affected by the final decision⟩ — see VOICE 1

vote *vb* to set before the mind for consideration ⟨I *vote* we quit working and go to lunch⟩ — see PROPOSE 1

vouch (for) *vb* to declare (something) to be true or genuine ⟨two people are required to *vouch for* a document⟩ — see CERTIFY 1

vow *n* a person's solemn declaration that he or she will do or not do something ⟨we need your *vow* that you won't damage anything while we're gone⟩ — see PROMISE

vow *vb* to make a solemn declaration of intent ⟨she *vowed* to love him forever⟩ — see PROMISE 1

voyage *n* a journey over water in a vessel ⟨a *voyage* across the English Channel⟩ — see SAIL

voyage *vb* **1** to take a trip especially of some distance ⟨*voyaged* across the country⟩ — see TRAVEL 1
2 to travel on water in a vessel ⟨*voyaging* on a cruise ship for the first time⟩ — see SAIL 1

vulgar *adj* **1** belonging to the class of people of low social or economic rank ⟨paintings that appeal to the *vulgar* taste⟩ — see IGNOBLE 1
2 depicting or referring to sexual matters in a way that is unacceptable in polite society ⟨a warning about the movie's *vulgar* language⟩ — see OBSCENE 1
3 held by or applicable to a majority of the people ⟨the *vulgar* opinion is that the nation is in decline⟩ — see GENERAL 3
4 lacking in refinement or good taste ⟨the kind of *vulgar* behavior shown by someone who's made a lot of money and wants everyone to know it⟩ — see COARSE 2
5 used in or suitable for speech and not formal writing ⟨Latin was once the language of scholars, and English the *vulgar* language used by the common people⟩ — see COLLOQUIAL 1

vulgarism *n* a disrespectful or indecent word or expression ⟨used *vulgarisms* that embarrassed his family⟩ — see SWEARWORD

vulgarity *n* **1** the quality or state of lacking refinement or good taste ⟨our cousins' general *vulgarity* and poor manners irritate my mother⟩
synonyms coarseness, commonness, crassness, crudeness, grossness, indelicacy, indelicateness, lowness, raffishness, roughness, rudeness, tastelessness
related words boorishness, churlishness, clownishness, loutishness; insensitivity, thoughtlessness; gracelessness, tackiness
near antonyms courtliness; elegance, grace, graciousness; consideration, sensitivity, thoughtfulness
antonyms cultivation, gentility, polish, refinement, tastefulness
2 the quality or state of being obscene ⟨the pointless *vulgarity* of the joke disgusted her⟩ — see OBSCENITY 1

vulnerability *n* **1** the quality or state of having little resistance to some outside agent ⟨*vulnerability* to infection⟩ — see SUSCEPTIBILITY
2 the state of being left without shelter or protection against something harmful ⟨the *vulnerability* of the car to vandalism when it's parked on the street⟩ — see EXPOSURE 1

vulnerable *adj* **1** being in a situation where one is likely to meet with harm ⟨I'm *vulnerable* to sunburn whenever I go out in the sun⟩ — see LIABLE 1
2 lacking protection from danger or resistance against attack ⟨*vulnerable* baby chicks⟩ — see HELPLESS 1

W

wackiness *n* lack of good sense or judgment ⟨what *wackiness* made you think this was a good idea?⟩ — see FOOLISHNESS 1

wacky *adj* **1** different from the ordinary in a way that causes curiosity or suspicion ⟨raised by an uncle with a rather *wacky* philosophy of parenting⟩ — see ODD 2
2 having or showing a very abnormal or sick state of mind ⟨a series of bizarre letters that the killer sent to the police, detailing his *wacky*, disturbed view of the world⟩ — see INSANE 1
3 showing or marked by a lack of good sense or judgment ⟨one club member whose *wacky* ideas for activities usually produced groans⟩ — see FOOLISH 1

wad *n* **1** a considerable amount ⟨a starlet who got a big *wad* of publicity because of her antics⟩ — see LOT 2
2 a small uneven mass ⟨a *wad* of gum stuck to the desk⟩ — see LUMP 1
3 a very large amount of money ⟨amassed—and lost—a *wad* playing the stock market⟩ — see FORTUNE 2

wad *vb* to form into a round compact mass ⟨she *wadded* up the paper and threw it in the wastebasket⟩
synonyms agglomerate, ball, roll, round
related words clump, lump; bead
near antonyms open, spread, unfold
antonyms unroll

waddle *vb* to move forward while swaying from side to side ⟨the toddler *waddled* back into the water⟩ — see STAGGER 1

wade (into) *vb* to start work on energetically ⟨*waded* deep *into* the repair project and didn't come out of it until four hours later⟩ — see ATTACK 3

waft *n* a slight or gentle movement of air ⟨*wafts* carrying the scent of spring flowers⟩ — see BREEZE 1

waft *vb* to rest or move along the surface of a liquid or in the air ⟨a feather *wafted* past us and settled on the grass⟩ — see FLOAT

wag *n* **1** a quick jerky movement from side to side or up and down ⟨the dog gave its tail a single *wag* before it flopped back down⟩
synonyms switch, waggle
related words oscillation, swing; flap, flutter, wave; jerk, shake, twitch, wiggle
2 a person (as a writer) noted for or specializing in humor ⟨some *wag* wrote a droll piece of political satire for the newspaper⟩ — see HUMORIST

wag *vb* to move from side to side or up and down with quick jerky motions ⟨the cat's tail *wagged* back and forth in annoyance⟩
synonyms switch, waggle
related words oscillate, swing; beat, flail, flap, flop, whip; flick, flicker, flutter, wave; jerk, shake, twitch, wiggle

wage *n, often* **wages** *pl* the money paid regularly to a person for labor or services ⟨the *wage* you earn is more than enough to support us comfortably⟩
synonyms emolument, hire, pay, payment, salary, stipend
related words minimum wage, take-home pay; compensation, recompense, remittance, remuneration, requital, return; check, commission, paycheck; recoupment, redress, reparation, restitution; reimbursement, repayment; profit, takings, yield

wager *n* the money or thing risked on the outcome of an uncertain event ⟨lost her *wager* when the horse dropped out of the race⟩ — see BET

wager *vb* to risk (something) on the outcome of an uncertain event ⟨*wagered* five dollars that his dog would win⟩ — see BET

wagerer *n* one that bets (as on the outcome of a contest or sports event) ⟨as a *wagerer* of very small amounts, my uncle regards a visit to the racetrack as simply a pleasant way to spend the afternoon⟩ — see BETTOR

waggery *n* **1** playful, reckless behavior that is not intended to cause serious harm ⟨tossing lighted firecrackers around is not the kind of harmless *waggery* that it might seem⟩ — see MISCHIEF 1
2 something said or done to cause laughter ⟨his latest *waggery* had us all doubled over with laughter⟩ — see JOKE 1

waggish *adj* tending to or exhibiting reckless playfulness ⟨a *waggish* disposition that often got him into trouble with the school's headmaster⟩ — see MISCHIEVOUS 1

waggle *n* a quick jerky movement from side to side or up and down ⟨a quick *waggle* of her head to indicate "no"⟩ — see WAG 1

waggle *vb* to move from side to side or up and down with quick jerky motions ⟨the rabbit *waggled* its ears and hopped away⟩ — see WAG

wagon *n* a wheeled usually horse-drawn vehicle used for hauling ⟨harness the horses up to the *wagon* so I can bring in the hay⟩ — see CART

wail *n* **1** a crying out in grief ⟨a prolonged *wail* arose from every corner of the city as the victims of the earthquake were unearthed from the rubble⟩ — see LAMENT 1
2 a long low sound indicating pain or grief ⟨rescuers heard a faint *wail* coming from the pile of rubble, a sure sign that one of the victims was still alive⟩ — see MOAN 1

wail *vb* **1** to express dissatisfaction, pain, or resentment usually tiresomely ⟨the state's residents are always *wailing* about their high taxes⟩ — see COMPLAIN
2 to make a long loud mournful sound ⟨the women stood beside the coffins, *wailing* for their fallen sons and daughters⟩ — see HOWL 1
3 to utter a moan ⟨the patient lay in her bed, occasionally softly *wailing* in pain⟩ — see MOAN 1

wail (for) *vb* to feel or express sorrow for ⟨grandfather asked us not to *wail for* him, saying that he had had a good life and was at peace⟩ — see LAMENT 1

wailing *adj* expressing or suggesting mourning ⟨a *wailing* quality in her voice that makes her a natural for country music⟩ — see MOURNFUL 1

wain *n* a wheeled usually horse-drawn vehicle used for hauling ⟨an antique *wain* that was once used for delivering milk⟩ — see CART

waist *n* the middle region of the human body ⟨bent at the *waist* to catch his breath⟩ — see MIDRIFF

waistline *n* the middle region of the human body ⟨used a belt to define her *waistline*⟩ — see MIDRIFF

wait *n* an instance or period of being prevented from going about one's business ⟨there was a long *wait* for the manager to come and help us⟩ — see DELAY

wait *vb* to remain in place in readiness or expectation of something ⟨hurry up, as your sisters are already at the door *waiting* for you⟩
synonyms await, bide, hold on, stay
related words hang around, linger, stick around; anticipate, expect
phrases bide one's time

waiter *n* a person who serves food or drink ⟨*waiters* at that restaurant must go through an extended training program⟩ — see SERVER

waiver *n* a document containing a declaration of an intentional giving up of a right, claim, or privilege ⟨before the hospital will treat you, you have to sign a *waiver* in which you give up your right to sue⟩
synonyms release
related words dispensation, exemption; abdication, relinquishment, renouncement; renunciation, surrender

wake *vb* **1** to cause to stop sleeping ⟨my banging around in the kitchen *woke* the cat⟩
synonyms arouse, awake, awaken, rouse, waken
related words raise, revive; reawake, reawaken; agitate, disturb, excite, provoke, stimulate, stir
near antonyms hypnotize, mesmerize; lay (down)
antonyms lull
2 to cease to be asleep ⟨I *woke* with a start when the door slammed⟩
synonyms arouse, awake, awaken, rouse, waken
related words arise, get up, rise, uprise; watch; revive; reawake, reawaken; shift, stir
near antonyms catnap, doze, drop (off), nap, nod, sleep, slumber, snooze; bed (down), couch, retire, turn in; oversleep

wakeful *adj* not sleeping or able to sleep ⟨the mother remained *wakeful* until her child returned home⟩
synonyms awake, sleepless, wide-awake
related words aroused, awakened, roused, wakened; aware, conscious; revived; reawakened
near antonyms drowsy, nodding, sleepy, slumberous (*or* slumbrous), somnolent; dreaming; hypnotized, mesmerized
antonyms asleep, dormant, dozing, napping, resting, sleeping, slumbering

waken *vb* **1** to cause to stop sleeping ⟨a sudden loud noise *wakened* us⟩ — see WAKE 1
2 to cease to be asleep ⟨she usually *wakens* when sunlight begins to stream through the windows⟩ — see WAKE 2

walk *n* a relaxed journey on foot for exercise or pleasure ⟨we went for a long *walk* outside because it was such a nice night⟩
synonyms constitutional, perambulation, ramble, range, saunter, stroll, turn
related words parade, promenade; expedition, hike, march, peregrination, tramp, travel, trek, trip; excursion, jaunt, junket, outing, sally, spin, tour; pilgrimage, progress, safari

walk *vb* to go on foot ⟨I *walked* slowly to school⟩
synonyms foot (it), hoof (it), leg (it), pad, step, traipse, tread
related words parade, promenade; march, pace, stride; hike, peregrinate, trek; amble, perambulate, ramble, saunter, stroll, wander; clump, stomp, stump, tramp, tromp; plod, trudge; hobble, limp; mince, prance, pussyfoot, tiptoe; stalk, strut, swagger; lumber, lurch, pound, shamble, shuffle, stagger; nip, trip, trot

walking out *n* the act of leaving a place ⟨your unexplained *walking out* like that was rude⟩ — see DEPARTURE

walkout *n* a work stoppage by a body of workers intended to force an employer to meet their demands ⟨after four weeks of the *walkout*, management gave in⟩ — see STRIKE 1

walk out *vb* **1** to leave a place often for another ⟨we simply *walked out* after waiting half an hour for someone to come and serve us⟩ — see GO 2
2 to refuse to work in order to force an employer to meet demands ⟨the salesclerks *walked out* upon learning of the second pay cut in six months⟩ — see STRIKE 1

wall *n* **1** a physical object that blocks the way ⟨an ancient *wall* that was built to block the invading barbarians⟩ — see BARRIER
2 means or method of defending ⟨investigators faced a *wall* of silence from the members of the police department⟩ — see DEFENSE 1

wall (in) *vb* to close or shut in by or as if by barriers ⟨a lake almost entirely *walled in* by mountains⟩ — see ENCLOSE 1

wallop *n* **1** a forceful coming together of two things ⟨felt the *wallop* of a car crashing into their front porch⟩ — see IMPACT 1
2 a hard strike with a part of the body or an instrument ⟨gave the ball a good *wallop* with the bat⟩ — see ¹BLOW

wallop *vb* **1** to strike repeatedly ⟨*walloped* the branches of the pear tree with a stick in an effort to knock down some fruit⟩ — see BEAT 1
2 to achieve a victory over ⟨finally *walloped* his fear of heights⟩ — see BEAT 2
3 to defeat by a large margin ⟨*walloped* their traditional rivals 20 to nothing⟩ — see WHIP 2
4 to deliver a blow to (someone or something) usually in a strong vigorous manner ⟨arrested for *walloping* a police officer⟩ — see HIT 1

wampum *n, slang* something (as pieces of stamped metal or printed paper) customarily and legally used as a medium of exchange, a measure of value, or a means of payment ⟨made some real *wampum* on that last business deal⟩ — see MONEY

wan *adj* lacking a healthy skin color ⟨she looks a little *wan* after all that tiring work⟩ — see PALE 2

wander *vb* to move about from place to place aimlessly ⟨we just went outside and *wandered* around until it was time to go⟩
synonyms gad (about), gallivant (*also* galavant), knock (about), maunder, meander, mooch, mope, ramble, range, roam, rove, traipse
related words amble, saunter, stroll; bum, hobo; straggle, stray; prowl, tramp, travel

wanderer *n* a person who roams about without a fixed route or destination ⟨a *wanderer* who reasoned that he could never be lost, as he didn't care where he was going⟩ — see NOMAD

wandering *adj* traveling from place to place ⟨a *wandering* carnival that visited small towns all over the South⟩ — see ITINERANT

wane *vb* to grow less in scope or intensity especially gradually ⟨in the course of the evening the storm steadily *waned*⟩ — see DECREASE 2

wangle *vb* to plan out usually with subtle skill or care ⟨*wangled* a way to get free tickets to the show⟩ — see ENGINEER

want *n* **1** the fact or state of being absent ⟨for *want* of a nail, the horse's shoe was lost during the race⟩ — see LACK 1

2 a falling short of an essential or desirable amount or number ⟨there's a notable *want* of teachers in that rural school district⟩ — see DEFICIENCY

3 a state of being without something necessary, desirable, or useful ⟨those children are in *want* of some good discipline⟩ — see NEED 1

4 the state of lacking sufficient money or material possessions ⟨grew up in extreme *want*⟩ — see POVERTY 1

want *vb* **1** to have an earnest wish to own or enjoy ⟨I *want* a new car so badly!⟩ — see DESIRE

2 to have as a requirement ⟨that stray cat *wants* food and a clean place to sleep⟩ — see NEED 1

3 to see fit ⟨do what you *want*⟩ — see CHOOSE 2

4 to wish to have ⟨I *want* some ice cream for dessert, please⟩ — see LIKE 1

wanting *adj* **1** falling short of a standard ⟨we tried her cooking and found it to be very *wanting*⟩ — see BAD 1

2 not coming up to a usual standard or meeting a particular need ⟨at this time of year food for many wild animals is *wanting*⟩ — see SHORT 3

3 not present or in evidence ⟨grass is almost entirely *wanting* in that arid wasteland⟩ — see ABSENT 2

wanting *prep* not having ⟨any application *wanting* the required photo will not be considered⟩ — see WITHOUT 1

wanton *adj* **1** depicting or referring to sexual matters in a way that is unacceptable in polite society ⟨that novel was once regarded as a *wanton* tale of forbidden love⟩ — see OBSCENE 1

2 having a strong sexual desire ⟨in earlier times, novelists usually portrayed *wanton* women as coming to a bad end⟩ — see LUSTFUL

3 having or showing the desire to inflict severe pain and suffering on others ⟨a *wanton* attack on unarmed civilians⟩ — see CRUEL 1

wantonness *n* the willful infliction of pain and suffering on others ⟨the barbaric *wantonness* with which the guards treated the prisoners of war⟩ — see CRUELTY

war *n* **1** a state of armed violent struggle between states, nations, or groups ⟨the United States declared *war* on Japan after the bombing of Pearl Harbor⟩
synonyms conflict, hostilities, hot war
related words civil war, cold war, holy war, limited war, world war; action, battle, engagement; combat, fighting, warfare; belligerency; wartime
near antonyms demilitarization, demobilization, disarmament; pacification; cease-fire, truce; calm, peacefulness, tranquillity (*or* tranquility)
antonyms peace

2 a lack of agreement or harmony ⟨the siblings always seemed to be at *war* with one another⟩ — see DISCORD

war (against) *vb* to oppose (someone) in physical conflict ⟨continually *warring against* their neighbors in an effort to expand their territory⟩ — see FIGHT 1

warble *n* a rhythmic series of musical tones arranged to give a pleasing effect ⟨whistled a cheerful *warble* as he strolled down the street⟩ — see MELODY

warble *vb* to sing with the alternation of two musical tones ⟨the skylark *warbled* prettily outside our window⟩
synonyms quaver, trill
related words slur; yodel; belt, carol, chant, chorus, croon, descant, harmonize, troll, vocalize; lilt, scat

ward *n* **1** means or method of defending ⟨frequent hand washing is an oft-recommended *ward* against the spread of common germs⟩ — see DEFENSE 1

2 responsibility for the safety and well-being of someone or something ⟨gained the *ward* of his cousin upon the death of her parents⟩ — see CUSTODY

ward *vb* to drive danger or attack away from ⟨vowed that he would take whatever measures were necessary to *ward* the nation's people⟩ — see DEFEND 1

warden *n* **1** a person or group that watches over someone or something ⟨in his role as *warden* of the school, a principal must provide a safe environment for the students⟩ — see GUARD 1

2 a person who takes care of a property sometimes for an absent owner ⟨served as *warden* for the country estate⟩ — see CUSTODIAN 1

warder *n* a person or group that watches over someone or something ⟨as *warder* of the velvet rope, he decides who gets into the fashionable nightclub and who doesn't⟩ — see GUARD 1

warehouse *n* a building for storing goods ⟨when the *warehouse* burned down, we lost most of our merchandise⟩ — see STOREHOUSE

wares *n pl* products that are bought and sold in business ⟨a merchant proudly displaying his *wares*⟩ — see MERCHANDISE

warfare *n* **1** a lack of agreement or harmony ⟨that troubled household seems to be almost constantly in a state of *warfare*⟩ — see DISCORD

2 an earnest effort for superiority or victory over another ⟨companies engaged in constant *warfare* for dominance in the market for home computers⟩ — see CONTEST 1

wariness *n* a close attentiveness to avoiding danger ⟨only her unceasing *wariness* saved the party of skiers from an avalanche⟩ — see CAUTION 1

warlike *adj* feeling or displaying eagerness to fight ⟨a seafarer's legend that the remote island was inhabited by a *warlike* and uncivilized tribe⟩ — see BELLIGERENT

warm *adj* **1** having or giving off heat to a moderate degree ⟨the pan was still *warm*, but no longer too hot to touch⟩
synonyms heated, lukewarm, tepid, toasty, warmed
related words thawed; broiling, burning, fiery, hot, piping hot, red-hot, roasting, scalding, scorching, searing, sultry, sweltering, torrid; overheated, roasted, superheated, sweltering; blazing, glowing, molten, sizzling; reheated
near antonyms arctic, bitter, bleak, chill, chilly, cold, freezing, frigid, frosty, glacial, ice-cold, iced, icy, nippy, polar, raw, sharp, snappy, snowy, subfreezing, subzero, wintry; unthawed; frosted; benumbed, nipped, numb
antonyms chilled, cool, cooled, refrigerated, unheated

2 having or expressing great depth of feeling ⟨a *warm* hug of welcome from our grandmother⟩ — see FERVENT

3 having or showing kindly feeling and sincere interest ⟨a *warm* inquiry after his parents' health⟩ — see FRIENDLY 1

4 showing or expressing acceptance or approval ⟨a movie that's been getting a *warm* reception from the critics⟩ — see POSITIVE

warm *vb* **1** to cause to have or give off heat to a moderate degree ⟨you'll need to *warm* the food in the microwave⟩
synonyms heat, toast
related words overheat, superheat; reheat; burn, char, fire, scald, scorch, sear
near antonyms freeze, frost, ice
antonyms chill, cool, refrigerate

2 to give satisfaction to ⟨my dance instructor's generous praise *warmed* my heart⟩ — see PLEASE

warm–blooded *adj* having or expressing great depth of feeling ⟨a *warm-blooded* defense of everyone's right to free speech⟩ — see FERVENT

warmed *adj* having or giving off heat to a moderate degree ⟨the *warmed* towels that the attendant handed us were a nice touch⟩ — see WARM 1

warmhearted *adj* **1** having or marked by sympathy and consideration for others ⟨a *warmhearted*, understanding pastor from whom many sought guidance⟩ — see HUMANE 1

2 having or showing kindly feeling and sincere interest ⟨a *warmhearted* welcome from the principal on the opening day of school⟩ — see FRIENDLY 1

warmness *n* the quality or state of being moderate in temperature ⟨the cozy *warmness* of a house can be so nice after an hour spent shoveling snow⟩ — see WARMTH 1

warmonger *n* one who urges or attempts to cause a war ⟨fortunately, the *warmongers* met with overwhelming opposition⟩

synonyms hawk, jingo, militarist

related words agitator, firebrand, fomenter, instigator, rabble-rouser; belligerent, combatant, militant; chauvinist

near antonyms peacemaker

antonyms dove, pacifist

warmth *n* **1** the quality or state of being moderate in temperature ⟨the cozy *warmth* of the inn's parlor was a welcome relief from the wintry weather outside⟩

synonyms lukewarmness, warmness

related words glow, radiance; heat, hotness, sultriness, stuffiness

near antonyms bitterness, bleakness, cold, coldness, frigidity, frostiness, iciness, rawness, sharpness; frost

antonyms chill, chilliness, coolness

2 depth of feeling ⟨I was surprised by the *warmth* of the greeting⟩ — see ARDOR 1

warn *vb* to give notice to beforehand especially of danger or risk ⟨Dad *warned* us that if we continued playing so rough, someone was sure to get hurt⟩

synonyms alert, caution, forewarn

related words augur, forecast, foretell, predict, presage, prognosticate, prophesy; advise, apprise, inform, notify; admonish; bode, forebode, portend

near antonyms imperil, risk

warning *adj* serving as or offering a warning ⟨usually gave a *warning* look when the children were getting out of hand⟩ — see CAUTIONARY

warning *n* **1** the act or an instance of telling beforehand of danger or risk ⟨she delivered a strict *warning* that anyone who was caught cheating would get expelled⟩

synonyms admonition, alarm, alert, caution, forewarning, notice

related words auguring, augury, forecasting, foretelling, predicting, prediction, presaging, prognosticating, prophecy, prophesying; apprising, informing, notification, notifying; advice, counsel, guidance, recommendation, suggestion; announcement, declaration

2 something that tells of approaching danger or risk ⟨the ominously darkening sky was a *warning* that a tornado was approaching⟩

synonyms caution, tocsin

related words omen, portent; notification; buoy, knell, sign, signal; foretaste, foretoken; announcement, declaration

warp *vb* **1** to change so much as to create a wrong impression or alter the meaning of ⟨the faulty English

translation really *warps* the meaning of the original text, which is in Russian⟩ — see GARBLE

2 to lower in character or dignity ⟨claims that violent movies *warp* the values of our young people⟩ — see DEBASE 1

3 to twist (something) out of a natural or normal shape or condition ⟨freezing *warped* the plastic, and now the cover won't fit⟩ — see CONTORT

warped *adj* having or showing lowered moral character or standards ⟨tired of his sick jokes and *warped* sense of humor⟩ — see CORRUPT

warping *n* the twisting of something out of its natural or normal shape or condition ⟨the *warping* of the doorframe over the years means there's always a draft now⟩ — see CONTORTION

warrant *vb* **1** to assume responsibility for the satisfactory quality or performance of ⟨the computer company unconditionally *warrants* all of its products for one full year⟩

synonyms guarantee

related words attest, authenticate, avouch, certify, testify (to), vouch (for), witness; assure, bond, contract, covenant; pledge, plight, swear, vow; adhere, assert, declare, insist; insure

2 to give official acceptance of something as satisfactory ⟨the state constitution *warrants* these measures⟩ — see APPROVE

3 to have as a requirement ⟨the situation *warrants* your immediate attention⟩ — see NEED 1

4 to state as a fact usually forcefully ⟨we'll all be dead before that happens, I *warrant*⟩ — see CLAIM 1

warranted *adj* being what is called for by accepted standards of right and wrong ⟨a *warranted* use of force⟩ — see JUST 1

warranty *n* a formal agreement to fulfill an obligation ⟨a one-year *warranty* for the refrigerator⟩ — see GUARANTEE 1

warrior *n* a person engaged in military service ⟨a program of tough training and discipline that turns untried civilians into *warriors*⟩ — see SOLDIER

wary *adj* having or showing a close attentiveness to avoiding danger or trouble ⟨kept a *wary* eye out for signs of the enemy⟩ — see CAREFUL 1

wash *vb* **1** to flow along or against ⟨crystal-clear waters gently *wash* the island's unspoiled beaches⟩

synonyms lap, lave, splash

related words gurgle, ripple, slosh

2 to flow in a broken irregular stream ⟨soapy water *washing* down the drain⟩ — see GURGLE

3 to make wet ⟨rain *washed* the countryside for days on end⟩ — see WET

4 to pour liquid over or through in order to cleanse ⟨*washed* the baby's hair⟩ — see FLUSH 1

washed *adj* containing, covered with, or thoroughly penetrated by water ⟨*washed* city streets glistened with the light of the lampposts⟩ — see WET

washed–out *adj* lacking intensity of color ⟨*washed-out* blond hair⟩ — see PALE 1

washed–up *adj* having lost forcefulness, courage, or spirit ⟨he felt rather *washed-up* after this latest failure⟩ — see EFFETE 1

washout *n* something that has failed ⟨her last project was a complete *washout*⟩ — see FAILURE 3

wash out *vb* **1** to be unsuccessful ⟨most of the participants in the tough training program *washed out*⟩ — see FAIL 2

2 to make white or whiter by removing color ⟨the bright lights of the TV studio *washed out* her facial features, making her look as white as a ghost⟩ — see WHITEN

3 to use up all the physical energy of ⟨that last illness *washed* the child *out* completely⟩ — see EXHAUST 1

washroom *n* a room furnished with a fixture for flushing body waste ⟨could you tell me where the *washroom* is?⟩ — see TOILET

waspish *adj* easily irritated or annoyed ⟨extremely *waspish*, she uses her wit viciously when irritated⟩ — see IRRITABLE

waspishness *n* readiness to show annoyance or impatience ⟨his eternal *waspishness* served to make those around him cranky as well⟩ — see PETULANCE

wassail *n* a bout of drinking ⟨woke up with a terrible headache from a wild *wassail* the night before⟩ — see CAROUSE

wastage *n* the state or fact of being rendered nonexistent, physically unsound, or useless ⟨the *wastage* of the surrounding countryside during the course of the war⟩ — see DESTRUCTION

waste *adj* producing inferior or only a small amount of vegetation ⟨*waste* acreage that was not fit for anything⟩ — see BARREN 1

waste *n* **1** an instance of spending money or resources without care or restraint ⟨it seems like a *waste* to spend my entire paycheck on a bigger TV⟩
synonyms extravagance, prodigality
related words indulgence, luxury, splurge; loss, wastage; generosity, liberality, openhandedness, profligacy; improvidence, shortsightedness; overindulgence; self-indulgence; excess, immoderacy, overkill; carelessness, heedlessness, imprudence, incautiousness; recklessness
near antonyms necessity; economizing, economy, frugality, saving, scrimping, skimping; austerity, moderation, restraint, temperance, temperateness
2 discarded or useless material ⟨gathered up the *waste* when he was finished sewing⟩ — see GARBAGE
3 land that is uninhabited or not fit for crops ⟨an area that was a barren *waste* after the strip-mining had ended⟩ — see WASTELAND
4 solid matter discharged from an animal's alimentary canal ⟨a local ordinance requiring dog owners to properly dispose of their pet's *waste*⟩ — see DROPPING 1

waste *vb* **1** to use up carelessly ⟨he *wasted* most of his allowance by buying comic books⟩
synonyms blow, dissipate, fritter (away), lavish, misspend, run through, spend, squander, throw away
related words splurge; consume, deplete, exhaust, impoverish; indulge, overindulge; disburse, expend, lay out
near antonyms economize, scrimp, skimp; preserve, protect, save; hoard, lay up
antonyms conserve
2 to bring to a complete end the physical soundness, existence, or usefulness of ⟨one country attempting to *waste* another⟩ — see DESTROY 1
3 to diminish the physical strength of ⟨endless hours of inactivity *wasted* him⟩ — see WEAKEN 1

waste (away) *vb* to lose bodily strength or vigor ⟨the tuberculosis resulted in her simply *wasting away*⟩ — see WEAKEN 2

wasted *adj* **1** lacking bodily strength ⟨a *wasted* frame—a shadow of the man he once was⟩ — see WEAK 1
2 suffering extreme weight loss as a result of hunger or disease ⟨a frail and *wasted* famine victim⟩ — see EMACIATED

wasteful *adj* given to spending money freely or foolishly ⟨my one *wasteful* child always seemed to run out of money by midweek⟩ — see PRODIGAL

wastefulness *n* the quality or fact of being free or wasteful in the expenditure of money ⟨his *wastefulness* is downright irresponsible⟩ — see EXTRAVAGANCE 1

wasteland *n* land that is uninhabited or not fit for crops ⟨with proper irrigation and fertilizer, they turned the desert *wasteland* into a fertile plain⟩
synonyms barren, desert, desolation, waste
related words badland; brush, bush; dust bowl; hinterland, upland; open, open air, outdoors, out-of-doors; nature, wild, wilderness

waster *n* someone who carelessly spends money ⟨we want you to get a job so that you'll be a *waster* of your own money and not ours⟩ — see PRODIGAL

wastrel *n* someone who carelessly spends money ⟨the black sheep of the family, he ended up being a *wastrel* and a drunkard⟩ — see PRODIGAL

watch *n* **1** a person or group that watches over someone or something ⟨the neighborhood crime *watch*⟩ — see GUARD 1
2 the act or state of being constantly attentive and responsive to signs of activity, opportunity, or danger ⟨kept a *watch* over the sick baby⟩ — see VIGILANCE

watch *vb* **1** to keep one's eyes on ⟨I turned my head to continue *watching* the bird as it flew away⟩
synonyms eye, observe
related words behold, look, regard, see, view; gape, gawk, gaze, glare, goggle, peer, rubberneck, stare; guard, wake, ward; monitor, read; spy; glance, glimpse, peek, peep
near antonyms blink, wink
2 to take notice of and be guided by ⟨*watch* what I do when I run into that kind of problem⟩ — see HEED 1
3 to pay continued close attention to (something) for a particular purpose ⟨*watched* the situation to see if it improved⟩ — see MONITOR
4 to have an interest or concern for ⟨*watched* the younger child while his mother worked⟩ — see CARE

watch (for) *vb* to believe in the future occurrence of (something) ⟨*watch for* all the latest news on this Web site⟩ — see EXPECT

watchful *adj* paying close attention usually for the purpose of anticipating approaching danger or opportunity ⟨under the *watchful* eye of several parents⟩ — see ALERT 1

watchfulness *n* the act or state of being constantly attentive and responsive to signs of opportunity, activity, or danger ⟨it was only her *watchfulness* that saved the boy from an accident⟩ — see VIGILANCE

watchman *n* **1** a person or group that watches over someone or something ⟨hired a *watchman* to patrol the factory at night⟩ — see GUARD 1
2 a person who takes care of a property sometimes for an absent owner ⟨a *watchman* lives next door to scare off prowlers⟩ — see CUSTODIAN 1

watch out (for) *vb* to be cautious of or on guard against ⟨*watch out for* hazards in the road⟩ — see BEWARE (OF)

watchword *n* **1** a word or phrase that must be spoken by a person in order to pass a guard ⟨the *watchword* is changed every day⟩ — see PASSWORD
2 an attention-getting word or phrase used to publicize something (as a campaign or product) ⟨their latest *watchword* turns up in every ad from that company⟩ — see SLOGAN

water *vb* to make wet ⟨*watered* the plants⟩ — see WET

water (down) *vb* to alter (something) for the worse with the addition of foreign or lower-grade substances ⟨*watered down* the cocktails while jacking up their prices⟩ — see ADULTERATE

water closet *n* a room furnished with a fixture for flushing body waste ⟨the first house in town to have an indoor *water closet*⟩ — see TOILET

watercourse *n* an open man-made passageway for water ⟨the Erie Canal was the first *watercourse* to connect the Hudson River with the Great Lakes⟩ — see CHANNEL 1

watercraft *n* a small buoyant structure for travel on water ⟨just about any kind of *watercraft* can be seen on the lake during the summer⟩ — see BOAT 1

watered *adj* containing, covered with, or thoroughly penetrated by water ⟨a *watered* lawn⟩ — see WET

waterfall *n* a fall of water usually from a great height ⟨I used to like to throw sticks in the stream and watch them go over the *waterfall*⟩
synonyms cascade, cataract, fall(s)
related words rapid(s), white water; eddy, riffle; undertow, vortex, whirlpool

waterless *adj* marked by little or no precipitation or humidity ⟨cacti prefer a nearly *waterless* environment⟩ — see DRY 1

waterlogged *adj* containing, covered with, or thoroughly penetrated by water ⟨*waterlogged* soil that caused the roots of the potted plant to rot⟩ — see WET

waterproof *n, chiefly British* a coat made of water-resistant material ⟨remember your *waterproof* if you're walking around London in the winter⟩ — see RAINCOAT

waterproof *adj* made of or treated with material that does not allow water to penetrate ⟨luckily, my backpack is *waterproof*, so my notes didn't get wet⟩
synonyms waterproofed, watertight
related words rainproof; water-repellent, water-resistant; nonabsorbent, nonporous
near antonyms absorbent, porous

waterproofed *adj* made of or treated with material that does not allow water to penetrate ⟨a *waterproofed* fabric that is used for outerwear⟩ — see WATERPROOF

waterspout *n* a pipe or channel for carrying off water from a roof ⟨the *waterspout* became clogged and then the roof leaked⟩ — see GUTTER 1

watertight *adj* made of or treated with material that does not allow water to penetrate ⟨don't wear a watch that isn't *watertight* into the tub!⟩ — see WATERPROOF

waterway *n* an open man-made passageway for water ⟨took a boat out on the *waterway*⟩ — see CHANNEL 1

watery *adj* **1** containing, covered with, or thoroughly penetrated by water ⟨the soft, *watery* earth of the marshland⟩ — see WET
2 having an overly soft liquid consistency ⟨*watery* oatmeal⟩ — see RUNNY
3 not containing very much of some important element ⟨*watery* lemonade⟩ — see WEAK 3

wave *n* a moving ridge on the surface of water ⟨the toddler was almost knocked down by the *waves* created by the speedboat⟩
synonyms billow, surge, swell
related words sea(s); breaker, whitecap; curl; comber, roller; eddy, riffle, ripple, wavelet; tidal wave, tsunami; undertow, vortex, whirlpool

wave *vb* to direct or notify by a movement or gesture ⟨*waved* them over to the side of the road⟩ — see MOTION

waver *vb* **1** to show uncertainty about the right course of action ⟨he's still *wavering* about whether to take the job⟩ — see HESITATE
2 to swing unsteadily back and forth or from side to side ⟨the steel tower *wavered* for a moment before falling over⟩ — see TEETER 1

wavering *n* the act or an instance of pausing because of uncertainty about the right course of action ⟨after a moment's *wavering*, she accepted his proposal⟩ — see HESITATION

wax *vb* **1** to become greater in extent, volume, amount, or number ⟨the noise level *waxed* as more people flooded into the stadium⟩ — see INCREASE 2
2 to coat (something) with a slippery substance in order to reduce friction ⟨*waxing* a surfboard⟩ — see LUBRICATE
3 to eventually have as a state or quality ⟨*waxed* poetic whenever he wrote to his girlfriend⟩ — see BECOME

way *n* **1** a passage cleared for public vehicular travel ⟨the town honored the local sports hero by naming after him a short *way* connecting two shopping centers⟩
synonyms artery, avenue, boulevard, drag, drive, expressway, freeway, highroad, highway, pass, passageway, pike, road, roadway, route, row, street, thoroughfare, trace, turnpike
related words causeway; alley, alleyway, bystreet, byway, catwalk, court, lane, place; approach, concourse, path, walkway; access; dead end; aisle, corridor, course, line; track, trail; channel; corduroy, tarmac; crossroad; bypass, overpass, underpass; cloverleaf, rotary
2 a usual manner of behaving or doing ⟨she's set in her *ways* and is not about to change⟩ — see HABIT
3 an established course for traveling from one place to another ⟨took the regular *way*⟩ — see PASSAGE 1
4 an established pattern of behavior ⟨that's just his *way*, so pay him no mind⟩ — see TENDENCY 1
5 an extent or area available for or used up by some activity or thing ⟨made *way* for them to pass⟩ — see ROOM 1
6 the direction along which something or someone moves ⟨go the same *way* that the school bus does⟩ — see PATH 1
7 the means or procedure for doing something ⟨figured out the best *way* to accomplish the task⟩ — see METHOD
8 the opening through which one can enter or leave a structure ⟨we came in the back *way*⟩ — see DOOR 2
9 the power, right, or opportunity to choose ⟨have it your *way*⟩ — see CHOICE 1
10 the space or amount of space between two points, lines, surfaces, or objects ⟨it's just a little *way* down the road⟩ — see DISTANCE

wayfarer *n* a person who roams about without a fixed route or destination ⟨one of the great *wayfarers* of American folklore, Johnny Appleseed wandered across the country, always planting apple seeds⟩ — see NOMAD

wayfaring *adj* traveling from place to place ⟨a *wayfaring* folksinger⟩ — see ITINERANT

waylay *vb* to lie in wait for and attack by surprise ⟨the robbers *waylaid* people on the road⟩ — see AMBUSH

way–out *adj* different from the ordinary in a way that causes curiosity or suspicion ⟨some new and *way-out* suggestions⟩ — see ODD 2

way station *n* a regular stopping place ⟨a *way station* for truck drivers⟩ — see STATION 2

wayward *adj* **1** given to resisting authority or another's control ⟨had always been the most *wayward* of their three children⟩ — see DISOBEDIENT
2 given to resisting control or discipline by others ⟨an institution to which *wayward* teens were often sent⟩ — see UNCONTROLLABLE
weak *adj* **1** lacking bodily strength ⟨the little boy was simply too *weak* to lift the box⟩
synonyms debilitated, delicate, effete, enervated, enfeebled, faint, feeble, frail, infirm, languid, low, prostrate, prostrated, sapped, slight, soft, softened, tender, torpid, unsubstantial, wasted, weakened, wimpy
related words challenged, disabled, incapacitated; paralyzed; broken-down, decrepit, worn out; impotent, powerless, puny; breakable, flimsy, fragile; dizzy, groggy, rocky, unsteady, woozy; exhausted, tired, weary; damaged, harmed, hurt, impaired, injured; resistless, susceptible, unresistant, vulnerable, yielding
near antonyms able-bodied, athletic, beefy, brawny, fit, husky, muscular, sinewy, strapping, virile; hard, hardy, lusty, robust, sturdy, tough; fortified, hardened, inured, strengthened, toughened; energetic, energized, invigorated, vigorous, vitalized; hale, healthy, sound; capable, competent; convalescing, recovering, recuperating
antonyms mighty, powerful, rugged, stalwart, stout, strong
2 lacking strength of will or character ⟨the opinion that overweight people are just *weak* individuals who easily give in to temptation⟩
synonyms characterless, effete, frail, invertebrate, nerveless, soft, spineless, weakened, wimpy, wishy-washy
related words forceless, ineffective, ineffectual; impotent, powerless; emasculated, unnerved; pliable, submissive; corrupt, unprincipled, unscrupulous, villainous; cowardly, craven, lily-livered
near antonyms ethical, good, moral, principled, right, righteous, upright, virtuous; determined, mettlesome, resolute; courageous, stalwart, stouthearted
antonyms backboned, firm, strong, tough
3 not containing very much of some important element ⟨the coffee came out too *weak* because I didn't put enough ground beans in⟩
synonyms dilute, diluted, thin, thinned, watery, weakened
related words adulterated, watered (down)
near antonyms enriched, fortified; concentrated, condensed, evaporated
antonyms full-bodied, rich, strong
4 not using or following good reasoning ⟨your argument is *weak*⟩ — see ILLOGICAL
5 unable to act or achieve one's purpose ⟨the vice president is a relatively *weak* official⟩ — see POWERLESS
weaken *vb* **1** to diminish the physical strength of ⟨several days of hardship in the desert had *weakened* them⟩
synonyms debilitate, enervate, enfeeble, prostrate, sap, soften, tire, waste
related words cripple, disable, incapacitate; deplete, depress, exhaust, impoverish, unman, wash out; damage, harm, hurt, impair, injure; break down, wear out; paralyze
near antonyms energize, invigorate, vitalize; harden, season, toughen
antonyms beef (up), fortify, recruit, strengthen
2 to lose bodily strength or vigor ⟨the bodybuilder *weakened* once she eased off on her workouts⟩

synonyms decay, droop, fail, flag, go, lag, languish, sag, waste (away), wilt
related words break down, wear out; yield
near antonyms convalesce, recover, recuperate; gain
2 to alter (something) for the worse with the addition of foreign or lower-grade substances ⟨*weakened* the juice with too much water⟩ — see ADULTERATE
weakened *adj* **1** containing foreign or lower-grade substances ⟨the pharmacist, motivated by pure greed, would pass off the *weakened* drugs to unsuspecting customers, some of whom had life-threatening illnesses⟩ — see IMPURE
2 lacking bodily strength ⟨left *weakened* by a prolonged illness⟩ — see WEAK 1
3 lacking strength of will or character ⟨the nation's people, *weakened* by years of tyranny, tended to automatically obey anyone with an authoritative manner⟩ — see WEAK 2
4 not containing very much of some important element ⟨some experts recommend that runners drink a *weakened* mixture of juice and water⟩ — see WEAK 3
weakening *n* a gradual sinking and wasting away of mind or body ⟨the all-too-apparent *weakening* of our grandfather was hard on our mother⟩ — see DECLINE 1
weakling *n* **1** a person lacking in physical strength ⟨he was a *weakling* until high school, when he started working out to put on muscle⟩
synonyms softy (*or* softie), wimp
related words pushover, sissy
antonyms powerhouse
2 a person without strength of character ⟨only a *weakling* would be willing to lie to save himself from punishment⟩
synonyms mollycoddle, wimp
related words coward, mouse
antonyms stalwart
weakly *adj* chronically or repeatedly suffering from poor health ⟨a *weakly* baby who required repeated hospitalizations⟩ — see SICKLY 1
weak–minded *adj* **1** not having or showing an ability to absorb ideas readily ⟨was written off as a *weak-minded* child until it was discovered that he was suffering from a learning disability⟩ — see STUPID 1
2 showing or marked by a lack of good sense or judgment ⟨a *weak-minded* decision to use all of their savings to buy lottery tickets in the hopes of hitting the jackpot⟩ — see FOOLISH 1
weakness *n* **1** the quality or state of lacking physical strength or vigor ⟨the flu left me with such *weakness* that I could hardly stand⟩
synonyms debilitation, debility, delicacy, delicateness, enfeeblement, faintness, feebleness, frailness, frailty, infirmity, languor, lowness
related words decay, decrepitude; breakdown, collapse, exhaustion, nervous breakdown, prostration; defenselessness, helplessness; softness, tenderness; disablement, incapacitation; damage, harm, hurt, impairment, injury
near antonyms energy, vitality; brawniness, fitness, huskiness, virility; hardness, ruggedness, stoutness, sturdiness, toughness; haleness, health, healthiness, soundness
antonyms hardihood, hardiness, robustness, strength, vigor
2 the quality or state of lacking strength of will or character ⟨in a moment of *weakness* he shoplifted the comic book⟩

synonyms frailness, frailty, softness, spinelessness
related words collapse; failing, flaw, peccadillo; evil, immorality, wickedness; corruption, corruptness
near antonyms discipline, self-discipline; goodness, morality, righteousness, rightness, uprightness, virtuousness
antonyms backbone, firmness, fortitude, mettle, resoluteness, strength
3 a defect in character ⟨his one *weakness* is his cock-eyed optimism about everything⟩ — see FAULT 1
4 the quality or state of having little resistance to some outside agent ⟨the devastating *weakness* of the immune system that is experienced by people with AIDS⟩ — see SUSCEPTIBILITY

weal *n* the state of doing well especially in relation to one's happiness or success ⟨the belief that somehow it is the nation's president who is responsible for the *weal* or woe of the people⟩ — see WELFARE

wealth *n* **1** the total of one's money and property ⟨her *wealth* increased to the point where she could afford several luxurious homes⟩
synonyms assets, capital, fortune, means, opulence, riches, substance, wherewithal
related words belongings, chattels, effects, holdings, paraphernalia, possessions, things; finances, money; king's ransom, mint, wad; abundance, affluence, prosperity, success; treasure, valuables; accession, acquisition, personalty, property; nest egg, reserve, resources, savings, treasury; collateral; heap, pile, pot; bonanza, mine, treasure trove
near antonyms debts, liabilities; indebtedness
2 a considerable amount ⟨a *wealth* of advice from all quarters on how they should spend their lottery winnings⟩ — see LOT 2
3 an amount or supply more than sufficient to meet one's needs ⟨a *wealth* of documentation to support her thesis⟩ — see PLENTY 1

wealthy *adj* having goods, property, or money in abundance ⟨a *wealthy* man who likes to collect antique cars⟩ — see RICH 1

wear *n* **1** the result of long and hard use ⟨after several years, the carpet was finally showing *wear*⟩
synonyms wear and tear
related words abrasion, corrosion, erasure, erosion; decomposition, disintegration
near antonyms fixing, mending, patching, rebuilding, reconditioning, reconstruction, renovation, repair, revamping
2 covering for the human body ⟨the latest in fashionable *wear*⟩ — see CLOTHING

wear *vb* **1** to use up all the physical energy of ⟨the job of running their own business *wears* them sometimes⟩ — see EXHAUST 1
2 to damage or diminish by continued friction ⟨all that walking every day *wore* the soles of my shoes very quickly⟩ — see ABRADE 1

wear and tear *n* the result of long and hard use ⟨my favorite jeans finally succumbed to *wear and tear* and had to be replaced⟩ — see WEAR 1

wearied *adj* **1** depleted in strength, energy, or freshness ⟨fell into bed *wearied* and desperate for sleep⟩ — see WEARY 1
2 having one's patience, interest, or pleasure exhausted ⟨Mom is *wearied* by your endless excuses for not having cleaned your room⟩ — see WEARY 2

weariless *adj* showing no signs of weariness even after long hard effort ⟨the *weariless* efforts to bring peace to that troubled region⟩ — see TIRELESS

weariness *n* **1** a complete depletion of energy or strength ⟨the kind of satisfying *weariness* that comes from a good day's labor⟩ — see FATIGUE
2 the state of being bored ⟨faces showing *weariness* and irritation at the long graduation speech⟩ — see BOREDOM

wearisome *adj* causing weariness, restlessness, or lack of interest ⟨a *wearisome* lecture on civic responsibility⟩ — see BORING

wear out *vb* to use up all the physical energy of ⟨keeping up with twin toddlers *wears* me *out*⟩ — see EXHAUST 1

weary *adj* **1** depleted in strength, energy, or freshness ⟨I am just too *weary* to do any more work tonight⟩
synonyms beat, burned-out (*or* burnt-out), bushed, dead, done in, drained, effete, exhausted, fatigued, jaded, limp, logy, played out, prostrate, spent, tired, tuckered (out), wearied, worn, worn-out
related words overtaxed, overworked; run-down; debilitated, enervated, enfeebled, sapped, weakened
phrases worn to a frazzle
near antonyms refreshed, rejuvenated, relaxed, rested, revitalized; active, energetic, invigorated, strengthened, strong, tireless, vitalized
antonyms untired
2 having one's patience, interest, or pleasure exhausted ⟨I am totally *weary* of this constant bickering⟩
synonyms bored, fed up, jaded, sick, tired, wearied
related words apathetic, disinterested, uninterested; glutted, sated, satiated, surfeited; dejected, demoralized, discouraged, disheartened, dispirited; beat, burned-out (*or* burnt-out), bushed, done in, drained, enervated, exhausted, fatigued, limp, played out, tuckered, worn-out; annoyed, frustrated, irritated; disgusted, nauseated, repulsed
near antonyms animated, energized, enlivened, excited, galvanized, invigorated, stimulated, vitalized; amused, entertained; beguiled, bewitched, captivated, charmed, enchanted, enthralled, fascinated, hypnotized, mesmerized; delighted, pleased, thrilled
antonyms absorbed, engaged, engrossed, gripped, interested, intrigued
3 causing weariness, restlessness, or lack of interest ⟨a *weary* march through a lot of boring facts and figures⟩ — see BORING

weary *vb* **1** to make weary and restless by being dull or monotonous ⟨these constant complaints are really *wearying* me⟩ — see ²BORE
2 to use up all the physical energy of ⟨a whole day of hard physical labor had thoroughly *wearied* her⟩ — see EXHAUST 1

wearying *adj* causing weariness, restlessness, or lack of interest ⟨a *wearying* effort to sort through years of records⟩ — see BORING

weather *vb* to come safely through ⟨we've *weathered* worse crises, and so we'll survive this one⟩ — see SURVIVE 1

weave *vb* to scatter or set here and there among other things ⟨a political commentator who slyly *weaves* lies into the truth⟩ — see THREAD 1

web *n* **1** something that catches and holds ⟨he was caught in the *web* of branches⟩ ⟨she was trapped by her own *web* of lies⟩
synonyms entanglement, net, snare
related words mesh, trap; knot, snarl, tangle; labyrinth, maze; cobweb, spiderweb
2 a device or scheme for capturing another by surprise ⟨an ingenious *web* that was spun by undercover agents going after drug dealers⟩ — see TRAP 1

wed *vb* **1** to give in marriage ⟨the king wished to *wed* his favorite daughter to the bravest knight in the realm⟩ — see MARRY 2

2 to perform the ceremony of marriage for ⟨the priest *weds* six to eight couples a week⟩ — see MARRY 1

3 to take a spouse ⟨she swore that she would never *wed*⟩ — see MARRY 4

4 to take as a spouse ⟨a true romantic, he intends to *wed* her on Valentine's Day⟩ — see MARRY 3

wedded *adj* of or relating to marriage ⟨living in *wedded* bliss⟩ — see MARITAL

wedding *n* a ceremony in which two people are united in matrimony ⟨they chose to have the *wedding* outdoors in the spring⟩

synonyms bridal, espousal, marriage, nuptial(s)

related words match, matrimony, wedlock; reception; engagement, hand, pledge, promise, proposal, troth

wedge *vb* to fit (something) into a tight space ⟨managed to *wedge* one last book onto the bookshelf⟩ — see CROWD 1

wedged *adj* firmly positioned in place and difficult to dislodge ⟨the pebble in the heel of his shoe was pretty well *wedged*⟩ — see TIGHT 2

wedlock *n* a union representing a special kind of social and legal partnership between two people ⟨hoped that her children would wait until they were older before entering *wedlock*⟩ — see MARRIAGE 1

wee *adj* very small in size ⟨a *wee* baby⟩ — see TINY

weedy *adj* growing thickly and vigorously ⟨*weedy* vegetation in the abandoned lot⟩ — see RANK 1

weep *vb* **1** to flow forth slowly through small openings ⟨water *weeping* through the basement wall⟩ — see EXUDE

2 to shed tears often while making meaningless sounds as a sign of pain or distress ⟨the child was *weeping* over a lost toy⟩ — see CRY 1

weeping *adj* expressing or suggesting mourning ⟨a *weeping* song about a long-lost love⟩ — see MOURNFUL 1

weigh *vb* **1** to be of importance ⟨evidence that will *weigh* heavily against the defendant⟩ — see MATTER

2 to give serious and careful thought to ⟨*weighed* the options for weeks before making a decision⟩ — see PONDER

weigh (on *or* upon) *vb* to push steadily against with some force ⟨the backpack *weighed upon* my back uncomfortably⟩ — see PRESS 1

weighed *adj* decided on as a result of careful thought ⟨a *weighed* decision to take the company in a new direction⟩ — see DELIBERATE 1

weight *n* **1** the amount that something weighs ⟨I'm not allowed to lift anything with a *weight* of over ten pounds⟩

synonyms heaviness, heft

related words mass; tonnage; deadweight; heftiness, massiveness, ponderousness, weightiness; solidity, solidness, substantiality; burdensomeness, cumbersomeness

2 the quality or state of being important ⟨a matter of little *weight*⟩ — see IMPORTANCE

3 a mass or quantity of something taken up and carried, conveyed, or transported ⟨those books are a heavy *weight* to have to carry around all day⟩ — see LOAD 1

4 a special notice or importance given to something ⟨put extra *weight* on the matter by putting it at the top of the agenda⟩ — see EMPHASIS 1

5 the main or greater part of something as distinguished from its appendages ⟨the *weight* of the evidence supports my conclusion⟩ — see BODY 1

6 the power to direct the thinking or behavior of others usually indirectly ⟨as a critic he has great *weight* in the theater world⟩ — see INFLUENCE 1

weight *vb* to place a weight or burden on ⟨*weighted* the car with a ton of furniture and then headed off for college⟩ — see LOAD 1

weightiness *n* **1** the state or quality of being heavy ⟨the *weightiness* of the bookcase made it difficult to move⟩

synonyms avoirdupois, heaviness, heftiness, massiveness, ponderousness

related words overweight; solidity, solidness, substantiality; bulk, bulkiness, hugeness; burdensomeness, cumbersomeness

near antonyms airiness, delicacy, etherealness; flimsiness, fluffiness, insubstantiality, slightness

antonyms lightness, weightlessness

2 the quality or state of being important ⟨first judged the *weightiness* of each issue⟩ — see IMPORTANCE

weightless *adj* having little weight ⟨the kitten seemed nearly *weightless* when I picked her up⟩ — see ¹LIGHT 1

weightlessness *n* the state or quality of having little weight ⟨the relative *weightlessness* of the suitcase surprised me⟩ — see ¹LIGHTNESS 1

weighty *adj* **1** having a matter of importance as its topic ⟨interrupted a *weighty* discussion with a silly question⟩ — see SERIOUS 2

2 having great meaning or lasting effect ⟨choosing a college is a *weighty* decision⟩ — see IMPORTANT 1

3 having great weight ⟨lifted the *weighty* sack and wondered what was in it⟩ — see HEAVY 1

4 not joking or playful in mood or manner ⟨the principal looked at me with a rather *weighty* expression⟩ — see SERIOUS 1

5 having power over the minds or behavior of others ⟨one of the *weightiest* figures in the field of medicine⟩ — see INFLUENTIAL 1

weird *adj* **1** different from the ordinary in a way that causes curiosity or suspicion ⟨always has a somewhat *weird* opinion of what's happening in the news⟩ — see ODD 2

2 fearfully and mysteriously strange or fantastic ⟨*weird* sounds from the woods just beyond our campsite⟩ — see EERIE

3 having seemingly supernatural qualities or powers ⟨a self-styled, contemporary witch, she sells herbal mixtures that she claims are *weird* potions⟩ — see MYSTIC 1

4 noticeably different from what is generally found or experienced ⟨a *weird* little plant that we found growing in the garden⟩ — see UNUSUAL 1

weirdo *n* a person of odd or whimsical habits ⟨one of the *weirdos* that the rest of the school always seemed to be talking about⟩ — see ECCENTRIC

welcome *adj* giving pleasure or contentment to the mind or senses ⟨a *welcome* chance to rest⟩ — see PLEASANT

welcome *n* an expression of goodwill upon meeting ⟨offered a warm *welcome* to the stranger⟩ — see HELLO

welcome *vb* receive or accept gladly or readily ⟨the eager recruits *welcomed* every new project with which they were presented⟩

synonyms embrace

related words adopt, espouse, take up; greet, hail; enjoy, like, prefer; choose, cull, decide (on), elect, handpick, name, opt (for), pick, select, single (out), take

near antonyms decline, refuse, reject, turn down

welfare *n* the state of doing well especially in relation to one's happiness or success ⟨the social worker was pleased at the improvement in the child's *welfare*⟩
synonyms good, interest, weal, well-being
related words prosperity, success, successfulness; fitness, health, healthiness, robustness, soundness, wellness, wholeness, wholesomeness; bliss, felicity, happiness, joy; advantage, benefit, gain, sake; content, contentedness, gratification, satisfaction
near antonyms unhealthiness, unsoundness; misery, sadness, unhappiness, wretchedness

well *adv* **1** in a satisfactory way ⟨our current system for dividing household chores works *well*, so let's keep it⟩
synonyms acceptably, adequately, all right, fine, good, nicely, OK (*or* okay), passably, satisfactorily, so-so, tolerably
related words appropriately, congruously, correctly, decently, decorously, felicitously, fittingly, meetly, rightly, seemly, suitably
near antonyms unbearably; inappropriately, incorrectly, indecently, unsuitably
antonyms bad, badly, inadequately, intolerably, poorly, unacceptably, unsatisfactorily
2 in a generous manner ⟨the warm and gracious couple always treats overnight guests *well*⟩
synonyms bountifully, generously, handsomely, liberally, munificently
related words considerately, courteously, hospitably, kindly, nicely, reasonably, thoughtfully; affably, amiably, cheerfully, cheerily, genially, good-naturedly, graciously
near antonyms contemptuously, disdainfully, rudely, scornfully; obnoxiously, provocatively; coldly, coolly, frigidly, hostilely; angrily, belligerently
antonyms stingily
3 in a skillful or expert manner ⟨she plays the piano very *well*⟩
synonyms ably, adeptly, capably, competently, expertly, masterfully, proficiently, skillfully
related words aptly; adroitly, deftly, dexterously
near antonyms inaptly
antonyms incapably, incompetently, inefficiently, ineptly, inexpertly, poorly, unskillfully
4 with good reason or courtesy ⟨we cannot *well* get out of going to your cousin's wedding⟩
synonyms considerately, courteously, kindly, nicely, reasonably, thoughtfully
related words pleasantly; excusably, justifiably
near antonyms contemptuously, disdainfully, rudely, scornfully
5 in a pleasing way ⟨the day went *well*, despite the rough beginning⟩
synonyms agreeably, delectably, deliciously, delightfully, dreamily, favorably, felicitously, gloriously, nicely, pleasantly, pleasingly, satisfyingly, splendidly, swimmingly
related words finely, grandly; advantageously, helpfully; fortunately, happily, luckily; prosperously, successfully
antonyms badly
6 to a full extent or degree ⟨we are *well* aware that this home renovation is going to be costly⟩ — see FULLY 1

well *adj* enjoying health and vigor ⟨my mother is quite *well*, thank you⟩ — see HEALTHY 1

well *interj* how surprising, doubtful, or unbelievable ⟨*well*, that is odd!⟩ — see NO

well–being *n* the state of doing well especially in relation to one's happiness or success ⟨we're only doing this for your own *well-being*⟩ — see WELFARE

wellborn *adj* of high birth, rank, or station ⟨the *wellborn* men among the colonists had no experience with physical labor⟩ — see NOBLE 1

well–bred *adj* showing consideration, courtesy, and good manners ⟨a *well-bred* young woman who was unfailingly polite to everyone⟩ — see POLITE 1

well–disposed *adj* having an easygoing and pleasing manner especially in social situations ⟨a bachelor who has a reputation for being *well-disposed*, especially towards the ladies⟩ — see AMIABLE

well–founded *adj* based on sound reasoning or information ⟨a *well-founded* complaint about the business's treatment of its customers⟩ — see GOOD 1

well–heeled *adj* having goods, property, or money in abundance ⟨the resort caters to a *well-heeled* clientele that demands the best and has the money to pay for it⟩ — see RICH 1

well–known *adj* widely known ⟨an anchorwoman so *well-known* that she passes for a local celebrity⟩ — see FAMOUS

wellness *n* the condition of being sound in body ⟨restored the patient to general *wellness*⟩ — see HEALTH

well–nigh *adv* very close to but not completely ⟨it was *well-nigh* dark, but I could still see a little⟩ — see ALMOST

well–off *adj* having goods, property, or money in abundance ⟨a *well-off* couple adopted the baby⟩ — see RICH 1

well–read *adj* having or displaying advanced knowledge or education ⟨any *well-read* person would recognize the quotation⟩ — see EDUCATED

well–spoken *adj* able to express oneself clearly and well ⟨a *well-spoken* advocate for the legal rights of the underprivileged⟩ — see ARTICULATE

well–to–do *adj* having goods, property, or money in abundance ⟨a doctor who is now quite *well-to-do* as a result of her successful medical practice⟩ — see RICH 1

welter *n* **1** a state of noisy, confused activity ⟨there was a *welter* of pushing and shoving as people rushed to grab the best seats for the outdoor concert⟩ — see COMMOTION
2 an unorganized collection or mixture of various things ⟨a *welter* of junk in the closet, most of which needed to be thrown out⟩ — see MISCELLANY 1

wet *adj* **1** containing, covered with, or thoroughly penetrated by water ⟨I left the car windows open while it rained, and the seats got all *wet*⟩
synonyms awash, bathed, doused, drenched, dripping, saturated, soaked, soaking, sodden, soggy, soppy, soused, washed, watered, waterlogged, watery
related words deluged, drowned, flooded, inundated, overflowed; submerged, swamped; hydrated; dipped, dunked, splashed; aqueous; steeped; flushed, irrigated, laved, rinsed, sluiced; clammy, damp, dank, humid, moist
near antonyms waterproof, water-resistant, water-repellent, watertight; baked, dehydrated, freeze-dried; droughty, parched, sere, sunbaked, thirsty; wrung
antonyms arid, dry, unwatered, waterless
2 marked by or abounding with rain ⟨a *wet* and dreary day⟩ — see RAINY

wet *n* a steady falling of water from the sky in significant quantity ⟨winced as he walked out into the *wet* without any protection⟩ — see RAIN 1

wet *vb* to make wet ⟨you need to *wet* your hair thoroughly first⟩
synonyms bathe, douse, drench, soak, souse, wash, water
related words damp, dampen, humidify, hydrate, moisten; deluge, drown, flood, inundate, overflow; submerge, swamp; splash; impregnate, saturate, steep; flush, irrigate, lave, rinse, sluice; dip, dunk
near antonyms bake, dehydrate, evaporate, freeze-dry, parch; wring; dehumidify
antonyms dry

whack *n* **1** an effort to do or accomplish something ⟨took a *whack* at solving the math problem⟩ — see ATTEMPT

2 a hard strike with a part of the body or an instrument ⟨gave the wasp's nest a good *whack* with the bat⟩ — see ¹BLOW

3 a loud explosive sound ⟨the *whack* echoed around the field⟩ — see CLAP 1

whack *vb* to deliver a blow to (someone or something) usually in a strong vigorous manner ⟨*whacked* the vending machine to get the candy bar to fall⟩ — see HIT 1

whacking *adj* unusually large ⟨harvested a *whacking* number of zucchini from the garden⟩ — see HUGE

whacking *adv* to a great degree ⟨the clown wore a *whacking* big pair of shoes⟩ — see VERY 1

whale *n* something that is unusually large and powerful ⟨a *whale* of a truck⟩ — see GIANT

whale *vb* **1** to deliver a blow to (someone or something) usually in a strong vigorous manner ⟨*whaled* the ball so hard that it sailed over the fence and into the neighbor's yard⟩ — see HIT 1

2 to strike repeatedly with something long and thin or flexible ⟨*whaled* the rug with a broom to knock the dirt out of it⟩ — see WHIP 1

3 to strike repeatedly ⟨mercilessly *whaled* the boy for stealing from her purse⟩ — see BEAT 1

wharf *n* a structure used by boats and ships for taking on or landing cargo and passengers ⟨tied the rowboat up at the *wharf*⟩ — see DOCK

what *interj* how surprising, doubtful, or unbelievable ⟨*what*! I can't believe we won!⟩ — see NO

wheedle *vb* to get (someone) to do something by gentle urging, special attention, or flattery ⟨*wheedled* him into doing their homework for them⟩ — see COAX

wheel *n* a rapid turning about on an axis or central point ⟨the *wheel* of the tape reel⟩ — see SPIN 1

wheel *vb* **1** to change the course or direction of (something) ⟨*wheeled* the bike around sharply to see what had fallen off⟩ — see TURN 2

2 to move (something) in a curved or circular path on or as if on an axis ⟨*wheeled* the bicycle's tires around to see if they were balanced⟩ — see TURN 1

3 to move in circles around an axis or center ⟨she *wheeled* around and around the pole until finally she got dizzy and fell down⟩ — see SPIN 1

4 to turn away from a straight line or course ⟨the highway *wheels* to the west as it forms an arc that bypasses the city⟩ — see CURVE 1

wheeze *vb* to breathe hard, quickly, or with difficulty ⟨he was *wheezing* after a hard run⟩ — see GASP

whelm *vb* to subject to incapacitating emotional or mental stress ⟨the news so *whelmed* them that they were stunned into silence⟩ — see OVERWHELM 1

when *conj* in spite of the fact that ⟨she quit writing *when* she could have been a fine author⟩ — see ALTHOUGH

where *adv* at, in, or to what place ⟨*where* will you be tonight?⟩
synonyms whereabouts (*also* whereabout), whither
related words wherever

whereabouts *also* **whereabout** *adv* at, in, or to what place ⟨*whereabouts* do you expect to be on your journey tonight?⟩ — see WHERE

whereas *conj* for the reason that ⟨*whereas* you chose to participate in this stupid prank, you will be held responsible as well⟩ — see SINCE

wherefore *adv* for this or that reason ⟨it was getting late, and *wherefore* we decided to move on⟩ — see THEREFORE

wherefore *n* something (as a belief) that serves as the basis for another thing ⟨demanded to know the whys and *wherefores* for the decision⟩ — see REASON 2

wherewithal *n* **1** available money ⟨had the *wherewithal* to pay cash for the car⟩ — see FUND 2

2 the total of one's money and property ⟨people with the *wherewithal* to be able to afford such a lavish lifestyle⟩ — see WEALTH 1

whet *vb* to make sharp or sharper ⟨*whetted* the knife using the stone⟩ — see SHARPEN

whetted *adj* having an edge thin enough to cut or pierce something ⟨I'll need a well-*whetted* axe to split the wood⟩ — see SHARP 1

whiff *vb* to become aware of by means of the sense organs in the nose ⟨*whiffed* the food cooking on the stove and announced that he was staying for dinner⟩ — see SMELL 1

while *conj* in spite of the fact that ⟨*while* this paper is very well done, it's still late⟩ — see ALTHOUGH

while *n* **1** an indefinite but usually short period of time ⟨we stayed at school for a *while* longer⟩
synonyms bit, space, spell, stretch
related words lapse; season, span; day, epoch, era; flash, instant, jiffy, minute, moment, second, shake, spurt, trice, twinkle, twinkling, wink; aeon (*or* eon), age, eternity; interim, interlude, intermission, interval
2 the active use of energy in producing a result ⟨it's not worth my *while* to fix it, so we'll get a new one⟩ — see EFFORT

whilom *adj* having been such at some previous time ⟨ignored the *whilom* friends who had turned on her⟩ — see FORMER

whilst *conj, chiefly British* in spite of the fact that ⟨*whilst* a good worker, he's not a very good manager⟩ — see ALTHOUGH

whim *n* a sudden impulsive and apparently unmotivated idea or action ⟨on a *whim*, we stopped at the roadside stand to get ice cream⟩
synonyms caprice, fancy, freak, notion, vagary, whimsy (*also* whimsey)
related words capriciousness, freakishness, whimsicality; conceit; concept, conception, image, impression, picture, thought; brainstorm, inspiration

whimper *vb* to utter feeble plaintive cries ⟨the dog *whimpered* to be let in⟩
synonyms mewl, pule
related words fuss, snivel, snuffle, whine; bawl, cry, weep; peep, squeak; yelp; mumble, murmur, mutter
near antonyms scream, screech, shriek, squeal; howl, squall, wail, yowl; call, caterwaul, squawk; bellow, roar

whimsical *adj* prone to sudden illogical changes of mind, ideas, or actions ⟨it's hard to make plans with my *whimsical* best friend⟩
synonyms capricious, freakish, impulsive

related words mercurial, moody, temperamental, volatile; eccentric, flaky, quirky; arbitrary, erratic, fickle, inconstant, irregular, willful (*or* wilful); impractical, quixotic, romantic

near antonyms equable; levelheaded, logical, practical, reasonable, sensible; fast, fixed, hard-and-fast, immutable, inflexible, invariable, unalterable, unchangeable; changeless, constant, established, set, settled, stable, steadfast, steady, unchanging, unvarying

whimsicality *n* an inclination to sudden illogical changes of mind, ideas, or actions 〈her *whimsicality* made her unpredictable〉

synonyms capriciousness, freakishness, impulsiveness

related words moodiness, volatility; eccentricity, flakiness; changeability, unpredictability; arbitrariness, fickleness, inconstancy, irregularity, willfulness; changeability, flexibility, mutability, variability

near antonyms levelheadedness, practicality, reasonableness; fastness, fixedness, immutability, inflexibility, invariability; changelessness, constancy, stability, steadfastness, steadiness

whimsy *also* **whimsey** *n* a sudden impulsive and apparently unmotivated idea or action 〈the pop singer's latest *whimsy* is that she has acting talent〉 — see WHIM

whine *vb* to express dissatisfaction, pain, or resentment usually tiresomely 〈for the whole of our vacation, the kids *whined* on and on about the weather〉 — see COMPLAIN

whiner *n* **1** a person who makes frequent complaints usually about little things 〈don't be a *whiner*—the hike's not that difficult〉 — see CRYBABY

2 an irritable and complaining person 〈among the hospital staff she had acquired a reputation for being a *whiner*〉 — see GROUCH

whinny *vb* to make the cry typical of a horse 〈the father *whinnied* and reared as his young daughter pretended to ride him〉 — see NEIGH

whip *n* a long thin or flexible tool for striking 〈please do not use your belt as a *whip*〉

synonyms flogger, lash, scourge, switch

related words blacksnake, cat-o'-nine-tails, cowhide, crop, knout, quirt, rawhide, strap; cane, club, cudgel, flail; stripe

whip *vb* **1** to strike repeatedly with something long and thin or flexible 〈*whipped* the animal when it did not move fast enough to please him〉

synonyms birch, cowhide, flagellate, flail, flog, hide, horsewhip, lash, rawhide, scourge, slash, switch, tan, thrash, whale

related words cane, club, cudgel; stripe; bang, bop, box, bust, clap, clip, clobber, clout, crack, cuff, hit, knock, lam, paste, punch, slap, slug, smack, smite, sock, spank, swat, swipe, thwack, wallop, whack; bash, batter, belt, bludgeon, buffet, bung, drub, hammer, lace, lambaste (*or* lambast), lick, mangle, maul, pelt, pound, pummel, rough, thump

2 to defeat by a large margin 〈we *whipped* them 13-0 in the last game〉

synonyms clobber, drub, rout, skunk, snow under, thrash, trim, trounce, wallop

related words beat, best, conquer, hurdle, lick, master, overbear, overcome, overmatch, prevail (over), subdue, surmount, throw, triumph (over), win (against), worst; crush, overpower, overthrow, subjugate, vanquish; exceed, outdo, surpass

3 to achieve a victory over 〈a bad habit that you need to *whip*〉 — see BEAT 2

4 to change the course or direction of (something) 〈any more complaints and I'm *whipping* this car around and heading back home〉 — see TURN 2

5 to move or cause to move with a striking motion 〈her hair *whipped* in the wind〉 — see FLAP

6 to strike repeatedly 〈threatened to *whip* them if they didn't behave〉 — see BEAT 1

whip (up) *vb* to cause or encourage the development of 〈*whipped up* protests against the proposed amendment to the state's constitution〉 — see INCITE 1

whipper *n* one that defeats an enemy or opponent 〈as the *whippers* of teams from much larger schools, our players have much to be proud of〉 — see VICTOR 1

whippersnapper *n* a person of no importance or influence 〈some young *whippersnapper* piped up with a pointless quibble〉 — see NOBODY

whipping *n* failure to win a contest 〈suffered a *whipping* that took them out of competition〉 — see DEFEAT 1

whipping boy *n* a person or thing taking the blame for others 〈used the government's economic policies as the *whipping boy* for every bad decision the company made〉 — see SCAPEGOAT

whir *also* **whirr** *vb* to fly, turn, or move rapidly with a fluttering or vibratory sound 〈the hummingbird *whirred* as it hovered over a flower〉 〈our tires *whirred* as we traveled over the rough road〉

synonyms buzz, drone, hum, whish, whiz (*or* whizz), zip, zoom

related words thrum; hiss, murmur, purr, rustle, sigh, whisper

whir *n* a monotonous sound like that of an insect in motion 〈a *whir* coming from the refrigerator〉 — see HUM

whirl *n* **1** a rapid turning about on an axis or central point 〈the *whirl* of the mechanical ride made him dizzy〉 — see SPIN 1

2 a state of mental uncertainty 〈so many changes at once had her all in a *whirl*〉 — see CONFUSION 1

3 a state of noisy, confused activity 〈lost an earring in the *whirl* of the party〉 — see COMMOTION

whirl *vb* **1** to cause (as a liquid) to move about in a circle especially repeatedly 〈*whirled* the chocolate syrup into the milk with a spoon〉 — see STIR 1

2 to move (something) in a curved or circular path on or as if on an axis 〈the figure skater *whirled* his partner with effortless grace〉 — see TURN 1

3 to move in circles around an axis or center 〈the gambler held his breath as the roulette wheel *whirled*〉 — see SPIN 1

4 to proceed or move quickly 〈cars *whirling* by on the highway〉 — see HURRY 2

5 to be in a confused state as if from being twirled around 〈my mind *whirled* from all of the excitement〉 — see SPIN 2

whirling *adj* having a feeling of being whirled about and in danger of falling down 〈still *whirling* from the amusement ride, I needed to sit down〉 — see DIZZY 1

whirlpool *n* water moving rapidly in a circle with a hollow in the center 〈in *The Odyssey*, Ulysses is trapped between the six-headed monster Scylla and Charybdis, a deadly *whirlpool* that threatens to suck his ship down〉

synonyms maelstrom, vortex

related words eddy, swirl, whirl

whirlwind *adj* moving, proceeding, or acting with great speed 〈after a *whirlwind* romance of only a few weeks, the couple decided to get married〉 — see FAST 1

whish *n* a sound similar to the speech sound \s\ stretched out 〈the *whish* of tires on wet pavement〉 — see HISS 1

whish *vb* **1** to fly, turn, or move rapidly with a fluttering or vibratory sound ⟨a baseball *whished* past my head⟩ — see WHIRR

2 to make a sound like that of stretching out the speech sound \s\ ⟨the match *whished* as it burst into flame⟩ — see HISS

whisk *vb* **1** to cause to move or proceed fast or faster ⟨the museum guide kept *whisking* us along, telling us there was much more we had to see⟩ — see HURRY 1

2 to move or proceed smoothly and readily ⟨now that the highway has been widened, traffic just *whisks* along⟩ — see FLOW 2

3 to proceed or move quickly ⟨*whisked* through the crowd and delivered the urgent message⟩ — see HURRY 2

whisper *n* a rumor or report of a personal or sensational nature ⟨there were *whispers* that the starlet was secretly married⟩ — see TALE 1

whisper *vb* to make (as a piece of information) the subject of common talk without any authority or confirmation of accuracy ⟨assistants *whispered* that the two singers were having a secret relationship⟩ — see RUMOR

whistling *adj* having a high musical pitch or range ⟨the *whistling* sound of missiles as they sped toward their targets⟩ — see SHRILL

whit *n* the smallest amount or part imaginable ⟨I care not a *whit* about what other people think⟩ — see JOT

white *adj* **1** lacking an addition of color ⟨dazzlingly *white* paint on the walls of the new house⟩ — see COLORLESS

2 not causing injury or hurt ⟨told a little *white* lie⟩ — see HARMLESS

whiten *vb* to make white or whiter by removing color ⟨years of sunlight had almost completely *whitened* the flag⟩

synonyms blanch, bleach, blench, decolorize, dull, fade, pale, wash out

related words brighten, lighten; dim, matte (*also* mat *or* matt); whitewash; frost, silver

near antonyms blacken; blotch, discolor, mottle, shade, splotch, spot, tarnish; color, dye, paint, stain, tinge, tint; burnish, polish, shine

antonyms darken, deepen

whitewash *vb* to make (something) seem less bad by offering excuses ⟨don't try to *whitewash* your rudeness by saying that you were having a bad day⟩ — see PALLIATE 1

whither *adv* at, in, or to what place ⟨*whither* are you going, my lady?⟩ — see WHERE

¹**whiz** *or* **whizz** *n* **1** a sound similar to the speech sound \s\ stretched out ⟨the *whiz* of an arrow flying by at an uncomfortably close range⟩ — see HISS 1

2 a monotonous sound like that of an insect in motion ⟨the irritating *whiz* of a bee in the room⟩ — see HUM

²**whiz** *n* **1** a person with a high level of knowledge or skill in a field ⟨the computer *whiz* whom we all go to when we're having problems⟩ — see EXPERT

2 a very smart person ⟨one of those *whizzes* who does very well in every subject⟩ — see GENIUS 1

whiz *or* **whizz** *vb* **1** to make a sound like that of stretching out the speech sound \s\ ⟨just hearing the bullets *whiz* as they fly by their heads must be terrifying for soldiers⟩ — see HISS

2 to fly, turn, or move rapidly with a fluttering or vibratory sound ⟨many vehicles were *whizzing* past us at breakneck speeds⟩ — see WHIRR

whole *adj* **1** not divided or scattered among several areas of interest or concern ⟨you'll need to put your *whole* effort into this project⟩

synonyms all, concentrated, entire, exclusive, focused (*also* focussed), undivided

related words absolute, complete, full, thorough, total; comprehensive, intact, integral, perfect

near antonyms deficient, fragmental, fragmentary, incomplete, partial

antonyms diffuse, divided, scattered

2 enjoying health and vigor ⟨*whole* and happy again after months of recuperation⟩ — see HEALTHY 1

3 not lacking any part or member that properly belongs to it ⟨the puzzle isn't quite *whole*, but close enough⟩ — see COMPLETE 1

whole *n* a complete amount of something ⟨the landlord eventually refunded the *whole* of our deposit⟩

synonyms aggregate, full, sum, summation, total, totality

related words gross; completeness, comprehensiveness, entirety; bulk, lion's share, mass

phrases the whole kit and kaboodle, the whole shebang

near antonyms net

wholehearted *adj* characterized by unqualified enthusiasm ⟨*wholehearted* praise for the novel by the leading critics⟩ — see HEARTY 1

wholeness *n* the condition of being sound in body ⟨young people who don't appreciate their *wholeness* and youthfulness while they have it⟩ — see HEALTH

whole number *n* a character used to represent a mathematical value ⟨today we'll learn how to add *whole numbers*⟩ — see NUMBER

wholesome *adj* **1** enjoying health and vigor ⟨a *wholesome* young woman in the prime of her life⟩ — see HEALTHY 1

2 good for the health ⟨trying to eat a more *wholesome* diet⟩ — see HEALTHFUL

wholesomeness *n* the condition of being sound in body ⟨after the physical exam the doctor commended me on my general *wholesomeness*⟩ — see HEALTH

wholly *adv* to a full extent or degree ⟨not *wholly* convinced by the evidence that the prosecutor presented⟩ — see FULLY 1

whoop *n* a loud vocal expression of strong emotion ⟨let out a *whoop* of joy⟩ — see SHOUT

whopper *n* **1** a statement known by its maker to be untrue and made in order to deceive ⟨told a *whopper* to get out of doing homework⟩ — see LIE

2 something that is unusually large and powerful ⟨a *whopper* of a fish that won first prize in the derby⟩ — see GIANT

whopping *adj* unusually large ⟨delivered a *whopping* ten-pound baby⟩ — see HUGE

whore *n* a woman who engages in sexual activities for money ⟨a historic district of the seaport that was once notorious for the *whores* who gathered there⟩ — see PROSTITUTE

why *interj* how surprising, doubtful, or unbelievable ⟨*why*, what a strange thing to say!⟩ — see NO

why *n* something (as a belief) that serves as the basis for another thing ⟨asked the *whys* behind the surprising decision⟩ — see REASON 2

wicked *adj* **1** not conforming to a high moral standard; morally unacceptable ⟨a *wicked* urge to steal just for the sake of stealing⟩ — see BAD 2

2 tending to or exhibiting reckless playfulness ⟨a *wicked* grin on his face when he said that⟩ — see MISCHIEVOUS 1

wickedly *adv* in a mean or spiteful manner ⟨whispered *wickedly* amusing comments about the other performers in the talent show⟩ — see NASTILY

wickedness *n* **1** playful, reckless behavior that is not intended to cause serious harm ⟨a couple of live wires who got into all kinds of *wickedness* during school vacations⟩ — see MISCHIEF 1

2 the state or quality of being utterly evil ⟨the movie featured a villain of unadulterated *wickedness*⟩ — see ENORMITY 1

wide *adj* **1** having a greater than usual measure across ⟨the river was so *wide* that it was impossible to cross it in less than a day⟩

synonyms broad, fat, thick

related words expansive, extensive; commodious, roomy, spacious

near antonyms fine, hairlike; elongated; needlelike; close, compressed, condensed, constricted, contracted, squeezed, tight, tightened

antonyms narrow, skinny, slender, slim, thin

2 having considerable extent ⟨a *wide* and detailed knowledge of the issue⟩ — see EXTENSIVE

wide–awake *adj* **1** not sleeping or able to sleep ⟨was *wide-awake* with worry for most of the night⟩ — see WAKEFUL

2 paying close attention usually for the purpose of anticipating approaching danger or opportunity ⟨investors who were *wide-awake* bought the stock as soon as it was offered⟩ — see ALERT 1

wide–eyed *adj* lacking in worldly wisdom or informed judgment ⟨a *wide-eyed* and trusting child⟩ — see NAIVE 1

widespread *adj* having considerable extent ⟨a *widespread* area of drought⟩ — see EXTENSIVE

width *n* an area over which activity, capacity, or influence extends ⟨surprised by the *width* of his power and influence in the oil business⟩ — see RANGE 2

wield *vb* to bring to bear especially forcefully or effectively ⟨*wields* considerable influence in the field of women's sports⟩ — see EXERT

wife *n* the female partner in a marriage ⟨a husband and *wife* who treat each other as equals in their marriage⟩

synonyms helpmate, helpmeet, lady

related words bride; consort, mate, partner, spouse; dowager, matron; homemaker, housewife

wiggle *vb* to make jerky or restless movements ⟨the baby *wiggled* in her sleep⟩ — see FIDGET

wight *n* a member of the human race ⟨what unfortunate *wight* would be out and about in such foul weather?⟩ — see HUMAN

wild *adj* **1** living outdoors without taming or domestication by humans ⟨*wild* animals can be shy or aggressive when confronted by humans⟩

synonyms feral, savage, unbroken, undomesticated, untamed

related words uncontrolled, unsubdued; bestial, brutal, brute; barbarous, uncivilized

near antonyms controlled, subdued; housebroken, trained; civilized, socialized

antonyms broken, busted, domestic, domesticated, tame, tamed

2 existing without human habitation or cultivation ⟨that land has been completely *wild* since the owners abandoned it⟩

synonyms natural, uncultivated, untamed

related words native; uninhabited; overgrown, untended; waste; undeveloped

near antonyms inhabited; developed

antonyms cultivated, tamed

3 marked by turmoil or disturbance especially of natural elements ⟨a *wild* night, full of wind and rain⟩

synonyms stormy, tempestuous, tumultuous, turbulent

related words blustery, rough, violent; brutal, harsh, severe; unsettled

near antonyms calm, halcyon, peaceful, placid, quiet, serene, tranquil

4 conceived or made without regard for reason or reality ⟨some *wild* claim that he was abducted by aliens⟩ — see FANTASTIC 1

5 different from the ordinary in a way that causes curiosity or suspicion ⟨public speakers in the park typically spout some *wild* ideas⟩ — see ODD 2

6 marked by great and often stressful excitement or activity ⟨the holidays were especially *wild* around here this year⟩ — see FURIOUS 1

7 not civilized ⟨ancient traces of a *wild* people who lived in mountain caves⟩ — see SAVAGE 1

wild *adv* in a confused and reckless manner ⟨as soon as the doors opened, early-morning bargain hunters ran *wild* through the store⟩ — see HELTER-SKELTER 1

wild *n* that part of the physical world that is removed from human habitation ⟨some animals aren't meant to live outside of the *wild*⟩ — see NATURE 2

wilderness *n* that part of the physical world that is removed from human habitation ⟨released the wolf back into the *wilderness*⟩ — see NATURE 2

wildly *adv* in a confused and reckless manner ⟨upon being dismissed, the students dashed *wildly* off in all directions⟩ — see HELTER-SKELTER 1

wile *n* **1** a clever often underhanded means to achieve an end ⟨had to use all of her *wiles* to convince her guests to stay⟩ — see TRICK 1

2 the use of clever underhanded actions to achieve an end ⟨it took both *wile* and cajolery to talk him into it⟩ — see TRICKERY

wile *vb* to attract or delight as if by magic ⟨her stories of the Old South could *wile* anyone⟩ — see CHARM 1

wiliness *n* **1** skill in achieving one's ends through indirect, subtle, or underhanded means ⟨admired the politician's *wiliness*, but questioned his ethics⟩ — see CUNNING 1

2 the inclination or practice of misleading others through lies or trickery ⟨her reputation for *wiliness* made people disinclined to trust her⟩ — see DECEIT

will *n* **1** the power to control one's actions, impulses, or emotions ⟨she kept her face still by sheer force of *will*⟩

synonyms restraint, self-containment, self-control, self-discipline, self-government, self-possession, self-restraint, willpower

related words self-denial; moderation, temperance; determination, nerve; command, control, discipline, mastery; aplomb, assurance, composure, confidence, coolness, equanimity, poise, self-confidence; discretion

near antonyms gratification, indulgence, self-indulgence; immoderacy, intemperance, overindulgence; demerit, failing, fault, feebleness, foible, frailty, shortcoming, vice, weakness

2 the act or power of making one's own choices or decisions ⟨you cannot force me to do anything against my own *will*⟩ — see FREE WILL

will *vb* **1** to give by means of a will 〈*willed* their house to their children〉 — see LEAVE 2

2 to see fit 〈do as you *will*〉 — see CHOOSE 2

willful *or* **wilful** *adj* **1** given to resisting authority or another's control 〈a particularly *willful* horse that took weeks to break to saddle〉 — see DISOBEDIENT

2 given to resisting control or discipline by others 〈finally the parents sought professional counseling for the *willful* child〉 — see UNCONTROLLABLE

3 having or showing a tendency to force one's will on others without any regard to fairness or necessity 〈a *willful* disregard for the rights of others〉 — see ARBITRARY 1

4 made, given, or done with full awareness of what one is doing 〈a *willful* attempt to cheat siblings out of their rightful inheritance〉 — see INTENTIONAL

5 sticking to an opinion, purpose, or course of action in spite of reason, arguments, or persuasion 〈the kind of *willful* person who can never bring himself to admit that he made a mistake〉 — see OBSTINATE

willfully *adv* with full awareness of what one is doing 〈*willfully* chose to risk pneumonia by jumping into a freezing lake〉 — see INTENTIONALLY

willfulness *n* **1** a steadfast adherence to an opinion, purpose, or course of action 〈her unceasing *willfulness* eventually wore down her critics and opponents〉 — see OBSTINACY

2 refusal to obey 〈*willfulness* was dealt with harshly at the orphanage〉 — see DISOBEDIENCE

willies *n pl* a sense of panic or extreme nervousness 〈spiders give me the *willies* for some reason〉 — see JITTERS

willing *adj* **1** having a desire or inclination (as for a specified course of action) 〈I'm a little confused, but perfectly *willing* to do as you ask〉

synonyms amenable, disposed, game, glad, inclined, ready

related words predisposed; agreeable, compliant, obedient, submissive; favorable, receptive; prepared, prompt, quick, responsive, swift

near antonyms averse, loath (*or* loth), reluctant

antonyms disinclined, unwilling

2 having or showing the ability to respond without delay or hesitation 〈she's always lent a *willing* hand whenever a neighbor needed help or a friend a favor〉 — see QUICK 1

3 done, made, or given with one's own free will 〈a *willing* sacrifice of her free time for a good cause〉 — see VOLUNTARY 1

willingly *adv* **1** by choice or preference 〈I would not *willingly* eat liver, but sometimes I have no choice〉 — see RATHER 1

2 of one's own free will 〈chose *willingly* to help her little brother with his homework〉 — see VOLUNTARILY

willingness *n* cheerful readiness to do something 〈his unhesitating *willingness* to take on the tough assignments has earned him the status of the president's right-hand man〉 — see ALACRITY

williwaw *n* a sudden brief rush of wind 〈a *williwaw* rose up seemingly out of nowhere and raised havoc with our campsite〉 — see GUST 1

willowy *adj* able to bend easily without breaking 〈the rattan's stems are split into *willowy* staves that are woven together to produce exquisite baskets〉

synonyms flexible, limber, lissome (*also* lissom), lithe, pliable, pliant, supple

related words adaptable, ductile, elastic, fluid, malleable, modifiable, plastic, variable, yielding; flaccid, floppy

near antonyms inelastic, nonmalleable, unyielding; breakable, brittle, fragile

antonyms inflexible, rigid, stiff

willpower *n* the power to control one's actions, impulses, or emotions 〈trying to summon the *willpower* to resist eating a huge piece of cake〉 — see WILL 1

wilt *vb* **1** to be limp from lack of water or vigor 〈the plants *wilted* after I forgot to water them for three whole days〉 — see DROOP 1

2 to lose bodily strength or vigor 〈she had *wilted* a bit after walking around the hot and humid city〉 — see WEAKEN 2

3 to lose liveliness, force, or freshness 〈after six solid hours of painting, his energy was starting to *wilt*〉 — see WITHER

wily *adj* clever at attaining one's ends by indirect and often deceptive means 〈a *wily* judge of character, she takes advantage of car buyers' insecurities to sell them a bigger machine than they really need〉 — see ARTFUL 1

wimp *n* **1** a person lacking in physical strength 〈just because you can't lift 300 pounds doesn't mean you're a *wimp*〉 — see WEAKLING 1

2 a person without strength of character 〈what kind of *wimp* would just give in to pressure?〉 — see WEAKLING 2

wimpy *adj* **1** lacking bodily strength 〈a *wimpy* person is not the best choice for a job with a moving company〉 — see WEAK 1

2 lacking strength of will or character 〈a *wimpy* effort to change the law that was doomed to failure〉 — see WEAK 2

win *n* an instance of defeating an enemy or opponent 〈a team with 12 *wins* and two losses〉 — see VICTORY

win *vb* **1** to achieve victory (as in a contest) 〈the kind of person who always has to *win*—even if the game is just for fun〉

synonyms conquer, prevail, triumph

related words overcome, sweep; squeak, squeeze; contend, vie; succeed

phrases carry the day

near antonyms collapse, fail, flop, fold, wash out; flounder, struggle; decline, slip, slump, wane

antonyms lose

2 to receive as return for effort 〈*win* a gold medal in swimming〉 — see EARN 1

3 to obtain (as a goal) through effort 〈*won* a substantial victory in the struggle for civil rights for all〉 — see ACHIEVE 1

win (against) *vb* to achieve a victory over 〈finally *won* against his father in a chess game〉 — see BEAT 2

win (over) *vb* to cause (someone) to agree with a belief or course of action by using arguments or earnest requests 〈a combination of solid reasoning and outright begging *won* my parents *over*, and I became an exchange student for a year〉 — see PERSUADE

wince *vb* to draw back in fear, pain, or disgust 〈*winced* at the awful smell〉 — see FLINCH

¹wind *n* **1** noticeable movement of air in a particular direction 〈there's a *wind* coming from underneath the front door〉

synonyms current, draft

related words blast, blow, flurry, gale, gust, head wind, squall, tail wind, tempest, tornado, windstorm; breath, breeze, puff, waft, zephyr

2 a prevailing or general movement or inclination 〈the *winds* of public opinion are changing on this issue〉 — see TREND 1

3 language that is impressive-sounding but not meaningful or sincere ⟨unfortunately the speech was nothing but *wind*⟩ — see RHETORIC 1

²wind *n* something that curves or is curved ⟨there's one last easterly *wind* to the river before it empties into the sea⟩ — see BEND 1

wind *vb* to follow a circular or spiral course ⟨flowering vines *wind* around the porch's graceful columns⟩
synonyms coil, curl, entwine, spiral, twine, twist
related words arc, arch, bend, crook, curve, hook, sweep, swerve, turn, veer, wheel; swirl, whirl; circle, encircle, interlace, intertwine, lace, loop; bow, bulge; meander, weave, zigzag
near antonyms straighten

windfall *n* something that provides happiness or does good for a person or thing ⟨hitting the lottery jackpot was a real *windfall* for the recently laid-off worker⟩ — see BLESSING 2

windiness *n* the use of too many words to express an idea ⟨he's a brilliant thinker, but his *windiness* tends to overwhelm his ideas⟩ — see VERBIAGE

winding *adj* **1** marked by a long series of irregular curves ⟨a long and *winding* path through the woods⟩ — see CROOKED 1
2 turning around an axis like the thread of a screw ⟨a *winding* staircase leads to the top of the lighthouse⟩ — see SPIRAL

windjammer *n* a boat equipped with one or more sails ⟨with no set course to follow, a *windjammer* sails wherever the wind and the captain's whim takes it⟩ — see SAILBOAT

windup *n* the last part of a process or action ⟨the marketing team then energetically launched into the *windup* of the presentation⟩ — see FINALE

wind up *vb* **1** to bring (an event) to a natural or appropriate stopping point ⟨try to *wind up* the performance, as we're almost out of time⟩ — see CLOSE 3
2 to come to an end ⟨her speeches usually *wind up* with one last joke⟩ — see CEASE 1

windy *adj* **1** marked by strong wind or more wind than usual ⟨one particularly *windy* day should shake the last of the autumn leaves from the trees⟩
synonyms blowy, blustery, breezy, gusty
related words drafty; stormy, tempestuous
near antonyms breathless, calm, motionless, still
2 marked by the use of impressive-sounding but mostly meaningless words and phrases ⟨gave his usual *windy* speech about working for the people⟩ — see RHETORICAL
3 using or containing more words than necessary to express an idea ⟨a *windy* saleswoman who told us a lot more than we wanted to know about vacuum cleaners⟩ — see WORDY

wing *n* a group of people acting together within a larger group ⟨the conservative *wing* of the party⟩ — see FACTION

wing *vb* to move through the air with or as if with outstretched wings ⟨watched the flocks of birds as they *winged* southward for the winter⟩ — see FLY 1

wink *n* **1** a short sleep ⟨I wasn't able to catch a *wink* during the entire flight⟩ — see ¹NAP
2 a very small space of time ⟨I turned to look away, and in a *wink* he was gone⟩ — see INSTANT

wink *vb* **1** to rapidly open and close one's eyes ⟨she *winked* several times to get the dust and grit out of her eyes⟩
synonyms blink

related words bat, flutter; squint
2 to shine with light at regular intervals ⟨a lighthouse was *winking* in the distance⟩ — see BLINK 1
3 to shoot forth bursts of light ⟨fireflies *winking* in the darkness⟩ — see FLASH 1
4 to secretly sympathize with or pretend ignorance of something improper or unlawful ⟨the whole sporting world seems to *wink* as untold sums are bet on the outcome of the Super Bowl⟩ — see CONNIVE

wink (at) *vb* to overlook or dismiss as of little importance ⟨I won't *wink at* misbehavior of any kind in my classroom⟩ — see EXCUSE 1

winner *n* **1** a person or thing that is successful ⟨the idea turned out to be a *winner*⟩ — see HIT 1
2 one that defeats an enemy or opponent ⟨the *winner* of any given war is usually the one who gets to write the history of that war⟩ — see VICTOR 1
3 the person who comes in first in a competition ⟨the other finalists graciously congratulated the *winner*⟩ — see CHAMPION 1

winning *adj* **1** having qualities that tend to make one loved ⟨a particularly pretty and *winning* child⟩ — see LOVABLE
2 likely to win one's affection ⟨flashed a *winning* smile that soon had us at her beck and call⟩ — see INGRATIATING

winsome *adj* likely to win one's affection ⟨gave her a *winsome* look⟩ — see INGRATIATING

wintry *adj* **1** having a low or subnormal temperature ⟨a *wintry* and snowy day⟩ — see COLD 1
2 lacking in friendliness or warmth of feeling ⟨the doorman gave the uninvited visitors a *wintry* smile and escorted them out⟩ — see COLD 2

wipe out *vb* to destroy all traces of ⟨a mistake that *wiped out* all possibility of their winning the championship⟩ — see ANNIHILATE 1

wire *n* a length of braided, flexible material that is used for tying or connecting things ⟨a telephone *wire*⟩ — see CORD

wisdom *n* **1** the ability to understand inner qualities or relationships ⟨with age and experience comes *wisdom*—hopefully⟩ ⟨neither book learning nor simple intelligence should be confused with *wisdom*⟩
synonyms discernment, insight, perception, perceptiveness, sagaciousness, sagacity, sageness, sapience
related words acuity, acumen, astuteness, penetration, perspicacity, sensitivity, understanding; appreciation, apprehension, comprehension, grasp; braininess, brain(s), brightness, brilliance, canniness, cleverness, gray matter, intellect, intelligence, judgment (or judgement), mentality, power, reason, sense, smartness, wit; discrimination, judiciousness, prudence, sanity; logic, rationality
near antonyms density, dullness (also dulness), obtuseness; brainlessness, folly, foolishness, idiocy, imbecility, mindlessness, silliness, simpleness, stupidity, witlessness; illogic, irrationality, unreasonableness, unsoundness; craziness, insanity, lunacy, madness; preposterousness, senselessness, silliness, zaniness
2 a body of facts learned by study or experience ⟨shared some of the *wisdom* that he had accumulated over 20 years as an oceanographer⟩ — see KNOWLEDGE 1
3 the ability to make intelligent decisions especially in everyday matters ⟨had overstayed her welcome and lacked the *wisdom* to know it⟩ — see COMMON SENSE

wise *adj* **1** having or showing deep understanding and intelligent application of knowledge ⟨a respected and *wise* old judge famous for her sensible rulings⟩
synonyms discerning, insightful, perceptive, sagacious, sage, sapient
related words acute, perspicacious; experienced; discriminating, discriminative; brainy, brilliant, bright, clever, intelligent, keen, nimble, quick, quick-witted, smart; cerebral, erudite, knowledgeable, learned, literate, scholarly; astute, sharp, shrewd; contemplative, reflective, thoughtful
near antonyms dense, dull, obtuse; brainless, dumb, feebleminded, foolish, idiotic, imbecilic, moronic, silly, simple, slow, stupid, thoughtless, unintelligent, witless; undiscriminating
antonyms undiscerning, unperceptive, unwise
2 having inside information ⟨they fooled everyone else, but I'd heard them talking and was *wise* to their true intentions⟩
synonyms hip, knowing
related words alerted, aware, clued, forewarned, informed, prepared, ready, warned; observant, observing, sharp, sharp-eyed; alert, attentive, open-eyed, vigilant, watchful
phrases in the know
near antonyms oblivious, unaware, unconscious, uninformed, unperceiving, unseeing, unwitting; heedless, unmindful, unobservant, unobserving; unprepared, unready, unwary
antonyms unknowing
3 suitable for bringing about a desired result under the circumstances ⟨selling the stock just before it plunged in value was a *wise* move on your part⟩ — see EXPEDIENT
wise (up) *vb* to give information to ⟨*wised* him *up* to some of the more effective tricks of salesmanship⟩ — see ENLIGHTEN 1
wiseacre *n* a person who likes to show off in a clever but annoying way ⟨a *wiseacre* who kept interrupting the class with his smart remarks⟩ — see SMART ALECK
wisecrack *n* something said or done to cause laughter ⟨a whispered *wisecrack* doubled them over in laughter⟩ — see JOKE 1
wisecrack *vb* to make jokes ⟨*wisecracked* to hide his nervousness during the auditions⟩ — see JOKE
wise guy *n* a person who likes to show off in a clever but annoying way ⟨don't be such a *wise guy*⟩ — see SMART ALECK
wish *vb* to see fit ⟨you're free to sit wherever you *wish*⟩ — see CHOOSE 2
wish (for) *vb* to have an earnest wish to own or enjoy ⟨I *wished for* a pony so badly⟩ — see DESIRE
wishy–washy *adj* **1** lacking in qualities that make for spirit and character ⟨this story is too *wishy-washy*; you need to add some verve to it⟩
synonyms banal, flat, insipid
related words unentertaining, unexciting, uninspiring, unrewarding, unsatisfying; bland, boring, drab, dreary, dry, dull, heavy, humdrum, jading, leaden, monotonous, pedestrian, ponderous, tedious, tiresome, tiring, uninteresting, wearisome, weary, wearying; inane; innocuous, inoffensive; mild, soft, subdued, tame, weak; common, commonplace, ordinary, stale, unexceptional
near antonyms piquant, poignant, pungent, racy, spicy; meaty, substantial; entertaining, exciting, galvanizing, inspiring, invigorating, thrilling

2 lacking strength of will or character ⟨in a time of crisis the nation can ill afford *wishy-washy* leaders⟩ — see WEAK 2
wit *n* **1** a person (as a writer) noted for or specializing in humor ⟨one of the most talented *wits* of his generation⟩ — see HUMORIST
2 the ability to make intelligent decisions especially in everyday matters ⟨he doesn't even have the *wit* to know when to come in out of the rain⟩ — see COMMON SENSE
3 the normal or healthy condition of the mental abilities ⟨scared out of her *wits*⟩ — see MIND 2
witch *n* **1** a woman believed to have often harmful supernatural powers ⟨in the old days women were sometimes accused of being *witches* and using evil magic to make the crops fail or an animal die suddenly⟩
synonyms enchantress, hag, hex, sorceress
related words charmer, conjuror (*or* conjurer), enchanter, necromancer, voodoo; magician, sorcerer, warlock, wizard
2 a mean or ugly old woman ⟨heaven help you if your ball lands on that *witch's* lawn⟩ — see CRONE
3 a person skilled in using supernatural forces ⟨freakish storms that were once thought to be the work of *witches*⟩ — see MAGICIAN 1
witchcraft *n* the power to control natural forces through supernatural means ⟨taught all of her daughters *witchcraft*⟩ — see MAGIC 1
witchery *n* **1** the power of irresistible attraction ⟨the movie star's violet eyes are frequently cited as the source of her cinematic *witchery*⟩ — see CHARM 2
2 the power to control natural forces through supernatural means ⟨used his newly acquired *witchery* to wreak revenge on his enemies⟩ — see MAGIC 1
with *prep* **1** as the result of ⟨cried *with* happiness⟩ — see BECAUSE OF
2 using the means or agency of ⟨was able to finish the project *with* her help⟩ — see BY 2
3 without being prevented by ⟨a very successful attorney even *with* her physical disability⟩ — see DESPITE
withal *adv* **1** in addition to what has been said ⟨a successful businessman and *withal* a major contributor to local charities⟩ — see MORE 1
2 in spite of that ⟨a homely face that was *withal* rather compelling⟩ — see HOWEVER
withdraw *vb* **1** to move back or away (as from something difficult, dangerous, or disagreeable) ⟨the army was forced to *withdraw* from the line of battle⟩ — see RETREAT 1
2 to solemnly or formally reject or go back on (as something formerly adhered to) ⟨*withdraw* the offer of surrender upon hearing the terms⟩ — see ABJURE
3 to take away from a place or position ⟨*withdrew* her hand from the table⟩ — see REMOVE 2
withdrawal *n* an act of moving away especially from something difficult, dangerous, or disagreeable ⟨*withdrawal* is sometimes the better part of valor⟩ — see RETREAT 1
wither *vb* to lose liveliness, force, or freshness ⟨shortly after the moon landing, interest in the space program *withered*⟩ ⟨the old man seemed to *wither* suddenly when he turned eighty⟩
synonyms dry, wilt
related words mummify, shrivel, wizen; decline, fade, wane; decrease, diminish, lessen
near antonyms freshen, revive; flourish, prosper, thrive; develop, grow, increase, wax; crest, peak, surge

withhold *vb* **1** to be unwilling to grant ⟨must *withhold* official approval until all proper forms have been submitted⟩ — see DENY 2

2 to continue to have in one's possession or power ⟨*withhold* some money for your own expenses⟩ — see KEEP 2

within *n* an interior or internal part ⟨structural decay had started from *within*⟩ — see INSIDE 1

without *prep* **1** not having ⟨spent two days *without* food⟩
synonyms minus, sans, wanting

2 out of the reach or sphere of ⟨a goal *without* our grasp⟩ — see BEYOND 2

withstand *vb* to refuse to give in to ⟨trying to *withstand* the temptation to skip school on such a beautiful day⟩ — see RESIST

witless *adj* **1** not having or showing an ability to absorb ideas readily ⟨a dog so *witless* that it instantly forgets every command it's been taught⟩ — see STUPID 1

2 showing or marked by a lack of good sense or judgment ⟨a *witless* decision to relocate to the other side of the country without even the prospect of a job⟩ — see FOOLISH 1

witlessness *n* **1** lack of good sense or judgment ⟨we will continue to berate you until you've stopped exhibiting such *witlessness*⟩ — see FOOLISHNESS 1

2 the quality or state of lacking intelligence or quickness of mind ⟨for sheer *witlessness* the movie's dialogue deserves some sort of award⟩ — see STUPIDITY 1

witness *n* something presented in support of the truth or accuracy of a claim ⟨sees violent entertainment as *witness* of the nation's moral decline⟩ — see PROOF

witness *vb* **1** to declare (something) to be true or genuine ⟨a notary public *witnessing* wills and other important documents⟩ — see CERTIFY 1

2 to make note of (something) through the use of one's eyes ⟨*witnessed* the crime⟩ — see SEE 1

3 to make a solemn declaration under oath for the purpose of establishing a fact ⟨I *witnessed* to the fact that I had seen them together that night⟩ — see TESTIFY

witticism *n* something said or done to cause laughter ⟨a drama critic who is best remembered for his biting *witticisms*⟩ — see JOKE 1

wittingly *adv* with full awareness of what one is doing ⟨*wittingly* lied before the entire assembly⟩ — see INTENTIONALLY

witty *adj* given to or marked by mature intelligent humor ⟨Susan is popular because she is so *witty* and fun-loving⟩ ⟨he's well-known for his *witty* retorts⟩
synonyms clever, facetious, humorous, jocular, smart
related words cerebral, highbrow, intellectual; bantering, frivolous, jesting, joking, joshing, teasing; antic, comic, comical, droll, farcical, funny, hysterical, laughable, ludicrous, ridiculous, riotous, risible, rollicking, screaming, side-splitting, uproarious; amusing, diverting, entertaining; mischievous, playful, prankish; jocose, jocund, jolly, jovial, laughing, merry, mirthful, sunny; scintillating, sparkling; flip, flippant, pert, smart-alecky (*or* smart-aleck); whimsical
near antonyms brainless, lowbrow, stupid, witless; corny, hackneyed, lame; humorless, uncomic, unfunny; earnest, grave, serious, sober, solemn, somber (*or* sombre); doleful, dolorous, lachrymose, plaintive, sorry, tearful, woeful

wizard *n* **1** a person skilled in using supernatural forces ⟨in the legend of King Arthur, Merlin serves both as a *wizard* and as a mentor to the idealistic king⟩ — see MAGICIAN 1

2 a person with a high level of knowledge or skill in a field ⟨a *wizard* at fixing cars⟩ — see EXPERT

3 a very smart person ⟨a *wizard* who never studied for tests⟩ — see GENIUS 1

wizardry *n* the power to control natural forces through supernatural means ⟨a movie about *wizardry* and bizarre creatures⟩ — see MAGIC 1

wobble *vb* **1** to make a series of small irregular or violent movements ⟨the patient's hand *wobbles* so much that he can scarcely hold a glass of water⟩ — see SHAKE 1

2 to make a series of unsteady side-to-side motions ⟨the table *wobbled* whenever I leaned on it⟩ — see ROCK 1

3 to show uncertainty about the right course of action ⟨we cannot afford to have the governor *wobble* at this critical time⟩ — see HESITATE

4 to swing unsteadily back and forth or from side to side ⟨the drunk stood up, *wobbled* for a moment, and fell forward⟩ — see TEETER 1

wobbling *adj* marked by or given to small uncontrollable bodily movements ⟨her *wobbling* gait is due to Parkinson's disease⟩ — see SHAKY 1

wobbling *n* the act or an instance of pausing because of uncertainty about the right course of action ⟨she had a brief moment of *wobbling* and then made her choice⟩ — see HESITATION

wobbly *adj* marked by or given to small uncontrollable bodily movements ⟨all *wobbly* from the chills associated with the flu⟩ — see SHAKY 1

woe *n* **1** a state of great suffering of body or mind ⟨a sad tale of *woe*⟩ — see DISTRESS 1

2 deep sadness especially for the loss of someone or something loved ⟨lost in *woe* ever since the death of her husband⟩ — see SORROW

woebegone *adj* feeling unhappiness ⟨the most *woebegone* people that I had ever seen in my life⟩ — see SAD 1

woeful *adj* **1** expressing or suggesting mourning ⟨the *woeful* expressions of the players after the humiliating loss⟩ — see MOURNFUL 1

2 feeling unhappiness ⟨never saw a more *woeful*-looking bunch than those campers sitting there in the drenching rain⟩ — see SAD 1

3 of a kind to cause great distress ⟨the restaurant patron made the *woeful* discovery that he had left his wallet at home⟩ — see REGRETTABLE

woefully *adv* with feelings of bitterness or grief ⟨*woefully* recounted the many injustices that the family had endured at the hands of the dictator⟩ — see HARD 2

woman *n* an adult female human being ⟨for a while, the toddler called every *woman* "mama"⟩
synonyms female, lady
related words dame, gentlewoman; madam, madame, senora (*or* señora); beauty, belle, chick [*slang*], damsel, doll, gal, girl, ingenue (*or* ingénue), lass, lassie, mademoiselle, maid, maiden, miss, senorita (*or* señorita)

womanish *adj* **1** having or displaying qualities more suitable for women than for men ⟨ancient warriors were not supposed to display any *womanish* qualms about slaughtering the enemy⟩ — see EFFEMINATE

2 of, relating to, or marked by qualities traditionally associated with women ⟨she had a *womanish* gentleness, especially when dealing with children, that he loved⟩ — see FEMININE 1

womanlike *adj* **1** having or displaying qualities more suitable for women than for men ⟨his buddies teased him about his *womanlike* attention to his personal appearance⟩ — see EFFEMINATE

2 of, relating to, or marked by qualities traditionally associated with women ⟨the novelist displays a *womanlike* sensitivity to the characters' feelings⟩ — see FEMININE 1

womanly *adj* **1** having or displaying qualities more suitable for women than for men ⟨his *womanly* walk was mimicked mercilessly around the barracks⟩ — see EFFEMINATE

2 of, relating to, or marked by qualities traditionally associated with women ⟨the wife had a *womanly* need to discuss their relationship that her husband never understood at all⟩ — see FEMININE 1

wonder *n* **1** something extraordinary or surprising ⟨the cunningly crafted miniature of our house is a *wonder*, perfect in every detail⟩
synonyms caution, flash, marvel, miracle, phenomenon, portent, prodigy, sensation
related words curiosity, sight, spectacle; apparition, appearance
2 the rapt attention and deep emotion caused by the sight of something extraordinary ⟨when we first saw the pyramids of Egypt, we gazed with openmouthed *wonder*⟩
synonyms admiration, amazement, astonishment, awe, wonderment
related words dread; fear; respect, reverence, veneration; curiosity, interest; shock, surprise; disbelief, incomprehension, incredulity; beguilement, bewitchment, captivation, enchantment, fascination; animation, enlightenment, enlivenment, excitement, invigoration, stimulation; absorption, engagement, engrossment, enthrallment, immersion, involvement
near antonyms apathy, disinterest, incuriosity, indifference, unconcern; boredom, doldrums, ennui, listlessness, restlessness, tedium, tiredness, weariness; cheerlessness, dispiritedness, joylessness, melancholy

wonderful *adj* **1** causing wonder or astonishment ⟨a country that's just filled with *wonderful* sights⟩ — see MARVELOUS 1

2 of the very best kind ⟨my mother makes *wonderful* meals⟩ — see EXCELLENT

wondering *adj* filled with amazement or wonder ⟨a child's *wondering* expression upon meeting Santa⟩ — see OPENMOUTHED

wonderment *n* the rapt attention and deep emotion caused by the sight of something extraordinary ⟨gazed in *wonderment* at the holiday decorations⟩ — see WONDER 2

wondrous *adj* causing wonder or astonishment ⟨what a *wondrous* discovery fire must have been⟩ — see MARVELOUS 1

wont *adj* being in the habit or custom ⟨she thanked the waitress profusely, as she is *wont* to do whenever anyone does her a favor⟩ — see ACCUSTOMED

wont *n* a usual manner of behaving or doing ⟨he got up early, as is his *wont*⟩ — see HABIT

woo *vb* to act so as to make (something) more likely ⟨unwilling to *woo* approval from the public⟩ — see COURT 1

wood *n* tree logs as prepared for human use ⟨a huge load of *wood* outside the furniture maker's factory⟩
synonyms lumber, timber
related words beam, brace, pile, post, ridgepole, sill, splint, stake, stave, stick; bar, billet, block; cordwood, firewood

wood *n, often* **woods** *pl* a dense growth of trees and shrubs covering a large area ⟨deer and mountain lions live in those *woods*⟩ — see FOREST

wooden *adj* lacking social grace and assurance ⟨an eminent scientist who was *wooden* in front of television cameras⟩ — see AWKWARD 1

woodland *n* a dense growth of trees and shrubs covering a large area ⟨the fires burned a large portion of the *woodland*⟩ — see FOREST

wooer *n* a man who courts a woman usually with the goal of marrying her ⟨of all her *wooers*, he was the only one who met with her father's approval⟩ — see SUITOR 1

wool *n* the hairy covering of a mammal especially when fine, soft, and thick ⟨the *wool* from cashmere goats is considered by many to be the finest available⟩ — see FUR 1

woolgathering *n* the state of being lost in thought ⟨my *woolgathering* was abruptly interrupted by a question from the teacher⟩ — see REVERIE

woolly *also* **wooly** *adj* **1** made of or resembling hair ⟨the dog's *woolly* coat will require a lot of grooming⟩ — see HAIRY 2

2 covered with or as if with hair ⟨still had a water bed and a *woolly* coverlet on top of it⟩ — see HAIRY 1

word *n* **1** a pronounceable series of letters having a distinct meaning especially in a particular field ⟨my doctor used all of these medical *words* that I didn't understand⟩
synonyms expression, term
related words linguistic form, monosyllable, morpheme; collocation, idiom, locution, phrase; archaism, coinage, colloquialism, euphemism, loan word, modernism, neologism
2 something that is said ⟨people who believe that the Bible is the literal *word* of God⟩
synonyms statement, utterance
related words communication, message; announcement, declamation, declaration, manifesto, proclamation, pronouncement
3 a report of recent events or facts not previously known ⟨what's the latest *word* on the airplane crash?⟩ — see NEWS
4 a person's solemn declaration that he or she will do or not do something ⟨I give you my *word* that I won't try to escape⟩ — see PROMISE
5 a statement of what to do that must be obeyed by those concerned ⟨her *word* is law inside the classroom⟩ — see COMMAND 1

word *vb* to convey in appropriate or telling terms ⟨tried to *word* the declaration exactly right⟩ — see PHRASE

wordbook *n* a reference book giving information about the meanings, pronunciations, uses, and origins of words listed in alphabetical order ⟨consulted the *wordbook* to see if he was using the word correctly⟩ — see DICTIONARY

wordiness *n* the use of too many words to express an idea ⟨*wordiness* will only detract from what you are trying to say⟩ — see VERBIAGE

wording *n* the way in which something is put into words ⟨it's important to get the *wording* of this law precisely correct⟩
synonyms diction, language, phraseology, phrasing
related words expression, formulation, locution; enunciation, phrase, speech, style, utterance, voice

wordless *adj* understood although not put into words ⟨a *wordless* fondness for each other⟩ — see IMPLICIT

wordy *adj* using or containing more words than necessary to express an idea ⟨your paper is two pages too long—it doesn't need to be so *wordy*⟩

synonyms circuitous, circumlocutory, diffuse, long-winded, prolix, rambling, verbose, windy

related words chatty, communicative, conversational, gabby, garrulous, loquacious, talkative, talky, voluble; redundant, repetitious, tautological; embellished, embroidered, exaggerated; bombastic, grandiloquent, highfalutin

near antonyms brief, short; aphoristic, epigrammatic, sententious; compendious, summary; abbreviated, abridged, condensed, shortened; abrupt, blunt, brusque, curt, laconic, snippy

antonyms compact, concise, crisp, pithy, succinct, terse

work *n* **1** a literary, musical, or artistic production ⟨this is my favorite *work* from that author⟩ — see COMPOSITION 1

2 something produced by physical or intellectual effort ⟨this book is the *work* of many talented people⟩ — see PRODUCT 1

3 the action for which a person or thing is specially fitted or used or for which a thing exists ⟨the *work* of a movie director is to tell a story through a series of striking images⟩ — see ROLE

4 the active use of energy in producing a result ⟨put a lot of *work* into the project⟩ — see EFFORT

5 the activity by which one regularly makes a living ⟨what kind of *work* do you do?⟩ — see OCCUPATION

6 works *pl* a building or set of buildings for the manufacturing of goods ⟨a glass *works* where stained glass is made⟩ — see FACTORY

work *vb* **1** to be the cause of (a situation, action, or state of mind) ⟨believed that he could *work* miracles⟩ — see EFFECT

2 to find an answer for through reasoning ⟨finally figured out how to *work* the math problem⟩ — see SOLVE

3 to have a certain purpose ⟨the human kidneys *work* as a kind of filtering system for the blood⟩ — see FUNCTION

4 to produce a desired effect ⟨this headache remedy takes half an hour to *work*⟩ — see ACT 2

5 to set or keep in motion ⟨this pump is *worked* by hand⟩ — see MOVE 2

6 to control the mechanical operation of ⟨show me how to *work* the machine⟩ — see OPERATE 1

7 to devote serious and sustained effort ⟨*worked* for 16 hours straight⟩ — see LABOR

work (for) *vb* to be a servant for ⟨*worked for* a rich and powerful family⟩ — see SERVE 1

work (in) *vb* to introduce in a gradual, secret, or clever way ⟨managed to *work in* several references to baseball in his paper on the merits of teamwork⟩ — see INSINUATE

workable *adj* **1** capable of being done or carried out ⟨a *workable* plan for attracting a minor league team to the city⟩ — see POSSIBLE 1

2 capable of being put to use or account ⟨found one *workable* tool in the whole pile of gadgets⟩ — see PRACTICAL 1

workaday *adj* **1** being of the type that is encountered in the normal course of events ⟨just a *workaday* guy living a *workaday* life⟩ — see ORDINARY 1

2 having to do with the practical details of regular life ⟨wished that she could afford servants so as not to be bothered with such *workaday* matters as cooking, cleaning, and grocery shopping⟩ — see MUNDANE 1

3 not designed for special occasions ⟨a *workaday* outfit that I could afford to get dirty⟩ — see CASUAL 1

worker *n* **1** a person who does very hard or dull work ⟨a champion of the rights of the farm *workers* who pick the nation's fruits and vegetables⟩ — see SLAVE 2

2 one who works for another for wages or a salary ⟨a factory owner who is known for his fair and generous treatment of his *workers*⟩ — see EMPLOYEE

working *adj* **1** being in effective operation ⟨the only *working* coal mine in the area⟩ — see ACTIVE 1

2 capable of being put to use or account ⟨only one *working* telephone in the house⟩ — see PRACTICAL 1

3 involved in often constant activity ⟨a boss who is of the opinion that a *working* employee is a needed employee, as idleness is a sign of dispensability⟩ — see BUSY 1

workmanlike *adj* accomplished with trained ability ⟨did a *workmanlike* job of fixing the faucet⟩ — see SKILLFUL 1

workout *n* something done over and over in order to develop skill ⟨a *workout* with dumbbells for building the muscles of the hands⟩ — see EXERCISE 2

work out *vb* **1** to find an answer for through reasoning ⟨by putting our two heads together, we were able to *work out* the problem⟩ — see SOLVE

2 to produce or bring about especially by long or repeated effort ⟨*worked out* a compromise between the warring factions⟩ — see HAMMER (OUT)

3 to turn out as planned or desired ⟨our plans for a ski vacation just didn't *work out*⟩ — see SUCCEED 1

4 to determine (a value) by doing the necessary mathematical operations ⟨after *working out* the cost of a college education, we've decided that it's never too early to start saving⟩ — see CALCULATE 1

workshop *n* a building or set of buildings for the manufacturing of goods ⟨a *workshop* for making toys⟩ — see FACTORY

world *n* **1** human beings in general ⟨the whole *world* is waiting to see how this crisis will play out⟩ — see PEOPLE 1

2 the celestial body on which we live ⟨worried about the effects of pollution on the *world*⟩ — see EARTH 1

3 the whole body of things observed or assumed ⟨theories about the origin of the *world*⟩ — see UNIVERSE

worldly *adj* **1** having a wide and refined knowledge of the world especially from personal experience ⟨she returned from her year as an exchange student a much more *worldly* person⟩ — see WORLDLY-WISE

2 having to do with life on earth especially as opposed to that in heaven ⟨preoccupied with *worldly* concerns⟩ — see EARTHLY

worldly–wise *adj* having a wide and refined knowledge of the world especially from personal experience ⟨having followed their father on his military assignments all over the world, the Johnson kids have become very *worldly-wise*⟩

synonyms cosmopolitan, smart, sophisticated, worldly

related words suave, urbane; civilized, cultivated, cultured, polished, refined; experienced, knowing, practiced (*or* practised), schooled, seasoned; bored, cynical, jaded, skeptical; down-to-earth, pragmatic (*also* pragmatical), realistic, sober

near antonyms callow, green, inexperienced, raw; parochial, provincial, rustic; philistine, uncivilized, uncultured, unrefined; childlike, simple, simpleminded; idealistic, impractical; uncritical, unknowing

antonyms ingenuous, innocent, naive (*or* naïve), unsophisticated, unworldly, wide-eyed

worm *vb* **1** to advance gradually beyond the usual or desirable limits ⟨settlements *worming* into lands reserved for the natives⟩ — see ENCROACH

2 to introduce in a gradual, secret, or clever way ⟨the swindler *wormed* himself into their trust⟩ — see INSINUATE

3 to move slowly with the body close to the ground ⟨the cat *wormed* along the ground as it snuck up on the bird⟩ — see CRAWL 1

worn *adj* depleted in strength, energy, or freshness ⟨she was feeling very *worn* after a long day at work⟩ — see WEARY 1

worn–out *adj* **1** depleted in strength, energy, or freshness ⟨*worn-out* tourists heading back to their hotel after a hard day of sightseeing⟩ — see WEARY 1

2 worn or torn into or as if into rags ⟨used *worn-out* clothes for dusting the furniture⟩ — see RAGGED 2

worried *adj* feeling or showing uncomfortable feelings of uncertainty ⟨he had a *worried* expression as he listened to the news⟩ — see NERVOUS 1

worrisome *adj* **1** causing worry or anxiety ⟨a *worrisome* leak in the basement⟩ — see TROUBLESOME

2 marked by or causing agitation or uncomfortable feelings ⟨the *worrisome* job of dealing with backstage crises during the performance⟩ ⟨the *worrisome* habit of fiddling with her hair⟩ — see NERVOUS 2

worry *n* an uneasy state of mind usually over the possibility of an anticipated misfortune or trouble ⟨she can only concentrate on something when she is free of *worry*⟩ — see ANXIETY 1

worry *vb* **1** to experience concern or anxiety ⟨they *worried* for days about the upcoming exam⟩

synonyms bother, fear, fret, stew, sweat, trouble

related words agonize; long, pine, yearn; chafe; despair

phrases care a hang, give a hang

near antonyms accept; abide, bear, endure, stick out, stomach, sustain, take, tolerate

2 to trouble the mind of; to make uneasy ⟨those strange noises *worry* me⟩ — see DISTURB 1

worsen *vb* to become worse or of less value ⟨the condition of the house *worsened* with every year of neglect⟩ — see DETERIORATE

worship *n* excessive admiration of or devotion to a person ⟨his *worship* of his big brother meant that he'd go to any extreme for his idol⟩

synonyms adulation, deification, idolatry, idolization, worshipping (*also* worshiping)

related words adoration, deference, glorification, reverence, veneration; idealization, romanticization; affection, fancy, favor, fondness, like, liking, love; appreciation, esteem, regard, respect; approval

near antonyms condemnation, disapproval, disfavor, dislike, dismissal, disregard, hatred, loathing, scorn

worship *vb* **1** to offer honor or respect to (someone) as a divine power ⟨the ancient Greeks *worshipped* many different gods⟩

synonyms adore, deify, glorify, revere, reverence, venerate

related words admire, honor, love, regard, respect; dignify, exalt, magnify; extol (*also* extoll), laud, praise; delight, gratify, please, satisfy

near antonyms blaspheme, desecrate, profane, violate; affront, dishonor, disrespect, insult, offend, outrage, pique, ridicule, scorn, slight; displease; defame, disparage, libel, malign, slander, slur, smear

2 to feel passion, devotion, or tenderness for ⟨he *worships* his daughter, and would do anything for her⟩ — see LOVE 2

3 to love or admire too much ⟨thought that some of her fellow senior citizens *worshipped* the old days too

much, observing that they weren't all good⟩ — see IDOLIZE

worshipful *adj* reflecting great admiration or devotion ⟨a movie fan's *worshipful* stare upon finally meeting her idol⟩ ⟨a teacher surrounded by *worshipful* little children⟩

synonyms adoring, adulatory, deifying, idolizing, worshipping (*also* worshiping)

related words glorifying, reverential, venerating; affectionate, fond, loving; appreciative, deferential, respectful; approving

near antonyms condemning, contemptuous, disapproving, hateful, loathing, scornful

worshipping *also* **worshiping** *n* excessive admiration of or devotion to a person ⟨feels that there is just too much *worshipping* of rock stars⟩ — see WORSHIP

worshipping *also* **worshiping** *adj* reflecting great admiration or devotion ⟨young men with a *worshipping* regard for professional athletes⟩ — see WORSHIPFUL

worst *vb* to achieve a victory over ⟨how humiliating for a tennis champ to be *worsted* by a player no one had ever heard of⟩ — see BEAT 2

worth *n* **1** the relative usefulness or importance of something as judged by specific qualities ⟨money alone cannot determine the true *worth* of some things⟩

synonyms account, merit, valuation, value

related words assessment, estimation, evaluation; excellence, greatness, perfection; consequence, importance, significance, weight; desirability

near antonyms emptiness, worthlessness; baseness, cheapness, inferiority, meanness, paltriness, pettiness, poorness; deficiency, inadequacy, insufficiency, unacceptability

2 the amount of money for which something will find a buyer ⟨one surefire way to determine the actual *worth* of a painting is to sell it at auction⟩ — see VALUE 1

worthless *adj* having no usefulness ⟨that expensive toy is *worthless* now that it's broken⟩

synonyms chaffy, empty, junky, no-good, null, valueless

related words base, cheap, inferior, lousy, low-grade, second-rate; bad, defective, flawed, imperfect, substandard, unsatisfactory; deficient, inadequate, insufficient, unacceptable

near antonyms invaluable, precious, priceless; cherished, esteemed, prized, treasured; choice, exceptional, fancy, high-grade, special

antonyms useful, valuable, worthy

worthy *adj* having sufficient worth or merit to receive one's honor, esteem, or reward ⟨made charitable contributions to the American Red Cross and other *worthy* causes⟩ ⟨a *worthy* opponent in a tennis match⟩

synonyms deserving, good, meritorious

related words admirable, commendable, creditable, laudable, praiseworthy; invaluable, priceless; cherished, prized, treasured; choice, excellent, exceptional, fancy, high-grade, primary, prime, special

near antonyms base, cheap, inferior, second-rate, substandard; bad, defective, flawed, imperfect; deficient, inadequate, insufficient, unacceptable, unsatisfactory

antonyms no-good, undeserving, valueless, worthless

wound *vb* **1** to cause bodily damage to ⟨an arrow had *wounded* the animal, but the vet was able to save it⟩ — see INJURE 1

2 to cause hurt feelings or deep resentment in ⟨that callous comment really *wounded* me⟩ — see INSULT

wraith *n* the soul of a dead person thought of especially as appearing to living people ⟨Ebenezer Scrooge is visited by the *wraith* of his old business partner⟩ — see GHOST

wrangle *n* an often noisy or angry expression of differing opinions ⟨she prefers to have a good *wrangle* and get it all out at once⟩ — see ARGUMENT 1

wrangle *vb* to express different opinions about something often angrily ⟨a town meeting at which local residents *wrangled* for hours about property taxes⟩ — see ARGUE 2

wrangler *n* a person who takes part in a dispute ⟨known as a petty, unrelenting *wrangler* who likes argument for the sake of argument⟩ — see DISPUTANT

wrap *vb* **1** to encircle or bind with or as if with a belt ⟨*wrapped* her waist with a colorful silk sash⟩ — see GIRD 1

2 to surround or cover closely ⟨a sinister darkness seemed to *wrap* the lonely cabin⟩ — see ENFOLD 1

wrap up *vb* **1** to bring (an event) to a natural or appropriate stopping point ⟨a grand parade will *wrap up* the week-long celebration⟩ — see CLOSE 3

2 to make into a short statement of the main points (as of a report) ⟨a reporter *wrapped up* the mayor's speech in a few sentences⟩ — see SUMMARIZE 1

wrath *n* **1** an intense emotional state of displeasure with someone or something ⟨waited until my initial *wrath* had eased before voicing my complaint⟩ — see ANGER

2 suffering, loss, or hardship imposed in response to a crime or offense ⟨the evangelist warned the gathering that unrepentant sinners would suffer the *wrath* of God⟩ — see PUNISHMENT

wrathful *adj* feeling or showing anger ⟨in a *wrathful* voice she demanded to know what had happened⟩ — see ANGRY

wrathfulness *n* an intense emotional state of displeasure with someone or something ⟨the *wrathfulness* with which he voiced his complaint was shocking⟩ — see ANGER

wreathe *vb* to scatter or set here and there among other things ⟨*wreathed* small flowers into the design for the wallpaper⟩ — see THREAD 1

wreck *n* **1** the portion or bits of something left over or behind after it has been destroyed ⟨found the *wreck* of the ship lying on the floor of the ocean⟩ — see REMAINS 1

2 the destruction or loss of a ship ⟨the *wreck* cost the insurance company millions of dollars⟩ — see SHIPWRECK

3 the violent coming together of two bodies into destructive contact ⟨a dangerous stretch of roadway that has been the scene of numerous car *wrecks*⟩ — see CRASH 1

wreck *vb* **1** to cause irreparable damage to (a ship) by running aground or sinking ⟨many an unwary captain has *wrecked* his ship on the shoals that surround the island⟩ — see SHIPWRECK

2 to bring to a complete end the physical soundness, existence, or usefulness of ⟨*wrecked* the toy by playing with it too roughly⟩ — see DESTROY 1

wreckage *n* **1** the state or fact of being rendered nonexistent, physically unsound, or useless ⟨the *wreckage* of those ancient statues represents a great loss to the art world⟩ — see DESTRUCTION

2 the portion or bits of something left over or behind after it has been destroyed ⟨the *wreckage* of the cathedral was kept as a memorial and as a reminder of war's terrible cost⟩ — see REMAINS 1

3 the destruction or loss of a ship ⟨debris floated ashore for weeks after the *wreckage*⟩ — see SHIPWRECK

wrecking *n* the destruction or loss of a ship ⟨the *wrecking* of the freighter was one of the worst disasters ever on the Great Lakes⟩ — see SHIPWRECK

wrench *n* **1** a forceful rotating or pulling motion for the purpose of dislodging something ⟨a sharp *wrench* only served to lodge the bent nail more securely into the wood⟩

synonyms twist, twisting, wrenching, wresting, wringing

related words draft, draw, extraction, pull, tug, yank; dislocation, displacement

2 the act or an instance of applying force on something so that it moves in the direction of the force ⟨with one final hard *wrench* I was able to pull the door open⟩ — see PULL 1

wrench *vb* **1** to move by or as if by a forceful rotation ⟨with one last sharp yank, he *wrenched* the cap off the medicine bottle⟩

synonyms twist, wrest, wring

related words draw, dredge (up), extract, jerk, lug, pluck, pull, tug, tweak, yank; jimmy, lever, pry; budge, dislocate, displace, disturb, remove; shift, transfer, transpose

2 to injure by overuse, misuse, or pressure ⟨*wrenched* her shoulder by all of that heavy lifting⟩ — see STRAIN 1

3 to separate or remove by forceful pulling ⟨*wrenched* the post out of the ground⟩ — see TEAR 2

wrenching *n* a forceful rotating or pulling motion for the purpose of dislodging something ⟨a firm *wrenching* dislodged the rock⟩ — see WRENCH 1

wrest *vb* **1** to draw out by force or with effort ⟨*wrested* a promise from them after days of pleading⟩ — see EXTRACT 1

2 to get (as money) by the use of force or threats ⟨vowed that the bully had *wrested* his lunch money from him for the last time⟩ — see EXTORT

3 to get with great difficulty ⟨farmers who were used to *wresting* a living from a harsh land⟩ — see EKE OUT

4 to move by or as if by a forceful rotation ⟨I need a strong arm to *wrest* the lid off this pickle jar⟩ — see WRENCH 1

5 to separate or remove by forceful pulling ⟨*wrested* open the stuck door of the cabinet⟩ — see TEAR 2

wresting *n* a forceful rotating or pulling motion for the purpose of dislodging something ⟨a sharp *wresting* got the rusty screw out⟩ — see WRENCH 1

wrestle *vb* to seize and attempt to unbalance one another for the purpose of achieving physical mastery ⟨the sisters *wrestled* on the floor over the last cookie⟩

synonyms grapple, scuffle, tussle

related words battle, clash (with), combat, contend, fight, war (against); duel; bash, batter, beat, buffet, hit, punch, slug, strike; box, spar; brawl, skirmish

wretch *n* a mean, evil, or unprincipled person ⟨what *wretch* stole this child's money?⟩ — see VILLAIN

wretched *adj* **1** extremely unsatisfactory ⟨this paper is simply *wretched*—you'll have to rewrite it⟩

synonyms atrocious, awful, execrable, lousy, punk, rotten, terrible

related words bad, deficient, inferior, off, poor, substandard, unsatisfactory, wanting; contemptible, miserable, shameful; defective, faulty, flawed; low-grade, mediocre, reprehensible, second-rate; bum, useless, valueless, worthless; inadequate, insufficient, lacking; abominable, odious, vile

near antonyms choice, excellent, exceptional, first-class, first-rate, premium, prime, superior; adequate, sufficient; acceptable, satisfactory

antonyms great, marvelous (*or* marvellous), wonderful

2 arousing or deserving of one's loathing and disgust ⟨a *wretched* lie⟩ — see CONTEMPTIBLE 1

3 causing or marked by an atmosphere lacking in cheer ⟨lived alone in a *wretched* room in a run-down hotel⟩ — see GLOOMY 1

4 falling short of a standard ⟨a *wretched* attempt at writing an original song⟩ — see BAD 1

5 feeling unhappiness ⟨she was *wretched* for weeks after breaking up with her boyfriend⟩ — see SAD 1

6 not following or in accordance with standards of honor and decency ⟨his *wretched* treatment of women earned him a bad reputation⟩ — see IGNOBLE 2

7 of low quality ⟨*wretched* goods that aren't even worth half of what the store is charging for them⟩ — see CHEAP 2

8 deserving of one's pity ⟨those *wretched* souls who cannot even afford a decent roof over their heads⟩ — see PATHETIC 1

wretchedly *adv* with feelings of bitterness or grief ⟨we're *wretchedly* disappointed in you for behaving so irresponsibly⟩ — see HARD 2

wriggle *vb* **1** to make jerky or restless movements ⟨*wriggling* in his seat all throughout the church service⟩ — see FIDGET

2 to move slowly with the body close to the ground ⟨a snake *wriggling* across the lawn⟩ — see CRAWL 1

wring *vb* **1** to get (as money) by the use of force or threats ⟨that bill collector is willing to do anything to *wring* money out of deadbeats⟩ — see EXTORT

2 to get with great difficulty ⟨managed to *wring* the information out of the tight-lipped suspect⟩ — see EKE OUT

3 to move by or as if by a forceful rotation ⟨I'm so mad I'd like to *wring* your neck off your shoulders⟩ — see WRENCH 1

wringing *n* a forceful rotating or pulling motion for the purpose of dislodging something ⟨a firm *wringing* of the shoe got it off⟩ — see WRENCH 1

wrinkle *n* **1** a small fold in a soft and otherwise smooth surface ⟨the old woman's face creased into *wrinkles* as she smiled⟩ ⟨the curtains cascaded onto the floor in ripples and *wrinkles*⟩

synonyms crease, crimp, crinkle, furrow

related words corrugation, layer, loop, plait, pleat, ply, pucker, seam, tuck; crow's-foot

2 something (as a device) created for the first time through the use of the imagination ⟨the latest *wrinkle* in digital photography⟩ — see INVENTION 1

wrinkle *vb* **1** to develop creases or folds ⟨if you don't fold clothes promptly after drying, they'll *wrinkle*⟩

synonyms crease, crinkle, furrow, rumple

related words collapse, crumple, double, fold

2 to create (as by crushing) an irregular mass of creases in ⟨sitting down on the bedspread *wrinkled* it⟩ — see CRUMPLE 1

write *vb* **1** to compose and set down on paper the words of ⟨*write* a theme in which you name your choice for the most important person in human history⟩

synonyms author, pen, pencil (in), scratch (out)

related words cast, compose, craft, draft, draw (up), formulate, frame, prepare; recast, redraft, revise, rewrite; letter, print, type, typewrite; record, take

down, transcribe; autograph, register, sign; couch, express, phrase, put, word

2 to engage in an exchange of written messages ⟨promise you'll *write* while you're away⟩ — see CORRESPOND 1

writer *n* a person who creates a written work ⟨a *writer* who is still trying to get published⟩ — see AUTHOR 1

write off *vb* **1** to express scornfully one's low opinion of ⟨don't *write off* the movie just yet—it gets better as it goes along⟩ — see DECRY 1

2 to lower the price or value of ⟨that one blunder will *write off* to nothing all the good will we've been building up⟩ — see DEPRECIATE 1

writhe *vb* to make jerky or restless movements ⟨*writhing* in pain from the disease⟩ — see FIDGET

wrong *adj* **1** falling short of a standard ⟨was told by the school snobs that her clothes and hair were all *wrong*⟩ — see BAD 1

2 having an opinion that does not agree with truth or the facts ⟨I'm sorry, but the latest research proves you *wrong*⟩ — see INCORRECT 1

3 not appropriate for a particular occasion or situation ⟨had a knack for saying just the *wrong* thing⟩ — see INAPPROPRIATE

4 not being in agreement with what is true ⟨some of the results are *wrong*⟩ — see FALSE 1

5 not conforming to a high moral standard; morally unacceptable ⟨was caught doing something *wrong*⟩ — see BAD 2

wrong *adv* off the desired or intended path or course ⟨all of our carefully laid plans went *wrong*⟩

synonyms afield, amiss, astray, awry

related words badly; faultily, improperly, inappropriately, incorrectly, mistakenly, wrongly; inadequately, insufficiently

near antonyms perfectly; auspiciously, favorably, promisingly; correctly, properly, rightly; appropriately, fittingly, suitably

antonyms aright, right, well

wrong *n* **1** that which is morally unacceptable ⟨the age at which we learn the difference between right and *wrong*⟩ — see EVIL 1

2 unfair or inadequate treatment of someone or something or an instance of this ⟨trying to right all the *wrongs* in the world⟩ — see DISSERVICE

wrongdoer *n* a person who commits moral wrongs ⟨believes that *wrongdoers* should be locked up forever⟩ — see EVILDOER 1

wrongdoing *n* **1** a breaking of a moral or legal code ⟨before pronouncing sentence, the judge read the long list of *wrongdoings* that the criminal had committed in his lifetime⟩ — see OFFENSE 1

2 improper or illegal behavior ⟨the police officer was found to be completely innocent of any *wrongdoing*⟩ — see MISCONDUCT

wrongful *adj* contrary to or forbidden by law ⟨charged with *wrongful* possession of narcotics⟩ — see ILLEGAL 1

wrongly *adv* in a mistaken or inappropriate way ⟨you have *wrongly* interpreted this passage in the Bible⟩

synonyms amiss, erroneously, faultily, improperly, inaccurately, inappropriately, inaptly, incorrectly, mistakenly, unsuitably

related words fallibly, imperfectly; extraneously, irrelevantly, meaninglessly, pointlessly, senselessly; inadequately, insufficiently; undesirably, unsatisfactorily; foolishly, unwisely

near antonyms infallibly, perfectly; meaningfully, pertinently, relevantly, sensibly; acceptably, adequately, satisfactorily, sufficiently; prudently, sagely, wisely

antonyms appropriately, aptly, correctly, fittingly, properly, right, rightly, suitably

wrongness *n* the quality or state of being unsuitable or unfitting ⟨the *wrongness* of your comment about the bride's weight can scarcely be described⟩ — see INAPPROPRIATENESS 1

wroth *adj* feeling or showing anger ⟨I've been waxing *wroth* all afternoon!⟩ — see ANGRY

XYZ

X (out) *vb* to show (something written) to be no longer valid by drawing a cross over or a line through it ⟨*x out* the names of the people who have already left⟩
  synonyms cancel, cross (out), delete, kill, scratch (out), strike (out), stroke (out)
  related words blot out, efface, erase, expunge, obliterate, rub out, wipe out; cut, excise, remove

yammer *vb* to express dissatisfaction, pain, or resentment usually tiresomely ⟨customers *yammered* on for what seemed like days about the billing mistake⟩ — see COMPLAIN

yank *n* the act or an instance of applying force on something so that it moves in the direction of the force ⟨had to give the shoe a good *yank* to get it off⟩ — see PULL 1

yank *vb* **1** to move or cause to move with a sharp quick motion ⟨she stupidly *yanked* the wheel while I was driving⟩ — see JERK 1
  2 to draw out by force or with effort ⟨*yanked* out a tooth with a pair of pliers⟩ — see EXTRACT
  3 to separate or remove by forceful pulling ⟨grab the other one, and let's see if we can't *yank* these two grocery carriages apart⟩ — see TEAR 2

yard *n* **1** an open space wholly or partly enclosed (as by buildings or walls) ⟨inmates are allowed an hour of exercise in the prison's inner *yard*⟩ — see COURT 2
  2 the area around and belonging to a building ⟨we're looking for a house with a big *yard*⟩ — see GROUND 1

yardstick *n* something set up as an example against which others of the same type are compared ⟨this essay will be the *yardstick* by which I grade the others⟩ — see STANDARD 1

yarn *n* **1** a brief account of something interesting that happened especially to one personally ⟨Grandpa likes to tell *yarns* about when he was young⟩ — see STORY 2
  2 a work with imaginary characters and events that is shorter and usually less complex than a novel ⟨a ripping *yarn* about space travel and alien monsters⟩ — see STORY 1

yaw *vb* to depart abruptly from a straight line or course ⟨the ship *yawed* when the waves hit it broadside⟩ — see SWERVE 1

yea *adv* **1** not merely this but also ⟨we will go to the new land, and, *yea*, we will be happy!⟩ — see EVEN
  2 used to express agreement ⟨I vote *yea* on the proposed increase in the school budget⟩ — see YES

yeah *adv* used to express agreement ⟨*yeah*, we'll be there⟩ — see YES

yearn (for) *vb* to have an earnest wish to own or enjoy ⟨*yearned for* a little house in the country⟩ — see DESIRE

yearning *n* a strong wish for something ⟨had a sudden *yearning* for something sweet⟩ — see DESIRE

yeast *n* something that arouses action or activity ⟨taxation without representation proved to be the *yeast* of rebellion⟩ — see IMPULSE

yell *n* a loud vocal expression of strong emotion ⟨the crowd gave a *yell* of approval⟩ — see SHOUT

yell *vb* **1** to cry out loudly and emotionally ⟨*yelled* with fear when she saw the "monster" under her bed⟩ — see SCREAM

2 to speak so as to be heard at a distance ⟨Mom *yelled* to the kids in the backyard that it was time to go home⟩ — see CALL 1

yellow *adj* having or showing a shameful lack of courage ⟨you'll come into the cave, unless you're *yellow*⟩ — see COWARDLY

yellowness *n* a shameful lack of courage in the face of danger ⟨the *yellowness* that his friend showed when faced with the school bully was embarrassing⟩ — see COWARDICE

yelp *vb* to cry out loudly and emotionally ⟨*yelped* with surprise when everything fell off the closet shelf and onto his head⟩ — see SCREAM

yen *n* a strong wish for something ⟨I have a strange *yen* to take the day off⟩ — see DESIRE

yes *adv* used to express agreement ⟨*yes*, I'll be ready for the test tomorrow⟩
  synonyms all right, alright, aye (*also* ay), OK (*or* okay), yea, yeah
  related words certainly, indeed, indisputably, undoubtedly, unquestionably
  antonyms nay, no, no way

yesterday *n* the events or experience of former times ⟨my grandparents are always reminiscing about *yesterday*⟩ — see PAST

yesteryear *n* the events or experience of former times ⟨the simple games of *yesteryear* that kept children entertained for hours⟩ — see PAST

yet *adv* **1** at a later time ⟨we may *yet* figure it out⟩
  synonyms eventually, finally, someday, sometime, ultimately
  phrases at last, at length, at long last
  near antonyms ne'er, never, nevermore
  2 in addition to what has been said ⟨offered *yet* another option for our planned tour of Europe⟩ — see MORE 1
  3 in spite of that ⟨the hikers were scared, and *yet* they continued to go deeper into the cave⟩ — see HOWEVER
  4 up to this or that time ⟨we have *yet* to win a single game⟩ ⟨she had *yet* to accomplish a single thing⟩ — see HITHERTO

yet *conj* if it were not for the fact that ⟨it feels like summer, *yet* according to the calendar we're still in early spring⟩ — see EXCEPT

yield *n* **1** an increase usually measured in money that comes from labor, business, or property ⟨the stock's *yield* has increased over the years⟩ — see INCOME
  2 something produced by physical or intellectual effort ⟨wheat farmers were able to increase the *yield* per acre substantially⟩ — see PRODUCT 1
  3 the total amount collected or obtained especially at one time ⟨the total *yield* for our trick-or-treating was staggering⟩ — see HAUL 1

yield *vb* **1** to give up and cease resistance (as to a liking, temptation, or habit) ⟨I finally *yielded* to temptation and had a bowl of ice cream⟩
  synonyms bow, give in, submit, succumb, surrender
  related words gratify, indulge, wallow; acquiesce (to), concede (to)
  near antonyms battle, breast, combat, confront, counter, defy, face, meet, object, oppose, repel; thwart, withstand
  antonyms hold off, resist

2 to produce as revenue ⟨I expect that stock to *yield* at least 14% profit this year⟩

synonyms give, pay, return

related words bring in, produce; afford, furnish, provide, supply

3 to cease resistance (as to another's arguments, demands, or control) ⟨after insisting that her answer was not incorrect, Mary *yielded* when her teacher threatened her with detention⟩

synonyms bow, budge, capitulate, concede, give in, knuckle under, quit, submit, succumb, surrender

related words acquiesce

near antonyms contend, fight

antonyms resist

4 to be the cause of (a situation, action, or state of mind) ⟨the sort of embarrassing question that seldom *yields* an honest answer⟩ — see EFFECT

5 to fall down or in as a result of physical pressure ⟨the door soon *yielded* to the battering ram⟩ — see COLLAPSE 1

6 to give (something) over to the control or possession of another usually under duress ⟨refusing to *yield* the city to enemy troops⟩ — see SURRENDER 1

yielding *adj* **1** receiving or enduring without offering resistance ⟨a person too *yielding* to even stand up for his own rights⟩ — see PASSIVE

2 not stiff in structure ⟨after sitting on a hard bench for hours, I was happy to sink into the sofa's *yielding* cushions⟩ — see LIMP 1

yoke *n* the state of being a slave ⟨a people able at last to throw off the *yoke* and to embrace freedom⟩ — see SLAVERY 1

yoke *vb* to put or bring together so as to form a new and longer whole ⟨*yoked* several ideas together to come up with a new theory⟩ — see CONNECT 1

yokel *n* an awkward or simple person especially from a small town or the country ⟨a lame comedy about the misadventures of *yokels* in the big city⟩ — see HICK

yon *adv* at or to a greater distance or more advanced point ⟨the belief that it is the destiny of the human race to explore our solar system and *yon*⟩ — see FARTHER

yonder *adv* at or to a greater distance or more advanced point ⟨look *yonder* and you'll see the skyline of the city⟩ — see FARTHER

yore *n* the events or experience of former times ⟨my favorite stories are about knights and fair maidens in the days of *yore*⟩ — see PAST

young *adj* being in the early stage of life, growth, or development ⟨a *young* cat requires more food than an older one⟩ ⟨a *young* tree that will eventually reach 50 feet tall⟩

synonyms adolescent, immature, juvenile, youngish, youthful

related words minor, underage; embryonic; callow, green, inexperienced, puerile, raw; babyish, childish, childlike, infantile; undeveloped, unfinished, unfledged, unformed, unripe, unripened; blooming, blossoming, burgeoning, flourishing, flowering

near antonyms aged, aging, elderly, old; full-blown, full-fledged; golden, mellow, ripe, ripened

antonyms adult, full-grown, mature, matured

youngish *adj* being in the early stage of life, growth, or development ⟨a *youngish* but surprisingly mature audience showed up to watch the serious film⟩ — see YOUNG

youngster *n* a young person who is between infancy and adulthood ⟨a herd of *youngsters* following their nature

guide like ducklings after a mother duck⟩ — see CHILD 1

youth *n* **1** a male person who has not yet reached adulthood ⟨a big, strapping *youth* who even at his relatively young age knew the meaning of hard work⟩ — see BOY

2 a young person who is between infancy and adulthood ⟨rounded up the neighborhood *youths* and formed them into a softball team⟩ — see CHILD 1

3 the state or time of being a child ⟨told the young people to enjoy their *youth* while they could⟩ — see CHILDHOOD

youthful *adj* being in the early stage of life, growth, or development ⟨it's still a *youthful* nation with a lot of promise and potential⟩ — see YOUNG

yowl *n* a loud vocal expression of strong emotion ⟨the cat gave a *yowl* of anger⟩ — see SHOUT

yowl *vb* to make a long loud mournful sound ⟨coyotes *yowling* at the moon⟩ — see HOWL 1

yo–yo *n* a person who lacks good sense or judgment ⟨some *yo-yo* cut the electricity off⟩ — see FOOL 1

yuletide *n* the season celebrating Christmas ⟨these days, as far as the stores are concerned, *yuletide* starts in September⟩

synonyms Christmastime, Noel

related words Advent; Christmas, nativity, Xmas, yule

yummy *adj* very pleasing to the sense of taste ⟨a *yummy* meal⟩ — see DELICIOUS 1

zaniness *n* lack of good sense or judgment ⟨what *zaniness* possessed you to skip class on a test day?⟩ — see FOOLISHNESS 1

zany *adj* showing or marked by a lack of good sense or judgment ⟨a *zany* plan to drive cross-country on a motorized scooter⟩ — see FOOLISH 1

zany *n* a comically dressed performer (as at a circus) who entertains with playful tricks and ridiculous behavior ⟨hired a *zany* to entertain the children⟩ — see CLOWN 1

zap *vb* to deliver a blow to (someone or something) usually in a strong vigorous manner ⟨*zapped* the annoying bug with a swatter⟩ — see HIT 1

zealot *n* one who is intensely or excessively devoted to a cause ⟨some people called John a *zealot* because he was always crusading for human rights⟩

synonyms crusader, fanatic, militant, partisan

related words activist; dreamer, visionary; cultist, disciple, follower, idolizer, votary; addict, aficionado, buff, bug, devotee, enthusiast, fan, fancier, fiend, freak, lover, maniac, nut; backer, patron, promoter, supporter; booster, rooter, well-wisher; faddist

near antonyms dabbler, dilettante

zenith *n* the highest part or point ⟨at the *zenith* of her career as a dancer⟩ — see HEIGHT 1

zephyr *n* a slight or gentle movement of air ⟨a summer *zephyr* gently stirred her hair⟩ — see BREEZE 1

zero *n* **1** the numerical symbol 0 or the absence of number or quantity represented by it ⟨anything multiplied by *zero* comes out to zero⟩

synonyms aught, cipher, goose egg, naught (*also* nought), nil, nothing, oh, zilch, zip

related words blank, void

2 a person of no importance or influence ⟨those snobs tried to make me feel like a complete *zero*⟩ — see NOBODY

zero hour *n* a time or state of affairs requiring prompt or decisive action ⟨we're at the *zero hour*, so someone has to make a decision⟩ — see EMERGENCY

zest *n* the quality or state of being stimulating to the mind or senses ⟨dumped in more spices to add some *zest* to the marinade⟩ — see PIQUANCY

zesty *adj* sharp and pleasantly stimulating to the mind or senses ⟨bland pasta that needs a *zesty* sauce⟩ — see PIQUANT

zigzag *vb* to move suddenly aside or to and fro ⟨the toy car *zigzagged* across the floor⟩ — see DODGE 1

zilch *n* **1** a person of no importance or influence ⟨a passive and retiring little *zilch* of a person⟩ — see NOBODY

2 the numerical symbol 0 or the absence of number or quantity represented by it ⟨the amount of money that we have coming in right now is *zilch*⟩ — see ZERO 1

zing *n* active strength of body or mind ⟨has the youthful, adventurous *zing* to go out and conquer mountains⟩ — see VIGOR 1

zip *n* **1** active strength of body or mind ⟨he has surprising *zip* for a man his age⟩ — see VIGOR 1

2 the numerical symbol 0 or the absence of number or quantity represented by it ⟨I've got *zip* as far as new ideas go⟩ — see ZERO 1

zip *vb* **1** to fly, turn, or move rapidly with a fluttering or vibratory sound ⟨a dragonfly *zipped* by my ear⟩ — see WHIRR

2 to make an irregular series of quick, sudden movements ⟨the fly *zipped* around the room, trying to find a way to the outside⟩ — see FLIT

3 to proceed or move quickly ⟨knowing that she was already late, she went *zipping* off to class⟩ — see HURRY 2

zippy *adj* having much high-spirited energy and movement ⟨a crowd of *zippy* children who'd been cooped up all day⟩ — see LIVELY 1

zone *n* **1** a broad geographical area ⟨a tropical *zone*⟩ — see REGION 2

2 a part or portion having no fixed boundaries ⟨at that point we were out of the danger *zone* for avalanches⟩ — see REGION 1

zoom *n* a monotonous sound like that of an insect in motion ⟨the *zoom* of a motorboat off in the distance⟩ — see HUM

zoom *vb* **1** to fly, turn, or move rapidly with a fluttering or vibratory sound ⟨a squadron of fighter planes *zooming* by over our heads⟩ — see WHIRR

2 to proceed or move quickly ⟨race cars *zooming* around a track at breakneck speeds⟩ — see HURRY 2

3 to rise abruptly and rapidly ⟨*zoomed* to a supervisory position after only a few months⟩ — see SKYROCKET

Additional Merriam-Webster References for Students—

Merriam-Webster's Elementary Dictionary
Grades 2–4
This colorfully illustrated and easy-to-use dictionary features short and clear definitions to enhance communication skills. Includes more than 32,000 entries, 600 illustrations, and 250 word history paragraphs.
0-87779-575-4, $15.95

Merriam-Webster's Intermediate Dictionary
Grades 5–8
This newly revised, illustrated dictionary is the ideal companion to the *Intermediate Thesaurus*, offering more than 70,000 entries, 15,000 usage examples, and 1,000 carefully drawn illustrations.
0-87779-579-7, $17.95

Merriam-Webster's School Dictionary
Grades 9–12
Recently updated, this illustrated reference features more than 100,000 entries, including thousands of new words and meanings, more than 15,000 usage examples, 530 synonym paragraphs, and 200 word history paragraphs.
0-87779-580-0, $18.95

Merriam-Webster's School Thesaurus
Grades 9–12
With more than 157,000 synonyms, antonyms, idiomatic phrases, and related and contrasted words, this alphabetically arranged thesaurus is an essential word choice tool for high school students.
0-87779-178-3, $15.95

Merriam-Webster OnLine
www.merriam-webster.com
One of the world's top ranking Web sites, Merriam-Webster OnLine offers free access to *Merriam-Webster's Online Dictionary*, *Online Thesaurus*, and *Word of the Day*.

Merriam-Webster's Word Central
www.WordCentral.com
A free, interactive reference site developed just for kids, featuring *Merriam-Webster's Student Dictionary* (ages 11–14), the *Daily Buzzword*, and a host of word games and activities.